Circulation Research

An Official Journal of the American Heart Association

VOLUME 56

January–June

1985

AMERICAN HEART ASSOCIATION, INC.

Circulation Research

An Official Journal of the American Heart Association

Circulation Research provides a medium for bringing together basic research on the cardiovascular system from various disciplines including biology, biochemistry, biophysics, morphology, pathology, physiology, and pharmacology. The Journal also will accept for publication manuscripts on clinical research that contribute to an understanding of fundamental problems.

Circulation Research

AN OFFICIAL JOURNAL OF THE AMERICAN HEART ASSOCIATION

VOLUME 56

January–June 1985

No. 1 (January)

Two Distinct Effects of Oxygen on Vascular Tone in Isolated Porcine Coronary Arteries.
Gabor Rubanyi and Richard J. Paul 1

Effects of Pressure Gradients between Branches of the Left Coronary Artery on the Pressure Axis Intercept and the Shape of Steady State Circumflex Pressure-Flow Relations in Dogs.
Louis M. Messina, Frank L. Hanley, Paul N. Uhlig, Robert W. Baer, Mark T. Grattan, and Julien I.E. Hoffman 11

Transmission of Intrathoracic Pressure to the Intracranial Space during Cardiopulmonary Resuscitation in Dogs.
Alan D. Guerci, An-Yun Shi, Howard Levin, Joshua Tsitlik, Myron L. Weisfeldt, and Nisha Chandra ... 20

Relationship between Myocardial Fiber Direction and Segment Shortening in the Midwall of the Canine Left Ventricle.
Gregory L. Freeman, Martin M. LeWinter, Robert L. Engler, and James W. Covell 31

Pulmonary Artery Constriction Produces a Greater Right Ventricular Dynamic Afterload Than Lung Microvascular Injury in the Open Chest Dog.
James E. Calvin, Jr., Robert W. Baer, and Stanton A. Glantz 40

Limitations of Tracer Oxygen Uptake in the Canine Coronary Circulation.
Colin P. Rose and Carl A. Goresky 57

The Role of Free Radical-Mediated Processes in Oxygen-Related Damage in Cultured Murine Myocardial Cells.
James A. Scott, Ban An Khaw, Elizabeth Locke, Edgar Haber, and Charles Homcy 72

The Economy of Isometric Force Development, Myosin Isoenzyme Pattern, and Myofibrillar ATPase Activity in Normal and Hypothyroid Rat Myocardium.
Ch. Holubarsch, R.P. Goulette, R.Z. Litten, B.J. Martin, L.A. Mulieri, and N.R. Alpert 78

A Dihydropyridine (Bay k 8644) That Enhances Calcium Currents in Guinea Pig and Calf Myocardial Cells: A New Type of Positive Inotropic Agent.
Gunter Thomas, Minn Chung, and Charles J. Cohen 87

Mechanism of Action of Angiotensin II and Bradykinin on Prostaglandin Synthesis and Vascular Tone in the Isolated Rat Kidney: Effect of Ca^{++} Antagonists and Calmodulin Inhibitors.
Christy L. Cooper, Joel E. Shaffer, and Kafait U. Malik 97

Vascular Adrenergic Neuroeffector Function Does Not Decline in Aged Rats.
Sue Piper Duckles, Bart J. Carter, and Cynthia L. Williams 109

Inhibitors of Prostaglandin Synthesis Augment β-Adrenergic Responsiveness in Canine Coronary Arteries.
Gabor Rubanyi and Paul M. Vanhoutte 117

BRIEF COMMUNICATIONS

Direct Analysis of β-Adrenergic Receptor Subtypes on Intact Adult Ventricular Myocytes of the Rat.
Iain L.O. Buxton and Laurence L. Brunton 126

Ryanodine as a Tool to Determine the Contributions of Calcium Entry and Calcium Release to the Calcium Transient and Contraction of Cardiac Purkinje Fibers.
Eduardo Marban and W. Gil Wier 133

Significance of Quiescent Smooth Muscle Migration in the Injured Rat Carotid Artery.
Alexander W. Clowes and Stephen M. Schwartz 139

Phospholipase D Produces Increased Contractile Force in Rabbit Ventricular Muscle.
G.A. Langer and T.L. Rich 146

INSTRUCTIONS TO AUTHORS 150

NEWS FROM THE AMERICAN HEART ASSOCIATION 154

No. 2 (February)

SPECIAL ARTICLE

The Accuracy of Inferring Left Ventricular Volume from Dimension Depends on the Frequency of Information Needed to Answer a Given Question.
Bryan K. Slinker and Stanton A. Glantz 161

Analysis of the Pressor Sympathetic Reflex Produced by Intracoronary Injections of Bradykinin in Conscious Dogs.
Massimo Pagani, Paolo Pizzinelli, Raffaello Furlan, Stefano Guzzetti, Ornella Rimoldi, Giulia Sandrone, and Alberto Malliani 175

Possible Mechanisms of Ventricular Arrhythmias Elicited by Ischemia Followed by Reperfusion: Studies on Isolated Canine Ventricular Tissues.
Gregory R. Ferrier, Margaret P. Moffat, and Anton Lukas 184

Fate of Intercellular Junctions in Isolated Adult Rat Cardiac Cells.
Francoise Mazet, Beatrice A. Wittenberg, and David C. Spray 195

Neurogenic Muscarinic Vasodilation in the Cat: An Example of Endothelial Cell-Independent Cholinergic Relaxation.
Joseph E. Brayden and John A. Bevan 205

Angiotensin II in Rat Brain Comigrates with Authentic Angiotensin II in High Pressure Liquid Chromatography.
M. Ian Phillips and Birgitta Stenstrom 212

Influence of Ribose, Adenosine, and "AICAR" on the Rate of Myocardial Tissue Adenosine Triphosphate Synthesis during Reperfusion after Coronary Artery Occlusion in the Dog.
M. Mauser, H.M. Hoffmeister, C. Nienaber, and W. Schaper 220

Sodium Pump Inhibition, Enhanced Calcium Influx via Sodium-Calcium Exchange, and Positive Inotropic Response in Cultured Heart Cells.
William H. Barry, Yonathin Hasin, and Thomas W. Smith 231

Dipyridamole Decreases Glomerular Filtration in the Sodium-Depleted Dog: Evidence for Mediation by Intrarenal Adenosine.
Lois J. Arend, Carl I. Thompson, and William S. Spielman 242

Optimal Power Generation by the Left Ventricle: A Study in the Anesthetized Open Thorax Cat.
G.J. van den Horn, N. Westerhof, and G. Elzinga 252

Effect of Reperfusion Late in the Phase of Reversible Ischemic Injury: Changes in Cell Volume, Electrolytes, Metabolites, and Ultrastructure.
Robert B. Jennings, Jutta Schaper, Mary L. Hill, Charles Steenbergen, Jr., and Keith A. Reimer 262

BRIEF COMMUNICATIONS

[^{125}I]Aminobenzyladenosine, A New Radioligand with Improved Specific Binding to Adenosine Receptors in Heart.
Joel Linden, Amrat Patel, and Samy Sadek 279

LETTERS TO THE EDITOR 285

ERRATUM 286

NEWS FROM THE AMERICAN HEART ASSOCIATION 287

No. 3 (March)

CONTROVERSIES IN CARDIOVASCULAR RESEARCH

Coronary Diastolic Pressure-Flow Relation and Zero Flow Pressure Explained on the Basis of Intramyocardial Compliance.
Jos A.E. Spaan 293

Coronary Pressure-Flow Relationships: Controversial Issues and Probable Implications.
Francis J. Klocke, Robert E. Mates, John M. Canty, Jr., and Avery K. Ellis 310

Identification and Characterization of Leukotriene C_4 Receptors in Isolated Rat Renal Glomeruli.
Barbara J. Ballermann, Robert A. Lewis, E.J. Corey, K. Frank Austen, and Barry M. Brenner 324

Real-Time Kinetics of Sarcomere Relaxation by Laser Diffraction.
Yves Lecarpentier, Jean-Louis Martin, Victor Claes, Jean-Paul Chambaret, Arnold Migus, André Antonetti, and Pierre-Yves Hatt 331

Postextrasystolic Potentiation of the Isolated Canine Left Ventricle: Relationship to Mechanical Restitution.
David T. Yue, Daniel Burkhoff, Michael R. Franz, William C. Hunter, and Kiichi Sagawa 340

Mechanisms of Augmented Segment Shortening in Nonischemic Areas during Acute Ischemia of the Canine Left Ventricle.
Wilbur Y.W. Lew, Zhengyu Chen, Brian Guth, and James W. Covell 351

Electrophysiological Study of Cardiovascular Neurons in the Rostral Ventrolateral Medulla in Rats.
D. Les Brown and Patrice G. Guyenet 359

Kinetics of Thallium Exchange in Cultured Rat Myocardial Cells.
David McCall, Lawrence J. Zimmer, and Arnold M. Katz 370

Ultrastructural Morphometric Analysis of Myocardium from Dogs, Rats, Hamsters, Mice, and from Human Hearts.
Jutta Schaper, Eckhardt Meiser, and Gerhard Stämmler 377

Changes in Cholinergic Parameters Associated with Failure of Conotruncal Septation in Embryonic Chick Hearts after Neural Crest Ablation.
Margaret L. Kirby, Robert S. Aronstam, and Jerry J. Buccafusco 392

α-Adrenergic Receptors in Cerebral Microvessels of Normotensive and Spontaneously Hypertensive Rats.
Hideyuki Kobayashi, Akihiko Wada, Futoshi Izumi, Maria-Sandra Magnoni, and Marco Trabucchi 402

Interactions of Vasopressin with the Area Postrema in Arterial Baroreflex Function in Conscious Rabbits.
Karl P. Undesser, Eileen M. Hasser, Joseph R. Haywood, Alan K. Johnson, and Vernon S. Bishop 410

Variables Controlling the Secretion of a Somatomedin-like Peptide by Cultured Porcine Smooth Muscle Cells.
David R. Clemmons 418

Calcium Sensitivity of Isometric Force in Intact and Chemically Skinned Aortas during the Development of Aldosterone-Salt Hypertension in the Rat.
E. Garwitz McMahon and R.J. Paul 427

Structural and Electrophysiological Changes in the Epicardial Border Zone of Canine Myocardial Infarcts during Infarct Healing.
Philip C. Ursell, Phyllis I. Gardner, Arline Albala, John J. Fenoglio, Jr., and Andrew L. Wit 436

BRIEF COMMUNICATIONS

The Effects of Ryanodine on Calcium-Overloaded Sheep Cardiac Purkinje Fibers.
M. Valdeolmillos and D.A. Eisner 452

Elevated Plasma Norepinephrine Concentrations in Decompensated Cirrhosis: Association with Increased Secretion Rates, Normal Clearance Rates, and Suppressibility by Central Blood Volume Expansion.
Kathleen M. Nicholls, Michael D. Shapiro, Vicki J. Van Putten, Rudiger Kluge, Hsiao-Min Chung, Daniel G. Bichet, and Robert W. Schrier 457

Subfornical Organ: Does It Protect against Angiotensin II-Induced Hypertension in the Rat?
Cathy A. Bruner, Michael L. Mangiapane, and Gregory D. Fink 462

NEWS FROM THE AMERICAN HEART ASSOCIATION 467

No. 4 (April)

BRIEF REVIEWS

New Studies of the Excitatory Sodium Currents in Heart Muscle.
Harry A. Fozzard, Craig T. January, and Jonathan C. Makielski 475

Carotid Baroreceptor Reflex Coronary Vasodilation in the Dog.
Bruce R. Ito and Eric O. Feigl 486

Evidence for a Specific Receptor Site for Lidocaine, Quinidine, and Bupivacaine Associated with Cardiac Sodium Channels in Guinea Pig Ventricular Myocardium.
Craig W. Clarkson and Luc M. Hondeghem 496

Calcium-Dependent Fluxes of Potassium-42 and Chloride-36 during Norepinephrine Activation of Rat Aorta.
Jacquelyn M. Smith and Allan W. Jones 507

Role of Adenosine in Coronary Blood Flow Regulation after Reductions in Perfusion Pressure.
William P. Dole, Nobuyuki Yamada, Vernon S. Bishop, and Ray A. Olsson 517

Differential Effects of Antihypertensive Drug Therapy on Vascular Smooth Muscle Cell Hypertrophy, Hyperploidy, and Hyperplasia in the Spontaneously Hypertensive Rat.
Gary K. Owens 525

The Significance of the Late Fall in Myocardial P_{CO_2} and Its Relationship to Myocardial pH After Regional Coronary Occlusion in the Dog.
Shukri F. Khuri, Robert A. Kloner, Stephanie A. Karaffa, William Marston, Arthur D. Taylor, N.C. Joseph Lai, Donald E. Tow, and Ernest M. Barsamian 537

Transmural Distribution of Isomyosin in Rabbit Ventricle during Maturation Examined by Immunofluorescence and Staining for Calcium-Activated Adenosine Triphosphatase.
Brenda R. Eisenberg, Joy A. Edwards, and Radovan Zak 548

Fibrosis, Lipids, and Calcium in Human Atherosclerotic Plaque: In Vitro Differentiation from Normal Aortic Walls by Ultrasonic Attenuation.
Eugenio Picano, Luigi Landini, Alessandro Distante, Antonio Benassi, Roberta Sarnelli, and Antonio L'Abbate 556

Differential Effects of Central Angiotensin II and Substance P on Sympathetic Nerve Activity in Conscious Rats: Implications for Cardiovascular Adaptation to Behavioral Responses.
Thomas Unger, Hans Becker, Margaret Petty, Gudrun Demmert, Bernhard Schneider, Detlev Ganten, and Rudolf E. Lang 563

Effect of Membrane Depolarization on Binding of [^{3}H]Nitrendipine to Rat Cardiac Myocytes.
Frank J. Green, Barbara B. Farmer, Gail L. Wiseman, Mimi J.L. Jose, and August M. Watanabe 576

Optimal Arterial Resistance for the Maximal Stroke Work Studied in Isolated Canine Left Ventricle.
Kenji Sunagawa, W. Lowell Maughan, and Kiichi Sagawa 586

Transient Analysis of the Canine Cerebrovascular Response to Carbon Dioxide.
David A. Wilson, Richard J. Traystman, and Carlos E. Rapela 596

BRIEF COMMUNICATIONS

Failure of Atriopeptin II to Cause Arterial Vasodilation in the Conscious Rat.
Rodney W. Lappe, Jos F.M. Smits, Joy A. Todt, Jacques J.M. Debets, and Robert L. Wendt 606

Effects of Acetylcholine on Action Potential Characteristics of Atrial and Ventricular Myocardium after Bilateral Cervical Vagotomy in the Cat.
Richard J. Kovacs and John C. Bailey 613

Comparative Vascular Pharmacology of the Atriopeptins.
Korekiyo Wakitani, Takeshi Oshima, Arthur D. Loewy, Sandra W. Holmberg, Barbara R. Cole, Steven P. Adams, Kam F. Fok, Mark G. Currie, and Philip Needleman 621

ERRATA 628

NEWS FROM THE AMERICAN HEART ASSOCIATION 629

No. 5 (May)

BRIEF REVIEWS

Molecular Characterization of Adrenergic Receptors.
Charles J. Homcy and Robert M. Graham 635

SPECIAL ARTICLES

Animal Models for Protecting Ischemic Myocardium: Results of the NHLBI Cooperative Study: Comparison of Unconscious and Conscious Dog Models.
Keith A. Reimer, Robert B. Jennings, Fred R. Cobb, Robert H. Murdock, Joseph C. Greenfield, Jr., Lewis C. Becker, Bernadine Healy Bulkley, Grover M. Hutchins, Richard P. Schwartz, Jr., Kent R. Bailey, and Eugene R. Passamani 651

Coronary Venous Perfusion of the Ischemic Myocardium during Acute Coronary Artery Occlusion in Isolated Rat Hearts.
Yuji Taira, Hideo Kanaide, and Motoomi Nakamura 666

Inotropic Effect, Binding Properties, and Calcium Flux Effects of the Calcium Channel Agonist CGP 28392 in Intact Cultured Embryonic Chick Ventricular Cells.
Stephane Laurent, Donghee Kim, Thomas W. Smith, and James D. Marsh 676

Effects of Coronary Artery Occlusion and Reperfusion on Cardiac Cycle-Dependent Variation of Myocardial Ultrasonic Backscatter.
Robert M. Glueck, Jack G. Mottley, James G. Miller, Burton E. Sobel, and Julio E. Pérez 683

Viscoelastic Behavior of the Thoracic Aorta of Dogs and Rabbits.
Brian J. Gentile and David R. Gross 690

The Effects of Antiarrhythmic Drugs, Stimulation Frequency, and Potassium-Induced Resting Membrane Potential Changes on Conduction Velocity and dV/dt_{max} in Guinea Pig Myocardium.
Jack W. Buchanan, Jr., Tomoaki Saito, and Leonard S. Gettes 696

Protection of Canine Cardiac Mitochondrial Function by Verapamil-Cardioplegia during Ischemic Arrest.
Seung Boo Yoon, Jeanie B. McMillin-Wood, Lloyd H. Michael, Robert M. Lewis, and Mark L. Entman . . . 704

Surface Densities of Diaphragmed Fenestrae and Transendothelial Channels in Different Murine Capillary Beds.
Anthony J. Milici, Nancy L'Hernault, and George E. Palade . . . 709

"Fade" of Hyperpolarizing Responses to Vagal Stimulation at the Sinoatrial and Atrioventricular Nodes of the Rabbit Heart.
Joseph J. Salata and Jose Jalife . . . 718

The Mechanism by Which Adenosine and Cholinergic Agents Reduce Contractility in Rat Myocardium. Correlation with Cyclic Adenosine Monophosphate and Receptor Densities.
Joel Linden, Cathy E. Hollen, and Amrat Patel . . . 728

Intramural Reentry as a Mechanism of Ventricular Tachycardia during Evolving Canine Myocardial Infarction.
Jeffrey B. Kramer, Jeffrey E. Saffitz, Francis X. Witkowski, and Peter B. Corr . . . 736

Effects of Propranolol on Atherogenesis in the Cholesterol-Fed Rabbit.
Aram V. Chobanian, Peter Brecher, and Catherine Chan . . . 755

BRIEF COMMUNICATIONS

Acetylcholine Release from Rat Atria Can Be Regulated through an α_1-Adrenergic Receptor.
Glenn T. Wetzel, David Goldstein, and Joan Heller Brown . . . 763

NEWS FROM THE AMERICAN HEART ASSOCIATION . . . 767

No. 6, (June)

Vol. 56 JUNE 1985 No. 6

CONTENTS

BRIEF REVIEWS

The Plasma Membrane Sodium-Hydrogen Exchanger and Its Role in Physiological and Pathophysiological Processes.
Rex L. Mahnensmith and Peter S. Aronson . . . 773

CONTROVERSIES IN CARDIOVASCULAR RESEARCH

Response to the Article by Klocke et al. on "Coronary Pressure-Flow Relationships: Controversial Issues and Probable Implications."
Jos A. E. Spaan . . . 789

Response to the Article by Spaan on "Coronary Diastolic Pressure-Flow Relation and Zero Flow Pressure Explained on the Basis of Intramyocardial Compliance."
Francis J. Klocke, Robert E. Mates, John M. Canty, Jr., and Avery K. Ellis . . . 791

Hemodynamic Response to Normovolemic Polycythemia at Rest and during Exercise in Dogs.
JoAnn Lindenfeld, John V. Weil, Victoria L. Travis, and Lawrence D. Horwitz . . . 793

Vascular and Adrenal Receptors for Atrial Natriuretic Factor in the Rat.
Ernesto L. Schiffrin, Lynn Chartier, Gaétan Thibault, Jean St-Louis, Marc Cantin, and Jacques Genest . 801

The Left Ventricular dP/dt_{max}-End-Diastolic Volume Relation in Closed-Chest Dogs.
William C. Little . . . 808

Characterization of a Kininogenase from Rat Vascular Tissue Resembling Tissue Kallikrein.
Hector Nolly, A. Guillermo Scicli, Gloria Scicli, and Oscar A. Carretero . . . 816

Differences in Norepinephrine Activation and Diltiazem Inhibition of Calcium Channels in Isolated Rabbit Aorta and Mesenteric Resistance Vessels.
Cynthia Cauvin, Scott Lukeman, John Cameron, Ok Hwang, and Cornelis van Breemen . . . 822

Cytoskeletal Features of Rat Aortic Cells during Development: An Electron Microscopic, Immunohistochemical, and Biochemical Study.
Olivier Kocher, Omar Skalli, Daniel Cerutti, Françoise Gabbiani, and Giulio Gabbiani . . . 829

Hyaluronidase Does Not Prevent Deterioration of Vascular Functional Integrity during Reperfusion after No-Flow Ischemia in Isolated Rabbit Hearts.
Ronald G. Tilton, Peter A. Cole, Kenneth B. Larson, Charles Kilo, and Joseph R. Williamson . . . 839

The Electromotive Force of the Ventricular Free Wall and Papillary Muscle Preparations.
Saburo Mashima, Kan Takayanagi, Georg Schmidt, and Akira Nozaki . . . 851

Action Potential Prolongation and Induction of Abnormal Automaticity by Low Quinidine Concentrations of Canine Purkinje Fibers: Relationship to Potassium and Cycle Length.
Dan M. Roden and Brian F. Hoffman **857**

The Calcium Channel Blocker Nitrendipine Blocks Sodium Channels in Neonatal Rat Cardiac Myocytes.
Atsuko Yatani and Arthur M. Brown **868**

Interaction between a Normoxic and a Hypoxic Region of Guinea Pig and Ferret Papillary Muscles.
Heinz Hofmann **876**

Stimulation of Hypertrophy of Cultured Neonatal Rat Heart Cells through an α_1-Adrenergic Receptor and Induction of Beating through an α_1- and β_1-Adrenergic Receptor Interaction: Evidence for Independent Regulation of Growth and Beating.
Paul Simpson **884**

BRIEF COMMUNICATIONS

The Independent Effects of Oxygen Radical Scavengers on Canine Infarct Size: Reduction by Superoxide Dismutase but not Catalase.
Steven W. Werns, Michael J. Shea, Edward M. Driscoll, Christopher Cohen, Gerald D. Abrams, Bertram Pitt, and Benedict R. Lucchesi **895**

Direct Observation of the "Oxygen Paradox" in Single Rat Ventricular Myocytes.
Michael D. Stern, Ann M. Chien, Maurizio C. Capogrossi, Don J. Pelto, and Edward G. Lakatta **899**

LETTERS TO THE EDITOR **904**

NEWS FROM THE AMERICAN HEART ASSOCIATION 906
VOLUME AUTHOR INDEX 912
VOLUME SUBJECT INDEX 914

Circulation Research JANUARY 1985 VOL. 56 NO. 1
An Official Journal of the American Heart Association

Two Distinct Effects of Oxygen on Vascular Tone in Isolated Porcine Coronary Arteries

Gabor Rubanyi and Richard J. Paul
From the Department of Physiology, University of Cincinnati, College of Medicine, Cincinnati, Ohio

SUMMARY. The relation between P_{O_2} and vessel tone was studied in isolated porcine left descending coronary artery rings. Porcine left descending coronary artery mounted isometrically and equilibrated in Krebs-bicarbonate solution (37°C, pH 7.4, when gassed with 95% oxygen + 5% carbondioxide) exhibited spontaneous basal tone. Decreasing bath P_{O_2} to 40%, 20%, and 12% elicited sustained increases in basal tension which were reversible, ranging between 10% and 20% of the contraction induced by 40 mM potassium chloride. Further decreases in P_{O_2} to near zero (anoxia) resulted in relaxation to baseline. Cyclooxygenase inhibitors indomethacin (5.5×10^{-6} M), aspirin (5×10^{-5} M), and meclofenamate (10^{-5} M) decreased vascular tone and totally prevented coronary vasoconstriction induced by lowering bath P_{O_2} to 12% or 40% but did not affect anoxic vasorelaxation. Neither basal tone nor the vasoconstriction induced by decreases in bath P_{O_2} were influenced by the antihistaminergic drug pyribenzamine (10^{5} M) or by the α-adrenergic blocker phentolamine (10^{-6}). Isoproterenol (10^{-9} to 10^{-8} M) or an elevation of the bath potassium concentration from 5.9 to 11 mM significantly augmented coronary vasoconstriction induced by lowering bath P_{O_2} from 95% to 40%. Elevation of the bath potassium chloride concentration to 40 mM further increased isometric force but inhibited the vasoconstriction in response to decreasing P_{O_2} from 95% to 40%. Anoxia relaxed contractions induced by 40 mM potassium chloride, histamine, or ouabain. The data suggest the existence of two distinct oxygen-sensitive mechanisms in porcine coronary arteries, both of which regulate vascular tone. One is activated at relative high P_{O_2} values (10–40%), and the vasoconstriction induced by this mechanism is mediated by vascular prostaglandin synthesis. The other is expressed at low P_{O_2} values (near zero), and the depression of mechanical activity by this mechanism may be related to limitation of oxidative energy metabolism. The first mechanism can be augmented by β-adrenoceptor stimulation indicative of an interaction between vascular prostaglandin synthesis and β-adrenergic mechanisms in the coronary artery wall. **(*Circ Res 56: 1–10, 1985*)**

It is well documented that mechanical tension in some vascular smooth muscle preparations is sensitive to organ bath oxygen tension (Carrier et al., 1964; Smith and Vane, 1966; Detar and Bohr, 1968; Fay, 1971; Gellai et al., 1973; Chance et al., 1977; Coburn, 1977; Coburn et al., 1979; Shepherd and Vanhoutte, 1979; Needleman and Isakson, 1980; Singer et al., 1981). Pittman and Duling (1973) provided data and a mathematical model which suggested that the oxygen sensitivity of in vitro artery strips is the result of an anoxic core within each strip in the muscle bath. Pittman and Duling's model is based on the premise that the anoxic core limits oxidative energy generation, which in turn limits the mechanical tension development. Coburn's experiments in rabbit aortic strips, however, produced evidence which was not consistent with the suggestion that the vascular oxygen sensor is the mitochondrial respiratory chain (Coburn, 1977; Coburn et al., 1979). Mechanical tension was still affected by alteration in organ bath P_{O_2} after inhibition of detectable oxygen uptake by cyanide treatment. It was suggested that there is an oxygen-sensitive system other than electron transport chain which regulates vascular smooth muscle tension. The nature of this oxygen sensitivity is still unknown.

There are various reports throughout the literature to the effect that, in response to changes in oxygen tension, alterations in the rate of prostaglandin (PG) biosynthesis within the vessel wall *appear* to be determinants of coronary arterial tone (Kalsner, 1975, 1976, 1977; Needleman et al., 1977; Roberts et al., 1981). These studies (though restricted to bovine coronary arteries only) support Coburn's theory that there is an oxygen sensitivity in the coronary vessel wall which is not related to the respiratory chain, and suggest that it may be linked to vascular prostagladin synthesis. However, because the responses observed in these studies to decreases in

Po_2 were in the direction of vasodilation, a separation of the underlying mechanism(s) is not straightforward. Thus, the existence of an oxygen-sensitive system different from the respiratory chain is yet controversial.

Based on preliminary experiments on the relation between muscle tension and bath Po_2 (Rubanyi and Paul, 1983), it appeared that the porcine coronary artery could be ideally suited to demonstrate distinct responses to oxygen. In the present study, the coexistence of two distinct responses to decreases in bath Po_2 is described in isolated porcine coronary artery rings. They were identified and separated from each other by the different bath Po_2 ranges, by the direction of mechanical responses, and by their differential sensitivity to cyclooxygenase inhibitor drugs.

An unusual and novel characteristic of the response at high Po_2 suggested by our results is that it not only involves vascular prostaglandin metabolism, but also involves interaction with β-adrenergic mechanisms. A characterization of this interaction between prostaglandin biosynthesis and β-adrenergic mechanisms suggested that it may underlie the "paradox" reversal of β-adrenergic responses under ischemic conditions (Moore and Parratt, 1973; Barcia et al., 1976; Vatner et al., 1977), and thus play a role in the development of coronary vasospasm.

Methods

Preparation of Arterial Rings

Pig hearts obtained promptly after slaughter were drained of blood and immersed in ice-cold (4°C) modified Krebs-bicarbonate solution. The distal portions of the left anterior descending coronary artery were carefully dissected out (maximum, within 30 minutes after slaughter) and placed in cold Krebs-bicarbonate solution in a Petri dish. Arteries were then cleaned of fat and adhering connective tissue. Care was taken to avoid stretching. Most of the arteries that were used had an outside diameter of 1.5–2.0 mm. The arteries were cut into rings 5 mm long.

Recording of Muscle Tension

Arterial rings were suspended in a water-jacketed muscle chamber filled with 70 ml of Krebs-bicarbonate solution maintained at 37°C and gassed with 95% O_2, 5% CO_2 from a fritted glass outlet at the bottom of the chamber. Each arterial ring was suspended on a pair of stainless-steel hooks, one of which was fixed to a plate inside the chamber and the other to a Kistler-Morse DSK force transducer. The transducer was attached to a rack and pinion device above the chamber in order to adjust the length of the muscle ring. Tension was measured isometrically and recorded (Linear instrument 585 recorder). The muscle chamber was filled with Krebs-bicarbonate solution at the top of the chamber and washing was accomplished by allowing solutions to drain at the bottom of the chamber.

Recording of Bath O_2-Tension

The Po_2 of the bathing medium was continuously measured using a Clark-type oxygen electrode (YSI 5331) immersed into the bathing solution and was recorded on the Linear Instrument recorder in parallel with isometric muscle tension. Note that the actual time course of changes in Po_2 is shown representatively in Figure 3 only, whereas Figures 1, 2, 4, and 5 schematically show the initial and steady state Po_2 values. The average response time to attain 90% of a new steady state Po_2 was 3.7 ± 0.3 minutes and to the steady state was 8.2 ± 0.5 minutes.

Equilibration of Arterial Rings

Arterial rings were equilibrated in Krebs-solution gassed with 95% O_2, 5% CO_2 for 2 hours at their optimal length [at a resting (unstimulated) tension of approximately 100 mN (10 g)]. We selected this load on the basis of preliminary experiments showing that rings equilibrated in this manner responded to high potassium (40 mM) depolarization with maximal active tension development. Since porcine coronary artery (PCA) rings undergo stress relaxation, they were restretched to obtain 100 mN at 30-minute intervals, at which time the chamber was filled with fresh Krebs-bicarbonate solution. Stress relaxation usually decreased within 1 hour.

Solutions

The modified mammalian Krebs-bicarbonate solution used for preparation of tissues and as the bathing medium had the following composition (mM): NaCl (118), KCl (4.7), $CaCl_2 \cdot H_2O$ (2.5), KH_2PO_4 (1.18), $MgSO_4$ (1.18), glucose (5.5), and $NaHCO_3$ (25). All the constituents (Sigma) were dissolved in distilled, demineralized water. Increasing extracellular K^+ concentration was carried out by adding KCl from a concentrate (3 M) to the muscle bath.

The bathing medium was gassed with mixtures containing 95% O_2, 5% CO_2; 40% O_2, 55% N_2, 5% CO_2; 20% O_2, 75% N_2, 5% CO_2; 12% O_2, 83% N_2, 5% CO_2 or 95% N_2, 5% CO_2, giving a pH of 7.4 in the Krebs-bicarbonate buffer solution at 37°C. When changing from one gas mixture to another, the solution in the muscle chamber was exchanged for one pre-equilibrated with the new gas mixture.

Chemicals

Stock solutions of reagent grade drugs were prepared as follows: acetylsalicyclic acid (ASA; aspirin, dissolved in Krebs solution, 1 mg/ml); histamine (dissolved in H_2O, 10^{-2} M); indomethacin (dissolved in Krebs-solution, 0.2 mg/ml); isoproterenol (dissolved in H_2O; 10^{-4} M); sodium meclofenamate (dissolved in H_2O; 10^{-2} M); sodium nitroprusside (dissolved in H_2O; 10^{-2} M); ouabain octahydrate (dissolved in H_2O; 5×10^{-3} M); papaverine HCl (dissolved in H_2O; 10^{-2} M); pyribenzamine (dissolved in H_2O, 10^{-2} M); phentolamine (dissolved in H_2O, 10^{-3} M); *l*-propranolol (dissolved in H_2O, 10^{-3} M); and *d*-propranolol (dissolved in H_2O, 10^{-3} M). Drugs were added to the muscle bath in aliquots up to 700 μl.

Calculations

Muscle contraction was measured as the increase in tension above the initial baseline. Responses were calculated as active force development related to cross-section of the vascular ring (mN/mm^2), or expressed as the percent of the 40 mM KCl-induced test contraction. At the end of an experiment, the rings were cut open and the length (l) and the width, as well as the blotted weight (blot wt), were measured. Vessel cross-section area was calculated as 2 × blot wt/l·1.06 (Paul, 1983). Data are reported as mean values with standard errors of the mean. Results were analyzed by Student's *t*-test with $P < 0.05$ considered statistically significant.

Results

Characteristics of Isometric Contraction in Porcine Coronary Arteries

During the equilibration period, after the tissue length for optimal force development (see Methods) had been adjusted, in many, but not all arteries (in 26 out of 35), a spontaneous development of force took place. This force is often referred to as "basal tone," which we take to mean that part of the total isometric force at a given length which is attributable to active force generation by the contractile elements in the absence of exogenous stimulation. The spontaneous force which developed during equilibration was variable. In the majority of cases ($n = 19$) it was small, averaging 22.5 ± 3.5% of the contractile force elicited by KCl (40 mM). However, in an appreciable number of cases ($n = 7$), this spontaneously developed force averaged 69.7 ± 7.7% of a KCl contracture. The basis for this difference is unknown. In all cases studied, however, the spontaneous force was abolished by prolonged anoxia, i.e., 2.4 ± 1.2% ($n = 7$) of the spontaneously developed force remained following prolonged (20–30 minutes) exposure to N_2. Similarly, isoproterenol (10^{-7} M) essentially abolished the spontaneously developed force with 2.5 ± 1.1% ($n = 10$) remaining following exposure. Similar results were obtained with papaverine (10^{-4} M) or sodium-nitroprusside (10^{-4} M). Because of these characteristics consistent with the definition given above, the spontaneously developed force will be referred to as basal tone.

The isometric force generated by 40 mM KCl above the existing basal tone was 39.6 ± 3.4 mN/mm^2 ($n = 29$), which is consistent with previously published values (Paul, 1983). It should be noted that other agonists can elicit up to twice this active force (Paul et al., 1979). Thus, basal tone is only in the order of 10% of the maximum isometric force. It is also noteworthy that the level of basal tone was only weakly correlated with the force elicited by KCl ($r = 0.48$; $P < 0.05$; $n = 19$).

Responses of Porcine Coronary Artery to Decreases in Bath P_{O_2}

Anoxia

Figure 1 depicts the typical responses of porcine coronary arterial rings to alteration in O_2 tension (P_{O_2}) of the Krebs-bicarbonate solution. When the P_{O_2} of the bathing medium was decreased by changing the gas mixture from 95% O_2 to 95% N_2 (anoxia), tension of the PCA ring increased transiently (phase 1). After approximately 5 minutes, tension began to fall (phase 2) and reached its lowest level in about 20 minutes (not shown in the figure, see Fig. 2). Similarly, after an initial transient augmentation, anoxia abolished contractions evoked by histamine (10^{-4} M), ouabain (10^{-5} M), or high K^+ (40 mM) (data not shown, five tissues studied for each case). Reoxygenation with 95% O_2 during phase 1 or shortly after the onset of phase 2 (i.e., before total relaxation of the ring), resulted in a brief relaxation (phase I) followed by contraction (phase II) to levels higher than the original basal tone and, finally, by relaxation to the original tone. The mean value of the peak vasoconstriction elicited by anoxia in 13 PCA rings in the absence of exogenous stimulation was 9.9 ± 1.5% ($P < 0.01$) of the control contracture induced by 40 mM KCl.

Hypoxia

When the P_{O_2} of the bathing medium was decreased by changing the gas mixture from 95% O_2 to 12% O_2 (hypoxia), tension of PCA rings increased as well (Fig. 1), but in contrast to anoxia, hypoxia induced a sustained contraction. Only when the gas mixture was returned back to 95% O_2 did the ring relax to the initial level of basal tone. The mean value of the hypoxia-induced vasoconstriction of 10 PCA rings was 11.3 ± 1.2% ($P < 0.01$) of the control contraction induced by addition of 40 mM KCl.

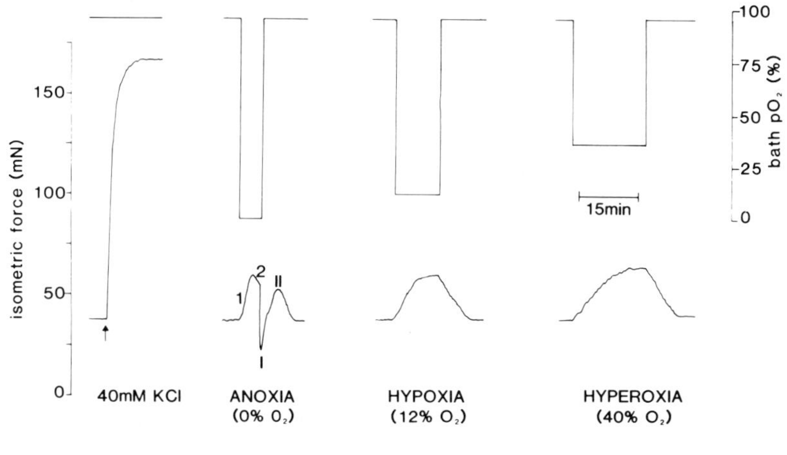

FIGURE 1. *Responses of porcine coronary artery rings to changes in bath P_{O_2}. Reduction in oxygen tension by gassing the bathing medium with 95% N_2, 5% CO_2 (anoxia) induced a transient contraction (phase 1) followed by relaxation (phase 2). Reoxygenation by 95% O_2, 5% CO_2 resulted in a relaxation (phase I) followed by contraction (phase II) above baseline. The decrease of bath P_{O_2} to 12% (hypoxia) or 40% elicited a sustained contraction (10–15% of 40 mM KCl-induced test contracture, lefthand side of the figure), which was reversible upon reoxygenation with 95% O_2.*

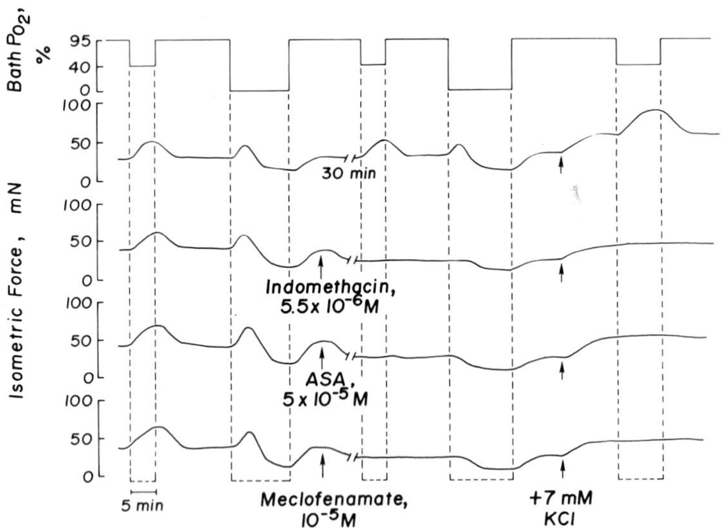

FIGURE 2. *Effect of inhibition of prostaglandin synthesis on mechanical responses of porcine coronary artery rings to changes in bath P_{O_2}. Treatment of the PCA rings with indomethacin (5.5×10^{-6}M), aspirin (ASA) (5×10^{-5} M) or meclofenamate (10^{-5} M) induced a relaxation of basal tone and prevented vasoconstriction induced by reducing bath P_{O_2} to 40%, but did not prevent anoxic vasorelaxation. Note that restoration of level of isometric force to the level of the previous basal tone by elevation of bath K^+ concentration from 5.9 to 12.9 mM did not restore the vasoconstriction induced by lowering bath P_{O_2} from 95 to 40%.*

Decrease in Bath P_{O_2} from 95% to 40%

To examine whether the transient (anoxia) or sustained (hypoxia) contraction of PCA rings induced by varying bath P_{O_2} was related to mitochondrial respiration limited by oxygen, we studied the effect on basal coronary tone of decreasing bath P_{O_2} from 95% to 40%. PCA rings responded to a decrease in bath P_{O_2} from 95% to 40% with a sustained contraction (Fig. 1). When the gas mixture was changed back to 95% O_2, the rings relaxed and reached the level of tone observed prior to the decrease in P_{O_2} to 40%. The average value of coronary vasoconstriction induced by the P_{O_2} change in 10 PCA rings was 14.9 ± 2.3% ($P < 0.01$) of the KCl-induced control contraction. These results were similar to the initial phase observed in the response to anoxia and the response to hypoxia. It is of interest to note that the magnitude of the response to a decrease in P_{O_2} was not correlated with the level of basal tone measured prior to the decrease in P_{O_2} ($r = 0.22$; NS; $n = 24$).

Effect of Cyclooxygenase, Adrenergic, and Histaminergic Inhibition on the Changes in Vascular Tone Induced by a Decrease of Bath P_{O_2}.

In five experiments, four rings cut from the same coronary artery were suspended in individual muscle baths. After P_{O_2} cycles of 95-40-95% and 95-0-95% (anoxia), rings number 2, 3, and 4 were treated with the cyclooxygenase inhibitors, indomethacin (5.5×10^{-6} M), aspirin (5×10^{-5} M), or meclofenamate (10^{-5} M), respectively, while the first ring served as control. As shown in a typical recording in Figure 2, all of the cyclooxygenase inhibitors decreased basal tone (by approximately 50%) and totally abolished the sustained vasoconstrictor response induced by a decrease in bath P_{O_2} from 95 to 40%, and the initial transient increase in tone during anoxia. None of the inhibitor drugs affected the vasorelaxation to baseline induced by prolonged anoxia (Fig. 2). Although basal tone was reduced by these agents, the complete inhibition of the vasoconstrictor response to decreasing bath P_{O_2} cannot be ascribed to a generalized inhibition of contractility since, in the presence of these agents, the magnitude of a KCl contracture was unaffected. Moreover, the restoration of tension to the previous basal tone levels by an elevation of bath K^+ concentration from 5.9 to 12.9 mM did not restore the vasoconstriction induced by decreasing bath P_{O_2} (Fig. 2).

To investigate the possible role of the release of other vasoconstrictor substances in the hypoxic mechanical response, we tested the effect of histamine and catecholamine inhibitors in five PCA rings. As shown in a typical recording in Figure 3, neither basal tone nor the reversible vasoconstrictor response to the change from 95% to 40% O_2 in the PCA strip was influenced by the antihistamine (H_1-receptor antagonist) pyribenzamine (10^{-5} M), or by the α-adrenergic inhibitor, phentolamine (10^{-6} M).

Isoproterenol and Increasing Extracellular K^+ Concentration Alter Coronary Vasoconstriction Induced by a Decrease in Bath P_{O_2} from 95 to 40%

Treatment of PCA rings with increasing doses (3×10^{-9} to 10^{-8} M) of isoproterenol (ISO) relaxed basal tension progressively and significantly augmented the vasoconstriction induced by decreasing bath P_{O_2}. The P_{O_2} response was depressed at a higher isoproterenol concentration (10^{-7} M) (Fig. 4). The potentiating effect of 10^{-8} M isoproterenol was statistically significant both when expressed as percent of control (Fig. 7) or as the absolute isometric force increment (Table 1).

Elevation of the K^+ concentration in the Krebs-bicarbonate solution from 5.9 to 11 mM increased isometric force, which reached a maximum approximately 20 minutes after the addition of KCl. The vasoconstrictor response of the PCA ring evoked by decreasing the bath P_{O_2} to near 0% (anoxia), 10%

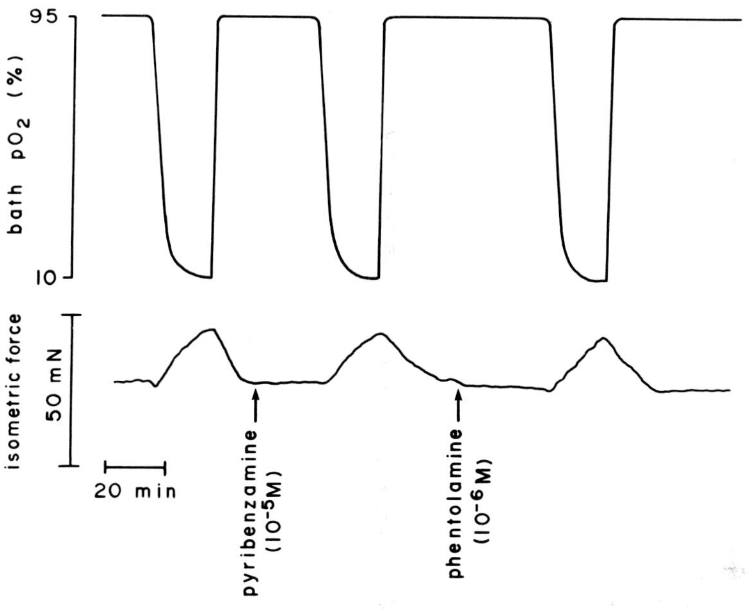

FIGURE 3. *Effect of histamine and adrenergic-receptor antagonists on mechanical responses of a porcine coronary artery ring to a decrease in bath* Po_2 *from 95 to 40%* O_2*. Pyribenzamine (histamine-antagonist) and phentolamine (α-adrenergic antagonist) did not influence basal tone or vasoconstriction induced by a decrease of bath* Po_2*.*

(hypoxia), and 40% was significantly higher under this condition (Fig. 5). Elevation of extracellular K^+ concentration to 40 mM caused a rapid contracture of the PCA ring. The response of the PCA ring to decreasing the bath Po_2 to 40%, 10%, and 0% in the presence of 40 mM K^+ was significantly diminished when compared to the response in the presence of 5.9 or 11 mM K^+. It should be noted that this diminished response is not due to a saturation of the absolute isometric force-generating capacity by 40 mM K^+. Histamine (10^{-4} M) for example, can substantially increase isometric force (+32.4 ± 2.9%; $n = 5$) when added to a 40 mM K^+-induced contracture. The mean values of the responses to a decrease in bath Po_2 from 95 to 40% of 10 PCA rings (expressed as percent of the control response or as the absolute force increment) in the presence of 11 mM K^+ and in the presence of 40 mM K^+ are summarized in Figure 7 and Table 1, respectively.

Addition of 10^{-7} M isoproterenol to the muscle bath in the presence of 40 mM K^+ relaxed the PCA ring (Fig. 6A). When relaxation attained a steady state (~ 20 minutes), the decrease in bath Po_2 from 95% to 40% was repeated. The vasoconstrictor response of the PCA ring to decreasing the bath Po_2 from 95% to 40% O_2 in the presence of 40 mM K^+ was significantly increased by isoproterenol (Fig. 6A). The mean value of the response of 10 PCA rings in the presence of 10^{-7} M isoproterenol and 40 mM K^+ are summarized in Figure 7 and Table 1.

In order to study the possible role of endogenous norepinephrine release on the increased response to a decrease in bath Po_2 from 95 to 40% elicited by elevation of bath K^+ concentration to 11 mM, we examined the effect of β-adrenergic receptor blockade by *l*-propranolol. Treatment of PCA rings with *l*-propranolol (10^{-6} M) caused partial relaxation of a contraction induced by 11 mM K^+ and, in addition, significantly decreased coronary vasoconstriction induced by the reduction of bath Po_2 (Fig. 6B). A similar concentration of *d*-propranolol was ineffective (Fig. 7). The mean values of the responses of five PCA rings are summarized in Figure 7 and Table 1.

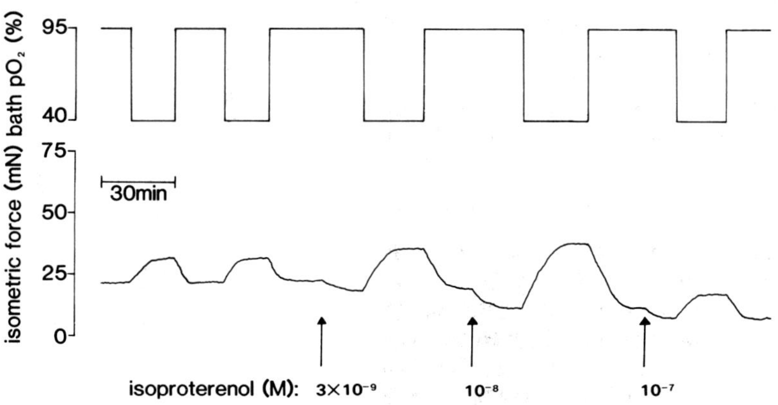

FIGURE 4. *Typical responses of an isolated porcine coronary artery ring to a decrease in bath* Po_2 *from 95 to 40%* O_2 *in the absence and presence of increasing concentrations (3 × 10^{-9} to 10^{-7} M) of isoproterenol.*

TABLE 1

Effect of $[K^+]_o$, Isoproterenol and *l*-Propranolol on Isometric Force and Vasoconstriction in Response to a Decrease in Bath Po_2 from 95 to 40% (Δforce) in Isolated Porcine Coronary Artery Rings

Experimental conditions	Force (95% O_2) (mN/mm^2)	ΔForce (95–40% O_2) (mN/mm^2)
5.9 mM K^+ (basal)	31.7 ± 5.5 (15)	+4.7 ± 0.9* (8)
5.9 mM K^+ + isoproterenol (10^{-8} M)	20.2 ± 3.5* (5)	+7.5 ± 1.1† (5)
11 mM K^+	41.4 ± 3.8* (14)	+8.4 ± 1.3† (12)
11 mM K^+ + *l*-propranolol (10^{-6} M)	34.2 ± 4.3 (5)	+4.2 ± 0.8 (5)
11 mM K^+ + *d*-propranolol (10^{-6} M)	40.5 ± 3.6* (5)	+8.1 ± 1.4† (5)
40 mM K^+	71.3 ± 6.2* (14)	+1.2 ± 0.3† (12)
40 mM K^+ + isoproterenol (10^{-7} M)	57.4 ± 3.5* (10)	+5.2 ± 0.6 (10)

Values are expressed as the mean ± SEM; numbers in parentheses represent numbers of experiments.

* Statistically significant difference ($P < 0.05$) from control (5.9 mM K^+) values.

† Statistically significant difference ($P < 0.05$) from Δforce obtained in the presence of 5.9 mM K^+.

Discussion

Coexistence of Two Distinct Oxygen Tension Responses in Porcine Coronary Arteries

In the present study, the coexistence of two distinct oxygen-sensitive responses was described in the isolated porcine coronary artery. If the Po_2 of the bathing solutions was decreased to near zero, the active mechanical tension developed under basal conditions (basal tone) or when stimulated by exogenous agents was relaxed.This vasorelaxation was not sensitive to cyclooxygenase inhibition, indicating it is unlikely that the effect of low Po_2 on vascular tone was mediated by vasodilator prostaglandins. The most probable explanation for this phenomenon is the "classical" mechanism which is coupled to the mitochondrial respiratory chain. According to this theory, the inhibition of mechanical tension development below a critical bath Po_2 level is the result of the development of an anoxic core in the preparation, which limits oxidative energy generation. Although ATP production via glycolysis continues under anoxic conditions in this tissue (Paul et al., 1979), Paul (1983) has shown recently that it provides energy primarily for active ion transport processes across the plasma membrane, and isometric force development is dependent on oxidative energy production in isolated porcine coronary artery rings. An alternative explanation is that anoxia-induced relaxation may be due to a stimulation of ouabain-sensitive electrogenic Na-K pump, as suggested by Detar (1980). This can be excluded, in so far as a decrease in bath Po_2 to near zero relaxed porcine coronary artery rings preincubated with 10^{-5} M ouabain (Rubanyi and Paul, unpublished observations).

The present experiments demonstrate the existence of another O_2-sensitive response in isolated PCA rings. The presence of this second oxygen-sensitive response in the vessel wall could be identified and separated from the first by the following characteristics: (1) it affects coronary vascular tone at relatively high Po_2 levels (well above the critical Po_2 value, see below), (2) the direction of vascular tone changes was opposite to that observed at low Po_2 (vasoconstriction vs. vasorelaxation), and (3) the vasoconstriction induced by this oxygen-sensitive system was abolished by cyclooxygenase inhibitors.

The sustained contraction observed on reduction of the Po_2 from 95 to 40% suggests the existence of an oxygen-sensitive system in the porcine coronary vascular wall which is different from the respiratory chain. Whereas the present studies cannot unequivocally rule out the respiratory chain, the observed effects occur in a Po_2 range that makes this unlikely. In porcine coronary artery stimulated with KCl, both force and the rate of oxygen consumption decline when the bath Po_2 is decreased below 7.8% (Paul

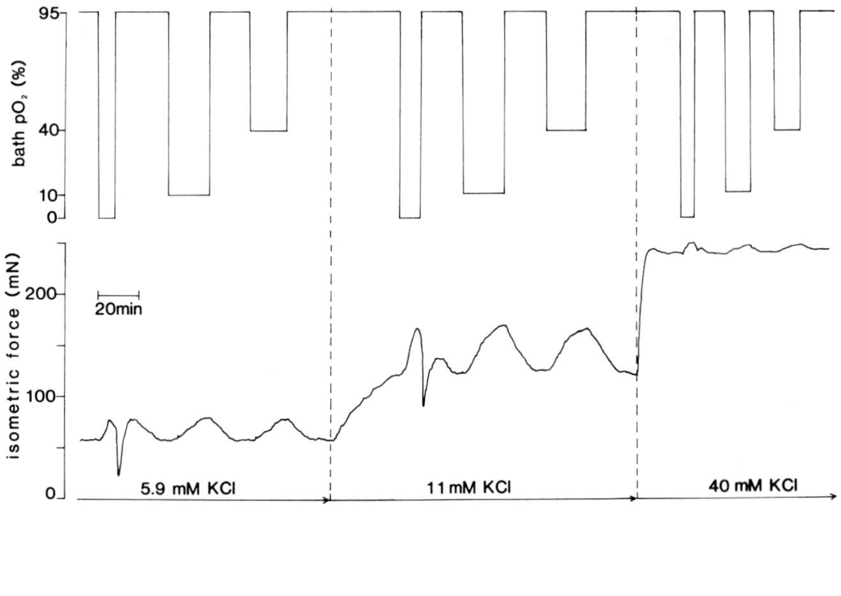

FIGURE 5. *Typical responses of an isolated porcine coronary artery ring to decreasing bath Po_2 [from 95 to 0 (anoxia), 10 (hypoxia), and 40% O_2] at various extracellular potassium concentrations (5.9, 11 and 40 mM).*

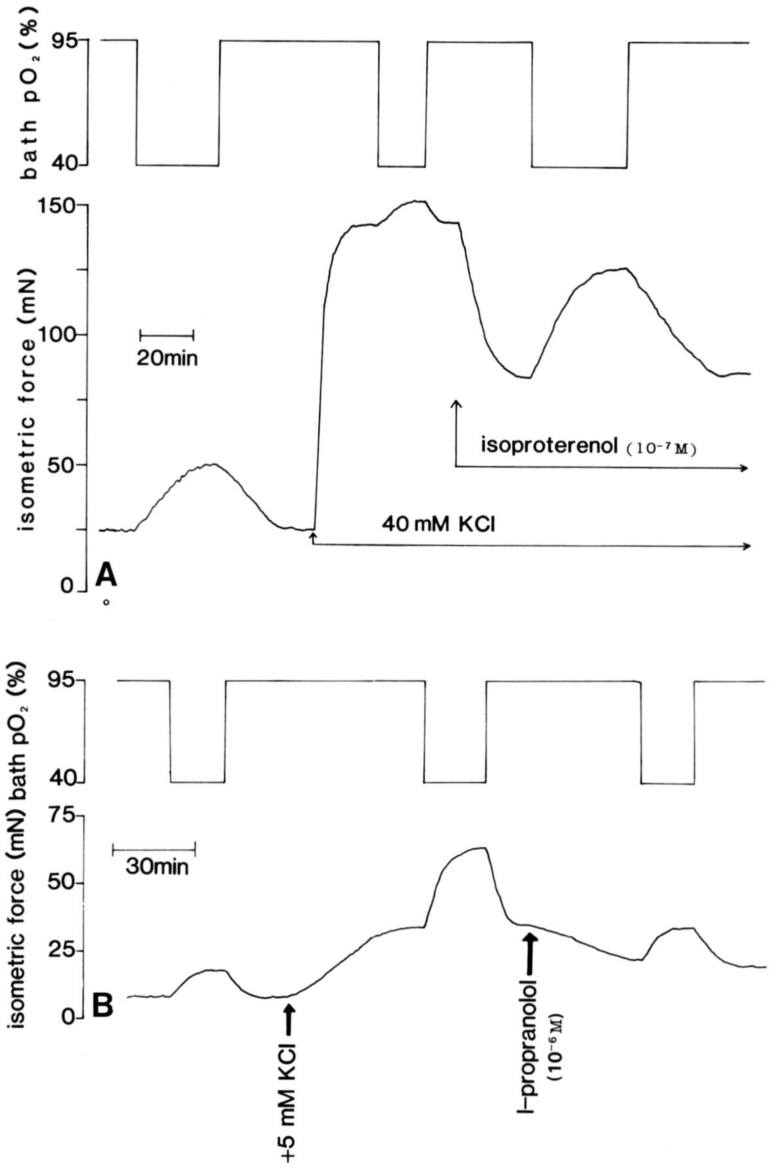

Figure 6. *A: experimental record showing that β-adrenergic receptor stimulation (isoproterenol; 10^{-7} M) restores the vasoconstriction induced by decreasing bath Po_2 (from 95% to 40% O_2) in the presence of 40 mM KCl in an isolated porcine coronary artery ring. B: β-adrenergic receptor blockade (l-propranolol; 10^{-6} M) eliminates the augmentation by elevation of K^+ concentration (from 5.9 to 11 mM) of the bath Po_2 decrease (from 95 to 40% O_2) induced vasoconstriction in an isolated porcine coronary artery ring.*

et al., 1979). A value in this range is consistent with the hypothesis that an anoxic core begins to develop at Po_2 levels below this value, the so-called "critical Po_2" (Pittman and Duling, 1973; Glück and Paul, 1977). Though the absolute value of the critical Po_2 may be subject to some uncertainty, for Po_2 levels in the range between 40% and 100%, the presence of anoxic regions is highly unlikely. In addition, tissue Po_2 can be calculated to be substantially higher than that reported to be rate limiting for mitochondrial respiration (Chance et al., 1977). Our present data support Coburn's hypothesis (Coburn, 1977; Coburn et al., 1979) and the observations of Hellstrand et al. (1977) that there is an oxygen-sensitive system other than the electron transport chain in the vessel wall which regulates vascular smooth muscle tone. Among the previous demonstrations of responses to decreases in Po_2, there is only one, in which the development of an anoxic core in the vascular tissue can likely be excluded. Kalsner (1977) observed vasorelaxation and an increased synthesis of prostaglandin-like material in isolated bovine coronary artery strips when Po_2 was decreased from 515 to 112 mm Hg. However, an increase in vascular tone by changes in Po_2 in this relatively high range has not been demonstrated.

In order to avoid a hypoxic core in isolated vascular preparations, the vast majority of such in vitro experiments are performed at high, unphysiological oxygen concentrations. The facts that (1) a distinct oxygen-sensitive response could be demonstrated at high O_2 concentrations, and (2) no further contractions were observed when Po_2 was decreased from the physiological 20% to 15 or 10% (data not shown), suggest that under physiological conditions this response is fully activated. Changes in conditions which may affect this oxygen-sensitive system, such as activation of phospholipase A_2 (cf. Franson et al., 1979), may thus contribute to the local regulation of coronary arterial tone. These findings at

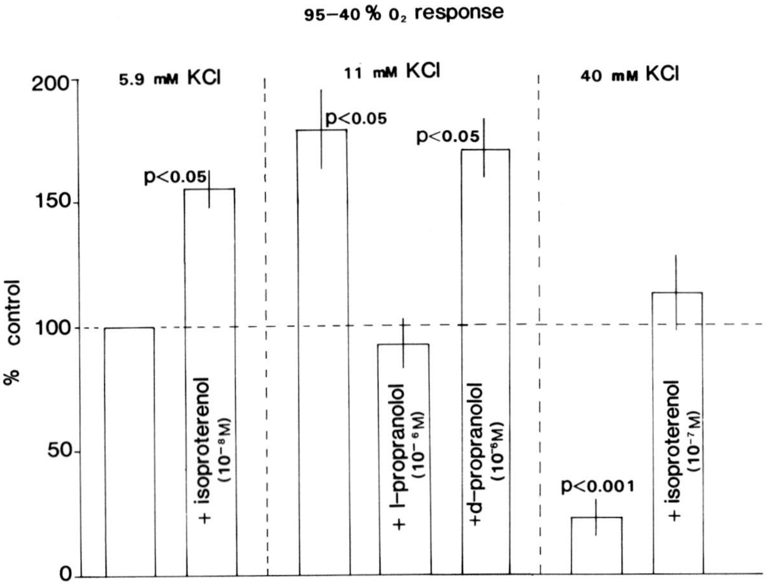

FIGURE 7. *Summary of the effects of β-adrenergic receptor stimulation (isoproterenol) and β-blockade (l-propranolol) on bath* Po_2 *decrease (from 95 to 40%* O_2*) induced vasoconstriction of isolated porcine coronary arteries in the presence of various extracellular potassium concentrations. The effects are expressed as a percent of the control response. Columns represent the mean of at least five experiments, and bars represent the* SEM.

the same time indicate that suppression of this mechanism by high O_2 concentrations should be considered when data obtained in in vitro experiments are related to physiological in vivo conditions.

Because the vasoconstriction induced by decreasing Po_2 from 95 to 40% could be totally prevented by indomethancin, aspirin, and meclofenamate, we suggest that this oxygen-sensitive response is related to vascular prostaglandin (PG) biosynthesis via the cyclooxygenase pathway. This is supported by the similar effects of these different cyclooxygenase inhibitors. The final experimental demonstration of this hypothesis, however, must await the chemical determination of endogenous arachidonic acid metabolites in the coronary arteries during changes in Po_2.

Previous studies on isolated bovine coronary artery preparations revealed that continuous synthesis and release of PGs (most probably PGI_2) contributes to the regulation of vascular tone in this vessel (Kalsner, 1975, 1976, 1977; Needleman et al., 1977; Needleman and Isakson, 1980; Roberts et al., 1981). These studies on only one (bovine) preparation lead to the generalized view that local production of PGs in coronary vascular tissue causes vasodilation (Needleman and Isakson, 1980) and inhibition or alteration of the prostaglandin release mechanism (by anoxia under in vitro conditions) was implicated in the etiology of coronary vasospasm (Kalsner, 1977; Needleman and Isakson, 1980).

Our data show that—in contrast to the results for bovine coronary artery—in porcine coronary rings, inhibition of PG synthesis leads to relaxation of basal tone, suggesting that a continuous release of vasoconstrictor cyclooxygenase product(s) contributes to maintenance of basal tone in PCA. In addition, our data suggest that a decrease in bath Po_2 could lead to an increased synthesis of this product resulting in vasoconstriction, as the vasoconstrictor response to Po_2 decreases could be prevented by indomethacin, aspirin, or meclofenamate. Although both basal tone and the vasoconstrictor response to a decrease in Po_2 were diminished by these PG synthesis inhibitors, control experiments indicated that this was not a reflection of a nonspecific inhibition of contractility. Neither initial basal tone nor the changes in basal tone induced by the antagonists were correlated with the responses to decreases in Po_2. Furthermore, the possibility that the cyclooxygenase inhibitors prevented coronary vasoconstriction due to a general reduction in force can be excluded because (1) restoration of force to the previous levels of basal tone in the presence of indomethacin, aspirin or meclofenamate did not restore the vasoconstriction induced by a decrease in Po_2, and (2) both a *decrease* in basal tone or the force induced by 40 mM KCl by isoproterenol and an *increase* in force by elevation of extracellular K^+ concentration (to 11 mM) significantly augmented the isometric force induced by lowering bath Po_2 from 95 to 40%. The present assumption of in situ synthesis and release of vasoconstrictor substance via cyclooxygenase pathway in PCA rings is substantiated by previous data, which showed that both the labile endoperoxides and the primary prostaglandins synthesized from them induce vasoconstriction in the porcine coronary artery (Needleman and Isakson, 1980).

Possible Interactions of Vascular Prostaglandin Synthesis and β-Adrenergic Mechanisms in the Coronary Arterial Wall

Pretreatment of PCA rings with phentolamine (α-adrenergic blockade) or with pyribenzamine (which inhibits histamine-induced contracture in this preparation) did not influence coronary vasoconstriction induced by decreasing bath Po_2 from 95% to 40%. However, stimulation of β-adrenoceptors by isoproterenol significantly augmented the coronary vasoconstriction induced by a decrease in bath Po_2. These findings suggest that stimulation of β-adrenergic receptors may have two opposite effects in this tissue: first, it induces the well known vasorelaxation, and, second, it potentiates the vasoconstriction induced by a decrease in bath Po_2. Previous reports of "paradox" reversal of β-adrenergic responses under ischemic conditions in the in situ coronary circulation (Moore and Parrat, 1973; Barcia et al., 1976; Vatner et al., 1977) support the hypothesis that stimulation of β-adrenergic receptors may favor the development of coronary vasospasm.

Theoretically, the following equally possible mechanisms may be responsible for this potentiation: (1) β-adrenoceptor stimulation may facilitate the production of vasoconstrictor cyclooxygenase metabolite(s); (2) β-adrenoceptor stimulation may augment vascular smooth muscle sensitivity to vasoconstrictor prostanoids; and (3) cyclooxygenase products may depress β-adrenergic relaxation which augments their direct vasoconstrictor action in the presence of isoproterenol. Although recent studies suggest that the latter mechanism may play a role (Rubanyi and Paul, 1984), the present experiments do not allow one to distinguish between these potential mechanisms. Interactions between O_2-sensitive changes in vascular tone and β-adrenergic mechanisms have already been reported for isolated canine coronary arteries (Henry et al., 1978; Borda et al., 1980). However, in contrast to the present observations, in this study, propranolol completely inhibited the vasoconstriction induced by anoxia. These results, however, could not be confirmed in recent experiments (Rimele and Vanhoutte, 1984). In addition, the vasoconstriction induced by anoxia in canine coronary arteries is not sensitive to cyclooxygenase inhibitors (Rimele and Vanhoutte, 1984) excluding the involvement of vasoconstrictor prostanoids in that response.

The present experiments have shown that an elevation of the bath K^+ concentration from 5.9 to 11 mM significantly potentiated, but high K^+ depolarization (40 mM K^+) inhibited the vasoconstriction induced by a reduction in bath Po_2 in PCA rings. Similar observations were made by DeMey and Vanhoutte (1983) on isolated canine femoral arteries. They found that a contraction induced by 25 mM K^+ was significantly augmented by hypoxia but responses to 50 mM K^+ were not. Both 11 and 40 mM K^+ caused an increase of vascular tone in PCA rings, but they had different properties; whereas the contraction induced by 11 mM K^+ developed slowly and could be partially inhibited by *l*-propranolol, 40 mM K^+ induced a rapid contraction which was insensitive to β-adrenergic receptor blockade. Similar observations were made by Borda et al. (1980) in the isolated canine coronary artery. They also showed that elevation of external K^+ concentration up to 12–15 mM stimulated the release of endogenous norepinephrine (^{3}H-NE), but higher concentrations (above 20 mM) inhibited ^{3}H-NE release. These authors suggested that coronary contraction elicited by an increase of K^+ up to 15 mM is mediated by the release of NE from adrenergic nerves, since it was accompanied by increase of ^{3}H-NE release and could be inhibited by denervation or β-adrenergic receptor blockade (Borda et al., 1977, 1980).

The present finding of a potentiation of the vasoconstrictor response to decreases in Po_2 induced by β-adrenergic receptor stimulation and these earlier observations indicate that the potentiation of hypoxic vasoconstriction in PCA rings by elevation of K^+ up to 12 mM is likely due to the release of endogenous NE and consequent stimulation of β-adrenergic receptors. This hypothesis is strengthened by the observation that both the vasoconstriction and potentiation of the oxygen sensitive response by 11 mM K^+ were significantly depressed by *l*-propranolol but not by *d*-propranolol in PCA rings. These data, in combination with the observations that, in open-chest animals subjected to coronary ligation, the potassium concentration in blood samples collected from venules in the ischemic zone may exceed 10 mM (Benzing et al., 1971; Downar et al., 1977; Schuchleib et al., 1976) indicate a potential role of hypoxic-ischemic K^+-release from cardiac and coronary vascular cells in the pathogenesis of coronary vasospasm.

The inhibition of coronary vasoconstriction induced by a reduction in bath Po_2 from 95 to 40% by higher K^+, on the other hand, may be explained by three classes of mechanisms: (1) Inhibition of endogenous NE release (as demonstrated by Borda et al., 1980) may decrease β-adrenergic tone, and similar to β-adrenergic blockade by *l*-propranolol can reduce this vasoconstriction response to Po_2 changes from 95 to 40% by eliminating the potentiation exerted by β-adrenergic mechanisms. (2) Depolarization of the vascular cell membrane by high K^+ may directly inhibit the synthesis and/or the vascular effect of the vasoconstrictor PG(s). (3) The cellular mechanism(s) involved in this Po_2 response may require a certain level of cell membrane polarization. The present finding that administration of isoproterenol to high K^+-treated coronary arteries can restore oxygen sensitivity supports the first class of mechanisms. However, these classes are not mutually exclusive, and further studies are needed to resolve the exact nature of high K^+-induced inhibition of this Po_2 response in isolated porcine coronary arteries.

The demonstration that this vascular PG synthesis mediates coronary vasoconstriction induced by a decrease of bath Po_2, and this vasoconstriction can be potentiated by β-adrenergic agonists may indicate that β-adrenergic mechanisms modulate the intrinsic PG-biosynthesis and/or the vascular action of PGs in coronary arteries. Although the exact nature of this interaction is not known, we suggest that under certain conditions (e.g., during hypoxia or ischemia when the coronary vasodilator reserve is maximally utilized) the PG-mediated vasoconstrictor action of β-adrenoceptor stimulation may dominate. This may provide an explanation for the earlier "paradox" findings that β-adrenergic blockade inhibits hypoxic and ischemic coronary vasospasm, and β-adrenergic stimulation causes vasoconstriction under hypoxic/ischemic conditions.

This work was supported in part by NIH 22619 and 23240. RJP is an Established Investigator of the American Heart Association.

Address for reprints: Gabor Rubanyi, M.D., Department of Physiology and Biophysics, Mayo Clinic and Foundation, Rochester, Minnesota 55905.

Received November 11, 1983; accepted for publication September 19, 1984.

References

Barcia F, Borer JS, Capurro N, Kent KM (1976) Propranolol mediated increase in collateral flow during acute myocardial infarction (abstr). Circulation **54 (suppl II):** 156

Benzing VH, Gebert G, Strohm M (1971) Ionenverschiebungen im Myokard des narkotissierten Hundes unter verschiedenen Bedingungen. Verh Dtsch Ges Krieslaufforschung **37:** 353–356

Borda LJ, Schuchleib R, Henry PD (1977) Effects of potassium on isolated canine coronary arteries. Circ Res **41:** 778–786

Borda L, Schuchleib R, Henry PD (1980) Hypoxic contraction of isolated canine coronary artery: Mediation by potassium-dependent exocytosis of norepinephrine. Circ Res **46:** 870–879

Carrier O Jr, Walker JR, Guyton AC (1964) Role of oxygen in autoregulation of blood flow in isolated vessels. Am J Physiol **206:** 951–954

Chance B, Oshino N, Sugano T, Mayevsky A (1977) Basic principles of tissue oxygen determination from mitochondral signals. *In* Oxygen Transport to Tissue, edited by M Reivich, RF Coburn, S Lahiri, B Chance. New York, Plenum Press, pp 277–291

Coburn RF (1977) Oxygen tension sensors in vascular smooth muscle. *In* Tissue Hypoxia and Ischemia, edited by M Reivich, RF Coburn, S Lahiri, B Chance. New York, Plenum Press, pp 101–115

Coburn RF, Grubb B, Aronson RD (1979) Effect of cyanide on oxygen tension dependent mechanical tension in rabbit aorta. Circ Res **44:** 368–378

De Mey JG, Vanhoutte PM (1983) Anoxia and endothelium dependent reactivity of the canine coronary arteries. J Physiol (Lond) **335:** 65–74

Detar R (1980) Mechanism of physiological hypoxia-induced depression of vascular smooth muscle contraction. Am J Physiol **238:** H761–H769

Detar R, Bohr DF (1968) Oxygen and vascular smooth muscle contraction. Am J Physiol **214:** 241–244

Downar E, Janse MJ, Durrer D (1977) The effect of "ischemic" blood on transmembrane potentials of normal porcine ventricular myocardium. Circulation **55:** 455–462

Fay FS (1971) Guinea pig ductus arteriosus. I. Cellular and metabolic basis for oxygen sensitivity. Am J Physiol **221:** 470–479

Franson RC, Pang DC, Weglicki WB (1979) Modulation of lipolytic activity in isolated canine cardiac sarcolemma by isoproterenol and propranolol. Biochem Biophys Res Commun **90:** 956–962

Gellai M, Norton JM, Detar R (1973) Evidence for direct control of coronary vascular tone by oxygen. Circ Res **32:** 279–289

Glück E, Paul RJ (1977) The aerobic metabolism of porcine carotid artery and its relationship to isometric force: Energy cost of isometric contraction. Pflugers Arch **370:** 9–18

Hellstrand P, Johansson B, Norberg K (1977) Mechanical, electrical and biochemical effects of hypoxia and substrate removal on spontaneously active vascular smooth muscle. Acta Physiol Scand **100:** 69–83

Henry PD, Yokoyama M, Fischer S (1978) Hypoxic coronary contraction mediated by $beta_2$-adrenergic receptors (abstr). Am J Cardiol **41:** 357

Kalsner S (1975) Endogenous prostaglandin release contributes directly to coronary artery tone. Can J Physiol Pharmacol **53:** 560–565

Kalsner S (1976) Intrinsic prostaglandin release. A mediator of anoxia-induced relaxation in an isolated coronary artery preparation. Blood Vessels **13:** 155–166

Kalsner S (1977) The effect of hypoxia on prostaglandin output and on tone in isolated coronary arteries. Can J Physiol Pharmacol **55:** 882–887

Moore GE, Parratt JR (1973) Effect of noradrenaline and isoprenaline on blood flow in the acutely ischemic myocardium. Cardiovasc Res **7:** 446–457

Needleman P, Isakson PC (1980) Intrinsic prostaglandin synthesis in blood vessels. *In* Handbook of Physiology, sec 2, The Cardiovascular System. II. Vascular Smooth Muscle, edited by DF Bohr, AP Somlyo, HV Sparks Jr. pp 613–633

Needleman P, Kulkarin PS, Raz A (1977) Coronary tone modulation: Formation and actions of prostaglandins, endoperoxides and thromboxanes. Science **195:** 409–412

Paul RJ (1983) The effects of isoproterenol and ouabain on oxygen consumption, lactate production and the activation of phosphorylase in coronary artery smooth muscle. Circ Res **52:** 683–690

Paul RJ, Bauer M, Pease M (1979) Vascular smooth muscle: Aerobic glycolysis linked to sodium and potassium transport process. Science **206:** 1414–1416

Pittman RN, Duling BR (1973) Oxygen sensitivity of vascular smooth muscle. I. In vitro studies. Microvasc Res **6:** 202–211

Rimele TJ, Vanhoutte PM (1984) Effects of inhibitors of arachidonic and metabolism and calcium entry on hypoxic-induced responses in the isolated canine coronary artery. *In* Calcium Antagonists, edited by N Sperelakis. Boston, Martinus Nijhoff, pp 303–316

Roberts AM, Messina EJ, Kaley G (1981) Prostacyclin (PGI_2) mediates hypoxic relaxation of bovine coronary arterial strips. Prostaglandins **21:** 555–569

Rubanyi G, Paul RJ (1983) Hypoxic vasoconstriction in porcine coronary artery: Characterization of a novel oxygen tension sensor (abstr). Fed Proc **42:** 1347

Rubanyi G, Paul RJ (1984) O_2-sensitivity of Beta-adrenergic responsiveness in isolated bovine and porcine coronary arteries. J Pharmacol Exp Ther **230:** 692–698

Schuchleib R, Borda L, Davis J, Henry P (1976) Effects of sustained increases in extracellular potassium on coronary resistance in intact dog hearts (abstr). Clin Res **24:** 240A

Shepherd JT, Vanhoutte PM (1979) The Human Cardiovascular System. Facts and Concepts. New York, Raven Press

Singer HA, Wagner JD, Duling B, Peach MJ (1981) Endothelial-smooth muscle interactions in rabbit thoracic aorta: muscarinic relaxation and hypoxic-induced contraction (abstr). Fed Proc **40:** 689

Smith DJ, Vane JR (1966) Effects of oxygen tension on vascular and other smooth muscle. J Physiol (Lond) **186:** 284–294

Vatner SF, Baig H, Manders WT, Ochs, H, Pagani M (1977) Effects of propranolol on regional myocardial function, electrograms, and blood flow in conscious dogs with myocardial ischemia. J Clin Invest **60:** 353–360

INDEX TERMS: Porcine coronary artery • Vascular smooth muscle • Oxygen • Prostaglandins • β-Adrenergic mechanisms

Effects of Pressure Gradients between Branches of the Left Coronary Artery on the Pressure Axis Intercept and the Shape of Steady State Circumflex Pressure-Flow Relations in Dogs

Louis M. Messina, Frank L. Hanley, Paul N. Uhlig, Robert W. Baer, Mark T. Grattan, and Julien I.E. Hoffman

From the Cardiovascular Research Institute and the Departments of Pediatrics, Physiology, and Surgery, University of California, San Francisco, California

SUMMARY. When steady state pressure-flow relations are studied in the circumflex coronary artery, pressure gradients develop between it and other branches of the left coronary artery. To assess the effects of these pressure gradients, we compared the pressure axis intercept and shape of steady state circumflex pressure-flow relations in the presence and absence of gradients after autoregulation was abolished, both in the beating heart and during long diastoles in dogs. We used peripheral coronary pressures and radionuclide-labeled microspheres to assess arterial collateral flow. In the beating heart, interarterial pressure gradients reduced the curvature at low circumflex pressures, and overestimated the mean pressure axis intercept by 7.8 mm Hg ($P <$ 0.05). The results were similar for the pressure-flow relations derived during long diastoles. This overestimation exaggerates the difference between the pressure axis intercept and coronary sinus pressure. The peripheral coronary pressure and microsphere results indicate that these effects are mediated largely by arterial collateral flow. **(*Circ Res 56: 11–19, 1985*)**

CORONARY arterial pressure-flow relations have been used to investigate the physical forces that regulate coronary blood flow (Cross et al., 1961; Downey and Kirk, 1975; Bellamy, 1978). The pressure axis intercept of these relations has been interpreted as the downstream pressure opposing forward flow in the coronary circulation; however, this pressure has greatly exceeded the coronary sinus pressure, which traditionally has been assumed to be the downstream pressure. The shape of these relations, found to be linear by some (Dole and Bishop, 1982; Eng et al., 1982) but curvilinear by others (L'Abbate et al., 1980; Klocke et al., 1981), is thought to convey information about the conductance of the coronary circulation. Because of this variability of the pressure axis intercept and the shape of coronary arterial pressure-flow relations, the physiological significance of both remains uncertain.

One factor that might account for this variability is the specific coronary artery in which the pressure-flow relation is obtained. In our laboratory, we have consistently found that the pressure axis intercept of a steady state circumflex pressure-flow relation (Verrier et al., 1980; Vlahakes et al., 1982) is much higher than that in a steady state left main coronary arterial pressure-flow relation (Rouleau et al., 1979; Uhlig et al., 1984). A possible explanation for the higher pressure axis intercept of the circumflex pressure-flow relation may be that when circumflex pressure is selectively lowered below that in the other branches of the left coronary artery, interarterial pressure gradients occur and are accompanied by collateral flow that is not measured by the upstream flow transducer. This error in measurement could underestimate total circumflex flow and thus overestimate the pressure axis intercept. Whether these pressure gradients also affect the shape of a circumflex pressure-flow relation is unknown.

To assess the effects of interarterial pressure gradients on the pressure axis intercept and the shape of steady state circumflex arterial pressure-flow relations, we compared circumflex pressure-flow relations in the presence and absence of left coronary interarterial pressure gradients, both in the beating heart and during long diastoles in dogs. In a second series of experiments, we used radionuclide-labeled microspheres to determine whether the effects of interarterial pressure gradients on steady state circumflex pressure-flow relations can be explained by collateral flow across those gradients.

To eliminate the confounding influences of changing smooth muscle tone on our results, we conducted all experiments in the absence of autoregulation.

Methods

Surgical Preparation

Experiments were done on 16 mongrel dogs weighing 26–38 kg. After anesthesia was induced by sodium thiopental (25 mg/kg, iv) each dog was ventilated with halothane (0.75%–1.0%) and oxygen was delivered by a Harvard respirator through a cuffed endotracheal tube. Pancuronium bromide (0.05 mg/kg, iv) was given for muscle relaxation. Arterial blood gases were analyzed frequently. Tidal volume and respiratory rate were adjusted to maintain the Pa_{CO_2} between 20 and 30 torr, the Pa_{O_2} at about 100 torr, and the pH between 7.39 and 7.45. Core temperature was kept at about 37.5°C by a heating blanket and an infrared lamp.

A left thoracotomy was performed, and the left main, septal, and proximal coronary arteries were carefully dissected free from surrounding connective tissue. After pacing electrodes were sewn to the right ventricular free wall, heart block was induced by injecting 40% formalin into the atrioventricular node (Steiner and Kovalik, 1968). Silastic pressure catheters (0.275 mm i.d., 0.625 mm o.d.) were inserted into the distal circumflex artery and into the coronary sinus by a modified Herd-Barger technique (Verrier et al., 1980). Solid state pressure transducers (Millar Instruments, 7F) were inserted into the descending aorta via the left femoral artery and into the left ventricle via a purse-string suture in the left atrial appendage.

After sodium heparin (10,000 U, iv) was given, blood was pumped from the right femoral artery into a pressurized reservoir by a Sarns roller pump (Fig. 1). Reservoir pressure was controlled by a Fairchild pressure regulator fed from a compressed air source. Arterial blood flowed from the reservoir through a segment of Tygon tubing into a stainless steel cannula that was inserted into the left main coronary artery via the left subclavian artery and secured with a silk ligature. While the cannula was being positioned, care was taken that the septal artery remained adequately perfused. Pressure was measured at the tip of the cannula through a small stainless steel tube fixed to its inner wall. The circumflex artery was ligated just distal to the bifurcation of the left main coronary artery and cannulated with a short stainless steel cannula; this cannula was connected to the common pressure reservoir by a segment of Tygon tubing containing a cannulating flow transducer (Howell Instruments).

The flow transducer was connected to a Narcomatic RT 500 flowmeter. All fluid-filled catheters were connected to Statham P23Db pressure transducers; zero was set at mid-chest level. Data were recorded on an eight-channel polygraph (Beckman R612) and simultaneously on FM magnetic tape. These tape-recorded signals were subsequently digitized at 5-msec intervals and analyzed (Horowitz and Glantz, 1979; Horowitz, 1980) by a digital computer (PDP 11/70, Digital Equipment Corporation).

After the surgical procedure was completed, chromonar (10 mg/kg, iv) was given to abolish autoregulation. Repeated tests for the absence of reactive hyperemia after a 15-second coronary occlusion were made throughout the experiment. Additional chromonar (5 mg/kg, iv) was given as needed.

Pressure-Flow Relation Protocol

In the pressure-flow relations studied when gradients were absent, pressures in all branches of the left coronary artery were altered simultaneously by changing common reservoir pressure. The small pressure drop across the inflow tubing was similar in each circuit, so a reduction in reservoir pressure decreased pressures similarly in the left main and the circumflex coronary arteries. In the pressure-flow relations studied when pressure gradients were present, circumflex pressure was changed independently by

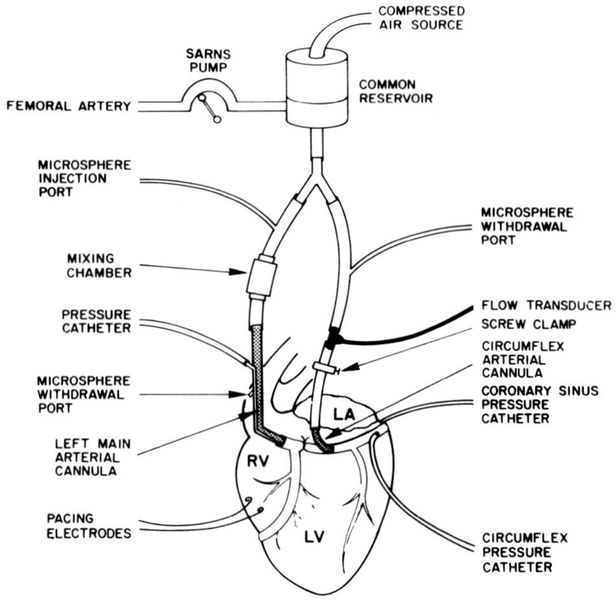

FIGURE 1. *Schematic representation of the surgical preparation*

adjusting a screw clamp on the circumflex perfusion circuit while left main pressure remained constant. Each pressure-flow relation consisted of 12 evenly distributed pressure-flow points obtained over a similar range of distal circumflex pressures, including low pressures and the pressure measured during a circumflex occlusion, namely, peripheral coronary pressure.

The effects of interarterial pressure gradients on steady state circumflex pressure-flow relations in the beating heart were examined in nine dogs. The ventricles were paced at 100 beats/min. To obtain each pressure-flow point, we first set the mean circumflex pressure to the desired level and then, after a steady state was reached, recorded the data. In each dog, one pressure-flow relation was obtained without interarterial pressure gradients and two were obtained when there were gradients, mean left main pressure was held constant first at 80 mm Hg and then at 100 mm Hg. If the preparation remained stable, additional pressure-flow relations were generated over a wide range of left main arterial pressures.

The effects of interarterial pressure gradients on steady state circumflex pressure-flow relations during long diastoles were examined in five dogs. We first set the mean circumflex pressure to the desired level and then arrested the heart by turning off the pacemaker; measurements were made after a steady state was reached, usually within 2–3 seconds. One pressure-flow relation was obtained without interarterial pressure gradients and the other when they were present while mean left main pressure was held constant at 100 mm Hg.

We noted a close correlation between the pressure axis intercept and the peripheral coronary pressure of the pressure-flow relations obtained when there were pressure gradients in our preliminary experiments. Because the peripheral coronary pressure is an indirect measurement of the collateral flow rate into the occluded bed (Kattus and Gregg, 1959) and depends on the perfusion pressure in the surrounding, normally perfused arteries, in each dog we determined the relationship between the circumflex peripheral coronary pressure and a wide range of left main arterial pressures by setting the left main coronary artery to a constant pressure, clamping the circumflex perfusion circuit, and then measuring the peripheral coronary pressure.

The occlusive zero of the flow transducer and zeros for the pressure channels were checked before and after each pressure-flow relation was determined. The cannulating flow transducer was calibrated by pumping the dog's blood through the perfusion circuit and timing the collection in a graduated cylinder.

Microsphere Protocol

To measure collateral flow rates, six mongrel dogs were studied; in four of these dogs pressure-flow relations during long diastoles had been examined. In each experiment, 3.0×10^5 to 5.0×10^5 microspheres 15 μm in diameter were injected into a port (Fig. 1) of the left main perfusion circuit, using standard techniques (Heymann et al., 1977). The microsphere injection port was distal to the origin of the circumflex perfusion circuit from the common reservoir, so no microspheres could enter the origin of the circumflex artery.

After chromonar was given to abolish autoregulation, mean left main and circumflex pressures were both set to 100 mm Hg, and the first set of microspheres was injected when left coronary interarterial pressure gradients were absent. For the subsequent injections, the left main coronary arterial pressure was kept at 100 mm Hg and the circumflex pressure was lowered independently by adjusting the screw clamp on the circumflex perfusion circuit. Six additional sets of microspheres were injected over the same range of left coronary interarterial pressure gradients as examined during the construction of a circumflex pressure-flow relation.

Starting immediately before and continuing for 2 minutes after the microsphere injection, a reference blood sample was collected from the most distal port of the left main cannula. In addition, starting immediately before and continuing for 3 minutes after the injection, a blood sample was collected from the circumflex perfusion circuit to verify that no microspheres entered the circumflex artery by reflux from their site of injection.

At the end of the experiment, the circumflex, left main, and right coronary arteries were cannulated separately and perfused with red, blue, and green dye, respectively, at a constant perfusion pressure of 100 mm Hg. The heart then was fixed in 10% formalin. When the heart was cut, the region supplied by the circumflex artery was identified by its red dye, and the center of this region was cut into pieces, placed in vials, and, along with the reference blood samples, counted in a well scintillation counter. The flow rates were calculated as previously described (Baer et al., 1984).

Analysis of Data

Linear and quadratic regressions of mean circumflex flow on mean circumflex pressure were determined for each pressure-flow relation, and the pressure axis intercepts were calculated both by linear regression and by determining the positive root of the best fit quadratic equation. The linear and quadratic regressions were compared by an analysis of variance.

Differences between the pressure axis intercepts of the pressure-flow relations in the beating heart were tested by a one-way analysis of variance and the Newman-Keuls test for multiple comparisons (Zar, 1974). Differences between the pressure axis intercepts of the pressure-flow relations measured during long diastoles were tested by a paired t-test.

All data are expressed as mean ± SD.

Results

In all circumflex pressure-flow relations curvature was seen over the entire range of circumflex perfusion pressures examined (Fig. 2), each curve being

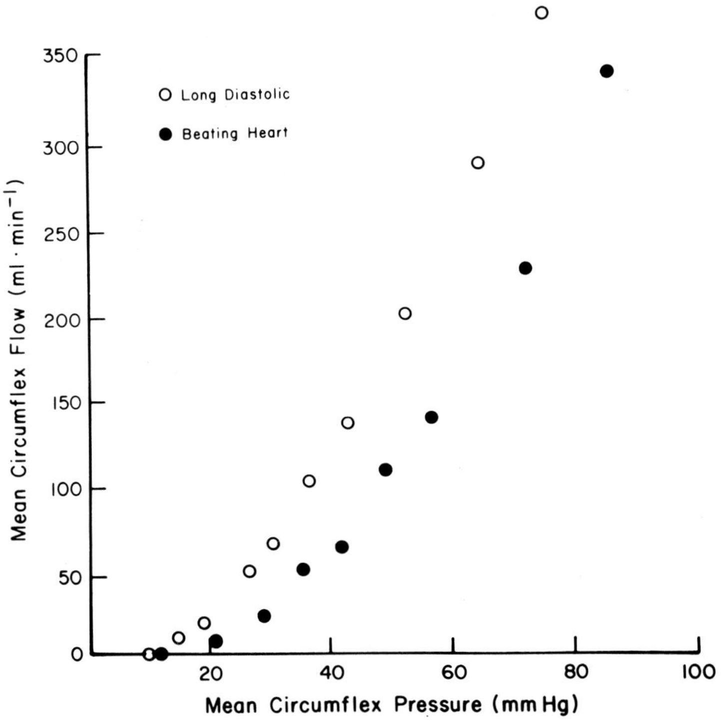

FIGURE 2. *Circumflex pressure-flow relations obtained when pressure gradients were absent, both in the beating heart and during long diastoles in the same dog. Although the pressure-flow relation during the long diastole has a slightly lower pressure axis intercept, it differs from the pressure-flow relation in the beating heart primarily by its slope.*

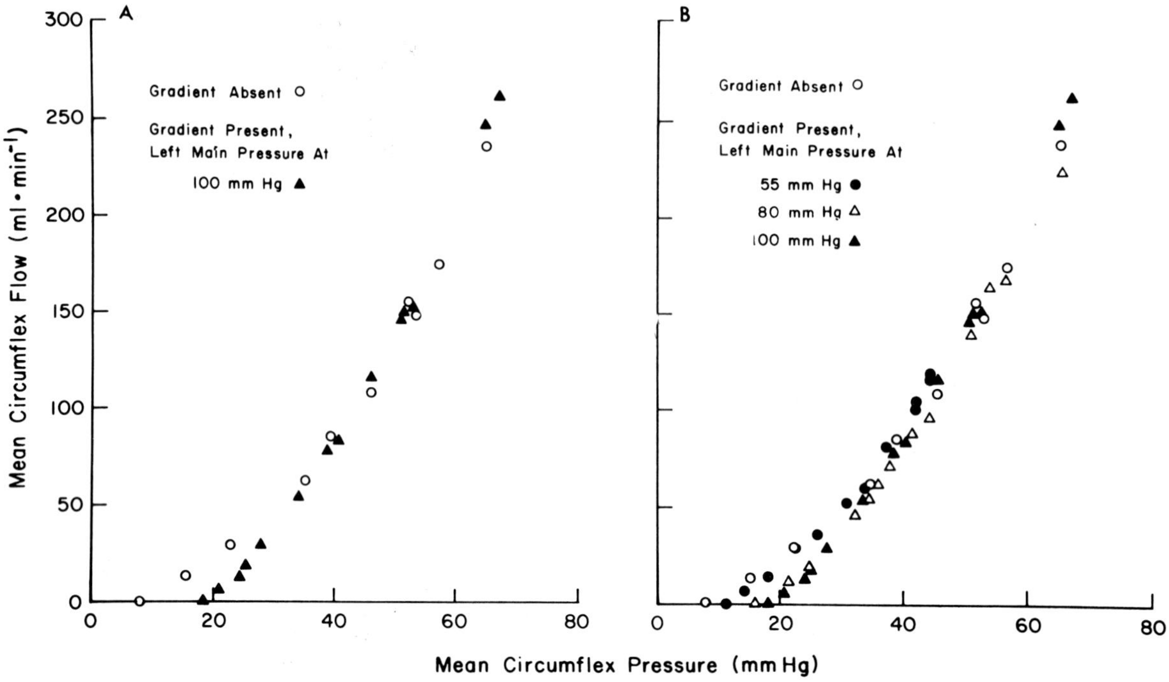

FIGURE 3. *Circumflex pressure-flow relations for the beating heart in one dog when interarterial pressure gradients were absent and when they were present. Panel A: the pressure-flow relation in the absence of gradients is more curved over the lower range of perfusion pressures and has a lower pressure axis intercept. Panel B: as constant left main pressure is increased, the corresponding pressure-flow relation has less curvature over the lower range of perfusion pressures and a higher pressure axis intercept.*

significantly better fit by a quadratic than by a linear regression equation ($P < 0.05$). The pressure axis intercept of a pressure-flow relation was consistently lower when calculated from its quadratic than from its linear regression equation. For the beating heart, the mean differences were 6.1 ± 2.1 mm Hg when interarterial gradients were absent and 4.6 ± 1.4 mm Hg when they were present; during long diastoles, the mean difference was 3.9 ± 1.3 mm Hg when gradients were absent and 2.1 ± 1.2 mm Hg when they were present. All pressure axis intercepts reported below were obtained from the quadratic regression equations.

Left coronary interarterial pressure gradients significantly affected the pressure axis intercept and the shape of the pressure-flow relations, both in the beating heart and during long diastoles (Fig. 3; Table 1). Over the higher range of circumflex arterial perfusion pressures, when interarterial pressure gradients were small, the pressure-flow relation obtained when pressure gradients were present was nearly superimposible on that obtained without them (Fig. 3A); however, below a perfusion pressure of about 40 mm Hg, when the interarterial pressure gradients were large, the two pressure-flow relations diverged. Less flow was measured at the same perfusion pressure when gradients were present than when they were absent, so that the pressure-flow relations had less curvature and intercepted the pressure axis at a higher pressure when pressure gradients were present (Fig. 3A; Table 1). This overestimation of the pressure axis intercept exaggerated the difference between the pressure axis intercept and coronary sinus pressure (Table 1).

As the set constant pressure of the left main cannula was increased, the corresponding pressure-flow relation had less curvature and a higher pressure axis intercept than did one obtained at a lower constant left main pressure (Fig. 3B; Table 1). In fact, the pressure axis intercept varied linearly with left main coronary arterial pressure, as can be inferred from the following relationships. For a given pressure-flow relation, the calculated pressure axis intercept was nearly identical to the peripheral coronary pressure, the plot of these variables approximating a line of identity (Fig. 4A). In turn, the peripheral coronary pressure varied linearly with the left main arterial pressure in each dog [mean correlation coefficient = 0.956 (0.092), mean slope = 0.13 (0.041)] (Fig. 4B).

In the microsphere experiments, collateral flow into the circumflex artery was found when forward flow was still present. Furthermore, collateral flow was measured over the same range of pressure gradients (60–85 mm Hg) in which the pressure-flow relations in the presence of gradients differed from those derived in their absence. In all dogs, as the gradient increased, the collateral flow rate also increased (Fig. 5). The mean collateral flow during occlusion for all six dogs was 0.13 ml/min per g. Finally, in the four dogs in which microspheres were given and pressure-flow relations during long dias-

TABLE 1
Pressure Axis Intercepts and Coronary Sinus Pressures for Circumflex Pressure-Flow Relations When Interarterial Pressure Gradients Were Absent and Present

	Gradients absent	Gradients present: Mean left main pressure 80 mm Hg	Gradients present: Mean left main pressure 100 mm Hg
In the beating heart			
No. of dogs	9	7	9
Pressure-axis intercept (mm Hg)	8.1 (1.1)*	12.8 (2.4)*	15.8 (2.9)*
Coronary sinus pressure (mm Hg)	3.1 (1.4)	5.1 (2.4)	5.8 (2.1)
During long diastoles			
No. of dogs	5		5
Pressure-axis intercept (mm Hg)	11.6 (1.9)		19.0 (5.1)†
Coronary sinus pressure (mm Hg)	8.4 (1.8)		10.3 (0.7)

Pressures are given as mean ± SD.
* All significantly different from each other, $P = 0.0005$.
† Significantly different from value with gradient absent, $P = 0.029$.

toles were determined, when the difference between intercepts was large, a high collateral flow rate was measured, and when this difference was small, a low collateral flow rate was measured.

Discussion

Critique of Methods

To avoid errors from assessing pressure axis intercepts by extrapolation (Klocke et al., 1981) we included in each pressure-flow relation points at very low pressures and flows, down to zero flow.

We excluded two potential sources of error in our collateral flow measurements. First, the dyeing technique and cutting scheme we used ensured that we were not counting microspheres in the normally perfused tissue bordering the collateral-dependent area. These procedures were effective because the mean collateral flow rate measured during acute circumflex occlusion in this study (0.13 ml/min per g) is even less than rates of 0.21 ml/min per g found by Gottwik et al. (1983), and similar to rates obtained in experiments in which the exclusion of the normally perfused tissues was confirmed by microscopic analysis of the cut tissues (Hirzel et al., 1976). Furthermore, studies by Gottwik et al. (1983) and Yellon et al. (1981) showed that, within the ischemic zone, the collateral flow rate per gram of tissue is similar from region to region, provided that the border zone has been excluded. Second, we believe that no microspheres entered the collateral-dependent bed of the circumflex artery anterograde by reflux from the site of injection because we did not detect radioactivity in the blood collected from the circumflex perfusion circuit. In addition, we detected no collateral flow during the microsphere injections made when the gradients were small (under 60 mm Hg) or absent.

At low collateral flows, the numbers of microspheres entering the circumflex vascular bed were often small: in seven flow measurements there were more than 400 microspheres, in nine there were

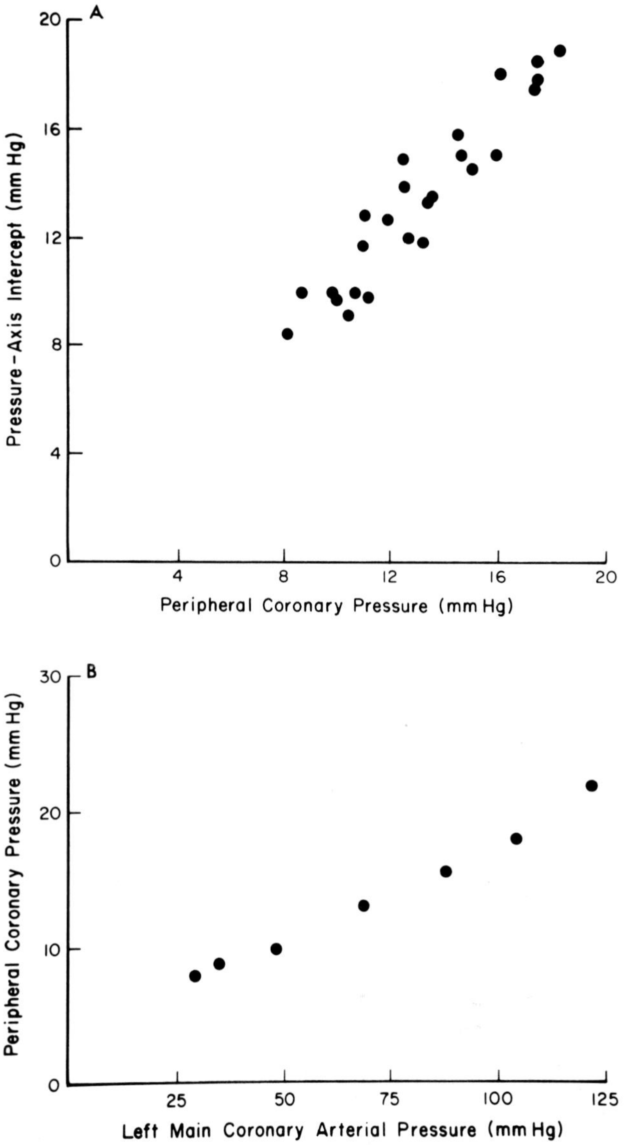

FIGURE 4. *Panel A: correlation between the pressure axis intercept and the peripheral coronary pressure of circumflex pressure-flow relations in dogs when interarterial pressure gradients were present. Data are from experiments in the beating heart (slope = 1.05, r = 0.943). Panel B: a representative correlation between the peripheral coronary pressure and the left main arterial pressure (slope = 0.15, r = 0.99).*

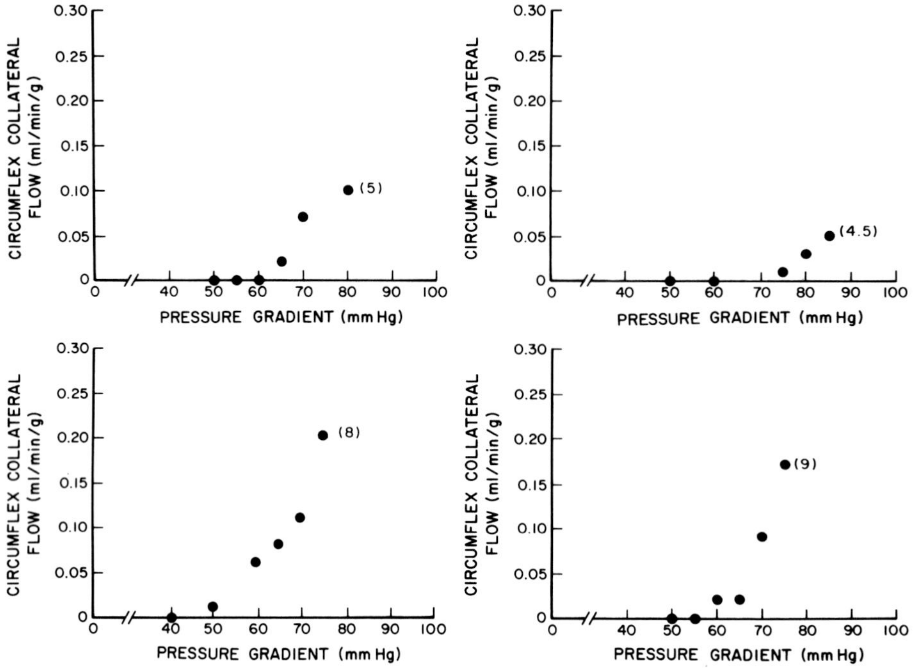

FIGURE 5. *Collateral flow rate as a function of the size of the interarterial pressure gradients in four of the six dogs in which microsphere studies were done. The highest collateral flow rate represents collateral flow during the circumflex occlusion. The lowest collateral flow rate indicates the minimal gradient at which a collateral flow rate was detected. The numbers in parentheses next to the highest collateral flow rates in each dog are the differences between pressure axis intercepts measured in the presence and the absence of interarterial pressure gradients in those dogs.*

between 100 and 400 microspheres, and in four there were under 100 microspheres. Although small numbers of microspheres decrease the precision of flow measurements (Buckberg et al., 1971) the results are unbiased. Furthermore the larger collateral flows at complete circumflex occlusion would have had the most precise measurements.

Although we did not control or measure collateral flow from the right coronary artery into the coronary artery, this flow is small (Murray and Vatner, 1980) and, therefore, unlikely to have affected our results. Furthermore, any differences due to collateral flow in our studies would have been even greater than those observed if we had excluded collateral inflow from the right coronary artery.

Finally, we believe that it is unlikely that the size of the vascular bed supplied by the circumflex artery changes when gradients are present and when they are absent because the collateral vessels enter the arterial tree upstream from the capillary bed (Schaper, 1971). In addition, the capillaries of a given vascular bed are end capillaries and do not anastomose with capillaries of adjacent beds (Okum et al., 1979).

Effects of Interarterial Pressure Gradients

Our results show that pressure gradients occurring during the determination of steady state circumflex pressure-flow relations in the absence of autoregulation cause overestimation of the pressure axis intercept and reduce the curvature of that relation both for the beating heart and during long diastoles (Fig. 3; Table 1). The magnitude of these changes depends on the perfusion pressure in the left main coronary artery (Fig. 3B; Table 1). When steady state circumflex pressure-flow relations are determined, the perfusion pressure in the other branches of the left coronary artery is usually not controlled, as it was in our experiments, but rather is the prevailing aortic pressure. Thus, in most experiments, the pressure axis intercept and the curvature of a steady state circumflex pressure-flow relation vary with the prevailing aortic pressure, thereby accounting for some of the variability of reported results.

The difference between peripheral coronary pressures or pressure axis intercepts obtained from the circumflex coronary artery when pressure gradients are present and from the left main coronary artery has not been discussed before. (It should be emphasized that the pressure axis intercepts and peripheral coronary pressures should be similar, as shown in Figure 3, because the pressure during complete coronary occlusion is indeed the lowest point on the pressure-flow curve.) In the isolated circumflex coronary artery, pressures of 14–30 mm Hg have been reported for peripheral coronary pressures (Mosher et al., 1964; Fam and McGregor, 1964; Elliot et al., 1968; Fam and McGregor, 1969; Elliot et al., 1974; Gould et al., 1975) and for pressure axis intercepts (Bellamy, 1978; Verrier et al., 1980; Vlahakes et al.,

1982; Dole and Bishop, 1982). On the other hand, in the left main coronary artery, Eng et al. (1982) found an average pressure axis intercept of 10.7 ± 2.4 mm Hg, close to our mean value of 8.1 mm Hg; had they used curvilinear rather than linear extrapolation, their intercept would have been even lower. Pressure-axis intercepts in this range were also described by Rouleau et al. (1979) and by Uhlig et al. (1984).

We believe that the most likely cause for the effects of the interarterial pressure gradients was the occurrence of collateral flow that entered the circumflex bed when pressure in the circumflex artery was selectively lowered below that in the other branches of the left coronary artery. Because this collateral flow entered the circumflex artery distal to the flow transducer, it was not recorded. Any collateral flow across these pressure gradients would increase circumflex arterial pressure, resulting in a higher pressure for the same flow as measured by the upstream flow transducer when gradients were present than when they were absent. Ultimately, the pressure axis intercept would appear to be raised above its true value and the curvature over the lower part of the pressure-flow relation would be reduced.

The above hypothesis is supported by several findings. First, collateral flow was found when there was still forward flow in the circumflex artery, and it occurred over the same range of pressure gradients as that over which the two types of pressure-flow relations diverged (Fig. 5). Second, the collateral flow rate was related to the difference between the intercepts of the pressure-flow relations derived in the absence and in the presence of gradients. Third, for the pressure-flow relations obtained when pressure gradients were present, peripheral coronary pressure, which is directly related to collateral blood flow (Fam and McGregor, 1964; Elliot et al., 1968, 1974) was closely correlated with the left main coronary pressure (Fig. 4B). Finally, support comes also from studies in swine which normally have very little collateral coronary flow (Fedor et al., 1978; Millard, 1980; Sjöquist et al., 1984). If our hypothesis about the influence of collateral flow on pressure axis intercept is correct, there should be little difference between pressure axis intercepts or peripheral coronary pressures in the left main coronary artery or in one of its branches in swine; Bellamy and O'Benar (1984) noted that flow stopped at a left main coronary arterial pressure of 13 ± 5 mm Hg, whereas Pantely et al. (1984) observed a pressure axis intercept of 12.1 ± 3.1 mm Hg in the left anterior descending coronary artery.

One question remaining is whether the collateral flow measured by the microspheres is sufficient to account for the entire difference between pressure-flow relations determined in the presence and in the absence of pressure gradients. We examined this question first by looking at maximal differences between flows for the two types of pressure-flow relations; this maximal difference occurs at the pressure at which the pressure-flow relation determined when gradients are present reaches zero flow, that is, at complete occlusion. Thus, in Figure 3A, in the pressure-flow relation determined when there were gradients, there was no flow at a circumflex pressure of 18 mm Hg, but there was a flow of 18 ml/min at the same circumflex pressure when gradients were absent. This implies that the collateral flow rate would have had to be 18 ml/min to account for the difference between the two pressure-flow relations. The mean maximal difference in flow rates for all the pressure-flow relations derived in the beating heart at a left main pressure of 100 mm Hg was 11 ml/min. Collateral flow rates of this magnitude in the acutely occluded canine circumflex artery have been described: 11.3 ml/min in dogs weighing 16 kg (Scheel et al., 1980), 20.8 ml/min in dogs weighing 16–24 kg (Schaper et al., 1976), and 21.1 (11.8) ml/min per 100 g (Gottwik et al., 1984) in dogs weighing 24–32 kg. In our microsphere experiments, the collateral flow rate was also of this magnitude. Because our microsphere measurements are in ml/min per g, we converted the mean flow rate of 11 ml/min to ml/min per g, as follows. Total heart weight, known for three of the six dogs studied, averaged 209 g. Because the canine circumflex coronary artery supplies on average 38.6 ± 3.6% of the myocardial mass (Scheel et al., 1982), in our dogs the circumflex coronary artery supplied an average of 80.7 g of myocardium. Therefore, the total collateral flow rate of 11 ml/min is equivalent to a collateral flow rate per gram of 0.14 ml/min per g, and this value was nearly identical to the value of 0.13 ml/min per g measured by the microspheres during circumflex occlusion.

In addition to this analysis of mean maximal collateral flow, in three dogs, we directly examined whether the collateral flow rates measured by the microspheres accounted for the difference between flow rates at the same perfusion pressure for the two pressure-flow relations over a wide range of pressure gradients. For each dog at each pressure gradient, we multiplied the observed collateral flow per gram by the estimated weight of myocardium supplied by the circumflex artery (Scheel et al., 1982). This total collateral flow rate was then compared with the differences between flow rates at the same perfusion pressure for the two pressure-flow relations. In two of the three dogs the microsphere measurements of collateral flow accounted almost entirely for the differences between flows for the two pressure-flow relations (Table 2).

We considered an alternative mechanism that might explain how altering the pressure in the rest of the left main coronary artery can influence the pressure axis intercept in the region supplied by the circumflex artery. When pressures and flows are very low in the circumflex vascular bed while the heart is beating, there will be changes of regional

Table 2
Comparison of Total Collateral Flow Rates (A) (B) and the Differences between Flow Rates of the Pressure-Flow Relations Determined in the Presence and in the Absence of Pressure Gradients in Three Dogs

Dog one			Dog two			Dog three		
Pressure gradient (mm Hg)	Flow rates (ml/min) 1	2	Pressure gradient (mm Hg)	Flow rates (ml/min) 1	2	Pressure gradient (mm Hg)	Flow rates (ml/min) 1	2
85	5.8	7.0	80	9.7	8.5	75	22.0	21.0
80	3.5	6.6	70	6.8	6.5	70	18.7	19.5
75	1.2	4.4	70	7.7	6.5	65	7.7	10.4
			65	2.0	4.3	60	8.8	9.1
						50	1.0	0.0

Microspheres were injected at lower gradients in each dog, but no collateral flow was detectable.
A = computed from microspheres; B = estimated difference in the flow rates at the same perfusion pressure between the pressure-flow relations derived in the presence and in the absence of gradients.

myocardial function due to ischemia, whether or not there are interarterial pressure gradients. However, when pressures are lowered in parallel in all branches of the left coronary artery, there will be global left ventricular ischemia, as well. We do not believe that our findings can be explained by the effects of global myocardial ischemia, because the differences between pressure-flow relations described when interarterial pressure gradients were present and were absent were similar in beating hearts and during diastolic arrest; in the latter, ischemia would be minimal or absent because the metabolic demand during cardiac arrest is only about 20% of that in the beating heart (McKeever et al., 1958; Monroe and French, 1960). There is no doubt that ischemia would have occurred at low flows in the beating heart, but even then it could not explain our results. Although global ischemia could influence flow in the circumflex vascular bed by raising left ventricular end-diastolic pressure, the effect of such increased preload is to raise, not lower, the pressure axis intercepts (Aversano et al., 1984).

Some previous studies in which circumflex preparations were used (Verrier et al., 1980; Klocke et al., 1981; Vlahakes et al., 1982) reported little or no significant effect of collateral flow on circumflex pressure-flow relations. These investigators lowered the pressure in the circumflex artery and then, after a steady state was reached, occluded the left anterior descending artery transiently to exclude collateral flow; they failed to find any resulting change in circumflex pressure or flow. This method, however, may yield misleading results. Occluding the left anterior descending artery would not exclude the substantial potential collateral contributions of the septal artery or of vessels proximal to the left anterior descending occluder or to the site of cannulation of the circumflex artery. Furthermore, the investigators also extrapolated over the lower range of perfusion pressures to obtain the pressure axis intercept and did not examine the range of perfusion pressures over which the effects of the collateral flow would have been the most prominent.

Conclusions

Our findings raise questions about the physiological significance of the shape and pressure axis intercept of steady state coronary arterial pressure-flow relations. When circumflex pressure-flow relations were studied when they were interarterial pressure gradients, there was a decrease in curvature and an overestimation of the pressure axis intercept, which exaggerated the difference between the pressure axis intercept and the coronary sinus pressure. In contrast, when the circumflex pressure-flow relations were determined without gradients, the mean difference between the pressure axis intercept and the coronary sinus pressure was 5.0 mm Hg for the beating heart and even less—3.2 mm Hg—during long diastoles. Thus our study suggests the need to reassess whether there is indeed a downstream pressure that is greatly above coronary sinus pressure opposing forward pressure in the coronary circulation.

We thank Mimi Zeiger for expert editorial assistance, Kathy Storer and Richard Truelove for preparation of the manuscript, Bruce Payne and Carl McWatters for preparation of the microspheres, and Jose Morales for technical assistance. We also thank Hoechst-Roussel Pharmaceuticals, Inc., for their generous donation of the chromonar used in this study.

This work was supported by Grant HL25847 from the National Heart, Lung, and Blood Institute.

Dr. Messina was supported by the American Heart Association, California Affiliate, Research Fellowship No. 82N6A, with funds contributed by the San Francisco and Long Beach Chapters.

Address for reprints: Julien I.E. Hoffman, M.D., 1403-HSE, University of California, San Francisco, California 94143.

Received August 15, 1983; accepted for publication August 30, 1984.

References

Aversano T, Klocke FJ, Mates RE, Canty JM Jr (1984) Preload-induced alterations in capacitance-free diastolic pressure-flow relations. Am J Physiol **246:** H410–H417

Baer RW, Payne BD, Verrier ED, Vlahakes GJ, Molodowitch D, Uhlig PN, Hoffman JIE (1984) Increased number of myocardial blood flow measurements with radionuclide-labelled microspheres. Am J Physiol **246:** H418–H434

Bellamy RF (1978) Diastolic coronary artery pressure-flow relations in the dog. Circ Res **43:** 92–101

Bellamy RF, O'Benar JD (1984) Cessation of arterial and venous flow at a finite driving pressure in porcine coronary circulation. Am J Physiol **246:** H525–H531

Buckberg GD, Luck JC, Payne B, Hoffman JIE, Archie JP, Fixler DE (1971) Some sources of error in measuring regional blood flow with radioactive microspheres. J Appl Physiol **31:** 598–604

Cross CE, Rieben PA, Salisbury PF (1961) Coronary driving pressure and vasomotor tonus as determinants of coronary blood flow. Circ Res **9:** 589–600

Dole WP, Bishop VS (1982) Influence of autoregulation and capacitance on diastolic coronary artery pressure-flow relationships in the dog. Circ Res **51:** 261–270

Downey M, Kirk ES (1975) Inhibition of coronary blood flow by a vascular waterfall mechanism. Circ Res **36:** 753–760

Elliot EC, Jones EL, Bloor CM, Leon AS, Gregg DE (1968) Day-to-day changes in coronary hemodynamics secondary to constriction of circumflex branch of left coronary artery in conscious dogs. Circ Res **22:** 237–250

Elliot EC, Khouri EM, Snow JA, Gregg DE (1974) Direct measurement of coronary collateral blood flow in conscious dogs by an electromagnetic flowmeter. Circ Res **34:** 374–383

Eng C, Jentzer JH, Kirk ES (1982) The effects of the coronary capacitance on the interpretation of diastolic pressure-flow relationships. Circ Res **50:** 334–341

Fam WM, McGregor M 1964) Effect of coronary vasodilator drugs on retrograde flow in areas of chronic myocardial ischemia. Circ Res **15:** 355–365

Fam WM, McGregor M (1969) Pressure-flow relationships in the coronary circulation. Circ Res **25:** 293–301

Fedor M, McIntosh DM, Rembert JC, Greenfield JC Jr (1978) Coronary and transmural myocardial blood flow responses in awake domestic pigs. Am J Physiol **235:** H435– H444

Gottwik M, Wüsten B, Hofmann M, Puschmanns, Nienaber C, Schaper W (1983) Development of collaterals. Application of external subcritical fixed constrictors in a canine model. Basic Res Cardiol **78:** 183–192

Gould KL, Lipscomb K, Calvert C (1975) Compensatory changes of the distal coronary vascular bed during progressive coronary constriction. Circulation **51:** 1085–1094

Heymann MA, Payne BD, Hoffman JIE, Rudolph AM (1977) Blood flow measurements with radionuclide-labeled particles. Prog Cardiovasc Dis **20:** 55–79

Hirzel HO, Nelson GR, Sonnenblick EH, Kirk ES (1976) Redistribution of collateral blood flow from necrotic to surviving myocardium following coronary occlusion in the dog. Circ Res **39:** 214–222

Horowitz SL (1980) An integrated, interactive user-oriented biomedical data acquisition, processing, and display system. Ph.D. Dissertation, University of California, Berkeley

Horowitz SL, Glantz SA (1979) Analog to digital data conversion and display. System Users Manual. University of California, San Francisco

Kattus AA, Gregg DE (1959) Some determinants of coronary collateral blood flow in the open-chest dog. Circ Res **7:** 628–642

Klocke FJ, Weinstein IR, Klocke JF, Ellis AK, Kraus DR, Mates RE, Canty JM, Anbar RD, Romanowski RR, Wallmeyer KW, Echt MP (1981) Zero-flow pressures and pressure-flow relationships during single long diastoles in the canine coronary bed before and during maximum vasodilation. Limited influence of capacitative effects. J Clin Invest **68:** 970–980

L' Abbate A, Marzilli M, Ballestra AM, Camici P, Trivella M, Pelosi G, Klassen GA (1980) Opposite transmural gradients of coronary resistance and extravascular pressure in the working dog's heart. Cardiovasc Res **14:** 21–29

McKeever WP, Gregg DE, Canney PC (1958) Oxygen uptake of the non-working left ventricle. Circ Res **6:** 612–623

Millard RW (1980) Changes in cardiac mechanics and coronary blood flow of regionally ischemic porcine myocardium induced by Diltiazem. Chest **78:** 193–199

Monroe RG, French G (1960) Ventricular pressure-volume relationships and oxygen consumption in fibrillation and arrest. Circ Res **8:** 260–266

Mosher P, Ross J Jr, McFate PA, Shaw RF (1964) Control of coronary blood flow by an autoregulatory mechanism. Circ Res **14:** 250–259

Murdock RH Jr, Harlan DM, Morris JJ III, Pryor WW Jr, Cobb FR (1983) Transitional blood flow zones between ischemic and non-ischemic myocardium in the awake dog. Circ Res **52:** 451–459

Murray PA, Vatner SF (1980) Fractional contributions of the right and left coronary arteries to perfusion of normal and hypertrophied right ventricles of conscious dogs. Circ Res **47:** 190–200

Okun EM, Factor SM, Kirk ES (1979) End-capillary loops in the heart: An explanation for discrete infarctions without border zones. Science **206:** 565–566

Pantely GA, Ladley HD, Bristow JD (1984) Low zero-flow pressure and minimal capacitance effect on diastolic coronary artery pressure-flow relations during maximum vasodilation in swine. Circulation **70:** 485–494

Rouleau J, Boerboom LE, Surjadhana A, Hoffman JIE (1979) The role of autoregulation and tissue diastolic pressures in the transmural distribution of left ventricular blood flow in anesthetized dogs. Circ Res **45:** 804–815

Schaper W (1971) The Collateral Circulation of the Heart. New York, Elsevier

Schaper W, Flameng W, Winkler B, Wüsten W, Türschmann G, Neugebauer G, Carl M, Pasyk S (1976) Quantification of collateral resistance in acute and chronic experimental coronary occlusion in the dog. Circ Res **39:** 371–377

Scheel KW, Wilson JL, Ingram LA, McGehee L (1980) The septal artery and its collaterals in dogs with and without circumflex occlusion. Am J Physiol **238:** H504–H514

Scheel KW, Ingram RA, Gordey RL (1982) Relationship of coronary flow and perfusion territory. Am J Physiol **243:** H738–H747

Sjöquist P-O, Duker G, Almgren O (1984) Distribution of the collateral blood flow at the lateral border of the ischemic myocardium after acute coronary occlusion in the pig and the dog. Basic Res Cardiol **79:** 164–175

Steiner C, Kovalik ATW (1968) A simple technique for production of complete heart block in dogs. J Appl Physiol **25:** 631–632

Uhlig PN, Baer RW, Vlahakes GJ, Hanley FL, Messina LM, Hoffman JIE (1984) Arterial and venous coronary pressure-flow relations in anesthetized dogs: Evidence for a vascular waterfall in epicardial coronary veins. Circ Res **55:** 238–248

Verrier ED, Edelist G, Consigny PM, Robinson S, Hoffman JIE (1980) Greater coronary vascular reserve in dogs anesthetized with halothane. Anesthesiology **53:** 445–459

Vlahakes GJ, Baer RW, Uhlig PN, Verrier ED, Bristow JD, Hoffman JIE (1982) Adrenergic influence in the coronary circulation of conscious dogs during maximal vasodilation with adenosine. Circ Res **51:** 371–384

Yellon DM, Hearse DJ, Crome R, Grannell J, Wyse RKH (1981) Characterization of the lateral interface between normal and ischemic tissue in the canine heart during evolving myocardial infarction. Am J Cardiol **47:** 1233–1239

Zar JH (1974) Biostatistical Analysis. Englewood Cliffs, NJ, Prentice-Hall

INDEX TERMS: Interarterial pressure gradients • Steady state circumflex pressure-flow relations • Radionuclide-labeled microspheres • Collateral blood flow • Peripheral coronary pressure

Transmission of Intrathoracic Pressure to the Intracranial Space during Cardiopulmonary Resuscitation in Dogs

Alan D. Guerci, An-Yun Shi, Howard Levin, Joshua Tsitlik, Myron L. Weisfeldt, and Nisha Chandra

From the Peter Belfer Laboratory for Myocardial Research, Cardiology Divisions and Department of Medicine, Johns Hopkins Hospital, and The Francis Scott Key Medical Center, Baltimore, Maryland

SUMMARY. Elevation of intrathoracic pressure during cardiopulmonary resuscitation generates carotid pressure and flow, but also increases intracranial pressure. This increase in intracranial pressure may limit cerebral blood flow. Therefore, we performed studies designed to quantify the extent of this transmission and to identify the mechanism of transmission of intrathoracic pressure to the intracranial space during cardiopulmonary resuscitation in dogs. Intracranial pressure increased during the chest compression phase of all modes of cardiopulmonary resuscitation tested. During simultaneous compression-ventilation cardiopulmonary resuscitation, change in intracranial pressure (mm Hg) = 0.33 change in intrathoracic pressure (mm Hg) + 2.02 ($r = 0.86$) and was not significantly different from the relationship observed during conventional cardiopulmonary resuscitation. The magnitude of transmission of intrathoracic pressure to the intracranial space was increased by binding the abdomen and by raising the baseline intracranial pressure. No single route accounted for transmission of intrathoracic pressure to the intracranial space during cardiopulmonary resuscitation. Intracranial pressure fluctuations were unrelated to either carotid arterial or jugular venous pressure, and were found instead to be the result of pressure transmission by blood in non-valved veins and by cerebrospinal fluid. This was determined by three maneuvers. First, obstruction of cerebrospinal fluid flow by ligation of the cervical spinal cord reduced intracranial pressure ($P < 0.001$) and made the change in intracranial pressure equivalent to pressure changes at the confluence of the intracranial venous sinuses, without affecting pressure changes at the confluence of the intracranial venous sinuses. Second, ligation of the cervical spinal cord and one of the two longitudinal vertebral veins adjacent to the cervical cord reduced the pressure changes in the intracranial space and at the confluence of the intracranial venous sinuses to about 60% of the levels observed when the cervical cord alone was ligated. Thus, the non-valved longitudinal vertebral veins appear to be the vascular channels of critical importance to pressure transmission. Finally, pressure changes in the thoracic cerebrospinal fluid were increased ($P < 0.05$) by cord ligation, even after exsanguination minimized pressure transmission via blood-filled channels, indicating direct transmission of intrathoracic pressure through intervertebral foramina to the cerebrospinal fluid. Thus, although non-valved veins and cerebrospinal fluid account for transmission of intrathoracic pressure to the intracranial space during cardiopulmonary resuscitation, this pressure transmission is modest except with abdominal binding or under conditions of increased intracranial pressure. **(*Circ Res 56: 20–30, 1985*)**

INTRACRANIAL pressure is known to increase during the chest compression phase of cardiopulmonary resuscitation (CPR) in humans as well as in dogs (Bircher and Safar, 1981; Koehler et al., 1983). This observation has dual significance. First, intracranial pressure appears to be the downstream pressure for cerebral perfusion during CPR (Koehler et al., 1983; Michael et al., 1984), as in the nonarrested state. Elevation of intracranial pressure during chest compression could therefore substantially limit brain blood flow. Second, several lines of evidence indicate that blood flow during CPR is the result of an increase in intrathoracic pressure rather than direct compression of the heart between the sternum and vertebral column (Rudikoff et al., 1980; Chandra et al., 1981a; Niemann et al., 1981). For the cerebral circulation, the increase in intrathoracic pressure produced by chest compression is efficiently transmitted to the carotid arteries, whereas transmission of intrathoracic pressure to the jugular veins is blocked by valves at the thoracic inlet (Niemann et al., 1980; Fisher et al., 1982). To the extent that intrathoracic pressure is in some manner transmitted to the intracranial space, a dilemma is created: transmission of intrathoracic pressure would then account for both the upstream and downstream pressures for cerebral perfusion. In particular, methods of CPR which raise intrathoracic pressure to high levels generate higher carotid pressure and flow (Chandra et al., 1980, 1981b), but could, as a result of transmission of intrathoracic pressure to the intracranial space, fail to improve cerebral perfusion.

Previous studies of the relationship of intracranial pressure fluctuations to intrathoracic pressure have been confined to the intact circulation and, in general, assess transmission to the intracranial space of arterial pulse pressure or airway pressure during positive pressure ventilation with positive end-expiratory pressure (PEEP). Carotid pulse pressure ordinarily produces only very small changes in intracranial pressure (usually less than 5 mm Hg); these fluctuations in intracranial pressure are increased under conditions of increased intracranial elastance (Lofgren et al., 1973a; Guinane, 1975) but not by PEEP. PEEP produces changes in jugular venous pressure which correlate closely with (and seem to determine) changes in intracranial pressure (Luce et al., 1982). As in the case of carotid pulse pressure, the resulting intracranial pressure fluctuations are influenced by intracranial elastance and are usually small.

Insofar as CPR can be defined as a system characterized by rapid and wide fluctuations in intrathoracic pressure, the observations of Hamilton et al. (1944) on lumbar cerebrospinal fluid pressure during coughing may be more relevant to the subject of intracranial pressure fluctuations during CPR. They reasoned that jugular and carotid pressure fluctuations during cough were not responsible for the observed increase in spinal canal pressure. During cough, spinal pressure increased by more than twice the increase in jugular pressure, a relationship that ruled out jugular pressure changes as the sole determinant of changes in intracranial pressure. Whereas increases in peak arterial and spinal canal pressure were of similar magnitude during cough, Hamilton and colleagues argued that these pressures were unrelated to each other, because only a tiny fraction of arterial pulse pressure is normally reflected in the cerebrospinal fluid pressure. Augmentation of arterial pulse pressure by coughing should not alter this relationship. They concluded by postulating direct transmission of intrathoracic and intraabdominal pressure through the intervertebral foramina to the cerebrospinal fluid.

The present studies were designed to assess the extent of transmission of changes in intrathoracic pressure to the intracranial space during CPR in dogs. We also determined the influence of different modes of CPR, abdominal binding, and the level of intracranial pressure itself on the magnitude of pressure transmission. Finally, we examined the route of transmission of intrathoracic pressure to the intracranial space in terms of the contributions to intracranial pressure fluctuations made by the cerebrospinal fluid and arterial, jugular, and other venous blood-filled channels.

Methods

Forty-eight large mongrel dogs (22–35 kg) were anesthetized with ketamine (15–20 mg, im) and pentobarbital (15 to 20 mg/kg, iv) and intubated through a tracheostomy. Fluid-filled catheters were advanced to the right atrium and thoracic aorta via femoral cutdown, and to the carotid artery and jugular vein through side branches in the neck. Catheter position was confirmed by characteristic prearrest pressure tracings and by postmortem examination. Zero pressure was obtained by exposing the catheter tip to air in situ at the end of each experiment. Intracranial pressure was measured through a 16-gauge cannula inserted into the lateral ventricle via a Burr hole. When necessary, this cannula was flushed with mock cerebrospinal fluid prepared by adding 2.4 mEq of sodium bicarbonate to 100 ml of 0.9% saline. Intracranial venous pressure was measured through a 16-gauge cannula inserted into a drill hole at the confluence of the sagittal and transverse sinuses. Cannula position was confirmed by the free return of venous blood and by the observation that elevation of intracranial pressure by infusion of mock cerebrospinal fluid had no effect on pressure at the confluence, whereas elevation of pressure at the confluence by large saline bolus raised intracranial pressure. Pressures were measured with Statham P23Db and P23ID transducers.

All pressures and flows were recorded on a Brush Mark 600 recorder. In these studies, we did not measure intrathoracic pressure directly, because we wanted to avoid any possibility of modification of intrathoracic pressure fluctuations during CPR by instrumentation of the pleural space. Instead, changes in right atrial pressure were taken as equivalent to changes in intrathoracic (pleural) pressure based on previous studies which showed an extremely close correlation between these pressures during CPR (Chandra et al., 1981a, 1981b).

All dogs received heparin, 2 mg/kg, prior to arrest. In some animals (see below), a Biotronix BL-2045 cannulating electromagnetic flow probe was inserted in the carotid artery, and flow was measured with a Biotronix BL-613 sine wave flowmeter.

After measurement of control pressures and flows, ventricular fibrillation was induced by passing 60 Hz alternating current through a right ventricular pacing wire. External chest compression was initiated within 30 seconds of fibrillation with a Michigan Instruments pneumatic chest compressor (Thumper). During conventional CPR, the chest was compressed 2.5–8.0 cm at a rate of 60 compressions/min. Compression duration was 0.6 second. After every fifth chest compression, the lungs were inflated to a pressure of 33 mm Hg. Simultaneous compression-ventilation (SCV) CPR consisted of chest compression with the Thumper and synchronized ventilation with a pressure-limited ventilator, as previously described (Chandra et al., 1981b). Compression and ventilation were maintained for the first 50% of each compression-release cycle. Compression force and ventilation pressure were varied so that we might explore intracranial pressure fluctuations over a wide range of intrathoracic pressures. Except where otherwise noted, SCV-CPR was performed at a rate of 40/min. All animals were ventilated with room air using a Harvard volume cycled ventilator prior to arrest and with 95% oxygen and 5% carbon dioxide during CPR in order to prevent arterial P_{CO_2} from falling to very low levels during SCV-CPR (when there is marked hyperventilation). The possibility of increased cerebrovascular tone due to profound hypocarbia was in this way avoided.

Determinants of the Magnitude of Transmission of Intrathoracic Pressure to the Intracranial Space

The extent of transmission of intrathoracic pressure to the intracranial space was evaluated sequentially in three ways. First, intrathoracic pressure was varied by changing chest compression force and, during SCV-CPR, airway pressure. Second, the influence of abdominal binding, a maneuver known to increase common carotid pressure and flow (Rudikoff et al., 1980), was assessed. Finally, the influence of baseline intracranial pressure on intracranial pressure fluctuations was determined by infusing mock cerebrospinal fluid (see above) into the lateral ventricle and studying intrathoracic-intracranial pressure relationships at elevated baseline intracranial pressure.

Mechanism of Elevation of Intracranial Pressure

Role of Cerebrospinal Fluid

To examine the role of thoracolumbar cerebrospinal fluid in the transmission of intrathoracic pressure to the intracranial space, laminectomies were performed in seven animals at the level of the fourth cervical vertebral body. Heavy silk suture was placed loosely around the spinal cord and fed into a snare. CPR was performed at variable chest compression force and airway pressure to establish baseline intrathoracic-intracranial pressure relationships and then repeated with the snare drawn tight. Pressure in the thoracic cerebrospinal fluid was measured in six of these animals by inserting an 18-gauge plastic cannula into the subarachnoid space on the caudal side of the snare.

Role of Vascular Channels

The role of vascular channels in the transmission of intrathoracic pressure to the intracranial space was examined in eight dogs. Animals were instrumented as described above, and baseline intrathoracic-intracranial pressure relationships were established during a brief period of CPR. The animals then were defibrillated and exsanguinated by opening additional large bore arterial catheters to atmosphere. Upon cessation of cardiac activity, CPR was reinstituted. Intracranial pressure was maintained at baseline by infusing mock cerebrospinal fluid into the lateral ventricle, and intrathoracic-intracranial pressure relationships were studied again. We assume that, under these conditions of acute, profound hypovolemia, with carotid and jugular pressure near zero, the vascular contribution to intrathoracic-intracranial pressure relationships was minimized.

The contribution of arterial pressure to intracranial pressure was examined in five animals by advancing a balloon-tipped catheter to the ascending aorta under fluoroscopy. When inflated, this balloon completely occluded the aorta. This method permitted study of the effect of abolition of extrathoracic arterial pressure on intracranial pressure fluctuations.

The role of the jugular vein in the transmission of intrathoracic pressure to the intracranial space was examined in two ways. The first consisted of rapid fluctuation of airway pressure during SCV-CPR performed at slow rates (10/min). This maneuver permitted careful inspection of phase and amplitude relationships in the jugular and intracranial pressures. In a second approach, large bore plastic tubing was inserted into the external jugular vein and advanced across the venous valves at the thoracic inlet in the course of resuscitative efforts in four dogs. In this way, the influence of the ensuing marked increase in jugular pressure fluctuations on intracranial pressure was studied.

Finally, the role of venous channels other than the jugular was examined in seven dogs by measuring pressure at the confluence of the sagittal and transverse venous sinuses. Laminectomies were performed at the level of the fourth cervical vertebral body. A snare was passed around the cervical spinal cord and one of the two longitudinal venous sinuses which lie on the ventral side of the spinal cord. Pressure was measured in the lateral ventricle and in the confluence of the sinuses before and after tightening the snare.

Data Analysis

Data were analyzed on CLINFO (sponsored by NIH Division of Resources Grant 5 M01 RR 35-20). Regression lines were constructed by least-squares analysis. Significance levels for correlation coefficients of regression equations follow each equation in parentheses. Standard error of the estimate ($Sy \cdot x$) also follows each equation, under the abbreviation SEE. Slopes of regression lines were compared by the method of Glantz (1981). Paired data were compared by *t*-test.

Results

Transmission of Intrathoracic Pressure to the Intracranial Space

Intrathoracic pressure was transmitted to the intracranial space in all animals studied. Figure 1 shows tracings obtained in one animal during conventional CPR and SCV-CPR. Carotid flow and pressures in jugular vein, aorta, right atrium, and lateral ventricle can be seen to rise and fall together in phase with each chest compression. Higher intrathoracic pressures were accompanied by increased intracranial pressure fluctuations during both forms of CPR. The relationship between changes in intrathoracic pressure and intracranial pressure during SCV-CPR with the abdomen bound and unbound is plotted in Figure 2. The relationship between changes in intrathoracic pressure (ΔITP) and intracranial pressure (ΔICP) with the abdomen unbound was fit by the following linear equation:

$$\Delta ICP\ (mm\ Hg) = 0.33\ \Delta ITP\ (mm\ Hg) + 2.0 \quad (1)$$

where $r = 0.86$ ($P < 0.001$), SEE = 4.74, and ΔITP ranged from 10 to 90 mm Hg.

Abdominal binding, previously shown to increase carotid pressure and flow during CPR (Rudikoff et al., 1980), increased the extent to which intrathoracic pressure was transmitted to the intracranial space. With the abdomen bound, the relationship was fit by a linear equation with a significantly different ($P < 0.01$) slope:

$$\Delta ICP\ (mm\ Hg) = 0.52\ \Delta ITP\ (mm\ Hg) + 2.7 \quad (2)$$

with $r = 0.84$ ($P < 0.001$), and SEE = 7.45.

During conventional CPR, the relationships for intracranial and intrathoracic pressure changes were similar.

Transmission of Intrathoracic Pressure to the Intracranial Space

The Role of Baseline Intracranial Pressure

To examine the influence of baseline intracranial pressure on the extent of transmission of intrathor-

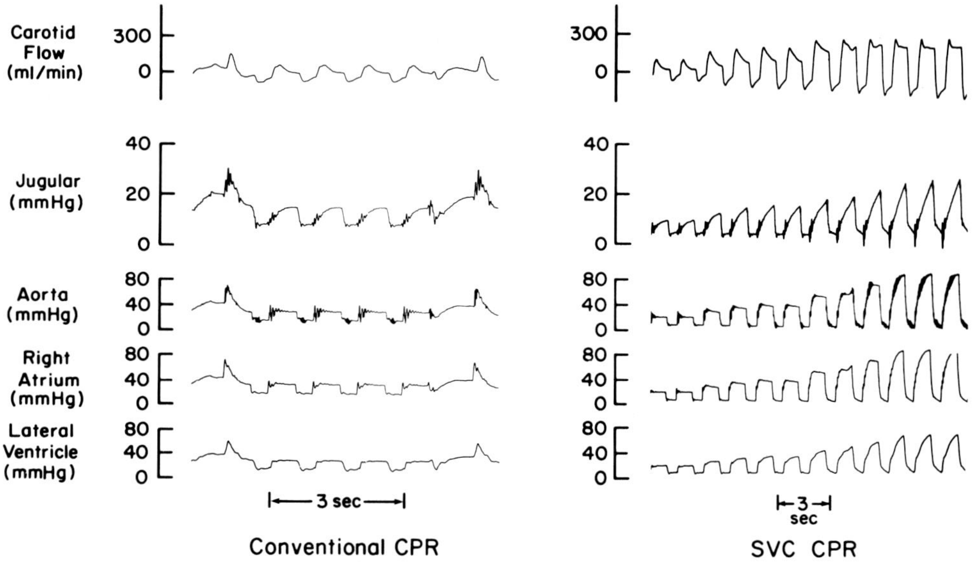

FIGURE 1. *Intracranial pressure during CPR. Panel on the left shows common carotid blood flow and pressures in the jugular vein, aorta, right atrium, and lateral ventricle during conventional CPR. Pressures and flow are greatest on the compressions following ventilation. The panel on the right shows pressures and flow in the same animal during SCV-CPR. Pressures and flow gradually increase because airway pressure is gradually increased. In both forms of CPR, intracranial pressure (lateral ventricle) rises and falls in phase with each chest compression.*

acic pressure to the intracranial space, mock cerebrospinal fluid was infused into the lateral ventricle, and SCV-CPR was performed with both normal and elevated baseline intracranial pressure in seven dogs. Elevation of baseline intracranial pressure increases the extent of transmission of intrathoracic pressure to the intracranial space. For baseline intracranial pressure between 12 and 16 mm Hg, the relationship between fluctuations in intrathoracic and intracranial pressure was fit by the equation:

$$\Delta ICP \text{ (mm Hg)} = 0.40\ \Delta ITP \text{ (mm Hg)} + 5.9 \quad (3)$$

where $r = 0.91$ ($P < 0.001$), and SEE = 3.71.

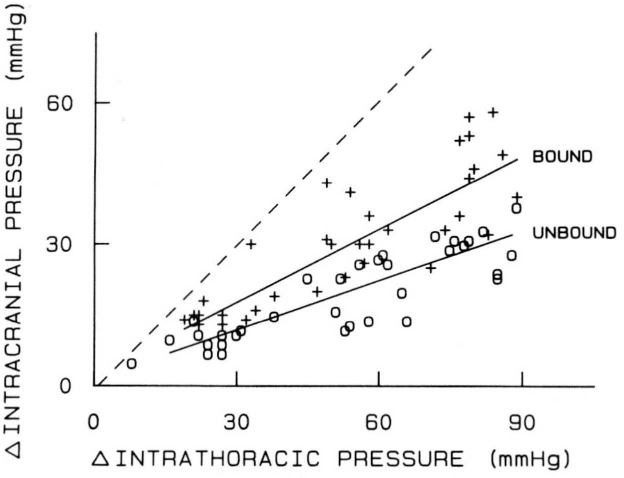

FIGURE 2. *Effect of abdominal binding on intracranial pressure fluctuations during SCV-CPR. Data points obtained with the abdomen bound (+); data points obtained with the abdomen unbound (O). The dashed line is a line of identity. Abdominal binding increases the extent to which intrathoracic pressure is transmitted to the intracranial space.*

Elevation of baseline intracranial pressure to the range of 22–30 mm Hg changed the relationship ($P < 0.001$ vs. Equation 3) to:

$$\Delta ICP \text{ (mm Hg)} = 0.77\ \Delta ITP \text{ (mm Hg)} + 2.4 \quad (4)$$

where $r = 0.95$ ($P < 0.001$) and SEE = 5.21.

Mechanism of Transmission of Intrathoracic Pressure to the Intracranial Space

Role of the Cerebrospinal Fluid

To evaluate the role of the cerebrospinal fluid as a medium by which intrathoracic pressure is transmitted to the intracranial space, pressure was measured in the thoracic subarachnoid space (ΔCSF_T) and lateral ventricle before and after spinal cord ligation in seven animals. Prior to cord ligation, pressure fluctuations were similar in the thoracic and intracranial cerebrospinal fluid:

$$\Delta CSF_T \text{ (mm Hg)} = 0.33\ \Delta ITP \text{ (mm Hg)} + 2.9 \quad (5)$$

where $r = 0.88$ ($P < 0.001$) and SEE = 3.49, and

$$\Delta ICP \text{ (mm Hg)} = 0.32\ \Delta ITP \text{ (mm Hg)} + 3.2 \quad (6)$$

where $r = 0.91$ ($P < 0.001$) and SEE = 2.67.

Following cord ligation, these relationships were no longer equivalent ($P < 0.002$):

$$\Delta CSF_T \text{ (mm Hg)} = 0.40\ \Delta ITP \text{ (mm Hg)} + 3.2 \quad (7)$$

where $r = 0.76$ ($P < 0.001$) and SEE = 6.34.

$$\Delta ICP \text{ (mm Hg)} = 0.22\ \Delta ITP \text{ (mm Hg)} + 2.4 \quad (8)$$

where $r = 0.82$ ($P < 0.001$) and SEE = 2.78.

Intracranial pressure fluctuations thus decreased

substantially (slope of equation 6 ≠ slope of equation 8, $P < 0.01$) following spinal cord ligation, indicating that cerebrospinal fluid is one medium by which intrathoracic pressure is transmitted to the intracranial space.

Mechanism of Transmission of Intrathoracic Pressure to the Intracranial Space

Role of Vascular Channels

The possibility of transmission of intrathoracic pressure to the intracranial space along vascular channels was investigated in several ways. First, eight dogs were fibrillated and SCV-CPR was performed briefly with the abdomen unbound to establish baseline intrathoracic-intracranial pressure relationships. The animals were then defibrillated, exsanguinated, and CPR was resumed. Prior to exsanguination, the relationship between intracranial and intrathoracic pressure fluctuations was

$$\Delta ICP \text{ (mm Hg)} = 0.31\ \Delta ITP \text{ (mm Hg)} + 1.5 \quad (9)$$

where $r = 0.95$ ($P < 0.001$) and SEE = 1.36.

After exsanguination, baseline intracranial pressure fell almost to zero and intracranial pressure fluctuations were virtually abolished. Because of the previously described dependence of intracranial pressure fluctuations on baseline pressure, mock cerebrospinal fluid was infused into the lateral ventricle until the original intracranial pressure was restored. Under conditions of acute hypovolemia with normal baseline intracranial pressure, the relationship was:

$$\Delta ICP \text{ (mm Hg)} = 0.06\ \Delta ITP \text{ (mm Hg)} + 1.8 \quad (10)$$

where $r = 0.56$ ($P < 0.01$) and SEE = 1.55.

This slope is less than that of Equation 9 ($P < 0.001$). Thus, even after restoration of normal baseline intracranial pressure, transmission of intrathoracic pressure to the intracranial space was markedly reduced by removal of blood from vascular channels. This indicates that blood-filled channels are necessary for the majority of pressure transmission.

To examine the contribution of extrathoracic arterial pressure fluctuation to changes in intracranial pressure, a balloon-tipped catheter large enough to occlude the aorta completely, when inflated, was advanced to the ascending aorta under fluoroscopy in five animals. In all animals, carotid pressure and flow fell immediately to zero with balloon inflation, but intracranial pressure fluctuations were not affected. Figure 3 shows a tracing during balloon inflation in one of the five animals. Intrathoracic pressure is not transmitted to the intracranial space along arterial channels.

The jugular veins were also examined as possible routes for transmission of intrathoracic pressure to the intracranial space during CPR. The rate of jugular pressure rise often lagged behind the rate of rise in intracranial pressure (Fig. 3) and marked discrepancies between peak jugular and intracranial pressures were occasionally observed. Because these findings suggested that jugular pressure changes did not determine intracranial pressure, two maneuvers were studied in an attempt to clearly dissociate intracranial and jugular pressure fluctuations.

The first maneuver consisted of rapid fluctuation of airway pressure (and, thus, intrathoracic pressure) during SCV-CPR performed at slow rates. In seven animals with the abdomen bound and high baseline intracranial pressure (21.6 ± 5.0 mm Hg), rapid fluctuation of airway pressure produced changes in intrathoracic pressure of 37.7 ± 5.5 mm Hg. During this same maneuver, intracranial pressure changed by 23.3 ± 8.4 mm Hg, whereas jugular pressure changed by only 2.4 ± 2.7 mm Hg ($P < 0.001$) (Fig. 4).

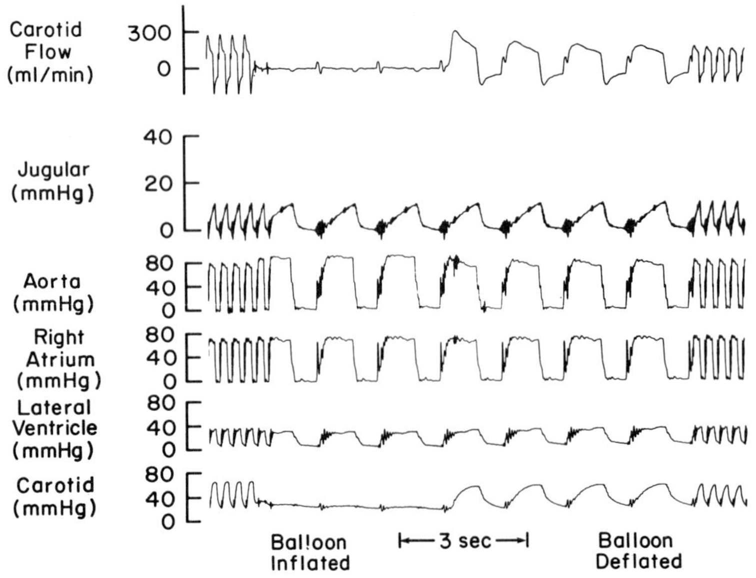

FIGURE 3. *Effect of balloon occlusion of the ascending aorta on intracranial pressure fluctuations during CPR. Carotid pressure and flow fall immediately toward zero with inflation of a balloon in the ascending aorta. Pressures in the jugular vein, aortic root, right atrium, and lateral ventricle are unaffected.*

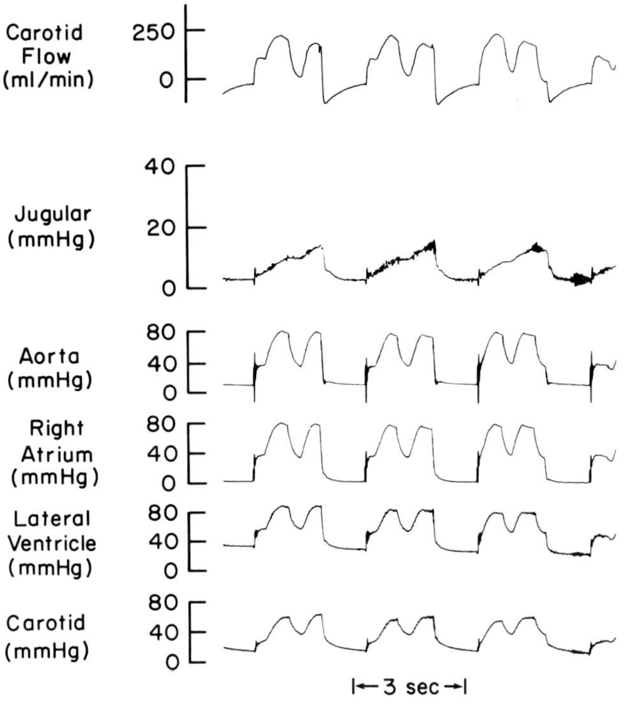

FIGURE 4. *Dissociation of jugular and intracranial pressure changes during CPR. Rapid fluctuation in airway pressure during SCV-CPR at low rates (10 cycles/min) is reflected by a change in aortic and right atrial pressure of more than 40 mm Hg. Intracranial pressure falls and rises by nearly 25 mm Hg during the same maneuver. Jugular pressure, which is lower than intracranial pressure throughout the maneuver, changes by less than 5 mm Hg.*

In the second maneuver, large bore plastic tubing was inserted into the external jugular vein and advanced across the venous valves at the thoracic inlet in the course of resuscitative efforts in four dogs. This maneuver resulted in a rise in jugular venous pressure to the level of right atrial pressure but had no effect on intracranial pressure (Fig. 5). Postmortem dissection of the jugular veins of these animals revealed a more distal set of venous valves at the level of the mandible in each animal, as previously described by Hegedus and Shackleford (1965).

Because jugular and intracranial pressures were not closely correlated and could be easily dissociated, pressure transmission along venous channels other than the jugular was examined in an additional seven dogs during SCV-CPR. Pressure fluctuations were measured at the confluence of the sagittal and transverse sinuses (ΔCon) as well as in the lateral ventricle and thoracic subarachnoid space before and after cord ligation. Prior to cord ligation, the relationships between ΔITP, ΔICP, and ΔCon were fit by the equations (Fig. 6a):

$$\Delta\text{ICP (mm Hg)} = 0.32\ \Delta\text{ITP (mm Hg)} + 3.2 \quad (6)$$

where $r = 0.91$ ($P < 0.001$) and SEE = 2.67.

$$\Delta\text{Con (mm Hg)} = 0.21\ \Delta\text{ITP (mm Hg)} + 3.5 \quad (11)$$

where $r = 0.81$ ($P < 0.001$) and SEE = 2.88.

Although quantitatively less than intracranial pressure changes (slope of Equation 6 ≠ slope of Equation 11, $P < 0.001$), the phase and direction of pressure changes at the confluence of the sinuses were always similar to intracranial pressure changes. This contrasts with the previously noted discrepancies between jugular and intracranial pressure changes and suggested that fluctuations at the confluence of the intracranial sinuses reflected the vascular contribution to intracranial pressure changes. After cord ligation, (Fig. 6b) with ΔITP again ranging from 10 to 80 mm Hg, the relationship was fit by a new set of equations:

$$\Delta\text{ICP (mm Hg)} = 0.22\ \Delta\text{ITP (mm Hg)} + 2.4 \quad (8)$$

where $r = 0.82$ ($P < 0.001$) and SEE = 2.78.

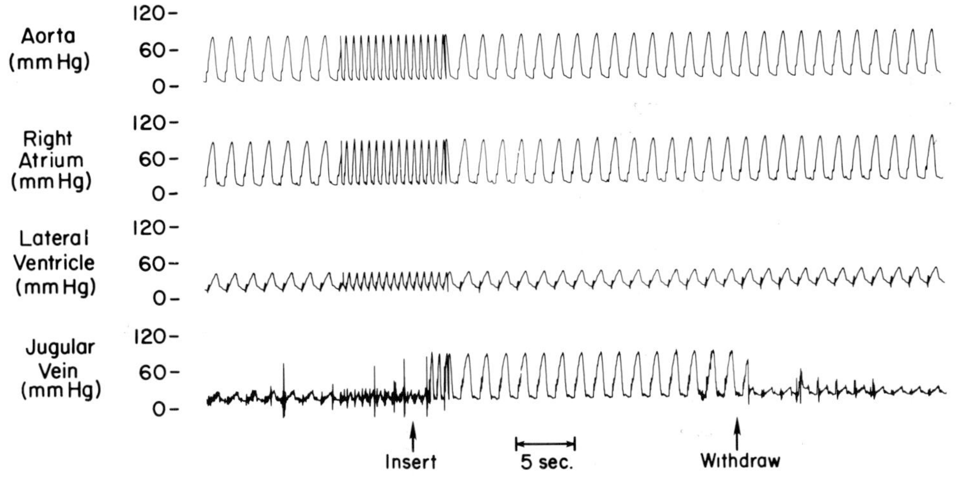

FIGURE 5. *Dissociation of jugular and intracranial pressure fluctuations with a jugular conduit. CPR is performed at constant chest compression force and airway pressure while a conduit is passed across the venous valve at the thoracic inlet. Conduit insertion makes jugular pressure fluctuations equivalent to right atrial fluctuations but has no effect on intracranial pressure.*

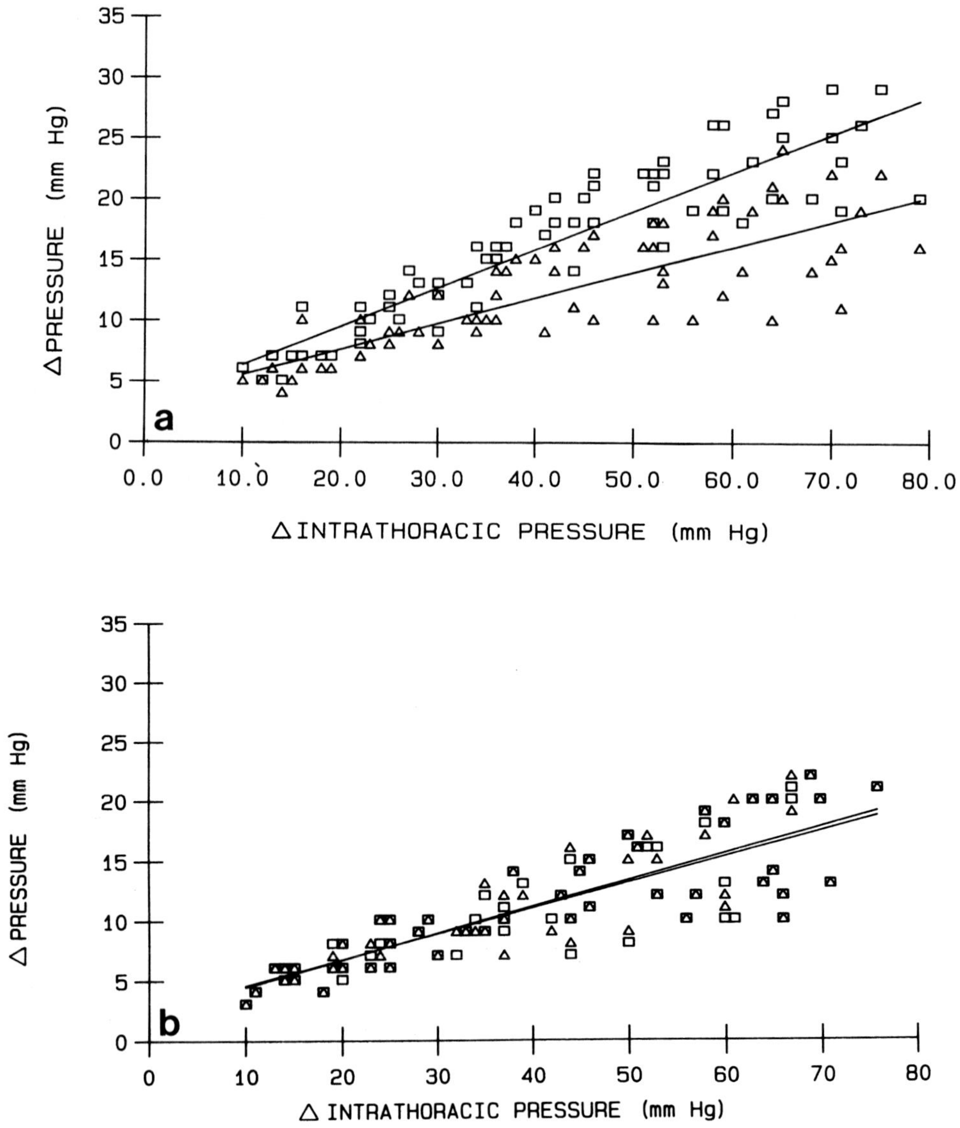

FIGURE 6. *Panel a: pressure fluctuations in the lateral ventricle (□) and at the confluence of the intracranial venous sinuses (Δ) prior to ligation of the cervical spinal cord. Panel b: pressure fluctuations in the lateral ventricle (□) and at the confluence of the intracranial venous sinuses (Δ) after ligation of the cervical spinal cord. Regression lines for both sets of data are not significantly different, and, furthermore, do not differ significantly from pressure fluctuations at the confluence of venous sinuses prior to cord ligation (c.f., Fig. 6a).*

$$\Delta Con\ (mm\ Hg) = 0.22\ \Delta ITP\ (mm\ Hg) + 2.2 \quad (12)$$

where $r = 0.84$ ($P < 0.001$) and SEE = 2.41.

These equations do not differ significantly from each other. Thus, once pressure transmission via cerebrospinal fluid was abolished by spinal cord ligation, intracranial pressure changes were dependent on and equivalent to changes in pressure at the confluence of the sinuses (Fig. 7).

Although pressure fluctuations in the thoracic cerebrospinal fluid did not increase significantly after cord ligation with the abdomen unbound, they did increase ($P < 0.01$) following cord ligation with the abdomen bound. This finding suggested the possibility of direct transmission of intrathoracic pressure to the thoracic subarachnoid space (in addition to pressurization of thoracic cerebrospinal fluid by blood in paraspinal veins which anastamose with the intercostal and azygous systems). To examine this process, pressure fluctuations were measured in the intracranial and thoracic subarachnoid spaces and at the confluence of the venous sinuses after exsanguination. Following exsanguination and prior to cord ligation,

$$\Delta CSF_T\ (mm\ Hg) = 0.06\ \Delta ITP\ (mm\ Hg) + 2.7 \quad (13)$$

where $r = 0.73$ ($P < 0.001$) and SEE = 1.0.

After cord ligation pressure changes in the thoracic cerebrospinal fluid were increased ($P < 0.05$) to:

$$\Delta CSF_T\ (mm\ Hg) = 0.11\ \Delta ITP\ (mm\ Hg) + 3.3 \quad (14)$$

where $r = 0.91$ ($P < 0.001$), SEE = 1.1, and ΔITP ranged from 10 to 80 mm Hg.

Because exsanguination virtually abolished pressure changes at the confluence of the venous sinuses, thoracic cerebrospinal fluid pressure fluctuations in the absence of vascular pressure fluctuations

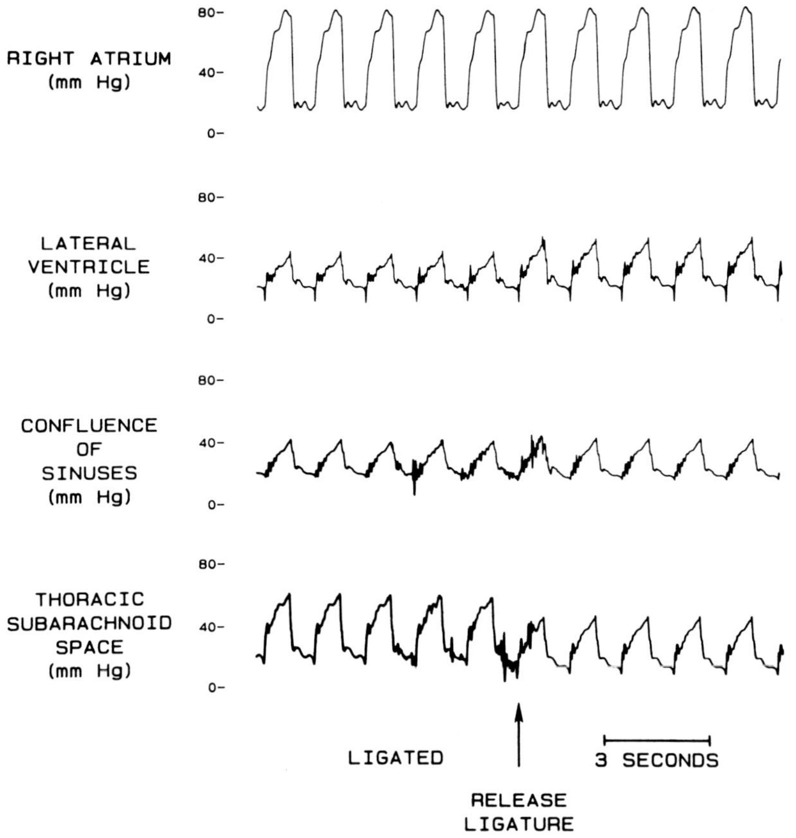

FIGURE 7. *Pressure fluctuations before and after release of a ligature around the cervical spinal cord. Intracranial (lateral ventricle) pressure changes are equivalent to pressure changes at the confluence of the intracranial venous sinuses during ligation and greater than venous sinus pressure after release of the ligature. Thoracic cerebrospinal fluid pressure fluctuations are greater than intracranial pressure during cord ligation and equal to intracranial pressure changes after release of the ligature. Venous sinus pressure is unaffected by ligation. This result demonstrates that (1) thoracic and intracranial cerebrospinal fluid pressures are in equilibrium when CSF flow is unobstructed, (2) pressure changes at the confluence of the venous sinus account entirely for intracranial pressure changes when transmission of pressure is eliminated (by cord ligation), and (3) thoracic cerebrospinal fluid pressure changes are increased by cord ligation, suggesting direct transmission of intrathoracic pressure to the thoracic subarachnoid space.*

indicate direct transmission of intrathoracic pressure to the spinal canal.

Finally, to determine whether the longitudinal vertebral veins participate in pressure transmission, a snare was passed around one of the two veins and the spinal cord. Before the snare was tightened,

$$\Delta ICP \text{ (mm Hg)} = 0.31\ \Delta ITP \text{ (mm Hg)} + 3.0 \quad (15)$$

where $r = 0.94$ ($P < 0.001$) and SEE = 2.2.

$$\Delta Con \text{ (mm Hg)} = 0.23\ \Delta ITP \text{ (mm Hg)} + 3.6 \quad (16)$$

where $r = 0.89$ ($P < 0.001$) and SEE = 2.2.

After the snare was tightened around the cervical cord and one of the longitudinal vertebral veins adjacent to the cord,

$$\Delta ICP \text{ (mm Hg)} = 0.10\ \Delta ITP \text{ (mm Hg)} + 4.8 \quad (17)$$

where $r = 0.66$ ($P < 0.01$) and SEE = 2.3.

$$\Delta Con \text{ (mm Hg)} = 0.09\ \Delta ITP \text{ (mm Hg)} + 5.0 \quad (18)$$

where $r = 0.62$ ($P < 0.01$) and SEE = 2.5.

Once again, intracranial venous sinus and lateral ventricular pressure changes were equivalent after obstruction of cerebrospinal fluid flow. However, with simultaneous ligation of one of the longitudinal vertebral veins, these pressure changes were significantly less than intracranial venous sinus pressure prior to ligation (slope of Equations 17 and 18 ≠ slope of Equation 16, $P < 0.01$). This result differs from that obtained by cord ligation alone, after which pressure fluctuations in the lateral ventricle and confluence were equivalent to pressure changes at the confluence prior to cord ligation, and suggests that the longitudinal vertebral veins participate in pressure transmission.

Discussion

These studies demonstrate that elevation of intracranial pressure is a consistent feature of CPR. At each of the baseline intracranial pressures studied, the proportion of intrathoracic pressure transmitted to the intracranial space was relatively constant over a wide range of changes of intrathoracic pressure during both conventional and SCV-CPR. In animals with normal baseline intracranial pressure, about one-third of the change in intrathoracic pressure was transmitted to the intracranial space during CPR with the abdomen unbound and about one-half of the intrathoracic pressure change was transmitted to the intracranial space during CPR with the abdomen bound.

Baseline intracranial pressure is a critical determinant of the extent to which intrathoracic pressure is transmitted to the intracranial space. When baseline intracranial pressure was raised from a range of 12 to 16 mm Hg to a range of 22 to 30 mm Hg by infusing a mock solution of cerebrospinal fluid into the lateral ventricle, transmission of intrathoracic pressure to the intracranial space nearly doubled (Fig. 3). The fact that transmission of intrathoracic pressure to the intracranial space is increased by raising intracranial pressure is in keeping with current understanding of intracranial elastance in both animals and humans in the non-arrest situation (Lofgren et al., 1973; Lofgren and Zwetnow, 1973; Guinane, 1975; Avezaat et al., 1979; Burchiel et al., 1981). Increased intracranial elastance is also a likely explanation for the marked increase in intracranial pressure reported by Rogers and colleagues (1979) during CPR in a patient with cerebral edema.

Vascular channels are responsible for the bulk of transmission of intrathoracic pressure to the intracranial space, as demonstrated by studies in which exsanguination reduced intracranial pressure fluctuations to low levels despite maintenance of baseline intracranial pressure. Ligation of the cervical spinal cord also decreased intracranial pressure fluctuations, but by a lesser amount than exsanguination. Because this maneuver eliminated pressure transmission by the cerebrospinal fluid, it indicates that cerebrospinal fluid also contributes to intracranial pressure fluctuations during CPR. In addition, thoracic cerebrospinal fluid pressure, in equilibrium with intracranial pressure before cord ligation, was increased following cord ligation (Fig. 7). The increase in thoracic cerebrospinal fluid pressure produced by cervical cord ligation, present even during acute, profound hypovolemia, demonstrates that intrathoracic pressure is transmitted to the spinal canal directly through intervertebral foramina as well as via vascular channels.

A major goal of these experiments was the identification of the specific vascular routes of transmission of intrathoracic pressure to the intracranial space. Intracranial pressure fluctuations were unaffected by ablation of carotid (and all other cephalic arterial) pressure changes during aortic occlusion. Clearly, then, the large arteries of the neck do not transmit intrathoracic pressure to the brain. The dissociation of jugular venous pressure and intracranial pressure can be explained by the presence of competent venous valves at the thoracic inlet and mandible (Hegedus and Shackleford, 1965; Niemann et al., 1980; Fisher et al., 1981), which prevented retrograde pressure transmission.

That neither the extrathoracic arteries nor the jugular veins account for transmission of intrathoracic pressure to the intracranial space does not rule out other vascular channels as routes of pressure transmission. As noted above, when CPR was performed at constant baseline intracranial pressure, exsanguination eliminated approximately 80% of intracranial pressure fluctuations. This result demonstrates that blood-filled vascular channels are essential for transmission of intrathoracic pressure to the intracranial space. Direct evidence in support of non-valved veins in the transmission of intrathoracic pressure to the intracranial space was provided by studies in which pressure was measured at the confluence of the transverse and sagittal sinuses. Before cord ligation, pressure changes at the confluence accounted for most of the intracranial pressure change (Eq. 11). After cord ligation, pressure changes at the confluence were unchanged and accounted for all of the intracranial pressure fluctuation (Eq. 12).

We did not examine directly blood pressure or flow in the vertebrobasilar system or the longitudinal vertebral veins. Nevertheless, these veins, which are not known to contain valves, must be regarded as loci for transmission of intrathoracic pressure to the intracranial space during CPR. The longitudinal vertebral veins are particularly attractive in this regard. Situated inside the vertebral column, the longitudinal vertebral veins communicate extensively with the azygous and intercostal veins and have direct access to the intracranial space via the foramen magnum (Reinhard et al., 1962) Indeed, when one of the two longitudinal sinuses were ligated, pressure fluctuations at the confluence of the sinuses and in the lateral ventricle fell.

In summary, at normal baseline intracranial pressure, a relatively constant proportion of intrathoracic pressure is transmitted to the intracranial space. The majority of pressure transmission occurs along venous channels other than the jugular. The longitudinal vertebral veins are the most important of several possible channels. Substantial pressure transmission is also mediated by cerebrospinal fluid as a consequence of transmission of intrathoracic pressure ITP to the thoracic CSF, most likely via the intervertebral foramina. Increased pressure transmission during abdominal binding is presumably due to the fact that abdominal binding increases lumbar spinal fluid pressure as well as intraabdominal pressure. Caudal run-off of blood and spinal fluid during chest compression is thereby impeded.

Increases in intracranial pressure during ventilation with positive end-expiratory pressure (PEEP) in dogs have been attributed to passive elevation of jugular venous pressure (Luce et al., 1982). These findings do not necessarily conflict with our own observations. Unlike PEEP, which is applied at low levels for long periods of time in animals with normal carotid and jugular flow, CPR consists of the application of high pressure for short time intervals with low blood flows. In relation to the brain, the jugular vein during CPR is a downstream segment, compartmentalized by valves, with a compliance great enough so that the small amount of antegrade and retrograde blood flow is accommodated with a pressure rise which may be considerably less than intracranial pressure fluctuations. The brevity of increases in intrathoracic pressure during CPR may not permit equilibration of jugular pressure with pressure in those non-valved veins which do transmit intrathoracic pressure to the intracranial space. This contrasts sharply with studies of PEEP, in which increases in intrathoracic venous pressure are so modest and so slow that the jugular valves may not close. If so, the jugular vein would remain in equilibrium with other craniovertebral veins during PEEP. As these studies demonstrate, this equilibrium is not necessarily reached during CPR.

The adequacy of cerebral blood flow during CPR has been an issue of major concern ever since the development of modern resuscitative techniques. Two recent papers (Koehler et al., 1983, Michael et al., 1984) show a clear correlation between cerebral perfusion and cerebral perfusion pressure gradients (mean carotid artery pressure—mean intracranial pressure) over a wide range of pressures and experimental conditions. Peak intrathoracic pressure ranged from 56 to 101 mm Hg during conventional and SCV-CPR in these studies, and mean carotid pressure varied from as little as 17 mm Hg during SCV-CPR with carotid collapse, to 71 mm Hg during SCV-CPR after collapse, had been reversed by epinephrine. In these studies, intracranial pressure fluctuations were minimally affected by carotid collapse for reasons made clear by Figure 3: intracranial pressure changes during CPR are unrelated to carotid arterial pressure. Intracranial pressure fluctuations were substantially increased by abdominal binding in the study by Michael et al. (1984), but this phenomenon did not alter the fundamental relationship between cerebral perfusion pressure and actual cerebral blood flow.

The major goals of CPR are maintenance of cerebral and coronary perfusion at levels compatible with cell survival until spontaneous effective circulation is restored. Viewed from the perspective of generation of cerebral perfusion pressure gradients, elevation of intrathoracic pressure is a two-edged sword. Transmission of intrathoracic pressure to the intracranial space, which limits cerebral flow, is ever present and increased by abdominal binding and under conditions of elevated baseline intracranial pressure. Nevertheless, elevation of intrathoracic pressure is a sword which may be wielded to advantage. Intracranial pressure fluctuations are proportional to intrathoracic pressure changes but unrelated to carotid artery pressure during CPR. Therefore, efforts designed to maintain peak carotid pressure at or near peak intrathoracic pressure should maximize the cerebral perfusion pressure gradient for any given change in intrathoracic pressure. Furthermore, to the extent that the efficiency of transmission of intrathoracic pressure to the carotid artery can be maximized, efforts aimed at the safe elevation of intrathoracic pressure to levels above those attained during conventional CPR will be rewarded by increased cerebral blood flow.

Supported by Grant P50-HL 17655-10 from the National Heart, Lung, and Blood Institute, National Institute of Health, and Grant 5T32 HL 07227-07 from the National Heart, Lung, and Blood Institute, Bethesda, Maryland.

Computational assistance provided by CLINFO (NIH Division of Resources Grant 5M01 RR 35-20).

Dr. Shi is a member of the faculty of the Peking Medical College, Peoples Republic of China.

Address for reprints: Nisha Chandra, M.D., Director, Coronary Care Unit, Francis Scott Key Medical Center, Baltimore, Maryland 21224.

Received July 19, 1983; accepted for publication September 19, 1984.

References

Avezaat CJJ, Van Eijndhoven JHM, Wyper DJ (1979) Cerebrospinal fluid pulse pressure and intracranial pressure relationships. J Neurol Neurosurg Psychiatry **42:** 687–700

Bircher N, Safar P (1981) Comparison of standard and new closed-chest CPR and open chest CPR in dogs. Crit Care Med **9:** 384–385

Burchiel KJ, Steege TD, Wyler AR (1981) Intracranial pressure changes in brain-injured patients requiring positive end-expiratory pressure ventilation. Neurosurgery **8:** 443–449

Chandra N, Rudikoff M, Weisfeldt ML (1980) Simultaneous chest compression and ventilation at high airway pressure during cardiopulmonary resuscitation. Lancet **1:** 175–178

Chandra N, Guerci A, Weisfeldt ML, Tsitlik J, LePor N (1981a) Contrasts between intrathoracic pressure during external chest compression and cardiac massage. Crit Care Med **9:** 789–792

Chandra N, Weisfeldt ML, Tsitlik J, Vaghaiwalla F, Snyder L, Hoffecker M, Rudikoff M (1981b) Augmentation of carotid flow during CPR in dogs by ventilation at high airway pressures simultaneous with chest compression. Am J Cardiol **48:** 1053–1063

Fisher J, Vaghaiwalla F, Tsitlik J, Levin H, Brinker J, Weisfeldt ML, Yin F (1982) Determinants and clinical significance of jugular venous valve competence. Circulation **65:** 188–196

Glantz SA (1981) Primer of Biostatistics. New York, McGraw-Hill

Guinane JE (1975) Cerebrospinal fluid pulse pressure and brain compliance in adult cats. Neurology **25:** 559–564

Hamilton WF, Woodbury RA, Harper HT (1944) Arterial, cerebrospinal and venous pressure in man during cough and strain. Am J Physiol. **141:** 42–50

Hegedus SA, Shackleford RT (1965) A comparative anatomical study of the craniocervical venous systems in mammals, with special reference to the dog. J Anat **116:** 375–386

Koehler RC, Chandra N, Guerci AD, Tsitlik J, Traystman RJ, Rogers MC, Weisfeldt ML (1983) Augmentation of cerebral perfusion by simultaneous chest compression and lung inflation with abdominal binding after cardiac arrest in dogs. Circulation **67:** 266–274

Lofgren L, Zwetnow N (1973) Cranial and spinal components of the cerebrospinal fluid pressure-volume curve. Acta Neurol Scand **49:** 575–596

Lofgren L, Von Essen C, Zwetnow N (1973) The pressure volume curve of the cerebrospinal fluid space in dogs. Acta Neurol Scand **49:** 557–574

Luce JM, Huseby JS, Kirk W, Butler J (1982) Mechanisms by which positive end-expiratory pressure increases cerebrospinal fluid in dogs. J Appl Physiol **52:** 231–235

Michael JR, Guerci AD, Koehler RC, Shi AY, Tsitlik J, Chandra N, Niedermeyer E, Rogers MC, Traystman RJ, Weisfeldt ML (1984) Mechanisms by which epinephrine augments cerebral and myocardial perfusion during cardiopulmonary resuscitation in dogs. Circulation **69:** 822–835

Niemann JT, Rosborough J, Hausknecht M, Brown D, Criley JM (1980) Cough CPR. Crit Care Med **8:** 141–146

Niemann JT, Rosborough J, Hausknecht M, Gardner D, Criley JM (1981) Pressure synchronized cineangiography during experimental cardiopulmonary resuscitation. Circulation **64:** 985–991

Reinhard KR, Miller ME, Evans HE (1962) The craniovertebral veins and sinuses of the dog. Am J Anat **11:** 67–87

Rogers MC, Nugent SK, Stidham GL (1979) Effects of closed-chest cardiac massage on intracranial pressure. Crit Care Med **7:** 454–456

Rudikoff MT, Maughan WL, Effron M, Freund P, Weisfeldt ML (1980) Mechanisms of blood flow during cardiopulmonary resuscitation. Circulation **61:** 345–352

INDEX TERMS: Cardiopulmonary resuscitation • Resuscitation • Intracranial pressure

Relationship between Myocardial Fiber Direction and Segment Shortening in the Midwall of the Canine Left Ventricle

Gregory L. Freeman, Martin M. LeWinter, Robert L. Engler, and James W. Covell
From the University of California, San Diego, School of Medicine, La Jolla, California

SUMMARY. Myocardial fiber orientation undergoes an orderly transition from the epicardium to the endocardium in the left ventricle, with circumferential fibers predominating in the middle one-third of the heart wall. How fibers lying at different depths in the myocardium, running in different directions, interact to produce local deformation is not known. To define the relationship between the orientation of uniaxial myocardial fibers and *local wall motion*, we placed three sets of ultrasonic dimension gauges in the middle one-third of the apex-to-base distance of the left ventricle of nine dogs. One pair was placed in line and two intentionally out of line with the presumed local fiber direction. The relative angle between the gauge and the local myofibers was determined by the use of postmortem radiography and histological techniques. Our results show that in the midwall of the left ventricle, myocardial segment shortening is maximal in the direction of local fibers; the shortening measured by gauges placed out of line with the local fiber axis by more than 30° was significantly less than the actual in-line fiber shortening which occurred. This suggests that functional tethering between midwall fibers and endocardial or epicardial fibers does not play a major role in the pattern of midwall deformation. We also documented that an external reference line can be used to predict midwall myofiber direction. Using this line as a guide, ultrasonic dimension gauges could be placed within an average of 12° (range: 0.5 to 18.5°) from the local fiber axis. **(*Circ Res 56: 31–39, 1985*)**

THE left ventricle of the mammalian heart has a complex morphology which has intrigued investigators for many years. Anatomic studies have demonstrated the manner in which individual myofibers are woven together to form the ventricular chamber (McCallum, 1900; Robb and Robb, 1942; Torrent-Guasp, 1973). Streeter (1979) has demonstrated that myocardial fiber orientation in the frontal plane undergoes an orderly transition from the epicardium to the endocardium, with circumferential fibers predominating in the middle one third of the heart wall. The way in which fibers lying at different depths in the heart wall and having different orientations interact during the cardiac cycle is not known. One theory holds that individual myocardial fibers act as "slippery skinned rods" which bear tension in only one direction and exert no force on the fibers oriented in other directions (Hort, 1957; Streeter, 1979). According to this theory, significant functional interaction does not occur between layers of myofibers lying in different depths of the heart wall. Another theory holds that such interaction, which some have termed "tethering," does occur. Using the technique of partial coronary occlusion, Gallagher et al. (1982) showed that the shortening behavior of epicardial segments is partially dependent on underlying fibers which are oriented in a markedly different direction. Meier et al. (1982) postulated a similar mechanism in the right ventricle of dogs. These and other studies (Dieudonne, 1969; Ingels et al., 1971; Arts et al., 1982) suggest an important functional linkage between successive myocardial layers. Moreover, the presence of an extensive collagenous network surrounding myocytes, collagen struts between myocytes, and microthreads (3–6 nm in diameter) between myocytes and between collagen struts demonstrates an anatomical framework for functional connections between layers (Caulfield and Borg, 1979; Robinson and Winegrad, 1981).

The net result of the complicated myofiber arrangement is to translate uniaxial sarcomere shortening into three-dimensional deformation of the ventricular cavity. In the absence of functional connections between fibers lying at different depths in the heart wall, local segment shortening would be greatest in a direction parallel to local fiber axis. This relation has been assumed by numerous investigators, who have used ultrasonic transit time-dimension gauges to study regional function, and aligned the gauges with the presumed fiber orientation. Techniques used to analyze ventricular function noninvasively, such as echocardiography, presume that, since most of the ventricular fibers are circumferential, the measurement of a linear dimension in this direction will reflect overall myofiber performance (Mitchell et al., 1969; Karliner et al., 1970;

Cooper et al., 1972). If fibers that are oriented in different directions do have important functional connections, systolic deformation will include both shortening along the axis of the fibers and motion related to such connections. The latter may be termed "lateral strain," since it is in effect sideways motion of the fibers. If lateral strain occurs, the behavior of linear segments will not depend solely on the local fiber orientation, but, to some extent, on a pattern of global ventricular deformation.

The purpose of this study was to determine how left ventricular midwall segment shortening is influenced by deformation in other layers by examining the relationship between local shortening and fiber direction. We were also interested in whether the orientation of local fibers could be predicted accurately from external landmarks in the intact, beating heart, and how closely ultrasonic dimension gauges could be aligned with the fiber axis.

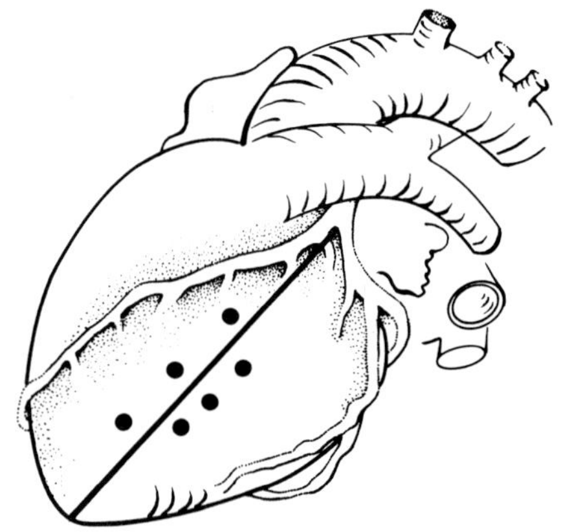

FIGURE 1. *The positions of the external long axis marker and ultrasonic dimension gauges. The middle set of crystals is perpendicular to the long axis, while both the apical and basal sets are at an angle to it.*

Methods

Nine mongrel dogs were anesthetized with pentobarbital, 25 mg/kg, iv. The animals were intubated and respiration was supported by a Harvard ventilator; supplemental anesthesia was administered as needed. A midline sternotomy and bilateral 5th interspace thoracotomy was performed, and the heart was suspended in a pericardial cradle. The azygos vein was ligated, and sutures were positioned around the caval veins, the hila, the ascending aorta, and the innominate, left carotid, and left subclavian arteries. These were left loosely in place. A 7F micromanometer-tipped catheter (Millar Instruments) was placed in the left ventricle via the left carotid artery and a fluid-filled 8F pigtail catheter was introduced into the left ventricle via the left femoral artery. The micromanometer-tipped red catheter was calibrated to the fluid-filled catheter, and the latter was then withdrawn to the ascending aorta.

Quantitative information on the direction of fibers in the left ventricular wall stems primarily from the extensive work of Streeter (1979). In those studies, an internal reference axis system was employed which is not directly accessible in the beating heart. The current studies required that pairs of piezoelectric crystals be inserted in the midwall of the ventricle in a known relationship to the local fibers. Accordingly, we developed an empirical technique to estimate the location of the internal reference axis from an external reference axis on the surface of the beating heart. A length of 3-0 silk suture was sewn to the epicardium over the apical dimple, passed over the surface of the LV by the shortest path and secured to the epicardium just below the bifurcation of the left coronary artery. This was left in place for the duration of the study. Three sets of ultrasonic dimension gauges were then placed in the midwall of the left ventricle. Polyethylene sheathes with a flange 0.5 cm from the gauge crystals aided in insertion into the midwall at a reproducible depth. All gauges were placed in the middle one-third of the apex-to-base distance of the ventricle. The middle set of crystals was placed in the direction of the local fiber axis as predicted from prior anatomic studies (i.e., perpendicular to the external reference axis). The other gauges were intentionally placed out of line with the predicted local fiber axis (Fig. 1).

In two additional dogs, the same protocol was carried out, but the three pairs of dimension gauges were placed in the most superficial layer of the epicardium. All recordings were made on a Brush-Clevite model 2000 oscillograph, at a paper speed of 200 mm/sec. Control aortic pressure, left ventricular pressure, and segment gauge signals were recorded with respiration suspended at end-expiration, and all values were averaged for three successive beats.

The segment length at onset of ejection (LOE) was defined as the length at the time in systole when the ventricular pressure became equal to the aortic pressure. The value of pressure at the rapid upstroke of the aortic tracing was noted, and transposed to the micromanometer tracing to account for the time lag between these two catheter systems. The end-systolic length (ESL) was defined at the time when LV pressure fell below aortic pressure, using a similar time lag correction. Ejection phase shortening was equal to (LOE−ESL)/LOE.

After instrumentation, recordings were made at control left ventricular end-diastolic pressure (LVEDP) which ranged from 7 to 10 mm Hg. Measurements were then repeated after infusion of normal saline to raise the LVEDP to approximately 15 mm Hg. Left ventricular pressures were then allowed to return to the control state, and measurements were made following a 2-mg iv bolus of calcium chloride. After return to the control state once more, measurements were repeated a final time at the time of peak response to a 2-μg iv bolus of isoproterenol.

At this point, the micromanometer-tipped catheter was removed, and the pigtail catheter was reintroduced into the ventricle. The previously placed sutures were tied, isolating the heart. After injection of KCl to arrest the heart, the LV pressure was adjusted to the control value (7–10 mm Hg) by infusion or withdrawal of saline, and the heart was fixed by rapid intracoronary injection using the technique of Yoran et al. (1973). Bouin's solution, which consists of 10 g of picric acid crystals, 50 ml of glacial acetic acid, and 250 ml of 37% formalin in 750 ml H_2O, was used as the fixative agent. The heart was excised, the right ventricle and atria dissected away, and the LV was cast with latex and immersed in Bouin's solution. When the latex was set a metal skewer (4.8 mm o.d.) was passed from the apical dimple to the mitral aspect of the

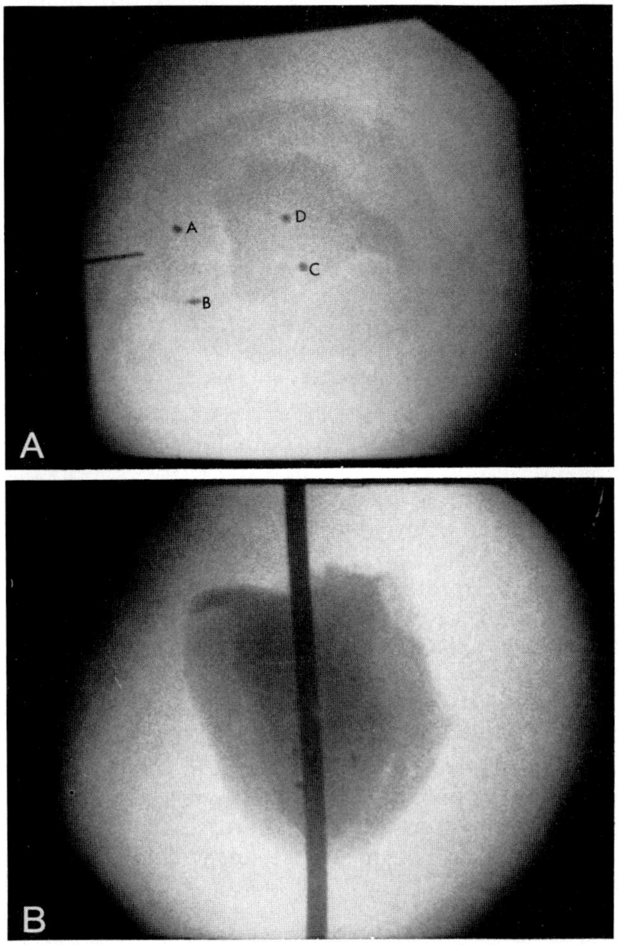

FIGURE 2. *Panel A: radiograph of a ventricular slice, showing that the crystals are in the midwall (points A and B). The marker on the left shows the location of external long axis. Point C marks the center of the x-ray beam and point D shows the location of the internal long axis marker. Panel B: a radiograph showing the internal long axis marker and dimension gauges. In this example, the external long axis marker overlies the internal marker, which also obscures the position of one crystal.*

aortic valve (the long axis used by Streeter). A fine wire marker was placed over the silk suture determining the external long axis. The heart was then positioned in a special holder, and radiographs were taken with the external marker lying in a plane perpendicular to the table (see Fig. 2). This allowed determination of angle between internal and external long axis markers.

After removal of the external marker, the ventricle was cut into rings, approximately 1 cm thick, perpendicular to the internal long axis, and radiographs were taken of these (see Fig. 2). Transmural blocks measuring approximately 1 × 1 cm which included each crystal were excised and were notched to identify their reference edge. The crystals were gently removed, and the tissue blocks were embedded in paraffin. Tissue shrinkage of 15–20% is expected using our processing technique (Humason, 1979). This was assumed to be homogeneous. Sections 10 μm thick were taken, beginning at and tangent to the epicardium, proceeding to the endocardium. Defects at the site of the crystals were clearly seen, and 15–20 sections were mounted from this region (Fig. 3).

A goniometer eyepiece (accurate ±0.25°) was used to determine the angle between the fiber direction and the reference edge in the six adjacent sections from each block in which the crystal defect had its largest diameter. An average value was calculated, and this value was used in the subsequent analysis. In two instances, sections were mounted through the entire course of the crystal (approximately 60 sections) to determine how much the local angle changed in this depth of the heart wall.

The angle between the intracrystal axis and the internal long axis was determined from the radiographs (Fig. 2A). The angle between the local fiber direction and the internal long axis was determined from the microscopic slides (Fig. 3). Together, the radiographic and histological measurements allowed calculation of the relative angle between local myofiber orientation and the intracrystal axis.

When the angle between the reference edge and the myofibers was different in the two crystals of a given pair, the average of these values was used.

Results

Figure 4A illustrates the construct used in our data analysis. The myofibers run in a direction parallel

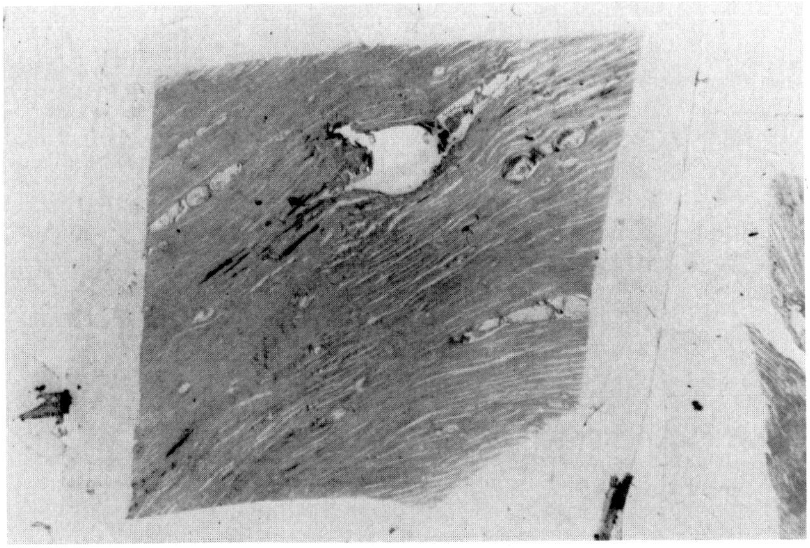

FIGURE 3. *Photomicrograph of histological section with the reference edge on top. The crystal defect is clearly visible.*

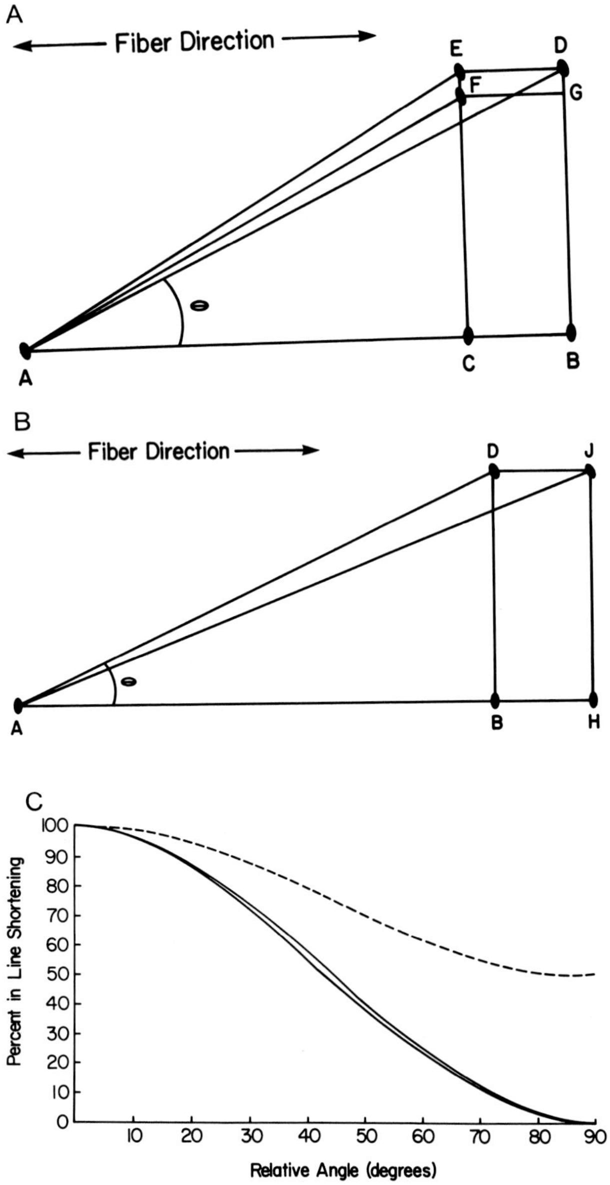

FIGURE 4. *Panel A: the geometric relation between the crystals and the fiber directions shown when relative angle = 0° (segment AB) and when relative angle = θ (segment AD). For clarity, all shortening is shown to occur at one end of the segment. See text for details. Panel B: effect of increasing end-diastolic segment length on geometric construct. Panel C: the ratio of measured shortening to in-line shortening as a function of the relative angle between the myofibers and the intragauge axis. Upper solid line shows the relation assuming 10% in-line shortening and no lateral strain. Lower solid line shows the relation assuming 30% in-line shortening and no lateral strain. Dashed line shows the relation assuming 10% in-line shortening and 5% lateral strain. See Appendix for the mathematical derivation of these relations, and text for details.*

to segment AB. For purposes of simplification, all shortening is shown to occur from one end of the segment, and whole body rotation affecting all points equally has been ignored; this simplification does not alter the geometry.

For the purposes of our analysis, we were interested in the relation between the in-line shortening, $\Delta\ell_I$, expressed as (AB-AC)/AB, and the shortening detected by the segment gauge, $\Delta\ell_m$. The latter would be (AD-AE)/AD in the absence of lateral strain, and (AD-AF)/AD in the presence of lateral strain. As shown in the Appendix, this relation is complex, being defined by the equation.

$$\left(\frac{1-\Delta\ell_m}{1-\Delta\ell_I}\right)^2 = \cos^2\theta + \left(\frac{1-\Delta\ell_s}{1-\Delta\ell_I}\right)^2 \sin^2\theta. \quad (1)$$

θ is the relative angle at the onset of shortening, <DAB, and $\Delta\ell_s$ is the shortening resulting from lateral strain (BD − BG)/BD.

The solid lines in Figure 4C depict the theoretical relation of measured shortening as a percent of in-line shortening as the angle θ goes from 0° to 90°, assuming that no lateral strain occurs ($\Delta\ell_s = 0$). As can be seen from Equation 1, the relation of measured to in-line shortening is dependent on the amount of in-line shortening which occurs; however, this factor plays a small role. The upper solid line in Figure 4C assumes in-line shortening to be 10% and the lower solid line assures in-line shortening to be 30%. Since a 3-fold increase in shortening would alter the ratio of $\Delta\ell_m/\Delta\ell_I$ by such a small amount, we have excluded this factor from subsequent analysis. Data on Figures 6 and 7 are plotted against the line assuming $\Delta\ell_I$ to be 10%, which is near the mean control value from our experiments (10.5%).

The dashed line in Figure 4C represents the relation of measured to in-line shortening, assuming that the in-line shortening is 10% and the shortening due to lateral strain is 5%. This plot demonstrates that, if lateral strain occurs, the measured shortening would fall above the line of prediction used in our construct, which assumes no lateral strain. Furthermore, the divergence of these two constructs is a function of relative angle: as relation angle increases, the influence of lateral strain becomes more pronounced.

We analyzed the relationship between the relative angle and shortening magnitude for each crystal pair. Values in each dog were normalized to the crystal pair with maximal shortening and expressed as a percent. Data from one segment gauge in each of two dogs was excluded for technical reasons.

To determine how the myofibers were oriented at the crystal site, we used the histological sections in which the crystal defect had its largest diameter. Through a 1- to 1.5-mm layer of the midwall (representing the diameter of the crystal), the fiber orientation undergoes some transition. In two instances, we analyzed sections taken every 50 μm throughout the depth of crystal defect. Figure 5 shows data from one of these. The mean fiber direction from the six sections with the maximal defect was within 2° of the average of the values of all 50 sections; in the other instance it was within

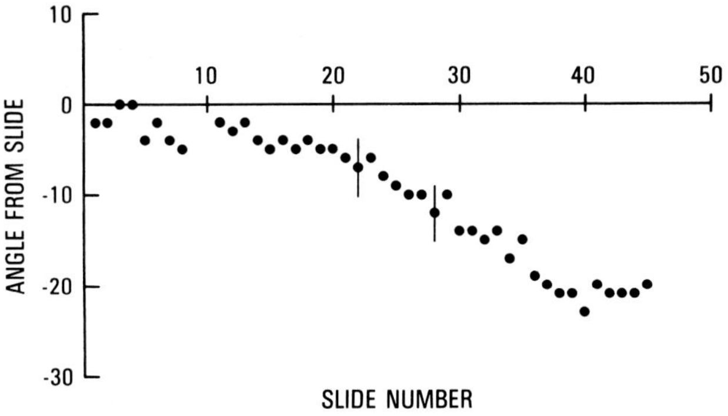

FIGURE 5. *Distribution of myofiber angles measured from histological sections taken throughout the depth of the crystal defect. Vertical bars mark sections when the crystal defect was largest.*

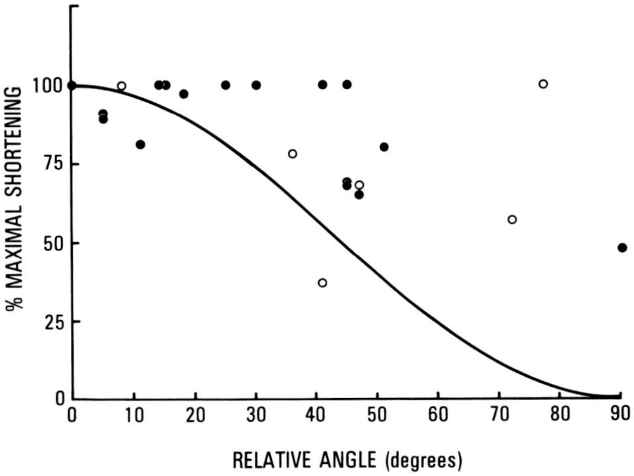

FIGURE 7. *Epicardial data from the animals studied by Gallagher et al. (1982) (solid circles) and our two animals (open circles). The percent maximal shortening is plotted against the relative angle. The solid line again represents the theoretical relation shown in Figure 4C. Data for this plot kindly provided by Dr. Gallagher.*

3°. These data indicate that the method of choosing sections for analysis from the maximal defect diameter approximates the average direction of the fibers acting on the entire crystal.

Shortening Data

The shortening values for all segments ranged between −2.5% and 18.6%. The peak value of control shortening ranged from 7.6 to 18.6% in these animals. As can be seen from the solid lines in Figure 4C, control shortening values in this range do not substantially alter the relation between measured shortening and relative angle.

Figure 6 shows our control data and the relation predicted assuming no lateral strain. As the relative angle became larger, the measured shortening value decreased. The points are distributed on both sides of the line of prediction. A linear regression of the relation between observed and predicted values revealed a correlation coefficient of 0.74. In every case where an animal had a segment with a relative angle greater than 30°, the shortening in that segment was less than that in the more well-aligned segments.

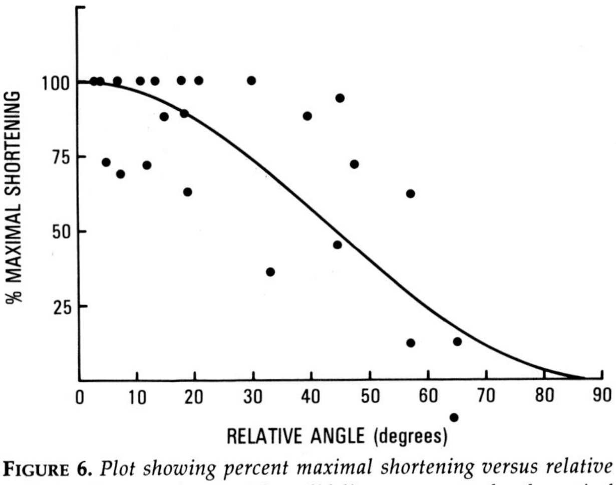

FIGURE 6. *Plot showing percent maximal shortening versus relative angle in the control state. The solid line represents the theoretical relation shown in Figure 4c.*

An unpaired *t*-test between segments with relative angle less than 30° and greater than 30° showed that the latter had lower shortening values ($P < 0.05$).

Volume infusion caused an increase in the percent maximal shortening at any given relative angle in 13 of 17 segments. Isoproterenol and calcium did not systematically alter the shortening to relative angle relation.

Data from the additional two dogs in which the dimension gauges were placed in the epicardium is shown in Figure 7 (open circles). In five of the six measurments, the relationship between relative angle and shortening falls above the line of prediction.

The projection of the external and internal long axis markers in eight dogs showed that the angle formed by them ranged from 0° to 6.5° with a mean of 1.7°, indicating that the external reference system accurately reflected the internal Z axis used in earlier studies to define myocardial fiber anatomy (Streeter, 1969).

In each dog, we attempted to place one set of crystals in line with the local fibers using the external reference system as a guide. In nine dogs, the average relative angle for this gauge, representing the error in alignment of the dimension gauge, ranged from 0.5° to 18.5° with a mean value of 12°.

Critique of the Method

The assessment of an in situ relative angle is technically difficult. Care was taken to fix the individual hearts at a pressure corresponding to the control LVEDP. Despite the use of specialized holders and knife guides, error of 1–2° may have been introduced when reference edges were cut. Also, use of 1-cm^2 samples for histological determination of local fiber direction necessitates the estimation of a precise fiber orientation for an area in which there is some geometric variability. The samples used by Streeter (1979) were considerably smaller, approximately 0.1 × 0.7 cm, ensuring less inherent variability. Use of small samples, however, would make verification of the crystal site impossible, and not allow an assessment of the average angle acting on the crystals, and thus was not practical for this study.

Another possible source of error is the difference in depth within the myocardium at which the crystals were placed. Although calibrated sheathes were used to insert each to the same depth, and although radiography showed the crystals to be in the midwall (Fig. 2B), slight differences in depth were unavoidable. When the crystals were at slightly different depths, there was a difference between the fiber angle at the center of each gauge (range 1° to 42°). The fiber angle was calculated as the average of these two values for each gauge. Despite the difference in fiber angle at each gauge, the entire gauge subtended up to a 20° range of angles, and there was always substantial overlap in fiber direction at the two gauges. However, the dispersion of fiber angles between the two gauges may have added to the scatter apparent in the data.

Figure 5 graphically depicts the fact that, even though the gauges were small in comparison to the thickness of the ventricular wall, fiber orientation was not the same at all points through the depth of the crystal. Our method of defining the local fiber direction took advantage of the spherical nature of the defect produced in the fixed tissue by quantifying the angle at the widest aspect of the defect. We demonstrated that this was within 3° of the average of the angles measured in serial sections produced for the entire depth of the crystal, and feel that it is a good estimation of the net direction of the fibers acting on the crystals. It is still possible that ± 3° error was introduced by this technique, and that this added to the variance of the data shown in Figure 6.

For our analysis, we assumed that circumferential shortening was the same at the three gauge sites in any one animal. Prior studies from our laboratory have shown modest regional differences in both systolic (LeWinter et al., 1975) and diastolic (Lew and LeWinter, 1983) deformation patterns at different sites in the left ventricle. These studies have compared widely disparate regions of the ventricle—the base vs. the apex or the anterior vs. lateral wall; there is no evidence for marked differences in deformation in areas as small as those analyzed in this study. Thus, we feel this assumption is justified.

Discussion

Our data demonstrate that, in the midwall of the left ventricle, shortening is maximal in the direction of the local myofiber, and thus supports the hypothesis that lateral strain introduced by functional connections to overlying muscle layers does not play a dominant role in this region. Thus, although anatomic linkage in the form of collagen network has been demonstrated between myocardial layers (Caulfield and Borg, 1979; Robinson and Winegrad, 1981), epicardial and endocardial influences do not reduce the dependence of shortening patterns in the midwall on local fiber orientation. Since midwall shortening is determined primarily by local fiber orientation, placement of segment gauges markedly out of line with the local fibers in this region will result in falsely low shortening values. This theoretical relation is illustrated by the solid lines in Figure 4C, and its mathematical derivation shown in the Appendix. It is sigmoidal in nature such that measured shortening becomes increasingly less accurate as relative angle becomes larger. Our data correspond to the theoretical relation, and indicate that gauges placed more than 30° off of the local fiber axis will report shortening that is substantially less than that of the local myofibers.

The mathematical relation between measured and in-line shortening, defined by Equation 1, is of interest for several reasons. The relation is complex, being dependent on the relative angle, θ, and the amounts of both in-line and lateral shortening. For our construct, we have assumed that no lateral strain occurs, or $\Delta\ell_2 = 0$. As can be seen from the equation, if lateral strain does occur, the ratio of measured to in-line shortening will be larger than that predicted by our construct. The dashed line in Figure 4C is a plot of the relation when lateral shortening occurs with a magnitude equal to half of the in-line shortening. The relation falls above the line predicted by our construct, deviating more from it as the relative angle approaches 90°. In the case in which lateral shortening is equal in magnitude to in-line shortening, the ratio of measured to in-line shortening will always be 1.0, indicating a concentric decrease in size of the heart from end-diastole to end-systole. Since our midwall data indicate that gauges placed substantially out of line with local fibers measure very low shortening values, it lends support to the concept that, at this depth in the left ventricular wall, lateral strain arising from fibers in the epi- and endocardium does not alter the dependence of local deformation on local fiber alignment, or, at the least, provides a balance and opposing effect.

We limited our study to the middle one third of the ventricular apex-to-base distance. At the apex, the wall is thinner, the fiber orientation is more curvilinear and the pitch angle is steeper. At the base, the fibrous skeleton could affect deformation. Whether the relation of local fiber direction to local segment shortening persists in these regions remains to be studied.

A number of clinical techniques used to evaluate ventricular function depend on measurement of linear dimensions during the cardiac cycle. Those which measure an internal diameter such as echocardiographic or cineangiographic analysis of diameters (mean circumferential fiber velocity) must assume that the chord used for analysis is aligned with the circumferential fibers, and that no regional differences of function are present. Although these assumptions cannot be directly verified in the individual hearts being studied, in the absence of obvious wall motion abnormalities they probably permit a reasonable estimate of the behavior of the midwall circumferential fibers. Our results suggest that other methods, particularly those which use a surface parameter to evaluate wall motion (Massie et al., 1978; Ingels et al., 1980; Karsch et al., 1980) will not directly reflect performance of the functional unit of the myocardium, the uniaxial myofiber.

Gallagher et al. (1982) showed that epicardial shortening behavior may be influenced by shortening which is occurring in the midwall fibers. These investigators directly measured the relation of local fiber orientation to intracrystal axis by in situ determination of the relative angle with a protractor. In their studies, significant epicardial deformation occurred in the circumferential direction, which was approximately 70° out of line with the local epicardial fiber direction. Coronary occlusion producing midwall and subendocardial but not epicardial ischemia eliminated the epicardial circumferential deformation. The solid circles in Figure 7 show an analysis of the pre-ischemic control data from those animals, using our construct. Clearly, most of the segments have shortening values that fall above the line of prediction, which assumes no lateral strain, and more closely approximate the relation illustrated by the dashed line in Figure 4C, where lateral strain is assumed to occur. Data from the two animals in which we placed epicardial gauges and directly measured fiber angle are also shown, and similarly fall above the line of prediction. Thus, unlike the midwall, the epicardium undergoes substantial lateral strain.

The reason for this seeming paradox may be that, since a preponderance of the myofibers in the left ventricular wall are oriented in the circumferential direction, most of the force leading to deformation has a circumferential vector, whereas a smaller fraction of total force is exerted by fibers lying in a more longitudinal direction. This would suggest that lateral strain would be more apparent in the epicardial (and presumably endocardial) layers than in the midwall layers. Furthermore, it is also possible that lateral stress introduced by epicardial fibers may be balanced by the effects of subendocardial fibers which are oriented in an opposite direction. This would predict that, under conditions of strictly subendocardial ischemia, lateral strain resulting from epicardial fibers would be unmasked in the midwall region. Likewise, if the influence of epicardial fibers could be selectively removed, the influence of subendocardial fibers on midwall deformation would become apparent.

Any long axis shortening which occurs must be a result of noncircumferential fibers in the epicardium and endocardium. The importance of helical fibers in determining ventricular performance was described mathematically by Sallin (1969). If the left ventricle is assumed to be an ellipse of revolution, circumferential shortening alone will not permit development of ejection fractions comparable to those observed in vivo. Shortening of helical fibers (anatomically, predominantly the endocardial and epicardial fibers) will lead to physiological ejection fractions. Meier et al. (1982) have demonstrated that motion of epicardial markers on the canine right ventricle confirms the importance of helical shortening patterns in ventricular ejection. Although one would think that this long axis deformation would lead to lateral strain in the midwall, it's overall magnitude is small: Mitchell et al. (1969) demonstrated that long axis shortening is on the order of 8–10%. Furthermore, although mathematical analysis has assumed uniform shortening behavior along the helical pathway it is possible that regional variations of long axis deformation may occur. In any case, our data suggest that this helical shortening pattern does not introduce substantial lateral strain in the midwall during ejection.

It is of interest to note that volume infusion caused an increase in the percent maximal shortening at any given relative angle in almost all of the segments. In Figure 4B, it can be seen that an increase in end-diastolic length would cause the angle θ to become smaller ($<$DAB greater than $<$JAB). Since the hearts were fixed at control volumes, the relative angle we measured would overestimate the angle present during the acquisition of increased volume data. Shortening values from that state should thus fall above the line of prediction based on control relative angles, as was the case.

The administration of calcium and isoproterenol, on the other hand, did not consistently change the results. Inotropic stimulation causes greater segment shortening from the same or lower end-diastolic length in the intact heart. An interesting facet of our geometric construct is that, although the relation between relative angle and measured shortening is dependent on the amount of in-line shortening, this effect is quite small (Fig. 4C). It is therefore understandable that the data did not show a consistent change in the relation between shortening and relative angle after inotropic interventions.

Our secondary goal was to determine whether gauges could be accurately placed in the fiber direction in the beating heart. The description of fiber orientation generally used as a reference system for gauge placement (Streeter et al., 1969) was based on an internal long axis which passed from the apical dimple to the mitral aspect of the aortic valve. Our radiographic data illustrate that the line passing from the apical dimple to the bifurcation of the left coronary artery is an excellent predictor of the internal long axis and can be used to predict local fiber orientation.

When using this reference system, we found a wide variability in the accuracy with which gauges could be implanted. In nine attempts to align a gauge with the circumferential fibers, the relative angle ranged from 0.5° to 18.5°, with a mean value of 12°. This variability probably relates to the difficulty in implanting crystals precisely in the moving heart, the presence of epicardial coronary arteries which limit insertion sites, and individual variations in the actual fiber geometry. Fortunately, the shortening measured by gauges falling within 18.5° of the fiber axis is reasonably close to the shortening along the fiber axis, preventing this from being a major source of error. Furthermore, in animal studies, the accurate placement of gauges in relation to the external long axis which closely predicts the internal long axis can be directly verified.

In conclusion, we have demonstrated that, in the anterior ventricular midwall, segment shortening is maximal in the orientation of the local myocardial fibers, indicating that lateral strain does not reduce the dependence of segment motion on the underlying myofiber orientation in this region during ejection. We have shown that the fiber orientation can be assessed accurately by means of a reproducible external reference system, and that segment gauges can be aligned to local myofiber direction with acceptable error.

Appendix

(see Figure 4A)

$\theta = \angle DAB$

In-line shortening $= \Delta\ell_I = (AB - AC)/AB$

Shortening due to lateral strain $= \Delta\ell_s = (BD - BG)/BD$

Measured shortening $= \Delta\ell_m = (AD - AF)/AD$

For any $\Delta\ell_I$, $AC = K_I \cdot AB$, where $K_I = 1 - \Delta\ell_I$

For any $\Delta\ell_s$, $BG = K_s \cdot BD$, where $K_s = 1 - \Delta\ell_s$

For any $\Delta\ell_m$, $AF = K_m \cdot AD$, where $K_m = 1 - \Delta\ell_m$

$\sin\theta = BD/AD$

$\cos\theta = AB/AD$

$AF^2 = AC^2 + CF^2 = AC^2 + BG^2$

By substitution

$(K_m \cdot AD)^2 = (K_I \cdot AB)^2 + (K_s \cdot BD)^2$

Rearranging terms demonstrates that

$$\left(\frac{K_m}{K_I}\right)^2 = \left(\frac{AB}{AD}\right)^2 + \left(\frac{K_s}{K_I}\right)^2 \cdot \left(\frac{BD}{AD}\right)^2,$$

or

$$\left(\frac{K_m}{K_I}\right)^2 = \cos^2\theta + \left(\frac{K_s}{K_I}\right)^2 \sin^2\theta.$$

By substitution

$$\left(\frac{1 - \Delta\ell_m}{1 - \Delta\ell_I}\right)^2 = \cos^2\theta + \left(\frac{1 - \Delta\ell_s}{1 - \Delta\ell_I}\right)^2 \sin^2\theta.$$

We would like to thank Dr. Kim Gallagher for making available original data of a previously published study (Gallagher et al., 1982) permitting us to examine the relationship between epicardial fiber direction and function.

Also, this study would not have been possible without the skilled technical help of Richard S. Pavelec and the secretarial skills of Jacqueline Covell, Gabriele Drumm, and Louise Williams.

This research was supported in part by National Heart, Lung, and Blood Institute Grants HL-07444 and HL-28644.

Address for reprints: Gregory L. Freeman, M.D., University of Texas Health Science Center, 7703 Floyd Curl Drive, San Antonio, Texas 78284.

Received November 3, 1983; accepted for publication September 21, 1984.

References

Arts T, Veenstra PC, Reneman RS (1982) Epicardial deformation and left ventricular wall mechanics during ejection in the dog. Am J Physiol **243:** H379–H390

Caulfield JB, Borg TK (1979) The collagen network of the heart. Lab Invest **40:** 364–372

Cooper R, Karliner JS, O'Rourke RA, Peterson KL, Leopold G (1972) Ultrasound determinations of mean fiber-shortening rate in man. Am J Cardiol **29:** 257–268

Dieudonne JM (1969) Gradients de directions et de deformations principales dans la paroi ventriculare gauche normale. J Physiol (Paris) **61:** 305–330

Gallagher KP, Osakada G, Hess OM, Koziol JA, Kemper WS, Ross J Jr (1982) Subepicardial segmental function during coronary stenosis and the role of myocardial fiber orientation. Circ Res **50:** 352–359

Hort W (1957) Mikro metrische untersucheungen an verscheiden weiten Meerschweinchenherzen. Verh Dtsch Ges Kreislaufforsch **23:** 343–346

Humason GL (1979) Animal Tissue Techniques. San Francisco, W.H. Freeman, p 34

Ingels NB Jr, Daughters GB, Davies SR, MacDonald IB (1971) Stereophotogrammetric studies on the dynamic geometry of the canine left ventricular epicardium. J Biomech **4:** 541–550

Ingels NB, Daughters GT, Stinson EB, Alderman EL (1980) Evaluation of methods for quantifying left ventricular segmental wall motion in man using myocardial markers as a standard. Circulation **61:** 966–972

Karliner JS, Gault JH, Eckberg D, Mullins CB, Ross J Jr (1970) Mean velocity of fiber shortening. A simplified measure of left ventricular myocardial contractility. Circulation **44:** 323–333

Karsch KR, Lamm U, Blanke H, Rentrop KP (1980) Comparison of nineteen models for assessment of localized left ventricular wall motion abnormalities. Clin Cardiol **3:** 123–128

Lew WYW, LeWinter MM (1983) Regional circumferential lengthening patterns in canine left ventricle. Am J Physiol **245:** H741–H748

LeWinter MM, Kent RS, Kroener JM, Carew TE, Covell JW (1975) Regional differences in myocardial performance in the left ventricle of the dog. Circ Res **37:** 191–199

Massie BM, Botvinick EH, Brundage BH, Greenberg B, Shames D, Gelberg H (1978) Relationship of regional myocarial perfusion to segmental wall motion. Circulation **58:** 1154–1163

McCallum JB (1900) On the muscular architecture and growth of the ventricles of the heart. Johns Hopkins Hospital Reports **9:** 307–335

Meier GD, Ziskin MC, Bove AA (1982) Helical fibers in myocardium of dogs change their pitch as they contract. Am J Physiol **243:** H1–H12

Mitchell JH, Wildenthal K, Mullins CB (1969) Geometrical studies on the left ventricle utilizing biplane cinefluorography. Fed Proc **28:** 1334–1343

Robb JS, Robb RC (1942) The normal heart. Anatomy and physiology of the structural units. Am Heart J **23:** 455–467

Robinson RF, Winegrad S (1981) A variety of intercellular connections in heart muscle. J Mol Cell Cardiol **13:** 185–195

Sallin EA (1969) Fiber orientation and ejection fraction in the human left ventricle. Biophys J **9:** 954–964

Streeter DD (1979) Gross morphology and fiber geometry of the heart. *In* Handbook of Physiology, The Cardiovascular System, edited by RM Berne. Washington, D.C., American Physiological Society, pp 61–112

Streeter DD, Hanna WT (1973) Engineering mechanics for successive states in canine left ventricular myocardium. II. Fiber angle and sarcomere length. Circ Res **33:** 656–664

Streeter DD, Spotnitz HM, Patel DP, Ross J Jr, Sonnenblick EH (1969) Fiber orientation in the canine left ventricle during diastole and systole. Circ Res **24:** 339–347

Torrent-Guasp F (1973) The Cardiac Muscle. The Juan March Foundation, Barcelona, Spain

Yoran C, Covell J, Ross J Jr (1973) Rapid fixation of the left ventricle: Continuous angiographic and dynamic recordings. J Appl Physiol **35:** 155–157

INDEX TERMS: Ventricular function • Fiber orientation • Segment shortening • Wall motion • Ultrasonic dimension gauge • Piezoelectric crystals

Pulmonary Artery Constriction Produces a Greater Right Ventricular Dynamic Afterload Than Lung Microvascular Injury in the Open Chest Dog

James E. Calvin, Jr., Robert W. Baer, and Stanton A. Glantz

From the Cardiovascular Research Institute, and Department of Medicine, University of California, San Francisco, San Francisco, California

SUMMARY. Investigators model noncardiogenic pulmonary hypertension by constricting the pulmonary artery to increase right ventricular afterload. To investigate this model's validity, we compared the right ventricular afterload, quantified as pulmonary input impedance, created by constricting the pulmonary artery and by inducing a pulmonary microvascular injury (with glass beads infused into the pulmonary circulation). The pulmonary injury constriction produced a different right ventricular afterload than the microvascular injury. The constriction increased both the input resistance and the characteristic impedance. Mircrovascular injury increased only input resistance. Physiological levels of lung inflation did not influence pulmonary impedance, but lung hyperinflation increased input resistance both before and while constricting the pulmonary artery or after producing microvascular injury. Total right ventricular power output and stroke work were unchanged during each vascular intervention. Pulmonary artery constriction did not affect power output distribution, whereas microvascular injury decreased oscillatory power and its relative contribution to total power. Lung hyperinflation dramatically reduced right ventricular power and left ventricular stroke work. These effects appeared mediated by right ventricular afterload increase uncompensated for by right ventricular preload increase. These observations help explain the hemodynamic consequences of acute pulmonary hypertension and the effects of lung hyperinflation with positive end-expiratory pressure respiration in such patients. **(*Circ Res 56: 40–56, 1985*)**

PULMONARY hypertension, manifest as elevated pulmonary artery pressure, and right ventricular dysfunction associated with noncardiogenic pulmonary edema are often fatal (Zapol and Snider, 1977; Sibbald et al., 1978; Sturm et al., 1979). Although many investigators have studied the lung's pathological and physiological response to pulmonary edema (Staub, 1981; Rinaldo and Rogers, 1982), there have not been studies of the heart's response to the pulmonary hypertension frequently associated with noncardiogenic edema. In noncardiogenic pulmonary edema, a pulmonary microvascular injury elevates pulmonary artery pressure, and so increases right ventricular afterload, which may make the right ventricle reduce its stroke volume and dilate. Previous investigators have studied the right ventricle's response to increased afterload by constricting the pulmonary artery (Kelly et al., 1971; Bemis et al., 1974; Stool et al., 1974; Pouleur, 1978; Olsen et al., 1983; Visner et al., 1983). Besides increasing right ventricular afterload, this intervention reduces left ventricular filling (preload) by reducing both pulmonary venous return and left ventricular distensability resulting from the dilated right ventricle competing for the available space within the pericardium (Glantz et al., 1978). We hypothesized that, since a pulmonary artery constriction reduces the distensability of the proximal arterial wall, and a downstream microvascular injury affects the small resistance vessels, these different interventions would impose different afterloads on the right ventricle. To test this hypothesis, we characterized the right ventricular dynamic afterload by computing the pulmonary artery input impedance and compared the impedance produced by constricting the main pulmonary artery with that produced by a microvascular injury. We determined the histological nature of the experimental microvascular injury to relate our findings to the clinical syndrome of noncardiogenic pulmonary edema (Lamy et al. 1976). We also compared both right and left ventricular performance during both interventions. The pulmonary artery constriction subjected the right ventricle to greater dynamic afterload than did a comparable microvascular injury.

Inflating normal lungs increases right ventricular afterload (Smith et al., 1982). When the lungs are injured, pulmonary artery pressure is elevated and the right ventricle is already stressed. Since patients with such problems are often treated by ventilation with positive end-expiratory pressure (PEEP), which results in increased lung volumes, we determined how lung inflation modulates right ventricular dynamic afterload during pulmonary artery constriction and microvascular injury. The dynamic afterload was unchanged during phasic respiration, expiration, and inspiration of a normal tidal volume, but hyperinflating lungs significantly increased right ventricular dynamic afterload and this increase depressed both right and left ventricular performance.

Methods

Preparation

We studied anesthetized open-chest mongrel dogs that weighed 19.3–25.7 kg. All dogs were premedicated with Benadryl (4 mg/kg) and morphine (2–4 mg/kg), then anesthetized with chloralose (50 mg/kg, iv) and morphine (2 mg/kg, im), with supplemental doses given as necessary to maintain anesthesia. Sodium bicarbonate was infused as necessary to keep the arterial blood pH between 7.35 and 7.45. The dogs were intubated and ventilated with a 350-ml tidal volume using a Harvard model 607 volume cycled ventilator at 18 breaths/min. These settings were adjusted as necessary to maintain the P_{CO_2} between 35 and 45 mm Hg. When necessary, supplemental oxygen was administered to keep the oxygen saturation above 85%.

We exposed the heart through a left lateral thoracotomy. We studied seven dogs with their hearts outside the pericardium and six dogs with their hearts inside the pericardium. In the first set, we opened the pericardium widely and rested the heart in a pericardium cradle. In the second group, we cut the pericardium vertically across the origin of the great vessels for a length extending from 1 cm superior to the aorta to 2 cm below the inferior margin of the left atrial appendage. This procedure allowed us to remove the heart gently while leaving most of the pericardial sac intact. After instrumenting the heart (as described below), we popped it back into the pericardial sac and loosely sutured the incision from its inferior margin to the level of the inferior border of the great vessels (Tyson et al., 1984).

We instrumented all hearts with two pairs of hemispheric sonomicrometer crystals sewn to the epicardium (Van Trigt et al., 1981). The first pair consisted of a crystal on the right ventricular posterior wall (right of the posterior descending artery near the apex) and one crystal on the anterolateral wall (distal to the right ventricular branch and proximal to the marginal branch of the right coronary artery). This pair of crystals provided a chord length along one of the right ventricle's principal directions of shortening (Meier et al., 1980). The second pair of crystals consisted of one on the left ventricular anterior wall (distal to the take-off of the first diagonal branch of the left anterior descending artery) and one on the posterior wall (left of the posterior descending artery midway between the apex and the atrioventricular groove). This position gave reproducible values and wave shapes during control conditions from dog to dog. The crystals were driven electrically by a four-channel sonomicrometer (Triton Corporation, model 120).

We advanced a 7F Millar micro-tipped pressure transducer (Millar Instruments Co. PC480 Houston, TX) into the pulmonary artery through a stab wound in the right ventricular outflow tract. Similar pressure transducers were advanced into the right and left ventricles from cutdowns on the right external jugular vein and carotid artery, respectively. In the dogs with an intact pericardium, we made this stab wound through a 4-mm slit in the pericardium. We attached all pressure transducers to a Validyne model CD19 solid state bridge amplifiers. The transducer-amplifier system has a flat frequency response to at least 1 kHz. The Millar pressure transducers were turned on and warmed to 37°C for at least 12 hours before the experiment. Repeated drift tests performed on the entire system showed that it drifts less than 0.5 mm Hg/5 hours after being warmed up. All transducers were calibrated and balanced to read zero when exposed to atmospheric pressure while at 37°C. This procedure was accomplished by placing the transducers in a tube partially filled with water that was submerged in a constant temperature water bath. To balance and calibrate the transducers, we located the tips just above the water in the tube and pressurized the tube to the desired level. Airway pressure was measured at the mouth from a Statham model P23Db strain gauge pressure transducer attached to the respirator circuit. All transducers were calibrated on the day of the experiment, with a mercury manometer.

A 7F Swan-Ganz catheter (Edwards) was advanced into the pulmonary artery from the external jugular vein to measure cardiac output by thermodilution with an Edwards model 9520A cardiac output computer. We used a large-bore Teflon catheter inserted into the right ventricle through a stab wound in the anterior wall to infuse glass beads into the lungs.

The pulmonary artery was carefully isolated by blunt dissection. A 45- or 50-mm circumference electromagnetic flow probe (Carolina Medical Instruments, model EP445C) driven by an electromagnetic flow meter (Carolina Medical Instruments, model 501) was placed around the proximal pulmonary artery about 3 cm above the valve. The flow measurement system has a flat frequency response to at least 100 Hz.

The pressure transducer was aligned to the proximal edge of the flow probe. The top part of the pericardial incision was left open in those dogs in which the pericardium was resutured to prevent kinking the vessel or obstructing the flow.

The flowmeter was initially zeroed by placing the flow probe in a beaker of saline, nulling it, then balancing it according to the manufacturer's specifications. Zero reference was rechecked during the experiment by assuming end-diastole to have zero flow. We further corrected for baseline drift by programming our computer to adjust the baseline in the digitized data to produce zero flow at end-diastole on a beat-to-beat basis. The flowmeter gain was set using the manufacturer's probe factor based on the dog's hematocrit. We checked the manufacturer's calibration by pumping blood of known hematocrit through an excised pulmonary artery at a known rate. The measured flow was always within 20% of the known flow rate. We also measured cardiac outputs in triplicate using the thermodilution technique throughout the experiment. The cardiac output obtained from the flow probe was consistently within the 80% confidence interval for the mean thermodilution cardiac output.

Protocol

We waited 15 minutes, after completing the instrumentation, for the dogs to stabilize. Data were recorded during phasic respiration, at end inspiration, at end expiration, and during a lung hyperinflation. The lung hyperinflation was produced by clamping the expiratory limb of the respiratory circuit and inflating the lung until we observed at least a 30% reduction in pulmonary artery flow (three to five respiratory cycles). To provide control data at the higher heart rates often observed during the pulmonary artery constriction and microvascular injury, we paced seven dogs from the right atrium at one to three different rates between 120 and 180 beats/min under basal conditions and recorded data during the all inflation states.

We constricted the pulmonary artery by tightening a snare around the pulmonary artery, 1–2 cm distal to the flow probe. We attempted to achieve a 50% increase in pulmonary artery pressure and a 25% reduction in ventricular output.

When the dog was in steady state, we recorded data during phasic respiration, end inspiration, end expiration and lung hyperinflation. We then loosened the snare and repeated measurements during phasic respiration. The dogs then were allowed to return to control steady state.

To produce a distal microvascular injury, we repeatedly injected 1- to 3-g doses of 150- to 200-μm glass beads (model G-2506, Sigma) through the right ventricular catheter. We recorded data after giving each dose of glass beads. We continued to inject glass beads, 1 g at a time, until the dog developed left ventricular systolic blood pressure under 60 mm Hg. Repeat measurements were taken at each dose during all lung inflation states.

All data were recorded continuously on FM analog tape, using a Honeywell model 5600C FM tape recorder, then digitized at 200 samples/sec (Horowitz and Glantz, 1979) for subsequent analysis. The tape recorder has a flat frequency response to at least 2 kHz. We were limited to recording only 20–30 seconds of data by the severe nature of some of the loads, by the fact that the respirator was turned off during most of the measurements.

Routine hemodynamic variables—including pulmonary artery mean, systolic and diastolic pressures, left and right ventricular end-diastolic and maximum pressures, left and right ventricular end-diastolic and end-systolic dimensions—were obtained from the digitized data. Figure 1 shows typical tracings during the control, pulmonary artery constriction, and microvascular injury. Both vascular interventions increased pulmonary artery pressures. Figure 1 also shows that the lung hyperinflation increases pulmonary diastolic pressures and reduces pulmonary artery flow.

Left and right ventricular dimension stroke work was calculated as

$$W = \int d\,(dP/dt)\,dt$$

where d and P denote the appropriate diameters or chord and pressures, and W denotes ventricular dimension stroke work, and the integration is over one beat.

Right ventricular stroke volume was calculated as the integral of the pulmonary artery flow. Right ventricular volume stroke work was calculated as

$$SW_R = SV(P_{Rmax} - P_{Red}).$$

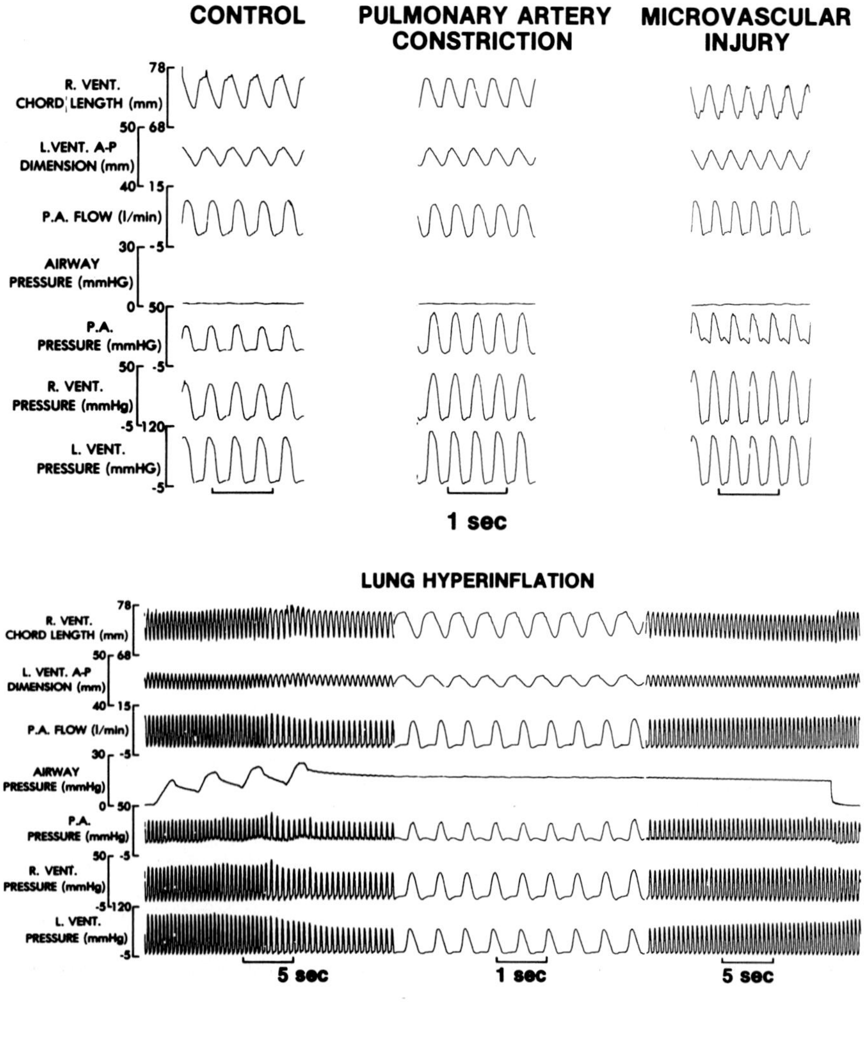

FIGURE 1. *Representative hemodynamic tracings during control, pulmonary artery constriction, and microvascular injury; recordings are at end-expiration (upper panels). The pulmonary artery systolic pressure is increased during both the pulmonary artery constriction and the mircrovascular injury. The pulmonary diastolic pressure is increased during the microvascular injury. Lung hyperinflation (lower panel) is associated with an increase in pulmonary diastolic pressure and a reduction in pulmonary artery flow. Left ventricular systolic pressure also falls. Right ventricular end-diastolic pressure is increased with little change in right ventricular chord length. Left ventricular dimensions fall.*

Left ventricular volume stroke work was calculated as

$$SW_L = SV\ (P_{Lmax} - P_{Led}),$$

where SV is the right ventricular stroke volume measured with the electromagnetic flow prob.

Complete hemodynamic measurements were obtained during baseline conditions and glass bead microvascular injury in all 13 dogs. Two dogs did not have a pulmonary artery constriction series to ensure that the effects observed during the microvascular injury were not confounded by application of the pulmonary artery constriction. Seven dogs were paced at rates between 120 and 180 during baseline conditions. Complete sets of data for lung hyperinflation were obtained in 10 dogs

Quantification of Right Ventricular Dynamic Afterload with Pulmonary Vascular Impedance

The pulmonary artery input impedance spectrum more completely characterizes the right ventricle's dynamic afterload than either pulmonary artery pressure or pulmonary vascular resistance. Impedance represents the pulsatile nature of the circulation, and all the factors that contribute to the arterial load (arterial wall distensibility, blood viscosity, cross-sectional area of vascular bed) that the right ventricle must overcome (Bergel and Milnor, 1965; Milnor, 1982). We estimated the pulmonary artery input impedance as the ratio of the Fourier transform of pulmonary artery pressure to the Fourier transform of the pulmonary artery flow,

$$Z(f)=P(f)/Q(f),$$

in which Z(f) is the pulmonary artery input impedance and P(f) and Q(f) are the Fourier transforms of the pulmonary artery pressure and flow, respectively. Z, P, and Q are complex-valued fractions of frequency, f. The magnitude of Z describes the relative magnitudes of the pressure and flow components at frequency f, and the phase of Z describes the phase difference between the pressure and flow components at frequency f.

Two values of impedance, Z(f), have special physiological significance. The input resistance is the pulmonary input impedance at O Hz, Z_O, the ratio of mean pressure to mean flow. Z_O depends on the cross-sectional area of the pulmonary vascular bed and the mean left atrial pressure. However, Z_O is not equal to commonly used pulmonary vascular resistance, which is mean pulmonary artery pressure minus mean left atrial pressure divided by mean pulmonary flow. The characteristic impedance, Z_{inf}, is the average magnitude of the impedance at high frequencies. (Many investigators use Z_O to denote the characteristic impedance, rather than Z_{inf}. We believe it is more logical to denote impedance at zero frequency by Z_O and impedance at high frequencies—the characteristic impedance—by Z_{inf}.) Z_{inf} represents the pulsatile component of the impedance. It depends on vascular wall compliance and blood inertia. Hence, changing proximal arterial wall stiffness (such as that produced by constricting the pulmonary artery) should alter the static component of impedance, Z_O, as well as the pulsatile component, Z_{inf}. In contrast, microvascular injury should increase Z_O without changing Z_{inf}.

Calculation of Pulmonary Vascular Impedance from Digitized Data

We estimated the Fourier transforms of pulmonary artery pressure and flow by computing Fast Fourier Transforms from our digitized data using the IMSL routine FFTRC (IMSL Library, 1980).

Our approach differs from that taken by many previous investigators, who implicitly assumed that the pressure and flow signals were strictly periodic, and used these data to compute a Fourier series. They then estimated the pulmonary input impedance by computing the ratio of the pressure and flow amplitudes at each harmonic of the heart rate. This classical method is a special case of the method we used, because, if the signal is strictly periodic, the Fourier series and Fourier transform will yield identical results, with all the information concentrated at the harmonics of the heart rate (Glantz, 1979). In other words, one could obtain a spectrum analogous to those reported by earlier workers from our results by simply choosing only those points that occur at the harmonics of the heart rate. Since the pulmonary input impedance values calculated at frequencies between the heart rate harmonics fall more-or-less along a smooth curve connecting the points obtained at the harmonics, our approach and the traditional Fourier series approach lead to similar conclusions. The advantages of the Fourier transform approach are that it avoids the necessity of assuming that the heart performs in a strictly periodic manner and that it yields information at frequencies between the harmonics of the heart rate, i.e., better frequency resolution.

There are several practical difficulties that one must address to obtain reliable estimates of the pressure and flow transforms (Brigham, 1974). The problem of aliasing, resulting when high frequency signals masquerade as low frequency signals, is minimized by a 200-Hz sampling rate, which is well above the rate required by the sampling theorem. We sampled two experiments at both 200 and 500 Hz and compared the results to ensure that the 200-Hz rate was adequate. To reduce extraneous noise further in our estimates of the pressure and flow spectra, we divided each 20-second data set into four subsets 5 seconds long, transformed each subset, then averaged the results. This procedure reduced the standard error of the estimated transform by 50%, but still maintained a frequency resolution of 0.2 Hz.

Leakage is another potential problem. This noise, introduced by sampling from a window that does not start and end at the same place in an approximately periodic signal, was minimized by choosing subsets of data that included an integral number of beats. For example, had we sampled from some point in mid-systole to end-diastole, we would have introduced a significant implied discontinuity in our data (Brigham, 1974). This problem would introduce unpredictable noise at all frequencies of the pressure and flow transforms. The following procedure was used to minimze leakage. Each data subset was started at end-diastole and terminated at the last end-diastole within 5 seconds. We then made each data subset the same length as the shortest subset by deleting points immediately preceding the last end-diastole. This procedure kept the frequency increments the same for all four transforms (so that they could be averaged), but avoided introducing significant leakage due to large implied discontinuities, because the pressure and flow are both changing slowly immediately before end-diastole.

One needs to be careful in applying this procedure, because if the shortest data subset is substantially shorter than the others, this algorithm could "back up" into systole in the last beat in the longer data subsets. It could also create a situation where the last beat is artificially shortened and, hence, would introduce artificial nonperiodici-

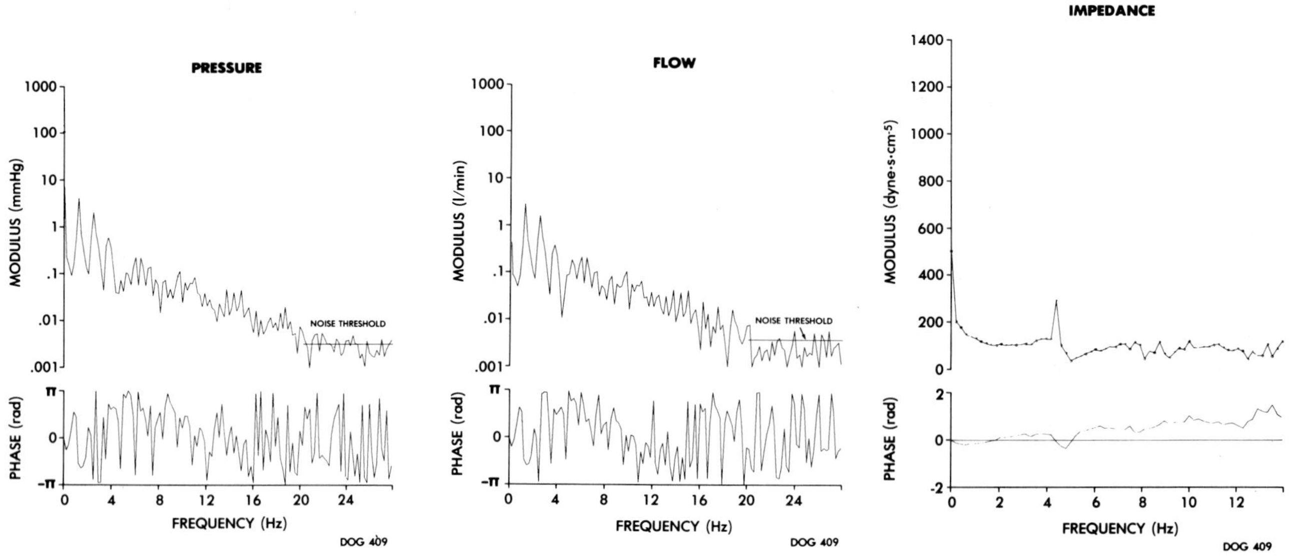

FIGURE 2. *Pulmonary artery pressure and flow transforms in the dog. Panel A is a representative pressure transform used in the calculation of the input impedence. Most of the energy is concentrated at multiples of the fundamental harmonic. The horizontal line at the right of the graph represents the threshold for including points in the impedance calculation. Panel B is the corresponding flow transforms. Panel C represents the pulmonary input impedance calculated from these two transforms.*

ties into the transform. In short, the very procedure we adopted to reduce leakage could create it. Therefore, we checked each set of data to see that there were only small differences in the lengths of the data subsets and the pressures and flows at the beginnings and ends of the data subsets. With the respirator off (at end expiration, held inspiration, or lung hyperinflation), the data subsets were shortened only by a few samples (median = 5 samples; 25th percentile = 1 sample; 75th percentile = 14 samples) which represents only 5% of an average beat duration (heart rate = 124 beat/min). Likewise, the variation in starting and ending pulmonary artery pressure was small, with a standard deviation below 1 mm Hg. As expected, there was more variation during phasic respiration (median samples deleted = 14, representing 14% of average heart rate; standard deviation in starting and ending pressure less than 2 mm Hg). The flow signals were always near zero at the start and end of the data segments. Thus, the procedure we adopted to minimize leakage did not inadvertently introduce it.

There is very little pressure or flow information at frequencies above 14 Hz, and the noise contribution in this range is considerable (Hammon et al., 1981). Figure 2 shows typical transforms of the pressure and flow data. Note that, since the pressure and flow pulses are nearly periodic, most of the energy is concentrated at harmonics of the heart rate. The spectra are displayed to 28 Hz, although, at the higher frequencies, the background noise obscures the signal. To avoid errors in the computed impedance due to dividing by very small numbers that are in the range of the noise, we used the pressure and flow tranforms to select a noise threshold that had to be exceeded for each point to be used in the impedance computation. We set this threshold at the top of the 90% confidence interval for the signal observed above 20 Hz on the assumption that all energy in this range represents noise. The horizontal lines at the right edges of the spectra in Figures 2, A and B, show this threshold for the data presented here. (The ability to set this threshold objectively for each data set is another advantage of using the Fourier transform. Figure 2C gives the impedance spectra calculated from these two transforms in panels A and B.

The characteristic impedance, Z_{inf}, cannot be measured directly because of the wave reflections caused by vascular branching and tapering. It can, however, be estimated by averaging the impedance moduli at high frequencies. Like Hammon et al. (1981), we estimated the characteristic impedance by averaging the impedance moduli between 7 and 14 Hz. There is very little information above this range that could be of use in this estimate.

Right Ventricular Power Output

To describe the right ventricle's response to the pulmonary artery constriction and the microvascular injury, we computed the right ventricle's power output. The total power output can be broken into steady flow power and oscillatory power (Milnor et al., 1966). The former represents the power generated to maintain cardiac output; the latter represents the extra power necessitated by the pulsatile nature of the cardiac pump. The steady flow power is the product of the mean pressure and the mean flow, given by their Fourier transforms at O Hz:

$$W_O = P(O)\, Q(O).$$

The pulsatile (oscillatory) power is the sum of the products of the pressure and flow transforms at all non-zero frequencies

$$W_P = \sum \mathrm{Re}[P(f)\, Q(f)] = \sum 1/2\ P(f)Q(f) \cos \phi(f)$$

in which ϕ is the phase offset between the pressure and flow transforms. The total power equals the sum of the steady flow power and pulsatile power,

$$W_T = W_O + W_P.$$

Assessment of Lung Injury

We measured lung water in eight dogs, using the method of Pearce et al. (1965) to determine the extent of lung injury created by injecting the glass beads. We also obtained control measurements from lungs of three dogs used for other experiments. A measured amount of water was added to the lungs, which were then homogenized. Duplicate aliquots of the homogenate were weighed and subsequently allowed to dry for 48 hours in an oven at 85%C. Another pair of homogenate samples were centrifuged at 1700 rpm for 1 hour, and the supernatant extract was also weighed and dried. Duplicate hemoglobin concentrations taken from a blood specimen collected from the pulmonary veins at the end of the experiment and from the supernatant samples were determined. The blood specimens were also weighed and then allowed to dry. The total mass of glass beads injected was subtracted from both the wet and dry weights of the lung (Malik and Van der Zee, 1978). The lung blood volume and lung extravascular water content were calculated from these data.

Postmortem lung and heart specimens were also obtained for routine histology to determine the microscopic nature of the microvascular injury created by the glass beads, and to verify that none of the beads lodged in the coronary circulation.

Statistical Analysis

Results are summarized as mean ± SD.

We averaged the impedance spectra from different dogs by accumulating the data into bins 0.2 Hz wide, then computing the means and standard deviations of the modulus and phase within each bin.

We used two different approaches to test hypothesis about our data. First, we used a repeated measures analysis of variance to compare values of the hemodynamic variables we observed at the spontaneous heart rate during baseline conditions, during pulmonary artery constriction, and following the dose of glass beads that came closest to doubling the pulmonary resistance. The presence or absence of the pericardium was taken as a grouping factor. The vascular intervention (baseline, pulmonary artery constriction, glass beads) and the lung inflation state (phasic respiration, held inspiration, held expiration, lung hyperinflation) were taken as trial factors. We also did repeated-measures analysis of variance on each pair of trial factors to compare each cell of the appropriate trial factor directly with others; differences were judged significant if P was less than 0.05 after applying a Bonferroni correction. The results of both the global analysis and the paired comparisons are reported in Table 1. All computations were done with BMDP2V (Dixon, 1981).

This approach has the advantage of being relatively straightforward and easy to summarize, but has the disadvantage of permitting us to use only a small fraction of the data we collected. It also ignores potential multivariate relationships between the variables of interest. Therefore, we also subjected our data collected at all doses of glass beads and all spontaneous and paced heart rates to a stepwise multiple linear regression analysis with BMDP2R (Dixon, 1981). We took the input impedance, characteristic impedance, and right ventricular stroke volume as dependent variables and dose of beads, right ventricular end-diastolic dimension, heart rate, and airway pressure as independent variables, along with dummy variables, to model the influence of the specific vascular conditions, the presence or absence of the pericardium, and between-dog variability. We also performed a regression analysis on data for each dog separately. The results of the dog-by-dog analysis and the analysis of the pooled data were similar.

Results were considered statistically significant when P was below 0.05.

Results

Nature and Severity of Lung Injury

The dose of glass beads necessary to double pulmonary input resistance was not significantly different for dogs with and without pericardia (6 ± 2 vs. 7 ± 3 g). Lung histology revealed an inflammatory response characterized by hyperemia and polymorphonuclear infiltration after glass bead infusion (Fig. 3). Intraalveolar hemorrhage also was observed. The lung water:dry weight ratio, corrected for the mass of infused glass beads, was significantly increased (3.9 ± 0.9 vs. 2.5 ± 1.4 for control lungs, $P < 0.05$ by unpaired t-test). These data show that the beads produced a significant microvascular injury with evidence of pulmonary inflammation and hemorrhage and an increased amount of lung water.

The microvascular injury also reduced lung compliance. Figure 4 shows a plot of airway pressure against tidal volume. This figure shows that microvascular injury produced higher airway pressures for a smaller tidal volume than during control. In contrast, constricting the pulmonary artery did not alter the relationship between tidal volume and airway pressure. Airway pressure was also increased at all levels of inflation during the microvascular injury (Table 1). Because the tidal volume was essentially constant throughout these experiments, the increase in airway pressure is further evidence that the microvascular injury decreased lung compliance consistent with an acute lung injury.

Effect of the Pericardium

Opening the pericardium significantly reduced left ventricular diastolic pressure. Whether the pericardium was open or closed did not significantly affect pulmonary input impedance or ventricular systolic function. As a result, the descriptive statistics represent data pooled from all experiments whether the pericardium was closed or open.

Effects of Vascular Interventions

Impedance

Figure 5 shows the pulmonary artery input impedance spectra averaged over all dogs for expiration and for lung hyperinflation during baseline, pulmonary artery constriction, and the microvascular injury. The dark lines show the mean impedance and the light lines one standard deviation above and below the mean impedance. The values for Z_O and Z_{inf}, as well as the phase information, we obtained during baseline were comparable to those reported by earlier investigators (Bergel and Milnor, 1965; Elkins and Milnor, 1971; Reubin et al., 1971; Elkins et al., 1974; Pouleur et al., 1978; Hopkins et al., 1979; Hammon et al., 1981). Figure 6 summarizes the results for all experimental conditions. Both pul-

TABLE 1
Hemodynamic Results

	Airway pressure (mm Hg)	$\overline{PAP}$ (mm Hg)	PAP_S (mm Hg)	PAP_D (mm Hg)	RVEDP (mm Hg)	LVEDP (mm Hg)	LVP_{max} (mm Hg)	SV (ml)	HR (beats/min)
Baseline									
Phasic respiration	4 ± 2	16 ± 3	28 ± 6	8 ± 2	6 ± 3	5 ± 3	93 ± 14	29 ± 9	118 ± 25
Inspiration	8 ± 3	16 ± 3	29 ± 5	9 ± 2	6 ± 3	5 ± 3	92 ± 12	29 ± 10	113 ± 24
Expiration	0 ± 2	15 ± 3	29 ± 5	7 ± 3	6 ± 3	5 ± 3	92 ± 12	29 ± 9	113 ± 25
Lung hyperinflation	17 ± 5	18 ± 4	29 ± 5	13 ± 4	7 ± 4	5 ± 3	67 ± 25	18 ± 8	110 ± 11
Pulmonary artery constriction									
Phasic respiration	4 ± 2	23 ± 6	46 ± 11	7 ± 4	7 ± 4	3 ± 4	90 ± 23	20 ± 13	136 ± 25
Inspiration	8 ± 4	24 ± 7	47 ± 15	9 ± 3	7 ± 4	3 ± 4	93 ± 21	20 ± 9	137 ± 26
Expiration	1 ± 2	24 ± 8	47 ± 16	8 ± 4	6 ± 4	3 ± 4	93 ± 22	20 ± 8	138 ± 26
Lung hyperinflation	17 ± 3	23 ± 10	41 ± 23	12 ± 4	8 ± 4	4 ± 4	57 ± 18	11 ± 10	129 ± 20
Microvascular injury									
Phasic	4 ± 2	28 ± 7	40 ± 11	20 ± 6	7 ± 4	4 ± 4	91 ± 28	20 ± 9	133 ± 28
Inspiration	9 ± 2	27 ± 6	38 ± 10	19 ± 5	7 ± 4	4 ± 4	87 ± 26	19 ± 9	133 ± 29
Expiration	2 ± 3	26 ± 6	38 ± 9	18 ± 5	7 ± 4	4 ± 4	92 ± 26	21 ± 9	129 ± 30
Lung hyperinflation	18 ± 7	25 ± 9	33 ± 12	19 ± 7	9 ± 6	4 ± 4	57 ± 30	10 ± 9	114 ± 27
*Results of repeated measures analysis of variance**									
All data	VL	V	V	VL	L	PL	L	VL	
Without lung hyperinflation	VL	V	V	VL		P		VL	
Baseline vs. PA constriction	L	V	V	L		VP	L	VL	V
Baseline vs. microvascular injury	VL	V	V	VL		P†	L	VL	
PA constriction vs. microvascular injury	L			V			L	L	

Results are expressed as mean ± SD. $n = 13$ for basal and microvascular injury, $n = 11$ for pulmonary artery constriction, $n = 10$ for lung hyperinflation, PAP = mean pulmonary artery pressure, PAP_S = systolic pulmonary artery pressure, PAP_D = diastolic pulmonary artery pressure, RVEDP = right ventrticular end-diastolic pressure, LVEDP = left ventricular end-diastolic pressure, SV = stroke volume, HR = heart rate, DSWL = left ventricular dimension stroke work, DSWR = right ventricular dimension stroke work, VSWR = right

* V = significant vascular effect; L = significant lung inflation effect; P = significant pericardial effect; $P < 0.05$.

† $P < 0.06$.

monary artery constriction and microvascular injury increased the input resistance, Z_O, but only pulmonary artery constriction elevated the characteristic impedance, Z_{inf}, to 140% of control. Lung hyperinflation during baseline, pulmonary artery constriction, and microvascular injury increased the input

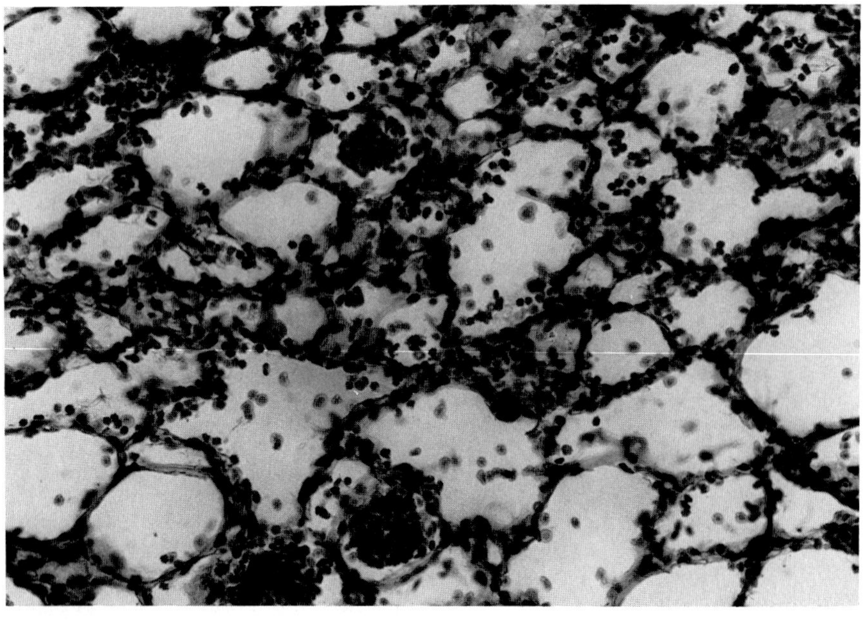

FIGURE 3. *Histology of a representative dog's lung after the microvascular injury. This section demonstrates an inflammatory response characterized by hyperemia and polymorphonuclear leukocyte infiltration. In addition, intraalveolar hemorrhage is observed.*

Table 1 (continued)

	VSWL (ml·mm Hg)	DSWL (mm·mm Hg)	DSWR (mm·mm Hg)	VSWR (ml·mm Hg)	LVEDD (mm)	LVESD (mm)	RVEDD (mm)	RVESD (mm)
Baseline								
Phasic respiration	2600 ± 1100	282 ± 143	81 ± 43	750 ± 290	56 ± 6	52 ± 5	55 ± 17	52 ± 15
Inspiration	2600 ± 1100	280 ± 123	84 ± 47	760 ± 300	56 ± 6	52 ± 5	55 ± 17	52 ± 15
Expiration	2600 ± 1100	289 ± 128	86 ± 52	730 ± 290	56 ± 6	53 ± 5	56 ± 17	53 ± 15
Lung hyperinflation	1200 ± 1000	150 ± 85	76 ± 99	410 ± 290	53 ± 6	52 ± 5	55 ± 17	50 ± 16
Pulmonary artery constriction								
Phasic respiration	1900 ± 1500	176 ± 90	108 ± 95	940 ± 790	54 ± 6	52 ± 5	55 ± 18	53 ± 16
Inspiration	1900 ± 1100	174 ± 90	87 ± 72	900 ± 660	54 ± 6	52 ± 5	55 ± 18	53 ± 16
Expiration	1900 ± 1200	183 ± 110	85 ± 80	920 ± 690	54 ± 6	53 ± 5	56 ± 18	54 ± 17
Lung hyperinflation	680 ± 770	89 ± 55	27 ± 33	350 ± 460	56 ± 6	51 ± 5	51 ± 18	51 ± 17
Microvascular injury								
Phasic	1800 ± 1200	240 ± 142	117 ± 99	770 ± 540	56 ± 7	53 ± 6	57 ± 17	54 ± 16
Inspiration	1700 ± 1200	234 ± 126	87 ± 97	690 ± 540	56 ± 8	53 ± 6	55 ± 16	53 ± 16
Expiration	1900 ± 1200	200 ± 207	103 ± 84	740 ± 460	56 ± 7	55 ± 11	56 ± 17	54 ± 16
Lung hyperinflation	870 ± 1200	150 ± 181	43 ± 44	420 ± 620	54 ± 6	53 ± 6	51 ± 16	50 ± 16
*Results of repeated measures analysis of variance**								
All data	L	LV†	L†	L	L	L		L
Without lung hyperinflation		V†				L	L	VP
Baseline vs. PA constriction	L	VL		L	L	VL	L	V
Baseline vs. microvascular injury	L	L†		L			L	
PA constriction vs. microvascular injury	L	L	L	L		L		

ventricular volume stroke work, LVIDD = left ventricular end-diastolic dimension, LVESD = left ventricular end-systolic dimension, RVEDD = right ventricular end-diastolic dimension, RVESD = right ventricular end-systolic dimension.

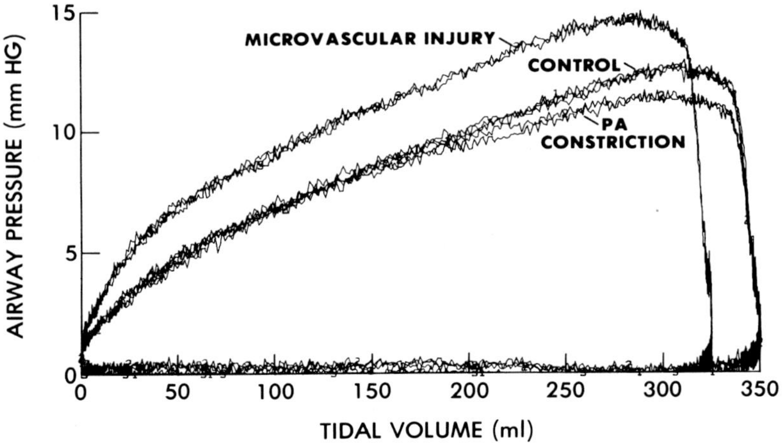

Figure 4. *Representative lung pressure-tidal volume loop during phasic respiration in a dog during each vascular intervention. Pulmonary artery constriction had no significant effect on the pressure-volume loop compared to control. Microvascular injury was associated with an increase in airway pressure at similar tidal volumes, suggesting reduced lung compliance.*

resistance even further, but did not affect characteristic impedance. The pulmonary artery constriction increased input resistance, Z_O, to 170% of control, and the microvascular injury increased it to 215% of control.

Neither impedance parameter changed with lung inflation state during physiological tidal volumes (phasic respiration, during held expiration, or held inspiration).

The absence of a preceding pulmonary artery constriction in two dogs did not affect the impedance spectra during the microvascular injury. Multiple linear regression analysis confirmed these results. Multiple linear regression analysis also confirmed that changes in heart rate during control conditions produced by pacing did not affect the impedance spectra. This same analysis also confirmed that characteristic impedance, Z_{inf}, increased significantly during pulmonary artery constriction but not during microvascular injury.

Table 2 summarizes the pulmonary input impedance spectra during held expiration under baseline

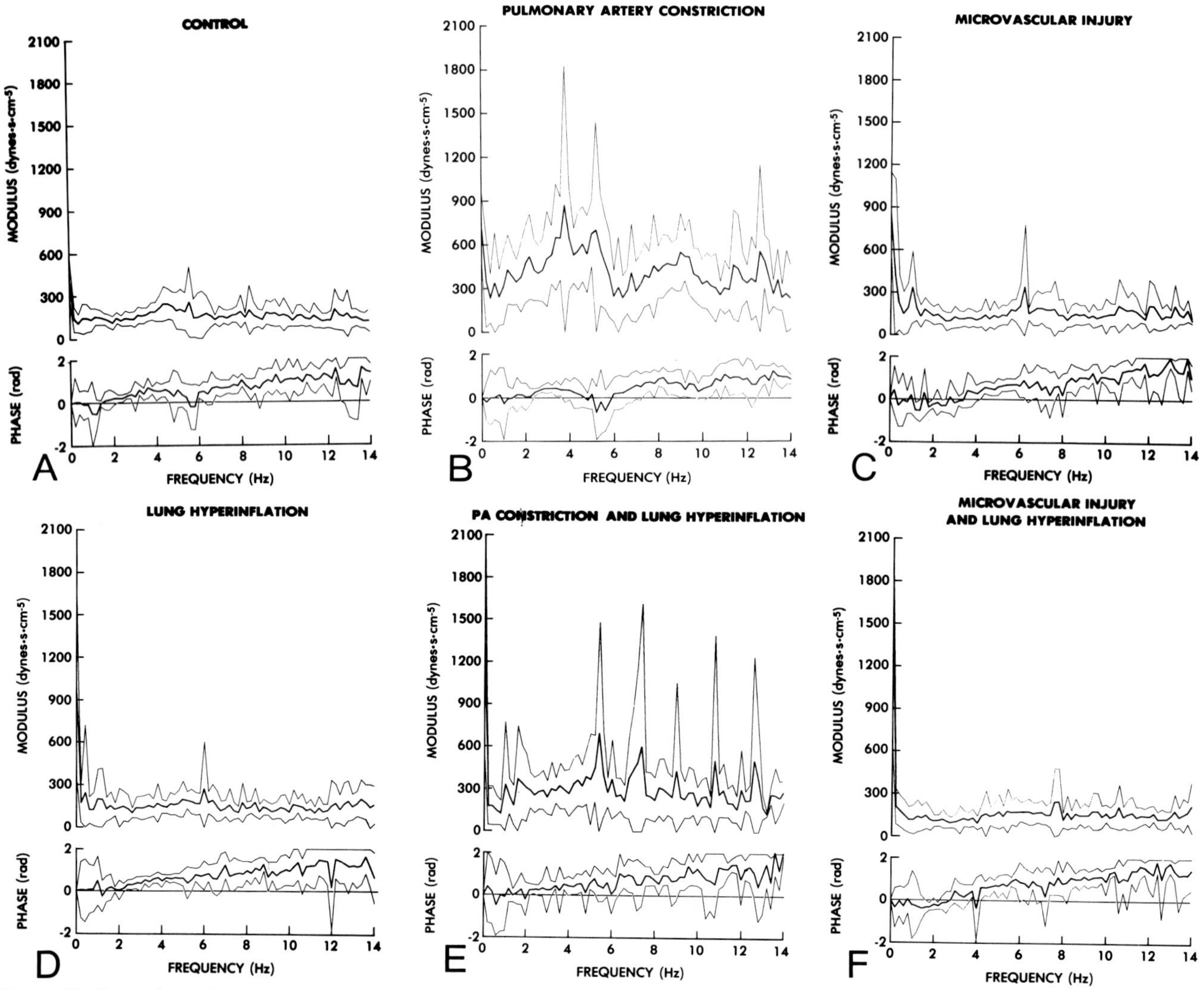

FIGURE 5. *The pooled pulmonary artery impedance spectra at expiration and lung hyperinflation during control, pulmonary artery constriction and microvascular injury. The dark line represents the mean value of impedance at each frequency. The light lines represent standard deviation above and below the mean. Panel A shows control pulmonary input impedance. Panel B shows that pulmonary artery constriction increases both the input resistance and characteristic impedance. Panel C shows that the microvascular injury increases the input resistance above control. Lung hyperinflation increases the input resistance further for the control state and each vascular intervention (panels D, E, and F). All data were recorded at end-expiration.*

conditions at different heart rates. Consistent with the findings of earlier investigators (Bergel and Milnor, 1965), multiple linear regression analysis demonstrated that changing heart rate did not significantly affect the impedance.

This result also provides additional support for the accuracy of the impedance spectra derived using the entire Fourier transform of the pressure and flow data, rather than just the peak values at the harmonics of the heart rate one obtains from a Fourier series. Earlier investigators who used Fourier series analysis increased their frequency resolution by pacing at a variety of heart rates; we were able to obtain the same information from data at a single heart rate using the Fourier transform. If leakage at the frequencies between the harmonics of the heart rate was a problem, the spectra computed using different heart rates (i.e., having the harmonics at different frequencies) would probably yield different results. The fact that the spectra from all the heart rates were similar is further evidence that the computational approach we used yielded accurate results.

Pressures

Both pulmonary artery constriction and microvascular injury increased the mean and systolic pulmonary artery pressures (to 149% and 171% of control, respectively; see Table 1 for actual values). Only microvascular injury increased the pulmonary artery diastolic pressure (to 150% of control). There was no significant change in the right ventricular end-diastolic pressure during either vascular intervention.

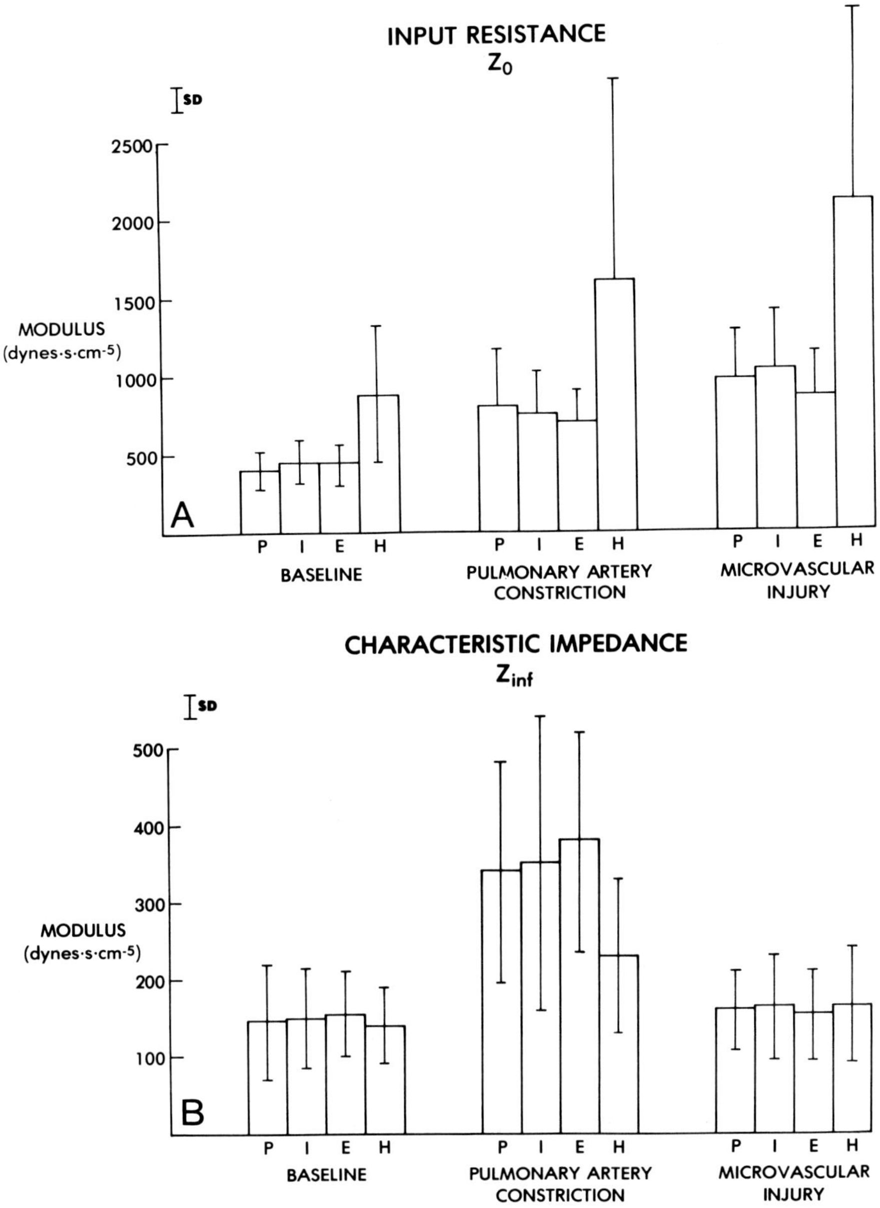

FIGURE 6. *Panel A: pulmonary input resistance, Z_0, at each lung inflation state (P = phasic respiration, I = end-inspiration, E = end-expiration, H = lung hyperinflation) during control, pulmonary artery constriction, and microvascular injury. Both pulmonary artery constriction and microvascular injury increase the input resistance for each lung inflation state. Lung hyperinflation always increases Z_0 even further. No significant changes were noted between phasic respiration, inspiration, or expiration during control or either vascular intervention. Panel B: pulmonary characteristic impedance, Z_{inf}, at each lung inflation state, during control pulmonary artery constriction, and microvascular injury. Only pulmonary artery constriction increased the characteristic impedance. Neither the microvascular injury nor lung hyperinflation had any effect on Z_{inf}.*

TABLE 2

Effect of Heart Rate on Pulmonary Input Impedance (dyne·sec·cm^{-5})

	Spontaneous heart rate												Pacing*									
	Phasic			Held insp			Held exp			Hyperinf				Phasic		Held insp		Held exp		Hyperinf	
Dog	HR†	Z_0	Z_{inf}	HR	Z_0	Z_{inf}	HR	Z_0	Z_{inf}	HR	Z_0	Z_{inf}	HR	Z_0	Z_{inf}	Z_0	Z_{inf}	Z_0	Z_{inf}	Z_0	Z_{inf}
409	90	382	78	83	431	76	76	362	91	114	697	80	160	388	80	576	56	538	68	940	60
410	98	654	323	96	603	30	87	693	186	97	599	153	130	559	136	579	165	552	232	1434	177
411	104	289	89	106	295	90	112	693	186	115	403	104	130	292	93	303	93	298	67	589	89
412	119	224	98	118	225	90	118	199	78	112	364	129	160	177	115	177	96	179	82	328	77
414	110	472	176	110	498	170	114	472	213	124	1072	188	160	602	129	657	113	627	127	670	122
415	84	399	136	77	397	144	83	389	143	96	782	83	160	366	93	406	82	395	63	1068	98
419	112	522	109	112	556	121	115	534	104	102	1530	150	160	501	108	609	181	485	89	2901	79

Held insp = held inspiration; Held exp = held expiration; Hyperinf = hyperinflation; Z_0 = pulmonary input resistance; Z_{inf} = pulmonary characteristic impedance.

* Table shows results for only one rate, even though several dogs were paced at two or three different rates. The statistical analysis used data for all rates.

† Heart rate in beats/min.

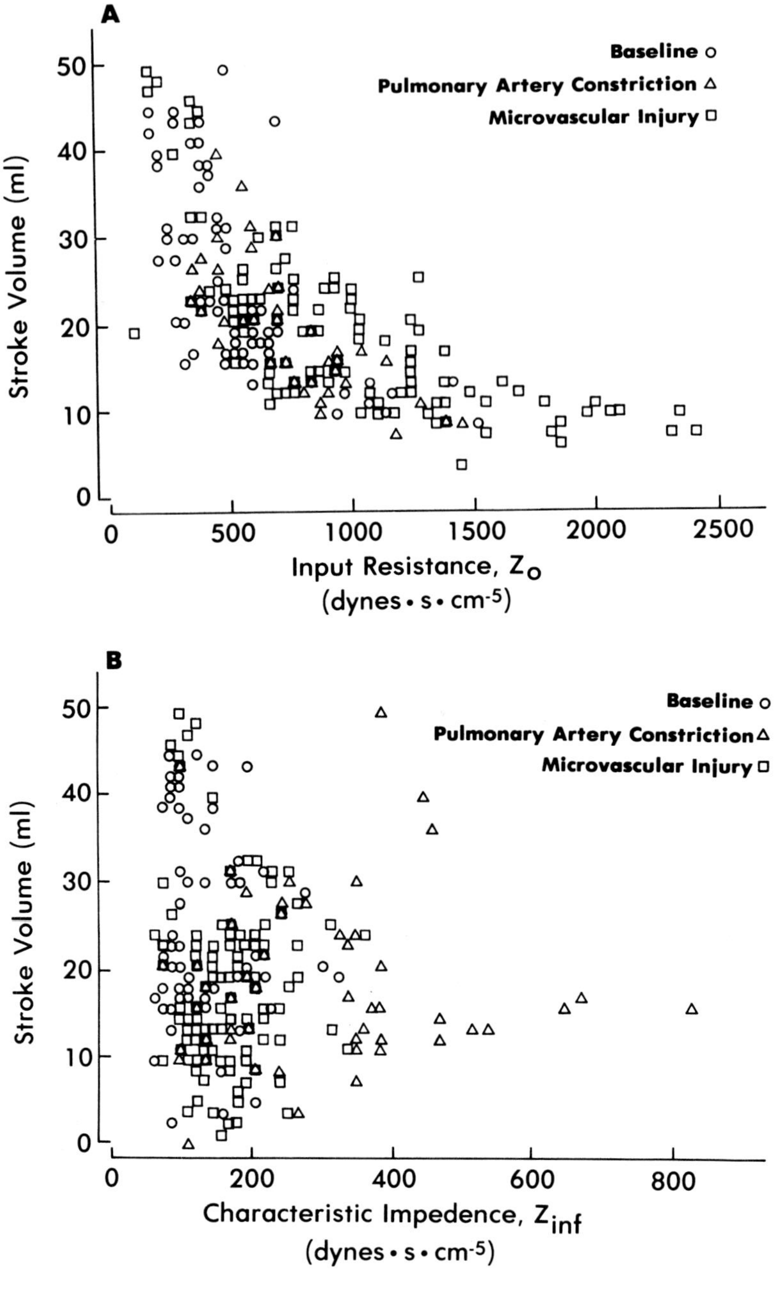

FIGURE 7. *The relationship between stroke volume and input resistance,* Z_0 *(A), and characteristic impedance,* Z_{inf} *(B), during all vascular interventions and all lung inflation states in all 13 dogs. Stroke volume is inversely related to input resistance, but is unrelated to the level of characteristic impedance.*

Ventricular Performance

Both pulmonary artery constriction and the microvascular injury decreased right ventricular stroke volume significantly and to a similar degree (to 70% of control). This decrease in stroke volume was inversely related to the input resistance ($r = 0.67$, $P < 0.05$ for SV vs. $1/Z_O$), regardless of the vascular intervention or lung inflation state (Fig. 7A). In contrast, right ventricular stroke volume was not related to the characteristic impedance Z_{inf} (Fig. 7B).

Right ventricular dimension and volume stroke work did not change significantly with either vascular intervention. Right and left ventricular end-diastolic dimensions did not change significantly with vascular intervention. Pulmonary artery constriction decreased left ventricular dimension stroke work (to 63% of control) but did not significantly affect volume stroke work; microvascular injury did not significantly affect either measure of left ventricular systolic function.

Right Ventricular Power Output

The right ventricular steady flow power increased slightly, but not significantly, during both the pulmonary artery constriction and microvascular injury (Fig. 8). The pulsatile power did not change during the pulmonary artery constriction, but fell significantly (to 66% of control) during the microvascular injury. The reduction of pulsatile power during microvascular injury meant that a smaller proportion of the total power output of the right ventricle was manifest as pressure and flow oscillation than during control or pulmonary artery constriction.

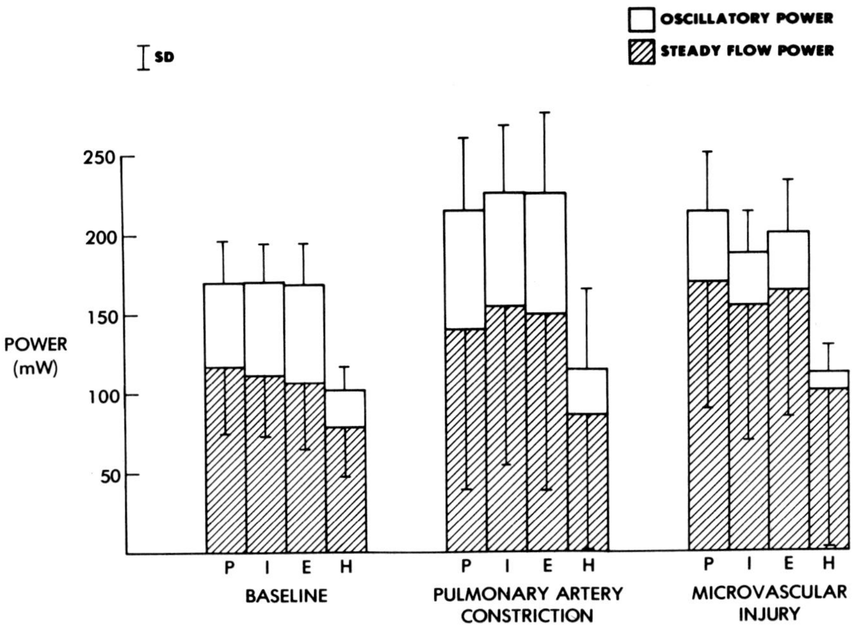

FIGURE 8. *Right ventricular steady flow power (dark bars) and oscillatory power (open bars) at each lung inflation state during control conditions, pulmonary artery constriction, and microvascular injury. Neither vascular intervention affects the absolute value of steady flow power, but microvascular injury reduces the oscillatory power and its relative contribution to the total power output. Lung hyperinflation reduces both steady flow and oscillatory power during control and during both vascular interventions.*

Effects of Lung Hyperinflation

Lung hyperinflation had dramatic effects over and above the effects observed during the pulmonary artery constriction or microvascular injury. Because these effects were not observed at physiological levels of lung inflation (phasic respiration, held inspiration, held expiration), they deserve special attention. All changes ascribed to lung hyperinflation are compared to the pooled observations of phasic respiration, expiration, and inspiration during each vascular intervention as their control.

Impedance

Lung hyperinflation dramatically increased pulmonary input resistance, Z_0, regardless of the nature of vascular intervention (to 203% of control during baseline, 213% of control during pulmonary artery constriction, and 225% of control during microvascular injury). In sharp contrast, lung hyperinflation did not significantly change the characteristic impedance, Z_{inf} (Figs. 5 and 6).

Pressures

Lung hyperinflation significantly increased pulmonary artery and right ventricular end-diastolic pressures. Right ventricular end-diastolic pressures increased during all conditions (to 124% of control during baseline, 126% of control during pulmonary artery constriction, and 131% of control during microvascular injury), whereas pulmonary artery diastolic pressure increased only during baseline and pulmonary artery constriction.

Ventricular performance

Lung hyperinflation reduced right ventricular stroke volume, right ventricular volume and dimension stroke work, and left ventricular dimension stroke work. It reduced right ventricular stroke volume to 62% of control during baseline, to 55% of control during pulmonary artery constriction, and to 50% with the microvascular injury (Table 1). It reduced right ventricular stroke work volume and dimension, especially when the pulmonary artery pressure was high from either vascular intervention. (Volume and dimension stroke work fell to 46% and 92%, respectively, of control during baseline, to 36% and 30% during the pulmonary artery constriction, and to 48% and 32% with the microvascular injury). Lung hyperinflation cut both left ventricular stroke work volume and dimension approximately in half with each intervention.

Lung hyperinflation had variable effects on left and right ventricular dimensions. Lung hyperinflation did not significantly change right ventricular end-diastolic dimension during baseline conditions. Lung hyperinflation significantly reduced right ventricular end-diastolic dimensions (to 94% of control) during pulmonary artery constriction and microvascular injury (to 96% of control). It consistently reduced left ventricular end-diastolic dimension when the pericardium was intact. Lung hyperinflation did not consistently change left ventricular end-diastolic dimension when the pericardium was open.

Right Ventricular Power Output

Lung hyperinflation significantly reduced both steady flow power (to 70% of control during baseline, 51% during pulmonary artery constriction, and 36% during microvascular injury) and pulsatile power (to 42% of control during baseline, 21% during pulmonary artery constriction, and 31% during the microvascular injury), resulting in a drastically lower total power output (Fig. 8). Despite this reduction in total power, lung hyperinflation per se did not affect the distribution of power between steady flow and pulsatile power.

Discussion

Malik and Van Der Zee (1978) first described the use of glass bead infusion to create a microvascular lung injury. They reported an increase in lung lymph flow and lung water following the injury, but did not describe the injury's histological nature. Our histological examination revealed a significant parenchymal lung injury. Evidence for both an inflammatory response (hyperemia and polymorphonuclear leukocyte infiltration) and intraalveolar hemorrhage were observed, and were similar to changes previously observed (Lamy et al., 1976) in adult respiratory distress syndrome. These findings, combined with the elevated lung water, reduced lung compliance, and reduced pulmonary hypertension, confirm that the glass bead injury resembles the clinical syndrome of noncardiogenic pulmonary edema well enough to provide a useful experimental model to study the hemodynamic responses to this disease.

We compared this model with pulmonary artery constriction to show that not all forms of pulmonary hypertension present this same dynamic afterload to the right ventricle. By quantifying afterload as pulmonary artery input impedance, we found that the dynamic afterload that the right ventricle faces during a proximal pulmonary artery constriction is greater than during a microvascular injury. When both interventions approximately doubled the input resistance, Z_O, only the pulmonary artery constriction increased the characteristic impedance, Z_{inf}. This increase in Z_{inf} means that the right ventricle had to expend more power overcoming the resistance to the pulsatile components of pressure and flow to maintain a given mean flow than during a comparable microvascular injury.

Both vascular interventions decreased right ventricular stroke volume without changing either the right ventricular dimension or volume stroke work or the total power output. Hence, both interventions had similar effects on right ventricular performance.

Neither pulmonary artery constriction nor microvascular injury depressed left ventricular volume stroke work. Pulmonary artery constriction depressed left ventricular dimension stroke work, however. This difference in responses of left ventricular volume and dimension stroke works suggests—but does not prove—that the pulmonary artery constriction is affecting left ventricular function by changing its geometry. Others (Kelly et al., 1971; Stool et al., 1974; Glantz et al., 1978; Olsen et al., 1983; Visner et al., 1983) have shown that pulmonary artery constriction changes left ventricular geometry by reducing septal-free wall diameter more than anterior-posterior diameter.

Our observations about left and right ventricular systolic function based on measurement of left ventricular anterior-posterior diameter and right ventricular chord length reflect regional function only. The volume stroke work for each ventricle probably gives a better view of overall ventricular work. The disparity between the left ventricular dimension and volume stroke work results might be explained by a change in cardiac geometry involving regional diameters or patterns of systolic wall thickening that is insufficient to depress volume stroke work. Whereas we have insufficient data to determine the exact nature of the altered left ventricular function, our data suggest some change during pulmonary artery constriction. We have no evidence of any change in left ventricular geometry or function during microvascular injury. Further experiments using both septal-free wall and anterior-posterior dimensions are needed to confirm that a microvascular injury did not alter ventricular geometry, before firm conclusions about ventricular function can be drawn. Unfortunately, limitations in the number of channels of data that could be recorded precluded measurement of both septal-free wall and anterior-posterior dimensions in the present study, so that the explanation of our results must remain tentative.

The distribution of right ventricular power output differs during pulmonary artery constriction and microvascular injury. The level of pulsatile power and its relative contribution to the total right ventricular power output were reduced, compared to control, during the microvascular injury, but were unchanged during the pulmonary artery constriction. Since oscillatory power is required because of pressure and flow pulsations, a reduction in its relative contribution preserves energy required to maintain cardiac output. This situation was not observed during pulmonary artery constriction.

The reduction in pulsatile (oscillatory) power observed during microvascular injury is likely, in part, to be secondary to the 10% increase in heart rate from control that we observed. Milnor et al. (1966) showed that pulsatile power falls as heart rate increases. They attributed this reduction in oscillatory power to two factors. First, the flow moduli fall steeply as the fundamental frequency (i.e., the heart rate) increases from 0 to 3 Hz, suggesting a rate-dependent change in the harmonic structure of flow waveform. Second, stroke volume decreases as heart rate increases, resulting in waveforms with smaller amplitude. Hence, smaller pulsations would require less energy to maintain a given cardiac output. During pulmonary artery constriction, we found that the magnitude of oscillatory power and its relative contribution to total power output was maintained near control values, despite an increase in heart rate similar to that observed during microvascular injury. We suspect that oscillatory power remains near control levels during the pulmonary artery constriction because the characteristic impedance increases. This increase in characteristic impedance, Z_{inf}, increases the oscillatory power while the accompanying increase in heart rate decreases oscillatory power. The net effect of these opposing influences is that the oscillatory power remains unchanged during pulmonary artery constriction.

The response of the pulmonary artery pressure

and flow waveforms to alterations in pulmonary input impedance is similar to the response of systemic waveforms observed in studies of the systemic impedance spectra using both isolated heart preparations (Imperial et al, 1961; Salisbury et al., 1962; Elzinga et al., 1973) and intact dogs (O'Rourke, 1967; Urschel et al., 1968; Walker, 1975; Levken and Kiil, 1975; Nichols et al.,1980). Increasing either aortic input resistance or characteristic impedance reduces left ventricular stroke volume and increases systolic aortic pressure; the mean and diastolic aortic pressure fall with increasing characteristic impedance (Nichols et al., 1980), but they increase with an increase in input resistance. Although the mean pulmonary artery pressure did not fall with the increase in characteristic impedance produced by the pulmonary artery constriction (because the pulmonary diastolic pressure did not change significantly), we have demonstrated that pulmonary waveforms have similar responses in systolic pulmonary pressure and right ventricular stroke volume. The peak systolic pulmonary pressure increased and the right ventricular stroke volume decreased when either characteristic impedance or input resistance was increased. The increase in input impedance produced by the microvascular injury also increased both the mean and the diastolic pulmonary artery pressure to a degree similar to the response noted in the systemic circulation. Therefore, changes in either the input resistance or characteristic impedance in the pulmonary circulation produce alterations in the pulmonary artery analogous to those seen in the systemic circulation.

Elkins et al. (1974) studied pulmonary artery input impedance in dogs with chronic pulmonary hypertension produced by embolizing 3 × 4-mm acrylic beads into the pulmonary artery. The values for pressures and pulmonary artery input impedance they observed under control conditions were similar to ours. Despite the fact that their intervention produced much more severe pulmonary hypertension than we did (mean pulmonary artery pressure was 44 mm Hg compared to 24 mm Hg in our study), their data do not show a significant increase in Z_{inf} ($P > 0.15$ by both unpaired *t*- and Mann-Whitney tests). In contrast to our results during microvascular injury, their data do not show a fall in either steady flow or pulsatile power. This difference may be due to the fact that the obstruction produced by Elkins et al., with their relatively large 3 × 4-mm beads, is more similar to a pulmonary artery constriction than the microvascular injury we produced with our 150- to 200-μm beads, which block more distal resistance vessels.

Pouleur et al. (1978) clamped a main branch of the pulmonary artery, resulting in an increase in the impedance spectra magnitude up to the first three harmonics. Our results are consistent with their study.

The influence of pharmacological agents on the pulmonary input impedance has been studied by Bergel and Milnor (1966), Reuben et al. (1971), and Hammon et al. (1981). The microvascular injury that we produced increased the input resistance without a change in the characteristic impedance. Our result differs from that of Hammon et al. (1981), indicating that both pulmonary input resistance and characteristic impedance increase when serotonin was infused. These authors suggested that the increase in characteristic impedance observed during the serotonin infusion was the result of increased vascular tone in the proximal artery bed. In contrast, we believe that the glass beads produced a more distal injury than the site of serotonin action, without any accompanying vasoconstriction of the proximal vasculature. Thus, only the input resistance was increased.

The pericardium has been shown to have a significant effect on the diastolic properties of the heart (Elzinga et al., 1974; Shirato et al., 1976; Glantz et al., 1978; Janicki and Weber, 1978; Stokland et al., 1980); we found that removing it significantly reduced left ventricular diastolic pressure. As would be expected from the findings of Misbach and Glantz (1979), we did not find that the pericardium had a significant influence upon either ventricle's systolic response to an afterload increase due to pulmonary artery constriction of microvascular injury.

Lung hyperinflation always increased input resistance because it reduced pulmonary flow and increased diastolic pressure. The increase in input resistance during lung hyperinflation is similar to the increase that Bergel and Milnor (1965) observed when they serially increased lung volume, and that Smith et al. (1982) observed during ventilation with positive end-expiratory pressure (PEEP). These investigators explained their results by proposing that increased intraalveolar pressure during lung hyperinflation exceeded both arterial and venous pressures and collapses small intraalveolar vessels (Howell et al., 1961; Permutt et al., 1961). We have demonstrated that this effect occurs not only in normal lungs, but also when the lungs are injured.

During lung hyperinflation, right ventricular stroke volume, steady flow power, and oscillatory power were drastically reduced, right ventricular end-diastolic dimension was unchanged, and right ventricular end-diastolic pressure was increased. Lung hyperinflation also reduced left ventricular volume and dimension stroke work and left ventricular end-diastolic dimension, and increased left ventricular end-diastolic pressure. Therefore, lung hyperinflation when pulmonary artery pressure is already high, due to pulmonary injury, and right ventricle is already stressed, may further reduce right ventricular output and work. Lung hyperinflation further increased right ventricular afterload, beyond the increase caused by pulmonary artery constriction or microvascular injury, and, in turn, further depressed both right and left ventricular systolic function.

Two main conclusions can be drawn from these observations. First, the dramatic reductions in right ventricular stroke volume and power during lung hyperinflation were brought about largely by an increase in the pulmonary input resistance without a compensatory increase in right ventricular end-diastolic size or preload. Ordinarily, one would expect right ventricular preload to increase to maintain output when the afterload is suddenly increased, but this adjustment does not occur with lung hyperinflation. Quite to the contrary, lung hyperinflation hampers the right ventricle's ability to adapt to the resulting increased afterload. This increase in right ventricular afterload without a compensatory increase in preload occurred regardless of the nature of the vascular intervention.

This observation has special relevance when treating a patient with respiratory failure and pulmonary hypertension with mechanical ventilation and positive end-expiratory pressure (PEEP). Because PEEP also increases lung volume, although not to the same extent as in our experimental preparation, our findings suggest that the reduction in cardiac output observed when positive end-expiratory pressure is instituted is not simply related to reduced right ventricular preload, but may be related more to the increase in right ventricular afterload and the accompanying inability of the right ventricle to compensate for it by increasing its preload. Therefore, we agree with Smith et al. (1982) and Rankin et al. (1982) that one of the primary mechanisms by which lung hyperinflation or PEEP decreases cardiac output is by depressiong right ventricular stroke volume because of the increased pulmonary input resistance.

Second, lung hyperinflation reduces left ventricular preload. It does this not only because the right ventricle's stroke volume is reduced, but, also, because it changes both ventricles' diastolic pressure-volume relations. Although we left our thoracotomy and both pleural spaces open to atmospheric pressure, we observed an increase in right ventricular end-diastolic pressure without an increase in right ventricular end-diastolic dimension and an actual decrease in left ventricular end-diastolic size. We believe that these changes probably were due to an increase in the contact pressure between the lungs and the heart when the lungs are hyperinflated such that both ventricles' diastolic pressure-volume curves were changed. Similar increases in extracardiac contact pressure have been reported during studies of PEEP (Prewitt et al., 1979; Fewell et al., 1980, 1981). We cannot rule out a direct interaction between both ventricles mediated by shifting of the interventricular septum, however, because we did not measure septal-free wall dimension.

Our data agree with those of Smith et al. (1982) and Cassidy et al. (1982), who suggested that left ventricular volumes are reduced with either a small or variable change in left ventricular dimensions during PEEP therapy. They conflict with those of Jardin et al. (1981), who suggested that the right ventricle dilates and causes left ventricular compression directly within an intact pericardium. We believe, rather, that the elevated right ventricular end-diastolic pressures that we observed during lung hyperinflation probably reflects a compressive force that the lungs exert directly on the heart. The associated reduction in left ventricular end-diastolic dimensions without a change in left ventricular end-diastolic pressure suggests that the distensibility of both ventricles is affected. Although lung hyperinflation increased the gas volume of the lungs more than that usually produced by PEEP, our dogs did have open chests and, hence, a greater lung volume is required to observe an effect. The airway pressure we generated by lung hyperinflation is comparable to that seen with high levels of PEEP.

We have demonstrated that the nature of the pulmonary vascular intervention cannot be characterized simply by its effect on pulmonary artery pressure. We found three differences in the effects of pulmonary artery constriction and microvascular injury. First, the pulmonary artery constriction increased with the resistive component and characteristic impedance of right ventricular dynamic afterload, whereas microvascular injury increased only the resistive component. Second, our data suggest that pulmonary artery constriction may have changed left ventricular geometry, whereas microvascular injury did not. Third, microvascular injury reduced the amount and proportion of right ventricular pulsatile power, a potentially beneficial adaptation to increased load not manifest during pulmonary artery constriction.

Lung hyperinflation imposes a further burden on the heart, regardless of vascular intervention, by both increasing the pulmonary input resistance and limiting any increase in right ventricular preload to compensate for it. Therefore, models of pulmonary hypertension based on pulmonary artery banding do not reflect accurately the conditions existing when the pulmonary hypertension is created by a microvascular injury. The injury induced by infusing glass beads into the pulmonary circulation is a good experimental model of the clinical syndrome of non-cardiogenic pulmonary edema for the study of cardiopulmonary interactions occurring in this situation.

We wish to thank Jahar Bhattacharya, J.I.E. Hoffman, W.W. Parmley, Peter Smith, Fernando Florenzano, Bryan Slinker, and Wilmor Nichols for their thoughtful criticism, Ed Stokes and Steve Sizemore for their programming assistance, Robert Battagin for designing custom electronics, Jim Stoughton for his diligent technical assistance, Mary Hurtado and Pat Nardella for typing the manuscript, and Mimi Zieger for reviewing the manuscript.

Supported by National Institutes of Health Research Grant HL-25869 and Training Grant HL-01792. Dr. Calvin was a fellow of the Medical Research Council of Canada, and Dr. Glantz held a National Institutes of Health Research Career Development Award.

Dr. Calvin's present address is: Department of Medicine, Division of Cardiology, University of Ottawa, Ottawa, Ontario, Canada. Dr.

Baer's present address is: Department of Physiology, Kirksville College of Osteopathic Medicine, Kirksville, Missouri 63501.

Address for reprints: Stanton A. Glantz, Associate Professor of Medicine, Room 1186 M, University of California, San Francisco, California 94143.

Received January 21, 1983; accepted for publication October 3, 1984.

References

Bemis CE, Serur JR, Borkenhager D, Sonnenblick EH, Urschel CW (1974) Influence of right ventricular filling pressure on left ventricular pressure and dimension. Circ Res **34:** 498–504

Bergel DH, Milnor WR (1965) Pulmonary vascular impedance in the dog. Circ Res **16:** 401–415

Brigham EO (1974) The Fast Fourier Transform. Englewood Cliffs, N.J., Prentice Hall

Cassidy SS, Mitchell JH, Johnson RL (1982) Dimensional analysis of right and left ventricles during positive pressure ventilation in dogs. Am J Physiol **242:** H549–H556

Dixon WJ (1981) BMDP Statistical Software, 1981. Berkeley, California, University of California Press

Elkins RC, Milnor WR (1971) Pulmonary vascular response to exercise in the dog. Circ Res **29:** 591–599

Elkins RC, Peyton MD, Greenfield LJ (1974) Pulmonary vascular impedance in chronic pulmonary hypertension. Surgery **76:** 57–64

Elzinga C, Westerhof NC (1973) Pressure and flow generated by the left ventricle against different impedances. Circ Res **32:** 178–186

Elzinga G, Van Grondelle R, Westerhof NC, van der Bos GC (1974) Ventricular interference. Am J Physiol **226:** 941–947

Fewell JE, Abendschein DR, Carlson CJ, Rapaport E, Murray JF (1980) Mechanism of decreased right and left ventricular volumes during continuous positive pressure ventilation in dogs. Circ Res **47:** 467–472

Fewell JE, Abendschein DR, Carlson CJ, Rapaport E, Murray JF (1981) Continuous positive pressure ventilation decreases right and left ventricular end-diastolic volume in the dog. Circ Res **46:** 125–132

Glantz SA (1979) Mathematics for Biomedical Applications chap 6, Fourier Analysis, Spectra, and Filters. Berkeley, California, University of California Press, pp 244–252

Glantz SA, Misbach GA, Moores WY, Mathey DG, Lekven J, Stowe DF, Parmley WW, Tyberg JV (1978) The pericardium substantially affects the left ventricular diastolic pressure volume relationship in the dog. Circ Res **42:** 433–441

Hamman JW, Smith PK, McHale PA, Vanbenthuysen KM, Anderson RW (1981) Analysis of pulsatile pulmonary artery blood flow in the unanesthetized dog. J Appl Physiol **50:** 805–813

Hopkins RA, Hammon JW Jr, McHale PA, Smith PK, Anderson RW (1979) Pulmonary vascular impedance analysis of adaption to chronically elevated blood flow in the awake dog. Circ Res **45:** 267–274

Horowitz S, Glantz SA (1979) Analog-to-digital data conversion and display system, UCSF (mimeo)

Howell JBL, Permutt S, Proctor DR, Riley RL (1961) Effect of inflation of the lung on different parts of pulmonary vascular bed. J Appl Physiol **16:** 71–76

Imperial ES, Levy MN, Zieske J (1961) Outflow resistance as an independent determinant of cardiac performance. Circ Res **9:** 1148–1155

IMSL Library (1980) IMSL, Inc., Houston, Texas, FFTRC-1-3

Janicki JS, Weber KT (1980) The pericardium and ventricular interaction, distensibility and function. Am J Physiol **238:** H494–H503

Jardin F, Farcot JC, Boisante L, Curien N, Margairaz A, Boudarias JP (1981) Influence of positive end-expiratory pressure on left ventricular performance. N Engl J Med **304:** 387–392

Kelly DT, Spotnitz HM, Beiser GD, Pierce JE, Epstein SE (1971) Effects of chronic right ventricular volume and pressure loading on left ventricular performance. Circulation **44:** 403–412

Lamy M, Fallat RJ, Koeniger E, Dietrich H-P, Ratliff JL, Eberhart RC, Tucker HJ, Hill JD (1976) Pathological features and mechanisms of hypoxemia in adult respiratory distress syndrome. Am Rev Resp Dis **114:** 267–284

Lekven J, Kiil F (1975) Myocardial function in general and regional left ventricular ischemic in dogs at control and high aortic pressure. Cardiovasc Res **9:** 373–382

Malik AB, Van Der Zee H (1978) Mechanisms of pulmonary edema induced by microembolization in dogs. Circ Res **42:** 72–79

Meier GD, Bove AA, Santamore WP, Lynch PR (1980) Contractile function in canine right ventricle. Am J Physiol **239:** H794–H804

Milnor WR (1982) Vascular impedance. *In* Hemodynamics. Baltimore, Williams & Wilkins, pp 157–191

Milnor WR, Bergel DH, Bargainer CJD (1966) Hydraulic power associated with pulmonary blood flow and its relation to heart rate. Circ Res **19:** 467–480

Misbach G, Glantz S (1979) Changes in the diastolic pressure-diameter relation alter ventricular function curves. Am J Physiol **237:** H664–H648

Nichols WW, Pepine CJ, Geiser EA, Conti CR (1980) Vascular load defined by the aortic input impedance spectrum. Fed Proc **39:** 196–201

Olsen CO, Tyson GS, Maier GW, Spratt JA, Davis JW, Rankin JS (1983) Dynamic ventricular interaction in the conscious dog. Circ Res **52:** 85–104

O'Rourke MF (1967) Steady and pulsatile energy losses in the systemic circulation under normal conditions and in simulated arterial disease. Cardiovasc Res **1:** 313–326

Patel DJ, Defreitas FM, Fry DL (1963) Hydraulic input impedance to aorta and pulmonary artery in dogs. J Appl Physiol **18:** 134–146

Pearce ML, Yamashita J, Beazell J (1965) Measurement of pulmonary edema. Circ Res **16:** 482–488

Permutt S, Howell JB, Proctor DF, Riley RL (1961) Effect of lung inflation on static pressure-volume characteristics of pulmonary vessels. J Appl Physiol **16:** 64–70

Pouleur H, Lefevre J, van Eyll C, Janmin PM, Charlier AA (1978) Significance of pulmonary input impedance in right ventricular performance. Cardiovasc Res **12:** 617–629

Prewitt RM, Wood LDH (1979) Effect of positive end-expiratory pressure on ventricular function in dogs. Am J Physiol **236:** H534–H544

Rankin JS, Arentzen CE, Anderson RW, McHale RA (1977) Viscoelastic prospectives of the left ventricle in the conscious dogs. Circ Res **41:** 37–45

Rankin JS, Olsen CO, Arentzen CE, Tyson GS, Maier B, Smith PK, Hammon JW, Davis JW, McHale PA, Anderson RW, Sagiston DC (1982) The effects of airway pressure on cardiac function in intact dogs and man. Circulation **66:** 108–120

Reuben SR, Swadling JP, Gershe BJ, Lee G deJ (1971) Impedance and transmission properties of the pulmonary arterial system. Cardiovasc Res **5:** 1–9

Rinaldo JE, Rogers RM (1982) Adult respiratory distress syndrome changing concepts of lung injury and repair. N Engl J Med **306:** 900–909

Salisbury PF, Cross CE, Reiben PA (1962) Ventricular performance modified by the elastic properties of the outflow system. Circ Res **11:** 319–328

Shirato K, Shabetai R, Bhargava V, Franklin D, Ross JR (1978) Alteration of the left ventricular diastolic pressure segment length relation produced by the pericardium: Effects of cardiac distension and afterload reduction in conscious dogs. Circulation **57:** 1191–1198

Sibbald WJ, Paterson NA, Holliday RL, Anderson RA, Lobb TR, Duff JH (1978) Pulmonary hypertension in sepsis: Measurement by the pulmonary arterial diastolic-pulmonary wedge pressure gradient and the influence of passive and active factors. Chest **73:** 583–591

Smith PK, Tyson GS, Hammon JW, Olsen CO, Hopkins RA, Maier GW, Sabiston DC, Rankin JS (1982) Cardiovascular effects of ventilation with positive end-expiratory pressure. Ann Surg **195:** 121–131

Staub NC (1981) Pulmonary edema due to increased microvascular permeability. Annu Rev Med **32:** 291–312

Stokland O, Miller MM, Lekven J, Ilebekk A (1980) The significance of the intact pericardium for cardiac performance in the dog. Circ Res **47:** 27–32

Stool EW, Mullin CB, Leshin SJ, Mitchell JH (1974) Dimensional changes of the left ventricle during acute pulmonary arterial hypertension in dogs. Am J Cardiol **33:** 868–875

Sturm JA, Lewis FR, Trentz O, Oestern HJ, Hempelman G, Tscherne H (1979) Cardiopulmonary parameters and prognosis after severe multiple trauma. J Trauma **19:** 305–318

Tyson GS, Maier GW, Olson CO, Davis JW, Rankin JS (1984) Pericardial influences on ventricular filling in the conscious dog: An analysis based on pericardial pressure. Circ Res **54:** 173–184

Urschel CW, Covell JW, Sonnenblick EH, Ross J, Braunwald E (1968) Effect of decreased aortic compliance on performance of the left ventricle. Am J Physiol **214:** 298–304

Van Trigt P, Bauer BJ, Olsen CO, Rankin JS, Wechsle AS (1981) An improved transducer for measurement of cardiac dimensions with sonomicrometry. Am J Physiol **240:** H664–H668

Visner MS, Arentzen CE, O'Conner MJ, Larson EV, Anderson RW (1983) Alterations in left ventricular three-dimensional dynamic geometry and systolic function during acute right ventricular hypertension in the conscious dog. Circulation **67:** 353–365

Walker WE (1975) The influence of changes of aortic input impedance on the dynamics of left ventricular performance. Ph.D. thesis, Baltimore, Md., The Johns Hopkins University

Zapol W, Snider MI (1977) Pulmonary hypertension in severe acute respiratory failure. N Engl J Med **296:** 476–480

INDEX TERMS: Cardiac mechanics • Impedance • PEEP • Systole • Diastole • Pericardium

Limitations of Tracer Oxygen Uptake in the Canine Coronary Circulation

Colin P. Rose and Carl A. Goresky

From the McGill University Medical Clinic, Montreal General Hospital, and the Departments of Medicine and Physiology, McGill University Medical School, Montreal, Quebec, Canada

SUMMARY. Theoretical models of oxygen transport in the myocardium have failed to account for low average tissue pO_2 relative to to coronary sinus pO_2, measured with pO_2 electrodes and myoglobin saturation, and for hypoxic contractile failure at relatively high coronary sinus pO_2 levels. These findings could be explained by either arteriovenous diffusional shunting or a limiting rate of transfer of oxygen from blood to tissue, or both. To gain new insights, we performed multiple indicator dilution tracer experiments across the coronary circulation in the dog, with $^{18}O_2$ as the oxygen tracer and ^{51}Cr-labeled red cells as the reference tracer for oxygen. ^{125}I-Albumin and $^{22}Na^+$ were included to provide the relative plasma flow rate. The tracer oxygen outflow curve consisted of a large early peak related to its reference red cell curve. No tracer emerged before the labeled red cells. The downslope, which contains the returning component of the tracer curve, decreased less steeply when oxygen consumption was reduced by propranolol. Fitting the tracer oxygen outflow curve with a distributed model including irreversible sequestration behind a resistance gave a transfer rate constant which was relatively small, and a relatively large rate constant for sequestration. Relative oxygen consumption (estimated from the arteriovenous difference) correlated closely with the rate constant for sequestration. Estimated average tissue oxygen concentrations were of the order of one-third blood concentration. Dimensional analysis indicates that the low transfer rate constant derives from hemoglobin-oxygen binding; this decreases fractional tracer oxygen transfer in proportion to the ratio of plasma:red cell oxygen pools (***Circ Res 56: 57–71, 1985***)

THE description of the distribution of oxygen to tissue began when Krogh, with Erlang (Krogh, 1919) devised a steady state model (without flow) in which a cylindrical source was visualized to feed oxygen to tissue where it was consumed and distributed in a spatially uniform fashion. In this model, the existence of resistance to oxygen transfer at the interface was not visualized. This initial formulation was designed to give some insight into the distribution of oxygen in resting skeletal muscle, where the distances between perfused capillaries are relatively large and where substantial gradients in oxygen concentration will then develop between perfused vessels. In subsequent decades, flow along the length and the appropriate conservation equations have been added to the model. This model has become the paradigm used to estimate the distribution of oxygen tensions in tissue and to predict physiological changes. The model has been explored numerically, with appropriate values for oxygen contents, diffusion coefficients, tissue dimensions, and flows. From these explorations, predicted sets of values for capillary and tissue oxygen tensions have been obtained.

The heart is a constantly working muscle, consuming substantial amounts of oxygen, in which the distances between perfused capillaries are very small in comparison with resting skeletal muscle. When numerical explorations of the type outlined above are carried out in a Krogh type (no resistance at the interface) model with dimensions corresponding to that of a capillary tissue unit in the heart, and when the expected decrease in oxygen tension from artery to coronary sinus is matched, the predicted decreases in pO_2 from capillary to tissue in the short distances available between capillaries, perpendicular to their long axes, are found to be relatively small, of the order of 2–3 mm Hg (Lübbers, 1982). When these predictions and the inferences which arise from them are compared to experimental observations, three major discrepancies are found. First, in both buffer-perfused (Schubert et al., 1978) and in situ (Whalen, 1971) hearts, tissue pO_2 values recorded with small pO_2 electrodes (tip diameter <5 μm) are substantially less than the venous pO_2, whereas Krogh-Erlang modeling of the kind cited above predicts much higher tissue values with an average tissue pO_2 for the cardiac capillary tissue unit intermediate between arterial and venous pO_2 values (Grunewald and Sowa, 1978; Lübbers, 1982). The introduction of model heterogeneity at the level of capillary flow did not improve the predicted values (Grunewald and Sowa, 1977). Second, tissue oxygen concentrations are also low in relation to venous effluent oxygen concentration in the hemoglobin-free isolated perfused rat heart, when these are estimated from myoglobin oxygen saturation by spectrophotometry. When the perfusate buffer is saturated with 95% O_2 (pO_2 approximately 680 torr), the pO_2 in the venous effluent at 37°C is approximately 300 torr (Neely et al., 1967), and the myocyte pO_2 is approximately 8 torr (Araki et al., 1983). The tissue levels are again lower than those expected on the basis of the Krogh-Erlang model. Third, there is at least an order of magnitude difference between the single cell and whole organ definitions of the pO_2 level at which limitation in the oxygen-consuming function occurs. The oxygen consumption of isolated cardiac myocytes does not decrease until the ambient pO_2 is lowered to 0.15 torr (Wittenberg and Robinson, 1981); whereas the in situ hypoxic heart begins to fail mechanically (the linkage to oxygen-consumption-based energy generation becomes inadequate) when blood oxygen input concentration is reduced to a level such that the coronary sinus pO_2 falls to 9–11 torr (Case, 1965).

There are two possible explanations for these discrepancies. Schubert et al. (1978) proposed that a large vessel diffusional arteriovenous shunt could explain observed high venous pO_2 values relative to average tissue pO_2. Such a shunt should lead to a drop in arterial pO_2 in the progression from large arteries to terminal arterioles [analogous to that observed by Duling and Berne (1970) in the longer vessels of the hamster cheek pouch] if a substantial amount of oxygen is transferred. This kind of change was not found by Weiss and Sinha (1978) when they measured the pO_2 values in the arterioles of frozen hearts, by use of microspectrophotometry. One should note, however, that their measurements extended only to arterioles down to 43 μm in size; the oxygen contents of the smallest arterioles were not measured. Large hemodynamic shunts, which could raise venous pO_2 without changing arterial pO_2, have been ruled out by previous microsphere studies [see, for example, Ziegler et al. (1971a)]. As an alternative explanation, one could postulate a resistance to oxygen transfer from blood to tissue. This would explain both the unexpectedly low steady state values for myocardial tissue pO_2 and the relatively high value of coronary sinus pO_2 at which mechanical failure begins, in the hypoxic heart.

The presence of such a resistance has not been expected, even though Pappenheimer et al. (1951) originally projected, on the basis of their studies, which indicated that only a small fraction of the capillary wall is available for the transfer of lipid insoluble molecules, that the corresponding calculated diffusion area appeared too small to account for the observed rates of transfer of oxygen across the capillary wall. They suggested that, because of its lipid solubility [the distribution ratio for oxygen between cottonseed oil and water at 37°C is 5:1 (Lawrence et al., 1946)], oxygen probably penetrates the whole endothelial surface. They inferred that its limitation at the capillary level might be small, but acknowledged that some new approach was needed to secure pertinent data. It is appropriate to note that substantial resistance to the transfer of highly lipid-soluble materials from blood to tissue may still be present in the heart. The rate of transfer at the capillary endothelium of free fatty acids, the major substrate of the heart, is so low that most of the free fatty acids remaining in the coronary veins (about 50% of arterial concentration) have not left the circulation (Rose and Goresky, 1977). The handling of this substrate also illustrates another effect. The rapid metabolism of the free fatty acids in the presence of limited transfer from capillary to tissue results in a predicted (Rose and Goresky, 1977) and measured (Van der Wusse et al., 1982) tissue-free fatty acid concentration which is only one-twentieth that simultaneously measured in the coronary sinus. Relatively low levels of tissue oxygen concentration thus could also be expected, in the face of its consumption, if resistance to oxygen transfer from blood to tissue were present (Goresky et al., 1983). Such a resistance could arise from either an intrinsically low permeability of the capillary itself or some inherent characteristic of hemoglobin binding which has not been perceived.

The permeability of continuous type systemic capillaries to oxygen has previously been measured in only one organ, the rete mirabile of the eel. In this organ, which consists only of capillaries, the capillary barrier has been shown, during countercurrent perfusion with oxygenated Krebs-Ringer buffer lacking red cells, to reduce the apparent diffusion coefficient of oxygen to 0.5% of its free diffusion coefficient in water (Rasio and Goresky, 1979). The concomitantly measured permeability was somewhat larger than that for labeled water; despite this, approximately one-third of the arterial oxygen was not transferred from arterial to venous capillaries, during steady perfusion. Mammalian capillaries are thin-walled rather than thick-walled, as in the rete. Nonetheless, if they offer a proportionately similar resistance to oxygen diffusion, it should be detectable at an experimental level.

We therefore designed a set of multiple indicator dilution tracer oxygen studies to examine the exchange of oxygen between blood and tissue in the heart. We thought that if these demonstrated a measurable resistance to the loss of tracer from blood to tissue, this new finding would need to be integrated into future models of the transfer of oxygen to tissue.

Methods

Mongrel dogs weighing between 15 and 25 kg were anesthetized with sodium pentobarbital. Fourteen animals were studied. In each, the carotid artery and jugular vein were exposed. Catheters then were inserted via these vessels into the coronary sinus and mainstem of the left coronary artery. We determined that catheters had been placed correctly by flushing an injection of Renographin through each catheter and monitoring its subsequent movement fluoroscopically. This procedure was repeated before each experiment to ensure that the catheters remained securely in place. The principle of a multiple indicator dilution study is that, for each substance studied, an appropriate reference is included and the two are injected together in a bolus. From a comparison of the outflow patterns of the two, deductions are made concerning events which have occurred within the microvascular bed of the organ to displace the outflow pattern of the study substance from that of its reference (Chinard et al., 1955).

While the catheterizations were proceeding, the labeled blood which was to serve as the injection mixture was prepared. This was designed to contain ^{125}I-labeled albumin, which served as a vascular plasma reference; ^{22}Na, a tracer for the interstitial space; ^{51}Cr-labeled red blood cells, which served as the vascular reference for the tracer oxygen; and the stable tracer $^{18}O_2$. After the addition of the radioactive tracers, the blood injectate, which was matched in hematocrit to arterial blood, was completely deoxygenated, and then reoxygenated to arterial levels with the $^{18}O_2$. The rate of entry of labeled sodium into dog red cells is low (Prankerd, 1961). Over the period required to prepare the injection mixture, less than 2% of the added labeled sodium will have entered the red cells. We have therefore neglected this.

When the animal had stabilized with respect to heart rate and blood pressure, and the injection mixture had been prepared, 0.75 ml of the injection bolus was rapidly injected into the coronary artery, and, simultaneously, an anaerobic collection of samples from the coronary sinus was begun at a rate of approximately one sample per 0.6 second. More frequent sampling was not feasible, in view of the size of the sample needed for mass spectrometry. Each sample contained about 0.5 ml of blood. Of this, 0.3 ml of blood was injected anaerobically into individual helium-filled sealed chromatographic vials which contained crystalline potassium ferricyanide and trichloroacetic acid, to induce the release of oxygen bound to hemoglobin into the overlying gas phase in the vial.

The headspace gas was sampled by withdrawing 150 μl with a 250-μl gas-tight syringe (Hamilton no. 1725N) that had been flushed immediately before with helium. The sample was analyzed on a Hewlett-Packard 5984 coupled gas chromatograph-mass spectrometer under the following conditions. The column was a 1 meter × 4 mm i.d. glass column packed with molecular sieve 5A, 80/100 mesh (Coast Engineering Laboratory), conditioned at 250°C for 6 hours and operated isothermally at 100°C with helium flow rates of 30 ml/min. A single stage helium jet separator operated at 250°C and the ion source, at 210°C, 70 eV. Ion currents were monitored at 32, 34, 36, and 28 daltons for 50 msec each, in a selected ion-monitoring mode. Under these conditions, oxygen and nitrogen had retention times of 10 seconds and 14 seconds, respectively. An appreciable current at 28 daltons in an analysis was interpreted to signal air contamination of that sample, and was cause for rejection of that result.

Prior to each batch of analyses, room air samples were analyzed to confirm that the proper $^{18}O_2$ and $^{16}O_2$ natural abundances could be determined. Artificial enrichment of the ambient room air used for this calibration check was prevented by carrying out the calibration immediately before the arrival of the enriched samples from the laboratory in another building where they were collected. The data system presented the analytical results in the form of time-integrated peak areas for the currents at 32, 34, and 36 daltons. There was no evidence of hardware-related isotopic discrimination, except in relation to retention times: $^{18}O_2$ [m/z (ratio of mass expressed in atomic mass units: charge expressed as multiples of an electron charge) = 36] was seen to elute slightly earlier than $^{16}O_2$ (m/z = 32), by about 1 second. This effect was considered to be of no consequence because peak areas were determined and used, not peak heights, which are progressively reduced with increasing retention time. The $^{18}O_2$ enrichment above background in each sample and in an aliquot of the injection mixture was determined from the mass peak area ratio 36/(32 + 34 + 36).

From the remaining 0.2 ml of blood in each sample, 0.1 ml was extracted and diluted with 1.5 ml of saline, pipetted into a counting tube, and assayed for radioactivity in a γ-ray spectrometer set for the photopeaks characteristic of ^{125}I and ^{51}Cr. The proteins were then precipitated with 0.2 ml of trichloroacetic acid, and 0.2 ml of the supernatant fluid was pipetted into a scintillation cocktail and assayed for ^{22}Na activity in a liquid scintillation β-counter. Cross-over standards (consisting of each radioactive species alone) and standards from the injection mixture were treated identically. From the activity of the cross-over standards in their primary channel and their spill into the various other channels, the activity in outflow samples due to each species was determined in its primary channel. To normalize the activity resulting from each of the radioactive tracers with respect to the others, the activity of each in the collected samples was divided by the total activity injected for that species. The resulting value is a fraction of the total injected per milliliter of venous blood (that is, an outflow fraction per milliliter, with the dimensions per ml).

Fourteen animals were studied. Two were studied in a baseline condition only, seven were studied 15 minutes after the injection of 1 mg/kg of the β-blocker propranolol, and five were paired baseline-propranolol runs. In the last group, the propranolol was administered 20 minutes after the first run.

Before each run, samples were collected from the coronary artery and coronary sinus and analyzed for blood gas tensions, and for oxygen content with a Lex O_2 Con-K analyzer (Lexington Instruments). These data were then utilized to convert the $^{18}O_2$ enrichment in each outflow sample to a fractional recovery per milliliter. To express the data in this fashion, the relative $^{18}O_2$ content of each coronary venous blood sample (the product of the $^{18}O_2$ enrichment and the O_2 content) was divided by the amount of $^{18}O_2$ injected (the product of the injection volume and the $^{18}O_2$ content of the injection mixture). That is,

$$FR_{36cs} = \frac{F_{36cs}}{F_{36pot}} \cdot \frac{C_{venous}}{C_{art}} \cdot \frac{1}{V}$$

where FR_{36cs} is the normalized $^{18}O_2$ coronary sinus outflow fractional recovery per milliliter blood (ml^{-1}), F_{36cs} is the enrichment of $^{18}O_2$ in the coronary sinus sample (dimensionless), F_{36pot} is the enrichment of $^{18}O_2$ in the injection mixture (dimensionless), C_{venous} is the coronary sinus oxygen content (ml/100 ml blood), C_{art} is the arterial oxygen content (ml/100 ml blood), and V is the injection volume (ml).

Analysis of Data

The characteristic values and parameters describing the present set of experiments (Tables 1 and 2) extend across

TABLE 1
Hemodynamic and Oxygen Content Data

Experiment no.	Propranolol administration	Heart rate (beats/min)	Systolic blood pressure (mm Hg)	Hematocrit	Arterial blood oxygen content (ml/100 ml)	Coronary venous oxygen content (ml/100 ml)
1a	+	111	160	0.40	16.8	6.02
2a	−			0.48	23.9	9.80
2b	+			0.48	22.2	8.16
3a	−	96	140	0.42	21.2	8.80
4a	−	96	130	0.42	15.1	5.50
4b	+	111	120	0.42	14.3	3.80
5a	+	126	210	0.55	22.9	11.30
6a	+	120	180	0.40	19.9	6.30
7a	−	90	190	0.37	20.1	7.23
7b	+	114	180	0.37	20.8	9.90
8a	−	93	150	0.42	21.2	5.99
8b	+	165	190	0.42	20.5	7.04
9a	+	126	190	0.40	18.4	6.14
10a	+	120	190	0.38	14.8	4.21
11a	−	96	150	0.38	17.9	4.20
11b	+	111	160	0.40	17.2	5.10
12a	−	72	120	0.43	18.2	5.20
13a	+	132	150	0.39	18.4	3.10
14a	+	132	150	0.47	18.7	8.90

a wide range of values for flow and oxygen consumption. The tracer oxygen curves are found to vary in form with oxygen consumption in reasonably consistent fashion, across this spectrum. Representative sets of data are illustrated below.

The results of typical higher flow-higher oxygen consumption (experiment 8a) and lower flow-lower oxygen consumption (experiment 8b) runs are presented in the upper panels of Figure 1 and in Table 3. The relations between the set of outflow dilution curves may be interpreted as follows. The diffusible tracer ^{22}Na is limited to the plasma fraction of blood. This indicator permeates the

TABLE 2
Parameters from Model Optimization

Experiment no.	ϕ_{Na}* (ml/sec per ml)	a′	b′ (per sec)	k_{cNa} (ml/sec per ml)	Oxygen consumption† (ml/min per ml)	$[k_{cO_2}]\frac{\gamma_{O_2}}{\gamma_{Na}}$ (ml/sec per ml)	$[k_{seq}]\frac{\gamma_{O_2}}{\gamma_{Na}}$ (ml/sec per ml)	$\frac{k_{cO_2}}{k_{cO_2}+k_{seq}}$
1a	0.0898	1.190	0.168	0.163	0.97	0.179	0.214	0.455
2a	0.2010	0.325	0.126	0.194	3.27	0.401	0.655	0.380
2b	0.0816	0.687	0.240	0.143	1.32	0.167	0.267	0.391
3a	0.0797	0.512	0.148	0.120	1.02	0.197	0.179	0.524
4a	0.1140	0.855	0.154	0.207	1.13	0.311	0.385	0.446
4b	0.1030	0.884	0.237	0.195	1.12	0.319	0.366	0.476
5a	0.0555	0.959	0.112	0.088	0.87	0.068	0.187	0.485
6a	0.0571	0.687	0.271	0.112	0.78	0.133	0.269	0.332
7a	0.1520	1.170	0.088	0.205	1.86	0.214	0.566	0.274
7b	0.0616	0.717	0.229	0.129	0.64	0.137	0.118	0.537
8a	0.1166	1.240	0.108	0.214	1.84	0.232	0.784	0.228
8b	0.0705	0.665	0.208	0.129	0.98	0.153	0.343	0.309
9a	0.2270	1.080	0.115	0.327	2.78	0.389	1.163	0.286
10a	0.0766	1.220	0.129	0.120	0.78	0.138	0.349	0.283
11a	0.0903	0.833	0.150	0.140	1.20	0.301	0.427	0.414
11b	0.1620	0.620	0.225	0.222	1.96	0.435	0.715	0.378
12a	0.1360	0.813	0.114	0.172	1.86	0.273	0.793	0.256
13a	0.0837	0.491	0.255	0.139	1.26	0.353	0.593	0.374
14a	0.1210	0.472	0.386	0.255	1.34	0.195	0.436	0.309

* ϕ values can be converted to plasma flow in ml/min per g by multiplying by 8.85.
† Oxygen consumption values will be expressed in ml/min per g when multipied by 8.85/60.

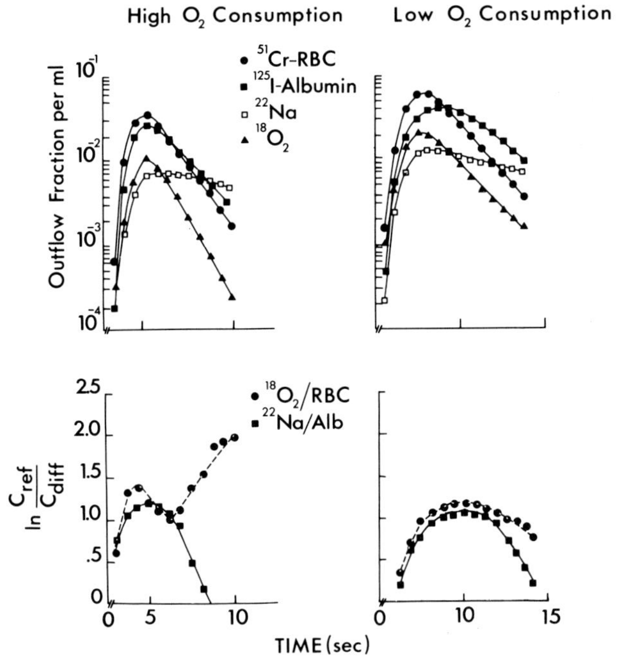

FIGURE 1. *Upper panels: normalized coronary sinus outflow fraction per milliliter vs. time curves, obtained from the same preparation, during higher flow-higher oxygen consumption and lower flow-lower oxygen consumption states (experiments 8a and 8b), the latter after propranolol. The ordinate scale is logarithmic and the abscissa, linear. The significant change in the oxygen curve in the lower oxygen consumption state is the large increment in tracer returning to the circulation later in time. The mean transit times for labeled red cells and albumin, corrected for catheter times, were, in the high flow-high oxygen consumption run, 6.14 and 6.88 seconds, respectively, and in the low flow-low oxygen consumption run, 8.82 and 10.31 seconds. Lower panels: logarithmic ratio time curves (that is,* $ln[C(t)_{Alb}/C(t)_{Na}]$ *and* $ln[C(t)_{RBC}/C(t)_{O_2}]$ *vs. time curves, where* $C(t)_{Alb}$, $C(t)_{Na}$, $C(t)_{RBC}$, *and* $C(t)_{O_2}$ *are the outflow fractions per ml for labeled albumin, sodium, red cells, and oxygen). These curves mirror, in a sense, the instantaneous loss (or extraction) of tracer sodium and oxygen from the vasculature, in relation to their appropriate reference. In the higher flow higher oxygen consumption run, the oxygen extraction continues to increase with time, whereas, in the lower flow lower oxygen consumption run, with the increased late return of tracer oxygen, the extraction later along the curve decreases with time.*

capillary wall in a barrier-limited fashion (Goresky et al., 1970; Ziegler and Goresky, 1971a; Rose et al., 1980), but is excluded from cardiac myocytes over the time of a single passage. Hence, it serves as an interstitial space marker. Since labeled albumin is also confined to the plasma fraction of blood, and since it does not leave the vasculature perceptibly during a single passage, it is the appropriate vascular reference for the labeled sodium. As the injected mass of tracers moves through the capillaries, some of the labeled sodium leaves the capillary and enters the interstitial space; this is why the labeled sodium curve is lower than the labeled albumin curve, early in time. Later, the outflow fraction per milliliter of labeled sodium rises above that of labeled albumin because the sodium which initially entered the interstitial space is now returning to the capillary. If samples were collected for long enough, eventually all of the injected tracer ^{22}Na would be recovered, since sodium is not metabolized in the myocardium. The relation between the labeled albumin and labeled sodium curves appears to be qualitatively the same in both runs, apart from the effect of the change in flow. Decreased flow is evident in the second run in this instance, after propranolol; the change with propranolol is what one would ordinarily expect to see in a sympathetically stimulated, but not in an unstimulated preparation (Heyndrickx et al., 1980; Cousineau et al., 1984). With the decrease in flow in the second run, the common area under the labeled albumin and sodium curves becomes larger and the curves are more spread out in time.

Now consider the labeled oxygen. Since red blood cells

TABLE 3
Representative Outflow Profiles in Higher and Lower Oxygen Consumption Regimes

	Higher oxygen consumption run (Outflow fraction per ml × 10^3)					Lower oxygen consumption run (Outflow fraction per ml × 10^3)			
Time (sec)	^{51}Cr-red cells (per ml)	^{125}I-albumin (per ml)	^{22}Na (per ml)	$^{18}O_2$ (per ml)	Time (sec)	^{51}Cr-red cells (per ml)	^{125}I-albumin (per ml)	^{22}Na (per ml)	$^{18}O_2$ (per ml)
2.76	0.00	0.00	0.00	0.00	4.84	0.00	0.00	0.00	0.00
3.40	0.64	0.19	0.05	0.33	5.48	1.53	0.45	0.23	1.03
4.04	9.72	4.97	1.46	1.94	6.12	12.15	9.96	2.61	6.25
4.68	28.51	15.63	4.76	5.47	6.76	39.49	15.10	7.17	14.16
5.32	34.50	26.07	7.50	10.24	7.40	59.61	27.56	11.18	20.29
5.96	25.57	24.60	7.38	8.29	8.04	63.54	36.26	13.04	19.96
6.60	17.23	22.07	7.36	6.26	8.68	47.02	40.58	12.53	16.44
7.24	12.00	16.74	7.09	3.84	9.32	35.00	40.05	12.75	12.92
7.88	8.57	11.60	7.22	2.18	9.96	25.98	33.21	11.34	9.16
8.52	6.06	8.36	6.85	1.27	10.60	19.00	29.87	9.87	6.16
9.16	4.31	5.95	6.40	0.71	11.24	13.50	24.11	9.96	4.47
9.80	2.58	4.67	6.22	0.40	11.88	9.40	19.12	9.56	3.52
10.44	1.70	3.41	5.31	0.23	12.52	6.80	14.42	8.91	2.44
					13.16	5.00	11.83	8.26	2.00
					13.80	3.30	9.72	7.78	1.45

are confined to the vascular compartment and normally about 98.5% of the oxygen in arterial blood is carried by hemoglobin inside the red blood cells, we will utilize the labeled red blood cells as an approximate description of the outflow kinetics the labeled oxygen pool would have had, in the absence of uptake. In doing this, we neglect the small initial labeled oxygen component in plasma. The labeled oxygen outflow curve encloses, in each case, an area much smaller than the labeled red cell curve (in these tracer experiments within a steady state, tracer oxygen is lost in proportion to the steady state extraction of bulk oxygen). With respect to the magnitude of the labeled red cell curve, the initial part of the labeled oxygen curve is relatively the same in each run of Figure 1. It is lower in magnitude than the reference-labeled red cell curve, and it progressively departs from this reference over the upslopes of the curves, on the semilogarithmic plots. The upslope similarity in the two runs is presumably because, in each case, the same relative proportion of the tracer oxygen moves along the capillary to the outflow without exchanging. With the decrease in demand in the lower blood flow-lower oxygen consumption case, one would expect that, of the tracer oxygen that does cross from the capillary to cellular space, a lesser proportion would be metabolically sequestered by the cells. With this kind of response, a larger proportion of the tracer oxygen would be expected to return to the capillary, later in time. This expected variation is embodied in the change in shape of the later parts of the tracer oxygen dilution curves illustrated in Figure 1. In the control run, the downslope segment of the tracer oxygen curve has a slightly steeper rate of decrease than the corresponding reference-labeled red cell curve. In contrast, after propranolol, the downslope of the tracer oxygen dilution curve is less steep than that of the corresponding reference-labeled red cell curve, due to an increased return of tracer oxygen from the tissue to the circulation. This relative kind of change in curve shape was found over the spectrum of the acquired data sets, varying in relatively systematic fashion with the level of oxygen consumption. The change, in general, reflected the level of oxygen consumption rather than the presence or absence of propranolol. This lack of systematic effect across the whole group with propranolol is what would have been expected, in the absence of a protocol designed to produce β-blockade in a preparation previously systematically highly sympathetically activated (Heyndrickx et al., 1980).

The relationship between the reference and permeable tracer curves (red cells and oxygen, and albumin and sodium) can also be described by plotting logarithmic ratio curves (Rose and Goresky, 1976). These are illustrated in the lower panels of Figure 1. The Naperian or natural logarithmic ratio curve relating labeled sodium to its reference, labeled albumin, in each case rises smoothly along the upslopes of the dilution curves to a peak and then exhibits a downslope, concomitant with return of tracer to the circulation. Since one can assume, in general, that the initial extractions of any substance along an outflow dilution curve are proportional to the time it has spent in the capillary, the data indicate an increase in capillary outflow transit times with time along the dilution curve, a heterogeneity of capillary transit times. The rate of increase in capillary transit time with time (the degree of heterogeneity) has previously been shown to vary with the coronary tone (Rose and Goresky, 1976; Rose et al., 1980). In this case, it was larger in the lower flow-lower oxygen consumption run. The log ratio (albumin:sodium) vs. time curve thus shows a slightly greater initial slope. There is, however, no other striking overall change. On the other hand, in the case of the log ratio curve relating tracer oxygen to labeled red cells, we see that there is a clear change in the relative form of the tracer oxygen outflow curves, from the high oxygen consumption to the low oxygen consumption state. Both runs show a common initial behavior. Specifically, the slope of the log (labeled red cell:oxygen) concentration ratio vs. time curve shows an initial rising slope, as for the albumin and sodium pair of labels, indicating a corresponding increasing upslope extraction (that is, passage into tissue) of the oxygen label with time. In the high oxygen consumption run, there is also an initial hump on the log ratio (red cell:oxygen) - time curve, which is followed by a later and more protracted rise in the curve (illustrated in the lower left panel of Fig. 1). The early hump was commonly present in the high oxygen consumption situation; the later rise could be interpreted to indicate that, late in time, the return of oxygen tracer from tissue in the high oxygen consumption state was not large enough to counteract the increased extraction along longer transit time capillaries. In contrast, in the low oxygen consumption state, the log ratio-time plot, after an initial increase, decreases with time (lower right panel of Fig. 1). More tracer oxygen is returning to the vasculature late in time along the curve than is leaving it. The late increased label return appears to correlate with the lower rate of cellular oxygen demand.

The shape of the oxygen curves provides a challenge. The relative shape change of the log ratio-time plots from the high oxygen to the low oxygen consumption states indicates that the change in the oxygen tracer curve with demand is principally in the later parts of the curve, rather than across the whole curve. Past explorations of the behavior of other substances can be used to gain insight into the kind of process which might underlie these observations. The absence of a barrier does not appear to correspond to the kind of change observed. In the liver, where flow-limited distribution of alcohol has been demonstrated, concomitant with removal, the removal effect is distributed in a monotonically increasing fashion across the whole dilution curve (Goresky et al., 1983b). The curve shape change observed might, on the other hand, be expected, if there were a resistance to exchange between blood and tissue. In the presence of such a resistance, the outflow profile consists of two parts, a vascular throughput and a later exchanging tail (Goresky et al., 1970), and tracer sequestration affects the profile only by reducing the magnitude of the latter (Ziegler and Goresky, 1971b; Rose et al., 1977; Goresky et al., 1983a). If such were present, one would expect to see only the later part of the curve augmented when the metabolic demand is lowered. The form of the data suggests that such a resistance may be present. Larger vessel countercurrent exchange might also be present, but the expectations associated with this have not yet been well clarified through explicit models. It is clear, however, that an early outflow precession of tracer oxygen with respect to labeled red cells would document the presence of this kind of diffusional shunting. At the level of resolution of our data, none was found. We have therefore considered it unlikely that this kind of countercurrent exchange has made a substantial contribution to the present set of labeled oxygen outflow profiles, obtained from the heart.

The Model Utilized to Analyze the Data

On the basis of the foregoing considerations, a barrier-limited model was utilized to analyze the tracer oxygen outflow dilution data. The model contains a bidirectional resistance to the free diffusion of oxygen at the interface between the vascular and extravascular space, and a unidirectional process sequestering oxygen at the cellular level. A very similar model has previously been used to describe the early interstitial removal of tracer rubidium by cardiac myocytes (Ziegler and Goresky, 1971b), the sequestration of tracer galactose within liver cells (Goresky et al., 1973), and neuronal uptake of tracer catecholamine from the interstitium of the heart (Cousineau et al., 1980).

The model of the coronary microvasculature is in the form of a system of partial differential equations. The solution to these equations will describe the exchange and uptake characteristics of the heart, and if the model represents the distribution of tracer oxygen in vivo, the solutions generated by the model should match the results obtained experimentally with the multiple indicator dilution technique. Implicit in the model are four assumptions: (1) there is plug flow in the capillary, (2) the effects of diffusion parallel to the capillary are negligible, (3) the radial gradient of tracer in the extravascular space is small, and (4) tracer oxygen uptake follows first order kinetics (see Discussion).

We will now describe mathematically the resistance to exchange between capillary and tissue, and the sequestration of oxygen at the cellular level. Let u and v represent the concentration of tracer in the capillary at a distance along the length x and at a time t after tracer entry, in the intravascular and extravascular spaces, respectively; W, the bulk flow velocity in the capillary; γ, the ratio of accessible extravascular to intravascular volumes; k_1 and k_2, the permeability surface products for efflux from and influx into the capillary per volume of accessible extravascular space (these are both equal when exchange is passive, as we might assume it to be here); and k_{seq}, the unidirectional rate constant for uptake of tracer oxygen by tissue cells per unit extravascular space. Since sodium is excluded from the muscle cells over short times, its k_{seq} is assumed to be zero. Two partial differential equations describe the distribution of tracer from the single capillary. The first is an equation of conservation,

$$\frac{\partial u}{\partial t} + W\frac{\partial u}{\partial x} + \gamma\frac{\partial v}{\partial t} + \gamma v k_{seq} = 0 \qquad (1)$$

and the second describes the rate of change of tracer concentration in the extravascular space with time,

$$\frac{\partial v}{\partial t} = k_1 u - k_2 v - k_{seq} v. \qquad (2)$$

The time domain solution of this system in response to an impulse injection has been described previously (Ziegler and Goresky, 1971b; Rose et al., 1977). When there is a constraint at the barrier, the solution consists of two parts: a vascular throughput, and a returning component. In the flow-limited extreme, when the constraint disappears, the solution converges on a single damped delayed wave, propagating in both vascular and extravascular spaces.

This modeling, complimented at the whole organ level with those expressions which have been developed to account for the heterogeneity of transit times in the heart (Rose and Goresky, 1976), was then utilized to fit both labeled sodium and labeled oxygen outflow dilution curves. The separable parameters obtained by virtue of the fit (Rose and Goresky, 1977) included the following:

1. For sodium, with labeled albumin as the intravascular reference:

k_{cNa} = the capillary permeability surface product per unit interstitial space (inverse seconds). Sodium exchange is assumed to occur passively, so that, in terms of the model, $k_{cNa} = k_1 = k_2$, for sodium,

ϕ = the plasma flow per unit interstitial space (with dimensions of inverse seconds). This is calculated as the reciprocal of the difference between the mean transit times of the labeled sodium and albumin curves. The parameter is independent of the rest of the fitting procedure and can be considered to be model independent.

a' and b' = the parameters which describe the heterogeneity of capillary transit times. These are the intercept (at the outflow appearance) and the initial slope of the natural logarithm of the ratio of albumin to sodium fractional outflow recovery vs. time plot.

2. For oxygen, with labeled red blood cells as the intravascular reference (note that, by virtue of the change in the reference, a new bulk velocity, that of the red cells, has been adopted):

k_{cO_2} = the capillary permeability surface product per unit extravascular space for tracer oxygen. Again, the exchange is assumed to be symmetrical, in terms of the barrier, so that $k_{cO_2} = k_1 = k_2$, for oxygen,

γ_{O_2}/γ_{Na} = the ratio of the extravascular:vascular space sizes for oxygen to the interstitial:plasma space sizes for sodium, and

k_{seq} = the rate constant for the unidirectional uptake of oxygen by myocardial cells per unit extravascular space (inverse seconds).

Note that, in this situation, where the labeled red cells are taken as the reference, a new definition of the barrier in the system appears. With the red cells as the reference, the barrier potentially includes the red cell membrane, the plasma space, the capillary wall, the interstitium, and the myocyte membrane. In any distributed system, the barrier between two exchanging pools is generally defined as an interface with no appreciable volume capacity for the tracer. In this instance, the relative capacities of these phases for oxygen is negligible, in relation to that of the hemoglobin in red cells and the myoglobin in the heart muscle cells. Thus, it is reasonable to regard the whole as the barrier and to try to differentiate the resistance of each of the elements on the basis of ancillary information from other kinds of experimental data. The two exchanging pools would then appear to be, on the vascular side, the oxygen pool bound to hemoglobin and, at the tissue level, the oxygen store bound to myoglobin and the cytochromes.

To determine the numerical values of the parameters, a digital PDP 11/23 computer was utilized to fit the modeling to the experimental data. First, smooth curves approximating the experimental albumin and sodium curves were obtained by manipulating the coefficients of a fifteenth order Laguerre polynominal representation of the curves. Then, by use of a frequency domain parameter optimization routine (Rose et al., 1980), the parameters k_{cNa}, and a′ and b′ were progressively optimized until a sodium curve calculated from the albumin reference curve by use of the model and the Rosenbrock optimization algorithm (Rosenbrock and Storey, 1966) fit the experimental sodium dilution curve as closely as possible (this usually required about 30 iterations). The procedure fit the whole labeled sodium curve, including the upslope, in a systematically optimal fashion (Rose and Goresky, 1976; Cousineau et al., 1983); throughput and returning components were resolved. Thus, polynomial representations of the red cell and oxygen curves were found. Then, with the a′ and b′ values obtained from the sodium fit, the parameters k_{cO2}, k_{seq}, and γ_{O_2}/γ_{Na} were optimized. In this case, a labeled oxygen curve calculated from the labeled red cell reference was fit to the observed outflow-labeled oxygen dilution curve. The best fit values obtained for the parameters were then interpreted as being the actual values that the parameters assume in vivo.

Since red cells have a slightly smaller transit time than plasma, the use of a′ and b′ from the sodium curve is not strictly correct (the lower panels of Figure 2 show that a′ and b′ will be slightly larger for the red cells). If, however, we can assume that the ratio of capillary transit times of red cells to plasma is relatively independent of flow, then this assumption will result only in a small constant underestimate of γ_{O_2}/γ_{Na} (the parameter optimized along the curve is the product of gamma and the capillary transit time).

Results

The main consequence of the presence of a substantive barrier to the distribution of oxygen will be that its tracer outflow profile will be expected to consist of two components. Some of the tracer oxygen will be carried along through the capillary without exchanging; this is the throughput component. The remainder of the tracer oxygen will enter the tissue space, and, of this, a proportion of the tracer which has not been metabolized by the myocardial cells will return to the vasculature. This is the returning component. If the apparent permeability of the barrier to the material being considered, tracer oxygen, were very high, and if the accessible extravascular space were reasonably large (and if red cell carriage of the label had no effect), one would initially expect a major decrement in the upslope of the curve [in the case of labeled water, for instance, upslope outflow fraction per ml values in the heart are of the order of 10% of the outflow fraction per ml values of simultaneously injected labeled red cells (Rose et al., 1977)]. The labeled oxygen profiles in the sets of normalized outflow dilution curves illustrated in Figure 1, in both high and low oxygen consumption states, on the other hand, initially appear to correspond to a relatively low permeability barrier-limited type of curve. The salient feature of each panel in the illustration is that a large proportion of the tracer oxygen emerges at the outflow concomitantly with its reference, labeled red cells. It is this feature which will preoccupy us, in our analysis of the curves. One would expect, on the basis of past data (Rasio and Goresky, 1979), the permeability of the myocardial capillary barrier to be higher for oxygen than for water. Yet, the form of the data initially appears to be such that these expectations are not capable of being fulfilled, if the capillaries are imposing a limitation on oxygen transport. In what follows, we show that this anomaly is more apparent than real, by using the information from all four curves in each set to gain insight into the dimensions of the underlying phenomenological constants. The second major feature of the data is the change in form of the outflow profile of tracer oxygen from the high to the low oxygen consumption state, the increase in the relative proportion of tracer oxygen recovered at the outflow, late in time.

Collated data from 19 technically satisfactory runs carried out in 14 animals are presented in tabular form: in Table 1, the hemodynamic and oxygen content data, and in Table 2, the optimized parameters describing the labeled sodium and oxygen curves. In Table 2, the optimized parameters for the oxygen curve are reported as the parameter products $k_{cO_2}(\gamma_{O_2}/\gamma_{Na})$ and $k_{seq}(\gamma_{O_2}/\gamma_{Na})$. In these forms, the parameter values are normalized in terms of the interstitial sodium space, and thus can be directly compared to k_{cNa} values; their expected relative impact can then be perceived immediately.

Figure 2 illustrates the optimized model analysis of the data illustrated in Figure 1. The model approximations to the tracer oxygen and sodium curves have been, in each case, resolved into throughput and returning components. The components of the labeled sodium curve are as expected. There is an early throughput component, with a later prolonged returning component. In the case of the tracer oxygen curves, the throughput components are relatively large; they are of the same order of magnitude as those of the labeled sodium [the $k_{cO_2}(\gamma_{O_2}/\gamma_{Na})$ values are of the same order as the k_{cNa} values]. The tracer oxygen throughput components make up a major proportion of each observed tracer oxygen outflow dilution curve. The returning components are, proportionately, quite small, in relation to those for labeled sodium; they are abbreviated in magnitude, particularly later in time. The model also accounts for the early hump illustrated on the baseline log (red cell:oxygen) ratio-time plot. It is the summation of the two resolved components which leads to this curious shape. At the level of the modeling, the effect of the sequestration of tracer oxygen on the contour of the tracer oxygen outflow curve can be perceived by setting the value for k_{seq} in the optimized parameter set equal to zero and then computing the resulting outflow curve. The difference between this and the observed curve is the sequestration effect. The k_{seq} zero curves have been added to the lower panels of Figure 2; the areas between these curves and the observed curves (the

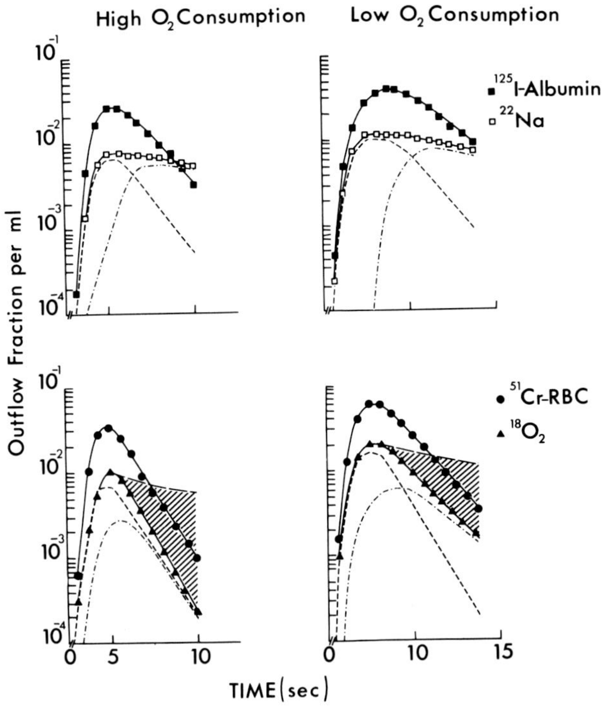

FIGURE 2. *The results of model analysis of the tracer sodium and oxygen dilution curves illustrated in Figure 1. Both throughput and returning components are illustrated for the tracer sodium and oxygen curves; and, in the case of the labeled oxygen curve, the shaded areas represent the sequestration effect.*

sequestration effect) have been shaded, to accentuate the changes.

From the analyzed curves it becomes possible to see in more detail the changes in shape with changes in oxygen consumption. In the lower oxygen consumption state, the throughput component of the tracer oxygen curve does not change in relation to the labeled red cell curve. This is presumably because the effect of demand is imposed at the level of the myocardial cells only; it would not be expected to change the nature of the resistance to the passage of tracer oxygen from the hemoglobin to the myoglobin-bound pool. The increased proportion of tracer oxygen returning to the vasculature in the lower oxygen consumption state is manifested both as an increased area under the returning component of the curve and a decrease in the shaded sequestration effect (the tail of the curve is seen to shift toward the shape expected with a lower degree of sequestration).

From the outflow fraction per ml vs. time curves, it is possible to estimate the outflow recovery of oxygen tracer relative to that for labeled red cells. This recovery should, of course, be equivalent to the ratio of venous:arterial oxygen contents. For the group of experiments as a whole, the average for the ratio was 0.999 ± 0.028 (SD). The values are essentially as expected.

Relative myocardial O_2 consumption in these experiments has been calculated by use of the following relation:

$$\dot{V}_{O_2} = \frac{1}{1 - \text{Hct}} \cdot \phi_{Na} \cdot (C_{O_2 art} - C_{O_2 cs}) \cdot \frac{60}{100} \quad (3)$$

where $\dot{V}_{O_2}$ is the myocardial oxygen consumption per unit interstitial space, expressed in units of ml/min per ml interstitial space; Hct is the hematocrit, expressed as a fraction; ϕ_{Na} is the plasma flow per unit interstitial space calculated from the inverse of the difference in the mean transit times of albumin and sodium, expressed as ml/sec per ml interstitial space; and $C_{O_2 art}$ and $C_{O_2 cs}$ are the oxygen contents of arterial and coronary sinus blood, respectively, in units of ml/100 ml blood.

For comparison with other experimental data, the parameter ϕ can be converted to coronary plasma flow in ml/min per g by multiplying its numeric value by 8.85 (Rose et al., 1980), a value corresponding to the product of 60 sec/min and an average of 0.1475 ml interstitial space/g; and that for $\dot{V}_{O_2}$ can be converted to oxygen consumption in ml/min per g by multiplying by 8.85/60. We have preferred to record the derived parameters in tabulating the results of our data analysis, rather than the converted values, since there may be minor variations in the interstitial space. It seems reasonable to assume that these will not be very large, however, so that values calculated by use of the above conversion factors should be close to correct.

Figure 3 shows the relation between the tracer-derived $k_{seq}(\gamma_{O_2}/\gamma_{Na})$ and the oxygen consumption calculated using Equation 3, which utilizes ϕ and the difference between arterial and coronary sinus oxygen contents. The one reflects the other, as expected. The relation consolidates the impression arising from the early inspection of the forms of the data.

The model-derived description of the tracer data can then be utilized to predict the underlying steady state, by calculating the response of the system with the fitted parameters to a prolonged steady infusion of parent material (in the fashion outlined in the Appendix to Goresky et al., 1973). The relation predicted from the model is that the ratio of the underlying steady state tissue to intravascular oxygen concentration at each point along the falling concentration profile in the capillary is in the ratio $k_{cO_2}/(k_{cO_2} + k_{seq})$. Knowing this ratio, one can then obtain some insight into the manner in which tissue oxygen tension has been regulated in these preparations, which one can presume is autoregulating, since this function is preserved even in preparations in which the chest had previously been opened (Rose et al., 1980). Figure 4 shows the relation between the calculated ratio of tissue to intravascular oxygen concentrations and oxygen consumption, over a wide range of tissue oxygen consumption rates. The significant feature of the relation is that it shows calculated tissue oxygen concentration levels

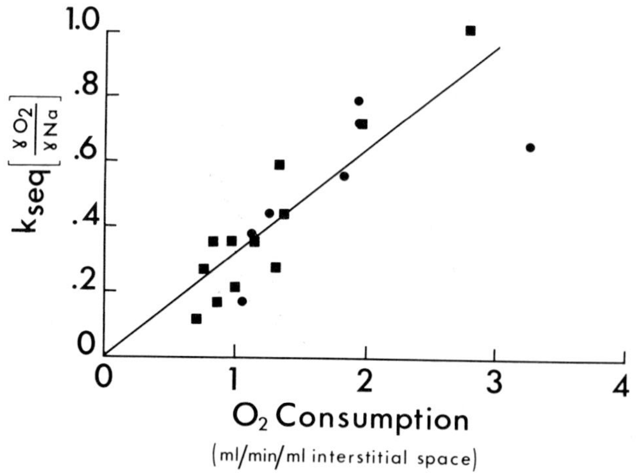

FIGURE 3. *Plot of the variation in the parameter product $k_{seq}[\gamma O_2/\gamma_{Na}]$ with oxygen consumption. The filled circles are baseline runs, and the filled squares, runs carried out after propranolol. Oxygen consumption values can be converted to more usually utilized values, in ml/min per g, by multiplying by 8.85/60 (Rose et al., 1980).*

of the order of one third of concomitmant vascular levels. There was no significant change in the ratio over the experimentally encountered range of oxygen consumption rates, but there was a tendency for the ratio to decrease slightly at higher levels of oxygen consumption. It appears that the increase in flow with increase in metabolic demand and the reservoir function of the myoglobin in the muscle cells underlie this response.

Figure 5 shows the expected increase in the capillary rate constant for tracer sodium; Figure 6 shows that for tracer oxygen, with increased oxygen consumption, an expected recruitment is seen to occur. Figure 7 shows that the capillary rate constant for tracer oxygen $k_{cO_2}[\gamma_{O_2}/\gamma_{Na}]$ increases concomitantly with the value of the simultaneously measured capillary rate constant for tracer sodium k_{cNa}. The correlation coefficient between the two values is 0.63.

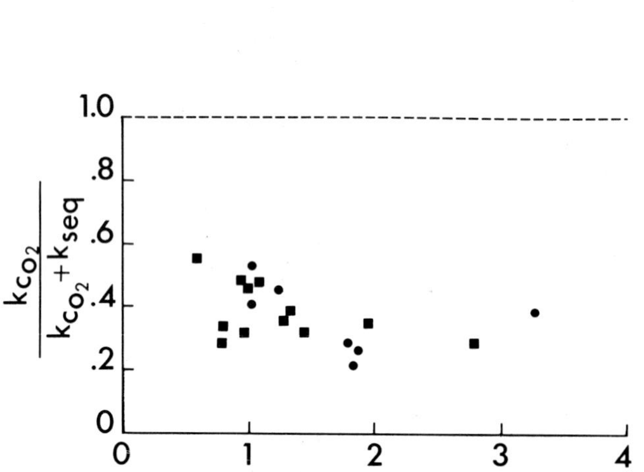

FIGURE 4. *Plot of $k_{cO_2}/(k_{cO_2} + k_{seq})$, the ratio of the underlying steady state concentration of oxygen in the extravascular to that in the intravascular space, versus oxygen consumption.*

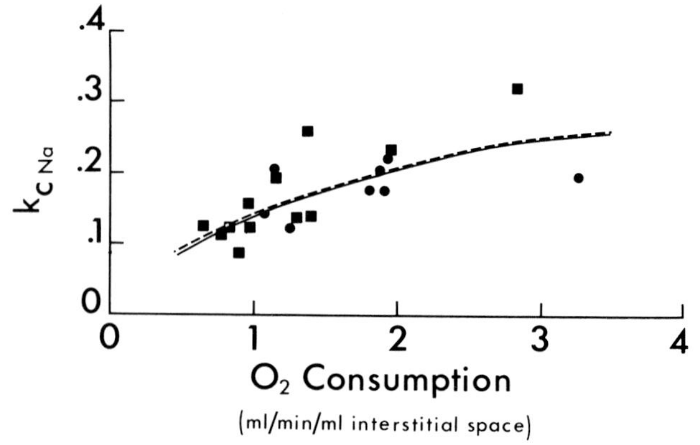

FIGURE 5. *Change in the capillary rate constant k_{cNa} for the exchange of tracer sodium with change in O_2 consumption. The k_{cNa} values can be converted to more usually expressed values, in ml/min per g, by multiplying by 8.85; and the oxygen consumption values, by multiplying by 8.85/60 (Rose et al., 1980). Saturating rising hyperbolic (dashed) or exponential (solid) profiles, fitted by least squares (Goresky et al., 1969), provide a better description of a mean locus through the data than a linear regression. The loci corresponding to the lines are*

$$k_{cNa} = \frac{0.40(O_2\ consumption)}{O_2\ consumption + 1.69}$$

and

$$k_{cNa} = 0.28(1 - e^{-0.74[O_2\ consumption]}).$$

The two loci correspond closely, over the range of the data.

The average value for the $k_{cO_2}[\gamma_{O_2}/\gamma_{Na}]/k_{cNa}$ ratio was 1.41 and the ratio was found not to vary systematically with either k_{cNa} or ϕ_{Na}.

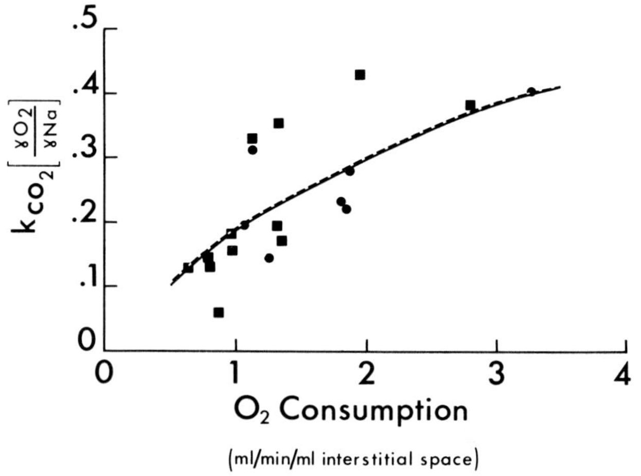

FIGURE 6. *Plot of the variation in the parameter product $k_{cO_2}[\gamma O_2/\gamma_{Na}]$ with oxygen consumption. Saturating hyperbolic (dashed) and rising exponential (solid) profiles, fitted to the data by least squares, are again displayed. The loci corresponding to the levels are*

$$k_{cO_2}\left[\frac{\gamma_{O_2}}{\gamma_{Na}}\right] = \frac{0.744(O_2\ consumption)}{O_2\ consumption + 2.71}$$

and

$$k_{cO_2}\left[\frac{\gamma_{O_2}}{\gamma_{Na}}\right] = 0.49(1 - e^{-0.098[O_2\ consumption]}).$$

The two again correspond reasonably closely, over the range of the data.

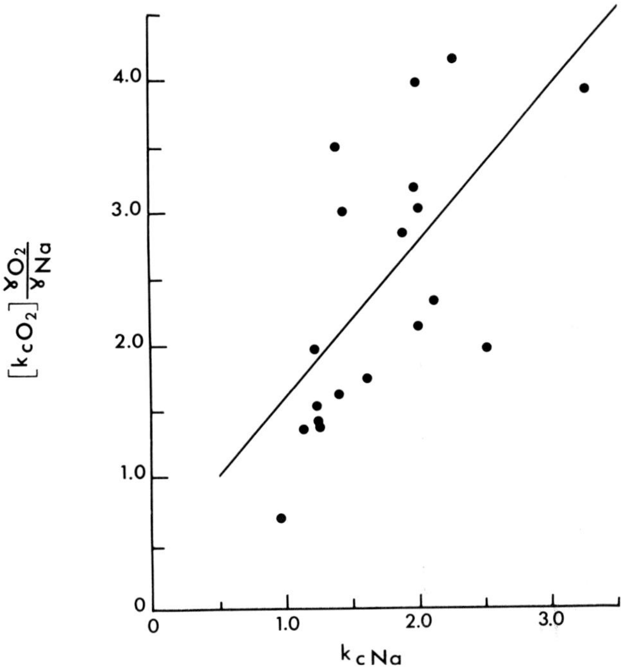

FIGURE 7: *The variation of* $k_{cO_2}[\gamma_{O_2}/\gamma_{Na}]$ *with* k_{cNa}. *The two parameters increase concomitantly. The solid line corresponding to the linear regression relating the two is* $k_{cO_2}[\gamma_{O_2}/\gamma_{Na}] = 1.13k_{cNa} + 0.047$.

Discussion

Why is the Rate Constant for Tracer Oxygen Transfer from Blood to Tissue So Low?

The data gathered in the present set of tracer experiments indicate that the rate of escape of tracer oxygen from blood to tissue is much lower than one might have expected, when one compares the calculated value with that for tracer sodium. The findings indicate, in preliminary fashion, that there is an anomalously high resistance to fractional tracer oxygen distribution at the level of the vasculature. The magnitude of the resistance and the nature of the phenomena leading to the resistance can be understood only by undertaking a dimensional analysis of the calculated parameters. The presence of this resistance appears to provide an explanation for both the relatively low tissue P_{O_2} levels and the disparity between the single cell and whole organ P_{O_2} levels at which limitation in the oxygen-consuming function is found.

Prior to carrying out this analysis, we need to examine the potential of various phenomena to contribute to this barrier function. In dealing with these, we continue to assume that there is no arteriovenous shunting (we deal with this assumption later in more detail). There would then seem to be only two plausible general sites at which the movement of tracer oxygen could be impeded: at the level of release from hemoglobin, or at the interface between the red cell pool and the muscle myoglobin reservoir (with the multiple potential barriers which this implies). The kinetics of bulk desaturation of sheep red cells are known from the work of Sirs (1966). At 20°C, the desaturation of red cell hemoglobin, assessed spectrophotometrically after sudden dilution with an oxygen-free isotonic medium, is more than 50% complete at 50 msec. Comparison of this set of values with those obtained with hemoglobin solutions indicates that the delay imposed by the red cell membrane is too small to be perceived, with this experimental approach. Since anatomical fractional volume measurements indicate that the average transit time of a myocardial capillary should be of the order of one-third of the total transit time (Bassingthwaighte et al., 1974), that is, 2–3 seconds (Ziegler and Goresky, 1971a), it is highly unlikely that bulk oxygen hemoglobin-unloading kinetics or a resistance at the red cell membrane could be responsible for the apparent kinetic limitation in the delivery of tracer oxygen to tissue. At the same time, if there were a substantial red cell oxygen release limitation, one would expect a reduction in the calculated capillary rate constant for tracer oxygen with increase in flow. The present data show, however, that the capillary rate constant for tracer oxygen increases with flow along with that for sodium, presumably due to capillary recruitment. Thus, if we can assume that hindering effects at the level of hemoglobin oxygen release kinetics and of the red blood cell membrane are not of major importance, we must conclude that the resistance to the distribution of tracer (and bulk) oxygen must be at the interface between the red cell and tissue myoglobin oxygen stores.

Dimensional analysis provides the insight needed to define the nature of the resistance to the loss of tracer from the vasculature. The low rate constant for tracer oxygen loss from the capillaries is based on a phenomenon which we will term the red cell pool effect. We gain insight into this by examining the ratio of $k_{cO_2}[\gamma_{O_2}/\gamma_{Na}]$ to k_{cNa}. The average value for this ratio is 1.41. Even though this value indicates that these rate constants are of relatively similar magnitude, so that the initial extractions of tracer oxygen and sodium are of the same order of magnitude, the estimated permeability surface (PS) products for these two substances are not similar. The ratio

$$\frac{k_{cO_2}}{k_{cNa}}\left[\frac{\gamma_{O_2}}{\gamma_{Na}}\right] = \frac{P_{O_2}S_{O_2}}{\text{Mgb } O_2 \text{ space}} \cdot \frac{\text{Na interstitial space}}{P_{Na}S_{Na}} \cdot \frac{\text{Mgb } O_2 \text{ space}}{\text{Hgb } O_2 \text{ space}} \cdot \frac{\text{capillary plasma space}}{\text{Na interstitial space}}$$

where Mgb is myoglobin and Hgb is hemoglobin

$$= \frac{P_{O_2}S_{O_2}}{P_{Na}S_{Na}}\left[\frac{\text{capillary plasma space}}{\text{Hgb } O_2 \text{ space}}\right].$$

The analysis can be carried further by assuming that all of the resistance to oxygen transfer between the hemoglobin and myoglobin pools is situated at the level of the capillary, so that $S_{O_2} = S_{Na}$. Permeability estimates for the capillary secured through this kind of analysis will be minimal, since one is attributing to the capillary all of the resistance between red cell and tissue. In that case, the ratio then

$$= \frac{P_{O_2}}{P_{Na}}\left[\frac{\text{capillary plasma space}}{\text{Hgb } O_2 \text{ space}}\right].$$

To provide appropriate dimensions, the Hgb O_2 space must be expressed in terms of equivalent ml of plasma. The ratio of the oxygen content of plasma: that of red cells in fully oxygenated blood is of the order of 0.3:20.0 = 0.015. Since the ratio of $k_{cO_2}[\gamma_{O_2}/\gamma_{Na}]$ to k_{cNa} averages 1.41, the permeability ratio $P_{O_2}/P_{Na} \approx 94$. The presence of the hemoglobin binding (the red cell capacity or the red cell pool effect) thus greatly magnifies the effect of any resistance to oxygen diffusion. It is this which accounts for the low rate constant for the loss of tracer oxygen from the vasculature. The large red cell pool consequent to hemoglobin binding expands the capillary oxygen capacity and, by virtue of this, decreases the relative rate of loss of tracer oxygen from the vasculature. It expands the space available in the red cell; the fractional exchange of red cell (and capillary) tracer oxygen is, as a direct consequence, much diminished in relation to what otherwise would occur.

The matter can be clarified further by examining the expected form of the damping factor leading to loss of tracer from the impulse function traveling along the capillary. It will be of the form $\exp[-(P_{O_2}S_{O_2}/V_{cO_2})\tau_c]$, where V_{cO_2} is the space of distribution for oxygen in the capillary and τ_c is the transit time of the reference in the capillary. In this instance, the red cell pool effect results in a large value for V_{cO_2}, and this, in consequence, diminishes the magnitude of the rate constant $P_{O_2}S_{O_2}/V_{cO_2}$, which controls the rate of loss of tracer from the capillary.

What is the Magnitude of the Apparent Permeability of the Capillary Bed to Tracer Oxygen?

The permeability value estimated from our calculated parameters is then found to be not low, but high. An estimate of the apparent capillary permeability to tracer oxygen can be obtained as follows. Since the maximum observed capillary permeability surface product values for sodium are of the order of 1.5 ml/min per g (Guller et al., 1975; Rose et al., 1980), and anatomical capillary surface area is of the order of 500 cm^2/g (Bassingthwaighte et al., 1974), the permeability of the myocardial capillaries to the sodium ion is of the order of 1.5/(500 × 60) = 5×10^{-5} cm/sec. Thus, from the estimated permeability ratio, the projected permeability of the cardiac capillaries to oxygen is calculated to be of the order of 4.6×10^{-3} cm/sec. This value is larger than that previously estimated for labeled water in the heart, 6×10^{-4} cm/sec (Rose et al., 1977).

The rank ordering of the myocardial capillary permeabilities to water and oxygen corresponds to that observed by Rasio and Goresky (1979) in the capillaries of the counterperfused rete mirabile of the eel, where the perfusion medium was a buffer solution containing no red cells. In that instance, the method for estimating relative permeability was straightforward, and required no difficult-to-accept assumptions. The estimated permeability to oxygen of the myocardial capillaries is thus of the order expected from the only other estimate available in a continuous systemic type capillary system. Two other considerations indicate that the permeability estimate may be high. The mean hemoglobin oxygen saturation in the cardiac capillary is lower than in the arterial blood, and the capillary hematocrit is lower than in the systemic vessels. Inclusion of these factors would reduce the permeability estimate somewhat.

The permeability value obtained for tracer oxygen is, of course, quite large. The notion that the diffusional resistance between blood and tissue oxygen-utilizing sites can be thought of as a barrier for oxygen is, in this case, founded on the reasonable presumption that the interface between the hemoglobin and myoglobin pools, although distributed in space, has such a low capacity in comparison to these, that it can be neglected; the region then fulfills the usual definition of a barrier. At the same time, one would wish to know the dimensions of a layer of plasma which would give an equivalent resistance, to determine whether the barrier function could be attributed simply to the dimensions of the structures involved, with no special resistance attributed to the nature of the intervening structures themselves (the resistance of which we have attributed to the capillary, in the dimensional analysis). This can be approximated in the following fashion. If the layer were only plasma (or material with an equivalent resistance), the oxygen permeability would be equal to the ratio of the diffusion coefficient for oxygen D_{O_2} and the thickness of the layer Δx, so that

$$\Delta x = \frac{D_{O_2}}{P_{O_2}}. \qquad (4)$$

The diffusion coefficient for oxygen in plasma is 2.1 × 10^{-5} cm^2/sec at 25°C (Goldstick et al., 1976). From this and the permeability estimate outlined above, the equivalent value for Δx is approximately 46 μm. This is of the order of six times the distance from the capillary to the middle of the cardiac muscle cell (and many times the thickness of the barrier between blood and the sarcoplasma). The calculation indicates, as one would have expected, that over some lesser thickness, there is a resistance substantially larger than that encountered in plasma. The site of the resistance is not clearly obvious but, in view of the measured resistance in the continuous capillaries in the rete mirabile, it seems likely that a substantial proportion of this resistance is localized to the capillary membrane. The finding of Araki et al. (1983) of tissue myocardial oxygen concentrations substantially lower than venous values in the absence of a red cell pool effect (red cell-free perfusion was used), reinforces the impression that a barrier effect is present in the heart.

Oxygen Consumption

Once the tracer oxygen has crossed this apparent barrier, we have presumed that its subsequent sequestration within myocardial cells follows first order kinetics—that is, that the proportion of tracer oxygen taken up irreversibly by the cells is directly proportional to the concentration of tracer oxygen at the site. These kinetics would lead to an exponentially decreasing concentration profile along the capillary. However, observations from isolated component systems indicate that, at the level of the oxygen tensions expected in tissue, cytochrome a_3 will be saturated with oxygen, and oxygen utilization in the presence of saturating substrate feed will be expected to be saturated, to follow zero order kinetics. In terms of tracer kinetics, one would then expect, with rise in the local bulk oxygen concentration, a compensatory decrease in the corresponding linearized tracer rate constant (Goresky et al., 1983a). The present experiments have not been carried out across a broad enough range of input oxygen concentrations to see such a change, and the utilization of oxygen in the normally functioning heart is modified by both work load and substrate availability. The whole is more complex than might be expected on the basis of the component parts.

To ascertain whether the model analysis provides an accurate representation of the actual in vivo events associated with the transport of oxygen, it is appropriate to determine whether any of the parameters determined by the fitting procedure can be correlated with other data, measured independently of the model. In this case we examined oxygen consumption. In our experiments, there were two ways to measure this. In the first, the oxygen consumption is calculated in a model-independent fashion, from knowledge of the steady state arterial and venous blood oxygen contents, the hematocrit, and the flow per unit interstitial space. The calculation of the flow per unit interstitial space is independent of the fitting procedure used to derive the rest of the parameter set needed to describe the labeled sodium curve, as indicated earlier; in that sense it is a model-independent measure. It should be noted that none of the parameters used to calculate oxygen consumption in this fashion are derived from the numerical fit to the oxygen curve. In the second approach, the oxygen consumption is formulated as the product of the sequestration rate constant for oxygen and the average local tissue oxygen concentration, both being derived from the fit to the oxygen curve. In the present situation, where the local tissue oxygen concentration remains reasonably constant, one would expect the rate constant to mirror the rate of oxygen consumption, i.e. the two independent calculations of the oxygen consumption to be directly related to each other. This is what was observed in Figure 3. The strong relation between the two provides major evidence that the projections arising from the model are sensible.

From the analytical solutions of the mathematical model, the ratio of the steady state concentrations of oxygen in the extravascular to that in the intravascular space (that is $v(x, \infty)/u(x, \infty)$) is equal to $k_1/(k_2 + k_{seq})$ (Goresky et al., 1973) or (since $k_1 = k_2$, in this case) to $k_1/(k_1 + k_{seq})$, for a steady state input of oxygen. Changes in the ratio $k_1/(k_1 + k_{seq})$ would be expected with change in k_{seq}, the rate constant indicative of oxygen uptake by the cells, unless a concomitant change in k_1, the flow-dependent parameter (Rose et al., 1980), also occurs. The variation in the ratio $k_1/(k_1 + k_{seq})$ with the oxygen consumption is plotted in Figure 4. From this figure, we see that in all experiments, the model predicts a tissue pO_2 of approximately one third of the vascular pO_2. There is thus a linkage in which k_1 (and k_2) change with k_{seq} in a fashion such as to preserve a relative constancy of the ratio $k_1/(k_2 + k_{seq})$.

Some of the experimental procedures were long and stressful, and undoubtedly provoked reasonably large-scale sympathetic (and, with this, metabolic) stimulation in some animals. Initial cardiac oxygen consumption rates in these animals then correspond to those found in animals highly activated sympathetically and metabolically by coronary sinus pacing (Cousineau et al., 1983). This background provided the kind of situation which yielded the large range of consumptions observed. If the kind of change observed here is to be studied in more detail in the future, coronary sinus pacing (Cousineau et al., 1984) might provide the required degree of background sympathetic and metabolic activation.

Analysis of the Data

The assumptions underlying the analysis need some reconsideration. Arteriovenous diffusional shunting has been excluded from the analysis but could still be present. We have assumed that it is not present in the heart in an important amount, because we have been unable to record a precession of tracer oxygen at the outflow with respect to simultaneously injected labeled red cells. The assumption of time precession is based on an expectation that arteriovenous diffusion times will be shorter than transit times through the vascular bed. This appears to be a reasonable expectation, but has not had a detailed model appraisal. Experimentally, even with labeled hydrogen, the most diffusible label one could utilize, the degree of precedence at the outflow over labeled red cells was found to be very small (0.1%) (Feigl and Roth, 1981). It was therefore not unexpected that we were unable to find precession of tracer oxygen at the outflow with reference to labeled red cells. The model utilized to analyze the data is, in other senses, incomplete. The barriers and spaces separating the red cell pool from the myoglobin-bound oxygen have not been modeled in a separable fashion and, in particular, the small plasma oxygen component, which moves more slowly than the red cells, has not been modeled in a fashion which defines its interaction. Although, in theory, this could be done, the plasma oxygen space appeared so small, relatively, that we thought it unlikely that we could recognize its influence, even in near perfect experiments with $^{18}O_2$. It seems likely that such interactions will be able to be defined only by another approach, by examining the behavior in the heart of radioactive oxygen (an alternate and more easily detected tracer), both when the perfusion fluid contains and lacks red cells.

General Considerations

The red cell pool effect imposed by hemoglobin in the microvasculature would initially seem to be a counterproductive constraint. The need for such a phenomenon can be understood, however, after consideration of the function and dimensions of capillaries. Capillaries are long, thin tubes which provide a large surface area over which exchange can occur. In the absence of a barrier, and at high rates of oxygen consumption, all the oxygen in the blood could diffuse into the tissue adjacent to the upstream end of the capillary and be utilized; blood then arriving at the downstream end of the capillary would have a marked reduced oxygen content, and the tissue adjacent to this portion of the capillary would become hypoxic (Goresky et al., 1983a). However, coronary sinus (and capillary) pO_2 levels virtually never drop below 20 torr, in the absence of restriction of coronary blood flow. The effect which we have found, a high (but not unlimited) permeability but low oxygen tracer fractional escape rate, due to the red cell pool effect, allows some oxygen to diffuse across the proximal end of the capillary and leaves some to be carried downstream, so that tissues at the downstream end of the capillary can also be oxygenated. This provides a desirable functional design. With this effect on oxygen transfer, less oxygen reaches the tissue at each point along the capillary, but all points along the capillary will ultimately be supplied with oxygen. The red cell pool effect counteracts what otherwise would occur in the presence of a high permeability, because of the poor geometry of the capillary circulation. Consumption beyond the resistance then creates a step-down in concentration to the lower levels in tissue.

We thank Dr. Orval Mamer, head of the McGill M.R.C Biomedical Mass Spectrometry Unit, for his inestimable help in the measurement of $^{18}O_2$ enrichment; Louise Gagnon, Eva Ibrahim, and Kay Lumsden for their superb technical assistance; Margaret Mulherin for typing this manuscript; and the referees for their invaluable comments, in the review of this manuscript.

Supported by grants from the Medical Research Council of Canada, the Quebec Heart Foundation, and the Fast Foundation.

Dr. Rose is a Chercheur Boursier of the Fonds de la Recherche en Santé du Québec and Dr. Goresky, a Career Investigator of the Medical Research Council of Canada.

Address for reprints: Dr. Carl A. Goresky, University Medical Clinic, Montreal General Hospital, 1650 Cedar Avenue, Montreal, Quebec H3G 1A4, Canada.

Received September 30, 1982; accepted for publication September 28, 1984.

References

Araki R, Tamura M, Yamazaki I (1983) The effect of intracellular oxygen concentration on lactate release, pyridine nucleotide reduction, and respiration rate in rat cardiac tissue. Circ Res **53:** 448–455

Bassingthwaighte JB, Yipintsoi T, Harvey RB (1974) Microvasculature of the dog left ventricular myocardium. Microvasc Res **7:** 229–249

Case RB (1965) Effects of low pO_2 on left ventricular function. *In* Cardiovascular and Respiratory Effects of Hypoxia, edited by JD Hatcher, DB Jennings. New York, Karger, pp 191–207

Chinard FP, Vosberg GJ, Enns T (1955) Transcapillary exchange of water and other substances in certain organs of the dog. Am J Physiol **183:** 221–234

Cousineau D, Rose CP, Goresky CA (1980) Labeled catecholamine uptake in the dog heart. Circ Res **47:** 329–338

Cousineau D, Rose CP, Lamoureux D, Goresky CA (1983) Changes in cardiac transcapillary exchange with metabolic coronary vasodilation in the intact dog. Circ Res **53:** 719–730

Cousineau D, Goresky CA, Bach GG, Rose CP (1984) The effect of beta adrenergic blockade on in vivo norepinephrine release in the canine heart. Am J Physiol **246:** H283–H292

Duling BR, Berne RM (1970) Longitudinal gradients in periarteriolar oxygen tension: a possible mechanism for the participation of oxygen in local regulation of blood flow. Circ Res **27:** 669–678

Feigl EO, Roth AC (1981) Diffusional shunting in the canine myocardium. Circ Res **48:** 470–480

Goldstick TK, Ciuryla VT, Zuckerman L (1976) Diffusion of oxygen in plasma and blood. *In* Oxygen Transport to Tissue II, edited by J Grote, D Reneau, G Thews. New York, Plenum, pp 183–190

Goresky CA, Cronin RFP, Wangel BE (1969) Indicator dilution measurements of extravascular water in the lungs. J Clin Invest **48:** 487–501

Goresky CA, Ziegler WF, Bach GG (1970) Capillary exchange modeling: Barrier-limited and flow-limited distribution. Circ Res **27:** 739–764

Goresky CA, Bach GG, Nadeau BE (1973) On the uptake of materials by the intact liver: The transport and net removal of galactose. J Clin Invest **52:** 991–1008

Goresky CA, Bach GG, Rose CR (1983a) Effects of saturating metabolic uptake on space profiles and tracer kinetics. Am J Physiol **244:** G215–G232

Goresky CA, Gordon ER, Bach GG (1983b) Uptake of monohydric alcohols by liver: Demonstration of a shared enzymic space. Am J Physiol **244:** G198–G214

Grunewald WA, Sowa W (1977) Capillary structures and O_2 supply to tissue. Rev Physiol Biochem Pharmacol **77:** 150–209

Grunewald WA, Sowa W (1978) Distribution of the myocardial tissue pO_2 in the rat and the inhomogeneity of the coronary bed. Pflugers Arch **374:** 57–66

Guller B, Yipintsoi T, Orvis AL, Bassingthwaighte JB (1975) Myocardial sodium extraction at varied coronary flows in the dog. Circ Res **37:** 359–378

Heyndrickx GR, Pannier JL, Muylaert P, Mabilde C, Leusen I (1980) Alterations in myocardial oxygen balance during exercise after β-adrenergic blockade in dogs. J Appl Physiol **49:** 28–33

Krogh A (1919) The number and distribution of capillaries in muscles with calculations of the oxygen pressure head necessary for supplying the tissue. J Physiol (Lond) **52:** 409–415

Lawrence JH, Loomis WF, Tobias CA, Turpin FH (1946) Preliminary observations of the narcotic effect of xenon with a review of values for solubilities of gases in water and oils. J Physiol (Lond) **105:** 197–204

Lübbers DW (1982) Oxygen supply to the myocardium. *In* Microcirculation of the Heart, edited by H Tillmanns, W Kubler, H Zebe. Berlin, Springer-Verlag, p 119

Neely JR, Liebermeister H, Battersby EJ, Morgan HE (1967) Effect of pressure development on oxygen consumption by isolated rat heart. Am J Physiol **212:** 804–814

Pappenheimer JR, Renkin EM, Borrero LM (1951) Filtration, diffusion, and molecular seiving through capillary membranes. A contribution to the pore theory of capillary permeability. Am J Physiol **167:** 13–46

Prankerd TAJ (1961) The Red Cell. Springfield, Illinois, Thomas, p 164

Rasio EA, Goresky CA (1979) Capillary limitation of oxygen distribution in the isolated rete mirabile of the eel (*Anguilla anguilla*). Circ Res **44:** 498–503

Rose CP, Goresky CA (1976) Vasomotor control of capillary transit time heterogeneity in the canine coronary circulation. Circ Res **39:** 541–554

Rose CP, Goresky CA (1977) Constraints on the uptake of labeled palmitate by the heart: the barriers at the capillary and sarcolemmal surfaces and the control of intracellular sequestration. Circ Res **41:** 534–545

Rose CP, Goresky CA, Bach GG (1977) The capillary and sarcolemmal barriers in the heart: An exploration of labeled water permeability. Circ Res **41:** 515–533

Rose CP, Goresky CA, Bélanger P, Chen M (1980) Effects of vasodilation and flow rate on capillary permeability surface product and interstitial space size in the canine coronary circulation: A frequency domain technique for modeling multiple dilution data with Laguere functions. Circ Res **47:** 312–328

Rosenbrock HH, Storey C (1966) Computational Techniques for Chemical Engineers. Oxford, Pergamon Press

Schubert RW, Whalen WJ, Nair P (1978) Myocardial pO_2 distribution: Relationship to coronary autoregulation. Am J Physiol **234:** H361–H370

Sirs JA (1966) The egress of oxygen from sheep erythrocytes. Biochim Biophys Acta **112:** 538–549

Van der Wusse GJ, Roeman THM, Prinzen FW, Coumans WA, Reneman RS (1982) Uptake and tissue content of fatty acids in dog myocardium under normoxic and ischemic conditions. Circ Res **50:** 530–546

Weiss HR, Sinha AK (1978) Regional oxygen saturation of small arteries and veins in the canine myocardium. Circ Res **42:** 119–126

Whalen WJ (1971) Intracellular pO_2 in heart and skeletal muscle. Physiologist **14:** 69–82

Wittenberg BA, Robinson TF (1981) Oxygen requirements, morphology, cell coat, and membrane permeability of calcium tolerant myocytes from hearts of adult rats. Cell Tissue Res **216:** 231–251

Ziegler WH, Goresky CA (1971a) Transcapillary exchange in the working left ventricle of the dog. Circ Res **29:** 181–207

Ziegler WH, Goresky CA (1971b) Kinetics of rubidium uptake in the working dog heart. Circ Res **29:** 208–220

INDEX TERMS: Oxygen transport in heart • Red cell pool effect on oxygen diffusion • Tracer oxygen transfer from blood to tissue • Intracellular oxygen sequestration • Limiting transfer rates for tracer oxygen

The Role of Free Radical-Mediated Processes in Oxygen-Related Damage in Cultured Murine Myocardial Cells

James A. Scott, Ban An Khaw, Elizabeth Locke, Edgar Haber, and Charles Homcy

From the Department of Radiology, and the Cardiac Unit, Massachusetts General Hospital, Harvard Medical School, Boston, Massachusetts

SUMMARY. A new approach to quantifying myocyte cell death utilizing fluorescence-activated sorting of antimyosin antibody-labeled cells was used to study the effects of oxygen-generated free radicals on cell survival. Uptake of antimyosin, reflecting sarcolemmal damage, increased under conditions which promoted elevated free radical formation and decreased in the presence of increased levels of free radical-scavenging agents. Superoxide dismutase decreased antimyosin uptake at pH 6.7 and 7.5. Mannitol decreased antimyosin uptake at pH 6.5 and 6.7 but not at pH 7.5, and dimethyl sulfoxide decreased antimyosin uptake at pH 6.4 but not at pH 7.5. These data suggest that a greater portion of hydroxyl radicals are produced at higher concentrations of hydrogen ion. Mannitol, a scavenger of hydroxyl radicals, was effective in reducing antimyosin uptake at pH 7.5 in the presence of ferrous sulfate, but had no effect on antimyosin uptake in the absence of ferrous sulfate, suggesting possible iron-mediated catalysis of hydroxyl radical formation. The data suggest that oxygen-derived free radicals can cause significant loss of membrane integrity in cultured myocytes, that the species of radical formed is dependent both on pH and the concentration of iron salts, and that this injury is, at least in part, preventable by the administration of exogenous radical scavenging agents **(*Circ Res 56: 72–77, 1985*)**

RECENT work has suggested a role for free radical-mediated processes in myocardial damage, especially with respect to the reoxygenation of hypoxic tissue (Guarnieri et al., 1978, 1980; Del Maestro, 1980; Schlafer et al., 1982). It is thought that the intracellular accumulation of reducing equivalents during hypoxia leads to the increased generation of oxygen radical species when ischemic tissue is reoxygenated. Certain antioxidant compounds (e.g., selenium and tocopherols) are capable of decreasing this reoxygenation damage, presumably by a mechanism involving free radical detoxification or "scavenging" (Guarnieri et al., 1978; Schlafer et al., 1982).

In a previous paper we presented a new technique involving laser-activated cell sorting of myocardial cells labeled with fluorescent antimyosin-antibody (Khaw et al., 1982). This method can detect membrane defects when fluorescent-labeled antibody binds to the intracellular protein, myosin, indicating a loss of cell membrane integrity. This provides an extremely sensitive and specific method for detecting and quantifying membrane damage to the myocardial cell in tissue culture. We now have examined the importance of free radical-mediated cellular damage in this tissue culture system, and the role of radical scavenging enzymes and the chemical scavengers, dimethyl sulfoxide and mannitol, in preventing this damage. The effectiveness of these agents in reducing antimyosin uptake was examined with respect to extracellular pH, since different radical species have been reported to predominate at varying pH values (Hess et al., 1982).

Methods

Cell Culture Preparation

Neonatal CD-1 mice (Charles River Breeding Laboratories) were exsanguinated, and the hearts treated with 0.125% trypsin-ethylenediamine tetraacetic acid (EDTA) and gently stirred until the cells were dissociated. The separated neonatal murine myocytes were then allowed to stabilize for 3–4 days in Dulbecco's minimal essential medium (DMEM)-10% fetal calf serum (FCS) (Gibco). Cells were incubated in a 7% CO_2 humid atmosphere at 37°C (Scott et al., 1981; Khaw et al., 1982).

Preparation of Antimyosin-Coupled Covaspheres

Cardiac myosin was extracted from the hearts of 100 CD-1 mice by the method of Katz et al. (1965). Purified cardiac myosin was used to immunize rabbits as previously described (Khaw et al., 1976). Antisera thus obtained were applied to a murine cardiac myosin-agarose immunoadsorbent prepared by the cyanogen bromide-activation method of Cuatrecasas (1970). Specific anticardiac myosin antibody was desorbed with a guanidine-HCl gradient and renatured by stepwise dialysis. Antimyosin antibody activity was determined by its binding capacity for ^{125}I-murine cardiac myosin. Purified antimyosin at 1 mg/ml was then coupled to 100 μl of preactivated Covaspheres (Covalent Technology). Between 100 and 150 μg antimyosin antibody was incorporated into 100 μl of the Covasphere suspension. Spheres were washed in

DMEM three times and then suspended in 1 ml of DMEM and stored at 4°C until used.

Interventions

Cells were incubated in DMEM-10% fetal calf serum for 24-hour periods after gassing with a 93% O_2-7% CO_2 mixture. The Po_2 was measured with an oxygen analyzer at the end of the incubation. Cells were incubated at various pH levels ranging from 6.7 to 7.5, effected by varying the CO_2 content in the culture chamber, or by adding dilute HCl to the incubation medium. Chemical buffering agents were not added, to avoid possible competing chemical mechanisms of radical scavenging. Readings of the pH were taken after 24-hour incubation periods. Measurements were taken on quadruplicate cultures of cells.

Bovine superoxide dismutase (3000 U/mg, Sigma Chemical Co.), mannitol (Sigma Chemical Co.), $FeSO_4$ (Sigma Chemical Co.), or dimethyl sulfoxide (DMSO, MCB Reagents) was added to culture medium prior to 24-hour incubation with antimyosin-labeled Covaspheres, at 37°C.

Separation of Labeled Cells

At the beginning of each 24-hour incubation period, each flask received 50 μl of antimyosin-labeled Covaspheres. After incubation, the medium was removed and saved. The cells were washed twice with fresh media and then treated with 0.25% trypsin-EDTA to dissociate the myocytes from the flasks. Exposure to trypsin was limited during cell preparations, since incubation of cells in the presence of trypsin for periods exceeding approximately 15 minutes (at 37°C) caused trypsin-related increases in sarcolemmal injury. Aliquots of 3 ml DMEM with 10% FCS were added to inactivate the trypsin. Unbound Covaspheres were separated by employing a fetal calf serum gradient and centrifuging at 100 *g* for 6 minutes. Cells with bound Covaspheres were recovered in the pellet, which was resuspended in 0.5 ml FCS. These preparations were examined with a fluorescence microscope. The remainder of each sample was used for cell sorting in a FACS III (Becton-Dickinson) sorter employing a 70-μm nozzle and a logarithmic amplifier. The laser settings were at the lowest level. The size and fluorescence parameters were held constant for each experiment to ensure valid comparison of high and low fluorescence populations. Ten thousand cells were counted in each culture. Triplicate or quadruplicate cultures were used to examine each intervention. The sorted cells were grouped into low (0–5 spheres/cell) and high (6–100 spheres/cell) populations. The instrument settings were determined by isolating the myocyte peak and bracketing the window settings to encompass the myocyte size range. Fluorescence settings were made with a logarithmic amplifier calibrated to correspond to the number of microspheres/cell. Results are expressed as the percentage of cells demonstrating greater than 5 microspheres/cell. This degree of uptake has previously been shown to correlate with irreversible cellular injury (Khaw et al., 1982). Selected cells were examined by the trypan blue exclusion test and plated in culture medium as a further test of viability.

Statistical Analysis

Data were expressed as irreversibly injured cells (cells containing greater than 5 spheres/cell divided by total cells counted) to conform to a Gaussian distribution. Analysis of variance was used in evaluating data followed by the performance of the *t*-test modified for multiple comparisons (Bonferroni's method). Results are expressed as mean ± 1 SEM.

We examined the effect of DMSO and superoxide dismutase in a cell-free antimyosin radioimmunoassay to determine the extent to which nonspecific competitive binding might interfere with our results in tissue culture. DMSO reduced maximal antigen binding from 75% in controls without added DMSO to 71% at 1% (vol/vol) DMSO, 70% at 2% (vol/vol) DMSO, and 66% at 5% (vol/vol) DMSO. The superoxide dismutase preparation used in these experiments was also examined in the radioimmunoassay system at a 0.5 mg/ml concentration with no evidence of interference with antimyosin binding.

Results

Effect of Oxygen Concentration on Cellular Injury

The effect of changing the concentration of environmental oxygen on cellular injury was examined. At an ambient Po_2 of 61 mm Hg, the percentage of irreversibly injured cells was 8.9 ± 2.8, whereas at a Po_2 of 140 mm Hg, the percentage was 27.7 ± 5.8 ($P < 0.05$), consistent with an effect of oxygen concentration on cellular injury. Overall, no significant change in cellular injury was seen as the Po_2 was increased from 140 to 300 mm Hg, suggesting that a relatively small increase in oxygen radical production occurs between these oxygen tensions, consistent with data reported in radiation experiments (Hall, 1978). We incubated cells at the higher oxygen concentration, however, to obtain optimal conditions for free radical production.

Effect of Radical Scavenging Agents on Cellular Injury

We examined the effect of superoxide dismutase and mannitol as examples of water-soluble radical scavenging agents. Both agents reduced cellular injury, although in the case of mannitol the reduction was pH dependent. Superoxide dismutase (0.5 mg/ml) decreased the number of irreversibly injured cells relative to control cultures at pH 6.7 ($P < 0.05$) and pH 7.5 ($P < 0.001$) as shown in Figure 1. Mannitol (20 mM) decreased the number of irreversibly injured cells at pH 6.5 ($P < 0.001$) and 6.7 ($P < 0.05$), but did not affect cellular injury at pH 7.5, as shown in Figure 1.

DMSO was examined as an example of a membrane-permeable radical scavenging agent with primary hydroxyl radical scavenging capacity (Dorfman and Adams, 1973). At a 5% (vol/vol) concentration, DMSO reduced cellular injury at pH 6.4 ($P < 0.05$), but not at pH 7.5, as shown in Figure 2. Figure 3 is a fluorescent-activated cell sorter (FACS) display which demonstrates alterations in forward light scatter, an indicator of cell volume, and fluorescence intensity in the presence of DMSO. In the control population, a fraction of cells scattering a greater degree of laser light is apparent. This

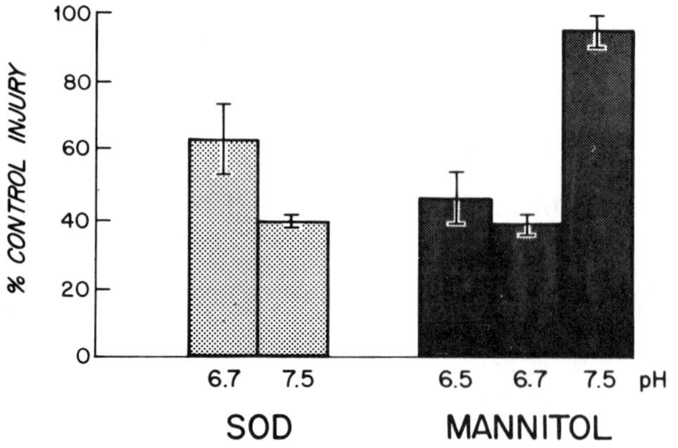

FIGURE 1. *The water-soluble radical scavengers superoxide dismutase (SOD) and mannitol each were effective in reducing cellular injury at pH 6.7 ($P < 0.05$), whereas only superoxide dismutase was effective at pH 7.5 ($P < 0.001$). Mannitol reduced antimyosin uptake at pH 6.5 ($P < 0.001$) and pH 6.7 ($P < 0.05$). The percentage of irreversibly injured cells in control cultures was 13.4 ± 5.7% in mannitol experiments and 12.3 ± 7.6% in superoxide dismutase experiments. The number of injured cells in treated preparations is expressed as a percentage of the number of injured cells in the control cultures.*

subgroup is absent in the DMSO-treated cells. Furthermore, this control group contains a subgroup of cells binding a greater number of antimyosin-coated spheres, as shown by the arrow. Gating with the FACS analyzer indicated that these highly fluorescent cells were those of greater apparent volume as measured by forward light scatter. DMSO treatment abolishes the majority of this population. This result was also typical for those cells treated with superoxide dismutase or mannitol when protection was demonstrable.

Effect of Ferrous Ions on Cellular Injury

We examined the effect of ferrous sulfate to assess the importance of the metal-catalyzed Haber-Weiss

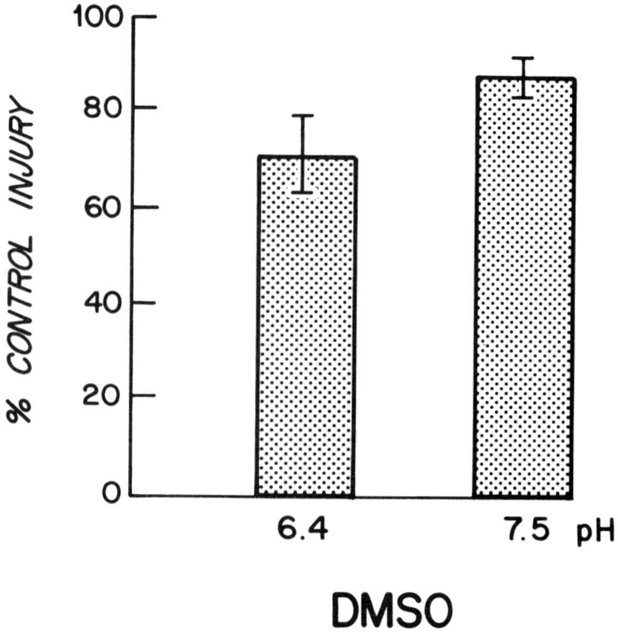

FIGURE 2. *DMSO, a membrane permeable hydroxyl radical scavenger (5% vol/vol), reduced cellular injury from control at pH 6.4 ($P < 0.05$) but not at pH 7.5. The percentage of irreversibly injured cells in control cultures was 12.2 ± 4.5%. The number of injured cells in treated preparations is expressed as a percentage of the number of injured cells in the control cultures.*

reaction in influencing cellular injury. This reaction, as outlined in the Discussion, provides a route for the formation of hydroxyl radicals from superoxide and hydrogen peroxide (Halliwell, 1982). Figure 4 illustrates the effect of 50 μM $FeSO_4$ in altering the distribution of free radicals at pH 7.5. Mannitol (20 mM) alone was ineffective in reducing cellular injury at this pH, consistent with a relative minority of hydroxyl radicals among the injurious radical spe-

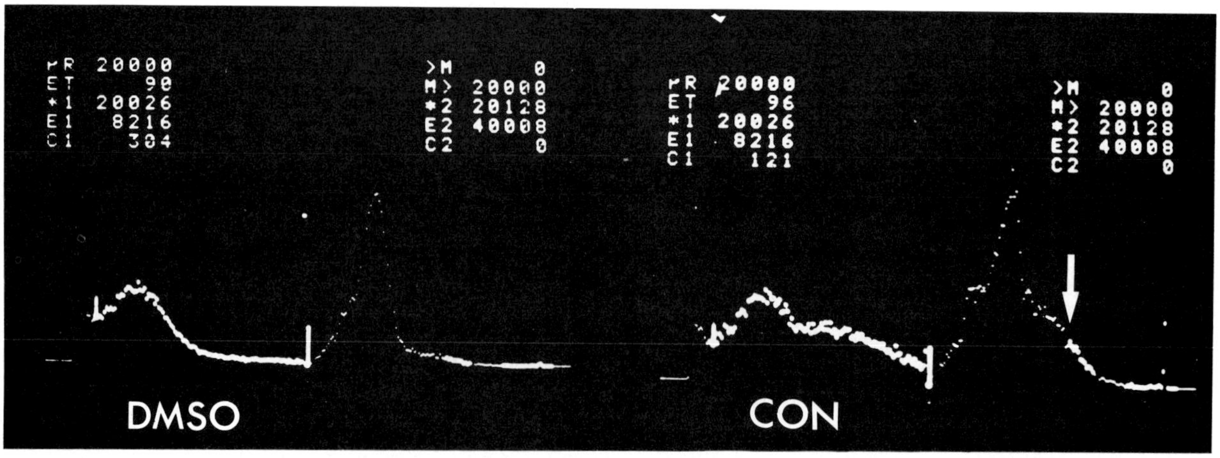

FIGURE 3. *Size and fluorescence plots are shown for control (CON) and 5% DMSO-incubated (DMSO) cultures. The lefthand portion of each figure displays the size distribution of cells, and the righthand portion displays the fluorescence distribution. Size and fluorescence are shown on the x axis, with the number of cells registering a particular size or fluorescence on the y axis. Note the shift of both size and fluorescence curves to the left in DMSO-incubated cultures, indicating less cellular swelling and antimyosin uptake in DMSO-incubated cultures relative to control. The arrow indicates a population of damaged cells (higher fluorescence) in the control cultures, which is not seen in the DMSO-incubated cultures.*

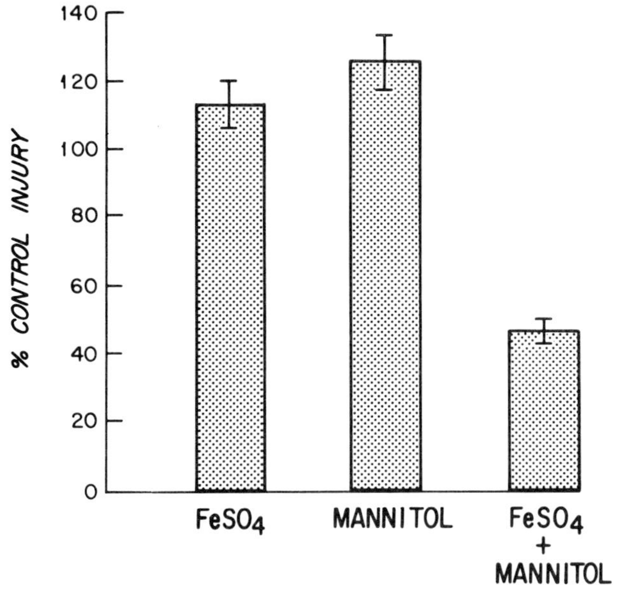

FIGURE 4. *Ferrous sulfate (50 μM) and mannitol (20 mM) are shown with respect to their effects, alone and in combination, on cellular injury a pH 7.5. Note that mannitol is effective in reducing cellular injury in the presence of ferrous sulfate ($P < 0.001$). Irreversible injury in control cultures was 18.0 ± 1.3%. The number of injured cells in treated preparations is expressed as a percentage of the number of injured cells in the control cultures.*

cies. $FeSO_4$ alone also has no effect on cellular injury, suggesting that, whereas iron salts catalyze the conversion of superoxide to hydroxyl radicals, they do not affect cellular injury, since both superoxide and hydroxyl radicals are injurious to the cell. Additionally, in the presence of both $FeSO_4$ and mannitol, $FeSO_4$-produced hydroxyl radicals (from the superoxide species) are now scavenged by mannitol, thus reducing cellular injury. Therefore, both $FeSO_4$ and mannitol are necessary for effective scavenging of the superoxide species.

Discussion

This work confirms and extends prior observations (Guarnieri et al., 1978, 1980; Del Maestro, 1980; Schlafer et al., 1982; Meerson et al., 1982) that free radical-mediated processes can play a significant role in the production of irreversible cellular injury, a finding of particular relevance in view of the hypothesized role for free radical injury during reoxygenation as postulated by Meerson et al. (1982). According to this hypothesis, normal cardiac tissue contains enzymatic chemical agents capable of detoxifying highly reactive free radical compounds derived mainly from molecular oxygen. During ischemia, several conditions prevail which lead to increased free radical formation upon reintroduction of oxygen. These include the intracellular accumulation of reducing equivalents, the conversion of xanthine dehydrogenase to xanthine oxidase, and the accumulation of by-products of ATP hydrolysis which act as substrates for free radical production through the action of xanthine oxidase (Hess et al., 1982; Rao et al., 1983). The subsequent reintroduction of oxygen during reperfusion leads to increased reduction of molecular oxygen and increased free radical levels. The cell, unable to detoxify this radical load, suffers irreversible injury, largely related to the peroxidation of membrane lipids. It has been suggested that an exogenous supply of radical scavenging agents prior to and during reperfusion of ischemic tissue can minimize this type of radical-mediated injury.

Since irreversible injury has been shown to be closely correlated with the loss of membrane integrity (Jennings and Reimer, 1981) and since oxygen radical-mediated injury is primarily directed at unsaturated lipid constituents of the cell membrane (Hess et al., 1982; Meerson et al., 1982), it seems likely that an assessment of membrane integrity would constitute an excellent marker for determining the extent of radical-mediated cellular injury. We have previously described a method of quantitatively assessing membrane integrity in the cultured myocardial cell using flow cytometry with fluorescent-tagged antimyosin (Khaw et al., 1982). Although the normal cell membrane is impermeable to a large molecule such as antimyosin antibody, the molecule can bind to intracellular myosin made available by damage to the cell membrane. By quantifying the degree of antimyosin uptake within the cell, the integrity of the sarcolemma can be directly assessed. The method has the advantages of examining individual cells rather than tissue aggregates (as in the isolated perfused heart or intact animal) and permitting simultaneous examination by light or fluorescence microscopy. It also affords the capability of sorting cells into populations based on surface-bound antimyosin. These sorted populations can be subsequently recultured and studied. The method is more sensitive to sarcolemmal injury than other traditional techniques of evaluating membrane integrity, such as trypan blue exclusion (Khaw et al., 1982) and, additionally, permits quantification of membrane injury unavailable from dye uptake techniques. We have previously determined that irreversible cellular injury is associated with the uptake of greater than five antimyosin microspheres/cell (Khaw et al., 1982), lesser degrees of uptake representing nonspecific adhesion of microspheres to the cell membrane. The ratio of cells containing greater than five microspheres/cell to all cells studied, therefore, provides a measure of the percentage of irreversibly injured cells.

Since an elevated oxygen tension should result in increased oxygen radical production (Hall, 1978), membrane damage (as evidenced by antimyosin uptake) should be related to ambient oxygen concentrations. The relationship between oxygen partial pressure and oxygen radical formation, however, is probably not linear. Theoretically, oxygen radical formation should rapidly increase between Po_2 values ranging from 0 to 30 mm and increase more slowly at higher concentrations (Hall, 1978). Experiments performed with yeast, bacteria, and mammalian cells in culture support this prediction (see Hall). Since this range corresponds to that expected in the ischemia-reoxygenation transition, oxygen radical levels can be expected to increase rapidly during the course of reperfusion. In our model, antimyosin antibody uptake increases in those cells exposed to environments with ambient Po_2 of 140 mm Hg as compared to Po_2 of 61 mm Hg, consistent with oxygen radical-mediated sarcolemmal injury. These data are consistent with results in other cell lines where increased plating efficiency of cells was observed at reduced (1–3% O_2) environmental oxygen concentrations in comparison with 20% O_2 (Richter et al., 1972). Although oxygen environments exceeding 140 mm Hg at times appeared to increase cellular injury in our system, this effect was not significant, suggesting that oxygen radical production is near maximal at ambient O_2 levels.

If oxygen radicals are a cause of membrane injury, then agents that detoxify these substances should have a protective effect on the myocardial cell. These protective agents can be classified as membrane-permeable (i.e., agents which can pass through the intact cell membrane and enter the interior of the cell, thus detoxifying both extracellular, intracellular, and intramembranous radicals) and membrane impermeable. DMSO (Szmant, 1975) is an example of the former type, whereas superoxide dismutase, catalase, and mannitol are examples of the latter type of agent. Although there is some evidence that the superoxide radical can pass through lipid bilayers (Fukuzawa and Gebicki, 1983), the high chemical reactivity of free radical species (especially the hydroxyl radical) suggests that scavenging processes will be most effective when the scavengers are located closest to the site of radical formation.

With regard to membrane-impermeable radical scavengers, we have examined the effects of superoxide dismutase (which catalyzes the production of hydrogen peroxide and water from the superoxide radical) and mannitol (which degrades the hydroxyl radical). Extracellularly administered superoxide dismutase decreased the percentage of dead cells relative to control at pH 7.5 ($P < 0.001$) and pH 6.7 ($P < 0.05$). This observation is in accordance with the results of other workers who have found the superoxide radical to be an important mediator of cellular injury, reporting protection of cells with extracellular superoxide dismutase (Hess et al., 1981; Guarnieri, 1981) and increased cellular damage in cells where endogenous superoxide dismutase levels are lowered by diethyldithiocarbamate (Guarnieri et al., 1981). A role for the hydroxyl radical at lower pH values is suggested by the observed inhibition of antimyosin uptake at pH 6.7 but not at pH 7.5 in the presence of 20 mM exogenous mannitol or 5% (vol/vol) DMSO, both hydroxyl radical scavengers. It is interesting that Hess and co-workers have also demonstrated a pH-dependent role for the hydroxyl radical in producing subcellular injury (Hess et al., 1982) consistent with these findings.

Previous work has suggested a role for DMSO in protecting ischemic heart muscle in intact animals (Finney et al., 1967; Leon et al., 1970; Schlafer et al., 1982) and as a scavenger of hydroxyl radicals (Dorfman and Adams, 1973; Repine et al., 1981). In our experiments, cells incubated with 5% DMSO showed significantly decreased cellular injury at pH 6.4 ($P < 0.05$) but not at pH 7.5. These findings are consistent with greater importance of the hydroxyl radical in producing cellular injury at lower pH values. The ability of DMSO to reduce cellular injury may in part relate to its ability to pass through the cell membrane and scavenge intracellular and intramembranous radicals in addition to radicals in the extracellular space. Caution must be taken with this interpretation, however, since, in addition to its hydroxyl radical-scavenging properties, DMSO possesses membrane-stabilizing effects possibly unassociated with radical scavenging (Szmant, 1975).

We investigated the importance of ferrous ions in producing sarcolemmal injury, since iron is a well-known catalyst of peroxidation reactions (Halliwell, 1982) and is present in human blood at concentrations of approximately 100 μg/100 ml. Iron species promote the formation of the highly reactive hydroxyl radical species by the metal-catalyzed Haber-Weiss reaction (Halliwell, 1982) as shown:

$$Fe\ (II) + H_2O_2 \rightarrow Fe\ (III) + OH^- + OH\cdot$$
$$Fe\ (III) + O_2^- + \rightarrow Fe\ (II) + O_2$$

Thus, iron catalyzes the formation of the hydroxyl radical from superoxide and hydrogen peroxide. Iron salts should reduce the concentration of the superoxide anion and increase the concentration of hydroxyl radicals as a result of this reaction. To elucidate the role of iron catalysis in our system, we examined the effect of mannitol and ferrous sulfate (50 μM) on antimyosin antibody uptake. Ferrous sulfate alone did not alter cellular injury relative to control cultures. Mannitol reduced cellular injury at pH 7.5 in the presence of $FeSO_4$ ($P < 0.001$) but not in its absence. This is consistent with the conversion of superoxide to hydroxyl radicals by $FeSO_4$ with scavenging of the latter species by mannitol, thus reducing the radical load to which the cell membrane is exposed.

These results support a role for free radical-mediated processes in the production of sarcolemmal injury in the myocardium. The ability of exogenously administered membrane-impermeable agents to reduce sarcolemmal injury is consistent with extracellular activity of injurious radical species. The marked reduction in uptake afforded by the membrane-permeable agent, DMSO, underlies the importance for intracellular radical activity in the generation of sarcolemmal injury (Hassan and Fridovich, 1980). Further work should lead to a greater understanding of the critical metabolic complexities in the heart's biochemical transformations of molecular oxygen.

We would like to thank K. Taylor for her assistance in the preparation of this manuscript, Susan Cahill and Gary Weil for technical assistance, and John Newell for statistical advice.

This work was supported in part by a grant from R.J. Reynolds Industries, Inc., and by Ischemia SCOR-HL-26215.

Dr. Scott is affiliated with the Department of Radiology; all other authors of this paper are affiliated with the Cardiac Unit.

Address for reprints: Charles Homcy, M.D., Cardiac Unit, Massachusetts General Hospital, Boston, Massachusetts 02114.

Received August 29, 1983; accepted for publication September 17, 1984.

References

Cuatrecasas P (1970) Protein purification by affinity chromatography. Derivitization of agarose and polyamide beads. J Biol Chem **245:** 3059–3065

Del Maestro RF (1980) An approach to free-radicals in medicine and biology. Acta Physiol Scand [Suppl] **492:** 153–168

Dorfman LM, Adams GE (1973) Reactivity of the hydroxyl radical in aqueous solutions. U.S. Department of Commerce, National Bureau of Standards, NSRDS-NBS no. 46

Finney JW, Urschel HC, Balla GA, Race GJ, Jay BE, Pingree HP, Dorman HL, Mallams JT (1967) Protection of the ischemic heart with dimethyl sulfoxide alone or dimethyl sulfoxide with hydrogen peroxide. Ann NY Acad Sci **141:** 231–241

Fukuzawa K, Gebicki JM (1983) Oxidation of alpha-tocopherol in micelles and liposomes by the hydroxyl, perhydroxyl and superoxide free radicals. Arch Biochem Biophys **226:** 242–251

Guarnieri C (1981) Influence of oxygen radicals on heart metabolism. J Mol Cell Cardiol (suppl) **13:** 34

Guarnieri C, Ferrari R, Visiolo O, Caldarera CM, Naylor WG (1978) Effect of tocopherol on hypoxic perfused and re-oxygenated rabbit heart muscle. J Mol Cell Cardiol **10:** 893–906

Guarnieri C, Flamigni F, Caldarera CM (1980) Role of oxygen in the cellular damage induced by re-oxygenation of hypoxic heart. J Mol Cell Cardiol **12:** 797–808

Guarnieri C, Flamigni F, Ventura C, Rossoni-Caldarera C (1981) Inhibition of rat heart superoxide dismutase activity by diethyldithiocarbamate and its effect on mitochondral function. Biochem Pharmacol **20:** 2174–2176

Hall EJ (1978) Radiobiology for the Radiologist. Philadelphia, Harper & Row, pp 85–87

Halliwell B (1982) Superoxide-dependent formation of hydroxyl radicals in the presence of iron salts is a feasible source of hydroxyl radicals in vivo. J Biochem **205:** 461–463

Hassan HM, Fridovich I (1980) Impermeability of the *E. coli* cell envelope to superoxide. *In* Biological and Clinical Aspects of Superoxide and Superoxide Dismutase, edited by WH Bannister, JV Bannister. New York, Elsevier, pp 57–71

Hess ML, Okabe E, Kantos HA (1981) Proton and free-oxygen radical interaction with the calcium transport system of cardiac sarcoplasmic reticulum. J Mol Cell Cardiol **13:** 767–772

Hess ML, Manson NH, Okabe E (1982) Involvement of free radicals in the pathophysiology of ischemic heart disease. Can J Physiol Pharmacol **60:** 1382–1389

Jennings RB, Reimer KA (1981) Lethal myocardial ischemic injury. Am J Pathol **102:** 241–255

Katz AM, Doris I, Repke CT, Rubin BB (1965) Adenosine-triphosphate activity of cardiac myosin. Circ Res **19:** 611–620

Khaw BA, Beller GA, Haber E, Smith TW (1976) Localization of cardiac anti-myosin-specific activity in myocardial infarction. J Clin Invest **58:** 439–446

Khaw BA, Scott J, Fallon JT, Cahill SL, Haber E, Homcy C (1982) Myocardial injury: Quantitation by cell sorting initiated with antimyosin fluorescent spheres. Science **217:** 1050–1053

Leon AS, Bluor CM, Pitt B (1970) The effects of dimethyl sulfoxide (DMSO) on the healing of experimental myocardial necrosis. Am Heart J **79:** 384–389

Meerson FZ, Kagan VE, Kozlov YP, Belkina LM, Archipenico V (1982) The role of lipid peroxidation in the pathogenesis of damage and antioxidant protection of the heart. Basic Res Cardiol **77:** 465–485

Rao PS, Cohen MV, Mueller HS (1983) Production of free radicals and lipid peroxides in early experimental myocardial ischemia. J Mol Cell Cardiol **15:** 713–716

Repine JE, Pfenninger OW, Talmadge DW, Berger EM, Pettijohn DE (1981) Dimethyl sulfoxide prevents DNA nicking mediated by ionizing radiation or iron/hydrogen peroxide generated hydroxyl radical. Proc Natl Acad Sci USA **78:** 10010–10033

Richter A, Sanford KK, Evans VJ (1972) Influence of oxygen and culture media on plating efficiency of some mammalian tissue cells. J Natl Cancer Inst **49:** 1705–12

Schlafer M, Kane PF, Kirsh MM (1982) Superoxide dismutase plus catalase enhances the efficacy of hypothermic cardioplegia to protect the globally ischemic reperfused heart. J Thorac Cardiovasc Surg **83:** 830–839

Scott JA, Lader CD, Miller SW, Kolodny GM (1981) Effect of radiographic contrast material on cultured myocardial cells. Invest Rad **16:** 141–151

Szmant HH (1975) Physical properties of dimethyl sulfoxide and its function in biological systems. Ann NY Acad Sci **243:** 20–23

INDEX TERMS: Tissue culture • Cell membrane • Oxygen toxicity • Free radicals

The Economy of Isometric Force Development, Myosin Isoenzyme Pattern and Myofibrillar ATPase Activity in Normal and Hypothyroid Rat Myocardium

Ch. Holubarsch, R.P. Goulette, R.Z. Litten, B.J. Martin, L.A. Mulieri, and N.R. Alpert
From the Institute of Physiology II, University of Tubingen, Tubingen, Federal Republic of Germany, and the Department of Physiology and Biophysics, University of Vermont, Burlington, Vermont

SUMMARY. Hypothyroidism was induced in Wistar-Kyoto rats by adding propylthiouracil to the drinking water (0.8 mg/ml). Initial heat, total activity-related heat, and resting heat rate were measured in left ventricular papillary muscle preparations of propylthiouracil-treated and control rats contracting isometrically at 12 beats/min (21°C), using Hill type, planar vacuum-deposited bismuth and antimony thermopiles. In the propylthiouracil preparations, relative to control, time-to-peak tension increased from 288 ± 27 (mean ± SD) to 411 ± 25 msec ($P < 0.001$), dp/dt_{max} decreased from 38.3 ± 9.5 to 20.4 ± 3.5 $g \cdot mm^{-2}$/sec ($P < 0.001$), and peak developed tension decreased from 6.11 ± 1.75 to 4.64 ± 0.89 $g \cdot mm^{-2}$ ($P < 0.05$). In the propylthiouracil preparations, initial heat was significantly ($P < 0.001$) reduced by 27 or 43% when normalized to peak twitch tension or tension-time integral, respectively. In experiments where the papillary muscles were tetanized, the slope of the linear function of total activity-related heat versus tension-time integral was decreased by 43% ($P < 0.001$) in the propylthiouracil preparations, indicating an improved economy of isometric tension maintenance. The predominant myosin isoenzyme of the left ventricular wall, as well as the papillary muscle myocardium, was the V_3 variety in the propylthiouracil animals, in contrast to V_1 in the controls. Myofibrillar actomyosin calcium-magnesium-stimulated adenosine triphosphatase activity was significantly ($P < 0.02$) decreased from 55 ± 18 (control) to 31 ± 8 nmol inorganic phosphate ion/mg·min (propylthiouracil). Correspondingly, the myofibrillar myosin calcium-stimulated adenosine triphosphatase activity was also significantly ($P < 0.01$) decreased from 294 ± 98 (control) to 85 ± 25 nmol inorganic phosphate ion/mg·min (propylthiouracil). The results give evidence of (1) increased economy of force generation and maintenance in propylthiouracil myocardium, which is paralleled by (2) structural changes of myosin (shifts in the isoenzyme pattern), and (3) associated changes of myofibrillar adenosine triphosphatase activity. We conclude that the observed myothermal data reflect slowed crossbridge cycling in propylthiouracil myocardium, which must not necessarily be interpreted as being detrimental, in view of the increased economy of force generation. **(*Circ Res 56: 78–86, 1985*)**

A POSITIVE correlation has been observed between contractile protein adenosine triphosphatase (ATPase) activity and shortening velocity across species in skeletal muscle (Barany, 1967) and as a function of age in the myocardium (Alpert et al., 1967). These observations were confirmed for the myocardium, using different species and a variety of temperatures (Delcayre and Swynghedauw, 1975; Hamrell and Low, 1978). The experiments relating contractile protein ATPase activity and mechanical V_{max} were extended to include cardiac hypertrophy secondary to pressure overload (Chandler et al., 1967; Alpert et al., 1974; Medugorac and Jacob, 1976; Hamrell and Alpert, 1977; Alpert and Mulieri, 1977; Jacob et al., 1977, 1980, 1983; Maughan et al., 1979). Furthermore, increases of both parameters due to experimentally induced hyperthyroidism have been reported (Goodkind et al., 1974; Yazaki and Raben, 1975; Banerjee et al., 1976; Rovetto et al., 1972). No significant increase of myosin ATPase activity was observed when thyroxine was administered to young rats, which, under normal conditions, exhibit a high level of cardiac myosin ATPase activity (Yazaki and Raben, 1975; Szabó et al., 1979). Decreases of myocardial contractile protein ATPase activity and mechanical V_{max} were observed in hypothyroid rats (Buccino et al., 1967; Korecky and Beznak, 1971; Yazaki and Raben, 1975; Strauer and Schulze, 1976; Hoh et al., 1977; Pope et al., 1980; Schwartz et al., 1981; Ebrecht et al., 1982).

These studies lead to the hypothesis that the intrinsic enzymatic properties of actomyosin regulate the velocity of muscle shortening, although the in vitro measured myosin ATPase activity need not necessarily reflect the true conditions in vivo. This problem was recently reviewed in detail (Scheuer and Bhan, 1979). To answer the question whether the general parallelism between biochemical and mechanical data is founded upon a causal connection, studies are required which link the biophysical and biochemical parameters in living muscle preparations.

Recently, a rapid myothermal technique was used to demonstrate that the tension-dependent heat per unit tension during an isometric contraction of rabbit papillary muscle is decreased by pressure overload and increased by thyrotoxicosis (Alpert and Mulieri, 1980, 1982; Alpert et al., 1979). In this method, measurements of liberated energy are utilized to distinguish between alterations of excitation-contraction coupling and intrinsic chemomechanical transduction economy of the contractile proteins in vivo. Thus, in the rabbit myocardium, the economy of force generation is inversely related to the contractile protein ATPase activity. The goal of the present study was to extend these observations to the rat myocardium to test the hypothesis that the economy of force development is inversely related to contractile protein ATPase activity. In these experiments, we exploit the sensitivity of the rat myocardium to the thyroid status where decreases in circulating thyroxine produce dramatic changes in contractile protein ATPase.

Because it has been suggested, recently, that changes in ATPase activity rely on structural changes of heavy chains of myosin (Hoh et al., 1977; Lompré et al., 1979; Pope et al., 1980; Rupp, 1982; Litten et al., 1982), we also analyzed the myosin isoenzyme pattern so that correlations between structural and functional data could be obtained.

Methods

Definition of Heat Terms

Total heat (T) is the sum of total activity-related heat (T_A) and basal heat (B). T_A is the sum of initial heat and recovery heat (Alpert and Mulieri, 1982). Initial heat is the heat production arising from calcium cycling (TIH—the tension-independent heat) plus crossbridge cycling (TDH—the tension-dependent heat). The recovery heat (R) arises from the metabolic resynthesis of high energy compounds from ADP. The ratio of recovery to initial heat (R:I) is the recovery ratio.

Animals and Preparations

All experiments were performed on left ventricular papillary muscles of rats obtained from a colony of Wistar-Kyoto rats maintained at the University of Vermont. The experimental animals were housed individually, and hypothyroidism was induced by adding 0.8 mg/ml propylthiouracil (PTU) to the drinking water over a period of 3 weeks. The treatment was started when the rats were between 6 and 7 weeks old. In a recent paper (Holubarsch et al., 1982), the methods, procedure of sacrifice, and papillary muscle preparation are described in detail.

Thermopile and Thermal Measurements

The exact details of producing and calibrating antimony-bismuth planar thermopiles were described previously (Mulieri et al., 1977). The experiments of the present study were performed on three different thermopiles which had the same design and exhibited almost equal values of temperature sensitivity (1.238 mV/°C, 1.311 mV/°C, 1.325 mV/°C) and heat loss coefficient (0.535 mcal/°C.s, 0.546 mcal/°C.s, 0.590 mcal/°C.s). The temperature sensitivity was evaluated according to the method of Hill and Woledge (1962), while heat loss coefficient was determined by a modification (Mulieri et al., 1977) of the method of Kretzschmar and Wilkie (1972). The voltage output of the thermopile was amplified by a galvanometer (Kipp, A 80) and a twin phototube (RCA 920). The signals from the galvanometer and the capacitance-type, isometric force transducer were displayed on a Tektronix 5103N oscilloscope and a chart recorder (Gould-Brush 2400).

For heat measurements, the Krebs-Ringer solution was drained; during that procedure, premoisturized, and temperature-equilibrated gas was admitted at the top of the chamber to avoid contamination by room air.

Experimental Procedure

During the 2-hour equilibration period, the muscle preparation was stimulated at 12/min about 20% above threshold. The optimum length (l_o) was found by increasing the muscle length in small steps (0.1–0.05 mm). To define resting tension, the muscle was released by 1.5 mm to establish mechanical zero. When steady state conditions were reached at l_o, the chamber was drained, and temperature and tension signals were recorded synchronously during repetitive stimulation at different paper speeds for analyzing initial heat, as described below. For the analysis of total activity-related heat, stimulation was stopped, and the decline of the temperature signal (cool-off curve after activity) was recorded until the signal was constant. This baseline represents the resting temperature. Under these resting conditions, the thermopile, including the preparation and adhering Krebs-Ringer solution, was heated by infra-red emitting diodes, and cool-off curves were recorded (Mulieri et al., 1977). This procedure was repeated three times, and the time constants of the cool-off curves, after infra-red heating, were analyzed by a computerized nonlinear least squares method. These time constants were used for calculating initial heat (see below).

To analyze the basal heat rate, we partially filled the chamber to submerge the lower part of the frame of the thermopile. This allowed the achievement of temperature-equilibration. The muscle preparation remained in the temperature-equilibrated moisturized gas environment. After a steady state rest period of 20 minutes, the muscle preparation and thermopile were submerged abruptly, and the deflection in temperature trace was taken as the resting temperature. The basal heat rate was determined from this deflection and the heat loss characteristics of the muscle and system. Resting tension was determined at this point, as described above.

Heat Calculations

The recorded temperature changes were converted into heat values as follows. Initial heat was calculated as the product of the peak temperature difference, the cool off constant, τ, and the heat loss coefficient (Alpert and Mulieri, 1982). Peak temperature difference corrected for heat loss was evaluated by extrapolating the cool off curve of the preceding twitch and measuring the temperature difference between the extrapolated curve and the peak temperature signal (arrows, Fig. 1). The shape of the extrapolated line was obtained by omitting the stimulus and recording the cool-off after the last twitch response in the series and then translating that curve back to the previous falling temperature excursion (see dotted lines on Fig. 1). The time constant, τ, was evaluated by means of a nonlinear least squares exponential fitting program

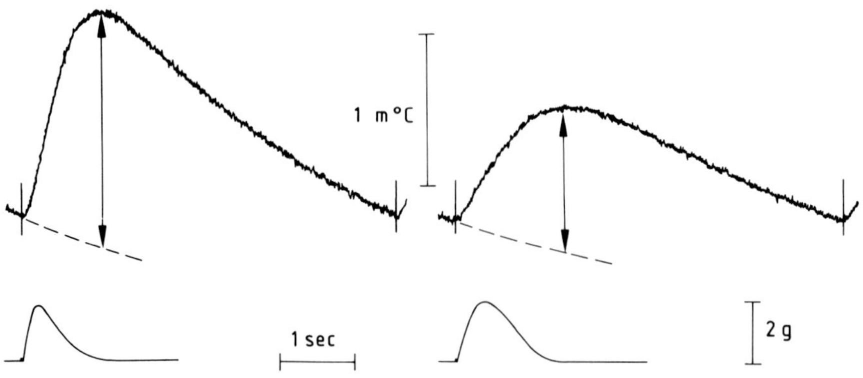

FIGURE 1. *Original recordings of temperature signal (upper trace) and isometric force signal (lower trace) of control rat myocardium (left) and PTU-treated rat myocardium (right). The arrows indicate the temperature difference between the peak temperature signal and the extrapolated temperature signal of the preceding twitch for analysis of initial heat (see Methods).*

from the cool-off curves after infra-red heating. The heat loss coefficient was defined as previously described (Kretzschmar and Wilkie, 1972; Mulieri et al., 1977). The total activity-related heat was calculated from the area between temperature base line during rest and the oscillating temperature signal during the steady state period of activity for one stimulus interval (Bugnard, 1934; Alpert and Mulieri, 1982; Holubarsch et al., 1982). Since the total activity-related heat is the sum of initial heat and recovery heat, the recovery:initial heat ratio equals $(T_A\text{-}I)/I$.

The temperature decrease when submerging the resting muscle preparation abruptly was multiplied by the heat loss coefficient and yielded the resting heat rate.

Experiments with Iodoacetic Acid (IAA) in N_2-CO_2 Atmosphere

In order to protect ourselves from the possibility that initial heat is contaminated with recovery heat, we performed experiments in control preparations incubated in IAA and 95% N_2-5% CO_2. In contrast to rabbit myocardium (Alpert and Mulieri, 1982), rat myocardium cannot tolerate long periods (90 minutes) of 0.1 mM IAA incubation. Therefore, the muscle preparations were soaked in 0.25 mM IAA and 95% N_2-5% CO_2 solution, for 5 minutes, and then drained and allowed to equilibrate for an additional 10 minutes. In untreated muscle in a single twitch following a 15-minute period without stimulation, the developed peak tension and initial heat per unit developed tension were not significantly different from values of paced twitches. The IAA and N_2-CO_2 treatment resulted in a 17 ± 9% reduction in peak developed tension. In this preparation, the recovery heat diminished by 89% ± 15%. The comparison of the ratio of measured initial heat to peak developed tension under control and IAA plus N_2-CO_2 conditions indicated that only 3.3 ± 2.5% (range between 1 and 6%) of initial heat represents contamination by recovery heat.

Measurements of Tension-Dependent Heat

The initial heat is the sum of the tension-dependent heat (TDH-crossbridge cycle) and tension-independent heat (TIH-calcium cycle). In order to separate TDH from TIH, the hyperosmotic mannitol method was used in half of all experiments (Hill, 1965). The muscle was incubated in 2- or 1.75-fold hyperosmotic Krebs-Ringer solution to abolish developed tension (Alpert and Mulieri, 1977, 1980; Holubarsch et al., 1982). During this treatment, lasting 20 minutes (2-fold mannitol) or 30 minutes (1.75-fold mannitol), no stimulus was applied to the muscle. When the stimulus was reapplied and developed tension was less than 5% of maximum twitch tension, the muscle chamber was drained and the oscillating temperature signal was recorded. Tension-independent heat was analyzed in the same manner as described for initial heat. Tension-dependent heat is the difference between initial heat and tension-independent initial heat.

Tetanizing Experiments

We tetanized the preparations after submerging the preparations into a Krebs-Ringer solution containing 7.5 mM caffeine and 11 mM calcium for a period of 15 minutes and then applying different numbers of stimuli at a frequency of 3.5 Hz (Gibbs and Loiselle, 1978). The numbers of stimuli were 1, 2, 3, 4, and 5, and then were varied between 6 and 24 (Fig. 2). A planimeter was used to measure the tension-time integral and the temperature-time integral; the latter was converted into heat by multiplying by the heat loss coefficient.

Measurements of Myosin Isoenzymes

Pyrophosphate Gel Electrophoresis

The left ventricle (free wall and septum) from each of the hearts from which papillary muscles were taken was frozen in liquid nitrogen, powdered, and stored at −75°C. Pyrophosphate gel electrophoresis was carried on 25 mg of the left ventricle. In some instances, electrophoresis was also carried out on left ventricular papillary muscles (1–5 mg) (Fig. 4). This method is used to separate the myosin isoenzymes V_1, V_2, and V_3 from the supernatant of crude heart extracts and is based on the procedure described by Hoh et al. (1977). The pyrophosphate gels were then scanned with a laser beam densitometer of our own design having high spatial resolution (Brayden and Halpern, 1983).

Quantification of the Relative Amounts of Myosin Isoenzymes

A special method for quantifying the relative amounts of V_1, V_2, and V_3 from the densitometer tracing was developed because of the potential problem from the overlapping of V_1, V_2, and V_3 peaks. The overlap may lead to erroneous evaluations of the concentration of V_1 and V_3. The percent V_1 isoenzyme was calculated from densitometer traces using the following equation:

$$\%\ V_1 = A_{V1}/A_T,$$

where A_{V1} equals the area under the V_1 peak and A_T equals the total sum of areas under V_1, V_2, and V_3 peaks. The V_1 peak area (A_{V1}) was determined by weighing the paper which makes up half the V_1 peak area (side away

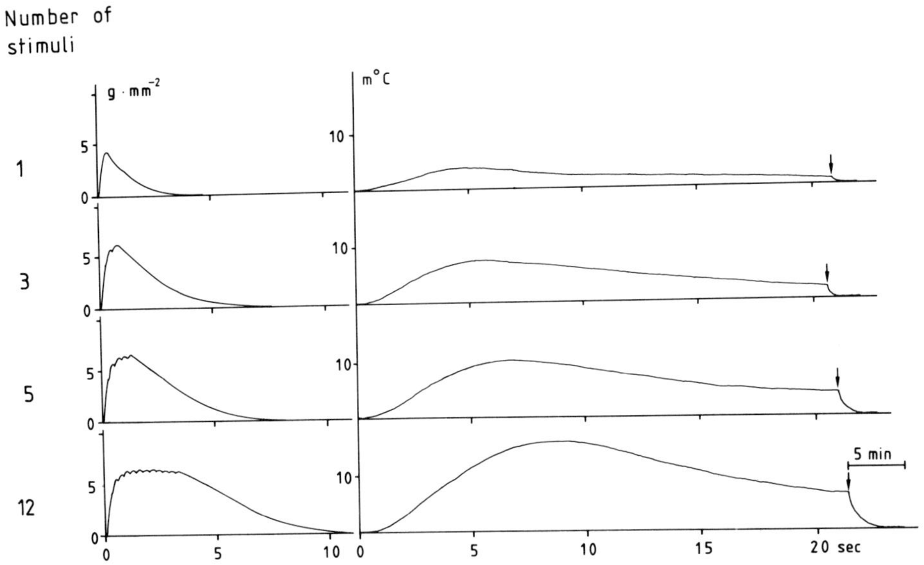

FIGURE 2. *Original recordings of force and temperature from the rat papillary muscle under conditions for producing tetanus. The preparations were incubated in caffeine (7.5 mM) and high calcium (11 mM) for 15 minutes without stimulation. After draining the chamber, different numbers of stimuli were applied at a frequency of 3.5 Hz. In the top trace, the response to one stimulus is shown as follows: the tension development is shown on the left and the temperature change on the right. In the two middle traces, the responses to three and five stimuli, respectively, are illustrated. In the bottom trace, 12 stimuli were applied. The arrows at the end of the temperature traces indicate a change in recording speed (note different time scales).*

from the V_2 peak) and multiplying by two. To obtain the half area, a line was drawn from the peak of V_1 through three points midway between the two sides of the upper portion of the peak where contamination by V_2 and V_3 isoenzymes was judged to be minimal. The total area was obtained by weighing the paper under the total scan of the V_1, V_2, and V_3 peaks. The percent V_3 was calculated in the same way as described above for V_1. Percent V_2, which is, in the models used in the present study, small and in some instances not measurable, was calculated indirectly by subtracting the areas of V_1 and V_3 from the total area.

Myofibrillar ATPase Activity

Myofibrillar Preparation

Cardiac myofibrils were prepared from the remaining left ventricle according to the following modification of the method of Pagani and Solaro (1984). All solutions used in the purification procedure contained the following protease inhibitors: 2 μg/ml pepstatin A (Sigma), 2 μg/ml leupeptin (Sigma), and 4 mM dichlorvos (serine protease inhibitor) (Bodwell and Meyer, 1981) (Vapona brand of 2,2-dichlorovinyl dimethyl phosphate from Shell Development Co.). The myofibrils were stored on ice overnight in 30 mM KCl, 30 mM imidazole (pH 7.0), 2 μg/ml leupeptin, 2 μg/ml pepstatin A, and 4 mM dichlorvos and used the next day to determine the myofibrillar ATPase activities.

Myofibrillar ATPase Activity Measurements

Myofibrillar actomyosin Ca^{++}-Mg^{++}-stimulated ATPase activity was measured in 30 mM KCl, 25 mM imidazole (pH 7.0), 7.5 mM $MgCl_2$, 5.0 mM Na_2ATP, 10 mM NaN_3, 1.0 mM $CaCl_2$, 0.5 mM EGTA [free Ca^{++} concentration = 3.35×10^{-4} M, using the program of Maughan et al. (1979)]. Myofibrillar myosin Ca^{++}-stimulated ATPase was assayed in 450 mM KCl, 51 mM imidazole (pH 7.5), 10 mM $CaCl_2$, 5 mM Na_2ATP, and 5 mM NaN_3. Assays were carried out at 21°C, and reactions were stopped by the addition of cold $HClO_4$. Precipitated protein was removed by centrifugation, and inorganic phosphate levels were determined by modified Fiske-Subbarow method (1925).

Myofibrillar ATPase assays were also carried out on myofibrils from fresh WKY rat heart (not frozen or stored). Under these circumstances, the myofibrillar ATPase activity was comparable to the myofibrils from frozen hearts.

Statistics

Unless stated otherwise, values are given as mean ±SD. Unpaired and paired Student's *t*-test was used to determine significant differences. Additionally, linear regression analysis was used, and the correlation coefficient was determined (Snedecor, 1956). A *P* value <0.05 was taken as statistically significant.

Results

Body and Heart Weight

The body weight at the time the animals were randomly selected for the control and treatment groups was 100 ± 11 g. Both groups received water and rat chow ad libitum. After 3 weeks, the weight of the control animals was 208 ± 29 g. The body weight of the experimental animals was reduced by 29% ($P < 0.001$) (Table 1). The heart weight and heart-to body-weight ratio for the control animals was 0.67 ± 0.04 g and 3.26 ± 0.42 g/kg, respectively. These were reduced in the PTU animals by 40% ($P < 0.001$) and 15% ($P < 0.05$), respectively (Table 1).

TABLE 1
Body Weight, Heart Weight, and Heart-to-Body Weight Ratio for Control and PTU-Treated Rat Preparations

Preparation	Body wt (g)	Heart wt (g)	Heart wt / Body wt (10^{-3})
Control ($n = 10$)	208 ± 29	0.67 ± 0.04	3.26 ± 0.42
PTU ($n = 40$)	147 ± 14†	0.40 ± 0.03†	2.77 ± 0.23*

* $P < 0.05$.
† $P < 0.001$.

TABLE 2
Mechanical Data of Control and PTU-Treated Rat Preparations

Preparation	Cross-sectional area (mm^2)	Optimum length (mm)	Peak twitch tension (g/mm^2)	Resting tension (g/mm^2)	Time-to-peak tension (msec)	dP/dt_{max} ($g/sec \cdot mm^2$)
Control ($n = 10$)	0.43 ± 0.13	6.00 ± 1.18	6.11 ± 1.75	1.15 ± 0.21	288 ± 27	38.3 ± 9.5
PTU ($n = 10$)	0.46 ± 0.07	6.11 ± 1.10	4.64 ± 0.89*	0.99 ± 0.25	411 ± 25†	20.4 ± 3.5†

* $P < 0.05$.
† $P < 0.001$.

Mechanical and Thermal Measurements

Time-to-peak tension was prolonged from 288 ± 27 to 411 ± 25 msec ($P < 0.001$) in the PTU rats, whereas peak twitch tension was decreased from 6.11 ± 1.75 (control) to 4.64 ± 0.89 g/mm^2 (PTU) ($P < 0.05$). Maximum dP/dt decreased from 38.3 ± 9.5 in control to 20.4 ± 3.5 $g/mm^2 \cdot sec$ in the PTU preparations ($P < 0.001$) (Table 2; Fig. 1). The active-to-resting tension ratio was 5.45 ± 1.68 and 4.85 ± 0.96 (NS) for the control and PTU papillary muscles, respectively.

Paced Twitches

Initial heat was 2.31 ± 0.69 in the control and 1.27 ± 0.25 mcal/g in the PTU preparations ($P < 0.001$) (Fig. 1; Table 3). Initial heat, normalized for peak twitch tension or the tension-time integral, was significantly ($P < 0.001$) diminished from 3.79 ± 0.42 in control to 2.75 ± 0.32 $\mu cal/g \cdot cm$ in PTU preparations, and from 6.76 ± 1.28 (control) to 3.85 ± 0.45 $\mu cal/g \cdot cm \cdot sec$ (PTU) ($P < 0.001$) (Table 3).

When recovery heat was taken into account, total activity-related heat per peak tension in the PTU preparations was not significantly different from the control (Table 3). In contrast, total activity-related heat per tension-time integral was significantly ($P < 0.05$) smaller in the PTU (8.60 ± 1.31 $\mu cal/g \cdot cm \cdot sec$) than in the control preparations (10.96 ± 2.40 $\mu cal/g \cdot cm \cdot sec$) (Table 3). The recovery to initial heat values were 0.63 ± 0.29 in control and 1.24 ± 0.23 in PTU preparations ($P < 0.001$) (Table 3).

The tension-independent heat as assessed by the hyperosmotic mannitol method was 0.154 ± 0.009 and 0.118 ± 0.025 mcal/g in the control and in PTU preparations, respectively ($P < 0.02$). Tension-dependent heat, normalized for peak twitch tension or tension-time integral, was depressed by 26% ($P < 0.01$) or 40% ($P < 0.01$), respectively, in the PTU preparations (Table 4).

Resting heat rate was reduced from 4.41 ± 1.19 mW/g in control to 3.68 ± 1.12 mW/g in PTU preparations ($n = 10$; NS).

Tetanic Contractions

The total activity-related heat was measured, along with the tension-time integral, where the tension-time integral was varied by changing the number of stimuli applied to the papillary muscle (Fig. 2). The correlation coefficients for the relation between total activity-related heat to tension-time integral varied between 0.96 and 0.99 as evaluated by linear regression analysis (Fig. 3). The slope of the linear regression equations was 43% ($P < 0.001$) lower in the PTU than the control preparations (Table 5).

Myosin Isoenzyme and Myofibrillar ATPase Analyses

Three-week treatment of PTU shifted the percent content of myosin V_1 in left ventricular wall myocardium from 85.0 ± 5.6% (control) to 3.9 ± 2.9% (PTU), while the myosin V_3 was increased from 6.6 ± 1.7% (control) to 90.4 ± 9.9% (PTU) (Table 5). Along with the shift in the myosin isozyme pattern,

TABLE 3
Myothermal Data of Control and PTU-Treated Rat Preparations

Preparation	Initial heat (mcal/g)	Recovery heat / Initial heat	Initial heat / Peak tension ($\mu cal/g \cdot cm$)	Initial heat / $\int \sigma \cdot t$ ($\mu cal/g \cdot cm \cdot sec$)	Total heat / Peak tension ($\mu cal/g \cdot cm$)	Total heat / $\int \sigma \cdot t$ ($\mu cal/g \cdot cm \cdot sec$)
Control ($n = 10$)	2.21 ± 0.69	0.63 ± 0.29	3.79 ± 0.42	6.76 ± 1.28	5.90 ± 0.84	10.96 ± 2.40
PTU ($n = 10$)	1.26 ± 0.25†	1.24 ± 0.23†	2.75 ± 0.32†	3.85 ± 0.45†	5.84 ± 0.89	8.60 ± 1.31*

* $P < 0.05$.
† $P < 0.001$.

TABLE 4
Tension-Dependent Heat (TDH) and Tension-Independent Heat (TIH) for Control (C) and PTU-Treated Rat Preparations

Preparation	TIH (mcal/g)	TDH (mcal/g)	TDH / Peak tension (μcal/g·cm)	TDH / $\int\sigma\cdot t$ (μcal/g·cm·sec)
Control ($n = 5$)	0.154 ± 0.009	1.97 ± 0.22	3.60 ± 0.42	5.90 ± 1.51
PTU ($n = 5$)	0.118 ± 0.025*	1.12 ± 0.24‡	2.65 ± 0.21†	3.52 ± 0.24†

* $P < 0.02$.
† $P < 0.01$.
‡ $P < 0.001$.

the myofibrillar actomyosin Ca^{++}-Mg^{++}-stimulated ATPase activity of the left ventricle was significantly ($P < 0.02$) decreased from 55 ± 17 (control) to 31 ± 8 nmol P_i/mg·min (PTU). Similarly, myofibrillar myosin Ca^{++}-stimulated ATPase activity was significantly ($P < 0.01$) decreased from 294 ± 98 (control) to 85 ± 25 nmol P_i/mg·min (PTU).

Before correlating the myosin isoenzyme pattern with heat data, it is necessary to ascertain that the isoenzyme pattern of the left ventricular wall myocardium corresponds to that of the papillary muscles. There is an excellent match between the percent values of all the myosin isoenzymes of the papillary muscle and the wall myocardium (Fig. 4). These data were obtained from a separate group of animals subjected to the identical treatment described in Methods.

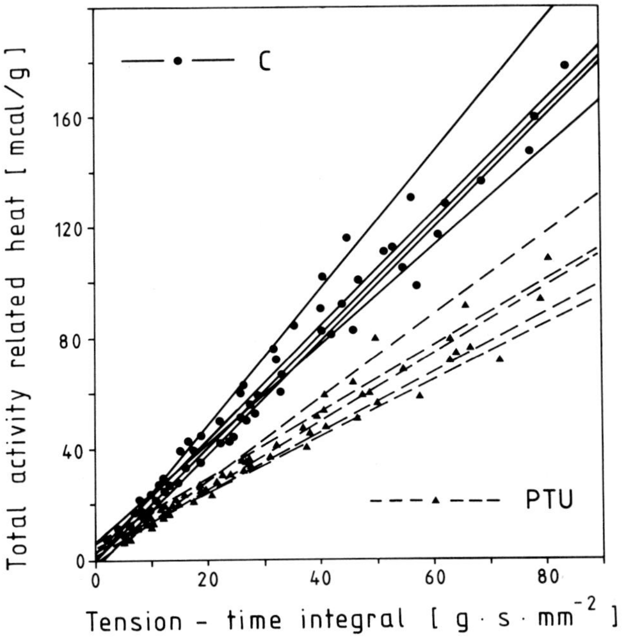

FIGURE 3. *The relationship of total activity-related heat and tension-time integral. Each line represents a separate experiment carried out under tetanizing conditions in which the tension-time integral is varied by changing the number of stimuli applied. The data are indicated by the following symbols: ●, control; ▲, PTU.*

Discussion

Comparison of Mechanics and Heat in Normal and Hypothyroid Rat Myocardium

The results of the present study demonstrate that a 3-week period of treatment by addition of PTU to the drinking water leads to an impairment of normal growth, diminished body weight, and reduced heart weight when compared to age-matched controls. The fact that growth of the heart is impaired more than that of the whole body is reflected in the reduced ratio between heart and body weight. These results are in good agreement with those of Minelli and Korecky (1969), Whitehorn (1971), and Loiselle et al. (1982), who induced hypothyroidism by hypophysectomy or application of a single dose of ^{131}I.

The effects of thyroid hormone deficiency on the contractile properties of the myocardium are also obvious. The 24% decrease of peak developed ten-

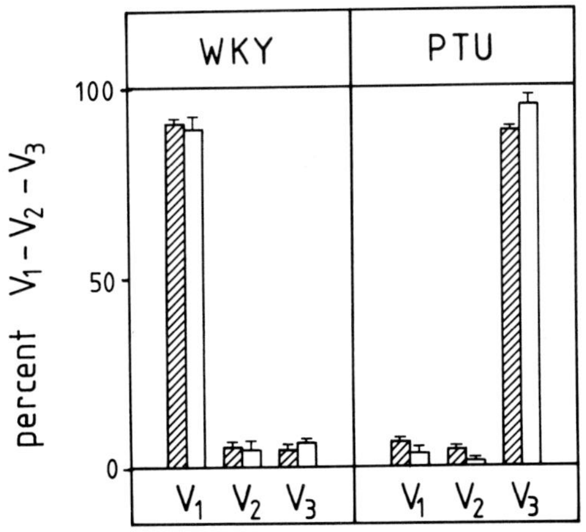

FIGURE 4. *Comparison between the content of V_1, V_2, and V_3 myosin isoenzymes of the rat myocardium from the left ventricle (cross-hatched columns) and left ventricular papillary muscles (white columns) of control WKY (left) and PTU-treated rats (right). Mean values ± SEM of percent content of V_1, V_2, and V_3 are given for five WKY and five PTU preparations, respectively. There was no significant difference between left ventricular wall and papillary muscle myocardium. Note, however, the dramatic change in isoenzyme distribution from control (WKY) to PTU preparations.*

TABLE 5
The Relationship between Total Activity-Related Heat (T_A) and Tension-Time Integral during Isometric Tetanus in Muscles with Varying Myosin Isoenzyme Ratios for Control (C) and PTU-Treated Rat Preparations

Preparation	Slope of T_A vs. $\int \sigma \cdot t$ (mcal/g/g·sec·mm^{-2})	Intercept (mcal/g)	Correlation coefficient	V_1 (%)	V_3 (%)
Control ($n = 5$)	2.09 ± 0.26	0.44 ± 3.90	0.98 ± 0.01	85.0 ± 5.6	6.5 ± 1.7
PTU ($n = 5$)	1.19 ± 0.19*	2.58 ± 3.00	0.99 ± 0.01	3.9 ± 2.9*	90.4 ± 9.9*

* $P < 0.001$.

sion in the PTU preparations is significant, and has already been shown in hypothyroidism (Buccino et al., 1967; Minelli and Korecky, 1969; Strauer and Schulze, 1976). In contrast to the latter papers, the prolongation of time-to-peak tension and the decrease of maximum rate of tension development were much more pronounced in the present study. This difference may be attributed to different experimental temperatures (37°C vs. 21°C). In the recent paper of Loiselle et al. (1982), an increase of peak-developed tension of papillary muscles from hypothyroid rats was found when hypothyroidism was induced by a single dose of ^{131}I in 1-year-old rats. These data are in contrast to all the papers cited above, and to our findings. The degree of hypothyroidism, as well as the age of the rats, may be responsible for these differences.

To acquire direct evidence on the process of ATP splitting in the intact myocardium during mechanical activity, the rapid myothermal method (Mulieri et al., 1977; Alpert and Mulieri, 1980, 1982) was applied to myocardium of normal and PTU rats. The heat liberated due to mechanical activity is analyzed in terms of I and T_A (T_A = initial plus recovery heat). Because legitimate objections may be raised against the experimental approach of separating initial and recovery heat by the Bugnard method, measurements were made using IAA treatment with an N_2-CO_2 atmosphere which, on the average, blocked recovery metabolism and heat by 89%. We found that initial heat, under these conditions, might have 3% (range 1–6%) contamination with recovery heat. This potential contamination does not influence our final conclusions.*

Heat liberated during a paced twitch was significantly reduced by PTU treatment, when I was related to peak twitch tension (Hill, 1965; Alpert and Mulieri, 1982) or tension-time integral (Gibbs and Gibson, 1970), or when T_A was related to tension-time integral. This indicates an improved economy of force generation. However, T_A per peak developed tension is not significantly different in PTU and control preparations. This lack of effect is brought about by the following two conditions: First, in control compared to PTU animals, a higher twitch tension is reached in a shorter time; thus control compared with PTU exhibits a significantly higher (24%) peak twitch tension, while there is no significant difference in the tension-time integral. Second, there was an increase in the recovery ratio from 0.63 in control to 1.24 in PTU rat myocardium, which has an off-setting effect on the decrease in initial heat. Accordingly, where T_A is normalized for peak twitch tension, there is no difference between the two groups of animals.

The difference in the R:I ratio for the normal and PTU preparations is of interest. We suggest an activity-related baseline shift, possibly due to alterations in average intracellular levels of ADP and calcium, which can explain the higher apparent R:I ratio in the PTU rat (Alpert and Mulieri, 1982). Alternatively, there may be a change in the energy cost of ATP resynthesis resulting from the treatment.

In order to evaluate how much of the observed differences between PTU and control rat myocardium are due to activation heat, i.e., excitation-contraction coupling, and to tension-dependent heat alterations, i.e., crossbridge cycling, the hyperosmotic mannitol method was used (Holubarsch et al., 1982). The 23% reduction of tension-independent heat in hypothyroid rat myocardium suggests that calcium release and uptake might be reduced. This could be explained by changed properties of the sarcoplasmic reticulum and/or sarcolemmal binding sites. It is interesting to note that Nayler et al. (1971) were able to verify reciprocal alterations of calcium uptake and binding by cardiac microsomal fractions in hyperthyroid dogs.

There is also a reduction in tension-dependent heat evident when tension-dependent heat is nor-

One could hypothesize that the difference between the recovery ratio of PTU myocardium (1.24) and that of control myocardium (0.63) results from an alteration in the time course of recovery heat. If it is assumed that the differences in the R:I ratios for the control (.63) and PTU (1.23) result from contamination of the initial heat by recovery heat in the control hearts, then to account for the differences in these rates, a contamination of 27% is needed. (R:I = (63 + 27)/(100 − 27) = 1.23. This value is four and one half times higher than the largest, and nine times greater than the average measured value of recovery heat contamination in IAA/N_2-CO_2, and, thus, represents an unlikely possibility.

malized for developed tension. A value of 3.60 ± 0.42 μcal/g·cm is calculated for control and 2.65 μcal/g·cm for PTU rat preparations (Table 4). These data indicate an improvement of economy of tension generation of the contractile proteins based on a change in the basic force generating process itself, i.e., crossbridge cycling. In a recent paper, Loiselle et al. (1982) show similar results by analyzing heat measurements on the basis of heat-stress relations: the slope of heat vs. stress is significantly decreased in hypothyroid myocardium when 1-year-old rats were made hypothyroid by ^{131}I. This finding is in good agreement with the demonstrated 26% decrease of tension-dependent heat in the PTU myocardium used in the present paper. However, Loiselle et al. reported increased activation heat, i.e., tension-independent heat, in their hypothyroid papillary muscles. Accordingly, the hypothyroid preparations of these authors showed an increase in peak developed tension when compared to controls. The differences in activation heat between the PTU preparations of the present paper and the hypothyroid preparations of Loiselle et al. (1982) may result from the following: (1) pharmacological vs. radioactive intervention, (2) the age of the rats, (3) the temperature at which the experiments were carried out, and (4) the method by which TIH was measured.

Heat vs. Myosin Isoenzymes and Myofibrillar ATPase

The present paper confirms the presence of the isoenzyme patterns shown by Hoh et al. (1977), Schwartz et al. (1981), and Ebrecht et al. (1982). In control myocardium of young rats, the V_1 variety is predominant, whereas in hypothyroid myocardium the predominant isoenzyme is the V_3 species. It was important to show that there were no significant differences of the myosin isoenzyme content in the myocardium of the papillary muscles and the left ventricular wall, as was also shown by Loiselle et al. (1982). This dramatic change of the isoenzyme pattern is associated with energetic changes, i.e., improved economy of force generation, on the one hand, and characteristic biochemical changes, i.e., slowed ATPase activity, on the other (see Results). The comparison demonstrates similar decreases in the PTU myocardium for heat per tension-time integral (43% reduction) and actomyosin ATPase activity (44% reduction), with associated changes in the isoenzyme pattern (shift from V_1 to V_3).

The parallels among changes in isoenzyme distribution, myofibrillar ATPase activity, and myothermal economy of the rat myocardium offer strong evidence for possible causal links between structural changes of myosin and functional changes in myosin ATPase and mechanical performance of the myocardium. Slowed mechanical V_{max} and lowered ATPase activity are manifestations of a slowed crossbridge cycling rate (Buccino et al., 1967; Strauer and Schulze, 1976; Schwartz et al., 1981; Ebrecht et al., 1982). The present demonstration of accompanying improved economy of force generation can be interpreted in terms of a combination of slowed cycling rate and an increased duration of the on-time of the crossbridge (Alpert and Mulieri, 1980).

In conclusion, the *fast* normal rat hearts seem to sacrifice economy of tension development for ability to eject blood at high velocity. Although the decreased economy of force development might have resulted in an increased myocardial oxygen demand, this is apparently compensated for by development of a more efficient production of ATP as manifested by the smaller R:I ratio in the euthyroid hearts (Table 3). The *slow* hypothyroid rat hearts, however, develop tension with high economy at the expense of speed. Under these conditions, the proposed oxygen demand for force development is low and can be met with a slower heart rate and velocity of shortening. Thus the normal rat heart is adapted for fast work, while the PTU rat heart is adapted for slow work.

Ch. Holubarsch greatly appreciates the support and advice of Prof. Dr. R. Jacob, Chairman, Institute of Physiology, University of Tubingen.

This work was presented in part at the 10th Heart Congress of the International Society for Heart Research, Moscow, U.S.S.R., September 1980 (Holubarsch et al., 1980).

This work was supported in part by U.S. Public Health Service Grants HL17592 and HL28001. The experimental part of this research was performed at the laboratory at the University of Vermont.

Ch. Holubarsch was supported by a fellowship from the Dr. Karl Kuhn-Stiftung, University of Tubingen. Present address: Department of Cardiology, University of Freiburg, Gugstellerstrass 55, 78 Freiburg, West Germany.

Address for reprints: Dr. N.R. Alpert, Department of Physiology and Biophysics, University of Vermont, Burlington, Vermont 05405.

Received February 17, 1984; accepted for publication October 3, 1984.

References

Alpert NR, Mulieri LA (1977) The partitioning of altered mechanics in hypertrophied heart muscle between the sarcoplasmic reticulum and the contractile apparatus by means of myothermal measurements. Basic Res Cardiol **72:** 153–159

Alpert NR, Mulieri LA (1980) The functional significance of altered tension dependent heat in thyrotoxic myocardial hypertrophy. Basic Res Cardiol **75:** 179–184

Alpert NR, Mulieri LA (1982) Increased myothermal economy of isometric force generation in compensated cardiac hypertrophy induced by pulmonary artery constriction in rabbit. A characterization of heat liberation in normal and hypertrophied right ventricular papillary muscles. Circ Res **50:** 491–500

Alpert NR, Gale HH, Taylor N (1967) The effect of age on contractile protein ATPase activity and the velocity of shortening. *In* Factors Influencing Myocardial Contractility, edited by RD Tanz, F Kaveler, J Roberts. New York, Academic Press, pp 127–133

Alpert NR, Hamrell BB, Halpern W (1974) Mechanical and biochemical correlates of cardiac hypertrophy. Circ Res **34/35** (suppl II): 71–82

Alpert NR, Mulieri LA, Litten RZ (1979) Functional significance of altered myosin adenosine triphosphatase activity in enlarged hearts. Am J Cardiol **44:** 947–953

Banerjee SK, Flink IL, Morkin E (1976) Enzymatic properties of native and N-ethylmaleimide-modified cardiac myosin from normal and thyrotoxic rabbits. Circ Res **39:** 319–326

Barany M (1967) ATPase activity of myosin correlated with speed of muscle shortening. J Gen Physiol **50:** 197–216

Bodwell JE, Meyer WL (1981) Purification and characterization of carboxypeptidase A from rat skeletal muscle. Biochemistry **20:** 2767–2777

Brayden JE, Halpern W (1983) A high spatial-resolution laser beam densitometer for quantitative analysis of polyacrylamide gels. Anal Biochem **130:** 9–13

Buccino RA, Spann JR Jr, Pool PE, Sonnenblick EH, Braunwald E (1967) Influence of the thyroid state on the intrinsic contractile properties and energy stores of the myocardium. J Clin Invest **46:** 1669–1682

Bugnard L (1934) The relation between total and initial heat in single muscle twitches. J Physiol **82:** 509–519

Chandler BM, Sonnenblick EH, Spann JF, Pool PE (1967) Association of depressed myofibrillar adenosine triphosphatase and reduced contractility in experimental heart failure. Circ Res **21:** 717–725

Delcayre C, Swynghedauw B (1975) A comparative study of heart myosin ATPase and light subunits from different species. Pflugers Arch **355:** 39–47

Ebrecht G, Rupp H, Jacob R (1982) Alterations of mechanical parameters in chemically skinned preparations of rat myocardium as a function of isoenzyme pattern of myosin. Basic Res Cardiol **77:** 220–234

Fiske CH, Subbarow Y (1925) The colorimetric determination of phosphorous. J Biol Chem **66:** 357–400

Gibbs CL, Gibson WR (1970) Effects of alterations in stimulus rate upon energy output, tension development and tension-time integral of cardiac muscle in rabbits. Circ Res **27:** 611–618

Gibbs C, Loiselle D (1978) The energy output of tetanized cardiac muscle: Species differences. Pflugers Arch **373:** 31–38

Goodkind MJ, Dambach GE, Thyrum PT, Luchi RJ (1974) Effect of thyroxine on ventricular myocardial contractility and ATPase activity in guinea pigs. Am J Physiol **226:** 66–72

Hamrell BB, Alpert NR (1977) The mechanical characteristics of hypertrophied rabbit cardiac muscle in the absence of congestive heart failure. Circ Res **40:** 20–25

Hamrell BB, Low RB (1978) The relationship of mechanical V_{max} to myosin ATPase activity in rabbit and marmot ventricular muscle. Pflugers Arch **377:** 119–124

Hill AV (1965) Trails and Trials in Physiology. London, E Arnold

Hill AV, Woledge RC (1962) An examination of absolute values in myothermic measurements. J Physiol **162:** 311–333

Hoh JFY, McGrath PA, Hale PT (1977) Electrophoretic analysis of multiple forms of rat cardiac myosin: Effects of hypophysectomy and thyroxine replacement. J Mol Cell Cardiol **10:** 1053–1076

Holubarsch C, Alpert NR, Goulette R, Mulieri LA (1980) Changes in energetic and mechanical behaviour of myocardium of propylthiouracil-treated rats. J Mol Cell Cardiol **12** (suppl 1): 60

Holubarsch C, Alpert NR, Goulette R, Mulieri LA (1982) Heat production during hypoxic contracture of rat myocardium. Circ Res **51:** 777–786

Jacob R, Ebrecht G, Kämmereit A, Medugorac I, Wendt-Gallitelli MF (1977) Myocardial function in different models of cardiac hypertrophy. An attempt at correlating mechanical, biochemical and morphological parameters. Basic Res Cardiol **72:** 160–166

Jacob R, Brenner B, Ebrecht G, Holubarsch C, Medugorac I (1980) Elastic and contractile properties of the myocardium in experimental cardiac hypertrophy of the rat. Methodological and pathophysiological considerations. Basic Res Cardiol **75:** 253–261

Jacob R, Ebrecht G, Holubarsch C, Rupp H, Kissling G (1983) Mechanics and energetics in cardiac hypertrophy as related to the isoenzyme pattern of myosin. *In* Perspectives in Cardiovascular Research: Myocardial Hypertrophy and Failure, vol 7, edited by NR Alpert. New York, Raven Press, pp 553–570

Korecky B, Beznak M (1971) Effect of thyroxine on growth and function of cardiac muscle. *In* Cardiac Hypertrophy, edited by NR Alpert. New York, Academic Press, pp 55–64

Kretzschmar KM, Wilkie DR (1972) A new method for absolute heat measurements, utilizing the Peltier effect. J Physiol (Lond) **224:** 18P–20P

Litten RZ III, Martin BJ, Low RB, Alpert NR (1982) Altered myosin isozyme pattern from pressure-overload and thyrotoxic hypertrophied rabbit hearts. Circ Res **50:** 856–864

Loiselle DS, Wendt IR, Hoh JFY (1982) Energetic consequences of thyroid-modulated shifts in ventricular isomyosin distribution in the rat. J Muscle Res Cell Motil **3:** 5–23

Lompré AM, Schwartz K, d'Albis A, Lacombe G, Van Thiem N, Swynghedauw B (1979) Myosin isoenzyme redistribution in chronic heart overload. Nature **282:** 105–107

Maughan DM, Low E, Litten R III, Brayden J, Alpert NR (1979) Calcium-activated muscle from hypertrophied rabbit hearts. Mechanical and correlated biochemical changes. Circ Res **44:** 279–287

Medugorac I, Jacob R (1976) Concentration and adenosinetriphosphatase activity of left ventricular actomyosin in Goldblatt rats during compensatory stage of hypertrophy. Hoppe Seylers Zeitschrift Physiol Chemie **357:** 1495–1503

Minelli R, Korecky B (1969) Effect of growth hormone and thyroxine on isometric contractile mechanics of cardiac muscle. Can J Physiol Pharmacol **47:** 545–552

Mulieri LA, Luhr G, Trefry J, Alpert NR (1977) Metal-film thermopiles for use with rabbit right ventricular papillary muscles. Am J Physiol **233:** C146–C156

Nayler WG, Merrillees NCR, Chipperfield D, Kurtz JB (1971) Influence of hyperthyroidism on the uptake and binding of calcium by cardiac microsomal fractions and on mitochondrial structure. Cardiovasc Res **5:** 469–482

Pagani ED, Solaro RJ (1984) Methods for measuring functional properties of sarcoplasmic reticulum and myofibrils in small samples of myocardium. *In* Methods in Pharmacology, vol 5, edited by A Schwartz. New York, Plenum Press, pp 49–69

Pope B, Hoh JFY, Weeds A (1980) The ATPase activities of rat cardiac myosin isoenzymes. FEBS Lett **118:** 205–208

Rovetto MJ, Hjalmarson AC, Morgan HE, Barrett MJ, Goldstein RA (1972) Hormonal control of cardiac myosin adenosine triphosphatase in the rat. Circ Res **31;** 397–409

Rupp H (1982) Polymorphic myosin as the common determinant of myofibrillar ATPase in different haemodynamic and thyroid states. Basic Res Cardiol **77:** 34–46

Scheuer J, Bhan AK (1979) Cardiac contractile proteins. Circ Res **46:** 1–12

Schwartz K, Lecarpentier Y, Martin JL, Lompré AM, Mercadier JJ, Swynghedauw B (1981) Myosin isoenzymic distribution correlates with speed of myocardial contraction. J Mol Cell Cardiol **13:** 1071–1075

Snedecor GW (1956) Statistical Methods, Iowa State University Press, Iowa

Strauer BE, Schulze W (1976) Experimental hypothyroidism: Depression of myocardial contractile function and hemodynamics and their reversibility by substitution with thyroid hormones. Basic Res Cardiol **71:** 624–644

Szabó J, Nosztray K, Takács J, Szegi J (1979) Thyroxine-induced cardiomegaly: Assessment of nucleic acid, protein content and myosin ATPase of rat heart. Acta Physiol Academiae Scientiarum Hungaricae, **54:** 69–79

Whitehorn WV (1971) Effects of hypophyseal hormones on cardiac growth and function. *In* Cardiac Hypertrophy, edited by NR Alpert. New York, Academic Press, pp 27–37

Yazaki Y, Raben MS (1975) Effect of the thyroid state on the enzymatic characteristics of cardiac myosin. A difference in behavior of rat and rabbit cardiac myosin. Circ Res **36:** 208–215

INDEX TERMS: Myocardium • Crossbridges • Economy • Hypothyroidism • Myosin isoenzymes • Heat measurements • Thermodynamics

A Dihydropyridine (Bay k 8644) That Enhances Calcium Currents in Guinea Pig and Calf Myocardial Cells

A New Type of Positive Inotropic Agent

Gunter Thomas, Minn Chung, and Charles J. Cohen

From the Institute of Pharmacology, Bayer AG, Wuppertal, Federal Republic of Germany, and the Miles Institute for Preclinical Pharmacology, New Haven, Connecticut

SUMMARY. Bay k 8644 is a structural analog of nifedipine with positive inotropic activity. The mechanism of drug action was evaluated by measuring the effects of Bay k 8644 on twitch tension, action potential configuration, and calcium channel currents in myocardial cells. Bay k 8644 increases twitch tension in guinea pig atria without changing the time course of tension development. The drug does not occlude the effect of isoproterenol on twitch tension. The effects of Bay k 8644 on atrial twitch tension are highly dependent on the frequency of stimulation. Maximal inotropic effects are observed at ~0.5 Hz, but no inotropic effect occurs at 0.003 Hz (a rested-state contraction). Since positive inotropic effects only occur with frequent electrical stimulation, they are not due to an intracellular action or to mechanisms that elevate cell calcium in quiescent muscle, such as inhibition of the Na,K-ATPase. Bay k 8644 increases the action potential duration of calf ventricular muscle and Purkinje fibers. Effects on action potential duration are occluded by 1 μM nisoldipine, which specifically blocks calcium channels. The interaction of Bay k 8644 with calcium channels in calf Purkinje fibers was studied using the two-microelectrode voltage clamp technique. Strontium was used as a charge carrier to minimize current through calcium-activated channels and to avoid changes in calcium conductance due to changes in intracellular calcium. Bay k 8644 increases strontium currents and alters the time- and voltage-dependence of channel opening. The greatest percent increase in strontium current occurs for weak depolarizations. For strong depolarizations, strontium current is increased most at the beginning of a test pulse. The drug-induced changes in calcium channel gating are inconsistent with a calcium- or cyclic adenosine monophosphate-mediated effect, and indicate a novel mechanism of action on calcium channels. Thus, Bay k 8644 is the first positive inotropic agent shown to act specifically and directly on calcium channels. **(*Circ Res 56: 87–96, 1985*)**

CALCIUM channels play an important role in excitation-contraction coupling in cardiac and vascular smooth muscle. Agents that block these channels produce vasodilation and depress cardiac contractility. The most potent and specific of the Ca^{++} channel blockers are the 1,4-dihydropyridines, typified by nifedipine (Vater et al., 1972). Recently, this laboratory reported on a nifedipine-derivative that acts as a positive inotropic agent (Schramm et al., 1983a, 1983b). The drug, Bay k 8644 (shown in Fig. 1), acts as a competitive antagonist of nifedipine in contractility experiments, suggesting that it acts by increasing Ca^{++} influx through voltage-gated Ca^{++} channels (Schramm et al., 1983a, 1983b). Other agents are known to exert positive inotropic effects by increasing Ca^{++} currents, but some of them, such as the cardiac glycosides, increase Ca^{++} currents indirectly by increasing intracellular Ca^{++} (Marban and Tsien, 1982; Lederer and Eisner, 1982). Consequently, tension measurements alone cannot define the primary site of drug action. For this reason, we have investigated the mechanism of drug action in greater detail by correlating the mechanical and electrical effects of Bay k 8644 on myocardial cells.

Four different categories of drug action were tested for by measuring the effects of Bay k 8644 on twitch tension, action potential configuration, and Ca^{++} channel currents: (1) an intracellular effect, such as increasing the Ca^{++} sensitivity of the myofibrils or altering Ca^{++} uptake and release by the sarcoplasmic reticulum; (2) elevation of cell Na^+, which results in increased cell Ca^{++} due to Na-Ca exchange; (3) a direct effect on Ca^{++} channels, resulting in increased Ca^{++} influx; and (4) prolongation of the action potential duration by an effect on Na^+ or K^+ channels, which indirectly increases current through Ca^{++} channels or increases Ca^{++} release from the sarcoplasmic reticulum. We found that Bay k 8644 directly interacts with Ca^{++} channels to promote Ca^{++} entry. No other site of action was detected. The drug represents a new type of positive inotropic agent because it affects Ca^{++} channels in a unique way.

Preliminary reports of parts of this work have

been published previously (Thomas et al., 1983a, 1983b; Cohen and Chung, 1984).

Methods

Preparations

Mechanical studies were performed on guinea pig left atria. Pirbright-white guinea pigs (250-300 g) of either sex were killed by a blow to the head. Electrophysiological experiments were performed on calf ventricular trabeculae or Purkinje fibers. Calf hearts were obtained from a local slaughterhouse and transported to the laboratory in ice-cold physiological saline. Voltage clamp experiments were performed on short segments of Purkinje fibers (~200 μm in diameter and 0.5–1.5 mm long) obtained from either ventricle.

Twitch Tension Measurements

Left atria were separated from the ventricle, suspended in an organ bath, and maintained under a constant resting tension of 0.5–1.0 g. Square pulse field stimuli were 2 msec and 16V (~2.5× threshold). Contractions were measured isometrically with Stratham UC2 strain gauges and recorded with a chart recorder (Hellige) and digital storage oscilloscope (Vuko VKS 22-16).

Voltage Clamp Measurements

Two microelectrode voltage clamp experiments were performed as previously described (Kass et al., 1979). Command pulses were rounded with a time constant of 100 μsec to reduce cell damage. Membrane current and voltage were filtered with an 8-pole low pass Bessel filter (Frequency Devices) and recorded with an LSI 11/23 computer. Cut-off frequencies and sampling rates are indicated in the appropriate figure legends. In order to equate membrane current with Ca^{++} channel current, all current pathways other than Ca^{++} channels must be blocked or inactivated. In particular, the transient outward and delayed rectifier currents must be blocked. Previous studies have shown that these currents can be minimized by loading the fibers with Cs^+ by using nystatin (Marban, 1981) or by injecting quaternary ammonium salts, such as tetrabutylammonium (Kass et al., 1982). We used a modification of these techniques: Cs^+ was injected into the fibers under voltage clamp using current-passing microelectrodes filled with 2.5 M Cs acetate plus 1.0 M CsCl. Cs^+ salts were used instead of tetrabutylammonium salts because they have a higher solubility and ionic mobility, so that outward currents could be passed more readily with unbeveled micropipettes. Cs^+ was iontophoresed into the fibers until block of outward currents was maximal (~15 minutes). In addition, extracellular Ca^{++} and K^+ were replaced by Sr^{++} and Cs^+ (see composition of solutions below). The Ca^{++}-dependent transient outward is only weakly activated by Sr^{++} (Siegelbaum and Tsien, 1980; Coraboeuf and Carmeliet, 1982). The use of Sr^{++} as a charge carrier also allowed us to determine whether drugs directly affect Ca^{++} channels (see Results).

Solutions and Drugs

Tension measurements were conducted in Krebs-Henseleit solution containing (mM): NaCl, 118; KCl, 4.8; $CaCl_2$, 1.8; $MgSO_4$, 1.2; KH_2PO_4, 1.2; $NaHCO_3$, 25; glucose, 10; pH, 7.4. Solutions were gassed with 95% O_2, 5% CO_2 and maintained at 30°C. Action potential measurements were made in (mM): NaCl, 150; KCl, 4; $CaCl_2$, 1.8; $MgCl_2$, 0.5; HEPES, 10; glucose, 5; pH, 7.4. Temperature was maintained at 35 ± 1°C. Voltage clamp experiments were conducted in (mM): NaCl, 134; CsCl, 20; $SrCl_2$, 5.4; $MgCl_2$, 0.5; HEPES, 10; glucose, 5; pH, 7.4. Temperature was maintained at 30 ± 1°C. Solutions for electrophysiological experiments were gassed with 100% O_2. Changes in divalent cation composition were made without compensating for the change in tonicity.

Bay k 8644 is methyl 1,4-dihydro-2,6-dimethyl-3-nitro-4-(2-trifluoromethylphenyl)-pyridine-5-carboxylate, and its structure is given in Figure 1. The structural formula for nifedipine is also shown to illustrate the close structural analogy of these compounds. Bay k 8644, nitrendipine (Bay e 5009), and nisoldipine (Bay k 5552) are all products of Bayer AG. They were dissolved in 40% dimethyl sulfoxide (DMSO) or polyethylene glycol 400 (Baker). Final solvent concentrations in these experiments were <0.03%. The solvents have no effect on Ca^{++} channel currents (Kass, 1982) or twitch tension at those low concentrations. Sodium vapor lights were used during experiments with dihydropyridines because the compounds are light sensitive. Isoproterenol sulfate was obtained from Boehringer Ingelheim.

Results

Positive Inotropic Effects

The effect of Bay k 8644 on twitch tension in guinea pig atria is shown in the top panel of Figure 2. Twitch tension is approximately doubled after a 5-minute exposure to 280 nM Bay k 8644, with little change in the time course of tension development. Bay k 8644 and elevated external Ca^{++} have similar effects on twitch tension (middle panel). In contrast, the β-adrenoceptor agonist, isoproterenol, shortens the time-to-peak tension and speeds the rate of relaxation (bottom panel). These results suggest that Bay k 8644 is not a sympathomimetic agent. Likewise, the positive inotropic effect of Bay k 8644 is unaffected by propranolol, a β-adrenoceptor antagonist (Thomas et al., 1983b).

Figure 3 further contrasts the inotropic effects of Bay k 8644 and β-adrenoceptor agonists. This figure shows that maximally effective doses of Bay k 8644 do not occlude the effect of isoproterenol on twitch tension. 1 μM Bay k 8644 was a maximally effective dose because increasing the concentration to 3 μM did not have an additional effect on tension. However, 10 nM isoproterenol further increased twitch tension. This result suggests that the two drugs do

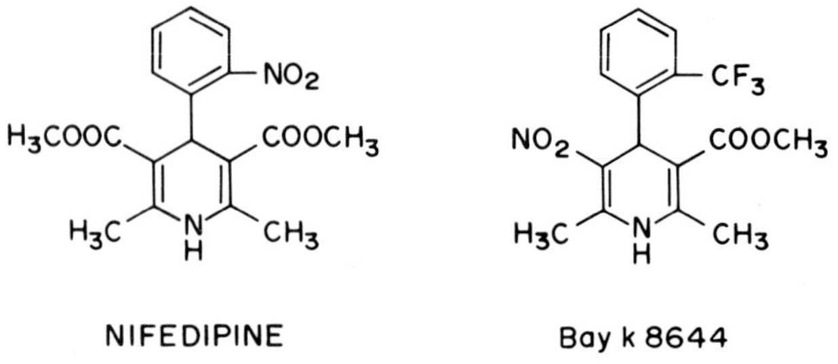

FIGURE 1. *Structure of nifedipine (Bay a 1040) and Bay k 8644.*

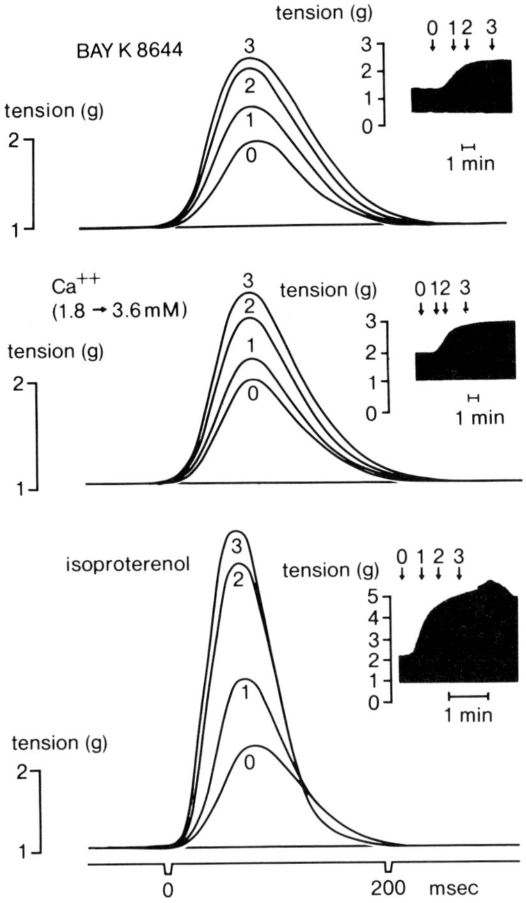

FIGURE 2. *Effect of Bay k 8644, increased Ca⁺⁺, and isoproterenol on twitch tension in guinea pig atria. The effects of each agent are shown on a slow time scale in the inset. The time course of single contractions during the development of the inotropic effect is superimposed for the times indicated in the insert. 1.0 Hz stimulation in all three experiments. Top panel: effect of 280 nM Bay k 8644; middle panel: effect of increasing external Ca⁺⁺ from 1.8 to 3.6 mM; bottom panel: effect of 300 nM isoproterenol. The experiments were performed on three different preparations. See text for further details.*

not share a common mechanism of action. It also indicates that the response to Bay k 8644 had a maximum that was not due to a mechanical limitation.

The positive inotropic effect of Bay k 8644 was studied under a wide range of concentrations and stimulation rates. Figure 4 shows that Bay k 8644 is a very potent positive inotropic agent during 1 Hz stimulation. Increases in cardiac contractility are consistently produced by 10 nM drug, and maximal effects are produced at 1 μM.

The inotropic effects of Bay k 8644 were evaluated in mammalian atrial cells, because insight into the mechanism of drug action is readily obtained from the dependence of inotropy on stimulation rate in this tissue. In these cells, the first contraction after a long rest period (a rested-state contraction) should be insensitive to agents that act primarily on Ca^{++} channels, but these contractions are enhanced by

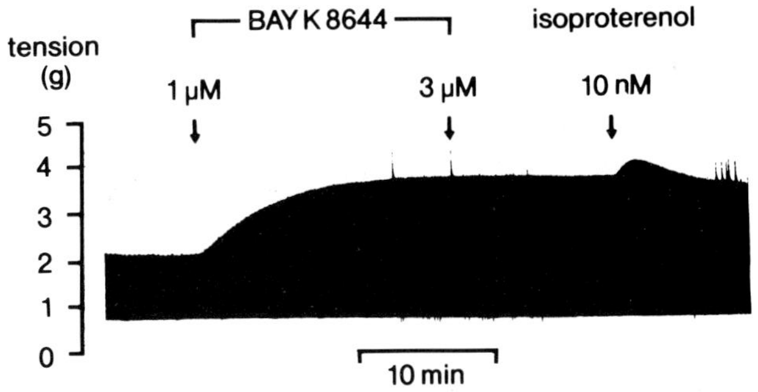

FIGURE 3. *Combined effect of isoproterenol and a maximally effective dose of Bay k 8644 on twitch tension in guinea pig atria: twitch tension was recorded during continuous stimulation at 1.0 Hz. The tissue was successively exposed to 1 μM Bay k 8644, 3 μM Bay k 8644, and 3 μM Bay k 8644 plus 10 nM isoproterenol at the times indicated by the arrows. Longer-lasting responses to isoproterenol were observed in other experiments in which oxidation of the drug was inhibited or when higher drug concentrations were used. However, higher doses of isoproterenol usually produced arrhythmias.*

positive inotropic agents that alter intracellular Ca^{++} release or load the cell with Ca^{++} during rest (see the discussion section for references). This behavior is illustrated in Figures 5 and 6.

The upper panels of Figure 5 show twitch tension when an atrium was rested for 10 minutes and then stimulated at 1.0 Hz. In each panel, a large rested-state contraction was followed by smaller contractions that progressively increased with further stimulation. The left panel shows the control response. The middle panel shows that 830 nM nitrendipine depresses steady state twitch tension for 1.0 Hz stimulation, but does not alter the rested-state contraction. In contrast, elevating external Ca^{++} in the

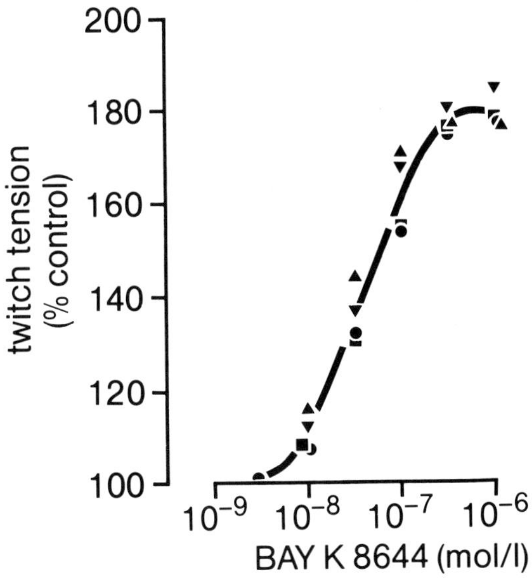

FIGURE 4. *Concentration dependence of the positive inotropic effect of Bay k 8644 on guinea pig atria. Results from four different experiments are shown (●-■-▲-▼). Each atrium was paced at 1.0 Hz and had a resting tension of 0.7 to 0.8 g. In each experiment, the concentration of Bay k 8644 was progressively increased. The curve was drawn by eye.*

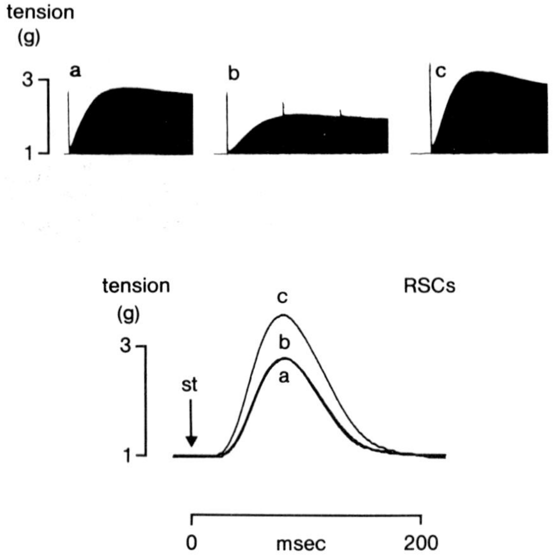

FIGURE 5. *Effect of nitrendipine and increased Ca^{++} on rested-state contractions and twitch tension during steady stimulation in a guinea pig atrium. Each of the upper panels is a tension recording from an atrium during 1 Hz stimulation under control conditions (a), after the addition of 830 nM nitrendipine (b), and in the presence of nitrendipine after increasing Ca^{++} from 1.8 to 3.6 mM (c). Each train was preceded by a rest period of >10 minutes. The train shown in panel b was the second one in the presence of nitrendipine. The rested-state contractions are reproduced on a fast time scale in the lower panel. The arrow marks the time of stimulation.*

continued presence of nitrendipine does alter the rested-state contraction (right panel). The rested-state contractions for all three panels are superimposed on an expanded time scale in the lower panel. Nitrendipine was studied because its specificity for blocking Ca^{++} channels in myocardial cells is well documented (Lee and Tsien, 1983; Shibata et al., 1984), but it alters Ca^{++} transport by the sarcoplasmic reticulum only at very high doses (Colvin et al., 1982; Chamberlain et al., 1984). In contrast, changes in external Ca^{++} result in changes in intracellular Ca^{++}, even in the absence of electrical stimulation (Sheu and Fozzard, 1982; Lakatta and Lappé, 1981).

Figure 6 shows the result when the same stimulation pattern is applied in the presence of 280 nM Bay k 8644. This dose increases the steady state twitch tension for 1.0 Hz stimulation (as shown in Fig. 2) and also increases the second twitch in a train by 20.4%, but does not affect the rested-state contraction (see the lower panel for an expanded time scale). This experiment suggests that the inotropic effect of Bay k 8644 is not due to an intracellular action, or to any mechanism that alters cell Ca^{++} at rest, such as inhibition of the Na,K-ATPase.

The effect of Bay k 8644 on the steady state force-frequency relationship is shown in Figure 7. Increasing the stimulation rate above 0.2 Hz normally produces a positive force staircase in mammalian atria (Koch-Weser and Blinks, 1963). Bay k 8644 shifts the positive staircase effect to lower frequencies of stimulation. Consequently, the maximal percent increase in twitch tension occurs for stimulation at about 0.5 Hz.

Electrophysiological Effects

The dependence of the mechanical effects of Bay k 8644 on continual electrical stimulation suggests that the drug alters a sarcolemmal ionic conductance. The nature of the conductance change was explored in electrophysiological studies on calf ventricular muscle and Purkinje fibers. Figure 8 shows

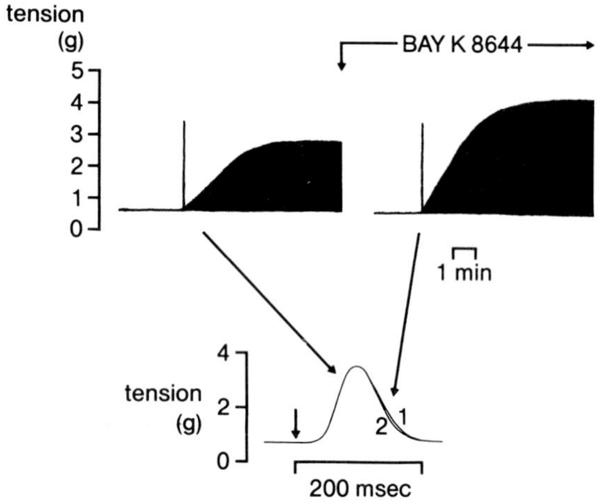

FIGURE 6. *Effect of 280 nM Bay k 8644 on rested-state contractions and twitch tension during steady stimulation in guinea pig atria. The pattern of stimulation is the same as in Figure 5. Bay k 8644 was applied immediately after the first train, and the second train was started 11 minutes later. The rested state contractions for the control run and in the presence of Bay k 8644 are labeled (1) and (2), respectively, in the lower panel. The arrow marks the time of stimulation.*

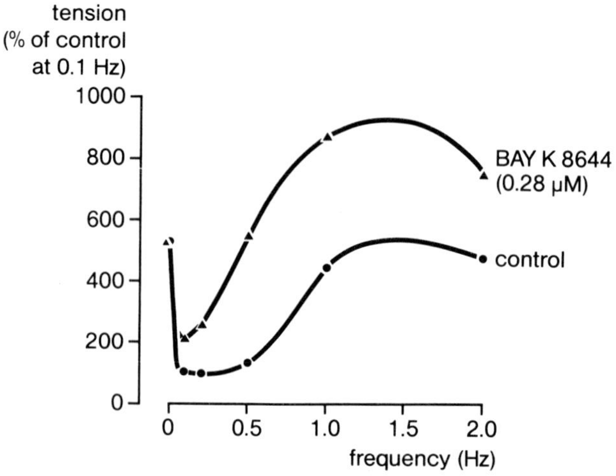

FIGURE 7. *Dependence of the positive inotropic effect of Bay k 8644 on frequency of stimulation. The ordinate is peak twitch tension during steady state stimulation, normalized to the control response at 0.1 Hz stimulation. The circles are control responses, and triangles are with 280 nM Bay k 8644. The slowest stimulation rate studied was 0.003 Hz. The curves were drawn by eye.*

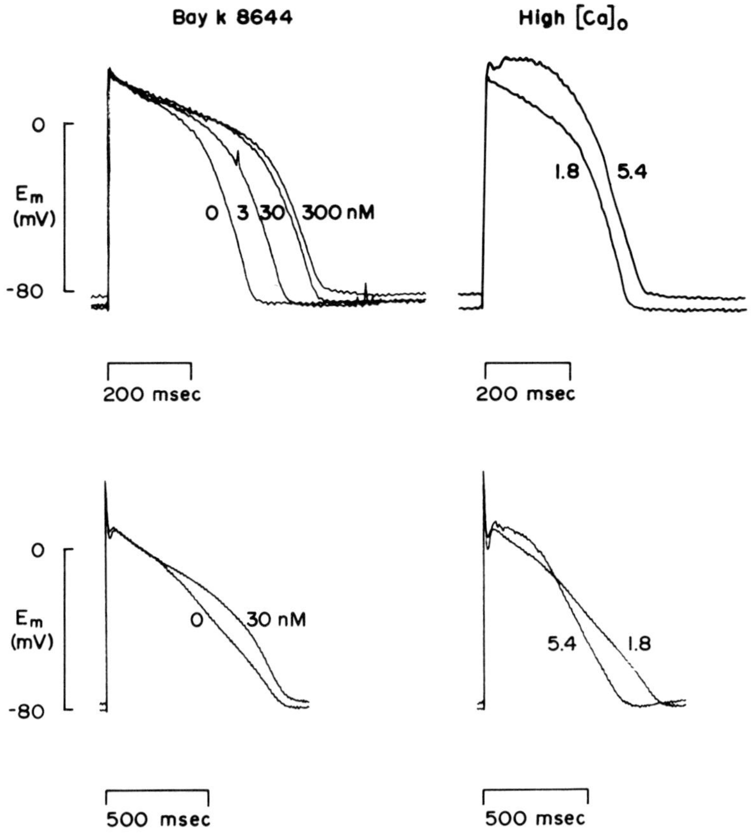

FIGURE 8. *Effect of Bay k 8644 and external Ca^{++} on the cardiac action potential. Upper panels: action potentials recorded in calf ventricular muscle when Bay k 8644 was progressively increased to 3, 30, and 300 nM. Larger increases in action potential duration were sometimes observed when Bay k 8644 was increased from 30 to 300 nM. At right, the effect of increasing external Ca^{++} from 1.8 to 5.4 mM in the same preparation. Stimulation at 0.5 Hz (50 V stimulus for 1.0 msec). T = 35.6 ± 1.0°C. Lower panels: effect of 30 nM Bay k 8644 on the action potential recorded in calf Purkinje fiber. At right, the effect of increasing external Ca^{++} from 1.8 to 5.4 mM. Stimulation at 1.0 Hz (20 V stimulus for 1.4 msec). T = 34.0 ± 0.4°C. All voltage measurements were sampled at 250 Hz. Please note the change in time scale between the upper and lower panels.*

the effect of Bay k 8644 on the cardiac action potential. The upper left panel shows that the action potential duration of ventricular muscle is progressively increased as the concentration of Bay k 8644 increases from 3 to 300 nM. The effects on action potential duration are similar to those of elevated external Ca^{++} (upper right panel), but the drug increases the plateau height less than elevated Ca^{++}. The lower left panel shows that Bay k 8644 also increases the action potential duration in Purkinje fibers. This action contrasts with the effect of increased external Ca^{++} (Dudel et al., 1966; Temte and Davis, 1967; Kass and Tsien, 1976; Colatsky and Hogan, 1980; but see Reuter, 1967) or β-adrenoceptor agonists (Tsien et al., 1972), which usually decrease the action potential duration. Similar effects of Bay k 8644 on the action potential were seen in one other calf Purkinje fiber and in one rabbit Purkinje fiber.

The effect of Bay k 8644 on action potential duration indicates a decrease in net outward current during repolarization. If the drug affects only inward Ca^{++} currents (and, indirectly, Ca^{++}-activated outward currents), then a high dose of the specific Ca^{++} channel blocker nisoldipine should eliminate the effect of Bay k 8644 on action potential configuration (Kazda et al., 1980; Kass, 1982). Figure 9 shows a test of this prediction. A Purkinje fiber was exposed to 1 μM nisoldipine, which shortened the action potential and depessed the plateau height (Kass, 1982). However, this dose does not alter the delayed rectifier current, I_x (Kass, 1982). 30 nM Bay k 8644 was then added in the continued presence of nisoldipine (a low dose was chosen so as not to reverse the nisoldipine block of Ca^{++} channels). No additional change in action potential was observed, in contrast to the result of Figure 8. A similar result was obtained in another calf Purkinje fiber.

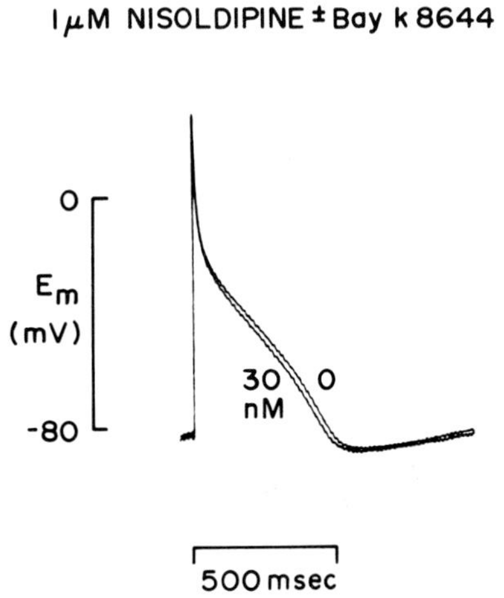

FIGURE 9. *Effect of 30 nM Bay k 8644 on the Purkinje fiber action potential in the presence of 1 μM nisoldipine. Action potentials recorded in 1 μM nisoldipine (labeled 0) and in 1 μM nisoldipine + 30 nM Bay k 8644 are superimposed. Steady state response during 1.0 Hz stimulation (28 V stimulus for 1.0 msec). T = 36.7 ± 0.1°C. The voltage measurements were sampled at 250 Hz.*

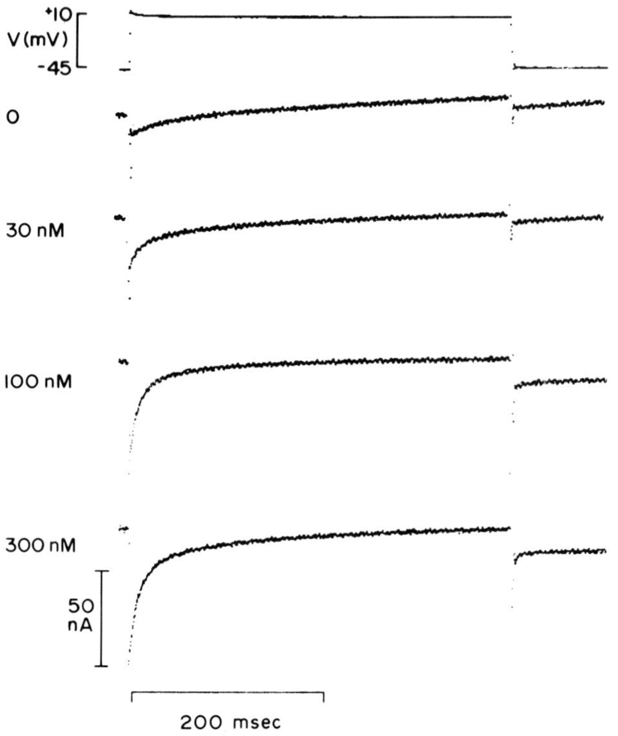

FIGURE 10. *Dose-dependent effect of Bay k 8644 on Ca^{++} channel currents: membrane currents in 0, 30, 100, and 300 nM Bay k 8644 are shown as well as the voltage step in 300 nM Bay k 8644. Bath solution contained 5.4 mM Sr^{++}. Leak currents were not subtracted. Each current recording is signal averaged from three successive voltage steps; 400-msec pulses were applied at 0.4 Hz. Voltage and current were low pass filtered with f_c = 1.0 kHz (0, 30 and 100 nM drug) or f_c = 1.5 kHz (300 nM) and sampled at 2 kHz. T = 31.8 ± 1.9°C.*

The results presented thus far indicate that Bay k 8644 enhances Ca^{++} currents in myocardial cells. Recent voltage clamp studies of I_{Ca} suggest that all positive inotropic agents may have this effect, because the Ca^{++} channel conductance often increases in parallel with intracellular Ca^{++} (Isenberg, 1977; Weingart et al., 1978; Noble and Shimoni, 1981; Marban and Tsien, 1982; Lederer and Eisner, 1982). This indirect drug effect on Ca^{++} conductance can be eliminated by using Sr^{++} as the charge carrier (Marban and Tsien, 1982). To determine whether Bay k 8644 acts directly on voltage-gated Ca^{++} channels to enhance Ca^{++} entry, we measured Sr^{++} currents with a two-microelectrode voltage clamp in calf Purkinje fibers. Purkinje fibers were used because the effects of other inotropic agents on Ca^{++} channels are well characterized in this tissue, and because run-down of Ca^{++} currents is negligible.

Figure 10 shows the effect of Bay k 8644 on Sr^{++} currents (I_{Sr}). I_{Sr} was elicited by stepping the membrane potential from −45 to +10 mV. The current recordings show (from top to bottom) the effect of 0, 30, 100, or 300 nM Bay k 8644. Bay k 8644 increases I_{Sr} and changes the time course of channel gating. I_{Sr} is most enhanced immediately after the voltage step, so that large increases in peak I_{Sr} are observed. The rate of current decay is speeded, so that only a small increase in I_{Sr} is observed at the end of the depolarization.

Bay k 8644 could increase peak I_{Sr} and speed the rate of channel inactivation by uniformly shifting the voltage-dependence of channel gating to more negative voltages. Figure 11 indicates that this is not the case. Comparison of the control record at −15 mV with the record at −30 mV in Bay k 8644 suggests a voltage shift of ~15 mV, but other pairwise comparisons indicate much larger effects on the voltage-dependence of channel gating. In general, the time course of I_{Sr} in the presence of 300 nM Bay k 8644 was unlike the current elicited by stronger depolarizations without drug. Figure 12 shows a plot of the peak current measured at each voltage. The maximal inward current was seen at more negative potentials in the presence of Bay k 8644, indicating that the largest percent increase in I_{Sr} was seen for weak depolarizations. This type of change in the current-voltage relationship can occur as an artifact of inadequate voltage control during the current measurement (Jack et al., 1975; chapter 12). However, the same change in the I-V relationship occurred when the effect of Bay k 8644 on peak current was offset by reducing external Sr^{++} from 5.4 to 1.8 mM. Similar effects of Bay k 8644 on the I-V relationship were observed in four other experiments.

Deactivation of Ca^{++} channels after repolarization is normally so fast that it occurs while the membrane capacitance is being discharged in this preparation. However, a slow component of this "tail current" can be seen in the presence of Bay k 8644 (this is most easily seen by comparing the two current recordings at +15 mV after repolarization in Fig. 11). These tail currents are blocked by nisoldipine with the same potency as the inward current during the test pulse, indicating that they are through Ca^{++} channels (unpublished results).

Discussion

Mechanism of Drug Action

Earlier contractility studies from this laboratory suggested that Bay k 8644 acts on the same Ca^{++} channels as nifedipine, but that the two dihydropyridines have a diametrically opposite effect on these channels: nifedipine blocks the channels, while Bay k 8644 enhances Ca^{++} entry (Schramm et al., 1983a, 1983b). The voltage clamp experiments presented in this paper provide direct experimental support for this idea. Bay k 8644 directly interacts with Ca^{++} channels to increase Ca^{++} entry into myocardial cells. Our findings are consistent with ligand binding studies with [^{3}H]-Bay k 8644, which indicate that the drug acts at the same site as nitrendipine and nifedipine (Bellemann, 1984; Janis et al., 1984). Similar electrophysiological findings have recently been reported by others (Hess et al., 1984; Sanguinetti and Kass, 1984; Ochi et al., 1984).

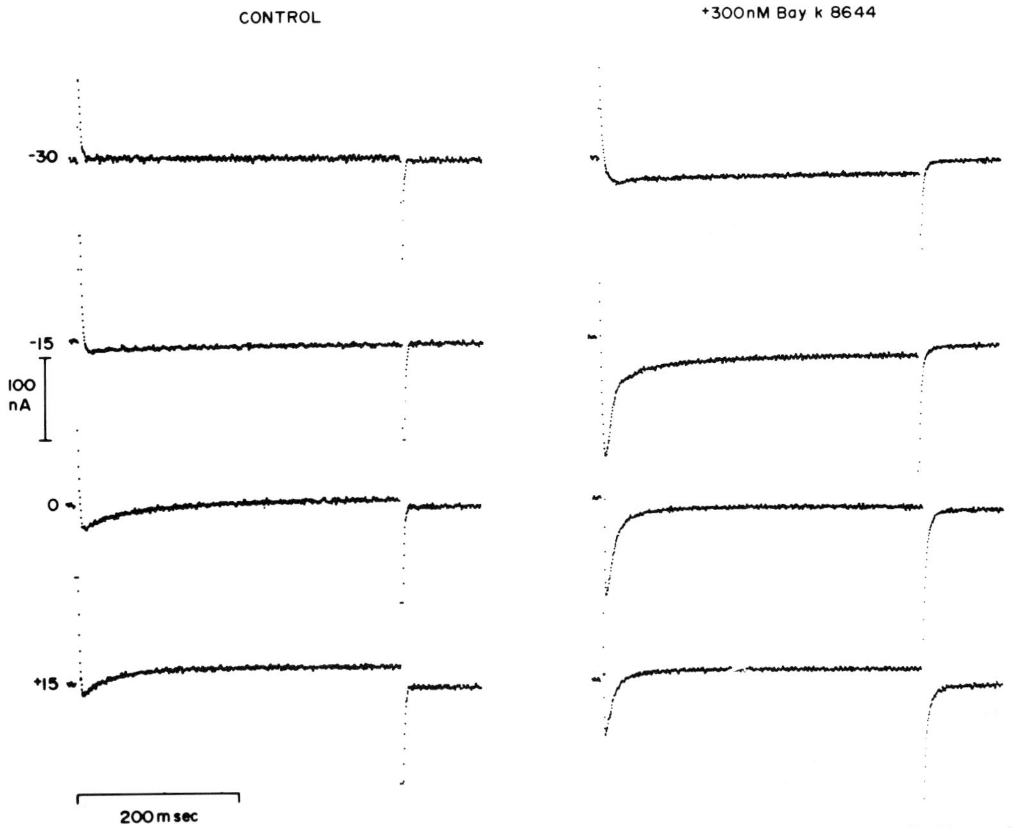

FIGURE 11. *Voltage-dependence of the effect of Bay k 8644 on Ca^{++} channel currents. Test pulses (400 msec) were applied from a holding potential of −45 mV to the potentials indicated at the left of the figure. The left column are currents measured in the absence of drug, and the right column are currents after adding 300 nM Bay k 8644. Bath solution contained 5.4 mM Sr^{++}. Leak currents were not subtracted. Each record is the average of three successive sweeps. Test pulses were applied at 0.4 Hz. Currents were low pass filtered with f_c = 1.5 kHz and sampled at 2.0 kHz. T = 29.9 ± 0.4°C.*

The lack of effect of Bay k 8644 on atrial rested state contractions indicates that the drug does not alter cell Ca^{++} in the absence of electrical activity. This distinguishes Bay k 8644 from cardiac glycosides, which increase these contractions (Koch-Weser and Blinks, 1962; Tuttle and Farah, 1962; Vincenzi, 1967), presumably because inhibition of the sodium pump increases intracellular Ca^{++} even at rest (Bers and Ellis, 1982; Sheu and Fozzard, 1982). It also distinguishes Bay k 8644 from a number of cardiotonic agents that alter the intracellular transport or binding of Ca^{++}, such as caffeine (Lewartowski et al., 1978), ryanodine (Frank and Sleator, 1975), metabolic inhibitors (Katzung et al., 1957), isoproterenol (G. Thomas, unpublished observations), and phosphodiesterase inhibitors (Reinhardt et al., 1977). Hence, the positive inotropic effect of Bay k 8644 is not due to inhibition of the Na,K-ATPase or to increased sensitivity of the myofibrils to Ca^{++}.

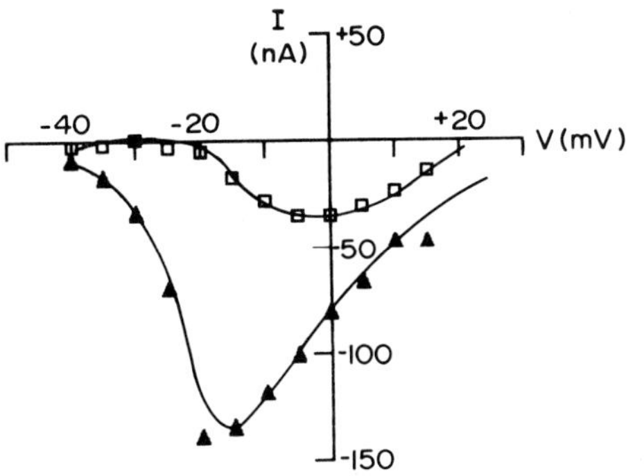

FIGURE 12. *Effect of 300 nM Bay k 8644 on the peak current-voltage relationship. Data are from the same experiment shown in Figure 11. Open squares are peak currents without drug, and filled triangles are currents in 300 nM Bay k 8644. Bath solution contained 5.4 mM Sr^{++}. Leak currents were not subtracted. The curves were drawn by eye.*

The effects of nitrendipine and Bay k 8644 on twitch tension further clarify the role of Ca^{++} channels in atrial muscle. Although tension development at physiological stimulation rates is sensitive to changes in I_{Ca}, this source of Ca^{++} seems to play a minor role in atrial rested-state contractions. For example, Ni^{++} has a small effect on rested-state contractions at concentrations that block a substantial fraction of I_{Ca} (Lewartowski et al., 1978). Nitrendipine is a more specific blocker of Ca^{++} channels than drugs previously used to characterize atrial rested state contractions. Nitrendipine, 830 nM, should block a significant fraction of I_{Ca} at all stimulation rates, although more block is likely at faster rates of stimulation (Lee and Tsien, 1983; Sanguinetti and Kass, 1984). This dose had no effect on rested-state contractions, but had a pronounced effect during 1 Hz stimulation (Fig. 5; Kass and Sanguinetti (1984) found that nitrendipine block of I_{Ca} is much less after rest in a well-polarized cell than during constant stimulation. This can account, in part, for the greater drug effect during 1 Hz stimulation). Hence, the activating Ca^{++} for atrial rested-state contractions is almost entirely from intracellular Ca^{++} stores. Either I_{Ca} is unimportant in supplying Ca^{++} for tension development in rested-state contractions, or a small fraction of I_{Ca} can trigger maximal Ca^{++} release from the sarcoplasmic reticulum in atrial cells (Fabiato and Fabiato, 1978). The lack of effect of Bay k 8644 on rested-state contractions is consistent with these ideas. Excitation-contraction coupling is qualitatively different in ventricular cells, where rested-state contractions are sensitive to changes in I_{Ca} (Lewartowski et al., 1978; G. Thomas, unpublished results).

Most agents that increase I_{Ca} exert their effect by increasing cyclic AMP. However, the electrical and mechanical effects of Bay k 8644 are not consistent with a cyclic AMP-mediated mechanism: (1) maximally effective doses of Bay k 8644 do not occlude the inotropic effects of isoproterenol (Fig. 3). This indicates that the two drugs do not share a common pathway for modifying Ca^{++} channel function. (2) Agents that increase cyclic AMP also speed the rate of Ca^{++} uptake by the sarcoplasmic reticulum (Fabiato and Fabiato, 1975b; Tada and Katz, 1982) and increase the delayed rectifier K^{+} channel current (I_x) (Tsien et al., 1972). Bay k 8644 does not speed the rate of relaxation of tension (Fig. 2), suggesting a lack of effect on Ca^{++} uptake by the sarcoplasmic reticulum. Furthermore, Bay k 8644 increases the action potential duration over a broad concentration range, but β-adrenoceptor agonists can decrease the action potential duration due to enhanced I_x (Tsien et al., 1972; Kass and Wiegers, 1982). (3) β-Adrenoceptor agonists or intracellular injection of cyclic AMP increase the magnitude of I_{Ca} with little change in the time- or voltage-dependence of channel gating [Noma et al., 1980; Isenberg and Klockner, 1982; Kass and Wiegers, 1982; but Bean et al. (1984) found that the rate of activation is slowed by isoproterenol, and the peak of the I-V is at more negative voltages]. Agents that increase I_{Ca} by changing cell Ca^{++} also produce a scalar increase in current (Marban and Tsien, 1982). In contrast, Bay k 8644 increases the peak Ca^{++} channel current, with the largest increases occurring at potentials where the probability for channel opening is normally very low. For stronger depolarizations (to potentials spanned by the plateau of the action potential), the rate of current decay is increased, so that the current is increased most at the beginning of a test pulse or action potential (see Figs. 10 and 11). The changes in the time and voltage dependence of Ca^{++} channel gating produced by Bay k 8644 indicate a novel mechanism of action on Ca^{++} channels.

Comparison with Other Cardiotonic Agents

The best characterized and most often used cardiotonic agents are the cardiac glycosides and sympathomimetic amines. Both classes of drugs, like Bay k 8644, increase cardiac contractility by altering sarcolemmal Ca^{++} transport. Serious questions have been raised about their usefulness in chronic therapy to increase cardiac output. The increase in intracellular Ca^{++} produced by these drugs can aggravate the effects of ischemia and cause arrhythmias (Smith, 1975; Braunwald et al., 1976, chapter 12; Hamer, 1979; Fleckenstein, 1983). Most of the currently available cardiotonic agents are plagued by the difficulties associated with Ca^{++} overload and, consequently, have a low therapeutic index. Katz has even suggested that this problem is inherent to positive inotropic agents, and questions the usefulness of new drugs of this type (Katz, 1978).

Bay k 8644 is a particularly interesting drug because it increases I_{Ca} in a unique way that should allow the extra Ca^{++} influx to be used very efficiently. Consequently, less Ca^{++} entry should be needed to achieve a given inotropic effect. As discussed above, Bay k 8644 increases Ca^{++} entry primarily during the first 50 msec of systole, with smaller increases taking place during the action potential plateau, and probably no increment in influx during diastole. Recent studies suggest that Ca^{++} entry at the beginning of an action potential has a greater effect on tension development than entry at other times.

Simultaneous measurements of tension and I_{Ca} under voltage clamp indicate that Ca^{++} entry throughout the action potential is important for tension development (Beeler and Reuter, 1970; Gibbons and Fozzard, 1975; Wier and Isenberg, 1982). However, two studies indicate that Ca^{++} entry during the action potential plateau is used for loading intracellular stores of Ca^{++} and affects tension development only on subsequent beats, whereas Ca^{++} release from these stores is determined only by the first few milliseconds of depolarization: (1) twitch tension is not increased when test pulses are made longer than 100 msec if the effects of prior electrical stimulation are eliminated by a long rest period (Gibbons and Fozzard, 1971); (2) a 50-msec depolarization elicits as much tension as a 500-msec depolarization immediately after a change in pulse duration (Wier and Isenberg, 1982; compare Fig. 5, a and d).

The Ca^{++} influx occurring during the first few milliseconds of a cardiac action potential is only a small fraction of the Ca^{++} that activates myofibrils (Wier and Isenberg, 1982; Fabiato, 1983; Malloy and Morad, 1984), but is likely to serve as a trigger for the intracellular release of Ca^{++} (Fabiato and Fabiato, 1975a). Ca^{++}-induced Ca^{++} release from the sarcoplasmic reticulum is a graded function of the activating Ca^{++} concentration, rather than an all-or-nothing process (Fabiato and Fabiato, 1975a; Fabiato, 1983). Hence, the increase in Ca^{++} entry produced by Bay k 8644 should be amplified by increased release of Ca^{++} from the sarcoplasmic reticulum.

Agents that alter I_{Ca} via cyclic AMP are prone to produce Ca^{++} overload for three reasons: (1) Ca^{++} entry is not preferentially increased at the beginning of systole, so that Ca^{++} release from the sarcoplasmic reticulum is not optimized; (2) the sensitivity of myofibrils to Ca^{++} is reduced, so that a greater increment in intracellular Ca^{++} must occur for a given inotropic effect [Ray and England, 1976; McClellan and Winegrad, 1978; Allen and Kurihara, 1980; Marban et al., 1980; but Fabiato and Fabiato (1975b) did not find this effect]; and (3) the positive inotropic effect of increased cyclic AMP is always accompanied by an increase in heart rate. Bay k 8644 has none of these effects, and, thus, offers a promising new way to increase cardiac output. Unfortunately, Bay k 8644 is not clinically useful because it increases coronary resistance, apparently by a direct effect on vascular smooth muscle (Schramm et al., 1983a, 1983b). Although it is uncertain whether the vasoconstrictor properties of these dihydropyridines can be eliminated, it is clear that the discovery of superior positive inotropic agents is, in principle, possible.

Bay k 8644 is the most specific positive inotropic agent for increasing Ca^{++} channel currents. As such, it should be a useful pharmacological tool for defining the role of Ca^{++} in physiological processes, complementing the use of the Ca^{++} channel blockers.

Note added in proof:

After this manuscript was submitted for publication, S. Kokubun and H. Reuter [Proc. Natl. Acad. Sci. (Wash.) **81:** 4824–4827 (1984)] and A. M. Brown et al. [Nature **311:** 570–572 (1984)] reported voltage clamp studies that demonstrated direct effects of Bay k 8644 on cardiac Ca^{++} channels.

Dr. Thomas is affiliated with the Institute of Pharmacology, Bayer, AG, and Mr. Chung and Dr. Cohen are affiliated with the Miles Institute for Mechanical Pharmacology.

Address for reprints: Dr. G. Thomas, Institute of Pharmacology, Pharma Research Center, Bayer AG, Postfach 10 17 09, D-5600 Wuppertal 1, Federal Republic of Germany.

Received May 3, 1984; accepted for publication October 10, 1984.

References

Allen DG, Kurihara S (1980) Calcium transients in mammalian ventricular muscle. Eur Heart J **1** (suppl A): 5–15

Bean BP, Nowycky MC, Tsien RW (1984) β-Adrenergic modulation of calcium channels in frog ventricular heart cells. Nature **307:** 371–375

Beeler GW Jr, Reuter H (1970) The relation between membrane potential, membrane currents, and activation of contraction in ventricular myocardial fibres. J Physiol (Lond) **207:** 211–299

Bellemann P (1984) Binding properties of a novel calcium channel activating dihydropyridine in monolayer cultures of beating myocytes. FEBS Lett **167:** 88–92

Bers DM, Ellis D (1982) Intracellular calcium and sodium activity in sheep heart Purkinje fibers. Effect of changes of external sodium and intracellular pH. Pflugers Arch **393:** 171–178

Braunwald E, Ross J Jr, Sonnenblick EH (1976) Mechanisms of Contraction of the Normal and Failing Heart, ed 2, Boston, Little, Brown

Chamberlain BK, Volpe P, Fleischer S (1984) Inhibition of calcium-induced calcium release from purified cardiac sarcoplasmic reticulum vesicles. J Biol Chem **259:** 7547–7553

Cohen CJ, Chung M (1984) A nifedipine-derivative (Bay k 8644) that increases Ca currents in myocardial cells: A novel positive inotropic agent (abstr). Biophys J **45:** 394a

Colatsky TJ, Hogan PM (1980) Effects of external calcium, calcium channel-blocking agents and stimulation frequency on cycle length-dependent changes in canine cardiac action potential duration. Circ Res **46:** 543–552

Colvin RA, Pearson N, Messineo FC, Katz AM (1982) Effects of Ca^{2+} channel blockers on Ca^{2+} transport and Ca^{2+} ATPase in skeletal and cardiac sarcoplasmic reticulum vesicles. J Cardiovasc Pharmacol **4:** 935–941

Coraboeuf E, Carmeliet E (1982) Existence of two transient outward currents in sheep cardiac Purkinje fibers. Pflugers Arch **392:** 352–359

Dudel J, Peper K, Trautwein W (1966) The contribution of Ca^{++} ions to the current voltage relation in cardiac muscle (Purkinje fibers). Pflugers Arch **288:** 262–28

Fabiato A (1983) Calcium-induced release of calcium from the cardiac sarcoplasmic reticulum. Am J Physiol **245:** C1–C14

Fabiato A, Fabiato F (1975a) Contractions induced by a calcium-triggered release of calcium from the sarcoplasmic reticulum of single skinned cardiac cells. J Physiol (Lond) **249:** 469–495

Fabiato A, Fabiato F (1975b) Relaxing and inotropic effect of cyclic AMP on skinned cardiac cells. Nature **253:** 556–558

Fabiato A, Fabiato F (1978) Calcium-induced release of calcium from sarcoplasmic reticulum of skinned cells from adult human, dog, cat, rabbit, rat and frog hearts and from fetal and newborn rat ventricles. Ann NY Acad Sci **307:** 491–522

Fleckenstein A (1983) Calcium Antagonism in Heart and Smooth Muscle. Experimental Facts and Therapeutic Prospects. New York, J Wiley

Frank M, WW Sleator (1975) Effect of ryanodine on myocardial calcium. Naunyn Schmiedebergs Arch Pharmacol **290:** 35–47

Gibbons WR, Fozzard HA (1975) Relationships between voltage and tension in sheep cardiac Purkinje fibers. J Gen Physiol **65:** 345–365

Gibbons WR, Fozzard HA (1971) Voltage dependence and time dependence of contraction in sheep cardiac Purkinje fibers. Circ Res **28:** 446–460

Hamer J (1979) The paradox of the lack of the efficacy of digitalis in congestive heart failure with sinus rhythm. Br J Clin Pharmacol **8:** 109–113

Hess P, Lansman JB, Tsien RW (1984) Modulation of single calcium channels by the calcium agonist Bay k 8644 (abstr). Biophys J **45:** 394a

Isenberg G (1977) Cardiac Purkinje fibres. The slow inward current under the influence of modified [Ca^{2+}]. Pflugers Arch **371:** 61–69

Isenberg G, Klockner U (1982) Calcium currents of isolated bovine ventricular myocytes are fast and of large amplitude. Pflugers Arch **395:** 30–41

Jack JJB, Noble D, Tsien RW (1975) Electric Current Flow in Excitable Cells. Oxford, Clarendon Press

Janis RA, Rampe D, Sarmiento JG, Triggle DJ (1984) Specific binding of a calcium channel activator, [^{3}H]BAY k 8644, to membranes from cardiac muscle and brain. Biochem Biophys Res Commun **121:** 317–323

Kass RS (1982) Nisoldipine: A new, more selective calcium current blocker in cardiac Purkinje fibers. J Pharmacol Exp Ther **223:** 446–456

Kass RS, Tsien RW (1976) Control of action potential duration by calcium ions in cardiac Purkinje fibers. J Gen Physiol **67:** 599–617

Kass RS, Wiegers SE (1982) The ionic basis of concentration-related effects of noradrenaline on the action potential of calf cardiac Purkinje fibres. J Physiol (Lond) **322:** 541–558

Kass RS, Siegelbaum SA, Tsien RW (1979) Three-microelectrode voltage clamp experiments in calf cardiac Purkinje fibres: Is slow inward current adequately measured? J Physiol (Lond) **290:** 201–225

Kass RS, Scheuer T, Malloy KJ (1982) Block of outward current in cardiac Purkinje fibers by injection of quaternary ammonium ions. J Gen Physiol **79:** 1041–1063

Katz AM (1978) A new inotropic drug: Its promise and a caution. N Engl J Med **299:** 1409–1410

Katzung B, Rosin H, Scheider F (1957) Frequency-force relationship in the rabbit auricle and its modificatin by some metabolic inhibitors. J Pharmacol Exp Ther **120:** 324–333

Kazda S, Garthoff B, Meyer H, Schlossmann K, Stoepel K, Towart R, Vater W, Wehinger E (1980) Pharmacology of a new calcium antagonistic compound, isobutyl methyl 1,4-dihydro-2,6-dimethyl-4-(2-nitrophenyl)-3,5-pyridine-dicarboxylate (nisoldipine, BAY k 5552). Arzneimittelforsch **30:** 2144–2162

Koch-Weser J, Blinks JR (1962) Analysis of the relation of the positive inotropic action of cardiac glycosides to the frequency of contraction of heart muscle. J Pharmacol Exp Ther **136:** 305–317

Koch-Weser J, Blinks JR (1963) The influence of the interval between beats on myocardial contractility. Pharmacol Rev **15:** 601–652

Lakatta EG, Lappé DL (1981) Diastolic scattered light fluctuation, resting force and twitch force in mammalian cardiac muscle. J Physiol (Lond) **315:** 369–394

Lederer WJ, Eisner DA (1982) The effects of sodium pump activity on the slow inward current in sheep cardiac Purkinje fibres. Proc R Soc Lond [Biol] **214:** 249–262

Lee KS, Tsien RW (1983) Mechanism of calcium channel blockade by verapamil, D600, diltiazem and nitrendipine in single dialysed heart cells. Nature **302:** 790–794

Lewartowski B, Prokopczuk A, Putkowski B (1978) Effect of inhibitors of slow calcium current on rested state contraction of papillary muscles and the post rest contractions of atrial muscle of the cat and rabbit hearts. Pflugers Arch **377:** 167–175

Malloy KJ, Morad M (1984) Photochemical unblocking of Ca^{2+}-antagonists in mammalian heart (abstr). Biophys J **45:** 134a

Marban E (1981) Inhibition of transient outward current by intracellular ion substitution unmasks slow inward current in cardiac Purkinje fibers. Pflugers Arch **390:** 102–106

Marban E, Tsien RW (1982) Enhancement of calcium current during digitalis inotropy in mammalian heart: Positive feedback regulation by intracellular calcium? J Physiol (Lond) **329:** 589–614

Marban E, Rink TJ, Tsien RW, Tsien RY (1980) Free calcium in heart muscle at rest and during contraction measured with Ca^{2+}-sensitive microelectrodes. Nature **286:** 845–850

McClellan G, Winegrad S (1978) The regulation of calcium sensitivity of the contractile system in mammalian cardiac muscle. J Gen Physiol **72:** 737–767

Noble S, Shimoni Y (1981) The calcium and frequency dependence of the slow inward current "staircase" in frog atrium. J Physiol (Lond) **310:** 57–75

Noma A, Kotake H, Irisawa H (1980) Slow inward current and its role mediating the chronotropic effect of epinephrine in the rabbit sinoatrial node. Pflugers Arch **388:** 1–9

Ochi R, Hino N, Niimi Y (1984) Prolongation of calcium channel open time by the dihydropyridine derivative BAY k 8644 in cardiac myocytes. Proc Jpn Acad **60B:** 153–156

Ray KP, England PJ (1976) Phosphorylation of the inhibitory subunit of troponin and its effect on the calcium dependence of cardiac myofibril adenosine triphosphate. FEBS Lett **70:** 11

Reinhardt D, Roggenbach W, Schmidt V, Schumann H-J (1977) The effect of papaverine on the frequency-force relationship in guinea-pig left atria. Eur J Pharmacol **41:** 123–132

Reuter H (1967) The dependence of slow inward current in Purkinje fibres on the extracellular calcium-concentration. J Physiol (Lond) **192:** 479–492

Sanguinetti MC, Kass RS (1984) Dihydropyridine derivatives: Voltage-dependent modulation of calcium channel current (abstr). Biophys J **45:** 394a

Schramm M, Thomas G, Towart R, Franckowiak G (1983a) Activation of calcium channels by novel 1,4-dihydropyridines. Arzneimittelforsch **33:** 1268–1272

Schramm M, Thomas G, Towart R, Franckowiak G (1983b) Novel dihydropyridines with positive inotropic action through activation of Ca^{2+} channels. Nature **303:** 535–537

Sheu SS, Fozzard HA (1982) Transmembrane Na^{+} and Ca^{2+} electrochemical gradients in cardiac muscle and their relationship to force development. J Gen Physiol **80:** 325–351

Shibata EF, Momose Y, Giles W (1984) Nitrendipine actions on atrial tissue in the heart. *In* Nitrendipine, edited by A Scriabine, S Vanov, and K Deck. Baltimore-Munich, Urban and Schwarzenberg pp 199–208

Siegelbaum SA, Tsien RW (1980) Calcium-activated outward current in calf cardiac Purkinje fibres. J Physiol (Lond) **299:** 485–506

Smith TW (1975) Digitalis toxicity: Epidemiology and clinical use of serum concentration measurements. Am J Med **58:** 470–476

Tada M, Katz AM (1982) Phosphorylation of the sarcoplasmic reticulum and sarcolemma. Annu Rev Physiol **44:** 401–423

Temte JV, Davis LD (1967) Effect of calcium concentration on the transmembrane potentials of Purkinje fibers. Circ Res **20:** 32–44

Thomas G, Schramm M, Franckowiak G (1983a) Dihydropyridines that exert positive inotropic effects in isolated cardiac muscle: Evidence for Ca channel modulation (abstr). Pharmacologist **25:** 206

Thomas G, Schramm M, Franckowiak G (1983b) From negative inotropic to positive inotropic dihydropyridines. Calcium channel modulation in isolated heart preparations. Naunyn Schmiedebergs Arch Pharmacol (abstr). **324:** R47

Tsien RW, Giles WR, Greengard P (1972) Cyclic AMP mediates the action of adrenaline on the action potential plateau of cardiac Purkinje fibres. Nature [New Biol] **240:** 181–183

Tuttle RS, Farah A (1962) The effect of ouabain on the frequency-force relation and on post-stimulation potential in isolated atrial and ventricular muscle. J Pharmacol Exp Ther **135:** 142–150

Vater W, Kroneberg G, Hoffmeister F, Kaler H, Meng K, Oberdorf A, Puls W, Schlossmann K, Stoepel K (1972) Zur pharmakologie von 4-(2′-nitrophenyl)-2,6-dimethyl-1,4-dihydropyridin-3,5-dicarbonsaure-dimethylester (nifedipin, BAY a 1040). Arzneimittelforsch **22:** 1–14

Vincenzi FF (1967) Influence of myocardial activity on the rate of onset of oubain action. J Pharmacol Exp Ther **155:** 279–287

Weingart R, Kass RS, Tsien RW (1978) Is digitalis inotropy associated with enhanced slow inward calcium current? Nature **273:** 389–392

Wier WG, Isenberg G (1982) Intracellular [Ca^{2+}] transients in voltage clamped cardiac Purkinje fibers. Pflugers Arch **392:** 284–290

INDEX TERMS: Positive inotropic dihydropyridines • BAY K 8644 • Calcium channel • Rested state contraction • Cardiac muscle • Nitrendipine

Mechanism of Action of Angiotensin II and Bradykinin on Prostaglandin Synthesis and Vascular Tone in the Isolated Rat Kidney

Effect of Ca^{++} Antagonists and Calmodulin Inhibitors

Christy L. Cooper, Joel E. Shaffer, and Kafait U. Malik

From the Department of Pharmacology, College of Medicine, University of Tennessee Center for the Health Sciences, Memphis, Tennessee

SUMMARY. We have studied the effect of angiotensin II and bradykinin on prostaglandin output and vascular tone during extracellular calcium depletion and administration of calcium antagonists and calmodulin inhibitors to elucidate the mechanism of action in the isolated rat kidney perfused with Tyrode's solution. Administration of angiotensin II (0.028–0.28 nmol) or bradykinin (0.28–2.8 nmol) enhanced the output of prostaglandin E_2 and 6-keto-prostaglandin $F_{1\alpha}$ in a dose-dependent manner. Angiotensin II, but not bradykinin, produced renal vasoconstriction. Omission of calcium from the medium or infusion of calcium entry blockers, diltiazem (60 μM), or nimodipine (47 μM), failed to alter prostaglandin output elicited by angiotensin II or bradykinin; however, the effect of angiotensin II to produce renal vasoconstriction was inhibited. If calcium was omitted from the medium, the intracellular calcium antagonists, 8-(diethylamino)octyl 3,4,5-trimethoxybenzoate hydrochloride (23 μM), dantrolene sodium (31 μM), or ryanodine (2 μM), attenuated prostaglandin output caused by angiotensin II but not bradykinin. Calmodulin inhibitors, trifluoperazine (2 μM), napthalene sulfonamide hydrochloride (2 μM), or calmidazolium (2 μM), diminished prostaglandin output elicited by angiotensin II, but not that caused by bradykinin. Trifluoperazine, but not naphthalene sulfonamide or calmidazolium, attenuated the renal vasoconstrictor effect of angiotensin II. Prostaglandin output induced by angiotensin II and bradykinin were inhibited by mepacrine and indomethacin, whereas, the prostaglandin output caused by exogenous arachidonic acid (33 nmol) was abolished by indomethacin but was unaltered by mepacrine, calcium antagonists, and calmodulin inhibitors. From these data, we conclude that angiotensin II produces renal vasoconstriction by a mechanism dependent on extracellular calcium but not calmodulin, whereas angiotensin II-induced prostaglandin output depends on intracellular calcium and calmodulin. In contrast, bradykinin appears to stimulate prostaglandin synthesis by a calcium/calmodulin-independent mechanism. **(*Circ Res 56: 97–108, 1985*)**

ANGIOTENSIN II (AII), an octapeptide, contracts vascular smooth muscle and causes renal vasoconstriction (Page and Bumpus, 1961), whereas bradykinin (BK), a nonapeptide, relaxes vascular smooth muscle and produces renal vasodilation in several mammalian species (Regoli and Barabé, 1980). Both peptides stimulate prostaglandin synthesis in several tissues, including renal cellular elements, renal medullary slices, as well as in the intact kidney in vitro and in vivo (McGiff, 1981). However, the mechanism by which AII and BK stimulate prostaglandin synthesis and produce alterations in vascular tone is poorly understood. The demonstration that Ca^{++} depletion from the medium or administration of Ca^{++} channel blockers attenuate the effect of AII or BK to stimulate prostaglandin synthesis in renal medullary slices, glomerular mesangial cells, or aortic and pulmonary endothelial cells in culture (Benabé et al., 1982; Whorton et al., 1982; Zenser et al., 1982; Crutchley et al., 1983; Scharschmidt and Dunn, 1983) and attenuate the effect of AII to cause vascular smooth muscle contraction (St. Louis et al., 1977) suggests that the peptides produce these biological actions by a mechanism involving extracellular Ca^{++}. However, the findings that removal of Ca^{++} from the medium in the absence or presence of EGTA and/or administration of agents that inhibit cellular entry of Ca^{++} do not completely prevent the action of AII or BK to stimulate prostaglandin synthesis (Juan, 1979; Simmet and Hertting, 1980) and of AII to produce vascular smooth muscle contraction (Kalsner et al., 1970; Deth and van Breeman, 1974) suggest that either Ca^{++} is not absolutely necessary, or that intracellular Ca^{++} is involved in these biological actions of the peptides. To test this hypothesis, we investigated the effects of altering the Ca^{++} concentration of the perfusion medium and the extracellular Ca^{++} antagonists, diltiazem (van Breeman et al., 1981) and nimodipine (Towart and Kazda, 1979; Towart, 1981), and the intracellular Ca^{++} antagonists, dantrolene sodium (Morgan and Bryant, 1977), ryanodine (Sutko and Kenyon, 1983), and TMB-8* (Chiou and Malagodi, 1975), on the AII and BK action on prostaglandin output and vascular tone in the isolated rat kidney perfused with or without Ca^{++}-containing Tyrode's solution. Since several biological actions of Ca^{++} are mediated by its interaction with calmodulin, we have investigated the effect of three structurally distinct calmodulin inhibitors, trifluoperazine (Levin and Weiss, 1976), W-7* (Hidaka et al., 1981), and calmidazolium (Van Belle, 1981), to determine the possible contribution of this Ca^{++}-binding protein to the actions of AII and BK on prostaglandin synthesis and vascular tone.

Methods

Male Sprague-Dawley rats (weighing 350–400 g), maintained on regular Purina chow diet, were anesthetized with ether, and the abdomen was opened by a midline laparotomy. The aorta was ligated proximal and distal to the left renal artery, and a catheter was inserted into the renal artery. The kidney was flushed with heparinized saline (100 U/ml), isolated from the animal, and perfused with Tyrode's solution at a constant flow rate of 5 ml/min, using a Harvard peristaltic pump as described previously (Malik and McGiff, 1975). The perfusion fluid was maintained at 37°C and gassed with a mixture of 95% O_2 and 5% CO_2. The renal perfusate was allowed to flow out of the cut ends of the renal vein and ureter, and was not recirculated. The composition of Tyrode's solution in mmol/liter was as follows: NaCl, 137; KCl, 2.7; $CaCl_2$, 1.8; $MgCl_2$, 1.1; $NaHCO_3$, 12; NaH_2PO_4, 0.42; and D(+)-glucose, 5.6. Perfusion pressure was measured with a pressure transducer (Statham P23 ID) and recorded on a physiograph (Esterline Angus). Since the flow rate was maintained constant, changes in perfusion pressure reflect alterations in renal vascular resistance.

Experimental Protocol

The following eight series of experiments were performed.

Series 1

The purpose of this series of experiments was to investigate the effects of AII, BK, and the Ca^{++} ionophore, A-23187, on the renal output of PGE_2 and 6-keto-$PGF_{1\alpha}$ and on vascular tone in kidneys perfused with and without added Ca^{++} in the absence or presence of EGTA (23 μM). In kidneys perfused with Tyrode's solution containing normal (1.8 mM), lower (0.6 mM), or higher (5.4 mM) Ca^{++}, drugs were administered during 35–125 minutes of perfusion, whereas in kidneys perfused with Ca^{++}-free Tyrode's solution, the drugs were given during 80–155 minutes of perfusion, since the basal output of prostaglandins was stable during these periods. Moreover, the basal output of prostaglandins and the perfusion pressure during these periods were also similar in kidneys perfused with or without Ca^{++}-containing Tyrode's solution. AII (0.028–0.28 nmol), BK (0.28–2.8 nmol), A-23187 (9.6 nmol), or their respective vehicles, were injected as a bolus at 15-minute intervals in a random order into the side port of the tubing leading to the renal artery. Changes in perfusion pressure were recorded and renal perfusate samples were collected for 2-minute periods just prior to and after the injections of AII, BK, A-23187, or their vehicles. The samples were frozen at −20°C for later analysis of prostaglandins.

Series 2

The effect of AII and BK on the renal output of prostaglandins and on vascular tone was examined in the presence of the Ca^{++} channel blockers, diltiazem (60 and 300 μM), nimodipine (47 and 235 μM), or their respective vehicles. After a 35-minute stabilization period, AII (0.097 nmol), BK (0.94 nmol), or their vehicles were injected at 15-minute intervals in a random order. Changes in perfusion pressures were recorded, and samples of the renal perfusate were collected for prostaglandin determination as described for series 1 experiments.

Series 3

This series of experiments was performed to investigate the effect of the intracellular Ca^{++} antagonists, dantrolene sodium, TMB-8, and ryanodine on the actions of AII and BK on prostaglandin synthesis and vascular tone in kidneys perfused with Tyrode's solution in the absence and presence of 1.8 mM Ca^{++}. Dantrolene sodium (31 μM), TMB-8 (2.3 μM), or ryanodine (2 μM) was added to the perfusion medium, and, after 80 minutes of stabilization, AII (0.097 nmol), BK (0.94 nmol), or their vehicles were injected into the kidney in a random order at 15-minute intervals. In an additional series of experiments, the kidneys were perfused with Tyrode's solution containing 0.9 or 0.6 mM Ca^{++} and TMB-8 (2.3 μM), and the effect of AII (0.097 nmol) on prostaglandin output and on renal vascular tone was determined.

Series 4

The effect of trifluoperazine, W-7, and calmidazolium was studied in concentrations reported to inhibit calmodulin activity (Levin and Weiss, 1976; Hidaka et al., 1981; Van Belle, 1981), on AII- and BK-induced prostaglandin output and on their vascular actions in the absence and presence of 1.8 mM Ca^{++}. Trifluoperazine (2 μM), W-7 (2 μM), calmidazolium (0.2 μM), or their vehicles were added to the perfusion fluid, and AII (0.097 nmol), BK (0.94 nmol), or their vehicles were injected into the renal arterial catheter at 15-minute intervals.

Series 5

The purpose of these experiments was to study the effect of the AII receptor antagonist [Sar^1,Ala^8]-AII on AII and BK actions on prostaglandin output and vascular tone in kidneys perfused without and with Ca^{++}-containing Tyrode's solution. [Sar^1,Ala^8]-AII (0.02 or 1.1 μM) was added to the perfusion medium. AII (0.097 nmol), BK (0.94 nmol), or their vehicles were injected at 15-minute intervals, and the perfusate was collected as described for series 1 experiments.

Series 6

The purpose of this series of experiments was to examine the effect of Ca^{++} antagonists, calmodulin inhibitors, and [Sar^1,Ala^8]-AII on arachidonic acid-induced prostaglandin output and alterations in vascular tone in kid-

* *TMB-8, 8-(diethylamino) octyl 3,4,5-trimethoxybenzoate hydrochloride; W-7, naphthalenesulfonamide hydrochloride.*

neys perfused with or without Ca^{++}-containing Tyrode's solution. Diltiazem (60 μM), nimodipine (47 μM), dantrolene sodium (31 μM), TMB-8 (2.3 μM), ryanodine (2 μM), trifluoperazine (2 μM), W-7 (2 μM), calmidazolium (0.2 μM), or their vehicles were added to the perfusion medium, and arachidonic acid (33 nmol), or its vehicle was injected into the kidney.

Series 7

This series of experiments was performed to determine the effect of a combined injection of AII and BK on prostaglandin output and on vascular tone in kidneys perfused with Ca^{++}-containing Tyrode's solution. AII (0.097 nmol) plus BK (0.94 nmol) or their vehicles were injected, and the renal perfusate samples were collected, by a protocol similar to that described in series 1.

Series 8

The effect of indomethacin and mepacrine on vascular tone and prostaglandin output elicited by AII, BK, and arachidonic acid was determined in the presence or absence of Ca^{++} (1.8 μM). The kidney was perfused with Tyrode's solution containing indomethacin (2.8 μM), mepacrine (21 μM), or their vehicles with or without Ca^{++}. AII (0.097 nmol), BK (0.94 nmol), arachidonic acid (33 nmol), or their vehicles were injected into the renal arterial catheter by a protocol similar to that described for series 1 experiments.

Determination of Prostaglandins

Prostaglandin E_2 and 6-keto-prostaglandin $F_{1\alpha}$ (the stable hydrolysis product of PGI_2) in the renal perfusate were measured by radioimmunoassay as described previously (Shaffer and Malik, 1982). The limit of detection of PG in our assay was: 2 pg for PGE_2 and 5 pg for 6-keto-$PGF_{1\alpha}$. The cross-reactivity for each antibody was less than 0.5% for other prostaglandins and their metabolites. Extraction blanks varied from 0 to 3 pg/tube. Specific binding ranged from 35 to 45% for each antibody, and nonspecific binding ranged from 2 to 3%. The intra-assay and interassay coefficient of variation was 5 and 12%, respectively. Recovery of prostaglandins, added to the perfusate before extraction, was 90 to 95%, and none of the drugs used in our experiments interfered with the radioimmunoassay.

Drugs

The following drugs used in this study were purchased: bradykinin diacetate (Protein Research Foundation, Minoh-Shi), angiotensin II (Beckman Instruments, Inc.), indomethacin, quinacrine dihydrochloride (mepacrine), and ethyleneglycol-bis-(β-amino-ethyl ether) N′,N′-tetraacetic acid (EGTA, Sigma Chemical Co.), arachidonic acid (Nu Cher Prep Inc.), 8-(diethylamino) octyl 3,4,5-trimethoxybenzoate hydrochloride (TMB-8, Aldrich Chemical Co.), naphthalene-sulfonamide hydrochloride (W-7, Rikaken Co.), calmidazolium (Janssen Pharmaceutical) and [Sar^1,Ala^8]-angiotensin II (Calbiochem). The drugs that were gratis are: dilitazem (Marion Labs), nimodipine (Pfizer Inc.), dantrolene sodium (Norwich Eaton Pharmaceuticals), trifluoperazine (Smith, Kline and French Labs), ryanodine (Merck, Sharp and Dohme), A-23187 (Eli Lilly Co.), unlabeled prostaglandins (Upjohn Company), and PGE_2 and 6-keto-$PGF_{1\alpha}$ antisera (Dr. L. Levine, Brandeis University).

AII and BK were dissolved in saline (1 mg/ml) and A-23187 in dimethyl sulfoxide (1 mg/ml) to prepare stock solutions, and were stored in small aliquots at −20°C and diluted with saline just before use. Arachidonic acid was dissolved in absolute ethanol (20 mg/ml) and divided in 5-μl aliquots and stored at −20°C in small vials protected from light. The contents of the vials were diluted with 0.1 ml Na_2CO_3 (1 mg/ml) and 0.9 ml of 0.15 M NaCl just before use. Solutions of AII, BK, A-23187, and arachidonic acid were injected in a volume of 0.1 ml into the renal arterial circuit. [Sar^1,Ala^8]-AII was dissolved in 0.15 M NaCl and nimodipine in polyethylene glycol 400 (2.5 mg/ml) and infused into the renal arterial circuit to obtain the final concentration. Since nimodipine is light sensitive, the solution and the perfusion apparatus were covered with aluminum foil during use. Dantrolene sodium was solubilized (5 mg/ml) in Tyrode's solution containing 25 μl of 1 N NaOH and added to the perfusion fluid. Diltiazem, TMB-8, dantrolene sodium, ryanodine, trifluoperazine, W-7, calmidazolium, and mepacrine were dissolved in small volumes of Tyrode's solution with or without Ca^{++}, depending upon the experimental protocol, and added to the perfusion fluid to obtain the final concentration.

Analysis of Data

The basal and the increase in prostaglandin output elicited by various agents is expressed as ng/min of immunoreactive PGE_2 and 6-keto-$PGF_{1\alpha}$. The basal output represents the amount of prostaglandins in the samples collected for a 2-minute period immediately before administration of a drug. The increase in the output of prostaglandins caused by a drug was calculated by subtracting the basal efflux of prostaglandins from that obtained during 2-minute periods immediately after the injection of a drug. The results are expressed as mean ± SEM. The data were analyzed by one-way analysis of variance, and Dunnett's test was applied to determine the difference between means and Student's *t*-test for unpaired observations. A correction factor was employed when Dunnett's test was used in the cases of unequal sample sizes (Zar, 1984). Differences between means were considered significant if the probability (P) of the null hypothesis being true was less than 0.05.

Results

Effect of AII, BK, and A-23187 on the Output of Prostaglandins and Vascular Tone in the Rat Kidney Perfused with or without Ca^{++} (1.8 mM)-Containing Tyrode's Solution (Figs. 1 and 2)

The basal perfusion pressure remained at a steady level (56 ± 4 mm Hg, $n = 6$) for 3–4 hours in kidneys perfused with or without Ca^{++}-containing Tyrode's solution. During this period of perfusion the wet weight of the kidney, which averaged 1.6 g (range 1.5–1.8 g), was unchanged. In kidneys perfused with Ca^{++} (1.8 mM) -containing Tyrode's solution, administration of AII (0.028–0.28 nmol) into the renal arterial circuit increased perfusion pressure and the output of PGE_2 and 6-keto-$PGF_{1\alpha}$. Injections of BK (0.28–2.8 nmol) into the kidney also increased the output of PGE_2 and 6-keto-$PGF_{1\alpha}$, but had no effect on perfusion pressure. The rise in perfusion pressure elicited by AII peaked in 30–40 seconds, whereas the output of prostaglandins caused by AII and BK reached maximal levels in 2 minutes and gradually

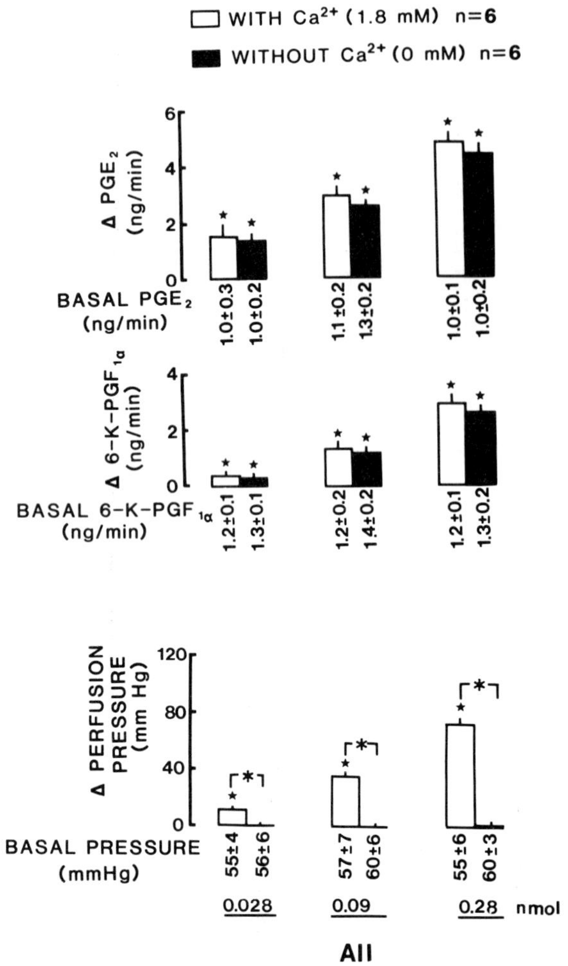

FIGURE 1. *Effect of AII on the output of* PGE_2 *(upper panel) and 6-keto-*$PGF_{1\alpha}$ *(6-K-*$PGF_{1\alpha}$*, shown in middle panel) and on the perfusion pressure (bottom panel) in the isolated rat kidney perfused with and without* Ca^{++}*-containing Tyrode's solution. ★ denotes values different from basal, whereas ∗ represents the difference between the values obtained in the presence and absence of* Ca^{++} *(*$P < 0.05$*).*

returned to the basal level within the next 5 minutes. With Ca^{++}-free Tyrode's solution, injections of AII (0.028–0.28 nmol) or BK (0.28–2.8 nmol) did not alter the perfusion pressure, but enhanced the output of prostaglandins. Addition of Ca^{++} (1.8 mM) to the perfusion medium restored the vasoconstrictor effect of AII to levels observed in kidneys perfused with normal Tyrode's solution. Both AII and BK produced a greater increase in the output of PGE_2 than 6-keto-$PGF_{1\alpha}$ in the presence, as well as in the absence, of Ca^{++}. In kidneys perfused with Ca^{++}-free Tyrode's solution containing EGTA, the basal output of prostaglandins (1.4 ± 0.3 ng/min PGE_2, and 1.2 ± 0.3 ng/min 6-keto-$PGF_{1\alpha}$) or the rise in prostaglandin output elicited by AII (0.097 nmol) (3.4 ± 0.2 ng/min PGE_2 and 1.9 ± 0.2 ng/min 6-keto-$PGF_{1\alpha}$) and by BK (0.94 nmol) (2.2 ± 0.3 ng/min PGE_2 and 1.3 ± 0.1 ng/min 6-keto-$PGF_{1\alpha}$) ($P <$

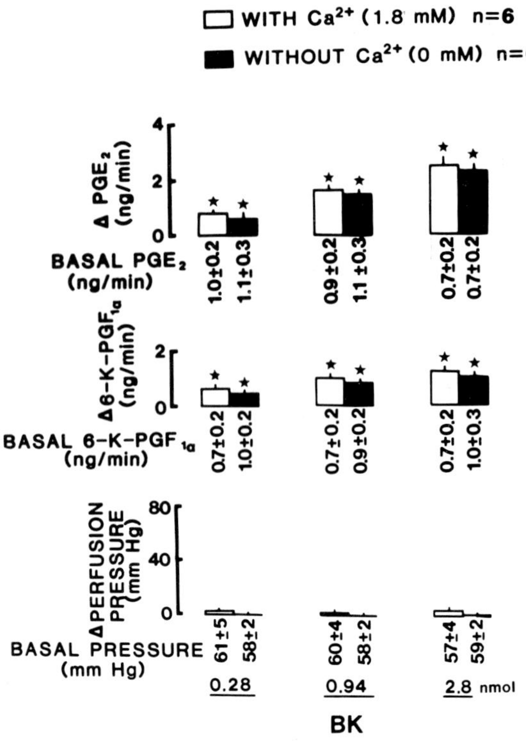

FIGURE 2. *Effect of BK on the output of* PGE_2 *(upper panel) and 6-keto-*$PGF_{1\alpha}$ *(middle panel) and on the perfusion pressure (bottom panel) in the isolated rat kidney perfused with and without* Ca^{++}*-containing Tyrode's solution. ★ denotes values different from basal (*$P < 0.05$*).*

0.05, $n = 4$) was the same as that observed in kidneys perfused with Ca^{++}-free Tyrode's solution in the absence of EGTA (Figs. 1 and 2) ($P > 0.05$).

In kidneys perfused with Tyrode's solution containing higher (5.4 mM) or lower (0.6 mM) Ca^{++}, the output of prostaglandins elicited by AII (0.097 nmol) or BK (0.94 nmol) was the same as that obtained in the presence of normal Ca^{++} (data not shown). However, the rise in perfusion pressure elicited by AII was significantly higher in the presence of 5.4 mM Ca^{++} (58 ± 9 mm Hg, $n = 6$) and lower in the presence of 0.6 mM Ca^{++} (18 ± 3 mm Hg, $n = 6$) than that observed during normal Ca^{++}, 1.8 mM (32 ± 6 mm Hg, $n = 6$) ($P < 0.05$). The basal output of prostaglandins or the perfusion pressure were not altered by raising or lowering Ca^{++} concentration in the perfusion medium.

Administration of A-23187 (9.6 nmol) into the kidney perfused with Ca^{++} (1.8 mM) -containing Tyrode's solution increased the output of PGE_2 and 6-keto-$PGF_{1\alpha}$ from 0.99 ± 0.20 to 3.11 ± 0.51 ng/min and 1.03 ± 0.15 to 2.72 ± 0.4 ng/min, respectively ($P < 0.05$, $n = 6$), but failed to alter perfusion pressure. In the absence of Ca^{++}, A-23187 failed to alter either the output of prostaglandins or perfusion pressure. Injections of each drug vehicle into the renal arterial circuit did not alter the output of prostaglandins or the perfusion pressure in the presence or absence of Ca^{++}.

Effect of Diltiazem and Nimodipine on the Actions of AII and BK on Prostaglandin Output and Vascular Tone (Figs. 3 and 4)

In kidneys perfused with Tyrode's solution containing diltiazem or nimodipine, administration of AII (0.097 nmol) increased the renal output of PGE_2 and 6-keto-$PGF_{1\alpha}$. The magnitude of this increase was not different from that obtained in the presence of the vehicles of these agents. The rise in perfusion pressure produced by AII was significantly attenuated during infusion of diltiazem or nimodipine (Fig. 3). The output of prostaglandins elicited by BK (0.94 nmol) was not altered by the Ca^{++} channel blockers (Fig. 4). During infusion of diltiazem or nimodipine, the basal output of prostaglandins or perfusion pressure was not altered. Increasing the concentration of the Ca^{++} channel blockers in the perfusion medium by 5-fold also failed to alter the rise in PG output elicited by AII or BK. In the presence of 5-fold higher concentrations of diltiazem or nimodipine, AII still significantly increased perfusion pressure from 54 ± 3 to 69 ± 2 mm Hg and from 55 ± 2 to 64 ± 3 mm Hg, respectively ($P < 0.05$, $n = 7$ and $n = 5$, respectively).

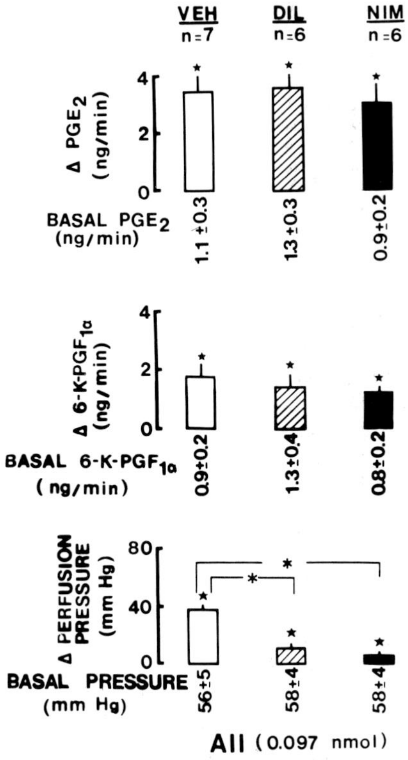

FIGURE 3. *Effect of the Ca^{++} channel blockers diltiazem, (DIL) 60 μM and nimodipine, (NIM) 47 μM, or their vehicles, (VEH) on the output of PGE_2 (upper panel) and 6-keto-$PGF_{1\alpha}$ (middle panel) and on the changes in perfusion pressure (bottom panel) elicited by AII in the isolated rat kidney perfused with normal Tyrode's solution (1.8 mM). ★ denotes values different from basal, whereas * denotes the difference between values in the presence of a Ca^{++} channel blocker and its vehicle ($P < 0.05$).*

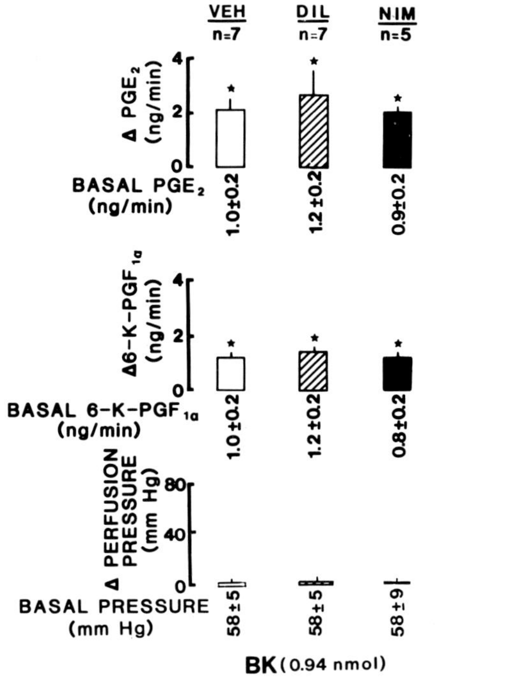

FIGURE 4. *Effect of the Ca^{++} channel blockers diltiazem, (DIL) 60 μM and nimodipine, (NIM) 47 μM or their vehicles (VEH) on the output of PGE_2 (upper panel) and 6-keto-$PGF_{1\alpha}$ (middle panel) and on the changes in perfusion pressure on (bottom panel) elicited by BK in the isolated rat kidney perfused with normal Tyrode's solution (1.8 mM). ★ denotes values different from basal ($P < 0.05$).*

Effect of Dantrolene Sodium, TMB-8, or Ryanodine on AII and BK Actions on Prostaglandin Output and Vascular Tone in the Absence and Presence of Ca^{++} (Figs. 5 and 6).

In kidneys perfused with Ca^{++}-free Tyrode's solution containing dantrolene sodium, TMB-8, or ryanodine, the effect of AII (0.097 nmol), but not that of bradykinin (0.94 nmol), to enhance the output of PGE_2 and 6-keto-$PGF_{1\alpha}$ was significantly reduced. Addition of Ca^{++} (1.8 mM) to the medium abolished the inhibitory effect of intracellular Ca^{++} antagonists on AII-induced prostaglandin output and renal vasoconstriction. In kidneys perfused with Tyrode's solution containing normal Ca^{++} (1.8 μM), the intracellular Ca^{++} antagonists also failed to alter AII- or BK-induced output of prostaglandins and the rise in perfusion pressure caused by AII. However, in kidneys perfused with solution containing 0.9 mM Ca^{++} and TMB-8, the output of prostaglandins was reduced, whereas the rise in perfusion pressure elicited by AII remained unaltered (Fig. 6). In the presence of 0.6 mM Ca^{++} addition of TMB-8 reduced both the prostaglandin output and the rise in perfusion pressure caused by AII (Fig. 6). The basal output of prostaglandins and the perfusion pressure were unaltered by variations in Ca^{++} concentrations and/or addition of intracellular Ca^{++} antagonists to the medium.

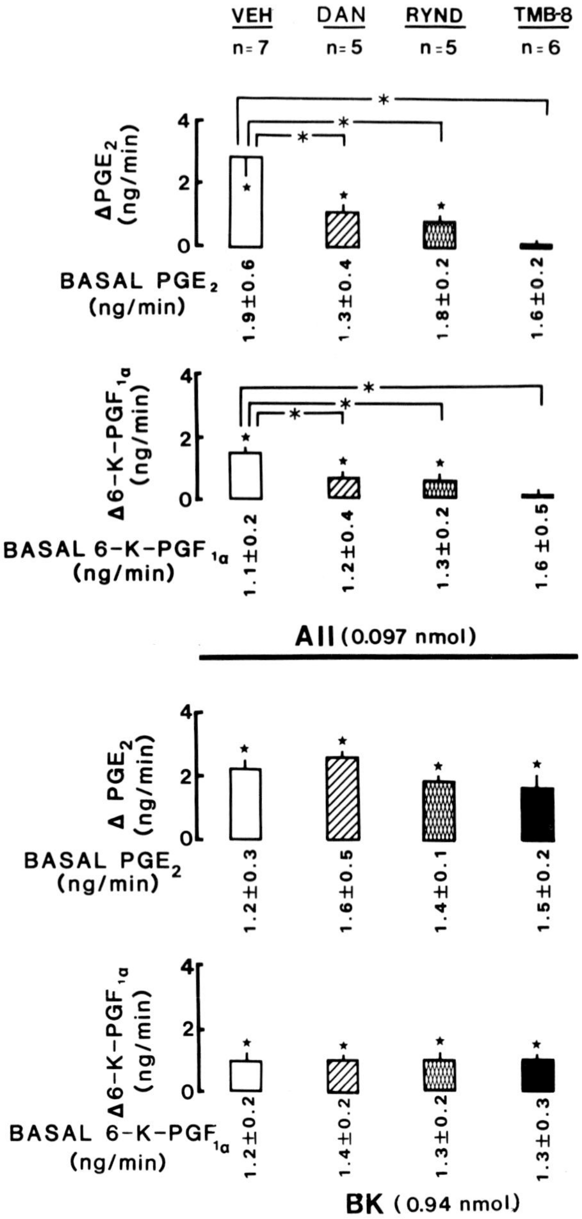

Figure 5. *Effect of dantrolene sodium, (DAN) 31 μM, ryanodine, (RYND) 2 μM, or TMB-8, 2.3 μM, or their vehicles (VEH) on PGE_2 output (upper panel for each respective drug) and 6-keto-$PGF_{1\alpha}$ output (lower panel for each respective drug) elicited by AII and BK in the isolated rat kidney perfused with Ca^{++}-depleted Tyrode's solution (0 mM). ★ denotes values different from basal, whereas * denotes the difference between values in the presence of a Ca^{++} antagonist and its vehicle ($P < 0.05$).*

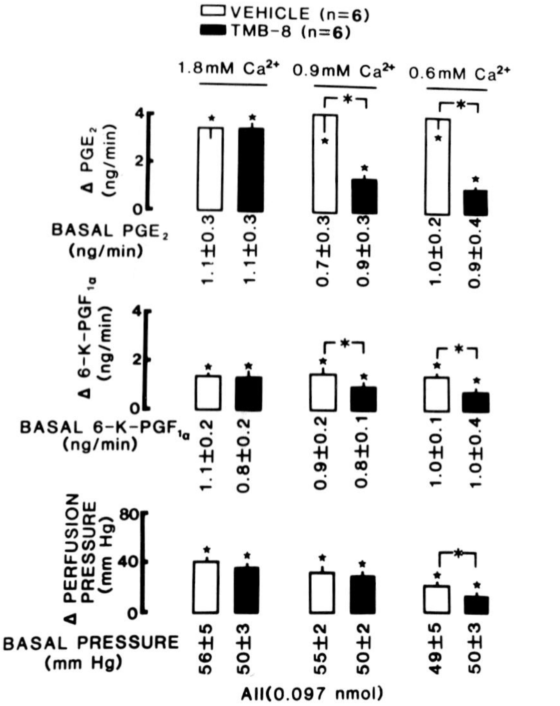

Figure 6. *Effect of AII on the output of PGE_2 (upper panel) and 6-keto-$PGF_{1\alpha}$ (middle panel) and on the perfusion pressure (bottom panel) in the isolated rat kidney perfused with Tyrode's solution containing normal Ca^{++} (1.8 mM), or low Ca^{++} (0.9 or 0.6 mM) in the presence of TMB-8, 2.3 μM. ★ denotes values different from basal, and * represents the difference between values obtained in the presence of the Ca^{++} antagonist, TMB-8, and its vehicle ($P < 0.05$).*

Effect of Trifluoperazine, W-7, and Calmidazolium on the Actions of AII and BK on Prostaglandin Output and Vascular Tone in the Presence or Absence of Ca^{++} (Figs. 7 and 8)

Infusion of trifluoperazine, W-7, or calmidazolium in the presence of Ca^{++} inhibited the output of both PGE_2 and 6-keto-$PGF_{1\alpha}$ elicited by AII. Trifluoperazine, but not W-7 or calmidazolium, attenuated the rise in perfusion pressure elicited by AII (0.097 nmol). In the absence of Ca^{++}, the calmodulin inhibitors also attenuated the rise in prostaglandin output produced by AII. The effect of BK (0.94 nmol) to increase the output of prostaglandins was unaltered by the calmodulin inhibitors in the presence or absence of Ca^{++}. The basal output of prostaglandins or perfusion pressure was also unaffected by the calmodulin inhibitors.

Effect of [Sar^1,Ala^8]-AII on the Actions of AII and BK on Prostaglandin Output and Vascular Tone in the Presence or Absence of Ca^{++} (Fig. 9)

In kidneys perfused with Ca^{++}-containing (1.8 mM) or Ca^{++}-free Tyrode's solution, infusion of [Sar^1,Ala^8]-AII reduced the effect of AII (0.097 nmol) to increase prostaglandin output and the perfusion pressure; the magnitude of decrease was the same in the absence as in the presence of Ca^{++}. Infusion of higher concentration of [Sar^1,Ala^8]-AII abolished both the output of prostaglandins and renal vasoconstriction produced by AII; the prostaglandin output elicited by BK (0.94 nmol) was not altered by either the low or high concentration of the AII receptor antagonist (data not shown). [Sar^1,Ala^8]-AII did not alter the basal output of prostaglandins or perfusion pressure in the presence or absence of Ca^{++}.

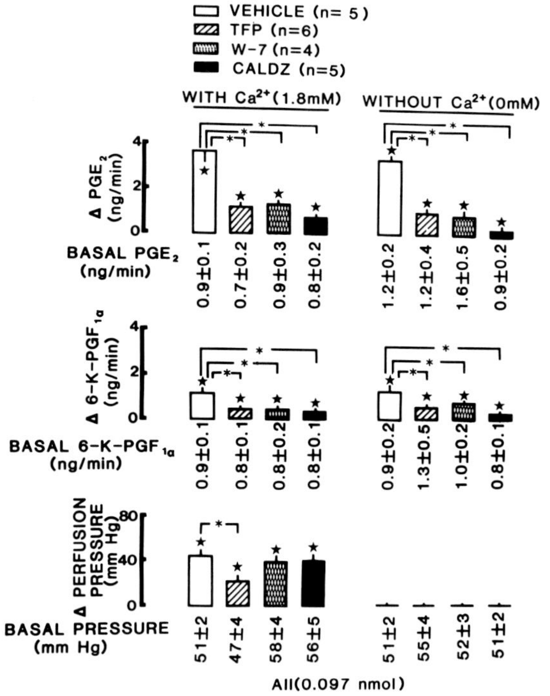

FIGURE 7. *Effect of the calmodulin inhibitors trifluoperazine, (TFP) 2 μM, W-7, 2 μM, or calmidazolium, (CALDZ) 0.2 μM, or their vehicles (VEH) on the output of PGE_2 (upper panel) and 6-keto-$PGF_{1\alpha}$ (middle panel) and the changes in perfusion pressure (bottom panel) elicited by AII in the isolated rat kidney perfused with normal (1.8 mM) and Ca^{++}-depleted Tyrode's solution.* ★ *denotes values different from basal, and* * *represents the difference between values obtained with a calmodulin inhibitor and its vehicle ($P < 0.05$).*

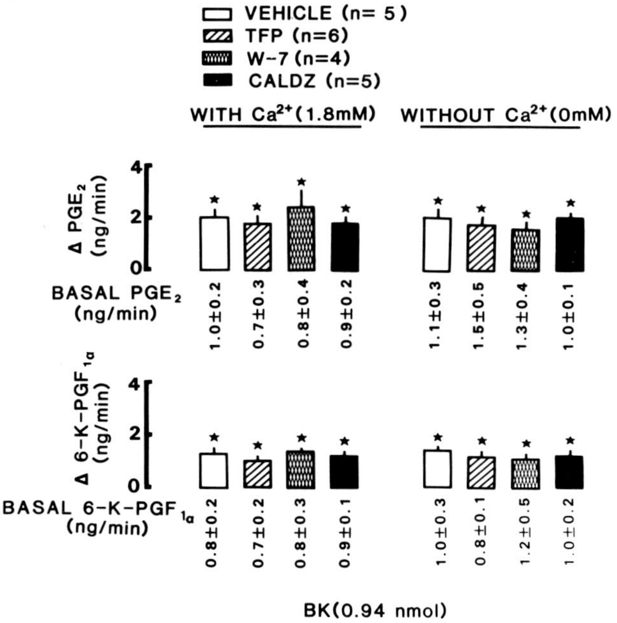

FIGURE 8. *Effect of calmodulin inhibitors trifluoperazine, (TFP) 2 μM, W-7, 2 μM, or calmidazolium, (CALDZ) 0.2 μM, or their vehicles (VEH) on the output of PGE_2 (upper panel) and the output of 6-keto-$PGF_{1\alpha}$ (middle panel) elicited by BK in the isolated rat kidney perfused with normal (1.8 mM) and Ca^{++}-depleted Tyrode's solution.* ★ *denotes values different from basal ($P < 0.05$).*

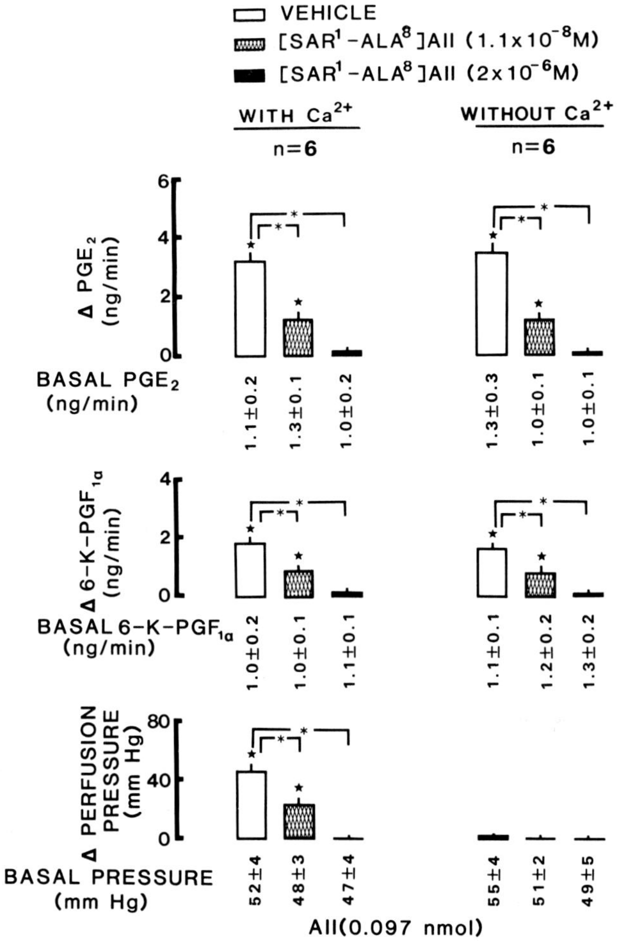

FIGURE 9. *Effect of [Sar¹,Ala⁸]-AII, 0.02 μM, or 1.1 μM, or its vehicle on the output of PGE_2 (upper panel) and 6-keto-$PGF_{1\alpha}$ (middle panel) and on the changes in perfusion pressure (bottom panel) elicited by AII in kidneys perfused with Ca^{++}-containing (1.8 mM) and Ca^{++}-depleted Tyrode's solution.* ★ *denotes values different from basal, and* * *represents the difference between values obtained with [Sar¹, Ala⁸]-AII and its vehicle ($P < 0.05$).*

Effect of Ca^{++} Depletion, Ca^{++} Antagonists, Calmodulin Inhibitors, and [Sar¹,Ala⁸]-AII on the Actions of Arachidonic Acid on Prostaglandin Output and Vascular Tone

Administration of arachidonic acid (33 nmol) enhanced the output of PGE_2 and 6-keto-$PGF_{1\alpha}$ from 1.42 ± 0.24 to 6.91 ± 0.80 ng/min and from 1.32 ± 0.11 to 6.21 ± 0.40 ng/min, respectively, and enhanced the perfusion pressure from 57 ± 4 to 69 ± 2 mmHg ($P < 0.05$, $n = 5$) in kidneys perfused with Ca^{++}-containing Tyrode's solution. In kidneys perfused with Ca^{++}-depleted solution, administration of arachidonic acid produced similar increases in the output of prostaglandins, but it failed to increase perfusion pressure. The effect of arachidonic acid to enhance prostaglandin synthesis was not altered by diltiazem, nimodipine, dantrolene sodium, TMB-8, ryanodine, trifluoperazine, W-7, calmidazolium or [Sar¹,Ala⁸]-AII. The increase in perfusion pressure elicited by arachidonic acid in the presence of Ca^{++}

was reduced by diltiazem (60 μM) from 18 ± 6 mmHg ($n = 6$) to 8 ± 1 mmHg ($n = 6$) ($P < 0.05$) and by nimodipine (47 μM) from 18 ± 6 mmHg ($n = 6$) to 13 ± 5 mmHg ($n = 7$) ($P < 0.05$) but not by other agents.

Effect of AII plus BK on the Output of Prostaglandins and Vascular Tone in the Presence of Ca^{++} (Table 1)

Administration of the combination of AII and BK into kidneys perfused with normal Tyrode's solution enhanced the output of PGE_2 and 6-keto-$PGF_{1\alpha}$. Prostaglandin output elicited by this combination was significantly greater than that elicited by the separate administration of AII or BK. The rise in perfusion pressure elicited by AII plus BK was not significantly different from that elicited by the injection of AII alone.

Effect of Indomethacin and Mepacrine on the Actions of AII, BK, and Arachidonic Acid on Prostaglandin Output and Vascular Tone in the Presence or Absence of Ca^{++} (Fig. 10)

During infusion of indomethacin, in the presence of Ca^{++}, AII (0.097 nmol), BK (0.94 nmol), or arachidonic acid (33 nmol)-induced prostaglandin output was completely prevented. Infusion of mepacrine abolished AII and BK but not arachidonic acid-induced output of PGE_2 and 6-keto-$PGF_{1\alpha}$. The basal prostaglandin output was reduced by indomethacin but not by mepacrine. The effect of indomethacin and mepacrine on prostaglandin output elicited by AII, BK, or arachidonic acid in the absence of Ca^{++} was similar as in the presence of Ca^{++} (data not shown). The increase in perfusion pressure elicited by AII or arachidonic acid in the presence of Ca^{++} was reduced during infusion of indomethacin or mepacrine (Fig. 10).

TABLE 1

Effect of AII and BK Alone and in Combination on PG Output and Perfusion Pressure in the Isolated Rat Kidney

Substance (nmol)	Increase in prostaglandin output: PGE_2 (ng/min)	Increase in prostaglandin output: 6-keto-$PGF_{1\alpha}$ (ng/min)	Increase in perfusion pressure
($n = 4$)			
AII (0.097)	2.5 ± 0.4	1.7 ± 0.3	47 ± 5
BK (0.94)	2.2 ± 0.2	1.1 ± 0.4	2.5 ± 0.4*
AII + BK (0.097 + 0.94)	4.24 ± 0.4†	3.3 ± 0.3†	43 ± 5
($n = 4$)			
AII (0.29)	6.45 ± 0.3	2.8 ± 0.3	61.2 ± 4
BK (2.8)	3.44 ± 0.2	1.6 ± 0.2	4.6 ± 1.8*
AII + BK (0.29 + 2.8)	10.6 ± 0.4†	4.1 ± 0.3†	60.4 ± 5

The basal output of PGE_2 was 1.2 ± 0.3 ng/min and of 6-keto-$PGF_{1\alpha}$ was 0.9 ± 0.2 ng/min. The basal perfusion pressure was 56 ± 5 mm Hg.

* All of the values in the table except those indicated by * were significantly greater than the basal values ($P < 0.05$).

† Denotes values significantly higher than the values obtained during administration of either AII or BK alone. n denotes the number of kidneys perfused.

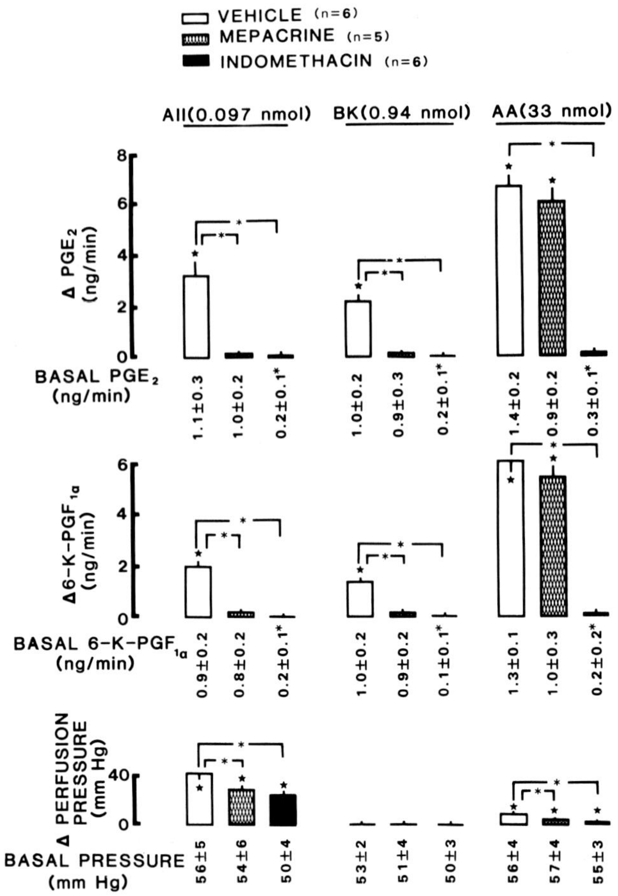

FIGURE 10. *Effect of mepacrine, 21 μM, and indomethacin, 2.8 μM, or their vehicles on the output of PGE_2 (upper panel) and 6-keto-$PGF_{1\alpha}$ (middle panel) and on the changes in perfusion pressure (bottom panel) elicited by AII, BK, and arachidonic acid (AA) in the isolated rat kidney perfused with normal Tyrode's solution. ★ represents values different from basal, whereas * represents the difference between values obtained in the presence of a drug and its respective vehicle ($P < 0.05$).*

Discussion

The present study in the isolated rat kidney perfused with Tyrode's solution indicates that AII requires extracellular Ca^{++} to produce renal vasoconstriction and intracellular Ca^{++} to stimulate prostaglandin synthesis. Only the stimulation of prostaglandin synthesis depends upon calmodulin, a Ca^{++}-binding protein (Cheung, 1980). In contrast, BK stimulates prostaglandin synthesis by a mechanism which appears to be independent of both extra- and intracellular Ca^{++} and calmodulin.

AII-Induced Vasoconstriction

In the isolated rat kidney perfused with Tyrode's solution containing Ca^{++}, administration of AII produced renal vasoconstriction and increased the output of PGE_2 and 6-keto-$PGF_{1\alpha}$, in a dose-related manner, a finding consistent with that reported in other species (Needleman et al., 1973; McGiff, 1981). Removal of Ca^{++} from the perfusion medium abolished AII-induced renal vasoconstriction but failed to alter prostaglandin output elicited by AII which suggests a selective requirement of extracellular Ca^{++} in the former but not in the latter action of the peptide. Loss of AII-induced renal vasoconstriction was not due to disruption of vascular smooth muscle contractile elements, since addition of Ca^{++} to the perfusion fluid restored the vasoconstrictor effect of AII. The selective involvement of extracellular Ca^{++} to the renal vasoconstriction and not to prostaglandin output elicited by AII was also suggested by our findings that (1) raising or lowering Ca^{++} concentrations in the perfusion medium augmented or reduced, respectively, the renal vasoconstriction but not the output of prostaglandins produced by AII and (2) two structurally dissimilar Ca^{++} antagonists, diltiazem, and nimodipine (Towart and Kazda, 1979; van Breeman et al., 1981; Towart, 1981), attenuated AII-induced renal vasoconstriction without altering its effect on prostaglandin output. These observations, taken together with the demonstration that AII increases uptake of ^{45}Ca into the vascular smooth muscle (Deth and van Breeman, 1974), suggest that AII produces renal vasoconstriction primarily by increasing the influx of extracellular Ca^{++}, a finding which is consistent with those reported in the rabbit aorta (Deth and van Breeman, 1974; St. Louis et al., 1977).

Our finding that [Sar^1,Ala^8]-AII, a selective AII receptor antagonist, abolished the renal vasoconstrictor effect of AII but not that of a structurally dissimilar peptide, arginine vasopressin (unpublished observation), suggests that AII increases the influx of Ca^{++} consequent to its interaction with a specific receptor. The interaction of AII with its receptor may enhance Ca^{++} influx by a mechanism coupled with membrane depolarization (voltage-operated channels) and/or by a nonelectrical mechanism (receptor-operated channels). Our demonstration that diltiazem and nimodipine, Ca^{++} entry blockers (Towart and Kazda, 1979; van Breeman et al., 1981; Towart, 1981), like nifedipine (Jover et al., 1982), attenuated AII-induced renal vasoconstriction suggests that AII could activate voltage-operated channels (Freer et al., 1976; Mironneau and Gargouil, 1979; Kass and Blair, 1981). Nevertheless, our observation that removal of Ca^{++} from the perfusion fluid was more effective than the Ca^{++} entry blockers in inhibiting the renal vasoconstrictor effect of AII suggests that the peptide is unlikely to increase Ca^{++} influx only through voltage-sensitive channels.

Enhanced influx of Ca^{++} through receptor- or voltage-operated channels consequent to AII-receptor interaction may release intracellularly bound Ca^{++} (Ford and Podolshky, 1972) or act directly to activate vascular smooth muscle contractile elements. In the present study, dantrolene sodium, ryanodine, or TMB-8—agents that inhibit release of Ca^{++} from intracellular sites (Chiou and Malagodi, 1975; Morgan and Bryant, 1977; Sutko and Kenyon, 1983)—failed to alter AII-induced renal vasoconstriction in the presence of extracellular Ca^{++} (1.8 mM), suggesting that intracellular Ca^{++} is not utilized in this action of the peptide. However, we cannot exclude a small contribution of intracellular Ca^{++} in the vasoconstriction elicited by AII, since, in the presence of low Ca^{++} (0.6 mM), TMB-8 attenuated AII-induced renal vasoconstriction.

Ca^{++} in the vascular smooth muscle may interact with calmodulin to increase the activity of myosin kinase which phosphorylates the light chain of myosin and allows the latter to interact with actin to initiate vascular smooth muscle contraction (Adelstein et al., 1982). Supporting this proposal is the demonstration that AII stimulates and chlorpromazine, a calmodulin inhibitor, attenuates myosin light chain phosphorylation in cultured vascular smooth muscle cells (Anderson et al., 1981). Moreover, agents that inhibit Ca^{++} calmodulin-dependent myosin kinase reduce the contraction of rabbit aorta produced by AII (Asano et al., 1982). However, much higher concentrations of the calmodulin inhibitors were required to reduce contraction of the vascular smooth muscle produced by AII than those caused by other agonists (Peach, 1981; Asano et al., 1982). In the present study, trifluoperazine attenuated AII-induced renal vasoconstriction; however, two structurally dissimilar and relatively more specific calmodulin inhibitors, W-7 (Hidaka et al., 1981) and calmidazolium (Van Belle, 1981), failed to alter the renal vasoconstrictor effect of this peptide. Thus, it appears that the AII-induced rise in cellular Ca^{++} concentration could increase myosin kinase activity and produce renal vasoconstriction by a mechanism unrelated to calmodulin.

BK Actions on Vascular Tone

Bradykinin, which is known to produce renal vasodilation in vivo in several species, and relaxation, contraction, or no effect in the isolated perfused vessels or arterial strips (Regoli and Barabé, 1980), enhanced the prostaglandin output but did not alter the renal vascular tone in our preparation in the presence of Ca^{++}. The inability of bradykinin to produce alterations in vascular tone in the present study could be due to loss of intrinsic tone in the in vitro Tyrode-perfused kidney. However, this is unlikely, since histamine, a renal vasodilator, at doses of 2.4, 4.8, and 24 nmol, reduced the perfusion pressure by 10, 18, and 28 mmHg, respectively (unpublished observation). Whether bradykinin requires the presence of some blood-borne factors for expression of its vasodilator action in the kidney in vitro is unknown.

AII- and BK-Induced Prostaglandin Output

An important finding in the present study was that depletion of Ca^{++} from the perfusion medium in the absence or presence of EGTA or addition of Ca^{++} entry blockers, which attenuated AII-induced renal vasoconstriction, did not alter the effect of AII and BK to enhance the output of prostaglandins. These findings, and our observation that a Ca^{++} ionophore, A23187, which increased the output of PGE_2 and 6-keto-$PGF_{1\alpha}$ without altering the vascular tone, failed to alter prostaglandin output in the absence of Ca^{++}, suggest that (1) the effect of AII to increase renal output of prostaglandins is not the result of alterations in vascular tone, and (2) both AII and BK stimulate renal prostaglandin output by a mechanism that does not require extracellular Ca^{++}. Juan (1979) has reported that, in the rabbit ear artery, the effect of bradykinin to stimulate the output of PGE_2 was not altered by removal of Ca^{++} from the medium and was reduced only by adding high amounts of EGTA to the Ca^{++}-depleted medium. In the rabbit portal vein, in the absence of Ca^{++} and in the presence of EGTA, the output of PGE_2 elicited by AII was not completely prevented (Simmet and Hertting, 1980). However, in the bovine pulmonary artery (Crutchley, 1983) and porcine aortic endothelial cells (Whorten et al., 1982), renal medullary slices (Benabé et al., 1982; Zenser et al., 1982), or glomerular mesangial cells in culture (Scharschmidt and Dunn, 1983), the effect of AII or BK to stimulate prostaglandin synthesis was abolished by the lack of Ca^{++} or by addition of Ca^{++} channel blockers in the medium. Loss of the effect of AII or BK to stimulate prostaglandin synthesis in these tissues, but not in the intact perfused kidney in the absence of Ca^{++}, could be due to differences in experimental conditions (incubation vs. perfusion and/or time of preincubation without Ca^{++}) and/or the response of various renal cellular structures (vascular and glomerular mesangium, medullary interstitium, cortical and medullary tubules) to the peptides. In spite of differences in the response of renal medullary slices or mesangial cells in culture and perfused kidney to AII or BK during removal of Ca^{++} for the medium, the profile of prostaglandins released by the peptides in the former tissues was similar to that obtained in the intact kidney.

Prostaglandin synthesis elicited by AII and BK in the rat kidney, as in the rabbit kidney (Needleman et al., 1973), was due to activation of two distinct types of receptors because [Sar^1,Ala^8]-AII, a selective AII receptor antagonist, inhibited the output of prostaglandins elicited by AII but not BK. Although the binding of AII with its receptor sites has been reported to be influenced by divalent cations (Wright et al., 1982), Ca^{++} in our study did not appear to alter the action of AII on its receptor to increase prostaglandin output for the following reasons. First, the effect of AII to increase the output of PGE_2 or 6-keto-$PGF_{1\alpha}$ was not affected by changes in Ca^{++} concentration or removal of Ca^{++} from the medium. Second, the magnitude of inhibition of AII-induced prostaglandin output by [Sar^1,Ala^8]-AII, in the absence of Ca^{++} was similar to that observed in the presence of Ca^{++}.

Prostaglandin synthesis elicited by AII and BK in the absence of extracellular Ca^{++} could be due to the mobilization of Ca^{++} from the cell membrane or intracellular structures, which may in turn cause activation of phospholipase A_2 or other lipases that release arachidonic acid from tissue phospholipids for prostaglandin synthesis. Our demonstration that an intracellular Ca^{++} antagonist, TMB-8 [which reduces thrombin and A23187-induced arachidonic acid or prostaglandin release from platelets (Rittenhouse-Simmons and Deykin, 1978; Brotherton and Hoak, 1982] and other intracellular Ca^{++} antagonists, dantrolene sodium and ryanodine (Chiou and Malagodi, 1975; Morgan and Bryant, 1977), abolished prostaglandin output elicited by AII, but not BK, suggests that the former but not the latter peptide acts by a mechanism requiring intracellular Ca^{++}. The possibility that BK stimulates prostaglandin synthesis by mobilizing Ca^{++} from intracellular sites that are resistant to blockade by the above intracellular Ca^{++} antagonists cannot be totally excluded. Alternatively, it is possible that BK promotes prostaglandin synthesis by activating a lipase that is distinct from that involved in the action of AII. That AII stimulates prostaglandin synthesis by a mechanism involving mobilization of intracellular Ca^{++} is also suggested by the demonstrated ability of this peptide to release Ca^{++} from microsomes in the aorta (Baudouin et al., 1972). The inhibitory action of the intracellular Ca^{++} antagonists on AII-induced prostaglandin synthesis in our study was not due to the action of these agents to interfere with the action of AII at its receptor, or due to a reduction in cyclooxygenase activity since: (1) in kidneys perfused with Tyrode's solution containing 0.9 mM Ca^{++}, the intracellular Ca^{++} inhibitor, TMB-8, attenuated the output of prostaglandins without altering the renal vasoconstriction elicited by AII, and (2) the output of PGE_2 and 6-keto-$PGF_{1\alpha}$ elicited by arachidonic acid was not altered by the intracellular Ca^{++} antagonists. These findings, together with our demonstration that increasing or decreasing the Ca^{++} concentration in the perfusion medium enhanced or reduced the renal vasoconstriction, respectively, without altering the output of prostaglandins elicited by AII, suggest that it is improbable that the extracellular Ca^{++} entering renal cells during interaction of the peptide with its receptor is the source of cellular Ca^{++} involved in the prostaglandin synthesis-stimulating action of AII.

An important finding in the present study was that trifluoperazine, W-7, and calmidazolium, in concentrations known to inhibit calmodulin activity (Levin and Weiss, 1976; Hidaka et al., 1981; Van Belle, 1981), attenuated the renal output of prostaglandins elicited by AII, but not that caused by exogenous arachidonic acid. This finding, and the demonstration that a phospholipase A_2-like activity was increased by Ca^{++}-calmodulin and inhibited by trifluoperazine in platelets (Wong and Cheung, 1979) and in renal medullary slices (Craven and DeRubertis, 1983), suggests that Ca^{++} released from intracellular storage sites by AII may stimulate deacylation by interacting with calmodulin. A Ca^{++}-calmodulin-mediated synthesis of prostaglandins has also been reported for arginine vasopressin in renal medullary slices (Craven and DeRubertis, 1981) and the isolated rat kidney (Cooper and Malik, 1984). It appears unlikely, from our study, that the reduction of AII-induced prostaglandin output by calmodulin inhibitors is due to their interference with intracellular Ca^{++} release, since the effect of the calmodulin inhibitors to attenuate AII-induced prostaglandin output was not altered by the addition of Ca^{++} to the medium, whereas the inhibitory effect of intracellular Ca^{++} antagonists on prostaglandin output elicited by AII was abolished by raising the Ca^{++} concentration to 1.8 mM. The calmodulin inhibitors failed to alter the effect of BK to enhance renal output of prostaglandins, which suggests that BK stimulates prostaglandin synthesis in the rat kidney by a mechanism independent of calmodulin. However, Crutchley et al. (1983), in bovine pulmonary artery, and Whorton et al. (1982), in porcine aortic cultured endothelial cells, have reported that Ca^{++} depletion or Ca^{++} channel blockers and trifluoperazine attenuated BK-induced output of prostaglandins. It remains to be determined whether these differences in the susceptibility of BK-induced prostaglandin synthesis to Ca^{++} antagonists and calmodulin inhibitors in the rat kidney and endothelial cells, are due to differences in the cell type and/or the lipase activated by the kinin.

AII and BK may release arachidonic acid for prostaglandin synthesis from tissue phospholipids by causing activation of an acylhydrolase, presumably phospholipase A_2 or phospholipase C (Kunze and Vogt, 1971; Bell et al., 1979; Billah et al., 1981; Prescott and Majerus, 1983). Our demonstration that mepacrine, a phospholipase A_2 and C inhibitor (Vargaftig and Coiron, 1971; Hoffmann et al., 1982), reduced the output of prostaglandins elicited by AII and BK, but not that caused by exogenous arachidonic acid, suggests that AII and BK stimulate prostaglandin synthesis by activating phospholipase A_2 and/or C. However, the finding that intracellular Ca^{++} antagonists and calmodulin inhibitors attenuated AII- but not BK-induced prostaglandin synthesis in the rat kidney suggests that the lipase involved in the action of AII but not BK is dependent upon Ca^{++} and calmodulin. Further evidence suggesting that BK stimulates prostaglandin synthesis by a mechanism distinct from that of AII resulted from our observation that the output of prostaglandins elicited by combined administration of AII and BK was approximately equal to the sum of the prostaglandin output produced by administration of these peptides alone. Although mepacrine, in our study, inhibited AII and BK-induced prostaglandin synthesis, it failed to alter the basal output of prostaglandins. Since, indomethacin, a cyclooxygenase inhibitor, reduced the basal and abolished AII and BK-induced prostaglandin output, it appears that arachidonic acid released in the absence of hormone stimulation arises from a distinct lipid pool, or the lipase that stimulates deacylation is insensitive to AII and BK (Schwartzman et al., 1981).

The present study in the isolated intact rat kidney indicates that AII produces renal vasoconstriction by a mechanism that requires extracellular Ca^{++} but not calmodulin, whereas the effect of AII to stimulate prostaglandin synthesis requires intracellular Ca^{++}, which appears to interact with calmodulin and, presumably, activates phospholipase A_2 and/or C. In contrast, BK enhances prostaglandin synthesis by stimulating a lipase that does not appear to require Ca^{++} and calmodulin.

We wish to thank Elizabeth Bordwell, Diane Overton, and Marie Hurt for their technical assistance and Christa Ingram for typing this manuscript. We also thank Dr. Lawrence Levine for the generous supply of PGE_2 and 6-keto-$PGF_{1\alpha}$ antibodies, and the pharmaceutical companies listed in Methods for providing various drugs for this study.

This work was presented in part at the Annual Meeting of the Society of Pharmacology and Experimental Therapeutics, August 1982, and at the Federation of American Societies for Experimental Biology, April 1983.

This study was supported by U.S. Public Health Service Grant HL 19134 from the National Heart, Lung, and Blood Institute.

This work was done in partial fulfillment of the requirements for the Ph.D. degree by C.L. Cooper.

Dr. J.E. Shaffer's present address: Department of Pharmaceutical Research, American Critical Care, 1600 Waukegan Road, McGraw Park, Illinois 60085.

Address for reprints: Dr. Kafait U. Malik, Professor of Pharmacology, Department of Pharmacology, College of Medicine, University of Tennessee, 874 Union Avenue, Crowe 100, Memphis, Tennessee 38163.

Received June 7, 1984; accepted for publication October 10, 1984.

References

Adelstein RS, Sellers JR, Conti MA, Pato MD, DeLanerolle P (1982) Regulation of smooth muscle contractile proteins by calmodulin and cyclic AMP. Fed Proc **41:** 2873–2878

Anderson JM, Gimbrone MA Jr, Alexander RW (1981) Angiotensin II stimulates phosphorylation of the myosin light chain in cultured vascular smooth muscle cells. J Biol Chem **256:** 4693–4696

Asano M, Suzuki Y, Hidaka H (1982) Effects of various calmodulin antagonists on contraction of rabbit aortic strips. J Pharmacol Exp Ther **220:** 191–196

Baudouin M, Meyer P, Fermandjian S, Morgat JL (1972) Calcium release induced by interaction of angiotensin in smooth muscle cell microsomes. Nature **235:** 336–338

Bell RL, Kennerly DA, Stanford N, Majerus PW (1979) Diglyceride lipase: A pathway for arachidonate release from human platelets. Proc Natl Acad Sci USA **76:** 3238–3241

Benabé JE, Spy LA, Morrison AR (1982) Effects of angiotensin II on phosphatidylinositol and polyphosphoinositide turnover in rat kidney. J Biol Chem **257:** 7430–7434

Billah MM, Lapetina EG, Cuatrecasas P (1981) Phospholipase A_2 activity specific for phosphatidic acid. J Biol Chem **256:** 5399–5403

Brotherton AFA, Hoak JC (1982) Role of Ca^{2+} and cyclic AMP in the regulation of the production of prostaglandins by the vascular endothelium. Proc Natl Acad Sci USA **79:** 495–499

Cheung WY (1980) Calmodulin plays a pivotal role in cellular regulation. Science **207:** 19–27

Chiou CY, Malagodi MH (1975) Studies on the mechanism of action of a new Ca^{2+} antagonist, 8-(*N,N*-diethylamino) octyl 3,4,5-trimethoxy-benzoate hydrochloride in smooth and skeletal muscles. Br J Pharmacol **53:** 279–285

Cooper CL, Malik KU (1984) Mechanisms of action of vasopressin on prostaglandin synthesis and vascular function in the isolated rat kidney: Effect of calcium antagonists and calmodulin inhibitors. J Pharmacol Exp Ther **229:** 139–147

Craven PA, DeRubertis FR (1981) Effects of vasopressin and urea on Ca^{2+}-calmodulin-dependent renal prostaglandin E. Am J Physiol **241:** F649–F658

Craven PA, DeRubertis FR (1983) Ca^{2+} calmodulin-dependent release of arachidonic acid for renal medullary prostaglandin synthesis. Evidence for involvement of phospholipases A_2 and C. J Biol Chem **258:** 4814–4823

Crutchley DJ, Ryan JW, Ryan US, Fisher GH (1983) Bradykinin-induced release of prostacyclin and thromboxanes from bovine pulmonary artery endothelial cells. Studies with lower homologs and calcium antagonists. Biochim Biophys Acta **751:** 99–107

Deth R, van Breeman C (1974) Relative contributions of Ca^{2+} influx and cellular Ca^{2+} release during drug induced activation of the rabbit aorta. Pflugers Arch **348:** 13–22

Ford LE, Podolshky RJ (1972) Intracellular calcium movements in skinned muscle fibres. J Physiol (Lond) **223:** 21–33

Freer RJ, Pappano AJ, Peach MJ, Bing KT, McLean ML, Vogeland S, Sperelakis N (1976) Mechanism for the positive inotropic effect of angiotensin II on isolated cardiac muscle. Circ Res **39:** 178–183

Hidaka H, Asano M, Tanaka T (1981) Activity structure relationship of calmodulin antagonists. Naphthalenesulfonamide derivatives. Mol Pharmacol **20:** 571–578

Hoffmann SL, Prescott SM, Majerus PW (1982) The effects of mepacrine and *p*-bromophenacyl bromide on arachidonic acid release in human platelets. Arch Biochem Biophys **215:** 237–244

Jover B, Casellas D, Dupont M, Mimran A (1982) Influence of nifedipine on vascular reactivity: Studies in the isolated perfused rat kidney. Eur Heart J **3:** 15–17

Juan H (1979) Role of calcium in prostaglandin E release induced by bradykinin and the ionophore A 23187. Naunyn Schmiedebergs Arch Pharmacol **37:** 177–183

Kalsner S, Nickerson M, Boyd GN (1970) Selective blockade of potassium-induced contractions of aortic strips by β-diethylamino ethyldiphenylpropylacetate (SKF 525A). J Pharmacol Exp Ther **174:** 500–508

Kass RS, Blair ML (1981) Effects of angiotensin II on membrane currentin cardiac Purkinje fibers. J Mol Cell Cardiol **13:** 797–809

Kunze H, Vogt W (1971) Significance of phospholipase A for prostaglandin formation. Ann NY Acad Sci **180:** 123–125

Levin RM, Weiss B (1976) Mechanism by which psychotropic drugs inhibit adenosine cyclic 3:5-monophosphate phosphodiesterase of brain. Mol Pharmacol **12:** 581–589

Malik KU, McGiff JC (1975) Modulation by prostaglandins of adrenergic transmission in the isolated perfused rabbit and rat kidney. Circ Res **36:** 599–609

McGiff JC (1981) Prostaglandins, prostacyclin, and thromboxanes. Annu Rev Pharmacol Toxicol **21:** 479–509

Mironneau J, Gargouil YM (1979) Action of indapamide on the excitation-contraction coupling in vascular smooth muscle. Eur J Pharmacol **56:** 57–67

Morgan KG, Bryant SH (1977) The mechanism of action of dantrolene sodium. J Pharamcol Exp Ther **201:** 138–147

Needleman P, Kauffman AH, Douglas JR Jr, Johnson EM Jr, Marshall GR (1973) Specific stimulation and inhibition of renal prostaglandin release by angiotensin analogs. Am J Physiol **224:** 1415–1419

Page I, Bumpus M (1961) Angiotensin. Physiol Rev **41:** 331–390

Peach MJ (1981) Molecular actions of angiotensin. Biochem Pharmacol **30:** 2745–2751

Prescott SM, Majerus PW (1983) Characterization of 1,2-diacylglycerol hydrolysis in human platelets. J Biol Chem **258:** 764–769

Regoli D, Barabé J (1980) Pharmacology of bradykinin and related kinins. Pharmacol Rev **32:** 1–46

Rittenhouse-Simmons S, Deykin D (1978) The activation by Ca^{2+} of platelet phospholipase A_2: Effects of dibutyryl cyclic adenosine monphosphate and 8-(*n,N*-diethylamino-octyl-3,45-trimethosybenzoate. Biochim Biophys Acta **543:** 409–422

Scharschmidt LA, Dunn MJ (1983) Prostaglandin synthesis by rat glomerular mesangial cells in culture. Effect of angiotensin II and arginine vasopressin. J Clin Invest **71:** 1756–1764

Schwartzman M, Liberman E, Raz A (1981) Bradykinin and angiotensin II activation of arachidonic acid deacylation and prostaglandin E_2 formation in rabbit kidney. J Biol Chem **256:** 2329–2333

Shaffer JE, Malik KU (1982) Enhancement of prostaglandin output during activation of beta-1 adrenoceptors in the isolated rabbit heart. J Pharmacol Exp Ther **223:** 729–735

Simmet T, Hertting G (1980) On the relation between contraction and prostaglandin release in rabbit mesenteric blood vessels. Eur J Pharmacol **65:** 325–331

St. Louis J, Regoli D, Barabe J, Park WK (1977) Myotropic actions of angiotensin and noradrenaline in strips of rabbit aorta. Can J Physiol Pharmacol **55:** 1056–1069

Sutko JL, Kenyon JL (1983) Ryanodine modification of cardiac muscle responses to potassium-free solutions. Evidence for inhibition of sarcoplasmic reticulum calcium release. J Gen Physiol **82:** 385–404

Towart R (1981) The selective inhibition of serotonin-induced contractions of rabbit cerebral vascular smooth muscle by calcium-antagonistic dihydropyridines. An investigation of the mechanism of action of nimodipine. Circ Res **48:** 650–657

Towart R, Kazda S (1979) The cellular mechanism of action of nimodipine (Bay 3 9736), a new calcium antagonist. Br J Pharmacol **67:** 409P–410P

Van Belle H (1981) R24 571 A potent inhibitor of calmodulin-activated enzymes. Cell Calcium **2:** 483–494

van Breeman C, Hwang O, Meisheri KD (1981) The mechanism of inhibitory action of diltiazem on vascular smooth muscle contractility. J Pharmacol Exp Ther **218:** 459–463

Vargaftig BB, Coiron M (1971) Detection de la phospholipase a de divers venins animax per ses effects sur la coagulation du jaune d'cenf et par la formation de "substance a contraction différée c." J Pharmacol (Paris) **2:** 155–173

Whorton AR, Young SL, Data JL, Barchowsky A, Kent RS (1982) Mechanism of bradykinin stimulated prostacyclin synthesis in porcine aortic endothelial cells. Biochim Biophys Acta **712:** 79–87

Wong PY-K, Cheung WY (1979) Calmodulin stimulates platelet phospholipase A_2. Biochem Biophys Res Commun **90:** 473–480

Wright GB, Alexander RW, Eckstein LS, Gimbrone MA Jr (1982) Sodium, divalent cations, and guanine nucleotides regulate the affinity of the rat mesenteric artery angiotensin II receptor. Circ Res **50:** 462–469

Zar JH (ed) (1984) Comparison of a control mean to each other group mean. Biostatistical Analysis, ed 2. Englewood Cliffs, N.J., Prentice-Hall, pp 194–195

Zenser TV, Rapp NS, Davis BB (1982) Independent mechanisms for bradykinin-mediated prostaglandin E_2 and cyclic GMP synthesis in rabbit renal inner medulla slices. J Pharmacol Exp Ther **221:** 532–535

INDEX TERMS: PGE_2 • 6-Keto-$PGF_{1\alpha}$ • Bradykinin • Angiotensin II • Renal vasoconstriction • Calcium depletion • Calcium channel blockers • Intracellular calcium antagonists • Calmodulin inhibitors

Vascular Adrenergic Neuroeffector Function Does Not Decline in Aged Rats

Sue Piper Duckles, Bart J. Carter, and Cynthia L. Williams

From the Department of Pharmacology, College of Medicine, University of Arizona, Health Sciences Center, Tucson, Arizona

SUMMARY. To investigate adrenergic control of blood vessels during aging, rats aged 6, 12, 20, and 27 months were studied using in vitro techniques. Accumulation of [^{3}H]norepinephrine, one index of adrenergic nerve density, did not alter with age in the femoral or renal arteries or renal vein. In the femoral vein [^{3}H]norepinephrine accumulation was greater at 6 and 27 months of age. Norepinephrine sensitivity was determined in both an innervated vessel, the femoral artery, and a non-innervated vessel, the carotid artery. In both cases, sensitivity to norepinephrine did not alter with age. In the renal and femoral arteries and veins, no significant changes in maximum responses to norepinephrine (10^{-5} M), potassium chloride, or transmural nerve stimulation were seen with advancing age. Furthermore, frequency response curves (2–16 Hz, 200 pulses) did not differ with age for any of the four vessels studied, with one exception. The response to stimulation at 4 Hz of the femoral vein from 6-month-old rats was significantly larger than responses at other ages. During nerve stimulation, the renal vein exhibited rapid contractions superimposed upon the maintained contractile response. This type of rapid contraction occurred only rarely (1 out of 5) in the renal vein from 27-month-old rats. In summary, neither adrenergic nerve density as reflected by [^{3}H]norepinephrine accumulation nor norepinephrine sensitivity decline with age. As the net effect of various components, the ability of vascular smooth muscle to respond to adrenergic nerve stimulation is also maintained during advancing age. **(*Circ Res 56: 109–116, 1985*)**

WHEREAS some authors maintain that the effectiveness of adrenergic stimulation on the cardiovascular system declines with advancing age (Lakatta, 1980; Wollner and Spalding, 1978), others have referred to the "hyperadrenergic state" of old age (Rowe and Troen, 1980). Most would agree, however, that adrenergic regulation of vascular smooth muscle may potentially play an important role in the pathophysiology and treatment of such age-related problems as postural hypotension, hypertension, and alterations in homeostatic thermoregulation (Balmagiya and Rozovski, 1983; Rowe, 1983; Wollner and Spalding, 1978; Conrad and Bressler, 1982).

Examination of the literature on this controversy over function of the adrenergic system in old age is less than conclusive, as most animal studies of the vasculature during aging have been hampered by methodological problems. For example, as reviewed by Fleisch (1980), few investigators have verified the specificity of alterations in α-adrenergic receptor responsiveness by testing another contractile agonist. Thus, alterations in the magnitude of maximum contractile responses could reflect changes in vessel elasticity or smooth muscle structure, rather than specific changes in the adrenergic system. Another problem with many studies of "aging" is that it has been difficult to obtain animals over a wide age range. Immature and adult animals have been compared, but truly senescent animals have not always been available (Duckles, 1983).

For these reasons, we have studied adrenergic responses of the vasculature of the Fischer 344 rat, from a colony maintained by the National Institutes of Aging. In a strain where the mean life span varies from 24 to 29 months depending on diet (Masoro, 1980), we chose to study animals aged 6, 12, 20, and 27 months. Density of adrenergic innervation has been assessed by measuring [^{3}H]norepinephrine ([^{3}H]NE) accumulation in a series of vessels. Sensitivity to exogenous NE as well as to transmural adrenergic nerve stimulation in vitro has been determined under carefully defined conditions in order to answer the question: does the function of the vascular adrenergic neuroeffector alter with advancing age?

Methods

Blood vessels from four groups of Fischer 344 rats were studied: 6, 12, 20, and 27 months of age. Mean weights (n = 6) were 324 ± 9, 403 ± 9, 394 ± 10, and 396 ± 6 g, respectively. The animals were obtained from the National Institutes of Health Aging Colony, housed in the Division of Animal Resources in stainless steel hanging cages, and fed with Wayne Lab-Blox rat chow. After being received at the University of Arizona, the animals were retained from 1 to 4 weeks before being studied.

After decapitation, the femoral artery and vein, the left renal artery and vein, and the carotid artery were carefully removed. The vessels were placed in Krebs' solution at room temperature which was composed as follows (mM): Na^+, 147.6; K^+, 6.4; Ca^{++}, 1.6; Mg^{++}, 1.2; Cl^-, 130; HCO_3^-, 26; SO_4^{--}, 1.2; $H_2PO_4^-$, 1.2; glucose, 11; disodium ethylenediamine tetraacetate, 0.027. Care was taken during dissection so that vessels were not stretched.

Norepinephrine Accumulation

Vascular segments were incubated in Krebs' solution containing 0.11 mM ascorbic acid and equilibrated with 95% O_2, 5% CO_2 at 37°C for 60 minutes. To measure non-neuronal accumulation, cocaine (10^{-4} M) was present during the last 30 minutes of the equilibration period and during incubation with norepinephrine. The initial equilibration was followed by incubation in Krebs' solution containing [7-^{3}H (*N*)]-1-NE (10^{-8} M, New England Nuclear, lot 1848-041, specific activity 17.2 Ci/mmol) for 30 minutes. At the end of this period, tissues were briefly rinsed in fresh Krebs' solution, blotted, and weighed. Tissues were solubilized in 0.5 ml soluene-100 (Packard), and radioactivity of solubilized tissues and a bath aliquot was determined by liquid scintillation counting. Accumulation was calculated as milliliters of bath fluid cleared per gram wet weight of tissue. Neuronal accumulation was calculated as total accumulation − accumulation in the presence of cocaine.

Contractile Studies

With the aid of a dissecting microscope, vessel segments were trimmed to a length of 4 mm, and two pieces of platinum wire (0.13 mm diameter) were passed through the lumen. One wire was connected to a Gould-Statham UC2 Universal transducing cell with microscale accessory for isometric recording of changes in force with a potentiometric recorder. The other wire was attached to a moveable plastic support for adjustment of the resting force. The entire apparatus was then placed in a tissue bath containing 50 ml of prewarmed (37°C), oxygenated (95% O_2, 5% CO_2) Krebs' solution.

Two parallel platinum electrodes (40 mm long) were placed on either side of the vessel segment approximately 5 mm apart for delivery of transmural nerve stimulation (TNS). Electrical stimulation (15 V, 0.3 msec) was delivered from a Grass stimulator and coupling device to provide a low source impedance (Duckles and Silverman, 1980). After equilibration for 60 minutes at 37°C, the bath solution was replaced. For determination of the optimal resting force, tissues were tested at a series of resting forces using a single standard TNS stimulus for 20 seconds at a frequency of 2, 4, or 8 Hz, depending on the responsiveness of the vessel segment. In the case of the carotid artery, 10^{-7} M NE was used as the standard stimulus. The resting force at which the largest response to the standard stimulus was produced was then maintained for the remainder of the experiment.

In studies of responses to transmural nerve stimulation, TNS at 2, 4, 8, and 16 Hz for a train duration of 200 pulses was delivered. Ten-minute rest periods were allowed between each stimulus train. This was followed by determination of the maximum contractile response at 16 Hz when vessels were stimulated for at least 2 minutes until a plateau response was obtained. For the renal artery, renal vein, and femoral vein, plateau responses at 32 Hz were smaller than at 16 Hz, 96 ± 4, 75 ± 6, and 71 ± 9% of plateau responses at 16Hz, respectively ($n = 3$). For the femoral artery, plateau responses at 32 Hz were somewhat larger than responses at 16 Hz, 118 ± 6% ($n = 3$). Thus maximum responses to TNS are somewhat underestimated by responses at 16 Hz in the femoral artery. In all cases, responses to TNS at 16 Hz were blocked by tetrodotoxin (10^{-6} M), confirming their neurogenic origin. After washout of the tetrodotoxin, deoxycorticosterone (10^{-7} M), desmethylimipramine (10^{-7} M), and propranolol (10^{-7} M) were added to block extraneuronal and neuronal metabolism and β-adrenergic receptors, respectively. Under these conditions the maximum contractile response to 10^{-5} M NE was evaluated as an index of maximum α-adrenergic responsiveness. After washout of the NE, 150 mM KCl was added to the bath.

For determination of sensitivity to NE, in a separate series of experiments, cumulative concentration response curves to NE were determined. Again deoxycorticosterone, 10^{-7} M, desmethylimipramine, 10^{-7} M and propranolol, 10^{-7} M, were present. Maximum responses to KCl (150 mM) were determined at the end of each experiment. EC_{50} values (concentration that produces 50% of the maximum response) were determined from concentration-response curves. Geometric means and confidence intervals were calculated (Fleming et al., 1972).

Drugs Used

The following drugs were used: deoxycorticosterone, Aldrich; tetrodotoxin, Calbiochem; *l*-norepinephrine bitartrate and *d,l*-propranolol, HCl, Sigma; desmethylimipramine, courtesy of USV Laboratories, Tuckahoe, NY.

Statistics

Means and standard errors are reported throughout. Analysis of variance was used for determination of differences between groups.

Results

[^{3}H]Norepinephrine Accumulation

Total, extraneuronal (+ cocaine), and neuronal [^{3}H]NE accumulation by the femoral artery and vein and renal artery and vein are illustrated in Figure 1. In the femoral artery and the renal artery and vein, there were no significant differences with age in either total or neuronal NE accumulation. In the femoral vein, however, both total and neuronal [^{3}H]NE accumulation in tissue from 6-month-old rats was significantly greater than in tissue from both 12- and 20-month-old rats ($P < 0.01$). Accumulation in the femoral vein of 27-month-old rats was significantly greater than in 12-month-old rats.

Resting Force

Resting force-response relationships are shown in Figures 2 and 3 for the vessels studied: the femoral artery and vein, the renal artery and vein, and the carotid artery. There were no significant differences with age in the optimum resting forces used, except for the femoral artery, where the optimum force for animals 6 months of age was smaller than the optimum resting forces for vessels from older animals.

Maximal Contractile Responses

There were no significant differences with age in the maximal contractile responses to TNS, NE, or KCl in the femoral and renal arteries and veins (Fig. 4). In the carotid artery, however, maximal re-

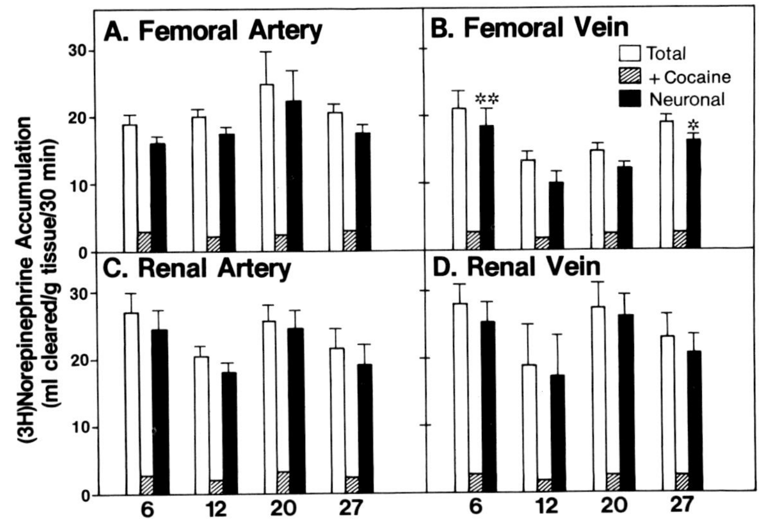

Figure 1. *[^{3}H]NE accumulation (total, + cocaine and neuronal) in four vessels from rats 6, 12, 20, and 27 months of age. Values are means ± SE (n = 6). ** different from 12 and 20 months; * different from 12 months (P < 0.01).*

sponses to NE were significantly smaller in the 6-month-old animals than 20-month-old ($P < 0.001$). Maximum responses to NE were 0.52 ± 0.04 g in vessels from 6-month-old rats and 0.63 ± 0.03, 0.77 ± 0.04, and 0.71 ± 0.06 from 12-, 20-, and 27-month-old animals, respectively. The maximal contractile response to TNS, expressed as a percent of the maximal response to NE is shown in Table 1. There were no significant differences with age, as tested by analysis of variance, for any of the four vessels studied. Overall, these findings demonstrate that ability of these vessels to respond maximally to either NE or adrenergic nerve stimulation does not decline with age.

Sensitivity to Exogenous Norepinephrine

Cumulative concentration response curves to NE were determined in an innervated vessel, the femoral artery, as well as in a non-innervated vessel, the carotid artery (Fig. 5). Lack of responsiveness of the carotid artery to transmural nerve stimulation was used as evidence of the lack of adrenergic innervation. As can be seen in Figure 5 and Table 2, sensitivity to NE did not change significantly with age as assessed by the EC_{50} value.

Sensitivity to TNS

Sensitivity to transmural nerve stimulation can be assessed from the frequency response curve as

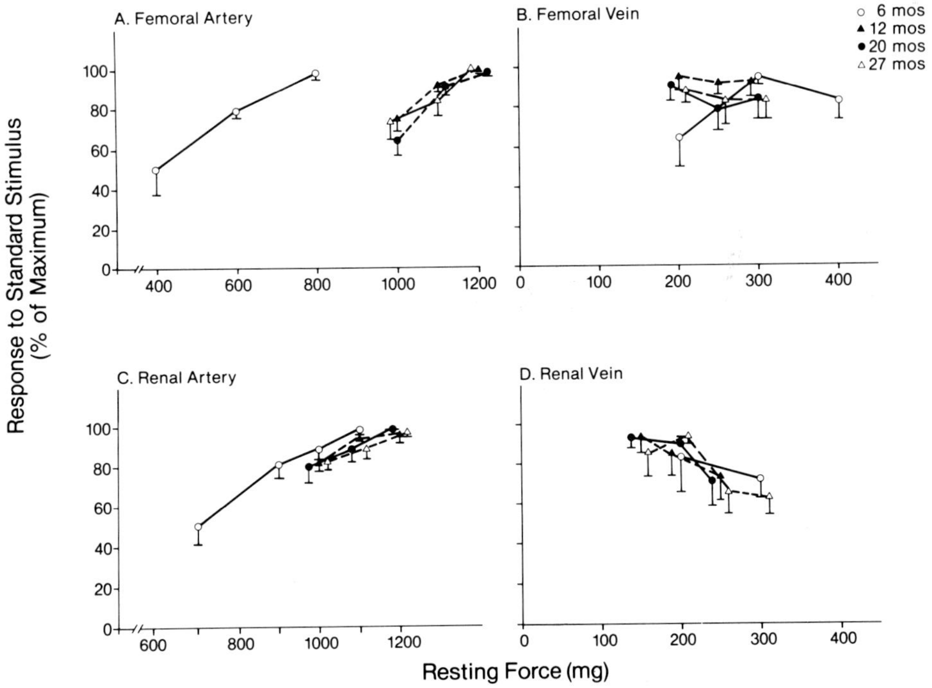

Figure 2. *Resting force-response relationship for four vessels studied for responses to TNS. As described in Methods, responses to a single standard frequency of TNS (2, 4, or 8 Hz for 20 seconds) were determined at various resting forces in each vessel segment. Values are means ± SE (n as in Table 1).*

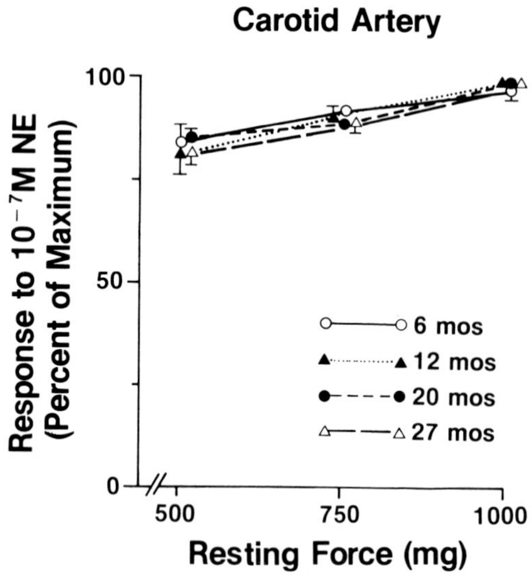

FIGURE 3. *Resting force-response relationship for the carotid artery. Responses to a standard concentration of NE (10^{-7} M) were determined at various resting forces in each vessel segment. Means ± SE are shown (n = 10).*

shown in Figure 6. Comparison of the responsiveness of vessels from animals of various ages demonstrates that, on the whole, adrenergic contractile responsiveness does not alter with age. However, there was one exception: the femoral vein from rats 6 months of age showed a greater response to stimulation at 4 Hz than femoral veins from older animals.

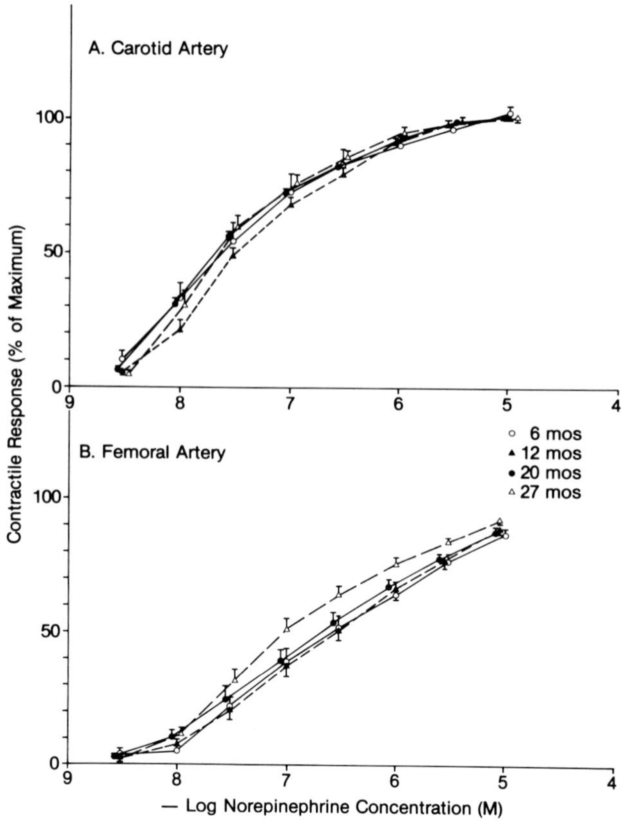

FIGURE 5. *Concentration-response curves to NE in the femoral artery and carotid artery from animals of four different ages. Responses to NE are expressed as a percent of the maximum NE response. Values are means ± SE (n = 5–8).*

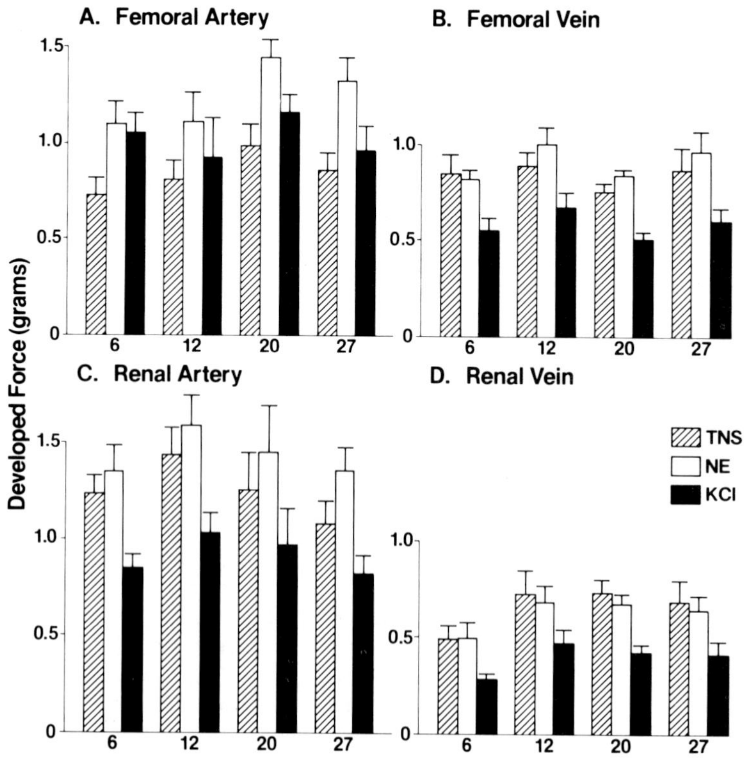

FIGURE 4. *Maximal contractile responses to transmural nerve stimulation (TNS), norepinephrine (NE), and KCl in the four vessels studied from rats 6, 12, 20, and 27 months old. Maximum responses to TNS were obtained by stimulating for at least 2 minutes at 16 Hz until a plateau contraction was obtained. Means ± SE are indicated; n values are listed in Table 1.*

TABLE 1
Maximal Contractile Response to Transmural Nerve Stimulation*

	Percent of maximal NE response in rats at age			
	6 mo	12 mo	20 mo	27 mo
Femoral artery	66 ± 4 (11)	74 ± 4 (6)	67 ± 6 (7)	67 ± 7 (6)
Femoral vein	101 ± 8 (8)	89 ± 4 (5)	90 ± 2 (5)	88 ± 4 (5)
Renal artery	95 ± 6 (8)	90 ± 3 (5)	87 ± 2 (6)	79 ± 5 (6)
Renal vein	103 ± 5 (5)	103 ± 10 (5)	109 ± 4 (6)	105 ± 7 (5)

Values are means ± SE. Numbers in parentheses = number of animals.
* % of maximal norepinephrine response.

Renal Vein Spiking

During adrenergic nerve stimulation or stimulation with exogenous NE, segments of the renal vein often exhibited rapid contractions superimposed upon the maintained contractile response (Fig. 7). The frequency and magnitude of these rapid contractions, which we have termed spikes, are summarized in Table 3. As can be seen in Table 3 and Figure 7, such spiking activity was common in renal veins from animals younger than 20 months of age, occurring in 13 out of 15 vessel segments studied. However, this type of rapid contraction was rarely seen in renal veins from the oldest group of animals, occurring in only one out of five vessels studied.

Discussion

A major conclusion of the present study is that the function of the adrenergic neuroeffector mechanism of vascular smooth muscle does not decline with age. We took care to circumvent methodological problems that have plagued previous approaches to this problem.

Animals that spanned the full age range from young adult to senescent were studied, using the resources of the National Institutes of Health aging colony. In addition, care was taken to ensure that each vessel segment was studied at the optimum point on the resting force-response curve. In addition, for each vessel studied, the contractile potential of the tissue was assessed using two approaches, maximum responses to both NE and KCl were determined at the end of each experiment. This made it possible to express our results as a percentage of the maximum contraction of which the tissue was capable (Table 1; Fig. 5), allowing us to assess adrenergic mechanisms, independent of possible changes in blood vessel structure or smooth muscle composition (Cox, 1977; Nagasawa et al., 1979). Thus, the major aim of this study was directly addressed, enabling us to conclude that the function of the vascular adrenergic neuroeffector shows only subtle changes with age.

TABLE 2
Norepinephrine EC_{50} in Vessels from Rats of Different Ages

Age (mo)	Femoral artery ($\times 10^{-7}$ M)	n	Carotid artery ($\times 10^{-8}$ M)	n
6	2.2 (1.0–5.1)	5	4.2 (2.0–8.5)	5
12	2.7 (1.1–6.6)	5	3.7 (2.2–6.2)	6
20	2.0 (0.7–6.0)	5	2.3 (1.8–3.0)	8
27	0.98 (0.5–2.0)	5	2.6 (1.7–3.8)	5

Geometric mean EC_{50} and confidence intervals are shown.

Perhaps the major alteration in adrenergic function seen with age was loss of the rapid pulsatile contractile response of the renal vein during adrenergic nerve stimulation. This loss did not appear to be progressive with age, but was apparent only in the 27-month-old rats. The physiological function and mechanism of this "spiking" response cannot be determined from our in vitro experiments. The simplest explanation for such a coordinated, relatively fast contractile response would be the presence of pacemaker cell(s) and coordinated electrical activity; however, an electrophysiological approach would be necessary to test this hypothesis.

The best studied vessel showing phasic contractile activity is the rat portal vein, in which multiple pacemaker sites apparently account for coordinated contractions (Hermsmeyer, 1973). In the portal vein phasic contractions occur spontaneously, not in the presence of adrenergic stimulation, as was true in the renal vein that we have studied. It is interesting that this loss of spiking contractions in the 27-month-old rat renal vein is not associated with a decline in maximum responses to nerve stimulation or a shift in the frequency response curve (Figs. 4 and 6). This is true even though, at a stimulation frequency of 4 Hz, the spikes account for as much as 30 or 40% of the total contractile response (Table 3).

For the most part, we saw no change with age in sensitivity to either exogenous NE or to transmural nerve stimulation and no apparent alteration in adrenergic nerve density as assessed by [^{3}H]NE accumulation. The single exception was the femoral vein, where both [^{3}H]NE accumulation and sensitivity to nerve stimulation were increased in vessels from the 6-month-old rats. [^{3}H]NE accumulation was also higher in the 27-month-old femoral vein, but sensitivity to nerve stimulation was not increased. We can only speculate about the reasons for this, which could include alterations in NE release, changes in smooth muscle sensitivity, etc. At any rate, this increased sensitivity to nerve stimulation in the 6-month-old femoral vein does not change our overall conclusion that adrenergic responsiveness does not

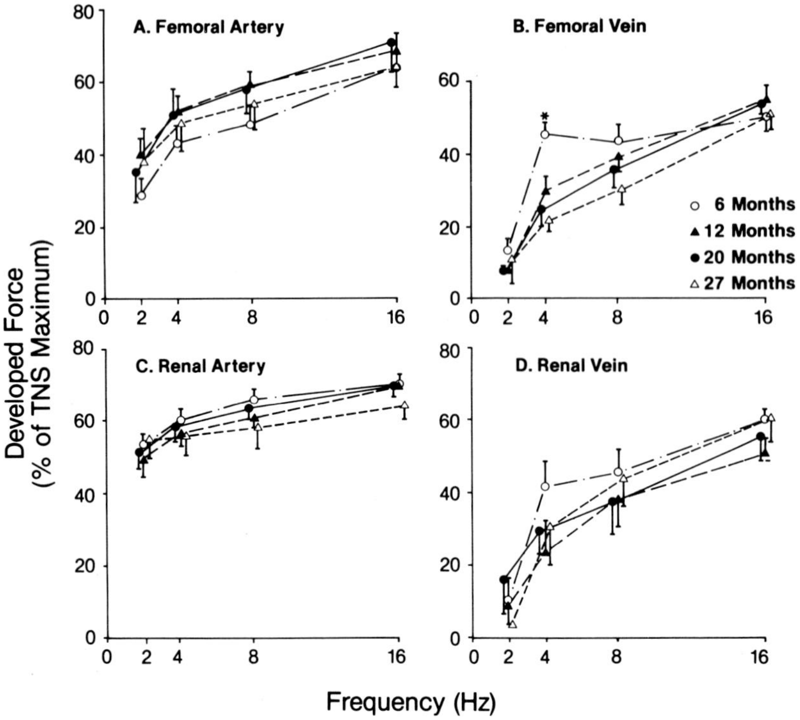

FIGURE 6. *Contractile responses of vessels from rats of four different ages to transmural nerve stimulation (200 pulses) at various frequencies. Results are expressed as a percent of the maximum response to TNS. Values shown are means ± SE. n values are identical to those listed in Table 1.*

decline with advancing age, as there was no progressive decline from 12 to 27 months and, as shown by animal weight, 6-month-old rats are not yet fully grown.

In comparing our results with those in the literature, one must keep in mind that function of the adrenergic neuroeffector junction per se has rarely been examined. As reviewed by Fleisch (1980), many authors have neglected to demonstrate that alterations in contractile function are specific to the adrenergic nervous sytem. In the large blood vessels that have usually been studied, such as the aorta, it is clear that profound structural changes occur with age, and an overall decline in contractile function is not unexpected (Tuttle, 1966; Cohen and Berkowitz, 1976; Simpkins et al., 1983; Yin et al., 1983).

Some authors have seen age-related changes in adrenergic responsiveness per se. For example, in the rabbit, indices of innervation density, NE content, and accumulation, did not change with age, but contractile responses to adrenergic nerve stimulation did decline with age (Duckles, 1983). However, this study compared young rabbits with adults, and did not really study a wide age span. Truly senescent animals have rarely been studied.

Several authors have reported that NE concentration in vascular smooth muscle declines with age in human vessels (Neubauer and Christensen, 1978;

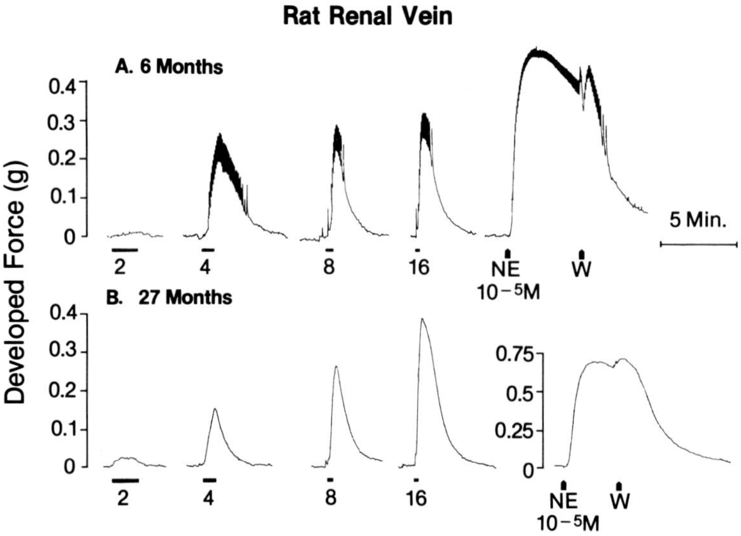

FIGURE 7. *Contractile responses of rat renal vein segments from animals of two ages: A, 6 months; B, 27 months. Frequency of nerve stimulation for 200 pulses is indicated. NE = norepinephrine; W = wash.*

TABLE 3
Renal Vein Spikes

Rat age (mo)	Fraction with spiking	Spike size mg 4 Hz	Spike size mg 16 Hz	Spike size % of total response 4 Hz	Spike size % of total response 16 Hz	Spike no.* 4 Hz	Spike no.* 16 Hz
6	4/5	72 ± 16	58 ± 3	31 ± 7	17 ± 1	18 ± 7	23 ± 7
12	4/5	111 ± 52	110 ± 35	39 ± 12	26 ± 8	4 ± 2	13 ± 3
20	5/5	55 ± 26	77 ± 23	29 ± 6	18 ± 5	6 ± 3	13 ± 5
27	1/5	5	5	7	6	72	60

* Total number of spikes in response to stimulation at 4 Hz for 50 seconds and 16 Hz for 12.5 seconds. Values were determined only from those vessels that did show spiking activity.

Waterson et al., 1974), as well as rat vessels (Embree et al., 1981). In contrast to these findings, our results suggest that one index of adrenergic nerve density, [^{3}H]NE accumulation, does not decline with age in vessels of the rat. Further studies will be necessary to determine that [^{3}H]NE accumulation does correlate with NE content, as well as stimulation-evoked NE release.

In support of our findings that the adrenergic responsiveness of vascular smooth muscle does not change with advancing age, it has recently been demonstrated that sensitivity to NE of isolated arteries from humans ranging from 30 to 83 years in age is similar (Scott and Reid, 1982). Furthermore, maximal contractile responses to NE expressed as a percentage of maximal responses to KCl did not change with age in these human vessels. This stability of vascular adrenergic responses with age also supports the findings of two recent clinical studies (MacLennan et al., 1980; Smith and Fasler, 1983). These suggested that postural hypotension in old age is not due to an alteration in adrenergic function per se, but can be accounted for primarily by arteriosclerosis.

This suggests an important point: the current study focuses on a very discrete aspect of the entire functional system for blood pressure control. It is possible that function of the vascular adrenergic neuroeffector mechanism is maintained in old age, but alterations at other sites, such as baroreceptor sensing, central control or ganglionic transmission, could cause a change in the overall function of adrenergic cardiovascular control.

The careful technical assistance of Sue Waite is gratefully acknowledged.

This work was supported by NIH Grant AGO3322. SPD is an Established Investigator of the American Heart Association, with funds provided in part by the Arizona Affiliate.

Address for reprints: Sue Piper Duckles, Ph.D., Department of Pharmacology, College of Medicine, University of Arizona, Health Sciences Center, Tucson, Arizona 85724.

Received April 3, 1984; accepted for publication October 17, 1984.

References

Balmagiya T, Rozovoski SJ (1983) Age-related changes in thermoregulation in male albino rats. Exp Gerontol **18:** 199–210
Cohen ML, Berkowitz BA (1976) Vascular contraction: Effect of age and extracellular calcium. Blood Vessels **13:** 139–154
Conrad KA, Bressler R (1982) Drug Therapy for the Elderly. St. Louis, Mosby
Cox RH (1977) Effects of age on the mechanical properties of rat carotid artery. Am J Physiol **233:** H256–H263
Duckles SP (1983) Age-related changes in adrenergic neuronal function of rabbit vascular smooth muscle. Neurobiol Aging **4:** 151–156
Duckles SP, Silverman RW (1980) Transmural nerve stimulation of blood vessels in vitro: A critical examination. Blood Vessels **17:** 53–57
Embree LJ, Roubein IF, Jackson DW, Ordway F (1981) Aging effect on the noradrenaline content of rat brain microvessels. Exp Aging Res **7:** 215–224
Fleisch JH (1980) Age-related changes in the sensitivity of blood vessels to drugs. Pharmacol Ther **8:** 477–487
Fleming WW, Westfall DP, DeLaLande IS, Jellett LB (1972) Log-normal distribution of equieffective doses of norepinephrine and acetylcholine in several tissues. J Pharmacol Exp Ther **181:** 339–345
Hermsmeyer K (1973) Multiple pacemaker sites in spontaneously active vascular muscle. Circ Res **33:** 244–251
Lakatta EG (1980) Age related alterations in the cardiovascular responses to adrenergic mediated stress. Fed Proc **39:** 3173–3177
MacLennan WJ, Hall MRP, Timothy JI (1980) Postural hypotension in old age: Is it a disorder of the nervous system or of blood vessels? Age Ageing **9:** 25–32
Masoro EJ (1980) Mortality and growth characteristics of rat strains commonly used in aging research. Exp Aging Res **6:** 219–233
Nagasawa S, Handa H, Okumura A, Naruo Y, Moritake K, Hayashi K (1979) Mechanical properties of human cerebral arteries. Part 1: Effects of age and vascular smooth muscle activation. Surg Neurol **12:** 297–304
Neubauer B, Christensen NJ (1978) The decrease in noradrenaline concentration in the posterior tibial artery with age. Gerontology **24:** 299–303
Rowe JW (1983) Systolic hypertension in the elderly. N Engl J Med **309:** 1246–1247
Rowe JW, Troen BR (1980) Sympathetic nervous system and aging in man. Endocrine Rev **1:** 167–179
Scott PJW, Reid JL (1982) The effect of age on the responses of human isolated arteries to noradrenaline. Br J Clin Pharmacol **13:** 237–239
Simpkins JW, Field FP, Ress RJ (1983) Age-related decline in adrenergic responsiveness of the kidney, heart and aorta of male rats. Neurobiol Aging **4:** 233–238

Smith SA, Fasler JJ (1983) Age-related changes in autonomic function: Relationship with postural hypotension. Age Ageing **12:** 206–210

Tuttle RS (1966) Age-related changes in the sensitivity of rat aortic strips to norepinephrine and associated chemical and structural alterations. J Gerontology **21:** 510–516

Waterson JG, Frewin DB, Soltys JS (1974) Age-related differences in catecholamine fluorescence of human vascular tissue. Blood Vessels **11:** 79–85

Wollner L, Spalding JMK (1978) The autonomic nervous sytem. *In* Textbook of Geriatric Medicine and Gerontology, ed 2, edited by JC Brocklehurst. New York, Churchill Livingstone, pp 245–267

Yin FCP, Spurgeon HA, Kallman CH (1983) Age-associated alterations in viscoelastic properties of canine aortic strips. Circ Res **53:** 464–472

INDEX TERMS: Transmural nerve stimulation • Norepinephrine • Fischer 344 rat • [^{3}H]Norepinephrine accumulation

Inhibitors of Prostaglandin Synthesis Augment β-Adrenergic Responsiveness in Canine Coronary Arteries

Gabor Rubanyi and Paul M. Vanhoutte

From the Department of Physiology and Biophysics, Mayo Clinic and Mayo Foundation, Rochester, Minnesota

SUMMARY. The effects of inhibition of endogenous prostaglandin synthesis on the release of norepinephrine from sympathetic nerves and on postjunctional adrenergic responsiveness were studied in isolated canine left circumflex coronary arteries. In rings, suspended for isometric tension recording and contracted with prostaglandin $F_{2\alpha}$, transmural electrical stimulation caused frequency-dependent relaxations, which were blocked by propranolol and augmented by indomethacin. In superfused strips, previously incubated with [^{3}H]norepinephrine, electrical stimulation (2 Hz) increased the overflow of tritiated neurotransmitter; indomethacin did not influence basal or evoked [^{3}H]norepinephrine overflow. Exogenous norepinephrine caused relaxations in rings contracted with prostaglandin $F_{2\alpha}$, but increases in tension in potassium-depolarized tissues which could be abolished by phentolamine; isoproterenol induced relaxations in both cases. Indomethacin significantly augmented the relaxation in response to exogenous norepinephrine (during contractions with prostaglandin $F_{2\alpha}$) and reversed norepinephrine-induced contractions (during potassium-depolarization) into relaxation. Other cyclooxygenase inhibitors had comparable effects. In the presence of propranolol, indomethacin did not diminish contractions evoked by norepinephrine in depolarized rings. Relaxations induced by sodium nitroprusside or acetylcholine during contractions caused by prostaglandin $F_{2\alpha}$ or potassium chloride were not affected by indomethacin. The augmentation of β-adrenergic responsiveness by indomethacin was abolished by exogenous prostacyclin. The prostacyclin synthetase inhibitor tranylcypromine and exogenous prostaglandin E_2 depressed β-adrenergic responsiveness. Indomethacin did not affect the facilitatory action of phosphodiesterase inhibition on β-adrenergic relaxation. The data suggest that endogenous prostaglandins (most probably prostacyclin and prostaglandin E_2) exert a "braking" effect on β-adrenergic responsiveness in coronary arterial smooth muscle. ***(Circ Res 56: 117–125, 1985)***

THE large coronary arteries of the canine heart contain adrenergic nerve terminals which release norepinephrine upon stimulation; under control conditions, the β-adrenergic effect of the released transmitter predominates, causing relaxation (Borda et al., 1977; Rorie and Shepherd, 1980; Cohen et al., 1983). The relaxations of the canine coronary artery induced by electrical stimulation of the adrenergic nerve endings or by the indirectly acting sympathomimetic amine, tyramine, are potentiated by the inhibitor of cyclooxygenase, indomethacin (Cohen et al., 1983). These observations suggest that endogenously formed prostaglandins impair adrenergic neuroeffector interaction in this preparation by either decreasing the release of norepinephrine from the adrenergic nerve endings, by accelerating the disposition of the transmitter, by increasing α-adrenergic responsiveness of the vascular smooth muscle or by reducing β-adrenergic relaxation. The present study demonstrates that inhibition of vascular prostaglandin synthesis augments the postjunctional β-adrenergic responsiveness of coronary arterial smooth muscle.

Methods

The heart was removed from mongrel dogs (15–25 kg) following anesthesia with sodium pentobarbital (30 mg/kg, iv). The left circumflex coronary artery (approximately 4 cm long and 2.0 mm in outside diameter) was dissected free.

Organ Bath Experiments

Rings of vessel, 4 mm in length, were placed in organ chambers (25 ml) filled with Krebs-Ringer-bicarbonate solution of the following millimolar composition: NaCl, 118.3; KCl, 4.7; $MgSO_4$, 1.2; KH_2PO_4, 1.2; $CaCl_2$, 2.5; $NaHCO_3$, 25.0; calcium EDTA, 0.026; and glucose 11.1. In certain experiments, the KCl concentration was increased by 20 mM. The solution was maintained at 37°C and gassed with a 95% O_2-5% CO_2 gas mixture. The rings were connected to a strain gauge (Gould model UC2) for measurement of isometric force. Before the actual experiments, they were placed at the optimal point of their length-tension relationship (Vanhoutte and Leusen, 1969) by repeated 3-minute exposures to 2×10^{-2} M KCl. Basal tension in the rings was increased gradually over a 90-minute period until contractions were maximal. The optimal basal tension was 12.5 ± 0.8 g for 144 rings from 18 dogs.

Drugs

The following pharmacological agents were used: acetylsalycilic acid (aspirin, Sigma); indomethacin (Sigma); isobutyl-methylxanthine (IBMX; Sigma); *d,l*-isoproterenol (Sigma); sodium meclofenamate (Parke-Davis); sodium nitroprusside (Sigma); levo[7-^{3}H(*N*)]norepinephrine, specific activity: 2.7 Ci/mmol (New England Nuclear); *l*-norepinephrine bitartrate (Sigma); phentolamine mesylate (Ciba-Geigy); *d,l*-propranolol (Sigma), prostacyclin (PGI_2, Sigma), prostaglandin E_2 (Sigma), prostaglandin $F_{2\alpha}$ (Sigma), and tranylcypromine sulfate (Smith, Kline and French Labs). Drugs were dissolved in distilled water such that volumes of less than 0.2 ml per dose were added to the organ chambers. The concentrations of drugs are expressed as final molar bath concentrations (M). Indomethacin was dissolved in 0.0005% Na_2CO_3. Blocking agents were added to the bath for at least 30 minutes prior to determining their effect on the response to agonists or electrical stimulation. The response of coronary rings in the presence of antagonists was always compared to that of a ring from the same vessel in which a response in the absence of antagonist was elicited simultaneously. To study relaxation, we contracted the rings with either prostaglandin $F_{2\alpha}$ (2×10^{-6} M) or with KCl (2×10^{-2} M). Contractions reached a maximum in 6–8 minutes; in time control experiments, the plateau response to both agonists was linear for 40 minutes. Inhibitory responses to electrical stimulation or drugs were elicited after the plateau was reached and were expressed as percent of the contraction induced by prostaglandin $F_{2\alpha}$ or KCl. ID_{50} is the concentration of agonist causing 50% inhibition of these contractions. All vascular rings analyzed in the present study contained endothelial cells as they all relaxed to 10^{-7} M acetylcholine (Furchgott and Zawadzki, 1980).

Electrical Stimulation

Adrenergic nerve endings of left circumflex coronary rings were stimulated electrically with parallel rectangular platinum electrodes (1 cm^2, 7-mm spacing), a stimulator (Grass SD9) and a d.c. current amplifier. Since supramaximal transmural stimulation of coronary artery rings results in non-neurogenic inhibitory responses (Brine et al., 1979; Toda, 1981; Rooke et al., 1982), the current-threshold for the non-neurogenic response was determined for each experiment. Rings were contracted with prostaglandin $F_{2\alpha}$ (2×10^{-6} M) in the presence of tetrodotoxin (10^{-7} M) and the maximal pulse duration (10 V, 16 Hz) which caused no relaxation was determined. After washout of tetrodotoxin, responses to these stimuli were then repeated after contraction with prostaglandin $F_{2\alpha}$ (2×10^{-6} M); relaxations were expressed as percent of the response to prostaglandin $F_{2\alpha}$. Frequency-response curves were obtained by allowing responses to reach maximum before increasing the frequency. The responses in the presence of indomethacin were obtained simultaneously with control responses in untreated rings from the same arteries.

[^{3}H]Norepinephrine Release by Electrical Stimulation

Longitudinal strips of left circumflex coronary artery (3–4 cm long, 2–3 mm wide, 34 ± 2.7 mg; n = 12) were incubated for 120 minutes in [^{3}H]norepinephrine (10^{-6} M). After incubation, the tissues were rinsed in fresh physiological salt solution, suspended at 4 g tension, and superfused, by means of a roller pump, with oxygenated physiological salt solution (3 ml/min; 37°C). For electrical stimulation, two platinum wires (0.3 mm in diameter, 10 cm long) were placed parallel to and in contact with the strips. Electrical impulses were 10 V, 0.2 msec in duration (Vanhoutte et al., 1973; Cohen et al., 1983).

After an initial washout period of 120 minutes, the superfusate was collected for 2-minute intervals (by means of a fraction collector) for estimation of the efflux of total radioactivity. Strips were electrically stimulated (S_1) for 6 minutes at 2 Hz, followed by a 48-minute washout period during which tritium efflux reached basal levels. A second stimulation (S_2) was applied in the presence or absence of indomethacin (5×10^{-6} M). The effect of the cyclooxygenase inhibitor (applied 40 minutes before S_2) was expressed as the ratio between the overflow of tritium evoked by S_1 and the overflow evoked by S_2.

Radioactivity Measurements

At the end of the experiments with [^{3}H]norepinephrine, the strips were blotted dry, weighed, and the tritiated compounds were extracted with 1 N acetic acid containing 0.03 mM disodium EDTA and 5 mM ascorbic acid (Verbeuren et al., 1978; Verbeuren and Vanhoutte,1982). Fractional release of tritiated compounds was calculated as the ratio of disintegrations per minute (dpm) released per unit time to the total dpm extracted plus dpm released.

To determine the amounts of intact [^{3}H]norepinephrine and its major metabolites in the superfusate, samples for column chromatographic analysis were obtained by pooling three of the 2-minute samples immediately before and after each period of electrical stimulation. In these samples, tritiated norepinephrine was separated from its major metabolites as described previously (Verbeuren et al., 1977, 1978). Evoked efflux of tritiated norepinephrine was calculated as stimulated minus basal efflux.

Samples (1 ml) of the incubation solutions, superfusate, the extraction medium, and the fractions obtained during the column chromatographic procedure were added to 10 ml scintillation fluid (Safety-Solve; Research Products International), and the radioactivity was measured in a liquid scintillation spectrometer (Beckman LS 6800); corrections for quenching were made by the external standard method. All samples were counted for 10 minutes or until 10,000 counts/min was reached.

Statistical Analysis

Unless otherwise noted, rings or strips from six animals were studied for each group of experiments. The data are expressed as means ± SEM. Statistical evaluation of the data was carried out by Student's two-tailed *t*-test. Differences were regarded as significant when *P* values were less than 0.05.

Results

Organ Bath Experiments

KCl (2×10^{-2} M) produced significantly greater contractions (7.4 ± 0.9 g; n = 15; $P < 0.01$) than prostaglandin $F_{2\alpha}$ (2×10^{-6} M) (3.9 ± 0.4 g; n = 16). In rings contracted with prostaglandin $F_{2\alpha}$, transmural electrical stimulation caused frequency-dependent relaxation which could be inhibited by propranolol (10^{-6} M) (Fig. 1). Norepinephrine caused concentration-dependent relaxations in rings contracted with prostaglandin $F_{2\alpha}$, and contractions in those exposed to KCl (Figs. 2 and 3).

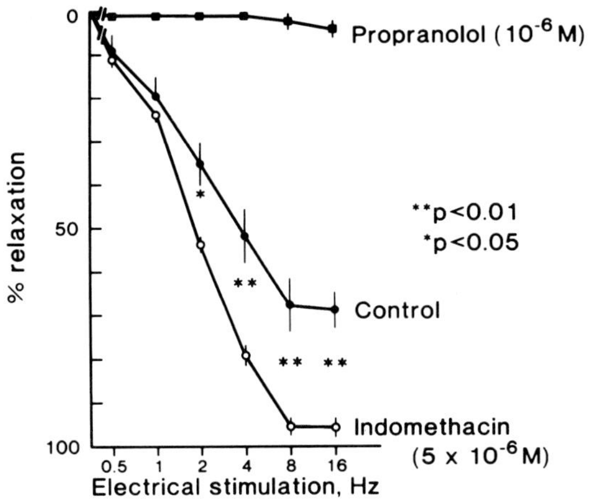

FIGURE 1. *Effect of indomethacin and propranolol on transmural electrical stimulation (10 V; 0.25 msec) evoked relaxations of isolated canine left circumflex coronary arteries during prostaglandin $F_{2\alpha}$ (2×10^{-6} M)-induced contractions. Each symbol represents the mean ± SEM of rings taken from six dogs. Control responses and those in the presence of antagonists were obtained simultaneously in separate rings from the same dog.*

The addition of indomethacin (5×10^{-6} M) to the organ bath increased basal tension (by 0.91 ± 0.25 g; $P < 0.05$; $n = 15$) and augmented prostaglandin $F_{2\alpha}$-induced contractions (from 3.5 ± 0.9 g to 7.3 ± 0.9 g; $P < 0.01$; $n = 9$). Indomethacin significantly augmented the relaxations due to electrical stimulation (in the 2–16 Hz frequency range; Fig. 1) and to norepinephrine (Figs. 2 and 3). Indomethacin did not influence the contractions evoked by KCl (8.9 ± 0.9 g in the absence, and 9.3 ± 1.4 g in the presence of indomethacin; $n = 9$), but reversed the increases in tension caused by norepinephrine (10^{-8} to 3×10^{-6} M) during these contractions into relaxations; at higher concentrations (10^{-5} to 10^{-4} M) of norepinephrine, tension tended to return toward control values (Figs. 2 and 3). During contractions caused by prostaglandin $F_{2\alpha}$ and KCl, sodium nitroprusside caused concentration-dependent relaxations, which were not affected by indomethacin during contractions evoked by prostaglandin $F_{2\alpha}$ (relaxations with 10^{-7} M sodium nitroprusside: 41.5 ± 4.1 and 41.8 ± 6.6% in the absence and presence of indomethacin, respectively) or KCl (20.4 ± 2.9 and 17.1 ± 5.8%, respectively. The endothelium-dependent relaxations to acetylcholine were not affected by the cyclooxygenase inhibitor (data not shown).

Acetylsalicyclic acid (5×10^{-5} M) and sodium meclofenamate (10^{-5} M) increased basal tone (by 0.6 ± 0.2 g and 0.8 ± 0.2 g, respectively) and augmented prostaglandin $F_{2\alpha}$-induced contractions (from 3.9 ± 0.2 to 7.1 ± 0.3 g and from 4.1 ± to 6.8 ± 0.4 g, respectively). In the presence of both drugs, the contractile responses to norepinephrine (3×10^{-8} to 3×10^{-6} M) were reversed to relaxation, whereas, at higher doses of the catecholamine, tension tended to return toward control values in KCl-contracted rings (Fig. 4). Sodium meclofenamate augmented the isoproterenol-induced relaxations in a fashion similar to that of indomethacin, but acetylsalycilic acid caused significant augmentation of β-adrenergic relaxations only at low concentrations (3×10^{-8}-3×10^{-7} M) of isoproterenol (Fig. 4).

In the presence of phentolamine (10^{-5} M), norepinephrine evoked dose-dependent relaxations during contractions caused by KCl (Fig. 5). In the presence of propranolol (10^{-6} M), the increases in tension caused by norepinephrine during KCl-induced responses were significantly greater (Fig. 5) than those obtained in the absence of the β-adrenergic blocker (Fig. 3). Phentolamine and propranolol did not significantly affect the KCl-induced contraction. Isoproterenol relaxed preparations contracted with KCl in a dose-dependent manner (ID_{50}: 4.8 ± 1.2 × 10^{-7} M; maximal effect at 10^{-5} M concentration: 45 ± 9.2% relaxation); this relaxation was significantly inhibited by propranolol (10^{-6} M). At 10^{-7} to 10^{-6} M it was significantly augmented by phentolamine (10^{-5} M; Fig. 5). After combined treatment with indomethacin and phentolamine (10^{-5} M), norepinephrine caused relaxation only during KCl-induced

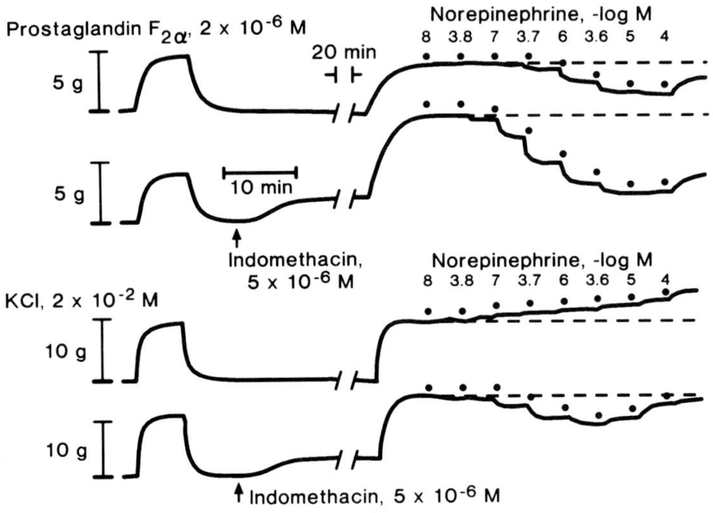

FIGURE 2. *Isometric tension recordings in rings of isolated canine coronary arteries. Responses to increasing concentrations of norepinephrine in the absence or presence of indomethacin during contractions with prostaglandin $F_{2\alpha}$ (upper two tracings) or with KCl (lower two tracings). Indomethacin augmented relaxation induced by norepinephrine during prostaglandin $F_{2\alpha}$-evoked contractions, and reversed the response to norepinephrine from contraction to relaxation in rings exposed to KCl.*

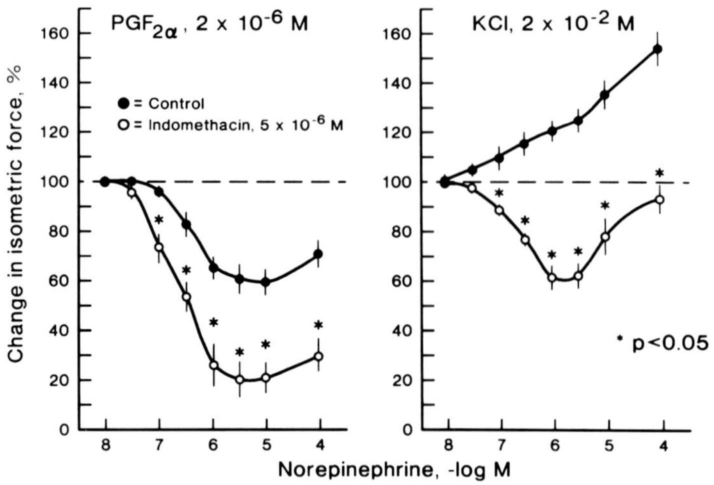

FIGURE 3. *Effect of indomethacin on changes in isometric force in response to norepinephrine in canine coronary arteries contracted with prostaglandin $F_{2\alpha}$ (left) or KCl (right). Symbols represent means ± SEM of rings from six dogs. Control responses and those in the presence of indomethacin were obtained simultaneously in separate rings from the same dog.*

contractions; the relaxations caused by 10^{-6} to 10^{-4} M norepinephrine were significantly greater than those observed in the presence of indomethacin alone (Fig. 5). The augmentation by indomethacin of the relaxations induced by isoproterenol was not influenced by the presence of phentolamine (10^{-5} M; Fig. 5). In the presence of propranolol (10^{-6} M) and indomethacin, increasing doses of norepinephrine caused contractions which were significantly greater in the 3×10^{-6} to 10^{-4} M concentration range (Fig. 5) than those observed under control conditions (Fig. 3), but similar to those obtained in the presence of propranolol alone (Fig. 5). Indomethacin augmented the relaxation induced by 10^{-4} M isoproterenol in the presence of the β-adrenoceptor antagonist (Fig. 5).

In another series ($n = 5$), four rings were studied in parallel; two were pretreated with 5×10^{-6} M indomethacin. After contraction with prostaglandin $F_{2\alpha}$ (2×10^{-6} M), one control and one indomethacin-treated ring were exposed to 10^{-8} M prostacyclin which caused relaxation (by 14 ± 4% in control rings, and 27 ± 5% in indomethacin-treated rings). When the effect of prostacyclin had stabilized (approximately 3 minutes), increasing concentrations (10^{-9} to 10^{-7} M) of isoproterenol were given (Fig. 6). Prostacyclin significantly reduced the relaxation induced by 3×10^{-9} to 10^{-8} M isoproterenol (Fig. 6). Indomethacin significantly augmented the relaxations to all doses of isoproterenol (Fig. 6); this augmentation was abolished by prostacyclin (Fig. 6).

The prostacyclin synthetase inhibitor tranylcypromine (10^{-4} M) augmented basal tension (by 1.0 ± 0.5 g; $n = 5$) and prostaglandin $F_{2\alpha}$-induced contraction (7.2 ± 0.6 g; $n = 5$). It significantly reduced the relaxation to isoproterenol in the concentration range of 3×10^{-9}–3×10^{-7} M (Fig. 7). Exogenous prostaglandin E_2 induced concentration-dependent (10^{-7} to 10^{-5} M) increases in isometric tension of intact coronary artery rings. At a concentration of 10^{-6} M, prostaglandin E_2 evoked concentrations (4.2 ± 0.4 g; $n = 5$) comparable to those induced by 2×10^{-6} M of prostaglandin $F_{2\alpha}$; the relaxations to increasing concentrations of isoproterenol (10^{-9} to 10^{-6} M) were significantly depressed (Fig. 7). A similar depression of β-adrenergic responsiveness was noted during contractions (5.6 ± 0.4 g; $n = 7$) caused by the combination of prostaglandin $F_{2\alpha}$ (2×10^{-6} M) and E_2 (2×10^{-7} M) (Fig. 7).

Rings contracted with prostaglandin $F_{2\alpha}$ were treated with isobutyl-methylxanthin (IBMX; 10^{-6} M). IBMX reduced the contractions (by 12 ± 4%) and

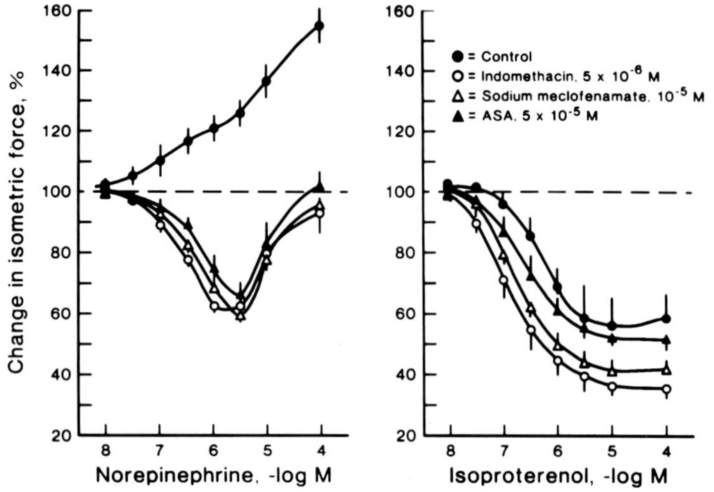

FIGURE 4. *Effect of various cyclooxygenase inhibitors [indomethacin, sodium meclofenamate, and acetylsalicylic acid (ASA)] on responses to norepinephrine (left) and isoproterenol (right) in canine coronary arteries contracted with KCl. Results are expressed as percent of the response to 2×10^{-2} M KCl. Symbols represent means ± SEM of five experiments. Control responses and those in the presence of antagonists were obtained simultaneously in four separate rings from the same dogs. The differences shown between responses to norepinephrine and isoproterenol in the absence or presence of cyclooxygenase inhibitors were statistically significant ($P < 0.05$), except at higher concentrations of isoproterenol (10^{-6} to 10^{-4} M) in the presence of acetylsalycilic acid.*

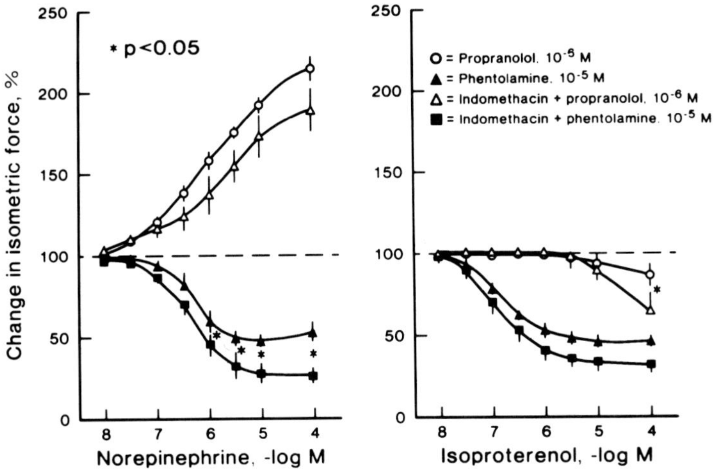

FIGURE 5. *Effect of propranolol and phentolamine on responses of canine coronary arteries to norepinephrine (left) and isoproterenol (right) in the presence and absence of indomethacin during contractions evoked by KCl. Results are expressed as percent of 2×10^{-2} M KCl-induced isometric contractions (7.4 ± 0.9 g; n = 15). Symbols represent means ± SEM of six experiments.*

significantly augmented the relaxation caused by isoproterenol, both in the absence and presence of indomethacin (Fig. 8).

[³H]Norepinephrine Overflow

In superfused left circumflex coronary artery strips, previously incubated with [³H]norepinephrine, transmural electrical stimulation at 2 Hz for 6 minutes (S_1) evoked an increase in tritium and [³H]norepinephrine overflow, but caused no change in basal tone of quiescent coronary artery strips (Fig. 9). A repeated stimulation (S_2) after 48 minutes of superfusion with physiological salt solution caused smaller increases in tritium and [³H]norepinephrine overflow (Fig. 9). In paired strips from the same coronary arteries studied in parallel, indomethacin (5×10^{-6} M; started 8 minutes after S_1) augmented basal tension but did not alter the fractional release

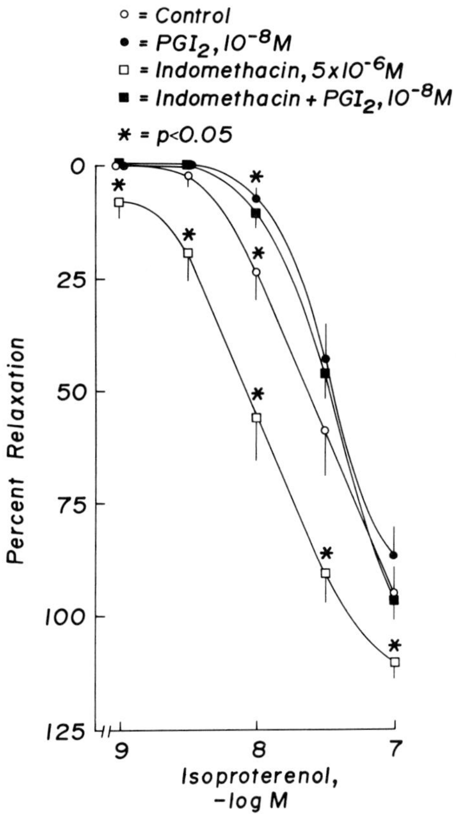

FIGURE 6. *Effect of exogenous prostacyclin on β-adrenergic relaxation in response to isoproterenol in canine coronary arteries contracted with prostaglandin $F_{2\alpha}$ (2×10^{-6} M) in the absence and the presence of indomethacin (5×10^{-6} M). Symbols represent the mean ± SEM of rings taken from five dogs. Control responses and those in the presence of prostacyclin and indomethacin were obtained simultaneously in four separate rings from the same dog.*

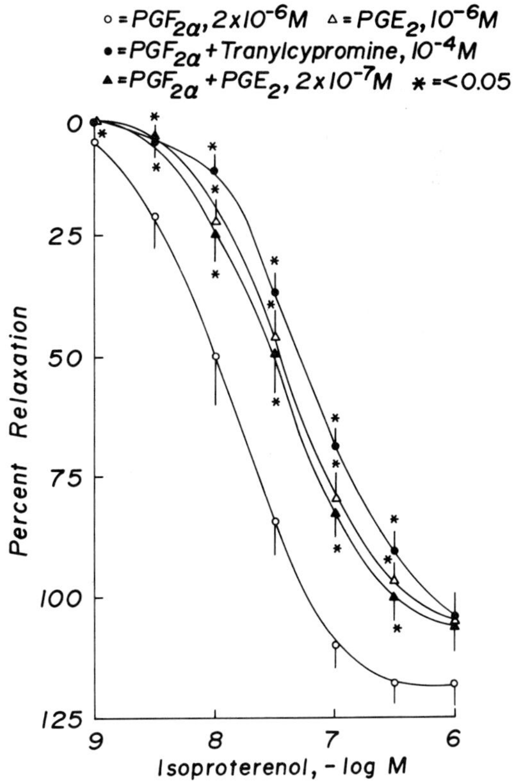

FIGURE 7. *Effect of exogenous prostaglandin E_2 and tranylcypromine on β-adrenergic relaxation in response to isoproterenol in canine coronary arteries. Symbols represent the mean ± SEM of rings taken from five dogs. Control responses and those in the presence of prostaglandin E_2 or tranylcypromine were obtained simultaneously in four separate rings from the same dog.*

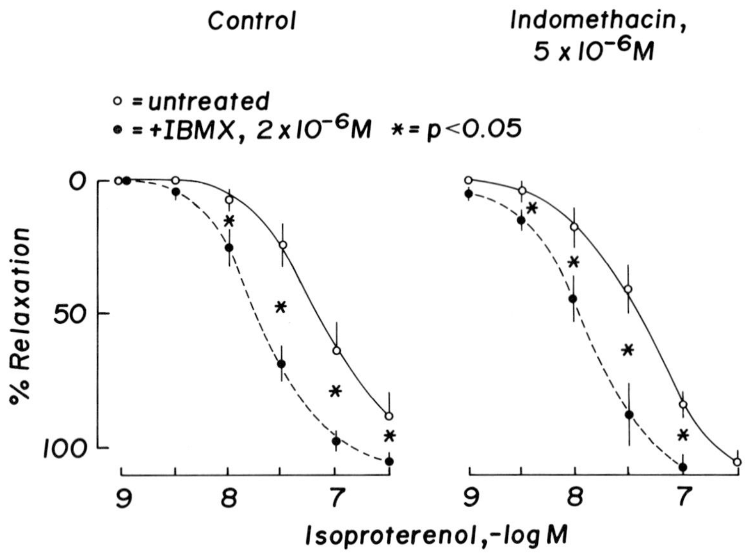

FIGURE 8. *Effect of the phosphodiesterase inhibitor drug isobutyl-methylxanthine (IBMX; 10^{-6} M) on isoproterenol-induced relaxations of canine coronary arteries contracted with prostaglandin $F_{2\alpha}$ (2×10^{-6} M), in the absence (left) and presence (right) of indomethacin (5×10^{-6} M). Symbols represent the mean ± SEM of rings taken from four dogs. Control responses and those in the presence of inhibitors were obtained in four separate rings from the same dog.*

of tritium or the [^{3}H]norepinephrine overflow under basal conditions or with repeated electrical stimulation (Fig. 9; Table 1). The ratio of S_2:S_1 in the presence of indomethacin was comparable to that obtained in its absence (Table 1). Similarly, indomethacin had no effect on basal or stimulation-evoked overflow of metabolites of norepinephrine (Table 1).

Discussion

The present study shows that indomethacin augments β-adrenergic relaxation caused by endogenous norepinephrine released by electrical stimulation of isolated canine coronary arteries, and demonstrates that these findings cannot be explained by a prejunctional action of the drug. Indeed, indomethacin does not affect basal or stimulation-evoked overflow of [^{3}H]norepinephrine, excluding the possibility that it facilitates the release of transmitter. Similarly, the fact that indomethacin did not influence the basal or stimulation-evoked overflow of the major metabolites of norepinephrine rules out the possibility that the drug enhances β-adrenergic relaxation because it inhibits the disposition of the released transmitter from the junctional cleft. Thus, indomethacin augments relaxation of canine coronary arteries during activation of the sympathetic nerve endings by acting at the postjunctional level. This conclusion is strengthened by the observed effects of indomethacin on the response to exogenous norepinephrine, during contractions evoked by prostaglandin $F_{2\alpha}$.

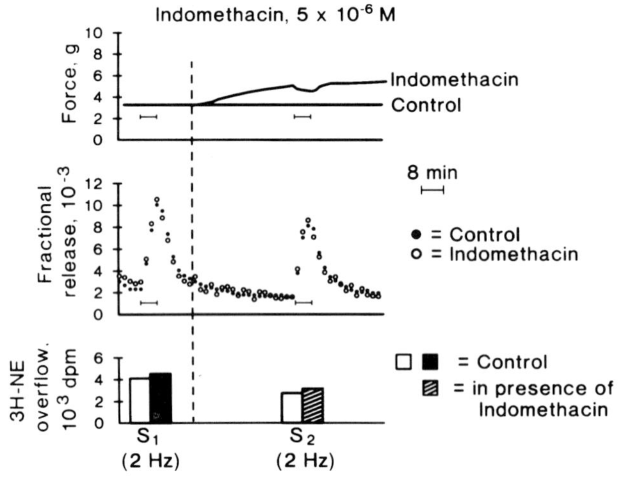

FIGURE 9. *Effect of indomethacin on tension, fractional release of tritiated compounds, and overflow of intact [^{3}H]norepinephrine under basal conditions and during electrical stimulation (10 V, 0.2 msec, 2 Hz for 6 minutes) of superfused canine coronary arteries. Control responses and those in the presence of indomethacin were obtained simultaneously in two separate strips from the same dog. Superfusate contained indomethacin (5×10^{-6} M) 40 minutes prior to the second stimulation period.*

In rings contracted with 20 mM KCl exogenous norepinephrine causes contraction rather than relaxation. Under normal conditions, the β-adrenergic effects of catecholamines predominate in coronary smooth muscle (Zuberbuhler and Bohr, 1965; Seidel et al., 1975; Cohen et al., 1983). However, during hypoxia (Borda et al., 1980) or ischemia (Moore and Parratt, 1975; Barcia et al., 1976; Vatner et al., 1977), the α-adrenergic component of their action, for unknown reasons, is augmented and overrules the β-adrenergic relaxation. The present experiments demonstrate, for norepinephrine, that a similar reversal from relaxation to contraction occurs when the coronary smooth muscle is exposed to high K^+. As myocardial hypoxia and ischemia cause accumulation of K^+ in the extracellular fluid (Benzing et al., 1971; Schuchleib et al., 1976; Downar et al., 1977), the paradoxical response to norepinephrine observed in the present studies in coronary rings contracted with K^+ may explain the reversal obtained in vivo in the hypoxic or ischemic heart. The present findings do not allow a conclusion as to the nature of the cellular mechanism underlying the K^+-induced reversal from β- to α-adrenergic predomi-

TABLE 1

Effect of Indomethacin on Overflow of ^{3}H-Norepinephrine and its Metabolites in Canine Coronary Arteries.

	Fractional ^{3}H release*	S_2/S_1†	^{3}H-NEΔ (dpm)‡	S_2/S_1†	DOPEGΔ	DOMAΔ	NMNΔ	VMAΔ	MOPEGΔ
Basal§									
Control	0.64 ± 0.06		128 ± 52		702 ± 126	228 ± 76	85 ± 44	177 ± 74	153 ± 125
Indomethacin (5 × 10^{-6} M)	0.78 ± 0.07		98 ± 38		951 ± 139	453 ± 123	87 ± 4107	328 ± 105	144 ± 121
Stimulation‖									
Control	2.12 ± 0.16	0.87 ± 0.06	4923 ± 470	0.85 ± 0.04	1037 ± 74	997 ± 254	2281 ± 101	649 ± 146	2242 ± 359
Indomethacin (5 × 10^{-6} M)	2.84 ± 0.47	0.88 ± 0.04	5375 ± 689	0.84 ± 0.03	1502 ± 305	1238 ± 324	2838 ± 774	697 ± 111	2311 ± 625

Results are expressed as means ± SEM (n = 5). Δ abbreviations: NE, norepinephrine; MOPEG, 3 methoxy, 4 hydroxyphenylglycol; VMA, 3-methoxy, 4-hydroxymandelic acid; NMN, normetanephrine; DOMA, 3,4-dihydroxymandelic acid; DOPEG, 3,4-dihydroxyphenylglycol.

* Results are given as percent fractional release of tritium (^{3}H) during 6-minute superfusion before (basal) or after (stimulation) electrical stimulation.

† S_2/S_1 = the ratio between the overflow of ^{3}H or ^{3}H-norepinephrine evoked by S_2 and that evoked by S_1.

‡ Results are given as dpm/15 ml superfusate (see Methods) collected for 6 minutes before (basal) and after (stimulation) electrical stimulation.

§ Superfusion with physiological salt solution (control) or with solution containing indomethacin (5 × 10^{-6} M).

‖ Transmural electrical stimulation: 10 V, 0.2 msec at 2 Hz for 6 minutes.

nance. One explanation would be that the high K^+ causes inhibition of Na^+,K^+-ATPase (Webb and Bohr, 1980; Cooke et al., 1984). The observation that inhibitors of cyclooxygenase reverse the effect of norepinephrine during contractions evoked by K^+ from contraction to relaxation, strongly suggests that endogenous prostanoids play an important role as well.

Postjunctional augmentation of relaxations induced by catecholamines in the presence of indomethacin could be explained if the drug were to inhibit the α-adrenergic activation of the coronary smooth muscle by the adrenergic transmitter (Zuberbuhler and Bohr, 1965; Feigl, 1968; Vatner et al., 1970; Seidel et al., 1975; Heyndrickx et al., Cohen et al., 1983). This interpretation is supported by the fact that α-adrenoceptor blockade with phentolamine (Seidel et al., 1975; Cohen et al., 1983) reverses the response to norepinephrine in arteries contracted with depolarizing solution. However, the fact that it is unlikely that indomethacin has an effect on α-adrenoceptors results from the following observations: (1) after pretreatment with propranolol, norepinephrine evoked comparable α-adrenergically mediated contractions in the absence and presence of indomethacin, and (2) indomethacin augmented the relaxation caused by the β-adrenoceptor agonist isoproterenol. The present findings in the canine coronary artery differ from the observations in rabbit kidney where one of the end-products of cyclooxygenase pathway, prostacyclin, was shown to inhibit α-adrenergic vasoconstriction postjunctionally (Hedqvist, 1979).

Another explanation for the augmented β-adrenergic relaxation would be that indomethacin acts as a phosphodiesterase inhibitor (Flores and Sharp, 1972; Flower, 1974). β-Adrenergically mediated relaxations of coronary arteries can be augmented by inhibitors of phosphodiesterase (Siedel et al., 1975; Kukovetz et al., 1981). However, the present finding that the phosphodiesterase inhibitor drug isobutylmethylxanthine was equally potent in augmenting β-adrenergic relaxations in the absence and the presence of indomethacin, may argue against this possibility. This conclusion is strengthened considerably by the fact that other inhibitors of cyclooxygenase, without inhibiting properties on phosphodiesterase, also augment β-adrenergic responsiveness in the canine coronary artery.

Since indomethacin augmented the contraction caused by prostaglandin $F_{2\alpha}$, the change in active tone rather than the inhibition of prostaglandin synthesis may result in augmentation of β-adrenergic relaxations. The following findings refute this possibility: (1) β-adrenergic responsiveness was increased by indomethacin and other cyclooxygenase inhibitors in K^+-depolarized rings, despite the fact that the inhibitors of prostaglandin synthesis did not augment KCl-induced contractions; and (2) sodium nitroprusside- or acetylcholine-evoked relaxations were not affected by indomethacin in prostaglandin $F_{2\alpha}$-contracted rings despite the augmentation of the contractile response. Thus, the most logical explanation for the postjunctional effect of indomethacin (and other cyclooxygenase inhibitors) is that the augmentation of β-adrenergically mediated coronary relaxation is due to inhibition of the synthesis of endogenous prostaglandins.

In isolated canine, porcine, and bovine coronary arteries, hypoxia, which stimulates prostaglandin-synthesis in the coronary artery wall (Kalsner, 1977; Roberts et al., 1981), inhibits β-adrenergically mediated relaxation (Borda et al., 1980). Exogenous prostaglandins inhibit, while inhibition of endogenous prostaglandin synthesis augments, coronary vasodilation caused by electrical stimulation of the adrenergic nerves and exogenous catecholamines in isolated cat hearts (Sunahara and Talesnik, 1974). These observations, taken in conjunction with the facilitatory action of three inhibitors of cyclooxygenase, strongly support the hypothesis that prostanoids generated within the coronary arterial wall exert a "braking" effect on β-adrenergic responsiveness.

The augmentation of basal tension by the cyclooxygenase inhibitors indicates that, in the canine coronary artery preparations, the dominant cyclooxygenase end-product is a vasodilator prostaglandin, most probably prostacyclin (Kalsner, 1977; Needleman and Isakson, 1980; Roberts et al., 1981). The prostacyclin synthetase inhibitor, tranylcypromine, and cyclooxygenase inhibitors caused comparable augmentations of basal tension and contractions induced by prostaglandin $F_{2\alpha}$. Exogenous prostacyclin abolishes the effect of indomethacin. These observations may suggest that endogenous prostacyclin is responsible for the reduction in β-adrenergic responsiveness. However, tranylcypromine depressed, rather than augmented, β-adrenergic relaxations. The other two major pharmacological actions of tranylcypromine, inhibition of monoamine-oxidase (Vanhoutte and Shepherd, 1969) and antagonism of α_2-adrenoceptors (unpublished observations) should enhance rather than depress the inhibitory effect of catecholamines. Thus, cyclooxygenase products other than prostacyclin may also be involved in the blunting of β-adrenergic responsiveness, especially when prostacyclin synthesis is inhibited. A likely candidate would be prostaglandin E_2, whose production may be increased in the presence of tranylcypromine. This prostanoid inhibits metabolic coronary vasodilatation in the perfused heart (Sunuhara and Talesnik, 1974). Furthermore, in the present study, exogenous prostaglandin E_2 depressed β-adrenergic responsiveness.

The inhibitory effect of the metabolite(s) of arachidonic acid on β-adrenergically mediated relaxation could be of importance in the pathogenesis of vasospasm of large coronary arteries (Maseri et al., 1979; Hillis and Braunwald, 1978; Sparks and Gorman, 1981), as it would favor α-adrenergic coronary vasoconstriction. This would be the case, in particular, under conditions (e.g., hypoxia or ischemia) when endogenous prostaglandin biosynthesis is accelerated (Berger et al., 1970; Kalsner, 1977; Needleman, et al., 1977; Roberts et al., 1981) the local release of norepinephrine is increased (Borda et al., 1980), and the main effect of catecholamines is shifted from β-adrenergic to α-adrenergic predominance (Moore and Parratt, 1973; Barcia et al., 1976; Vatner et al., 1977). These findings in isolated coronary arteries may help to explain why, in intact cats and dogs, hypoxia and ischemia inhibit coronary vasodilation evoked by β-adrenoceptor stimulation.

Supported in part by Research Grant HL05883 from the National Institutes of Health.

Address for reprints: Paul M. Vanhoutte, M.D., Department of Physiology and Biophysics, Mayo Clinic, Rochester, Minnesota 55905.

Received January 5, 1984; accepted for publication October 10, 1984.

References

Barcia F, Borer JS, Capurro N, Kent KM (1976) Propranolol mediated increase in collateral flow during acute myocardial infarction (abstr). Circulation **54** (suppl II): 156

Benzing VH, Gebert G, Strohm M (1971) Ionenverschiebungen im Myokard des narkotisierten Hunden unter verschiedenen Bedingungen. Verh Dtsch Ges Kreislanfforschung **37:** 353–356

Berger HJ, Zaret BL, Speroff L, Cohen LS, Wolfson S (1976) Regional cardiac prostaglandin release during myocardial ischemia in anesthetized dogs. Circ Res **36:** 566–571

Borda L, Schuchleib R, Henry PD (1977) Effects of potassium on isolated coronary arteries. Modulation of adrenergic responsiveness and release of norepinephrine. Circ Res **41:** 778–786

Borda L, Shuchlieb R, Henry PD (1980) Hypoxic contraction of isolated canine coronary artery: Mediation by potassium-dependent exocytosis of norepinephrine. Circ Res **46:** 870–879

Brine F, Cornish EJ, Miller RC (1979) Effects of uptake inhibitors on response of sheep coronary arteries to catecholamines and sympathetic nerve stimulation. Br J Pharmacol **67:** 553–561

Cohen RA, Shepherd JT, Vanhoutte PM (1983) Prejunctional and postjunctional actions of endogenous norepinephrine at the sympathetic neuroeffector junction in canine coronary arteries. Circ Res **52:** 16–25

Cooke JP, Shanley T, Shepherd JT, Vanhoutte PM (1984) Ouabain reverses beta-adrenergic predominance in isolated canine coronary arteries. Fed Proc **43:** 430

Downar E, Janse MJ, Durrer D (1977) The effect of "ischemic" blood on transmembrane potentials of normal porcine ventricular myocardium. Circulation **55:** 455–462

Feigl EO (1968) Carotid sinus reflex control of coronary blood flow. Circ Res **23:** 223–237

Flores AGA, Sharp GWG (1972) Endogenous prostaglandins and osmotic water flow in the toad bladder. Am J Physiol **223:** 1392–1397

Flower RJ (1974) Drugs which inhibit prostaglandin synthesis. Pharmacol Rev **26:** 33–63

Furchgott RF, Zawadzki JV (1980) The obligatory role of endothelial cells in the relaxation of arterial smooth muscle by acetylcholine. Nature **288:** 373–376

Gorman MN, Sparks HV Jr (1982) Progressive coronary vasoconstriction during relative ischemia in canine myocardium. Circ Res **51:** 411–420

Hedqvist P (1979) Actions of prostacyclin (PGI_2) on adrenergic neuroeffector transmission in the rabbit kidney. Prostaglandins **17:** 249–258

Heyndrickx GR, Muylaert P, Pannier JL (1982) α-Adrenergic control of oxygen delivery to myocardium during exercise in conscious dogs. Am J Physiol **242:** H805–H809

Hillis LD, Braunwald E (1978) Coronary-artery spasm. N Engl J Med **299:** 695–702

Kalsner S (1977) The effect of hypoxia on prostaglandin output and on tone isolated coronary arteries. Can J Physiol Pharmacol **55:** 882–887

Kukovetz WR, Pöch G, Holzmann S (1981) Cyclic nucleotides and relaxation of vascular smooth muscle. *In* Vasodilatation, edited by PM Vanhoutte, I Leusen. New York, Raven Press, pp 339–353

Maseri A, L'Abbate A, Chierchia S, Parodi O, Severi S, Biagini A, Distante A, Marzilli M, Ballestra AM (1979) Significance of spasm in the pathogenesis of ischemic heart disease. Am J Cardiol **44:** 788–792

Moore GE, Parratt JR (1973) Effect of noradrenaline and isoproterenol on blood flow in the acutely ischemic myocardium. Cardiovasc Res **7:** 446–457

Needleman PG, Isakson PC (1980) Intrinsic prostaglandin synthesis in blood vessels. *In* Handbook of Physiology, sec 2, The Cardiovascular System, II. Vascular Smooth Muscle, edited by DF Bohr, AP Somlyo, HV Sparks. Washington, D.C., American Physiological Society, pp 613–633

Needleman PG, Kulkarni PS, Raz A (1977) Coronary tone modulation: Formation and actions of prostaglandins, endoperoxides and thromboxanes. Science **195:** 409–412

Roberts AM, Messina EJ, Kaley G (1981) Prostacyclin (PGI_2) mediates hypoxic relaxation of bovine coronary arterial strips. Prostaglandins **21:** 555–569

Rooke T, Cohen RA, Verbeuren TJ, Vanhoutte PM (1982) Non-neurogenic inhibitory effect of electrical impulses in isolated canine coronary arteries. Eur J Pharmacol **80:** 251–254

Rorie DK, Shepherd JT (1980) Norepinephrine content, release and distribution in isolated dog coronary artery. Proc Soc Exp Biol Med **165:** 384–390

Schuchleib R, Borda L, Davis J, Henry P (1976) Effects of sustained increases in extracellular potassium on coronary resistance in intact dog hearts (abstr). Clin Res **24:** 246A

Seidel CL, Schnarr RL, Sparks HV (1975) Coronary artery cyclic AMP content during adrenergic receptor stimulation. Am J Physiol **229:** 265–269

Strong CG, Bohr DF (1967) Effects of prostaglandins E_1, E_2, A_1 and $F_{2\alpha}$ on isolated vascular smooth muscle. Am J Physiol **213:** 725–733

Sunahara FA, Talesnik J (1974) Prostaglandin inhibition of metabolically induced coronary vasodilatation. J Pharmacol Exp Ther **188:** 135–147

Toda N (1981) Response of isolated monkey coronary arteries to catecholamines and to transmural electrical stimulation. Circ Res **49:** 1228–1236

Vanhoutte PM, Leusen I (1969) The reactivity of isolated venous preparations to electrical stimulation. Pflugers Arch **306:** 341–353

Vanhoutte PM, Shepherd JT (1969) Activity and thermosensitivity of canine cutaneous veins after inhibition of monoamine oxidase and catechol-O-methyl transferase. Circ Res **25:** 456

Vanhoutte PM, Lorenz RR, Tyce GM (1973) Inhibition of norepinephrine-^3H release from sympathetic nerve endings in veins by acetylcholine. J Pharmacol Exp Ther **185:** 386–394

Vatner SF, Franklin D, Van Citters RL, Braunwald E (1970) Effects of carotid sinus nerve stimulation on the coronary circulation of the conscious dog. Circ Res **27:** 11–21

Vatner SF, Baig H, Manders WT, Ochs H, Pagani M (1977) Effects of propranolol on regional myocardial function, electrograms and blood flow in conscious dogs with myocardial ischemia. J Clin Invest **60:** 353–360

Verbeuren TJ, Vanhoutte PM (1982) Deamination of released ^3H-noradrenaline in the canine saphenous vein. Naunyn Schmiedebergs Arch Pharmacol **318:** 148–157

Verbeuren TJ, Coen E, Vanhoutte PM (1977) Determination of ^3H-norepinephrine and its metabolites in superfusate from isolated blood vessels. Arch Int Pharmacodyn Ther **227:** 171–174

Verbeuren TJ, Janssens WJ, Vanhoutte PM (1978) Effect of moderate acidosis on adrenergic neurotransmission in canine saphenous veins. J Pharmacol Exp Ther **206:** 105–114

Webb RC, Bohr DF (1981) Relaxation of vascular smooth muscle by isoproterenol dibutyryl-cyclic AMP and theophylline. J Pharmacol Exp Ther **217:** 26–35

Zuberbuhler RC, Bohr DF (1965) Responses of coronary smooth muscle to catecholamines. Circ Res **16:** 431–440

INDEX TERMS: Canine coronary artery • Sympathetic nerve activation • β-Adrenergic receptors • Endogenous prostaglandins • Prostaglandin $F_{2\alpha}$ • Prostacyclin • Prostaglandin E_2 • Indomethacin • Cyclooxygenase inhibitors • Sodium nitroprusside • Tranylcypromine • Vasospasm

BRIEF COMMUNICATIONS

Direct Analysis of β-Adrenergic Receptor Subtypes on Intact Adult Ventricular Myocytes of the Rat

Iain L.O. Buxton and Laurence L. Brunton

From the Divisions of Cardiology and Pharmacology, Department of Medicine, M-013H, University of California, San Diego, La Jolla, California

SUMMARY. β_1- and β_2-Adrenergic receptors co-exist in the adult rat ventricle. We have employed radioligand binding and cell purification techniques to determine the cellular origin of these receptors. The β-adrenergic antagonist ligand (±)-[^{125}I]iodocyanopindolol binds to 2×10^5 receptors per purified adult rat cardiomyocyte, with a dissociation constant of 70 pM. The subtype-selective antagonists betaxolol (β_1), practolol (β_1), and zinterol (β_2) compete for [^{125}I]iodocyanopindolol-binding sites on intact myocytes in monophasic manners with dissociation constants of 46, 845, and 923 nM, respectively. [^{125}I]iodocyanopindolol binding to membranes prepared from nonmyocyte elements of rat ventricle occurs with a dissociation constant of 43 pM and a capacity of 88 fmol/mg membrane protein. Computer analysis of competition of [^{125}I]iodocyanopindolol binding by betaxolol, practolol, and zinterol in nonmyocyte membranes demonstrates biphasic curves that comprise binding to both β_1- and β_2-receptors. These data demonstrate that purified adult ventricular myocytes possess only β_1-receptors, and that the β_2-receptors found in rat ventricle are located on nonmyocyte cell types **(*Circ Res 56: 126–132, 1985*)**

EVIDENCE for the co-existence of β_1- and β_2-receptors for catecholamines in the mammalian myocardium comes from both physiological and radioligand binding studies. Carlsson et al. (1972, 1977) present evidence that the inotropic and chronotropic responses of the cat heart to catecholamines are differentially antagonized by subtype-specific β-antagonists. Studies in guinea pig heart lead to the same conclusion (Dreyer and Offermeir, 1975). Radioligand binding studies, employing heterogeneous membranes prepared from homogenized hearts, reveal the presence of both β-receptor subtypes in rat (Minneman et al., 1979a, 1979b), kitten (Kaumann et al., 1983) and human heart (Stiles et al., 1983; Waelbroeck et al., 1983). Although these data demonstrate the presence of both β_1- and β_2-receptors in mammalian heart, they do not describe the distribution of β-adrenergic receptor subtypes among different cell types within the ventricle.

In the course of our own work on the hormonal regulation of cardiac function and metabolism, we have wondered whether specific hormone receptors (and, hence, distinct responses) can be assigned to particular cell types within the heart. In particular, we have considered whether β_1- and β_2-receptors co-exist on ventricular myocytes. To approach these questions experimentally, we have combined the techniques of radioligand binding and cell purification. Specifically, we have measured the distribution of β-receptor subtypes on purified cardiomyocytes from adult rat ventricle and on the nonmyocyte elements of ventricle by employing the subtype nonselective β-adrenergic antagonist (±)-[^{125}I]iodocyanopindolol ([^{125}I]ICYP), the β_1 subtype-selective antagonists, betaxolol and practolol, and the β_2-selective antagonist, zinterol.

Methods

Preparation of Ventricular Cardiomyocytes

Male Sprague-Dawley rats were given heparin (1500 U/kg, ip) and sodium pentobarbital (12 mg, ip), and were killed 10 minutes later. Hearts were rapidly removed and immediately perfused with Ca^{++}-free basal medium Eagle (BME, 18°C) via the aorta to stop spontaneous beating and to remove blood cells. Hearts were trimmed of extraneous tissue including pericardium, and mounted via the aorta in a recirculating perfusion apparatus. Ventricular myocytes were prepared by collagenase perfusion in the absence of Ca^{++} by a method we have previously described in detail (Buxton and Brunton, 1983). For experiments, purified myocytes were resuspended in BME containing $CaCl_2$ (1 mM) and BSA (0.01% wt/vol). Viability of myocytes was determined by their capacity to exclude trypan blue (1 volume of cells plus 9 volumes of 0.3% trypan blue). Myocytes were routinely 80–90% rod-shaped cells excluding trypan blue. Myocytes were used in experiments 15–20 minutes after their purification.

Preparation of Ventricular Membranes

Rat hearts were removed and handled in a manner identical to that used to prepare myocytes, except that enzyme perfusion was omitted. Ventricles were dissected away from atrial and valvular tissue and immediately frozen, using Wallenberger clamps precooled in liquid nitrogen. Membranes were prepared from frozen tissue as described below.

Preparation of Myocyte, Nonmyocyte, and Liver Membranes

Tissue determined to be "nonmyocyte" in origin included tissue pieces remaining after filtration of enzyme-released myocytes, as well as cells contained in the first supernatant from myocyte purification. Microscopic examination of this material confirmed the presence of numerous small nonmuscle cells, damaged myocytes, and collagen fibers. Thus, while not devoid of myocyte membrane, this material was enriched for nonmyocyte cell types present in rat ventricle. Both purified myocytes and nonmyocytes were collected by centrifugation (1000 $g \times$ 2 minutes) and quick-frozen in liquid nitrogen. Whole rat ventricle and liver were freeze-clamped at the temperature of liquid nitrogen. For the preparation of membranes, frozen tissues and frozen cell pellets were powdered at −70°C and then homogenized (50 mM Tris, 10 mM $MgCl_2$, 1 mM EDTA, pH 7.5, 4°C) in glass-glass homogenizing tubes (Kontes) and filtered through Nitex cloth (149 μm). Membranes were collected by centrifugation (3000 $g \times 5$ minutes) and suspended in homogenizing buffer at 1–2 mg protein/ml. Protein was determined by the method of Bradford (1976).

Radioligand Binding Assay

Radioiodinated cyanopindolol was the generous gift of Dr. Paul Insel, and was prepared as described previously (Engle et al., 1981). Binding assays were performed in triplicate by incubating 2–3 × 10^3 myocytes, or 30–50 μg of membrane suspension with 0.1 ml of [^{125}I]ICYP (2200 Ci/mmol) and 0.1 ml of various β-adrenergic antagonists or diluent in a final volume of 1.0 ml in polypropylene test tubes (16 × 105 mm Sarstedt, washed). Assays were initiated by the addition of myocytes or membranes diluted in BME immediately prior to addition to the assay. All tubes containing myocytes were gassed with O_2/CO_2 (95%/5%) and capped. Equilibrium binding was carried out for 60–90 minutes at 34°C in a rotary water bath at 120 rpm. Assays were terminated with the addition of 10 ml of cold (4°C) hypotonic buffer (10 mM Tris, 1 mM EDTA, pH 7.5). Bound and free [^{125}I]ICYP were separated by rapid filtration over glass fiber filters (Whatman GF/C). Filters were washed with an additional 10 ml of hypotonic buffer at 4°C. Radioactivity retained on filters was determined using a gamma counter at 86% efficiency. Replicate variation was less than 5% in all experiments. Nonspecific binding for both membranes and intact myocytes was determined by [^{125}I]ICYP binding in the presence of 1 μM *l*-propranolol. The subtraction of nonspecific binding from total binding yielded specific binding which was routinely 60% for intact myocytes and 70% for membranes at 100 pM [^{125}I]ICYP.

Incubation of both intact cells and membranes with [^{125}I]ICYP resulted in the rapid appearance of specific binding that reached equilibrium in 45 minutes and was appropriately reversed by propranolol (1 μM). Binding was linear with increasing myocyte number or amount of membrane protein. Viability of myocytes maintained under identical conditions during binding assays remained between 90 and 95% of starting figures.

Data Analysis

The equilibrium dissociation constant (K_D) and maximal number of binding sites (B_{max}) for [^{125}I]ICYP, a nonselective β-adrenergic antagonist, on ventricular myocytes and ventricular nonmyocyte and liver membranes were determined from Scatchard analysis (Scatchard, 1949) of saturation binding isotherms. Competition curves employing β-subtype-specific antagonists were analyzed by means of a computer program that performs iterative, nonlinear regression (Munson and Rodbard, 1980). This program fits the binding data to equations describing the laws of mass action for one or two classes of binding sites and determines whether the two-site model is statistically better than the one-site fit of the data.

The affinity (K_D) of the nonselective antagonist radioligand [^{125}I]ICYP was determined separately in each competition experiment with subtype-selective antagonists and either intact myocytes or membranes, and was entered in the computer analysis as a constant. Computer-generated fits of competition data provide estimates of the affinity constant (K_I) of subtype-specific antagonists and of the concentration of each receptor subtype. Further, computer analysis determined nonspecific binding from data obtained at high competitor concentrations which was indistinguishable from simultaneous measurements of binding in the presence of 1.0 μM *l*-propranolol. The likelihood that more than one receptor subtype was present was decided by comparison of the residual variances obtained, assuming either one or two classes of binding sites (Munson and Rodbard, 1980). The limitation of this computer method to detect small numbers of β_2-receptors on the ventricular myocyte derives from both precise measurements of binding at a given antagonist concentration (replicate variation <5%) and a large difference in the affinities (K_I) of subtype-selective agents for β_1- vs. β_2-receptors (Delean et al., 1981, and data of Table 1).

Results

Distribution of β-Receptors in Myocardial Membranes

As a starting point to verify our techniques, we determined the distribution of β_1- and β_2-receptors in a membrane fraction of an homogenate of rat heart ventricle.

The kinetics of binding of [^{125}I]ICYP to whole ventricle membranes showed a large degree of high affinity binding (K_D = 23 pM, B_{max} = 91 fmol/mg protein) that was readily competed for by β-adrenergic antagonists. Based on such competition of [^{125}I]ICYP binding with the β-subtype-specific agents, practolol and zinterol, we calculated a distribution of β-receptors of 65–70% β_1 and 30–35% β_2 for whole ventricle (Fig. 1). This relatively high proportion of β_2-receptors suggested to us that we might reasonably expect to detect the appearance of even a moderate fraction of either receptor subtype in more purified fractions of cardiac tissue.

Characteristics and Distribution of β-Receptors in Purified Myocytes

Binding of [^{125}I]ICYP to the intact myocyte was saturable with increasing radioligand concentration (5–1000 pM). Scatchard analysis of saturation isotherms yielded linear plots indicating that [^{125}I]ICYP bind to a single class of sites on the myocyte (Fig. 2). The ability of the nonselective β-adrenergic antagonist propranolol to compete for [^{125}I]ICYP bind-

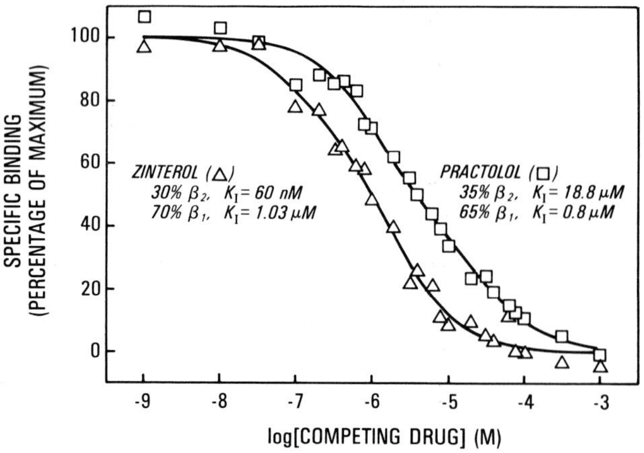

FIGURE 1. *Competition of [^{125}I]ICYP binding sites in membranes of rat whole ventricle. Membranes were prepared from rat whole ventricle and incubated at 32°C with [^{125}I]ICYP (40 pM) and increasing concentrations of the β-receptor subtype-selective antagonists practolol (β_1) and zinterol (β_2). Data are expressed as a percentage of maximal specific binding in the absence of competitor. Curves are computer-generated best fits representing two classes of binding sites and thir proportions (see Methods). Values are the mean of triplicate determinations in a single representative experiment.*

ing, as well as the capacity of the (*l*)-isomer of the β-agonist isoproterenol to compete for [^{125}I]ICYP binding with a greater affinity (K_I = 80 nM) than the *d*-isomer (K_I = 2500 nM) confirmed that [^{125}I]ICYP was binding to β-adrenergic receptors on the myocytes. Characteristics of the cardiomyocyte β-receptor from Scatchard analyses of several experiments are listed in Table 1.

To determine the relative proportion of β_1- and β_2-receptor subtypes on intact ventricular cardiomyocytes, we employed the β_1-selective antagonists betaxolol and practolol and the β_2-selective agent zinterol to compete for [^{125}I]ICYP binding to these intact adult muscle cells. Competition for [^{125}I]ICYP binding by each antagonist resulted in monophasic curves, demonstrating a single class of β-adrenergic binding sites (Fig. 3). The K_I value for both betaxolol (46 nM) and practolol (800 nM) is consistent with competition of these drugs for binding to a β_1-receptor, whereas the K_I value calculated for zinterol binding (1.2 μM) to the same receptor demonstrates a much lower affinity than would be predicted for the binding of zinterol to a β_2-receptor [20 nM (Minneman et al., 1979a, 1979b, and Table 1)].

Similar results were obtained in membranes prepared from freshly purified myocytes. Myocyte membranes bound [^{125}I]ICYP with high affinity (K_D = 52 pM) to a large number of sites, 188 fmol of receptor/mg membrane protein. This density agrees well with our estimate of 2.1 × 10^5 receptors/cell, given that each cell has a measured membrane protein content of 2.2 ng. Practolol competed for this binding in a monophasic manner with an affinity (K_I) of 780 nM. This affinity is in excellent agreement with data for competition of [^{125}I]ICYP binding to intact myocytes, shown above. Thus, the results with myocyte membranes confirm our finding a single subtype of β-receptor (β_1) on intact myocytes.

Distribution of β-Receptor Subtypes in Nonmyocyte Membranes

Because we detected only β_1-receptors on ventricular myocytes, we anticipated that membranes prepared from the nonmyocyte components of the ventricle would reveal the presence of β_2-adrenergic receptors. Saturation isotherms produced under conditions identical to those used to assay [^{125}I]ICYP binding to purified myocytes gave linear Scatchard curves (Fig. 4), indicating that the nonselective radiolabeled antagonist recognizes a single class of binding sites in nonmyocyte membranes (kinetic parameters summarized in Table 2). However, competition of [^{125}I]ICYP binding to nonmyocyte membranes by betaxolol, practolol and zinterol occurred over a broader concentration range than expected for a single component interaction, indicating the presence of both β_1- and β_2-receptors (Fig. 5). Data of competition for [^{125}I]ICYP binding by betaxolol and practolol were best satisfied by a two-site fit

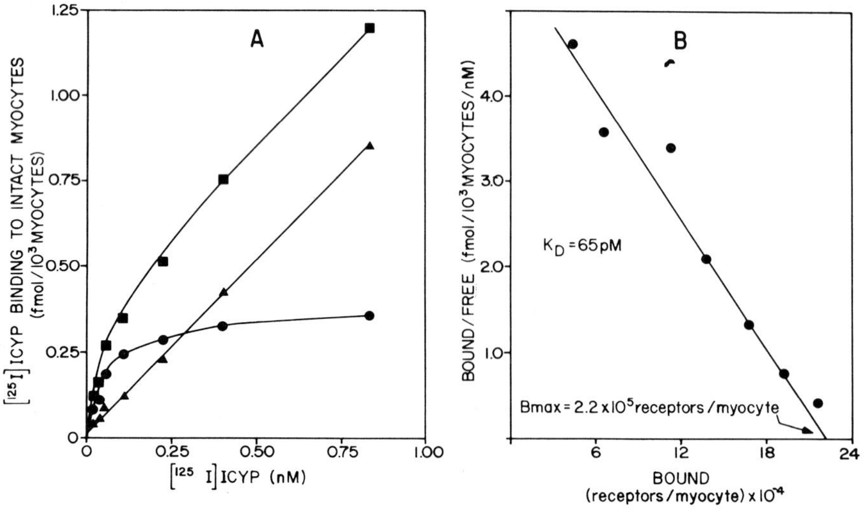

FIGURE 2. *Binding of [^{125}I]ICYP to intact cardiac myocytes. Panel A: purified myocytes were incubated with increasing concentrations of [^{125}I]ICYP (10–840 pM) in the presence and absence of propranolol (10^{-6} M). Specifically bound radioactivity (●) was determined by subtracting from total binding (■) the [^{125}I]ICYP bound in the presence of propranolol (▲). The Hill slope calculated for specific binding = 0.99. Panel B: Scatchard plot of specific binding.*

TABLE 1
β-Adrenergic Receptors on Myocytes and Nonmyocytes

Tissue	Characteristics of [^{125}I]ICYP binding: K_D (pM)	Characteristics of [^{125}I]ICYP binding: Receptor density	Distribution of β-adrenergic receptor subtypes: Receptor subtype	Receptor prevalance (%): Practolol	Receptor prevalance (%): Zinterol	Dissociation constant (μM): Practolol	Dissociation constant (μM): Zinterol
Nonmyocyte membranes	43 ± 1.6	126 ± 17 (fmol/mg protein)	β_1	51.5 ± 8.5	46.5 ± 8.5	0.66 ± 0.14	1.19 ± 0.42
Purified myocytes	70 ± 12	162 ± 16 (fmol/mg protein)	β_1	100	100	0.85 ± 0.06	0.92 ± 0.21
		2.1 ± 0.2 × 10^5 (receptors/cell)	β_2	None	None		

Radiolabled antagonist affinity (K_D) and receptor density were determined by incubating tissue with increasing concentrations of [^{125}I]ICYP (5–1000 pM) in the presence and absence of 1 μM (−)-propranolol. Data obtained with [^{125}I]ICYP and the subtype-selective agents practolol (β_1) and zinterol (β_2) were analyzed by computer as described in Methods. Values are the mean ± SE of four to six experiments. Measurements of protein refer to membrane protein.

with 40% β_2-receptors (K_D: betaxolol 0.3 μM, practolol 12.2 μM). The balance (60%) of receptors interacted with both betaxolol and practolol with the high affinity (0.004 and 0.5 μM, respectively) expected for binding to a β_1-receptor. Competition [^{125}I]ICYP binding to the nonmyocyte membranes by the β_2-selective antagonist zinterol revealed two components of binding in the proportion β_2:β_1, 45:55. The dissociation constants for the interactions of these receptors with zinterol were 40 nM (β_2) and 800 nM (β_1). The ability of zinterol to compete with high affinity for a large fraction (45%) of [^{125}I]ICYP binding to nonmyocyte membranes is not the result of the absence of added guanine nucleotide (GTP). When zinterol competition of [^{125}I]ICYP binding to these membranes was compared with and without 100 μM added GTP, the guanine nucleotide caused only a small rightward shift in the high and low affinity components of binding. This slight shift caused no change in the estimation of proportions of β_1- and β_2-receptors present (Fig. 6).

The resolution of β_1- and β_2-receptors by betaxolol, practolol, and zinterol, the appropriateness of their affinities, and the excellent agreement on the relative densities of the receptor subtypes determined by these agents, demonstrate convincingly that the nonmyocyte fraction contains β_2- as well as β_1-receptors.

Confirmation of the ability of methods applied here to detect β_2-adrenergic receptors was provided by identical studies performed on a tissue known to be a homogeneous source of β_2-adrenergic receptors (Minneman et al., 1979c). Binding of [^{125}I]ICYP to rat liver membranes showed a single class of high affinity sites (K_D = 25 pM; B_{max} = 69 fmol/mg membrane protein). Competition of [^{125}I]ICYP binding to liver membranes by subtype-specific antagonists gave monophasic curves with affinities for zinterol and practolol appropriate for a β_2-receptor (15 and 760 nM, respectively).

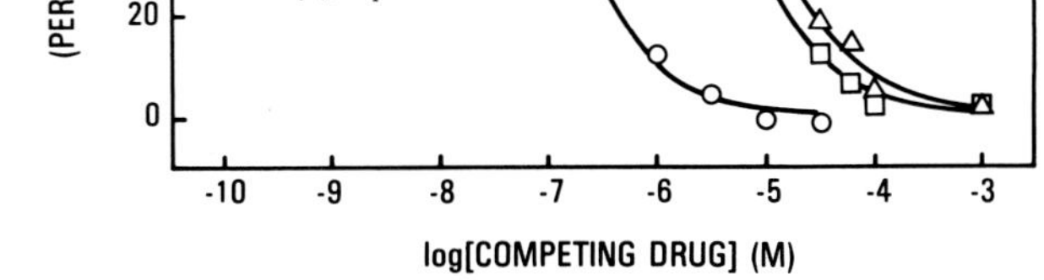

FIGURE 3. *Subtype specificity of β-receptors on intact cardiac myocytes. Purified myocytes were incubated at 32°C with [^{125}I]ICYP (50 pM) and increasing concentrations of the β-receptor subtype-specific antagonists betaxolol and practolol (β_1) and zinterol (β_2), as described in Methods. Data are expressed as the percent of maximal specific [^{125}I]ICYP binding occurring in the absence of competitor. Values are the mean of triplicate determinations in a single representative experiment. Curves are computer-generated best fits of a single class of sites (see Methods).*

Discussion

We have employed radioligand-binding techniques to investigate the distribution of β-adrenergic receptors in rat myocardium, a tissue known to contain both β_1- and β_2-receptors (Minneman, 1979a, 1979b, and Table 1). Our work differs from previous studies in two principal ways. First, we have purified ventricular myocytes from rat heart and are thus able to compare receptor binding data from whole ventricle, purified cardiomyocytes, myocyte membranes, and the nonmyocyte fraction of ventricle. Second, we provide data on β-adrenergic receptors present on fully differentiated, intact car-

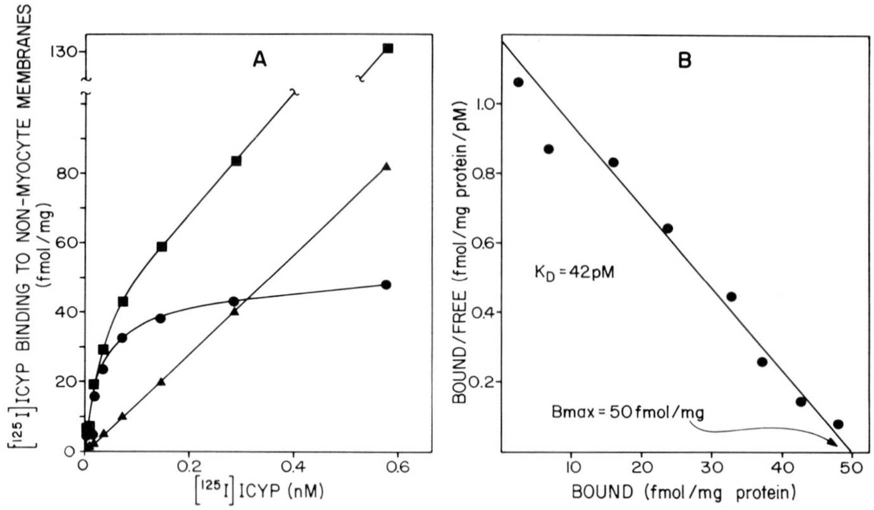

FIGURE 4. *Binding of [^{125}I]ICYP to the nonmyocyte fraction of rat ventricle. Panel A: membranes prepared from the nonmyocyte fraction of rat ventricle were incubated with increasing concentrations of [^{125}I]ICYP (5–580 pM) in the presence (nonspecific binding, ▲) and absence (total binding, ■) of propranolol (10^{-6} M). Specific binding (●) was determined as the difference of nonspecific and total binding. The Hill slope for specific binding was 0.97. Panel B: Scatchard plot of specific binding.*

diomyocytes freshly prepared from adult animals, in contrast to an earlier study employing fetal myoblasts adapted to tissue culture (Lau et al., 1980).

Employing antagonists selective for β_1- or β_2-receptors and the β-specific radioligand [^{125}I]ICYP, we find a single class of β_1-receptors on purified ventricular myocytes. In the nonmyocyte fraction, however, approximately 50% of β-receptors are of the β_2-subtype, data consistent with reports of as many as 24% β_2-receptors in rat heart ventricle (Table 1, and Minneman et al., 1979a, 1979b), since our preparation represents a purification of both myocyte (all β_1) and nonmyocyte elements (contributing β_2-receptors). Indeed, it seems likely to us that many of the β_1-receptors identified in the nonmyocyte fraction of ventricle are contributed by damaged myocytes that are excluded during myocyte purification.

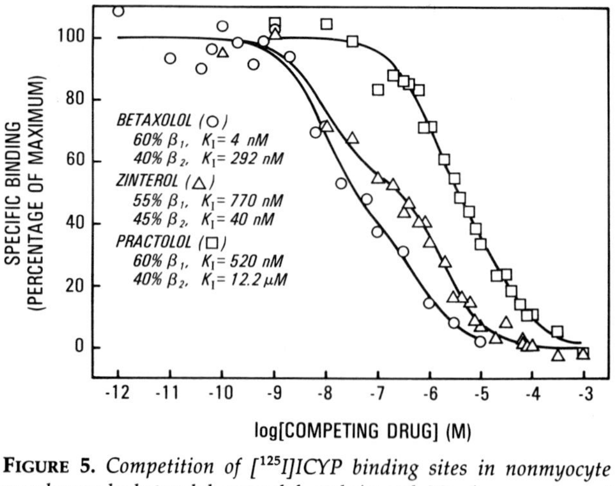

FIGURE 5. *Competition of [^{125}I]ICYP binding sites in nonmyocyte membranes by betaxolol, practolol, and zinterol. Membranes prepared from the nonmyocyte fraction of rat ventricle were incubated at 32°C with [^{125}I]ICYP (45 pM) and increasing concentrations of betaxolol, practolol, or zinterol. Data are expressed as a percentage of maximal specific [^{125}I]ICYP binding in the absence of competitor. Values are the mean of triplicate determinations in a single representative experiment. Curves are computer-generated best fits of two classes of binding sites (see Methods).*

It is, of course, possible that cardiomyocytes have a small fraction of β_2-receptors that we failed to detect. Applying the analysis described by DeLean et al. (1981), we can estimate the limits of our ability to discern a small population of β_2-receptors. In using a subtype-specific antagonist with a nonspecific labeled ligand in a competitive binding assay, one needs an antagonist that exhibits a selectivity between β_1- and β_2-receptors of ~50 to detect as few as 10% β_2-receptors. In our experiments, the selectivities of the compounds were ~20 for practolol and zinterol and ~60 for betaxolol. Thus, within these limits (10% β_2-receptors), which are the likely limits imposed by experimental error, we do not detect β_2-receptors on the adult cardiomyocyte.

The number of β_1-receptors found on each adult myocyte, $\sim 2 \times 10^5$, seems, at first glance, large. This high density of receptor on the intact myocyte manifests itself as an appropriately high content of receptors in isolated membranes, ~162 fmol/mg pro-

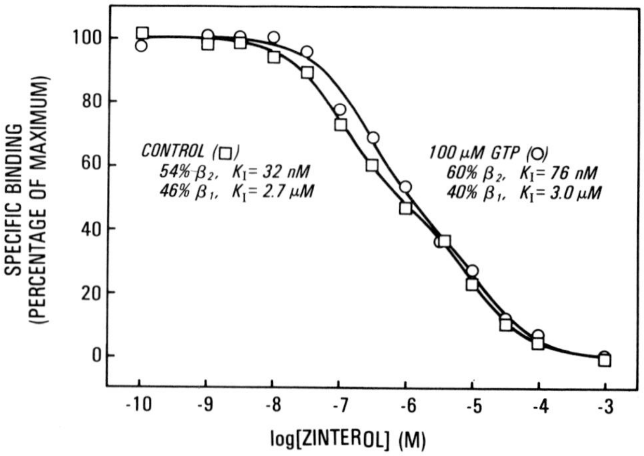

FIGURE 6. *Effect of GTP on zinterol competition of [^{125}I]ICYP binding to nonmyocyte membranes. Nonmyocyte membranes were incubated with 50 pM [^{125}I]ICYP and increasing concentrations of zinterol in the presence (○) or absence of (□) of 100 μm GTP. Data, determined in triplicate, are expressed as a percentage of maximal specific binding in the absence of competitor. Curves are computer generated best-fits of the data modeled to two binding sites (see Methods).*

tein. Our estimate compares favorably with that of Moustafa et al. (1978), who found 360,000 binding sites for [^{3}H]dihydroalprenolol per rat cardiomyocyte. The report of Lau et al. (1980) of 7500 β-receptors per myocyte in primary cultures of fetal heart is probably not a relevant comparison, since those cells were immature, far smaller than the adult cells that we isolate, and possibly contaminated by other cell types. Densities of 10^3 to 10^4 receptors per cell are routine in many prototypic cell systems (for β-receptors: S49 cells, ~1200 cell; avian red cells, ~600/cell; BC3H-1 cells, 9000/cell; C6 glioma cells, ~9400/cell). When expressed as a function of cell size, the density of β-receptors on myocytes falls in this range. Myocytes are large cells; ours average 20 μm × 90 μm. Assuming that the myocyte is a cylinder of those dimensions, the surface density is 33 β_1-receptors per μm^2, compared to ~3 receptors/μm^2 for S49 lymphoma cells, ~1 receptor/μm^2 for pigeon red cells, 42 receptors/μm^2 for C6 glioma cells (Dibner et al., 1981), and 20 receptors/μm^2 for the BC3H-1 smooth muscle cell (calculated from data of Hughes et al. (1982) and Brown et al. (1984). Thus, the prevalence of β-adrenergic receptors per unit area of myocyte membrane is not unusually high. Furthermore, if surface receptor density is a way in which cells regulate their adrenergic responsiveness (Shear et al., 1976), then this number of β-receptors in a highly responsive tissue such as heart seems reasonable.

The presence of β_1- but not β_2-receptors on rat myocytes implies that the metabolic and contractile response of rat ventricular muscle to β-agonists results exclusively from occupation of β_1-receptors. This conclusion varies from that reached by Robberecht et al. (1983) and Waelbroeck et al. (1983). These workers have recently offered evidence that human cardiac tissue has equal contents of β_1- and β_2-receptors, and that only the β_2-adrenergic receptors are coupled to adenylate cyclase. These studies must be accepted with caution, however, since the tissues employed were largely atrial and were from patients who had been receiving β-blockade therapy. In addition, these human tissues, removed during surgical repair of coronary insufficiency or valvular disease, very likely represent diseased rather than normal tissue and were certainly a population of mixed cell types. The sort of study that we have performed emphasizes the utility of a purified cell population and provides a direct test of the proposal of Waelbroech and colleagues (1983).

This work was supported by NSF Grant PCM 78-81-10116, AHA Grant-in-Aid 83-740, PHS Training Grant HL 0-7444, and RCDA Grant HL 00935 (to L.L. Brunton).

Address for reprints: Dr. Laurence L. Brunton, Divisions of Cardiology and Pharmacology, Department of Medicine, M-013H, University of California, San Diego, La Jolla, California 92093.

Received December 19, 1983; accepted for publication September 7, 1984.

References

Bradford MM (1976) A rapid and sensitive method for the quantitation of microgram quantities of protein utilizing the principle of protein-dye binding. Anal Biochem **72:** 248–254

Brown RD, Berger KD, Taylor PW (1984) Alpha$_1$-adrenergic receptor activation mobilizes cellular Ca^{++} muscle cell line. J Biol Chem **259:** 7554–7562

Buxton ILO, Brunton LL (1983) Compartments of cyclic AMP and protein kinase in mammalian cardiomyocytes. J Biol Chem **258:** 10233–10239

Carlsson E, Ablad B, Brandstrom A, Carlsson B (1972) Differential blockade of the chronotropic effects of various adrenergic stimuli in the cat heart. Life Sci **11:** 953–958

Carlsson E, Dahlof CG, Hedberg A, Tangstrand B (1977) Differentiation of cardiac chronotropic and ionotropic effects of β-adrenoceptor agonists. Naunyn Schmiedebergs Arch Pharmacol **300:** 101–105

DeLean A, Hancock AA, Lefkowitz RJ (1982) Validation and statistical analysis of a computer modeling method for quantitative analysis of radioligand binding data for mixtures of pharmacological receptor subtypes. Mol Pharmacol **21:** 5–16

Dibner M, Wolfe RA, Insel PA (1981) Replacement of serum with defined medium increases -adrenergic receptor number of cultured glioma cells. Exp Cell Res **131:** 424–427

Dreyer AC, Offermeir J (1975) Indications for the existence of two types of cardiac beta-adrenergic receptors. Pharmacol Res Commun **7:** 151–161

Engle G, Hoyer D, Berthold R, Wagner H (1981) (±)-[^{125}Iodo] cyanopindolol, a new ligand for β-adrenoceptors: Identification and quantitation of subclasses of β-adrenoceptors in guinea pig. Naunyn Schmiedebergs Arch Pharmacol **317:** 277–285

Fertuck HC, Salpeter MM (1976) Quantitation of junctional and extrajunctional acetylcholine receptors by electron microscope autoradiography after ^{125}I-α-bungarotoxin binding of mouse neuromuscular junctions. J Cell Biol **69:** 144–158

Hayes JS, Brunton LL, Mayer SE (1980) Selective activation of particular cAMP-dependent protein kinase by isoproterenol and prostaglandin E_1. J Biol Chem **255:** 5113–5119

Hughes RJ, Boyle MR, Brown RD, Taylor P, Insel PA (1982) Characterization of coexisting alpha$_1$- and beta$_2$-adrenergic receptors on a cloned muscle cell line, BC3H-1. Mol Pharmacol **22:** 258–266

Kaumann AJ, Morris TH, Bojar H (1983) Heart β-receptors: On the functional role of heterogeneous binding sites. J Receptor Res **3:** 61–70

Lau YH, Robinson RB, Rosen MR, Bilezikian JP (1980) Subclassification of β-adrenergic receptors in cultured rat cardiac myoblasts and fibroblasts. Circ Res **47:** 41–48

Minneman KP, Hegstrand LR, Molinoff PB (1979a) The pharmacological specificity of beta-1 and beta-2 adrenergic receptors in rat heart and lung in vitro. Mol Pharmacol **16:** 21–33

Minneman KP, Hegstrand LK, Molinoff PB (1979b) Simultaneous determination of beta-1 and beta-2 adrenergic receptors in tissues containing both receptor subtypes. Mol Pharmacol **16:** 34–36

Minnemann KP, Hedberg H, Molenoff PB (1979c) Comparison of beta adrenergic receptor subtypes in mammalian tissues. J Pharmacol Exp Ther **211:** 502–508

Moustafa E, Giachetti A, Downey HF, Bashour FA (1978) Binding of (^{3}H)dihydroalprenolol to beta adrenoceptors of cells isolated from adult rat heart. Naunyn Schmiedebergs Arch Pharmacol **303:** 107–109

Munson PJ, Rodbard D (1980) LIGAND: A versatile computerized approach for characterization of ligand-binding systems. Anal Biochem **107:** 220–239

Robberecht P, Delhaye M, Taton G, DeNeef P, Waelbroeck M, De Smet JM, Leclerc JL, Chatelain P, Christophe J (1983) The human heart beta-adrenergic receptors. I. Heterogeneity of the binding sites: Presence of 50% beta$_1$- and 50% beta$_2$-adrenergic receptors. Mol Pharmacol **24:** 169–173

Scatchard G (1949) The attractions of proteins for small molecules and ions. Ann NY Acad Sci USA **51:** 660–672

Shear M, Insel PA, Melmon KL, Coffino P (1976) Agonist-specific refractoriness induced by isoproterenol. J Biol Chem **251:** 7572–7576

Stiles GL, Taylor S, Lefkowitz RS (1983) Human cardiac beta-adrenergic receptors: Subtype heterogeneity delineated by direct radioligand binding. Life Sci **33:** 467–473

Waelbroeck M, Taton G, Delhaye G, Chatelain P, Camus JC, Pochet R, Leclerc JL, DeSmet JM, Robberecht P, Christophe J (1983) The human heart beta-adrenergic receptors. II. Coupling of $beta_2$-adrenergic receptors with the adenylate cyclase system. Mol Pharmacol **24:** 174–182

INDEX TERMS: β-Adrenergic receptors • Purified ventricular myocytes • Subtype-specific β-antagonists • Iodocyanopindolol

Ryanodine as a Tool to Determine the Contributions of Calcium Entry and Calcium Release to the Calcium Transient and Contraction of Cardiac Purkinje Fibers

Eduardo Marban and W. Gil Wier

From the Department of Physiology, University of Maryland at Baltimore, and the Division of Cardiology, Department of Medicine, The Johns Hopkins Hospital, Baltimore, Maryland

SUMMARY. Our object was to assess the relative roles of transsarcolemmal calcium entry and intracellular calcium release in the contraction of cardiac Purkinje fibers. We observed intracellular calcium transients, membrane potential, and contraction in aequorin-injected canine cardiac Purkinje fibers exposed to highly selective pharmacological modifiers of excitation-contraction coupling. To influence selectively the release of calcium from the sarcoplasmic reticulum, we used the plant alkaloid, ryanodine. To influence calcium entry, selectively, we used either the calcium channel antagonist, nitrendipine, or the calcium channel agonist, Bay k 8644. Ryanodine alone (1 μM) reduced both components of the intracellular aequorin luminescence signal (L_1 and L_2). In three muscles, the luminescence signals were 3% of control in amplitude (standard error of the mean, 2%) without two distinct components and the twitch tension was 2% of control (standard error of the mean, 3%), whereas the action potential was prolonged. The aequorin signal and twitch remaining in ryanodine were abolished by the calcium antagonist nitrendipine (10 μM), which also lowered the action potential plateau, consistent with the block of functional calcium channels. In two experiments, the calcium-channel agonist, Bay k 8644, in the presence of ryanodine, increased the aequorin luminescence and the contraction, but only to a very small fraction of their control values. Sodium withdrawal in potassium-free, ryanodine-containing solution produced large slow increases in calcium and tension, showing that tension could still be produced, that aequorin remained functional, and that sodium/calcium exchange was not inhibited by ryanodine. Caffeine increased intracellular calcium, showing that calcium stores were not depleted. In summary, the negative inotropic effect of ryanodine is due to a decrease in the calcium released from internal stores, and calcium entry normally contributes only a very small fraction of the total activator calcium. ***(Circ Res 56: 133–138, 1985)***

ALTHOUGH a rise in intracellular calcium (Ca^{++}) is known to initiate contraction in cardiac muscle (Allen and Blinks, 1978), the sources of that Ca^{++}, particularly in mammalian tissues, remain unclear. Two concepts are widely held. The first is that insufficient Ca^{++} enters the cell to account *completely* for the activation of contraction; estimates of the contribution of entering Ca^{++} to the activation of contraction vary from none (Fabiato, 1983) to 30% (Morad and Goldman, 1973). The second concept is that the small amount of Ca^{++} that enters, triggers a much larger release of Ca^{++} from the sarcoplasmic reticulum (SR) (see Fabiato, 1983).

Support for the idea that entering Ca^{++} contributes measurably to contractile activation came from voltage-clamp studies in Purkinje fibers (Gibbons and Fozzard, 1975) and ventricular tissue (New and Trautwein, 1972). The first studies on intracellular Ca^{++} transients in Purkinje fibers (Wier, 1980; Wier and Isenberg, 1982) also suggested that Ca^{++} entering the cell via surface membrane Ca^{++} channels accounted for a small component of contraction and an early, rapid rise in aequorin luminescence (component L_1 of the aequorin signal). Ca^{++} currents are now known to be larger than previously thought [in multicellular preparations (Marban, 1981), and in single cells (Isenberg and Klockner, 1982)], further supporting the idea that entering Ca^{++} may have a significant role in activating contraction.

Nevertheless, recent data (Hess and Wier, 1984) suggest that the L_1 component of the aequorin signal may not directly reflect Ca^{++} entry, and thus the contribution of entering Ca^{++} remains uncertain. Because caffeine strongly reduces L_1 and not slow inward current, Hess and Wier suggested that L_1 might arise from Ca^{++} released from SR that makes junctional contact with surface membrane. (L_2 would arise from Ca^{++} released, via Ca^{++}-induced Ca^{++} release, from SR deep in the muscle.) The Ca^{++} that enters would have to be bound rapidly or be taken up by the SR, as suggested by Isenberg (1982) and Fabiato (1983).

To investigate this question further, we attempted to block selectively the release of Ca^{++} from the SR and to observe the remaining intracellular Ca^{++} transients. We used the putative blocker of SR calcium release, ryanodine (Jenden and Fairhurst, 1969; Sutko and Kenyon, 1983), on the assumption that this would minimize the contribution of released Ca^{++} to the Ca^{++} transient. Ryanodine appears well-suited as a tool for this dissection of the Ca^{++} transient: whereas it blocks Ca^{++} release from the SR, entry pathways such as Ca^{++} channels and Na-Ca exchange are not inhibited (Sutko and Kenyon, 1983; Mitchell et al., 1984). We used Ca^{++} channel antagonists in the presence of ryanodine to confirm that Ca^{++} channels remained functional. We used Ca^{++} channel agonists, also in the presence of ryanodine, to increase Ca^{++} current in order to observe more clearly any signal directly related to Ca^{++} entry.

Methods

Biological Preparation

Adult mongrel dogs of either sex were anesthetized with T-61 Euthanasia Solution (0.5 ml/kg, iv bolus; American Hoechst Corp.). Each milliliter of this solution contains: 200 mg of *N*-[2-(m-methoxy-phenyl)-2-ethyl-butyl-(1)]-γ-hydroxybutyramide; 50 mg of 4,4′-methylene-bis(cyclohexyl-trimethyl-ammonium iodide); 5 mg of tetracaine hydrochloride; 0.6 ml of dimethylformamide in distilled water. The hearts were quickly removed through a left lateral thoracotomy and immediately rinsed with Tyrode's solution. Purkinje fibers of 200–450 μm external diameter and 1–2 mm length were dissected from the endocardial surface of the right ventricle and mounted on fine stainless steel hooks, one end fixed to a pedestal in the bath chamber and the other to a tension transducer (Akers 801 element). The bath chamber, heated by a Peltier device to 35°C, was perfused with standard physiological saline of the following composition (in mM): Na^+, 144; K^+, 2.7; Ca^{++}, 2.7; Mg^{++}, 2.0; HCO_3^-, 24; Cl^-, 132.1; dextrose, 5. Solutions were equilibrated with 95% O_2/5% CO_2 to pH = 7.4 at 35°C. Field stimulation with 1 msec pulses was applied at a frequency of 1 Hz. K^+-free solution was made by simply omitting KCl. K^+-free, low Na^{++} solution had the following composition (in mM): Na^+, 24; Ca^{++}, 2.7; Mg^{++}, 2.0; HCO_3^{--}, 24; Cl^+, 9.4; sucrose, 245; dextrose, 5.

Measurement of Aequorin Luminescence and Membrane Potential

By means of previously described techniques (Allen and Blinks, 1978; Wier and Hess, 1984), 10–20 superficial cells were micro-injected with aequorin (purchased from Dr. John Blinks, Rochester, Minn.). A 3M KCl-filled microelectrode then was used to measure membrane potential while luminescence was conducted, via a Lucite light guide, onto a photomultiplier tube (EMI 9893) positioned beneath the preparation. Luminescence was collected by photon-counting techniques, and signals were averaged when necessary to improve signal-to-noise ratio, as described by Wier et al. (1983). Maximal luminescence (L_{max}) was determined from Triton X-100 lysis at the end of the experiment, and this value was used to calculate fractional luminescence (L/L_{max}). Membrane potential and tension were recorded continuously on magnetic tape (Hewlett-Packard 3964A recorder). A sufficient number of aequorin signals was averaged to obtain an acceptable signal-to-noise ratio.

Materials

Ryanodine, a plant-derived alkaloid of molecular weight 495 daltons, was obtained from Penick Corp., and stored at 10°C as 1 mM aqueous stock solution. Nitrendipine and Bay k 8644, supplied by Miles Pharmaceuticals, were kept as 1 mM stock solutions in polyethylene glycol in opaque containers. Drug-containing experimental solutions were prepared immediately before use by appropriate dilution of the stock solutions, or, in the case of caffeine, by addition of drug in powder form and solubilization in the experimental solution.

Results

Effects of Ryanodine on Membrane Potential, Aequorin Luminescence, and Tension

Figure 1A shows an example of the simultaneously recorded action potential, aequorin luminescence, and twitch tension before the addition of drug. Ryanodine (10 nM) decreased twitch tension and aequorin luminescence (Fig. 1B). The aequorin luminescence signal not only decreased in amplitude, but also changed in shape. The two components, L_1 and L_2, are readily apparent in the presence of ryanodine (Fig. 1B). A selective inhibition of

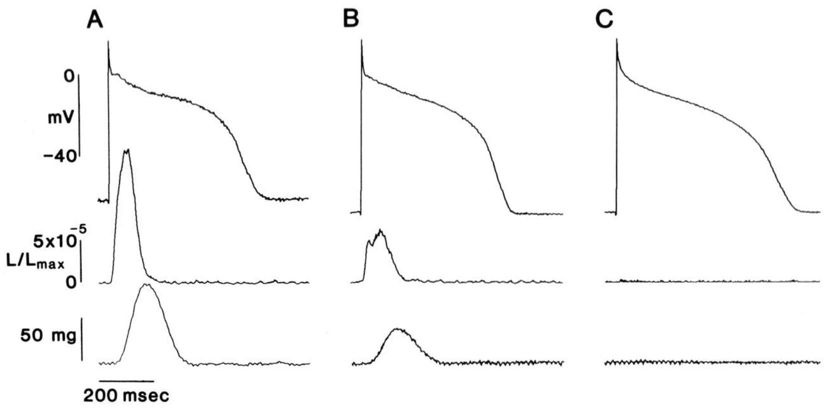

FIGURE 1. *Membrane potential, fractional aequorin luminescence and tension in response to ryanodine. Panel A: no drug. L/L_{max} signals are the average of 97 sweeps. Panel B: 20 minutes after washing on 10 nM ryanodine. 57 sweeps averaged. The notch in the aequorin signal separates components L_1 and L_2. Panel C: Steady state effect (20 min) of 1 μM ryanodine. 528 sweeps averaged. Preparation 1–5.*

release of Ca^{++} from the SR can explain the progression from Figure 1A to 1B: the underlying L_1 was "unmasked" by a selective decrease in L_2. On this basis, further increase in ryanodine concentration should selectively abolish L_2, but not L_1. When the ryanodine concentration was increased to 1 μM (Fig. 1C), the aequorin luminescence transient and twitch tension were markedly reduced. Thus, the idea that L_1 reflects Ca^{++} entry is not supported by these data. Similar effects of ryanodine on twitches and aequorin signals were observed in all other (nine) experiments.

There were three changes in the action potential: (1) a slight increase in the maximum diastolic potential, due at least in part to improved membrane potential recording stability as tension declined; (2) a genuine decrease in the rate of phase 1 repolarization and in the associated "notch" (Kenyon and Gibbons, 1979); and (3) a lengthening of plateau depolarization. The changes in rapid repolarization and in the plateau are consistent with known effects of ryanodine to decrease transient outward current (Sutko and Kenyon, 1983) and to slow the inactivation of Ca^{++} current (Mitchell et al., 1984), both of which are attributable (Siegelbaum and Tsien, 1980; Tsien and Marban, 1982) to the observed decrease in Ca^{++}.

Although the Ca^{++} transient and the twitch appear to be abolished by ryanodine, closer inspection of averaged signals reveals tiny Ca^{++} transients and twitches, as shown in Figures 2A and 3A. In three muscles, the mean maximal amplitude of the aequorin signals was 3% ± 2% (SEM) of control, whereas the mean peak contraction tension was 2% ± 3% of control (note the change in gain of the calibration bars), making them much smaller than the previously identified L_1 or L_2. The kinetics of these signals also distinguish them from either L_1 or L_2: luminescence rises rapidly, but then declines slowly (most evident in Fig. 2A). Correspondingly, twitch relaxation is prolonged.

Relationship to Ca^{++} Entry Via Ca^{++} Channels or Na-Ca Exchange

To investigate the possible relationship of these signals to surface membrane Ca^{++} conductance, we exploited the new highly specific dihydropyridine Ca^{++} channel agonist, Bay k 8644 (Schramm et al., 1983), and antagonist, nitrendipine (Lee and Tsien, 1983). Figure 2 shows the effects of nitrendipine (10 μM) on membrane potential, aequorin luminescence, and tension during exposure to ryanodine (1 μM). The action potential plateau is markedly depressed by nitrendipine, as expected from the blockade of functional Ca^{++} channels. Concomitantly, the luminescence and tension signals become undetectable during exposure to nitrendipine (Fig. 2B). Our conclusion that Ca^{++} channels remain functional in ryanodine agrees with the results of voltage clamp experiments in calf Purkinje fibers (Sutko and Kenyon, 1983) and in rat ventricular cells (Mitchell et al., 1984).

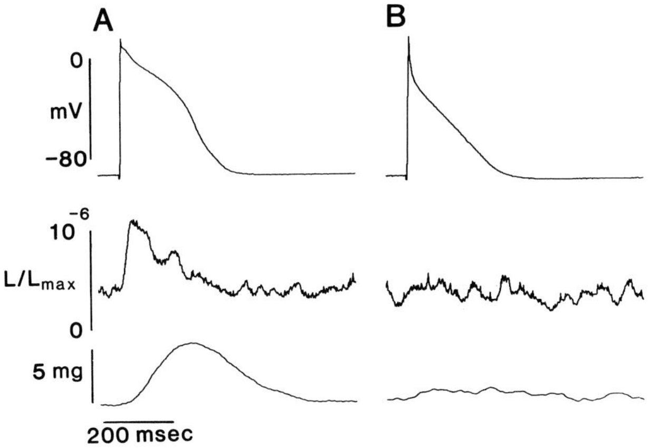

FIGURE 2. *Effect of Ca^{++} channel blockade during ryanodine exposure. Vertical order of records as in Figure 1. Panel A: steady state effect of 1 μM ryanodine. Luminescence and tension records averaged over 1450 sweeps. Panel B: steady state nitrendipine (10 μM) effect in continuing presence of ryanodine. 649 sweeps averaged. Note the changes in the L/L_{max} and tension gains relative to Figure 1. Preparation 1–17.*

In two experiments, the effects of an increase in Ca^{++} influx were tested using Bay k 8644, an agonist compound known to increase Ca^{++} current in Purkinje fibers (Sanguinetti and Kass, 1984; Cohen and Chung, 1984). In preliminary dose-response experiments, we found that 300 nM Bay k 8644 maximized twitch tension. With ryanodine present, this concentration of Bay k 8644 elevates the action potential plateau and augments the luminescence transient and tension (Fig. 3).

Although Na-Ca exchange is generally believed to extrude Ca^{++} from heart cells, under certain conditions the mechanism can reverse and actually cause Ca^{++} entry (e.g., Coraboueuf et al., 1981).

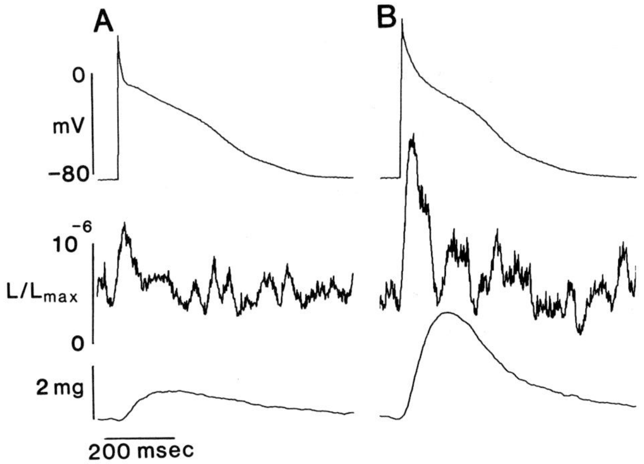

FIGURE 3. *Effect of Ca^{++} channel agonist Bay k 8644 in the presence of ryanodine. Panel A: steady state effect of 1 μM ryanodine. 4000 sweeps averaged. Panel B: steady state Bay k 8644 (300 nM) effect in continuing presence of ryanodine. 1500 sweeps averaged. Preparation 3–14.*

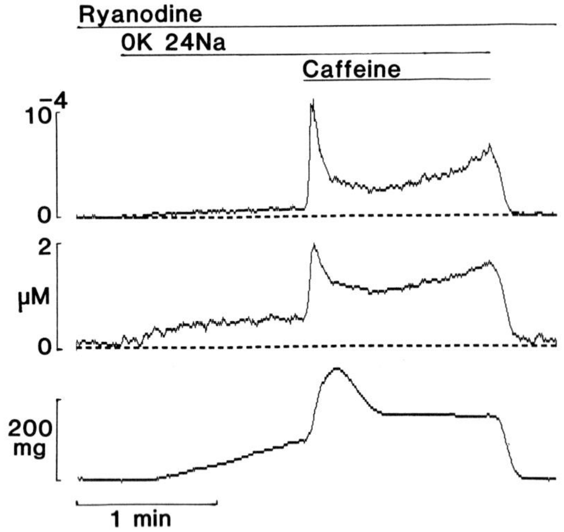

FIGURE 4. *Luminescence, calculated* $[Ca^{++}]_i$, *and tension during a sodium withdrawal contracture in the presence of ryanodine (1 μM). After a steady state was reached in ryanodine, the fiber was exposed to* K^+*-free solution for 3 minutes just prior to washing in* K^+*-free, low-*Na^+ *solution. After 1 minute, caffeine (10 mM) was added. Luminescence,* $[Ca^{++}]$, *and tension decreased when the fiber was re-exposed to physiological saline solution.*

Ryanodine does not affect Na-Ca exchange as measured in sarcolemmal membrane vesicles (Sutko and Kenyon, 1983), but we sought independent confirmation that this mechanism remains functional in our preparation. Figure 4 shows aequorin luminescence, derived Ca^{++}, and force during exposure to K^+-free, low-Na^+ solution (see Wier et al., 1983) in the presence of ryanodine (1 μM). The rise in Ca^{++}, evident as the low-Na^+ solution washes in, reflects Ca^{++} influx via a functional Na-Ca exchange mechanism (Coraboeuf et al., 1981).

Another feature of Figure 4 should also be noted. In other systems (e.g., Chapman, 1974; Fabiato and Fabiato, 1975), caffeine has been used as a tool to "dump" Ca^{++} from the SR to determine its level of Ca^{++} loading. Using the same strategy, 10 mM caffeine was applied to the fiber in Figure 4. Caffeine evoked a large increase in Ca^{++} and force, above and beyond those induced by Na^+ withdrawal alone. Under these conditions, the SR appears to contain a large amount of Ca^{++} even in the presence of ryanodine, which has been suggested (under different conditions) to decrease the Ca^{++} loading of the SR (Hilgemann et al., 1983). Similar effects of Na^+ withdrawal in the presence of ryanodine were seen in six other preparations; the caffeine effect was confirmed in one other fiber.

Upper-Limit Estimates for Ca^{++} Transients in Ryanodine

If aequorin is uniformly distributed throughout the cytoplasm, the observed luminescence sets an upper limit (Blinks et al., 1982) on the spatial average $[Ca^{++}]$. In three experiments, luminescence signals of the type shown in Figure 2A, when referred to a standard calibration curve (Wier and Hess, 1984), corresponded to a mean peak $[Ca^{++}]$ of 109 ± 25 nM (SEM).

Discussion

We find that Ca^{++} entry results in only a very small rise in Ca^{++} in the presence of ryanodine. It is not immediately clear that this is true under control conditions, since in the absence of ryanodine (control) the amount of entering Ca^{++} and/or its intracellular distribution will be somewhat different than in its presence, as discussed below.

At least one factor will tend to increase Ca^{++} entry in the presence of ryanodine, compared to control. Recent voltage clamp experiments indicate that Ca^{++} influx is *increased* by ryanodine (Mitchell et al., 1984), perhaps as a consequence of reduced inactivation of Ca^{++} current by Ca^{++}. This may explain the increased depletion of extracellular Ca^{++} caused by ryanodine (Hilgemann et al., 1983).

Other factors will tend to reduce the Ca^{++} transient due to Ca^{++} entry in ryanodine compared to that in control. For example, an important factor that influences the Ca^{++} transient, and which may be different in ryanodine compared to control is the Ca^{++}-buffering capacity of the cytoplasm. Ryanodine is not itself a Ca^{++} buffer, as it does not affect Ca^{++} activity in solution (Jones et al., 1979), but it may have indirect effects on Ca^{++} buffering. Ca^{++} released from the SR under normal conditions will compete with entering Ca^{++} for buffer sites. In the presence of ryanodine, more of the entering Ca^{++} will be buffered, because more Ca^{++}-binding sites will be available. However, we calculate that this effect is small: even if sufficient Ca^{++} is released from the SR to elevate free $[Ca^{++}]$ to 10^{-6} M, then the additional $[Ca^{++}]$ increment resulting from entry could be at most twice that in the absence of Ca^{++} release from the SR (assuming steady state buffering, calculated from data in Table 4 of Fabiato, 1983). A second factor to be considered is that, in the absence of the release process, the SR may have a somewhat increased ability to take up the Ca^{++} that enters, because it may not be loaded with Ca^{++}, as suggested by Hilgemann et al. (1983). However, this would require a fairly large leak of Ca^{++} from the SR in the presence of ryanodine, a phenomenon for which we can find no supporting evidence. Furthermore, the experiment in Figure 4 shows that the SR can contain Ca^{++} when ryanodine is present (although the conditions for Ca^{++} loading in this experiment are quite different than during twitches). Consistent with our observations, there is no direct effect of ryanodine on Ca^{++} ATPase activity in SR vesicles (Sutko et al., 1979).

On balance, the data support the conclusion that, under control conditions, only a very small fraction of the Ca^{++} transient could be due directly to Ca^{++} entry. Thus, the components of the aequorin signal, L_1 and L_2, may arise from Ca^{++} released from intracellular storage sites. This possibility had already been raised, based on the effects of caffeine, another inhibitor of SR function which decreases L_1 and L_2 while not blocking Ca^{++} channels (Hess and Wier, 1984). However, the effects of caffeine are difficult to interpret, in that it not only affects the SR, but also sensitizes the myofilaments to Ca^{++} (Wendt and Stephenson, 1984; Hess and Wier, 1984) thereby increasing Ca^{++} buffering.

The small aequorin signal that remains in the presence of ryanodine could be due to Ca^{++} entry, or it could be due to an incomplete effect of ryanodine to inhibit Ca^{++} release from the SR. In either case, the figure of 100 nM (see Results) is an upper-limit on the increase in cytoplasmic $[Ca^{++}]$ which is due to Ca^{++} entry. This result agrees reasonably well with estimates of Ca^{++} influx based on contemporary measurements of Ca^{++} current. Using voltage clamp data from Cs^{+} loaded calf Purkinje fibers (Marban and Tsien, 1982), Fabiato and Baumgarten (1984) have calculated that total Ca^{++} rises approximately 1 μM during the first 20 msec of maximal Ca^{++} current. When intracellular Ca^{++} buffering is considered, the maximum $[Ca^{++}]$ increase in this time interval should be equal to or less than 100 nM.

Implications for Excitation-Contraction Coupling

Would Ca^{++} transients of the magnitude measured in ryanodine suffice to trigger Ca^{++}-induced Ca^{++} release under normal conditions? Our upper-limit estimate for spatial average $[Ca^{++}]$ due to Ca^{++} entry is lower than the minimum concentration (400 nM) required to trigger Ca^{++}-induced Ca^{++} release in skinned dog Purkinje cells (Fabiato, 1982). A number of factors might explain the apparent discrepancy. The Ca^{++} transient we detect could arise from a subcellular compartment in which local $[Ca^{++}]$ exceeds spatial average $[Ca^{++}]$. Some of the entering Ca^{++} does reach the myofilaments, however, as twitches invariably accompany our luminescence signals. Furthermore, Ca^{++}-induced Ca^{++} release may propagate along the SR; if so, only a fraction of the SR need be exposed to the "trigger" $[Ca^{++}]$. Finally, even a small absolute rise in $[Ca^{++}]$ may suffice to trigger release, if the rate of change of $[Ca^{++}]$, $\Delta[Ca^{++}]/\Delta t$ is important, as suggested by Fabiato (1983).

A small increment of 100–200 nM $[Ca^{++}]$ would not produce much force when added on to the low resting $[Ca^{++}]$, but the steepness of the Ca^{++}-tension relation at higher $[Ca^{++}]$ predicts that such an increment would result in more force if superimposed on the $[Ca^{++}]$ rise associated with release from the SR.

Finally, we noted a tendency for estimated diastolic $[Ca^{++}]$ to be lower in ryanodine than in control. If real, such a decrease in diastolic $[Ca^{++}]$ could be due to a decrease in the basal Ca^{++} "leak" from the SR and would agree with the observation that ryanodine decreases Ca^{++}-dependent phosphorylase a activity in cardiac muscle (Jones et al., 1979).

Ryanodine does not affect the amphibian heartbeat (Chapman, 1979), and only partially inhibits the twitch of mammalian ventricular muscle (Sutko et al., 1979). Additional experiments will be required to establish whether the effect of ryanodine on the SR is less complete, or if, as expected (Morad et al., 1983), Ca^{++} entry is relatively more important in these tissues.

We thank David Yue for his comments on the manuscript.

Financial support was obtained from the Miles Institute for Preclinical Pharmacology, and from U.S. Public Health Service Grant 29473.

Dr. Marban is affiliated with the The Johns Hopkins Hospital.

Address for reprints: Dr. W.G. Wier, Department of Physiology, University of Maryland School of Medicine, 660 W. Redwood St., Baltimore, Maryland 21201.

Received July 20, 1984; accepted for publication October 10, 1984.

References

Allen DG, Blinks JR (1978) Calcium transients in aequorin-injected frog cardiac muscle. Nature **273:** 509–513

Blinks JR, Wier WG, Hess P, Prendergast F (1982) Measurement of Ca^{++} concentration in living cells. Prog Biophys Mol Biol **40:** 1–114

Chapman R (1979) Excitation-contraction coupling in cardiac muscle. Prog Biophys Mol Biol **35:** 1–52

Cohen CJ, Chung M (1984) A nifedipine-derivative (Bay k 8644) that increases Ca currents in myocardial cells: A novel positive inotropic agent (abstr). Biophys J **45:** 394a

Coraboeuf E, Gautier P, Guiraudou P (1981) Potential and tension changes induced by sodium removal in dog Purkinje fibres: Role of an electrogenic sodium-calcium exchange. J Physiol (Lond.) **311:** 605–622

Fabiato A (1982) Calcium release in skinned cardiac cells: variations with species, tissues, and development. Fed Proc **41:** 2238–2244

Fabiato A (1983) Calcium-induced release of calcium from the cardiac sarcoplasmic reticulum. J Physiol (Lond) **245:** C1–C14

Fabiato A, Baumgarten CM (in press) Methods for detecting calcium release from the sarcoplasmic reticulum of skinned cardiac cells and the relationships between calculated transarcolemmal calcium movements and calcium release. *In* Function of the Heart in Normal and Pathological States, edited by N Sperelakis. Nijhoff, The Hague

Fabiato A, Fabiato F (1975) Contractions induced by a calcium-triggered release of calcium from the sarcoplasmic reticulum of single skinned cardiac cells. J Physiol (Lond) **249:** 469–495

Gibbons WR, Fozzard HA (1975) Relationships between voltage and tension in sheep cardiac Purkinje fibers. J Gen Physiol **65:** 345–365

Hess P, Wier WG (1984) Excitation-contraction coupling in cardiac Purkinje fibers: Effects of caffeine on the intracellular $[Ca^{++}]$ transient, membrane currents and contraction. J Gen Physiol **83:** 417–433

Hilgemann DW, Delay MJ, Langer GA (1983) Activation-dependent cumulative depletions of extracellular free calcium in guinea pig atrium measured with antipyrylazo III and tetramethylmurexide. Circ Res **53:** 779–793

Isenberg G (1982) Ca entry and contraction as studied in isolated bovine ventricular myocytes. Z Naturforsch **37c:** 502–512

Isenberg G, Klockner U (1982) Calcium currents of isolated bovine ventricular myocytes are fast and of large magnitude. Pflugers Arch **395:** 30–41

Jenden DJ, Fairhurst AS (1969) The pharmacology of ryanodine. Pharmacol Rev **21:** 1–25

Jones LR, Besch HR, Sutko JL, Willerson JT (1979) Ryanodine-induced stimulation of net Ca^{++} uptake by cardiac sarcoplasmic

reticulum vesicles. J Pharmacol Exp Ther **209:** 48–55
Kenyon JL, Gibbons WR (1979) Influence of chloride, potassium and tetraethylammonium on the early outward current of sheep cardiac Purkinje fibers. J Gen Physiol **73:** 117–138
Lee KS, Tsien RW (1983) Mechanism of calcium channel blockade by verapamil, D600, diltiazem, and nitrendipine in single dialyzed heart cells. Nature **302:** 790–794
Marban E (1981) Inhibition of transient outward current by intracellular ion substitution unmasks slow inward calcium current in cardiac Purkinje fibers. Pflugers Arch **290:** 102–106
Marban E, Tsien RW (1982) Effects of nystatin-mediated intracellular ion substitution on membrane currents in calf Purkinje fibres. J Physiol (Lond) **329:** 569–587
Mitchell MR, Powell T, Terrar DA, Twist VW (1984) Ryanodine prolongs Ca-currents while suppressing contraction in rat ventricular muscle cells. Br J Pharmacol **81:** 13–15
Morad M, Goldman Y (1973) Excitation-contraction coupling in heart muscle: Membrane control of development of tension. Prog Biophys Mol Biol **27:** 257–313
Morad M, Goldman YE, Trentham DR (1983) Rapid photochemical inactivation of Ca^{++}-antagonists shows that Ca^{++} entry directly activates contraction in frog heart. Nature **304:** 635–638
New W, Trautwein W (1972) Inward membrane currents in mammalian myocardium. Pflugers Arch **334:** 1–23
Sanguinetti MC, Kass RS (1984) Dihydropyridine derivatives: Voltage-dependent modulation of calcium channel current (abstr). Biophys J **45:** 394a
Schramm M, Thomas G, Towart R, Franckowiak G (1983) Novel dihydropyridines with positive inotropic action through activation of Ca^{++} channels. Nature **303:** 535–537
Siegelbaum SA, Tsien RW (1980) Calcium-activated transient outward current in cardiac Purkinje fibres. J Physiol (Lond) **299:** 485–506
Sutko JL, Kenyon JL (1983) Ryanodine modification of cardiac muscle responses to potassium free solutions: Evidence for inhibition of sarcoplasmic reticulum calcium release. J Gen Physiol **82:** 385–404
Sutko JL, Willerson JT, Templeton GH, Jones LR, Besch HR (1979) Ryanodine: Its alteration of cat papillary muscle contractile state and responsiveness to inotropic interventions and a suggested mechanism of action. J Pharmacol Exp Ther **209:** 37–47
Tsien RW, Marban E (1982) Digitalis and slow inward current in heart muscle: Evidence for regulatory effects of intracellular calcium on calcium channels. *In* Advances in Pharmacology and Therapeutics, vol 3. Oxford, Pergamon, pp 217–225
Wendt IR, Stephenson DG (1983) Effects of caffeine on Ca-activated force production in skinned cardiac and skeletal muscle fibres of the rat. Pflugers Arch **398:** 210–216
Wier WG (1980) Calcium transients during excitation-contraction coupling in mammalian heat: Aequorin signals of canine Purkinje fibers. Science **207:** 1085–1087
Wier WG, Isenberg G (1982) Intracellular $[Ca^{++}]$ transients in voltage-clamped cardiac Purkinje fibers. Pflugers Arch **392:** 284–290
Wier WG, Hess P (1984) Excitation-contraction coupling in cardiac Purkinje fibers: Effects of cardiotonic steroids on the intracellular $[Ca^{++}]$ transient, membrane potential and contraction. J Gen Physiol **83:** 395–416
Wier WG, Kort AA, Stern MD, Lakatta EG, Marban E (1983) Cellular calcium fluctuations in mammalian heart: Direct evidence from noise analysis of aequorin signals in Purkinje fibers. Proc Natl Acad Sci USA **80:** 7367–7371

INDEX TERMS: Ryanodine • Calcium transients • Purkinje fibers • Nitrendipine • Bay k 8644

Significance of Quiescent Smooth Muscle Migration in the Injured Rat Carotid Artery

Alexander W. Clowes and Stephen M. Schwartz
From the Departments of Surgery and Pathology, University of Washington School of Medicine, Seattle, Washington

SUMMARY. Cellular accumulation in the intima of injured artery has generally been attributed to smooth muscle cell proliferation. Since smooth muscle cells in normal artery are found mainly in the media, migration of smooth muscle cells into the intima has been considered a necessary prerequisite for subsequent myointimal thickening. The nondividing medial cells would appear to have no role in the reparative process. We have investigated in the rat ballooned carotid the possibility that nondividing cells might also contribute to injury-induced intimal thickening. All proliferating smooth muscle cells were labeled by ^{3}H-thymidine given by continous intraperitoneal infusion. The amounts of ^{3}H-thymidine used were not toxic and did not inhibit smooth muscle cell proliferation. Autoradiograms performed on histological cross-sections showed a progressive decrease in the fraction of unlabeled cells at 3, 7, and 14 days after carotid injury. However, the actual number of nondividing cells remained constant. The calculated growth fraction for the 14-day period was 40%. A substantial number of unlabeled cells was observed in the intima. These data have led us to conclude that only a small fraction of smooth muscle cells in an artery proliferate in response to the injury stimulus, and do so shortly after injury, or not at all. Furthermore, nondividing, as well as proliferating smooth muscle cells, can migrate and contribute, in a substantial way, to the increase in intimal smooth muscle cell number. **(*Circ Res 56: 139–145, 1985*)**

THE way in which smooth muscle cells (SMC) accumulate in arterial intima is of considerable importance to our understanding of atherogenesis and arterial wound repair. The generally accepted dogma, at least for injured arteries, is that SMC respond to the injury stimulus by migrating out of the media and proliferating to form a thickened intima. Tritiated thymidine pulse-labeling experiments from our laboratory demonstrate SMC proliferation occurring as early as 2 days after injury in the media (thymidine index ca 30–50%/24 hr) and at 4 days in the intima (thymidine index ca 70%/24 hr) (Clowes et al., 1983a). Similarly, Thomas et al. (1979) have demonstrated in a pig model of atherosclerosis that arterial plaques enlarge on account of cell replication in preexisting intimal cell masses. These data have provided support for the concept that the response to injury and atherosclerosis is principally a proliferative one.

Under circumstances of injury, proliferation and subsequent intimal thickening depend upon early migration of SMC from the media to the intima, as suggested by Hassler (1979) and Webster et al. (1974). SMC migration in response to a variety of stimulants has been studied in vitro (Thorgeirsson et al., 1979; Grotendorst et al., 1981; Ihnatowicz et al., 1981; Seppa et al., 1982; Bernstein et al., 1982; Nakao et al., 1982). The results of these investigations demonstrate that SMC proliferation and directed migration are separable phenomena. For example, although SMC proliferate in response to epidermal growth factor (EGF), fibroblast growth factor (FGF), insulin, and platelet-derived growth factor (PDGF), SMC exhibit chemotaxis only in response to PDGF (Grotendorst et al., 1981; Ihnatowicz et al., 1981). Furthermore, SMC migration does not appear to depend on proliferation; SMC require both PDGF and other serum factors for proliferation, but require PDGF alone for migration (Bernstein et al., 1982; Weinstein et al., 1981). Since PDGF and other mitogens are probably present at the surface of injured artery in variable amounts, SMC might in some instances be expected to migrate and proliferate, and, in others, to respond by directed migration alone. We have investigated this possibility in injured rat carotid and show that a significant proportion of SMC responding to the injury stimulus can enter the intima without ever proliferating.

Methods

Male Sprague-Dawley rats (500 g; 5 months old) were subjected to left carotid injury by the balloon technique as previously described (Clowes et al., 1983a, 1983b). In brief, under general anesthesia (pentobarbitol), a 2F balloon embolectomy catheter was introduced into the external branch of the left common carotid artery and passed along the common carotid in an inflated state. This procedure effectively strips endothelium off of the luminal surface. During the same anesthesia, an osmotic infusion pump (Alza, Alzet Corp.) containing 2 ml of ^{3}H-thymidine (6.7 Ci/mm, 1 mCi/ml, ICN) was inserted into the peritoneal cavity. This pump infuses continuously at a rate of approximately 5 μl/hr.

At 1 hour and 3, 7, and 14 days, animals were killed and both carotids were retrieved. Two 5-mm segments were cut from the central portion of each carotid for DNA determinations (Clowes et al., 1983a) and a third piece removed, fixed in 2.5% glutaraldehyde in 0.1 M phosphate-buffered saline, pH 7.4, and embedded in methacrylate. Cross-sections (2 μm) were cut and autoradiograms prepared (Clowes et al., 1983a) by dipping the slides in Kodak NTB-2 emulsion and storing them in light-tight boxes at 4°C. The autoradiograms were developed after
2 weeks and the thymidine index (%) determined for intimal and medial SMC separately and for entire cross-sections (2 sections/animal). The "unlabeled cell index" (%) for the entire cross section was equal to (100-thymidine index) and the unlabeled SMC DNA at any time point was equal to 1/100 × (unlabeled cell index × total DNA).

The "non-dividing fraction" for each time period (t) was then:

Nondividing fraction (%)

$$= \frac{\text{unlabeled cell index}_t \times \text{DNA}_t^c}{\text{DNA}_0^c}$$

Where DNA^c (corrected or normalized DNA content)

$$= \frac{\text{DNA}_{\text{left carotid}}}{\text{DNA}_{\text{right carotid}}}$$

Growth fraction (%) = 100 − nondividing fraction.

This formulation of the growth fraction corrects for inter-animal variation in normal carotid DNA content and is reasonably accurate as long as the DNA/nondividing cell and nondividing cell volume remain constant. In previous studies, we have shown that the mean DNA/cell remains constant between 0 and 12 weeks after injury (Clowes et al., 1983a). This method of measuring growth fraction also is not influenced by the means used to mark proliferating cells, since ^{3}H-thymidine will not be taken up by nondividing cells. Nevertheless, the possibility that ^{3}H-thymidine infused chronically would alter total SMC accumulation in injured artery was eliminated by including a group of control animals subjected to left carotid injury and receiving continuous pump infusion of lactated Ringer's solution intraperitoneally. Furthermore, we confirmed that the pumps provided continuous infusion of ^{3}H-thymidine by performing autoradiography on intestine and skin wounds made the day before sacrifice.

A calculation of unlabeled SMC DNA was made for the intima and the media separately at 7 and 14 days after injury. Since the total DNA content of the left carotid could not readily be partitioned into medial and intimal DNA, we made the approximation that $\text{DNA}_{\text{media}} = \text{DNA}_{\text{right carotid}}$ and $\text{DNA}_{\text{intima}} = \text{DNA}_{\text{left carotid}} - \text{DNA}_{\text{right carotid}}$. This approximation was validated by showing that the number of nuclei in the left carotid media per cross-section was the same as in the right carotid media [at 3 days (n = 4): left carotid media—288 ± 22 (SD); right carotid media—270 ± 45; at 14 days (n = 5): left carotid media—285 ± 48; right carotid media 265 ± 34]. The unlabeled SMC DNA of the media = 1/100 × (unlabeled cell index$_{\text{media}}$ × DNA$_{\text{right carotid}}$) and unlabeled SMC DNA of the intima = 1/100 × [unlabeled cell index$_{\text{intima}}$ × (DNA$_{\text{left carotid}}$ − DNA$_{\text{right carotid}}$)].

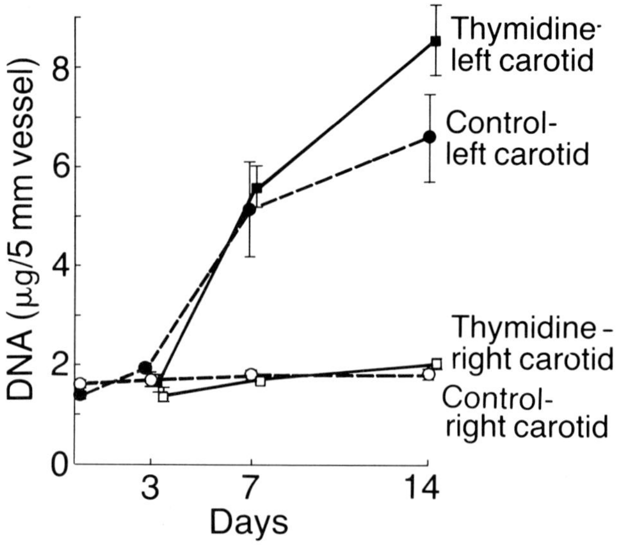

FIGURE 1. *Graphic representation of DNA content (µg DNA/5 mm vessel ± SEM) of right and left carotids of animals killed at intervals between 0 and 14 days after surgery. Control animals received continuous intraperitoneal infusion of lactated Ringer's solution, and experimental animals received ^{3}H-thymidine. The differences between control and experimental carotids are not significant (paired t-test).*

Results

Endothelium was completely removed from the left carotid artery by the balloon catheter, leaving only media containing SMC behind. At 7 and 14 days, circumferential intimal thickening was evident. Continuous infusion of ^{3}H-thymidine produced no discernible toxic effect upon the hyperplastic response of the artery to the experimental injury as measured by the increase in DNA content (Table 1; Fig. 1). Satisfactory minipump function was documented at all times out to 14 days by demonstrating labeled cells in fresh skin wounds

TABLE 1
DNA Content of Injured Carotids

Type of infusion	Time after injury: 1 hr	3 days	7 days	14 days
^{3}H-Thymidine		1.65 ± 0.37 (4)	5.62 ± 0.79 (5)	8.57 ± 1.57 (5)
Lactated Ringer's solution	1.40 ± 0.12 (3)	1.95 ± 0.15 (4)	5.15 ± 1.40 (4)	6.63 ± 1.80 (4)

Results are expressed as mean ± SD (µg DNA/5 mm). Numbers in parentheses = number of animals in each group. The differences between ^{3}H-thymidine and lactated Ringer's groups are not significant (t-test).

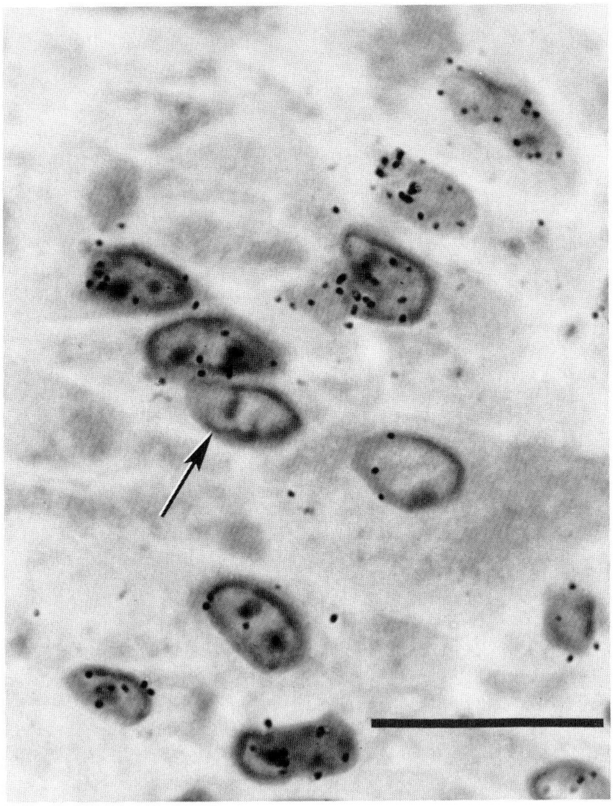

FIGURE 2. *Autoradiogram of histological cross-section at 14 days. Note unlabeled nucleus (arrow) in intima surrounded by labeled nuclei. Bar = 10 μm.*

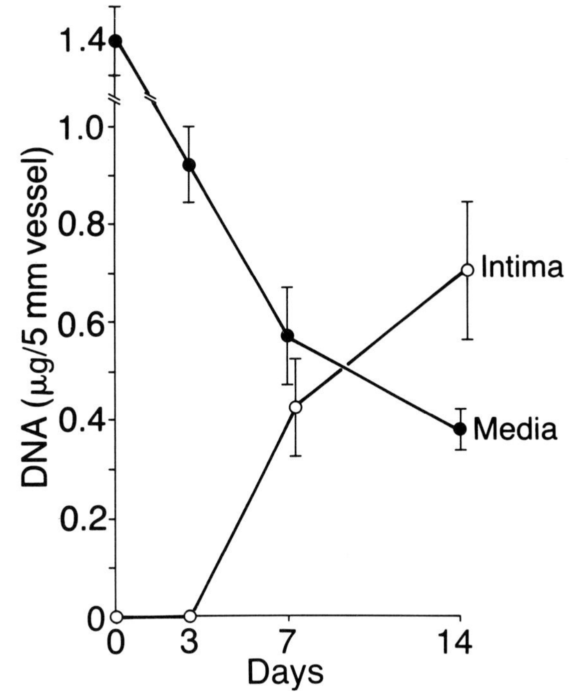

FIGURE 3. *Graph demonstrating changes in nondividing DNA of media and intima cell mass (μg DNA/5 mm vessels ± SEM) in the left carotid as a function of time. The decrease in medial unlabeled (or nondividing) DNA between 0 and 3 days is due to entry of cells into S phase; the decrease between 3 and 14 days is due mainly to migration of unlabeled cells from the media into the intima. At the start of the experiment, and at 3 days, there are no smooth muscle cells in the intima.*

made just before sacrifice and by evidence of continuous labeling cells in the epithelial lining of the crypts in gut (data not shown).

Unlabeled cells were observed in both the media and the intima at 7 and 14 days (Fig. 2). The number of unlabeled cells, as estimated from the DNA measurements, in the media declined, and the number of unlabled intimal cells increased during this period of time (Fig. 3). The possibility that an artefact (asymmetric ^{3}H-thymidine (^{3}H-TDR) distribution in the nucleus, inadequate thymidine labeling) could account for the unlabeled cells was eliminated by preparing autoradiagrams on cell dispersions (from collagenase-elastase digested intima alone) and by increasing the concentration of tritiated thymidine in the osmotic pump; in each instance, comparable proportions of unlabeled intimal cells were observed (data not shown). The fraction of unlabeled cells (intima + media) declined from 56% at 3 days to 13% at 14 days (Fig. 4) but the absolute amount of unlabeled cell DNA and the nondividing fraction remained constant (Fig. 5). The calculated growth fraction increased slightly over the time interval (range: 23–39%), but the changes were not significant.

If we multiply the unlabeled fraction by the final left carotid DNA content (normalized for each animal by dividing by right carotid DNA), the result will be the DNA that has not replicated during the 2-week interval of the study. That unlabeled DNA, divided by the amount of DNA at the start of the experiment, provides a measure of the fraction of the cells that never undergo replication. By subtraction from 100%, we obtain an estimate of the growth fraction. Whereas the calculation does make some assumptions regarding DNA content per cell and cell death, these factors should have only slight impact on the estimate of growth fraction. For example, changes in the tetraploid population should be apparent only in the labeled population of SMC—not in the unlabeled cell population, upon which our calculations are based. Since dead, nonreplicating cells would disappear from our estimate of unlabeled DNA, cell death would be expected to produce a falsely low estimate of the nonreplicating population. In summary, our approach produces a minimum estimate of the frequency of nondividing migrating cells.

We estimated the minimum number of cell divisions required to produce the marked increase in DNA content of the left carotid at 14 days. If we use an average growth fraction of 30%, an initial $DNA_{left\ carotid}$ of 1.4 μg (just after injury), a final $DNA_{left\ carotid}$ of 8.57 μg (at 14 days) and we assume no cell death, then each cell would be required to undergo four divisions. Since our previous pulse

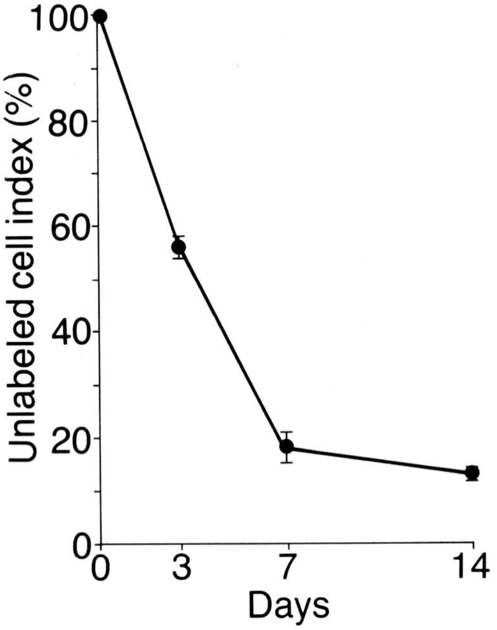

FIGURE 4. *Graph of the unlabeled cell index (± SEM) of the entire left carotid (intima and media) between 0 and 14 days after injury.*

label studies indicate that at least the first round of proliferation occurs in the media, no more than three additional divisions could occur in the intima. If the unlabeled intimal DNA mass at 14 days is 0.7 μg (Fig. 3) and the total intimal DNA mass is 6.5 μg (Fig. 1: $DNA_{left\ carotid} - DNA_{right\ carotid}$), then three divisions (8-fold increase) of an intimal cell mass equal to 0.7 μg would account for the increase. An alternative—but, in view of earlier pulse-labeling data (Clowes et al., 1983a), less likely—possibility is that all the proliferation takes place in the media, and labeled daughter cells migrate into the intima. Thus, we can account for 8/9 of the increase in DNA content of the intima by three rounds of cell replication. The remainder of the DNA must be due to migration without replication. Since the number of these nondividing cells does not increase, we can conclude that, at a minimum, approximately 50% of SMC migrating into the intima subsequently do not proliferate (Fig. 6).

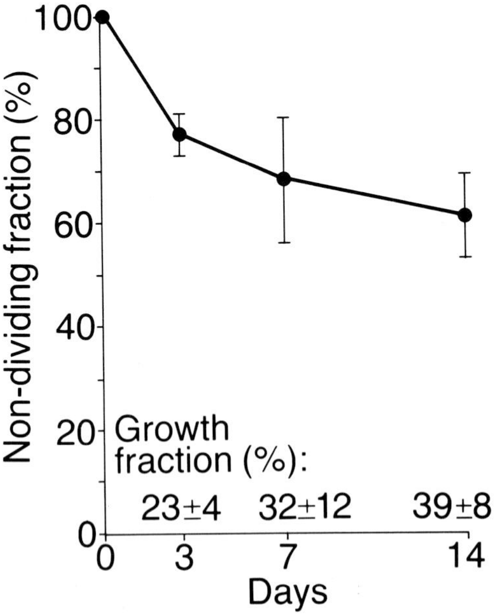

FIGURE 5. *Graph of the nondividing fraction (± SEM) for the entire left carotid for each time period. The growth fraction for each period is recorded below.*

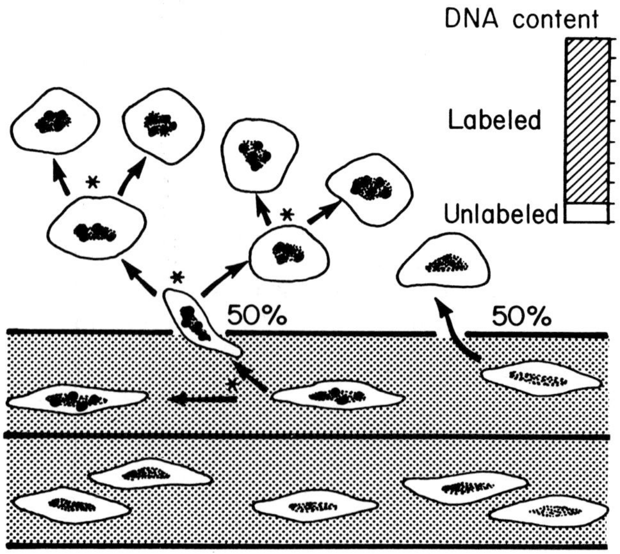

FIGURE 6. *Schematic diagram suggesting how SMC accumulate in the intima by migration and proliferation (50%) or migration alone (50%). One-ninth of the DNA content of the intima at 14 days (bar graph) is accounted for by nondividing SMC. Pulse label experiments (Clowes et al., 1983a) indicate that SMC proliferation in the media is maximal at 2 days after carotid injury, and then declines rapidly thereafter. Therefore, it is likely that, after the first round of medial SMC proliferation, daughter cells migrate and continue to proliferate in the intima; an alternative and less likely possibility is that SMC continue to proliferate mainly in the media and daughter cells then migrate into the intima.*

Discussion

In the past, migration from the media through the internal elastic lamina has been considered a necessary prerequisite for introducing SMC into the intima (Hassler, 1970; Webster et al., 1974; Spaet et al., 1975). We now demonstrate that migration alone without proliferation can account for part of the intimal SMC accumulation. Approximately 50% of the cells that migrate into lesions never divide. As the population of intimal nondividing SMC increases the medial nondividing population decreases. The absolute number of nondividing cells in the vessel wall remains relatively constant in the period between 3 and 14 days after injury, indicating that if SMC are going to respond to the injury stimulus, they do so immediately. Even though the rat carotid artery is thin (three to five medial elastic layers), the SMC growth fraction induced by extensive injury is only between 20 and 40%.

All cells proliferating in response to injury were labeled by ^{3}H-thymidine (^{3}H-TdR). In vitro continuous labeling, either with ^{3}H-TdR or bromodeoxyuridine, has allowed for measurement of the nondividing fraction over long periods of time (Ross et al., 1978; Matsumara et al., 1979; Rabinovitch, 1983). Although both ^{3}H-TdR and bromodeoxyuridine can produce toxic effects and inhibit cell proliferation, the nondividing fraction should not be altered, since nondividing cells do not take up these molecules. The proportion of the original population of cells in the tissue that never enter the cell cycle can be obtained by dividing the total number of unlabeled cells at the end of the experiment by the number of cells at the beginning of the experiment. Similar studies in vivo have not been possible before, because a method for continuous ^{3}H-TdR administration in small animals was lacking. Since we have quantitative data for DNA accumulation in response to the injury with and without labeled DNA, we can conclude that this dose is not harmful to the normal hyperplastic response. A similar method has been used in vitro by Rabinovitch (1983) to examine the effects of serum and aging upon the human fibroblast growth fractions and transition probabilities out of G_0. In vivo, this approach permits a precise measurement of growth fraction, especially as it changes with time and has been used, for example, to quantify proliferation in hepatocytes and oval cells in regenerating liver (Tatematsu et al., 1984).

For the purposes of this study, quiescent SMC in the arterial wall can be considered synchronized in G_0–G_1. Based on our earlier studies we would expect that the majority of the proliferating cells would enter the growth cycle between 24 and 72 hours after injury (Clowes et al., 1983a). The present data demonstrate that the population of nondividing SMC remains relatively constant between 3 and 14 days after injury, thereby demonstrating that if SMC are going to proliferate, they do so immediately after injury.

The observation that unlabeled cells are present in the intima suggests that SMC can migrate from the media without proliferating. An alternative explanation is that some other nondividing cell type has entered the intima from the blood; however, in injured normolipemic rat arteries (Clowes et al., 1983b; Fishman et al., 1975; Schwartz et al., 1975), only SMC have been observed in the thickened intima. If the unlabeled cells are SMC, then several questions are raised. Do the nondividing intimal SMC have different properties from proliferating SMC which allow for only a limited response (migration only) to mitogens? Are these cells the same as the rest, but because there is a large accumulation of migratory stimulant in the wall compared to mitogen, they migrate without dividing? Are there several different factors introduced into the wall as a consequence of injury—some controlling migration, and, others, proliferation?

At present, there are no data from animal experimentation to discriminate between these possibilities. SMC migrate and proliferate in response to extensive arterial endothelial injury, yet they do not, when the injury is limited (Reidy and Schwartz, 1981). In both circumstances, endothelium is stripped away and the denuded surface covered with platelets. The reason for the difference in response of the medial SMC to these two forms of injury is not known. One possible explanation provided by the studies of Castellot et al. (1982) is that, in the limited-injury model, endothelium adjacent to the narrow denuded strip produce sufficient amounts of heparin-like glycosaminoglycans to inhibit SMC proliferation. Migration might also be affected by these molecules. We have recently demonstrated that SMC migration in vitro is inhibited by heparin (Majack and Clowes, 1984). This effect is dose-dependent, reversible, and specific for SMC, since endothelial cells are not affected.

In cell culture, a variety of mitogens stimulate SMC growth and undirected migration (chemokinesis), but only platelet-derived growth factor (PDGF) induces directed migration (chemotaxis) in a Boyden chamber (Grotendorst et al., 1981). Other factors generated as part of the injury process (platelet factor 4, thromboglobulin, lymphokines, macrophage factors, fibronectin, and collagen fragments) might also play a role (Postlethwaite et al., 1976, 1978, 1981; Gauss-Muller et al., 1980; Wahl and Wahl, 1981; Seppa et al., 1981; Senior et al., 1983). Whole blood serum, but not plasma-derived serum, contains both growth- and migration-stimulating factors for SMC. At least one of these is PDGF. Whether PDGF is important for SMC migration and proliferation in injured artery remains to be determined. Although PDGF induces directed migration in vitro, we do not know whether the concept of chemotaxis is important in vivo in the movement of SMC from the media through the internal elastic lamina to the intima. An alternative possibility is that medial SMC exhibit increased chemokinetic activity in response to the injury stimuli, randomly move about, and occasionally cross into the intima.

We need to consider the possible significance of migration by itself as a mechanism for formation of atherosclerotic lesions. First, the balloon lesion does not appear to be able to provide a model for the monoclonality of human lesions (Benditt and Benditt, 1973). As shown by Pearson et al. (1979), lesions in ballooned hares are polyclonal. This is consistent with the view that randomly migrating medial cells are the source for the cells in the intimal lesion. This leaves open the possibility that occasional migration of individual cells, perhaps occurring during vascular differentiation, could produce a single cell focus in the intima. Such a focus could form intimal cell masses of the sort identified by Thomas et al. (1979) as the site of origin of atherosclerotic lesions in swine or the preatherosclerotic intimal cell masses identified in human coronary arteries by the Velicans (1979). Second, the reasons for migration without proliferation remain unclear. The Campbells (1981) and, more recently, Gabbiani et al. (1984) have proposed that the loss of contractile phenotype occurs as an early event in lesion formation and is a prerequisite for smooth muscle cell entry into the growth cycle. Perhaps this phenotypic change is necessary for migration but not sufficient for proliferation. The mitogenic stimulus in the balloon model may be present only transiently. Cells that have undergone the requisite changes after this interval may migrate but not proliferate. Perhaps most intriguing is the possibility that some migrating smooth muscle cells, like striated muscle cells (Caplan et al., 1983), may be post-mitotic and lack the ability to divide.

In summary, these experiments provide support for the hypothesis that the injury process stimulates a small proportion of the medial SMC to enter the growth cycle. Although proliferation accounts for much of the intimal accumulation of SMC, migration of both dividing and nondividing cells is also important. This migratory step is probably regulated by promoting and inhibiting factors carried in the blood (e.g., PDGF) and generated locally in the wall (e.g., heparan sulfate).

This work was supported by Grants HL27769 and HL03174 and Research Career Development Award (to A.W.C.) HL01108 from the National Institutes of Health, U.S. Public Health Service.

Address for reprints: Alexander W. Clowes, M.D., Department of Surgery, University of Washington, School of Medicine, RF-25, Seattle, WA 98195.

Received May 24, 2984; accepted for publication October 3, 1984.

References

Benditt EP, Benditt JM (1973) Evidence for a monoclonal origin of human atherosclerotic plaques. Proc Natl Acad Sci USA **70:** 1753–1756

Bernstein LR, Antoniades H, Zetter BR (1982) Migration of cultured vascular cells in response to plasma and platelet-derived factors. J Cell Sci **56:** 71–82

Caplan AI, Fizman MC, Eppenberger HM (1983) Molecular and cell isoforms during development. Science **221:** 921–927

Castellot JJ, Favreau LV, Karnovsky MJ, Rosenberg RD (1982) Inhibition of vascular smooth muscle growth by endothelial cell-derived heparin. J Biol Chem **257:** 11256–11260

Chamley-Campbell JH, Campbell GR (1981) What controls smooth muscle phenotype? Atherosclerosis **40:** 347–357

Clowes AW, Reidy MA, Clowes MM (1983a) Kinetics of cellular proliferation after arterial injury. I. Smooth muscle growth in the absence of endothelium. Lab Invest **49:** 327–333

Clowes AW, Reidy MA, Clowes MM (1983b) Mechanisms of stenosis after arterial injury. Lab Invest **49:** 208–215

Fishman JA, Ryan GB, Karnovsky MJ (1975) Endothelial regeneration in the rat carotid artery and the significance of endothelial denudation in the pathogeneis of myointimal thickening. Lab Invest **32:** 339–351

Gabbiani G, Kocher O, Bloom WS, Vanderkerchove J, Weber K (1984) Actin expression in smooth muscle cells of rat aortic intimal thickening, human atheromatous plaque and cultured rat media. J Clin Invest **73:** 148–152

Gauss-Muller V, Kleinman HK, Martin GR, Schiffmann E (1980) Role of attachment factors and attractants in fibroblast chemotaxis. J Lab Clin Med **96:** 1071–1080

Grotendorst GR, Seppa HEJ, Kleinman HK, Martin GR (1981) Attachment of smooth muscle cells to collagen and their migration toward platelet-derived growth factor. Proc Natl Acad Sci USA **78:** 3669–3672

Hassler O (1970) The origin of the cells constituting arterial intimal thickening: An experimental autoradiographic study with the use of ^{3}H-thymidine. Lab Invest **22:** 286–293

Ihnatowycz IO, Winocour PD, Moore S (1981) A platelet-derived factor chemotatic for rabbit smooth muscle cells in culture. Artery **9:** 316–317

Majack RA, Clowes AW (1984) Inhibition of vascular smooth muscle cell migration by heparin-like glycosaminoglycans. J Cell Physiol **118:** 253–256

Matsumara T, Pfendt EA, Hayflick L (1979) DNA synthesis in the human diploid cell strain WI-38 during in vitro aging: An autoradiography study. J Gerontol **34:** 323–327

Nakao J, Ooyama T, Chang WC, Murota S, Orimo H (1982) Platelets stimulate aortic smooth muscle cell migration in vitro. Involvement of 12-L-hydroxy-5,8,10,14-eicosatetranoic acid. Atherosclerosis **43:** 143–150

Pearson TA, Dillman J, Williams KJ, Wolff JA, Adams R, Solez K, Heptinstall RH, Malmros H, Steinby N (1979) Clonal characteristics of experimentally induced "atherosclerotic" lesions in the hybrid hares. Science **206:** 1423–1425

Postlethwaite AE, Snyderman R, Kang AH (1976) The chemotactic attraction of human fibroblasts to a lymphocyte-derived factor. J Exp Med **144:** 1188–1203

Postlethwaite AE, Seyer JM, Kang AH (1978) Chemotactic attraction of human fibroblasts to type I, II, and III collagens and collagen-derived peptides. Proc Natl Acad Sci USA **75:** 871–875

Postlethwaite AE, Keski-Oja J, Balian G, Kang AH (1981) Induction of fibroblast chemotaxis by fibronectin. Localization of the chemotactic region to a 140,000 molecular weight non-gelatin-binding fragment. J Exp Med **153:** 494–499

Rabinovitch PS (1983) Regulation of human fibroblast growth rate by both noncycling cell fraction and transition probability is shown by growth in 5-bromodeoxyuridine followed by Hoechst 33258 flow cytometry. Proc Natl Acad Sci USA **80:** 2951–2955

Reidy MA, Schwartz SM (1981) Endothelial regeneration. III. Time course of intimal changes after small defined injury to rat aortic endothelium. Lab Invest **44:** 301–308

Ross R, Nist C, Kariya B, Rivest MJ, Raines E, Callis J (1978) Physiological quiescence in plasma-derived serum: Influence of platelet-derived growth factor on cell growth in culture. J Cell Physiol **97:** 497–508

Schwartz SM, Stemerman MB, Benditt EP (1975) The aortic intima. II. Repair of the aortic lining after mechanical denudation. Am J Pathol **81:** 15–42

Senior RM, Griffin GL, San Huang J, Walz DA, Duel TF (1983) Chemotactic activity of platelet alpha granule proteins for fibroblasts. J Cell Biol **96:** 382–385

Seppa HEJ, Yamada KM, Seppa ST, Silver MH, Kleinman HK, Schiffman E (1981) The cell binding fragment of fibronectin is chemotactic for fibroblasts. Cell Biol Int Rep **5:** 813–819

Seppa H, Grotendorst G, Seppa S, Schiffmann E, Martin G (1982) Platelet-derived growth factor is chemotactic for fibroblasts. J Cell Biol **92:** 584–588

Spaet TH, Stemerman M, Veith FJ, Lejnieks I (1975) Intimal injury and regrowth in the rabbit aorta: Medial smooth muscle cells as a source of neointima. Circ Res **36:** 58–70

Tatematsu M, Ho RH, Kaku T, Ekem JK, Farber E (1984) Studies on the proliferation of and fate of oval cells in the liver of rats treated with 2-acetylaminofluorene and partial hepatectomy. Am J Pathol **114:** 418–430

Thomas WA, Reiner JM, Florentin RA, Scott RF (1979) Population dynamics of arterial cells during atherogenesis. VIII. Separation of the roles of injury and growth stimulation in early aortic atherogenesis in swine originating in pre-existing intimal smooth muscle cell masses. Exp Mol Pathol **31:** 124–144

Thorgeirsson G, Robertson AL, Cowan DH (1979) Migration of human vascular endothelial and smooth muscle cells. Lab Invest **41:** 51–62

Velican D, Velican CA (1979) Study of fibrous plaques occurring in the coronary arteries of children. Atherosclerosis **33:** 201–215

Wahl SM, Wahl LM (1981) Modulation of fibroblast growth and function by monokines and lymphokines. Lymphokines **2:** 179–201

Webster WS, Bishop SP, Geer JC (1974) Experimental aortic intimal thickening. I. Morphology and source of intimal cells. Am J Pathol **76:** 245–260

Weinstein R, Stemerman MB, Maciag T (1981) Hormonal requirements for growth of arterial smooth muscle cells in vitro: An endocrine approach to atherosclerosis. Science **212:** 818–820

INDEX TERMS: Tritiated thymidine • Smooth muscle cell • Migration • Arteriosclerosis • Growth fraction

Phospholipase D Produces Increased Contractile Force in Rabbit Ventricular Muscle

G.A. Langer and T.L. Rich

From the Departments of Medicine and Physiology, and the American Heart Association, Greater Los Angeles Affiliate, Cardiovascular Research Laboratories, University of California, Los Angeles, School of Medicine, Center for the Health Sciences, Los Angeles, California

SUMMARY. Inclusion of phospholipase D (*Streptomyces chromofuscus*, 5 U/ml) in the medium perfusing rabbit papillary muscles increased peak force development by 78% and peak dF/dt by 89%. The maximal contractile response occurred 40–50 minutes after addition of the enzyme to the perfusate. As peak contractile response developed, aftercontractions appeared in most muscles. The inotropic response was slowly reversible, with disappearance of aftercontractions, upon discontinuation of the enzyme. Phospholipase D produces a specific increase of phosphatidic acid in the sarcolemma and, therefore, an increase in net anionic charge on the membrane. It has been shown previously that phospholipase D induces a large increase in sarcolemmal calcium binding. We propose, on the basis of the present study, that phospholipid-bound calcium may play a significant role in the control of contractile force in mammalian myocardium. **(*Circ Res 56: 146–149, 1985*)**

IT has been proposed that calcium (Ca^{++}) bound to sarcolemmal sites of mammalian myocardium plays a major role in control of force development by the heart (Bers and Langer, 1979; Langer and Nudd, 1983). Previous work indicates that, at physiological concentrations of Ca^{++}, 80–85% of Ca^{++} bound to sarcolemma is bound to phospholipid (Philipson et al., 1980). A major fraction of this binding is presumed to be at anionic sites on the hydrophilic ends of the amphiphilic phospholipid molecules (Langer and Nudd, 1983). Studies on purified cardiac sarcolemma and cultured myocardial cells show Ca^{++} displacement by the specific cationic probe for anionic phospholipid sites, polymyxin B (PXB), and large increases of Ca^{++} binding after exposure to phospholipase D (PLD) (Burt and Langer, 1983; Burt et al., 1983; Burt et al., in press). Finally, it has been shown that PLD treatment of purified sarcolemmal vesicles increases Na^{+}-Ca^{++} exchange by 300–400% (Philipson and Nishimoto, 1984). Therefore, there is considerable evidence that Ca^{++} binding at the sarcolemma can be predictably manipulated by alteration of anionic phospholipid sites, and that the activity of the Na^{+}-Ca^{++} exchanger is linked, by an undefined mechanism, to Ca^{++} at these sites. An important question which remains is whether alteration in phospholipid Ca^{++} binding produces an inotropic response in whole, functional myocardium, and the present study is directed to that question.

Methods

A total of 24 papillary muscles dissected from the right ventricle of adult New Zealand rabbits was mounted in a Lucite chamber with one end connected to a capacitance transducer in order to measure isometric force and its first derivative (dF/dt). After dissection and mounting in the chamber, the muscles were perfused for 60 minutes with a solution of the following composition (mM): 140 NaCl, 4 KCl, 1.0 $CaCl_2$, 1.0 $MgCl_2$, 22 $NaHCO_3$, 10 glucose with 10 mU/ml insulin. The perfusate was equilibrated to a mixture of 95% O_2-5% CO_2 by passage of the solution through a gas exchanger prior to its entry into the chamber. The pH of the solution was 7.4. After initial equilibration, 8 μM bovine serum albumin and 0.5% glycerol were added to the perfusate, and an additional 25–30 minutes of equilibration was allowed. The PLD used in these studies was the enzyme purified from *Streptomyces chromofuscus* (Calbiochem). This enzyme, in contrast to that derived from cabbage, is active at physiological Ca^{++} concentration and pH (Imamura and Horiuti, 1979). It is stabilized by albumin and stored in glycerol and was added to the muscle perfusate with these agents present to give a final concentration of 5 U/ml PLD. The albumin/glycerol additive, by itself, caused a slow decline in muscle force over the 25- to 30-minute equilibration period. Experiments were performed between 36 and 37°C with field stimulation at 1.25–1.50 times threshold at 30 beats/min.

Results

The pattern of the response to PLD is shown in Figure 1. Twenty one of 24 muscles demonstrated a latency period in the force response with a mean delay of 20.2 ± 3.1 (SE) minutes for the entire group. The molecular weight of the enzyme is 50 K daltons. Although the papillary muscles were selected for minimum radius (0.42 ± 0.03 mm), it is expected that time would be required for the large molecule to diffuse through the endocardium and subendocardial connective tissue of the muscles. The peak contractile response usually occurred between 20 and 30 minutes after onset, or between 40 and 50

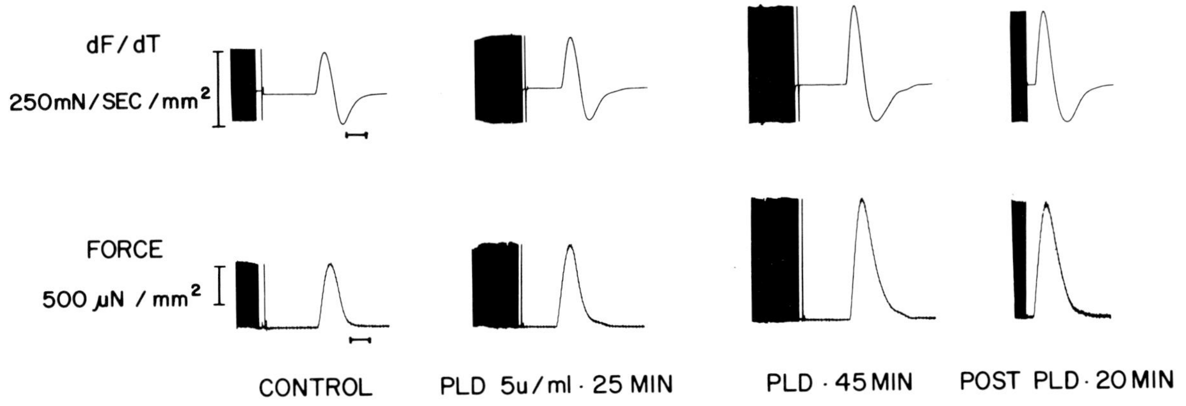

FIGURE 1. *Force development and its first derivative in rabbit papillary muscle. Active force envelope is indicated by solid black at slow chart speed, followed by single beats at rapid chart speed (time bars = 200 msec for rapid speed). Muscle was stimulated at 30 beats/min. Response to addition of 5 U/ml PLD to the perfusate is shown 25 and 45 minutes after addition and 20 minutes after removal of the enzyme. At 45 minutes, both force and dF/dt increased by 2-fold. Twenty minutes after removal of PLD, force and dF/dt had decreased by 10% from peak value.*

minutes after first exposure to PLD. The increase in peak force after PLD was 1.78 ± 0.11-fold with a 1.89 ± 0.13-fold increase in dF/dt.

As the peak force response continued to increase, aftercontractions appeared and resting tension began to rise, as shown in Figure 2, which represents the response of another muscle. The aftercontractions and rise in resting force are clear indications of increased Ca^{++} loading by the cells (Orchard et al., 1983). Removal of PLD is followed by a decline in resting force and disappearance of the aftercontractions over the course of 30 minutes, at which time active force is little changed and dF/dt has declined by 12%. The inotropic response to PLD was slowly reversible upon removal of the enzyme. In the experiment shown in Figure 2, the increment in force declined by 50% over the course of 100 minutes after the enzyme had been removed (not shown).

All of the activity of the enzyme is lost when heated to 80°C for 15 minutes (Imamura and Horiuti, 1979). Perfusion of papillary muscle which had demonstrated a 111% increase in force after application of active enzyme lost all of its positive inotropy within 30 minutes after substitution of heat-inactivated enzyme in the perfusate.

Finally, it was of interest to explore the possibility that PLD, through creation of additional anionic surface charge, would produce accumulation of cations, such as Ca^{++}, in the aqueous diffuse double layer (McLaughlin, 1977). Such an accumulation of Ca^{++} could conceivably produce the demonstrated positive inotropy without the requirement that additional Ca^{++} actually binds to the anionic sites created by PLD treatment. A specific probe has been developed for investigation of the diffuse double layer (McLaughlin et al., 1983). Dimethonium (ethane-bis-trimethylammonium) is a divalent cation of molecular weight 306 that replaces inorganic cations in the diffuse double layer but does not bind to the membrane. Therefore it will compete with Ca^{++}, as well as other cations in the double layer, but not with Ca^{++} bound to the membrane. The effectiveness of dimethonium as a displacer of Ca^{++}

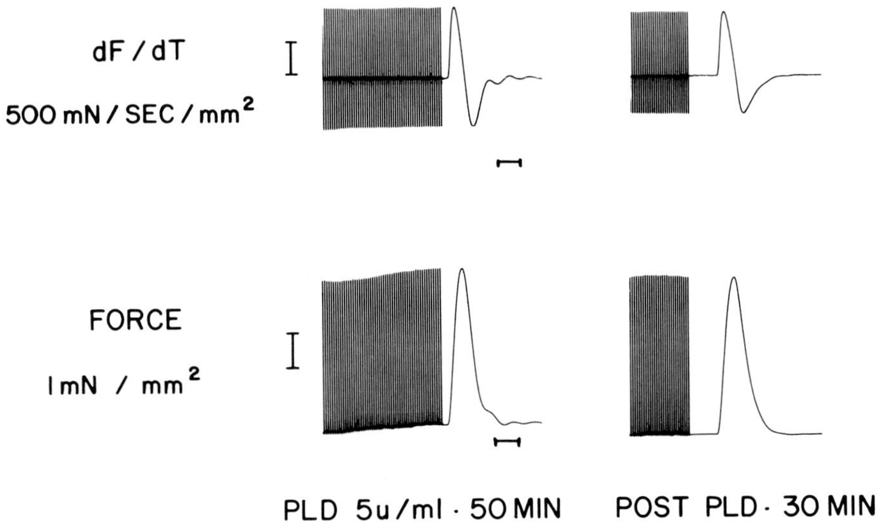

FIGURE 2. *Force envelope and its first derivative, as in Figure 1. Fifty minutes after addition of 5 U/ml PLD to the perfusate force and dF/dt had increased 2-fold above control, and as shown in the force record, resting force had begun to increase. At this time, prominent aftercontractions can be seen. Thirty minutes after removal of the enzyme, resting force had returned to control and aftercontractions had disappeared. At this time, peak force had not declined and dF/dt had decreased by 12%. Muscle was stimulated at 30 beats/min. Time bar = 200 msec rapid chart speed.*

in the diffuse double layer has been proven in tissue culture studies (Fintel et al., unpublished data). It has also been shown to produce a small but significant negative inotropic effect on the positive inotropy induced by sucrose-substituted low sodium perfusion in whole tissue. Substitution of neutral sucrose for sodium induces a large increase in diffuse double layer Ca^{++}. The negative inotropic response to dimethonium ion under these conditions indicates that it gains access to the double layer in whole tissue. Application of 10 mM dimethonium ion to a papillary muscle which had developed an increase of 50% in force after PLD exposure resulted in no decrease in the positive inotropy.

Discussion

PLD cleaves the nitrogenous base from phospholipids, producing phosphatidic acid, and thereby increasing the net anionic charge on the membrane. Philipson and Nishimoto (1984) found that PLD treatment (0.4 U/ml) of sarcolemmal vesicles increased the phosphatidic acid level from 0.9 to 8.9% of total phospholipid content. This increase in phosphatidic acid should provide additional binding sites for cations, particularly Ca^{++}. Such increased binding after PLD treatment has been demonstrated in sarcolemma prepared from rat cardiac myocyte culture (Langer and Nudd, 1983) where 0.1 U/ml PLD (cabbage) caused a 56% increase in sarcolemma Ca^{++} binding.

Details of Ca^{++} movement subsequent to binding have not been defined. Ohsako and Deguchi (1981) found that exogenous as well as endogenous phosphatidic acid stimulated Ca^{++} influx in neuroblastoma and in cultured heart cells. Salmon and Honeyman (1980) proposed that increased phosphatidate may mediate the increased cellular Ca^{++} levels produced by cholinergic stimulation and noted that phosphatidate at concentrations as low as 10^{-8} M produced contractions in isolated smooth muscle cells. Phosphatidic acid has been proposed as a Ca^{++} ionophore in the promotion of Ca^{++} uptake in isolated nerve terminals (Harris et al., 1981) and in liposomes (Serhan et al., 1982). By contrast, an ionophoretic action of phosphatidic acid could not be demonstrated in another liposomal membrane model (Holmes and Yoss, 1983). Pertinent to the possibility of ionophoretic action is the demonstration by Philipson and Nishimoto (1984) that, in sarcolemmal vesicles, phosphatidic acid formation increased Na^{+}-Ca^{++} exchange activity by 300–400%. In the vesicle system, the enhanced Ca^{++} uptake is Na^{+} gradient-dependent and results in an outwardly directed Ca^{++} gradient. As they point out, this eliminates the possibility, in the vesicle system, that the PLD-induced increase in Ca^{++} uptake is due to an ionophoretic action of phosphatidic acid.

The present study, in association with the demonstration of increased phosphatidic acid levels in sarcolemmal vesicles (Philipson and Nishimoto, 1984) clearly shows that such increase is associated with a marked positive inotropy, and there is other evidence that the inotropy might be related to Na^{+}-Ca^{++} exchange. It is possible that augmented Ca^{++} uptake with increased force development is dependent only on a net increase in anionic sarcolemmal charge and not, specifically, to an increase of phosphatidic acid. Evidence for this possibility comes from previous PXB studies (Burt and Langer, 1983; Burt et al., 1983). PXB is an amphiphilic peptidolipid with a highly charged cationic head group and a lipophilic tail. It has been shown to bind only to artificial membranes which contain negatively charged phospholipid or to zwitterions like phosphatidylethanolamine at pH > 7.2 (Feingold et al., 1974; Imai et al., 1975; Teuber and Miller, 1977). The cationic head of PXB therefore interacts with several anionic phospholipids and is a potent displacer of Ca^{++} from isolated sarcolemma (Burt and Langer, 1983) and cultured cardiac cells (Burt et al., 1983). We have also demonstrated that it is negatively inotropic (unpublished observation). The conclusion from the PXB studies is that a variety of negatively charged phospholipids may contribute to the supply of Ca^{++} which crosses the sarcolemma upon excitation.

Another effect of increase of anionic surface charge would be to augment movement of cations, including Ca^{++}, into the diffuse double layer. If such movement contributed to increased Ca^{++} influx, increased force development would be expected. The fact that 10 mM dimethonium ion produced no decrease in the PLD-induced inotropy indicates that double layer Ca^{++} does not contribute significantly to the response. In addition, the fact that PXB removes most of the PLD-induced increment of Ca^{++} from cultured cells (Burt et al., 1984) supports the proposal that Ca^{++} binding is augmented. If such is the case, then the increased anionic charge produced by PLD-induced phosphatidate production would be neutralized by the increased bound Ca^{++}. Therefore, net surface charge would not be altered at a time when post-PLD steady state had been reached, and any effects which might be attributed to a nonspecific increase in surface charge would not apply.

Factors other than changes in charge on phospholipid head groups play a role in cation binding. One of these is fluidity of lipids in the membrane. There is an enhancement in cation affinity with increased lipid fluidity (Puskin and Martin, 1979). Fluidity changes of the membrane usually occur, however, by change in cholesterol content or by modification of the fatty acid chains of the phospholipids. PLD alters neither of these, and it is unlikely that its modification of head group charge would have significant effects on the fluidity of the in vivo membrane. Therefore, we believe the evidence supports the proposal that negatively charged phospholipids at the external sarcolemmal surface bind the Ca^{++} which may supply the systems responsible for transsarcolemmal movement of Ca^{++}. Philipson and Nishimoto (1984) have already shown stimulation of Na^{+}-Ca^{++} exchange by elevation of the sarcolemmal phosphatidic acid level. There are, as yet, no experimental data directed to possible effects of phosphatidic acid-mediated or other anion-mediated Ca^{++} binding on slow inward current. However, it is clear, from the present study, that increase in at least one negatively charged phospholipid, phosphatidic acid, is associated with large reversible increases in myocardial contractile force mediated by increased Ca^{++} uptake.

It might be expected that phosphatidate once formed by PLD would persist, and the inotropy might be sustained after removal of the enzyme. It has been found, however, that sarcolemmal membrane contains an endogenous phosphatidate hydrolase (Philipson and Nishimoto, 1984). The action of this enzyme may account for the slow return to control levels of force upon removal of PLD.

Supported by U.S. Public Health Service Grant HL28539-02 and the Castera Foundation.

Address for reprints: Glenn A. Langer, M.D., Cardiovascular Research Labs, A3-381 CHS, UCLA School of Medicine, Los Angeles, California 90024.

Received April 30, 1984; accepted for publication October 18, 1984.

References

Bers DM, Langer GA (1979) Uncoupling cation effects on cardiac contractility and sarcolemmal Ca^{2+} binding. Am J Physiol **237:** H332–H341

Burt JM, Langer GA (1983) Ca^{2+} displacement by polymyxin B from sarcolemma isolated by "gas dissection" from cultured neonatal rat myocardial cells. Biochim Biophys Acta **729:** 44–52

Burt JM, Duenas CJ, Langer GA (1983) Influence of polymyxin B, a probe for anionic phospholipids, on calcium binding and calcium and potassium fluxes of the cultured cardiac cells. Circ Res **53:** 679–687

Burt JM, Duenas CJ, Langer GA (in press) Phospholipase D produces increased cell surface Ca-binding and positive inotropy in rat heart. Am J Physiol

Feingold DS, HsuChen CC, Sud IJ (1974) Basis for the selectivity of action of the polymycin antibiotics as cell membranes. Ann NY Acad Sci **235:** 480–492

Harris RA, Schmidt J, Hitzemann BA, Hitzemann J (1981) Phosphatidate as a molecular link between depolarization and neurotransmitter release in the brain. Science **212:** 1290–1291

Holmes RP, Yoss NL (1983) Failure of phosphatidic acid to translocate Ca^{2+} across phosphatidylcholine membranes. Nature **305:** 637–638

Imai M, Inoue K, Nojima, S (1975) Effect of polymyxin B as liposomal membranes derived from *Escherichia coli* lipids. Biochim Biophys Acta **375:** 130–137

Imamura S, Horiuti Y (1979) Purification of *Streptomyces chromofuscus* phospholipase D by hydrophobic affinity chromatography on palmitoyl cellulose. J Biochem 85: 79–95

Langer GA, Nudd LM (1983) Effects of cations, phospholipases and neuraminidase on calcium binding to "gas dissected" membranes from cultured cardiac cells. Circ Res **53:** 482–490

McLaughlin S (1977) Electrostatic potentials of membrane solution interfaces. Curr Top Membr Transp **9:** 71–144

McLaughlin A, Eng W, Varo G, Wilson T, McLaughlin S (1983) Dimethonium, a divalent cation that exerts only a screening effect on the electrostatic potential adjacent to negatively charged phospholipid bilayer membranes. J Membr Biol **76:** 183–193

Ohsako S, Deguchi T (1981) Stimulation by phosphatidic acid of calcium influx and cyclic AMP synthesis in neuroblastoma cells. (1981) J Biol Chem **256:** 10945–10948

Orchard CH, Eisner DA, Allen DG (1983) Oscillations of intracellular Ca^{2+} in mammalian cardiac muscle. Nature **304:** 735–738

Philipson KD, Nishimoto AY (1984) Stimulation of Na^{+}-Ca^{2+} exchange in cardiac sarcolemmal vesicles by phospholipase D. J Biol Chem **259:** 16–19

Philipson KD, Bers DM, Nishimoto AY (1980) The role of phospholipids in the Ca^{2+} binding of isolated cardiac sarcolemma. J Mol Cell Cardiol **12:** 1159–1173

Puskin JS, Martin T (1979) Divalent cation binding to phospholipid vesicles. Dependence on temperature and lipid fluidity. Biochim Biophys Acta **552:** 53–65

Salmon DM, Honeyman TW (1980) Proposed mechanism of cholinergic action in smooth muscle. Nature **284:** 344–345

Serhan CN, Fridovich J, Goetzl EJ, Dunham PB, Weissman G (1982) Leukotriene B_4 and phosphatidic acid are calcium ionophores. Studies employing arsenazo III in liposomes. J Biol Chem **257:** 4746–4752

Teuber M, Miller IR (1977) Selective binding of polymyxin B to negatively charged lipid monolayers. Biochim Biophys Acta **467:** 280–289

INDEX TERMS: Phospholipase D • Calcium binding • Phosphatidic acid • Sarcolemmal anionic sites • Calcium flux

Instructions to Authors*

GENERAL EDITORIAL POLICY

MANUSCRIPTS

Circulation Research accepts for publication definitive and comprehensive manuscripts that present the unpublished results of significant cardiovascular research. First priority is given to research that provides a better understanding of mechanisms that influence normal or abnormal function of the cardiovascular and related systems. Low priority is given to reports that confirm published work, that present a new method or a modification of an existing method without applying it to a biological problem, or that describe preliminary or incomplete studies. The number of papers that can be published each year is limited. Only those that receive a high priority will be accepted for publication.

One complete long manuscript is preferred to several fragmented, interdependent manuscripts.

Manuscripts are generally reviewed by two or more referees who are members of the Editorial Board or consultants. Each review and the editor's letter to the authors usually are sent to the other reviewers as are the authors' responses to reviews. *If an author's prior work, published or in press, provides information essential to the reviewer's understanding of a submitted manuscript, three copies of that work should accompany the manuscript.* Also, if the author has closely related work, in press or under review, three copies of that work should be sent along with the original manuscript or with any of the revised versions as the case may be. Acceptance of manuscripts is based on scientific content and presentation of the material. Clarity, conciseness, and correct grammatical construction are essential. Use of the active voice rather than the passive in expository writing is precise, emphatic, and unambiguous. The process of review and evaluation usually requires six to eight weeks. The copy of all accepted manuscripts is edited. The editors may make changes to eliminate ambiguity and to improve communication between author and reader. Dates of receipt and acceptance are published with each paper. In accord with the U.S. Copyright Act of 1976, release forms that transfer copyright from the author(s) to the publisher will be mailed to the principal author for all authors' signatures.

Submit manuscripts to:

Dr. Francois M. Abboud, Editor
Circulation Research
Cardiovascular Center
University of Iowa College of Medicine
Iowa City, Iowa 52242

In the letter of transmittal, the author should indicate that the work has not been published and is not being considered for publication elsewhere in whole or in part (except as an abstract). The letter of transmittal should indicate that all coauthors have read and approved the submission of the manuscript.

* Revised January 1985.

SPECIAL CATEGORIES

In addition to regular manuscripts, several other categories of articles may be considered.

Brief Communications—Well-documented experimental results of unusual interest but circumscribed scope may be published under the category of *Brief Communications.* These communications should not exceed 2000 words and have no more than 20 references. A maximum of 4 display items (Tables and/or Figures) are permitted.

If a manuscript is rejected for publication under the category, *Brief Communications,* it may be resubmitted only as a regular, more comprehensive article. Authors must indicate whether their manuscripts are being submitted as *Brief Communications* or as regular articles.

Brief Reviews—The purpose of *Brief Reviews* is to present, for some broad aspect of the cardiovascular or related systems, a timely analysis of its present state, existing problems, and future directions of research. These reviews are usually invited and should be written for the general readership of *Circulation Research;* hence, the use of highly specialized terminology should be avoided.

Brief Reviews will be considered for publication and will be evaluated in the same manner as manuscripts describing original research.

Special Articles—These should be an appraisal of the present state, existing problems, and future directions of research but for a more specific area of cardiovascular investigation than that addressed by *Brief Reviews.* They should be more focused than a *Brief Review,* and address research topics which are of recent interest or in which the number of existing publications is relatively limited.

Controversies in Cardiovascular Research—The purpose of these articles is to present two divergent views about an area of research in which there is major disagreement about data or their interpretation. Two authors, or groups of authors, are invited to submit manuscripts, each in support of different or opposing opinions. Authors are expected to restrict their presentations to arguments that advance our understanding of a subject and the reasons for disagreement about it. Manuscripts will be reviewed by referees in the usual way. After manuscripts are selected for publication, each manuscript will be sent to the authors of the other manuscript. Each will be asked to write a brief comment on, or a rebuttal to the paper presenting the opposing view.

Letters to the Editor—These provide an opportunity to express views about a specific paper or papers published in *Circulation Research.* They also provide a means to present points of scientific interest that do not require extended treatment. If a letter refers to a published paper, the senior author of that paper will be given an opportunity to read the letter and to reply. If acceptable, and after editorial review, both letters will be published.

PREPARATION OF MANUSCRIPT

Submit manuscripts in triplicate, except for *Brief Reviews,* for which we require an original plus three copies. The original must be typed on $8\frac{1}{2} \times 11$ inch bond paper of good quality (not "erasable"); if your paper is larger, trim it to size before typing. USE DOUBLE SPACING THROUGHOUT (text, tables, references, and legends) AND ALLOW AMPLE MARGINS (1½ inches on sides, top, and bottom). The second copy should be clear and legible and should not be on onionskin paper. Begin the following sections on separate pages; title, summary, text, reference list, individual tables, figure legends, and footnotes to text. Number *all pages* in sequence in the upper righthand corner and do not staple them.

Title—The title should be informative for the reader and indexer. Do not sacrifice clarity for brevity. ***Include the species studied.*** If possible, indicate what you measured and what you found.

On the title page also state (1) names of authors, including first names, (2) department and institution at which the work was done, (3) city, state, and zip code, (4) notice of grant support (if appropriate), (5) abbreviated title (50 letters and spaces or less), (6) name, address and telephone number for correspondence and mailing proofs, and (7) name and address for requesting reprints (if such a footnote is desired).

Summary—Furnish in *one paragraph* a summary of *no more than 250 words.* The summary should be intelligible to one who has not read the text and should state concisely the purpose of the study, the methods used, the results (summarizing important numerical data), and the conclusions. It should emphasize new and important aspects of the work. Use complete sentences and *do not use* abbreviations.

Index Terms—Four or five key words which are suitable for use in indexing should be included.

Introduction—Clearly state what was studied and why. Provide a concise summary of the background for your study. Include only major references and, when possible, cite recent reviews in place of long lists of individual reports.

Methods—Identify the methods, apparatus, and preparations used in enough detail so that an experienced researcher can repeat your experiments. If you used a well-known method, include a reference to it. For a published method that is not well known, give a reference and brief description. If you have modified a method, or developed a new method, provide a complete and explicit description and critical evaluation. Include information on the errors or limitations of all critical methods and on their accuracy, reproducibility, and sensitivity.

Describe your experimental protocol clearly. If it or your experimental methods are based on certain assumptions, state the assumptions clearly and discuss their validity in relation to your work.

Identify precisely any special chemicals used. Give their source and purity. Do not use abbreviations without first giving the official name of the chemical. Use the generic or officially accepted trivial name of drugs; include the widely used proprietary or popular name or abbreviation in parentheses the first time a drug is mentioned. State clearly the form in which the drug was used (salt or base), the amount given in relation to body weight, and the route of administration. If injected, state the volume and the rate of injection. State the frequency and the time of additional doses. If the drug was added to fluid in a bath or a reservoir, give the final concentration. Include information on diluents or preservatives.

Give a careful description of the statistical method used and a reference to a published description of it.

Guidelines for Animal and Human Research: For experimental animals, state the species, strain, number used, and other pertinent descriptive characteristics. For human subjects or patients, describe their characteristics. When describing surgical procedures on animals, identify the preanesthetic and anesthetic agents used, and state the amount or concentration and the route and frequency of administration for each. The use of paralytic agents, such as curare or succinylcholine, is not an acceptable substitute for anesthetics. For other invasive procedures on animals, report the analgesic or tranquilizing drugs used; if none were used, provide justification for such exclusion. When reporting studies on unanesthetized animals or on humans, indicate that the procedures followed were in accordance with institutional guidelines.

Results—Present your results in logical sequence in the text, tables, and illustrations. Do not *repeat* in the *text* data contained in tables or illustrations, although you may wish to summarize or call special attention to important data presented numerically in the tables or graphically in the illustrations.

Tables: Type each table on a separate sheet with a *brief* title at the top and footnotes at the bottom. Design each table to fit within the column or page size of the Journal. Double space, allowing 1½-inch margins on all four sides. Keep horizontal ruled lines to a minimum and omit vertical ruled lines. If you use abbreviations in column headings, define them in a footnote. The order in which footnote symbols are used is determined by reading horizontally across the table. Use standard symbols in the following order: *, †, ‡, §, ‖, ¶. In a series of related tables, present data in consistent form. Try to arrange tables so that variables are listed sequentially in the boxheads and the values for a given variable are presented vertically under the relevant boxhead. In tables that present means ± SE, limit the number of boxheads for such double rows of figures to no more than seven or eight. When more columns of tabulated statistics need to be presented, divide the material into two tables. Probability values, or other correlations, should be presented without the use of large brackets, as these have to be drawn in by hand. Abbreviations used in tables should be the same as those used in the text and figure legends; abbreviations used for the first time in tables should be defined in table footnotes. Do not present the same data in tables and figures unless the latter emphasize special relationships. Do not submit lengthy tables or data from each experiment unless it is impossible or inadvisable to summarize. If the editors so recommend, the Journal will file complete tables of data permanently with the National Auxiliary Publication Services, which supplies photocopies or microfilm for a fee.

Illustrations: Submit duplicate copies of unmounted, glossy, high-contrast, black and white photographic prints not larger than 8½ × 11 or smaller than 5 × 7 inches, and a set of photocopies. Trim prints of photomicrographs to leave only the area to be published. Indicate special features with arrows (white on black or black on white) and explain in the legend. To indicate magnification, draw the scale *directly* on the print. Cover electron micrographs with transparent paper and indicate on the overlay the critical lines or areas that must be reproduced with greatest fidelity.

Illustrations should be prepared for reduction to 3 inches in width. On occasion the illustration may be reduced to only 6 inches in width. Make sure that lettering within all illustrations is uniform with respect to size and type face and that the illustrations are consistent in overall format and size. Conventional printing is required on figures. The height and thickness of letters and numbers in illustrations must be legible when the figures are reduced. To ensure adequate size, it is advisable to make symbols 3 mm high and letters 5 mm high on a 5 × 7 photograph and symbols 6 mm high and letters 10 mm high on a 8½ × 11 photograph. *If it appears that, after reduction, the symbols and letters will be too small, the illustration will be returned to the author for modification.* Use only standard symbols for points: □ ○ ■ ● △ ▲ ×. If possible, explain symbols in the legend. When photographing graphs, eliminate grid lines unless they are essential. Label each axis with the quantity measured and the units of measurements. Do not print a title on the figure. Abbreviations, symbols, words, etc., used in illustrations should be identical to those used in the corresponding section of the text. As the editors will change British spelling to American in the *text*, please be sure that American spelling is used on illustrations to coincide with the text.

Identify each print on the back with a typed label or mark it lightly with a *soft* pencil. Include the figure number, name of the first author, and (abbreviated) title of the article. Also indicate the top of the figure, especially when it is a radiological or histological photograph. Enclose each set of figures in a separate envelope; do not use paper clips or staples. The Journal does not return illustrations of published papers.

Number figures consecutively as cited in the text. If composites are submitted, they should be grouped for consecutive citation also.

For figures in color, supply color transparencies properly trimmed or marked to indicate the part to be reproduced; in addition, supply positive color prints *in duplicate* to assist referees in making recommendations. Color figures are published only if the author assumes the costs of engraving and printing.

Legends: Type legends double spaced in sequence. Do not paste the legend to the back or bottom of figures. Legends should be as concise as possible. Keep the title brief; it should not be repeated in lettering at the top of the figure. Include experimental details in the text. Explain in the legends all symbols and all abbreviations used for the first time. If abbreviations are repeated in a series of figures, define them only in the legend of the first figure in the series.

If a figure has been published previously, acknowledge its source and submit written permission of author and publisher. The previously published source should also be included in the list of references (see References, below).

Powers of Ten in Tables and Figures: Use of multipliers by powers of 10 in tables and figures may be confusing. It is preferable to use an appropriate unit prefix rather than a power of 10 multiplier (e.g., mM instead of $M \times 10^{-3}$). If this is impractical, the following convention should be followed. A value of 0.003 for a certain quantity K may be entered as 0.30 under the heading "10^2K"; in other words, $10^2K = 0.30$, or $K = 0.3/10^2 = 0.003$. An entry of 0.30 under a column heading "$10^{-2}K$" or "$K \times 10^{-2}$" is not an acceptable way of expressing the value 0.003 for K.

Formulas and Equations. A line of type containing a built-up fraction $\frac{a}{b}$ requires an additional line of space: reduce formulas and equations to a single line when possible by using the solidus fraction (a/b). Type each equation in the appropriate place in the text and separate built-up equations from the text by three or four interlinear spaces. Be sure that equations are correct; changes in galley or page proof are costly, require time, and may delay publication. Define all abbreviations and symbols. Clearly indicate mathematical symbols and Greek and script letters in the margin of the manuscript opposite the line in which they first appear. Identify the number 1 (one) and letter l (el) and zero versus the letter O (oh).

In accord with the rule of the International Union of Pure and Applied Chemistry, the mass number of an atom should be written as a superior prefix, e.g., ^{14}C, not C^{14}. In designating isotopically labeled compounds, write the mass number as a superior prefix to the atomic symbol, not to an abbreviation. The symbol of the isotope, and if necessary a prefix denoting the number and the position of the isotopically substituted atoms, should be enclosed in square brackets immediately after the name of the compound, e.g., leucine[carboxyl-^{14}C]. The symbol U denotes uniform labeling, e.g., glucose[$^{14}C(U)$].

Abbreviations and Terminology: Avoid abbreviations in the title and in the summary. Keep abbreviations in text, tables, and figures to a minimum; use them only for long and cumbersome words that are repeated often. When more than a few abbreviations are essential, group them in a glossary and define them precisely. Use standard abbreviations when possible and *define each* when first used. Once an abbreviation is introduced, it should be used as consistently as possible throughout the text. In the text itself, try to avoid the use of symbols that contain subscripts. For acceptable abbreviations, terminology, usage, and units of measurement, refer to the Council of Biology Editors Style Manual, 5th ed., 1983 (Council of Biology Editors, Inc., 9650 Rockville Pike, Bethesda, Maryland 20814).

Discussion—Do not use the discussion to repeat your results; use it to interpret them, to point out relationships and implications, and to discuss the meaning and importance of your observations. Include hypotheses when applicable and speculation when warranted, but clearly label them as such. Present arguments both for and against your hypotheses. When your results differ from those of previous investigators, attempt to explain the discrepancy. Check original reports to be sure that you have quoted previous workers accurately. If there is a question about the meaning of published statements, communicate with the author(s) if possible to be sure your interpretation is accurate. If you refer to the *unpublished* work of others, include a letter of permission from the responsible investigator. Do not refer to work that is planned or in progress.

Acknowledgment—When expressing appreciation to another scientist for assistance with your research or manuscript, enclose written permission, since such an acknowledgment may imply endorsement of your data and conclusions.

References—Accuracy is the author's responsibility. In *text citations,* give (in parentheses) the author(s)' name(s) and year of publication, e.g. (Doe, 1973) or (Doe and Doe, 1977). When there are more than two authors, include only the first author's name followed by *"et al."* and the date. When several references are *cited* together, list chronologically, with earliest publication first.

The reference *list* should be double spaced and on a separate page after the text. Arrange the list *alphabetically by author and do not number it*. If you cite two or more references by the *same* author(s) in the *same* year, then (in order cited) add "a," "b," etc., to the year, both in text citations and in the reference list (*see Sample*). *Note preferred* ***punctuation*** *in Sample*. Include in the reference list the surnames and initials of all authors, the year of publication in parentheses, the complete title of the article, the name of the journal, volume number, and inclusive pages. If it is an abstract, please so indicate. Abbreviate journal names according to listings in *Index Medicus*.

For books, also name all editors, the place of publication, publisher, and page range, if applicable.

Sample—Journal References

Green G (1970) Hemodynamic variables in the primate during . . . Circ Res **140:** 220–228
Green G (1973a) etc.
Green G (1973b) etc.
Green G, Black A (1968) etc.
Green G, Black A (1970) etc.
Green G, White W (1960) etc.
† Green G, White W, Black B (1968) etc.
† Green G, Brown B, Black B (1970a) etc.
† Green G, Black B, Brown B (1970b) etc.

Sample—Book References

When alluding to entire book:

Hill AV (1970) First and Last Experiments in Muscle Mechanics, London, Cambridge University Press

When alluding to chapter or section of edited book:

Rajan KS, Manian AA, Davis JM, Stripkus A (1974) Studies on the metal chelation of chlorpromazine and its hydroxylated metabolites. *In* The Phenothiazines and Structurally Related Drugs, ed 2, vol 1, edited by IS Forrest, CJ Carr, E Usdin. New York, Raven Press, pp 571–591

Only published papers and those already accepted for publication may be included in the reference list. If "in press," indicate the name of the journal. Personal communications and unpublished observations should not appear in the reference list but may be cited in the text. In that case, obtain written permission from the author(s). Citation of abstracts is discouraged; when unavoidable, the citation should be so marked after the title (*abstr*).

The reference list should be limited to those references needed to provide adequate background, to describe methods, and to present fairly any opposing evidence of concepts; recent review articles may be cited to provide historical background.

MANUSCRIPT PROCESSING AND PUBLICATION CHARGES

In keeping with the policy of the Publications Committee of the American Heart Association for AHA Journals, a manuscript processing fee of $50 should be submitted to the Journal at the time of initial submission of the manuscript. If the cost represents a hardship to an author, it will be waived without prejudicing the review process. The check should be made out to *The American Heart Association*.

Authors will be assessed a charge per printed page for papers published in *Circulation Research*. The ability to pay page charges is in no way related to consideration of a manuscript for publication. The author bears the cost of color illustrations as well as the cost of any reprints ordered. If the manuscript includes complex tables, the author will be asked to share the cost of their publication. If the number of illustrations is excessive, the author will be asked to eliminate some of them. A charge will be made for author alterations in galley proof and for changes in figures once engravings have been made.

† *A special problem arises in the list when there are several papers by (e.g.) Green et al. in the same or over several years. Whereas the list could be in strict* ***alphabetical*** *order of the full reference, the reader will find no clue in text (citing Green et al.) to the* ***alphabetical*** *status of the names of the second and subsequent authors. It is therefore recommended that all papers by, e.g., Green et al. (by Green and more than one co-author) be arranged, irrespective of the names of the other authors, in* ***chronological*** *order, and if published the same year, that those references be listed in the order cited in the text, adding "a," "b," etc., to the year, as noted above.*

News from the American Heart Association

7320 Greenville Avenue, Dallas, Texas 75231
Telephone: 214 750-5300

Conference on Stroke, New Orleans, Feb. 21–23, To Hold NMR Symposium

A Symposium on nuclear magnetic resonance in stroke will open the 10th International Joint Conference on Stroke and Cerebral Circulation, Feb. 21–23, in New Orleans.

Dr. J. Donald Easton of San Antonio is chairman, and chairmen of the symposium on Thursday, Feb. 21, will be Drs. K.M.A. Welch of Detroit and S.K. Hilal of New York. Other speakers will be Drs. M. Chopp of Detroit, M. Brandt-Zawadski of San Francisco, L. N. Hopkins of Buffalo, S.K. Hilal, J. E. Pritchard of New Haven and K.M.A. Welch.

Thursday's program will conclude with the feature lecture "Cerebral Vascular Clinical-Pathologic Potpourri," by Dr. C. Miller Fisher of Harvard Medical School.

A breakfast seminar on management of asymptomatic carotid disease will begin Friday's program with Drs. C.B. Shields and W.S. Moore as chairmen. It will continue with presentation of abstracts on experimental aspects. Abstracts on epidemiological and clinical aspects will continue Friday.

Saturday's session will open with a breakfast seminar on ischemic disease and the eye and continue with abstracts on carotid plaques and surgical aspects. Abstracts on experimental and clinical aspects will conclude the Conference on Saturday.

Sixty-four abstracts of the Conference are published in the January-February issue of STROKE.

Editors are Appointed for 2 AHA Publications

New Editors have been named for the AHA publications MODERN CONCEPTS OF CARDIOVASCULAR DISEASE and CURRENT CONCEPTS OF CEREBROVASCULAR DISEASE/STROKE.

They are Shahbudin H. Rahimtoola, M.D., professor of medicine at the University of Southern California, Los Angeles, for the monthly MODERN CONCEPTS. He succeeds Frank I. Marcus, M.D., of Tucson whose term has concluded. Louis R. Caplan, M.D., Professor and Chairman of the Department of Neurology at Tufts University, succeeds Frank Yatsu of Houston whose term as Editor of the bimonthly CURRENT CONCEPTS has ended.

Dr. Rahimtoola

Dr. Rahimtoola, who is also chief of the Section of Cardiology at the LAC/USC Medical Center, has won the AHA Citation for International Service for work as a visiting teacher in Thailand and the Award of Merit of the Greater Los Angeles AHA affiliate. He attended medical school in Pakistan and is a Fellow of the Royal College of Physicians, a former Fulbright Scholar, a former Mayo Foundation Fellow in Physiology, and a Fellow of the Royal Postgraduate Medical School of London. He is a member of the Editorial Board of CIRCULATION and four other journals. With associates, he has published 240 papers in scientific journals.

Dr. Caplan

Dr. Caplan is a Summa Cum Laude graduate of the University of Maryland School of Medicine and a member of Phi Beta Kappa. He was a resident in Neurology at Boston City Hospital and has been a Fellow at Guys Hospital, London, Harvard Medical School, and Massachusetts General Hospital. He is also a Fellow of the American College of Physicians and the American Academy of Neurology. He was Chairman of the Department of Neurology at Beth Israel Hospital, Boston, and, at Michael Reese Hospital, Chicago. He is also Neurologist-in-Chief at the New England Medical Center. With associates, he is the author of 110 scientific papers.

1986 Xth World Congress On Cardiology Organizes

Seven former presidents of the American Heart Association have joined the committee which is organizing the Xth World Congress of Cardiology to be held Sept. 14–19, 1986, in Washington, DC.

The AHA is host for the Congress and the organizers include Dr. Thomas N. James of the University of Alabama Medical Center in Birmingham, president.

A former president of AHA, he is joined on the committee by six other former presidents. They are Drs. Donald C. Harrison of Stanford University, Harriet P. Dustan of the University of Alabama, Elliot Rapaport of the University of California, James A. Schoenberger of Rush-Presbyterian-St. Luke's Medical Center, Chicago, John T. Shepherd of Mayo Foundation, and Paul N. Yu of Strong Memorial Hospital, Rochester, NY. Ross Reid of New York City, a former AHA Board Chairman, is World Congress Treasurer.

A World Congress is held every four years and was last held in this country in 1954.

Regional Vice Presidents Elected by AHA Delegates

Eight regional vice presidents were elected by delegates to the American Heart Association Assembly in Miami Beach.

They were:

Robert C. Talley, M.D., Ph.D., Sioux Falls, SD, *Great Plains Region*; William T. Herzog, Chapel Hill, NC, *Mid-*

dle Atlantic; Joseph R. Welch, Randolph, MA, *New England*; Frederick J. Wenzel, Marshfield, WI, *North Central*; Robert J. Boroughs, Seattle, *Northwest Rocky Mountain*; Reagan H. Bradford, M.D., Ph.D., Oklahoma City, *Southern*; Herbert Mark, M.D., White Plains, NY, *Upper Atlantic*; Rodman D. Starke, M.D., San Francisco, *Southwest.*

Other vice presidents elected were:

Robert M. Daugherty, Jr., M.D., Ph.D., Reno, NV, *Program*; Saul Winegrad, M.D., Philadelphia, *Research*; Robert A. O'Rourke, M.D., San Antonio, *Councils*; and William K. Van't Hof, Grand Rapids, MI, *Development*.

Pediatric Cardiology Examination July 12

The Sub-Board of Pediatric Cardiology of the American Board of Pediatrics will hold its next certifying examination on Friday, July 12.

To sit for the examination, applicants must have certification by the American Board of Pediatrics, two years of full-time graduate training in an accredited pediatric cardiology program, and verification of training and recommendation by the Pediatric Cardiology Program Director.

Candidates who achieve a qualifying score on the written exam will be eligible for the oral examination in October in San Antonio, TX.

Registration will extend until February 28, 1985, at the American Board of Pediatrics, 111 Silver Cedar Court, Chapel Hill, NC 27514-1651. Tel. 919-929-0461.

In-training Exam

The Sub-Board will also offer an in-training exam to residents, Fellows, and interested physicians on July 24. The purpose is to allow future candidates for the cardiology certifying exam to familiarize themselves with the content and complexity of the questions used. It will also provide physicians in practice with a self-assessment exercise.

The exam will be offered only at those institutions where the pediatric cardiology program director agrees to monitor the exam. Residents and Fellows should express their interest to their program director. Physicians in practice should get in touch with the program director at the institution closest to them.

Registration for this exam will begin May 1 and continue through June 15.

2 New Laboratories Created by NINCDS

Two new laboratories have been added to the intramural research program of the National Institute of Neurological and Communicative Disorders and Stroke. They are the Laboratory of Neurobiology and the Laboratory of Experimental Neuropathology.

Directing these new units are Drs. Thomas S. Reese and Henry deF. Webster, former section chiefs at the Laboratory of Neuropathology and Neuroanatomical Sciences.

Dr. Reese supervises the Laboratory of Neurobiology which contains two sections: 1) Structural Cell Biology which has developed cryogenic techniques for stopping and examining cellular processes, thus making possible study of a variety of nervous system functions such as synaptic transmission, synaptic spine function and axoplasmic transport. The second section on Structural Plasticity studies the responses of the mammalian central nervous system to injury and regeneration by using the techniques developed in the structural cell biology section.

Dr. Webster's Laboratory of Experimental Neuropathology has sections on cellular neuropathology and neurotoxicity. The cellular section is studying cellular mechanisms of myelin formation. Human demyelinating diseases and virus-induced demyelination are special interests. The Neurotoxicology Section conducts basic research on how toxins induce disease in the central and peripheral nervous systems.

The two new laboratories bring the total number of NINCDS intramural Research Program units to 8 branches and 11 laboratories.

Neural Mechanisms/CVD At Italian Symposium

An international symposium on neural mechanisms and cardiovascular disease will be held May 1–3 in Santa Margherita Ligure, near Genoa, Italy.

The meeting is organized by the Istituto di Ricerche Cardiovascolari G. Sisini and the Cattedra Patologia Medica, Centro Fidia per lo Studio della Innervazione Cardiovascolare, and the Ospedale L. Sacco, University of Milan. Dr. C. Bartorelli of Milan will be president of the symposium.

The program includes discussions of cardiovascular reflexes and their possible pathophysiological significance, central organization of reflexes, neural mechanisms and arterial blood pressure variability, computer-assisted analysis and assessment of CV function, neural mechanisms in cardiac arrhythmias, and experimental vs. human pathophysiology.

Thirteen U.S. physicians are listed among the speakers and the official language will be English.

Inquiries may go to A. Malliani, Istituto Ricerche Cardiovascolari, Via Bonfadini, 214, 20138 Milano, Italy. Tel. 02-5063984 (p.m.).

Subscriptions Due

Subscriptions for many readers of CIRCULATION, CIRCULATION RESEARCH, HYPERTENSION, STROKE and ARTERIOSCLEROSIS are now due for the year 1985. Renewals should be sent with payment. Subscribers in Japan should go through Nankodo Co. Ltd., 42-5 Hongo 3-Chome, Bonkyo-Ku, Tokyo, Japan; all orders from Europe should go through Bailliere Tindall, 1st Anne's Road, Eastbourne, East Sussex BN21 3UN, England.

Other orders should go to the AHA Scientific Journal Subscriptions Department, 7320 Greenville Ave., Dallas, TX 75231.

Subscriptions to CIRCULATION RESEARCH are $86 in the U.S. and $105 outside U.S.

1985 Catalog Lists AHA Journals, Books

The 1985 catalog of AHA Scientific Journals and Books has been issued listing two monthly and three bimonthly journals as well as 49 monographs in print.

The catalog also lists the bimonthly RECURRING BIBLIOGRAPHY of HYPERTENSION, the monthly MODERN CONCEPTS OF CARDIOVASCULAR DISEASE and the bimonthly CARDIO-VASCULAR NURSING and CURRENT CONCEPTS OF CEREBROVASCULAR DISEASE-STROKE.

Copies of the catalog may be obtained from Heart Association affiliates (ask for 74-006-A) or from the National Center, Dallas.

ICHD Report Is Reprinted As Atherosclerosis Guide

"Optimal Resources for Primary Prevention of Atherosclerotic Diseases," a report of the Inter-Society Commission for Heart Disease Resources, has been published as a pamphlet by AHA to serve as a guide for physician and public health policy.

The report, originally published in CIRCULATION (**70**, July, 1984) is now available from Heart Association affiliates and the National Center (ask for 72-112-A).

The statement is an update of the 1970 report, "Primary Prevention of the Atherosclerotic Diseases." The Study Group was charged to assess relevant new data and, where the evidence is less than definitive, to formulate conclusions and recommendations based on best judgement. Current developments are reviewed, and issues that were raised in response to the earlier recommendations are considered.

Members of the Study Group were Drs. William B. Kannel, chairman, Joseph T. Doyle, Adrian M. Ostfeld, David Jenkins, Lewis Kuller, Richard N. Podell, and Jeremiah Stamler.

Medical Device Deaths To Be Reported to FDA

The U.S. Food and Drug Administration has ordered manufacturers and importers of medical devices, including artificial heart valves, x-ray machines, surgical equipment, and artificial joints, to report deaths and serious injuries linked to them.

The order, issued under a 1976 law, is similar to the requirement on reporting dangerous drugs which has been in effect.

An FDA spokesman said that the rules require companies to report device-related deaths and serious injuries by phone as soon as possible. Failure to do so could result in seizure of the product and revocation of marketing approval.

AHA Briefs . . .

• **Modern Concepts of Cardiovascular Disease** for January is "Right Ventricular Infarction—Pathophysiology, Diagnosis, Clinical Course, and Treatment" by Henri E. Kulbertus, M.D., Pierre Rigo, M.D., and V. Legrand, M.D., of Liège, Belgium.

• **Current Concepts of Cerebrovascular Disease/Stroke** for January/February is "Cognitive and Behavioral Deficits After Right Hemisphere Stroke" by Robert W. Stein, M.D., Daniel B. Hier, M.D., and Louis R. Caplan, M.D., of Michael Reese Hospital, Chicago.

• The 6th Scientific Meeting of the **Inter-American Society of Hypertension** will be held May 19–23 in Cleveland, OH. Inquiries may go to the Coordinator, IASH Meeting, Research Division FF2-49, 9500 Euclid Ave., Cleveland, OH 44106. Tel. 216-444-5837.

• Members of the AHA Nutrition Committee and staff members have met with **meat industry** representatives to establish a dialogue. AHA volunteers explained the rationale of dietary recommendations and described community programs in nutrition. Meat industry representatives explained their production and marketing operations.

• The first **International Congress on Hospital Laws, Procedures, and Ethics** will be held Sept. 8–12 in Tel Aviv, Israel. Judge Amnon Carmi is chairman of the organizing committee. Inquiries may go to Hospitalaw, 28 Ahad Ha'am St., POB 394, Tel Aviv 61003, Israel. Tel. 03-650862. Telex 33803 TLV. Cable PELTOURS TELAVIV

• **Patricia M. McNamara**, assistant director of the **Framingham Heart Study**, has retired after 39 years of government service. She served 35 years with the Study, the longest service of any staff member. She developed the CVD Event Outcome Data File which gave pertinent information on over 6,000 cardiovascular events and the cause of death among the 5,209 study participants.

• The **toposcopic catheter**, developed by Dr. Seth Goldstein and Daniel Shook of the Biomedical Engineering and Instrumentation Branch of NIH was cited by *Research and Development Magazine* as one of the most significant new products of 1984. The toposcopic catheter uses a flexible everting tube to move through long, narrow, curving body passages. This allows localized removal or infusion of fluid in areas beyond obstruction that cannot be passed with conventional catheters.

• The 11-acre tract, formerly owned by the Sisters of the Visitation and purchased by the National Institutes of Health, has been dedicated as the **Mary Woodard Lasker Center for Health Research and Education.** Mrs. Lasker has been for more than 40 years an advocate of funds for health research. The Center will house the cooperative program of the Howard Hughes Medical Institute and NIH to increase the vigor of American biomedical research. A new wing will be added to the building.

• **Dr. Michael I. Goldberg** has joined the American Society for Microbiology as executive director. He was formerly Associate Director for Program Planning and Evaluation of the National Institutes of Health. With an active membership of over 31,000, the ASM is believed to be the oldest and largest single biological life science organization.

• The Division of Blood Diseases and Resources of the NHLBI has invited grant applications to determine **fac-**

tors that produce refractoriness to transfused platelets and to identify methods to improve platelet support for refractory patients. Applications are due by Feb. 15. Inquiries may go to Dr. Luiz H. Barbosa, Federal Bldg. Rm. 5C10, NIH, Bethesda, MD 20205.

Meetings Calendar

1985

Jan. 20–25: **Basic Principles of Pacing and Electrophysiology**—Dual Chamber and Antitachycardia Pacing. Princess **Cruise to Caribbean**. Sponsored by Cardiostim America. Course Director, S. Furman, M.D. Inquiries: Cardiostim America, POB 428, Mount Kisco, NY 10549. Tel. 914-241-3295. Telex 42-0170 (via ITT).

Jan. 27–30: **Cardiac Doppler 3rd International Tutorial and Symposium.** San Diego. Sponsored by the International Cardiac Society and the Institute of Applied Physiology and Medicine. Inquiries: Director Med. Ed., 701 16th Ave., Seattle, WA 98122. Tel. 206-442-7330.

Jan. 28–30: **The Clinical Laboratory in the New Era: Quality, Cost, and Diagnostic Demands**. Hotel Del Coronado, San Diego. 8th Annual Arnold O. Beckman Conference. Sponsored by the American Association for Clinical Chemistry. Inquiries: AACC, 1725 K St., NW Washington, DC 20006. Tel. 202-857-0717.

Jan. 28–30: **Doppler-Echocardiography–1985: State of the Art.** Holy Cross Hospital, Fort Lauderdale, FL. Inquiries: Professional Medical Services, Suite 527, POB 6010, Sherman Oaks, CA 91403.

Jan. 28–31: **3rd Annual Cardiology Update Symposium.** Sheraton-Waikiki, Honolulu. Sponsored by Straub Clinic and Hospital, University of Hawaii, John A. Burns School of Medicine, and Institute for Medical Studies. Inquiries: Inst. for Med. Studies, 30131 Town Center Drive, Suite 215, Laguna Niguel, CA 92677.

Jan. 28–Feb. 8: **Introduction to Echocardiography.** Bowman Gray School of Medicine, Winston-Salem, NC. Inquiries: Center for Medical Ultrasound, Bowman Gray School of Medicine of Wake Forest University, 300 S. Hawthorne Rd., Winston-Salem, NC 27103. Tel. 919-748-4505.

Jan. 30–Feb. 1: **Management of Heart Disease.** University of Arizona, Tucson. 28th Annual Session of Arizona Heart Association. Sponsored by the American College of Physicians. Inquiries: ACS, 4200 Pine St., Philadelphia, PA 19104.

Feb. 8–10: **Pathophysiology and Techniques of Cardiopulmonary Bypass: V.** Sheraton Harbor Island East, San Diego. Sponsored by the Cardiothoracic Research & Education Foundation. Joe R. Utley, M.D., course director. Inquiries: CREF, POB 33185, San Diego, CA 92103. Tel. 619-692-9115.

Feb. 11–13: **NIH Consensus Development Conference on Health Implications of Obesity.** Masur Auditorium, Bethesda, MD. Sponsored by National Heart, Lung, and Blood Institute, National Institute of Arthritis, Diabetes, and Digestive and Kidney Disease, and NIH Office of Medical Applications of Research. Inquiries: Michele Dillon, Prospect Associates, Suite 401, 2115 East Jefferson St., Rockville, MD 20852. Tel. 301-468-6555.

Feb. 19–22: **Cardiac Rehabilitation: Status '85.** Hotel Intercontinental, Houston. Sponsored by Universal Services Rehab. and Development, Texas Heart Institute, American College of Sports Medicine. Inquiries: M. L. Pollock, Ph.D., USRD, Travis Center, Suite 500, 6655 Travis, Houston, TX 77030. Tel. 713-630-6525.

Feb. 21–23: **10th International Joint Conference on Stroke and Cerebral Circulation.** New Orleans. Inquiries: Coordinator, Scientific Sessions, AHA, 7320 Greenville Ave., Dallas, TX 75231. Tel. 214-750-5439.

Feb. 24–March 1: **7th Annual Cardiology at Big Sky.** Big Sky MT. Sponsored by Burns Clinic, Petoskey, MI, AHA Council on Clinical Cardiology and AHA Montana Affiliate. Sidney Goldstein, M.D., course director. Inquiries: Dr. S. Goldstein, Henry Ford Hospital, Div. CV Med., 2799 W. Grand Blvd., Detroit, MI 48202.

Feb. 25–28: **Critical Care Medicine, 23rd Annual Symposium.** MGM Grand Hotel, Las Vegas, NV. Inquiries: Assoc. Dean, USC School of Medicine, PG Div., 2025 Zonal Ave., KAM 307, Los Angeles, CA 90033. Tel. 213-224-7051.

March 3–8: **Annual Meeting American Society for Microbiology.** Las Vegas, NV. Inquiries: ASM, 1913 I St., NW, Washington, DC 20005.

March 7–9: **American Heart Association 25th Annual Conference on Cardiovascular Disease Epidemiology.** Doubletree Inn, Tucson, AZ. Inquiries: G. Wilson, AHA, 7320 Greenville Ave., Dallas, TX 75231. Tel. 214-750-5437.

March 8–12: **Advances in Nutrition Therapy II and Digestive Disease Review V.** Caribe Hilton, San Juan, Puerto Rico. Sponsored by Puerto Rican Society of Gastroenterology and Norwalk, CT, Hospital. Inquiries: Dept. Medicine, Norwalk Hospital, Norwalk, CT 06856.

March 10–14: **American College of Cardiology Scientific Session.** Anaheim, CA. Inquiries: ACC, 9111 Old Georgetown Rd., Bethesda, MD 20814. Tel. 301-897-5400.

March 14–16: **Symposium on the Thanatology Curriculum for Schools of Medicine, Nursing, and Related Health Professions.** Columbia-Presbyterian Medical Center, New York City. Sponsored by Foundation of Thanatology and Columbia Univ. School of Nursing. Inquiries: Dr. A. H. Kutscher, 630 W. 168th St., New York, NY 10032.

March 28–30: **86th Annual Meeting, American Society for Clinical Pharmacology and Therapeutics.** Hilton Palacio del Rio, San Antonio, TX. Inquiries: Mrs. E. Galasso, 1718 Gallagher Rd., Norristown, PA 19401. Tel. 215-825-3838.

March 29–31: **8th Annual Intensive Clinical Neurology Course for Non-Neurologists.** New York City. Inquiries: L. P. Levitt, M.D., 12120 S. Cedar Crest Blvd., Allentown, PA 18103. Tel. 215-433-6474.

April 2–6: **3rd Annual Interventional Radiology Seminar.** Buena Vista Palace, Lake Buena Vista, Florida (Walt Disney World Village Plaza). Sponsored by Dept. Radiology, U. of South Florida College of Medicine. Inquiries: C. Krissman, 12901 N. 30 St., Tampa, FL 33612. Tel. 813-974-2538.

April 10–12: **26th National Student Research Forum.** University of Texas Medical Branch, Galveston. Inquiries: Student Research Forum, POB 54, Station 1, UTMB, Galveston, TX 77550. Tel. 409-761-3762.

April 11–12: **Oak Ridge Conference on Advanced Analytical Concepts for the Clinical Laboratory.** Sheraton Charlestown, SC. Sponsored by American Association for Clinical Chemistry. Inquiries: AACC, 1725 K St., SW, Washington, DC 20006. Tel. 202-857-0717.

April 21–26: **Federation of American Societies for Experimental Biology.** Anaheim, CA. Inquiries: 9650 Rockville Pike, Bethesda, MD 20014.

April 28–30: **National Conference on High Blood Pressure Control.** Palmer House, Chicago. Inquiries: NCHBP, 1501 Wilson Blvd., Suite 600, Arlington, VA 22209. Tel. 202-944-3176.

May 3–4: **Perspectives on the Management of Chronic Congestive Heart Failure.** Baltimore, MD. Sponsored by Div. of Cardiology, University of Maryland School of Medicine. Inquiries: Program of Cont. Ed., University of Maryland School of Medicine, 10 S. Pine St., Rm. 300, Baltimore, MD 21201. Tel. 301-528-3956.

May 6–7: **Symposium on Leukotrienes in Cardovascular and Pulmonary Function.** Philadelphia. Inquiries: Allan M. Lefer, Ph.D., Dept. of Physiology, Jefferson Medical College, 1020 Locust St., Philadelphia, PA 19107.

May 12–15: **6th Annual Meeting, Society for Clinical Trials.** New Orleans. Inquiries: Curt Furberg, MD, SCT, 600 Wyndhurst Ave., Baltimore, MD 21210.

May 12–15: **Annual Meeting, American Thoracic Society.** Anaheim, CA. Slide and poster presentations. Inquiries: ATS, 1740 Broadway, New York, NY 10019. Tel. 212-245-8000, Ext. 570.

May 17–18: **Clinical Concerns in Hemodialysis Therapy.** Sheraton Harbor Island East Hotel, San Diego. Program Chairman, Richard A. Sherman, M.D. Sponsored by American Kidney Fund and Nephrology Society of New Jersey. Inquiries: Dr. R. A. Sherman, Academic Health Science Center, CN 19, New Brunswick, NJ 08903. Tel. 1-800-922-0130.

May 19–23: **6th Scientific Meeting Inter-American Society of Hypertension.** Cleveland. Inquiries: 6th Meeting IASH, Research Division FF2-49, 9500 Euclid Ave., Cleveland, OH 44106. Tel. 216-444-5837.

May 23–24: **Vascular Surgery 1985. Current State of the Art. 2nd International Vascular Symposium.** Waldorf-Astoria Hotel, New York City. John B. Chang, M.D., program chairman. Inquiries: A. J. Boehme, Long Island Jewish-Hillside Medical Center, New Hyde Park, NY 11042. Tel. 212-470-2114.

May 24–27: **7th Annual Meeting American Section of the International Society for Heart Research.** Houston. Inquiries: Dr. J. Allen, Dept. Cell Biophysics, Baylor College of Med., Houston, TX 77025.

June 2–6: **2nd World Congress of Pediatric Cardiology.** New York City. Inquiries: V. Herlitz, 404 Park Ave. S., New York, NY 10016.

June 10–12: **Surgery for Coronary Artery Disease.** Durham, NC. Sponsored by Duke University Medical Center and American College of Cardiology. R. H. Jones, M.D., program director. Inquiries: ACC, 9111 Georgetown Rd., Bethesda, MD 20814. Tel. 301-897-5400, Ext. 228.

June 17–18: **Today's Therapy in Nephrology.** Resorts International Hotel, Atlantic City, NJ. Sponsored by American Kidney Fund and Nephrology Society of New Jersey. Inquiries: See May 17–18, Dr. Sherman.

July 12: **Certifying Examination, Sub-Board of Pediatric Cardiology.** Chapel Hill, NC. Registration until Feb. 28. Inquiries: American Board of Pediatrics, 111 Silver Cedar Court, Chapel Hill, NC 27514-1651. Tel. 919-929-046.

July 21–26: **37th Annual Meeting American Association of Clinical Chemistry.** Georgia World Congress Center, Atlanta. Inquiries: AACC, 1725 K St., NW, Washington, DC 20006. Tel. 202-857-0717.

Oct. 11–12: **4th Southern Biomedical Engineering Conference.** Jackson MS. Deadline for papers March 1. Inquiries: Dr. Barry W. Sauer, SBEC, Div. Cont. Health Prof. Ed., University of Mississippi Medical Center, 2500 N. State St., Jackson, MS 39216-4505.

Nov. 11–14: **58th Annual Scientific Sessions, American Heart Association, Washington, DC. Inquiries: Coordinator Scientific Sessions, AHA, 7320 Greenville Ave., Dallas, TX 75231. Tel. for Abstracts: 214-750-5439; for housing and reservations 214-750-5425.**

Nov. 12–13: **Subspecialty Boards in Cardiovascular Disease.** Philadelphia. Registration to April 1. Inquiries: American Board of Internal Medicine, 3624 Market St., Philadelphia, PA 19104. Tel. 215-243-1500.

1986

Sept. 13–20: **Xth World Congress of Cardiology.** Washington, DC. Inquiries: Secretariat, 7320 Greenville Ave., Dallas, TX 75231. Tel. 214-750-5429. Cable Tencard, Dallas, TX.

Abroad

1985

Feb. 12–16: **First Philippine Heart Center for Asia International Symposium on Valvular Heart Diseases.** Manila Hotel, Philippines. Inquiries: PHCA Symposium, 5th Floor, Medical Arts Bldg., PHCA, East Ave., Quezon City, Philippines. Tel. 98-04-21-2620. Telex 42032 TOWMED PM

March 24–27: **2nd International Congress on Essential Fatty Acids and Prostaglandins.** Egham, near London, England. Multidisciplinary sessions and poster presentations. Inquiries: Prostaglandin Congress, c/o Zoological Society, London, NW1 4RY, United Kingdom.

March 29–31: **International Symposium on Ambulatory Monitoring.** Clinica Medica I, University of Padua, Italy. Prof. C. Dal Palù president of symposium. Inquiries: A. C. Pessina, Clinica Medica I-Policlinico, University of Padua, Via Giustiniani, 2, 35100 Padova, Italy.

April 1–3: **PTCA Course II.** Geneva Switzerland. Drs. Bernhard Maier and Wilhelm Rutishauser, course directors. Live demonstrations of percutaneous transluminal coronary angiography and lectures in English. Inquiries: Dr. Bernhard Meier, Center for Cardiology, University Hospital, CH-1211, Geneva 4, Switzerland.

April 22–26: **International Symposium 1985 Cardiovascular Pharmacotherapy.** Geneva, Switzerland. Inquiries: Interconference SA., 58 rue Ernest-Bloch, CH-1207, Geneva, Switzerland.

May 1–3: **International Symposium on Neural Mechanisms and Cardiovascular Disease.** Santa Margharita Ligure, (near Genoa), Italy. Dr. C. Bartorelli, symposium president. Inquiries: A. Malliani, Istituto Ricerche Cardiovascolari, Via Bonfadini, 214, 20138 Milano, Italy. Tel. 02-5063984 (p.m.)

May 8–10: **4th Congress Southern African Hypertension Society.** Johannesburg, South Africa. Inquiries: Prof. Clive Rosendorff, Dept. Physiology, Univ. Witwatersrand Medical School, York Rd., Parktown 2193, South Africa.

May 10–12: **International Symposium on Sports Cardiology.** Knokke, Belgium. Inquiries: Dr. I. Bekaert, Alg. Ziekenhuis St. Jozef, Steenweg op Merksplas 44, 2300 Turnout, Belgium. Tel. 014-4104-51.

May 23–25: **Unstable Angina Revisited.** Rotterdam, the Netherlands. Organized by the Thoraxcenter of Erasmus University, Rotterdam, the Netherlands Interuniversitary Cardiological Institute, the Netherlands, and the Toronto General Hospital, Toronto, Canada. Inquiries: Prof. P.G. Hugenholtz, M.D., Thoraxcenter Bd 406, Erasmus University, Rotterdam. POB 1738, 3000 DR Rotterdam, the Netherlands.

June 1–8: **Frontiers in Imaging and Cardiopulmonary Diagnosis.** England. (Also in Scotland, June 9–15). Eric N. C. Milne, M.D., program director. Faculty from U.S.A., 3 British and 2 Scottish medical schools. Inquiries: Ryals, POB 610203, DFW Airport, Texas 75261, U.S.A. 214-659-9590.

June 8–20: **2nd Advanced Ten Day Seminar on Epidemiology and Prevention.** Ireland. Sponsored by Council of Epidemiology and Prevention, International Society and Federation of Cardiology in cooperation with WHO. Inquiries: Rose Stamler, Room 1-615, 303 E. Chicago Ave., Chicago, IL 60611.

June 9–14: **International Congress of Angiology.** Athens, Greece. Inquiries: Prof. P. Balas, 17 Sisini St., 115 28 Athens (612) Greece.

June 16–20: **12th Symposium, International Society of Cerebral Blood Flow—"Brain: 85."** Ronneby Brunn Hotel. Lund, Sweden. Inquiries: K. Dahlgren, Dept. Clinical Neurophysiology, University Hospital, S-221 85 Lund, Sweden. Tel. +46-46-10-33-70.

June 16–21: **12th International Congress of Cardiology.** Vancouver, B.C., Canada. Inquiries: Dr. Henry Mizgala, Suite 1704, 1200 Alberni St., Vancouver, B.C., Canada V6E 1A6. Tel. 604-681-5226. Cable: Venuvan.

June 23–26: **International Conference on Preventive Cardiology.** Sovincenter, Moscow, USSR. Sponsored by WHO, International Society and Federation of Cardiology. Official languages English and Russian. Inquiries: A. A. Stepanenko, International Conference on Prevention Cardiology, Institute of Preventive Cardiology, 10 Petroverigsky Lane 101837 Moscow, USSR. Telex 411355. Cable USSR MOSCOW K-62, Preventive Cardiology. Tel. 221-93-47.

June 26–28: **6th Symposium on Echocardiology With a Postgraduate Course on Doppler Cardiography.** Rotterdam, the Netherlands. Sponsored by Erasmus University Thoraxcenter. Inquiries: PG Med. Ed., Erasmus University, Rotterdam, PBO 1738, 3000 DR Rotterdam, the Netherlands. Tel. 010-635011/635013.

July 15–19: **4th Meeting, World Federation on Ultrasound in Medicine and Biology.** Sydney, Australia. Inquiries: WFUMB, POB 1441 GPO, Sydney, NSW, Australia 2001.

Aug. 31–Sept. 7: **Diagnosis of Diseases of the Chest.** Italy. (Also in Greece, Sept. 8–14). 2nd Great Teachers Foundation International Postgraduate Medical Education Program. Eric N. C. Milne, M.D., program director. Inquiries: Ryals (see June 1–8 above).

Aug. 31–Sept. 7: **11th Congress of International Society of Hypertension.** Heidelberg, Federal Republic of Germany. Organized by German Institute of High Blood Pressure Research and German Hypertension League. Dr. Detlev Ganten, Congress chairman. Inquiries: GKV, Frankfurter Str. 57, D-6050 Offenbach 1, Heidelberg, FRGermany.

Sept. 1–6: **13th World Congress of Neurology.** Hamburg, Germany. Inquiries: Dr. T. Stober, Dept. Neurology, Faculty of Med., University of Saarland, D-6650 Homburg/Saar, FRG.

Sept. 1–7: **3rd Postgraduate International Course on Pain Therapy.** Vicenza, Italy. Inquiries: Ruggiero Rizzi, M.D., Ospedale Generale Regionale, 36100 Vicenza, Italy.

Sept. 3–6: **European Nuclear Medicine Congress.** Barbican Centre, London, England. Incorporates 23rd Meeting Society of Nuclear Medicine, Europe, 8th Meeting European Nuclear Medicine Society, 13th Meeting British Nuclear Medicine Society. Inquiries: Congress, Institute of Nuclear Medicine, Middlesex Hospital Medical School, Mortimer St., London, W1N 8AA, United Kingdom. Tel. OI-631 1066.

Sept. 7–9: **3rd International Brain Heart Conference.** Trier, Germany. Inquiries: Dr. T. Stober, Dept. Neurology, Faculty of Med. University of Saarland, D-6650, Homburg/Saar, Federal Republic of Germany.

Sept. 8–12: **1st International Congress on Hospital Laws, Procedures, and Ethics.** Tel Aviv, Israel. Judge Amnon Carmi, organizing chairman. Inquiries: Hospitalaw, 28 Ahad Ha'am St., POB 394, Tel Aviv 61003, Israel. Tel. 03-650862. Telex 33803 TLV. Cable PELTOURS TELAVIV.

Oct. 6–10: **7th International Symposium on Atherosclerosis.** Melbourne, Australia. Inquiries: Dr. P. J. Nestel, Baker Medical Research Inst., Commercial Rd., Prahran, Vic., Australia 3181.

Oct. 27–30: **3rd Asian Pacific Symposium on Cardiac Pacing and Electrophysiology.** Hilton Hotel, Melbourne, Australia. Sponsored by Cardiac Society of Australia and New Zealand under auspices of International Cardiac Pacing Society. Inquiries: 3rd Asian Pacific Symposium on Cardiac Pacing and Electrophysiology, Suite 3.5, Epworth Medical Centre, 62 Erin St., Richmond, Vic. 3131, Australia.

Nov. 28–30: **7th Biennial Congress of Cardiology.** Rawalpindi/Islamabad, Pakistan. Inquiries: Pakistan Cardiac Society, Brig. Muhammad Zulfiqar Ali Khan, AFIC/NIHD, Rawalpindi, Pakistan. Tel. 64946, 61-31113, 61-33911.

AHA Scientific Sessions Future Meeting Dates

1985	Washington, DC	Nov. 11–14
1986	Dallas, TX	Nov. 17–20
1987	Anaheim, CA	Nov. 16–19

Xth World Congress of Cardiology, 1986

The Xth World Congress of Cardiology will be held in Washington, DC, Sept. 13–20, 1986. Official languages English, Spanish, and French. Inquiries: Secretariat, Xth World Congress Cardiology, 7320 Greenville Ave., Dallas, TX 75231. Tel. 214-750-5429. Cable: Tencard, Dallas.

Circulation Research

FEBRUARY 1985
VOL. 56 NO.2

An Official Journal of the American Heart Association

SPECIAL ARTICLE

The Accuracy of Inferring Left Ventricular Volume from Dimension Depends on the Frequency of Information Needed to Answer a Given Question

Bryan K. Slinker and Stanton A. Glantz

From the Cardiovascular Research Institute and Department of Medicine, University of California, San Francisco, California

SUMMARY. Left ventricular volume is an important variable in cardiovascular physiology. Because volume cannot be transduced directly, by necessity people measure one or more cardiac dimensions, then implicitly or explicitly estimate volume. Despite its common use, this practice has never been adequately justified. Previous validations of the use of left ventricular dimensions to infer volume have ignored the complexity of the relation between dimensions and volume, particularly over a broad range of hemodynamic states, and have not considered the frequency content of the volume signal needed to answer a given physiological question. We show that, strictly speaking, the assumptions underlying this practice are false. The resulting errors are of little practical consequence under many circumstances, whereas they can be quite important under other circumstances. We consider the frequency content of the volume signal to organize our examples and findings. In this general framework, we find that, for most assessments of volume change from dimension change at or below a frequency of about the heart rate (e.g., beat-to-beat end-diastolic volume), there is no limitation, provided all relevant dimensions are measured. However, for information at frequencies above the heart rate (i.e., rapid changes in volume or dimension), it is probably not possible to draw accurate conclusions about left ventricular volume from dimension data. **(*Circ Res 56: 161–174, 1985*)**

LEFT ventricular volume is an important determinant of cardiac function. The left ventricle adapts to chronic alterations in its mechanical load (e.g., pressure or volume overload) by increasing its size through dilation and hypertrophy. The Frank-Starling mechanism relates left ventricular systolic performance to end-diastolic volume (i.e., sarcomere length) on a beat-to-beat basis (Frank, 1895; Starling, 1918). To understand individual beats in terms of pressure-volume loops (Sagawa, 1978), time-varying systolic volume elastance (Suga and Sagawa, 1974a), or diastolic pressure-volume curves (Glantz and Parmley, 1978), one must have knowledge of continuous left ventricular volume throughout a beat. To estimate the contribution of viscous forces to diastolic pressures (Rankin et al., 1977; Pouleur et al., 1979; Hess et al., 1983) one must have knowledge of the rate of volume change. Thus, study of left ventricular function emphasizes left ventricular volume changes occurring over a broad range of time scales, from slow changes during chronic adaptation to fast changes that determine the magnitude of viscous forces during filling.

The time-varying left ventricular volume can be considered a signal, and so can be decomposed into a sum of sine waves of various frequencies using Fourier analysis. Viewed in the frequency domain, the diverse volume information required to study different aspects of left ventricular function can be simply restated: Studies of chronic adaptation in left ventricular size require low frequency volume information, while studies of viscous forces during diastole require high frequency information. Transforming diameter data into the frequency domain allows us to define the limitations of such measurements as indicators of left ventricular volume relative to the fundamental frequency of cardiac activity, the heart rate.

Because there is no perfect volume transducer applicable to intact human or animal studies, left ventricular volume must be estimated. Most investigators measure one or more left ventricular dimensions, using techniques such as angiography (Rushmer and Thal, 1951; Dodge et al., 1966), ultrasonic crystals (Rushmer et al., 1956; Horwitz et al., 1968; Bugge-Asperheim et al., 1969; Sasayama et al., 1976; Rankin et al., 1976; Hintze et al., 1982), radiopaque markers (Carlsson and Milne, 1967; Mitchell et al., 1969), or echocardiography (Feigenbaum, 1972), then relate these dimensions to volume by using the dimension as a surrogate for volume without explicitly stating the relationship between dimension(s) and volume, or by combining the measured dimensions with some explicit mathematical function to estimate left ventricular volume. Because all these methods require a linear measurement between two points in the left ventricular wall, such as diameters across the cavity or segment lengths tangent to the wall, we will focus on dimensions obtained with pairs of piezoelectric crystals. Regardless of the technology used to obtain the dimension data, these two approaches to relating dimension to volume are fundamentally similar; both assume a single, fixed relationship between left ventricular dimension(s) and volume.

Past attempts to justify the use of left ventricular dimensions to assess volume have not adequately evaluated the assumption of a fixed relationship between dimensions and volume. Good correlations ($r > 0.90$) between dimensions and known volume have been demonstrated in excised beating (Suga and Sagawa, 1974b) and postmortem (Bishop and Horwitz, 1970; Levken et al., 1972; Rankin et al., 1976) left ventricles, or a left ventricular volume estimated by indicator dilution (Bishop and Horwitz, 1970; Levken et al., 1972). Others have shown similar correlations between change in dimension or some product of dimensions during systole and a stroke volume determined from aortic flow measurement with an electromagnetic flow probe (Wilson et al., 1967; Bishop and Horwitz, 1970; Horwitz and Bishop, 1972; Bugge-Asperheim et al., 1972; Rankin et al., 1976; Olsen et al., 1983) or by indicator dilution (Kirkpatrick et al., 1976). Although these studies provide evidence of a reasonable relationship between left ventricular dimension and volume, they do not clearly delineate the limitations involved in using dimensions to assess volume for two reasons. First, these studies have reported validations using predominantly low frequency volume change, even though some investigators have studied high frequency volume change. Second, the volume standards, particularly postmortem left ventricles, angiography, and indicator dilution methods, are themselves subject to considerable error.

In this paper, we systematically examine the assumption of a fixed relationship between left ventricular dimensions and volume. This examination covers a wide range of hemodynamic states and the whole cardiac cycle. We will show that, *as a rule of thumb*, the ability of dimensions to represent left ventricular volume accurately decreases as the frequency of left ventricular volume information required to answer the physiological question at hand increases. Although the frequency of the heart rate is not an absolute delimiter, the variability of the relationship between left ventricular dimension(s) and volume does not importantly limit most uses of left ventricular dimensions to assess left ventricular volume for the study of left ventricular function during chronic adaptation or beat-to-beat changes in function. In contrast, important limitations exist for detailed studies of left ventricular function during short periods of the cardiac cycle or studies of viscous effects, which require the derivatives of dimension or volume.

Methods

To collect the original data included in this paper, we used a total of 10 male mongrel dogs (weight 21–26 kg). All dogs were preanesthetized with morphine sulfate and diphenhydramine (1 mg/kg each). General anesthesia was induced with intravenous thiopental sodium (0.75 mg) and was maintained with methoxyflurane delivered in a 60:40 mixture of oxygen and nitrous oxide by a Ventimeter (Airshields). Blood gases and pH were monitored at 30- to 60-minute intervals, and ventilation was adjusted and sodium bicarbonate given to maintain p_{O_2} greater than 80 mm Hg, p_{CO_2} at 40 ± 5 mm Hg, pH at 7.4 ± 0.05, and HCO_3^- at 24 ± 4 mmol.

Two different preparations were used.

For preparation 1, seven dogs were instrumented with 5 MHz epicardial hemispherical crystals (Van Trigt et al., 1981) placed to measure base-to-apex dimension (B) and anterior-to-posterior minor axis diameter (A) (sutured on the anterior and posterior left ventricle free walls adjacent to the ventral and dorsal interventricular sulci approximately ¾ of the distance from the apex to the circumflex artery) (Rankin et al., 1976). Wall thickness (h) was measured on the lateral free wall at midventricle, using a 2-mm flat plate crystal tunneled obliquely through the wall to lie against the endocardium and a 5-mm flat plate crystal sutured to the overlying epicardium. Intercrystal transit-time dimensions were measured using a Triton Technology sonomicrometer. Left ventricular volume (V) was calculated by the method of Rankin et al. (1976):

$$V = \pi/6(A - 2h)^2(B - 1.1h). \quad (1)$$

The instrumentation of these dogs was completed by placing electromagnetic flow probes (Carolina Medical Electronics) snugly on the aortic root and main pulmonary artery, balloon occluders around pre- and post-cavae, a balloon catheter in the pulmonary artery, an umbilical tape snare around the descending thoracic aorta, and 8F Millar (Millar Instruments) pressure catheters in the right (via a small stab incision in the outflow tract) and left (via a carotid artery) ventricles.

For preparation 2, three additional dogs were instrumented only with 5 MHz epicardial hemispherical crystals to measure several closely spaced anterior-posterior left ventricle diameters. One set of crystals was placed as described above, and an additional crystal was placed approximately 1 cm (crystal center to crystal center) away from each of the original pair. In some dogs, one or two additional crystals were placed on the anterior free wall (about 1 cm intercenter distances). A total of four to seven dimensions between crystal pairs was measured (only two dimensions were measured simultaneously). Balloon catheters were placed on both the pre- and post-cavae. One dog prepared as in preparation 1 was also used for this preparation, bringing the total to four dogs.

Data Recording and Analysis

All data were recorded on FM magnetic tape (Honeywell 5600C) and later digitized (Horowitz et al., 1984) at a 200-Hz sampling rate and stored on digital tape. Specific

TABLE 1
Equations for Commonly Used Left Ventricular Model Shapes

Ellipsoid (Fig. 1A)	$V_e = \pi/6\ A^2B$
Half ellipsoid (Fig. 1B)	$V_{he} = \pi/6\ A^2B$
Half ellipsoid + cylinder (Fig. 1C)	$V_{he+c} = [(3 - \phi)/2]\pi/6\ A^2B$
Truncated ellipsoid (Fig. 1D)	$V_{te} = [(3\phi - 1)/(2\phi^2)]\pi/6\ A^2B$

A = time-varying left ventricular anterior-posterior diameter. B = time-varying left ventricular base-apex diameter. $\phi = b/B$, where b is the semimajor axis of the ellipse. Under the assumption of a single fixed relationship between diameter and volume, ϕ is a constant. V = volume.

analyses will be described in the appropriate sections below.

Influence of Model Shape

To estimate left ventricular volume from measured dimensions, one must choose a model shape and derive the mathematical relationship between the dimensions in the model and its volume. Table 1 lists the equations of the commonly used model shapes shown in Figure 1.

The equations associated with commonly used prolate model shapes with circular cross-sections (Table 1) are all of the general form

$$V_c(t) = F_i(\phi)A^2(t)B(t) \tag{2}$$

where $F_i(\phi)$ scales the product of dimensions to produce a volume estimate for the different model shapes. $F_i(\phi)$ depends on the specified model shape, and ϕ is the ratio of the semimajor axis of the ellipsoid to the total base-apex diameter (Fig. 1). A(t) is time-varying left ventricular anterior-posterior diameter, and B(t) is time-varying left ventricular base-apex diameter. Similar derivations for the corresponding general ellipsoidal model shapes with elliptical cross-section yield

$$V_e(t) = F_i(\phi)A(t)S(t)B(t) \tag{3}$$

where S(t) is time-varying left ventricle septal-free wall diameter.

Of the determinants of time-varying volume described by Equations 2 and 3, only the diameters are time-varying. The scaling factor $F_i(\phi)$ does not depend on time. Thus, assuming a fixed relationship between left ventricular diameter and volume, any of the shapes examined (for a given set of diameters) will give equally valid relative volumes. Estimated left ventricular volume change over time results from measured diameter changes over time. The model shape contributes nothing to the relative time variation of the left ventricular volume estimate.

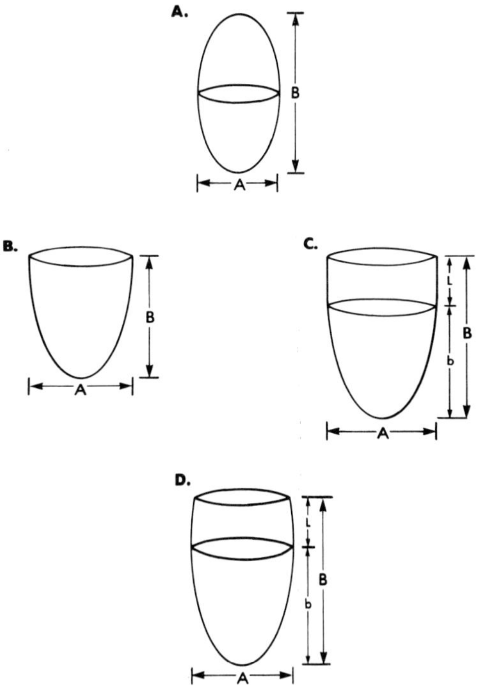

FIGURE 1. *Four commonly used left ventricle model shapes. Shape A: full prolate spheroid with minor axis, A, and major axis B. Shape B: half prolate spheroid with minor axis, A, and semimajor axis, B. Shape C: half prolate spheroid with minor axis, A, and semimajor axis b plus cylindrical segment with diameter, A, and height, L. Shape D: truncated prolate spheroid with minor axis, A, semimajor axis, b, and truncated semimajor axis, L. A = anterior-posterior diameter; B = base-apex diameter. See Table 1 for equations.*

Information Content of Diameter Changes at Different Frequencies

Table 2 shows the magnitudes (average and standard deviations) at each harmonic of the Fourier transforms of epicardial-to-epicardial anterior-posterior diameters measured in the four preparation 2 dogs. The diameter signals contain clearly identifiable information out to the fifth or sixth harmonic before exhibiting the relatively flat spectrum associated with the underlying noise in the measuring system. This finding is consistent with reports by Vayo (1967) and Rankin et al. (1976). The zero frequency component represents the mean diameter, and the first harmonic represents the basic sinusoidal variation as the heart beats. The higher harmonics include the information necessary to describe progressively faster changes in the diameter waveform, as well as the fine details of the observed wave shape, and become especially important if

TABLE 2
Average Magnitude Spectra Obtained from Several Closely Spaced Left Ventricle Anterior-Posterior Diameter Measurements in Dogs

			Magnitude (mm) at harmonic					
Dog	*n*	HR	0	1 (HR)	2	3	4	5
607	7	150	58.9 ± 6.7	0.40 ± 0.09	0.06 ± 0.06	0.05 ± 0.01	0.02 ± 0.01	0.02 ± 0.01
611	6	129	47.5 ± 5.7	0.50 ± 0.13	0.11 ± 0.06	0.16 ± 0.02	0.13 ± 0.04	0.09 ± 0.02
612	4	111	47.5 ± 2.7	1.23 ± 0.20	0.12 ± 0.07	0.30 ± 0.08	0.09 ± 0.06	0.10 ± 0.03
613	4	113	64.5 ± 1.8	0.95 ± 0.10	0.11 ± 0.02	0.09 ± 0.04	0.08 ± 0.02	0.03 ± 0.01

Values are mean ± SD of the frequency magnitude spectra obtained from fast Fourier transforms of *n* closely spaced left ventricular anterior-posterior diameters. HR = heart rate.

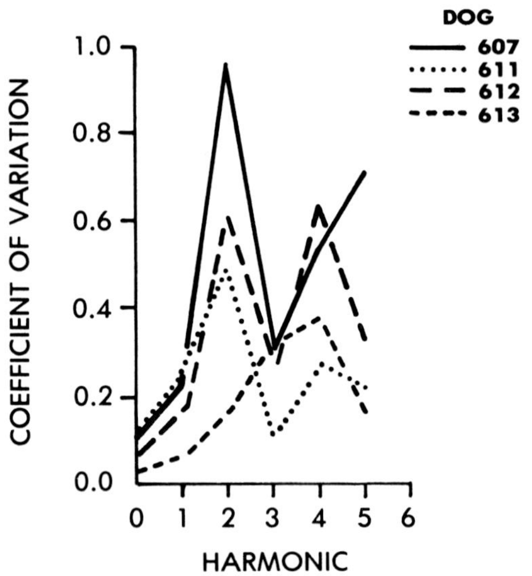

FIGURE 2. *The coefficient of variation (standard deviation/mean) as a function of harmonic (multiples of heart rate, HR). The increase in coefficient of variation with increase in frequency indicates that the variability in information content of the diameters increases relative to the mean, suggesting that diameter is less reliably related to volume at higher frequencies of volume change. The jump between harmonics 1 (heart rate) and 2 suggests that the heart rate is the frequency that divides reliable inference about volume from less reliable inference about volume.*

one is interested in computing the derivative of the waveform.

The mean magnitude, as well as the standard deviation, of the sinusoid at each harmonic falls as harmonic number (frequency) increases (Table 2). To get a better idea of the variability between the slightly different diameters, we computed the coefficient of variation (standard deviation/mean) in amplitude at each harmonic; this procedure quantifies the variability normalized for the amplitude of the signal at that harmonic. Figure 2 shows that, although between-site variation is relatively small for the mean diameters (0th harmonic) and first harmonic (at the heart rate), it increases rapidly at the second harmonic. The overall trend over the frequency range of 0 Hz to the third or fourth harmonic is one of increasing coefficients of variation. The coefficients of variation decrease above the third or fourth harmonic as the signal approaches the noise of the measuring system, which is small and varies little among experiments. This trend means that, at the important harmonics above the heart rate, the variation in information between closely spaced sites is large compared with the components of the signal at those frequencies. In other words, although the gross appearances of the signals were similar (because of similar amplitudes of the low frequency components), the detailed structure of the waveforms was variable. This fact precludes drawing strong conclusions about questions that depend on relating the fine structure of the diameter waveform to the fine structure of volume change.

Examining the Assumptions

To facilitate the investigation of the assumption of a single fixed relationship between left ventricular dimensions and volume, we state the component assumptions that are implicit when assuming a fixed relationship:

Regional Invariance: There is no regional variation among possible left ventricular dimension measurements; for example, a segment length or diameter measured near the apex of the left ventricle is as representative of left ventricular volume as one measured near the base.

Cycle Invariance: The relationship between any given left ventricular dimension and volume does not vary throughout the cardiac cycle.

Although we concentrate on the inference of left ventricular volume from dimensions measured with ultrasonic crystals, the analysis applies to any means of obtaining a left ventricular dimension. In addition, it is important to emphasize that the conclusions we reach apply, even if a dimension could be measured with no error.

Regional Invariance

For a dimension to be used, accurately, as a substitute for, or estimate of, left ventricular volume (particularly when comparing diameters among subjects or among different laboratories), it must convey the same information about left ventricular volume change no matter where it is measured on the left ventricle. Regional variation in the relation between left ventricular dimension and volume can be considered on two levels. First, gross variation arises because the left ventricle consists of several anatomical regions: anterior free wall, posterior free wall, lateral free wall, septum, base, and apex. Thus, some choice of representative regions is required. Second, local variation arises from differences in site of trans ducer placement because it is difficult to define clearly the boundaries of a particular anatomical region of interest, such as a segment length measured on the anterior free wall midway between the base and apex or an anterior-posterior diameter measured in the plane of the left ventricle minor axis. Placement with reference to relatively fixed landmarks on the left ventricle (e.g., LeWinter et al., 1975) can minimize placement errors within a laboratory, but among different laboratories there are certain to be errors on the order of several millimeters in what are ostensibly the same placement sites. This difficulty is compounded by the all-too-brief descriptions of crystal placement given by most investigators.

If dimensions that are different on either a gross or local scale respond differently to a given change in intrinsic left ventricular function, left ventricular volume, or mechanical load on the left ventricle, the selection of a dimension may have important consequences for interpreting left ventricular function.

Segment Lengths

There are gross variations in the way left ventricular segment lengths change during the cardiac cycle in a baseline state. Data from different articles (Bugge-Asperheim et al., 1969, 1972; Lekven et al., 1972; LeWinter et al., 1975; Hagl et al., 1977; Theroux et al., 1977; Hurlbut et al., 1978; Kumada et al.,

1979; Sabbah et al., 1981; Badke, 1982), which are nominally representative of normal physiological function, show wide variation. For example, average diastolic filling rates (our calculations) range from 1 mm/sec (Bugge-Asperheim et al., 1969) to 70 mm/sec (Theroux et al., 1977). This wide range reflects, in part, different physiological conditions, different initial lengths due to variable separation between the pairs of crystals, and different orientation of the axis between the crystal pair with respect to myocardial fiber angle. However, when controlling for such differences by examining regional data reported in a single paper or in a variety of papers originating from the same laboratory, average rates of change are seen to vary by as much as a factor of 10. This large variation supports the work of several investigators who have reported regional variation among segment lengths (Bugge-Asperheim et al., 1969; Bugge-Asperheim and Kiil, 1973; LeWinter et al., 1975; Kent et al., 1978; Lew and LeWinter, 1983).

Regional variation on a local scale can also be demonstrated. Lekven et al. (1972) show data which relate segment length, S, cubed to postmortem left ventricular volume, V, in five dogs. These segment lengths were measured on the anterior free wall of each left ventricle. (It is reasonable to assume that Lekven et al. attempted to place the pair of crystals at the same site on the free wall of each ventricle. However, because no explicit assurance is given by these authors that this was the case, the possibility remains that the variations in placement are larger than we assume.) Although the five segment length-volume relationships are linear with correlation coefficients of 0.91 to 0.99, the five slopes differ by an order of magnitude (Fig. 3A). A given volume change produces only small variation in S^3 in some dogs, but large variation in others. Hence, in the absence of a volume calibration standard, the segment length data from these different dogs would not be directly comparable.

In lieu of calibration against a known volume, segment lengths are commonly normalized as percent change from a baseline state. Consider two identical left ventricles, one in which segment length relates to volume by

$$S^3 = 210 + 2.4V \quad (4)$$

and a second for which segment length relates to volume by

$$S^3 = 1100 + 26V. \quad (5)$$

These two equations represent the smallest and largest slopes of the lines in Figure 3A. Assume the end-diastolic volume in each ventricle is 60 ml and stroke volume is 30 ml. Percent segment length shortening during systole is 7% for the first ventricle and 11% for the second. Because volume change is the same in both ventricles, there should be no discrepancy. Thus, percent change normalizations can yield large differences in segment length change, when, in fact, there are no differences in volume change. The converse is also easily demonstrable. A 10% segment shortening from an end-diastolic length of 7 mm, for the ventricle described by Equation 4, represents a 38-ml stroke volume and 0.69 ejection fraction, whereas a 10% shortening from an end-diastolic length of 13.5 mm, for the ventricle described by Equation 5, represents a 25-ml stroke volume and 0.48 ejection fraction. Hence, equal percent shortenings of segments on two hypothetically similar ventricles do not translate into equal levels of ventricular function.

Percent change only accounts for scaling differences in the mean level of a signal. Alternatively, z score normalization computed as

$$z_i = (x_i - \bar{x})/s \quad (6)$$

where i is the ith data point, $\bar{x}$ is the mean, and s the standard deviation, can be used to normalize the

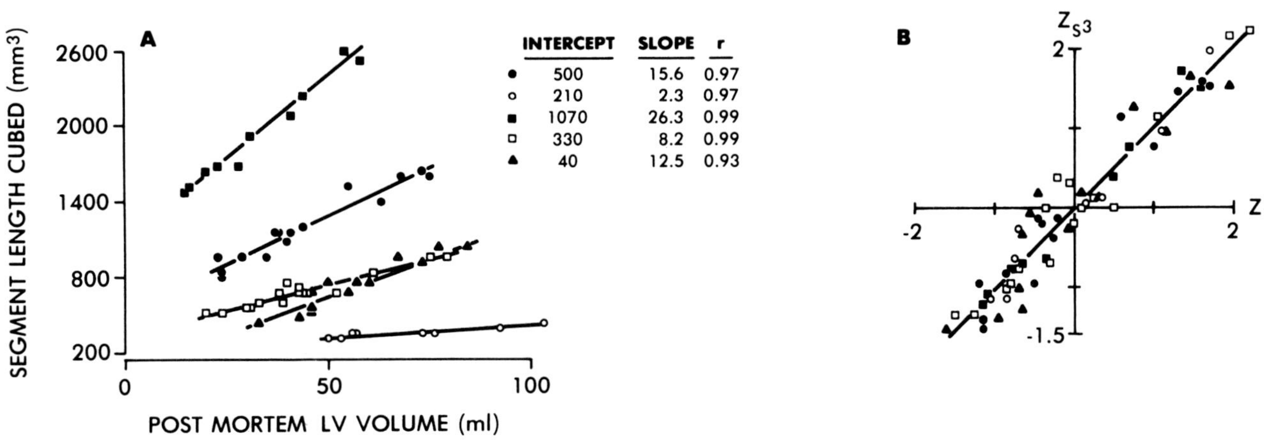

FIGURE 3. *Panel A: the cube of segment length as a function of postmortem left ventricular volume. The linear regression coefficients, slopes, intercepts, and correlation coefficients, r, are shown at upper right. The data were extracted from Figure 4 of Lekven et al. (1972). Panel B: following normalization of both segment length cubed, and volume as z-scores, the five different relationships of panel A superimpose with a common slope of 0.97 and intercept of zero, closely matching the line of identity drawn on the figure.*

segment lengths by accounting for both the mean and the variability about the mean. We calculated the mean and standard deviation for the S^3 and volume data from each of the five dogs in Figure 3A. After z normalization of S^3 and left ventricular volume, the five very different slopes [$P < 0.001$ by analysis of covariance (Zar, 1974)] of the relations between raw S^3 and left ventricular volume superimpose with a common slope of 0.97 ($P > 0.5$) (Fig. 3B). The common slope of about 1.0 indicates that a change of one standard deviation in volume produces a change of one standard deviation in segment length. Thus, the raw segment lengths, which show different degrees of variability in response to a given volume change, can now be compared by taking into account the variability (quantified as the standard deviation), as well as the mean, of the segment length. The fundamental relationship between the five different raw segment lengths and slow changes in volume in a nonbeating left ventricle (Fig. 3A) is the same from dog to dog.

Regional variation has also been shown in the responses of segment length changes to alterations in hemodynamic state or contractility. LeWinter et al. (1975) report that percent segment length shortening measured basally on the left ventricle decreased after a sudden aortic constriction, but that shortening measured at midventricular or apical sites did not change significantly. A recent report from the same laboratory (Lew and LeWinter, 1983) showed differences in rapid and slow segment lengthening (normalized as strain relative to minimum diastolic length at a baseline end-diastolic pressure of 5 mm Hg) during filling among anterior segment lengths measured at midwall depth at basal, midventricular, and apical sites. Hurlbut et al. (1978) showed that systolic segment shortening near the base was not appreciably changed by either positive (isoprenaline) or negative (propranolol) inotropic interventions, whereas segment shortening near the left ventricle apex was markedly changed. In this case, two entirely different interpretations are possible, depending on the region chosen to represent global left ventricular volume. However, these regional differences may be of interest in terms of the segment length itself. Our conclusions do not apply in studies where no volume inference (either implicit or explicit) is made from the segment lengths.

Diameters

Gross Variation

There is well-accepted evidence for regional differences among various left ventricular diameters. The base-apex diameter contributes relatively little to left ventricular volume change compared to the minor axis diameters (Hawthorne, 1961; Mitchell and Mullins, 1967; Wilson et al., 1967; Bishop and Horwitz, 1970; Rankin et al., 1976; Walley et al., 1982; Grover and Glantz, 1983). The two commonly measured minor axis diameters, the septal-free wall and the anterior-posterior, respond differently when a pulmonary artery constriction increases right ventricular afterload (Bemis et al., 1974; Stool et al., 1974; Glantz et al., 1978; Badke, 1982; Kingma et al., 1983; Olsen et al., 1983; Visner et al., 1983) because of direct ventricular interaction. The septal-free wall diameter decreases, whereas the anterior-posterior diameter remains constant or decreases slightly. Similarly, Cassidy et al. (1982) showed that positive end-expiratory pressure respiration affects these two minor axis diameters differently. Conversely, these two minor axis diameters both fall when a vena caval constriction reduces inflow to both ventricles.

The different responses in septal-free wall and anterior-posterior diameters to pulmonary artery constriction and positive end-expiratory pressure respiration are the result of a left ventricular shape change. Thus, the choice of diameter will always influence interpretation of experimental results. Both septal-free wall and anterior-posterior diameters are required for correct assessment of left ventricular volume when experiments involve interventions that affect the two ventricles differently.

Local Variation at Baseline Volumes

Given that appropriate diameters have been chosen, how important are small differences in transducer placement? For example, it is difficult to determine precisely where anterior-posterior diameter measurements are made from descriptions and diagrams in published papers. Most investigators seem to measure the minor axis from 60% to 85% of the distance along the apex-to-base circumference (apex = 0% and base = 100%), a variation in crystal placement of about 25 mm. Given the complexity of left ventricular cavity deformation, this local variation is of potential importance because diameters do not all respond identically to volume change.

Figure 4 shows epicardial-to-epicardial anterior-posterior diameters recorded in the seven preparation 1 dogs. These diameters are grossly similar: they are nearly maximum at end diastole, nearly minimum at end systole, and have similar mean values and amplitudes. However, the fine details, including rates of change and the location and timing of various small, quick changes in diameter, differ from dog to dog. Comparison of waveforms displayed in many published papers yields similar findings. For example, average rates of diameter change (our calculations) vary widely (Horwitz and Bishop, 1972; Stinson et al., 1974; Mahler et al., 1975; Rankin et al., 1976; Sasayama et al., 1976; Boettcher et al., 1978; Carew et al., 1979; Ling et al., 1979; Pouleur et al., 1979; Olsen et al., 1981; Hintze et al., 1982) and the diameters increase (Mitchell and Mullins, 1967; Pouleur et al., 1979), decrease (Bishop and Horwitz, 1970; Rankin et al., 1976; Boettcher et al., 1978; Sabbah et al., 1981; Hintz et al., 1982) or

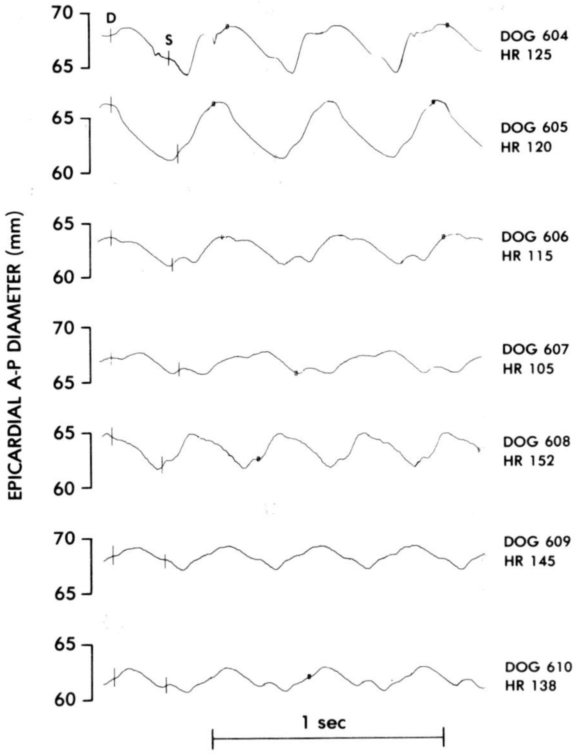

FIGURE 4. *Baseline recordings of epicardial-to-epicardial anterior-posterior (A-P) diameters from seven dogs. The waveform shapes are grossly similar, but the timing and rate of diameter changes at various points in the cardiac cycle are dissimilar. D = end diastole, S = end systole.*

remain nearly constant (Ling et al., 1979; Olsen et al., 1983) during isovolumic contraction. Whether we consider diameters similar or dissimilar depends on the frequency of diameter change of interest. Low frequency components—mean levels, value at end diastole, or diameter change between maximum diameter and minimum diameter—are similar, whereas high frequency components—the fine details of waveform shape and rates of change—are dissimilar. This observation agrees with our earlier demonstration that, as a rule of thumb, variability among similarly located diameters increases at frequencies greater than the heart rate.

To examine whether different possible anterior-posterior minor axis diameters in the same heart contain the same information about left ventricular volume, we used the four to seven different epicardial anterior-posterior diameters measured in each of four preparation 2 dogs. Measuring multiple diameters (Fig. 5A) in each dog means that any differences are largely attributable to different relationships between left ventricular diameter and volume. Figure 5B shows six different anterior-posterior diameters in one ventricle. This example is typical of the four dogs studied. Except for large mean (0 Hz) differences, the low frequency aspects of the diameter waveforms are similar. In contrast, the amounts and rates of change during the cardiac cycle are variable. Some of the differences in Figure 5B could be due to changes in volume (end-diastolic pressures ranged from 4.4 to 7.7 mm Hg). Volume effects are likely to be minimal for the following reasons. For each simultaneously measured pair of diameters volume was identical. In addition, variation in end-diastolic pressure was smaller in the other dogs [11.7 to 12.9 mm Hg, 12.2 to 12.8 mm Hg (for one dog, entrapment of the pressure transducer prohibited comparison of pressure)]. Finally, the similarity of the results from all dogs (Fig. 2; Table 2) suggest that volume changes play a minor role.

The low frequency similarities become more apparent after the diameters are normalized. To remove scale effects due to different distances between crystal pairs (Fig. 6A), we computed both percent change (Fig. 6B) and z (Fig. 6C) normalizations. Normalization produces a remarkable match between the low frequency components of these two widely different raw diameter signals. This result confirms that low frequency signal content is very similar among different anterior-posterior diameter measurements. Therefore, for most practical purposes, left ventricular volume and diameter have a fixed relationship at frequencies of volume change less than or equal to approximately the heart rate.

In contrast, the fine details of the waveform do

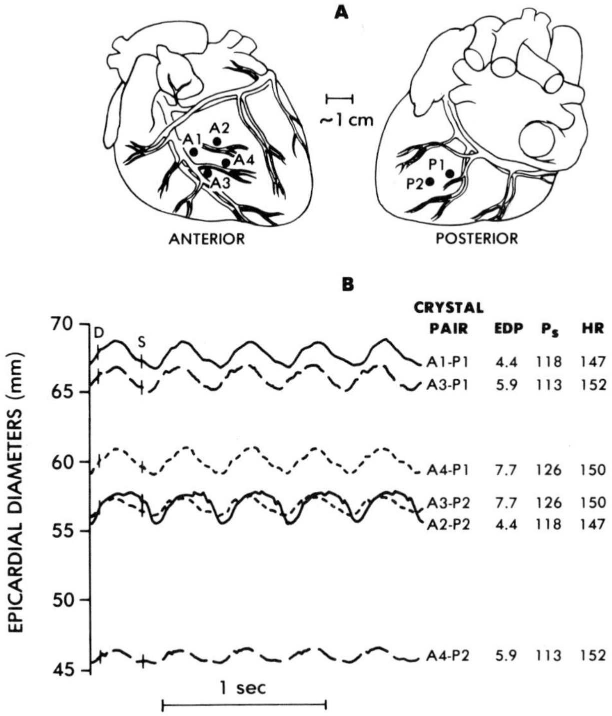

FIGURE 5. *Panel A: location of epicardial crystal placements on the anterior free wall (left) and posterior free wall (right). Panel B: three pairs of the measured epicardial anterior-posterior diameters from one dog are shown (the crystal pair designations for each diameter can be referenced to panel A). Each diameter pair was measured simultaneously. The different pairs were measured under similar conditions. The variation in EDP in this example is the largest seen in the four dogs studied. EDP = end-diastolic pressure; P_s = peak systolic pressure; HR = heart rate; D = end diastole; S = end-systole.*

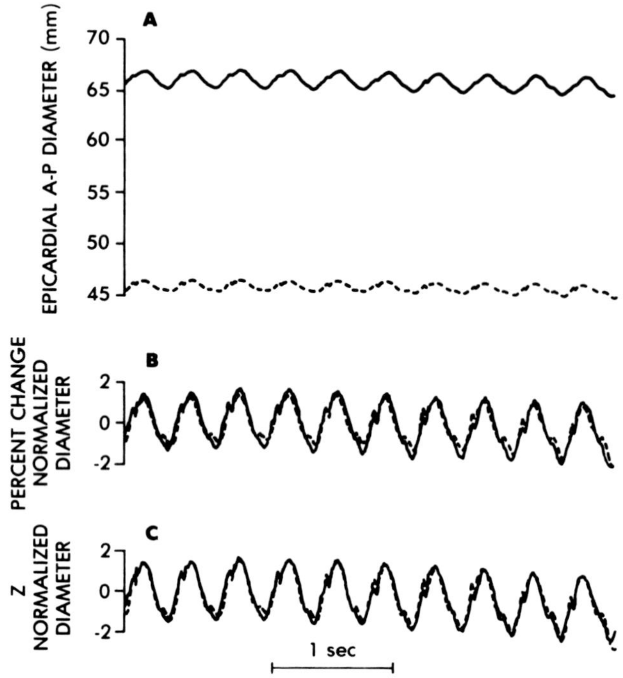

FIGURE 6. *One pair of the diameter measurements shown in Figure 5B is redrawn in panel A. After normalization as percent change from control, these raw diameters nearly superimpose (panel B). After z normalization, the superimposition is slightly improved (panel C).*

not always match. When present, this mismatch is particularly obvious for differences in timing and rate of lengthening and shortening during different portions of the cardiac cycle. Ling et al. (1979) reported similar results when comparing two simultaneously measured epicardial-to-epicardial anterior-posterior diameters, one measured near the apex and one measured at midventricle. These two diameters had similar average magnitude and magnitude of change when normalized as a strain relative to minimum end-diastolic length when the vena cavae were constricted, but the rates and timing of diameter change during different portions of diastole were different. Because left ventricular volume change was identical, these differences in the high frequency components indicate that diameter and volume cannot be considered to be related by a fixed relationship at frequencies of volume change substantially greater than the heart rate. Hence, relatively small differences in diameter location will influence inferences made regarding higher frequency left ventricular volume change.

Local Variation as Volume Changes

The previous examples considered different, but closely spaced, diameters when left ventricular volume was changing around a stable baseline. To examine similar regional responses to hemodynamic perturbations, we used percent change and z scores to normalize several different epicardial anterior-posterior diameters after a vena caval constriction (Fig. 7B). The waveforms were normalized, using the mean and standard deviation during the baseline before the constriction.

Both the percent change and z normalized waveforms consistently diverged as left ventricular volume decreased from its baseline value (Fig. 7, C and D) because the scaling between means and variations about means that existed between the diameters in the baseline state was not the same as the scaling that existed between the diameters following a vena caval constriction. For a fixed model shape, the scaled diameters should continue to superimpose as left ventricular volume decreases. Because they do not, the left ventricle shape must have changed. Hence, there is not a fixed model shape relating diameter to volume.

The relationship between diameter and volume is most affected at low left ventricular volumes. In the four dogs in which simultaneous comparisons of anterior-posterior diameter measurements were made, the divergence was near the minimum diameter in 10 of 13 pairwise comparisons. Likewise, data in various reports from Rankin and his coworkers (Rankin et al., 1976; Olsen et al., 1981, 1983) show that, as left ventricular volume gets very small,

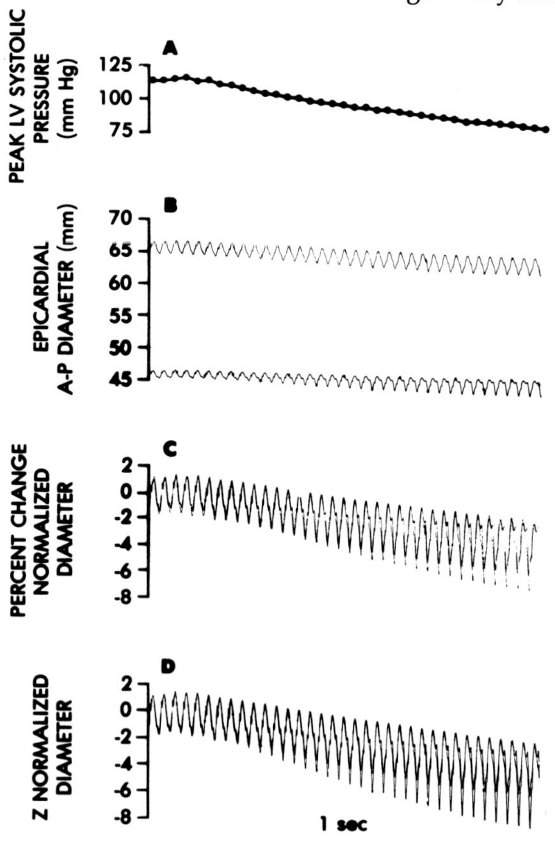

FIGURE 7. *Response of peak systolic pressure (panel A), raw diameters (panel B), percent change normalization (panel C), and z normalizations (panel D) of the same diameter pair shown in Figure 6 to a vena caval constriction. The normalizations are relative to the mean (percent change) or mean and standard deviation (z score) of the first 2 seconds of data. The divergence of the normalized diameters as volume decreases was typically seen in the four dogs in which simultaneous diameter measurements were made.*

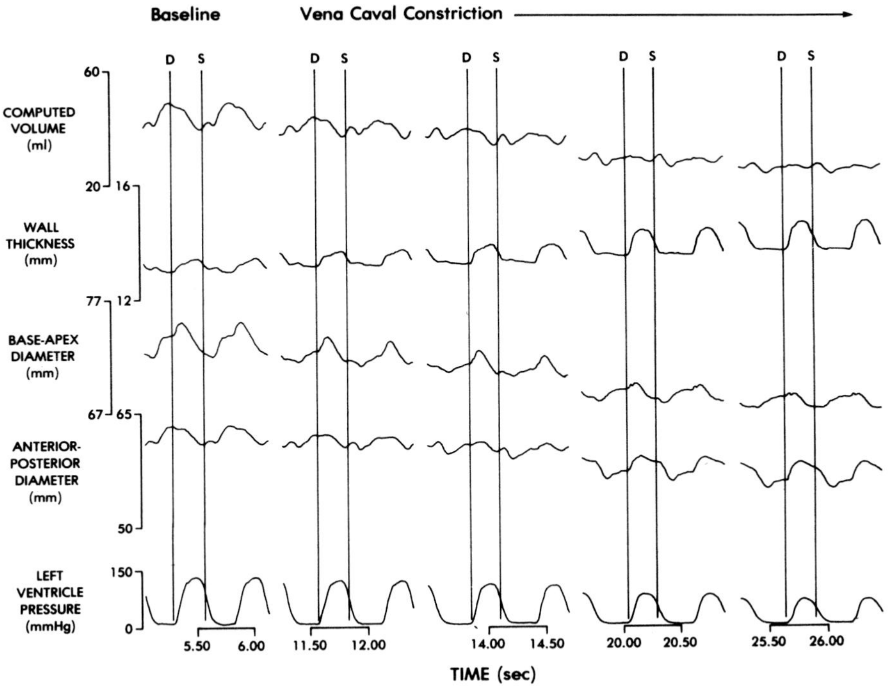

FIGURE 8. *Estimated left ventricular volume (volume = $\pi/6[(A - 2h)^2(B - 1.1h)]$, where A = anterior-posterior diameter, B = base-apex diameter, and h = wall thickness), wall thickness, base-apex diameter, anterior-posterior diameter, and left ventricular pressure are shown at various times before (baseline) and after vena caval constriction. The anterior-posterior diameter paradoxically lengthens at low volumes—so much so that negative volume changes are computed.*

the epicardial-to-epicardial diameter actually lengthens during ejection. This pattern is commonly seen in our data (Fig. 8) (at present, we do not know whether endocardial-to-endocardial diameters change in a similar manner at low left ventricular volumes). These paradoxical changes in diameter can result only if the relationship that existed between diameter and volume at baseline has changed as left ventricular volume decreases.

Some investigators (Rankin et al., 1976; Hess et al., 1983; Olsen et al., 1983) have combined observed diameters with a mathematical model for volume and differentiated the result to calculate flow into and out of the left ventricle. We compared flows, computed as the negative derivative of estimated volume, with aortic flows measured using an electromagnetic flow probe following vena caval constriction, pulmonary artery constriction, and aortic constriction in six of the preparation 1 dogs. Although the measured and calculated flow signals did not precisely superimpose under any conditions, the flow calculated at low left ventricular volume produced by a vena caval constriction has a different magnitude and time course, relative to the measured

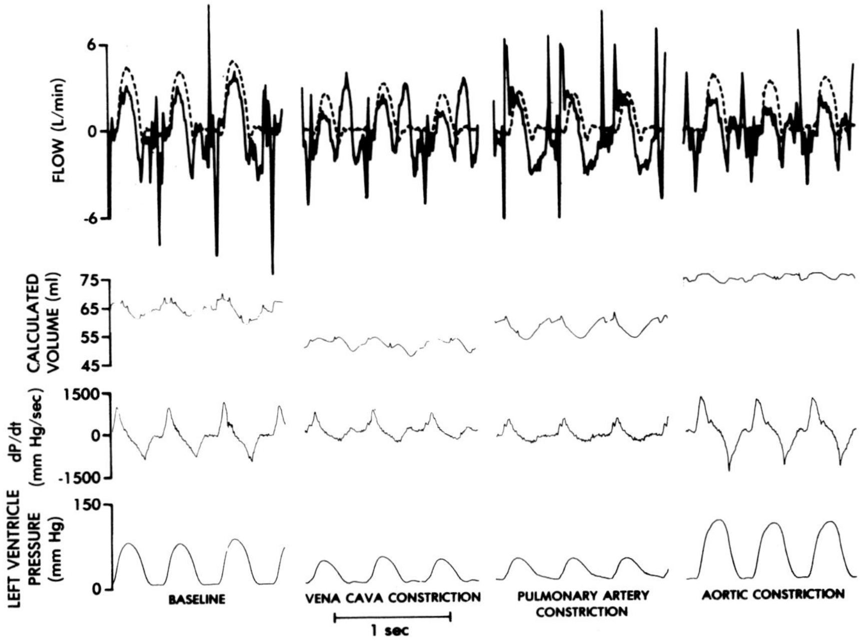

FIGURE 9. *Computed left ventricular outflow (------) and aortic flow measured electromagnetically (– – – –) (upper strip), calculated left ventricular volume (see equation in legend, Fig. 8), dP/dt, and left ventricular pressure during baseline state (far left), vena caval constriction (middle left), pulmonary artery constriction (middle right), and aortic constriction (far right).*

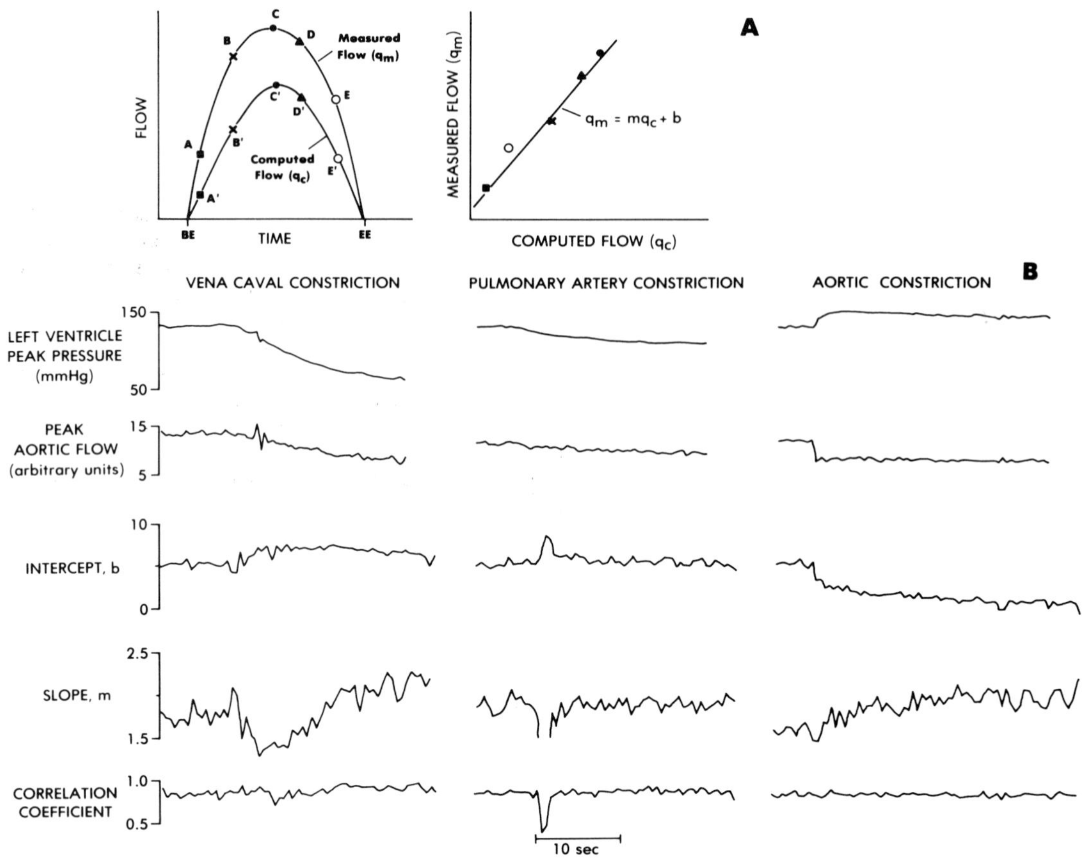

FIGURE 10. *Panel A: a schematic depiction of the regression analysis used to compare measured (q_m) and calculated (q_c) aortic flows. On the left is shown a pair of beats, with points A, B, C, D, E, and A', B', C', D', E' indicated. The regression is performed by regressing A, B, C, D, E, etc., on A', B', C', D', E', etc., as shown on the right. Because this is a schematic, the points plotted in the right panel do not necessarily correspond with points plotted with the same symbol in the left panel. Panel B: an example of the beat-to-beat regression of measured flow on computed flow is shown for a vena caval constriction (left), pulmonary artery constriction (middle), and aortic constriction (right). The slope (m), intercept (b), correlation coefficient (r), peak left ventricular pressure, and peak aortic flow are shown as functions of time.*

aortic flow, than that calculated during the baseline state (Fig. 9). To quantify this change in relationship between left ventricular diameter and volume we regressed (Fig. 10A) the measured instantaneous flow on the calculated instantaneous flow, both sampled every 5 msec during the ejection period of each heart beat. The ejection period was judged in reference to the measured flow. The correlation coefficient values between the predicted and measured flow during ejection were high (greater than 0.85) and remained nearly constant throughout the multiple beats during the occlusions (Fig. 10B). However, the regression slope and intercept change as left ventricular volume is changed by vena caval constriction, pulmonary artery constriction, and aortic constriction (Fig. 10B). In the different experiments, we observed both increases and decreases in slope and intercept.

When comparing two waveforms of the same shape, a relative change in magnitude without a shift in the onset of one waveform relative to the other waveform would produce a constant zero intercept and change only the slope. A shift in the onset of one waveform relative to the other would change both intercept and slope, and reduce the correlation coefficient. Also, if the shapes of the signals change relative to one another, slope, intercept, and correlation coefficient would change. Thus, the trends seen in the data of Figure 10B are mostly due to magnitude shifts between the measured and calculated flows, because shifts in the onset of one waveform relative to the other, or shape change between the measured and calculated ejection flow, would also change the correlation coefficient (as in the middle panel of Fig. 10B). However, a small effect due to shape changes or shifts in the onset of one waveform relative to the other is suggested by the changes in intercept.

The trends seen in response to vena caval constriction and pulmonary artery constriction could be due to change in flow probe contact with the aorta when pressure drops. However, we observed both increases and decreases in slope and intercept. A change in the quality of the flow probe signal is not likely to produce a shift in the onset of the measured flow relative to the calculated flow. Additionally, trends in regression coefficients were observed in response to aortic constriction, where pressure increased. Thus, the slope and intercept trends observed as left ventricular volume and pressure changes from baseline mean that the relationship between left ventricular diameters and volume is not constant.

This interpretation is supported by the results obtained by Wilson et al. (1967), who empirically determined the constant (i.e., the model shape) that best related epicardial-to-epicardial anterior-posterior and base-apex diameters to known left ventricular volume. This constant was $\pi/6$ in the standing dog, slightly less in the recumbent dog, and about $\pi/8$ during exercise. The model shape which describes the relationship between left ventricular diameter and volume at a normal left ventricular volume changes as hemodynamic state, particularly left ventricular volume, changes.

As before, whether the changing relationship between left ventricular diameter and volume is important depends on the use intended for a left ventricular diameter measurement. The mean diameter or value at any given point in the cardiac cycle, for example, end diastole, shows a monotonic decrease following vena caval constriction and pulmonary artery constriction, or increase following aortic constriction. These trends in low frequency events are useful for evaluating left ventricular volume change, and it matters little that the relation between diameter and volume change is not constant. However, for finer details of left ventricular diameter signals (i.e., higher frequency information), the paradoxical diameter changes at low left ventricular volume prohibit the use of diameter to represent or estimate volume.

Above what left ventricular volume are diameter measurements acceptable? We cannot answer this question precisely. One cannot simply say that the cutoff between acceptable and unacceptable data is the volume where obviously spurious results (e.g., lengthening during ejection) begin. These spurious results do not appear suddenly; they gradually appear as left ventricular volume decreases. There is an important practical implication of this shape change as volume decreases. The resulting paradoxical diameter changes suggest that a minimum diastolic diameter measurement at very low volumes may not, as has been assumed by some investigators (Rankin et al., 1977; Ling et al., 1979; Pouleur et al., 1979), represent the left ventricle's unstressed volume.

Although if one begins at higher volumes (e.g., using conscious dogs, or after volume loading in acute experiments) there will be a wider range of volumes for which diameter relates well to volume, doing so will not *eliminate* the problem. Hence, any attempt to compute diastolic viscous properties (e.g., Rankin et al., 1977; Pouleur et al., 1979; Hess et al., 1983) or to demonstrate shifts or nonlinearity of end-systolic pressure-diameter relations (e.g., Crozatier et al., 1981) as left ventricular volume decreases from normal values may be uninterpretable. Such attempts should not be made unless the investigator clearly demonstrates the range of left ventricular volumes over which the relation between diameter and volume is fixed.

Cycle Invariance

For the use of dimensions to represent or estimate left ventricular volume to make sense under all circumstances, the relationship between left ventricular dimension and volume must remain fixed throughout the cardiac cycle.

Segment Lengths

Most segment length waveforms displayed in published reports are maximum at end diastole, minimum at end systole, and show few high frequency changes during the isovolumic portions of the cardiac cycle. However, it has been noted that there can be shortening or lengthening of a segment during isovolumic contraction and relaxation (Bugge-Asperheim et al., 1969). Such length changes when left ventricular volume is constant represent a disassociation between volume and segment length changes during the isovolumic portions of the cardiac cycle. Thus, strictly speaking, the assumption of cycle invariance in the relationship between segment length and volume is false.

Diameters

Figure 11 shows that there is hysteresis in the relationship between endocardial-to-endocardial anterior-posterior diameter and left ventricular volume in an isolated ventricle preparation (Suga and Sagawa, 1974b). There can be a difference of as much as 7 ml in left ventricular volume at a given anterior-posterior diameter depending on whether the left ventricle is ejecting or filling—a large error compared to the 19 to 20-mm stroke volume ejected. This hysteresis is incompatible with the assumption

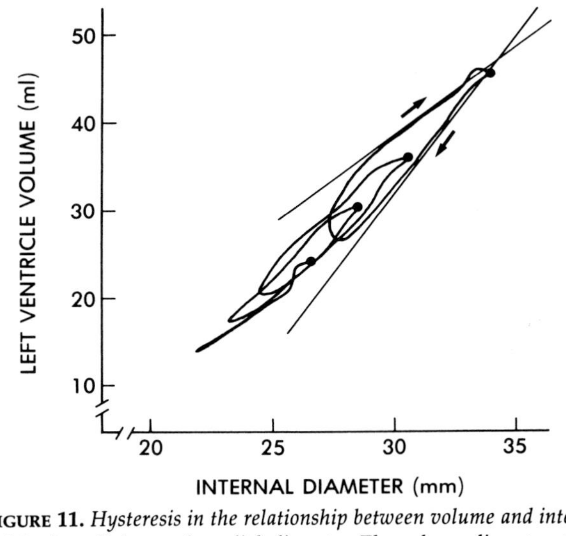

FIGURE 11. *Hysteresis in the relationship between volume and internal (endocardial-to-endocardial) diameter. The volume-diameter plot is redrawn from Figure 3 of Suga and Sagawa (1974b) (with permission of the American Physiological Society). The lines drawn tangent to two points on the upper loop show that dV/dD (the slope of the tangent lines) is not constant.*

of a constant relationship between left ventricular diameter and volume throughout the cardiac cycle.

According to the chain rule for differentiation

$$\frac{dV}{dt} = \frac{dV}{dD}\frac{dD}{dt}$$

The assumption of a fixed functional relationship between left ventricular volume, V, and diameter, D, dictates that dV/dD (the rate of change of volume with respect to diameter) be constant. The hysteresis (Fig. 11) illustrates that dV/dD is not constant. Therefore, the cycle invariance assumption is false.

A variety of published papers and our results from open-chest anesthetized dogs provide additional support for this conclusion. In ejecting contractions, diameter changes during isovolumic contraction and relaxation. In fact, several investigators have shown that rates of diameter change can be large (Stinson et al., 1974; Mahler et al., 1975; Kirkpatrick et al., 1976), or even maximal (Pouleur et al., 1979), during isovolumic portions of the cardiac cycle. Such changes in left ventricular diameter during isovolumic contraction and relaxation result in spurious estimated flows out of or into the left ventricle (Fig. 9). The relative magnitudes and time courses of calculated and measured flow change as volume changes. For example, the estimated flow during isovolumic relaxation and early filling becomes the dominant event of the cardiac cycle after vena caval constriction.

Figure 12 shows that non-ejecting contractions also show a disassociation between diameter and volume. Epicardial-to-epicardial anterior-posterior diameter changes continuously during non-ejecting contractions after an extrasystole. Anterior-posterior diameter lengthened approximately 1.4 mm during a non-ejecting systole. This is a large change relative to the 2.5 mm shortening during an ejecting contraction. Similarly, Suga and Sagawa (1974b) show a 1-mm change in endocardial-to-endocardial anterior-posterior diameter during an isovolumic contraction, which is large relative to the 3- to 4-mm change shown during an ejecting contraction. Hence, during non-ejecting contractions and during isovolumic portions of ejecting contractions, both endocardial-to-endocardial and epicardial-to-epicardial diameters change by large amounts relative to the amount they change during an ejection.

Two important practical issues arise out of this consideration of cycle invariance. The first concerns the validation of dimensions as a substitute for volume. Diastolic volume change is often inferred from diastolic diameter changes. However, validations done in beating hearts to support this practice use ejection phase standards like aortic flow (Bishop and Horwitz, 1970; Rankin et al., 1976). The falsity of the cycle invariance assumption implies that a validation during ejection may not hold during filling, because the relationships between diameter and volume are different. This is not a problem for low frequency changes in volume, but is a problem for high frequency changes in volume. The second issue concerns selection of an interval of the cardiac cycle for study. Although, the spurious computed outflow during isovolumic relaxation returns to zero just before or at the time of minimum diastolic pressure, we have no way of judging when the obviously spurious relation between left ventricular diameter and volume during isovolumic relaxation ends and an assumed good relation begins during early diastole. Hence, we advise against the practice of analyzing higher frequency diastolic diameter data only after the time of minimum pressure (Rankin et al., 1977; Pouleur et al., 1979).

Conclusion

To relate dimensions to volume, one must assume that there is a single fixed relationship between dimension and volume. It does not matter what the relationship (i.e., model shape) is, when determining

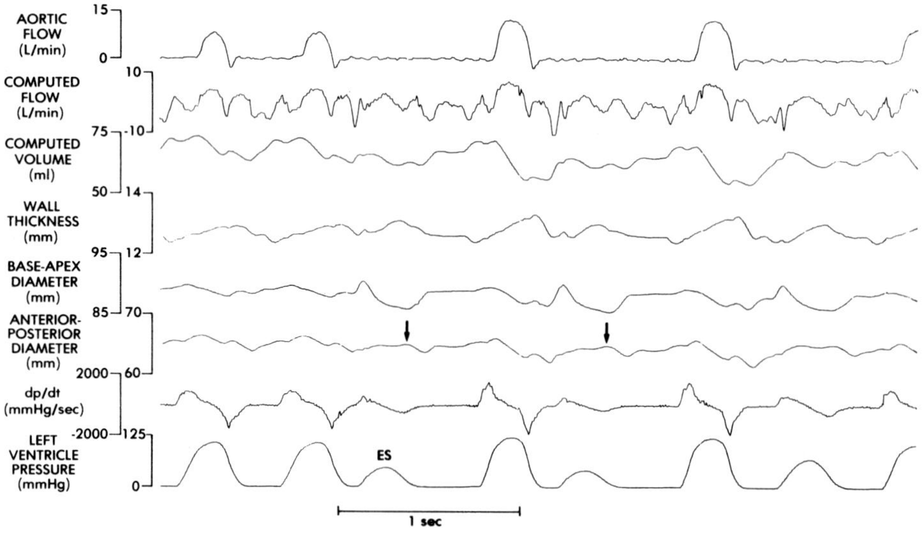

FIGURE 12. *Measured aortic flow, computed flow (negative derivative of computed volume), computed volume, left ventricular wall thickness, base-apex diameter, anterior-posterior diameter, and pressure following an extrasystole (ES). In the alternans that followed the ES, diameter changes a large amount during non-ejecting beats (arrows).*

relative changes in volume, but whatever the relationship is, it must remain constant over all hemodynamic states of interest and at all times during the cardiac cycle. Strictly speaking, because the left ventricle shape changes as cavity volume changes, this assumption is false. The frequency content of ventricular dimension and volume signals is a unifying element for considering whether it is valid to infer global volume change from measured local dimension change.

In general, the ability to relate dimension to volume accurately decreases as the frequency of the information one needs increases. As a rule of thumb, we separate accurate inferences regarding volume from inaccurate ones at approximately the heart rate frequency. Although frequency analysis of the information content of diameter measurements, as well as the various examples showing regional and cycle variation in the relationship between dimension and volume, all suggest the frequency of the heart rate as a good break point, there is a "gray area" around the frequency of the heart rate.

For changes in volume that occur at frequencies less than or equal to the heart rate, the falsity of the assumption of a fixed relationship between dimension and volume usually does not limit inferring volume from dimension (Two exceptions are using dimension change between end diastole and end systole as a substitute for stroke volume at very low ventricular volumes, and the requirement that both septal-free wall and anterior-posterior diameters are measured if hemodynamic interventions such as pulmonary artery constriction or positive end-expiratory pressure respiration are used to study left ventricular function). Fortunately, most applications fall into this low frequency range. In contrast, for changes in volume at frequencies greater than the heart rate, the falsity of this assumption limits the use of dimension change to infer volume change. In particular, one should not attempt to make inferences based on derivatives of dimension or on subtle changes in the fine details of dimension change when the intent, either implicit or explicit, is to relate this dimension change to global volume change.

Thus, some past reports in the literature may require reinterpretation, and future use of this necessary practice of relating dimension measurements to volume should consider the guidelines we present. In particular, validation of an adequate relationship between dimension and volume must consider the frequency content of the volume information required to answer the question of interest, and must cover the range of hemodynamic states and left ventricular volumes over which the left ventricle is to be evaluated.

We thank James Stoughton for excellent technical assistance in conducting the experiments, Steve Sizemore for computer programming assistance, and Susan Quan and Les Harmon for preparing the illustrations. We are grateful for the many helpful criticisms made by Paul Daly, Fernando Florenzano, Julien Hoffman, Joel Karliner, Martin LeWinter, and William Parmley.

This work was supported by NIH Research Grant HL-25869. Dr. Slinker was supported by NIH Training Grant HL-07192.

Address for reprints: Bryan K. Slinker, D.V.M., Ph.D., or Stanton A. Glantz, Ph.D., Cardiology Division, 1186 Moffitt, University of California, San Francisco, CA 94143.

Received March 5, 1984; accepted for publication November 28, 1984.

References

Badke FR (1982) Left ventricular dimensions and function during right ventricular pressure overload. Am J Physiol **242:** H611–H618

Bemis CE, Serur JR, Borkenhagen D, Sonnenblick EH, Urschel CW (1974) Influence of right ventricular filling pressure on left ventricular pressure and dimension. Circ Res **34:** 498–504

Bishop VS, Horwitz LD (1970) Left ventricular transverse internal diameter: Value in studying left ventricular function. Am Heart J **80:** 507–514

Bishop VS, Horwitz LD, Stone HL, Stegall HF, Engelken EJ (1969) Left ventricular internal diameter and cardiac function in conscious dogs. J Appl Physiol **27:** 619–623

Boettcher DH, Vatner SF, Heyndrickx GR, Braunwald E (1978) Extent of utilization of the Frank-Starling mechanism in conscious dogs. Am J Physiol **234:** H338–H345

Bugge-Asperheim B, Kiil F (1973) Preload, contractility and afterload as determinants of stroke volume during elevation of aortic blood pressure in dogs. Cardiovasc Res **7:** 528–541

Bugge-Asperheim B, Leraand S, Kiil F (1969) Local dimensional changes of the myocardium measured by ultrasonic technique. Scand J Clin Lab Invest **24:** 361–371

Bugge-Asperheim B, Lekven J, Kiil F (1972) Effect of saline infusion on stroke volume and end-systolic volume at various levels of adrenergic activity in dogs. Scand J Clin Lab Invest **29:** 15–24

Carew TE, Covell JW (1978) Left ventricular function in exercise-induced hypertrophy in dogs. Am J Cardiol **42:** 82–88

Carlsson E, Milne ENC (1967) Permanent implantation of endocardial tantalum screws: A new technique for functional studies of the heart in the experimental animal. J Can Assoc Radiol **18:** 304–309

Cassidy SS, Mitchell JH, Johnson RL Jr (1982) Dimensional analysis of right and left ventricles during positive-pressure ventilation in dogs. Am J Physiol **242:** H549–H556

Crozatier B, Caillet D, Jouannot P, Hatt PY (1979) Pulsus alternans in regionally hypoxic ventricles of open-chest dogs: Regional mechanical alternation of potentiation and attenuation of the inotropic state. Basic Res Cardiol **74:** 639–648

Crozatier B, Caillet D, Thuillez C, Chevrier JL, Peronneau P, Hatt PY (1981) Preload changes modify systolic pressure-diameter relations in the conscious dog. Am J Physiol **240:** H354–H360

Dodge HT, Sandler H, Baxley WA, Hawley RR (1966) Usefulness and limitations of radiographic methods for determining left ventricular volume. Am J Cardiol **18:** 10–24

Feigenbaum, H (1972) Clinical application of echocardiography. Prog Cardiovasc Dis **14:** 531–558

Frank O (1895) On the dynamics of cardiac muscle. Z Biol **32:** 370–447 (English translation by CB Chapman, E. Wasserman. Am Heart J **58:** 282–317 and Am Heart J **58:** 467–478, 1959)

Glantz SA, Parmley WW (1978) Factors which affect the diastolic pressure-volume curve. Circ Res **42:** 171–180

Glantz SA, Misbach GA, Moores WY, Mathey DG, Lekven J, Stowe DF, Parmley WW, Tyberg JV (1978) The pericardium substantially affects the left ventricular diastolic pressure-volume relationship in the dog. Circ Res **42:** 433–441

Grover M, Glantz SA (1983) Endocardial pacing site affects left ventricular end-diastolic volume and performance in the intact anesthetized dog. Circ Res **53:** 72–85

Hagl S, Heimisch W, Meisner H, Erben R, Baum M, Mendler N (1977) The effect of hemodilution on regional myocardial function in the presence of coronary stenosis. Basic Res Cardiol **72:** 344–364

Hawthorne EW (1961) Instantaneous dimensional changes of the left ventricle in dogs. Circ Res **9:** 110–119

Hawthorne EW (1966) Dynamic geometry of the left ventricle. Am J Cardiol **18:** 566–573

Hess OM, Osakada G, Lavelle JF, Gallagher KP, Kemper WS, Ross J Jr (1983) Diastolic myocardial wall stiffness and ventricular relaxation during partial and complete coronary occlusions in the conscious dog. Circ Res **52:** 387–400

Hintze TH, Vatner SF (1982) Cardiac dynamics during hemorrhage: Relative unimportance of adrenergic inotropic responses. Cir Res **50:** 705–713

Horowitz SL, Sizemore SR, Glantz SA (1984) Biomedical waveform processing system user manual. UCSF Mimeo

Horwitz LD, Bishop VS (1972) Left ventricular pressure-dimension relationships in the conscious dog. Cardiovas Res **6:** 163–171

Horwitz LD, Bishop VS, Stone HL, Stegall HF (1968) Continuous measurement of internal left ventricular diameter. J Appl Physiol **24:** 738–740

Hurlbut TA III, Scales F, Buja LM, Willerson JT (1978) Use of chronically implanted ultrasonic crystals in the intact heart of the cat. Cardiovasc Res **12:** 387–390

Ilebekk A, Miller MM, Kiil F (1979) Cardiac performance: Independent effects of inotropy and preload at high heart rate. Am J Physiol **236:** H568–H576

Kent RS, Carew TE, LeWinter MM, Covell JW (1978) Comparison of left ventricular free wall and septal diastolic compliance in the dog. Am J Physiol **234:** H392–H398

Kingma I, Tyberg JV, Smith ER (1983) Effects of diastolic transeptal pressure gradient on ventricular septal position and motion. Circulation **68:** 1304–1314

Kirkpatrick SE, Pitlick PT, Naliboff J, Friedman WF (1976) Frank-Starling relationship as an important determinant of fetal cardiac output. Am J Physiol **231:** 495–500

Kumada T, Karliner JS, Pouleur H, Gallagher KP, Shirato K, Ross J Jr (1979) Effects of coronary occlusion on early ventricular diastolic events in conscious dogs. Am J Physiol **237:** H542–H549

Lekven J, Bugge-Asperheim B, Kiil F (1972) Relationship between local myocardial dimensions and left ventricular volume in dogs. Scand J Clin Lab Invest **29:** 5–14

Lew WYW, LeWinter MM (1983) Regional circumferential lengthening patterns in canine left ventricle. Am J Physiol **245:** H741–H748

LeWinter MM, Kent RS, Kroener JM, Carew TE, Covell JW (1975) Regional differences in myocardial performance in the left ventricle of the dog. Circ Res **37:** 191–199

Ling D, Rankin JS, Edwards CH II, McHale PA, Anderson RW (1979) Regional diastolic mechanics of the left ventricle in the conscious dog. Am J Physiol **236:** H323–H330

Mahler F, Covell JW, Ross J Jr (1975) Systolic pressure-diameter relations in the normal conscious dog. Cardiovasc Res **9:** 447–455

Mitchell JH, Mullins CB (1967) Dimensional analysis of left ventricular function. *In* Factors Influencing Myocardial Contractility, edited by RD Tanz, F Kavaler, J Roberts. New York, Academic Press, pp 177–188

Mitchell JH, Wildenthal K, Mullins CB (1969) Geometrical studies of the left ventricle utilizing biplane cinefluorography. Fed Proc **28:** 1334–1343

Molaug M, Stokland O, Ilebekk A, Lekven J, Kiil F (1981) Myocardial function of the interventricular septum: effects of right and left ventricular pressure loading before and after pericardiotomy in dogs. Circ Res **49:** 52–61

Olsen CO, Van Trigt P, Rankin JS (1981) Dynamic geometry of the intact left ventricle. Fed Proc **40:** 2023–2030

Olsen CO, Tyson GS, Maier GW, Spratt JA, Davis JW, Rankin JS (1983) Dynamic ventricular interaction in the conscious dog. Circ Res **52:** 85–104

Pouleur H, Karliner JS, LeWinter MM, Covell JW (1979) Diastolic viscous properties of the intact canine left ventricle. Circ Res **45:** 410–419

Rankin JS, McHale PA, Arentzen CE, Ling D, Greenfield JC Jr, Anderson RW (1976) The three-dimensional dynamic geometry of the left ventricle in the conscious dog. Circ Res **39:** 304–313

Rankin JS, Arentzen CE, McHale PA, Ling D, Anderson RW (1977) Viscoelastic properties of the diastolic left ventricle in the conscious dog. Circ Res **41:** 37–45

Rushmer RF, Thal N (1951) Mechanics of ventricular contraction: A cinefluorographic study. Circulation **4:** 219–228

Rushmer RF, Franklin DL, Ellis RM (1956) Left ventricular dimensions recorded by sonocardiometry. Circ Res **4:** 684–688

Sabbah HN, Marzilli M, Stein PD (1981) The relative role of subendocardium and subepicardium in left ventricular mechanics. Am J Physiol **240:** H920–H926

Sagawa K (1978) The ventricular pressure-volume diagram revisited. Circ Res **43:** 677–687

Sasayama S, Ross J Jr, Franklin D, Bloor CM, Bishop S, Dilley RB (1976) Adaptations of the left ventricle to chronic pressure overload. Circ Res **38:** 172–178

Schiller NB, Skioldebrand CG, Schiller EJ, Mavroudis CC, Silverman NH, Rahimtoola SH, Lipton MJ (1983) Canine left ventricular mass estimation by two-dimensional echocardiography. Circulation **68:** 210–216

Shirato K, Shabetai R, Bhargava V, Franklin D, Ross J Jr (1978) Alteration of the left ventricular diastolic pressure-segment length relation produced by the pericardium: Effects of cardiac distension and afterload reduction in conscious dogs. Circulation **57:** 1191–1198

Starling EH (1918) Linacre Lecture on the Law of the Heart. London, Longmans Group

Stinson EB, Rahmoeller G, Tecklenberg PL (1974) Measurement of internal left ventricular diameter by a tracking sonomicrometer. Cardiovasc Res **8:** 283–289

Stool EW, Mullins CB, Leshin SJ, Mitchell JH (1974) Dimensional changes of the left ventricle during acute pulmonary arterial hypertension in dogs. Am J Cardiol **33:** 868–875

Suga H, Sagawa K (1974a) Instantaneous pressure-volume relationships and their ratio in the excised, supported canine left ventricle. Circ Res **35:** 117–126

Suga H, Sagawa K (1974b) Assessment of absolute volume from diameter of the intact canine left ventricular cavity. J Appl Physiol **36:** 496–499

Theroux P, Ross J Jr, Franklin D, Covell JW, Bloor CM, Sasayama S (1977) Regional myocardial function and dimensions early and late after myocardial infarction in the unanesthetized dog. Circ Res **40:** 158–165

Van Trigt P III, Bauer BJ, Olsen CO, Rankin JS, Wechsler AS (1981) An improved transducer for measurement of cardiac dimensions with sonomicrometry. Am J Physiol **240:** H664–H668

Vayo HW (1967) Fourier series analysis of ventricular dimensions. *In* Factors Influencing Myocardial Contractility, edited by RD Tanz, F Kavaler, J Roberts. New York, Academic Press, pp 141–148

Visner MS, Arentzen CE, O'Conner MJ, Larson EV, Anderson RW (1983) Alterations in left ventricular three-dimensional dynamic geometry and systolic function during acute right ventricular hypertension in the conscious dog. Circulation **67:** 353–365

Walley KR, Grover M, Raff GL Jr, Benge JW, Hannaford B, Glantz SA (1982) Left ventricular dynamic geometry in the intact and open chest dog. Circ Res **50:** 573–589

Wilson MF, Ninomiya I, Caldwell WM (1967) Left ventricular dimension-flow relations in unanesthetized dogs. *In* Factors Influencing Myocardial Contractility, edited by RD Tanz, F Kavaler, J Roberts. New York, Academic Press, pp 149–161

Zar JH (1974) Biostatistical Analysis. Englewood Cliffs, N.J., Prentice-Hall, pp 230–232

INDEX TERMS: Diameter • Segment length • Sonomicrometer • Left ventricle geometry • Hemodynamics • Cardiac mechanics • Ventricular function

Analysis of the Pressor Sympathetic Reflex Produced by Intracoronary Injections of Bradykinin in Conscious Dogs

Massimo Pagani, Paolo Pizzinelli, Raffaello Furlan, Stefano Guzzetti, Ornella Rimoldi, Giulia Sandrone, and Alberto Malliani

From Istituto Ricerche Cardiovascolari, CNR; Patologia Medica, Ospedale "L.Sacco"; Università Milano, Italy

SUMMARY. The reflex hemodynamic effects of intracoronary bradykinin were tested in 20 conscious instrumented dogs. When the experiments were performed after full recovery from surgery and anesthesia, graded doses (10–300 ng/kg) of bradykinin always produced graded pressor responses, in the absence of any pain reaction. At the maximum pressor response obtained with 100 ng/kg, mean arterial pressure rose 28 ± 3% from 89 ± 4 mm Hg, left ventricular pressure 20 ± 3% from 121 ± 2 mm Hg, heart rate 30 ± 4% from 88 ± 5 beats/min, rate of change of left ventricular pressure 18 ± 3% from 2812 ± 65 mm Hg/sec ($P < 0.01$). Higher doses of bradykinin did not produce greater responses. The magnitude of the response was similar when the injection was performed in either the left anterior descending (change in mean arterial pressure 29 ± 3%) or circumflex (change in mean arterial pressure 27 ± 2%) coronary artery. The reflex nature of the response was proved by its disappearance after appropriate pharmacological blockades; moreover, after vagotomy, the pressor rise was maintained, the heart rate response was reduced (change in heart rate 10 ± 2%), and the inotropic response was enhanced (rate of change of left ventricular pressure 24 ± 3%). This suggested that the afferent pathway of the pressor reflex was in the sympathetic nerves and that a subordinate vagal depressor reflex was also operative. No pain reaction was obtained even when injecting very large amounts (1000–2000 ng/kg) of bradykinin, which, instead, induced arterial hypotension. Pain reactions (as inferred by agitation and vocalization) were observed in three out of nine dogs studied during the first week after surgery. This reaction was no longer present when the same animals were tested later on, at the time of complete recovery. In five of the nine dogs studied during the first week after surgery, the intracoronary injection of bradykinin produced a depressor (change in mean arterial pressure −31 ± 6%) response, which, however, reverted to a pressor effect (change in mean arterial pressure 22 ± 4%) later, when recovery was complete. In five additional dogs, the pressor response observed after full recovery from surgery was no longer present when the injection of bradykinin was repeated under anesthesia. The present experiments in conscious dogs show that the chemical stimulation of the fully innervated heart with intracoronary bradykinin can initiate pressor reflexes independent of pain and in the presence of intact buffering mechanisms. **(*Circ Res 56: 175–183, 1985*)**

BRADYKININ is a natural compound capable of exciting both vagal (Kaufman et al., 1980) and sympathetic (Uchida and Murao, 1974; Nishi et al., 1977; Baker et al., 1980; Lombardi et al., 1981) cardiac sensory endings. In anesthetized dogs, epicardial administration of bradykinin induced only excitatory reflex cardiovascular responses (Staszewska-Barczak et al., 1976; Staszewska-Barczak and Dusting, 1977) or either excitatory or inhibitory responses in sinoaortic denervated vagotomized dogs (Felder and Thames, 1982). On the other hand, intracoronary injections of bradykinin in anesthetized cats elicited either excitatory or inhibitory reflex responses, the former being mediated by cardiac sympathetic afferent fibers and the latter by cardiac vagal afferents (Reimann and Weaver, 1980; Lombardi et al., 1982).

It is likely that the differences in the "central excitatory state" (Sherrington, 1929) of various circuits, as affected by anesthesia and by the specific experimental conditions or animal model, might explain these contrasting observations.

Thus, the primary goal of this study in conscious dogs was to assess the effects of the simultaneous stimulation with bradykinin of the vagal and sympathetic sensory supply of the heart in the absence of anesthesia and recent surgery.

Next, we assessed the effects of anesthesia and recovery from surgery, as well as the effects of vagotomy on the observed responses.

Finally, we examined the effects of different pharmacological blockades on the hemodynamic responses to intracoronary bradykinin.

The results indicate that, in conscious dogs, the

intracoronary injection of bradykinin consistently initiates a dose-dependent pressor sympathetic reflex, requiring as the most crucial factor a full recovery from surgery. In the latter circumstances, signs of pain never accompanied the pressor reflex.

Methods

Under aseptic conditions and pentobarbital anesthesia (30 mg/kg, iv), 28 mongrel dogs of either sex (24–32 kg body weight) underwent thoracotomy in the 5th left intercostal space. A heparin-filled Tygon catheter was implanted in the descending thoracic aorta through a puncture and secured with a suture. In a first group of 25 dogs, after the pericardium had been opened, either the left anterior descending (eight dogs) or circumflex coronay artery (17 dogs) was carefully dissected 2–3 cm from its bifurcation so as to avoid any damage to the pericoronary nerves, and a small silicone (Dow Corning) catheter was implanted by the technique described by Herd and Barger (1964). In 14 of these dogs, a miniature pressure transducer (Konigsberg) was implanted within the left ventricle through a stab wound in the apex. In these dogs, a second Tygon catheter was implanted in the left atrium.

In a second group of three dogs, a pressure catheter was implanted in the aorta and a catheter for injections was positioned within the pericardial sac and secured with a purse string suture. After the thoracotomy had been sutured, the catheters and the wire were exteriorized at the base of the neck.

Recorded Variables

Aortic and left atrial pressures were measured with the catheters implanted in the aorta and the left atrium, respectively, using pressure transducers (Statham Instruments). Aortic mean pressure was obtained with an RC filter with a 2-second time constant. Left ventricular pressure was measured with the implanted miniature pressure gauge, which was calibrated statically in vitro and dynamically in vivo, using the left atrial and aortic pressures. The time derivative of left ventricular pressure (LVP) (i.e., dP/dt) was obtained from the LVP signal with an operational amplifier with a frequency response of 0.5–700 Hz.

A triangular signal with known slope was used to calibrate the differentiator. Heart rate was measured continuously with a cardiotachometer, triggered by the R wave of the ECG (lead II) obtained with an AC amplifier.

Data were recorded on a multichannel FM-type recorder (Racal Store 7) and played back on a direct writing recorder (Brush Gould).

Protocol

Experiments were performed 2–3 weeks postoperatively, when the dogs were apparently well and had recovered from the operation, as judged by their normal behavior, body temperature, and hematocrit. While the trained dogs were lying quietly on a recording table, aortic blood pressure, left ventricular pressure and dP/dt, and heart rate were recorded continuously before, during, and after the intracoronary injection of graded doses of bradykinin (BRS 640 Sandoz, molecular weight 1060.25). This substance was freshly prepared for every experiment, with normal saline. Doses injected were 10–300 ng/kg in a volume of 0.5–1.0 ml. In seven dogs, larger doses 1000–2000 ng/kg were also employed. To assess the role of incomplete recovery from surgery on animal responsiveness, we also studied nine dogs the first week postoperatively. As the animals during this period could easily exhibit life-threatening arrhythmias, they were studied only once, until complete recovery.

The role of anesthesia was assessed in a group of five dogs that were studied first after complete recovery from surgery, and, later, on a different day, under thiopental sodium anesthesia (20 mg/kg, iv, followed by booster doses 5 mg/kg, iv, every 30 minutes).

At the autopsy, the intracoronary position of the catheter, the patency of the coronary artery and the lack of infarction of the myocardium perfused by it were verified.

The role of the route of administration of bradykinin was assessed in a group of three conscious dogs with an intrapericardial catheter. In these animals, doses of bradykinin of 150–300 ng/kg (in 2–3 ml of saline) were injected through the implanted catheter, into the pericardial sac. After 5–10 minutes, the drug was washed away with repeated (3–4 times) injections and withdrawals of 20 ml of 37°C saline.

α-Adrenergic receptor-mediated responses were blocked with phentolamine, 1 mg/kg, iv; β-adrenergic receptor-mediated responses were blocked with propranolol 1 mg/kg, iv; and muscarinic receptor mediated responses were blocked with atropine 0.2 mg/kg, iv. The completeness of α-adrenergic receptor blockade was verified by the abolition of a pressure response to a test injection of 0.1–0.3 μg/kg norepinephrine, iv; β-adrenergic receptor blockade was verified by the lack of heart rate or dP/dt response to 0.08 μg/kg of iv isoproterenol. Muscarinic receptor blockade was verified by the lack of a further increase in heart rate following a booster dose of 0.1 mg/kg of iv atropine. Ganglionic transmission was blocked with trimethaphan (Arfonad, Roche) infused iv at a dose of 5–10 μg/kg per min.

To study the afferent limb of the reflex, we planned experiments in which the vagi were severed in the neck, thus leaving intact only the sympathetic portion of cardiac afferent innervation. To minimize the problems related to acute hypertension and respiratory depression that can follow vagotomy, this intervention was performed in two steps (Pagani et al., 1982). Thus, in five dogs under thiopental anesthesia (20 mg/kg, iv), the cervical vagi were moved to a subcutaneous position, and 3–5 days later, the response to intracoronary bradykinin was studied. Following this, under light transient thiopental sodium anesthesia (5–10 mg/kg, iv) and local infiltration with Xylocaine (Byk Gulden), both vagi were cut in the neck. The response to intracoronary bradykinin was again determined after a recovery period of 24–48 hours.

Statistics

The results are expressed as means ± SEM. Each individual animal underwent several (4–10) trials, the responses in each dog were calculated at their early peak, and the average was used to compute the group means. The significance of the responses to intracoronary bradykinin was assessed with the *t*-test for paired observations. One-way analysis of variance was used to assess the differences of responses obtained with and without pharmacological blockades, using the Scheffè test for multiple comparisons. Differences were considered significant with a *P* value <0.05 (Armitage, 1971).

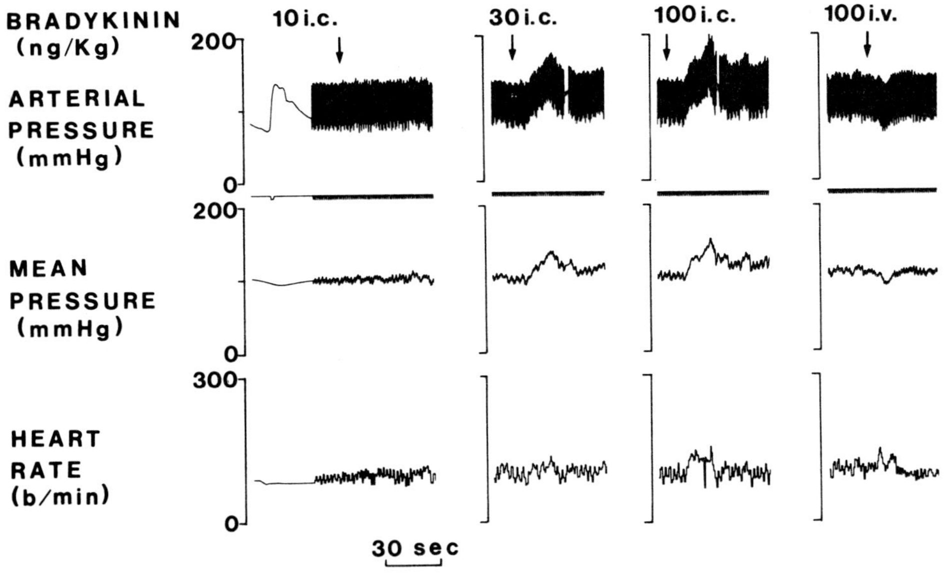

FIGURE 1. *Progressive pressor responses to graded injections of freshly prepared bradykinin into the cannulated circumflex coronary artery of a conscious dog. Note that hypotension and tachycardia are produced by intravenous injections (100 ng/kg, right panel).*

Results

In the conscious dog, the intracoronary (ic) injection of bradykinin at doses devoid of direct hemodynamic effects produced a cardiovascular reflex that was always pressor in nature. As shown in Figure 1, graded injections of bradykinin, in doses ranging from 10 to 100 ng/kg, into the circumflex coronary artery induced gradual increases in arterial pressure and heart rate. The pressor response begins 15 ± 1 seconds after the injection and reaches a peak in 26 ± 2 seconds, after which both pressure and heart rate slowly return to baseline levels.

Moreover, it is important to notice that pressor responses of the same magnitude were obtained from injections into either the left anterior descending or circumflex coronary artery. In fact, 100 ng/kg of bradykinin into the left anterior descending coronary artery ($n = 7$) increased mean arterial pressure 29 ± 3% from 86 ± 6 mm Hg and heart rate 31 ± 8% from 86 ± 2 beats/min, while a similar injection into the circumflex coronary artery ($n = 13$) increased mean arterial pressure 27 ± 2% from 92 ± 3 mm Hg and heart rate 31 ± 4% from 88 ± 2 beats/min. Hence, in the following sections of the paper, the results of the experiments will be presented together, irrespective of the specific site of the injection.

Dose-Response Analysis

As shown in Figure 2, a clear dose-response curve was detectable starting from a threshold dose of 10 ng/kg. With increasing doses of ic bradykinin, the response rose up to a maximum, which was obtained with 100 ng/kg, after which, even the use of greater doses produced no further increase in the response.

At the peak of the response to 100 ng/kg, the increase in mean arterial pressure was 28 ± 3% from 89 ± 4 mm Hg, in left ventricular pressure 20 ± 3% from 121 ± 2 mm Hg, in heart rate 30 ± 4% from 88 ± 5 beats/min, and in left ventricular dP/dt maximum 18 ± 3% from 2812 ± 65 mm Hg/sec.

It should be noticed that, when injected iv, the vasodilatory properties of the drug became apparent only with high doses. For instance, whereas 10 ng/kg was the approximate threshold dose for intracoronary effects, 100 ng/kg was the smallest dose which consistently caused a transient hypotension (−21 ± 2%) and tachycardia (41 ± 11%) when injected iv (Fig. 1).

During the experiments, the animals remained calm or somnolent on the recording table, and did not manifest any discernible pain reaction (vocalization, struggling) to the intracoronary injections of bradykinin; however, they could show an increase in depth of respiration.

Since the absence of a pain reaction was surprising (Guzman et al., 1962), we planned experiments to elicit behavioral reactions in a limited number of animals. In seven dogs, we injected very large amounts of bradykinin into the cannulated coronary artery (1000–2000 ng/kg) to excite the afferent fibers from the corresponding area of myocardium maximally. Even with this dose, no reaction was observed which could be attributed to pain, whereas the vasodilatory action of the drug induced hypotension (−38 ± 3%) and tachycardia (47 ± 8%).

Effects of Recovery from Surgery

In a second series of experiments, we injected bradykinin into the coronary bed of nine dogs during the first week after surgery, hence, before a complete recovery. Five of these dogs exhibited an early depressor response (Fig. 3, III day) which reverted to the usual pressor effect at a time of complete recovery from surgery (Fig. 3, XX day; Table 1).

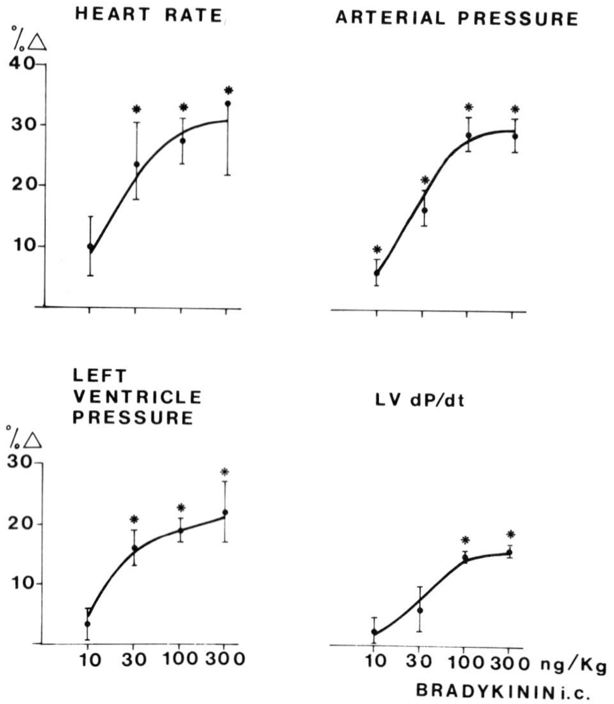

FIGURE 2. *Dose-response analysis of the hemodynamic effects of intracoronary injections of bradykinin in conscious dogs. Doses of bradykinin are in ng/kg, hemodynamic responses are indicated as % change from control.*

Out of the nine dogs, three animals exhibited vocalization and agitation, suggesting a pain reaction, in response to the bradykinin injection performed during the first week after surgery: this reaction was no longer present when the animals were tested during the course of the third week. The presumable pain reactions were accompanied in two cases by hypertension and tachycardia, and in one case by hypotension and bradycardia (Fig. 3, III day).

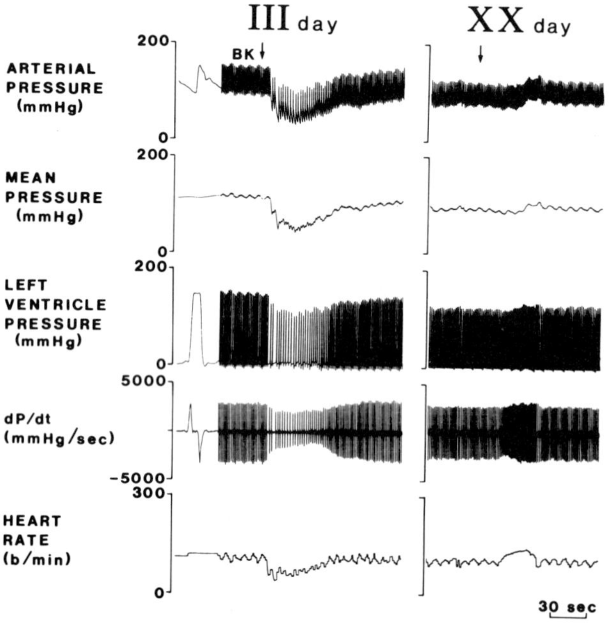

FIGURE 3. *Contrasting effects of intracoronary bradykinin (100 ng/kg) in a conscious dog when examined early (left panel) and late after surgery (right panel). Note that while a depressor response was obtained in the III day postoperatively, it reverted to a pressor one at the time of complete recovery from surgery (XX day postoperatively).*

Effects of Anesthesia

The acute effects of barbiturate anesthesia were tested in a group of five animals by comparing the hemodynamic response to ic bradykinin obtained in the conscious state, after full recovery from surgery, with that observed, in a following day, under anesthesia (see Methods). Thus, the pressor (20 ± 4% from 96 ± 7 mm Hg) and heart rate response (28 ± 4% from 90 ± 3 b/min) were drastically reduced in the anesthetized state, as mean arterial pressure was no longer significantly increased by ic bradykinin (8 ± 6% from 98 ± 8 mm Hg) and the tachycardia response was reduced (9 ± 2% from 138 ± 8 beats/min).

Effects of Various Blockades (Table 2, Fig. 4)

α-Adrenergic receptor blockade with phentolamine (1 mg/kg, iv) reduced mean arterial pressure to 77 ± 3 mm Hg and increased heart rate to 139 ± 11 beats/min and left ventricular dP/dt to 3016 ± 291 mm Hg/sec. Under these conditions, the pressor response to ic bradykinin (100 ng/kg) was virtually abolished, while the heart rate response was preserved and the increase in left ventricular dP/dt was slightly enhanced.

The increase in heart rate was reduced either by β-adrenergic receptor blockade with propranolol (1 mg/kg, iv) or by muscarinic blockade with atropine (0.2 mg/kg, iv) and was abolished by their combination, while the pressor response was preserved. The dP/dt response was abolished by β-adrenergic receptor blockade. In a group of four conscious dogs, the effects of intracoronary bradykinin were tested during ganglionic transmission blockade obtained with an infusion of trimethaphan 5–10 μg/kg/min, iv. Under these conditions (Fig. 4; Table 2), the pressor and heart rate response was no longer observed.

Effects of Intrapericardial Bradykinin

In a group of three conscious dogs, we obtained a consistent pressor (20 ± 5% from 97 ± 8 mm Hg) and heart rate response (18 ± 2% from 113 ± 7 beats/min) when injecting bradykinin (150–300 ng/kg) into the pericardial sac. This response was maintained for periods of 5–10 minutes until the injected bradykinin was washed from the pericardial sac with warm saline.

Effects of Vagotomy

The role of the vagi was assessed in five animals in which the effects of intracoronary bradykinin was examined before and 1–3 days after vagotomy.

As shown in Figure 5, the pressor response was

TABLE 1
Contrasting Effects of Intracoronary Bradykinin (100 ng/kg) in Five Conscious Dogs when Examined Early and Late in the Postoperative Period

	Mean arterial pressure (mm Hg)	Left ventricle pressure (mm Hg)	Left ventricle dP/dt (mm Hg/sec)	Heart rate (beats/min)
Early response				
Control	87 ± 3	118 ± 10	2115 ± 220	96 ± 8
%Δ	−31 ± 6*	−16 ± 3*	−17 ± 4*	−34 ± 9*
Late response				
Control	85 ± 5	109 ± 3	3119 ± 404	93 ± 4
%Δ	22 ± 4*†	11 ± 2*†	17 ± 2*†	49 ± 9*†

* Results are expressed as mean ± SEM. Note that the depressor response observed in these animals during the first week after surgery reverted to a pressor one, later, at the time of complete recovery.
* Significantly different from control ($P < 0.05$).
† Early response significantly different from late response ($P < 0.05$).

essentially unmodified by vagotomy: mean arterial pressure increased 23 ± 1% from 98 ± 4 mm Hg before vagotomy and 20 ± 1% from 88 ± 3 mm Hg after vagotomy. The heart rate response was reduced: 25 ± 4% from 90 ± 4 beats/min before vagotomy and 10 ± 2% from 120 ± 1 beats/min after vagotomy. Finally, the increase in left ventricular dP/dt maximum was enhanced: 13 ± 2% from 2547 ± 308 mm Hg/sec before vagotomy and 24 ± 3% from 2728 ± 271 mm Hg/sec after vagotomy.

TABLE 2
Effects of Various Blockades on the Reflex Response to Intracoronary Bradykinin in Conscious Dogs

	Mean arterial pressure (mm Hg)	Left ventricle pressure (mm Hg)	Left ventricle dP/dt (mm Hg/sec)	Heart rate (beats/min)
Control				
Baseline	89 ± 4	121 ± 2	2812 ± 65	88 ± 5
%Δ	28 ± 3*	20 ± 3*‡	18 ± 3*‡	30 ± 4*
$n = 20$				
α-Blockade				
Baseline	77 ± 3	106 ± 2	3016 ± 291	139 ± 11
%Δ	−5 ± 3†	−1 ± 5†	22 ± 6*	17 ± 3*
$n = 6$				
β-Blockade				
Baseline	94 ± 5	125 ± 5	2199 ± 197	86 ± 2
%Δ	19 ± 2*	15 ± 1*	4 ± 3†	11 ± 2*†
$n = 5$				
Muscarinic blockade				
Baseline	93 ± 6	116 ± 7	2890 ± 234	168 ± 7
%Δ	21 ± 4*	17 ± 3*	16 ± 4*	9 ± 2*†
$n = 7$				
β-plus muscarinic block				
Baseline	98 ± 8	123 ± 11	2385 ± 286	125 ± 3
%Δ	16 ± 3*†	13 ± 3†	4 ± 2†	1 ± 4†
$n = 5$				
Ganglionic blockade				
Baseline	61 ± 9	85 ± 10	2675 ± 395	126 ± 6
%Δ	−2 ± 2†	−3 ± 3†	−5 ± 5†	1 ± 2†
$n = 4$				

* Significantly different from control ($P < 0.05$).
† Significantly different from control response ($P < 0.05$).
‡ $n = 4$.

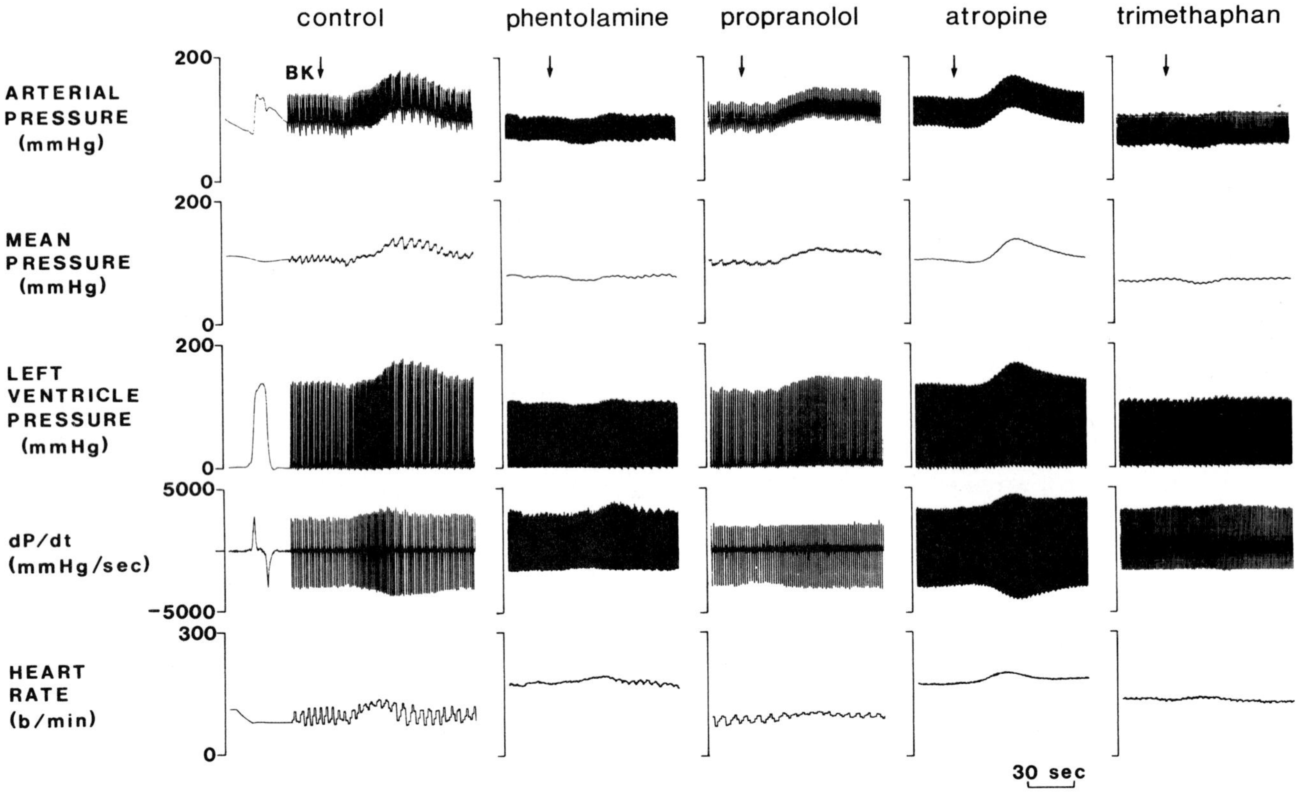

FIGURE 4. *Hemodynamic effects of intracoronary bradykinin in a conscious dog in control conditions and during various autonomic blockades. Injections (100 ng/kg), indicated by the arrow, are performed in separate days.*

Discussion

In the conscious dog, the chemical stimulation with bradykinin of the sensory supply of the heart elicits a pressor sympathetic reflex characterized by a rise in arterial blood pressure, in left ventricular pressure and dP/dt, and in heart rate. When the animals were studied after full recovery from surgery, the pressor response was constantly obtained, in absence of any pain reaction. After vagotomy, a similar pressor reflex could still be elicited and its inotropic component was even enhanced.

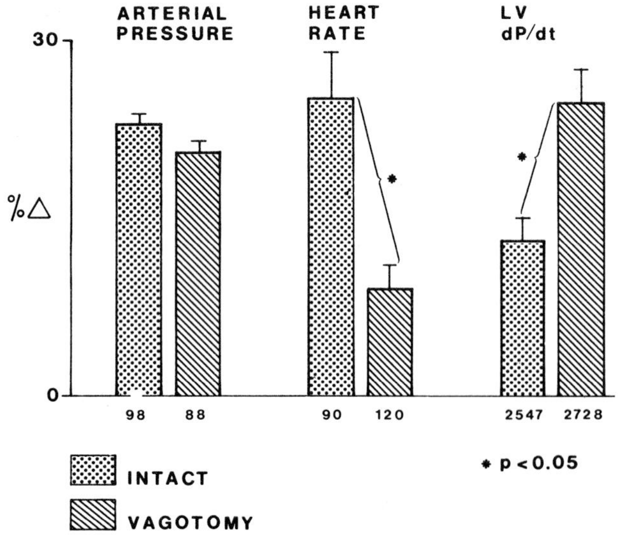

FIGURE 5. *Comparison of the effects of intracoronary bradykinin (100 ng/kg) in five conscious dogs before and after vagotomy. Note the greater inotropic and smaller chronotropic responses after vagotomy. Control values before injections are shown at the base of the bars.*

Reflex Nature of the Response

The reflex nature of the response to the ic injection of bradykinin was proved by its disappearance after appropriate pharmacological blockades. Pretreatment with phentolamine, which blocks α-adrenergic receptor-mediated responses, abolished the rise in arterial pressure, while maintaining the increase in heart rate and left ventricular dP/dt. Pretreatment with propranolol, which blocks β-adrenergic receptor-mediated responses, maintained the pressor, reduced the heart rate, and abolished the inotropic response to ic bradykinin.

Muscarinic receptor blockade drastically reduced the heart rate response, while sparing the increase in arterial pressure and in left ventricular dP/dt. As already pointed out (Pagani et al., 1982), it is difficult to ascertain the relative contribution of an efferent sympathetic excitation and of a parasympathetic withdrawal in determining the tachycardia component of an excitatory reflex in the intact conscious animal. Apart from the complexity of the interaction between vagal and sympathetic neurotransmitters

(Levy, 1971; Vatner et al., 1979), it has been proved that the ic bradykinin, being capable of exciting vagal (Kaufman et al., 1980) and sympathetic (Uchida and Murao, 1974; Nishi et al., 1977; Baker et al., 1980; Lombardi et al., 1981) cardiac sensory endings, can simultaneously activate reflexes mediated by cardiac vagal and sympathetic afferent fibers (Reimann and Weaver, 1980; Felder and Thames, 1982; Lombardi et al., 1982). In terms of neural circuits, this corresponds, at the very least, to vago-vagal, vago-sympathetic, sympatho-sympathetic and sympatho-vagal reflexes (Malliani, 1982), in addition to possible baroreceptive modulatory influences. An additional complication in interpreting the results following atropine administration consists of the fact that, in such experimental conditions, the baseline heart rate is greatly elevated and, hence, it might be difficult for it to increase further. Yet a small heart rate response to intracoronary bradykinin could still be observed during muscarinic blockade, together with a significant increase in arterial blood pressure and myocardial contractility.

The absence of hemodynamic effects of ic injections of bradykinin during ganglionic blockade gives greater support to the conclusion that the observed responses are reflex in nature and are not dependent upon direct effects of bradykinin on the efferent nerve endings or on the myocardium.

As to the afferent limb of the reflex, the observation that the pressor, the heart rate, and the inotropic responses were maintained after vagotomy, i.e., when the only innervation to and from the heart is via the sympathetic nerves, strongly suggests that the afferent pathway is in the sympathetic nerves (Coleridge and Coleridge, 1979). This contention is supported by recent experiments in anesthetized cats by Lombardi et al. (1982) showing that the afferent pathway of the excitatory reflexes that are initiated by ic bradykinin after vagotomy is via the cardiac sympathetic afferents, as it is abolished by sympathetic deafferentation. Moreover, excitatory reflexes mediated by cardiac sympathetic afferent fibers have been described in acute (Malliani et al., 1969, 1972, 1973; Brown and Malliani, 1971; Peterson and Brown, 1971) and chronic conditions (Barron and Bishop, 1982) in the absence of functioning vagi.

Finally, it should be pointed out that our results are not in contrast with experiments showing cardio-cardiac depressor reflexes mediated by the vagi, induced by injections of veratridine in the coronary artery (Barron and Bishop, 1982) or by coronary artery occlusion (Peterson and Bishop, 1974) in conscious dogs. Indeed, the present study suggests the operation of a subordinate vagal depressor reflex, modulating the inotropic response. This modulation might well occur at the level of spinal interneurones, as the excitation of spinothalamic cells induced by sympathetic afferent activation from the heart is depressed by the stimulation of afferent vagal fibers (Ammons et al., 1983).

Adequacy of the Stimulus

Although it has been proved that bradykinin is released into the coronary venous blood during experimental myocardial ischemia (Kimura et al., 1973) and that doses of comparable magnitude administered ic can excite cardiac sympathetic sensory endings (Lombardi et al., 1981), admittedly, the abrupt stimulation used in the present experiments cannot be considered as duplicating a natural pathophysiological condition.

However, our specific purpose was to analyze, in the conscious state, the result of the simultaneous stimulation of vagal and sympathetic cardiac afferent fibers, and to explore the mechanisms underlying the prevailing type of the reflex response, i.e., inhibitory or excitatory.

The results showed that fundamental differences characterize the anesthetized and the conscious state. In fact, ic administration of bradykinin in anesthetized animals elicits either pressor or depressor reflexes (Staszewska-Barczak et al., 1976; Staszewska-Barczak and Dusting, 1977; Reimann and Weaver, 1980; Felder and Thames, 1982; Lombardi et al., 1982). The inhibitory reflexes have been interpreted as mediated by cardiac vagal (Reimann and Weaver, 1980; Lombardi et al., 1982) or by cardiac sympathetic afferent fibers (Felder and Thames, 1982).

In the experiments on conscious dogs reported here, only pressor responses were observed. However, an inhibitory response was elicited in a small group of animals during the early phase of their recovery from the operation: response which reverted to a pressor one, in the same animals, later, when the recovery from surgery was complete. Moreover, the importance of anesthesia in altering the normal cardiovascular control mechanisms (Vatner and Braunwald, 1975) is further emphasized by the near abolition during anesthesia of the pressor response to ic bradykinin. Hence, it would appear that the acute effects of anesthesia and recent surgery emphasize the efficacy of depressor reflexes. These alterations in responsiveness might be less important in other species, such as the cat, where excitatory cardio-cardiac reflexes may be easier to obtain, even during anesthesia.

Finally, it should be pointed out that no differences were noticed, whether the drug was injected into the left anterior descending or circumflex coronary artery, an observation which is in keeping with data obtained in conscious animals subjected to either anterior or posterior experimental myocardial infarction (Karlsberg et al., 1979) but which does not parallel the preferential ventricular distribution of sources for inhibitory or excitatory reflexes described on anesthetized dogs (Walker et al., 1978). However, the pathophysiology of the hyperacute phases of myocardial infarction indicate that a hemodynamic picture suggestive of a depressor reflex is more commonly associated with inferior wall infarcts, whereas pressor reflexes are more commonly observed during anterior wall infarcts, (Webb et al., 1972; Pantridge, 1978). Although it is difficult to compare the reflex effects of the chemical stimulation of the intact heart with those observed in the course of acute experimental ischemia (Peterson and Bishop, 1974), one could suggest that, from the healthy heart, the prevalence of excitatory reflex mechanisms initiated by intracoronary bradykinin might be capable of masking possible opposite influences.

Excitatory Reflexes and Pain

The evidence against the possibility that pain, as a conscious experience, contributed to the pressor reflexes observed is 3-fold. First, dose-response curves were obtained, indicating a progressive buildup of excitation. Second, behavioral changes indicating a pain reaction were never observed. Third, in the few instances in which a pain reaction was obtained during recovery from surgery, it could be associated with either a pressor or depressor response, as in the case of Figure 5. In short, the simple coupling between hypertension and pseudoaffective reactions (Woodsworth and Sherrington, 1904) may not apply to the complexity of the conscious state. On the other hand, in previous experiments, we had already observed that an intense stimulation of aortic sympathetic mechanoreceptors leading to pressor reflexes was not associated with pain reactions (Pagani et al., 1982).

Moreover, our observations, whatever may be the peripheral algogenic neural code from the heart (Malliani and Lombardi, 1982; Malliani et al., 1984), seem to refute the existence of specific cardiac nociceptors (Baker et al., 1980). In such a case, we should have confirmed the findings by Guzman et al. (1962), obtained on animals recovering from surgery and anesthesia, indicating a constant relationship between intracoronary bradykinin administration and pain reactions.

Pathophysiological Implications

It has been increasingly recognized that electrocardiographic changes typical of ischemic episodes can occur in concomitance of (1) increases in arterial pressure and heart rate (Lewis, 1931; Roughgarden, 1966; Guazzi et al., 1971, 1975; Littler et al., 1973; Maseri et al., 1978; Figueras et al., 1979; Chierchia et al., 1980), (2) decreases in arterial pressure and rises in heart rate (Guazzi et al., 1971, 1975; Maseri et al., 1978), (3) decreases in arterial pressure and in heart rate (Guazzi et al., 1971). In each of these cases, hemodynamic and electrocardiographic alterations can precede pain or occur in the absence of it. These circulatory changes suggest a various participation of pressor, depressor, and baroreceptive reflex mechanisms (Peterson and Bishop, 1974) associated with the direct striking depressing effects of ischemia on ventricular function (Pagani et al., 1978).

The present experiments in dogs, in which the depressant action of ischemia was avoided, show the potentiality of pressor reflexes arising from the intact heart and how they can manifest, in the conscious state, independently of pain and in the presence of functioning buffer mechanisms.

We wish to thank U. Boccaccini for his technical help and Y. Stewart for typing the manuscript.

Address for reprints: Dr. Massimo Pagani, Istituto Ricerche Cardiovascolari, Via Bonfadini 214, 20138 Milano, Italy.

Received November 28, 1983; accepted for publication October 3, 1984.

References

Ammons SN, Blair RW, Foreman RD (1983) Vagal afferent inhibition of spinothalamic cell responses to sympathetic afferents and bradykinin in the monkey. Circ Res **53:** 603–612

Armitage P (1971) Statistical Methods in Medical Research. Oxford, Blackwell

Aviado DM Jr, Schmidt CF (1955) Reflexes from stretch receptors in blood vessels, heart and lungs. Physiol Rev **35:** 247–300

Bainbridge FA (1915) The influence of venous filling upon the rate of the heart. J Physiol (Lond) **50:** 65–84

Baker DG, Coleridge HM, Coleridge JCG, Nerdrum T (1980) Search for a cardiac nociceptor: Stimulation by bradykinin of sympathetic afferent nerve endings in the heart of the cat. J Physiol (Lond) **306:** 519–536

Barron KW, Bishop VS (1981) The influence of vagal afferents on the left ventricular contractile response to intracoronary administration of catecholamines in the conscious dog. Circ Res **49:** 159–169

Barron KW, Bishop VS (1982) Reflex cardiovascular changes with veratridine in the conscious dog. Am J Physiol **242:** H810–H817

Bezold A von, Hirt L (1867) Uber die physiologischen Wirkungen des essigsauren Veratrins. Untersuch Physiol Lab Würzburg **1:** 73–156

Bishop VS, Lombardi F, Malliani A, Pagani M, Recordati G (1976) Reflex sympathetic tachycardia during intravenous infusions in chronic spinal cats. Am J Physiol **230:** 25–29

Brown AM, Malliani A (1971) Spinal sympathetic reflexes initiated by coronary receptors. J Physiol (Lond) **212:** 685–705

Chierchia S, Brunelli C, Simonetti I, Lazzari M, Maseri A (1980) Sequence of events in angina at rest: Primary reduction in coronary flow. Circulation **61:** 759–768

Coleridge JCG, Coleridge HM (1979) Chemoreflex regulation of the heart. *In* Handbook of Physiology 2, The Cardiovascular System, Vol 1, The Heart, edited by RM Berne, N Sperelakis, SR Geiger. Washington, D.C., American Physiological Society, pp 653–676

Costantin LR (1963) Extracardiac factors contributing to hypotension during coronary occlusion. Am J Cardiol **11:** 205–217

Cyon E, Ludwig C (1866) Die Reflexe eines der sensiblen Nerven des Herzen auf die motorischen der Blutefässe. Ber Sächs Ges (Akad) Wiss **18:** 307–328

De Waele D, Van de Velde J (1940) Sur un réflexe hypertenseur des oreillettes. Arch Int Physiol **50:** 33–53

Felder RB, Thames MD (1979) Interaction between cardiac receptors and sinoartic baroreceptors in the control of efferent cardiac sympathetic nerve activity during myocardial ischemia in dogs. Circ Res **45:** 728–736

Felder RB, Thames MD (1981) The cardiocardiac sympathetic reflex during coronary occlusion in anesthetized dogs. Circ Res **48:** 685–692

Felder RB, Thames MD (1982) Responses to activation of cardiac sympathetic afferents with epicardial bradykinin. Am J Physiol **242:** H148–H153

Figueras J, Singh BN, Ganz W, Charuzi Y, Swan HJC (1979)

Mechanism of rest and nocturnal angina: observations during continuous hemodynamic and electrocardiographic monitoring. Circulation **59:** 955–968
Guazzi M, Polese A, Fiorentini C, Magrini F, Bartorelli C (1971) Left ventricular performance and related haemodynamic changes in Prinzmetal's variant angina pectoris. Br Heart J **33:** 84–94
Guazzi M, Polese A, Fiorentini C, Magrini F, Olivari MT, Bartorelli C (1975) Left and right heart haemodynamics during spontaneous angina pectoris. Comparison between angina with ST segment depression and angina with ST segment elevation. Br Heart J **37:** 401–413
Guzman F, Braun C, Lim RKS (1962) Visceral pain and the pseudoaffective response to intra-arterial injection of bradykinin and other algesic agents. Arch Int Pharmacodyn **136:** 353–384
Herd JA, Barger AC (1964) Simplified technique for chronic catheterization of blood vessels. J Appl Physiol **19:** 791–792
Karlsberg RP, Penkoske PA, Cryer PE, Corr PB, Roberts R (1979) Rapid activation of the sympathetic nervous system following coronary artery occlusion: relationship to infarct size, site, and haemodynamic impact. Cardiovasc Res **13:** 523–531
Kaufman MP, Baker BG, Coleridge HM, Coleridge JCG (1980) Stimulation by bradykinin of afferent vagal C-fibers with chemosensitive endings in the heart and aorta of the dog. Circ Res **46:** 476–484
Kimura E, Hashimoto K, Furukawa S, Hayakawa H (1973) Changes in bradykinin level in coronary sinus blood after the experimental occlusion of a coronary artery. Am Heart J **85:** 635–647
Langley JN (1903) The autonomic nervous system. Brain **26:** 1–26
Levy MN (1971) Sympathetic-Parasympathetic interactions in the heart. Circ Res **29:** 437–445
Lewis T (1931) Angina pectoris associated with high blood pressure and its relief by amyl nitrite; with a note on Nothnagel's syndrome. Heart **15:** 305–327
Linden RJ (1973) Function of cardiac receptors. Circulation **48:** 463–480
Littler WA, Honour J, Sleight P, Stott FD (1973) Direct arterial pressure and electrocardiogram in unrestricted patients with angina pectoris. Circulation **48:** 125–134
Lombardi F, Della Bella P, Casati R, Malliani A (1981) Effects of intracoronary administration of bradykinin on the impulse activity of afferent sympathetic unmyelinated fibers with left ventricular endings in the cat. Circ Res **48:** 69–75
Lombardi F, Patton CP, Della Bella P, Pagani M, Malliani A (1982) Cardiovascular and sympathetic responses reflexly elicited through the excitation with bradykinin of sympathetic and vagal cardiac sensory endings in the cat. Cardiovasc Res **16:** 57–65
Lombardi F, Casalone C, Della Bella P, Malfatto G, Pagani M, Malliani A (1984) Global versus regional myocardial ischaemia: differences in cardiovascular and sympathetic responses in cats. Cardiovasc Res **18:** 14–23
Malliani A (1982) Cardiovascular sympathetic afferent fibers. Rev Physiol Biochem Pharmacol **94:** 11–74
Malliani A, Lombardi F (1982) Considerations of the fundamental mechanisms eliciting cardiac pain. Am Heart J **103:** 575–578
Malliani A, Schwartz PJ, Zanchetti A (1969) A sympathetic reflex elicited by experimental coronary occlusion. Am J Physiol **217:** 703–709
Malliani A, Peterson FD, Bishop VS, Brown AM (1972) Spinal sympathetic cardiocardiac reflexes. Circ Res **30:** 158–166
Malliani A, Parks M, Tuckett RP, Brown AM (1973) Reflex increases in heart rate elicited by stimulation of afferent cardiac sympathetic nerve fibers in the cat. Circ Res **32:** 9–14
Malliani A, Pagani M, Lombardi F (1984) Visceral versus somatic mechanisms. *In* Textbook of Pain, edited by Wall and Melzack. Edinburgh, Churchill-Livingstone, pp 100–109
Maseri A, Severi S, De Nes M, L'Abbate A, Chierchia S, Marzilli M, Ballestra AM, Parodi O, Biagini A, Distante A (1978) Variant angina: One aspect of a continuous spectrum of vasospastic myocardial ischemia. Am J Cardiol **42:** 1019–1035
Nishi K, Sakanashi M, Takenaka F (1977) Activation of afferent cardiac sympathetic nerve fibers of the cat by pain producing substances and noxious heat. Pflugers Arch **372:** 53–61
Pagani M, Schwartz PJ, Banks R, Lombardi F, Malliani A (1974) Reflex responses of sympathetic preganglionic neurons initiated by different cardiovascular receptors in spinal animals. Brain Res **68:** 215–225
Pagani M, Vatner SF, Baig H, Braunwald E (1978) Initial myocardial adjustments to brief periods of ischemia and reperfusion in the conscious dog. Circ Res **43:** 83–92
Pagani M, Pizzinelli P, Furlan R, Guzzetti S, Rimoldi O, Malliani A (1981) A sympathetic hypertensive reflex from the heart of conscious dogs. Clin Sci **61:** 181s–183s
Pagani M, Pizzinelli P, Bergamaschi M, Malliani A (1982) A positive feedback sympathetic pressor reflex during stretch of the thoracic aorta in conscious dogs. Circ Res **50:** 125–132
Pantridge JF (1978) Autonomic disturbance at the onset of acute myocardial infarction. *In* Neural Mechanisms in Cardiac Arrhythmias, edited by PJ Schwartz, AM Brown, A Malliani, A. Zanchetti. New York, Raven Press, pp 7–17
Peterson DF, Brown AM (1971) Pressor reflexes produced by stimulation of afferent cardiac nerve fibers in the cardiac sympathetic nerves of the cat. Circ Res **28:** 605–610
Peterson DF, Bishop VS (1974) Reflex blood pressure control during acute myocardial ischemia in the conscious dog. Circ Res **34:** 226–232
Reimann KA, Weaver LC (1980) Contrasting reflexes evoked by chemical activation of cardiac afferent nerves. Am J Physiol **239:** H316–H325
Roughgarden JW (1966) Circulatory changes associated with spontaneous angina pectoris. Am J Med **41:** 947–961
Sherrington CS (1929) Some functional problems attaching to convergence. Proc R Soc Lond [Biol] **105B:** 332–362
Staszewska-Barczak J, Dusting GJ (1977) Sympathetic cardiovascular reflex initiated by bradykinin-induced stimulation of cardiac pain receptors in the dog. Clin Exp Pharmacol Physiol **4:** 443–452
Staszewska-Barczak J, Ferreira SH, Vane JR (1976) An excitatory nociceptive cardiac reflex elicited by bradykinin and potentiated by prostaglandins and myocardial ischaemia. Cardiovasc Res **10:** 314–327
Taquini AC, Aviado DM (1961) Reflex stimulation of heart induced by partial occlusion of pulmonary artery. Am J Physiol **200:** 647–650
Uchida Y, Murao S (1974) Bradykinin-induced excitation of afferent cardiac sympathetic nerve fibers. Jpn Heart J **15:** 84–91
Vatner SF, Braunwald E (1975) Cardiovascular control mechanisms in the conscious state. N Engl J Med **293:** 970–976
Vatner SF, Rutherford JD, Ochs HR (1979) Baroreflex and vagal mechanisms modulating left ventricular contractile responses to sympathomimetic amines in conscious dogs. Circ Res **44:** 195–207
Walker JL, Thames MD, Abboud FM, Mark AL, Klopfenstein HS (1978) Preferential distribution of inhibitory cardiac receptors in left ventricle of the dog. Am J Physiol **235:** H188–H192
Webb SW, Adgey AA, Pantridge JF (1972) Autonomic disturbance at onset of acute myocardial infarction. Br Med J **3:** 89–92
White JC (1957) Cardiac Pain. Anatomic pathways and physiologic mechanisms. Circulation **16:** 644–655
Woodsworth RS, Sherrington CS (1904) A pseudoaffective reflex and its spinal path. J Physiol (Lond) **31:** 234–243

INDEX TERMS: Sympathetic afferents • Vagal afferents • Pressor reflexes • Cardiac pain • Conscious dogs

Possible Mechanisms of Ventricular Arrhythmias Elicited by Ischemia followed by Reperfusion

Studies on Isolated Canine Ventricular Tissues

Gregory R. Ferrier, Margaret P. Moffat, and Anton Lukas
From the Department of Pharmacology, Dalhousie University, Halifax, Canada

SUMMARY. The purpose of this study was to develop an isolated tissue model in which arrhythmic activity could be generated in response to conditions encountered in ischemia followed by reperfusion, and in which intracellular recordings could be used to identify and study arrhythmogenic mechanisms. Isolated canine Purkinje fiber-papillary muscle preparations were superfused with modified Tyrode's solutions. Tissues were exposed to conditions observed in ischemia (hypoxia, acidosis, elevated lactate, zero substrate for 40 minutes). Superfusion with Tyrode's solution of "normal" composition was then reinstituted. Transmembrane recordings from Purkinje and muscle tissues were made, using standard microelectrode techniques. Ischemic conditions caused loss of membrane potential, shortened action potentials, depressed excitability, and progressive bidirectional conduction block between muscle and Purkinje tissues. Spontaneous activity, probably reentrant in origin, was observed. Return to nonischemic conditions resulted in a multiphasic sequence of responses in Purkinje fibers: prompt hyperpolarization, progressive depolarization to unresponsiveness, and final repolarization to control. The depolarization phase was accompanied by oscillatory afterpotentials which initiated extrasystoles. Final repolarization included a phase of automaticity at low membrane potentials, during which Purkinje tissue functioned as a parasystolic focus. Elevation of potassium concentration to 10 mM during the ischemic period did not alter the sequence of electrophysiological events during ischemic conditions or upon reperfusion. This study demonstrates that ischemia followed by reperfusion elicits an orderly sequence of electrophysiological events which may constitute important mechanisms of arrhythmia in vivo. **(*Circ Res 56: 184–194, 1985*)**

CORONARY ligation in the dog leads to arrhythmias with early and late phases (Tennant and Wiggers, 1935; Harris and Rojas, 1943; Harris, 1950). However, reperfusion of previously ischemic myocardium also leads to a rapid increase in arrhythmias including ventricular fibrillation (Harris and Rojas, 1943; Harris, 1950). Mechanisms of arrhythmias during the two periods may differ (Corbalan, 1976). Arrhythmias during the early phase following coronary ligation may be caused by reentry (Lazzara et al., 1978). However, injury currents at the junction of ischemic and normal tissues also may enhance automaticity during this phase (Janse et al., 1980). Arrhythmias in response to reperfusion may involve enhanced automaticity, possibly in addition to reentry (Penkoske et al., 1978; Murdock et al., 1980; Kaplinsky et al., 1981). Possible mechanisms of automaticity include phase 4 depolarization characteristic of ventricular Purkinje fibers, or abnormal mechanisms such as oscillatory afterpotentials (delayed afterdepolarizations) or depolarization-induced automaticity (early afterdepolarizations).

The purpose of this study was to develop an in vitro model in which arrhythmic activity could be generated in response to ischemia and reperfusion, and in which intracellular recordings could be utilized to differentiate between the mechanisms. We studied the endocardial aspect of ventricular preparations because both muscle and Purkinje tissues are accessible and because all, except the most superficial layers of large bundles of Purkinje fibers, may be subjected to adverse conditions in response to ischemic episodes in vivo (Lazzara et al., 1974). Also, we wished to study effects of ischemia and reperfusion on conduction across the Purkinje-myocardial junction. A preliminary report of this work has been published in abstract form (Ferrier, 1983).

Methods

Experiments were performed on cardiac tissues excised from adult mongrel dogs (15–20 kg) of either sex. Hearts were rapidly removed from animals anesthetized with sodium pentobarbital (30–35 mg/kg, iv). The hearts were fibrillated electrically, and papillary muscles with attached branches of the specialized conducting system (false tendons) were excised from either ventricle and mounted in a tissue bath for study. The tissues were superfused with a modified Tyrode's solution which was equilibrated with a 95% O_2/5% CO_2 gas mixture and maintained at 37°C.

Stimulation was accomplished through bipolar silver electrodes which were applied either to the false tendon or to the apex of the papillary muscle. Stimuli were rectangular pulses, 3 msec in duration, and were 1.5 times the threshold voltage. Pulses were obtained by an optically isolated digital stimulator (Pulsar 4I and 6I, Frederick Haer and Co.). Preparations were stimulated with patterns of stimulation consisting of trains of 10 or 15 pulses followed by 3-second pauses. The basic cycle length (BCL) was usually 500 msec, but could be varied, so that we might study effects on subsequent activity in the pause.

Transmembrane activity was recorded at two sites, using glass microelectrodes filled with 2.7 M KCl (resistance 15–30 MΩ). One microelectrode was impaled in the free-running segment of a false tendon, the other was usually impaled in a muscle fiber in the apical one-third of the papillary muscle. The microelectrode recordings and record of stimulus pattern were displayed on an oscilloscope (Tektronix 5110) and photographed with a Grass camera.

The experimental protocol included an initial equilibration period of 1–2 hours, during which the tissues were superfused with control Tyrode's solution with the following millimolar composition: NaCl, 129.0; KCl, 4.0; NaH_2PO_4, 0.9; $NaHCO_3$, 20.0; $CaCl_2$, 2.5; $MgSO_4$, 0.5; and dextrose, 5.5. The pH was 7.4 when the solution was gassed with 95% O_2/5% CO_2 and warmed to 37°C. After equilibration, control activity was recorded. The preparations then were superfused for 40 minutes with Tyrode's solution with a composition which had been further modified to mimic several of the conditions occurring in ischemia (Elharrar and Zipes, 1977). The millimolar composition of the "ischemic" Tyrode's solution was: NaCl, 123.0; KCl, 4.0: NaH_2PO_4, 0.9; $NaHCO_3$, 6.0; $CaCl_2$, 2.5; $MgSO_4$, 0.5; and sodium lactate, 20.0. This solution was gassed with 95% N_2/5% CO_2, resulting in a final Po_2 of 48 mm Hg measured in the tissue bath. The pH of the solution at 37°C was 6.8. Thus, the test solution mimicked hypoxia, acidosis, lactate accumulation, and substrate deprivation. In one series of six experiments, the effects of elevating the concentration of potassium during the "ischemic" period were studied. In those experiments, the concentration of KCl was 10 mM. This potassium concentration was selected to correspond to the mean plateau level reported by Hill and Gettes (1980) for extracellular myocardial potassium levels during coronary occlusion. In all experiments, the preparations were exposed to test solution for 40 minutes. Superfusion with control Tyrode's solution was then reinstated, and the effects were monitored for 1 hour. Control and test solutions were delivered to the tissue chamber via separate conduits at a flow rate of 10 ml/min. The bath volume was 10 ml. Thus, transition from one solution to another was rapid, although not instantaneous.

Results

The effects of exposing false tendon-papillary muscle preparations to conditions of ischemia followed by reperfusion proved to be complex but reproducible. Description of these effects is facilitated by considering periods of ischemia and reperfusion separately.

The effects of ischemic conditions in two representative experiments are illutrated in Figure 1. Panels A and B were recorded before exposure to

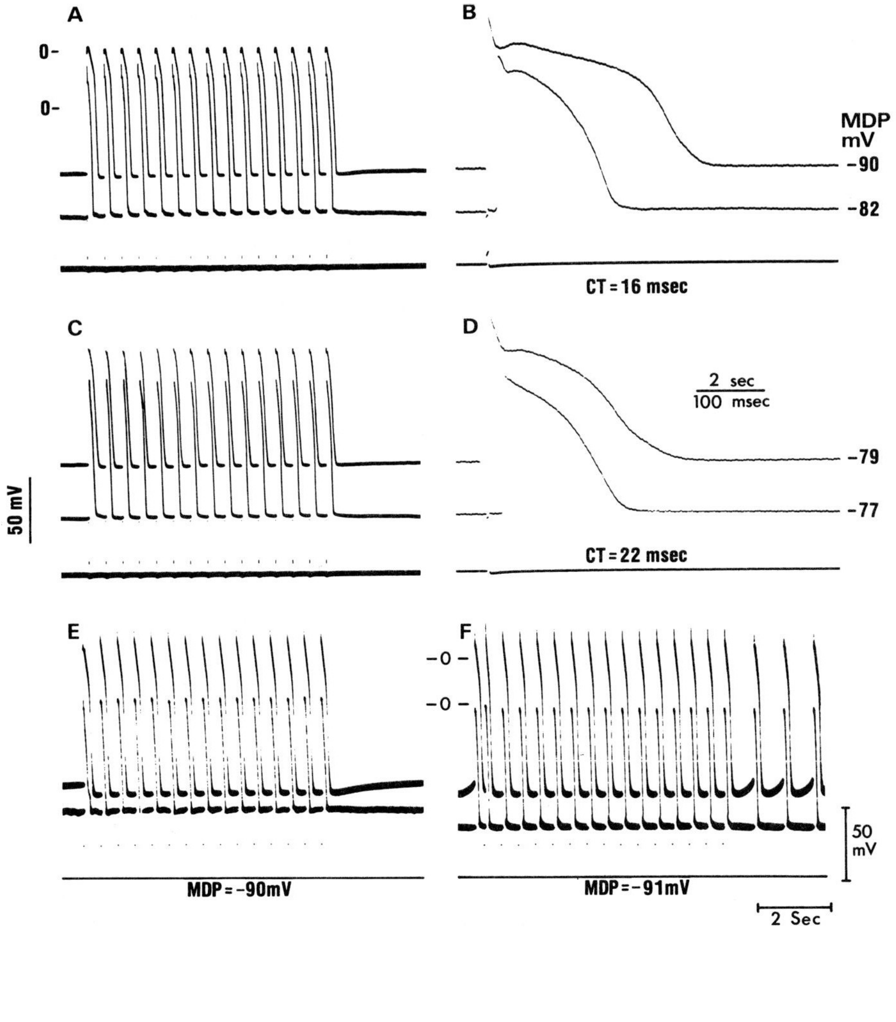

FIGURE 1. *Effects of ischemic conditions on the electrophysiological characteristics of canine Purkinje and muscle tissues. In each panel, the top trace is a microelectrode recording from false tendon (Purkinje tissue), the second trace is a recording from papillary muscle, and the bottom trace is a record of stimulation delivered to the false tendon. Panels A and B were recorded during the control, nonischemic period. Panels C and D were recorded after exposure to conditions of ischemia for 35 minutes. MDP = maximum diastolic potential; CT = conduction time. The time calibration for panels A–D (shown in panel D) equals 2 seconds for panels A and C, and 100 msec for panels B and D. The voltage calibration for panels A–D is given beside panel C, and zero reference potentials for microelectrode recordings are given in panel A. Panels E and F, from another preparation, show transient enhancement of pacemaker activity in Purkinje tissue by conditions of ischemia. Panel E was recorded during the control period. Panel F was recorded after a 10-minute exposure to ischemic conditions. Time and voltage calibrations, and zero reference potentials are indicated in panel F. In panels E and F, MDP = maximum diastolic potential in Purkinje tissue.*

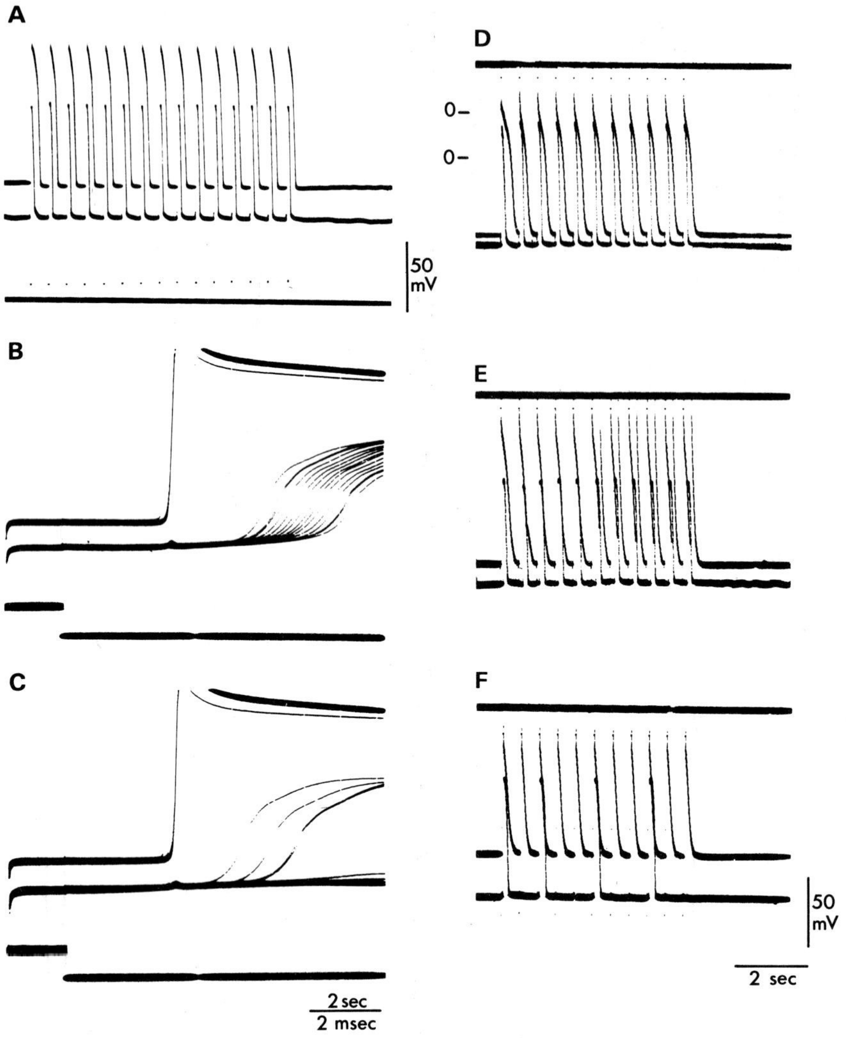

FIGURE 2. *Patterns of conduction block between Purkinje and muscle tissues induced by conditions of ischemia. Panels A–C show second-degree block with Wenckebach periodicity. The identity of traces is the same as in Figure 1. The time calibration below panel C represents 2 seconds for panel A and 2 msec for panels B and C. The voltage calibration is indicated in panel A. The cycle length of stimulation during the train was 500 msec in panels A and B and 300 msec in panel C. Panels D–F illustrate a bigeminal rhythm and second-degree conduction block between Purkinje and muscle tissues induced by conditions of ischemia. In each panel, the top trace is a record of the pattern of stimulation. The middle and bottom traces are microelectrode recordings from false tendon and papillary muscle, respectively. Voltage and time calibrations are indicated in panel F.*

ischemic conditions. In Purkinje tissue (panel A, top record), a train of 15 driven responses was followed by slow diastolic depolarization which failed to initiate activity within a 3-second pause in stimulation. Panel B illustrates the configurations of the potentials recorded from Purkinje and muscle tissues. The maximum diastolic potentials (MDP) recorded in Purkinje and muscle tissues respectively were −90 and −82 mV. Panels C and D were recorded after exposure to ischemic conditions for 35 minutes. In nine preparations in which stable impalements were maintained the MDP in Purkinje decreased 12.5 ± 3.9 mV (SE). Stable impalements were maintained in muscle in six experiments. Here, the decrease in MDP was 9.6 ± 4.3 mV (SE). The decrease in MDP was accompanied by changes in action potential configuration (panel D). In Purkinje fibers, ischemia caused the APD at 25, 50, and 95% of repolarization to decrease by 55.4 ± 10.7 (SE), 57.0 ± 10.3, and 14.0 ± 10.6 msec, respectively. In muscle, the corresponding abbreviations were 21.0 ± 7.7 (SE), 21.1 ± 10.3, and 4.9 ± 4.7 msec. Thus, in both tissues, the time to complete repolarization was not greatly altered. However, the plateau was markedly depressed, and the action potential duration early in phase 3 repolarization was abbreviated.

In two of nine experiments, automaticity was transiently enhanced by exposure to ischemic conditions for approximately 10 minutes. Recordings from one experiment are shown in Figure 1 (E and F). Before exposure to ischemic conditions, driven activity in Purkinje tissue was followed by phase 4 depolarization which failed to reach threshold (panel E). Panel F was recorded from the same fiber after exposure to ischemic conditions for 10 minutes. The slope of phase 4 depolarization was greatly enhanced and, during the pause in stimulation, three spontaneous beats were generated and propagated to muscle. After 90 seconds, automaticity stopped (not illustrated), and the slope of phase 4 depolarization gradually declined with further exposure to ischemic conditions. Automaticity was absent in all experiments at the end of the "ischemic period."

Ischemic conditions consistently depressed conduction between Purkinje and muscle tissues. Figure 1 shows an example of first-degree block. Conduction time from the recording site on the false tendon to the site on muscle (determined from enlarged projections of film records) increased from 16 msec during the control period (panel B) to 22 msec when the preparation was exposed to ischemic conditions (panel D).

Conduction block frequently progressed to second-degree block resembling either Mobitz type I or II patterns. Figure 2 (A–C), recorded after exposure to ischemic conditions for 12 minutes, shows an example of type I or Wenckebach periodicity. Panel A, recorded at a slow sweep speed, demonstrates one-to-one conduction from Purkinje tissue (top trace) to muscle when the BCL was 500 msec. Panel B shows only the upstrokes of the action potentials recorded under the same conditions. In panel B, the earliest upstroke recorded from muscle (lower) corresponds to the first beat of the train. The conduction time from Purkinje tissue to muscle increased progressively with each sequential beat. When the BCL was shortened to 300 msec (panel C), conduction time increased with the first 3 to 4 beats. Conduction then failed for the remainder of the train. Conduction resumed with the beginning of each new train (not illustrated).

Panels D, E, and F of Figure 2 were recorded from another preparation, after exposure to ischemic conditions for 8, 28, and 40 min, respectively. Panel D was recorded before any major depression of conduction and all beats propagated from Purkinje tissue D (top) to muscle (bottom). Panel E was recorded after the conduction delay between Purkinje and muscle sites began to increase progressively through each train (as in panels A and B). Midway through the train, a bigeminal rhythm developed at the recording site in Purkinje tissue. The fixed coupling and degree of prematurity of the spontaneous activity suggests, but does not prove, that the thythm was reentrant in origin. The abrupt cessation of the arrhythmia with termination of pacing also is compatible with this interpretation. With further exposure of the tissues to the test solution, a higher degree of block appeared and the bigeminal rhythm stopped (panel F). The pattern of second-degree block in panel F is that of Mobitz type II. In the complete series of experiments, depression of conduction was accompanied by nondriven activity ranging from isolated extrasystoles to salvos and short runs of potentials with brief intervals.

Effects of Reperfusion with Normal Tyrode's Solution

Several distinct phases of arrhythmic activity occurred in sequence when preparations were reexposed to control, oxygenated Tyrode's solution. The successive appearance of these phases was closely related to a reproducible cyclic change in MDP. Figure 3 shows a typical example of the changes in MDP that occurred in Purkinje tissue during ischemic conditions and the return to nonischemic conditions. Ischemic conditions resulted in prompt decrease in MDP, followed by a period (approximately 30 minutes), during which the MDP remained relatively stable. Near the end of the 40-minute exposure to ischemic conditions, the MDP decreased further. Return to control Tyrode's solution resulted in a rapid repolarization which, in two experiments, resulted in hyperpolarization of the Purkinje tissues relative to the control MDP. Maximum repolarization of the tissues was achieved within 2–4 minutes of reperfusion, and was followed by rapid depolarization to membrane potentials of −55 to −60 mV. The false tendons remained severely depolarized or recovered very slowly for 15–30 minutes. Following this period, recovery progressed more rapidly. Stable membrane potentials −80 mV or greater were achieved within 50–60 minutes of reperfusion with control Tyrode's solution. Essentially identical phasic changes in membrane potential were seen in all nine preparations in which stable impalements were maintained throughout the experiment. Impalements in muscle were seldom maintained throughout the period of reperfusion. The discontinous recordings which were collected indicate that muscle exhibited qualitatively similar, but greatly attenuated, phasic changes in MDP.

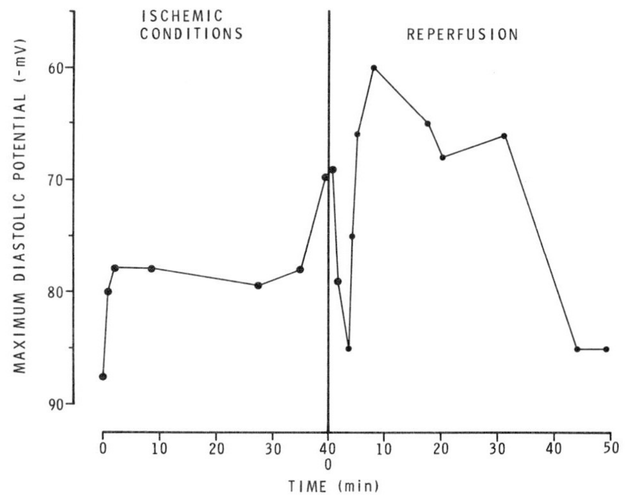

FIGURE 3. *Effects of exposure to ischemic conditions followed by return to nonischemic conditions on maximum diastolic potential in Purkinje tissue. The ordinate indicates the maximum diastolic potential in mV as a function of duration of exposure to ischemic conditions (to left of vertical line) and duration of superfusion after return to control Tyrode's solution (to right of vertical line).*

Several different mechanisms or potential mechanisms of arrhythmia appeared in response to return to nonischemic conditions. The sequence of their appearance and the relationship to the changes in MDP are illustrated in Figure 4. Except where noted, the top microelectrode recording is from the Purkinje site and the bottom record is from muscle. The MDP recorded in Purkinje tissue is given for each panel. Panel A, identical to panel F of Figure 2, was recorded at the end of the period of ischemic conditions. The MDP of Purkinje tissue had decreased to

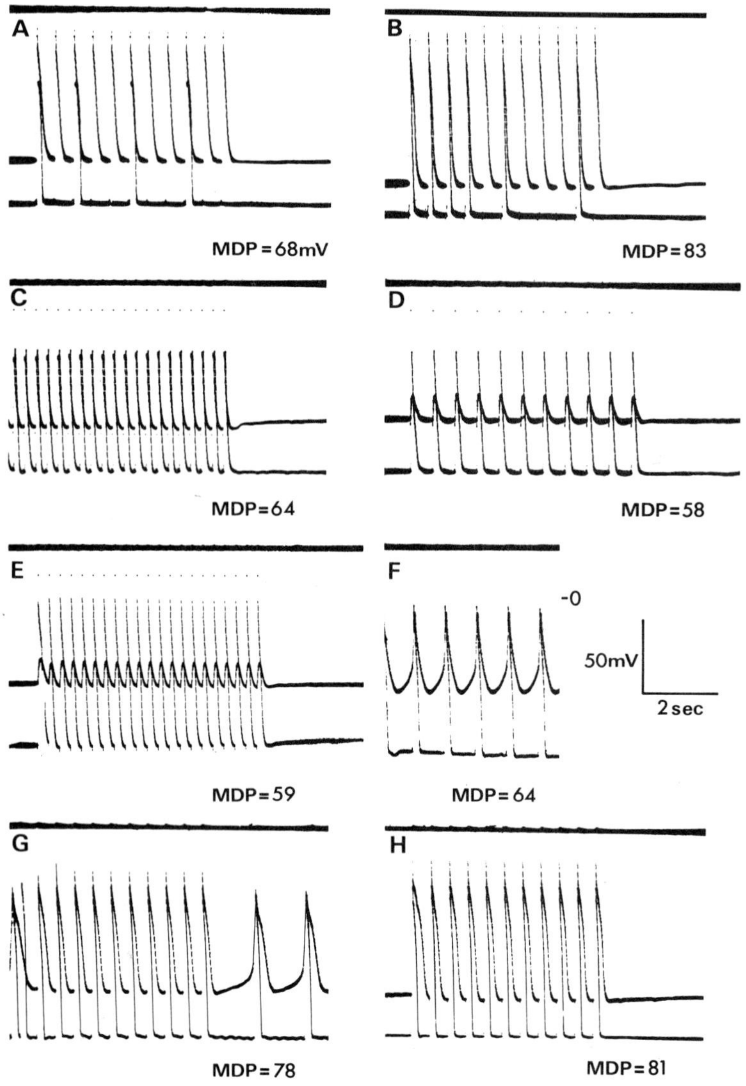

FIGURE 4. *Effects of reperfusion with control Tyrode's solution on electrophysiological activity of Purkinje and muscle tissue previously exposed to ischemic conditions for 40 minutes. In each panel, the top trace is a record of stimulation. The identity of the microelectrode traces and sequence of events is indicated in the text. Voltage and time calibrations are in panel F. MDP = the maximum diastolic potential recorded in Purkinje tissue following the last driven action potential in that panel.*

−68 mV and second-degree conduction block had developed. In panel B, recorded 3.5 minutes after return to control Tyrode's solution, second-degree conduction block was still evident. However, the MDP in Purkinje tissue had increased to −83 mV. The MDP in muscle had also increased slightly. Immediately after the traces in panel B were recorded, the Purkinje fibers began to depolarize. Panel C was recorded 7.5 minutes after return to control Tyrode's solution. The MDP had decreased to −64 mV. During this period of progressive depolarization, oscillatory afterpotentials (OAP) appeared in Purkinje tissue but not in muscle. An OAP can be seen following the last driven action potential in the record from Purkinje tissue in panel C. OAP were observed at this phase of progressive depolarization in eight of nine preparations.

The preparation continued to depolarize following the sequence illustrated in panel C. After 8.5 minutes of reperfusion, the MDP had decreased to −58 mV (panel D). The preparation could no longer be driven by stimuli applied to the false tendon. Therefore, stimulation was then delivered to the apex of the papillary muscle. Active responses were still elicited in muscle, but no longer propagated to the recording site on the false tendon. In panel D, the muscle action potentials cross over the trace from Purkinje tissue. The responses in Purkinje tissue are represented by the much slower electrotonic (passive) deflections with amplitudes of approximately 20 mV. Panel E, recorded after 11 minutes of reperfusion, is similar to panel D, except that the rate of stimulation is faster and the microelectrode that was previously impaled in muscle had been reimpaled in a site in subendocardial Purkinje tissues. Activity clearly propagated from muscle to subendocardial Purkinje fibers. Failure of conduction occurred between the subendocardial layer of Purkinje fibers and the false tendon which continued to exhibit only electronic deflections. In five experiments, the second microelectrode was used to impale numerous sites on the false tendon during this stage. All sites were found to be depolarized to levels similar to those seen at the continuously impaled site. These observations plus the finding that the preparations could not be driven by stimuli applied to the false tendon, indicate that most, if not all, of the fibers within the false tendon were similarly depolarized.

Reperfusion with control Tyrode's solution was followed by depolarization, inexcitability, and failure of conduction in false tendons in all experiments. The membrane potential initially recovered very slowly following this phase. In all experiments, gradual increase in MDP was accompanied by the appearance of pacemaker activity at membrane potentials characterized by "slow response" or calcium-mediated action potentials. This activity has been described in Purkinje tissue (Hauswirth et al., 1969; Imanishi, 1971) and muscle where it has been referred to as depolarization-induced automaticity (DIA) (Katzung and Morgenstern, 1977). An example is shown in panel F of Figure 4, recorded 36 minutes after initiation of reperfusion. The MDP in the Purkinje fiber had increased to −64 mV, and the fiber had become continuously automatic. Stimulation had been discontinued temporarily. There was a smooth transition between the pacemaker potential and the upstroke of the action potential. The lower trace, recorded from a site in muscle, demonstrates that the spontaneous activity originating in Purkinje tissue propagated to the muscle. Automaticity characteristically persisted as the MDP gradually recovered. Panel G was recorded 47 minutes after initiation of reperfusion. The MDP in Purkinje tissue had increased to −78 mV. The train of action potentials starting at the left of this panel represents driven activity initiated by stimuli delivered to a site on muscle. The driven action potentials successfully propagated to the Purkinje site. Pacemaker activity was still exhibited during the pauses in driven activity, but occurred at membrane potentials associated with normal pacemaker activity and sodium-mediated action potential upstrokes. Transition from automaticity at low membrane potentials to the activity shown in panel G was gradual and continuous. Automaticity stopped in all preparations before 60 minutes of reperfusion had elapsed. Panel H was recorded after 50 minutes of reperfusion. The MDP in Purkinje tissue had increased to −81 mV, and automaticity no longer appeared in the pauses in driven activity.

In the present study, reperfusion regularly elicited two mechanisms of abnormal automaticity, OAP and DIA. Although OAP were regularly observed, complete characterization of this abnormal mechanism of automaticity was hindered by the continuously changing response of the tissues. OAP showed a progressive increase in amplitude during the period of depolarization that followed maximum hyperpolarization. This is illustrated in Figure 5A. The panel at the extreme left was recorded at the peak of hyperpolarization following reperfusion with

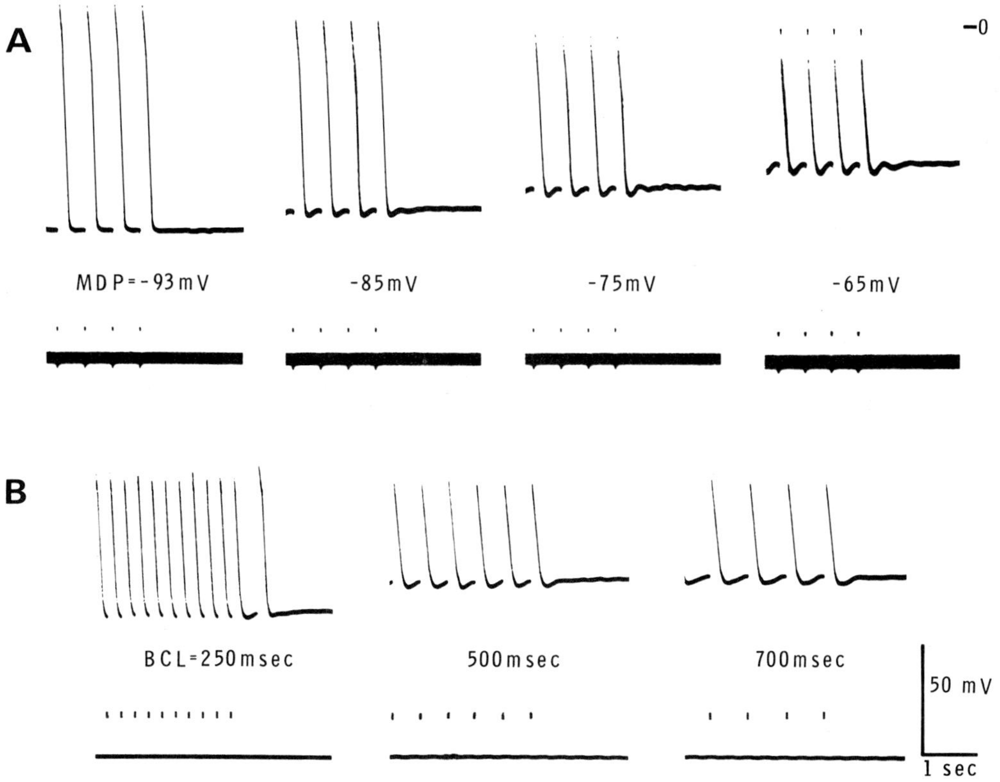

FIGURE 5. *Oscillatory afterpotentials induced in Purkinje tissue by return to nonischemic conditions. Panels in 5A illustrate the appearance and progressive increase in amplitude of OAP. The three panels in 5B were recorded from Purkinje tissue in a different experiment from 5A. The basic cycle length (BCL) of stimulation was varied and is indicated in each panel. In the center and right panels, all action potentials were stimulated. The trains of activity were followed by subthreshold OAP. In the left panel, the OAP reached threshold and induced an extrasystole (last action potential). MDP = maximum diastolic potential immediately following the last driven action potential.*

normal Tyrode's solution. This recording from Purkinje tissue shows that the last four driven beats of a train of 15. The MDP at the end of the train was −93 mV. OAP were not visible at this time. The remaining three panels in Figure 5A were recorded from the same impalement and show that the MDP decreased progressively to −85, −75, and −65 mV. OAP appeared following the trains of driven activity, and increased in amplitude as the MDP decreased. The upstrokes of OAP visible in the diastolic intervals between action potentials exhibited a similar increase. The preparation became inexcitable following the sequence illustrated. It is not clear from the present experiments whether the progressive increase in the amplitude of OAP is caused by the progressive decrease in MDP or another mechanism. The amplitude of digitalis-induced OAP increases with depolarization over the same range of membrane potentials (Ferrier, 1980; Wasserstrom and Ferrier, 1981). A similar voltage dependence has been demonstrated for an oscillatory current in sheep Purkinje fiber in the absence of cardiotonic agents (Vassalle and Mugelli, 1981).

The amplitude and interval of OAP induced by digitalis also change in response to the BCL of preceding driven activity (Ferrier et al., 1973). The BCL of driven activity also was varied in the present experiments when OAP were exhibited. Figure 5B shows traces recorded from a Purkinje fiber in a representative experiment. The three panels show progressive depolarization as in Figure 5A. However, the BCL of driven activity was 250, 500, and 700 msec (left to right). When the BCL was 700 msec, the ascending limb of OAP could be seen developing between driven responses throughout the train. A distinct OAP was evident following the last driven response. The interval at which the peak of the OAP followed the upstroke of the last driven response was approximately equal to the preceding BCL. When the BCL was 500 msec, the interval of the OAP was shorter and the amplitude was less. In the experiment illustrated, the OAP reached threshold and initiated an extrasystole when the BCL was 250 msec. In the present experiments, the amplitude of OAP appeared to be least following trains of beats at intermediate BCL (400–500 msec) and increased with either shorter (250–300 msec) or longer BCL (600–700 msec). This relationship appeared qualitatively similar to that documented for digitalis-induced OAP, but could not be quantified in the present study because of the additional effects of continuously decreasing MDP.

Depolarization-induced automaticity also occurred regularly in response to reperfusion with control Tyrode's solution. This abnormal mechanism of automaticity was observed only in Purkinje tissue. The papillary muscles, however, were not markedly depolarized at this time. Previous studies have shown that depolarized cardiac tissues, exhibiting DIA and connected to more normally polarized tissues, may function as parasystolic foci (Ferrier and Rosenthal, 1980; Rosenthal and Ferrier, 1983; Ferrier and Shoukair, 1981). Therefore, the possibilities that false tendons depolarized by ischemic conditions followed by reperfusion would function as parasystolic foci and exhibit electrotonic modulation of spontaneous cycle length were examined in the present study. Figure 6 (A and B) shows traces recorded during reperfusion. The top trace shows that the Purkinje fibers had depolarized and become automatic. The lower microelectrode recording was from muscle and indicates one-to-one exit conduction

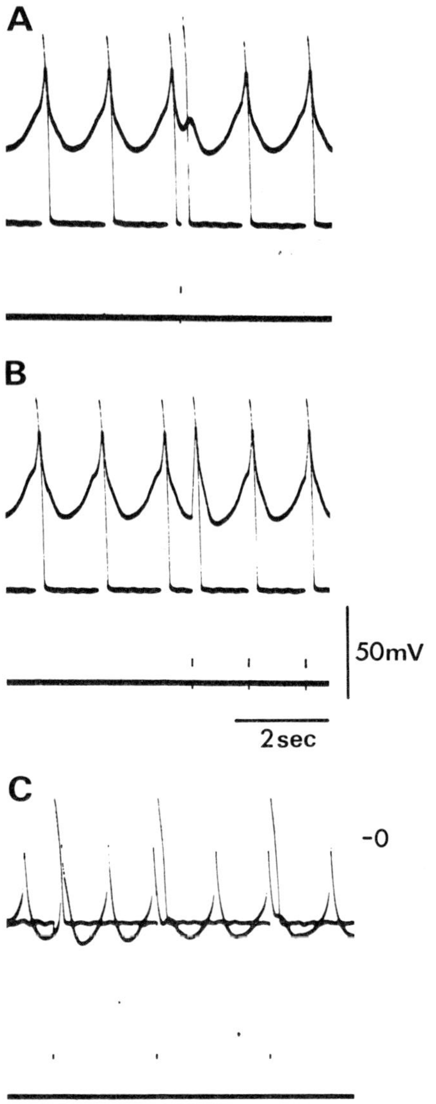

FIGURE 6. *Panels A and B: modulated parasystolic activity with exit conduction induced by reperfusion. In each panel, the top trace is a microelectrode record from Purkinje tissue, the middle trace is a microelectrode record from muscle, and the bottom trace is a record of stimuli applied to muscle. Panel C: modulated parasystolic activity with complete exit block. Traces are identified in the text. All three large amplitude rapidly rising action potentials recorded from the surface of the papillary muscle were driven. Voltage and time calibrations are in panel B.*

TABLE 1
Incidence and Time Course of Reperfusion Effects in Canine Purkinje Tissues Exposed to Ischemic Conditions with Normal or Elevated Potassium Levels

[K+]		Hyperpolarization*	OAP	Depolarization to inexcitability†	DIA	Modulated parasystole	Recovery**
4 mM	Incidence (n = 9)	9	8	9	9	7	9
	Time (min ± SD)	2.3 ± 0.6§	5.3 ± 1.3§	9.4 ± 3.1‡	25.4 ± 6.3‡		52.7 ± 4.7‡
10 mM	Incidence (n = 6)	6	2	5	5	4	6
	Time (min ± SD)	3.3 ± 1.6§	6.3§ (9.5, 3.0)	11.0 ± 8.3‡	31.8 ± 5.7‡		42.5 ± 13.1‡

Time: time elapsed since the start of reperfusion; §time at peak; ‡time at onset. OAP: oscillatory afterpotential; DIA: depolarization-induced automaticity. Differences in time course between [K+] = 4 or 10 mM are not statistically significant (two-sided *t*-test).
* Greater than 10 mV relative to end of ischemic period.
† Depolarization to −50 to −60 mV, inexcitable and quiescent.
** Membrane potentials ≥ −80 mV and cessation of automaticity.

from the focus of automaticity. Of nine preparations examined, six demonstrated exit conduction and three demonstrated third-degree exit block. In Figure 6A, a stimulus was delivered to muscle following the third spontaneous beat. The stimulus elicited an action potential in muscle. The action potential failed to propagate to the recording site in Purkinje tissue. However, it imposed an electrotonic depolarization and caused a marked delay in the next spontaneous firing of the Purkinje fiber. Thus, the false tendon exhibited entrance block to test beats interpolated early in the pacemaker cycle. When test beats were interpolated later with respect to the cycle of the pacemaker, the beats captured the automatic site and, thus, accelerated the discharge of the tissue. An example is shown in panel B. The last three beats in panel B were initiated by stimuli delivered to muscle. The first of these occurred after approximately 40% of the pacemaker cycle had elapsed, and successfully discharged the fiber. The following two driven beats arrived near the expiration of the respective pacemaker cycles and discharged the pacemaker only slightly prematurely. Similar phases of delay and acceleration were demonstrated in seven of nine preparations.

Modulation of pacemaker activity also occurred in preparations exhibiting complete exit block, as shown in Figure 6C. The traces in this example overlap. The trace showing pacemaker potentials graduating smoothly into the upstrokes of action potentials was recorded from the false tendon during reperfusion. The remaining trace was recorded from the surface of the papillary muscle. All three action potentials apparent in the latter trace were elicited by stimuli delivered to the papillary muscle. None of the spontaneous beats generated in the false tendon propagated to the papillary muscle. The driven beats at the middle and right of panel C caused electrotonic depolarizations which delayed the subsequent spontaneous firings of the false tendon. The test beat at the left of panel C occurred late in the spontaneous cycle and accelerated the next firing of the false tendon.

Effects of Elevating Potassium Concentration during Ischemic Conditions

The preceding results were collected in experiments in which the potassium concentrations of the superfusate were 4 mM during both the "ischemic" and reperfusion periods. It is well known that extracellular potassium concentration rises during ischemia (Harris et al., 1954). Our results suggest that elevated potassium is not necessary to elicit a strong reperfusion response in Purkinje tissue. However, elevated levels of extracellular potassium during ischemia might modify or even abolish the reperfusion response elicited in Purkinje tissue. Therefore, in six experiments, we studied the effects of the same sequence of "ischemic" conditions followed by reperfusion, but the potassium concentration was elevated to 10 mM during the "ischemic" period and returned to 4 mM during reperfusion. The high potassium concentration corresponds to the mean plateau level reported for extracellular myocardial potassium levels during coronary occlusion by Hill and Gettes (1980).

The responses of tissues to this modified protocol were similar to those in which potassium was not elevated. The maximum diastolic potential in Purkinje tissue decreased from −87.8 ± 1.69 (SE) mV to −62.5 ± 2.6 (SE) mV when the tissues were exposed to ischemic conditions. The decrease in membrane potential (25.3 ± 1.9 mV) was significantly greater than that observed in response to ischemic conditions at 4 mM KCl (12.5 ± 3.9 mV; $P < 0.02$, unpaired *t*-test). Two preparations exposed to ischemic conditions with 10 mM KCl also exhibited an initial increase in automaticity similar to that seen in experiments using 4 mM KCl (see Fig. 1F). The response of the tissues to reperfusion with normal Tyrode's solution also was nearly identical to that observed following ischemic conditions with 4 mM KCl. The reperfusion responses of tissues exposed to both protocols are summarized in Table 1. The greatest difference observed was that OAP occurred in only two of six of the Purkinje tissues exposed to 10 mM KCl, whereas eight of nine preparations exhibited OAP when the potassium concentration was 4 mM. In addition, although all preparations exhibited a secondary depolarization following the initial hyperpolarization, in one preparation exposed to ischemic conditions with elevated potassium, action potentials initiated by stimulation of muscle continued to propagate into the false tendon throughout the reperfusion period. In the remaining five preparations, depolarization resulted in complete failure of conduction into the false tendon. In these five experiments, DIA also appeared as the preparations began the final recovery phase. Entrance block with modulation of the cycle length of the DIA was demonstrated in four of these preparations (indicated as modulated parasystole in Table 1). All six preparations recovered maximum diastolic potentials greater than −85 mV within 60 minutes of initiation reperfusion. No statistically significant differences in the time courses of the responses were observed with the two concentrations of potassium.

Discussion

The present study demonstrates that canine false tendon-papillary muscle preparations exposed to ischemic conditions followed by return to nonischemic conditions exhibit an orderly sequence of major mechanisms of arrhythmia. As many as five mechanisms may occur in a single ischemia-reperfusion sequence. During exposure to ischemic conditions, Purkinje fibers showed an initial moderate but rapid decline in MDP. This was associated with a transient appearance of automaticity in 25% of preparations. The automatic activity occurred at high membrane potentials (greater than −70 mV) and was therefore presumably generated by normal pacemaker activity characteristic of Purkinje fibers. Continued exposure to ischemic conditions resulted in progressive impairment of conduction across the Purkinje-muscle junction. Spontaneous activity associated with this phase was dependent on an initiating beat for its appearance, and was closely coupled to the initiating beat. The behavior observed is most compatible with a reentrant mechanism, although automatic mechanisms cannot be excluded (Moe et al., 1977). The remaining three mechanisms of arrhythmia occurred in response to return to nonischemic conditions. Reperfusion characteristically resulted in rapid hyperpolarization followed by depolarization in Purkinje fibers. OAP occurred during the depolarizing phase. OAP were observed when the MDP was between −60 and −85 mV. This range corresponds approximately to the range in which OAP induced by digitalis characteristically appear (Ferrier, 1980; Wasserstrom and Ferrier, 1981). It also is similar to the range of membrane potentials over which an oscillatory current (I_{os}) has been reported in sheep Purkinje fibers not treated with digitalis (Vassalle and Mugelli, 1981). Whether the transmembrane current causing OAP upon reperfusion is identical to the current (TI) underlying digitalis-induced OAP (Kass et al., 1978a, 1978b) remains to be determined. The amplitude of the most prominent OAP following a train of driven beats varied with changes in preceding BCL. This relationship also was similar to the cycle length dependence of the amplitude of digitalis-induced OAP (Ferrier et al., 1973). With the conditions of the present study, OAP generated only single extrasystoles. Whether repetitive firing similar to that seen with digitalis-induced OAP (Ferrier et al., 1973) or in 24-hour infarcts (El-Sherif et al., 1983) can be demonstrated with slightly different conditions, remains to be investigated.

The appearance of OAP was followed by progressive depolarization until conduction failed in Purkinje tissue. The MDP of fibers within the false tendon decreased to approximately −55 mV, and the tissue was inexcitable to extracellular stimuli applied directly to the false tendon. In experiments in which one microelectrode was used to impale various sites, the thin subendocardial layer of Purkinje fibers on the surface of the papillary muscle was frequently found to be excitable and less severely depolarized than tissue within the false tendon. Thus, the underlying muscle may provide a protective effect on very nearby Purkinje fibers by acting as a polarizing current source. Failure of conduction also appeared to be restricted to free-running false tendons and thick bundles of Purkinje fibers on the surface of the papillary muscle. This phase of electrical disturbance might be expected to result in macroreentry, or at least disruption of the normal sequence of activation and contraction, if it occurred in the whole heart.

The final recovery of membrane potential in false tendons began with the appearance of automaticity in the depolarized tissue in 14 of a total of 15 preparations. The MDP at this time was approximately −60 mV. Thus the automatic activity was most likely identical to DIA which involves the slow inward (calcium) current as the main inward current (Imanishi, 1971). This mechanism of automaticity exhibits several characteristics which suggest that it may function as an important mechanism of arrhythmia. We have shown that DIA is not subject to overdrive suppression (Ferrier and Rosenthal, 1980). This observation has been confirmed recently (Dangman and Hoffman, 1983). Also, tissues exhibiting DIA, and which are connected to normally polarized tissues, frequently exhibit entrance block and electrotonic modulation of cycle length, as in the present study (Ferrier and Rosenthal, 1980; Ferrier and Shoukair, 1981; Rosenthal and Ferrier, 1983). Modulation and entrainment of the resulting parasystolic focus can generate a wide range of complex arrhythmias, including those with fixed coupling (Jalife and Moe, 1979; Moe et al., 1977).

Experiments which incorporated elevated levels

of potassium as one of the ischemic conditions differed little from those in which potassium was not altered. These observations indicate that elevation of potassium levels is not essential to elicit a potentially arrhythmogenic response during ischemic conditions or upon reperfusion. Downar et al. (1977) also concluded that elevated potassium was neither essential nor sufficient to elicit the electrophysiological changes observed during coronary occlusion in the pig. In the present study, we observed transient enhancement of automaticity during ischemia in one-third of preparations, even in the presence of 10 mM KCl. This may represent strong enhancement of automaticity by lactate and low pH similar to that demonstrated by Coraboeuf et al. (1976). Incorporation of elevated potassium as one of the ischemic conditions in the present study also had little effect on the response during reperfusion. The greatest change we observed was a decreased incidence of OAP. OAP occurred very early in reperfusion, and it is possible that they may have been suppressed in some preparations by slow washout of the higher concentration of potassium.

The responses we have observed to conditions mimicking ischemia followed by reperfusion are not observed in canine false tendon-papillary muscle preparations removed from apparently healthy hearts and exposed only to normal Tyrode's solution. The protocol including initial equilibration, exposure to ischemic conditions, and reexposure to normal Tyrode's solution represents a total duration of 3–4 hours. In various experimental protocols, we have regularly observed preparations exposed to normal Tyrode's solution for periods of up to 10–12 hours. Purkinje tissues which achieved a MDP of −80 mV or greater within 1 hour of dissection were never observed to depolarize spontaneously or exhibit OAP or DIA. Preparations which failed to repolarize following dissection, or exhibited spontaneous beats during control equilibration were excluded from this study. Thus, the observations reported represent the effects of the experimental intervention and are not observed spontaneously.

The conditions incorporated in our model were selected to inhibit energy metabolism in both Purkinje and muscle tissues. Hypoxia was selected to inhibit aerobic metabolism. Substrate exclusion, mimicking near complete substrate extraction in poorly perfused tissue, would aid inhibition of aerobic metabolism, at least in muscle. Purkinje tissue contains large stores of glycogen which could still be utilized anaerobically. Therefore, low pH and elevated lactate were included because they have been shown to inhibit anaerobic metabolism (Rovetto et al., 1975). All of these factors have been demonstrated in ischemic myocardium (Downar et al., 1977; Elharrar and Zipes, 1977). This model is obviously incomplete, since various metabolites (e.g., adenosine, etc.) that would accumulate in the interstitial compartment in a perfusion model must quickly wash out of at least the superficial layers of tissue. On the other hand, the superfusion model has the advantages that one may determine which components are both sufficient and necessary to yield a model that generates recognized mechanisms of arrhythmia, and one can record from both Purkinje and muscle tissues.

In a study of Downar et al. (1977), porcine ventricular tissues exposed to blood from ischemic myocardium in vitro exhibited rapid uneventful recovery upon "reperfusion" with control Tyrode's solution. The reason for absence of marked reperfusion effects could reflect a species difference, differences in exact levels of O_2, pH, etc., or perhaps the duration of exposure to ischemic conditions. In their study, isolated preparations were exposed to ischemic conditions for 12 minutes. In preliminary experiments, we have found that 10-minute periods of ischemic conditions are followed by greatly attenuated reperfusion effects.

The main phases of arrhythmogenesis seen in the present study resemble those seen upon occlusion and release of coronary vessels in the in situ canine heart. It is well established that arrhythmias occur during coronary occlusion and that they occur, frequently with greater severity, upon release of the occluded vessel (Harris, 1950; Corbalan et al., 1976; Penkoske et al., 1978; Murdock et al., 1980; Kaplinsky et al., 1981). Arrhythmias occurring early in ischemia are believed to be caused by reentry (Lazzara et al., 1978), and may be subdivided into very early and later periods (Kaplinsky et al., 1979). Arrhythmic mechanisms also occurred in two phases in our model. However, the early phase was related to enhanced automaticity rather than reentry. The significance of this phase is unknown. Late in the ischemic period, activity that appeared to be reentrant was observed.

Our observations are compatible with the occurrence of a major period of arrhythmogenesis upon return to nonischemic conditions. The combination of three different major mechanisms of arrhythmia, OAP, profound conduction block in specialized conducting tissue, and modulated parasystole, may well explain the severity of arrhythmias seen in response to reperfusion following coronary occlusion. Abnormal mechanisms of automaticity may play a major role following reperfusion. Penkoske et al. (1978) studied the effects of 35-minute occlusions of the left anterior descending coronary artery in the cat. Reperfusion was accompanied by improved conduction but marked elevation of idioventricular rate. Enhancement of automaticity may depend on the duration of the ischemic period. Murdock et al. (1980) studied 10-minute occlusions in dogs and did not find an elevation of ventricular rate on reperfusion.

Reperfusion arrhythmias also have been divided by Kaplinsky et al. (1981) into two categories. These authors described an immediate burst of arrhythmic activity during the initial 1–2 minutes. The activity occurred at a time corresponding to the rapid hyperpolarization seen in our in vitro model. If the rapid hyperpolarization occurred at slightly different times in adjacent tissues, it would be expected to result in marked disparities in excitability and refractoriness and thereby provide conditions favoring arrhythmic activity (Han and Moe, 1964).

We wish to thank Claire Guyette for excellent technical assistance provided throughout the study.

This study was supported in part by grants from the Nova Scotia and New Brunswick Heart Foundations. Dr. Moffat is a Fellow of The Medical Research Council of Canada. Dr. Lukas is a Fellow of the Canadian Heart Foundation.

Address for reprints: Dr. Gregory R. Ferrier, Department of Pharmacology, Sir Charles Tupper Medical Building, Dalhousie University, Halifax, Nova Scotia, Canada, B3H 4H7.

Received October 10, 1983; accepted for publication October 24, 1984.

References

Coraboeuf E, Deroubaix E, Hoerter J (1976) Control of ionic permeabilities in normal and ischemic heart. Circ Res **38** (suppl I): 92–98

Corbalan R, Verrier RL, Lown B (1976) Differing mechanisms for ventricular vulnerability during coronary artery occlusion and release. Am Heart J **92:** 223–230

Dangman KH, Hoffman BF (1983) Studies on overdrive stimulation of canine cardiac Purkinje fibers: maximum diastolic potential as a determinant of the response. J Am Coll Cardiol **2:** 1183–1190

Downar E, Janse MJ, Durrer D (1977) The effect of "ischemic" blood on transmembrane potentials of normal porcine ventricular myocardium. Circulation **55:** 455–462

Elharrar V, Zipes DP (1977) Cardiac electrophysiologic alterations during myocardial ischemia. Am J Physiol **233:** H329–H345

El-Sherif NE, Gough WB, Zeiler RH, Mehra R (1983) Triggered ventricular rhythms in 1-day old myocardial infarction in the dog. Circ Res **52:** 566–579

Ferrier GR (1977) Digitalis arrhythmias: role of oscillatory afterpotentials. Prog Cardiovasc Dis **19:** 459–474

Ferrier GR (1980) Effects of transmembrane potential on oscillatory afterpotentials induced by acetylstrophanthidin in canine ventricular tissues. J Pharmacol Exp Ther **215:** 332–341

Ferrier GR (1983) Mechanisms of cardiac arrhythmias elicited by conditions of ischemia followed by reperfusion (abstr). Circulation **68** (suppl III): 20

Ferrier GR, Rosenthal JE (1980) Automaticity and entrance block induced by focal depolarization of mammalian ventricular tissue. Circ Res **47:** 238–248

Ferrier GR, Shoukair SM (1981) Parasystole induced by digitalis in isolated canine ventricular tissues (abstr). Circulation **64** (suppl IV): 24

Ferrier GR, Saunders JH, Mendez C (1973) Cellular mechanism for the generation of ventricular arrhythmias by acetylstrophanthidin. Circ Res **32:** 600–609

Han J, Moe GK (1964) Non-uniform recovery of excitability in ventricular muscle. Circ Res **14:** 44–60

Harris AS (1950) Delayed development of ventricular ectopic rhythms following experimental coronary occlusion. Circulation **1:** 1318–1328

Harris AS, Rojas AG (1943) The initiation of ventricular fibrillation due to coronary occlusion. Exp Med Surg **1:** 105–122

Harris AS, Bisteni A, Russel RA, Brigham JC, Firestone JE (1954) Excitatory factors in ventricular tachycardia resulting from myocardial ischemia: Potassium a major excitant. Science **119:** 200–203

Hauswirth O, Noble D, Tsien RW (1969) Tthe mechanism of oscillatory activity at low membrane potentials in cardiac Purkinje fibers. J Physiol (Lond) **200:** 255–265

Hill JL, Gettes LS (1980) Effect of acute coronary artery occlusion on local myocardial extracellular K^+ activity in swine. Circulation **61:** 768–778

Imanishi S (1971) Calcium-sensitive discharges in canine Purkinje fibers. Jpn J Physiol **21:** 443–463

Jalife J, Moe GK (1979) A biological model of parasystole. Am J Cardiol **43:** 761–772

Janse MJ, Van Capelle FJL, Morsink H, Kléber AG, Wilms-Schopman F, Cardinal R, D'Alnoncourt CN, Durrer D (1980) Flow of "injury" current and patterns of excitation during early ventricular arrhythmias in acute regional myocardial ischemia in isolated porcine and canine hearts. Circ Res **47:** 151–165

Kaplinsky E, Ogawa S, Balke BA, Dreifus LS (1979) Two periods of early ventricular arrhythmia in the canine acute myocardial infarction model. Circulation **60:** 397–403

Kaplinsky E, Ogawa S, Michelson EL, Dreifus LS (1981) Instantaneous and delayed ventricular arrhythmias after reperfusion of acutely ischemic myocardium: evidence for multiple mechanisms. Circulation **63:** 333–340

Kass RS, Lederer WJ, Tsien RW, Weingart R (1978a) Role of calcium ions in transient inward currents and aftercontractions induced by strophanthidin in cardiac Purkinje fibers. J Physiol (Lond) **281:** 187–208

Kass RS, Tsien RW, Weingart R (1978b) Ionic basis of transient inward current induced by strophanthidin in cardiac Purkinje fibers. J Physiol (Lond) **281:** 209–226

Katzung BG, Morgenstern JA (1977) Effects of extracellular potassium on ventricular automaticity and evidence for a pacemaker current in mammalian ventricular myocardium. Circ Res **40:** 105–111

Lazzara R, El-Sherif N, Scherlag BJ (1974) Early and late effects of coronary artery occlusion on canine Purkinje fibers. Circ Res **35:** 391–399

Lazzara R, El-Sherif N, Hope RR, Scherlag BJ (1978) Ventricular arrhythmias and electrophysiological consequences of myocardial ischemia and infarction. Circ Res **42:** 740–749

Moe GK, Jalife J, Mueller WJ, Moe B (1977) A mathematical model of parasystole and its relation to clinical arrhythmias. Circulation **56:** 968–979.

Murdock DK, Loeb JM, Euler DE, Randall WC (1980) Electrophysiology of coronary reperfusion. A mechanism for reperfusion arrhythmias. Circulation **61:** 175–182

Penkoske PA, Sobel BE, Corr PB (1978) Disparate electrophysiological alterations accompanying dysrhythmia due to coronary occlusion and reperfusion in the cat. Circulation **58:** 1023–1035

Rosenthal JE, Ferrier GR (1983) Contribution of variable entrance and exit block in protected foci to arrhythmogenesis in isolated ventricular tissues. Circulation **67:** 1–8

Rovetto MJ, Lamberton WF, Neely JR (1975) Mechanisms of glycolytic inhibition in ischemic rat hearts. Circ Res **37:** 742–751

Tennant R, Wiggers CJ (1935) The effect of coronary occlusion on myocardial contraction. Am J Physiol **112:** 351–361

Vassalle M, Mugelli A (1981) An oscillatory current in sheep cardiac Purkinje fibers. Circ Res **48:** 618–631

Wasserstrom JA, Ferrier GR (1981) Voltage dependence of digitalis afterpotentials, aftercontractions, and inotropy. Am J Physiol **241:** H646–H653

INDEX TERMS: Arrhythmias • Ischemia-reperfusion • Automaticity • Reentry

Fate of Intercellular Junctions in Isolated Adult Rat Cardiac Cells

Francoise Mazet, Beatrice A. Wittenberg, and David C. Spray
From the Departments of Neuroscience and Physiology, Albert Einstein College of Medicine, Bronx, New York

SUMMARY. Freeze fracture and thin section techniques have revealed morphological changes in gap junctions and intercalated discs of adult rat myocytes following enzymatic dissociation. Cell separation leaves behind small vesicular remnants of formerly adjacent cells connected to the intact cell by gap junctions; in contrast, desmosomes cleave at the region of intercellular contact. Apparently, the next step in gap junction breakdown is internalization of the remnants. In thin section, lanthanum penetration reveals that the cleft of some apparently internalized gap junctions is in contact with the sarcolemma, while that of others is not. In freeze fracture replicas, cytoplasmic gap junctions frequently possess hexagonally packed domains of E-face pits separated by smooth regions that may correspond to separations of membranes of internalized junctions found in thin section. Study of material maintained overnight at 37°C showed no surface junctional remnants; topologies of cytoplasmic gap junctions were generally complex, and concentric membrane vesicles were common. These observations suggest that enzymatic dissociation initiates a progressive, defined sequence of junctional internalization that begins with attached cell remnants and may have as the last determinable step the separation into single membranes inside the intact cell. **(*Circ Res 56: 195–204, 1985*)**

FRESHLY dissociated cells are becoming preparations of choice for many physiological and biochemical studies. Interpretation of data from these studies depends on the extent to which the morphological and physiological properties of the dissociated cells correspond to those of the intact tissue, an issue addressed in heart by recent reviews by Dow et al. (1981a, 1981b). Of particular interest to us is the fact that many cells are connected by intercellular junctions in situ: therefore, the dissociation process must alter the specialized regions of intercellular contact. Junctional breakdown in these cases begins with abrupt disruption of intercellular contact, and is synchronized to within 3 hours, the duration of the dissociation procedure. Thus, disappearance might be detected readily after cell dissociation, and these studies might reveal a rapid time course of junctional removal that would allow us to detect new expression of junctional proteins by reassociated cells.

Previous studies have shown that the fate of the gap junction depends on the medium used for the dissociation procedure, and perhaps also on the tissue examined. When the tissue is treated with hypertonic sucrose or solutions with calcium buffered to submicromolar levels with chelators, gap junctions of heart (Dewey and Barr, 1965) and liver (Goodenough and Gilula, 1974; Hirokawa and Heurser, 1982) apparently split along the region of cell contact, leaving "hemichannels" in membranes of each of the previously connected cells. Alternatively, when tissue is dissociated with peptidases and solutions with calcium concentrations in the range 1–20 μM, gap junctions of heart (Muir, 1967; Severs and Powell, 1980), exocrine pancreas (Amsterdam and Jamieson, 1974), and perhaps most other tissues remain attached to one of the previously connected cells, generally with remnants of the nonjunctional membrane of the other cell attached.

We show here morphological changes that occur in gap junctions and desmosomes when cardiac myocytes from the adult rat ventricle are dissociated by collagenase digestion in lowered extracellular calcium. Freeze fracture replicas and thin section images suggest that dissociation initiates a progressive process of gap junction breakdown. First, we see small enclosed remnants of the neighboring cell connected to the intact cell by gap junctions, then gap junctional breakdown proceeds through endocytosis to internalization of the junctional membranes. Junctional membranes then separate, and the process presumably ends with lysosomal destruction. In contrast, desmosomes appear to come apart during dissociation, and circular profiles of hemidesmosomes are seen within the cytoplasm. Gap junctions and desmosomes seem therefore to have similar fates, although they or their attachment to nonjunctional membranes are differentially sensitive to the dissociation process employed.

A preliminary report of this work has appeared (Mazet et al., 1982).

Methods

Adult rat myocardium was separated enzymatically into single cells by a modification of the procedure of Wittenberg and Robinson (1981). Briefly, this procedure began with perfusion of intact heart with low calcium medium buffered with 4-(2-hydroxyethyl)-1 piperazine ethanesulfonic acid (HEPES) and containing collagenase. The perfused tissue was minced, and dissociation was completed by repeated incubations in medium to which 0.3 mM calcium chloride was added. Separation of intact cells from damaged cells and subcellular debris was achieved by centrifugation through Percoll.

After several hours, this technique yields 12–15 million cells, of which about 10 million are calcium tolerant, as shown by their quiescence and shape in solutions containing 1–3 mM external Ca^{++}. Isolated myocytes were maintained at room temperature at the end of the isolation procedure in an isosmotic medium at pH 7.2 containing (mM): NaCl (97), $CaCl_2$ (0.3–1.0), KCl (4.7), NaH_2PO_4 (8.4), $MgCl_2$ (1.6), $NaHCO_3$ (4.0), HEPES (17.4), glucose (9.69), taurine (10), and creatine (20).

For electron microscopic examination of thin sections, suspensions of freshly dissociated cells were centrifuged at low speed (34 *g*) for 30 seconds, the supernatant solution was discarded, and the pellet was resuspended in a solution containing 2.5% glutaraldehyde with or without lanthanum nitrate (1%) in 0.1 M cacodylate buffer. After a brief rinse in buffer with or without lanthanum, the cell pellets were postfixed for 1 hour with 1% OsO_4 in the same buffer with or without lanthanum. Some samples without lanthanum were treated for 1 hour after postfixation with 4% uranyl acetate in veronal acetate buffer. Samples were then dehydrated through a graded series of ethanols and embedded in Epon. Thin sections of specimens fixed with lanthanum were observed unstained; other sections were poststained with uranyl acetate and lead citrate (Venable and Coggeshall, 1965).

Samples for freeze-fracture were also fixed immediately after dissociation. Cell pellets were resuspended in a solution containing 3% glutaraldehyde in 0.2 M cacodylate buffer (pH = 7.3). They were treated with 25% buffered glycerol at room temperature and were then frozen in liquid nitrogen-cooled Freon 22. The samples were fractured using the Balzers device (Balzers high vacuum freeze-etch unit BA 360M), at −135°C. The replicas were cleaned in bleach, after which they were rinsed in several changes of distilled water. Electron microscopic examination of thin sections and replicas was carried out on a Philips 300 transmission electron microscope at 60 kV. All

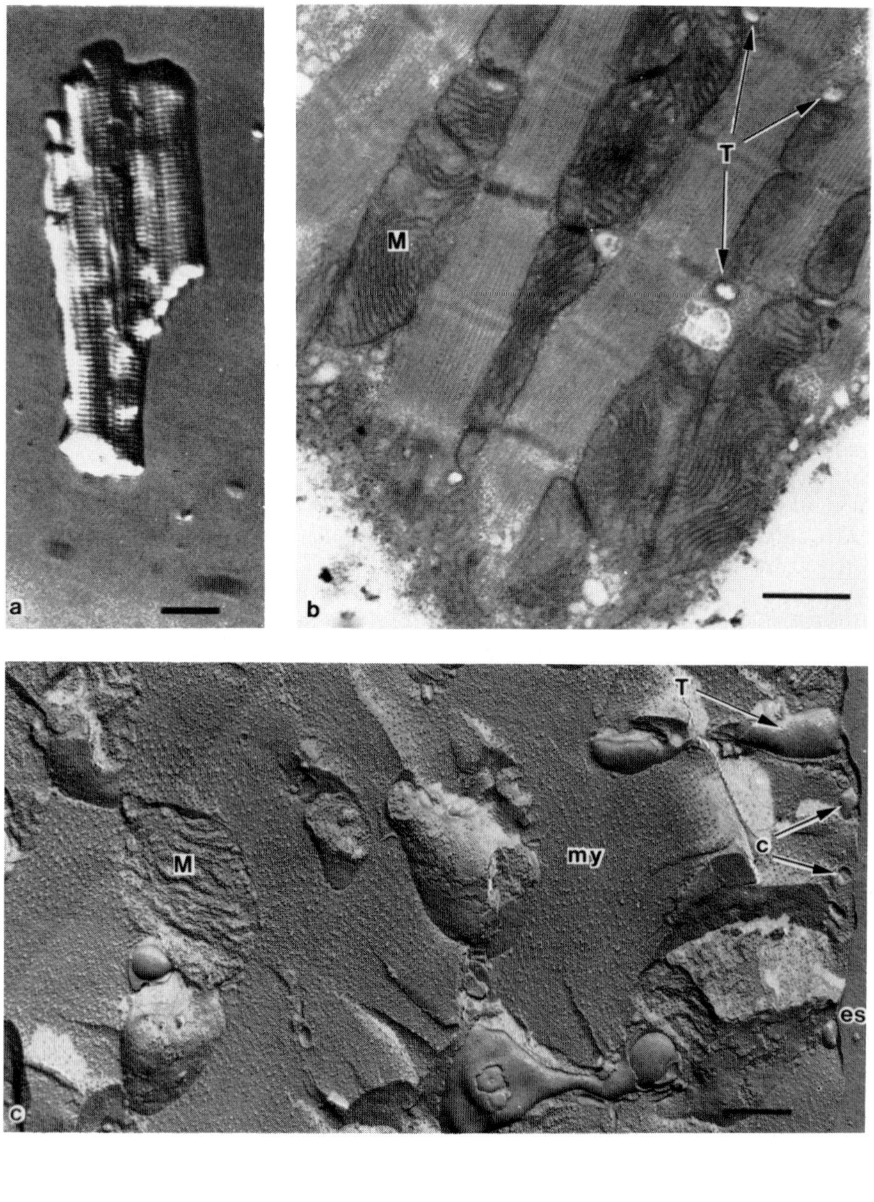

FIGURE 1. *Panel a: light micrograph of an adult rat ventricular myocyte dissociated according to the techniques of Wittenberg and Robinson (1981). Freshly dissociated cells display irregular, stepped edges in the regions of former cell contact. Dissociation is virtually complete, with fewer than 0.1% of the myocytes associated with an adjacent cell after the dissociation procedure. Bar = 20 μm. Panel b: longitudinal thin section of an isolated rat myocyte. Mitochondria (M) are apparent, which are interspersed between the myofilaments and have tightly packed cristae. Sarcomere length in this micrograph is 1.35 μm. At the Z-band level, T-tubules (T) are observed. Caveolae are also present near the surface membrane. Bar = 0.5 μm. Panel c: another aspect of cytoplasmic structure is shown in a freeze fracture replica, with a T-tubule (T) opening onto the surface membrane which is bounded by extracellular space (es). Along the sarcolemma, small caveolae (c) are present. Within the cytoplasm, myofilaments (my), and mitochondria (M) appear. Bar = 0.5 μm.*

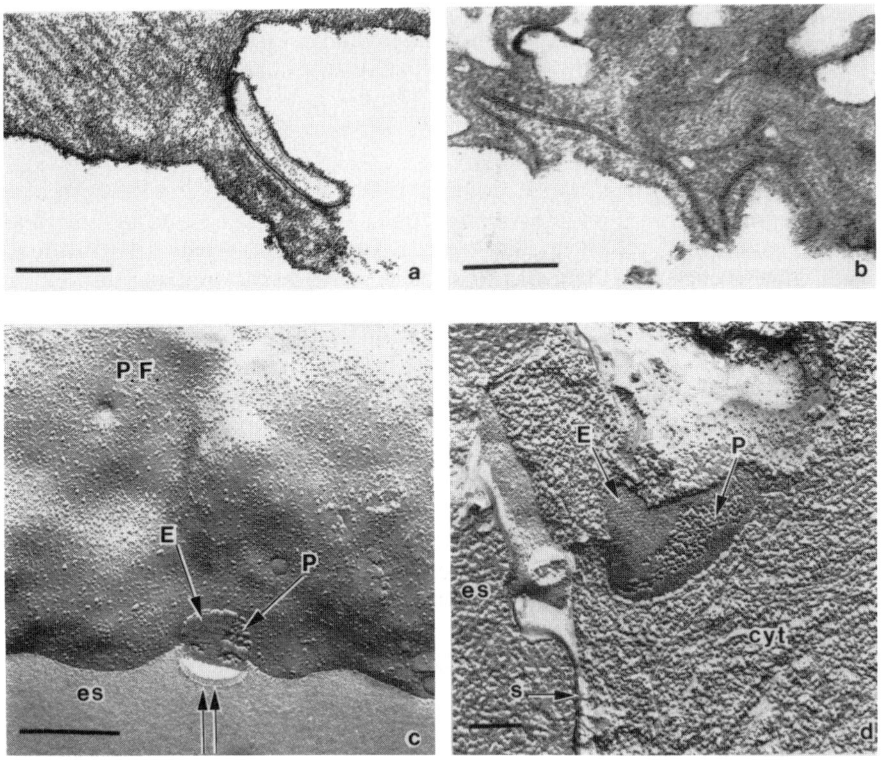

FIGURE 2. *Micrographs of thin sections (panels a and b) and freeze fracture replicas (panels c and d) of freshly dissociated rat ventricular myocytes. In panel a, a small vesicle formed by the lateral nonjunctional membrane is attached to an isolated myocyte via a gap junction. The extracellular space is filled with lanthanum. The gap junction remnant is closed, and contains no cellular organelles. In panel b, a similar vesicle shows the beginning of an infolding in the cytoplasm of the myocyte. Panel c shows a freeze fracture view of a superficial gap junction. On the P-fracture membrane (PF), a small gap junction with both P- and E-face views included is observed (near the double arrows). It appears that the junction involves a bleb and that the fracture plane has fortuitously crossed this junctional vesicle (double arrows). Bars in panels a, b, and c correspond to 0.25 μm. Panel d: on this micrograph, the fracture plane passes through the cytoplasm of an isolated myocyte. Near the sarcolemma (s) within the cytoplasm (cyt) a gap junction vesicle is observed. Pits occur on the E-fracture face (E), and particles are found on the P-fracture face (P). Bar = 0.5 μm.*

freeze fracture images have been mounted so that the shadow direction is from the bottom to the top of the figure.

Results

General Appearance of Dissociated Cells

The typical light microscopic appearance of individual rat ventricular myocardial cells a few hours after isolation, but before fixation, is shown in Figure 1a (see also Wittenberg and Robinson, 1981). The myocytes obtained by this procedure are usually binucleate (not shown) and are generally elongated with irregular stepped edges, confirming that separation of each cell from its neighbors has occurred by cleavage at the intercalated discs, as well as at transverse branch points. These cells possess normal permeability barriers to extracellular calcium and sodium ions (Gupta and Wittenberg, 1983), and the sarcomere length at rest (about 1.9 μm) is independent of extracellular Ca^{++} concentration (from 0.1 to 3 mM). The sarcolemma of dissociated cells is both intact and functional: the normal glycocalyx is preserved (Wittenberg and Robinson, 1981; Fig. 1b, present study), distribution of the dye acridine orange indicates an intact pH permeability barrier (not shown), and electrophysiological studies indicate that the cells generate resting and action potentials of normal amplitudes [at least −70 and 115 mV, respectively (White et al., 1983)].

The general ultrastructural appearance of dissociated myocytes has been described (Kao et al., 1980; Robinson et al., 1980; Dow et al., 1981b; Wittenberg and Robinson, 1981; Severs et al., 1982). Figure 1, b and c, compares the general appearance of cells used in this study in thin section and using the freeze fracture technique. Mitochondria (M) and T-tubules (T) are interspersed among myofilaments (my), and caveloae (c) are observed just below the sarcolemmal surface.

Appearance of Gap Junctions on the Surface of Dissociated Cells

Small enclosed membranes (less than a few μm in diameter) in contact with the sarcolemma were seen frequently in thin sections of freshly dissociated cells (Fig. 2, a and b). The extracellular membrane vesicles presumably represented the remnants of formerly adjacent cells. They were connected to the surface membrane by gap junctions, as shown in Figure 2, a and b, by the penetration of lanthanum into the region of contact of the two membranes. In some sections, closure of cell remnants was not unambiguously demonstrated (Fig. 2b). As considered in the Discussion, this result would be expected if the plane of the section was tangential to the nonjunctional membrane. Surface vesicles were remarkably free of normal cytoplasmic inclusions; apparently, cytoplasmic material was lost before the nonjunctional membrane resealed.

Freeze fracture examination of the P-fracture face of isolated myocytes revealed gap junctions on the sarcolemmal surface (e.g., Fig. 2c, double arrow) that presumably corresponded to the extracellular membrane vesicles seen in thin section (Fig. 2, a and 2, b). Presumably, these gap junctions were remnants of a formerly interconnected neighboring cell.

The P-fracture face of isolated myocytes was characterized by high particle density compared to the E-face, as was the case in the intact heart (data not shown). Gap junctions are unambiguously identified by junctional particles on the P-face (characteristically about 9 nm in our study) and complementary E-face pits. The example illustrated shows a fortuitous cross-section of the junctional membrane (Fig. 2c, double arrows) which is presumably broken off during the process of freeze fracture and corresponds to the thin section views above.

Subsurface Gap Junctions in Dissociated Myocytes

Thin sections revealed that gap junction remnants frequently were invaginated into the surface of the intact cell (Fig. 2b). In freeze fracture replicas with the fracture plane passing through the cytoplasm, apparently subsurface gap junctions were encountered (Fig. 2d), which were close to the sarcolemma and thus may correspond to the longitudinal views provided by thin section. Within the cytoplasm, the gap junction vesicle was easily identified as a prominent structure bounded by two membranes: one characterized by the junctional P-face particles and the other by typical complementary E-face pits (Fig. 2d). It was strikingly different in appearance compared to the much smoother T-tubule membrane, which exhibited no E-face pits (Fig. 1c).

Intracytoplasmic gap junction vesicles observed in both freeze fracture and thin section had an average diameter of 0.32 ± 0.024 μm (SE, $n = 34$); true maximal diameters, the measurement of which would require serial sections, presumably are larger. The invaginated gap junction vesicles could be found at various distances from the cell surface, the average distance being in thin section 0.23 ± 0.091 μm (SE, $n = 6$) and in freeze fracture 0.46 ± 0.067 μm (SE, $n = 35$). In some cases, apparently cytoplasmic gap junctions were found as far as 1 or 2 μm below the surface.

Individual thin sections and freeze fracture replicas provide only a two-dimensional view of these spheroidal structures, and cannot resolve whether the vesicles were in contact with the sarcolemma. To determine whether the clefts of either deep or superficial cytoplasmic gap junctions were continuous with extracellular space, we added colloidal lanthanum to the fixative. The external surface of the sarcolemma was diffusely outlined by lanthanum binding to the glycocalyx; lanthanum also penetrated T-tubules, producing staining that was particulate and diffuse. Lanthanum also outlined the gap junctions in some membrane vesicles within the cytoplasm (Fig. 3, double arrow). The staining with lanthanum sometimes emphasized small dilations within the intermembrane space (not illustrated) which could represent the empty spaces that were observed devoid of pits in freeze fracture (Fig. 5, b, d, and f). The fact that lanthanum sometimes permeated the space between the membranes of the gap junction vesicles (as in Fig. 3) indicates that this space was in continuity with extracellular space. The vesicle bearing this gap junction was thus invaginated into the sarcoplasm but was still connected to the surface. The membrane leaflet enclosed inside the bimembranous vesicle (Fig. 3, arrowhead) could correspond to the nonjunctional membrane of the adjacent cells infolded during the invagination of the junction within the cytoplasm.

Other subsurface gap junctions, even in the same preparation, did not show lanthanum outlining the formerly extracellular space (Fig. 4, a and b). In these figures, lanthanum was found within caveolae (arrowhead, Fig. 4b), but did not permeate the intermembrane "gap" region between the two membranes of the gap junction vesicle. Unlabeled vesicles thus were presumably gap junctions completely internalized within the cytoplasm, in which contact with the extracellular space was restricted or absent. In one of these micrographs, the membranes of the unlabeled vesicle have separated, forming an involuted concavity within the vesicle (Fig. 4b). [It is tempting to suggest that the smaller separation points between the junctional membranes comprising this vesicle (arrows, Fig. 4b) might correspond to the smooth aisles surrounding domains of pits on the E fracture face of cytoplasmic vesicles observed

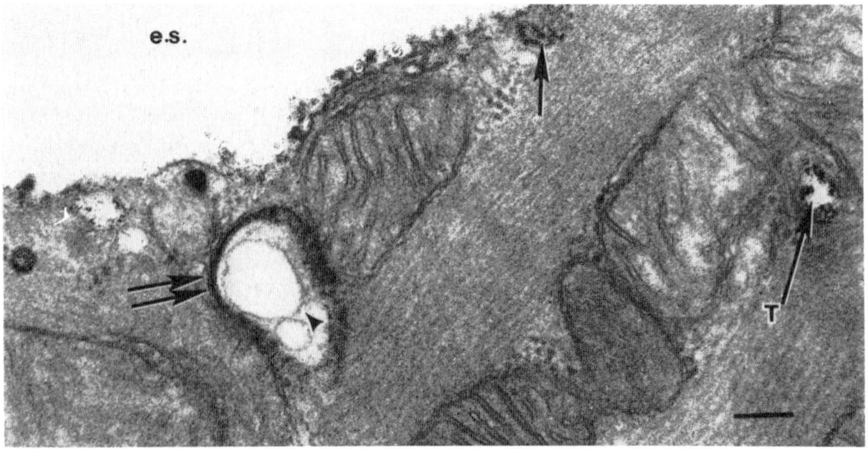

FIGURE 3. *Thin section of a lanthanum-labeled isolated myocyte, showing an annular gap junction (double arrow) with the intermembrane "gap" region filled with lanthanum. A T-tubule (T), caveola (arrow), and the glycocalyx covering the sarcolemma are labeled with lanthanum. The arrowhead indicates a region of nonjunctional membrane infolded into the gap junction vesicle. Bar = 0.1 μm.*

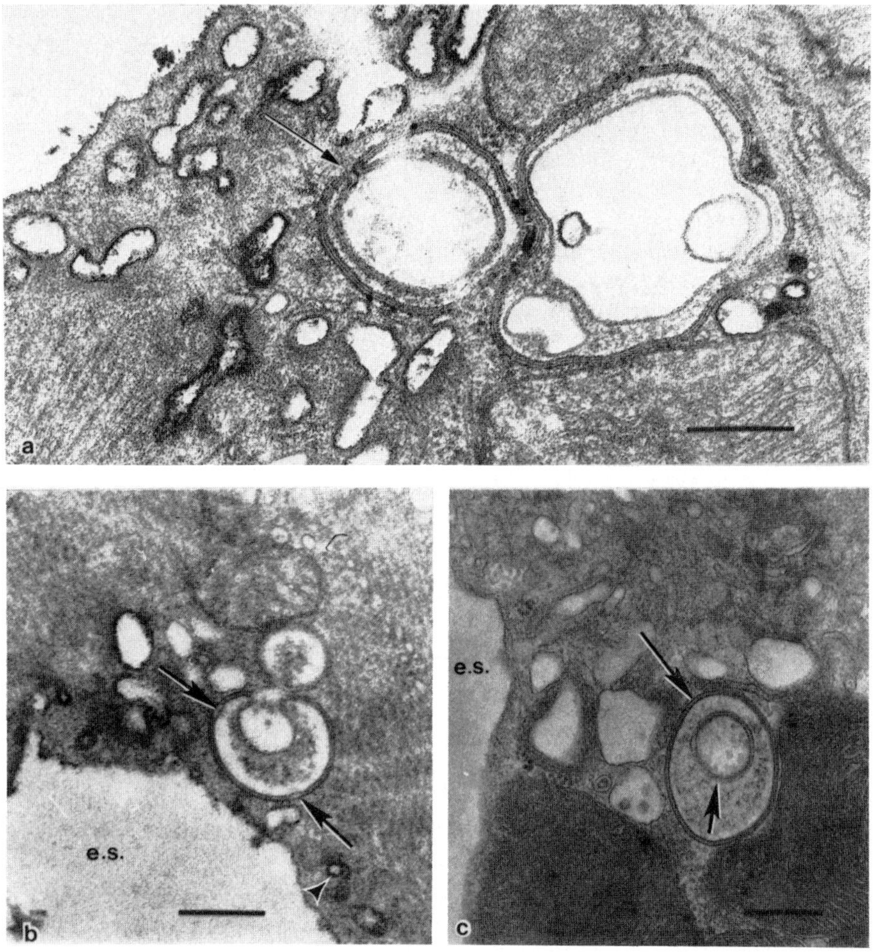

FIGURE 4. *In panels a and b, thin section of the same lanthanum-labeled preparation as in Figure 3, but showing an unlabeled gap junction vesicle. Panel a: the circular gap junction vesicle appears to involute within itself (arrow). In panel b, one of the membranes of the unlabeled gap junction vesicle begins to be involuted into the vesicle itself. The arrows indicate two separation points between the junctional membrane comprising this vesicle. Note the caveola (arrowhead) containing lanthanum within formerly extracellular space (es). In panel c, a thin section of dissociated cells maintained overnight at 37°C shows two concentric annular junctional profiles (arrows). Bars in panels a, b, and c correspond to 0.25 μm.*

in freeze-fracture (Fig. 5d). Although this would be consistent with the apparent association between thin section and freeze fracture images of vesicles where there is a larger expanse of separated junctional membranes (see below), the argument is less strong for short range irregularities in spacing of pits, which could be due to normal heterogeneity.] Internalized junctions that were not stained with lanthanum often exhibited profiles suggesting unusual topologies, as shown in Figure 4a, where some cytoplasmic vesicles were encircled within additional septilaminar structures. The single membranes observed in the multilamellar vesicle on the right presumably represent a further stage in junctional degradation.

Such complex membrane structures were common in preparations maintained for longer periods after dissociation (Figs. 4c and 5). In these preparations, the dissociated cells were maintained overnight at 37°C before fixation for thin section or freeze fracture. The medium contained penicillin (250 IU/ml) and streptomycin (250 μg/ml) in a humid, 5% CO_2 environment. Figure 5 shows various appearances of the internalized gap junction in thin sections and freeze fracture images that presumably correspond. The regular intermembrane "gap" region comprising the annular gap junction observed in thin section (Fig. 5a) apparently corresponded to the random distribution of P-particles and closely packed E-face pits on the membrane surface of a gap junction vesicle within the cytoplasm (Fig. 5b). The annular profile shows dilations of the intermembrane space at various points along the vesicle circumference (Fig. 5c) which could correspond (see above) to the empty spaces existing between the E-face pit clusters observed in freeze fracture replicas of cytoplasmic gap junction vesicles (Fig. 5d). In Figure 5e, an annular gap junction is shown in which the two membranes are separated; this may correspond to a gap junction vesicle exhibiting P-junctional particles on only half of its membrane in freeze fracture replicas (Fig. 5f).

Appearance of Desmosomes in Dissociated Myocytes

In heart muscle, most gap junctions are located in specialized regions, the intercalated disks (McNutt and Fawcett, 1974) which contain other types of intercellular contacts: fasciae adherens and desmosomes. These contacts are usually considered to function as intercellular attachment devices (Farquar and Palade, 1963). In thin sections of isolated myocytes, hemidesmosomes were observed at the

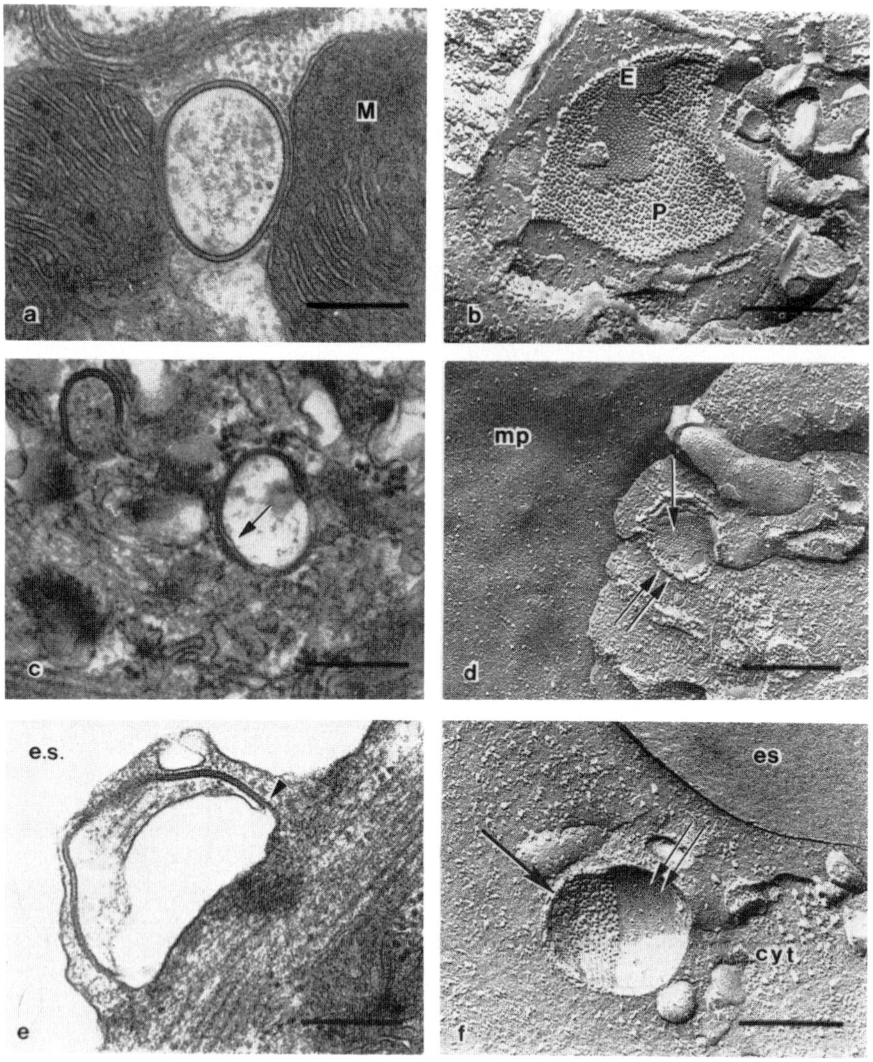

FIGURE 5. *Internalized gap junctions are observed in thin section (panels a, c, and e) and freeze fractures (panels b, d, and f) of dissociated cells maintained overnight at 37°C. The thin sections were obtained from material stained en bloc with uranyl acetate after fixation. In panel a, a circular junctional profile is shown, with a continuous bimembranous leaflet. M: mitochondrion. This image seems comparable to the freeze fracture image in panel b, which shows a gap junction vesicle surrounded by cytoplasm. Note the P-fracture face particles of the inner leaflet and the complementary E-fracture face pits on the outer leaflet. In panel c, an annular junctional profile is shown with a small separation between the two membranes (arrow). In a presumably corresponding freeze fracture view (panel d), a gap junction vesicle is indicated by a double arrow. This gap junction is characterized by a regular cluster of E-face pits separated by empty spaces (arrow). mp, plasma membrane. Bars = 0.25 μm. Panel e: annular junctional profiles in thin section often showed splitting of the junctional membranes (arrowhead), which could correspond to the freeze fracture image in panel f. The arrow in panel f indicates a gap junction vesicle in which half of its membrane (double arrow) is devoid of particles. cyto: cytoplasm; es: extracellular space, Bars = 0.25 μm.*

ends of the cells (Fig. 6a). Such structures were composed of single membranes with filaments, presumably actin, attached to the cytoplasmic surface. Progressively, over several hours, the area of the intercalated disc became smooth and regular in shape and appeared to be sealing off (compare Fig. 6a, b, and c), although serial sections would be required to establish this. The ends of the fibers were smooth and rounded and surface hemidesmosomes were no longer present (Fig. 6, b and c). Flattening of the circular hemidesmosome profiles was striking, at later times, due perhaps to reassociation of formerly extracellular aspects of the hemidesmosome. Desmosomes at the intercalated discs thus apparently separated, and each half of the desmosome was then internalized by each cell, as has been described in other tissues (Overton, 1968; Risinger and Larsen, 1981).

Discussion

The abundance of intercellular junctions in heart could conceivably prevent dissociation of the tissue into viable cells. Early attempts to dissociate cells resulted in myocytes that were not calcium tolerant, and from which electrophysiological properties like those of normal cells could not be demonstrated (cf. Fry et al., 1979). These difficulties have been attributed to leaks in the sarcolemma, either due to damage with inadequate resealing or to hypothesized patency of the gap junction channels exposed to external solution by the dissociation process. Gap junctions are resistant to mechanical stress (Muir, 1967; Goodenough and Revel, 1970; Amsterdam and Jamieson, 1974). As a result of this stability, when cells are forced apart after enzymatic treatment in low calcium, gap junctions are torn from the membranes of formerly adjacent cells and remain attached to one cell by small vesicles of nonjunctional membranes. (The question of what happens to the cells that lose their junctions also arises. Based on recovery of total protein and myoglobin content, we estimate that our yield of rectangular cells is 30–50%. Since some cells are no doubt lost in the process of mincing the tissue and, in the intact heart, each cell is connected to at least four others, our high yield argues that at least some cells recover after gap junctions have been ripped from their membranes.) Thin sections of intact myocyte sarcolemma with attached remnants of another cell sometimes suggested that the nonjunctional remnant might not be resealed, which could be attributed to oblique membrane section. Alternatively, resealing of the remnants may be slower than or independent of the closure of junctional channels, as would be expected if viability and sarcolemmal integrity of dissociated cells depended upon two distinct processes, junctional channel closure and membrane resealing. In intact heart, the recovery of gap junctional coupling after mechanical injury has been termed "healing over" and has been shown to depend upon submillimolar concentrations of divalent cations, cytoplasmic pH, and certain drugs (cf. Barr and Dewey, 1964; Dreifuss et al., 1966; DeMello, 1982). Sorting out the quantitative interaction of these effects is complicated by the complex geometry of cardiac tissue and by the participation of more than one process in the phenomenon of "healing over." In Purkinje fiber strands, the pH dependence of longitudinal resistance has been shown to be similar to that of gap junctional resistance of embryonic cells (compare Reber and Weingart, 1982, with Spray et al., 1981). The use of isolated myocyte pairs (White et al., 1982) should allow quantification of divalent cation effects on gap junctional conductance similar to that achieved in other systems (Spray et al., 1982).

Whether attributable to minimizing sarcolemmal injury or to rapid closing of the exposed gap junctions, recent improvements in the techniques of dissociation have provided cells which possess properties typical of the tissues in vivo (cf. Dow et al., 1981a, 1981b). These viable, calcium-tolerant myocytes provide a tissue for morphological examina-

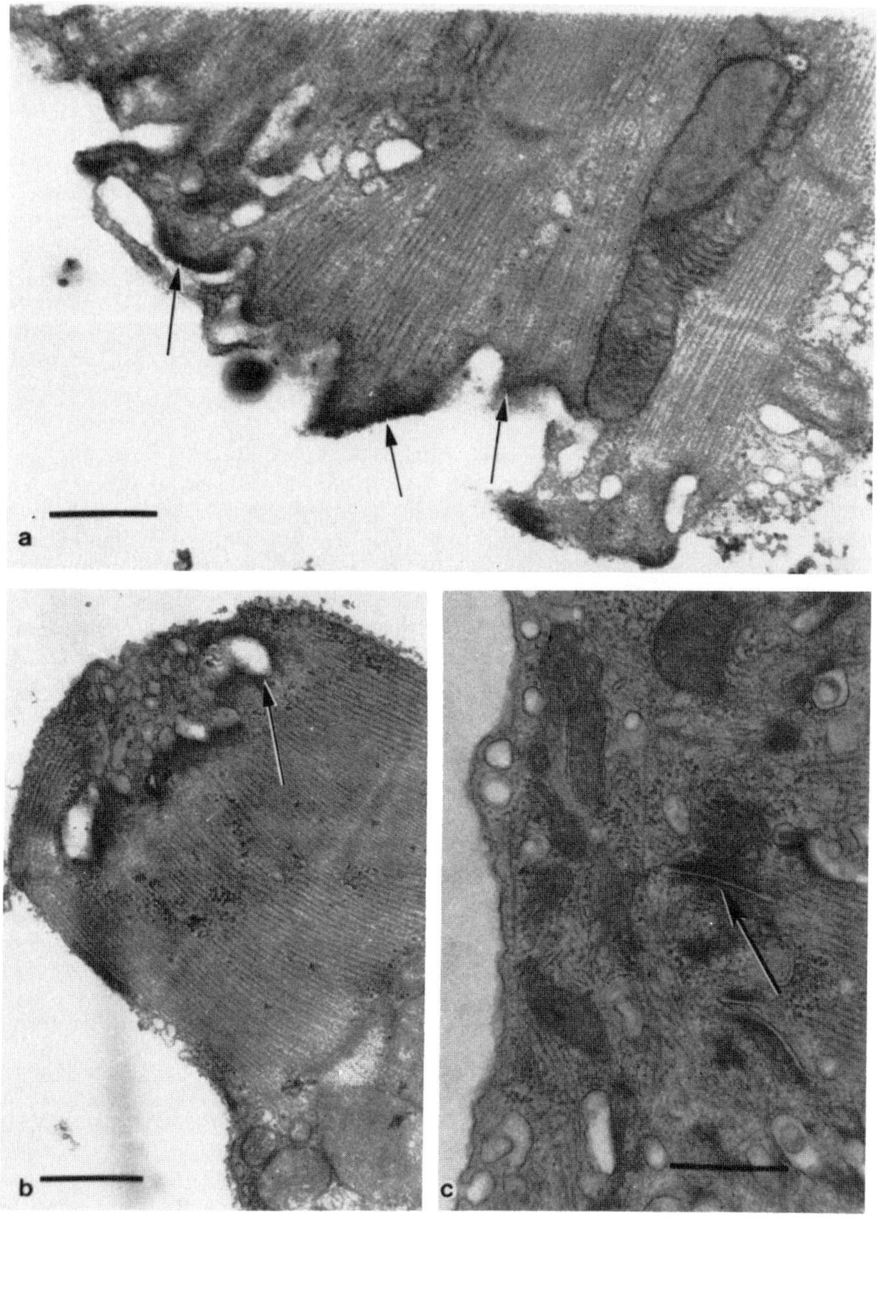

FIGURE 6. *Fate of desmosomes after dissociation. Panel a: soon after the cells are separated, thin sections show hemidesmosomes (arrows) in the region of the former intercalated disc. Parallel myosin filaments terminate within 0.1 μm from the hemidesmosomes. Panels b and c: after incubation overnight at 37°C, no surface hemidesmosomes are present, but subsurface vesicles (panel b) and apparently similar compressed structures (panel c, arrow) are observed that are similar to the formerly surface hemidesmosomes in possessing dense material attached to the cytoplasmic side of the membrane. The intercalated disc region of the cell is smooth and round after overnight incubation with myofilaments running parallel to the sarcolemma at the end of the fiber. In panels b and c, which are from the same preparation, small vesicles underlie the sarcolemma. Bars = 0.5 μm.*

tion in which separation of junctional membranes is known to occur within a span of 2 or 3 hours. Although resolution of the timing of membrane separation is coarse in these studies, the subsequent events are also slow, allowing the determination of a plausible sequence in junctional removal.

Examination of freeze-fracture replicas and thin section revealed that gap junctions were not split between adjacent plasma membranes, but remained attached to one cell after myocyte dissociation (Fig. 2). This form of retention of gap junction was first described for dissociated heart cells (Muir, 1967), and subsequent investigations using heart and other cell types have confirmed these observations (Amsterdam and Jamieson, 1974; Fry et al., 1979; Severs and Powell, 1980; Preus et al., 1981).

The superior viability of our dissociated adult cardiac cells (cf. Wittenberg and Robinson, 1981) has allowed us to follow the course of gap junction removal. After dissociation, our studies reveal subsurface vesicles containing gap junctions. Using only freeze fracture, it is not possible to determine whether the intracytoplasmic gap junctional vesicles correspond to invagination or to complete internalization of these junctions. We have examined thin sections of preparations where colloidal lanthanum was used as an electron opaque tracer to identify the extracellular space. Some circular gap junction profiles within the cytoplasm were labeled with lanthanum, indicating direct contact with extracellular space (Fig. 3). However, lanthanum was absent from other intracytoplasmic gap junction vesicles in the same section suggesting that the membranes of those vesicles were not continuous with the extracellular space (Fig. 4b). These unlabeled gap junction vesicles thus correspond to internalized gap junctions, which presumably arose from the pinching off of invaginated junctional blebs. Enclosed gap junctional structures have been observed in other tissues after dissociation (cf. Larsen, 1977, 1983), in dissociated carcinoma cells (Dunia et al., 1979), and during differentiation (cf. Ginzberg and Gilula, 1979), and have been similarly interpreted as representing a late stage in the process of gap junction removal from the surface membrane.

Among the unlabeled, presumably internalized, gap junction vesicles, several profile types were found in addition to the common circular shape (Fig. 4). These complex profiles might result from the involution of the internalized gap junction within itself. The progressive involution seems to involve the separation of the double membrane, and may thus correspond to the final stage of junctional breakdown. This membrane separation may represent the pit-free regions observed on the E-face of freeze fracture replicas of cytoplasmic gap junction vesicles (Fig. 5).

The process of dissociation used for these studies required about 3 hours, and some surface or labeled subsurface junctional vesicles were found at the end of this procedure. Synchronization of junctional disruption therefore is imprecise, and presumably not all gap junctions were being internalized at the same time. In order to interpret these findings in terms of the sequence of events, we assume that surface remnants are from newly dissociated cells and that internalized junctions are from junctions disrupted earlier in the procedure. This assumption is at least partially justified by our examination of cells 12 hours later, which revealed no surface remnants. Instead, sections of these cells show internalized, involuted bimembranous structures and abundant circular profiles of single membranes (cf. Fig. 5) whose origin is unknown but which may correspond to a final stage in gap junction dissolution.

The sequence of events that we envision to follow the disruption of junctional contact between ventricular myocytes is shown in Figure 7. In the first step, the nonjunctional membrane of one or the other cell is broken but remains attached to the other cell via the region of the gap junction. These junctions may be either open or closed, depending on pH or Ca^{++} concentrations near the cytoplasmic mouths of the channels. Our initial and final perfusion solutions contained 0.01 and 0.3 mM Ca^{++}, respectively. These Ca^{++} concentrations straddle the

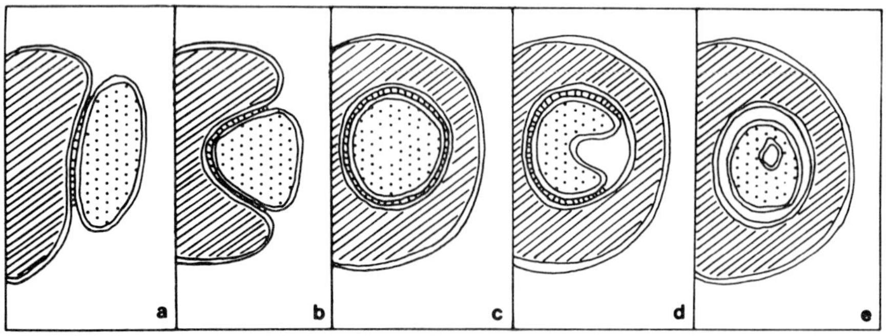

FIGURE 7. *Depiction of possible sequence of events in disappearance of gap junctions from the sarcolemma of dissociated myocytes. Mechanical dissociation leaves single cells with membrane remnants from formerly adjacent cells attached to the surface by gap junctions (horizontal lines, panel a). The surface remnants are subsequently internalized (panels b–d), a process that may involve involution into complex concentric structures. Finally, junctional membranes separate (panel d), a process that presumably results in concentric vesicles, each of which is formed by a single membrane (panel e). Shaded and dotted areas represent cytoplasms of the intact and formerly adjacent cell, respectively.*

levels to which junctions respond in other systems (Rose and Loewenstein, 1975; Spray et al., 1982).

The nonjunctional membranes then seal (Fig. 7), a process that is also dependent upon divalent cation concentration in the extracellular fluid (DeMello, 1982), and the enclosed vesicles begin to invaginate into the sarcolemma. Invagination is progressive (Fig. 7b, c) until the vesicle, composed of a double membrane connected in part by gap junctional particles, is totally enclosed within the cytoplasm and no longer communicates with the extracellular space. Finally, the bimembranous leaflet separates (Fig. 7d), producing sometimes complex membrane profiles that are totally surrounded by cytoplasm (Fig. 7e). Because the intercellular connection provided by gap junctions is inaccessible to proteolytic enzymes (cf. Kensler and Goodenough, 1980), we suggest that this final stage in breakdown may be caused either by hypertonicity of the solution within the enclosed junctional vesicle or by the very low levels of Ca^{++} activity achieved by cytoplasmic Ca^{++} binding. Hypertonic extracellular solutions split hepatocyte and cardiac junctions (cf. Dewey and Barr, 1964; Goodenough and Gilula, 1974), and gap junctions separate in the presence of high concentrations of calcium chelators (Campbell and Albertini, 1981; Hirokawa and Heuser, 1982). While there is no reason to hypothesize large osmotic differences across the gap junction vesicles, abundant evidence indicates that cytoplasmic calcium activity is normally about 0.1 μM, less than that found necessary extracellularly to maintain contact between junctional membranes. Exchange within bound cytoplasmic pools might therefore be responsible for eventual separation of membranes of cytoplasmic gap junctions.

We conclude from this study that the adult rat heart, which is composed of cells connected by gap junctions, no longer poses any particular problem to dissociation for study of individual cells. Over a time course of at most several hours, gap junctions disappear from the surface membrane and, over a longer time course, are eventually degraded. Internalized gap junction profiles have been seen in developing cardiac tissue (cf. Legato, 1979), but the extent to which the sequence outlined here occurs in vivo is unknown. Studies are now underway to examine the time course of reestablishment of gap junctional contact between myocytes in which surface junctions are no longer present. These studies should allow the assessment of whether reformation is accelerated by pharmacological treatments, and may shed new light on cardiac pathology involving death of small numbers of myocytes.

We are grateful for the space and equipment made available for this work by Dr. P.G. Model, for criticisms of drafts of this manuscript and for helpful discussions with R.D. Ginzberg, M.V.L. Bennett, and E.A. Morales. We are especially indebted to C.F. Wong for technical assistance in cell dissociation and to J. Zavilowitz for assistance in maintaining cells overnight in culture.

Dr. Mazet was a Visiting Fellow supported in part by the Centre National de la Recherche Scientifique (France); work was also supported in part by a Grant-in-Aid from the American Heart Association (DCS), a McKnight Development Award (DCS), and NIH Grants NS 16524 and NS 07512 (DCS) and HL19299 (BW).

Dr. Mazet's present address is: Laboratoire de Physiologie Comparee et de Physiologie Cellulaire Associe au CNRS. Universite Paris X1 Centre d'Orsay, 91405, Orsay, France.

Address for reprints: David C. Spray, Ph.D., Department of Neuroscience, Albert Einstein College of Medicine, 1410 Pelham Parkway South, Bronx, New York 10461.

Received March 26, 1984; accepted for publication October 31, 1984.

References

Amsterdam A, Jamieson, JD (1974) Studies on dispersed pancreatic exocrine cells. I. Dissociation technique and morphologic characteristics of separated cells. J Cell Biol **63:** 1037–1056

Barr L, Dewey MM, Berger W (1965) Propagation of an action potential and the structure of the nexus in cardiac muscle. J Gen Physiol **48:** 797–823

Campbell KL, Albertini DF (1981) Freeze-fracture analysis of gap junction disruption in rat ovarian granulosa cells. Tissue Cell **13:** 651–668

DeMello WC (1982) Intercellular communication in cardiac muscle. Circ Res **51:** 1–8

Dewey MM, Barr L (1964) A study of structure and distribution of the nexus. J Cell Biol **23:** 553–585

Dow JW, Harding NG, Powell T (1981a) Isolated cardiac myocytes: I. Preparation of adult myocytes and their homology with intact tissue. Circ Res **15:** 483–514

Dow JW, Harding NG, Powell T (1981b) Isolated cardiac myocytes: II. Functional aspects of mature cells. Circ Res **15:** 549–579

Dreifuss JJ, Girardier L, Forsmann WG (1966) Etude de la propagation de l'excitation dans le ventricule de rat au moyen de solutions hypertoniques. Pflugers Arch **292:** 13–33

Dunia I, Nicolas JF, Jakob H, Benedetti EL, Jacob F (1979) Junctional modulation in mouse embryonal carcinoma cells by Fab fragments of rabbit anti-embryonal carcinoma cell serum. Proc Natl Acad Sci USA **76:** 3387–3391

Farquhar MG, Palade GE (1963) Junctional complexes in various epithelia. J Cell Biol **17:** 375–412

Fry DM, Scales D, Inesi G (1979) The ultrastructure of membrane alterations of enzymatically dissociated cardiac myocytes. J Mol Cell Cardiol **11:** 1151–63

Ginzberg RD, Gilula NB (1979) Modulation of cell junctions during differentiation of the chicken otocyst sensory epithelium. Develop Biol **68:** 110–129

Goodenough DA, Gilula NB (1974) The splitting of hepatocyte gap junctions and zonulae occludentes with hypertonic dissacharides. J Cell Biol **61:** 575–590

Goodenough DA, Revel JP (1970) A fine structural analysis of intercellular junctions in the mouse liver. J Cell Biol **45:** 272–290

Gupta RK, Wittenberg BA (1983) NMR observation of the effect of extracellular calcium on intracellular Na+ ions in isolated cardiac myocytes (abstr). Fed Proc **42:** 2065

Hirokawa N, Heuser J (1982) The inside and outside of gap-junction membranes visualized by deep etching. Cell **30:** 395–406

Kao RL, Christman EW, Luh SL, Krauhs JM, Tyers GFO, Williams EH (1980) The effects of insulin and anoxia on the metabolism of isolated mature rat cardiac myocytes. Arch Biochem Biophys **203:** 587–599

Kensler RW, Goodenough DA (1980) Isolation of mouse myocardial gap junctions. J Cell Biol **86:** 755–764

Larsen WJ (1977) Structural diversity of gap junctions: A review. Tissue Cell **9:** 373–394

Larsen WJ (1983) Biological implications of gap junction structure, distribution and composition: A review. Tissue Cell **15:** 645–671

Legato MJ (1979) Cellular mechanisms of normal growth in the mammalian heart. I. Qualitative and quantitative features of ventricular architecture in the dog from birth to five months of age. Circ Res **44:** 250–262

Mazet F, Wittenberg BA, Spray DC, Model PG (1982) Gap junction structure in isolated cardiac myocytes (abstr). J Cell Biol **95:** 90a

McNutt NS, Fawcett DW (1974) Myocardial ultrastructure. *In* The Mammalian Myocardium, edited by GA Langer, AJ Brady. New York Wiley, pp 1–49

Muir AR (1967) The effects of divalent cations on the ultrastructure of the perfused rat heart. J Anat **101:** 239–262

Overton J (1968) The fate of desmosomes in trypsinized tissue. J Exp Zool **168:** 203–214

Preus D, Johnson R, Sheridan JD (1981) Gap junctions between Novikoff hepatoma cells following dissociation and recovery in the absence of cell contact. J Ultrastruct Res **77:** 248–262

Reber WR, Weingart R (1982) Ungulate cardiac Purkinje fibers: The influence of intracellular pH on the electrical cell-to-cell coupling. J Physiol (Lond) **328:** 87–104

Risinger MA, Larsen WJ (1981) Endocytosis of cell-cell junctions and spontaneous cell dissagregation in a cultured human ovarian adenocarcinoma (colo 316). Tissue Cell **13:** 413–430

Robinson TF, Hayward BS, Krueger JW, Sonnenblick EH, Wittenberg BA (1980) Isolated heart myocytes: Ultrastructural case study technique. J Microscop **124:** 135–142

Rose B, Loewenstein WR (1975) Permeability of cell junction depends on local cytoplasmic calcium activity. Nature (Lond) **254:** 250–252

Severs NJ, Powell T (1980) Sarcolemma structure in isolated rat myocytes. *In* Electron Microscopy, vol 2, edited by P Brederoo, W De Priester. Leiden, Seventh European Congress on Electron Microscopy Foundation, pp 134–135

Severs NJ, Slade AM, Powell T, Twist VW, Warren RL (1982) Correlation of ultrastructure and function in calcium-tolerant myocytes isolated from the adult rat heart. J Ultrastruct Res **81:** 222–239

Spray DC, Harris AL, Bennett MVL (1981) Gap junctional conductance is a simple and sensitive function of intracellular pH. Science **211:** 712–715

Spray DC, Stern JH, Harris AL, Bennett MVL (1982) Comparison of sensitivities of gap junctional conductance to H and Ca ions. Proc Natl Acad Sci USA **79:** 441–445

Venable JH, Coggeshall R (1965) A simplified lead citrate stain for use in electron microscopy. J Cell Biol **25:** 407–408

White RL, Carvalho AC, Spray DC, Wittenberg BA, Bennett MVL (1983) Gap junctional conductance between isolated pairs of ventricular myocytes from rat (abstr). Biophys J **41:** 217a

Wittenberg BA, Robinson TF (1981) Oxygen requirements, morphology, cell coat and membrane permeability of calcium-tolerant myocytes from hearts of adult rats. Cell Tissue Res **216:** 232–251

INDEX TERMS: Gap junctions • Nexus • Desmosomes • Intercalated disks • Dissociated cardiac myocytes

Neurogenic Muscarinic Vasodilation in the Cat

An Example of Endothelial Cell-Independent Cholinergic Relaxation

Joseph E. Brayden and John A. Bevan

From the Department of Pharmacology, University of Vermont, College of Medicine, Burlington, Vermont

SUMMARY. Nerve-mediated and acetylcholine-induced dilator behavior of feline posterior auricular arteries was studied in vitro. We evaluated the muscarinic nature and endothelial cell-dependence of the vasodilations and attempted to determine if there are inhibitory muscarinic receptors located directly on the smooth muscle cells in this artery. Transmural nerve stimulation of arteries which were pretreated with guanethidine (5×10^{-6} M) and constricted with prostaglandin $F_{2\alpha}$ (3×10^{-6} M) caused a frequency-dependent, tetrodotoxin-sensitive relaxation of up to 50% of induced tone. Atropine (10^{-7} M) blocked more than 95% of this response at all frequencies. Removal of the endothelium by rubbing the intimal surface did not affect the magnitude of the response, but prolonged it slightly. Neurogenic relaxations in rubbed preparations were atropine-sensitive, although less so than control at higher stimulation frequencies. Relaxation of this artery to the calcium ionophore A23187 was completely endothelial cell-dependent. However, exogenous acetylcholine caused dose-dependent relaxations both in control and rubbed preparations. We conclude that the posterior auricular artery is an example of a blood vessel which has muscarinic receptors located directly on its smooth muscle cells which, when activated by acetylcholine released from perivascular nerves, mediate a smooth muscle cell relaxation. This finding contrasts with models of the vascular smooth muscle cell which indicates an excitatory role for muscarinic receptors. **(*Circ Res 56: 205–211, 1985*)**

ALTHOUGH adrenergically mediated neural control of blood vessels is established and widespread within the cardiovascular system of most animals (Bevan et al., 1980; Vanhoutte et al., 1981), evidence for a functional cholinergic neural supply to arteries and veins is less common and less convincing. Tissues such as the lung (Fisher, 1965), heart (Brown, 1968), uterus (Bell, 1968), skeletal muscle (Bulbring and Burn, 1935) and kidneys (Stinson et al., 1968) are thought to receive a neurogenic, cholinergic vasodilator input. However, many of the conclusions are based on histological evidence of acetylcholinesterase activity, a measure which is no longer considered to be conclusive evidence for cholinergic nerves (Koelle, 1955; Barajas and Wang, 1975). Other studies have examined the effects of exogenously applied acetylcholine as an index of cholinergic innervation. As muscarinic receptors are known to occur in many blood vessels where there is no evidence of cholinergic innervation, the latter type of evidence is without value. Perhaps some of the best evidence for cholinergic vasodilator nerves comes from studies of the cerebral and extracerebral cephalic circulation (Pinard et al., 1979; Bevan et al., 1982a) where at least part of nerve-mediated vasodilation seems to be under muscarinic control. In addition to pharmacological evidence for cholinergic innervation in cephalic vascular beds, biochemical indices of a cholinergic nerve supply, including high choline acetyltransferase levels (Bevan et al., 1982b) and a high affinity choline uptake system (Florence and Bevan, 1979), have been found in these arteries.

As is now clear, largely from the work of Furchgott et al. (1983), a wide variety of blood vessels dilate upon exposure to exogenous acetylcholine through a mechanism which is endothelial cell-dependent. Acetylcholine acts upon muscarinic receptors located on the endothelial cells. These cells in turn release an as yet unidentified endothelium-derived relaxing factor which leads ultimately to relaxation of the vascular smooth muscle cells. In those arteries so far examined, removal of the endothelium abolishes the vascular relaxation caused by acetylcholine (Furchgott and Zawadzki, 1980; De Mey et al., 1982). It is not known whether cholinergic neurogenic vasodilation is dependent upon the endothelium or whether it is mediated through muscarinic receptors located at postjunctional sites on the vascular smooth muscle cells themselves. In the present study, we have characterized the neurodilator behavior of one vessel from the cephalic circulation, the feline posterior auricular artery. The neural relaxation in this artery is almost completely cholinergic. Our intent was to evaluate the endothelial cell dependence of a muscarinic vasodilator response which clearly is mediated by nerves and, as a corollary, to determine whether or not there are inhibitory muscarinic receptors located directly on the vascular smooth muscle cells in this artery.

Methods

Cats weighing 3–4 kg and of either sex were anesthetized with sodium pentobarbital (50 mg/kg) and exsanguinated. The posterior auricular artery, a branch of the proximal external carotid artery, was then rapidly removed and placed in oxygenated Krebs bicarbonate solution of the following composition (mM): Na^+, 144.2; K^+, 4.9; Ca^{++}, 1.6; Mg^{++}, 1.2; Cl^-, 126.7; HCO_3^-, 25.0; SO_4^{--}, 1.99; glucose, 11.1; and disodium ethylenediamine tetraacetate, 0.023.

After removal of surrounding connective tissue, 4-mm-long cylindrical segments of artery having unstretched lumen diameters of approximately 0.8 mm were mounted between two wires, one of which was connected to an isometric force transducer and the other to a micrometer displacement device. Tissues were then immersed in organ baths containing 50 ml of oxygenated Krebs solution (pH 7.4), and changes in tone were measured as previously described (Bevan et al., 1982a). In brief, after temperature equilibration for 15 minutes at 37°C, resting tension was adjusted to 1.0 g, which in pilot studies was found to be an optimal pre-load for force development, and platinum-stimulating electrodes were positioned, one on either side of the artery. After a 60-minute equilibration period, vessels were exposed to an EC_{70} dose of norepinephrine (3×10^{-6} M) and then washed. Guanethidine (5×10^{-6} M) was added to the tissue bath and replaced after every wash to block adrenergic constriction. Blockade occurred in all experiments and was verified by a lack of constriction in response to transmural nerve stimulation after 30 minutes of exposure to guanethidine. Dilator responses to nerve stimulation were examined after induction of tone by prostaglandin $F_{2\alpha}$ ($PGF_{2\alpha}$, 3×10^{-6} M). Transmural nerve stimulation was applied as 20-second trains of 0.3-msec pulses at a current strength of 70 mA. Stimulation frequencies ranging from 1 to 16 Hz were used. In every experiment, the dilator responses to such stimulation were shown to be tetrodotoxin-sensitive (3×10^{-7} M) at all frequencies of stimulation. Frequency-response characteristics and effects of various drugs were determined at least 30 minutes after washout of the tetrodotoxin. Peak dilation was expressed as percentage decrease in the level of active tone.

In experiments designed to test the effect of disruption of the endothelium, arteries were rubbed briefly over the entire intimal surface, using a short length of stainless steel tubing, 0.2 mm in diameter, and then were mounted as usual in the organ bath. Destruction of endothelial cells was verified by means of a pharmacological criterion—absence of relaxation to the calcium ionophore A23187—and, at the end of experiments, by direct observation of the intimal surface after en face silver staining (Poole et al., 1958).

Dose-response relationships to acetylcholine and calcium ionophore A23187 were obtained by cummulative addition of the agents to the organ bath following induction of tone with $PGF_{2\alpha}$.

Data are presented as mean ± SEM, and statistical comparisons were made using Student's *t*-test.

Results

Evidence for Removal of Endothelial Cells

Removal of endothelial cells was confirmed pharmacologically by loss of dilator action of the calcium

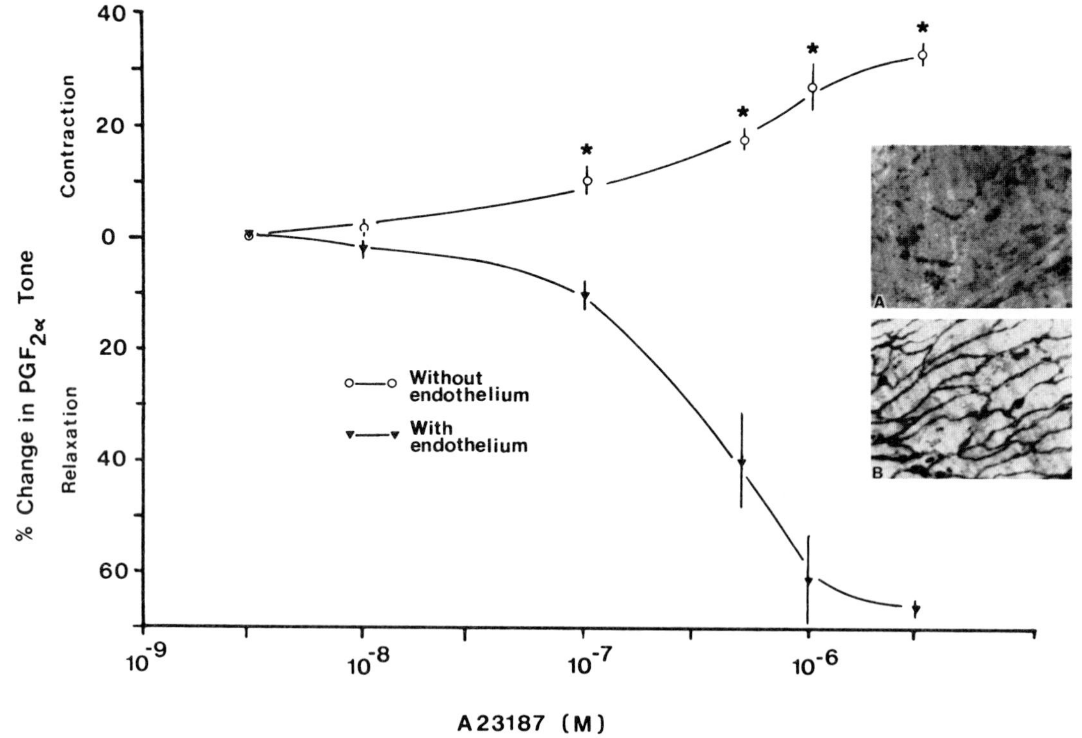

FIGURE 1. *Calcium ionophore A23187 dose-response relationships of control (n = 5) and rubbed posterior auricular arteries (n = 5). Data are expressed as percent change in $PGF_{2\alpha}$-induced tone. Arteries with endothelium dilated due to this agent at a threshold dose of 10^{-8} M. Arteries without endothelial cells showed only a constrictor response to A23187. *P < 0.001 vs. control. Insets: examples of en face silver-stained preparations of rubbed (inset A) and control (inset B) posterior auricular arteries following in vitro experiments.*

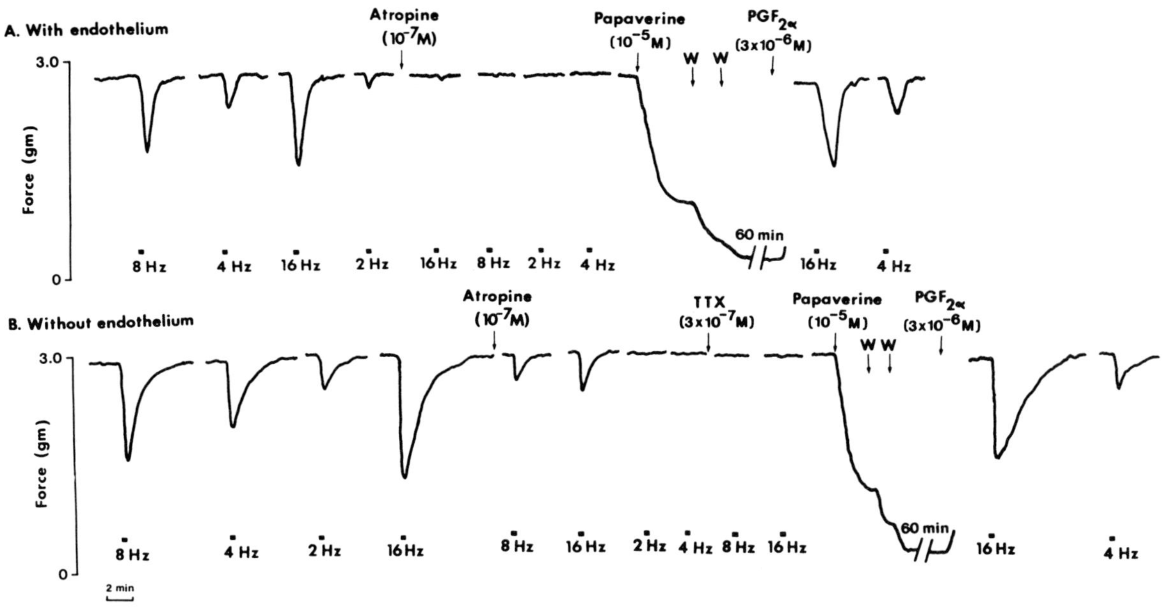

FIGURE 2. *Typical pattern of dilator responses of posterior auricular arteries with (panel A) and without (panel B) endothelium. Active tone was induced with* $PGF_{2\alpha}$ *(3 × 10⁻⁶ M) in the presence of guanethidine (5 × 10⁻⁷ M). Time of stimulation is indicated by bar above frequency labels. Intervals between stimulations are 10 minutes, except where indicated. Ten-minute treatment with atropine (10⁻⁷ M) blocked more than 95% of the response at all frequencies when the endothelium was present, and more than 60% of the response when the endothelium was absent.*

ionophore A23187 in rubbed preparations (Fig. 1). Although intact preparations underwent a dose-dependent relaxation to concentrations of this agent ranging from 3×10^{-9} to 3×10^{-6} M, rubbed vessels did not respond to doses less than about 10^{-7} M, and contracted at higher doses. In addition, the state of the endothelium was routinely examined histologically at the conclusion of experiments. After 3–4 hours in the organ bath, vessels which were not subjected to the rubbing procedure maintained an intact endothelium (inset, Fig. 1) over nearly all of the intimal surface, with the exception of those areas which had been in continual contact with the mounting wires. Arterial segments that had been intentionally rubbed were, in all cases, completely devoid of endothelial cells (inset, Fig. 1).

Dilator Responses of Intact Arteries

Traces of the typical pattern of dilator responses of an intact posterior auricular artery are shown in Figure 2A. Responses to transmural nerve stimulation were frequency dependent and reached a maximum during the 20-second stimulation or within a few seconds after the stimulus was removed. Redevelopment of tone to prestimulation levels also was rapid and generally occurred within the 60 seconds following cessation of stimulation. Ten minutes after treatment with atropine (10^{-7} M), the effect of transmural nerve stimulation was nearly abolished at all stimulation frequencies (Fig. 2A). Dilator responses to papaverine (10^{-5} M, Fig. 2A) were not affected by the presence of atropine. After washout of drugs,

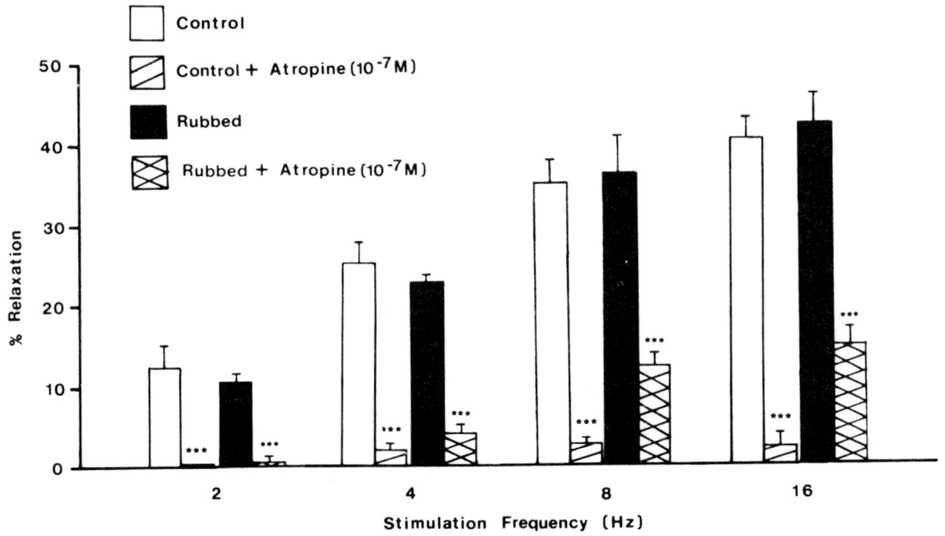

FIGURE 3. *Summary of effects of atropine (10⁻⁷ M) on neurogenic relaxations of posterior auricular arteries with (n = 8) and without (n = 8) endothelium. Data are expressed as percent decrease in* $PGF_{2\alpha}$*-induced tone following transmural nerve stimulation at 2,4,8, and 16 Hz. Error bars are standard errors. ***P < 0.001 vs. responses prior to addition of atropine.*

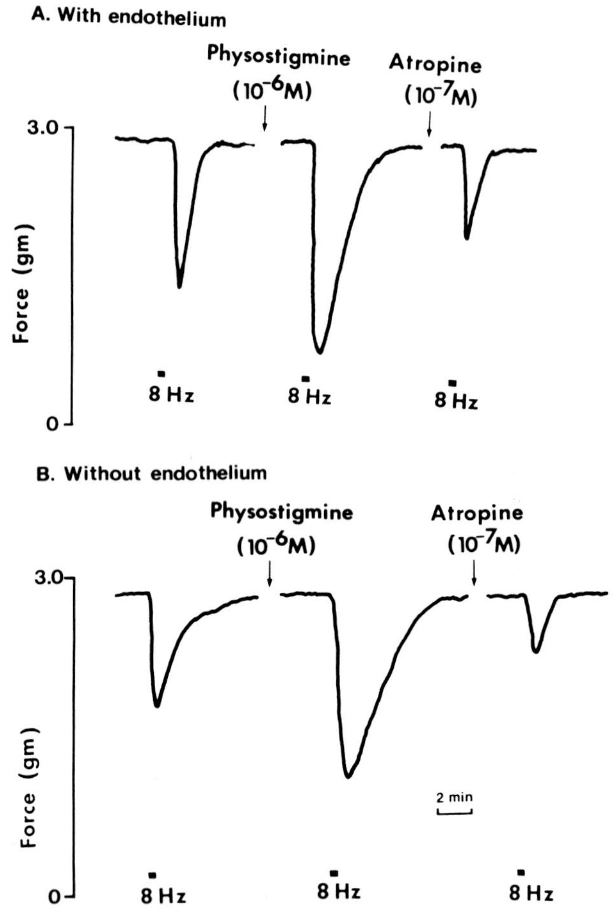

FIGURE 4. *Effects of physostigmine and subsequent addition of atropine (10^{-7} M) on relaxations of posterior auricular arteries at 8 Hz stimulation frequency. Physostigmine potentiated and prolonged the relaxations, and atropine reversed the effect of physostigmine in control and rubbed preparations.*

constrictor and dilator responses could be induced which were equivalent to those elicited at the onset of the experiments, thus indicating the stability of these preparations with time (Fig. 2A).

Relaxations of up to 45% of induced tone were common at higher frequencies of stimulation, and in all cases responses were inhibited nearly completely by atropine (Fig. 3). As would be predicted for a classical muscarinic response, physostigmine (10^{-6} M) increased both the magnitude and duration of the dilator response (Fig. 4A), and the subsequent addition of atropine reversed this effect.

Effects of Endothelial Cell Removal

Removal of the endothelium had no significant effect on the ability of the posterior auricular artery to contract to $PGF_{2\alpha}$ (Table 1, legend). The magnitudes of the neurogenic dilator responses of rubbed arterial segments were not different from those of intact preparations (Figs. 2B, 3, and 4B; Table 1). The potentiating effect of physostigmine also was not different in rubbed arteries compared with control (Fig. 4B; Table 1).

Nevertheless, some differences in dilator behavior of the two preparations were apparent (Table 1). The $t_{1/2}$ for recovery of relaxations to prestimulation levels of tone in vessels lacking endothelial cells was significantly greater than that for control vessels at all frequencies of stimulation. In addition, an atropine-resistant component ranging from 20% to 40% of the total relaxation was observed in rubbed vessels at stimulation frequencies of 4,8 and 16 Hz. Increased concentrations of atropine up to 5×10^{-6} M did not effect this response.

In three experiments, 10 minutes of exposure to indomethacin (10^{-5} M) or 5,8,11,14-eicosatetraynoic acid (3×10^{-5} M), a lipoxygenase and cycloxygenase inhibitor, did not alter the atropine-resistant component (data not shown). Atropine-reisistant relaxations were tetrodotoxin-sensitive, again indicating their neurogenic origin (Fig. 2B). Relaxations of rubbed arteries to papaverine occurred in the presence of atropine and tetrodotoxin. The effects of all drugs were reversible, and the dilator capability of rubbed preparations did not decline during the

TABLE 1
Summary of Transmural Nerve Stimulation-Induced Relaxations in Presence (+) and Absence (−) of Endothelium

Parameter	Stimulation frequency							
	2 Hz		4 Hz		8 Hz		16 Hz	
	(+)	(−)	(+)	(−)	(+)	(−)	(+)	(−)
Peak dilator response (g)	0.4 ± 0.1	0.3 ± 0.1	0.8 ± 0.1	0.7 ± 0.1	1.1 ± 0.1	1.2 ± 0.2	1.2 ± 0.1	1.3 ± 0.1
$T_{1/2}$ for recovery of initial tone (sec)	23 ± 3	50 ± 5†	22 ± 1	48 ± 3‡	27 ± 3	51 ± 6†	28 ± 3	52 ± 4†
Atropine-resistant dilation (% of total dilation)	0 ± 0	9.9 ± 9.8	4.2 ± 2.3	22.1 ± 8.1*	4.8 ± 2.8	40.6 ± 5.4‡	3.1 ± 3.1	37.0 ± 5.2‡
Peak dilator response in presence of physostigmine (g)	0.8 ± 0.5	0.9 ± 0.3	1.5 ± 0.3	1.3 ± 0.3	2.0 ± 0.2	1.8 ± 0.3	ND	ND

* $P < 0.05$ vs. control; † $P < 0.01$ vs. control; ‡ $P < 0.001$ vs. control. $n = 4$ for experiments testng effects of physostigmine. For other parameters, $n = 10$ for control experiments and $n = 8$ for experiments testing effects of endothelial cell removal. Peak constrictor responses to $PGF_{2\alpha}$ (3×10^{-6}) were 2.9 ± 0.2 g and 3.2 ± 0.2 g in control ($n = 10$) and rubbed vessels ($n = 8$), respectively, and were not significantly different from each other. ND: not determined.

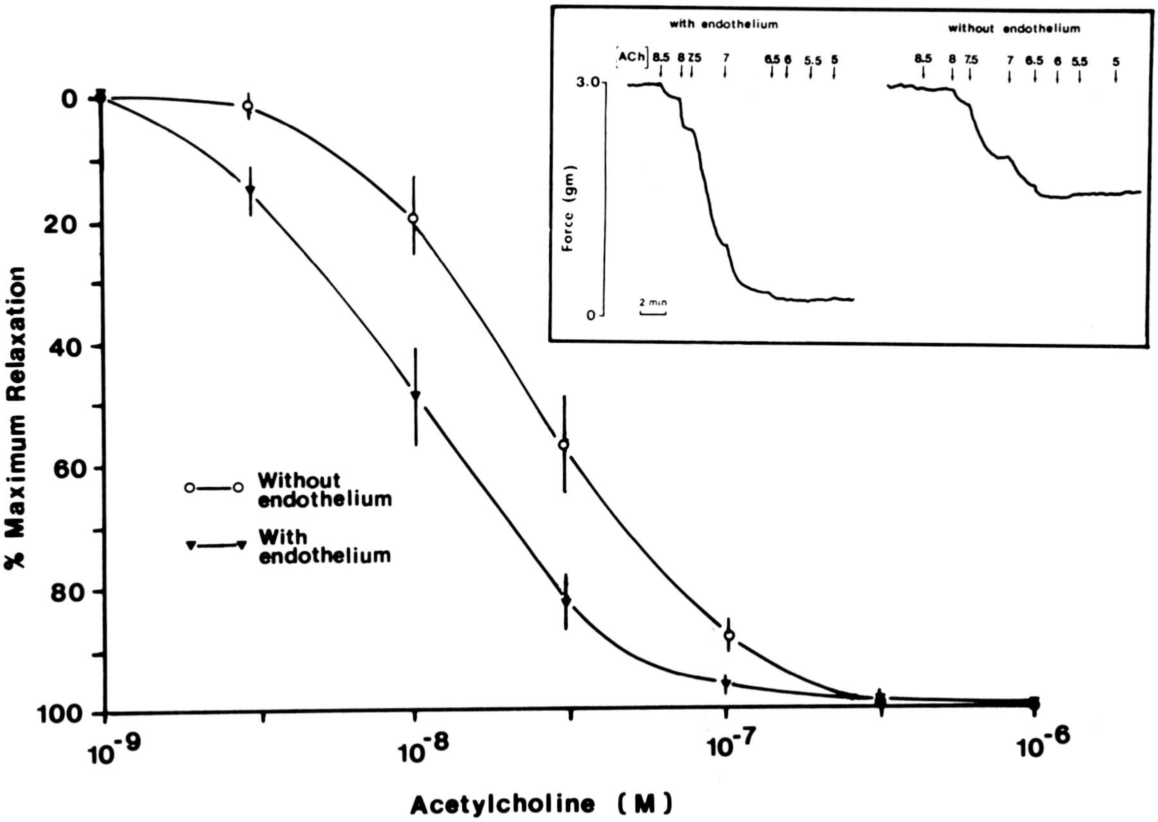

FIGURE 5. *Acetylcholine dose-response relationships with (n = 6) and without (n = 6) endothelium. Data are expressed as percent of the maximum response to acetylcholine. Maximum relaxations (% of active tone) were 83.9 ± 3.9% with endothelium and 58.6 ± 4.1% (P < 0.001 vs. unrubbed) without endothelium. Negative log EC_{50} values (mean with 95% confidence intervals) were 7.99 (7.80–8.33) with endothelium and 7.56 (7.36–7.95) (P < 0.05 vs. unrubbed preparations) without endothelium. Inset: tracings of typical responses to exogenous acetylcholine of arteries with and without endothelium. Numbers above arrows are negative log acetylcholine values.*

course of the experiments, as indicated by the responses to nerve stimulation at the end of experiments (Fig. 2B).

Responses to Exogenous Acetylcholine

Addition of exogenous acetylcholine to both rubbed and intact arteries caused a dose-dependent relaxation (Fig. 5). The peak dilator response occurred at an acetylcholine concentration of 3×10^{-6} M in both control and rubbed preparations. The EC_{50} for this effect of acetylcholine in rubbed vessels was significantly different from that for control vessels (Fig. 5, legend). In addition, the maximum acetylcholine-induced relaxation of $PGF_{2\alpha}$-induced tone in rubbed vessels was significantly less than relaxation of control arteries (Fig. 5, legend).

Discussion

The results from this study support the notion that cephalic vessels are subject to inhibitory neural inputs which could have significant effects on vascular resistance and distribution of blood flow. Many examples of neurogenic dilator responses of cerebral blood vessels have been described (D'Alecy, 1977; Lee, 1982). In the extracerebral cephalic circulation, the tongue (Eccles and Wallis, 1974), nasal mucosa (Anggard, 1974), eye (Stjernschantz and Bill, 1980), and salivary glands (Lundberg, 1981) all receive well-documented vasodilator innervation. Previous reports from this laboratory (Bevan et al., 1982a) have demonstrated that neurodilator responses of many feline cephalic arteries consist of two components, one of which is cholinergic, mediated through muscarinic receptors, and that the contribution of this component can vary considerably from vessel to vessel. The posterior auricular artery apparently falls at one end of this spectrum, since its neural dilator mechanism is mediated predominantly by one transmitter substance, i.e., acetylcholine.

The ability of the posterior auricular artery to relax upon activation of its perivascular nerves does not seem to be dependent on the presence of endothelial cells. Peak dilator responses were nearly identical in magnitude in arteries with and without endothelial cells. This finding is in agreement with similar studies of feline cerebral arteries (Lee, 1982) in which transmural nerve stimulation caused relaxations of nearly 50% of developed tone in arteries with and without endothelium, although, in this case, the dilation, since it was resistant to atropine, was not cholinergic.

In the present study, nerve-mediated relaxations of posterior auricular arteries were atropine-sensitive, both in control and in rubbed preparations. Thus, these experiments suggest that acetylcholine released from perivascular nerves can act directly on the smooth muscle cells to cause relaxation via a muscarinic receptor. In preliminary experiments, dilator responses also were examined after induction of tone with 5-hydroxytryptamine (10^{-6} M). Identical neurogenic dilator behavior was observed, regardless of the agonist used to induce tone. This finding argues against the involvement of dilator mechanisms which may be specific to $PGF_{2\alpha}$ or its receptors. Responses to $PGF_{2\alpha}$ were maintained for longer periods of time than those to 5-hydroxytryptamine, and, hence, the prostaglandin was used throughout these studies.

It is not clear whether or not the nerve-released acetylcholine, in addition to having a direct effect on smooth muscle cells, caused arterial relaxation by inducing secondary release of a relaxing factor from the endothelial cells. The actual magnitude of the atropine-sensitive relaxation, i.e., that remaining after the atropine-insensitive component is subtracted from the total response, is decreased in rubbed arteries. This would indicate a possible endothelial cell contribution to the cholinergic relaxation in intact preparations. In a recent study, Angus and co-workers (1983) showed that acetylcholine applied to the adventitial side of canine femoral arteries in vivo was able to traverse the arterial wall and cause an endothelium-dependent relaxation. Thus, it is conceivable that acetylcholine release from nerves could diffuse through the vessel wall and reach the endothelial cell layer, although evidence to the contrary also has been presented (Cohen et al., 1984).

The mechanism by which endothelial cell removal unmasked the atropine-insensitive dilator response in this artery is not known. It is possible that transmural nerve stimulation caused a tetrodotoxin-sensitive release of a constrictor substance from the endothelial cells (De Mey and Vanhoutte, 1983) which offset the effects of a noncholinergic dilator transmitter substance. Removal of endothelial cells might then have revealed the atropine-insensitive relaxation. The lack of effect of indomethacin and 5,8,11,14-eicosatetraynoic acid argues against the involvement of arachidonic acid metabolites in the atropine-resistant vasodilator response.

Furchgott and Zawadzki (1980) first reported that removal of endothelial cells from rabbit aortic strips completely abolished the relaxation responses of this preparation to acetylcholine and, in later work (Furchgott et al., 1983), to ATP, bradykinin and the calcium ionophore A32187. These authors also found that both control and rubbed preparations constricted when high concentrations of acetylcholine (>10^{-6} M) were applied. Subsequent work by others has confirmed these findings in a variety of blood vessels (Altura and Chand, 1981; De Mey et al., 1982). As a result of these studies, current models of the vascular smooth muscle cell imply that activation of muscarinic receptors located on this cell leads to constriction (Furchgott et al., 1981, Vanhoutte, 1981). The present study represents an example of a blood vessel where this clearly is not the case. Arteries lacking endothelial cells still undergo significant relaxation in response to low doses of exogenous acetylcholine. This finding indicates that muscarinic receptors which mediate smooth muscle cell relaxation to exogenous acetylcholine indeed are present on the vascular smooth muscle cells. The dilator response of the posterior auricular artery to the calcium ionophore A23187 showed the same endothelial dependence as has been seen in other blood vessels (Furchgott et al., 1983). This suggests that, although the dilator response of the posterior auricular artery to acetylcholine is unique when compared to that seen in all other vessels so far examined, it is unlikely that this artery is unusual in other respects. Indeed, the greater relaxation response of control posterior auricular arteries to exogenous acetylcholine compared with the response in arteries which have been rubbed probably is due to the combined effects of an endothelial-derived relaxation factor, as well as the direct relaxant effect of acetylcholine on the smooth muscle cells.

The functional implications of this cholinergic outflow are not clear. The posterior auricular artery supplies middle ear structures, as well as skeletal muscle near the ears (Crouch, 1969). It has been suggested that dilator innervation in arteries supplying other feline cephalic structures may be activated during times of thermal stress (Bevan et al., 1981, Gibbins et al., in press). However, based on the nature of the tissues supplied by the posterior auricular artery, a thermoregulatory role for these nerves seems unlikely. It is possible that this system is analagous to the sympathetic, muscarinic dilator innervation which has been demonstrated in arteries supplying other skeletal muscles (Bulbring and Burn, 1935), but, pending further work, a specific role for this particular dilator outflow must remain speculative. Regardless of the physiological conditions which might lead to activation of these dilator nerves, the direct muscarinic inhibitory response which occurs in this artery upon activation of its neural input is pronounced, and is sufficient to play an important role in determining blood flow in the tissues supplied by this artery.

Supported by U.S. Public Health Service Grants HL 32383 and HL 06804.

Address for reprints: Joseph E. Brayden, Ph.D., Department of Pharmacology, University of Vermont, College of Medicine, Burlington, Vermont 05405.

Received June 14, 1984; accepted for publication November 8, 1984.

References

Altura BM, Chand N (1981) Bradykinin-induced relaxation of renal and pulmonary arteries is dependent upon intact endothelial cells. Br J Pharmacol **74:** 10–11

Anggard A (1974) The effects of parasympathetic nerve stimulation on the microcirculation and secretion in the nasal mucosa of the cat. Acta Otolaryngol **78:** 98–105

Angus JA, Campbell GR, Cocks TM, Manderson JA (1983) Vasodilatation by acetylcholine is endothelium-dependent: A study by sonomicrometry in canine femoral artery in vivo. J Physiol (Lond) **344:** 209–222

Barajas LP, Wang P (1975) Demonstration of acetylcholinesterase in the adrenergic nerves of renal glomerular arterioles. J Ultrastruct Res **53:** 244–253

Bell C (1968) Dual vasoconstrictor and vasodilator innervation of the uterine arterial supply in the guinea-pig. Circ Res **23:** 279–289

Bevan JA, Bevan RD, Duckles SP (1980) Adrenergic regulation of vascular smooth muscle. *In* Handbook of Physiology: The Cardiovascular System, edited by DF Bohr, AP Somlyo, HV Sparks. Washington, D.C., American Physiological Society, pp 515–566

Bevan JA, Bevan RD, Buga G, Florence VM, Jope CA, Jope RS, Moritoki H (1981) The cranial neural vasodilator outflow. *In* Vasodilatation, edited by PM Vanhoutte, I Leusen. New York, Raven Press, pp 19–26

Bevan JA, Buga GM, Jope CA, Jope RS, Moritoki H (1982a) Further evidence for a muscarinic component to the neural vasodilator innervation of cerebral and cranial extracerebral arteries of the cat. Circ Res **51:** 421–429

Bevan JA, Buga GM, Florence VM, Gonsalves A, Snowden A (1982b) Distribution of choline acetyltransferase in cerebral and extracerebral cranial arteries of the cat: Its relationship to neurogenic atropine-sensitive dilation. Circ Res **50:** 470–476

Brown AM (1968) Motor innervation of the coronary arteries of the cat. J Physiol (Lond) **198:** 311–328

Bulbring E, Burn JH (1935) The sympathetic dilator fibers in the muscles of the cat and dog. J Physiol (Lond) **83:** 483–501

Cohen RA, Shepherd JT, Vanhoutte PM (1984) Neurogenic cholinergic prejunctional inhibition of sympathetic beta adrenergic relaxation in the canine coronary artery. J Pharmacol Exp Ther **229:** 417–421

Crouch JE (1969) Text-Atlas of Cat Anatomy. Philadelphia, Lee & Febiger

D'Alecy (1977) Adrenergic and cholinergic influence on CBF as determined with the venous outflow method. *In* Neurogenic Control of the Brain Circulation, edited by C Owman, L Edvinsson. Oxford, Pergamon Press, pp 327–330

De Mey JG, Vanhoutte PM (1983) Anoxia and endothelium dependent reactivity of the canine femoral artery. J Physiol (Lond) **335:** 65–74

De Mey JG, Claeys M, Vanhoutte PM (1982) Endothelium-dependent inhibitory effects of acetylcholine, adenosine triphosphate, thrombin and arachidonic acid in the canine femoral artery. J Pharmacol Exp Ther **222:** 166–173

Eccles R, Wallis DI (1974) Vasomotor responses of the tongue and nose of the cat recorded by plethysmography. J Physiol (Lond) **241:** 77–78p

Fisher AWF (1965) The intrinsic innervation of the pulmonary vessels. Acta Anat **60:** 481–496

Florence VM, Bevan JA (1979) Biochemical determinations of cholinergic innervation in cerebral arteries. Circ Res **45:** 212–218

Furchgott RF (1983) Role of endothelium in responses of vascular smooth muscle. Circ Res **53:** 557–573

Furchgott RF, Zawadzki JV (1980) The obligatory role of endothelial cells in the relaxation of arterial smooth muscle by acetylcholine. Nature **288:** 373–376

Furchgott RF, Zawadzki JV, Cherry PD (1981) Role of the endothelium in the vasodilator response to acetylcholine. *In* Vasodilatation, edited by PM Vanhoutte, I Leusen. New York, Raven Press, pp 49–66

Furchgott RF, Cherry PD, Zawadzki JV (1983) Endothelium-dependent relaxation of arteries by acetylcholine, bradykinin and other agents. *In* Vascular Neuroeffector Mechanisms: 4th International Symposium, edited by JA Bevan, M Fujiwara, RA Maxwell, K Mohri, S Shibata, N Toda. New York, Raven Press, pp 37–43

Gibbins IL, Brayden JE, Bevan JA (in press) Perivascular nerves with immunoreactivity to vasoactive intestinal polypeptide in cephalic arteries of the cat: Distribution, possible origins and functional implications. Neuroscience

Koelle GP (1955) The histochemical identification of acetylcholinesterase in cholinergic, adrenergic and sensory neurons. J Pharmacol Exp Ther **114:** 167–184

Lee TJ (1982) Cholinergic mechanism in the large cat cerebral artery. Circ Res **50:** 870–879

Lundberg JM (1981) Evidence for the existence of vasoactive intestinal polypeptide (VIP) and acetylcholine neurons in cat exocrine glands. Morphological, anatomical and functional studies. Acta Physiol Scand [Suppl] **496:** 1–57

Poole JCF, Sanders AG, Florey HW (1958) The regeneration of aortic endothelium. J Pathol Bacteriol **75:** 133–143

Stinson JM, Barnes AB, Zakheim RM, Chimoskey JE, Spinelli FR, Barger AC (1968) Cholinergic vasodilatation during renal artery constriction in the unanesthetized dog. Fed Proc **27:** 630–638

Stjernschantz J, Bill A (1980) Vasomotor effects of facial nerve stimulation: noncholinergic vasodilation in the eye. Acta Physiol Scand **109:** 45–50

Vanhoutte PM (1981) Why is acetylcholine a vasodilator? *In* Vasodilatation, edited by PM Vanhoutte, I Leusen. New York, Raven Press, pp 67–72

Vanhoutte PM, Verbeuren TJ, Webb RC (1981) Local modulation of adrenergic neuroeffector interaction in the blood vessel wall. Physiol Rev **61:** 151–247

INDEX TERMS: Vasodilation, neurogenic • Vasodilation, cholinergic • Vasodilation, muscarinic • Endothelium

Angiotensin II in Rat Brain Comigrates with Authentic Angiotensin II in High Pressure Liquid Chromatography

M. Ian Phillips and Birgitta Stenstrom
From the Department of Physiology, University of Florida, Gainesville, Florida

SUMMARY. Indirect evidence has implicated a role for central angiotensin II in blood pressure control. To answer directly the question of whether angiotensin II exists in the brain, independent of blood-borne angiotensin, and to quantify the amounts in different parts of the central nervous system, a sensitive radioimmunoassay was used to measure extracts of male adult rat brain hypothalamus and cortex after purification with high pressure liquid chromatography with a high recovery. The fractions coeluted with authentic angiotensin. Rats were nephrectomized bilaterally, and 24 hours later the brains were extracted in acetic acid and boiled. SepPak C-18 purification preceded reverse phase high pressure liquid chromatography. High pressure liquid chromatography revealed two peaks, one which comigrated precisely with [Ile^5] angiotensin II, and another smaller peak which overlapped with [Ile^5] angiotensin III. The highest levels were found in the hypothalamus (125 pg/g tissue), pituitary (190 pg/g tissue), spinal cord (199 pg/g tissue), and lower levels were found in cortex (60 pg/g tissue). The results demonstrate that the antibody which was previously used in the immunocytochemical localization of angiotensin in the hypothalamus detects authentic angiotensins. However, the study did not depend on just one antibody. A second antibody which we developed gave the same results. Molecular sieving using Sephadex G-25 with acetic acid revealed a distinct peak in the 1000 MW range and a smaller, higher molecular weight peak which needs further investigation. Spontaneously hypertensive rats did not have higher concentrations of hypothalamic angiotensin II than normotensive rats. The present data provide evidence for angiotensin in the central nervous system, and the implications of an independent brain angiotensin for control of blood pressure and water balance can be explored with this procedure. **(*Circ Res 56: 212–219 1985*)**

THE proposal has been advanced that angiotensin II (AII) in the brain plays an important role in cardiovascular control, but the presence or absence of a brain renin-angiotensin system has been debated since the presence of renin in the brain was first proposed in 1971 (Fischer-Ferraro et al., 1971; Ganten et al., 1971). Major arguments for the existence of such a system include the following: the presence of all the components of the system have been demonstrated directly or indirectly in the brain (Yang and Neff, 1972; Hirose et al., 1978; Phillips, 1978; Printz et al., 1980), the distribution of AII-like immunoreactivity in the brain (Ganten et al., 1978; Phillips et al., 1979), the potent action of angiotensin on the brain in producing blood pressure and drinking responses (Fitzsimons, 1972; Severs and Daniels-Severs, 1973), the finding of the renin-angiotensin components in neuroblastoma (Fishman et al., 1981; Inagami et al., 1982), and the synthesis of angiotensin in brain cells in culture (Raizada et al., 1983). However, major arguments against the existence of brain renin were that cathepsin D had been confused with renin (Reid, 1979), that AII immunoreactivity is not distributed in the same brain areas as other components of the renin-angiotensin system (Reid and Brownfield, 1982), and that a conclusive demonstration of the presence of angiotensin in brain or cerebral spinal fluid was lacking. Although it is now clear that renin can be separated from cathepsin D and exist in the brain (Hirose et al., 1978), convincing proof of the existence of a brain renin-angiotensin system requires that authentic AII is formed in the brain. Several investigators have used radioimmunoassays to measure AII concentration in cerebral spinal fluid, but the results have been conflicting (Semple et al., 1980; Hermann et al., 1982) or they have not characterized the AII (Ganten et al., 1971; Fischer-Ferraro et al., 1971; Hutchinson and Csicsmann, 1978). Part of the problem is that large quantities or large proportions of AII in brain tissue are difficult to extract. A preliminary study by Meyer et al. (1982) indicated that only 10% of AII immunoreactivity coeluted with AII. It was concluded that further studies needed to be done. This paper is a report of 20 replications and a procedure with high recovery to quantify and characterize the AII immunoreactivity in the brain. We have now developed an extraction procedure with very high recovery rates (>95%), a high titer antibody, and we report here finding measurable amounts of AII in the hypothalamus, pituitary, and cortex of rat brains that comigrate with authentic [Ile^5] AII using high pressure liquid chromatography (HPLC). We have further characterized the extract by molecular sieving and found the purified extract was the same molecular weight as AII. Since the rats were previously nephrectomized and blood levels of AII were at or below measurable levels, the results offer proof of AII being present in the brain. A preliminary report of this finding was presented (Phillips and Stenstrom, 1983). The levels of this brain AII in spontaneously hypertensive rats (SHR) were similar to those of normotensive rats, and this leads to further consideration of the action of brain AII in hypertension.

Methods

Subjects

Adult male Sprague-Dawley rats, spontaneously hypertensive rats of the Okomoto strain (SHR), and Wistar-Kyoto rats (WKY) (250–350 g) were used. Each rat was housed with ab libitum food and water available. The animal room was on a 6 a.m. to 6 p.m. light and 6 p.m. to 6 a.m. dark cycle at least 1 week before the experiment.

Surgery

Bilateral nephrectomy was performed under chloral hydrate anesthesia. All animals were in good condition after surgery, as judged by their coats and behavioral activity. Twenty-two to 24 hours later, each rat was swiftly decapitated and the brain rapidly dissected. An area including the hypothalamus with parts of the septum, thalamus, and midbrain (but not the pituitary) was dissected out, and a piece of cortex was removed from the same brain.

Extraction

Brain Tissue

The samples were either extracted immediately or first frozen on dry ice and then stored at −20°C for no more than 1 week. Brain parts were dissected out, weighed, and put in 8–10 volumes of 1 M acetic acid (containing 15 mM EDTA and 1.25 mM *o*-phenanthroline) and put in a boiling water bath for 15 minutes to denature proteins and prevent hydrolysis. For the fresh tissue, the maximum time between decapitation and boiling was 4 minutes. Frozen pieces were dropped into boiling 1 M acetic acid. A series of pilot experiments showed that there was no difference in AII levels with the two procedures.

Hypothalamic blocks weighed an average of 146.0 mg, and cortex, 190.0 mg. Two samples of these tissues were pooled together. Pituitary tissue weighed <10 mg per rat, and 20 pituitaries had to be pooled. Two samples from 40 rats were assayed. All samples were homogenized on a Potter-Elvehjem homogenizer at 4°C. The homogenates were spun for 20 minutes at 3,000 *g* at 4°C. The supernatant was collected and the pellet was reextracted with half of the original volume of 1 M acetic acid and spun 20 minutes at 10,000 *g*.

Supernatant extracts were pooled and defatted with equal volumes of petroleum ether. The aqueous phase was dried under an airstream on a hot plate (60°C) in bovine serum albumin (BSA)-coated polyethylene scintillation vials.

Blood

One milliliter of blood containing 15 mM EDTA and 1.25 mM *o*-phenanthroline was extracted with 6.4 ml 85% acetone and spun for 15 minutes at 1,000 *g* at 4°C. The supernatant was collected and the pellet reextracted with 3.6 ml 65% acetone and spun for 15 minutes at 1,000 *g*. The supernatants were pooled and dried under an airstream on a hot plate in BSA-coated polyethylene scintillation vials, and later purified on an ion exchange column, as described under Chromatography.

Chromatography

For preparation of blood samples for radioimmunoassay, SP-Sephadex C-25 was used. SP-Sephadex was swollen and washed five times, first with 0.5 M sodium acetate, pH 5.0, and second, in 0.05 M sodium acetate, pH 5.0. Both buffers had 0.01% sodium azide added. Gel [7 cm (3 ml)] was packed in Kontes disposable columns, 0.8 × 20 cm, and stopped with cotton wool. Columns were washed with 30 ml 0.05 M sodium acetate, pH 5.0. Each sample was dissolved in 2 ml 0.05 M sodium acetate, pH 5.0, vortexed, left 15 minutes, and applied to the column, and the vial was rinsed with 3 ml of the same buffer. Three milliliters of 0.05 M sodium acetate, pH 5.0, were added to the column, and then AII was eluted with 5 ml of 0.05 M sodium acetate, pH 7.4, with 0.005% sodium azide. AII was collected in BSA-coated scintillation vials and dried under air, as before. Recovery for AII in this chromatography procedure was 93.2%. This was used for the blood samples, since it provided a more rapid method without involving HPLC.

SepPak C-18 Purification

For preparation of tissue for HPLC, SepPak C-18 cartridges were used for initial purification. SepPak cartridges (Waters Associates) were moistened with 3 ml of methanol and washed with 10 ml of 1% trifluoroacetic acid (TFA) in water, then coated with 1 ml of 1% Polypep solution (Sigma) in water to protect against nonspecific absorption of angiotensin on the cartridge, and washed with 10 ml of methanol, water, and TFA (80/19/1, vol/vol), followed by 10 ml of 1% TFA in water.

Dried brain extract was dissolved in 5 ml of 0.001 M HCl and applied to the SepPak cartridge, and the vial was rinsed with 5 ml of 0.001 M HCl, which was also applied. The cartridge was washed with 2 × 5 ml of 1% TFA/1% NaCl (1/1, vol/vol), and 2 ml of methanol/water/TFA (30/69/1, vol/vol). Peptides retained in the cartridge were eluted with methanol/water/TFA (70/29/1, vol/vol). The eluate was dried under air in BSA-coated polypropylene tubes on a warm plate.

High Pressure Liquid Chromatography

Angiotensins were further purified on a Beckman HPLC model 332 (2 110A pumps, 420 controller, coupled to a variable wavelength detector) with a reverse phase column (Brown Lee Spheri-5 C-8 column, 4.6 mm inner diameter × 250 mm length, filled with 5-μm beads) was used. The elution solutions were 10 mM ammonium acetate (pH 4.15) and methanol. Two gradients were used: (a) a linear gradient 30–80% methanol in 35 minutes, and (b) a gradient of 30–50% methanol for 8 minutes, staying at 50% for 20 minutes, and 50–80% methanol in 10 minutes. This was found to give a better separation of AII and AIII than gradient (a). Another elution system using acetonitrile and

0.26 M formic acid with triethylamine, pH 6.5, was also tried. This system started with 16% acetonitrile for 12 minutes, followed by a gradient of 16–50% acetonitrile for 30 minutes. The flow rate in each case was 1 ml/min. One-milliliter fractions were collected in BSA-coated tubes and dried under air on a warm plate for radioimmunoassay.

Recovery

To measure the recovery of AII with this purification procedure, unlabeled AII (30–200 pg) was added to brain tissue homogenates. After extraction, SepPac purification, and high pressure liquid chromatography, the amounts were measured by radioimmunoassay and the levels in pure brain tissue were subtracted from the levels obtained in brain tissue with exogenous AII added.

Radioimmunoassay

Samples were dissolved in 0.05 M Tris-buffer, pH 7.5. ^{125}I-AII and antibody were dissolved in 0.05 M Tris buffer, pH 7.5, containing 1% bovine γ-globulin.

Two antibodies were used. One was the antibody Celine, a gift from Dr. Ganten. It cross-reacts 100% with AIII and with AII (3–8) hexapeptide, <1% with AI, and less than 0.01% with rat angiotensinogen and saralasin. Cross-reactivity to peptides unrelated to angiotensin is <0.001% (Hermann et al., 1982). The second was an antibody developed in our laboratory which has high sensitivity (ED_{50} 9 pg). This antibody (Ab-2) was tested for cross-reactivity to the following peptides: AIII, 100%; AI, 0.5%; saralasin, 0.004%; AII tetrapeptide, 0.003%; AII tripeptide, 0.0007%; oxytocin, <0.0005%; bradykinin, <0.0005%; somatostatin, <0.0005%; metenkephalin, <0.0005%; substance P, <0.0005%; BSA, <0.0005%; and vasopressin, 0.003%. Measurements of the same samples by two assays with the different antibodies showed close similarity in results.

^{125}I-AII was prepared by iodination of AII, using the chloramine-T method, and purified on a DEAE-Sephadex A-25 column, by a slight modification of the method of Dusterdieck and McElwee (1971). The specific activity was 1600 μCi/μg. Aliquots of 10 μCi/ml were stored at −80°C and diluted immediately before each assay.

Standard curves were made with 3.9–250 pg unlabeled [Ile^5] AII (Peninsula). A stock solution of 1 ng/μl was stored in aliquots at −80°C and diluted immediately before each assay. The buffer solution used was 0.05 M Tris buffer, pH 7.5.

Duplicates of the samples and of the standard solutions were mixed with antibody (Celine) at a final dilution of 1:450,000 and Ab-2 to 1:300,000 and 6000 counts/min ^{125}I-AII, and incubated 20–24 hours at 4°C.

To separate the unbound AII from the AII which was bound to antibody, polyethyleneglycol in a final concentration of 12.5% was added to all tubes. The tubes were spun for 45 minutes at 1000 g, the supernatant aspirated, and the pellet counted in a Beckman 5500 γ-counter at an efficiency of 79% for ^{125}I.

Gel Filtration

Sephadex G-25 was used to determine the approximate molecular weight of the immunoreactive angiotensin.

Two elution systems were used with Sephadex G-25: (A) 0.012 M Tris-HCl, pH 8.0, column dimension 2 × 90 cm, flow rate 0.5 ml/min, fraction size 2 ml, and (B) 0.2 M acetic acid, column dimension 1.7 × 75 cm, flow rate 0.5 ml/min, fraction size 2 ml. Eluted fractions were collected in BSA-coated tubes.

Nonpurified hypothalamic extracts were dissolved in 2 ml of the respective elution buffer and applied to the column. The eluted fractions from the column utilizing system A were assayed directly (measured for AII content by RIA), whereas the fractions from system B, which could not be directly assayed until the acid was removed, were first dried under air on a warm plate.

Finally, the AII-containing peak after HPLC purification of hypothalamic extract was also subjected to gel filtration using system B with Sephadex G-25.

Statistics

Least squares linear regression analysis was applied to the data for determination of slopes and their degree of parallelity.

Results

Preliminary experiments, using an ion exchanger for purification as described for blood samples in methods, showed that hypothalamic blocks were higher in AII content than any other part of the brain studied. This was anticipated from immunohistochemical studies, and, therefore, we concentrated on the hypothalamic area with the cortex for comparison and purified the extracts with SepPak C18 and high pressure liquid chromatography to see whether the immunoreactive material was indeed authentic AII. Shown in Figure 1 is a typical elution pattern of purified hypothalamic area extract. There is a distinct peak of immunoreactive extract eluting with the same fractions as synthetic angiotensin AII, and there seems to be a peak in the area of AIII. However, the levels in the AIII area are very low and might not be significant.

Hypothalamus contained 158 ± 29 pg/g tissue in 14 experiments with SepPak C18 and HPLC (or 139

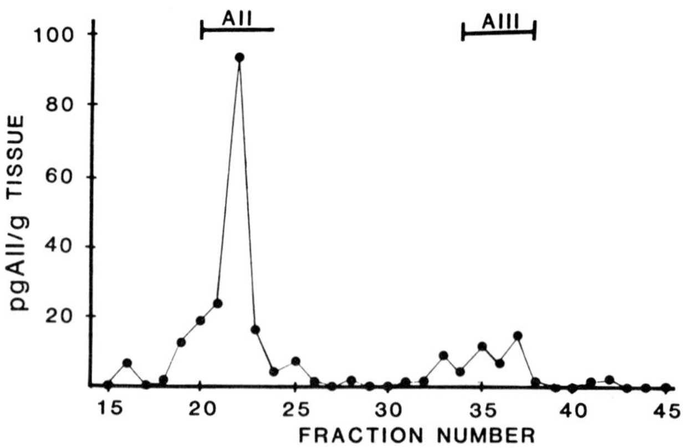

FIGURE 1. *HPLC elution profile of brain extract. This figure shows the result of extracting AII from blocks of hypothalamus from the brains of rats nephrectomized 24 hours previously. The tissue was extracted in acetic acid and passed through a SepPak C18 cartridge for initial purification followed by reversed phase HPLC. Solvent system (b) was used. The results show a distinct peak of a substance coeluting with AII (and a second peak in the area of AIII). The amount extracted from the tissue as measured by the radioimmunoassay from 14 different experiments was 158 ± 29 pg/g tissue.*

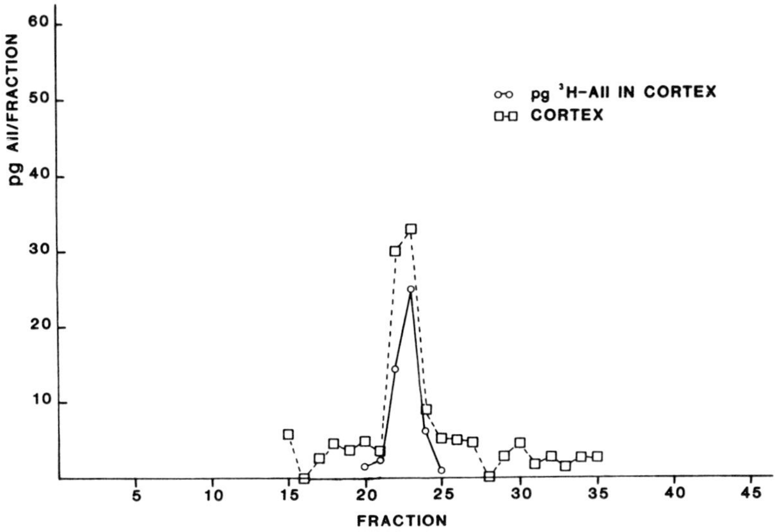

FIGURE 2. *HPLC elution profile of [³H]angiotensin. To confirm the coelution of an angiotensin-like peptide in the brain with synthetic AII, cortical tissue was extracted and purified with and without the addition of tritiated AII. The figure demonstrates that the AII-like material coeluted with labeled AII on the reverse phase HPLC.*

± 20 pg/g when SP-Sephadex was used in 20 separate experiments), and cortex 61 ± 15 pg/g in 12 separate experiments. Another brain site containing high AII levels was the pituitary (116 and 265 pg/g in two experiments with 20 pooled pituitaries in each sample). Spinal cord contained 199 ± 110 pg/g in six experiments. Synthetic AII, [^{3}H]AII, and synthetic AIII were used to calibrate the HPLC system. Gradient system (b) gave good separation between AII and AIII in the HPLC system. Gradient system (a) gave less separation. With the acetotrile elutions system, no AII was recovered. AII was collected from a peak, but the peak shifted in successive replications. The methanol gradient (2) was stable over many replications. Adding [^{3}H]AII cortex homogenate gave the elution pattern in Figure 2. This shows that co-elution of [^{3}H]AII and endogenous AII comigrate to the same fractions and have exactly the same peak. Since cortex had smaller amounts of peptide, no peak for AIII was detected.

In a series of six recovery experiments performed as described in Methods, we found the recovery of our purification procedure to be 95 ± 5% ($n = 6$) (or 95 ± 2 SE). As the recovery of AII is virtually complete, we do not adjust our values for recovery.

The radioimmunoassay developed to measure the AII has a high sensitivity and good reproducibility. The standard deviations are small over 16 replications (Fig. 3), and the ED_{50} is 27.9 ± 2.5 pg and the slope = 1.06 ± 0.05. The useful range of the assay is between 3.9 and 250 pg/incubate. Blood samples of the nephrectomized rats were <4 pg/ml/rat.

Extracts from the HPLC and purification procedures did not interfere with the radioimmunoassay. Different AII concentrations of a sample were compared to the standard curve. From a 1-ml extract of

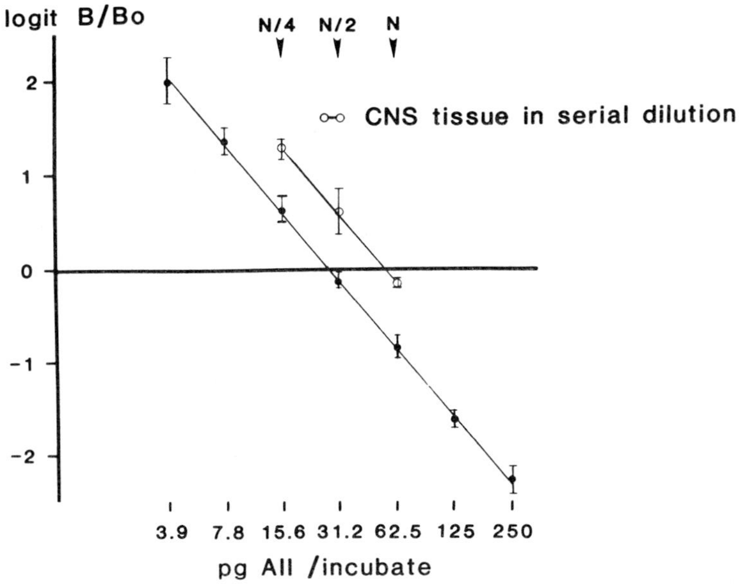

FIGURE 3. *Standard curve for AII radioimmunoassay. To make sure there was no nonspecific interference from the brain tissue, a purified extract was serially diluted and, after a log-logit transformation, the slope of the sample was compared to that of the standard curve. Serial dilution of a purified sample gives a slope parallel to that of the standard curve. (Least squares linear regression analysis of the slope for the standard curve is −2.38 and for the dilution curve −2.36.) The standard deviations at each point in the standard curve represent 16 replications indicating reproducibility.*

HPLC-purified neural tissue, three samples were tested: one was 400 μl, the second 200 μl plus 200 μl buffer, and the third 100 μl plus 300 μl buffer. Shown in Figure 3 is the result of such a serial dilution curve compared to the log-logit transformed standard curve of the assay. As can be seen, it is parallel with the standard curve. This parallelism was confirmed by comparing the slopes after least square analysis. The slope of the standard curve was −2.38 and the slope of the dilution curve was −2.36.

There was no interference between the peptide and the tissue. We determined if a fixed quantity of exogenous AII added to different amounts of tissue would give a line parallel to that of tissue without exogenous AII. The levels were measured after HPLC purification and are shown in Figure 4. The results showed that after adding 62.5 pg exogenous AII to tissue, there is linearity of concentration of AII up to 240 mg tissue, but with higher amounts of tissue there was a decline in recovery of the peptide. The slope of the upper curve was 0.11, and of the lower curve, 0.10, up to 240 mg tissue. For the experiments, we were therefore constrained to 200-mg tissue sample series, and we did not investigate this problem further.

Table 1 shows that, in the different strains of rats used, there was not a significant difference between Sprague-Dawley, SHR, or WKY. In SHR, hypothalamic levels were 125 ± 25 pg/g, and in normotensive Sprague-Dawley, 126 ± 23 pg/g. Although the WKY appeared to have higher levels, there was much wider variation than with the other two strains.

To examine the molecular weight of the AII in the present study, we investigated both crude and HPLC-purified hypothalamic extract with Sephadex G-25 gel filtration, using two different buffers. The elution profile of a crude extract in Tris-buffer showed all the immunoreactive material elutes in the void volume, suggesting a molecular weight above 5000. However, elution of crude extract in acetic acid reveals a completely different profile, and unmasks the 1000 MW AII peak. There is a distinct peak in the same fractions in which the [^{3}H]AII eluted. There was a much reduced peak in the higher molecular weight fractions (Fig. 5). However, the peak remained, even after passing the extract from the Sephadex G-25 through the HPLC (Fig. 6). It should be noted that the AII was within the fractionation range, as opposed to [^{3}H]tyrosine which was in the fully retained volume. Further tests with ^{125}I-AI (MW 1420) and ^{125}I-AII (MW 1170) showed a complete separation of peaks. [^{3}H]AIII (MW 932) had a peak that was distinct from [^{3}H]AII, but with overlap of the curves. These results indicate that the Sephadex G-25 in these studies was able to fractionate AII (MW 1026).

TABLE 1
Levels of Angiotensin II (pg/g tissue) in Bilaterally Nephrectomized Rats*

Rat strain	*n*	Hypothal.	*n*	Cortex
Sprague-Dawley	32	125 ± 25	14	60 ± 17
SHR (Okomoto)	7	126 ± 23	3	37 ± 23
WKY	4	237 ± 165	4	105 ± 104

* Mean ± SE of amounts calculated as area under the curve in the radioimmunoassay of chromatography fractions compared with standard samples.

Discussion

The results clearly demonstrate that there are detectable levels of AII in the hypothalamus, cortex, and pituitary of rat brain. The AII extracted from hypothalamic and cortical tissue appears in the same fraction as the peak of radioimmunoactivity for authentic AII. Control tubes which were tested without the presence of tissue contained no AII. Cortex which was treated in the same way as the hypothalamic tissue showed a reduced amount of angioten-

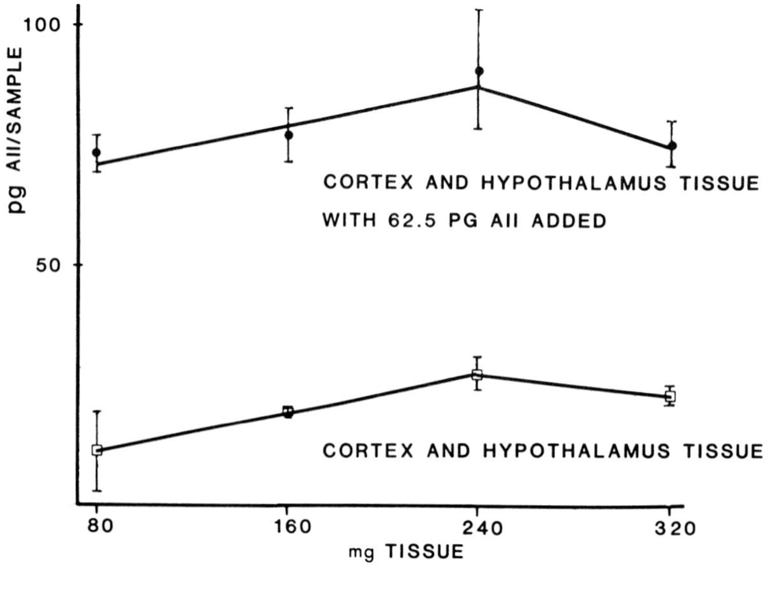

FIGURE 4. *Sample size limitation curve. To test whether the tissue contains substances that would interfere with the assay, a fixed amount of AII (62.5 pg) was added to different amounts of cortex and hypothalamus tissue homogenates. The samples were then extracted and purified with HPLC. The squares indicate the amount of AII found in the tissue. The circles indicate the amount of AII detected after 62.5 pg exogenous AII were added. The results show that, up to 240 mg tissue, the curves were parallel, indicating that there was no interference from the tissue. Above 240 mg tissue, an interference was detected by the lower amount of AII recovered. (Slope of the lower curve = 0.10 with an intercept of 3 pg/AII, and the slope of the upper curve = 0.11 with an intercept of 63 pg/AII. The curves were fitted by least squares fit.)*

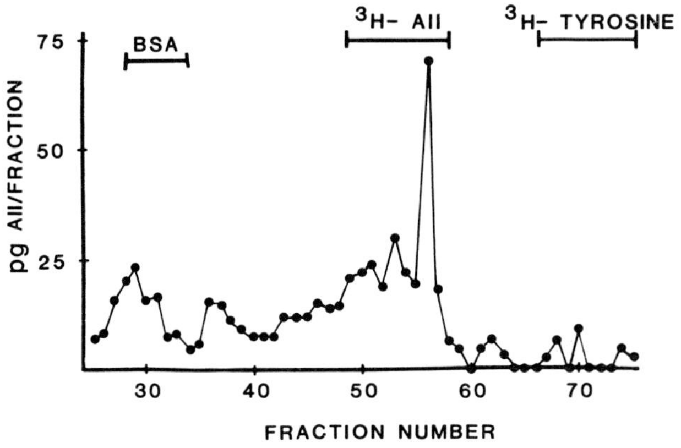

FIGURE 5. *Molecular sieving on brain extract. The result of passing hypothalamus extract through the Sephadex G-25 column equilibrated with acetic acid. In this figure, it can be seen that there may be a small peak for a high molecular weight substance, but a very clear peak for a peptide with the same molecular weight as AII. These data were based on a crude hypothalamic extract. The result with a HPLC-purified hypothalamic extract is shown in Figure 6.*

sin, but there was still a detectable peak in the same fractions. At a slightly longer retention time, there was some overlap with AIII, but not enough to provide a distinct peak. Since neither of the two antibodies cross-reacted with AI, the system could not detect the precursor. This was an advantage, in that AII did not need to be separated from AI in the gel filtration.

We have previously shown the distribution of immunoreactive AII, using the immunohistochemical method in brain cells and fibers of the rat, monkey, and human, and found the greatest levels in the hypothalamus (Phillips et al., 1979, 1980; Quinlan and Phillips, 1981). However, the immunocytochemistry technique shows only immunoreactivity, and does not allow one to state that authentic AII was being stained exclusively. In these three species, the distribution is very similar, and the major cell localization is in the supraoptic and periventricular nuclei of the hypothalamus. The most concentrated fiber bundles are in the median eminence. These results were confirmed later by two independent studies (Zimmerman et al., 1980; Brownfield et al., 1982), one using a different antibody (Zimmerman et al., 1980). For this reason, we chose the hypothalamus as the tissue in which to measure AII on HPLC. In addition, we measured cortex, pituitary, and spinal cord.

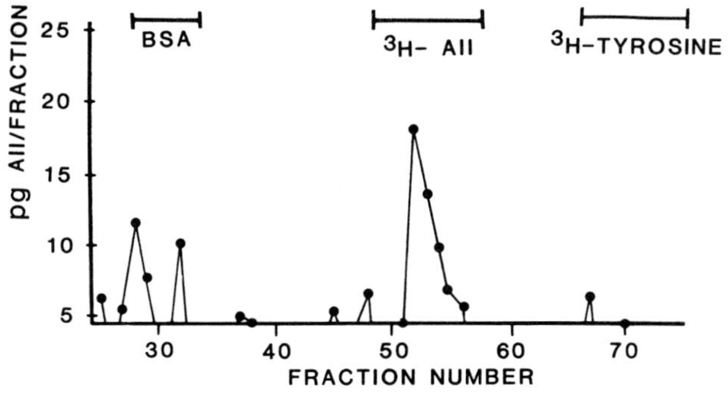

FIGURE 6. *The elution profile of HPLC-purified hypothalamic tissue after it had been passed through Sephadex G-25. The distribution of one peak in the 1000 MW range coelutes with [^{3}H]AII.*

Immunohistochemical staining of cells in the anterior pituitary has also been reported (Steele et al., 1982). The present results lead us to conclude that in the immunohistochemical studies, authentic AII was being labeled.

The question of whether this AII is formed by a renin-angiotensin system or not is still an open one. Although all the components for the renin angiotensin system appear to exist in the brain, their distribution does not overlap in all respects, as one might expect if the presence of angiotensin depended on the activity of renin and angiotensinogen to form AI and its conversion by converting enzyme to form AII (Reid and Brownfield, 1982).

It may be that brain AII is made "on demand" and does not reach high levels, or that it reaches high levels only at certain times because of circadian rhythms. Having described a procedure to measure AII by HPLC, it should be possible to study the physiology of brain AII by experiments with renin and converting enzyme inhibitors, by incorporation of the labeled amino acids, isoleucine and valine, and by inhibiting synthesis at various stages. Preliminary results in brain cell cultures indicate that there is synthesis of brain angiotensin involving at least conversion of AI to AII (Raizada et al., 1983).

Earlier, we found AII levels of up to 76 ± 5 pg/g wet weight of tissue when extracted by 2 M acetic acid, but only 10% coeluted with AII on HPLC (Meyer et al., 1982). The elution system used acetonitrile. When we repeated the use of acetonitrile in the present study, we were unable to obtain AII. However, by using methanol, we found measurable quantities of AII. Therefore, the reason for the small yield reported previously may have been the use of acetonitrile. Acetonitrile produces too much lability in the system, and in the Meyer et al. (1982) report, the peaks for synthetic AII were in different fractions, depending on pH. Hermann and Ganten (1982) also found acetonitrile to be inconsistent and, like us, used methanol (Ganten et al., 1983). For the Meyer et al. study, two pools of five whole brains were pooled and homogenized. We have now found that more than 240 mg tissue interferes with the AII assay and, therefore, those five whole brains may have also interfered with the assay. Molecular sieving with a Varian Micropak TSK 200 column at pH 7.0 indicated that only a high molecular weight substance was present (Meyer et al., 1982). We now find that with acetic acid as an elution buffer in Sephadex G-25, a clear peak at low molecular weight is revealed. We felt that the methodology of the Meyer et al. (1982) report was useful in establishing an extraction procedure, but required further development and more replications because, with each new method of extraction, the amount of angiotensin detected increased. In the acetic acid extraction procedure, the recovery was 48 ± 4%, and with methanol, recovery was 60 ± 1%. The present report supercedes this previous report, and the current data represent the strongest supporting evidence for the existence of endogenous brain angiotensin. Our data and those obtained independently by Hermann et al. (1982) on rat brain tissue and cerebrospinal fluid (CSF) angiotensin support this conclusion. They used similar methods and one of the two antibodies that we have used. They did not, however, test for molecular weight of the AII. Recently, Husain et al. (1983) have found a family of higher molecular weight AI in dog CSF. As yet, we have not completely studied the molecular weight of the higher molecular weight AII found in the void volume of the Sephadex G-25 fractions, and further tests are necessary. The clinical significance of the present finding has been alluded to in studies of spontaneously hypertensive rats where blood pressure can be lowered by blockade of AII in the brain with saralasin or captopril, even though the blood levels of angiotensin or renin are normal or low (Phillips et al., 1977; McDonald et al., 1980). Therefore, an important action of brain angiotensin may be in maintaining blood pressure. Excess amounts of AII in SHR were not found in this study, as shown in Table 1. Highest levels occurred in WKY brains, but the variation was too large to make this significant. Only a part of the brain has been analyzed so far, and further studies are necessary to define total levels, but the more important factor may be turnover of AII and the interaction of brain angiotensin levels and receptor sensitivity.

Increased angiotensin receptor sensitivity to existing amounts may contribute to hypertension. Alternatively, lack of down-regulation of receptors to constant amounts of AII in the brain could equally maintain high blood pressure. Ganten et al. (1983) have recently reported that icv captopril significantly decreased AII brain levels in SHR stroke prone (SHRSP), but not in WKY, and concluded from this that in SHRSP, there is a higher activity of brain renin angiotensin.

We have used bilateral nephrectomy throughout this experiment to avoid contamination with blood-borne angiotensin. A method for calculating the contamination of plasma-borne substances has been proposed by Gregory et al. (1982) utilizing tritiated inulin as a marker of cerebral vascular space. In their study, they found that there were no net alterations in regional brain angiotensinogen in the first 24 hours after nephrectomy, although there was a 2-fold increase in plasma angiotensinogen in the absence of plasma renin. At 32 hours postnephrectomy, certain areas of the rat hypothalamus exhibited significant elevations in angiotensinogen content. Since, in our experiment, the brains were taken 22–24 hours after nephrectomy, the levels of angiotensinogen should not have been elevated, according to the results of Gregory et al. (1982).

However, nephrectomy by itself may have caused some action on the brain angiotensin system. Earlier, we found that angiotensin injected into the ventricles has a prolonged pressor action after nephrectomy (Hoffman and Phillips, 1976). Therefore, further experiments will be needed to separate the action of nephrectomy in lowering renin levels from any action that it has on brain angiotensin levels. This does not detract, however, from the main result of this paper, which is a demonstration that angiotensin exists in the brain with the same retention times on HPLC as authentic AII, and that there are measurable differences between the content of cortex, hypothalamus, pituitary, and spinal cord. The levels found are within a range that is effective when injected directly into specific brain areas to produce drinking and a blood pressure increase (Phillips, 1978; Simpson, 1981). Finally, since the levels of AII in the blood were at or below detectable levels of the radioimmunoassay, we may conclude that the brain levels of AII represent an independent source of the peptide.

We are particularly grateful to Steve Childers, Department of Pharmacology, for use of his HPLC apparatus, and for numerous helpful suggestions. Our colleagues, C. Sumners, E. Richards-Sumners, and K. Hermann, have been most helpful in reviewing the manuscript. Carolyn Gabbard is thanked for typing the manuscript and its revisions.

The worked was supported by NIHLBI Grant HL-27334-03.

Address for reprints: Dr. M. Ian Phillips, Department of Physiology, Box J-274, JHMHC, University of Florida, Gainesville, Florida 32610.

Received May 20, 1983; accepted for publication October 30, 1984.

References

Brownfield MS, Reid IA, Ganten D, Ganong WF (1982) Differential distribution of immunoreactive angiotensin and angiotensin-converting enzyme in rat brain. Neuroscience **7:** 1759–1769

Dusterdieck G, McElwee G (1971) Iodination of angiotensin II and purification of the labelled hormone. *In* Radioimmunoassay Methods, edited by KE Kirkham, WM Hunter. London, Churchill-Livingston Press, pp 24–30

Fischer-Ferraro C, Nahmod VE, Goldstein DJ, Finkielman S (1971) Angiotensin and renin in rat and dog brain. J Exp Med **133:** 353–361

Fishman MC, Zimmerman EA, Slater EE (1981) Renin and angiotensin II: The complete system within the neuroblastoma and glioma. Science **214:** 922–923

Fitzsimons JT (1972) Thirst. Physiol Rev **52:** 408–559

Ganten D, Minnich JL, Granger P, Hayduk K, Brecht HM, Barbeau A, Boucher R, Genest J (1971) Angiotensin-forming enzyme in brain tissue. Science **173:** 64–65

Ganten D, Fuxe K, Phillips MI, Mann JFE, Ganten U (1978) The brain isorenin-angiotensin system: Biochemistry, localization and possible role in drinking and blood pressure regulation. *In* Frontiers in Neuroendocrinology, edited by WF Ganong, L Martini. New York, Raven Press, pp 61–99

Ganten D, Hermann K, Bayer C, Unger T, Lang RE (1983) Angiotensin synthesis in the brain and increased tumors in hypertensive rats. Science **221:** 869–871

Gregory TJ, Wallis CJ, Printz MP (1982) Regional changes in rat brain angiotensinogen following bilateral nephrectomy. Hypertension **4:** 827–838

Hermann K, Ganten D, Bayer C, Unger T, Lang RE, Rascher W (1982) Definite evidence for the presence of [Ile[5]]angiotensin I and [Ile[5]]angiotensin II in the brain of rats. *In* The Renin Angiotensin System in the Brain, edited by D Ganten, M Printz, MI Phillips, BA Scholkens. Heidelberg, Springer-Verlag, pp 192–207

Hirose S, Yokosawa H, Inagami T (1978) Immunochemical identification of renin in rat brain and distinction from acid proteases. Nature **274:** 392–393

Hoffman WE, Phillips MI (1976) A prolonged pressor response to intraventricular angiotensin II following bilateral nephrectomy. Life Sci **19:** 1323–1330

Husain A, Bumpus FM, Smeby RR, Brosnihan KB, Khosla MC, Speth RC, Ferrario CM (1983) Evidence for the existence of a family of biologically active angiotensin I-like peptides in the dog central nervous system. Circ Res **52:** 460–464

Hutchinson JS, Csicsmann J (1978) The distribution of immunoreactive angiotensins I and II extracted from rat brain. Acta Med Acad Sci Hung **35:** 277–285

Inagami T, Okamura T, Hirose S, Clemens D, Celio MR, Naruse K, Takii Y, Yokosawa H (1982) Identification, characterization and evidence for interneuronal function of renin in the brain and neuroblastoma cells. *In* The Renin Angiotensin System in the Brain, edited by D Ganten, M Printz, MI Phillips, BA Scholkens. Heidelberg, Springer-Verlag, pp 64–75

McDonald WJ, Wickre C, Aumann S, Ban D, Moffitt B (1980) The sustained antihypertensive effect of chronic cerebroventricular infusion of angiotensin antagonist in spontaneously hypertensive rats. Endocrinology **107:** 1305–1308

Meyer DK, Phillips MI, Eiden L (1982) Studies on the presence of angiotensin II in rat brain. J Neurochem **38:** 816–920

Phillips MI (1978) Angiotensin in the brain. Neuroendocrinology **25:** 354–377

Phillips MI, Stenstrom B (1983) Angiotensin II and III in rat hypothalamus and cortex shown by HPLC (abstr). Soc Neurosci **9:** 444

Phillips MI, Mann JFE, Haebara H, Hoffman WE, Dietz R, Schelling P, Ganten D (1977) Lowering of hypertension by central saralasin in the absence of plasma renin. Nature **270:** 445–447

Phillips MI, Weyhenmeyer J, Felix D, Ganten D, Hoffman WE (1979) Evidence for an endogenous brain renin-angiotensin system. Fed Proc **38:** 2260–2266

Phillips MI, Quinlan JT, Weyhenmeyer J (1980) An angiotensin-like peptide in the brain. Life Sci **27:** 2589–2594

Printz MP, Lewicki JA, Wallis CJ (1980) Brain angiotensinogen: Origin and evidence for an influence by adrenal corticosteroids. *In* Enzymatic Release of Vasoactive Peptides, edited by F Gross, G Vogel. New York, Raven Press, pp 193–207

Quinlan JT, Phillips MI (1981) Immunoreactivity for an angiotensin II-like peptide in the human brain. Brain Res **205:** 212–218

Raizada MK, Phillips MI, Gerndt JS (1983) Primary cultures from fetal rat brain incorporate [^{3}H]isoleucine and [^{3}H]valine into immunoprecipitable angiotensin II. Neuroendocrinology **36:** 64–67

Reid IA (1979) The brain renin-angiotensin system: A critical analysis. Fed Proc **38:** 2255–2259

Reid IA, Brownfield MS (1982) The brain renin angiotensin system: Some unresolved problems. *In* the Renin Angiotensin System in the Brain, edited by D Ganten, M Printz, MI Phillips, BA Scholkens. Heidelberg, Springer-Verlag, pp 792–207

Semple PF, MacRae WA, Morton JJ (1980) Angiotensin II in human cerebrospinal fluid may be an immunoassay artifact. Clin Sci **59:** 61s–64s

Severs WB, Daniels-Severs AE (1973) Effects of angiotensin on the central nervous system. Pharmacol Rev **25:** 415–449

Simpson JB (1981) The circumventricular organs and the central actions of angiotensin. Neuroendocrinology **32:** 248–256

Steele MK, Brownfield MS, Ganong WF (1982) Immunocytochemical localization of angiotensin immunoreactivity in gonadotrops and lactotrops of the rat anterior pituitary gland. Neuroendocrinology **35:** 155–158

Yang HYT, Neff NH (1972) Distribution and properties of angiotensin converting enzyme of rat brain. J Neurochem **19:** 2243–2250

Zimmerman EA, Krupp L, Hoffman DL, Matthew E, Nilaver G (1980) Exploration of peptidergic pathways in brain by immunocytochemistry: A ten-year perspective. Peptides **1:** 3–10

INDEX TERMS: Brain angiotensin II • Radioimmunoassay • Hypothalamus • Pituitary • Spinal cord • High pressure liquid chromatography

Influence of Ribose, Adenosine, and "AICAR" on the Rate of Myocardial Adenosine Triphosphate Synthesis during Reperfusion after Coronary Artery Occlusion in the Dog

M. Mauser, H.M. Hoffmeister, C. Nienaber, and W. Schaper

From the Max-Planck-Institute, Department of Experimental Cardiology, Bad Nauheim, Federal Republic of Germany

SUMMARY. Recovery of adenosine triphosphate after myocardial ischemia is limited by the slow adenine nucleotide de novo synthesis and the availability of precursors of the nucleotide salvage pathways. We determined the adenine nucleotide de novo synthesis in the dog by infusion of [^{14}C]glycine and the acceleration of adenine nucleotide built up by intracoronary infusion of ribose together with [^{14}C]glycine or radiolabeled 5-amino-4-imidazolcarboxamide riboside or adenosine in the same animal model and with the same dosage of substrates (9 mmol) in postischemic and nonischemic myocardial tissue. After 45 minutes of occlusion of a side branch of the left coronary artery, the ischemic area was reperfused for 3 hours, and needle biopsies were taken for biochemical analysis. Adenine nucleotide de novo synthesis was found to be very slow (1.5 nmol/g wet weight per hour). The rate was doubled after ischemia. Adenine nucleotide synthesis was accelerated 5-fold by ribose, the basic substrate of the adenine nucleotide de novo synthesis, 9-fold by 5-amino-4-imidazolcarboxamide riboside, an intermediate of the adenine nucleotide de novo synthesis and 90-fold by adenosine, a substrate of the nucleotide salvage pathway. Therefore, only adenosine infusion resulted in a measurable increase of adenosine triphosphate levels after 3 hours of reperfusion, but over a longer time period, ribose or 5-amino-4-imidazolcarboxamide riboside also can be expected to replenish reduced myocardial adenosine triphosphate faster than adenine nucleotide de novo synthesis. Studies with radiolabeled 5-amino-4-imidazolcarboxamide riboside showed significant incorporation of radioactivity into 5-amino-4-imidazolcarboxamide ribose triphosphate which had also risen measurably during 5-amino-4-imidazolcarboxamide ribose infusion, and which is not normally found in heart muscle. **(*Circ Res 56: 220–230, 1985*)**

IT is a well-established fact that ischemia leads to a depletion of adenosine triphosphate (ATP) (Chang, 1938; Burdette, 1956; Berne, 1963; Gerlach et al., 1963) which is not readily reversible upon reoxygenation of tissue, especially when the coronary occlusion (or other forms of oxygen deprivation) lasted longer than 10 minutes (Danforth et al., 1960; Kammermeier et al., 1963, 1964; Isselhard et al., 1964, 1970a; Schaper et al., 1979). The slow rate of ATP synthesis after ischemia (Zimmer et al., 1973) is mainly the result of two factors. (1) The conversion of glucose-6-phosphate to ribose-5-phosphate proceeds extremely slowly in mammalian heart muscle (Zimmer and Gerlach, 1978; Ibel et al., 1982). (2) Substrates for the salvage pathways, notably adenosine, but possibly also inosine and hypoxanthine, are rapidly washed out of the tissue upon reflow and are hence lost for salvage (Katori and Berne, 1966; Fox et al., 1979).

Clinical efforts to reestablish blood flow in acute myocardial infarction by fibrinolysis (Schmutzler et al., 1966; Rentrop et al., 1981) were reported to be successful, but mechanical function of the reperfused segment often returns only after a long delay. This effect is known from animal experiments (Kloner et al., 1981). Other probable metabolic effects of ischemia and reperfusion that cannot be measured in human patients may also be dependent on ATP. A fast restitution of ATP levels during reflow after ischemia appears highly desirable. We report here in a comparative study the three most promising substances, i.e., ribose, 5-amino-4-imidazolcarboxamide riboside (AICAR), and adenosine, for repletion of purine nucleotides.

Methods

Experimental Design

Thirty-eight dogs of either sex weighing approximately 28 kg were anesthetized with subcutaneous piritramide (5 kg) and intravenous sodium pentobarbital (15 mg/kg). They were artificially respired with a Bird respirator system using a gas mixture containing 30% nitrous oxide, 70% oxygen. The oxygen concentration was adjusted to give an arterial Po_2 between 100 and 120 mm Hg. The Pco_2 varied between 38 and 45 mm Hg. A Millar catheter tip manometer was advanced into the left ventricle via the left carotid artery, aortic blood pressure was monitored with a catheter (via the right femoral artery) that was connected to a Statham P23 pressure transducer. A venous line was established via the left femoral vein. Under fluoroscopic control, a Flexo pulmocath catheter (F4) was advanced into the descending branch of the left coronary artery (LAD) via a transfemoral guiding catheter for intracoronary infusion. The dogs were anticoagulated at the beginning with 5000 IU heparin, intravenously, followed by the same dose after 2 hours. Left thoracotomy and exposure of the heart was performed via the 5th intercostal space and a side branch of the LAD was prepared at its origin. A snare was placed around the artery for occlusion and reperfusion. The whole preparation was allowed to stabilize for 30 minutes. After 45 minutes of occlusion of the LAD sidebranch, the ischemic area was reperfused for 3 hours. Reperfusion was documented by fluoroscopic control. Nine millimoles (1 ml/min of a 50 mM solution) of ribose (seven dogs), AICAR (seven dogs), or adenosine (eight dogs) were infused via the intracoronary catheter into the LAD proximal to the previously occluded vessel. One group with saline infusion (seven dogs) served as a control.

Radiolabeled nucleosides (5-amino-2-^{3}H diazole-4-carboxamidriboside, [^{3}H]AICAR, or 2-[^{3}H]adenosine) were added to "cold" nucleosides to obtain a specific activity of 4.5 mCi in 9 mmol total amount infused (n = 3 dogs for each nucleoside).

Ribose incorporation was measured by infusion of 9 mmol ribose for 3 hours, together with 1-[^{14}C]glycine (specific activity 55.4 mCi/mmol) with an infusion rate of 0.8 mCi/hr (n = 3).

Purine de novo synthesis was measured by intracoronary infusion of 1-[^{14}C]glycine (specific activity 55.4 mCi/mmol) for 3 hours with an infusion rate of 0.8 mCi/hr (n = 3 dogs).

Needle biopsies (Tru-Cut) for biochemical analysis of nucleotides, nucleosides, and creatine phosphate were taken before any intervention, at the end of 45 minutes of regional ischemia, and after 3 hours of reperfusion. In dogs that received ribose, AICAR, or adenosine infusion, biopsies after 3 hours of reperfusion were obtained from the previous ischemic area, from nonischemic areas distal to the intracoronary substrate infusion, and from nonischemic areas that received the substrate via recirculation (posterior of the heart). The experiment was terminated after the last biopsy with 10 ml of concentrated potassium chloride, the heart was removed, sliced in bread-loaf fashion, and myocardial rings were incubated in *p*-nitroblue tetrazoliumchloride to exclude hearts with marked subendocardial infarctions. Since we occluded only a sidebranch of the LAD, no infarction occurred within 45 minutes of ischemia which would have occurred if the whole LAD had been occluded for the same time period.

ECG, left ventricular pressure, LV dP/dt, and aortic pressure were recorded on a direct-writing inkjet recorder. Instantaneous myocardial oxygen consumption was calculated on-line according to Bretschneider's equation (Bretschneider et al., 1970) by a digital computer, and kept in a range between 6 and 7 ml O_2/100 g per min. In dogs receiving AICAR, blood samples from the left atrium and the inferior vena cava were obtained before ischemia and in short intervals during AICAR infusion.

Tissue Sampling and Biochemical Analysis

Extraction Procedures

Biopsies (10–25 mg) were frozen immediately (2–3 seconds) in liquid nitrogen and weighed on a Kettler balance in precooled vials. The frozen tissue was homogenized in ice cold 0.6 M perchloric acid (400 μl) with an ultrasound homogenizer (Sonicator Cell Disruptor W-225 R) for 10 seconds. The homogenate was centrifuged at 12,000 rpm for 3 minutes, and 350 μl of the supernatant were neutralized with the required volume of 6 N KOH, resulting in a total volume of about 420 μl. The supernatant was decanted and stored in liquid nitrogen until it was analyzed, within the next 3 days. Blood samples were immediately centrifuged at 3000 rpm for 5 minutes, and 200 μl of serum were added to 500 μl of 0.6 N perchloric acid. The supernatant extract was neutralized with 6 N KOH and stored at −36°C.

Nucleotide and Nucleoside Analyses

ATP and creatine phosphate values were determined using bioluminiscence, as described by Ellis and Gardner (1980). Normal ATP values in the dog are reported to be 4 μmol/g wet weight with this method. ADP, AMP, IMP, NAD, and AICAR-monophosphate were separated and quantified by high performance liquid chromatography (HPLC), using a Varian 5000 gradient controller combined with a Dupont spectrophotometer and a Dupont integrator. A 50-μl sample of the undiluted supernatant extract was injected onto a Zorbax-NH_2 column (Dupont) and developed isocratically with 5 mM $NH_4H_2PO_4$ (pH 2.8) for 15 minutes, followed by a linear gradient of 5 mM to 750 mM $NH_4H_2PO_4$ (pH 4.5) at a flow rate of 2 ml/min.

Nucleosides and AICAR were separated on a Dupont ODS column using a linear gradient of 0 to 30% methanol-water (vol/vol) within 25 minutes. Uric acid and AICAR in plasma were separated on a Dupont ODS column using a linear gradient of 30 mM KH_2PO_4 (pH 3.5) to 30% methanol diluted in 30 mM KH_2PO_4 (pH 3.5) within 25 minutes.

The peaks found at 254 nm were identified by comparison of retention times with external standards. Peak areas were quantified by using peaks of known concentration and expressed in nmol/g or μmol/g wet weight. Since Reimer (Reimer et al., 1981) showed that tissue water after regional ischemia changes in the first hours of reperfusion by only 3%, no dry weight determinations were made.

For separation of amino acids in myocardial tissue, 20 μl of a solution containing 800 mg *o*-phtalaldehyde and 200 μl mercaptoethanol in 10 ml methanol were added to 150 μl of the sample for pre-column derivatization. A linear gradient of 30 minutes was established between solution A (tetrahydrofuran, methanol, 0.05 M sodium acetate, pH 5.9, 0.8/19.2/80, vol/vol/vol) and solution B (methanol, 0.05 M sodium acetate, pH 5.9, 80/20, vol/vol) on a Waters Radial Compression System using a C-18 column. Amino acids were detected with a fluorescence spectrophotometer (Kratos) at an emission wavelength of 228 nm and a 470 nm cut-off filter.

Analysis of [^{3}H]AICAR, [^{3}H]Adenosine, and [^{14}C]Glycine Incorporation

Four biopsies were extracted together in one vial, as described above, to obtain larger amounts of nucleotides. Fifty microliters of the supernatant extract were injected onto a DuPont ODS column and developed by means of a paired ion gradient system. A linear gradient was established, using 5 mM tetrabutylammonium phosphate with 30 mM KH_2PO_4 (pH 5.5) and 2% to 40% acetonitrile within 40 minutes. This resulted in a good separation of guanosine triphosphate (GTP), AICAR-triphosphate, and ATP. There was no coelution of ADP and adenylsuccinate which occurs with the ion-exchange method used for quantification of the nucleotides. AICAR triphosphate was identified as described by Sabina et al. (1982). We sampled AMP, ADP, IMP, ATP, and, if present, AICAR triphosphate by collecting the outflow of the HPLC column for the entire peak into scintillation vials containing 10 ml xylene scintillation fluid (Packard Instruments). Radioactivity was counted on a Packard Tri-Carb liquid scintillation counter and expressed in counts/min per 100 mg wet weight. To verify that radioactivity is not found in any other compound of the chromatogram, the column outflow of one biopsy of each experiment was sampled continuously in 30s fractions. No loss or interchange of the tritium atoms from [^{3}H]AICAR or [^{3}H]adenosine was detected, since the radioactivity baseline was always low and stable, and radioactivity was found only in anabolic or catabolic products of AICAR or adenosine.

For quantification of [^{3}H]AICAR and [^{3}H]adenosine incorporation into the nucleotides, the specific activity of the substrates in the infusate was determined by quantification of the substrate concentration by HPLC. The column outflow during the substrate peak was sampled, and radioactivity was counted in a liquid scintillation counter, as described above. Since there is no measurable AICAR content and only a minimal adenosine content in reperfused myocardial tissue, the specific activity of the infused substrates equals that of the tissue, and radioactivity incorporated into nucleotides can directly be converted into concentration.

In the experiments with [^{14}C]glycine as a marker of the nucleotide synthesis, specific activity of myocardial tissue glycine was measured directly, by the HPLC separation method, as described above. A total of 43.3 μmol of glycine was infused intracoronary within the 3-hour period. This increases plasma glycine levels by only 2.5%, assuming a 50 ml/min flow in the LAD. Because of the dilution of the intracoronary infusate in the whole body fluid, the recirculating radioactive glycine can be neglected, as compared to the activity in the intracoronary blood, i.e., the specific activity of glycine in the peripheral venous plasma was under 3%, compared to the calculated specific activity in the intracoronary plasma. Furthermore, the specific activity of myocardial tissue glycine in myocardial areas that received [^{14}C]glycine only via recirculation was only 7% compared to areas of intracoronary [^{14}C]glycine infusion.

Therefore, because of the rapid exchange of glycine between blood and cells (Elwyn et al., 1972), a constant tissue-specific activity can be expected within minutes of the 3-hour infusion period and can be maintained over the infusion period.

Chemicals

AICAR, adenosine, ribose, $NH_4H_2PO_4$, KH_2PO_4, tetrabutylammonium phosphate, and all nucleotides and nucleosides for HPLC-standards were obtained from Sigma Chemicals. [^{3}H]Adenosine and [^{14}C]glycine were made by Amersham Inc. [^{3}H]AICAR was made to our specification by Amersham, Inc. Fireflyluciferase was obtained by Lumac and creatine kinase by Boehringer Mannheim.

Statistics

Statistics were done by paired or unpaired *t*-test. All values are expressed as means ± SE, unless otherwise mentioned.

TABLE 1
Hemodynamics

		Saline	Ribose	AICAR	Adenosine
HR (beats/min)	Control	110.5 ± 8.0	91.8 ± 6.2	86.4 ± 6.5	99.5 ± 8.7
	Ischemia (45 min)	94.3 ± 5.7	80.5 ± 9.1	86.4 ± 6.1	95.6 ± 7.1
	Reflow (180 min)	102.0 ± 6.2	83.6 ± 8.1	106.0 ± 7.1	113.0 ± 6.9*
LVPsys (mm/Hg)	Control	129.0 ± 5.2	126.0 ± 7.2	119.0 ± 3.2	137.0 ± 9.4
	Ischemia (45 min)	120.0 ± 6.0	125.0 ± 4.4	120.0 ± 2.9	129.0 ± 7.7
	Reflow (180 min)	117.0 ± 5.1	124.0 ± 8.2	106.0 ± 7.1	118.0 ± 9.2*
$\dot{M}VO_2$ (ml/100 g per min)	Control	8.74 ± 0.41	6.51 ± 0.56	6.28 ± 0.33	7.71 ± 0.51
	Ischemia (45 min)	7.29 ± 0.43	6.08 ± 0.51	6.84 ± 0.48	7.41 ± 0.54
	Reflow (180 min)	6.98 ± 0.31	6.50 ± 0.62	7.41 ± 0.37	8.24 ± 0.57*

Results (in all tables) are expressed as means ± SE.
* $P < 0.05$ (compared to control) (paired *t*-test).

Results

Hemodynamics

Global hemodynamic parameters, such as heart rate, left ventricular pressure, and aortic pressure, remained unchanged over the entire experiment in the control-, ribose-, and AICAR-treated group (Table 1). In the adenosine-treated group, heart rate was significantly higher and aortic mean pressure lower during adenosine infusion, which is due to the peripheral vasodilating effect of adenosine. The hemodynamic changes were larger during the first hour of reperfusion and changed toward normalization during the following 2 hours of adenosine infusion, resulting in an 11% reduction of aortic mean pressure and a 10% increase of heart rate after 3 hours of adenosine infusion (Table 2). Subsequently, the instantaneous myocardial oxygen consumption (MVO_2) was found to be stable in a range between 6 and 7 ml O_2/min per 100 g in the control-, ribose-, and AICAR-treated group, but increased during adenosine infusion.

Effects of Ischemia on High-Energy Phosphates

In our experimental model, 45 minutes of regional ischemia led to a marked depression of tissue ATP by 50% (Fig. 1) and creatine phosphate by 80–90% (Table 3). AMP concentrations were doubled and ADP concentration remained unaltered. The breakdown products of AMP, like adenosine, inosine, and hypoxanthine/xanthine, were markedly increased. NAD was decreased by 24.6% (Table 3).

TABLE 2

Heart Rate (HR) and Mean Aortic Pressure (AOP_m) after 45 Minutes of Ischemia and during 3 Hours of Reperfusion with Intracoronary Adenosine Infusion (3 mM/hr)

	HR	AOP_m
Control	99.5 ± 8.7	113.0 ± 7.3
Ischemia (45 min)	95.6 ± 7.1	109.5 ± 5.7
Reflow (60 min)	132.1 ± 7.2*	83.4 ± 8.8*
Reflow (120 min)	123.2 ± 6.8†	92.6 ± 7.6†
Reflow (180 min)	113.4 ± 6.9†	99.0 ± 9.3†

* $P < 0.02$.
† $P < 0.05$.

Effect of Reperfusion on High Energy Phosphates

ATP de Novo Synthesis

Adenine nucleotide de novo synthesis was measured by 1-[^{14}C]glycine incorporation into nucleotides. Specific activity of [^{14}C]glycine in myocardial tissue after 3 hours of [^{14}C]glycine infusion is shown in Table 4. From the known specific activity and the detected radioactivity in the ATP and ADP, the nucleoside synthesis rates were calculated (Table 5). Basic ATP synthesis rate in nonischemic tissue was found to be very slow (3.74 nmol/g wet weight per

TABLE 3

Nucleotides, Nucleosides, and Creatine Phosphate Levels after 45 Minutes of Ischemia and 3 Hours of Reperfusion with Different Substrate Infusion

	Control	45 Min of Ischemia	Reperfusion: Saline	Reperfusion: AICAR	Reperfusion: Adenosine
ADP (nm/g wet wt)	1120 ± 61	980 ± 82	822 ± 81*	912 ± 57*	748 ± 102*
AMP (nm/g wet wt)	68.1 ± 3.0	144.0 ± 9.0*	41.0 ± 3.1*	42.3 ± 2.8*	54.8 ± 17.1
IMP (nm/g wet wt)	7.1 ± 4.3	7.4 ± 5.1	ND	67.0 ± 10.0*	8.8 ± 4.3
Adenosine (nm/g wet wt)	9.0 ± 0.9	65.7 ± 15.4†	8.1 ± 0.9	7.3 ± 1.7	174.1 ± 36.8†
Inosine (nm/g wet wt)	9.2 ± 3.5	1131 ± 249†	5.2 ± 1.6	5.9 ± 1.7	212 ± 42.0†
Hypoxanthine (nm/g wet wt)	ND	261 ± 24.1	ND	ND	55.1 ± 9.9
AICAR (nm/g wet wt)	ND	ND	ND	985 ± 266	ND
AICAR-MP (nm/g wet wt)	ND	ND	ND	572 ± 91	ND
NAD (nm/g wet wt)	691 ± 83	522 ± 71*	543 ± 43*	580 ± 25*	498 ± 72*
CP (μM/g wet wt)	9.25 ± 0.73	2.75 ± 0.25†	12.26 ± 0.49*	12.94 ± 0.53*	10.52 ± 0.38
n	8	8	7	7	8

* $P < 0.01$; † $P < 0.001$ compared to control (paired *t*-test).

TABLE 4
Glycine Levels and Glycine Specific Activity after 3 Hours of ^{14}C-Glycine Intracoronary Infusion in Postischemic and Nonischemic Myocardial Tissue

	Postischemic	Nonischemic
Glycine level (nmol/g wet wt)	815.2 ± 62.3	1041.5 ± 83.5
Specific activity (counts/min per nmol)	3830.2 ± 262.5	3974.3 ± 296.3

3 hr). Within the first 3 hours of reperfusion of previously ischemic tissue, the rate was doubled (7.48 nmol/g wet weight per 3 hr) (Table 5). The synthesis rates of adenine nucleotides were 3.07 nmol/g wet weight per hr in postischemic and 1.50 nmol/g wet weight per hr in nonischemic myocardium (Table 6). This slow synthesis rate would lead only to nonmeasurable increases of ATP within 3 hours of reperfusion. Therefore, the ATP levels in the control group with 45 minutes of ischemia and 3 hours of reperfusion remained depressed to 50% of normal (Fig. 1). AMP, adenosine, and inosine, and hypoxanthine levels returned to normal values. Creatine phosphate concentrations showed a marked increase compared to ischemic levels to a value of 15% above normal ("overshoot") (Table 3).

Ribose as a Substrate for ATP Synthesis

The synthesis rate of adenine nucleotides (AN) with ribose-infusion was determined in the same way as the AN de novo synthesis, by infusing ribose together with [^{14}C]glycine. The synthesis rate was found to be 15.1 nmol/g wet weight per hr in postischemic and 9.8 nmol/g wet weight per hr in nonischemic tissue (Table 6). This results in a 5- to 6-fold increase of AN de novo synthesis. This increase is far too low to be measured in overall tissue ATP levels, and therefore no increase of ATP could be shown within 3 hours of reperfusion (Fig. 1). Creatine phosphate concentration showed the same "overshoot" phenomenon as in the saline-treated control group (control, 9.7 ± 0.6 μmol/g wet weight;

TABLE 6
Purine Nucleotide de Novo Synthesis and Accelerated Synthesis Rates after 3 Hours of Intracoronary Substrate Infusion in Previously Ischemic and Nonischemic Myocardium*

	de Novo	Ribose	AICAR	Adenosine
Postischemic	3.07 ±0.26	15.06 ±0.39	27.4 ±3.3	268.5 ±45.2
Nonischemic	1.50 ±0.31	9.77 ±0.49	28.5 ±4.2	218.7 ±36.0

* In nmol/g wet weight per hour.

180 minutes of reperfusion, 12.2 ± 1.7 μmol/g wet weight).

AICAR as a Substrate of ATP Synthesis

AICAR was taken up by the myocardial cell and was phosphorylated to AICAR-monophosphate (AICAR-MP) (Fig. 2). At the same tissue AICAR concentration, the phosphorylation rate was higher in previously ischemic compared to nonischemic myocardium. Since AICAR concentrations were twice as high (previous ischemic areas) or 4-fold as high (nonischemic areas) as AICAR-MP concentration, phosphorylation seemed to be rate limiting. Areas that received AICAR only via blood recirculation in a 70-fold lower plasma concentration showed a 15-fold lower AICAR tissue concentration and a lower AICAR-MP concentration compared to infusion areas. This demonstrates a dose-dependent AICAR uptake and AICAR-MP formation (Fig. 2). Transformation of AICAR-MP to inosine monophosphate (IMP) is shown by the 9-fold increase of IMP in the tissue (Table 3) and the incorporation of ^3H into IMP in [^3H]AICAR-treated dogs (Fig. 3a; Table 7). This incorporation is dependent on the AICAR-MP levels. Only 15% of the AICAR-MP activity was found in IMP. A similar percentage was found in the increase of tissue levels of AICAR-MP and IMP. Further incorporation into the adenine nucleotide pool is shown by ^3H incorporation into ADP and ATP (Table 7; Fig. 3, a and b). There are also linear

TABLE 5
Incorporation of Radioactivity into ATP and ADP within 3 Hours of ^{14}C-Glycine Intracoronary Infusion with or without Addition of Ribose (3 mM/hr) and Calculated Synthesis Rates

		[^{14}C]Glycine		[^{14}C]Glycine + ribose	
		Radioactivity (counts/min per g wet wt × 10^3)	Synthesis rate (nM/g wet wt per 3 hr)	Radioactivity (counts/min per g wet wt × 10^3)	Synthesis rate (nM/g wet wt per 3 hr)
ATP	I	28.6 ± 4.4	7.48 ± 1.15	122.9 ± 5.7	32.09 ± 1.49
	NI	14.9 ± 4.3	3.74 ± 1.08	85.5 ± 6.7	21.50 ± 1.68
ADP	I	6.7 ± 1.3	1.74 ± 0.33	47.3 ± 8.6	12.34 ± 2.31
	NI	3.0 ± 1.3	0.76 ± 0.32	31.1 ± 7.5	7.82 ± 1.89

I = previously ischemic myocardium; NI = nonischemic myocardium.

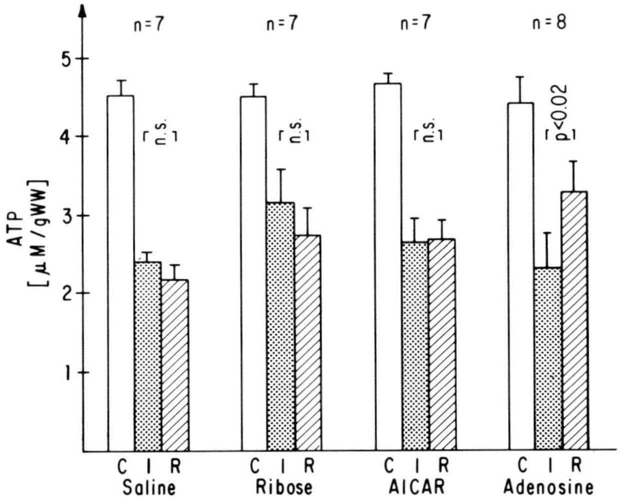

FIGURE 1. *Tissue ATP levels before ischemia (C), after 45 minutes of regional ischemia (I), and after 3 hours of reperfusion (R) with intracoronary infusion of ribose, AICAR, or adenosine. A group with saline infusion served as a control. Within 3 hours, only adenosine infusion leads to a significant increase in tissue ATP levels.*

correlations between the [^{3}H]AICAR-MP levels and radiolabel incorporation into ADP and ATP (Fig. 3, a and b). The net ATP synthesis can be calculated from the ^{3}H incorporation into ATP and from the known specific activity of infused AICAR. It results in a rate of ATP synthesis of 19 nmol/g wet weight per hr in areas of intracoronary AICAR infusion (Table 7). This increase is too small to be detected in overall tissue ATP-levels after 3 hours of reperfusion. Consequently, there was no difference between the endischemic ATP values and those, after 3 hours of reperfusion with AICAR (Fig. 1). A marked percentage of the AICAR-MP activity was found in AICAR triphosphate (AICAR-TP) which is synthesized in preference to ATP with high AICAR concentrations (Fig. 3b). Tissue AICAR-TP concentrations calculated from these data ranged between 0.15 and 0.3 μmol/g wet weight in the areas with intracoronary AICAR infusion. Inosine and hypoxanthine tissue levels stayed within normal limits during AICAR infusion (Table 3). Creatine phosphate showed the same postischemic overshoot as the control group.

Adenosine as a Substrate of ATP Synthesis

After [^{3}H]adenosine infusion, radioactivity was found in AMP, ADP, and in large amounts in ATP, resulting in an adenine nucleotide synthesis rate of 268 nmol/g wet weight per hr (Table 7). A similar synthesis rate (323 nmol/g wet weight per hr) was calculated from the directly measured increase in tissue ATP concentrations (Fig. 1). Tissue adenosine levels were higher during adenosine infusion compared to values at the end of ischemia, demonstrating that the infused adenosine is only partially deaminated until it reaches the reperfused postischemic myocardium (Table 3).

Catabolism of AICAR and Adenosine

With AICAR infusion, no rise in tissue inosine or hypoxanthine concentrations was found (Table 3). Plasma uric acid concentrations increased with time with no difference between left atrial and vena cava inferior blood (Fig. 4a). A marked difference in AICAR levels between caval and left atrial blood but no difference in uric acid levels indicates peripheral uptake of AICAR and renal elimination of nonmetabolized AICAR (Fig. 4b).

Adenosine infusion is followed by high tissue inosine and hypoxanthine (Table 3) and high hypoxanthine levels in plasma (control, 0.18 ± 0.01 mg/liter; 3 hours of adenosine infusion, 1.21 ± 0.49 mg/liter), showing fast deamination of adenosine in blood and tissue. No adenosine was found in vena cava inferior blood. Uric acid levels were twice as high as after AICAR infusion (11.32 ± 0.25 mg/liter).

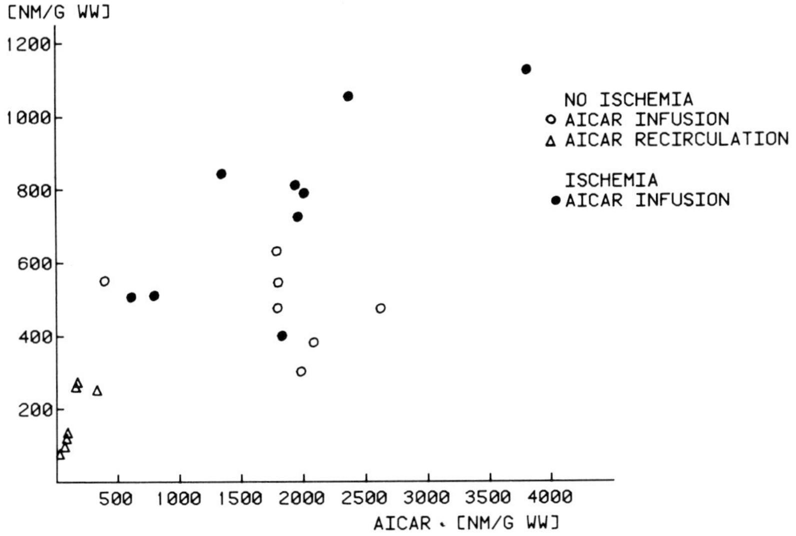

FIGURE 2. *AICAR phosphorylation is shown by plotting the content of AICAR vs. AICAR monophosphate of single biopsies obtained from different sites of the heart. Comparison of ischemic (closed circles) and nonischemic (open circles) intracoronary infusion areas demonstrates a higher phosphorylation rate in previously ischemic areas, and comparison of infusion areas to areas that received AICAR via recirculation shows a dose-dependent build-up of AICAR-monophosphate.*

TABLE 7
Incorporation of [^{3}H]AICAR or Adenosine into Nucleotides* and Calculated Nucleotide Synthesis Rates†

		[^{3}H]AICAR		[^{3}H]Adenosine	
		Radioactivity (counts/min per g wet wt × 10^3)	Synthesis rate (nmol/g wet wt per 3 hr)	Radioactivity (counts/min per g wet wt × 10^3)	Synthesis rate (nmol/g wet wt per 3 hr)
IMP	I	16.4 ± 4.5	37.2 ± 9.6		
	NI	16.2 ± 6.2	36.8 ± 12.1		
AMP	I			8.5 ± 1.7	18.94 ± 3.1
	NI			6.7 ± 1.3	14.72 ± 1.9
ADP	I	11.2 ± 2.9	25.5 ± 6.2	48.6 ± 5.2	108.0 ± 11.6
	NI	11.2 ± 5.2	27.9 ± 8.4	39.4 ± 2.8	86.4 ± 19.6
ATP	I	24.8 ± 4.9	56.7 ± 11.5	306.6 ± 53.2	678.3 ± 115.3
	NI	25.5 ± 5.4	57.3 ± 10.6	252.8 ± 39.7	554.7 ± 91.5
AICAR-TP	I	81.8 ± 11.9	186.0 ± 22.6		
	NI	80.1 ± 13.4	178.5 ± 26.4		

I = previously ischemic myocardium; NI = nonischemic myocardium.
* Within 3 hours of reperfusion.
† Specific activity of infused compounds: AICAR, 439.8 counts/min per nmol; adenosine, 451.9 counts/min per nmol.

Discussion

The slow recovery of the depleted adenine nucleotide pool, especially of ATP, following a period of potentially reversible ischemia is well recognized (DeBoer et al., 1980; Reimer et al., 1981; Swain et al., 1982b). Since the fall of ATP during ischemia is not accompanied by a rise in ADP, we must conclude that ADP is quickly transformed to AMP, which is found to be doubled after ischemia in our experiments. The myokinase reaction and dephosphorylation of AMP by 5′-nucleotidase leads to adenosine which is deaminated to inosine. Both nucleosides can leave the cell. During reflow, the nucleotide degradation products are washed out of the interstitial space (Katori and Berne, 1966; Fox et al., 1979) and are unavailable for the nucleotide salvage pathways (Maguire et al., 1972; Parker et al., 1976). The cell is now dependent on the very slow and energy-consuming de novo synthesis. Our experiments and those of Zimmer et al. (1973) showed a doubling of the AN de novo synthesis during recovery from oxygen deprivation, but, in our dog experiments, the de novo synthesis rate was only 38% (3 nmol/g wet weight per hr) compared to the rate measured in rats. Therefore, it would have taken about 14 days to synthesize 1.0 μmol/g wet weight of ATP. There are two reasons for this. First, ribose-5-phosphate, the basic substrate of AN de novo synthesis was shown to be in short supply after ischemia (Zimmer et al., 1973). Second, the energy-consuming assembly of the purine structure by successive attachment of C-fragments to phosphoribosylpyrophosphate is slow in energy-depleted cells. It was already shown by Zimmer (1980) that exogenous supply of ribose can speed up ATP synthesis 3- to 4-fold in the rat heart. In our dog model, ribose infusion leads to similar results by accelerating AN de novo synthesis 4- to 6-fold. This acceleration is far too slow to achieve a measurable increase of ATP within 3 hours of reperfusion. These results also show that the acceleration of AN synthesis by AICAR or adenosine cannot be due to a splitting of the molecule and incorporation of the ribose moiety of the molecule, because acceleration rates of AN synthesis are higher with AICAR and adenosine, as compared to ribose.

Studies with AICAR

A new approach bypassing several steps of the AN de novo synthesis pathway was the infusion of AICA-riboside (AICAR) as shown by Sabina et al. (1982). AICAR is the dephosphorylated form of the AN de novo synthesis intermediate, AICAR monophosphate (AICAR-MP). It enters the biosynthetic pathway distal to the major control points (Wyngarden and Ashton, 1959) and needs only one molecule of ATP and GTP to form AMP. Swain et al. (1982a) showed a 25% increase of ATP (from a postischemic 70–95% of normal) within 24 hours of AICAR infusion in the dog. In our study, with a more severe ischemia and a reduction of ATP to 50% of normal, we demonstrated incorporation of tritium-labeled AICAR into ATP representing a 9-fold increase of AN synthesis within the first 3 hours of reperfusion compared to the de novo synthesis that was measured by [^{14}C]glycine incorporation and a 20-fold increase of AN synthesis in nonischemic tissue. This acceleration is twice that for ribose, but is still too small to be detected from overall tissue ATP levels within 3 hours of reperfusion. There are two reasons for the still insufficient acceleration of ATP synthesis by AICAR. First, uptake, especially in postischemic tissue, and phosphorylation of AICAR to AICAR monophosphate by myocytes, is slow: AICAR con-

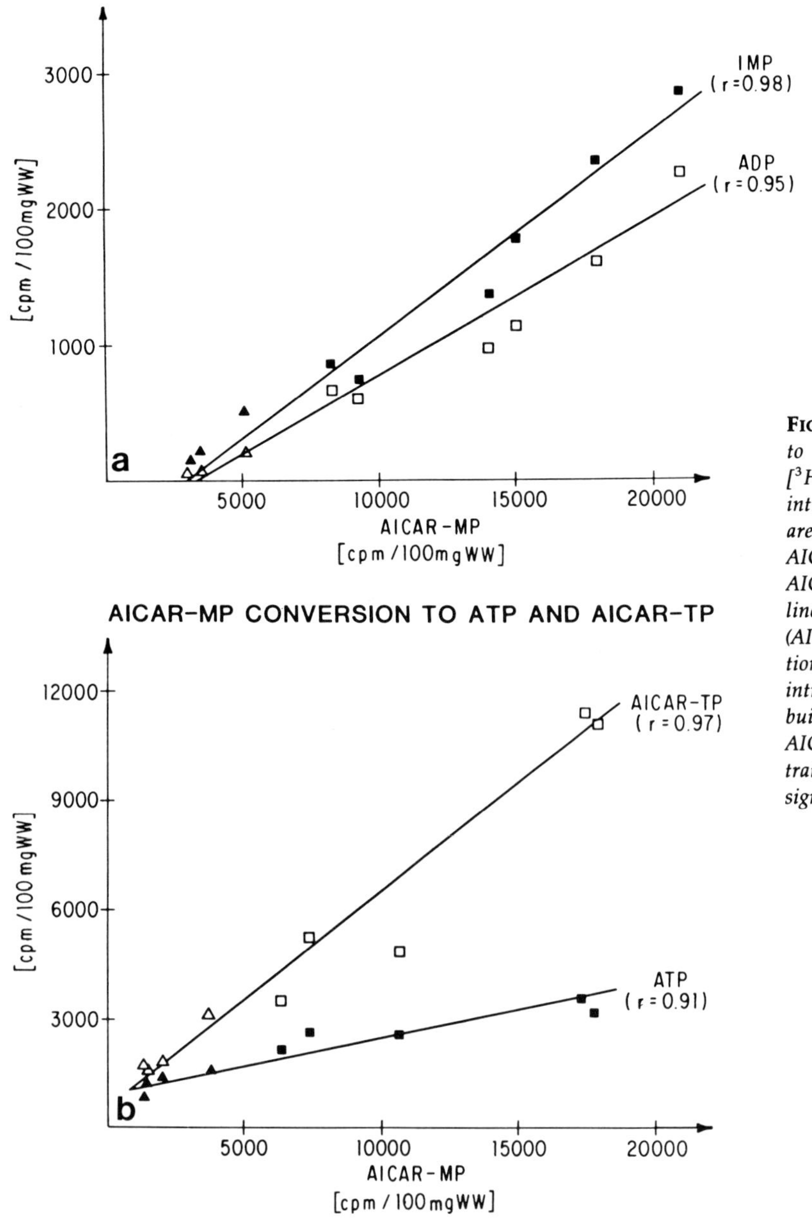

FIGURE 3. *Panel a: AICAR-monophosphate is converted to IMP and ADP, as shown by incorporation of [^{3}H]AICAR. Radioactivity found in IMP and ADP in intracoronary infusion areas (squares) and recirculation areas (triangles) is linearly correlated to the content of AICAR monophosphate. Panel b: incorporation of [^{3}H] AICAR into ATP and AICAR triphosphate (AICAR-TP) is linearly correlated to the levels of AICAR monophosphate (AICAR-MP) over a wide range of AICAR-MP concentration. With higher AICAR-MP concentrations, in areas of intracoronary AICAR infusions (squares), AICAR-TP is built up in preference to ATP. In areas that received AICAR via recirculation (triangles) in much lower concentrations, incorporation into ATP and AICAR-TP is not significantly different.*

centrations are twice as high as AICAR-MP concentrations in previously ischemic tissue, and four times higher in nonischemic tissue. Second, with higher AICAR monophosphate concentrations, the preferred metabolic pathway is the transformation of AICAR-MP to AICAR triphosphate. AICAR triphosphate formation from AICAR has also been shown by Zimmerman and Deeprose (1978) in erythrocytes, by Bochner et al. (1982) in cells after 10-tetrahydrofolate deficiency, and in small amounts by Sabina et al. (1982) in the heart after intraatrial AICAR infusion. The AICAR triphosphate levels reported by Sabina are in the same range as the levels we found in myocardial areas that received AICAR via recirculation. In these areas, AICAR triphosphate formation and ATP buildup is equal. With higher AICAR-MP levels in areas that received AICAR via intracoronary infusion, AICAR triphosphate formation becomes predominant and leads to AICAR triphosphate levels of 0.15–0.3 μmol/g wet weight within 3 hours of reperfusion. A reported inhibition of the enzyme adenylosuccinate lyase by AICAR-MP (Sabina et al., 1982), which catalyses the transformation of IMP to AMP, could not be observed in our study, since there was a linear correlation between AICAR concentrations and ATP built up over a 20-fold range encompassing myocardial areas that received AICAR only via recirculation and myocardial areas that received AICAR via intracoronary infusion. From our data, we cannot decide whether the metabolism of AICAR to ATP is linear during the 3-hour infusion period. However, the constant increase of uric acid in plasma shows a linear catabolism of infused AICAR. The slow time-dependent increase of uric acid in plasma with no differences between left atrial and

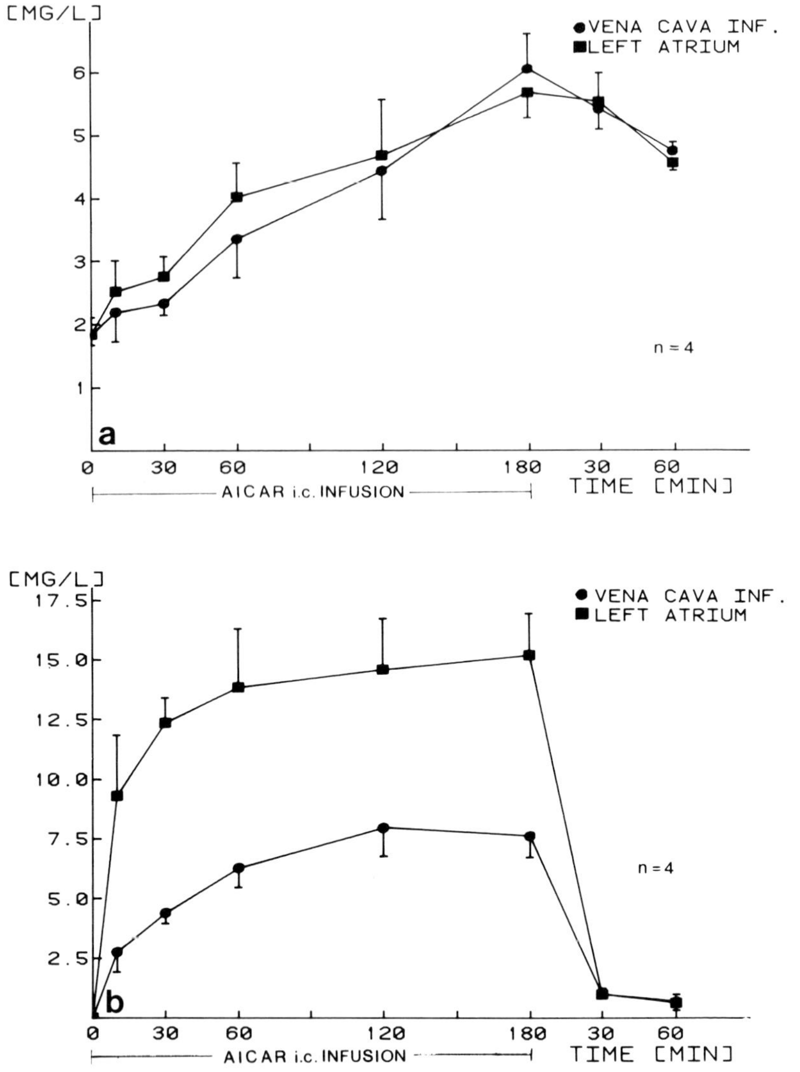

FIGURE 4. *Panel a: AICAR infusion leads to a slow time-dependent increase of plasma uric acid levels with no statistical difference in left atrial and vena cava inferior levels. After stopping AICAR infusion, uric acid is slowly eliminated. (Statistics: 10 minutes and 30 minutes of AICAR infusion, $P < 0.002$ compared to control; 60–180 minutes of AICAR infusion, $P < 0.001$ compared to control.) Panel b: with intracoronary AICAR infusion, plasma AICAR levels rise within the first hour of infusion. A marked difference between left atrial and vena cava inferior AICAR concentrations under steady state conditions with no difference in uric acid levels suggests peripheral uptake and kidney elimination of unmetabolized AICAR. Stopping AICAR infusion leads to a sharp fall of plasma AICAR concentrations.*

venous concentrations over the whole infusion period is indicative of a slow catabolism of AICAR. The very high plasma levels of AICAR are also a parameter for the slow metabolism, and the great difference between left atrial plasma levels and vena cava inferior plasma levels under steady state conditions after 1 hour of AICAR infusion can be explained by uptake in peripheral tissue and renal excretion of nonmetabolized AICAR. The time-dependent increase of plasma uric acid concentration after AICAR infusion would suggest IMP formation. Since IMP is a crossroad of three metabolic pathways (IMP to AMP, IMP to GTP, IMP to inosine), we are not surprised to find a much lower radiolabel incorporation into ATP as compared to adenosine: most of the newly formed IMP is probably degraded to uric acid. The complete absence of a rise in inosine and hypoxanthine above normal levels in tissue and plasma with AICAR infusions is, however, difficult to explain, and would suggest the possibility of a route from AICAR to uric acid not encompassing IMP. It also shows that the AICAR dose used is appropriate for investigation of the effects of AICAR. A further increase of AICAR-MP concentration with higher AICAR concentrations would lead only to a minimal increase in ATP formation. A decrease in AICAR concentration leads to a decrease in ATP formation as shown.

Studies with Adenosine

An increase of ATP in postischemic myocardium is reported with adenosine as a precursor (Reibel and Rovetto, 1979; Isselhard et al., 1980; Foker et al., 1980). Since most of these studies have been done in isolated rat or guinea pig hearts, no addition of an inhibitor of adenosine deaminase for preventing adenosine deamination in blood (van Belle 1969) was necessary. In a whole animal preparation, acceleration of ATP synthesis was successful only when intravenous adenosine was given together with EHNA (erythro-g-(2-hydroxy-3-nonyl)-adenine, a potent adenosine deaminase blocker. As far as we know, adenosine was therefore not used to replenish decreased ATP pools rapidly in regionally ischemic and reperfused myocardium in the dog heart. Foker's study (Foker et al., 1980) was done in the totally and globally ischemic heart within the context of a cardioplegic study. Isselhard et al. (1970b, 1980) studied adenosine either in postasphyxic rabbit hearts or in normal dog hearts. The intracoronary administration of adenosine has the advantage of partially bypassing the adenosine deamination by blood which is correlated with contact time (van Belle, 1969). It leads only to minimal adenosine concentrations in the peripheral tissues after passing through the lungs, i.e., it does not recirculate. This allows high local adenosine concentrations with only minor peripheral hemodynamic changes. It cannot be ruled out that these hemodynamic changes may influence ATP catabolism; however, Isselhard (1980, 1984, in press) has shown recently that the hemodynamic changes produced by adenosine do not affect ATP synthesis. Since myocardial oxygen consumption increases slightly after adenosine infusion, due to an increase of heart rate, there is probably an increase in ATP turnover. This may lead to a small underestimation of accelerated ATP synthesis by adenosine. High tissue adenosine levels demonstrate the uptake of adenosine from the blood. Increased inosine and hypoxanthine tissue levels show that part of the adenosine is rapidly deaminated. The ^{3}H incorporation found in ATP after infusion of [^{3}H]adenosine, as well as the increase of total ATP from 50% postischemic to 75% of normal within 3 hours of reperfusion results in a 90-fold increase of ATP synthesis compared to the de novo synthesis. These incorporation rates are comparable to those reported in studies with isolated perfused hearts (Reibel and Rovetto, 1979; Isselhard et al., 1980). Adenosine transformation to AMP is catalyzed by the enzyme adenosine kinase which is not an enzyme of the purine de novo synthesis pathway. Incorporation of both ribose and AICAR is dependent on the pre-existent purine de novo synthesis pathway. However, ribose enters this pathway after being converted to ribose-5-phosphate and phosphoribosylpyrophosphate, at the beginning, and AICAR enters after conversion to AICAR-MP, near the end, of this pathway.

There seemed to be several rate-limiting steps. One is the availability of phosphoribosylpyrophosphate which can be overcome by the infusion of ribose. However, this can speed up the synthesis only by a factor of five to six, which is minimal compared to adenosine incorporation. Because of the big difference in the incorporation rate of AICAR and adenosine, there must also be a rate-limiting step in the conversion of AICAR-MP to AMP. Since there is no increase of AICAR-MP after ribose infusion, the capacity of the conversion of ribose-5-phosphate to AICAR-MP seems also to be limited. The conversion of phosphoribosylpyrophosphate to IMP is dependent on ATP, which is needed at several steps of this pathway. This seems to be no problem, not even for the ATP-depleted cell, because ribose incorporation is doubled in postischemic tissue with lower ATP levels and there is no big difference in the incorporation of ribose and AICAR, whereas AICAR enters this pathway distal to the ATP-dependent steps.

Each of the three tested substrates is able to restore postischemic reduced myocardial ATP levels significantly faster than ATP-de novo synthesis, but there are big differences in the extent of incorporation of these precursors into the adenine nucleotide pool. Adenosine is rapidly incorporated and leads to a fast increase of tissue ATP levels within hours.

Incorporation of ribose or AICAR is much slower, and a measurable increase of ATP levels in dog myocardium would only be expected after 1–2 days.

The ability of fast restoration of ATP levels leads to two questions that have to be resolved in further experiments, i.e., (1) will reduced contractile function improve with higher ATP levels? and (2) will partially restored myocardial ATP levels protect the heart against recurrent episodes of ischemia?

Address for reprints: Dr. Manfred Mauser, Max-Planck-Institute for Physiological and Clinical Research, Department of Experimental Cardiology, Benekestrasse 2, D-6350 Bad Nauheim, Federal Republic of Germany.

Received May 20, 1983; accepted for publication October 31, 1984.

References

Belle van H (1969) Uptake and deamination of adenosine by blood: Species differences, effect of pH, ions, temperature, and metabolic inhibition. Biochim Biophys Acta **192:** 124–132

Berne RM (1963) Cardiac nucleotides in hypoxia: Possible role in regulation of coronary flow. Am J Physiol **204:** 317–322

Bochner B, Ames BN (1982) ZTP (5-amino-4-imidazole carboxamide riboside 5′-triphosphate): A proposed alarmone for 10-formyl-tetrahydrofolate deficiency. Cell **29:** 929–937

Bretschneider HJ, Cott LA, Hensel I, Kettler D, Martel J (1970) Ein neuer komplexer haemodynamischer Parameter aus 5 additiven Gliedern zur Bestimmung des O_2-Bedarfs des linken Ventrikels. Pflugers Arch **319:** 14

Burdette WJ (1956) Adenosine nucleotide levels in cardiac arrest. Am Heart J **52:** 193–197

Chang I (1938) Effect of asphyxia on the adenosinetriphosphate content of the rabbit heart. Q J Exp Physiol **28:** 3

Danforth WH, Naegele S, Bing RJ (1960) Effect of ischemia and reoxygenation on glycolytic reactions and adenosinetriphosphate in heart muscle. Circ Res **7:** 965–971

DeBoer LMV, Ingwall JS, Kloner RA, Braunwald E (1980) Prolonged derangements of canine myocardial purine metabolism after a brief coronary artery occlusion not associated with anatomic evidence of necrosis. Proc Natl Acad Sci USA **77:** 5471–5474

Ellis RJ, Gardner C (1980) Determination of myocardial high-energy phosphate using bioluminiscence. Anal Biochem **105:** 354–360

Elwyn DH, Launder WJ, Parikh HC, Wise Jr EM (1972) Roles of plasma and erythrocytes in interorgan transport of amino acids in dogs. Am J Physiol **222:** 1333–1342

Foker JE, Einzig E, Wang T (1980) Adenosine metabolism and myocardial preservation. J Thorac Cardiovasc Surg **80:** 506–516

Fox AC, Reed GE, Meilman H, Silk BB (1979) Release of nucleosides from canine and human hearts as an index of prior ischemia. Am J Cardiol **43:** 52

Gerlach E, Deuticke B, Dreisbach RH (1963) Der Nukleotidabbau im Herzmuskel bei Sauerstoffmangel und seine mögliche Bedeutung für die Coronardurchblutung. Naturwissenschaft **50:** 228–234

Hunkapillar MW, Hood LE (1978) Direct microsequence analysis of polypeptides using an improved sequenator, a nonprotein carrier (polybren), and high pressure liquid chromatography. Biochemistry **17:** 2124–2133

Ibel H, Steinkoff G, Zimmer HG (1982) Comparative studies on the myocardial hexose monophosphate shunt in different animal species (abstr). Pflugers Arch **394:** R13

Isselhard W, Pohl W, Berghoff WJW, Schmerbauch D, Schuler HW (1964) Versuche zur Verbesserung der Energiebereitstellung im künstlich stillgestellten Herzen und in der Erholung bei Reperfusion. Verh Dtsch Ges Herz Kreislaufforsch **30:** 216–221

Isselhard W, Mäurer W, Stremmel W, Krebs J, Schmitz H, Neuhof H, Esser A (1970a) Stoffwechsel der Kaninchenherzen in situ während Asphyxie und in der postasphyxtischen Erholung. Pflugers Arch **316:** 164–193

Isselhard W, Hinzen D, Geppert E, Maurer W (1970b) Beeinflussung des post-asphyktischen Wiederaufbaus der Adeninnukleotide im Kaninchenherzen in vivo durch Substratangebot. Pflugers Arch **320:** 195–209

Isselhard W, Eitenmüller J, Mäurer W, DeVreese A, Reineke H, Czerniak A, Sturz J, Herb HG (1980) Increase in myocardial adenine nucleotides induced by adenosine: Dosage, mode of application and duration, species differences. J Mol Cell Cardiol **12:** 619–634

Isselhard W, Hamaji M, Mäurer W, Erkens H, Walter H (in press) Adenosine-induced increase in myocardial adenine nucleotides without adenosine-induced systemic hypotension. Basic Res Cardiol **6**

Kammermeier H (1964) Verhalten von Adenin-Nukleotiden und Kreatinphosphat im Herzmuskel bei funktioneller Erholung nach länger dauernder Asphyxie. Verh Dtsch Ges Herz Kreislaufforsch **30:** 206–211

Kammermeier H, Karitzky D (1963) Verhalten von ATP und Kreatinphosphat bei der Wiederbelebung des Myokards nach länger dauernder Asphyxie. Pflugers Arch **178:** 101

Katori M, Berne RM (1966) Release of adenosine from anoxic heart: Relationship to coronary flow. Circ Res **19:** 420

Kloner RA, Lawrence W, DeBoer V, Darsee JR, Ingwall JS, Hale S, Tumas J, Braunwald E (1981) Prolonged abnormalities of myocardium salvaged by reperfusion. Am J Physiol **241:** H591–H599

Maguire MH, Lukas MC, Rettie JF (1972) Adenine nucleotide salvage synthesis in the rat heart, pathways of adenosine salvage. Biochim Biophys Acta **262:** 108–115

Parker JC, Smith EE, Jones CE (1976) The role of nucleoside and nucleobase metabolism in myocardial adenine nucleotide regeneration after cardiac arrest. Circ Shock **3:** 11–20

Reibel DK, Rovetto MJ (1979) Myocardial adenosine salvage rates and restoration of ATP content following ischemia. Am J Physiol **237:** H247–H252

Reimer KA, Hill ML, Jennings RB (1981) Prolonged depletion of ATP and of the adenine nucleotide pool due to delayed resynthesis of adenine nucleotides following reversible myocardial ischemic injury. J Mol Cell Cardiol **13:** 229–239

Rentrop P, Blanke H, Karsch KR, Kaiser H, Koestering H, Leitz K (1981) Selective intracoronary thrombolysis in acute myocardial infarction and unstable angina pectoris. Circulation **63:** 307–317

Sabina RL, Kernstine KH, Boyd RL, Holmes EW, Swain JL (1982) Metabolism of 5-amino-4-imidazole carboxamide riboside in cardiac and skeletal muscle. J Biol Chem **257:** 10178–10183

Schaper J, Mulch J, Winkler B, Schaper W (1979) Ultrastructural, functional and biochemical criteria for estimation of reversibility of ischemic injury: A study on the effects of global ischemia on the isolated dog heart. J Mol Cell Cardiol **11:** 521–541

Schmutzler R, Heckner F, Koertge P, van de Loo J, Pezold FA, Poliwoda H, Praetorius F, Zekoth D (1966) Zur thrombolytischen Therapie des frischen Herzinfarktes. Dtsch Med Wochenschr **91:** 581–587

Swain JL, Hines JJ, Sabina RL, Holmes EW (1982a) Accelerated repletion of ATP and GTP pools in postischemic canine myocardium using a precursor of purine de novo synthesis. Circ Res **51:** 102–105

Swain JL, Sabina RL, McHale PA, Greenfield JC, Holmes EW (1982b) Prolonged myocardial nucleotide depletion after brief ischemia in the open-chest dog. Am J Physiol **242:** H818–H826

Wyngarden A, Ashton DM (1959) Regulation of activity of phosphoribosylpyrophosphate amido-transferase by purine ribonucleotides: Potential feedback control of purine biosynthesis. J Biol Chem **234:** 1492–1496

Zimmer HG (1980) Restitution of myocardial adenine nucleotides: acceleration by administration of ribose. J Physiol (Paris) **76:** 769–775

Zimmer HG, Gerlach E (1978) Stimulation of myocardial adenine nucleotide biosynthesis by pentose and pentitols. Pflugers Arch **376:** 223–227

Zimmer HG, Trendelenburg C, Kammermeier H (1973) De-novo-synthesis of myocardial adenine-nucleotides in the rat. Acceleration during recovery from oxygen deficiency. Circ Res **32:** 635–642

Zimmerman PT, Deeprose RD (1978) Metabolism of 5-amino-1-β-D-ribofuranosyl imidazole-4-carboxamide and related five-membered heterocycles to 5-triphosphates in human blood and L 5178 Y cells. Biochem Pharmacol **27:** 709–716

INDEX TERMS: Adenosine • AICAR • Ribose • ATP • Reperfusion

Sodium Pump Inhibition, Enhanced Calcium Influx via Sodium-Calcium Exchange, and Positive Inotropic Response in Cultured Heart Cells

William H. Barry, Yonathin Hasin, and Thomas W. Smith

From the Cardiovascular Division, Brigham and Women's Hospital, and the Departments of Medicine, Brigham and Women's Hospital and Harvard Medical School, Boston, Massachusetts

SUMMARY. The effects of sodium pump inhibition produced by exposure to the cardiac glycosides, ouabain or dihydroouabain, or by reduction in extracellular potassium to 1.0 mM, on contractile state and sodium-calcium exchange were studied in primary monolayer cultures of chick embryo ventricular cells. Ouabain, 10^{-6} M, dihydroouabain, 5×10^{-5} M, and extracellular potassium of 1.0 mM all induced similar and prominent positive inotropic effects. These effects were accompanied, in each case, by 40–50% inhibition of the rate of active uptake of ^{42}K and by similar increases in steady state sodium content. Stimulation of the rate of ^{45}Ca uptake on exposure to zero extracellular sodium occurred in response to extracellular potassium (1.0 mM) or to glycoside concentrations that induced a positive inotropic effect and sodium-potassium pump inhibition. Reactivation of the sodium pump after return from 1.0 to 4.0 mM extracellular potassium was rapid and was associated with membrane hyperpolarization and slowing of spontaneous beating rate. With pump reactivation under these circumstances, the time course of disappearance of stimulation of sodium-calcium exchange on exposure to zero extracellular sodium was similar to the time course of loss of the positive inotropic effect. Under physiological conditions (4.0 mM extracellular potassium), exposure to positively inotropic but nontoxic concentrations of ouabain or dihydroouabain caused a small but consistent increase in unidirectional calcium influx, but had no discernible effect on calcium efflux. Since similar inotropic effects were produced for comparable degrees of glycoside or low extracellular potassium-induced sodium pump inhibition and increases in cellular sodium content, sodium pump inhibition rather than a glycoside-specific change in calcium binding appears to underlie the inotropic response. These findings are further consistent with the view that the primary mechanism of the positive inotropic effects of digitalis and low extracellular potassium in this experimental preparation is sodium pump inhibition resulting in increased intracellular sodium. We suggest that increased calcium influx via sodium-calcium exchange is the principal mechanism whereby increased intracellular sodium results in enhanced calcium availability to the myofibrils, but an additional effect on calcium efflux is not excluded. **(*Circ Res 56: 231–241, 1985*)**

IT has been recognized for some time that cardiac glycosides bind to and inhibit the membrane-bound monovalent cation transport system known as Na^+,K^+-ATPase (Glynn, 1964; Schwartz, 1976). However, the mechanisms whereby this interaction of digitalis with the sodium pump in a myocardial cell results in an increase in the intracellular Ca^{++} transient during systole (Allen and Blinks, 1978; Morgan and Blinks, 1982) and the resulting increase in contractile force have not been completely determined. On the basis of studies of perfused squid axons, Baker et al. (1969) proposed that an increase in intracellular Na^+ ($[Na^+]_i$) as a consequence of Na pump inhibition could produce an increase in Ca^{++} influx via a Na-Ca exchange mechanism. It has also been proposed that glycosides may induce an increase in the affinity for Ca^{++} of Na^+,K^+-ATPase (Gervais et al., 1977) or an associated membrane macromolecule (Lüllmann and Peters, 1979), resulting in an increase in superficial membrane-bound Ca^{++} (Nayler, 1973, Bailey and Fawzi, 1982). We, and many other investigators (for discussion, see Biedert et al., 1979; Barry et al., 1981) have shown close quantitative relationships among the degree of glycoside-induced sodium pump inhibition, increases in exchangeable cellular Na^+ and Ca^{++} contents, and the positive inotropic response. In addition, Sheu and Fozzard (1982) have recently reported proportional elevations in intracellular Na^+ and Ca^{++} activities measured with ion-specific microelectrodes after exposure of myocardium to glycoside concentrations producing graded increases in inotropic state. These findings are consistent with the hypothesis that altered Na^+-Ca^{++} exchange is causally related to the positive inotropic effect of digitalis (Langer, 1977; Brody and Akera, 1977). However, these data do not allow determination of whether the changes in intracellular $[Ca^{++}]$ occur because of enhanced Ca^{++} influx or decreased Ca^{++} efflux via the Na^+-Ca^{++} exchange system, nor has the relative importance of sodium pump inhibition vs. alteration of superficial Ca^{++} binding been defined.

We have recently reported techniques for measuring Ca^{++} influx and efflux and quantifying Na^+-Ca^{++} exchange in monolayer cultures of chick embryo ventricular cells (Barry and Smith, 1982). In the present studies, we have utilized these methods to examine the effects of cardiac glycosides on unidirectional Ca^{++} fluxes and Na^+-Ca^{++} exchange. In addition, we have compared the effects of glycoside-induced sodium pump inhibition with effects of exposure to low $[K^+]_o$ on contractility, Na^+ content, and altered Na^+-Ca^{++} exchange during onset and washout of sodium pump inhibition. Our results using this experimental preparation indicate that cardiac glycosides induce their direct myocardial positive inotropic effect by alteration of Na^+-Ca^{++} exchange, as a consequence of increased $[Na^+]_i$ resulting from Na^+ pump inhibition.

Methods

Tissue Culture

Cultures of beating chick embryo ventricular cells were prepared as described previously (Barry et al., 1980). Briefly, 10-day-old chick embryo hearts were removed under sterile condition, and the ventricles were cut into 0.5-mm fragments and placed in Ca^{++}- and Mg^{++}-free Hanks' solution. The ventricular fragments were gently agitated in 10 ml 0.025% (wt/vol) trypsin in Ca^{++}- and Mg^{++}-free Hanks' solution at 37°C for 4 cycles of 7 minutes each. The supernatant suspensions containing cells dissociated by these cycles were placed in 20 ml of cold trypsin inhibitor medium. This suspension was centrifuged at 2000 rpm for 10 minutes, the supernatant phase was discarded, and the cells were resuspended in culture medium consisting of 6% heat-inactivated fetal calf serum, 40% medium 199 (Grand Island Biological Co.), 0.1% penicillin-streptomycin antibiotic solution, and 54% balanced salt solution containing (in mM): NaCl, 116; NaH_2PO_4, 1.0; $MgSO_4$, 0.8; KCl, 1.18; and $NaHCO_3$, 26.2. Final concentrations (in mM) were: Na^+, 144; K^+, 4.0; HCO_3^-, 17; Ca^{++}, 0.97; Cl^-, 131; Mg^{++}, 1.0; and glucose, 5. The suspension of cells was diluted to 4×10^5 cells/ml and placed in plastic tissue culture petri dishes containing 25-mm circular coverslips (VWR-VanLab thickness no. 2). Cultures were incubated in a humidified 5% CO_2-95% air atmosphere at 37°C. Confluent layers two to three cells thick in which 70–80% of the cells were synchronously contracting developed by 2–3 days. Contractility studies were done on day 3 of culture. Plastic microspheres 2–3 μm in diameter (3M Co.) were added to the cultures on day 2 of the culture. The plastic microspheres became attached to cell surfaces and were moved by contraction of individual cells in the layers. This provided an improved image for contraction measurement and recording.

Measurement of Contractility

A glass coverslip with attached cultured heart cells was placed in a chamber provided with inlet and exit ports for culture perfusion. The chamber was placed on the stage of an inverted phase contrast microscope (Leitz Diavert) enclosed in a Lucite box with controlled temperature (37°C). The inlet to the perfusion chamber was connected by polyethylene tubing to several syringe pumps so that the culture could be sequentially perfused with medium containing various K^+ concentrations or cardiac glycosides. During continuous perfusion, medium bathing a cell in the center of a coverslip exchanged with a time constant of 15 seconds at a flow rate of 0.96 ml/min. The optical apparatus was supported by an air table to damp building vibrations, and the cells were magnified using a ×40 objective. The image was monitored by a low-light-level TV camera (Dage 650 SSX) attached to the microscope observation tube using a ×2 coupler. The TV camera had an interlace defeat so that the image was composed of 262 raster lines. The motion detector monitored a selected raster-line segment and provided new position data every 16 msec for an image border of a microsphere within the cell layer moving along the raster line. The analog voltage output from the motion detector was filtered at 15 Hz with a 48 dB/octave low-pass filter and calibrated to indicate actual μm of motion. The first derivative was obtained electronically and recorded as velocity of motion in μm/sec. Cultured heart cells used in the experiments described contracted spontaneously at rates varying from 70 to 120 beats/min. Rate, amplitude, and velocity of contraction remained stable for several hours during control perfusion.

Ion Fluxes and Contents

Approximately 140 25-mm circular glass coverslips with attached myocytes were obtained from each culture. Twenty-four hours before their use in ion uptake and content experiments, cells were exposed to medium containing L-(4,5-^{3}H,*N*)-leucine (0.2 μCi/ml, [leucine] = 28 mg/liter). [^{3}H]Leucine was incorporated into cell protein, and subsequent determination of ^{3}H counts permitted normalization of Na^+, K^+, or Ca^{++} isotope counts relative to mg of cell protein for each coverslip, after the relationship between ^{3}H counts and protein concentration was determined. To facilitate consistent labeling and washing of individual coverslips, small Lucite baskets were constructed which held 10 coverslips each. Glass coverslips were loaded into these baskets from the petri dishes, care being taken not to damage the cells. The cells on eight to 10 coverslips were equilibrated for 30 minutes in tissue culture medium at 37°C in a 5% CO_2 atmosphere. By means of a thin wire handle, a basket containing coverslips was then immersed in isotope uptake medium (5 μCi/ml) at 37°C. After the desired uptake period, ranging from 1 second to 2 hours, coverslips were removed from the uptake medium and washed for 4 seconds each in four 50-ml volumes of balanced salt solution at 4°C. This was found to be adequate to remove more than 99% of the rapidly exchanging ^{51}Cr after labeling the cells to asymptote in 2 μCi/ml of the extracellular space marker [^{51}Cr]-EDTA.

After washing as described above, the monolayer was scraped off the coverslip, and the cells were placed in 2 ml of a solution containing 1% sodium dodecyl sulfate and 10 mM sodium borate. Over a 2-hour period, complete cell dissolution was accomplished. A 1.6-ml aliquot of the dissolved cell mixture was placed in 15 ml Aquasol liquid scintillation fluid (New England Nuclear). From a quarter of the samples, 0.2 ml was used for determination of protein content (Lowry et al., 1951). Simultaneous counting of ^{24}Na, ^{42}K, or ^{45}Ca and ^{3}H counts in dissolved cells from each coverslip was performed with a Packard Liquid scintillation spectrometer. From the ^{3}H counts per min per mg protein ratio for the culture, the mg protein for each coverslip was determined. A known volume (50 μl) of uptake medium containing a specific isotope was placed in a 1.6-ml sample of dissolved cells not exposed to any isotope. From the counts/min observed from this sample and the known ion concentration of the uptake medium, the counts/min · nmol for each ion were determined. For normalization of each coverslip, the data were calculated as nmol/mg protein. For ion content studies, cells were labeled to asymptote [30 minutes for ^{24}Na (Biedert et al., 1979), 2 hours for ^{45}Ca (Barry and Smith, 1982)]. When the effects of interventions were assessed (e.g., resupply of K^+, washout of glycoside), cells were maintained in ^{24}Na of the same specific activity as the labeling solution.

For ^{45}Ca efflux experiments, coverslips of cells placed vertically in a Lucite basket were labeled for 2 hours with isotope. The basket was then immersed in 37°C efflux medium containing no isotope, and individual coverslips removed at 20-second time intervals, washed, and the cells dissolved and counted as described above. For determination of the rate constants for rapid efflux, ^{45}Ca loss from 0 to 80 seconds was determined. Each data point was an average of at least six coverslips.

Membrane Potential Recording

Intracellular potentials were measured using 80–90 MΩ glass capillary microelectrodes (1.2 mm o.d., extruded fiber 30-31-1; Frederick Haer). Electrodes were pulled on an Industrial Sciences Associates model M1 puller. Cell penetration was achieved with a Burleigh Inchworm Controller mounted on a conventional micromanipulator. Potentials were obtained from the same cell or immediately adjacent to the cell from which motion was recorded. The zero level of potential was established before cell penetration; recordings in which this potential changed by more than 5 mV after intracellular recordings were made were discarded.

Solutions

All experiments were done using solutions with a Ca^{++} concentration of 0.6 mM, to provide more sensitive detection of inotropic effects (Biedert et al., 1979). Both bicarbonate-buffered (Barry et al., 1981) and HEPES-buffered (Barry et al., 1978) salt solutions to which 1% fetal calf serum was added were utilized (pH 7.35). HEPES-buffered solutions were employed for electrophysiological studies, and zero $[Na^+]_o$ uptake experiments. For zero $[Na^+]_o$-Ca^{++} uptake experiments, Na^+ was substituted on a molar basis with choline chloride (+1 mM atropine) or KCl (Barry and Smith, 1982), and the 1% fetal calf serum was omitted.

Results

We initially sought to determine concentrations of ouabain, dihydroouabain, and $[K^+]_o$ which produced an equivalent positive inotropic response. In previous studies (Biedert et al., 1979; Barry et al., 1981) 10^{-6} M ouabain and 5×10^{-5} M dihydroouabain (DHO) both produced 40–50% inhibition of ^{42}K uptake, and a prominent positive inotropic effect. In preliminary studies of the effects of low $[K^+]_o$, we found that a $[K^+] = 1.0$ mM produced a near maximal inotropic effect. We therefore compared the sequential inotropic effects of 1.0 mM $[K^+]$, DHO 5×10^{-5} M, and ouabain 10^{-6} M on amplitude of contraction of the same cells. The results are shown in Figure 1. These two glycoside concentrations and this $[K^+]_o$ all induced a similar degree of positive inotropy, although the time course of onset and offset of effects differed; changes in $[K^+]_o$ and DHO exposure and washout produced more rapid changes in inotropic state than ouabain. As indicated in the figure legend, low $[K^+]_o$ also induced a more prominent chronotropic effect in these cells.

Given the fact that these glycoside concentrations and this $[K^+]_o$ produced an equivalent degree of positive inotropy, if all the inotropic effect of glycoside were due to Na pump inhibition, one would predict that this reduction of $[K^+]_o$ would produce a decrease in Na pump activity comparable to that caused by glycoside exposure. We therefore measured the degree of depression of active ^{42}K uptake induced by a $[K^+]_o$ of 1.0 mM. These data are shown in Figure 2. Correcting for the fact that the low $[K^+]_o$ alters the passive K^+ uptake (non-pump-mediated K^+ uptake), and assuming that Na^+ influx remains the same under these conditions, a $[K^+)]_o$ of 1.0 mM caused a 41% inhibition of active K^+ uptake, a degree of pump inhibition comparable to that achieved with 10^{-6} M and ouabain (Biedert et al., 1979) and 5×10^{-5} M DHO (Barry et al., 1981).

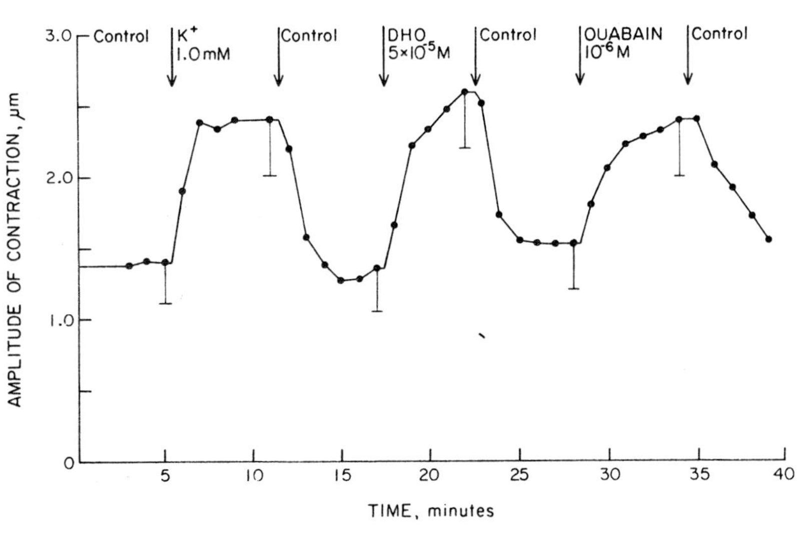

FIGURE 1. *Effects of glycosides and low $[K^+]_o$ on contractility of cultured myocardial cells. Amplitude of contraction (means ± SEM, n = 5) is plotted as a function of time. At each vertical arrow, the perfusion solution bathing the cells was switched to the indicated $[K^+]$ or glycoside concentration. The $[K^+]_o$ of the control solution was 4.0 mM. Rate of contraction increased from 90.8 ± 12.9 to 142.2 ± 5.0 beats/min on exposure to K^+ = 1.0 mM, from 92.1 ± 11.8 to 106.8 ± 12.6 after DHO, and from 79.8 ± 7.7 to 93.5 ± 6.6 on exposure to ouabain in these cells.*

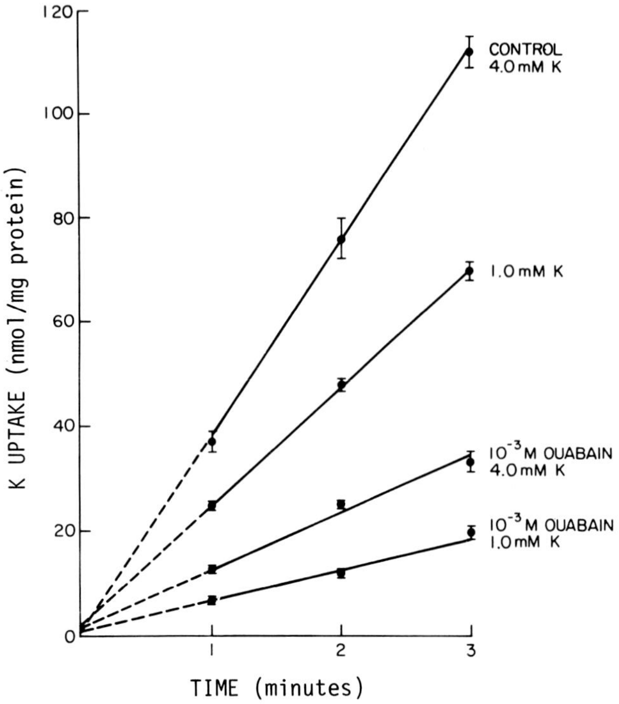

FIGURE 2. *Depression of active uptake of K^+ by exposure to reduced $[K^+]$ = 1.0 mM. Control active Na pump-mediated uptake (27 nmol/mg protein per minute) is calculated from the differences in the slope of the uptake in 4.0 mM K^+ (upper line) and the slope of uptake in the presence of 10^{-3} M ouabain, a concentration that completely inhibits the Na pump (Biedert et al., 1979), and 4 mM K^+. Active uptake in the presence of K^+ = 1.0 mM is the difference between the slopes of K^+ uptake in 1.0 mM K^+, and in 1.0 mM K^+ and 10^{-3} M ouabain (16 nmol/mg protein per minute). Thus, 1.0 mM K^+ reduced active K^+ uptake by 41%, a degree of inhibition of the Na pump comparable to that achieved with ouabain 10^{-6} M and DHO 5 × 10^{-6} M (Barry et al., 1981; Biedert et al., 1979). Points plotted indicate means ± SEM; n = 13.*

These data are consistent with the findings of Glitsch et al. (1978) and Gadsby (1980) regarding the relationship of Na pump activity to $[K^+]_o$ in other myocardial preparations, and suggest that these interventions cause a positive inotropic effect in this system by a common mechanism, i.e., a decrease in the activity of the Na pump.

To test this hypothesis further, we measured changes in steady state cellular Na^+ content produced by these interventions. As shown in Figure 3, ouabain 10^{-6} M, DHO 5 × 10^{-5} M, and $[K^+]_o$ = 1.0 mM all produced a similar increase in Na^+ content (zero time point). Assuming a cell H_2O content of 7.5 μl/mg protein (Barry et al., 1981), this corresponds to an increase in $[Na^+]_i$ from about 15 to 21 mM. On washout of drugs and restoration of $[K^+]_o$ to 4.0 mM, Na^+ content returned to normal somewhat more slowly than the fall in contractility (see Fig. 1). This finding is consistent with our previous results (Barry et al., 1981) and suggests that changes in total cellular Na^+ content lag behind cytoplasmic $[Na^+]$, possibly because of a relatively slowly exchanging intracellular Na^+ compartment (Biedert et al., 1979).

To examine this issue directly would require a Na^+-sensitive microelectrode recording of Na^+ activity (a^i_{Na}) under these experimental conditions. However, because of the small size and delicateness of the tissue-cultured cells, use of ion-sensitive microelectrodes is not currently possible. Eisner et al. (1981) have recently shown that in voltage-clamped sheep Purkinje fibers, following reactivation of the Na pump, the electrogenic Na pump current is linearly related to cytoplasmic a^i_{Na}. We therefore measured changes in membrane potential and ^{42}K uptake on abrupt resupply of 4.0 mM K^+ in cells previously exposed to 1.0 mM K^+ to estimate the time course of fall in a^i_{Na} under these conditions. Figure 4 shows effects on contractility and membrane potential caused by resupply of 4.0 mM $[K^+]_o$ to a cell in which positive inotropy was induced by exposure to $[K^+]_o$ = 1.0 mM. Decline of amplitude of contraction was rapid in this cell and was complete in 1 minute. Reactivation of the Na pump was associated with transient (<1 min.) hyperpolarization and with slowing of rate of contraction. The slowing in rate of contraction and rate of loss of inotropy were

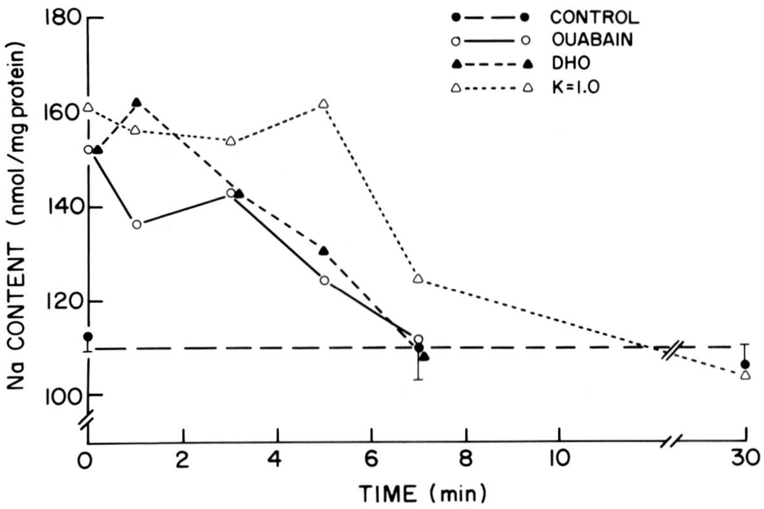

FIGURE 3. *Increases in Na^+ content induced by K^+ = 1.0 mM, ouabain = 10^{-6} M or DHO = 5 × 10^{-5} M, and time course of return to baseline of Na^+ content on resupply of normal medium. Cells were labeled for 30 minutes in ^{24}Na-containing medium. The control Na^+ contents (solid circles) were approximately 110 nmol/mg protein, and remained stable over the duration of the experiment. Exposure of cells to ouabain, DHO, and $[K^+]_o$ = 1.0 mM all produced an equivalent increase in Na^+ content (time = 0). Cells were then placed in ^{24}Na-containing media without glycoside or with a $[K^+]$ = 4.0 mM, and changes in Na^+ content measured as a function of time. By 7 minutes, Na^+ content had returned to normal, although recovery of Na^+ content tended to lag behind loss of inotropy (see text). Each point indicates the means, n = 9 to 24. SEM are shown for control cells only, but were similar for other points plotted.*

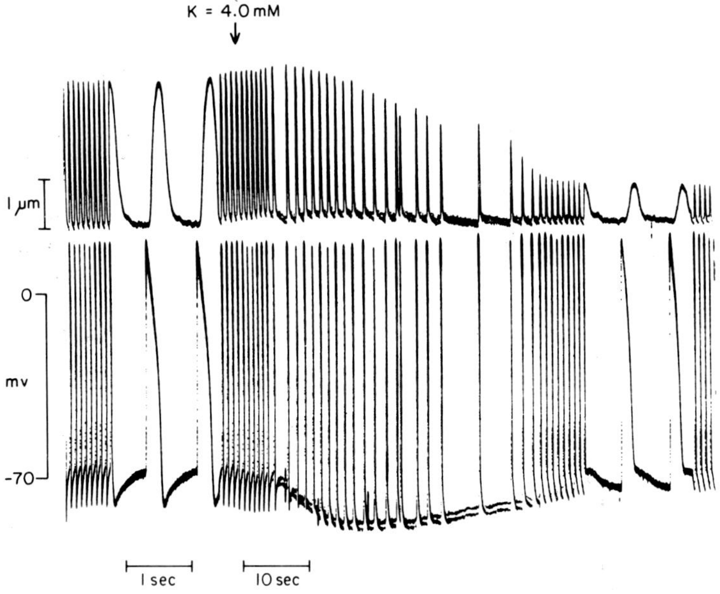

FIGURE 4. *Effect of resupply of K^+ on contraction and membrane potential. Amplitude of cell motion is shown on the upper trace, and membrane potential on lower trace. On the left, cells were perfused with $[K^+]_o$ of 1.0 mM, which resulted in a positive inotropic effect. At the vertical arrow, the cells were perfused with culture medium containing a normal $[K^+]_o$ = 4.0 mM. This resulted in transient hyperpolarization and a concomitant return to baseline inotropic state, complete within 60 seconds. Although rate of contraction was not controlled in this experiment, possibly altering slightly the time course of changes in these parameters, we estimated a time constant of 28.9 seconds for loss of inotropy, and of 33.2 seconds for loss of hyperpolarization.*

greater when Na pump reactivation was produced by resupply of $[K^+]_o$ than by washout of glycoside.

To investigate further whether reactivation of the Na pump was responsible for the rapid loss of inotropy and hyperpolarization with slowing in beating rate after resupply of $[K^+]_o$, we studied the rate of uptake of ^{42}K under these conditions. These results are shown in Figure 5. When cells in $[K^+]_o$ = 1.0 mM were abruptly reexposed to media containing a normal $[K^+]_o$, there was stimulation of the rate of uptake of ^{42}K which lasted 1–2 minutes, consistent with the duration of slowing and hyperpolarization noted previously, further supporting the view that the dissipation of inotropy is due to reactivation of the Na pump and subsequent fall in cytoplasmic a^i_{Na} concentration.

Thus, both a reduced $[K^+]_o$ and glycosides produced at steady state a similar inotropic effect for a given degree of pump inhibition and increase in cellular Na^+ content. This is consistent with the hypothesis that Na pump inhibition with resulting increase in $[Na^+]_i$ is the cause of glycoside-induced inotropy rather than glycoside-induced changes in superficial cell calcium binding, since low K_o^+ and glycoside exposure would not be expected to alter calcium binding by an equal amount. We next examined the question of how an increase in $[Na^+]_i$ induces an inotropic effect in these cells.

Our recent experiments (Barry and Smith, 1982) indicate that Ca^{++} influx via Na^+-Ca^{++} exchange in these cells is very sensitive to the transsarcolemmal $[Na^+]$ gradient, and is greatly magnified by increases in $[Na^+]_i$ and/or decreases in $[Na^+]_o$. The work of Coraboeuf et al. (1981) and Horackova and Vassort (1979) indicate that this process is electrogenic. If so, calcium influx should be stimulated by cell depolarization. We therefore compared rapid Ca^{++} influx in control cells with that in cells previously treated with ouabain for 7 minutes, upon exposure to zero $[Na^+]_o$-KCl solution. This concentration of K^+ (137 mM) results in membrane depolarization, in addition to reduction of $[Na^+]_o$ concentration to zero, thereby enhancing any effect of an increase in $[Na^+]_i$ on Ca^{++} influx via Na^+-Ca^{++} exchange. The

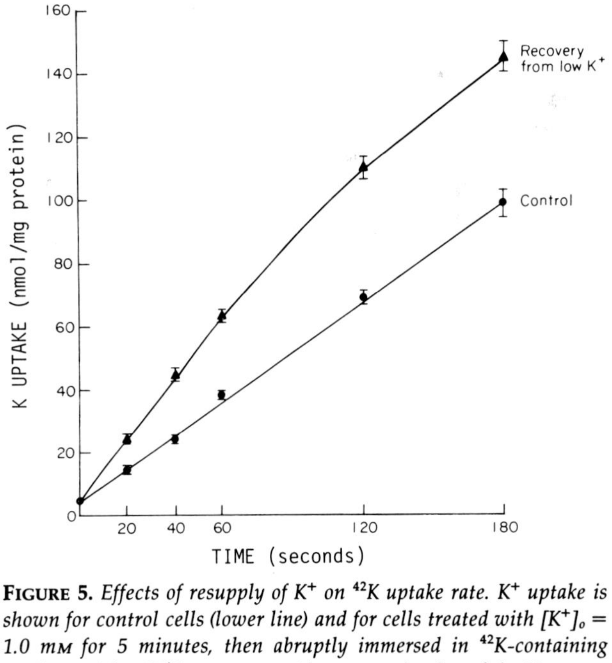

FIGURE 5. *Effects of resupply of K^+ on ^{42}K uptake rate. K^+ uptake is shown for control cells (lower line) and for cells treated with $[K^+]_o$ = 1.0 mM for 5 minutes, then abruptly immersed in ^{42}K-containing medium with a $[K^+]_o$ = 4.0 mM. Abrupt reactivation of the Na pump in this experiment resulted in the stimulation of K^+ uptake above the control level, and was most prominent for the first 60 seconds after exposure to a $[K^+]_o$ of 4.0 mM. In comparing the time course of hyperpolarization and loss of inotropy (Fig. 4) and resupply of $[K^+]_o$ to the time course of reactivation of K^+ uptake, it should be remembered that in the perfusion experiments the exact moment of resupply of a $[K^+]_o$ = 4 mM is not sharply defined, because the perfusion chamber exchanges with a time constant of 15 seconds (see text). Each point plotted is a mean ± SEM for seven to eight coverslips.*

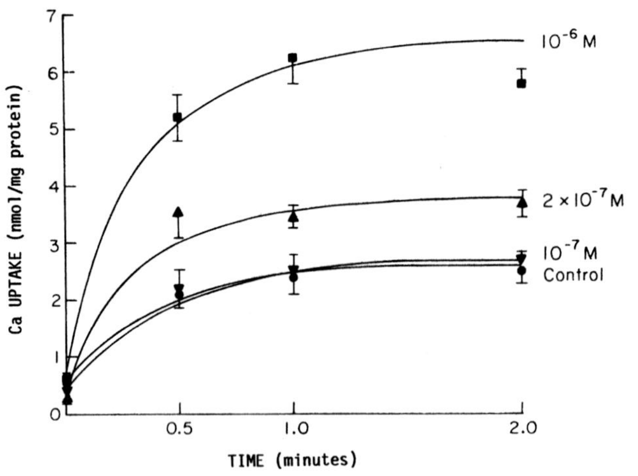

FIGURE 6. *Dose-response relationship for ouabain-induced stimulation of Ca^{++} uptake in zero $[Na^+]_o$-KCl. Cells were treated with ouabain 10^{-6} M, 2×10^{-7} M, or 10^{-7} M for 7 minutes, then immersed in zero $[Na^+]_o$-KCl solution. Only concentrations of ouabain which produced a positive inotropic effect in these cells (2×10^{-7} to 10^{-6} M) produced a stimulation of Ca^{++} uptake relative to control cells. Each point equals mean ± SEM, n = 9 to 12.*

results are shown in Figure 6. Ouabain, 10^{-7} M, caused neither measurable stimulation of Na^+-Ca^{++} exchange nor a positive inotropic response. A concentration of ouabain (2×10^{-7} M) previously shown to cause threshold inhibition of ^{42}K uptake and positive inotropy in these cells (Biedert et al., 1979) caused stimulation of Ca^{++} uptake observed on abrupt exposure to zero $[Na^+]_o$, presumably due to enhanced Na^+-Ca^{++} exchange. This effect was ouabain concentration-dependent; the maximal stimulation of Ca^{++} uptake in zero $[Na^+]_o$ seen with positively inotropic but nontoxic concentrations of ouabain (10^{-6} M) was only about 20% that obtained after complete pump inhibition with 10^{-3} M ouabain (Barry and Smith, 1982).

The time course of disappearance of stimulation of Ca^{++} influx in zero $[Na^+]_o$-KCl after washout of ouabain is shown in Figure 7. The rate of dissipation of this effect was similar to the time course of loss of positive inotropic effect under these conditions. Thus, stimulation of Ca^{++} uptake in zero $[Na^+]_o$-KCl correlates well with positive inotropy developing after exposure to glycosides. These results support the hypothesis that increased Ca^{++} influx via this mechanism is responsible for the enhanced intracellular $[Ca^{++}]$ transient. However, although cells are depolarized fully during a portion of the normal contraction-relaxation cycle, a zero $[Na^+]_o$-KCl external medium does not occur under physiological conditions, and in the presence of zero $[Na^+]_o$, a contracture develops in these cells (Barry and Smith, 1984). Furthermore, the possibility exists that this Na^+-Ca^{++} exchange system functions to extrude Ca^{++} in the presence of a normal transsarcolemmal $[Na^+]$ gradient (Reuter and Seitz, 1968; Sheu and Fozzard, 1982). We therefore measured the effects of positively inotropic concentrations of glycoside on unidirectional Ca^{++} fluxes under physiological conditions.

As shown in Figure 8, exposure to near-maximal inotropic but nontoxic concentrations of glycoside (in the example shown, 5×10^{-5} M DHO) produced a consistent small increase in Ca^{++} influx and in rapidly exchanging Ca^{++} content (measured at 5 minutes). This effect could not be detected at submaximally inotropic glycoside concentrations and was of borderline statistical significance. As reported by Kazazoglou et al. (1983), a substantial concentration-dependent increase in ^{45}Ca influx occurs in cultured heart cells after exposure to nontoxic, positively inotropic concentrations of ouabain if cells are initially incubated in medium with low $[Ca^{++}]_o$. Experiments in our own laboratory show that after a 5-minute exposure to medium containing 0.1 mM EGTA, the positively inotropic but nontoxic ouabain concentration of 2×10^{-6} M increased Ca^{++} uptake in normal $[Ca^{++}]$, normal $[Na^+]$ medium from 1.75 ± 0.05 to 2.15 ± 0.08 nmol/mg protein·30 seconds ($n = 8$; $P < 0.01$) (Kim and Smith, unpublished data). As shown in the inset to Figure 8, exposure

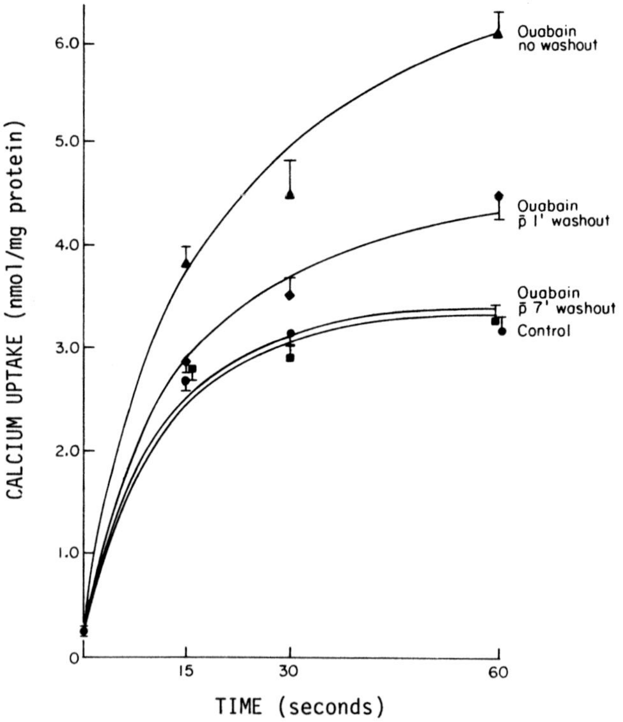

FIGURE 7. *Effect of zero $[Na^+]_o$-KCl on Ca^{++} uptake in cells treated with ouabain, and after ouabain washout. One group of cultured cells was exposed to 10^{-6} M ouabain for 7 minutes to establish a stable augmentation of contractile state (triangles). Two additional groups of cells similarly exposed to 10^{-6} M ouabain were then washed free of ouabain in normal medium for 1 minute (diamonds) or for 7 minutes (squares). Each group of cells was then abruptly exposed to zero $[Na^+]_o$-KCl solution containing ^{45}Ca, and ^{45}Ca uptake was determined (points plotted as means ± SEM; n = 9 to 12). Exposure to ouabain 10^{-6} M for 7 minutes resulted in an increase in rapid Ca^{++} uptake in zero $[Na^+]_o$-KCl (triangles) relative to control cells (circles). This effect was partially dissipated in 1 minute, and fully dissipated in 7 minutes of ouabain washout, consistent with the time course of loss of the positive inotropic effect.*

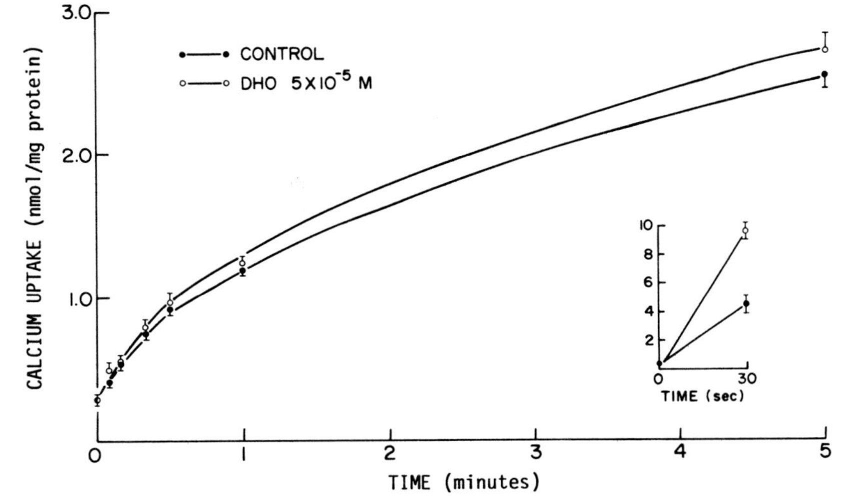

FIGURE 8. *The effects of dihydroouabain (DHO) on Ca^{++} uptake. Cells were incubated for 5 minutes in DHO 5×10^{-5} M and then immersed in ^{45}Ca containing physiological solution for times indicated. Influx of Ca^{++} was slightly increased above control levels by this concentration of glycoside, but this did not achieve statistical significance (0.05 < P < 0.10). In the inset, cells from the same culture were treated in an identical way, but Ca^{++} uptake was performed during abrupt immersion in zero $[Na^+]_o$-KCl solution. This resulted in a marked amplification of the increase in rapid Ca^{++} uptake by DHO-treated cells compared with controls. Points plotted are mean ± SEM, n = 9 to 10.*

of cultured cells to zero $[Na^+]_o$-KCl produced a much more marked amplification of the small increase in Ca^{++} influx detectable after ouabain exposure.

Additional experiments showed no significant effect of exposure of these cells to maximally positive inotropic concentrations of glycosides on unidirectional Ca^{++} efflux. Using the equation $y = C + Ae^{-Kt}$ to fit the rapid phase (first 80 seconds) of Ca^{++} efflux, we determined a control weighted mean value for K^+ of 3.40 ± 0.58/minute; after exposure to 5×10^{-5} M dihydroouabain, $K^+ = 3.04 \pm 0.56$ ($n = 4$, mean ± SEM, $P > 0.90$ by ANOVA). Furthermore, subsequent experiments have shown that in these cultured cells, abrupt removal of extracellular Na^+ results in an *increase* in Ca^{++} efflux (Barry and Smith, 1984). Interpretation of these results is complicated by an undefined component of Ca^{++}-Ca^{++} exchange. Nevertheless, it appears that significant Ca^{++} efflux occurs in these cells via a mechanism other than Na^+-Ca^{++} exchange (see also, Eisner et al., 1984). We suspect that the primary effect of an increase in $[Na^+]_i$ subsequent to partial Na pump inhibition is to amplify the increase in Ca^{++} influx via Na^+-Ca^{++} exchange that occurs to a smaller degree during the normal depolarization cycle (Eisner et al., 1983), resulting cumulatively in a slight increase in Ca^{++} content in the sarcoplasmic reticulum (Biedert et al., 1979; Barry et al., 1981). However, an additional small effect on Ca^{++} efflux is not excluded.

Heart cell cultures prepared as described here contain 20–30% fibroblasts (Barry et al., 1981). To determine the possible contribution of nonmyocardial cells to observed Ca^{++} uptake, we prepared monolayer cultures of fibroblasts by preplating trypsin-dissociated suspensions of intact ventricles, and culturing preplated fibroblast-enriched cultures for three passages. Fibroblasts showed only minimal stimulation of Ca^{++} uptake in zero $[Na^+]_o$-KCl solution, even after exposure to very high concentrations of ouabain (10^{-3} M). For example, Ca^{++} content measured at 60 seconds of uptake in zero $[Na^+]_o$-KCl solution was 2.17 ± 0.60 (SEM) nmol/mg protein in control fibroblast cells and increased only slightly to 2.80 ± 0.45 after exposure to 10^{-3} M ouabain for 5 minutes. This should be contrasted with the 10-fold increase in Ca^{++} content measured at 60 seconds in *myocardial* cell cultures treated in an identical fashion (Barry and Smith, 1982). This finding is consistent with the results of Wakabayashi and Goshima (1981), who found that nonmyocardial cells show very little stimulation of calcium uptake by Na^+-Ca^{++} exchange with increases in intracellular Na^+ concentration, and further suggests that essentially all of this phenomenon is attributable to the predominant myocyte component of our cultures. In addition, we found that incubation of myocardial cells in a Na^+-free medium (choline chloride) *during* exposure to glycoside completely prevented the subsequent stimulation of Ca^{++} uptake in zero $[Na^+]_o$-KCl medium. We have previously shown that this uptake of Ca^{++} is not inhibited by high concentrations of verapamil (Barry and Smith, 1982). Thus, this enhanced uptake appears to be due primarily to increased Ca^{++} influx due to Na^+-Ca^{++} exchange in the myocytes as a consequence of Na pump inhibition.

An increased uptake of Ca^{++} via Na^+-Ca^{++} exchange was also observed after sodium pump inhibition induced by low $[K^+]_o$. As shown in Figure 9, after exposure of cells to $K^+ = 1.0$ mM for 5 minutes, Ca^{++} uptake in zero $[Na^+]_o$ was markedly stimulated. On resupply of a 4.0 mM $[K^+]_o$, within 1 minute this stimulation of Ca^{++} uptake had almost completely disappeared. These results are entirely consistent with the time course of hyperpolarization, stimulation of ^{42}K uptake, and fall in contractile amplitude noted previously after resupply of 4.0 mM $[K^+]_o$, and suggest that cytoplasmic a^i_{Na} in these cells is modulating pump rate, Na^+-Ca^{++} exchange, and contractility. This result also suggests that changes in bulk Na^+ content lag behind changes in a^i_{Na} after reactivation of the pump (compare Figs. 3, 7, and 9).

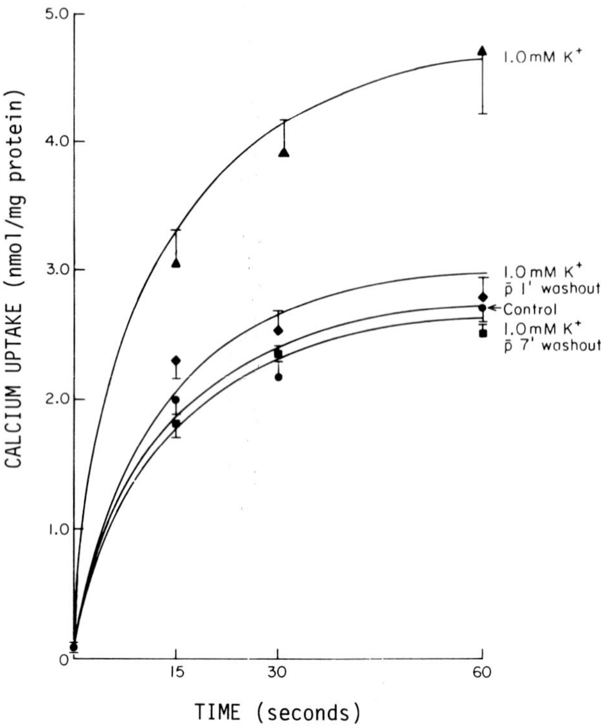

FIGURE 9. *Stimulation of Ca^{++} uptake in zero $[Na^+]_o$ after low $[K^+]_o$ exposure and also after resupply of $K^+ = 4.0$ mM. Cells were abruptly immersed in ^{45}Ca-containing medium with zero $[Na^+]_o$ (choline chloride substitution) at time zero. Ca^{++} uptake by control cells under these conditions is shown by the solid circles. Treatment of cells for 5 minutes with 1.0 mM K^+ prior to exposure to zero $[Na^+]_o$ resulted in a marked increase in Ca^{++} uptake (upper curve, triangles). The next group of cells was exposed to $K^+ = 1.0$ mM for 5 minutes, then placed in normal medium containing 4.0 mM K^+ for 1 minute (diamonds) or 7 minutes (squares) before uptake in zero $[Na^+]_o$ was measured (see legend for Fig. 7). Points plotted indicate means ± SEM, $n = 6$.*

A lower Ca^{++} uptake in zero $[Na^+]_o$ for low $[K^+]_o$-treated cells as compared with glycoside-treated cells was consistently observed (compare Figs. 6, 7, 8, and 9). To avoid reactivation of the Na pump during exposure to zero $[Na^+]_o$-KCl solution, choline chloride substitution was used to produce a zero-$[Na^+]_o$ solution in the low $[K^+]_o$ experiments. It seemed possible that the reduced Ca^{++} uptake in zero $[Na^+]_o$ noted after exposure to low $[K^+]_o$ reflected a lesser degree of stimulation of Ca^{++} influx via Na^+-Ca^{++} exchange in choline chloride as compared with KCl, since the degree of increase in Na^+ content achieved by exposure to low K^+ and glycoside was comparable. We therefore determined the effects of choline chloride and KCl zero $[Na^+]_o$ solutions on Ca^{++} uptake in cells with the same degree of Na pump inhibition. Ca^{++} uptake by cells exposed to 10^{-6} M ouabain for 7 minutes, then immersed for 30 seconds in zero $[Na^+]_o$-KCl ^{45}Ca solution was 3.61 ± 0.28 nmol/mg protein vs. 2.65 ± 0.09 for cells immersed for the same time period in $[Na^+]_o$-choline chloride solution (means ± SEM, $n = 7$, $P < 0.01$). This enhanced uptake of Ca^{++} in zero $[Na^+]_o$-KCl vs. zero $[Na^+]_o$-choline chloride solution probably reflects a greater degree of membrane depolarization, and thus greater stimulation of electrogenic Na^+-Ca^{++} exchange, induced by KCl. This phenomenon was not detected in our previous study of Ca^{++} uptake via Na^+-Ca^{++} exchange (Barry and Smith, 1982) because the relative effects of choline chloride and KCl substitution were not determined under conditions of an increased $[Na^+]_i$, and fewer early time points of uptake were determined.

Discussion

In 1969, Baker and co-workers showed that an increase in $[Na^+]_i$ of a perfused squid axon preparation enhanced Ca^{++} influx via a Na^+-Ca^{++} exchange mechanism, and proposed that this effect of Na_i^+ might be involved in producing the positive inotropic effect of cardiac glycosides. Glitsch et al. (1970) demonstrated that $[Na^+]_i$ affected Ca^{++} influx in guinea pig atria, and Langer and Serena (1970), working with an arterially perfused rabbit septal preparation, demonstrated that toxic, contracture-producing concentrations of strophanthidin caused an increase in Ca^{++} content without any decrease in Ca^{++} efflux, consistent with an increase in Ca^{++} influx as a consequence of Na pump inhibition. Reiter and colleagues (1971) showed that the positive inotropic effect of a reduction in extracellular K^+ concentration in guinea pig papillary muscle was dependent on the presence of extracellular Na^+, and proposed that the mechanism of low $[K^+]_o$-induced inotropy is an increase in Ca^{++} influx via enhanced Na^+-Ca^{++} exchange.

Subsequently, much work has shown a correlation between Na pump inhibition and inotropy (see Biedert et al., 1979; Barry et al., 1981), and studies using ion-specific microelectrodes for measurement of a^i_{Na} and a^i_{Ca} (Ellis, 1977; Lee et al., 1980; Eisner et al., 1981; Cohen et al., 1982; Sheu and Fozzard, 1982) have supported the hypothesis that an increase in a^i_{Na} is causally related to the development of positive inotropy due to Na pump inhibition. However, based largely on the work of Reuter and Seitz (1968) suggesting that the $[Na^+]$ gradient across the cardiac cell membrane influences the rate of Ca^{++} extrusion via Na^+-Ca^{++} exchange, investigators have proposed (Cohen et al., 1982; Sheu and Fozzard, 1982) that increased $[Na^+]_i$ causes an increase in $[Ca^{++}]_i$ by virtue of a decreased Ca^{++} efflux rather than an increased Ca^{++} influx. Others (Bailey and Fawzi, 1982; Burt and Langer, 1982) have suggested that an alteration of superficially bound Ca^{++} associated with or as a consequence of glycoside-induced pump inhibition may also be involved.

Our results bear directly on these issues. First, our findings suggest that in cultured heart cells, an increase in $[Na^+]_i$ induced by Na pump inhibition results in an increase in Ca^{++} content by increasing Ca^{++} influx rate, in addition to or rather than by decreasing the rate constant for Ca^{++} efflux. We find no decrease in the Ca^{++} efflux rate constant produced by a decrease in the transmembrane $[Na^+]$ gradient resulting either from an increase in $[Na^+]_i$ (this paper) or by a decrease in $[Na^+]_o$ (Barry and Smith, 1982, 1984). These results are consistent with the findings of Goshima and Wakabayashi (1981), who noted no effects of toxic concentrations of ouabain on Ca^{++} efflux from cultured myocardial cells, and with the results of Langer and Serena (1970). As discussed by Mullins (1981), the direction of Ca^{++} flux via Na^+-Ca^{++} exchange will depend on the stoichiometry of the exchange process, membrane concentration gradients for Na^+ and Ca^{++}, and membrane potential. Estimates of the stoichiometry in ventricular myocardium sarcolemmal vesicles (Pitts, 1980), in cultured myocardial cells (Wakabayashi and Goshima, 1981), and in intact rabbit ventricle (Bridge and Bassingthwaighte, 1983), suggest a 3 Na^+-to-1 Ca^{++} ratio. Thus, the exchange process would be expected to be electrogenic, and the reversal potential, $E_{rev} = 3E_{Na} - 2E_{Ca}$. Assuming that $E_{Na} = 60$ mV, and $E_{Ca} = 120$ mV (Coraboeuf et al., 1981), $E_{rev} = -60$ mV. Thus, Na^+ entry with Ca^{++} extrusion would occur only at membrane potentials more negative than -60 mV, and Ca^{++} influx via this mechanism should increase with membrane depolarization above -60 mV. This hypothesis is supported by the results of Coraboeuf et al. (1981) and Horackova and Vassort (1979), and is consistent with our findings of an enhanced effect of zero $[Na^+]_o$-KCl as compared with zero $[Na^+]_o$-choline chloride on Ca^{++} uptake. Thus, it appears likely that Ca^{++} enters the cell during systole in greater amounts via Na^+-Ca^{++} exchange after Na^+ pump inhibition (Eisner et al., 1983). Decreased Ca^{++} efflux appears to play a less important role in glycoside-induced inotropy in our cultured heart cell preparation, since there appears to be an alternate system for Ca^{++} extrusion, presumably a sarcolemmal ATP-dependent Ca^{++} pump.

Although effects on Ca^{++} entry seem to predominate over effects on Ca^{++} extrusion in our cultured heart cell preparation, in more mature myocardial cells with a lower contraction frequency, a^i_{Na} could be lower and the reversal potential for Na^+-Ca^{++} exchange (Mullins, 1979) less negative, favoring Ca^{++} efflux via Na^+-Ca^{++} exchange. In such circumstances, exposure to cardiac glycosides resulting in elevation of a^i_{Na} might decrease Ca^{++} extrusion via Na^+-Ca^{++} exchange, and thus produce an increase in cell Ca^{++} content and the positive inotropic effect by this mechanism. The recent work of Siegl et al. (1984), however, shows that 3′,4′-dichlorobenzamil in concentrations (20–40 μM) that inhibit Na^+-Ca^{++} exchange produces a negative inotropic effect in adult guinea pig ventricle. This finding suggests that the *net* effect of the Na^+-Ca^{++} exchange process in this tissue favors Ca^{++} entry.

Previous investigators have raised the possibility that an alteration of Ca^{++} binding by superficial myocardial cell sites might account for some of the positive inotropic effects of glycosides. Recently, Burt and Langer (1982) reported an increase in "La-displaceable Ca" in cultured neonatal rat heart cells after exposure to toxic concentrations of ouabain or low $[K^+]_o$, which they attribute to binding to superficial sites. However, this increase in Ca^{++} after pump inhibition was not present if cells were disrupted prior to exposure to glycoside or low K^+, indicating that an intact cell was required for this effect. Our own previous results demonstrating more rapid inhibition of Ca^{++} influx than efflux by La^+ in cultured heart cells (Barry and Smith, 1982) suggest that exposure to La^+ in the presence of ^{45}Ca would produce a decrease in Ca^{++} content by immediately stopping Ca^{++} influx, while Ca^{++} efflux continues for 1–2 minutes. Thus, the "La-displaceable" pool might actually contain in part an intracellular Ca^{++} component. This could explain why intact cells were required for the effect noted by Burt and Langer. We have no direct evidence that superficial Ca^{++} binding is not altered by glycosides in myocardial cells at nontoxic concentrations, since the methods we have employed do not detect superficially bound ^{45}Ca (Barry and Smith, 1982). However, the similarity of effects on the Na pump, contractility, Na^+ content, and Na^+-Ca^{++} exchange by glycosides and low $[K^+]_o$ make a glycoside-specific effect on superficial calcium binding less likely as a primary inotropic mechanism.

Because of the more pronounced chronotropic effects of low $[K^+]_o$ exposure in these cells, caution must be used in making quantitative comparisons of the degree of inotropy produced relative to the degree of pump inhibition achieved by low $[K^+]_o$ compared to glycosides. However, the cells used in these experiments do not show a positive treppe response in this contraction frequency range. For example, in separate experiments in which cultured cells were electrically paced, with extracellular microelectrodes, at 90/min amplitude of contraction was 1.51 ± 0.15 μm; at 120/min, 1.44 ± 0.14 μm; and at 150 /min, 1.19 ± 0.13 μm (means ± SEM, n = 5). These findings support the view that the positive inotropic effect observed was related to an increase in $[Na^+]_i$ secondary to pump inhibition, rather than to an increase in spontaneous contraction frequency.

The data reported here support the view that Na pump inhibition produces a sustained increase in subsarcolemmal $[Na^+]$ which, in turn, enhances Ca^{++} influx via Na^+-Ca^{++} exchange, although reduced Ca^{++} efflux via this mechanism cannot be excluded. This enhanced influx may result in an increased storage of calcium within the sarcoplasmic reticulum, appearing as an increase in rapidly exchanging Ca^{++} content (Biedert et al., 1979; Barry et al., 1981; Maitland et al., 1982). This increased "priming" of the sarcoplasmic reticulum by enhanced Na^+-Ca^{++} exchange could produce an inotropic effect by increasing the amount of Ca^{++} released with each action potential from this intracellular storage site (Fabiato, 1981; Wier and Isenberg, 1982). We attribute the delay in return to normal of bulk Na^+ content in these cells after reactivation of the pump (Fig. 3) relative to decay of inotropic effects to some degree of intracellular binding of Na^+, perhaps in mitochondria or sarcoplasmic reticulum. Thus, bulk Na^+ content appears to reflect changes in a^i_{Na} at steady state, but to lag behind a^i_{Na} changes after abrupt reactivation of the pump. Further elucidation of this point will require measurements of a^i_{Na} with sodium-sensitive microelectrodes in cultured heart cell monolayers.

Our data do not argue against an effect of increased $[Ca^{++}]_i$ induced by pump inhibition on the slow inward Ca^{++} current (Weingart et al., 1978; Marban and Tsien, 1982; Lederer and Eisner, 1982). Furthermore, it must be acknowledged that in intact myocardial tissue, many effects of cardiac glycosides on inotropic state and Na pump activity may be influenced by modulation of sympathetic and parasympathetic nervous system activities (Lechat et al., 1983). Nevertheless, the close correspondence of stimulation of Na^+-Ca^{++} exchange in these cells to inotropic effects due to pump inhibition, both temporally and quantitatively, makes it likely in our view that alteration of Ca^{++} influx via Na^+-Ca^{++} exchange is the major mechanism of the direct positive inotropic effect of cardiac glycosides.

We are indebted to Louise A. Liechty and Denise Beaudoin for excellent technical assistance.

Supported in part by National Institutes of Health Grants HL 23893 and HL 18003.

Dr. Hasin was a Research Fellow of the American Heart Association, Northeastern Massachusetts Chapter.

Address for reprints: Thomas W. Smith, M.D., Cardiovascular Division, Brigham and Women's Hospital, 75 Francis Street, Boston, Massachusetts 02115.

Received April 12, 1983; accepted for publication October 31, 1984.

References

Allen DG, Blinks JR (1978) Calcium transients in aequorin-injected frog cardiac muscle. Nature **273:** 509–513

Bailey LE, Fawzi AB (1982) The role of superficially bound calcium in the regulation of myocardial contractility and the positive inotropic response to ouabain. Can J Physiol Pharmacol **60:** 568–575

Baker PF, Blaustein MP, Hodgkin AL, Steinhardt PA (1969) The influence of Ca on Na efflux in squid axons. J Physiol (Lond) **200:** 431–458

Barry WH, Smith TW (1982) Mechanisms of transmembrane calcium movement in cultured chick embryo ventricular cells. J Physiol (Lond) **325:** 243–260

Barry WH, Smith TW (1984) Movement of Ca^{2+} across the sarcolemma: Effects of abrupt exposure to zero external Na concentration. J Mol Cell Cardiol **16:** 155–164

Barry WH, Goldminz D, Kimball T, Fitzgerald JW (1978) Influence of cell dissociation and culture on inotropic responses to calcium and lanthanum. J Mol Cell Cardiol **10:** 967–979

Barry WH, Pober J, March JD, Frankel SR, Smith TW (1980) Effects of graded hypoxia on contraction of cultured chick embryo ventricular cells. Am J Physiol **239:** 651–657

Barry WH, Biedert S, Muira DS, Smith TW (1981) Changes in cellular Na^+, K^+, and Ca^{2+} contents, monovalent cation transport rate, and contractile state during washout of cardiac glycosides from cultured chick heart cells. Circ Res **49:** 141–149

Biedert S, Barry WH, Smith TW (1979) Inotropic effects and changes in sodium and calcium contents associated with inhibition of monovalent cation active transport by ouabain in cultured myocardial cells. J Gen Physiol **74:** 479–494

Bridge JHB, Bassingthwaighte JB (1983) Uphill sodium transport driven by an inward calcium gradient in heart muscle. Science **219:** 178–179

Brody TM, Akera T (1977) Relations among Na^+,K^+,-ATPase activity, sodium pump activity, transmembrane sodium movement, and cardiac contractility. Fed Proc **36:** 2219–2224

Burt JM, Langer GA (1982) Ca^{++} distribution after Na pump inhibition in cultured neonatal rat myocardial cells. Circ Res **51:** 543–550

Cohen CJ, Fozzard HA, Sheu SS (1982) Increase in intracellular sodium ion activity during stimulation in mammalian cardiac muscle. Circ Res **50:** 651–662

Coraboeuf E, Gautier P, Guirandou P (1981) Potential and tension changes induced by sodium removal in dog Purkinje fibers: Role of an electrogenic sodium-calcium exchange. J Physiol (Lond) **311:** 605–622

Eisner DA, Lederer WJ, Vaughan-Jones RD (1981) The dependence of sodium pumping and tension on intracellular sodium activity in voltage-clamped sheep Purkinje fibers. J Physiol (Lond) **312:** 163–187

Eisner DA, Lederer WJ, Vaughan-Jones RD (1983) The control of tonic tension by membrane potential and intracellular sodium activity in the sheep cardiac Purkinje fibre. J Physiol (Lond) **335:** 723–743

Eisner DA, Orchard CH, Allen DG (1984) Control of intracellular ionized calcium concentration by sarcolemmal and intracellular mechanisms. J Mol Cell Cardiol **16:** 137–146

Ellis D (1977) The effects of external cations and ouabain on the intracellular sodium activity of sheep heart Purkinje fibers. J Physiol (Lond) **273:** 211–240

Fabiato A (1981) Myoplasmic free calcium concentration reached during the twitch of an intact isolated cardiac cell and during calcium-induced release of calcium from the sarcoplasmic reticulum of a skinned cardiac cell from the adult rat or rabbit ventricle. J Gen Physiol **78:** 457–497

Gadsby DC (1980) Activation of electrogenic Na^+ K^+ exchange by extracellular K^+ in canine cardiac Purkinje fibers. Proc Natl Acad Sci USA **77:** 4035–4039

Gervais A, Lane LK, Anner BM, Lindenmayer GE, Schwartz A (1977) A possible molecular mechanism of the action of digitalis: Ouabain action on calcium binding to sites associated with a purified Na-K activated ATPase from kidney. Circ Res **40:** 8–14

Glitsch HG, Reuter H, Scholz H (1970) The effect of the internal sodium concentration on calcium fluxes in isolated guinea pig auricles. J Physiol (Lond) **209:** 25–43

Glitsch HG, Grabowski W, Thiehen J (1978) Activation of the electrogenic sodium pump in guinea pig atria by external potassium ions. J Physiol (Lond) **276:** 515–524

Glynn IM (1964) The action of cardiac glycosides on ion movements. Pharmacol Rev **16:** 381–407

Goshima K, Wakabayashi S (1981) Involvement of an Na^+-Ca^+ exchange system in genesis of ouabain-induced arrhythmias of cultured myocardial cells. J Mol Cell Cardiol **13:**489–509

Horackova M, Vassort G (1979) Sodium-calcium exchange in regulation of cardiac contractility. Evidence for an electrogenic voltage dependent mechanism. J Gen Physiol **73:** 403–424

Kazazoglou T, Renaud J-F, Rossi B, Lazdunski M (1983) Two classes of ouabain receptors in chick ventricular cardiac cells and their relation to (Na^+,K^+)-ATPase inhibition, intracellular Na^+ accumulation, Ca^{2+} influx, and cardiotonic effect. J Biol Chem **258:** 12163–12170

Langer GA (1977) Relationship between myocardial contractility and the effects of digitalis on ionic exchange. Fed Proc **36:** 2231–2234

Langer GA, Serena SD (1970) Effects of strophanthidin upon contraction and ionic exchange in rabbit ventricular myocar-

dium: Relation to control of active state. J Mol Cell Cardiol **1:** 65–90
Lechat P, Malloy CR, Smith TW (1983) The direct and indirect effects of ouabain on monovalent cation active transport and inotropic state in guinea pig left atrium. Circ Res **52:** 411–422
Lederer WJ, Eisner DA (1982) The effects of sodium pump activity on the slow inward current in sheep cardiac Purkinje fibers. Proc R Soc Lond [Biol] **214:** 249–269
Lee CO, Kang DH, Sokol JH, Lee KS (1980) Relation between intracellular Na ion activity and tension of sheep cardiac Purkinje fibers exposed to dihydroouabain. Biophys J **29:** 315–330
Lowry DH, Rosebrough NJ, Farr AL, Randall RJ (1951) Protein measurement with the Folin phenol reagent. J Biol Chem **193:** 265–275
Lüllmann H, Peters T (1979) Action of cardiac glycosides on excitation-contraction coupling in heart muscle. Prog Pharmacol **3:** 5–57
Maitland PC, Lamont SV, Barrit GJ (1982) Evidence that concentrations of ouabain which induce positive inotropic effects in the perfused guinea pig heart increase the amount of calcium in a rapidly-exchangable cellular compartment. Biochem Pharmacol **31:** 2471–2478
Marban E, Tsien RW (1982) Enhancement of calcium current during digitalis inotropy in mammalian heart: Positive feedback regulation by intracellular calcium? J Physiol (Lond) **329:** 589–614
Morgan JP, Blinks JR (1982) Intracellular Ca^{2+} transients in the cat papillary muscle. Can J Physiol Pharmacol **60:** 524–528
Mullins LJ (1981) Ion Transport in Heart. Raven Press, New York
Mullins LJ (1979) The generation of electric currents in cardiac fibers by a Na-Ca exchange. Am J Physiol **236:** C103–C110
Nayler WG (1973) An effect of ouabain on the superficially located stores of calcium in cardiac muscle cells. J Mol Cell Cardiol **5:** 101–110
Pitts BJR (1979) Stoichiometry of sodium-calcium exchange in cardiac sarcolemmal vesicles. J Biol Chem **254:** 6232–6235
Reiter M, Seiber K, Stickel FJ (1971) Sodium dependence of the inotropic effect of a reduction in extracellular potassium concentration. Naunyn Schmiedebergs Arch Pharmacol **268:** 361–378
Reuter H, Seitz H (1968) The dependence of calcium efflux from cardiac muscle on temperature and external ion composition. J Physiol (Lond) **195:** 451–470
Schwartz A (1976) Is the cell membrane Na^+,K^+-ATPase enzyme the pharmacological receptor for digitalis? Circ Res **39:** 2–7
Sheu SS, Fozzard HA (1982) Transmembrane Na^+ and Ca^{2+} electrochemical gradients in cardiac muscle and their relationship to force development. J Gen Physiol **80:** 325–351
Siegl PKS, Cragoe EJ Jr, Trumble MJ, Kaczorowski GJ (1984) Inhibition of Na^+/Ca^{2+} exchange in membrane vesicle and papillary muscle preparations from guinea pig heart by analogs of amiloride. Proc Natl Acad Sci USA **81:** 3238–3242
Wakabayashi S, Goshima K (1981) Kinetic studies of sodium-dependent calcium uptake by myocardial cells and neuroblastoma cells in culture. Biochim Biophys Acta **642:** 158–172
Weingart R, Kass RS, Tsien RW (1978) Is digitalis inotropy associated with enhanced slow inward Ca current? Nature **273:** 389–392
Wier WG, Isenberg G (1982) Intracellular [Ca^{2+}] transients in voltage clamped cardiac Purkinje fibers. Pflugers Arch **392:** 284–290

INDEX TERMS: Na^+-Ca^{++} exchange • Inotropy • Digitalis

Dipyridamole Decreases Glomerular Filtration in the Sodium-Depleted Dog

Evidence for Mediation by Intrarenal Adenosine

Lois J. Arend, Carl I. Thompson, and William S. Spielman
From the Department of Physiology, Michigan State University, East Lansing, Michigan

SUMMARY. To determine the renal effects of inhibiting the uptake and subsequent metabolism of endogenous adenosine, dipyridamole, a nucleoside transport inhibitor, was infused intrarenally into anesthetized dogs. Dipyridamole (24 μg/kg per min) inhibited the cellular extraction of [^{14}C]adenosine (72 ± 3% vs. 9 ± 3%) and elevated the excretion of endogenous adenosine (0.60 ± 0.08 to 1.70 ± 0.21 nmol/min, $P < 0.05$). The action of exogenous adenosine to decrease glomerular filtration rate is known to be enhanced by sodium depletion, and is minimal or absent in sodium-loaded animals. To ascertain whether dietary sodium intake alters the renal effects of elevated endogenous adenosine, dipyridamole was infused into sodium-depleted and sodium-loaded dogs. In the sodium-depleted dogs ($n = 9$), dipyridamole infusion decreased the glomerular filtration rate by 59 ± 7% (20 ± 1 to 8 ± 2 ml/min, $P < 0.05$) which returned to control levels within 30 minutes after stopping infusion of dipyridamole. Renal vascular resistance was unchanged during dipyridamole infusion. In the sodium-loaded dogs ($n = 5$), dipyridamole had no effect on glomerular filtration rate (22 ± 4 vs. 25 ± 3 ml/min) or renal vascular resistance. In a separate series of sodium-depleted dogs ($n = 8$), the dipyridamole-induced decrease in glomerular filtration rate was completely reversed or inhibited by theophylline, an adenosine receptor antagonist. These experiments demonstrate that inhibition of cellular uptake of adenosine elevates adenosine levels, that dipyridamole decreases glomerular filtration rate in sodium-depleted but not sodium-loaded dogs, and that the decrease in glomerular filtration rate is inhibited by theophylline. We conclude that the decrease in glomerular filtration rate during dipyridamole administration is mediated by increased endogenous adenosine. **(*Circ Res 56: 242–251, 1985*)**

WORK in several laboratories has raised the possibility that intrarenally produced adenosine plays a role in the intrinsic control of glomerular filtration rate (GFR) and renin release (Spielman and Thompson, 1982). It has been postulated that extracellular adenosine, produced from cellular 5′-adenosine monophosphate (5′-AMP), presumably, but not necessarily, as a product of the adenosine triphosphate (ATP) hydrolysis associated with active transepithelial transport, acts to alter renal function. Stated simply, increased active solute reabsorption, secondary to an increased GFR, would increase adenosine production which would, in turn, act to constrict the afferent arteriole and dilate the efferent arteriole (Osswald et al., 1978b) and thereby reduce glomerular capillary hydrostatic pressure and GFR. Evidence in support of this hypothesis has come from studies that have evaluated the renal action of exogenously administered adenosine (Osswald et al., 1975; Spielman et al., 1980) or, in a few cases, with the use of methylxanthines as adenosine antagonists (Osswald et al., 1980; Gerkens et al., 1983). For the most part, however, only circumstantial evidence has been obtained that supports a role for endogenously produced adenosine in the control of renal function. A more direct assessment of the actions of intrarenal adenosine would be to elevate endogenous levels of adenosine, through pharmacological or physiological perturbations, while monitoring renal function.

In a variety of nonrenal tissues, extracellular adenosine has been reported to enter cells by facilitated diffusion through a nucleoside uptake mechanism, where it is deaminated and phosphorylated to inosine and 5′-AMP (Arch and Newsholme, 1978). This nucleoside uptake mechanism is inhibitable by a variety of pharmacological agents (Paterson, 1979). The hypothesis tested in this study was that inhibition of cellular uptake of adenosine increases the extracellular levels of adenosine, which in turn alters renal function. The present investigation was thus undertaken (1) to identify the presence of a renal uptake mechanism for adenosine, (2) to determine whether its inhibition leads to the elevation of extracellular adenosine, and (3) to determine whether the elevation of endogenous levels of adenosine by inhibition of cellular uptake results in changes in renal function that mimic the effects of exogenously administered adenosine.

Methods

Preparation

Experiments were performed on dogs of either sex, weighing 12–20 kg. The animals were allowed free access to water and were deprived of food 24 hours before the experiment. On the day of the experiment, the animals were anesthetized with sodium pentobarbital (30 mg/kg, iv) and maintained with periodic small doses as needed. The trachea was exposed and cannulated, and each animal was mechanically ventilated with a Harvard respirator. Minute volumes were initially selected from the nomogram of Kleinman and Radford (1964). Body temperature was monitored with a rectal temperature probe and maintained at 37°C by a circulating water-heating pad and a radiant heat lamp, when necessary. Catheters (PE 240) were placed in the femoral arteries for measurement of blood pressure (Statham strain gauge, P23Db, Hewlett-Packard recorder, 7754B) and for blood sampling, and in the femoral veins for systemic infusions and anesthetic administration.

A retroperitoneal flank incision was made to expose the left renal artery for placement of a noncannulating electromagnetic flow probe (Zepeda Instruments). The flow probe was calibrated by renal artery cannulation at the end of each experiment. A small curved infusion needle (22-gauge) was placed into the renal artery distal to the flow probe. The patency of the needle was maintained by a constant infusion at a rate of 1.38 ml/min. Another small curved needle (20-gauge) was placed in the renal vein for sampling of the renal venous effluent. The dogs were then placed in a metal frame which held them in a position approximating their normal standing posture. After the completion of all surgical procedures, at least 1 hour was allowed for attainment of steady state, as determined by the stability of blood pressure, renal blood flow, and blood gas measurements.

Analytical

Inulin concentrations in plasma and urine were determined by the anthrone method described by Davidson and Sackner (1963). Plasma and urine sodium and potassium concentrations were determined by flame photometry.

One and one-half milliliter aliquots of plasma and urine taken during each clearance period were processed and analyzed for adenosine as follows. The blood samples (3–4 ml) were immediately diluted in 300 μl of a solution containing 32 μM dipyridamole and 3μM erythro-9-(2-hydroxy-3-nonyl)adenine (EHNA), an inhibitor of adenosine deaminase. The blood samples were then centrifuged and a 1.5-ml plasma aliquot was removed and placed in 60 μl of 70% perchloric acid. Similarly, 1.5-ml aliquots of urine were placed in 60 μl perchloric acid. All samples were then centrifuged at 10,000 *g* for 30 minutes to remove the protein precipitate. A 1.2-ml aliquot of the perchloric acid extract was removed and neutralized with a concentrated solution of potassium carbonate (7 M). The potassium perchlorate precipitate was removed by centrifugation and a 200-μl aliquot of the neutralized acid extract was used for high-pressure liquid chromatography (HPLC) analysis of adenosine. Four control tubes were prepared from a single arterial or venous blood sample and processed with each sample set. Two tubes received known amounts of adenosine, and the third was used to measure endogenous levels. In the final tube, the collecting solution was replaced with 2–5 units of adenosine deaminase activity in saline. The adenosine values of these tubes were used to ensure the identity of the adenosine peak and to calculate the recovery of adenosine for each experiment.

The neutralized acid extract was injected (WATERS-WISP) onto a C18 reverse-phase column (Beckman Ultrasphere ODS) and eluted using an isocratic (9–12% of a 70% solution, balance was 4 mM K_2HPO_4) elution (1–1.5 ml/min). A fraction (±2.5 min) of the eluate containing adenosine, as determined by the retention time of standards (and verified by the recovery tubes), was collected using a timer (ChronTrol), valve (The Lee Co. #LFAA1201418A), and fraction collector (Eldex Universal) system. The adenosine fraction was concentrated to dryness under reduced pressure using a vortex evaporator (Buchler Instruments). The samples were resuspended in 1 ml of water and the adenosine converted to inosine by the addition of 0.5 unit of adenosine deaminase and incubated for 15 minutes at room temperature. The adenosine deaminase was inactivated by the addition of 1 ml of HPLC grade methanol, and the samples were once again concentrated to dryness under reduced pressure, reconstituted in a small volume (typically 220–250 μl), and a 200-μl aliquot was injected on a C18 reverse-phase column and eluted as described above. We quantified the inosine peak by measuring the area under the curve (WATERS data module) and relating this to standards run under the same condition. Recoveries for all experiments were 100 ± 7%, and individual values were not corrected for recovery.

Indicator Dilution Curves

The [U-^{14}C]-adenosine (278 mCi/mmol) was obtained from Amersham. The 9-β-D-arabino-furanosyl-[adenine-2-^{3}H] (ara-A) (32.6 Ci/mmol) was obtained from ICN. The ara-A was converted to 9-β-D-arabino-furanosyl hypoxanthine-[2-^{3}H] (ara-H) by treatment with adenosine deaminase (Sigma Chemical) and subsequent purification on a HPLC reverse phase column. Injectate containing [^{3}H]ara-H (2 μCi/ml) and [^{14}C]adenosine (0.34 μCi/ml) was made up in 1.5 ml of normal saline. The bolus was quantified by diluting 100 μl of the injectate with 900 μl saline and counted for radioactivity. Bolus injections (2–4 sec) of 1 ml were made directly into the renal artery cannula while a constant infusion rate of 1.38 ml/min was maintained to flush the cannula. Immediately before initiation of the bolus injection, sampling was begun from both ureters and the renal vein. Before each injection, renal vein plasma and urine samples were obtained for determination of blank activity. Urine samples were collected for an average of 30 seconds (range 15–60 sec) to obtain approximately 1 ml of urine per sample depending on urine flow. Contiguous 10-second withdrawals via the renal vein catheter (average 20 ml/min) were made starting with the injection and lasting 2 minutes after completion of the injection. All samples were corrected for the blank values immediately before the injection, and results were normalized as the plasma or urine concentration (% of injectate/ml).

Urine samples (0.7–1.2 ml) for radioactivity determinations were collected directly into preweighed scintillation vials. After sample collection, the volume was determined gravimetrically. In a few cases where the sample volume was less than 0.7 ml, 0.5 ml of saline was added after volume determination.

Statistical

Statistical analysis was performed by analysis of variance using the Student-Newman-Keuls test for multiple comparisons and by Student's paired *t*-test when appropriate. A *P* value of <0.05 was considered statistically significant. All data are presented as mean ± 1 SEM.

Experimental

Group I—Effect of Dipyridamole on the Renal Uptake of Adenosine and the Concentration of Adenosine in Plasma and Urine (n = 5)

To determine whether renal adenosine uptake is blocked by dipyridamole, we employed a single-injection, multiple-tracer, indicator-dilution technique. The uptake of adenosine was compared with that of a nonmetabolized analog of adenosine, 9-β-D-arabinofuranosyl hypoxanthine (ara-H), used as an extracellular reference. A group of dogs maintained on a normal laboratory diet were prepared as described above, with the following additions. A right flank incision was made to expose the right ureter, which was cannulated with PE 240 tubing. The incision was then closed to prevent excess fluid loss. After the surgical preparation, the animals were given a saline volume expansion of 5% of body weight to initiate a brisk urine flow. An intravenous infusion of saline (4–5 ml/min) was given to maintain urine flow rate at approximately 2 ml/min. After at least 60 minutes had been allowed for stabilization of the animal preparation, renal adenosine uptake studies were performed, and samples for adenosine concentration were taken, as described above, during a control period, and after 45 minutes of dipyridamole infusion into the renal artery at 24 μg/kg per min.

Group II—Effects of an Adenosine Uptake Inhibitor, Dipyridamole, on Renal Function in Dogs Maintained on a Low-Sodium (Group IIa, n = 9) or a High-Sodium Intake (Group IIb, n = 5)

To determine whether the elevation of endogenous adenosine by inhibition of cellular uptake produced renal effects similar to those resulting from the intrarenal infusion of exogenous adenosine, we studied renal function before, during, and after the intrarenal infusion of dipyridamole. Because the effects of exogenous adenosine on renal function are enhanced by sodium depletion and attenuated or blocked by sodium loading (Osswald et al., 1978a), dogs were divided into two groups and either sodium-depleted or sodium-loaded to determine whether the renal effects of elevation of endogenous adenosine by inhibition of uptake are also influenced by dietary sodium intake.

One group of dogs (group IIa) was given 100 mg of furosemide (iv) on the first day of the dietary regimen, and maintained on a low-sodium diet (<2 mEq/day) for 10–14 days before the experiment. Dogs were allowed water ad libitum. On the day of the experiment, animals were prepared as described above. During the experiment, dextrose (5.5% in water) was infused (1.38 ml/min) into the renal artery for the control period. Urine was collected for two or three 15-minute clearance periods, and midpoint systemic arterial and renal venous blood samples were taken. This procedure was repeated during the infusion of dipyridamole (24 μg/kg per min in 5.5% dextrose) and again during dextrose infusion for the recovery period. A period of 30 minutes was allowed after the onset and termination of the dipyridamole infusion before beginning the dipyridamole and recovery clearance periods, respectively.

Another group of dogs (group IIb) was given 15 mg deoxycorticosterone acetate each day and fed the same low-sodium food as the previous group to which had been added 200 mEq sodium (as NaCl). This dietary regimen was continued for 10–14 days. The experimental procedure for group IIb dogs was identical to the procedure outlined above for group IIa except that saline (0.9%) was used in place of dextrose for the control and recovery periods and was used as vehicle for the dipyridamole.

In both groups, bolus injections of adenosine (5 and 10 nmol) were given into the renal artery during the control and dipyridamole periods to test for enhancement of the renal vasoconstriction to exogenous adenosine by dipyridamole.

Group III—Effect of Dipyridamole on Renal Function in the Sodium-Depleted Dog, during Constant Renal Perfusion Pressure (n = 5)

To determine whether the renal actions of dipyridamole in the low-sodium dog (group IIa) were a consequence of the fall in arterial blood pressure, another group of dogs was sodium-depleted and prepared as described above, except that a clamp was placed around the abdominal aorta cephalad to the left renal artery. Two clearance periods were conducted during the infusion of 5.5% dextrose at the animals' ambient blood pressure. The aortic clamp was then tightened to lower the renal perfusion pressure (RPP) to 100 mm Hg, which is in the autoregulatory range and was near the average mean arterial pressure (MAP) of the dogs in group IIa during steady state dipyridamole infusion. The dextrose infusion was continued, and clearance periods were conducted. Maintaining RPP at 100 mm Hg, dipyridamole was infused and clearance periods were conducted after 30 minutes of equilibration. The dipyridamole was replaced by dextrose, and RPP was maintained at 100 mm Hg for the recovery clearance periods.

Group IV—Effect of an Adenosine Antagonist, Theophylline, on the Dipyridamole-Induced Changes in Renal Function in the Sodium-Depleted Dog (n = 8)

To determine whether the renal effects of dipyridamole could be inhibited or reversed by an adenosine antagonist, a group of dogs (group IV) was sodium-depleted and prepared as described above. In five dogs (group IVa) dextrose was infused (2.76 ml/min) into the renal artery and control urine and blood samples were collected. The dipyridamole infusion was then started (24 μg/kg per min, 1.38 ml/min) while the dextrose continued (1.38 ml/min). After a 30-minute equilibration period, blood and urine samples were collected. The dextrose infusion was replaced by theophylline (5 μmol/min) while the dipyridamole continued, and another equilibration period was allowed before samples were collected again. In a group of three dogs (group IVb), the above procedure was followed, except that the theophylline and dipyridamole periods were reversed. Theophylline (5 μmol/min) was infused during a dextrose infusion for the second set of samples, and then the dextrose was replaced by dipyridamole (24 μg/kg per min).

In both groups, bolus injections of adenosine (5 and 10 nmol) were given into the renal artery to test for enhancement and attenuation of the renal vasoconstriction by dipyridamole and theophylline, respectively.

Results

Group I—Effects of Dipyridamole on the Renal Uptake of Adenosine and the Concentration of Adenosine in Plasma and Urine

The cumulative venous recovery of labeled adenosine and ara-H was 15.6 ± 2.7 and 50.5 ± 7.6%,

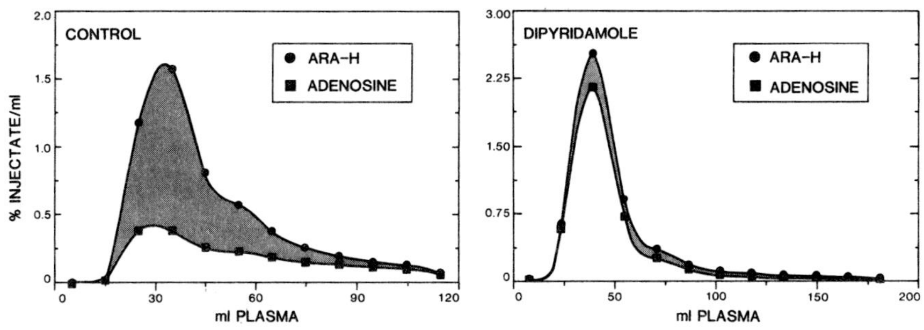

FIGURE 1. *Dilution curves for adenosine and ara-H from a representative single-injection, multiple-tracer experiment are shown. Data in the left panel were collected during saline infusion, and in the right panel, during dipyridamole infusion. Each datum point represents the concentration of tracer, normalized as percent of injected dose, recovered in the venous effluent. The curves were generated by fitting the data with a cubic function. Total sampling time was 2 minutes.*

respectively, during control. In the presence of dipyridamole, the recovery of adenosine increased to 48.1 ± 8.9% ($P < 0.05$ compared to control) and was not different from the venous recovery of ara-H (56.4 ± 10.5%, NS) during dipyridamole. The ratio of adenosine to ara-H in the first eluting samples averaged 0.28 ± 0.03 compared to 0.91 ± 0.03 during dipyridamole ($P < 0.05$), indicating that the cellular uptake of adenosine was inhibited in the presence of dipyridamole. Representative dilution curves for the venous effluent before and during dipyridamole are shown in Figure 1.

The control urinary excretions following injection of labeled adenosine and ara-H were 10.8 ± 1.2 and 19.8 ± 1.7% of the amount injected. Excretion of the adenosine label was increased in the presence of dipyridamole to 15.2 ± 2.2% and was not different from ara-H excretion (20.1 ± 2.5%, NS). The adenosine:ara-H ratio in the early eluting samples was 0.57 ± 0.03 in control and increased to 0.82 ± 0.01 during dipyridamole ($P < 0.05$). These results, similar to those obtained with renal venous plasma, indicate that this level of dipyridamole blocked the cellular uptake of tracer adenosine. Representative dilution curves for the urinary effluent before and during dipyridamole are shown in Figure 2.

The renal venous concentration of endogenous adenosine increased from 48 ± 9 nM in control to 108 ± 25 nM during dipyridamole. The urinary excretion of endogenous adenosine similarly increased from 595 ± 77 pmol/min to 1695 ± 207 pmol/min during dipyridamole ($P < 0.05$). The concentration of endogenous adenosine in arterial blood also increased during dipyridamole, however, due to the variability of the response (in two of the five dogs studied, arterial adenosine decreased) this increase was not statistically significant (73 ± 26 vs. 165 ± 59 nM, NS).

Group II—Effects of an Adenosine Uptake Inhibitor, Dipyridamole, on Renal Function in Dogs Maintained on a Low-Sodium or a High-Sodium Intake

The intrarenal infusion of dipyridamole caused a decrease in GFR in the dogs maintained on the low-sodium diet but produced no significant change in GFR when infused into the dogs that had been maintained on the high-sodium diet (Fig. 3; Table 1). GFR was decreased in the low-sodium dogs (group IIa) by an average of 58.6% (19.8 ± 1.1 vs. 8.2 ± 1.5 ml/min, $P < 0.05$), and returned to control levels in the recovery period (20.3 ± 1.1 ml/min). In the high-sodium dogs (group IIb), the average GFR during the infusion of dipyridamole was not significantly different from the control GFR (22.3 ± 3.9 vs. 25.1 ± 3.4 ml/min, NS). The intrarenal infusion of dipyridamole in the low-sodium dogs consistently produced a small and transient increase in renal blood flow at the onset of the infusion, which waned, and during the steady state was lower than the control blood flow (145 ± 10 vs. 117 ± 10 ml/min, $P < 0.05$). Steady state blood flow during the infusion of dipyridamole was also somewhat lower in the high-sodium dogs, albeit, not significantly (178 ± 24 vs. 157 ± 18 ml/min, NS).

The intrarenal infusion of dipyridamole had no effect on the renal perfusion pressure in the dogs maintained on the high-sodium diet. In contrast, the infusion of dipyridamole resulted in a fall of renal perfusion pressure in the low-sodium dogs (121 ± 5 to 101 ± 6 mm Hg, $P < 0.05$). Renal vascular resistance (RVR) was not significantly different in

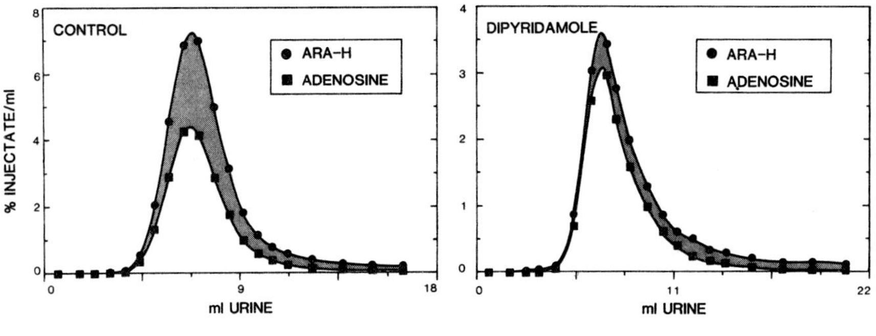

FIGURE 2. *Dilution curves for adenosine and ara-H in the urinary effluent are shown. See legend for Figure 1 for explanation. Total sampling time was 10 minutes.*

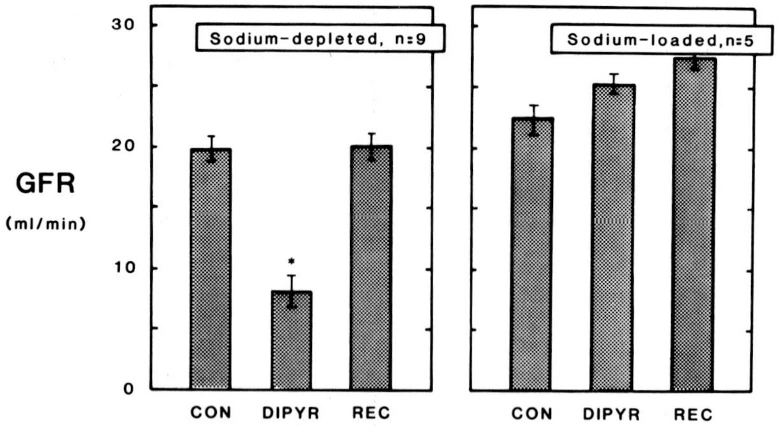

FIGURE 3. *Comparison of glomerular filtration rate (GFR) before, during, and after the intrarenal infusion of dipyridamole (24 μg/kg per min) in sodium-depleted and sodium-loaded dogs. Each bar represents the mean ± SEM for the group. Individual animal values were taken as the mean of three clearances in each period. Asterisk indicates $P < 0.05$.*

either group of dogs during the infusion of dipyridamole. Filtration fraction (FF) decreased significantly in the sodium-depleted dogs (0.28 ± .03 vs. 0.13 ± 0.02, $P < 0.05$) during the infusion of dipyridamole, but was not significantly different in the sodium-loaded dogs.

Fractional excretion of sodium and the plasma concentrations of sodium and potassium were not significantly different from control values during the infusion of dipyridamole.

In group IIa dogs (low-sodium), injections of 5 and 10 nmol of adenosine resulted in 45 ± 8 and 56 ± 10% decreases in renal blood flow (RBF) during the infusion of dextrose; during the infusion of dipyridamole, the decreases in RBF in response to 5 and 10 nmol adenosine were significantly greater (66 ± 11 and 74 ± 11%, respectively; $P < 0.05$). In the high-sodium group, RBF decreased by 14 ± 3

TABLE 1

Group	GFR (ml/min)	RBF (ml/min)	RPP (mm Hg)	FF	RVR (mm Hg/min per ml)	FE_{Na} (%)	Plasma Na^+ (mEq/liter)	Plasma K^+ (mEq/liter)
IIa: sodium-depleted ($n = 9$*)								
Control	19.8 ± 1.1	145 ± 10	121 ± 5	0.28 ± 0.03	0.91 ± 0.10	0.23 ± 0.15	134.4 ± 1.0	3.34 ± 0.10
Dipyridamole	8.2 ± 1.5†	117 ± 10†	101 ± 6†	0.13 ± 0.02†	0.95 ± 0.14	0.15 ± 0.05	130.7 ± 1.9	3.57 ± 0.12
Recovery	20.3 ± 1.1	135 ± 17	117 ± 5	0.27 ± 0.03	0.93 ± 0.13	0.44 ± 0.05	121.4 ± 3.1	3.52 ± 0.25
IIb: sodium-loaded ($n = 5$)								
Control	22.3 ± 3.9	178 ± 24	102 ± 8	0.24 ± 0.03	0.62 ± 0.09	2.60 ± 0.68	148.3 ± 4.9	2.17 ± 0.41
Dipyridamole	25.1 ± 3.4	157 ± 18	99 ± 9	0.29 ± 0.03	0.69 ± 0.12	2.09 ± 0.50	159.3 ± 3.9	2.34 ± 0.45
Recovery	27.3 ± 3.4	133 ± 19†	123 ± 11†	0.39 ± 0.07	1.02 ± 0.15	2.41 ± 0.46	162.9 ± 4.7	2.59 ± 0.47
III: sodium-depleted, constant pressure ($n = 5$‡)								
Initial	25.7 ± 3.4	165 ± 27	133 ± 3	0.30 ± 0.05	0.89 ± 0.13	0.77 ± 0.54	139.5 ± 3.4	3.65 ± 0.35
Control	24.4 ± 4.1	163 ± 34	100	0.32 ± 0.06	0.77 ± 0.21	0.16 ± 0.09†	135.7 ± 3.1	3.89 ± 0.36
Dipyridamole	15.0 ± 3.6†	167 ± 43	100	0.22 ± 0.06†	0.86 ± 0.27	0.15 ± 0.09	130.9 ± 3.6	4.22 ± 0.41
Recovery	24.1 ± 3.4	181 ± 42	100	0.31 ± 0.07	0.74 ± 0.21	0.10 ± 0.03	128.2 ± 3.5	4.35 ± 0.55
IVa: sodium-depleted ($n = 5$)								
Control	21.9 ± 1.0	154 ± 14	124 ± 8	0.29 ± 0.04	0.85 ± 0.14	0.31 ± 0.20	137.5 ± 2.7	3.31 ± 0.10
Dipyridamole	7.9 ± 2.5†	119 ± 15†	99 ± 8†	0.12 ± 0.03†	0.86 ± 0.07	0.18 ± 0.06	132.5 ± 3.4	3.41 ± 0.11
Dipyr/Theo	25.7 ± 1.9	157 ± 11	112 ± 7	0.31 ± 0.03	0.72 ± 0.07	0.85 ± 0.29	126.4 ± 1.9	3.22 ± 0.11
IVb: sodium-depleted ($n = 3$)								
Control	31.3 ± 5.2	165 ± 7	117 ± 6	0.38 ± 0.08	0.71 ± 0.05	0.28 ± 0.08	135.5 ± 3.7	3.44 ± 0.25
Theophylline	30.6 ± 4.9	175 ± 15	107 ± 3	0.36 ± 0.08	0.61 ± 0.04	0.74 ± 0.10†	125.5 ± 3.6	3.39 ± 0.18
Theo/Dipyr	25.5 ± 3.5	174 ± 23	96 ± 6†	0.29 ± 0.05	0.57 ± 0.06	0.74 ± 0.05	125.9 ± 3.6	3.74 ± 0.24

GFR = glomerular filtration rate; RBF = renal blood flow; RPP = renal perfusion pressure; FF = filtration fraction; RVR = renal vascular resistance; FE_{Na} and FE_k = fractional excretion of sodium and potassium, respectively.

* FE_{Na}, $n = 3$.

‡ FE_{Na}, plasma Na^+, and plasma K^+, $n = 3$.

† $P < 0.05$.

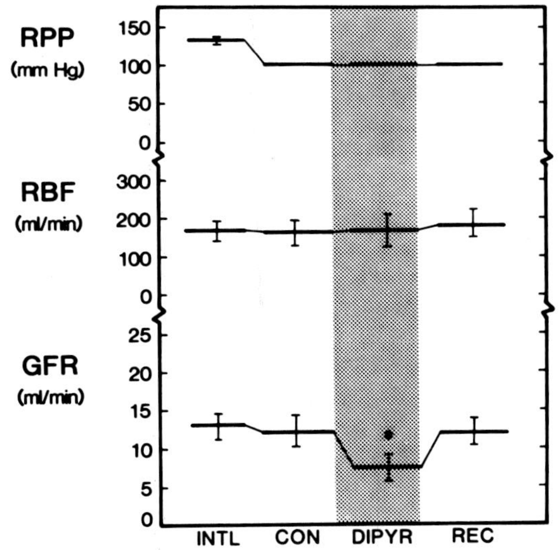

FIGURE 4. *Renal perfusion pressure (RPP), renal blood flow (RBF), and glomerular filtration rate (GFR) in five sodium-depleted dogs before, during, and after the intrarenal infusion of dipyridamole (24 μg/kg per min) while renal perfusion pressure was maintained at 100 mm Hg. Each value represents the mean ± SEM for the group. Individual animal values were taken as the mean of three clearances in each period. Asterisk indicates P < 0.05.*

and 25 ± 8% during the control saline infusion and by 28 ± 5% ($P < 0.05$) in response to 5 nmol adenosine and 39 ± 6% (NS) in response to 10 nmol adenosine during the dipyridamole infusion.

In some preliminary experiments, dipyridamole was infused into the femoral vein. With systemic administration, the effects on renal function were the same as that seen in the intrarenal infusion.

Group III—Effect of Dipyridamole on Renal Function during Constant Renal Perfusion Pressure

An initial clearance period was performed in each animal at its ambient arterial pressure. The average initial RPP for five dogs was 133 ± 3 mm Hg. Initial GFR was 25.7 ± 3.4 ml/min, and RBF was 165 ± 27 ml/min. Filtration fraction was 0.30 ± 0.05 and fractional sodium excretion was 0.77 ± 0.54% (Fig. 4).

There was no effect of decreasing renal perfusion pressure (RPP) to 100 mm Hg on GFR (25.7 ± 3.4 vs. 24.4 ± 4.1, ml/min, NS) or RBF (165 ± 27 vs. 163 ± 34 ml/min, NS). Filtration fraction and vascular resistance remained constant as well (Table 1). With the fall in RPP fractional excretion of sodium decreased significantly from 0.77 ± 0.54 to 0.16 ± 0.09% ($P < 0.05$).

With RPP maintained at 100 mm Hg, dipyridamole infusion resulted in a fall in GFR from 24.4 ± 4.1 to 15.0 ± 3.6 ml/min ($P < 0.05$). There was no change in RBF with dipyridamole infusion (167 ± 43 ml/min, NS); consequently, filtration fraction decreased from 0.32 ± 0.06 to 0.22 ± 0.06 ($P < 0.05$). Vascular resistance and fractional sodium excretion did not change significantly from the previous period.

During the recovery period, (i.e., 30 minutes after stopping dipyridamole infusion), GFR and filtration fraction both returned to their respective control values (GFR: 24.1 ± 3.4 ml/min; FF: 0.31 ± 0.07). There was no significant change in RBF, vascular resistance, or fractional sodium excretion.

Group IV—The Effect of Theophylline on the Renal Actions of Dipyridamole

The intrarenal infusion of dipyridamole in group IV resulted in changes similar to those described for group II dogs (Table 1; Fig. 5). GFR decreased from 21.9 ± 1.0 to 7.9 ± 2.5 ml/min ($P < 0.05$); likewise, RBF decreased from the control level of 154 ± 14 ml/min to 119 ± 15 ml/min ($P < 0.05$). Filtration fraction also decreased from 0.29 ± 0.04 to 0.12 ± 0.03 ($P < 0.05$). As with group II, MAP decreased during the dipyridamole infusion from 124 ± 8 to 99 ± 8 mm Hg ($P < 0.05$). Injections of adenosine during the control dextrose infusion resulted in decreases in RBF of 35 ± 10 and 42 ± 11% for 5 and 10 nmol adenosine, respectively. In response to the same doses during the dipyridamole infusion, the decreases in RBF were significantly greater (51 ± 14% and 60 ± 12%; $P < 0.05$). The concomitant infusion of theophylline resulted in the reversal of all of these effects (Fig. 5). GFR increased to 25.7 ± 1.9 ml/min and RBF increased to 157 ± 11 ml/min. Neither increase was significantly different from the respective control values. The filtration fraction returned to the control level (0.31 ± 0.03) during theophylline infusion as well. Renal perfusion pressure increased from 99 ± 8 to 112 ± 7 mm Hg, a value which was not statistically different than the control value of 124 ± 8 mm Hg. The decreases in RBF in response to adenosine injections were 31 ± 15 and 43 ± 20% during the theophylline infusion, and were not significantly different than the control responses.

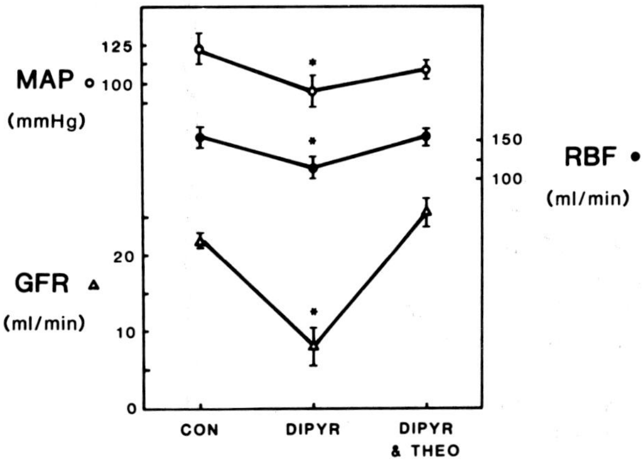

FIGURE 5. *Mean arterial pressure (MAP), renal blood flow (RBF), and glomerular filtration rate (GFR), in five sodium-depleted dogs before and during the intrarenal infusion of dipyridamole (24 μg/kg per min), and during the intrarenal infusion of theophylline (5 μmol/min) and dipyridamole, simultaneously. Each value represents the mean ± SEM for the group. Individual animal values were taken as the mean of three clearances in each period. Asterisk indicates P < 0.05.*

In an additional three dogs, theophylline was infused prior to dipyridamole to determine if the effects of dipyridamole on renal function could be inhibited by the presence of theophylline. Theophylline infusion alone did not significantly change GFR from the control level (31.3 ± 5.2 vs. 30.6 ± 4.9 ml/min, NS). Likewise, RBF did not change in the steady state (165 ± 7 vs. 175 ± 15 ml/min, NS), although there was an initial tendency of blood flow to increase immediately after theophylline infusion was begun. Renal perfusion pressure was also not affected by theophylline (117 ± 6 vs. 107 ± 3 mm Hg, NS). Fractional sodium excretion increased from 0.28 ± 0.08 to 0.74 ± 0.10% ($P < 0.05$). Theophylline infusion did not affect renal vascular resistance or filtration fraction (Table 1). The infusion of theophylline attenuated the decreases in RBF to adenosine injections as compared to control. Injections of adenosine (5 and 10 nmol) during the dextrose infusion resulted in 44 ± 3 and 52 ± 6% decreases in RBF. During the theophylline infusion, the decreases in RBF in response to adenosine were significantly less (19 ± 5% and 33 ± 3%, $P < 0.05$).

In the presence of theophylline, the infusion of dipyridamole did not significantly affect GFR (30.6 ± 4.9 vs. 25.5 ± 3.5 ml/min, NS) or RBF (175 ± 15 vs. 174 ± 23 ml/min, NS). Filtration fraction did not change from the value during theophylline infusion alone (0.36 ± 0.08 vs. 0.29 ± 0.05, NS). Likewise, dipyridamole infusion in the presence of theophylline had no effect on renal perfusion pressure (107 ± 3 vs. 96 ± 6 mm Hg, NS); however, this was significantly different from the control value of 117 ± 6 mm Hg ($P < 0.05$). Vascular resistance and fractional sodium excretion were not changed with the infusion of dipyridamole (Table 1). Adenosine injections (5 and 10 nmol) during the theophylline/dipyridamole infusion resulted in 33 ± 17 and 47 ± 21% decreases of RBF which were not significantly different than the control responses.

Discussion

The reported actions of adenosine—namely, the production of a marked fall in GFR (Tagawa and Vander, 1970), alteration of cortical distribution of blood flow (Spielman et al., 1980), a decrease in renin release (Tagawa and Vander, 1970)—form the basis of the hypothesis that intrarenally produced adenosine, as the active extracellular metabolite of the ATP hydrolysis associated with transepithelial transport, is the mediator of the intrinsic regulation of renal function. However, the majority of the previous studies have involved the use of exogenous adenosine, and, whereas these studies provide important support for the role of adenosine as a regulator of renal function—alone, this evidence can be considered as merely suggestive. The use of dipyridamole, a nucleoside uptake blocker, in the present study more directly allows for the investigation of the role that endogenous adenosine may play in the regulation of renal function. The hypothesis tested in the present study was that inhibition of the cellular uptake of adenosine increases the extracellular level of endogenous adenosine, which, in turn, alters renal function. We therefore sought to determine the effect of dipyridamole on (1) the renal uptake of adenosine, (2) the plasma and urinary levels of adenosine, and (3) renal function.

For any substance to have a role as a regulatory intercellular mediator, it must have a system for inactivation, through uptake and/or metabolism. Nucleoside uptake is known to occur by facilitated diffusion in a variety of cell types (Berlin and Oliver, 1975), and is inhibitable pharmacologically (Paterson et al., 1975). Dipyridamole has been shown to block the uptake of adenosine by a number of cell types, including erythrocytes, platelets, and myocardial cells (Feigl, 1983). In the present study, to determine whether renal adenosine uptake is blocked by dipyridamole, we employed a single-injection, multiple-tracer, indicator-dilution technique. This technique involves the simultaneous injection of radiolabeled adenosine, together with a radiolabeled reference, in this case a nontransported, nonmetabolized analog of adenosine, ara-H, and collection of serial samples of the urinary and renal venous effluents. Comparison of the tracer adenosine to the reference in urine and renal venous blood yields important information about the renal handling of adenosine (Thompson et al., in press). Based on knowledge of adenosine transport in other tissues, we hypothesized that injected adenosine can leave the vascular compartment by simple diffusion into the interstitial space, as well as by facilitated diffusion into cells via the nucleoside carrier, whereas the reference, ara-H, can leave the vascular compartment only by simple diffusion. Thus, the difference in the recovery of tracer adenosine and the recovery of the reference was taken as the uptake and metabolism of adenosine by cells (Thompson et al., in press). The difference between the recovery of adenosine and that of the reference is virtually abolished during the infusion of dipyridamole (Figs. 1 and 2), and indicates that the cellular uptake of adenosine is blocked. This inhibition of the cellular uptake is apparent in both the renal venous and urinary effluents, leading to the conclusion that the kidney possesses a dipyridamole-sensitive cellular uptake mechanism for adenosine in both the vascular and tubular compartments.

Once in the cell, adenosine is metabolized to inosine or 5′-AMP by adenosine deaminase or adenosine kinase, respectively. Because adenosine metabolism is primarily intracellular (Berne and Rubio, 1974) and its physiological actions are primarily extracellular (Arch and Newsholme, 1978), exogenous administration of adenosine during pharmacological inhibition of the cellular uptake is generally expected to result in increased extracellular levels and, hence, increase its biological activity. In the heart, dipyridamole enhances the coronary vasodilation produced by adenosine (Feigl, 1983). Likewise, the renal vasoconstriction produced by the intrarenal injection of adenosine is augmented in the presence of dipyridamole (Sakai et al., 1981). In the present study, bolus injections of adenosine produced transient vasoconstrictions which were enhanced during the infusion of dipyridamole.

The knowledge that dipyridamole blocks the uptake and potentiates the action of exogenously administered adenosine has led investigators to use dipyridamole to enhance events suspected to be mediated by elevated levels of endogenous adenosine (Feigl, 1983). However, because the mechanism by which intracellular adenosine exits the cell remains to be defined, and because the dipyridamole-inhibitable, facilitated diffusion is presumably a bidirectional process (Plagemann and Wohlhueter, 1980), release, as well as cellular uptake, may be inhibited in the presence of dipyridamole. Thus, it is important to ascertain whether blocking cellular uptake is actually associated with levels of adenosine.

In general, it can be assumed that the concentration of adenosine in venous blood and urine can be used as an indication of the concentration of adenosine in the extracellular fluid. Measurements of adenosine in the plasma and urine before and during the administration of dipyridamole indicate that extracellular adenosine levels are indeed elevated by dipyridamole. The concentration of adenosine in arterial blood also increased during dipyridamole, and this is presumably due to the effect of dipyridamole on adenosine uptake in other tissues, a finding not surprising in light of the fall in arterial blood pressure. The increases in venous and urinary adenosine concentration were not, however, dependent on an increase in extrarenal adenosine levels, since the rise in venous and urinary adenosine was also seen in two of the five experiments in which the arterial levels were decreased or unchanged. In addition, the arterial concentration of adenosine was increased, on the average, to slightly more than 100 nM, and the changes in renal function that occurred would require, in an infusion of exogenous adenosine, a concentration of 5 μM, or 50 times the concentration observed with the dipyridamole infusion, suggesting that the functional changes were probably elicited by increases in intrarenal adenosine levels.

Having established that (1) cellular uptake of adenosine is blocked by dipyridamole in the kidney, and (2) adenosine levels are elevated during the administration of dipyridamole, we then sought to determine the effects of elevated endogenous adenosine on renal function. The renal actions of adenosine are influenced by the dietary sodium intake of the animal (Osswald et al., 1978a). That is, the intrarenal infusion of adenosine results in a decrease in GFR in sodium-depleted rats and dogs, but has relatively little, if any, effect when infused into sodium-loaded animals. Likewise, the effect of exogenous adenosine to produce a redistribution of renal cortical blood flow is influenced by the dietary sodium intake of the animal (Spielman et al., 1980). The mechanism responsible for these differences in response to adenosine is unknown at present, although the enhanced renin-angiotensin system and increased renal nerve activity present in the sodium-depleted animal are possibilities. Several recent studies have been aimed at clarifying the role of angiotensin in the renal actions of adenosine. The reduction in RBF following a brief occlusion of the renal artery—which is thought to be mediated by adenosine—as well as the decrease in RBF in response to an injection of adenosine, has been attenuated by high concentrations of the angiotensin II antagonist [Sar[1], Ile[8]] AII (Spielman and Osswald, 1979), suggesting an adenosine-AII interaction. However, measurements of renal lymph AII, used as an indication of interstitial AII levels, have shown that intrarenal AII did not increase, but actually decreased, during an adenosine infusion (Spielman, 1984). Therefore, whereas an adenosine-AII interaction appears to exist, it may be more complicated than has been postulated previously.

To determine the renal effects of elevated endogenous adenosine and the influence of sodium intake on these actions, we studied the effects of dipyridamole administration in sodium-depleted and sodium-loaded dogs, thereby comparing the renal effects of endogenous to exogenous adenosine. Animals maintained on a diet low in sodium were found to have a reversible fall in the GFR in response to the dipyridamole infusion, whereas GFR did not change upon infusion of dipyridamole in the sodium-loaded dogs.

In addition to the fall in GFR, renal blood flow was also reduced during the dipyridamole infusion in the sodium-depleted dog. There was, however, no calculated change in the renal vascular resistance as mean arterial blood pressure was concomitantly reduced. The filtration fraction was markedly reduced during the dipyridamole infusion, indicating that the fall in GFR was proportionally greater than the fall in renal plasma flow. No hemodynamic changes were observed during the infusion of dipyridamole in the sodium-loaded dogs. These effects are similar in many ways to the effects of the intrarenal infusion of adenosine, but the fall in the arterial blood pressure, an effect not seen during the infusion of adenosine, makes the comparison somewhat complicated.

To compare the effects of dipyridamole to the effects of exogenous adenosine more directly, and to determine what contribution the fall in arterial pressure had on the decrease in GFR, we infused dipyridamole into another series of sodium-depleted animals in which renal perfusion pressure was held constant. When renal perfusion pressure was held constant at 100 mm Hg, dipyridamole infusion still produced a marked fall in GFR (−38%), indicating that the effect of dipyridamole is, for the most part, independent of the fall in arterial pressure. It should be noted here that, whereas mean arterial pressure fell during the dipyridamole infusion and was a major contributing factor to the decrease in RBF, systemic pressure did not fall below the autoregulatory range of the kidney and should not have been expected to result in a decrease in RBF. These findings suggest that dipyridamole, or endogenous adenosine, may cause an impairment of autoregulation in sodium-depleted animals. The mechanism by which this interference might occur is unknown, and may be of sufficient importance to merit further investigation.

The ability of theophylline to antagonize the actions of adenosine is well documented. In the kidney, theophylline has been shown to act as a competitive inhibitor of adenosine's actions to produce a vasoconstriction (Osswald, 1975), decrease GFR, and inhibit renin secretion (Spielman, 1984). Furthermore, this action of theophylline has been shown to occur at doses well below those required for an inhibitory effect on cyclic nucleotide phosphodiesterase (Spielman, 1984). To ascertain whether the decrease in GFR resulting from dipyridamole infusion in the sodium-depleted dog was mediated by elevated adenosine levels, theophylline was infused before and after the dipyridamole infusion. Theophylline was able to reverse, as well as inhibit, the dipyridamole-induced decrease in GFR, suggesting that elevated endogenous adenosine was responsible for the fall in GFR.

In summary, we found that, in the anesthetized dog, dipyridamole blocked the cellular uptake of adenosine, elevated the extracellular concentration of adenosine, and decreased GFR in the sodium-depleted but not the sodium-loaded dog, and the effect on GFR was blocked by the adenosine antagonist, theophylline. Elevation of endogenous adenosine by inhibition of cellular uptake resulted in a fall in GFR in the sodium-depleted animal, a condition known to enhance the actions of adenosine. Although the intent of this investigation was to evaluate the renal effects of elevated endogenous adenosine through pharmacological inhibition of its cellular uptake, the marked effect of dipyridamole to decrease GFR in the sodium-depleted animal raises important issues concerning the clinical use of dipyridamole in situations where extracellular fluid volume is reduced. These findings indicate that, given an appropriate physiological or pathophysiological situation (e.g., sodium-depletion), elevated levels of endogenous adenosine have the capability of altering GFR. Whereas the present findings are consistent with a role for intrarenally produced adenosine in the regulation of renal function, it remains to be determined whether endogenous adenosine elevated by circumstances other than pharmacological (i.e., physiological or pathophysiological) will result in similar changes in renal function.

We wish to acknowledge the technical assistance of Cindy DeLonjay and the secretarial assistance of Rosa Manlove. We also wish to thank Boehringer Ingelheim for the generous supply of dipyridamole.

Supported by National Science Foundation Grant PCM-8110588, and by a grant from the American Heart Association of Michigan.

Dr. Spielman is the recipient of Research Career Development Award HL-01010.

Address for reprints: Dr. William S. Spielman, Department of Physiology, Michigan State University, East Lansing, Michigan 48824-1101.

Received July 9, 1984; accepted for publication November 24, 1984.

References

Arch JRS, Newsholme EA (1978) The control of the metabolism and the hormonal role of adenosine. *In* Essays in Biochemistry, vol 14, edited by PN Campbell, F Dickens. New York, Academic Press, pp 82–124

Berlin RD, Oliver JM (1975) Membrane transport of purine and pyrimidine bases and nucleosides in animal cells. Int Rev Cytol **42:** 287–336

Berne RM, Rubio R (1974) Adenine nucleotide metabolism in the heart. Circ Res **34 35** (suppl III): 109–120

Davidson WD, Sackner MA (1963) Simplification of the anthrone method for determination of inulin in clearance studies. J Lab Clin Med **62:** 351–356

Feigl ED (1983) Coronary physiology. Physiol Rev **63:** 1–205

Gerkens JF, Heidemann HT, Jackson EK, Branch RA (1983) Aminophylline inhibits renal vasoconstriction produced by intrarenal hypertonic saline. J Pharmacol Exp Ther **225:** 611–615

Kleinman LI, Radford EP (1964) Ventilation standards for small mammals. J Appl Physiol **19:** 360–362

Osswald H (1975) Renal effects of adenosine and their inhibition by theophylline. Naunyn Schmiedebergs Arch Pharmacol **288:** 79–86

Osswald H, Schmitz HJ, Heidenreich O (1975) Adenosine response of the rat kidney after saline loading, sodium restriction and hemorrhagia. Pflugers Arch **357:** 323–333

Osswald H, Schmitz HJ, Kemper R (1978a) Renal action of adenosine: Effect on renin secretion in the rat. Naunyn Schmiedebergs Arch Pharmacol **303:** 95–99

Osswald H, Spielman WS, Knox FG (1978b) Mechanism of adenosine-mediated decrease in glomerular filtration rate in dogs. Circ Res **43:** 465–469

Osswald H, Nabakowski G, Hermes H (1980) Adenosine as a possible mediator of metabolic control of glomerular filtration rate. Int J Biochem **12:** 263–267

Paterson ARP (1979) Adenosine transport. *In* Physiological and Regulatory Functions of Adenosine and Adenine Nucleotides, edited by HP Baer, GI Drummond. New York, Raven Press, pp 305–313

Paterson ARP, Kim SC, Bernard O, Cass CE (1975) Transport of nucleosides. Ann NY Acad Sci **255:** 402–410

Plagemann PGW, Wohlhueter RM (1980) Permeation of nucleosides, nucleic acid bases, and nucleotides in animal cells. *In* Current Topics in Membranes and Transport, vol 14, Carriers and Membrane Transport Proteins, edited by F Bronner, A Kleinzeller. New York, Academic Press, pp 225–330

Sakai K, Aono J, Haruta K (1981) Species differences in renal vascular effects of dipyridamole and in the potentiation of adenosine action by dipyridamole. J Cardiovasc Pharmacol **3:** 420–430

Spielman WS (1984) Antagonistic effect of theophylline on the adenosine-induced decrease in renin release. Am J Physiol **247:** F246–F251

Spielman WS, Osswald H (1979) Blockade of the postocclusive renal vasoconstriction by an angiotensin II antagonist: Evidence for an angiotensin-adenosine interaction. Am J Physiol **237:** F463–F467

Spielman WS, Thompson CI (1982) A proposed role for adenosine in the regulation of renal hemodynamics and renin release. Am J Physiol **242:** F423–F435

Spielman WS, Britton SL, Fiksen-Olsen MJ (1980) Effect of adenosine on the distribution of renal blood flow in dogs. Circ Res **46:** 449–456

Tagawa H, Vander AJ (1970) Effects of adenosine compounds on renal function and renin secretion in dogs. Circ Res **26:** 327–338

Thompson CI, Sparks HV, Spielman WS (in press) The renal handling of plasma adenosine: Relative contribution of arterial adenosine to the renal effluent. Am J Physiol

INDEX TERMS: Renal function • Theophylline • Nucleoside uptake • Persantine

Optimal Power Generation by the Left Ventricle

A Study in the Anesthetized Open Thorax Cat

G. J. van den Horn, N. Westerhof, and G. Elzinga
From the Laboratory for Physiology, Free University, Amsterdam, The Netherlands

SUMMARY. We studied the interaction of the left ventricle and the systemic arterial bed in the open thorax cat. In the steady state, the ventricle can be characterized by the pump function graph (i.e., the relationship between mean left ventricular pressure and mean outflow). From this pump function graph, the apparent source resistance of the heart is found. Apparent source resistance is defined as the ratio of the difference between maximal and actual mean left ventricular pressure, and mean outflow. The arterial system can be characterized by the ratio of mean aortic pressure and mean flow (peripheral resistance). The pressure and flow at which the heart operates is defined as the working point. We have investigated whether the ventricle in the intact cat is working optimally, i.e., that it cannot increase work output further at the end-diastolic volume, contractile state, and prevailing heart rate. This condition is considered as "matching" of ventricle and load. It could be shown that optimal power is transferred when the ratio of peripheral and apparent source resistance equals twice the ratio of mean aortic and mean left ventricular pressure (the matching principle). In four cats, we observed that mean aortic and mean left ventricular pressures are proportionally related. Mean external power (the time intergral of the product of pressure and flow divided by cycle length) and steady power (the product of mean pressure and mean flow) were found to be proportional as well. These proportionalities allow for the calculation of peripheral resistance and mean external power from the pump function graph. Pump function graphs were determined in three groups: control ($n = 9$), atrial pacing ($n = 8$), and halothane ($n = 5$). We compared the ratio of peripheral and source resistance at the working point and at the point of optimal work output (expressed in steady ventricular power). It could be shown that, in all investigated groups, the power optimum and the working point coincide. It was concluded that circulatory control in the intact anesthetized cat keeps the ventricle at optimal work output under the conditions studied. **(*Circ Res 56: 252–261, 1985*)**

IN this study, we investigated the interaction between the left heart and the systemic arterial bed in the anesthetized open thorax cat. In our approach, the heart is regarded as a source (pump), loaded by the arterial system. The pumping ability of the heart can be described quantitatively by the pump function graph (Elzinga and Westerhof, 1973, 1978, 1979). This graph relates mean left ventricular pressure and mean flow and allows for determination of the (apparent) source resistance. The arterial system is described by its peripheral resistance, i.e., the ratio of mean aortic pressure and mean flow. We attempt to answer the following questions: (1) Does the heart in the anesthetized open thorax cat pump at optimal external power under control conditions? (2) Do changes in heart rate and inotropic state move the working point (i.e., the mean pressure and mean flow value at which the heart operates) closer to or further away from the point where external power is optimal? (3) Can we derive quantitative relations between (apparent) source resistance of the heart and peripheral resistance as a basis for a "matching" principle?

Methods

Surgical Procedure

Male cats (2.8–4.2 kg) anesthetized with sodium pentobarbital (Nembutal), 40 mg/kg, were artificially ventilated with a mixture of room air and oxygen (2:1). During surgery, halothane (1.5 vol%) was added to the ventilatory gas mixture. Oxygen and carbon dioxide content of the expired air were continuously monitored by a capnograph (Datex Normocap), and kept constant at 23–27 and 3.5–3.8 vol%, respectively, by adjusting the room air:oxygen ratio and the tidal volume. In this way, it was possible to maintain blood gas values stable within the normal ranges for the anesthetized cat, i.e., pH 7.32–7.42, arterial P_{CO_2} 28–32 mm Hg, and arterial $P_{O_2} > 100$ mm Hg (Fink and Schoolman, 1963). Body temperature was maintained at 37°C with a heating pad. A midline sternotomy was performed. All wound edges were cauterized carefully to minimize blood loss. The pericardium was opened longitudinally in the midline, and the edges sutured to the thoracic wall. The ascending aorta was then dissected free from surrounding structures, up to the root of the right brachiocephalic trunk. Two concentric purse-string sutures were put in the ventral wall of the ascending aorta, 1–1.5 cm cranial from the aortic valves. A stiff polyethylene catheter was introduced into the left ventricular cavity through the apex to obtain left ventricular pressure. The animals were heparinized with 1000 IU/kg. From this point onward, two different procedures were followed.

Pressure and Power Experiments

In four cats, a stiff polyethylene catheter was introduced through the purse-string sutures into the proximal aorta. The catheter tip was positioned approximately 0.5 cm distal to the aortic valves. This catheter was used to measure aortic pressure. A perivascular flow probe put around the root of the ascending aorta completed the instrumentation. These experiments were used to relate mean left ventricular pressure to mean aortic pressure, and to investigate how mean external power and steady power compare.

Experiments Relating Heart and Arterial System

In 22 cats, the ascending aorta was partially clamped with an atraumatic side clamp (Cooley). A hole was punched in the ventral aortic wall in the center of the purse-string sutures. Then the clamp was put more dorsally, obstructing the blood flow toward the periphery completely. During this procedure, femoral artery pressure was measured. The cannula of the artificial load (see below) was introduced through the hole in the aortic wall. Both purse-string sutures were immediately tightened, and the Cooley clamp removed. The duration of complete flow obstruction was less than 10 seconds. The aortic occluder (Fig. 1) was then put in place, just distal to the cannula. A femoral vein was cannulated for reinfusion of blood ejected into the reservoir of the artificial load. Finally, a perivascular electromagnetic flow probe was put around the root of the ascending aorta.

The Artificial Load

To obtain left ventricular pump function graphs in the open thorax cat, we measured left ventricular pressure and flow while the left ventricle was made to eject against different artificial loads, imposed on a beat-to-beat basis. This beat-to-beat approach was used to avoid changes in left ventricular filling and inotropic state. To provide different loads to the left heart on a beat-to-beat basis, a combination of two devices was used, as shown in Figure 1. Normally, device A was closed, and device B open; the heart then was loaded by the animal's arterial system. When ejection against an artificial load was desired, device B occluded the aorta just proximal to the right brachiocephalic trunk, while, at the same time, the valve in device A was opened. In this situation, the heart ejected through device A against an adjustable resistance, into a reservoir from which the blood was returned to the animal. Changes from normal to artificial load were performed in selected diastoles by a trigger pulse, derived from the cardiotachometer (see below). The devices were reset after the beat studied, so that the normal periphery loaded the heart except during the selected beats with artificial load. This procedure enabled us to obtain heartbeats under different loading conditions for a constant inotropic state and filling.

Measurements and Recordings

During all experiments, left ventricular, ascending aortic, and femoral artery pressures were measured with Statham P23Db transducers. The pressure transducers were calibrated before and after each experiment against a Wallace and Tiernan precision manometer. In the experiments relating the heart and the arterial system, it was verified that mean aortic and mean femoral artery pressures were comparable, which means that the devices caused no obstruction of the ascending aorta. Heart rate was obtained from left ventricular pressure via a cardiotachometer. Trigger pulses derived from the cardiotachometer were used to activate the artificial load (if present). These pulses were also recorded to control sampling during off-line A to D conversion of the pressure and flow signals. Flow in the ascending aorta was measured by a perivascular cuff probe (Skalar Transflow 601 system). Zero drift was corrected for by automatic zero control during diastole (Dijkema and Elzinga, 1973). Flow through the artificial load was measured by a cannulating electromagnetic flow probe made in our workshop. Flow probes were connected to Skalar flowmeters (Transflow 601). Both flow-measuring systems were calibrated in vitro with saline. All signals were recorded on an eight-channel ink writer (Elema Schoenander, type EMT 81), and on analog tape (SE 7000).

Experimental Protocol

Pressure and Power Experiments

The following interventions were used to obtain a wide range of pressures and flows: (1) halothane (0.5–3.5 vol%), (2) norepinephrine (0.2–0.8 mg/kg per min), (3) atrial

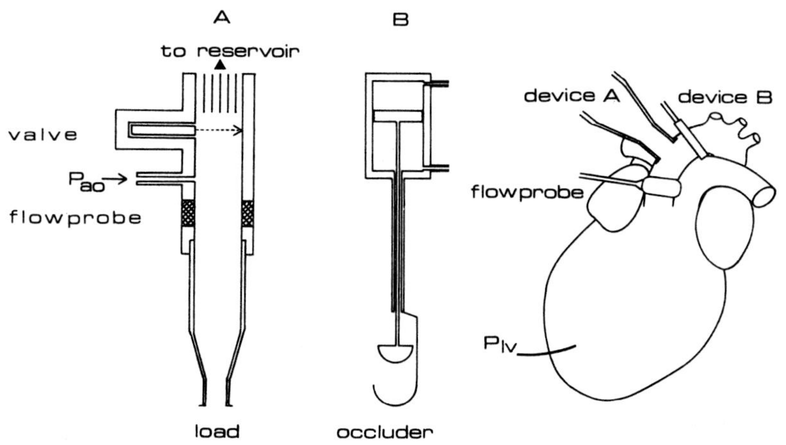

FIGURE 1. *Devices used to apply different artificial loads to the left ventricle on a beat-to-beat basis. Device A consists of a cannula, which is normally closed by a pneumatic valve. An adjustable outflow resistor mounted at the distal end of the cannula constitutes the actual artificial load. By opening the valve and closing the aortic occluder (device B) in a selected diastole, the left ventricle faces this load during the next systole. A cannulated flow probe permits measurement of blood flow. Via a side opening in the cannula, proximal aortic pressure can be measured continuously. The bore of the cannula is 6 mm, except at the very proximal end, where it is 3 mm. Device B is a pneumatic occluder, used to obstruct all flow to the arterial system when an artificial load was applied. Both devices could be controlled separately. At the right hand side, both devices are shown in situ.*

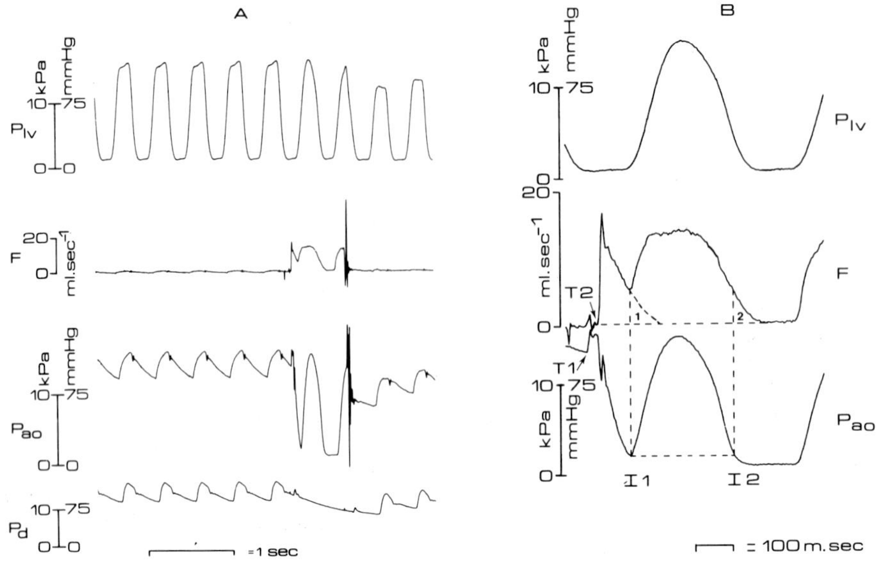

Figure 2. *Panel A: example of pressures and flow in the steady state and a beat with an artificial load. Panel B: example of digitized tracings of a beat against an artificial load. Sampling was performed at a rate of 500 Hz. From top to bottom: left ventricular pressure (P_{lv}), device flow (F), and proximal aortic pressure (P_{ao}). T1 and T2 indicate the moments that the aortic occluder closes and the valve in device A opens, respectively. Integration was performed between I_1, and I_2. At these moments the amount of blood contained in the proximal aorta is the same (same aortic pressure). No ejection flow is present after moment I2 when the decays of flow in the phases marked 1 and 2 are identical. The differences in the decays were small. For further explanation, see text.*

pacing (120–200 beats/min), (4) infusions of Haemaccel at 37°C (10–20 ml), and (5) combinations of 1–4.

During each intervention, left ventricular pressure, aortic pressure, and aortic flow were recorded after a steady state had been reached.

Experiments Relating Heart and Arterial System

Each experimental run consisted of 12–24 beats, during which the left ventricle faced a different artificial load. The time between two such beats amounted to 2 or 3 minutes. This time was sufficient to reach the stable control condition again. At the start and end of an experimental run, an isometric beat was imposed by closing the outflow resistor in device A completely. After each ejection into the artificial load, the blood was returned from the reservoir to the animal. Normal heart beats, i.e., the heart ejecting into the animal's own arterial system, were recorded in the steady state. These normal beats were used to calculate peripheral resistance.

We studied the interaction between the heart and the arterial system during control ($n = 9$) and for two interventions: (1) changes in heart rate ($n = 8$), and (2) reduction of contractility and decrease of peripheral resistance ($n = 5$). These interventions were brought about by increasing the pace frequency, and by administration of halothane to thc animal. Except for the control series, the hearts were paced from the right atrium.

Experimental runs were accepted if mean left ventricular pressure of the isometric beats at the start and at the end of the run differed less than 10%.

Data Analysis

Data analysis was performed off-line, from analog tape, with a DEC PDP 11/34 computer. Heart rate, left ventricular pressure, ascending aortic pressure, flow through the artificial load (in the experiments of type B only), and ascending aortic flow signals were converted from analog into digital form. In the type A experiments, A to D conversion was carried out over exactly one heart period. In the type B experiments, the signal driving the aortic occluder was used to control the period of sampling by the computer. Sampling was performed at a rate of 500 Hz. The digitized tracings were visualized one by one by plotting every signal as a function of its sample number on a storage oscilloscope (Tektronix 611). An example of a graphic representation taken from an experiment of series B is shown in Figure 2B. The original recording is shown in Figure 2A.

At the start of the tracings in Figure 2B, the heart is in diastole; the aortic valves are closed, and aortic pressure exceeds left ventricular pressure. At the moment the tracings start, the pulse to close the aortic occluder has been given, but closure is effected after a mechanical delay of about 60 msec. The moment of actual closure can be seen from the pressure oscillations in the tracing of aortic pressure (moment T1). Until then, the valve in device A remained closed. Hence, flow is zero per definition. This initial flow level is used as the zero value during the analysis. Then, about 20 msec later, the valve in device A is opened, while the heart is still in diastole (moment T2). Since the blood in the proximal aorta is under pressure, blood is expelled through device A, a positive flow is measured, and aortic pressure falls (emptying of proximal aortic windkessel). When systole starts, left ventricular pressure rises, the aortic valves open, and the heart ejects into the artificial load. Shortly after the onset of the next systole, the valve in device A is closed again, and the aortic occluder (B) is opened, reestablishing the natural load conditions to the heart (not shown in Fig. 2B).

Calculations

Mean pressures were obtained by integration of the respective signals over the heart period, and dividing by this period. However, in the experiments of type B, it is not correct to integrate the measured flow signal over the whole cardiac cycle due to (partial) changes in the blood volume stored in the proximal aorta. This amount of blood stored is assumed to depend only on pressure in the ascending aorta. Therefore, the integration period was taken between isobaric points, starting at the onset of pressure rise (i.e., between moments I1 and I2, Fig. 2B). Following this procedure, it is implicit that no ejection should occur after moment I2. When the decays of flow in the phases marked 1 and 2 (Fig. 2B) are identical, no ejection flow is present, since the same windkessel discharges. The differences in the decays were small. The volume corresponding to area 2 was no larger than 15%

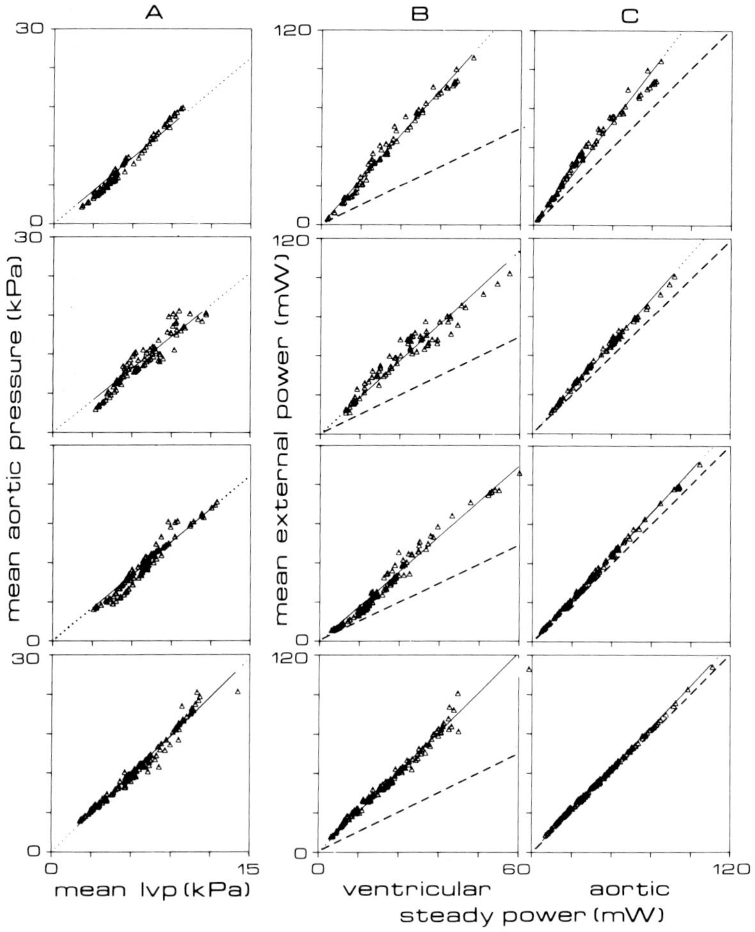

FIGURE 3. *Relationships between mean aortic pressure and mean left ventricular pressure (panels A), between mean external power and left ventricular steady power (panels B), and between mean external power and aortic steady power (panels C) in four cats. All data were fitted with straight lines through the origin. The dashed lines in panels B and C are lines of identity, and the differences between the data and these lines are equal to oscillatory power. Ventricular oscillatory power is a large part of mean external power; aortic oscillatory power is a small fraction. See Table 1 for details.*

of stroke volume in any experiment. All integrations were carried out numerically, using Simpson's rule.

Left ventricular end-diastolic pressure (LVEDP) was determined at 20 msec before the onset of rise of the dP/dt curve. Left ventricular dP/dt was determined by differencing the digitized tracing of the left ventricular pressure curve.

Pump function graphs were fitted (Marquardt, 1963) with a parabolic function (Eq. A1). $\overline{P}_{max}$ and $\overline{F}_{max}$ are the intercepts of the graph with the pressure and flow axis. The optimum of mean left ventricular power (Eq. A9) is found when flow is equal to $\overline{F}_{max}/\sqrt{3}$.

Results

Pressure and Power Experiments

Figure 3A shows mean aortic pressure in four cats, plotted as a function of mean left ventricular pressure for a wide range of values (mean P_{lv} from 15 to 100 mm Hg). The data are fitted (Marquardt, 1963) with a straight line through the origin. Numbers of data points, coefficients of correlation, and regression coefficients are given in Table 1. The observed proportionality (constant a) makes it possible to couple the pump function graph and the systemic arterial pressure-flow relation. Peripheral resistance can now be calculated (Eq. A12) for any point on the pump function graph.

The relations between mean external power and steady ventricular power, and between mean external power and steady aortic power (for definitions see Appendix, Eqs. A4, A5, and A6) are shown in Figure 3, B and C. Again, proportional relationships are found between the steady powers and mean external power. From Table 1, it can be seen that a reliable description of the data in Figure 3 is given by a single coefficient characterizing each experiment. From the slopes of the relationship between mean external power and aortic steady power (Fig. 3C), it can be seen that aortic oscillatory power (i.e.,

TABLE 1
Proportionality Constants

Cat	n	a = $\overline{P}_{ao}/\overline{P}_{lv}$	r	b = $\overline{W}_{ext}/(\overline{P}_{lv}\cdot\overline{F})$	r	c = $\overline{W}_{ext}/(\overline{P}_{ao}\cdot\overline{F})$	r
1	74	1.70	0.98	2.32	0.99	1.33	0.98
2	73	1.63	0.95	1.88	0.96	1.16	0.99
3	96	1.68	0.97	1.79	0.99	1.07	0.99
4	123	1.96	0.99	2.02	0.99	1.06	0.99

n = number of data points; r = correlation coefficient; a, b, and c = proportionality constants (c = b/a). $\overline{P}_{lv}$ and $\overline{P}_{ao}$ = mean left ventricular and mean aortic pressures; $\overline{W}$ = mean flow; $\overline{W}_{ext}$ = mean external power.

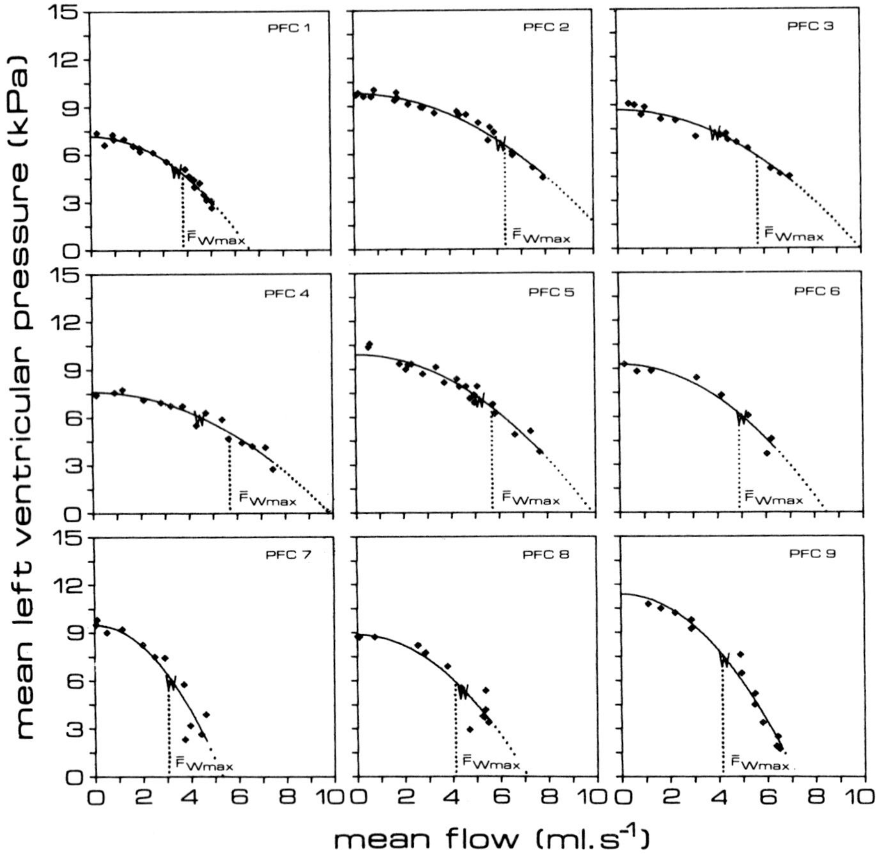

FIGURE 4. *Pump function graphs from nine experiments on open thorax cats. These graphs were all determined with the hearts beating at their natural rate and filling. The working point in each graph is indicated by W; the mean flow value for which external power transfer by the heart would be optimal ($\bar{F}_{Wmax}$; c.f. Fig. 5) is indicated by the dotted lines.*

the difference between the line of identity and the line through the data points) is small. In our experiments, aortic oscillatory power amounted to 13% (average value) of mean external power.

The finding that mean external power is proportional to left ventricular steady power makes it possible to obtain mean external power from the pump function graph. Even without knowing the value of the proportionality factor, we can locate the point of optimum external power from the pump function graph.

In summary, we now have the tools to determine, from the pump function graph, the point of optimum external power, the working point, and peripheral and apparent source resistances.

TABLE 2
Control Pump Function Graphs

Exp	*n*	*r*	2a	Rp:Rs at WP	W_{lvst} at WP
PFC1	20	0.99	3.68	4.14	99.8%
PFC2	24	0.98	3.82	3.94	100.0%
PFC3	15	0.98	3.54	8.54	89.1%
PFC4	15	0.97	3.36	6.18	94.5%
PFC5	21	0.97	3.62	4.46	99.3%
PFC6	8	0.98	3.06	2.70	99.7%
PFC7	12	0.93	3.38	2.78	99.3%
PFC8	13	0.94	2.48	3.38	98.4%
PFC9	15	0.99	3.74	3.78	100.0%
Mean			3.41	4.43	97.8
SD			0.42	1.85	3.7

n = number of data points; *r* = correlation coefficient; a = ratio of mean aortic and mean left ventricular pressure; Rp = peripheral resistance; Rs = source resistance; W_{lvst} = left ventricular steady power, indicated as a percentage of its maximum. WP = working point.

Experiments Relating Heart and Arterial System

Control

Figure 4 shows pump function graphs obtained from experiments in nine cats. The hearts of these cats were allowed to pump at their own rates. Apart from the anesthetic agent, no drugs or fluids were administered. The data are fitted with the parabola of equation A1.

Number of data points, correlation coefficients, and intercept values are shown in Table 2. Coefficients of variation of heart rate, left ventricular dP/dt, and LVEDP in these experiments were 0.65%, 2.52%, and 7.94%, respectively (average values), reflecting the stability of the preparation during the determination of the pump function graphs.

From the pump function graph, left ventricular steady power can be derived as a function of mean flow (Eq. A7). An example of the "fit" of this derived curve to the actual left ventricular steady power data is given in Figure 5. Optimal left ventricular steady power and the mean flow value for which it oc-

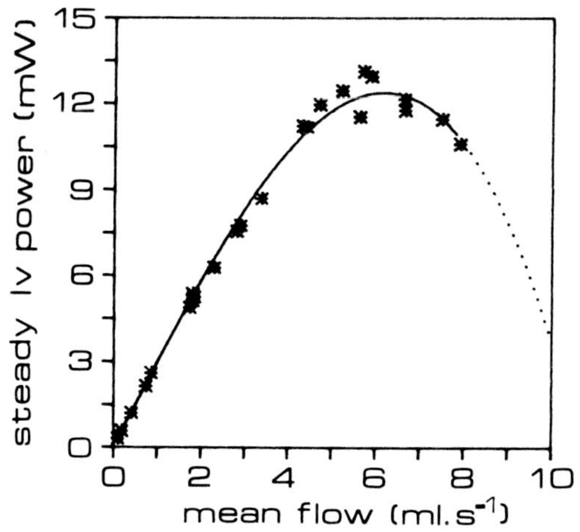

FIGURE 5. *Left ventricular steady power as a function of mean flow. The curve was derived from the equation of the pump function graph, using the same values of $\bar{P}_{max}$ and $\bar{F}_{max}$. The mean flow value for which the optimum value of steady power is found ($\bar{F}_{Wmax}$) corresponds to the position of the dotted lines in Figure 4. (Data from experiment PFC2.)*

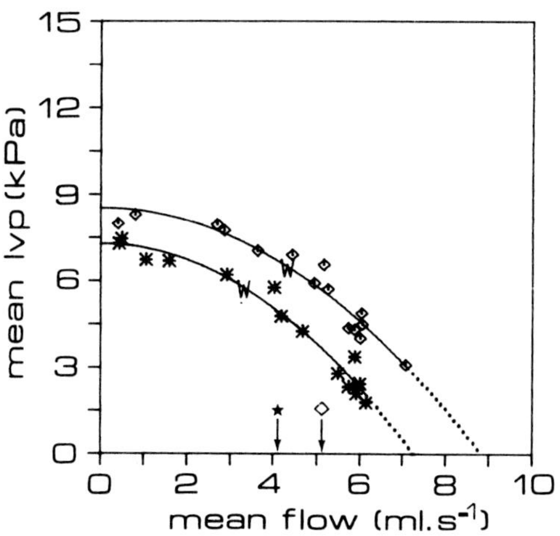

FIGURE 6. *Example of an experiment (HR3) where two pump function graphs were determined in the same cat at two different heart rates imposed by atrial pacing. Working point (W) and mean flow value where external power is optimal ($\bar{F}_{Wmax}$) are indicated. ◇: HR = 180 beats/min; *: HR = 200 beats/min.*

curred were calculated according to Equations A8 and A9. This flow value ($\bar{F}_{Wmax}$) is indicated in each pump function graph; the working point is indicated by W (Fig. 4). In all nine experiments, the ratio between mean aortic pressure and mean left ventricular pressure was determined from beats recorded when the animal's own periphery loaded the heart. The Rp:Rs ratio in the point of optimal mean external power can be obtained (see Appendix), and is found to be equal to twice the proportionality constant (a) between mean aortic pressure and mean left ventricular pressure:

$$Rp:Rs = 2a \qquad (\bar{F} = \bar{F}_{Wmax}) \qquad (A14)$$

Rp:Rs ratios were calculated at the working point, and at the power optimum of each experiment. Table 2 shows the individual ratios and the mean and standard deviations at working points and power optima. Rp:Rs ratios at the working point could not be shown to differ significantly from those at the point of optimal external power (paired *t*-test, $P > 0.10$). When power at the working point is expressed as a percentage of optimal power, an average value of 97.8% is found. Individual percentages are shown in Table 2 as well.

Interventions

Changes in Heart Rate. In eight cats, experimental runs to determine the pump function graph were carried out at two different heart rates. Of these two, the one with the lower heart rate was regarded as control. Figure 6 shows an example of such an experiment.

In Table 3, the relative changes in heart rate, $\bar{P}_{max}$, and $\bar{F}_{max}$ are given for each experiment. It can be seen that the relative changes in $\bar{P}_{max}$ and $\bar{F}_{max}$ are about equal, indicating a parallel shift of the pump function graph. Also, the sign of the changes is negative, indicating an inward shift of the graph due to pacing at increased frequency. In experiments on the isolated cat heart, it was found that, for constant filling, an increase of heart rate causes the graph to shift outward (Elzinga and Westerhof, 1980); an outward shift was also found for increased filling at constant heart rate (Elzinga and Westerhof, 1978). In our experiments, an increase in heart rate resulted in a reduction of left ventricular end-diastolic pressure (LVEDP). (The small values of LVEDP led to large changes percentage-wise. The actual control values were 0.76, 0.94, 0.97, 0.92, 0.98, 1.05, and 0.56 kPa, respectively.) Apparently, heart rate changes and changes in LVEDP counteract in these experiments.

The effect of atrial pacing on the arterial system is also shown in Table 3. Except in experiment 4, aortic pressure and flow at the working point were

TABLE 3
Relative Changes (%) in Cardiac Function and Setting of the Arterial System due to Pacing at Increased Heart Rate

	Heart				Arterial system		
Cat	$\bar{P}_{max}$	$\bar{F}_{max}$	HR	LVEDP	$\bar{F}$	$\bar{P}$	Rp
HR1	−17	−15	+14	−9	−4	−30	−17
HR2	−9	−2	+11	−17	−14	+1	+17
HR3	−15	−18	+11	−27	−23	−11	+15
HR4	−0	+2	+13	−14	+4	+2	−2
HR5	−12	−13	+13	−30	−22	−2	+25
HR6	−18	−16	+20	−24	−17	−18	−1
HR7	−20	−17	+13	−29	−14	−31	−20
HR8	+13	−12	+20	+170	−6	−8	−3
Mean	−10	−11	+14		−12	−12	+2
SD	11	7	4		9	13	16

$\bar{P}_{max}$ and $\bar{F}_{max}$ = pressure and flow axis intercepts; HR = heart rate; LVEDP = left ventricular end-diastolic pressure; $\bar{F}$ = flow at working point; $\bar{P}$ = aortic pressure at working point; Rp = peripheral resistance.

TABLE 4
Heart Rate Experiments*

Cat	Lower heart rate Rp:Rs at WP	Rp:Rs at PO	W_{lvst} at WP	Increased heart rate Rp:Rs at WP	Rp:Rs at PO	W_{lvst} at WP
HR1	3.76	3.44	99.9	2.48	3.38	98.4
HR2	4.16	3.74	99.8	6.02	3.76	96.6
HR3	5.32	3.48	97.2	6.28	3.50	94.8
HR4	4.90	3.48	98.1	4.80	3.58	98.6
HR5	2.96	3.52	99.5	4.04	3.54	99.7
HR6	3.00	3.52	99.6	3.10	3.48	99.8
HR7	2.88	3.52	99.3	2.30	3.20	98.1
HR8	3.06	3.48	99.7	2.18	3.08	98.0
Mean	3.76	3.52	99.1	3.90	3.44	98.0
SD	0.95	0.09	1.0	1.65	0.22	1.6

* Rp:Rs ratios are at the working points (WP) and at the points of optimal external power (PO). Left ventricular steady power (W_{lvst}) is indicated as a percentage of its maximum.

reduced. Statistical analysis could not demonstrate a significant change in peripheral resistance (*t*-test, $P > 0.20$). These findings agree with the parallel inward shift of the pump function graph in all experiments; in experiment 4, where aortic pressure and flow remained practically unchanged, the pump function graph did not shift either.

Table 4 shows the individual ratios of peripheral resistance and apparent source resistance, both at the working point and at the power optimum. Neither under control conditions nor during increased heart rate could statistically significant differences be demonstrated between the ratios of peripheral and apparent source resistances at the working point and at the point of optimal external power ($P > 0.20$).

Halothane. In a series of five experiments, pump function graphs were determined both with and without halothane. This drug is known to depress

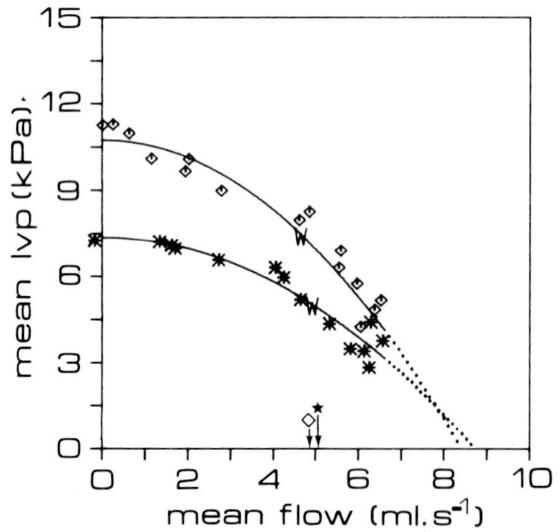

FIGURE 7. *Pump function graphs both before and after addition of halothane to the ventilatory gas mixture in the same cat (experiment HAL1). Heart rate was kept constant by right atrial pacing. Working points, etc., as in Figure 6. ◇: control; *: halothane.*

TABLE 5
Relative Changes (%) in Cardiac Function and Setting of the Arterial System due to Halothane

Cat	Heart $\overline{P}_{max}$	$\overline{F}_{max}$	Arterial system $\overline{F}$	$\overline{P}$	Rp
HAL1	−31	+4	+6	−34	−27
HAL2	−36	−7	−11	−27	−18
HAL3	−32	0	−3	−27	−24
HAL4	−42	−1	−4	−40	−37
HAL5	−34	0	−9	−25	−17
Mean	−35	−1	−4	−31	−17
SD	4	4	7	6	8

$\overline{P}_{max}$ and $\overline{F}_{max}$: pressure and flow axis intercepts; $\overline{F}$ = flow at working point; $\overline{P}$ = aortic pressure at working point; Rp = peripheral resistance.

blood pressure both by its negative inotropic and chronotropic effects on the heart and by reducing peripheral resistance. Heart rate was kept constant by pacing during both runs. After determination of the pump function graph during control, halothane (2 vol%) was added to the ventilatory gas mixture. The animals were allowed to stabilize for approximately 20 minutes before a new series of artificial loads was applied to the heart.

Figure 7 shows an example of an experiment from this series. Relative changes of $\overline{P}_{max}$ and $\overline{F}_{max}$ due to halothane are given in Table 5. It appears that the flow axis intercept, $\overline{F}_{max}$, does not change after halothane (paired *t*-test, $P > 0.20$). However, the pressure axis intercept, $\overline{P}_{max}$, is affected markedly (paired *t*-test, $P < 0.001$): on the average, $\overline{P}_{max}$ is reduced by more than 30%. This effect on the pump function graph can be described as an anti-clockwise rotation around the flow axis intercept. LVEDP did not change after halothane intervention (paired *t*-test, $P > 0.20$).

The data describing the effect of halothane on the arterial system are also given in Table 5. Mean flow at the working point was relatively little affected (average reduction: 4%), whereas aortic pressure was reduced in all cases (average reduction: 31%). In all experiments, peripheral resistance was reduced as well (17–37%).

The Rp:Rs ratios at the working point and at the power optimum were determined both before and during halothane. These values and the percentage of optimal steady power at the working point are given in Table 6. Statistical analysis (paired *t*-test) shows that the working point and the power optimum coincide. This holds true both with ($P > 0.10$) and without ($P > 0.20$) halothane.

Discussion

We have demonstrated in this study that the left heart of the anesthetized open thorax cat pumps at optimal external power output. This holds both under control conditions and after changes in heart rate and inotropic state. We found that pumping at

TABLE 6
Halothane Experiments*

	Without halothane			Halothane		
Cat	Rp:Rs at WP	Rp:Rs at PO	W_{lvst} (%)	Rp:Rs at WP	Rp:Rs at PO	W_{lvst} (%)
HAL1	3.76	3.44	99.9	3.50	3.40	100.0
HAL2	2.82	3.16	99.8	3.52	3.48	100.0
HAL3	3.64	3.26	99.8	4.16	3.36	99.3
HAL4	3.58	2.94	99.4	3.94	2.96	98.7
HAL5	2.12	3.09	97.8	2.96	3.06	100.0
Mean	3.18	3.18	99.3	3.62	3.25	99.6
SD	0.70	0.19	0.9	0.46	0.23	0.6

* Rp:Rs ratios are at the working points (WP) and at the points of optimal external power (PO). Left ventricular steady power (W_{lvst}) is indicated as a percentage of its maximum.

optimal power output implies that peripheral and apparent source resistance are related, such that their ratio equals twice the ratio of mean aortic and mean left ventricular pressure (Eq. A14).

We were able to obtain these results from the pump function graph alone, due to the quantitative relationships we found to exist between mean aortic and mean left ventricular pressures and between mean external power and left ventricular steady power (Fig. 3). To a good approximation, both relationships appear to be proportional. The proportionality is not essential for our approach, since any unique relationship would enable us to relate peripheral and source resistances, and to indicate the power maximum on the pump function graph. The proportionality, however, simplifies the calculations considerably.

In two of the control animals (PFC3 and PFC4), the ratio of peripheral resistance and apparent source resistance at the working point is found to be large. This is due to the fact that the ratio Rp:Rs changes nonlinearly with flow (see Eq. A13). When the working point is located to the left of the power optimum, the ratio varies more than when it is located to the right. In Table 2, Rp:Rs ratios deviate more from 2a for smaller flows, than for larger flows. Although not statistically significant, the working point is more often found to the left of the optimum power than to the right. When the working point is located to the left of the power optimum, the heart behaves as a pressure source, i.e., pressure changes little for changes in flow. Such a source would have the possibility of "flow reserve."

Piene and Sund (1979) showed, for a simple analog model, that the ratio $\overline{P}_{lv}:\overline{P}_{ao}$ would approximate the ratio of cardiac cycle time and ejection time if the compliance of the load approached infinity. Using an analog in which the load consists of a three-element windkessel, which is a more accurate representation of the arterial system (Westerhof et al., 1971), we were able to calculate the ratio $\overline{P}_{ao}:\overline{P}_{lv}$ as a function of peripheral resistance (Rp) and arterial compliance (C). In this model, we found a constant ratio $\overline{P}_{ao}:\overline{P}_{lv}$ equal to about 0.75 × T/Te (T and Te are cycle time and ejection time, respectively), for a wide range of resistance values, provided that the RpC time of the windkessel amounted to more than 300 msec for heart rates from 2 to 4 Hz (the range in which the cat heart operates). In the pressure and power experiments (A), the RpC time of the arterial system was estimated from the diastolic decay of the aortic pressure curve and was found to be between 900 and 1200 msec. Moreover, replotting mean aortic pressure as a function of mean left ventricular pressure times the ratio T/Te yielded almost straight lines through the origins ($r > 0.99$), with slopes of 0.72, 0.74, 0.74, and 0.80, respectively.

With respect to the proportional relationship between mean aortic and mean left ventricular pressures, it is of interest to note that Sagawa (1967) suggested that one could characterize ventricular pump function by a graph relating mean aortic pressure and cardiac output. In experiments on isolated cat hearts, where compliance and resistance of the loading system were changed independently (Elzinga and Westerhof, 1973), proportional relationships between mean aortic and mean left ventricular pressures can be demonstrated as long as compliance does not fall below half of the control value. Therefore, for smaller compliance values, ventricular pump function can be described only by relating mean left ventricular pressure and output. Although, by itself, Sagawa's concept is limited, his approach is useful in intact animals in view of the results presented here.

Our finding that, under normal conditions, the heart operates at optimal external power is in agreement with that of Wilcken et al. (1964), who showed that acute changes of the load resulted in a diminution of external work in the dog.

A feedback system responsible for such an optimization should operate unambiguously. However, detection of external power is ambiguous, since the same value of external power is found for two different pressures and flows. Moreover, power receptors are not known to exist.

Several authors (O'Rourke, 1965; Kenner and Estelberger, 1976; Yamashiro et al., 1978; Milnor, 1979) proposed that minimization of oscillatory power is a criterion governing the interaction between heart and arterial system. We found oscillatory power in the systemic circulation to be only about 13% of mean external power, which is in agreement with the 10% mentioned by McDonald (1974). From the standpoint of overall cardiac energy turnover, considering that the heart is about 25% efficient (Elzinga and Westerhof 1980), minimization of oscillatory power (13% of 25% energy turnover) seems hardly important.

Wilcken et al. (1964) reported that, if the intraaortic balloon they used to increase the load to the heart was kept inflated for 30 seconds and then released, external power always increased. This indicates that, during those 30 seconds, the hearts were not working at their power optimum. This could mean that the mechanism responsible to achieve optimal power output needs more than half a minute. Therefore, mechanisms other than neural may be involved in this interaction. The fact that, in our experiments, the hearts could be demonstrated to operate at optimal external power transfer during halothane indicates that the depth of narcosis does not disturb the control mechanism. This may also point toward a nonneural mechanism.

What mechanisms may lead to a setting of the cardiovascular system so that external power is optimal? In most mammals, blood pressure is about the same. On the other hand, the tissues require a certain blood flow. Both requirements are satisfied at a finite external power value (Stein and Sabbah, 1976; Schultz et al., 1980; Elzinga, 1983). For a given setting of the arterial system, this can be achieved by an infinite number of settings of the heart, but there is only one setting such that external power is optimal for that heart. This is illustrated in Figure 8, where three pump function graphs are shown, all delivering equal pressure, equal flow, and equal external power. Without assuming other criteria, it is not clear why the heart chooses to pump at its power optimum. Such a criterion might be minimization of the rate of energy turnover of the heart.

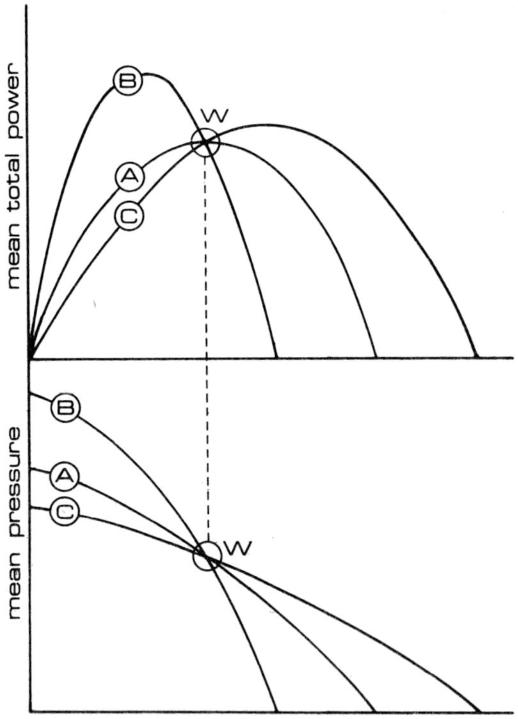

FIGURE 8. *Schematical drawing of three different pump function graphs. These hearts deliver equal pressure, equal flow, and equal external power at the working point (W). Only the heart characterized by curve A pumps at its power optimum.*

Finally, one may raise the question whether the observation that ventricle and arterial systems work together to keep power output optimal, can be regarded as a matching principle. The word "matching" suggests here that certain properties of ventricle and arterial system are closely connected and change together in order to achieve a common goal. Within this context, optimization of power output may be regarded as the matching principle for the left ventricle and the systemic circulation.

Appendix

Pump function graphs were fitted (Marquardt, 1963) through the obtained pressure and flow data, using a parabolic function of the form:

$$\overline{P}_{lv} = \overline{P}_{max}\cdot(1 - \overline{F}^2/\overline{F}^2_{max}), \quad \text{(A1)}$$

where $\overline{P}_{lv}$ is mean left ventricular pressure, $\overline{F}$ is mean flow, and $\overline{P}_{max}$ and $\overline{F}_{max}$ are the pressure axis and flow axis intercepts of the pump function graph.

Apparent source resistance (Rs), is a function of mean flow. We can derive Rs from the pump function graph:

$$Rs = (\overline{P}_{max} - \overline{P}_{lv})/\overline{F} = \overline{F}\cdot\overline{P}_{max}/\overline{F}^2_{max}. \quad \text{(A2)}$$

Peripheral resistance (Rp) is calculated from mean aortic pressure (P_{ao}) and mean flow data in the control beats as:

$$Rp(\overline{F}) = \overline{P}_{ao}/\overline{F}. \quad \text{(A3)}$$

Mean external power ($\overline{W}_{ext}$) is defined (McDonald, 1974) as:

$$\overline{W}_{ext} = \frac{1}{T}\cdot\int_0^T P(t)\cdot F(t)\,dt, \quad \text{(A4)}$$

and can be calculated, either from aortic or from left ventricular pressure, leading to essentially the same result. The heart period is T. Steady power is calculated from mean values of pressure and flow.

Aortic steady power (W_{aost}) is defined as:

$$W_{aost} = \overline{P}_{ao}\cdot\overline{F}. \quad \text{(A5)}$$

Left ventricular steady power (W_{lvst}), is:

$$W_{lvst} = \overline{P}_{lv}\cdot\overline{F}, \quad \text{(A6)}$$

and can be obtained directly from the pump function graph as a function of mean flow (Eqs. A1 and A6):

$$W_{lvst}(\overline{F}) = \overline{P}_{max}\cdot(\overline{F} - \overline{F}^3/\overline{F}^2_{max}). \quad \text{(A7)}$$

Maximal left ventricular steady power is found when the derivative of Equation A7 with respect to mean flow is zero:

$$d[W_{lvst}(\overline{F})]/d\overline{F} = \overline{P}_{max}\cdot(1 - 3\overline{F}^2/\overline{F}^2_{max}) = 0 \quad \text{(A8)}$$

This optimum is (reached for flow $F_{W_{max}}$:

$$\overline{F}_{W_{max}} = \overline{F}_{max}/\sqrt{3}. \quad \text{(A9)}$$

Finally, we define oscillatory powers (W_{aos} and W_{lvos}) as the differences between mean external power and steady powers:

$$W \quad = \overline{W} \quad - W_{aost} \qquad (A10)$$

and

$$W_{lvos} = \overline{W}_{ext} - W_{lvst}. \qquad (A11)$$

It will be clear that aortic oscillatory power is much smaller than ventricular oscillatory power, whereas ventricular steady power is much smaller than aortic steady power.

When mean left ventricular and mean aortic pressures can be assumed to be proportional, as shown in the series of experiments called A, we can write:

$$Rp = a \cdot \overline{P}_{lv}/\overline{F}. \qquad (A12)$$

From Equations A1, A2, and A12, we can calculate the ratio of peripheral resistance and apparent source resistance:

$$Rp{:}Rs = a \cdot (\overline{F}^2_{max}/\overline{F}^2 - 1), \qquad (A13)$$

so that, at optimal external power (Eq. A9),

$$Rp{:}Rs = 2a. \qquad (A14)$$

Part of this work has been presented at the FASEB Meeting, Chicago, 1983.

Address for reprints: Prof. Dr. G. Elzinga, Laboratory for Physiology, Free University, Van der Boechorststraat 7, 1081 BT Amsterdam.

Received March 6, 1984; accepted for publication October 25, 1984.

References

Dijkema FK, Elzinga G (1973) Integrator for aortic and pulmonary artery flow signals, with automatic zero adjustment and beat-to-beat flow computation. Cardiovasc Res **7:** 572–576

Elzinga G (1983) Cardiac oxygen consumption and the production of heat and work. *In* Cardiac Metabolism, edited by AJ Drake-Holland, MIM Noble. New York, John Wiley, pp 173–194

Elzinga G, Westerhof N (1973) Pressure and flow generated by the left ventricle against different impedances. Circ Res **32:** 178–186

Elzinga G, Westerhof N (1978) The effect of an increase in inotropic state and end-diastolic volume on the pumping ability of the feline left heart. Circ Res **42:** 620–628

Elzinga G, Westerhof N (1979) How to quantify pump function of the heart. Circ Res **44:** 303–308

Elzinga G, Westerhof N (1980) Pump function of the feline left heart changes with heart rate and its bearing on the energy balance. Cardiovasc Res **14:** 81–92

Fink BR, Schoolman A (1963) Arterial blood acid-base balance in unrestrained waking cats. Proc Soc Exp Biol Med **112:** 328–330

Kenner T, Estelberger W (1976) Zur Frage der optimalen Abstimmung der Herzkontraktion an die Eigenschaften des Arteriensystems. Verh Dtsch Ges Kreislaufforsch **42:** 132–135

Marquardt DW (1963) An algorithm for least squares estimation of non-linear parameters. J Soc Ind Appl Math **11:** 431–441

McDonald DA (1974) Blood Flow in Arteries. London, Arnold, pp 384–388

Milnor WR (1979) Aortic wavelength as a determinant of the relation between heart rate and body size in mammals. Am J Physiol **237:** R3–R6

O'Rourke MF (1965) Pressure and flow in arteries. MD Thesis, University of Sidney, Australia

Piene H, Sund T (1979) Flow and power output of right ventricle facing load with variable input impedance. Am J Physiol **237:** H125–H130

Sagawa K (1967) Analysis of the CNS ischemic feedback regulations of the circulation. *In* Physical Basis of Circulatory Transport, edited by EB Reeve, AC Guyton. Philadelphia, Saunders, pp 141–149

Schultz DL, Tan LB, Lee G de J, Rajagopalan B, Cherry GW, Gundel WD, Schipperheyn JJ, Huisman P (1980) Pump function and its interaction with the systemic load. *In* Cardiac Dynamics, edited by J Baan, AC Arntzenius, EL Yellin. The Hague/Boston/London, Nijhoff, pp 231–247

Stein PD, Sabbah HN (1976) Rate of change of ventricular power: An indicator of ventricular performance during ejection. Am Heart J **91:** 219–227

Westerhof N, Elzinga G, Sipkema P (1971) An artificial system for pumping hearts. J Appl Physiol **31:** 776–781

Wilcken DEL, Charlier AA, Hoffman JIE, Guz A (1964) Effects of alterations in aortic impedance on the performance of the ventricles. Circ Res **14:** 283–293

Yamashiro SM, Daubenspeck JA, Bennett FM, Edlemann SK, Grodins FS (1978) Optimal control analysis of left ventricular ejection. *In* Cardiovascular System Dynamics, edited by J Baan, A Noordergraaf, J Raines. Cambridge, MIT Press, pp 427–431

INDEX TERMS: Matching • External power • (Apparent) source resistance • Peripheral resistance

Effect of Reperfusion Late in the Phase of Reversible Ischemic Injury

Changes in Cell Volume, Electrolytes, Metabolites, and Ultrastructure

Robert B. Jennings, Jutta Schaper, Mary L. Hill, Charles Steenbergen, Jr., and Keith A. Reimer

From the Department of Pathology, Duke University Medical Center, Durham, North Carolina, and the Max Planck Institut, Bad Nauheim, West Germany

SUMMARY. The acute effects of reperfusion on myocardium reversibly damaged by 15 minutes of severe ischemia in vivo, were studied. Changes in the adenine nucleotide pool, cell volume regulation, myocardial calcium, and ultrastructure were studied at the end of 15 minutes of ischemia and after 0.5, 3.0, and 20 minutes of reflow. Before reperfusion, adenosine triphosphate and the adenylate pool decreased by 63% and 44% of control, respectively, and the adenylate charge was reduced to 0.65. After 3 minutes of reperfusion, the adenylate charge was restored to control by the rephosphorylation of adenosine mono- and diphosphate, but adenosine triphosphate was still reduced by 45%. Mild tissue edema was detected after 0.5 minute of reflow and persisted throughout 20 minutes of reperfusion. The increased tissue water was accompanied by a slight increase in sodium and a marked increase in tissue potassium. Although massive calcium accumulation develops when irreversibly injured tissue is reperfused, no calcium overload was detected during early reperfusion of reversibly injured myocytes. Reperfusion for 3 minutes exaggerated the mitochondrial swelling induced by 15 minutes of ischemia but after 20 minutes of reperfusion, myocardial ultrastructure was essentially normal except for rare swollen, or disrupted, mitochondria. Thus, the cellular abnormalities associated with brief periods of ischemia persist for variable periods of time after reperfusion of reversibly injured myocytes. First: although adenine nucleotide repletion occurs very slowly, the adenylate charge was restored after 3 minutes, indicating rapid resumption of mitochondrial adenosine triphosphate production. Second: calcium overload was not detected, but myocardial edema and increased potassium persisted throughout the 20 minutes of reperfusion. Third: the ultrastructural consequences of ischemia were nearly reversed after 20 minutes of reperfusion. **(*Circ Res 56: 262–278, 1985*)**

ALTHOUGH reperfusion prevents the death of ischemic, but still viable (reversibly injured) myocytes, recent evidence suggests that the ischemic cells do not immediately return to their preischemic state. For example, they exhibit persistent depression of the adenine nucleotide pool (ΣAd pool) (Reimer et al., 1981a; Swain et al., 1982a, 1982b; Kloner et al., 1983b), persistent contractile dysfunction (Heyndrickx et al., 1975; Weiner, et al., 1976; Hess et al., 1979) and perhaps residual ultrastructural monuments to the ischemic episode (Kloner et al., 1983a). With the advent of acute reperfusion therapy in man via lysis of arterial thrombi, better understanding of the response of reversibly injured myocytes to reperfusion is required. Moreover, changes exhibited during the early phase of reperfusion might provide clues to the nature of the molecular event or events which cause ischemic myocytes to die. In this study, we have investigated the effect of 0.5, 3.0, and 20 minutes of reperfusion on the adenine nucleotide pool, cell volume regulation, myocardial Ca^{++}, and ultrastructure in myocardium previously injured by 15 minutes of severe regional ischemia in the open-chest anesthetized dog.

The results show that, although adenine nucleotide repletion is slow, after 3 minutes of reperfusion, aerobic metabolism has resumed and has restored the adenylate charge, apparently by resynthesizing 0.6–0.8 μmol of ATP from the AMP and ADP of the damaged tissue. The reperfused tissue becomes edematous and gains both K^+ and Na^+. However, although Ca^{++} overload has been proposed as a potential cause of cell death or cellular dysfunction in ischemia (Shen and Jennings, 1972; Jennings et al., 1975; Farber and El-Mofty, 1975; Shine et al., 1978; Nayler et al., 1979; Bourdillon and Poole-Wilson, 1981; Farber, 1982; Jennings, 1984), an increase in myocardial calcium was not detected after any of the periods of reperfusion studied. Alterations in ultrastructure induced by ischemia essentially disappeared after 20, but not after 3 minutes of reperfusion. Thus, successful reperfusion salvages myocytes which almost have been killed by an episode of ischemia, but does not immediately restore the damaged myocytes to their control preischemic state. Metabolic, ionic, and ultrastructural defects persist in the damaged myocytes for variable periods of time.

Methods

Healthy mongrel dogs of either sex and weighing 30–40 pounds were used. Each dog was anesthetized with 30–40 mg/kg of sodium pentobarbital and was intubated and ventilated with room air on a Harvard model 607 respirator at a rate of 200 ml/kg per min. The respirator rate was adjusted, and supplemental oxygen was given to maintain arterial blood gases at physiological levels. Using a Gould model 2400 recorder, lead II of the electrocardiogram was monitored and peripheral blood pressure was recorded with a Statham model DB23 pressure transducer connected to a polypropylene catheter in the right femoral artery. A left thoracotomy was done, using aseptic techniques, and the circumflex artery was isolated beneath the left atrial appendage.

Twenty-seven dogs were subjected to 15 minutes of ischemia induced by occluding the circumflex artery with a silk snare. Twenty-six dogs survived the period of occlusion, and three of these were studied without reperfusion. Of the remaining 23 dogs, nine survived reperfusion without fibrillating. Of these, five were studied after 3 minutes, and four after 20 minutes of reperfusion. The remaining 14 dogs developed ventricular fibrillation (VF) upon reperfusion, so-called reflow VF. We attempted to defibrillate the first nine of these dogs, of which only one attempt was successful. These nine dogs have been excluded. No attempt was made to defibrillate the last five fibrillating hearts; these five hearts were excised very quickly with a cut across the base of the ventricles and were placed in ice-cold KCl within 8 seconds of the onset of VF. Each of these five dogs had developed VF between 20 and 30 seconds, and they have been combined to form an early reperfusion group. The same rapid excision technique was used in three dogs in the permanent ischemia group, in three of five dogs in the 3-minute group, and in two of four dogs in the 20-minute reflow group. In the remaining dogs, cardiac excision was slower (15–90 seconds).

The ultrastructural changes associated with permanent ischemia or ischemia with brief reperfusion were assessed in all of the hearts included in this experiment. Nonischemic control myocardium also was examined by electron microscopy in all hearts in this study. Previously unreported ultrastructural data from nine dogs subjected to 60 minutes, 24 hours, or 4 days of reperfusion also are included in this paper. The metabolite data from the latter experiments, the design of which was identical to the studies reported here, have been reported previously (Reimer et al., 1981a).

Areas which were severely ischemic, or which had been severely ischemic, were identified by injecting intravenously, the fluorescent dye thioflavine S (TS) (1.0 ml/kg of a freshly centrifuged 4% solution in normal saline), 10–15 seconds before excision of the heart (Jennings et al., 1978). In the reperfusion groups, the circumflex artery was reoccluded just prior to administration of the dye. Ten seconds after TS injection, each heart was excised quickly and was cooled rapidly with stirring in 750 ml of ice-cold (0°C) isotonic KCl. The atria and ventricles were opened widely after the first minute of cooling to assure rapid cooling of the endocardial region. After cooling to 10–15°C, the heart was removed from the cold KCl and placed under ultraviolet light to distinguish between non-ischemic or mildly ischemic (TS fluorescent) and severely or totally ischemic (non-fluorescent) areas of the anterior and posterior papillary (AP and PP) muscles, respectively. Only non-fluorescent areas of the posterior papillary muscle were included in ischemic samples; contamination of samples by non-ischemic or mildly ischemic tissue was thereby avoided. This sampling technique can be done quickly enough to permit accurate measurements of the adenine nucleotide pool, but does not preserve the creatine phosphate content of ischemic tissue (Jennings et al., 1978). In all samples, any attached endocardium or epicardium was removed.

Thioflavine S (TS) could not be used for sampling in dogs which developed VF; ischemic tissue in these dogs was obtained from the upper one-half (portion to which chordae tendinae are attached) of the PP muscle based on the distribution of ischemia observed in prior experiments using the thioflavine S technique. Nonischemic samples were obtained from the mid-portion of the AP muscle.

Adenine Nucleotides

Two myocardial slices from each papillary muscle were used for adenine nucleotide assays. Each was weighed quickly on a Cahn model DTL microbalance and transferred to 3.6% ice cold (0°) perchloric acid. The entire process of slicing and weighing the cold tissue took 30–60 seconds. The slices were homogenized with a Tri-R homogenizer and centrifuged. The supernatant was neutralized to pH 5.0 to 6.0 with K_2CO_3 and KOH, and was frozen. Later, the samples were centrifuged to remove $KClO_4$ and were assayed either by enzymatic methods or by high pressure liquid chromatography (HPLC). Enzymatic methods for measuring ATP, glucose-6-phosphate (G-6-P), creatine phosphate (CP), and lactate are those given in Jennings et al. (1978). Adenosine triphosphate (ATP), adenosine diphosphate (ADP), adenosine monophosphate (AMP), hypoxanthine (HX), xanthine (X), inosine (I), nicotinamide adenine dinucleotide (NAD), and adenosine (ADO) were measured by HPLC, by a modification of the methods of Anderson and Murphy (1976). HPLC was performed with a Waters model 6000A solvent delivery system, a model 680 gradient controller, a model U6K sample injector system, an 8-mm (i.d.) × 10 cm μ-Bondapak reverse phase C18 radial pak cartridge (10 μm) in a Z-module (Waters), and a model 440 absorbance detector set at a wavelength of 254 μm. The flow rate was 0.5 ml/min. In previous studies (Reimer et al., 1981a), an isocratic method using ammonium phosphate buffer (0.05 M, pH 6.0) was used; nucleosides, particularly adenosine, were eluted slowly and had broad peaks. To hasten the elution of adenosine and to sharpen peaks, the procedure was modified in this study by addition of methanol to the solvent. The extracts were chromatographed initially with a gradient controller to change the mobile phase from 100% ammonium phosphate buffer to 95% ammonium phosphate buffer and 5% methanol after 5 minutes. The gradient had a concave shape, with half of the change occurring in the last minute. ATP was eluted first, between 2 and 2.5 minutes, when there was virtually no methanol present. ADP was eluted shortly after ATP, followed by HX, X, AMP, I, NAD, and ADO. However, in many instances, the I and NAD peaks overlapped. Therefore, the chromatography procedure was refined further to separate I and NAD. The proportion of methanol was increased from 0% to 2% during the first 5 minutes with a concave gradient; the composition of the mobile phase was maintained at 2% methanol from 5 minutes to 12 minutes; and the proportion of methanol was increased from 2% to 8% between 12 and 15 minutes with a concave gradient. This modification resulted in good separation of

I and NAD and a sharp ADO peak at approximately 18 minutes. Where there was sufficient extract remaining after the enzymatic assays and the initial chromatography, repeat chromatography was performed to measure I. Levels of the nucleotides in the repeat chromatograms were indistinguishable from those found in the original chromatograms. A standard solution of each compound was prepared and the concentration was determined with a Gilford model 250 spectrophotometer by ultraviolet absorbance at the wavelength of the molar extinction coefficient. The concentrations of nucleotides, nucleosides, and bases in tissue samples were determined using a Waters data module to calculate peak areas. The data module was calibrated with the standard solutions, and the peak areas in tissue samples were converted to tissue contents using the ratio of concentration to peak area in the standard. Inosine contents were determined by direct measurement using the modified HPLC procedure and by calculation from the combined I and NAD peaks. Subtraction of the I + NAD peak area in nonischemic tissue from the corresponding peak area in ischemic samples from the same heart provided an estimate of the increase in I content in the ischemic tissue. This calculation is valid as long as NAD content is constant. In this and previous studies (Jennings et al., 1981), when NAD was measured separately from I, brief periods of ischemia with or without reperfusion had no effect on tissue NAD content. Tissue nucleotide, nucleoside, or base contents were expressed as μmol/g wet weight, and the total adenine nucleotide pool (ΣAd) was calculated as the sum of ATP, ADP, and AMP content. Each extract was chromatographed one to three times, and mean values for each sample were calculated.

Total Tissue Water and Electrolytes

Total tissue water (TTW) was measured in four to six additional slices of each papillary muscle and subjacent tissue. These slices were weighed and then dried overnight at 105°C. The dry slices were reweighed and the TTW was expressed as ml H_2O/100 g dry tissue.

Electrolytes were extracted from each of two dried slices in 5 ml of 0.75 N HNO_3, according to techniques described previously (Jennings et al., 1978). Briefly, Mg^{++}, Na^+, and K^+ were determined in a dilution containing 5000 ppm of RbCl. Ca^{++} was determined in a one to ten dilution containing 10,000 ppm La^{+++}. These dilutions were done in ion-free glassware, verified prior to use to have no detectable sodium. All four electrolytes were measured with an IL 351 atomic absorption spectrophotometer interfaced with a Tektronix model 31 computer calculator. Standard curves were prepared for all four ions, and two standards and two reagent blanks were analyzed with every series of unknowns. Electrolyte contents were expressed as mmol/100 g dry tissue.

Estimation of Calcium and Plasma Content of Normal and Damaged Myocardium with ^{45}Ca

In some dogs, approximately 5.0 μCi of ^{125}I-labeled human serum albumin (RISA) (Mallinckrodt) was injected intra-arterially 50 minutes before coronary occlusion to estimate the content of plasma/g wet heart. This was done so that tissue calcium content could be corrected for possible changes in the vascular space of the damaged tissue which might be increased because of reactive hyperemia during reperfusion.

Twenty-five minutes after injection of RISA (and 25 minutes before coronary occlusion, 50–100 μCi of $^{45}CaCl_2$ was injected with 5.0 ml normal saline intra-arterially. Blood samples were taken at 5 and 1 minutes prior to occlusion and 5, 10, and 14 minutes after occlusion. In the 20-minute reflow group, additional blood samples were taken after 10 and 19 minutes of reperfusion. Serum samples were counted immediately for ^{125}I albumin and for ^{45}Ca according to the methods described below. (Virtually all of the plasma ^{45}Ca and ^{125}I activity was found in the serum.) A least square regression line was used to estimate exact plasma activity of RISA at the time the myocardium was sampled.

Following ischemia with or without reperfusion, the heart was excised as described above. After sampling for metabolite analysis, additional samples were weighed and were placed in a gamma counting tube to determine RISA activity or were dried to constant weight for water and electrolytes or ^{45}Ca assays.

The tissue and plasma RISA activity was counted in a model 5912 Packard multichannel gamma counter. Tissue samples weighing from 0.04–0.50 g were used and appropriate background corrections made. The amount of plasma trapped in the myocardium then was expressed in ml plasma/g wet weight.

Electrolyte or ^{45}Ca assays were done on samples of damaged and control myocardium weighing between 0.030 and 0.125 g. The samples were placed in thoroughly washed and rinsed (deionized water) scintillation vials (Scientific Products) and were dried to constant weight. The TTW was measured in 3–6 samples from nonischemic and damaged areas in each heart. The dried tissue for ^{45}Ca activity measurement was solubilized with 1.0 ml of Soluene 350 (Packard), and ^{45}Ca activity was counted in a Packard model 3255 liquid scintillation counter using data from an automatic external ^{226}Ra source to convert cpm to dpm. The ^{45}Ca activity in 1.0 ml of serum was determined using 0.1-ml aliquots of serum solubilized with 1.0 ml of soluene. The logarithmic curve of decreasing ^{45}Ca concentration was plotted, and the plasma ^{45}Ca activity at the time of coronary occlusion and at the termination of the experiment was estimated from this curve. The ^{45}Ca channel on the scintillation counter was set to minimize contamination from ^{125}I in the samples.

The ^{45}Ca activity in myocardium was referred to the plasma activity of ^{45}Ca/ml plasma. After 25 minutes, ^{45}Ca had fully equilibrated between the serum and myocardial pools, even though the activity of ^{45}Ca in both compartments declined slowly (Shen and Jennings, 1972b).

Tissue ^{45}Ca content was corrected for plasma trapped in the tissue, as follows. The plasma-free tissue content of ^{45}Ca activity per gram wet weight was calculated by subtracting plasma ^{45}Ca activity in the tissue from the total tissue ^{45}Ca activity. This calculation was done using the plasma content per gram of tissue measured with RISA in each sample and the known ^{45}Ca activity/ml of plasma at the time of sampling. Tissue ^{45}Ca activity then was normalized to plasma activity.

Ultrastructure

Thin slices of nonischemic AP and of severely ischemic or ischemic reperfused PP were processed for electron microscopic examination using techniques previously described (Jennings et al., 1978). Briefly, multiple cubes measuring 1 mm or less in diameter were cut under glutaraldehyde with a sharp razor blade and were transferred to 20–30 ml of 4% glutaraldehyde in 0.1 M cacodylate buffer. After 1–4 hours of fixation, the blocks were post-osmicated, dehydrated in a graded ethanol series, rinsed in propylene oxide, and embedded in Epon 812. Thick sections from six or more blocks of control and damaged tissue were examined by light microscopy. Ultrathin sections were cut from at least three representative blocks of each slice of control and damaged tissue, were stained with uranyl acetate/lead citrate, and were examined in a Hitachi HS-8 electron microscope. At least three grids from each block were examined and the changes recorded. Representative areas were photographed.

Statistics

Tabulated results are reported as means ± SEM. For each experimental group, differences between nonischemic vs. ischemic or ischemic/reperfused samples within the same heart have been analyzed by Student's paired *t*-test. In addition, where indicated, differences between experimental groups were analyzed by one-way analysis of variance to determine whether the groups are significantly different, followed by individual comparisons using Student's paired or nonpaired *t*-test.

Results

All dogs reported in this paper developed evidence of regional ischemia within 20–30 seconds after the occlusion of the circumflex artery. These changes included cyanosis of the circumflex vascular region, mild to marked elevation of the S-T segment in lead II, and a mean decrease in systolic pressure of about 10%. Most dogs developed multiple premature ventricular contractions (PVC) beginning 12–13 minutes after occlusion which persisted with variable intensity through the 15th minute. Reperfusion was associated with disappearance of cyanosis and the appearance of a hyperemic blush.

The ischemic or reperfused tissue was grossly indistinguishable from control myocardium. However, following injection of thioflavine S 10–15 seconds before excision of the heart, the zone of severe ischemia was detected easily as dark nonfluorescent tissue when illuminated with ultraviolet light. (In the reperfused hearts, the circumflex artery was reoccluded during the thioflavine injection.) The nonfluorescence invariably was subendocardial and sometimes extended into the midmyocardium or was transmural. In about 20% of hearts, the tip of the AP and some of the subjacent free wall of the left ventricle also was severely ischemic. However, this ischemic tissue always was excluded from the AP samples used as nonischemic control tissue.

Metabolites and Adenylate Charge Late in the Reversible Phase of Severe Ischemia and after Brief Periods of Reperfusion

Fifteen minutes of severe ischemia caused marked depletion of the ATP and ΣAd pool (Tables 1 and 2). The individual ATP levels after 15 minutes of ischemia in 11 dogs reported earlier (Reimer et al., 1981a), are plotted in Figure 1 together with the results from the three dogs added in the present study. The ATP averaged 2.06 ± 0.166 μmol/g wet weight (range 1.16–3.26); the mean reduction in ATP in these 14 hearts was 63%.

Reperfusion for 3 or 20 minutes permitted repletion of ATP from ADP and AMP and the adenylate charge (AC) was restored to control levels (Table 2). The mean increase in ATP after 3 minutes of reperfusion was 0.8 μmol/g wet heart and was correlated with a decrease of 0.4 μmol/g of ADP and 0.5 μmol/g of AMP. After 20 minutes of reperfusion, the increase in ATP was slightly greater but the difference between 3 and 20 minutes of reperfusion was not statistically significant. In previous studies, fur-

TABLE 1
ATP and Lactate of Ischemic Tissue and of Ischemic Reperfused Tissue

Minutes of ischemia and of reperfusion	μmol/g wet wt			
	ATP		Lactate	
	AP	PP	AP	PP
15 + 0 (7)*	5.32 ± 0.22	1.95 ± 0.27[c]	9.22 ± 1.06	30.21 ± 1.89[c]
15 + 0.5 (5)	5.18 ± 0.30	1.78 ± 0.20[c]	8.64 ± 0.75	29.61 ± 2.60[c]
15 + 3 (5)	5.09 ± 0.24	2.75 ± 0.12[c]	7.30 ± 0.97	6.52 ± 1.39
15 + 20 (4)	5.40 ± 0.22	3.06 ± 0.25[c]	4.79 ± 0.42	5.19 ± 0.74

Metabolite levels were measured by enzymatic techniques. AP = nonischemic anterior papillary muscle; PP = ischemic myocardium or ischemic-reperfused myocardium from the posterior papillary muscle. The results are means ± SEM. Statistical comparisons between control and damaged tissue from the same hearts were made using a two-tailed paired *t*-test. *a*: $P < 0.05$; *b*: $P < 0.01$; *c*: $P < 0.001$ as compared with nonischemic values. One-way analysis of variance for the PP metabolites shows that the groups are significantly ($P < 0.005$) different and non-paired *t*-tests were used to compare the non-reperfused group to the groups with reperfusion and to compare groups with 3 vs. 20 minutes of reperfusion. The increase in ATP and decrease in lactate induced by 3 or 20 minutes of reperfusion was significant ($P < 0.001$) vs. the effects of 15 minutes of ischemia without reperfusion. There was no significant change in these metabolites between 3 and 20 minutes of reperfusion.

* Numbers in parentheses = number of dogs in each group.

TABLE 2

Adenine Nucleotides, Nucleosides, and Bases of Control, Ischemic, and Reperfused Tissue

Minutes of ischemia	Minutes of reperfusion	μmol/g wet wt									
		AC	ATP	ADP	AMP	ΣAd	ADO	I‡	HX	X	ΣNS
0* (20)†	0	0.84 ±0.01	4.92 ±0.14	1.49 ±0.05	0.30 ±0.03	6.71 ±0.15	0.038 ±0.012	0.072 ±0.037	0.053 ±0.011	0.021 ±0.015	0.18
15 (7)	0	0.65 ±0.03^{c}	1.87 ±0.25^{c}	1.20 ±0.08^{b}	0.67 ±0.08^{c}	3.73 ±0.31^{c}	0.37 ±0.06^{c}	2.36 ±0.19^{c}	0.28 ±0.03^{c}	0.13 ±0.02^{c}	3.14
15 (5)	0.5	0.71 ±0.03^{c}	1.75 ±0.17^{c}	1.05 ±0.06^{c}	0.37 ±0.06^{d}	3.16 ±0.13^{c}	0.27 ±0.04^{c}	1.96 ±0.31	0.35 ±0.05^{c}	0.18 ±0.03^{c}	2.76
15 (5)	3.0	0.85 ±0.01^{f}	2.58 ±0.19^{c}	0.80 ±0.12^{c,d}	0.16 ±0.05^{a,f}	3.55 ±0.35^{c}	0.046 ±0.016^{f}	0.82 ±0.24	0.20 ±0.06^{c}	0.056 ±0.011^{b,d}	1.12
15 (4)	20.0	0.86 ±0.01^{f}	2.85 ±0.26^{c,d}	0.76 ±0.06^{c,e}	0.16 ±0.03^{a,e}	3.76 ±0.35^{c}	ND	0.02 ±0.02	0.015 ±0.010^{f}	ND	0.04

Nonischemic control tissue was taken from the anterior papillary muscles, and ischemic or reperfused ischemic samples were obtained from the posterior papillary muscles in the same 21 hearts as in Table 1. The control samples from one heart were lost in processing. The control values were pooled because they were virtually indistinguishable. All results are means ± SEM. One-way analysis of variance demonstrated significant ($P < 0.005$) differences between the five experimental groups for each metabolite. Individual comparisons were performed by Student's non-paired *t*-test. *a*: $P < 0.05$, compared with control (nonischemic) values; *b*: $P < 0.01$, compared with control; *c*: $P < 0.001$, compared with control; *d*: $P < 0.05$, compared with 15 minutes of ischemia and no reflow (15 + 0) values; *e*: $P < 0.01$, compared with 15 + 0; *f*: $P < 0.001$, compared with 15 + 0. There is no significant difference in any of these parameters between 3 and 20 minutes of reperfusion. AC (adenylate charge) = (ATP + 1/2 ADP)/ΣAd; ΣAd = ATP + ADP + AMP; ADO = adenosine; I = inosine; HX = hypoxanthine; X = xanthine; ΣNS = ADO + I + HX + X; ND = none detectable.

* Control nonischemic.

† Numbers in parentheses = number of dogs in each group.

‡ I: In many of the initial chromatograms, there was overlap between I and NAD. As described in Methods, a slight modification in the HPLC procedure improved the separation. Where sufficient extract was available, I was remeasured using the modified procedure. This was possible in two 15 + 0 hearts, one 15 + 0.5 heart, one 15 + 3 heart, and three 15 + 20 hearts. Thus, seven control values were determined, and, in addition, there was previously reported data (Jennings et al., 1981) to compute I contents for the control and 15 + 0 conditions. These are presented in the table. For the other conditions, I values were calculated from the combined I and NAD peaks by subtracting the corresponding peak area measured in control samples from the same heart. Thus, these values are an estimate of the difference in inosine content between experimental and control tissue from the same heart, assuming that NAD content is constant. This assumption is warranted, since, in the hearts where NAD was measured, control and experimental tissue had the same amounts, which is in agreement with previous data (Jennings et al., 1981). Comparison of I values calculated from the combined I and NAD peaks and I values measured by modified HPLC procedure shows good agreement. In the 15 + 0 group, calculated I is 2.47 ± 0.15 and measured I is 2.36 ± 0.19; in the 15 + 0.5 group, measured I is 2.06; in the 15 + 3 group, measured I is 0.59; and in the 15 + 20 group, no I was detected in three samples.

ther restoration of the ATP that had been degraded to nucleosides and bases required at least 4 days (Reimer et al., 1981a). Adenine nucleosides and bases were reduced by 3 minutes and were negligible after 20 minutes of reperfusion (Table 2). Although the rate of adenine nucleotide repletion from nucleosides and bases is very slow, it is not possible to determine the rate of synthesis in the present acute studies because the period of reperfusion was too short.

Although the AC had recovered after 3 minutes of reperfusion, no significant change in the adenylate charge or in ATP of the damaged tissue was detected at 0.5 minute (Table 2). The reason for the apparent lack of ATP production during the first 30 seconds is not known. The return of the S-T segment toward control, loss of cyanosis, and the increase in TTW, and sodium in the damaged tissue (Table 3) is evidence that reperfusion had occurred but the failure to wash out lactate and nucleosides and bases is evidence that early subendocardial reperfusion was sluggish or inhomogeneous (Tables 1 and 2). Whether sluggish reperfusion and/or slow restoration of aerobic metabolism would have been observed in dogs which did not die of reflow VF is unknown. Although not statistically significant, the greater degree of adenine nucleotide depletion in the hearts that fibrillated may indicate either that the probability of reflow VF is greater when the degree of ischemia is greater or that VF accelerates adenine nucleotide breakdown.

NAD is a critical cofactor in glycolysis as well as

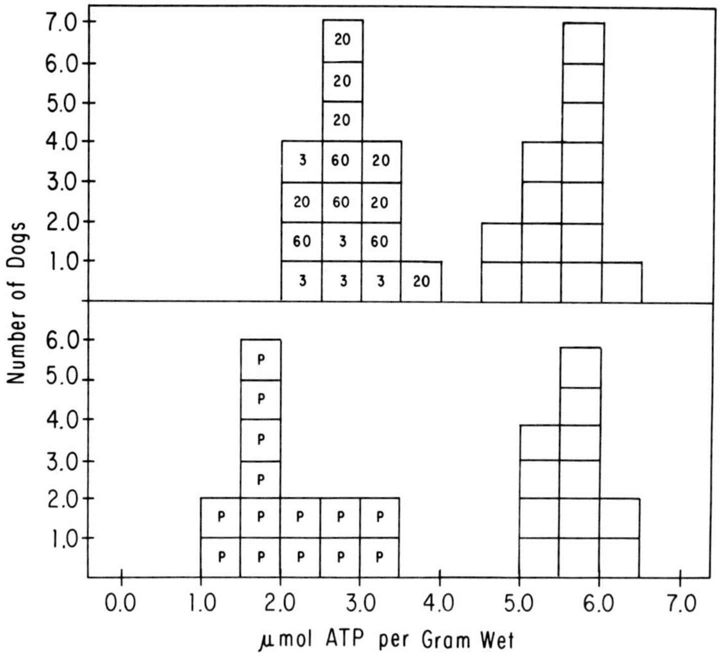

FIGURE 1. *The top panel shows the ATP of the posterior papillary muscle (PP) of individual dog hearts after 15 minutes of ischemia and 3, 20, or 60 minutes of reperfusion. Four of the 20-minute reperfusion group and all of the 60-minute reperfusion group were reported previously (Reimer et al., 1981a). The open squares represent the ATP of nonischemic anterior papillary muscle (AP) samples from the same hearts. The ATP of severely ischemic PP samples of 14 dogs at the end of 15 minutes of ischemia but no reperfusion (labeled P) are shown in the bottom half of the figure. This group includes three dogs which are part of the present study and 11 dogs studied previously by the same experimental protocol (Reimer et al., 1981a). In all samples, the ATP was measured enzymatically. The reperfused tissue, taken together, clearly contained more ATP than the permanently ischemic tissue. The median ATP content of the permanently ischemic samples was about 2.0 μmol/ATP per g wet, whereas none of the reperfused samples were below this value.*

in mitochondrial metabolism. This intermediate is known not to be broken down to a significant extent after as much as 90 minutes of total ischemia (Jennings et al., 1981). In those samples in the present study where NAD was measured separately from I, neither ischemia nor reperfusion altered myocardial NAD content.

Electrolyte Changes in Severely Ischemic Reversibly Injured Muscle with and without Reperfusion

Fifteen minutes of severe ischemia had no detectable effect on the TTW or ion levels of the myocardium (Table 3). Although the ions may be redistrib-

TABLE 3
Electrolytes and Water in Ischemic and Nonischemic Left Ventricle after Brief Episodes of Reperfusion

Minutes of ischemia and of reperfusion	ml/100 g dry				
	TTW	Na^+	K^+	Mg^{++}	Ca^{++}
0 + 0* (17)†	364.7 ± 3.0	14.47 ± 0.39	40.03 ± 0.60	4.69 ± 0.06	0.37 ± 0.02
15 + 0 (3)	369.0 ± 2.4	16.02 ± 0.37	38.18 ± 0.79	5.11 ± 0.20	0.42 ± 0.03
15 + 0.5 (5)	384.2 ± 5.0[b]	16.80 ± 0.43[b]	37.31 ± 0.73	4.65 ± 0.12	0.39 ± 0.05
15 + 3 (5)	400.7 ± 3.5[c]	17.53 ± 0.57[a]	42.06 ± 1.87	4.68 ± 0.09	0.40 ± 0.03
15 + 20 (4)	399.8 ± 13.0[a]	16.15 ± 0.99	43.68 ± 0.84[b]	4.20 ± 0.10	0.46 ± 0.02

The ischemic and nonischemic tissue used are posterior and anterior papillary muscles, respectively, trimmed free of endocardium. All values are means ± SEM. One-way analysis of variance shows that there are significant differences in total tissue water (TTW) ($P < 0.005$), Na^+ content ($P < 0.005$), and K^+ content ($P < 0.01$) among the experimental groups. The control left ventricle water and electrolyte values were pooled because there was no significant difference between any of the groups. The statistics, however, are paired two-tailed *t*-tests run against individual nonischemic left ventricular values of the individual heart in each group. *a:* $P < 0.05$; *b:* $P < 0.01$; *c:* $P < 0.001$. The means of the water and electrolytes were essentially identical after 3 vs. 20 minutes of reperfusion. Although the number of hearts used for electrolyte analysis in the 15 + 0 group in this study is small, the same results are obtained if previous data—some of which were published elsewhere (Reimer et al., 1981a)—are included. Mean values from 15 samples of myocardium subjected to 15 minutes of permanant ischemia are TTW 367 ± 2.90, Na^+ 15.46 ± 0.75, K^+ 39.15 ± 0.80, Mg^{++} 5.12 ± 0.07, and Ca^{++} 0.45 ± 0.02. These data are not substantially different from present results.

* Control nonischemic.

† Numbers in parentheses = number of dogs in each group.

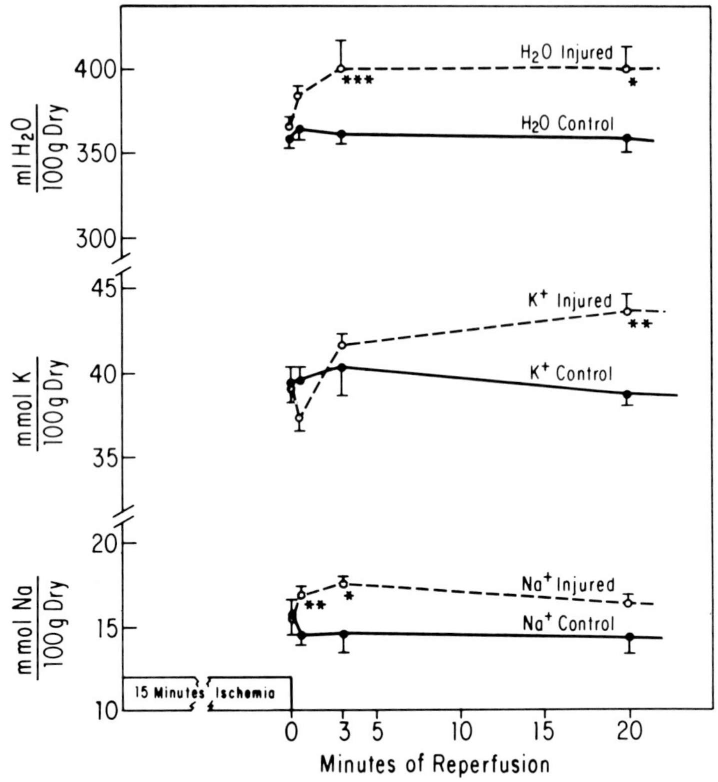

FIGURE 2. *The effect of various periods of reperfusion on TTW, Na^+, and K^+ in the damaged and control myocardium are plotted as a function of the period of reperfusion. As expected, because of the very low collateral flow in the PP, 15 minutes of ischemia produced no change in TTW, Na^+, or K^+ (Whalen et al., 1974). After reperfusion, both Na^+ and H_2O increased promptly and remained elevated. However, after 30 seconds of reperfusion, the K^+ of the damaged tissue was slightly lower than control (not significant). Thereafter, tissue K^+ rose to much higher levels than control. At 20 minutes, the injured tissue had restored its normal ultrastructure and adenylate charge but still showed a marked increase in K^+ and smaller increases in Na^+ and H_2O. In other studies (Reimer et al., 1981a), these changes were still present after 60 minutes but not after 1440 minutes of reperfusion.*

uted within the tissue (Hirche et al., 1979; Hill and Gettes, 1980), the data in Table 3 and Figure 2 shows that they neither leave nor enter the ischemic tissue during a brief episode of severe ischemia. We attribute this absence of shifts to the low collateral flow (Reimer and Jennings, 1979). After 20–30 seconds of reperfusion, both tissue H_2O and Na^+ increased. By the time 3 minutes of reperfusion had passed, this small change was maximal (Fig. 2) and was on the order of 9% for water and 13% for Na^+. K^+, on the other hand, was decreased after 20–30 seconds of reperfusion and thereafter increased by a mean of 5 mmol/100 g dry weight. In experiments reported previously (Reimer et al., 1981a), we found that the increase in K^+ persisted for 60 minutes but not for 24 hours of reperfusion.

TABLE 4
^{45}Ca Activity in Damaged and Control Left Ventricular Myocardium after 15 Minutes of Ischemia Followed by 3 Minutes of Reperfusion

Tissue site	Plasma-free tissue Ca^{++}: ^{45}Ca dpm/g wet / ^{45}Ca dpm/ml plasma — Injured	Control	Plasma-free tissue Ca^{++}: mmol Ca^{++}/100 g dry — Injured	Control	TTW (ml/100 g dry) — Injured	Control	Myocardial plasma content (ml/100 g dry) — Injured	Control	ATP (μmol/g wet) — Injured	Control
Subendocardial	0.302 ±0.012	0.272 ±0.022	0.379	0.313	402.0 ±6.2[b]	360.2 ±2.6	20.2 ±3.5	18.5 ±2.8	2.81 ±0.23[b]	5.22 ±0.25
Mid-myocardial	0.294 ±0.002	0.293 ±0.008	0.358	0.339	387.0 ±14.0	363.0 ±4.9	22.3 ±4.4	14.4 ±0.5	3.63 ±0.10[b]	
Subepicardial	0.298 ±0.009	0.285 ±0.017	0.344	0.331	361.3 ±8.6	364.0 ±1.0	18.1 ±1.8	21.2 ±2.8	4.10 ±0.29[a]	

Data from three dog hearts. All samples are free of endocardium and epicardium. The subendocardial samples are from the posterior and anterior papillary muscles. The mid-myocardial and subepicardial samples are from the inner and outer one-half of the free wall of the left ventricle under each papillary muscle. The ^{45}Ca results have been corrected for the ^{45}Ca contributed by the plasma. TTW = total tissue water. All results are given as mean ± SEM. The probability that the means are different by a two-tailed nonpaired *t*-test is: a, $P < 0.05$ and b, $P < 0.01$. The water and ATP data show a transmural gradient of injury, with the subendocardial layer being the most injured and the mid- and subepicardial layers demonstrating progresively less injury. However, ^{45}Ca was not accumulated at any site in the damaged tissue. Plasma content was slightly increased in the ischemic-reperfused tissue as compared with control, but this change was not significant after 3 minutes of reperfusion. Plasma-free tissue Ca^{++} was converted from units of tissue dpm per gram wet weight divided by plasma dpm/ml to mmol/100 g dry using a plasma calcium of 2.5 mM and the appropriate TTW for wet weight to dry weight conversion. Inclusion of plasma calcium would increase tissue calcium by approximately 0.05 mmol/100 g dry.

Although total tissue water was increased, at no time was there a significant increase in tissue Ca^{++}. These chemical data fit well with the ^{45}Ca uptake data shown in Table 4. Thus, there is no direct chemical evidence of an increased net uptake of Ca^{++} occurring during short intervals of reperfusion of reversibly injured ischemic myocardium.

A partial explanation for the increased tissue water and variable shifts in electrolytes (Table 3) in the reversibly injured reperfused tissue is provided by analysis of the plasma content of the tissue. Reactive hyperemia could cause increased quantities of plasma and erythrocytes to be trapped within the tissue. In dogs subjected to 15 minutes of ischemia and 20 minutes of reflow, the mean plasma content was 22.4 ± 0.5 ml/100 g dry heart in the nonischemic AP and 32.5 ± 1.4 ml in the reperfused ischemic PP. This yields a mean increase of about 10 ml of plasma or 9.2 ml of H_2O. Thus, about 26% of the 36 ml maximum increase in H_2O detected in these experiments could be accounted for as increased plasma content of the damaged tissue. If one assumes that the capillary hematocrit in myocardium is 40% and that 80% of erythrocytes is water, then hyperemia could account for as much as 40% of the observed increase in TTW. However, little increase in plasma was observed after 3 minutes of reflow despite a large increase in TTW.

Similar calculations for the contributions of cations suggest that increases in Na^+, Ca^{++}, Mg^{++}, and K^+ of 1.4, 0.025, 0.02, and 0.04 mmol/100 g dry weight, respectively, could have occurred because of increased plasma in the tissue. These calculations do not take into account the contribution of erythrocyte cations. The maximum observed increase in mean Na^+ and K^+ in the damaged tissue was 3.0 and 3.7 mmol/100 g dry weight. Thus, only about 25–40% of the maximum increase in tissue water and Na^+ can be accounted for by reactive hyperemia; some of the Na^+ and much of the K^+ shifts must have occurred via a different mechanism.

^{45}Ca Distribution after 15 Minutes of Ischemia and Variable Periods of Reflow

The effect of 15 minutes of permanent ischemia on the ^{45}Ca activity in myocardium was assessed by injecting the isotope 25 minutes before occluding the circumflex artery, which allowed for equilibration between tissue and serum prior to the onset of ischemia. The heart was excised and ^{45}Ca activity was assessed in control and experimental tissue after 15 minutes of ischemia had passed. Since there is virtually no collateral flow to permit further equilibration between the severely ischemic papillary muscle and serum, the ^{45}Ca content of the ischemic myocardium was referred to the serum level with which this tissue was last in equilibrium, i.e., the serum ^{45}Ca at the onset of occlusion (25 minutes after ^{45}Ca injection), whereas the activity of ^{45}Ca in the nonischemic control tissue was referred to the level found at the time of excision (40 minutes after ^{45}Ca injection). No significant difference in ^{45}Ca activity between ischemic and nonischemic myocardium was detected. The damaged tissue contained 0.269 ± 0.007 and the control tissue 0.252 ± 0.003 dpm/g per dpm per ml plasma.

Reperfusion for 3 minutes resulted in no increase in ^{45}Ca activity in the damaged muscle (Table 4). This conclusion was based on serum ^{45}Ca activity at the end of this brief period of reperfusion (rather than on the higher serum ^{45}Ca at the onset of occlusion). Thus, there was no detectable Ca^{++} overload. Also, it took only 3 minutes of reperfusion for the damaged tissue to come into equilibrium with the new lower circulating level of ^{45}Ca (Table 4). Instead of accumulating Ca^{++}, the damaged myocytes lost more ^{45}Ca than they gained. Moreover, although there is a transmural gradient of ischemia (Reimer and Jennings, 1979) such that ATP depletion and cellular injury are increasingly more severe as one progresses from epicardium to endocardium (Table 4), there was no accompanying gradient of Ca^{++} activity in either the ischemic or nonischemic muscle.

Ultrastructure Late in Reversible Phase of Ischemia; Effect of Reperfusion

The changes found late in the reversible phase of regional ischemia without reperfusion have been summarized elsewhere (Jennings and Ganote, 1974; Jennings et al., 1978). Four dog hearts were studied in detail, and are reported in this paper. The changes observed in three of the four are typical of those seen previously (Fig. 3); however, one heart showed slightly more marked changes than those seen in the past (Fig. 4). In all hearts, the ischemic tissue showed glycogen depletion, moderate margination of the chromatin of the nucleus, marked relaxation of myofibrils, and mild alterations in mitochondrial structure (Figs. 3 and 4). The matrix granules which were present in many of the mitochondria of control tissue were absent in the ischemic tissue; in addition, variable degrees of mitochondrial swelling with disorganization of the cristae, and a mild increase in the matrix space were detectable in a few mitochondria (Fig. 3). However, most mitochondria were indistinguishable from those of control heart. In the fourth heart studied in this experiment, the mitochondrial swelling was much more marked (Fig. 4). Virtually all mitochondria clearly showed an increase in the matrix space (Fig. 4B), and mitochondria with disorganized cristae (Fig. 4B) or absent cristae were not uncommon (Fig. 4C). An occasional tiny osmiophilic structure which might be an early stage of an amorphous matrix density also was present in the matrix space of some of the mitochondria. All hearts showed prominent I-bands and two of the four showed N-bands in the wide I-bands, a finding generally attributed to superstretching of the sarcomeres. In all cases, the sarcolemma was intact (Fig. 4C).

The effect of reperfusion on the ultrastructural

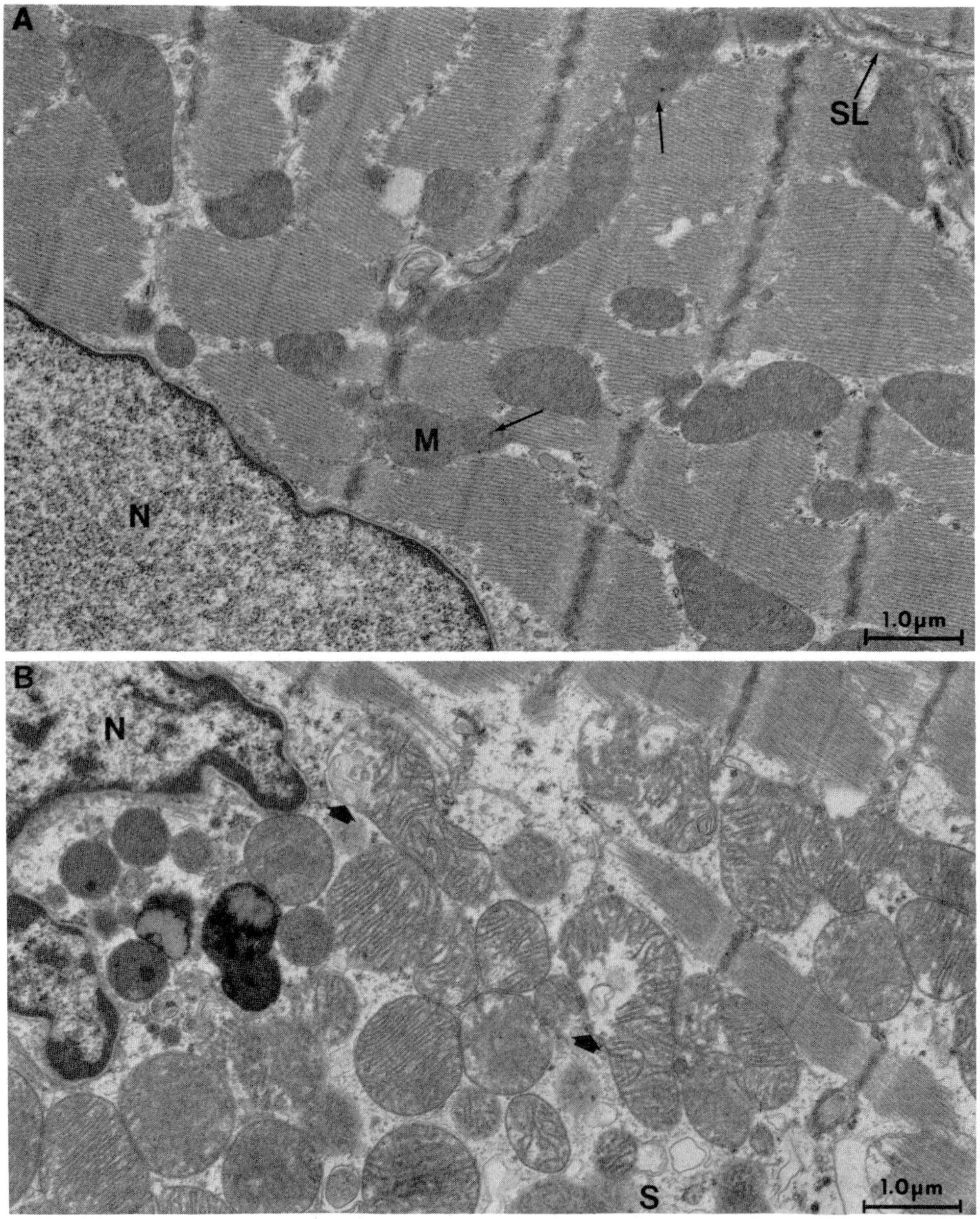

FIGURE 3. *Fifteen minutes of ischemia with no reperfusion. The typical structural changes induced by 15 minutes of severe ischemia in the projecting portion of the PP are shown in panel B, and should be contrasted to a representative nonischemic myocyte of the AP of the same heart (panel A). Note that the chromatin of the nucleus (N) is peripherally aggregated in the ischemic tissue. Also, the sarcoplasm (S) of the damaged myocyte is clearer than control and contains less granular glycogen. The cristae of the mitochondria (M) are densely packed in control; the matrix is scanty and contains occasional tiny matrix granules (arrows), whereas the ischemic tissue shows an increased matrix space in some mitochondria, as well as focal swelling (thick arrows). Although not illustrated in the ischemic tissue, the sarcolemma (SL) was indistinguishable from control. The ATP of the ischemic tissue was reduced by 67% to 1.85 μmol/g wet. Glutaraldehyde osmium fixation. Panels A and B: 15,750 ×.*

changes produced by ischemia was studied in five dogs given 20–30 seconds, five dogs given 3 minutes, and in groups of four dogs each given 20, 60, and 1440 minutes, and three hearts given 4 days of reperfusion. Twenty to 30 seconds of reperfusion had no significant effect on ultrastructure. On the other hand, 3 minutes of reperfusion (Fig. 5) increased the degree of swelling of many of the mitochondria. In addition, the nuclear chromatin of most damaged myocytes appeared to be more evenly distributed than it was at the end of 15 minutes of permanent ischemia. There still was less glycogen in the sarcoplasm than in the control tissue and the myofibrils remained relaxed.

At the end of 20 minutes of reperfusion, the damaged myocytes were virtually indistinguishable from control. An occasional swollen mitochondria (Fig. 6) was the only monument to the episode of ischemia. Glycogen was present; the nuclear chromatin was evenly distributed, the myofibrils of some myocytes were contracted, while, in others, they were relaxed. Most mitochondria were indistin-

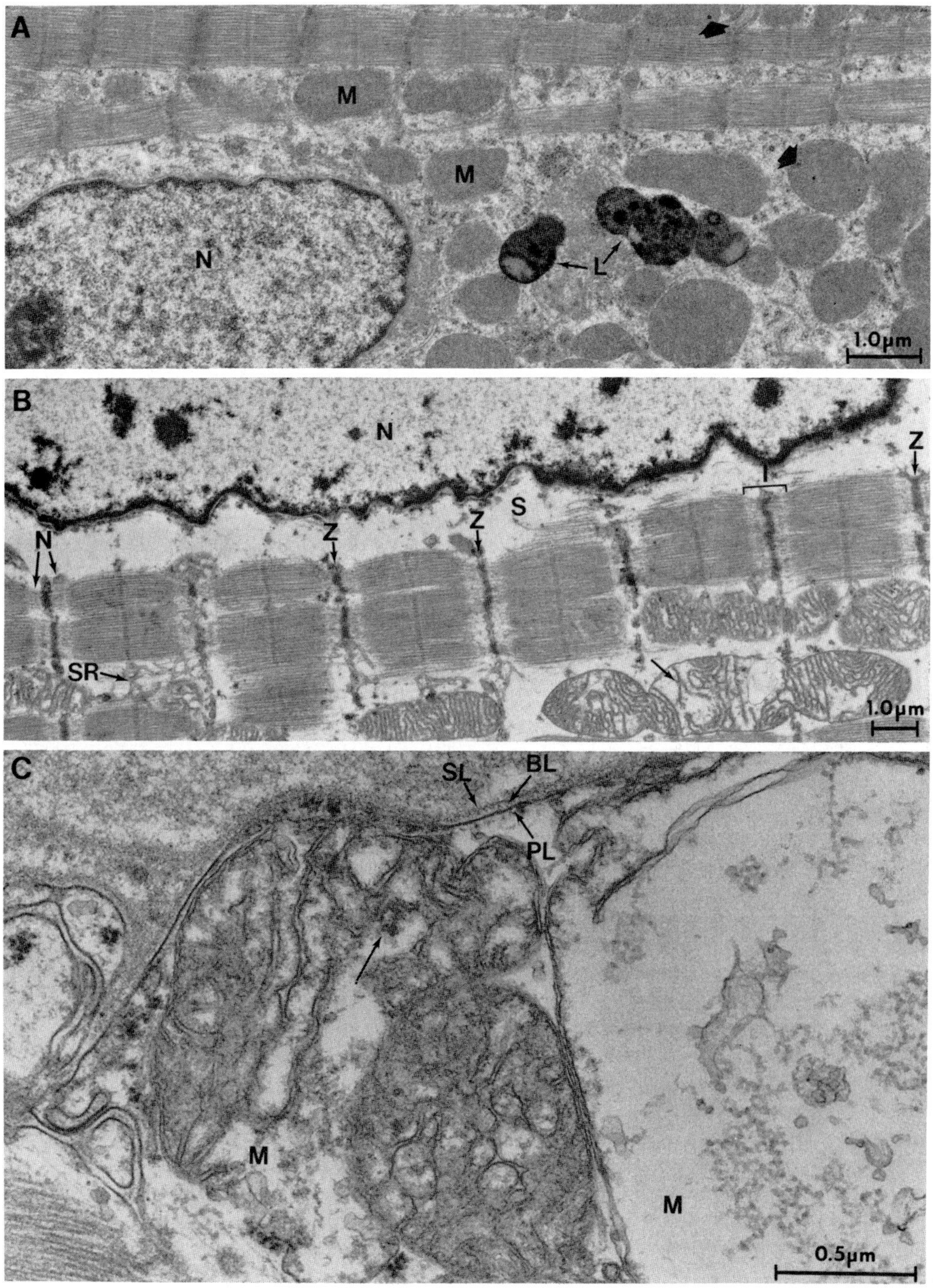

Figure 4. *Fifteen minutes of ischemia with no reperfusion. These micrographs illustrate the most severe ultrastructural changes observed in this experiment as a consequence of 15 minutes of severe low-flow ischemia. This heart had the lowest ATP and one of the highest lactate levels observed. Panel A in this figure is a control nonischemic myocyte from the AP. The structure of this myocyte is virtually identical to that seen in Figure 3A. The nuclear chromatin (N) is evenly distributed; the myofibrils are contracted; the sarcoplasm (S) contains granular glycogen and dense mitochondria (M) as well as lipofuscin pigment granules (L). Dense matrix granules (thick arrows) are present in some mitochondrial profiles. A representative damaged myocyte is shown in panel B. The chromatin of the nucleus is markedly aggregated peripherally, as in Figure 3B. The sarcoplasm (S) is clear and contains very little glycogen. The myofibrils are relaxed and contain N-bands (N) and prominent I-bands on either side of the Z-line (Z). The sarcoplasmic reticulum (SR) is intact. The matrix space of virtually all mitochondria is increased, and the cristae are occasionally disorganized (arrow). Panel C is a high power view of sarcolemma (SL) with an intact glycocalyx (GL) and plasmalemma (PL). Under it are two swollen mitochondria (M). A structure at the arrow in one of the swollen mitochondria may be an early form of an amorphous matrix density. The mitochondria in panel C are representative of the most severely involved mitochondria detected in this experiment in permanently ischemic tissue. Glutaraldehyde fixation with post-osmication. Panel A: 7,750×; panel B: 12,500×; panel C: 50,000×.*

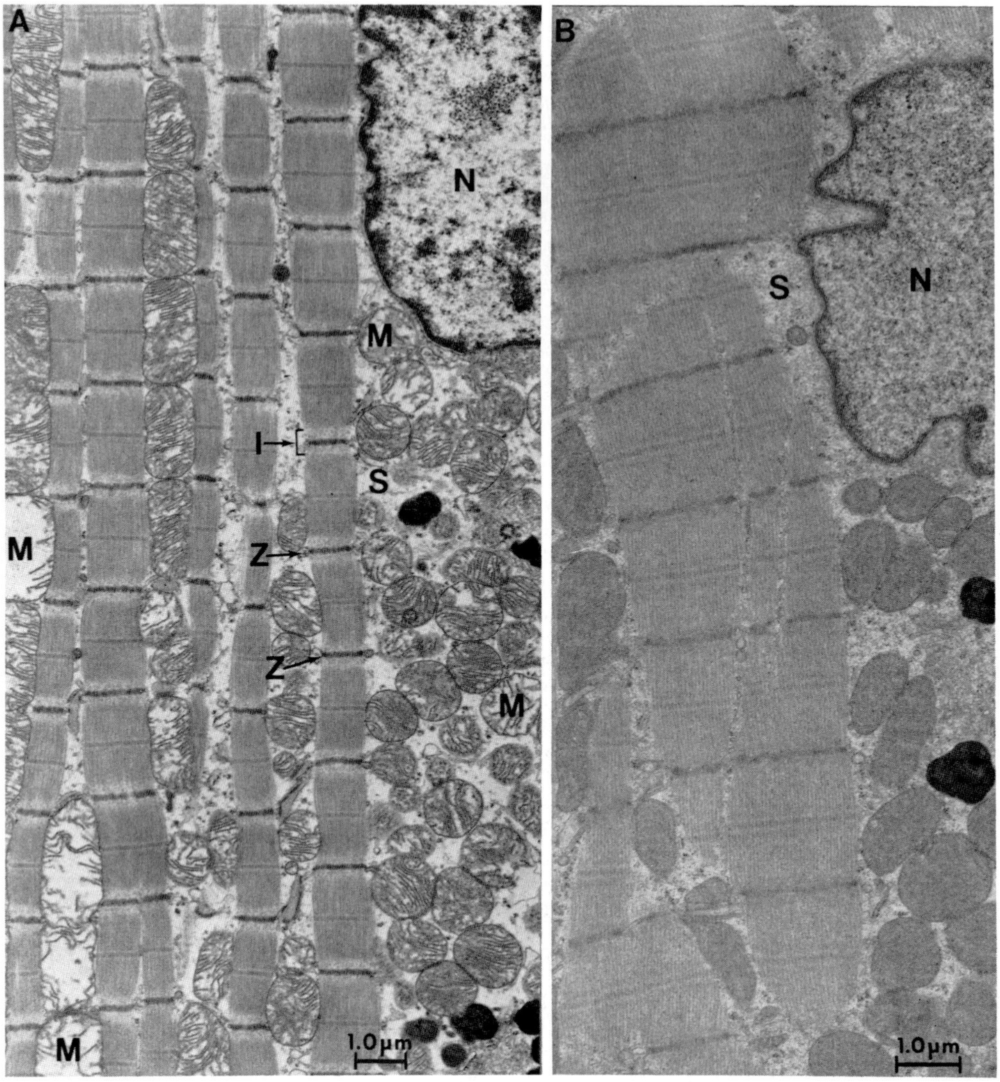

FIGURE 5. *Fifteen minutes of ischemia with 3 minutes of perfusion. Each of the five hearts studied after 3 minutes of reperfusion showed changes similar to those illustrated in panel A. Marked swelling was noted in some mitochondria; those labeled M are representative of the badly swollen variety. The remaining mitochondria were less markedly involved. The chromatin of the nucleus (N) still is aggregated peripherally. The sarcoplasm (S) is less dense and contains little granular glycogen. The myofibrils are relaxed; they demonstrate large I-bands, in contrast to the myocytes of control, which are contracted. The damage shown in panel A is as marked as we observed after 3 minutes of reperfusion. Three of the five dogs studied showed this degree of change. Panel B is from the nonischemic AP of the same dog and is presented as a control to compare to panel A. The appearance is similar to control tissue presented in Figures 3A and 4A. Glutaraldehyde fixation with post-osmication. Panel A: 7,750×; panel B: 10,075×.*

guishable from control; no swelling persisted; the cristae were tightly packed and small matrix granules occasionally were detected.

The changes found after 1, 24, or 96 hours of reflow were similar to those seen after 20 minutes of reperfusion. An occasional swollen mitochondrion still was present at 24 (Fig. 7) or 96 hours.

The capillary endothelium at all times, whether at the end of 15 minutes of ischemia or after variable periods of reperfusion, was indistinguishable from control. Pinocytotic vesicles persisted and tight junctions remained intact. Granulocytes occasionally were noted in the lumen of capillaries, but not in the interstitial space. Adherence of the granulocytes to the endothelium was not detected in the sections. No granulocytes were seen in control tissue.

Discussion

The experiments reported in this paper were done to assess the response of severely ischemic myocytes which were on the verge of death, to reperfusion with arterial blood. It was known that reperfusion would salvage myocytes (Jennings and Reimer, 1982); however, the acute reactions occurring within them as they reverted from anaerobic glycolysis to aerobic metabolism and resumed life in a perfused, oxygenated environment were unknown or poorly understood.

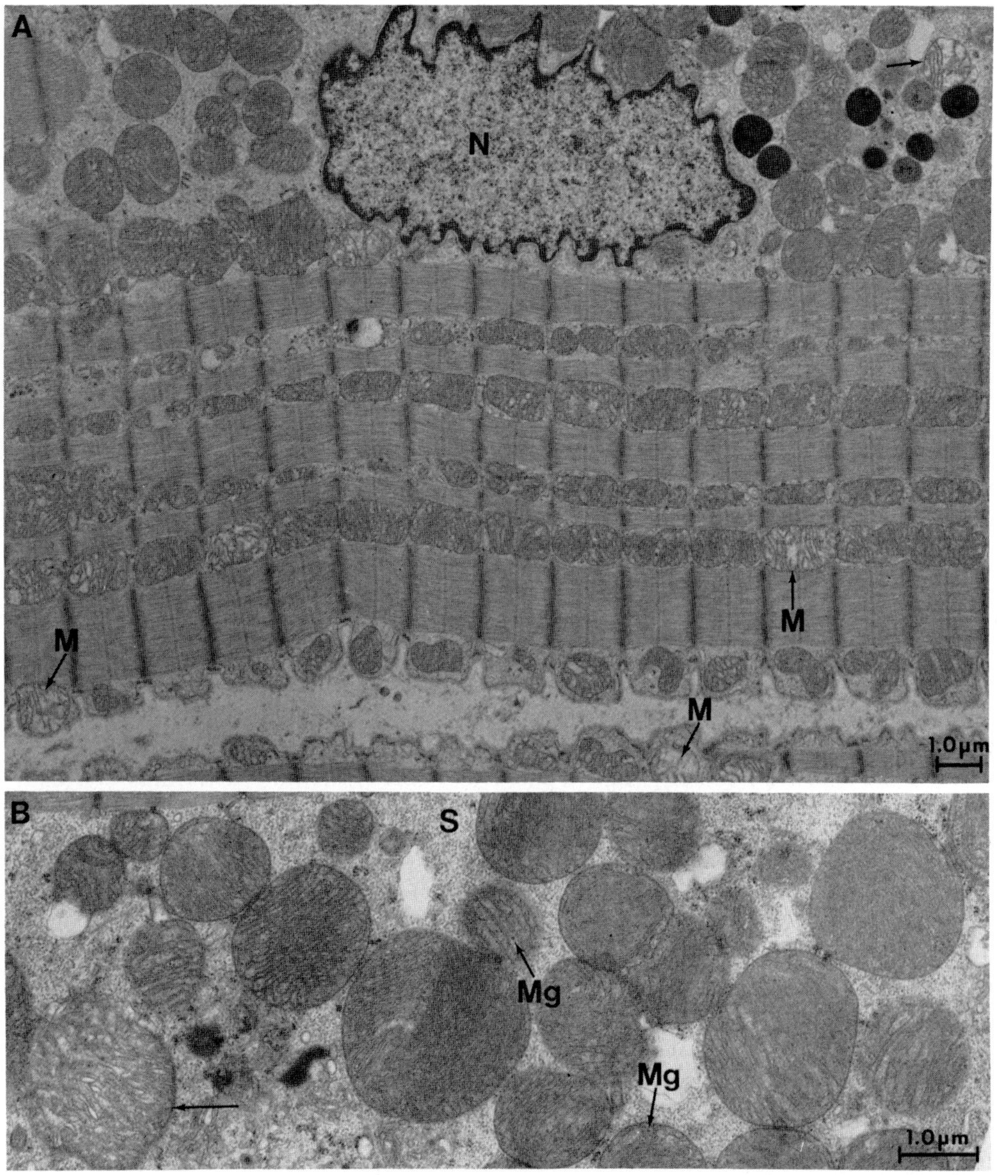

Figure 6. *Fifteen minutes of ischemia with 20 minutes of reperfusion. The lower power view (panel A) shows that the architecture of the myocytes is well preserved. Myocytes are virtually indistinguishable from the typical control myocytes shown in Figures 3A, 4A, and 5B. The chromatin of the nucleus (N) is evenly distributed. An occasional swollen mitochondrion (M) is detected. The myofibrils are contracted. Panel B is a higher power view of typical mitochondria; except for one swollen mitochondrion (arrow), they are indistinguishable from control. Note that there is abundant glycogen in the sarcoplasm (S). Matrix granules (Mg) are present but tiny. Glutaraldehyde fixation with post-osmication. Panel A: 7,000×; panel B: 13,000×.*

Effect of Ischemia with or without Reperfusion on the Adenine Nucleotide Pool and Its Catabolites

In the experiments reported in this paper, the metabolite levels found after 15 minutes of ischemia, but immediately prior to reperfusion were in the range reported earlier (Jennings et al., 1978, 1981; Reimer et al., 1981a). About 65% of the ATP was gone. ADP levels were depressed as well, and AMP more than doubled. As a result, the AC was markedly depressed and the total pool of adenine nucleotides was depressed to nearly 50% of control. Moreover, the lost adenine nucleotides were accounted for as ADO, I, HX, and X. Finally, the lactate was increased to 30 μmol/g. The above depletion of ATP was about two-thirds of the ATP depletion that has previously been associated with irreversible injury (Jennings et al., 1978).

Many other investigators such as Kloner et al. (1983b) and Swain et al. (1982a, 1982b), have also observed rapid ATP depletion or adenine nucleotide depletion in myocardial ischemia. However, the degree of these changes varies as a function of intrinsic variation among animals and of sampling techniques. Even with the precise sampling employed in our study, the degree of depression of ATP varied from 50–80% and ΣAd from 40–60%. Additional variation may be induced if moderately ischemic or nonischemic tissue is included in the sample by blind biopsy procedures (Kloner et al., 1981; Swain et al., 1982a, 1982b; Allison and Holsinger, 1983). Any such contamination would increase the ATP level of the ischemic tissue. Studies based on cardiac biopsies have shown less marked metabolic changes compared to those reported in this paper (Swain et al., 1981; Heinrichs et al., 1983; Kloner et al., 1983b). In one study, Allison and Holsinger (1983) have failed to find persistent depression in the ΣAd after 20 minutes of ischemia in the open-chest anesthetized dog when the biopsy technique was used for sampling.

Reperfusion of the ischemic myocardium for 20–30 seconds produced no detectable effects. The adenylate charge remained depressed. Tissue lactate, AMP, I, HX, etc., all remained high and the ultrastructure was unaltered. However, after 3 or 20 minutes of reperfusion, the AC had returned to control levels as a consequence of conversion of AMP and ADP to ATP. About 0.8–1.0 μmol ATP was gained in the process. These results suggest that, even though adenine nucleotide content requires several days to recover completely (Reimer et al., 1981a), mitochondria retain the capacity to quickly generate ATP from the ADP available for high energy phosphate (HEP) synthesis.

It is of interest that studies using implanted crystals to measure the contractile properties of the ischemic reperfused myocardium have shown that contractility is depressed for 24 hours or more after 5 to 15 minutes of ischemic injury (Heyndrickx et al., 1975; Weiner et al., 1976; Hess et al., 1979). Although depressed ATP could be the explanation for the depressed contractility, Hoffmeister et al. (1983) have successfully accelerated ATP repletion during ischemia without accelerating recovery of contractile function. Thus, the explanation for the delayed recovery of contractility remains unknown. Other studies have shown that the reversibly injured reperfused tissue has markedly increased levels of CP (Swain et al., 1982; Kloner et al., 1983b; Allison and Holsinger, 1983), an observation which indicates that net energy production in the damaged tissue exceeds energy utilization.

Changes in Myocardial Tissue Ca^{++} Due to Ischemia with or without Reperfusion

Previous studies have shown that enormous increases in myocyte Ca^{++} occurred when myocytes irreversibly injured by 40 minutes of ischemia were reperfused with arterial blood (Shen and Jennings, 1972a; Whalen et al., 1974). The increases in Ca^{++} occurred within 2 minutes (Whalen et al., 1974), and were due chiefly to increased entry of extracellular Ca^{++} into the sarcoplasm where it was actively accumulated by the mitochondria and was precipi-

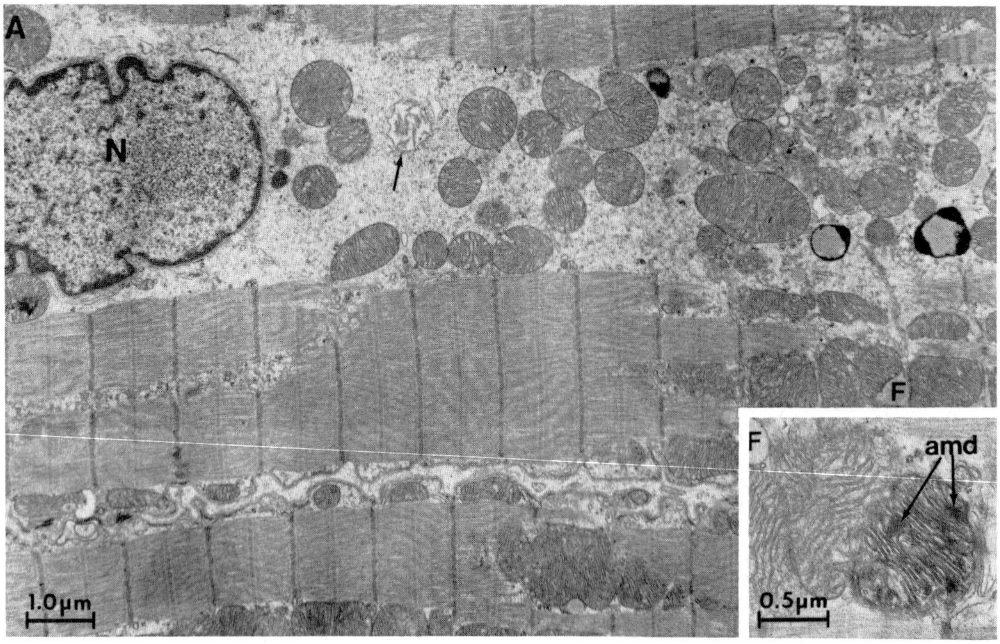

FIGURE 7. *Fifteen minutes of ischemia with 24 hours of reperfusion. Panel A shows a typical myocyte of PP. Except for the occasional swollen (arrow) or disrupted mitochondrion (inset), this myocyte is essentially indistinguishable from the control myocytes. The chromatin of the nucleus (N) is evenly distributed. The mitochondria are similar to control mitochondria, but matrix granules were less prominent in the mitochondria of the damaged tissue. A small para-mitochondrial vacuole is present adjacent to a mitochondrion to the left of the insert. Such vacuoles have been observed in reversibly injured myocardium previously, but their significance is uncertain (Kloner et al., 1983a). The mitochondrion in the inset was the only damaged mitochondrion in another myocyte. It contains prominent amorphous matrix densities (amd). Glycogen is prominent in both control and damaged tissue. Occasional droplets (F) of triglyceride are detected, but they are not increased in amount in the damaged tissue. Glutaraldehyde fixation with post-osmication. Panel A: 10,750×; Inset: 22,000×.*

tated as calcium phosphate (Shen and Jennings, 1972b). This massive loading with calcium was detected by several techniques including: (1) direct measurement of the calcium content of the myocardium (Shen and Jennings, 1972a; Whalen et al., 1974) (2) detection of ^{45}Ca accumulation from the plasma reperfusing the tissue (Shen and Jennings, 1972b), and (3) ultrastructural studies which showed massive loading of calcium phosphate in the mitochondria of the damaged myocytes (Shen and Jennings, 1972a).

In contrast, previous studies have shown that myocardium injured by 15 minutes of ischemia and reperfused for 20 minutes with arterial blood neither loaded Ca^{++} nor developed contraction-band necrosis (Reimer et al., 1981a), a finding which suggested that badly damaged myocytes reperfused late in the phase of reversible injury either did not develop massive mitochondrial loading with Ca^{++}, or that, if it did occur, it was transient.

In the present study, ^{45}Ca was used as a more sensitive means to detect calcium uptake from the plasma pool (Shen and Jennings, 1972b) during the first few minutes of reperfusion. The sensitivity of this detection system for calcium uptake is not well defined, but the technique should permit detection of a 15–25% increase in the level of ^{45}Ca in the damaged myocardium (see Fig. 2 in Shen and Jennings, 1972b). No such increase was detected. Since we failed to detect any increased entry of Ca^{++} into badly injured myocytes, some of which were approaching the point of no return, after aerobic metabolism was restored (3 minutes of reflow), the results of our experiments do not support the idea that myocytes develop an inability to control Ca^{++} homeostasis prior to the onset of irreversible myocardial ischemic injury (Jennings, 1984). The absence of a generalized increase in net Ca^{++} in the myocytes late in the reversible phase of injury does not rule out the development of defective Ca^{++} homeostasis occurring after slightly more injury. However, we cannot answer the question of whether slightly more ischemic injury would be associated with entry of calcium into reversibly injured myocytes in the model used for these experiments because some of the myocytes become irreversibly injured and die after only another 4 to 5 minutes of ischemia (Jennings and Reimer, 1983). A marked increase in calcium in a few dead cells could not be differentiated from a generalized increase in Ca^{++}.

The massive Ca^{++} entry observed in irreversibly injured cells is closely related to membrane damage. Neither membrane damage (Jennings et al., 1978; Jennings and Reimer, 1981), nor Ca^{++} entry was detectable at 15 minutes in our experiments. However, once severe membrane damage is present, the large downhill gradient for Ca^{++} from the extracellular to the intracellular space plus the steady massage, by contraction, of the myocytes involved, would lead to the entry of much Ca^{++} into the sarcoplasm. After 40 minutes of ischemia, when many irreversibly injured myocytes are present, the ^{45}Ca activity can increase by 20 times during 20 minutes of reperfusion (Shen and Jennings, 1972b). The increased intracellular Ca^{++} causes massive contracture of the myofibrils and accelerates the evolution of the necrotic process (Jennings, 1984).

Most of the experiments in which Ca^{++} entry has been shown to occur early in ischemia have employed hearts or portions of heart perfused in vitro under conditions of anoxia or with episodes of low or absent flow (ischemia) (Shine et al., 1978; Nayler et al., 1979; Bourdillon and Poole-Wilson, 1981). The results of these studies on perfused hearts are not necessarily comparable to those we have found in regional ischemia in vivo, because in vivo ischemia differs in a number of potentially significant ways from in vitro ischemia or anoxia. These include: (1) ATP and high energy phosphate depletion are more profound and more rapid in vivo than in vitro (Jennings et al., 1981); (2) extracellular oncotic pressure is maintained in vivo by protein in the capillaries and is virtually absent in vitro in hearts perfused with crystalloidal solutions; (3) much of the available extracellular Ca^{++} is bound to protein in vivo, in contrast to its generally ionized state in crystalloidal solutions; and (4) the extracellular fluid volume available in severe or total ischemia in vivo is very much smaller than that found in the usual perfused preparation (Jennings et al. 1983b). Thus, injury during in vivo ischemia may be different from injury during in vitro anoxia or ischemia. Furthermore, because tissue Ca^{++} is very scant under control conditions but can increase by nearly an order of magnitude in irreversibly damaged myocytes, a modest increase in tissue Ca^{++} could arise from either massive Ca^{++} uptake in a small proportion of lethally injured myocytes or slightly enhanced Ca^{++} influx in all myocytes. These two mechanisms of Ca^{++} gain cannot be distinguished unless a method is available to detect the fact that some myocytes are lethally injured. Therefore, the significance of the observed modest increases in tissue Ca^{++} in the in vitro anoxia and ischemia models remains to be established, as does the relevance of these observations to cell injury in in vivo ischemia.

Effect of Reperfusion on Myocardial Electrolytes and Water

Following irreversible myocardial cell injury, the acute changes in myocardial ion and water content after reperfusion include massive swelling, marked accumulation of Na^+, Cl^-, Ca^{++}, and phosphate, and loss of K^+ and Mg^{++} (Shen and Jennings, 1972; Whalen et al., 1974). The increase in Ca^{++} is especially marked. The ion and water changes observed in the reversibly injured tissue reported in Table 3 were definite, but of much smaller magnitude, and sometimes were in a different direction. For example, there was a relatively small increase in Na^+ and

TTW, no change in Ca^{++}, and an unexpected increase in tissue K^+. Thus, viable, but damaged, reperfused tissue has a characteristic electrolyte distribution which differs greatly from the changes seen in reperfused irreversibly injured tissue.

The slight but significant increase in TTW and Na^+ was partially accounted for by the increase in the quantity of plasma trapped in the hyperemic reperfused tissue. Based on the ultrastructural observations of mitochondrial enlargement and mild vacuolization of the sarcoplasm, it seems likely that some or much of the remainder of the increased TTW was due to intracellular edema. However, the cause of the intracellular edema is unknown. The cell swelling may be due to increased intracellular osmolarity due to the accumulation of lactate, H^+, ADO, inorganic phosphate, glycolytic intermediates, etc., in the sarcoplasm prior to reperfusion. However, although increased intracellular osmolarity may explain the initial swelling, it will not explain the persistence of swelling, because the metabolites which could cause increased osmolarity are washed from the tissue by 20 minutes of reperfusion.

The explanation of the increased K^+ content of the tissue also is unknown. Together with the increase in TTW, it clearly is a highly characteristic feature of reperfused reversibly damaged myocardium. The change is transient; it persists for 60 minutes but not for 24 hours of reperfusion (Reimer et al., 1981a). The increases in tissue contents of K^+, as well as Na^+, after 20 minutes of reperfusion can be accounted for without requiring any change in extracellular or intracellular concentration of either ion if 25% of the increase in TTW is extracellular and 75% is intracellular, assuming that extracellular volume is 20% of TTW in control myocardium. This is consistent with the measurements of plasma volume during reperfusion, which suggested an increase in extracellular volume of less than half of the increase in TTW. Alternatively, a K^+ overshoot could have occurred due to accelerated Na^+, K^+-ATPase activity occasioned by intracellular Na^+ accumulation during the period of ischemia. The data suggest that ion gradients are reestablished early during reperfusion of reversibly injured ischemic myocardium, but that abnormalities of cell volume regulation do not resolve as rapidly.

Ultrastructural Changes Due to Ischemia with or without Reperfusion

The ultrastructural changes observed after 15 minutes of ischemia varied from heart to heart. All hearts showed loss of glycogen, peripheral aggregation of nuclear chromatin, and generally mild mitochondrial changes. In some hearts, swollen mitochondria were prominent, whereas other hearts showed virtually all intact or only slightly swollen mitochondria. Irrespective of the condition of the mitochondria, fully developed amorphous matrix densities, which are a hallmark of irreversible injury, were absent.

After 20 minutes of reperfusion, the ultrastructure of the damaged tissue essentially was indistinguishable from control. The only abnormalities detectable were occasional swollen mitochondria. The latter change apparently persisted for as long as 96 hours, since disrupted mitochondria, sometimes in lysosomes, still were detectable after this prolonged interval of reperfusion. Presumably, the abnormal mitochondria persisting in the reperfused tissue included some or all of the badly swollen mitochondria noted at the end of 3 minutes of reperfusion. The mitochondrial matrix granules that had disappeared after 15 minutes of ischemia were restored by 20 minutes of reperfusion with oxygenated blood.

The structural manifestations of reversible regional ischemia largely reflect the altered metabolism and contractile function of the tissue. Thus, loss of particulate glycogen in the sarcoplasm is a reflection of glycogen utilization, whereas stretching and the appearance of I-bands in the myofibrils are correlated with cessation of contraction of the ischemic tissue and paradoxical stretching of sarcomeres during systole. The explanation for the margination of the nuclear chromatin observed in ischemia is not known. This change was essentially reversed after only 3 minutes of reperfusion. After 20 minutes of reperfusion, the nuclei are indistinguishable from control.

The mitochondrial changes of well developed acute irreversible ischemic injury in vivo include swelling, disorganization of cristae, and the appearance of mitochondrial amorphous matrix densities in virtually every mitochondrial profile (Jennings and Ganote, 1974). These changes are first detectable in a significant number of cells when 92% or more of the ATP has been depleted and when anaerobic glycolysis is slowing or has stopped (Jennings and Reimer, 1981). In the experiments reported in this paper, 64% of the ATP was depleted, lactate accumulation had not reached maximum levels, and mitochondrial changes associated with irreversibility were not observed. Nevertheless, when ATP and lactate changes were marked, mitochondrial swelling was marked as well (Fig. 4). Conversely, less severe metabolic consequences of ischemia were associated with less severe mitochondrial swelling. Reperfusion produced transient swelling of virtually all mitochondria when ATP levels were low, and of a smaller number of mitochondria when ATP levels were higher. It is not known whether the swelling is related to ATP content per se, but it is known that mitochondrial volume regulation is an energy dependent process. Nevertheless, except for a rare disrupted mitochondrion, only 20 minutes of reperfusion are required to restore mitochondrial structure to normal.

No change in the ultrastructure of the plasmalemma of the reversibly injured tissue was noted, a finding which is consistent with the hypothesis that membrane integrity must be maintained if the myocytes are to survive (Jennings and Reimer, 1981). The hypothesis that reperfusion induces membrane damage by free radical production (McCord and Fridovich, 1978; Jolly et al., 1984) is not supported by our results, even though the conditions for free radical generation were optimal after 15 minutes of ischemia (e.g., via the action of xanthine oxidase on hypoxanthine). The tissue contained about 0.3 μmol HX, and became hyperemic (well oxygenated) with the onset of reperfusion. Moreover, the HX was only slowly washed out by reperfusion. Nevertheless, no membrane damage detectable by alterations in structure, increases in the inulin diffusible space (Reimer et al., 1981b) or Ca^{++} uptake, occurred in our experiments. Thus, free radicals, if generated, produced no detectable effect late in the reversible phase of ischemic injury.

The relationship of ATP availability to various ultrastructural changes in ischemic tissue has been a subject of investigation in ischemia (Jennings et al., 1978). The results of the experiments reported here clearly establish that tissue ATP levels as low as 1.9 μmol/g wet weight are associated with an essentially normal ultrastructure after 20 or more minutes of reperfusion.

Conclusions:

The results show clearly that myocardium that has been badly but reversibly damaged by ischemia, survives, if it is reperfused. Nevertheless, the tissue does not return to control conditions for minutes, hours, or days, depending upon which alteration is being considered. For example, the adenylate charge is restored to control levels after 3 minutes, and the ultrastructure—except for isolated abnormal mitochondria—is restored to control after 20 minutes of reoxygenation, but the adenine nucleotide pool remains markedly depressed for 24 hours, and still is not restored completely after 4 days of reperfusion (Reimer et al., 1981a). In addition, there are persistent alterations in volume control with edema persisting for 24 hours of reperfusion (Reimer et al., 1981a) and a significantly elevated tissue K^+ level persisting for at least 60 minutes (but not 24 hours) of reperfusion.

This work was supported in part by Grants HL23138 and HL27416 from the National Heart, Lung, and Blood Institute of the National Institutes of Health.

Dr. Schaper is affiliated with the Max Planck Institute.

Address for reprints: Dr. Robert B. Jennings, Department of Pathology, Duke University Medical Center, Durham, North Carolina 27710.

Received March 26, 1984, accepted for publication November 15, 1984.

References

Allison TB, Holsinger JW (1983) Myocardial metabolism and regional myocardial blood flow in the canine left ventricle following twenty minutes of circumflex artery occlusion and reperfusion. J Mol Cell Cardiol **15:** 151–161

Anderson FS, Murphy RC (1976) Isocratic separation of some purine nucleotide, nucleoside, and base metabolites from biological extracts by high-performance liquid chromatography. J Chromatog **121:** 251–262

Bourdillon PDV, Poole-Wilson PA (1981) Effects of ischaemia and reperfusion on calcium exchange and mechanical function in isolated rabbit myocardium. Cardiovasc Res **XV:** 121–130

Farber JL (1982) Biology of disease: Membrane injury and calcium homeostasis in the pathogenesis of coagulative necrosis. Lab Invest **47:** 114–123

Farber JL, El-Mofty SK (1975) The biochemical pathology of liver cell necrosis Am J Pathol **81:** 237–250

Henrichs KJ, Matsuoka H, Schaper W (1983) Enhanced post-ischemic ATP-repletion by pharmacological inhibition of nucleoside washout and catabolism. Circulation **68** (suppl III): 389

Hess ML, Barnhart GR, Crute S, Komwatana P, Krause S, Greenfield LJ (1979) Mechanical and biochemical effects of transient myocardial ischemia. J Surg Res **26:** 175–184

Heyndrickx GR, Millard RW, McRitchie RJ, Maroko PR, Vatner SF (1975) Regional myocardial functional and electrophysiological alterations after brief coronary artery occlusion in conscious dogs. J Clin Invest **56:** 978–985

Hill JL, Gettes LS (1980) Effect of acute coronary artery occlusion on local myocardial extracellular K^+ activity in swine. Circulation **61:** 68–78

Hirche H, Franz C, Bös L (1979) Ion-selective electrodes in cardiac ischemia. *In* Brain and Heart Infarct II, edited by KJ Zülch, W Kaufmann, K-A Hossman, V Hossman. Berlin, Springer-Verlag, pp 104–111

Hoffmeister HM, Mauser M, Schaper W (1983) Regional function during accelerated ATP depletion after myocardial ischemia. Circulation **68** (suppl III): 193

Jennings RB (1984) Calcium ions in ischemia. *In* Calcium Antagonists and Cardiovascular Disease, edited by LH Opie. New York, Raven Press, pp 85–95

Jennings RB, Ganote CE (1974) Structural changes in myocardium during acute ischemia. Circ Res **35** (suppl III): 156–172

Jennings RB, Reimer KA (1981) Lethal myocardial ischemic injury. Am J Pathol **102:** 241–255

Jennings RB, Reimer KA (1983) Factors involved in salvaging ischemic myocardium: Effect of reperfusion of arterial blood. Circulation **68** (suppl I): 25–36

Jennings RB, Ganote CE, Reimer KA (1975) Ischemic tissue injury. Am J Pathol **81:** 179–198

Jennings RB, Hawkins HK, Lowe JE, Hill ML, Klotman S, Reimer KA (1978) Relation between high energy phosphate and lethal injury in myocardial ischemia in the dog. Am J Pathol **92:** 187–214

Jennings RB, Reimer KA, Hill ML, Mayer SE (1981) Total ischemia, in dog hearts, in vitro. I. Comparison of high energy phosphate production, utilization and depletion and of adenine nucleotide catabolism in total ischemia in vitro vs. severe ischemia in vivo. Circ Res **49:** 892–900

Jennings RB, Reimer KA, Jones RN, Peyton RB (1983a) High energy phosphates, anaerobic glycolysis and irreversibility in ischemia. *In* Myocardial Ischemia, edited by JJ Spitzer. New York, Plenum, pp 403–419

Jennings RB, Steenbergen C Jr, Kinney RB, Hill ML, Reimer KA (1983b) Comparison of the effect of ischaemia and anoxia on the sarcolemma of the dog heart. Eur Heart J **4:** (suppl H): 123–137

Jolly SR, Kane WJ, Bailie MB, Abrams GD, Lucchesi BR (1984) Canine myocardial reperfusion injury: Its reduction by the combined administration of superoxide dismutase and catalase. Circ Res **54:** 277–285

Kloner RA, Ellis SG, Carlson NV, Braunwald E (1983a) Coronary reperfusion for the treatment of acute myocardial infarction: Postischemic ventricular dysfunction. Cardiology **70:** 233–246

Kloner RA, Ellis SG, Lange R, Braunwald E (1983b) Studies of experimental coronary artery reperfusion. Effects on infarct size, myocardial function, biochemistry, ultrastructure, and microvascular damage. Circulation **68:** I8–I15

McCord JM, Fridovich I (1978) The biology and pathology of oxygen radicals. Ann Intern Med **89:** 122–127

Nayler WG, Poole-Wilson PA, Williams A (1979) Hypoxia and

calcium. J Mol Cell Cardiol 11: 683–706
Reimer KA, Jennings RB (1979) The "wavefront phenomenon" of myocardial ischemic cell death. II. Transmural progression of necrosis within the framework of ischemic bed size (myocardium at risk) and collateral flow. Lab Invest 40: 633–644
Reimer KA, Hill ML, Jennings RB (1981a) Prolonged depletion of ATP and of the adenine nucleotide pool due to delayed resynthesis of adenine nucleotides following reversible myocardial ischemic injury in dogs. J Mol Cell Cardiol 13: 229–239
Reimer KA, Jennings RB, Hill ML (1981b) Total myocardial ischemia, in vitro. 2. High energy phosphate depletion and associated defects in energy metabolism, cell volume regulation, and sarcolemmal integrity. Circ Res 49: 901–911
Shen AC, Jennings RB (1972a) Myocardial calcium and magnesium in acute ischemic myocardial injury. Am J Pathol 67: 417–440
Shen AC, Jennings RB (1972b) Kinetics of calcium accumulation in acute myocardial ischemic injury. Am J Pathol 67: 441–452
Shine, KI, Douglas AM, Ricchiuti NV (1978) Calcium, strontium, and barium movements during ischemia and reperfusion in rabbit ventricle. Implications for myocardial preservation. Circ Res 43: 712–720
Swain JL, Hines JJ, Sabina RL, Holmes EW (1982a) Accelerated repletion of ATP and GTP pools in postischemic canine myocardium using a precursor of purine de novo synthesis. Circ Res 51: 102–105
Swain JL, Sabina RL, McHale PA, Greenfield JC Jr, Holmes EW (1982b) Prolonged myocardial nucleotide depletion after brief ischemia in the open chest dog. Am J Physiol 242: H818–H826
Weiner JM, Apstein CS, Arthur JH, Pirzada FH, Hood WB (1976) Persistance of myocardial injury following brief periods of coronary occlusion. Cardiovasc Res 10: 678–686
Whalen DA Jr, Hamilton DG, Ganote CE, Jennings RB (1974) Effect of a transient period of ischemia on myocardial cells. I. Effects on cell volume regulation. Am J Pathol 74: 381–398

INDEX TERMS: Ischemia, myocardial • Reversible cell injury • Calcium overload in ischemia • Adenine nucleotides in ischemia • Reperfusion of ischemic myocardium

BRIEF COMMUNICATIONS

[^{125}I]Aminobenzyladenosine, a New Radioligand with Improved Specific Binding to Adenosine Receptors in Heart

Joel Linden, Amrat Patel, and Samy Sadek
From the Oklahoma Medical Research Foundation, Oklahoma City, Oklahoma

SUMMARY. The density of adenosine receptors in membranes derived from rat hearts is 25 times lower than the density of receptors in rat brain membranes. Consequently, adenosine radioligands which are useful in brain such as *l*-[^{3}H]phenylisopropyladenosine, [^{3}H]cyclohexyladenosine, [^{3}H]-2-chloroadenosine and *l*-[^{125}I]hydroxyphenylisopropyladenosine are of limited usefulness in heart, due to a high ratio of nonspecific to specific binding. We have synthesized a new radioligand, [^{125}I]-N^6-4-aminobenzyladenosine, which binds to rat heart membranes with one-sixth the nonspecific binding of the other radioligands. [^{125}I]-N^6-4-aminobenzyladenosine bound to rat ventricle membranes with a K_D equivalent to that of *l*-[^{125}I]hydroxyphenylisopropyladenosine and a B_{max} of 15.2 fmol/mg protein. [^{125}I]-N^6-4-aminobenzyladenosine bound with a higher affinity to brain (K_D = 1.93 nM) than to heart membranes (K_D = 11.6 nM). At the radioligand K_D, 60% of the total [^{125}I]-N^6-4-aminobenzyladenosine bound to heart membranes was specifically bound. Iodination of aminobenzyladenosine increased its affinity for the adenosine receptor by 22-fold, possibly due to a steric or hydrophobic effect of iodine. The new ligand was found to be a full adenosine agonist based on its ability to inhibit cyclic adenosinemonophosphate accumulation in isolated embryonic chick heart cells and rat adipocytes. [^{125}I]-N^6-4-Aminobenzyladenosine bound to a single affinity site and was displaced from cardiac and brain adenosine receptors by other adenosine analogues with a potency order of *l*-phenylisopropyladenosine > 5′-*N*-ethylcarboxamide adenosine. These characteristics suggest that the radioligand binds to an R_i adenosine receptor. **(*Circ Res 56: 279–284, 1985*)**

RADIOLIGAND binding to adenosine receptors in membranes derived from tissues rich in adenosine receptors (brain and testes) has been convincingly demonstrated using [^{3}H]cyclohexyladenosine, *l*-[^{3}H]phenylisopropyladenosine, and [^{3}H]-2-chloroadenosine (reviewed by Daly, 1982). Other adenosine radioligands which have been shown to bind to adenosine receptors include [^{3}H]-5′-*N*-ethylcarboxamide adenosine (Daly et al., 1979), [^{3}H]diethylphenylxanthine (Yeung and Green, 1984), and [^{125}I]hydroxyphenylisopropyladenosine (HPIA) (see Munshi and Baer, 1982; Schwabe et al., 1982; Linden, 1984). Inotropic effects by adenosine and adenosine analogues on heart have been studied extensively (Shrader et al., 1977; Dobson, 1978; Belardinelli et al., 1982), but it has been difficult to characterize adenosine receptors in heart membranes because the sparsity of receptors results in a high ratio of nonspecific to specific binding. Our initial attempts to measure adenosine receptors in heart membranes using tritiated compounds were only marginally successful. For the purposes of this study, two iodinated radioligands, *l*-[^{125}I]HPIA and new compound [^{125}I]-N^6-4-aminobenzyladenosine ([^{125}I]ABA), were tested as cardiac adenosine receptor radioligands. Both compounds bound specifically to adenosine receptors with similar K_D's in the nanomolar range, but the latter compound displayed one-sixth of the lower nonspecific binding and is therefore the more useful radioligand.

Methods

Synthesis of N^6-4-Nitrobenzyladenosine

The N^6-4-nitrobenzyl derivative of adenosine was prepared by a modification of the method of Fleysher et al. (1969). Adenosine (10.7 g, 40 mmol) was added to 140 ml of dimethylformamide and stirred at 80°C under N_2 until a clear solution resulted. The solution was cooled to 21°C, and *p*-nitrobenzylbromide (25.92 g, 120 mmol; Aldrich) was added. After being stirred at room temperature under nitrogen for 24 hours, the resultant N^1-substituted adenosine derivative was rearranged to the N^6-substituted compound and crystallized. The structure of this and other compounds was confirmed by UV and NMR spectra.

Synthesis of N^6-4-Aminobenzyladenosine (ABA)

N^6-4-Nitrobenzyladenosine (NBA) (3.62 g, 9 mmol) was dissolved in acetone and 10% NaOH (pH 10). Sodium dithionite (5.22 g, 30 mmol) was added, and the mixture was heated with stirring at 40–50°C for 1 hour. The product was cooled to room temperature and adjusted to pH 7–8 with HCl. The mixture was not allowed to become acidic, since hydrolysis in acid leads to formation of the free base (Jones and Robins, 1963). The product was extracted with ethyl acetate several times and dried by adding Na_2SO_4. After filtration, the product was concentrated and then crystallized by the addition of hexane and cooling to 4°C for 18 hours. The crystals were filtered, washed with ethyl acetate, and stored desiccated at −20°C.

HPLC Method for Purification of N^6-Benzyladenosine Derivatives

N^6-Benzyladenosine derivatives were applied to a 4.5 × 20 mm octadecyl (C18) reverse phase column and eluted with chromatography buffer (MeOH/50 mM ammonium formate, pH 8; 1:1) isocratically at a flow rate of 1 ml/min using an IBM LC/9533. UV absorption of the eluate was monitored at 271 nm. Fractions of the column eluate were collected at 30-second intervals using a Gilson 201 fraction collector. The fractions containing ^{125}I-labeled products were counted in a Beckman 5500 γ-counter.

Preparative Iodination of ABA

One milligram of ABA was dissolved in 2.5 ml of 0.3 N KH_2PO_4 (pH 7.5). To this solution, 0.25 ml of 10 mM KI and 10 μCi Na ^{125}I (Amersham) were added, followed by 0.5 ml of chloramine T (2 mg/ml in H_2O). After mixing for 60 seconds, the iodination reaction was stopped by the addition of 1 ml of sodium metabisulfite (10 mg/ml in H_2O). The product was extracted five times with 0.5 ml of ethyl acetate. The pooled extracts, which contained 60% of the added radioactive iodide, were evaporated to dryness under nitrogen and dissolved in chromatography buffer. IABA was separated from ABA and I_2ABA by HPLC, as described above. There was a 1:1 ratio of iodine to ABA in IABA based on the ratio of OD:tracer ^{125}I.

Synthesis of Carrier-Free [^{125}I]ABA

One millicurie of Na ^{125}I, in 100 μl of 0.3 N KH_2PO_4 (pH 7.5) was added to 100 μl of 0.1 mM ABA, followed by 5 μl of chloramine T (1 mg/ml in water). The mixture was mixed for 60 seconds, and the iodination reaction was stopped with 50 μl of sodium metabisulfite (5 mg/ml in H_2O). The products were extracted 5 times with 200 μl of ethyl acetate, evaporated to dryness under N_2, and dissolved in chromatography buffer. [^{125}I]ABA was purified by HPLC, as described above.

Radioligand Binding Assays

l-[^{125}I]Hydroxyphenylisopropyladenosine ([^{125}I]HPIA) synthesis, binding assays, and protein determinations were conducted as described by Linden (1984). Equilibrium binding assays with either [^{125}I]ABA or [^{125}I]HPIA, were conducted for 2 hours at 21°C and terminated by filtration over 25-mm glass fiber filters (Gelman A/E). Nonspecific binding was assessed by the addition of 0.1 mM *l*-phenylisopropyladenosine (PIA). Membranes were preincubated with 1 U/ml of adenosine deaminase at 37°C for 20 minutes. Fifty microliters of membranes were added to 50 μl of radioligand prepared in Tris buffer (50 mM Tris-Cl, 15 mM $MgCl_2$, and 0.1 mM EDTA, pH 7.3, at 25°C). The radioligand concentrations were held constant between 50 and 150 pM and diluted with various concentrations of unlabeled ligands between 0.1 and 25 nM.

Preparation of Membranes

Rat brains or heart ventricles were homogenized with a Polytron tissue disruptor in 25 volumes of ice-cold HEPES-sucrose buffer (mM): HEPES, 10; EDTA, 10; benzamide, 0.1; dithiothreitol, 1; sucrose, 292. The homogenates were centrifuged at 2,000 *g* for 20 minutes. The pellets were resuspended in 25 volumes of ice-cold sucrose-free HEPES buffer, incubated on ice for 15 minutes, and centrifuged at 20,000 *g* for 30 minutes. The final pellet was resuspended in five volumes of HEPES buffer containing 20% glycerol and frozen at −70°C. The brain membranes were diluted 10-fold with HEPES buffer for binding assays, heart membranes were used undiluted. Glycerol slightly reduced the amount (20%) but had no effect on the affinity of radioligand binding.

Preparation of Adipocytes and Heart Cells

Epididymal fat pads from 200 to 300-g male Sprague-Dawley rats were minced in Eagle's spinner-modified minimal essential medium buffered with 10 mM Na-HEPES (pH 7.4) containing 1% bovine serum albumin and 1 mg/ml collagenase. After incubation at 37°C for 45 minutes in a shaker bath, loosely adherent cells were separated upon being pipetted through 250 μM nylon mesh. The cells were resuspended in HEPES medium and maintained at 21°C until used. Ventricles obtained from 10-day-old embryonic white Leghorn chicks were dispersed in Ca^{++}- and Mg^{++}-free phosphate-buffered saline containing 0.05% collagenase and 0.01% trypsin. Cells were harvested at 5-minute intervals. Cells were washed and maintained at 21°C in HEPES-buffered (10 mM, pH 7.4) Ham's F12 medium until used.

cAMP Measurements

Adipocytes and heart cells were incubated in a volume of 100 μl with 1 U/ml adenosine deaminase, 1 mM Ro7-2956 (a phosphodiesterase inhibitor), 1 mM ascorbate, and in some cases adenosine analogues or 1 μM (−)-isoproterenol for 90 seconds at 37°C. Cells were lysed by the addition of 400 μl of 0.1 N HCl. Succinyl cAMP tryosyl methyl ester was iodinated and purified by paper and anion exchange chromatography as described by Brooker et al. (1979). Tissue extracts of cAMP were acetylated and assayed by Gammaflo automated radioimmunoassay (Brooker et al., 1976).

Results and Discussion

Physical Properties of NBA, ABA, and IABA

Alkylation of adenosine with *p*-nitrobenzylbromide gave the N^1-substituted derivative which was rearranged in base to give the N^6-substituted compound, NBA. Both NBA and its reduced products,

TABLE 1
Properties of N^6-Nitrobenzyl, -Aminobenzyl, and -Iodoaminobenzyl Adenosines

Compound	UV_{max}* ($\epsilon \times 10^{-3}$)† This report	UV_{max}* ($\epsilon \times 10^{-3}$)† Dutta et al., 1975	HPLC elution time (min)
Adenosine	260 (15.1)		2.4
Nitrobenzyladenosine	269 (22.4)	269 (22.2)	6.9
Aminobenzyladenosine	268 (20.2)	268 (20.7)	3.5
Iodoaminobenzyl adenosine	269 (20.6)		7.5

* Wavelength of maximum UV absorption (nm).
† Extinction coefficient (m^{-1} cm^{-1}).

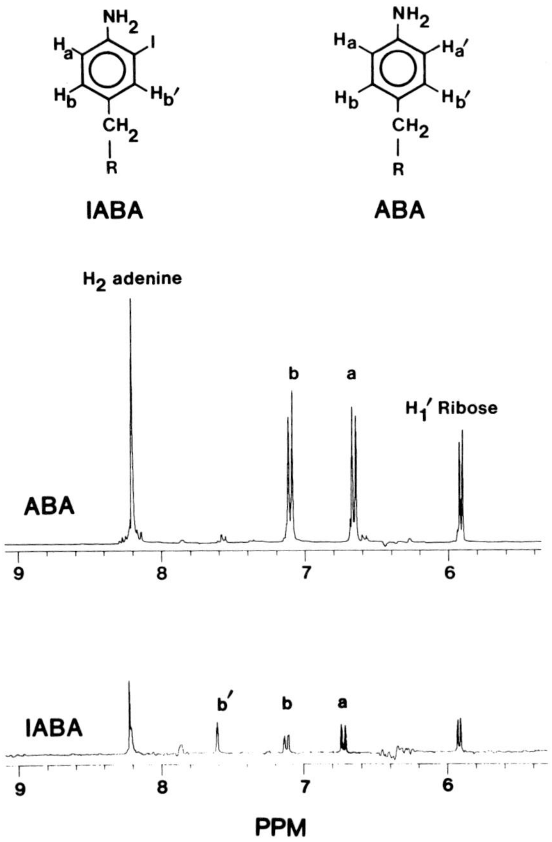

FIGURE 1. *NMR of ABA and IABA. Compounds were scanned in a 300-MHz Fourier-transform NMR. The methyl peak of the solvent (methanol) was used as an internal standard. For the ABA tracing, the doublet labeled a represents H_a and $H_{a'}$ in the ABA molecule shown above, and the doublet labeled b represents H_b and $H_{b'}$. For the IABA tracing, doublets labeled a, b, and b′ represent H_a, H_b, and $H_{b'}$, respectively, in the IABA molecule. R = adenosine.*

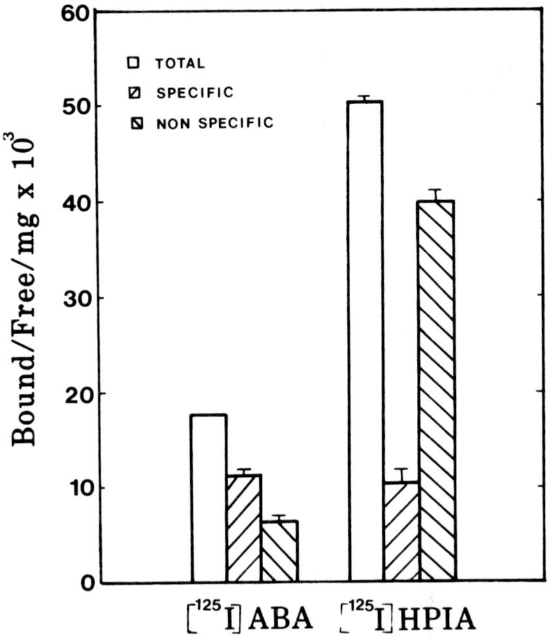

FIGURE 2. *[^{125}I]ABA and [^{125}I]HPIA binding to heart membranes. [^{125}I]ABA (120 pM) and [^{125}I]HPIA (145 pM) were incubated with the same preparation of rat ventricle membranes (460 μg) for 2 hours at 21°C. The concentrations of both radioligands were less than 10% of their K_D, in which case the ratio of specifically bound to free radioligand is proportional to the receptor affinity for the radioligand. Since this ratio was approximately equal for both radioligands, we conclude that they have nearly identical K_D. In contrast, nonspecific [^{125}I]HPIA binding was 6.2 times greater than nonspecific [^{125}I]ABA binding. Data points represent the mean ± SEM, n = 4.*

ABA and IABA, could be readily resolved from each other by HPLC. The UV absorption spectra of NBA and ABA agreed with previously published results (Table 1). NMR confirming the structures of ABA and IABA are illustrated in Figure 1.

Binding of [^{125}I]HPIA and [^{125}I]ABA to Heart Membranes

Figure 2 compares the specific and nonspecific equilibrium binding of [^{125}I]HPIA and [^{125}I]ABA to heart membranes. Both radioligands bound with about the same affinity, but [^{125}I]ABA displayed one-sixth the nonspecific binding.

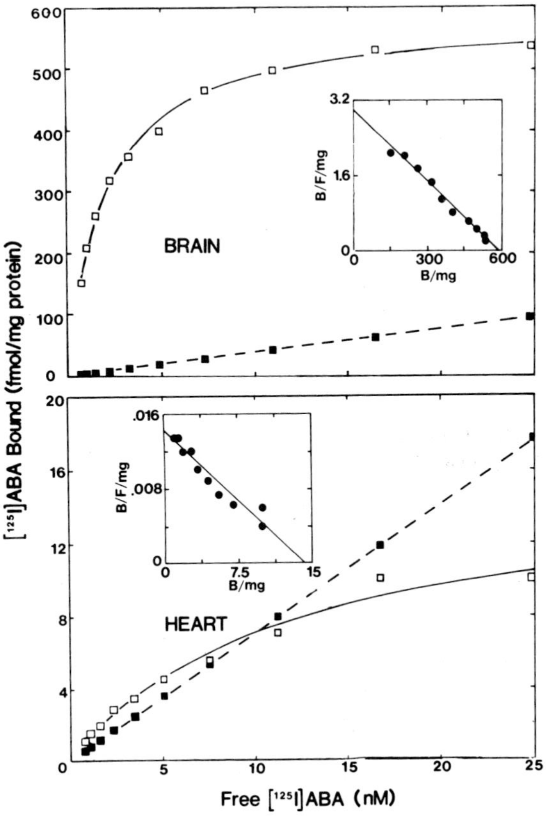

FIGURE 3. *Equilibrium binding of [^{125}I]ABA to brain and heart membranes. Various concentrations of [^{125}I]ABA were incubated with brain (57 μg protein) or heart (403 μg protein) membranes for 2 hours before filtration over glass fiber filters. Each point represents the mean of three closely agreeing replicates. Opened and closed squares represent specific and nonspecific binding, respectively. Binding parameters were estimated by Scatchard plots shown as insets, and then fit to an untransformed single-site binding equation using a nonlinear least squares technique as described in Linden (1984). Binding parameters (B_{max}, fmol/mg protein; and K_D, nM) were 585, 1.93, and 15.2, 11.6 for brain and heart, respectively. Similar results were observed in two additional experiments.*

Figure 3 shows the results of [^{125}I]ABA equilibrium-binding assays to brain and heart membranes. Specific radioligand binding to heart membranes exceeded nonspecific binding at radioligand concentrations below its K_D. [^{125}I]ABA bound with higher affinity to brain membranes (K_D = 1.93 nM) than heart membranes (K_D = 11.6 nM), possibly reflecting a difference in receptors. It is notable in this regard that [^{3}H]cyclohexyladenosine binds with higher affinity to bovine (K_D = 0.7 nM) than guinea pig brains

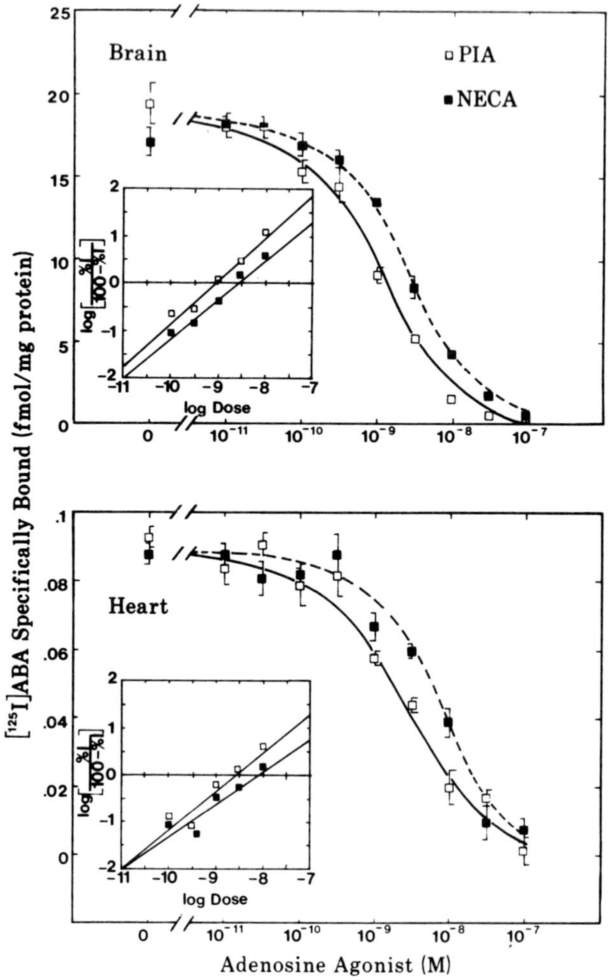

FIGURE 4. *Displacement of [^{125}I]ABA from brain and heart adenosine receptors by PIA and NECA. Brain (72 μg) and heart membranes (451 μg) were incubated with 80 pM [^{125}I]ABA and various concentrations of PIA or NECA. The ED_{50} for PIA, calculated from the x-axis intercepts of the Hill plot shown in the insets, were 0.92 and 2.7 nM for brain and heart, respectively. The ED_{50} for NECA were 2.7 and 8.1 nM for brain and heart, respectively. Hill coefficients ranged between 0.7 and 0.9. Data points represent the mean ± SEM, n = 3.*

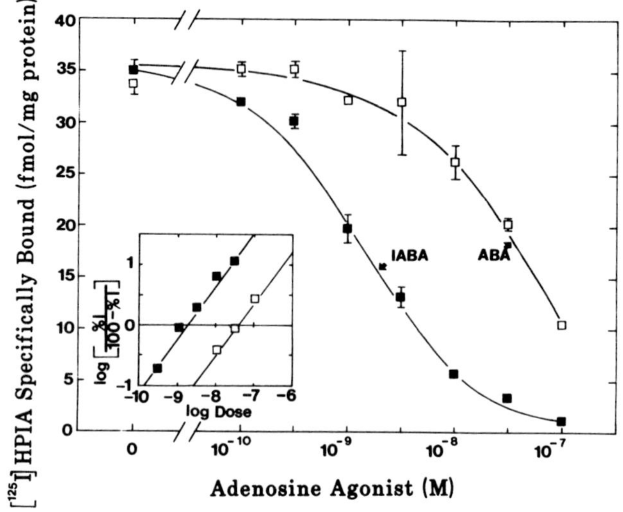

FIGURE 5. *Displacement of [^{125}I]HPIA from brain adenosine receptors by ABA and IABA. Brain membranes (165 μg protein) were incubated with 160 pM [^{125}I]HPIA and various concentrations of ABA and IABA. The ED_{50} were calculated from the x-axis intercepts of Hill plots shown in the inset. The ED_{50} for IABA, 1.79 nM, was 22 times lower than the ED_{50} for ABA, 39 nM. Hill coefficients were 0.85 and 0.88 for ABA and IABA, respectively; n = 3. Similar results were attained in a second experiment.*

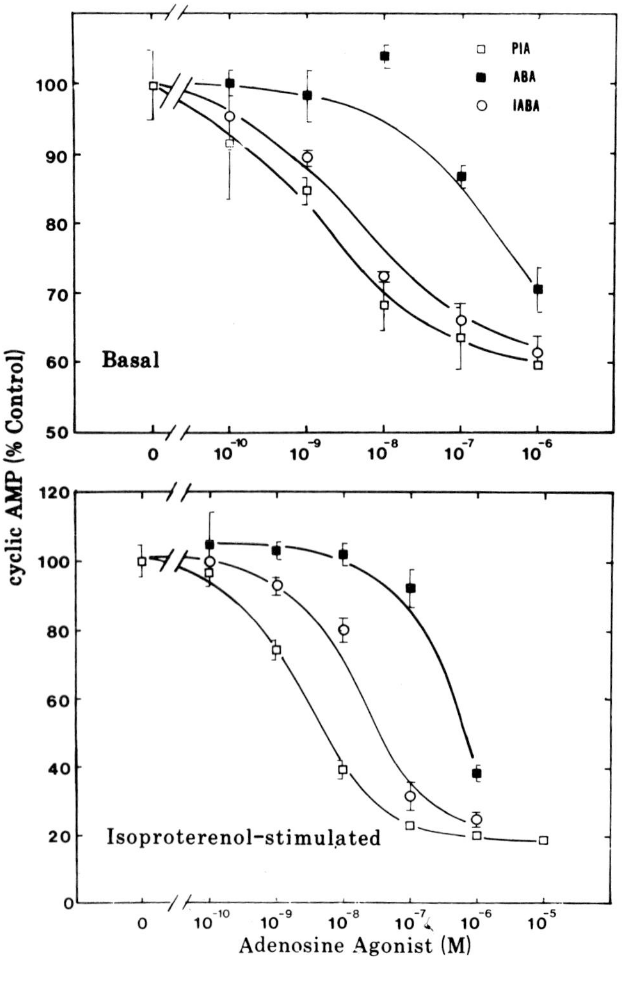

FIGURE 6. *Effect of adenosine analogues on the cAMP content of adipocytes. Freshly prepared adipocytes (70 μg protein) were incubated with 1 U/ml adenosine deaminase, 1 mM ascorbate, 1 mM Ro7-2956, and adenosine analogues without (top) or with (bottom) 1 μM l-isoproterenol for 90 seconds, and then lysed with HCl (see Methods). In the basal condition, 100% corresponds to 24 pmol/mg protein; in the l-isoproterenol-stimulated condition, 100% corresponds to 121 pmol/mg protein. Data points represent the mean ± SEM, n = 4.*

(K_D = 6 nM; Bruns et al., 1980). The ability of PIA and 5′-*N*-ethylcarboxamide adenosine (NECA) to compete with [^{125}I]ABA for binding to brain and heart membranes is illustrated in Figure 4. In both cases, NECA was less potent than PIA, indicative of binding to R_i receptors (Yeung and Green, 1983).

The high affinity of [^{125}I]ABA for adenosine receptors was surprising in view of the relatively low affinity of N^6-benzyladenosine compared to N^6-substituted isopropyl and phenyl compounds (Daly, 1982). Displacement of [^{125}I]HPIA by ABA or IABA from binding to brain membranes (Fig. 5) indicates that the iodinated compound has a much greater affinity for adenosine receptors in brain than the uniodinated compound. The increase in affinity upon iodination may be due to a steric or hydrophobic effect of the iodine atom.

Effect of ABA and IABA on Adipocyte and Heart Cell Cyclic AMP Content

The addition of three adenosine analogs, PIA, IABA, and ABA, to isolated adipocytes resulted in a 40 and 80% decrease, respectively, in the basal- and *l*-isoproterenol-stimulated cAMP content of isolated adipocytes (Fig. 6). These experiments confirm that IABA is a full adenosine agonist with an efficacy equivalent to PIA. Also, as was the case in radioligand binding assays, IABA was found to be over 20 times more potent than ABA. PIA and IABA also decreased isoproterenol-stimulated cAMP accumulation in embryonic chick heart cells (Fig. 7). The maximum response of heart cells to adenosine agonists, 30%, was considerably less than the maximum response in adipocytes. In the absence of isoproterenol, adenosine analogs has no detectable effect on the cAMP content of heart cells. Assays were conducted in the presence of 1 mM Ro7-2956 and 1 U/ml of adenosine deaminase. cAMP levels for basal, PIA-treated (1 μM for 90 seconds), and IABA-treated heart cells were 11.74 ± 0.39, 11.10 ± 0.37, and 12.17 ± 0.41 pmol/mg protein, respectively (mean ± SEM, n = 10).

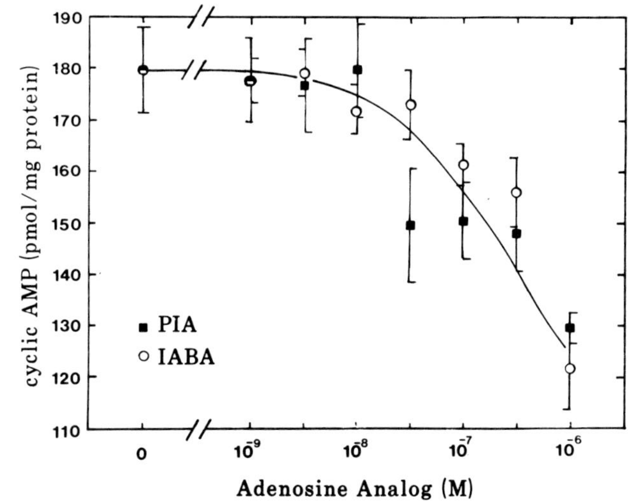

FIGURE 7. *Effect of adenosine analogues on the AMP content of embryonic chick heart cells. Freshly prepared heart cells (89 μg protein) were incubated with adenosine deaminase, ascorbate, Ro7-2956, and l-isoproterenol, as described in the legend for Figure 6. Data points represent the mean ± SEM, n = 5.*

Additional Uses of [^{125}I]ABA

In brain and testes, the density of adenosine receptors is in excess of 1 pmol/g wet weight, and currently available radioligands are adequate for measuring R_i receptors. However, [^{125}I]ABA may represent an important improvement in detection of adenosine receptors in other tissues which contain fewer than 0.3 pmol/g wet weight of adenosine receptors. These include heart, lung, kidney, adrenal, fat, stomach, small intestine, pancreas, thyroid, skeletal muscle, vas deferens, ovary, and submandibular gland (Murphy and Snyder, 1981).

We gratefully acknowledge the expert technical assistance of Sheryl Christofferson and Pamela Brett. We also thank Robert Robinson for his help with NMR, and Karen Bagby and Erma Dulin for their help in preparing this manuscript.

This research was supported in part by Grants OK-83-G-17 from the American Heart Association and HL-31432 from the National Institutes of Health.

Dr. Sadek's present address is: Department of Nuclear Medicine, Faculty of Medicine, University of Kuwait, Kuwait.

Address for reprints: Joel Linden, Cardiovascular Program, Oklahoma Medical Research Foundation, 825 N.E. 13th Street, Oklahoma City, Oklahoma 73104.

Received July 2, 1984; accepted for publication November 9, 1984.

References

Belardinelli L, Fenton RA, West A, Linden J, Althaus JS, Berne RM (1982) Extracellular action of adenosine and the antagonism by aminophylline on the atrioventricular conduction of isolated perfused guinea pig and rat hearts. Circ Res **51:** 569–579

Brooker G, Terasaki WL, Price MG (1976) Gammaflo: A completely automated radioimmunoassay system. Science **194:** 270–276

Brooker G, Harper JF, Terasaki WL, Moylan RD (1979) Radioimmunoassay of cyclic AMP and cyclic GMP. Adv Cyclic Nucleotide Res **10:** 1–34

Bruns RE (1980) Adenosine receptor activation in human fibroblasts: Nucleoside agonists and antagonists. Can J Physiol Pharmacol **28:** 673–691

Bruns RE, Daly WJ, Snyder SH (1980) Adenosine receptors in brain membranes: Binding of N^6-cyclohexyl[^{3}H]adenosine and 1,3-diethyl-8-[^{3}H]phenylxanthine. Proc Natl Acad Sci USA **77:** 5547–5551

Daly JW (1982) Adenosine receptors: Targets for future drugs. J Med Chem **25:** 197–207

Dobson JG Jr (1978) Reduction by adenosine of the isoproterenol-induced increase in cyclic adenosine 3′,5′-monophosphate formation and glycogen phosphorylase activity in rat heart muscle. Circ Res **43:** 785–792

Dutta SP, Tritsch GL, Cox C, Chheda GB (1975) Synthesis and biological activities of some N^6-(nitro-and-aminobenzyl) adenosines. J Med Chem **18:** 780–783

Fleysher MH, Bloch A, Hakala MT, Nichol CA (1969) Synthesis and biological activity of some new N^6-substituted purine nucleosides. J Med Chem **12:** 1056–1061

Jones JW, Robins RK (1963) Purine nucleosides. III. Methylation studies of certain naturally occurring purine nucleosides. J Am Chem Soc **85:** 193–201

Linden J (1984) Purification and characterization of (−)[^{125}I] hydroxyphenylisopropyladenosine, an adenosine R-site radioligand. Mol Pharmacol **26:** 414–423

Munshi R, Baer HP (1982) Radioiodination of *p*-hydroxyphenylisopropyladenosine: development of a new ligand for adenosine receptors. Can J Physiol Pharmacol **60:** 1320–1322

Murphy KMM, Snyder SH (1981) Adenosine receptors in rat testes: Labeling with ^{3}H-cyclohexyladenosine. Life Sci **28:** 917–920

Schwabe Y, Lenschow V, Ukena D, Ferry DR, Glassman H (1982) [^{125}I]N^6-*p*-Hydroxyphenylisopropyladenosine, a new ligand for R_i adenosine receptors. Naunyn Schmiedebergs Arch Pharmacol **321:** 84–87

Shrader J, Baumann G, Gerlach E (1977) Adenosine as inhibitor of myocardial effects of catecholamines. Pflugers Arch **372:** 29–35

Yeung S-MH, Green RD (1983) Agonist and antagonist affinities for inhibitory adenosine receptors are reciprocally affected by 5′-guanylylimidodiphosphate or *N*-ethylmaleimide. J Biol Chem **258:** 2334–2339

Yeung S-MH, Green RD (1984) [^{3}H]-5′-*N*-ethylecarboxamide adenosine binds to both R_a and R_i adenosine receptors in rat striatum. Naunyn Schmiedebergs Arch Pharmacol **325:** 218–225

INDEX TERMS: Adenosine receptors • [^{125}I]N^6-4-Aminobenzyladenosine • cAMP

LETTERS TO THE EDITOR

Comments on *"Biochemical Properties of Membranes Isolated from Calcium-Depleted Rabbit Hearts"* which appeared in *Circ. Res. 54: 217–226, 1984*

The "calcium paradox" and perfusion with calcium-free solutions may indeed have nothing in common with the pathophysiology of ischemic myocardial injury. However, the conclusion of Lamers et al. that, in contrast to ischemia, "the specific activity of the Na^+-Ca^{++} antiporter is not affected by Ca^{++} depletion of the heart," may be incorrect. In sarcolemmal vesicles isolated from rabbit hearts made ischemic for 1 hour, the initial rate of Na^+-Ca^{++} exchange, measured at 1 second, and the calculated V_{max} for Na^+-Ca^{++} exchange were both 50% of control (Bersohn et al., 1982). Plateau level of Na_i^+-dependent Ca^{++} uptake was not affected by ischemia, and no significant differences were measured after 2.7 seconds of the Ca^{++}-uptake reaction (Bersohn et al., 1982; Figs. 3 and 4). The earliest time point reported by Lamers et al. (1984) (Fig. 2) is 15 seconds. Therefore, if the effects of Ca^{++}-free perfusion on Na^+-Ca^{++} exchange were similar to those of ischemia, they would not be detected by the experiment reported.

Lamers et al. are appropriately concerned about selective purification of unrepresentative sarcolemma. The experiments of Bersohn et al. utilized sarcolemmal preparations from ischemic hearts with a 15% yield of K^+-*p*-nitrophenylphosphatase (K^+-*p*NPPase) and an 8% yield of Na^+, K^+-ATPase compared to crude homogenate. In subsequent unpublished experiments, I measured Na^+-Ca^{++} exchange in a crude membrane fraction containing 45–50% of the homogenate K^+-*p*NPPase activity for the ischemic samples. Na_i^+-dependent Ca^{++} uptake measured after 1 second in 40 μM Ca^{++} was 58% of control after 1 hour of ischemia. Therefore, selective purification of more damaged sarcolemma is a less probable explanation for the effects of ischemia on Na^+-Ca^{++} exchange. Whether the calcium overload produced by Ca^{++} depletion and reperfusion is a good model for the calcium overload of ischemia and reperfusion remains unclear at present.

Malcolm M. Bersohn, M.D.
Department of Medicine
UCLA School of Medicine
Veterans Administration Medical Center
16111 Plummer Street
Sepulveda, California 91343

References

Bersohn MM, Philipson KD, Fukushima JY (1982) Sodium-calcium exchange and sarcolemmal enzymes in ischemic rabbit hearts, Am J Physiol **242**: C288–C295
Lamers JMJ, Stinis JT, Ruigrok TJC (1984) Biochemical properties of membranes isolated from calcium-depleted rabbit hearts. Circ Res **54**: 217–226

INDEX TERMS: Cardiac ischemia • Sarcolemma • Sodium-calcium exchange

Reply to the Preceding Letter

It was not our intention (Lamers et al., 1984) to show that the calcium paradox (calcium depletion followed by calcium repletion) has nothing in common with the ischemia-reperfusion model. It is true that the consequences of ischemia and calcium depletion are totally different in many respects. Ischemia, for example, leads to a decrease of the high-energy phosphate levels of the myocardium, whereas these levels are not lowered, but are even increased, during calcium-free perfusion (Boink et al., 1976). However, energy-dependent reactions as a consequence of uncontrolled entry of calcium into the cells may be involved in the development of both reperfusion- and calcium repletion-induced myocardial cell damage. The purpose of our study was not to investigate whether calcium overload produced by calcium depletion and repletion is a good model for the calcium overload that occurs during ischemia-reperfusion, but to detect changes in sarcolemmal calcium transport systems due to calcium depletion that could explain the severity of the calcium paradox damage.

It remains possible that measurement at a time point earlier than 15 seconds would have resulted in different values for the initial rate of Na_i^+-dependent Ca^{++} uptake in sarcolemmal vesicles (Lamers et al., 1984). However, as has been demonstrated by Reeves and Sutko (1979), using a similar subcellular preparation, measurements made after 7 seconds give a good indication of initial rates of the Na^+-Ca^{++} antiporter. That the initial rate of 0.1–0.5 nmol/sec per mg in these studies (see also, Daly et al., 1984) is much lower than the 6.5 nmol/sec per mg observed by Bersohn et al. (1982) may be a consequence of different vesicle properties: purity of the preparation, permeability for monovalent cations of the vesicles, total Ca^{++} uptake capacity (intravesicular volume), degree of Ca^{++}-calmodulin-dependent phosphorylation, membrane potential of the vesicles, and steepness of the applied Na^+ gradient. In addition, different initial rates of the Na^+-Ca^{++} antiporter can be seen with the use of sarcolemmal vesicles isolated from nonperfused or perfused rabbit heart (Lamers et al., 1984).

It is interesting that, even in a crude membrane fraction containing 45–50% activity yield of a sarcolemmal enzyme marker, a depressed Na^+_i-dependent Ca^{++} was measured after 1 hour of ischemia (Bersohn, 1985). Thus, workers in this field need not to be unduly concerned about selective purification of unrepresentative sarcolemma from the ischemic myocardium. At the moment, we do not know whether this is also true for a high yield sarcolemmal preparation from the Ca^{++}-depleted heart. With respect to the frequently observed separation of the glycocalyx after Ca^{++}-free perfusion of the heart, a recent report of Frank et al. (1984) is particularly relevant. These authors demonstrated that sarcolemmal membranes isolated by a conventional method had lost a portion of the external lamina. Therefore, it appears that not only selective purification of unrepresentative sarcolemma, but also removal of essential membrane components during the isolation procedure, should be taken into consideration.

Jos M. J. Lamers, M.D.
Department of Biochemistry I
Medical Faculty
Erasmus University
P.O. Box 1738, 3000 DR
Rotterdam, The Netherlands

Tom J. C. Ruigrok, M.D.
Department of Cardiology
University Hospital
3500 CG Utrecht
The Netherlands

References

Bersohn MM (1985) Letter to the Editor. Circ Res 56: 000–000

Bersohn MM, Philipson KD, Fukushima JY (1982) Sodium-calcium exchange and sarcolemmal enzymes in ischemic rabbit hearts. Am J Physiol **242:** C288–C295

Boink ABTJ, Ruigrok TJC, Maas AHJ, Zimmerman ANE (1976) Changes in high-energy phosphate compounds of isolated rat hearts during Ca^{2+}-free perfusion and reperfusion with Ca^{2+}. J Mol Cell Cardiol **8:** 973–979

Daly MJ, Elz JS, Nayler WG (1984) Sarcolemmal enzymes and Na^+-Ca^{2+} exchange in hypoxic, ischemic, and reperfused rat hearts. Am J Physiol **247:** H237–H243

Frank JS, Philipson KD, Beydler S (1984) Ultrastructure of isolated sarcolemma from dog and rabbit myocardium; comparison to intact tissue. Circ Res **54:** 414–423

Lamers JMJ, Stinis JT, Ruigrok TJC (1984) Biochemical properties of membranes isolated from calcium-depleted rabbit heart. Circ Res **54:** 217–226

Reeves JP, Sutko JL (1979) Sodium-calcium ion exchange in cardiac membrane vesicles. Proc Natl Acad Sci USA **76:** 590–594

INDEX TERMS: Heart • Sarcolema • Na^+-Ca^{++} antiporter • Ca^{++} paradox • Ischemia-reperfusion • Ca^{++} overload

Erratum

RE: D. Kim, J.D. Marsh, W.H. Barry, and T.W. Smith. Effects of Growth in Low Potassium Medium or Ouabain on Membrane Na,K-ATPase, Cation Transport, and Contractility in Cultured Chick Heart Cells (*Circ. Res. 55: 39–48, 1984*)

We wish to correct a literature citation that appeared in our paper in the July 1984 issue of *Circulation Research.* As originally published, the introduction includes a statement conveying the incorrect impression that the abstract of Anderson, Henry, and Lieberman (J. Gen. Physiol. 82: 18a, 1983) reported the effects of low $[K^+]_o$ growth conditions on HeLa cells, when, in fact, the study was on chick embryo heart cells. Anderson et al. reported that growth of chick embryo heart cells in tissue culture for 24 hours in the presence of 0.5 mM K^+ caused an 80% increase in the number of sodium pump sites present in the cell membrane, as judged by $[^3H]$ouabain binding, accompanied by a 74% increase in Na,K-ATPase activity.

News from the American Heart Association

7320 Greenville Avenue, Dallas, Texas 75231
Telephone: 214 750-5300

Research Applications Are Invited by Heart; Most Due by July 1

Applications for four types of research awards in the cardiovascular field, including stroke, are invited by the American Heart Association. Deadlines for three programs are July 1; for the fourth, Grants-in-Aid, the deadline is October 1.

Research awards are:

Clinician-Scientist: To encourage young physicians to investigative careers. Awardees are supported for one to three years of research training and during subsequent period of independent investigation. Awards are for three years with possible extension two more years. U.S. citizenship and an M.D. or Ph.D. degree are required.

Established Investigator: A five-year stipend award for young physicians and scientists to conduct independent research. Applicants should have three years of post-doctoral research experience and, ordinarily, be under age 50 at application. U.S. citizenship and doctoral degrees required. Negotiated stipend is based on institutional standing and is up to an AHA maximum of $30,000 annually at entry.

British-American Research Fellowship: Jointly supported by AHA and the British Heart Foundation. One year stipend awards for U.S. citizen physicians and scientists, ordinarily under age 35 at application, who are seeking additional research training best available in British institutions. Applications should show evidence of potential for a research career. Stipend is $12,000 with dependency and travel allowances. Doctoral degree required.

Grants-in-Aid: Deadline for applications is Oct. 1. One to three year research projects in non-profit institutions are supported, based primarily on scientific excellence. Offered for research activities broadly related to cardiovascular function and disease or related basic study. Doctoral degrees required.

Information on all National Research Awards may be obtained from the Director of Research Awards, AHA, 7320 Greenville Ave., Dallas, TX 75231. Telephone: 214-750-5300.

Conference on Stroke Opens in New Orleans

The 10th International Joint Conference on Stroke and Cerebral Circulation will be held in New Orleans, Feb. 21–23.

A symposium on nuclear magnetic resonance in stroke will open the sessions with Dr. J. Donald Easton of San Antonio as chairman. A feature lecture—"Cerebral Vascular Clinical Pathological Potpourri," by Dr. C. Miller Fisher of Harvard, will also be given Thursday, Feb. 21.

Other highlights of the program will include a breakfast seminar on management of symptomatic carotid disease and a breakfast symposium on ischemic disease and the eye. Sixty-four papers on experimental aspects of stroke, epidemiological, clinical, carotid plaques, and surgery in stroke will be delivered. Abstracts were published in the January/February issue of STROKE, a Journal of Cerebral Circulation.

The sessions are sponsored by the AHA Stroke Council, Cerebrovascular Surgery Section of the American Association of Neurological Surgeons, the Canadian Stroke Society of the Canadian Heart Foundation, the American Neurological Association and the Society for Vascular Surgery.

Scientific Sessions To Meet Nov. 11–14

The 58th AHA Scientific Sessions will be held in Washington, D.C., Nov. 11–14, 1985. Abstracts are due in Dallas in early May.

The Scientific Sessions Committee, with Dr. Bernadine Healy Bulkley, of the Johns Hopkins Medical School, chairman, met in January to review the 1984 sessions and begin planning for 1985.

Forms for abstracts may be obtained from the Scientific Sessions Section, AHA, 7320 Greenville Ave., Dallas, TX, 75231. Tel. 1-245-750-5441.

Four Revised Statements Are Published by Heart

Four new or revised scientific statements on stroke, cigarette smoking, prevention of rheumatic fever, and prevention of bacterial endocarditis have been published in the AHA scientific journals CIRCULATION and STROKE.

The statements, representing Association policy, were first introduced in press conferences at the November, 1984, Scientific, Sessions in Miami Beach.

Stroke Risk Factors

"Risk Factors in Stroke," a statement for physicians by the Subcommittee on Risk Factors and Stroke of the Stroke Council, (published in STROKE, Nov./Dec. 1984—**15**, No. 6, 1105–1111) updated a statement published in 1971. Since then the "impressive" rate of decline in cerebrovascular and heart disease mortality have occurred. "Circumstantial evidence," the sub-committee states, "suggests that the change was related chiefly to more effective treatment of hypertension. However, other factors may also have contributed to the decline."

Listed among Risk Factors in Stroke in the statement were Single Risk Factors, well documented, treatment not feasible or value not established: *age and gender, familial factors, race, diabetes mellitus, prior stroke, and asymptomatic carotid bruits.* Treatable: *hypertension, cardiac disease, transient ischemic attacks, elevated hematocrit, sickle cell disease.*

Other Risk Factors

The statements also continues by listing less well documented risk factors where treatment is not feasible or value not established and those treatable but value not established. Further listed are multiple risk factors (Framingham Profile and Paffenbarger and Williams Criteria).

Members of the Subcommittee were Drs. Mark L. Dyken and Philip A. Wolf, co-chairmen, H.J.M. Barnett, John J. Bergan, William K. Hass, William B. Kannel, Lewis Kuller, John F. Kurtzke, and Thoralf M. Sundt. Copies of the statement may be obtained from the Heart Association in Dallas (ask for No. 71-022-A).

Cigarettes and CVD

The statement on Cigarette Smoking and Cardiovascular Disease (published in CIRCULATION, Dec., 1984–**70**, No. 6, 1114A-1117A), updated a 1977 publication. It called cigarette smoking "the most important preventable cause of premature death in the United States" and noted its relationship to atherosclerotic CV disease, cancer, and chronic obstructive pulmonary disease.

With hypertension and hypercholesterolemia, cigarette smoking was included in the three major, independent CHD risk factors, the statement said. It pointed to the concurrent use by women of oral contraceptives and cigarettes as a risk factor, and also the risk of malignant hypertension, renovascular hypertension, high-density/low density lipoprotein cholesterol, and smoking and familial predisposition. Other topics discussed in the statement are pathology, clinical correlations, pathophysiology, types of smoking, cessation, and patient management recommendations.

Statement Authors

Authors of the statement (available from AHA, Dallas—ask for No. 71-001-C) were Drs. John H. Holbrook, chairman, Scott M. Grundy, Charles H. Hennekens, William B. Kannel, and Jack P. Strong. They were a Task Force appointed by the Steering Committee of AHA.

Rheumatic Fever

The revised "Prevention of Rheumatic Fever," a statement for health professionals by the Committee on Rheumatic Fever and Infective Endocarditis of the Council on CV Disease in the Young, updates a 1977 publication. (Published in CIRCULATION: **70**, No. 6, December, 1984, 1118A-1122A).

Rheumatic fever, the statement said, can usually be prevented and "changes (in this statement) from previous recommendations reflect the current rarity of acute rheumatic fever in most areas of the United States." However, there are areas in the world and in the U.S. where the disease is prevalent and may lead to rheumatic heart disease, the statement said.

Authors of the report were Drs. Stanford T. Shulman, chairman, Don P. Amren, Alan L. Bisno, Adnan S. Dajani, David T. Durack, Michael L. Gerber, Edward L. Kaplan, H. Dean Millard, W. Eugene Sanders, Richard H. Schwartz, and Chatrchai Watanakunakorn.

The Report may be obtained from AHA, Dallas (ask for No. 71-005-C).

Bacterial Endocarditis

The Report on Prevention of Bacterial Endocarditis was also prepared by the Committee on Rheumatic Fever and Infective Endocarditis of the Council on Cardiovascular Disease in the Young. It updates a 1977 publication and is published in Dec., 1984 CIRCULATION (**70**, 6, 1123A-1127A).

The statement points out the danger of dental treatment, surgical procedures or instrumentation involving mucosal surfaces or contaminated tissue causing bacterial endocarditis or endarteritis. Since it is impossible to predict development of the infection, the statement recommends prophylactic antibiotics for patients at risk. Physicians and dentists are warned that antibiotics must be administered *shortly* before (and not several days before) a procedure. The statement also stresses that "antibiotic regimens used to prevent recurrences of acute rheumatic fever are inadequate for the prevention of bacterial endocarditis."

A reprint may be obtained from AHA, Dallas (ask for 71-005-C).

Scientific Councils Name 3 New Chairmen

Robert A. O'Rourke, M.D., of San Antonio, has been elected Vice President for Councils and three new chairmen for the 14 Scientific Councils were named. They are:

Aram Van Chobanian, M.D., chairman of the *High Blood Pressure Council.*

L. Henry Edmunds, Jr., M.D., chairman of the *Council on Cardiovascular Surgery.*

Mark L. Dyken, M.D., chairman of the *Stroke Council.*

Other Council chairmen whose terms continue are:

Council on Arteriosclerosis: Edwin L. Bierman, M.D.; *Council on Basic Science*: Howard E. Morgan, M.D.; *Council on Cardiopulmonary*: Robert L. Johnson, Jr., M.D.; *Council on Cardiovascular Disease in the Young*: Elizabeth W. Nugent, M.D.; *Council on Cardiovascular Nursing*: Caroline L. Murdaugh, R. N., Ph.D.; *Council on Cardiovascular Radiology*: Lewis Wexler, M.D.; *Council on Circulation*: Allyn L. Mark, M.D.; *Council on Clinical Cardiology*: Robert C. Schlant, M.D.; *Council on Epidemiology*: H. Alfred Tyroler, M.D.; *Council on the Kidney in CV Disease*: Darrell D. Fanestil; *Council on Thrombosis*: John C. Hoak, M.D.

Dr. Richard E. Hurley Heads Congress Staff

Richard E. Hurley, M.D., has retired as senior medical advisor of the American Heart Association after 24 years service and has joined the staff of the Xth World Congress of Cardiology as executive vice president. The World Congress will be held in Washington, D.C., September 14–19, **1986**. The AHA will be host for the scientific meeting last held in this country in 1954.

Dr. Hurley has been liaison with the Congress organizing committee which includes Dr. Thomas N. James of Birmingham, AL, as president, and Dr. Donald C. Harrison of Palo Alto, CA, as secretary general. The Congress secretariat is in the AHA National Center in Dallas.

Congress vice presidents include Drs. Harriet P. Dustan, Charles Fisch, Elliot Rapaport, James A. Schoenberger, John T. Shepherd and Paul N. Yu. Ross Reid is treasurer.

HYPERTENSION Supplement On Central BP Regulation

"Central Alpha-Adrenergic Blood Pressure Regulating Mechanisms" has been published as a supplement to September/October HYPERTENSION. It is edited by William B. Abrams M.D. and Charles S. Sweet, Ph.D.

The symposium "stems from an extramural research program generated and sponsored by the Merck Sharp & Dohme Research Laboratories to acquire more information about the central mechanism" of methyldopa action, Dr. Abrams said. "Although acknowledged for the past 15 years to exert its anti-hypertensive effects via the brain, information . . . has not been precise. The central mechanism of clonidine, although synthesized more recently, has been investigated more thoroughly because of its direct and immediate effects," Dr. Abrams said. Studies on clonidine helped identify the role of brain alpha-adrenergic mechanisms in blood pressure regulation and confirmed earlier concepts of methyldopa action.

The supplement is also printed as AHA Monograph No. 109 (No. 73-095A) and is available from the Scientific Publishing Section, AHA, Dallas.

Subscriptions Due

Subscriptions for many readers of CIRCULATION, CIRCULATION RESEARCH, HYPERTENSION, STROKE and ARTERIOSCLEROSIS are now due for 1985. Renewals should be requested with payment.

Subscribers in Japan should order through Nankodo Co. Ltd., 42-5 Hongo 3-Chome, Bonkyo-Ku, Tokyo, Japan. All orders from Europe should go through Bailliere Tindall, 1st Anne's Road, Eastbourne, East Sussex BN23 3UN, England.

Other orders should go to the AHA Scientific Journals Subscription Dept., 7320 Greenville Ave., Dallas, TX 75231.

Subscriptions to CIRCULATION RESEARCH are $86 in the U.S.; $105 outside the U.S.

AHA Briefs . . .

• The National Heart, Lung, and Blood Institute has announced that it will hold a conference on **"Treatment of the Elderly with Coronary Heart Disease"** in Bethesda, MD, in the Spring (no date set yet). Inquiries may go to E. Kelner-Schron, R.N., M.S., NHLBI, Federal Bldg.—Rm. 216, Bethesda. Tel. 1-301-496-3107.

• **Dr. Donald A.B. Lindberg** has been sworn in as Director of the National Library of Medicine. He succeeded Dr. Martin N. Cummings who retired. Dr. Lindberg was formerly director of the Information Sciences Group and professor of pathology at the University of Missouri School of Medicine in Columbia, MO.

• The NIH Recombinant DNA Advisory Committee has unanimously **rejected a proposal to ban experiments** in which genes from higher animals, including man, are transferred into animals of other species. The panel, including scientists, physicians, lawyers, ethicists and lay members, advises the NIH Director on federally funded genetic engineering experiments.

• An International Symposium on **Ultrasound Diagnosis of Cerebrovascular Disease** will be held May 13–15 in Seattle, WA. It will be preceded by a basic course (May 10–12) in cerebrovascular ultrasound (Doppler and B-scan). Merrill P. Spencer, M.D., program chairman. Inquiries may go to Dept. Med. Ed., IAPM, 701 16th Ave., Seattle, WA 98122. Tel. 1-206-442-7330.

• **"Hemodynamics and Atherosclerosis"** will be discussed Oct. 3–4 in Wellington, New Zealand. Coverage will include hemodynamics, effect of hemodynamic stress on the blood vessel wall, hemodynamic localization of atherosclerosis and the complications of atherosclerosis and hemodynamics in the pathogenesis of thrombosis. Inquiries may go to Dr. W. E. Stehbens, Dept. of Pathology, Wellington Clinical School of Medicine, Wellington 2, New Zealand.

• A comprehensive literature review and evaluation covering the last 10 years is being conducted of **smoking cessation** methods, techniques, programs, and smoking prevention programs for adults and children. The review is sponsored by the National Cancer Institute. Published or unpublished articles, papers, or reports are invited by Dr. Jerry Schwartz, 746 Hawthorn Lane, Davis, CA 95616.

• The 1st **Latin American Congress of Cardiac Pacing** will be held in Buenos Aires, Argentina, Oct. 8–10. Dr. Alejandro Dussaut is president of the organizing committee. Inquiries may go to Congresos Internacionales S.A., Moreno 584-9° piso, 1091 Buenos Aires, Argentina. Tel. 14-3216/3408/3283. Telex 22036 JECON AR.

• An **International Symposium on Cardiogenic Reflexes**, Sept 16–20, is planned for the University of Leeds, England. It is organized by the Dept. of Cardiovascular Studies, University of Leeds, under the auspices of the Commission on Cardiovascular Physiology of the International Union of Physiological Science. Inquiries may go to Dr. R. Hainsworth, Dept. CV Studies, Univ. Leeds, Leeds LS2 93T, England.

Meetings Calendar 1985

Feb. 21–23: **10th International Joint Conference on Stroke and Cerebral Circulation.** New Orleans. Inquiries: Coordinator, Scientific Sessions, AHA, 7320 Greenville Ave., Dallas, TX 75231. Tel. 214-750-5439.

Feb. 24–March 1: **7th Annual Cardiology at Big Sky.** Big Sky MT. Sponsored by Burns Clinic, Petoskey, MI, AHA Council on Clinical Cardiology and AHA Montana Affiliate. Sidney Goldstein, M.D., course director. Inquiries: Dr. S. Goldstein, Henry Ford Hospital, Div. CV Med., 2799 W. Grand Blvd., Detroit, MI 48202.

Feb. 25–28: **Critical Care Medicine, 23rd Annual Symposium.** MGM Grand Hotel, Las Vegas, NV. Inquiries: Assoc. Dean, USC School of Medicine, PG Div., 2025 Zonal Ave., KAM 307, Los Angeles, CA 90033. Tel. 213-224-7051.

March 3–8: **Annual Meeting American Society for Microbiology.** Las Vegas, NV. Inquiries: ASM, 1913 I St., NW, Washington, DC 20005.

March 7–9: **American Heart Association 25th Annual Conference on Cardiovascular Disease Epidemiology.** Doubletree Inn, Tucson, AZ. Inquiries: G. Wilson, AHA, 7320 Greenville Ave., Dallas, TX 75231. Tel. 214-750-5437.

March 8–12: **Advances in Nutrition Therapy II and Digestive Disease Review V.** Caribe Hilton, San Juan, Puerto Rico. Sponsored by Puerto Rican Society of Gastroenterology and Norwalk, CT, Hospital. Inquiries: Dept. Medicine, Norwalk Hospital, Norwalk, CT 06856.

March 10–14: **American College of Cardiology Scientific Session.** Anaheim, CA. Inquiries: ACC, 9111 Old Georgetown Rd., Bethesda, MD 20814. Tel. 301-897-5400.

March 14–16: **Symposium on Thanatology Curriculum for Schools of Medicine, Nursing, and Related Health Professions.** Columbia-Presbyterian Medical Center, New York City. Sponsored by Foundation of Thanatology and Columbia Univ. School of Nursing. Inquiries: Dr. A. H. Kutscher, 630 W. 168th St., New York, NY 10032.

March 18–20: **Critical Care Medicine: Update 1985.** The Johns Hopkins Medical Institutions, Baltimore. Sponsored by Dept. Anesthesiology/Critical Care Medicine. Inquiries: C. Kearney, OCE, Rm 19 Turner, 720 Rutland Ave., Baltimore, MD 21205. Tel. 1-301-955-3168.

March 28–30: **86th Annual Meeting, American Society for Clinical Pharmacology and Therapeutics.** Hilton Palacio del Rio, San Antonio, TX. Inquiries: Mrs. E. Galasso, 1718 Gallagher Rd., Norristown, PA 19401. Tel. 215-825-3838.

March 29–31: **8th Annual Intensive Clinical Neurology Course for Non-Neurologists.** New York City. Inquiries: L. P. Levitt, M.D., 12120 S. Cedar Crest Blvd., Allentown, PA 18103. Tel. 215-433-6474.

April 2–6: **3rd Annual Interventional Radiology Seminar.** Buena Vista Palace, Lake Buena Vista, Florida (Walt Disney World Village Plaza). Sponsored by Dept. Radiology, U. of South Florida College of Medicine. Inquiries: C. Krissman, 12901 N. 30 St., Tampa, FL 33612. Tel. 813-974-2538.

April 10–12: **26th National Student Research Forum.** University of Texas Medical Branch, Galveston. Inquiries: Student Research Forum, POB 54, Station 1, UTMB, Galveston, TX 77550. Tel. 409-761-3762.

April 11–12: **Oak Ridge Conference on Advanced Analytical Concepts for the Clinical Laboratory.** Sheraton Charlestown, SC. Sponsored by American Association for Clinical Chemistry. Inquiries: AACC, 1725 K St., SW, Washington, DC 20006. Tel. 202-857-0717.

April 21–26: **Federation of American Societies for Experimental Biology.** Anaheim, CA. Inquiries: 9650 Rockville Pike, Bethesda, MD 20014.

April 28–30: **National Conference on High Blood Pressure Control.** Palmer House, Chicago. Inquiries: NCHBP, 1501 Wilson Blvd., Suite 600, Arlington, VA 22209. Tel. 202-944-3176.

May 1–2: **21st Annual Cardiovascular Symposium.** Hunt Memorial, Hartford, CT, Medical Society. Sponsored by Cardiology Section, St. Francis Hosp. and Medical Center. Inquiries R. M. Jeresaty, M.D., Cardiology, St. Francis Hosp./Medical Center, 114 Woodland St., Hartford, CT 06105. Tel. 1-289-548-4820.

May 3–4: **Perspectives on the Management of Chronic Congestive Heart Failure.** Baltimore, MD. Sponsored by Div. of Cardiology, University of Maryland School of Medicine. Inquiries: Program of Cont. Ed., University of Maryland School of Medicine, 10 S. Pine St., Rm. 300, Baltimore, MD 21201. Tel. 301-528-3956.

May 12–15: **6th Annual Meeting, Society for Clinical Trials.** New Orleans. Inquiries: Curt Furberg, MD, SCT, 600 Wyndhurst Ave., Baltimore, MD 21210.

May 12–15: **Annual Meeting, American Thoracic Society.** Anaheim, CA. Slide and poster presentations. Inquiries: ATS, 1740 Broadway, New York, NY 10019. Tel. 212-245-8000, Ext. 570.

May 13–15: **International Symposium: Ultrasound Diagnosis of Cerebrovascular Disease.** Seattle. (May 10–12: Pre-symposium Basic Course in Cerebrovascular Ultrasound—Doppler and B-Scan). Sponsored by Institute of Applied Physiology and Medicine. Merrill P. Spencer, M.D., program chairman. Inquiries: Dept. Med. Ed., Inst. Applied Physiology and Med., 701 Sixteenth Ave., Seattle, WA 98122. Tel. 1-206-442-7330.

May 16–18: **Practical Applications of Echo and Doppler Techniques in Cardiology.** Cleveland Marriott Inn-Airport Hotel. Inquiries: Professional Medical Seminars, POB 5400, Sherman Oaks, CA 91413.

May 17–18: **Clinical Concerns in Hemodialysis Therapy.** Sheraton Harbor Island East Hotel, San Diego. Program Chairman, Richard A. Sherman, M.D. Sponsored by American Kidney Fund and Nephrology Society of New Jersey. Inquiries: Dr. R. A. Sherman, Academic Health Science Center, CN 19, New Brunswick, NJ 08903. Tel. 1-800-922-0130.

May 17–22: **UCSD-Anesthesiology Review.** Vacation Village, San Diego. Sponsored by Dept. Anesthesiology, University of California, San Diego School of Medicine. Inquiries: K. Naughton, Dept. Anesthesia (M-029), UCSD, La Jolla, CA 92093. Tel. 1-619-452-3865.

May 19–23: **6th Scientific Meeting Inter-American Society of Hypertension.** Cleveland. Inquiries: 6th Meeting IASH, Research Division FF2-49, 9500 Euclid Ave., Cleveland, OH 44106. Tel. 216-444-5837.

May 23–24: **Vascular Surgery 1985. Current State of the Art. 2nd International Vascular Symposium.** Waldorf-Astoria Hotel, New York City. John B. Chang, M.D., program chairman. Inquiries: A. J. Boehme, Long Island Jewish-Hillside Medical Center, New Hyde Park, NY 11042. Tel. 212-470-2114.

May 24–27: **7th Annual Meeting American Section of the International Society for Heart Research.** Houston. Inquiries: Dr. J. Allen, Dept. Cell Biophysics, Baylor College of Med., Houston, TX 77025.

June 2–6: **2nd World Congress of Pediatric Cardiology.** New York City. Inquiries: V. Herlitz, 404 Park Ave. S., New York, NY 10016.

June 10–12: **Surgery for Coronary Artery Disease.** Durham, NC. Sponsored by Duke University Medical Center and American College of Cardiology. R. H. Jones, M.D., program director. Inquiries: ACC, 9111 Georgetown Rd., Bethesda, MD 20814. Tel. 301-897-5400, Ext. 228.

June 17–18: **Today's Therapy in Nephrology.** Resorts International Hotel, Atlantic City, NJ. Sponsored by American Kidney Fund and Nephrology Society of New Jersey. Inquiries: See May 17–18, Dr. Sherman.

July 12: **Certifying Examination, Sub-Board of Pediatric Cardiology.** Chapel Hill, NC. Registration until Feb. 28. Inquiries: American Board of Pediatrics, 111 Silver Cedar

Court, Chapel Hill, NC 27514-1651.

July 21–26: **37th Annual Meeting American Association of Clinical Chemistry.** Georgia World Congress Center, Atlanta. Inquiries: AACC, 1725 K St., NW, Washington, DC 20006. Tel. 202-857-0717.

July 22–26: **Interdisciplinary Symposium on Plant Flavonoids in Biology and Medicine.** Biochemical, Pharmacological, and Structure-Activity Relationships. Buffalo, NY. Inquiries: Dr. Elliott Middleton, Jr., Dept. Med., Buffalo General Hospital, 100 High St., Buffalo, NY 14203. Tel. 1-716-845-2985.

Oct. 11–12: **4th Southern Biomedical Engineering Conference.** Jackson MS. Deadline for papers March 1. Inquiries: Dr. Barry W. Sauer, SBEC, Div. Cont. Health Prof. Ed., University of Mississippi Medical Center, 2500 N. State St., Jackson, MS 39216-4505.

Nov. 11–14: **58th Annual Scientific Sessions, American Heart Association, Washington, DC. Inquiries: Coordinator Scientific Sessions, AHA, 7320 Greenville Ave., Dallas, TX 75231. Tel. for Abstracts: 214-750-5439; for housing and reservations 214-750-5425.**

Nov. 19–20: **Subspecialty Boards in Cardiovascular Disease.** Philadelphia. Registration to April 1. Inquiries: American Board of International Medicine, 3624 Market St., Philadelphia, PA 19104. Tel. 215-243-1500. (New date.)

1986

Sept. 13–20: **Xth World Congress of Cardiology.** Washington, DC. Inquiries: Secretariat, 7320 Greenville Ave., Dallas, TX 75231. Tel. 214-750-5429. Cable Tencard, Dallas, TX.

Abroad

1985

Feb. 12–16: **First Philippine Heart Center for Asia International Symposium on Valvular Heart Diseases.** Manila Hotel, Philippines. Inquiries: PHCA Symposium, 5th Floor, Medical Arts Bldg., PHCA, East Ave., Quezon City, Philippines. Tel. 98-04-21-2620. Telex 42032 TOWMED PM

March 24–27: **2nd International Congress on Essential Fatty Acids and Prostaglandins.** Egham, near London, England. Multidisciplinary sessions and poster presentations. Inquiries: Prostaglandin Congress, c/o Zoological Society, London, NW1 4RY, United Kingdom.

March 29–31: **International Symposium on Ambulatory Monitoring.** Clinica Medica I, University of Padua, Italy. Prof. C. Dal Palù, president of symposium. Inquiries: A. C. Pessina, Clinica Medica I-Policlinico, University of Padua, Via Giustiniani, 2, 35100 Padova, Italy.

April 1–3: **PTCA Course II.** Geneva, Switzerland. Drs. Bernhard Meier and Wilhelm Rutishauser, course directors. Live demonstrations of percutaneous transluminal coronary angiography and lectures in English. Inquiries: Dr. Bernhard Meier, Center for Cardiology, University Hospital, CH-1211, Geneva 4, Switzerland.

April 19–21: **6th Cardiological Meeting Congressi Italo-Monegaschi.** San Remo, Italy. Inquiries: Dr. G. Reforzo, Centro Cardiologico Fondazione Don C. Gnocchi, 18038, San Remo, Italy.

April 22–25: **13th European Congress on Non-Invasive Cardiovascular Dynamics.** Brescia, Italy. Sponsored by European Society for Noninvasive Cardiovascular Dynamics. C. Rusconi, M.D., chairman. Inquiries: G. Orlando, M.D., St. Orsola Hospital, Via Vittorio Emanuele No. 27, 25122 Brescia, Italy. Tel. 030/47061

April 22–26: **International Symposium 1985 Cardiovascular Pharmacotherapy.** Geneva, Switzerland. Inquiries: Interconference SA., 58 rue Ernest-Bloch, CH-1207, Geneva, Switzerland.

May 1–3: **International Symposium on Neural Mechanisms and Cardiovascular Disease.** Santa Margharita Ligure, (near Genoa), Italy. Dr. C. Bartorelli, symposium president. Inquiries: A. Malliani, Istituto Ricerche Cardiovascolari, Via Bonfadini, 214, 20138 Milano, Italy. Tel. 02-5063984 (p.m.)

May 8–10: **4th Congress Southern African Hypertension Society.** Johannesburg, South Africa. Inquiries: Prof. Clive Rosendorff, Dept. Physiology, Univ. Witwatersrand Medical School, York Rd., Parktown 2193, South Africa.

May 10–12: **International Symposium on Sports Cardiology.** Knokke, Belgium. Inquiries: Dr. I. Bekaert, Alg. Ziekenhuis St. Jozef, Steenweg op Merksplas 44, 2300 Turnhout, Belgium. Tel. 014-4104-51.

May 22: **Symposium on Coronary Arteriography.** Rotterdam, the Netherlands. Organized by Working Group on Coronary Blood Flow and Angina Pectoris, on behalf of the European Society of Cardiology. Inquiries: Prof. P. G. Hugenholtz, M.D., Thoraxcenter BD 406, Erasmus Univ., Rotterdam, POB 1738, 3000 DR Rotterdam, the Netherlands.

May 23–25: **Unstable Angina Revisited.** Rotterdam, the Netherlands. Organized by the Thoraxcenter of Erasmus University, Rotterdam, the Netherlands Interuniversitary Cardiological Institute, the Netherlands, and the Toronto General Hospital, Toronto, Canada. Inquiries: Prof. P.G. Hugenholtz, M.D., Thoraxcenter Bd 406, Erasmus University, Rotterdam. POB 1738, 3000 DR Rotterdam, the Netherlands.

June 1–8: **Frontiers in Imaging and Cardiopulmonary Diagnosis.** England. (Also in Scotland, June 9–15). Eric N. C. Milne, M.D., program director. Faculty from U.S.A., 3 British and 2 Scottish medical schools. Inquiries: Ryals, POB 610203, DFW Airport, Texas 75261, U.S.A. 214-659-9590.

June 8–20: **2nd Advanced Ten Day Seminar on Epidemiology and Prevention.** Ireland. Sponsored by Council of Epidemiology and Prevention, International Society and Federation of Cardiology in cooperation with WHO. Inquiries: Rose Stamler, Room 1-615, 303 E. Chicago Ave., Chicago, IL 60611.

June 9–14: **International Congress of Angiology.** Athens, Greece. Inquiries: Prof. P. Balas, 17 Sisini St., 115 28 Athens (612) Greece.

June 11–14: **3rd International Symposium on Body Surface Mapping.** Nijmegen, the Netherlands. Inquiries: Dr. R. Th. van Dam, Dept. Cardiology, Geert Grooteplein Zuid 8, 6525 AG Nijmegen, the Netherlands.

June 16–20: **12th Symposium, International Society of Cerebral Blood Flow—"Brain: 85."** Ronneby Brunn Hotel, Lund, Sweden. Inquiries: K. Dahlgren, Dept. Clinical Neurophysiology, University Hospital, S-221 85 Lund, Sweden. Tel. +46-46-10-33-70.

June 16–21: **12th International Congress of Cardiology.** Vancouver, B.C., Canada. Inquiries: Dr. Henry Mizgala, Suite 1704, 1200 Alberni St., Vancouver, B.C., Canada V6E 1A6. Tel. 604-681-5226. Cable: Venuvan.

June 23–26: **International Conference on Preventive Cardiology.** Sovincenter, Moscow, USSR. Sponsored by WHO, International Society and Federation of Cardiology. Official languages English and Russian. Inquiries: A. A. Stepanenko, International Conference on Prevention Cardiology, Institute of Preventive Cardiology, 10 Petroverigsky Lane 101837 Moscow, USSR. Telex 411355. Cable USSR MOSCOW K-62, Preventive Cardiology. Tel. 221-93-47.

June 26–28: **6th Symposium on Echocardiology With a Postgraduate Course on Doppler Cardiography.** Rotterdam, the Netherlands. Sponsored by Erasmus University Thoraxcenter. Inquiries: PG Med. Ed., Erasmus University, Rotterdam, PBO 1738, 3000 DR Rotterdam, the Netherlands. Tel. 010-635011/635013.

July 15–19: **4th Meeting, World Federation on Ultrasound in Medicine and Biology.** Sydney, Australia. Inquiries:

WFUMB, POB 1441 GPO, Sydney, NSW, Australia 2001.

Aug. 31–Sept. 7: **Diagnosis of Diseases of the Chest.** Italy. (Also in Greece, Sept. 8–14). 2nd Great Teachers Foundation International Postgraduate Medical Education Program. Eric N. C. Milne, M.D., program director. Inquiries: Ryals (see June 1–8 above).

Aug. 31–Sept. 7: **11th Congress of International Society of Hypertension.** Heidelberg, Federal Republic of Germany. Organized by German Institute of High Blood Pressure Research and German Hypertension League. Dr. Detlev Ganten, Congress chairman. Inquiries: GKV, Frankfurter Str. 57, D-6050 Offenbach 1, Heidelberg, FRGermany.

Sept. 1–6: **13th World Congress of Neurology.** Hamburg, Germany. Inquiries: Dr. T. Stober, Dept. Neurology, Faculty of Med., University of Saarland, D-6650 Homburg/Saar, FRG.

Sept. 1–7: **3rd Postgraduate International Course on Pain Therapy.** Vicenza, Italy. Inquiries: Ruggiero Rizzi, M.D., Ospedale Generale Regionale, 36100 Vicenza, Italy.

Sept. 3–6: **European Nuclear Medicine Congress.** Barbican Centre, London, England. Incorporates 23rd Meeting Society of Nuclear Medicine, Europe, 8th Meeting European Nuclear Medicine Society, 13th Meeting British Nuclear Medicine Society. Inquiries: Congress, Institute of Nuclear Medicine, Middlesex Hospital Medical School, Mortimer St., London, W1N 8AA, United Kingdom. Tel. OI-631 1066.

Sept. 7–9: **3rd International Brain Heart Conference.** Trier, Germany. Inquiries: Dr. T. Stober, Dept. Neurology, Faculty of Med. University of Saarland, D-6650, Homburg/Saar, Federal Republic of Germany.

Sept. 8–12: **1st International Congress on Hospital Laws, Procedures, and Ethics.** Tel Aviv, Israel. Judge Amnon Carmi, organizing chairman. Inquiries: Hospitalaw, 28 Ahad Ha'am St., POB 394, Tel Aviv 61003, Israel. Tel. 03-650862. Telex 33803 TLV. Cable PELTOURS TELAVIV.

Sept. 16–20: **International Symposium on Cardiogenic Reflexes.** University of Leeds, England. Organized by Dept. of CV Studies, Univ. Leeds, and Commission on CV Physiology of International Univ. of Physiological Sciences. Inquiries: Dr. R. Hainsworth, Dept. CV Studies, University of Leeds, Leeds LS2 93T, England.

Oct. 3–4: **Hemodynamics and Atherosclerosis.** Wellington, New Zealand. Inquiries: Dr. W.E. Stehbens, Dept. Pathology, Wellington Clinical School of Med., Wellington, 2, New Zealand.

Oct. 6–10: **7th International Symposium on Atherosclerosis.** Melbourne, Australia. Inquiries: Dr. P. J. Nestel, Baker Medical Research Inst., Commercial Rd., Prahran, Vic., Australia 3181.

Oct. 8–10: **1st Latin American Congress of Cardiac Pacing.** Buenos Aires, Argentina. Operated by Latin American Society of Cardiac Pacing and Argentine Chamber of Cardiac Pacing. Dr. Alejandro Dussaut, president organizing committee. Inquiries: Congresos Internacionales S.A., Moreno 854—9° piso, 1091 Buenos Aires, Argentina. Tel. 14-3216/3408/3283. Telex 22036 JECON AR.

Oct. 27–30: **3rd Asian Pacific Symposium on Cardiac Pacing and Electrophysiology.** Hilton Hotel, Melbourne, Australia. Sponsored by Cardiac Society of Australia and New Zealand under auspices of International Cardiac Pacing Society. Inquiries: 3rd Asian Pacific Symposium on Cardiac Pacing and Electrophysiology, Suite 3.5, Epworth Medical Centre, 62 Erin St., Richmond, Vic. 3131, Australia.

Nov. 28–30: **7th Biennial Congress of Cardiology.** Rawalpindi/Islamabad, Pakistan. Inquiries: Pakistan Cardiac Society, Brig. Muhammad Zulfiqar Ali Khan, AFIC/NIHD, Rawalpindi, Pakistan. Tel. 64946, 61-31113, 61-33911.

AHA Scientific Sessions Future Meeting Dates

1985	Washington, DC	Nov. 11–14
1986	Dallas, TX	Nov. 17–20
1987	Anaheim, CA	Nov. 16–19

Xth World Congress of Cardiology, 1986

The Xth World Congress of Cardiology will be held in Washington, DC, Sept. 13–20, 1986. Official languages English, Spanish, and French. Inquiries: Secretariat, Xth World Congress Cardiology, 7320 Greenville Ave., Dallas, TX 75231. Tel. 214-750-5429. Cable: Tencard, Dallas.

Circulation Research MARCH 1985 VOL. 56 NO. 3

An Official Journal of the American Heart Association

CONTROVERSIES IN CARDIOVASCULAR RESEARCH

The first two articles in this issue of CIRCULATION RESEARCH by Jos A. E. Spaan and Francis J. Klocke et al. address various aspects of coronary pressure-flow relationships which have been a matter of some controversy in recent years. Issues such as the physiological significance of zero flow pressure and the role of intramyocardial compliance are important for our understanding of the regulation of coronary blood flow. We plan to publish responses from each author in a later issue of the journal.

The Editors.

Coronary Diastolic Pressure-Flow Relation and Zero Flow Pressure Explained on the Basis of Intramyocardial Compliance

Jos A.E. Spaan

From the Departments of Physiology and Physiological Physics, Leiden University Medical Centre, Leiden, and of Mechanical Engineering, Delft University of Technology, Delft, The Netherlands

SUMMARY. In the controversy about the mechanisms determining the high zero flow pressures and the further interpretation of coronary diastolic pressure flow relations, this paper takes a stand in favor of intramyocardial compliance as the primary cause of the high zero flow pressures. An attempt has been made to estimate the compliance distribution within the coronary circulation and to show the specific effect of intramyocardial compliance on arterial and venous pressure-flow relations. Since no data are available on the distensibility of coronary arterioles and capillaries, these data were taken from studies on mesenteric vessels. Based on these data, it is shown that, depending on the transmural pressure, smooth muscle tone may either increase or decrease arteriolar compliance. A compliance distribution has been proposed based on assumed pressure, volume, and distensibility distributions. For all but the venous division of the circulation, experimental data on volume could be found in the literature. Based on this compartmental analysis, it is predicted that overall intramyocardial compliance may exceed epicardial arterial compliance by a factor 45. The literature presenting functional evidence for intramyocardial compliance effects has been reviewed. Experimental results on venous outflow during long diastoles have been analyzed. $P_{f=0}$ coronary pressure at zero flow, is higher when measured later in diastole. It is shown that this may be explained by charging of intramyocardial compliance in the period before flow ceases. The discrepancy between results on pressure-flow relations in the fully dilated bed and autoregulated bed are related to the differences in pressure, resistance, and compliance distributions. **(*Circ Res 56: 293–309, 1985*)**

THE beating of the heart impedes the blood flow through the heart muscle. It is tempting to assume that the effect of cardiac contraction on coronary flow is restricted to systole. Diastole, then, may be considered as the period in which the myocardium, but in particular the subendocardium, is perfused (e.g., Downey and Kirk, 1975; Archie, 1975; Hoffman and Buckberg, 1976). This is why the coronary diastolic pressure flow relation has received so much attention. In the concept of Gregg and Green (1940), at the end of diastole the vascular bed within the myocardium is free of all mechanical effects related to systole. The coronary resistance could then be characterized by the ratio of the difference between end-diastolic arterial pressure and right atrial pressure and end-diastolic coronary arterial flow (see Fig. 1). This ratio was called end-diastolic resistance. Many studies have used the end-diastolic resistance since then, as an index to characterize the coronary bed.

The discovery by Bellamy (1978) that diastolic flow may cease at a coronary pressure far above

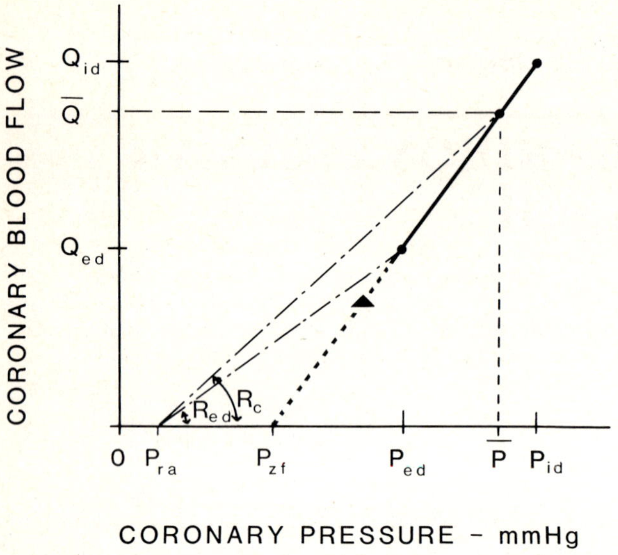

FIGURE 1. *Schematic of coronary pressure flow relation. P = coronary pressure, Q = coronary flow. Indices: id = initial diastole, ed = end diastole, zf = zero flow, ra = right atrium.* $\bar{P}$ *= mean coronary pressure,* $\bar{Q}$ *= mean coronary flow. The diastolic pressure flow relation is represented by the heavy line. The normal trajectory is indicated by the unbroken part. During a long diastole, the pressure-flow line intercepts the pressure axis at* $P_{f=0}$*. (*P_{zf} *on the figure is the same as* $P_{f=0}$ *in the text). Overall coronary resistance,* R_c*, is defined as* $(\bar{P} - P_{ra})/\bar{Q}$*. End-diastolic resistance is defined as* $(P_{ed} - P_{ra})/Q_{ed}$*. If diastole were to be prolonged suddenly, pressure and flow would decrease to lower values indicated by ▲ on the pressure flow line. End-diastolic resistance would then be higher.*

right atrial pressure has forced a reexamination of the end-diastolic resistance concept. Bellamy's discovery was made while examining coronary flow tracings from chronically instrumented dogs in Dr. Gregg's laboratory. Figure 1 illustrates the discussion regarding coronary resistance. The heavy line represents the pressure-flow relation measured by Bellamy (1978) during a long diastole. It is now clear that, normally, the end-diastolic resistance value depends on a factor which is not mechanically related to the coronary system at all, namely, the duration of diastole and, hence, heart rate. Obviously, the interpretation of the overall coronary resistance, defined in Figure 1, depends also on the mechanism responsible for the diastolic pressure-flow relation and, in particular, for the high zero flow pressure (Bellamy, 1980; Klocke and Ellis, 1980).

The two hypotheses which represent the two extremes in thought as to the cause of the high intercept pressure are: (1) Coronary flow stops at high pressures because of a Starling resistor effect in the resistance vessels (Permutt and Riley, 1963; Bellamy, 1978; Riley, 1982). $P_{f=0}$ equals the pressure needed to push these vessels open before any flow may pass, and is thought to be caused by summation of the pressure exerted by the smooth muscle and the extravascular pressure. (2) Coronary flow ceases because of the compliance effect of the intramyocardial vessels. In diastole, intramyocardial blood volume and blood pressure change more slowly than arterial pressure due to large time constants for charging and discharging the intramyocardial compliance. Blood flow ceases when arterial pressure becomes equal to intramyocardial blood pressure.

The theme of this presentation is that the high $P_{f=0}$ is not due to a Starling resistor, but is a function of intramyocardial blood volume, compliance, and time constants. To demonstrate this, information will be provided about the blood volume and compliance of different segments of the coronary circulation; then functional evidence for intramyocardial compliance will be offered as a basis for a simple distributed model of intramyocardial compliances and resistances; and, finally, the effects of these intramyocardial compliances during long diastoles will be analyzed to show how they explain many of the features observed in pressure-flow relations in the coronary artery.

The compliance of intramyocardial vessels has received little attention in the past (e.g., Feigl, 1983). Especially single vessel studies are lacking, due to the experimental problems involved in this kind of study. Moreover, it is only recently that data became available on the distensibility of capillaries (Smaje et al., 1980) which were, for a long time, considered as rigid tunnels. In general, pressure-vessel diameter relations are nonlinear and, if present, are smooth muscle tone dependent. To assess the importance of these characteristics and the lack of coronary studies, we have used data from different types of vessels, obtained from organs other than the heart. Hence, the reader is requested to be very careful in his own application of numbers derived in this study.

Based on the analysis presented below, it is advised that one use the overall coronary resistance as the index to quantify coronary tone. If possible, epicardial venous or coronary sinus pressure should be used as downstream pressure. The diastolic pressure-flow lines and $P_{f=0}$ are characteristics of the coronary circulation, but their practical use has yet to be established. In the fully dilated coronary bed, resistance and compliance will be pressure dependent. In this case, the concept of coronary resistance has only *little* practical value and, when used, detailed information about other parameters should be provided.

Distribution of Coronary Compliance Assessed from Single Vessel and Coronary Compartment Studies

The pressure-volume relation may be considered as constitutional for the hemodynamic characteristics of a vessel or division of the circulation. The compliance of a vessel at a certain pressure equals the slope of the pressure-volume relation at that pressure. Often, compliance is estimated by measuring a volume change dV as a result of a pressure

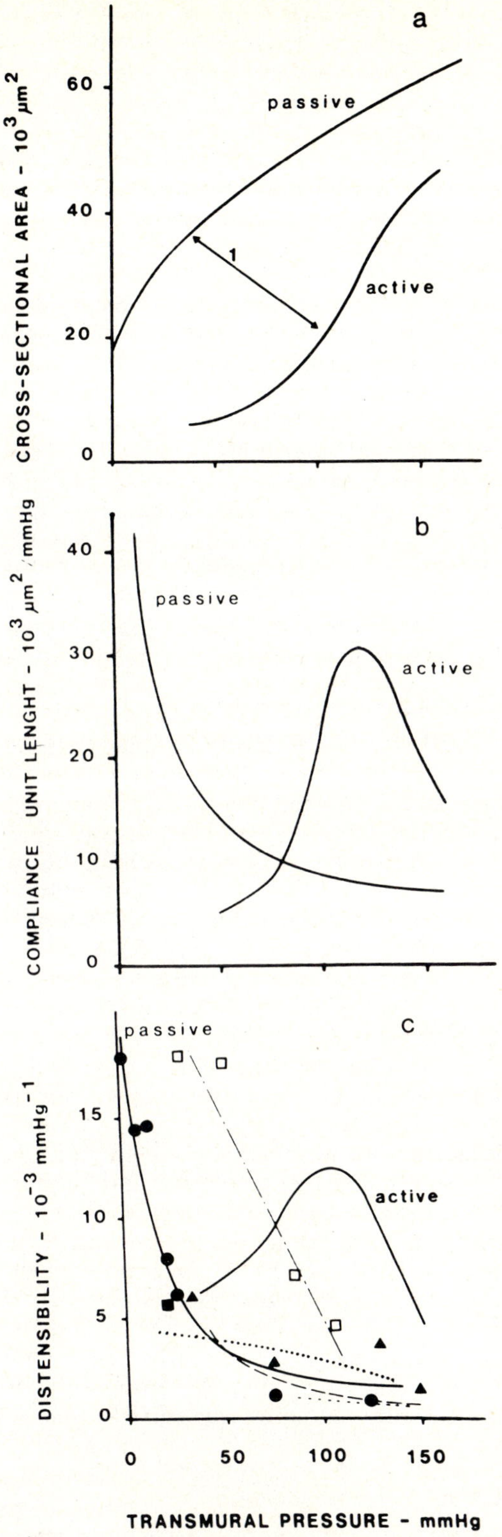

FIGURE 2. *Vessel mechanics. Panel a: corrected active and passive relationship of a 50-µm arteriole measured with a myograph by Mulvany et al. (1977, 1984). The pressure axis is scaled such that the passive experimental data agree with data of Wiederhielm (see text). Line 1 indicates the cross-sectional area-transmural pressure relation at autoregulation (decreasing resistance with decreasing pressure). Panel b: compliance per unit length vs. transmural pressure as calculated from panel a. Panel c: the heavy lines represent distensibility vs. transmural pressure calculated from panel a. Other data from the literature: ●, Wiederhielm (1965), ▲, Patel et al. (1970), ■ Smaje et al. (1980), (· · · ·) Gregg et al. (1935), (– – – –) Arts et al. (1979), (· · · ·) Douglas and Greenfield (1970). The midcapillary distensibility after 3 minutes of pressure change from Bouskela and Wiederhielm (1979) are represented by □ and (— · — · — ·).*

change dP or vice versa. It will be assumed that dV/dP will be an approximation of compliance at the pressure midway in the pressure change dP. The specific compliance is defined as the compliance normalized by the actual volume. However, in single vessel studies, often the diameter-pressure relations are measured. If the possible variations of vessel length are neglected, volume and volume variations will be proportional to cross-sectional area, A, and its variations, respectively. The compliance per unit length is defined as the cross-sectional area change due to a change in transmural pressure, dA/dP. The distensibility of a vessel is defined as the relative change in cross-sectional area as a result of a small change in pressure. The cross-sectional stiffness is the inverse of the distensibility. Note that when cross-sectional area is indeed proportional to volume, specific compliance equals distensibility. An estimate of a compliance of a division of the circulation can be made by multiplying the distensibility by the volume of the division.

One distinguishes dynamic and static compliances and distensibilities (e.g., Cox, 1982). Dynamic values are obtained with pressure variations of 1 Hz or more. Static values are obtained after pressure alterations lasting many seconds. First, the dynamic parameters will be discussed.

Below, the distribution of coronary compliance is estimated from the distribution of coronary volume and the distensibility of the different kinds of vessels.

Distensibility and Compliance of Small Arteries

The coronary compartment containing the smaller arteries and arterioles clearly has a key role in determining coronary flow. However, very little is known about the wall mechanics and the effect of smooth muscle tone on it. To assess the compliant behavior of this compartment the results of Wiederhielm (1965) and Mulvany et al. (1977, 1984) will be combined. Wiederhielm (1965) measured the pressure-volume relation of small arteries with fully relaxed smooth muscle. From his Figure 3, the distensibility was calculated as function of transumral pressure. The results are shown in our Figure 2c. Mulvany et al. (1977, 1984) measured force-length relations of fully relaxed and maximally activated small artery (0–50 µm) rings mounted in a myograph. The discrepancy between ring and vessel segment studies (Cox, 1983) was overcome by using Wiederhielm's curve as the standard. The pressure axis of the calculated pressure-distensibility curves of Mulvany et al. (1977, 1984) were reduced so that the passive pressure-distensibility curves coincide at the point of maximal tension development. From the corrected data of Mulvany, it has been calculated how cross-sectional area, compliance per unit length, and distensibility depend on transmural pressure. These relations are depicted in Figure 2. Note that area is proportional to volume, compliance per unit length is proportional to compliance, and that distensibility equals specific compliance.

The curves in Figure 2, although derived from measurements on mesenteric arterioles, illustrate what one may expect with regard to the basic influence of transmural pressure and smooth muscle tone on the coronary circulation. The cross-sectional area (Fig. 2a) may be reduced by a factor 6, due to an increase in tone when the pressure is around 60 mm Hg. According to the law of Poiseuille, the resistance of these small vessels may vary by a factor of 36. This illustrates the ability of arterioles to regulate flow. It is also clear from Figure 2a that the volume of the arteriolar division is dependent on the same factors. During autoregulation, as a result of arterial pressure decrease, both transmural pressure and resistance decrease. Under these conditions, the area-pressure relationship will follow a direction indicated by line 1.

The essential characteristic of a compliant compartment is that flow into, q_{in}, and out of q_{out}, the compartment may differ because of volume changes: $q_{in} - q_{out} = C \cdot dP/dt$ where P equals the transmural pressure and C the compliance. The curves in Figure 2b are obtained from the first derivatives of the respective curves in Figure 2a. As is clear from Figure 2b, the passive vessel compliance increases with decreasing pressure. However, in the presence of smooth muscle tone, the compliance-transmural pressure relation shows a completely different course. It may exhibit a maximum at a certain pressure. Moreover, depending on the transmural pressure, smooth muscle tone may cause either an increase or a decrease of compliance. Because of normalization, the specific compliance or distensibility becomes more or less independent of the actual volume of a vessel. At least in the passive case, the distensibility-transmural pressure relationship unifies to a certain extent the data obtained with different kinds of vessels. Note that in the trajectory measured by Mulvany et al., the distensibility was increased by smooth muscle tone.

Distensibility of Capillaries and Venules

From earlier studies on the distensibility of capillaries, it was concluded that capillaries behave as rigid tunnels (Burton, 1954; Baez et al., 1960; Fung et al., 1966). However, more recently, distensibility measurements have been reported by Smaje et al. (1980), who used pressure variations within the physiological range. From their results one can calculate distensibility values of 0.0055 and 0.005/mm Hg for the capillary and venulary distensibility, respectively. Since flow within the capillaries and venules was obstructed distally, one may assume that those values were estimated at pressures higher than normal. Moreover, venular distensibility may have been underestimated because of damping of the pressure-pulse in the capillaries. However, a similarity between capillary and venulary distensibilities is not surprising, since the walls of venules with a diameter of up to 30 μm are not very much different from the walls of capillaries (Brown, 1965). The distensibility of the mesenteric capillary may be explained by the mechanics of the basement membrane (Smaje et al., 1980). However, Borg and Caulfield (1981) reported on collagen struts connecting the coronary capillary walls with myocytes. Papillary muscle was fixed either in systole or in diastole and studied with a scanning electron microscope. The struts were stretched in the systolic fixed muscle, whereas, in the diastolic fixed muscle, they were somewhat wavy. The authors concluded that the tension on the struts in systole "may play a role in maintaining capillary patency in the presence of very high wall tensions." Hence, capillary compliance in systole may be different from that in diastole.

Distensibility of the Larger Arteries

Distensibility of the larger coronary arteries has been studied by several investigators (see Fig. 2c). The inverse of distensibility (= cross-sectional stiffness) was determined in an elegant way by Arts et al. (1979) from wave velocity measurements in vivo. Distensibility from the other studies reported on below have been recalculated according to the present definition. Gregg et al. (1935) measured the pressure-volume relations on the coronary arterial tree with the aid of mercury. Douglas and Greenfield (1970) cannulated the coronary artery and obstructed the coronary bed with beads, 200 μm in diameter. At certain resting pressures, they rapidly injected an amount of blood and measured the resulting increase in pressure. One should note that the transient of pressure during and immediately after cessation of the rapid injection was not fully in agreement with the model used to calculate compliance. Patel et al. (1970) determined pressure-volume relations of segments of isolated coronary arteries.

One should note that smooth muscle tone was not defined in these studies. According to Figure 2c, one may assume that tone was small in these experiments.

Static Elastic Measurements

If vessels are subjected to a pressure step for a long time, the ultimate increase of cross-sectional area will be much larger than the rapid responses discussed above (e.g., Gow et al., 1974). Douglas and Greenfield (1970) found for the epicardial arteries at a pressure of 100 mm Hg a static distensibility of 0.002/mm Hg compared with a dynamic distensibility of 0.7×10^{-3}/mm Hg. Bouskela and Wiederhielm (1979) measured capillary diameter changes in the bat wing after 3 minutes of a combined increase of arterial and venous pressure. The pressure increases were maintained for 3 minutes. The distensibility of mid-capillaries was calculated from their report, and plotted in Figure 2c, assuming that control transmural pressure in the capillaries was 20 mm Hg. The static distensibility is much higher than the dynamic distensibility. Coronary flow after prolonged adenosine infusion exceeds peak reactive hyperemic flow after 30 seconds of coronary occlusion (L'Abbate et al., 1981). This finding fits with the larger static distensibility compared to the dynamic one. If the microvasculature is exposed to a higher pressure for a period of time, the diameters of microvessels will increase to a larger extent, and their resistance will be lower.

It has not been reported how dynamic distensibility is influenced after static deformations. However, this point is very relevant with respect to studies on the fully dilated coronary bed.

Overall Coronary Volume

To get some insight in the distribution of compliance from the pressure-distensibility relationship, one must know the volume distribution within the coronary circulation. This analysis will focus on the autoregulating heart perfused at an arterial pressure of 100 mm Hg. These conditions have to be specified because they influence coronary blood volume and, probably, its distribution. According to Salisbury et al. (1961) and Morgenstern et al. (1973), total coronary volume varies by 0.075 ml/100 g LV per mm Hg arterial pressure change in the normal pressure range. Moe et al. (1939) report a value of 0.08 ml/100 g LV per mm Hg. The dependency of coronary volume on arterial pressure will be discussed in more detail below.

In most studies on coronary blood volume, in fact, residual volume after excision of the heart was determined. The results vary over a wide range, e.g.: 8.4 ml/100 g LV (Klein, 1945), 6.6 ml/100 g LV (Gibson, 1946) and 4.8 ml/100 g LV (Salisbury et al., 1961; Crystal et al., 1981; Eliasen et al., 1982). In the last three studies, the hearts were blotted before the determination of blood volume, implying that larger arteries and veins were empty. Since residual coronary volume is underestimated in this way, the total coronary blood volume at higher pressures, 14 ml/100 g LV at Pa = 100 mm Hg, calculated by Salisbury et al. (1961), must be underestimated, as well. However, using the mean transit time technique, Hirche and Lochner (1962) and Morgenstern et al. (1973) estimated a total coronary volume of the dog heart in situ around 12.5 ml/100 g LV.

Coronary Arterial Volume

The volume of the larger coronary arteries has been determined by the casting method. Douglas and Greenfield (1970) injected silicone into the left main coronary artery of a dog, after having first blocked the coronary circulation with 200-μm beads. The authors found a correlation between volume and total heart weight. At a weight of 120 g, coronary volume was 1.5 ml at an arterial pressure of 100 mm Hg. This value is in reasonable agreement with the measurements of Arts (1978) who used an araldite casting method. For hearts with a total weight of 123 g, he measured a value of 1.12 ml for the left anterior descending and circumflex arterial trees (total left coronary arterial tree minus septal branch), including vessels down to a diameter of 400 μm. Taking into account a right heart free wall weight fraction of 15%, one may conclude from this study that the volume of the arterial tree with vessel diameter down to 200 μm equals 1.6 ml/100 g LV.

The volume of intramural small arteries and arterioles was determined by Wüsten et al. (1977). A radioactive barium-gelatin method was used. These authors state explicitly that epicardial and larger intramural arteries are excluded from their measurements. The reported value is 3.6 ml/100 g LV. On the one hand, this value may overestimate small arterial volume because of the higher transmural pressure and vasodilation. Assuming that peak reactive hyperemia is maximally four times control flow, small arterial volume may be overestimated by a factor of two due to vasodilation (since resistance is inversely proportional to volume). On the other hand, the barium-gelatin mixture may not have filled the smallest arterioles. Quite arbitrarily, the value of 2.7 ml/100 g LV will be chosen as a compromise value for small arterial volume.

Volume of Capillary Compartment

No direct measurements of the volume of the myocardial capillary compartment in vivo have been reported. However, capillary volume in the postmortem dog heart has been determined by O'Keefe et al. (1978). They reported a capillary volume fraction in the heart of 27%. This is higher than the total coronary volume fraction measured by more direct means.

The capillary cross-sectional area fraction in a virtual plane perpendicular to the capillaries equals the product between capillary density and capillary cross-sectional area. This fraction equals the capillary blood volume fraction of a space bounded by two such planes. Hence, estimates for capillary blood volume may be derived from measured values of capillary density and capillary diameters. However, values of capillary density, expressed in number per mm^2, vary widely. For rat hearts, Buss et al. (1981) reported 2100 and Martini and Honig (1969), 2200. Roberts and Wearn (1941) measured 3343 on the postmortem human heart. Bassinghtwaigthe et al. (1974) reported 3170 for the dog heart.

The large variation in numbers may be due in part to differences in techniques used. For example, the rheological properties of blood and structure of capillary network may lead to a very heterogeneous distribution of capillary flow (e.g., Wieringa et al.,

TABLE 1
Data on Capillary Diameter

Method	Diameter (μm)	Species	References
a	5.6	Dog	Bassinghtwaigthe et al. (1974)
a	5.14	Rat	Potter and Groom (1983)
a	5.3	Rat	Tomanek et al. (1982)
a	7.2–8.9	Rat	Buss et al. (1981)
b	4.1*–6.3†	Dog	Tillmanns et al. (1974)
b	6–6.4	Rat	Steinhausen et al. (1978)
c	4*–5†	Rat	Henquell et al. (1976)

Methods: a = casting, b = fluorescence microscopy, c = stop-motion micro-cinematography.
* In systole.
† In diastole.

1982; Damon and Duling, 1984). It is not unlikely that, as a result, dye or casting media will not fill all the capillaries. Consequently, one may expect that the higher values are closer to reality. For this study, a value of 3200 cap/mm^2 will be used.

Published values of capillary diameters within the heart vary between 4 and 9 μm. A review of measured capillary diameters in the heart is given in Table 1. In further calculations, a value of 5 μm has been assumed for the diameter of the capillaries in the beating heart. This volume is in the range of the in vivo measurements. Together with the assumed value of 3200 cap/mm^2 for the capillary density, we arrive at a capillary volume fraction of 0.063.

Conclusion with Respect to the Distributions of Distensibility, Volume, and Compliance

As has been discussed above, little adequate information is available on the blood volume distribution within the heart. Even less is known about vascular wall properties of the myocardial microcirculation. Moreover, in the analysis of the cross-sectional area-transmural pressure relationship, the influence of longitudinal stress and strain in the vessel wall (e.g., Tickner and Sacks, 1967) has been neglected. However, by lack of more quantitative information, the data collected above will be used to estimate the distribution of compliance over the coronary bed.

The parameter that unifies to a certain extent the characteristics of the different kinds of vessels is distensibility. For the vessels with relaxed, or without, smooth muscle, a strong nonlinear pressure-distensibility relation holds. Normally, the activation of smooth muscle in the larger vessels is low, resulting in distensibilities close to those of the resting vessel wall. The distensibilities of the capillary and venular compartments are large, which is a consequence of the low transmural pressures under normal physiological conditions. Increasing vasomotor tone at constant pressure may result in a decreasing or increasing compliance. Little is known about the distribution of blood volume within the heart. The influence of the beating of the heart on this distribution is a yet-unexplored field of research.

Table 2 gives a review of assumed and estimated values of the distributions of pressure, volume, distensibility, and compliance within the coronary circulation. Because of a lack of direct measurements on the venous circulation, it was assumed that the volumes of small and large veins would be twice the volumes of small and large arteries, respectively. Note that the sum of the compartmental volumes exceeds the published values on total coronary volume. Recently, Eng and Kirk (1983) reported a preliminary study on the compliance of the coronary arterial tree down to 25-μm vessels. The values found were in the order of 0.016 ml/mm Hg per 100 g LV. This tallies very reasonably with the predicted value of the sum of small artery in large artery compliances given in Table 2.

It will be clear that more experiments on the distribution of these quantities are needed to clarify the discrepancies in the analyses given above. However, we may conclude that the intramyocardial compliance exceeds the epicardial arterial compliance, many times. Moreover, the distribution of compliance will depend strongly on the perfusion conditions of the heart.

TABLE 2
Estimate of Coronary Compliance Distribution Based on Assumptions Explained in Text

Compartment	Pressure (mm Hg)	Volume (ml/100 g LV)	Distensibility (10^{-3}/mm Hg)	Compliance (ml/mm Hg per 100 g LV)
Art > 200 μm	100	1.6	1.4	0.0022
Small arteries	35	2.7	4.5	0.013
Capillaries	20	6.3	5.5	0.035
Small veins	12	5.4*	8	0.043*
Large veins	8	3.2*	14	0.045*
Total		19.2		0.138
Intramyocardial		14.4		0.091

* These data are based on the *assumption* that coronary venous volume equals twice the coronary arterial volume and consequently should be applied with care.

Functional Evidence for Intramyocardial Compliance

Compression of Intramyocardial Compliant Vessels by the Beating of the Heart

The influence of heart contraction on intramyocardial blood volume and coronary flow has been studied for centuries. An accessible review of the earlier literature, starting with Scaramucci's paper of 1689, was presented by Porter (1898). Compression of the microvessels within the ventricle wall was part of Porter's own work, as well. He studied the pulsatile nature of the coronary flow by observing spurts of blood from incised arteries and veins. In the context of the present controversy, it is worth noting that Porter used long diastoles, obtained by vagal stimulation, to study the coronary circulation, albeit to enhance the venous outflow in the next beat. Due to the compliance of the intramural vessels and their volume reduction in systole, energy is stored in the vessel walls that is turned into labor during diastole. This results in suction of blood from both the arterial and venous side (e.g., Wiggers, 1954). In fact, one may consider the intramyocardial blood compartment to be analogous to the ventricle cavity. Both are compressed by systole. However, because of the absence of valves, the intramyocardial pump action cannot cause a net flow, and because of the high resistance of the small intramyocardial vessels, the ejection fraction of this pump is small (Spaan et al., 1981a, 1983). However, intramyocardial pumping may result in retrograde coronary arterial flow (Spaan et al., 1981b; Chilian and Marcus, 1982).

Mean intramyocardial blood volume depends on cardiac contraction. Increase of ventricular pressure and/or contractility decreases intramyocardial blood volume (Salisbury et al., 1961). A weight decrease of the ventricular wall as a result of the injection of adrenaline has been shown by Stubbs and Widdas (1959a). However, they concluded that this was due, in significant part, to loss of interstitial fluid. The authors perfused the hearts with Locke's solution. Salisbury et al. (1961) claimed that, in their similar experiments, a fluid shift did not occur because they perfused the hearts with blood. They may be correct in this regard, since their estimates of the dependency of coronary blood volume on arterial pressure are very close to those obtained by Morgenstern et al. (1973), using the mean transit time method. Stubbs and Widdas (1959b) also showed a step-wise increase in heart muscle weight when the heart was arrested by potassium citrate.

Diameter changes of intramyocardial vessels during the cardiac cycle have been reported by Tillmanns et al. (1974). They found the capillary diameter to be 4.1 μm in systole and 5.3 μm in diastole. Measurements were obtained from vessels 100 μm below the epicardium of the dog heart. According to the calculation discussed above, the capillary volume fraction would be 0.042 in systole and 0.099 in diastole. If these numbers would apply to a whole left ventricle weighing 100 g, capillary blood volume alone would vary 5.7 ml during the cardiac cycle. As is discussed in Appendix B, this volume variation is four times larger than likely, as based on the diastolic-systolic variations in coronary arterial and venous flow. Since the reported variations of arteriolar and venular diameters are not incorporated in these calculations, and most likely extravascular compression at the endocardium exceeds that at the epicardium, one must conclude that the reported cyclic diameter variations are at odds with the cyclic variations in overall coronary flow.

Assessment of Distribution of Compliance and Resistance

The effects of distributed compliance and resistance may be analyzed with the aid of models that have a discrete number of compartments. Each model compartment describes analogously the hemodynamic characteristics of a division of the circulation. In the compartmental analysis discussed above, the following sequence of compartments was considered: arteries - arterioles (or small arteries) - capillaries - venules (or small veins) - veins. The model compartments may be presented by using electical circuit elements or hydrodynamic elements (Fig. 3). Capacitances or windkessels represent the

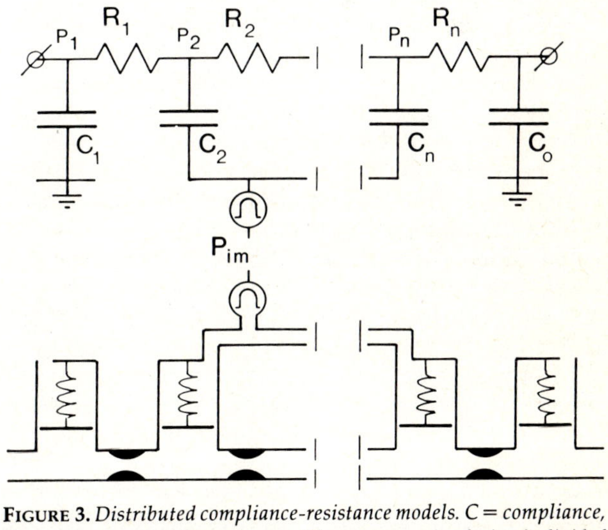

FIGURE 3. *Distributed compliance-resistance models. C = compliance, R = resistance, and P = pressure. The coronary circulation is divided into a number of n compartments. The compliances are represented by capacitances (upper panel) or windkessels (lower panel). Epicardial arterial and epicardial venous compliance, C_1 and C_o, respectively, are connected to zero pressure. The compliances representing the intermyocardial compartments, C_2-C_n, are loaded by cardiac contraction represented by the intramyocardial pressure, P_{im}. The resistances represent the hydrodynamic resistances of the intramyocardial compartments. The first resistances will be influenced by smooth muscle tone. All resistances may be transmural pressure dependent (Arts, 1978). The simplest form of the intramyocardial pump model is when all intramyocardial compliance is lumped into one capacitance. Hence, R_2 is then directly connected to C_o.*

compliant behavior of the vessels. The electrical or hydrodynamic resistances represent the overall resistance of a division of the coronary circulation. The resistances and compliances within each compartment may be linked in many ways to form a circuit (e.g., Linehan et al., 1982). However, in general, most compartment models may be represented by the general model depicted in Figure 3. Each model element, except the last, contains a windkessel and outflow resistance. However, apart from the first and last windkessels, representing clearly the epicardial arterial and epicardial venous compliances, respectively, the relation between circuit elements and physiological compartments is now obscured. For example, R_1 will be related to the resistances of both epicardial arteries and small intramural arteries. The outside of each windkessel compartment is connected to the extravascular space. For the epicardial vessels, the extravascular pressure will be the intrathoracal pressure. The extravascular pressure for the intramyocardial vessels will be the tissue pressure (Arts, 1978), which will vary across the myocardial wall. In the model, no parallel resistance-compliance elements representing, e.g., viscoelastic properties of the vessel walls, are included. This would complicate the present analysis even more.

Resistance and compliance are continuously, though not homogeneously, distributed over the circulation. The number of model elements needed to study the impact of this distribution on coronary flow mechanics depends on the hemodynamic phenomena of interest. For example, the high frequency input impedance (frequencies >2 Hz) of the circuit depicted in Figure 3 will reflect only the characteristics of C_1 and R_1. Interpretation of the relation between pressure and flow in the coronary artery varying at a rate corresponding to frequencies lower than 1 Hz requires information on compliances located more downstream. When studying the dynamic interaction between arterial and venous flow and/or pressure, information on the complete circuit is needed. In general, one may state that the more distributed the model (i.e., more compartments), the better the distribution of phasic flow and pressure in the circulation may be described. However, there is a practical limit to the number of compartments that can be defined quantitatively. The information on distribution of compliance over the coronary bed is too limited, as has been shown above. Evaluation of models of the kind in Figure 3 normally requires measurements from both the inflow and outflow side of the circulation (Sagawa, 1972). In the case of the coronary circulation, this requirement is difficult to meet because of the absence of a unique outflow channel.

Distribution of Resistance and Compliance

Models containing two compliance-resistance elements were evaluated for the dog hindlimb by Sato et al. (1971) and for the dog lung lobe by Linehan et al. (1982). No experimental studies directed to the distribution of compliance in the coronary circulation have been reported. Some indirect conclusions can be drawn from a study of Spaan et al. (1981a). Autoregulation was intact in this study. R_1 could be correlated with the quotient (P_{map} -Pw)/CBF where P_{map} = mean arterial pressure, Pw = wedge pressure after 15 seconds of occlusion, and CBF = mean coronary blood flow. It was found that $R_1 = 0.63*Rc-12.9$ mm Hg·sec/ml. Sato (1971) found a ratio of 0.7 between first resistance and overall resistance for the dog hindlimb. It was also shown by Spaan et al. (1981a) that the decay of the coronary peripheral pressure after abrupt occlusion of the arterial flow was compatible with two capacitance resistance elements in series. The intramyocardial compliance was estimated as 0.07 ml/mm Hg per 100 g LV, which agrees reasonably with the overall estimate calculated from microvascular properties, as shown above. However, if the downstream resistance had been smaller than the estimated 30% of overall resistance, a higher value for the intramyocardial compliance would have been found. From experiments in which both arterial and coronary sinus pressure were manipulated (Scharf et al., 1973), one may indeed conclude that the resistance distal to the intramyocardial compliance is much smaller than the proximal resistance.

In terms of the two-element model, the change of pressure, ΔP_2, over the intramyocardial compliance is related to a change in arterial pressure, ΔP_a, according to: $\Delta P_2 = \Delta P_a \times R_2/(R_1 + R_2)$. As reviewed above, coronary volume changes proportional to arterial pressure by 0.075 ml/mm Hg per 100 g LV. Epicardial arterial compliance is about 50 times too low to explain this number. If $R_2/(R_1 + R_2) = 0.37$, as concluded above, then intramyocardial compliance would be 0.20 ml/mm Hg per 100 g LV. This is about twice the intramyocardial compliance calculated from the estimation of volume and distensibility distribution in the coronary circulation. The interpretation of the results of experiments in which coronary volume has been measured as function of arterial pressure may be complicated by the volume change of the small arteries and arterioles. Due to autoregulation, arteriolar resistance increases when arterial pressure increases, and vice versa (e.g., Burrows and Johnson, 1981). This effect is illustrated in Figure 2a by curve 1. Cross-sectional area and arteriolar volume will decrease until maximal smooth muscle tone is achieved. Thereafter, volume will increase with pressure.

Variation of smooth muscle tone must also be taken into account when interpreting the results of the constant flow experiment of Morgenstern et al. (1973). At constant coronary flow, arterial pressure was lowered by infusion of adenosine. Since flow was constant, one may expect that pressures in and distal to the capillaries remained constant as well.

Coronary volume changed by 0.05 ml/mm Hg per 100 g LV. This number is approximately 3 times the estimated compliance of smaller arteries and arterioles. The difference may be even larger, due to a change in smooth muscle tone. This is illustrated by curve 1 in Figure 2a. Pressure decreased at constant flow: hence, coronary resistance decreased as a result of increasing arteriolar volume.

One has to conclude that a significant compliance is distributed over the coronary bed. However, the magnitude of the compliances at the different levels in the coronary circulation remains uncertain. The intramyocardial pump model with two resistance-capacitance elements (Spaan, 1981a) seems, for the time being, suitable enough to assess the characteristic influence of intramyocardial compliance on arterial and venous coronary flow. However, one should bear in mind that a more distributed model would explain the measured phenomena in more detail.

Intramyocardial Compliance Effects during Long Diastoles

Coronary Venous Flow

When measuring coronary-arterial and venous flow concomitantly, the intramyocardial compliance effects become very clear. Preliminary reports on this matter have been presented by Chilian et al. (1982), Tomonaga et al. (1983), and Spaan (1983). In the first two studies, the coronary arteries were perfused from the aorta. In experiments from our laboratory, which will be described in more detail below, the main coronary artery of the goat was cannulated and perfused (Spaan et al., 1981). The great cardiac vein was cannulated via the hemiazygos vein and drained into a container. The pressure within the container was regulated in such a way that epicardial venous pressure in the area that was drained, remained constant. This pressure was measured with a catheter introduced by the Herd-Barger (1964) technique. The outside diameter of the intravascular part of the catheter was 0.6 mm. The His bundle was destroyed by the injection of formalin. The long diastoles were obtained by cessation of right ventricular pacing.

Figure 4 depicts the results of a typical experiment. Perfusion pressure was maintained during the diastole for a certain time, after which the perfusion line was abruptly occluded. Although coronary arterial inflow continued after cardiac arrest, venous outflow ceased for a second or so. This is in agreement with the findings of Porter (1898) and Wiggers (1954), namely, that coronary venous outflow is restricted to systole. It should be mentioned, however, that some diastolic coronary venous flow was found by Stein et al. (1968). After the initial drop, venous outflow increased and reached a plateau. In cases in which perfusion pressure was maintained, the pattern of venous outflow mimicked that of

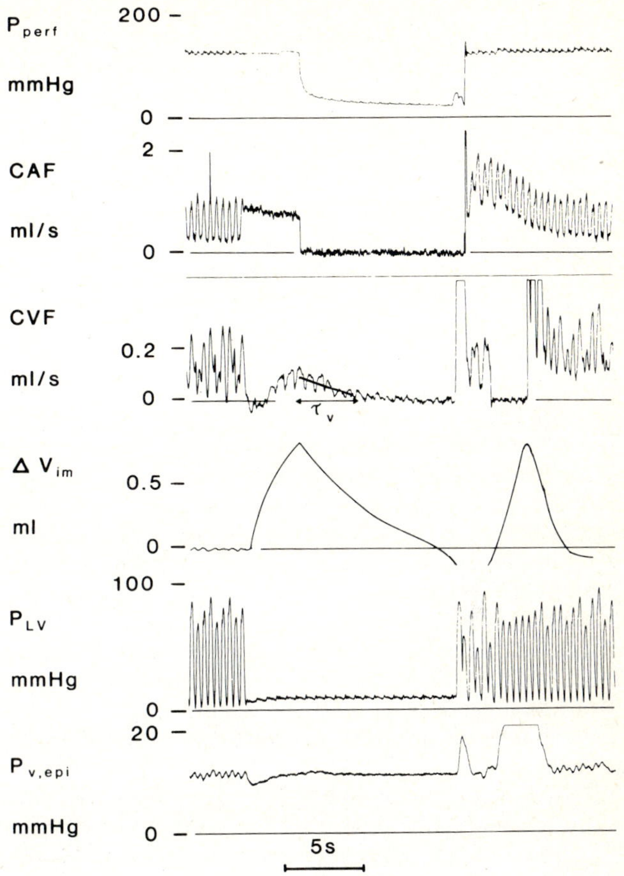

FIGURE 4. *Arterial occlusion late in a long diastole.* P_{LV} = *left ventricular pressure;* $P_{v,epi}$ = *epicardial venous pressure;* P_{perf} = *perfusion pressure or equals coronary peripheral pressure,* P_{cp}, *at arterial occlusion. CAF = coronary arterial flow; CVF = coronary venous flow. Note the rapid decrease of venous outflow and of epicardial venous pressure at cardiac arrest. During the period of arterial inflow, intramyocardial blood volume increased by* ΔV_{im}. *After arterial occlusion, both* ΔV_{im} *and venous outflow decayed simultaneously with* P_{cp}, *as expected from a discharging intramyocardial compliance. The time constant for venous outflow* τ_v *was determined by linearizing the CVF curve after arterial occlusion by eye.*

arterial inflow if the latter decreased due to metabolic vasoconstriction (Spaan, 1983). When inflow was abruptly stopped (Fig. 4), venous outflow decreased. The absence of venous outflow during the first part of the long diastole can be explained by the relaxation of extravascular pressure which has a sucking effect on the blood. In general, it is assumed that the systolic-diastolic variation of extravascular pressure is much larger in the subendocardium than in the subepicardium. It is therefore not unlikely that, in diastole, epicardial venous blood is sucked into the subendocardium.

Inflow without outflow means an increase of blood volume in the vessels between both the cannulas, and a charging of the intramyocardial compliance. The venous flow signal after arterial occlusion shows the discharging of intramyocardial compliance. By assuming that the pattern of venous cannula flow represents the pattern of total coronary venous flow, it is possible to calculate intramyocardial blood volume variations. A new steady blood volume was reached after 4 seconds of steady perfusion pressure during cardiac arrest in the long diastole obtained just prior to the one shown in Figure 4. The time constant for venous outflow decay after arterial occlusion was 4 seconds. This must also represent the characteristic time of pressure decay within the intramyocardial compliance. Note that vasomotor tone was present but not constant throughout the period of arrest.

The advantage of the great cardiac vein is that it may be easily cannulated, at least in the goat. Moreover, in this way, the coronary sinus, which has a large blood storage capacity and, presumably, a large compliance which complicates the study of transients in venous flow, is excluded from the outflow circuit. The disadvantage is that great cardiac venous flow is not necessarily representative of total coronary venous flow. An increase of coronary venous pressure forces blood to flow via alternative routes. A model describing the partition of coronary venous flow has been presented by Scharf et al. (1971). Essential to this model is a Starling resistor behavior of the venous part of the coronary circulation. Partition of venous outflow from one channel to the other occurs only if venous pressure exceeds the Starling resistor pressure, which is between 5 and 10 mm Hg. Moreover, a Starling resistor effect with a similar threshold pressure has been shown to exist in the coronary sinus (Uhlig et al., 1984). Should the venous cannula pressure have been above this critical value, cannula flow would have been retrograde at the end of the period of arterial occlusion.

Peripheral Coronary Pressure

Peripheral coronary pressure, P_{cp}, is defined as the pressure measured distal to a coronary occlusion. When the heart is beating, P_{cp} does not fall to right atrial pressure after sudden arterial occlusion (Gregg et al., 1940; Spaan et al., 1981a). Figure 4 shows an arterial occlusion in a long diastole (e.g., Eng et al., 1982; Hori, 1982). Note that, after 7 seconds, P_{cp} is above venous pressure but still decaying. The coronary peripheral pressure and $P_{f=0}$, estimated from diastolic P-F lines, must relate to the same phenomena, since both regard the condition of zero arterial flow. The peripheral coronary pressure decay curves obtained within the autoregulating bed could not be fitted with a single exponential model. However, the basic course of the peripheral coronary pressure decay is easily explained by a model with two or more compliance-resistance elements in series (Fig. 3). Just prior to arterial occlusion, all compliances are charged. After occlusion, flow will occur from each compliance into the venous direction, and the pressure in each compartment will decrease. The multi-exponential nature of the peripheral pressure

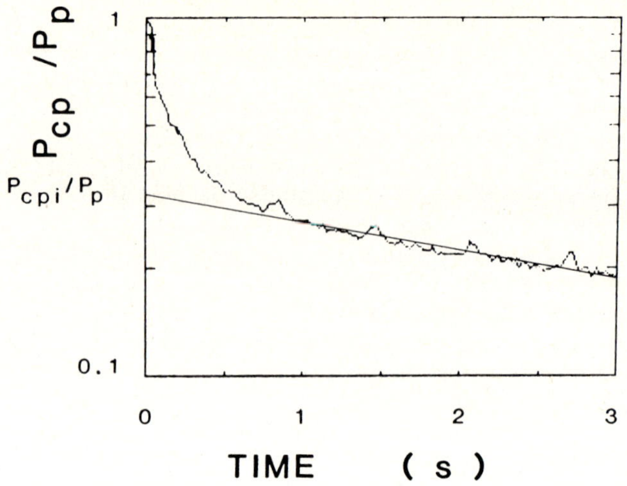

FIGURE 5. *Logarithmic peripheral coronary pressure decay curve obtained from the top panel of Figure 4. P_{cpi}/P_p is obtained from linearization of the curve between 0.5 and 3 seconds.*

decay curve is also clear from Figure 5, where $\log_{10} P_{cp}/P_p$ has been plotted vs. time. P_p is the perfusion pressure before occlusion. It was chosen to characterize the peripheral coronary pressure in the following manner. In $\log_{10} P_{cp}/P_p$ vs. time curves, as plotted in Figure 5, a line was fitted by eye through the data points between 0.5 and 3 seconds after occlusion. The intersection of this line with the vertical axis at $t = 0$ times P_p resulted in the initial peripheral coronary pressure, P_{cpi}. P_{cpi} is the estimate of the pressure within the first compliance prior to arterial occlusion.

The estimated initial peripheral coronary pressure, P_{cpi}, was determined from arterial occlusions within 0.4 second, and later than 3.4 seconds after cardiac arrest. P_{cpi} is higher with the late diastolic occlusion than with the early diastolic occlusion, as shown in Figure 6. This difference may be attributed to the charging of compliance in the period of diastolic arterial inflow. Both early and late diastolic P_{cpi} values depend on pre-occlusion perfusion pressure. In terms of the model of Figure 3, this may be explained by vasomotor tone dependency of the resistor(s) downstream from the first intramyocardial compliance.

Modeling P-F Lines with the Intramyocardial Pump Model

The intramyocardial pump model, although being a simplification, may be helpful in understanding the basic effects of intramyocardial compliance on arterial P-F relations. The initial conditions for a long diastole are determined by the steady beating heart. In order to bring out the basic role of intramyocardial compliance, the epicardial compliance has been neglected. Moreover, the intramyocardial tissue pressure has been approximated by a square wave, giving an angular profile to the waveform of the tracings (Fig. 7). The model equations are pre-

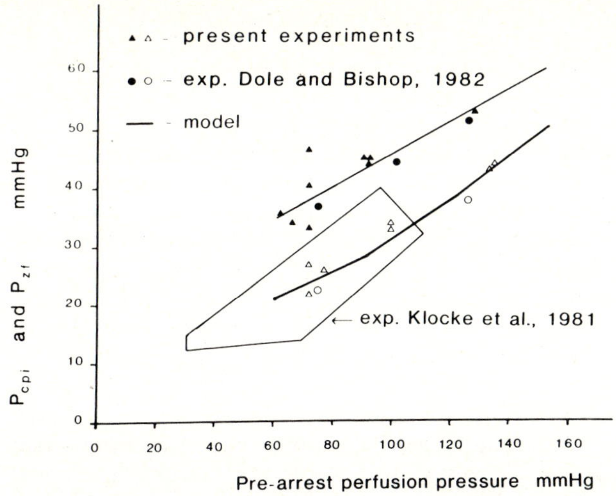

FIGURE 6. *Initial peripheral coronary pressure, P_{cpi}, compared with theoretical predictions of the intramyocardial pump model and experiments on $P_{f=0}$ by Dole and Bishop (1982a) and Klocke et al. (1981). ▲ and Δ represent P_{cpi} obtained from occlusions later than 3.4 seconds and before 0.4 second after cardiac arrest, respectively. $P_{f=0}$ values of Dole and Bishop (1982a) were obtained with decaying coronary arterial pressure (●), and with the constant pressure technique (○). The encircled area indicates $P_{f=0}$ results of Klocke et al. obtained with decaying coronary arterial pressure. The solid lines are the predictions of the intramyocardial pump model. The upper line is the prediction of P_{cpi} in late diastole, the bottom line of P_{cpi} in early diastole.*

sented in Appendix A. In the steadily beating situation, the model predicts variations of intramyocardial blood pressure, P_{ib}, inflow, and outflow around a mean value. Note, however, that venous outflow increases after the initial drop, and then decays. In this respect, in- and outflow show the same characteristics as the measured arterial inflow and venous outflow when vasoconstriction in the long diastole occurs (Spaan, 1983). With an inflow occlusion at the onset of cardiac arrest (Fig. 7b), both P_{ib} (which is now equivalent to peripheral pressure) and outflow decay from a very low value following the initial drop. When arterial inflow is stopped later in diastole (Fig. 7c), P_{ib} decays from a higher value after the initial drop, in agreement with the experimental results of Figure 4. In Figure 7b (broken curves), simulation results are shown when perfusion pressure decays from the onset of cardiac arrest. As can be concluded from the course of P_{ib}, intramyocardial blood volume initially increases. However, inflow soon becomes too low, and P_{ib} decreases. Outflow follows the course of P_{ib}. The simulation of outflow strongly resembles the coronary venous outflow curve measured by Chilian et al. (1982) and Tomonaga et al., (1983) with decaying coronary inflow pressure. At the time that $P_a = P_{ib}$, inflow is zero, and by definition $P_a = P_{f=0}$ ($P_{f=0}$ = pressure at zero flow). When P_a decays below P_{ib}, arterial flow becomes negative, which agrees with the experimental results of Kirkeeide et al. (1981) and Klocke et al. (1981). The amount of backflow is determined in part by the assumed value of intramyocardial compliance. When the decay of arterial pressure starts later in diastole, intramyocardial compliance charges to a higher value (Fig. 7c). As a

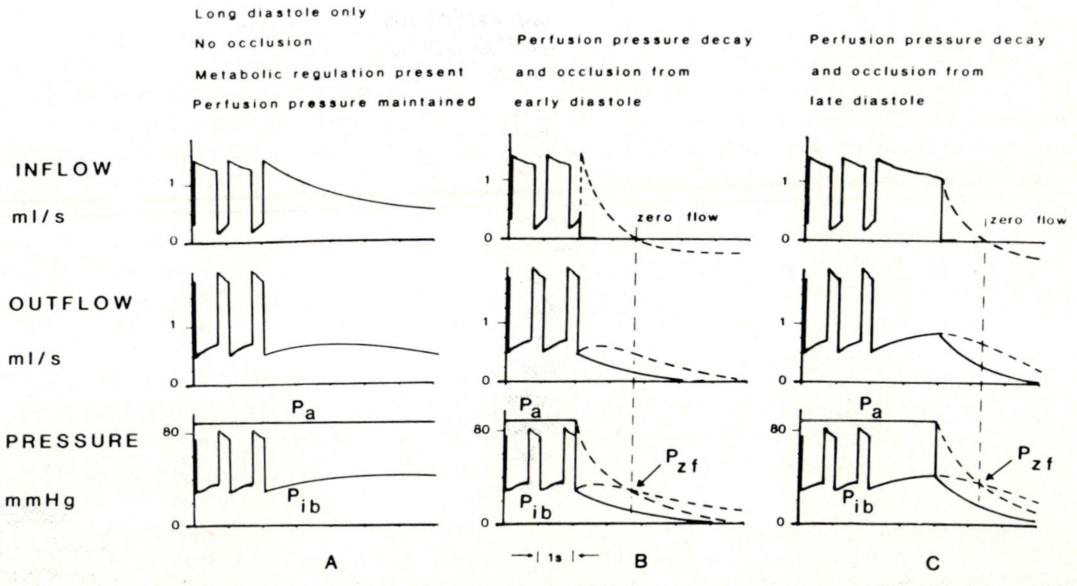

FIGURE 7. *Model simulation of arterial inflow, venous outflow, and intramyocardial blood pressure, P_{ib}. Panel A: perfusion pressure, P_a, is constant. Arterial inflow decreases because of charging of the intramyocardial compliance and metabolic vasoconstriction due to the relationship between R_{in} and $R_{in} + R_{out}$ (see Appendix A). Panel B: the coronary artery is occluded at cardiac arrest. Venous outflow and intramyocardial blood pressure ($P_{ib} = P_a$ after occlusion) decay to zero. The broken curves simulate the case of exponentially decaying arterial pressure. Panel C: arterial occlusion 2 seconds after cardiac arrest. Intramyocardial blood pressure increases during arterial inflow. As a result, P_{cpi} will be higher than with early diastolic occlusion. Compare the curves with the results of Figure 4. The broken curves simulate the experiments with decreasing arterial pressure.*

result, $P_{f=0}$ is higher than in the case where decay of P_a starts at cardiac arrest. The predicted values for the initial peripheral coronary pressure (P_{cpi}) at different pre-arrest values of arterial pressure are shown in Figure 6. Values for early diastolic occlusion, as well as late diastolic occlusion, are shown by the heavy lines. As explained above, P_{cpi} is higher when the pressure switch is made later in diastole.

Conclusions on Intramyocardial Compliance Effects during Long Diastole

Intramyocardial compliance effects become very clear from the venous outflow signal when coronary venous pressure is kept constant to exclude epicardial venous compliance effects. Several seconds are required for venous outflow to adjust to new steady states in either heart rate (from beating to cardiac arrest) or coronary flow (arterial occlusion). These findings could be explained by a simple intramyocardial pump model. This model contains a compliance with a magnitude in the order of values predicted for the overall intramyocardial compliance from other studies. The model also predicts the higher coronary peripheral pressure found with occlusions later in diastole. The dependency of initial peripheral coronary pressure, P_{cpi}, on pre-occlusion perfusion pressure will be discussed in the next section.

Interpretation of Diastolic Pressure Flow Lines

Coronary Tone and Entrance Compliance Effects

Pressure-flow lines may appear to be linear over a significant range of pressure, despite the fact that coronary tone is changing in time (Spaan, 1979; Dole and Bishop, 1982b). Shape and course of the P-F lines depend on a possible variation of coronary tone and on the shape of the arterial pressure decay curve. However, the direction of change of vasomotor tone during coronary pressure decay is not obvious. If coronary flow decreases too rapidly, vasodilation might occur, as is illustrated by the reactive hyperemia after occlusion in the long diastole (Fig. 4). An increase of tone during long diastoles at constant perfusion pressure has been reported by Klocke et al. (1981), Spaan and Laird (1981), and Eng et al. (1982). In these studies, the His bundle was destroyed. Long diastoles were obtained by cessation of pacing. In the study by Dole and Bishop (1982a, 1982b), long diastoles were obtained by vagal stimulation, and coronary flow remained constant for periods up to 5 seconds.

The possibility that compliance might result in an overestimation of $P_{f=0}$ was analyzed by Eng et al. (1981, 1982). The proposed model consists of only one compliance-resistance element, as defined in Figure 3. The compliance relates only to the larger arteries, as there is no proximal resistance in the model. However, as noted by Hori et al. (1982), the coronary decay constant found by Eng et al. (1982) would require a compliance 50 times larger than the compliance of epicardial arteries. Moreover, using the ratio between aortic time constant and coronary time constant found by the authors, arterial inflow should drop considerably (about 37%) at the onset of pressure decay. Measurements obtained by Dole and Bishop (1982a, 1982b) do not show a sudden drop in flow. Other discrepancies between this simplified model and experimental results have been noted by Hoki et al. (1982) and Braakman et al. (1982).

The single RC model has been evaluated by Mates et al. (1983) by the Fourier technique for frequencies higher than 1 Hz. They concluded that the model is adequate as a high frequency input impedance model (frequency >1 Hz) with epicardial compliance values. However, the larger intramyocardial compliances affect the input impedance only for lower frequencies.

Diastolic Pressure-Flow Relations in the Coronary Bed with Autoregulation

At present, two methods of obtaining P-F lines can be distinguished. The first is the technique where perfusion pressure decays more or less exponentially. With the other technique, introduced by Eng et al. (1981, 1982), P-F lines are constructed by changing pressure stepwise to different values in successive diastoles. With the constant-pressure technique, P-F relations are obtained free of entrance compliance effects. What is more important, the method standardizes the pressure changes and eliminates the low frequency content of the arterial pressure signal. According to compliance models, as shown in Figure 3, the inverse of the slope of the P-F line obtained with the constant pressure technique will represent the first resistance of the model, and $P_{f=0}$ the pressure in the first intramyocardial compliance at the moment the arterial pressure is switched to a different value. This technique results in lower $P_{f=0}$ values than does the decaying pressure technique. The difference is in the same order of magnitude as found between late and early diastolic P_{cpi} values. As illustrated by the model calculations above, this may be explained by charging of the intramyocardial compliance during the period of pressure decay. One may wonder, however, why the $P_{f=0}$ values obtained by Klocke et al. (1981) with the decaying pressure technique are lower than those obtained by Dole and Bishop (1982a) obtained with a similar technique. One of the factors may be that the pressure decay of Klocke et al. started immediately at the beginning of cardiac arrest, whereas Dole and Bishop maintained perfusion pressure for 1 or 2 seconds before pressure was changed.

In autoregulated hearts, P_{cpi} and $P_{f=0}$ depend on the initial perfusion pressure. P_{cpi} and $P_{f=0}$ are far above the normal capillary pressure values at higher initial perfusion pressures. These features may be explained on the basis of the windkessel analog of the small artery compartment. Consider the $R_1C_2R_2$ circuit part to be the model for this compartment. $P_{f=0}$ and P_{cpi} reflect the pressure in C_2, P_2. This pressure has been built up in the control condition and may be written as

$$P_2 = P_3 + (P_1 - P_3) \times R_2/(R_1 + R_2),$$

where P_1 = pressure in the control condition, and P_3 = the capillary pressure. A change in coronary tone will effect both R_1 and R_2, and, hence, the ratio $R_2/(R_1 + R_2)$ is relatively independent of coronary tone. This conclusion fits with the analysis of the pulsatile nature of coronary flow by Spaan et al. (1981a). As a result, P_2 (and, hence) $P_{f=0}$, and P_{cpi} relate to perfusion pressure in the control condition. This explanation requires a significant compliance of the smaller arteries and arterioles. As has been discussed above, some evidence for this has been presented by Morgenstern et al. (1973), Wüsten et al. (1977), and Eng and Kirk (1983). One should note that P_{cpi} is not very sensitive to the magnitude of C_2 in the model of Figure 3. However, if $P_{f=0}$ is determined by changing the perfusion pressure continuously, the rate by which C_2 discharges into the compliance more downstream becomes relevant. Moreover, the shape of the curve becomes unpredictable because of the possible changes of coronary tone and continuous changing charge of the intramyocardial compliance.

Diastolic P-F Relations in the Pharmacologically Dilated Coronary Bed

The main characteristic of P-F lines in the pharmacologically dilated coronary bed is that $P_{f=0}$ is independent of initial perfusion pressure. However, the value of $P_{f=0}$ is not the same in all studies. Eng et al. (1982) reported 10–14 mm Hg, Klocke et al. (1981) 15 mm Hg, and Dole and Bishop (1982a) 23 mm Hg. Since Dole and Bishop changed perfusion pressure later in diastole, their higher value for $P_{f=0}$ might be the result of charging of intramyocardial compliance.

At first, the independency of $P_{f=0}$ of initial perfusion pressure, and, therefore, of initial coronary flow, seems to be at odds with an intramyocardial compliance model containing a downstream resistance. According to such a model, $P_{f=0}$ should represent the pressure within the intramyocardial compliance. This pressure should depend on flow before pressure is varied to determine $P_{f=0}$. Moreover, the low value of $P_{f=0}$ suggests that arterial pressure equalizes rapidly with the pressure at the venular or capillary level. However, these results may be explained by the altered vessel wall mechanics due to the pharmacological dilation. To begin with, one should note that during long diastoles, the venous outflow in the fully dilated bed showed a pattern similar to the one in the autoregulated bed (Chilian, 1982; Tomonaga et al., 1983). Hence, intramyocardial compliance effects are also manifest in the dilated coronary bed. After vasodilation, the vessel wall mechanics of the smaller arteries may be described by the passive curves in Figure 2. Furthermore, the pressure distribution from epicardial arteries to epicardial veins will be quite different from the distribution in the autoregulated bed. In the latter case, most of the pressure drop will occur across the very small arterioles. However, without autoregulation, the pressure drops more gradually (Murphy, 1980). Moreover, as a result of the higher coronary flow, capillary pressure and arteriolar pressure will be much higher in the dilated bed than in the autoregulated bed at the same perfusion pressure. It is conceivable that if perfusion pressure is above a certain level, microvascular pressure will be such that distensibility and compliance become very small. As a result, arteriolar compliance becomes negligible. Therefore, if arterial pressure is decreased to measure the P-F relation, intramyocardial blood pressure will fall very rapidly to the level where the compliance becomes significant. In this respect, it is important to have detailed information about the way the P-F relation is constructed. Usually, with the constant pressure technique, there is a wait of a few tenths of a second after the perfusion pressure is being changed before the pressure and flow data are taken. The RC-time constant of intramyocardial pressure changes in the autoregulated heart is in the order of seconds (Figs. 4 and 7). However, in the fully dilated bed, microvascular pressure will be increased and both resistance and compliance are decreased. If both are changed by a factor of three, the time constant for initial intramyocardial pressure changes will be reduced by a factor of nine. After lowering the pressure, the time constants may increase again.

An extra complication is that the resistance downstream of the intramyocardial compliance may be pressure dependent. So, at the higher flow rate, this resistance will be lower, resulting in a relatively lower pressure within the intramyocardial compliance.

Conclusions

In this paper, the evidence for intramyocardial compliance has been summed up. It was concluded that vessels of all types, including capillaries, are distensible. Except for the larger coronary arteries, no quantitative data on single vessel distensibilities of the coronary circulation are available. Therefore, data from other organ vessels were used. Consequently, one has to be very careful in applying values of parameters based solely on these distensibilities. They were produced in this paper to make the intramyocardial compliance plausible. Coronary blood volume depends on arterial and venous pressure, and also on heart contraction. Moreover, the venous outflow during long diastoles manifests the intramyocardial compliance. However, it has also been discussed that compliance of vessels are transmural pressure, and, if present, smooth muscle tone dependent. Obviously, resistance and its distribution with respect to the distribution of compliance depends on the same factors. These factors are determined by the functioning of the heart and the conditions by which the coronary bed is perfused.

Let us consider the value and meaning of the concept of coronary resistance. Resistance is defined as the ratio between driving pressure and flow. The driving pressure should be taken as the difference between arterial pressure and epicardial venous pressure. Because of a Starling resistor effect, this pressure may be higher than right atrial pressure (Uhlig et al., 1984). The use of the resistor concept is to predict flow at an arbitrary driving pressure knowing the flow at a different driving pressure. However, the coronary resistance in the fully dilated bed of the arrested heart is driving pressure dependent (Hanley et al. 1984), which may not be surprising in view of the distensibility of the blood vessels. In part, this may explain the curve linearity of pressure-flow lines at low pressures. When the heart beats, the situation is even more complicated because of the large intramyocardial blood volume variations (see Appendix B). Resistance and compliance distribution will vary during the heart cycle. Hence, one must conclude that when the coronary bed is fully dilated, the coronary resistance concept is of little value. When used anyhow, the hemodynamic conditions should be reported in detail.

Within the autoregulated state, however, coronary flow variations seem to be linearly related to arterial pressure and ventricular pressure variations (Spaan et al., 1981a; Saint Felix and Demoment, 1982). Hence, one may consider the resistances and compliances to be constant during the cardiac cycle. As a result, compliances in circuits, as depicted in Figure 3, do not influence mean flow-mean pressure relationships. This linear behavior may not be present under all circumstances. However, as long as more detailed information on coronary compliance behavior is not available, the overall coronary resistance, as defined in Figure 1, should be preferred as the index to quantify coronary vascular smooth muscle tone.

It has been shown that the observations of the last decennium on pressure-flow relations and zero flow pressure during long diastoles are compatible with the concept of a compliant microvasculature within the heart. Studies on the diastolic coronary pressure-flow relations clearly may reveal some essential properties of the coronary circulation. Because of intramyocardial compliance effects, one has to advise against the decaying pressure technique when the decay time constant is in the order of seconds. With the constant pressure technique, one should be very careful in defining both the control conditions and moment of pressure change. The practical value of diastolic pressure-flow relations and $P_{f=0}$ will depend on the outcome of these studies.

Essential in understanding the relation between $P_{f=0}$ and arterial pressure under control conditions are the pressure-volume relationships of the arteriolar compartment at different levels of coronary tone. Especially at this point, the data are very scarce. No attention has been paid in this paper to the possibility of a Starling resistor effect within arterioles. This is the topic of the other part of the controversy. However, the compliance effects of all vessels are undeniable and of such a magnitude that these may not be neglected in model studies in which Starling resistors are incorporated. Reports trying to bridge both concepts have already been presented (Westerhof et al., 1983; Downey et al., 1983). The author's personal opinion, however, is that a Starling resistor mechanism in the autoregulated heart is not likely at other than venous levels. Convincing evidence for this mechanism may be the observation of narrow gaps (diameter in the order of micrometers) within arterioles or other microvessels. These gaps are required on physical principles to form the Starling resistor. However, up until now, myocardial microcirculatory studies do not report observations on local vessel collapse (e.g., Nellis et al., 1981; Tillmanns et al., 1981).

The intramyocardial compliance may be functional, since it results in a diastolic sucking action on arterial blood as a result of the previous systole. In this way, diastolic flow will be increased to compensate for the lower or even retrograde systolic flow. An arteriolar Starling resistor would uncouple the microvascular pressure from the arterial pressure. In this case, compensation for systolic restriction of microvascular flow would require a decreased diastolic resistance. In other words, with diastolic suction as a result of systolic compression, a lower vasodilatory capacity of the coronary bed is needed to allow a certain net coronary flow.

It has been argued that the coronary flow mechanics of the fully dilated bed differ considerably from the autoregulated bed. Hence, one should be very careful in applying interpretations of results obtained in the dilated bed to the autoregulated bed, and vice versa. More research should be directed to the distribution of resistance and compliance in the coronary bed under different conditions. Insight into these distributions are of crucial importance for understanding the mechanics of coronary flow.

Appendix A

We have calculated the results shown in Figure 7 by using two resistance-capacitance elements in series (Fig. 3), and by assuming $C_1 = 0$. This last assumption simplifies the calculations considerably, and accentuates the role of intramyocardial compliance. The venous pressure $P_v = 10$ mm Hg. The overall coronary resistance, $R_1 + R_2$, was calculated as the ratio between difference $P_1 - P_2$ and mean coronary flow $\overline{CBF}$. $\overline{CBF}$ was assumed to equal 1 ml/sec, independent of arterial pressure. P_1, R_1, and R_2 were calculated from the overall coronary resistance and the correlation $R_1 = 0.66(R_1 + R_2) - 10$ mm Hg sec/ml (Spaan et al., 1981a). Coronary flow decreases during cardiac arrest at constant perfusion pressure. This behavior was simulated by decreasing the overall coronary conductance, $1/(R_1 + R_2)$ exponentially with time. Since the correlation between R_1 and $R_1 + R_2$ was found to be independent of coronary tone in the steady beating heart, this correlation was assumed to remain during cardiac arrest. The value of intramyocardial compliance, C_1, was assumed to be 0.07 ml/mm Hg per 100 g LV. The extravascular pressure, P_{im}, was approximated by a square wave with a systolic value of 50 mm Hg and diastolic value of 5 mm Hg.

The following equations describe the dynamic and static behavior of the model:

$$V_{ib} = C_1(P_1 - P_{im})$$

$$dV_{ib}/dt = q_1 - q_2$$

$$q_1 = (P_1 - P_2)/R_1$$

$$q_2 = (P_2 - P_v)/R_2$$

where V_{ib} = intramyocardial blood volume or the charge of C_1, and q_1 and q_2 = arterial inflow and venous outflow, respectively. The equations were solved numerically using Euler integration. For the calculations, an Epson HX20 microcomputer was used.

Appendix B

Coronary Blood Volume Variations during a Heart Cycle

The coronary blood volume variation during a heart cycle has not been investigated systematically. However, a rough estimate can be made from the cyclic variation in the integral of the difference between inflow and outflow, since $dV/dt = q_{in} - q_{out}$. It will be assumed that q_{in} and q_{out} are block-waves and that q_{out} is only systolic and q_{in} is only diastolic. Moreover, only the case that diastole and systole have the same duration, T, will be considered. This is the case at a heart rate of about 2 beats/sec, and consequently, T = 0.25 sec. With these assumptions, the systolic-diastolic flow differences of both q_{in} and q_{out} will be twice the mean coronary flow, q_m. Consequently, the coronary volume variation, ΔV, will be:

$$\Delta V = 2q_m T.$$

In hearts with autoregulation, q_m is in the order of 1.5 ml/sec per 100 g. Consequently, the estimation of the overall coronary volume variation is 0.75 ml, about 5% of total coronary volume at an arterial pressure of 100 mm Hg. The absolute volume variation at the arterial side of the circulation will be lower because the arterial diastolic-systolic flow difference was overestimated (e.g., Spaan, 1981a, 1981b). However, the relative volume variations may be similar because of the lower arterial volume.

In the pharmacologically dilated coronary bed, and at a perfusion pressure of 70 mm Hg, mean coronary flow may be five times higher than in the autoregulated bed. Consequently, the cyclic volume variations may be 25% of total coronary volume. Since coronary resistance is proportional to the inverse of the volume squared, cyclic resistance variations may be of the order of 10% in the autoregulated bed, but 50% in the dilated bed. One therefore may not be surprised that characteristics of coronary flow in the beating heart are not the same in both cases.

This study obtained its present form after many discussions with the Physiological Physics group of the University of Leiden. I wish to express my appreciation for this support. I especially wish to mention Peter Wieringa, who surveyed for me the literature on capillary density and capillary diameter. I would also like to acknowledge the support of Aart Boekee in preparing the figures, and of Guusje de Jong and Heleen Bronsveld for preparing the manuscript.

Supported by grants from the Foundation for Medical Research (FUNGO) and the Dutch Heart Foundation.

Address for reprints: Prof. Dr. Ir. J.A.E. Spaan, Laboratorium voor Fysiologie, Wassenaarseweg 62, 2300 RC Leiden, The Netherlands.

References

Archie JP (1975) Intramyocardial pressure: Effect of preload on transmural distribution of systolic coronary blood flow. Am J Cardiol **35:** 904–911

Arts MGJ (1978) A mathematical model of the dynamics of the left ventricle and the coronary circulation. Ph.D. Thesis, State University of Limburg, Maastrict, The Netherlands

Arts T, Kruger RTI, van Gerven W, Lambregts JAC, Reneman RS (1979) Propagation velocity and reflection of pressure waves in the canine coronary artery. Am J Physiol **237:** H469–H474

Baez S, Lamport H, Baez A (1960) Pressure effects in living microscopic vessels. *In* Flow Properties of Blood, edited by AL Copley, G Stainsby. London, Pergamon, pp 122–136

Bassinghtwaigthe JB, Yipintsoi T, Harvey RB (1974) Microvasculature of the dog left ventricular myocardium. Microvasc Res **7:** 229–249

Bellamy RF (1978) Diastolic coronary artery pressure-flow relations in the dog. Circ Res **43:** 92–101

Bellamy RF (1980) Calculation of coronary vascular resistance. Cardiovasc Res **14:** 261–269

Borg TK, Caulfield JB (1981) The collagen matrix of the heart. Fed Proc **40:** 2037–2041

Bouskela E, Wiederhielm C (1979) Viscoelastic properties of capillaries (abstr). Microvasc Res **17:** S1

Braakman R, van den Horn JJ, van Huis GA, Krams R, Langewouter GJ, Sipkema P, Westerhof N (1982) Letter to the Editor. Circ Res **51:** 822

Brown RE (1965) The pattern of the microcirculatory bed in the ventricular myocardium of domestic mammals. Am J Anat **116:** 355–374

Burrows ME, Johnson PC (1981) Diameter, wall tension, and flow in mesenteric arterioles during autoregulation. Am J Physiol **241:** H829–H837

Burton AC (1954) Relation of structure to function of the tissues of the wall of blood vessels. Physiol Rev **34:** 619–642

Buss DD, Hyde DM, Stovall MY (1981) Application of stereology to coronary microcirculation. Basic Res Cardiol **76:** 411–415
Chilian WM, Marcus ML (1982) Phasic coronary blood flow velocity in intramural and epicardial coronary arteries. Circ Res **50:** 775–781
Chilian WM, Bohling BA, Marcus ML (1982) Interpretations of zero-flow pressures in the coronary circulation (abstr). Circulation **66** (suppl II): 43
Cox RH (1982) Mechanical properties of the coronary vascular wall and the contractile process. *In* The Coronary Artery, edited by S Kalsner. London, Croom Helm Ltd., pp 59–90
Cox RH (1983) Comparison of arterial wall mechanics using ring and cylindrical segments. Am J Physiol **244:** H298–H303
Crystal GJ, Downey HF, Bashour FA (1981) Small vessel and total coronary blood volume during intracoronary adenosine. Am J Physiol **241:** H194–H201
Damon DH, Duling BR (1984) Distribution of capillary blood flow in the microcirculation of the hamster: An in vivo study using epifluorescent microscopy. Microvasc Res **27:** 81–95
Dole WP, Bishop VS (1982a) Influence of autoregulation and capacitance on diastolic coronary artery pressure-flow relationships in the dog. Circ Res **51:** 261–270
Dole WP, Bishop VS (1982b) Regulation of coronary blood flow during individual diastoles in the dog. Circ Res **50:** 377–385
Douglas JE, Greenfield JC (1970) Epicardial coronary artery compliance in the dog. Circ Res **27:** 921–929
Downey JB, Kirk ES (1975) Inhibition of coronary blood flow by a vascular waterfall mechanism. Circ Res **36:** 753–760
Downey JM, Lee J, Chambers PE (1983) Location and magnitude of the coronary artery capacitance. *In* Mechanics of the Coronary Circulation, edited by RE Mates, RM Nerem, PD Stein. New York, The American Society of Mechanical Engineers, pp 45–48
Eliasen P, Amtorp O, Tondevold, Haunso S (1982) Regional blood flow, microvascular blood content and tissue hematocrit in canine myocardium. Cardiovasc Res **16:** 593–598
Eng C, Kirk ES (1983) The arterial component of the coronary capacitance. *In* Mechanics of the Coronary Circulation, edited by RE Males, RM Nevem, PD Stein. New York, The American Society of Mechanical Engineers, pp 49–50
Eng C, Jentzer JH, Kirk ES (1981) Coronary capacitive effects on estimates of diastolic critical closing pressures. Basic Res Cardiol **76:** 559–593
Eng C, Jentzer JH, Kirk ES (1982) The effects of the coronary capacitance on the interpretation of diastolic pressure-flow relationships. Circ Res **50:** 334–341
Feigl EO (1983) Coronary physiology. Physiol Rev **63:** 1–205
Fung YC, Zweifach BW, Intaglietta M (1966) Elastic environment of the capillary bed. Circ Res **19:** 441–461
Gibson JG II, Seligman AM, Peacock WC, Aub JC, Fine J, Evans RD (1946). J Clin Invest **25:** 848–857
Gow BS, Schonfeld D, Patel DJ (1974) The dynamic elastic properties of the canine left circumflex coronary artery. J Biomech **7:** 389–395
Gregg DE, Green HD (1940) Registration and interpretation of normal phasic inflow into a left coronary artery by an improved differential manometric method. Am J Physiol **130:** 114–125
Gregg DE, Green HD, Wiggers CJ (1935) Phasic variations in peripheral coronary resistance and their determinants. Am J Physiol **112:** 362–373
Hanley FL, Messina LM, Grattan MT, Hoffman JIE (1984) The effect of coronary inflow pressure on coronary vascular resistance in the isolated dog heart. Circ Res **54:** 760–772
Henquell L, La Celle PLL, Honig CR (1976) Capillary diameter in rat heart in situ: Relation to erythrocyte deformability, O_2 transport and transmural O_2 gradients. Microvasc Res **12:** 259–274
Herd JA, Barger AC (1964) A simplified technique for chronic catheterization of blood vessels. J Appl Physiol **19:** 791–792
Hirche H, Lochner W (1962) Messung der Durchblutung und der Blutfülling des coronaren Gefüssbetles mit der Teststoffinjektionsmethode am narkotisierten Hund bei geschlossenem Thorax. Pflugers Arch **274:** 624–632
Hoffman JIE, Buckberg GD (1976) Transmural variations in myocardial perfusion. Prog Cardiol **5:** 37–89
Hoki N, Tomonaga G, Kajiya F (1982) Letter to the Editor. Circ Res **51:** 821
Hori S (1982) Letter to the Editor. Circ Res **51:** 819–821
Kirkeeide R, Puschmann S, Schaper W (1981) Diastolic coronary pressure-flow relationships investigated by induced long-wave pressure oscillations. Basic Res Cardiol **76:** 564–569
Klein JR (1945) Estimation of blood in tissue. Arch Biochem **8:** 421–424
Klocke FJ, Ellis AK (1980) Control of coronary blood flow. Annu Rev Med **31:** 489–508
Klocke FJ, Weinstein IR, Klocke JF, Ellis AK, Kraus DR, Mates RE, Canty JM, Anbar RD, Romanowski RR, Wallmeyer KW, Echt MP (1981) Zero-flow pressure and pressure-flow relationship during single long diastoles in the canine coronary bed before and during maximum vasodilation. J Clin Invest **68:** 970–980
L'Abbate A, Camici P, Trivella MG, Pelosi G, Davies GJ, Ballestra AM, Taddei L (1981) Time-dependent response of coronary flow to prolonged adenosine infusion: Doubling of peak reactive hyperaemic flow. Cardiovasc Res **15:** 282–286
Linehan JH, Dawson CA, Rickaby DA (1982) Distribution of vascular resistance and compliance in a dog lung lobe. J Appl Physiol **53:** 158–168
Mates RE, Burns T, Caby JM, Greenberg R, Nelson J (1983) Modelling diastolic impedance to coronary blood flow. *In* Mechanics of the Coronary Circulation, edited by RE Males, RM Nevem, PD Stein. New York, The American Society of Mechanical Engineers, pp 41–44
Martini J, Honig CR (1969) Direct measurement of intercapillary distance in beating rat heart in situ under various conditions of O_2 supply. Microvasc Res **1:** 244–256
Moe GK, Wood EH, Visscher MB (1939) Aortic pressure and the diastolic volume law of energy output in cardiac contraction. Proc Soc Exp Biol Med **40:** 460–463
Morgenstern C, Höljes U, Arnold G, Lochner W (1973) The influence of coronary pressure and coronary flow on intracoronary blood volume and geometry of the left ventricle. Pflugers Arch **340:** 101–111
Mulvany MJ (1985) Determinants of vascular hemodynamic characteristics. Hypertension III-13–III-18
Mulvany MJ, Halpern W (1977) Contractile properties of small arterial resistance vessels in spontaneously hypertensive and normotensive rats. Circ Res **41:** 19–26
Murphy RA (1980) Mechanics of vascular smooth muscle. *In* Handbook of Physiology, sec 2, The Cardiovascular System, vol. II, Vascular Smooth Muscle, edited by DF Bohr, AP Somlijo, HV Sparks. Washington, D.C., The American Physiological Society, pp 325–351
Nellis SH, Liedtke AJ, Whitesell L (1981) Small coronary vessel pressure and diameter in an intact beating rabbit heart using fixed-position and free-motion techniques. Circ Res **49:** 342–353
O'Keefe DD, Hoffman JIE, Cheitlin R, O'Neill MJ, Allard JR, Shapkin E (1978) Coronary blood flow in experimental canine left ventricular hypertrophy. Circ Res **43:** 43–51
Patel DJ, Janicki JS (1970) Static elastic properties of the left coronary circumflex artery and the common carotid artery in dogs. Circ Res **2:** 149–158
Permutt S, Riley RL (1963) Hemodynamics of collapsible vessels with tone: The vascular waterfall. J Appl Physiol **18:** 924–932
Porter WT (1898) The influence of the heart-beat on the flow of blood through the walls of the heart. Am J Physiol **1:** 145–163
Potter RF, Groom AC (1983) Capillary diameter and geometry in cardiac and skeletal muscle studied by means of corrosion casts. Microvasc Res **25:** 68–84
Riley RL (1982) A postscript to circulation of the blood: Men and ideas. Circulation **66:** 683–688
Roberts JT, Wearn JT (1941) Quantitative changes in the capillary muscle relationship in human hearts during normal growth and hypertrophy. Am Heart J **21:** 617–633
Sagawa K (1972) The use of control theory and systems analysis in cardiovascular dynamics. *In* Cardiovascular Fluid Dynamics, vol I, edited by DH Bergel. New York, Academic Press, pp 115–171

Saint-Felix D, Demoment G (1982) Pressure-flow relationship in the canine left coronary artery: Study of linearity and stationarity using a time-domain representation and estimation methods. Med Biol Eng Comp **20:** 231–239

Salisbury PF, Cross CE, Rieben PA (1961) Physiological factors influencing coronary blood volume in isolated dog hearts. Am J Physiol **200:** 633–636

Sato T, Yamashiro SM, Grodins FS (1971) Measurement of peripheral vascular properties by a frequency response method. Am J Physiol **220:** 1640–1650

Scharf SM, Bromberger-Barnea B, Permutt S (1971) Distribution of coronary venous flow. J Appl Physiol **30:** 657–662

Scharf SM, Bromberger-Barnea B (1973) Influence of coronary flow and pressure on cardiac function and coronary vascular volume. Am J Physiol **224:** 918–925

Smaje LH, Fraser PA, Clough G (1980) The distensibility of single capillaries and venules in the cat mesentery. Microvasc Res **20:** 358–370

Spaan JAE (1979) Does coronary resistance change only during systole? Circ Res **45:** 838–839

Spaan JAE (1983) Evidence of intramyocardial compliance loaded by cardiac contraction in the dog and goat. J Physiol (Lond) **345:** 45P

Spaan JAE, Laird JD (1981) Coronary vasoconstriction in long diastoles (abstr). Circulation **64** (suppl IV): p 39

Spaan JAE, Breuls NPW, Laird JD (1981a) Diastolic-systolic coronary flow differences are caused by intramyocardial pump action in the anesthetized dog. Circ Res **49:** 584–593

Spaan JAE, Breuls NPW, Laird JD (1981b) Forward coronary flow normally seen in systole is the result of both forward and concealed back flow. Basic Res Cardiol **76:** 582–586

Spaan JAE, Bruinsma P, Laird JD (1983) Coronary flow mechanics of the hypertrophied heart. *In* Cardiac Left Ventricular Hypertrophy, edited by HEDJ ter Keurs, JJ Schipperheijn. Boston, Martinus Nijhoff, pp 171–191

Stein PD, Badeer HS, Schuetle WH, Glaser JF (1969) Pulsatile aspects of coronary sinus blood flow in closed-chest dogs. Am Heart J **78:** 331–337

Steinhausen M, Tillmanns H, Thederan H (1978) Microcirculation of the epimyocardial layer of the heart. I. A method for in vivo observation of the microcirculation of superficial ventricular myocardium of the heart and capillary flow pattern under normal and hypoxic conditions. Pflugers Arch **378:** 9–14

Stubbs J, Widdas WF (1959a) Extravascular fluid losses in the perfused isolated rabbit heart. J Physiol (Lond) **148:** 393–402

Stubbs J, Widdas WF (1959b) The interrelationship of weight change and coronary flow in the isolated perfused rabbit heart. J Physiol (Lond) **148:** 403–416

Tickner EG, Sacks AH (1967) A theory for the static elastic behavior of blood vessels. Biorheology **4:** 151–168

Tillmanns H, Ikeda S, Hansen H, Sarma JSM, Fauvel J-M, Bing RJ (1974) Microcirculation in the ventricle of the dog and turtle. Circ Res **34:** 561–569

Tillmanns H, Steinhausen M, Leinberger H, Thederan H, Kübler W (1981) Pressure measurements in the terminal vascular bed of the epimyocardium of rats and cats. Circ Res **49:** 1201–1211

Tomanek RJ, Searls JC, Lachenbruch PA (1982) Quantitative changes in the capillary bed during developing, peak, and stabilized cardiac hypertrophy in the spontaneously hypertensive rat. Circ Res **51:** 295–304

Tomonaga G, Tsujioka K, Ogasawara Y, Goto M, Nakai M, Tadaoka S, Kajiya F (1983) Evaluation of phasic blood flow velocity in peripheral coronary vein by laser doppler velocimeter (abstr). Circulation (suppl III): 203

Uhlig PN, Baer RW, Vlahakes GJ, Hanley FL, Messina LM, Hoffman JIE (1984) Arterial and venous coronary pressure-flow relations in anesthetized dogs: Evidence for a vascular waterfall in epicardial coronary veins. Circ Res **55:** 238–248

Westerhof N, Sipkema P, van Huis GA (1983) Coronary pressure-flow relations and the vascular waterfall. Cardiovasc Res **17:** 162–169

Wiederhielm CA (1965) Distensibility characteristics of small blood vessels. Fed Proc **24:** 1075–1084

Wieringa PA, Spaan JAE, Stassen HG, Laird JD (1982) Heterogeneous flow distribution in a three-dimensional network simulation of the myocardial microcirculation. Microcirculation **2:** 195–216

Wiggers CJ (1954) The interplay of coronary vascular resistance and myocardial compression in regulating coronary flow. Circ Res **2:** 271–279

Wüsten B, Buss DD, Deist H, Schaper W (1977) Dilatory capacity of the coronary circulation and its correlation to the arterial vasculature in the canine left ventricle. Basic Res Cardiol **72:** 636–650

INDEX TERMS: Intramyocardial compliance • Coronary artery zero flow pressure • Coronary artery diastolic pressure-flow curves • Myocardial microcirculation • Models of coronary circulation

Coronary Pressure-Flow Relationships

Controversial Issues and Probable Implications

Francis J. Klocke, Robert E. Mates, John M. Canty, Jr. and Avery K. Ellis
From the Departments of Medicine, Physiology, and Mechanical and Aerospace Engineering, State University of New York at Buffalo, Buffalo, New York

Background

In studies in which impedance flow through a vascular bed is calculated, driving pressure has traditionally been taken as the difference between inflow and outflow pressures, with the latter often assumed to be equal to right atrial pressure and, therefore, negligible in magnitude. In the coronary bed, ventricular diastolic pressure has sometimes been substituted for right atrial pressure, and has been taken as an index of intramyocardial forces presumed to influence the "back pressure" opposing coronary inflow.

These approximations have continued, despite publications dating back at least 50 years which suggest that inflow in several vascular beds ceases at pressures considerably in excess of right atrial or ventricular diastolic pressure. Values of this so-called "zero-flow pressure" ($P_{f=0}$) as high as 45 mm Hg were reported in the isolated hindlimb of dogs in the 1930's (Whittaker and Winton, 1933; Gomez and Veil, 1936). Influences of vasomotor tone, viscosity, and vessel distention and recruitment were addressed in the 1940's, and nonlinear pressure-flow relationships were identified experimentally (Pappeheimer and Maes, 1942; Green et al. 1944). A possible causative role of active tension in vascular smooth muscle was further emphasized in the early 1950's (Burton, 1951; Nichol et al., 1951). Permutt and colleagues' classical studies of pulmonary pressure-flow relationships in the early 1960's called attention to extravascular compressive forces, as well as vasomotor tone, and proposed a "vascular waterfall" as another explanation for higher-than-expected minimum pressures for forward flow (Permutt et al., 1962; Permutt and Riley, 1963).

Mosher et al. (1964) were among the first to describe pressure-flow relations in the coronary circulation. Steady state relationships obtained in five beating hearts by reducing perfusion pressure in step-wise fashion and measuring inflow 30 seconds to 2 minutes later indicated that inflow ceased at an average pressure of 23 mm Hg. Instantaneous relationships obtained by abruptly reducing pressure and measuring flow after only 1–2 seconds (presumably before autoregulatory changes could occur) showed higher values, suggesting in retrospect that $P_{f=0}$ varied with inflow pressure and that changes in $P_{f=0}$ were involved in autoregulatory adjustments of flow to changes in pressure. Later, a systolic waterfall was suggested by Downey and Kirk (1975).

Recent Coronary Studies

Interest in coronary pressure-flow relationships was rekindled by Bellamy's retrospective analysis of records of phasic coronary pressure and inflow in conscious dogs in the laboratory of the late Dr. Donald Gregg (Bellamy, 1978). During prolonged diastoles related to marked sinus arrhythmia, coronary inflow ceased at coronary arterial pressures as high as 40–50 mm Hg. For individual diastoles, flow was considered a linear function of inflow pressure. $P_{f=0}$ was taken as the pressure-axis intercept of the extrapolated relationship, and resistance as the reciprocal of its slope. Interventions associated with coronary vasodilation (e.g., reactive hyperemia postocclusion, adenosine administration) resulted in substantial decreases in both estimated $P_{f=0}$ and resistance.

Bellamy's report (1978) prompted a number of related studies of pressure-flow relationships. $P_{f=0}$ derived from measurements during single long diastoles remained higher than right atrial or left ventricular diastolic pressure, even when possible overestimates related to extrapolation of data terminating at pressures higher than $P_{f=0}$ were obviated (Klocke et al., 1981). On the basis of apparent shifts in $P_{f=0}$ following coronary sinus occlusion, Bellamy and colleagues (1980) suggested that $P_{f=0}$ results from a "modified" waterfall influenced by extravascular forces and vasomotor tone, with venous pressure being a determinant of perivascular tissue pressure. Inconsistencies in the use of coronary outflow pressure (rather than $P_{f=0}$) in calculations of driving pressure and resistance were pointed out (Bellamy, 1980). Other groups agreed that diastolic $P_{f=0}$ was less during vasodilation than with tone intact, and varied directly with inflow pressure when tone was operative (Klocke et al., 1981; Dole and Bishop, 1982a). In a study pertinent to viscous effects, it was found that conductance increased substantially, but that $P_{f=0}$ decreased insignificantly, in response to hemodilution during maximum vasodilation (Baer et al., 1981). Ventricular systole was reported by three laboratories to increase $P_{f=0}$ above diastolic values (Panerai et al., 1979; Bellamy and Lowenson, 1980; Taylor et al., 1981).

Currently Controversial Issues

Although implications of these studies have been discussed widely, there remains controversy as to whether the effective back pressure opposing coronary flow is greater than coronary outflow or left ventricular diastolic pressure and, if so, by how much. The relative magnitude of $P_{f=0}$ in vasodilated and vasoactive beds is at particular issue. There is also uncertainty about variations of $P_{f=0}$ within the myocardium, and increasing appreciation of the need to deal with the contour as well as the pressure-axis intercept of pressure-flow relationships. Among the important points underlying these issues are the effects of reactive (i.e., nonresistive) components of coronary impedance and the differences among—and/or vagaries of—individual experimental preparations used to study pressure-flow relationships. Effects of reactive components relate importantly to the magnitude and distribution of coronary capacitance, and, in particular, to the question of what portion of total intravascular capacitance affects diastolic pressure-flow relationships. The present discussion will attempt to clarify the implications of currently available studies by addressing four topics: reactive components of coronary input impedance, construction and interpretation of diastolic pressure-flow relationships which are free of reactive effects, persisting complexities in studies in nonvasodilated beds, and models of coronary pressure-flow behavior.

Reactive Components of Impedance

When discussions of $P_{f=0}$ in the coronary bed intensified in the late 1970's and early 1980's, Eng et al. (1982) called attention to reactive elements of impedance, particularly capacitance. Because of capacitive effects, inflow measured in a proximal artery necessarily underestimates flow in more distal portions of a vascular bed as inflow pressure falls (e.g., Hochberger and Zweifach, 1968). Conversely, measured inflow exceeds more distal flow when inflow pressure is increasing. The important questions in the coronary bed are the magnitude of this capacitive flow and its effects on the intercept and contour of experimentally determined pressure-flow relationships.

Characteristics of Coronary Input Impedance

Recent attempts to elucidate effects of capacitive flow on diastolic pressure-flow relationships identified a need for information about in vivo coronary input impedance. In a system with reactive as well as resistive components, input impedance is frequency-dependent and normally expressed in terms of modulus of impedance and phase angle. At zero frequency, the modulus of impedance is the vascular resistance calculated from mean flow and mean pressure gradient. At higher frequencies, the modulus falls, due to interactions of elastic, viscous, and inertial elements.

The conventional technique for determining input impedance involves resolving pulsatile pressure and flow waveforms into sinusoidal components by Fourier transformation. The coronary circulation is complex, not only in that pressure and flow are pulsatile, but also in that impedance may vary during the cardiac cycle. Systolic increases in resistance and/or $P_{f=0}$ related to mechanical effects of cardiac contraction are suggested by the reductions in mean coronary flow observed when heart rate is increased during pharmacological vasodilation (Raff et al., 1972; Domenech and Goich, 1976; Bache and Cobb, 1977). Such variations in impedance preclude the determination of coronary input impedance by Fourier transformation of pressure and flow waveforms taken over the entire cardiac cycle (Canty et al., 1985).

Using a programmable pressure control system (Canty and Mates, 1982), our laboratory has introduced sinusoidal pressure oscillations of constant amplitude and varying frequency at constant mean pressure levels during prolonged diastoles produced by cessation of pacing in heart-blocked dogs (Canty et al., 1985). The findings are qualitatively similar to those observed in other peripheral vascular beds: (1) as frequency is increased, the modulus of input impedance falls due to elastic properties of the coronary vessels; (2) at higher frequencies, the modulus of impedance levels off, probably due to inertia of the blood and viscoelastic effects; (3) the modulus of impedance decreases more rapidly with frequency as distending pressure decreases, both before and during vasodilation; (4) at any given pressure and frequency, input impedance modulus is smaller during vasodilation than with vasomotor tone active; (5) phase angles are negative, with flow leading pressure. Thus, in vivo diastolic coronary input impedance is a function of both distending pressure and vasomotor tone.

Reported Values of Coronary Capacitance

Coronary capacitance in this discussion is defined as a change in volume for a given change in pressure, i.e., $\Delta V/\Delta P$. The derivation of values of capacitance from impedance data requires some form of impedance modeling. As reflected by the numerous models of the coronary circulation proposed in recent years, the possibilities are virtually limitless!

Our initial approach to impedance modeling has been to examine systematically a number of lumped parameter models, incorporating viscoelastic and inertial elements, as well as resistance and capacitance, and using a standard optimization technique to determine the best least-squares fit to the measured impedance data (Mates et al., 1983). Over the frequency range 1–5 Hz, which includes the pressure decay rates encountered during long diastoles, a simple lumped RC parallel model has been surprisingly adequate. Above 5 Hz, data fits have been improved by adding a Voigt viscoelastic element

TABLE 1
Quantitative Estimates of Coronary Capacitance

Study	Preparation	Model	Mean distending pressure (mm Hg)	10³ Capacitance (ml/mm Hg per 100 g) Tone present	Tone absent	Pressure-dependent
1. Lewi and Schaper, 1971	In vivo: inflow pressure perturbation	RC	NS	0.4, 3[a]	0.9, 12[a]	
2. Canty et al., 1985	In vivo: inflow pressure perturbation	RC	30–110	1.6–6.0	2.7–14	Yes
3. Downey et al., 1983	In vivo: inflow pressure perturbation	RCR	NS	12[b]	59[b]	
4. Eng and Kirk, 1983	In vivo: 25-μm emboli	None[c]	<73[d]		14–17	No
5. Douglas and Greenfield, 1970	In vitro: 200-μm emboli	RC	90–150[e]		1.1–1.6[f]	Yes
6. Spaan et al., 1981	Arterial pressure decay following inflow occlusion	"Pump"	90	70[g]		
7. Spaan, 1982	Venous outflow following arterial occlusion	None	NS	100–250[h]		

NS = not stated.

[a] Values have been calculated for the two animals illustrated in Figures 3 and 4. Capacitance was taken as the reciprocal of the modulus of volume elasticity, with pressure expressed as mm Hg rather than dynes/cm^2. Since weights of the perfused circumflex segments were not given, these two sets of values are expressed as ml/mm Hg rather than ml/mm per 100g.

[b] Whereas these values are noticeably higher than those in studies 1 and 2, it should be noted that capacitance was calculated from a different model.

[c] The cannulated artery of a bed occluded with 25-μm spheres was opened to a preselected back pressure. Capacitive flow was taken as the amount by which backflow during the first 30 seconds exceeded flow during subsequent 30-second periods (with the latter presumed to represent steady state collateral flow).

[d] Distending pressures averaged 73 ± 10 (SD) mm Hg prior to 11–90 mm Hg step reductions produced by opening the embolized anterior descending artery to preselected back pressures.

[e] 0.1-ml increments in volume were superimposed on initial distending pressures of 60–120 mm Hg. From the data in Figure 2 and Table 1, we estimate pressure increments associated with the volume increments to have averaged 60 mm Hg. Mean distending pressure has therefore been taken as 30 mm Hg greater than initial distending pressure.

[f] Calculated from the data in Table 1, assuming the left main, anterior descending, and circumflex beds to constitute 83, 32, and 39%, respectively, of total cardiac mass (Marcus, 1983, p. 7).

[g] Estimate based on time constant of 3 seconds derived from the pattern of arterial pressure decay following inflow occlusion in a bed with vasomotor tone operative (Fig. 7). As discussed in the present text and by Downey et al. (1982), autoregulatory vasodilation probably occurred during the pressure decay, causing the reported time constant to reflect variations in resistance as well as capacitive effects. In addition, the model used to calculate capacitance appears to assume that resistance is constant throughout the cardiac cycle. As noted in the present text, systolic increases in resistance related to mechanical effects of cardiac contraction seem likely on the basis of the reductions in mean coronary flow observed when heart rate is increased during pharmacological vasodilation (Raff et al., 1972; Domenech and Goich, 1976; Bache and Cobb, 1977).

[h] Great cardiac vein outflow was collected for 5–10 seconds after left main coronary occlusion in an autoregulating bed and related to the mass of the left anterior descending bed. Anterior descending drainage reaching the coronary sinus through marginal veins rather than the great cardiac vein (Nakazawa et al., 1978) was presumably not included.

(Canty et al., 1983a, 1985). Table 1 summarizes our studies and six other reports from which quantitative estimates of capacitance have been, or can be, derived. Three points are of interest:

1. Two of three studies (nos. 2 and 5) in which capacitance was examined at different levels of distending pressure find capacitance to vary inversely with pressure. The lack of such variation in the third study (no. 4) may relate to technical limitations of the experimental procedure (see third and fourth footnotes in Table 1). In our own laboratory, the degree of variation of capacitance was 3- to 4-fold over the pressure range ordinarily encountered during long diastoles.

2. Studies in which measurements were made before and during pharmacological vasodilation (nos. 1, 2, and 3) indicate that capacitance at any given pressure is at least twice as large in the vasodilated bed as in the bed with tone intact.

3. Values of capacitance reported by studies employing inflow pressure perturbation (nos. 1, 2, and 3) are of the same order of magnitude as those measured in a model-independent fashion by opening the cannulated artery of a bed occluded with 25-μm spheres to predetermined back pressures (no. 4). However, these values are 1–2 orders of magnitude smaller than those derived from measurements of venous outflow following arterial occlusion (no. 7). The values in studies 1–4 also reflect only a small fraction of the heart's total intravascular volume, which has most frequently been estimated at 6–15 ml/100 g (Marcus, 1983, p. 17).

The last of these points bears importantly on the question of what portion of total capacitance influences diastolic pressure-flow relationships. We shall come back to this question in our consideration of models of pressure-flow behavior.

Effects of Rate of Change of Inflow Pressure on Capacitive Flow

Capacitive flow (CF) during long diastoles depends on the instantaneous rate at which transmural pressure is changing (dP/dt), as well as on capacitance (C), i.e., CF = C · dP/dt. This point is illustrated in Figure 1, which shows instantaneous pressure-flow relationships in a vasodilated bed during a long diastole in which coronary inflow pressure was made to decline linearly at three constant rates. At any given pressure level, measured inflow varies inversely with the absolute value of dP/dt, i.e., capacitive flow increases as dP/dt increases. The figure supports the view that values of capacitance are pressure-dependent, since the separation between any two relationships increases as pressure falls. It also calls attention to the variability in intercept and contour of pressure-flow relationships that can result from differences in capacitive effects produced by different patterns of inflow pressure decay. This latter point will be discussed further.

Capacitance-Free Diastolic Relationships

Because of the potential importance of capacitive effects when changing pressure and flow are used to construct diastolic pressure-flow relationships, experimental approaches which can define and compensate for capacitive flow have been of interest. If a coronary artery in a vasodilated bed is

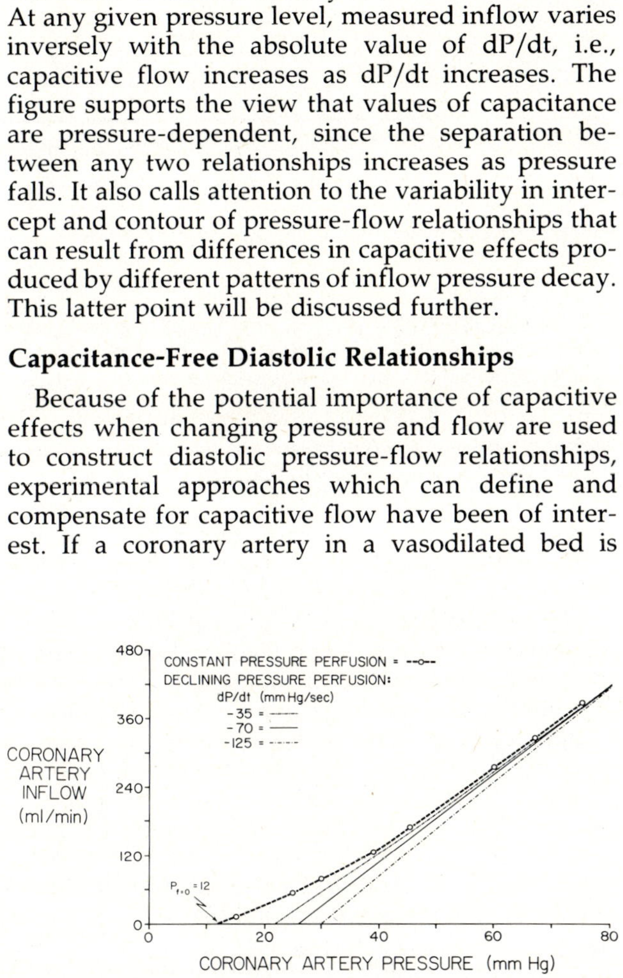

FIGURE 1. *Influence of reactive elements of impedance on diastolic pressure-inflow relationships in a canine circumflex bed vasodilated with adenosine. The thin lines represent instantaneous relationships recorded at 20-msec intervals during a single long diastole in which coronary inflow pressure was controlled by a programmable source (Canty and Mates, 1982) and made to decrease linearly at rates of −35, −70, and −125 mm Hg/sec. The open circles represent steady state flows during eight additional long diastoles in which coronary inflow pressure was held constant at each of eight preselected levels. The curvilinear dashed line connecting the eight points is taken to be free of reactive effects and to represent the purely resistive pressure-flow relationship. The −35 mm Hg/sec data are better described by a second- than first-order fit (P < 0.01), whereas the −70 and −125 mm Hg/sec data sets are linear.*

perfused at a constant pressure during a long diastole, reactive effects should disappear after an initial transient, with the steady state flow level representing the purely resistive component of impedance. Flow during later stages of a long diastole in an autoregulating bed should be relatively free of reactive effects if the time constant for the initial transient is short in relation to the time constant for autoregulation. If flows are measured during several long diastoles in which the level of constant pressure is varied, data from the several diastoles can presumably be combined to obtain a capacitance- and inertia-free pressure-flow relationship (Fig. 1).

Capacitance-Free Values of $P_{f=0}$

We are aware of four comparisons of pressure-flow relationships constructed in the fashion just described with those obtained during declining inflow pressure (Klocke et al., 1981; Downey et al., 1981; Eng et al., 1982; Dole and Bishop, 1982a). All four studies confirm that coronary capacitance results in an overestimate of $P_{f=0}$ when the latter is taken as the pressure-axis intercept of a pressure-flow relationship constructed during a period of declining inflow pressure. Salient points of these studies, including capacitance-free values of $P_{f=0}$, are summarized in Table 2.

Of particular interest (Table 2) is the fact that all three reports in which $P_{f=0}$ was measured during pharmacologically induced maximum vasodilation (nos. 1, 2, and 3) find a back pressure to flow during long diastoles which is modestly but systematically greater than coronary outflow or diastolic intraventricular pressure. Average capacitance-free values of $P_{f=0}$ in the three studies were 11–15 mm Hg. Values of right atrial and left ventricular diastolic pressures immediately prior to long diastoles averaged 3–5 and 7–9 mm Hg in the two studies in which they were reported (nos. 1 and 3). Using a different experimental approach to deal with capacitive effects, Kirkeeide et al. (1981) reported a similar effective back pressure during vasodilation, averaging 10 mm Hg. More recent studies in which pressure-flow relationships have been constructed during vasodilation from points measured during long diastoles a few seconds after onset of constant-pressure perfusion also report that $P_{f=0}$ exceeds coronary outflow and ventricular intracavitary pressures by at least a few mm Hg (Canty et al., 1983; Messina et al., 1983; Uhlig et al., 1984*).

* *In the study by Uhlig et al. (1984), the coronary sinus was cannulated and $P_{f=0}$ at high coronary sinus pressures was less than coronary sinus pressure. However, uncannulated coronary venous pathways remained at lower pressures during these measurements and values of $P_{f=0}$ exceeded pressures in the uncannulated pathways. Backflow into the coronary sinus was noted frequently at high coronary sinus pressures. Retrograde coronary sinus inflow presumably exited through the uncannulated venous pathways, thereby interacting with normal antegrade flow and further complicating the interpretation of the pressures recorded at the point of arterial inflow cessation.*

TABLE 2
Values of $P_{f=0}$ Derived from Flow Measurements during Several Long Diastoles Employing Different Levels of Constant-Pressure Perfusion

Study	Preparation: Chest open/closed	Preparation: Artery perfused	Tone present: Time of flow measurement (sec)[c]	Tone present: P_{cor} before long diastoles (mm Hg)	Tone present: $P_{f=0}$ (mm Hg)	Vasodilated: Vasodilating agent	Vasodilated: $P_{f=0}$ (mm Hg)
1. Klocke et al., 1981	Open[a]	LC	1–4[d]	126 ± 15 / 86 ± 15	22 ± 4	Carbocromen	11
2. Dole and Bishop, 1982a	Closed[b]	LC	0.5–1.0	75	21 ± 5	Adenosine	15 ± 2
				125	37 ± 5		
3. Eng et al., 1982	Open[a]	LM, LC	<0.2	NS[e]	11 ± 3	Carbocromen	11 ± 2
4. Downey et al., 1981	Open[a]	LM	0.2	50	18 ± 4		
				130	27 ± 6		

Average values are mean ± 1 SD. LC = left circumflex coronary artery, LM = left main coronary artery, P_{cor} = pressure in perfused coronary artery, NS = not stated.

[a] These studies employed barbiturate anesthesia and acutely induced heart block, with long diastoles being produced by sudden cessation of ventricular pacing.

[b] This study employed chloralose anesthesia and produced long diastoles by vagal stimulation following intracoronary atropine.

[c] After establishment of each constant-pressure level.

[d] Eng and Kirk (1982) have called attention to Figure 9 in that report, pointing out that instantaneous inflow 1 second after a sudden reduction in inflow pressure was sometimes negative. As mentioned in the text of the report, such momentary backflow was felt to result from backward capacitive discharge from vessels downstream to the in-line electromagnetic flowmeter. The time course of the backward discharge probably reflected inertial effects of sudden flow reversal as well as the RC charcteristics of the coronary artery cannula and constant-pressure reservoir perfusion circuit. The failure of backward flow to be sustained has been taken as evidence against a collateral flow effect. A similar, somewhat briefer flow transient in a vasodilated bed is shown in Figure 3. In addition, Dole et al. have illustrated a negative flow transient in response to a sudden reduction of inflow pressure in an autoregulating bed (Dole et al., 1984, Fig. 4)

[e] Mean aortic pressures averaged 91 ± 14 mm Hg. However, Figure 3 shows a gradient of ~30 mm Hg across the coronary perfusion circuit in a nonvasodilated bed, indicating that coronary pressure was, at least in some cases, substantially less than aortic pressure.

Thus, all laboratories studying the point seem to agree that the back pressure to coronary flow during long diastoles is systematically greater than right atrial and/or left ventricular diastolic pressure during pharmacological vasodilation. The traditional formulation of coronary driving pressure is therefore inappropriate. Whereas the magnitude of the error involved in its use may be small under some experimental conditions, the need for improved definition and understanding of the mechanisms which govern coronary back pressure is apparent. A recent report from our laboratory indicates that capacitance-free values of $P_{f=0}$ rise appreciably in the vasodilated bed when left ventricular preload is increased (Aversano et al., 1984). Bellamy's coronary sinus occlusion study (in which capacitive effects were not evaluated directly and vasodilation was produced by temporarily occluding the coronary artery prior to diastolic arrest) suggested that $P_{f=0}$ is also sensitive to elevations in coronary outflow pressure (Bellamy et al., 1980). Uhlig and co-workers (1984) have reported a vascular waterfall in the epicardial venous system of open-chest dogs which appears capable of influencing arterial as well as venous coronary flow, and have suggested that effects of increasing diastolic pressure may be mediated through such a waterfall.

Three of the four studies (1, 2, and 4) summarized in Table 2 report that the magnitude of capacitance-free values of $P_{f=0}$ is influenced by vasomotor tone, as well as non-tone-dependent factors, and that $P_{f=0}$ varies with coronary pressure prior to diastolic arrest when tone is operative. Average values of $P_{f=0}$ were appreciably higher than during vasodilation, varying between 18 and 37 mm Hg. The lower values of $P_{f=0}$ and absence of a demonstrable influence of vasomotor tone on $P_{f=0}$ in study no. 3 may relate to factors such as relatively low levels of coronary pressure prior to long diastoles (see fifth footnote in Table 2). In addition, since constant-pressure perfusion data in this study were sometimes taken within 200 msec of the onset of diastole in autoregulating beds, constant-pressure flow measurements in such instances probably included the transient related to refilling of vessels emptied during the preceding systole described by Downey et al. (1983).

The quantitative implications of $P_{f=0}$ levels of 20–40 mm Hg have caused the measurements of this magnitude with vasomotor tone operative to be regarded with particular skepticism. Concern has most frequently centered on effects of capacitive flow. As discussed earlier, capacitive flow—and, therefore, the degree of capacitance-related overestimate of $P_{f=0}$ during declining pressure measurements—depends on the absolute value of capacitance and the instantaneous rate of change of transmural pressure. Depending on experimental conditions, substantial overestimates are clearly possible.

When flow is measured with an in-line flowmeter in an external perfusion circuit, the capacitance of the circuit between the flowmeter and the coronary artery is added to the capacitance of the coronary vessels themselves. Potential effects of dP/dt at the time of inflow cessation are illustrated in Figure 1, in which overestimates of $P_{f=0}$ exceed the capacitance-free value of 12 mm Hg by 83–150% as dP/dt at inflow cessation increases in magnitude from −35 to −125 mm Hg/sec. To our knowledge, values of dP/dt at the point of zero inflow have not been evaluated systematically in any published study of $P_{f=0}$ employing declining inflow pressure. Perfusion circuit capacitance and/or a high dP/dt at the time of inflow cessation could be involved in occasional marked discrepancies between the capacitance-free value of $P_{f=0}$ and $P_{f=0}$ derived from a declining pressure measurement (e.g., Eng et al., 1982, Fig. 4).

On the other hand, even though absolute values of capacitance increase substantially over the range of spontaneous pressure decay during a typical long diastole, capacitive flow may be quite small at the time of inflow cessation because of large reductions in dP/dt as diastole proceeds. In our own experience to date, pressure-flow relationships recorded during a steady decline of inflow pressure at −3 mm Hg/sec have corresponded closely to capacitance-free relationships in vasodilated beds (Aversano et al., 1984, Fig. 4). An example of particular interest is Bellamy's widely reproduced record of a diastole lasting ~2.5 seconds in a conscious dog with vasomotor tone intact (Bellamy, 1978, Fig. 1). Although the rate of decrease of circumflex inflow pressure was ~60 mm Hg/sec at the onset of diastole, it had fallen to ~3 mm Hg/sec at the point at which a $P_{f=0}$ of 45 mm Hg was recorded. Assuming capacitance to be 0.003–0.005 ml/mm Hg per 100 g at this pressure, capacitive flow at the point of inflow cessation would be estimated at <0.5 ml/min for a 50-g circumflex bed. The overestimate of $P_{f=0}$ related to this small capacitive flow would be only a few mm Hg. In their paper calling attention to effects of capacitance, Eng et al. (1982) used a parallel RC model and assumed an exponential decay of aortic pressure and constant values of R and C to estimate the shift in $P_{f=0}$ caused by capacitance. If their model is applied to Bellamy's data near the point of inflow cessation, using C = 0.005 ml/mm Hg, R = 3 mm Hg/ml per min, and dP/dt = −3 mm Hg/sec, a shift of only 3 mm Hg is predicted.† Thus, unless one postulates values of capacitance which are an order of magnitude larger than indicated by studies 1–5 in Table 1, Bellamy's $P_{f=0}$ of 45 mm Hg seems difficult to explain as an artifact of undetected capacitive flow.

† *Limitations of this model have been discussed by several workers (Dole and Bishop, 1982a; Hori, 1982; Hoki, 1982; Braakman et al., 1982) and acknowledged by its proponents (Eng and Kirk, 1982).*

The issue of $P_{f=0}$ in beds with vasomotor tone operative will be commented upon further when considering complexities in the experimental determination of the contour of pressure-flow relationships in beds with tone active, and when discussing pressure-flow modeling. On the basis of the capacitance-free values of $P_{f=0}$ in Table 2 and the considerations just discussed, the conclusion that $P_{f=0}$ is higher in autoregulating beds than vasodilated beds, and pressure-dependent when tone is operative, seems persuasive.

Possible Effects of Collateral Flow on Measured Values of $P_{f=0}$

As controversial points about coronary pressure-flow relationships have become more focused, questions have arisen about possible effects of collateral flow on even capacitance-free values of $P_{f=0}$. Of particular concern is the possibility that reported values of $P_{f=0}$ are artificially high in preparations in which the test coronary artery is cannulated because of unmeasured collateral flow into the cannulated bed. Concern about effects of collateral flow is heightened in canine preparations, in which flows as high as 0.1–0.2 ml/min per g are sometimes recorded in the central core of myocardial segments a few minutes after regional inflow occlusion.

Recent reports make two points about acute studies in previously unmanipulated canine coronary beds: (1) a minimum interarterial pressure gradient of 40–70 mm Hg is required before any collateral flow is detected (Messina et al., 1983; Messina et al., personal communication); (2) collateral flow within the low-pressure portion of the bed requires a minimum arterial pressure of ~20 mm Hg in the collateralized segment (Eng and Kirk, 1984).

The issue of effects of collateral flow highlights subtle but potentially important differences among superficially similar experimental approaches used to determine the low pressure portion of pressure-flow relationships. When interarterial pressure gradients are not present, as in canine left main preparations (e.g., Eng et al., 1982; Messina et al., 1983; Uhlig et al., 1984), collateral flow is not an issue (unless there is reason to expect unusual collateralization from the nondominant right coronary artery). In cannulated preparations, potential effects of collateral flow on $P_{f=0}$ measured during long diastoles are minimized by the spontaneous decline in aortic pressure (and corresponding reduction in pressure gradient between the noncannulated and cannulated beds at low cannula pressures) as diastole proceeds (e.g., Klocke et al., 1981; Dole and Bishop, 1982a). Even when arterial pressure in the cannulated bed exceeds 20 mm Hg and an interarterial pressure gradient >40 mm Hg is present, there is also the question of the time required for preexisting collateral channels to open (Khouri et al., 1971). Collateral flow may be greater during studies in which these conditions are established a minute or two before a pressure-flow data point is obtained (e.g., Mosher et al., 1964; Messina et al., 1983) rather than a few seconds before (e.g., Klocke et al., 1981; Canty et al., 1983; Aversano et al., 1984). Finally, pressure-flow relationships derived from measurements of arterial inflow in situations in which collateral flow is likely assume that the size of the bed perfused by the cannulated artery does not change as the pressure gradient between the cannulated and noncannulated beds is varied.

Despite these differences among experimental approaches, it remains noteworthy that laboratories recently studying coronary pressure-flow relationships—including one studying swine, in which collateral effects would be expected to be less prominent than in dogs (Pantely et al., 1984)—all report that $P_{f=0}$ in vasodilated beds normally exceeds coronary venous and left ventricular diastolic pressures by at least a few mm Hg. The studies discussed above indicating that $P_{f=0}$ is higher with tone operative than during vasodilation also seem difficult to "explain away" on the basis of collateral flow.

Possible Effects of Myocardial Ischemia on Measured Values of $P_{f=0}$

Hoffman (1981) has called attention to possible effects of myocardial ischemia when determining the lower-pressure portion of pressure-flow relationships. Values of $P_{f=0}$ derived from measurements of full-cycle flow in the beating heart (which "cancel" reactive effects within the cardiac cycle) may include effects of ischemia-induced reductions in impedance caused by decreased myocardial contractility (Marzilli et al., 1979). If heart rate changes as perfusion pressure is lowered, additional changes in time-averaged impedance are possible. Although the critical level of pressure required to avoid myocardial ischemia is no doubt rate- and afterload-dependent, levels below 40 mm Hg—which are crucial in the determination of $P_{f=0}$—may be a problem even in pharmacologically dilated beds when heart rate is rapid. Additionally, when measurements are made during a long diastole after a period of reduced pressure with the heart beating, it is possible that diastolic myocardial properties have been altered by the preceding period of reduced flow.

Contour of Capacitance-Free Relationships

It is apparent that capacitive flow can affect the contour as well as the intercept of diastolic pressure-flow relationships. This consideration is pertinent, not only to values of resistance (or conductance) derived from pressure-flow relationships, but also to disagreement among laboratories as to whether diastolic pressure-flow relationships are linear or nonlinear. The issue of curvilinearity was raised initially in regard to relationships constructed during periods of declining inflow pressure. Although our own laboratory's initial reports employed linear data fits (Ellis and Klocke, 1979; Canty and Klocke, 1979), we found as our experience increased (Klocke et al., 1981) that relationships were fit better by a second- than first-order process (despite linear correlation coefficients averaging 0.95–0.96), and became hesitant to infer specific values of resistance.

In retrospect, the contours of all diastolic pressure-flow relationships obtained during declining inflow pressure have been influenced by capacitive flow. The degree of influence no doubt varied from study to study, and is difficult to characterize quantitatively. Attempts to do so would have to deal with both instantaneous dP/dt (Fig. 1) and pressure-dependent changes in capacitance (Table 1). Apparent linearity of some previously reported relationships may reflect a combination of the effects of variations in dP/dt and capacitance. For example, in Figure 1, the capacitance-free relationship is curvilinear, whereas the relationships at high dP/dt levels are linear. Although there is no question that the changes in contour of pressure-flow relationships are independent of capacitive effects during interventions such as pharmacological vasodilation, modest changes in contour in studies employing declining inflow pressure need to be interpreted cautiously. Capacitive effects seem likely to limit the amount of new information that can be obtained in future studies of pressure-flow relationships in which inflow pressure is allowed to change in an undefined fashion.

More recent studies employing constant-pressure perfusion during several long diastoles, or other approaches for eliminating reactive effects, indicate that capacitance-free pressure-flow relationships in the vasodilated bed of open-chest dogs and isolated vented dog hearts are indeed curvilinear (Canty et al., 1983; Messina et al., 1983; Aversano et al., 1984; Hanley et al., 1984). Although, potentially, collateral flow can affect the contour of pressure-flow relationships, as well as their pressure-axis intercepts (Klocke et al., 1984), the curvilinearity of capacitance-free relationships has been equally apparent in left main (Messina et al., 1983; Hanley et al., 1984) and left circumflex (Canty et al., 1983; Aversano et al., 1984) preparations. The degree of curvilinearity can be substantial, particularly in the lower pressure range,‡ and appears to vary with preload and outflow pressure. As coronary arterial pressure was reduced from 65 to 20–30 mm Hg in an open-chest canine preparation, conductance decreased by ~30% at normal levels of left ventricular diastolic pressure, and by ~50% at left ventricular diastolic pressures of 30–35 mm Hg (Aversano et al., 1984). Similarly, in an isolated empty heart preparation, the slope of the relationship between flow and the logarithm of inflow pressure decreased

‡ *Although extreme degrees of curvilinearity, with flow "hugging" the pressure axis, can be difficult to exclude experimentally (Aversano et al., 1984), they would have limited physiological meaning because of the very low flows associated with them.*

by 35% as transcoronary driving pressure was reduced from 30 to 10 mm Hg (Hanley et al., 1984).

Dole and colleagues continue to find capacitance-free pressure-flow relationships to be linear in both vasoactive and pharmacologically dilated beds of closed-chest dogs (Dole and Bishop, 1982a; Dole et al., 1984). In their preparation, the circumflex artery is perfused through a metal cannula wedged in the proximal circumflex artery, and long diastoles are produced by vagal stimulation following intracoronary atropine. The basis for the difference in contour between their studies and those of other laboratories remains unclear, but could relate to differences between closed- and open-chest preparations or other experimental features just noted. Collateral flow effects at high coronary (and low aortic) pressures and other factors which may cancel curvature produced by changing resistance (Dole and Bishop, 1982; Hanley et al., 1984) also deserve consideration.

Whereas the basis for curvilinearity of pressure-flow relationships must involve pressure-dependent changes in the caliber of open vascular channels (Hanley et al., 1984), alterations in the number of perfused channels also seem likely. As pointed out by several groups, if $P_{f=0}$ varies within the heart, the pressure-axis intercept of a pressure-flow relationship represents the minimum value of $P_{f=0}$ associated with a measurable conductance in a distribution of $P_{f=0}$ within the myocardial wall. In such a distribution, the number of open vascular channels increases with perfusion pressure and contributes to curvilinearity. Three studies have suggested that $P_{f=0}$ varies transmurally (Archie, 1978; Rouleau et al., 1979; Ellis and Klocke, 1980), but each has experimental limitations. A preliminary report indicating that $P_{f=0}$ does not vary transmurally (Firmin et al., 1982) involves assumptions that are difficult to validate. In our recent study of effects of preload (Aversano et al., 1984), pressure-axis intercepts exceeded left ventricular diastolic pressure when the latter was 17 mm Hg or less, but were less than ventricular diastolic pressure at higher levels of preload. Increases in ventricular diastolic pressure were also accompanied by increases in coronary resistance at all levels of inflow pressure. These findings are compatible with a vascular waterfall in which higher values of $P_{f=0}$ are concentrated in the inner myocardial layers. The preload-related increases in resistance may reflect not only a shift in minimum $P_{f=0}$, but also a broadening of the overall distribution of $P_{f=0}$ (and, therefore, a diminished number of functionally open channels at any inflow pressure). Although microsphere studies by Hanley et al. (1984) did not show a sequential dropout of vessels by transmural layer as inflow pressure was reduced, these workers were careful to note that their findings were directly applicable only to the isolated empty heart, and that transmural flow patterns would likely be altered in a working heart preparation.

In summary, the inherently nonlinear relationship between coronary pressure and flow needs to be taken into account in future attempts to quantify resistance and/or $P_{f=0}$, and to identify changes in these parameters in response to interventions. The reductions in resistance which occur as inflow pressure is raised reflect increases in vessel radius, and probably vessel recruitment as well. More definitive studies of intramyocardial variations of $P_{f=0}$ (both transmural and nontransmural) in working hearts are needed.

Confounding Effects in Nonvasodilated Beds

Autoregulatory effects remain a difficult confounding point in attempts to define $P_{f=0}$ and/or the contour of diastolic pressure-flow relationships in beds that are not maximally dilated. Normal autoregulatory processes allow coronary flow to vary directly with myocardial metabolic demand at a constant coronary arterial pressure, and to remain relatively constant when inflow pressure is altered in the face of constant metabolic demand (Mosher et al., 1964). These metabolically induced and/or pressure-induced autoregulatory effects have long been agreed to involve changes in coronary vascular resistance, i.e., vasoconstriction and vasodilation. Three of the studies in Table 2 (1, 2, and 4) suggest that changes in $P_{f=0}$ can also be involved, in that the values of $P_{f=0}$ obtained from constant-pressure diastoles appear to vary with levels of diastolic pressure immediately prior to the determination of $P_{f=0}$. Dole and Bishop (1982a) have studied the point most extensively, concluding that pressure-induced autoregulation involves important changes in $P_{f=0}$, as well as coronary resistance.

Reports from at least five laboratories confirm that autoregulatory changes in flow occur during long diastoles in which the coronary bed is not dilated by pharmacological or other means. Our laboratory (Klocke et al., 1981) noted substantial time-dependent reductions in flow during long diastoles with constant inflow pressures $\geq$60 mm Hg. The time required for a 50% decrease in flow was ~4 seconds and seemed consistent with the 10- to 15-second total autoregulatory time noted by Mosher et al. (1964) following abrupt changes in perfusion pressure at constant metabolic demand in beating hearts. Time-dependent changes in flow were smaller at pressures <60 mm Hg, suggesting that autoregulatory changes during long diastoles may affect the contour of a pressure-flow relationship to a greater degree than its intercept. Half-times of flow reduction similar to those reported by our laboratory were noted by Spaan and Laird (1981). Reductions in circumflex inflow of as much as 50 ml/min have been observed following a step increase in inflow pressure shortly after the onset of a long diastole (Klocke et al., 1984). In the constant-pressure perfusion experiments of Eng et al. (1982), the decision to use flow measurements taken within 200 msec of the onset of long diastoles in nondilated beds was based on reductions in flow as diastole proceeded. Dole and Bishop (1982) illustrated substantial changes in diastolic flow (at constant coronary pressure) in response to intracoronary adenosine injection, sudden cessation of pacing, and reactive hyperemia coupled with a marked reduction in heart rate at the moment of reflow. They felt it was possible, however, to maintain an essentially constant level of flow during long diastoles as long as such interventions were avoided (Dole and Bishop, 1982a). This assumption was importantly involved in their relatively detailed measurements of autoregulatory changes in resistance and $P_{f=0}$ (Dole and Bishop, 1982a).

Because of probable time-dependent changes in resistance and/or $P_{f=0}$ during long diastoles in nonvasodilated beds, we feel that the detailed interpretation of even pressure-flow relationships obtained using constant-pressure perfusion remains less clear than when vasodilation has been induced. Additional studies clarifying the nature of, and basis for, time-dependent changes in flow at constant pressure during long diastoles in autoregulating beds are highly desirable. As noted earlier, the conclusion that $P_{f=0}$ is higher in autoregulating than in vasodilated beds, and pressure-dependent when tone is operative, currently seems persuasive.

Modeling Coronary Pressure-Flow Behavior

The traditional concept of the coronary circulation as a resistive bed supplied by aortic pressure and drained at right atrial pressure is clearly not adequate to describe the pressure-flow relationships elucidated by experimental studies. Three findings must be reconciled in attempts to model coronary pressure-flow behavior:

1. The instantaneous pressure-flow relationship at any time during the cardiac cycle has a pressure-axis intercept greater than right atrial pressure. Studies during diastole discussed above indicate that the magnitude of $P_{f=0}$ depends on the level of smooth muscle tone in the vascular bed, as well as tone-independent factors. Studies during systole are more limited and less definitive. Recent reports suggesting that pressure-axis intercepts are higher during systole than diastole (Panerai et al., 1979; Bellamy and Lowensohn, 1980; Taylor et al., 1981) seem importantly limited by capacitive effects related to the two points listed below and/or by the magnitude of corrections applied to instantaneous recordings of coronary pressure and perfusion circuit flow to correct for reactive effects. Nevertheless, the possibility that $P_{f=0}$ is higher in systole than diastole requires consideration.

2. The phasic pattern of coronary venous outflow shows a peak related to systolic contraction while coronary inflow is reduced during systole and peaks during diastole. Capillary red cell velocity patterns appear to follow those in veins, rather than arterioles (at least in superficial vessels) (Tillmans et al., 1974). There is evidence that venous outflow persists after cessation of arterial inflow in at least some experimental circumstances (Chilian and Marcus, 1982; Spaan, 1982; Bellamy and O'Benar, 1984).

3. When inflow pressure is reduced, arterial backflow can occur during systole (Spaan et al., 1981; Chilian and Marcus, 1982).

Although various explanations of one or more of these phenomena have been proposed, two have received particular attention. Following earlier models of the pulmonary circulation (Permutt and Riley, 1963), several groups have considered a vascular waterfall a possible basis for experimentally observed pressure-flow relationships. Spaan and colleages (1981) have proposed an intramyocardial pump, capacitively coupled to the circulation, as an explanation for patterns of phasic outflow and systolic backflow.

Waterfall-Pump Model

Figure 2 shows a model incorporating both the waterfall and the intramyocardial pump (Mates, 1984) which appears consistent with available experimental findings. Aortic pressure is represented by P_a and coronary venous (right atrial) pressure by P_v. The intramyocardial or extravascular pressure, which drives the pump, is shown as P_e. P_s represents an effective component of extravascular pressure due to vascular smooth muscle tone. P_e is assumed to vary during the cardiac cycle as ventricular pressure rises and falls, as suggested by Spaan et al. (1981). P_s is also time-varying, but with a longer time constant (several seconds). The waterfall (WF) regulates pressure under the influence of P_e and P_s (shown by dotted lines) by partial vascular collapse, producing an effective back pressure to coronary inflow (P_b). If pressures proximal and distal to the waterfall are above the effective back pressure, the waterfall has no effect. If distal pressure falls below the effective back pressure, the waterfall will produce whatever pressure drop is necessary to maintain the back pressure.

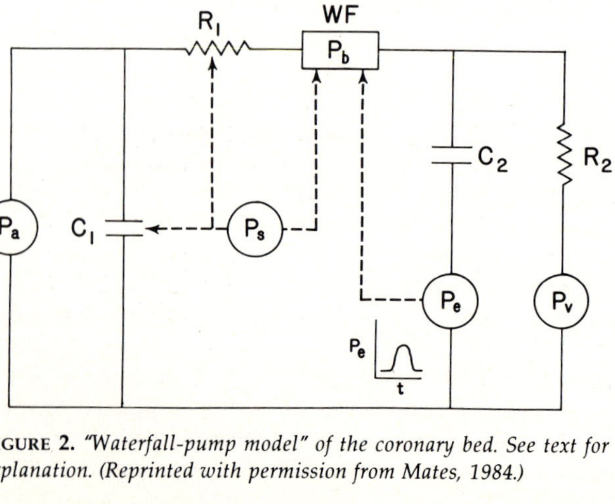

FIGURE 2. *"Waterfall-pump model" of the coronary bed. See text for explanation. (Reprinted with permission from Mates, 1984.)*

In this model, the resistance of the coronary bed is divided into two lumped components, R_1 and R_2. Similarly, capacitance is divided into a proximal component (C_1) and distal component (C_2). The lumped model is an obvious simplification, since, in reality, resistance and capacitance are distributed throughout the bed. The formulation in Figure 2 also ignores possible transmural variations in impedance which have been referred to above. Extravascular pressure is assumed to affect the waterfall. As mentioned earlier, changes in mean flow with heart rate in vasodilated beds suggest that R_1 may also be influenced by P_e. Smooth muscle tone appears to influence not only the waterfall pressure but also the proximal resistance and capacitance R_1 and C_1.

Let us examine the model in relation to the experimental findings cited above:

1. Experimentally observed diastolic pressure-flow relationships are consistent with the model as long as the waterfall pressure P_b is considered to be tone-dependent. However, the distal capacitance C_2 also tends to regulate pressure between R_1 and R_2 during diastole. Spaan has suggested that a waterfall is not necessary (at least in the autoregulating bed) to explain the implication of diastolic pressure-flow relationships that pressure at some intermediate point in the circulation is regulated separately from venous pressure (Spaan and Laird, 1983). His hypothesis is that C_2 is sufficiently large so that the time constant for charging this capacitance (R_1C_2) is long compared to the time of diastole. Inflow recordings following step changes in inflow pressure during long diastoles in vasodilated beds in our own laboratory and in that of Downey show reactive time constants <100 msec, with no subsequent variation in inflow for at least 5–10 seconds (as long as coronary outflow and intraventricular pressures are kept constant) (Canty and Mates, 1982; Downey et al., 1982, 1983; Klocke et al., 1984). Figure 3 illustrates this type of response, with inflow remaining constant for 12 seconds after the initial transient following a reduction in inflow pressure. If one postulates a capacitance discharging at a sufficiently slow rate to be inapparent in this type of record, we find the capacitance required to be much larger than any reported values and inconsistent with estimates of total myocardial blood volume.

In a regulating bed, as noted above, it is more difficult to sort out the transient effects following a step change in pressure. However, unless some fundamental change occurs in the model during pharmacological vasodilation, it seems unlikely that the higher values of $P_{f=0}$ observed with tone operative can be explained entirely on the basis of intramyocardial capacitance. Preliminary reports from Downey et al. (1982, 1983) indicate that the early diastolic overshoot in coronary flow during constant-pressure perfusion in dogs with vasomotor tone operative decays exponentially with a time constant of 55 msec (which is even less than during vasodilation). The short time constant would lead to the conclusion that reactive effects related to intramyocardial capacitance are completed early in diastole in beds with tone active, as well as in beds which have been dilated pharmacologically. In addition, Dole and colleagues have illustrated a 6-second period of apparent zero inflow in an autoregulating bed following a sudden reduction in inflow pressure from 125 to 27 mm Hg during a long diastole (Dole et al., 1984, Fig. 4).

As also noted above, it seems plausible that backflow pressures are higher during systole than during

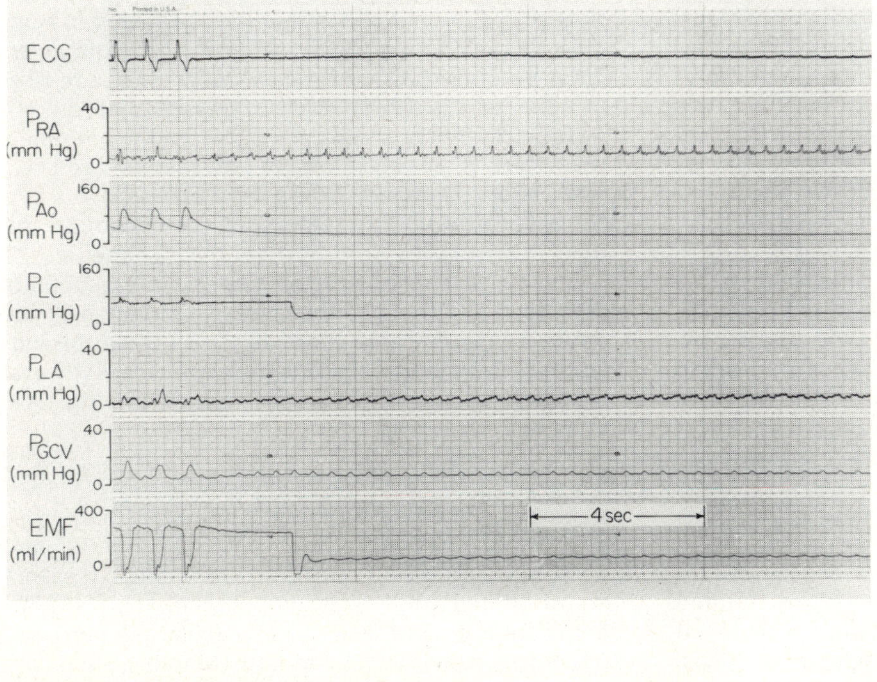

FIGURE 3. *Response of coronary inflow to a reduction in inflow pressure during a long diastole in a heart-blocked dog in which the coronary bed was vasodilated with carbocromen. Following cessation of pacing, right, and left atrial reservoirs are opened, to keep coronary outflow and left ventricular pressures constant. The decay in inflow during the first second of diastole may relate to these initial adjustments in intracavitary pressures (see Aversano et al., 1984, Fig. 3), as well as to the effects of refilling of vessels compressed during the previous systole (see present text). When pressure in the cannulated left circumflex artery is subsequently reduced from 61 to 21 mm Hg, circumflex inflow stabilizes at 35 ml/min following an initial transient related to reactive effects and remains at this level for the next 12 seconds. (ECG = electrocardiogram; $P_{RA, Ao, LC, LA, GCV}$ = pressures in the right atrium, aorta, left circumflex artery, left atrium, and great cardiac vein; EMF = phasic left circumflex inflow, measured with an electromagnetic flowmeter.)*

diastole. This could be due to an influence of P_e on the waterfall back pressure P_b.

2. The phasic pattern of venous outflow is explained by the intramyocardial pump. During systole, the extravascular pressure, P_e, rises as left ventricular pressure increases. The resulting pressure difference across capacitor C_2 causes blood to be discharged through resistance R_2 into the right atrium. As the ventricle relaxes and P_e falls, venous outflow drops and the capacitor C_2 is recharged. If R_2 remains constant during the cardiac cycle, the pressure proximal to this resistance and to capacitance C_2 will rise during systole and fall during diastole in phase with the measured venous outflow. This explanation for venous outflow patterns would hold whether or not a waterfall is present upstream of C_2.

3. The intramyocardial pump also can explain systolic back flow. The original coronary waterfall model proposed by Downey and Kirk (1975) contained an electrical diode as part of the waterfall, preventing backflow. However, a collapsible tube will permit backflow if the distal pressure is higher than the effective backflow pressure. Thus, backflow is expected when the pressure proximal to R_2 exceeds inflow pressure. The observation of systolic backflow neither confirms nor precludes the existence of a waterfall.

Whereas Figure 2 provides a plausible model to explain a variety of experimental findings, the anatomic interpretation of model elements remains in question because it is presently possible to measure phasic pressures and flows only in the relatively proximal coronary arteries and distal coronary veins. Lacking detailed pressure and flow measurements at the microcirculatory level, one can only speculate on the anatomic location of individual lumped elements. The dependence of apparent back pressure on smooth muscle tone suggests that the waterfall, if it exists, lies upstream of the capillaries at the level at which primary flow regulation occurs. With this interpretation, R_1 would represent the lumped precapillary resistance and R_2 the resistance distal to this point. Similarly, C_1 would lump all of the precapillary capacitance, while C_2 would represent the capacitance of the capillary and venous beds. The fact that we were unable to identify two capacitive elements in perturbing inlet pressure and flow with a sine wave (Mates et al., 1983) is consistent with a location of C_2 distal to the major portion of coronary resistance. As indicated in Table 1, capacitance influenced by inflow pressure perturbation appears to increase 2-fold when the bed is pharmacologically vasodilated. This would be compatible with a significant portion of C_1 being located in the smaller precapillary vessels.

The anatomic distribution of capacitance bears importantly on the question of what portion of total capacitance influences diastolic pressure-inflow relationships. Since the capacitance C_2 is located downstream to the point of regulated pressure, it need not be involved in inflow regulation. Thus, persistence of coronary venous outflow beyond the point of inflow cessation during a long diastole (Chilian et al., 1982; Spaan, 1982; Bellamy and O'Benar, 1984) does not exclude a point of regulated pressure at the arteriolar-precapillary level. The capacitance values in Table 1 estimated from inflow perturbation and arterial embolization (studies 1–5) presumably reflect C_1, whereas those obtained from venous outflow (study 7) represent primarily C_2.

Long Diastoles vs. Normal Cardiac Cycles

Although resistive components of coronary impedance can be separated from reactive ones in studies of pressure-flow relationships during long diastoles, the applicability of findings during long diastoles to the normal cardiac cycle remains to be demonstrated. Whereas the preponderance of coronary flow occurs during diastole, normal diastoles may not be quasi-steady. In the model shown in Figure 2, the vessels emptied during systole, represented by C_2, must be recharged during the early stage of diastole.

This systolic-diastolic interaction could influence the magnitude and distribution of flow (Hoffman, 1983). The extravascular pressure P_e in Figure 2 probably varies transmurally with ventricular stresses, being highest at the endocardium. In addition, the diastolic time course of P_e has not been established. Although the original model suggested that P_e is proportional to left ventricular pressure (Spaan et al., 1981), Bellamy's "modified" waterfall concept (Bellamy et al., 1980) suggests that myocardial blood content may play a role in regulating P_e as expanding blood vessels compress surrounding tissue. If P_e does depend on blood volume, as well as P_{LV}, its diastolic time course may differ from P_{LV}, being lower during early diastole and then increasing more rapidly as vessels are refilled. In such a setting, the maximum driving pressure for coronary flow (P_{Ao}-P_e) would be higher than expected in early diastole, and would decrease during diastole as arterial pressure falls and extravascular pressure rises (Klocke et al., 1984). Measurements that do not include the initial stage of diastole might not detect this effect. It also seems likely that systolic compression causes some redistribution of blood flow across the myocardium, an effect which could not be appreciated in inflow and outflow measurements.

Further studies of systolic-diastolic interaction are of interest, although their interpretation will no doubt be complicated (particularly in the autoregulating bed) by the numerous transients involved and the current lack of techniques for measuring local phasic pressure and flow.

Limitations of Resistance Calculations

As the preceding discussion has indicated, coronary input impedance is a complex quantity, and attempts to represent impedance by a single measure are of limited value. Marcus points out that at least ten different approaches for calculating coronary resistance have been proposed (Marcus, 1983, pp.

107–109). Calculations of resistance have been employed by most investigators to provide a measure of coronary vascular smooth muscle tone, to assess vasodilator reserve, and/or to define changes in vascular tone as a result of various interventions. Both mean and instantaneous values of pressure and flow have been used in the calculations. The fundamental difficulty in all such approaches is, of course, that the relationship between coronary arterial pressure and flow depends not only on vascular tone but also on several additional independent variables.

Figure 4 schematically illustrates some of these confounding factors in diastolic measurements of pressure and flow. Flow in the microcirculation is higher than inflow, since capacitive elements in the circulation are discharging as aortic pressure drops. As noted earlier, the magnitude of the capacitive flow depends on the instantaneous rate of change of pressure and absolute value of capacitance. In the hope of minimizing reactive effects (including early diastolic refilling of vessels emptied during systole), calculations of diastolic resistance have sometimes employed values of end-diastolic pressure and flow, rather than mean diastolic pressure and flow. End-diastolic resistance derived from these values and coronary outflow pressure (R) differs from the actual resistance at end-diastole (R′), not only because measured inflow differs from microcirculatory flow, but also because the actual back pressure to flow—which is itself dependent on ventricular diastolic and coronary venous pressures—is higher than venous pressure. Finally, coronary resistance varies

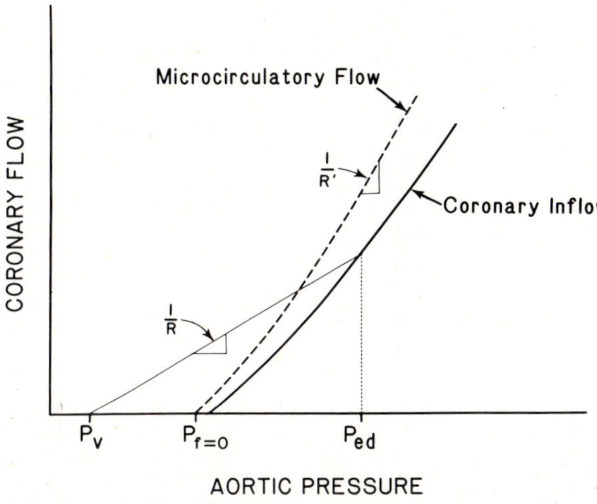

FIGURE 4. *Complexities of attempts to quantify diastolic resistance from measurements of arterial pressure and coronary inflow. Diastolic coronary inflow measured during declining aortic pressure is shown by the solid line, and flow at the microcirculatory level by the dashed line. P_{ed} represents end-diastolic pressure, P_v coronary venous pressure, and $P_{f=0}$ the capacitance-free zero-flow pressure. R = end-diastolic resistance derived from end-diastolic aortic pressure and coronary flow and coronary venous pressure. R′ = actual resistance at end-diastole, derived from the slope of the microcirculatory pressure-flow relationship at end-diastolic aortic pressure. (Redrawn from Klocke et al., 1984, and reprinted with permission.)*

inversely with pressure, as reflected by the nonlinear pressure-flow relationship.

Whereas capacitive effects can be minimized by utilizing mean full-cycle values of pressure and flow rather than end-diastolic values (Vlahakes et al., 1982), the resistance derived from the full-cycle values is influenced by effects of back pressure and curvature of the pressure-flow relationship, as well as by heart rate and contractility and the possibility that back pressure and/or conductance differ in systole and diastole.

The most desirable approach for quantifying vascular conductance would seem to be to establish (at a normal level of arterial pressure) the slope of a diastolic pressure-flow curve which is free of reactive effects. This is not an easy task experimentally. Phasic recordings of coronary inflow and inflow pressure would be required. Pressure-flow data in early diastole, which include capacitive refilling of vessels emptied during the preceding systole, cannot presently be corrected for this effect in any quantitative sense. If systolic-diastolic interactions are assumed to be negligible in later diastole, there is the possibility of applying currently available estimates of coronary capacitance and directly measured central aortic dP/dt to calculate the amount of unmeasured capacitive flow which needs to be added to measured inflow. If capacitive flow is small in relation to measured inflow, and similar in magnitude before and during an intervention, the correction might be practical. Changes in outflow pressure and/or ventricular diastolic pressure sufficient to alter conductance would also need to be considered. Finally, a relatively slow heart rate would be required to allow data to be collected over a sufficient pressure range to allow a meaningful slope calculation.

Because of the limitations of all currently available approaches for determining resistance (or conductance), we agree with Marcus that modest changes in this parameter must continue to be interpreted with considerable caution (Marcus, 1983, pp. 107–109). In attempting to define mechanisms of flow adjustment, one must consider the back pressure to coronary flow as well as resistance. However, as pointed out by Vlahakes et al. (1982), shifts in pressure-flow relationships can sometimes be noteworthy, even when underlying mechanisms cannot be clarified.

Summary

On the basis of the material discussed, our current assessments of the controversial points mentioned at the beginning of this article may be summarized as follows:

1. $P_{f=0}$, the minimum back pressure to coronary flow associated with a measurable conductance, is indeed greater than coronary outflow pressure (and usually left ventricular diastolic pressure, as well). $P_{f=0}$ needs to be taken into account in attempts to determine coronary driving pressure.

2. In maximally vasodilated beds, $P_{f=0}$ derived from diastolic pressure-flow relationships exceeds coronary outflow pressure by at least a few mm Hg. $P_{f=0}$ varies with coronary outflow and/or diastolic ventricular cavity pressure. When left ventricular preload is elevated, $P_{f=0}$ exceeds outflow pressure by increasing amounts.

3. $P_{f=0}$ appears to be systematically higher and pressure-dependent in beds in which vasomotor tone is operative. An improved understanding of the nature of, and basis for, time-dependent changes in resistance and/or $P_{f=0}$ during long diastoles in nonvasodilated beds is needed.

4. The contour of pressure-flow relationships which are free of reactive effects is curvilinear rather than linear. The degree of curvilinearity is substantial and can change with interventions. Curvilinearity is accentuated at lower pressures and may reflect changes in the number of perfused vascular channels as well as the caliber of individual channels.

5. Capacitive effects need to be dealt with quantitatively in studies of pressure-flow relationships. Values of the capacitance which is involved in these effects vary with both pressure and tone. Capacitive flow also depends upon the instantaneous rate of change of pressure, which has not usually been defined in published studies.

6. Although intramyocardial capacitance is large and plays an important role in systolic-diastolic flow interactions, a controlling role in diastolic coronary arterial pressure-flow relationships has not been established experimentally. In vasodilated beds, inflow remains remarkably constant for several seconds after the brief transient associated with a step-change in the level of constant pressure perfusion during a long diastole.

7. Calculations of coronary vascular resistance (by whatever method) remain of limited value, particularly when changes in response to an intervention are modest. Because of the curvilinear diastolic pressure-flow relationship, resistance is pressure-dependent and, at any given pressure, is probably best defined by establishing the slope of a diastolic pressure-flow curve which is free of reactive effects.

8. A modified vascular waterfall seems a plausible explanation for experimental findings indicating a regulated pressure within the coronary bed which is higher than outflow pressure. Any model of the coronary circulation describing flow throughout the cardiac cycle needs to deal with systolic-diastolic interactions, as well as $P_{f=0}$ and reactive effects. More definitive evaluation of waterfall or other models which appear compatible with existing data will require additional experimental studies which test the models' implications (and expose their inadequacies) more fully.

Supported by grants from the National Heart, Lung, and Blood Institute (2-P01-HLB-15194, 1-K08-HLB-01168), American Heart Association (83-717), and The Alexandrine and Alexander L. Sinsheimer Fund.

Address for reprints: Francis J. Klocke, M.D., Room CC-169, SUNYAB Center, Erie County Medical Center, 462 Grider Street, Buffalo, New York 14215.

References

Archie JP Jr (1978) Transmural distribution of intrinsic and transmitted left ventricular diastolic intramyocardial pressure in dogs. Cardiovasc Res **12:** 255–262

Aversano T, Klocke FJ, Mates RE, Canty JM Jr (1984) Preload-induced alterations in capacitance-free diastolic pressure-flow relationships. Am J Physiol **246:** H410–H417

Bache RJ, Cobb FR (1977) Effect of maximal coronary vasodilation on transmural myocardial perfusion during tachycardia in the awake dog. Circ Res **41:** 648–653

Baer RW, Vlahakes GJ, Uhlig PN, Hoffman JIE (1981) Effect of increased hematocrit on maximal coronary vascular conductance and O_2 delivery (abstr). Fed Proc **40:** 602

Bellamy RF (1978) Diastolic coronary artery pressure-flow relations in the dog. Circ Res **43:** 92–101

Bellamy RF (1980) Calculation of coronary vascular resistance. Cardiovasc Res **14:** 261–269

Bellamy RF, Lowensohn HS (1980) Effect of systole on coronary pressure-flow relations in the right ventricle of the dog. Am J Physiol **238:** H481–H486

Bellamy RF, O'Benar JD (1984) Cessation of arterial and venous flow at a finite driving pressure in porcine coronary circulation. Am J Physiol **246:** H525–H531

Bellamy RF, Lowensohn HS, Ehrlich W, Baer RW (1980) Effect of coronary sinus occlusion on coronary pressure-flow relations. Am J Physiol **239:** H57–H64

Braakman R, vd Horn FJ, v Huis GA, Krams R, Langewouters GJ, Sipkema P, Westerhof N (1982) Letter to the editor. Circ Res **51:** 822

Burton AC (1951) On the physical equilibrium of small blood vessels. Am J Physiol **164:** 319–329

Canty JM, Klocke FJ (1979) Beat-to-beat changes in driving pressure and vascular resistance during reactive hyperemia (abstr). Circulation **60** (suppl II): 101

Canty JM, Mates RE (1982) A programmable pressure control system for coronary flow studies. Am J Physiol **243:** H796–H802

Canty JM Jr, Mates RE, Klocke FJ (1983) Rapid determination of capacitance-free pressure-flow relationships during single diastoles (abstr). Fed Proc **42:** 1092

Canty JM Jr, Mates RE, Klocke FJ (1983a) Viscoelastic behavior of in vivo coronary artery capacitance (abstr). Physiologist **26:** A-44

Canty JM Jr, Klocke FJ, Mates RE (in press) Pressure and tone dependence of coronary diastolic input impedance and capacitance. Am J Physiol

Chilian WP, Bohling BA, Marcus ML (1982) Interpretations of zero-flow pressures in the coronary circulation (abstr). Circulation **66** (suppl II): 43

Dole WP, Bishop VS (1982) Regulation of coronary blood flow during individual diastoles in the dog. Circ Res **50:** 377–385

Dole WP, Bishop VS (1982a) Influence of autoregulation and capacitance on diastolic coronary artery pressure-flow relationships in the dog. Circ Res **51:** 261–270

Dole WP, Alexander GM, Campbell AB, Hixson EL, Bishop VS (1984) Interpretation and physiological significance of diastolic coronary artery pressure-flow relationships in the canine coronary bed. Circ Res **55:** 215–226

Domenech RJ, Goich J (1976) Effect of heart rate on regional coronary blood flow. Cardiovasc Res **10:** 224–231

Douglas JE, Greenfield JC Jr (1970) Epicardial coronary artery compliance in the dog. Circ Res **27:** 921–929

Downey JM, Kirk ES (1975) Inhibition of coronary blood flow by a vascular waterfall mechanism. Circ Res **36:** 753–760

Downey J, Lee J, Chambers D (1981) Coronary critical closing pressure corrected for coronary capacitance effects (abstr). Physiologist **24:** 26

Downey J, Lee J, Chambers D (1982) Capacitive time constant of the coronary artery (abstr). Circulation **66** (suppl II): 42

Downey JM, Lee J, Chambers DE (1983) Location and magnitude of the coronary artery capacitance. *In* Mechanics of the Coronary Circulation, edited by RE Mates, RM Nerem, PD Stein. New York, American Society of Mechanical Engineers, pp 45–48

Ellis AK, Klocke FJ (1979) Coronary flow autoregulation with and without changes in coronary vascular resistance (abstr). Circulation **60** (suppl II): 259

Ellis AK, Klocke FJ (1980) Effects of preload on the transmural distribution of perfusion and pressure-flow relationships in the canine coronary vascular bed. Circ Res **46:** 68–77

Eng C, Kirk ES (1982) Reply to letters to the editor. Circ Res **51:** 822–825

Eng C, Kirk ES (1983) The arterial component of the coronary capacitance. *In* Mechanics of the Coronary Circulation, edited by RE Mates, RM Nerem, PD Stein. New York, American Society of Mechanical Engineers, pp 49–50

Eng C, Kirk ES (1984) Flow into ischemic myocardium and across coronary collateral vessels is modulated by a waterfall mechanism. Circ Res **55:** 10–17

Eng C, Jentzer JH, Kirk ES (1982) The effects of the coronary capacitance on the interpretation of diastolic pressure-flow relationships. Circ Res **50:** 334–341

Firmin RK, Uhlig PN, Baer RW, Messina LM, Hanley FL, Turley K, Hoffman JIE (1982) Transmural pressure-flow (PF) relations in canine left ventricular hypertrophy (LVH) (abstr). Circulation **66** (suppl II): 44

Gomez D-M, Veil C (1936) Sur la limite statique de la pression arterielle. C R Soc Biol (Paris) **123:** 957–959

Green HD, Lewis RN, Nickerson ND, Heller AL (1944) Blood flow, peripheral resistance and vascular tonus with observation on the relationship between blood flow and cutaneous temperature. Am J Physiol **141:** 518–536

Hanley FL, Messina LM, Grattan MT, Hoffman JIE (1984) The effect of coronary inflow pressure on coronary vascular resistance in the isolated dog heart. Circ Res **54:** 760–772

Hochberger AI, Zweifach BW (1968) Analysis of critical closing pressure in the perfused rabbit ear. Am J Physiol **214:** 962–968

Hoffman JIE (1981) Why is myocardial ischaemia so commonly subendocardial? Clin Sci (Lond) **61:** 657–662

Hoffman JIE, Baer RW, Hanley FL, Messina LM, Grattan MT (1983) Regulation of transmural myocardial blood flow. *In* Mechanics of the Coronary Circulation, edited by RE Mates, RM Nerem, PD Stein. New York, American Society of Mechanical Engineers, pp 1–17

Hoki N (1982) Letter to the editor. Circ Res **51:** 821–822

Hori S (1982) Letter to the editor. Circ Res **51:** 819–821

Khouri EM, Gregg DE, McGranahan GM Jr (1971) Regression and reappearance of coronary collaterals. Am J Physiol **220:** 655–661

Kirkeeide R, Puschmann S, Schaper W (1981) Diastolic coronary pressure-flow relationships investigated by induced long-wave pressure oscillations. Basic Res Cardiol **76:** 564–569

Klocke FJ, Weinstein IR, Klocke JF, Ellis AK, Kraus DR, Mates RE, Canty JM, Anbar RD, Romanowski RR, Wallmeyer KW, Echt MP (1981) Zero-flow pressures and pressure-flow relationships during single long diastoles in the canine coronary bed before and during maximum vasodilation: Limited influence of capacitive effects. J Clin Invest **68:** 970–980

Klocke FJ, Canty JM Jr, Mates RE (1984) Evolving concepts of coronary pressure-flow relationships. *In* Functional Aspects of the Normal, Hypertrophied and Failing Heart, edited by FL Abel, WH Newman. Boston, Martinus Nijhoff, pp 40–56

Lewi PJ, Schaper WKA (1971) The estimation of coronary volume elasticity in the beating heart of the dog. Pflügers Arch **325:** 191–198

Marcus ML (1983) The Coronary Circulation in Health and Disease. New York, McGraw-Hill

Marzilli M, Goldstein S, Sabbah HN, Lee T, Stein PD (1979) Modulating effect of regional myocardial performance on local myocardial perfusion in the dog. Circ Res **45:** 634–641

Mates RE (in press) Modeling coronary blood flow. *In* Encyclopedia of Systems and Control, edited by M Singh. Oxford, Pergamon Press

Mates RE, Burns T, Canty JM, Greenberg R, Neeson J (1983) Modeling diastolic impedance to coronary blood flow. *In* Mechanics of the Coronary Circulation, edited by RE Mates, RM Nerem, PD Stein. New York, American Society of Mechanical Engineers, pp 41–44

Messina LM, Hanley FL, Hoffman JIE (1983) Comparison of left main and circumflex coronary artery pressure-flow relations (abstr). Fed Proc **42:** 1092

Mosher P, Ross J Jr, McFate PA, Shaw RF (1964) Control of coronary blood flow by an autoregulatory mechanism. Circ Res **14:** 250–259

Nakazawa HK, Roberts DL, Klocke FJ (1978) Quantitation of anterior descending vs. circumflex venous drainage in the canine great cardiac vein and coronary sinus. Am J Physiol **234:** H163–H166

Nichol J, Girling F, Jerrard W, Claxton EB, Burton AC (1951) Fundamental instability of the small blood vessels and critical closing pressures in vascular beds. Am J Physiol **164:** 330–344

Panerai RB, Chamberlain JH, Sayers BMcA (1979) Characterization of the extravascular component of coronary resistance by instantaneous pressure-flow relationships in the dog. Circ Res **45:** 378–390

Pantely GA, Ladley HD, Bristow JD (1984) Low zero-flow pressure and minimal capacitance effect on diastolic coronary arterial pressure-flow relationships during maximum vasodilation in swine. Circulation **70:** 485–494

Pappenheimer JR, Maes JP (1942) A quantitative measure of the vasomotor tone in the hindlimb muscles of the dog. Am J Physiol **137:** 187–199

Permutt S, Riley RL (1963) Hemodynamics of collapsible vessels with tone: The vascular waterfall. J Appl Physiol **18:** 924–932

Permutt S, Bromberger-Barnea B, Bane HN (1962) Alveolar pressure, pulmonary venous pressure and the vascular waterfall. Med Thorac **19:** 239–260.

Raff WK, Kosche F, Lochner W (1972) Extravascular coronary resistance and its relation to microcirculation. Am J Cardiol **29:** 598–603

Rouleau J, Boerboom LE, Surjadhana A, Hoffman JIE (1979) The role of autoregulation and tissue diastolic pressures in the transmural distribution of left ventricular blood flow in anesthetized dogs. Circ Res **45:** 804–815

Spaan JAE (1982) Intramyocardial compliance studied by venous outflow at arterial occlusion (abstr). Circulation **66** (suppl II): 42

Spaan JAE, Laird JD (1981) Coronary vasoconstriction in long diastoles (abstr). Circulation **64** (suppl IV): 39

Spaan JAE, Laird J (1983) High zero-flow pressures in autoregulated coronary beds during long diastoles can be explained by intramyocardial compliance (abstr). Circulation **68** (suppl III): 307

Spaan JAE, Breuls NPW, Laird JD (1981) Diastolic-systolic coronary flow differences are caused by intramyocardial pump action in the anesthetized dog. Circ Res **49:** 584–593

Taylor WR, Wise RA, Bromberger-Barnea B (1981) Autoregulation of coronary blood flow: Instantaneous systolic and diastolic coronary artery pressure-flow relationships (abstr). Circulation **64** (suppl IV): 39

Tillmans H, Ikeda S, Hansen H, Sarma JSM, Fauvel JM, Bing RJ (1974) Microcirculation in the ventricle of the dog and turtle. Circ Res **34:** 561–569

Uhlig PN, Baer RW, Vlahakes GJ, Hanley FL, Messina LM, Hoffman JIE (1984) Arterial and venous coronary pressure-flow relations in anesthetized dogs: Evidence for a vascular waterfall in epicardial coronary veins. Circ Res. **55:** 238–248

Vlahakes GJ, Baer RW, Uhlig PN, Verrier ED, Bristow JD, Hoffman JIE (1982) Adrenergic influence in the coronary circulation of conscious dogs during maximal vasodilation with adenosine. Circ Res **51:** 371–384

Whittaker SRF, Winton FR (1933) The apparent viscosity of blood flowing in the isolated hindlimb of the dog and its variation with corpuscular concentration. J Physiol (Lond) **78:** 339–369

INDEX TERMS: Coronary pressure-flow relationships • Zero-flow pressure • Coronary vascular resistance • Coronary capacitance • Impedance modeling

Identification and Characterization of Leukotriene C_4 Receptors in Isolated Rat Renal Glomeruli

Barbara J. Ballermann, Robert A. Lewis, E.J. Corey, K. Frank Austen, and Barry M. Brenner

From the Department of Medicine, Harvard Medical School, the Departments of Medicine and Rheumatology/Immunology, Brigham and Women's Hospital, Boston, Massachusetts; and the Department of Chemistry, Harvard University, Cambridge, Massachusetts

SUMMARY. The immediate reduction of renal blood flow and glomerular filtration rate in response to intravenous infusion of leukotriene C_4 in the rat prompted an analysis of isolated rat renal glomeruli for the presence of specific receptors for leukotriene C_4. Specific binding of [^{3}H]leukotriene C_4 to glomeruli increased in a time-dependent manner, reached equilibrium after 60 minutes of incubation at 4°C, and was 80% reversible upon addition of excess unlabeled leukotriene C_4 at equilibrium. Specific binding of [^{3}H]leukotriene C_4 to glomeruli increased in a dose-dependent manner, approaching saturation at concentrations of 40–60 nM. Inhibition of binding of [^{3}H]leukotriene C_4 with increasing concentrations of unlabeled leukotriene C_4 was dose dependent. The equilibrium dissociation constant for [^{3}H]leukotriene C_4 binding to glomeruli, calculated from saturation and competitive binding-inhibition studies, was 25 ± 7 nM and 35 ± 16 nM (mean ± SEM), respectively, and glomerular leukotriene C_4 receptor density was 8.5 ± 1.5 and 9.0 ± 3.0 pmol/mg protein, respectively. The other natural vasoactive sulfidopeptide leukotrienes, leukotriene D_4 and leukotriene E_4, the chemotactic agent, leukotriene B_4, and the sulfidopeptide leukotriene antagonist, FPL 55712, competed for the receptor at concentrations 2–3 orders of magnitude higher than the homoligand, leukotriene C_4. The binding and specificity characteristics of the glomerular leukotriene C_4 receptor are similar to those previously reported for the DDT_1 nonvascular smooth muscle cell line derived from hamster vas deferens, for guinea pig ileum smooth muscle, and for a subcellular fraction of rat lung homogenate, and represent the first characterization of such a receptor in a vascular tissue. **(*Circ Res 56: 324–330, 1985*)**

THE oxidative metabolism of arachidonic acid via 5-lipoxygenase forms 5-hydroperoxy-6-*trans*-8,11,14-*cis*-eicosatetraenoic acid (5-HPETE), which is enzymatically converted to 5,6-oxido-7,9-*trans*-11,14-*cis*-eicosatetraenoic acid (LTA_4). LTA_4 is processed by an epoxide hydrolase to 5*S*,12*R*-dihydroxy-6,14-*cis*-8,10-*trans*-eicosatetraenoic acid (LTB_4), or by a glutathione-*S*-transferase to 5*S*-hydroxy-6*R*-S-glutathionyl-7,9-*trans*-11,14-*cis*-eicosatetraenoic acid (LTC_4). From LTC_4, sequential cleavage of glutamic acid by γ-glutamyl transpeptidase and of glycine by a dipeptidase forms 5*S*-hydroxy-6*R*-S-cysteinylglycyl-7,9-*trans*-11,14-*cis*-eicosatetraenoic acid (LTD_4) and 5*S*-hydroxy-6*R*-S-cysteinyl-7,9-*trans*-11,14-*cis*-eicosatetraenoic acid (LTE_4), respectively (Samuelsson, 1983). LTC_4 and LTD_4 are potent spasmogens for some nonvascular smooth muscles in vitro, as exemplified by the response of guinea pig ileum and both upper and lower guinea pig airways (Drazen et al., 1980; Lewis et al., 1981). LTC_4 and LTD_4 are likewise effective as airway smooth muscle constrictors when inhaled as aerosols by guinea pigs (Leitch et al., 1983) and humans (Weiss et al., 1982). Vascular activities of the sulfidopeptide leukotrienes have been demonstrated upon intradermal injection into guinea pigs (Drazen et al., 1980) or topical application to the hamster cheek pouch (Dahlén et al., 1981), where LTC_4 and LTD_4 cause constriction of arterioles, followed by leakage of plasma from postcapillary venules. Intracoronary injection of LTC_4 in sheep (Michelassi et al., 1982) or bolus administration intravenously of LTC_4 or LTD_4 in ventilated rats (Pfeffer et al., 1983) causes coronary artery constriction and a reduction in cardiac output. Infusion of LTC_4 and LTD_4 into the renal artery of isolated, perfused rat kidneys causes a marked, dose-dependent increase in renal vascular resistance (Rosenthal and Pace-Asciak, 1983). When infused systemically into the intact, anesthetized rat, LTC_4 produces immediate vasoconstriction of the peripheral, coronary, and renal circulations, followed by a significant reduction of plasma volume, presumably on the basis of enhanced vascular permeability and activation of the renin-angiotensin system (Badr et al., 1984).

Specific receptors for LTC_4 have been characterized in nonvascular smooth muscle cells and tissues (Krilis et al., 1983, 1984), and in crude membrane fractions of rat lung homogenate (Pong et al., 1983). In view of the reported vascular effects of LTC_4, and specifically those on renal vascular resistance and glomerular filtration rate (Badr et al., 1984), receptors for LTC_4 are now demonstrated in renal glomeruli isolated from normal rats.

Methods

Leukotrienes C_4, D_4, E_4, and B_4 were prepared synthetically (Corey et al., 1980a, 1980b) and were stored under argon at −80°C in 0.05 M phosphate buffer, pH 6.8, containing 20% ethanol. $[^3H\text{-}C_{14,15}]LTC_4$ (35.7–40 Ci/mmol) was supplied by New England Nuclear, and FPL55712 by Fisons. High performance liquid chromatography (HPLC) grade methanol (Fisher Scientific Co.), L-serine, *N*-2-hydroxyethyl-piperazine-*N'*-2-ethane sulfonic acid (HEPES), reduced glutathione, sodium tetraborate, arachidonic acid (Sigma Chemical Corp.), and prostaglandin E_2 (Seragen) were purchased from the manufacturers.

Isolation of Glomeruli

Male Sprague-Dawley rats, 250–300 g (Gofmoor Farms), were decapitated and exsanguinated, and the kidneys were removed and placed in ice-cold phosphate-buffered saline (PBS), pH 7.4; all subsequent steps were carried out at 4°C. Glomeruli were isolated by the following method modified from that of Misra (1972). The kidneys were bisected longitudinally and the medulla, papilla, capsule, and any visible connective tissue were removed by macroscopic dissection. The remaining cortical rims were then minced with a razor blade and pressed through a stainless steel sieve of 90-μm pore size. The resulting suspension was sequentially poured through sieves with pore sizes of 180, 150, and 90 μm, respectively. The glomeruli were retained on the 90-μm sieve and were washed extensively; the glomeruli were then rinsed from the surface of the sieve into a 50-ml centrifuge tube, sedimented at 100 *g* for 2 minutes, and resuspended in 20 mM HEPES buffer, pH 7.4, containing 125 mM NaCl and 5 mM $CaCl_2$. Sedimentation and resuspension were repeated twice. Two 50-μl portions of the final suspension were examined microscopically for each preparation. Glomeruli were largely intact, devoid of Bowman's capsule and afferent or efferent arterioles, and routinely of better than 98% purity as assessed by light microscopy. Between 1 and 2×10^4 glomeruli were usually obtained from each rat, representing 1.8–3.6 mg of protein, as determined by the method of Lowry et al. (1951).

To determine the influence of any retained blood products on LTC_4 binding, rats were anesthetized with ether, and the aorta was cannulated below the renal arteries and cross-clamped between the renal arteries. The left kidney was immediately perfused with 50 ml of ice-cold saline to produce complete blanching, while the right kidney continued to be perfused by the systemic circulation. Both kidneys then were removed, and their glomeruli were isolated separately. The binding of $[^3H]LTC_4$ to rat ileal segments was also examined, using conditions identical to those utilized to define receptor binding to guinea pig ileal segments (Krilis et al., 1984).

Radioligand Binding

Because glomeruli were found to adhere to polyethylene tubes under the assay conditions to be described, binding experiments were carried out in borosilicate glass tubes in which retention of glomerular protein was less than 5%. Unless otherwise stated, between 500 and 1000 glomeruli were incubated in duplicate or triplicate with constant concentrations of $[^3H]LTC_4$ in 0.5 ml of assay buffer consisting of 20 mM HEPES, pH 7.4, 125 mM NaCl, 5 mM $CaCl_2$, and 1 mM serine-borate complex at 4°C for 60 minutes on a rotary shaking platform. Serine-borate complex was included to prevent LTC_4 metabolism by peptide cleavage (Tate and Meister, 1978; Örning and Hammarström, 1980). Bound radioactivity was separated from free by suction-filtration through prewetted glass-fiber filters (Boehringer-Mannheim) on a single Hoeffer filtration manifold, followed by four successive washings with 2.5-ml portions of ice-cold assay buffer; the filtration step and all of the washes were complete within 10 seconds. Timed experiments ($n = 2$), each done in triplicate, at 10-second intervals, demonstrated that total and nonspecific, and thus also specific $[^3H]LTC_4$ binding, did not change during 40 seconds of continuous washing with ice-cold assay buffer. Filters were placed into scintillation vials with 1 ml of ethanol:water, 4:1 (vol/vol) at room temperature for 12–16 hours. Five milliliters of Aquasol (NEN) were added and, after an additional 2–4 hours of incubation at room temperature, bound radioactivity was determined in a Tracor scintillation counter with 50% counting efficiency for tritium. Total radioactivity per assay tube was determined in buffer solution replicates without glomeruli; two 100-μl portions of the mixture were added directly to scintillation vials containing 1 ml of 80% ethanol, and were processed and counted in parallel with the filters. Specific binding was defined as bound radioactivity which was inhibited by 3 μM unlabeled LTC_4. Nonspecific binding was found to be 2–3% of the total radioactivity added, and ranged from 10–20% of the total bound radioactivity in competition experiments; in saturation studies, nonspecific binding reached 30–50% at the highest $[^3H]LTC_4$ concentrations used.

The time course of specific $[^3H]LTC_4$ binding to glomeruli was assessed in six separate experiments for concentrations of $[^3H]LTC_4$ of 0.3, 0.6, 1.0, 3.3, 6.7, and 8.5 nM. Glomeruli were incubated with these concentrations of $[^3H]LTC_4$ with and without 3 μM unlabeled LTC_4 for periods from 1–120 minutes at 4°C. In four experiments, we assessed reversibility of the binding at equilibrium by adding 3 μM unlabeled LTC_4 after 60 minutes of incubation with $[^3H]LTC_4$ and determining remaining bound radioactivity as a function of time.

Specific $[^3H]LTC_4$ binding as a function of increasing glomerular concentration was assessed at fixed concentrations of $[^3H]LTC_4$. In four separate experiments in which the $[^3H]LTC_4$ concentration was 1.9, 2.5, 5.0, and 7.7 nM, the glomerular concentration was varied in each from 200–2000/ml. The influence of Ca^{++} on $[^3H]LTC_4$ binding to glomeruli was examined at concentrations of 1, 2, 5, and 10 mM, added as its chloride salt by comparison to specific binding in the absence of added divalent cations. The heat sensitivity of the glomerular LTC_4-binding site was determined by boiling glomeruli for 15 minutes before assessing specific and nonspecific $[^3H]LTC_4$ binding.

To determine the saturability, affinity, and density of LTC_4-binding sites, 250–300 glomeruli were incubated with increasing concentrations of $[^3H]LTC_4$ (0.5–60 nM) in an incubation volume of 250 μl for 60 minutes at 4°C. Total and nonspecific binding were determined for each concentration of $[^3H]LTC_4$. Data were analyzed using the LIGAND program (Munson and Rodbard, 1980).

We carried out competitive binding-inhibition studies by incubating a fixed number of glomeruli with $[^3H]LTC_4$ in a volume of 0.5 ml in the presence of increasing concentrations of unlabeled LTC_4 (0.1–3000 nM). Data for competition by unlabeled LTC_4 were analyzed with the LIGAND program to determine the number of distinct sites, binding affinity, and receptor density. Competition of LTD_4 (0.01–100 μM), LTE_4 (0.01–100 μM), LTB_4 (0.01–100 μM), FPL 55712 (0.1–100 μM), reduced glutathione (0.001–10 mM), prostaglandin E_2 (0.001–10 mM), or arachidonic acid (0.001–10 mM) for [^{3}H]LTC_4 binding was also determined.

Bioconversion and/or oxidative inactivation of [^{3}H]LTC_4 was examined by incubating [^{3}H]LTC_4 in the absence and presence of glomeruli for 90 minutes at 4°C. Glomeruli were separated by centrifugation in a Beckman microfuge at 8,000 *g* for 30 seconds at 4°C, and the supernatant extract was removed. The glomeruli were resuspended and incubated for 30 minutes at 4°C with buffer containing 3 μM unlabeled LTC_4 in order to displace bound [^{3}H]-LTC_4; the glomeruli were then sedimented with the microfuge, and the eluate supernatant was removed. The residual tissue-associated radioactivity was determined as usual and compared with replicates in which specific binding of [^{3}H]LTC_4 to glomeruli was determined in the routine fashion. Solutions of [^{3}H]LTC_4 incubated without glomeruli, the glomerular [^{3}H]LTC_4 supernatant, and the glomerular eluate each were adjusted to the solvent for reverse-phase-HPLC, namely, methanol:assay buffer:acetic acid (65:34.9:0.1, vol/vol/vol, pH 5.6). Each sample was injected individually with 200–500 ng of unlabeled LTC_4 standard onto an Altex C_{18} reverse-phase HPLC column (Rainin) and eluted isocratically at a flow rate of 1 ml/min with methanol:water:acetic acid (65:34.9:0.1, vol/vol/vol, pH 5.6). One-milliliter fractions were collected in scintillation vials, mixed with 5 ml aquasol, and assessed for radioactivity. The retention times of synthetic LTC_4, and of LTD_4 and LTE_4, which were chromatographed separately, were determined by on-line monitoring of the UV absorbance at 280 nm.

Protein was determined by the method of Lowry et al. (1951) after the glomeruli were washed three times by centrifugation in PBS to remove HEPES buffer and were digested in 1 N NaOH at 60°C for 30 minutes.

Data are presented as means ± SEM with n = 3 being the minimum number of separate experiments for any experimental condition; data for triplicate determinations within a single experiment are presented as means ± SD.

Results

Time-course and Reversibility of [^{3}H]LTC_4 Binding at 4°C

Specific binding of [^{3}H]LTC_4, at all concentrations (0.3–8.5 nM) tested, increased in a time-dependent manner at 4°C, reached binding equilibrium by 60 minutes of incubation, and remained stable for up to 120 minutes. Nonspecific binding reached its maximum at 5 minutes of incubation and remained stable thereafter. In four time-course experiments, an excess 3 μM unlabeled LTC_4 was added at binding equilibrium, resulting in rapid reversal of specific [^{3}H]LTC_4 binding which was 86 ± 4% (mean ± SEM) complete 60 minutes later. A representative time-course of [^{3}H]LTC_4 binding and reversal by displacement is shown in Figure 1.

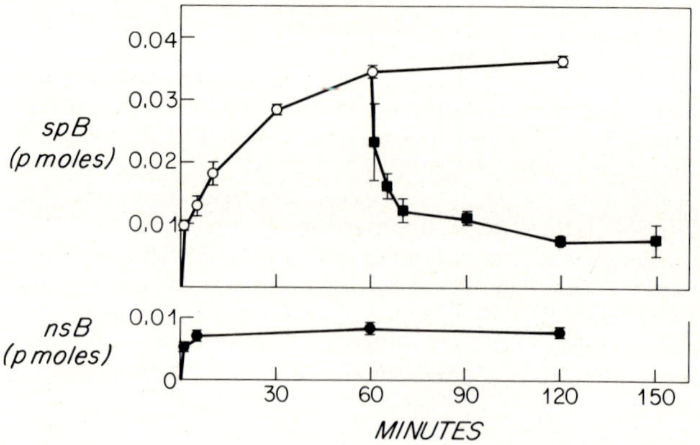

FIGURE 1. *Time course of specific (spB) (○) and nonspecific (nsB) (●) binding of 1.0 nM [^{3}H]LTC_4 to isolated glomeruli. At 60 minutes, 3 μM unlabeled LTC_4 was added, and the [^{3}H]LTC_4 remaining specifically bound was determined (■). Each point represents the mean ± SD of triplicate determinations.*

Effect of Ca^{++} Concentration, Renal Perfusion, Heat Treatment, and Varying Glomerular Concentration on Specific [^{3}H]LTC_4 Binding

Specific [^{3}H]LTC_4 binding relative to no added calcium was 94 ± 4% at a calcium ion concentration of 1 mM, and at 2, 5, and 10 mM, 103 ± 7, 105 ± 4, and 105 ± 3% (mean ± SEM, *n* = 4), respectively. As these differences were not significant, further experiments were arbitrarily carried out with 5 mM Ca^{++} in the buffer.

Specific [^{3}H]LTC_4 binding to glomeruli from saline-perfused kidneys was identical at 105 ± 7% (mean ± SEM, *n* = 3) to that obtained with glomeruli isolated from nonperfused kidneys, which was expressed as 100%. Hence, there was specific [^{3}H]LTC_4 binding to glomerular tissue, and not to retained blood products.

Specific [^{3}H]LTC_4 binding in glomeruli which were boiled for 15 minutes was reduced to 5.1 ± 2.4% (*n* = 3) of that of control glomeruli, demonstrating that the specific LTC_4-binding site in glomeruli is heat sensitive.

Specific [^{3}H]LTC_4 binding to glomeruli increased linearly when the glomerular concentration was varied from 200–2000/ml. Regression analysis of this relationship for four separate experiments yielded a correlation coefficient of 0.988 ± 0.004 (mean ± SEM). An experiment that is representative of this linear relationship is shown in Figure 2.

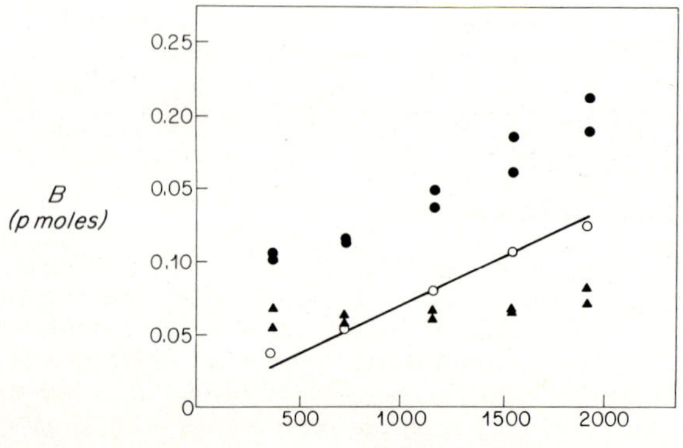

FIGURE 2. *Total (●), nonspecific (▲), and specific (○) binding (B) of 5 nM [^{3}H]LTC_4 with increasing glomerular concentrations.*

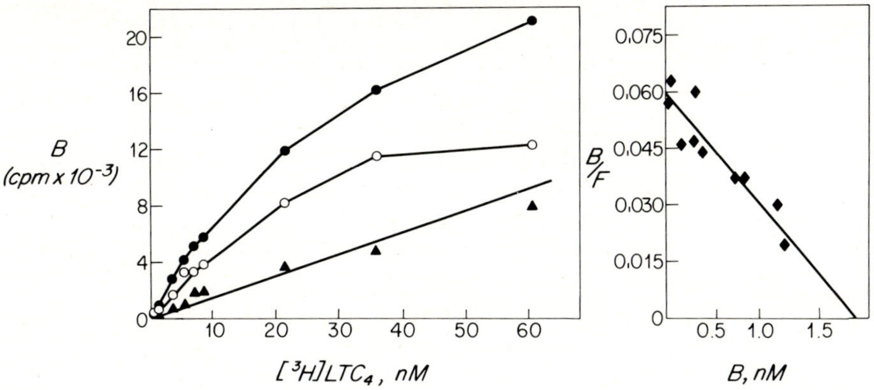

FIGURE 3. *Total (●), nonspecific (▲), and specific (○) binding (B) of increasing concentrations of [^{3}H]LTC_4 to isolated glomeruli. All points are means of duplicate determinations. The right hand panel shows Scatchard transformation of these data. B/F, bound/free.*

Binding of [^{3}H]LTC_4 to Rat Ileum Smooth Muscle

With a radioligand concentration of 2.22 nM, rat ileal longitudinal smooth muscle strips bound 37 ± 4 fmol [^{3}H]LTC_4/mg protein in the absence of unlabeled LTC_4, and 79 ± 11 fmol/mg protein in the presence of 0.3 μM unlabeled LTC_4. In glomeruli from the same rats, which were processed concurrently, total [^{3}H]LTC_4 binding was 568 ± 69 fmol/mg protein in the absence of unlabeled LTC_4, and 252 ± 23 fmol/mg in the presence of 0.3 μM unlabeled LTC_4. Thus, specific binding of radiolabeled LTC_4 was not observed in rat ileal smooth muscle, a tissue known not to contract in response to LTC_4 (Goldenberg and Subers, 1982).

Equilibrium Binding Parameters Derived from [^{3}H]LTC_4 Binding as a Function of Increasing Concentrations of Radioligand

Specific [^{3}H]LTC_4 binding to isolated glomeruli with increasing concentrations of [^{3}H]LTC_4 ranging from 0.5–60 nM reached a plateau between 40 and 60 nM in a representative experiment (Fig. 3), demonstrating saturability of the glomerular LTC_4-binding site. Scatchard transformation of these data (Fig. 3) resulted in a linear plot, indicating the detection of one population of binding sites. Equilibrium-binding parameters derived by Scatchard analysis were: an equilibrium dissociation constant (K_d) of 23.5 nM and a receptor density (R_o) of 8.4 pmol/mg glomerular protein. Saturation-binding data from six separate experiments were consistently found to best fit a one-site binding curve when analyzed by the LIGAND program. The binding parameters derived by computer analysis were K_d = 25 ± 7 nM (mean ± SEM) and glomerular LTC_4 receptor density = 7.8 ± 2.0 ± 10^8 sites/glomerulus or 8.0 ± 1.5 pmol/mg protein.

Competitive Binding Inhibition Studies

Incubation of glomeruli with 0.5–1 nM [^{3}H]LTC_4 in the presence of increasing concentrations of unlabeled LTC_4 (0.1–3000 nM) resulted in dose-dependent displacement of [^{3}H]LTC_4 from its binding site (n = 5), as illustrated in Figure 4A. Because increasing the concentration of unlabeled LTC_4 above 3 μM did not result in further inhibition of [^{3}H]LTC_4 binding, [^{3}H]LTC_4 binding in the presence of 3 μM unlabeled LTC_4 was taken as nonspecific binding. Competitive binding-inhibition data from five separate experiments depicted in Figure 4A were best resolved by a one-site binding curve. Binding parameters for the five experiments were

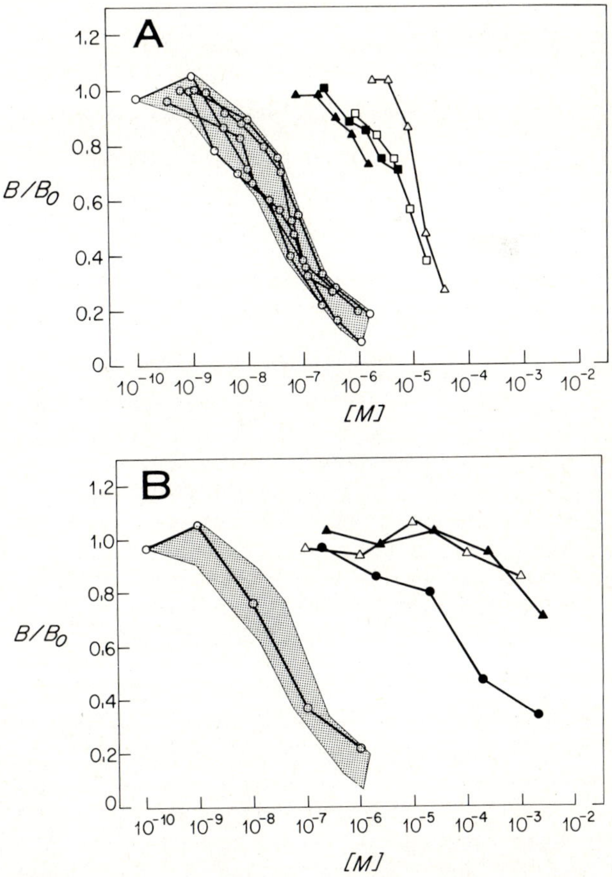

FIGURE 4. *Competitive inhibition of [^{3}H]LTC_4 binding to glomeruli. B_o refers to binding of [^{3}H]LTC_4 in the absence of a competing substance, and B/B_o is the fraction of [^{3}H]LTC_4 that remains bound in the presence of a competing ligand. Panel A, competition by unlabeled LTC_4 (○) (n = 5) enclosed in the shaded area. Competition by LTD_4 (■), LTE_4 (□), LTB_4 (▲), and FPL55712 (△). Panel B, competition by unlabeled LTC_4 (○), arachidonic acid (●), prostaglandin E_2 (△), and reduced glutathione (▲).*

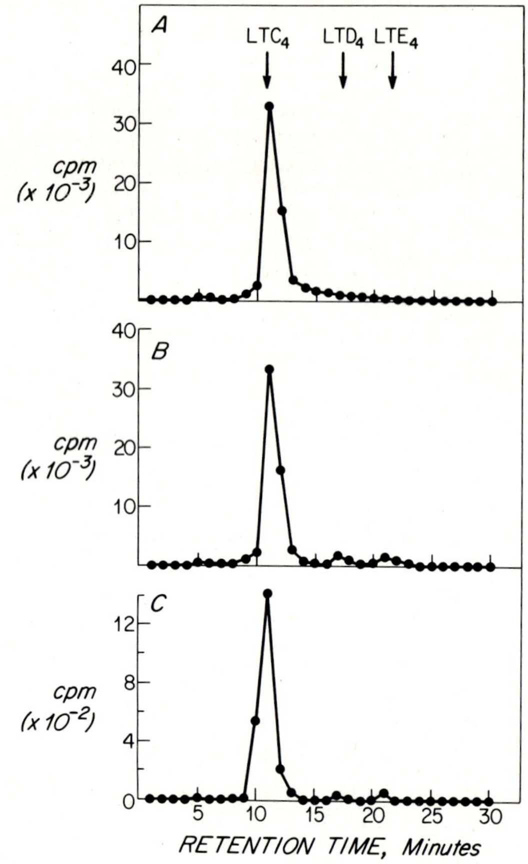

FIGURE 5. *RP-HPLC profile of [^{3}H]LTC_4 after 90 minutes of incubation of 1.1 nM LTC_4 in assay buffer alone (panel A), in the glomerular supernatant (panel B), and [^{3}H]LTC_4 after elution from the glomerular receptor (panel C). The retention times of synthetic leukotriene standards are indicated by the arrows in panel A.*

K_d = 35 ± 16 nM and R_o = 14.1 ± 8.0 × 10^8 sites/glomerulus, or 9.0 ± 3.0 pmol/mg protein. LTD_4, LTE_4, and LTB_4 were found to compete for [^{3}H]LTC_4 binding at concentrations 2.5–3 orders of magnitude higher than LTC_4. Similarly, the sulfidopeptide leukotriene antagonist FPL55712 competed for the glomerular LTC_4-binding sites at concentrations of 10^{-5} M or greater (Fig. 4A). Displacement of 50% of specifically bound [^{3}H]LTC_4 by LTD_4 and LTE_4 occurred at concentrations for LTD_4 of 8.0 and 5.6 μM and for LTE_4 of 9.0 and 18 μM in two experiments, and was not reached with either ligand in a third. Similarly, FPL55712 inhibited 50% of specific [^{3}H]-LTC_4 binding to glomeruli at 20 and 77 μM in two experiments, whereas, in a third experiment, competition was not demonstrated for concentrations up to 4 μM. Prostaglandin E_2 and reduced glutathione did not achieve 50% inhibition of [^{3}H]LTC_4 binding at concentrations of 1 and 3 mM, respectively (Fig. 4B).

[^{3}H]LTC_4 Degradation during and after Receptor Binding

[^{3}H]LTC_4 incubated in assay buffer alone at 4°C for 90 minutes co-eluted with the synthetic LTC_4 standard when subjected to reverse-phase HPLC with a recovery of 73 ± 5% (mean ± SEM, n = 3) of the applied counts. [^{3}H]LTC_4 incubated in the presence of glomeruli and [^{3}H]LTC_4 previously bound to glomeruli and then dissociated by excess unlabeled LTC_4 each eluted at the retention time of authentic LTC_4 with less than 2% of the radioactivity appearing at the retention times of LTD_4 and LTE_4 standards (Fig. 5). Overall recovery of [^{3}H]LTC_4 in the supernatant and eluate of glomeruli was 74 ± 15% (mean ± SEM, n = 6).

Discussion

Radioligand-binding techniques were used to identify and characterize specific binding sites for LTC_4 in isolated rat renal glomeruli. Association of [^{3}H]LTC_4 at 4°C with the glomerular binding site was time-dependent and reached equilibrium at 60 minutes of incubation for concentrations of [^{3}H]LTC_4 ranging from 0.3 nM to 8.5 nM, and was stable for at least 60 minutes thereafter (Fig. 1). Specific [^{3}H]LTC_4 binding to isolated renal glomeruli was rapidly reversible when excess unlabeled LTC_4 was added at equilibrium, showing that the association of [^{3}H]LTC_4 with glomeruli is not merely due to incorporation of this polar lipid into the phospholipid bilayer of plasma membranes. Because equilibrium conditions were verified for even the lowest concentrations of radioligand used in subsequent saturation and competitive binding studies, calculation of equilibrium-binding parameters was feasible with the LIGAND program (Munson and Rodbard, 1980).

Specific [^{3}H]LTC_4 binding was to glomerular tissue and not to retained blood elements, since specific [^{3}H]LTC_4 binding was identical in glomeruli isolated from saline-perfused and nonperfused kidneys within the same animal. Specific [^{3}H]LTC_4 binding was nearly undetectable in glomeruli that had been boiled for 15 minutes before the binding studies, indicating that the binding site is heat sensitive. Specific [^{3}H]LTC_4 binding to isolated glomeruli increased linearly with increasing glomerular concentration (Fig. 2), and was saturable with increasing [^{3}H]LTC_4 concentrations (Fig. 3), fulfilling two of the criteria that are usually required for a binding site to be considered as a receptor.

Because of the previous observation that guinea pig ileal segments (which are routinely used in the bioassay of slow-reacting substance of anaphylaxis) express specific LTC_4 receptors (Krilis et al., 1984), rat intestinal tissue, which does not respond to LTC_4 (Goldenberg and Subers, 1982), was used for comparison, with negative results.

With the LIGAND program, saturation data were consistently (n = 6) found to best fit a one-site binding model, indicating one population of LTC_4 receptors with a single affinity in isolated glomeruli. The linear Scatchard plot shown for one such experiment with increasing concentrations of [^{3}H]LTC_4

best illustrates that receptors with a single affinity are being detected (Fig. 3). Competitive binding-inhibition studies with increasing concentrations of unlabeled LTC_4 allowed analysis over a wider range of LTC_4 concentrations (0.5–3000 nM) (Fig. 4) than studies with increasing concentrations of radiolabeled LTC_4 (0.5–60 nM). Computer analysis of competition data also resolved only one class of receptors with a single affinity, thus ruling out a second, low-affinity site which might have been missed if only increasing concentrations of $[^3H]LTC_4$ had been used. Equilibrium-binding parameters were derived directly by LIGAND analysis and were similar for saturation and competition studies with equilibrium K_d = 25 ± 7 nM (mean ± SEM) and 35 ± 16 nM, respectively, and R_o = 8.0 ± 1.5 pmol/mg protein and 9.0 ± 3.0 pmol/mg protein, respectively. These values are likely to represent true K_d and R_o values for the glomerular LTC_4 receptor under these conditions, as LTC_4 was shown to remain intact during the binding studies (Fig. 5).

The K_d for the glomerular LTC_4 receptor is about one-half order of magnitude greater than that of LTC_4 receptors in guinea pig ileal smooth muscle segments, K_d = 7.6 nM (Krilis et al., 1984), and of cultured DDT_1 cells, K_d = 5.0 nM (Krilis et al., 1983), indicating a lower affinity of glomerular receptors for LTC_4. It is unlikely that this difference is due to variations in assay conditions, as the temperature, pH, and length of incubation were the same, and calcium was used as the divalent cation in all three of these studies, albeit at a higher concentration of 5 mM with glomeruli, as compared to 1 mM in the other studies. Na^+, at concentrations of 125 mM, has been reported to inhibit LTD_4 binding to a subcellular fraction of guinea pig lung (Pong and DeHaven, 1983), but not LTC_4 binding to a subcellular fraction of rat lung (Pong et al., 1983). NaCl at this concentration was required to preserve isotonicity in the studies with intact glomeruli, and would be present during any response of cell membrane receptors in vivo. The LTC_4 receptor affinity (K_d = 41 nM) previously reported for rat lung particulate fractions (Pong et al., 1983) more closely resembles that found in isolated rat glomeruli, suggesting that LTC_4 receptors may exhibit a degree of heterogeneity in different tissues or, perhaps, across species.

Competitive binding-inhibition studies demonstrated a high degree of specificity of the glomerular LTC_4-binding site for LTC_4, as structurally related sulfidopeptide leukotrienes LTD_4 and LTE_4 were able to compete for the receptor only at concentrations 2.5–3 orders of magnitude greater than LTC_4 (Fig. 4). The fact that LTD_4 and LTE_4—and LTB_4, which does not contain a thiopeptide domain—all displaced $[^3H]LTC_4$ with similar potencies, indicates that these other naturally occurring leukotrienes interact with the glomerular LTC_4 receptor in a rather nonspecific manner. FPL55712, an agent previously shown to partially inhibit LTD_4 but not LTC_4 constrictor effects in lung parenchymal strips (Drazen et al., 1980), is a very weak competitive inhibitor of $[^3H]LTC_4$ binding in glomeruli with only a 10-fold greater affinity than arachidonic acid, which displaced 50% of specifically bound $[^3H]LTC_4$ at a concentration of 0.56 mM. The high degree of specificity of LTC_4 for glomerular receptors is very similar to the findings of DDT_1 cells (Krilis et al., 1983), guinea pig ileum (Krilis et al., 1984), and rat lung particulate fractions (Pong et al., 1983), where LTD_4, LTE_4, LTB_4, and FPL55712 were also relatively ineffective in displacing $[^3H]LTC_4$.

Whole rat glomeruli consist of at least three cell types, endothelial cells, contractile smooth muscle-like mesangial cells, and epithelial cells; the exact cell type(s) expressing the LTC_4 receptor is not known. Mesangial cell contraction is known to occur in response to vasopressin and angiotensin II (Ausiello et al., 1980), and glomerular mesangial and epithelial cells release several prostaglandins in response to stimulation with the calcium ionophore A23187 (Kreisberg et al., 1982). Knowledge of functional responses of single populations of vascular cells to LTC_4 is presently limited to the report that cultured endothelial cells from human umbilical veins are induced by LTC_4 to produce prostacyclin (Cramer et al., 1983). The responses of microvascular beds to LTC_4, i.e., arteriolar constriction and augmented venular permeability (Drazen et al., 1980; Dahlen et al., 1981), should relate to an effect on smooth muscle and endothelial cells, respectively.

The demonstration of specific LTC_4 receptors in isolated renal glomeruli and previous indications of direct renal vasoconstrictor effects of LTC_4 (Rosenthal and Pace-Asciak, 1983; Badr et al., 1984) raise the question of the circumstances under which LTC_4 might be expected within the microenvironment of the renal glomerulus. Evaluations of lipoxygenase activities from isolated rat glomeruli (Jim et al., 1982) and from human and murine glomeruli (Baud et al., 1983; Sraer et al., 1983) have shown production of 12-HETE, 15-HETE, and smaller quantities of 8- or 9-HETE, but not of 5-HETE. However, infusion of either the calcium ionophore A23187 into isolated, perfused rat kidneys or antigen into the same preparation from rats previously sensitized with ovalbumin released LTC_4 and LTD_4 into the renal venous effluent (Pirotzky et al., 1984). The bioavailability of these particular 5-lipoxygenase products from their undefined renal source or from infiltrating inflammatory cells such as macrophages (Holdsworth et al., 1978; Lewis and Austen, 1984) or eosinophils (Galpin et al., 1978; Weller et al., 1983) would establish relevance for the effects of LTC_4 infusion on renal glomerular function. The present report defining the existence of specific renal glomerular receptors for LTC_4 therefore provides an additional and critical indication that this compound could act as a local mediator in certain renal inflammatory diseases that adversely affect local microvascular function.

This work was suported in part by Grants AI-07722, AI-20081, AM-05577, AM-30410, HL-17382, and RR-05669 from the National Institutes of Health, and in part by a grant from the National Science Foundation.

Address for reprints: Barbara J. Ballermann, M.D., Laboratory of Kidney and Electrolyte Physiology, Brigham and Women's Hospital, 75 Francis Street, Boston, Massachusetts 02115.

Received July 2, 1984; accepted for publication December 7, 1984.

References

Ausiello DA, Kreisberg JI, Roy C, Karnovsky MJ (1980) Contraction of cultured rat glomerular cells of apparent mesangial origin after stimulation with angiotensin II and arginine vasopressin. J Clin Invest **65:** 754–760

Badr KF, Baylis C, Pfeffer JM, Pfeffer MA, Soberman RJ, Lewis RA, Austen KF, Corey EJ, Brenner BM (1984) Renal and systemic hemodynamic responses to intravenous infusion of leukotriene C_4 in the rat. Circ Res **54:** 492–499

Baud L, Hagege J, Sraer J, Rondeau E, Perez J, Ardaillou R (1983) Reactive oxygen production by cultured rat glomerular mesangial cells during phagocytosis is associated with stimulation of lipoxygenase activity. J Exp Med **158:** 1836–1852

Corey EJ, Clark DA, Goto G, Marfat A, Mioskowski C, Samuelsson B, Hammarström S (1980a) Stereospecific total synthesis of a "slow reacting substance" of anaphylaxis, leukotriene C-1. J Am Chem Soc **108:** 1436–1439; correction **108:** 3663

Corey EJ, Clark DA, Marfat A, Goto G (1980b) Total synthesis of slow reacting substances (SRS), "leukotriene C-2" (11-*trans*-leukotriene C), and leukotriene D. Tetrahedron Lett **21:** 3143–3146

Cramer EB, Pologe L, Pawlowski NA, Cohn ZA, Scott WA (1983) Leukotriene C promotes prostacyclin synthesis by human endothelial cells. Proc Natl Acad Sci USA **80:** 4109–4113

Dahlén S-E, Bjork J, Hedqvist P, Arfors K-E, Hammarström S, Lindgren J-Å, Samuelsson B (1981) Leukotrienes promote plasma leakage and leukocyte adhesion in postcapillary venules: In vivo effects with relevance to the acute inflammatory response. Proc Natl Acad Sci USA **78:** 3887–3891

Drazen JM, Austen KF, Lewis RA, Clark DA, Goto G, Marfat A, Corey EJ (1980) Comparative airway and vascular activities of leukotrienes C-1 and D in vivo and in vitro. Proc Natl Acad Sci USA **77:** 4354–4358

Galpin JE, Shinaberger JH, Stanley TM, Blumenkrantz MJ, Bayer AS, Freidman GS, Montgomerie JZ, Guze LB, Coburn JW, Glassock RJ (1978) Acute interstitial nephritis due to methicillin. Am J Med **65:** 756–765

Goldenberg MM, Subers EM (1982) The reactivity of rat isolated gastrointestinal tissues to leukotrienes. Eur J Pharmacol **78:** 463–466

Holdsworth SR, Thomson NM, Glasgow EF, Dowling JM, Atkins RC (1978) Tissue culture of isolated glomeruli in experimental crescentic glomerulonephriits. J Exp Med **147:** 98–109

Jim K, Hassid A, Sun F, Dunn MJ (1982) Lipoxygenase activity in rat kidney glomeruli, glomerular epithelial cells and cortical tubules. J Biol Chem **257:** 10294–10298

Kreisberg JI, Karnovsky MJ, Levine L (1982) Prostaglandin production by homogeneous cultures of rat glomerular epithelial and mesangial cells. Kidney Int **22:** 355–359

Krilis S, Lewis RA, Corey EJ, Austen KF (1983) Specific receptors for leukotriene C_4 on a smooth muscle cell line. J Clin Invest **72:** 1516–1519

Krilis S, Lewis RA, Corey EJ, Austen KF (1984) Specific binding of leukotriene C_4 to plasma membrane and subcellular receptors of ileal smooth muscle cells. Proc Natl Acad Sci USA **81:** 4529–4533

Leitch AG, Corey EJ, Austen KF, Drazen JM (1983) Indomethacin potentiates the pulmonary response to aerosol leukotriene C_4 in the guinea pig. Am Rev Respir Dis **128:** 639–643

Lewis RA, Austen KF (1984) The biologically active leukotrienes: biosynthesis, metabolism, receptors, functions, and pharmacology. J Clin Invest **73:** 889–897

Lewis RA, Drazen JM, Corey EJ, Austen KF (1981) Structural and functional characteristics of the leukotriene components of slow reacting substance of anaphylaxis (SRS-A). *In* SRS-A and Leukotrienes, vol 1, edited by PJ Piper. London, Wiley, pp 101–117

Lowry OH, Rosebrough NJ, Farr AL, Randall RJ (1951) Protein measurement with the Folin phenol reagent. J Biol Chem **193:** 265–275

Michelassi F, Landa L, Hill RD, Phil D, Lowenstein E, Watkins WD, Petkau AJ, Zapol WM (1982) Leukotriene D_4: A potent coronary artery vasoconstrictor associated with impaired ventricular contraction. Science **217:** 841–843

Misra RP (1972) Isolation of glomeruli from mammalian kidneys by graded sieving. Am J Clin Pathol **58:** 135–139

Munson PJ, Rodbard D (1980) LIGAND: A versatile computerized approach for charcterization of ligand binding systems. Anal Biochem **107:** 220–239

Örning L, Hammarström S (1980) Inhibition of leukotriene C and leukotriene D biosynthesis. J Biol Chem **255:** 8023–8026

Pfeffer MA, Pfeffer JM, Lewis RA, Braunwald E, Corey EJ, Austen KF (1983) Systemic hemodynamic effects of leukotrienes C_4 and D_4 in the rat. Am J Physiol **244:** 4628–4633

Pirotzky E, Bidault J, Burtin C, Gubler MC, Benveniste J (1984) Release of platelet activating factor, slow reacting substance and vasoactive amines from isolated rat kidneys. Kidney Int **25:** 404–410

Pong S-S, DeHaven RN (1983) Characterization of a leukotriene D_4 receptor in guinea pig lung. Proc Natl Acad Sci (USA) **80:** 7415–7419

Pong S-S, DeHaven RN, Kuehl FA Jr, Egan RW (1983) Leukotriene C_4 binding to rat lung membranes. J Biol Chem **258:** 9616–9619

Rosenthal A, Pace-Asciak CR (1983) Potent vasoconstriction of the isolated perfused rat kidney by leukotrienes C_4 and D_4. Can J Physiol Pharmacol **61:** 325–328

Samuelsson B (1983) Leukotrienes: mediators of immediate hypersensitivity reactions and inflammation. Science (Wash) **220:** 568–575

Sraer J, Rigand M, Bens M, Rabinovitch H, Ardaillou R (1983) Metabolism of arachidonic acid via the lipoxygenase pathway in human and murine glomeruli. J Biol Chem **258:** 4325–4330

Tate SS, Meister A (1978) Serine-borate complex as a transition-state inhibitor of γ-glutamyl transpeptidase. Proc Natl Acad Sci USA **75:** 4806–4809

Weiss JW, Drazen JM, Coles NC, McFadden ER Jr, Weller PF, Corey EJ, Lewis RA, Austen KF (1982) Bronchoconstrictor effects of leukotriene C in humans. Science **216:** 196–198

Weller PF, Lee CW, Foster DW, Corey EJ, Austen KF, Lewis RA (1983) Generation and metabolism of 5-lipoxygenase pathway leukotrienes by human eosinophils: Predominant production of leukotriene C_4. Proc Natl Acad Sci USA **80:** 7626–7630

INDEX TERMS: Sulfidopeptide leukotrienes • Inflammatory mediator • Glomerular function • Glomerulonephritis

Real-Time Kinetics of Sarcomere Relaxation by Laser Diffraction

Yves Lecarpentier, Jean-Louis Martin, Victor Claes, Jean-Paul Chambaret, Arnold Migus, André Antonetti, and Pierre-Yves Hatt

From the I.N.S.E.R.M., U.275, Laboratoire d'Optique Appliquée, E.N.S.T.A.-Ecole Polytechnique, Palaiseau, France, and I.N.S.E.R.M., U.2, Hôpital Léon Bernard, Limeil-Brévannes, France

SUMMARY. Kinetics of sarcomere movement were studied in real-time by laser diffraction. Instantaneous sarcomere shortening was measured during afterloaded twitches simultaneously with instantaneous shortening and tension of the whole trabecula excised from rat right ventricle. Resting sarcomere length at optimal length was 2.20 ± 0.02 μm (mean ± SEM). Maximum amplitude of sarcomere shortening was 0.30 ± 0.01 and 0.16 ± 0.01 μm, respectively, in twitches loaded with preload only, and in "isometric" twitches. When the isotonic load (expressed as a percentage of maximum isometric force TF) increased, the maximum velocity of sarcomere relaxation max Vr (μm/sec) decreased: max Vr = $-4 \exp(-2.5 \times 10^{-2}$ % TF); $r = 0.95$. The time course of sarcomere relaxation appeared to be progressively delayed when the total load increased from preload only up to "isometric" load. Sarcomere relaxation occurred in two successive exponential phases, a rapid phase [time constant (msec): τ_1] followed by a slower one (time constant: τ_2). When the total load increased, τ_1 increased and τ_2 decreased according to the linear relations: % TF = 0.2 τ_1 + 4.8 ($r = 0.83$) and % TF = -0.1 τ_2 + 157 ($r = 0.95$). The relative predominance of both the time course and the amplitude of these two phases depended upon the level of total load. The rapid process predominated at low load, the slow one at high load. The role of load and/or shortening in the time course of these two phases is discussed. **(*Circ Res 56: 331–339, 1985*)**

SARCOMERE movement in intact cardiac muscle has usually been studied under isometric conditions during the relaxation phase (Krueger and Strobeck, 1978; Krueger and Farber, 1980). Little is known about real-time sarcomere dynamics recorded simultaneously with the mechanical behavior of the whole muscle either contracting at various levels of isotonic load or after rapid modifications of loading conditions. Different mechanisms interact to control both isotonic lengthening and isometric tension decay, and their interdependence is not well established. Despite the fact that sarcoplasmic calcium concentration plays a major role in several steps of excitation-contraction coupling involved in force generation, this concentration has been shown, by aequorin technique, to be considerably lowered at the time of peak isometric tension (Ashley and Ridgway, 1970; Taylor et al., 1975; Allen and Blinks, 1978; Blinks et al., 1978; Gordon and Ridgway, 1978). Thus, uncertainties remain concerning the intracellular mechanisms governing the slow decline of isometric tension under conditions of low sarcoplasmic calcium concentration. Moreover, relaxation has recently been shown to be sensitive to the level of external load in both mammalian heart muscle (Brutsaert et al., 1978b, 1980) and in spontaneously beating single cardiac cells (Lecarpentier et al., 1979) in which the sarcoplasmic reticulum was still functional. Intracellular calcium-sequestering systems, particularly the sarcoplasmic reticulum, have been assumed to account partially for this property, which disappears in mammalian heart muscle treated with caffeine (Lecarpentier et al., 1979; Poggesi et al., 1979), and which is not observed in frog myocardium (Brutsaert et al., 1978b). The present study extends these observations by examining sarcomere kinetics during cardiac relaxation, in both "isotonic" and "isometric" contractions, and demonstrates that two mechanisms are involved during cardiac relaxation. The first, which is a rapid process, prevails at low load, whereas, the second, which is slow, prevails at high load.

Methods

Experimental System and Mounting Procedure

Adult Wistar rats ($n = 10$) were anesthetized with ether. The heart was quickly removed and transferred to a dissection chamber filled with a physiological oxygenated saline solution. The aorta was cannulated and perfused with the same salt solution at a flow rate of 5 ml/min. The physiological solution used during dissection and experiments consisted of the following components in mM: NaCl, 118; KCl, 4.7; $NaHCO_3$, 24; $MgSO_4 \cdot 7H_2O$, 1.2; KH_2PO_4, 1.1; $CaCl_2 \cdot 6H_2O$, 2.5; and glucose, 4.5. This solution was in equilibrium with 95% O_2 and 5% CO_2 (pH = 7.4) and was maintained at 24°C.

Small, ribbon-shaped trabeculae or thin papillary muscles were rapidly excised from the right ventricle and

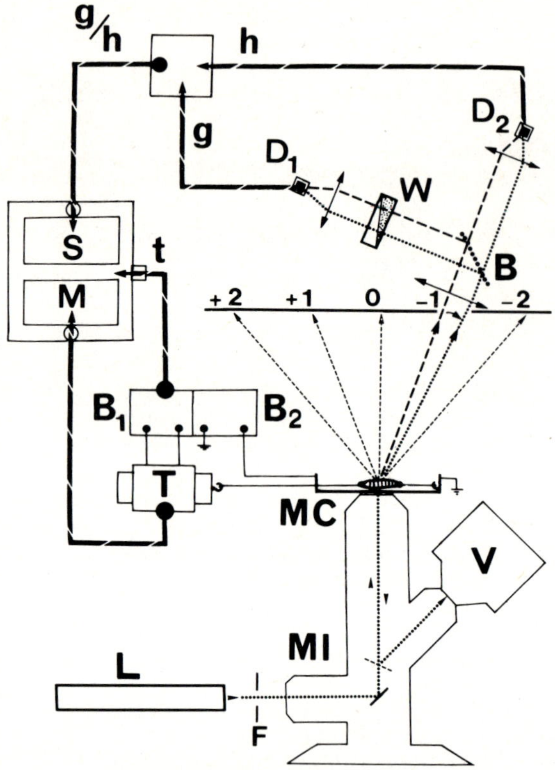

FIGURE 1. *Experimental set-up. Abbreviations are: L, laser; MI, microscope; V, video camera; MC, muscle chamber; B, beam splitter; W, densitometric wedge; F, split; D_1 and D_2, diodes; g and h, optical signals electronically converted by D_1 and D_2 respectively; g/h, signal function of sarcomere length; T, electromagnetic transducer; B_1, stimulator; M, muscle tension and shortening curves vs. time (t); S, instantaneous sarcomere length curve vs. time (t).*

mounted horizontally in a rectangular (1 × 5 cm) perfusion chamber. The glass bottom (0.2 mm thick) allowed visual observation under an inverted Reichert microscope (Fig. 1). The preparations were stimulated by means of an electrical field with two parallel silver electrode wires delivering 5-msec square pulses at a voltage slightly above threshold, and at 12 beats/min. After a one-half hour stabilization period, L_{max}, i.e., the initial length at the apex of the length-tension curve, was determined. The remainder of the experiment was carried out with preload corresponding to L_{max}.

Dimensions of trabeculae and papillary muscles (length, width, thickness, and cross-sectional area) were measured at L_{max}. The dimensions of specimens reported here were as follows: average length, 2.6 ± 0.2 (SEM) mm (range 2.1–3.5 mm); average width, 389 ± 34 μm (range 270–520 μm); average thickness, 167 ± 15 μm (range 90–210 μm). The cross-sectional area (s) of the muscles was calculated by considering muscle width and thickness as the major and minor axes of an ellipse (s = width × thickness × $\pi/4$): s = 0.052 ± 0.008 mm^2 (range 0.025–0.085 mm^2). Criteria for selection of specimens were: diffraction pattern with sharp first-order line, all or no response to electrical stimulation, stable mechanical performance and the resting force/total force ratio <20%. Three of the 10 muscles in which the resting force was more than 20% of total force at L_{max} were discarded from calculations. Mean value of resting force/total force at L_{max} was 17 ± 2%. Average resting force/mm^2 was 16.4 ± 1.4 mN/mm^2. The muscles developed at L_{max} 105 ± 6 mN/mm^2 or 5.4 ± 0.8 mN.

Optical Techniques

A 5-mW Helium-Neon laser (L) transilluminated a right ventricular rat trabecula or a thin papillary muscle horizontally mounted in the experimental chamber on the stage of an inverted microscope (Fig. 1). Thin cardiac muscle of this type acts as a tridimensional grating due to the regular array of sarcomeres, and diffracts the laser lines along several orders (at least ±1 and, in some cases, ±2). The spacing between zero and first-order of the Fraunhofer diffraction pattern was calculated according to the equation $SL = \lambda/\sin\theta$ where SL is the mean sarcomere length, $\lambda = 0.6328$ μm the wavelength of the laser, and θ the angular separation of the first-order diffraction line relative to the zero-order reference line. The laser beam passed through an adjustable slit and a 45-mm focal length lens, and was then collected with a 63× objective. The slit (F) was positioned in front of the lens so that its image (40 × 200 μm) was focused on the focal plane of the objective and could be superimposed onto the image of the trabecula. Both images were simultaneously observed through the microscope ocular or on the monitor of a video camera.

A region in the midlength of the specimen containing about 50–100 sarcomeres in series, was exactly superimposed onto the laser spot whose outline was determined by the adjustable slit. The diffraction pattern was then examined above the muscle chamber. A typical diffraction pattern is presented in Figure 2.

From the meridional diffraction pattern (Fig. 1), we selected the first-order line through an aperture and collected it through a lens which induced a parallel output. The beam then was split (B) into two equal parts. One beam was focused onto the PIN 10 diode D_2 producing the signal h which represented the variation of intensity of the first-order line. The other beam passed through an optical density wedge (W) whose transmission was related to the lateral shift of the beam and, consequently, to the

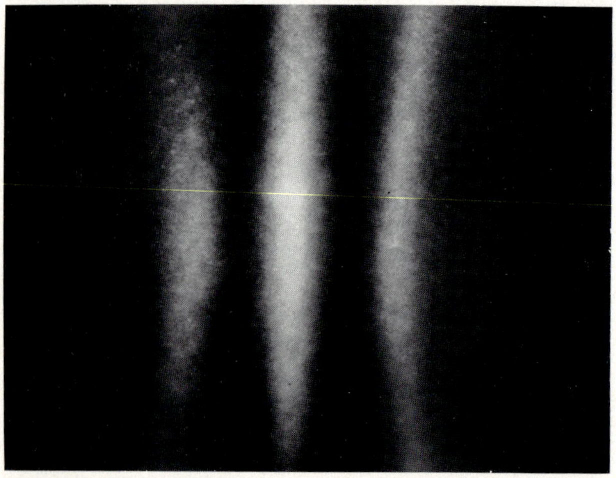

FIGURE 2. *Diffraction spectra obtained from a thin, right-ventricular rat trabecula. The two first-order diffracted lines (±1) were symmetrically spaced on either side of the central bright line of nondiffracted light (zero order). The distance between the zero-order line and the first-order lines are inversely related to sarcomere length.*

grating constant due to variations in the diffraction angle. This beam was then collected and focused onto the PIN 10 diode D_1 giving the signal g which represented the product of the variation of intensity of the first-order diffraction line and the variation of intensity due to the beam's lateral movement on the densitometric wedge. These signals were normalized so that initially g/h equals 1. During the twitch, the electronic system computed in real-time, the ratio g/h which is directly related to the instantaneous sarcomere length (SL) through the relationship $SL = SL_0/(1 + \alpha \log g/h)$ where SL_0 is the resting sarcomere length at L_{max} and α a constant characteristic of the optical set-up. In our experimental conditions, this expression can be linearized: $SL = SL_0 [1 + \alpha (1 - g/h)]$. Calibration of the sarcomere length at rest was checked by replacing the trabecula with gratings of known spacing positioned in the muscle plane. The accuracy of the apparatus was 1%, which corresponds to a change in sarcomere length of 200 Å. When the laser beam illuminated a different region in the midlength of the trabecula, the intensity variations (h) were modified but not the ratio g/h, i.e., the variations in sarcomere length during contraction. The ratio g/h, which is a function of the mean length value of about 50–100 sarcomeres illuminated by the laser beam, was independent of the position of the slit on the central segment of the muscle. The noise in the SL vs. time trace was minimized by diminishing background light. g/h was recorded with a low-pass filter (cut-off frequency: 2 kHz).

Computation was used to determine the function which best fitted sarcomere relaxation. The biphasic time course of sarcomere relaxation could not be fitted by a single exponential function. Figure 3 shows the time course of a twitch loaded with moderate afterload. Two exponential functions, whose time constants were respectively τ_1 and τ_2, were found to fit the whole time course of sarcomere relaxation of the experimental curves. A linear fit might also be used for both the two phases of sarcomere relaxation, especially at low load, where τ_1 appeared to be very short and τ_2 very long. However, the exponential fit accounted for most of the curves, particularly at middle and high loads, and often at low load. The onset (t_0) of the first exponential fit occurred at the onset of rapid sarcomere lengthening, soon after the time-to-peak sarcomere shortening (see Fig. 3: arrow 1 and t_0). The onset of the second exponential fit corresponded approximately to the isotonic-isometric transition where the slope of sarcomere relaxation suddenly decreased (see Fig. 3: arrow 2). Peak velocities of sarcomere shortening and lengthening were expressed graphically as the positive and negative maximum slopes of the SL vs. time curve. Maximum velocity of sarcomere lengthening (max.Vr) was also calculated from the equation of the first exponential fit; this calculated value is:

$$\frac{\Delta SL}{\tau_1} \exp\left(-\frac{t_0}{\tau_1}\right) = \frac{\Delta SL}{\tau_1}$$

where ΔSL is the amplitude of sarcomere elongation at t_0, t_0 the time at the onset of the first exponential fit, i.e., $t_0 = 0$, and τ_1 the time constant of the first exponential fit (Fig. 3).

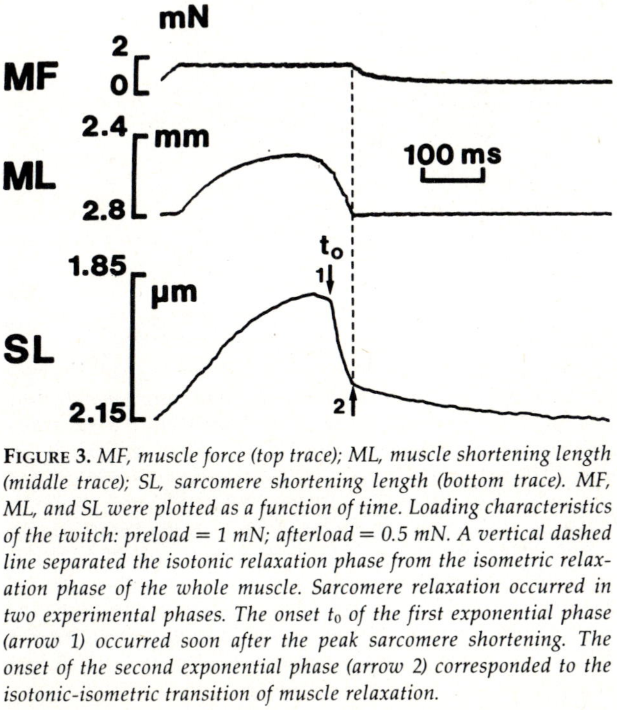

FIGURE 3. *MF, muscle force (top trace); ML, muscle shortening length (middle trace); SL, sarcomere shortening length (bottom trace). MF, ML, and SL were plotted as a function of time. Loading characteristics of the twitch: preload = 1 mN; afterload = 0.5 mN. A vertical dashed line separated the isotonic relaxation phase from the isometric relaxation phase of the whole muscle. Sarcomere relaxation occurred in two experimental phases. The onset t_0 of the first exponential phase (arrow 1) occurred soon after the peak sarcomere shortening. The onset of the second exponential phase (arrow 2) corresponded to the isotonic-isometric transition of muscle relaxation.*

Electromagnetic Lever System

A miniature panel meter (Eagle-Picher Industries, Inc.; sensitivity = 100 µA; internal resistance = 600 ohms) with center zero was adapted by replacing the pointer with a stainless steel tube and two small aluminum supports. This part was attached to the coil by epoxy cement. The rod was bent into the shape of a hook. The equivalent moving mass of the whole system (lever and coil) was 40 mg. The displacement of the lever was measured by means of an opto-electronic system mounted in the panel meter. The light beam of a miniature infra-red light-emitting diode (LS 600) was modulated by a small shutter on the lever and captured by a small photodiode (H 35). The resulting signal was amplified and linearized by operational amplifier circuits. The linear range was 1 mm with a linearity of 1%. The displacement signal was filtered with a third-order Raynter low pass-filter (optimal transient response cut-off frequency = 100 Hz). The filtered signal was differentiated using an active differentiator circuit. The RC constant was set to 0.1 second.

Force Generation and Measurement

The coil of the lever system was suspended within the field of a permanent magnet. The torque on the lever and, hence, the load imposed on the preparation, was proportional to the current through the coil when the lever was within the linear displacement range. The current was generated by a current source and set by means of decade switches in calibrated steps of 0.05 and 1 mN up to a total of 10 mN. Load alterations were performed by switching the current to a second level controlled by a second set of decade switches.

A unilateral force-sensing feedback circuit controlled the current source. This method is described elsewhere (De Clerck et al., 1978), and only a short overview is given here. The unfiltered displacement signal was compared to a present reference level, representing the position of an "electronic stop." If the length signal was higher than this level, no feedback occurred, and the preparation carried the load set by means of the decade switches. When it became lower, the lever was held in that position by the

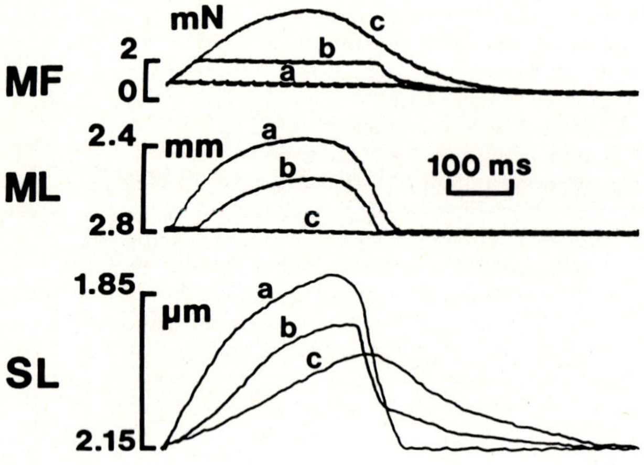

FIGURE 4. *Real-time kinetics of sarcomere and whole cardiac trabecula. Muscle force MF (top trace), muscle shortening length ML (middle trace), and sarcomere shortening length SL (bottom trace) were plotted as a function of time. A series of three superimposed contractions (twitches a, b, and c) can be seen against various loads, i.e., from isotonic twitch a with preload only (1 mN), then with various total loads (twitch b: 2 mN); up to a full "isometric" twitch c. These three contractions were similarly preloaded at L_{max} with 1 mN. During "isometric" twitch c, ML did not shorten, although SL decreased 7% of its resting length value at L_{max} (SL_0). When the afterload increased in twtiches b and c, the mechanical parameters of sarcomere (i.e., maximum amplitude of sarcomere shortening, peak velocities of shortening and of lengthening) decreased, and further time courses of sarcomere relaxation appeared progressively delayed. Mechanical characteristics of this typical trabecula at L_{max} and at rest: MF = 1 mN; ML, 2.80 mm; SL_0 = 2.15 μm; width, 360 μm; thickness, 180 μm; cross-sectional area, 0.05 mm².*

feedback mechanism, and the current through the coil was proportionally decreased and represented the load carried by the preparation. By adjusting this reference level, resting length and preload could be set. If the preparation developed a higher force than the load set with the decade switches, isotonic shortening occurred. In the course of an isometric contraction, the lever moved a very small amount (proportional to the force developed). This static compliance amounted to 1.2 μm/mN, and the dynamic compliance was negligible. The force signal was filtered and differentiated with the same kind of circuits as those of the length signal to minimize relative phase errors.

TABLE 1
Mechanical Parameters of Sarcomere Shortening

	Twitch with preload only	"Isometric" twitch
Sarcomere length at rest (SL_0) (μm)	2.20 ± 0.02	2.20 ± 0.02
Final sarcomere length at peak shortening (μm)	1.90 ± 0.02	2.04 ± 0.02
Maximum amplitude of sarcomere shortening (μm)	0.30 ± 0.01	0.16 ± 0.01
Percentage of maximum sarcomere shortening amplitude (% SL_0)	13.6 ± 0.4	7.0 ± 0.5

Data are shown as mean ± SEM. This table shows the mechanics of sarcomere during the twitch loaded with preload only and during "isometric" twitch.

Results

Mechanical Parameters of Sarcomere Kinetics

Sarcomere relaxation behavior was tested by either loading the muscle at various levels, or modifying the total load with load clamp steps during isotonic shortening. Real-time sarcomere shortening (SL) was recorded simultaneously with muscle shortening (ML) and with muscle force (MF). Figure 4 shows SL, ML, and MF in a typical muscle, contracting at three increasing levels of total load. Sarcomere kinetics clearly depended upon the loading conditions. When the load was increased from preload only (twitch a) up to isometric load (twitch c), there was a progressive decrease in the maximum amplitude of sarcomere shortening and in the peak velocities of shortening and of lengthening. Hereafter, the term "isometric" will refer exclusively to the mechanical behavior of the whole trabecula: indeed, when the total load became high enough, no external shortening of the whole muscle oc-

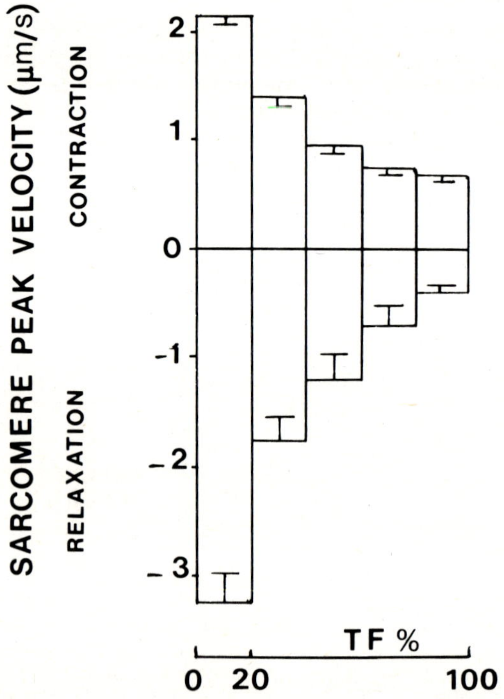

FIGURE 5. *Relationship between total load and maximum sarcomere velocity during contraction (max V_c) and relaxation (max V_r). Maximum sarcomere velocity was graphically determined by the maximum slope of the SL vs. time curve. Total load was expressed in terms of percentage of maximum isometric force at L_{max} (TF). Mean values of sarcomere velocity were calculated at five increasing levels of % TF: 0–20% TF, 21–40% TF, 41–60% TF, 61–80% TF, and 81–100% TF. Maximum velocity of sarcomere (μm/sec) exponentially decreased when % TF increased according to the equations max $V_c = 2.2 \exp(-1.4 \times 10^{-2}$ % TF) (r = 0.95) during the contraction phase and max $V_r = -4 \exp(-2.5 \times 10^{-2}$ % TF) (r = 0.95) during the relaxation phase.*

TABLE 2
Maximum Sarcomere Velocity

	Twitch with preload only (A)	"Isometric" twitch (B)	A/B ratio
Peak velocity of contraction (C)	2.09 ± 0.11 μm/sec	0.84 ± 0.11 μm/sec	2.76 ± 0.41
Peak velocity of relaxation (D)	3.95 ± 1.13 μm/sec	0.51 ± 0.12 μm/sec	8.95 ± 1.40
D/C ratio	2.00 ± 0.51	0.62 ± 0.13	

Graphic maximum sarcomere velocity during the twitch loaded with preload only (A) and during the "isometric" twitch (B). Peak velocity of contraction (C) and of relaxation (D) was calculated during (A) and (B). The A/B and D/C ratios are, respectively, listed in the third column and in the third line of this table. Data are shown as mean ± SEM. D/C and A/B ratios ± SE represent the mean values of the D/C and A/B ratios of each preparation, respectively.

curred. This contrasts with the internal sarcomere shortening observed in such "isometric" loading conditions (Fig. 4, twitch c).

Values of mechanical sarcomere parameters during both twitch with preload only and "isometric" twitch are expressed as mean ± SEM in Tables 1 and 2. Average resting length of sarcomere at L_{max} (SL_0) was 2.20 ± 0.02 μm (Table 1). When the trabecula was preloaded only, maximum amplitude of sarcomere shortening reached 0.30 ± 0.01 μm, which represented 13.6 ± 0.4% of SL_0 (Table 1). During the "isometric" twitch, the maximum amplitude of sarcomere shortening was 0.16 ± 0.01 μm and corresponded to 7.0 ± 0.5% of SL_0 (Table 1). Figure 5 shows the relationship between graphically determined sarcomere peak velocity and muscle force expressed as a percentage of the maximum isometric force at L_{max} (TF). Peak velocity of sarcomere shortening (max V_c) decreased exponentially when the muscle force increased according to the equation max $V_c = 2.2 \exp(-1.4 \times 10^{-2}$ % TF); the coefficient of regression $r = 0.95$. When muscle force increased, peak velocity of sarcomere lengthening [max V_r (graphic)] decreased more rapidly than max V_c, according to the equation: max $V_r = -4 \exp(-2.5 \times 10^{-2}$ % TF); the coefficient of regression $r = 0.95$. Maximum speed of sarcomere shortening was 2.09 ± 0.11 μm/sec in twitch with preload only and 0.84 ± 0.11 μm/sec in the "isometric" twitch (Table 2). Peak velocities of sarcomere relaxation were, respectively, 3.95 ± 1.13 μm/sec and 0.51 ± 0.12 μm/sec in twitch preloaded only and in the "isometric" twitch (Table 2). The ratio of these two values (Table 2: A/B ratio) was 8.95 ± 1.40 during the relaxation phase, although the A/B ratio was only 2.76 ± 0.41 during the contraction phase. Thus, the range of maximum speed variation of sarcomeres was broader during lengthening than during shortening. At preload only, sarcomere peak lengthening velocity was higher than sarcomere peak shortening velocity (Table 2: D/C ratio: 2.00 ± 0.51); the inverse was observed at "isometric" load (Table 2: D/C ratio = 0.62 ± 0.13).

The time course of sarcomere shortening differed strikingly from that of sarcomere lengthening according to the loading conditions. In a series of afterloaded twitches with similar preload (Fig. 4), sarcomere shortening initially presented a common pathway whose duration increased with total load, although the sarcomere vs. time curves appeared to be distinct from each other during the overall time course of relaxation phase (Fig. 4, twitches a, b, and c). When total load increased from twitch a with preload only up to isometric twitch c (Fig. 4), time-to-peak sarcomere shortening barely increased, and further time course of sarcomere relaxation appeared to be progressively delayed. The higher the total load, the later a given degree of sarcomere lengthening occurred. Twitch a with preload only rapidly reached its initial resting length. Sarcomere relaxation of the afterloaded twitches (twitch b in Fig. 4 and the twitch in Fig. 3) displayed two distinct and successive phases of auxotonic relaxation. First, a short and rapid phase, during which the main part of sarcomere lengthening was achieved (from arrow 1 to arrow 2 in Fig. 3). Second, a slow phase occurred, during which sarcomeres lengthened and reached their initial resting length (after arrow 2 in Fig. 3). In afterloaded twitches, the rapid phase of sarcomere lengthening corresponded in time to the isotonic relaxation phase of the whole muscle and the slow phase to the isometric relaxation phase. The bending from the rapid phase to the slow phase occurred approximately at the transition between the successive isotonic and isometric relaxation-phases of muscle force (MF) (arrow 2, Fig. 3). When the load increased, the amplitude of sarcomere lengthening decreased during the rapid phase and increased during the slow phase. In Figure 4, at any given moment of the rapid phase of sarcomere relaxation, the lower the load, the higher the instantaneous speed of sarcomere lengthening. Inversely, at any given moment in the slow phase, the higher the load, the higher the instantaneous velocity of sarcomere lengthening.

Modeling of sarcomere lengthening vs. time was fitted with two exponential functions. The time constants τ_1 and τ_2 of exponential fits of the fast and slow phases, respectively, were expressed as percentages of the maximum isometric force (TF) at L_{max} (Fig. 6). τ_1 and τ_2 were linearly related to the total load according to the equations: % TF = 0.2 τ_1 + 4.8 (coefficient of linear regression $r = 0.83$) and % TF = −0.1 τ_2 + 157 (coefficient of linear regression $r = 0.95$). When total load increased, the linear increase in τ_1 appeared to be associated with a linear decrease in τ_2. This load-dependent balance between the two phases τ_1 and τ_2 depended upon the level of load. At low load, the rapid phase predominated, and at high load the slower phase predominated. In the twitch with only the preload, only the fast phase was observed (Fig. 4, twitch a). In the

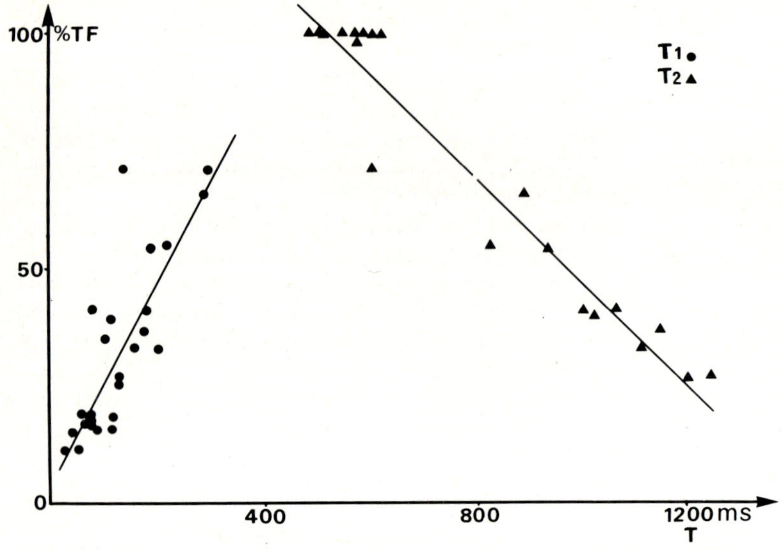

FIGURE 6. *Relationship between total load and time constants τ_1 (rapid phase) and τ_2 (slow phase). Total load was expressed in terms of the percentage of the maximum isometric force at L_{max} (% TF); τ_1 and τ_2 were linearly related to the % TF by the following equations: % TF = 0.2 τ_1 + 4.8 (r = 0.83) and % TF = −0.1 τ_2 + 157 (r = 0.95). The rapid process predominated at low load, the slow one at high load. The transition between the two phases was more precisely determined at low load than at high load, where τ_1 and τ_2 were not strikingly different ($\tau_1/\tau_2 \simeq 0.5$ at 70% TF).*

"isometric" twitch (Fig. 4, twitch c), the rapid phase disappeared and only the slow phase was observed. The relaxation time course of the "isometric" twitch c was markedly delayed, compared with that of twitches a and b.

Maximum velocity of sarcomere lengthening was also calculated from the maximum value of the exponential fit: max V_r (calculated) = $-\Delta SL/\tau_1$. This was then compared with max V_r (graphic): max V_r (calculated) = 1.08 max V_r (graphic) − 0.02 (coefficient correlation $r = 0.95$). Statistical analysis shows that the slope of this linear relationship did not differ significantly from 1.

Load Sensitivity of Sarcomere Relaxation

The load-bearing capacity of sarcomeres was also tested during isotonic contractions by triggering small, abrupt modifications in load (load clamp steps) of various amplitude and at different times during the twitch. In Figure 7, two afterload twitches b and c were rapidly load-clamped from 1 mN to a final total load of 2 mN, which was the total load of the control twitch a. When the load step occurred during the last third of the shortening phase as in twitches b and c (Fig. 7), the time course of sarcomere relaxation became markedly abbreviated. For a given isotonic load, the onset of isometric relaxation

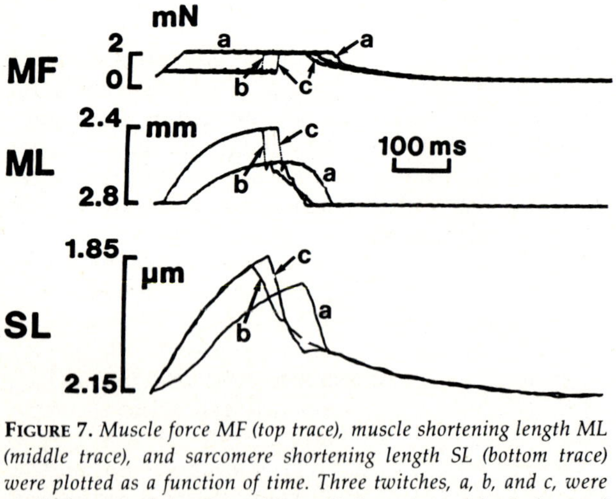

FIGURE 7. *Muscle force MF (top trace), muscle shortening length ML (middle trace), and sarcomere shortening length SL (bottom trace) were plotted as a function of time. Three twitches, a, b, and c, were similarly preloaded at L_{max} with 1 mN. Isotonic total load of control twitch a was maintained at 2 mN during the overall contraction. Total load of twitches b and c was 1 mN at the beginning of the contraction phase. An abrupt load clamp step of 1 mN was imposed during twitches b and c, at two different times during the last third of the contraction phase, in such a way that their final total load was similar to that of control twitch a (2 mN). The subsequent time course of twitches b and c was strikingly abbreviated. Mechanical characteristics of the trabecula were similar to those of Figure 4.*

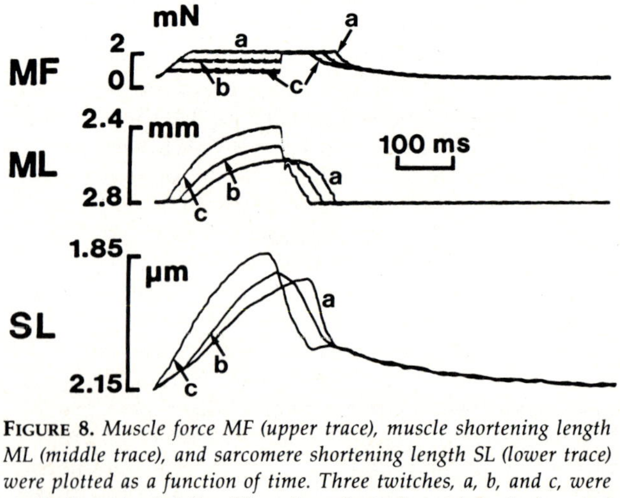

FIGURE 8. *Muscle force MF (upper trace), muscle shortening length ML (middle trace), and sarcomere shortening length SL (lower trace) were plotted as a function of time. Three twitches, a, b, and c, were similarly preloaded (1 mN) at L_{max}. Isotonic total load of control twitch a was maintained at 2 mN during the overall duration of the twitch. Two load clamp steps of various amplitude (0.5 mN in twitch b and 1 mN in twitch c, respectively) were imposed at the same time in such a way that the final total load was similar to that of control twitch a (2 mN). These load clamps were triggered at the same time as that imposed during twitch c in Figure 7. The higher the load step, the shorter the overall duration of the contraction. Mechanical characteristics of the trabecula: similar to those of Figure 4.*

of the whole trabecula depended upon the timing of load clamp steps. In the load-clamped twitches b and c, sarcomere relaxation occurred in two successive rapid and slow phases, as was observed in control twitch a. For the three twitches a, b, and c (Fig. 7), the sarcomere relengthening level which was measured at the "MF isotonic-isometric transition" corresponded to the end of the rapid phase of relaxation and appeared scarcely influenced by the time at which the load clamp was triggered. Thus, the onset and the end of the rapid phase of sarcomere relaxation clearly depended either on the level of total load (Figs. 3 and 4), or on the moment at which the final level of total load was reached after the load clamp steps (Fig. 7). Later, the slow phase of sarcomere relaxation of twitches a, b, and c (Fig. 7) exhibited a common pathway when returning to the resting length; this pathway was independent of the time at which the load clamps were imposed.

These results, which test the influence of the load on the time course of sarcomere relaxation, were also corroborated by those shown in Figure 8. Load clamp steps of various amplitude were imposed at the same moment during the last third of the shortening phase. These modified the load-bearing capacity of the muscle and the time course of sarcomere relaxation. As in Figure 7, sarcomere relaxation presented a rapid phase followed by a slow one. The higher the amplitude of the load clamp step, the sooner the rapid phase occurred. The end of the rapid phase corresponded to the "MF isotonic-isometric transition." The slow phases of sarcomere relaxation of twitches a, b, and c (Fig. 8) presented a similar time course. The sarcomere resting length was reached at the end of the common pathway of the slow phase.

In summary, real-time kinetics of sarcomere during relaxation lead to the following conclusions. Sarcomere lengthening occurred in two successive exponential phases. The time constants τ_1 and τ_2 of these two phases were linearly related to the total force imposed on the muscle. The rapid and the slow phases can be modulated independently: for a given final level of total load, the onset and the end of the rapid phase depended on loading changes previously imposed during the twitch, i.e., the timing (Fig. 7) and/or the amplitude (Fig. 8) of load clamp steps. On the contrary, the time course of the common pathway of the slow phase appeared to be independent of these loading modifications.

Discussion

Dynamics of Sarcomere Shortening and Lengthening

This paper focuses on the mechanical behavior of sarcomeres during relaxation at various levels of load. These results reveal the complex influence that the level of instantaneous load has upon intracellular mechanisms involved in sarcomere contraction and relaxation processes. Dimensions of the trabeculae and the maximum isometric force at L_{max} per cross-sectional area were quite similar to those observed by Pollack and Huntsman (1974), Krueger and Pollack (1975), ter Keurs et al. (1980), and Gordon and Pollack (1980). Sarcomere velocity and sarcomere shortening shown in Tables 1 and 2 appeared to be of a comparable order of magnitude to those observed by other investigators. In twitches where the load represented a small fraction of isometric load, Pollack and Krueger (1976) observed that the maximum unloaded sarcomere velocity reaches 10 μm/sec in rat cardiac trabecula. Similar values have been found by Krueger et al. (1980) in isolated cardiac cells during unloaded contraction. In our study, however, the maximum speed of sarcomere shortening was measured in the preloaded twitch which represented 17 $\pm$ 2% of maximum "isometric" tension. This preloaded twitch differs somewhat from unloaded conditions and accounts for the fact that we obtained lower values as compared with those of Pollack and Krueger (1976). This also explains why the average sarcomere length at peak shortening of the preloaded twitch was 1.90 $\pm$ 0.02 μm (Table 1) rather than the 1.6 μm found in unloaded contraction by Pollack and Krueger (1976), ter Keurs (1978) in intact papillary muscle, and Krueger et al. (1980) in single cardiac cell. During the isometric twitch, we found the same internal sarcomere shortening (7% of the resting sarcomere length at L_{max}) as previously measured by Krueger and Pollack (1975). This internal sarcomere shortening observed during "isometric" contraction has been shown to be due to high compliance in the extremities of the preparation (Krueger and Pollack, 1975).

Time Course of Sarcomere Relaxation Occurring in Two Phases

Sarcomere relaxation was characterized by two successive exponential phases whose relative importance was "balanced" by the general loading conditions (Fig. 6). The rapid phase corrsponding to the isotonic phase of the whole muscle lengthening contributed to the major part of relengthening. The slow phase terminated sarcomere lengthening and corresponded to the slow final decay of isometric tension. The onset and duration of the first rapid phase of sarcomere relaxation appeared to be modulated by the level of load, the amplitude of load variations, and the time at which a given level of final total load was triggered (Figs. 4, 7, and 8). In twitches load-clamped to the same final total load, the relengthening level of the sarcomere at the end of the rapid phase was slightly modified as compared with the varying times at which the "MF isometric" relaxation began (Figs. 7 and 8). In these twitches, the slow phase presented a common trajectory slowly reaching the initial resting sarcomere length. The relative role of the two phases during sarcomere relaxation appeared to be a function of the level of load. At low load, the rapid phase was predominant, while the second phase became predominant at heavy load. The "transition" between these two phases was quite evident, particularly at low load, when their time constants τ_1 and τ_2 were very different (Fig. 6). At heavy load, this transition appeared less precise because the difference between τ_1 and τ_2 was much smaller than at low load (Fig. 6). The fact that these two phases could not be fitted with a single exponential function argues in favor of two different mechanisms. This was corroborated by the fact that the time course of the rapid phase could be modified by changing the loading conditions without any change in the time constant of the slow phase (Figs. 7 and 8). It was also substantiated by the observation of the rapid phase only, during the preloaded twitch, and of the slow phase only, during the "isometric" twitch (Fig. 4).

Other investigators have shown that sarcomere relaxation in mammalian muscle could be characterized by two distinct phases. In unloaded single cardiac cells, Krueger et al. (1980) have found that sarcomere lengthening successively presents a rapid relaxation phase followed by a very slow one. Moreover, a biphasic curve has been observed in intact cardiac muscle in which relaxation is terminated by a slow phase of isometric tension decline (Krueger and Farber, 1980). These phases have been assumed to be governed by distinct mechanisms (Krueger and Strobeck, 1978) as suggested by the opposite effects of calcium on isometric and isotonic relaxation (Strobeck et al., 1975). Various hypotheses have been proposed to explain rapid sarcomere lengthening. The afterload pulling on the muscle contributes to rapid lengthening. Restoring forces occur at sarcomere length below the slack length (1.90 μm), where one might expect a significant effect on sarcomere relaxation. In our study, sarcomere length at peak shortening in twitch with preload reached only 1.90 $\pm$ 0.02 μm (Table 1), and internal restoring forces could hardly be involved in the rapid phase of sarcomere relaxation.

Biochemical and mechanical arguments have previously emphasized the role of the sarcoplasmic reticulum on intracellular calcium movements during both contraction and relaxation. The Ca^{++}-induced release of Ca^{++} from the sarcoplasmic reticulum is well-developed in adult rat ventricle and absent in frog myocardium and in newborn rat ventricle (Fabiato and Fabiato, 1978). Moreover, cardiac relaxation has been shown to be sensitive to the loading conditions (Brutsaert et al., 1978a, 1978b; Lecarpentier et al., 1979). This mechanical property expresses the possibility of modifying the timing of the isotonic-isometric transition according to the level of total load and requires the presence of an efficient sarcoplasmic reticulum. Thus, it disappears in mammalian single cardiac cells after pretreatment with the detergent BRIJ-58 (Brutsaert et al., 1978a), which destroys both sarcolemma and sarcoplasmic reticulum (Orentlicher et al., 1974; Fabiato and Fabiato, 1975). Load sensitivity also disappears in a caffeine medium (Lecarpentier et al., 1979; Poggesi et al., 1979) which partially inhibits the sarcoplasmic reticulum (Weber and Herz, 1968). Furthermore, load sensitivity of relaxation is not observed in the frog ventricular strip (Brutsaert et al., 1978b) where the sarcoplasmic reticulum is scarcely developed (Staley and Benson, 1968), nor in newborn rat myocardium (personal observation) in which the sarcoplasmic reticulum is not yet functional (Fabiato and Fabiato, 1978). Influence of the load on relaxation appears to be of physiological and pathological relevance because it can be observed in intact heart muscle (Raff and Glantz, 1981) and because it disappears after hypoxia (Chuck et al., 1981) but persists during cardiac hypertrophy (Lecarpentier et al., 1982). All these arguments suggest a partial involvement of the sarcoplasmic reticulum in the time course regulation of the rapid phase of sarcomere relaxation.

On the other hand, intracellular mechanisms governing cardiac relaxation at high load are not yet clearly understood. As previously discussed by Krueger and Farber (1980), relaxation is terminated by a slow phase during isometric tension decline. The slow final lengthening could be due to the force in the series elastic elements being relieved gradually. The free calcium concentration, studied with the aequorin technique, has been shown to return almost to its level at rest, long before isometric tension decay (Taylor et al., 1975; Gordon and Ridgway, 1978). The molecular mechanism of this isometric force decline at low calcium concentration remains uncertain, but might be explained by subtle interactions between actin and myosin filaments or by a cooperative effect modifying myofilament calcium affinity (Bremel et al., 1973; Taylor et al., 1975). Moreover, additional evidence supports a link between the calcium binding properties of troponin C and load and/or length changes (Endo, 1973; Allen and Kurihara, 1982; Housmans et al., 1983). Our results appear to be compatible with such a hypothesis: at high load or slight amplitude of sarcomere shortening, the calcium affinity of troponin C would seem to be higher than at low load, and vice versa. This may be confirmed by further experiments. In conclusion, sarcomere relaxation seems to occur in two successive phases, a rapid phase followed by a slower one, the respective time courses of which depend upon the general loading conditions.

We wish to acknowledge the technical assistance of Armindo Dos Santos, the secretarial expertise provided by M.-T. Dronne and S. Babilotte, and the use of laboratory facilities, generously provided by A. Orszag.

This work was supported by a grant from the Institut National de la Santé et de la Recherche Médicale (CRL 82 50 45) and ATP 63 78 95.

Address for reprints: Yves Lecarpentier, M.D., I.N.S.E.R.M. U 275, Laboratoire d'Optique Appliquée, E.N.S.T.A.-Ecole Polytechnique, 91120 Palaiseau, France.

Received November 11, 1982; accepted for publication November 8, 1984.

References

Allen DG, Blinks JR (1978) Calcium transients in aequorin-injected frog cardiac muscle. Nature (Lond) **273:** 509–513

Allen DG, Kurihara S (1982) The effects of muscle length on intracellular calcium transients in mammalian cardiac muscle. J Physiol (Lond) **327:** 79–94

Ashley CC, Ridgway EB (1970) On the relationships between membrane potential, calcium transient and tension in single barnacle muscle fibres. J Physiol (Lond) **209:** 105–130

Blinks JR, Rüdel R, Taylor SR (1978) Calcium transients in isolated amphibian skeletal muscle fibres: Detection with aequorin. J Physiol (Lond) **277:** 291–323

Bremel RD, Murray JM, Weber A (1973) Manifestations of cooperative behavior in the regulated actin filament during actin-activated ATP hydrolysis in the presence of calcium. *In* Symposia on Quantitative Biology, vol 37, edited by J Gordon. New York, Cold Spring Harbor Laboratory, Cold Spring Harbor, pp 267–275

Brutsaert DL, Claes VA, De Clerck NM (1978a) Relaxation of mammalian single cardiac cells after pretreatment with the detergent BRIJ-58. J Physiol (Lond) **283:** 481–491

Brutsaert DL, De Clerck NM, Goethals MA, Housmans PR (1978b) Relaxation of ventricular cardiac muscle. J Physiol (Lond) **283:** 469–480

Brutsaert DL, Housmans PR, Goethals MA (1980) Dual control of relaxation: Its role in the ventricular function in the mammalian heart. Circ Res **47:** 637–652

Chuck LH, Goethals MA, Parmley WW, Brutsaert DL (1981) Load-insensitive relaxation caused by hypoxia in mammalian cardiac muscle. Circ Res **48:** 797–803

De Clerck NM, Claes VA, Brutsaert DL (1977) Force velocity relations of single cardiac muscle cells. Calcium dependency. J Gen Physiol **69:** 221–241

Endo M (1973) Length dependence of activation of skinned muscle fibres by calcium. *In* Symposia on Quantitative Biology, vol 37, edited by J Gordon. New York, Cold Spring Harbor Laboratory, Cold Spring Harbor, pp 505–510

Fabiato A, Fabiato F (1975) Contractions induced by a calcium-triggered release of calcium from the sarcoplasmic reticulum of single skinned cardiac cells. J Physiol (Lond) **249:** 469–495

Fabiato A, Fabiato F (1978) Calcium-induced release of calcium from the sarcoplasmic reticulum of skinned cells from adult human, dog, cat, rabbit, rat, and frog hearts and from fetal and new-born rat ventricles. Ann NY Acad Sci **307:** 491–522

Gordon AM, Pollack GH (1980) Effects of calcium on the sarcomere length-tension relation in rat cardiac muscle. Circ Res **47:** 610–619

Gordon AM, Ridgway EB (1978) Calcium transients and relaxation in single muscle fibers. Eur J Cardiol **7** (suppl): 27–34

Housmans PR, Lee NK, Blinks JR (1983) Active shortening retards the decline of the intracellular calcium transient in mammalian heart muscle. Science **221:** 159–161

Krueger JW, Farber S (1980) Sarcomere length "orders" relaxation in cardiac muscle. Eur Heart J **1** (suppl A): 37–47

Krueger JW, Pollack GH (1975) Myocardial sarcomere dynamics during isometric contraction. J Physiol (Lond) **251:** 627–643

Krueger JW, Strobeck JE (1978) Sarcomere relaxation in intact cardiac muscle. Eur J Cardiol **7** (suppl): 79–96

Krueger JW, Forletti D, Wittenberg BA (1980) Uniform sarcomere shortening behavior in isolated cardiac muscle cells. J Gen Physiol **76:** 587–607

Lecarpentier YC, Chuck LHS, Housmans PR, De Clerck NM, Brutsaert DL (1979) Nature of load dependence of relaxation in cardiac muscle. Am J Physiol **237:** H455–H460

Lecarpentier YC, Martin JL, Gastineau P, Hatt PY (1982) Load dependence of mammalian heart relaxation during cardiac hypertrophy and heart failure. Am J Physiol **242:** H855–H861

Orentlicher M, Reuben JP, Grundfest H, Brandt PW (1974) Calcium binding and tension development in detergent treated muscle fibres. J Gen Physiol **63:** 168–186

Poggesi C, Ricciardi L, Reggiani C, Minelli R (1979) Isometric relaxation in rat myocardium: Load dependence and influence of caffeine. Experientia **35:** 1615–1616

Pollack GH, Huntsman LL (1974) Sarcomere length-active force relations in living mammalian cardiac muscle. Am J Physiol **227:** 383–389

Pollack GH, Krueger JW (1976) Sarcomere dynamics in intact cardiac muscle. Eur J Cardiol **4** (suppl): 53–65

Raff GL, Glantz SA (1981) Volume loading slows left ventricular isovolumic relaxation rate. Circ Res **48:** 813–824

Staley NA, Benson ES (1968) The ultrastructure of frog ventricular cardiac muscle and its relationship to mechanisms of excitation-contraction coupling. J Cell Biol **38:** 99–113

Strobeck JE, Bahler AS, Sonnenblick EH (1975) Isotonic relaxation in cardiac muscle. Am J Physiol **229:** 646–651

Taylor SR, Rüdel R, Blinks JR (1975) Calcium transients in amphibian muscle. Fed Proc **34:** 1379–1381

ter Keurs HEDJ, Bloot R, Rijnsburger WH, Nagelsmit MJ (1978) The influence of sarcomere length on tension development in rat heart muscle (abstr). Biophys J **21:** 86a

ter Keurs HEDJ, Rijnsburger WH, Heuningen R Van, Nagelsmit MJ (1980) Tension development and sarcomere length in rat cardiac trabeculae; Evidence of length-dependent activation. Circ Res **46:** 703–714

Weber A, Herz R (1968) Relationship between caffeine contracture of intact muscle and the effect of caffeine on reticulum. J Gen Physiol **52:** 750–759

INDEX TERMS: Laser diffraction • Sarcomere length • Cardiac relaxation

Postextrasystolic Potentiation of the Isolated Canine Left Ventricle

Relationship to Mechanical Restitution

David T. Yue, Daniel Burkhoff, Michael R. Franz, William C. Hunter, and Kiichi Sagawa

From the Department of Biomedical Engineering, The Johns Hopkins University School of Medicine, Baltimore, Maryland

SUMMARY. We established, for the isolated, isovolumically beating canine left ventricle, a comprehensive description of postextrasystolic contractile strength (dP/dt_{max}) as a function of extrasystolic and postextrasystolic stimulus intervals. In contrast to previous studies of postextrasystolic beats in in situ hearts, these isolated ventricles contracted isovolumically so that dP/dt_{max} was not affected by fluctuations in preload and afterload and was therefore considered to be a reliable index of intrinsic contractility. With the interval preceding extrasystoles constant, postextrasystolic contractile strength increased monoexponentially to a plateau as the interval preceding postextrasystoles lengthened, with a mean time constant (±SD) of 182 ± 44 msec ($n = 53$). The onset of this increase in postextrasystolic contractile strength coincided with repolarization of the extrasystolic action potential. With the interval preceding postextrasystoles held constant and long (1200 msec), postextrasystolic contractile strength decreased according to a monoexponential function as the interval preceding extrasystoles lengthened [mean time constant (±SD) of 176 ± 18 msec ($n = 10$)]. These phenomena could be quantitatively summarized by a single equation description of postextrasystolic contractile strength which involved monoexponential functions with one time constant. The mathematical form of this description led us to a simple interpretation of these phenomena in terms of currently proposed excitation-contraction coupling models of the heart. **(*Circ Res 56: 340–350, 1985*)**

THE MARKED INFLUENCE of changes in stimulation pattern upon the contractile strength of extrasystoles and postextrasystoles has long fascinated both the physiologist and the physician (Cranefield, 1965). For the physiologist, these phenomena appear to be fundamental manifestations of the beat-to-beat kinetics of activator calcium (Morad and Goldman, 1973), whereas, for the physician, they represent relationships which may prove to be sensitive indicators of contractility and disease state (Reichel et al., 1974; Anderson et al., 1979).

Despite such long-standing interest in these phenomena, their quantitative characterization at the ventricular level has remained incomplete. Information regarding the dependence of extrasystolic and postextrasystolic contractile strength upon preceding stimulus intervals has been primarily derived from superfused, isolated muscle (Johnson, 1979). Far less is known at the ventricular level mainly because of the uncertainty in determining whether changes in observed pressure reflect alterations in stimulation pattern or the associated fluctuations in preload and afterload (Anderson et al., 1976; Burkoff et al., 1984a).

These difficulties were recently surmounted by the use of an isolated, perfused canine ventricle in our study of the force-interval relationship of extrasystoles (Burkhoff et al., 1984a). In this preparation, preload and afterload could be held constant by making the isolated ventricle contract isovolumically, thereby rendering contractile strength a direct function of preceding stimulus intervals. In addition, the atria could be removed, thus facilitating the ability to pace the ventricle as desired over a broad range of intervals. We demonstrated for the isovolumically beating ventricle that extrasystoles exhibited the phenomenon known from isolated muscle studies as mechanical restitution (Braveny and Kruta, 1958). Specifically, extrasystolic ventricular contractile strength rose with a monoexponentially increasing time course as the interval preceding extrasystoles was gradually lengthened.

The purpose of the present study was to extend our previous work with extrasystoles and establish, in the isolated heart, a comprehensive description of postextrasystolic contractile strength. The strength of postextrasystoles was a function of both the interval preceding extrasystoles (ESI) and the interval preceding postextrasystoles (PESI). With ESI constant, postextrasystolic strength increased as PESI was lengthened (postextrasystolic mechanical restitution), and, with PESI fixed, postextrasystolic strength increased as ESI was shortened (postextrasystolic potentiation). These phenomena could be quantitatively summarized by a single equation which describes postextrasystolic contractile strength. The simplicity of the description led us to a novel interpretation of these phenomena in terms of currently proposed excitation-contraction (e-c) coupling models of the heart.

Methods

Surgical Preparation

A total of 14 isolated, perfused canine hearts were studied. The procedures used to isolate and support a canine heart were similar to those described by Suga and Sagawa (1974). A pair of mongrel dogs was anesthetized with sodium pentobarbital (30 mg/kg, iv). The femoral arteries and veins of one dog (support dog) were cannulated and connected to a perfusion system that was used to supply oxygenated blood to the isolated heart. The chest of the second dog (donor dog) was opened under artificial respiration. The left subclavian artery was cannulated with the arterial line of the perfusion system. The brachiocephalic artery was cannulated to monitor the coronary perfusion pressure. The azygous vein, superior and inferior vena cavae, descending aorta, and lung hili were ligated. The heart was then removed from the donor dog. Left and right atria were completely excised to eliminate spontaneous supraventricular rhythms and thereby facilitate the exploration of a wide range of stimulated pacing intervals. All chordae tendiniae were freed from the mitral valve leaflets. A metal adapter that held isolated heart to the ventricular-volume servo-pump system was sutured to the mitral ring. When the surgical preparation was complete, the isolated heart was positioned such that a water-filled, latex balloon was inside the left ventricular cavity. Accumulation of blood in the space between the balloon and ventricular wall was avoided by venting.

The ventricles were made to contract isovolumically throughout a given protocol by holding balloon volume, and therefore left ventricular volume, constant at a single level set between 15 and 35 ml. In all experiments, the coronary perfusion pressure was maintained constant at a selected level between 80 and 100 mm Hg by a servo-controlled perfusion pump (Harvard Apparatus, model 1215). The temperature of the perfusate was maintained between 35° and 37°C. Since the atria had been excised

TABLE 1
Definition of Experimental Variables

Variable: Type	Variable: Name	Definition	
Pacing intervals	SSI	Steady state cycle length: interval between steady state stimuli	
	ESI	Extrasystolic stimulus interval: interval between extrasystolic and last steady state stimuli	
	PESI	Postextrasystolic stimulus interval: interval between extrasystolic and postextrasystolic stimuli	
Measured quantities	dP/dt_{max} (SS)	Steady state beats	Maximum rate of rise of pressure
	dP/dt_{max} (ES)	Extrasystolic beats	
	dP/dt_{max} (PES)	Postextrasystolic beats	
	$MAPD_{90}$	Duration of monophasic action potentials, measured at 90% repolarization	
Force-interval relations	MRC_{es}	Extrasystolic mechanical restitution curve: normalized dP/dt_{max} of extrasystoles plotted vs. ESI	
	MRC_{pes}	Postextrasystolic mechanical restitution curve: normalized dP/dt_{max} of postextrasystoles plotted vs. PESI, with ESI held constant	
	PESPC	Postextrasystolic potentiation curve: normalized dP/dt_{max} of fully restituted postextrasystoles plotted vs. ESI	
	Extrasystolic Mechanical Restitution Curve (MRC_{es})		
Parameters characterizing force-interval relations	$CR_{max,es}$	Maximum extrasystolic contractile response: plateau value	
	$T_{mrc,es}$	Time constant	
	$t_{o,es}$	ESI-axis intercept value	
	Postextrasystolic Mechanical Restitution Curve (MRC_{pes})		
	$CR_{max,pes}$	Maximum postextrasystolic contractile response: plateau value	
	$T_{mrc,pes}$	Time constant	
	$t_{o,pes}$	PESI-axis intercept value	
	Postextrasystolic Potentiation Curve (PESPC)		
	A	Amplitude	
	B	Plateau value	
	T_{pespc}	Time constant	

and, therefore, could not be used as a pacing site, the hearts were stimulated, instead, with one bipolar electrode placed near the AV node, and the other at the apex. This electrode placement was chosen in an attempt to activate the ventricle through the His-Purkinje system.

Variables

To describe accurately the force-interval relation of extra- and postextrasystoles, we found it necessary to use a number of variables. Although these will be carefully defined in the text, they are also compiled and described briefly in Table 1.

Measurements

The left ventricular pressure was measured by a catheter-tip pressure transducer (Millar 300) placed inside the latex balloon within the left ventricle. The left ventricular pressure was electronically differentiated (Gould model 13-4615-71, corner frequency 30 Hz). The maximum rate of rise of left ventricular pressure (dP/dt_{max}) was used to quantify contractile strength.

A cardiac surface electrogram was recorded by placing one electrode at the base of the right ventricle and another at the base of the left ventricle. By examining the shape of this signal, we could identify ventricular escape and aberrantly conducted beats which were then excluded from analysis.

To measure the durations of local myocardial depolarization, we recorded monophasic action potentials (MAP) from the epicardial surface of the left ventricle using a new contact-electrode recording technique (Franz et al., 1983). The recording device consisted of two electrodes (sintered Ag-AgCl) mounted on the distal end of an L-shaped cantilever. One electrode, placed at the tip of the cantilever, was pressed against the epicardium by a spring-loading mechanism. The other electrode was positioned 5 mm proximal to the tip. Electrical contact between the proximal electrode and the heart was made through a small saline-soaked piece of foam rubber. The voltage across the two electrodes was differentially amplified to obtain the MAP signal. The time duration from the upstroke of the MAP to 90% repolarization will be referred to as the $MAPD_{90}$.

Protocols and Representation of Data

A digital computer (Intel, model iSBC 86/12A) controlled a pacer which supplied current to the electrodes. The computer was programmed to produce two types of pacing paradigms.

The first type of pacing pattern is shown by the set of schematized pacing spikes at the top of Figure 1A. During the "priming period," ventricles were paced by a series of 15–20 regularly timed stimuli delivered at a rate of 130 beats/min (equivalent to a steady state cycle length of 460 msec). The priming period was long enough so that the mechanical and electrical responses to stimulation had been at a steady state for at least 8 beats before an altered stimulus interval was imposed. If an escape or aberrantly conducted beat occurred during this time, such that a steady state was not observed for at least the last 5 beats of the priming period, another set of regularly timed stimuli was delivered before proceeding further. An extrasystolic stimulus followed the last regularly timed stimulus of the priming period by an interval called the extrasystolic interval(s) (ESI). A postextrasystolic stimulus was then delivered which followed the extrasystolic stimulus by an

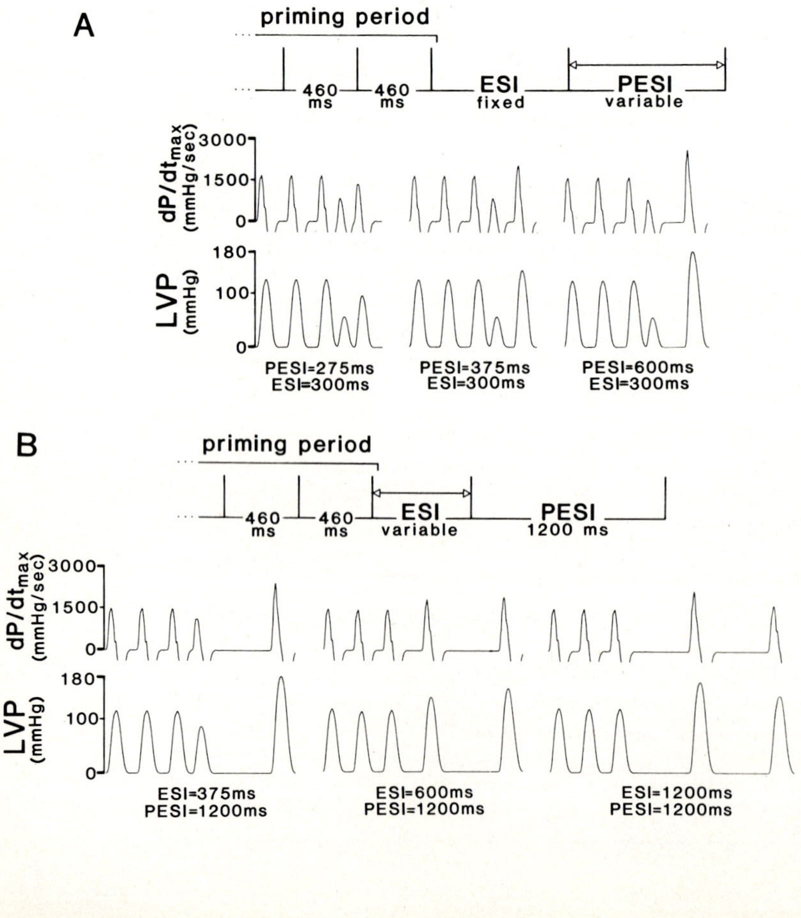

FIGURE 1. *Original records from a single, isovolumically beating isolated heart. Each frame shows three steady state responses, an extrasystolic response, and a postextrasystolic response for various stimulus intervals. Left ventricular volume was 23 ml. Panel A: top; schematized pacing spikes illustrating the stimulation protocol used to determine postextrasystolic mechanical restitution curves (see text for details). The extrasystolic interval (ESI) is the interval between the last stimulus in the priming period and the extrasystolic stimulus. The postextrasystolic interval (PESI) is the interval between extrasystolic and postextrasystolic stimuli. Bottom: ventricular responses illustrating recovery of postextrasystolic contractile strength as PESI was increased with ESI constant at 300 msec. LVP is left ventricular pressure. Panel B: top; schematized pacing spikes illustrating the stimulation protocol used to determine postextrasystolic potentiation curves and extrasystolic mechanical restitution curves simultaneously (see text for details). Bottom: ventricular responses illustrating simultaneous decline of postextrasystolic contractile strength and recovery of extrasystolic contractile strength with lengthening ESI.*

interval called the postextrasystolic interval(s) (PESI). This sequence was repeated with ESI held constant while PESI was changed with each repetition. The longest PESI was either 1200 msec, or, if this was not possible, that interval which was determined by the timing of ventricular escape beats. The shortest PESI was that which elicited a postextrasystolic contraction just after complete relaxation of the extrasystolic contraction. If PESI were shortened beyond this point, postextrasystolic beats became fused to extrasystoles so that the contractile strength of postextrasystoles, independent of the contribution from incompletely relaxed extrasystoles, could not be determined. By not allowing PESI to be this short, we excluded such fused beats from analysis.

The ventricular responses to the first type of stimulation protocol, illustrated by the original records in Figure 1A, were used to determine postextrasystolic mechanical restitution curves (defined below). When PESI was short, postextrasystolic dP/dt_{max} and left ventricular pressure (LVP) were small (leftmost frame of Figure 1A with PESI = 275 msec). As PESI was lengthened, postextrasystolic dP/dt_{max} and pressure increased monotonically (middle and rightmost frames of Figure 1A with PESI equal to 375 and 600 msec, respectively). The recovery of postextrasystolic contractile strength with lengthening PESI was graphically represented by postextrasystolic mechanical restitution curves (MRC_{pes}) which were constructed by plotting postextrasystolic dP/dt_{max} (normalized by the last preceding steady state dP/dt_{max} and expressed in %) as a function of PESI. Note that since ESI was fixed (ESI = 300 msec in the particular example shown in Figure 1A), extrasystolic dP/dt_{max} did not change with each repetition of the stimulation sequence.

The second type of pacing pattern (top of Fig. 1B) was similar to the first, except that, with each repetition of the sequence, ESI was varied while PESI was held constant at an interval of 1200 msec. The shortest ESI was that which elicited an extrasystolic contraction just after complete relaxation of the last steady state contraction, thereby excluding from analysis those extrasystoles which were "fused" to steady state beats. The longest ESI was 1200 msec.

The mechanical responses to the second type of stimulation pattern, illustrated by the original records in Figure 1B, were used to simultaneously determine extrasystolic mechanical restitution curves and postextrasystolic potentiation curves (both defined below). When ESI was short, the dP/dt_{max} and pressure of extrasystoles were small, whereas those indices for postextrasystoles were large (leftmost frame of Figure 1B with ESI = 375 msec). As ESI was lengthened, the contractile strength of extrasystoles increased while that of postextrasystoles decreased (middle and rightmost frames of Figure 1B with ESI equal to 600 and 1200 msec, respectively). The recovery of extrasystolic contractile strength with lengthening ESI was represented by extrasystolic mechanical restitution curves (MRC_{es}) which were constructed by plotting extrasystolic dP/dt_{max} (normalized by the last steady state dP/dt_{max} and expressed in %) as a function of ESI. The simultaneous decline of postextrasystolic contractile strength with lengthening ESI was graphically represented by postextrasystolic potentiation curves (PESPC). PESPC were constructed by plotting the dP/dt_{max} of postextrasystoles following long PESI equal to 1200 msec (normalized by the last steady state dP/dt_{max} and expressed in %) as a function of ESI.

Analysis

Monoexponential functions were fitted to the three types of curves discussed above (MRC_{pes}, MRC_{es}, and PESPC) by the Taylor series method of nonlinear least-squared error estimation (Draper and Smith, 1981).

The quality of the fit was estimated by the root mean squared error normalized by the magnitude of the exponential (RMSNE) and expressed in percent.

Ninety-five percent confidence intervals were determined for the time constants associated with the fitted monoexponential functions by using a linearized estimate of the variance-covariance matrix (Draper and Smith, 1981). Differences between two time constants were considered statistically significant ($P < 0.05$) when their 95% confidence intervals did not overlap.

Results

Effect of Different Extrasystolic Intervals on Postextrasystolic Mechanical Restitution

To establish a comprehensive description of postextrasystolic contractile strength as a function of both ESI and PESI, we determined a number of postextrasystolic mechanical restitution curves (MRC_{pes}) corresponding to a wide range of different ESI. Four major properties of postextrasystolic mechanical restitution were demonstrated by all 11 ventricles studied in this series. These properties are illustrated by the MRC_{pes} in Figure 2, which were measured from a single, representative ventricle. The four curves were obtained in a sequential manner over a period of 20–30 minutes and correspond to ESI values of 300, 350, 460, and 1200 msec. The

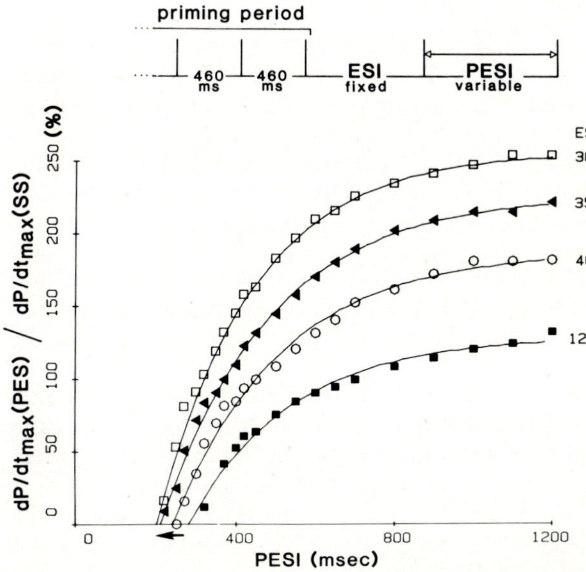

FIGURE 2. *Top: stimulation protocol used to determine postextrasystolic mechanical restitution curves (MRC_{pes}). Bottom: four MRC_{pes}s measured from a single ventricle. dP/dt_{max}(PES) and dP/dt_{max}(SS) are the extrasystolic and steady state dP/dt_{max}s. The four curves were obtained with ESI set equal to 300 (open square), 350 (filled triangle), 460 (open circle), and 1200 (filled square) msec. Solid curves are least-squares fitted monoexponential functions.*

stimulation pattern ("first type") used to obtain these curves is reproduced at the top of Figure 2.

First, the curves were well-described by a monoexponential rise to a plateau level, termed the "maximum postextrasystolic contractile response ($CR_{max,pes}$)." The solid curves in Figure 2 are monoexponential functions of the form:

$$\frac{dP/dt_{max}(PES)}{dP/dt_{max}(SS)} = CR_{max,pes}\{1-\exp[-(PESI-t_{o,pes})/T_{mrc,pes}]\}, \quad (1)$$

where $dP/dt_{max}(PES)$ and $dP/dt_{max}(SS)$ are defined in Table 1; $t_{o,pes}$ is the PESI-axis intercept of the fitted curve; and $T_{mrc,pes}$ is the time constant of postextrasystolic mechanical restitution. For each curve, $CR_{max,pes}$, $t_{o,pes}$ and $T_{mrc,pes}$ were chosen to provide the best least-squares fit to the data. The quality of the fit for the four MRC_{pes} in Figure 2 was quantified by root-mean-squared normalized errors (RMSNE) which were 1.54, 1.47, 2.60, and 3.10%, corresponding to ESI values of 300, 350, 460, and 1200 msec, respectively. Monoexponentials were fitted to the 53 MRC_{pes} obtained from all 11 ventricles in this series and the mean RMSNE (±SD) was 2.00 ± 0.63%, indicating that MRC_{pes} were well-fitted by the monoexponential form.

Second, $T_{mrc,pes}$ varied little with alterations in ESI, as illustrated by the four sequentially determined curves in Figure 2. Their time constants were 243, 278, 276, and 255 msec, corresponding to ESI of 300, 350, 460, and 1200 msec, respectively. More generally, there was no statistical significance ($P >$ 0.05) to the differences in time constant among the MRC_{pes} within 9 of 12 sequentially determined sets of curves (from 11 ventricles). In the other three sets of curves, there was only one MRC_{pes} whose time constant differed significantly ($P < 0.05$) from those of the other curves in each set. Furthermore, the variation of $T_{mrc,pes}$ with changes in ESI was small in all 12 sets of curves. This is demonstrated by normalizing the $T_{mrc,pes}$ of each set of curves with the $T_{mrc,pes}$ corresponding to an ESI of 460 msec, and noting that the mean normalized time constant (±SD) was 101 ± 12% (n = 41) (time constants of curves with ESI = 460 msec not included in the mean). Finally, there was no significant trend to the minor variations of normalized time constant that did exist. For each set of curves, the line of regression between normalized $T_{mrc,pes}$ and ESI was determined, and the average slope of this regression (±SD) was −0.02 ± 0.07%/msec (n = 12). The mean $T_{mrc,pes}$ (±SD) corresponding to an ESI of 460 msec was 181 ± 41 msec (n = 12).

The third general property was a leftward shift of the MRC_{pes} as ESI was reduced, as denoted by the arrow drawn in Figure 2. To quantify the amount of shift as a function of ESI, we plotted the PESI-axis intercept ($t_{o,pes}$) vs. ESI for each of the 12 sets of curves in this series (Fig. 3). For 52 of 53 curves

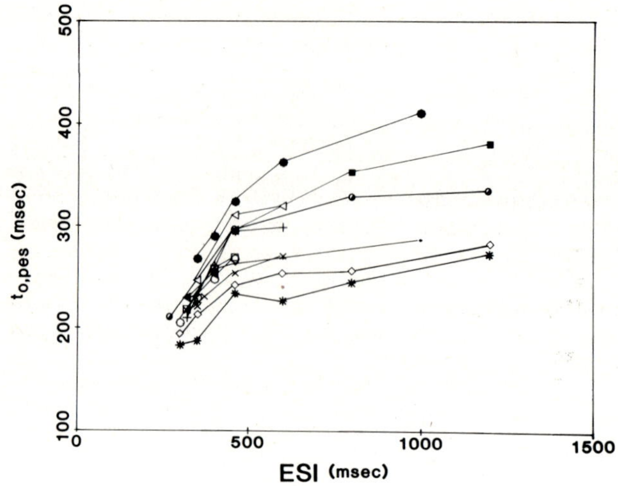

FIGURE 3. *Time-axis intercept of MRC_{pes} ($t_{o,pes}$) plotted as a function of ESI. The relationship demonstrates the "leftward shift" of MRC_{pes} along the PESI axis as ESI is shortened. Each symbol type corresponds to curves comprising a sequentially determined set of MRC_{pes} measured from within a single ventricle. Data from 12 sets of curves are shown.*

measured in this series, $t_{o,pes}$ declined every time ESI decreased.

Finally, the fully-restituted plateau value of the MRC_{pes} ($CR_{max,pes}$) increased as ESI was reduced in all 12 sets of curves. In Figure 2, for example, $CR_{max,pes}$ was 258, 228, 189, and 129% corresponding to ESI levels of 300, 350, 460, and 1200 msec. The details of this property will be deferred to the last section of the Results.

With regard to extrasystolic mechanical restitution, the MRC_{es} (defined in Methods in connection with the "second type" of pacing protocol) is equivalent to an MRC_{pes} with ESI set equal to the steady state cycle length, SSI (460 msec in this study). Then, from the first and second properties discussed above, we know that the MRC_{es} will rise monoexponentially with a time consant virtually equal to that of any MRC_{pes}.

Relationship between PESI-Axis Intercept and Action Potential Duration of Extrasystoles

To determine whether the leftward shift of MRC_{pes} with decrease in ESI was associated with the shortening of the extrasystolic action potential, we simultaneously determined the PESI-axis intercepts ($t_{o,pes}$) of MRC_{pes} and the duration of monophasic action potentials of extrasystoles in three ventricles. If a reduction of $t_{o,pes}$ is taken as a quantitative indicator of the amount of leftward shift, then a correlation between $t_{o,pes}$ and the duration of extrasystolic monophasic action potentials would suggest that the leftward shift and the shortening of extrasystolic action potentials were interrelated.

For each ventricle, $\Delta t_{o,pes}$ (defined as the difference of a given $t_{o,pes}$ from the $t_{o,pes}$ when ESI = 460 msec) was plotted vs. $\Delta MAPD_{90}$ (defined as the difference of an extrasystolic $MAPD_{90}$ from the steady state $MAPD_{90}$) (Fig. 4). The line of regression between $\Delta t_{o,pes}$ and $\Delta MAPD_{90}$ was determined for the pooled data from the three ventricles (slope = 1.32; y-axis intercept = −3.34 msec; $r = 0.88$; $n = 18$), and the results indicate that, as the extrasystolic action potential shortened, the MRC_{pes} shifted leftward by a comparable amount. Furthermore, the absolute values of steady state $MAPD_{90}$ and $t_{o,pes}$ when ESI was 460 msec were similar; their respective mean values (±SD) were 227 ± 21 and 246 ± 15 msec ($n = 3$). Hence, our results are consistent with the hypothesis that the onset of postextrasystolic mechanical restitution coincided with and may have been causally linked to repolarization of the extrasystolic action potential.

Dependence of $CR_{max,pes}$ upon ESI: Relationship to Extrasystolic Mechanical Restitution

To ascertain directly the variation of the maximum postextrasystolic contractile response of MRC_{pes} ($CR_{max,pes}$) as a function of ESI and determine whether this function was related to the mechanical restitution curve of extrasystoles, we simultaneously determined postextrasystolic potentiation curves (PESPC) and extrasystolic mechanical restitution curves (MRC_{es}) in this series of 10 ventricles. The stimulation protocol used to determine these curves ("second type") is reproduced at the top of Figure 5. Notice, with reference to the results shown in Figure 2, that all postextrasystoles arising from the long

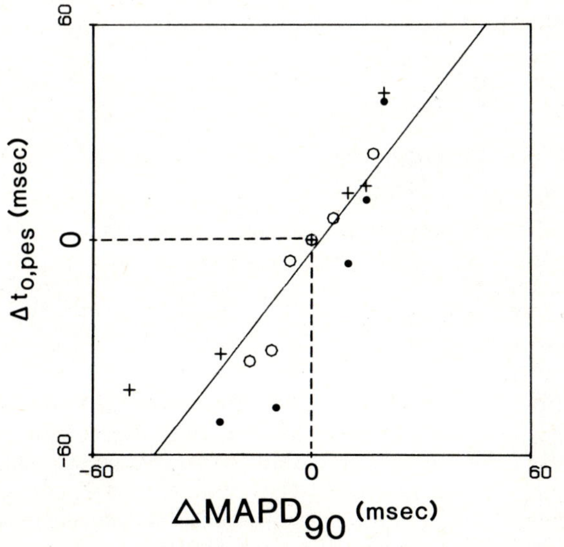

FIGURE 4. *Relation between changes in the minimum required PESI for $dP/dt_{max}(PES)$ to reach zero ($\Delta t_{o,pes}$) and changes in the duration of the extrasystolic monophasic action potential ($\Delta MAPD_{90}$). $\Delta t_{o,pes}$ is equal to the difference of the PESI-axis intercept of a given MRC_{pes} from that of an MRC_{pes} determined with ESI = 460 msec. Each symbol type corresponds to curves comprising a sequentially determined set of MRC_{pes} measured from within a single ventricle. Data from three ventricles are shown.*

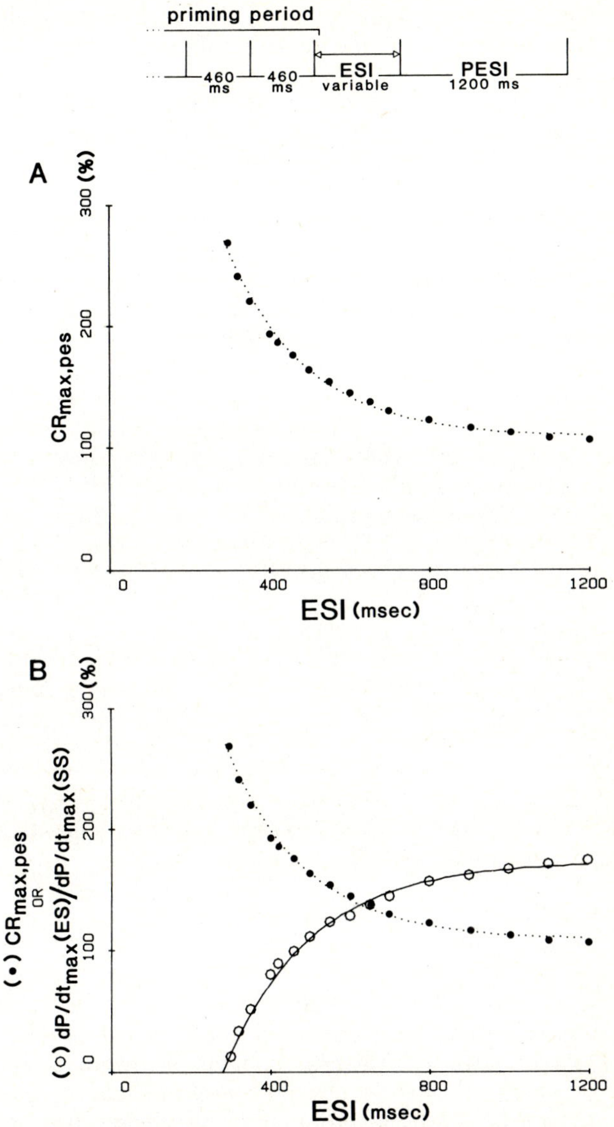

FIGURE 5. *Top: stimulation protocol used to obtain a postextrasystolic potentiation curve and extrasystolic mechanical restitution curve, simultaneously. Panel A: postextrasystolic potentiation curve (PESPC) demonstrating tendency for decline in postextrasystolic contractile strength with lengthening ESI. $CR_{max,pes}$ is the fully restituted postextrasystolic dP/dt_{max} normalized by $dP/dt_{max}(SS)$ and expressed in percent. The dotted curve is a least-squares fitted monoexponetial function. Panel B: simultaneously determined extrasystolic mechanical restitution curve (MRC_{es}) (open circles and solid curve) and PESPC replotted from panel A (filled circles and dotted curve), illustrating that the time course of postextrasystolic potentiation and of mechanical restitution are governed by similar time constants. $dP/dt_{max}(ES)$ is the dP/dt_{max} of extrasystoles. The solid curve is a least-squares fitted monoexponential function.*

PESI in this protocol (1200 msec) would manifest almost fully-restituted plateau levels of contractile strength. Therefore, postextrasystolic contractile strength was nearly equivalent, after normalization by the steady state response and expressed in percent, to $CR_{max,pes}$.

The PESPC (Fig. 5A) and the MRC_{es} (open circles,

Fig. 5B), which were simultaneously obtained from a single, representative ventricle, illustrate three major results.

First, postextrasystolic potentiation curves decreased monoexponentially to a plateau level as described by a function of the form:

$$CR_{max,pes} = B + A\,(\exp[-(ESI-t_{o,es})/T_{pespc}]), \quad (2)$$

where B is the plateau level and A expresses the amplitude of the PESPC; $t_{o,es}$ is the ESI-axis intercept for the simultaneously determined MRC_{es}; and T_{pespc} is the time constant of the PESPC. The dotted curve fitted to the PESPC in Figure 5A is derived from Equation 2 with A, B, and T_{pespc} chosen to provide the best least-squares fit to the data. In this ventricle, A = 171%, B = 108%, and T_{pespc} = 199 msec, with a root-mean-squared normalized error (RMSNE) of 2.59%. Monoexponentials of the form in Equation 2 were fitted to all 10 PESPC obtained from the 10 ventricles in this series and the mean RMSNE (±SD) was 2.59 ± 0.87%, demonstrating that all PESPC were essentially monoexponential in shape. The mean value for the time constant of the PESPC (T_{pespc}) (±SD) was 176 ± 18 msec. The mean value (±SD) for A was 168 ± 32%, and for B was 105 ± 13%.

Second, as noted earlier in the Results, extrasystolic mechanical restitution curves (MRC_{es}) are a subset of MRC_{pes}, so that MRC_{es} could be described by a function of the form:

$$\frac{dP/dt_{max}(ES)}{dP/dt_{max}(SS)} = CR_{max,es}\,\{1-\exp[-(ESI-t_{o,es})/T_{mrc,es}]\}, \quad (3)$$

where $dP/dt_{max}(ES)$ and $dP/dt_{max}(SS)$ are defined in Table 1; $CR_{max,es}$ is the plateau level of the curve; $t_{o,es}$ is the ESI-axis intercept for the fitted curve; and $T_{mrc,es}$ is the time constant of extrasystolic mechanical restitution. The solid curve fitted to the MRC_{es} in Figure 5B (open circles) represents Equation 3 with $CR_{max,es}$, $t_{o,es}$, and $T_{mrc,es}$ chosen to provide the best least-squares fit to the data. In this case, $CR_{max,es}$ = 173%, $t_{o,es}$ = 276 msec, and $T_{mrc,es}$ = 216 msec. The root-mean-squared normalized error (RMSNE) for this curve was 1.80%. Monoexponentials of the form in Equation 3 were fitted to the 10 MRC_{es} obtained from the 10 ventricles in this series and the mean RMSNE (±SD) was 1.93 ± 0.40%. The mean parameter values (±SD) were: $T_{mrc,es}$ = 189 ± 30 msec, $CR_{max,es}$ = 166 ± 23%, $t_{o,es}$ = 284 ± 32 msec.

Third, PESPC and MRC_{es} were closely interrelated in that the time constants of curves obtained from the same ventricle were nearly identical. This interrelationship is visually emphasized in Figure 5B which displays on the same set of axes the PESPC (filled circles and dotted curve replotted from Fig. 5A) and the simultaneously measured MRC_{es} (open circles and solid curve). In Figure 5B, the time constant of the MRC_{es} ($T_{mrc,es}$) was 216 msec, whereas that for the PESPC (t_{pespc}) was 199 msec. The mean difference between the two time constants (±SD) for pairs of curves measured in the same ventricle ($T_{mrc,es} - T_{pespc}$) was only −13 ± 23 msec (n = 10). The small difference in time constant between simultaneously obtained MRC_{es} and PESPC was not statistically significant ($P > 0.05$) in 9 of the 10 ventricles studied.

Discussion

We showed, for the isolated canine ventricle, that the dependence of postextrasystolic contractile strength upon preceding stimulus intervals was determined by four quantitative properties:

1. Postextrasystolic mechanical restitution follows a monoexponential rise to a plateau (Eq. 1, Fig. 2).
2. The time constant of postextrasystolic mechanical restitution ($T_{mrc,pes}$) was invariant with changes in ESI, and was virtually the same as the time constant of restitution following steady state beats ($T_{mrc,es}$).
3. The time to the onset of postextrasystolic mechanical restitution ($t_{o,pes}$) decreased as extrasystoles became more premature (Fig. 3). This decrease was correlated with the shortening of extrasystolic action potentials (Fig. 4).
4. The maximum postextrasystolic contractile response ($CR_{max,pes}$) is a decreasing monoexponential function of ESI (Eq. 2, Fig. 5A), and the time constant of this decrease (T_{pespc}) was approximately equal to the time constant of extrasystolic mechanical restitution ($T_{mrc,es}$).

We will focus upon three aspects of these results: first, the synthesis of the above properties into a single equation which describes postextrasystolic potentiation; second, the relationship of our results to past work, both at the muscle and ventricular levels; and third, the interpretation of our results in terms of currently proposed e-c coupling models.

Single-Equation Description of Postextrasystolic Contractile Strength

The properties listed above can be condensed into a single equation which provides a comprehensive description of postextrasystolic contractile strength following pacing at a given steady rate (130 beats/min, in our study). Based upon the second and fourth properties outlined above, we can make the approximation that all the time constants ($T_{mrc,pes}$, $T_{mrc,es}$ and T_{pespc}) are equal, so that, henceforth, we will refer to only one time constant designated T. Then, upon combining Equations 1 and 2, we have the following simple expression which describes the normalized contractile strength of *any* postextrasystolic beat preceded by intervals within the ranges explored in this study:

$$\frac{dP/dt_{max}(PES)}{dP/dt_{max}(SS)} = \{A\,(\exp[-(ESI-t_{o,es})/T]) + B\} \times \{1-\exp[-(PESI-t_{o,pes})/T]\}, \quad (4)$$

where $t_{o,pes}$ varies in parallel with the $MAPD_{90}$ of extrasystolic beats (Fig. 4), and $t_{o,es}$ has been shown to correlate closely with $MAPD_{90}$ of steady state beats (Burkhoff et al., 1984a). This equation describes a provocative phenomenon: interval-dependent postextrasystolic contractile behavior dominated by essentially one time constant.

Since it has been shown in the isolated canine heart (Burkhoff et al., 1984a) and in isolated muscle (Rumberger and Reichel, 1972) that the time constant of extrasystolic mechanical restitution is independent of the steady state stimulation rate, we believe that our description for postextrasystoles (Eq. 4) will hold for priming period rates other than 130 beats/min. Only the particular values for A, B, and $t_{o,es}$ would differ for different priming period rates.

Relationship to Past Work

Our results are very similar to phenomena which have been observed, at least in part, in isolated mammalian cardiac muscle. Unfortunately, a full comparison is not possible because either some of the protocols required for our description have not been pursued, or comparable quantitative analysis of the data has not been performed.

Postextrasystolic mechanical restitution curves, MRC_{pes}, have been measured in isolated papillary muscles or ventricular trabeculae of the cat (Hoffman et al., 1956), rabbit (Johnson et al., 1964; Wohlfart, 1979), and dog (Anderson et al., 1976). Qualitatively, these MRC_{pes} appear as if they could have been described by a monoexponential time course whose time constant was insensitive to changes in ESI; however, explicit analysis to determine these properties was not performed. Johnson and coworkers (1964) did quantify their data by fitting functions to their MRC_{pes}. However, since they used nested exponential functions to describe their curves, it is difficult to determine whether monoexponential functions with a single time constant would have fit their data as well.

Postextrasystolic potentiation curves (PESPC) and extrasystolic mechanical restitution curves (MRC_{es}) were simultaneously determined in isolated papillary muscles of the cat (Bass, 1975) and rabbit (Wohlfart, 1979). PESPC declined with a time course approximately equal to that of the rise of MRC_{es} with lengthening ESI, but there was no quantitative analysis to determine whether this was actually the case. In earlier work, Hoffman et al. (1956) and Braveny and Kruta (1958) measured curves that were similar to our PESPC, except that the PESI was varied with changing ESI such that ESI + PESI = 2 × SSI. Their "pseudo PESPC" appeared to decline in a fashion reciprocal to the rise of MRC_{es}.

The leftward shifts of MRC_{pes} that we observed in the ventricle with shortening of ESI were probably observed in isolated cardiac muscle by Johnson et al. (1964) and Anderson et al. (1976), but they did not specifically demonstrate this phenomenon. Even so, the ventricular behavior might have been anticipated on the basis of previous electrophysiological studies on isolated muscle. Voltage clamp studies with sheep Purkinje fibers (Gibbons and Fozzard, 1971; Lipsius et al., 1982) and with cat ventricular tissue (Tritthart et al., 1973; Trautwein et al., 1975) suggested that the processes of mechanical restitution are voltage dependent and proceed at appreciable rates only after the membrane has repolarized beyond a certain potential range (~ −35 to −60 mV). Then, shortening of extrasystolic action potentials with increased prematurity (Boyett and Jewell, 1978) would allow mechanical restitution to begin sooner and thereby cause a leftward shift of MRC_{pes}. In our previous studies with isolated canine ventricles (Burkhoff et al., 1984a) and in humans (Franz et al., 1983), we were able to verify a similar prediction that the leftward shifts of extrasystolic mechanical restitution curves (MRC_{es}) correlated with the shortening of steady state action potentials when the heart rate used in the priming period was increased. That $\Delta t_{o,pes}$ and $\Delta MAPD_{90}$ were not exactly equal may relate to the fact that $\Delta t_{o,pes}$ is a global, ventricular property, whereas $\Delta MAPD_{90}$ is a local epicardial property. Then, with slight regional variations of action potential duration and time of activation (Watanabe et al., 1983), $\Delta t_{o,pes}$ might differ somewhat from $\Delta MAPD_{90}$.

Our description of postextrasystolic potentiation also appears to be in general agreement with the results obtained from in situ canine ventricular preparations. Anderson et al. (1976) measured MRC_{pes} which rise monotonically to a plateau. Elzinga et al. (1981) measured PESPC which decline monotonically to a plateau. However, in either case, no quantitative analysis was directed at determining whether the curves were monoexponential.

Even if more extensive protocols and analysis had been performed in these in situ studies, the quantitative comparison of in situ ventricular data to our results would remain problematic. Those in situ ventricles were ejecting and filling, not isovolumically contracting, so that measured contractile strength (usually dP/dt_{max}) was not only a function of stimulus interval, but also of changing preload (Starling mechanism) and afterload (variable severity of dP/dt_{max} attenuation by ejection) (Burkoff et al., 1984a). In situ force-interval relations using a preload and afterload insensitive index of contractile strength, such as E_{es} (Sagawa, 1981), will have to be determined before a direct quantitative comparison of our results to the in situ ventricle can be made.

Interpretation of Results

The simplicity of our phenomenological results—that the functions which describe extra- and post-extrasystolic contractile strength (MRC_{es}, MRC_{pes}, and PESPC) are all monoexponential with the same time constant—suggested that it might be relatively simple to understand the mechanism underlying these phenomena. Yet, it was not at all clear whether currently proposed models of e-c coupling (Wood et al., 1969; Beeler and Reuter, 1970; Gibbons and Fozzard, 1971; Morad and Goldman, 1973; Edman and Johannsson, 1976; Wohlfart, 1979) could provide a straightforward explanation for our findings.

This was because these hypotheses were proposed as a set of qualitative descriptions of individual e-c coupling events, while prediction of the PESPC and its relationship to the MRC_{es} or MRC_{pes} would require quantitative integration of the results of many individual steps occurring over two cardiac cycles. We therefore developed the following quantitative formulation of an e-c coupling model which makes it possible to visualize clearly how the monoexponential nature (with identical time constants) of our descriptive functions (MRC_{es}, MRC_{pes}, PESPC) could, in fact, represent the net, ensemble behavior of the individual steps which comprise those currently proposed e-c coupling hypotheses.

Figure 6A depicts a model cardiac cell whose e-c

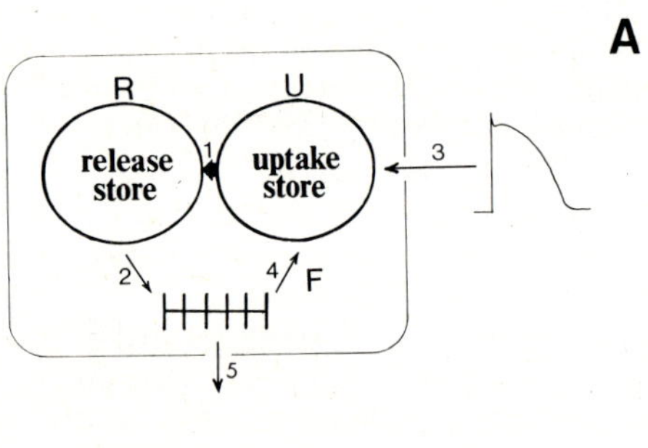

FIGURE 6. *Hypothesized e-c coupling events within a single cardiac cell. Panel A: calcium fluxes during a single cardiac cycle. The internal store is functionally divided into an uptake store (U) and release store (R) between which sequestered calcium gradually "moves" during the repolarized interval between beats. The myofilaments are represented by the cross-hatched line. F is the recirculation fraction. Panel B: intracellular events which relate most directly to the determination of extrasystolic contractile strength. R(es) is the amount of calcium released to the myoplasm during an extrasystole. U(es) is the amount of calcium left in the internal store at the time of the extrasystolic stimulus. Panel C: intracellular events which contribute most directly to the determination of postextrasystolic contractile strength. I(es) is the amount of calcium which enters the cell to be sequestered by the uptake store during an extrasystole.*

coupling properties are a representative composite of those currently proposed in the literature. The general attributes of such a model are developed below.

A common feature of the models cited above which is crucial for the prediction of our results is that the internal store of calcium, presumably the sarcoplasmic reticulum, has the property that sequestered calcium gradually becomes more releasable in the interim between beats. In the present formulation, this is *functionally represented* by splitting the internal store into an "uptake store" (labeled U) and "release store" (labeled R). Calcium sequestered by the internal store first enters the U store, and then "moves" slowly to the R store with a monoexponential time course characterized by an invariant time constant T (Fig. 6A, 1). *The two compartments and the movement of calcium between them need not be interpreted in an anatomical sense; they could just as well be considered a convenient representation for the recovery of releaseability from a single internal store compartment* [one example of which might be the recovery of sensitivity to Ca^{++}-induced Ca^{++} release from sarcoplasmic reticulum (Fabiato, 1983)].

Upon stimulation, the calcium in the R store is completely released into the myoplasmic space (Fig. 6A, 2), and an action potential is elicited which gives rise to calcium entry into the cell (Fig. 6A, 3). Most of this entry calcium is thought to enter the U store directly, while contractile strength in that beat is assumed to reflect primarily the amount of internally released calcium (Fozzard, 1977). Accordingly, in this formulation, contractile strength and the amount of released calcium are related by a constant of proportionality. The assumption of linearity is supported by the finding in aequorin-injected canine Purkinje fibers that the relation between dF/dt_{max} and estimated peak intracellular [Ca^{++}]-resting intracellular [Ca^{++}] is approximately linear for variably restituted contractions (Yue et al., 1984), and the approximation that ventricular pressure relates linearly to muscle stress (see Discussion in Burkhoff et al., 1984b).

Calcium bound to the myofilaments and in the myoplasm is removed through two pathways. A "recirculation fraction" (F) of the released calcium "recirculates" back to the U store (Fig. 6A, 4) (Morad and Goldman, 1973). The remainder of the released calcium is extruded from the cell (Fig. 6A, 5). Finally, it is postulated that there is no movement of calcium from U to R stores until the membrane is repolarized beyond a certain range. This idea is based upon our leftward shift results and the voltage clamp data discussed in connection with these phenomena.

Having discussed the general features of the model, we now specify the particular form of the events associated with the determination of extrasystolic contractile strength (Fig. 6B). Let $R_{max}(ss)$ be the amount of calcium in the U store just before any calcium moves from U to R stores following the steady state contraction which precedes an extrasystole. The amount of calcium released on the extrasystolic beat (R(es)) is therefore equal to $R_{max}(ss)$ multiplied by an exponential factor:

$$R(es) = R_{max}(ss)\ \{1-\exp[-(ESI-t_{o,es})/T]\}. \quad (5a)$$

Since calcium is assumed to move from uptake to release stores only after the membrane has repolarized, the numerator of the argument of the exponential is proportional to ESI − $t_{o,es}$, where $t_{o,es}$ approximates the action potential duration in the preceding steady state beat (Burkhoff, 1984a). The amount of calcium left in the uptake compartment at the time of the extrasystolic stimulus [U(es)] must be the difference between $R_{max}(ss)$ and R(es) (Eq. 5b):

$$U(es) = R_{max}(ss)\ \{\exp[-(ESI-t_{o,es})/T]\}. \quad (5b)$$

Recalling that we have assumed that contractile strength and amount of released calcium are linearly related, and defining R(ss) as the amount of calcium released on a steady state beat, we obtain Equation 5c as the model's expression for an extrasystolic mechanical restitution curve (MRC_{es}):

$$\frac{dP/dt_{max}(ES)}{dP/dt_{max}(SS)} = \frac{R_{max}(ss)}{R(ss)} \times \{1-\exp[-(ESI-t_{o,es})/T_{mrc,es}]\}. \quad (5c)$$

Having described the state of the internal store when the extrasystole occurs, we next explore the details of events which contribute most directly to postextrasystolic contractile strength. There are three sources of calcium for postextrasystoles (Fig. 6C). Consider first the amount of calcium [I(es)] which enters the cell via the extrasystolic action potential to be sequestered by the U store. A number of investigators have provided evidence suggesting that the magnitude of the slow inward Ca^{++} current is inversely related to the amount of calcium released (Edmands et al., 1968; Hiraoka and Sano, 1976; Simurda et al., 1976; Tsien and Marban, 1982). To account for this, I(es) is assumed to vary inversely with R(es) such that:

$$I(es) = I_{max} - hR(es), \quad (6)$$

where I_{max} is a positive constant equal to the maximum possible value of I(es) and h is a positive constant equal to the intensity of the inverse relation. The second calcium source which contributes to the postextrasystole is the amount of calcium which recirculated back to the U store, F × R(es). Finally, there is the amount of calcium which was left in the U store at the time of the extrasystolic stimulus [U(es) in Eq. 5b]. If we consider only fully restituted postextrasystolic responses, there is sufficient time for all the calcium in the internal store—the calcium which came into the U store through the membrane, the recirculated calcium, and the calcium that was in the U store at the time of the extrasystolic stimulus—to move to the R store by the time of the postextrasystolic stimulus. Thus, the amount of calcium released on fully restituted postextrasystoles would be simply:

$$F\ R(es) + U(es) + I(es). \quad (7)$$

Substituting into Equation 7 for R(es), U(es), and I(es) from Equations 5a, 5b, and 6, respectively, and normalizing the result by R(ss), we have the following model prediction for a postextrasystolic potentiation curve (PESPC):

$$CR_{max,pes} = \underbrace{\left[\frac{R_{max}(ss)}{R(ss)}(F-h) + \frac{I_{max}}{R(ss)}\right]}_{B} + \underbrace{\left[\frac{R_{max}(ss)}{R(ss)}(1-F+h)\right]}_{A}\left(\exp\left[\frac{-(ESI-t_{o,es})}{T}\right]\right). \quad (8)$$

After integrating the events of the past two cardiac cycles, we see in Equation 8 that the e-c coupling model of Figure 6 predicts exactly the experimentally determined PESPC form (Eq. 2), with the indicated model interpretations for the constants B and A. The important predictions of the model (contained in Eqs. 5c and 8) are: (1) not only should the MRC_{es} follow a monoexponential time course, but also the PESPC, and (2) the time constants characterizing the MRC_{es} and PESPC should be the same.

Furthermore, it is simple to show from Equation 8, that the model accurately predicts the experimentally derived form of the MRC_{pes}. Calcium movement from U to R stores during the repolarized period preceding postextrasystoles is also postulated to follow a monoexponential time course with time constant T. Then, the model prediction for a MRC_{pes} is simply Equation 8 multiplied by an exponential time function which increases from zero to unity as a function of the repolarized interval (approximated by PESI-$t_{o,pes}$):

$$\frac{dP/dt_{max}(PES)}{dP/dt_{max}(SS)} = \{A(\exp[-(ESI-t_{o,es})/T]) + B\} \times \{1-\exp[-(PESI-t_{o,pes})/T]\}, \quad (9)$$

where the model predictions for A and B are given in Equation 8. Equation 9 agrees with the experimentally derived form for the MRC_{pes} (Eq. 4).

In summary, interval dependence of extrasystolic and postextrasystolic contractile strength that is described by essentially a single time constant (Eq. 4) can be quantitatively explained by an e-c coupling model in which calcium releaseability from an internal store increases with a monoexponential time course, provided that other processes involved in determining contractile strength (e.g., Eq. 6) relate linearly to the amount of calcium released. If such an interpretation is correct, then mechanical restitution and postextrasystolic potentiation curves represent macroscopic phenomena which bear a direct and interpretable relation to events on a much smaller scale. As such, these curves may provide valuable insights into the intracellular events of the heart in both health and disease.

We acknowledge the inspiration and encouragement of Prof. Dr. Jochen Schaefer. We gratefully thank Dr. Joe Alexander, Jr., Dr. Robert O. Oikawa, and Dr. Eduardo Marban for their perceptive editorial advice. Kenneth Rent's excellent surgical skills aided greatly in this study.

This work was presented in part at the American Heart Association Annual Scientific Sessions, Anaheim, California, November 1983 (Yue et al., 1983).

This work was supported by U.S. Public Health Service Research Grants RO1-HL-14903 and HL-30552.

D. T. Yue was supported by Medical Scientist Training Program Grant 5T32GM070309007, D. Burkhoff was supported by Biomedical Engineering Training Grant 5T32GM07057, and M. R. Franz was supported by a Research Fellowship Grant from the Deutsche Forschungsgemeinschaft.

Address for reprints: David T. Yue, Traylor Building, Room 223, Department of Biomedical Engineering, The Johns Hopkins University, School of Medicine, 720 Rutland Avenue, Baltimore, Maryland 21205.

Received April 21, 1984; accepted for publication December 5, 1984.

References

Anderson PAW, Rankin JS, Arentzen CE, Anderson RW, Johnson EA (1976) Evaluation of the force-frequency relationship as a descriptor of the inotropic state of canine left ventricular myocardium. Circ Res **39:** 832–839

Anderson PAW, Manring A, Serwer GA, Benson DW, Edwards SB, Armstrong BE, Sterba RJ, Floyd RD (1979) The force-interval relationship of the left ventricle. Circulation **60:** 334–348

Bass BG (1975) Enhanced contractility during relaxation of cat papillary muscle. Am J Physiol **228:** 1708–1716

Beeler GW, Reuter H (1970) The relation between membrane potential, membrane currents and activation of contraction in ventricular myocardial fibers. J Physiol (Lond) **207:** 211–229

Boyett MR, Jewell BR (1978) A study of the factors responsible for rate-dependent shortening of the action potential in mammalian ventricular muscle. J Physiol (Lond) **285:** 359–380

Braveny P, Kruta V (1958) Dissociation de deux facteurs: Restitution et potentiation dans l'action de l'amplitude de la contraction du myocarde. Arch Int Physiol Biochim **66:** 633–652

Burkhoff D, Yue DT, Franz MR, Hunter WC, Sagawa K (1984a) Mechanical restitution of canine left ventricles. Am J Physiol **246:** H8–H16

Burkhoff D, Yue DT, Franz MR, Hunter WC, Sunagawa K, Maughan WL, Sagawa K (1984b) Quantitative comparison of the force-interval relationships of the canine right and left ventricles. Circ Res **54:** 468–473

Cranefield PF (1965) The force of contraction of extrasystoles and potentiation of force of the postextrasystolic contraction: A historical review. Bull NY Acad Med **41:** 419–427

Draper NR, Smith H (1981) Applied Regression Analysis, ed 2. New York, Wiley-Interscience, pp 94, 462–468, 472

Edman KAP, Johannsson M (1976) The contractile state of rabbit papillary muscle in relation to stimulation frequency. J Physiol (Lond) **254:** 565–581

Edmands RE, Greenspan K, Fisch C (1968) Electrophysiological correlates of contractile change in mammalian and amphibian myocardium. Cardiovasc Res **3:** 252–260

Elzinga G, Lab MJ, Noble MIM, Papadoyannis DE, Pidgeon J, Seed A, Wohlfart B (1981) The action-potential duration and contractile response of the intact heart related to the preceding interval and the preceding beat in the dog and cat. J Physiol (Lond) **314:** 481–500

Fabiato A (1983) Calcium-induced release of calcium from cardiac sarcoplasmic reticulum. Am J Physiol **245:** C1–C14

Fozzard HA (1977) Heart: Excitation-contraction coupling. Annu Rev Physiol **39:** 201–220

Franz MR, Schaefer J, Schottler M, Seed AW, Noble MIM (1983) Electrical and mechanical restitution of the human heart at different rates of stimulation. Circ Res **53:** 815–822

Gibbons WR, Fozzard HA (1971) Voltage dependence and time dependence of contraction in sheep cardiac Purkinje fibers. Circ Res **28:** 446–460

Hiraoka M, Sano T (1976) Role of slow inward current in the genesis of ventricular arrhythmia. Jpn Circ J **40:** 1419–1427

Hoffman BF, Bindler E, Suckling EE (1956) Postextrasystolic potentiation of contraction in cardiac muscle. Am J Physiol **185:** 95–102

Johnson EA (1979) Force-interval relationship of cardiac muscle. *In* Handbook of Physiology. The Cardiovascular System, vol I, edited by SR Geiger, RM Berne. Washington, D.C., American Physiological Society, pp 475–496

Johnson EA, Rowe MJ, Vaughan PC (1964) A quantitative description of short term changes in the force of contraction of rabbit papillary muscle with the pattern of stimulation. Aust J Exp Biol Med Sci **42:** 197–208

Lipsius SL, Fozzard HA, Gibbons WR (1982) Voltage and time dependence of restitution in heart. Am J Physiol **243:** H68–H76

Morad M, Goldman Y (1973) Excitation-contraction coupling in heart muscle: Membrane control of development of tension. Prog Biophys Mol Biol **27:** 257–313

Reichel H, Rumberger E, Schaefer J, Schwarzkopf HJ (1974) Frequency potentiation in the human myocardium. Basic Res Cardiol **69:** 11–20

Rumberger E, Reichel H (1972) The force-frequency relationship: A comparative study between warm- and cold-blooded animals. Pflugers Arch **332:** 206–217

Sagawa K (1981) Editorial. The end-systolic pressure-volume relation of the ventricle: Definition, modifications and clinical use. Circulation **63:** 1223–1227

Simurda J, Simurdova M, Braveny P, Sumbera J (1976) Slow inward current and action potentials of papillary muscles under non-steady state conditions. Pflugers Arch **362:** 209–218

Suga H, Sagawa K (1974) Instantaneous pressure-volume relationships and their ratio in the excised, supported canine left ventricle. Circ Res **35:** 117–126

Trautwein W, McDonald TF, Tripathi O (1975) Calcium conductance and tension in mammalian ventricular muscle. Pflugers Arch **534:** 55–74

Tritthart H, Kaufmann R, Volkmer HP, Bayer R, Krause H (1973) Ca- movement controlling myocardial contractility. I. Voltage, current and time dependence of mechanical activity under voltage clamp conditions (cat papillary muscles and trabeculae). Pflugers Arch **338:** 207–231

Tsien RW, Marban E (1982) Digitalis and slow inward current in heart muscle: Evidence for regulatory effects of intracellular calcium on calcium channels. *In* Advances in Pharmacology and Therapeutics II, vol 3, Cardio-Renal and Cell Pharmacology, edited by H Yoshida, Y Hagihara, S Ebashi. Oxford, Pergamon Press, pp 217–225

Watanabe T, Rautaharju PM, McDonald TF (1983) Regional differences in the action potential of guinea pig ventricle (abstr). Circulation **68** (suppl III): 85

Wohlfart B (1979) Relationship between peak force, action potential duration and stimulus interval in rabbit myocardium. Acta Physiol Scand **106:** 395–409

Wood EH, Heppner RL, Weidmann S (1969) Inotropic effects of electric currents. Circ Res **24:** 409–445

Yue DT, Burkhoff D, Franz MR, Hunter WC, Sagawa K (1983) Relationship of postextrasystolic potentiation to mechanical restitution in isolated, blood-perfused canine ventricles (abstr). Circulation **68:** (suppl III): 370

Yue DT, Wier WG, Sagawa K (1984) Direct measurement of the intracellular $[Ca^{2+}]$ transients underlying the cardiac force-interval relationship (abstr). VIth Proceedings of the Cardiovascular Systems Dynamics Society

INDEX TERMS: Cardiac force-interval relationship • Postextrasystolic potentiation • Mechanical restitution • Excitation-contraction coupling • Isolated ventricle

Mechanisms of Augmented Segment Shortening in Nonischemic Areas during Acute Ischemia of the Canine Left Ventricle

Wilbur Y.W. Lew, Zhengyu Chen, Brian Guth, and James W. Covell
From the Cardiovascular Division, Department of Medicine, University of California, San Diego, and San Diego Veterans Administration Medical Center, San Diego, California

SUMMARY. To examine the interaction between normal and nonischemic areas of the left ventricle during acute ischemia, we implanted midwall ultrasonic segment length gauges in the ischemic zone and in nonischemic areas of the canine left ventricle. During acute ischemia, end-diastolic pressure and segment length in the nonischemic areas increased. There was no change from control in the segment length at the time of aortic valve opening and closure. Thus, in nonischemic areas, total segment shortening, as measured by the percent change in segment length from the time of end-diastole to aortic valve closure, increased. This was due to an increase in isovolumic shortening (end-diastole to aortic valve opening) with no change in ejection shortening (aortic valve opening to closure). The progressive increase in isovolumic shortening in nonischemic areas over time was directly paralleled by the progressive development of the isovolumic lengthening or bulge in the ischemic zone. Nonischemic areas, whether adjacent, on the opposite wall, or distant to the ischemic zone, all behaved similarly. Adrenergic blockade did not qualitatively alter these findings. We conclude that acute ischemia induces a mechanical disadvantage which is greater than just the loss of contractile function by the ischemic segment. Despite the apparent hyperfunction of nonischemic areas, the increased total segment shortening is expended in stretching the ischemic zone during isovolumic systole. As a result, there is no significant "compensatory" increase in ejection shortening in nonischemic areas. The results from the present study indicate that augmented total segment shortening in nonischemic areas is due to a combination of the Frank-Starling mechanism and regional intraventricular unloading of the nonischemic into the ischemic areas. **(*Circ Res 56: 351–358, 1985*)**

DURING acute ischemia of the left ventricle, an increase in systolic shortening has been measured in nonischemic areas in experimental animals by a variety of techniques, including ultrasonic segment gauges (Theroux et al., 1974, 1976, 1977; Heyndrickx et al., 1975; Molaug et al., 1983), epicardial strain gauges (Nakano, 1966; Pashkow et al., 1977), ultrasonic wall thickness gauges (Savage et al., 1981; Nakamura et al., 1982) and echocardiography (Kerber et al., 1976). Some studies using epicardial strain gauges did not find an apparent hyperfunction of nonischemic areas (Banka and Helfant, 1974; Vokonas et al., 1976; Wyatt et al., 1976), indicating that the effects may not always be reflected transmurally. An increase in systolic motion in nonischemic areas has been noted in patients by echocardiography (Corya et al., 1975; Nieminen and Heikkila, 1976) and angiography (Rigaud et al., 1979; Stack et al., 1983; Sheehan et al., 1983).

The hyperfunction of nonischemic areas is thought to be due primarily to utilization of the Frank-Starling mechanism (Theroux et al., 1974; Molaug et al., 1983), although some have suggested increased sympathetic stimulation as the primary mechanism (Nakano, 1966; Pashkow et al., 1977; Rigaud et al., 1979). The increased segment shortening by nonischemic areas is thought to compensate for the loss of systolic function in the ischemic zone. This study was undertaken to clarify the mechanisms and effectiveness of the apparent hyperfunction in nonischemic areas during acute ischemia, and to define the nature of the interaction between ischemic and nonischemic segments.

Methods

Instrumentation

Ten mongrel dogs of either sex weighing between 13 and 30 kg were anesthetized with intravenous sodium pentobarbital (25 mg/kg), intubated, and respiration was supported with a Harvard respirator. The heart was exposed through a midline sternotomy and bilateral 5th interspace thorocotomy, and supported in a pericardial cradle. A 7F high fidelity micromanometer-tipped (Millar, model PC 574) catheter was advanced into the left ventricle from the left carotid artery. A 100-cm 7F fluid-filled pigtail catheter, attached to a Statham P23 DB transducer, was advanced into the left ventricle from the left femoral artery. Pressures from the two catheters were matched, then the fluid-filled catheter was withdrawn into the

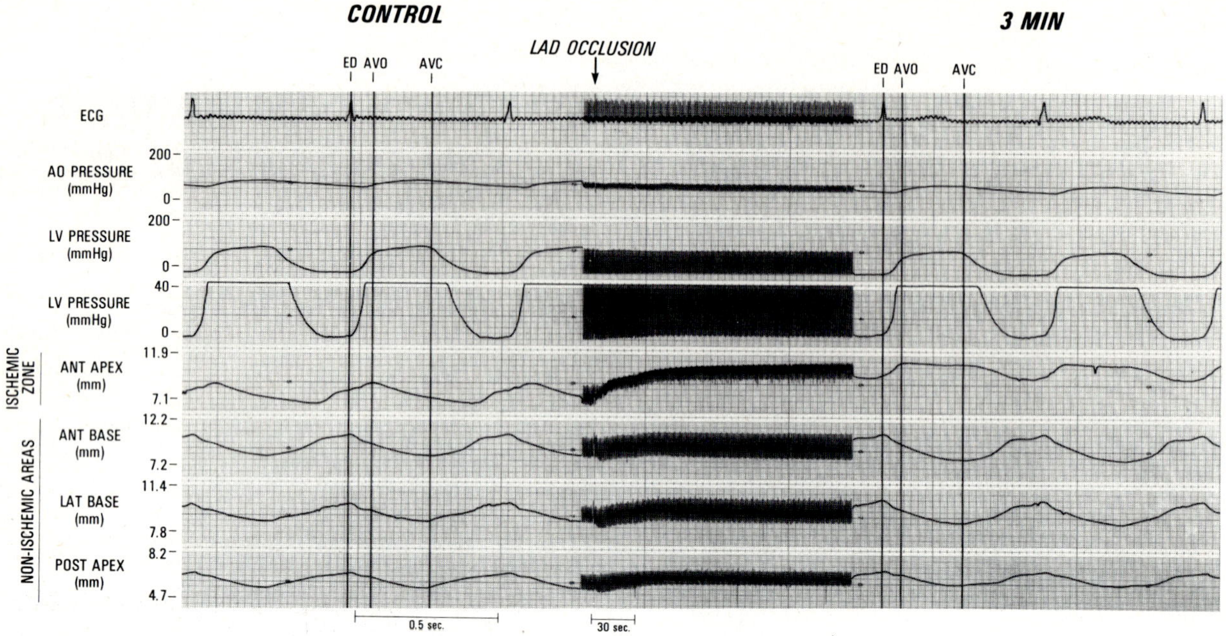

FIGURE 1. *Typical continuous recording from a dog with the electrocardiogram (ECG) and pressures in the aorta (AO) and left ventricle (LV), and segment length gauge signals from the anterior (ANT) apex and base, lateral (LAT) base, and posterior (POST) apex. The left panel is a control period. The middle panel at slow paper speed records 3 minutes of acute ischemia in the anterior apex, produced by occlusion of the mid-left anterior descending (LAD) coronary artery (arrow). The panel on the right is after 3 minutes of ischemia. Time scales are at the bottom. See text for discussion.*

ascending aorta for measurement of central aortic pressure.

Limb leads for an electrocardiogram (ECG) were placed for monitoring. The left anterior descending coronary artery was dissected free beyond the first or second large diagonal branch. A brief 1- to 2-minute test occlusion of the coronary artery was performed while an epicardial ECG lead was used to define the location of maximal ST segment elevation. The epicardial ECG lead also was used to confirm that areas subsequently to be designated as nonischemic had no significant epicardial ST segment deviation. After release of the coronary artery occlusion, the animal was allowed to recover for at least 45 minutes.

Ultrasonic segment gauges, composed of two 5-mHz piezoelectric crystals (2 mm in diameter) were implanted through small stab wounds to a depth of 4–6 mm from the epicardial surface, approximately 1 cm apart, and oriented in the circumferential or hoop axis fiber direction (Streeter et al., 1969). Such an orientation was achieved in the anterior wall by placing the segment gauge perpendicular to the external long axis as defined by a line from the bifurcation of the left main coronary artery to the apical dimple. In the posterior wall, the external long axis was defined from the inferior pulmonary vein to the apical dimple. The external long axis of the lateral wall was defined by a line midway between the anterior and posterior external long axes and also with an end-point at the apical dimple.

In all animals, one gauge was placed in the ischemic zone of the anterior apex (in the region of maximal ST segment elevation during the test occlusion of the coronary artery), and a second gauge (pair of crystals) was placed directly opposite in the posterior apex, in a nonischemic area. Six of the 10 animals were used to determine whether the location of the nonischemic area in relation to the ischemic zone influenced its response. In all six of these animals, an additional segment gauge was placed in the lateral base, and, in four of the six animals, a fourth gauge was placed in the anterior base. All gauges in nonischemic areas were placed in areas without ST segment elevation and clearly away from visible cyanosis or dyskinesis during the trial occlusion. Gauges in the anterior base were separated from the ischemic zone (anterior apex) by at least one or two normally perfused acute diagonal branches of the left anterior descending coronary artery.

The electrocardiogram, central aortic pressure, left ventricular pressure, and ultrasonic segment length gauge signals were recorded on a forced ink (Brush Clevite) 8-channel polygraph at a paper speed of 200 mm/sec and on FM magnetic tape for subsequent playback with analog-to-digital conversion. Recordings were made with respiration transiently suspended at end-expiration during a control period and 3 and 15 minutes after coronary artery occlusion.

Experimental Protocol

In all 10 animals, regional ventricular function was measured during a control period, then continuously for 3 minutes after acute occlusion of the mid-left anterior descending coronary artery (see Fig. 1). In five animals, the coronary artery occlusion was released after 3 minutes, and the animals were allowed to recover for 45 minutes. During this recovery period, bilateral vagotomy was performed and intravenous propranolol (0.5–1.0 mg/kg) was administered. This was followed by a repeat 3-minute occlusion of the coronary artery. In four animals, the initial coronary artery occlusion was maintained for 15 minutes, and in two of these animals, it was maintained for 46 to 67 minutes.

Data Analysis

All data were played back from FM tape for analog-to-digital conversion at 5 msec intervals with at least 15 consecutive beats averaged. For purposes of timing cardiac events, end-diastole was defined by the inflection point following atrial contraction in the high gain left ventricular pressure tracing, or, if this was not obvious, from the peak of the R wave of the electrocardiogram. Aortic valve opening was defined by transposing the central aortic pressure at onset of systole onto the high fidelity left ventricular pressure tracing, thus correcting for the inherent signal delay from the fluid-filled catheter system. Similarly, aortic valve closure was defined by transposing the central aortic pressure of the dicrotic notch onto the left ventricular pressure tracing (see Fig. 1).

Total segment shortening was defined as the percent change in segment length from end-diastole to aortic valve closure. This was divided into two components. Isovolumic shortening was the percent change in segment length from end-diastole to aortic valve opening. Ejection phase shortening was calculated as the total segment shortening minus isovolumic shortening, thus measuring the change in segment length from aortic valve opening to closure.

Statistical Analysis

Changes in hemodynamic, segment length, and segment shortening measurements were compared by repeated measure analysis of variance (Winer, 1971). In all cases, a P value of less than 0.05 was considered statistically significant.

Results

Hemodynamic Measurements

Three minutes after acute occlusion of the mid-left anterior descending coronary artery, the heart rate of 122 ± 9 beats/min (mean ± 1 SE) was not significantly different from the control value of 118 ± 9 beats/min. Left ventricular end-diastolic pressure increased significantly from 6.0 ± 0.8 mm Hg during control to 8.0 ± 0.7 mm Hg after 3 minutes of ischemia. There was a slight but significant decrease in mean aortic pressure from 114 ± 5 to 109 ± 5 mm Hg after 3 minutes of ischemia. In the four animals measured after 15 minutes of ischemia, there was no significant change in heart rate or ventricular pressure between 3 and 15 minutes.

Segment Lengths

In the anterior apex (ischemic zone), segment lengths throughout the cardiac cycle increased significantly 3 minutes after occlusion of the coronary artery. End-diastolic segment length of the anterior apex increased in the 10 animals, from 10.6 ± 0.9 mm to 12.2 ± 1.1 mm after 3 minutes of ischemia. The segment length at aortic valve opening increased from 10.8 ± 0.9 mm to 13.6 ± 1.2 mm and at aortic valve closure from 9.0 ± 0.8 mm to 13.5 ± 1.2 mm.

In the posterior apex (nonischemic area), the segment length at end-diastole increased significantly in the 10 animals, from a control value of 11.8 ± 1.1 mm to 12.3 ± 1.2 mm after 3 minutes of ischemia. However, there was no significant change in segment length at aortic valve opening (11.7 ± 1.1 mm control, 11.8 ± 1.2 mm after 3 minutes of ischemia) or aortic valve closure (10.5 ± 0.9 mm control, 10.6 ± 1.0 mm after 3 minutes of ischemia). There was an initial tendency for the aortic valve closure segment length to be smaller than control, but this was a transient change only during the first 10–15 seconds of ischemia (Fig. 1).

In other nonischemic areas, a similar pattern was observed. In the six animals with lateral base measurements, end-diastolic segment length increased significantly from 10.1 ± 0.6 mm to 10.4 ± 0.7 mm after 3 minutes of ischemia, but there was no significant change in aortic valve opening or closure segment lengths. In the four animals with anterior base measurements, end-diastolic segment length increased significantly from 8.4 ± 1.2 mm to 8.7 ± 1.2 mm, also without change in aortic valve opening or closure segment lengths.

In four animals, measurements were obtained during 15 minutes of acute ischemia. There were no significant changes in segment lengths in the ischemic zone (anterior apex) or nonischemic area (posterior apex) between 3 and 15 minutes. In two of these animals, segment lengths remained stable after 46 and 67 minutes of ischemia.

Regional Segment Shortening

During the control period, total segment shortening in the anterior apex (ischemic zone) of the 10 animals was 13.1 ± 3.4% and was predominantly due to shortening during the ejection phase (16.4 ± 3.0%), with little contribution by segment length changes during isovolumic systole (−2.3 ± 1.3%). After 3 minutes of ischemia, total segment shortening was replaced by total segment lengthening of −11.0 ± 3.3%, now predominantly due to lengthening during isovolumic systole (−11.4 ± 1.9%), with little contribution by segment length changes during the ejection phase (0.5 ± 1.6%). All changes in segment shortening in the anterior apex with acute ischemia were significant.

In the nonischemic posterior apex, 3 minutes of acute ischemia resulted in a significant increase in total segment shortening in the 10 animals from 10.3 ± 1.3% to 12.6 ± 1.3%, entirely due to a significant increase in isovolumic shortening from 0.4 ± 1.1% to 3.4 ± 1.0%, whereas there was no significant change in ejection phase shortening (9.9 ± 1.0% control, 9.2 ± 1.1% after 3 minutes of ischemia). These results reflect the increased end-diastolic segment length and unchanged segment lengths at aortic valve opening and closure observed in nonischemic areas (see above).

Pressure-segment length loops were drawn from digitized data obtained at 5-msec intervals (Fig. 2). In the ischemic zone, marked increases in segment length occurred throughout the cardiac cycle 3 min-

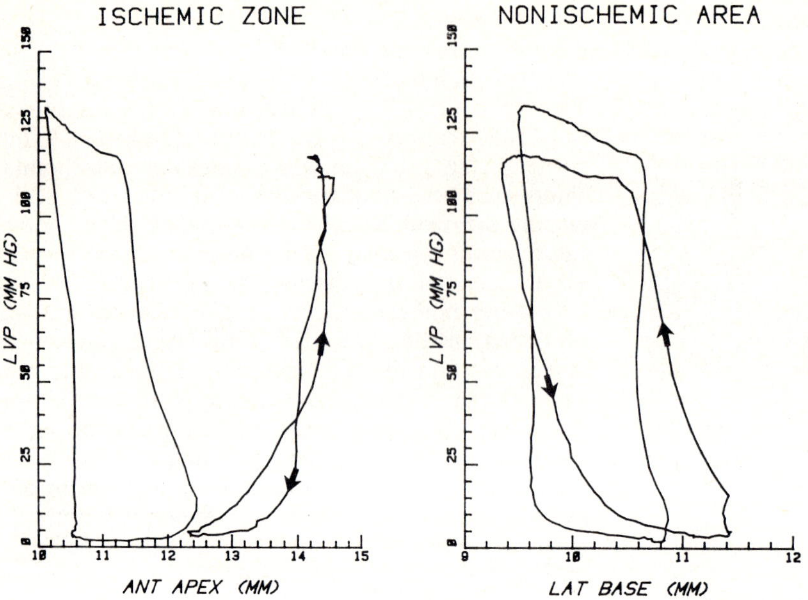

FIGURE 2. *Pressure-segment length loops are plotted for the anterior (ANT) apex (ischemic zone) and the lateral (LAT) base (nonischemic area). Loops were obtained by averaging data at 5-msec intervals from 20 cardiac cycles. In both panels, the loop on the left (without arrows) is during a control period and the loop on the right (with directional arrows) is 3 minutes after coronary occlusion. See text for discussion.*

utes after coronary artery occlusion. There was segment lengthening during isovolumic systole (isovolumic bulge), with little change in segment length or akinesis during the ejection phase. In the nonischemic area, there was an increase in end-diastolic segment length 3 minutes after ischemia, due to an increase in end-diastolic pressure. However the segment length at aortic valve opening and closure were unchanged, and thus the ejection phase shortening was unchanged. Total segment shortening, measured from end-diastole to aortic valve closure, was increased, entirely due to an increase in isovolumic shortening from end-diastole to aortic valve opening. This occurred at the same time as the isovolumic bulge in the ischemic segment.

The temporal sequence of changes in shortening patterns from 30 seconds to 3 minutes is demonstrated in Figure 3 for the six animals with simultaneous measurements in the anterior apex (ischemic zone), lateral base, and posterior apex (two nonischemic areas). In all animals, the progressive isovolumic lengthening or bulge in the ischemic zone was paralleled by a progressive increase in isovolumic shortening in the nonischemic areas. There were no regional differences in the response of nonischemic areas to acute ischemia. Similar changes were seen in the lateral base, posterior apex, and in the anterior base (a third nonischemic area measured simultaneously in four of these animals).

Regional shortening patterns were stable between 3 and 15 minutes of ischemia, as examined separately in four animals. In these four animals, there was no significant change in the anterior apex (ischemic zone) from 3 to 15 minutes for total segment lengthening (−9.6 ± 3.2% to −8.9 ± −3.8%), isovolumic segment lengthening (−11.6 ± 2.8% to −11.0 ± 2.7%), or ejection phase shortening (2.0 ± 1.4% to 2.1 ± 1.5%). Similarly, in the nonischemic posterior apex, total segment shortening (13.5 ± 1.3% to 13.1 ± 1.4%), isovolumic shortening (2.8 ± 1.6% to 2.8 ± 1.4%), and ejection shortening (10.6 ± 1.9 to 10.3 ± 1.5%) did not change significantly from 3 to 15 minutes of ischemia. In two of these

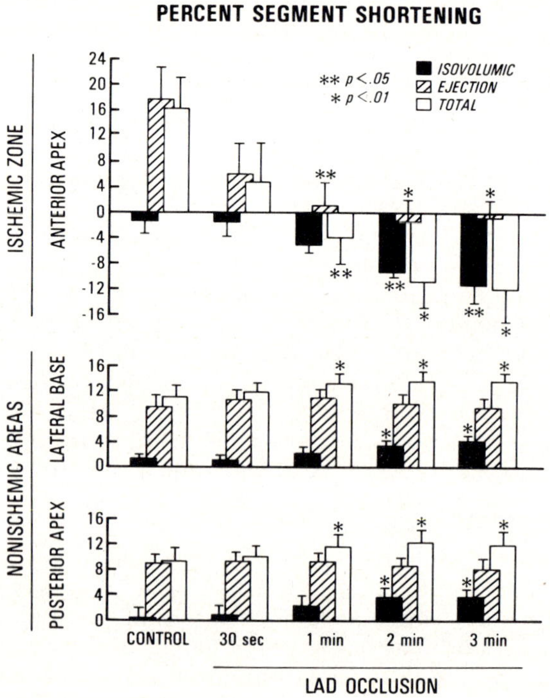

FIGURE 3. *Mean values from six animals are given for percent segment shortening in the anterior apex (ischemic zone), lateral base, and posterior apex (two nonischemic areas) during a control period, then at 30 seconds, 1, 2, and 3 minutes after occlusion of the mid-left anterior descending (LAD) coronary artery. Bars denote one standard error of the mean. Total segment shortening is the sum of isovolumic shortening and ejection shortening. Statistical comparisons are given for each type of shortening when compared to the same measure in the same region during the control period. See text for discussion.*

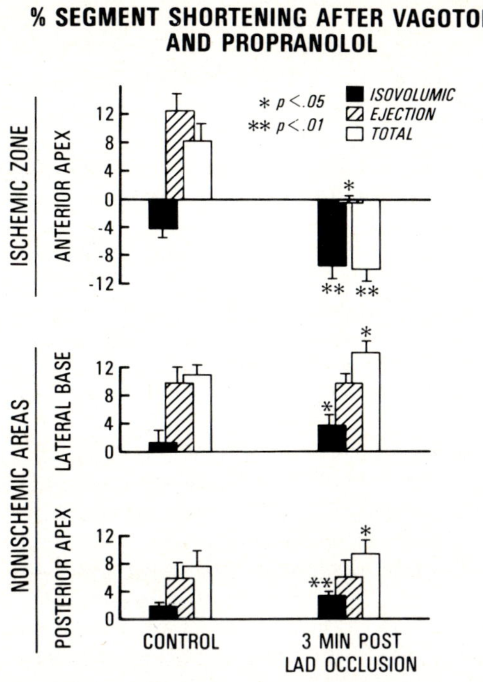

FIGURE 4. *Percent segment shortening after vagotomy and intravenous propranolol in five animals during a control period and 3 minutes after occlusion of the mid-left anterior descending (LAD) coronary artery. Format is identical to Figure 3, except that only two time periods are given. See text for discussion.*

animals, regional segment length changes remained stable to 46 and 67 minutes of ischemia.

In five animals, the effects of 3 minutes of ischemia were compared before and after vagotomy and intravenous propranolol. There was a 10–45% decrease in total and ejection phase segment shortening in all areas during the control period after adrenergic blockade. Nevertheless, changes in shortening patterns in response to acute ischemia were qualitatively similar, before and after vagotomy and intravenous propranolol (see Fig. 4). After 3 minutes of ischemia, there was replacement of total segment shortening with lengthening in the ischemic zone (anterior apex), primarily due to isovolumic lengthening, while there was akinesis during the ejection phase. In the nonischemic areas, there was an increase in total segment shortening due to an increase in isovolumic shortening, with no change in ejection phase shortening. Both nonischemic areas (lateral base and posterior apex) behaved similarly.

Discussion

During acute regional ischemia of the left ventricle, shortening in the ischemic zone decreases progressively, then is replaced by paradoxical systolic expansion, as described in the classic study by Tennant and Wiggers (1935). Nakano (1966) first described an increase in contractile force in nonischemic areas, as measured by epicardial strain gauges. Increased fiber shortening in nonischemic areas was predicted by Hood (1970a) based on postmortem measurements of animals following myocardial infarction. Theroux et al. (1974), using subendocardial ultrasonic segment gauges, demonstrated increased end-diastolic segment length, segment shortening, and work in control (nonischemic) areas during 5-minute coronary artery occlusions. Increases in segment shortening of nonischemic areas has since been shown by others (Heyndrickx et al., 1975; Kerber et al., 1976; Theroux et al., 1976, 1977; Pashkow et al., 1977; Rigaud et al., 1979; Savage et al., 1981; Nakamura et al., 1982; Molaug et al., 1983), and has been thought to represent a compensatory response produced by utilization of the Frank-Starling mechanism or by generalized increased sympathetic stimulation. The goals of the current study were, first, to clarify the mechanisms of this apparent hyperfunction response of nonischemic areas and, second, to determine its effectiveness in compensating for loss of systolic function by the ischemic zone.

The current study demonstrated a progressive replacement of systolic shortening in the ischemic zone by lengthening during isovolumic systole (isovolumic bulge), and with akinesis during the ejection phase. Increased end-diastolic length in the nonischemic areas produced increased total segment shortening by the Frank-Starling mechanism. However, this increase was entirely attributed to increased shortening during isovolumic systole, whereas ejection shortening did not change. The increase in isovolumic shortening in nonischemic areas directly paralleled the development of isovolumic bulging in the ischemic zone. Thus, part of the increased total segment shortening produced by the nonischemic areas was "dissipated" into the ischemic zone during isovolumic systole, counteracting any potential (compensatory) increase in systolic function during the ejection phase. After 2–3 minutes of ischemia, regional shortening patterns remained stable for up to 15 minutes (and in two animals for 46 and 67 minutes). The location of the nonischemic area in relation to the ischemic zone did not influence its interaction with the ischemic zone. Thus, areas within the same circumferential hoop but directly opposite the ischemic zone (i.e., the posterior apex) demonstrated the same findings as sites which were distant (lateral base) or adjacent (anterior base) to the ischemic zone. The anterior base measurements in this study were obtained in a nonischemic area separated from the ischemic zone (anterior apex) by one or two normally perfused diagonal branches of the left anterior descending coronary artery, proximal to the site of occlusion. Thus, this nonischemic area was not the same as the marginal or border segments investigated in other studies, i.e., the area directly adjacent to the ischemic zone which demonstrates a reduction in systolic function despite normal coronary artery perfusion (Theroux et al., 1974, 1976, 1977; Roan et al., 1979).

When acute ischemia was produced after removal of adrenergic influences, total segment shortening in nonischemic areas still increased, due to an increase in isovolumic shortening with no change in ejection shortening. Thus, changes in adrenergic tone may influence the extent of increase in shortening but not its distribution during systole. In these animals, the effects of an initial 3 minutes of ischemia were compared to a repeat 3-minute episode of ischemia 45 minutes later (after vagotomy and intravenous propranolol). The rationale for this protocol was based on prior studies which demonstrated full return of regional systolic and diastolic function 30–45 minutes after release of 5-minute occlusions of the coronary artery (Theroux et al., 1976), whereas abnormalities of subendocardial blood flow and function may persist for over 3 hours after release of 15-minute occlusions (Heyndrickx et al., 1975, 1978). Findings from the current study indicate that the apparent hyperfunction of nonischemic areas during acute ischemia is a mechanical phenomenon, due to a combination of utilization of the Frank-Starling mechanism and regional intraventricular unloading into ischemic segments.

The direct measurements of the current study demonstrated a significant interaction between ischemic and nonischemic segments. This interaction was envisioned by Tennant and Wiggers (1935) as "a struggle between forces causing shortening and those tending to lengthen the fibers" in the ischemic segments. Several investigators have examined the mechanical consequences of such an interaction between "weak and strong" muscles linked in series, such as with isolated strips of hypoxic and normal myocardium placed in series (Tyberg et al., 1969; Wiegner et al., 1978), ventricular aneurysms (Parmley et al., 1973; Janz and Waldron, 1978), asynchrony of ventricular contraction with pacing (Badke et al., 1980), or theoretical models of regionally ischemic ventricles (Elings et al., 1977; Laird and Vellekoop, 1977; Bogen et al., 1980). The magnitude of the mechanical disadvantage produced by the interaction of ischemic and nonischemic segments is thought to be related directly to the size and inversely related to the stiffness of the ischemic area (Elings et al., 1977; Laird and Vellekoop, 1977; Bogen et al., 1980) or of the aneurysmal tissue (Parmley et al., 1973). Although this was not systematically examined in our study, we did note that, with smaller zones of ischemia, there was less of an increase in segment shortening by nonischemic areas.

Our findings were importantly dependent on the presence of systolic lengthening in the ischemic zone, particularly during isovolumic systole. It is probable that our findings would be present for several hours beyond the period of acute ischemia studied. This hypothesis is based on the observations that the majority of changes in regional function occur in the first 5 minutes of infarction, with relatively little further change until 24 hours (Theroux et al., 1977; Roan et al., 1979), and the magnitude of aneurysmal bulging is stable for several hours (Pirzada et al., 1976; Vokonas et al., 1976; Savage et al., 1981). Indirect evidence that this interaction between ischemic and nonischemic areas is still present several hours after the acute event is provided by two clinical studies (Stack et al., 1983; Sheehan et al., 1983). After successful reperfusion of the infarcted zone with intracoronary streptokinase, as regional wall motion of the ischemic zone improved, wall motion in the nonischemic areas, which had been hyperkinetic, decreased to normal. Although our results may be applicable during the acute period of ischemia (minutes to hours), we would not extrapolate our results to the later periods (days). The increased stiffness of the ischemic zone (Hood et al., 1970b), and additional long-term compensatory mechanisms, such as hypertrophy of nonischemic areas (Theroux et al., 1977: Sasayama et al., 1981), may influence the interaction between ischemic and nonischemic areas to an uncertain extent.

The mechanical phenomena observed in the current study are probably not unique to our preparation of anterior wall ischemia. Several investigators have demonstrated an increase in nonischemic area segment shortening or wall thickening following occlusion of the left circumflex coronary artery (Heyndrickx et al., 1975; Kerber et al., 1976; Theroux et al., 1976, 1977; Savage et al., 1981; Nakamura et al., 1982). Although these investigators did not distinguish between isovolumic and ejection phase changes, the increase in nonischemic area total segment shortening in the study by Theroux et al. (1976, Fig. 3) was due primarily to an increase in isovolumic shortening.

Extrapolation of our results to the conscious animal, and, thus, the clinical application to man, is more difficult. Differences in the initial cardiac volume, shape, and contraction patterns between the conscious animal and anesthetized open-chest preparations (Rushmer, 1954; Leshin et al., 1972; Rankin et al., 1976) may influence the interaction between ischemic and nonischemic areas. Although increased nonischemic area segment shortening and wall thickening following coronary artery occlusion has been demonstrated in the conscious animal, the magnitude and time course of these changes are complex. Kumada et al. (1979) found no increase in nonischemic area segment shortening after a brief 1-minute coronary artery occlusion. Hess et al. (1982) found no change in nonischemic area wall thickening after a 2-minute occlusion, although in this study left ventricular end-diastolic pressure did not increase. In contrast, Theroux et al. (1976) found a significant increase in left ventricular end-diastolic pressure and nonischemic area segment shortening after a 2-minute coronary artery occlusion. Of note, the magnitude of these changes in this conscious dog study were less than those found in their previous study in the anesthetized dog (Theroux et al.,

1974). Velocity of nonischemic area segment shortening has been shown to increase at 5 and 15 minutes after coronary artery occlusion (Heyndrickx et al., 1975) but not after 1 hour (Cox and Vatner, 1982). Savage et al. (1981) found a significant increase in wall thickening in the nonischemic area at 15 minutes, 1, 24, and 48 hours after coronary artery occlusion. In a more prolonged study, Theroux et al. (1977) found an increase in nonischemic area segment shortening which was significant only at 1, 2, and 3 weeks following coronary artery occlusion. In contrast to their earlier acute study (Theroux et al., 1976), left ventricular end-diastolic pressure did not increase, which may explain the lack of increased nonischemic area shortening during the acute phase. Finally, Sasayama et al. (1981) demonstrated a tendency for nonischemic area segment shortening and wall thickening to increase after coronary artery occlusion, but only the increase in segment shortening after 3 weeks was significant. In this study, left ventricular end-diastolic pressure did not increase significantly until 2 and 3 weeks after coronary artery occlusion, which may in part explain the lack of change in nonischemic area function during the acute period of ischemia.

Acute ischemia in the conscious animal also is associated with a significant increase in heart rate (Heyndrickx et al., 1975; Theroux et al., 1976, 1977; Kumada et al., 1979; Savage et al., 1981; Sasayama et al., 1981; Hess et al., 1982), a reflex response which was blunted in our anesthetized open-chest preparation. Although such reflex changes may modify the magnitude of the interaction between ischemic and nonischemic areas, the qualitative findings in the current study were not significantly influenced by adrenergic factors. Thus, an apparent hyperfunction in the nonischemic area and regional intraventricular unloading effects during isovolumic systole were seen both before and after adrengeric blockade.

Thus, in the conscious animal, acute coronary artery occlusion may not be associated with a significant increase in nonischemic area function if the occlusion is brief (less than 2 minutes), or if left ventricular end-diastolic pressure does not increase. When an apparent hyperfunction in the nonischemic area is noted in the conscious animal, the magnitude of this change may be less than in the anesthetized preparation (Theroux et al., 1976). Furthermore, with similar periods of coronary artery occlusion, wall thickening measurements may not yield precisely the same information as segment shortening measurements (Theroux et al., 1976; Sasayama et al., 1981; Hess et al., 1982). Therefore, extrapolation of our results to the conscious animal and to more prolonged periods of ischemia must be made cautiously. The magnitude and time course of functional interactions between ischemic and nonischemic areas during isovolumic systole remain to be determined in the conscious animal.

Finally, the results from this study have implications concerning the clinical evaluation of regional ventricular function. Many methods such as echocardiography and angiography determine regional cardiac dimensions or volume at end-diastole and end-systole to calculate a regional ejection fraction. This ejection fraction is similar to the measure of total segment shortening as defined in this study, and will include changes which occur during both isovolumic systole and the ejection phase. Under normal circumstances, there is little contribution from isovolumic shortening to total segment shortening. Thus, total segment shortening will be a good approximation of ejection phase shortening. However, with acute ischemia, our results suggest that measurement of total segment shortening or the clinically used regional ejection fraction may not accurately reflect the regional contributions to the forward ejection of blood. Under these circumstances, an index of ejection phase shortening would be preferable.

In conclusion, during acute ischemia of the left ventricle, there is a reciprocal interaction between ischemic and nonischemic segments. Ischemic segments are stretched passively by pressure and volume generated from nonischemic areas during isovolumic systole. In nonischemic segments, utilization of the Frank-Starling mechanism produces increased total segment shortening. However, since most of this increased shortening is expended in stretching the dyskinetic ischemic segments during isovolumic systole, there is no true compensatory increase in ejection shortening. If the Frank-Starling mechanism is not utilized, the unloading of nonischemic segments into ischemic segments during isovolumic systole would result in a decrease in the amount of segment shortening available for ejecting blood. If these findings can be extrapolated to man, it would suggest that the immediate survival from an acute myocardial infarction will in part depend on the contractile reserve of nonischemic segments, which must be adequate to provide sufficient forward cardiac output while overcoming the mechanical disadvantages imposed by the ischemic zone.

We gratefully acknowledge the assistance of Elizabeth Gilpin in the statistical analysis and Janeen McCracken for word processing.

Supported by National Institutes of Health Grants HL-28644 and Research Training Grant HL-07444 and by the Research Service of the Veterans Administration.

Address for reprints: Wilbur Y.W. Lew, M.D., Cardiovascular Division 111A, Veterans Administration Medical Center, 3350 La Jolla Village Drive, San Diego, California 92161.

Dr. Chen's current address is: Department of Medicine, Teaching Hospital of Sichuan Medical College, Chengdu, Sichuan Province, Peoples Republic of China.

Received February 8, 1984; accepted for publication December 20, 1984.

References

Badke FR, Boinay P, Covell JW (1980) Effects of ventricular pacing on regional left ventricular performance in the dog. Am J Physiol **238:** H858–H867

Banka VS, Helfant RH (1974) Temporal sequence of dynamic contractile characteristics in ischemic and nonischemic myocardium after acute coronary ligation. Am J Cardiol **34:** 158–163
Bogen DK, Rabinowitz SA, Needleman A, McMahon TA, Abelmann WH (1980) An analysis of the mechanical disadvantage of myocardial infarction in the canine left ventricle. Circ Res **47:** 728–741
Corya BC, Rasmussen S, Knoebel SB, Feigenbaum H (1975) Echocardiography in acute myocardial infarction. Am J Cardiol **36:** 1–10
Cox DA, Vatner SF (1982) Myocardial function in areas of heterogeneous perfusion after coronary artery occlusion in conscious dogs. Circulation **66:** 1154–1158
Elings VB, Jahn GE, Vogel JHK (1977) A theoretical model of regionally ischemic myocardium. Circ Res **41:** 722–729
Heikkilä J, Tabakin BS, Hugenholtz PG (1972) Quantification of function in normal and infarcted regions of the left ventricle. Cardiovasc Res **6:** 516–531
Hess OM, Osakada G, Lavelle JF, Gallagher KP, Kemper WS, Ross J Jr (1982) Left ventricular geometry during partial and complete coronary occlusion in the conscious dog. Int J Cardiol **1:** 387–403
Heyndrickx GR, Millard RW, McRitchie RJ, Maroko PR, Vatner SF (1975) Regional myocardial functional and electrophysiological alterations after brief coronary artery occlusion in conscious dogs. J Clin Invest **56:** 978–985
Heyndrickx GR, Baig H, Nellens P, Leusen I, Fishbein MC, Vatner SF (1978) Depression of regional blood flow and wall thickening after brief coronary occlusions. Am J Physiol **234:** H653–H659
Hood WB Jr (1970a) Experimental myocardial infarction. III. Recovery of left ventricular function in the healing phase. Contribution of increased fiber shortening in noninfarcted myocardium. Am Heart J **79:** 531–538
Hood WB Jr, Bianco JA, Kumar R, Whiting RB (1970b) Experimental myocardial infarction. IV. Reduction of left ventricular compliance in the healing phase. J Clin Invest **49:** 1316–1323
Janz RF, Waldron RJ (1978) Predicted effect of chronic apical aneurysms on the passive stiffness of the human left ventricle. Circ Res **42:** 255–263
Kerber RE, Marcus ML, Wilson R, Ehrhardt J, Abboud FM (1976) Effects of acute coronary occlusion on the motion and perfusion of the normal and ischemic interventricular septum: An experimental echocardiographic study. Circulation **54:** 928–935
Kumada T, Karliner JS, Pouleur H, Gallagher KP, Shirato K, Ross J Jr (1979) Effects of coronary occlusion on early ventricular diastolic events in conscious dogs. Am J Physiol **237:** H542–H549
Laird JD, Vellekoop HP (1977) Time course of passive elasticity of myocardial tissue following experimental infarction in rabbits and its relation to mechanical dysfunction. Circ Res **41:** 715–721
Leshin SJ, Mullins CB, Templeton GH, Mitchell JH (1972) Dimensional analysis of ventricular function: Effects of anesthetics and thoracotomy. Am J Physiol **222:** 540–545
Molaug M, Geiran O, Kiil F (1983) Compensatory cardiac mechanisms evoked by septal ischemia in dogs. Am J Cardiol **51:** 201–206
Nakamura M, Sasayama S, Takahashi M, Ohyagi A, Yamamoto A, Lee JD, Kawai C (1982) Regional dysfunction of the interventricular septum during acute coronary artery occlusion. Cardiovasc Res **16:** 144–150
Nakano J (1966) Effect of changes in coronary arterial blood flow on the myocardial contractile force. Jpn Heart J **7:** 78–86
Nieminen M, Heikkilä J (1976) Echoventriculography in acute myocardial infarction. III. Am J Cardiol **38:** 1–8
Parmley WW, Chuck L, Kivowitz C, Matloff JM, Swan HJC (1973) In vitro length-tension relations of human ventricular aneurysms. Relation of stiffness to mechanical disadvantage. Am J Cardiol **32:** 889–894
Pashkow F, Holland R, Brooks H (1977) Early changes in contractility and coronary blood flow in the normal areas of the ischemic porcine heart. Am Heart J **93:** 349–357
Pirzada FA, Ekong EA, Vokonas PS, Apstein CS, Hood WB Jr (1976) Experimental myocardial infarction. XIII. Sequential changes in left ventricular pressure-length relationships in the acute phase. Circulation **53:** 970–975
Rankin JS, McHale PA, Arentzen CE, Ling D, Greenfield JC Jr, Anderson RW (1976) The three-dimensional dynamic geometry of the left ventricle in the conscious dog. Circ Res **39:** 304–313
Rigaud M, Rocha P, Boschat J, Farcot JC, Bardet J, Bourdarias JP (1979) Regional left ventricular function assessed by contrast angiography in acute myocardial infarction. Circulation **60:** 130–139
Ringertz HG, Carlsson E, Tyberg JV (1976) A method for the study of regional ischemic dysfunction in the intact dog. Invest Radiol **11:** 556–562
Roan P, Scales F, Saffer S, Buja LM, Willerson JT (1979) Functional characterization of left ventricular segmental responses during the initial 24h and 1 wk after experimental canine myocardial infarction. J Clin Invest **64:** 1074–1088
Rushmer RF (1954) Shrinkage of the heart in anesthetized thoracotomized dogs. Circ Res **2:** 22–27
Sasayama S, Gallagher KP, Kemper WS, Franklin D, Ross J Jr (1981) Regional left ventricular wall thickness early and late after coronary occlusion in the conscious dog. Am J Physiol **240:** H293–H299
Savage RM, Guth B, White FC, Hagan AD, Bloor CM (1981) Correlation of regional myocardial blood flow and function with myocardial infarct size during acute myocardial ischemia in the conscious pig. Circulation **64:** 699–707
Sheehan FH, Mathey DG, Schofer J, Krebber HJ, Dodge HT (1983) Effect of interventions in salvaging left ventricular function in acute myocardial infarction: A study of intracoronary stretokinase. Am J Cardiol **52:** 431–438
Stack RS, Phillips HR III, Grierson DS, Behar VS, Kong Y, Peter RH, Swain JL, Greenfield JC Jr (1983) Functional improvement of jeopardized myocardium following intracoronary stretokinase infusion in acute myocardial infarction. J Clin Invest **72:** 84–95
Streeter DD Jr, Spotnitz HM, Patel DP, Ross J Jr, Sonnenblick EH (1969) Fiber orientation in the canine left ventricle during diastole and systole. Circ Res **24:** 339–347
Tennant R, Wiggers CJ (1935) The effect of coronary occlusion on myocardial contraction. Am J Physiol **112:** 351–361
Theroux P, Franklin D, Ross J Jr, Kemper WS (1974) Regional myocardial function during acute coronary artery occlusion and its modification by pharmacologic agents in the dog. Circ Res **35:** 896–908
Theroux P, Ross J Jr, Franklin D, Kemper WS, Sasayama S (1976) Regional myocardial function in the conscious dog during acute coronary occlusion and responses to morphine, propranolol, nitroglycerin, and lidocaine. Circulation **53:** 302–314
Theroux P, Ross J Jr, Franklin D, Covell JW, Bloor CM, Sasayama S (1977) Regional myocardial function and dimensions early and late after myocardial infarction in the unanesthetized dog. Circ Res **40:** 158–165
Tyberg JV, Parmley WW, Sonnenblick EH (1969) In-vitro studies of myocardial asynchrony and regional hypoxia. Circ Res **25:** 569–579
Tyberg JV, Forrester JS, Wyatt HL, Goldner SJ, Parmley WW, Swan HJC (1974) An analysis of segmental ischemic dysfunction utilizing the pressure-length loop. Circulation **49:** 748–754
Vokonas PS, Pirzada FA, Hood WB Jr. (1976) Experimental myocardial infarction. XII. Dynamic changes in segmental mechanical behavior of infarcted and non-infarcted myocardium. Am J Cardiol **37:** 853–859
Wiegner AW, Allen GJ, Bing OHL (1978) Weak and strong myocardium in series: Implications for segmental dysfunction. Am J Physiol **235:** H776–H783
Winer BJ (1971) Statistical Principles of Experimental Design. New York, McGraw-Hill
Wyatt HL, Forrester JS, da Luz PL, Diamond GA, Chagrasulis R, Swan HJC (1976) Functional abnormalities in nonoccluded regions of myocardium after experimental coronary occlusion. Am J Cardiol **37:** 366–372

INDEX TERMS: Acute myocardial infarction • Regional ventricular function • Frank-Starling mechanism • Hyperkinesis • Isovolumic systole

Electrophysiological Study of Cardiovascular Neurons in the Rostral Ventrolateral Medulla in Rats

D. Les Brown and Patrice G. Guyenet
From the Department of Pharmacology, University of Virginia, School of Medicine, Charlottesville, Virginia

SUMMARY. In urethane-anesthetized rats, electrophysiological recordings of spontaneously active neurons in the vasopressor area of the rostral ventrolateral medulla were analyzed for participation in cardiovascular regulation. A total of 138 units were found which were inhibited by transient increases in mean arterial pressure elicited by intravenous injection of norepinephrine, aortic occlusion, or electrical stimulation of the hypothalamus, with 100% inhibition occurring at 148 mm Hg. Histograms of postsystolic activity showed that these units had pulse-synchronous rhythms which grew more prominent as arterial pressure increased. Furthermore, electrical stimulation of the superior laryngeal nerve, which elicited a vasodepressor response, strongly inhibited these units. Thus, these neurons were termed negatively correlated cardiovascular units. At least half of these cells project to or through the thoracic spinal cord. In addition, arterial pressure sensitivity is conveyed through carotid sinus and aortic arch afferents. Approximately half of the cardiovascular units are also excited by hypothalamic stimulation. Finally, analysis of neighboring cells showed that it is possible to distinguish between cardiovascular and respiratory units. These data are consistent with the concept of a medullary center which supports tonic sympathetic vasomotor tone and which mediates baroreceptor reflexes, as well as vascular responses of the defense reaction. **(*Circ Res 56: 359–369, 1985*)**

THE importance of the rostral ventrolateral medulla oblongata in cardiovascular regulation has been demonstrated repeatedly. Tonic arterial pressure maintenance requires the integrity of this area (Reis and Cuenod, 1965; Dampney and Moon, 1980). Electrical and chemical stimulation of the area elicits a powerful vasopressor response comprised, in part, of femoral and renal vasoconstriction (Dampney and Moon, 1980; Ross et al., 1984a). Microinjection of muscimol, an agonist at receptors for γ-aminobutyric acid (GABA), in the vasopressor area of the rostral medulla reduces arterial pressure to basal levels (Willette et al., 1983). Finally, anatomical evidence indicates that reticulospinal neurons of the area project specifically to the intermediolateral cell column and the central autonomic area of the spinal cord (Amendt et al., 1983; Ross et al., 1984b).

Similarly, the rostral ventrolateral medulla participates in baroreceptor reflex control of arterial pressure. Application of glycine to the surface of the medulla just ventral to the rostral pressor area not only reduces resting arterial pressure, but also greatly reduces the vasoconstrictor response to carotid occlusion (Winnergren and Oberg, 1980). Furthermore, microinjection of muscimol into the vasopressor area blocks the depressor response to aortic nerve stimulation (Willette et al., 1983).

In addition, the rostral ventrolateral medulla integrates cardiovascular responses originating in the hypothalamus. Microinjection of bicuculline methiodide, an antagonist at receptors for GABA, into the vasopressor area enhances pressor responses elicited by anterior hypothalamic stimulation (Willette et al., 1984). Topical applications of glycine to the medullary surface greatly attenuates the vasoconstrictor components of the defense reaction (Hilton et al., 1984). Because of the concomitant reduction of resting arterial pressure, Hilton et al. proposed that the same pool of medullary neurons that integrates the defense reaction also provides basal sympathetic tone; they also suggested that the medullary neurons are tonically excited by hypothalamic drive.

Electrophysiological recordings in the intermediate portion of the nucleus paragigantocellularis lateralis have shown the existence of neurons with axonal projections to the thoracic spinal cord and with pulse-synchronous rhythms (Brown and Guyenet, 1984). These cells are also acutely sensitive to pharmacologically induced changes in arterial pressure. Thus, these neurons were proposed to be cardiovascular neurons mediating baroreceptor signals to the spinal preganglionic neurons. The purpose of the present study was to further examine the role of these cardiovascular neurons in baroreceptor reflexes and in the integration of hypothalamic vasopressor responses.

Methods

Experiments were performed, unless otherwise specified, on male Sprague-Dawley rats (320–420 g), anesthetized with urethane (1.5 g/kg). This single dose provided adequate anesthesia for the duration of the experiment because unparalyzed animals remained unresponsive to hindlimb toe pinch until termination of the experiment, at which time the animals were killed with a bolus injection of a saturated solution of potassium chloride. The animals were placed on a heating pad to maintain rectal temperature at 37°C. After tracheal intubation, the animals were respirated with a minute volume of 600–780 ml/kg. End tidal CO_2 was continuously monitored and regulated between 3.5 and 5.0% by adjusting tidal volume. Arterial pressure was monitored through a catheter in the femoral artery or the brachial artery in experiments utilizing aortic occlusion. The tapered tip of a second large catheter which housed five smaller catheters was placed in the femoral vein or into the tubing of a butterfly catheter inserted into a tail vein; this catheter was used for the injection of small boluses (10–50 μl) of norepinephrine (150 μg/ml) or the vasodilator, sodium nitroprusside (0.5 mg/ml).

The right marginal mandibular branch of the facial nerve was exposed and the tip of a concentric bipolar stimulating electrode (David Kopf Instruments, NE100) was implanted in the fascia surrounding the nerve. Typical stimulation parameters for antidromic activation of the facial nerve were: 1–2 mA, 200 μsec, 1 Hz. At this intensity, orthodromic activation of muscles underlying the vibrissae (several centimeters distal) was observed and provided an index for successful stimulation of the nerve. Direct activation of muscles adjacent to the electrode usually required a stronger stimulus.

For hypothalamic stimulation, a small opening was drilled in the parietal bone 5.7 mm rostral to lambda. This permitted placement of an electrode in the ipsilateral dorsomedial hypothalamus at 1.0 mm lateral to the midline and 9.0 mm below the cerebral surface, according to the atlas of Paxinos and Watson (1982). The location of the electrode could be confirmed by the large pressor response—up to 100 mm Hg—produced by electrical stimulation (5 sec train, 250 μA, 100 Hz, 500 μsec). Stimulation sites were verified histologically.

Another stimulating electrode was implanted in the spinal cord, following a laminectomy at thoracic (T3-T4) levels. The tip of the electrode was placed 0.5–1.0 mm lateral to the midline and 1.0–1.5 mm below the dorsal surface of the spinal cord. These coordinates approximate the location of the intermediolateral cell column; however, histological verification was not attempted. Stimulation parameters were maximal (5 mA, 200 μsec, 1.5 Hz) until a reticulospinal unit was detected; then, intensity was reduced to just above threshold level for antidromic activation of the unit (0.2–2.0 mA). Prior to spinal cord stimulation, pancuronium bromide (Pavulon; 100 μg/kg) was administered to block neuromuscular transmission.

In experiments in which the superior laryngeal nerve was stimulated, a midline incision was made on the ventral surface of the neck. The sternohyoidus and omohyoidus muscles, as well as the end of the trachea distal to the cannula, were transected and retracted to reveal the right superior laryngeal nerve at its junction with the nodose ganglion. The segment of the nerve adjacent to the nodose ganglion was placed on a bipolar silver electrode. Just before stimulation, the nerve was raised above the surrounding tissue with a micromanipulator, and the area was then flooded with mineral oil. Next, the esophagus was ligated, transected, and retracted rostrally, and the longus capitis muscles were resected bilaterally, revealing the basal occipital bone. An opening was drilled in the bone and the dura was carefully cut away from the ventral surface of the right rostral medulla. A pressure foot, made of a small plastic ring glued to a steel support rod, was pressed against the surface of the brain with a micromanipulator to minimize movement. Through this window a recording electrode (see below) was lowered into the medulla.

For all experimental procedures other than superior laryngeal nerve stimulation, a dorsal approach to the brainstem was used. In these experiments, a portion of the interparietal bone and the dura overlying the right hemicerebellum was removed to permit advancement of a recording electrode. Single-unit recordings were made with glass microelectrodes (W.P.I. Omega Dot) filled with 2 MNaCl containing 1% fast green at pH 7.5. Impedances were commonly 4–8 MΩ, measured at 400 Hz. Signals were filtered (bandpass: 200–4000 Hz), monitored on an oscilloscope, and recorded on a tape recorder (Vetter model B Instrumentation Recorder), along with arterial pressure and tidal CO_2. The signal, digitized by a window discriminator, was counted during intervals of 1 or 2 seconds and recorded as an integrated activity histogram.

In two experiments, baroreceptor nerves were transiently blocked with a local anesthetic. Bilaterally, catheters were gently inserted into the nerve sheath of the vagosympathetic nerve trunk and pushed rostrally to the region of the nodose ganglion. Then the carotid sinuses were denervated and the superior laryngeal nerves were transected. After identification of a cardiovascular neuron, 50 μl of chloroprocaine (Nesacaine, 20 mg/ml) was superfused onto the region of the nodose ganglion. Several washes with normal saline (1 ml total) through the same catheter over the next 30 minutes was sufficient for recovery of properties of cardiovascular neurons. The animals in these experiments were initially anesthetized with ether, rapidly tracheotomized and intubated, and subsequently anesthetized with halothane (Fluothane, 0.8%) and maintained areflexive to hindlimb toe pinch.

In one experiment, the brainstem was hemisected with a retractable wire knife lowered on a micromanipulator. The transection was made at the midcollicular level. Postmortem examination of the brain confirmed the completeness of the transection.

At the end of an experiment, a deposit of fast green dye was made by passing a 20-μA current for 20 minutes. Subsequent histological processing permitted location of the recording sites, which were then mapped on standardized sections adapted from an atlas (Paxinos and Watson, 1982).

Post-event histograms of unit activity and averaged arterial pressure or tidal CO_2 waveforms were generated with a computer (Tracor Northern TN-1505). The latter was triggered with the gate output of an oscilloscope which was itself triggered from the arterial pressure or tidal CO_2 signals. Cardiac electrical activity could be evaluated by electrocardiogram (ECG) waveforms generated by signal averaging the recording electrode signal over more than 200 cycles. Statistical comparisons were made using analysis of variance techniques (Yamane, 1964). Values are reported as mean ± SD.

Results

Electrophysiological Location of the Vasopressor Center in the Ventrolateral Medulla Oblongata

Stimulation of the facial nerve elicited a field potential with a latency of 2 msec (peak) in the nucleus of the facial nerve (Fig. 1). This field poten-

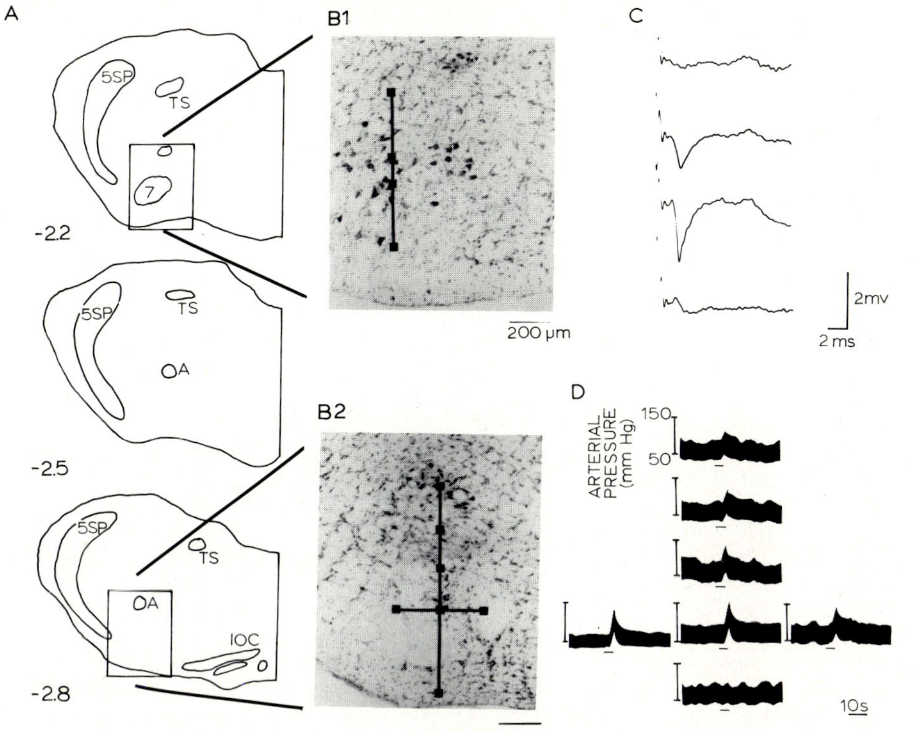

Figure 1. *Electrophysiological localization of pressor area of the rostral ventrolateral medulla. Panel A: transverse sections of the medulla ranging from 2.2–2.8 mm caudal to the interaural line. Panel B1: vertical line marks electrode track through the nucleus of the seventh cranial nerve and squares mark four recording sites, with corresponding antidromic field potentials in panel C. Panel B2: seven stimulation sites (■) delineate the center of the pressor area, with corresponding arterial pressure responses in panel D. The largest response occurs at approximately the intersection of the horizontal and vertical lines. Stimulus: 8 μA, 0.2 msec, 50 Hz, 3-sec train. Anatomical abbreviations: 5SP, spinal nucleus of the trigeminal nerve; 7, nucleus of the seventh nerve; A, nucleus ambiguus; IOC, inferior olivary complex; TS, tractus solitarius.*

tial was used to map the medial, lateral, ventral, and posterior boundaries of the facial nucleus. The stereotaxic coordinates of these boundaries permitted reliable location of the powerful "vasopressor" area which lies immediately caudal to the facial nucleus, close to the ventral surface of the medulla. Stimulation of this area with recording electrodes using 12.7 ± 3.2 μA (0.2 msec, 50 Hz for 3 sec) (Fig. 1) produced increases in mean arterial pressure of 33.3 ± 4.7 mm Hg (n = 3). Neurons with cardiovascular properties (described below) were found in a region which coincided precisely with the focus of this vasopressor region, within a column approximately 400 μm in diameter and 600 μm long, extending from the caudal end of the facial nucleus to the rostral end of the inferior olivary complex. The middle panel of Figure 1A shows the rostral end of the recording area. At this level, a few motorneurons of facial nucleus can still be seen.

Cardiovascular Neurons of the Vasopressor Center

Single-unit recordings identified a total of 138 cardiovascular neurons, characterized by their immediate and complete decrease in activity (as a result of either inhibition or disfacilitation) during the rapid rise of arterial pressure produced by a bolus injection of norepinephrine and by the recovery of activity to basal levels that followed closely in time the return of arterial pressure to resting levels (Fig. 2A). Figure 2B shows the response curve of a typical unit: there is a relatively linear region of high sensitivity to changes in mean arterial pressure and a cut-off pressure above which the unit is completely silenced. When arterial pressure was reduced below resting levels with vasodilator drugs, unit activity reached a maximum at pressures of 60–85 mm Hg and did not increase further, as pressure decreased. These cardiovascular neurons were called "negatively correlated" because of the negative slope of the pressure sensitive portion of the response curve.

A second characteristic of these cardiovascular neurons was a cardiac rhythm manifested only at elevated arterial pressures, which shifted unit activity to the highly sensitive portion of its response curve (Fig. 2D). At lower pressures, for which unit activity lies in its pressure-insensitive region, pulse-synchronous rhythms were diminished or absent (Fig. 2C). Maximal inhibition of unit activity occurred at 74.3 ± 7.8 msec after the R-wave, with 80% inhibition occurring approximately 8 msec earlier (n = 21).

Three cardiovascular neurons were analyzed for pulse-synchronous rhythms when impulses in nerves carrying baroreceptor signals were transiently blocked. In animals with bilateral carotid sinus denervation and superior laryngeal nerve transection, the remaining baroreceptor nerves—vagus, aortic nerve, and sympathetic chain—were anesthetized with chloroprocaine. The cells lost virtually all sensitivity to changes in arterial pressure and displayed only slight pulse-synchronous activity in one case (Fig. 3B) and none in two other cases. Activity which was both pressure-sensitive and pulse-synchronous returned after washing out the anesthetic (Fig. 3C).

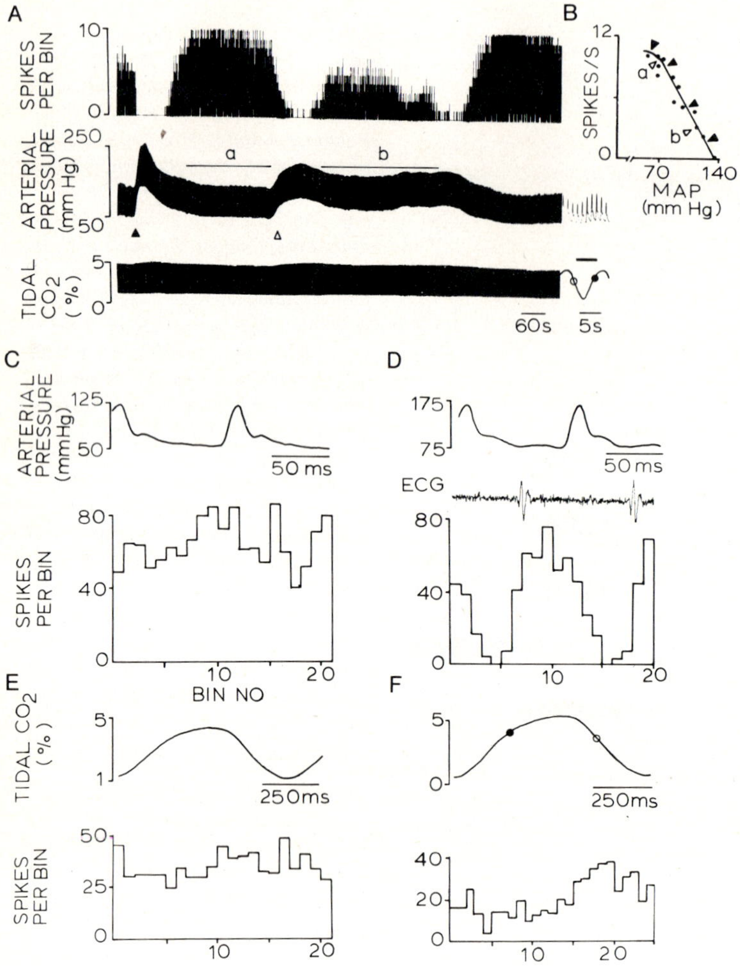

FIGURE 2. *Identification of a cardiovascular neuron. Panel A: responses to bolus injection (▲) and slow infusion (Δ) of norepinephrine. Analysis of cardiac cycle and respiratory cycle synchrony of unit activity was made during periods of low (line a) and high (line b) arterial pressures. Expanded time scale at the end of the arterial pressure trace shows the modulation of pressure during the respiratory cycle. Panel B: response curve relating unit activity and mean arterial pressure (MAP). Upper pair of arrows (▲) mark range of unit activity associated with respiratory modulation of pressure at low (a) mean arterial pressures. Lower pair of arrows (▲) associated with range of activity at high (b) mean arterial pressures. Histograms of unit activity during cardiac cycle, at low and high arterial pressures in panels C and D, respectively. Electrocardiogram (ECG) is shown for reference. Histogram of unit activity during respiratory cycle at high and low arterial pressures in panels E and F, respectively. Peak (●) and nadir (○) mean arterial pressures during respiratory cycle shown in expanded traces in panel A.*

Respiratory Neurons

Neurons with prominent rhythms synchronized to the respiratory cycle were commonly encountered in the region 200–300 μm dorsal to the region where the cardiovascular neurons were found (Fig. 4B). These cells commonly showed an acute sensitivity to plasma CO_2 levels. Because these cells are located in the region of well-defined respiratory cell groups and have a prominent sensitivity to events linked to respiration, we have classified them as respiratory units. The response of respiratory cells to changes in arterial pressure was highly variable between cells (Fig. 4A). Frequently, activity decreased when arterial pressure increased, but with a generally poor temporal correlation of the two events. Furthermore, unit activity never displayed any cardiac rhythm, even when examined at elevated pressures (Fig. 4C).

Cardiovascular neurons were examined for possible involvement in respiration. At resting arterial pressures, these cells never showed any detectable respiratory rhythm (Fig. 2E). At elevated arterial pressures, an apparent respiratory modulation of unit activity appeared (Fig. 2F). However, closer examination revealed that arterial pressure was modulated during the respiratory cycle (Fig. 2F) and that the change in unit activity was appropriate for the respiration-related changes in arterial pressure at the new operating point on the response curve (Fig. 2B). These observations were confirmed for five cardiovascular units, and suggest that the respiratory modulation of unit discharge is a result of respiratory modulation of arterial baroreceptor activity.

Responses to Aortic Occlusion

Occlusion of the abdominal aorta with a snare produced a rapid, transient rise in arterial pressure. This stimulus was used to examine the responses of six cardiovascular units; all units showed a decreased activity, proportional to the increased pressure (Fig. 5A). Moreover, the activity-pressure response curve for the snare coincided with the response curve generated with a bolus injection of norepinephrine (Fig. 5B). In the immediate vicinity of the cardiovascular neurons, the responses of four non-respiratory, non-cardiovascular units were examined; these cells did not respond to the snare-induced pressure rise (Fig. 5C).

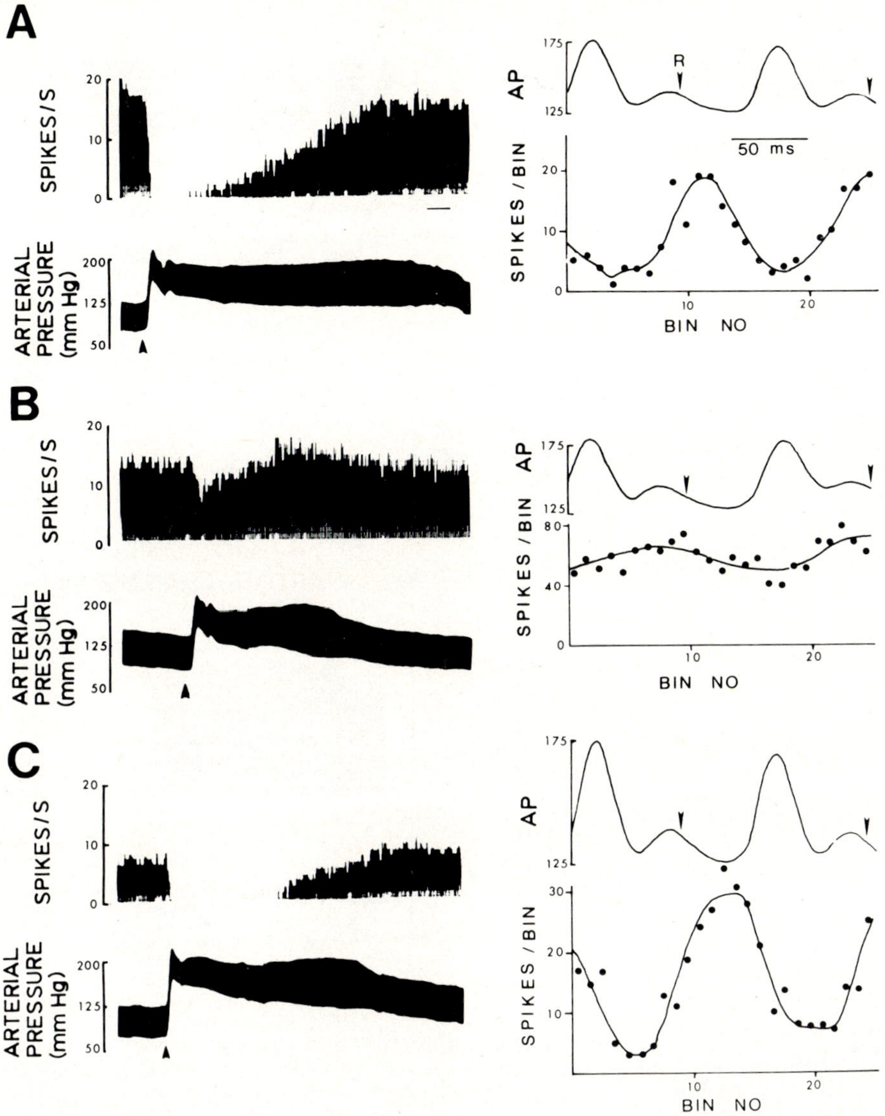

FIGURE 3. *Origin of pressure sensitivity and pulse-synchronous rhythm. Panel A: left panel shows integrated unit histogram of activity in response to bolus injection of norepinephrine (▲). Right panel shows post-systole histogram of activity during a subsequent infusion of norepinephrine. ▼ marks R-wave of ECG. Panel B: integrated unit histogram and post-systole histograms immediately after superfusion of lidocaine onto baroreceptor nerves. Panel C: recovery of pressure sensitivity and cardiac rhythm after washout of lidocaine, 30 minutes after lidocaine superfusion. Calibration bar: 30 sec.*

Responses to Superior Laryngeal Nerve Stimulation

A total of 18 units were studied for responses to a short electrical stimulation of the superior laryngeal nerve (2–5 sec train, 100–400 μA, 100 Hz, 200 μsec), which caused an immediate, transient decrease in arterial pressure to approximately 50–60 mm Hg. Nine cardiovascular neurons were tested, and all responded with an immediate reduction of activity, ranging from 70–100% (Fig. 6A). Five respiratory neurons were tested and all were unresponsive. Four neurons that did not have respiratory rhythms and were not sensitive to norepinephrine-induced changes in arterial pressure were also tested: three were unresponsive (Fig. 6B) and one was excited.

The Effects of Selective Deafferentation on Cardiovascular Neurons

Arterial baroreceptor fibers are known to travel in the vagus/aortic nerve/cervical sympathetic chain complex, carotid sinus and superior laryngeal nerves (Krieger and Marseillan, 1964). Cardiovascular neurons were studied in three different groups of partially baroreceptor-innervated animals: (1) carotid sinus afferents intact (vagus/aortic nerve/sympathetic chain complex, and superior laryngeal nerve transected); (2) aortic arch afferents partially intact and carotid sinus afferents intact (vagus/aortic nerve/sympathetic chain complex transected); (3) vagus/aortic nerve/sympathetic chain afferents intact (carotid sinus denervated). In all cases, cardiovascular neurons could be identified; however, many cells could not be fully silenced at pressures obtained by bolus injection of norepinephrine. For these cells, cut-off pressures were estimated by extrapolating the highly pressure-sensitive portion of the curve to the abscissa. With only carotid sinus afferents intact, cut-off pressure was 178.5 ± 32.7 mm Hg (n = 10). With carotid sinus and superior laryngeal nerve afferents intact, cut-off pressure was 169.8 ± 16.6 mm Hg (n = 10). In both groups of

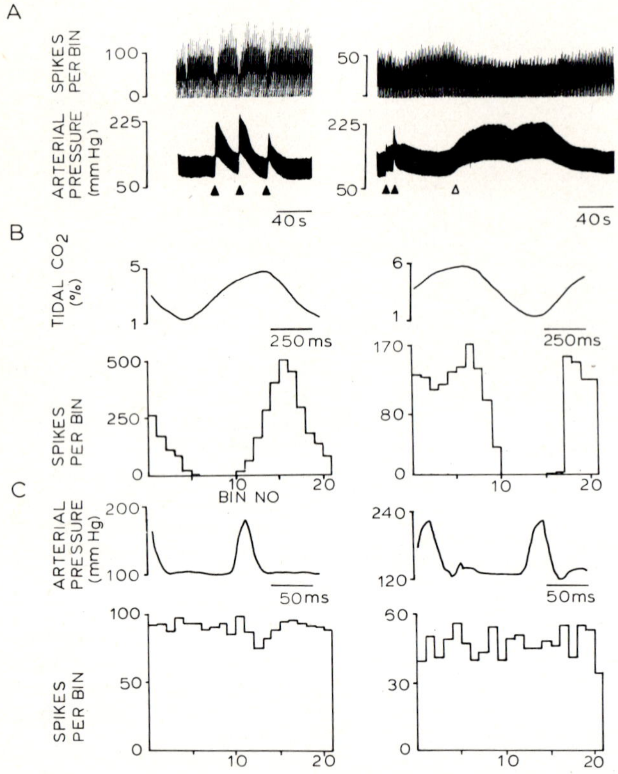

FIGURE 4. *Identification of two respiratory neurons. Panel A: unit activity changes with bolus injection (▲) and slow infusion (Δ) of norepinephrine. Panel B: histograms of unit activity during respiratory cycle. Panel C: histograms of unit activity during cardiac cycle.*

vagotomized animals, cardiovascular neurons displayed prominent pulse-synchronous rhythms when histograms of post-systolic activity during elevated arterial pressure were examined. With only carotid sinus afferents denervated, cut-off pressure was 142 ± 20.3 mm Hg (n = 3). In fully innervated animals cut-off pressure was 148.3 ± 21.3 mm Hg (q.v. Table 1).

Responses to Hypothalamic Stimulation and Midbrain Transection

Stimulation of the dorsomedial hypothalamus at moderate intensities (less than 250 μA) caused large increases in arterial pressure. All cardiovascular neurons tested were inhibited subsequent to the pressure increase, with a time course similar to that seen with pharmacological pressor responses (Fig. 7A). During the stimulus train, however, some units (10 of 19) were excited (Figs. 7A, 10C), and other units (9 of 19) were either inhibited (Fig. 10D) or unaffected. Respiratory neurons were uniformly excited by the same stimulation, and the excitation lasted several seconds beyond the stimulation (Fig. 7B).

Five cardiovascular neurons were identified in one animal with a midcollicular transection. Maximal firing rates ranged from 10–42 spikes/sec, and cut-off pressures ranged from 124–152. These values were similar to those found in animals with intact neuraxes.

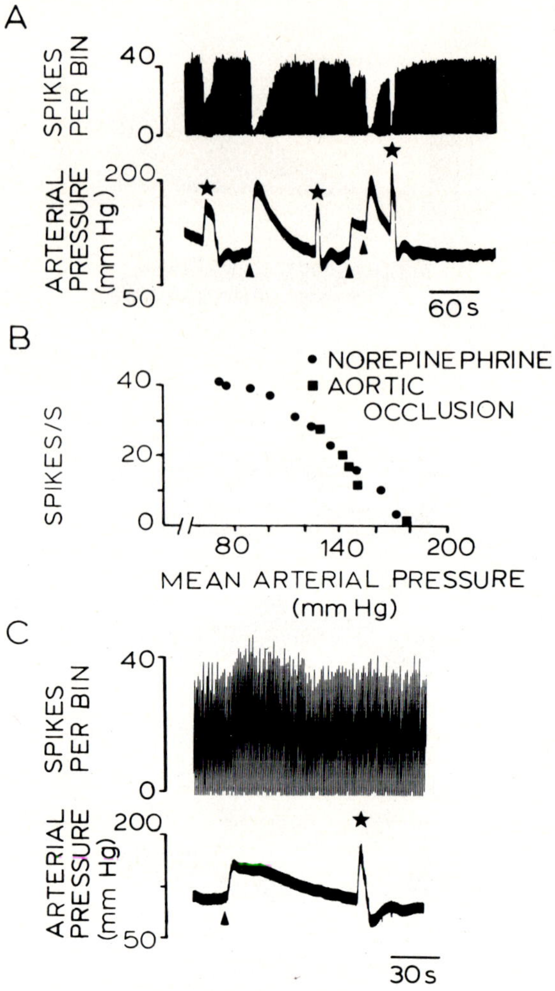

FIGURE 5. *Responses of neurons to aortic occlusion. Panel A: unit activity of a cardiovascular neuron in response to arterial pressure changes produced by injection of norepinephrine (▲) or occlusion of the abdominal aorta (★). Panel B: relationship of unit activity and mean arterial pressure during pharmacological and mechanical manipulations of pressure. Panel C: unit activity of unidentified cell in the vicinity of cardiovascular neurons during pharmacological and mechanical changes in arterial pressure.*

Electrophysiological Characteristics of Cardiovascular Neurons

The recorded spikes of cardiovascular neurons commonly displayed biphasic (positive/negative) waveforms. Frequently, constant latency spikes were evoked by electrical stimulation of the upper thoracic spinal cord; these spikes followed high frequency stimulation. A total of 84 negatively correlated cardiovascular neurons were tested for antidromic activation from the thoracic spinal cord: 44 were identified as antidromically activated (52%) on the basis of collision of spontaneous spikes and evoked spikes. Latencies were quite variable between cells, ranging from 4.5–95 msec. A natural consequence of the high level of activity of many of these cells was the collision of most antidromic impulses with spontaneous impulses. Only when

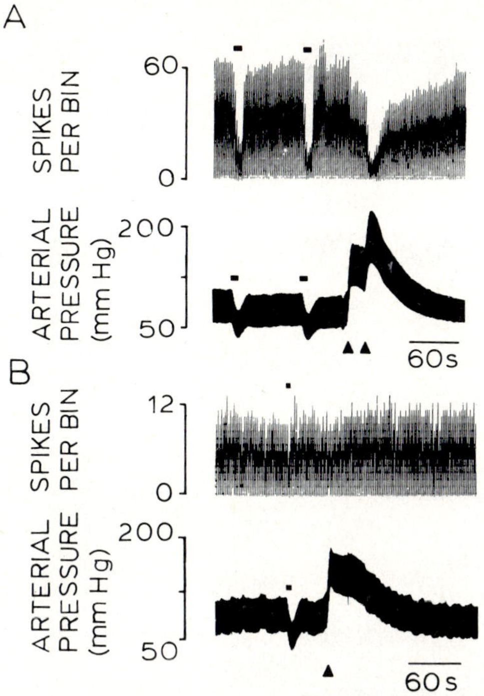

FIGURE 6. *Responses of neurons to superior laryngeal nerve stimulation. Panel A: unit activity of cardiovascular neuron decreases during ipsilateral superior laryngeal nerve stimulation (bar; 5-sec train, 300 μA, 100 Hz, 200 μsec) and norepinephrine injection (▲). Panel B: unit activity of an unidentified neuron shows no response to nerve stimulation or arterial pressure changes.*

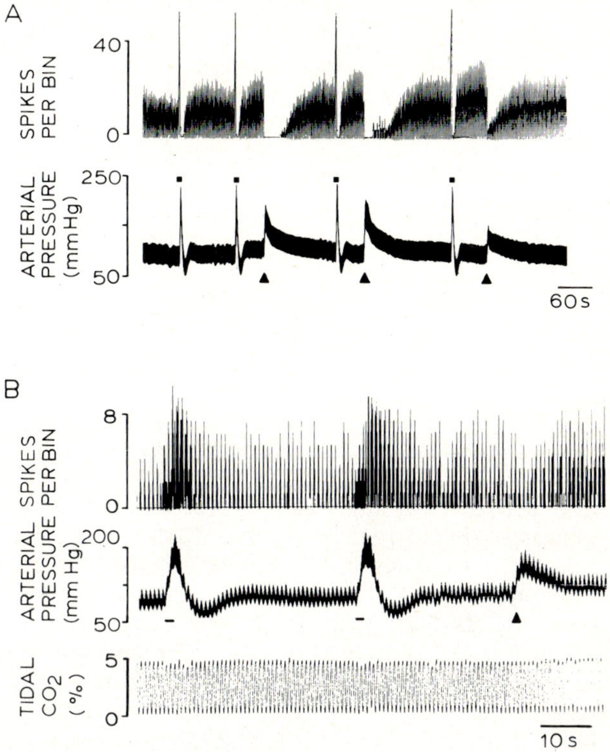

FIGURE 7. *Responses of neurons to hypothalamic stimulation. Panel A: unit activity of a cardiovascular neuron shows a pronounced increase during hypothalamic stimulation (bar; 5-sec train, 250 μA, 100 Hz, 500 μsec) followed by complete cessation during large, transient arterial pressure increase evoked by stimulation. Responses to norepinephrine injections are also shown (▲). Panel B: unit activity of a respiratory neuron shows excitation during and after hypothalamic stimulation (2-sec train).*

the cells were tested at elevated pressures were antidromic impulses reliably observed.

Calculated axonal conduction velocities varied from 0.4–8.5 m/sec (Fig. 8). This wide range of conduction velocities is not characteristic of any single fiber type. Indeed, a natural division of conduction velocities appeared between 1.1 and 2.0 m/sec, suggesting that at least two fiber types may be represented in the data. Thus, the data were further analyzed on the basis of this arbitrary division (Table 1). The maximal firing rates and sensitivities of the two groups were markedly different. Cut-off pressures were not different. These results are illustrated in Figure 9 with response curves based on the averaged data. Threshold pressures (the arterial pressure at which inhibition is first apparent) can be estimated from the response curves: 62 mm Hg for group 1 and 88 mm Hg for group 2.

Spike Amplitude Modulation

A striking and consistent characteristic of the cardiovascular neurons was the modulation of spike amplitude according to the on-going activity of the units (Fig. 10). Spike amplitude was minimal when

TABLE 1
Electrophysiological Properties of Antidromically Identified Cardiovascular Neurons

Group	Conduction velocity (m/sec)	Maximal firing rate (spikes/sec)	Sensitivity (spikes/sec per mm Hg)	Cut-off pressure (mm Hg)
Pooled	2.33 ± 2.04	19.1 ± 12.5	0.27 ± 0.19	148.3 ± 21.3
(*n*)	(44)	(120)	(125)	(128)
1	0.64 ± 0.21*	13.0 ± 9.8*	0.15 ± 0.10*	149.1 ± 17.8
(*n*)	(20)	(20)	(20)	(20)
2	3.83 ± 1.75*	23.9 ± 10.5*	0.37 ± 0.16*	153.1 ± 18.7
(*n*)	(24)	(24)	(24)	(24)

Results are expressed as mean ± SD.
* $P < 0.05$, comparing group 1 and group 2.

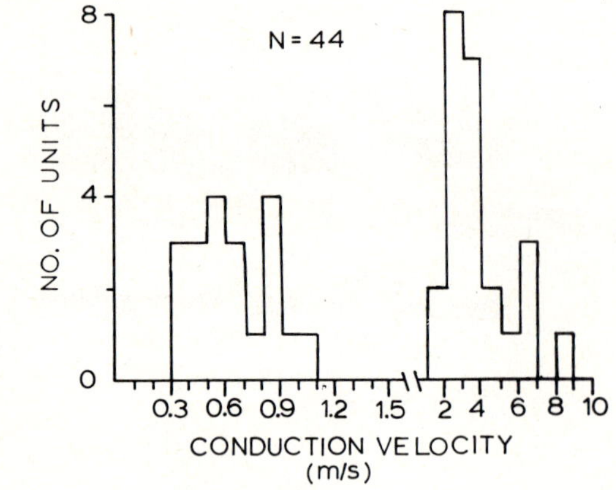

FIGURE 8. *Frequency histogram of calculated axonal conduction velocities of antidromically identified cardiovascular neurons.*

unit activity was high as a result of low arterial pressures (Fig. 10A). When hypothalamic stimulation further increased the activity of cardiovascular units, further reduction in spike amplitude was seen (Fig. 10C). In contrast, spike amplitude increased whenever unit activity decreased. This situation was observed without exception: when pressure was increased by norepinephrine injections or by hypothalamic stimulation (Fig. 10, A and C); when stimulation of the superior laryngeal nerve reduced arterial pressure (Fig. 10E); when hypothalamic stimulation reduced unit activity prior to pressure changes (Fig. 10D). Finally, a train of high frequency antidromic spikes showed the same gradual reduction in amplitude between initial and final spikes, whether at resting or elevated arterial pressures (Fig. 10, F–H).

Discussion

This study demonstrates that, within the potent vasopressor region of the rostral ventrolateral me-

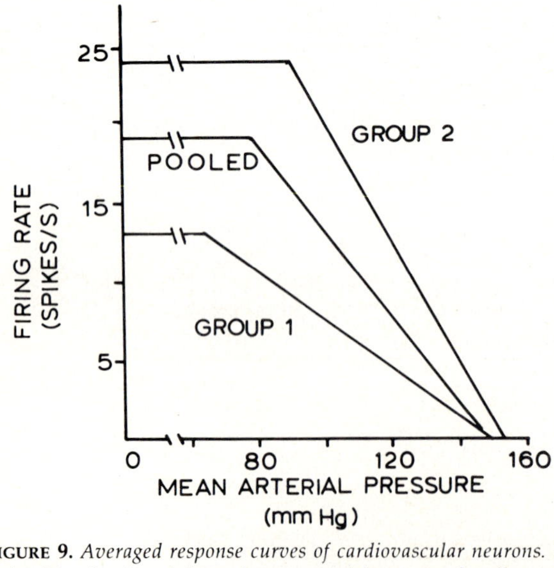

FIGURE 9. *Averaged response curves of cardiovascular neurons. Relationship of unit activity and mean arterial pressure for all neurons (pooled), for those with slower axonal conduction velocity (group 1) and for those with faster axonal conduction velocity (group 2).*

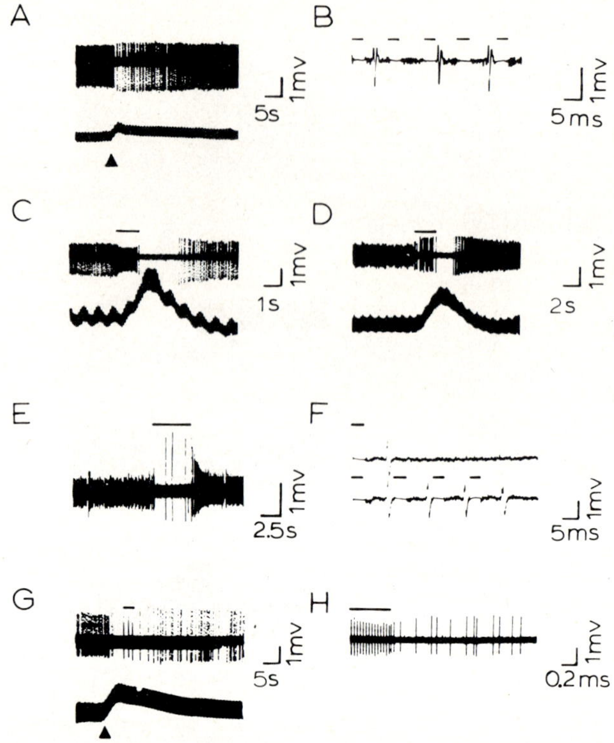

FIGURE 10. *Spike amplitude modulation. Panel A: slight spike amplitude increase (upper trace) during modest increase in arterial pressure (25 mm Hg) induced by norepinephrine (▲). Panel B: unit activity during hypothalamic stimulation train (100 Hz) showing filtering of stimulus artifacts (bars). Panel C: unit activity increases and spike amplitude decreases during hypothalamic stimulation (bar; 2-sec train, 100 Hz). Stimulation increases arterial pressure which silences unit; spike amplitude is increased and slowly declines as unit activity recovers. Panel D: hypothalamic stimulation (bar) decreases unit activity prior to the increase in arterial pressure; spike amplitude increases as unit activity decreases. Panel E: unit is nearly silenced during superior laryngeal nerve stimulation (bar; 5-sec train, 100 Hz). Spike amplitude increases threefold during decreased activity and recovers gradually after stimulation. Panel F: spinal cord stimulation (bar; 500 μA, 200 μsec, with artifact suppressed) elicits a single antidromic spike (upper trace) at elevated arterial pressures. Four stimulations at 50 Hz (lower trace) showing decline in successive antidromic spike amplitude. Panel G: bar marks three trains (at 1-sec intervals) of four antidromic spikes at 50 Hz (with artifact suppressed) during a period of silence at elevated arterial pressure. Spike amplitude fails to recover between trains. Note that individual spikes within trains are superimposed at this frequency. Panel H: train of 14 stimulations at 25 Hz (bar, artifact suppressed) elicits antidromic spikes at resting arterial pressure; note slight decrease in spike amplitude during stimulation and recovery of amplitude thereafter.*

dulla, there exists a group of neurons that are spontaneously active, are strongly inhibited by increases in arterial pressure, and project to the spinal cord. The pressure sensitivity is observed within the cardiac cycle, as well as in transient changes in mean arterial pressure. Moreover, these cells have properties that are distinctly different from respiratory neurons in the same vicinity. Because the cells are found in close association with the region of the medulla which controls basal vasomotor tone, have spinal projections, are acutely baro-sensitive in a wide variety of circumstances, and do not display any significant respiration-linked properties; they are likely candidates for cardiovascular neurons controlling sympathetic vasomotor outflow.

The question of artifact in evaluating arterial pressure sensitivity and pulse-synchronous activity must be considered. That such propeties arise from peripheral baroreceptors is indicated by four types of data. First, the response curves of the cardiovascular cells show 100% modulation of activity over a range of 65–85 mm Hg and exhibit threshold pressures at which inhibition is first detectable (Fig. 9); similar thresholds for baroreceptor activity have been described (Yao and Thoren, 1983). Furthermore, the response curves can be established by several independent methods: pharmacological or mechanical maneuvers (Figs. 2A, 5B, 9). Second, these cells have cardiac rhythms that also show threshold pressure characteristics appropriate for baroreceptor signals (Fig. 2, C and D). This rhythm and pressure sensitivity are reversibly reduced or eliminated by anesthetizing the peripheral nerves carrying baroreceptor afferents (Fig. 3). Third, partial elimination of baroreceptor afferents shifts the pressure-activity response curve to the right, indicating a decrease in the potency of arterial pressure in inhibiting the cells. Finally, these cells are strongly inhibited by electrical stimulation of the superior laryngeal nerve (Fig. 6A), a nerve known to carry baroreceptor fibers from the aortic arch and which buffers arterial pressure changes (Faber and Brody, 1983).

These data show that not only is baroreceptor inhibition mediated through the cardiovascular neurons of the nucleus paragigantocellularis lateralis, but also that baroreceptor signals from both carotid sinus and aortic arch regions converge on this descending pathway. Whether the convergence occurs at the level of these cells, or at some earlier synaptic junction, cannot be answered from our data. Baroreceptors are also found in the cardiopulmonary region; whether signals from such baroreceptors also converge on these cells is unknown. The present data do indicate that vagal afferents are not essential for the pressure sensitivity or pulse-synchronous activity of these neurons.

There have been many studies attempting to identify neurons in the brainstem which relay baroreceptor information to the sympathetic nervous system (q.v. Koepchen, 1975). Salmoiraghi (1962) identified a few units which he described as population-one and population-two cardiovascular neurons, based on their responses to pharmacological and reflex changes in arterial pressure. The cardiovascular neurons reported here are similar to the population-two neurons, with activities correlated negatively with mean arterial pressure levels (Fig. 2B). The term "cardiovascular" is broad and can imply the source of afferent signals or the destination of efferent outflow. With the paucity of present knowledge concerning specific pathways for integration of afferent and efferent cardiovascular information within the brain, it is justifiable to retain the term cardiovascular to describe interneurons which integrate cardiovascular sensory information. Although, in the present case, the targets to which the cardiovascular cells relay baroreceptor information are not known, recent evidence shows that the spinal cord projections from the same area terminate exclusively in the autonomic nuclei of the spinal cord (Ross et al., 1984b). The results of lesion and stimulation experiments involving this portion of the medulla suggest that these neurons do relay excitatory signals to vasculature (Ross et al., 1984a). The possibility of projections to preganglionic neurons involved in regulation of targets other than vasculature is not precluded.

In spite of the general similarity of cardiovascular neuron responses to changes in arterial pressure, significant diversity exists within the cardiovascular cell group (Table 1). Two types of descending pathways from the cardiovascular neurons are suggested by these data: unmyelinated fibers (group 1 in Table 1) characterized by a lower threshold pressure for baroreceptor inhibition and small myelinated fibers (group 2) with a higher threshold. Similarly, a broad spectrum of baroreceptor fibers has been described (Coleridge et al., 1980). Although there is little quantitative agreement about the specific properties of various fiber types, there is clearly consensus that different fiber types are characterized by different threshold pressures for activation. The most detailed comparative data (for a single species, using uniform techniques for analyzing the various fibers) indicates that large, myelinated fibers have a lower threshold—less than 60 mm Hg. Unmyelinated fibers have a higher threshold—greater than 84 mm Hg (Yao and Thoren, 1983). These threshold and fiber type relationships are opposite those of the cardiovascular neurons; thus, there is no apparent preservation of information, such as baroreceptor threshold, through fiber type specificity of central pathways.

Anatomical studies of the ventrolateral medulla have indicated the presence of as many as seven morphological cell types (Andrezik et al., 1981). Furthermore, many potential neurotransmitters have been found in cells in the general vicinity: epinephrine (presumed, due to the presence of phenylethanolamine-*N*-methyltransferase), serotonin, substance P, neuropeptide Y (Hökfelt et al., 1974, 1978, 1983; Steinbusch, 1981). In rats, some of these neurons have been demonstrated to project to the spinal cord and, specifically, to the intermediolateral cell column and central autonomic area (Bowker et al., 1982; Ross et al., 1984b). Thus, it is possible that the cardiovascular cell group of the ventrolateral medulla comprises a variety of cell types, with different transmitters subserving different functions.

The observed spike amplitude modulations raise the issue of recording artifact. Traditionally, amplitude constancy has been cited as evidence for recording stability. Conversely, inconstancy has been assumed to indicate electrode movement with respect to the unit recorded. There are many reasons to believe that the demonstrated modulations in amplitude were due to real changes in extracellular spike amplitude and not to artifactual changes in recorded spikes. The changes were highly systematic: amplitude *always* increased whenever unit activity decreased. When blood pressure was increased—whether due to mechanical, pharmacological, or central stimulation—unit activity was decreased, presumably via baroreceptor reflexes as blood pressure increased (Fig. 10, A and C). On the other hand, superior laryngeal nerve stimulation decreased unit activity and arterial pressure, presumably due to direct baroreceptor stimulation—yet, spike amplitude still increased (Fig. 10E). Thus, when unit activity decreased, spike amplitude increased. Conversely, as unit activity increased, amplitude decreased, as illustrated in the recovery period following reflex inhibition of the unit (Fig. 10, A, C, and D), or during excitation of the unit by hypothalamic stimulation (Fig. 10C). In the latter situation, spike amplitude changed before any change occurred in arterial pressure. Finally, the spikes produced by high frequency antidromic activation at stable pressures (high or low) showed a gradual reduction in amplitude (Fig. 10, G and H).

Another type of possible recording artifact could occur in situations such as illustrated in Figure 10C: the recording might comprise the spikes of two units—one before the silent period, and one after. This possibility can be ruled out because antidromic excitation of many units could be demonstrated at any time during the silent period. Furthermore, the envelope of the spike amplitude made a gradual transition between maximum and minimum amplitudes (Fig. 10, A, C, and D), indicating that the recording electrode was not shifting from one unit to another.

Thus, the systematic increases and decreases in spike amplitude cannot be attributed to any systematic movement of the recording electrode toward or away from the cardiovascular unit. The clearest correlation of amplitude modulation is with unit activity. In fact, the greatest amplitude changes (2-fold, or more) occurred with the fastest firing cells which could be fully silenced (Fig. 10E). One possible interpretation of the amplitude modulation is that, at low levels of activity, regenerative channels which are involved in spike generation may have sufficient time to recover between spikes; more active channels during a spike would allow more charge movement, measured as a larger spike. Alternatively, the cell may be relatively depolarized at high levels of activity and relatively hyperpolarized at low levels of activity. The depolarized state would provide less electrical driving force for charge movement during spikes. This hypothesis would require that the antidromically elicited spikes would produce a negative afterpotential or would receive subthreshold excitation from other units activated by spinal cord stimulation. The elucidation of the mechanism of amplitude modulation, however, must await intracellular recordings. Recent experiments with the dopaminergic neurons of the substantia nigra support the correlation between spike amplitude and the level of hyperpolarization (Grace and Bunney, 1983).

The existence in the rostral ventrolateral medulla of neurons which are involved in tonic sympathetic vasomotor control, as well as baroreceptor reflex regulation, has been suggested by many studies using a host of pharmacological agents (Feldberg and Guertzenstein, 1972; Wennergren and Oberg, 1980; Dampney et al., 1982; Willette et al., 1983; Hilton et al., 1984; Farlow et al., 1984; Ross et al., 1984a). The spontaneous activity of spinally projecting cardiovascular neurons is consistent with a center for tonic vasomotor control. The ventrolateral medulla has also been described as an important integration area for pressor responses emanating from the hypothalamus (Willette et al., 1984). Hilton et al. (1984) have further proposed that the same ventrolateral medullary neurons responsible for tonic sympathetic vasomotor drive are also a relay for hypothalamic defense reaction. Indeed, the cardiovascular neurons reported in the present study do respond to electrical stimulation of hypothalamic areas associated with the defense reaction. The two types of responses—some units powerfully excited (Figs. 7A and 10C), others inhibited (Fig. 10D)—are consistent with the two patterns of vasomotor responses in the defense reaction: powerful, general systemic vasoconstriction and hindlimb vasodilation, in part due to decreased sympathetic tone. However, the fact that these cells can maintain a high activity following midcollicular transection indicates that tonic excitatory drive from the hypothalamus is not essential to their activity, in contrast to the proposal of Hilton et al. Whether the activity of the cardiovascular neurons arises from an excitatory synaptic input or is due to an inherent pacemaker-like activity cannot be determined from the present experiments.

In summary, the negatively correlated cardiovascular neurons of the intermediate portion of the nucleus paragigantocellularis are a major souce of descending excitatory drive to spinal levels. Although the target organs of these neurons remain to be determined more precisely, these cells are likely to be involved in tonic vasomotor tone setting, as well as baroreceptor and defense reaction vasomotor responses. However, this does not diminish the possible importance of other areas of the brain in integrating various vasomotor functions (Hilton et al., 1984), nor does it preclude the existence of other descending vasomotor pathways (Morrison and Gebber, 1984; Byrum et al., 1984; Guyenet, 1984).

The technical assistance of Megan Borror and the careful review of this manuscript by Dr. Christopher Byrum are gratefully acknowledged.

Supported by HL28785 and NIH RCDA HL01128 to P.G.G.

Address for reprints: Dr. Patrice G. Guyenet, Department of Pharmacology, University of Virginia, School of Medicine, Charlottesville, Virginia 22908.

Received August 16, 1984; accepted for publication December 20, 1984.

References

Amendt K, Czachurski J, Dembowski K, Seller H (1979) Bulbospinal projections to the intermediolateral cell column: A neuroanatomical study. J Auton Nerv Syst **1:** 103–117

Andrezik JA, Chan-Palay V, Palay SL (1981) The nucleus paragigantocellularis lateralis in the rat. Conformation and cytology. Anat Embryol **161:** 355–371

Bowker RM, Westlund KN, Sullivan MC, Coulter JD (1982) Organization of descending serotonergic projections to the spinal cord. Prog Brain Res **57:** 239–265

Brown DL, Guyenet PG (1984) Cardiovascular neurons of the brainstem with projections to the spinal cord. Am J Physiol **247:** R1009–R1016

Byrum CE, Stornetta RL, Guyenet PG (1984) Electrophysiological properties of spinally-projecting neurons. Brain Res **303:** 15–29

Coleridge HM, Coleridge JCG, Kaufman MP, Dangel A, Baker DG (1980) Aortic baroreceptors in dogs: In vivo sensitivity and short term resetting. *In* Arterial Baroreceptors and Hypertension, edited by P Sleight. Oxford, Oxford Press, pp 53–58

Dampney RAL, Moon EA (1980) Role of the ventrolateral medulla in vasomotor response to cerebral ischemia. Am J Physiol **239:** H349–H358

Dampney RAL, Goodchild AK, Robertson LG, Montgomery W (1982) Role of the ventrolateral medulla in vasomotor regulation: A correlative anatomical and physiological study. Brain Res **249:** 223–235

Faber JE, Brody MJ (1983) Reflex hemodynamic response to superior laryngeal nerve stimulation in the rat. J Auton Nerv Syst **9:** 607–622

Farlow DM, Goodchild AK, Dampney RAL (1984) Evidence that vasomotor neurons in the rostral ventrolateral medulla project to the spinal sympathetic outflow via the dorsomedial pressor area. Brain Res **298:** 313–320

Feldberg WS, Guertzenstein PG (1972) A vasopressor effect of pentobarbitone sodium. J Physiol (Lond) **224:** 83–103

Grace AA, Bunney BS (1983) Intracellular and extracellular electrophysiology of nigral dopaminergic neurons 1. Identification and characterization. Neuroscience **10:** 301–315

Guyenet PG (1984) Baroreceptor-mediated inhibition of A5 noradrenergic neurons. Brain Res **303:** 30–41

Hilton SM, Marshall JM, Timms RJ (1984) Ventral medullary relay neurons in the pathway from the defence areas of the cat and their effect on blood pressure. J Physiol (Lond) **345:** 149–166

Hökfelt T, Fuxe K, Goldstein M, Johansson O (1974) Immunohistochemical evidence for the existence of adrenaline neurons in the rat brain. Brain Res **66:** 235–251

Hökfelt T, Ljungdahl A, Steinbusch H, Verhofstad A, Nilsson G, Brodin E, Pernow B, Goldstein M (1978) Immunohistochemical evidence of substance P-like immunoreactivity in some 5-hydroxytryptamine-containing neurons in the rat central nervous system. Neuroscience **3:** 517–538

Hökfelt T, Lundberg JM, Tatemoto K, Mutt V, Terenius L, Polak J, Bloom S, Sasek C, Elde R, Goldstein M (1983) Neuropeptide Y (NPY)- and FMRFamide neuropeptide-like immunoreactivities in catecholamine neurons of the rat medulla oblongata. Acta Physiol Scand **117:** 315–318

Koepchen HP, Langhorst P, Seller H (1975) The problem of identification of autonomic neurons in the lower brain stem. Brain Res **87:** 375–393

Krieger EM, Marseillan RF (1963) Aortic depressor fibers in the rat: An electrophysiological study. Am J Physiol **205:** 771–774

Morrison SF, Gebber GL (1983) Raphe neurons with sympathetic-related activity: Baroreceptor responses and spinal connections. Am J Physiol **246:** R338–R348

Paxinos G, Watson C (1982) The Rat Brain in Stereotaxic Coordinates. New York, Academic Press

Reis DJ, Cuenod M (1965) Central neural regulation of carotid baroreceptor reflexes in the cat. Am J Physiol **209:** 1267–1269

Ross CA, Ruggiero DA, Park DH, Joh TH, Sved AF, Fernandez-Pardal J, Saavedra JM, Reis DJ (1984a) Tonic vasomotor control by the rostral ventrolateral medulla: Effect of electrical or chemical stimulation of the area containing C1 adrenaline neurons on arterial pressure, heart rate, and plasma catecholamines and vasopressin. J Neurosci **4:** 474–494

Ross CA, Ruggiero DA, Joh TH, Park DH, Reis DJ (1984b) Rostral ventrolateral medulla: Selective projections to the thoracic autonomic cell column from the region containing C1 adrenaline neurons. J Comp Neurol **228:** 168–185

Salmoiraghi GC (1962) "Cardiovascular" neurones in brain stem of cat. J Neurophysiol **25:** 182–197

Steinbusch HWM (1981) Distribution of serotonin-immunoreactivity in the central nervous system of the rat; Cell bodies and terminals. Neuroscience **6:** 557–618

Wennergren G, Oberg O (1980) Cardiovascular effects elicited from the ventral surface of medulla oblongata in the cat. Pflugers Arch **387:** 189–195

Willette RN, Krieger AJ, Barcas PP, Sapru HN (1983) Medullary γ-aminobutyric acid (GABA) receptors and the regulation of blood pressure in the rat. J Pharmacol Exp Ther **226:** 893–899

Willette RN, Gatti PA, Sapru HN (1984) GABAergic mechanisms in the ventrolateral medulla alter vasopressor responses from the anterior hypothalamus. J Cardiovasc Pharmacol **6:** 476–482

Yamane T (1964) Statistics: An Introductory Analysis. New York, Harper & Row

Yao T, Thoren P (1983) Characteristics of brachiocephalic and carotid sinus baroreceptors with non-medullated afferents in rabbit. Acta Physiol Scand **117:** 1–8

INDEX TERMS: Rostral ventrolateral medulla • Baroreceptor reflexes • Defense reaction • Vasomotor center • Reticulospinal neurons • Rat

Kinetics of Thallium Exchange in Cultured Rat Myocardial Cells

David McCall, Lawrence J. Zimmer, and Arnold M. Katz

From the Cardiology Sections, Department of Medicine, University of Connecticut Health Center, Farmington, Connecticut, and Department of Medicine, University of Nebraska Medical Center, Omaha, Nebraska

SUMMARY. The kinetics of thallium exchange in cultured rat myocardial cells were studied and compared to those of potassium in the same tissue. Studies were carried out using low concentrations (10 nM to 5 μM) of thallium-204, approximating those likely to be encountered during clinical myocardial scintigraphy. Both thallium uptake and release could be described by a single exponential with a half-time of exchange which was approximately half that of potassium and which was largely independent of extracellular thallium concentration. Some 60% of thallium uptake occurred via an "active" or ouabain-inhibitable mechanism which, in the absence of extracellular potassium, could be activated by low concentrations (10 nM to 5 μM) of thallium. The apparent K_m for thallium on this active transport mechanism was 2–7 μM. Increasing extracellular potassium from 0–10 mM caused significant, concentration-dependent decreases in both the total and the active component of the thallium influx. Similarly nonradioactive thallium (0.10 μM to 0.10 mM) caused a concentration-dependent decrease in active potassium influx. Analysis of these results by both Lineweaver-Burk plots and Dixon plots confirmed competitive inhibition, potassium on thallium influx and vice versa, for the active component of the fluxes, and noncompetitive in the remainder. These findings indicate that active transport accounts for the greater portion of the influx of thallium and potassium, and that this active transport occurs via a common mechanism. If, as the results suggest, the receptor for thallium and potassium is the same, then the analysis by Dixon plots would indicate that the affinity of the receptor for thallium is 260 to 900 times greater than for potassium. This would therefore explain the rapid accumulation of thallium-201 by the myocardium, in vivo, from the low circulating concentrations of the isotope.
(*Circ Res 56: 370–376, 1985*)

THALLIUM-201 myocardial imaging has become an accepted diagnostic tool in cardiology, impairment of thallium-201 uptake commonly being used to detect and assess the extent of myocardial ischemia. Thallium ions (Tl^+) and potassium ions (K^+) are generally considered to behave in an analogous manner in a variety of biological systems (Mullins and Moore, 1960; Gehring and Hammond, 1964; Britten and Blank, 1968; Kashket, 1979), and Tl^+ can both activate (Britten and Blank, 1968) and be transported by (Landowne, 1975; Skulskii et al., 1978) membrane Na^+,K^+-ATPase. However, the K_m for Tl^+ of Na^+,K^+-ATPase, 0.16 mM (Britten and Blank, 1968), is considerably smaller than that for K^+. Most studies to date have examined the kinetics of Tl^+ transport when applied in concentrations between 0.01 and 1.0 mM to various enzyme or membrane systems, and little attention has been paid to myocardial thallium kinetics and exchange when the ion is used in concentrations (<1 μM) likely to be encountered during thallium-201 scintigraphy.

We therefore conducted the present study to examine the characteristics of cellular Tl^+ exchange, using low concentrations of the ion (10 nM to 5 μM), in cultured rat heart cells. The preparation used was chosen because of the presence of a single, rapidly exchangeable, extracellular compartment, which greatly facilitates flux determination, and because many of the cell's membrane characteristics (McCall, 1979; Wheeler et al., 1982) are similar to those of other myocardial preparations.

Methods

Myocardial Cell Cultures

Primary cultures of rat myocardial cells were prepared from the hearts of 1- to 2-day-old rats as previously described (McCall, 1979). Using only ventricular tissue, to obtain as nearly as possible a homogeneous population, the hearts were each cut into approximately six pieces and disaggregated to single cells by repeated trypsinization. After separation of fibroblasts (McCall, 1979) the cell suspension was seeded in Petri dishes, 6 cm in diameter (Falcon), and incubated at 37°C in an atmosphere of 5% CO_2 in air. All studies on the myocardial cells were carried out after 4–5 days growth in minimum essential medium containing 10% calf serum. By this time each Petri dish contained a synchronously contracting monolayer of some 1.0–1.5 × 10^6 cells. In all cultures used, myocardial cells accounted for at least 80% of the total cell population (McCall, 1979).

Ion flux studies were carried out with cultures whose initial intrinsic concentraction frequency lay in range 120–140/minute to minimize a rate-dependent effect. The values for cell surface area, cell volume, and volume of cell water previously reported (McCall, 1979) were used for all flux calculations.

Solutions Used

Because the pH of the growth medium depends on an atmosphere of 5% CO_2 in air, it could not be kept constant during the flux experiments, when cultures were continually being removed from, and replaced in, the incubator. All experiments were therefore carried out with the cells in a modified balanced salt solution (BSS) containing (mM): Na^+, 136.80; K^+, 5.35; Ca^{++}, 2.25; Mg^{++}, 1.03; Cl^-, 148.22; PO_4^{---}, 0.43; glucose 11.10; plus calf serum, 5%, and phenol red, 0.0002% (pH 7.2). The cells were allowed to equilibrate in BSS, which could maintain cell viability for at least 24 hours, for 2–3 hours before any measurements were made.

The K^+-free solutions used were obtained by omitting the K^+ salts and using dialyzed calf serum. No osmotic replacement for the K^+ salts was required, and during the K^+-free flux studies, the solution was continuously replaced to prevent accumulation of K^+ which could leak from the cells. Tl^+ solutions were prepared with Tl NO_3, because of its greater solubility; the final concentrations represent the combination of ^{204}Tl and the nonradioactive ion.

Ion flux Measurements

The technique employed in determining ionic content and fluxes in the cells have been described in detail elsewhere (Lamb and McCall, 1972; McCall, 1979). The K^+ and Tl^+ contents were measured after equilibration in BSS containing ^{42}K or ^{204}Tl. After cell loading, an isotonic Na^+- and K^+-free calcium-sorbitol solution at 0°C was used to wash the cells free of extracellular tracer, thereby permitting determination of intracellular radioactivity (McCall, 1979).

Influx determinations for K^+ were made and calculated as previously described (McCall, 1979). Initial studies of Tl^+ exchange showed that, like K^+, the uptake and release of Tl^+ could be described by a single exponential. The half-time of Tl^+ exchange was around 5 minutes compared to 12 minutes in the case of K^+. Subsequent determinations of Tl^+ influx were therefore made in the same way as for K^+ fluxes—in this case, after the cells had been exposed for 2 minutes to ^{204}Tl.

Separation of each influx into its "active," or ouabain-sensitive, and passive components was achieved from parallel measurements made in the presence and absence of 10^{-2} M ouabain (McCall, 1979). In each case, the cells were pretreated with ouabain for 10 minutes prior to the influx determination (Lamb and McCall, 1972) to ensure adequate Na pump inhibition. Efflux was measured by equilibrating the cells with the appropriate isotope tracer and then observing its loss into a nonradioactive solution by measuring the amount left in the cells at various times (McCall, 1979). For these studies, the nonradioactive solution at 37°C was continually replaced at 30–60 ml/min, which was not rate limiting to the efflux process. All flux determinations were made at 37°C (McCall, 1979).

Materials

^{204}Tl (5 Ci/g of Tl^+) was purchased from New England Nuclear. For the present study, ^{204}Tl was used because of its longer half-life and, as a consequence, its easier handling. Biologicals were from Flow Laboratories, and all chemicals from Mallinckrodt were of analytical grade.

Statistical Analysis

Student's *t*-tests for paired data were used to test for significant differences between groups. Linear regression analysis was done by least-squares fit. All results are presented as mean ± SEM.

Results

Thallium Uptake and Exchange

The uptake of Tl^+ by cultured myocardial cells, over the range of Tl^+ concentrations tested (10 nM to 10 μM), could be described by a single exponential. The half-time of uptake in the absence of extracellular K^+ was largely independent of the Tl^+ concentration, and the mean half-time of the exchange was 4.95 ± 0.51 minutes. This value is considerably less than the half-time of exchange for K^+ in the same preparation, which has a mean value of 12.05 minutes (McCall, 1979). The curve describing Tl^+ uptake was clearly asymptotic, intracellular Tl^+ reaching an equilibrium value within 20–40 minutes of exposure of the cells to the tracer.

Equilibration of intracellular Tl^+ ($[Tl^+]_i$) with respect to extracellular Tl^+ ($[Tl^+]_o$) is confirmed by the determination of the rate of loss of previously accumulated ^{204}Tl from the cells into a nonradioactive solution. These studies showed, over the range of Tl^+ concentrations tested and under equilibrium conditions, that the net Tl^+ efflux was almost identical to the net Tl^+ influx, mean half-time of ^{204}Tl loss being 5.09 ± 0.46 minutes (n = 15). Like the Tl^+ influx, the rate of Tl^+ loss under these conditions was unaffected by the concentration of Tl^+ to which the cells had been exposed during the loading period, and could be fitted to a single exponential.

Effect of Ouabain on Tl^+ Influx

The possibility that all or part of the Tl^+ uptake by myocardial cells could occur via the Na pump was assessed by measuring ^{204}Tl influx (2-minute exposure method) in the presence of ouabain, 10^{-9} to 10^{-3} M. As shown in Figure 1, ouabain effected a concentration-dependent decrease in Tl^+ uptake, very similar to that on the K^+ influx. None of the concentrations of ouabain used had any demonstrable effect on the Tl^+ efflux rate. Half-maximal inhibition of the Tl^+ influx was produced by 2×10^{-5} M ouabain, and the drug maximally inhibited some 60% of the total Tl^+ influx (Fig. 1). These findings are very similar to those found with the K^+ influx (McCall, 1979) where ouabain maximally inhibited 75% of the flux, with half-maximal inhibition occurring at a concentration of 10^{-6} M. The inhibitory effect of ouabain on the Tl^+ influx was significant ($P < 0.001$) for all concentrations of ouabain in excess of 10^{-7} M. This pattern of inhibition held true for all concentrations of Tl^+ tested, up to and including, in this case, 0.1 mM.

This finding strongly suggests that 60% of the Tl^+ influx represents active transport via the Na pump,

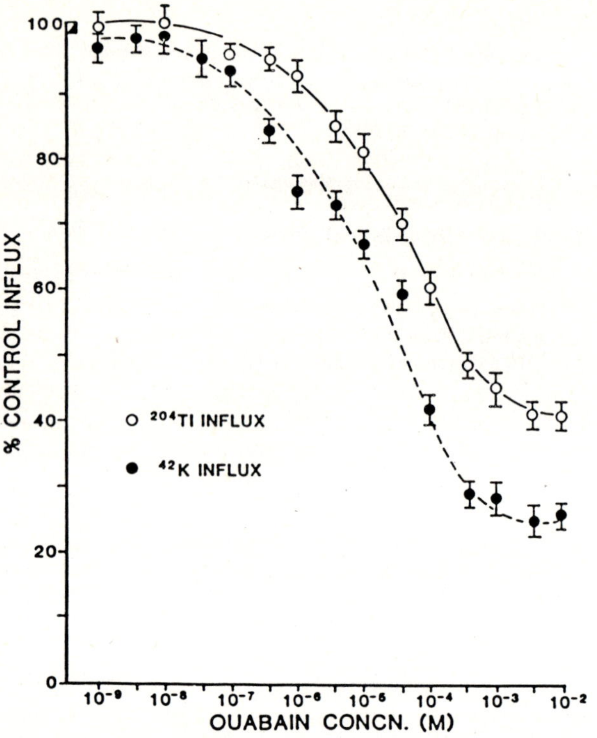

FIGURE 1. *Dose-response curve of ouabain (10^{-9} M to 10^{-2} M) on ^{42}K and ^{204}Tl influx myocardial cells at 37°C. Results expressed as mean + SEM for each n = 6.*

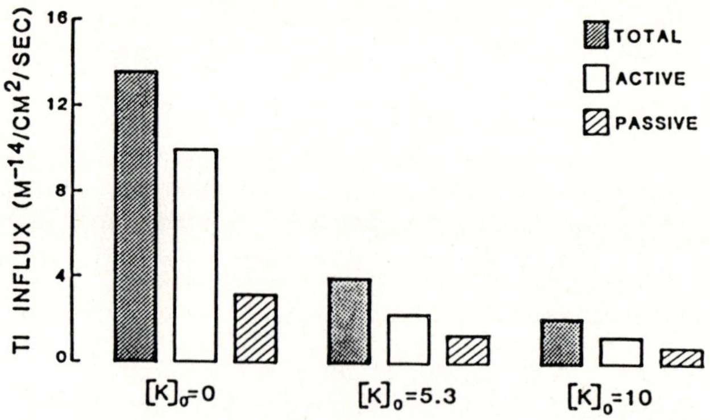

FIGURE 2. *Effect of extracellular K^+ on ^{204}Tl influx, myocardial cells at 37°C. Passive influx represents that measured in presence of 10^{-2} M ouabain and active influx was obtained by subtraction of passive from total influx. Bars represent mean of six observations. M^{-14} used in figures is mol^{-14}.*

so that in all subsequent studies the flux was divided into its "active" and passive components on the basis of ouabain sensitivity.

Effect of $[K^+]_o$ on Tl Exchange

Although the rate constant of Tl^+ uptake was independent of $[Tl^+]_o$, it was markedly affected by changes in $[K^+]_o$. The rate constant, λ, of Tl^+ uptake in the absence of extracellular K^+ was 0.14 ± 0.02 min^{-1} ($n = 5$). Increasing $(K^+)_o$ to 2 mM and 5 mM, for example, decreased λ to 0.09 ± 0.01 and 0.06 ± 0.02/min respectively (for each $n = 5$), both values being significantly ($P < 0.001$) less than the control. Similar progressive decreases in the rate constant were seen as $[K^+]_o$ was increased toward 10 mM.

Separation of the Tl^+ influx into its constituent components (Fig. 2) revealed that $[K^+]_o$ had a significant effect on all three components, total, active and passive, of the flux. For example (Fig. 2), using a $[Tl^+]_o$ of 2 μM, the total Tl^+ influx (mol^{-14}/cm^2 per sec) declined from a control (K^+-free conditions) of 13.56 ± 0.59 ($n = 10$) to 3.88 ± 0.11 ($n = 10$) and 2.10 ± 0.15 ($n = 5$) in 5.3 mM and 10 mM K^+, respectively (for each $P < 0.001$). At the same time, the passive or ouabain-insensitive influx (mol^{-14}/cm^2 per sec) declined from 2.86 ± 0.07 ($n = 10$ to 1.49 ± 0.04 ($n = 10$) and 0.84 ± 0.05 ($n = 5$), again in both cases the difference from the control being highly significant. By subtraction, this gives a net "active" Tl^+ influx (mol^{-14}/cm^2 per sec) of 10.70 in the absence of extracellular K^+, 2.40 at $[K^+]_o = 5.3$ mM, and 1.26 at $[K^+]_o = 10$ mM. The inhibitory effect of extracellular K^+ on both active and passive Tl^+ influx was apparent for all concentrations of Tl^+ tested in this way (0.1–2.0 μM).

The principal effect of changes in $[K]_o$ on Tl^+ exchange was to modify the Tl^+ influx. Increasing $[K^+]_o$ from 0 to 5 mM or 10 mM had little or no effect on the rate constants describing the loss of previously accumulated ^{204}Tl from the myocardial cells.

Tl^+ and K^+ Interrelationship in Myocardial Cells

From the above data, it is apparent that more than half of the cellular Tl^+ uptake, like that of K^+, occurs via a ouabain-sensitive mechanism, presumably the Na pump. Further, it is apparent that extracellular K^+ can act as an inhibitor of Tl^+ uptake, suggesting that both ions may enter the cell by a common pathway. It has also been shown previously (Britten and Blank, 1968) that Tl^+ is capable of functioning as an activator of Na^+,K^+-ATPase. For these reasons, it was felt that attempts to analyze the above data by Lineweaver-Burk, or double-reciprocal plots, where $[Tl^+]_o = S$ and Tl^+ influx = V, could be helpful in further clarifying the interaction of the two ions.

Using Lineweaver-Burk, or double reciprocal, plots to analyze the data for total Tl^+ influx, with K^+ as inhibitor, we obtained a pattern representative of mixed inhibition. Similar treatment of the non-ouabain-sensitive fluxes produced data in keeping with noncompetitive inhibition. However, when the active or ouabain-sensitive Tl^+ influx data were subjected to this analysis (Fig. 3), the results were in keeping with strictly competitive inhibition of the Tl^+ influx by K^+. From the data presented in Figure 3, the intercept on the y axis, representing the reciprocal of the maximum active Tl^+ influx, gives a value of 0.05, suggesting a maximal ouabain-sensitive Tl^+ influx of 20 mol^{-14}/cm^2 per sec. The x intercept of the $[K^+]_o = 0$ line (Fig. 3) would represent the reciprocal of the Michaelis constant (K_m) of Tl^+ on the active Tl^+ influx. The value for K_m obtained in the

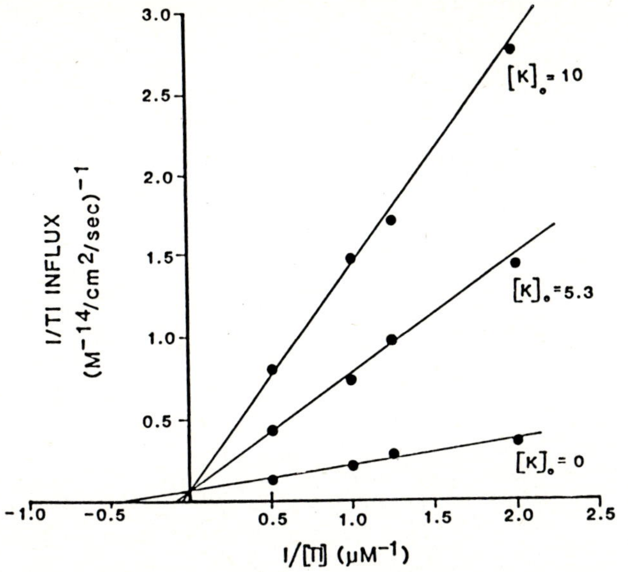

FIGURE 3. *Double-reciprocal plot of $[Tl^+]_o$ and active Tl^+ influx, myocardial cells at 37°C in the absence ($K^+ = 0$) and presence of two concentrations (5.3 and 10 mM) K^+. Each point is the mean of six observations, and lines shown are calculated linear regression lines, for each $r > 0.94$ ($P < 0.001$).*

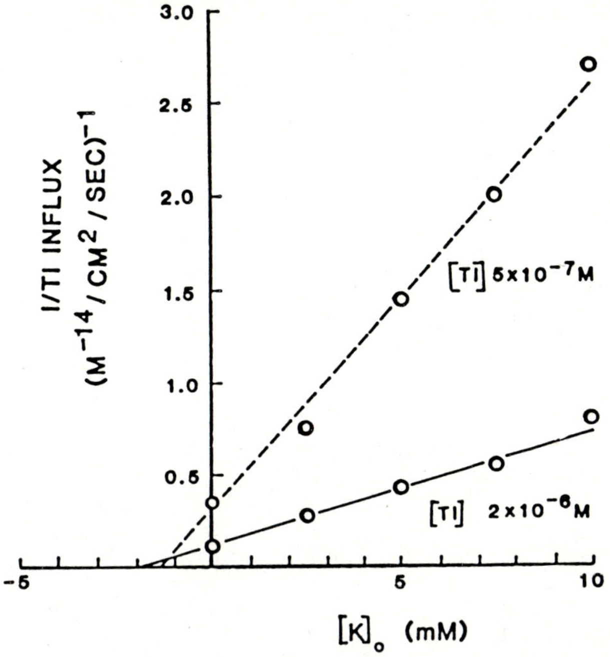

FIGURE 4. *Dixon plot of active Tl^+ influx, from two concentrations of Tl^+, and various concentrations of $[K^+]_o$. Each point is mean of six observations and lines shown are calculated linear regression lines ($r > 0.95$; $P < 0.001$).*

present study was therefore of the order of 2 μM. This latter value was rather surprising in light of previously reported values (Britten and Blank, 1969) for the K_m of Tl^+ on Na^+, K^+-ATPase (0.16 mM).

In view of the apparent differences between the present findings and those previously reported, further studies were carried out to determine the relationship between $[Tl^+]_o$ and active Tl^+ influx over the range of Tl^+ concentrations from 10 nM to 0.1 mM. This showed, in the absence of extracellular K^+, a sigmoid relationship reaching saturation at around 0.1 mM Tl^+ with a maximum active Tl^+ influx of 30 mol^{-14}/cm^2 per sec. This latter value is some 50% higher than the calculated maximum active Tl^+ influx (Fig. 3), and the apparent K_m is of the order of 7 μM compared with the previously calculated value of 2 μM.

The Tl^+:K^+ interrelationship in the myocardial cells was further explored using a Dixon plot (Dixon, 1953) of the inhibitor (K^+) against the reciprocal of the active, or ouabain-sensitive, Tl^+ influx (Fig. 4). This also confirmed competitive inhibition between K^+ and Tl^+ with respect to the active Tl^+ influx, and also permitted the calculation of the inhibitor constant (K_i) for K^+, the K^+ concentration at the point of intersection of the graphed lines being $-K_i$. The value for the $-K_i$ of K^+ on the active Tl^+ influx was found to be 1.2 mM (Fig. 4), which compares very favorably with the calculated K_m of K^+ on the active K^+ influx (Fig. 5) at 1.8 mM. The values used in Figure 5 were derived from the ^{42}K influx from solutions containing various concentrations of K^+ from 1–5.4 mM, measured in the presence and absence of 10^{-2} M ouabain.

Effect of $[Tl^+]_o$ on K Influx

To test the competitive nature of the Tl^+:K^+ interrelationship further, the effect of varying concentrations of nonradioactive Tl^+ on the ^{42}K uptake was determined. As in the other studies, the K^+ influx was separated into its active and passive components using 10^{-2} M ouabain. It was found that Tl^+ in concentrations from 0.10 μM to 0.10 mM produced a concentration-dependent decrease in both total and active K^+ influx (Fig. 6), the decrease being significant ($P < 0.01$) at 1 μM and highly significant ($P < 0.001$) at all concentrations in excess of 1 μM. Thallium-induced decreases in K^+ influx could be

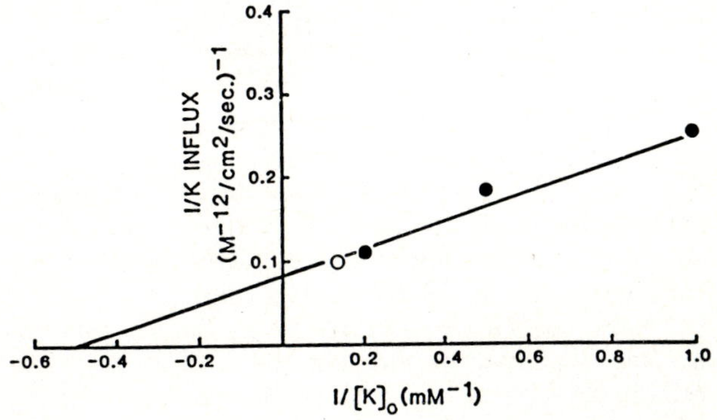

FIGURE 5. *Double reciprocal plot of active ^{42}K influx and $[K^+]_o$, myocardial cells at 37°C. Each point is mean of 5–10 observations, and the line shown is the calculated linear regression line ($r = 0.97$; $P < 0.001$). Open symbol from data previously reported (McCall, 1979).*

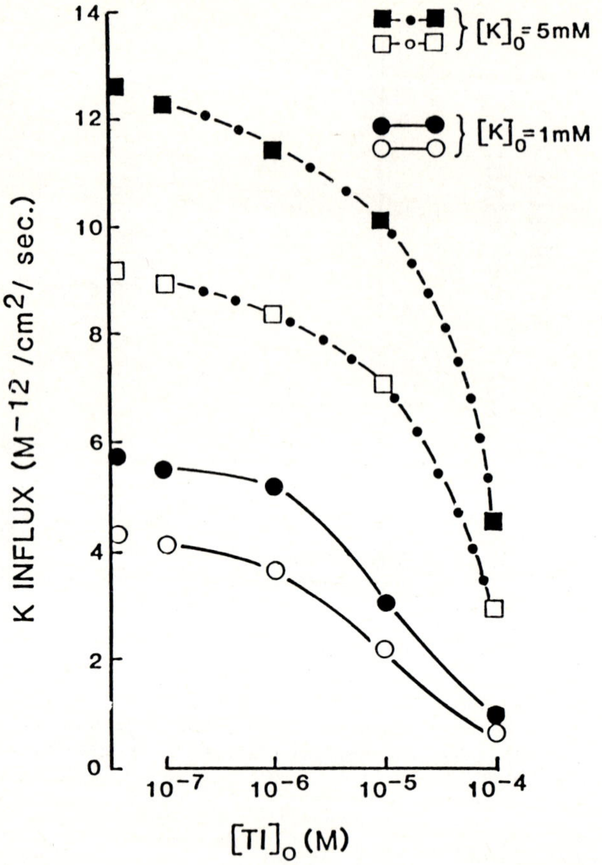

FIGURE 6. *Effect of nonradioactive Tl⁺ on ⁴²K influx, myocardial cells at 37°C. Closed symbols represent total influx and open symbols represent active or ouabain-sensitive influx. For each n = 5; lines fitted to points by eye.*

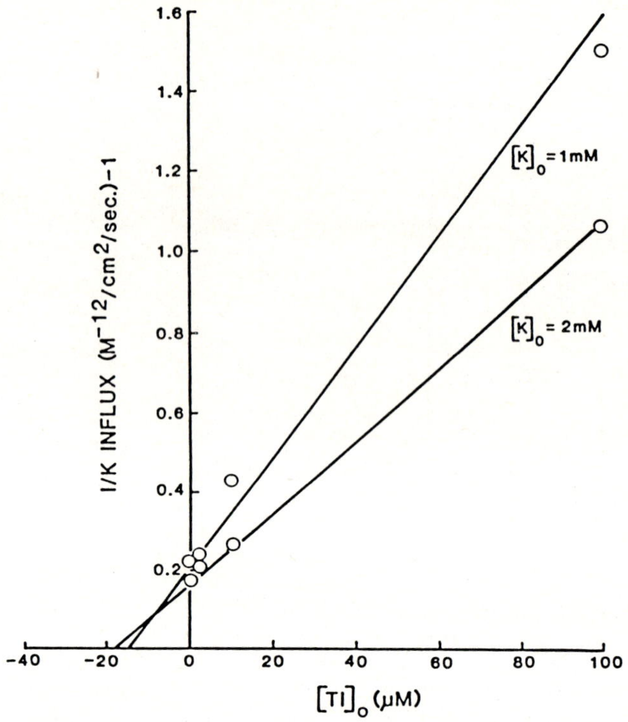

FIGURE 7. *Dixon plot of active ⁴²K influx and [Tl⁺]o, myocardial cells at 37°C. Data obtained from studies shown in Figure 6. Each point is mean of five observations, and lines shown are calculated linear regression lines (r > 0.95; P < 0.001).*

observed in the presence of each level of $[K^+]_o$ tested, from 1–5 mM.

By subjecting these data to the same analysis as that used for the Tl^+ flux data, we were able to confirm the presence of competitive inhibition by Tl^+ on K^+ influx (Fig. 7). The K_i of Tl^+ for the K^+ influx at 6 μM was similar to the apparent K_m of Tl^+ on the active Tl^+ influx (Fig. 3) described above.

The possibility that Na^+ loading, or changes in contraction frequency, during K^+-free treatment of the cells, modified Tl^+ influx, was evaluated in a series of studies in which both ^{24}Na content and contraction frequency were measured at various times after exposure to K^+-free or K^+-free + 1 μM Tl^+ BSS (Fig. 8). In K^+-free solution, there was a rapid gain in intracellular ^{24}Na, the initial rate of which was in keeping with previously reported Na^+ flux data (McCall, 1979). After 5 minutes, however, the rate of Na^+ accumulation declined, possibly indicating activation of alternative pathways of Na^+ extrusion, such as Na^+-Ca^{++} exchange, or a concentration-dependent decline in Na^+ influx. In the presence of 1 μM Tl^+ (Fig. 8), the gain in cellular Na^+ was much less rapid, in keeping with, or supporting, the contention that low concentrations of Tl^+ can at least partially activate the Na pump. A similar pat-

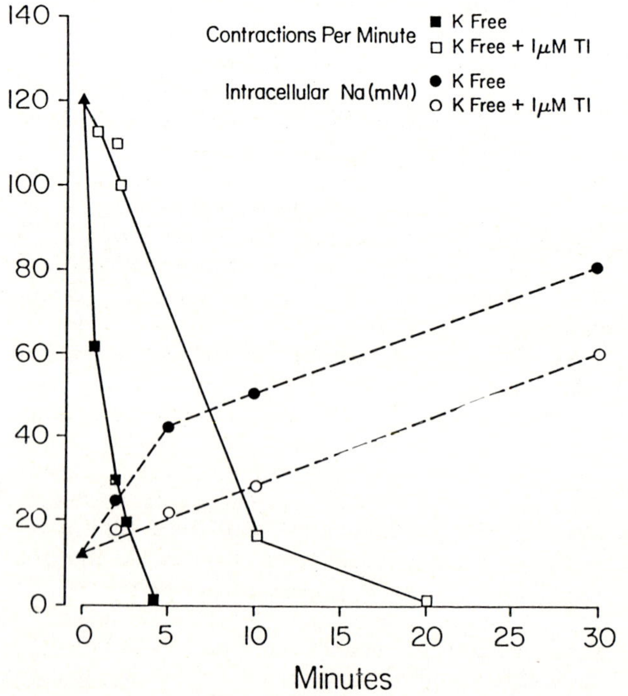

FIGURE 8. *Effect of treatment with K⁺-free BSS (closed symbols) and K⁺-free BSS containing 1 μM Tl⁺ (open symbols) on [Na⁺]i and contraction frequency, myocardial cells at 37°C. Each point is mean of five observations. Note: no correction has been made for possible cell volume changes at higher [Na⁺]i values.*

TABLE 1
Tl^+ Influx after Various Times in K^+-Free BSS ± 1 μM Tl^+

	30 sec	2 min	10 min	30 min
K^+-free	7.25 ± 0.17	7.16 ± 0.26	7.03 ± 0.16*	6.73 ± 0.28†
K^+-free + 1 μM Tl^+	7.14 ± 0.25	7.09 ± 0.31	7.10 ± 0.59	6.88 ± 0.13†

Tl^+ influx (M^{-14}/cm^2 per sec) expressed as mean ± SEM, for each $n = 5$. Using 30-sec and influx from either solution as baseline, * $P < 0.05$ and † $P < 0.01$.

tern was observed in the effects of the two solutions on contraction frequency (Fig. 8) in that the response to a K^+-free solution was much more immediate than that to a solution containing 1 μM Tl^+.

Since most determinations of Tl^+ influx were made over a 2-minute period, it is unlikely that either Na^+ loading or contraction frequency had a significant bearing on Tl^+ influx since, in the presence of 1 μM Tl^+, $[Na^+]_i$ had risen from 12.3 ± 0.3 mM to only 16.9 ± 0.5 mM ($n = 5$) during this time, and contraction frequency had declined by less than 10%. Nonetheless, determinations of ^{204}Tl influx after 30 seconds (using a 30-second influx measurement), 2 minute (using a 2-minute influx measurement) and 30 minutes (2-minute influx) of exposure to either a K^+-free or K^+-free + 1 μM Tl^+ solution were made. The results are summarized in Table 1.

Although there was a modest, but significant (Table 1), decline in ^{204}Tl influx after 30 minutes of treatment with either solution, it is unlikely that either Na^+ loading or contraction frequency significantly influenced the results, since most Tl^+ influx determinations were made over a 2-minute period, and following, at most, 10 minutes of Na pump inhibition (ouabain experiments). The data from Table 2 also serves to validate further the 2-minute ^{204}Tl influx measurements, since the values obtained are not significantly different from those obtained from a 30-second ^{204}Tl influx determination.

Discussion

The present study represents an attempt to define the kinetics of Tl^+ exchange in cultured myocardial cells, using concentrations of Tl^+ more closely approximating those likely to be encountered during clinical myocardial scintigraphy. Prior evaluations of Tl^+ exchange (Mullins and Moore, 1960; Gehring and Hammond, 1964; Britten and Blank, 1968; Kashket, 1979) have, in most instances, used concentrations of Tl^+ between 0.01 and 1.0 mM. By calculation from the specific activity of ^{201}Tl, as supplied by New England Nuclear (5–50 Ci/g Tl^+), and assuming an average extracellular volume of 15 liters, the administration of 1.5 mCi ^{201}Tl (Okada, 1980) would result in an extracellular Tl^+ concentration of between 0.1 and 1.0 μM. For this reason, the cellular exchange characteristics of this ion were explored at these lower concentrations (10 nM to 5 μM) used in the present study.

In the absence of extracellular K^+, Tl^+ was found to exchange twice as rapidly as K^+ ($t_{1/2}$ Tl^+ exchange = 5 minutes vs. $t_{1/2}$ K^+ exchange = 12 minutes). Over the range of concentrations tested the rate constant was unaffected by $[Tl^+]_o$. Both Tl^+ influx and efflux could be described by a single exponential, suggesting that intracellular Tl^+ is contained within a single compartment. In several ways, the characteristics of Tl^+ uptake described in the present study are similar to those found in red blood cells (Gehring and Hammond, 1964; Skulskii et al., 1978.), *Streptococcus* (Kashket, 1979), frog skeletal muscle (Mullins and Moore, 1960), and squid axon (Landowne, 1975). In addition, it is worth noting that the absolute values obtained for Tl^+ fluxes in the present study are very similar to those found by Mullins and Moore (1960) in skeletal muscle.

In the present study, myocardial cells accumulated Tl^+ rapidly until a steady state with respect to $[Tl^+]_i$ was reached within 20–30 minutes. Under these steady state conditions, net Tl^+ influx and Tl^+ efflux were equal. Equilibration times appear to be longer in both skeletal muscle (Mullins and Moore, 1960) and red cells (Gehring and Hammond, 1964), the difference in both tissues being attributable to a small, slowly exchanging component not seen in the myocardial cells or in *Streptococcus lactis* (Kashket, 1979). At equilibrium, the cells contained significantly higher concentrations of Tl^+ than that in the incubation medium, confirming that myocardial tissue, like other tissues, is capable of concentrating the ion. For all concentrations of $[Tl^+]_o$ tested, the $[Tl^+)_i$:$[Tl^+]_o$ ratio, at equilibrium and in the absence of extracellular K^+, was approximately 50:1 (Table 2). Gehring and Hammond (1964) found a ratio, $[Tl^+]_i$:$[Tl^+]_o$, at equilibrium of 8.66:1, whereas a much higher ratio, 500:1, was demonstrated in *S. lactis* preparations (Kashket, 1979). Although the reason for these differences is not clear, the lower ratio in erythrocytes may reflect the much lower Na pump density in these cells, compared to cultured heart cells (McCall, 1979), and/or the lower membrane potential of the cells.

Ouabain (10^{-2} M) maximally inhibited approxi-

TABLE 2
$[Tl^+]_i$:$[Tl^+]_o$ Ratios in Cultured Heart Cells at Equilibrium

$[Tl^+]_o$ (μM)	$[Tl^+]_i$ (μM)	$[Tl^+]_i$:$[Tl^+]_o$
10	459.4	46:1
5	233.2	46:1
1	56.6	56:1
0.5	23.6	47:1
0.1	5.0	50:1

Each value of $[Tl]_i$ represents mean of five observations.

mately 60% of the Tl^+ influx in cultured heart cells, a finding similar to that in both squid axon (Landowne, 1975) and red blood cells (Skulskii et al., 1978). Although not infallible (Baker et al., 1969), ouabain sensitivity is generally accepted to be the most reliable indication that an ion flux is dependent on Na pump activity. As such, it can therefore be assumed that the greater part of myocardial Tl^+ influx is dependent on membrane Na^+,K^+-ATPase. Further, the present study shows that the putative Na pump-dependent Tl^+ movement can be activated by low concentrations (10 nM to 5μM) of Tl^+ in the absence of extracellular K^+.

Although no direct measurements of Na^+,K^+-ATPase activity were made in the present study, certain inferences regarding the activity of the enzyme can be made. If all of the ouabain-inhibitable Tl^+ influx represents Na^+,K^+-ATPase activity, then the results of this study would give an apparent K_m for Tl^+ on the enzyme activity of 2–7 μM. This is considerably different than the K_m of Tl^+ on renal Na^+,K^+-ATPase of 0.17 mM found by Britten and Blank (1968) and Grisham et al. (1974). The latter authors, however, noted K_m of Tl^+ on Na^+,K^+-ATPase of 29 μM in the absence of Mn^{++}, a value not greatly different from that of the present study. Since isolated and purified ATPase was not studied in this preparation, the results are not strictly comparable. Nonetheless, it is clear that the K_m of Tl^+ for the active Tl^+ influx presented here is considerably less than that for the isolated enzyme system (Britten and Blank, 1968; Grisham et al., 1974). Several explanations could account for the difference, (1) the present experiments were carried out at 37°C compared to 21–23°C for the others (2) much lower concentrations of Tl^+ were used in the present studies (3) the preparation, having a single, rapidly exchangeable extracellular compartment, allows accurate flux determinations without contamination from trapped inhibitors such as K^+, and, finally, (4) the active transport properties of the preparation itself could be unique. The last factor is least likely since it has been shown (McCall, 1979; Wheeler et al., 1982) that cation transport by cultured myocardial cells is similar to that in other myocardial preparations. This is further supported by the observation in this study that the K_m of K^+ on the active K^+ influx is 1.8 mM, identical to that for both Na pump activity and ATPase activity (Glynn, 1968; Glitsch et al., 1978, Gadsby, 1980) in a wide variety of tissues. It seems most likely, therefore, that the present observation stems from a combination of the very low concentrations of Tl^+ used and the ability to measure fluxes accurately, free from inhibitor. Whatever the reason, the very low value for K_m of Tl^+ in the present study is consistent with the myocardial Tl^+ uptake observed in vivo in which the heart is exposed to very low concentrations of this ion.

An interrelationship between Tl^+ and K^+ has been shown in a variety of preparations (Mullins and Moore, 1960; Gehring and Hammond, 1964, 1967; Landowne, 1975; Kashket, 1979). This study has defined a competitive inhibition of active Tl^+ influx by K^+, and also of active K^+ influx by Tl^+. These findings suggest that active transport of both ions occurs via a common pathway, presumably the Na pump, and further suggests a common receptor for both on the enzyme system. The present data therefore support the concept that Tl^+ behaves as a K^+ analog in cultured myocardial cells.

We wish to acknowledge the technical assistance of Lisa D'Addabbo, Kevin Whitney, and Greg Prorok and the expert secretarial services of Donna Wallace in the preparation of this manuscript.

Supported by Grants HL-22568 and HL-22135 from the National Heart, Lung, and Blood Institute, and the Connecticut Heart Association.

Address for reprints: David McCall, M.D., Cardiology Section, University of Texas Health Science Center at San Antonio, 7703 Floyd Curl Drive, San Antonio, Texas 78284.

Received December 22, 1983; accepted for publication December 19, 1984.

References

Baker PF, Blaustein MP, Keynes RD, Manil J, Shaw TI, Steinhardt RA (1969) The ouabain-sensitive fluxes of sodium and potassium in squid giant axons. J Physiol (Lond) **200:** 459–496

Britten JS, Blank M (1968) Thallium activation of the ($Na^+ + K^+$)-activated ATPase of the rabbit kidney. Biochim Biophys Acta **159:** 160–166

Dixon M (1953) The determination of enzyme inhibitor constants Biochem J **55:** 170–171

Gadsby DC (1980) Activation of electrogenic Na^+/K^+ exchange by extracellular K^+ in canine cardiac Purkinje fibers. Proc Natl Acad Sci USA **77:** 4035–4039

Gehring PJ, Hammond PB (1964) The uptake of thallium by rabbit erythrocytes. J Pharmacol Exp Ther **200:** 215–221

Gehring PJ, Hammond PG (1967) The interrelationship between thallium and potassium in animals. J Pharmacol Exp Ther **155:** 187–201

Glitsch HG, Grabowski W, Thielen J (1978) Activation of the electrogenic sodium pump in guinea-pig atria by external potassium ions. J Physiol (Lond) **276:** 515–524

Glynn IM (1968) Membrane adenosine triphosphatase and cation transport. Br Med Bull **24:** 165–169

Grisham CM, Gupta RJ, Barnett RE, Mildvan AS (1974) Thallium-205 nuclear relaxation and kinetic studies of sodium and potassium ion activated adenosine triphyosphatase. J Biol Chem **249:** 6738–6744

Kashket ER (1979) Active transport of thallous ions by *Streptococcus lactis*. J Biol Chem **254:** 8129–8131

Lamb JF, McCall D (1972) Effect of prolonged ouabain treatment on Na, K, Cl and Ca concentrations and fluxes in cultured human cells. J Physiol (Lond) **225:** 599–617

Landowne D (1975) A comparison of radioactive thallium and potassium fluxes in the giant axon of the squid. J Physiol (Lond) **252:** 79–96

McCall D (1979) Cation exchange and glycoside binding in cultured rat heart cells. Am J Physiol **236:** C87–C95

Mullins LJ, Moore RD (1960) The movement of thallium ions in muscle. J Gen Physiol **43:** 759–773

Okada RD, Boucher CA, Strauss HW, Pohost GM (1980) Exercise radionuclide imaging approaches to coronary artery disease. Am J Cardiol **46:** 1188–1204

Skulskii JA, Manninen J, Jarnefelt J (1978) Factors affecting the relative magnitudes of the ouabain-sensitive and ouabain-insensitive fluxes of thallium ion in erythrocytes. Biochim Biophys Acta **506:** 233–241

Wheeler DM, Horres CR, Lieberman M (1982) Sodium tracer kinetics and transmembrane flux in tissue-cultured heart cells. Am J Physiol **243:** C169–C176

INDEX TERMS: Cultured myocardial cells • Na pump • Cation exchange • Myocardial thallium scintigraphy

Ultrastructural Morphometric Analysis of Myocardium from Dogs, Rats, Hamsters, Mice, and from Human Hearts

Jutta Schaper, Eckhardt Meiser, and Gerhard Stämmler
From the Max-Planck-Institute, Department of Experimental Cardiology, Bad Nauheim, Federal Republic of Germany

SUMMARY. Volume densities of mitochondria, myofibrils, and unspecified cytoplasm were measured by ultrastructural morphometry in myocardium from dogs, rats, hamsters, mice, and in biopsied tissue from human hearts. Human myocardium was composed of 23% mitochondria, 59% myofibrils, and 18% cytoplasm. Volume densities for mitochondria were 22% for dogs, 28% for rats and hamsters, and 32% for mice. Myofibrillar volume densities were highest in dogs with 63%, 57% for rats and hamsters, and 49% for mice. Differences were significant between all except man and dog, and rat and hamster. In an extensive analysis of canine myocardium, it could be shown that the quantitative composition of tissue from the left ventricular free wall (anterior, lateral, posterior) and the papillary muscles was identical. There were also no differences between subepi- and subendocardium as well as the midmyocardium. Volume densities from longitudinal sections were identical to those from transversal sections. Fixation with glutaraldehyde by perfusion or immersion provided identical results. There were no differences between volume densities in samples from the left ventricular free wall (anterior, lateral, and posterior) in rats, hamsters, and mice. It is concluded that each mammalian species is characterized by a very typical quantitative composition of the myocardium. The increase in mitochondrial volume correlated well with the increase in heart rate and oxygen consumption in smaller animals. These quantitative data are regarded as the morphological correlate of the differing functional capacity of hearts from different species. **(*Circ Res 56: 377–391, 1985*)**

THE quantitative distribution of cellular organelles in myocytes can be measured accurately by morphometric techniques developed for biological research during the last three decades (for review see Weibel 1969). These data can then be used to calculate the biochemical composition of the myocytes when results of quantitative biochemical techniques, such as absolute enzyme activity measurements, are available. They may then be related with and checked against the absolute amount of the particular cellular organelle in which the enzyme is located. Obviously, quantitative morphology also contributes significantly to morphological research on processes involved in the pathogenesis of cardiac diseases, such as the development of myocardial hypertrophy and many others. The most extensively studied tissue has been the rat heart, whereas only a limited number of morphometric data are available from the hamster, mouse, and dog heart (for summary of the pertinent literature, see Tables 9 and 10). Human myocardium obtained in vivo has been studied even less frequently (David et al., 1978; Laguens et al., 1979; Fleischer et al., 1978; 1980; Schaper and Schaper, 1983). It is obvious from the literature that morphometric data for one single species vary greatly (see Table 10), between authors, and that the morphometric techniques vary widely as well.

Studies comparing the quantitative composition of different species are very rare. Bossen et al. (1978) compared mouse and finch left ventricles, and they were able to obtain information on functional differences between species.

The present study contains a comparison of the quantitative composition of the left ventricular myocardium from several of the most widely used laboratory animals: dog, rat, hamster, mouse. Information on normal human myocardium will also be furnished. Furthermore, morphometric data from these different species were correlated with the most obvious functional differences between these hearts, i.e., with regard to heart rate (ranging from 60 beats/min in dogs to 600 beats/min in mice) and oxygen consumption. This study also presents an attempt to clarify questions concerning morphometric techniques in cardiac tissue.

Methods

Species

Myocardium from four widely used laboratory animals (i.e., dogs, rats, hamster, and mice) were quantitatively investigated. The animals, all healthy, were kept in animal quarters. Additionally, nonhypertrophied nonischemic human myocardium was included in this study.

Dogs

1. *Perfusion Fixation.* Two mongrel dogs, both of them females with a body weight of 20.0 kg, were anesthetized

by injection of piritramide (5 mg/kg body weight) and sodium pentobarbitol (10 mg/kg body weight). The animals were artifically ventilated with a Bird Mark 7 respirator and the thorax was opened in the 5th intercostal space. The femoral artery was prepared free, a catheter was introduced and advanced into the ascending aorta. Through this catheter the coronary vascular system was retrogradely perfused with 3 liters of a well-oxygenated Tyrode's solution (20°C, 400 mOsm) at a mean arterial pressure of 80 mm Hg. An incisure into the right atrial wall served as outflow route for the perfusion fluid. After about 3 minutes, when all blood elements had been removed from the coronary circulatory system, perfusion with 2% glutaraldehyde buffered with 0.1 M sodium cacodylate (20°C, pH 7.4, 400 mOsm) at the same pressure was begun. The hearts stopped beating, and turned a brown-yellow color. Perfusion fixation was terminated after 5 minutes of total fixative perfusion, the hearts were removed from the thorax, and tissue sampling was initiated. All hearts were transversally cut through the midline between left ventricular apex and base. The upper parts of the papillary muscles remained with the upper part of the heart, which was discarded. From the lower part, a slice was prepared and tissue samples were taken from the anterior (LA), lateral (LL), and posterior (LP) left ventricular wall, as well as from the anterior (AP) and posterior (PP) papillary muscle. All five samples were subdivided into subendocardial, midmyocardial, and subepicardial pieces, and from each of these 15 samples, small tissue probes with either longitudinal or transversal arrangement of myofibrils were prepared. As shown in Figure 1, a total of 30 tissue samples from each dog heart were thus prepared. The tissue was further processed as described below.

2. *Immersion Fixation.* Sixteen mongrel dogs, 10 females and 6 males, with an average body weight of 20.0 kg, were anesthetized as described above. After the thorax had been opened, a needle biopsy (Travenol Tru-cut needle) was removed from the left ventricular anterior wall and, after separation into a subendocardial, midmyocardial, and subepicardial tissue sample, immediately fixed by immersion in 2% 0.1 M cacodylate-buffered glutaraldehyde (4°C, pH 7.4, 400 mOsm). The dogs then were used further in various hemodynamic pathophysiological experiments. The tissue was further processed for electron microscopy, as described below.

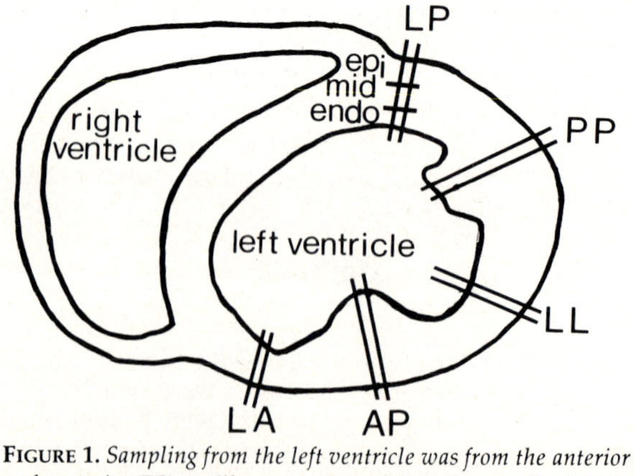

FIGURE 1. *Sampling from the left ventricle was from the anterior (AP) and posterior (PP) papillary muscle, and from the anterior (LA), lateral (LL), and posterior (LP) left ventricular free wall. All samples were subdivided into subendo- (endo), subepi- (epi), and midmyocardial (mid) pieces of tissue.*

Rats, Hamsters, Mice

Three adult animals of each species were anesthetized by intraperitoneal injection of sodium pentobarbital (3 mg/100 mg body weight). The abdominal aorta was cannulated and the right atrium opened. After 2 minutes of retrograde myocardial perfusion through the abdominal catheter (80 mm Hg perfusion pressure) with oxygen-saturated Tyrode's solution (pH 7.4, 400 mOsm), hearts were perfused for 5 minutes with 2% glutaraldehyde (20°C, pH 7.4, 400 mOsm). The hearts obtained the yellowish-brown color typical of tissue fixed by glutaraldehyde perfusion. After removal of the hearts from the animals' thorax, transmural tissue samples were taken from the anterior, lateral, and posterior left ventricular free wall. A total of three samples per animal and of nine samples per species were further processed for electron microscopy, as described below.

Human Hearts

Informed consent was obtained from all patients for the biopsies. Needle biopsies (1–2 mm in diameter) were taken from the outer half of the left ventricular free wall of six patients undergoing open-heart surgery for correction of an atrial septal defect. All patients had normal nonhypertrophied left ventricles, (as determined by standard clinical procedures) from which the tissues were taken during surgery before induction of cardiac arrest. All biopsies were taken from the area between left coronary descending artery and its r. marginalis. In the operating room, the tissue was immediately fixed by immersion in cold 2% glutaraldehyde buffered with 0.1 M cacodylate buffer (4°C, pH 7.4, 400 mOsm), and after transfer to the electron microscopic laboratory, were processed as described in the next paragraph.

Preparation of Tissue for Electron Microscopy

Tissue samples from perfusion-fixed hearts were immersed in 2% glutaraldehyde for 2 more hours. Tissues obtained as needle biopsies were fixed by immersion in 2% glutaraldehyde for a total of 6 hours. After fixation, all tissue samples were treated identically. After frequent rinsing with 0.1 M cacodylate buffer with 7.5% saccharose (4°C, pH 7.4, 400 mOsm), postfixation by immersion for 1 hour in 2% osmium tetroxide buffered with 4% veronal-acetate buffer (4°C, ph 7.4, 400 mOsm) was carried out. After frequent rinsing with the same veronal-acetate buffer to which 7.5% saccharose was added at room temperature, the tissue was dehydrated in a graded ethanol series. Substitution of ethanol by propylene oxide was followed by incubation of the tissue in a 50%:50% mixture of propylene oxide and epon. After 12 hours, the tissue was embedded in epon and polymerized for 3 days at 55°C. Sections 50 nm thick were prepared, mounted on uncovered copper grids, stained with aqueous uranyl acetate and lead citrate, and viewed in a Philips 300 electron microscope.

Electron Microscopy and Morphometry

From each grid, six sequential squares were selected. From each of these, four tissue areas situated close to the square corners free of nuclei, extracellular space, and microvessels were photographed on a 70-mm film at a magnification of 10,000. This selection corresponds to the "arbitrary sampling" method advocated by Weibel (1969).

For morphometric measurements, we used our own method, as described by Winkler et al. (1976). All micro-

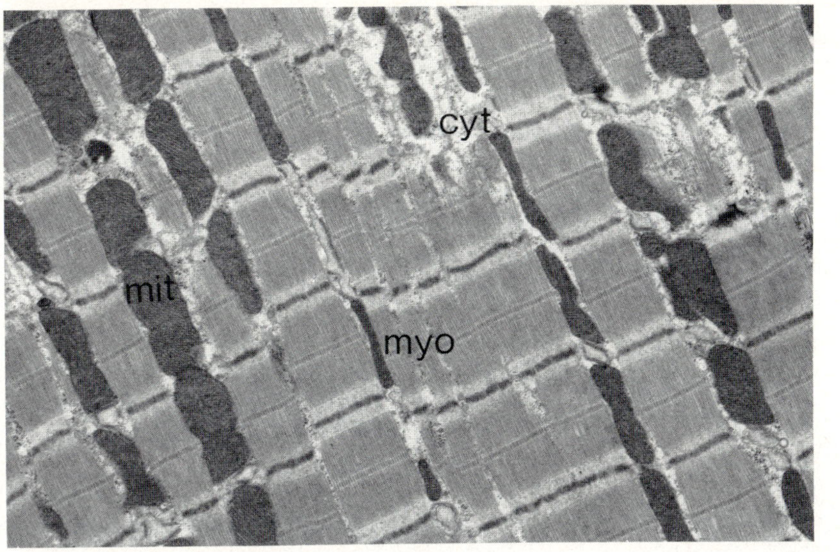

FIGURE 2. *Myocardium fixed by perfusion fixation with glutaraldehyde. mit = mitochondria, myo = myofibrils, cyt = cytoplasm. The sarcomeres are in relaxation with distinct I-bands. 17,000 ×.*

graphs were projected as negatives on an electronic tablet (Tektronix 4953) at a final magnification of 30,000.

With an electronic pen, mitochondria and contractile material were delineated and the data stored on a Dec-tape. The volume densities of mitochondria (V_{vmit}), myofibrils (V_{vmyo}) and cytoplasm (V_{vcyt}) were calculated, using well established morphometric principles (Weibel, 1969).

Statistics

All data stored on tape were analyzed with a PDP 11/45 Dec-computer. Means and standard errors were determined from each sample. Statistical tests (Mann and Whitney or Kruskal and Wallis) were used for analysis of differences between groups (Weber, 1972). Linear regression analysis was used to determine the relationship between physiological and morphometric data. The level of statistical significance was $P < 0.05$.

Results

Canine Myocardium

The typical appearance of normal myocardium fixed by perfusion is shown in Figure 2. All volume densities for mitochondria (V_{vmit}), myofibrils (V_{vmyo}), and nonspecified cytoplasm (V_{vcyt}) obtained from a total of 60 tissue samples from two dog hearts are indicated in Table 1.

On the basis of these data, the possible existence of differences between values from (1) different sampling sites (free wall vs. papillary muscles, anterior, lateral, or posterior part of the left ventricular free wall) (2) different layers of the myocardium (subendocardium, midmyocardium, subepicardium) and (3) different modes of tissue sectioning (transversal vs. longitudinal) were evaluated by multiple analysis of variance.

Influence of Sampling Site

Table 2 shows that no statistically significant differences existed between V_{vmit}, V_{vmyo}, or V_{vcyt} from any sampling site of the left ventricular wall. Even though some significant differences existed between certain sample regions, e.g., V_{vmit} in LP and LA in subepicardium and midmyocardium ($P < 0.001$ and $P < 0.01$, respectively), the pattern of significances showed a random distribution, i.e., no systematic differences were apparent. It also becomes evident that there was a high variability of volume densities from one sample to the other, which may be seen from the rather high standard errors.

Influence of Sampling from Different Myocardial Layers

Table 3 shows that no sytematic differences existed between the volume densities of the subendocardial, midmyocardial, and subepicardial layers. The statement made with regard to the data presented in Table 2 also applies to Table 3. Although there are some significant differences between values from different myocardial layers, these significances are randomly distributed and only reflect the great variability of individual values. V_{vmit} was highest in the subendocardial layer, but differences were insignificant. Table 5 shows that this difference existed only in dog 1, indicating individual variability.

Influence of Direction of Tissue Sectioning

A multiple analysis of variance showed that the direction of tissue sectioning had no statistically significant influence on volume density determinations (Table 4). Only eight tissue samples (indicated by *) from these two dogs showed greater volume densities in longitudinally than in transversally cut sections, but six others (indicated by †) showed opposite changes. As has been shown earlier by Weibel (1969), the anisotropic structure of the myocardial cell apparently does not influence cellular volume fraction measurement.

Influence of Fixation

Figure 3 shows the typical appearance of normal myocardium fixed by immersion. Table 5 shows that there were no statistically significant differences between the mitochondrial volume densities obtained

TABLE 1
Morphometric Data from Canine Cardiac Muscle

	Dog 1			Dog 2		
	V_{vmit} (%)	V_{vmyo} (%)	V_{vcyt} (%)	V_{vmit} (%)	V_{vmyo} (%)	V_{vcyt} (%)
LAL epi	19.7 ± 1.1	67.7 ± 1.4	12.6 ± 0.7	19.7 ± 2.7	63.2 ± 2.6	17.1 ± 1.3
mid	21.9 ± 1.0	68.1 ± 1.3	10.0 ± 0.9	18.2 ± 1.5	64.9 ± 1.5	16.9 ± 1.3
endo	26.3 ± 1.6	61.7 ± 1.9	12.0 ± 0.8	19.6 ± 2.1	67.0 ± 1.9	13.4 ± 1.0
LAT epi	22.5 ± 1.0	65.0 ± 1.4	12.5 ± 1.0	20.6 ± 0.7	62.5 ± 1.5	16.9 ± 1.3
mid	24.3 ± 0.7	66.7 ± 1.1	9.0 ± 1.0	20.6 ± 0.9	69.4 ± 1.3	10.0 ± 1.2
endo	25.9 ± 1.1	60.2 ± 1.6	13.9 ± 1.2	22.7 ± 1.0	65.3 ± 1.1	12.0 ± 1.0
LLL epi	23.3 ± 2.7	66.0 ± 3.1	10.7 ± 1.2	21.0 ± 1.1	60.2 ± 1.7	20.3 ± 1.6
mid	23.9 ± 1.8	67.5 ± 1.8	8.6 ± 0.8	21.7 ± 1.8	60.5 ± 2.1	17.8 ± 1.2
endo	29.4 ± 2.1	61.3 ± 2.1	9.3 ± 0.8	24.9 ± 1.1	60.0 ± 1.6	15.1 ± 0.9
LLT epi	20.1 ± 0.8	72.7 ± 1.1	7.1 ± 1.2	21.0 ± 1.1	59.9 ± 1.8	19.1 ± 1.4
mid	22.3 ± 0.8	71.7 ± 1.2	6.5 ± 1.2	22.7 ± 0.9	67.0 ± 1.4	10.3 ± 1.2
endo	23.0 ± 0.8	68.0 ± 0.9	8.9 ± 0.6	20.8 ± 1.1	62.2 ± 1.6	16.9 ± 1.3
LPL epi	16.2 ± 0.8	58.9 ± 1.8	16.0 ± 1.1	22.5 ± 1.4	62.1 ± 1.4	15.3 ± 0.7
mid	26.1 ± 1.7	68.2 ± 2.3	11.8 ± 1.0	22.1 ± 1.8	63.2 ± 2.1	14.7 ± 1.1
endo	23.7 ± 2.0	63.5 ± 2.1	12.9 ± 0.9	25.1 ± 2.0	62.3 ± 2.0	12.6 ± 1.1
LPT epi	16.2 ± 0.8	58.9 ± 1.8	24.9 ± 1.8	26.1 ± 0.9	55.7 ± 0.9	22.8 ± 1.0
mid	18.5 ± 1.0	58.2 ± 2.3	23.2 ± 2.3	22.0 ± 1.3	63.0 ± 1.6	14.9 ± 1.3
endo	21.6 ± 1.2	48.9 ± 1.4	29.5 ± 1.7	23.2 ± 1.4	63.3 ± 1.3	13.5 ± 1.0
APL epi	21.5 ± 1.0	67.9 ± 1.3	11.0 ± 0.8	23.2 ± 1.7	62.9 ± 1.9	13.9 ± 1.0
mid	26.9 ± 2.3	63.7 ± 2.7	9.8 ± 0.9	19.2 ± 1.0	59.9 ± 1.8	20.9 ± 1.7
endo	29.0 ± 1.4	61.3 ± 1.6	9.7 ± 0.9	22.0 ± 1.4	58.7 ± 1.5	19.3 ± 1.3
APT epi	19.2 ± 0.9	66.2 ± 1.4	14.7 ± 1.5	21.8 ± 1.0	68.4 ± 1.3	9.8 ± 1.0
mid	24.3 ± 0.9	64.7 ± 1.3	11.0 ± 1.2	22.4 ± 1.3	62.7 ± 1.4	14.9 ± 0.9
endo	24.4 ± 1.0	66.3 ± 1.2	9.3 ± 1.0	21.7 ± 1.2	60.3 ± 1.4	18.0 ± 1.3
PPL epi	20.5 ± 1.1	69.1 ± 1.2	10.3 ± 0.8	24.3 ± 2.9	57.8 ± 3.3	17.8 ± 1.6
mid	27.6 ± 2.4	63.4 ± 2.5	9.0 ± 0.9	22.3 ± 2.3	57.4 ± 2.1	20.2 ± 1.7
endo	23.4 ± 1.2	68.7 ± 1.4	7.9 ± 1.0	20.1 ± 2.5	60.4 ± 2.5	19.4 ± 1.2
PPT epi	21.9 ± 0.8	67.3 ± 1.4	11.3 ± 1.6	23.7 ± 1.1	63.6 ± 1.4	12.7 ± 0.9
mid	19.7 ± 0.6	67.3 ± 0.9	13.0 ± 0.9	28.1 ± 1.1	60.3 ± 1.6	11.6 ± 1.2
endo	19.9 ± 1.4	69.2 ± 1.4	11.0 ± 0.8	22.8 ± 1.1	59.4 ± 1.4	17.8 ± 1.3

Volume fractions of myocardial tissue from dog 1 and dog 2. Each value represents the means ± SE obtained from 24 micrographs. LA = left anterior free wall, LL = left lateral free wall, LP = left posterior free wall, AP = anterior papillary muscle, PP = posterior papillary muscle, last letter L = longitudinal, last letter T = transversal direction of sectioning.

from perfusion-fixed myocardium and from immersion-fixed needle biopsies from canine hearts (n = 16 dogs). V_{vmyo} and V_{vcyt} were not evaluated in the latter group because these data originated from a study on the effects of ischemia on mitochondrial volume and surface densities and were used for a doctoral thesis in our institute (Pinkowski, 1983). The mode of tissue removal and fixation seems to have only a very limited influence on morphometric measurements, provided the number of animals is high enough in those experiments in which perfusion fixation cannot be applied.

Myocardial Cellular Volume Densities in the Dog Heart

Table 5 shows representative values for perfusion-fixed as well as for immersion-fixed left ventricular canine myocardium. From this table, it is evident that individual differences exist between individual canine hearts with regard to the subcellular composition of myocardial cells, that the mean values of V_{vmit} from the two perfusion-fixed dog hearts correspond to the mean value obtained by averaging mitochondrial volume densities from a different group of 16 dogs, and that canine myocardial cells consist of 22.4% mitochondria, 63.7% myofibrils, and 14.1% nonspecified cytoplasm.

Human Myocardium

The values obtained from six human hearts are also indicated in Table 5. Human myocardial cells consisted of 22.8% mitochondria, 61.8% myofibrils, 15.4% of unspecified cytoplasm. These values are similar to those obtained for canine myocardium, the only difference being a somewhat lower content of myofibrils in human myocardium.

Myocardial Cellular Volume Densities in the Rat, Hamster, and Mouse Heart

Table 6 shows the data obtained for the smaller animals used in this study. It is obvious that the rat

Table 2
Influence of Sampling Site on Morphometric Data

	Subepicardial layer					Midmyocardial layer					Subendocardial layer				
	LA	LL	LP	AP	PP	LA	LL	LP	AP	PP	LA	LL	LP	AP	PP
Dog 1															
LA V_{vmit}	*	NS	NS	NS	NS	*	NS	NS	NS	NS	*	NS	NS	NS	NS
V_{vmyo}		NS	NS	NS	NS		NS	NS	NS	NS		NS	NS	NS	NS
V_{vcyt}		NS	NS	NS	NS		NS	NS	NS	NS		NS	NS	NS	0.05
LL V_{vmit}	NS		NS	NS	NS	NS		NS	NS	NS	NS		NS	NS	NS
V_{vmyo}	0.01		NS	NS	NS	NS		NS	NS	NS	0.05		NS	NS	NS
V_{vcyt}	NS		0.025	NS	NS	NS		NS	NS	NS	NS		NS	NS	NS
LP V_{vmit}	0.001	NS		NS	NS	0.01	NS		NS	NS	NS	NS		NS	NS
V_{vmyo}	NS	0.001		NS	NS	NS	0.001		NS	NS	NS	0.001		NS	NS
V_{vcyt}	0.025	0.001		0.05	0.01	0.001	0.001		NS	NS	0.01	0.001		NS	0.025
AP V_{vmit}	NS	NS	NS		NS	NS	NS	0.01		NS	NS	NS	NS		NS
V_{vmyo}	NS	0.05	NS		NS	NS	0.025	NS		NS	NS	NS	0.001		NS
V_{vcyt}	NS	0.025	NS		NS	NS	NS	0.025		NS	NS	NS	0.001		NS
PP V_{vmit}	NS	NS	0.01	NS		0.01	NS	NS	0.025		0.025	NS	NS	NS	
V_{vmyo}	NS	NS	0.05	NS		NS	NS	NS	NS		0.025	NS	0.001	NS	
V_{vcyt}	NS	NS	0.001	NS		NS	0.01	NS	NS		NS	NS	0.001	NS	
Dog 2															
LA V_{vmit}	*	NS	NS	NS	NS	*	NS	NS	NS	NS	*	NS	NS	NS	NS
V_{vmyo}		NS	NS	NS	NS		NS	NS	NS	NS		NS	NS	0.025	NS
V_{vcyt}		NS	NS	NS	NS		NS	NS	NS	NS		NS	NS	0.05	0.025
LL V_{vmit}	NS		NS	NS	NS	NS		NS	NS	NS	NS		NS	NS	NS
V_{vmyo}	NS		NS	NS	NS	NS		NS	NS	NS	NS		NS	NS	NS
V_{vcyt}	NS		NS	NS	NS	NS		NS	NS	NS	NS		NS	NS	NS
LP V_{vmit}	NS	NS		NS	NS	NS	NS		NS	NS	NS	NS		NS	NS
V_{vmyo}	0.025	NS		NS	NS	NS	NS		NS	NS	NS	NS		NS	NS
V_{vcyt}	NS	NS		NS	NS	NS	NS		NS	NS	NS	NS		0.01	0.01
AP V_{vmit}	NS	NS	NS		NS	NS	NS	NS		NS	NS	NS	NS		NS
V_{vmyo}	NS	0.025	0.001		NS	NS	NS	NS		NS	NS	NS	NS		NS
V_{vcyt}	0.025	0.001	0.001		NS	NS	NS	NS		NS	0.05	NS	NS		NS
PP V_{vmit}	NS	NS	NS	NS		0.001	NS	0.025	0.01		NS	NS	NS	NS	
V_{vmyo}	NS	NS	0.01	NS		0.01	0.05	NS	NS		0.05	NS	NS	NS	
V_{vcyt}	NS	NS	0.001	NS		NS	NS	NS	NS		0.05	NS	NS	NS	

Statistically significant differences are randomly distributed between samples. NS = not significant. Numbers indicate the levels of statistical difference between longitudinal and transversal values.

* Values to the right of the diagonal rule are longitudinal; values to the left are transversal. The site of sampling from the left ventricle has no influence on the morphometric data. Abbreviations are explained in the footnote to Table 1.

and hamster heart contained a larger volume fraction of mitochondria than the dog heart, and that this value was even higher in the mouse heart.

Table 7 shows a comparison of all data from the different species. It is evident from this table that significant differences in V_{vmit} and V_{vmyo} existed between all species investigated, with only two exceptions: canine and human myocardium were similar, as well as rat and hamster cardiac tissue.

A close correlation existed between V_{vmit} and heart rate, as well as oxygen consumption, in all five species, as shown in Figure 4, a and b, and Table 8. An inverse relationship was observed between V_{vmyo} and these physiological variables, i.e., V_{vmyo} fell with increasing heart rate.

Discussion

The aim of this study was not only to establish and compare the quantitative composition of myocardial cells from hearts of different species, but also to investigate the influence of several methodological factors on morphometric data obtained from cardiac tissue. The question of methodology was investigated in the two perfusion-fixed dog hearts. After completion of this study, we carried out similar measurements in a group of four more mongrel dogs of about 20.0 kg body weight that were used as control animals in a different experimental series. All hearts were fixed by perfusion with glutaraldehyde. The results with regard to sampling site were

TABLE 3
Influence of Sampling from Different Myocardial Layers on Morphometric Data

	Dog 1			Dog 2		
	epi	mid	endo	epi	mid	endo
LA	*			*		
epi V_{vmit}		NS	0.01		NS	NS
V_{vmyo}		NS	NS		NS	NS
V_{vcyt}		NS	NS		NS	NS
mid V_{vmit}	NS		NS	NS		NS
V_{vmyo}	NS		NS	0.01		NS
V_{vcyt}	NS		NS	0.01		NS
endo V_{vmit}	NS	NS		NS	NS	
V_{vmyo}	NS	0.025		NS	NS	
V_{vcyt}	NS	0.025		0.05	NS	
LL	*			*		
epi V_{vmit}		NS	NS		NS	0.05
V_{vmyo}		NS	NS		NS	NS
V_{vcyt}		NS	NS		NS	NS
mid V_{vmit}	NS		NS	NS		NS
V_{vmyo}	NS		NS	0.025		NS
V_{vcyt}	NS		NS	0.001		NS
endo V_{vmit}	NS	NS		NS	NS	
V_{vmyo}	0.01	0.05		NS	NS	
V_{vcyt}	NS	0.01		NS	0.01	
LP	*			*		
epi V_{vmit}		NS	0.05		NS	NS
V_{vmyo}		NS	NS		NS	NS
V_{vcyt}		0.05	NS		NS	NS
mid V_{vmit}	NS		NS	NS		NS
V_{vmyo}	NS		NS	0.001		NS
V_{vcyt}	NS		NS	0.001		NS
endo V_{vmit}	0.01	NS		NS	NS	
V_{vmyo}	0.01	0.01		0.001	NS	
V_{vcyt}	NS	NS		0.001	NS	
AP	*			*		
epi V_{vmit}		0.05	0.01		NS	NS
V_{vmyo}		NS	NS		NS	NS
V_{vcyt}		NS	NS		0.01	0.05
mid V_{vmit}	0.01		NS	NS		NS
V_{vmyo}	NS		NS	0.05		NS
V_{vcyt}	NS		NS	0.025		NS
endo V_{vmit}	0.01	NS		NS	NS	
V_{vmyo}	NS	NS		0.001	NS	
V_{vcyt}	0.05	NS		0.001	NS	
PP	*			*		
epi V_{vmit}		0.025	NS		NS	NS
V_{vmyo}		NS	NS		NS	NS
V_{vcyt}		NS	NS		NS	NS
mid V_{vmit}	NS		NS	0.01		NS
V_{vmyo}	NS		NS	NS		NS
V_{vcyt}	NS		NS	NS		NS
endo V_{vmit}	NS	NS		NS	NS	
V_{vmyo}	NS	NS		NS	NS	
V_{vcyt}	NS	NS		NS	0.01	

The morphometric composition of the subendo- and the midmyocardium is identical in the normal canine heart. Statistically significant differences are randomly distributed. For abbreviations, see Tables 1 and 2.

* Values to the right of the diagonal rules are longitudinal; values to the left are transversal.

Table 4
Influence of the Direction of Sectioning on Morphometric Data

	V_{vmit}		V_{vmyo}		V_{vcyt}	
	L	T	L	T	L	T
			Dog 1			
LA epi	NS		NS		NS	
mid	NS		NS		NS	
endo	NS		NS		NS	
LL epi	NS		NS		0.025	L > T
mid	NS		NS		* 0.01	L > T
endo	* 0.05	L > T	0.025	L < T	NS	
LP epi	NS		* 0.001	L > T	* 0.001	L < T
mid	NS		0.001	L > T	* 0.001	L < T
endo	NS		0.001	L > T	0.001	L < T
AP epi	NS		NS		NS	
mid	NS		NS		NS	
endo	0.025	L > T	0.025	L < T	NS	
PP epi	NS		NS		NS	
mid	† 0.001	L > T	NS		† 0.01	L < T
endo	† 0.05	L > T	NS		0.025	L < T
			Dog 2			
LA epi	NS		NS		NS	
mid	NS		NS		0.001	L > T
endo	0.05	L < T	NS		NS	
LL epi	NS		NS		NS	
mid	NS		0.025	L < T	* 0.001	L > T
endo	* 0.025	L > T	NS		NS	
LP epi	NS		* 0.001	L > T	* 0.001	L < T
mid	NS		NS		NS	
endo	NS		NS		NS	
AP epi	NS		0.025	L < T	0.025	L > T
mid	NS		NS		0.01	L > T
endo	NS		NS		NS	
PP epi	NS		NS		0.05	L > T
mid	† 0.001	L < T	NS		† 0.001	L > T
endo	† 0.05	L < T	NS		NS	

The quantitative tissue composition is identical when measured in sections cut longitudinally (L) or transversally (T).
* Volume densities larger in longitudinal (L) than in transversal (T) sections.
† Examples where volume densities in longitudinal (L) sections are smaller than in transversal (T) sections from identical sampling sites. It is evident, from this table, that all differences are randomly distributed. For further explanation, see text.

identical, compared to those from the two canine hearts, which are therefore considered as representative, and sufficient for the investigation of methodological factors.

Sampling from the Left Ventricle

It is well known that differences exist in the cytoplasmic composition between left and right ventricles of rats (Laguens, 1971; Imamura et al., 1979; Olivetti et al., 1980; Anversa et al., 1982), and also between atrial and ventricular tissue (Anversa et al., 1975; Hirakow, 1980; Bossen et al., 1980). Imamura et al. (1978) reported mitochondrial and myofibrillar volume densities in the left ventricular free wall of the same rats in which Kawamura et al. (1976) had investigated the posterior papillary muscle 2 years earlier. The values obtained by both authors seem to be different (see Table 9), but this difference was not commented upon. Herbener et al. (1973) reported widely differing mitochondrial volume fractions from four different sampling sites of the mouse heart. Mall et al. (1978) prefer to use the posterior papillary muscle for technical reasons. By comparing his data with those of others, Mall et al. (1978) came to the conclusion that there exists a genuine quantitative difference between left ventricular papillary muscles and chamber wall muscle, probably especially in small animals. Most authors, however, prefer random sampling, which is a well-established principle in morphometry (Weibel 1969), although no systematic study has yet shown whether or not the differences in mechanical performance between

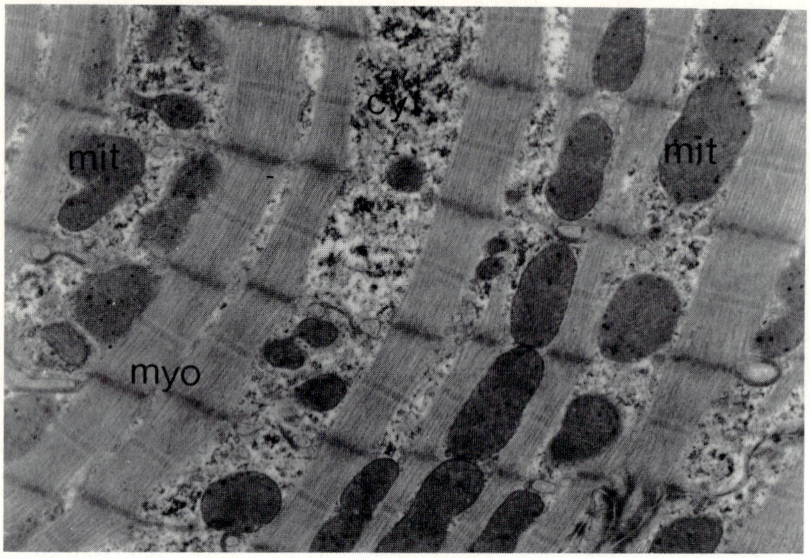

FIGURE 3. *Myocardium fixed by immersion fixation in glutaraldehyde. mit = mitochondria, myo = myofibrillar material, cyt = cytoplasm. Mitochondria and myofibrils are well aligned; the sarcomeres are in contraction. The quality of fixation is optimal, as shown by the presence of the dark matrix granules within the mitochondria. 20,000 ×.*

papillary muscles and the left ventricular free wall have a structural quantitative equivalent. However, from our earlier data (Winkler et al., 1977), and from the data presented here, it may be concluded that all parts (or regions) of the left ventricle possess a similar quantitative composition and that, therefore, random sampling may be applied.

Sampling from Myocardial Layers

It is a well-established fact that, after coronary artery occlusion, the subendocardium is much more susceptible to ischemic injury than the subepicardium (for review of the literature, see J. Schaper, 1979). Furthermore, after initiation of cardiac hypertrophy by constriction of one renal artery, the subepicardial region has been reported to show a more progressed stage of hypertrophy, whereas subendocardial enlargement lagged behind (Anversa 1978). It has been reported that differences exist in myocyte size and capillary densities between the subepi- and the subendocardium in the dog heart (Gerdes et al., 1980; Martorana et al., 1983), as well as in rat myocardium (Anversa et al., 1978; Gerdes et al., 1979). Tomanek et al. (1979) found in rat hearts a higher mitochondrial and lower myofibrillar fraction in the subendocardium than in the subepi-

TABLE 5
Volume Density of Mitochondria, Myofibrils, and Cytoplasm in Canine and Human Myocardium

	V_{vmit} (%)	V_{vmyo} (%)	V_{vcyt} (%)
Dog 1			
epi	20.19 ± 1.1	66.78 ± 1.5	13.24 ± 1.2
mid	22.95 ± 1.3	65.95 ± 1.7	11.19 ± 1.1
endo	24.66 ± 1.4	62.91 ± 1.6	12.24 ± 1.0
Mean	22.60 ± 1.5	65.21 ± 1.6	12.25 ± 1.1
Dog 2			
epi	22.24 ± 1.5	61.63 ± 1.8	16.57 ± 1.2
mid	21.93 ± 1.4	61.83 ± 1.7	15.22 ± 1.2
endo	22.29 ± 1.4	61.89 ± 1.6	15.80 ± 1.1
Mean	22.15 ± 1.4	62.12 ± 1.7	15.86 ± 1.2
Dog (n = 2)			
Mean values	22.4 ± 1.3	63.7 ± 1.6	14.1 ± 1.2
Dog (n = 16)			
Mean values	23.9 ± 1.0		
Human hearts (n = 6)			
Mean values	22.8 ± 1.4	61.8 ± 1.8	15.4 ± 1.2

This table shows V_{vmit}, V_{vmyo}, and V_{vcyt} for canine myocardium. All values are means ± SE. Hearts from dogs 1 and 2 were fixed by perfusion. Immersion fixation of left ventricular biopsies produced similar values for mitochondrial volume densities in 16 dogs. Human hearts show a quantitative tissue composition similar to that of dogs.

TABLE 6
Volume Densities of Mitochondria, Myofibrils, and Cytoplasm from the Rat, Hamster, and Mouse

	V_{vmit} (%)	V_{vmyo} (%)	V_{vcyt} (%)
Rat			
LA	27.6 ± 1.3	58.1 ± 1.6	14.7 ± 0.9
LL	29.5 ± 1.0	56.7 ± 1.7	13.8 ± 0.8
LP	27.7 ± 1.5	58.6 ± 1.8	14.4 ± 1.1
Mean	28.3 ± 1.3	57.8 ± 1.7	14.3 ± 1.0
Hamster			
LA	29.5 ± 1.5	55.5 ± 1.8	14.9 ± 1.1
LL	29.5 ± 1.5	53.8 ± 2.0	16.7 ± 0.9
LP	26.5 ± 1.6	59.5 ± 1.9	12.3 ± 1.1
Mean	28.5 ± 1.5	56.3 ± 1.9	14.6 ± 1.1
Mouse			
LA	32.5 ± 2.0	50.5 ± 2.2	16.9 ± 1.2
LL	32.2 ± 1.9	49.0 ± 1.9	18.7 ± 1.1
LP	31.9 ± 2.0	48.9 ± 1.8	19.0 ± 1.4
Mean	32.2 ± 2.0	49.4 ± 1.9	18.2 ± 1.2

All values are mean ± SE from three animals in each group. Differences between sampling sites are absent, but rat and hamster mean values are significantly different from those of mice (see Table 7).

TABLE 7
Comparison of Volume Densities between Species

	Dog	Rat	Hamster	Mouse	Man
Dog		0.001	0.001	0.001	NS
Rat	0.001		NS	0.025	0.001
Hamster	0.001	NS		0.025	0.001
Mouse	0.001	0.001	0.001		0.001
Man	NS	0.001	0.001	0.001	

Table 7 illustrates that volume densities are significantly different ($P < 0.025$ or $P < 0.001$) between all species except between canine and human hearts and between rat and hamster cardiac tissue. This comparison applies for mitochondrial (above diagonal rule) as well as myofibrillar (below diagonal rule) volume densities.

cardial layer, but the differences were not indicated as being significant. Our finding of a similar quantitative composition in myocytes from all three layers of canine left ventricles are in agreement with the data reported by Gerdes et al. (1980) and Anversa et al. (1978). Under pathological conditions, as, for example, hypertrophy (Anversa et al., 1979) or chronic ischemia (J. Schaper, own observations), significant differences may occur in the cytoplasmic composition of myocytes from the inner and outer myocardial layer.

Direction of Sectioning

Myocardial cells are composed of geometrically anisotropic tissue elements which do not have random orientation in space. Anisotropy does not influence the determination of volume densities, according to Delesse's principle (Weibel, 1969), which, in the present study is confirmed by comparing volume densities obtained from either longitudinally or transversally cut sections. However, anistropy and, therefore, the direction of sectioning the tissue, may influence the determination of surface densities, i.e., membrane profiles within a reference volume (Mall et al., 1978).

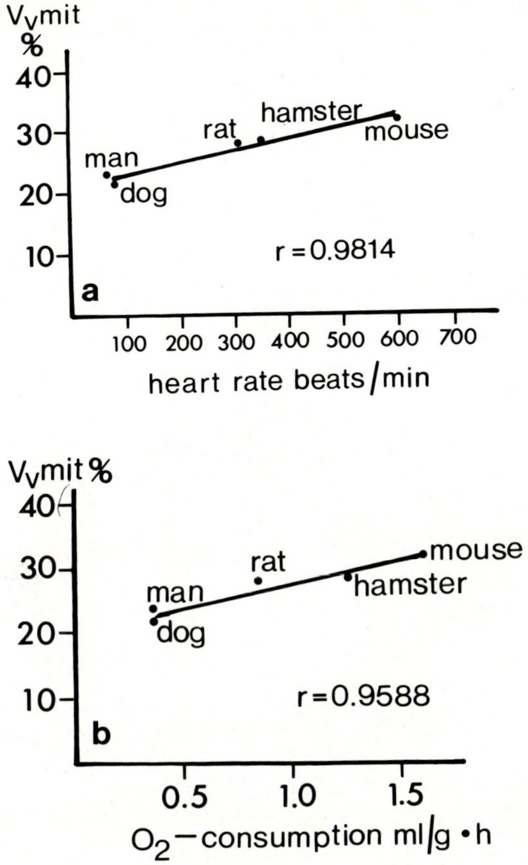

FIGURE 4. *Panel a: a close correlation exists between heart rate and V_{vmit} in all species investigated. Panel b: a close correlation exists between O_2 consumption and V_{vmit} in all species investigated.*

Mode of Tissue Fixation and Preparation

The choice of the fixative and its osmolarity may influence quantitative morphological data (Eisenberg and Mobley, 1975; Hayat, 1981). Shrinkage of the tissue may be as high as 45% of the original volume (Eisenberg and Mobley, 1975). Bossen et al.

TABLE 8
Physiological Data from Different Species

	Dog	Rat	Hamster	Mouse	Man
Body wt (kg)	20.0 ± 0.1	0.3 ± 0.01	0.15 ± 0.05	0.030 ± 0.002	70.0
Heart wt (g)	160.0 ± 8.0	0.9 ± 0.05	0.45 ± 0.04	0.15 ± 0.02	300.0
Heart rate (beats/min)	75	310	350	600	70
O_2 consumption (ml/g per hr)	0.36	0.84	1.24	1.59	0.40
HW:BW (g/kg)	8.0	3.0	3.0	5.0	4.0
HW:BW × V_{vmit} (g)	1.76	0.84	0.84	1.6	0.88

Body and heart weights were actually measured in this study, except in humans, where standard values were used. Body weight was lean body mass; heart weight includes both atria and both ventricles. Values are mean ± SD. The heart weight:body weight ratio (HW:BW) was calculated accordingly. Values for heart rate and O_2 consumption were taken from the Biology Data Book by Altman (1974). HW:BW × V_{vmit} has been calculated from our own data and is an indicator of the amount of mitochondria present in heart muscle per 1 kg body weight.

TABLE 9

Quantitative Analysis of Myocardial Composition of Human Hearts, Dogs, Rats, Hamsters, and Mice: 1968—Present

Author	Year	V_{vmit} (%)	V_{vmyo} (%)	Fixation
Man				
Fleischer	1978	34.5	47.1	I glut.
Schaper (present study)		22.8	61.8	I glut.
Dog				
Partin	1972	25.0	–	I OsO_4
Papadimitrou	1974	25.4	–	I glut.
Legato	1975	24.0	48.6	I glut.
McCallister	1978	26.0	54.0	P Karn.
Gerdes	1980	endo 25.4	endo 57.4	P glut.
		epi 24.1	epi 57.8	
Goldstein	1983	20.0–23.5	–	I Karn.
Schaper (present study)		22.0	63.0	P glut.
		23.4	–	I glut.
Rat				
Arcasoy	1968	28.5	–	I OsO_4
Poche	1968	40.2	59.8	I OsO_4
Schmalbruch	1970	27.0	55.0	P Karn.
Laguens	1971	36.6	–	I OsO_4
Friedman	1973	36.0	64.0	P glut.
Reith	1973	31.8	36.1	I OsO_4
Datta	1975	38.0	52.0	I glut.
Kawamura	1976	40.2	50.4	P glut.
Nakata	1977	35.5	56.7	I Karn.
Hatt	1978	31.1	58.7	P glut.
Iwamura	1978	37.2	57.1	P glut.
Lund	1978	endo 32.5	endo 62.7	
		epi 31.3	epi 62.0	P Karn.
David	1979	32.8	55.7	I Karn.
Tomanek	1979	endo 33.0	endo 59.5	
		epi 30.5	epi 63.0	P glut.
Tomanek	1979	endo 32.7	endo 61.8	
		epi 30.7	epi 63.1	P glut.
Wendt-Galitelli	1979	33.0	63.0	P glut.
Baranski	1980	43.2	–	I glut.
Craft-Cormney	1980	31.5	60.3	P Karn.
Hirakow	1980	34.1	61.1	P glut.
Lund	1982	34.0	60.0	P glut.
Frenzel	1981	29.0	53.0	P glut.
Guski	1981	31.4	48.4	I Karn.
Tomanek	1981	endo 29.9	endo 59.2	P glut.
		epi 30.3	epi 60.5	
Tomanek	1982	endo 32.7	endo 61.0	P Karn.
		epi 30.7	epi 62.4	
Tomanek	1982	epi 31.7	epi 56.8	P glut.
		endo 31.6	endo 57.8	P glut.
Schaper (present study)		28.3	57.8	P glut.
Hamster				
Lazarus	1976	28.2	45.9	P glut.
Bozner	1977	37.0	49.0	?
Colgan	1978	31.8	37.3	P glut.
Martorana	1979	28.7	69.6	P glut.
Schaper (present study)		28.6	56.2	P glut.
Mouse				
Herbener	1973	47.0	–	I glut.
Herbener	1976	47.7	–	I glut.
Tate	1976	53.8	–	I glut.
Bossen	1978	37.5	54.3	P glut.
Kainulainen	1979	43.7	44.3	I glut.
Schaper (present study)		32.2	49.4	P glut.

Table 9 shows the quantitative data available in the literature. I = immersion, P = perfusion, glut. = glutaraldehyde, Karn. = fixative according to Karnovski. Data from Page et al., Mall et al., and Anversa et al. are separately listed in Table 10.

TABLE 10
Quantitative Analysis of Rat Myocardium by Three Different Groups of Investigators

Author	Year	V_{vmit} (%)	V_{vmyo} (%)	Fixation
Page	1972	34–37	46–50	P OsO_4
Page	1973	35.5	47.6	P OsO_4
McCallister	1973	32.0	50.0	P OsO_4
Page	1974	35.1	46.7	P OsO_4
Smith	1976	35.0–36.0	—	P OsO_4
McCallister	1979	29.0	55.0	P Karn.
Mall	1980	33.8	55.4	P glut
Mall	1980	25.2	61.2	P glut
Mattfeldt	1983	26.9	62.3	P glut
Anversa	1971	outer 33.7	60.9	P glut
		mid 34.3	59.7	
		inner 34.6	59.2	
Anversa	1976	35.3	47.8	I Karn.
Anversa	1978	endo 33.8	53.8	
		epi 32.9	54.5	P glut
Anversa	1979	34.8	53.6	I Karn.
Wiener	1979	endo 33.8	53.8	
		epi 32.9	54.5	P glut
Anversa	1983	32.7	53.9	P glut

This table demonstrates the variability of quantitative data published by three different groups of investigators. P = perfusion; I = immersion.

(1978, 1981), therefore, caution against comparing stereological data obtained by different methods. Gerdes et al. (1982), using isolated myocytes, have shown that variations in tissue preparation may cause changes in cellular and tissue geometry, and they reported that an iso-osmolar fixative provides reproducible quantitative results. Legato (1979), on the other hand, believes that a varying osmolarity of solutions does not have a significant influence on quantitative data, whereas the choice of the primary fixative may significantly alter cell volume. On the basis of our own results and the work of many other investigators compiled in Tables 9 and 10, we would like to present a slightly different view. It is not necessarily the different fixative that influences stereological data. From the widely varying data on volume densities in rat myocardium, as indicated in Tables 9 and 10, it becomes evident that there exists no relationship between the fixative used and the level of volume densities determined. Furthermore, choice of fixation of the tissue by vascular perfusion or by immersion also seems to be without any substantial influence, as confirmed by the similarity of our own data obtained from perfusion- or immersion-fixed dog myocardium. It should be mentioned, however, that immersion fixation produces reliable reproducible results only when all preparatory conditions are optimal, i.e., if there is no time lag in fixation caused by specimens too large in size, or requiring special dissection procedures. Immersion fixation certainly is not the method of choice because of its uncertain fixing qualities, but it may provide useful data when handled properly in cases in which perfusion fixation is not applicable. As long as the fixation procedure has produced optimal tissue preservation, including avoidance of intracellular edema, and as long as cell volume fractions are being measured, as opposed to absolute values, cellular shrinkage seems to be a minor problem. Errors in stereological measurements are much more likely to be induced by the mode of tissue sampling, by the number of animals, samples, and micrographs investigated, and by the actual morphometric procedure. All these factors are handled in a nonuniform way throughout the literature, and their variation may explain the many deviations for one single species.

Experimental Results

This study shows that each of the four investigated animal species and the human heart has its own characteristic quantitative composition of myocardial cells.

Human Myocardium

Clinically normal human left ventricles contained 23% mitochondria, 62% myofibrils, and 15% cytoplasm. Only few data are available in the literature on human myocardium. David et al. (1978) reported mitochondrial to myofibrillar volume ratios in myocardium from children with Fallot's tetralogy or with a ventricular septum defect but values for normal nondiseased human myocardium were not indicated. Laguens et al. (1979) reported 24.4% mitochondria in three patients with progressive angina, between 28.6 and 36.0% mitochondria for patients in various stages of coronary insufficiency, and 38.2% mitochondria in mitral stenosis. Values for nondiseased human myocardium were not given in this study. Our group (Schaper et al., 1980; Schwarz et al., 1980; Schaper et al., 1981; Schaper and Schaper, 1983) has published several papers on morphometric data in hypertrophied or ischemic human myocardium. Fleischer et al. (1978, 1980) found in patients with apparently normal left ventricles a mitochondrial volume of 34%, independent of the age of the patients. The myofibrillar volume, on the other hand, was 47% in young patients (5–15 years) but 52% in older individuals (more than 45 years). Unverferth et al. (1981) measured the size of the mitochondrial surface and indicated 0.25 μm^2 as the normal value.

Our data on normal human myocardium are similar to those previously published (Schaper and Schaper, 1983) as control data in a morphometric study on hypertrophy of human left ventricles. In the aforementioned study by Schaper and Schaper, and in the present study, nonhypertrophied myocardial tissue was obtained from patients who underwent closure of an atrial septal defect during open-heart surgery. Because of the obvious difficulties in obtaining normal myocardium from humans, we considered this tissue to be the optimal approximation to normal conditions. Sampling of the myocardium by the needle biopsy technique and fixation by immersion in glutaraldehyde evidently did not influence these morphometric data, as shown by the similarity of results obtained in both studies. The quantitative data presented in this study obtained in canine myocardium fixed by perfusion or immersion confirm this finding.

Dogs

Normal dog hearts contained 22% mitochondria and 63% myofibrils in myocytes from the left ventricle. Papadimitrou et al. (1974) and McCallister et al. (1978) obtained slightly higher values for mitochondrial volume densities, and McCallister et al. (1978) reported a lower amount of contractile material (54%). Partin et al. (1972) reported 25% mitochondria in the normal dog heart; Legato (1975), 24% mitochondria and 48% myofibrils; Gerdes et al. (1980, 25% mitochondria and 57% myofibrils; and Goldstein (1983), 23% mitochondria. It is interesting to note that the mitochondrial volume densities are in rather close agreement in all the studies cited here, but the values for myofibrillar and therefore also for cytoplasmic densities are very divergent. Since the contractile material is a diffuse structural entity, not delineated by a membrane such as the mitochondria, errors in the definition of myofibrils while counting for volume fractions seem to be possible. In micrographs from truly randomly sampled areas, the amount of contractile material varies much more than that of mitochondria, which, if only a smaller number of micrographs were evaluated, could be a further source of error.

The data from Legato's (1979) study on normal growth of myocytes in dogs are difficult to compare, because the volume densities are indicated as points but not as percentages. Quantitative studies have shown that the composition of myocardial cells changes during fetal and postnatal development in the mouse (Herbener, 1976), hamster (Colgan et al., 1978), and rat (Page et al., 1974; Anversa et al., 1975; David et al., 1979; Olivetti et al., 1980; Hirakow et al., 1980) hearts; this was also found by Legato (1979) to be true in dog hearts.

Rats

The largest variations in myocardial volume densities are evident in the rat, the laboratory animal used most frequently in morphometric studies. We obtained 28% of mitochondrial and 57% of myofibrillar volume density in normal rats, which result is in agreement with the data obtained by Arcasoy (1968), Mall et al. (1980), Tomanek and Hovanec (1981), McCallister (1979), and Mattfeldt et al. (1983). Reith and Fuchs (1973), Tomanek et al. (1979, 1982), and Craft-Cormney and Anversa et al. (1983) measured mitochondrial volume densities around 32%, i.e., slightly higher than our values, but many authors (see Tables 9 and 10) have much higher values for mitochondrial volume fractions. Again, it is interesting to note that the values for myofibrillar volume densities vary widely, without relationship to the level of the mitochondrial volume. Table 10 shows volume densities for normal rat myocardium published by three different groups during the last 10 years. It is evident from this table that the different experimental series, even from one group of investigators, showed a differing quantitative composition of left ventricular myocytes, independent of the mode of fixation as well as of the choice of the primary fixative. The greatest consistency of results may be found in the data published by Anversa's group (Table 10), but, even there, a variability from 32–35% is evident. Variations are present in both mitochondrial and myofibrillar densities, but they are more pronounced in the latter. These variations in control values are indicative of an individual deviation from the mean value characteristic for one particular species. Our own data confirm this view. The individual animals from all our species showed a somewhat different quantitative composition of myocardial cells, and even the values for the various sampling sites within one particular animal varied slightly. It is believed that this is caused by a biological variability which warrants the preparation of a new control series with each new experimental setting.

Hamster

In hamster hearts, we found 28% mitochondria and 56% contractile material. Lazarus et al. (1976) reported 28% for mitochondrial volume density, and Martorana et al. (1979) also measured 28%, whereas Bozner and Dostal (1977) obtained 37%. The values for myofibrillar densities varied from 45% (Lazarus et al., 1976) to 69% (Martorana et al., 1979).

Mouse

In our mice, mitochondrial volume density was 32%, which is lower than the data found in the literature (Herbener 1973, 1976; Tate et al., 1976; Bossen et al., 1978; Kainulainen et al., 1979; see also Table 9).

Functional Importance of Morphometric Data

Mitochondrial volume densities showed differences that were statistically significant for all species except the human vs. the canine, and the rat vs. the hamster heart. Despite the biological variability between data from individual hearts, each of these mammalian species was found to possess a very specific and characteristic quantitative composition of myocardial cells. A close correlation existed between body weight and heart weight. The ratio between both [the relative heart weight (g/kg)] is also characteristic for each particular species, and decreases with decreasing size of the animals (Clark 1927). However, within one particular species, some variations in the heart weight:body weight ratio may exist because of differences between individuals in age, physical activity, and/or nutritional state (Clark, 1927; Brody 1945), or because of pathological factors.

Dogs exhibit the highest relative heart weight (Herrman 1925), i.e., gram heart weight per kg body weight, among all of the species investigated in this study (see Table 8). Both canine and human hearts possess 22–23% of mitochondria. It can then be calculated that 8-g relative heart weight consisting of 22% mitochondria contains 1.76 g mitochondria. This then also means that dog hearts contain 1.76 g mitochondria per kilogram body weight. In normal humans, 4 g heart per kilogram body weight are present which, when in the presence of 22% mitochondria per unit heart weight, then means that humans have only 0.88 g cardiac mitochondria per kilogram body weight. The fact that dogs have twice as much heart—and, therefore, more mitochondria—per kilogram body weight, than humans, may explain the fact that—in the presence of an almost identical quantitative composition of heart muscle cells—the endurance and speed performances of dogs are much higher than those of man.

With decreasing animal size, the heart rate increases drastically (Table 8), and an increased myocardial metabolic rate parallels the elevated heart rate. Basal metabolic rate is also higher in smaller animals (Altman, 1974). The morphological correlate of a high oxygen consumption because of a higher metabolic rate appears to be the increased volume density of mitochondria, i.e., the presence of more mitochondria in each heart muscle cell of small animals. Consequently, the amount of contractile material decreases. The number of cristae and, therefore, of respiratory chains might be a limiting factor for the metabolic rate (Weibel et al., 1981; Hoppler et al., 1981). Weibel et al. (1981) proposed the term "symmorphosis" to express the general principle of a regulated morphogenesis adapted to functional needs. Mathieu et al. (1981), in a morphometric study of skeletal muscle, found a close correlation between total mitochondrial mass and maximal oxygen consumption (Vo_{2max}). These findings are in agreement with our data showing an increased V_{vmit} in the presence of a higher Vo_{2max} in small animals. We therefore believe that the quantitative analysis of the mitochondrial content in myocardial cells is a measure of the oxidative capacity of cardiac muscle.

In summary, it has been shown that neither the site of sampling nor the direction of sectioning influences the determination of volume densities in normal cardiac muscle. Each of the animal species, including man, showed a characteristic quantitative composition of its myocardial cells. In rats, hamsters, and mice, V_{vmit} was significantly higher than in dogs or man. V_{vmit} correlated well with the specific Vo_{2max}, in each species. It is postulated that the amount of mitochondria in myocardial cells reflects the oxidative capacity of cardiac muscle.

Address for reprints: Jutta Schaper, M.D., Max-Planck-Institute for Physiological and Clinical Research, Department of Experimental Cardiology, Benekestrasse 2, D-6350 Bad Nauheim, Federal Republic of Germany.

Received October 21, 1983; accepted for publication December 12, 1984.

References

Altman PL, Dittmer DS (1974) Biological Data Book, vol 3. Bethesda, MD, Federation of the American Society on Experimental Biology

Anversa P (1983) Morphometry of exercise-induced right ventricular hypertrophy. Circ Res **52:** 57–64

Anversa P, Vitali-Mazza L, Visioli O, Marchetti G (1971) Experimental cardiac hypertrophy: A quantitative ultrastructural study in the compensatory stage. J Mol Cell Cardiol **3:** 213–221

Anversa P, Vitali-Mazza L, Loud AV (1975) Morphometric and autoradiographic study of developing ventricular and atrial myocardium in fetal rats. Lab Invest **33:** 696–705

Anversa P, Loud AV, Vitali-Mazza L (1976) Morphometry and autoradiography of early hypertrophic changes in the ventricular myocardium of adult rat. Lab Invest **35:** 475–483

Anversa P, Loud AV, Giacomelli F, Wiener J (1978) Absolute morphometric study of myocardial hypertrophy in experimental hypertension. II. Ultrastructure of myocytes and interstitium. Lab Invest **38:** 597–609

Anversa P, Olivetti G, Melissari M, Loud AV (1979) Morphometric study of myocardial hypertrophy induced by abdominal aortic stenosis. Lab Invest **40:** 341–349

Anversa P, Beghi C, Levicki V, McDonald SL, Kikkawa Y (1982) Morphometry of right ventricular hypertrophy induced by strenuous exercise in the rat. Am J Physiol **242:** H856–H861

Arcasoy M (1968) Ultrastructural alterations induced by therapeutic doses of digitoxin in cardiac and hepatic cells of rats. Aegean Med J **1:** 167–175

Baranski S, Kujawa M, Kaplanski A (1980) Ultrastructural qualitative and quantitative evaluation of cytoplasmatic structures of heart muscle of rats living aboard biosputnik Kosmos 936. Physiologist **23** (suppl): 38–40

Bossen EH, Sommer JR, Waugh RA (1978) Comparative stereology of the mouse and finch left ventricle. Tissue Cell **10:** 773–

Bossen EH, Sommer JR, Waugh RA (1981) Comparative stereology of mouse atria. Tissue Cell **13:** 71–77

Bozner A, Dostal J (1977) Table 643: Volume percent of myofibrils and mitochondria of the golden hamster heart during differentiation. *In* Quantitative Ultrastructural Data of Animal and Human Cells, by H David. New York, Stuttgart, Gustav Fischer Verlag, p 400

Brody S (1945) Bioenergetics and Growth. New York, Reinhold

Clark AJ (1927) Comparative Physiology of the Heart. Cambridge, University Press

Colgan JA, Lazarus ML, Sachs HG (1978) Post-natal development of the normal and cardiomyopathic hamster heart: A quantitative electron microscopic study. J Mol Cell Cardiol **10:** 43–54

Craft-Cormney C, Hansen JT (1980) Early ultrastructural changes in the myocardium following thyroxine induced hypertrophy. Virchows Arch [Cell Pathol] **33:** 267–273

Datta BN, Silver MD (1975) Cardiomegaly in chronic anemia in rats. An experimental study including ultrastructural, histometric and stereologic observations. Lab Invest **32:** 503–514

David H, Oldag D, Schubel B, Warnke H, Behrisch D (1978) Elektronenmikroskopische Befunde der Herzmuskulatur beim Morbus Fallot und Ventrikelseptumdefekt. Zentralbl Pathol **122:** 34–42

David H, Meyer R, Marx I, Guski H, Wenzelides K (1979) Morphometric characterisation of left ventricular myocardial cells of male rats during postnatal development. J Mol Cell Cardiol **11:** 631–638

David H (1979) Some recent results of the quantitative characterization of heart muscle cells. Z Mikrosk Anat Forsch **93:** 113–137

Eisenberg BR, Mobley BA (1975) Size changes in single muscle fibers during fixation and embedding. Tissue Cell **7:** 383–387

Fleischer M, Warmuth H, Backwinkel KP, Themann H, Achatzky RS, Dittrich H (1978) Feinstrukturell-morphometrische Befunde an der Kammerwand des nichtbelasteten menschlichen linken Ventrikels bei jungen und alten Patienten. Virchows Arch [Pathol Anat] **380:** 123–133

Fleischer M, Wippo W, Themann H, Achatzky RS (1980) Ultrastructural morphometric analysis of human myocardial left ventricles with mitral insufficiency. A comparison with normally-loaded and hypertrophied human left ventricles. Virchows Arch [Pathol Anat] **389:** 205–210

Frenzel H, Höltermann W, Schnurch HG, Novi A, Hort W (1981) Experimentelle morphologische und biochemische Untersuchungen am Herzen während der Rückbildung einer Hypertrophie (abstr). Verh Dtsch Ges Pathol **65:** 481

Gerdes AM, Callas G, Kasten FH (1979) Differences in regional capillary distribution and myocyte sizes in normal and hypertrophic rat hearts. Am J Anat **156:** 523–531

Gerdes AM, Kasten FH (1980) Morphometric study of endocardium and epicardium of the left ventricle in adult dogs. Am J Anat **159:** 389–394

Gerdes AM, Krisemann J, Bishop SP (1982) Morphometric study of cardiac muscle. Lab Invest **46:** 271–274

Goldstein MA, Murphy DL (1983) A morphometric analysis of ischemic canine myocardium with and without reperfusion. J Mol Cell Cardiol **15:** 325–334

Guski H, Meerson FZ, Wassilew G (1981) Comparative study of ultrastructure and function of the rat heart hypertrophied by exercise or hypoxia. Exp Pathol **20:** 108–120

Hayat MA (1981) Fixation for Electron Microscopy. New York, Academic Press

Herbener GH, Swigart RH, Lang CA (1973) Morphometric comparison of the mitochondrial populations of normal and hypertrophic heart. Lab Invest **28:** 96–103

Herbener GH (1976) Age-dependent changes in mitochondria. J Gerontol **31:** 8–12

Herrmann GR (1925) Experimental heart disease. 1. Methods of dividing hearts with sectional and proportional weights and ratios for two hundred normal dog hearts. Am Heart J **1:** 213–218

Hirakow R, Gotoh T, Watanabe T (1980) Quantitative studies on the ultrastructural differentiation and growth of mammalian cardiac muscle cells. I. The atria and ventricles of the rat. Acta Anat (Basel) **108:** 144–152

Hoppeler H, Mathieu O, Krauer R, Claassen H, Armstrong RB, Weibel ER (1981) Distribution of mitochondria and capillaries in various muscles. Respir Physiol **44:** 87–111

Imamura K (1978) Ultrastructural aspect of left ventricular hypertrophy in spontaneously hypertensive rats: A qualitative and quantitative study. Jpn Circ J **42:** 979–1002

Imamura K, Kawamura K, Takatsu T, Kashii C (1979) Ultrastructural study on hypertrophied myocardium in spontaneously hypertensive rats. A qualitative and quantitative comparison of left and right ventricle. Jpn Heart J **20:** 700

Kainulainen H, Pilström L, Vihko V (1979) Morphometry of myocardial apex in endurance trained mice of different ages. Acta Physiol Scand **107:** 109–114

Kawamura K, Kashii C, Imamura K (1976) Ultrastructural changes in hypertrophied myocardium of spontaneously hypertensive rats. Jpn Circ J **40:** 1119

Laguens R (1971) Morphometric study of myocardial mitochondria in the rat. J Cell Biol **48:** 673–676

Laguens RP, Weinschelbaum R, Favaloro R (1979) Ultrastructural and morphometric study of the human heart muscle cell in acute coronary insufficiency. Human Pathol **10:** 695–705

Lazarus M, Colgan JA, Sachs HG (1976) Quantitative light and electron microscopic comparison of the normal and cardiomyopathic syrian hamster heart. J Mol Cell Cardiol **8:** 431–441

Legato MJ (1975) Ultrastructural changes during normal growth in the dog and rat ventricular myofiber. *In* Development and Physiological Correlates of the Cardiac Muscle, edited by M Lieberman, T Sano. New York, Raven Press

Legato M (1979) Cellular mechanisms of normal growth in the mammalian heart. I. Qualitative and quantitative features of ventricular architecture in the dog from birth to five months of age. Circ Res **44:** 250–262

Lund DD, Tomanek RJ (1978) Myocardial morphology in spontaneously hypertensive and aortic-constricted rats. Am J Anat **152:** 141–151

Lund DD, Tomanek RJ (1980) The effects of chronic hypoxia on the myocardial cell of normotensive and hypertensive rats. Anat Rec **196:** 421–430

Mall G, Reinhard H, Kayser K, Rossner JA (1978) An effective morphometric method for electron microscopic studies on papillary muscles. Virchows Arch [Pathol Anat] **379:** 219–228

Mall G, Mattfeldt T (1980) Ultrastructural morphometric study on the rat heart after chronic ethanol feeding. Virchows Arch [Pathol Anat] **389:** 59–77

Martorana PA, Schaper J, van Even P (1979) The effect of physical exercise on elastase-induced emphysema in hamsters. Annu Rev Resp Dis **120:** 1209–1213

Martorana PA, van Even P, Wüsten B, Schaper J (1984) Increased myocardial capillary density in dogs with experimental emphysema. Lab Invest **50:** 592–596

Mathieu O, Krauer R, Hoppeler H, Gehr P, Lindstedt SL, Alexander RM, Taylor CR, Weibel ER (1981) Design of the mammalian respiratory system. VII. Scaling mitochondrial volume in skeletal muscle to body mass. Respir Physiol **44:** 113–128

Mattfeldt T, Mall G, Volk B (1980) Morphometric analysis of rat heart mitochondria after chronic ethanol treatment. J Mol Cell Cardiol **12:** 1311–1319

Mattfeldt T, Mall G (1983) Dipyridamole-induced capillary endothelial cell proliferation in the rat heart: A morphometric investigation. Cardiovasc Res **17:** 229–237

McCallister LP, Page E (1973) Effects of thyroxin on ultrastructure of rat myocardial cells. A stereological study. J Ultrastruct Res **42:** 136–155

McCallister LP, Dariello DC, Tyers GFO (1978) Morphometric observations of the effects of normothermic ischemic arrest on dog myocardial ultrastructure. J Mol Cell Cardiol **10:** 67–80

McCallister LP, Trapukdi S, Neely JR (1979) Morphometric observations on the effects of ischemia in the isolated perfused rat heart. J Mol Cell Cardiol **11:** 619–630

Olivetti G, Anversa P, Loud AV (1980) Morphometric study of early postnatal development in the left and right ventricular myocardium. II. Tissue composition, capillary growth and sarcoplasmic alterations. Circ Res **46:** 503–512

Page E, Polimeni PI, Zak R, Earley J, Johnson M (1972) Myofibrillar mass in rat and rabbit heart muscle. Correlation of microchemical and stereological measurements in normal and hypertrophic hearts. Circ Res **30:** 430–439

Page E, McCallister LP (1973) Quantitative electron microscopic description of heart muscle cells. Application to normal, hypertrophied and thyroxin-stimulated heart. Am J Cardiol **31:** 172–181

Page E, Early J, Power B (1974) Normal growth of ultrastructures in rat left ventricular myocardial cells. Circ Res **34/35** (suppl II): 12–16

Papadimitrou JM, Hopkins BE, Taylor RR (1974) Regression of left ventricular dilation and hypertrophy. Circ Res **35:** 127–135

Partin JS, Benzing G, Partin JC (1972) Quantitative fine structural changes in dog heart following cardiopulmonary bypass. J Mol Cell Cardiol **4:** 345–355

Pinkowski E (1983) Veränderungen am ischämisch geschädigten Herzmuskel während der Reperfusionsphase. Thesis, Universität Giessen

Poche R, de Mello-Mattos CM, Rembarz HW, Stoepel S (1968) Über das Verhältnis Mitochondrien:Myofibrillen in der Herzmuskelzelle der Ratte bei Druckhypertrophie des Herzens. Virchows Arch [Pathol Anat] **344:** 100–110

Reith A, Fuchs S (1973) The heart muscle of the rat under the influence of triiodothyronine and riboflavin deficiency with special reference to mitochondria. A morphologic and morphometric study by electron microscopy. Lab Invest **29:** 229–235

Sachs HG, Colgan JA, Lazarus ML (1977) Ultrastructure of the aging myocardium: a morphometric approach. Am J Anat **150:** 63–71

Schaper J (1979) Ultrastructure of the myocardium in acute ischemia. *In* The Pathophysiology of Myocardial Perfusion, edited by W Schaper. Amsterdam, Oxford, New York, Elsevier/North-Holland Biomedical Press, pp 581–673

Schaper J, Schwarz F, Kittstein H, Becker V, Winkler B (1980) Myocardial subcellular correlates of failure in human heart disease. Circulation **62** (suppl III): 14

Schaper J, Schwarz F, Hehrlein F (1981) Ultrastrukturelle Veränderungen im menschlichen Myokard bei Hypertrophie durch Aortenklappenfehler und deren Beziehung zur linksventrikulären Masse und Auswurffraktion. Herz **6:** 217–225

Schaper J, Schaper W (1983) Ultrastructural correlates of reduced cardiac function in human heart disease. Eur Heart J **4** (suppl A): 35–42

Schwarz F, Kittstein H, Winkler B, Schaper J (1980) Quantitative ultrastructure of the myocardium in chronic aortic valve disease. Basic Res Cardiol **75:** 109–117

Smith HE, Page E (1976) Morphometry of rat heart mitochondrial subcompartments and membranes: Application to myocardial cell atrophy after hypophysectomy. J Ultrastruct Res **55:** 31–41

Tate EL, Herbener GH (1976) A morphometric study of the density of mitochondrial cristae in heart and liver of aging mice. J Gerontol **31:** 129

Tomanek RJ (1979) The role of prevention or relief of pressure overload on the myocardial cell of the spontaneously hypertensive rat: A morphometric and stereological study. Lab Invest **40:** 83–91

Tomanek RJ, Davies JW, Anderson SC (1979) The effects of alpha-methyldopa on cardiac hypertrophy in spontaneously hypertensive rats: Ultrastructural, stereological, and morphometric analysis. Cardiovasc Res **13:** 173–182

Tomanek RJ, Hovanec JM (1981) The effects of long-term pressure overload and aging on the myocardium. J Mol Cell Cardiol **13:** 471–488

Tomanek RJ, Bhatnagar RK, Schmid P, Brody MJ (1982) Role of catecholamines in myocardial cell hypertrophy in hypertensive rats. Am J Physiol **242:** H1015–1021

Tomanek RJ (1982) Selective effects of alpha-methyldopa on myocardial cell components independent of cell size in normotensive and genetically hypertensive rats. Hypertension **4:** 499–506

Unverferth DV, Masorien RD, Unverferth BP, Talley RL, Balcerzak SP, Baba N (1981) Human myocardial morphologic and functional changes in the first 24 h after doxorubicin administration. Cancer Treat Rep **65:** 1093–1097

Weber E (1972) Grundriss der Biologischen Statistik. Jena, Gustav Fischer Verlag

Weibel ER (1969) Stereological principles for morphometry in electron microscopic cytology. Int Rev Cytol **26:** 235–248

Weibel ER, Taylor CR, Gehr P, Hoppeler H, Mathieu O, Maloiy GMO (1981) Design of the mammalian respiratory system. IX. Functional and structural limits for oxygen flow. Respir Physiol **44:** 151–164

Wendt-Galitelli MT, Erbrecht G, Jacob R (1979) Morphological alterations and their functional interpretation in the hypertrophied myocardium of Goldblatt hypertensive rats. J Mol Cell Cardiol **11:** 275–287

Wiener J, Giacomelli F, Loud AV, Anversa P (1979) Morphometry of cardiac hypertrophy induced by experimental renal hypertension. Am J Cardiol **44:** 919–929

Winkler B, Schaper J, Thiedemann KU, Wüsten B (1976) Application of a Computerized System for the Morphometric Analysis of Biological Material, vol 2 Proceedings Sixth European Congress Electron Microscopy TAL. Jerusalem, International Publishing Company, pp 146–147

Winkler B, Schaper J, Thiedemann KU (1977) Hypertrophy due to volume overloading in the dog heart. A morphometric study. Basic Res Cardiol **72:** 222–227

INDEX TERMS: Ultrastructure • Heart • Morphometry • Animals • Man

Changes in Cholinergic Parameters Associated with Failure of Conotruncal Septation in Embryonic Chick Hearts after Neural Crest Ablation

Margaret L. Kirby, Robert S. Aronstam, and Jerry J. Buccafusco

From the Departments of Anatomy, Pharmacology, and Toxicology, and Psychiatry, Medical College of Georgia, Augusta, Georgia, and the Department of Psychiatry, Veterans Administration Medical Center, Augusta, Georgia

SUMMARY. Cells from the neural crest over occipital somites migrate to the heart, where they give rise to parasympathetic postganglionic neurons as well as ectomesenchymal elements which contribute to conotruncal septation. With a microcautery needle, the neural crest over occipital somites was ablated bilaterally in chicken embryos at an early stage of development. Histological examination on incubation day 15 revealed conotruncal malformations, involving malformation or absence of the conotruncal septum in all embryos. Two peaks of embryo mortality were observed. One peak (incubation days 6–8) occurred at the same time as conotruncal septal closure; the second peak (incubation days 11–13) was concurrent with the onset of functional parasympathetic innervation. A disruption of parasympathetic innervation was indicated by: (1) a decrease in acetylcholinesterase staining, (2) a decrease (27%) in the number of ganglion cells in the conotruncus, (3) decreases in the acetylcholine content of atrium (31%) and ventricle (39%), and (4) a decrease (21%) in muscarinic acetylcholine receptor density on incubation day 15. Radiolabeled ligand-binding studies revealed no change in the affinity of cardiac muscarinic receptors for [^{3}H]methylscopolamine (K_D = 0.17–0.21 nM). Agonist-binding affinity and sensitivity to guanine nucleotides were similarly unaffected. The reasons for the limited extent of the parasympathetic lesion are unclear, but may involve recruitment of precursor cells from other regions of the neural crest, partial regeneration of the neural crest following surgical removal, or an alteration in the contribution of incoming sympathetic or preganglionic parasympathetic elements. No such plasticity was associated with neural crest contributions to the structural development of the conotruncus. Malformations were observed in all lesioned embryos. **(*Circ Res 56: 392–401, 1985*)**

NEURONS of the peripheral autonomic ganglia and their supporting cells arise from various levels of the neural crest (Horstadius, 1950; LeDouarin and Teillet, 1974). Neural crest is produced from ectoderm in the avian embryo after the neural folds appose each other to form the primitive neural tube. Kirby and Stewart (1983) used orthotopic transplantation of occipital neural crest from quail donors to chick embryo hosts to identify the origin of neural crest cells which provide parasympathetic postganglionic innervation of the heart. The parasympathetic postganglionic neurons, commonly referred to as cardiac ganglion cells, were found to arise bilaterally from the neural crest over somites 1–3 and to migrate toward the heart while it is still a simple tube. Removal of the neural crest over these somites decreased high affinity choline uptake (a marker for cholinergic nerve terminals) by 60% on day 10 of incubation, suggesting a depletion of cardiac ganglion neurons (Kirby and Stewart, 1983). Neural crest removal also produced a variety of conotruncal malformations (Kirby et al., 1983), which is thought to reflect the loss of ectomesenchymal, rather than neuronal, derivatives of the neural crest.

The present study was undertaken to characterize biochemical alterations in cardiac cholinergic systems in response to depletion of parasympathetic innervation. Many trophic interactions occur between motor neuron terminals and skeletal muscle cells during development (Fambrough, 1979; Holyday, 1980). Comparable interactions of developing autonomic terminals with their end organs have not been demonstrated. It was recently shown that the density of cardiac muscarinic receptors can be altered by atropine treatment on days 12–14 of incubation (Kirby and Aronstam, 1983). This period corresponds to the onset of cholinergic function in the heart (Pappano and Skowronck, 1974). In the present paper, we report the consequences of occipital neural crest ablation: a 20–30% decrease in the number of ganglion cells in the area of the outflow tract associated with a 31–39% decrease in acetylcholine concentration in the atrium and ventricle, as well as a 21% reduction of muscarinic acetylcholine receptors in whole hearts. A second point of interest is the relationship between the neuronal and ectomesenchymal contributions of neural crest to cardiac development. In contrast to the rather modest decreases in biochemical markers of cholinergic systems which suggest compensatory mechanisms in the patterns of cardiac innervation, heart malformations were observed in *every* embryo in which the neural crest over the occipital somites was removed.

Methods

Tissue Preparations and Microsurgery

Fertile Arbor Acre chicken eggs were purchased from Central Soya and stored at 15–20°C. Incubation was initiated in forced-draft incubators maintained at 38°C and 97% relative humidity. The eggs were opened at stages 8–9 [about 30 hours of incubation (Hamburger and Hamilton, 1951)] and prepared for microsurgery according to the method reported by Narayanan (1970). The neural folds over somites 1 and 2, 1 through 3, and 1 through 4 were ablated bilaterally by means of a microcautery unit developed in collaboration with the Biomedical Engineering Department of the Medical College of Georgia. The neural fold consists of the presumptive dorsal part of the neural tube, the neural crest, and some adjacent surface ectoderm (Noden, 1975; Tosney, 1982). Only the neural crest migrates from this region. Ablation of the neural fold was accomplished in a very circumscribed area without damage to the ventral neural tube or underlying mesoderm. The neural crest was ablated in a total of 319 embryos; 123 control embryos were processed in parallel. For control embryos, the eggs were opened, sealed, and returned to the preoperative incubator at the same time as experimental eggs.

After microsurgery, the eggs were sealed and returned to the preoperative incubator until the circulatory system was well-established (about 72 hours of total incubation). The viable eggs were transferred to a second incubator maintained at 37°C and 70% relative humidity. The eggs were monitored for viability daily until day 15 (total incubation). At that time, the hearts were removed and divided into atrial, ventricular, and conotruncal pieces. The atria and ventricles were frozen in liquid nitrogen until processed for measurement of acetylcholine concentration *or* muscarinic acetylcholine receptor content.

Histological and Histochemical Examination

The conotruncal regions were fixed in Perfix, embedded in paraffin, serially cross-sectioned, and stained with thionin. The number of cardiac ganglion cells was counted in every 10th section of the conotruncal region between the base of the semilunar valves and the first branches of the aorta. Malformations of the outflow tract were catalogued as the cardiac ganglion neurons were counted. The individual who analyzed these sections did not know whether the embryos were experimental or control.

Acetylcholinesterase histochemistry was used to visualize the cardiac ganglia remaining in the heart after neural crest extirpation. The method of Rickenbacher and Muller (1979) for developing whole hearts was used on the 12th or 15th day of incubation in lesioned and control embryos. Briefly, the embryos were perfused intracardially with cold 10% neutral-buffered formalin. The hearts were removed and postfixed for 2–6 hours at 4°C and washed in distilled water. Cholinesterase was demonstrated by Koelle and Friedenwald's modification of Gomori's method as reported by Thompson (166).

[^{3}H]Choline Uptake

[^{3}H]choline uptake in 15-day atria was measured as described previously (Kirby and Stewart, 1983). The atrial wall was rapidly isolated, minced, and placed in cold Krebs' buffer. Half of the pieces were incubated at 37°C in Kreb's buffer containing 10^{-4} M hemicholinium-3. The other half of the tissue was incubated similarly, except that hemicholinium-3 was excluded from the medium. After 5 minutes, the tissue was transferred into Kreb's buffer at 37°C containing 10^{-6} M choline chloride and 1 μCi/ml [^{3}H]choline chloride (77 Ci/mmol, Amersham).

The tissue was incubated with shaking for a total of 20 minutes, which had been shown previously to represent the time needed for saturation of choline uptake under these conditions. After the 20-minute incubation, the tissue was transferred through two 10-minute washes in Kreb's buffer and was blotted, weighed, placed in scintillation vials containing 1–2 ml ethanol, and shaken vigorously for several seconds. Scintillation cocktail was added and radioactivity was measured, using a Beckman LS 8000 with a tritium-counting efficiency of 38%. Radioactivity was determined in a 10-μl sample of each incubation well. To standardize the results from assay to assay, uptake was corrected for the counts per minute (counts/min) of specific neuronal uptake per million counts available in the incubation well. Neuronal uptake was obtained by subtracting the uptake in the presence of hemicholinium-3 (nonneuronal uptake) from the total uptake.

Acetylcholine Measurements

Atrial and ventricular samples were weighed and homogenized in 1.0 ml (ventricle) or 0.5 ml (atrium) of 1 N formic acid:acetone (15:85, vol/vol). The homogenates were centrifuged at 5000 *g* for 15 minutes, and 0.2-ml aliquots of the supernatants were evaporated to dryness in a vacuum centrifuge. The extracts were reconstituted in 0.2 ml of 10 mM phosphate-buffered saline, pH 7.4, containing 20 μM physostigmine, and were centrifuged at 12,000 *g* for 15 minutes. Endogenous acetylcholine was determined in 30-μl (ventricle) or 50-μl (atrium) aliquots of supernatant, by a radioimmunoassay procedure developed by Spector et al. (1978). Heart extracts or serial dilutions of a standard solution of ACh (1.6–100 pmol) were incubated with 100 μl of antiserum (final dilution 1:250) in buffered saline containing 0.125% bovine γ-globulin, 0.5% serum albumin, and 100 μl of [^{3}H]acetylcholine (80 Ci/mmol, Amersham; final dilution 1:4500) in a total volume of 0.5 ml. Antibody-bound [^{3}H]acetylcholine was precipitated by the addition of 0.5 ml of saturated ammonium sulfate. After centrifugation, the pellet was dissolved in water, and aliquots were removed for determination of radioactivity content by liquid scintillation counting. Several samples from atria and ventricles of control and experimental animals were adjusted to pH 11 and heated to 80°C for 15 minutes to hydrolyze endogenous acetylcholine. These hydrolyzed extracts did not displace antibody-bound tritium.

Muscarinic Receptor-Binding Measurements

Cardiac tissues were weighed and homogenized in 10 volumes of 50 mM Tris-HCl, pH 7.4, containing 1 mM $MgCl_2$ and 0.1 mM phenylmethylsulfonyl fluoride (to prevent proteolysis). This homogenate was filtered through cheesecloth to remove undisrupted material, and then centrifuged at 20,000 *g* for 20 minutes. The pellet was resuspended in fresh buffer and used without further treatment. Protein content was estimated by the method of Lowry et al. (1951).

Muscarinic receptor binding was measured using [^{3}H]-*N*-methylscopolamine ([^{3}H]MS; 80 Ci/mmol, Amersham). Cardiac tissue (10–15 μg protein/ml) was incubated with [^{3}H]MS for 60 minutes at room temperature in 50 mM Tris-HCl, pH 7.4, containing 1 mM $MgCl_2$ in a total volume of 5 ml. The suspension was then filtered under vacuum through glass fiber filters (Whatman GF/B). The filters were washed once with 5 ml of buffer and removed for determination of radioactivity content by liquid scintillation counting using a toluene-based cocktail (4 liters of toluene, 1.22 g of 1,4-bis-[4-methyl-5-phenyl-2-oxazolyl] benzene, 180 g of 2.5 diphenyloxazole, 150 ml of BioSolv-3). Nonspecific binding was determined by including 1 μM atropine in a parallel series of incubation media. All experimental points were determined in triplicate.

The number of muscarinic receptors and their affinity for [^{3}H]MS was determined in hearts pooled from 5–6 embryos. [^{3}H]MS binding was measured at nine concentrations between 0.032 and 3.2 nM. Binding parameters were determined by nonlinear regression analysis, using a mass action expression for ligand binding to a single population of non-interacting sites, as follows:

$$B = B_{max} \cdot C/(C + K_D),$$

where B is binding, B_{max} is the concentration of binding sites, C is the concentration of [^{3}H]MS, and K_D is the dissociation constant. Nonlinear regression was performed using procedures available in the Statistical Package for the Social Sciences. The number of muscarinic binding sites was measured further in 49 different hearts (24 control, 25 experimental). Since there wasn't enough tissue to obtain complete binding curves from single hearts, receptor concentrations were determined by measuring [^{3}H]MS binding at two near-saturating concentrations of [^{3}H]MS (3.2 and 5.6 nM). Receptor concentration was calculated assuming 95% and 97% receptor occupancy levels at these [^{3}H]MS concentrations. These measurements were performed in quadruplicate, including quadruplicate determinations of nonspecific binding. The validity of this approach to estimating the number of receptors is supported by the close adherence of [^{3}H]MS binding under these conditions to single-site mass action kinetics and by the absence of any significant differences between [^{3}H]MS affinity for muscarinic receptors in hearts from control and experimental animals.

Carbamylcholine binding was inferred from its inhibition of 0.1 nM [^{3}H]MS binding. Binding curves were resolved into high- and low-affinity components by nonlinear regression analysis and a model incorporating two independent binding sites, as follows:

$$B = R_H \cdot C/(C + K_{DH}) + (1\text{-}R_H) \cdot C/(C + K_{DL}),$$

where B is binding, C is the concentration of carbamylcholine, K_{DH} and K_{DL} are the carbamylcholine dissociation constants associated with the high- and low-affinity binding sites, and R_H and (1-R_H) are the fractions of receptors displaying high- and low-affinity carbamylcholine binding, respectively. In certain experiments 10 μM 5′-guanylylimidodiphosphate (Gpp(NH)p), a stable analogue of GTP, was included in the binding incubation media.

Statistical Methods

Summary data are presented as mean ± SEM. Statistical significance of ganglion cell counts, [^{3}H]choline uptake, acetylcholine levels, and receptor concentrations and binding parameters were determined by Students' *t*-test.

Results

Neural Crest Lesions

A microcautery lesion of the neural crest over somites 1 and 2 is illustrated in Figure 1. The lesion was created at stage 10 (about 35 hours of incubation). The histological examination was made about 5 hours later (i.e., in early stage 11). The neural fold was removed without causing damage to the ventral neural tube or underlying mesoderm (Fig. 1D). The neural tube continued to develop normally both cranial and caudal to the lesion (Figure 1, C and E). Most of the embryos were grossly normal throughout the incubation period, i.e., no external malformations of the beak, eyes, trunk, or limbs were apparent. Approximately 10% of the experimental embryos had defects in the skin and skull over the occiput. Thoracic wall defects were seen in approximately 20% of the experimental embryos. This type of defect is present in higher incidence after any surgical manipulation of the embryo, and does not have a significant correlation with heart defects (Kirby, unpublished data). The experimental embryos were slightly smaller than controls, although the developmental stage of experimental embryos was comparable to that of controls on the day of harvest.

Neural crest lesions over somites 1–2, 1–3, or 1–4 caused conotruncal malformations in every embryo. The only conotruncal abnormality which could be identified in serial sections of the conotruncal region was common outflow (comparable to persistent truncus), indicating a failure of high ventricular and aorticopulmonary septation. Common outflow was seen in 77% on the hearts analyzed from serial sections of the outflow area. If an experimental heart had a less severe form of septal defect (i.e., double outlet right ventricle), it would have appeared essentially normal in our serial sections, since the ventricles below the semilunar valves were removed prior to histological processing for biochemical measurements. It should be noted, however, that all of the hearts from experimental embryos appeared grossly abnormal, as has been described previously (Kirby et al., 1983).

The degree of ganglion cell depletion was the same, whether neural crest over somites 1–2 or 1–3 was removed (Table 1). Removal of neural crest over somites 1–4 resulted in a total ganglion cell count that was not significantly less than control. The outflow tract in embryos with somite 1–4 lesions was significantly longer than outflow tracts from embryos with somite 1–2 or 1–3 lesions or controls. This resulted in a significant decrease in density of ganglion cells following somite 1–4 lesions (Table 1).

A grossly elongated heart taken from a 15-day embryo is shown in Figure 2. Serial section analysis of the entire heart revealed that both of the great vessels arose from the right ventricle. A small

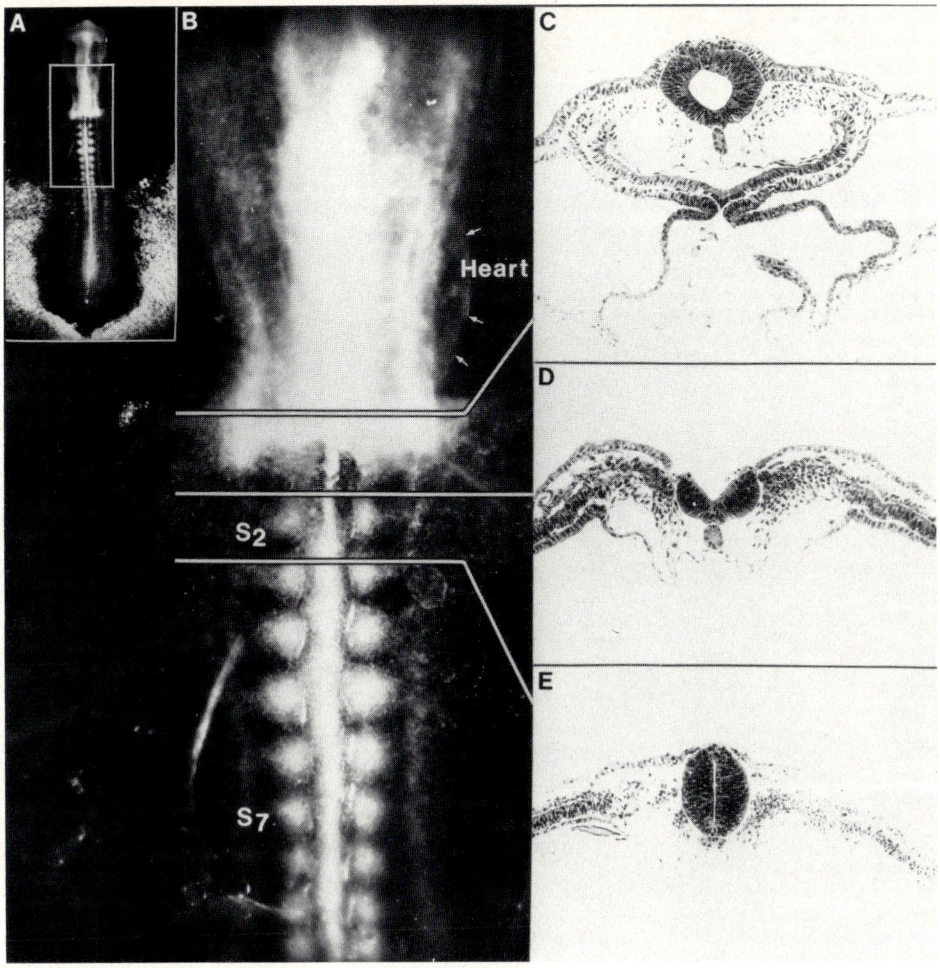

FIGURE 1. *A microcautery lesion of the neural folds at the level of somites 1 and 2 in an early stage 11 embryo. The lesion was made in the embryo early in stage 10. After a 5-hour recovery period, the embryo was fixed in ovo (Karnovsky's) for 5 minutes, and then removed from the egg and immersion-fixed for 1 hour. The embryo was photographed, by dark field illumination, and subsequently processed for light microscopy in glycol methacrylate. Panel A shows the whole stage 11 embryo with a total of 12 somites. The outlined area is enlarged (40×) in panel B. The area of the lesion can be seen in the dorsal neural tube adjacent to somites 1 and 2. The notochord is the light structure in the center of the lesioned area. The notochord is clearly visible in this area because the dorsal part of the neural tube is not present. Panels C, D, and E are cross-sections of the same embryo at the levels indicated (140×). Panel C is cranial to the lesion, panel D is at the level of the lesion, and panel E is caudal to the lesion. In panel D, removal of the neural folds caused loss of the dorsal part of the neural tube and some ectoderm; however, the mesoderm lateral to the neural tube was not damaged. The relationship of the developing heart to the position of the lesion can be visualized in panel B.*

aorticopulmonary septal defect was also present. Histochemical staining for acetylcholinesterase (Fig. 2) revealed a paucity of cholinesterase-positive nerves and ganglia in the cardiac plexus on both the dorsal and ventral surfaces of the heart, compared with hearts from control embryos.

Two peaks of mortality were observed in the lesioned embryos which survived the immediate postoperative period (Fig. 3). One peak lasted from incubation days 6 through 8, the second from incubation days 11 through 13. Control embryos also displayed a slight increase in mortality on days 7 and 8 of incubation. The survival to day 15 of incubation (at which time all hearts were harvested) was 19% for experimental and 54% for control embryos.

Ganglion Cell Population

The number of ganglion cells in the conotruncal region of normal embryos rose linearly from 71 ± 7 ($n = 5$) on incubation day 8 to 980 ± 156 ($n = 5$) on day 18 (Fig. 4). Regression analysis revealed that the

TABLE 1
Ganglion Cell Content and Length of Cardiac Outflow Tract* after Depletion of Parasympathetic Innervation by Neural Crest Lesions

Lesion	Ganglion cells	Length of outflow tract (μm)	Ganglion cell density (ganglion cells/unit length)	n
S 1–2	448 ± 30†	1707 ± 80	0.26†	29
S 1–3	433 ± 61†	1713 ± 120	0.25†	14
S 1–4	615 ± 51	1941 ± 100†	0.32†	19
Control	681 ± 34	1643 ± 40	0.41	47

* (Semilunar valve to the base of the first branches of the great vessels).
† Different from control $P < 0.025$.

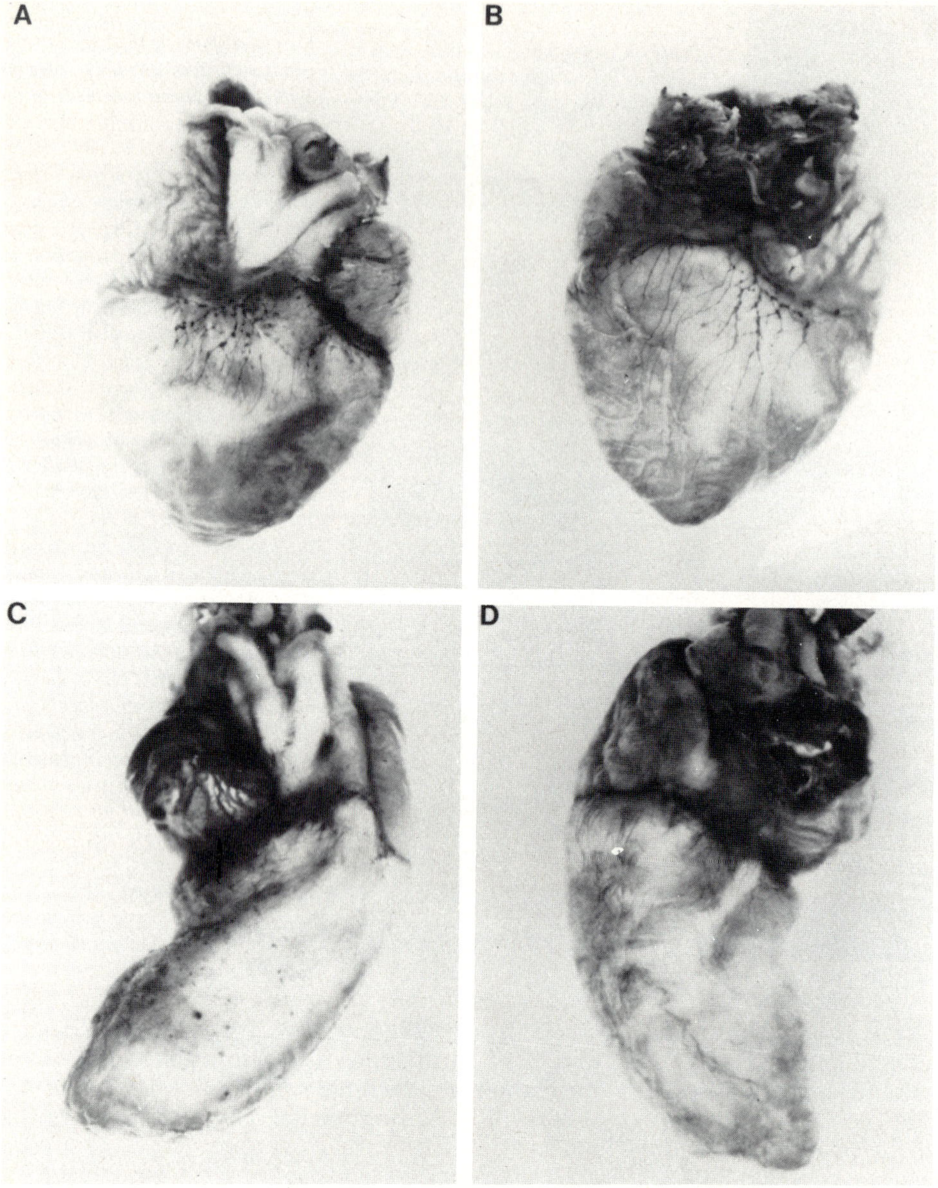

FIGURE 2. *Acetylcholinesterase-stained whole hearts from embryos on day 15 of incubation. The cholinesterase-positive structures (black) are the parasympathetic portion of the cardiac plexus. Panels A and B are the ventral and dorsal surfaces of a heart from a control embryo, whereas panels C and D are the ventral and dorsal surfaces of a heart from an embryo with a neural fold lesion similar to the one shown in Figure 1. The experimental heart has reduced parasympathetic innervation and is grossly malformed; serial cross-sections revealed that the aorta and pulmonary arteries arose from the right ventricle.*

mean number of neurons was highly correlated with age between 8 and 18 days of incubation ($r = 1.00$). On incubation day 20 (just prior to hatching), the number of cells decreased sharply to 663 ± 54 (n = 8).

In embryos with neural crest lesions over somites 1–2 or 1–3, the number of ganglion cells was 34–36% less than in controls on incubation day 15.

As presented above, the total number of ganglion cells after somite 1–4 lesion did not decrease significantly from control; however, the density of ganglion cells in the outflow area was significantly less than control. The depletion of total number of ganglion cells at day 10 after somite 1–3 lesions was about 50%, indicating that some recovery occurred between days 10 and 15.

[^{3}H]Choline Uptake

[^{3}H]Choline uptake was measured in seven atria from 15-day embryos with neural crest lesions over somites 1–3. The counts/min of [^{3}H]choline uptake per mg atrium (corrected for the number of counts available) were 435 ± 114. The mean uptake in eight control atria was 661.5 ± 125.8 counts/min. This represents a 34% decrease from control and correlates quite well with the decrease seen in total number of ganglion cells in the outflow tract at the same age and following the same lesion.

Acetylcholine Content

The acetylcholine content of 15-day incubation atrium and ventricle was measured in hearts from 23 control and 26 experimental embryos. Acetylcholine levels ranged from 1.5—4.5 nmol/mg protein, and were 31% lower in atria ($P < 0.02$) and 39% lower in ventricles ($P < 0.01$) from experimental animals (Table 2). In the same series of animals, the ganglion cell content was 31% lower in the experimental animals. Lesions over somites 1–2, 1–3, and

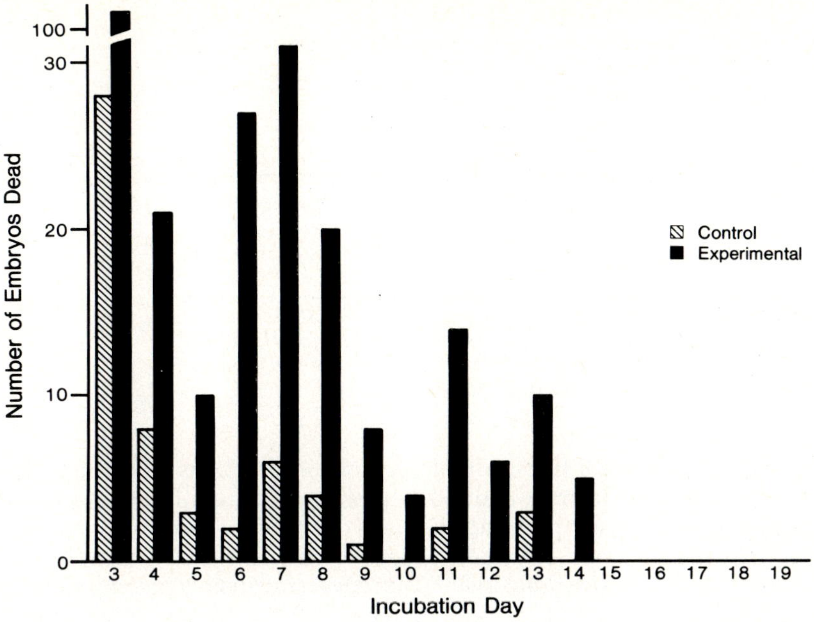

FIGURE 3. *Mortality of control and experimental embryos following ablation of neural crest over somites 1–3 on day 1. The number of embryos which died on each day of incubation is shown. A total of 319 experimental and 123 control embryos were used.*

1–4 were equally effective in reducing acetylcholine content, and only the grouped data are presented.

Muscarinic Receptors

[^{3}H]MS bound to muscarinic receptors in control and experimental embryos with the same high affinity (K_D = 0.17 - 0.21 nM; Fig. 5, Table 3). In three

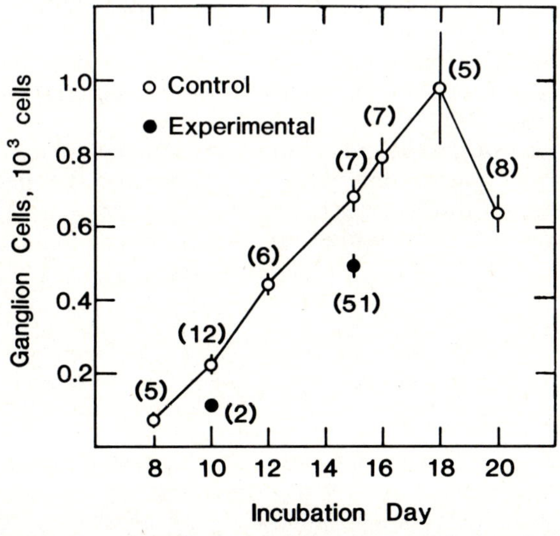

FIGURE 4. *Ganglion cell content of the conotrunus in experimental and control embryos. The number of ganglion cells in the conotruncal region between the base of the semilunar valves and the first branches of the aorta was measured at the indicated incubation day in hearts from control (○) and experimental (●) embryos in which the neural crest over somites 1–3 had been removed at an early stage of development. The symbols and lines indicate the mean number of cells and the* SEM; *the number of embryos examined is indicated in the parentheses. The number of ganglion cells was lower ($P < 0.05$) on day 15 in the experimental compared to the control embryos. The value given for the number of ganglion cells in lesioned embryos on day 10 is the average from two observations (80 and 138 ganglion cells).*

samples of pooled hearts, the number of [^{3}H]MS-binding sites was 22% lower ($P < 0.01$) in the experimental animals with neural crest lesions over somites 1–3.

Muscarinic receptor content of the whole heart (atria and ventricles) was also estimated separately in two series of 24–25 embryos. The ganglion cell content of the conotruncus was 24% lower in embryos with neural crest lesions ($P < 0.01$), whereas the muscarinic receptor content was 21% lower ($P < 0.001$; Table 3). Lesions over somites 1–2, 1–3, and 1–4 were equally effective in reducing muscarinic receptors, and only the grouped data are presented.

Carbamylcholine binding was measured in competition experiments with 0.1 nM [^{3}H]MS (Fig. 6). Carbamylcholine was resolved into high- and low-affinity components by iterative nonlinear regression procedures (Table 3). In experiments with hearts pooled from five to six embryos, neural crest lesions did not alter cardiac muscarinic receptor affinity of carbamylcholine (of either the high- or low-affinity sites) or the fractions of receptors which displayed high- and low-affinity carbamylcholine binding. Moreover, muscarinic receptors in hearts from control and experimental embryos were equally sensitive to inclusion of 10 μM Gpp(NH)p in the binding assay media (Fig. 6; Table 4). Gpp(NH)p decreased the apparent number and affinity of high-affinity binding sites; Gpp(NH)p increased the number of low-affinity binding sites without affecting their affinity for carbamylcholine (Table 3).

Discussion

The purpose of these experiments was to create parasympathetically aneural hearts by removing neural crest anlage of cardiac ganglion cells. Such a preparation would permit the evaluation of trophic

TABLE 2
Acetylcholine Content of Developing Chick Heart after Depletion of Parasympathetic Innervation by Neural Crest Lesions

	Ganglion cells	Acetylcholine		n
		Atrium	Ventricle	
Control	680 ± 32	4.04 ± 0.38	3.06 ± 0.25	23
Experimental	473 ± 41	2.79 ± 0.32	1.89 ± 0.25	26
% Change	−31%	−31%	−39%	
t-test	$P < 0.001$	$P < 0.02$	$P < 0.01$	

Results are expressed as means ± SEM. All measurements were made in hearts from 15-day embryos. The neural crest over somites 1–2, 1–3, or 1–4 was removed at stage 9 or 10 in the experimental embryos. Acetylcholine content is expressed as nmol/mg protein. Acetylcholine content in atria vs. ventricles is different ($P < 0.05$) in both control and experimental embryos.

parasympathetic nerve-cardiac muscle interactions. We were not successful in this attempt, for reasons which are not immediately clear. Our failure suggests some hitherto unappreciated flexibility in the development of the neuronal component of the neural crest that is not shared by ectomesenchymal neural crest elements.

The relationship between the heart and the nerves that innervate it is difficult to study in the adult, where the constituent structures cannot be separated. In the present study, advantage was taken of the natural temporal separation of elements in the developing chick heart in order to produce a heart with diminished parasympathetic innervation. The neural crest which seeds cardiac ganglion cells was removed before the cells migrated to the heart. These lesions resulted in substantial, although incomplete, depletions of molecular components of the cardiac parasympathetic system.

Previously, denervation of the heart was attempted in two different ways: (1) by transplanting the heart and, thereby, severing the nerves, and (2) by using various drugs which either create lesions in, or disrupt the function of, the cardiac nerves. Neither of the approaches provides an ideal model for the study of neuronal interactions with the heart. In transplanted hearts, both sympathetic and parasympathetic divisions of the autonomic nervous system are disrupted, and the heart itself sustains considerable insult. Moreover, intrinsic parasympathetic ganglion cells remain intact. On the other hand, drugs are likely to produce a variety of nonspecific and/or secondary effects which create difficulties in interpreting results from these studies.

Effects of Neural Crest Lesions on the Development of Parasympathetic Innervation

To identify the origin of neural crest cells that provide parasympathetic innervation of the heart, Kirby and Stewart (1983) used orthotopic transplantation of occipital neural crest from quail donors to chick embryo hosts. The parasympathetic postganglionic neurons (i.e., the cardiac ganglion cells) were found to arise *exclusively* from the neural crest over somites 1–3.

This raises the crucial question of why the depletion of parasympathetic innervation of the heart obtained in the present study was incomplete. The lesions were designed to remove *all* anlagen of

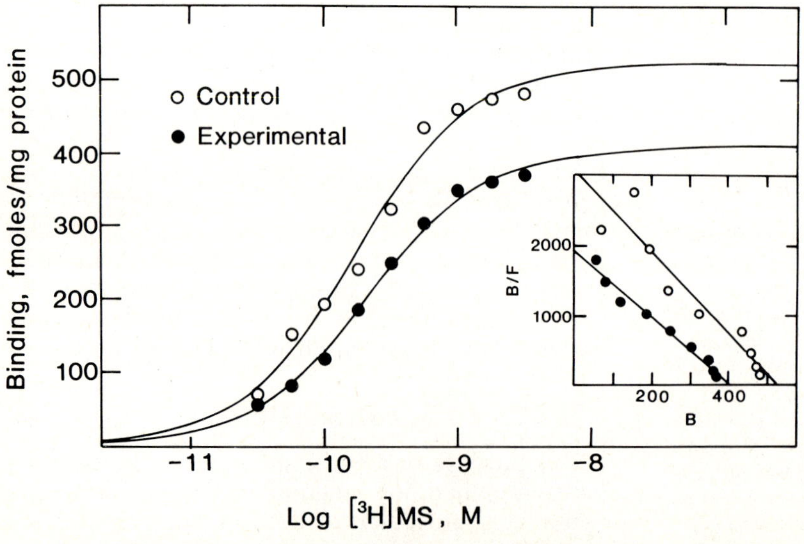

FIGURE 5. *[^{3}H]MS binding to muscarinic acetylcholine receptors in hearts from 15-day chick embryos. Specific (atropine-sensitive) binding in hearts from control (○) chicks and from chicks in which the neural crest over somites 1–3 was removed at stage 10 (●) is shown. The lines are drawn according to parameters obtained in nonlinear regression analyses using a single binding site model. The dissociation constants were 0.17 ± 0.03 and 0.21 ± 0.04 nM (n = 3) in the control and experimental hearts, respectively. The numbers of binding sites in control and experimental hearts were 524 ± 22 and 407 ± 11 (n = 3) fmol/mg protein, respectively (P < 0.01). Each point is the mean from three measurements performed with hearts pooled from five or six embryos. Inset: Scatchard plot of the binding data. B [^{3}H]MS bound in fmol/mg protein; F concentration of free [^{3}H]MS in nM.*

TABLE 3
Muscarinic Acetylcholine Receptor Content of Developing Chick Hearts after Depletion of Parasympathetic Innervation by Neural Crest Lesions

	Ganglion cells	Muscarinic receptors	*n*
Control	682 ± 36	340 ± 12	24
Experimental	521 ± 36	267 ± 14	25
% Change	−24%	−21%	
t-test	$P < 0.01$	$P < 0.001$	

Results are expressed as means ± SEM. All measurements were made in hearts from 15-day embryos. The neural crest over somites 1–2, 1–3, or 1–4 was removed at stage 9 or 10 in the experimental embryos. Muscarinic receptor content is expressed as fmol of [^{3}H]MS-binding sites per mg particulate protein.

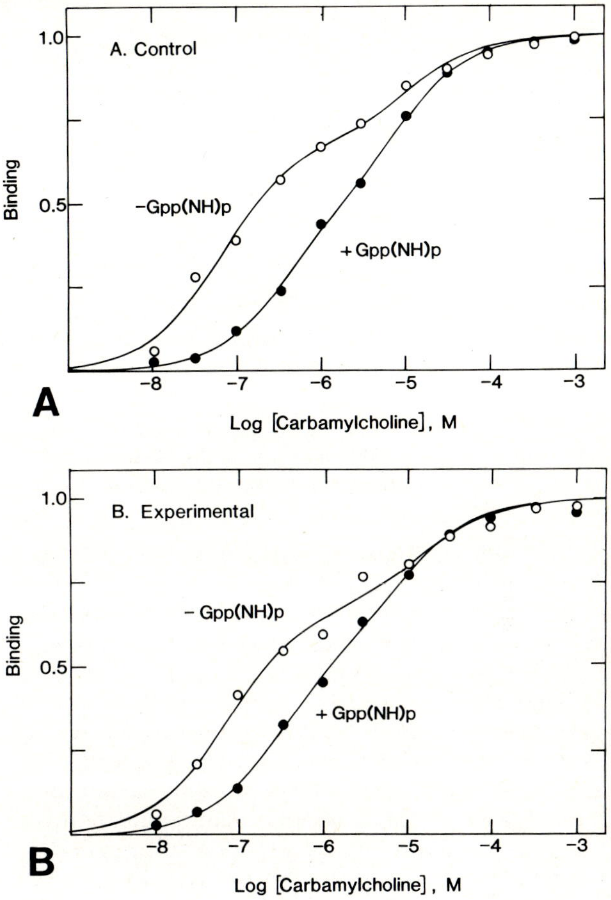

FIGURE 6. *Carbamylcholine binding to muscarinic acetylcholine receptors in hearts from 15-day chick embryos. In each experiment, hearts were pooled from five or six control (panel A) or experimental (panel B) hearts in which the neural crest over somites 1–3 had been removed at stage 9 or 10. Carbamylcholine binding was determined in competition studies with 0.1 nM [^{3}H]MS in the absence (○) and presence (●) of 10 μM Gpp(NH)p. Binding data were fitted by nonlinear regression analysis to a two binding-site model, and the binding parameters are presented in Table 3. Each point represents the mean from three experiments. Binding measurements varied by less than 10% of total specific binding measured in the absence of carbamylcholine.*

cardiac ganglion cells, and histological analysis immediately after surgery supported the effectiveness of the procedure. However, the number of cardiac ganglion cells on day 15 was reduced by only 24–31%.

There are several possible explanations for the apparent persistance of cardiac ganglion cell populations. It is possible that, after creating the lesions, adjacent cranial and caudal areas of the neural crest are recruited to contribute migrating cells (or to replace the cells that were removed). In the chimera experiments, quail cells replaced the chick neural crest cells over the lesioned somites. Therefore, any ability of adjacent areas to contribute to parasympathetic innervation of the heart would be masked. A second possibility is that the dorsal neural tube is replaced by dividing cells from the surviving ventral neural tube. Another possibility is that, in the absence of normal parasympathetic cardiac innervation, neuronal elements from the neural crest over somites 10–20, which normally give rise to the sympathetic innervation of the heart (Kirby and Stewart, 1984), provide cells morphologically indistinguishable from ganglion cells. A fourth possibility is that a few ganglion cells from the neural crest over somites 1–3 survive the lesion and migrate to the heart. The linear increase in ganglion cells between days 8 and 18 demonstrates the dynamic production of new neurons during this period. Heathcote and Sargent (in press) have shown a very similar pattern with frog atrial ganglion cells. In such a flexible situation, a few cells may be capable of seeding a full complement of ganglion cells. The fact that the somite 1–4 lesion caused a less significant depletion in ganglion cells in the conotruncus than lesions of neural crest over somites 1–2 or 1–3 suggests that the surviving but injured neural tube may be responsible for replacement of cardiac ganglion cells. Further work is required to evaluate these possibilities.

The limited decreases in pre- and postsynaptic biochemical markers of cholinergic synapses are perhaps less unexpected, due to the multiplicity of cholinergic elements within the heart. Acetylcholine content decreased 31–39%, whereas the number of muscarinic receptors decreased 21%. In a previous study (Kirby and Stewart, 1983), a second presynaptic indication of cholinergic neurons, high-affinity [^{3}H]choline uptake, was decreased 60% by similar neural crest lesions. However, choline uptake was measured on days 9 and 10 of incubation and, as we have shown here, there is a considerable change between days 10 and 15. Muscarinic cholinergic receptors are located on ganglion cells, myocardial membranes, and on the terminals of postganglionic cholinergic, and, possibly, adrenergic, neurons (Higgins et al., 1973; Nomura et al., 1979; Raiteri et al., 1981). Whereas it is frequently assumed that most muscarinic receptors are located on myocardial cell surfaces, it is not clear which cells contribute to the

TABLE 4
Muscarinic Receptor Binding Parameters after Depletion of Parasympathetic Innervation by Neural Crest Lesions

	[^{3}H]MS		Carbamylcholine		
	K_D (nM)	B_{max}	K_{DH} (μM)	K_{DL} (μM)	R_H
Control	0.17 ± 0.03	524 ± 22	0.063 ± 0.015	11 ± 3	0.68 ± 0.05
Control Gpp(NH)p			0.35 ± 0.07	9 ± 2	0.49 ± 0.05
Experimental	0.21 ± 0.04	407 ± 11*	0.070 ± 0.009	14 ± 4	0.67 ± 0.04
Control Gpp(NH)p			0.26 ± 0.06	8 ± 2	0.54 ± 0.05

Results are expressed as means ± SEM ($n = 3$).
* Different from control value, $P < 0.01$. All measurements were made in hearts pooled from five or six embryos on incubation day 15. The neural crest over somites 1–2, 1–3, or 1–4 was removed at stage 9 or 10 in the experimental embryos. K_D, [^{3}H]MS dissociation constant in nM; B_{max}, concentration of [^{3}H]MS-binding sites in fmol/mg protein. Carbamylcholine binding was resolved into high- and low-affinity components with dissociation constants K_{DH} and K_{DL} (in μM), respectively. R_H is the fraction of receptors which displayed high-affinity agonist binding.

changes reported here. It should also be noted that, in mature tissues, a disruption of muscarinic transmission with receptor blockers results in an *increase* (an up-regulation) of cholinergic receptors (Wise et al., 1980; Westlind et al., 1981).

Ganglion cells are also not the sole source of acetylcholine or choline uptake in the heart. A considerable amount of acetylcholine and choline uptake would be expected to be present in terminals of the vagus. The behavior of preganglionic neurons in the face of a diminished ganglion cell population has not been ascertained. To address these questions, it would be useful to produce a more complete depletion of the cardiac ganglion cell population and to eliminate preganglionic parasympathetic innervation of the heart.

Neural crest lesions did not alter the affinity of cardiac muscarinic receptors for antagonists or agonists. Agonist binding had multiple components; two-thirds of the receptors displayed high-affinity carbamylcholine binding in hearts from both control and experimental animals. Cardiac muscarinic receptors are coupled to a guanine nucleotide-dependent regulatory protein which plays a role in the elaboration of postsynaptic muscarinic responses. One indication of this coupling is a decrease in agonist-binding affinity in the presence of guanine nucleotides (Berrie et al., 1979; Rosenberger et al., 1979; Wei and Sulakhe, 1980). In the present experiments, neural crest lesions did not alter the sensitivity of agonist binding to guanine nucleotides: An increase in the fraction of receptors displaying low-affinity carbamylcholine binding was always observed. A conversion of high- to low-affinity receptors is consistent with the results of others (e.g., Galper et al., 1982; Waelbroeck et al., 1982; Birdsall et al., 1984; Dunlap and Brown, 1984). In addition, the apparent affinity for carbamylcholine of the high-affinity receptor population was markedly reduced. The reason for this alteration is not clear. It is possible that high-affinity receptors are converted to a novel low-affinity state different from that of the low-affinity receptors observed in the absence of guanine nucleotides.

Connective tissue derivatives of the neural crest are necessary for the development of the heart and great vessels, as well as a number of other structures derived from the embryonic pharyngeal apparatus (Kirby and Bockman, 1984). Removal of the neural crest causes a variety of developmental defects in these structures; these defects are analogous to those seen in human babies. The lesions created in the present study produced cardiac malformations in every embryo. Thus, there is a dissociation of the consequences of depletion of the connective tissue vs. neuronal contribution of the neural crest to the developing heart. The possibilities for rearrangement and compensation of the neural elements appears to be much more extensive. In clinical application, this suggests that children with conotruncal abnormalities would not necessarily have abnormal vagal control of the heart.

Many reports have appeared which characterize changes in nicotinic acetylcholine receptors in developing skeletal muscle (Fambrough, 1979). This is the first report showing the influence of parasympathetic postganglionic denervation on muscarinic acetylcholine receptors and acetylcholine content in an end organ.

Supported by National Institutes of Health Grants HD 17063, HL 31518, and NS 17429, and a grant-in-aid from the Georgia Affiliate of the American Heart Association. M.L.K. is an Established Investigator of the American Heart Association.

Address for reprints: Dr. Margaret L. Kirby, Department of Anatomy, Medical College of Georgia, Augusta, Georgia 30912.

Received July 23, 1984; accepted for publication December 13, 1984.

References

Berrie CP, Birdsall NJM, Burgen ASV, Hulme EC (1979) Guanine nucleotides modulate muscarinic receptor binding in the heart. Biochem Biophys Res Commun **87:** 1000–1005

Birdsall NJM, Hulme EC, Stockton JM (1984) Muscarinic receptor heterogeneity. Trends Pharmacol Sci **5S:** 4–8

Dunlap J, Brown JH (1984) Differences and similarities in muscarinic receptors of rat heart and retina: Effects of agonists, guanine nucleotides, and *N*-ethylmaleimide. J Neurochem **43:** 214–220

Fambrough DM (1979) Control of acetylcholine receptors in skeletal muscle. Physiol Rev **59:** 165–227

Galper JB, Dziekan LC, O'Hara DS, Smith TW (1982) The biphasic response of muscarinic cholinergic receptors in cultured heart cells to agonists. Effects on receptor number and affinity in intact cells and homogenates. J Biol Chem **257:** 10344–10356

Hamburger V, Hamilton HL (1951) A series of normal stages of the chick embryo. J Morphol **88:** 49–62

Heathcote DR, Sargent PB (in press) The genesis and differentiation of neurons in a frog parasympathetic ganglion. Dev Biol

Higgins CB, Vatner SF, Braunwald E (1973) Parasympathetic control of the heart. Pharmacol Rev **25:** 119–155

Hollyday M (1980) Motoneuron histogenesis and the development of limb innervation. *In* Current Topics in Developmental Biology, vol 15, Neural Development, Part I: Emergence of specificity in neural histogenesis, edited by RK Hunt. New York, Academic Press, pp 181–215

Horstadius S (1950) The Neural Crest. London, Oxford University Press

Kirby ML, Aronstam RS (1983) Atropine-induced alterations of normal development of muscarinic receptors in the embryonic chick heart. J Mol Cell Cardiol **15:** 685–696

Kirby ML, Bockman DE (1984) Neural crest and normal development: A new perspective. Anat Rec **209:** 1–6

Kirby ML, Stewart DE (1983) Neural crest origin of cardiac ganglion cells in chick embryo: Identification and extirpation. Dev Biol **97:** 433–443

Kirby ML, Stewart DE (1984) Adrenergic innervation of the developing chick heart: Neural crest, ablations to produce sympathetically aneural hearts. Am J Anat **171:** 295–305

Kirby ML, Gale TF, Stewart DE (1983) Neural crest cells contribute to normal aorticopulmonary septation. Science **220:** 1059–1061

LeDouarin NM, Teillet MA (1974) Experimental analysis of the migration and differentiation of neuroblasts of the autonomic nervous system and of neurectodermal mesenchymal derivatives using a biological cell marking technique. Dev Biol **41:** 162–184

Lowry OH, Rosebrough NJ, Farr AL, Randall RJ (1951) Protein measurement with the Folin phenol reagent. J Biol Chem **193:** 265–275

Narayanan CH (1970) Apparatus and current techniques in the preparation of avian embryos for microsurgery and for observing embryonic behavior. Bioscience **20:** 868–871

Noden DM (1975) An analysis of the migratory behavior of avian cephalic neural crest cells. Dev Biol **42:** 106–130

Nomura Y, Kajiyama H, Segawa T (1979) Decrease in muscarinic cholinergic response to the rat heart following treatment with 6-hydroxydopa. Eur J Pharmacol **60:** 323–327

Pappano AJ (1977) Ontogenetic development of autonomic neuroeffector transmission and transmitter reactivity in embryonic and fetal hearts. Pharmacol Rev **29:** 3–33

Pappano AJ, Skrowronck CA (1974) Reactivity of chick embryo heart to cholinergic agonists at the onset of cholinergic transmission. J Pharmacol Exp Ther **191:** 109–118

Raiteri M, March, M, Paudice P (1981) Adaptation of presynaptic acetylcholine autoreceptors following long-term drug treatment. Eur J Pharmacol **74:** 109–110

Richenbacher J, Muller E (1979) The development of cholinergic ganglia in the chick embryo heart. Anat Embryol **155:** 253–258

Rosenberger LB, Roeske WR, Yamamura HI (1979) The regulation of muscarinic cholinergic receptors by guanine nucleotides in cardiac tissues. Eur J Pharmacol **56:** 179–180

Spector S, Flex A, Semenuk G, Finberg JPM (1978) Development of a specific radioimmunoassay for acetylcholine. J Neurochem **30:** 685–689

Thompson SW (1966) Selected Histochemical and Histopathological Methods. Springfield, IL, Thomas, pp 673–676

Tosney KW (1982) The segregation and early migration of cranial neural crest cells in the avian embryo. Dev Biol **98:** 13–24

Waelbroeck M, Robberecht P, Catelain P, Christophe J (1982) Rat cardiac muscarinic receptors. I. Effects of guanine nucleotides on high- and low-affinity binding sites. Mol Pharmacol **21:** 581–588

Wei J-W, Sulakhe RV (1979) Agonist-antagonist interactions with rat atrial muscarinic cholinergic receptor sites: Differential regulation by guanine nucleotides. Eur J Pharmacol **58:** 91–92

Westlind A, Grynfarb M, Hedlund B, Bartfai T, Fuxe K (1981) Muscarinic supersensitivity induced by septal lesion or chronic atropine treatment. Brain Res **225:** 131–141

Wise BC, Shoji M, Kuo JF (1980) Decrease or increase in cardiac muscarinic cholinergic receptor number in rats treated with methacholine or atropine. Biochem Biophys Res Commun **92:** 1136–1142

INDEX TERMS: Acetylcholine • Parasympathetic innervation • Chick heart • Muscarinic receptors • Cardiac malformations • Neural crest • Development

α-Adrenergic Receptors in Cerebral Microvessels of Normotensive and Spontaneously Hypertensive Rats

Hideyuki Kobayashi, Akihiko Wada, Futoshi Izumi, Maria Sandra Magnoni, and Marco Trabucchi

From the Department of Pharmacology, University of Occupational and Environmental Health, School of Medicine, Kitakyushu, Japan, and the Department of Pharmacology and Pharmacognosy, University of Milan, Milan, Italy

SUMMARY. In rat cerebral microvessels, we characterized α_1- and α_2-adrenergic receptors, using [^{3}H]prazosin and [^{3}H]-*p*-amino-clonidine as radioligands. [^{3}H]Prazosin binding to the cerebral microvessels was saturable and of high affinity (dissociation constant of 78 pM), with a maximum binding of 48 fmol/mg protein. [^{3}H]Prazosin binding reached equilibrium within 15 minutes and was dissociated by the addition of 10 μM phentolamine. The inhibitory effects of isomers of norepinephrine and epinephrine on the binding showed that *l*-isomers were over 10 times more potent than *d*-isomers. [^{3}H]-*p*-Amino-clonidine binding to the cerebral microvessels was saturable and of high affinity (K_D = 0.61 nM) with a B_{max} of 73 fmol/mg protein. The binding reached equilibrium within 30 minutes, and was dissociated by the addition of 100 μM *l*-norepinephrine. *l*-Isomers of norepinephrine and epinephrine were over 10 times more potent than *d*-isomers in displacing the binding. Thus, both [^{3}H]prazosin and [^{3}H]-*p*-amino-clonidine bindings to the cerebral microvessels were characterized by saturability, high affinity, reversibility, and stereospecificity. Furthermore, the specificity of both binding sites was pharmacologically evaluated by the inhibitory effects of various adrenergic agonists and antagonists on the bindings. These data indicate the existence of α-adrenergic receptors in the cerebral microvessels and are consistent with the hypothesis that the cerebral microcirculation is regulated by adrenergic innervation. Furthermore, the receptors were measured in cerebral microvessels of spontaneously hypertensive rats and Wistar-Kyoto controls. The number of α_1-receptors in the cerebral microvessels of spontaneously hypertensive rats was significantly higher than that of Wistar-Kyoto rats, without any difference in the affinity constant to the ligands. No difference in α_2-receptors was observed between spontaneously hypertensive and Wistar-Kyoto rats. These results suggest that the neuronal regulatory mechanisms of the cerebral microcirculation are altered in hypertension. ***(Circ Res 56: 402–409, 1985)***

VARIOUS experimental observations suggest that brain microvasculature is under neuronal control of the central adrenergic system. In fact, morphological studies show that brain capillary endothelium is closely associated with adrenergic fibers originating from the locus coeruleus (Swanson et al., 1977), whereas physiological data indicate that α- and β-adrenergic receptors are involved in regulatory mechanisms of brain microvasculature. In particular, it is suggested that the two populations of receptors play an important role in mediating changes of cerebral blood flow and blood-brain barrier (BBB) permeability to molecules such as water and glucose (Raichle et al., 1975; MacKenzie et al., 1976 a, 1976b; Bates et al., 1977; Grubb et al., 1978; Schwartz, 1978; Abraham et al., 1979). Furthermore, biochemical experiments demonstrated the presence of norepinephrine, its synthesizing and catabolizing enzymes (Lai et al., 1975), and adrenergic receptors in cerebral microvessels. β-Adrenergic receptors linked to adenylate cyclase in the microvessels were well characterized (Herbst et al., 1979; Nathanson and Glaser, 1979; Kobayashi et al., 1981a, 1981b, 1982a, 1982b, 1982c). The existence of α-adrenergic receptors was also reported (Peroutka et al., 1980; Kobayashi et al., 1982a); however, the properties of the receptors were not fully analyzed.

On the other hand, several studies indicate that hypertension affects cerebral microvessel functions. In particular, increased BBB permeability and impairment of cerebral blood flow autoregulation have been described (Johansson, 1976; Strangaard et al., 1973, Hatzinikolau et al., 1981). Recently, we reported that the number of β-receptors located in the cerebral microvessels is decreased by about 30% in both genetic and experimental hypertensive rats (Magnoni et al., 1983). To investigate further the involvement of the adrenergic system in brain microvascular regulatory mechanisms in hypertension, we have measured α_1- and α_2-adrenergic receptors in the cerebral microvessels of normotensive and spontaneously hypertensive rats.

Methods

Male Sprague-Dawley rats weighing 200–300 g, adult (14–15-week-old) male spontaneously hypertensive rats (SHR), and age-matched Wistar-Kyoto control rats (WKY) were purchased from Charles River, Japan. Systolic blood pressure, measured by the tail cuff method, was 190 ± 5 mm Hg in SHR and 120 ± 3 mm Hg in WKY (means ± SEM, $n = 7$).

Brain microvessels were prepared as described previously (Kobayashi et al., 1981a). In each experiment, 20–40 rats per group were used. Rats were killed by decapitation. Gray matter of cerebral cortices was rapidly cleaned from pial membrane and white matter, minced by scissors, and homogenized by hand in a Teflon-glass homogenizer in gassed (95% O_2, 5% CO_2) Ringer's solution that consisted of 137 mM NaCl, 5 mM KCl, 3 mM $CaCl_2$, 1.2 mM $MgCl_2$, 12 mM $NaHCO_3$, 5 mM glucose, 1% bovine serum albumin (BSA), and 15 mM HEPES (pH 7.4). The homogenate was passed through 700-, 200-, and 100-μm nylon meshes and centrifuged at 1,000 *g* for 10 minutes. The pellet was suspended in the same solution, now containing 30% BSA, and centrifuged at 1,000 *g* for 15 minutes. The resulting small pellet was suspended in Ringer's solution. The floated thick layer was suspended in the supernatant and recentrifuged at 1,000 *g* for 15 minutes. The pellet was suspended in Ringer's solution and combined with the first suspension. The suspension was passed through a column of glass beads (0.2–0.5 mm in diameter) and washed extensively with Ringer's solution. The microvessels attached to the glass beads were released by gentle agitation in Ringer's solution, collected, and washed three times by centrifugation in the buffer used for binding assay.

α_1-Adrenergic receptors were measured as described previously (Barnes et al., 1979; Kobayashi et al., 1982a). The microvessels were incubated in triplicate with various concentrations of [^{3}H]prazosin in 50 mM Tris-HCl buffer (pH 7.5) at 25°C for 15 minutes. [^{3}H]Prazosin bound to the microvessels was separated from free ligand by filtration through GF/B glass fiber filter (Whatman), and the filters were washed four times with 5 ml of cold 50 mM Tris-HCl buffer. The filtration step was accomplished within 15 seconds. The radioactivity was measured in toluene base scintillation cocktail with an efficiency of 43%. The specific binding of [^{3}H]prazosin was defined as total binding minus nonspecific binding which was determined in the presence of 10 μM phentolamine.

α_2-Adrenergic receptors were measured using [^{3}H]-*p*-amino-clonidine ([^{3}H]PAC; Rouot and Snyder, 1979; Kobayashi et al., 1982a). The assay mixture consisted of various concentrations of [^{3}H]PAC, 0.001% ascorbic acid, 50 mM Tris-HCl buffer (pH 7.5), and the microvessels. Incubation was carried out at 25°C for 30 minutes. The specific binding of [^{3}H]PAC was defined as total binding minus nonspecific binding which was determined in the presence of 100 μM *l*-norepinephrine.

γ-Glutamyltranspeptidase (γ-GTP), a marker enzyme of brain capillary, was measured according to the method of Orlowski and Meister (1965), using γ-glutamyl-*p*-nitroanilide as a substrate. The samples were incubated in a reaction mixture composed of 5 mM L-γ-glutamyl-*p*-nitroanilide, 10 mM $MgCl_2$, and 100 mM Tris-HCl buffer (pH 9.0), in a final volume of 1 ml. After 60 minutes of incubation at 37°C, the reaction was terminated by the addition of 2 ml of 1.5 M acetic acid. The enzymatic reaction leads to the formation of *p*-nitroaniline which was determined by direct spectrophotometric measurement. The absorbance, at 410 nm, was recorded against a reference solution containing the same components except substrate.

Protein concentration was measured according to the method of Lowry et al. (1951).

The maximum binding and the dissociation constant values of the specific binding of [^{3}H]prazosin and [^{3}H]-PAC to the cerebral microvessels were analyzed by a linear least squares regression method on the Scatchard analysis.

Clonidine was kindly donated by Boehringer Ingelheim, phentolamine was from Ciba Geigy, and prazosin was from Pfizer. [^{3}H]Prazosin (20.2 Ci/mmol) was purchased from Amersham and [^{3}H]-*p*-amino-clonidine (56.6 Ci/mmol) was from New England Nuclear. *d*-Norepinephrine was from Adams Chemical and *d*-epinephrine was from ICN Pharmaceuticals. Other drugs were from Nakarai Chemicals.

Results

The purity of the cerebral microvessls of Sprague-Dawley rats was checked by phase-contrast microscopy and by measurement of γ-glutamyltranspeptidase activity, and they were highly purified as described previously (Kobayashi et al., 1981a).

The specific binding of [^{3}H]prazosin to the cerebral microvessels was a linear function of amount of protein in the preparation up to 250 μg/tube (data not shown). A higher concentration of protein interfered with the binding assay by slowing the passage of the incubation medium through the filter.

The specific binding of [^{3}H]prazosin to the cerebral microvessels is saturated at 500 pM of the ligand (Fig. 1a). Scatchard analysis of the data (Fig. 1b) showed that the [^{3}H]prazosin binding to the cerebral microvessels was characterized by high affinity with dissociation constant (K_D) of 78 ± 5 pM ($n = 5$, mean ± SEM) and maximum binding (B_{max}) of 48 ± 4 fmol/mg protein.

The time course of the [^{3}H]prazosin binding to the cerebral microvessels is shown in Figure 2. Equilibrium was attained within 15 minutes. After addition of phentolamine at the final concentration of 10 μM, the binding was dissociated with a half-time of 10 minutes showing the reversibility of [^{3}H]prazosin binding to the cerebral microvessels. From the data, association rate (K_{on}) of 0.00098/pM · min and dissociation rate (K_{off}) of 0.072/min were calculated. The K_D value obtained by the equation $K_D = K_{off}/K_{on}$ was 73 pM. This value is in good agreement with the K_D value calculated by the Scatchard analysis (Fig. 1b).

The specific binding of [^{3}H]PAC to the cerebral microvessels was saturated at 5 nM of [^{3}H]PAC concentration (Fig. 3a). The K_D value calculated by the method of Scatchard was 0.61 ± 0.03 nM ($n = 4$), and the B_{max} value was 74 ± 2 fmol/mg protein, indicating the high affinity characteristic of the binding (Fig. 3b). Further increases in [^{3}H]PAC concentration, up to 20 nM, did not produce any increase in the specific binding, indicating the [^{3}H]PAC labeled single class of receptors in the cerebral microvessels.

The time course of the [^{3}H]PAC binding to the cerebral microvessels is shown in Figure 4. Equilibrium was attained within 30 minutes. After the addition of *l*-norepinephrine at the final concentra-

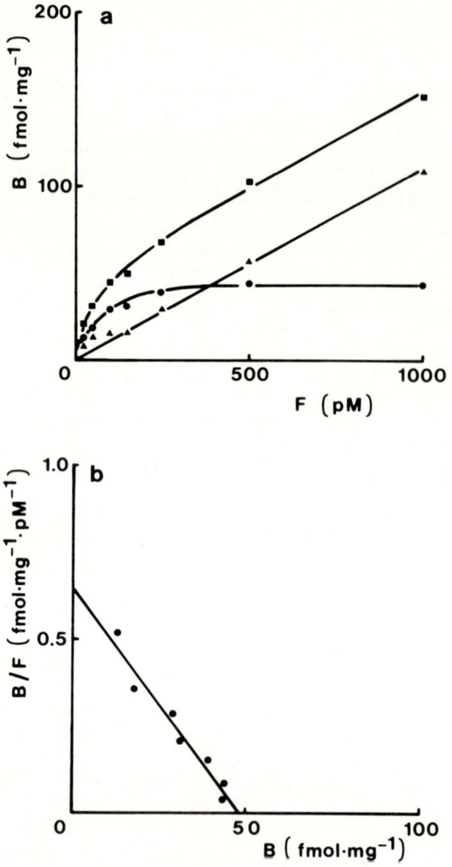

FIGURE 1. *Saturation curve (panel a) and Scatchard plot (panel b) of [^{3}H]prazosin binding to cerebral microvessels. Values are representative of five separate experiments with Sprague-Dawley rats, and are the means of triplicate determinations which varied less than 10%. ■, total binding; ▲, nonspecific binding; ●, specific binding; F, free concentration of [^{3}H]prazosin; B, [^{3}H]prazosin binding to the cerebral microvessels.*

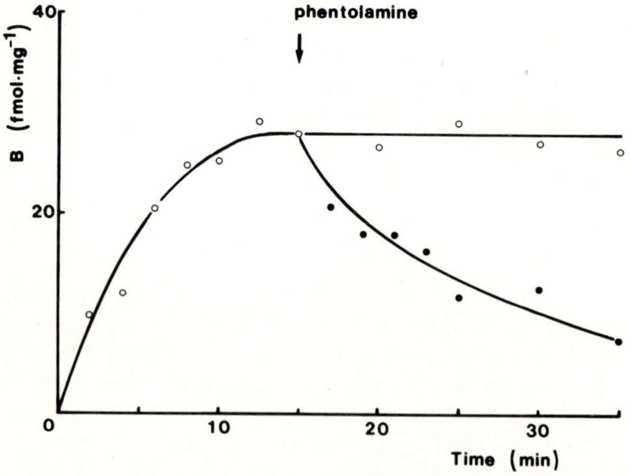

FIGURE 2. *Time course of specific [^{3}H]prazosin binding to cerebral microvessels. The concentration of [^{3}H]prazosin was 100 pM. Incubation was started by the addition of cerebral microvessel preparation of Sprague-Dawley rats, and was terminated by filtration at the times indicated (○). Dissociation (●) was started by adding 10 μM phentolamine, after equilibrium had been reached. Each point is the mean of three to five separate experiments with standard errors ranging from 5 to 20%.*

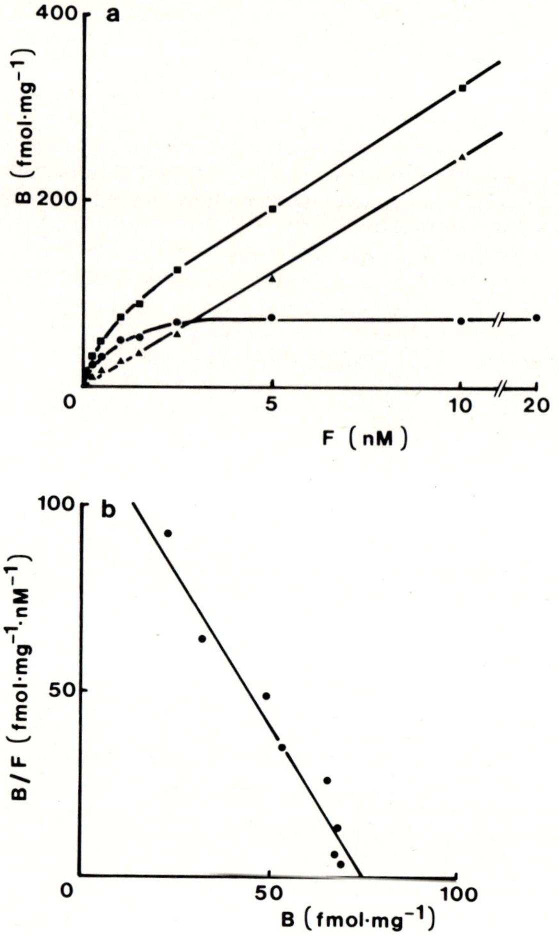

FIGURE 3. *Saturation curve (panel a) and Scatchard plot (panel b) of [^{3}H] PAC binding to cerebral microvessels. Values are representative of four separate experiments with Sprague-Dawley rats, and are the means of triplicate determinations which varied less than 10%. ■, total binding; ▲, nonspecific binding; ●, specific binding; F, free concentration of [^{3}H]PAC; B, [^{3}H]PAC binding to the cerebral microvessels.*

tion of 100 μM, the binding was dissociated with a half-time of 17 minutes, indicating that the [^{3}H]PAC binding to the cerebral microvessels is reversible. From the data, K_{on} of 0.194/nM · min and K_{off} of 0.095/min were calculated. The K_D value obtained by K_{off} division by K_{on} was 0.49 nM. This value was comparable with the K_D value calculated by the Scatchard analysis (Fig. 3b).

To characterize the stereospecificity of the binding sites, the inhibitory effect of *l*- or *d*-isomers of norepinephrine and epinephrine on [^{3}H]prazosin and [^{3}H]PAC bindings to the cerebral microvessels was investigated (Table 1). *l*-Norepinephrine was 17 times more potent than its *d*-isomer, and *l*-epinephrine was 22 times more potent than its *d*-isomer in inhibiting the [^{3}H]prazosin-specific binding to the cerebral microvessels. The inhibitory effect of *l*-norepinephrine to the [^{3}H]PAC binding to the microvessels was 38 times more potent than its *d*-isomer, and *l*-epinephrine was 17 times more potent than that its *d*-isomer. Thus, both the [^{3}H]prazosin

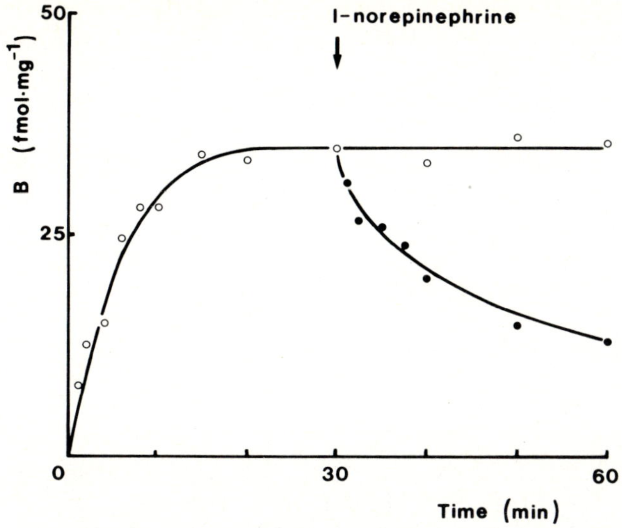

FIGURE 4. *Time course of specific [³H]PAC binding to cerebral microvessels. The concentration of [³H]PAC was 0.7 nM. Incubation was started by the addition of cerebral microvessels of Sprague-Dawley rats, and was terminated by filtration at the time indicated (○). Dissociation (●) was started by adding 100 μM l-norepinephrine after equilibrium had been reached. Each point is the mean of three to five separate experiments with standard errors ranging from 5 to 20%.*

and [³H]PAC bindings to the cerebral microvessels were characterized by their stereospecificity.

Inhibitory effects of various adrenergic agonists and antagonists on [³H]prazosin and [³H]PAC bindings to the cerebral microvessels were shown in Table 1. [³H]Prazosin binding was inhibited by prazosin > phentolamine > yohimbine > epinephrine > clonidine, and > norepinephrine, whereas [³H]-PAC binding was inhibited by phentolamine > clonidine > epinephrine > norepinephrine > yohimbine > and > prazosin. Ratio between the inhibitory constant (K_i) value for [³H]prazosin binding and the K_i value for [³H]PAC binding of each drug was calculated to demonstrate the characteristics of each ligand binding. The α_1-selective antagonist, prazosin, was 40,000 times more potent in inhibiting [³H]prazosin binding than in inhibiting [³H]PAC binding to the cerebral microvessels, whereas the α_2-selective agonist, clonidine, was 182 times more potent in inhibiting [³H]PAC binding than in inhibiting [³H]prazosin binding. These data indicate that [³H]prazosin bound to the cerebral microvessels with characteristics of α_1-adrenergic receptors, and [³H]-PAC bound with characteristics of α_2-adrenergic receptors.

The purity of the cerebral microvessel preparations from WKY and SHR was controlled by phase-contrast microscopy (Fig. 5). The preparations were practically free from neuronal and glial elements. At this level of magnification, no morphological difference between the preparations from WKY and SHR is detectable. Table 2 shows that γ-GTP activities of WKY and SHR are comparable, both in the brain homogenate and in the microvessel preparation. γ-GTP activity was more than 30 times higher in the microvessels than in the brain homogenate, indicating that both preparations were highly purified. There was no difference between WKY and SHR in recovery of the microvessels per unit of tissue weight.

Figure 6a shows the specific binding of [³H]prazosin to the cerebral microvessels from WKY and SHR. At various concentrations of [³H]prazosin, binding is higher in the preparation from SHR than in that from WKY. Scatchard analysis (Fig. 6b) shows that the B_{max} value for SHR is 50% higher than that of WKY, without a change in K_D value: B_{max}, 43 ± 3 and 66 ± 5 fmol/mg protein ($P < 0.01$); K_D, 81 + 5 and 83 ± 7 pM, for WKY and SHR, respectively.

TABLE 1
Inhibition of [³H]Prazosin and [³H]PAC Binding by Adrenergic Agonists and Antagonists

Drugs	K_i for [³H]prazosin binding (a)	K_i for [³H]PAC binding (b)	a/b
Agonists			
l-Norepinephrine	540 ± 40	20 ± 5	27
d-Norepinephrine	9000 ± 1100†	750 ± 80†	12
l-Epinephrine	200 ± 50	3.3 ± 0.3	61
d-Epinephrine	4300 ± 900*	55 ± 14†	78
Clonidine	310 ± 60	1.7 ± 0.3	182
Antagonists			
Prazosin	0.045 ± 0.008	1800 ± 600	0.000025
Phentolamine	2.1 ± 0.4	1.4 ± 0.4	1.5
Yohimbine	110 ± 50	30 ± 8	3.7

The IC_{50} values were determined graphically, and the K_i values were calculated from the equation, $K_i = IC_{50}/(1 + S/K_D)$, where S is the concentration of [³H]prazosin (100 pM) or [³H]PAC (0.7 nM) used in the assay, and K_D is the dissociation constant calculated by the Scatchard analysis (78 pM for [³H]-prazosin binding and 0.61 nM for [³H]PAC binding, as indicated in the text). The values given are expressed as nM and are the means ± SEM of three to six separate experiments, performed in triplicate, using Sprague-Dawley rats.

* $P < 0.01$, † $P < 0.001$ significant difference from value for its *l*-isomer analyzed by the method of Cochran and Cox (1959) for two groups of different variance.

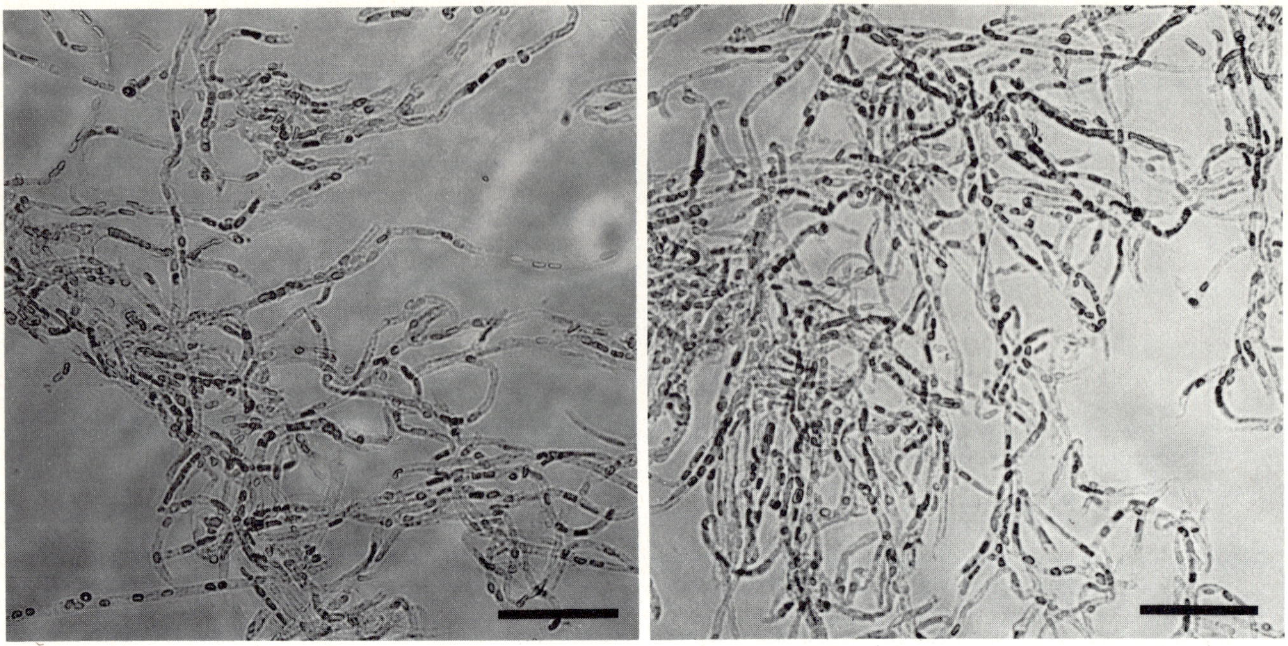

FIGURE 5. *Phase-contrast microscope observation of cerebral microvessel preparations of WKY and SHR. Left, WKY; right, SHR. Bars show 50 μm.*

TABLE 2
Recovery and γ-GTP Activity in Cerebral Microvessels Prepared from WKY and SHR

	WKY	SHR
Recovery	420 ± 35	395 ± 42
γ-GTP activity		
Brain homogenate	95 ± 12	106 ± 9
Microvessels	3980 ± 35	3850 ± 50

Recovery was expressed as μg protein of microvessels per g of cerebral cortex. γ-GTP activity was expressed in nmol product per mg protein per hr. The data are means ± SEM of four separate experiments.

Figure 7 shows the specific binding of [^{3}H]PAC to the microvessel preparations. No difference in [^{3}H]-PAC binding between WKY and SHR is observed: B_{max}, 70 ± 6 and 75 ± 6 fmol/mg protein; K_D, 0.64 ± 0.04 and 0.69 ± 0.05 nM for WKY and SHR, respectively.

The binding of [^{3}H]prazosin to the cerebral microvessels prepared from normotensive Wistar rats (B_{max}, 47 ± 3 fmol/mg protein; K_D, 78 ± 5 pM, n = 3) and the binding of [^{3}H]PAC (B_{max}, 73 ± 5 fmol/mg protein; K_D, 0.63 ± 0.04 nM, n = 3) were not different from the values of WKY (data not shown in figure).

Discussion

Our data show the existence of α_1- and α_2-adrenergic receptors in the rat cerebral microvessels which are labeled by [^{3}H]prazosin and [^{3}H]PAC, respectively. Both binding sites were characterized by saturability, high affinity, reversibility, and stereospecificity. Furthermore, the specificities of

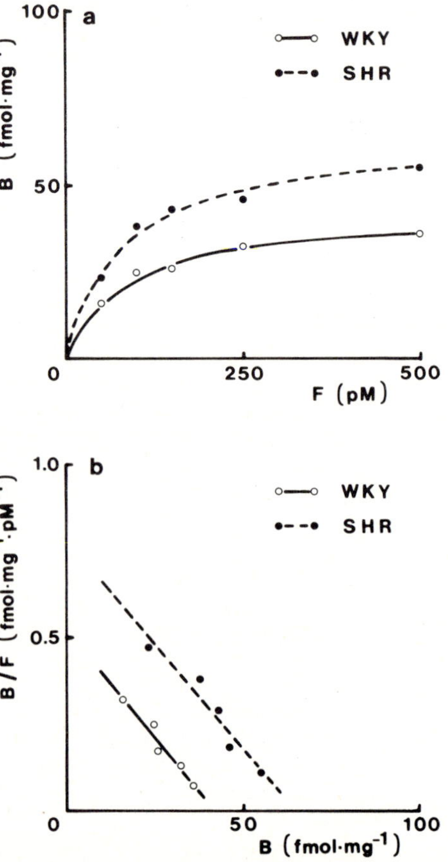

FIGURE 6. *[^{3}H]Prazosin-specific binding to cerebral microvessels (panel a) and its Scatchard plot (panel b) of WKY and SHR. The assay conditions are described in Methods. ○, WKY; ●, SHR. Each point shows the mean of four experiments which varied less than 10%.*

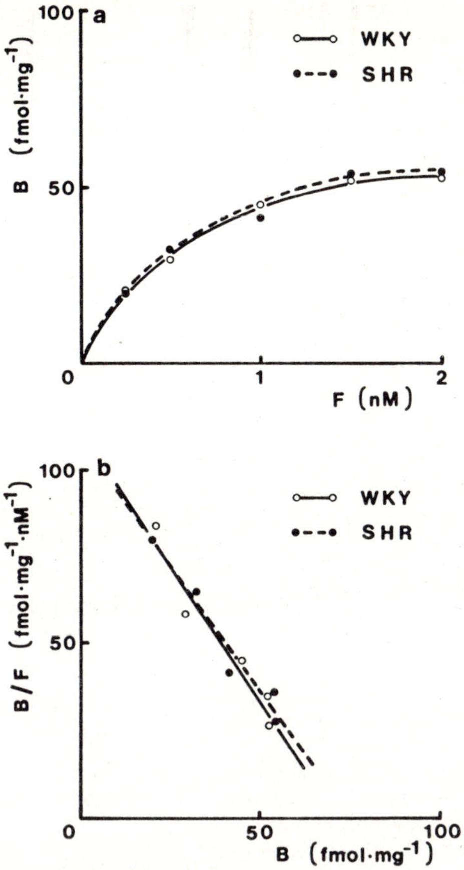

FIGURE 7. *[^{3}H]PAC-specific binding to cerebral microvessels (panel a) and its Scatchard plot (panel b) of WKY and SHR. The assay conditions are described in Methods.* ○, *WKY;* ●, *SHR. Each point shows the mean of four experiments which varied less than 10%.*

both binding sites were pharmacologically evaluated by the inhibitory effect of various adrenergic agonists and antagonists on the bindings. [^{3}H]Prazosin binding to the cerebral microvessels showed the pharmacological properties of α_1-adrenergic receptors, and [^{3}H]PAC binding satisfied the properties of α_2-adrenergic receptors. Harik et al. (1980) reported the existence of β-adrenergic receptors in the cerebral microvessels of the rat and pig, whereas they did not find the α_1-adrenergic receptor sites by use of [^{3}H]-WB4101. However, Peroutka et al. (1980) demonstrated the presence of a considerable number of α_1-receptor sites in the bovine cerebral microvessels, using the same radioligand, and we also reported the existence of α_1-receptors which were labeled by [^{3}H]prazosin (Kobayashi et al., 1982a). Characterization of the [^{3}H]prazosin-binding sites in this report ascertains the existence of the α_1-adrenergic receptors in the cerebral microvessels. These results, together with reports of the existence of β-adrenergic receptor sites (Kobayashi et al., 1981a, 1981b, 1982a–c; Peroutka et al., 1980) and β-adrenergic-sensitive adenylate cyclase activity (Herbst et al., 1979; Nathanson and Glaser, 1979) in the cerebral microvessels, are consistent with the hypothesis that functions of the brain microvessels are controlled by adrenergic innervation.

In a previous report, it was found that [^{3}H]-clonidine bound to the α_2-receptors with different affinity components (U'Prichard et al., 1979), whereas [^{3}H]PAC bound to the receptors uniformly (Rouot and Snyder, 1979). In our system, the straight line in the Scatchard analysis showed that [^{3}H]PAC labeled α_2-receptors of the cerebral microvessels with one affinity component, as in other tissues (Rouot and Snyder, 1979).

Preskorn et al. (1980) reported that tricyclic antidepressants, which are the blockers of the neuronal uptake of norepinephrine, increased the permeability for water from blood to the brain, and this blood-brain permeability of water was decreased by the α-adrenergic antagonist, phentolamine (Raichle et al., 1975). These results suggest that α-receptors located on the cerebral microvessels are involved in the regulation of blood-brain barrier functions.

The number of [^{3}H]prazosin-binding sites in SHR was significantly higher than in control, indicating an increase of α_1-receptors, whereas no difference in α_2-receptors labeled by [^{3}H]PAC was observed between SHR and WKY. Furthermore, a reduction of β-receptor density in the cerebral microvessels of SHR and DOCA-salt hypertensive rats has been demonstrated previously (Magnoni et al., 1983).

Morphological changes of the capillaries, such as increased diameter, endothelial cell degeneration, and deposition of collagen, were reported in experimental hypertensive animals and in humans with essential hypertension (Garcia et al., 1981). Physiological experiments indicate that the acute elevation of systolic blood pressure induces a disruption of the blood-brain barrier, characterized by increased cerebral blood flow, extravasation of markers which normally do not pass the blood-brain barrier, and cerebral edema (Johansson et al., 1970, Johansson, 1976; Heistad and Marcus, 1979). Impaired capacity of cerebral blood flow autoregulation and cerebral edema also have been described in patients with severe hypertension (Byrom, 1954; Strangaard et al., 1975; Healton et al., 1982).

In this report, we suggest the possibility that changes of α_1- and β-adrenergic receptors in the cerebral microvessels may be involved in the derangements of cerebral microvasculature observed in hypertension.

Catecholamines are implicated in the pathogenesis of hypertension. In fact, changes in the functions of peripheral adrenergic neurons and increased plasma catecholamine levels have been reported in hypertension, as well as alterations in the central nervous system (Reid et al., 1975; Nagaoka and Lovemberg, 1976, 1977; Brody et al., 1980). Synthesis, content, and turnover of catecholamines are modified in various brain regions of hypertensive rats (Nakamura et al., 1971 a, 1971 b; Goldberg et al., 1975; Versteeg et al., 1976; Nagaoka et al., 1977; Gianutsos and Moore, 1978; Saavedra et al., 1978), in concomitance with changes in adrenergic receptors (Cantor et al., 1981; Myers et al., 1981). Alterations in hypertension of both central and peripheral adrenergic system may therefore concur in determining the changes of α- and β-receptors in the brain capillaries.

It is interesting to note that the number of α_1- and β-adrenergic receptors is modified in opposite directions, indicating that the two populations may be independently regulated. Experimental observations show that α- and β-receptors mediate opposite effects in cerebral microvasculature. β-Receptor stimulation increases and α-receptor stimulation decreases cerebral blood flow and glucose uptake into the brain (Raichle et al., 1975; MacKenzie et al., 1976b; Schwarts, 1978; Abraham et al., 1979). The same events have been described, in the rat auditory system (Savaki et al., 1978). In this line, the higher level of α_1-receptors and the reduced level of β-receptors in the cerebral microvessels of hypertensive rats could produce the same functional changes in response to catecholamine system. These events may be the consequence of specific changes in neuronal regulatory mechanisms of cerebral microvasculature induced by hypertension.

This work was supported, in part, by a grant from the Ministry of Educaton, Science, and Culture of Japan.

Drs. Kobayashi, Wada, and Izumi are affiliated with the University of Occupational and Environmental Health, Japan, and Drs. Magnoni and Trabucchi with the University of Milan, Italy.

Address for reprints: Dr. Hideyuki Kobayashi, Department of Pharmacology, University of Occupational and Environmental Health, School of Medicine, Yahatanishi-ku, Kitakyushu 807, Japan.

Received February 8, 1983; accepted for publication December 17, 1984.

References

Abraham WC, Delanoy RL, Dunn AJ, Zornetzer SF (1979) Locus coeruleus stimulation decreases deoxyglucose uptake in ipsilateral mouse cerebral cortex. Brain Res **172:** 387–392

Barnes P, Karliner J, Hamilton C, Dollery C (1979) Demonstration of α_1-adrenoceptors in guinea pig lung using ^{3}H-prazosin. Life Sci **25:** 1207–1214

Bates D, Weinshilboum RM, Campbell RJ, Sundt TM Jr (1977) The effect of lesions in the locus coeruleus on the physiological responses of the cerebral blood vessels in cats. Brain Res **136:** 431–443

Brody MJ, Haywood JR, Touw KB (1980) Neuronal mechanisms in hypertension. Annu Rev Physiol **42:** 441–453

Byrom FB (1954) Pathogenesis of hypertensive encephalopathy and its relation to the malignant phase of hypertension experimental evidence from hypertensive rat. Lancet **2:** 201–211

Cantor EH, Abraham S, Spector S (1981) Central neurotransmitter receptors in hypertensive rats. Life Sci **28:** 519–526

Cochran WG, Cox GM (1959) Experimental Designs. New York, Wiley & Sons

Garcia JH, Ben-David E, Conger KA, Geer JC, Hollander W (1981) Arterial hypertension injures brain capillaries. Stroke **12:** 410–413

Gianutsos G, Moore KE (1978) Epinephrine contents of sympathetic ganglia and brain regions of spontaneously hypertensive rats of different ages. Proc Soc Exp Biol Med **153:** 45–49

Goldberg ME, Milmore JE, Haubrich MK, Haubrich DR (1975) Increased susceptibility to seizures and decreased catecholamine turnover in spontaneously hypertensive rats. Eur J Pharmacol **33:** 389–393

Grubb RL, Raichle ME, Eichling JO (1978) Peripheral sympathetic regulation of brain water permeability. Brain Res **144:** 204–207

Harik SI, Sharma VK, Wetherbee JR, Warren RH, Banerjee SP (1980) Adrenergic receptors of cerebral microvessels. Eur J Pharmacol **61:** 207–208

Hatzinikolau P, Brecher P, Gavras H (1981) Chronic hypertension increases tyrosine transport across the blood-brain barrier in the rat. Life Sci **29:** 1657–1660

Healton EB, Brust JC, Feinfeld DA, Thomson GE (1982) Hypertensive encephalopathy and the neurologic manifestations of malignant hypertension. Neurology **32:** 127–132

Heistad DD, Marcus ML (1979) Effect of sympathetic stimulation on permeability of the blood-brain barrier to albumin during acute hypertension in cats. Circ Res **45:** 331–338

Herbst TJ, Raichle ME, Ferrendelli JA (1979) β-Adrenergic regulation of adenosin 3′,5′-monophosphate concentration in brain microvessels. Science **204:** 330–332

Johansson B (1976) Brain barrier pathology in acute arterial hypertension. Adv Exp Med Biol **69:** 517–527

Johansson B, Li C-L, Olsson Y, Klatzo I (1970) The effect of acute arterial hypertension on the blood-brain barrier to protein tracers. Acta Neuropathol **16:** 117–124

Kobayashi H, Memo M, Spano PF, Trabucchi M (1981a) Identification of β-adrenergic receptor binding sites in rat brain microvessels, using [^{125}I]iodohydroxybenzylpindolol. J Neurochem **36:** 1383–1388

Kobayashi H, Maoret T, Ferrante M, Spano PF, Trabucchi M (1981b) Subtypes of β-adrenergic receptors in rat cerebral microvessels. Brain Res **220:** 194–198

Kobayashi H, Cazzaniga A, Spano PF, Trabucchi M (1982a) Ontogenesis of α- and β-receptors located on cerebral microvessels. Brain Res **242:** 358–360

Kobayashi H, Maoret T, Spano PF, Trabucchi M (1982b) Effect of age on β-adrenergic receptors on cerebral microvessels. Brain Res **244:** 374–377

Kobayashi H, Frattola L, Ferrarese C, Spano PF, Trabucchi M (1982c) Characterization of β-adrenergic receptors on human cerebral microvessels. Neurology **32:** 1384–1387

Lai FM, Udenfriend S, Spector S (1975) Presence of norepinephrine and related enzymes in isolated brain microvessels. Proc Natl Acad Sci USA **72:** 4622–4625

Lowry OH, Rosenbrough NJ, Farr AC, Randall RJ (1951) Protein measurement with Folin phenol reagent. J Biol Chem **193:** 265–275

MacKenzie ET, McCulloch J, O'Keane M, Pickard JD, Harper AM (1976a) Cerebral circulation and norepinephrine relevance of the blood-brain barrier Am J Physiol **231:** 483–488

MacKenzie ET, McCulloch J, Harper AM (1976b) Influence of endogeneous norepinephrine on cerebral blood flow and metabolism. Am J Physiol **231:** 489–494

Magnoni MS, Kobayashi H, Cazzaniga A, Izumi F, Spano PF, Trabucchi M (1983) Hypertension reduces the number of beta-adrenergic receptors in rat brain microvessels. Circulation **67:** 610–613

Myers MM, Whittemore SR, Hendley ED (1981) Changes in catecholamine neuronal uptake and receptor binding in the brains of spontaneously hypertensive rats (SHR). Brain Res **220:** 325–338

Nagaoka A, Lovemberg W (1976) Plasma norepinephrine and dopamine-beta-hydroxylase in genetic hypertensive rats. Life Sci **19:** 29–34

Nagaoka A, Lovemberg W (1977) Regional changes in the activities of aminergic biosynthetic enzymes in the brains of hypertensive rats. Eur J Pharmacol **43:** 297–306

Nakamura K, Gerold M, Thoenen H (1971a) Experimental hypertension of the rat: Reciprocal changes of norepinephrine turnover in heart and brain-stem. Naunyn Schmiedbergs Arch Pharmakol **268:** 125–139

Nakamura K, Gerold M, Thoenen H (1971b) Genetically hypertensive rats: Relationship between the development of hypertension and the changes of norepinephrine turnover of peripheral and central adrenergic neurons. Naunyn Schmiedebergs Arch Pharmakol **271:** 157–169

Nathanson JA, Glaser GH (1979) Identification of β-adrenergic-sensitive adenylate cyclase in intracranial blood vessels. Nature **278:** 567–569

Orlowski M, Meister A (1965) Isolation of γ-glutamyl tramspeptidase from hog kidney. J Biol Chem **240:** 338–347

Peroutoka SJ, Moskowitz MA, Reinhard JF Jr, Snyder SH (1980) Neurotransmitter receptor binding in bovine cerebral microvessels. Science **208:** 610–612

Preskorn SH, Hartman BK, Raichle ME, Clark HB (1980) The effect of dibenzazepines (tricyclic antidepressants) on cerebral capillary permeability in the rat in vivo. J Pharmacol Exp Ther **213:** 313–320

Raichle ME, Hartman BK, Eichling JO, Sharpe LG (1975) Central noradrenergic regulation of cerebral blood flow and vascular permeability. Proc Natl Acad Sci USA **72:** 3726–3730

Reid JL, Zivin JA, Kopin IJ (1975) Central and peripheral adrenergic mechanisms in the development of deoxycorticosterone-saline hypertension in rats. Circ Res **37:** 569–579

Rouot BR, Snyder SH (1979) [^{3}H]-*para*-amino-clonidine: A novel ligand which binds with high affinity to α-adrenergic receptors. Life Sci **25:** 769–774

Saavedra JM, Grobecker H, Axelrod J (1978) Changes in central catecholaminergic neurons in spontaneously (genetic) hypertensive rat. Circ Res **42:** 529–534

Savaki HE, Kadekaro M, Jehle J, Sokoloff L (1978) α- And β-adrenoceptor blockers have opposite effects on energy metabolism of the central auditory system. Nature **276:** 521–523

Schwartz WJ (1978) 6-Hydroxydopamine lesions of rat locus coeruleus alter brain glucose consumption as measured by the 2-deoxy-D-[^{14}C]-glucose tracer technique. Neurosci Lett **7:** 141–150

Strangaard S, Olesen J, Skinhoj E, Lassen NA (1973) Autoregulation of brain circulation in severe arterial hypertension. Br Med J **1:** 507–510

Swanson LW, Connelly MA, Hartman BK (1977) Ultrastructural evidence for central monoaminergic innervation of blood vessels in the paraventricular nucleus of the hypothalamus. Brain Res **136:** 166–173

U'Prichard DC, Bechtel WD, Rouot BM, Snyder SH (1979) Multiple apparent alpha-noradrenergic receptor binding sites in rat brain: Effect of 6-hydroxydopamine. Mol Pharmacol **16:** 47–60

Versteeg DHG, Palkovits M, Van der Gugten J, Wijnen HLJM, Smeets GMW, De Jong W (1976) Catecholamine content of individual brain regions of spontaneously hypertensive rats (SH-rats). Brain Res **112:** 429–434

INDEX TERMS: Cerebral microvessels • α-Adrenergic receptors • Brain microcirculation • Neuronal regulation • Spontaneously hypertensive rats

Interactions of Vasopressin with the Area Postrema in Arterial Baroreflex Function in Conscious Rabbits

Karl P. Undesser, Eileen M. Hasser, Joseph R. Haywood, Alan K. Johnson, and Vernon S. Bishop

From the Department of Pharmacology, The University of Texas Health Science Center at San Antonio, San Antonio, Texas

SUMMARY. This study compares the effect of arginine-vasopressin with phenylephrine on arterial pressure, heart rate, and renal sympathetic nerve activity in conscious rabbits with and without functional arterial baroreflexes and in rabbits with lesions of the area postrema. In intact rabbits, progressive infusions of arginine-vasopressin result in large decreases in renal sympathetic nerve activity and heart rate for a given increase in blood pressure as compared to progressive infusions of phenylephrine. In sinoaortic-denervated rabbits, the responses of arterial pressure on heart rate and renal sympathetic nerve activity to both arginine-vasopressin and phenylephrine are markedly attenuated, indicating the necessity for afferent baroreceptor activity in this response. This observation indicates that arginine-vasopressin is acting centrally to enhance the baroreflex. A central site of action of circulating vasopressin may be the area postrema, since it is the only circumventricular organ in the hindbrain. Lesioning the region of the area postrema resulted in a normalization of the responses evoked with arginine-vasopressin and phenylephrine. There was no difference in the phenylephrine responses of arterial pressure on renal sympathetic nerve activity or heart rate in area postrema-lesioned animals, compared to control rabbits. Therefore, we conclude that the area postrema or its surrounding tissue is either a site of action of circulating arginine-vasopressin or contains fibers of passage from another site where arginine-vasopressin acts to enhance baroreflex activity. **(*Circ Res 56: 410–417, 1985*)**

ALTHOUGH arginine-vasopressin (AVP) has been shown to be a potent vasoconstrictor agent (Altura and Altura, 1977; Cowley et al., 1974), increases in mean arterial pressure (MAP) have often been shown to be less than those observed with other vasoconstrictor agents when administered to animals with intact reflexes. A number of studies (Cowley et al., 1974; Montani et al., 1980; Liard et al., 1981; Guo et al., 1982) have indicated that AVP interacts in the central nervous system to modify arterial baroreflexes. It has been postulated that the central action of AVP results in increases in the gain of the arterial baroreflexes (Cowley et al., 1974; Montani et al., 1980). The resulting enhanced inhibition would result in a greater fall in sympathetic activity for any given increase in MAP. On the other hand, microinjections of AVP into the nucleus tractus solitarius results in increases in arterial pressure and heart rate (Matsuguchi et al., 1982), while administration of AVP into the 4th cerebral ventricle causes bradycardia (Varma et al., 1969). Although the effects of AVP appear to be dependent upon the site or route of administration, data from these studies suggest that AVP can act centrally to alter the control of the circulation.

Liard et al. (1981) demonstrated that intravertebral infusions of AVP, in concentrations which do not exert a peripheral effect, result in a decrease in cardiac output and heart rate, suggesting that the hindbrain is involved in the AVP interaction with the baroreflex. The area postrema may be such a site, since it is the only area in the hindbrain devoid of a blood-brain barrier. The area postrema has also been implicated in modifying baroreflex control to increase sympathetic outflow for another circulating neuropeptide, angiotensin II (Ferrario et al., 1972).

The purpose of this study was to examine reflex changes in renal sympathetic nerve activity and heart rate in response to the two pressor agents, AVP and phenylephrine. In addition, this study identifies a site which normalizes the differences seen in response to AVP and phenylephrine.

Methods

Experiments were performed on male New Zealand white rabbits weighing between 2 and 3 kg. Rabbits were anesthetized with sodium-pentobarbital (25 mg/kg). Through a midcervical incision, two catheters were inserted into the right jugular vein for administration of drugs, one for phenylephrine and one for arginine-vasopressin. A catheter was also inserted into the right femoral artery for monitoring arterial pressure. The left kidney was exposed retroperitoneally. Renal sympathetic nerves were isolated and two stainless steel electrodes were placed around the nerve. Electrodes for measuring renal sympathetic nerve activity were fabricated from seven

This manuscript from the University of Iowa was sent to John T. Shepherd, Consulting Editor, for review by expert referees, for editorial decision, and final disposition.

strands of wire (0.002" in diameter) over quad Teflon (0.009") (Medwire Corp.). The nerves and electrodes were covered with a silicone gel (Wackersilicone 604A and 604B mixed in a 9:1 ratio) and the gel was allowed to harden before closure (Schad and Sellers, 1975). The electrodes and catheters were exteriorized through the back of the neck. Rabbits were allowed to recover until the following day before the experimental protocol was begun.

On the day of the experiment, rabbits were placed in a shielded holding unit. Arterial pressure was monitored via the aortic catheter connected to a Gould Statham (P23Db) pressure transducer. Systemic arterial pressure and heart rate were displayed on a Beckman Dynograph. Renal sympathetic nerve activity (RSNA) was amplified by a Grass RPS 107 A.C. preamplifier, and whole nerve activity was obtained by rectifying and integrating the action potentials. Background noise was determined when nerve activity was eliminated either by increasing arterial pressure or by ganglionic blockade. Heart rate (HR) was determined with a Beckman cardiotachometer (9857B) which was triggered from the arterial pulse pressure.

Intact Animals

In nine rabbits, control curves were produced by progressive infusions of either phenylephrine (0.5–12 μg/kg per min) or arginine-vasopressin (2–50 mU/kg per min). Infusions were maintained for 3-minute periods to allow RSNA, HR, and MAP to stabilize before values were recorded. Flow rates ranged from 0.02–0.5 ml/min. Rabbits were allowed to recover a minimum of 30 minutes after an infusion before the other drug was administered. Recovery was considered to be complete once MAP, HR, and RSNA had returned to levels comparable to preinfusion values. The two drugs were administered randomly, and the order of administration had no effect on the HR, MAP, and RSNA responses.

Sinoaortic Denervation

Animals were anesthetized with sodium-pentobarbital (25 mg/kg). The aortic depressor and carotid sinus nerves were exposed through a midcervical incision. Aortic depressor nerves were identified both electrophysiologically and anatomically. The aortic depressor nerves were cut at the level of the nodose ganglion.

The bifurcation of the external and internal carotid artery was isolated and stripped of all nerve fibers in this region. The internal carotid artery was ligated and cut. The region of the carotid sinus was painted with 10% phenol. All animals were allowed to recover for a minimum of 7 days before renal nerve electrodes and catheters were implanted.

A total of six rabbits were sinoaortic denervated. Denervation was considered complete when heart rate did not decrease more than 12 beats/min in response to a 40 mm Hg increase in MAP, and RSNA did not decrease more than 15% when pressure was raised 30 mm Hg. In one of the rabbits, RSNA decreased 35% when pressure was raised 30 mm Hg. Following the experimental protocol, vagotomy abolished this decrease. Similar doses and infusion rates of phenylephrine and arginine-vasopressin were used in both sinoaortic-denervated and intact rabbits.

Area Postrema Lesion

In nine rabbits, the region of the area postrema (and surrounding tissue) was lesioned. Three of these had incomplete lesions of the area postrema, and these rabbits were not included in this study. The animals were anesthetized with sodium-pentobarbital and placed in a stereotaxic head holder. An incision was made between the ears and the muscle was dissected apart to expose the cisterna magnum. The atlanto-occipital membrane was cut and removed with a scalpel to expose the 4th ventricle at the level of the obex. A heating element in the shape of a triangle was placed on the area postrema under a dissecting microscope and the tissue was coagulated. Rabbits were allowed to recover for a minimum of 7 days before electrodes and catheters were implanted.

In five rabbits, sham lesions were made. The animals underwent a protocol similar to that of the area postrema-lesioned animals, except no heat was applied to the lesioning unit. The doses of phenylephrine and arginine-vasopressin used in sham and area postrema-lesioned rabbits were similar to those used in intact rabbits.

Histology

After experimentation, the animals were anesthetized with sodium-pentobarbital, and, in each, the chest was opened via a midsternal incision so as to expose the heart. The descending aorta was ligated at the level of the heart and the ascending aorta was ligated just as it leaves the heart. An 18-gauge needle was inserted into the ascending aorta for administration of the perfusion fluids. An incision was made in the right atrium to allow the perfusion fluids to leave the system.

The brain then was perfused with 100 ml of 27°C saline, followed by a 10% buffered formalin (37–40% formalin, 100 ml; distilled water, 900 ml; sodium monophosphate, 4 g; sodium diphosphate, 6.5 g). The brainstems were removed and stored in buffered formalin. Paraffin (15-μm) sections were cut serially, mounted, and stained by the Kluver-Barrera procedure (Kluver and Barrera, 1953). In some cases, alternate paraffin sections were stained with cresyl violet or Weil stain. Microscopic examinations of the sections were performed to localize and determine the extent of each lesion.

Statistical Analysis

The arterial pressure, heart rate, and renal nerve activity responses to progressive infusions of drugs were analyzed by one-way analysis of variance with repeated measures (Snedecor et al., 1967). All values are shown with SEM. Dose-response curves were analyzed by two-way analysis of variance with repeated measures (Winer, 1971) or linear regression analysis. Differences in slopes were determined by unpaired *t*-test. Significant differences revealed by analysis of variance were identified using the Newman-Keul's multiple range test (Winer, 1971). Differences between responses produced by either AVP or phenylephrine were analyzed by Students' paired *t*-test (Snedecor et al., 1967). Statistical significance was considered to be a probability level of less than 0.05.

Results

Intact Rabbits

No significant differences in the heart rate and renal sympathetic nerve activity responses to increases in arterial pressure produced with either AVP or phenylephrine were noted between intact and sham-lesioned rabbits ($n = 5$). Therefore, sham-lesioned rabbits will be referred to as intact rabbits. An analog recording comparing the effects of AVP and phenylephrine on arterial pressure and RSNA is seen in Figure 1. At equal pressor doses, vasopressin completely abolished nerve activity, whereas phenylephrine reduced nerve activity approximately 25%. Elimination of nerve activity with phenylephrine required that arterial pressure be raised to a substantially higher level.

The effects of increasing MAP with progressive infusions of AVP and phenylephrine on the percent change in RSNA and HR in nine rabbits are shown in Figure 2. A marked difference is seen between the effects of AVP and phenylephrine when the RSNA and HR responses to changes in MAP are compared. With phenylephrine infusion, increases in MAP of 10 mm Hg reduced RSNA by 58 ± 11%. In all rabbits, when MAP was increased by 30 mm Hg with phenylephrine, RSNA approached zero. With AVP infusions, RSNA was reduced 58% before detectable increases in MAP were observed; RSNA was abolished when MAP had increased by 7 mm Hg. Thus, for any given increase in MAP, there was a greater inhibition of RSNA with AVP, compared to phenylephrine. A similar response is seen when comparing ΔMAP vs. ΔHR. With AVP, there is a much greater fall in HR for any given increase in MAP, compared to the response produced with phenylephrine (Fig. 2).

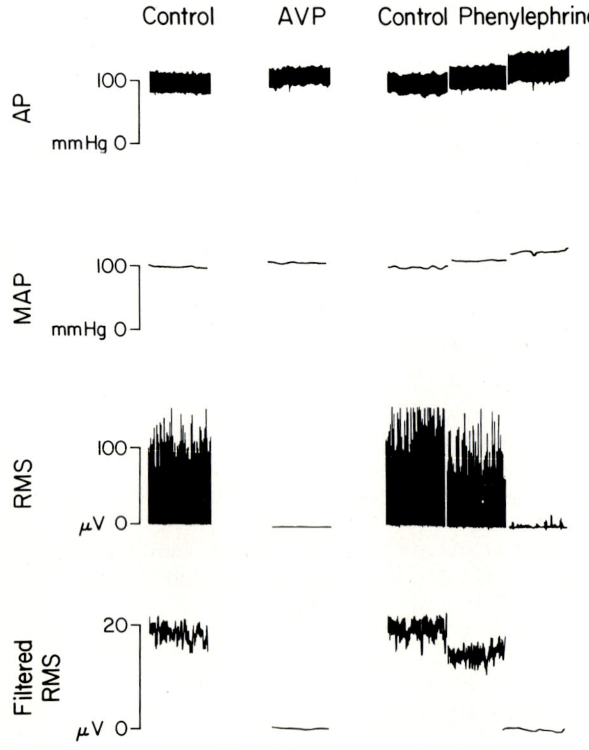

FIGURE 1. *Analog recording comparing infusions of AVP and phenylephrine on arterial pressure (AP) and renal sympathetic nerve activity (RSNA). Small increases in AP with infusions of AVP eliminate RSNA when compared to phenylephrine. (MAP = mean arterial pressure; RMS = root mean square of nerve potentials; filtered RMS = RMS filtered at 0.08 Hz; AVP = arginine-vasopressin.)*

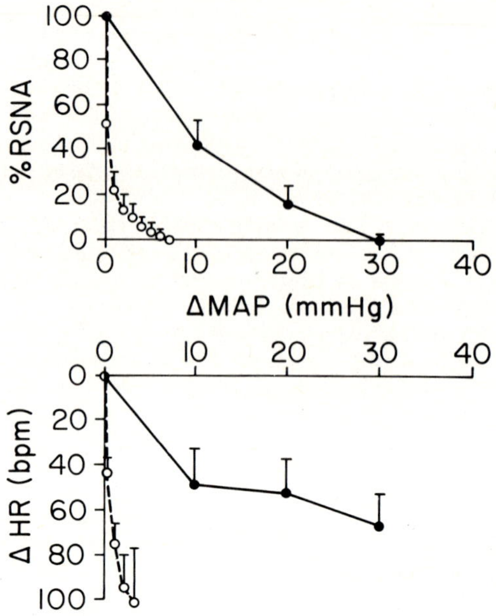

FIGURE 2. *Effect of increasing arterial pressure with progressive infusions of AVP or phenylephrine on RSNA (top) and HR (bottom). All values are significantly different ($P < 0.05$) between groups and from control. (n = 9, %RSNA = renal sympathetic nerve activity represented as a percent of control; ΔHR = change in heart rate; ΔMAP = change in mean arterial pressure; ●, phenylephrine; ○, AVP.)*

Sinoaortic-Denervated Rabbits

In six sinoaortic-denervated rabbits (SAD), increases in MAP with either phenylephrine or AVP produced similar effects on RSNA (Fig. 3). Resting values for MAP and HR are shown in Table 1. No

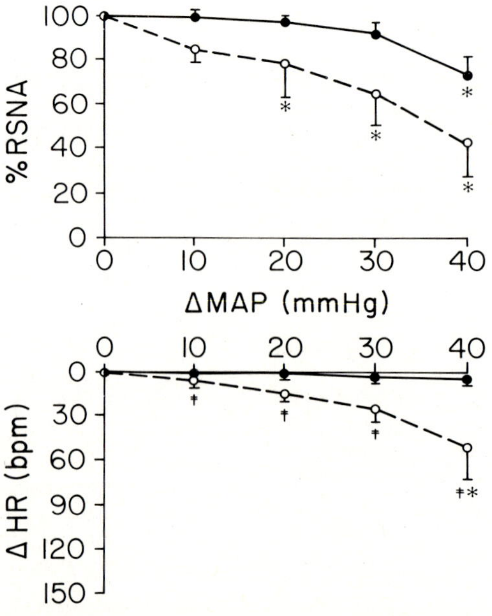

FIGURE 3. *Effect of increasing arterial pressure with progressive infusions of AVP or phenylephrine on RSNA (top) and HR (bottom) in sinoaortic-denervated rabbits. (n = 6; ●, phenylephrine; ○, AVP; *$P < 0.05$ difference from control; †$P < 0.05$ difference between groups.)*

TABLE 1
Resting Values for Arterial Pressure (MAP) and Heart Rate (HR)*

	Control	SAD	AP lesion
MAP	83 ± 4 $n = 9$	83 ± 4 $n = 6$	86 ± 4 $n = 6$
HR	289 ± 11 $n = 9$	339 ± 10† $n = 6$	306 ± 7 $n = 6$

* In control, sinoaortic-denervated (SAD), and area postrema-lesioned (AP lesion) rabbits. In the SAD rabbits, the resting heart rate is significantly higher than in the other groups.

† Significantly different from control and AP-lesioned groups ($P < 0.05$).

significant difference was seen between decreases in RSNA to increases in MAP with either AVP or phenylephrine. Significant decreases in RSNA were seen when MAP was increased 20 mm Hg with AVP, or 40 mm Hg with phenylephrine. In two SAD rabbits, vagotomy prevented the decrease in RSNA during phenylephrine and AVP infusions. Significant decreases in heart rate from control were seen only when MAP was increased by 40 mm Hg with AVP, and no decrease was seen with phenylephrine. At all values, the decrease in heart rate produced with AVP was greater than that produced with phenylephrine.

SAD rabbits exhibited no significant decreases in heart rate when MAP was increased with phenylephrine. However, as pressure was increased with AVP, there was a significant decrease in HR, suggesting a differential effect on HR and RSNA with phenylephrine but not with AVP.

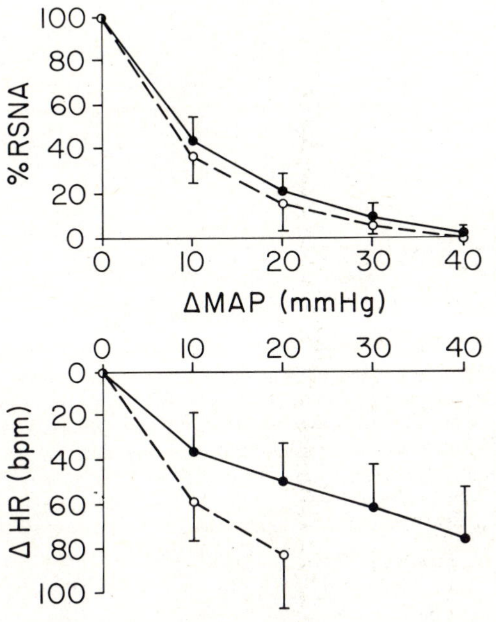

FIGURE 4. *Effect of increasing arterial pressure with progressive infusions of AVP or phenylephrine on RSNA (top) and HR (bottom) in area postrema-lesioned rabbits. All values are significantly different (P < 0.05) than control. There is no difference between AVP and phenylephrine values. (n = 6; ●, phenylephrine; O, AVP).*

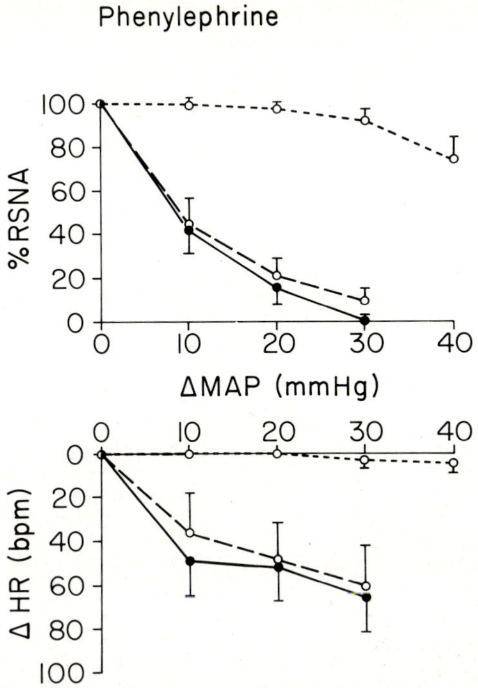

FIGURE 5. *Effect of increasing arterial pressure with progressive infusions of phenylephrine on RSNA (top) and HR (bottom) in intact, sinoaortic-denervated, or area postrema-lesioned rabbits. (●——●, intact; O— — —O, area postrema lesioned; O- - -O, sinoaortic denervated.)*

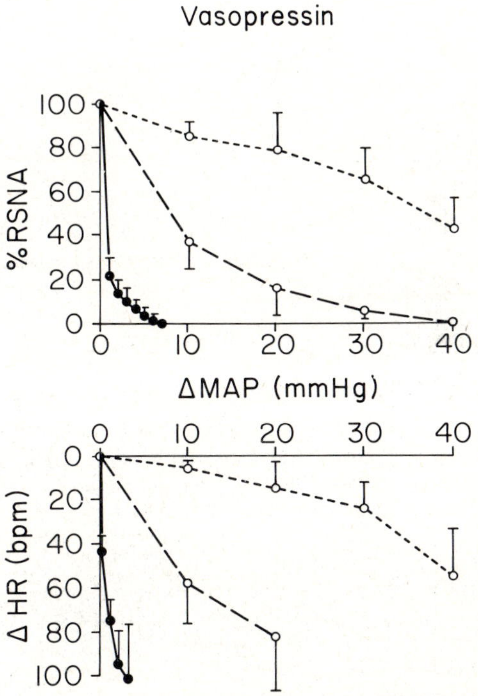

FIGURE 6. *Effect of increasing arterial pressure with progressive infusions of AVP on RSNA (top) and HR (bottom) in intact, sinoaortic-denervated, or area postrema-lesioned rabbits. (●——●, intact; O— — —O, area postrema lesioned; O- - -O, sinoaortic denervated.)*

Area Postrema-Lesioned Rabbits

In six rabbits, lesion of the area postrema had no effect on resting MAP or HR (Table 1). However, lesion of the area postrema abolished the differential response between phenylephrine and AVP (Fig. 4). After ablation of the area postrema, the ΔMAP vs. %RSNA relationship obtained with AVP infusion was shifted to approximate the relationship obtained with phenylephrine infusions in either intact or sham-lesioned animals. There was no significant difference in the ΔMAP vs. %RSNA or MAP-HR relationship during phenylephrine infusions between intact, sham-lesioned, or area postrema-lesioned animals. Also, as shown in Figure 4, after lesion of the area postrema, the ΔMAP-ΔHR responses produced with AVP were similar to those observed with phenylephrine in intact, sham lesion, or lesion rabbits.

Figures 5 and 6 summarize the HR and RSNA responses to increases in MAP produced with phenylephrine and AVP infusions. During AVP infusion, lesions of the area postrema shifted RSNA and HR responses to the right, during increases in MAP, but

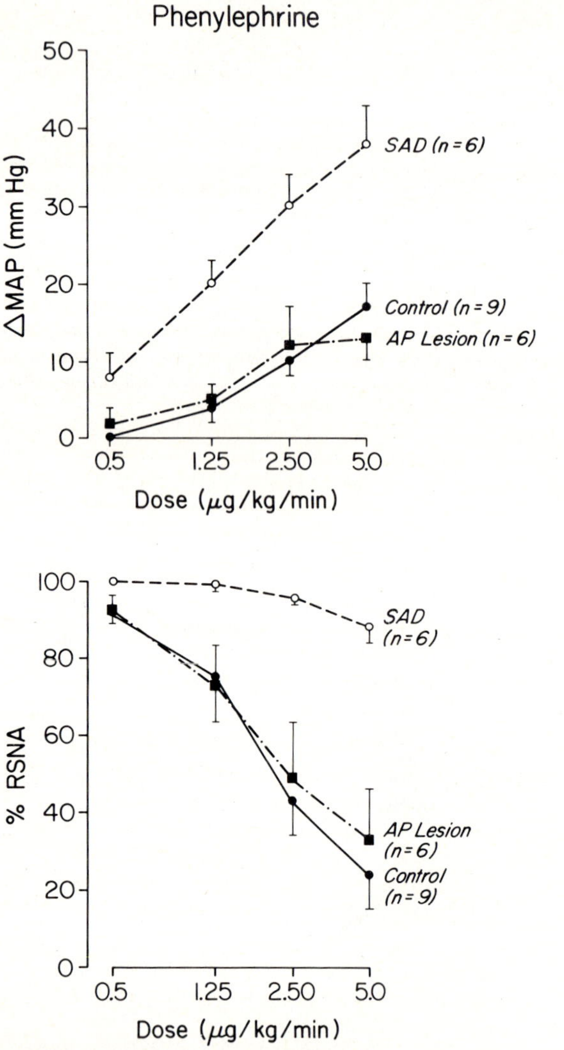

FIGURE 7. *Dose-response curves of increases in arterial pressure produced with progressive doses of phenylephrine in control, sinoaortic-denervated (SAD) or area postrema-lesioned (AP lesion) rabbits. Arterial pressure (ΔMAP) increases significantly ($P < 0.05$) with increasing doses of phenylephrine in control, lesioned, and sinoaortic-denervated rabbits. No difference is seen between control and lesioned rabbits, however, sinoaortic-denervated rabbits are different ($P < 0.05$) from both control and lesioned rabbits. Renal sympathetic nerve activity (RSNA) decreases significantly ($P < 0.05$) with increasing doses of phenylephrine in control and area postrema-lesioned rabbits. The slopes of the control and area postrema-lesioned animals are not different from one another and they are both different from sinoaortic-denervated rabbits ($P < 0.05$).*

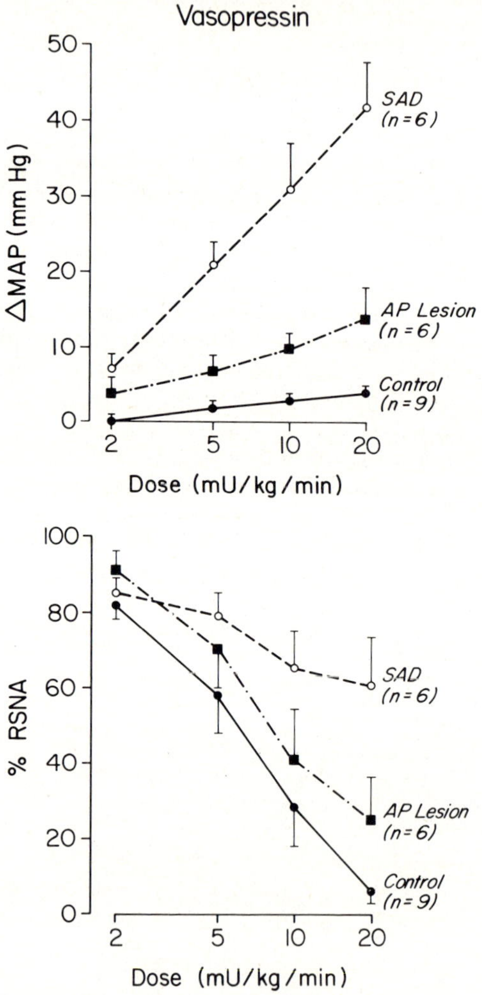

FIGURE 8. *Dose-response curves of increases in arterial pressure produced with progressive doses of AVP in control, sinoaortic-denervated (SAD), or area postrema-lesioned (AP lesion) rabbits. Arterial pressure (ΔMAP) increases significantly ($P < 0.05$) with increasing doses of AVP in lesioned and sinoaortic-denervated but not control rabbits. Lesioned rabbits are different ($P < 0.05$) from control and sinoaortic-denervated rabbits. Sinoaortic-denervated rabbits are also different ($P < 0.05$) from control rabbits. Renal sympathetic nerve activity (RSNA) decreases significantly ($P < 0.05$) with increasing doses of AVP in control and area postrema-lesioned but not sinoaortic-denervated rabbits. The slopes of the control and area postrema-lesioned rabbits are not different from one another, but both are different from sinoaortic-denervated rabbits ($P < 0.05$). At the higher doses of AVP, RSNA is significantly different between the control and area postrema-lesioned rabbit ($P < 0.05$).*

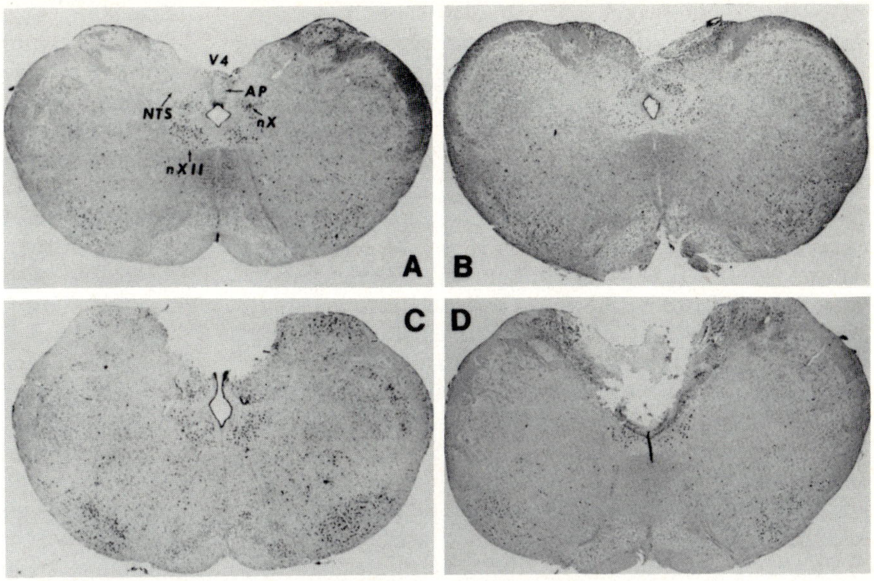

FIGURE 9. *Coronal sections of the hindbrain at the level of the obex in a control (panel A) and area postrema-lesioned rabbits. Panel B: minimum lesion which normalized the vasopressin and phenylephrine responses. Panel C: average lesion of area postrema-lesioned rabbits. Four rabbits had lesions comparable to this one. Panel D: maximum lesion used in this analysis which did not alter the arterial baroreflex response to phenylephrine. (nXII = hypoglossal nucleus; nX = dorsal motor nucleus; NTS = nucleus of tractus solitarii; V4 = fourth cerebral ventricle; AP = area postrema.)*

did not alter these responses during phenylephrine infusions. Sinoaortic denervation essentially abolished the RSNA and HR responses to increases in MAP during phenylephrine infusions. However, some residual effects were noted at higher MAP during AVP infusion.

Dose-Response Curves

MAP and RSNA dose-response curves for AVP and phenylephrine in intact, sinoaortic-denervated, and area postrema-lesioned rabbits are shown in Figures 7 and 8. Increasing doses of either pressor agent caused a dose-related increase and decrease in MAP and RSNA, respectively. Because, with either agent, the maximum dose tested was the dose that resulted in reducing RSNA to zero in the intact animal, the dose-response curves do not reach an asymptote. The MAP dose-response curve during phenylephrine infusion was unaltered after lesion of the area postrema. However, sinoaortic denervation resulted in a significant shift of the dose-response relationship to the left.

In intact rabbits, AVP infusion resulted in only small increases in MAP. However, lesions of the area postrema shifted the dose-response curve to the left, resulting in a greater increase in MAP for any given dose, compared to intact rabbits. Sinoaortic denervation also resulted in a large shift in the MAP dose-response curve to AVP. However, area postrema lesions shifted the AVP dose-response substantially to the left, resulting in a difference between the SAD and area postrema AVP dose-response curve which was similar to that observed between the SAD and control phenylephrine dose-response curve.

RSNA decreases comparable amounts to increasing doses of phenylephrine in both area postrema and control rabbits. In SAD rabbits, the decrease in RSNA to increasing doses of phenylephrine is abolished by vagotomy. The slopes of the AVP dose %RSNA relationship for control and area postrema-lesioned rabbits are not different from one another, and both are different from those of SAD rabbits. The decrease in RSNA seen in SAD rabbits is eliminated by vagotomy. At the higher dose of AVP, the amount of RSNA remaining is greater in the area postrema-lesioned rabbits, than in control.

Verification of Lesions

Lesions that normalized the differences between responses produced with phenylephrine and AVP destroyed the area postrema and variably damaged tissue lateral and ventral to the site of maximum damage (Fig. 9). Lesions ranged from minimal damage of the area postrema to removal of the entire area postrema and surrounding tissue, including portions of the NTS and dorsal motor nucleus. In one rabbit, the medial portion of the nucleus tractus solitarius (NTS) was damaged; however, in this animal, the reflex response produced with phenylephrine was not altered from that of control rabbits. In three rabbits that had incomplete lesions of the area postrema, the responses produced with phenylephrine and AVP were not normalized. These three rabbits were not included in our analysis. Baroreflex responses to phenylephrine were not altered in any animals subjected to lesions as compared to control.

Discussion

The purposes of this study were to evaluate the effects of AVP and phenylephrine on renal sympathetic efferent nerve activity and to localize a site of action of AVP in the central nervous system. Three conclusions are drawn from this study. (1) The reflex response to increases in MAP produced by progressive infusions of AVP was greater than that produced with phenylephrine. For any given increase in MAP, there was a greater decrease in RSNA or HR with AVP, compared to phenylephrine; (2) Sinoaortic denervation abolished the response to phenylephrine, whereas the response to AVP was markedly attenuated, but not completely abolished. (3) The difference seen between AVP and phenylephrine infusions was normalized by lesioning of tissue of the area postrema and its surrounding tissue.

Our observation that increases in mean arterial pressure with infusion of AVP produced greater inhibition of RSNA than similar increments in mean arterial pressure with phenylephrine is consistent with the results of previous studies. Results from separate laboratories have shown that AVP interacts with the arterial baroreflexes to increase the inhibitory influence of the reflex (Cowley et al., 1974; Montani et al., 1980; Guo et al., 1983). Cowley et al. (1974) noted that, in SAD dogs, pressor responses to norepinephrine were increased only 5-fold, whereas pressor responses to AVP increased 100-fold. They concluded that AVP potentiates the arterial baroreflexes. More recently, using anesthetized rabbits, Guo et al. (1982) observed a substantially greater inhibition of lumbar sympathetic nerve activity for a given increase in arterial pressure with AVP, compared to phenylephrine. In the above studies, functional arterial baroreflexes were necessary for the effects of AVP. However, in our study, sinoaortic deafferentation greatly attenuated but did not completely abolish the effects of AVP. In the conscious rabbit, following sinoaortic deafferentation, the mean arterial pressure dose-response curve to phenylephrine was shifted significantly to the left, and the reflex heart rate and RSNA nerve responses to increases in pressure of 30 mm Hg were abolished. Compared to the effects on the phenylephrine dose-response curve, sinoaortic denervation caused a greater shift in the arterial pressure/dose-response curve to AVP. However, sinoaortic deafferentation did not completely abolish the HR and RSNA reflex responses to increases in arterial pressure. Vagotomy after sinoaortic deafferentation abolished the reflex responses to large increases in pressure (40 mm Hg) during phenylephrine infusion, as well as those during AVP infusion. The decrease in RSNA and HR with AVP during large increases in MAP in SAD rabbits may be due to several causes. First, AVP has been shown to interact with the cardiopulmonary reflexes to inhibit sympathetic outflow (Hasser et al., 1984). Thus, the resulting activation of cardiopulmonary afferents with distension of the heart during exposure to elevations in MAP may lead to a greater inhibition of sympathetic outflow when MAP is increased with AVP, compared to that obtained with phenylephrine. Second, it is possible that AVP may have a greater effect on venous compliance than phenylephrine. For a given increase in MAP, AVP may cause a greater increase in filling pressure, resulting in a greater activation of cardiopulmonary afferents as compared to phenylephrine.

Various investigators have suggested that AVP acts at a central site to increase baroreflex sensitivity (Cowley et al., 1974; Montani et al., 1980; Hasser et al., 1983). Additional support for a central site of action was provided by Liard et al. (1981). AVP infused via the vertebral artery, as opposed to intravenous infusion, produced a greater inhibitory effect, suggesting that the central site for the action of AVP was in the region perfused by the vertebral arteries. Since the area postrema, which is the only circumventricular organ in the hindbrain, has been implicated as the site of action of angiotensin II to increase sympathetic outflow (Ferrario et al., 1972), we reasoned that the area postrema may also be involved in the central action of AVP.

In rabbits with lesions of the area postrema, the effects of AVP to increase the inhibitory influence of the arterial baroreflex on RSNA and heart rate were abolished. Since the arterial baroreflex responses to pressor challenges induced with phenylephrine were unaltered, lesions of the area postrema normalized the difference between the reflex responses to AVP and phenylephrine. Although the extent of the lesions varied among rabbits, the area postrema was the single area that was consistently destroyed in the rabbits exhibiting a normalized arterial baroreflex response between phenylephrine and AVP. In the majority of these rabbits, tissue surrounding the area postrema was also damaged. The largest lesion included a portion of the NTS and the dorsal motor nucleus. However, none of the lesioned rabbits displayed an altered arterial baroreflex control of heart rate or RSNA to increases in pressure with phenylephrine. Furthermore, lesions of the area postrema did not alter the magnitude or lability of arterial pressure (Nathan and Reis, 1977; Buchholz and Nathan, 1984). Thus, the damage produced by the lesions to other structures did not interfere with the normal arterial baroreflexes.

The relative difference between the AVP dose-response curve in area postrema-lesioned rabbits and sinoaortic-deafferentated rabbits was similar to the difference observed between the phenylephrine dose-response curves determined in intact rabbits and sinoaortic-deafferentated rabbits. Thus, the area postrema lesion, by abolishing the effects of AVP on the arterial baroreflex, normalized the AVP-arterial pressure dose-response curve.

In the intact rabbit, infusions of AVP decreased RSNA by 80% and heart rate by 40 beats/min before increases in MAP were detected. Even though intact baroreflexes were necessary to demonstrate this effect, the data suggest that the apparent buffering effect of AVP is related to dose, as well as to changes in MAP. After lesion of the area postrema and surrounding tissue, decreases in RSNA and HR during AVP infusions were similar to that observed with phenylephrine (Fig. 4). In this situation, the stimulus for the decrease in RSNA and HR appeared to be dependent upon MAP. Analysis of the AVP dose-response curves for RSNA shows that there is little difference between the intact and lesion groups (Fig. 8). However, in intact animals, the data indicate that, at the doses of AVP administered, the decrease in sympathetic outflow exactly counterbalanced the vasoconstrictor effects of AVP, suggesting an extremely fine regulation of MAP.

Previous studies in the dog have indicated that the area postrema is the site for the central actions of angiotensin II to increase sympathetic outflow. Our data indicate that it is also important in mediating the central effects of AVP to increase the apparent gain of the arterial baroreflex in conscious rabbits. Thus, these two observations suggest that the area postrema plays an important role in the modulation of the sympathetic outflow.

In summary, our results show that AVP acts via the area postrema, or surrounding tissue, to increase the arterial baroreflex inhibition of RSNA and heart rate in conscious rabbits.

We gratefully acknowledge the help of LuAnn Laubach and R. Allen Buchholz in preparing and interpreting the histology; we also thank Linda Stahl and Judith Smith for their expert technical assistance, Teri Mason and Nancy Ball for their assistance in statistical analysis, and Janet Wall for secretarial assistance in preparing the manuscript.

Supported by National Institutes of Health Grant HL-12415.

Dr. Johnson was a Visiting Professor from the Department of Psychology and the Cardiovascular Center, University of Iowa, Iowa City, Iowa, during the time this work was carried out.

Address for reprints: Vernon S. Bishop, Ph.D., Department of Pharmacology, University of Texas Health Science Center, 7703 Floyd Curl Drive, San Antonio, Texas 78284.

Received April 2, 1984; accepted for publication December 17, 1984.

References

Altura BM, Altura BT (1977) Vascular smooth muscle and neurohypophysial hormones. Fed Proc **36:** 1853–1860

Buchholz RA, Nathan MA (1984) Chronic lability of the arterial blood pressure produced by electrolytic lesions of the nucleus tractus solitarii in the rat. Circ Res **54:** 227–238

Cowley AW Jr, Monos E, Guyton AC (1974) Interaction of vasopressin and the baroreceptor reflex system in the regulation of arterial blood pressure in the dog. Circ Res **34:** 505–514

Ferrario CM, Gildenberg PL, McCubbin JW (1972) Cardiovascular effects of angiotensin mediated by the central nervous system. Circ Res **30:** 257–262

Guo GB, Sharabi FM, Abboud FM and Schmid PG (1982) Vasopressin augments baroreflex inhibition of lumbar sympathetic nerve activity in rabbits. Circulation **66:** (suppl II): 35

Hasser EM, Haywood JR, Johnson AK, Bishop VS (1984) Interaction of vasopressin and the sympathetic nervous system during vagal block in the conscious dog. Circ Res **55:** 454–462

Kluver H, Barrera E (1953) A method for the combined staining of cells and fibers in the nervous system. J Neuropathol Exp Neurol **12:** 400–403

Liard JR, Deriaz O, Tschopp M, Schoen J (1981) Cardiovascular effects of vasopressin infused into the vertebral circulation of conscious dogs. Clin Sci **61:** 345–347

Matsuguchi H, Sharabi FM, Gordon FJ, Johnson AK, Schmid PG (1982) Blood pressure and heart rate responses to microinjections of vasopressin into the nucleus tractus solitarius region of the rat. Neuropharmacology **21:** 687–693

Montani JP, Liard JF, Schoum J, Möhring J (1980) Hemodynamic effects of exogenous and endogenous vasopressin at low plasma concentrations in conscious dogs. Circ Res **47:** 346–355

Nathan MA, Reis DJ (1977) Chronic labile hypertension produced by lesions of the nucleus tractus solitarii in the cat. Circ Res **40:** 72–81

Schad H, Sellers H (1975) A method for recording autonomic nerve activity in anesthetized, freely moving cats. Brain Res **100:** 425–430.

Snedecor GW, Cochran WG (1967) Statistical Methods, ed 6. Ames, Iowa, Iowa State University Press

Varma S, Jatu BP, Bhargava KP (1969) Mechanism of vasopressin-induced bradycardia in dogs. Circ Res **24:** 787–792

Winer BJ (1971) Statistical Principles in Experimental Design, ed 2. New York, McGraw-Hill

INDEX TERMS: Sinoaortic denervation • Renal sympathetic nerves • Nerve recording • Phenylephrine • Dose response

Variables Controlling the Secretion of a Somatomedin-like Peptide by Cultured Porcine Smooth Muscle Cells

David R. Clemmons

From the Department of Medicine, University of North Carolina, School of Medicine, Chapel Hill, North Carolina

SUMMARY. Somatomedin-C, a peptide growth factor that is also termed insulin-like growth factor I, stimulates smooth muscle cell replication; however, these cells proliferate in somatomedin-C-deficient medium. We postulated, therefore, that these cells might release a somatomedin-like molecule into the surrounding culture medium. Porcine aortic smooth muscle cells that were exposed to serum-free Dulbecco's modified minimum essential medium for 24 hours were found to release a somatomedin-like molecule that could be detected by a specific radioimmunoassay for somatomedin-C. Several variables in the design of tissue culture conditions were found to regulate the secretion of the somatomedin-like peptide. There was an inverse relationship between somatomedin-like peptide secretion and culture density. Cultures grown to a density of 110,000 cells/well secreted 0.18 ± 0.02 U/ml per 10^5 cells, whereas cultures grown to 38,000 cells/well secreted 0.59 ± 0.06 U/ml per 10^5 cells ($P < 0.001$). Serum deprivation and days of preincubation before initiation of an experiment were found to influence somatomedin-like peptide secretion significantly. Platelet-derived growth factor, which stimulates smooth muscle cell replication, was a potent stimulant of somatomedin-like peptide secretion. Exposure to a concentration of 500 ng/ml platelet-derived growth factor induced a 2.8-fold increase in somatomedin-like peptide secretion over basal levels, (i.e., 0.37 ± 0.05 to 0.98 ± 0.7 U/ml, $P < 0.001$). The effect of platelet-derived growth factor was enhanced (41% increase) by concomitant incubation with 1% somatomedin-C-deficient platelet poor plasma. Transient exposure to platelet-derived growth factor followed by exposure to 1% somatomedin-C-deficient platelet-poor plasma caused a sustained increase in somatomedin-like peptide production even after platelet-derived growth factor had been removed from the culture dish. In contrast to platelet-derived growth factor, hormones and growth factors that circulate in plasma and do not stimulate smooth muscle cell replication after transient exposure, did not stimulate quiescent cultures to secrete the somatomedin-like peptide. However, if the cultures were transiently exposed to platelet-derived growth factor, then exposed to either insulin, epidermal growth factor, or thyroxine, each stimulated somatomedin secretion. Since these hormones were inactive when added to quiescent cultures, it is postulated that entry into the cell cycle is required to achieve stimulation with these substances. The production of this somatomedin-like peptide may be linked to smooth muscle cell replication, since many factors which stimulate replication also facilitate production and release of this material. **(*Circ Res 56: 418–426, 1985*)**

SOMATOMEDIN-C/insulin-like growth factor I (Sm-C/IGF-I), a peptide growth factor that circulates in plasma, is mitogenic for many cell types, including vascular smooth muscle cells (Pfeifle et al., 1982). Sm-C/IGF-I plasma concentrations are dependent upon pituitary growth hormone secretion, and Sm-C/IGF-I has been postulated to stimulate coordinated growth among multiple target tissues in vivo (Zapf et al., 1978; Clemmons and Van Wyk, 1981a). The somatomedins have been classified into two groups. Based on their isoelectric points, Sm-C/IGF-I is basic, whereas insulin-like growth factor II (human) or multiplication-stimulating activity (MSA) (rat) are neutral peptides. The addition of Sm-C/IGF-I alone to smooth muscle cultures will not completely eliminate the need for other plasma and serum mitogens, and multiple peptides that are contained in serum have been found to stimulate smooth muscle cell replication (Weinstein et al., 1981). Investigators have demonstrated that specific mitogens, such as platelet-derived growth factor (PDGF) and growth factors in platelet-poor plasma (PPP), may work together to facilitate cultured smooth muscle cell replication (Rutherford and Ross, 1976; Ross and Vogel, 1978), and when added in combination, their effects are often greater than the sum of the individual actions induced by each. This identification of synergistic effects among peptide growth factors has made it possible to design synthetic media containing defined components rather than serum to support cell growth (Weinstein et al., 1981).

Previous studies have reported that cultured human fibroblasts can proliferate in medium that is deficient in Sm-C/IGF-I; however, Sm-C/IGF-I stimulates fibroblast replication (Moses et al., 1978; Clemmons and Van Wyk, 1981b). These discrepant observations were clarified when it was reported that cultured fibroblasts produced a peptide growth factor that had biological and immunochemical characteristics similar to Sm-C/IGF-I (Atkison et al., 1980). Secretion of the somatomedin-like peptide by fibroblasts has been shown to be stimulated by human growth hormone and PDGF. Since smooth muscle cells have growth factor requirements similar to those of fibroblasts, and can proliferate in medium that is deficient in Sm-C, these studies were undertaken to determine whether cultured porcine aortic smooth muscle cells produce a somatomedin-like peptide. A secondary purpose was to determine whether other growth factors, such as PDGF, could stimulate the production and release of this substance.

Methods

Porcine aortic smooth muscle cells were isolated from young piglets by a previously published method (Ross, 1971). The abdominal aorta was removed from a 3-week-old animal, and the tissue was dissected to remove the endothelium and adventitia. Explants (2 × 2 mm) of the remaining subendothelial tissue were washed twice with PBS, then plated in 10-cm dishes (Falcon 3001, Falcon Labware Division, Becton Dickinson) in Dulbecco's modified Eagle's medium (DMEM) (Flow laboratories) supplemented with 10% fetal calf serum (FCS), (Grand Island Biological Company) (GIBCO), penicillin (100 U/ml), and streptomycin (100 μg/ml) (GIBCO). After a 2-week incubation period, the cells that had migrated from the explants were removed by trypsinization (0.5% trypsin, 0.02% EDTA) (GIBCO) and replated, using a split ratio of 1:3, in the same medium. Stock cultures were maintained in a humidified incubator containing 5% CO_2. The medium was changed every 3rd day until growth was confluent (usually 8–11 days). At that time, the cells were harvested by trypsinization and replated (passage dilution 1:4). Plating efficiences were determined to be greater than 88% for each trypsinization. All stock cultures were tested for mycoplasma contamination and were not contaminated (Chen, 1977). Cultures between the 4th and 9th passage were used in all the experiments.

Preparation of Growth Factors

Human Sm-C/IGF-I used for iodination in these studies was purified to homogeneity as determined by multiple criteria; and was a gift of Dr. Judson J. Van Wyk. Epidermal growth factor was purchased from Collaborative Research. Porcine insulin (lot #PJ5682) was a gift from the Eli Lilly Company. PDGF was purified by modification of previously described methods (Antoniades et al., 1979; Heldin et al., 1979). The material had an activity of approximately 1800 U/mg, 1 unit being equal to the quantity of PDGF necessary to stimulate nuclear labeling equal to 10% human serum. This PDGF preparation was estimated to be 14% pure. The PDGF preparation was tested for Sm-C content and, at a PDGF concentration of 50 μg/ml, there was no cross-reactivity with anti-Sm-C antibody. Somatomedin-C-deficient PPP was obtained from growth hormone-deficient donors by placing freshly drawn blood into prechilled (4°C) plastic tubes. The plasma was prepared by a previously described method (Clemmons et al., 1983). The Sm-C/IGF-I content was less than 4 ng/ml. The platelet factor 4 content of this plasma was less than 15 ng/ml by radioimmunoassay (White and Marouf, 1981).

Determination of Somatomedin-like Peptide Secretion

Porcine aortic smooth muscle cells were subcultured in 24 multiwell plates (Falcon 3008) in DMEM containing 10% FCS, with a plating density of 7000 cells/cm^2, unless otherwise noted. The medium was changed after 3 days, and confluent growth was reached after an additional 3–4 days of incubation. Before each experiment, serum-containing medium was removed by aspiration, the cells were washed three times with 0.5 ml serum-free DMEM [no immunoreactive somatomedin (Sm) was detected in the third wash], and the cultures were exposed to 0.5 ml of this medium. The duration of incubation in serum-free DMEM was 24 hours, unless otherwise noted. If cell density was the variable to be tested, the cells were plated at densities varying between 8,000 and 90,000 cells/well and cultured for 3 days. At that time, they were washed extensively and exposed to 0.5 ml of serum-free DMEM for 24 hours. After aspiration of the medium, the cells were detached by trypsinization and the cell number was determined in triplicate wells, with a particle data counter (Coulter model #ZBI). If the days since a prior medium change or plating was a variable to be tested, DMEM containing 10% FCS was added to cultures 3 days after plating, and the incubation continued without a further medium change until the day the experiment was to be performed.

Quantification of Immunoreactive Somatomedin-like Peptide Content in Medium

Medium samples for Sm-like peptide determination were removed at the time indicated, and each sample was stored at −20°C until it was assayed. The samples were prepared for radioimmunoassay by a previously described method (Clemmons et al., 1981). Pure Sm-C/IGF-I, 10,000 U/mg, was iodinated to a specific activity between 140 and 210 μCi/μg and purified by affinity chromatography. The radioimmunoassay used anti-human Sm-C/IGF-I antibody at a final dilution of 1 to 12,000 (Copeland et al., 1980). This assay is highly specific for Sm-C/IGF-I and shows little cross-reactivity with somatomedin-A, MSA, and IGF-II (Van Wyk et al., 1979). The radioimmunoassay was performed with 0.5% Tween detergent in the assay buffer. Under these conditions, dose-response curves obtained with unextracted conditioned medium were parallel to pure Sm-C/IGF-I standard. In addition, recovery of pure Sm-C/IGF-I from the medium preparation was 77%; therefore, the quantity of the somatomedin-like peptide that was present was slightly underestimated. Binding of [^{125}I]Sm-C/IGF-I to the smooth muscle cells was measured by a previously described method (Clemmons et al. 1981).

A partially purified preparation of the somatomedin-like peptide was prepared by the following method. Subconfluent cultures were washed and exposed to serum-free DMEM for 24 hours, and the medium aspirated was then concentrated by ultrafiltration, with an Amicon YM-5 membrane. The pooled concentrates from 500 ml of medium were dialyzed against 10 liters of 0.05 M Tris buffer, pH 5.0. CM Sephadex (1 g) was added to the

TABLE 1
Effect of Frequent Medium Changes, Time of Incubation, and Cyclohexamide on Sm-like Peptide Production

Test substance	Time of incubation (hr)	No. of medium changes	Immunoreactive Sm-C concentrations* (U/ml per 10^5 cells)
Serum-free DMEM	12		0.04 ± 0.01
Serum-free DMEM	24		0.07 ± 0.01
Serum-free DMEM	36		0.11 ± 0.02
Serum-free DMEM	48		0.13 ± 0.01
Serum-free DMEM	72		0.18 ± 0.04
Serum-free DMEM	96		0.17 ± 0.02
Serum-free DMEM	72	6	0.19 ± 0.02
Serum-free DMEM + cycloheximide (50 μM)	12		Undetectable
	24		Undetectable
Serum-free DMEM (preincubated 72 hr with 10% Sm-C/IGF-I-deficient serum)	24		0.09 ± 0.01

* The results represent the mean ± 1 SD of triplicate cultures obtained during two separate experiments.

dialysate, and the mixture was stirred overnight at 4°C. The mixture was poured into a 5 × 10 cm column, and the column was washed with three column volumes of 0.05 M Tris, pH 6.5, at 2.0 ml/min. The proteins were eluted using a linear NaCl gradient (0.1–1.0 M) in 0.05 M Tris, pH 8.0, at 1.0 ml/min. The somatomedin content of each 3.0-ml fraction was determined by RIA, and the active fractions were pooled, dialyzed, and lypophilized to dryness. The residue was reconstituted in 4.0 ml of 0.05 M ammoniun acetate, pH 3.7, containing 1% CHAPS detergent and applied to a 1.6 × 110 cm Sephadex G-150 column. The column was eluted with the same buffer at a flow rate of 13 ml/hr, and the active fractions were determined. The biological activity of the partially purified Sm-like peptide was determined by transiently exposing confluent, quiescent BALB/c 3T3 fibroblasts to PDGF (50 ng/ml) for 5 hours, followed by 5% Sm-C/IGF-I-deficient PPP and test quantities of pure Sm-C/IGF-I or the partially purified Sm-like peptide. After a 36-hour incubation, [^{3}H]thymidine incorporation was determined as previously described (Clemmons and Shaw, 1983). Under these conditions, BALB/c 3T3 fibroblasts are sensitive to the effects of Sm-like growth factors, but this bioassay is not specific for somatomedins.

Results

Quiescent, confluent porcine aortic smooth muscle cells secreted a peptide* into the medium in a quantity sufficient to be detected by the Sm-C radioimmunoassay. The release of this peptide into the medium was associated with a progressive increase for approximately 72 hours; it plateaued, thereafter, and no further increase over time was noted beyond that point (Table 1). To eliminate the possibility that the cells had taken up Sm-C from the FCS and released it during the 72-hour incubation, the following experiments were performed. The media were changed at 12-hour intervals for a 72-hour incubation period, the Sm-like peptide content was determined, and the results were summed. Although there was no significant increase in the apparent immunoreactive Sm-like peptide concentration compared to cultures incubated continuously for 72 hours, the immunoreactive Sm-like peptide concentration that was released was 2.4-fold greater than that present in 10% FCS (Table 1). Additional cultures were incubated with cycloheximide (50 μM) for 72 hours. As shown in Table 1, the cultures exposed to cycloheximide had no detectable immunoreactive Sm-like material. In another experiment, triplicate cultures were preincubated in MEM containing 10% Sm-C/IGF-I-deficient serum (final concentration = 0.2 ng/ml) for 3 days. The quantity of Sm-like peptide that was released was 22% greater than cultures exposed to 10% FCS. In addition, when [^{125}I]Sm-C/IGF-I (2 ng/ml) was exposed to the cultures for 48 hours at 37°C, then removed and reexposed to fresh cells, specific binding of the labeled peptide had been reduced by greater than 90%, indicating that most of the growth factor had been degraded.

Since PDGF is a potent stimulant of porcine aortic smooth muscle cell replication, it was of interest to determine the effect of this growth factor on Sm-like peptide production. Increasing concentrations of partially purified PDGF, that had no detectable Sm-C by radioimmunoassay, were added to quiescent smooth muscle cell cultures, and secretion of the Sm-like peptide was determined (Fig. 1). Under basal conditions, the cultures released 0.37 ± 0.05 U/ml in 24 hours, and this increased to 0.98 ± 0.07

** Evidence that this material is a peptide was obtained by proteolysis. Exposure of the Sm-like material to Protease® (Sigma) for 60 minutes at 37°C resulted in complete loss of immunoreactivity. As a control an additional sample was exposed for 60 minutes at 37°C to a protease preparation that had been heated previously to 90°C for 30 minutes. This material had full immunoreactivity.*

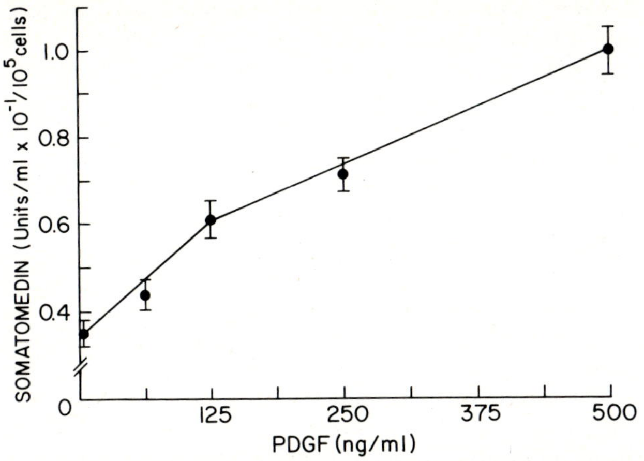

FIGURE 1. *PDGF stimulation of Sm-like peptide secretion by smooth muscle cells. Increasing concentrations of PDGF were added with 0.5 ml of serum-free DMEM to quiescent porcine aortic smooth muscle cell cultures. Control cultures received only serum-free DMEM. After 24 hours of incubation at 37°C, the medium samples were aspirated, and the Sm-like peptide content was determined by RIA. The results are the ± 1 SD of triplicate wells and are exposed as U/ml per 10^5 cells.*

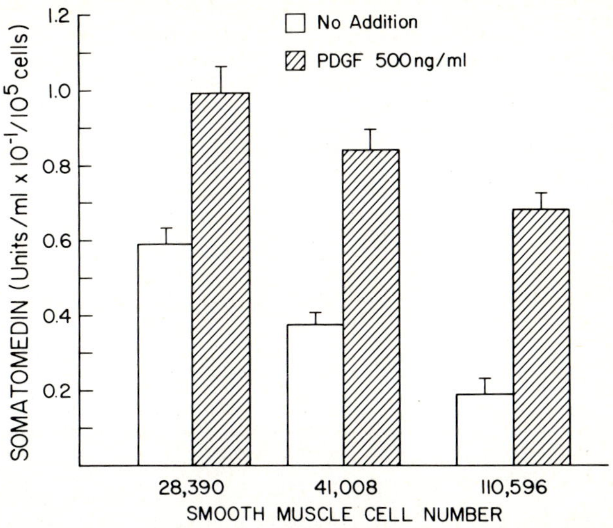

FIGURE 2. *The effect of culture density on Sm-like peptide secretion. Smooth muscle cells were plated at densities between 0.75 and 7.0 × 10^4 cells per cm^2 surface area. After a 3-day incubation period, the cultures were washed three times with serum-free DMEM and exposed to 0.5 ml serum-free DMEM with or without 500 ng/ml PDGF. After 24 hours of incubation at 37°C, medium samples were aspirated and the Sm-like peptide content and cell number determined as in Figure 1. The results are expressed as the mean of triplicate well ± 1 SD.*

U/ml when exposed to 500 ng/ml partially purified PDGF. Even at the lowest concentration of PDGF used (i.e., 62.5 ng/ml), there was a statistically significant ($P < 0.05$), increment in the concentration of Sm-like peptide released by the PDGF-treated cultures when compared to the nonstimulated cultures. Repetition of this experiment using pure PDGF (obtained from Cellular Products) showed that pure material could stimulate a 3.4-fold increase in Sm-like peptide release at a concentration of 14 ng/ml.

Increasing culture density is associated with a diminution in the growth rate of porcine aortic smooth muscle cells. To determine whether changes in Sm-like peptide secretion were associated with changes in culture density, smooth muscle cell cultures were plated at densities varying between 15,000 and 70,000 cells/well, and 3 days after plating, Sm-like peptide secretion was determined. Cell density had a significant effect on somatomedin secretion (Fig. 2). The basal secretion decreased from 0.58 ± 0.06 U/ml at 28,000 cells/well to 0.21 ± 0.05 U/ml at 110,000 cells/well ($P < 0.001$). Additionally, the effect of PDGF was attenuated by high culture density, although the percent stimulation inducible by PDGF increased as the culture density increased. To document the reproducibility of this relationship, we performed 11 experiments on separate days, using separate 24-well plates that had been plated at different culture densities. The basal rate of somatomedin secretion was compared for each density; cell density is plotted as function of somatomedin-like peptide concentration (Fig. 3). There was a highly significant correlation between density and Sm-like peptide secretion, $r = 0.88$, $P < 0.01$.

Other parameters that significantly influence somatomedin secretion are listed in Table 2. Varying the day of the last medium change had an effect on the release of the Sm-like peptide from the cells. Smooth muscle cells were plated at a high density between 1.12 × 10^5 cells/well in DMEM supplemented with 10% FCS. After incubation intervals of between 3 and 10 days without a medium change, the cultures were washed and exposed to serum-free DMEM for 24 hours. Each incubation interval between days 5 and 10 showed statistically significant increments in Sm-like secretion, compared to day 3 cultures, and by day nine there had been a

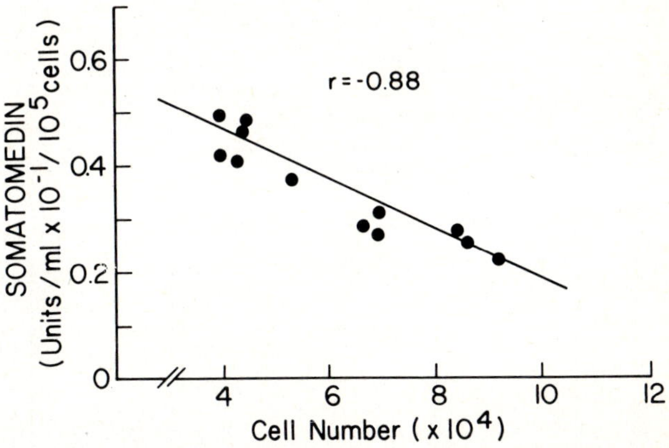

FIGURE 3. *Correlation between culture density and Sm-like peptide secretion. Smooth muscle cells were plated at 11 different densities and incubated for 3 days in DMEM supplemented with 10% FCS. At that time, the cultures were washed three times with serum-free DMEM and 0.5 ml of that medium added to triplicate cultures. After a 24-hour incubation period the Sm-like peptide content and cell number were determined as in Figure 1.*

TABLE 2
Effect of Varying the Day Since the Last Medium Change and Serum Deprivation on Sm-like Peptide Production

Day	Sm concentration (U/ml per 10^5 cells)
3	0.06 ± 0.01
4	0.06 ± 0.02
5	0.10 ± 0.01*
7	0.14 ± 0.02*
9	0.17 ± 0.04*
10	0.17 ± 0.03*
Serum supplement	
0.5% FCS	0.10 ± 0.02
10% FCS	0.17 ± 0.01

Results are expressed as mean ± 1 SD.
* Compared to day 3, $P < 0.01$.

2.9-fold increase in the Sm-like peptide concentrations. To determine whether this increase was due to serum deprivation, smooth muscle cell cultures were preincubated for 3 days in DMEM supplemented with either 0.5% or 10% FCS. The cultures that had been incubated in 0.5% FCS had a 49% increase in Sm-like peptide secretion. Since a 2.9-fold increase was demonstrable after 9 days in culture, the effect of time in culture appeared to predominate. Other parameters that were examined were passage number, number of medium changes during the first 48-hour incubation period, and the effect of protease inhibitors. None of these appeared to have statistically significant effects on Sm-C secretion (data not shown).

Multiple growth factors that circulate in plasma were tested for their capacity to stimulate the secretion of this peptide. When incubated in the presence of Sm-C deficient PPP, epidermal growth factor, thyroxine, and insulin all failed to induce significant increments in Sm-like peptide secretion (Fig. 4, left panel). In contrast, if PDGF (100 ng/ml) and 0.5% Sm-C-deficient PPP were co-incubated with each of these factors, each substance induced a statistically significant increment in Sm-like peptide secretion. The variables that were necessary for insulin to be an effective stimulant were analyzed, using two different experimental designs. Quiescent cells were transiently exposed to PDGF followed by Sm-C-deficient PPP, plus increasing concentrations of insulin. Compared to identical cultures that were transiently exposed to PDGF followed by insulin in serum-free DMEM, there was a marked increase in the concentration of Sm-like peptide that was released (Fig. 5). This suggests that other factors in Sm-C deficient PPP are required to obtain the maximal stimulation of Sm-like peptide secretion. However, since the combination of insulin plus Sm-C-deficient PPP (Fig. 4, left panel) caused no increase in Sm-like peptide secretion, it appears that these factors are active only in cells that had prior exposure to PDGF. To analyze this dependency upon PDGF exposure further, 500 ng/ml of PDGF were added to quiescent smooth muscle cells simultaneously with 1% Sm-C-deficient PPP and variable concentrations of insulin. There was a concentration-dependent increase in the amount of Sm-like peptide secreted in response to insulin (Fig. 6). In contrast, when the cultures were exposed to epidermal growth factor (20 ng/ml) and 1% Sm-C-deficient PPP, the rate of Sm-like peptide secretion following stimulation by identical concentrations of insulin was greatly reduced.

To determine whether the Sm-like peptide that was secreted was biologically active we tested a partially purified preparation of this material for its capacity to stimulate replication in BALB/c 3T3 fibroblasts. For comparison, additional cultures received 5% Sm-C/IGF-I-deficient PPP and increasing concentrations of pure Sm-C/IGF-I. The Sm-like peptide stimulated significant increases in DNA synthesis (Table 3). Based on RIA units, the most highly

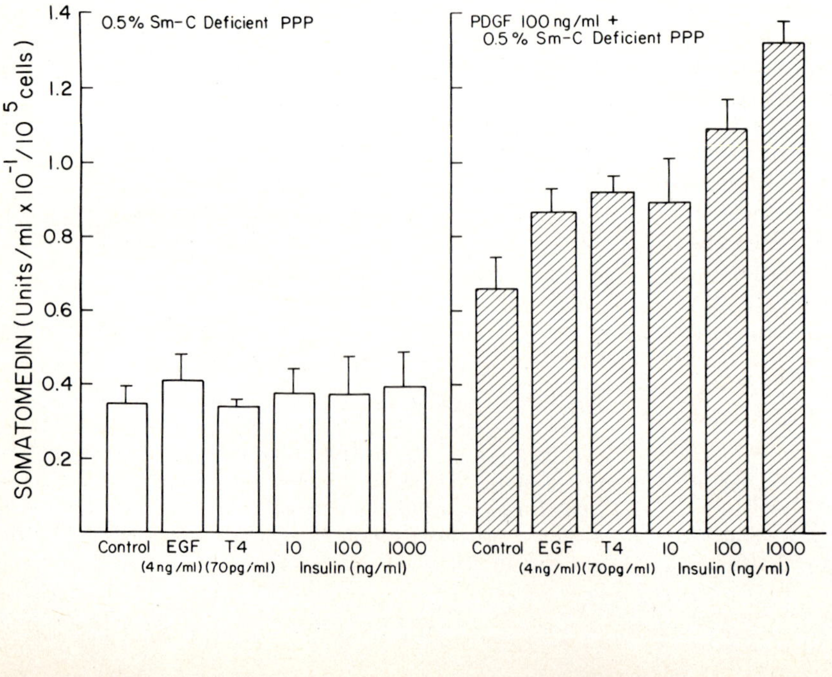

FIGURE 4. *Stimulation of Sm-like peptide secretion by plasma growth factors. EGF, thyroxine, and insulin were added at the concentrations listed to quiescent smooth muscle cell cultures in 0.5 ml of DMEM supplemented with 0.5% Sm-C-deficient PPP in the presence ▨ or absence □ of PDGF. Following 24-hours of incubation at 37°C, the medium samples were removed, and the Sm-like peptide concentration and cell number were determined as in Figure 1. The results are expressed as the mean ± 1 SD of triplicate determinations.*

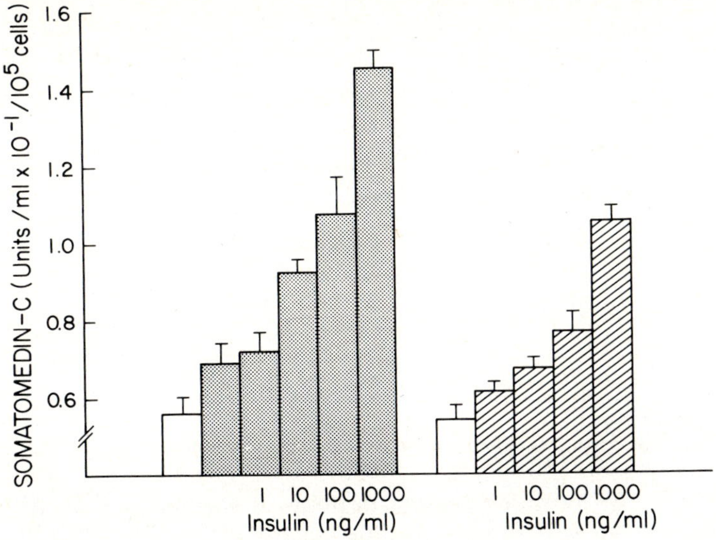

FIGURE 5. *Effect of Sm-C deficient PPP on Sm-like peptide secretion in response to insulin. Quiescent smooth muscle cell cultures (6.2–6.8 × 10^4 cells/well) were transiently exposed to 0.5 ml DMEM and PDGF (100 ng/ml). After a 5-hour incubation period, variable concentrations of insulin (1–1000 ng/ml) were added in 0.5 ml DMEM in the presence ▨ or absence ▨ of 0.5% Sm-C-deficient PPP. After a 24-hour incubation period Sm-like peptide secretion was determined as previously described for Figure 1.*

purified material was less potent than pure Sm-C/IGF-I.

Discussion

Sm-C/IGF-I stimulates replication in multiple types of cultured cells, including smooth muscle cells (Pfeifle et al., 1982). The observation that smooth muscle cells can replicate in medium that is deficient in Sm-C/IGF-I, however, raised an important question. Was this growth factor required for smooth muscle cell replication? Like smooth muscle cells, cultured human fibroblasts are capable of replicating in Sm-C/IGF-I-deficient medium. Fibroblasts produce a growth factor with immunochemical and biological properties similar to Sm-C (Clemmons et al., 1981), and it has been proposed that the secretion of this peptide enables fibroblasts to replicate in Sm-C-deficient medium (Clemmons and Van Wyk, 1981). In addition, the production of the Sm-like peptide by fibroblasts can be stimulated by other growth factors, such as PDGF, and this appears to be one mechanism by which PDGF can stimulate fibroblast replication.

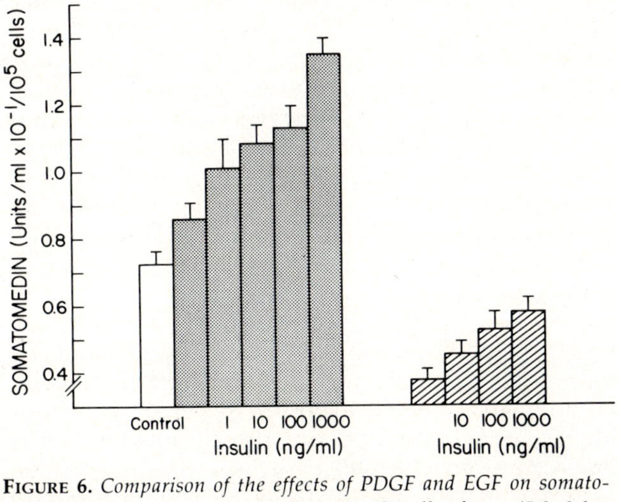

FIGURE 6. *Comparison of the effects of PDGF and EGF on somatomedin-like peptide secretion. Smooth muscle cell cultures (5.9–6.6 × 10^4 cells) were washed 3 times with serum-free DMEM and exposed to PDGF ▨ (100 ng/ml) plus 0.5% Sm-C-deficient PPP. Additional cultures were exposed to EGF ▨ (20 ng/ml), plus 0.5% Sm-C-deficient PPP, and both groups were incubated with these reagents for 24 hours at 37°C. The results are expressed as the mean ± 1 SD of triplicate determinations.*

Since smooth muscle cells have some growth characteristics that are similar to fibroblasts, these experiments were conducted to determine whether they secreted an Sm-like peptide. Both quiescent and smooth muscle cells that had been stimulated to enter the cell cycle released into the medium a peptide that has immunochemical properties similar to Sm-C/IGF-I. The results support the conclusion that the smooth muscle cell cultures are producing a Sm-C/IGF-I-like peptide and are not just taking it up from fetal calf serum and releasing it into the medium, although the results provide only indirect evidence of synthesis. Attempts to confirm biosynthesis of the peptide using radiolabeled amino acids have been unsuccessful, due to the small amount of Sm-like peptide that secreted relative to the total amount of protein.

The material that is secreted is a peptide. The partially purified peptide is biologically active and mimicks the effect of pure Sm-C/IGF-I, using the BALB/C 3T3 cell bioassay test system. The BALB/C 3T3 cell bioassay test system is not specific for Sm-C, and it is possible that a mitogen that co-purifies with the Sm-like peptide could account for the bioactivity. Recent studies in our laboratory have demonstrated that addition of a specific monoclonal anti-Sm-C antibody that binds the Sm-like peptide to PDGF-stimulated smooth muscle cell cultures results in inhibition of [^{3}H]thymidine incorporation (Clemmons and Van Wyk, personal communication). Since the antibody binds specifically to Sm-C and to the partially purified Sm-like peptide, this finding strengthens our conclusion that the Sm-like peptide is the active component of the partially purified material. These observations support the conclusion that the secreted form of this material

TABLE 3
Biological Activity of the Smooth Muscle Cell Media

Test substance	Protein concentration (μg/ml)	Sm-C/IGF-I concentration* (U/ml)	[^{3}H]Thymidine incorporation† (counts/min)
5% Sm-C/IGF-I deficient PPP			15,460 ± 530
5% normal PPP			106,300 ± 210
Somatomedin-like peptide			
30% Crude conditioned medium	16	0.03	46,930 ± 950
CM Sephadex purified	4.4	0.05	51,880 ± 720
G-150 Sephadex purified	0.7	0.05	52,910 ± 190
Sm-C/IGF-I		0.03	41,860 ± 1,340
		0.12	78,970 ± 1,100
		0.48	99,200 ± 1,480

* These results were determined by radioimmunoassay.
† The results represent the mean ± 1 SD of duplicate samples obtained from two separate experiments.

may act locally to stimulate smooth muscle cell replication.

Further support for the hypothesis that the release of this peptide is closely linked to the control of smooth muscle cell replication is provided by analysis of the variables that control its release. High-density cultures were shown to release decreased amounts of Sm-like peptide per cell. The mechanism for this decrease is unknown. It is possible that diminished Sm-like peptide production at high density merely reflects a diminution in the rate of total cellular protein synthesis (Levine et al., 1965). Our laboratory has previously reported that Sm-like peptide production per cell was reduced 4-fold in high-density fibroblasts cultures, whereas there was only a 1.7-fold reduction in total protein synthesis (Clemmons and Shaw, 1983). Cultures at high density also have diminished rates of pinocytosis (Davies and Ross, 1980), decreased peptide growth factor receptors (Holley et al., 1977), and decreased proteoglycan accumulation (Peitilia and Nakkari, 1982). It is possible that reduction in Sm-C secretion per cell in high-density cultures is part of a more generalized metabolic response to confluent growth.

Time in culture and serum deprivation were important modulators of Sm-like peptide secretion. Time in culture was relatively more important, but both parameters need to be standardized to permit valid comparisons between the results of two or more experiments. Serum deprivation prior to initiation of an experiment leads to increased rates of replication after the addition of fresh serum supplements or growth factors (Pledger et al., 1978). The enhanced rates of Sm-like peptide secretion noted in these studies after serum deprivation may be linked to this increase in replication.

Paritally purified PDGF was a potent stimulant of Sm-like peptide secretion. Likewise, pure PDGF was stimulatory, indicating that PDGF is an important component of the biological activity in our partially purified preparations. This study did not determine whether this effect of PDGF was specific for the Sm-like peptide. Since PDGF stimulates the synthesis of many cellular proteins, it is possible that this effect is related to this general property of PDGF. High-density cultures could also be stimulated by PDGF exposure. Previous studies have shown that maximal cell density is directly proportional to PDGF concentration in the medium (Vogel et al., 1980). It is possible that stimulation of Sm-like peptide secretion by PDGF in high-density cultures is a mechanism by which PDGF can overcome the negative effects of culture density on cell growth.

PDGF causes rapid initiation of ion and amino acid transport (Owen et al., 1982) and an immediate increase in the rates of protein synthesis in cultured cells (Cochran et al., 1981). Since PDGF is capable of stimulating quiescent smooth muscle cells to enter the cell cycle (Rutherford and Ross, 1976), it is possible that stimulation of Sm-like peptide secretion by PDGF is one of the early events that lead to cell cycle entry. Conversely, since transient exposure to PDGF followed by exposure to Sm-C-deficient plasma leads to a sustained increase in Sm-like peptide secretion, the PDGF-induced increase may be secondary to the fact that the cells are no longer quiescent, and in that state will intrinsically secrete more Sm-like peptide. However, continuous exposure of cycling cells to PDGF is definitely associated with higher rates of Sm-like peptide secretion, suggesting that PDGF is continuing to stimulate the synthesis of this Sm-like material, even in cycling cells.

Cell cycle timing is an important determinant of the DNA synthesis response of cells to growth factors contained in plasma. In this study, none of the plasma growth factors could stimulate Sm secretion without simultaneous exposure to PDGF. This finding suggests that smooth muscle cells must leave the quiescent state to be able to increase Sm-like peptide secretion in response to these growth factors and hormones. Whether these factors act to stimulate a PDGF-dependent effect on Sm-like peptide secretion, or whether they are effective simply because the cells have been stimulated to enter the cell cycle, cannot be determined from these studies.

Detailed chemical analysis of the Sm-like peptide was not carried out in these studies; however, the peptide has immunochemical properties similar to Sm-C, since it cross-reacts with both polyclonal antisera used in these studies and a highly specific monoclonal anti-Sm-C antibody. These results imply structural homology at several antigenic sites. Studies of the biological response to this peptide show that the partially purified peptide is biologically active and the activity is retained through two purification steps. Based upon RIA units, its activity is comparable to pure human Sm-C/IGF-I, although—due to probable species differences in the primary structure—an exact equivalent relationship cannot be determined. Furthermore, until molecular weight and isoelectric point determinations are made, it will not be possible to know the exact chemical relationship between this growth factor and Sm-C/IGF-I.

Several investigators have reported the production and release into the medium of growth factors by cells maintained in tissue culture. Dulak and Temin (1973) and, more recently, Nissley and Rechler (1977) have reported the production of rat somatomedin (MSA) by cultured buffalo rat liver cells. Acquaviva et al. (1982) have used this system to study the biosynthesis of this somatomedin-like peptide. Although several studies have reported the conditioning of medium by the cellular secretion of growth factors (Young et al., 1975; Millis et al., 1978) this phenomenon has taken on new significance with the proposal of a model for the autocrine regulation of cell growth. Delarco and Todaro (1978) have reported that spontaneously and virally transformed cell lines have the capacity to secrete transforming growth factors into the medium. More importantly, they and others (Kaplan and Ozanne, 1982) have demonstrated that these peptides can regulate cell growth. Several investigators have reported the production of specific growth factors by cultured fibroblasts (Atkison et al., 1980; Clemmons et al., 1981), and recently Canalis et al. (1980) have reported the production of growth factors by normal cartilage and bone cells. These studies support the hypothesis that the smooth muscle cell is an additional cell type that is capable of autocrine growth regulation.

Analysis of the mechanisms that control the secretion of these factors may have important implications for understanding fundamental biochemical reactions that control the response to vascular wall injury and the development of atherosclerosis. Since PDGF release appears to be an important component of the acute response to vascular injury, it is possible that the rapid increase in Sm-like peptide release induced by PDGF is a growth regulatory event. Secretion of this material in selective areas could stimulate regional proliferation of the subendothelium and leave areas adjacent to the injury unaffected. Therefore, the elucidation of the factors that control this somatomedin autocrine regulatory system may further our understanding of atherosclerosis.

I wish to thank Debra Shaw and Todd Brown for their technical assistance and Geri Cox for preparing and editing the manuscript. I thank Drs. Judson Van Wyk and Louis Underwood for their gift of somatomedin-C, and Dr. Robert Reddick who prepared electron micrographs of the smooth muscle cells.

This work was supported by U.S. Public Health Service Research Grant HL26309. Dr. Clemmons is supported in part by General Clinical Research Center Grant RR00046.

Address for reprints: David R. Clemmons, M.D., Department of Medicine, University of North Carolina, School of Medicine, Chapel Hill, North Carolina 27514.

Received October 17, 1983; accepted for publication December 28, 1984.

References

Acquaviva AM, Bruni CB, Nissley SP, Rechler MM (1982) Cell free synthesis of rat insulin-like growth factor II. Diabetes **31:** 656–658

Antoniades HN, Scher CD, Stiles CD (1979) Purification of human platelet derived growth factor. Proc Natl Acad Sci USA **79:** 1809–1813

Atkison PR, Weidman ER, Bhaumick B, Bala RM (1980) Release of somatomedin-like activity by cultured WI-38 human fibroblasts. Endocrinology **106:** 2006–2012

Canalis E, Peck WA, Raisz LG (1980) Stimulation of DNA and collagen synthesis by autologous growth factor in cultured fetal rat calvaria. Science **210:** 1021–1023

Chen TR (1977) In situ detection of mycoplasma contamination in cell culture by fluorescent Hoescht #33258 stain. Exp Cell Res **104:** 255–260

Clemmons DR, Shaw DS (1983) Variables controlling somatomedin production by cultured human fibroblasts. J Cell Physiol **115:** 137–142

Clemmons DR, Van Wyk JJ (1981a) Somatomedin: Physiological control and effects on cell proliferation. *In* Handbook of Experimental Pharmacology, edited by R Baserga. New York, Springer Verlag, pp 161–208

Clemmons DR, Van Wyk JJ (1981b) Somatomedin-C and platelet derived growth factor stimulate human fibroblast replication. J Cell Physiol **106:** 361–367

Clemmons DR, Underwood LE, Van Wyk JJ (1981) Hormonal control of immunoreactive somatomedin production by cultured human fibroblasts. J Clin Invest **67:** 10–17

Clemmons DR, Isley WL, Brown MT (1983) Dialyzable factor in human serum of platelet origin stimulates endothelial replication and growth. Proc. Natl Acad Sci USA **80:** 1641–1645

Cochran BH, Lillquist JS, Stiles CD (1981) Post-transcriptional control of protein synthesis in BALB/3T3 cells by platelet derived growth factor and platelet poor plasma. J Cell Physiol **109:** 429–438

Copeland KC, Underwood LE, Van Wyk JJ (1980) Induction of immunoreactive somatomedin-C in human serum by growth hormone: Dose response relationships and effect on chromatographic profiles. J Clin Endocrinol Metab **50:** 690–697

Davies PF, Ross R (1980) Growth mediated density dependent inhibition of endocytosis in cultured arterial smooth muscle cells. Exp Cell Res **129:** 329–336

DeLarco JE, Todaro GJ (1978) A human fibrosarcoma cell line producing multiplication stimulation activity (MSA)-related peptides. Nature **272:** 356–358

Dulak NC, Temin HM (1973) Multiplication stimulation activity for chick embryo fibroblasts from rat liver cell conditioned medium: A family of small peptides. J Cell Physiol **81:** 161–170

Heldin CH, Westermark B, Wasteson A (1979) Platelet derived growth factor: Purification and partial characterization. Proc Natl Acad Sci USA **76:** 3722–3726

Holley RW, Amour R, Baldwin JH, Brown KD, Yeh YC (1977) Density dependent regulation of growth of BS1-C cells in culture: Control of growth by serum factors. Proc Natl Acad Sci USA **74:** 5046–5050

Kaplan PL, Ozane B (1982) Transforming growth factors enable transformed and normal cells to grow in serum free medium. *In* Growth of Cells in Hormonally Defined Medium. Cold Spring Harbor, New York, Cold Spring Harbor Laboratory, pp 333–344

Levine EM, Rechler V, Brooks CB, Eagle H (1965) Contact inhibition, macromolecular synthesis and polyribosomes in cultured diploid human fibroblasts. Proc Natl Acad Sci USA **53:** 350–356

Millis AJ, Hoyle M, Field B (1978) Human fibroblast conditioned media contains growth promoting activities for low density cells. J Cell Physiol **93:** 17–24

Moses AC, Cohen KL, Johnsonbaugh R, Nissley SP (1978) Contribution of human somatomedin activity to the growth of human skin fibroblasts and chick embryo fibroblasts in culture. J Clin Endocrinol Metab **46:** 937–946

Nissley SP, Rechler MM (1977) Multiplication stimulating activity (MSA): A somatomedin-like polypeptide from cultured rat liver cells. *In* Third Dicennial Review Conference: Cell Tissue and Organ Cultures, NCI monograph #48, pp 167–178

Owen AJ, Geyer RP, Antoniades HN (1982) Human platelet-derived growth factor stimulates amino acid transport and protein synthesis of human diploid fibroblasts in plasma free media. Proc Natl Acad Sci USA **79:** 3202–3207

Peitilia K, Nikkari T (1982) Effect of cell density on the incorporation of [^{3}H]proline into collagen by rabbit aortic smooth muscle cells in culture. Artery **10:** 72–79

Pfeifle B, Ditschuneit HH, and Ditschuneit H (1982) Binding and biologic actions of insulin-like growth factors on human arterial smooth muscle cells. Horm Metab Res **14:** 409–414

Pledger WJ, Stiles CD, Antoniades HN, Scher CD (1978) An ordered sequence of events is required for BALB/c 3T3 cells to become committed to DNA synthesis. Proc Natl Acad Sci USA **75:** 2839–2843

Ross R (1971) Smooth muscle cell. II. Growth of smooth muscle in culture and formation of elastic fibers. J Cell Biol **50:** 172–186

Ross R, Vogel A (1978) The platelet derived growth factor. Cell **14:** 203–210

Rutherford RB, Ross R (1976) Platelet factors stimulate fibroblasts and smooth muscle cells quiescent in plasma to proliferate. J Cell Biol **69:** 196–202

Van Wyk JJ, Svoboda ME, Underwood LE (1979) Evidence from radioligand assays that somatomedin-C and insulin-like growth factor-I. J Clin Endocrinol Metab **50:** 206–208

Vogel A, Ross R, Raines E (1980) Role of serum components in density-dependent inhibition of growth in 3T3 cells: Platelet derived growth factor is the major serum determinant of saturation density. J Cell Biol **85:** 377–385

Weinstein R, Stemmerman MB, Maciag T (1981) Hormonal requirements for growth of arterial smooth muscle cells in vitro: An endocrine approach to atherosclerosis. Science **212:** 818–820

White GC, Marouf AF (1981) Platelet factor 4 levels in patients with coronary artery disease. J Lab Clin Med **97:** 369–378

Young M, Oyer J, Blanchard MH, Asdovrian H, Amos H, Arnason BGW (1975) Secretion of nerve growth factor by primary chick fibroblast cultures. Science **187:** 361–362

Zapf K, Rinderknecht E, Humbel RE, Froesch ER (1978) Nonsuppressible insulin-like activity (NSILA) from human serum: Recent accomplishments and their physiologic implications. Metabolism **27:** 1803–1828

INDEX TERMS: Somatomedin-C • Replication • Growth factor • Platelets • Atherosclerosis

Calcium Sensitivity of Isometric Force in Intact and Chemically Skinned Aortas during the Development of Aldosterone-Salt Hypertension in the Rat

E. Garwitz McMahon and R.J. Paul
With the technical assistance of Glenn E. Doerman
From the Department of Physiology, University of Cincinnati, Cincinnati, Ohio

SUMMARY. We investigated the role of altered vascular calcium handling in the development of aldosterone-salt hypertension in the rat. The calcium sensitivity of isometric force in response to 50 mM KCl was compared in aortic rings from control and aldosterone-hypertensive rats. Over the entire range of calcium concentrations studied, responses in aortas from the hypertensives were significantly depressed compared to controls [ED_{50}: aldosterone-hypertensive rats (n = 6), 0.739 ± 0.137; controls (n = 7), 0.141 ± 0.021 mM; $P < 0.001$]. However, calcium sensitivity in response to 1 μM norepinephrine was similar in aortas from both hypertensives and controls [ED_{50}: aldosterone-hypertensive rats (n = 7), 0.196 ± 0.022; controls (n = 7), 0.180 ± 0.024 mM]. The calcium sensitivity of Triton X-100 skinned aortic rings from aldosterone-hypertensive rats was likewise not significantly different from sensitivity in controls [ED_{50}: aldosterone-hypertensive rats (n = 9), $3.61 \times 10^{-7} \pm 0.57$; controls ($n$ = 8), $3.89 \times 10^{-7} \pm 0.64$ M]. Therefore, the observed decrease in calcium sensitivity in response to membrane depolarization in aortas from aldosterone-hypertensive rats probably is not due to a change in calcium sensitivity of the contractile system itself. The time course for development of changes in calcium handling in vessels from the aldosterone-hypertensive rats was found to be quite different from the time course for changes in monovalent ion metabolism. Whereas increases in monovalent ion permeability reportedly appear as early as one week after the start of aldosterone-salt treatment, significant alterations in calcium handling were not apparent until after four weeks of treatment. After one week of aldosterone-salt treatment, calcium sensitivity in response to 50 mM KCl was similar in aortas from the aldosterone-treated rats compared to controls. After two weeks, the ED_{50} for calcium sensitivity in response to 50 mM KCl was slightly increased in the aldosterone-treated group, compared to controls. Therefore, the trend appears to be a progressive decrease in calcium sensitivity in aortic smooth muscle during the development of aldosterone-salt hypertension in the rat. This reduction in calcium sensitivity appears to be primarily a membrane phenomenon; it is unlikely that it reflect alterations in the contractile system itself. **(*Circ Res 56:427–435, 1985*)**

THERE is general agreement that the calcium-handling properties of arterial smooth muscle from experimental hypertensive animals are altered compared to arteries from normotensive control animals. However, the nature and extent of these alterations and the possible role of altered calcium metabolism in the development of hypertension remain a matter of dispute. Early work in this area supported the view that calcium sensitivity in response to both norepinephrine (NE) and high potassium was increased significantly in vessels from hypertensives. Hinke (1966) was the first to demonstrate enhanced calcium sensitivity in response to NE and KCl in isolated perfused tail artery from deoxycorticosterone acetate (DOCA) hypertensive rats. An increase in membrane permeability to calcium in vessels from the hypertensives was proposed as a possible mechanism underlying this enhanced responsiveness. Holloway and Bohr (1973) reached similar conclusions, based on their study of the membrane-stabilizing effect of high calcium solutions in femoral artery strips from spontaneously hypertensive rats (SHR), DOCA, and renal hypertensive rats. These alterations in calcium metabolism were later shown to reflect a primary functional change in the vascular smooth muscle membrane itself, rather than a secondary alteration in response to an increase in wall stress (Hansen and Bohr, 1975).

In contrast to these early consistent findings, most subsequent work has generated conflicting results. In 1978, Pedersen and coworkers reported a reduced sensitivity to calcium in response to both NE and KCl in aortas from SHR compared to normotensive Wistar controls. More recently, reduced sensitivity to extracellular calcium in response to NE has been reported in large mesenteric arteries from DOCA-hypertensive rats (Moreland et al., 1982), whereas cerebral arteries from SHR were found to be less sensitive to extracellular calcium in response to KCl depolarization (Winquist and Bohr, 1983). Others have reported that aortas from SHR are leakier to extracellular calcium (Webb and Bhalla, 1976; Noon et al., 1978). A recent study by Mulvany and Nyborg (1980) using small mesenteric resistance vessels from SHR indicated that small vessel sensitivity to calcium in hypertension differs substantially from large vessel responsiveness. Mesenteric resistance vessels from SHR were found to be more sensitive to calcium than controls, when stimulated with NE, but not when stimulated with high potassium. These findings suggest an abnormality in receptor-operated calcium channel function but normal potential-sensitive activation processes in SHR resistance vessels. It is not clear to what extent abnormalities in calcium handling might contribute to the elevated pressure in this form of experimental hypertension.

An alteration in calcium sensitivity in vessels from hypertensives could be the result of a change at a number of possible sites in the excitation-contraction coupling scheme. A change in membrane permeability to calcium might be considered a logical candidate, since vascular permeability to monovalent ions—sodium, potassium, and chloride—has been shown to be increased significantly in large arteries from hypertensive animals (Jones, 1983). Changes in cytoplasmic calcium removal mechanisms—calcium uptake into the sarcoplasmic reticulum and active calcium transport via a sarcolemmal Ca^{++} ATPase—may also lead to an alteration in calcium responsiveness. There is some evidence from work using isolated microsomal membrane fractions that calcium removal mechanisms in arteries from hypertensives might be inadequate (Moore et al., 1975; Twietmeyer et al., 1978; Kwan et al., 1979). Alternatively, a change in the calcium sensitivity of the regulatory mechanisms for the contractile system may underlie the alteration in calcium sensitivity in vessels from hypertensives. This possibility can be directly tested by measuring calcium sensitivity in a chemically skinned vascular preparation that is devoid of functional plasma membrane and intracellular calcium pools. In such a system, the calcium sensitivity of the contractile system itself can be directly evaluated.

This approach was recently utilized by Nghiem and Rapp (1983) to evaluate calcium sensitivity in tail artery from SHR. They reported that calcium sensitivity in skinned SHR tail artery was similar to that in a skinned preparation from Dahl salt-resistant rats. These results would suggest that alterations in calcium sensitivity in the SHR are not the result of an altered calcium responsiveness of the contractile system itself. However, this conclusion is not straightforward, because interpretation of data from the SHR model is known to be quite sensitive to the type of control animal used (Seidel, 1979).

The present study was undertaken to determine whether the calcium handling properties of aortas from aldosterone-salt hypertensives rats (AHR) are altered during the development of this form of experimental hypertension. This model of mineralocorticoid-dependent hypertension is of particular interest, in that hypertension is produced with physiological doses of aldosterone (Garwitz and Jones, 1982a). Aorta from AHR have been shown to have substantially altered membrane permeabilities to sodium, potassium, and chloride (Garwitz and Jones, 1982a, 1982b), as well as a significantly elevated basal oxygen consumption rate (McMahon and Paul, 1984). In this study, the calcium sensitivity of both intact and chemically skinned aortas from AHR was determined, so that the role of altered calcium metabolism in the development of this form of experimental hypertension could be assessed.

Methods

Animals and Tissues

The aldosterone-hypertensive rat model has been described in detail elsewhere (Garwitz and Jones, 1982a, 1982b). Briefly, the left kidney was removed from anesthetized male Sprague-Dawley rats (150–200 g). An osmotic mini-pump (Alza) containing *d*-aldosterone (Sigma) dissolved in polyethylene glycol, or vehicle only for the control group, was implanted subcutaneously in the animals. Aldosterone was infused into the rats at 0.25 μg/hr. Control rats were given a 1% (wt/vol) NaCl solution to drink, whereas the aldosterone-treated animals also received a supplement of KCl (0.3% wt/vol) in the NaCl solution to aid in the maintenance of body weight. Systolic blood pressure was measured using a tail cuff technique (Friedman and Freed, 1949).

On the morning of the experiment, the rats were killed and the thoracic aortas were rapidly removed. The aortas were cleaned of adventitia and adherent fat and then cut transversely into rings. One 6-mm ring was mounted isometrically in a glass chamber (volume = 1.8 ml) for measurement of force. A second ring (approximately 1 mm) was mounted in a system used for measurement of isometric force in chemically skinned vascular smooth muscle. At the end of each experiment, the segments were cut open longitudinally, and muscle dimensions (segment length and circumference) were then measured by microscopy, using an ocular scale. The tissues were then gently blotted and weighed.

Intact Vascular Preparation

The physiological solution (PSS) had the following composition (mM): Na^+, 146.2; K^+, 5.0; Mg^{++}, 1.2; Ca^{++}, 2.5; Cl^-, 143.9; HCO_3^-, 13.5; $H_2PO_4^-$, 1.2; and glucose, 11.4. Ca^{++}-free PSS was similar to PSS with the exclusion of $CaCl_2$ and the addition of 0.2 mM ethyleneglycol-bis (β-amino-ethyl ether)-*N,N'* tetraacetic acid (EGTA). Solutions were gassed with a mixture of 95% O_2/5% CO_2 at 37°C. The measured pH of these solutions was typically between 7.3. and 7.4. Solutions of norepinephrine (L-norepinephrine bitartrate; Sigma) were made by dissolving NE in PSS. Ethylenediamine tetraacetic acid (EDTA, 0.026 mM) was added to these solutions to delay oxidation of the drug. Depolarization-induced contractions were elicited by the addition of KCl (45 μl) from a concentrate (2 M) to increment the bath concentration by 50 mM.

Isometric measurements of force were made on intact vessel segments with a Kistler-Morse transducer (compliance = 0.1 μm/mN). Vessel cross-sectional area was calculated according to A = 2 × wet weight/1.06 × C, where

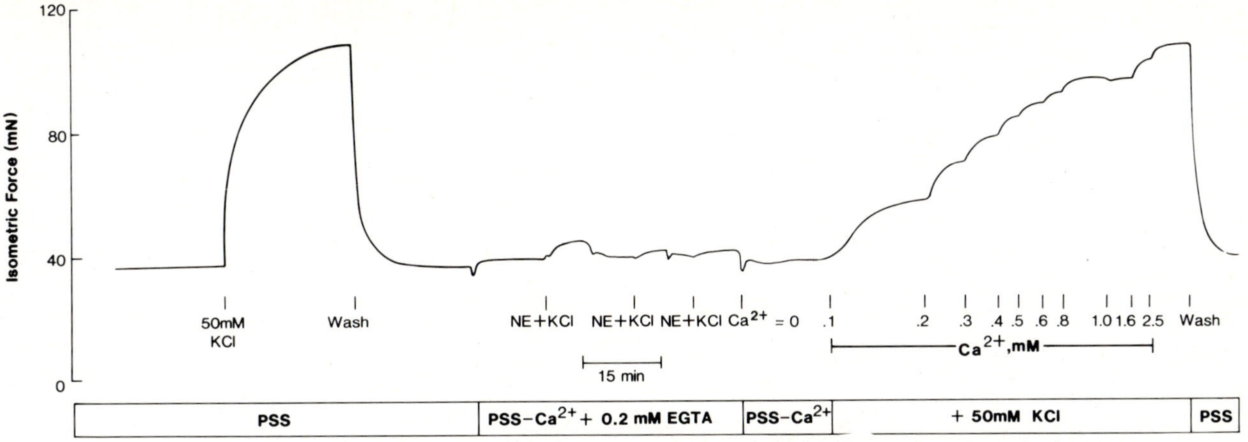

FIGURE 1. *Protocol used to measure calcium sensitivity in response to 50 mM KCl in thoracic aorta from a control rat. Following a test contracture to 50 mM KCl, intracellular stores of calcium were first depleted by repeated exposure to 1 μM NE and 50 mM KCl in Ca^{++}-free solution containing 0.2 mM EGTA. Calcium was then added back cumulatively in the presence of 50 mM KCl to determine the calcium dose-response relationship.*

1.06 g/cm^3 is used as an estimate of tissue density and C is vessel circumference.

Skinned Vascular Preparation

A 1-mm aortic ring was mounted horizontally between a movable and fixed post, the movable end attached to a force transducer (AME 801, Aksjeselskapet Mikro-elektronik). The ring was bathed initially in a morpholinopropane sulfonic acid (MOPS)-buffered PSS solution in a 0.4-ml Lucite bath. The ionic species in MOPS-PSS were similar to that of the bicarbonate-buffered PSS, with the exclusion of $NaHCO_3$ and the addition of 2 mM MOPS. Experiments were conducted with solutions equilibrated with room air at 37°C.

The aortic rings were chemically skinned by a modification of the procedure described by Rüegg and Paul (1982). The following solutions were used for skinned fiber experiments at 25°C: *presoak solution (PS)*—20 mM imidazole, 5 mM EGTA, 50 mM KCl, and 150 mM sucrose (pH 7.4); *skinning solution*—PS + 5% Triton X-100, 0.5 mM dithioerythritol (DTE), 1 mM phenylmethyl sulfonyl fluoride (PMSF); *relaxing solution (RS)*, containing (mM) – K^+, 21; Na^+, 36; Mg^{++}(total), 10; EGTA, 4; ATP, 7.5; imidazole, 20; Cl, 35; azide 1; an ATP-regenerating system consisting of 10 mM phosphocreatine, and 10 U/ml of creatine phosphokinase, pH 6.7; *contracting solution (CS)*—EGTA was partly replaced with Ca^{++}-EGTA to increase the free Ca^{++}. The concentration of free Ca^{++} was calculated by means of the calculator program provided by Fabiato and Fabiato (1979). The absolute stability constants used in the program are those compiled by Fabiato (1981).

Statistical Methods

Values are presented as the mean ± SEM. Significance was determined by Student's *t*-test; a probability of less than 0.05 was regarded as statistically significant.

Experimental Protocol

Tissues were equilibrated initially for a period of 2 hours in PSS at 37°C. During equilibration, the tissues were stretched in a step-wise fashion until a stable force of approximately 7–10 mN/mm segment length was achieved. We have previously determined that a passive tension of this magnitude occurs at a length that is optimal for active force development in aortas from both the control and hypertensive rats (McMahon and Paul, 1984). Calcium sensitivity in the intact vessels was determined in response to both potassium depolarization (50 mM KCl) and norepinephrine stimulation (1 μM NE). The protocol used to measure calcium sensitivity in response to potassium depolarization is illustrated in Figure 1, using an aorta from a control rat. Figure 2 illustrates the same protocol conducted with an aorta from an aldosterone-

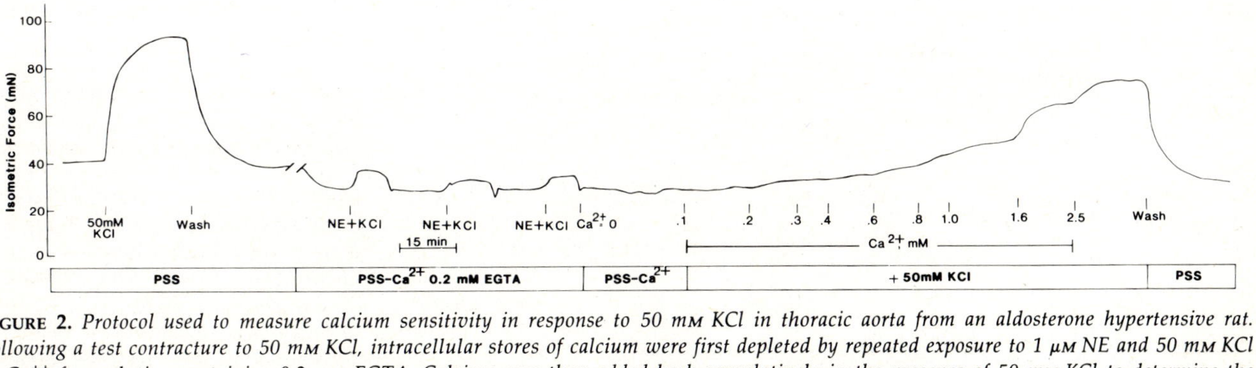

FIGURE 2. *Protocol used to measure calcium sensitivity in response to 50 mM KCl in thoracic aorta from an aldosterone hypertensive rat. Following a test contracture to 50 mM KCl, intracellular stores of calcium were first depleted by repeated exposure to 1 μM NE and 50 mM KCl in Ca^{++}-free solution containing 0.2 mM EGTA. Calcium was then added back cumulatively in the presence of 50 mM KCl to determine the calcium dose-response relationship.*

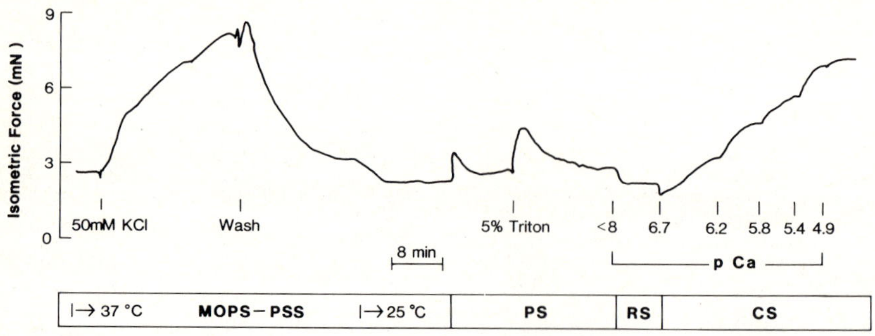

FIGURE 3. *Protocol for measuring calcium sensitivity in Triton X-100 skinned rings of thoracic aorta from a control rat. Before skinning, the isometric tension response to the addition of 50 mM KCl was measured in the intact tissue at 37°C. After the bath temperature was lowered to 25°C, the ring was exposed to a 5% Triton solution for 10 minutes, then rinsed briefly in "relaxing solution" (see Methods). The isometric tension response to increasing concentrations of free Ca^{++} was then recorded to obtain the Ca^{++} dose-response relationship.*

hypertensive rat. Following a test contracture with 50 mM KCl, the vessels were exposed to calcium-free solution containing 0.2 mM EGTA, then repeatedly stimulated with 50 mM KCl and 1 μM NE. This procedure effectively depletes the tissue of intracellular calcium stores, as indicated by the small response to the third application of NE + KCl in Figures 1 and 2. The vessel was then depolarized with 50 mM KCl in calcium-free solution (no EGTA), and the isometric tension response to increasing concentrations of calcium was recorded. The isometric tension responses to the cumulative addition of calcium were considerably slower in the aorta from the AHR (Fig. 2) compared to the control aorta (Fig. 1). However, responses to each concentration of calcium were allowed to reach a steady state level before exposure to the next calcium concentration. Calcium sensitivity in response to NE was measured subsequent to depletion of internal calcium, as in Figures 1 and 2. The vessels then were exposed to a given concentrations of calcium for 5–10 minutes, followed by activation with 1 μM NE. The vessel was then relaxed in Ca^{++}-free PSS and this sequence was repeated with increasing concentrations of calcium. For both KCl and NE, the response to 2.5 mM Ca^{++} was considered maximal. The concentration of calcium required to give the half-maximal response (ED_{50}) was determined by linear interpolation for individual aortas, then averaged.

The protocol for measuring calcium sensitivity in chemically skinned aortic rings is illustrated in Figure 3, using an aorta from a control rat. Figure 4 illustrates the same protocol conducted with an aorta from an aldosterone-hypertensive rat. Prior to the skinning procedure, the intact aortic rings were equilibrated for 2 hours in MOPS-PSS at 37°C. The isometric tension response to the addition of 50 mM KCl was then recorded for comparison with subsequent measurements of isometric force in the skinned preparation. Note, for comparison with results in Figures 1 and 2, where 6-mm rings were used, that in the experiments illustrated in Figures 3 and 4, 1-mm rings were used. After washout of KCl, and relaxation, the bath temperature was lowered to 25°C for the remainder of the experiment. The skinning procedure was initiated by exposing the ring to presoak solution, followed by a 10-minute exposure to 5% Triton X-100. After a rinse in presoak solution to wash out the Triton X-100, the ring was placed in relaxing solution. A lack of response to maximal doses of norepinephrine and caffeine in control experiments verified that the fibers were completely skinned. A cumulative dose-response relationship to Ca^{++} was then obtained by exposing the tissue to increasing concentrations of free Ca^{++}. The ED_{50} for calcium was calculated as the free calcium concentration required to give 50% of the response achieved at pCa = 4.9.

Results

After 4 weeks of infusion, systolic blood pressure in the aldosterone-salt treated group was elevated substantially compared to controls (Table 1). The calcium sensitivity of aortas from these animals was investigated using the protocol depicted in Figures 1 and 2. After depletion of internal calcium stores, the isometric tension response to increasing extracellular calcium concentrations was recorded in depolarized vessels. The results from a series of these experiments are summarized in Figure 5. Isometric tension responses in both the controls and hypertensives have been normalized to the force attained at 2.5 mM Ca^{++} in each group. Maximal active stress in response to 2.5 mM Ca^{++} was similar in controls and hypertensives [C: (n = 7), 30.00 ± 2.62; AHR: (n = 5), 27.90 ± 2.41 mN/mm^2]. Active stress values for each experimental series are henceforth included in the figure legends. Over the entire range of calcium concentrations studied, responses in aortas from the aldosterone hypertensives were significantly depressed when compared to controls. In addition, the shape of the two curves was quite

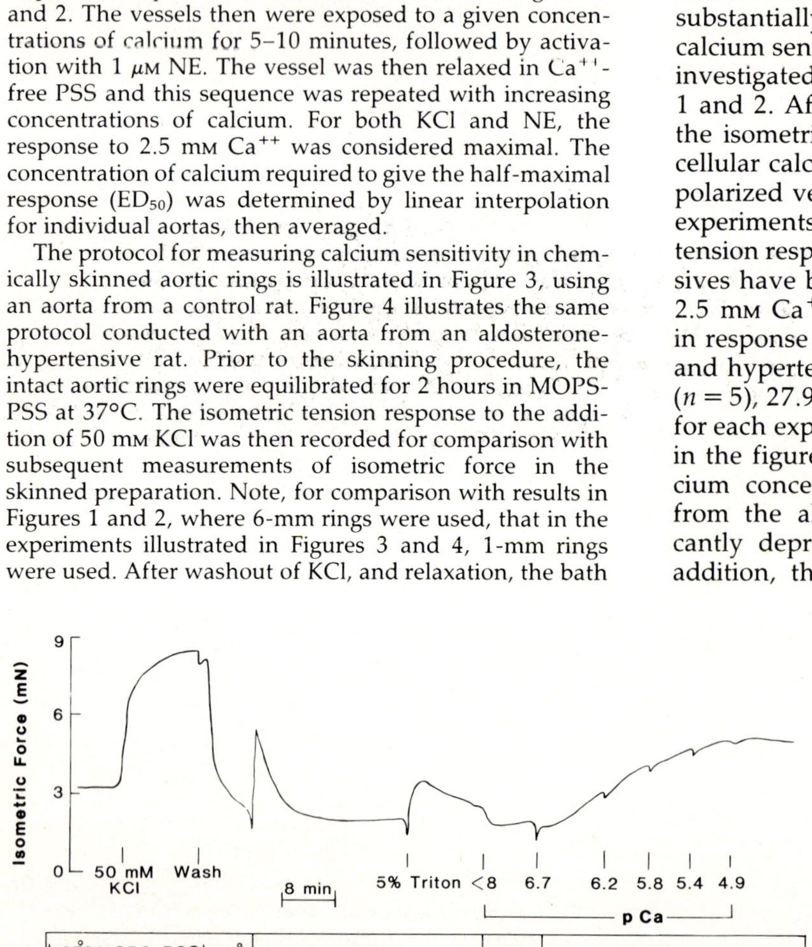

FIGURE 4. *Protocol for measuring calcium sensitivity in Triton X-100 skinned rings of thoracic aorta from an aldosterone-hypertensive rat. Before skinning, the isometric tension response to the addition of 50 mM KCl was measured in the intact tissue at 37°C. After the bath temperature was lowered to 25°C, the ring was exposed to a 5% Triton solution for 10 minutes, then rinsed briefly in "relaxing solution" (see Methods). The isometric tension response to increasing concentrations of free Ca^{++} was then recorded to obtain the Ca^{++} dose-response relationship.*

TABLE 1
Systolic Blood Pressure and Calcium Sensitivity in Intact and Chemically Skinned Aortas during the Development of Aldosterone-Salt Hypertension

	Systolic blood pressure (mm Hg)	Ca^{++} ED_{50} Intact aorta, 50 mM KCl (mM)	Skinned aorta (μM)
Control, 1 wk	118 ± 5 (6)	0.099 ± 0.014 (6)	0.53 ± 0.087 (6)
Aldosterone, 1 wk	133 ± 2* (6)	0.110 ± 0.014 (6)	0.52 ± 0.081 (6)
Control, 2 wk	115 ± 2 (5)	0.114 ± 0.012 (5)	0.44 ± 0.058 (4)
Aldosterone, 2 wk	157 ± 5† (6)	0.192 ± 0.036 (6)	0.50 ± 0.059 (4)
Control, 4 wk	119 ± 2 (14)	0.141 ± 0.021 (7)	0.36 ± 0.057 (9)
Aldosterone, 4 wk	214 ± 6† (14)	0.739 ± 0.137* (6)	0.39 ± 0.081 (8)

Values are means ± SEM for the number of animals given in parentheses.
* $P < 0.025$.
† $P < 0.001$.

different. Responses in the controls reached a plateau level at low concentrations of Ca^{++}, while steady state tension responses in the hypertensives increased in an almost linear fashion over the entire range of extracellular calcium levels tested. The ED_{50} for calcium in aortas from the hypertensives rats was increased 5-fold compared to controls (Table 1). These results indicate that the sensitivity to extracellular calcium induced by membrane depolarization was reduced in vessels from hypertensives compared to controls.

To determine whether calcium sensitivity was similarly altered in vessels from the hypertensives under conditions in which receptor-operated channels are thought to mediate contraction, we examined the dependence of isometric force on extracellular calcium in response to a maximal dose of norepinephrine (1 μM) as described above (see Experimental Protocol). As shown in Figure 6, calcium sensitivity in response to 1 μM NE was similar in aortas from the control and hypertensive rats. The ED_{50} for calcium in controls [($n = 7$) 0.180 ± 0.024 mM] was not significantly different from the value calculated for the hypertensive group [($n = 7$) 0.196 ± 0.022 mM].

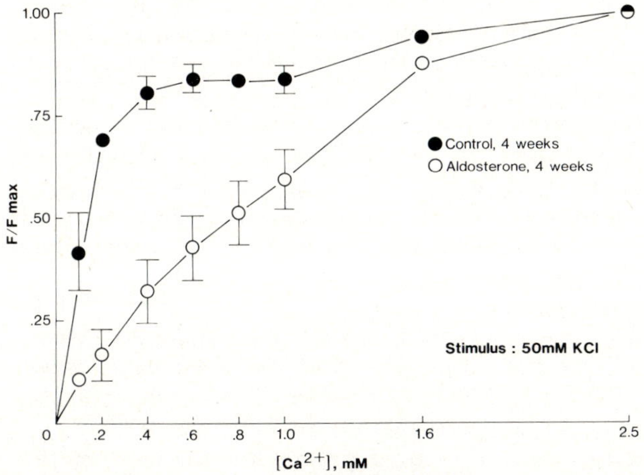

FIGURE 5. *Calcium dose-response relationship in response to 50 mM KCl in aortic rings from control (●, n = 7) and aldosterone-hypertensive rats (○, n = 6). Isometric tension responses have been normalized to the force obtained at 2.5 mM Ca^{++} in each vessel [C: (n = 7), 30.00 ± 2.62; AHR: (n = 5), 27.90 ± 2.41 mN/mm^2]. Each symbol represents the mean value ± SEM, except where the size of the symbol exceeds the SEM.*

The reduced calcium sensitivity in response to depolarization in vessels from hypertensives may reflect an alteration in the excitation-contraction coupling scheme at numerous possible sites. One possibility is that the change in calcium sensitivity is due to altered calcium responsiveness of the contractile system itself. This can be evaluated by measuring calcium responsiveness in a chemically skinned vascular preparation in which the ability of the plasmalemma and other intracellular organelles to buffer cytoplasmic calcium levels has been removed. In such a system, isometric tension responses to increases in extracellular calcium will reflect the calcium sensitivity of the contractile system itself. The protocol for detergent skinning used in this study was detailed previously (see Experimental Protocol, Figs. 3 and 4). As shown in Figure 7, skinned aortic rings contracted substantially in response to an increase in extracellular calcium concentration. Tension responses in skinned aortas from AHR tended to be slightly lower than responses in controls, although maximal force at pCa = 4.9 was not significantly different in the two groups (Fig. 7).

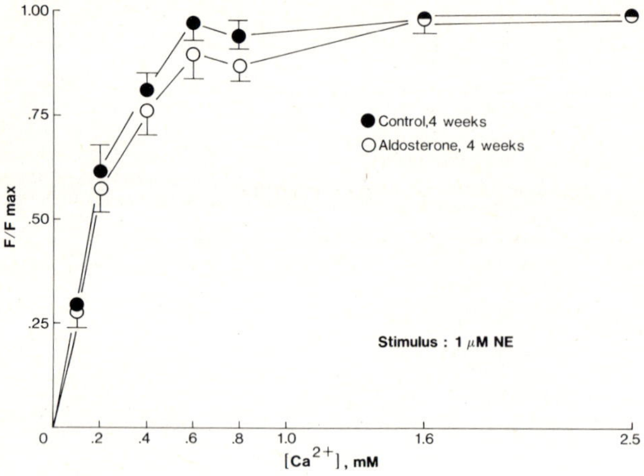

FIGURE 6. *Calcium dose-response relationship in response to 1 μM norepinephrine in aortic rings from control (●, n = 7) and aldosterone-hypertensive rats (○, n = 7). Isometric tension responses have been normalized to the force obtained at 2.5 mM Ca++ in each vessel [C: (n = 7), 24.44 ± 2.54; AHR: (n = 7), 20.96 ± 2.65 mN/mm²]. Each symbol represents the mean ± SEM except where the symbol size exceeds the SEM.*

These maximal responses in the skinned aortas represented 88 ± 12% (AHR, $n = 7$) and 127 ± 29% (C, $n = 6$) of responses to KCl obtained in intact aortic rings before skinning. The ED_{50} for calcium in skinned aortas from the AHR was not significantly different from the value obtained in controls (Table 1). These results indicate that the calcium sensitivity

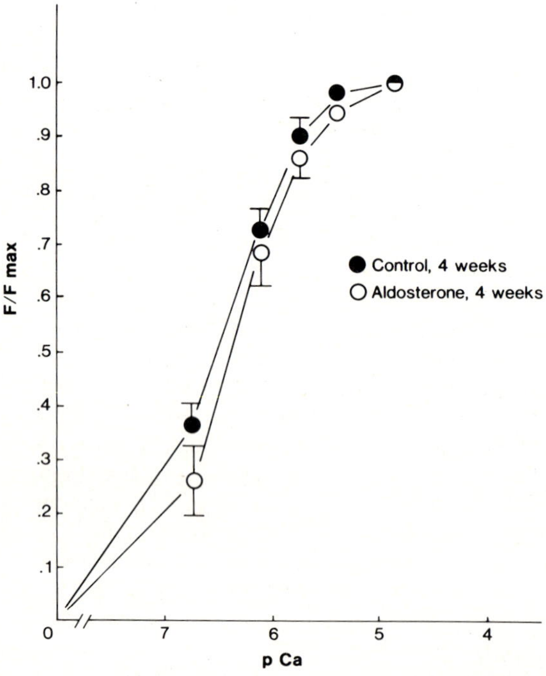

FIGURE 7. *Calcium-dose response relationship in chemically skinned aortic rings from control (●, n = 9) and aldosterone hypertensive rats (○, n = 8). Isometric tension responses have been normalized to the force obtained at pCa = 4.9 in each vessel [C: (n = 9), 4.08 ± 0.36; AHR: (n = 8), 3.99 ± 0.35 mN]. Each symbol represents the mean ± SEM, except where the symbol size exceeds the SEM.*

of the contractile system is similar in aortas from control and hypertensive rats. Therefore, the observed decrease in calcium sensitivity in response to depolarization in intact vessels from hypertensives is not due to a change in the sensitivity of the contractile system, itself, to calcium.

Vascular permeability to monovalent ions has been reported to be increased significantly in aortas from aldosterone-hypertensive rats as early as 1 week after the start of aldosterone-salt treatment (Garwitz and Jones, 1982b). If changes in membrane permeability to calcium follow a similar time course, then calcium permeability may likewise be increased early in the course of the hypertension development. Therefore, the decrease in calcium sensitivity in response to KCl depolarization observed after 4 weeks of aldosterone treatment in the present study may be compensatory to early increases in calcium influx. To investigate this possibility, we measured calcium sensitivity in response to 50 mM KCl in aortas from rats receiving the aldosterone-salt treatment for 1 week and compared it with aortas from age-matched controls receiving 1% NaCl for a similar period of time. After 1 week, systolic blood pressure was marginally elevated in rats receiving aldosterone, compared with controls (Table 1). Although this elevation in pressure was statistically significant, a systolic pressure of 133 mm Hg is similar to previously published values for controls (Jones et al., 1977; Garwitz and Jones, 1982a), and is considered to fall within the normal range for the rat. As shown in Figure 8, calcium sensitivity in response to 50 mM KCl in aortas from the aldosterone-treated rats was similar to controls over the entire range of extracellular calcium concentrations studied. The ED_{50} in the aldosterone-treated group was not significantly different from controls (Table 1).

A second group of animals received the aldosterone-salt treatment for a period of 2 weeks. Systolic blood pressure in these animals was significantly elevated compared with controls receiving 1% NaCl for 2 weeks (Table 1). However, calcium sensitivity in response to 50 mM KCl was not significantly different in aortas from the two groups (Fig. 9). Although the ED_{50} for calcium was slightly increased in the hypertensives compared with controls (Table 1), this difference was not statistically significant. These results do not support the hypothesis that the decrease in calcium permeability under KCl-depolarizing conditions observed after 4 weeks of aldosterone infusion is compensatory to early increases in vascular permeability to calcium. Rather, the trend appears to be a progressive decrease in this calcium permeability during the course of hypertension development.

Aortic segments from the 1- and 2-week aldosterone-treated and control rats were also subjected to detergent treatment, and calcium sensitivity in these skinned aortic preparations was determined by the protocol previously described. The results from

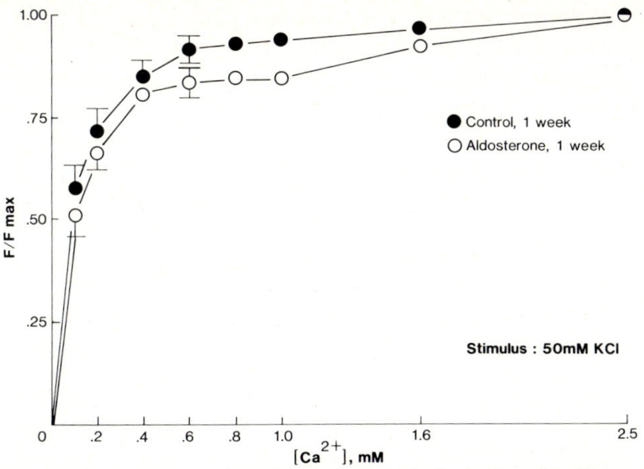

FIGURE 8. *Calcium dose-response relationship in response to 50 mM KCl in aortic rings from controls (●, n = 6) and rats infused with aldosterone for 1 week (○, n = 6). Isometric tension responses have been normalized to the force obtained at 2.5 mM Ca++ in each vessel [C: (n = 6), 25.79 ± 3.97; A: (n = 6), 27.49 ± 3.59 mN/mm²]. Each symbol represents the mean ± SEM, except where the symbol size exceeds the SEM.*

these experiments are summarized on Table 1, along with systolic blood pressure data and calcium ED_{50} levels in intact aortas from the 1-, 2-, and 4-week groups. As with the 4-week animals, after 1 and 2 weeks of aldosterone-salt treatment, the ED_{50} for calcium in the skinned aortas was similar to the value obtained in aortas from age-matched normotensive controls. In addition, these values were similar to values obtained in aortas from rats receiving aldosterone for 4 weeks. Therefore, at no time during the course of hypertension development was there an alteration in the calcium sensitivity of the contractile system itself.

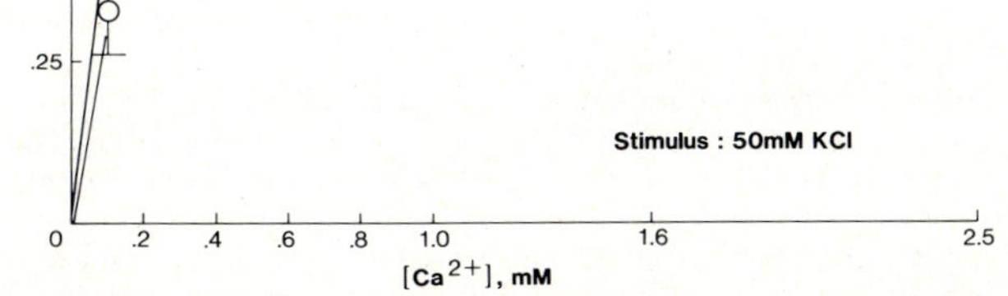

FIGURE 9. *Calcium dose-response relationship in response to 50 mM KCl in aortic rings from controls (●, n = 5) and rats infused with aldosterone for 2 weeks (○, n = 6). Isometric tension responses have been normalized to the force obtained at 2.5 mM Ca++ in each vessel [C: (n = 5), 27.01 ± 3.13; A: (n = 6), 36.69 ± 4.81 mN/mm²]. Each symbol represents the mean ± SEM, except when the symbol size exceeds the SEM.*

Discussion

The calcium sensitivity of isometric force in response to membrane depolarization with high potassium was significantly reduced in aortas from AHR compared to controls. This reduction in sensitivity was not due to an altered calcium sensitivity of the contractile system itself, since calcium sensitivity was similar in chemically skinned aortas from control and hypertensive rats. Furthermore, in response to a maximal dose of norepinephrine, the dependence of isometric force on extracellular calcium in intact aortas from AHR was not significantly different from the calcium sensitivity in aortas from control rats.

It has been proposed that, in smooth muscle, calcium influx stimulated by KCl depolarization occurs through potential-operated calcium channels, whereas NE receptor occupation stimulates calcium influx through a distinct receptor-operated pathway (Bolton, 1979; Van Breemen et al., 1982). In addition, NE receptor occupation stimulates release of calcium from intracellular stores (Van Breemen et al., 1980). Meisheri and coworkers (1981) demonstrated that the NE-stimulated influx of Ca^{++} was additive to that induced by KCl-depolarization, and was not as sensitive to blockade by Ca^{++} antagonists. These data suggest that calcium influx through potential-operated and receptor-operated calcium channels occurs through two distinct pathways. Therefore, the reduction in calcium sensitivity in response to KCl-depolarization in aortas from the AHR suggests an alteration exclusively in potential-operated calcium handling in these vessels. Since calcium sensitivity in response to NE in AHR aortas was similar to that of controls, it is unlikely that intracellular calcium storage and release mechanisms are involved. The reduced level of calcium sensitivity in response to membrane depolarization is thus likely to result from either a reduction in the potential-mediated calcium influx and/or an enhanced rate of calcium efflux in the AHR aorta.

Two calcium extrusion mechanisms have been proposed to operate in vascular smooth muscle, active calcium transport via Ca^{++}-ATPase and Na^{+}-Ca^{++} exchange (Van Breemen et al., 1979). It is currently a matter of debate which mechanism is more crucial to the maintenance of cellular calcium homeostasis, although the bulk of experimental evidence appears to favor the former mechanism (Van Breemen et al., 1982). An enhanced rate of calcium pumping as a mechanism responsible for the reduced calcium sensitivity in AHR would be consistent with previously documented metabolic changes in aortas from AHR (McMahon and Paul, 1984). We have demonstrated that the rate of both basal and stimulated ATP utilization in aortas from AHR are enhanced significantly compared to controls, and that it is unlikely that these increases are due to enhanced Na^{+}-K^{+} transport or inefficient energy utilization by the contractile machinery. An elevated rate of calcium extrusion via a Ca^{++}-ATPase is a possible factor underlying this enhanced energy utilization in AHR, although further study is required to test this hypothesis adequately. On the other hand, it is not possible to rule out decreased calcium influx in response to membrane depolarization as a potential factor underlying the reduced calcium sensitivity in aortas from the hypertensives. Calcium flux studies would be required to assess this possibility adequately.

This study indicates that the time course and directionality of changes in calcium metabolism during the development of aldosterone-salt hypertension in the rat differ substantially compared to alterations in monovalent ion metabolism. Passive membrane permeability to potassium and chloride in rat aorta is increased as early as 1 week after the initiation of aldosterone-salt treatment, and permeability increases steadily as the hypertension progresses (Garwitz and Jones, 1982b). In contrast, calcium sensitivity in response to membrane depolarization, while unchanged after 1 week of aldosterone-salt treatment, decreased progressively during the development of hypertension. Thus, changes in calcium handling appear to lag somewhat behind changes in monovalent ion metabolism. This result suggests that a resetting of membrane excitation mechanisms through changes in passive permeability to Na^+, K^+, and Cl^- might play a more important causal role in the development of aldosterone-salt hypertension than changes in calcium-handling properties.

In contrast to most previous reports on calcium sensitivity in arteries from mineralocorticoid hypertensive rats, our study demonstrates that the development of this form of hypertension is not always accompanied by an enhancement of arterial calcium sensitivity. Whereas calcium responsiveness to NE remained unchanged during the course of hypertension development in AHR aorta, potential-mediated calcium sensitivity actually decreased compared to controls. This reduction in calcium sensitivity in aortas from AHR may not be unique to mineralocorticoid-dependent hypertension, since Pedersen and coworkers (1978) report a similar reduction in SHR aortas, although others have reported an enhanced calcium sensitivity (Holloway and Bohr, 1973; Noon et al., 1978; Mulvany and Nyborg, 1980). These discrepant results obtained in studies using vessels from SHR may partially reflect the diverse ages of the SHR used, as well as the control animal utilized. In mineralocorticoid-dependent models in the rat, the divergent results may be due to differences in the artery chosen for study, since caudal artery (Hinke, 1966) has been compared to femoral (Holloway and Bohr, 1973), carotid (Bohr, 1974), and mesenteric arteries (Kwan et al., 1979). Although a consensus on the importance of alterations in calcium handling in hypertension is not possible at this time, it is clear that responses in a particular type of hypertension may be quite different compared to responses in other forms of the disease. Moreover, within a given model of hypertension, calcium-handling responses in different arteries may also be unique. Our results indicate that the altered level of calcium sensitivity in response to membrane depolarization in aortas from AHR is primarily a membrane phenomenon and probably does not reflect alterations in the regulatory mechanisms of the contractile system itself.

Supported in part by: NIH 23240; HL 06769 (EGM); Southwest Ohio Chapter of the American Heart Association; an Established Investigatorship (RJP) of the AHA.

Address for reprints: Dr. Ellen G. McMahon, Department of Physiology, 231 Bethesda Avenue, University of Cincinnati, Cincinnati, OH 45267-0576.

Received August 6, 1984; accepted for publication December 20, 1984.

References

Bohr DF (1974) Reactivity of vascular smooth muscle from normal and hypertensive rats: Effect of several cations. Fed Proc **33:** 127–132

Bolton TB (1979) Mechanisms of action of transmitters and other substances in smooth muscle. Physiol Rev **3:** 606–718

Fabiato A (1981) Myoplasmic free calcium concentration reached during the twitch of an intact isolated cardiac cell and during calcium-induced release from the sarcoplasmic reticulum of a skinned cardiac cell from the adult rat or rabbit ventricle. J Gen Physiol **78:** 457–497

Fabiato A, Fabiato F (1979) Calculator programs for computing the composition of the solutions containing multiple metals and ligands used for experiments in skinned muscle cells. J Physiol (Paris) **75:** 463–505

Friedman M, Freed SC (1949) Microphonic manometer for indirect determination of systolic blood pressure in the rat. Proc Soc Exp Biol Med **70:** 670–672

Garwitz ET, Jones AW (1982a) Aldosterone infusion into the rat and dose-dependent changes in blood pressure and arterial ionic transport. Hypertension **4:** 374–381

Garwitz ET, Jones AW (1982b) Altered arterial ion transport and its reversal in aldosterone hypertensive rat. Am J Physiol **243:** H927–H933

Hansen TR, Bohr DF (1975) Hypertension, transmural pressure, and vascular smooth muscle responses in rats. Circ Res **36:** 590–598

Hinke JAM (1966) Effect of Ca^{++} upon contractility of small arteries from DOCA-hypertensive rats. Circ Res **18/19** (suppl I): I23–I34

Holloway ET, Bohr DF (1973) Reactivity of vascular smooth muscle in hypertensive rats. Circ Res **33:** 678–685

Jones AW (1974) Altered ion transport in large and small arteries from spontaneously hypertensive rats and the influence of calcium. Circ Res **34** (suppl I): 117–122

Jones AW (1983) Vascular smooth muscle-arterial tissue cations. *In* Hypertension: Physiopathology and Treatment, edited by J Genest, O Kuchel, P Hamet, M Cantin. New York, McGraw-Hill, pp 488–498

Jones AW, Sander PD, Kampschmidt DL (1977) The effect of norepinephrine on aortic ^{42}K turnover during deoxycorticosterone acetate hypertension and antihypertensive therapy in the rat. Circ Res **41:** 256–260

Kwan CY, Belbeck I, Daniel EE (1979) Abnormal biochemistry of vascular smooth muscle plasma membrane as an important factor in the initiation and maintenance of hypertension in rats. Blood Vessels **16:** 259–268

McMahon EG, Paul RJ (1984) Metabolic and mechanical properties of aortas from aldosterone-salt hypertensive rats. Circ Res **55:** 349–357

Meisheri KD, Hwang O, Van Breemen C (1981) Evidence for two separate Ca^{2+} pathways in smooth muscle plasmalemma. J Membr Biol **59:** 19–25

Moore L, Hurwitz L, Davenport GR, Landon EJ (1975) Energy-dependent calcium uptake activity of microsomes from the aorta of normal and hypertensive rats. Biochim Biophys Acta **413:** 432–443

Moreland RS, Webb RC, Bohr DF (1982) Vascular changes in DOCA hypertension-influence of a low protein diet. Hypertension **4** (suppl III): 99–107

Mulvany MJ, Nyborg N (1980) An increased calcium sensitivity of mesenteric resistance vessels in young and adult spontaneously hypertensive rats. Br J Pharmacol **71:** 585–596

Nghiem CX, Rapp JP (1983) Responses to calcium of chemically skinned vascular smooth muscle from spontaneously hypertensive rats. Clin Exp Hyper Theory Practice **A5:** 849–856

Noon JP, Rice PJ, Baldessarini RJ (1978) Calcium leakage as a cause of the high resting tension in vascular smooth muscle from the spontaneously hypertensive rat. Proc Natl Acad Sci USA **75:** 1605–1607

Pedersen OL, Mikkelsen E, Andersson KE (1978) Effects of extracellular calcium on potassium and noradrenaline induced contractions in aorta of spontaneously hypertensive rats: Increased sensitivity to nifedipine. Acta Pharmacol Toxicol **43:** 137–144

Rüegg JC, Paul RJ (1982) Calmodulin and cyclic AMP-dependent protein kinase alter calcium sensitivity in porcine carotid skinned fibers. Circ Res **48:** 539–548

Seidel CL (1979) Aortic actomyosin content of maturing normal and spontaneously hypertensive rats. Am J Physiol **237:** H34–H39

Twietmeyer TA, Bhalla RC, Maynard JA (1978) Acid and alkaline phosphatase activities and calcium transport in aortic smooth muscle from DOCA hypertensive rats. J Mol Cell Cardiol **10:** 1131–1140

Van Breemen C, Aaronson P, Loutzenhiser R (1979) Na-Ca interactions in mammalian smooth muscle. Pharmacol Rev **30:** 167–208

Van Breemen C, Aaronson P, Loutzenhiser R, Meisheri K (1980) Ca^{2+} movements in smooth muscle. Chest **78:** 1575–1655

Van Breemen C, Aaronson P, Loutzenhiser R, Meisheri K (1982) Calcium fluxes in isolated rabbit aorta and guinea pig *Tenia coli*. Fed Proc **41:** 2891–2897

Webb RC, Bhalla RC (1976) Altered calcium sequestration by subcellular fractions of vascular smooth muscle from spontaneously hypertensive rats. J Mol Cell Cardiol **8:** 651–661

Winquist RJ, Bohr DF (1983) Structural and functional changes in cerebral arteries from spontaneously hypertensive rats. Hypertension **5:** 292–297

INDEX TERMS: Vascular smooth muscle • Hypertension • Aldosterone • Salt (NaCl) • Chemical skinning • Calcium sensitivity

Structural and Electrophysiological Changes in the Epicardial Border Zone of Canine Myocardial Infarcts during Infarct Healing

Philip C. Ursell, Phyllis I. Gardner, Arline Albala, John J. Fenoglio, Jr., and Andrew L. Wit
From the Departments of Pathology and Pharmacology, College of Physicians and Surgeons of Columbia University, New York, New York

SUMMARY. Structural and electrophysiological properties of the epicardial muscle which survives on the surface of transmural infarcts of the canine heart (epicardial border zone) were studied at different times after occlusion of the left anterior coronary artery (LAD). Isolated preparations were superfused in vitro, transmembrane potentials recorded, and impulse propagation mapped. In preparations from subacute infarcts (1 and 5 days), resting potential, action potential amplitude, upstroke velocity, and duration were all significantly reduced. Well-defined directional differences in propagation occurred. Propagation was more rapid in the direction perpendicular to the left anterior coronary artery than in the direction perpendicular to the base of the heart, because of the uniform anisotropic structure of the surviving muscle fibers which were arranged in tightly packed bundles oriented perpendicular to the left anterior coronary artery. The only ultrastructural abnormalities found in these muscle fibers was an accumulation of large amounts of lipid droplets. As the infarcts healed, resting potential, action potential amplitude, and upstroke velocity returned to normal by 2 weeks, although action potential duration decreased further. Lipid droplets had disappeared, and connective tissue had invaded the epicardial border zone, separating the muscle bundles. By 2 months, action potentials were normal, but the muscle fibers were widely separated and disoriented by the connective tissue (parallel bundles no longer were found). In these regions with a nonuniform anisotropic structure, the well-defined directional differences in impulse propagation were lost. However, activation was very slow, perhaps because of diminished connections between cells. The persistence of slow conduction in healed infarcts may contribute to the occurrence of chronic arrhythmias. **(*Circ Res 56: 436–451, 1985*)**

A BORDER zone of muscle cells survives on the epicardial surface of transmural canine infarcts caused by complete occlusion of the left anterior descending coronary artery (LAD). The importance of this region stems from the observation that reentrant excitation occurs here, causing ventricular tachycardia during the first week, and possibly later, following the coronary occlusion (El-Sherif et al., 1977a, 1977b, 1981; Wit et al., 1982; Mehra et al., 1983). The goal of our study was to characterize some of the electrophysiological, histological, and ultrastructural properties of muscle cells in this epicardial border zone and to determine whether these properties change with time as the infarct heals (Ursell et al., 1982a, 1982b). Definition of the evolution of electrophysiological and structural properties may help to elucidate underlying mechanisms causing reentry in this region.

Methods

Surgical Production of Myocardial Infarction

Myocardial infarction was produced in 47 mongrel dogs weighing 10–15 kg by a two-stage ligation of the LAD, by the technique described by Harris (1950). A detailed description of our surgical procedure has been given in previously published reports (Friedman et al., 1973a, 1973b). The chest then was closed in layers, and an airtight seal was established. Thirty-one dogs survived the occlusion. These dogs developed ventricular arrhythmias consisting of multiple premature depolarizations or ventricular tachycardia by 20–24 hours after the surgical procedure. The spontaneously occurring arrhythmias subsided by the 3rd day.

At various times, ranging from 1 day to 18 months after coronary occlusion, the surviving dogs were reanesthetized with sodium pentobarbital (15–30 mg/kg, iv) for the electrophysiological study. Five animals were studied at 1 day, eight at 5 days, six at 2 weeks, seven at 2 months, and four at 8–18 months. We chose these times because they represent periods during the subacute (1–5 days), healing (2 weeks), and healed (2–18 months) phases of myocardial infarction. We characterized the anatomical and electrophysiological properties of the muscle on the epicardial surface of the infarct at each of these different stages. In addition, three sham-operated dogs that had undergone the identical surgical procedure, including coronary artery dissection, but without occlusion, were included in the study. Five normal dogs that had not undergone any previous surgery served as controls.

In Vitro Electrophysiological Studies

After induction of anesthesia on the day of the study, electrocardiograms were taken from all the dogs. The heart then was exposed through a thoracotomy on the left side, between the 5th and 6th ribs. A 20 × 20 × 3-mm piece of myocardium was then excised rapidly with a sharp scalpel blade from the epicardial aspect of the infarcted left ventricle while it was still in situ. The infarcted region was visually identified by its mottled appearance. The excised myocardium was immediately pinned to the waxed base of a 25-ml superfusion chamber, epicardial surface upward, and superfused with oxygenated Tyrode's solution at a rate of 50–75 ml/min. The composition of the Tyrode's solution was (in mM/liter); NaCl, 137; $NaHCO_3$, 24; dextrose, 5.5; NaH_2PO_4, 1.8; $MgCl_2$, 0.5; $CaCl_2$, 2.5; and KCl, 4.0. The solution was briskly gassed with a 95% O_2-5% CO_2 mixture, both in the reservoir and in the bath. The pH of the Tyrode's solution in the tissue bath under these conditions was 7.30–7.35. The temperature was maintained constant at 36.5 ± 0.5°C. The isolated preparations were stimulated through Teflon-coated bipolar silver wire electrodes with isolated square pulses 1–2 msec in duration, at twice diastolic threshold. The stimuli were generated by a Devices gated pulse generator (type 2521). The basic stimulus cycle length was 1000 msec for all experiments.

After an initial equilibration period of 60 minutes, transmembrane action potentials were recorded from subepicardial fibers at 25–35 sites over the entire epicardial surface of the preparations with glass capillary microelectrodes filled with 3 M KCl. The tip resistances of the microelectrodes were 10–30 megohms, and tip potentials were less negative than 5 mV. At each recording site, action potentials were recorded from the most superficial subepicardial fiber, i.e., the first transmembrane potential recorded as the microelectrode was advanced downward by the micrometer drive of the micromanipulator. Action potentials were also recorded from underlying fibers. Membrane potentials were recorded between the microelectrode—which was coupled through a silver/silver chloride junction to a high input impedance amplifier with capacitance neutralization—and a reference half-cell (Ag/AgCl black pellet) which connected the bath to ground. Membrane potentials were displayed on a Tektronix 565 oscilloscope, along with a reference bipolar electrogram which was recorded with Teflon-coated silver wire electrodes. Membrane potentials and electrograms were photographed with a Grass C4 oscilloscope camera. Action potentials were displayed simultaneously at oscilloscopic sweep speeds of 50 and 1–0.2 msec/cm. Resting membrane potential, amplitude, and duration of the action potential at 50% and 90% repolarization were calculated from photographs taken at the 50 msec/cm sweep speed, whereas $\dot{V}_{max}$ of phase 0 (slope of the most vertical tangent to the upstroke) was calculated from photographs taken at the 1–0.2 msec/cm sweep speeds. The depth of the fluid over the preparation was maintained at a minimal level (<5 mm) to minimize capacitance in the recording system. Capacitance neutralization of the amplifier was adjusted when necessary (Friedman et al., 1973a).

We determined the mean value for each of the measured parameters in each preparation. For the control and each time period, the mean of the mean values for each preparation within the group was calculated. We then compared the mean values of the different groups. A statistical difference was evaluated first by using an analysis of variance F-test on the groups of data and then by either an unpaired Student's *t*-test or a modified *t*-test for populations of unequal variance (Snedecor and Cochran, 1967). All results are presented as mean ± SD; *P* values less than 0.05 were considered significant. An effort was made to collect data equally from all regions of each preparation. However, the increased thickness of the endocardium in the healed infarct preparations sometimes prevented recordings from being obtained at some sites.

To elucidate whether the changes in transmembrane potentials and structure which occur during the healing process influenced conduction characteristics, we mapped impulse propagation while stimulating the preparations at a regular rate from different sites. Extracellular waveforms were recorded through unipolar or bipolar Teflon-coated silver wire electrodes with a 0.3-mm tip diameter. When unipolar recordings were obtained, the indifferent electrode was located in the bath, approximately 3 cm from the recording electrode. Activation maps were constructed from electrogram recordings obtained at 70–100 sites within regions measuring approximately 200 mm^2. In our initial experiments, we recorded electrograms sequentially by moving a "roving" recording electrode in 1-mm intervals with the micrometer drive of the micromanipulator. Activation time at each site was measured in relation to a fixed reference electrode near the stimulation site and plotted on a diagrammatic representation of the preparation. Periodically, while activation sequence was being determined, the "roving" electrode was returned to sites at which electrical activity had previously been recorded to verify that activation time and electrogram waveform morphology had not changed; if they had, the experiment was not continued and the data were discarded. With this technique, it took 20–30 minutes to complete a map. Later experiments were done with a multiple electrode-recording system which enabled us to record unipolar electrograms simultaneously from 96 sites. An electrode array resembling a bristle brush was constructed by embedding 96 Teflon-coated silver wires in a sheet of 2-mm-thick plexiglass, 2.5 × 2.5 cm. Each wire extended about 2 mm through the plexiglass sheet, thus forming the bristles of this "brush." Each electrode contact was 1 mm from the others. The "brush" was attached with an aluminum rod to the mechanical stage of a micromanipulator and positioned on the surface of the tissue preparations. Each electrode lead was fed into one of a group of 96 preamplifiers with automatic gain controlled by a microprocessor. The input has a bandwidth of 10–1000 Hz. The signals were multiplexed and sampled at a frequency of 4000 samples/sec (each signal sampled at a 0.25-msec interval) and digitized by an 8-bit analog-to-digital converter. The digitized signals were converted to Miller[2] code by means of an Ampex pulse code modulation system, and were stored on wide-band tape (Ampex). The digitized signals were then put on the disk of a PDP 11/34 computer and the electrograms displayed in groups of seven on a Tektronix 4012 graphics terminal. The moments of activation were marked by hand with the cursor. Activation times in relation to a reference time were then calculated by the computer, and activation maps displayed. Placement of the electrode brush on the tissue did not hinder adequate superfusion, which occurred through the bristles. Stable electrograms were recorded throughout the experimental period. With this multiple electrode array, a complete activation map of a single stimulated impulse could be readily constructed. As a consequence, the electrode was in position on the tissue for less than 5 minutes at a time.

We also mapped activation in some of the preparations from healed infarcts with a microelectrode. This was done when electrograms showed a high degree of fractionation (contained multiple components) (Gardner et al., 1982), making it difficult to assign a moment of activation to them, or when impulse propagation was studied in very small regions. Transmembrane potentials were recorded sequentially from multiple sites, as described above for the "roving" extracellular electrode. Activation at each site was measured in relation to a reference electrode near the stimulation site.

Electron Microscopy and Histology

Tissue for electron microscopy was obtained at two different times during each experiment. First, fresh tissue directly adjacent to the patch of epicardial muscle removed for the electrophysiological study was excised from the in situ beating heart, blocked, and cut into 1-mm^3 pieces, and fixed immediately. Tissue for electron microscopy was also obtained from some of the Tyrode's superfused preparations after the microelectrode studies had been completed. Samples were cut from the epicardial surface in either of two ways: (1) a 3 × 3-mm sample of tissue, 1–2 mm thick, was excised and cut into 1-mm^3 pieces, or (2) a core of tissue 1.5 × 1.5 mm, approximately 4 mm deep, was cut and divided into superficial (epicardial) and deep portions. All tissue was fixed and embedded as previously described (Friedman et al., 1975; Fenoglio et al., 1976). Care was then taken to orient tissue in the embedding mold so that sectioning would occur perpendicular to the plane of the epicardial surface. When oriented in this way, the epicardial surface formed one margin of the section.

Ultrathin sections were cut with diamond knives on a Porter-Blum MT-2 ultramicrotome, stained with lead citrate and uranyl acetate, and examined in a Siemens Elmiskop electron microscope. The epicardium could be identified in each section, and thus the location of ventricular muscle cells relative to the epicardial surface was known. In sections from deeper blocks not containing the epicardial surface, identification of the infarct by its ultrastructural characteristics enabled us to determine the relationship of surviving muscle to necrotic muscle.

After excision of tissue for electron microscopy, the entire preparation of epimyocardium which had been studied in the superfusion chamber was fixed in 10% neutral buffered formaldehyde. The side that had been closest to the LAD was marked with India ink. After fixation, the entire tissue was sliced into five pieces cut perpendicular to the LAD border and perpendicular to the plane of the epicardium. The slices then were processed for histology according to routine methods. Five-micron-thick sections were cut from the face of each paraffin-embedded block. Each histological section, stained with hematoxylin-phloxine-saffron, showed the full thickness of the tissue preparation from the epicardial surface to where the muscle was cut from the ventricular wall. From these sections, we determined the thickness of the epicardial sheet of ventricular muscle that survived over the infarcts in these hearts, as well as the orientation of the muscle fibers. In five experiments on subacute infarcts, the number of surviving (intact) muscle cell layers that constituted this sheet was determined at 40–50 equidistant points along the length of each section. This analysis was done on sections cut at three different levels in each block, i.e., 15 sections per experiment. We then plotted the number of surviving layers on a graphic representation of the ventricular epicardial surface to provide a topographic map of the surviving epicardial muscle.

Results

In this paper, we report only data from those infarcts which were transmural, because reentrant excitation has been mapped on the epicardial surface of this type of infarct (El-Sherif et al., 1981; Wit et al., 1982; Mehra et al., 1983). The infarcts were present in similar locations on the anterior left ventricle in all dogs. The medial border was adjacent to the LAD and extended from near the apex, approximately 5 cm toward the base. The infarcts often extended to the lateral free wall of the left ventricle.

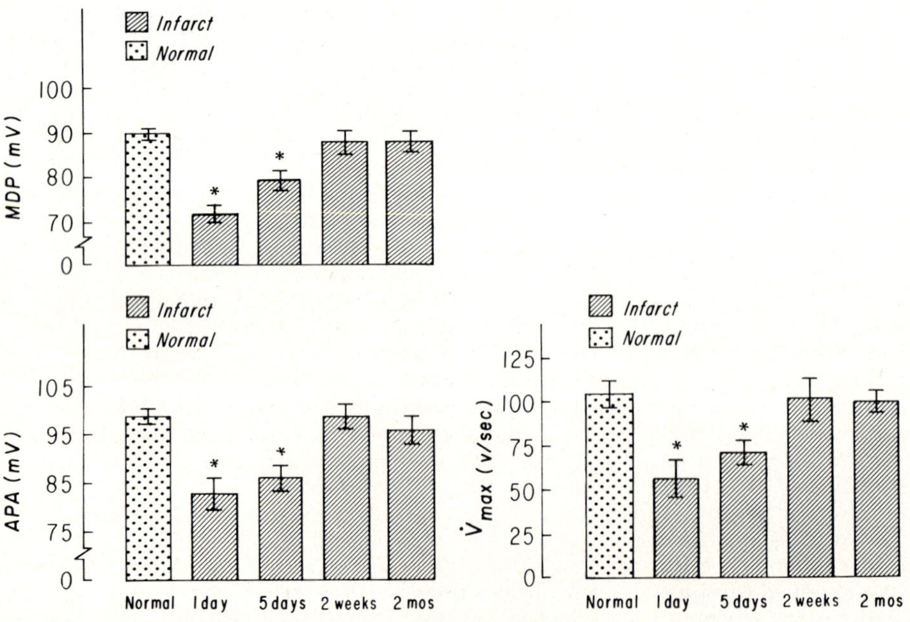

FIGURE 1. *Changes in maximum diastolic potential (MDP), total action potential amplitude (APA), and rate of phase 0 depolarization ($\dot{V}_{max}$) of surviving epicardial muscle fibers with increasing time after coronary occlusion. Column heights represent mean values for the first "layer" of muscle fibers beneath the epicardial surface in preparations from noninfarcted hearts (stippled columns) and in each group of infarcted preparations (ruled columns) studied at the time indicated on the abscissa. Brackets indicate ± standard deviation. The number of impalements from which mean values were calculated in this and Figure 2 are noninfarcted—353 impalements in eight preparations; 1-day infarcts—295 impalements in five preparations; 5-day infarcts—283 impalements in eight preparations; 2 week infarcts—169 impalements in six preparations; 2-month infarcts—180 impalements in seven preparations. Asterisks denote values significantly different from controls ($P < 0.01$).*

Characteristics of Epicardial Muscle, 1 and 5 Days after Coronary Artery Occlusion (the Subacute Phase)

Transmembrane Potentials

At any one site in the *noninfarcted* preparations, transmembrane potentials could be recorded from at least five to eight cells as the microelectrode was advanced downward. The mean values for maximum diastolic potential, action potential amplitude, phase 0 $\dot{V}_{max}$, and action potential duration of the control, normal ventricular muscle in the first epicardial muscle cell layer are shown by the control bars in the graphs in Figures 1 and 2. The transmembrane potentials recorded from subepicardial ventricular muscle fibers of the three sham-operated dogs were no different from the normals, which had had no prior surgery. The data from the sham-operated animals, therefore, were combined with the nonoperated normals for comparisons with the infarct preparations.

At many of the recording sites in the infarcted preparations, transmembrane potentials could only

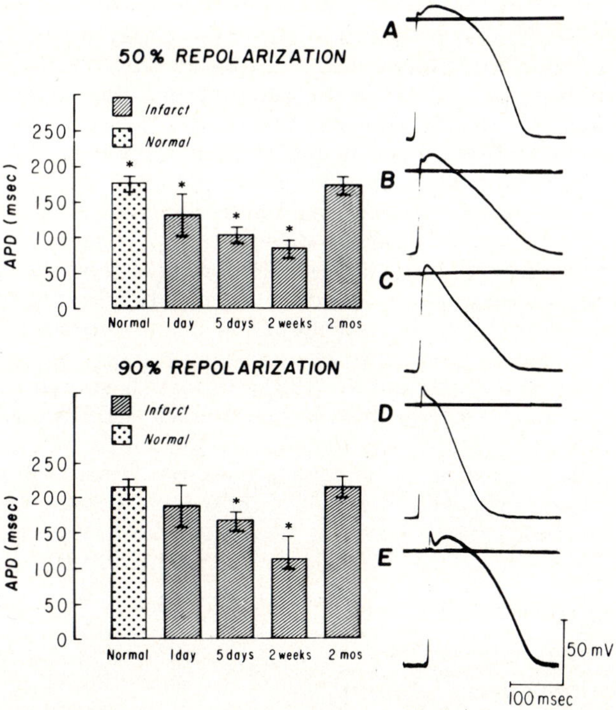

FIGURE 2. *Changes in action potential duration (APD) measured to 50% repolarization (above left) and 90% repolarization (below left) of epicardial muscle fibers with increasing time after coronary artery ligation. Column heights represent mean values for the first layer of muscle fibers beneath the epicardial surface in normal noninfarcted preparations (stippled columns) and in each group of infarcted preparations (ruled columns) studied at the times indicated on the abscissa. Brackets indicate ± standard deviation. Asterisks denote values significantly different from control. At the right are shown representative transmembrane potential recordings; A is normal, B is 1 day, C is 5 days, D is 2 weeks, and E is 2 months.*

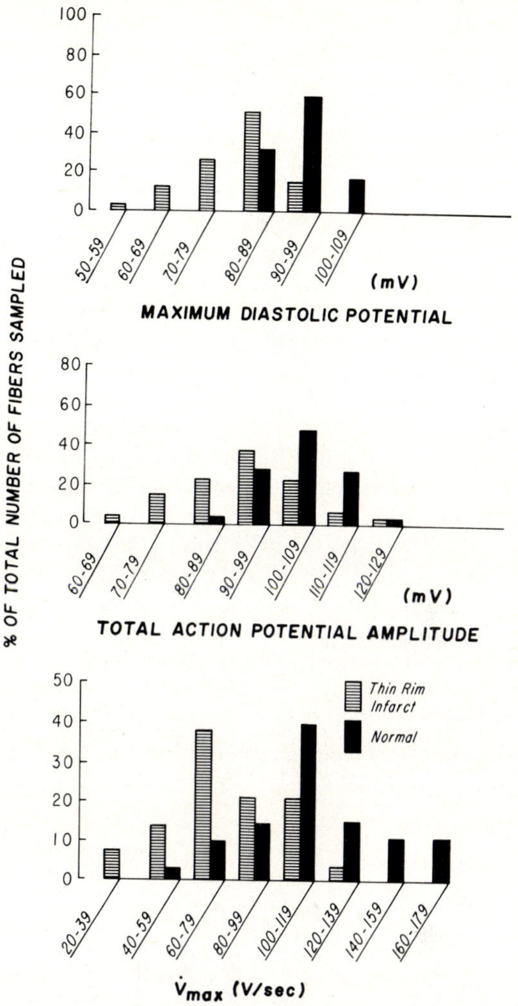

FIGURE 3. *Frequency distribution of values for maximum diastolic potential, action potential amplitude, and $\dot{V}_{max}$ from epicardial muscle fibers in normal, noninfarcted preparations (solid columns) and in preparations from hearts with 5-day-old infarcts (ruled columns). The values on the ordinate represent the percent of the total number of fibers impaled, having values within the defined intervals indicated on the abscissa. Note that most fibers in normal preparations had maximum diastolic potentials of 90 mV or more and amplitudes of 100 mV or more, whereas a large percentage of fibers in the infarcted preparations had much lower values.*

be recorded from one to three cells, as the microelectrode was advanced downward. Only the transmembrane potential characteristics of the first cell layer were quantified in the graphs shown in Figures 1–4, but there did not seem to be major differences in action potential characteristics that were dependent on how far into the subepicardium the microelectrode was advanced. The transmembrane potentials of the surviving epimyocardial fibers 1 and 5 days after coronary occlusion were different from those muscle fibers in normal preparations. Figure 1 shows that the mean values for maximum diastolic potential, action potential amplitude, and $\dot{V}_{max}$ of phase 0 were significantly reduced ($P < 0.001$). Only the maximum diastolic potential at 1 day was significantly less than at 5 days. A change that was particularly striking was that the action potentials had little plateau phase during repolarization, and the action potential duration was decreased, more so in 5-day-old than in 1-day-old infarcts (Fig. 2). Although this characteristic can result from acute anoxia caused by diminished Po_2 in the superfusion solution (Carmeliet, 1978), acute anoxia was not the cause here, since, under these experimental conditions, a well-defined plateau was recorded from muscle in normal preparations. These characteristics remained relatively stable over the 2- to 3-hour time period of the experiment.

There was variability in the transmembrane potential characteristics from one recording site to another. This variability for the 5-day infarcts is illustrated in Figures 3 and 4; similar variability also was found for 1-day infarcts. Severely depressed diastolic potentials (<-70 mV) and action potential upstrokes ($\dot{V}_{max}$ <60 V/sec) were sometimes seen under our experimental conditions. We did not encounter action potentials that had the characteristics of slow responses, as defined by Cranefield (1975).

Conduction

We determined activation patterns by mapping impulse propagation 1–3 hours after the preparations were isolated. The preparations were first driven from electrodes on the LAD margin (margin located adjacent to the left anterior descending coronary artery prior to excision from the heart) and then from electrodes on the basal margin (margin toward the base of the heart prior to excision). The activation patterns from the two different stimulation sites were compared. Identical results were obtained with the different techniques for mapping, described in Methods. The characteristics of conduction in the 1- and 5-day-old infarcts were similar. Figure 5 shows data from representative experiments on 5-day infarct preparations. The map at the top left shows activation of the epicardial muscle when the stimulating electrode was at the LAD margin, and the map at the bottom left shows activation of the same region when the stimulating electrode was at the basal margin. As is evident in the figure, the isochrones are widely spaced when activation occurred in the direction perpendicular to the LAD margin (top left), and are close together when activation occurred in the direction perpendicular to the basal margin (bottom left). Thus, the speed of activation is dependent on the direction of activation. The panel at the right in the figure shows the apparent conduction velocities (calculated in directions perpendicular to the isochrones) for another similar preparation. The most rapid apparent conduction velocity of 0.25 m/sec was in the direction perpendicular to the LAD margin; the slowest apparent conduction velocity of 0.07 m/sec was in the direction perpendicular to the basal margin. The conduction velocity also varied monotonically between these two axes. Although apparent conduction velocities varied in different preparations, this pattern was always found with a ratio of most rapid to slowest apparent conduction velocity of between 2.5 and 4.0:1. These conduction characteristics are those of a uniformly anisotropic structure, as described by Spach et al. (1981). In fact, as shown by the results of the histological studies described in the next section, the structure of the surviving epicardial muscle in the subacute infarcts is uniformly anisotropic. The direction of most rapid conduction in these experiments was always parallel to the long axis of myocardial fiber orientation; the direction of slowest conduction was perpendicular to the long axis.

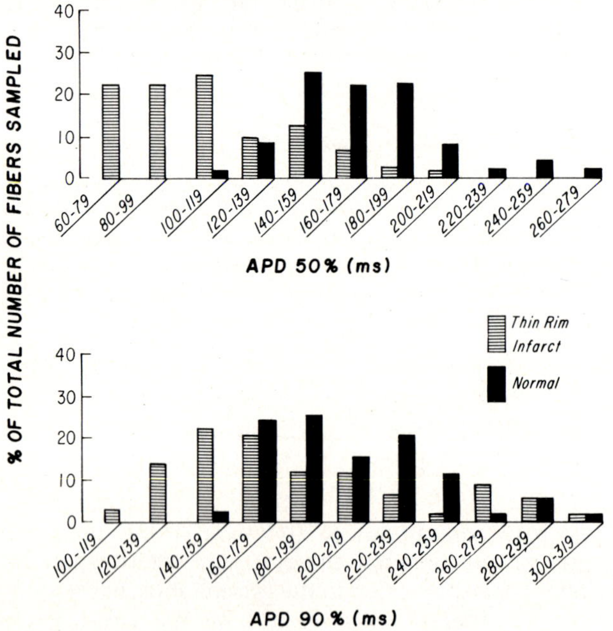

FIGURE 4. *Frequency distribution of time to 50% repolarization (APD_{50}) (top) and time to 90% repolarization (bottom) of epicardial muscle fibers in normal noninfarcted preparations (solid columns) and in preparations from hearts with 5-day-old infarcts (ruled columns). The values on the ordinate represent the percent of the total number of fibers having values within the defined intervals indicated on the abscissa. Note that most of the action potentials recorded from noninfarcted preparations had durations to 50% repolarization of 140–200 msec and that most epicardial muscle fibers surviving over infarcts had durations less than 120 msec, indicating the absence of the plateau.*

Histology and Ultrastructure

The infarcts on which the electrophysiological studies were done were transmural; they extended from the subendocardium to the subepicardium. Beneath the epicardium was a rim of normal-appearing ventricular muscle cells overlying the infarct zone (Fig. 6). Within the infarct zone at 1 day (and beneath the normal-appearing cells), the myocardial fibers were separated by interstitial edema and, in a few cases, hemorrhage. These fibers were somewhat hyperchromatic and lacked nuclei, histological char-

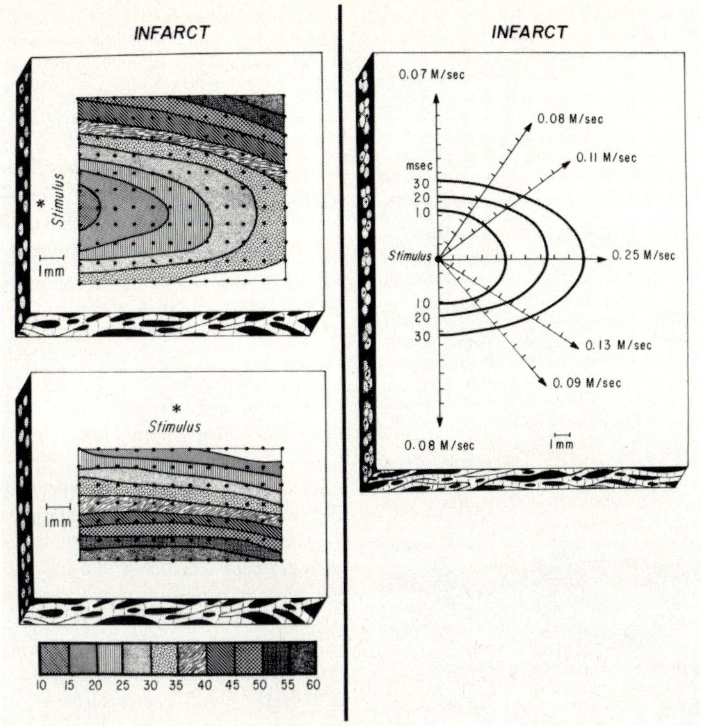

FIGURE 5. *Activation maps of an epicardial preparation from a 5-day-old infarct. At the top left is shown the pattern of activation when the stimulus site (indicated by the asterisk) was on the LAD margin. At the bottom left is shown the pattern of activation of the same region when the stimulus site (indicated by the asterisk) was moved to the margin toward the base of the heart. Each dot on the maps indicates a point at which an activation time was measured. Activation times are indicated by the pattern of shading according to the scale below. A 1-mm distance calibration is also shown. At the right, the apparent conduction velocities are shown for each direction of propagation in another similar preparation.*

acteristics of necrotic myocardial cells. A few scattered polymorphonuclear leukocytes were present. Tongues of necrotic cells extended from the bulk of the infarct deep within the ventricular wall up toward the epicardium, reaching to within 100–200 myocardial cell layers, and, occasionally, to within 10 cell layers, of the epicardial surface. At 5 days, there was a marked interstitial inflammatory infiltrate composed of polymorphonuclear leukocytes and mononuclear cells, including lymphocytes, plasma cells, macrophages, and scattered fibroblasts. The epicardium contained a mixed mononuclear and polymorphonuclear cell inflammatory infiltrate, as well as fibrinous exudate, indicative of postinfarction pericarditis. The infarcted myocardial cells were shrunken and hyperchromatic, containing an intensely acidophilic homogeneous cytoplasm without cross-striations (Fig. 6). Myocardial cell nuclei were absent. Many myocardial cells were undergoing phagocytosis by adjacent macrophages. There were no histologically normal bundles of myocardial fibers within the infarct. By 5 days, virtually every infarct extended to within 1–30 muscle cell layers of the epicardium, and in six preparations, extended directly to the epicardial surface in focal areas.

At both 1 and 5 days, the normal-appearing muscle fibers overlying the infarct were characterized by intact cell membranes, pink cytoplasm exhibiting cross-striations, and ovoid centrally oriented nuclei with evenly dispersed chromatin (Fig. 6). These were the muscle fibers from which transmembrane potentials and electrograms were recorded. As noted above, at 1 day, the rim of surviving tissue was variable in thickness (10–200 cell layers), but by 5 days it was much more uniformly thin, consisting of from 1–30 myocardial cell layers. Figure 7 shows the topography of this zone in one of the 5-day hearts. The number of cell layers that made up this rim of muscle varied slightly from one region to another. In the example shown in Figure 7, it was only 4–20 cell layers thick. The number of surviving cell layers increased toward the margin with normal myocardium. In six of the 5-day hearts, the infarct extended to the epicardial surface in focal areas where there were no surviving ventricular muscle cells.

The intact myocardial fibers comprising this epicardial zone of surviving muscle at 1 and 5 days were always arranged in parallel in closely packed fascicles (Fig. 6). Many of the individual myocardial cells were separated by interstitial edema. The long axis of the fibers was perpendicular to the left anterior descending coronary artery and extended from the coronary artery toward the lateral left ventricle and apex, the same orientation as epicardial muscle fibers in the noninfarcted anterior left ventricle (Greenbaum et al., 1981). Therefore, the epicardial border zone has a uniformly anisotropic structure (Spach et al., 1981). As mentioned previously, the most rapid conduction velocities which were found during mapping studies, such as the one shown in Figure 5, were in a direction parallel to the long axis of the myocardial fibers; the slowest conduction velocities were in a direction perpendicular to the long axis.

Ultrastructurally, these surviving ventricular mus-

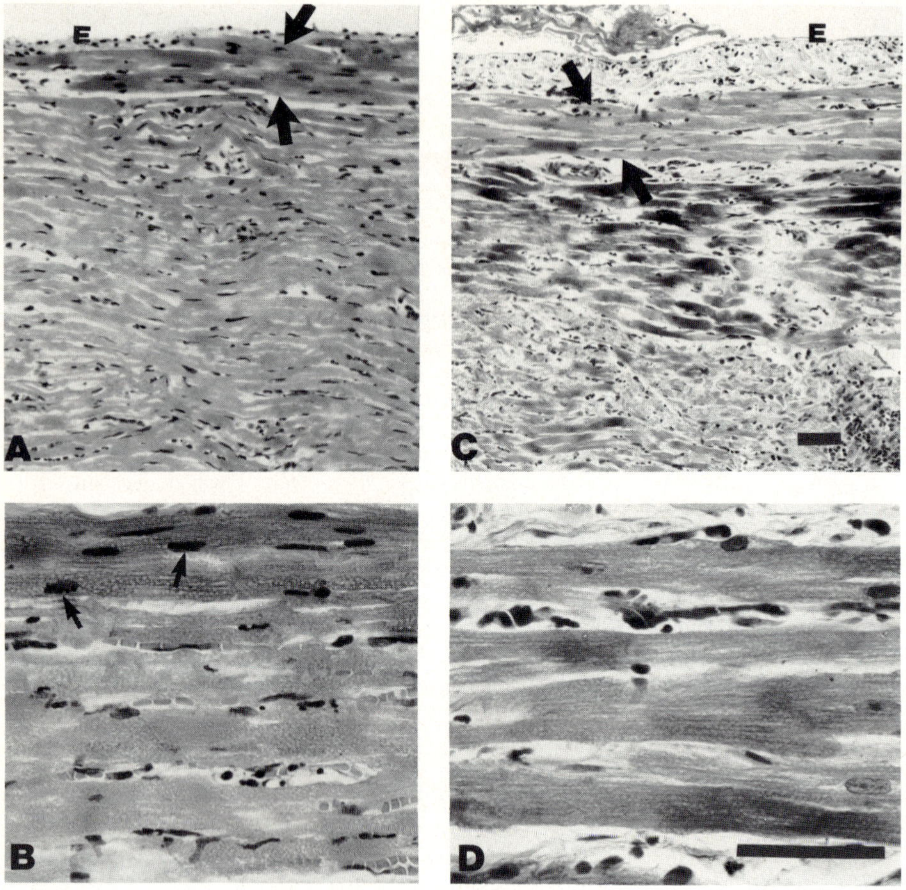

FIGURE 6. *Surviving subepicardial muscle fibers in 1- and 5-day infarcts. Panels A and B show a section of epimyocardium 1 day after coronary occlusion. At low magnification (panel A), there are a few scattered inflammatory cells in the epicardium (E). Directly subjacent to the epicardium is a thin rim of parallel-oriented intact myocardial fibers (delimited by arrows). Deep to the epicardial surface are many layers of muscle cells largely devoid of nuclei. There are foci of wavy fibers, as well as mild interstitial edema, scattered inflammatory cells, and hemorrhage, histological features of recent infarction. At high power magnification (panel B), the subepicardial rim of myocardium consists of two or three layers of cells that have intact cell membranes, cross-striations, and central ovoid nuclei (arrows). Beneath these surviving fibers are dying muscle cells without nuclei or with pyknotic nuclei. At 5 days (panels C and D), the histological appearance is similar but better defined. In panel C, a fibrinous pericarditis is well-developed. The thin rim of surviving myocardium (arrows) is sharply demarcated from the subjacent myocardial cells separated by interstitial edema and a marked inflammatory infiltrate. At high-power magnification (panel D), the intact myocardial cells of the thin rim appear normal. The bars represent 50 μm. Hematoxylin-phloxine-saffron.*

cle cells, although viable, were affected by the ischemia caused by the coronary artery occlusion. Muscle cells at both 1 and 5 days showed similar changes. The major abnormality identified was the presence of numerous nonmembrane-bound lipid droplets within the sarcoplasm of the epicardial muscle cells (Fig. 8). Although we did not quantify the amount of lipid, more than 90% of the muscle cells contained more than 10 droplets per cell. (Lipid droplets in normal ventricular muscle cells in the subepicardium were scarce.) The number of droplets varied from cell to cell, but, overall, increased progressively in number from muscle cells adjacent to the epicardium to muscle cells adjacent to the frankly necrotic region. Lipid droplets filled major portions of the intact muscle fibers adjacent to the infarcted cells, whereas, at the epicardial surface, the droplets were fewer, and were scattered. Other ultrastructural features of the surviving epicardial muscle were normal. The sarcolemmae of these cells were intact. The intercalated discs, including numerous normal nexi, coursed stepwise transversely between muscle cells. Numerous side-to-side disc connections between the parallel-oriented fibers were also apparent. Cell nuclei contained fine chromatin and large nucleoli. The sarcoplasm contained normal-appearing contractile elements, abundant glycogen, and numerous mitochondria (Fig. 8). T-tubules were present, and Z-bands appeared normal. Scattered dilated segments of sarcoplasmic reticulum and occasional osmiophilic dense bodies were present in some cells. The interstitium contained variable amounts of proteinaceous material separating the surviving myocardial fibers in the thin rim overlying the infarct. The branching nature of the fibers was accentuated due to the edema.

There was always a distinct sharp but irregular boundary between the intact muscle cells overlying the infarct and the ventricular muscle cells within the infarct (Fig. 8). The muscle cells within the infarct showed characteristics of irreversible ischemia—discontinuous sarcolemmae and intramitochondrial dense deposits of calcium. Scattered cells were frankly necrotic, with disintegrating cell organelles and masses of coagulated protein. Some of the necrotic cells were being phagocytized by macrophages.

Characteristics of Epicardial Muscle 2 Weeks to 18 Months after Coronary Artery Occlusion (the Healing and Healed Phases)

As the infarcts healed, there were significant changes in the transmembrane potentials, conduc-

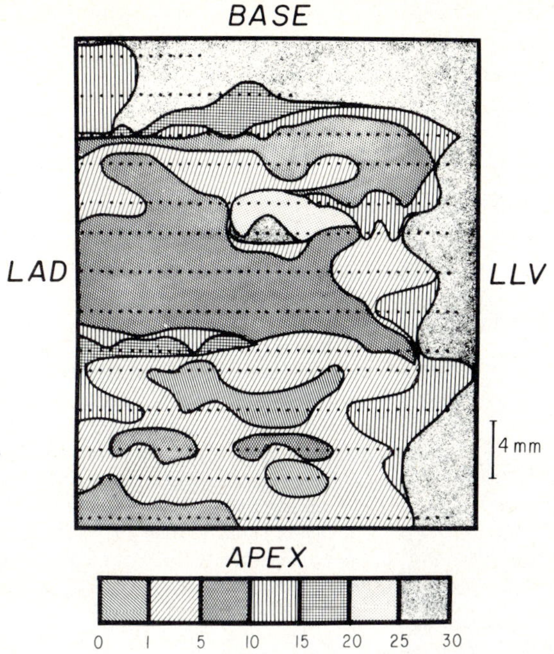

FIGURE 7. *Graphic depiction of the thickness of the surviving epicardial sheet of muscle over an infarct. The rectangle represents the block of tissue excised from the epicardial surface on the anterior left ventricle. The top margin is toward the base, the bottom toward the apex, the left toward the LAD, and the right toward the lateral left ventricle. Each pattern of shading indicates the number of surviving epicardial muscle cell layers (thickness) according to the key at the bottom of the figure.*

tion characteristics, and structure of the muscle fibers surviving in the epicardial border.

Transmembrane Potentials

Transmembrane potentials could be recorded from one to two cell layers at many epicardial sites in the preparations isolated from the hearts with healing or healed infarcts. We did not attempt to advance the microelectrode any further through the subepicardium. It was more difficult to impale the myocardial cells in these preparations, probably because of the increased amounts of connective tissue on the epicardial surface of the infarcts at these times (see below). At sites where membrane potentials were not recorded, we could not be certain that there were no viable muscle fibers; the thick connective tissue may have prevented us from recording action potentials.

The maximum diastolic potential, action potential amplitude, and $\dot{V}_{max}$ of phase 0 of the surviving epicardial muscle at 2 weeks and 2 months were not significantly different from normal ($P > 0.05$) (Fig. 1). Fibers with values less than 2 standard deviations from the mean were rarely found. In contrast, the action potential duration at both 50% and 90% repolarization was even shorter at 2 weeks than at 5 days ($P < 0.01$), and there was very little evidence of a plateau phase (Fig. 2). The action potential duration and configuration of the surviving muscle fibers in 2-month-old infarcts were not significantly different from those of muscle fibers in noninfarcted preparations ($P > 0.05$) (Fig. 2). There was no difference between the characteristics of the transmembrane potentials recorded from the older infarcts, and those from the 2-month infarcts (based on analysis of 105 action potentials in four preparations).

Conduction

The preparations from the 15-day-old infarcts still showed the directional differences in activation that were found in the 1- and 5-day-old infarct preparations (see Fig. 5). There was, however, a marked difference in conduction characteristics in preparations from the 2- to 18-month healed infarcts, compared to the subacute infarcts. The protocol used to study activation in some of the experiments was similar to the one used for the experiments on the subacute infarcts. Activation maps during stimulation at different margins of the preparations were constructed from the timing of electrogram deflections. The maps from a representative experiment on a 16-month-old infarct are shown in Figure 9; similar maps were obtained from healed infarcts of all ages. It is apparent that in part of the preparation there are no longer the marked directional differences in activation time; uniform anisotropy is no longer evident. In the top panel, which shows activation during stimulation at the LAD margin, activation away from this margin occurs relatively rapidly at the left of the preparation, but much more slowly at the right, where the isochrones are closely bunched (compare this with Fig. 5, top panel, where activation across the whole preparation in this direction occurred relatively rapidly). Stimulation from the apical margin (bottom panel) resulted in activation of the left of the preparation that was slower than during stimulation at the LAD margin. This directional difference in activation was not apparent in the right half of the preparation, where activation time was as long as that shown in the top panel.

The absence of the clear directional differences in activation time which characterized the 1- and 5-day infarcts was particularly apparent in the preparations that had a large number of fractionated electrograms—electrograms with long durations of 10–70 msec consisting of multiple deflections. (Gardner et al., Circulation, submitted). In these preparations, we did not construct activation maps from electrogram recordings because of the difficulty in assigning an activation time to the electrograms. We therefore used recordings of transmembrane action potentials. An activation map of a preparation from a 2-month infarct is shown in Figure 10. The orientation is the same as in the other figures. The isochrones are not uniformly distributed in any direction, closely bunched isochrones occur in all directions, and there is no direction of rapid

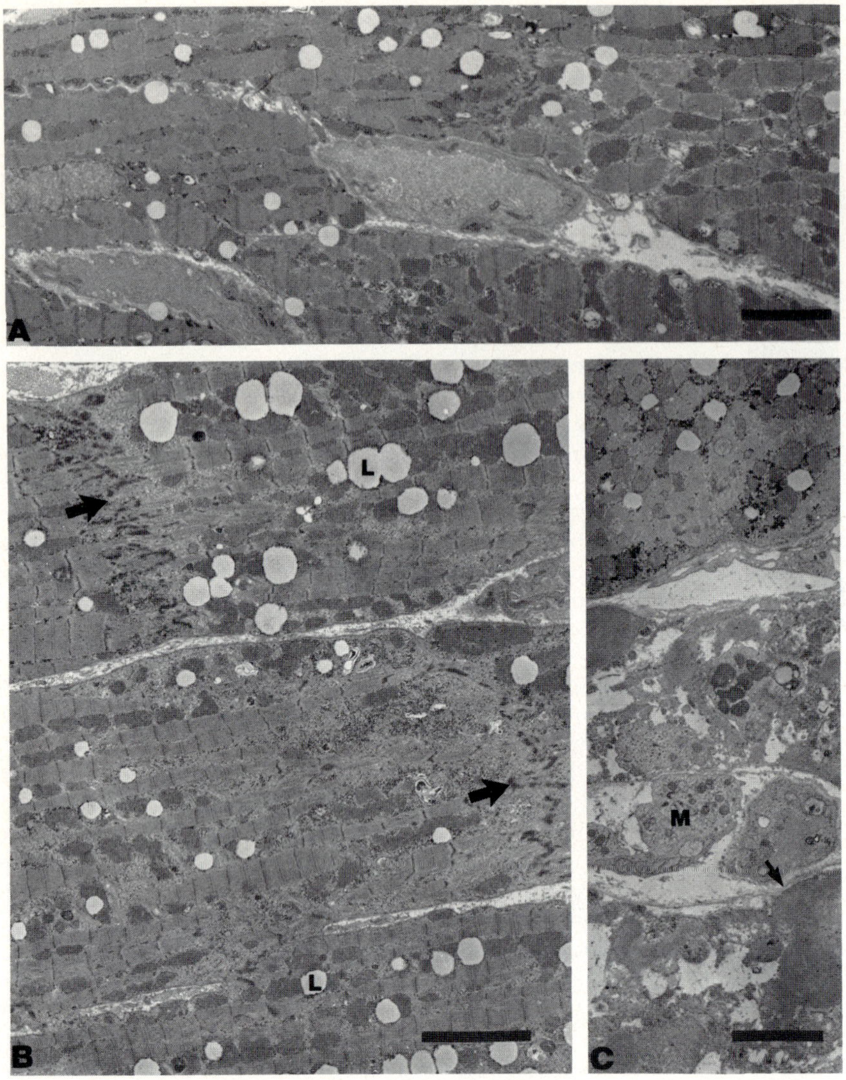

FIGURE 8. *Ultrastructure of muscle fibers in the surviving epicardial rim of 1 day (panel A) and 5 day (panel B) infarcts. The only ultrastructural abnormality detected at these times was the presence of intrasarcoplasmic lipid droplets (L). The contractile elements, mitochondria, and intercalated discs (arrows) appear normal. The sarcolemmae are intact. In these fields, there is only mild interstitial edema, but in other fields there was more extensive extracellular edema. The myocardial cells, however, were always oriented in parallel array. The bars represent 5 μm. The interface between surviving subepicardial muscle and necrotic muscle was sharp (panel C, 5-day infarct). The cell at the top is a viable cell with abundant lipid, whereas the cells at the bottom are necrotic, demonstrating ultrastructural features of irreversible cell injury—namely, discontinuous sarcolemmae (arrow) and intramitochondrial deposits of calcium. There is abundant interstitial edema and numerous macrophages (M). The bar represents 3 μm.*

activation similar to the subacute infarct preparations. It is also apparent from this figure that activation occurs much more slowly than in the preparations from the subacute infarcts. It took the impulse 90 msec to reach the right border, a distance of 3 mm—an apparent conduction velocity of 0.03 meter/sec. However, the parameters of the transmembrane potentials used to construct this map were not significantly different from our normal values. These parameters are shown in the bar graph (experiment 1) in Figure 10. Similar data were obtained in two other experiments in which mapping was done with microelectrodes (Fig. 10, experiments 2 and 3); slow activation with normal action potentials was found.

Histology and Ultrastructure

At 2 weeks, the infarct was composed of granulation tissue with scattered mononuclear cells and small blood vessels. Overlying the infarcts, the epicardium was thickened by dense fibrous tissue, indicative of healed postinfarction pericarditis. There were no intact ventricular muscle cells within the infarcts.

At the epicardial surface, there was still a thin rim of 1–30 layers of histologically intact ventricular muscle cells (Fig. 11). The intact cells were characterized by distinct cell membranes and acidophilic cytoplasm with cross-striations. The cells contained large central ovoid nuclei with evenly dispersed chromatin. The myocardial fiber bundles still had the parallel orientation which was evident at 5 days, probably accounting for the prominent directional differences in activation which were still present at this time. There was increased fibrous tissue adjacent to the healing infarct in this subepicardial region, sometimes separating individual myocardial fibers along their length (Fig. 11). The separation of myocardial fibers was particularly marked at the margin between infarct and intact muscle, but was also apparent all the way up to the epicardial surface.

The surviving epimyocardial cells at 2 weeks displayed a range of ultrastructural appearances rang-

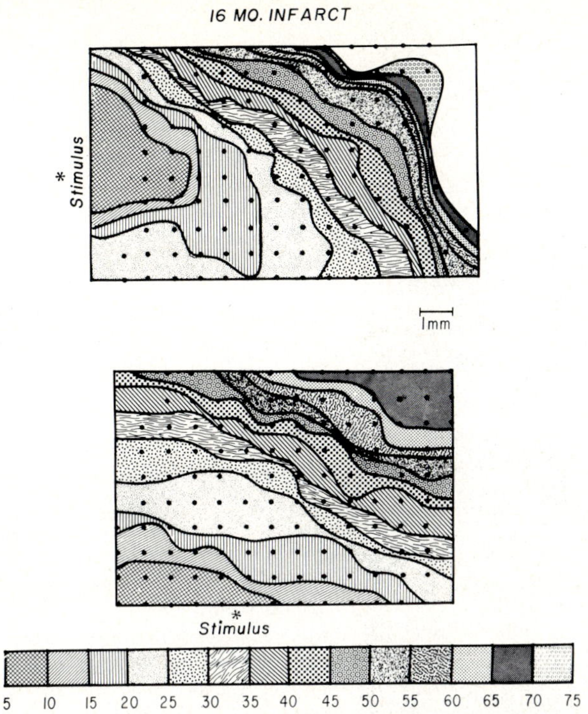

FIGURE 9. *Activation of an epicardial preparation from a 16-month-old infarct. At the top is shown the pattern of activation when the stimulus site (indicated by the asterisk) was on the LAD margin. At the bottom is shown the pattern of activation of the same region when the stimulus site (indicated by the asterisk) was moved to the margin near the apex. Each dot on the map indicates a point at which an activation time was measured from an extracellular electrogram. Activation times are indicated by the pattern of shading according to the scale below. A distance scale of 1 mm is also shown.*

ing from normal to highly abnormal. Some cells immediately subjacent to the epicardium (i.e., farthest from the infarct) appeared normal. The sarcolemmae were intact, and the contractile elements were normal. Intercalated discs contained numerous normal nexi and coursed transversely across fibers. However, in most (50–90%) of the cells throughout the entire thickness of this surviving epimyocardial zone in each infarct, there were striking changes in ultrastructure (Fig. 12). Although these cells also had intact sarcolemmae and normal-appearing nuclei, suggesting that they were viable, they showed a moderate-to-marked loss of contractile elements and concomitant loss of T-tubules. The myofibrils that remained were in disarray, and there was loss of myofilament registry. In cells with only a few remaining contractile elements, these elements were oriented at the periphery of the cell (Fig. 12). Contractile elements were replaced by large pools of glycogen and numerous normal-appearing mitochondria. The sarcoplasm also contained numerous osmiophilic dense bodies and dilated segments of sarcoplasmic reticulum. A few scattered lipid droplets remained in some cells. However, no cells contained the extensive amount of lipid that was present in the majority of the cells at 5 days.

There was a relatively small, well-defined scar on the anterolateral surface of the hearts with 2- to 18-month-old healed infarcts. Cross-sections of the ventricular wall showed variable thinning, with the wall being only one-half to one-quarter the normal thickness. Large amounts of adipose tissue were found in the scar tissue of the 4- to 18-month infarcts, but not in the 2-month infarcts. The thin rim of surviving 1–30 layers of intact muscle cells still persisted, trapped on the epicardial surface of the dense scar (Fig. 11). The organization of the muscle fibers, in regions where they were present in relatively large numbers (20–30 cell layers), was similar to the 15-day infarcts, i.e., parallel-oriented fibers separated by increased connective tissue. In these regions, directional differences in conduction similar to those seen at 1 day to 2 weeks were found. For example, the left side of the preparation from which the maps in Figure 9 were constructed had 20–30 layers of parallel-oriented fibers. In the regions where there were fewer cell layers, the myocardial fibers were markedly separated from each other along their length to such an extent that we could not be certain whether there were side-to-side connections between bundles (Fig. 11). In addition, the individual cells and their orientation were markedly deformed by the ingrowth of fibrous tissue

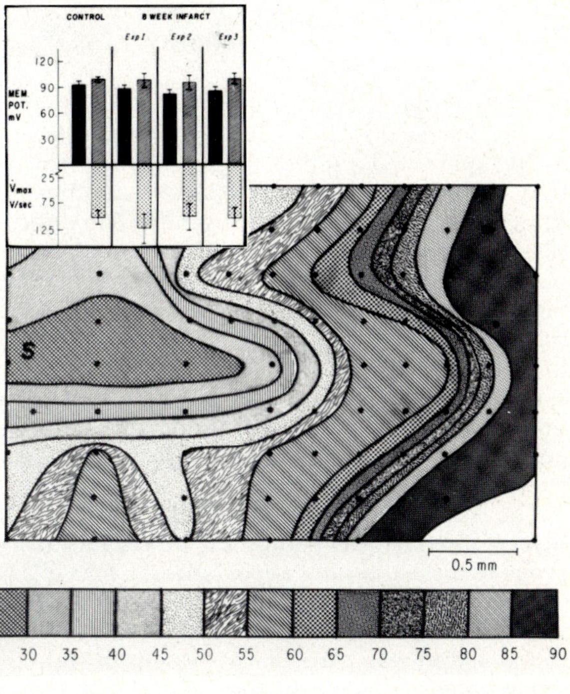

FIGURE 10. *Activation of an epicardial preparation from a 2-month-old infarct. The stimulus site is shown by the S. Each dot indicates the site at which an action potential was recorded. Activation times are indicated by the pattern of shading according to the scale below. A 0.5-mm distance calibration is also shown. Above are bar graphs comparing the resting membrane potential (solid bars), action potential amplitude (striped bars), and $\dot{V}_{max}$ (stippled bars) of the transmembrane potentials recorded in this experiment (experiment 1) and two others (experiments 2 and 3), with control (noninfarcted) preparations.*

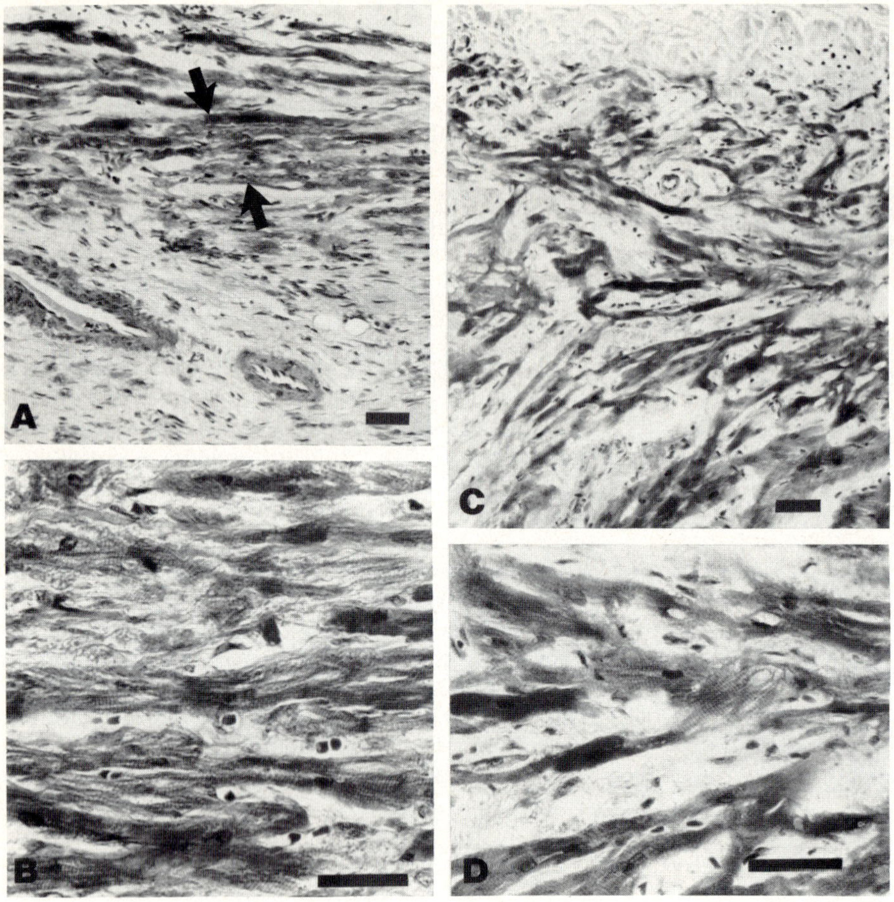

FIGURE 11. *Surviving epicardial muscle fibers in a 2-week-old infarct (panels A and B) and in a 2-month-old infarct (panels C and D). In panel A, the thin rim at 15 days (arrows) consists of several layers of ventricular muscle cells between the epicardium and the granulation tissue of the healing infarct. These surviving cells were separated by fibrous tissue, especially adjacent to the infarct. The parallel orientation of the fibers, however, was generally retained. At high magnification (panel B), these myocardial cells appear to be intact with distinct cross-striations. In panel C, the disorganization of the surviving myocardial cells in the thin rim at 2 months is evident. The cells are widely separated and disoriented because of the ingrowth of fibrous tissue from the adjacent infarct. At high magnification (panel D), the myocardial cells have distinct cross-striations and central nuclei. The bars represent 50 μm. Hematoxylin-phloxine-saffron.*

from the healed infarct. These myocardial fibers no longer presented a uniformly anisotropic structure–they were no longer parallel to one another—but, rather, were oriented in many different directions (Fig. 11) (Spach et al., 1982). This type of structure was found in the right side of the preparation in Figure 9 and the preparation in Figure 10. Neither region showed the prominent directional differences in conduction characteristic of the subacute infarcts. As in the 5-day-old infarcts, several of the healed infarcts extended to the epicardial surface in focal areas, leaving no intact muscle cells adjacent to the epicardium.

The surviving rim of epicardial muscle in the healed infarcts was comprised of cells showing a range of ultrastructural appearances, from cells with normal shape and intracellular components to cells with a markedly distorted shape (Fig. 13). The distorted shape was particularly evident in those cells immediately adjacent to the infarct, but was also seen in cells just beneath the epicardium. The distortion occurred because the interstitium was expanded by abundant collagen which separated and isolated individual cells and portions of cells. The bizarre configurations of some cells severely limited cell-to-cell interfaces. Attenuated projections of muscle cells were apposed through very short intercalated discs containing numerous nexi. As a result, the total extent of cell-to-cell connections appeared to be decreased. Despite their abnormal shape, the distorted cells contained abundant glycogen, normal mitochondria, and a normal number of contractile elements organized in registry (Fig. 13). Normal appearing T-tubules were distributed throughout the sarcoplasmic reticulum. Intrasarcoplasmic lipid droplets were not present in abnormal amounts. Ventricular muscle cells with reduced numbers of contractile elements were rarely identified. All cells had a completely intact sarcolemma and normal-appearing nuclei. None of the cells had the ultrastructural abnormalities which were present in surviving fibers in 2-week-old infarcts.

Discussion

Epicardial Muscle Survives Transmural Myocardial Infarction

In their studies on ventricular arrhythmias in the canine heart with subacute myocardial infarction caused by LAD occlusion, El-Sherif et al. (1977a, 1977b) recorded continuous electrical activity from the epicardial surface of infarcts during tachycardias. These results not only verified Harris' original observation that subepicardial muscle did not infarct (Harris, 1950) but suggested that reentrant excitation occurred in this muscle to cause tachycardia (El-

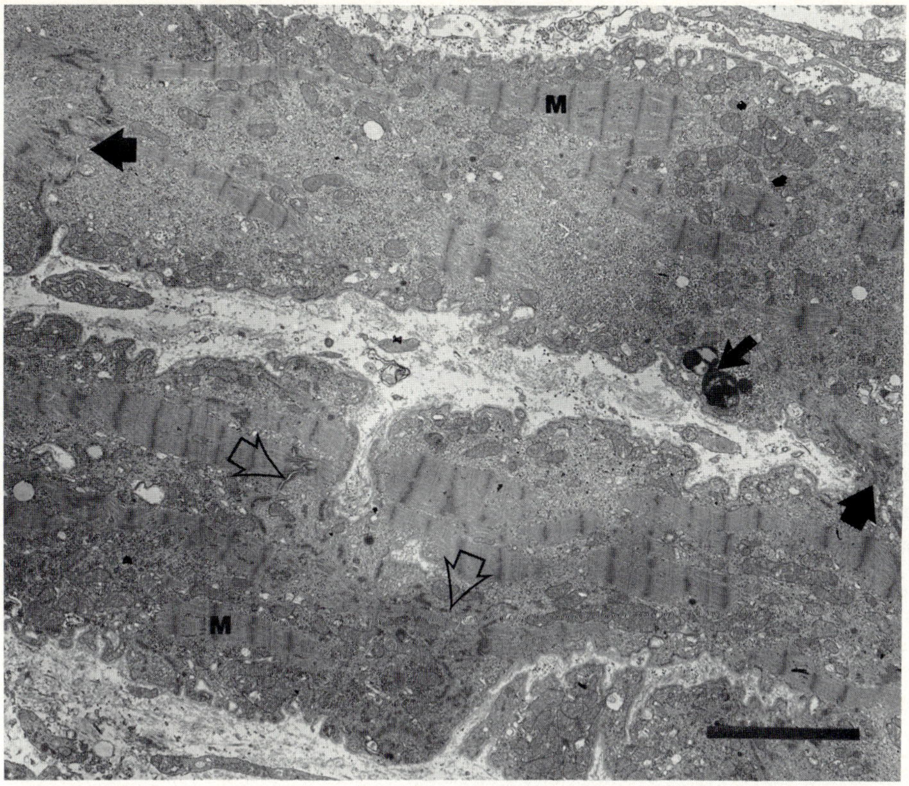

FIGURE 12. *Ultrastructure of muscle fibers in surviving epicardial rim over a 2-week-old infarct. At this time, although scattered myocardial cells were misshapen, especially adjacent to the healing infarct, the majority were oriented in parallel. The most striking ultrastructural abnormalities of the myocardial cells at this time were changes reminiscent of degeneration, characterized by loss of contractile elements (M) and replacement by large collections of monoparticulate glycogen and mitochondria. In severely affected cells, the few remaining contractile elements were adjacent to the sarcolemmae. Many cells contained osmiophilic dense bodies (thin arrow) and dilated segments of sarcoplasmic reticulum. Although several intercalated discs had unusually serpiginous configurations (open arrows) the majority of the intercalated discs (both end-to-end and side-to-side) appear normal (thick arrows). The sarcolemmae were intact, indicating cell viability. The bar represents 5 μm.*

Sherif et al., 1977a, 1977b). Subsequently, impulse propagation in the surviving epicardial muscle was mapped by techniques that enabled electrograms to be recorded simultaneously from a large number of sites. The results of these studies verified that reentrant excitation occurs in the surviving epicardial muscle (El-Sherif et al., 1981, 1982; Wit et al., 1982; Mehra et al., 1983).

The rim of surviving epicardial muscle is what remains after the wavefront of injury—that is, the sequential progression of myocardial damage from endocardium to epicardium (Reimer et al., 1977)—has stopped advancing toward the epicardial surface. Since we found more surviving muscle cell layers at 1 day (up to several hundred) than at 5 days (1–30), it appears that ischemic injury is still progressing between these two times. Not condemned to inevitable death, as has previously been claimed (Hearse and Yellon, 1981), this muscle probably survives and forms a border zone of the infarct because the epicardial region is supplied by collateral branches of both the LAD and left circumflex coronary arteries (Schaper, 1971). After coronary occlusion, blood flow is redistributed from dying intramyocardial regions to the subepicardium (Rivas et al., 1976).

Structural and Electrophysiological Properties of Surviving Epicardial Muscle: Possible Relationships to Arrhythmogenesis

We found a reduction in resting membrane potential, action potential amplitude, and upstroke velocity and action potential duration in the surviving ventricular muscle cells of the thin epicardial border zone, 1–5 days after occlusion. Other investigators have reported similar results (Hope et al., 1980; Lazzara and Scherlag, 1980; Spear et al., 1983). Action potential duration was shorter at 5 days than at 1 day, also suggesting more ischemic damage by the later time. The only ultrastructural abnormality of the myocardial cells was the presence of intracellular lipid deposits which appeared similar at 1 and 5 days. Since all of the abnormalities in transmembrane potentials persisted after several hours of superfusion in well-oxygenated Tyrode's solution, the prolonged period of ischemia in situ prior to the study probably caused alterations in membrane properties which are not totally dependent on an abnormal extracellular environment.

The significance of the lipid within the myocardial cells in relation to the abnormal transmembrane potentials is unclear. Lipid droplets have been identified previously in surviving muscle and Purkinje cells adjacent to experimental myocardial infarcts (Wartman et al., 1956; Friedman et al., 1975; Fenoglio et al., 1979; Page and Polimeni, 1977; Bilheimer et al., 1978; Vokonas et al., 1978). Presumably, the lipid is related to ischemia; it has been suggested that, during hypoxia, lipid droplets are derived from circulating plasma lipids which can no longer be metabolized by the mitochondria (Wartman et al., 1956; Page and Polimeni, 1977; Bilheimer et al., 1978). Whether the lipid droplets are the cause of the electrophysiological abnormalities we found at

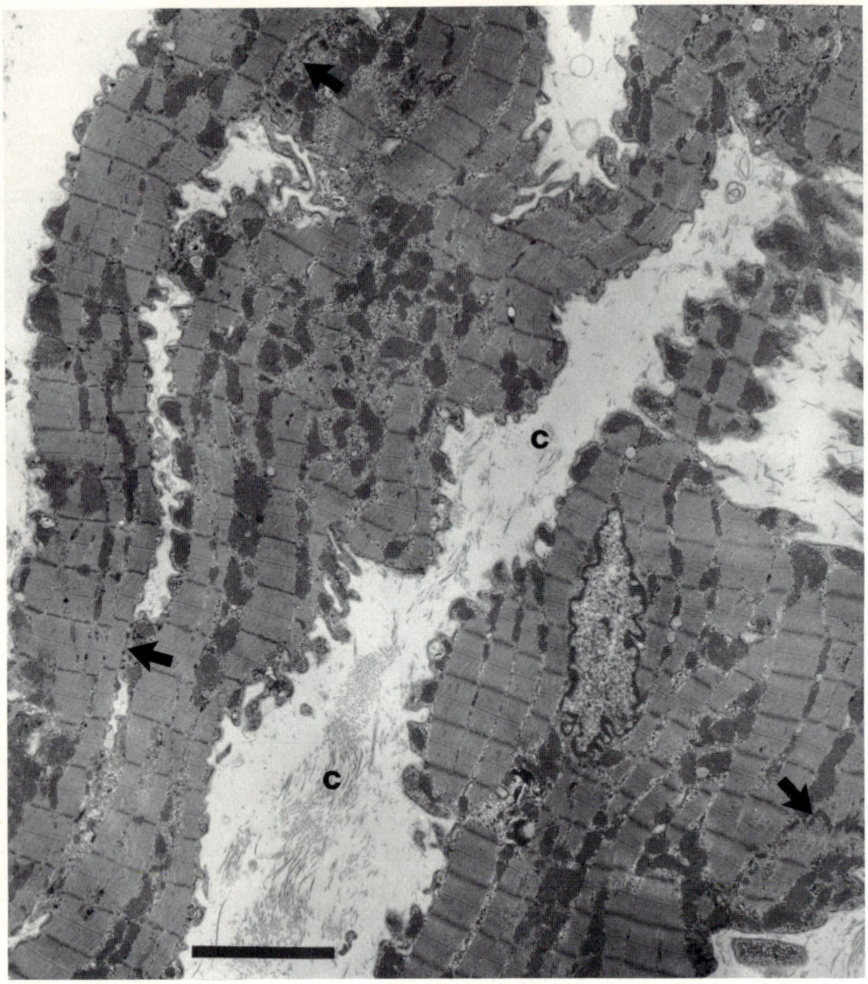

FIGURE 13. *Ultrastructure of muscle fibers in surviving epicardial rim over a 2-month-old infarct. At this time, the myocardial cells are markedly deformed. Abundant collagen (C) in the interstitium separates the cells and accentuates their branching nature. Only short segments of intercalated discs (arrows) are evident; the junctions of the intercalated discs, appear normal. The intracellular components—contractile elements, mitochondria and glycogen—are intact. The bar represents 5 μm.*

1 and 5 days, or merely an independent association, cannot be answered by this study. That large amounts of intracellular and extracellular lipid may be arrhythmogenic has been suggested (Opie, 1972).

The abnormalities in the transmembrane potentials at 1–5 days may contribute to the occurrence of reentry. The decrease in resting potential and upstroke velocity may, in part, explain the slowed conduction that occurs in the epicardial muscle during tachycardia (El-Sherif et al., 1977a,1977b, 1981, 1982; Lazzara and Scherlag, 1980; Wit et al., 1982). The short action potential duration, if accompanied by a decrease in refractory period, might also facilitate the occurrence of reentry. During reentry, reexcitation of the epicardial muscle has occurred within 100–130 msec, suggesting a shortening of the refractory period (Wit et al., 1982). However, studies will still be required to determine the exact relationship of the abnormalities in the transmembrane potentials recorded from in vitro muscle to the in situ arrhythmias.

The structure of the rim of surviving epicardial muscle may also contribute to the occurrence of reentry. The surviving ventricular muscle cells in the epicardial border zone of transmural infarcts constitute a thin sheet overlying the infarct. This viable muscle is often connected to normal myocardium only at its periphery; connections with underlying intramural bundles of surviving muscle are only rarely present. Hence, impulses cannot activate the epicardial muscle from below, and thereby prevent circus movement. Conduction of impulses is confined to an essentially two-dimensional plane on the epicardial surface (Wit et al., 1982; Mehra et al., 1983). At 1–5 days, the muscle fibers in the thin rim were parallel-oriented, making this region a uniformly anisotropic structure. This architecture influences conduction of impulses (Clerc, 1976). Spach et al. (1981) have shown that conduction velocity perpendicular to the long axis of fiber orientation in atria or ventricles is slowed sufficiently to cause reentry. We have also shown in this study that very slow conduction occurs in this epicardial region when activation occurs perpendicular to the long axis of fiber orientation, whereas it is more rapid parallel to the long axis. The slow conduction caused by anisotropy may also contribute to the occurrence of reentrant ventricular tachycardia (Gardner et al., 1981).

There is not yet sufficient data to indicate whether

or not reentry occurs in the surviving epicardial muscle at 2 weeks to 18 months after permanent coronary occlusion, although ventricular tachycardias can sometimes be induced by programmed stimulation at these times (A.L. Wit, unpublished observations). Nevertheless, the further changes in structure and electrophysiology that accompany healing of the infarct may have some relationship to arrhythmogenesis. By 2 weeks after occlusion, the myocardial fibers are separated by an ingrowth of connective tissue. Many of the cells also show ultrastructural features suggestive of degeneration (Maron et al., 1975). These changes are nonspecific, implying no particular etiology. They may reflect ongoing ischemia in the muscle cells or may be a residuum of the initial ischemic event. Alternatively, they may not be related to ischemia, but may be a response to local factors such as lingering proteases from the adjacent myocardial infarct or encroachment by fibrous tissue of the healing infarct. The role of the pericarditis which occurs after infarction is also unknown. Whatever the cause, these degenerative changes in no way predict the fate of the muscle cells. By structural criteria, these cells are viable; they may recover and resynthesize their normal components, or they may further degenerate and die. That many of the cells recover is suggested by the fact that by 2 months the muscle cells remained misshapen, but appeared otherwise structurally normal.

The ultrastructural changes that we found at 2 weeks were associated with repolarization further accelerated from that recorded at 1–5 days. Resting potential and upstroke velocity, however, had returned to normal. Spear et al. (1983) also found similar changes in transmembrane potentials of epicardial muscle cells over infarcts caused by coronary occlusion and reperfusion. Since we did not ultrastructurally mark individual cells from which transmembrane action potentials were recorded, we cannot determine whether some of these potentials were recorded from the muscle cells with abnormal structure or mainly from cells with normal structure.

At 2–18 months, the muscle fibers are markedly distorted and the epicardial border zone no longer has a uniform anisotropic structure. The intercellular contacts are also attenuated. The intracellular ultrastructure and the transmembrane potentials are not significantly different from normal. Recovery may be due to the development of collateral vessels.

Myerburg et al. (1977) have also determined transmembrane potential characteristics of muscle cells surviving in healed infarcts up to 6 months old in feline hearts. The muscle fibers that they studied were in the subendocardium and presented a histological picture similar to the epicardial surface of canine hearts. Although many of the surviving muscle fibers had normal transmembrane potentials, action potentials with abnormal characteristics also were found.

Because of the distortion of the muscle fibers which no longer have a parallel orientation in healed infarcts, the well-defined directional differences in activation time seen in the subacute infarct preparations did not occur in some regions. Activation of the epicardial border zone in the healed infarcts was still very slow, despite the normal transmembrane potentials. We have not yet determined why activation is so slow. Conduction velocity might be normal, but activation may occur over circuitous pathways caused by the distortion of muscle fiber orientation, giving the impression of a slow conduction velocity. On the other hand, conduction velocity might be slowed as a result of decreased coupling between cells caused by their separation by connective tissue.

Border Zones of Myocardial Infarcts

There has been considerable controversy as to whether a border zone (a zone of viable but damaged muscle fibers with abnormal physiological properties) exists adjacent to a myocardial infarct (Hearse and Yellon, 1981). A number of studies using histological, biochemical, or histochemical staining techniques have concluded that there is a sharp interface between necrotic and normal tissue on the lateral aspect of infarcts during the first 24 hours after coronary occlusion, and thus no border zone (Hirzel et al., 1977; Factor et al., 1978, 1981; Janse et al., 1979; Yellon et al., 1981). However, others suggest that there is a narrow lateral border zone less than 3 mm wide (Cox et al., 1968; Harken et al., 1978; Gottlieb et al., 1981; Koyanagi et al., 1982). Some studies show biochemical abnormalities and low blood flows in this lateral border zone, but it is difficult to distinguish between intermediately damaged cells and interdigitating normal cells and dead cells by some of the techniques that have been used (Hearse and Yellon, 1981). Muscle fibers in this region on the lateral aspect of infarcts do have some structural features that are similar to the epicardial border zone which we described. Their histology appears normal, but numerous lipid droplets are present during the first several days after coronary occlusion (Vokonas et al., 1978; Fishbein et al., 1980; Gottlieb et al., 1981). Besides the lipid, the only other ultrastructural abnormality which has been described is sarcomere relaxation (Gottlieb et al., 1981).

The morphological changes in the lateral border zone in the weeks and months following myocardial infarction (during infarct healing) have not been well documented. There are some data indicating that biochemical abnormalities may persist (Schwartz et al., 1973), although there are the same difficulties in interpreting these data as there are for the studies on more acute infarcts (Hearse and Yellon, 1981). Dusek et al. (1971) have described structural changes in the lateral regions of infarcts which are similar to those that we found on the epicardial surface. They describe the occurrence of a progressive increase in interstitial connective tissue 1–4 weeks after myocardial infarction, and this collagenization led to deformation of the surviving cells. They found, as we did at 2 weeks, that the deformed muscle cells were largely devoid of contractile elements, and that they contained primarily glycogen and scattered mitochondria. Whether cells with normal intracellular ultrastructure were located on the lateral aspect of older infarcts, as we found, is not apparent. It has not been possible to determine whether the electrophysiological properties (action potentials and conduction) of the cells on the lateral aspects of infarcts are abnormal—a finding which would help to establish the existence of a lateral border zone.

Supported by the following grants from the Heart, Lung, and Blood Institute: Program Project Grants HL-12738 and HL-30557, Cardiovascular Training Grant T32 HL 07271, and Postdoctoral Fellowship 5F32 HL 06272.

Address for reprints: Dr. Andrew L. Wit, Department of Pharmacology, College of Physicians and Surgeons, Columbia University, 630 West 168th Street, New York, New York 10032.

Received September 19, 1983; received in revised form November 12, 1984; accepted for publication December 13, 1984.

References

Bilheimer DW, Buja LM, Parker RW, Bonke FJ, Willerson JT (1978) Fatty acid accumulation and abnormal lipid deposition in peripheral and border zones of experimental myocardial infarcts. J Nucl Med **19:** 276–283

Carmeliet E (1978) Cardiac transmembrane potentials and metabolism. Circ Res **42:** 577–587

Clerc L (1976) Directional differences of impulse spread in trabecular muscle from mammalian heart. J Physiol (Lond) **255:** 335–346

Cox JL, McLaughlin VW, Flowers NC, Horan LG (1968) The ischemic zone surrounding acute myocardial infarction. Its morphology as detected by dehydrogenase staining. Am Heart J **76:** 650–659

Cranefield PF (1975) The Conduction of the Cardiac Impulse. Mt. Kisco, N.Y., Futura

Dusek J, Rona G, Kahn DS (1971) Healing process in the marginal zone of an experimental myocardial infarct. Findings in the surviving cardiac muscle cells. Am J Pathol **62:** 321–338

El-Sherif N, Scherlag BJ, Lazzara R, Hope RR (1977a) Reentrant venticular arrhythmias in the late myocardial infarction period. 1. Conduction characteristics in the infarction zone. Circulation **55:** 686–702

El-Sherif N, Hope RR, Scherlag BJ, Lazzara R (1977b) Re-entrant ventricular arrhythmias in the late myocardial infarction period. 2. Patterns of initiation and termination of re-entry. Circulation **55:** 702–719

El-Sherif N, Smith A, Evans K (1981) Canine ventricular arrhythmias in the late myocardial infarction period. 8. Epicardial mapping of reentrant circuits. Circ Res **49:** 255–265

El-Sherif N, Mehra R, Gough WB, Zeiler RH (1982) Ventricular activation patterns of spontaneous and induced ventricular rhythms in canine one-day-old myocardial infarctions: Evidence for focal and reentrant mechanisms. Circ Res **51:** 152–166

Factor SM, Sonnenblick EH, Kirk ES (1978) The histologic border zone of acute myocardial infarction—islands or peninsulas? Am J Pathol **92:** 111–124

Factor SM, Okun EM, Kirk ES (1981) The histological lateral border zone of acute canine myocardial infarction. A function of microcirculation. Circ Res **48:** 640–649

Fenoglio JJ Jr, Albala A, Silva FG, Friedman PL, Wit AL (1976) Structural basis of ventricular arrhythmias in human myocardial infarction: A hypothesis. Hum Pathol **7:** 547–563

Fenoglio JJ Jr, Karagueuzian HS, Friedman PL, Albala A, Wit AL (1979) Time course of infarct growth toward the endocardium after coronary artery occlusion. Am J Physiol **326:** H356–H370

Fishbein MC, Hare CA, Gissen SA, Spadero J, MacLean D, Moroko PR (1980) Identification and quantification of histochemical border zones during the evolution of myocardial infarction in the rat. Cardiovasc Res **14:** 41–49

Friedman PL, Fenoglio JJ Jr, Wit AL (1975) Time course for reversal of electrophysiological and ultrastructural abnormalities in subendocardial Purkinje fibers surviving extensive myocardial infarction in dogs. Circ Res **36:** 127–144

Friedman PL, Stewart JR, Fenoglio JJ Jr, Wit AL (1973a) Survival of subendocardial Purkinje fibers after extensive myocardial infarction in dogs: In vitro and in vivo correlations. Circ Res **33:** 597–611

Freidman PL, Stewart JR, Wit AL (1973b) Spontaneous and induced cardiac arrhythmias in subendocardial Purkinje fibers surviving extensive myocardial infarction in dogs. Circ Res **33:** 612–626

Gardner PI, Ursell PC, Fenoglio JJ Jr, Allessie MA, Bonke FIM, Wit AL (1981) Structure of the epicardial border zone in canine infarcts is a cause of reentract excitation (abstr). Circulation **64:** (suppl IV): 320

Gardner PI, Ursell PC, Fenoglio JJ Jr, Wit AL (1982) Anatomical and electrophysiological basis for electrograms showing fractionated activity (abstr). Circulation **66** (suppl II): 78

Gottlieb GJ, Kubo SH, Alonso DR (1981) Ultrastructural characterization of the border zone surrounding early experimental myocardial infarcts in dogs. Am J Pathol **103:** 292–303

Greenbaum RA, Gibson DG, Becker AE, Anderson RH (1981) Left ventricular fiber architecture in man. Br Heart J **45:** 248–263

Harken AH, Barlow CH, Harden WR III, Chance B (1978) Two and three dimensional display of myocardial ischemic "border zone" in dogs. Am J Cardiol **42:** 954–959

Harris AS (1950) Delayed development of ventricular ectopic rhythms following experimental coronary occlusion. Circulation **1:** 1318–1328

Hearse DJ, Yellon DM (1981) The "border zone" in evolving myocardial infarction: Controversy or confusion? Am J Cardiol **47:** 1321–1334

Hirzel HO, Sonnenblick EH, Kirk ES (1977) Absence of a lateral border zone of intermediate creatine phosphokinase depletion surrounding a central infarct 24 hours after acute coronary occlusion in the dog. Circ Res **41:** 673–683

Hope RR, Scherlag BJ, Lazzara R (1980) Excitation of ischemic myocardium: Altered properties of conduction, refractoriness and excitability. Am Heart J **99:** 753–765

Janse MJ, Cinca J, Morena H, Fiolet JWT, Kleber AG, deVries GP, Becker AE, Durrer D (1979) The "border zone" in myocardial ischemia. An electrophysiological, metabolic and histochemical correlation in the pig heart. Circ Res **44:** 576–588

Koyanagi S, Eastham CL, Harrison DG, Marcus ML (1982) Transmural variation in the relationship between myocardial infarct size and risk area. Am J Physiol **242:** H867–H874

Lazzara R, Scherlag BJ (1980) Role of the slow current in the generation of arrhythmias in ischemic myocardium. *In* The Slow Inward Current and Cardiac Arrhythmias, edited by DP Zipes, JC Bailey, V Elharrar. The Hague, Martinus Nijhoff, pp 339–416

Maron BJ, Ferrans VJ, Roberts WC (1975) Ultrastructural features of degenerating cardiac muscle in patients with cardiac hypertrophy. Am J Pathol **79:** 387–434

Mehra R, Zeiler RH, Gough WB, El-Sherif N (1983) Reentrant ventricular arrhythmias in the late myocardial infarction period. Electrophysiologic-anatomic correlation of reentrant circuits. Circulation **67:** 11–23

Myerburg RJ, Gelband H, Nilsson K, Sung RJ, Thurer RJ, Morales AR, Bassett AL (1977) Long-term electrophysiological abnormalities resulting from experimental myocardial infarction in cats. Circ Res **41:** 73–84

Opie LH (1972) Metabolic response during impending myocardial infarction. I. Relevance of studies of glucose and fatty acid metabolism in animals. Circulation **45:** 483–490

Page E, Polimeni PI (1977) Ultrastructural changes in the ischemic zone bordering experimental infarcts in rat left ventricles. Am J Pathol **87:** 81–104

Reimer KA, Lowe JE, Rasmussen MM, Jennings RB (1977) The wavefront phenomenon of ischemic cell death. I. Myocardial infarct size vs. duration of coronary occlusion in dogs. Circulation **56:** 786–794

Rivas F, Cobb FR, Bache RJ, Greenfield JC Jr (1976) Relationship between blood flow to ischemic regions and extent of myocardial infarction. Serial measurements of blood flow to ischemic regions in dogs. Circ Res **38:** 439–447

Schaper W (1971) The Collateral Circulation of the Heart. New York, American Elsevier, pp 30–38

Schwartz A, Wood JM, Allen JC, Bornet EP, Entman ML, Goldstein MA, Sordahl LA, Suzuki M, Lewis RM (1973) Biochemical and morphologic correlates of cardiac ischemia. I. Membrane systems. Am J Cardiol **32:** 46–61

Snedecor GW, Cochran WG (1967) Statistical Methods. Ames, Iowa, Iowa University Press, p 114

Spach M, Miller WT, Geselowitz DB, Barr RC, Kootsey JM, Johnson EA (1981) The discontinuous nature of propagation in normal canine cardiac muscle: Evidence for recurrent discontinuities of intracellular resistance that affect the membrane currents. Circ Res **48:** 39–54

Spach MS, Miller WT, Dolber PC, Kootsey JM, Sommer JR, Mosher CE Jr (1982) The functional role of structural complexities in the propagation of depolarization in the atrium of the dog. Cardiac conduction disturbances due to discontinuities of effective axial resistivity. Circ Res **50:** 175–191

Spear JF, Michelson EL, Moore EN (1983) Cellular electrophysiologic characteristics of chronically infarcted myocardium in dogs susceptible to sustained ventricular tachyarrhythmias. J Am Coll Cardiol **1:** 1099–1110

Ursell PC, Gardner PI, Wit AL, Fenoglio JJ Jr (1982a) Are structural and electrophysiologic changes in the epicardial border zone related to infarct healing? (abstr) Fed Proc **41:** 381

Ursell PC, Gardner PI, Wit AL, Fenoglio JJ Jr (1982b) Is there a border zone of viable but abnormal muscle cells in canine myocardial infarcts? (abstr) Am J Cardiol **49:** 1017

Vokonas PS, Malsky PM, Paul SJ, Robbins SL, Hood WB Jr (1978) Radioautographic studies in experimental myocardial infarction: Profiles of ischemic blood flow and quantification of infarct size in relation to magnitude of ischemic zone. Am J Cardiol **42:** 67–75

Wartman WB, Jennings RB, Yokoyama HO, Clabaugh GF (1956) Fatty changes of the myocardium in early experimental infarction. Arch Pathol **62:** 318–323

Wit AL, Allessie MA, Bonke FIM, Lammers W, Smeets J, Fenoglio JJ Jr (1982) Electrophysiologic mapping to determine the mechanism of experimental ventricular tachycardia initiated by premature impulses. Am J Cardiol **49:** 166–185

Yellon DM, Hearse DJ, Crome R, Grannell J, Wyse RKH (1981) Characterization of the lateral interface between normal and ischemic tissue in the canine heart during evolving myocardial infarction. Am J Cardiol **47:** 1233–1239

INDEX TERMS: Ischemia • Transmembrane potentials • Anisotropy • Conduction • Arrhythmias

BRIEF COMMUNICATIONS

The Effects of Ryanodine on Calcium-Overloaded Sheep Cardiac Purkinje Fibers

M. Valdeolmillos and D. A. Eisner

From the Department of Physiology, University College London, Gower Street, London, United Kingdom

SUMMARY. Prolonged exposure to high concentrations of strophanthidin produces an initial increase followed by a subsequent decrease of twitch tension. The slow decrease is termed calcium overload. The aim of the present work was to investigate the effects of ryanodine (an inhibitor of calcium release from the sarcoplasmic reticulum) on calcium-overloaded sheep cardiac Purkinje fibers. The fibers were voltage-clamped, and tension was measured while monitoring the intracellular calcium concentration with the photoprotein aequorin. When strophanthidin (10 μM) was applied to produce calcium overload, a depolarizing pulse produced twitch, and tonic components of tension and repolarization produced an aftercontraction. These components of tension were accompanied by corresponding increases of aequorin light. Ryanodine (1 μM) gave a transient increase of twitch tension. The twitch then decreased to very low levels. The aftercontraction and its corresponding aequorin light signal decreased monotonically on application of ryanodine. It has been suggested that the fall of force in calcium overload may be due to random diastolic release of calcium from the sarcoplasmic reticulum interfering with subsequent systolic calcium release. We suggest that the positive inotropic effect of ryanodine can be explained if ryanodine decreases the diastolic release of calcium. The transient positive inotropic effect of ryanodine reported here is therefore consistent with the hypothesis that the fall of force in calcium overload is due to diastolic calcium oscillations. **(*Circ Res 56: 452–456, 1985*)**

THE plant alkaloid ryanodine has been shown to interfere with excitation-contraction coupling in a variety of cardiac preparations. In general, it depresses contraction, and this effect has been attributed to inhibition of Ca^{++} release from the sarcoplasmic reticulum (SR) (Sutko et al., 1979; Sutko and Willerson, 1980; Sutko and Kenyon, 1983). This inhibition of Ca^{++} release has been demonstrated in isolated SR, albeit at much higher concentrations than those which affect contraction in intact tissues (Jones et al., 1979). Ryanodine can therefore be used as a probe to investigate the contribution of the SR to the various components of tension in cardiac muscle. This is particularly important, since the response of cardiac muscle to depolarization of the surface membrane is complicated, and there is considerable controversy as to the origin of the activating Ca^{++}. For example, when the Na-K pump is inhibited, the following components of tension are seen (Eisner and Lederer, 1979): (1) a phasic twitch that is thought to be produced largely by Ca^{++} release from the SR, (2) a component of tonic tension that is maintained during a depolarization lasting for several seconds and that has been attributed to Ca^{++} entry into the cell from the extracellular fluid, and (3) an oscillatory aftercontraction seen on repolarization that is produced by the oscillatory release of Ca^{++} from the SR. Sutko and Kenyon (1983) have investigated the effects of ryanodine under these conditions, and, in support of the postulated origin of the various components, found that ryanodine abolished the twitch and aftercontraction but did not decrease the tonic tension.

When the Na-K pump is inhibited for a prolonged period, there is an initial increase in twitch tension followed by a slow fall of twitch tension which is accompanied by an increase of tonic tension and aftercontraction (Vassalle and Lin, 1979; Eisner et al., 1984b). This slow decrease of twitch tension has been described as "Ca-overload" (Vassalle and Lin, 1979); however, its mechanism is still controversial. To examine this Ca^{++} overload further, we have studied the effects of ryanodine on it. We find that, under these conditions of Ca^{++} overload, ryanodine can *increase* the twitch tension while decreasing the aftercontraction. This observation is important, not only for studying the actions of ryanodine, but also for the information it gives on the mechanism of Ca^{++} overload.

Methods

The experiments were performed on sheep cardiac Purkinje fibers obtained from a local abbatoir. The fibers were removed from the heart, shortened to 2 mm in length, and connected to a tension transducer in the experimental bath. The membrane potential was controlled with a con-

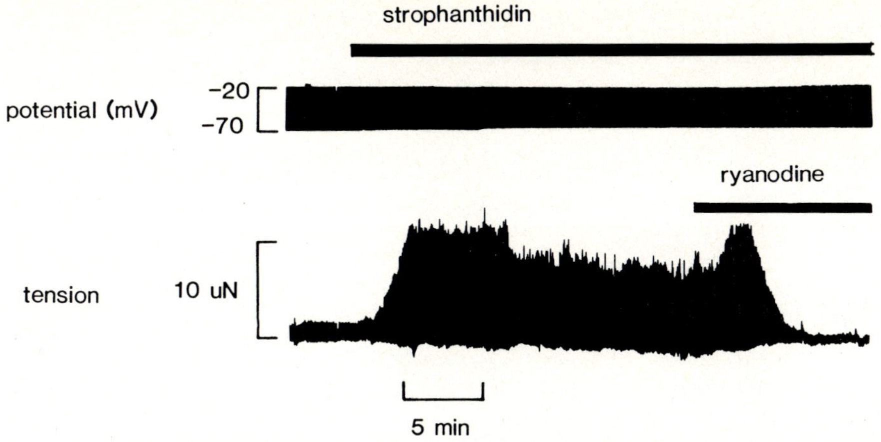

FIGURE 1. *The effects of strophanthidin and ryanodine on the contraction of a voltage-clamped cardiac Purkinje fiber. Traces show: top, membrane potential; bottom, tension (0.1–10 Hz). Strophanthidin (10 μM) and ryanodine (1 μM) were applied for the periods shown. Throughout the experiment, the membrane potential was held at −68 mV, and a 1-second duration pulse to −20 mV was applied at 0.33 Hz.*

ventional two-microelectrode voltage clamp. The general methods for measuring force in voltage-clamped fibers have been published previously (Eisner and Lederer, 1979). In Figures 1 and 2, the tension records have been high pass filtered to remove the effects of baseline drifts.

This paper shows that ryanodine produces a transient increase of twitch tension. When changing solutions with a conventional valve, it is often difficult to avoid artefacts due to transient changes of solution level, temperature, etc. Ryanodine was therefore added as a concentrated solution directly to the bottle containing the superfusing solution. This produced a delay due to the length of the tubing which has been allowed for.

In the present experiments, $[Ca^{++}]_i$ was measured with the photoprotein aequorin. This was microinjected into 20–30 cells (see Wier and Isenberg, 1982; Blinks et al., 1982; Allen and Orchard, 1983, for further details). The light emitted from aequorin was collected by a photomultiplier tube mounted below the bath and connected to the base of the bath (made from a coverslip) by a Lucite light guide. A shutter could be closed in front of the photomultiplier to correct for background counts (Cannell and Allen, 1983). To minimize the dark counts from the photomultiplier tube, the output from the tube was connected to a discriminator amplifier (Princeton Applied Research 1121A). The records shown were obtained from a rate meter and were averaged from several voltage clamp pulses, using a microprocessor.

The experimental solutions contained (in mM): NaCl, 145; $CaCl_2$, 5; $MgCl_2$, 2; KCl, 5; glucose, 10. It was buffered with 5 mM Tris-HEPES (pH 7.3). All experiments were performed at 35 ± 1°C. Strophanthidin (Sigma) was kept as a stock solution (10^{-2} M in ethanol) and was added as required. Ryanodine was a generous gift of Dr. J. Kenyon (University of Texas at Dallas). It was kept frozen in a solution of 10 mM in H_2O.

Results

Figure 1 shows a record from an experiment in which a voltage-clamped sheep cardiac Purkinje fiber was exposed to strophanthidin for a prolonged period. This produced an increase of force which developed over a period of about 5 minutes, and then subsequently declined. This secondary fall of force has been observed previously and has been termed Ca^{++} overload (Vassalle and Lin, 1979). At this stage, ryanodine (1 μM) was added. This produced an initial rise of tension which lasted for 2 minutes before tension eventually fell to a low level. Control experiments showed that, as expected, if ryanodine was added in the absence of strophanthidin, there was no initial increase of tension and the twitch declined monotonically. Furthermore, if ryanodine was added in the presence of strophanthidin before the twitch had begun to decline, there was no increase of twitch. The effects of ryanodine were examined in seven fibers which were Ca^{++} overloaded, as judged by the fact that twitch tension had begun to decline. In five of these, there was a transient increase of tension which had a mean value of 42 ± 6% (SEM). In the remaining two experiments, there was no significant increase of twitch tension and the twitch declined slowly.

The time courses of onset and decay of the positive inotropic effect of ryanodine are shown in more detail in Figure 2, which is taken from a similar experiment. The preparation had been exposed to strophanthidin for 45 minutes at the start of the record shown. When ryanodine was subsequently added, the twitch first increased, before decreasing to a very low value. In this experiment, the photoprotein aequorin had been previously injected into the fiber in order to measure $[Ca^{++}]_i$. Specimen aequorin and tension records from this experiment are shown in Figure 3. Figure 3A shows a control record obtained before the exposure to strophanthidin shown in Figure 2. Depolarization produces a small increase of $[Ca^{++}]_i$ and tension. The other records were obtained at the times indicated on Figure 2. The addition of strophanthidin (panel B) increased the twitch tension and produced a component of tonic tension which developed during the depolarizing pulse. Repolarization produced oscillatory aftercontractions. The various components of tension are accompanied by corresponding changes of $[Ca^{++}]_i$, as shown by the aequorin light. In particular, it should be noted that the diastolic level of

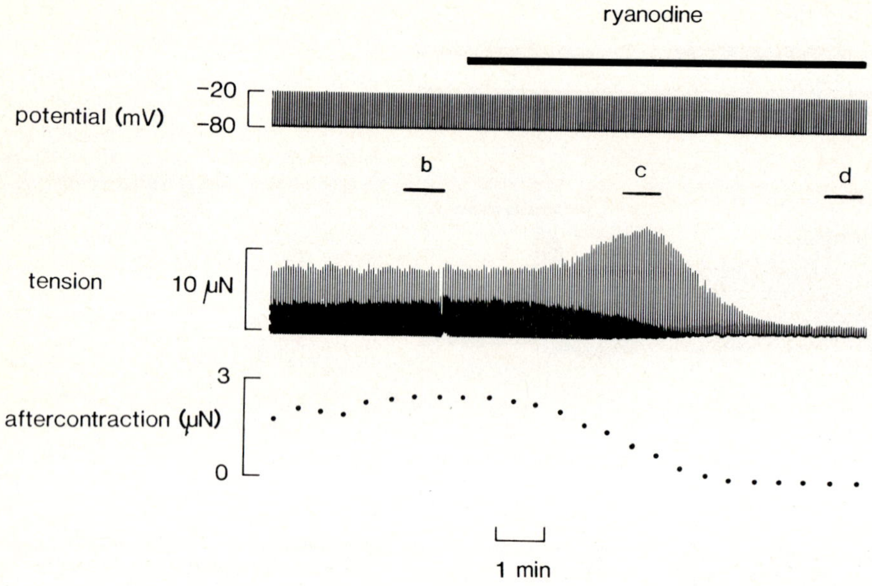

FIGURE 2. *Time course of onset of the effects of ryanodine on a Ca++-overloaded cardiac Purkinje fiber. Traces show: top, membrane potential; middle, tension (0.1–10 Hz); bottom, aftercontraction magnitude as measured from an unfiltered tension record. The preparation had been exposed to strophanthidin (10 μM) for 45 minutes before the beginning of the record shown. Ryanodine (1 μM) was applied for the period indicated. The membrane potential was held at −80 mV and a 500 msec duration pulse to −20 mV was applied at 0.33 Hz.*

aequorin light emission is increased, and that, following the transient increase, light falls to below the diastolic level before increasing during the pulse. This undershoot of aequorin light in Ca^{++} overload has been reported previously (Orchard et al., 1983; Wier and Hess, 1984) and appears to result from a temporary decrease of spontaneous calcium oscillations following stimulation (Stern et al., 1983). Figure 3C was obtained during the period of increased twitch tension shortly after ryanodine was added. It is clear that, although the twitch is increased, the aftercontraction is smaller than that shown in Figure 3B. Furthermore, the second aftercontraction which was present in panel B is now abolished. There is a corresponding decrease in the oscillations of $[Ca^{++}]_i$. It should also be noted that the increase of twitch tension is accompanied by a decrease of the peak aequorin light. Figure 3D shows the effects of prolonged exposure to ryanodine. The twitch and aftercontraction have been completely abolished, as have the corresponding changes of $[Ca^{++}]_i$. Depolarization now produces only a tonic increase of tension. The changes of aftercontraction magnitude are plotted below the tension record of Figure 2. It is evident that the aftercontraction begins to decline at almost exactly the same time as the twitch increases.

Discussion

The present work shows that, in Ca^{++}-overloaded Purkinje fibers, ryanodine produces a transient increase of twitch tension. This transient increase of twitch tension occurs at the same time as the aftercontraction starts to decrease. The transient positive inotropic effect of ryanodine is seen only in preparations that have been exposed to strophanthidin long enough for the twitch to decline (i.e., Ca^{++} overloaded). As previously reported (Sutko and Kenyon, 1983), when ryanodine is applied before Ca^{++} overload occurs, only a fall of twitch tension is seen. Although the negative ionotropic effect of Ca^{++} overload produced by prolonged exposure to strophanthidin is well known, there is no agreed explanation for its cause. Recent work has shown that the decrease of force is not accompanied by a

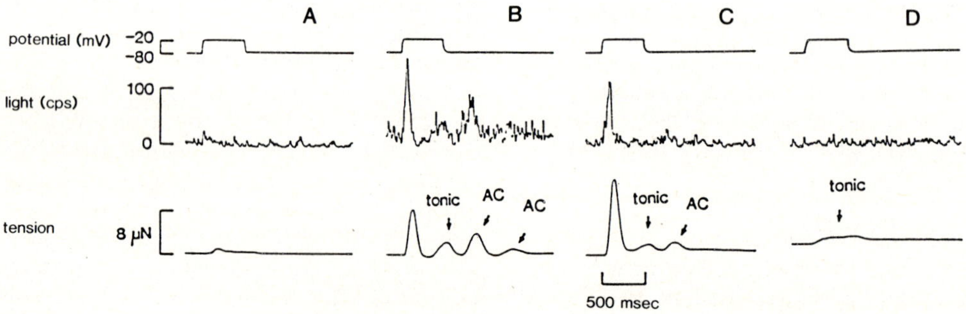

FIGURE 3. *Specimen records of the effects of strophanthidin and ryanodine on aequorin light and tension. Data from the experiment of Figure 2. In each panel, traces show: top, membrane potential; middle, aequorin light; bottom, tension. All records are the average of 16 pulses. Panels show: A, control, obtained before the application of strophanthidin shown in Figure 2; B, after 48 minutes of exposure to strophanthidin; C, 3 minutes after adding ryanodine (1 μM); D, 7 minutes after adding ryanodine (1 μM). The points at which records B–D were obtained are shown in Figure 2.*

decrease of systolic $[Ca^{++}]_i$ as measured by aequorin (Wier and Hess, 1984; Allen et al., 1984). The present work shows that the transient *increase* of force produced by ryanodine is not accompanied by a rise of $[Ca^{++}]_i$. It is therefore likely that the *positive* inotropic effect of ryanodine is related to the mechanism of the *negative* inotropic effect of Ca^{++} overload, since in neither case does force change in the same direction as peak systolic aequorin light.

Two explanations have been suggested for the fall of force in Ca^{++} overload. (1) The sensitivity of the contractile apparatus to $[Ca^{++}]_i$ may be decreased during the period of Ca^{++} overload. For example, it is known that exposure to strophanthidin decreases intracellular pH (Deitmer and Ellis, 1978; Vaughan-Jones et al., 1983) and this acidification will decrease force (Fabiato and Fabiato, 1978; Allen and Orchard, 1983). (2) The decrease of systolic force may be due to the spontaneous diastolic Ca^{++} oscillations which are present in strophanthidin intoxicated preparations. Kort and Lakatta (1984) have suggested that these oscillations will deplete the sarcoplasmic reticulum of Ca^{++} and thereby interfere with systolic Ca^{++} release. Since the oscillations can be out of phase in different cells, the systolic Ca^{++} release will vary from cell to cell. The less activated cells will add an extra compliance which will allow the more activated ones to shorten, thus decreasing the force produced by the preparation (Eisner et al., 1984a). On the other hand, if the *mean* systolic $[Ca^{++}]_i$ remains constant, the increased *variance* of systolic $[Ca^{++}]_i$ will increase the peak systolic aequorin light, since the light emission is approximately proportional to $[Ca^{++}]^{2.5}$. Furthermore, even if the mean systolic $[Ca^{++}]_i$ decreases, if its variance increases sufficiently, the mean aequorin signal will increase. Therefore, diastolic Ca^{++} oscillations may be able to decrease total systolic force even though the mean Ca^{++} signal as detected by aequorin increases (Eisner et al., 1984a). A similar discrepancy between changes of light and tension has been discussed previously (Orchard et al., 1983; Wier et al., 1983). It is worth reemphasizing that the above considerations mean that the aequorin light records of Figure 3 cannot be interpreted simply as being related to the mean $[Ca^{++}]_i$.

If the fall of force in Ca^{++} overload is due to Ca^{++} oscillations, it is easy to see how ryanodine can increase the twitch tension. Ryanodine will decrease SR Ca^{++} release, and will therefore decrease the Ca^{++} oscillations. This reduction of oscillations also leads to the reduction in the aftercontraction magnitude. The effects of ryanodine on the twitch will be the combination of two factors. First, ryanodine will decrease the diastolic Ca^{++} oscillations and thereby increase the systolic release of Ca^{++} and, hence, the twitch. Second, ryanodine will directly decrease the Ca^{++} release that produces the twitch. The balance of these two factors could produce the phasic increase of twitch tension seen in the present work. The transient positive inotropic effect of ryanodine is therefore consistent with the hypothesis that the fall of force in Ca^{++} overload is due to diastolic Ca^{++} oscillations. Furthermore, if in some cases the two factors cancel out, one can explain the lack of an initial positive inotropic effect in two of the overloaded fibers studied.

It is also necessary to consider whether the present results can be accounted for by other explanations. For example, the acidification produced by Ca^{++} overload has been shown to be due to an increase of $[Ca^{++}]_i$ (Vaughan-Jones et al., 1983). Therefore, the removal of these Ca^{++} oscillations by ryanodine may well produce an intracellular alkalinization and thence increase force. One problem with this hypothesis, however, is that an intracellular alkalinization will increase not only the twitch, but also the tonic tension (Eisner et al., 1982). Therefore, this hypothesis cannot explain the result of Figure 3, B and C, where ryanodine increases twitch tension with no increase of tonic tension. This lack of an increase of tonic tension also excludes other explanations in which the transient increase in twitch tension produced by ryanodine is ascribed to an increase of Ca^{++} sensitivity of the contractile apparatus. It should, however, be noted that these results do not exclude the possibility that a part of the fall in force of Ca^{++} overload is due to an intracellular acidification.

In conclusion, we suggest that the positive inotropic effect of ryanodine seen in Ca^{++}-overloaded preparations involves a removal of the Ca^{++} oscillations which may produce the fall of tension in Ca^{++} overload.

We are indebted to Dr. D.G. Allen for advice on the use of aequorin. We thank him and Dr. S.C. Wray for reading an earlier version of this paper. We thank Dr. J. R. Blinks for supplying us with aequonin which was purified in his laboratory with support from NIH Grant HL12186.

Supported by grants from the British Heart Foundation. M.V. was in receipt of a grant from the Fondo de Investigaciones de la Seguridad Social (Spain).

Address for reprints: D. A. Eisner, University College London, Gower Street, London WC1E 6BT, United Kingdom.

Received August 27, 1984; accepted for publication November 15, 1984.

References

Allen DG, Orchard CH (1983) The effects of changes of pH on intracellular calcium transients in mammalian cardiac muscle. J Physiol (Lond) **335:** 555–567

Allen DG, Eisner DA, Pirolo JS, Smith GL (1984) Calcium transients during "calcium overload" in ferret ventricular muscle (abstr). J Physiol (Lond) **357:** 57P

Blinks JR, Wier WG, Hess P, Prendergast FG (1982) Measurement of $[Ca^{2+}]$ concentrations in living cells. Prog Biophys Mol Biol **40:** 1–114

Cannell MB, Allen DG (1983) A photomultiplier tube assembly for the detection of low light levels. Pflugers Arch **398:** 165–168

Deitmer JW, Ellis D (1980) Interactions between the regulation of the intracellular pH and sodium activity of sheep cardiac Purkinje fibers. J Physiol (Lond) **304:** 471–488

Eisner DA, Lederer WJ (1979) Inotropic and arrhythmogenic effects of potassium-depleted solutions on mammalian cardiac muscle. J Physiol (Lond) **294:** 255–277

Eisner DA, Lederer WJ, Vaughan-Jones RD (1982) The relationship between intracellular pH and contraction in sheep cardiac Purkinje fibres. J Physiol (Lond) **334:** 106P–107P

Eisner DA, Allen DG, Pirolo JS, Smith GL (1984a) How does increasing $[Ca^{2+}]_o$ decrease force in Ca-overloaded cardiac muscle? (abstr). J Muscle Res Cell Motil **6** [part 2]

Eisner DA, Lederer WJ, Vaughan-Jones RD (1984b) The quantitative relationship between twitch tension and intracellular sodium activity in sheep cardiac Purkinje fibres. J Physiol (Lond) **335:** 251–266

Fabiato A, Fabiato F (1978) Effects of pH on the myofilaments and the sarcoplasmic reticulum of skinned cells from cardiac and skeletal muscles. J Physiol (Lond) **276:** 233–255

Jones LR, Besch HR, Sutko JL, Willerson JT (1979) Ryanodine-induced stimulation of net Ca^{++} uptake by cardiac sarcoplasmic reticulum vesicles. J Pharmacol Exp Ther **209:** 48–55

Kort AA, Lakatta EG (1984) Calcium-dependent mechanical oscillations occur spontaneously in unstimulated mammalian cardiac tissues. Circ Res **54:** 396–404

Orchard CH, Eisner DA, Allen DG (1983) Oscillations of intracellular Ca^{2+} in mammalian cardiac muscle. Nature **304:** 735–738

Stern MD, Kort AA, Bhatnagar GM, Lakatta EG (1983) Scattered-light intensity fluctuations in diastolic rat cardiac muscle caused by spontaneous Ca^{++}-dependent cellular mechanical oscillations. J Gen Physiol **82:** 119–153

Sutko JL, Kenyon JL (1983) Ryanodine modification of cardiac muscle responses to potassium-free solutions. Evidence for inhibition of sarcoplasmic reticulum calcium release. J Gen Physiol **82:** 385–404

Sutko JL, Willerson JT (1980) Ryanodine alteration of the contractile state of rat ventricular myocardium. Comparison with dog, cat, and rabbit ventricular tissues. Circ Res **46:** 332–343

Sutko JL, Willerson JT, Templeton GH, Jones LR, Besch HR (1979) Ryanodine: Its alterations of cat papillary muscle contractile state and responsiveness to inotropic agents and a suggested mechanism of action. J Pharmacol Exp Ther **209:** 37–47

Vassalle M, Lin CI (1979) Effect of calcium on strophanthidin-induced electrical and mechanical toxicity in cardiac Purkinje fibers. Am J Physiol **236:** H689–H697

Vaughan-Jones RD, Lederer WJ, Eisner DA (1983) Ca^{2+} ions can affect intracellular pH in mammalian cardiac muscle. Nature **301:** 522–524

Wier WG, Hess P (1984) Excitation-contraction coupling in cardiac Purkinje fibers. Effects of cardiotonic steroids on the intracellular $[Ca^{2+}]$ transient, membrane potential, and contraction. J Gen Physiol **83:** 395–415

Wier WG, Isenberg G (1982) Intracellular $[Ca^{2+}]$ transients in voltage clamped cardiac Purkinje fibers. Pflugers Arch **392:** 284–290

Wier WG, Kort AA, Stern MD, Lakatta EG, Marban E (1983) Cellular calcium fluctuations in mammalian heart: Direct evidence from noise analysis of aequorin signals in Purkinje fibers. Proc Natl Acad Sci USA **80:** 7367–7371

INDEX TERMS: Calcium-overload • Ryanodine • Strophanthidin • Cardiac muscle

Elevated Plasma Norepinephrine Concentrations in Decompensated Cirrhosis

Association with Increased Secretion Rates, Normal Clearance Rates, and Suppressibility by Central Blood Volume Expansion

Kathleen M. Nicholls, Michael D. Shapiro, Vicki J. Van Putten, Rudiger Kluge, Hsiao-Min Chung, Daniel G. Bichet, and Robert W. Schrier

From the Department of Medicine, University of Colorado Medical School, Denver, Colorado

SUMMARY. Plasma norepinephrine concentrations are elevated in patients with decompensated cirrhosis, and correlate inversely with urinary sodium and water excretion. Increased plasma norepinephrine concentrations may result from a decreased metabolic clearance rate or an increased secretion rate, possibly in response to a decreased "effective arterial blood volume." If the latter hypothesis is correct, plasma norepinephrine might be expected to be suppressed when central blood volume is expanded by head-out water immersion. In the present study, plasma norepinephrine secretion and clearance rates were determined by infusion of tritiated norepinephrine. Norepinephrine secretion rates were elevated in eight cirrhotic patients as compared to control subjects (1.50 ± 0.25 vs. 0.26 ± 0.08 $\mu g/m^2$ per min, $P < 0.001$), whereas clearance rates were similar (3.13 ± 0.48 vs. 2.60 ± 0.28 liters/min, NS). Baseline plasma norepinephrine concentrations were markedly elevated in the cirrhotic patients (830 ± 136 vs. 185 ± 12 pg/ml, $P < 0.001$). Head-out water immersion significantly suppressed plasma concentrations of both norepinephrine (704 ± 72 to 475 ± 70 pg/ml, $P < 0.005$) and epinephrine (121 ± 33 to 57 ± 10 pg/ml, $P < 0.05$) in all seven patients studied. We conclude that the high circulating catecholamine concentrations in cirrhosis are secondary to increased secretion, rather than to decreased metabolic clearance, and are suppressible by central blood volume expansion. **(*Circ Res 56: 457–461, 1985*)**

RECENT studies in which a sensitive radioenzymatic method was used have demonstrated elevated concentrations of plasma norepinephrine (NE) in decompensated cirrhotic patients (Henriksen et al., 1981; Bichet et al., 1982; Ring Larsen et al., 1982). Results of such studies have also demonstrated that the inability to excrete a water load provides a reliable means to delineate those cirrhotic patients who will have the highest plasma concentrations of NE (Bichet et al., 1982). These so-called "non-excretor" patients also have other hormonal indicators of a decrease in effective arterial blood volume (EABV), including elevated plasma concentrations of renin, aldosterone, and vasopressin (Bichet et al., 1982).

These findings have supported the "underfilling" hypothesis of sodium and water retention in cirrhosis (Better and Schrier, 1983). Moreover, since considerable experimental results indicate that the nonosmotic release of vasopressin is mediated by alterations in baroreceptor activity, it has been proposed that diminished afferent vagal and glossopharyngeal neural traffic to the central nervous system initiates both vasopressin release (Schrier et al., 1979) and increased efferent sympathetic activity. Since it has been demonstrated that neural alterations in baroreceptor activity in normal subjects are associated with parallel changes in plasma NE (Grossman et al., 1982), the proposal has been made that the elevated plasma concentrations of NE in cirrhotic patients result from increased NE secretion rates.

Alternatively, diminished NE clearance rates may account for, or substantially contribute to, the increased plasma NE concentrations in non-excretor cirrhotic patients. The viability of this possibility is supported by the observation that these "non-excretor" patients with decompensated cirrhosis exhibit a significantly higher incidence of ascites and hypoalbuminemia than the cirrhotic patients who can excrete a water load normally (Bichet et al., 1982). Thus, at least the hepatic component of NE clearance could theoretically be substantially diminished in the non-excretor patients. However, studies by Ring Larsen et al. (1982) documented normal hepatic NE extraction in decompensated cirrhotic patients.

The present study was therefore undertaken to examine the whole-body NE secretion and clearance rates in non-excretor cirrhotic patients. Since volume and/or baroreceptor-mediated increases in NE plasma concentrations should diminish during improvement in EABV, the effect of head-out water immersion (HWI) on plasma catecholamine concentrations was also examined.

Methods

Eight patients with decompensated cirrhosis (clinical ascites present) were admitted to the Clinical Research Center of the University of Colorado Health Sciences Center. Their ages ranged from 36 to 63 years, mean 52.8 ± 2.9 years. Seven of the patients were male. Five days prior to study, all drugs were discontinued and the patients were placed on a 40 mEq/day sodium diet. Fluid intake was unrestricted. The normal subjects were 7 healthy volunteers (6 male), on no medication, and ranged in age from 22 to 48 years (mean 30 ± 3.2 years). Informed consent was obtained from all subjects, and the research protocol was approved by the Human Research Committee of this institution.

NE kinetics were determined by a method slightly modified from that of Esler et al. (1980). Tritiated NE, levo [7,8^{3}H;N]3,4-$(OH)_2C_6H_3CH(OH)CH_2NH_2$, with specific activity 20–40 Ci/mmol (New England Nuclear) was diluted in 0.02 N sterile acetic acid and sterilized by millipore filtration. A 100-μCi aliquot of this solution was added to 150 ml of sterile 5% dextrose in water and infused intravenously at a constant rate of 0.35 μCi/m^2 per min for 90 minutes. The average total tritiated NE dose was 54 μCi. The dose of NE given was 0.002 μg/min, an amount insufficient to elevate blood pressure, heart rate, or total plasma NE level. Serial 6-ml blood samples were drawn at 10-minute intervals during the [^{3}H]NE infusion from an indwelling intravenous catheter in the contralateral forearm, and were assayed for total NE and [^{3}H]NE. The mean of these 10 determinations was taken as the baseline NE concentration for each subject.

During steady state conditions, the infusion rate of [^{3}H]NE equals its rate of removal from the plasma. Since the infusion dose is assumed to be too low to affect endogenous clearance rate, the clearance rate of endogenous NE equals the clearance of [^{3}H]NE, which is expressed by the following equation:

$$\text{Clearance} = \frac{[^3\text{H}]\text{NE infusion rate (dpm/min)}}{\text{Steady state plasma } [^3\text{H}]\text{NE (dpm/ml)}}.$$

The apparent secretion rate (ASR) of NE into the plasma is calculated as:

$$\text{ASR} = \frac{[^3\text{H}]\text{NE infusion rate (dpm/min)}}{\text{Specific activity of plasma } [^3\text{H}]\text{NE (dpm/pg)}}$$

where specific activity of plasma [^{3}H]NE (dpm/pg) = [plasma ^{3}H-NE (dpm/ml)]/[total plasma NE (pg/ml)].

Plasma [^{3}H]NE activity for clearance rate and apparent secretion rate calculations was derived by alumina extraction of the plasma obtained at 70, 80, and 90 minutes (Esler et al., 1980). [^{3}H]NE concentration was determined by liquid scintillation counting of the perchloric acid extract. The counting efficiency of the Packard liquid scintillation counter was 60%, and [^{3}H]NE concentrations (cpm/ml) were corrected to obtain dpm/ml. Mean percent recovery of [^{3}H]NE from the plasma was 64.0 ± 2.5%. Endogenous plasma NE concentrations and the NE concentrations of the perchloric acid extracts were measured by a modification (Bichet et al., 1982) of the radioenzymatic method of Peuler and Johnson (1977).

The effect of HWI on plasma NE and epinephrine (E) concentrations was studied in seven decompensated cirrhotics, including five of the above patients. Each patient served as his own control, and was studied on two occasions in the same semirecumbent position, at the same time of day. On each occasion, the patient received a standard 20 ml/kg water load intravenously over 30 minutes, before study. On one of the two occasions, in a random sequence, the patient was studied during HWI for 5 hours. Blood for NE and E determinations was drawn hourly during the two experiments. The plasma NE and E concentrations were then compared in the same patient with and without increased EABV secondary to HWI.

Statistical Analysis

Unpaired Student's t test was used to compare baseline NE levels, NE clearance, and secretion rates in cirrhotic patients with those of normal subjects. Paired Student's t test was utilized to compare catecholamine levels with and without water immersion. The results are expressed as the mean ± SEM. The null hypothesis was rejected if the P value was less than 0.05.

Results

Water Load Excretion

The mean percent excretion of the 20 ml/kg water load during control conditions in the eight cirrhotic patients was 33 ± 10% in 5 hours. The range was 9.0–60.0%. Therefore, each of the patients fulfilled the criterion for being labeled as a "non-excretor" (Bichet et al., 1982); that is, none of the patients were able to excrete 80% of the administered water load within 5 hours.

Plasma NE Concentrations

The mean plasma NE concentration in the seven normal subjects was 185 ± 12 pg/ml, and was 830 ± 136 pg/ml in the eight cirrhotic patients, $P <$ 0.001 (Fig. 1).

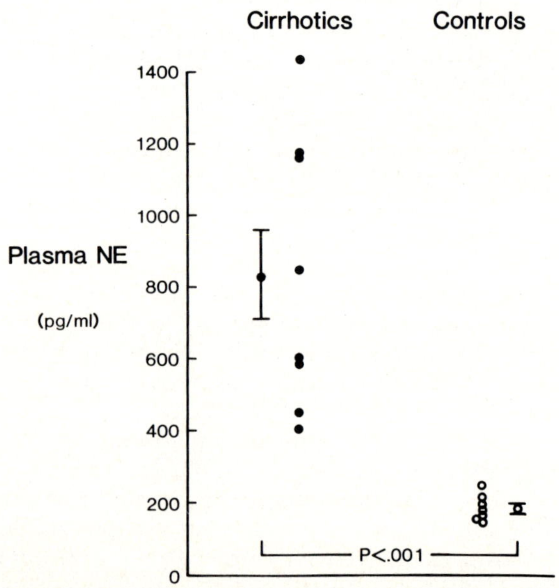

FIGURE 1. *Plasma norepinephrine (NE) concentrations under baseline conditions in cirrhotic patients and normal subjects.*

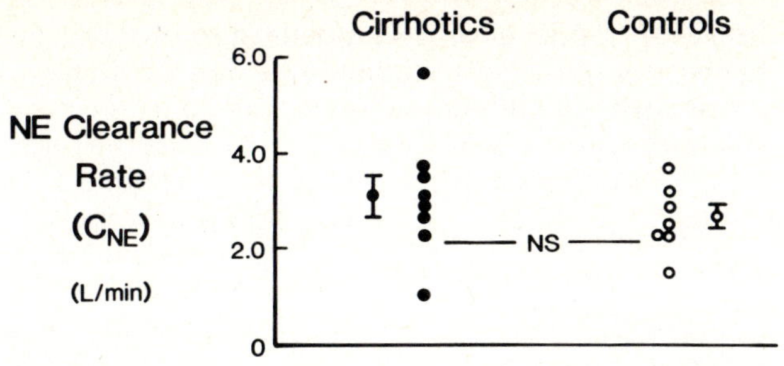

FIGURE 2. *Plasma NE clearance rates are comparable in cirrhotic patients and normal subjects.*

Plasma NE Clearance Rates

In Figure 2 are shown the plasma NE clearance rates in the normal subjects and the cirrhotic patients. The mean clearance rate in the normal subjects was 2.60 ± 0.28 liters/min and was 3.13 ± 0.48 liters/min in the cirrhotic patients; these values were not significantly different.

Plasma NE Secretion Rates

The plasma NE secretion rates in the normal subjects and cirrhotic patients are shown in Figure 3. The mean NE secretion rate was 0.26 ± 0.08 $\mu g/m^2$ per min for the control subjects and was 1.50 ± 0.25 $\mu g/m^2$ per min for the cirrhotic patients, $P <$ 0.001. There was a significant correlation between plasma NE concentrations and NE secretion rates as analyzed by linear regression analysis. In the 15 subjects (seven control and eight cirrhotic patients), the r value was 0.68 and the P value was <0.01. (plasma [NE] = 760 × apparent secretion rate − 180.)

Effect of HWI on Plasma NE

In each of seven patients studied, plasma NE concentrations were suppressed during HWI (Fig. 4). The mean plasma NE concentrations were suppressed from 704 ± 72 to 475 ± 70, $P < 0.005$. The plasma E concentrations were also suppressed by HWI from 121 ± 33 to 57 ± 10 pg/ml, $P < 0.05$ (Fig. 5). Furthermore, HWI resulted in an increase in the percent excretion of the administered water

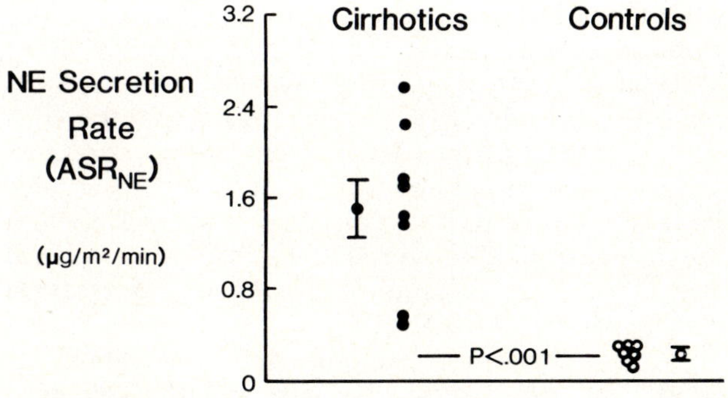

FIGURE 3. *Plasma NE secretion rates are significantly greater in cirrhotic patients than in normal subjects.*

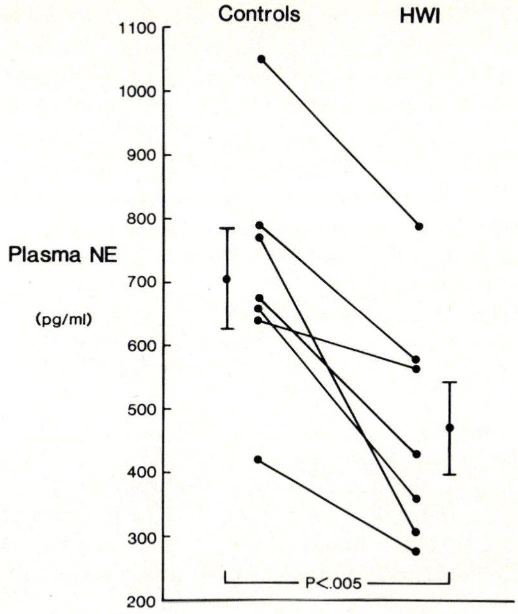

FIGURE 4. *Suppression of plasma NE during head-out water immersion (HWI) in cirrhotic patients. Each patient functioned as his own control.*

load to 65.7 ± 6.0% in 5 hours ($P < .05$), consistent with our previous experience (Bichet et al., 1982; Shapiro et al., 1984).

Discussion

Although there have been conflicting results in early studies in which less sensitive methods were used (Shaldon, 1962; Joly et al., 1967), more recent studies of cirrhotic patients by sensitive radioenzymatic technique have demonstrated significantly increased plasma NE concentrations (Henriksen et al., 1981; Bichet et al., 1982; Ring Larsen et al., 1982; Epstein, 1983). Moreover, decompensated cirrhotic patients have the highest NE levels, and also demonstrate more hyponatremia and higher plasma concentrations of arginine vasopressin, renin, and al-

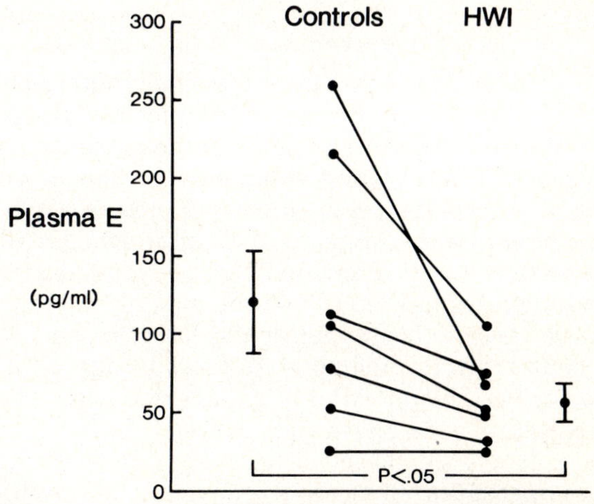

FIGURE 5. *Suppression of plasma epinephrine (E) during HWI in cirrhotic patients. Each patient functioned as his own control.*

dosterone than compensated cirrhotics who excrete a water load normally (Bichet et al., 1982). The results of the present investigation confirm those of previous studies from our laboratory in demonstrating significantly elevated plasma NE concentrations in non-excretor cirrhotic subjects. This study also extends these findings in delineating the relative contributions of altered NE clearance and secretion to the elevated plasma NE concentrations found in these patients.

Since the normal liver contains large quantities of monoamine oxidase and catechol-*o*-methyl transferase, decompensated cirrhotic patients might be expected to have a deficiency of these enzymes and, thus, impaired catecholamine clearance. Alternatively, or in addition, if the peripheral vasodilation, splanchnic venous pooling, and diminished oncotic pressure mediate a decrease in EABV in decompensated cirrhosis, then volume- and/or baroreceptor-mediated increases in NE secretion may cause an increase in plasma NE concentrations.

The results demonstrate that NE clearance is not diminished in patients with advanced cirrhosis, compared to normal subjects. Our clearance data are concordant with the results of Ring Larsen et al. (1982), who found normal hepatic extraction of NE in cirrhotic patients. In contrast, NE secretion rates were significantly increased in these decompensated cirrhotic patients. The elevated plasma NE concentrations in these patients are therefore more compatible with increased adrenergic activity and NE release, rather than diminished hepatic NE clearance. Moreover, in concert with the aforementioned elevations of plasma renin, aldosterone, and vasopressin, these results provide further support for the underfilling hypothesis of sodium and water retention in advanced cirrhosis. These findings are consistent with the findings of others (Ring Larsen et al., 1982; DiBona, 1984) which suggest that efferent sympathetic nerve activity is enhanced in decompensated cirrhosis, as a response to a decreased "EABV." This increased sympathetic tone seems likely to contribute to the renal vasoconstriction that characterizes this disorder (Better and Schrier, 1983; DiBona, 1984).

The underfilling hypothesis was examined further in the present study by measuring plasma NE concentrations in the same patients in the presence and absence of central blood volume expansion. If volume- and/or baroreceptor-mediated increases in adrenergic activity are triggered by a diminished EABV and account for the increased plasma NE concentrations, then central blood volume expansion should tend to reverse this sequence and lower plasma NE concentration. In preliminary studies in our laboratory, central blood volume expansion using HWI decreased plasma NE in four patients (Bichet et al., 1983). However, these results were not confirmed in a larger group of cirrhotic patients from another laboratory (Epstein et al., 1983). In the latter study, however, the level of decompensation of these patients was not rigidly defined. As indicated above, those cirrhotic patients who are unable to excrete a standard water load normally demonstrate the highest plasma NE concentrations, as well as other hormonal evidence of a decreased EABV. In the present study, each of the seven non-excretor patients demonstrated a suppression of plasma NE during HWI, a technique that has been previously documented to increase intracardiac pressures and cardiac index, presumed evidence of enhanced EABV (Bichet et al., 1983; Shapiro et al., 1984).

Although advancing age has been noted to increase plasma NE levels, its contribution appears to be quantitatively small (Ziegler et al., 1976). Specifically, Lake et al. (1977) reported that plasma NE levels increased by approximately 25% between the ages of 30 and 50 years, in a population of 67 hypertensive and 84 normotensive subjects. In the present studies, although the normal subjects were younger than the cirrhotic patients by the approximate margin noted above, the difference in plasma NE levels was much more pronounced than that anticipated from age alone. It therefore seems reasonable to maintain that the age difference between the cirrhotic and normal subjects cannot account for the 300–400% higher mean NE level in the cirrhotic group.

Although accepted as a valid index of overall sympathetic activity (Grossman et al., 1982), the plasma NE concentration does not delineate either the stimulus to secretion or its organ source. Sympathetic nervous discharge to different organs is non-uniform, and determinations of organ-specific sympathetic nervous function, via measurement of NE across isolated vascular beds, provides more specific information (Folkow et al., 1983; Esler, 1984). Ring Larsen et al. (1982) have measured renal arteriovenous differences of NE and have detected higher renal arterial-to-venous increments, as well as lower renal blood flows, in decompensated cirrhotic patients compared to normal subjects. Thus, the importance of the contribution of efferent renal sympathetic nerve activity to the renal vasoconstriction and, hence, sodium and water avidity of decompensated cirrhosis, has become increasingly evident (DiBona, 1984).

Our studies were designed to examine total peripheral activity rather than the secretion or clearance of NE across specific vascular beds. In this regard, Goldstein (1983) has proposed that the concept of venous plasma NE concentration, representing a mean sympathetic activity of multiple vascular beds, is analogous to total peripheral resistance, a useful index of the overall status of the peripheral circulation, but lacking in regard to information about specific vascular beds.

In summary, non-excretor decompensated cirrhotic patients consistently demonstrate increased plasma NE concentrations. These elevated NE concentrations are associated with increased NE secretion rates and normal NE clearance, as compared to normal subjects. The suppressibility of plasma NE and E with HWI provides further evidence that a decreased EABV is the stimulus for enhanced NE secretion in decompensated cirrhosis.

We are indebted to the staff of the Clinical Research Unit at the University of Colorado Health Science Center for their exemplary care of our patients, to Linda M. Benson for secretarial assistance, and to Carolyn Burke for expert technical assistance.

This work was supported by Grant RR-00051 from the General Clinical Research Center Program of the Division of Research Resources, NIH. Dr. M.D. Shapiro is supported by National Institutes of Health Training Grant AM07135.

Address for reprints: Dr. Robert W. Schrier, Medicine, B178, University of Colorado Medical School, 4200 E. 9th Avenue, Denver, Colorado 80262.

Received May 23, 1984; accepted for publication November 30, 1984.

References

Better O, Schrier RW (1983) Disturbed volume homeostasis in patients with cirrhosis of the liver. Kidney Int **23:** 303–311

Bichet DG, Van Putten VJ, Schrier RW (1982) Potential role of increased sympathetic activity in impaired sodium and water excretion in cirrhosis. N Engl J Med **307:** 1552–1557

Bichet DG, Groves BM, Schrier RW (1983) Mechanisms of improvement of water and sodium excretion by immersion in decompensated cirrhosis. Kidney Int **24:** 788–794

DiBona GF (1984) Renal neural activity in hepatorenal syndrome. Kidney Int **25:** 841–853

Epstein M (1983) Increased sympathetic activity in cirrhosis (letter). N Engl J Med **308:** 1030

Epstein M, Larios O, Johnson G (1983) Dissociation of plasma norepinephrine and renal sodium and water handling in cirrhosis (abstr). Am Soc Nephrol p 191A

Esler M (1984) How can we measure sympathetic nervous system "tone" in patients. Aust NZ J Med **14:** 4–5

Esler M, Jackman G, Kelleher D, Skews H, Jennings G, Bobik A, Korner P (1980) Norepinephrine kinetics in patients with idiopathic autonomic insufficiency. Circ Res **46:** 547–548

Folkow B, DiBona G, Hjemdahl P, Thoren P, Wallin BG (1983) Measurements of plasma norepinephrine concentrations in human primary hypertension—a word of caution concerning their applicability for assessing neurogenic contribution. Hypertension **5:** 399–402

Goldstein D (1983) Commentary. Hypertension **5:** 402–403

Grossman SH, Davis D, Gunnells JC, Shand DG (1982) Plasma norepinephrine in the evaluation of baroreceptor function in humans. Hypertension **4:** 566–571

Henriksen JH, Christensen NJH, Ring Larsen H (1981) Noradrenaline and adrenaline concentrations in various vascular beds in patients with cirrhosis. Relation to hemodynamics. Clin Physiol **1:** 293–304

Joly JG, Leduc J, Bernier J, Lavoie P, Viallet A (1967) Catecholamine levels in portal, hepatic and systemic venous blood in portal hypertension. Lancet **2:** 121–123

Lake RC, Ziegler MG, Coleman MD, Kopin IJ (1977) Age-adjusted plasma norepinephrine levels are similar in normotensive and hypertensive subjects. N Engl J Med **296:** 208–209

Peuler JD, Johnson GA (1977) Simlutaneous single isotope radioenzymatic assay of plasma norepinephrine, epinephrine and dopamine. Life Sci **21:** 625–636

Ring Larsen H, Hesse B, Henriksen JH, Christensen NJ (1982) Sympathetic nervous activity and renal and systemic hemodynamics in cirrhosis. Plasma norepinephrine concentration, hepatic extraction, and renal release. Hepatology **2:** 304–310

Schrier RW, Berl T, Anderson RJ (1979) Osmotic and nonosmotic control of vasopressin release. Am J Physiol **236:** F321–F332

Shaldon C (1962) Dynamic aspects of portal hypertension. Ann R Col Surg Engl **31:** 308–329

Shapiro M, Nicholls K, Groves B, Kluge R, Chung H-M, Bichet D, Schrier R (1984) Evidence for decreased effective blood volume in the sodium and water retention of cirrhotic man (abstr). IXth International Congress of Nephrology, p 127A

Ziegler MG, Lake RC, Kopin IJ (1976) Plasma noradrenaline increases with age. Nature **261:** 333–335

INDEX TERMS: Catecholamine kinetics • Cirrhosis • Head-out water immersion

BRIEF COMMUNICATIONS

Subfornical Organ

Does It Protect against Angiotensin II-Induced Hypertension in the Rat?

Cathy A. Bruner, Michael L. Mangiapane, and Gregory D. Fink

From the Department of Pharmacology and Toxicology, Michigan State University, East Lansing, Michigan, and the Department of Pharmacology, School of Medicine and Dentistry, University of Rochester, Rochester, New York

SUMMARY. The purpose of this study was to examine the contribution of the subfornical organ to the chronic hypertension produced by intravenous angiotensin II infusion in rats. Male rats were instrumented with permanent arterial and venous catheters and housed in metabolism cages for daily measurement of arterial pressure, heart rate, water intake, water balance, and urinary electrolyte excretion. Angiotensin II was infused intravenously at a rate of 10 ng/minute for 5 consecutive days, preceded by 2 control days, and followed by 2 recovery days. Normal rats with an intact subfornical organ ($n = 7$), and rats with an electrolytic lesion placed such that greater than 80% of the subfornical organ was destroyed ($n = 9$), were studied using this infusion protocol. An additional group of eight rats did not receive angiotensin II, and, thus, served as a time control. Both groups of rats receiving angiotensin II exhibited significant elevations in arterial pressure during the 5-day hormone infusion period, but pressure in rats with subfornical organ lesions (Δ23–29 mm Hg) was increased significantly more than that of intact rats (Δ14–20 mm Hg). Water intake was significantly increased on the 3rd, 4th, and 5th days of angiotensin II infusion only in rats with lesions in the subfornical organ. In contrast to previous studies showing that an intact subfornical organ is required for normal pressor and drinking responses to acute elevations in circulating angiotensin II in the rat, the current experiments indicate that the presence of the subfornical organ actually inhibits these same responses during more chronic increases in plasma angiotensin II levels. **(*Circ Res 56: 462–466, 1985*)**

CIRCULATING angiotensin II (AII) is believed to produce several physiological effects which are mediated at least in part through a direct action of the hormone on the central nervous system (Brody and Johnson, 1980; Ramsay, 1982; Reid, 1984). Such effects include drinking, increased arterial blood pressure, release of vasopressin, and release of adrenocorticotrophic hormone. The location of the receptor sites at which blood-borne AII interacts with the brain to cause these physiological changes is a matter of some controversy (Hartle and Brody, 1984; Reid, 1984). The circumventricular organ(s) (CVO)—structures which lack a blood-brain barrier and are situated on the luminal surface of the cerebral ventricles—have been proposed as neural sensors for blood-borne AII. The CVO include the organum vasculosum of the lamina terminalis (OVLT), the subfornical organ (SFO), and the area postrema. The median preoptic nucleus, intimately connected to the SFO and OVLT, may also be AII-sensitive (Lind and Johnson, 1982; Mangiapane et al., 1983; Hartle and Brody, 1984).

Although there is evidence for all the above structures, most recent evidence strongly suggests that, in the rat, circulating AII exerts many of its acute central actions via stimulation of receptor elements in the SFO. In vitro binding techniques (Sirett et al., 1977) have revealed receptors for AII in high concentration in the SFO, and in vivo studies have shown high-affinity binding sites for blood-borne or cerebrospinal fluid-borne AII in the SFO (Van Houten et al., 1980, 1983). Neurons within the SFO are excited by iontophoretic application of AII (Phillips and Felix, 1976), and electrolytic destruction of the structure in rats blocks or reduces the dipsogenic and pressor responses to short-term (minutes to hours) intravenous infusion of AII (Simpson et al., 1978; Mangiapane and Simpson, 1980a). In addition, microinjection of AII directly into the SFO provokes pressor responses within seconds and water ingestion within 1 minute postinjection (Mangiapane and Simpson, 1980b). Intravenous or intracerebroventricular injection of AII is a potent stimulus for vasopressin release in normal rats, but this release of vasopressin is blocked or attenuated in SFO-ablated rats (Knepel et al., 1982; Mangiapane et al., 1984). Dehydration, which causes a marked increase in plasma AII concentration (Abdelaal et al., 1976; Mann et al., 1980), stimulates cellular metabolism in the SFO as determined by the 2-deoxyglucose technique (Gross et al., 1983).

These studies have provided ample evidence supporting the postulate that blood-borne AII acts at the SFO in rats to elicit drinking behavior and bring about a centrally mediated pressor response. Nonetheless, all of the preceding studies have involved measuring physiological responses to AII during rather short-term (minutes to a few hours) increases in blood levels of the hormone. The purpose of the present experiment was to investigate the contribution of the SFO to a model of hypertension involving chronic increases in plasma AII concentration.

Methods

Animals

Male Sprague-Dawley rats weighing 300–400 g were studied. Before entering the experimental protocol, all rats were group housed (two rats per cage) in temperature-controlled and light-cycled quarters and were fed standard rat chow. All surgical procedures were carried out under sodium pentobarbital anesthesia (50 mg/kg, ip).

Infusion Protocol

In a preliminary operation, permanent polyvinyl-silicone rubber catheters were placed in the abdominal vena cava and aorta via the femoral vessels. The free ends of the catheters were tunneled subcutaneously to the skull and anchored there with dental acrylic. A flexible protective spring connected to a hydraulic swivel also was attached to the skull. Mounting the swivel above a standard metal metabolic cage allowed the rat unrestricted movement within the cage. Both catheters exited the metabolic cage inside the protective metal spring attached to the swivel. The venous catheter was attached to a Harvard infusion pump via the swivel to allow continuous (24 hr/day) iv infusion of fluids. The arterial catheter was filled with a heparinized solution and plugged when not in use. The plugged end of the arterial catheter rotated freely above the cage except during the recording of arterial pressure. The rats were fed a commercial sodium-deficient diet (12–15 g/day; 0.002 mEq Na^+, 0.3 mEq K^+/g) for the remainder of the experiment. The rats also received 40 ml/day of isotonic saline via intravenous infusion for the duration of the experiment (daily Na^+ intake = 6.2 mEq). Distilled water was available ad libitum from calibrated drinking tubes. All rats received twice daily injections of ampicillin (10 mg iv) after being housed in the metabolism cages.

Three days after placement of the rats in metabolism cages, the experimental protocol was started. This consisted of 2 control days, 5 days during which angiotensin II amide (Hypertensin) was infused continuously, iv, at a rate of 10 ng/min, then 2 postinfusion recovery days. Daily measurements included: (1) arterial pressure and heart rate obtained by connecting the arterial catheter to a low volume displacement pressure transducer (Statham P50) for 10–30 minutes each morning, (2) water intake calculated by adding the 40-ml infused volume to voluntary drinking volume obtained from a calibrated drinking tube, (3) urine volume obtained by quantitative collection from the metabolic cage, and (4) urinary sodium and potassium excretions calculated by multiplying urine volume by electrolyte concentrations (flame photometry).

Groups

Three groups of rats were studied in the preceding protocol. The first group (n = 7) received only saline during the 5-day "hormone infusion" period. The second group of rats (n = 8) received AII (10 ng/min) during the same 5-day infusion period. A third group (n = 9) was subjected to electrolytic destruction of the SFO 2–4 weeks prior to a 5-day infusion of AII (10 ng/min).

Lesion of the SFO

Rats were anesthetized with a pentobarbital-chloral hydrate mixture and immobilized in a Kopf stereotaxic instrument. A trephine hole was drilled in the skull dorsal to the lesion site, and a 30-gauge Teflon-insulated monopolar tungsten electrode was lowered to the lesion site. Because the anterior stalk of the SFO is quite ventral to the posterior stalk, three electrode penetrations were required. A total of 21 millicoulombs (mC) (1 mA for 21 sec) of anodal current was passed, with 7 mC passed per penetration. All penetrations were made in the midline after the superior sagittal sinus had been retracted. The first penetration was to 5.0 mm ventral to the dura, and 0.3 mm posterior to bregma. Each successive penetration was made to a point 0.3 mm posterior and 0.2 mm dorsal to the preceding one. After surgery, each rat received 100,000 IU of procaine penicillin (im) and was returned to its home cage. Control rats (second and third groups) were age and weight matched and treated identically to rats with SFO lesions throughout the study, except that they did not undergo surgery 2–4 weeks prior to AII infusion.

Lesions were produced in 22 rats in the laboratory of one of the authors (M.M.), after which the animals were sent to another laboratory (G.F.) for AII infusion. At the end of the infusion protocol, the brain of each rat was perfused with buffered formalin, coded, and returned to the original laboratory for a blind histological analysis of lesion size and location. Frozen sections (35 μm) were cut through the lesion site and stained with cresyl violet. The sections then were examined carefully in a light microscope to determine the location of the lesion; the examiner had no knowledge of the data for any particular animal. Only after confirmation that the lesion destroyed >80% of the SFO was a given rat included in the "SFO lesion" group. Sixteen rats completed the AII infusion protocol, and nine of these had >80% destruction of the SFO. These nine were included in the analysis. None of these had damage to the median preoptic nucleus (nucleus medianus). As is typical of SFO lesions (Mangiapane et al., 1984), all sustained a minor degree of damage to the fornical commissure, triangular septal nucleus, and paraventricular nucleus of the thalamus. Photomicrographs of the normal SFO and a representative SFO lesion are shown in Figure 1.

Statistical Analyses

The data were analyzed by a mixed design analysis-of-variance followed by the "protected" least significance difference test for individual group comparisons. A P value of less than 0.05 was the criterion for statistical significance.

Results

The results of 5 days of continuous AII infusion (10 ng/min, iv) in the three groups of rats are illustrated in Figure 2. Mean arterial pressure (MAP), heart rate (HR), water intake (WI), urinary sodium excretion ($U_{Na}V$), and urinary potassium excretion (U_KV) were unchanged during the 5-day infusion

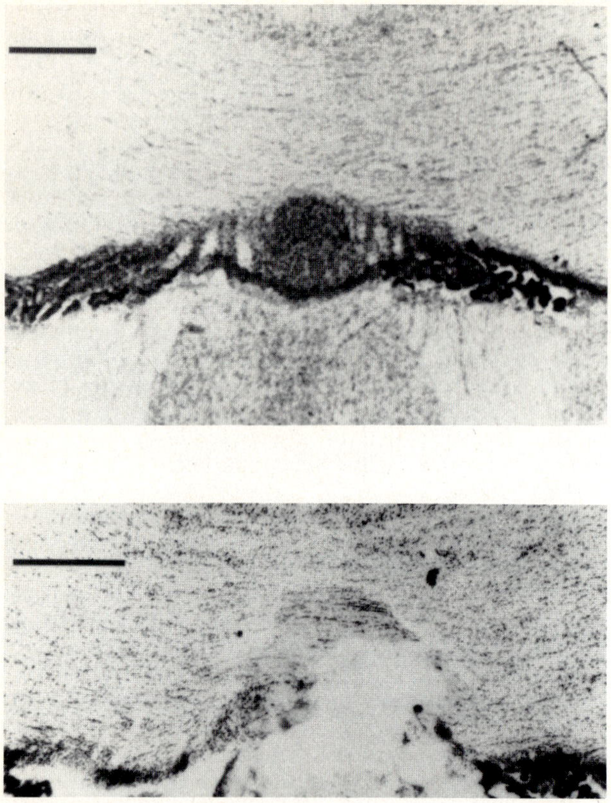

FIGURE 1. *Unretouched photomicrographs of coronal sections of rat brain at the level of the interventricular foramina. Top: normal subfornical organ is the dark-staining structure in the center of the photograph, and is flanked by fronds of the choroid plexus. Bottom: subfornical organ lesion. The scale bars are each 0.5 mm long.*

period in rats receiving only saline, compared to control period values. In normal (SFO intact; SFOI) rats receiving AII, MAP was increased significantly throughout the 5 days of infusion and returned to the control range by 24 hours after termination of the infusion. In rats with SFO lesions (SFOX), MAP also was increased significantly during the AII period and returned to a normal range by 24 hours after termination of the infusion. Moreover, MAP was greater in SFOX rats than in SFOI animals throughout the AII infusion period; however, this difference was statistically significant only on days 1, 4, and 5. SFOI rats exhibited a gradual increase in HR which was statistically significant by the 5th day of AII administration, and HR remained elevated for 48 hours after the infusion was stopped. No significant change in HR was observed in SFOX rats at any time during the protocol. The administration of AII did not produce changes in WI in SFOI rats, whereas WI was significantly increased by the 3rd day in SFOX rats, and remained significantly elevated for the remainder of the AII infusion period. Water intake returned to normal within 24 hour after AII infusion in SFOX rats was stopped. In all three groups of rats, urine output paralleled water intake; therefore, water balance remained unchanged throughout the experiment (not shown). Neither $U_{Na}V$ nor U_KV was significantly changed by AII infusion in either SFOX or SFOI rats.

During the control and recovery periods, MAP, WI, and U_KV were the same in all rats. Likewise, HR and $U_{Na}V$ did not differ in the three groups of rats during the control period. In SFOI rats, HR was significantly higher during the recovery period than in either saline-infused rats or SFOX rats. During the recovery period, $U_{Na}V$ was higher in SFOX rats than in saline-infused or SFOI rats.

Discussion

In the present experiments, the effect of chronic iv infusion of AII on arterial pressure and fluid/

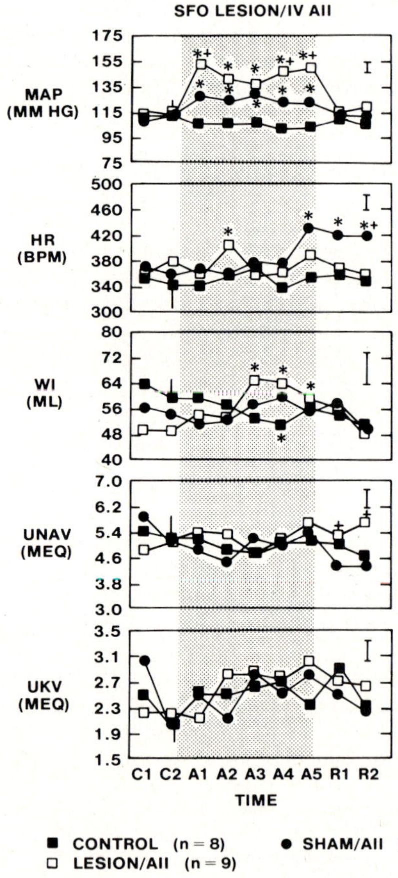

FIGURE 2. *Cardiovascular and fluid/electrolyte changes during 5-day intravenous infusion of angiotensin II (10 ng/min) in rats. Time intervals are in days, where C = control days, A = angiotensin infusion days, and R = recovery days. Shading further represents the interval during which angiotensin II was infused. Measured variables include mean arterial pressure (MAP), heart rate (HR), water intake (WI), urinary sodium excretion ($U_{Na}V$), and urinary potassium excretion (U_KV). Vertical lines on the C2 data symbols represent the standard error from the analysis of variance for any overtime comparison. Bars to the right of each box represent the average standard error from the analysis of variance for any between group comparison at a given time. Asterisks indicate a significant difference from the average of the two control day measurements, whereas crosses indicate a significant difference between the sham rats receiving angiotensin II (SHAM/AII) and the SFO-ablated rats receiving angiotensin II (LESION/AII).*

electrolyte homeostasis was assessed in rats. It is important to point out that the AII infusion rate utilized here (10 ng/min) has been shown previously to produce blood concentrations of AII in the rat roughly equivalent to those found during 24–48 hours of water deprivation (Mann et al., 1980). Thus, these experiments explored cardiovascular changes produced by blood levels of AII well within the "physiological" range.

The response of normal rats under the conditions of this study to chronic iv AII infusion was largely cardiovascular. Arterial pressure was significantly elevated throughout the 5-day infusion period, and a slowly developing tachycardia occurred. The delayed increase in heart rate observed here is a common, but not invariable, finding in this model and may be related to the known ability of circulating AII to interfere with baroreflex-mediated vagal activation and sympathoinhibition (Lumbers et al., 1979; Guo and Abboud, 1984). Water intake, water balance, and urinary electrolyte excretions were unchanged during AII infusion. This pattern of responses to iv AII is typical of many similar studies carried out in recent years in this laboratory (unpublished results). Although others have reported that chronic iv AII infusion produces transient urinary sodium retention and increased drinking behavior in the dog (Cowley et al., 1981), neither phenomenon occurs consistently in the rat at the doses of AII used in this experiment. Furthermore, despite the perception of AII as a hormone involved in the conservation of body water, none of the published studies on chronic AII infusion, including this one, have reported sustained positive water balance during AII infusion.

The primary issue examined in this study was the extent to which the SFO is necessary for cardiovascular and fluid/electrolyte responses to chronically elevated blood levels of AII. The large body of evidence indicating a significant contribution of the SFO to the major effects of AII on the central nervous system—that is, increased arterial pressure, drinking, and vasopressin release—was outlined in the introduction. However, in the current experiment, when rats with greater than 80% of the SFO destroyed received chronic iv infusions of AII, they responded with an even larger increment in MAP than did normal rats with an intact SFO. Furthermore, although normal rats did not increase water intake during the 5-day AII infusion, rats with SFO lesions exhibited a significant increase in drinking in response to the same infusion. Neither SFO-ablated rats nor normal rats exhibited changes in water balance or urinary electrolyte excretion during AII infusion. These results, in contrast to those obtained in studies utilizing acute AII stimulation, clearly indicate that AII receptors of the SFO are not required for pressor responses to circulating AII in our 5-day infusion model. If anything, the opposite is true: the presence of the SFO appears to retard the increases in arterial pressure and water turnover observed in association with chronically elevated plasma AII levels. Although this result appears to conflict with the finding (Buggy, 1981) that SFO-ablated rats are protected against chronic hypertension development in the presumably renin-dependent two-kidney, one-clip renal hypertension model, it should be noted that in Buggy's study, rats with lesions of the SFO had blood pressures markedly below control rats only more than 3 weeks after renal artery constriction. There is considerable dispute as to whether this model of hypertension remains "renin-dependent" after the first few weeks (Buggy and Fink, 1982).

There are a number of possible explanations for the disparities between our results and those from previous studies utilizing more short-term protocols. First, sodium intake may influence the neural response to circulating AII. In the current experiments all rats were receiving a high sodium intake (6.2 mEq/day), since this has been shown to augment greatly the hypertensive response to chronic iv infusion of AII (Fink et al., 1982). In fact, in this laboratory, it has proven impossible to produce sustained hypertension with iv AII in rats on "normal" (1–2 mEq/day) sodium intake (Fink et al., 1982). Previous short-term studies have used rats on a "normal" sodium intake. Since some CVO (e.g., OVLT) stimulated by AII also are known to be osmosensitive (Brody and Johnson, 1980; Thrasher et al., 1982) it is possible that a high sodium intake alters the *relative* sensitivity of the circumventricular organs to circulating AII. Thus, blood-borne AII may act to a greater extent at the SFO in rats on "normal" sodium intake, but preferentially at other CVO during concomitant osmotic stimulation accompanying higher sodium intakes.

A second possible explanation is that the cerebral receptors mediating thirst and the central component of the pressor response to elevated blood concentrations of AII are simply different during acute vs. chronic increases in blood hormone levels. Physiological stimuli that increase AII levels in blood can be either relatively acute (i.e., hemorrhage, water deprivation) or more chronic (sodium depletion, unilateral renal artery stenosis). Perhaps different cerebral mechanisms are activated, via different neural pathways, under these two different temporal conditions.

On the other hand, the finding here that SFO lesions actually potentiate the drinking and pressor response to chronic iv AII also requires examination. One explanation for this finding is based on the assumption that an acute electrolytic lesion placed in a structure bordering the cerebral ventricles might disrupt the normal blood-brain barrier and allow passage of blood-borne AII into sensitive brain areas to which it normally does not have access. However, this is an unlikely factor in the present experiments, since the lesions were placed 2–4 weeks prior to AII infusion, thus allowing adequate time for healing. A more likely explanation can be postulated based on recent neuroanatomical studies of the SFO. An efferent neural pathway which exhibits AII-like immunoreactivity has been identified (Lind and Johnson, 1982) passing from the SFO to the median preoptic region. The destruction of this pathway by SFO lesions might render AII receptors in the median preoptic region supersensitive to the hormone. If circulating AII exerts some of its neural actions on the median preoptic region, as has been proposed (Hartle and Brody, 1984), then receptor supersensitivity in this region could explain the augmented responses of SFO-ablated rats to chronic iv infusion of AII.

The present chronic, and previous acute, studies are in agreement that rats with SFO destruction do not respond normally to elevated plasma AII levels. A final possibility to be considered in view of all studies to date is that both excitatory and inhibitory neural pathways pass through, or originate, in the SFO, and can be influenced by circulating AII. Qualitatively different abnormalities in pressor responses and drinking behavior during acute and chronic elevations of plasma AII in rats with SFO lesions may reflect a different temporal pattern of engagement of such excitatory and inhibitory systems.

In conclusion, although the underlying mechanisms for the results obtained in these experiments remain highly speculative, it is clear that chronic elevation of blood AII levels, within a physiological range, can produce sustained hypertension without increasing water intake and in the absence of cerebral pressor mechanisms activated through the SFO.

Supported by National Institutes of Health Grant R01-HL24111.

Address for reprints: Gregory D. Fink, Ph.D., Department of Pharmacology and Toxicology, Michigan State University, East Lansing, Michigan 48824-1317.

Received September 17, 1984; accepted for publication December 20, 1984.

References

Abdelaal AE, Mercer PF, Mogenson GJ (1976) Plasma angiotensin II levels and water intake following β-adrenergic stimulation, hypovolemia, cellular dehydration and water deprivation. Pharmacol Biochem Behav **4:** 317–321

Brody MJ, Johnson AK (1980) Role of the anteroventral third ventricle (AV3V) region in fluid and electrolyte balance, arterial pressure regulation and hypertension. *In* Frontiers in Neuroendocrinology, vol 6, edited by WF Ganong, L Martini. New York, Raven Press, pp 249–292

Buggy J (1981) Prevention of renal but not DOC-salt hypertension after subfornical organ lesion (abstr). Fed Proc **40:** 390

Buggy J, Fink GD (1982) Experimental renal hypertension. *In* Hypertension Research: Methods and Models, edited by FM Radziahowski. New York, Dekker, pp 343–390

Cowley AW, Switzer SJ, Skelton MM (1981) Vasopressin, fluid and electrolyte response to chronic angiotensin II infusion. Am J Physiol **240:** R130–R138

Fink GD, Haywood JR, Owen JM, Bruner CA (1982) Sodium and the central nervous system in chronic angiotensin-induced hypertension in the rat (abstr). Fed Proc **41:** 1585

Gross PM, Kadekaro M, Sokoloff L, Holcomb HH, Saavedra JM (1983) Glucose metabolism of neural substrates for thirst (abstr). Fed Proc **42:** 611

Guo GB, Abboud FM (1984) Angiotensin II attenuates baroreflex control of heart rate and sympathetic activity. Am J Physiol **246:** H80–H89

Hartle DK, Brody MJ (1984) The angiotensin II pressor system of the rat forebrain. Circ Res **54:** 355–366

Knepel W, Nutto D, Meyer DK (1982) Effect of transection of subfornical organ efferent projections on vasopressin release induced by angiotensin or isoprenaline in the rat. Brain Res **248:** 180–184

Lind RW, Johnson AK (1982) Central and peripheral mechanisms mediating angiotensin-induced thirst. *In* The Renin-Angiotensin System in the Brain, edited by D Ganten, M Printz, MI Phillips, BA Scholkens. New York, Springer-Verlag, pp 353–364

Lumbers ER, McCloskey DI, Potter EK (1979) Inhibition by angiotensin II of baroreceptor-evoked activity in cardiac vagal nerves in the dog. J Physiol **294:** 69–80

Mangiapane ML, Simpson JB (1980a) Subfornical organ lesions reduce the pressor effect of systemic angiotensin II. Neuroendocrinology **31:** 380–384

Mangiapane ML, Simpson JB (1980b) Subfornical organ: Forebrain site of pressor and dipsogenic action of angiotensin II. Am J Physiol **239:** R382–R389

Mangiapane ML, Thrasher TN, Keil LC, Simpson JB, Ganong WF (1983) Deficits in drinking and vasopressin secretion after lesions of the nucleus medianus. Neuroendocrinology **37:** 73–77

Mangiapane ML, Thrasher TN, Keil LC, Simpson JB, Ganong WF (1984) Role for the subfornical organ in vasopressin release. Brain Res Bull **13:** 43–47

Mann JFE, Johnson AK, Ganten D (1980) Plasma angiotensin II. Dipsogenic levels and angiotensin-generating capacity of renin. Am J Physiol **238:** R372–R377

Phillips MI, Felix D (1976) Specific angiotensin II receptive neurons in the cat subfornical organ. Brain Res **109:** 531–540

Ramsay DJ (1982) Effects of circulating angiotensin II on the brain. *In* Frontiers in Neuroendocrinology, vol 7, edited by WF Ganong, L Martini. New York, Raven Press, pp 263–285

Reid IA (1984) Actions of angiotensin II on the brain: Mechanisms and physiologic role. Am J Physiol **246:** F533–F543

Simpson JB, Epstein AN, Camardo JS Jr (1978) Localization of angiotensin II in the subfornical organ of the rat. J Comp Physiol Psychol **92:** 581–608

Sirett NE, McClean AS, Bray JJ, Hubbard JI (1977) Distribution of angiotensin II receptors in rat brain. Brain Res **122:** 299–312

Thrasher TN, Keil LC, Ramsay DJ (1982) Lesions of the organum vasculosum of the lamina terminalis (OVLT) attenuate osmotically induced drinking and vasopressin secretion in the dog. Endocrinology **110:** 1837–1839

Van Houten M, Schiffrin EL, Mann JFE, Posner BI (1980) Radioautographic localization of specific binding sites for blood-borne angiotensin in the rat brain. Brain Res **186:** 480–485

Van Houten M, Mangiapane ML, Reid IA, Ganong WF (1983) (sar^1, ala^8) Angiotensin II in cerebrospinal fluid blocks the binding of blood-borne ^{125}I-angiotensin II to the circumventricular organs. Neuroscience **10:** 1421–1426

INDEX TERMS: Circumventricular organs · Renin-angiotensin system · Blood pressure · Drinking

News from the American Heart Association

7320 Greenville Avenue, Dallas, Texas 75231
Telephone: 214 750-5300

Grants-in-Aid Awards Are Listed by Heart; Total 384 for 1984–5

New and continuing research Grants-in-Aid totalling $11,728,000 for the 1984–5 year have been announced by the American Heart Association.

There were 100 new grants at $3,148,000 and 284 continuing grants totalling $8,580,000.

The Grants-in-Aid announcement completed the research awards granted for the year 1984–5. Fellowships totalling $11,965,700 were announced earlier (Circulation **69:** April, 1984, Ad pages 9 and 21–26).

Names of those awarded Grants-in-Aid 1984–5 are printed in the March issue of CIRCULATION (News From the American Heart Association section).

$43 Million Allocated By AHA to 1984 Research

The American Heart Association committed more than $43 million to its research programs in 1984—30.6% of the budget—the officers announced in the Annual Report. This brought to more than $565 million funds invested in research since 1949.

The officers, Dr. Antonio M. Gotto, Jr., president, and J. Franklin Smith, chairman of the board, also pointed to the 28% reduction in deaths from cardiovascular disease from 1972 to 1982.

Anti-Smoking Bill

"In 1984," the Report said, "the American Heart Association authored a bill that became the toughest legislation in history governing cigarette advertising." The requirement that cigarette companies mention heart disease and other specific ills of smoking in their advertisements and on package labels signalled the growth of influence of AHA voluntary leadership and its allies in the Coalition on Smoking, the Report added.

CPPT Trials

AHA has warned against elevated levels of cholesterol for three decades, the officers noted, and in 1984 results of the 10-year landmark Coronary Primary Prevention Trials (CPPT) provided significant new evidence that lowering serum cholesterol reduces heart disease risk.

Diet Guidelines

Also in 1984 AHA provided physicians with new guidelines for the dietary treatment of patients who had hyperlipidemia.

Public Support

The Report stressed that public support increased for AHA as evidenced by increased income of almost 39% in the past five years. (A 1984 Gallup Poll showed that more than 92% of those surveyed were aware of the Heart Association).

Membership in the Association affiliates has risen to over 120,000 professional and laymen who provided guidance for almost 2 million other volunteers. Fourteen Scientific Councils, the medical arm of AHA, had 12,500 members.

Public Programs

Other program activities mentioned by the Report were continuing education for physicians and nurses, public education on risk factors, screening people for high blood pressure, and educating the public on cardiopulmonary resuscitation. Program activities also help people stop smoking and adopt more healthful diets, lose weight, and return to productive lives after heart attack or stroke.

1984 Medical Education Efforts Reported by AHA

The AHA 1984 Annual Report listed the following professional activities:

- More than 16,000 persons—including 9,000 physicians, nurses, medical students, and other health professionals—attended the 56th Scientific Sessions (1983) in Anaheim.
- There were 1,752 presentations at the 56th Sessions, an increase of 232 over the previous year.
- More than 1,200 medical students and physicians attended 24 "how to" seminars.
- AHA Scientific Councils conducted annual conferences that attracted more than 1,200 participants. Through affiliates and local universities the Councils co-sponsored 24 postgraduate courses.
- More than 400,000 subscription copies of five AHA Scientific Publications were distributed by the National Center. More than 1.7 million copies of other professional journals were distributed by affiliates.

Atherosclerosis Symposium Sets Up Program Oct. 6–10

Details of the preliminary program for the 7th International Symposium on Atherosclerosis at the Regent Melbourne Hotel in Melbourne, Australia, Oct. 6–10, have been announced by the International Atherosclerosis Society.

Also announced were plans for a satellite symposium, "Cell Biology of the Artery Wall," to be held at Hayman Island, Great Barrier Reef, Australia, Oct. 11–15.

Another meeting on Hemodynamics and Atherosclerosis will be held Oct. 3–4 in Wellington, New Zealand, under the direction of Dr. W. E. Stehbens, Dept. of Pathology, Wellington Clinical School of Med., Wellington 2, NZ.

7th Symposium

The 7th International Symposium, supported by the American Heart Association among 11 other national societies, will open Oct. 7 with four speakers (three from the U.S.) on Epidemiology and Intervention Trials. They will be Drs. A. Motulsky, H. Blackburn, G. Assman, (Germany) and H. Tyroler. Dr. R. Levy is organizing chairman.

Workshop sessions will be held on "Cell Biology of Atherogenesis," Dr. O. Stein of Israel, chairwoman; "Regression of Atherosclerosis," Dr. A. Olsson, Sweden, chairman; "HDL and Atherosclerosis," Drs. E. Bierman of the U.S.A., and P. Barter of Australia, chairmen; "Inherited Lipoproteinemias and Atherosclerosis," Dr. H. Brewer, U.S.A., chairman, "New Pharmaceutical Developments," Dr. A. Kriesmann, West Germany, chairman.

October 8

Tuesday's program will begin with a plenary session on "Pathogenesis of Atherosclerosis" with Dr. R. Ross of U.S.A. as organizing chairman and Drs. D. Steinberg of U.S.A., M. Gimbrone of U.S.A. and J. Sixma of Holland. Workshop sessions in the afternoon will include "Microphages and Lipoprotein Transport," Dr. A. Chait, U.S.A., chairman; "Diabetes and Atherosclerosis", Dr. G. Crepaldi of Italy, chairman; "Genetic Regulation of Apolipoprotein Synthesis," Dr. J. Breslow, U.S.A. chairman; "Lipoprotein Structure and Function," Dr. A. Gotto, U.S.A., chairman; "Thrombosis, Prostanoids, and Atherosclerosis," Dr. C. Chesterman, Australia, chairman; "Cerebrovascular Disease," Dr. J. Geer, U.S.A., chairman.

October 9

Wednesday will include a plenary session on "Regulation of Lipoproteins" with Dr. R. Havel of U.S.A. as organizing chairman and Drs. Y. Stein of Israel, R. Mahley of U.S.A., S. Grundy of U.S.A., M. Brown of U.S.A. and P. Nestel of Australia as speakers.

October 10

The concluding session on "Perspectives and Future Directions" will be held Oct. 10. Dr. M. Oliver of the United Kingdom is organizing chairman and Drs. J. Goldstein of U.S.A. and F. G. Schettler of West Germany as speakers. Workshop sessions in the afternoon will include "Growth Factors and Atherosclerosis," Dr. D. Goodman, U.S.A., chairman; "Nutritional Factors," Dr. B. Lewis, U.K., chairman; "Preventive Epidemiology," Dr. B. Rifkind, U.S.A., chairman; "Arterial Extracellular Matrix and Lipoproteins," Dr. M. Bihari-Varga, Hungary, chairwoman; "Triglyceride-Rich Lipoproteins," Dr. S. Eisenberg, Israel, chairman; "Apolipoprotein Functions," Dr. N. Fidge, Australia, chairman.

Inquiries on the 7th International Symposium may go to the Secretariat, 7th Symposium, Baker Medical Research Institute, Commercial Road, Prahran, Melbourne, Vic. 3181, Australia.

Cell Biology

Applications for the limited registration for the Cell Biology symposium at Hayman Island may go (airmail) to Dr. Gordon R. Campbell, Dept. Anatomy, University of Melbourne, Parkville, 3052, Australia.

Radioactive Tracer Study Of ICHD Reprinted by AHA

"Optimal Resources for Radioactive Tracer Studies of the Heart and Circulation," the final report of the Inter-Society Commission for Heart Disease Resources, has been reprinted by AHA as a pamphlet and may be obtained from affiliates or the National Office in Dallas (ask for 72-101-B)

The report, reprinted from CIRCULATION (**70**, Sept. 1984 pp 525A-536A), suggests guidelines for the physical and human resources required for providing optimal services for radioactive tracer studies. Included are recommendations for manpower, space, equipment, and radiopharmaceuticals.

Abstracts of 57th SS

For physicians and scientists who were unable to attend the Scientific Sessions or do not subscribe to CIRCULATION, the Abstracts, containing 554 pages (1,793 abstracts), are now available from affiliates or the National Office (ask for 73-093A).

For Patients

Educational materials for patients now available from affiliates or the National Office include:

Grocery Guide—Tips on Wise Food Selection (50-068-A). Food products for following AHA dietary guidelines.

Dining Out—2 Pocket Folder. One side accomodates the Dining Out booklet with recommendations on diet; the other side can hold a restaurant guide generated from a local survey.

Fact Sheet on Heart Attack, Stroke and Risk Factors (51-024-1) Includes risk factors, emergency procedures, warning signals, and preventive measures.

Heart Facts 1985 (55-005-1): and *Calendar Wallet Cards—1985*, Heart Facts reflects latest information on CVD and offers a glossary of heart terms and statistical charts. The pocket calendar card notes early warning signals of heart attack and a plan for subsequent action.

HBP Control Conference In Chicago, April 28–30

The National Conference on High Blood Pressure Control will meet in the Palmer House, Chicago, April 28–30. The program will include workshops, roundtables, panels, papers, educational sessions, exhibits, posters and presentation of awards.

The conference will open with concurrent educational sessions: New Drugs in the Treatment of High Blood Pressure; Community Programs: Successes and Near Misses; Nursing Symposium.

3 Workshops Monday

Monday will include a plenary session on Unresolved Issues in HBP Control and concurrent workshop presentations on HBP in Asian/Pacific Populations; Implications of the 1984 Joint National Committee Report; and Unresolved Issues in HBP Control: Dialogue with the Experts. There will also be concurrent workshop presentations on HBP in Pediatrics; Case Studies: Resistant Patient Groups; Patient Adherence-Cost Elements; Unresolved Issues in HBP Control: Dialogue with the Experts. Another workshop session will consider Case Studies—Mild and Moderate HBP; HBP and Nutrition; Making the Media Work for You, HBP in Black and Hispanic Populations.

Tuesday Program

On Tuesday there will be a plenary session on Comprehensive HBP Control and workshop presentations on Use of Computers in HBP Control; Evaluation of Community Programs; and Technology Transfer: 5-Site Demonstration Project.

Inquiries may go to the National Conference on HBP Control, 2121 Wisconsin Ave., NW, Washington, DC 20007.

Peptides, Ion Transport April Symposium in Italy

An International Symposium on Peptides and Ion Transport will be held in Florence, Italy, April 24–26, sponsored by the Fondazione Giovanni Lorenzini and the European Membrane Club.

Ten additional scientific groups are sponsoring the meeting for which Drs. J. Axelrod of the U.S.A. and H.W. Kosterlitz of Aberdeen, Scotland, are honorary chairmen.

Seventeen speakers have been invited and the official language will be English.

Inquiries may go to Fondazione Giovanni Lorenzini, Via Monte Napoleone, 23, 20121 Milan, Italy. Tel. (02) 70.22.67 and 78.38.68. Cable LORENZFOUND

Heart Valve Symposium In Düsseldorf May 1–4

An international symposium—"Controversies in Heart Valve Replacement" has been organized for May 1–4 in Düsseldorf, Germany. It is sponsored by the European Society of Cardiology in cooperation with the Working Group on Valvular Prostheses.

The symposium will consider diagnosis and prognosis of valvular heart disease, indications and contraindications for surgical intervention, operative treatment and choice of valve, and treatment after heart valve surgery.

The scientific committee includes Drs. D. Horstkotte, of Düsseldorf, H. P. Krayenbühl of Zurich, and F. Loogen of Düsseldorf. Inquiries may go to Dr. Horstkotte, Dept. of Med. B., University of Düsseldorf, Moorenstrasse 5, D-4000 Düsseldorf, Germany, Tel. 049-211-3118278. Telex: 8587348 uni d.

Plan Brain/HBP Control Symposium Tokyo October

An International Symposium on Brain and Blood Pressure Control will be held in Kikai-Shinkoh Hall, Shiba Park, Tokyo Oct. 25–27. Abstract deadline is May 31. The meeting is organized by the Department of Pharmacology, Nippon Roche Research Center, Kamakura 247, Japan. Dr. Keiji Nakamura is organizing chairman and the organizing committee of 17 includes two Americans—Drs. Walter Lowenberg of NIH and Donald J. Reis of Cornell.

The program calls for 40 papers on the topics of cerebral integration of baro- and chemo-receptor reflexes, cerebral neurotransmitter and neuropeptide control of blood pressure, cerebral neuroanatomy related to blood pressure control, and cerebral mechanism related to development of hypertension and drug treatment.

Inquiries may go to Dr. Nakamura, Dept. Pharmacology, Nippon Roche Research Center, Kamakura 247, Japan. Tel. 0467-45-3191, Ext. 380,381. Telex 2222861 PANROCHE J

Subscription Renewal

Subscriptions for many readers of CIRCULATION, CIRCULATION RESEARCH, HYPERTENSION, STROKE, and ARTERIOSCLEROSIS are now due. Subscriptions that have not been renewed three months after expiration will be dropped. Renewals should be requested with payment included.

Subscriptions in Japan should be sent through Nankodo Co., Ltd., 42-5 Hongo 3-Chome, Bonkyo-Ku, Tokyo. All orders from Europe should go through Balliere Tindall, 1st Anne's Road, Eastbourne, East Sussex BN23 3UN, England.

Other orders should go to the AHA Scientific Journals Subscription Dept., 7320 Greenville, Ave., Dallas, TX 75231.

Rates for 1985 are:

	U.S.	Outside U.S.
CIRCULATION	$56	$ 72
CIRCULATION RESEARCH	86	105
HYPERTENSION	55	70
STROKE	50	65
ARTERIOSCLEROSIS	60	75

AHA Briefs...

- **Modern Concepts of Cardiovascular Disease** for March is "Role of Thrombolytic Therapy for Evolving Myocardial Infarction," by Bernard J. Gersh, M.B., Ch.B., D. Phil. of Mayo Clinic and Foundation.

• **Current Concepts of Cerebrovascular Disease/ Stroke** for March/April is "Hemorheology of the Cerebral Circulation in Stroke," by James H. Wood, M.D. and David B. Kee, Jr., M.D., of Emory University School of Medicine, Atlanta.

• The National Heart, Lung, and Blood Institute announces the availability of the 5-year **Preventive Cardiology Academic Award** for U.S. schools of medicine and osteopathy. Stipends have been increased to $40,000 annually. The program seeks to foster preventive cardiology curricula by stimulating research and careers in prevention and treatment. Deadline for application is April 1, 1985, for awards starting July 1, 1986. (Curt D. Furberg, M.D., DECA, NHLBI, NIH, Federal Bldg.-Rm. 6A-14, 7550 Wisconsin Ave., Bethesda, MD 20205. Tel. 303-496-1706).

• **The National Emergency Cardiac Care Conference for Volunteers** to consider standards will be held July 11–13 at the Dallas Fort Worth Hilton Hotel. Registration is limited to 250 and AHA affiliates are asked to send volunteers. Standards will be published in JAMA in January, 1986, and will be followed by regional meetings to review recommendations.

• "Modern Concepts in Hypertension," part one of the **3rd Annual Horizons in Cardiology** will be held March 22–24 at Keystone Resort, Keystone CO. Norman Kaplan, M.D. will be featured speaker. Part two of "Horizons" will be held April 12–13 in Pueblo, CO. Speakers will include Drs. Frederick Abrams and Charles Bedard and Donald Blanchard, J.D., Patricia King, J.D., and Rita Payton, D.A., on the topic "Financing Medical Ethics: Who Lives or Dies?" (James A. Sbarbaro, M.D., St. Mary-Corwin Hospital, 1008 Minnequa Ave., Pueblo, CO 81004-9988. Tel. 303-560-5340).

• **Dr. Millicent W. Higgins** has been appointed associate director for the Epidemiology and Biometrics Research Program in the National Heart, Lung, and Blood Institute Division of Epidemiology and Clinical Applications. A former faculty member at the University of Michigan, she is a member of the AHA research committee. The NHLBI Division of Epidemiology was established recently to foster research in this area.

• Seventy runners, most of them cardiologists, entered the first **Monitored Run/Jog** in Miami Beach, Nov. 13 during the 57th Scientific Sessions. More than half carried Holter monitors. Winners were Drs. Gordon Blackburn, Cleveland, O, David Branch, Boca Raton, FL, and William Phillips, Sayre, PA. Drs. Margo Tolins, St. Paul, MN, Karen Eddings, Boston, and Marta Sayers, Roanoke VA, were female division winners. The event was sponsored by Merck Sharp & Dohme.

• **Dr. Charles A. Sanders**, executive vice president of Squibb Corporation, received an award of appreciation for a new fellowship for CV research sponsored jointly by Squibb and AHA. The award was presented at the 57th Scientific Sessions in Miami by Mrs. Barney Clark, AHA National Residential Chairwoman.

• A symposium on **Skin Blood Flow Measurement and the Microcirculation** will be held March 22 at Ninewells Hospital, Dundee, Scotland. Organized by the Biological Engineering Society Blood Flow Group. (Biological Engineering Society, c/o Royal College of Surgeons, Lincoln's Inn Fields, London WC2A 3PN, United Kingdom).

• The Division of Lung Diseases, NHLBI, has solicited proposals from small business to **study physician practice behavior related to the prevention of lung diseases.** Information collected will provide baseline data for the Clinical Trial on Early Intervention for Chronic Obstructive Pulmonary Diseases. The trial seeks to determine the effects on pulmonary function during special care, compared to usual care, in a population of cigarette smokers having mild abnormalities in pulmonary function. (Douglas M. Frye, NHLBI, 5333 Westbard Ave.—Rm. 654, Bethesda, MD 20205. Tel. 301-496-7334).

Meetings Calendar 1985

March 28–30: **86th Annual Meeting, American Society for Clinical Pharmacology and Therapeutics.** Hilton Palacio del Rio, San Antonio, TX. Inquiries: Mrs. E. Galasso, 1718 Gallagher Rd., Norristown, PA 19401. Tel. 1-215-825-3838.

March 29–31: **8th Annual Intensive Clinical Neurology Course for Non-Neurologists.** New York City. Inquiries: L. P. Levitt, M.D., 12120 S. Cedar Crest Blvd., Allentown, PA 18103. Tel. 1-215-433-6474.

April 2–6: **3rd Annual Interventional Radiology Seminar.** Buena Vista Palace, Lake Buena Vista, Florida (Walt Disney World Village Plaza). Sponsored by Dept. Radiology, U. of South Florida College of Medicine. Inquiries: C. Krissman, 12901 N. 30 St., Tampa, FL 33612. Tel. 1-813-974-2538.

April 10–12: **26th National Student Research Forum.** University of Texas Medical Branch, Galveston. Inquiries: Student Research Forum, POB 54, Station 1, UTMB, Galveston, TX 77550. Tel. 1-409-761-3762.

April 11–12: **Oak Ridge Conference on Advanced Analytical Concepts for the Clinical Laboratory**. Sheraton Charlestown, SC. Sponsored by American Association for Clinical Chemistry. Inquiries: AACC, 1725 K St., SW, Washington, DC 20006. Tel. 1-202-857-0717.

April 11–12: **Right Heart Failure.** Hyatt Regency Hotel, Phoenix, AZ. Sponsored by St. Luke's Heart Lung Center. Inquiries: C. Campbell, St. Luke's Medical Center, 1800 E. Van Burne, Phoenix, AZ 85006. Tel. 1-602-251-8402.

April 21–26: **Federation of American Societies for Experimental Biology.** Anaheim, CA. Inquiries: 9650 Rockville Pike, Bethesda, MD 20014.

April 28–30: **National Conference on High Blood Pressure Control.** Palmer House, Chicago. Inquiries: NCHBP, 1501 Wilson Blvd., Suite 600, Arlington, VA 22209. Tel. 1-202-944-3176.

April 29–May 1: **American Association for Thoracic Surgery.** Hilton Hotel, New Orleans. Inquiries: W. T. Maloney, 13 Elm St., Manchester, MA 01944.

April 29–May 4: **20th Annual Family Practice Symposium.** Medical College of Georgia, Augusta. Inquiries: Div. Cont. Ed., Medical College of Georgia, Augusta, GA 30912. Tel. 1-404-828-3967.

April 30–May 3: **Exercise and Heart Disease: Prevention and Rehabilitation: 8th Cardiac Rehabilitation Symposium.** Red Carpet Hotel, Milwaukee, WI. Sponsored by Univ. of Wis.—Milwaukee Clinical Campus, Mount Sinai Medical Center (CV Dis. Sect.). Inquiries: S. Z. Aslakson, CME, 465B WARF Bldg, 610 Walnut St., Madison, WI 53705. Tel. 1-608-263-2856.

May 1–2: **21st Annual Cardiovascular Symposium.** Hunt Memorial, Hartford, CT, Medical Society. Sponsored by Cardiology Section, St. Francis Hosp. and Medical Center. Inquiries R. M. Jeresaty, M.D., Cardiology, St. Francis Hosp./Medical Center, 114 Woodland St., Hartford, CT 06105. Tel. 1-289-548-4820.

May 3–4: **Perspectives on the Management of Chronic Congestive Heart Failure.** Baltimore, MD. Sponsored by Div. of Cardiology, University of Maryland School of Medicine. Inquiries: Program of Cont. Ed., University of Maryland School of Medicine, 10 S. Pine St., Rm. 300, Baltimore, MD 21201. Tel. 1-301-528-3956.

May 3–6: **Annual Meeting American Federation for Clinical Research, American Society for Clinical Investigation, and Association of American Physicians.** Sheraton Hotel, Washington, DC. Inquiries Slack Inc., 6900 Grove Rd., Thorofare, NJ 08086.

May 6–7: **Symposium on Leukotrienes in Cardiovascular and Pulmonary Function.** Philadelphia. Inquiries: Allen R. Lefer, Ph.D., Dept. Physiology, Jefferson Medical College, 1020 Locust St., Philadelphia, PA 19107.

May 12–15: **6th Annual Meeting, Society for Clinical Trials.** New Orleans. Inquiries: Curt Furberg, MD, SCT, 600 Wyndhurst Ave., Baltimore, MD 21210.

May 12–15: **Annual Meeting, American Thoracic Society.** Anaheim, CA. Slide and poster presentations. Inquiries: ATS, 1740 Broadway, New York, NY 10019. Tel. 1-212-245-8000, Ext. 570.

May 13–15: **International Symposium: Ultrasound Diagnosis of Cerebrovascular Disease.** Seattle. (May 10–12: Pre-symposium Basic Course in Cerebrovascular Ultrasound—Doppler and B-Scan). Sponsored by Institute of Applied Physiology and Medicine. Merrill P. Spencer, M.D., program chairman. Inquiries: Dept. Med. Ed., Inst. Applied Physiology and Med., 701 Sixteenth Ave., Seattle, WA 98122. Tel. 1-206-442-7330.

May 16–18: **Practical Applications of Echo and Doppler Techniques in Cardiology.** Cleveland Marriott Inn-Airport Hotel. Inquiries: Professional Medical Seminars, POB 5400, Sherman Oaks, CA 91413.

May 17–18: **Clinical Concerns in Hemodialysis Therapy.** Sheraton Harbor Island East Hotel, San Diego. Program Chairman, Richard A. Sherman, M.D. Sponsored by American Kidney Fund and Nephrology Society of New Jersey. Inquiries: Dr. R. A. Sherman, Academic Health Science Center, CN 19, New Brunswick, NJ 08903. Tel. 1-800-922-0130.

May 17–22: **UCSD-Anesthesiology Review.** Vacation Village, San Diego. Sponsored by Dept. Anesthesiology, University of California, San Diego School of Medicine. Inquiries: K. Naughton, Dept. Anesthesia (M-029), UCSD, La Jolla, CA 92093. Tel. 1-619-452-3865.

May 19–23: **6th Scientific Meeting Inter-American Society of Hypertension.** Cleveland. Inquiries: 6th Meeting IASH, Research Division FF2-49, 9500 Euclid Ave., Cleveland, OH 44106. Tel. 1-216-444-5837.

May 23–24: **Vascular Surgery 1985. Current State of the Art. 2nd International Vascular Symposium.** Waldorf-Astoria Hotel, New York City. John B. Chang, M.D., program chairman. Inquiries: A. J. Boehme, Long Island Jewish-Hillside Medical Center, New Hyde Park, NY 11042. Tel. 1-212-470-2114.

May 24–27: **7th Annual Meeting American Section of the International Society for Heart Research.** Houston. Inquiries: Dr. J. Allen, Dept. Cell Biophysics, Baylor College of Med., Houston, TX 77025.

May 30–June 1: **Three Days in Cardiology.** Boston, Dr. Michael D. Freed program director. Sponsored by Children's Hospital, Boston, Cosponsored by AHA Council on Cardiovascular Diseases in the Young, and Children's Hospital, Boston. Inquiries: J. Cartier, Dept. Cardiology, the Children's Hospital, 300 Longwood Ave., Boston, MA 02115. Tel. 1-617-735-7893.

June 2–6: **2nd World Congress of Pediatric Cardiology.** New York City. Sponsors: American Academy of Pediatrics, American College of Cardiology, American Heart Association, Asian-Pacific Society of Cardiology, Asian Society of Pediatric Cardiology, Association of European Pediatric Cardiologists, Interamerican Society of Cardiology, International Society and Federation of Cardiology, New York Heart Association, Sociedad Latina de Cardiologia Pediatrica. Cosponsored by the Councils on Cardiovascular Diseases in the Young, and Cardiovascular Surgery of the AHA. Inquiries: V. Herlitz, 404 Park Ave. S., New York, NY 10016. Tel. 1-212-532-9400. Cable: HERLIMED.

June 10–12: **Surgery for Coronary Artery Disease.** Durham, NC. Sponsored by Duke University Medical Center and American College of Cardiology. R. H. Jones, M.D., program director. Inquiries: ACC, 9111 Georgetown Rd., Bethesda, MD 20814. Tel. 1-301-897-5400, Ext. 228.

June 10–13: **16th Annual Internal Medical Symposium.** Kiawah Island Inn, Kiawah Island, SC. Sponsored by the School of Medicine, Medical College of Georgia. Inquiries: Div. Cont. Ed., Medical College of Georgia, Augusta, GA 30912. Tel. 1-404-828-3867.

June 10–13: **Coronary Angiography 1985:** New Developments in Diagnostic Techniques, PTCA, and Thrombolytic Therapy. Boston. Dr. David C. Levin program director. Sponsored by The Harvard Medical School. Cosponsored by the AHA Council on Cardiovascular Radiology. Inquiries: Dept. Cont. Ed., Harvard Medical School, 25 Shattuck St., Boston, MA 02115. Tel. 1-617-732-6265.

June 17–18: **Today's Therapy in Nephrology.** Resorts International Hotel, Atlantic City, NJ. Sponsored by American Kidney Fund and Nephrology Society of New Jersey. Inquiries: See May 17–18, Dr. Sherman.

July 12: **Certifying Examination, Sub-Board of Pediatric Cardiology.** Chapel Hill, NC. Registration until Feb. 28. Inquiries: American Board of Pediatrics, 111 Silver Cedar Court, Chapel Hill, NC 27514-1651.

July 15–18: **Clinical Cardiology.** Hilton Head Inn, Hilton Head Island, SC. Sponsored by the School of Medicine, Medical College of Georgia. Inquiries: See Div. Cont. Ed., June 10–13.

July 18–21: **Pulmonary Diseases.** Kiawah Island Inn, Kiawah Island, SC. Sponsored by School of Medicine, Medical College of Georgia. Inquiries: See Div. Cont. Ed., 10–13.

July 21–26: **37th Annual Meeting American Association of Clinical Chemistry.** Georgia World Congress Center, Atlanta. Inquiries: AACC, 1725 K St., NW, Washington, DC 20006. Tel. 202-857-0717.

July 22–26: **Interdisciplinary Symposium on Plant Flavonoids in Biology and Medicine.** Biochemical, Pharmacological, and Structure-Activity Relationships. Buffalo, NY. Inquiries: Dr. Elliott Middleton, Jr., Dept. Med., Buffalo General Hospital, 100 High St., Buffalo, NY 14203. Tel. 1-716-845-2985.

July 24–28: **Critical Care Medicine.** Kiawah Island Inn, Kiawah Island, SC. Sponsored by School of Medicine, Medical College of Georgia. Inquiries: See Div. Cont. Ed., June 10–13.

Oct. 11–12: **4th Southern Biomedical Engineering Conference.** Jackson MS. Inquiries: Dr. Barry W. Sauer, SBEC, Div. Cont. Health Prof. Ed., University of Mississippi Medical Center, 2500 N. State St., Jackson, MS 39216-4505.

Oct. 13–18: **Clinical Congress, American College of Surgeons.** Chicago. Inquiries: ACS, 55 East Erie St., Chicago, IL 60611.

Oct 25: **Annual Meeting, Society of Neurological Anesthesia and Neurological Supportive Care.** San Francisco. Inquiries: Society of Neurological Anesthesia, POB 238, Univ. of Virginia Medical Center, Charlottesville, VA 22908.

Nov. 11–14: **58th Annual Scientific Sessions, American Heart Association, Washington, DC. Inquiries: Coordinator Scientific Sessions, AHA, 7320 Greenville Ave., Dallas, TX 75231. Tel. for Abstracts: 1-214-750-5439; for housing and reservations 1-214-750-5425. Commercial exhibits: 1-214-750-5388.**

Nov. 19–20: **Subspecialty Boards in Cardiovascular Disease.** Philadelphia. Registration to April 1. Inquiries: American Board of International Medicine, 3624 Market St., Philadelphia, PA 19104. Tel. 215-243-1500. (New date.)

1986

Jan 24–25: **Current Controversies and Techniques in Congenital Heart Surgery.** Baltimore, MD. (Immediately prior to Annual Meeting Society of Thoracic Surgeons, Washington, DC). Sponsored by Div. of Thoracic and Cardiovascular Surgery, University of Maryland School of Medicine. Inquiries: Program Cont. Ed., University of Maryland School of Medicine, 10 South Pine St., Suite 300, Baltimore, MD 21201. Tel. 301-528-3956.

Sept. 13–20: **Xth World Congress of Cardiology.** Washington, DC. Inquiries: Secretariat, 7320 Greenville Ave., Dallas, TX 75231. Tel. 214-750-5429. Cable Tencard, Dallas, TX.

Abroad

1985

April 1–3: **PTCA Course II.** Geneva, Switzerland. Drs. Bernhard Meier and Wilhelm Rutishauser, course directors. Live demonstrations of percutaneous transluminal coronary angiography and lectures in English. Inquiries: Dr. Bernhard Meier, Center for Cardiology, University Hospital, CH-1211, Geneva 4, Switzerland.

April 19–21: **6th Cardiological Meeting Congressi Italo-Monegaschi.** San Remo, Italy. Inquiries: Dr. G. Reforzo, Centro Cardiologico Fondazione Don C. Gnocchi, 18038, San Remo, Italy.

April 22–25: **13th European Congress on Non-Invasive Cardiovascular Dynamics.** Brescia, Italy. Sponsored by European Society for Noninvasive Cardiovascular Dynamics. C. Rusconi, M.D., chairman. Inquiries: G. Orlando, M.D., St. Orsola Hospital, Via Vittorio Emanuele No. 27, 25122 Brescia, Italy. Tel. 030/47061

April 22–26: **International Symposium 1985 Cardiovascular Pharmacotherapy.** Geneva, Switzerland. Inquiries: Interconference SA., 58 rue Ernest-Bloch, CH-1207, Geneva, Switzerland.

April 24–26: **International Symposium, Peptides and Ion Transport.** Florence, Italy. Inquiries: Organizing Secretariat, Peptides, Fondazione Giovanni Lorenzini, Via Monte Napoleone 23, 20121 Milan, Italy. Tel. 02.70.22.67 and 78.38.68. Cable: LORENZFOUND.

May 1–3: **International Symposium on Neural Mechanisms and Cardiovascular Disease.** Santa Margharita Ligure, (near Genoa), Italy. Dr. C. Bartorelli, symposium president. Inquiries: A. Malliani, Istituto Ricerche Cardiovascolari, Via Bonfadini, 214, 20138 Milano, Italy. Tel. 02-5063984 (p.m.)

May 1–4: **Controversies in Heart Valve Replacement.** Hotel Rheinpark Plaza, Düsseldorf, West Germany. Sponsored by European Society of Cardiology and Working Group on Valvular Prostheses. Inquiries: Dr. D. Horstkotte, Dept. Med. B, Univ. Düsseldorf, Moorenstrasse 5, D-4000 Düsseldorf, Germany. Tel. 049-211-3118278. Telex: 8587348 uni d.

May 2–4: **International Congress on Advanced Age.** Villa Marigola, San Terenzo di Lenci (SP) (near La Spezia). Official languages Italian and English. Topics: Advanced age and medical, surgical, physiopathological, and social problems. Inquiries: D. Valentini, XIX U.S.I. Spezzino, Via XXIV Maggio, 139, I-19100 La Spezia. Tel. (0187)533503.

May 8–10: **4th Congress Southern African Hypertension Society.** Johannesburg, South Africa. Inquiries: Prof. Clive Rosendorff, Dept. Physiology, Univ. Witwatersrand Medical School, York Rd., Parktown 2193, South Africa.

May 10–12: **International Symposium on Sports Cardiology.** Knokke, Belgium. Inquiries: Dr. I. Bekaert, Alg. Ziekenhuis St. Jozef, Steenweg op Merksplas 44, 2300 Turnhout, Belgium. Tel. 014-4104-51.

May 20–22: **Two Dimensional and Doppler Echocardiography.** Bisceglie (Bari), Italy. Drs. Navin C. Nanda and Paolo Rizzon, directors. Cosponsored by Cardiology Division of Alabama in Birmingham and University of Bari. Inquiries: Secretariat, Inter Centre, Via Principe Amedeo, 93, 70122 Bari, Italy.

May 22: **Symposium on Coronary Arteriography.** Rotterdam, the Netherlands. Organized by Working Group on Coronary Blood Flow and Angina Pectoris, on behalf of the European Society of Cardiology. Inquiries: Prof. P. G. Hugenholtz, M.D., Thoraxcenter BD 406, Erasmus Univ., Rotterdam, POB 1738, 3000 DR Rotterdam, the Netherlands.

May 23–25: **Unstable Angina Revisited.** Rotterdam, the Netherlands. Organized by the Thoraxcenter of Erasmus University, Rotterdam, the Netherlands Interuniversitary Cardiological Institute, the Netherlands, and the Toronto General Hospital, Toronto, Canada. Inquiries: Prof. P.G. Hugenholtz, M.D., Thoraxcenter Bd 406, Erasmus University, Rotterdam. POB 1738, 3000 DR Rotterdam, the Netherlands.

June 1–8: **Frontiers in Imaging and Cardiopulmonary Diagnosis.** England. (Also in Scotland, June 9–15). Eric N. C. Milne, M.D., program director. Faculty from U.S.A., 3 British and 2 Scottish medical schools. Inquiries: Ryals, POB 610203, DFW Airport, Texas 75261, U.S.A. 214-659-9590.

June 8–20: **2nd Advanced Ten Day International Teaching Seminar on Epidemiology and Prevention.** Ireland. Sponsored by Council of Epidemiology and Prevention, International Society and Federation of Cardiology in cooperation with WHO. Inquiries: Rose Stamler, Room 1-615, 303 E. Chicago Ave., Chicago, IL 60611.

June 9–14: **International Congress of Angiology.** Athens, Greece. Inquiries: Prof. P. Balas, 17 Sisini St., 115 28 Athens (612) Greece. (New date).

June 11–14: **3rd International Symposium on Body Surface Mapping.** Nijmegen, the Netherlands. Inquiries: Dr. R. Th. van Dam, Dept. Cardiology, Geert Grooteplein Zuid 8, 6525 AG Nijmegen, the Netherlands.

June 16–20: **12th Symposium, International Society of Cerebral Blood Flow—"Brain: 85."** Ronneby Brunn Hotel. Lund, Sweden. Inquiries: K. Dahlgren, Dept. Clinical Neurophysiology, University Hospital, S-221 85 Lund, Sweden. Tel. +46-46-10-33-70.

June 16–21: **12th International Congress of Cardiology.** Vancouver, B.C., Canada. Inquiries: Dr. Henry Mizgala, Suite 1704, 1200 Alberni St., Vancouver, B.C., Canada V6E 1A6. Tel. 604-681-5226. Cable: Venuvan.

June 20: **Doppler Ultrasound Techniques in Cardiology.** St. Bartholomew's Hospital, London, U.K. Inquiries: Biological Engineering Society, c/o Royal College of Surgeons, Lincoln's Inn Fields, London WC2A 3PN, United Kingdom.

June 23–26: **International Conference on Preventive Cardiology.** Sovincenter, Moscow, USSR. Sponsored by WHO, International Society and Federation of Cardiology. Official languages English and Russian. Inquiries: A. A. Stepanenko, International Conference on Prevention Cardiology, Institute of Preventive Cardiology, 10 Petroverigsky Lane 101837 Moscow, USSR. Telex 411355. Cable USSR MOSCOW K-62, Preventive Cardiology. Tel. 221-93-47.

June 26–28: **6th Symposium on Echocardiology With a Postgraduate Course on Doppler Cardiography.** Rotterdam, the Netherlands. Sponsored by Erasmus University Thoraxcenter. Inquiries: PG Med. Ed., Erasmus University, Rotterdam, PBO 1738, 3000 DR Rotterdam, the Netherlands. Tel. 010-635011/635013.

July 15–19: **4th Meeting, World Federation on Ultrasound in Medicine and Biology.** Sydney, Australia. Inquiries: WFUMB, POB 1441 GPO, Sydney, NSW, Australia 2001.

Aug. 31–Sept. 7: **Diagnosis of Diseases of the Chest.** Italy. (Also in Greece, Sept. 8–14). 2nd Great Teachers Foundation International Postgraduate Medical Education Program. Eric N. C. Milne, M.D., program director. Inquiries: Ryals (see June 1–8 above).

Aug. 31–Sept. 7: **11th Congress of International Society of Hypertension.** Heidelberg, Federal Republic of Germany. Organized by German Institute of High Blood Pressure Research and German Hypertension League. Dr. Detlev Ganten, Congress chairman. Inquiries: GKV, Frankfurter Str. 57, D-6050 Offenbach 1, Heidelberg, FRGermany.

Sept. 1–6: **13th World Congress of Neurology.** Hamburg, Germany. Inquiries: Dr. T. Stober, Dept. Neurology, Faculty of Med., University of Saarland, D-6650 Homburg/Saar, FRG.

Sept. 1–7: **3rd Postgraduate International Course on Pain Therapy.** Vicenza, Italy. Inquiries: Ruggiero Rizzi, M.D., Ospedale Generale Regionale, 36100 Vicenza, Italy.

Sept. 3–6: **European Nuclear Medicine Congress.** Barbican Centre, London, England. Incorporates 23rd Meeting Society of Nuclear Medicine, Europe, 8th Meeting European Nuclear Medicine Society, 13th Meeting British Nuclear Medicine Society. Inquiries: Congress, Institute of Nuclear Medicine, Middlesex Hospital Medical School, Mortimer St., London, W1N 8AA, United Kingdom. Tel. OI-631 1066.

Sept. 7–9: **3rd International Brain Heart Conference.** Trier, Germany. Inquiries: Dr. T. Stober, Dept. Neurology, Faculty of Med. University of Saarland, D-6650, Homburg/Saar, Federal Republic of Germany.

Sept. 8–12: **1st International Congress on Hospital Laws, Procedures, and Ethics.** Tel Aviv, Israel. Judge Amnon Carmi, organizing chairman. Inquiries: Hospitalaw, 28 Ahad Ha'am St., POB 394, Tel Aviv 61003, Israel. Tel. 03-650862. Telex 33803 TLV. Cable PELTOURS TELAVIV.

Sept. 9–12: **8th Annual European Conference on Lipoproteins.** Evangelische Akademie, Tutzing (near Munich), West Germany. Apoliprotein mutants and dyslipoproteinemias; cellular processing of lipoproteins. Sponsored by European Lipoprotein Club. Abstracts by May 1. Inquiries: Dr. J. Shepherd, Secretary European Lipoprotein Club, Dept. Pathological Biochemistry, Royal Infirmary, Glasgow, Scotland, G4 OSF.

Sept. 11–14: **Acute Brain Ischemia 1985: Medical and Surgical Therapy.** University of Siena, Italy. Satellite of 13th World Congress of Neurology, Sept. 1–6, Hamburg, Germany. Prof. Noè Battistini, organizer. Inquiries: GIBI S.a.s., M. P. Gerini, Via Orlona, 7, 00198 Rome, Italy.

Sept. 16–20: **International Symposium on Cardiogenic Reflexes.** University of Leeds, England. Organized by Dept. of CV Studies, Univ. Leeds, and Commission on CV Physiology of International Univ. of Physiological Sciences. Inquiries: Dr. R. Hainsworth, Dept. CV Studies, University of Leeds, Leeds LS2 93T, England.

Oct. 3–4: **Hemodynamics and Atherosclerosis.** Wellington, New Zealand. Inquiries: Dr. W.E. Stehbens, Dept. Pathology, Wellington Clinical School of Med., Wellington, 2, New Zealand.

Oct. 6–10: **7th International Symposium on Atherosclerosis.** Melbourne, Australia. Inquiries: Dr. P. J. Nestel, Baker Medical Research Inst., Commercial Rd., Prahran, Vic., Australia 3181.

Oct. 8–10: **1st Latin American Congress of Cardiac Pacing.** Buenos Aires, Argentina. Operated by Latin American Society of Cardiac Pacing and Argentine Chamber of Cardiac Pacing. Dr. Alejandro Dussaut, president organizing committee. Inquiries: Congresos Internacionales S.A., Moreno 854—9° piso, 1091 Buenos Aires, Argentina. Tel. 14-3216/3408/3283. Telex 22036 JECON AR.

Oct. 11–18: **Cell Biology of the Artery Wall.** Hayman Island, Great Barrier Reef, Australia. Satellite of 7th International Symposium on Arteriosclerosis, Oct. 6–10, Melbourne. Inquiries: Dr. Gordon H. Campbell, Dept. Anatomy, University of Melbourne, Parkville, 3052, Australia.

Oct. 25–27: **International Symposium on Brain and Blood Pressure Control.** Kikai-Shinkoh Hall, Shiba Park, Tokyo, Japan. Dr. Keiji Nakamura organizing chairman. Abstracts by May 31. Inquiries: Brain and Blood Pressure, Dept. of Pharmacology, Nippon Roche Research Center, Kamakura 247, Japan. Tel. 0467-45-3191-Ext. 380 or 381. Telex 2222861 PANROCHE J.

Oct. 27–30: **3rd Asian Pacific Symposium on Cardiac Pacing and Electrophysiology.** Hilton Hotel, Melbourne, Australia. Sponsored by Cardiac Society of Australia and New Zealand under auspices of International Cardiac Pacing Society. Inquiries: 3rd Asian Pacific Symposium on Cardiac Pacing and Electrophysiology, Suite 3.5, Epworth Medical Centre, 62 Erin St., Richmond, Vic. 3131, Australia.

Nov. 28–30: **7th Biennial Congress of Cardiology.** Rawalpindi/Islamabad, Pakistan. Inquiries: Pakistan Cardiac Society, Brig. Muhammad Zulfiqar Ali Khan, AFIC/NIHD, Rawalpindi, Pakistan. Tel. 64946, 61-31113, 61-33911.

AHA Scientific Sessions Future Meeting Dates

1985	Washington, DC	Nov. 11–14
1986	Dallas, TX	Nov. 17–20
1987	Anaheim, CA	Nov. 16–19
1988	Locale not set	Nov. 14–17
1989	New Orleans	Nov. 13–16
1990	Dallas	Nov. 12–15

Xth World Congress of Cardiology, 1986

The Xth World Congress of Cardiology will be held in Washington, DC, Sept. 13–20, 1986. Official languages English, Spanish, and French. Inquiries: Secretariat, Xth World Congress Cardiology, 7320 Greenville Ave., Dallas, TX 75231. Tel. 214-750-5429. Cable: Tencard, Dallas.

Circulation Research

APRIL 1985
VOL. 56 NO. 4

An Official Journal of the American Heart Association

BRIEF REVIEWS

New Studies of the Excitatory Sodium Currents in Heart Muscle

Harry A. Fozzard, Craig T. January, and Jonathan C. Makielski

From the Departments of Medicine and the Pharmacological and Physiological Sciences, The University of Chicago, Chicago, Illinois

EXCITATION and conduction in the heart are crucial to normal cardiac function, but these electrical events are not yet well understood at the cellular and molecular level. The reason for our poor understanding is that the principal excitatory current—the Na^+ current—has been difficult to study as a consequence of the geometrical complexity of cardiac tissue. The failure to characterize Na^+ currents in cardiac muscle has led to a dependence on data obtained from the more easily studied squid giant axon, interpreted for the different conditions in the heart through mathematical modeling.

Although cardiac muscle has profited from progress in understanding excitation and conduction in nerve, several important differences distinguish cardiac muscle from others in the family of excitable cells, and they limit the applicability of noncardiac models. Some of these differences are:

1. The cardiac action potential has a complex waveform and a long duration because more than the two dominant types of membrane current found in squid axon are involved in cardiac electrogenesis.
2. The cell membranes of cardiac tissue form a complex geometrical network. The tissue is made up of large numbers of relatively small and short cells, which are interconnected electrically by gap junctions.
3. Conduction velocity is a crucial variable in the electrical integration of the normal heartbeat, and even small changes could be of vital importance in setting the stage for serious, life-threatening arrhythmias.
4. Pacemaker properties are inherent in the function of several types of cardiac cells.
5. Membrane depolarization triggers cardiac contraction (as in skeletal muscle), and cellular mechanisms modulate the strength of contraction (in contrast to motor unit recruitment to control skeletal muscle contraction strength).
6. Interaction of excitability-altering drugs with cardiac cells appears to be different from the effects of these drugs in nerve cells.

The reason that direct study of ionic mechanisms in heart muscle has been difficult is because the essential tool—the voltage clamp—has been inadequate. The multicellular nature of the tissue has made it difficult to establish control of membrane potential rapidly and uniformly, especially for the excitatory Na^+ current (Johnson and Lieberman, 1971; Fozzard and Beeler, 1975; Beeler and McGuigan, 1978). The narrow intercellular spaces have resulted in local accumulation or depletion of ions, altering the ionic gradients that must be known or controlled if quantitative studies are to be made (Baumgarten and Isenberg, 1977; Levis et al., 1983). These problems have not prevented identification of such important properties as the Ca^{++} current (Reuter, 1973), but the problems with the voltage clamp technique have certainly contributed substantially to confusion over the factors controlling conduction velocity, repolarization, and pacemaking.

In the absence of quantitative studies of Na^+ current in heart muscle, models have been very helpful in understanding conduction. Weidmann's (1952) use of the cable model for passive membrane study was highly successful. The cable concept has been expanded and explored by Hunter et al. (1975) and Levin and Fozzard (1981). The efforts of Noble and others to synthesize the ionic currents into a mathematical model of the membrane action potential (Noble, 1962; McAllister et al., 1975; Beeler and Reuter, 1977) have contributed greatly to our understanding. However, experimental studies continue to show the limitations of these models (Spach et al., 1981, 1982; Walton and Fozzard 1983a, 1983b; Joyner et al., 1984). One of the more controversial topics has been the use of the maximal upstroke velocity to estimate the available Na^+ conductance (Weidmann, 1955; Baer et al., 1976; Cohen and Strichartz, 1977; Hondeghem, 1978; Walton and Fozzard, 1979; Bean et al., 1982; Cohen et al., 1984; Grant et al., 1984).

Quantitative voltage clamp study of Na^+ currents is now possible through the use of very small groups of cardiac cells or single isolated cells. With single cells, it is also possible to control the intracellular ionic environment. Single channels may be studied by clamping a small patch of membrane. Biochemical isolation and characterization of membrane components has been successful to the point that it is possible to reincorporate functional sodium channels into artificial membranes. Because of these dramatic advances in methodology, it seems certain that the next decade will belong to the experimentalists. With barely restrained enthusiasm, we describe in this brief review these new approaches in cardiac membrane electrophysiology.

New Preparations for Voltage Clamping

Until the last few years there were only two serious efforts to study Na^+ currents in heart cells, both using multicellular preparations that were shortened to minimize longitudinal loss of voltage control. Dudel and Rüdel (1970) reduced the temperature in order to slow the Na^+ currents in short sheep Purkinje strands, and controlled the transmembrane voltage by a two-micropipette method. Beeler and Reuter (1970) used a single sucrose gap to clamp short ventricular muscle bundles at 35°C. Although these studies provided evidence that the cardiac Na^+ current generally resembled that found in nerve, the voltage clamp methods were not able to control the membrane potential sufficiently to permit accurate quantitative studies.

Use of short multicellular preparations reduces longitudinal voltage non-uniformity, but radial non-uniformity of voltage control remains because of current flow in the narrow extracellular spaces between the closely packed cells (Attwell and Cohen, 1977; Schoenberg and Fozzard, 1979; Haas and Brummundt, 1980). Colatsky and Tsien (1979) were able to improve voltage control in a multicellular preparation by using a short Purkinje strand from the rabbit, which has rather wide intercellular spaces, and by using low temperature and low extracellular Na^+ concentrations. Ebihara et al. (1980, 1983) and Ebihara and Johnson (1980) used a very small spherical aggregate of cultured embryonic chick heart cells for a two-micropipette voltage clamp at 37°C and with normal extracellular Na^+. Although these studies suffered from some of the same problems as were seen with other multicellular preparations, they made it apparent that the activation of the Na^+ current could occur within a millisecond and that the Na^+ current does not always fit the original Hodgkin-Huxley mathematical model.

Single cardiac cells were available for biochemical studies for a number of years, but they were not usable for physiological studies because they often could not survive exposure to normal levels of extracellular Ca^{++}. Powell and others undertook to develop cell isolation procedures that would preserve Ca^{++} tolerance and normal electrical properties (Powell et al., 1980). The Powell technique, as well as similar methods of others, includes exposure of atrial or ventricular muscle or Purkinje fibers to a collagenase or trypsin solution with subsequent cell dispersion. The resulting single cells appear to have normal resting membrane potentials, action potentials, and contractions. Their membrane characteristics resemble those obtained from intact tissue (Table 1). Whereas we cannot yet state that their membrane properties are entirely normal, the principal electrical characteristics of normal cells are preserved. The single cells are important for electrical studies because they are amenable to rapid and nearly uniform voltage control, and because it may be possible to control their intracellular ionic environment.

Determination of the area of membrane under voltage control has been especially difficult in multicellular preparations of cardiac muscle because of the complex cell geometry (Mobley and Page, 1972; Hellam and Studt, 1974; Eisenberg and Cohen, 1983). This problem is not completely obviated by the use of single cells, because of membrane folding that is beyond the resolution of conventional microscopes used during the experimental studies. An alternative approach is to measure the membrane capacity, which should be linearly correlated with the membrane surface under appropriate conditions. The cardiac membrane capacity probably is constant with a value near 1 $\mu F/cm^2$,* similar to other cell membranes (Fozzard, 1979; Levis et al., 1983). Therefore, by measuring the charge delivered to the membrane during the capacity current, we can relate measured currents to the surface area being clamped.

New Techniques for Voltage Clamping

The ideal voltage clamp is one that controls the voltage and measures the current across a known area of cell membrane, with completion of a voltage change well before any voltage-dependent alteration in membrane properties. The transient inward currents carried by Na^+ and Ca^{++} pose the greatest technical challenge, because they activate rapidly after a suprathreshold step, and because the Na^+

* *The capacity of the membrane is the amount of charge required per unit of voltage change ($C = Q/V$). Na^+ channels are themselves charged structures, and their charges move in the membrane field. Consequently, for depolarization that activates Na^+ channels, additional charges are required to offset the channel "gating charge," which is additive to the membrane capacity. Hodgkin (1975) analyzed the effect of this increase in membrane capacity around excitation threshold on conduction in a model of the squid axon. He found that an increase in density of Na^+ channels would increase conduction velocity up to about 1000 channels per μm^2, but further increase in channel density would reduce conduction velocity because of this additional charging. His estimate of the capacity equivalent of a single channel is 8×10^{-18} F. We subsequently offer evidence that channel density is about 5 per μm^2. This would add less than 1% to the charge required to depolarize cardiac membranes, so it may be ignored. For other membranes where Na^+ channel density is several hundred per μm^2, this factor could be important.*

TABLE 1
Membrane Properties of Isolated Single Heart Cells

	Tissue	Temperature (°C)	V_m (mV)	Input resistance (MΩ)	R_m (KΩ-cm²)	τ_m (msec)	C_m (μF cm^{-2})
Powell et al. (1980)	Adult rat ventricular cells	37	−78.4 ± 9.7 (0.5 mM Ca^{++})	50	3.2	8	3.3
Brown et al. (1981)	Adult rat ventricular cells	20–22	−80 ± 10 (1.0 mM Ca^{++})	44.5 ± 4.6	0.6	16.2 ± 0.6	5.0
Hume and Giles (1981)	Adult bullfrog atrial cells	20	−88.6 ± 1.7 (2.5 mM Ca^{++})	219.8 ± 77.4		19.7 ± 7.3	2.3
Sheets et al. (1983)	Adult canine Purkinje cells	20–22	−80.0 ± 5.0 (1.8 mM Ca^{++})	21 ± 8	2.8	7.0 ± 1.9	2.7
Callewaert et al. (1984)	Adult sheep Purkinje cells	36–37	−70.8 ± 5.0 (1.8 mM Ca^{++})	66	13.6	26.8 ± 5.1	2.0

V_m is mean resting membrane potential and its standard deviation. R_m is the specific membrane resistance estimated from the input resistance and a calculation of the cell surface area assuming a smooth surface. τ_m is the membrane time constant in response to a current step. C_m is the specific membrane capacity obtained from the relation τ_m = RC, and is also dependent on the estimate of surface area. In this calculation, membrane folding is not included.

current is large. Adequate voltage control is necessary for any study of the voltage-dependent properties of membrane currents. During earlier studies in heart muscle, the requirement of good voltage control was avoided by asking only that the event under study has changed little during the period of poor control (see Fozzard and Beeler, 1975; Beeler and McGuigan, 1978). For example, cardiac electrophysiologists have claimed that poor voltage control during the first few milliseconds did not interfere with measurement of the Ca^{++} current, since it reached a peak only after several milliseconds. It is now clear that this argument was wrong. The Ca^{++} current activates quickly, when it is measured under better voltage control in single myocytes (Tsien, 1983; Josephson et al., 1984), so that we must judge previous measurements in multicellular preparations to be misleadingly slow.

The ionic current that changes most rapidly is the Na^+ current. In nerve, this current is fully activated in less than a millisecond at voltages near 0 mV. To compare the Na^+ channel in cardiac muscle to that of nerve, it is necessary that we record the Na^+ current with equivalent accuracy. As already noted, the best voltage clamp in a naturally occurring multicellular mammalian preparation was obtained in rabbit Purkinje strands (Colatsky and Tsien, 1979; Colatsky, 1980), where, typically, more than a millisecond was required to achieve voltage control. This is clearly too slow to permit study of activation, and the delay may also affect the value of peak Na^+ currents. Achievement of even this level of control required stringent conditions of low temperature and low Na^+ concentrations, which may influence the applicability of the results to the normal state. It must be pointed out that the investigators using the rabbit Purkinje strands fully realized the limitations of their voltage clamp, and used it only to study steady state properties and slow recovery from inactivation. Voltage clamp studies in aggregated embryonic chick heart cells (Ebihara et al., 1980; Ebihara and Johnson, 1980) also have shown evidence of quite rapid voltage control.

The first successful voltage clamp of the Na^+ current of single ventricular cells was reported by Lee et al. (1979; see also Brown et al., 1981a, 1981b), using a suction pipette method developed for voltage clamping of single neuronal cells (Lee et al., 1978; see also Kostyuk et al., 1975). The best control of Na^+ currents was accomplished by connecting two glass suction pipettes, 10–15 μm in diameter, to the myocyte, one to record voltage and one to pass current (Brown et al., 1981a). After the pipette sealed to the surface of the cell, the patch of membrane within its tip was ruptured by a pressure transient, allowing equilibration of the cytoplasm with the pipette-filling solution through the membrane tear. The resistance to the cell interior was 500–800 KΩ, permitting low impedance access for voltage recording and current passage. A similar method was used by Hume and Giles (1983) to connect to bullfrog atrial cells, except that, because of their smaller size, the amphibian cells required use of a single 2- to 4-μm tip diameter glass pipette for recording voltage and injecting current. This smaller pipette probably exchanges its content with cells only slowly, so that the intracellular environment is not as well controlled. A brief report of voltage clamp measurements of Na^+ currents in single canine Purkinje cells has appeared by Sachs and Specht (1981), who introduced current through a fine-tipped micropipette. As yet unreported in cardiac tissue is use of the "loose patch" technique of Almers et al. (1983).

An alternative method of connecting to the cell interior that has been used by three investigative groups is a flow-through polyethylene suction pipette developed by Kostyuk et al. (1975; see also Kostyuk, 1984) for voltage clamp and internal perfusion of single neuronal cells. Bodewei et al. (1982; see also Hering et al., 1983) have used this method to study rat ventricular cells, and Bustamante and MacDonald (1983) have used it to study human atrial cells. Makielski et al. (1983; see also Fozzard et al., 1984) have used this flow-through suction pipette for internal perfusion and voltage clamping of single canine cardiac Purkinje cells.

Voltage Control in Single Cardiac Cells

Voltage control can be assessed directly by monitoring the membrane potential with an independent microelectrode (one that is not part of the feedback circuit). In spite of the value of this test, it is rarely accomplished in cardiac muscle studies because of the difficulty in maintaining an additional microelectrode impalement. Such recordings in older two-micropipette voltage clamp studies showed failure to control the membrane potential during the Na^+ currents, with control achieved only after several milliseconds (New and Trautwein, 1972; Fozzard and Hiraoka, 1973). Good voltage control in a voltage-clamped single myocyte has been directly demonstrated by Josephson et al. (1984) during flow of Ca^{++} current. Independent membrane potential recording to confirm adequate voltage control during membrane current flow is an essential prerequisite to the quantitative interpretation of the experimental results.

Several indirect methods for assessing voltage control are available, including the characteristics of the capacity-charging current, the shape of the current-voltage relationship, the envelopes of tail currents, and the turn-off characteristics of currents by return of the voltage to holding potential levels during peak current flow. Some information is available from these indirect tests of voltage control in single myocytes.

Provided that the resistance in series with the cell membrane is low, the capacity current in response to a voltage step should peak quickly and decline rapidly as a single exponential in cells without t-tubules. It should be obvious that the voltage change across the membrane is not completed until the capacity current is over. Consequently, the time constant of the capacity current decline is a useful guide to the speed of voltage control. One of the best voltage clamps of single cardiac cells is that of Brown et al. (1981a, 1981b), who used rat ventricular myocytes. They showed time constants for decay of capacity current of about 100 μsec (when using one sealed glass pipette to measure voltage and a second to pass current). Using the flow-through suction pipette, Bodewei et al. (1982), Bustamonte and MacDonald (1983), and Makielski et al. (1983) also report rapid achievement of membrane voltage, with time constants for the decay of capacity current of around 100 μsec.

A severe test of voltage control is the ability to turn off the Na^+ current by clamping the membrane back to its resting level at the time of peak Na^+ current, and Brown et al. (1981a) were able to do this successfully. Makielski et al. (1983) also could rapidly terminate the Na^+ current at its peak by clamping back to the holding potential at the peak of the Na^+ current.

Brown et al. (1981a, 1981b) found that calculations of Na^+ conductance made from tail currents agreed with the values obtained during a prolonged voltage step. In addition, they found that scaling of currents that were varied by a factor of four [by lower $[Na^+]_o$ or tetrodotoxin (TTX) exposure] yielded similar current-voltage relations. Both of these tests are supportive of satisfactory control of voltage during their experiments.

In single heart cells, a voltage step can be completed within about 100 μsec, which is at least an order of magnitude improvement over that of multicellular preparations. However, it still may be insufficient for study of the earliest phases of activation of Na^+ currents or for recording of the very small Na^+ channel gating currents. Improvement in the speed of voltage control can be anticipated for several reasons. The suction pipette technique permits study of a fraction of a cell by pulling most of it into the opening at the pipette tip before sealing the cell to the pipette. The part of the cell within the pipette is amputated, thereby reducing the membrane area requiring control. Changes in the construction and shape of the pipette may reduce the series resistance to improve the speed of voltage control. As already mentioned, difficulties in the control of the peak Na^+ current can also be reduced by lower Na^+ concentrations and lower temperatures.

The Upstroke Velocity of the Action Potential

One of the major concerns with older measurements of Na^+ currents is that the peak recorded currents in the voltage clamp were small, not large enough to explain the rapid upstroke velocity of the cardiac action potential or its conduction velocity. Consequently, it is important to know if the newer studies can resolve this problem.

Most of the new observations of peak Na^+ currents in heart cells have been made with reduced extracellular Na^+ and at temperatures lower than 37°C. Brown et al. (1981b) found peak currents in rat ventricular cells at room temperature of around 0.5 mA/μF. Similar values were measured by Bustamante and MacDonald (1983) in human atrial cells and by Makielski et al. (1983) in canine Purkinje cells. These values are much larger than the 70 μA/μF reported by Bodewei et al. (1982) in rat ventricular cells. Those investigators attempted to clamp Na^+ currents while perfusing the interior of the cells with solution containing no Na^+, so their peak currents may have been lower as the result of loss of voltage control under these circumstances. Hume and Giles (1983) measured 70 μA/μF in frog atrial cells, and Ebihara et al. (1980a) measured 130 μA/μF in chick embryonic cells at 37°C. These much lower values could have been the result of tissue differences in Na^+ channel density, as well as some loss of voltage clamp control. The higher values of peak Na^+ current of 0.5 mA/μF can be used to estimate a Na^+ permeability ($\bar{P}_{Na}$) of at least 3–4 $\times 10^{-5}$ cm/sec. This is dramatically lower than the $\bar{P}_{Na}$ of 16 $\times 10^{-4}$ cm/sec, estimated by Hille and Campbell (1976) for frog skeletal muscle, or 2 $\times 10^{-3}$ cm/

sec measured by Frankenhauser (1959) for node of Ranvier.

These values of peak currents can be used to estimate the maximal upstroke velocity that could be achieved by the Na^+ currents in cardiac cells. The measured Na^+ currents of Brown et al. (1981b) and Makielski et al. (1983) are equivalent to 500 V/sec, substantially more than the normal action potential upstrokes at room temperature. It is to be expected that the largest possible current is never achieved during a triggered action potential, because of partial inactivation and/or progressive fall in Na^+ driving force (Walton and Fozzard, 1983; Cohen et al., 1984). We can conclude that the currents measured in the single cell voltage clamp may indeed be close to the maximal currents achievable.

Perfusion of the Inside of the Cell

One of the most powerful tools for the study of nerve cells has been the internally perfused axon (e.g., Baker et al., 1962). Cardiac cells can be dialyzed through glass pipettes sealed to the cells by exchange of the cytoplasm with the solution in these pipettes. Brown et al. (1981b) showed that it is even possible to use a microperfusion system to change the pipette contents and, thereby, change the cytoplasmic ion concentrations during the course of an experiment. They could alter intracellular Na^+ in a period of 2–8 minutes. The flow-through pipette may be even better for internal exchange. Makielski et al. (1983) were able to alter intracellular Na^+ within 2–3 minutes, as monitored by a change in the reversal potential of the Na^+ current. Control of other intracellular ions such as Ca^{++} has not been reported and may prove to be more difficult (Byerly and Moody, 1984).

This opportunity to control the intracellular ion concentrations and to apply drugs intracellularly offers a powerful tool for the study of cardiac cells. However, it should be pointed out that we do not yet know how to maintain the normal internal environment. Bodewei et al. (1982) used 140 mM Tris-phosphate, and Makielski et al. (1983) used Tris-glutamate at pH 7.2 with EGTA and variable amounts of Na^+. Brown et al. (1981a, 1981b) used KH_2PO_4, or cesium aspartate with $NaHCO_3$ and glucose. Bustamante and McDondald (1983) used cesium fluoride with a HEPES buffer. We have every reason to expect that the metabolic health of the cells, as well as the membrane channels, will depend on the detailed composition of these solutions, and little systematic information is yet available for cardiac cells.

Recording from Single Na^+ Channels

The behavior of a single membrane channel can now be recorded directly using a method developed by Neher and his colleagues (Hamill et al., 1981). They isolate a small patch of membrane, 1–5 μm^2 in area, by sealing a small-bore glass pipette to the membrane. The walls of the pipette seal tightly to the patch of membrane (gigaohm resistance to the bath), so that one can record the current required to hold the membrane patch at a chosen voltage. The presence of a channel in the isolated patch is manifested by a sudden increase in the current when the channel opens, and a sudden drop in current when the channel closes. This method allows study of the behavior of a single channel, or of a few channels, at rest, or in response to voltage steps. Sodium channels were first studied in skeletal muscle myotubes (Sigworth and Neher, 1980; Horn and Patlak, 1980), and in chromaffin cells (Fenwick et al., 1981).

Five investigative groups have reported some studies regarding cardiac Na^+ channels. Cachelin et al. (1983) have provided the most complete description of cardiac Na^+ channels, using cultured chick myocytes, and Ten Eick et al. (1982, 1984) used the same tissue type. Grant et al. (1983) studied rabbit ventricular myocytes and Kunze and Brown (1982) and Patlak (1984) studied rat ventricular myocytes.

From the limited data available from cardiac Na^+ channel studies (Table 2), we can draw the following conclusions:

1. Na^+ channel density is 2–10/μm^2. Whether the distribution of channels is random or localized is not yet known (Almers et al., 1983).
2. Under certain defined conditions, a single Na^+ channel has a conductance of about 15 pS, which is about 10^7 ions/sec per channel. With an open time of 1 msec, a single channel event is recorded by the movement of about 10,000 Na^+ ions.
3. Na^+ channel current-voltage relations do not appear to be linear, but bend toward a constant current at voltages negative to −50 mV. This may be related to an interaction with Ca^{++} (Yamamoto et al., 1984), although other technical problems, such as bandwidth of recording, may also contribute.
4. The Na^+ current changes its magnitude upon depolarization by increased probability of opening and by a somewhat longer mean open time.
5. Cachelin et al. (1983), Ten Eick et al. (1984), and Patlak (1984) have offered evidence that there may be two populations of Na^+ channels, based on channel currents, kinetics, and/or response to TTX.

Do Voltage Clamp and Patch Clamp Data Support the Hodgkin-Huxley Model?

The classical Hodgkin-Huxley model describes the Na^+ current as activating (opening of Na^+ channels) and inactivating (closing of Na^+ channels). These events are modeled as separate voltage-dependent processes that change their rates instantly as a function of voltage.

There has been evidence for some years that the behavior of the sodium channel in nerve is more complex than the model initially proposed by Hodgkin and Huxley. Activation occurs with a lag, thought to reflect the intermediate state that the channel must pass through, on the way to opening (Meves, 1978; Armstrong 1981; Horn et al., 1981;

TABLE 2
Properties of Single Cardiac Sodium Channels

Tissue	Measurement: γ	n	V_{th} (mV)	$\bar{t}_o$ (msec)	Mean closing rate
Adult rabbit ventricular cells [Grant et al. (1983)]	20 pS*	2–5/μm^2	~−45	1.2–2.1	680/sec
Cultured chick myocytes [Cachelin et al. (1983)]	15 pS	2–4/μm^2	~−50	0.9–2.3	
Adult rat ventricular cells [Kunze and Brown (1982)]	12 pS†	Several/μm^2	~−50		
Cultured chick myocytes [Ten Eick et al. (1982)]	10 pS‡				685/sec
Adult rat ventricular cells [Patlak (1984)]	10 pS§	2–10/μm^2	~−70	2.54	

γ is the single channel conductance. n is the estimated number of channels per unit area. V_{th} is the most negative membrane voltage at which single channels were seen to open. $\bar{t}_o$ is the mean open time for a channel.

* 1.2 pA at −10 mV (assume E_{Na} = +50 mV).
† 1.1 pA at −50 mV (assume E_{Na} = +40 mV).
‡ At two voltages of −40 and −20 mV.
§ 0.8 pA at −40 mV (assume E_{Na} = +40 mV).

Patlak and Horn, 1982). Inactivation also occurs with a lag, consistent with the idea that channels open before they can inactivate (Goldman, 1976; Armstrong, 1981; Bean, 1981). Inactivation often occurs with more than one time constant (Chiu, 1977; Bezanilla and Armstrong, 1977), as does recovery from inactivation (Schauf, 1974; Chiu, 1977). These investigators have suggested that the channel may have more than one inactivated state.

In heart cells, Brown et al. (1981b), Fozzard et al. (1984), and Patlak (1984) find at least two time constants to Na^+ current decay. The first two groups also showed a lag before recovery from inactivation, similar to the findings in myelinated nerve. Clark and Giles (1984) have found evidence of a delay before onset of inactivation in bullfrog atrial cells. Such a lag before onset of inactivation could be very important in heart muscle, because the current involved in generating the conducted action potential upstroke requires about 100–200 μsec to develop. A very slow phase of recovery from inactivation has also been seen in heart muscle (Cohen et al., 1981; Ebihara et al., 1983), which is influenced by the duration of depolarization or the presence of channel-active (antiarrhythmic) drugs.

Although the number of studies in heart muscle is small, it seems that the Hodgkin-Huxley mathematical model is not sufficient to describe the behavior of Na^+ current in nerve or in heart muscle. In turn, this casts some doubt on insights derived from models of excitation and conduction that use the Hodgkin-Huxley mathematical formulation. Whereas information generated with the Hodgkin-Huxley model may still be correct in specific instances, it is clearly necessary to determine in greater detail the behavior of Na^+ currents in the heart in order to develop the proper model for studies of excitation.

A Markovian chain model of sodium channel behavior has been useful in understanding experimental results (Fig. 1). It has evolved (for example, Bezanilla and Armstrong, 1977; Jakobson 1978; French and Horn, 1983; Aldrich et al., 1983) from

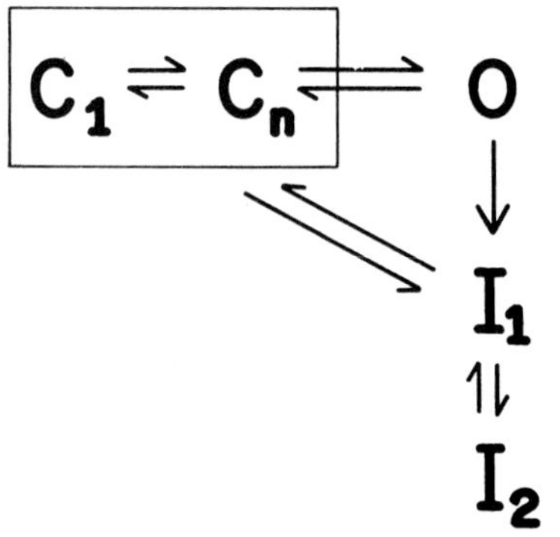

FIGURE 1. *A model of the Na^+ channel. The channel exists in three states, closed (C), open or conducting (O), and inactivated (I). There are several closed or nonconducting substates, illustrated here by $C_1 \rightleftharpoons C_n$. In response to a voltage step, channels in the C_1 state will be modified to some other closed state, from which they may open, or they may move directly to the inactivated state. Recovery is return to the C state, and it is indicated by the entire set of C_n, because no information is available to indicate to which C state the I state is transferred. See text for further explanation.*

voltage clamp and single channel studies in nerve, skeletal muscle, and heart because it explains results that differ in important ways from the original Hodgkin-Huxley model. The time course of the rise and decline of Na^+ current in response to a membrane depolarization will be given by the time- and voltage-dependent transitions of Na^+ channels between the closed (C), open (O), and inactivated (I) states. The transitions can be described by either rate constants or probability functions which are dependent upon voltage and time. The closed state is the state of the channel in the resting membrane. Upon depolarization of the membrane, the channel may go to the open state, and then to the inactivated state (C to O to I), or it may go directly to the inactivated state (C to I) from which it must return to the closed state (I to C) before further opening can occur. It seems likely that there are two or more closed states ($C_1, \ldots, C_n$) producing a lag before opening of the channel (C_n to O). Gating charge movement could occur during the C_1 to C_n transition (Armstrong and Bezanilla, 1974), from which the channel may open or inactivate. The Hodgkin-Huxley model assumes that activation (C to O), and inactivation (any transition to I) are independent; inactivation could occur from any state and the rate of inactivation is independent of the initial state. However, experimental results (Hoyt and Adelman, 1970; Goldman and Schauf, 1972; Bezanilla and Armstrong, 1977) show a delay in the development of inactivation, indicating that this assumption of Hodgkin-Huxley may be incorrect. The model in Figure 1 allows for a delay in the development of inactivation by permitting transitions from C_1 to C_n before transition to I. Complex behavior in the development of inactivation would also occur if the C_n to I transition and the C_n to O to I transitions occurred with different rates after a depolarization.

The Hodgkin-Huxley model also assumed that activation was much faster than inactivation, and that both were strongly voltage dependent. Some results of single sodium channel studies (Aldrich et al., 1983) suggest that inactivation of the open channel (O to I) is relatively fast ($t = 0.5$ msec) and not strongly voltage dependent, and that activation (C_n to O) is relatively slow ($t = 1$–2 msec). Other experimental results (Horn and Vandenberg, 1984; Vandenberg and Horn, 1984) suggest rate constants based on this model that differ in regard to the relative speeds and voltage dependencies of the activation and inactivation steps. Whether the kinetic differences are the result of species variation in Na^+ channels or of differences in experimental conditions is not yet clear.

The model in Figure 1 has the additional feature of two inactivated states (I_1 and I_2), which may explain such behavior as a two-exponential time course in the development of inactivation in response to a depolarization, and a lag in the onset of recovery from inactivation when the membrane is repolarized (Chiu, 1977; Fozzard et al., 1984). The explanation for these results in terms of the model is similar to the one above that accounts for the delay in activation, i.e., an intermediate state intervenes between the starting and end states in response to a membrane voltage change.

Late Na^+ Currents

Because low doses of TTX (10^{-7} M) shorten the plateau of the cardiac Purkinje fiber without affecting the upstroke velocity, Coraboeuf et al. (1979) suggested that there is a sodium current that is different from the one underlying the action potential upstroke. Several possible explanations exist for this effect of TTX. First, as already mentioned, there could be a second population of Na^+ channels. They could inactivate with time constants of several hundred msec and be particularly sensitive to TTX. This suggestion is supported by demonstration of a small, slowly inactivating component of Na^+ current in rabbit Purkinje strands (Gintant et al., 1984; Carmeliet, 1984). Second, there might be voltage-dependent, time-independent Na^+ channels that provide inward current at plateau voltages (Attwell et al., 1979). Third, some TTX-sensitive Na^+ channels could be independent of both voltage and time, and provide a background inward current important to the resting potential, as well as the plateau. Coraboeuf et al. (1979) noted that TTX also often caused a 5- to 7-mV hyperpolarization of the resting potential, and Sheu et al. (1980) found that Na_o removal produced a large hyperpolarization. TTX reduces intracellular Na^+ activity by about 1 mM (Dietmer and Ellis, 1980; January and Fozzard, 1984; Vassalle and Lee, 1984), as one would expect from a change in resting Na^+ permeability.

The problem that faces investigators who study these slowly decaying or steady Na^+ currents is their small size. It is in the range of currents that could be generated by membrane transport processes that depend on Na^+ but are not gated channels. Candidates include the electrogenic Na-K pump and the Na^+-Ca^{++} exchange system, and possibly Na^+-H^+ or NaCl-K^+ transport systems, if the latter are electrogenic. These transport systems are not yet well enough understood to permit quantitative study with the detail that is possible for the passive Na^+ channel. The late Na^+ currents probably have no role in excitation and conduction, although they could be important in other respects.

The Number of Na^+ Channels

Knowledge of the size of the patch clamp pipette and the apparent number of Na^+ channels that can be activated in the patch permits an estimate of the density of Na^+ channels. It is not exact, because the true area of the functional membrane in the patch is not exactly the area of the pipette opening, and because some channels may not open in ways that permit them to be unequivocally counted. For heart muscle, the number of Na^+ channels estimated from patch clamp sampling is 2–10/μm^2. It is interesting to compare this estimate with the maximal currents that can be recorded with the single cell voltage clamps. The peak currents of Brown et al. (1981b) and Makielski et al. (1983) are 0.5 mA/cm^2 (assuming 1 $\mu F/cm^2$) around −20 mV. Typical single channel currents at −20 mV are about 1 pA, yielding an estimate of 5 channels/μm^2 that is close to the number suggested by patch clamp measurement. These numbers must be compared to 200–500/μm^2 in squid axon (Levinson and Meves, 1975; Strichartz et al., 1979), 2,000–10,000/μm^2 in nodes of Ranvier (Rogart, 1981), and 200–300/μm^2 in the surface membrane of mammalian skeletal muscle (Richie and Rogart, 1977). These estimates of numbers of Na^+ channels are from TTX and saxitoxin (STX) binding, and equivalent measurements are complicated in heart muscle because of the low affinity of the toxins for the channel (Rogart et al., 1983; Renaud et al., 1983). If the present estimate of cardiac Na^+ channel density is correct, then the efforts to isolate and purify Na^+ channels from the heart (Doyle and Page, 1984) may appear to have a poor yield.

Isolation and Reconstitution of Na^+ Channels

An important and different approach to the study of Na^+ channels is their biochemical isolation. The functional state of these isolated channels can be studied by their incorporation into artificial bilayers. Good progress has been made in the chemical isolation of Na^+ channels (Catterall and Nirenberg, 1973; Goldin et al., 1980; Barchi et al., 1980; Agnew, 1984). At least two subunits have been identified, one of 270,000 and the other of 39,000 daltons (Beneski and Catterall, 1980). The 270,000 dalton unit is called α, and it has been shown to undergo phosphorylation by a cAMP-dependent protein kinase (Costa et al., 1982). Channels have been successfully incorporated into liposomal vesicles, where open channel fluxes can be measured (Goldin et al., 1980; Tanaka et al., 1983). These liposomal vesicle studies have serious limitations, because their small volume make flux studies less quantitative than we would like (Miller, 1984), and because the transmembrane voltage can only be estimated approximately and controlled crudely. These problems can be avoided by reconstitution of the channels in planar bilayers (Miller and Racker, 1976; Coronado and Latorre, 1982; Krueger et al., 1983; Hanke et al., 1984), where control of voltage is straightforward. Some success has been reported by Coronado and Latorre (1982), using sarcolemmal materials from heart muscle, but these investigators saw few Na^+ channels. Nelson et al. (1984) successfully reconstituted cardiac Na^+ channels in planar bilayers, but they, as well as others, have needed to treat the channels with batrachotoxin (BTX) to prevent inactivation.

A Role for Na^+ Channels in Modulating Contraction Strength

Intracellular Na^+ activity (a^i_{Na}) in heart muscle is a balance between Na^+ entry, partly through the Na^+ channels, and Na^+ exit via the Na-K pump. Stimulated fibers have a higher level of a^i_{Na} than resting fibers (Deitmer and Ellis, 1980; Cohen et al., 1982; Lee and Dagostino, 1983). The magnitude of the increase depends on the frequency and the duration of stimulation (Cohen et al., 1982). January and Fozzard (1984) studied this effect in voltage-clamped cardiac Purkinje fibers, showing that blockade of the Na^+ channels by TTX or steady depolarization to −50 mV prevented the stimulation-induced rise in a^i_{Na} and they proposed an important role for Na^+ channels. Falk and Cohen (1984) came to a similar conclusion by studying electrogenic pump current, but they also found some evidence for participation of Ca^{++} channels. This stimulation-dependent change in a^i_{Na} is thought to affect contraction through the Na^+-Ca^{++} exchange mechanism. In support of this idea, January (1984) has recently shown that TTX treatment also blocked the tension staircase (Bowditch phenomenon) and markedly depressed the frequency-force relationship in voltage-clamped cardiac fibers. The importance of this role of Na^+ channel in the overall control of contraction in the heart is uncertain, and it raises the possibility that modification of Na^+ channel behavior (e.g., antiarrhythmic drugs) could alter cardiac contraction.

Summary

After decades of frustration with inadequate methods, cardiac electrophysiologists have developed new techniques for superior control of membrane potential by use of single cells, and they have begun careful study of cardiac Na^+ currents. Direct recordings of the behavior of single Na^+ channels have been made by the newly developed patch clamp technique. Biochemists have made excellent progress purifying and characterizing the Na^+ channel proteins, and there has been some initial success in reconstituting these partially purified channels into lipid bilayers, where their function can be studied.

Even at this early stage of development of these new techniques, several conclusions are warranted:

1. The cardiac Na^+ currents are not accurately described by the original Hodgkin-Huxley mathematical formulation, making undesirable the further use of this model for study of cardiac excitation and conduction. We need to keep an open mind as to the kinetic behavior of Na^+ channels, until the newer experimental techniques provide a more complete picture.
2. Although the cardiac Na^+ channel strongly resembles Na^+ channels in other excitable tissues, important differences remain, reinforcing the idea that the detailed molecular structure of the cardiac

Na^+ channel will be different from its close relatives in other excitable cells.

3. The density of Na^+ channels in heart cell membranes is much less than in nerve and fast twitch skeletal muscle.

4. The Na^+ channels are the focus of action of many drugs and pathological processes.

5. The tools are at hand for a complete description of the Na^+ channel, including its gating and its molecular structure. We can expect considerable progress in this decade.

Address for reprints: Harry A. Fozzard, M.D., Department of Medicine—Box 249, The University of Chicago, 5841 South Maryland Avenue, Chicago, Illinois 60637.

References

Agnew WS (1984) Voltage-regulated sodium channel molecules. Annu Rev Physiol **46:** 517–530

Aldrich RW, Corey DP, Stevens CF (1983) A reinterpretation of mammalian sodium channel gating based on single channel recording. Nature **306:** 436–441

Almers W, Stanfield PR, Stühmer W (1983) Lateral distribution of sodium and potassium channels in frog skeletal muscle: Measurements with a patch-clamp technique. J Physiol (Lond) **336:** 261–284

Armstrong CM (1981) Sodium channels and gating currents. Physiol Rev **61:** 644–683

Armstrong CM, Bezanilla F (1974) Charge movement associated with the opening and closing of the activation gates of the Na channels. J Gen Physiol **63:** 533–552

Attwell D, Cohen I (1977) The voltage clamp of multicellular preparations. Prog Biophys Mol Biol **31:** 201–245

Attwell D, Cohen I, Eisner D, Ohba M, Ojeda C (1979) The steady-state TTX-sensitive ("window") sodium current in cardiac Purkinje fibers. Pflugers Arch **379:** 137–142

Baer M, Best PM, Reuter H (1976) Voltage-dependent action of tetrodotoxin in mammalian cardiac muscle. Nature (Lond) **263:** 344–345

Baker PF, Hodgkin AL, Shaw TI (1962) The effects of changes in internal ionic concentrations on the electrical properties of perfused giant axons. J Physiol (Lond) **164:** 355–374

Barchi RL, Cohen SA, Murphy LE (1980) Purification from rat sarcolemma of the saxitoxin-binding component of the excitable membrane sodium channel. Proc Natl Acad Sci USA **77:** 1306–1310

Baumgarten CM, Isenberg G (1977) Depletion and accumulation of potassium in the extracellular clefts of cardiac Purkinje fibers during voltage clamp hyperpolarization and depolarization. Pflugers Arch **386:** 19–31

Bean BP (1981) Sodium channel activation in the crayfish giant axon. Must channels open before inactivating? Biophys J **35:** 595–614

Bean BP, Cohen CJ, Tsien RW (1982) Block of cardiac sodium channels by tetrodotoxin and lidocaine: Sodium currents and $\dot{V}_{max}$ experiments. *In* Normal and Abnormal Conduction in the Heart: Biophysics, Physiology, Pharmacology, and Ultrastructure, edited by A Paes de Carvalho, BF Hoffman, M Lieberman. New York, Futura, pp 189–209

Beeler GW, McGuigan JAS (1978) Voltage clamping of multicellular myocardial preparations: Capabilities and limitations of existing methods. Prog Biophys Mol Biol **34:** 219–254

Beeler GW, Reuter H (1977) Reconstruction of the action potential of ventricular myocardial fibres. J Physiol (Lond) **268:** 177–210

Beeler GW, Jr, Reuter H (1970) Voltage clamp experiments on ventricular myocardial fibres. J Physiol (Lond) **207:** 165–190

Beneski DA, Catterall WA (1980) Covalent labeling of protein components of the sodium channel with a photoactivable derivitive of scorpion toxin. Proc Natl Acad Sci USA **77:** 639–643

Bezanilla F, Armstrong CM (1977) Inactivation of the sodium channel. I. Sodium current experiments. J Gen Physiol **70:** 549–566

Bodewei R, Hering S, Lemke B, Rosenshtraukh LV, Undrovinas AI, Wollenberger A (1982) Characterization of the fast sodium current in isolated rat myocardial cells: Simulation of the clamped membrane potential. J Physiol (Lond) **325:** 301–315

Brown AM, Lee KS, Powell T (1981a) Voltage clamp and internal perfusion of single rat heart muscle cells. J Physiol (Lond) **318:** 455–477

Brown AM, Lee KS, Powell T (1981b) Sodium currents in single rat heart muscle cells. J Physiol (Lond) **318:** 479–500

Bustamante JO, McDonald TF (1983) Sodium currents in segments of human heart cells. Science (Wash) **220:** 320–321

Byerly L, Moody WJ (1984) Intracellular calcium ions and calcium currents in perfused neurons of the snail *Lymnaes stagnalis.* J Physiol (Lond) **352:** 637–652

Cachelin AB, de Peyer JE, Kokubun S, Reuter H (1983) Sodium channels in cultured cardiac cells. J Physiol (Lond) **340:** 389–402

Callewaert G, Carmeliet E, Vereecke J (1984) Single cardiac Purkinje cells: General electrophysiology and voltage-clamp analysis of the pace-maker current. J Physiol (Lond) **349:** 643–661

Carmeliet E (1984) Slow inactivation of the sodium current in rabbit cardiac Purkinje fibres (abstr). J Physiol (Lond) **353:** 125P

Catterall WA, Nirenberg M (1973) Sodium uptake associated with the activation of action potential ionophores of cultured neuroblastoma and muscle cells. Proc Natl Acad Sci USA **70:** 3759–3763

Chiu SY (1977) Inactivation of sodium channels: second order kinetics in myelinated nerve. J Physiol (Lond) **273:** 573–596

Clark RB, Giles WR (1984) Na current inactivation develops with a delay in bullfrog atrial myocytes (abstr). J Physiol (Lond) **358:** 56P

Cohen IS, Strichartz GR (1977) On the voltage-dependent action of tetrodotoxin. Biophys J **17:** 275–279

Cohen CJ, Bean BP, Colatsky TJ, Tsien RW (1981) Tetrodotoxin block of sodium channels in rabbit Purkinje fibers. J Gen Physiol **78:** 383–411

Cohen CJ, Fozzard HA, Sheu S-S (1982) Increase in intracellular sodium ion activity during stimulation in mammalian cardiac muscle. Circ Res **50:** 651–661

Cohen CJ, Bean BP, Tsien RW (1984) Maximal upstroke velocity as an index of available sodium conductance. Circ Res **54:** 636–651

Colatsky TJ (1980) Voltage clamp measurements of sodium channel properties in rabbit cardiac Purkinje fibers. J Physiol (Lond) **305:** 215–234

Colatsky TJ, Tsien RW (1979) Sodium channels in rabbit cardiac Purkinje fibres. Nature (Lond) **278:** 265–268

Coraboeuf E, Deroubaix E, Coulombe A (1979) The effect of tetrodotoxin on action potentials of the conducting system in the dog heart. Am J Physiol **236:** H561–H567

Coronado R, Latorre R (1982) Detection of K^+ and Cl^- channels from calf cardiac sarcolemma in planer lipid bilayer membranes. Nature (Lond) **298:** 849–852

Costa MRC, Casnellie JE, Catterall WA (1982) Selective phosphorylation of the alpha subunit of the sodium channel by cAMP-dependent protein kinase. J Biol Chem **257:** 7918–7921

Deitmer JW, Ellis D (1980) The intracellular sodium activity of sheep heart Purkinje fibers: Effects of local anesthetics and tetrodotoxin. J Physiol (Lond) **300:** 269–282

Doyle DD, Page E (1984) Measurement of ^3H-saxitoxin binding sarcolemmal Na channels in sheep and rat heart (abstr). Circulation **70** (suppl II): 74

Dudel J, Rüdel R (1970) Voltage and time dependence of excitatory sodium current in cooled sheep Purkinje fibers. Pflugers Arch **315:** 136–158

Ebihara L, Johnson EA (1980) Fast sodium current in cardiac muscle. A quantitative description. Biophys J **32:** 779–790

Ebihara L, Shigeto N, Lieberman M, Johnson EA (1980) The initial inward current in spherical clusters of chick embryonic heart cells. J Gen Physiol **75:** 437–456

Ebihara L, Shigeto N, Lieberman M, Johnson EA (1983) A note on the reactivation of the fast sodium current in spherical clusters of embryonic chick heart cells. Biophys J **42:** 191–194

Eisenberg BR, Cohen IS (1983) The ultrastructure of the cardiac Purkinje strand in the dog: A morphometric analysis. Proc R Soc Lond [Biol] **217:** 191–213

Falk R, Cohen IS (1984) Membrane current following activity in canine cardiac Purkinje fibers. J Gen Physiol **83:** 771–799

Fenwick EM, Marty A, Neher E (1982) Sodium and calcium channels in bovine chromaffin cells. J Physiol (Lond) **331:** 599–635

Fozzard HA (1979) Conduction of the action potential. *In* Handbook of Physiology, sec 2, The Cardiovascular System, vol. I. The Heart. Washington, D.C., The American Physiological Society, pp 335–356

Fozzard HA, Beeler GW, Jr (1975) The voltage clamp and cardiac electrophysiology. Circ Res **37:** 403–413

Fozzard HA, Hiraoka M (1973) The positive dynamic current and its inactivation properties in cardiac Purkinje fibres. J Physiol (Lond) **234:** 569–586

Fozzard HA, Friedlander I, January CT, Makielski JC, Sheets MF (1984) Second-order kinetics of Na^+ channel inactivation in internally dialysed canine cardiac Purkinje cells (abstr). J Physiol (Lond) **353:** 72P

Frankenhaeuser B (1959) Steady state inactivation of sodium permeability in myelinated nerve fibres of *Xenopus laevis.* Physiol (Lond) **148:** 671–676

French RJ, Horn R (1983) Sodium channel gating: Models, mimics, and modifiers. Annu Rev Biophys Bioeng **12:** 319–356

Gintant GA, Datyner NB, Cohen IS (1984) Slow inactivation of a tetrodotoxin-sensitive current in canine cardiac Purkinje fibers. Biophys J **45:** 509–512

Goldin SM, Rhoden V, Hess EJ (1980) Molecular characterization, reconstitution, and "transport-specific fractionation" of the saxitoxin binding protein/Na^+ gate of mammalian brain. Proc Natl Acad Sci USA **77:** 6884–6888

Goldman L (1976) Kinetics of channel gating in excitable membranes. Q Rev Biophys **9:** 491–526

Goldman L, Schauf CL (1972) Inactivation of the sodium current *Myxicola* giant axons. J Gen Physiol **50:** 659–675

Grant AO, Starmer CF, Strauss HC (1983) Unitary sodium channels in isolated cardiac myocytes of rabbit. Circ Res **53:** 823–829

Grant AD, Starmer CF, Struss HC (1984) Antiarrhythmic drug action: Blockade of inward current. Circ Res **55:** 427–439

Haas HG, Brommundt G (1980) Influence of intracellular clefts on potential and current distribution in a multifiber preparation. Biophys J **30:** 327–349

Hamill OP, Marty A, Neher E, Sakmann B, Sigworth FJ (1981) Improved patch-clamp techniques for high-resolution current recording from cells and cell-free membrane patches. Pflugers Arch **391:** 85–100

Hanke W, Boheim G, Barhanin J, Pauron D, Lazdunski M (1984) Reconstitution of highly purified saxitoxin-sensitive Na^+-channels into planar lipid bilayers. EMBO J **3:** 509–515

Hellam DC, Studt JW (1974) A core-conductor model of the cardiac Purkinje fibre based on structural analysis. J Physiol (Lond) **243:** 637–660

Hering S, Bodewei R, Wollenberger A (1983) Sodium current in freshly isolated and in cultured single rat myocardial cells: Frequency and voltage-dependent block by mexiletine. J Mol Cell Cardiol **15:** 431–444

Hille B, Campbell DT (1976) An improved vaseline gap voltage clamp for skeletal muscle fibers. J Gen Physiol **67:** 265–293

Hodgkin AL (1975) The optimum density of sodium channels in an unmyelinated nerve. Phil Trans R Soc Lond [Biol] **270:** 297–300

Hondegham LM (1978) Validity of $\dot{V}_{max}$ as a measure of the sodium current in cardiac and nervous tissues. Biophys J **23:** 147–152

Horn R, Patlak J (1980) Single channel currents from excised patches of muscle membrane. Proc Natl Acad Sci USA **77:** 6930–6934

Horn R, Vandenberg CA (1984) Statistical properties of single sodium channels. J Gen Physiol **84:** 505–534

Horn R, Patlak J, Stevens CF (1981) Sodium channels need not open before they inactivate. Nature (Lond) **291:** 426–427

Hoyt RC, Adelman WJ (1970) Sodium inactivation experimental test of two models. Biophys J **10:** 610–617

Hume JR, Giles W (1981) Active and passive electrical properties of single bullfrog atrial cells. J Gen Physiol **78:** 19–42

Hunter PJ, McNaughton PA, Noble D (1975) Analytical models of propagation in excitable cells. Prog Biophys Mol Biol **30:** 99–144

Jakobsson E (1978) A fully coupled transient excited state model for the sodium channel. J Math Biol **5:** 121–142

January CT (1984) Role of intracellular sodium in the regulation of cardiac contractility (abstr). Clin Res **32:** 474a

January CT, Fozzard HA (1984) The effects of membrane potential, extracellular potassium, and tetrodotoxin on the intracellular sodium ion activity of sheep cardiac muscle. Circ Res **54:** 652–665

Johnson EA, Lieberman M (1971) Heart: Excitation and contraction. Annu Rev Physiol **33:** 479–532

Josephson IR, Sanchez-Chapula J, Brown AM (1984) A comparison of calcium currents in rat and guinea pig single ventricular cells. Circ Res **54:** 144–156

Joyner RW, Veenstra R, Rawling D, Chorro A (1984) Propagation through electrically coupled cells. Biophys J **45:** 1017–1025

Kostyuk PG (1984) Intracellular perfusion of nerve cells and its effects on membrane currents. Physiol Rev **64:** 435–454

Kostyuk PG, Krishtal OA, Pidoplichko VI (1975) The effect of internal flouride and phosphate on membrane currents during intracellular dialysis of nerve cells. Nature (Lond) **257:** 691–693

Krueger BR, Worley JF, III, French RJ (1983) Single sodium channels from rat brain incorporated into planar bilayer membranes. Nature (Lond) **303:** 172–175

Kunze DL, Brown AM (1982) Unitary sodium currents in mammalian ventricular cells (abstr). Physiologist **25:** 300

Lee CO, Dagostino M (1982) Effect of strophanthidin on intracellular Na ion activity and twitch tension of constantly driven canine cardiac Purkinje fibers. Biophys J **40:** 185–198

Lee KS, Akaike N, Brown AM (1978) Properties of internally perfused, voltage-clamped, isolated nerve cell bodies. J Gen Physiol **71:** 489–508

Lee KS, Weeks TA, Kao RL, Akaike N, Brown AM (1979) Sodium current in single heart muscle cells. Nature (Lond) **278:** 269–270

Levin DN, Fozzard HA (1981) A cleft model for cardiac Purkinje strands. Biophys J **33:** 383–408

Levinson SR, Meves H (1975) The binding of tritiated tetrodotoxin to squid giant axons. Phil Trans R Soc Lond [Biol] **270:** 349–352

Levis RA, Mathias RT, Eisenberg RS (1983) Electrical properties of sheep Purkinje strands. Biophys J **44:** 225–248

Makielski JC, January CT, Sheets MF, Undrovinas AI (1983) Single cardiac Purkinje cells for internal perfusion and voltage clamp (abstr). Biophys J **41:** 404a

McAllister RE, Noble D, Tsien RW (1975) Reconstruction of the electrical activity of cardiac Purkinje fibres. J Physiol (Lond) **251:** 1–59

Meves H (1978) Inactivation of the sodium permeability in squid giant nerve fibres. Prog Biophys Mol Biol **33:** 207–230

Miller C (1984) Ion channels in liposomes. Annu Rev Physiol **46:** 549–558

Miller C, Racker E (1976) Ca induced fusion of fragmented sarcoplasmic reticulum with artificial planar bilayers. J Memb Biol **30:** 283–300

Mobley BA, Page E (1972) The surface area of sheep cardiac Purkinje fibres. J Physiol (Lond) **220:** 547–563

Nelson MT, Reinhardt R, Lederer WJ (1984) Sodium channels from mammalian heart muscle incorporated into planar lipid bilayers. Biophys J **45:** 185a

New W, Trautwein W (1972) Inward membrane currents in mammalian myocardium. Pflugers Arch **334:** 1–23

Noble D (1962) A modification of the Hodgkin-Huxley equations applicable to Purkinje fibre action and pace-maker potentials. J Physiol (Lond) **160:** 317–352

Patlak J (1984) Two components of single Na channel inactivation in patch recordings from dissociated cells (abstr). Biophys J **45:** 185a

Patlak J, Horn R (1982) Effect of *N*-bromoacetamide on single sodium channel currents in excised membrane patches. J Gen Physiol **79:** 333–351

Powell T, Terrar DA, Twist VW (1980) Electrical properties of individual cells isolated from adult rat ventricular myocardium. J Physiol (Lond) **302:** 131–153

Renaud J-F, Kazazoglou T, Lombet A, Chicheportiche R, Jaimovich E, Romey G, Lazdunski M (1983) The Na^+ channel in mammalian cardiac cells. J Biol Chem **258:** 8799–8805

Reuter H (1973) Divalent cations as charge carriers in excitable membranes. Prog Biophys Mol Biol **26:** 1–43

Richie JM, Rogart RB (1977) The binding of labeled saxitoxin to the sodium channels in normal and denervated mammalian muscle and in amphibian muscle. J Physiol (Lond) **269:** 341–354

Rogart RD, Regen LJ, Dziekan LC, Galper JB (1983) Sodium channel subtypes in chick heart and brain. Proc Natl Acad Sci USA **80:** 1106–1110

Rogart R (1981) Sodium channels in nerve and muscle membrane. Annu Rev Physiol **43:** 711–725

Sachs F, Specht P (1981) Sodium currents in single cardiac Purkinje cells (abstr). Biophys J **33:** 123a

Schauf CL (1974) Sodium currents in Myxicola axons: Nonexponential recovery from the inactive state. Biophys J **14:** 151–154

Schoenberg M, Fozzard HA (1979) The influence of intercellular clefts on the electrical properties of sheep cardiac Purkinje fibers. Biophys J **25:** 217–234

Sheets MF, January CT, Fozzard HA (1983) Isolation and characterization of single canine Purkinje cells. Circ Res **53:** 544–548

Sheu S-S, Korth M, Lathrop D, Fozzard HA (1980) Intra- and extracellular K^+ and Na^+ activities and resting membrane potential in sheep cardiac Purkinje strands. Circ Res **47:** 692–700

Sigworth FJ, Neher E (1980) Single Na^+ channel currents observed in rat muscle cells. Nature (Lond) **287:** 447–449

Spach MS, Miller WT, Geselowitz DB, Barr RC, Kootsey JM, Johnson EA (1981) The discontinuous nature of propagation in normal canine cardiac muscle. Evidence for recurrent discontinuities of intracellular resistance that affect membrane currents. Circ Res **48:** 39–54

Spach MS, Miller WT, Dolber PC, Kootsey JM, Sommer JR, Mosher CE, Jr (1982) The functional role of structural complexities in the propagation of depolarization in the atrium of the dog. Cardiac conduction disturbances due to discontinuities of effective axial resistivity. Circ Res **50:** 175–191

Strichartz GR, Rogart RB, Richie JM (1979) Binding of radioactively labeled saxitoxin to the squid giant axon. J Membr Biol **48:** 357–364

Tanaka JC, Eccleston JF, Barchi RL (1983) Cation selectivity characteristics of the reconstituted voltage-dependent sodium channel purified from rat skeletal muscle sarcolemma. J Biol Chem **258:** 7519–7526

Ten Eick R, Matsuki N, Quandt F, Yeh J (1982) Na channels in cultured embryonic chick ventricle: Single channel conductance and open time: effect of TTX (abstr). Physiologist **25:** 198

Ten Eick R, Yeh J, Matsuki N (1984) Two types of voltage dependent Na channels suggested by differential sensitivity of single channels to tetrodotoxin. Biophys J **45:** 70–73

Tsien RW (1983) Calcium channels in excitable cell membranes. Annu Rev Physiol **45:** 341–358

Vandenberg CA, Horn R (1984) Inactivation viewed through single sodium channels. J Gen Physiol **84:** 535–564

Vassalle M, Lee CO (1984) The relationship among intracellular sodium activity, calcium, and strophanthidin inotropy in canine cardiac Purkinje fibers. J Gen Physiol **83:** 287–307

Walton M, Fozzard HA (1979) The relation of $\dot{V}_{max}$ to I_{Na}, $\overline{G}_{Na}$, and h_∞ in a model of the cardiac Purkinje fiber. Biophys J **25;** 407–420

Walton MK, Fozzard HA (1983) Experimental study of the conducted action potential in cardiac Purkinje strands. Biophys J **44:** 1–8

Walton MK, Fozzard HA (1983) The conducted action potential: Models and comparison to experiments. Biophys J **44:** 9–26

Weidmann S (1952) The electrical constants of Purkinje fibres. J Physiol (Lond) **118:** 348–360

Weidmann S (1955) The effect of the cardiac membrane potential on the rapid availability of the sodium-carrying system. J Physiol (Lond) **127:** 213–224

Yamamoto D, Yeh JZ, Narahashi T (1984) Voltage-dependent calcium block of normal and tetramethrin-modified single sodium channels. Biophys J **45:** 337–344

INDEX TERMS: Heart muscle • Voltage clamp • Cardiac electrophysiology • Sodium currents • Sodium channels • Hodgkin-Huxley model

Carotid Baroreceptor Reflex Coronary Vasodilation in the Dog

Bruce R. Ito and Eric O. Feigl
From the Department of Physiology and Biophysics, University of Washington School of Medicine, Seattle, Washington

SUMMARY. The hypothesis that neurally mediated coronary vasodilation occurs as part of the carotid baroreceptor reflex was investigated. The left main coronary artery was cannulated and perfused at constant pressure (100 mm Hg) in closed-chest, chloralose-anesthetized dogs. The heart was paced at a constant rate between 60 and 70 beats/min after atrioventricular heart block. Propranolol (1 mg/kg) was given to prevent β-receptor-mediated alterations in contractility. Aortic blood pressure was stabilized with a blood reservoir. The aortic depressor nerves were cut bilaterally to prevent the buffering influence of aortic arch baroreceptors on the carotid baroreceptor reflex. The carotid sinuses were vascularly isolated and perfused with arterial blood at controlled pressures. Under these conditions, a step change in carotid sinus pressure from 70 to 210 mm Hg produced a 0.29 ml/min per g increase in coronary flow above control and a 10 mm Hg increase in coronary sinus blood oxygen tension. A step in carotid sinus pressure from 70 to 150 mm Hg resulted in a flow increase of 0.13 ml/min per g and a coronary sinus oxygen tension increase of 5.3 mm Hg relative to prestimulation values. Atropine (0.5 mg/kg, iv) blocked most of the reflex coronary vasodilation, indicating a parasympathetic component, and the addition of adrenergic α-receptor blockade with phenoxybenzamine (0.25 mg/kg, ic) abolished the remaining response, demonstrating sympathetic participation. The reflex nature of the coronary response was confirmed with carotid sinus denervation and vagotomy. It is concluded that carotid sinus hypertension results in a graded reflex neural coronary vasodilation independent of myocardial metabolic factors. The major component is due to activation of parasympathetic coronary vasodilator fibers, but there is also inhibition of sympathetic vasoconstrictor fibers. **(*Circ Res 56: 486–495, 1985*)**

PREVIOUS studies have demonstrated that adrenergic α-receptor coronary vasoconstriction can be reflexly elicited by carotid sinus hypotension (Feigl, 1968, 1983; DiSalvo et al., 1971; Limet et al., 1975; Powell and Feigl, 1979; Ely et al., 1981). However, the reflex response to carotid sinus hypertension is less clear. Both coronary vasoconstriction (DiSalvo et al., 1971) and coronary vasodilation (Limet et al., 1975) have been observed during acute elevations in carotid sinus pressure. Coronary vasodilation during the elevation of aortic pressure has also been attributed to the carotid baroreflex (White et al., 1976). Electrical stimulation of the afferent carotid sinus nerve has been employed to mimic carotid sinus hypertension, and either coronary vasoconstriction (Falicov et al., 1970) or vasodilation (Vatner et al., 1970; Hackett et al., 1972; Religa et al., 1972; Solti et al., 1975) has been observed. However, it is difficult to equate a given nerve stimulation frequency with a carotid sinus pressure stimulus that physiologically activates baroreceptors. Furthermore, electrical stimulation of carotid sinus baroreceptor afferent fibers produces both excitatory and inhibitory reflex effects on cardiac vagal efferent fibers (McCloskey and Potter, 1981), in contrast to only excitatory effects reported with functional pressure stimulation of baroreceptors (Potter, 1981). It is also possible that much of the conflicting coronary flow data can be explained by alterations in myocardial metabolism, secondary to changes in heart rate and aortic pressure, in response to activation of the baroreceptor reflex. Large changes in myocardial metabolism would tend to mask the reflexly activated direct neural effect on coronary vascular resistance.

The present study was designed to determine the reflex response of the coronary vascular bed to carotid sinus hypertension and to identify the neural mechanisms involved. Large changes in myocardial metabolism were prevented by a combination of cardiac pacing, adrenergic β-receptor blockade, and stabilization of aortic pressure. Coronary blood flow was measured during constant perfusion pressure during acute pressure elevations in the isolated carotid sinuses, before and after interruption of various components of the baroreflex arc. Carotid sinus hypertension resulted in reflex coronary vasodilation primarily mediated by activation of parasympathetic vasodilator fibers, but also by inhibition of sympathetic vasoconstrictor fibers.

Methods

General Preparation

Adult mongrel dogs (23–30 kg) of either sex were premedicated with morphine sulfate (2.5 mg/kg, sc) and anesthetized with α-chloralose (100 mg/kg, iv). The dogs were intubated with a cuffed endotracheal tube and ventilated with a positive displacement respiration pump (Harvard 607) with an end-expiratory pressure of 3 cm H_2O. Ventilatory rate was adjusted to give an end-expiratory carbon dioxide content of 4.5%–5%, as continuously measured with an infrared analyzer (Beckman LB-2). Rectal temperature was held at 37°C with a heating pad and temperature controller (Yellow Springs 73A). A continuous intravenous drip (5 ml/kg per hr) of a sodium bicarbonate solution (1.5%) reduced the metabolic acidosis common with chloralose anesthesia (Arfors et al., 1971). Anesthesia was maintained with a continuous α-chloralose infusion (10 mg/kg per hr) plus 0.5 g supplements, as needed. Arterial blood pressure was measured with a strain gauge manometer (Statham P23Dd) through a polyethylene catheter (PE 160) inserted in the aorta via the left brachial artery. Anticoagulation was achieved with sodium heparin (750 U/kg, iv) followed by a continuous intravenous drip of 250 U/kg per hr. Three extracorporeal circuits were utilized, as described in separate sections below (Fig. 1).

Aortic Baroreceptor Denervation

To prevent the buffering influence of aortic arch baroreceptors on carotid sinus baroreceptor-mediated reflexes, the cervical aortic depressor nerves were cut bilaterally (Edis and Shepherd, 1971; Ito and Scher, 1973). The vagosympathetic trunks were dissected free from the common carotid arteries. With the aid of a dissecting microscope, the cervical aortic depressor nerves were located within the sheath of the vagosympathetic trunks just

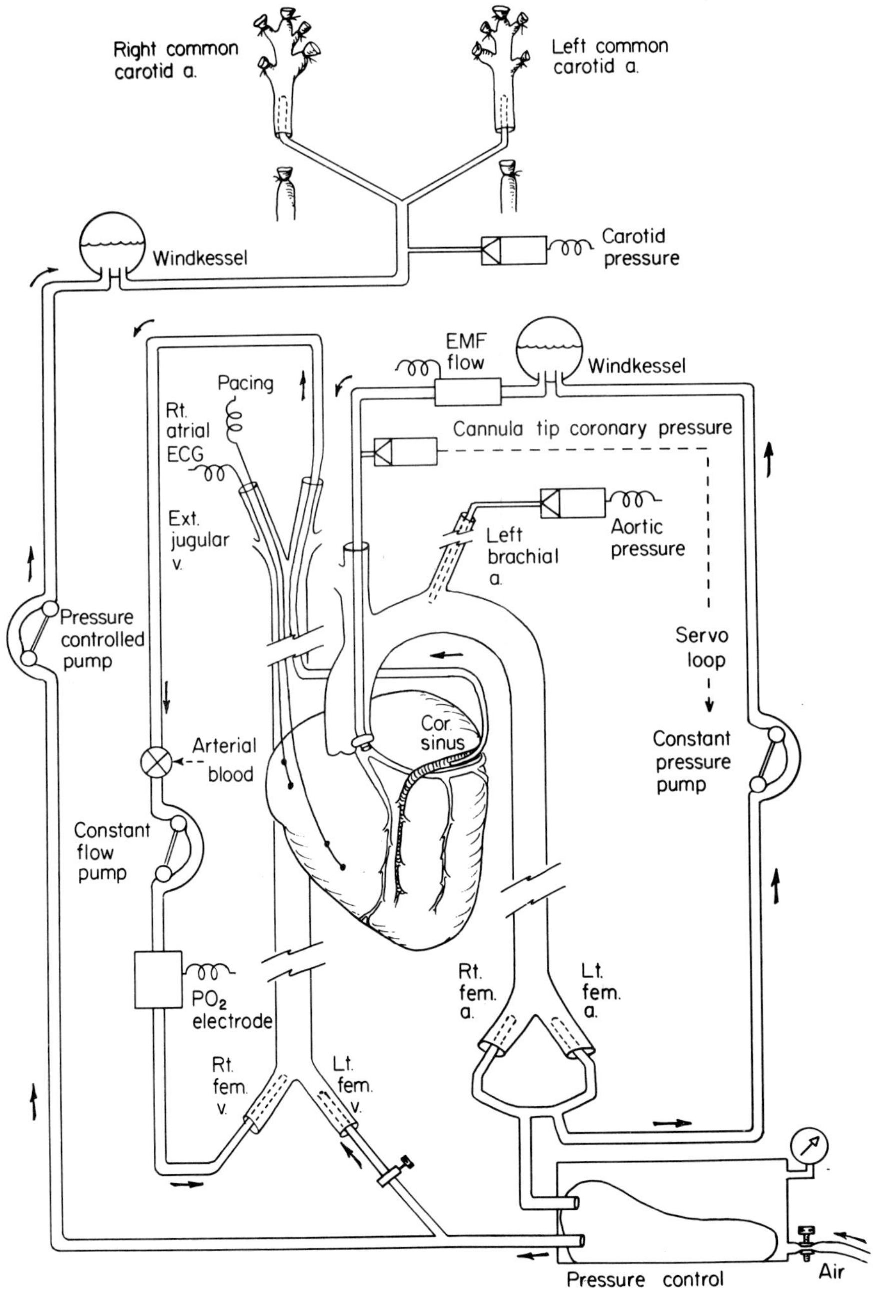

FIGURE 1. *Schematic of the closed-chest experimental preparation. The ventricles were paced at a constant rate while reflex changes in the atrial rate were recorded with an atrial electrocardiogram. The aortic pressure was stabilized with a pressurized reservoir. The left main coronary artery was perfused through a cannula inserted via the right carotid artery. Pressure at the cannula tip was maintained at 100 mm Hg with the servo-controlled pump while coronary flow was measured with an electromagnetic flowmeter in the perfusion line. A coronary sinus blood sample was continuously withdrawn for determination of myocardial venous oxygen tension. The isolated carotid sinuses were presented with step increases in distending pressure with a nonpulsatile roller pump.*

below the bifurcation of the common carotid arteries (Hasimoto and Hirohata, 1936). Identification of the aortic depressor nerve was verified by extracellular nerve recording with bipolar silver electrodes and a differential amplifier (Grass P15) prior to cutting.

Heart Block and Ventricular Pacing

Complete atrioventricular heart block was produced closed-chest by the injection of formalin into the AV node region with a fluoroscope (Ito and Feigl, 1983). A pacing catheter (USC #5651) was placed in the right ventricle via the right external jugular vein. The ventricles were paced at a constant rate (between 60 and 70 beats/min in different experimental animals) with 3- to 5-V, 0.3-msec pulses (Grass SD9 stimulator). An electrode placed in the right atrium via the left external jugular vein allowed recording of cardiac potentials relative to an indifferent electrode positioned subcutaneously in the neck. Analog filtering of this signal (Hewlett-Packard 8811A) resulted in an electrocardiogram with enhanced atrial depolarizations relative to the paced ventricular depolarizations. This atrial electrocardiogram was also used to confirm that the baroreceptor reflex was intact, as indicated by atrial bradycardia during carotid sinus hypertension.

Aortic Pressure Stabilization

To minimize changes in aortic pressure during carotid sinus hypertension, the arterial system was connected to an external pressurized reservoir via both femoral arteries. The reservoir consisted of a 1-liter intravenous solution bag within an acrylic chamber connected to a pressurized air source. Pressure within the chamber was monitored and could be adjusted to buffer aortic pressure changes during baroreceptor reflex peripheral vasodilation. To avoid stagnant blood accumulating in the reservoir bag, blood was continuously circulated through the bag via a small catheter in the right femoral vein.

Isolated Carotid Sinus Perfusion

Both carotid sinus regions were vascularly isolated by ligation of the major branches (internal carotid, external carotid, lingual, occipital, superior laryngeal, and ascending pharyngeal arteries) of the common carotid arteries downstream from the carotid bifurcation. Care was taken to avoid damage to the carotid sinus nerves and the venous drainage from the carotid bodies (Chungcharoen et al., 1952). The carotid sinus regions were perfused through a Y-shaped cannula inserted into the common carotid arteries (Fig. 1). Carotid sinus pressure was measured from a side port in the cannula (Statham P23ID) and was controlled by a non-pulsatile perfusion pump (Mohrman, 1980) in a servo feedback configuration. Rapid programmed changes in carotid sinus pressure were achieved by externally offsetting the control signal to the pump with a voltage source. A 30-ml Windkessel in the perfusion line served to damp out excessive pressure overshoots. Arterial blood from the femoral arteries was used as the perfusion source.

Left Coronary Artery Perfusion

The left main coronary artery was cannulated with a balloon-tipped stainless steel cannula (Smith et al., 1974; Mohrman and Feigl, 1978) via the right common carotid artery, without opening the chest. Coronary artery pressure was measured at the tip of the cannula via an inner steel tube and strain gauge manometer (Statham P23ID). Coronary pressure was held constant at 100 mm Hg with a servo-controlled roller pump (Sarns 3500). The seal between the balloon and the coronary ostium was checked by stopping inflow and measuring distal pressure. The seal was considered satisfactory if coronary pressure fell to 20–25 mm Hg. The cannula seal was further tested at the termination of the experiment with the pump running and the heart beating. Coronary pressure was set to 50 mm Hg above mean aortic pressure, and crystal violet dye was injected into the perfusion line. Leaks were readily demonstrated by dye stains in the aorta. Experiments with evidence of leaks were discarded. The crystal violet dye injection was also used to demarcate the region of perfused myocardium, which was excised and weighed postmortem. Coronary flow was measured with an extracorporeal electromagnetic flow transducer (Zepeda SWF-3) in the perfusion line. Mean coronary blood flow was obtained with an averaging circuit with a 2.0-second time constant. Occlusive zero flow records were obtained repeatedly during the experiment, and the flowmeter was calibrated with blood at the end of the experiment.

Coronary Sinus Cannulation

In 14 dogs, the coronary sinus was cannulated with a Sones catheter (USCI #5423) using fluoroscopy (Goodale et al., 1948). Myocardial venous blood was continuously sampled by withdrawal at constant flow (Cole-Parmer pump 4420). Blood was returned to the dog via a femoral vein. In four dogs, the coronary sinus was cannulated with a double-lumen, balloon-tipped cannula that allowed the collection of coronary sinus effluent. A flexible polyethylene tube down the center of the cannula was extended beyond the tip of the cannula for continuous coronary venous sampling. This cannula allowed collection of coronary sinus blood during the intracoronary infusion of phenoxybenzamine, thus diminishing systemic α-receptor blockade. When phenoxybenzamine was not being infused, blood was shunted into the right atrium.

With both techniques, verification was made postmortem that the tip of the sampling catheter was more than 20 mm into the coronary sinus measured from the ostium. Blood was withdrawn at a rate of less than 10 ml/min to avoid right atrial venous admixture (Koberstein et al., 1969).

Oxygen Tension Measurement

Coronary sinus blood oxygen tension was continuously measured with an in-line oxygen electrode (Feigl and D'Alecy, 1971) and meter (Instrumentation Labs 125A). The tubing transit time was determined at the end of each experiment. This value varied between 13 and 19 seconds in the different dogs. The appropriate time delay has been subtracted from all reported oxygen tension values. The oxygen tension measurements shown as original records have also been corrected by an appropriate shift of the time axis. The oxygen electrode was calibrated with pure nitrogen and a known nitrogen-oxygen mixture at the beginning and end of each experimental run.

Experimental Design

All animals were given propranolol, 1 mg/kg, iv, plus 0.5 mg/kg per hour, iv, to minimize adrenergic β-receptor-mediated changes in cardiac contractility. Activation of the carotid sinus baroreceptor reflex was achieved by presenting step changes in pressure to the carotid sinuses. After propranolol control runs, animals were subjected to one of four treatment protocols to determine the afferent and efferent reflex mechanisms involved in mediating the observed coronary response. (1) In the "atropine-first" group (six dogs), atropine (0.5 mg/kg, iv) was administered to block the parasympathetic cholinergic pathway to coronary vessels. Phenoxybenzamine [0.25 mg/kg, intracoronary (ic)] was then administered to block the sympathetic α-receptor pathway to coronary vessels. This intracoronary dose of phenoxybenzamine was chosen because it effectively blocks α-receptor-mediated coronary effects of the carotid sinus reflex (Mohrman and Feigl, 1978) and infused norepinephrine (Buffington and Feigl, 1983). (2) In the "phenoxybenzamine-first" group (seven dogs), the phenoxybenzamine (0.25 mg/kg, ic) was given first, followed by atropine (0.5 mg/kg, iv). (3) In the "vagotomy-first" group (two dogs), both vagi were sectioned in the neck, and the baroreceptor stimulus was repeated. Phenoxybenzamine (0.25 mg/kg, ic) was then administered and the stimulus repeated. (4) In the "carotid denervation" group (three dogs), deafferentation of the carotid sinus regions was produced by stripping the adventitia of the sinus regions, followed by topical application of phenol (10%). The carotid pressure stimulus was then repeated.

Experimental Protocol

Control experimental runs were obtained following propranolol but before additional autonomic blockade. Prior to the beginning of an experimental run, the external reservoir air pressure was adjusted to allow the accumulation of 100–150 ml of blood in the reservoir bag to provide sufficient volume for buffering the reflex peripheral vasodilation during carotid baroreceptor stimulation. Each experimental animal was presented with a 140 mm Hg step in carotid sinus pressure from 70 to 210 mm Hg. In 14 animals, an 80 mm Hg step from 70 to 150 mm Hg was also given.

The protocol for an experimental run consisted of an oxygen electrode calibration, a 20-second control period, 30 seconds of carotid hypertension, and 2 minutes of recovery, followed by an oxygen electrode calibration. The experimental period was limited to 30 seconds, because it was not possible to sequester sufficient blood in the reservoir for longer runs without inducing hypotension. When practicable, runs were repeated for each experimental condition.

Data Analysis

Analog records were digitized (Numonics 2400) at 5-second intervals for a 20-second period preceding the start of carotid sinus pressure elevation, and then every second for the duration of the stimulus (30 sec) and the post-stimulus recovery period (45 sec). At each time point, mean coronary blood flow, carotid sinus pressure, mean aortic pressure, and coronary sinus oxygen tension were read.

The experiment was designed to have each dog serve as its own control. The prestimulus control value for an individual dog for each experimental condition was obtained by taking the average of the values 20, 15, 10, and 5 seconds before the onset of the carotid pressure stimulus. For the coronary blood flow, coronary sinus oxygen tension and aortic pressure data, all measurements are expressed as the difference from the average prestimulus control value. The averages of these values for all dogs in each experimental group are shown in the figures. The standard error of the mean values given in the figures and text are measures of the variability between dogs and were derived from data sets containing one value from each dog studied in any given experimental group ($n - 1$ degrees of freedom). When multiple runs were obtained under the same experimental conditions, the average of these gave a single value for that dog in the overall data analysis.

Two-tailed paired t-tests were used to determine the statistical significance of the differences in the responses following each intervention in all experimental groups.

Results

Under control conditions (propranolol only), step increases in carotid sinus pressure resulted in atrial bradycardia and increases in left main coronary artery blood flow and coronary sinus blood oxygen tension (Fig. 2). With step elevations in carotid sinus pressure from 70 to 210 mm Hg ($n = 18$), average coronary flow increased 0.29 ± 0.04 (SEM) ml/min per g above the prestimulation value of 0.36 ± 0.03 ml/min per g (Fig. 3). Average oxygen tension in the coronary sinus rose by 10.0 ± 0.9 mm Hg above the prestimulation value of 20.5 ± 0.8 mm Hg. Step elevations in pressure from 70 to 150 mm Hg ($n = 14$) resulted in an average coronary flow increase of 0.13 ± 0.03 ml/min per g above the prestimulus value of 0.38 ± 0.03 ml/min per g and a coronary sinus oxygen tension increase of 5.3 ± 0.6 mm Hg above the prestimulation value of 20.4 ± 0.9 mm Hg.

Atropine-First Group

Average values for six dogs that were subjected to the atropine-first protocol are shown in Figure 4. In the propranolol control condition, coronary flow increased 0.28 ± 0.03 ml/min per g above the prestimulation value of 0.39 ± 0.06 ml/min per g, and coronary sinus oxygen tension increased by 9.6 ± 1.6 mm Hg from the prestimulation value of 22.6 ± 1.9 mm Hg following the step elevation in carotid sinus pressure from 70 to 210 mm Hg. After cholinergic blockade with atropine, the same step change in carotid sinus pressure resulted in a reduced coronary response ($P < 0.01$). Coronary flow increased 0.08 ± 0.01 ml/min per g above the prestimulation value of 0.44 ± 0.06 ml/min per g, and coronary sinus oxygen tension rose by 2.6 ± 0.6 mm Hg above the prestimulation value of 26.1 ± 2.6 mm Hg. The addition of α-receptor blockade with phenoxybenzamine further decreased the remaining changes in coronary flow and coronary sinus oxygen tension ($P < 0.01$) from the prestimulation values of 0.57 ± 0.10 ml/min per g and 31.3 ± 2.1 mm Hg (Fig. 4). The increase in prestimulation coronary blood flow from 0.44 to 0.57 ml/min per g following phenoxybenzamine indicates there was sympathetic vasoconstrictor coronary tone. In all three conditions, reflex changes in mean aortic pressure during the carotid sinus stimulus were less than 15 mm Hg (Fig. 4).

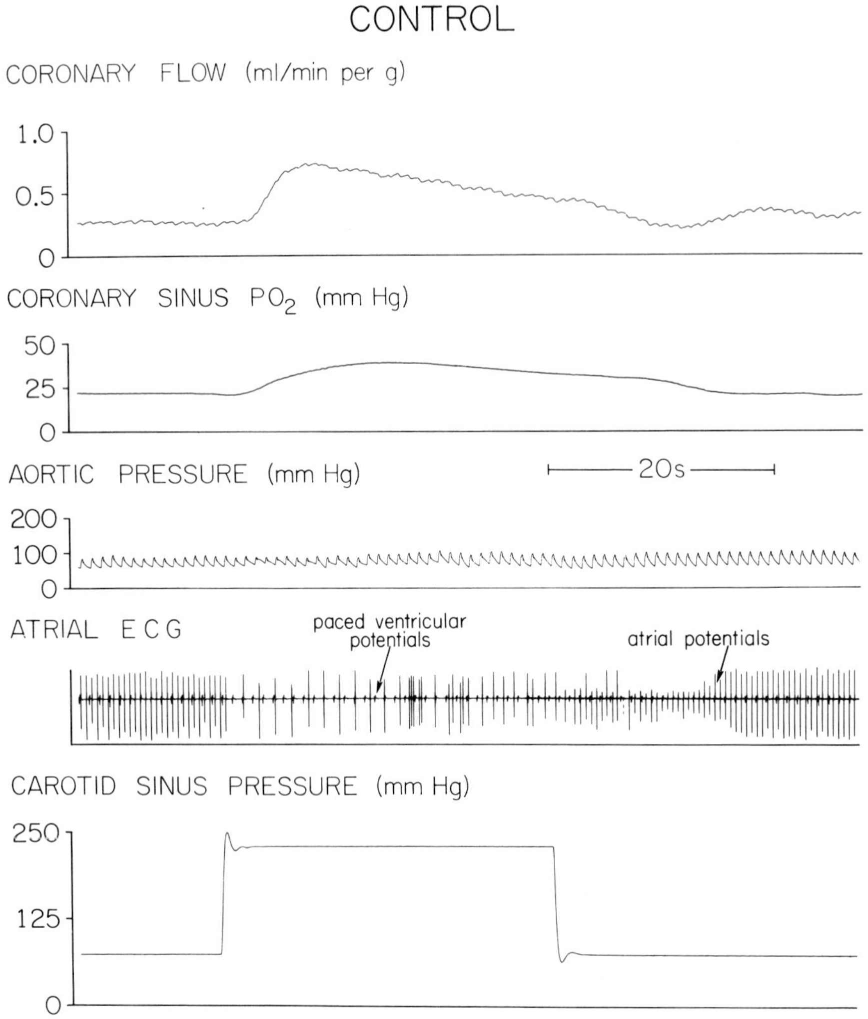

FIGURE 2. *Effects of carotid sinus hypertension after β-receptor blockade, with the heart paced at constant rate and the coronary artery perfused at constant pressure. A step change in carotid sinus pressure produced reflex coronary vasodilation and atrial bradycardia.*

Phenoxybenzamine-First Group

Average values for seven dogs that were subjected to the phenoxybenzamine-first protocol are shown in Figure 5. In the propranolol control condition for these animals, coronary flow increased 0.36 ± 0.09 ml/min per g above the prestimulation value of 0.39 ± 0.03 ml/min per g, and coronary sinus oxygen tension rose by 10.0 ± 2.0 mm Hg from the prestimulation value of 19.1 ± 0.6 mm Hg. After α-receptor blockade, the same step stimulus resulted in a coronary flow increase of 0.34 ± 0.09 ml/min per g above the prestimulation value of 0.61 ± 0.06 ml/min per g and an increase in coronary sinus oxygen tension of 6.4 ± 1.5 mm Hg above the prestimulation value of 28.1 ± 2.2 mm Hg. The increase in prestimulation coronary blood flow from 0.39 to 0.61 ml/min per g by phenoxybenzamine indicates there was sympathetic vasoconstrictor coronary tone. The response in coronary flow and coronary sinus oxygen tension were not different compared to the propranolol control condition ($P > 0.10$). After the addition of atropine, reflex changes in coronary flow and coronary sinus oxygen tension from the prestimulation values of 0.59 ± 0.05 ml/min per g and 26.6 ± 2.0 mm Hg were significantly reduced ($P < 0.01$) (Fig. 5).

Vagotomy-First Group

The parasympathetic role in the coronary response to carotid sinus hypertension was verified in two animals by cutting the vagus nerves in the neck. Vagotomy gave results similar to those achieved with atropine. Before vagotomy, a step change in carotid sinus pressure from 70 to 210 mm Hg resulted in a 0.17 ml/min per g increase in coronary flow above the prestimulation value of 0.25 ml/min per g. Average oxygen tension in the coronary sinus rose 11.4 mm Hg from the prestimulation value of 19.0 mm Hg. Vagotomy reduced this vasodilator response in coronary flow to 0.07 ml/min per g above the prestimulation value of 0.27 ml/min per g, and the response in coronary sinus oxygen tension to 4.1 mm Hg above the prestimulation value of 22.4 mm Hg. Completion of autonomic blockade with phenoxybenzamine further attenuated these responses in coronary flow and oxygen tension.

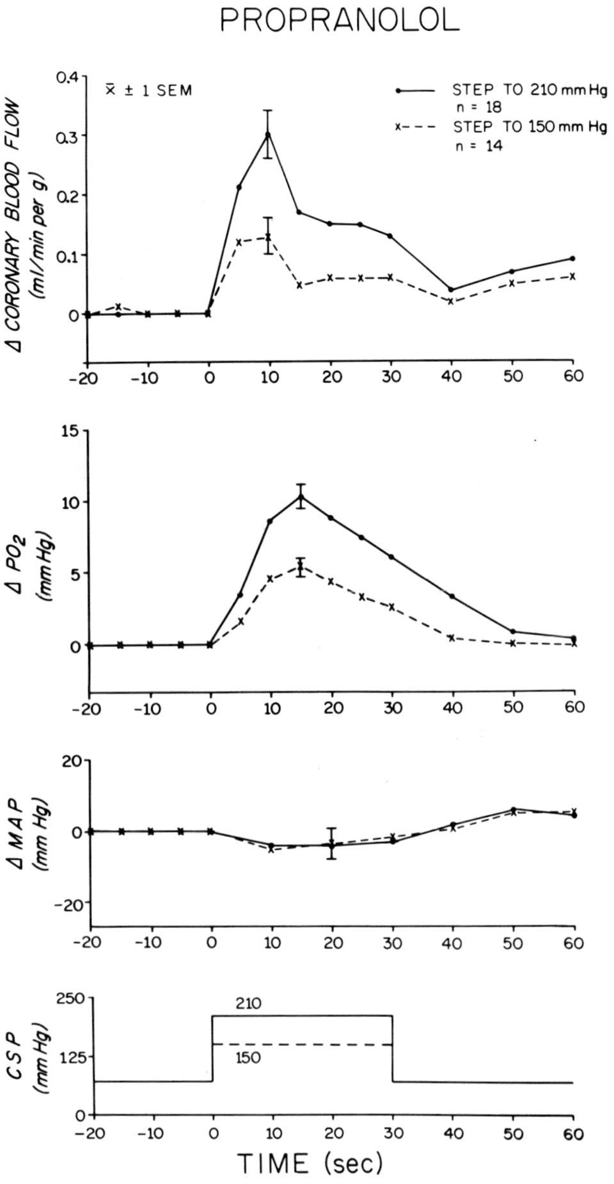

FIGURE 3. *Average responses to carotid sinus pressure (CSP) elevations from 70 to 210 mm Hg (n = 18) and from 70 to 150 mm Hg (n = 14) from the propranolol control trials. The response in coronary flow and coronary sinus oxygen tension (P_{O_2}) was significantly less (P < 0.01) at the lower level of carotid sinus hypertension. Data are expressed as the differences from the average of the values 20, 15, 10, and 5 seconds before the stimulus onset. The prestimulus values before the step to 210 mm Hg were: coronary blood flow 0.36 ± 0.03 (SEM) ml/min per g; coronary sinus oxygen tension 20.5 ± 0.80 mm Hg; mean aortic pressure (MAP) 79.1 ± 3.0 mm Hg. The prestimulus values before the step to 150 mm Hg were: coronary blood flow 0.38 ± 0.03 ml/min per g; coronary sinus oxygen tension 20.4 ± 0.9 mm Hg; mean aortic pressure 83.1 ± 3.7 mm Hg. The statistical significance between the responses at the two stimulus levels was determined using an unpaired t-test at the time point indicated by the ±1 SE bars.*

Carotid Sinus Denervation

To verify that the carotid sinus was the origin of the reflex, the carotid sinuses were surgically and chemically denervated following completion of the

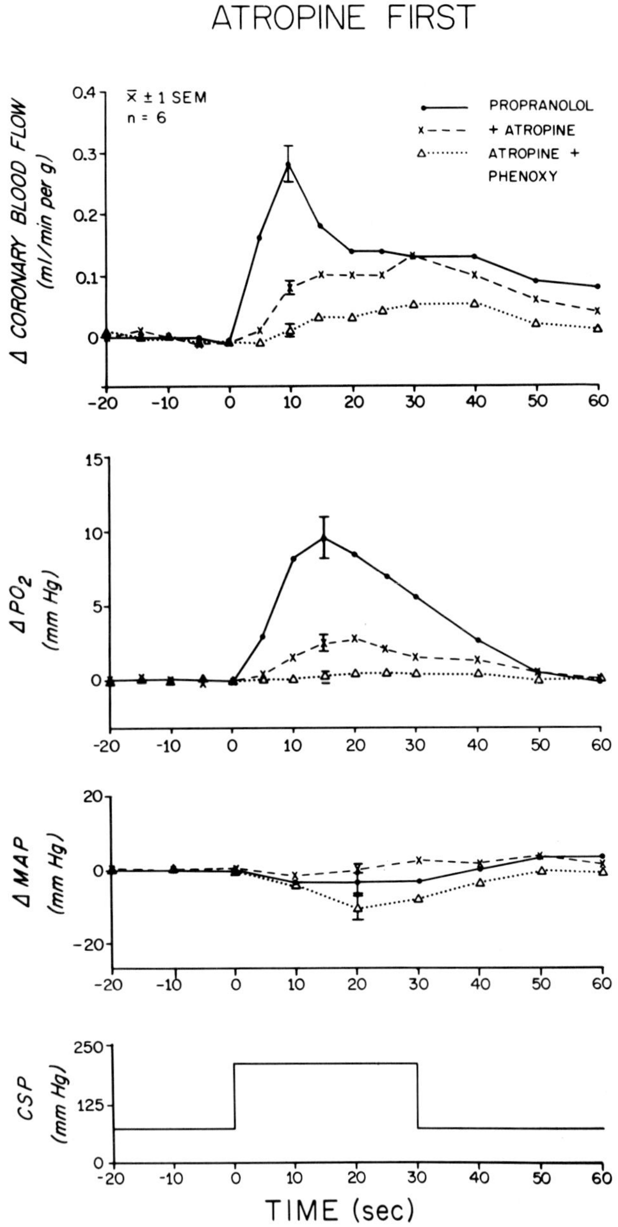

FIGURE 4. *Effects of carotid sinus pressure (CSP) elevation in the atropine-first group. The control responses (propranolol) in coronary flow and coronary sinus oxygen tension (P_{O_2}) were greatly attenuated (P < 0.01) by the administration of atropine. The addition of phenoxybenzamine after atropine further reduced these changes (P < 0.01). Data are expressed as differences from the average of the values 20, 15, 10, and 5 seconds before the stimulus onset. Each point represents the average of values obtained in six dogs. The prestimulus control values for the propranolol control trial were: coronary flow 0.39 ± 0.06 (SEM) ml/min per g; coronary sinus oxygen tension 22.6 ± 1.9 mm Hg; mean aortic pressure (MAP) 80.9 ± 5.9 mm Hg. The prestimulus values for the atropine trial were: coronary blood flow 0.44 ± 0.06 ml/min per g; coronary sinus oxygen tension 26.1 ± 2.6 mm Hg; mean aortic pressure 77.5 ± 6.3 mm Hg. The prestimulus values for the atropine + phenoxybenzamine trial were: coronary blood flow 0.57 ± 0.10 ml/min per g; coronary sinus oxygen tension 31.3 ± 2.1 mm Hg; mean aortic pressure 70.2 ± 4.9 mm Hg. The statistical significance between the responses after each treatment was calculated using a paired t-test at the time point indicated by the ±1 SE bars.*

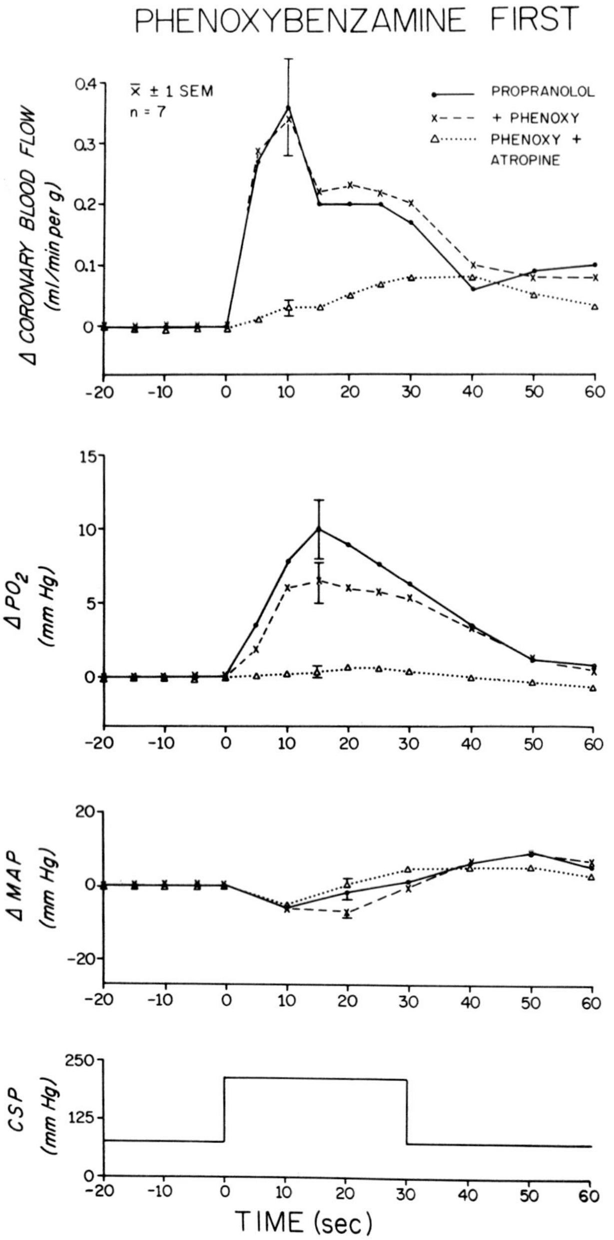

FIGURE 5. *Effects of carotid sinus pressure (CSP) elevation in the phenoxybenzamine-first group. Reflex coronary vasodilation was not significantly reduced ($P > 0.1$) by the administration of phenoxybenzamine. The addition of atropine after phenoxybenzamine significantly reduced the responses in coronary flow and coronary sinus oxygen tension (Po_2) ($P < 0.01$). Data are expressed as differences from the average of the values 20, 15, 10, and 5 seconds before the stimulus onset. Each point represents the average of values obtained in seven dogs. The prestimulus values for the propranolol control trial were: coronary blood flow 0.39 ± 0.03 (SEM) ml/min per g; coronary sinus oxygen tension 19.1 ± 0.06 mm Hg; mean aortic pressure (MAP) 82.2 ± 4.8 mm Hg. The prestimulus values for the phenoxybenzamine trial were: coronary blood flow 0.61 ± 0.06 ml/min per g; coronary sinus oxygen tension 28.1 ± 2.2 mm Hg; mean aortic pressure 70.6 ± 2.7 mm Hg. The prestimulus values for the phenoxybenzamine + atropine trial were: coronary blood flow 0.59 ± 0.05 ml/min per g; coronary sinus oxygen tension 26.6 ± 2.0 mm Hg; mean aortic pressure 73.8 ± 1.2 mm Hg. The statistical significance between the responses after each treatment was calculated using a paired t-test at the time point indicated by the ±1 SE bars.*

propranolol control runs in three animals. Before denervation, a step change in carotid sinus pressure from 70 to 210 mm Hg resulted in a 0.27 ml/min per g increase in coronary blood flow above the prestimulation value of 0.31 ml/min per g. Average oxygen tension in the coronary sinus rose 9.5 mm Hg above the prestimulation value of 20.7 mm Hg. After denervation, the same step elevation in carotid sinus pressure produced no change in coronary flow or coronary sinus oxygen tension from the prestimulation values of 0.32 ml/min per g and 23.8 mm Hg.

Discussion

These data indicate that stimulation of carotid sinus baroreceptors with a pressure stimulus produces reflex vasodilation of the coronary vascular bed by activation of parasympathetic vasodilator fibers and inhibition of sympathetic vasoconstrictor fibers. The data confirm the results obtained with electrical stimulation of the carotid sinus nerve and extend the observations to reflexes produced by functional pressure stimulation. The results may be conveniently discussed in relation to the major factors that influence coronary blood flow: (1) coronary perfusion pressure, (2) extravascular compression of coronary vessels, (3) local metabolic control, and (4) neural control.

Perfusion Pressure

The left main coronary artery perfusion pressure was held constant at 100 mm Hg with a servo-controlled pump. Therefore, the observed increase in coronary flow during carotid sinus hypertension was probably not due to changes in perfusion pressure.

Extravascular Compression

During each cardiac systole, the contracting myocardium compresses the coronary vessels and increases their resistance to flow above that during diastole. The magnitude of this extravascular component of coronary resistance is related to heart rate, systolic pressure, and myocardial contractility (Feigl, 1983). In the present experiments, the ventricles were paced at a constant rate and aortic pressure was stabilized. Therefore, the possibility that alterations in these two variables could explain the observed results is slight.

A reflex negative inotropic effect of carotid baroreceptor stimulation has been well described (Sarnoff et al., 1960; DeGeest et al., 1964; Levy et al., 1966a) and is due to both inhibition of sympathetic discharge (Sarnoff et al., 1960; DeGeest et al., 1964) and parasympathetic activation (Levy et al., 1966a). The observation that the negative inotropic effect of parasympathetic activation is accentuated by simultaneous cardiac sympathetic excitation (Hollenberg et al., 1965; Levy et al., 1966b; Levy and Zieske, 1969) suggests that an interaction between the autonomic pathways may also be involved. Cholinergic prejunctional inhibition of sympathetic norepinephrine release is a suggested mechanism for this effect (Vanhoutte and Levy, 1979; Vanhoutte, 1981). In the present study, sympathetically mediated alterations in inotropic state were avoided by β-receptor blockade with propranolol at the outset of all experiments.

The possibility that there was a direct negative parasympathetic inotropic effect, independent of sympathetic mechanisms, cannot be ruled out in the present experiments. However, the parasympathetic inotropic effect is small when sympathetic activation is low or absent (Hollenberg et al., 1964; Levy et al., 1966a, 1966b). Also, relatively large reductions in cardiac contractile state have minor effects on the extravascular component of coronary resistance (Snyder et al., 1975). Thus, it seems unlikely that a reflex decrease in systolic myocardial compression was primarily responsible for the observed coronary vasodilation.

Metabolic Control

Cardiac metabolism is a major influence on coronary blood flow through a local regulatory mechanism. The two major correlates of myocardial oxygen consumption are heart rate and systolic pressure (Rooke and Feigl, 1982). In the present experiments, the heart was paced at a constant rate and aortic pressure was stabilized. Sympathetically mediated changes in contractility were minimized by β-receptor blockade. Although the reflex decrease in aortic pressure due to peripheral vasodilation was blunted with the blood reservoir, small decreases in aortic pressure could not be prevented (Fig. 3). A decrease in cardiac afterload (aortic pressure) would result in a diminished myocardial metabolism and a secondary coronary vasoconstriction, rather than the observed vasodilation. A change in coronary sinus oxygen tension may be interpreted as an alteration in the balance between coronary blood flow and oxygen metabolism. The increase in coronary sinus oxygen tension observed during carotid sinus hypertension (Fig. 3) indicates that coronary blood flow increased more than any concomitant change in metabolism. Therefore, the reflex coronary vasodilation observed in the present study was probably not secondary to an augmented cardiac metabolism.

Neural Control

Direct parasympathetic cholinergic coronary vasodilation and sympathetic α-receptor vasoconstriction have been demonstrated in numerous laboratories (Feigl, 1983). These neural pathways can be reflexly activated by several stimuli. Parasympathetic coronary vasodilation is part of the Bezold-Jarisch reflex (Feigl, 1975) and the carotid body chemoreflex (Hackett et al., 1972; Vatner and McRitchie, 1975; Murray and Vatner, 1983; Murray et al., 1984). Reflex sympathetic α-receptor coronary vasoconstriction in response to carotid sinus hypotension has been reported in preparations with β-receptor blockade (Feigl, 1968; DiSalvo et al., 1971; Powell and Feigl, 1979) and without β-receptor blockade (Mohrman and Feigl, 1978).

Electrical stimulation of the afferent carotid sinus nerve has been shown to produce inhibition of coronary sympathetic constrictor tone (Vatner et al., 1970; Religa et al., 1972) and parasympathetic cholinergic coronary vasodilation (Hackett et al., 1972). However, it is difficult to equate a given nerve stimulation frequency with a carotid sinus pressure that physiologically stimulates baroreceptors. The present results confirm the previous results obtained with electrical stimulation of the carotid sinus nerve and demonstrate that baroreceptor activation with functional pressure stimuli produces a reflex coronary vasodilation.

Parasympathetic coronary vasodilation has been observed with elevations in carotid sinus pressure from 30 to 110 mm Hg in dogs with right heart bypass (Limet et al., 1975). However, this result is clouded by the observation that carotid body chemoreceptor activity is increased at carotid sinus pressures below 50–60 mm Hg (Biscoe et al., 1970). White et al. (1976) stimulated carotid and aortic baroreceptors with increased arterial pressure by inflating a balloon in the thoracic aorta of paced, heart-blocked dogs. The increase in cardiac afterload produced by this maneuver complicates the interpretation of direct reflex involvement in the response, since coronary vascular resistance changes secondary to altered cardiac metabolism may have been involved. White et al. (1976) observed an increase in coronary conductance that could be partially reduced by methscopolamine, suggesting a reflex parasympathetic cholinergic vasodilation. α-Receptor blockade further reduced the coronary conductance increase, indicating that inhibition of sympathetic constrictor tone to coronary vessels also was involved. However, deafferentation of the arterial baroreceptors abolished only the parasympathetic component of the coronary response, leaving open the possibility that reflexes from other receptors may have been involved. The present results confirm baroreceptor reflex parasympathetic coronary vasodilation.

The abolition of the reflex response in coronary flow and sinus oxygen tension after denervation of the carotid sinus region indicates that the reflex originates from the carotid sinus. Although a carotid body chemoreceptor reflex influence on coronary vessels has been demonstrated (Hackett et al., 1972; Vatner and McRitchie, 1975; Murray and Vatner, 1983; Murray et al., 1984), these receptors have been shown to be relatively insensitive to arterial pressure in the range of 60–220 mm Hg (Biscoe et al., 1970; Mancia, 1975). Thus, the reflex observed in the present study most likely originated from carotid sinus baroreceptors.

The efferent path for reflex coronary vasodilation includes both the sympathetic and parasympathetic divisions of the autonomic nervous system. Vagal parasympathetic vasodilation appears to be the predominant pathway, as was shown by the large reduction or abolition of the response in coronary flow and coronary sinus oxygen tension by the administration of atropine or vagotomy (Figs. 4 and 5). α-Receptor blockade blunted the reflex coronary flow and coronary sinus oxygen tension responses to carotid sinus hypertension (Fig. 4). This indicates that inhibition of sympathetic vasoconstrictor tone in coronary vessels is part of the carotid sinus reflex. Although the sympathetic component appears to be smaller than the parasympathetic component, its magnitude is dependent upon the level of pre-existing sympathetic tone. In the "phenoxybenzamine-first" experiments, the administration of phenoxybenzamine did not significantly alter the control coronary response to carotid hypertension (Fig. 5). Hackett et al. (1972) observed that the early abrupt reflex coronary vasodilation was due to parasympathetic activation, whereas the delayed response was due to sympathetic inhibition. The present results confirm this, and it is likely that the faster onset and greater magnitude of parasympathetic vasodilation (Fig. 4) masked the smaller, more slowly developing sympathetic component. Thus, only when the parasympathetic component was first removed was the sympathetic mechanism revealed (Fig. 4).

The coronary vasodilation observed in response to carotid hypertension was graded (Fig. 3). Step increases in carotid sinus pressure from 70 to 150 mm Hg resulted in increases in coronary flow and coronary sinus oxygen tension that equaled approximately 50% of the response elicited with the step to 210 mm Hg. This graded feature of the baroreceptor reflex has been demonstrated in the reflex control of heart rate and the vascular resistance of many peripheral beds (Kendrick et al., 1972; Kirchheim, 1976). The vasodilation in the present experiments peaked approximately 10 seconds after the beginning of the reflex, and was followed by a lower plateau until the end of the stimulus (Fig. 3). The reasons for the peak and decline are not elucidated by the present experimental design; conceivably, adaptation of any of the elements involved in the reflex could give this effect. Adaptation to steps in nonpulsatile pressure has been described for baroreceptors (Sleight et al., 1977) and for the pathway from carotid sinus baroreceptors to cardiac vagal efferent fibers (Potter, 1982). It is also probable that there was a competition between neural vasodilation and local metabolic coronary control that reduced the flow following the peak response.

In conclusion, carotid sinus hypertension elicits a graded baroreceptor reflex coronary vasodilation that is independent of myocardial metabolic mechanisms. The coronary vasodilation is primarily mediated by activation of parasympathetic vasodilator fibers, but also involves inhibition of sympathetic α-receptor vasoconstrictor fibers to coronary vessels.

We thank Fellner Smith and Stephanie Lathrop for expert technical assistance in these studies.

Supported by National Institutes of Health Grants HL 16910 and HL 07090.

Dr. Ito's present address is: Max Planck Institute, Parkstrasse 1, Bad Nauheim, West Germany.

Address for reprints: Dr. Eric O. Feigl, Department of Physiology and Biophysics, University of Washington SJ-40, Seattle, Washington 98195.

Received November 11, 1983; accepted for publication January 2, 1985.

References

Arfors K-E, Arturson G, Malmberg P (1971) Effect of prolonged chloralose anesthesia on acid-base balance and cardiovascular functions in dogs. Acta Physiol Scand **81:** 47–53

Biscoe TJ, Bradley GW, Purves MJ (1970) The relation between carotid body chemoreceptor discharge, carotid sinus pressure and carotid body venous flow. J Physiol (Lond) **208:** 99–120

Buffington CW, Feigl EO (1983) Effect of coronary artery pressure on transmural distribution of adrenergic coronary vasoconstriction in the dog. Circ Res **53:** 613–621

Chungcharoen D, Daly MdeB, Schweitzer A (1952) The blood supply of the carotid body in cats, dogs and rabbits. J Physiol (Lond) **117:** 347–358

DeGeest H, Levy MN, Zieske H Jr (1964) Carotid sinus baroreceptor reflex effects upon myocardial contractility. Circ Res **15:** 327–342

DiSalvo J, Parker PE, Scott JB, Haddy FJ (1971) Carotid baroreceptor influence on coronary vascular resistance in the anesthetized dog. Am J Physiol **221:** 156–160

Edis AJ, Shepherd JT (1971) Selective denervation of aortic arch baroreceptors and chemoreceptors in dogs. J Appl Physiol **30:** 294–296

Ely SW, Sawyer DC, Anderson DL, Scott JB (1981) Carotid sinus reflex vasoconstriction in right coronary circulation of dog and pig. Am J Physiol **241:** H149–H154

Falicov RE, Resnekov L, Kocandrle V, King S, Little CF (1970) Circulatory effects of carotid sinus nerve stimulation in dogs with reference to coronary flow and resistance. Circulation **41/42** (suppl II): 172–178

Feigl EO (1968) Carotid sinus reflex control of coronary blood flow. Circ Res **23:** 223–237

Feigl EO (1975) Reflex parasympathetic coronary vasodilation elicited from cardiac receptors in the dog. Circ Res **37:** 175–182

Feigl EO (1983) Coronary physiology. Physiol Rev **63:** 1–205

Feigl EO, D'Alecy LG (1971) Cuvette for continuously measuring blood oxygen tension. J Appl Physiol **30:** 909–911

Goodale WT, Lubin M, Eckenhoff JE, Hafkenschiel JH, Banfield WG Jr (1948) Coronary sinus catheterization for studying coronary blood flow and myocardial metabolism. Am J Physiol **152:** 340–355

Hackett JG, Abboud FM, Mark AL, Schmid PG, Heistad DD (1972) Coronary vascular responses to stimulation of chemoreceptors and baroreceptors. Evidence for reflex activation of vagal cholinergic innervation. Circ Res **31:** 8–17

Hasimoto K, Hirohata S (1936) On the aortic nerves in dogs. Tohoku J Exp Med **28:** 245–259

Hollenberg M, Carriere S, Barger AC (1965) Biphasic action of acetylcholine on ventricular myocardium. Circ Res **16:** 527–536

Ito BR, Feigl EO (1983) Technique for producing heart block in closed-chest dogs without electrical recording. Pflugers Arch **397:** 160–163

Ito CS, Scher AM (1973) Arterial baroreceptor fibers from the aortic region of the dog in the cervical vagus nerve. Circ Res **32:** 442–446

Kendrick E, Öberg B, Wennergren G (1972) Extent of engagement of various cardiovascular effectors to alterations of carotid sinus pressure. Acta Physiol Scand **86:** 410–418

Kirchheim HR (1976) Systemic arterial baroreceptor reflexes. Physiol Rev **56:** 100–176

Koberstein RC, Pittman DE, Klocke FJ (1969) Right atrial admixture in coronary venous blood. Am J Physiol **216:** 531–535

Levy MN, Zieske H (1969) Effect of enhanced contractility on the left ventriclar response to vagus nerve stimulation in dogs. Circ Res **24:** 303–311

Levy MN, Ng M, Lipman RI, Zieske H (1966a) Vagus nerves and baroreceptor control of ventricular performance. Circ Res **18:** 101–106

Levy MN, Ng M, Martin P, Zieske H (1966b) Sympathetic and parasympathetic interactions upon the left ventricle of the dog. Circ Res **19:** 5–10

Limet R, Fourny J, Kennedy JH (1975) Effects of the carotid sinus reflex upon coronary vessel tone. J Surg Res **19:** 199–207

Mancia G (1975) Influence of carotid baroreceptors on vascular responses to carotid chemoreceptor stimulation in the dog. Circ Res **36:** 270–276

McCloskey DI, Potter EK (1981) Excitation and inhibition of cardiac vagal motoneurones by electrical stimulation of the carotid sinus nerve. J Physiol (Lond) **316:** 163–175

Mohrman DE (1980) A servo-controlled roller pump for cardiovascular research. Am J Physiol **238:** H269–H274

Mohrman DE, Feigl EO (1978) Competition between sympathetic vasoconstriction and metabolic vasodilation in the canine coronary circulation. Circ Res **42:** 79–86

Murray PA, Vatner SF (1983) Reflex cardiovascular responses to chemoreceptor stimulation in conscious dogs with cardiac hypertrophy. Am J Physiol **245:** H871–H879

Murray PA, Lavallee M, Vatner SF (1984) α-Adrenergic-mediated reduction in coronary blood flow secondary to carotid chemoreceptor reflex activation in conscious dogs. Circ Res **54:** 96–106

Potter EK (1982) Adaptation of cardiac vagal responses to baroreceptor stimuli in the dog. J Physiol (Lond) **329:** 411–423

Powell JR, Feigl EO (1979) Carotid sinus reflex coronary vasoconstriction during controlled myocardial oxygen metabolism in the dog. Circ Res **44:** 44–51

Religa Z, Trzebski A, Religa A, Glowienko A (1972) Effect of the stimulation of afferent fibers in Hering's nerve on the blood flow and resistance in the coronary vessels of dogs. Pol Med J **11:** 632–641

Rooke GA, Feigl EO (1982) Work as a correlate of canine left ventricular oxygen consumption, and the problem of catecholamine oxygen wasting. Circ Res **50:** 273–286

Sarnoff SJ, Gilmore JP, Brockman SK, Mitchell JH, Linden RJ (1960) Regulation of ventricular contraction by the carotid sinus. Its effect on atrial and ventricular dynamics. Circ Res **8:** 1123–1136

Sleight P, Robinson JL, Brooks DE, Rees PM (1977) Characteristics of single carotid sinus baroreceptor fibers and whole nerve activity in the normotensive and the renal hypertensive dog. Circ Res **41:** 750–758

Smith FD, D'Alecy LG, Feigl EO (1974) Cannula-tip coronary blood flow transducer for use in closed-chest animals. J Appl Physiol **37:** 592–595

Snyder R, Downey JM, Kirk ES (1975) The active and passive components of extravascular coronary resistance. Cardiovasc Res **9:** 161–166

Solti F, Juhász-Nagy S, Szabó Z, Iskum M, Krasznai I (1975) Effect of the carotid sinus nerve stimulation on nutritive myocardial blood flow in regional cardiac ischaemia. Basic Res Cardiol **70:** 531–536

Vanhoutte PM, Levy MN (1979) Cholinergic inhibition of adrenergic neurotransmission in the cardiovascular system. *In* Integrative Functions of the Autonomic Nervous System, edited by CMcC Brooks, K Koizumi, A Sato. Tokyo, University of Tokyo Press, pp 159–176

Vanhoutte PM, Verbeuren TJ, Webb RC (1981) Local modulation of adrenergic neuroeffector interaction in the blood vessel wall. Physiol Rev **61;** 151–247

Vatner SF, McRitchie RJ (1975) Interaction of the chemoreflex and the pulmonary inflation reflex in the regulation of coronary circulation in conscious dogs. Circ Res **37:** 664–673

Vatner SF, Franklin D, Van Citters RL, Braunwald E (1970) Effects of carotid sinus nerve stimulation on the coronary circulation of the conscious dog. Circ Res **27:** 11–21

White SW, Porges WL, Reid JVO, Bhagat CI (1976) Baroreflex control of coronary conductance in normotensive and renal hypertensive conscious dogs with complete heart block. Clin Sci Mol Med **51** (suppl 3): 361–364

INDEX TERMS: Autonomic blockade • Parasympathetic cholinergic pathway • Sympathetic α-receptor pathway • Coronary blood flow • Carotid baroreceptor reflex

Evidence for a Specific Receptor Site for Lidocaine, Quinidine, and Bupivacaine Associated with Cardiac Sodium Channels in Guinea Pig Ventricular Myocardium

Craig W. Clarkson and Luc M. Hondeghem
From the Department of Pharmacology, University of California San Francisco, San Francisco, California

SUMMARY. According to the modulated receptor hypothesis, sodium channels have a specific receptor site for local anesthetic and antiarrhythmic drugs. Thus, in the presence of a high concentration of two drugs, competitive displacement of one drug by another may occur. Furthermore, if a drug that has relatively rapid post-stimulation recovery kinetics (e.g., lidocaine) displaces another drug with relatively slow recovery kinetics (i.e., quinidine or bupivacaine), then a net reduction in sodium channel blockade is expected at certain stimulation rates. We tested this prediction, using the maximum upstroke velocity of the ventricular action potential as an indicator of drug-free sodium channels. A single sucrose gap technique was used to stimulate guinea pig papillary muscles, and to control membrane voltage at all times except during the action potential upstroke. Drug-induced inhibition of maximum upstroke velocity increased as the stimulation rate was increased, and was significant ($P < 0.05$) at stimulation rates between 2.5 and 4 Hz in the presence of 43 μM lidocaine ($n = 5$), and between 0.15 and 4 Hz in the presence of 3.5 μM bupivacaine ($n = 4$). The addition of 43 μM lidocaine to a perfusate containing 3.5 μM bupivacaine resulted in a net increase in maximum upstroke velocity that was significant at rates between 1 and 3.3 Hz, with a maximum increase of 25 ± 6% at 1.6 Hz. In contrast, addition of 43 μM lidocaine to a perfusate containing 15 μM quinidine did not result in a significant change in maximum upstroke velocity at driving rates between 0.05 and 3.3 Hz ($P > 0.2$; $n = 4$). However, evidence for displacement of quinidine by lidocaine could be demonstrated by measuring post-stimulation recovery after a conditioning train of 19 10-msec pulses applied at 28 Hz. With this stimulation protocol, 41 ± 4% of maximum upstroke velocity recovered slowly from block with a time constant of 3.7 ± 1.2 seconds at −100 mV in the presence of 15 μM quinidine ($n = 5$). In the presence of a mixture of 43 μM lidocaine and 15 μM quinidine, this slow component was significantly reduced to 16 ± 7% ($n = 5$; $P < 0.01$), while 71 ± 13% of maximum upstroke velocity recovered with a time constant of 115 ± 21 msec, typical of lidocaine-blocked channels. A two-drug version of the modulated receptor theory was formulated. The effects of drug mixtures could be accounted for by this model. Our results provide strong support for the modulated receptor postulate that bupivacaine, quinidine, and lidocaine bind to a common receptor site.
(*Circ Res 56: 496–506, 1985*)

BUPIVACAINE has become a popular local anesthetic because of its excellent sensory anesthesia, long duration of action, and in obstetrics, its lack of adverse neonatal neurobehavioral effects (Scanlon et al., 1976). Unfortunately, bupivacaine can precipitate serious arrhythmias and death if it accidently gains access to the cardiovascular system (Albright, 1979; Kotelko et al., 1984). Bupivacaine-induced arrhythmias are commonly associated with symptoms of depressed cardiac conduction such as wide QRS complexes (Kotelko et al., 1984). These results, as well as those obtained in vitro (Courtney, 1984; Clarkson and Hondeghem, 1985) suggest that excessive block of cardiac sodium channels may be an important mechanism underlying bupivacaine cardiotoxicity.

We have found that bupivacaine avidly binds to inactivated sodium channels in ventricular myocardium during the action potential plateau ($K_d \cong 0.9$ μM), but has a relatively low affinity for both open and rested channels (Clarkson and Hondeghem, 1985). At normal diastolic potentials, bupivacaine dissociates relatively slowly from the sodium channel receptor ($\tau = 1$–2 seconds) (Clarkson and Hondeghem, 1985). These characteristics make bupivacaine a potent sodium channel blocker in cardiac tissue.

Bupivacaine block may be minimized by slowing heart rate, by shortening the action potential duration, and by inducing diastolic hyperpolarization to increase the rate of recovery (Clarkson and Hondeghem, 1985). Unfortunately, such changes cannot be satisfactorily carried out under clinical conditions. To explore an alternative approach for reducing bupivacaine cardiotoxicity, we investigated the effects of adding lidocaine to a ventricular muscle preparation depressed by bupivacaine. According to the modulated receptor hypothesis, different local anesthetic and antiarrhythmic drugs block sodium channels by binding to a common receptor site (Hille, 1977; Hondeghem and Katzung, 1977). If this is true, then high concentrations of lidocaine (≥20 μM) should be able to bind to and mask a substantial fraction of receptor sites during the upstroke and plateau of the cardiac action potential before bupivacaine binding to inactivated channels can substantially develop. Since lidocaine dissociates more rapidly from the sodium channel receptor during diastole than does bupivacaine (Grant et al., 1980; Clarkson and Hondeghem, 1985), displacement of bupivacaine by lidocaine should result in a net increase in maximum action potential upstroke velocity ($\dot{V}_{max}$) at normal heart rates (e.g., 1–2 Hz). Such an effect could be beneficial in reducing bupivacaine cardiotoxicity.

In addition to sodium channel block, bupivacaine has a potent negative inotropic effect which may also contribute to its cardiotoxicity (Block and Covino, 1981; Courtney, 1984; Kotelko et al., 1984). Since the inotropic effects of adding lidocaine to a bupivacaine-treated preparation may be of clinical relevance, we also investigated the effect of bupivacaine and lidocaine mixtures on twitch tension.

Finally, to gain further insight into the interaction of two heavily used clinical antiarrhythmics, we also investigated the effects of combinations of lidocaine and quinidine. Since quinidine primarily blocks open channels (Hondeghem and Katzung, 1977; Colatsky, 1982), and dissociation between beats is very slow (time constant of 4–7 seconds) (Grant et al., 1982; Weld et al., 1982), lidocaine should be much less effective in displacing quinidine than it is in displacing bupivacaine.

The test of these predictions should provide further insight into the electrophysiological effects of different drug mixtures, as well as provide a critical test of the hypothesis that local anesthetic and antiarrhythmic drugs block cardiac sodium channels by binding to a common receptor site. A preliminary report of part of this work has been published in a brief communication (Clarkson and Hondeghem, 1984).

Methods

Dissection and Mounting of Muscles

Guinea pigs of either sex weighing 250–450 g were killed by cervical dislocation. The thorax was opened and hearts were quickly removed. Papillary muscles with a diameter of 0.2–0.8 mm and length of 3.0–5.0 mm were dissected free from the right ventricle and mounted in a tissue bath divided into three chambers (posterior, central, and anterior) by two rubber membranes. The methods used were similar to those used by Beeler and Reuter (1970). Once mounted, the base of the papillary muscle was placed in the posterior chamber, a 2-mm segment in the central chamber, and the tip (less than 0.5 mm long) in the anterior chamber.

Solutions and Drugs

The anterior chamber was perfused with a HEPES-buffered salt solution of the following composition (in mM): NaCl, 143; KCl, 4; $CaCl_2$, 1.8; $MgCl_2$, 1.1; *d*-glucose, 5; and HEPES, 5. The solution was titrated to a pH of 7.38 ± 0.01 with approximately 3 mM NaOH, equilibrated with 100% oxygen, and maintained at 36 ± 0.2°C. The middle chamber was perfused with an isotonic sucrose solution to which glucose (5 mM) and $CaCl_2$ (40 μM) had been added. The posterior chamber was perfused with a HEPES solution similar to that perfusing the anterior chamber, with the exception that all NaCl had been replaced with an equimolar amount of KCl. Drugs (quinidine gluconate, lidocaine hydrochloride, and bupivacaine hydrochloride) were dissolved directly into the HEPES solution perfusing the anterior chamber. After the addition of either lidocaine or bupivacaine, an equilibration period of 30 minutes was allowed for drug effects on $\dot{V}_{max}$ to approach steady state. Since quinidine's effect on $\dot{V}_{max}$ takes somewhat longer to approach steady state, the minimum equilibration period used with this drug was 50 minutes.

Electrophysiological Techniques

To measure transmembrane potential, we used conventional glass microelectrodes filled with 3 M KCl and attached them to a high input impedance voltage follower with input capacitance compensation. Current used for stimulation and voltage clamping the tissue in the anterior chamber was applied from the posterior chamber and across the sucrose gap. Command pulses were generated by a microprocessor-based stimulator. Action potential upstrokes were elicited by current pulses, 1 msec long. The intensity of the current pulse was adjusted to maintain a constant latency between the stimulus and the time at which the maximum upstroke velocity ($\dot{V}_{max}$) of the action potential was achieved. $\dot{V}_{max}$ was measured by electronic differentiation of the action potential upstroke (Hondeghem and Cotner, 1978), and recorded on a Grass model 7 polygraph. During voltage clamp, membrane potential was controlled at all times except during the initial 5 msec of the action potential (the upstroke during which $\dot{V}_{max}$ was measured, and a few milliseconds of plateau) as well as the 20-second rest periods separating successive clamp protocols. Different voltage clamp pulse protocols (illustrated in the insets of Figures 1, 3, and 5) were used to determine the time course of recovery from block, and rate dependence of block.

Limitations of Methods

$\dot{V}_{max}$ was used as an indicator of drug-free sodium channels. All results reported in this study were obtained from muscles in which a single impalement was maintained between paired measurements. Furthermore, all muscles had $\dot{V}_{max}$ values of 150–350 V/sec in the absence of drug, and a less than 5% variation in $\dot{V}_{max}$ as stimulus to maximum upstroke velocity latency was varied within a window of 1 msec. There is some controversy as to whether $\dot{V}_{max}$ is linearly related to peak sodium conductance (Cohen and Strichartz, 1977; Hondeghem, 1978; Cohen, 1979; Walton and Fozzard, 1979; Cohen et al., 1984). This controversy can only be resolved when $\dot{V}_{max}$ and peak sodium current have been measured under identical physiological conditions. However, a correct interpretation of the results of the present study requires only that $\dot{V}_{max}$ be a monotonic function of peak sodium current, so that a decrease in $\dot{V}_{max}$ reflects a decrease in peak sodium current. Recent studies suggest that this is a valid assumption (Walton and Fozzard, 1979, 1983; Bean et al., 1983; Cohen et al., 1984).

Measurements of Twitch Tension

Papillary muscles were placed in a single-chambered tissue bath perfused with HEPES-buffered solution. Muscles were stimulated by a pair of bipolar extracellular electrodes placed in the bottom of the bath. The tip of each muscle was attached to a Grass force-displacement transducer by a silk suture (6-0), and the base was fixed to the Sylgard bottom of the bath with several fine pins. Muscles were preloaded to the length at which they developed maximal isometric tension. Before experiments were begun, muscles were paced at 0.5 Hz for 30 minutes to allow them to stabilize. During each experiment, papillary muscles were driven at stimulation rates between 0.2 and 3 Hz. After a change in stimulation rate, measurements were taken when twitch tension had reached steady state. This usually required about 2 minutes.

Data Analysis

The time course of recovery from block was defined using a least-square-error nonlinear exponential-fitting routine. To determine whether a single or double exponential function provided a better fit, we fit the data by both a single exponential function (of the form: $y = A \exp[-t/\tau] + B$) and a double exponential function (of the form: $y = A \exp[-t/\tau] + B \exp[-t/\tau] + C$). The double exponential fit was accepted as the fit of choice whenever it had a mean square error that was at least one-third that obtained with a single exponential.

$\dot{V}_{max}$ values are expressed as either a fraction or percentage of control $\dot{V}_{max}$ at 0.05 Hz. Paired comparisons were evaluated for statistical significant difference using Student's *t*-test. Comparisons between more than two groups were evaluated by one-way analysis of variance (ANOVA) and Scheffe's test for critical difference. Differences were considered significant if values of $P < 0.05$ were obtained. Results are represented as mean ± SEM.

Modeling

The modulated receptor model (Hondeghem and Katzung, 1977) was expanded to describe the effects of a mixture of two drugs. The differential equations for this drug-mixture model were incorporated into a computer program written in the C programming language, and run on a PDP 11/34A computer. The modulated receptor parameters used in the drug-mixture model are shown in Table 2. The parameters for lidocaine and quinidine are similar to those estimated by Hondeghem and Katzung (1977). However, a few of the parameters were changed in order to provide an adequate fit of the effects of individual drugs in the present experiments. No systematic attempt was made to determine whether other parameter values could fit the data equally well (or better). Simulation of the time course of block during a single action potential required about 3 minutes of computer time.

Results

Effects of Lidocaine, Quinidine, and Bupivacaine on $\dot{V}_{max}$

Before investigating the effects of drug mixture, we first determined what drug concentrations would produce a substantial level of block during a train of pulses at a high rate (3.3 Hz), as well as the relative rates of recovery from block at normal diastolic potentials (e.g., −85 mV). Pacing a papillary muscle at 3.3 Hz under control conditions resulted in only a small reduction of $\dot{V}_{max}$ (Fig. 1A) which may be largely ascribed to accumulation of slow inactivation (Saikawa and Carmeliet, 1982; Clarkson et al., 1984). However, in the presence of either bupivacaine (3.5 μM), lidocaine (43 μM), or quinidine (15 μM), the same pulse pattern resulted in a marked use-dependent accumulation of block which approached a steady state level by the end of a 19-beat pulse train (Fig. 1A). This steady state level of block results from the fact that block development during each action potential is approximately equal to the amount of recovery from block which occurs between each beat. The accumulated block slowly dissipated, after this pulse train, if the muscle was allowed to rest (Fig. 1B). In the absence of drug, $\dot{V}_{max}$ recovers from inactivation with an exponential time course having a time constant of less than 30 msec at −85 mV (Gettes and Reuter, 1974) (Fig. 1B). In the presence of drug, an additional slower exponential component representing recovery of drug-blocked channels can be observed. The time constant of this recovery process is different for channels blocked by different drugs (see Fig. 1B). At −85 mV, channels blocked by lidocaine recover with a time constant of 184 ± 17 msec ($n = 6$), channels blocked by bupivacaine recover with a time constant of 1.1 ± 0.2 seconds ($n = 5$), and channels blocked by quinidine recover with a time constant of 4.0 ± 0.8 seconds ($n = 4$). Characterization of the time course of recovery of drug-blocked channels and extrapolation of this process back to zero time (the y-intercept) provides an estimate of the fraction of channels blocked by drug at the end of the conditioning train (Khodorov et al., 1976; Bean et al., 1983). Using a least-squares fit of the time course of $\dot{V}_{max}$ recovery, we estimated the level of use-dependent block at the end of the 19th beat to be 63 ± 4% ($n = 5$) in the presence of 3.5 μM bupivacaine, 82 ± 7% in 43 μM lidocaine ($n = 6$), and 51 ± 8% in 15 μM quinidine ($n = 4$). The fast component representing recovery of drug-free channels from inactivation was not measurable in the presence of 43 μM lidocaine, since virtually all channels were blocked by drug, and was usually ignored when defining the time course of recovery in the presence of bupivacaine or quinidine by measuring $\dot{V}_{max}$ only after a recovery interval greater than 100 msec.

Effects of Mixing Lidocaine and Bupivacaine

Rate-Dependent Effects on $\dot{V}_{max}$

To determine the effects of drugs and drug mixtures on $\dot{V}_{max}$ at steady state at different stimulation rates, we clamped the action potential plateau to +20 mV for 180 msec at all stimulation rates, and clamped the diastolic potential to −85 mV (as illustrated in Fig. 1A). In the presence of 3.5 μM bupi-

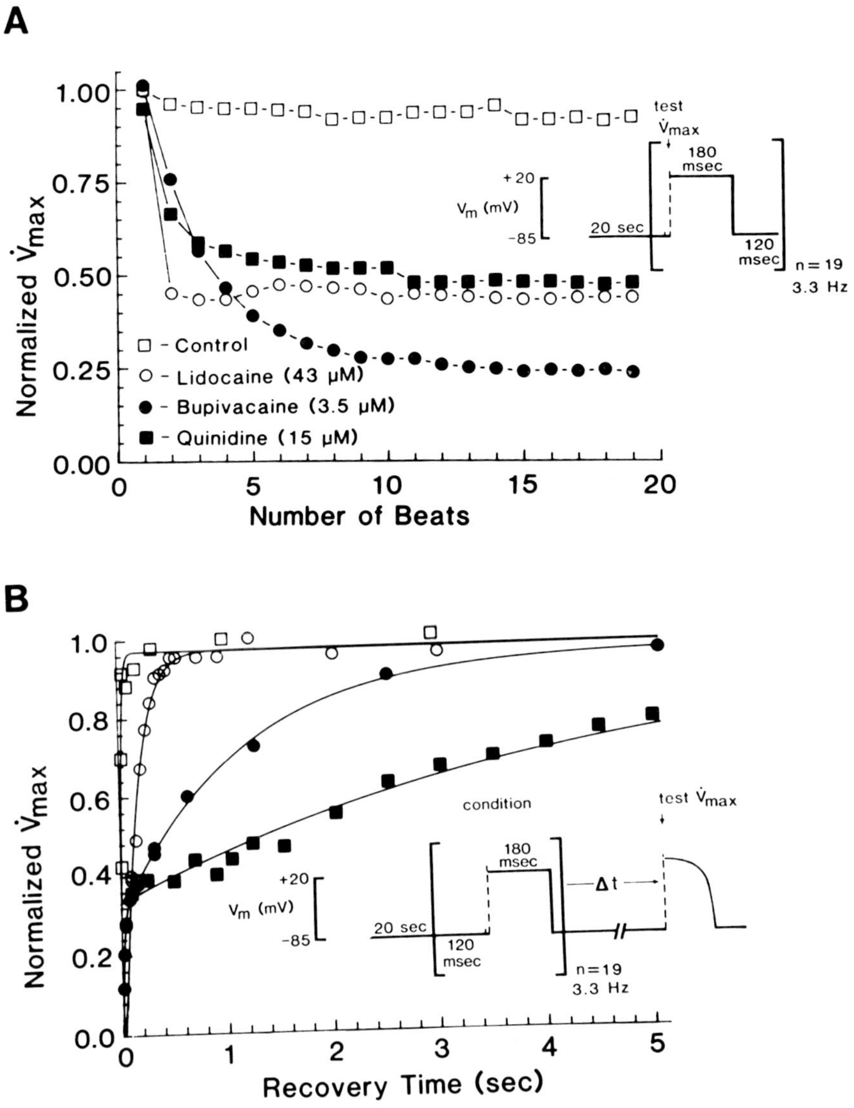

FIGURE 1. *Time course of development and recovery from use-dependent block of $\dot{V}_{max}$. The pulse protocols are shown as insets. The dotted vertical line in each inset indicates a free-running 5-msec action potential upstroke evoked by a 1-msec current stimulus. The interpulse period (120 msec) includes the time for the current stimulus and upstroke. The graphs show $\dot{V}_{max}$ normalized to its value under control conditions at 0.05 Hz. Part A shows the effect of a 19-beat pulse train at 3.3 Hz on $\dot{V}_{max}$ under control conditions, and in the presence of either 15 μM (5 μg/ml) quinidine, 43 μM (10 μg/ml) lidocaine, or 3.5 μM (1 μg/ml) bupivacaine. Part B shows the time course of $\dot{V}_{max}$ recovery under control conditions, and in the presence of drug. The curves represent nonlinear least-squares fits to the data points. The equations of fit for the normalized data were: 0.97 − 0.97 exp (−t/0.021 sec) for control; 0.97 − 0.97 exp (−t/0.140 sec) for lidocaine; 0.96 − 0.66 exp (−t/1.137 sec) − 0.39 exp (−t/0.020 sec) for bupivacaine; and 0.95 −0.62 exp (−t/4.419 sec) for quinidine. The fast component (τ = 10–30 msec) representing recovery of drug-free channels was not resolved in the presence of quinidine or lidocaine.*

vacaine alone, the steady state level of $\dot{V}_{max}$ decreased progressively as the stimulation rate was increased from 0.05 to 4 Hz (Fig. 2). This decrease was significant at all stimulation rates between 0.15 and 4 Hz ($P < 0.01$). Lidocaine (43 μM) also reduced $\dot{V}_{max}$ in a rate-dependent manner, but this reduction was significant only at stimulation rates between 2.5 and 4 Hz ($P < 0.05$). In addition, the extent of $\dot{V}_{max}$ reduction by lidocaine was significantly less than that produced by bupivacaine at all rates below 4 Hz ($P < 0.05$).

In four experiments, switching the superfusate solution from one containing 3.5 μM bupivacaine to one containing a mixture of 3.5 μM bupivacaine and 43 μM lidocaine resulted in a significant net increase in $\dot{V}_{max}$ (reduction of block) at stimulation rates between 1 and 3.3 Hz ($P < 0.05$) (see Fig. 2). The net increase in $\dot{V}_{max}$ was maximal at 1.67 Hz (100 beats/min), where addition of lidocaine resulted in an increase of $\dot{V}_{max}$ from 57 ± 3% to 82 ± 3% of control $\dot{V}_{max}$ ($P < 0.02$; $n = 4$). The level of $\dot{V}_{max}$ block in the presence of a mixture of 43 μM lidocaine and 3.5 μM bupivacaine was not significantly different than that obtained in 43 μM lidocaine alone, over a range of stimulation rates of 0.015 to 4 Hz ($P > 0.3$, one-way ANOVA) (see Fig. 2).

The effect of mixing lower concentrations of lidocaine (13 or 21 μM) with 3.5 μM bupivacaine were also determined in two additional experiments. The effects were qualitatively similar to those obtained with 43 μM lidocaine, except that the net increase in $\dot{V}_{max}$ was smaller. For example, the net increase in $\dot{V}_{max}$ at 1.6 Hz 30 minutes after we had switched from a bupivacaine perfusate to a perfusate containing a mixture of bupivacaine and lidocaine, was 9% when 13 μM lidocaine was used, and 12% with 21 μM lidocaine, compared to 25% with 43 μM lidocaine.

Recovery Kinetics

To determine whether the change in $\dot{V}_{max}$ observed upon addition of lidocaine to a bupivacaine-depressed preparation resulted from a reduction in bupivacaine-blocked channels, we characterized the

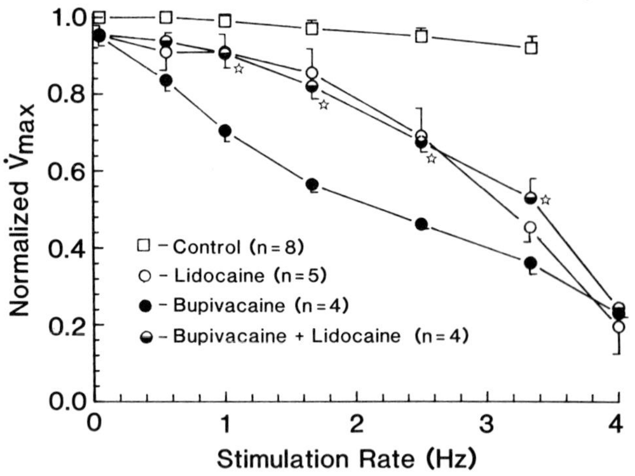

FIGURE 2. *Dependence of $\dot{V}_{max}$ upon stimulation rate under control conditions, and in the presence of 43 μM lidocaine, 3.5 μM bupivacaine, or a mixture of 3.5 μM bupivacaine plus 43 μM lidocaine. Data indicate mean values of $\dot{V}_{max}$ normalized to control at 0.05 Hz, and vertical bars indicate SEM. $\dot{V}_{max}$ values obtained in bupivacaine and the mixture of bupivacaine plus lidocaine were acquired from the same four preparations. Stars indicate values of $\dot{V}_{max}$ that were significantly increased ($P < 0.05$, one way ANOVA) 30 minutes after lidocaine was added to the bupivacaine perfusate. The $\dot{V}_{max}$ values obtained in the drug mixture were not significantly different from those obtained in lidocaine alone ($P > 0.3$; one-way ANOVA). In these experiments, the action potential plateau was clamped to +20 mV for 180 msec following the initial 5 msec of the upstroke, and the diastolic potential was clamped to −85 mV.*

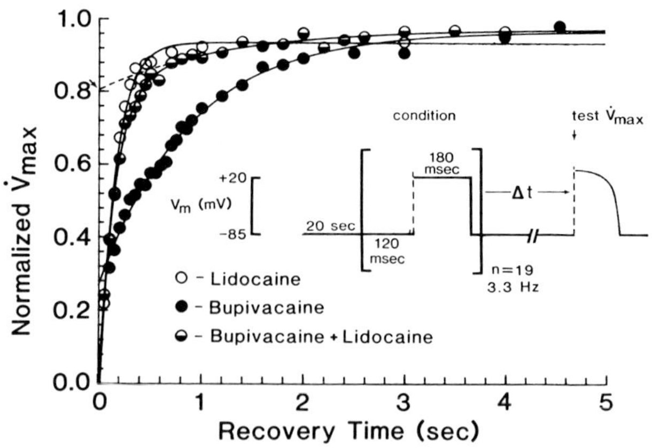

FIGURE 3. *The time course of recovery from block in the presence of 3.5 μM bupivacaine, 43 μM lidocaine, and a mixture of 3.5 μM bupivacaine plus 43 μM lidocaine. The pulse protocol is shown in the inset. The dotted vertical line in the inset indicates a free-running 5-msec action potential upstroke. The interpulse period (120 msec) includes the time for the current stimulus and upstroke. $\dot{V}_{max}$ has been normalized to its control value at 0.05 Hz. The curves represent nonlinear least-squares exponential fits of the data. The equations of fit were: $0.97 - 0.70 \exp(-t/0.894 \text{ sec})$ in bupivacaine; $0.94 \pm 0.94 \exp(-t/0.154 \text{ sec})$ in lidocaine; and $0.98 - 0.17 \exp(-t/1.219 \text{ sec}) - 0.83 \exp(-t/0.152 \text{ sec})$ in the mixture of bupivacaine plus lidocaine. The slow component of recovery in the presence of the drug mixture has been extrapolated (dashed line) to the ordinate, and its intercept is indicated by an arrow.*

time course of recovery from use-dependent block. In the presence of a mixture of 43 μM lidocaine and 3.5 μM bupivacaine, recovery from block contained two definable exponential components (Fig. 3). The fast component (83 ± 5% of control $\dot{V}_{max}$) had a time constant of 179 ± 40 msec ($n = 5$). Neither the amplitude nor the time constant of the fast component was significantly different from that obtained in the presence of 43 μM lidocaine alone ($P > 0.7$). The slow component had a time constant of 1.2 ± 0.1 seconds ($n = 5$), and was not significantly different from that obtained in the presence of bupivacaine alone (1.1 ± 0.2 seconds) ($P > 0.7$). However, the amplitude of the slow component (11 ± 6% of control $\dot{V}_{max}$) was significantly smaller than that obtained in the presence of bupivacaine alone (63 ± 4%) ($P < 0.001$; $n = 5$).

Contractility

In the presence of bupivacaine alone, twitch tension was significantly reduced at stimulation rates between 0.2 and 3 Hz (Table 1). However, the negative inotropic effect of bupivacaine was not significantly rate-dependent over this range of stimulation rates ($P > 0.10$, one-way ANOVA), in marked contrast to its effect on $\dot{V}_{max}$ (compare Table 1 and Fig. 2). Addition of lidocaine did not result in a significant change in twitch tension at stimulation rates between 0.2 and 0.5 Hz (see Table 1). However, addition of lidocaine did result in a significant further decrease in twitch tension at 1 and 2 Hz ($P < 0.02$). Thus, lidocaine does not reduce bupiva-

TABLE 1
Effect of Bupivacaine and Mixture of Bupivacaine and Lidocaine on Twitch Tenson*

Drug	Stimulation rate (Hz) 0.2	0.5	1.0	2.0	3.0
3.5 μM Bupivacaine†	63 ± 14	61 ± 11	61 ± 8	52 ± 6	48 ± 2
(n)	(4)	(4)	(5)	(5)	(4)
3.5 μM Bupivacaine + 43 μM lidocaine	54 ± 6	47 ± 6	36 ± 3‡	31 ± 5‡	
(n)	(3)	(3)	(4)	(4)	

* Twitch tension expressed as percent of control (mean ± SEM).

† Bupivacaine reduction of twitch tension was not significantly different at different stimulation rates ($P > 0.6$; one-way ANOVA).

‡ Significant additional depression after lidocaine was added to bupivacaine ($P < 0.02$; Scheffe's test).

caine's depressive effect on contractility, in contrast to its ability to attenuate bupivacaine's effect on $\dot{V}_{max}$.

Effects of Mixing Lidocaine and Quinidine

Steady State $\dot{V}_{max}$

Quinidine (15 μM) progressively reduced $\dot{V}_{max}$ in a rate-dependent manner as the stimulation rate was increased from 0.05 to 3.3 Hz (see Fig. 4). However, addition of 43 μM lidocaine to the quinidine perfusate did not significantly affect the steady state $\dot{V}_{max}$ obtained at rates between 0.5 and 3.3 Hz ($P > 0.2$) (Fig. 4).

Recovery Kinetics

Quinidine's ability to block open sodium channels rapidly during the action potential upstroke, in combination with its slow rate of dissociation between beats (i.e., similar to an "irreversible antagonist"), may make quinidine difficult to displace. To provide more favorable conditions for observing reduction of quinidine block by lidocaine, we used a conditioning train of 19 10-msec pulses (5 msec for latency and upstroke followed by 5 msec at +20 mV). Each pulse was separated by a diastolic interval of 25 msec at −100 mV (illustrated in Fig. 5). This pulse protocol was designed to minimize dissociation of lidocaine-blocked channels between beats, yet provide nearly complete recovery from fast inactivation of drug-free channels, and negligible accumulation of slow inactivation (Clarkson et al., 1984). In the presence of 15 μM quinidine alone, 41 ± 4% of control $\dot{V}_{max}$ recovered with a time constant of 3.7 ± 1.2 seconds at −100 mV following this rapid pulse train ($n = 5$). In the presence of a mixture of 43 μM lidocaine and 15 μM quinidine, recovery from block contained two definable components (Fig. 5). One component (71 ± 13% of control $\dot{V}_{max}$) had a time

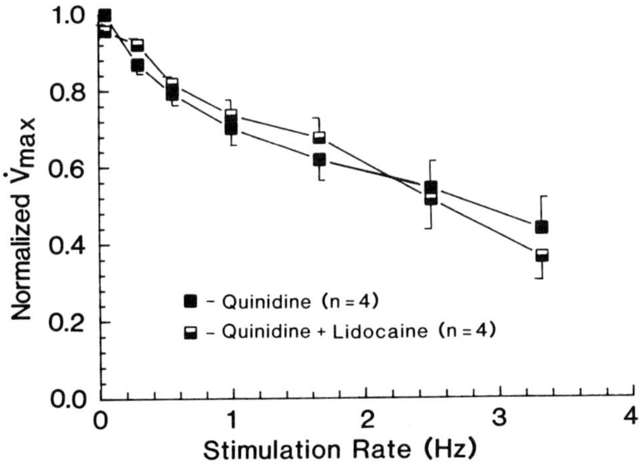

FIGURE 4. *The dependence of $\dot{V}_{max}$ upon stimulation rate in the presence of 15 μM quinidine, and a mixture of 15 μM quinidine plus 43 μM lidocaine. Values of $\dot{V}_{max}$ have been normalized to control at 0.05 Hz. Values of $\dot{V}_{max}$ obtained in the presence of quinidine were not significantly different ($P > 0.2$) than those obtained 30 minutes after switching to a perfusate containing quinidine plus lidocaine.*

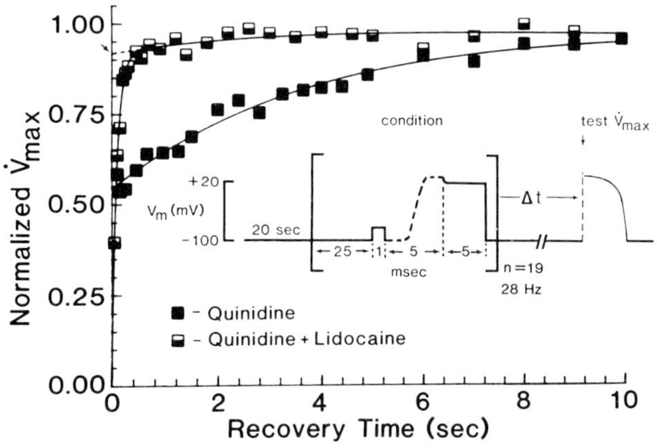

FIGURE 5. *The time course of recovery of $\dot{V}_{max}$ in the presence of 15 μM quinidine and 30 minutes after switching to a mixture of 15 μM quinidine plus 43 μM lidocaine. $\dot{V}_{max}$ has been normalized to its control value at 0.05 Hz. The pulse protocol is shown in the inset. An action potential upstroke was evoked by a 1-msec current stimulus. After the initial 5 msec of a free-running action potential upstroke (during which $\dot{V}_{max}$ was measured), the membrane was then clamped to +20 mV for 5 msec. Each pulse pattern during the conditioning train was separated by a 25-msec step to −100 mV. The curves represent nonlinear least-squares fits of the data. The equations of fit were: 1.01 − 0.47 exp (−t/3.933 sec) in quinidine; and 1.0 − 0.08 exp (−t/3.003 sec) − 0.94 exp (−t/0.092 sec) in the mixture of quinidine plus lidocaine. The slow component of recovery in the presence of the drug mixture has been extrapolated (dashed line) to the ordinate, and its intercept indicated by an arrow.*

constant of 115 ± 21 msec, and probably reflects recovery of lidocaine-blocked channels ($n = 5$). The other component had a time constant of 3.0 ± 0.7 seconds ($n = 5$), which was not significantly different from that observed in the presence of quinidine alone ($P > 0.5$). However, the amplitude of the slow component in the presence of the lidocaine-quinidine drug mixture was significantly reduced from 41 ± 4% to 16 ± 7% of control $\dot{V}_{max}$ ($P < 0.01$; $n = 5$) (see Fig. 5).

Discussion

Evidence for a Specific Drug Receptor

Our results clearly demonstrate that lidocaine can, under certain conditions, reduce the fraction of sodium channels blocked by either bupivacaine or quinidine. These results indicate that one drug can displace another from its site of action, and suggests that local anesthetic and antiarrhythmic drugs exert their effects by binding to a common receptor site (Hille, 1977; Hondeghem and Katzung, 1977). Evidence for competitive interactions between different local anesthetic drugs has also been recently obtained in nerve tissue (Rimmel et al., 1978; Schmidtmayer and Ulbricht, 1980; Pichon et al., 1981). This evidence for competitive drug interactions and displacement also provides strong evidence against hypotheses which propose that local anesthetic and antiarrhythmic drugs block sodium channels by a nonspecific effect on the cell membrane (Seeman, 1972; Lee, 1976). Unless there is a saturable receptor

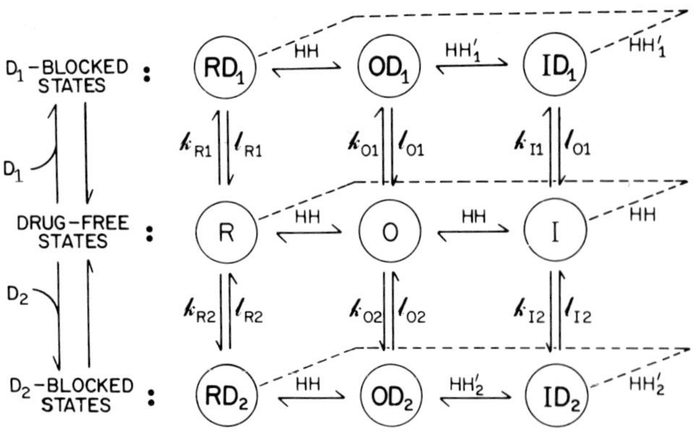

FIGURE 6. *A schematic diagram of the two-drug mixture version of the modulated receptor model. Drug-free states of the sodium channel are indicated by R (rested), O (open), and I (inactivated). Transitions between these three states are governed by Hodgkin-Huxley rate constants (HH). Drugs D_1 and D_2 may bind to each drug-free state with different rate constants. k_{R1}, k_{R2}, k_{O1}, k_{O2}, k_{I1}, and k_{I2} indicate drug association rate constants, while l_{R1}, l_{R2}, l_{O1}, l_{O2}, l_{I1}, and l_{I2} represent drug dissociation rate constants. The voltage dependence for inactivation of drug-associated (blocked) states are shifted to more negative potentials by an amount ΔV_1 or ΔV_2, resulting in different rate constants HH'_1 and HH'_2. For further discussion, see Appendix, and Hondeghem and Katzung (19j77).*

site for these drugs, an increase in total drug concentration produced by mixing two drugs together should always result in an enhancement of block, and not a decrease in block.

Modulated Receptor Theory for a Mixture of Two Drugs

The modulated receptor hypothesis has been shown to describe well the effects of numerous local anesthetic and antiarrhythmic drugs on sodium channels in nerve and cardiac tissue (Hondeghem and Katzung, 1984). Since it was not known whether this model could adequately describe the effects of drug mixtures as well, we therefore adapted the mathematical model of Hondeghem and Katzung (1977) to simulate the behavior of $\dot{V}_{max}$ in the presence of a mixture of two drugs.

In the drug-mixture model (illustrated in Fig. 6) we made the following assumptions. (1) In the absence of drug, sodium channels can exist in three primary states, rested (R), open (O), or inactivated (I), with the transitions between each state being governed by the same differential equations used in the original version of the modulated receptor model (see Hondeghem and Katzung, 1977). (2) Each drug competes for a single common receptor associated with the sodium channel. This receptor has state-dependent association (k_{R1}, k_{R2}, k_{O1}, k_{O2}, k_{I1}, k_{I2}) and dissociation (l_{R1}, l_{R2}, l_{O1}, l_{O2}, l_{I1}, l_{I2}) rate constants which can be different for each drug (D_1 and D_2). (3) Drug-associated channels do not conduct and have their inactivation parameters offset by a voltage shift of ΔV_1 or ΔV_2. A mathetmatical description of this model is provided in the Appendix.

To test the ability of the model to predict displacement of bupivacaine and quinidine by lidocaine, we

TABLE 2
Modulated Receptor Constants

	Bupivacaine	Lidocaine	Quinidine
k_R (per msec · M)	500	1	0
l_R (per msec)	1	1	0.05
k_O (per msec · M)	1	50,000	12,000
l_O (per msec)	1	2	2.7
k_I (per msec · M)	375	5,500	0
l_I (per msec)	0.00025	0.02	0.000154
ΔV* (mV)	28	35	48

* Drug-induced voltage shift of inactivation.

computed state-dependent rate constants and voltage shifts which could well describe the effect of each drug alone (see Table 2 and Fig. 7). Using these parameters and the drug-mixture model, we then simulated the predicted outcome of mixing lidocaine with either bupivacaine or quinidine. As shown in Figure 7, the model simulations (solid curves) have time courses very similar to the dashed curves which represent the time courses predicted from the exper-

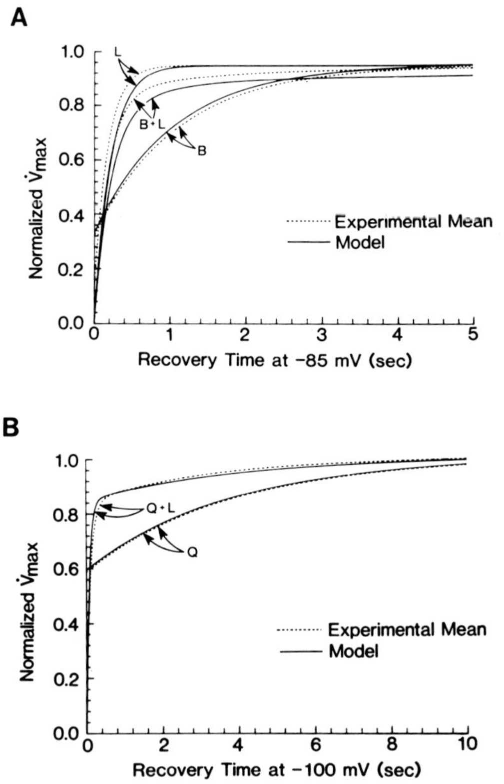

FIGURE 7. *Post-stimulation recovery of $\dot{V}_{max}$ in the presence of drug and drug mixtures. The dashed lines represent the time course of $\dot{V}_{max}$ recovery estimated from the mean experimental data (time constants and amplitudes), and the solid lines indicate the time course of $\dot{V}_{max}$ predicted by the model using the rate constants and voltage shifts shown in Table 2. Part A shows the time course of $\dot{V}_{max}$ recovery at −85 mV after a 19-beat train of action potentials at 3.3 Hz. The action potential duration was 185 msec. L = 43 μM lidocaine, B = 3.5 μM bupivacaine. Part B shows the time course of $\dot{V}_{max}$ recovery at −100 mV after a 19-beat train of action potentials at 28 Hz. The action potential duration was 10 msec. L = 43 μM lidocaine, Q = 15 μM quinidine.*

imental data (using mean values of time constants and levels of block). We therefore conclude that the effects of drug mixtures are qualitatively consistent with the predictions made by the modulated receptor hypothesis. However, we cannot rule out the possibility that other models may also adequately describe the data.

The Modulated Receptor Hypothesis as a Tool for Understanding Drug Interactions

The modulated receptor hypothesis may be a useful tool for predicting the electrophysiological effects of drug mixtures. In a beating heart, drug-receptor interactions do not typically achieve equilibrium, but rather change dynamically throughout the cardiac cycle. During an action potential, sodium channels cycle through a minimum of three different states (rested, open, and inactivated). Most local anesthetic and antiarrhythmic agents have a very low affinity for the receptor site when the channel is in the rested state, but have a high affinity for the receptor when the channel is open or inactivated (Hondeghem and Katzung, 1984). Consequently, block develops during each action potential, and then dissipates when the channels return to the rested state at the beginning of diastole. For many drugs (e.g., quinidine and bupivacaine), the rate of drug dissociation is slow enough so that block does not fully dissipate between beats even at very slow heart rates (e.g., 1 Hz).

In the presence of a mixture of two drugs, each drug will compete for a limited number of receptor sites during each action potential. When drug concentrations are very low, mixing two drugs is expected to result in more block than is produced by either drug alone, since the probability that two drugs will attempt to interact simultaneously with the same receptor is relatively low. However, when drug concentrations are raised to levels at which each drug is capable of binding to a large fraction of channels, then each of the two drugs will progressively interfere with the other's binding. If both drugs have similar affinities for different sodium channel states, as well as similar rates of binding and dissociation, then the competition between the drugs will be of little electrophysiological consequence. However, if one drug has substantially different characteristics, e.g., much faster kinetics for diastolic recovery from block, then the competitive interactions may become quite noticeable at certain driving rates. This is illustrated by the effect of adding lidocaine to a bupivacaine-depressed preparation. Displacement of bupivacaine by lidocaine will result in a progressively larger fraction of channels becoming free from block inbetween beats. The model predicts that at slow stimulation rates the fraction of channels blocked by bupivacaine will be small, and hence there can be relatively little improvement in $\dot{V}_{max}$ due to displacement (see Fig. 2). However, as the driving rate is increased, block by bupivacaine increases, and the addition of lidocaine will therefore result in a larger amount of displacement, and subsequent increase in $\dot{V}_{max}$. At even faster rates (e.g., >3 Hz), the diastolic interval between beats will not be long enough for block by lidocaine to dissipate. Thus, although fewer channels may be blocked by bupivacaine, a net increase in $\dot{V}_{max}$ will not be observed because of the rate-dependent block by lidocaine.

The time dependence and state dependence of drug-channel interaction appear to be important factors which can influence drug interactions. For example, lidocaine can bind to both open and inactivated channels (Hondeghem and Katzung, 1977; Hondeghem and Matsubara, 1984), in contrast to bupivacaine, which almost exclusively binds to inactivated channels (Clarkson and Hondeghem, 1985). High concentrations of lidocaine (e.g., 43 μM) will sequester a very large fraction of sodium channel receptors during the upstroke of the action potential and early during the plateau, prior to the time that bupivacaine binding (at concentrations $\leq$3.5 μM) can become appreciable (Clarkson and Hondeghem, 1985). These factors give lidocaine a distinct advantage in competing against bupivacaine.

In contrast to bupivacaine, quinidine avidly binds to open sodium channels (Colatsky, 1982; Weld et al., 1982; Hondeghem and Matsubara, 1984). As a result, lidocaine will have to compete with quinidine for available receptors during the upstroke. In addition, quinidine dissociates from its receptor very slowly at normal diastolic potentials (τ = 4 – 7 seconds) (Grant et al., 1982; Weld et al., 1982). Consequently, this drug will be difficult to displace, since there is little cycling between drug-free and quinidine-associated states at normal heart rates. This can account for lidocaine's inability to significantly alter steady state $\dot{V}_{max}$ in preparations depressed by 15 μM quinidine (see Fig. 4).

Bupivacaine's Negative Inotropic Effect is Neither Rate Dependent nor Reversed by Lidocaine

The mechanism underlying bupivacaine's negative inotropic effect is not clear. Possible mechanisms include: reduction of calcium influx due to calcium channel blockade (Eisner et al., 1979), reduction of calcium influx due to shortening of action potential duration (Gibbons and Fozzard, 1971; Ten Eick et al., 1976), inhibition of calcium efflux from the sarcoplasmic reticulum (Herbette et al., 1982), or reduction of intracellular calcium due to reduced intracellular sodium activity and the Na-Ca exchange mechanism (Lee et al., 1980; Eisner et al., 1981; Daut, 1982; Wasserstrom, 1983; Im and Lee, 1984).

The finding that bupivacaine's negative inotropic effect is not strongly rate dependent (Table 1), in contrast to its effect on $\dot{V}_{max}$ (Fig. 2), suggests that this drug does not exert its negative inotropic by reduction of sodium ion influx alone. The observation that lidocaine increased $\dot{V}_{max}$ in the presence of bupivacaine without reversing bupivacaine's negative inotropic effect is also consistent with this hypothesis. However, since we did not voltage clamp the action potential plateau during the contractility experiments, we cannot rule out the possibility that a partial reversal of bupivacaine's negative inotropic effect attributable to increased sodium ion influx by lidocaine was not attenuated by a lidocaine-induced shortening of the action potential duration.

Clinical Implications

The above-described drug interactions of lidocaine and quinidine have two possible clinical implications. First, lidocaine is not expected to be very effective in improving conduction in cardiac tissue that is severely depressed by quinidine. This does not, of course, rule out the possibility that lidocaine could have beneficial effects due to mechanism(s) other than drug displacement (e.g., lidocaine-induced decrease of ectopic pacemaker automaticity). Second, even though lidocaine may not be able to effect steady state $\dot{V}_{max}$ substantially, in the presence of a high concentration of quinidine, it can nevertheless provide an extra depression of early extrasystoles by blocking those channels that are not occupied by quinidine. This has been demonstrated in vitro by Hondeghem and Katzung (1980) and Moyer and Hondeghem (1980). The beneficial effects of combining antiarrhythmic drugs having slow and rapid recovery kinetics for suppression of extrasystoles has also been verified in two clinical studies (Breithardt et al., 1981; Duff et al., 1983).

Bupivacaine cardiotoxicity can be a serious and even lethal clinical condition (Albright, 1979; Food and Drug Administration, 1983). Signs of bupivacaine cardiotoxicity commonly include signs of depressed conduction (Kotelko et al., 1984). Consequently, therapeutic maneuvers which result in improved cardiac conduction may be beneficial in reducing bupivacaine cardiotoxicity.

Lidocaine appears quite effective in improving $\dot{V}_{max}$ when it is depressed by excessive bupivacaine concentrations in vitro. More important, this reversal of $\dot{V}_{max}$ appears to be maximal at clinically relevant heart rates (1–2 Hz or 60–120 beats/min) (see Fig. 2). These results suggest that lidocaine might be effective in treating bupivacaine-induced arrhythmias that result from slow intraventricular or intraatrial conduction. In support of this hypothesis, two recent reports have demonstrated that administration of lidocaine can be effective in terminating bupivacaine-induced arrhythmias in both cats (deJong and Davis, 1981) and man (Davis and deJong, 1982). Whereas the results of this study, as well as those of deJong and Davis, appear to provide a strong experimental basis for the use of lidocaine in treating bupivacaine cardiotoxicity, there are several questions that need to be answered. For example, intravenous administration of lidocaine could conceivably displace bupivacaine bound to plasma proteins (Gohneim and Pandya, 1974), and thereby worsen toxicity. Second, our contractility results suggest that lidocaine does not reduce bupivacaine's negative inotropic effect, and in high concentrations may further depress contractility (see Table 1). It is not yet clear to what extent the depression of contractility (pump failure) may contribute to bupivacaine mortality. Finally, although therapeutic levels of lidocaine (13–21 μM) produce a measurable increase in $\dot{V}_{max}$ in cardiac tissue depressed by a toxic concentration of bupivacaine (3.5 μM), it is not clear that the increase in $\dot{V}_{max}$ (cardiac conduction) produced by therapeutic concentrations of lidocaine is large enough to produce a beneficial therapeutic effect. Thus, further studies must be performed to determine whether lidocaine is an effective or safe treatment for bupivacaine cardiotoxicity.

Appendix

In the drug-mixture version of the modulated receptor hypothesis (illustrated in Fig. 6), the total population of sodium channels is set equal to one:

$$R + O + I + RD_1 + OD_1 + ID_1 + RD_2 + OD_2 + ID_2 = 1.$$

There are three major channel pools, a drug-free pool and pools blocked by either drug D_1 or D_2. The fraction of channels in the drug-free pool is given by the sum of:

$$R + O + I,$$

and the two drug-blocked pools (B_1 and B_2) are given by:

$$B_1 = RD_1 + OD_1 + ID_1$$
$$B_2 = RD_2 + OD_2 + ID_2.$$

The total fraction of all drug-blocked channels is:

$$B_T = B_1 + B_2.$$

If activation is described by the standard "m" variable, and absence of inactivation for drug-free and drug-associated channels is represented by h, h_1', and h_2', then the following equations hold:

$$R = h - O$$
$$RD_1 = h_1' - OD_1$$
$$RD_2 = h_2' - OD_2$$
$$O = m^3 \cdot h$$
$$OD_1 = m^3 \cdot h_1'$$
$$OD_2 = m^3 \cdot h_2'$$
$$I = 1 - B_T - h$$
$$ID_1 = B_1 - h_1'$$
$$ID_2 = B_2 - h_2'.$$

Based upon the association and dissociation rate constants shown in Figure 6, the rate of change in

B_T can be described by the following differential equation:

$$\begin{aligned} dB_T/dt = {} & (k_{r1}\cdot R + k_{O1}\cdot O + k_{I1}\cdot I)\,[D_1] \\ & + (k_{R2}\cdot R + k_{O2}\cdot O + k_{I2}\cdot I)\,[D_2] \\ & - (1_{R1}\cdot RD_1 + 1_{O1}\cdot OD_1 + 1_{I1}\cdot I_{D1}) \\ & - (1_{R2}\cdot RD_2 + 1_{O2}\cdot OD_2 + 1_{I2}\cdot I_{D2}). \end{aligned}$$

The activation parameter 'm' is described in the conventional fashion:

$$dm/dt = \alpha_m(1 - m) - \beta_m$$

where α_m and β_m are voltage-dependent functions:

$$\alpha_m = f_1(V)$$
$$\beta_m = f_2(V).$$

The functions $f_1(V)$ and $f_2(V)$ can be found in Hondeghem and Katzung (1977). The inactivation parameters can also be defined by a set of differential equations:

$$\begin{aligned} dh/dt = {} & \alpha_h\cdot I + 1_{R1}\cdot RD_1 + 1_{R2}\cdot RD_2 + 1_{O1}\cdot OD_1 \\ & + 1_{O2}\cdot OD_2 - \beta_h\,(R + O) - (k_{R1}\cdot R \\ & + k_{01}\cdot O)\,[D_1] - (k_{R2}\cdot R \\ & + k_{O2}\cdot O)\,[D_2] \\ dh_1'/dt = {} & \alpha'_{h1}\cdot ID_1 + (k_{R1}\cdot RD_1 + k_{O1}\cdot OD_1)\,[D_1] \\ & - \beta'_{h1}(RD_1 + OD_1) - (1_{R1}\cdot RD_1 \\ & + 1_{O1}\cdot OD_1) \\ dh_2'/dt = {} & \alpha'_{h2}\cdot ID2 + (k_{R2}\cdot RD_2 + k_{O2}\cdot OD_2)\,[D_2] \\ & - \beta'_{h2}(RD_2 + OD_2) \\ & - (1_{R2}\cdot RD_2 + 1_{O2}\cdot OD_2), \end{aligned}$$

where α_h and β_h are voltage-dependent functions defined by Hondeghem and Katzung (1977):

$$\alpha_h = f_3(V)$$
$$\beta_h = f_4(V)$$

and α'_{h1}, α'_{h2}, β'_{h1} and β'_{h2} are identical voltage-dependent functions, but shifted along the voltage axis by an amount ΔV_1 or ΔV_2, i.e.:

$$\alpha'_{h1} = f_3(V + \Delta V_1)$$
$$\alpha'_{h2} = f_3(V + \Delta V_2)$$
$$\beta'_{h1} = f_4(V + \Delta V_1)$$
$$\beta'_{h2} = f_4(V + \Delta V_2).$$

The functions $f_3(V)$ and $f_4(V)$ are the same as those defined by Hondeghem and Katzung (1977).

We are greatly indebted to Dr. J. Moyer for developing the software for data analysis and graphics, and for advice and assistance in developing the drug mixture computer model. We also thank Charles Lee for help with the illustrations, and Dr. B. Katzung for a critical reading of the manuscript.

This work was supported in part by National Institutes of Health Grant HL-21672. Dr. Hondeghem is an Established Investigator of the American Heart Association.

Address for reprints: Craig W. Clarkson, Department of Pharmacology, Tulane University School of Medicine, 1430 Tulane Avenue, New Orleans, Louisiana 70112.

Received August 27, 1984; accepted for publication January 10, 1985.

References

Albright GA (1979) Cardiac arrest following regional anesthesia with etidocaine or bupivacaine. Anesthesiology **51:** 285–287

Bean BP, Cohen J, Tsien RW (1983) Lidocaine block of cardiac sodium channels. J Gen Physiol **81:** 613–642

Beeler GW Jr, Reuter H (1970) Voltage clamp experiments on ventricular myocardial fibres. J Physiol (Lond) **207:** 165–190

Block A, Covino BG (1981) Effect of local anesthetic agents on cardiac conduction and contractility. Regional Anesthesiol **6:** 55–61

Breithardt G, Seipel L, Abendroth RR (1981) Comparison of the antiarrhythmic efficacy of disopyramide and mexiletine against stimulus-induced ventricular tachycardia. J Cardiovasc Pharmacol **3:** 1026–1037

Clarkson CW, Hondeghem LM (1984) Electrophysiological evidence that local anesthetics and antiarrhythmic drugs bind to a specific receptor site in cardiac sodium channels: Displacement of bupivacaine by lidocaine. Proc West Pharmacol Soc **27:** 23–25

Clarkson CW, Hondeghem LM (in press) Mechanism for bupivacaine depression of cardiac conduction: Fast block of sodium channels during the action potential with slow recovery from block during diastole. Anesthesiology

Clarkson CW, Matsubara T, Hondeghem LM (1984) Slow inactivation of $\dot{V}_{max}$ in guinea pig ventricular myocardium. Am J Physiol **247:** H645–654

Cohen I (1979) Some experimental difficulties in the use of $\dot{V}_{max}$ as a measure of G_{Na}. Circ Res **44:** 309–311

Cohen IS, Strichartz GR (1977) On the voltage-dependent action of tetrodotoxin. Biophys J **17:** 275–279

Cohen CJ, Bean BP, Tsien RW (1984) Maximal upstroke velocity as an index of available sodium conductance: comparison of maximal upstroke velocity and voltage clamp measurements of sodium current in rabbit Purkinje fibers. Circ Res **54:** 636–651

Colatsky TJ (1982) Quinidine block of cardiac sodium channels is rate- and voltage-dependent (abstr). Biophys J **37:** 343a

Courtney KR (1983) Quantifying antiarrhythmic drug blocking during action potentials in guinea-pig papillary muscle. J Mol Cell Cardiol **15:** 749–757

Courtney KR (1984) Relationship between excitability block and negative inotropic actions of antiarrhythmic drugs. Proc West Pharmacol Soc **27:** 181–184

Daut J (1982) The role of intracellular sodium ions in the regulation of cardiac contractility. J Mol Cell Cardiol **14:** 189–192

Davis NL, de Jong RH (1982) Successful resuscitation following massive bupivacaine overdose. Anesth Analg (Cleve) **61:** 62–64

de Jong RH, Davis NL (1981) Treating bupivacaine arrhythmias. Preliminary report. Regional Anesth **6:** 99–103

Duff HJ, Roden D, Primm RK, Oates JA, Woosley RL (1983) Mexiletine in the treatment of resistent ventricular arrhythmias: Enhancement of efficacy and reduction of dose-related side effects of combination with quinidine. Circulation **67:** 1124–1128

Eisner DA, Lederer WJ, Noble D (1979) Caffeine and tetracaine abolish the slow inward current in cardiac Purkinje Fibers. J Physiol (Lond) **293:** 76–77P

Eisner DA, Lederer WJ, Vaughan-Jones RD (1981) The dependence of sodium pumping and tension on intracellular sodium activity in voltage-clamped sheep Purkinje fibers. J Physiol (Lond) **317:** 189–205

Food and Drug Administration (1983) Adverse reactions with bupivacaine. FDA Drug Bulletin **13:** 23

Gettes LS, Reuter H (1974) Slow recovery from inactivation of inward currents in mammalian myocardial fibers. J Physiol (Lond) **240:** 703–724

Ghoneim MM, Pandya H (1974) Plasma protein binding of bupivacaine and its interaction with other drugs in man. Br J Anaesthiol **46:** 435–438

Gibbons WR, Fozzard HA (1971) Voltage dependence and time dependence of contraction in sheep cardiac Purkinje fibers. Circ Res **28:** 446–460

Grant AO, Strauss LJ, Wallace AG, Strauss HC (1980) The

influence of pH on the electrophysiologic effects of lidocaine in guinea pig myocardium. Circ Res **47:** 542–550

Grant AO, Trantham JL, Brown KK, Strauss HC (1982) pH-dependent effects of quinidine on the kinetics of dV/dt_{max} in guinea pig ventricular myocardium. Circ Res **50:** 210–217

Herbette L, Messineo FC, Katz AM (1982) The interaction of drugs with the sarcoplasmic reticulum. Annu Rev Pharmacol Toxicol **22:** 413–434

Hille B (1977) Local anesthetics: Hydrophilic and hydrophobic pathways for the drug-receptor reaction. J Gen Physiol **69:** 497–515

Hondeghem LM (1978) Validity of $\dot{V}_{max}$ as a measure of the sodium current in cardiac and nervous tissues. Biophys J **23:** 147–152

Hondeghem LM, Cotner CL (1978) Measurement of $\dot{V}_{max}$ of the cardiac action potential with a sample/hold peak detector. Am J Physiol **234:** H312–H314

Hondeghem LM, Katzung BG (1977) Time- and voltage-dependent interactions of antiarrhythmic drugs with cardiac sodium channels. Biochim Biophys Acta **472:** 373–398

Hondeghem LM, Katzung BG (1984) Antiarrhythmic agents: The modulated receptor mechanism of action of sodium and calcium channel-blocking drugs. Annu Rev Pharmacol Toxicol **24:** 387–423

Hondeghem LM, Matsubara T (1984) Quinidine and lidocaine: Activation and inactivation block. Proc West Pharmacol Soc **27:** 19–21

Im W-B, Lee CO (1984) Relationship between twitch tension and intracellular sodium ion activity during positive and negative inotrophy of canine cardiac Purkinje fibers (abstr). Biophys J **45:** 52a

Khodorov BI, Shishkova L, Peganov E, Revenko S (1976) Inhibition of sodium currents in frog Ranvier node treated with local anesthetics. Role of slow sodium inactivation. Biochim Biophys Acta **433:** 409–435

Kotelko DM, Shnider SM, Dailey PA, Brizgys RV, Levinson G, Shapiro WA, Koike M, Rosen MA (1984) Bupivacaine-induced cardiac arrhythmias in sheep. Anesthesiology **60:** 10–18

Lee AG (1976) Model for action of local anaesthetics. Nature **262:** 545–548

Lee CO, Kang DH, Sokol JH, Lee KS (1980) Relation between intracellular Na ion activity and tension of sheep cardiac Purkinje fibers exposed to dihydro-ouabain. Biophys J **29:** 315–330

Moyer JW, Hondeghem LM (1980) Effects of the combination of quinidine and lidocaine on the upstroke velocity of the cardiac action potential. Proc West Pharmacol Soc **23:** 159–161

Pichon Y, Schmidtmayer J, Ulbricht W (1981) Mutually exclusive blockage of sodium channels of myelinated frog nerve fibres by benzocaine and the indole alkaloid ervatamine. Neurosci Lett **22:** 325–330

Rimmel C, Walle A, Kessler H, Ulbricht W (1978) Rates of block by procaine and benzocaine and the procaine-benzocaine interaction at the node of Ranvier. Pflugers Arch **376:** 105–118

Saikawa T, Carmeliet E (1982) Slow recovery of the maximal rate of rise ($\dot{V}_{max}$) of the cardiac action potential in sheep Purkinje fibers. Pflugers Arch **394:** 90–93

Scanlon JW, Ostheimer GW, Lurie AO, Brown WU Jr, Weiss JB, Alper MH (1976) Neurobehavioral response of newborn infants after material epidural anesthesia. Anesthesiology **45:** 400–405

Schmidtmayer J, Ulbricht W (1980) Interaction of lidocaine and benzocaine in blocking sodium channels. Pflugers Arch **387:** 47–54

Seeman P (1972) The membrane action of anesthetics and tranquilizers. Pharmacol Rev **24:** 583–655

Ten Eick R, Nawrath H, McDonald TF, Trautwein W (1976) On the mechanism of the negative inotropic effect of acetylcholine. Pflugers Arch **361:** 207–213

Walton M, Fozzard HA (1979) The relation of $\dot{V}_{max}$ to I_{Na}, G_{Na}, and h_{∞}, in a model of the cardiac Purkinje fiber. Biophys J **25:** 407–420

Walton M, Fozzard HA (1983) Experimental study of the conducted action potential in cardiac Purkinje strands. Biophys J **44:** 1–8

Wasserstrom JA (1983) Intracellular sodium ion activity in rat ventricular myocardium. (abstr) Fed Proc **42:** 1113

Weld FM, Coromilas J, Rottman JN, Bigger JT (1982) Mechanisms of quinidine-induced depression of maximum upstroke velocity in ovine cardiac Purkinje fibers. Circ Res **50:** 369–376

INDEX TERMS: Lidocaine • Quinidine • Bupivacaine • Antiarrhythmic receptor • Modulated receptor hypothesis • Drug interactions

Calcium-Dependent Fluxes of Potassium-42 and Chloride-36 during Norepinephrine Activation of Rat Aorta

Jacquelyn M. Smith and Allan W. Jones
From the Department of Physiology, University of Missouri, Columbia, Missouri

SUMMARY. This study was designed to determine whether α-receptor-stimulated monovalent ionic fluxes in rat aorta required calcium, and, if so, whether both extracellular calcium and cellularly stored calcium are active. Calcium removal in the presence of 10 mM magnesium (to maintain membrane stability) inhibited the norepinephrine-stimulated increase in potassium-42 and chloride-36 efflux. However, the norepinephrine-stimulated increase in sodium-24 influx was relatively resistant to calcium depletion. Protocols were designed to measure the time course for the changes in potassium-42 efflux and contraction when calcium was removed or replaced in the presence of norepinephrine. The dose-dependent effect of a calcium antagonist (diltiazem) was also measured. A close correlation ($r = 0.94$) was found between inhibition of contraction and potassium-42 effluxes which followed the regression: % potassium-42 response = 1.0 × (% contraction) + 1.8%). The slope of 1.0 and intercept near zero suggests the hypothesis that norepinephrine-stimulated potassium-42 efflux and contraction are codependent on cellular calcium concentration. This co-dependence held for short phasic responses (~1 minute), as well as longer tonic responses (≥5 minutes). It appears that calcium-dependent potassium-42 effluxes can be supported by both the influx of extracellular calcium and release of cellular stores. It is concluded that calcium-dependent potassium channels (and possibly chloride channels) are operative in rat aorta and are an important component of the graded membrane response to norepinephrine. The sodium channels, however, do not appear to share this same calcium dependency. **(*Circ Res 56: 507–516, 1985*)**

EXCITATION of arterial smooth muscle by catecholamines is associated with increases in fluxes of ions down their electrochemical gradients (Jones, 1980). Much attention has been given to measures of Ca^{++} fluxes in a variety of arteries and species during excitation-contraction coupling (Cauvin et al., 1983; Daniel et al., 1983), and the concept has been developed that α-receptor activation of arterial smooth muscle increases both Ca^{++} influx and release from cellular sites (Van Breemen et al., 1980). These preparations generally respond to such stimuli with graded depolarization (Somlyo et al., 1969; Hermsmeyer, 1976); hence, they have been classified as a tonic type of smooth muscle. The timing and magnitude of the changes in K^+ conductance which accompany α-receptor activation appear to be important determinants of the tonic response. Large dose-dependent increases in ^{42}K efflux accompanied α-receptor activation in arteries from rats (Jones, 1973) and rabbits (Droogmans, et al., 1977; Martin and Gordon, 1983). The changes reflected alterations in K^+ permeability since they exceeded the changes in efflux predicted for a simple reduction of the electrochemical driving force (Jones, 1980). Inhibition of K^+ conductance by tetraethylammonium ion (TEA) resulted in the generation of action potentials in previously tonic arterial smooth muscle (Droogmans et al., 1977; Harder, 1982). These observations indicate that the coupling between conductances which tend to depolarize smooth muscle (Ca^{++}, Na^+, Cl^-) and that which hyperpolarizes (K^+), is a critical determinant of the type of response.

The coupling between α-receptor occupancy and subsequent changes in ionic events is not well understood. Bolton (1979) suggested that receptors could operate ionic channels directly. Separation of events modulated by receptors from those secondary to changes in membrane potential is not complete. In general, the α-receptor-controlled influx of Ca^{++} was additive to that induced by depolarization, and was not as sensitive to blockade by Ca^{++} antagonists (Meisheri et al., 1981). It is unclear to what extent α-receptor-related changes in the movements of Na^+, K^+, and Cl^- fall directly under the control of receptors or are secondary events. We reported that cAMP-dependent inhibition of norepinephrine (NE)-induced contraction in rat aorta was closely related to parallel inhibition of α-receptor-induced increases in ^{42}K and ^{36}Cl efflux (Jones et al., 1984). One explanation for this parallel inhibition is that elevated cAMP results in maintenance of cytoplasmic Ca^{++} at levels below those needed for contraction and to open Ca^{++}-dependent ionic channels.

The Ca^{++} dependence of K^+ movements has been observed in a wide variety of tissues. Gardos (1958) reported that the net efflux of K^+ from red blood cells was increased by cellular Ca^{++}. This observation has been confirmed in red cells with analyses of unidirectional fluxes of isotopes (Yingst and Hoffman, 1984) and by patch clamp methods (Grygorczyk et al., 1984). Ca^{++}-dependent activation of K^+-channels has also been observed in excitable cells such as nerve (Meech, 1978) and skeletal muscle (Barrett et al., 1982). Relatively few studies of Ca^{++}-dependent K^+-conductance have been published for smooth muscle. Recently, Singer and Walsh (1984) have used patch clamp methods to identify a Ca^{++}-dependent K^+-conductance in membranes from the stomach muscle of the *Bufo marinus*. Den Hertog (1981) observed that the sustained hyperpolarization induced in guinea pig *Taeni caeci* by α-receptor activation required extracellular Ca^{++}, as did the increase in ^{42}K efflux. These smooth muscles represent the intestinal, phasic type in which α-receptor activation tends to inhibit contraction. One study is available on arterial smooth muscle in which a possible Ca^{++} dependency was observed during norepinephrine (NE) stimulation of ^{86}Rb efflux and contraction (Martin and Gordon, 1983).

It was the purpose of this investigation to determine whether α-receptor-stimulated ^{42}K efflux required Ca^{++}. If such a dependence existed, it was of further interest to determine whether extracellular Ca^{++} and/or cellularly sequestered Ca^{++} are able to activate the ^{42}K efflux. Correlations were made between the Ca^{++}-dependent changes in ^{42}K efflux and in contractile response to test the hypothesis that a Ca^{++}-dependent K^+ channel is operative in arterial smooth muscle of the tonic type.

A preliminary communication of this study has been made (Jones et al., 1984).

Methods

Animals and Tissues

Male Sprague-Dawley rats (200–250 g wt) were decapitated, and the thoracic aorta was prepared according to a standardized method described previously (Jones, 1973; Jones et al., 1984). We removed the endothelial cells from the strips (flux studies) and rings (contractile studies) by lightly stroking the intimal surface with filter paper while the tissues were in the dissection solution. The tissues were mounted on stainless steel holders, followed by a 3-hour incubation at 37°C before initiation of the protocols.

Solutions

The normal physiological solution had the following composition (in mM): Na^+, 146.2; K^+, 5.0; Mg^{++}, 1.2; Ca^{++}, 2.5; Cl^-, 143.9; HCO_3^-, 13.5; $H_2PO_4^-$, 1.2; and glucose, 11.4. Solutions were gassed with a 97% O_2-3% CO_2 mixture to obtain a pH of 7.4. Propranolol (3 μM, Sigma), ethylenediaminetetracetic acid (0.025 mM), and ascorbic acid (1 mM, Sigma) were added to all solutions for β-receptor blockade and to inhibit oxidation of catecholamines. Aqueous stock solutions were prepared for NE (Sigma) and diltiazem, (gift from Marion Laboratores). The 0 Ca^{++} solutions were prepared with no Ca^{++}, 10 mM Mg^{++} (as Cl^- salt), and 2 mM ethyleneglycol-bis-(β-aminoethyl ether)*N,N'*-tetraacetic acid (EGTA). The corresponding control solutions contained elevated Mg^{++} (10 mM) and Ca^{++} = 2.5. In one series, 4.5 mM Ca^{++} (Cl^- salt) was added to the 0 Ca^{++} solution to compensate for the 2 mM EGTA.

Isotope Fluxes

Routine equilibration and washout methods were used (Jones, 1973, 1981). For efflux analyses, open strips were incubated for 3 hours at 37°C in solution containing ^{42}K (20 μCi/ml, University of Missouri Research Reactor) or ^{42}K plus ^{36}Cl (2 μCi/ml, ICN). After a 2-second rinse, each tissue was passed through a series of vigorously gassed tubes containing nonradioactive solution. Solution changes, e.g., drugs, 0 Ca^{++}, temperature, can be made quickly with this method, and diffusional delays can be maintained to a minimum (Jones, 1980). Washout curves were computed (IBM) by sequentially adding the tissue and tube radioactivity (measured by standard gamma and liquid scintillation methods) in reverse order and by normalization in terms of initial activity. Corrections for isotopic decay were also made. The fraction of the isotope exchanged per minute which represents the rate constant, k (per min), was calculated for each washout period and was used to compare the effects of drugs and ionic changes.

The influx of ^{24}Na (University of Missouri Research Reactor) was done on tissues that had been equilibrated 3 hours at 37°C in the normal physiological solution. The strips then were transferred to either 0 Ca^{++} solution or a high Mg^{++} (10 mM) physiological solution for either 5 or 20 minutes. Half the strips were exposed to NE for an additional half-minute, or for 5 minutes. The strips then were transferred into the same solution ($\pm Ca^{++}$, $\pm$NE) with ^{24}Na added (10 μCi/ml) for a 1-minute period. The influx was terminated by quickly transferring the tissues to the physiological solution chilled to 1°C. After several rinses, the tissues were removed at 10 minutes, blotted, dried for 2 hours at 110°C, then weighed. Previous studies have shown that the 10-minute wash at 1°C is sufficient to remove ^{24}Na from the extracellular space without reducing greatly the slowly exchanging (cellular) component (Jones, 1981). The ^{24}Na was released by adding 0.5 ml H_2O_2 (30% wt/vol) to each tissue, followed by 10-minute treatment in a microwave oven. The sample was extracted into a 0.1 M solution of HNO_3 for 10 minutes, then neutralized, and 10 ml of liquid scintillation cocktail were added. Standards were prepared similarly from the ^{24}Na incubation media, with Na^+ concentration verified by flame photometry. The counts were corrected for background and isotopic decay, and the data are presented as μEq Na^+/g dry wt per min. The relatively short exposure to ^{24}Na (1 minute) resulted in the exchange of less than 20% of the cellular contents. Because this exchange represents only a 10% average over the period for the influx, back flux corrections were not applied.

Contraction

The rings were prepared and mounted according to a standardized procedure (Jones et al., 1984). The rings were stretched to 1.3 times their resting diameter and isometric force was measured in response to agonists added to the bath. The responses during the various protocols were normalized in terms of the force developed during an initial control response. The response at 1 minute was used to measure the relatively fast, phasic component which was reported to depend mostly on the release of cellular Ca^{++} (Deth and Van Breemen, 1977). The response after 5 minutes was used to measure the tonic component which required extracellular Ca^{++} for its maintenance (Deth and Van Breemen, 1977).

Statistics

Results are presented as means ±SE, and significance was determined by Student's t-test, with $P < 0.05$ deemed to be significant. Standard linear regression methods were used in one series.

Results

Ca^{++} Removal and Antagonism

Removal of Ca^{++} (0 Ca^{++} solution), or addition of diltiazem, a Ca^{++} antagonist (Triggle and Swamy, 1980) inhibited the contractile response to NE in rat aorta, as shown in Figure 1A. Both the initial fast (phasic) response and the slow (tonic) response were inhibited by prolonged exposure to 0 Ca^{++} and diltiazem (DZ). Similar treatment also inhibited the NE-induced increase in ^{42}K efflux (Fig. 1B). As in the case of the contractile response (Fig. 1A), inhibition was more complete by 0 Ca^{++} than by DZ ($P < 0.001$). Because removal of Ca^{++} from physiological solution (Mg^{++} = 1.2 mM) was associated with a major increase in ^{42}K efflux (Jones, 1974), raising the Mg^{++} was an important adjustment to maintain membrane stability in 0 Ca^{++}. After a preliminary study, Mg^{++} = 10 mM was chosen because it maintained the resting ^{42}K efflux within 30% of the basal level and had little effect on the maximal ^{42}K response to NE in the presence of Ca^{++} ($\Delta k = 0.012 \pm 0.001$/min, n = 12 for both Mg^{++} = 1.2 and 10 mM). Higher concentrations of Mg^{++} maintained the resting ^{42}K effluxes closer to basal levels in 0 Ca^{++}, but significantly inhibited contractile and ionic flux responses to NE (data not shown).

Increases in ^{36}Cl effluxes (Fig. 2B) which accompanied ^{42}K efflux during NE stimulation (Fig. 2A) also exhibited Ca^{++} dependency. About 50% of the initial phasic response (time ≤1 minute) was inhibited by 10 minutes of exposure to 0 Ca^{++} (Table 1). However, the tonic response at 4.5 minutes was completely inhibited by 0 Ca^{++} (Table 1). These differential effects may reflect an ability for stored Ca^{++} released by NE (Deth and Casteels, 1977; Deth and Van Breemen, 1977) to stimulate ^{42}K and ^{36}Cl effluxes for a brief period.

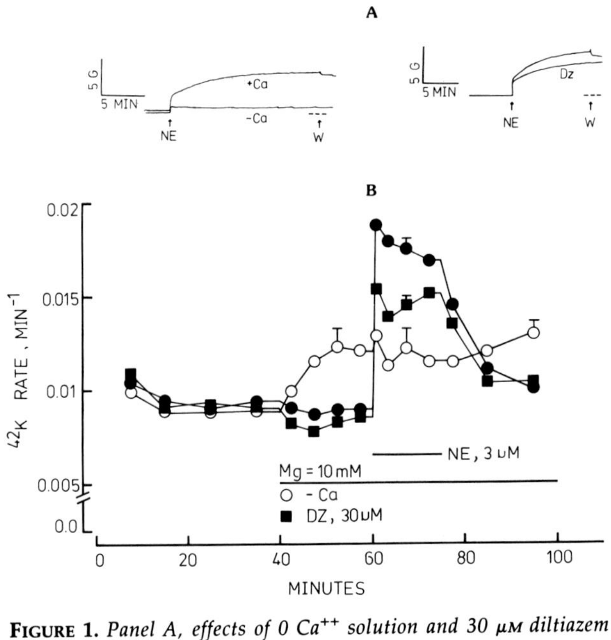

FIGURE 1. *Panel A, effects of 0 Ca^{++} solution and 30 μM diltiazem (DZ) on a typical contractile response of rat aorta to a supermaximal concentration of 3 μM NE. Control responses are from the same ring. The DZ and 0 Ca^{++} were applied 20 minutes before NE. W indicates washout of NE from controls. The dashed line represents the basal tension before NE. All responses were measured in Mg^{++} = 10 mM. Panel B, effects of 0 Ca^{++} and DZ on ^{42}K efflux responses to NE. Means plus SE (representative values) of the rate constants are plotted. After 40 minutes, tissues were placed in either a control solution (●) (Ca^{++} = 2.5 mM, Mg^{++} = 10 mM, n = 11 rats), 0 Ca^{++} solution (○) (EGTA = 2 mM, Mg^{++} = 10 mM, n = 5 rats), or DZ (■) (Ca^{++} = 2.5 mM, Mg^{++} = 10 mM, n = 6 rats). Time is in minutes. Horizontal lines indicate the period of application for the treatments.*

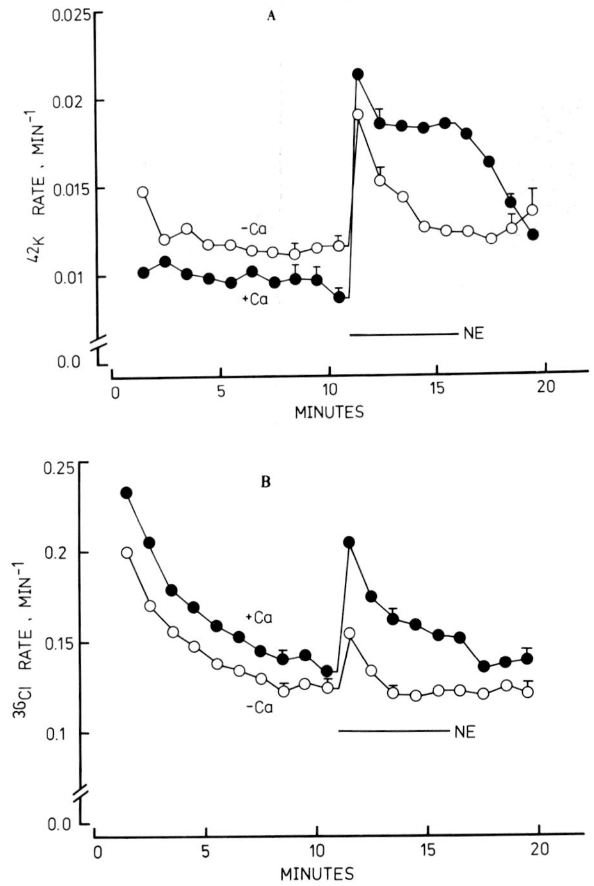

FIGURE 2. *Effect of 0 Ca^{++} (○) on NE stimulation of ^{42}K and ^{36}Cl efflux. Panel A, ^{42}K efflux plotted as in Figure 1B (n = 6 rats). The 0 Ca^{++} solution was applied at time = 0, and the composition of the 0 Ca^{++} and control solution (●) are the same as Figure 1B. Panel B, ^{36}Cl efflux measured simultaneously with the ^{42}K efflux in panel A.*

TABLE 1
Effects of 0 Ca^{++} Solution (10 minutes) on NE (3 μM)-Stimulated Increase in the Rate (Δk) of ^{42}K and ^{36}Cl Efflux Measured Simultaneously from Rat Aorta (n = 6) and on Contraction (n = 6)

	^{42}K		^{36}Cl		Contraction (%)	
Minutes in NE	0.5	4.5	0.5	4.5	0.5	4.5
Ca^{++} (Δk per min)	0.012 ±0.001	0.010 ±0.001	0.071 ±0.008	0.020 ±0.009	100	100
0 Ca^{++} (Δk per min)	0.007 ±0.001	0.001 ±0.001	0.032 ±0.008	−0.002 ±0.003	33 ±6	17 ±1
P	<0.02	<0.001	<0.01	<0.05	<0.001	<0.001

If the NE-induced increases in ion fluxes are dependent on free intracellular Ca^{++}, then a close relation would be expected between alterations in the efflux response and contraction. Systematic investigations were made to test the closeness of this relation. Protocols were designed to measure (1) the concentration-dependent effect of DZ on NE-stimulated ^{42}K efflux and contraction, (2) the time course for changes in ^{42}K efflux and contraction when Ca^{++} was replaced in 0 Ca^{++} + NE, and (3) the time course for changes in NE-stimulated ^{42}K efflux and contraction when Ca^{++} was removed.

Diltiazem Concentration

Diltiazem inhibited the NE-induced changes in both ^{42}K efflux and contraction in a similar manner (Fig. 3). The inhibitory responses were evaluated at 1-minute exposure to NE for the phasic response and at 10 minutes for the tonic response. The percent inhibition at 1 and at 10 minutes was similar for each concentration of DZ. At a DZ concentration of 30 μM, the inhibitory effect on NE-stimulated contraction and on ^{42}K efflux was relatively small compared to the inhibition of KCl-induced changes in ^{42}K efflux and contraction (Fig. 3). This contractile effect is consistent with the report of Triggle and Swamy (1980) that Ca^{++} antagonists were more potent inhibitors of KCl-induced contractions than of NE contractions in arterial smooth muscle. Similar to the results of Saida and Van Breemen (1983), extremely high concentrations of DZ could produce almost complete inhibition of NE contractions (Fig. 3). This inhibition also extended to NE-induced changes in ^{42}K efflux (Fig. 3).

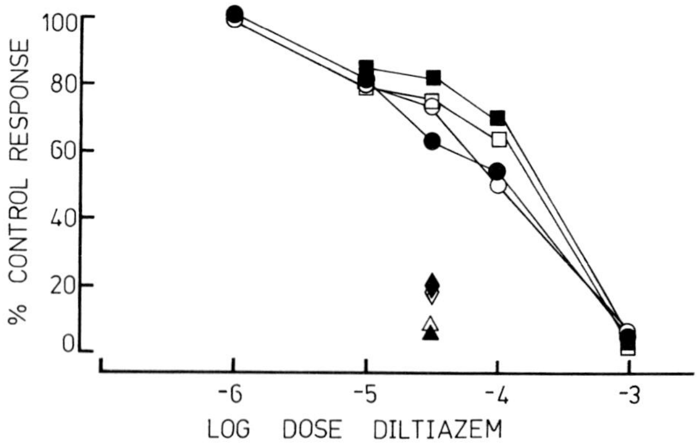

FIGURE 3. *Effects of various concentrations of DZ (log molar scale) on the NE stimulation of rat aorta. All tissues were exposed to DZ for 20 minutes before stimulation. Effects on ^{42}K efflux (n = 6 rats) at 1 minute (●) and after 10 minutes (○) in NE are plotted with equivalent analyses of effects on contraction (n = 5 rats) at 1 (■) and 10 minutes (□). KCl (85 mM) was used as a stimulus at DZ = 30 μM. Effects on ^{42}K efflux (n = 6 rats) at 1 (▲) and after 10 minutes (△) in KCl are plotted with equivalent effects on contraction (n = 5 rats) at 1 (◆) and 10 minutes (◇). The standard errors were of the order ±5%.*

Ca^{++} Replacement

The addition of Ca^{++} to 0 Ca^{++} solution containing NE caused a contraction which approached that developed when NE was added to a Ca^{++}-containing solution (Fig. 4A). The ^{42}K efflux response to replacement of Ca^{++} in the presence of NE (Fig. 4B) was similar to the contractile response. NE increased ^{42}K efflux transiently in 0 Ca^{++}, followed by a return toward basal rates, in sharp contrast to the response in the presence of Ca^{++}. Ca^{++} replacement after 15 minutes in 0 Ca^{++} + NE resulted in an increase in ^{42}K efflux ($P < 0.001$) to the levels achieved by tissues that had been exposed to NE and Ca^{++} throughout (Fig. 4B). The response to Ca^{++} replacement would be expected to be in the opposite direction if its major effect were to stabilize the membrane.

The time courses for the return of the responses after Ca^{++} replacement appear in Figure 5. The effect on ^{42}K efflux reached a maximum before contraction, but good agreement was noted overall. The return of both ^{42}K efflux and contraction when Ca^{++} was replaced in the presence of NE indicates that the availability of cellular Ca^{++}, rather than α-receptor activation alone, determined the ^{42}K efflux response.

Ca^{++} Removal

The transient stimulation of ^{42}K efflux by NE in 0 Ca^{++} is consistent with the hypothesis that $[Ca^{++}]_{cell}$ is elevated by the release of Ca^{++} from a cellular pool of limited capacity (Deth and Casteels, 1977; Karaki and Weiss, 1979). This hypothesis was tested further by varying the time in 0 Ca^{++} before expo-

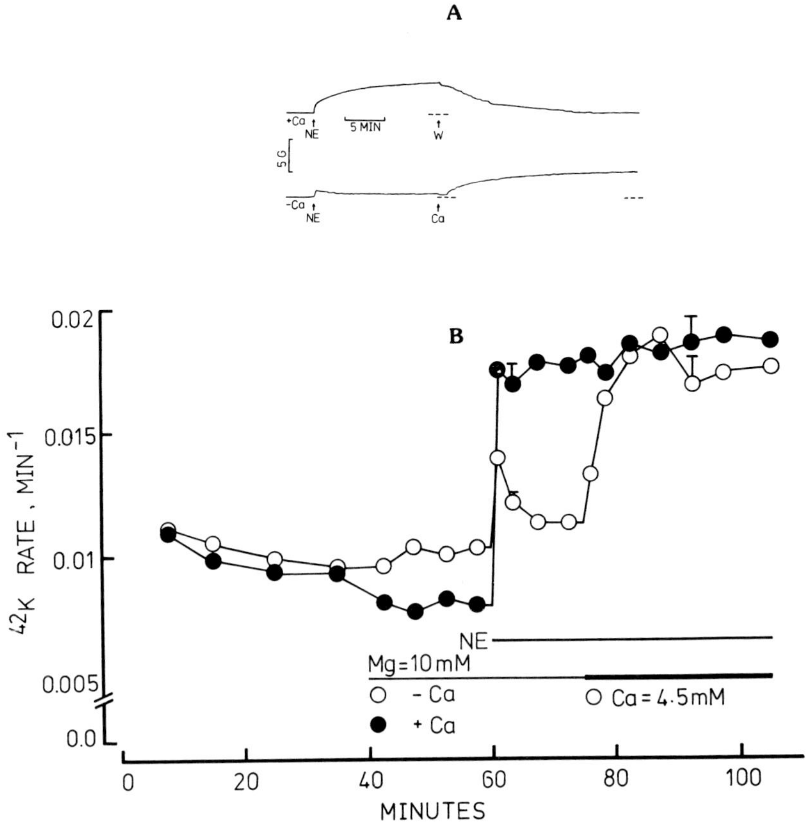

FIGURE 4. *Panel A, effects of 0 Ca^{++} solution (20 minutes before NE) and replacement of Ca^{++} on a typical contractile response in rat aorta. The data are plotted as in Figure 1A. Panel B, effects on 0 Ca^{++} solution and Ca^{++} replacement (○) on NE stimulation of ^{42}K efflux (n = 7 rats for each set). Controls (●) were exposed to Ca^{++} throughout. Data are plotted as in Figure 1B.*

sure to NE. The phasic contractile response (1 minute in NE) was reduced as the time in 0 Ca^{++} was increased (Fig. 6). Only a small tonic contraction remained after 12.5 minutes in 0 Ca^{++} + NE (Fig. 6). The initial response of ^{42}K efflux to NE (k at 1 minute) also showed a reduction which depended on the time the tissue was preincubated in 0 Ca^{++}

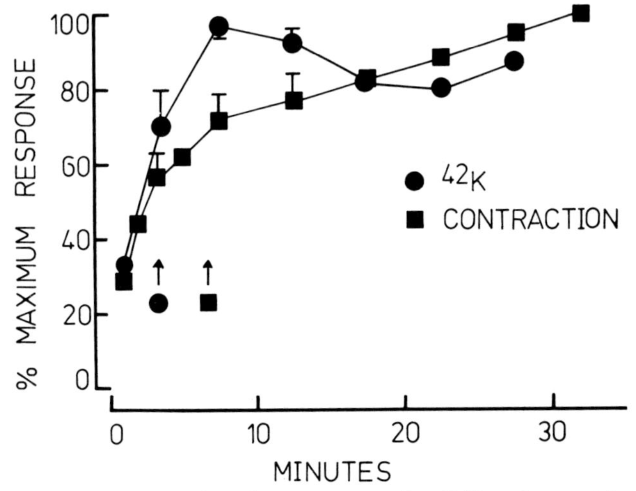

FIGURE 5. *Percent of maximum response after Ca^{++} replacement in the presence of NE for ^{42}K efflux (●) (n = 7 rats) and contraction (■) (n = 5 rats). Arrows indicate the representative rise times required to reach 63% maximum response, (●) 3.3 ± 0.6 and (■) 6.6 ± 2.0 minutes (not significant). The* SE *(representative values) are shown by vertical bars. The only significant difference ($P < 0.01$) occurred at 7.5 minutes.*

(Fig. 7). For instance, when the tissue was simultaneously placed in 0 Ca^{++} plus NE, approximately 90% of the control response occurred, while 40 minutes in 0 Ca^{++} removed any vestiges of a phasic response to NE (Fig. 7). The ^{42}K efflux returned toward basal levels with continued exposure to 0 Ca^{++} + NE (Fig. 7). The decrement of the contractile and ^{42}K responses was closely related over a range of times which led to almost complete inhibition (Fig. 8). However, there was a tendency for contraction to decrease more rapidly over the initial period and to retain some long-term residual response in comparison to ^{42}K efflux (Fig. 8).

Correlation of ^{42}K Efflux and Contraction

The hypothesis that both NE-induced changes in ^{42}K efflux and in contraction were dependent on the same factor, $[Ca^{++}]_{cell}$, was tested by correlating the average responses derived from the three protocols (Figs. 3, 5 and 8). The correlation was close to 1 and highly significant ($P < 0.001$). Moreover, the slope of 1.0 and intercept near zero indicated a co-dependence which may reside in a common dependency on $[Ca^{++}]_{cell}$. This observation suggests the hypothesis that the established role of $[Ca^{++}]_{cell}$ as a controller of contraction extends to the activation of ^{42}K efflux during NE stimulation.

Ca^{++} Dependency of ^{24}Na Influx

The ^{24}Na influx was measured under basal conditions and during NE treatment in the presence

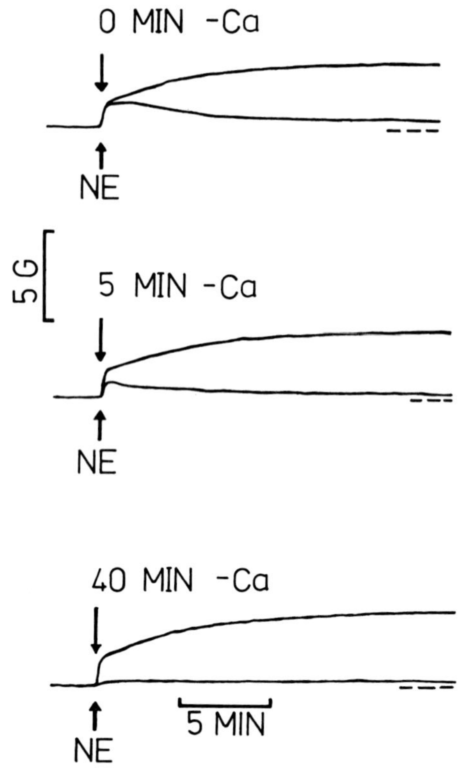

FIGURE 6. *Effects of the time in 0 Ca^{++} solution on typical contractile responses to NE. Data are plotted as in Figure 1A.*

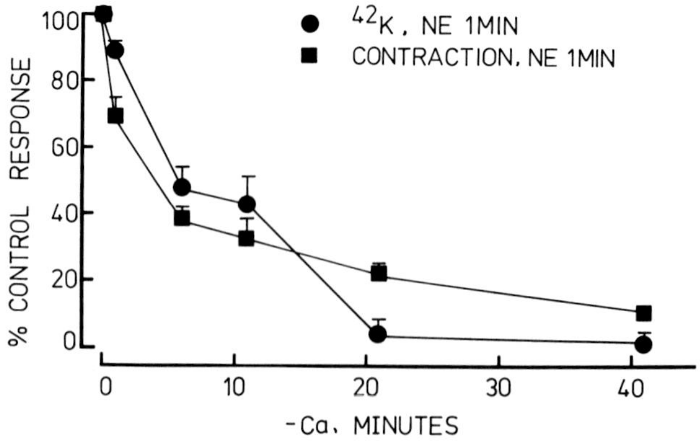

FIGURE 8. *Percent of control response to NE at various times after removal of Ca^{++}. Data for ^{42}K efflux (●) (n = 6 rats) and contraction (■) (n = 6 rats) are plotted + SE. Significant differences ($P < 0.05$) occurred at 1, 21, and 41 minutes.*

and absence of Ca^{++} (Table 2). The basal ^{24}Na influx was increased in the 0 Ca^{++} solution ($P < 0.001$). Ca^{++} depletion for 5 minutes did not greatly inhibit the NE-stimulated ^{24}Na influx. At 1.0 minutes in NE, the stimulated influxes were similar in 0 Ca^{++} and controls (+Ca^{++}), whereas 4.5 minutes of additional exposure to 0 Ca^{++} led to only a 30% reduction in NE-stimulated influx, compared to the response in the presence of Ca^{++}. This reduction is in sharp contrast to the attenuation (>80%) of contraction (Fig. 6) and ^{42}K efflux (Fig. 7) in 0 Ca^{++} 5 minutes, plus 5 minutes in 0 Ca^{++} + NE. Prolonged exposure to 0 Ca^{++} (20 minute) before NE did not reduce the initial ^{24}Na influx (1.0 minutes in NE), but did inhibit the response after an additional 4.5 minutes in 0 Ca^{++} plus NE. Under this latter condition, the contractile response (Fig. 4A) and ^{42}K efflux (Fig. 4B) were more than 90% inhibited. The NE-stimulated influx of ^{24}Na appears to be resistant to depletion of Ca^{++}, except under conditions of almost complete removal of extracellular and cellular sources for contractile responses.

Discussion

Ca^{++}-Dependent K^+ Channels

The results of the three protocols, which were designed to alter cellular Ca^{++}, showed that a close relation exists between force development and ^{42}K efflux from rat aorta during α-receptor stimulation. Since little evidence exists for a cause-and-effect relation between these two events, it is reasonable to conclude that both responses are controlled by a common factor, e.g., $[Ca^{++}]_{cell}$. Force development in skinned arterial smooth muscle was dependent on $[Ca^{++}]$, with half maximal stimulation achieved

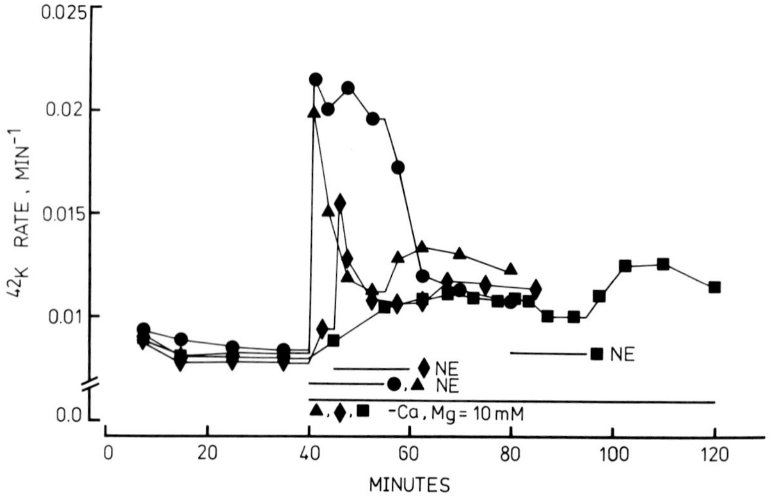

FIGURE 7. *Effects of the time in 0 Ca^{++} solution on ^{42}K efflux and response to NE. Data are plotted as in Figure 1B (n = 6 rats for each protocol). Note that, in three series, 0 Ca^{++} solution was applied at the same time (40 minutes), and that NE was applied at 0 (▲), 5 (◆), and 40 minutes (■) later. Controls (●) were incubated in Ca^{++}-containing solution throughout.*

TABLE 2
Influx of ^{24}Na in Rat Aorta and the Effects of NE (3 μM) and 0 Ca^{++} Solution Applied at Various Times

n	Time in 0 Ca^{++} (min)	Basal (−NE) ^{24}Na influx (μEq/g d.w./min)	*P**	Time in NE (min)	+ NE ^{24}Na influx (μEq/g d.w./min)	Δ ^{24}Na influx (NE) (μEq/g dry wt per min)	*P*†	*P*‡
12	0 (+Ca^{++})	1.91 ±0.14		1.0	2.40 ±0.13	0.49 ±0.19	0.03	
7	0 (+Ca^{++})	1.96 ±0.11		5.5	2.89 ±0.12	0.93 ±0.09	0.001	
11	5	3.04 ±0.21	0.001	1.0	3.56 ±0.24	0.52 ±0.25	0.07	>0.5
9	5	3.10 ±0.18	0.001	5.5	3.70 ±0.21	0.63 ±0.11	0.001	0.05
7	20	3.04 ±0.26	0.005	1.0	4.26 ±0.45	1.22 ±0.42	0.03	>0.1
6	20	3.47 ±0.03	0.001	5.5	3.69 ±0.41	0.22 ±0.37	>0.5	0.1

* Comparison between +Ca^{++} and 0 Ca^{++} conditions −NE.
† Comparison between −NE and +NE conditions with no change in Ca^{++}.
‡ Comparison between +Ca^{++} and 0 Ca^{++} on Δ ^{24}Na influx at equivalent time in NE.

at 0.8 to 6 × 10^{-7} M and maximal responses at 1–3 μM (Ruegg and Paul, 1982; Chatterjee and Murphy, 1983). Studies that employed patch clamp techniques have demonstrated Ca^{++} dependency of K^{+} channels (as well as voltage dependency) in a variety of types of cells. (Miller, 1983; Schwarz and Passow, 1983). At zero or slightly negative membrane potentials, however, [Ca^{++}] of 1 μM or greater was required to increase the time that K^{+} channels were open in red blood cells (Grygorcyzk et al., 1984; Yingst and Hoffman, 1984) and in skeletal muscle (Barrett et al., 1982; Latorre et al., 1982). A unique study on membrane patches from smooth muscle also used high [Ca^{++}] to increase the open time of K^{+} channels (Singer and Walsh, 1984). If our hypothesis is correct, then we would predict that the open time of Ca^{++}-dependent K^{+} channels in arterial smooth muscle would increase with similar [Ca^{++}] (0.1–3 μM) as contraction in the presence of physiological membrane potentials [E_m = −25 to −45 mV in NE (Jones, 1980; Haeusler, 1983). K^{+} channels from skeletal muscle required 5 μM Ca^{++} (or higher) to open at E_m = −20 to −40 mV (Barrett et al., 1982; Latorre et al., 1982). These comparisons are based on skeletal muscle, because the conductances of Ca^{++}-activated K^{+} channels in smooth muscle (Singer and Walsh, 1984) were similar to those in skeletal muscle [200–300 pS (Barrett et al., 1982; Schwarz and Passow, 1983)], in contrast to red blood cells which were 10-fold lower (Schwarz and Passow, 1983; Grygorsczyk et al., 1984). The difference in Ca^{++} dependence between isolated patches and intact cells may reside in the availability of a cofactor such as calmodulin which would be lost when cellular structures are exposed to experimental solutions (Ruegg and Paul, 1982). This explanation needs experimental verification.

The Ca^{++} activation and K^{+} effluxes during NE stimulation in this study is consistent with observations that increased membrane conductance occurred at constant membrane potential during NE stimulation (Haeusler, 1982, 1983). Treatment with TEA reduced the conductances resulting in depolarization and ability to generate action potentials (Casteels, et al., 1977; Haeusler, 1983). Ca^{++} activation of K^{+} channels (and contractile response) with increasing levels of NE could account for much of the voltage-independent change in conductance. It is also possible that the Ca^{++} dependency of K^{+} channels in the tonic type of smooth muscle requires lower [Ca^{++}] than the phasic type; hence, regenerative action potentials would be more readily inhibited. A shift to higher [Ca^{++}] for activation of K^{+} channels (at a given membrane potential) would allow a larger inward current to be unopposed by an increase in K^{+} conductance, and hence a regenerative response (action potential) would be more likely to occur. Action potentials tend to be conducted in smooth muscle and result in relatively large contractile responses (Golenhofen, 1981) consistent with propulsive motility. Closer coupling of inward Na^{+} and Ca^{++} currents with K^{+} efflux would result in graded changes in membrane potential and in contraction (Somlyo et al., 1969; Harder, 1982; Haeusler, 1983). Such graded responses can sustain a continuous opposition to distending forces, e.g., blood pressure, with less expenditure of energy than phasic contractile events (Chatterjee and Murphy, 1983).

Much of the above analyses of Ca^{++}-dependent

K^+ efflux was based on the assumption that force development quantitatively reflects changes in $[Ca^{++}]_{cell}$, and that Ca^{++} activation of the K^+ channel (increased probability of being open) occurred quickly with little inactivation (alteration in the probability of being open during constant stimulation). The first assumption is reasonable, although not entirely correct. Hysteresis has been observed between the $[Ca^{++}]$ dependence of contraction induced by increasing $[Ca^{++}]$ and relaxation resulting from reduction of $[Ca^{++}]$ in skinned arterial smooth muscle (Chatterjee and Murphy, 1983). Approximately 10 times lower $[Ca^{++}]$ was required for force maintenance than for force development. This difference may underlie some of the differences in the time courses for changes in ^{42}K efflux and contraction (Figs. 5 and 8). These discrepancies are relatively small, however, in comparison to the correlation derived over the whole range of responses (Fig. 9).

Opening of Ca^{++}-activated channels occurs much more rapidly than the resolution of the ^{42}K efflux method (Barrett et al., 1982). Likewise, inactivation of these channels during constant stimulation was not a dominant feature (Barrett et al., 1982; Latorre et al., 1982). The assumptions that the opening is rapid and stable appear to be reasonable approximations. Some fade occurred in the response of ^{42}K efflux to NE (Jones 1973; Fig. 2a). It is not clear whether this fade reflected slow inactivation of Ca^{++}-activated K^+ channel or represented a decay of $[Ca^{++}]_{cell}$ during force maintenance (Morgan and Morgan, 1982; Kato et al., 1984). Such transients could result from the acute influx and release of Ca^{++} from a pool of limited capacity, followed by α-receptor stimulated influx of Ca^{++} operating alone in the presence of increased Ca^{++} efflux. If it can be confirmed by direct measures than the Ca^{++}-activated K^+ channel has a stable dependence on voltage and $[Ca^{++}]$, once the membrane has reached a stable voltage, then the time course for the α-receptor-stimulated ^{42}K efflux may reflect that for $[Ca^{++}]_{cell}$.

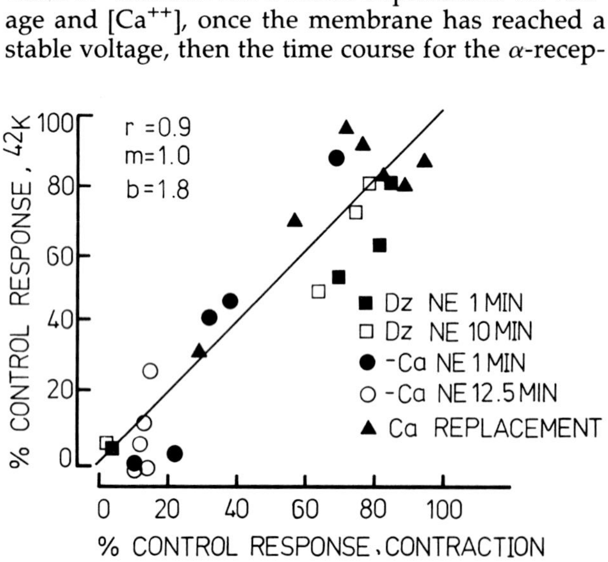

FIGURE 9. *Correlation between % control responses for ^{42}K efflux and for contraction when Ca^{++} was altered by DZ (■, □), Ca^{++} removal (●, ○), or replacement (▲). The line represents the linear regression, % ^{42}K = 1.0 × (% contraction) + 1.8%, with a correlation coefficient, r = 0.94 (P < 0.001).*

Our finding of Ca^{++}-dependent increases in ^{42}K efflux during NE stimulation are in general agreement with those of Martin and Gordon (1983), with one notable exception. They showed a close relation between NE-induced increases in ^{86}Rb efflux and tension development by rabbit aorta. As in our study, these two events were partially inhibited by a Ca^{++} antagonist. It was also noted that the increase in ^{86}Rb efflux during Ca^{++} removal could be reversed by elevating Mg^{++}. On the other hand, La^{+++} had a differential action on the NE-stimulated contracture and ^{86}Rb efflux. A transient contraction occurred, consistent with the release of stored Ca^{++}, but no related change occurred in ^{86}Rb efflux. The authors' interpretation, that increased $[Ca^{++}]$ from release had no effect on ^{86}Rb effluxes, has an alternate explanation. Various types of K^+ channels can be blocked by divalent and trivalent ions, such as Ba^{++}, Cu^{++}, Cd^{++}, and La^{+++} (Takata et al., 1967; Miller, 1983). Treatment with La^{+++} may have directly blocked K^+ channels and, hence, the ^{86}Rb response to NE. Despite this point, we feel that it is likely that Ca^{++}-dependent K^+ channels are operative in both rat and rabbit aorta, and are an important factor for the modulation of the membrane potential during NE stimulation.

Ca^{++}-Dependent Cl^- Efflux

NE also increased ^{36}Cl efflux from vascular smooth muscles with a computed increase in permeability that exceeded that for K^+ (Table 8, in Jones, 1980). As in the case of ^{42}K, removal of Ca^{++} greatly inhibited the phasic response and abolished the later tonic response (Table 1). Based on the parallelism with the Ca^{++} dependency of ^{42}K efflux, it is speculated that a Ca^{++}-dependent Cl^- channel is operative in rat aortic smooth muscle. There is additional basis for this speculation, in that a Ca^{++}-dependent Cl^- current has been observed in at least one cell, the *Xenopus* oocyte (Barish, 1983). The Cl^- equilibrium potential, E_{Cl}, in the oocyte was significantly less than the membrane potential ($E_{Cl} = -24$ mV vs. $E_m = -60$ to -90 mV), a characteristic it shares with arterial smooth muscle which also exhibited a significant difference between E_{Cl} and E_m (-30 mV vs. -55 mM, Jones, 1980).

It is unlikely that Cl^- and K^+ share the same channel. The peak Cl^- efflux exceeded that for K^+ by 2-fold (Jones, 1980), and single channel analyses indicated that Ca^{++}-dependent K^+ channels from skeletal muscle were impermeant to Cl^- (Latorre et al., 1982). Although little evidence is available concerning Ca^{++} dependency of Cl^- fluxes, more detailed investigations of, e.g., single channel behavior, may be a productive endeavor.

NE-Stimulated Na^+ Influx

The influx of ^{24}Na was stimulated by NE, in addition to the stimulation of ^{42}K and ^{36}Cl effluxes. Previously, NE effects were measured on ^{24}Na effluxes from Na^+-loaded arteries (Droogmans et al., 1977; Jones, 1980). The percent increases (25–50%) above basal levels were in agreement with the results of this study. The increase in ^{24}Na influx was maintained for at least 5 minutes in NE plus Ca^{++}, which indicated that α-receptor stimulation led to simultaneous increases in ^{24}Na, ^{42}K, and ^{36}Cl fluxes down their electrochemical gradients. Given the limitations of measuring rapid fluxes in tissues strips (Jones, 1980) it was not possible to determine whether increases in ^{24}Na influx occurred before changes in ^{42}K and ^{36}Cl efflux during the initial application of NE. The NE stimulation of ^{24}Na influx was more resistant to Ca^{++} removal than the ^{42}K and ^{36}Cl effluxes. Only under the extreme condition used (20 minutes in 0 Ca^{++} plus 5.5 minutes in NE) was the NE-stimulated ^{24}Na influx inhibited. It appears, however, that the increase in ^{24}Na influx falls more directly under the control of the α-receptor than ^{42}K or ^{36}Cl effluxes, which are linked with changes in cellular Ca^{++}.

The basal ^{24}Na influx increased in 0 Ca^{++} in contrast to the NE-stimulated influx. The basal and NE-stimulated influx of ^{24}Na exceeded the ^{45}Ca influx reported for rat aorta (Godfraind, 1976). The basal ^{45}Ca influx was only one-tenth (molar basis) that for Na^+; thus, the elevation in Na^+ influx in 0 Ca^{++} solution was beyond any reduction in Ca^{++} influx. This elevation may result from increased Na^+ permeability (despite the 10 mM Mg^{++}), or perhaps removal of adsorbed Ca^{++} which had occupied sites for the membrane transport of Na^+.

Control of Excitation

The observation that ionic events during α-receptor stimulation were controlled by $[Ca^{++}]_{cell}$ alters the interpretation of some previous work. Haeusler (1983) proposed that a combination of voltage- and Ca^{++}-dependent processes are operative in arteries during NE stimulation. It is probably not realistic to separate the responses into independent voltage- and Ca^{++}-regulated events (channels), since it is established that the Ca^{++}-dependent K^+ channels in several cell types exhibit a marked voltage dependency (Miller, 1983). The Ca^{++} sensitivity of the K^+ channels (high-conductance type) increased as the inside of the membrane was made more positive (depolarization). Electromechanical coupling and pharmacomechanical coupling (Somlyo and Somlyo, 1970) would therefore be an interactive process during NE stimulation of polarized arterial smooth muscle. It would be difficult to achieve an isolated electromechanical event, since the Ca^{++} entering during depolarization, e.g., KCl treatment, would itself alter membrane conductance. That is—in addition to controlling E_m, it is necessary to control $[Ca^{++}]_{cell}$ in order to define membrane channel characteristics. The development of a comprehensive model for excitation of arterial smooth muscle will therefore be even more complex than previously thought. The application of recent improvements in electrophysiological and biochemical techniques to the study of vascular smooth muscle may provide the required definitive approach.

We thank Nilam Dheri and Anthony Sanchez for capably conducting many of the protocols. We also thank Susanna Harwood for technical assistance. Diltiazem was a gift from Marion Laboratories.

This work was supported in part by DHHS Grant HL 15852 and postdoctoral support from DHHS HL 07094.

Address for reprints: Dr. Jacquelyn M. Smith, Department of Physiology, University of Missouri, Columbia, Missouri 65212.

Received August 28, 1984; accepted for publication January 17, 1985.

References

Barish M (1983) A transient calcium-dependent chloride current in the immature *Xenopus* oocyte. J Physiol (Lond) **342:** 309–325

Barrett JN, Magleby KL, Pallotta BS (1982) Properties of single calcium-activated potassium channels in cultured rat muscle. J Physiol (Lond) **331:** 211–230

Bolton TB (1979) Mechanisms of action of transmitters and other substances on smooth muscle. Physiol Rev **59:** 606–718

Casteels R, Kitamura K, Kuriyama H, Suzuki H (1977) The membrane properties of the smooth muscle cells of the rabbit main pulmonary artery. J Physiol (Lond) **271:** 41–61

Cauvin C, Loutzenhiser R, Van Breemen C (1983) Mechanisms of calcium antagonist-induced vasodilation. Annu Rev Pharmacol **23:** 373–396

Chatterjee M, Murphy RA (1983) Calcium-dependent stress maintenance without myosin phosphorylation in skinned smooth muscle. Science **221:** 464–466

Daniel EE, Grover AK, Kwan CY (1983) Calcium. *In* Biochemistry of Smooth Muscle, edited by NL Stephens. Boca Raton, Florida, CRC Press, pp 1–88

Den Hertog A (1981) Calcium and the α-action of catecholamines on guinea pig *Taenia caeci.* J Physiol (Lond) **316:** 109–125

Deth R, Casteels R (1977) A study of releasible Ca^{++} fractions in smooth muscle cells of the rabbit aorta. J Gen Physiol **69:** 401–416

Deth R, Van Breemen C (1977) Agonist induced release of intracellular Ca^{++} in the rabbit aorta. J Membr Biol **30:** 363–380

Droogmans G, Raeymaekers L, Casteels R (1977) Electro- and pharmacomechanical coupling in the smooth muscle cells in the rabbit ear artery. J Gen Physiol **70:** 129–148

Gardos G (1958) The function of calcium in the potassium permeability of human erythrocytes. Biochim Biophys Acta **30:** 653–654

Godfraind T (1976) Calcium exchange in vascular smooth muscle, action of noradrenaline and lanthanum. J Physiol (Lond) **260:** 21–35

Golenhofen K (1981) Differentiation of calcium activation processes in smooth muscle using selective antagonists. *In* Smooth Muscle: An Assessment of Current Knowledge, edited by E Bulbring, AF Brading, AW Jones, T Tomita. London, Edward Arnold, pp 157–170

Grygorcyzyk R, Schwarz W, Passow H (1984) Ca^{2+}-activated K^+ channels in human red cells: Comparison of single-channel currents with ion fluxes. Biophys J **45:** 693–698

Haeusler G (1982) α-Adrenoceptor mediated contractile and electrical responses of vascular smooth muscle. J Cardiovasc Pharmacol **4:** S97–S100

Haeusler G (1983) Contraction, membrane potential, and calcium fluxes in rabbit pulmonary arterial muscle. Fed Proc **42:** 263–268

Harder DR (1982) Membrane electrical activation of arterial smooth muscle. *In* Vascular Smooth Muscle: Metabolism, Ionic and Contractile Mechanisms, edited by MF Crass, III, CD Barnes. New York, Academic Press, pp 71–97

Hermsmeyer K (1976) Electrogenesis of increased norepinephrine sensitivity of arterial vascular smooth muscle in hypertension. Circ Res **38:** 362–367

Jones AW (1973) Altered ion transport in vascular smooth muscle from spontaneously hypertensive rats and influence of aldosterone, norepinephrine and angiotensin. Circ Res **33:** 563–572

Jones AW (1974) Altered ion transport in large and small arteries from spontaneously hypertensive rats and the influence of calcium. Circ Res **34:** (suppl 1): 117–122

Jones AW (1980) Content and fluxes of electrolytes. *In* Handbook of Physiology, The Cardiovascular System, vol II, Vascular Smooth Muscle, edited by DF Bohr, AP Somlyo, HV Sparks. Washington, D.C., Am Physiological Society, pp 253–299

Jones AW (1981) Kinetics of active sodium transport in aortae from control and deoxycorticosterone hypertensive rats. Hypertension **3:** 631–640

Jones AW, Smith JM, Dheri N (1984) Calcium activation of ionic fluxes during norepinephrine stimulation of arterial smooth muscle (abstr). Fed Proc **43:** 168A

Karaki H, Weiss GB (1979) Alteration in high and low affinity binding of ^{45}Ca in rabbit aortic smooth muscle by norepinephrine and potassium after exposure to lanthanum and low temperature. J Pharmacol Exp Ther **211:** 86–92

Kato S, Osa T, Ogasawara T (1984) Kinetic model for isometric contraction in smooth muscle on the basis of myosin phosphorylation hypothesis. Biophys J **46:** 35–44

Latorre R, Vergara C, Hidalgo C (1982) Reconstitution in plasma lipid bilayers of a Ca^{++}-dependent K^+ channel from transverse tubule membranes isolated from rabbit skeletal muscle. Proc Natl Acad Sci USA **79:** 805–809

Martin W, Gordon JL (1983) Differential calcium dependence of contractile response and ^{86}Rb efflux from rabbit aorta induced by vasoactive stimuli. J Cell Physiol **115:** 46–52

Meech RW (1978) Calcium-dependent potassium activation in nervous tissues. Annu Rev Biophys Bioeng **7:** 1–18

Meisheri KD, Hwang O, Van Breemen C (1981) Evidence for two separate Ca^{2+} pathways in smooth muscle plasmalemma. J Membr Biol **59:** 19–25

Miller C (1983) Integral membrane channels: Studies in model membranes. Physiol Rev **63:** 1209–1242.

Morgan JP, Morgan KG (1982) Vascular smooth muscle: The first recorded Ca^{2+} transients. Pflugers Arch **395:** 75–77

Ruegg JC, Paul RJ (1982) Vascular smooth muscle, calmodulin and cyclic AMP-dependent protein kinase alter calcium sensitivity in porcine carotid skinned fibers. Circ Res **50:** 394–399

Saida K, Van Breemen C (1983) Mechanisms of Ca^{++} antagonist-induced vasodilation, intracellular actions. Circ Res **52:** 137–142

Schwarz W, Passow H (1983) Ca^{2+}-activated K^+ channels in erythrocytes and excitable cells. Annu Rev Physiol **45:** 359–374

Singer JJ, Walsh JV (1984) Large conductance Ca^{++}-activated K^+ channels in smooth muscle cell membrane, reduction in unitary currents due to internal Na^+ ions. Biophys J **45:** 68–70

Somlyo AP, Somlyo AV (1970) Vascular smooth muscle. II. Pharmacology of normal and hypertensive vessels. Pharmacol Rev **22:** 249–353

Somlyo AV, Vinall P, Somlyo AP (1969) Excitation-contraction coupling and electrical events in two types of vascular smooth muscle. Microvasc Res **1:** 354–373

Triggle DJ, Swamy VC (1980) Pharmacology of agents that affect calcium, agonists and antagonists. Chest **78:** 174s–179s

Van Breemen C, Aaronson P, Loutzenhiser R, Meisheri K (1980) Ca^{2+} movements in smooth muscle. Chest **78:** 157s–165s

Yingst DR, Hoffman JF (1984) Ca^{++}-induced K^+ transport in human red blood cell ghosts containing arsenazo III. J Gen Physiol **83:** 19–45

INDEX TERMS: Rat aorta • ^{42}K, ^{36}Cl, ^{24}Na fluxes • Contraction • Ca^{++} antagonist • Ca^{++}-dependent K^+ channel • Ca^{++}-dependent Cl^- channel • Norepinephrine • Arterial smooth muscle.

Role of Adenosine in Coronary Blood Flow Regulation after Reductions in Perfusion Pressure

William P. Dole, Nobuyuki Yamada, Vernon S. Bishop, and Ray A. Olsson
With the assistance of Daniel M. Nuno

From The Department of Internal Medicine (Cardiovascular Division), University of Iowa, Iowa City, Iowa, and the University of South Florida School of Medicine, Tampa, Florida

SUMMARY. We employed intracoronary infusion of adenosine deaminase to test the hypothesis that endogenous adenosine contributes to regulation of coronary blood flow following acute reductions in coronary artery pressure. In 16 closed-chest anesthetized dogs, we perfused the left circumflex coronary artery from a pressurized arterial reservoir and measured coronary blood flow following changes in perfusion pressure before and 10 minutes after the start of intracoronary adenosine deaminase, 5 U/min per kg body weight. Parallel studies showed that this dose of enzyme resulted in cardiac lymph adenosine deaminase concentrations of 3.2 ± 0.4 U/ml. Adenosine deaminase abolished the vasodilator response to intracoronary adenosine, 4 and 8 μg, but had no effect on the vasodilator response to intracoronary papaverine, 200 and 300 μg, demonstrating enzyme efficacy and specificity. Additional experiments demonstrated that adenosine deaminase reversibly attenuated myocardial reactive hyperemia following 5- and 10-second coronary occlusions by 30% ($P < 0.05$), evidence that the infused enzyme effectively degraded endogenous adenosine. However, adenosine deaminase did not alter the time course for coronary autoregulation or the steady state autoregulatory flow response over the pressure range between 125 and 75 mm Hg. Further, adenosine deaminase did not alter steady state coronary flow when perfusion pressure was reduced below the range for effective autoregulation (60–40 mm Hg). Such results show that adenosine is not essential for either coronary autoregulation or for the maintenance of coronary vasodilation when autoregulatory vasodilator reserve is expended. (*Circ Res 56: 517–524, 1985*)

CORONARY autoregulation is the intrinsic ability of the heart to maintain its blood supply relatively constant in the face of fluctuations in perfusion pressure (Mosher et al., 1964; Cross, 1964). The mechanism underlying this fundamental adaptive flow response is unknown. According to the metabolic hypothesis, coronary autoregulation is initiated by flow-dependent changes in tissue levels of a metabolic substrate or a metabolite (Johnson, 1964; Rubio and Berne, 1975; Belloni, 1979; Feigl, 1983). Several studies have demonstrated increased adenosine production and release during conditions in which oxygen supply is reduced (Katori and Berne, 1966; Rubio and Berne, 1969; Rubio et al., 1974; Schrader et al., 1977). In one of these studies (Schrader et al., 1977), tissue adenosine content and adenosine release increased when perfusion pressure was lowered over the autoregulation range in isolated buffer-perfused guinea pig hearts. As the investigators point out, such a correlation only suggests, but does not prove, that adenosine is the primary determinant of changes in coronary resistance during autoregulation.

This study tests the hypothesis that endogenous adenosine is an essential mediator of coronary autoregulation. The hypothesis predicts that destroying interstitial adenosine should abolish autoregulation. Extending this inquiry to pressures below the autoregulation range tests a second hypothesis, namely, that endogenous adenosine mediates coronary flow only when autoregulatory vasodilator reserve is expended. In both sets of experiments, an intracoronary infusion of adenosine deaminase was used to destroy interstitial adenosine. Adenosine deaminase did not alter coronary pressure-flow relationships in either instance, new evidence that adenosine is not essential for coronary autoregulation.

Methods

Animal Preparation

Experiments were performed in 16 healthy closed-chest adult mongrel dogs (weight 25–35 kg). Animals were given morphine sulfate (3 mg/kg, sc) and anesthetized with α-chloralose (50 mg/kg, iv), with additional doses of chloralose given as needed throughout the experiment. The dogs were ventilated with oxygen-enriched room air by a positive pressure respirator to keep arterial oxygen tension between 100 and 125 mm Hg and carbon dioxide tension at 35 ± 5 mm Hg. Arterial pH was maintained at 7.40 ± 0.05 by an intravenous infusion of sodium bicarbonate (150 mM, 5 ml/kg per hr, iv) (Arfors et al., 1971).

This manuscript from the University of Iowa was sent to John T. Shepherd, Consulting Editor, for review by expert referees, for editorial decision, and final disposition.

The hematocrit averaged 38 ± 2%. Systemic pressure was measured in the aorta with a catheter passed retrograde from the femoral artery and a strain gauge pressure transducer. Rectal temperature was held at 37°C with heating pads. Heart rate was measured continuously with a cardiotachometer triggered from the electrocardiogram.

Coronary Perfusion System

Pressure in the circumflex artery was controlled by an extracorporeal perfusion circuit (Dole et al., 1981). The circumflex artery was perfused from a pressurized arterial reservoir through a metal cannula advanced through the right carotid artery into the ascending aorta and wedged in the proximal circumflex artery under pressure and flow monitoring as described by Smith et al. (1974). The reservoir was heated to maintain the temperature of the blood entering the cannula at 37°C. Coronary artery pressure was measured at the cannula tip through an external auxiliary tube opening at the distal end of the perfusion cannula. Blood passed from the reservoir through an electromagnetic flow probe before entering the coronary cannula. The pressure in the reservoir was controlled by means of two compressed air tanks connected in parallel, permitting arbitrary alterations in perfusion pressure. The seal between the cannula tip and circumflex artery was confirmed by observing the response of cannula tip pressure to inflow occlusion and by injecting saturated Evans blue solution into the coronary cannula at the end of the experiment as described previously (Dole et al., 1981). The dye injection also served to delineate the area of perfused myocardium which was removed and weighed in order to calculate coronary flow per unit of muscle mass. Blood coagulation in the extracorporeal perfusion circuit was prevented by infusion of sodium heparin (initial dose 500 U/kg, iv, then 250 U/kg, iv, every hour). The flow meter zero was determined by frequent coronary inflow occlusions. The flow probe was calibrated by timed blood volume collections after each experiment with blood from the experimental animal.

We have previously shown that this perfusion system does not alter systemic hemodynamics. Furthermore, coronary reactive hyperemia and autoregulation are not impaired with the cannula in place (Dole et al., 1981).

Penetration of ^{131}I-Adenosine Deaminase into Cardiac Interstitium

Experiments in five dogs evaluated the concentration of ^{131}I-adenosine deaminase in cardiac lymph during the intracoronary infusion of this enzyme. In these experiments, we used mongrel dogs anesthetized with sodium thiamylal, 18 mg/kg, iv, and maintained in surgical anesthesia by ventilation with O_2-enriched air containing 0.5% halothane. Surgical preparation entailed thoracotomy through the left 5th intercostal space to expose the heart for the transepicardial insertion of a 20-gauge angiocath into the left anterior descending coronary artery near its origin. A C-shaped piece of PE 10 tubing about 5 cm long was inserted into a lymphatic channel coursing over the left anterior descending coronary artery. Cyanoacrylate cement anchored both catheters. The experiments consisted of the intracoronary infusion of ^{131}I-adenosine deaminase, (Daddona and Kelley, 1977), specific activity 2950–3700 counts/min per U, for 20 minutes at a rate of 5 U/min per kg body weight. During the ^{131}I-adenosine deaminase infusion and for up to 30 minutes after its completion, we collected serial samples of lymph directly into capillary tubes certified to contain 50 ± 1 μl. The ^{131}I activity in this lymph and the ^{131}I and enzymatic activity of the infusate served for calculation of lymph adenosine deaminase (ADA) concentration by the formula:

$$\text{lymph ADA (U/ml)} = \frac{\text{infusate ADA (U/ml)} \times \text{lymph } ^{131}\text{I (counts/min per ml)}}{\text{infusate } ^{131}\text{I (counts/min per ml)}}.$$

Since the assay of adenosine deaminase activity is carried out at 25°C, but the cardiac interstitium is at 37°C, we compared initial rates of deamination of 0.1 mM adenosine at these two temperatures. At 37°C, the catalytic activity of adenosine deaminase was 1.95 times higher than the activity at 25°C.

Functional Activity of Adenosine Deaminase

Calf intestinal adenosine deaminase, type I, was obtained from Sigma as a suspension in 3.2 M $(NH_4)_2SO_4$, pH 6. The enzyme solution for intracoronary infusion consisted of 4000 U adenosine deaminase and 12 mmol Na_2HPO_4 in a total volume of 30 ml 0.14 M NaCl. The pH of the enzyme solution was 7.4. This solution was filtered through a 0.44-μm cellulose acetate membrane immediately prior to use. A solution containing the same proportions of $(NH_4)_2SO_4$ and Na_2HPO_4 in 0.14 M NaCl was infused into the coronary circulation during all control observations.

Two tests assessed the functional enzymatic activity of the adenosine deaminase. First, we determined the vasodilator response to a 4- and 8-μg intracoronary bolus of adenosine before, during, and at 120 minutes after the end of the adenosine deaminase infusion. Such a test ensures that the adenosine deaminase is catalytically active in our preparation. Second, we measured reactive hyperemic flow responses following 2-, 5-, and 10-second coronary inflow occlusions before, during, and at 60 minutes after discontinuing the adenosine deaminase infusion. The order of occlusions was randomized and each observation was the average of two occlusions for each duration. Occlusions were separated by at least 3 minutes. Such a test documents the penetration of the enzyme into the cardiac interstitial space. To allow the enzyme time to penetrate into the cardiac interstitium, all experimental observations began 10 minutes after the start of the adenosine deaminase infusion.

We assessed the specificity of adenosine deaminase for adenosine in four animals by comparing the effects of intracoronary injections of adenosine and papaverine before and during adenosine deaminase infusion. Attenuation of coronary vasodilator responses to adenosine but not to papaverine would provide evidence for enzyme specificity.

Since attenuation of vasodilator responses to intracoronary adenosine by adenosine deaminase could be due to exogenous enzyme in the blood, in five animals we compared vasodilator responses in the coronary bed to those in the femoral bed before, during, and at 120 minutes after discontinuing the infusion of the enzyme. Selective inhibition of adenosine-induced vasodilation in the coronary bed would indicate that the effect of adenosine deaminase was due to enzyme retained in the heart and not to enzyme in the blood which should affect adenosine responses in both the femoral and coronary beds. In these experiments, the left femoral artery was cannulated and perfused through an extracorporeal circuit with blood from the dog's left common carotid artery. The circuit contained an in-line electromagnetic flow probe for measuring femoral blood flow.

Experimental Protocol

After the preparation had stabilized for 30–45 minutes, we recorded control heart rate, mean aortic pressure, coronary blood flow at a coronary perfusion pressure of 100 mm Hg, the coronary flow response to intracoronary adenosine, the coronary flow response to intracoronary papaverine, coronary reactive hyperemia after 2-, 5-, and 10-second inflow occlusions, and coronary artery pressure-flow curves. In nine animals, steady state coronary flow was determined at pressures of 125, 100, and 75 mm Hg. In seven of these animals, the dynamic flow response to a step changes in pressure between 125 and 75 mm Hg was also recorded. In seven separate animals, steady state coronary artery pressure-flow relationships were obtained over the range of 100–40 mm Hg by decreasing pressure in 20 mm Hg steps. Flow was allowed to stabilize at least 2 minutes between each pressure change.

Following control measurements, adenosine deaminase was infused into the circumflex coronary bed at a rate sufficient to deliver 5 U/min per kg. At the 10th minute of enzyme infusion, we repeated all of the experimental observations. The adenosine deaminase infusion then was stopped and a final set of measurements of all experimental parameters was obtained 1 hour later. The responses to intracoronary injections of adenosine were also recorded at 120 minutes after infusion was discontinued.

At the completion of the experiment, Evans blue was injected into the perfusion cannula at the maximum coronary artery pressure used during the experiment, and the animal was killed by intravenous injection of saturated potassium chloride. The heart then was removed and the stained area weighed.

Quantification of Autoregulation

The degree of autoregulation was quantified by calculating the closed loop gain of the system (Norris et al., 1979) as

$$G_A = 1 - (\Delta F/F)/(\Delta P/P)$$

where F is the steady state flow at pressure P, and ΔF is the change in flow for a given change in pressure ΔP. Values for G_A greater than zero indicate the degree of autoregulation with a maximum value of 1. Values of $G_A \leq 0$ indicate a lack of autoregulation, i.e., a passive vascular bed.

We characterized the time course of the autoregulatory response by measuring $t_{1/2}$, the time for mean coronary flow to return 50% of the way to control after a step change in pressure, and also by measuring the time for flow to reach a steady state.

Data Analysis

Hemodynamic data before and after adenosine deaminase were compared by Student's *t*-test for paired observations. Differences in pressure-flow data, responses to drugs, and reactive hyperemic flow responses before, during, and after adenosine deaminase were assessed by analysis of variance and Tukey's test for multiple comparisons (Snedecor and Cochran, 1980).

Reactive hyperemic flow—defined as the volume of flow greater than control flow rate—and peak reactive hyperemic flow were determined, and the data from two occlusions for each duration were averaged and expressed as a percent change from the control response.

Differences between means were considered to be statistically significant when *P* was less than 0.05. All data are expressed as mean ± SEM.

Results

Control hemodynamic parameters for all 16 animals at a circumflex perfusion pressure of 100 mm Hg were: heart rate 132 ± 7 beats/min, mean aortic pressure 115 ± 6 mm Hg, and mean coronary flow 78 ± 3 ml/min per 100 g. The corresponding values during infusion of adenosine deaminase were 128 ± 8 beats/min, 116 ± 6 mm Hg, and 77 ± 3 ml/min per 100 g; at 60 minutes after discontinuing adenosine deaminase, they were 130 ± 8 beats/min, 113 ± 8 mm Hg, and 80 ± 4 ml/min per 100 g. These changes are not significant.

Effects of Adenosine Deaminase on Coronary Autoregulation

Figure 1 shows the effects of adenosine deaminase on steady state coronary flow over the pressure range of 125 to 75 mm Hg in nine animals. Control flow averaged 80 ml/min per 100 g at a pressure of 100 mm Hg and was not altered by adenosine deaminase. The autoregulatory gain for a step reduction in pressure from 125 to 100 mm Hg averaged 0.53 ± 0.04 during the control period prior to adenosine deaminase and 0.50 ± 0.05 during adenosine deaminase infusion. These values were not significantly different. The control gain for a reduction in pressure from 100 to 75 mm Hg averaged 0.56 ± 0.06 and was not altered during adenosine deaminase infusion (G_A = 0.58 ± 0.06).

Figure 2 shows the effects of adenosine deaminase on the coronary flow response to a step change in pressure between 125 and 75 mm Hg. Following a reduction in pressure, coronary flow initially decreased and then returned toward control, reaching

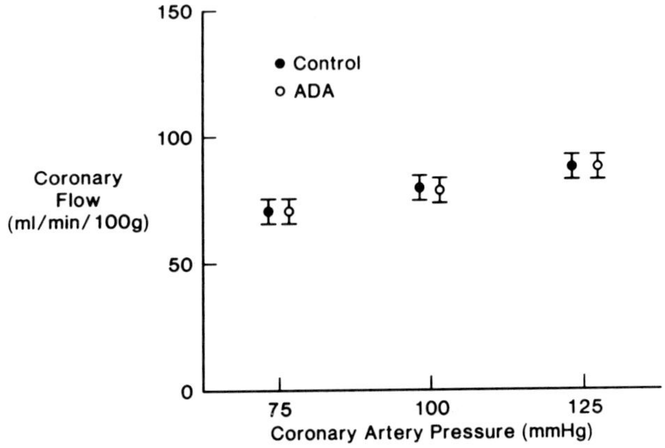

FIGURE 1. *Effects of adenosine deaminase (ADA) on coronary autoregulation. Closed circles indicate pre-ADA control flow values. Open circles indicate flow values during ADA infusion. ADA did not alter the steady state flow response following 25 mm Hg changes in pressure within the autoregulation range. Values are mean ± SEM, n = 9.*

a new steady state within 36 seconds. Following an increase in pressure, coronary flow rose transiently and then declined, reaching a new steady state within 25 seconds. Table 1 summarizes the effects of adenosine deaminase on the time course of coronary autoregulation in seven animals. Adenosine deaminase did not affect the dynamic flow response to a pressure change in either direction.

Effects of Adenosine Deaminase on Coronary Pressure Flow Relations below the Autoregulatory Range

Figure 3 shows the effects of adenosine deaminase on steady state coronary flow responses to 20 mm Hg reductions in pressure over the range between 100 and 40 mm Hg in seven animals. Whereas there was no difference in control flow when pressure was reduced from 100 to 80 mm Hg, pressure reductions below 80 mm Hg resulted in a progressive decrease in flow. Adenosine deaminase did not alter

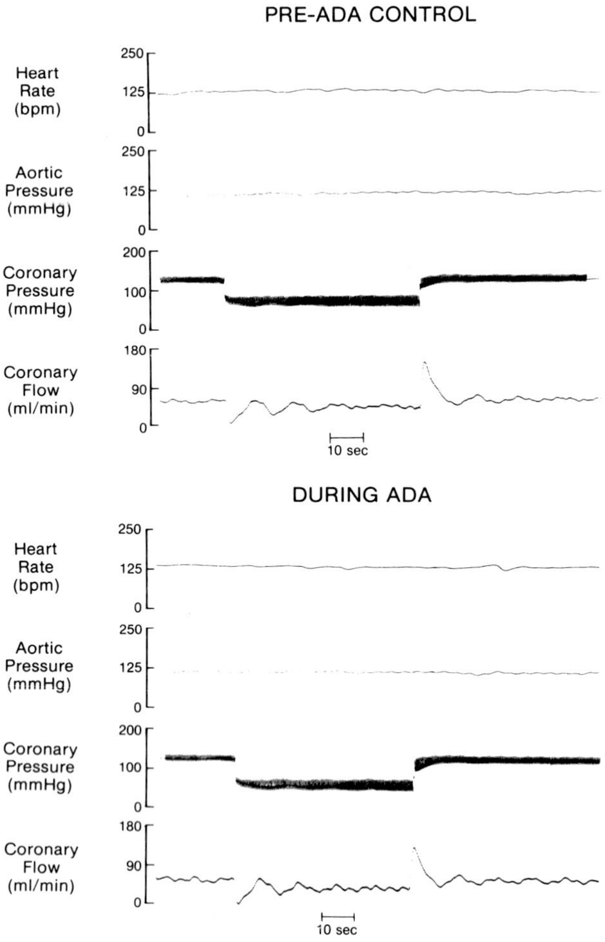

Figure 2. *Effects of adenosine deaminase (ADA) on the time course of coronary autoregulation following abrupt changes in perfusion pressure. The upper panel shows the pre-ADA control coronary flow response to 50 mm Hg step changes in pressure between 125 and 75 mm Hg. The lower panel shows the flow response to such pressure changes during infusion of ADA. ADA did not alter the dynamic flow response to pressure change in either direction.*

Table 1
Effects of Adenosine Deaminase on the Time Course of Coronary Autoregulation

	ΔP (mm Hg): 125 to 75		ΔP (mm Hg): 75 to 125	
	$t_{1/2}$ (sec)	Duration (sec)	$t_{1/2}$ (sec)	Duration (sec)
Control	2.7 ± 0.3	34.2 ± 2.2	2.5 ± 0.2	24.6 ± 2.7
ADA	2.6 ± 0.2	34.2 ± 2.1	2.4 ± 0.2	24.1 ± 2.9

Results are expressed as mean ± SEM, $n = 7$. Abbreviatons: ΔP, step change in pressure; ADA, adenosine deaminase; $t_{1/2}$, time for flow to return 50% of the way to control after ΔP.

the flow response to pressure change even at pressures below the autoregulation range.

Figure 4 plots the degree of autoregulation expressed as the gain, G_A, for each pressure step before and during adenosine deaminase infusion. There was a decrease in the degree of autoregulation when initial pressure was lowered from 100 to 80 mm Hg. Between 60 and 40 mm Hg, autoregulation was totally abolished, as indicated by the negative gain. Despite the progressive reduction in the degree of autoregulation, adenosine deaminase had no effect on the flow response to pressure change.

Cardiac Lymph ^{131}I-Adenosine Deaminase

Lymph flow rate varied between about 6 and 20 μl/min as judged by the time necessary to fill a 50-μl capillary pipette. Accordingly, the number of lymph samples collected during the 20 minutes of ^{131}I-adenosine deaminase infusion was three in 2 dogs, five in 2 dogs, and eight in 1 dog. As shown in Figure 5, lymph ^{131}I-adenosine deaminase activity rose throughout the period of infusion, reaching an average value of 3.2 ± 0.4 U/ml (range 2.2–4.5 U/ml). The time course of lymph ^{131}I-adenosine deaminase activity showed an initial rapid rise followed by an asymptotic approach to the maximum

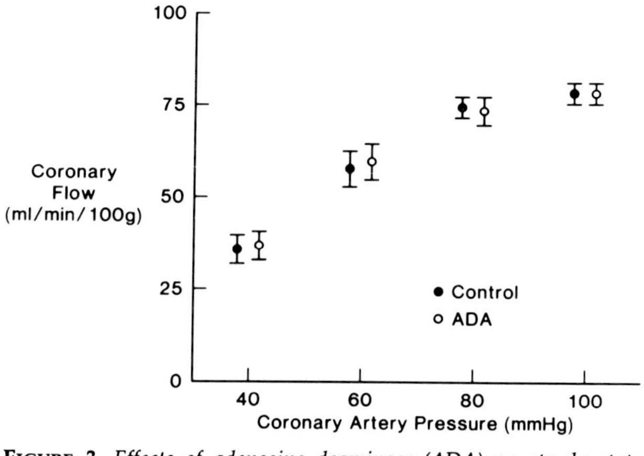

Figure 3. *Effects of adenosine deaminase (ADA) on steady state coronary flow responses to reductions in perfusion pressure below the autoregulatory range. Closed circles indicate pre-ADA control flow values. Open circles indicate flow values during ADA infusion. ADA did not alter coronary flow at pressures below the effective range for autoregulation. Values are mean ± SEM, $n = 7$.*

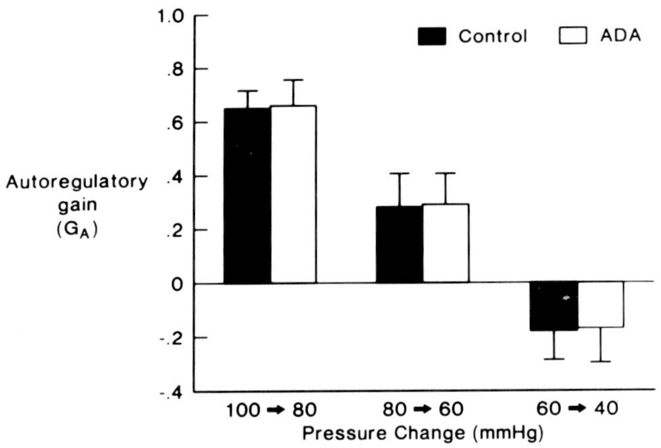

FIGURE 4. *Effects of adenosine deaminase (ADA) on the autoregulatory gain G_A, for 20 mm Hg reductions in perfusion pressure over the range between 100 and 40 mm Hg. Closed bars indicate pre-ADA control values. Open bars indicate values during ADA infusion. ADA had no effect on G_A despite a progressive reduction in the degree of autoregulation at the lower initial pressures. Values are mean ± SEM, n = 7.*

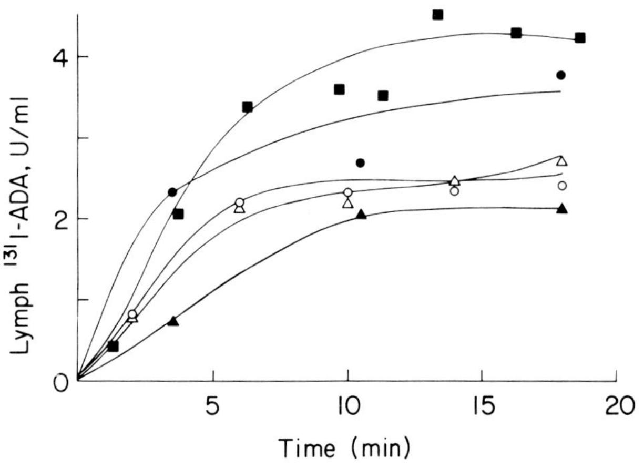

FIGURE 5. *Time course of ^{131}I-adenosine deaminase (^{131}I-ADA) activity in the cardiac lymph. Symbols represent data from individual dogs.*

value. Thus, by the 10th minute of enzyme infusion, lymph ^{131}I-adenosine deaminase concentration averaged 84% of maximum (range 74–95%). Lymph ^{131}I activity declined rapidly after the end of the enzyme infusion, but levels were still appreciable, approximately 0.5 U/ml, 20 minutes later (data not shown).

Functional Activity of Adenosine Deaminase

Figure 6 (panels A and B) summarizes the effects of adenosine and papaverine in the coronary bed before, during, and after intracoronary administration of adenosine deaminase. During control conditions, adenosine (4 and 8 μg) increased coronary flow by 124 ± 9% and 200 ± 24%, respectively. Adenosine deaminase totally abolished the vasodilator response to intracoronary adenosine during the enzyme infusion and for as long as 120 minutes after discontinuing the enzyme infusion. Papaverine in doses of 200 and 300 μg increased control coronary flow by 90 ± 15% and 120 ± 22%, respectively. The coronary vasodilator response to papaverine was unchanged during infusion of adenosine deaminase, demonstrating enzyme specificity. The intra-arterial injection of 10- and 20-μg doses of adenosine into the femoral bed increased mean femoral flow by 79 ± 14% and 118 ± 14%, respectively. In contrast to responses in the coronary bed, the vasodilator response to adenosine in the femoral bed (Fig. 6, panel C) was attenuated only during the enzyme infusion, and returned to control levels 120 minutes after the enzyme infusion was stopped. Thus, the prolonged inhibition of adenosine-induced coronary vasodilation was not due to adenosine deaminase still circulating in the blood, but rather reflected the action of residual enzyme in the heart.

The effects of adenosine deaminase on coronary reactive hyperemia are summarized in Table 2. During control conditions, the ratio of peak reactive hyperemic flow to basal flow averaged 1.5 ± 0.1 for 2-second occlusions, 2.4 ± 0.1 for 5-second occlusions, and 3.3 ± 0.3 for 10-second occlusions. Peak reactive hyperemic flow was modestly reduced (10%, $P < 0.05$) only with 5-second occlusions. Adenosine deaminase reduced reactive hyperemic flow by approximately 30% ($P < 0.05$) following 5- and 10-second coronary occlusions and by 8% ($P < 0.05$) following 2-second occlusions.

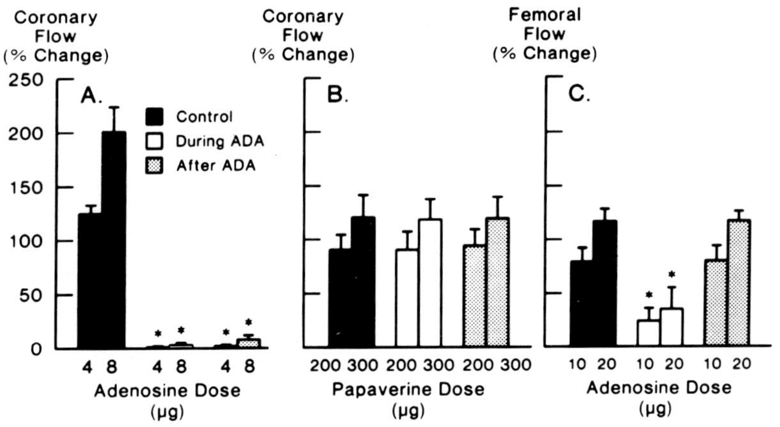

FIGURE 6. *Functional enzymatic activity of intracoronary adenosine deaminase (ADA). Panel A: coronary flow responses to intracoronary adenosine expressed as percent change. Closed bars indicate pre-ADA control values. Open bars indicate values during ADA infusion. Stippled bars indicate values obtained 120 minutes after stopping the ADA infusion. Values are mean ± SEM, n = 16. * Significantly different from respective control responses, P < 0.05. Panel B: coronary flow responses to intracoronary papaverine before ADA (closed bars), during ADA (open bars), and 120 minutes after stopping ADA (stippled bars). Panel C: femoral flow responses to intra-arterial injections of adenosine before intracoronary ADA (closed bars), during ADA (open bars), and 120 minutes after stopping ADA (stippled bars).*

TABLE 2
Effects of Adenosine Deaminase on Coronary Reactive Hyperemia

Duration of occlusion (sec)	Peak RH flow rate (%Δ from control)		RH flow (%Δ from control)	
	During ADA	After ADA (60 min)	During ADA	After ADA (60 min)
2	−2 ± 2	0 ± 1	−8 ± 3*	−3 ± 5
5	−10 ± 3*	−4 ± 3‡	−29 ± 3*†	−12 ± 2*‡
10	−2 ± 2	−2 ± 2	−32 ± 3*†	−17 ± 5*‡

Results are expressed as mean ± SEM, $n = 9$. Abbreviations: RH, reactive hyperemia; ADA, adenosine deaminase.

* Significantly different from zero, $P < 0.05$.

† Significantly different from 2-second occlusion during ADA, $P < 0.05$.

‡ Significantly different from corresponding values during ADA, $P < 0.05$.

Discussion

The major finding in this study is that intracoronary infusion of adenosine deaminase at a concentration sufficient to attenuate myocardial reactive hyperemia did not affect the coronary artery pressure-flow relationship when pressure was reduced over the autoregulation range or to levels even below this range.

Additional experiments demonstrated that adenosine deaminase was efficacious, selective, and had penetrated into the cardiac interstitial space. An intracoronary infusion of the enzyme abolished the coronary vasodilator response to adenosine but did not alter the response to papaverine, evidence of enzyme efficacy and specificity. Further, a comparison of the vasodilator responses to exogenous adenosine in the coronary and femoral beds 2 hours after the intracoronary adenosine deaminase infusion had been discontinued showed that the coronary response was still markedly attenuated, whereas the femoral response was fully restored. This finding indicated that suppression of the coronary response resulted from enzyme retained in the heart rather than from enzyme in the blood. The observation that adenosine deaminase attenuated myocardial reactive hyperemia following 5- and 10-second occlusions by 30%, provides functional evidence that infused enzyme penetrated into the cardiac interstitium. Finally, the studies of ^{131}I-adenosine deaminase confirm quantitatively that during intracoronary adenosine deaminase infusion, substantial amounts of the enzyme penetrate into the cardiac interstitium.

The collection of lymph from an epicardial lymphatic channel probably is the most direct way to probe the composition of the interstitial space of the perfusion field receiving ^{131}I-adenosine deaminase. Unlike lymph sampled at more remote sites, the lymph is unlikely to be diluted by lymph draining from regions not receiving enzyme directly, and thus more nearly represents the true value. Nevertheless, we believe that our measurements of lymph adenosine deaminase concentration are a minimum estimate of the catalytic activity of the enzyme in the interstitial space. Owing to the transit time of ^{131}I-adenosine deaminase from the interstitium to the sampling site and the averaging effect of sample collections lasting several minutes, the concentration in lymph at any moment will be less than that in the interstitium. Additionally, lymph adenosine deaminase activity does not reflect the extent to which enzyme binds to adenosine deaminase binding proteins (Daddona and Kelley, 1977; Schrader and Stacy, 1977) on the surface (Kornfield, 1983) of the cells which constitute the boundary of the interstitial space. Adenosine deaminase thus bound retains catalytic activity and augments that of enzyme in solution. Finally adenosine deaminase activity is, by convention, measured at 25°C. The catalytic activity in interstitium at 37°C was 1.95 times higher.

The use of adenosine deaminase to probe the participation of adenosine in coronary autoregulation raises a critical question: Does enough enzyme penetrate into the interstitial space to destroy adenosine as fast as it is formed? We do not know of a method for directly measuring the rate of release of adenosine into the cardiac interstitium. However, it is possible to calculate how much adenosine production would have to increase in order to maintain adenosine concentrations constant in the presence of adenosine deaminase. Such calculations make allowances for the temperature differential between the cardiac interstitium and the in vitro assay, assume that the interstitial space volume is 0.217 ml/g (Frank and Langer, 1974), and accept the basal interstitial adenosine concentration of 0.2 μM (Olsson et al., 1982). To maintain the adenosine concentration of 0.2 μM in the presence of 3.2 U adenosine deaminase per ml, the average of our measurements, adenosine production would have to increase substantially by 9.3 nmol/min per g of left ventricle. Because, under these conditions, the enzyme is operating at a substrate concentration of only 0.7% of K_m, any increase in the rate of adenosine production will elicit a proportional increase in catalytic activity such that adenosine concentration will remain essentially constant. The catalytic activity of the enzyme will not begin to limit the rate of degradation until the substrate concentration is well above the K_m of the adenosine deaminase, 29 μM (Rockwell and Maquire, 1970). We know of no evidence that cardiac interstitial adenosine concentrations ever attain such high levels. Accordingly, the finding that adenosine deaminase affected neither the static nor the dynamic autoregulatory flow response implies that adenosine is not essential for coronary autoregulation. Furthermore, since adenosine deaminase did not alter the coronary pressure-flow relationship when pressure was reduced below the autoregulatory range, it seems unlikely that adenosine is essential for the maintenance of coronary vasodilation at these lower perfusion pressures.

In these experiments, circumflex artery pressure was regulated independently of aortic pressure; thus, pressure gradients could have resulted in intracoronary collateral flow. Although early work by Driscol et al. (1964) demonstrated that the pattern of coronary flow in response to changes in perfusion pressure was not altered by sizeable pressure gradients between major vessels, more recent data suggest that collateral flow may influence the steady state pressure-flow relationship in the circumflex artery at low perfusion pressures (Messina et al., 1983). Although coronary flow may have been underestimated at the lower perfusion pressures in the present study, the gradient for collateral flow was the same before and during adenosine deaminase infusion. Thus, the failure of adenosine deaminase to alter coronary flow responses to pressure change cannot be attributed to differences in collateral flow.

Our experiments in blood perfused in situ dog hearts lead to a conclusion diametrically opposite to that reached by Schrader et al. (1977) who studied isolated, buffer-perfused guinea pig hearts. Differences in the characteristics of autoregulation, perhaps related to the preparations or to the species, and also a fundamental difference between the experimental designs, may explain the discordant conclusions. Coronary autoregulation in the guinea pig preparation occurred between pressures of 60 and 20 cm H_2O (44–15 mm Hg), which is below the pressure range for autoregulation which we and others have obsrved in the blood-perfused dog heart (Mosher et al., 1964; Cross, 1964; Guyton et al., 1977; Rouleau et al., 1979; Dole et al., 1981, 1982). An inverse correlation between adenosine release rate and coronary perfusion pressure in the guinea pig was the major element of support for the hypothesis that adenosine mediates coronary autoregulation. In our study, destruction of cardiac interstitial adenosine provides a direct test of the role of this nucleoside in coronary autoregulation.

Our conclusion that adenosine is not essential for coronary vasodilation following reductions in perfusion pressure is consistent with recent work by Gewirtz et al. (1983) in a closed chest conscious pig model. In that study an intracoronary infusion of adenosine deaminase had no effect on regional myocardial perfusion beyond a flow-limiting coronary stenosis which reduced post stenotic pressure to 77 mm Hg at a mean aortic pressure of 117 mm Hg. These authors point out that measurements of steady state coronary pressure and flow do not exclude the possibility that the effect of adenosine is transitory and might be essential in initiating but not maintaining coronary vasodilation. The present study shows that such is not the case, since adenosine deaminase did not alter the time course of coronary autoregulation.

A recent preliminary report by Hanley et al. (1984) also showed that adenosine deaminase does not alter coronary autoregulation. In addition, these investigators estimated interstitial adenosine concentrations by means of an epicardial well technique (Hanley et al., 1983) and found that adenosine concentration was the same at high and low perfusion pressures within the plateau of the coronary pressure-flow curve.

The attenuation of canine myocardial reactive hyperemia by intracoronary adenosine deaminase in the present study confirms a previous report by Saito et al. (1981) and indicates that adenosine can account for at least 30% of the hyperemic flow following coronary occlusions ≥5 sec. The additional finding that adenosine deaminase had little effect on reactive hyperemia following 2-second occlusions suggests that adenosine does not play a major role in flow regulation following relatively short coronary occlusions.

There is a potential limitation to the interpretation of experiments designed to assess the contribution of a single mediator to a physiological response which is the resultant of several, interacting mediators. In such a case, blocking or destroying one mediator could elicit a compensatory increase in the contribution of another such that the response is unaltered. Accordingly, we recognize the possibility that coronary autoregulation or myocardial reactive hyperemia may result from the concerted action of adenosine and other, as yet unidentified, vasodilator mechanisms which are capable of compensating when adenosine is destroyed.

Supported by National Institutes of Health Grant HL31860-02 and The American Heart Association, Iowa Affilitate.

Preliminary reports of this work were presented at the 56th Session of the American Heart Association, November 14, 1983, and at the 68th annual meeting of the Federation of American Societies for Experimental Biology, April 1, 1984.

Address for reprints: William P. Dole, M.D., University of Iowa, Department of Internal Medicine, Cardiovascular Division, Iowa City, Iowa 52242.

Received April 20, 1984; accepted for publication January 17, 1985.

References

Andy RJ, Kornfeld R (1982) The adenosine deaminase binding protein of human skin fibroblasts is located on the cell surface. J Biol Chem **257:** 7922–7925

Arfors KE, Artwison G, Malmberg P (1971) Effect of prolonged chloralose anesthesia on acid base balance and cardiovascular function in dogs. Acta Physiol Scand **81:** 47–53

Belloni FL (1979) The local control of coronary blood flow. Cardiovasc Res **13:** 63–85

Cross CE (1964) Influence of coronary arterial pressure on coronary vasomotor tonus. Circ Res **15** (suppl 1): 87–93

Daddona PE, Kelly WN (1978) Human adenosine deaminase binding protein: Assay, purification, and properties. J Biol Chem **253:** 4617–4623

Dole WP, Bishop VS (1982) Influence of autoregulation and capacitance on diastolic coronary artery pressure-flow relationships in the dog. Circ Res **51:** 261–270

Dole WP, Montville WJ, Bishop VS (1981) Dependency of myo-

cardial reactive hyperemia on coronary artery pressure in the dog. Am J Physiol **240:** H709–H715
Driscol TE, Moir TW, Eckstein RW (1964) Autoregulation of coronary blood flow: Effect of interarterial pressure gradients. Circ Res **15:** 103–111
Feigl EO (1983) Coronary physiology. Physiol Rev **63:** 1–205
Frank JS, Langer GA (1974) The myocardial interstitium, its structure and its role in ionic exchange. J Cell Biol **60:** 586–601
Gewirtz H, Brautigan DL, Olsson RA, Brown P, Most AS (1983) Role of adenosine in the maintenance of coronary vasodilation distal to a severe coronary artery stenosis: Observations in conscious domestic swine. Circ Res **53:** 42–51
Guyton RA, McClenathan JH, Newman GE, Michaelis LL (1977) Significance of subendocardial ST segment evaluation caused by coronary stenosis in the dog. Am J Cardiol **40:** 373–380
Hanley F, Messina LM, Baer RW, Uhlig PN, Hoffman JIE (1983) Direct measurement of left ventricular interstitial adenosine. Am J Physiol **245:** H327–H335
Hanley FL, Grattan MT, Stevens MB, Hoffman JIE (1984) The role of adenosine in coronary autoregulation (abstr). Fed Proc **43:** 308
Johnson PC (1964) Review of previous studies and current theories of autoregulation. Circ Res **15** (suppl): 2–9
Katori M, Berne RM (1966) Release of adenosine from anoxic hearts: Relationship to coronary flow. Circ Res **19:** 420–425
Messina LM, Hanley FL, Hoffman JIE (1983) Comparison of left main and circumflex coronary artery pressure-flow relations (abstr). Fed Proc **42:** 1092
Mosher P, Ross J Jr, Mcfate PA, Shaw RF (1964) Control of coronary blood flow by an autoregulatory mechanism. Circ Res **14:** 250–259
Norris CP, Barnes GE, Smith EE, Granger HJ (1979) Autoregulation of superior mesenteric flow in fasted and fed dogs. Am J Physiol **237:** H174–H177
Olsson RA, Saito D, Steinhart CR (1982) Compartmentalization of adenosine pool of dog and rat hearts. Circ Res **50:** 617–626
Rouleau J, Boerboom LE, Surjadhana A, Hoffman JIE (1979) The role of autoregulation and tissue diastolic pressures in the transmural distribution of left ventricular blood flow in anesthetized dogs. Circ Res **45:** 804–815
Rubio R, Berne RM (1969) Release of adenosine by the normal myocardium in dogs and its relationship to regulation of coronary resistance. Circ Res **25:** 407–415
Rubio R, Berne RM (1975) Regulation of cornary blood flow. Prog Cardiovasc Dis **18:** 105–122
Rubio R, Wiedmeier VT, Berne RM (1974) Relationship between coronary flow and adenosine production and release. J Mol Cell Cardiol **6:** 561–566
Saito D, Steinhart CR, Nixon DG, Olsson RA (1981) Intracoronary adenosine deaminase reduces canine myocardial reactive hyperemia. Circ Res **49:** 1262–1267
Schrader J, Haddy FJ, Gerlach E (1977) Release of adenosine, imosine and hypoxanthine from the isolated guinea pig heart during hypoxia, flow-autoregulation, and reactive hyperemia. Pflugers Arch **369:** 1–6
Schrader WP, Stacy AR (1977) Purification and subunit structure of adenosine deaminase from human kidney. J Biol Chem **252:** 6409–6415
Simon LN, Bauer RJ, Tolman RL, Robins RK (1970) Calf intestine adenosine deaminase. Substrate specificity. Biochemistry **9:** 573–577
Smith FD, D'Alecy LG, Feigl EO (1974) Cannula-tip coronary blood flow transducer for use in closed-chest animals. J Appl Physiol **37:** 592–595
Snedecor GW, Cochran WG (1980) Statistical Methods. Ames, Iowa, Iowa State University Press

INDEX TERMS: Adenosine • Coronary autoregulation • Adenosine deaminase • Myocardial reactive hyperemia

Differential Effects of Antihypertensive Drug Therapy on Vascular Smooth Muscle Cell Hypertrophy, Hyperploidy, and Hyperplasia in the Spontaneously Hypertensive Rat

Gary K. Owens

From the Department of Physiology, University of Virginia, Charlottesville, Virginia

SUMMARY. The present report extends our previous studies of smooth muscle cell hypertrophy, hyperploidy, and hyperplasia in the 5-month-old spontaneously hypertensive and Wistar-Kyoto rats to include analyses of 3- and 7-month-old rats and explores the effects of antihypertensive drug treatment on the accelerated growth of vascular smooth muscle in aortas of spontaneously hypertensive vs. Wistar-Kyoto rats. Drug-treated rats were administered a combination of reserpine, hydralazine, and chlorathiazide in their drinking water, either between 3 and 5 months or between 5 and 7 months of age. Drug treatment decreased the blood pressure of spontaneously hypertensive rats to values at or below those of Wistar-Kyoto rats for both age-treatment groups. Smooth muscle growth was evaluated by morphometric analyses of aortic smooth muscle content, flow cytometric and microdensitometric measurements of the frequency of polyploid smooth muscle cells, biochemical estimates of aortic medial smooth muscle cell number, and microdensitometric measurements of individual smooth muscle cell protein content. The following results were obtained. (1) Aortic medial smooth muscle content was not significantly increased in 3-month spontaneously hypertensive compared to Wistar-Kyoto rats, indicating that aortic smooth muscle hypertrophy occurred post-3 months, as well as after blood pressure was elevated. (2) In 5-month-old spontaneously hypertensive and Wistar-Kyoto rats, medial smooth muscle hypertrophy could be accounted for by cellular hypertrophy without hyperplasia; in contrast, medial hypertrophy in 7-month-old spontaneously hypertensive rats involved both cellular hypertrophy and hyperplasia. (3) Antihypertensive treatment prevented the accelerated growth of vascular smooth muscle that occurred in spontaneously hypertensive rats via cellular hypertrophy and hyperploidy, but it did not prevent an increase in smooth muscle cell number in spontaneously hypertensive rats between 5 and 7 months of age. Furthermore, it had no effect on the parallel increases in aortic medial smooth muscle cell number that occurred in both spontaneously hypertensive and Wistar-Kyoto rats between 3 and 5 months of age. (4) Whereas drug treatment prevented accelerated development of smooth muscle cell polyploidism in spontaneously hypertensive rats, in no case (spontaneously hypertensive or Wistar-Kyoto rats) did it reverse changes in ploidy that existed at the time of initiation of drug treatment, although it did cause cellular atrophy in smooth muscle cells of each ploidy class. (5) Reductions in vascular smooth muscle content with drug treatment were due to reductions in smooth muscle cell size, not to reductions in cell number. The differential effects of blood pressure lowering on hypertrophic vs. hyperplastic smooth muscle cell growth clearly suggests that the mediating factors for these two growth processes are different. Data support the hypothesis that hypertrophic smooth muscle cell growth represents a response to increased blood pressure or wall stress, but suggest that factors other than elevated blood pressure per se are responsible for smooth muscle cell hyperplasia. **(*Circ Res 56: 525–536, 1985*)**

ACCELERATED smooth muscle cell (SMC) growth is a characteristic feature in arteries of hypertensive animals (Wolinsky, 1970; Bevan, 1976; Owens et al., 1981; Lee et al., 1983) and man (Furuyama, 1962). Whereas many investigators regarded this as an adaptive response to normalize wall stress (Wolinsky, 1970; Mulvany et al., 1978; Warshaw et al., 1980), Folkow and others (Folkow et al., 1973; Lundgren et al., 1974) suggested, based on hemodynamic evidence, that an increase in vascular smooth muscle mass in resistance vessels may itself be the cause of the hypertension. Others (Wolinsky, 1970; Bevan, 1976) attempted to relate the accelerated smooth muscle growth associated with hypertension to the increased incidence of atherosclerotic disease observed in hypertensive patients.

The studies cited above underscore the importance of understanding the cellular growth mechanisms responsible for medial hypertrophy in hypertensive vessels. Our previous studies (Owens et al.,

1981; Owens and Schwartz, 1982) and those of Olivetti et al. (1982) showed that the increased mass of smooth muscle in aortas of spontaneously hypertensive rats (SHR) or Goldblatt hypertensive rats (Owens and Schwartz, 1983) compared to normotensive controls was due to SMC hypertrophy without detectable hyperplasia. Furthermore, we demonstrated that SMC hypertrophy was accompanied by an increase in DNA ploidy with up to 40% of the SMC population in chronic hypertensive animals being polyploid. In both SHR and Goldblatt rats, the frequency of polyploid cells increased with the duration and severity of hypertension, although ploidy also increased moderately in normotensive rats with age.

The distinction between SMC growth by cellular hypertrophy and hyperploidy as opposed to cellular hyperplasia is significant for several reasons. (1) It may have important implications with regard to understanding mechanisms that initiate SMC growth in hypertension and in understanding how accelerated vascular smooth muscle (VSM) cell growth in hypertension might relate to the increased incidence of atherosclerotic disease observed in hypertensive patients (Kannel et al., 1969). (2) Whereas an increase in cell number would not be expected to result in a change in individual cell function, there is evidence suggesting that cellular hypertrophy may be associated with functional and/or structural alterations in smooth (Gabella, 1979; Berner et al., 1981) and cardiac (Alpert and Mulieri, 1982) muscle). (3) Since DNA does not turnover, changes in SMC ploidy may represent a fixed change related to establishment of a chronic hypertensive state. Finally, (4) in light of the known role of SMC proliferation in atherogenesis (Ross and Glomset, 1976), it is critical that the specific effects of drug treatment on accelerated SMC growth in hypertension be understood. Whereas previous studies have demonstrated that changes in medial smooth muscle mass could be prevented or reversed by treatment (Brecher et al., 1978; Warshaw et al., 1980; Ehrhart and Ferrario, 1981) or reversal of hypertension (Wolinsky, 1971), they have not established the specific effects of drug treatment on SMC hypertrophy, hyperploidy, and hyperplasia. Thus the principal objectives of the present investigation were: (1) to extend previous studies of SMC hypertrophy, hyperploidy, and hyperplasia in 5-month SHR and Wistar-Kyoto (WKY) rats to include analysis of animals at 3 and 5 months of age; and (2) to examine the effects of lowering of blood pressure by antihypertensive drug treatment on aortic SMC hypertrophy, hyperploidy, and hyperplasia in SHR and WKY rats.

Methods

Animals

Male SHR and WKY rats used in this study were supplied by the Core Breeding Colony (NIH Program Project HL 19242) of the University of Virginia. This colony was derived from stock provided by the National Institutes of Health, and rats have growth characteristics and pressure relationships comparable to other SHR colonies (Table 1).

Systolic blood pressure was determined in conscious rats by a photoelectric tail cuff pulse detector (IITC, Inc.). Ambient temperature was maintained at 27°C. Animals were conditioned to the restraining cages before pressure measurements were attempted. Rats were identified by number and the blood pressure technician was not aware of experimental groupings. A minimum of three blood pressure measurements were made before initiation of drug treatment experiments, and at weekly intervals thereafter.

TABLE 1
Heart Weight, Body Weight, and Heart Weight:Body Weight Ratios of Drug-Treated and Untreated (control) SHR and WKY Rats

	Body wt (g)		Heart wt (g) (dry)		Heart wt (g) × 10^{-4} / body wt (g) ratio	
Age group	SHR	WKY	SHR	WKY	SHR	WKY
7-mo control	429 ± 5 (A, B) $n = 26$	449 ± 8 (A) $n = 10$	0.371 ± 0.006 (A)	0.332 ± 0.009 (B, C)	8.77 ± 0.13 (A)	7.37 ± 0.21 (D)
5–7-mo treated	408 ± 5 (B, C, D) $n = 29$	430 ± 8 (A, B) $n = 11$	0.330 ± 0.006 (B, C)	0.304 ± 0.009 (C, D)	8.10 ± 0.12 (B, C)	7.19 ± 0.21 (D)
5-mo control	397 ± 5 (C, D) $n = 27$	417 ± 6 (B, C) $n = 18$	0.355 ± 0.006 (A, B)	0.312 ± 0.007 (C, D)	8.94 ± 0.13 (A)	7.47 ± 0.15 (D)
3–5-mo treated	388 ± 6 (D) $n = 16$	419 ± 7 (B, C) $n = 13$	0.313 ± 0.007 (C, D)	0.313 ± 0.008 (C, D)	8.06 ± 0.16 (B, C)	7.48 ± 0.18 (D)
3-mo control	341 ± 10 (E) $n = 6$	327 ± 10 (E) $n = 6$	0.292 ± 0.012 (D)	0.247 ± 0.012 (E)	8.57 ± 0.27 (A, B)	7.55 ± 0.26 (D, C)

Results are expressed as means ± SE. Sample sizes (n) for heart weights and heart weight:body weight ratios were the same as for body weight. Means with the same letter (in parentheses) are not significantly different ($P > 0.05$, analysis of variance and Duncan's multiple range test).

The following antihypertensive agents were added to the drinking water of drug-treated rats: chlorothiazide (Diuril, courtesy of Merck, Sharp and Dohme), 500 mg/liter; hydralazine (Apresoline HCl, courtesy of Ciba-Geigy), 40 mg/liter; and reserpine (Serpasil, courtesy of Ciba-Geigy), 7 mg/liter (Freis et al., 1972). Drug-containing water was changed daily. This multiple drug-treatment regimen was chosen for its efficacy in normalizing blood pressure in the SHR, although this compromised data interpretation in terms of the mechanisms of drug-action. Animals were treated from 3 to 5 months or from 5 to 7 months of age. The 3- to 5-month group was chosen primarily to see whether changes in SMC ploidy were preventable. In previous studies (Owens and Schwartz, 1982), we observed that the rate of increase in polyploidism was the greatest during this age interval. We selected the second age group to evaluate the reversibility of polyploidism, since large numbers of polyploid cells are present in 5-month-old SHR (Owens and Schwartz, 1982).

Rats were killed by CO_2 asphyxia and the chest cavity was opened. The thoracic aorta was measured at its in situ length between the diaphragm and the descending arch of the aorta. This same segment and the heart were excised, perfused with Hank's solution (GIBCO), and placed in fresh Hank's solution. Hearts were cleaned of loose connective tissue, dried for 48 hours, and weighed. After measuring the length of the thoracic aorta in vitro, we removed 2-mm segments from each end and fixed them in 2% glutaraldehyde, 1% paraformaldehyde in Hank's buffer (pH 7.40) for morphometric evaluations. An intima-medial preparation of the remaining aortic segment then was made by carefully dissecting away the adventitia and intercostal arteries (Wolinsky and Daly, 1970). The endothelium was scraped off with a piece of Teflon. Resultant medial preparations were used for subsequent isolation of vascular SMC, flow cytometric and microdensitometric measurements of SMC DNA ploidy, and evaluation of aortic medial DNA content and SMC number.

Evaluation of Aortic Hypertrophy

Alterations in aortic and smooth muscle mass (or content) were determined by morphometric evaluation of medial cross-sectional area and smooth muscle volume density (Vv_{SMC}), i.e., the fraction of tissue occupied by smooth muscle) from light and transmission electron micrographs (Owens and Schwartz, 1982). Randomly selected pairs of fixed aortic segments from animals in each experimental group were selected for morphometric evaluations. These were postfixed in osmium tetroxide for 2 hours, dehydrated, en bloc stained with 3% uranyl acetate, and embedded in Epon. Thick (1-μm) sections were cut and stained with toluidine blue for light microscopic evaluation of medial cross-sectional area. Thin sections for transmission electron microscopy were cut and post-stained with uranyl acetate and Reynolds' lead citrate. Medial cross-sectional area and vessel lumenal diameter were determined by planimetry using a Zeiss Videoplan System. Multiple sections of the segments from each end of the thoracic aorta were evaluated. The average of these values was then taken as an estimate of the mean cross-sectional area of the thoracic aorta. Vv_{SMC} was determined on electron micrographs by standard point-counting techniques (Weibel and Bolender, 1973). A minimum of 15 electron micrographs (approximately 1325 μm^2/micrograph) were analyzed from each animal. Using this sampling method, the variability between electron micrographs from individual animals (expressed as the standard error divided by the mean) was determined as 5.0%, and between animals as 3.8%. A quantitative estimate of aortic smooth muscle content (per unit length) was obtained by multiplying aortic medial cross-sectional area by Vv_{SMC}. Smooth muscle content per thoracic aorta was calculated by multiplying this value by aortic length.

Analysis of the Frequency of Polyploid and Binucleate Vascular Smooth Muscle Cells

SMC nuclei were prepared for flow cytometric evaluation of DNA ploidy as previously described (Owens et al., 1981). In brief, SMC were enzymatically dissociated from medial preparations of thoracic aortas, and nuclei were extracted and stained for DNA with diamidinophenylindole. Measurement, acquisition, and analysis of DNA content was done on a FACS IV fluorescent-activated cell sorter (Becton-Dickinson). Diploid and tetraploid compartments were estimated by an adaptation of the method of Dean and Jett (1974). The results obtained with this assay agreed closely with those obtained by Feulgen-DNA microdensitometric analysis in tissue sections (Owens and Schwartz, 1982). Thus, this flow cytometric assay provides a valid measure of the frequency of polyploid smooth muscle nuclei in the intact aorta.

Aortic SMC used for microdensitometric evaluation of SMC ploidy and protein content and for determination of the fraction of binucleate cells were enzymatically dissociated from aortic medial preparations (Owens and Schwartz, 1982). Freshly isolated cells were fixed in 6% neutral-buffered formalin for 2 hours, washed with distilled water, and cell smears were made on glass slides and air-dried. Cells were stained for Feulgen DNA determinations by the method of Fand (1970) and counterstained with the protein stain, naphthol yellow S (Gaub et al., 1975) to facilitate identification of multinucleated cells (Fig. 1) and for the cellular protein measurements described below. Microspectrophotometric measurements were made at the Feulgen DNA absorption maximum of 565 nm with a Zeiss-Zonax scanning integrating microdensitometer. Standards of chick red blood cells (2.5 pg

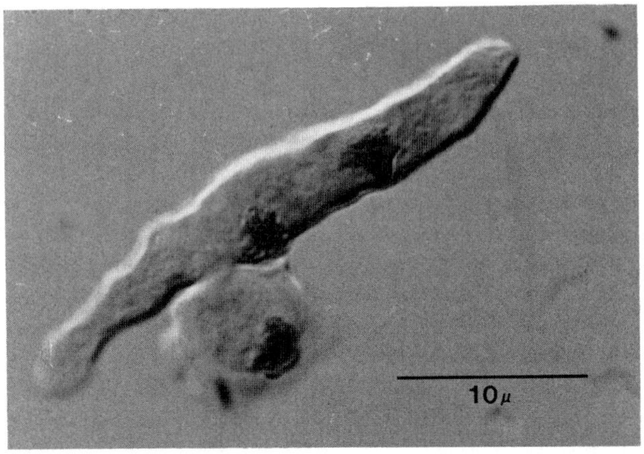

FIGURE 1. *A binucleate aortic vascular smooth muscle cell as visualized by Normarski optics. Cells were enzymatically dissociated from rat aortas, fixed, and cell smears stained for cellular protein (naphthol yellow S) and DNA (Feulgen's reagent) content as described in the text. Visualization in this manner permitted distinction between binucleate cells and closely adherent mononucleate cells. Determinations of the frequency of binucleate cells were included in calculations of the average DNA content of smooth muscle cells.*

DNA) were processed simultaneously to permit calculation of the DNA content of individual SMC nuclei. A minimum of 200 cells per animal were analyzed.

Determination of the frequency of binucleate SMC required a definitive means to assess that two nuclei were present in a single cell rather than in two adjacent cells that appear as one. This was achieved by examining Feulgen-DNA and naphthol yellow S-stained cell smears with Nomarski optics (Fig. 1). This permitted high resolution examination of cell surfaces and allowed us to resolve closely adjacent cells clearly. A random sample of at least 500 cells was evaluated from each animal.

Measurements of Smooth Muscle Cell Hypertrophy: Combined Protein-DNA Microdensitometry

Simultaneous microdensitometric determinations of the protein and DNA content of individual SMC were done to examine the relationship between SMC hypertrophy and hyperploidy, and to provide a quantitative measure of the degree of cellular hypertrophy (Owens and Schwartz, 1982). In brief, SMC smears were prepared and stained as described above. Microspectrophotometric measurements of cellular protein were made at the naphthol-yellow S absorption maximum of 445 nm, while DNA measurements were made at 565 nm. Standards of chick red blood cells (2.5 pg DNA) and cultured pig aortic endothelial cells were processed simultaneously. Cellular protein content of standards was determined by the method of Lowry et al. (1951). By comparison to standards, the DNA and protein content of individual SMC was calculated.

Determination of Medial DNA Content and Smooth Muscle Cell Number

The DNA content of thoracic aortic medial preparations was measured using the fluorometric assay of Labarca and Peigen (1980). DNA content was expressed on the basis of vessel length (in vitro) as well as on a per aorta basis. Total aortic medial DNA content was calculated as the product of vessel length × DNA/length. Aortic medial SMC number was determined by dividing medial DNA content by the average DNA content per SMC determined by a combination of Feulgen-DNA microspectrophotometry, flow cytometry, and binucleate counts.

Statistical Analyses

Data for each parameter from all of the experimental groups were first examined for differences across all groups using a one-way analysis of variance calculated from a general linear model (GLM procedure, Statistical Analysis System, SAS Institute, Inc.). These results then were incorporated in Duncan's multiple range test, which permitted the examination of individual, group-by-group differences in the context of a multiple comparison test; the pooled variability obtained by analysis of variance was used.

Least-squares methods were used for curve fitting in regression analyses. The significance of the slope, and intercept (i.e., testing the null hypothesis that they equal 0) were evaluated using a t-statistic (Mendenhall, 1979). A P level of 0.05 was considered significant.

Results

Blood Pressure and Heart Weights

Blood pressures of both SHR and WKY rats decreased to levels at or below that of untreated WKY controls ($P < 0.05$) within 7 days of initiation of antihypertensive drug treatment and were maintained at reduced levels during the remainder of the treatment period (Fig. 2). As shown, treatment between 3 and 5 months was effective in lowering blood pressure of the SHR below that of untreated WKY ($P < 0.05$), whereas treatment between 5 and 7 months lowered blood pressure of SHR to that of untreated WKY. Both the absolute fall and the percentage decrease in blood pressure were greater in treated SHR (3- to 5-month SHR, 36%, 5- to 7-month SHR, 24%) than treated WKY (3- to 5-month WKY, 16%; 5- to 7-month WKY, 10%). In addition, drug treatment decreased blood pressure in the 3- to 5-month SHR group more than in the 5- to 7-month group ($P < 0.05$).

Drug treatment had no apparent adverse effects on the animals with regard to respiratory disease, lethargy, or general appearance. Drug treatment significantly reduced heart weights and heart weight:body weight ratios of treated SHR compared to untreated SHR for both age groups studied. Similar reductions in heart weight:body weight ratios from pretreatment levels were not observed in WKY rats.

Evaluation of Aortic Smooth Muscle Content

Results of measurements of aortic medial cross-sectional area, smooth muscle volume density (Vv_{SMC}, i.e., fraction of aortic media occupied by smooth muscle), and aortic smooth muscle content are presented in Table 2. In addition, smooth muscle content data (per thoracic aorta) are also presented in Figure 3 to facilitate intergroup comparisons.

Results showed that aortic medial cross-sectional

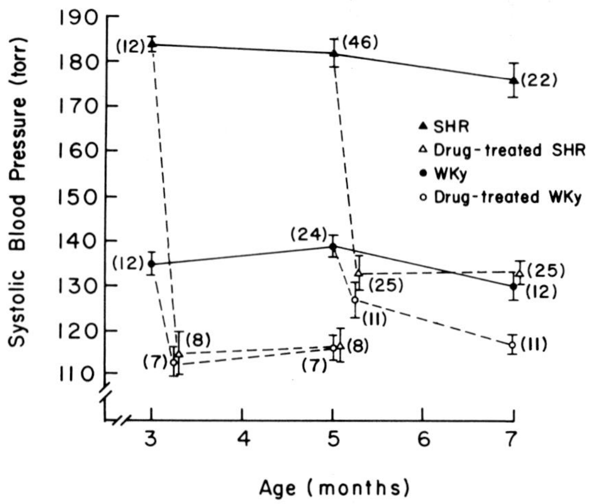

FIGURE 2. *Systolic blood pressure in drug-treated and untreated SHR and WKY rats as determined by a tail-cuff method in conscious rats. Drug-treated animals were administered a combination of reserpine, hydralazine, and chlorothiazide in their drinking water, as described in the text. Each data point represents the mean value (±SE) at each respective time point. The values in parentheses indicate the number of animals measured (n). The dotted lines connect blood pressures of drug-treated groups with those of the appropriate pretreatment groups.*

TABLE 2

Morphometric Evaluation of Medial Smooth Muscle Content, Cross-Sectional Area, and Smooth Muscle Volume Density ($V_{V_{smc}}$) in Thoracic Aortas of Drug-Treated (tx) and Untreated SHR and WKY Rats

Group	Aortic-medial cross-sectional area (mm^2)	Smooth muscle Vv_{smc}	Smooth muscle content (mm^3) / mm aortic length	Smooth muscle content (mm^3) / thoracic aorta
7-mo SHR $n = 6$	0.653 ± 0.033 (A)	0.345 ± 0.010 (A, B)	0.225 ± 0.012 (A)	8.16 ± 0.51 (A)
5–7-mo SHR_{tx} $n = 6$	0.580 ± 0.013 (B)	0.214 ± 0.007 (D)	0.125 ± 0.007 (D, E)	4.08 ± 0.25 (B, C, D, E)
5-mo SHR $n = 6$	0.630 ± 0.027 (A, B)	0.369 ± 0.018 (A)	0.228 ± 0.016 (A)	7.50 ± 0.62 (A)
3–5-mo SRH_{tx} $n = 6$	0.491 ± 0.006 (C)	0.351 ± 0.005 (A, B)	0.171 ± 0.003 (B)	5.27 ± 0.22 (B)
3-mo SHR $n = 5$	0.508 ± 0.006 (C)	0.285 ± 0.014 (C)	0.144 ± 0.007 (B, C, D)	3.99 ± 0.20 (C, D, E)
7-mo WKY $n = 5$	0.518 ± 0.010 (C)	0.320 ± 0.011 (B, C)	0.164 ± 0.002 (B, C)	5.09 ± 0.04 (B, C)
5–7-mo WKY_{tx} $n = 5$	0.425 ± 0.021 (D)	0.248 ± 0.012 (D)	0.106 ± 0.011 (E)	3.21 ± 0.21 (E)
5-mo WKY $n = 6$	0.426 ± 0.012 (D)	0.339 ± 0.015 (A, B)	0.145 ± 0.010 (B, C, D)	4.46 ± 0.37 (B, C, D)
3–5-mo WKY_{tx} $n = 6$	0.397 ± 0.008 (D)	0.344 ± 0.012 (A, B)	0.136 ± 0.004 (C, D, E)	4.28 ± 0.24 (B, C, D, E)
3-mo WKY $n = 5$	0.398 ± 0.024 (D)	0.313 ± 0.012 (B, C)	0.125 ± 0.011 (D, E)	3.48 ± 0.34 (D, E)

Results are expressed as means ± SE. Means with the same letter (in parentheses) are not significantly different (P >0.05, analysis of variance and Duncan's multiple range test).

area and smooth muscle content were significantly increased ($P < 0.001$) in SHR compared to WKY at 5 and 7 months of age. However, whereas cross-sectional area was significantly increased in SHR at

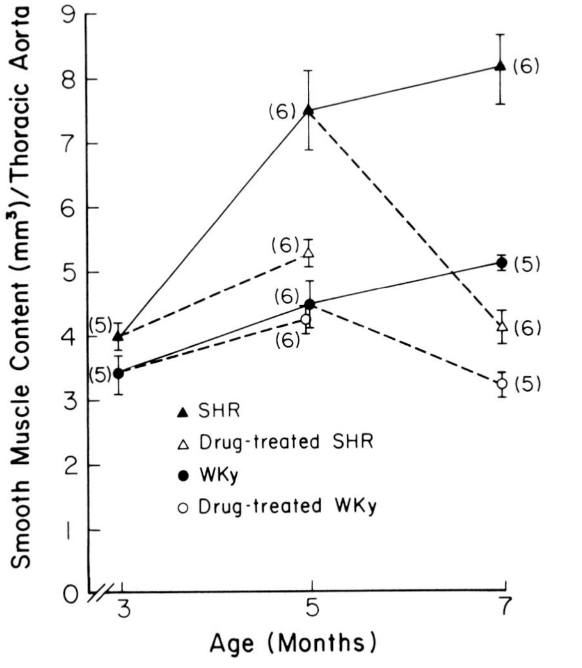

FIGURE 3. *Results of morphometric analyses of aortic smooth muscle content (mm³/thoracic aorta) in drug-treated and untreated SHR and WKY rats. Dotted lines indicate when drug-treatment was initiated. Means ± SE are shown. Values in parentheses indicate the number of vessels (animals) evaluated (n).*

3 months; smooth muscle content was not. In untreated SHR, there was a 88% increase in smooth muscle content (Fig. 3) between 3 and 5 months of age. Drug treatment of SHR during this interval significantly reduced this increase, although smooth muscle content and aortic medial cross-sectional area were still significantly greater ($P < 0.05$) than in WKY. The cellular fraction of the aortic media (i.e., $V_{V_{SMC}}$) increased significantly ($P < 0.05$) between 3 and 5 months of age in both treated and untreated SHR but not in WKY. The fact that both $V_{V_{SMC}}$ and smooth muscle content increased in treated SHR, but cross-sectional area remained unchanged from pretreatment values, implies that drug-treatment was more effective in decreasing extracellular volume than smooth muscle content during this interval. This was directly confirmed by evaluating extracellular aortic volume [i.e. $(1-V_{V_{SMC}})$ times the medial cross-sectional area, data not shown].

Whereas drug-treatment of rats between 3 and 5 months was effective in reducing only those increases in smooth muscle content that normally occur during this interval, treatment of SHR and WKY from 5 to 7 months old reduced aortic smooth muscle content below that of 5-month (pretreated) SHR or WKY ($P < 0.01$). The decrease in $V_{V_{SMC}}$ in 7-month treated SHR and WKY indicates that drug treatment during this age interval was more effective in reducing the cellular fraction of the wall than the extracellular fraction.

In summary, morphometric results showed: (1) aortic SM content was not increased in 3-month

SHR compared to WKY but was increased by 68% and 60%, respectively, in 5-month and 7-month SHR compared to age-matched WKY; (2) drug treatment in rats between 3 and 5 months old effectively reduced increases in smooth muscle content that normally occur in SHR during this interval, but did not reduce smooth muscle content below pretreatment levels in either SHR or WKY; (3) drug treatment of rats between 5 and 7 months significantly reduced aortic smooth muscle content but not extracellular volume below pretreatment levels in both SHR and WKY rats.

Smooth Muscle Cell Polyploidism

As observed previously (Owens et al., 1981; Owens and Schwartz, 1982), the frequency of tetraploid aortic SMC nuclei was significantly ($P < 0.01$) greater in SHR than WKY for all age groups studied (Fig. 4). The frequency of tetraploidy increased by more than 200% in SHR between 3 and 5 months old, and by 75% in WKY rats. In addition, tetraploidy also increased significantly in SHR between 5 and 7 months of age, $P < 0.05$) but not in WKY. Antihypertensive drug-treatment prevented further increases in tetraploidy in SHR for both age groups studied ($P < 0.001$), but in no case did it reduce tetraploidy below pretreatment levels. In contrast, drug treatment had no significant effect on the frequency of tetraploid SMC nuclei in WKY rats for either treatment interval, and, thus, did not prevent the increase in ploidy that occurred between 3 and 5 months in this group. Antihypertensive treatment thus appeared to prevent, but not reverse, changes in ploidy that occur in SHR. In addition, treatment did not prevent normal age-associated increases in ploidy in 3- and 5-month-old normotensive WKY rats.

Results of measurements of the frequency of octaploid and binucleate SMC are presented in Table 3. Cells were assessed by microdensitometric analysis of Feulgen-DNA-naphthol yellow S-stained cell smears. Due to time restraints on the number of cells that could reasonably be measured (i.e., measurements take about 1 minute per cell), statistical comparisons between groups with very low frequencies of octaploid and binucleate cells were compromised by high sample variances. Despite these limitations, significant differences were observed between several experimental groups. Binucleate cells and octaploid cells were more frequent in SHR than age-matched WKY rats, and their frequency appeared to increase with age in SHR. No significant differences in the frequency of octaploid or binucleate cells were evident in any of the WKY groups, although sample variances were high. Octaploid cells were extremely rare in WKY rats with only two cells detected in approximately 5800 cells measured. Drug treatment resulted in a significant decrease in the fraction of binucleate cells in 3- to 5-month treated SHR compared to 5-month untreated SHR, but appeared to have no effect in the 5- to 7-month treated group. Differences in the frequency of octaploid cells between treated and untreated SHR were not statistically significant, although mean frequencies for both the 3- to 5-month and 5- to 7-month treated SHR groups were lower than the corresponding untreated SHR groups.

Based on Feulgen-DNA microdensitometric measurements of binucleate and octaploid cells (Table 3) and flow cytometric evaluations of the frequency of tetraploid nuclei (Fig. 4) the average DNA content per SMC was calculated for animals from each experimental group for subsequent cell number calculations (Table 3). Average DNA per cell was greater in all SHR groups than in their corresponding age-matched, treatment-matched WKY controls.

Analysis of Aortic Medial DNA Content and Smooth Muscle Cell Number

To determine whether differences in aortic smooth muscle content between experimental groups (Table 2; Fig. 3) were due to changes in cell number or cell size, aortic medial DNA content and SMC number were analyzed for each experimental group (Table 3). Cell number data are also presented in Figure 5 to facilitate intergroup comparisons. As observed in previous studies (Owens et al., 1981; Owens and Schwartz, 1982), no detectable differences in cell number were observed between SHR and WKY rats at 5 months, even though smooth muscle content was increased in SHR by 68% ($P < 0.001$; Fig. 3). These results thus confirm previous observations that the hypertrophy of smooth muscle in 5-month-old SHR was due to cellular hypertrophy without detectable hyperplasia. In 3-month SHR, DNA content was increased, but no differences in cell number or smooth muscle content (Fig. 3) were apparent, thus indicating that neither SMC hypertrophy nor hyperplasia was detectable at this age. In contrast, SMC number was significantly increased in 7-month SHR, compared both to WKY and to 5-month SHR, demonstrating that SMC hyperplasia contributed to the medial smooth muscle hypertrophy at this age. However, observations that the increase in cell number (33%) could account for only a portion of the increase in smooth muscle content (60%) in SHR vs. WKY at this age suggests that cellular hypertrophy was present as well.

Drug-treatment of SHR did not prevent the increase in cell number between 5 and 7 months, although it clearly prevented further development of polyploidism (Fig. 4) and decreased aortic smooth muscle content (Fig. 3). The fact that smooth muscle content was decreased in 7-month treated SHR despite an increase in cell number means that individual cell size must have been decreased (i.e., cellular atrophy). This was confirmed directly by microdensitometric measurements of cellular protein content (Fig. 6). These analyses showed that the mean cellular protein content of SMC from treated 7-month-old SHR was reduced by 23% and 30%, respectively, compared to the untreated 5- and 7-month SHR

TABLE 3

Aortic Medial DNA Content, Smooth Muscle Cell Number, and the Frequency of Octaploid and Binucleate Smooth Muscle Cells in Drug-Treated (tx) and Untreated SHR and WKY Rats

Group	% Binucleate SMC	% Octaploid SMC	Average* DNA (pg) cell	DNA (μg) / cm aortic media	SMC no. / cm aortic media × 10^6	SMC no. / thoracic aorta × 10^6
7-mo SHR $n = 13$	2.49±0.27 (A)	1.03±0.19 (A)	8.54±0.11 (A)	19.70±0.51 (A)	2.23±0.06 (A)	7.67±0.25 (A)
5–7-mo SHR_{tx} $n = 13$	2.55±0.25 (A)	0.78±0.13 (A, B)	8.22±0.09 (B)	18.29±0.41 (A, B)	2.24±0.05 (A)	6.92±0.24 (A)
5-mo SHR $n = 12$	1.22±0.16 (B)	0.43±0.09 (B, C, D)	8.02±0.05 (B)	16.58±0.58 (B, C)	2.07±0.07 (B)	6.44±0.21 (B, C)
3–5-mo SHR_{tx} $n = 8$	0.47±0.12 (C)	0.19±0.13 (C, D)	7.70±0.11 (C)	16.13±0.30 (C, D)	2.09±0.04 (A, B)	6.11±0.35 (B, C)
3-mo SHR $n = 6$	0.32±0.05 (C)	0.52±0.14 (B, C)	7.32±0.03 (D)	12.97±0.38 (E)	1.77±0.05 (C, D)	4.92±0.41 (D, E)
7-mo WKY $n = 8$	0.44±0.13 (C)	0 (D)	7.44±0.08 (C, D)	13.83±0.50 (E)	1.86±0.07 (B, C)	5.75±0.38 (C, D)
5–7-mo WKY_{tx} $n = 7$	0.29±0.13 (C)	0 (D)	7.37±0.09 (D)	13.11±0.59 (E)	1.78±0.08 (C, D)	5.42±0.45 (C, D)
5-mo WKY $n = 10$	0.07±0.04 (C)	0 (D)	7.25±0.06 (D)	13.78±0.82 (E)	1.90±0.11 (B, C)	5.75±0.35 (C, D)
3–5-mo WKY_{tx} $n = 6$	0.23±0.11 (C)	0.09±0.09 (C, D)	7.29±0.07 (D)	14.17±0.71 (D, E)	1.94±0.10 (B, C)	5.53±0.41 (C, D)
3-mo WKY $n = 6$	0.04±0.04 (C)	0.07±0.07 (C, D)	6.94±0.02 (E)	10.58±0.43 (F)	1.52±0.06 (D)	4.25±0.41 (E)

Results are expressed as means ± SE. Means with the same letter (in parentheses) are not significantly different ($P > 0.05$, analysis of variance and Duncan's multiple range test).

* Calculations based on flow microflorometric and microdensitometric analyses, assuming 6.64 pg DNA per diploid nucleus.

groups. Drug treatment produced similar effects in WKY rats treated during this interval. Smooth muscle content was reduced by 37% ($P < 0.05$; Fig. 3) in treated vs. untreated 7-month WKY, whereas cell number was unchanged, thus indicating that reductions in individual cell size occurred in treated WKY rats as well.

Whereas cell number was not different between

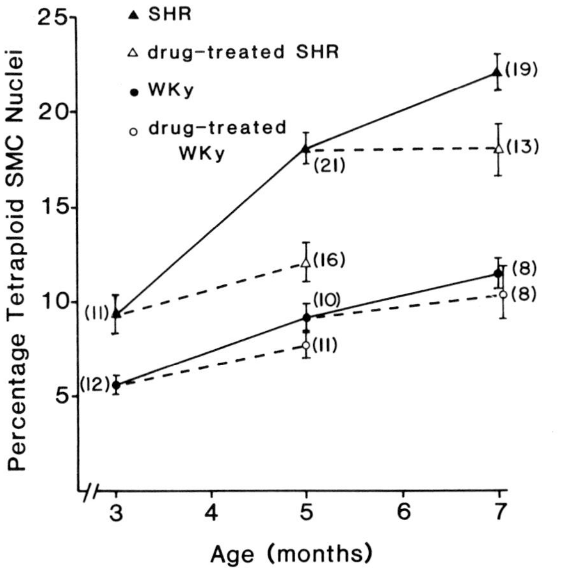

FIGURE 4. *Frequency of tetraploid aortic smooth muscle cell (SMC) nuclei in treated and untreated SHR and WKY rats as determined by flow microfluorimetric analysis of diamidinophenylindole-stained nuclei. Dotted lines indicate when antihypertensive drug-treatment was initiated. The values in parentheses indicate the number of animals evaluated (n).*

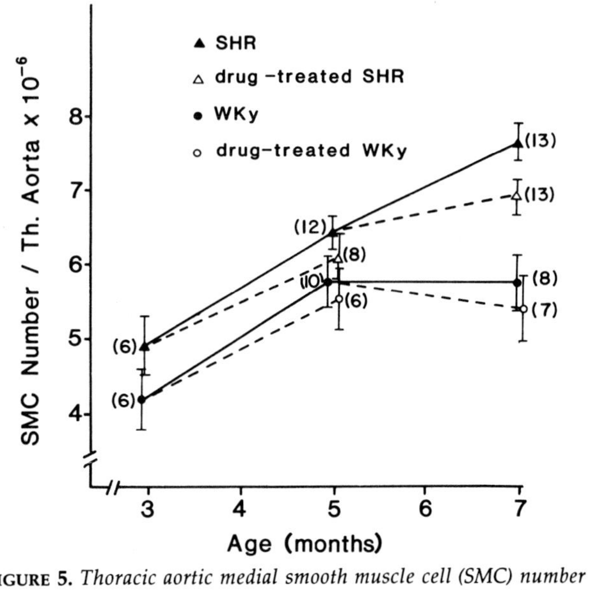

FIGURE 5. *Thoracic aortic medial smooth muscle cell (SMC) number of drug-treated and untreated SHR and WKY rats. SMC number was calculated by dividing the DNA content of thoracic aortic medial preparations by the average DNA content of SMC determined by flow microfluorimetric and microdensitometric evaluation of cellular DNA content. Dotted lines indicate when antihypertensive drug treatment was initiated. The results of statistical comparisons between groups are presented in Table 2. The number of animals evaluated (n) is given in parentheses.*

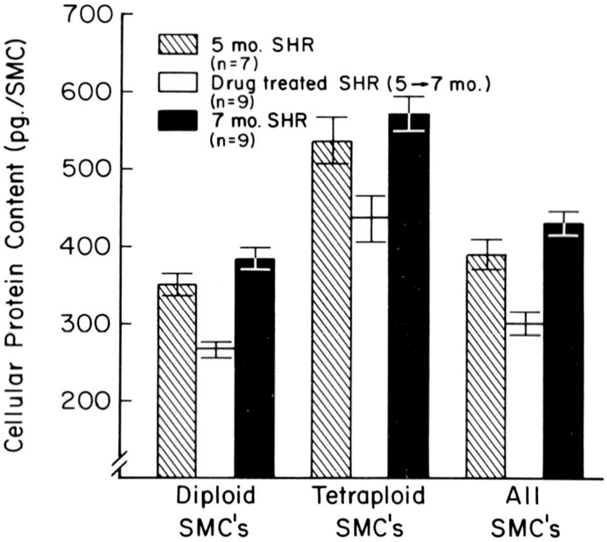

FIGURE 6. *Summary of cytospectrophotometric determinations of the protein and DNA content of individual aortic smooth muscle cells from drug-treated and untreated SHR. Protein contents (mean ± SE) of diploid and tetraploid smooth muscle cells are shown as well as the mean cellular protein content of randomly selected cells (i.e., all cells). At least 40 cells from each rat were analyzed. Results confirm previous observations showing an increase in cellular protein content in tetraploid vs. diploid cells, and show that drug treatment causes significant reductions in cell mass in each respective ploidy class.*

SHR and WKY rats at either 3 or 5 months of age, there were parallel increases in cell number in both strains during this interval (Table 3; Fig. 5). As observed in 5 - to 7-month treated SHR, drug treatment of SHR and WKY between 3 and 5 months did not prevent these increases in cell number, although it did inhibit increases in aortic smooth muscle content (Fig. 3) and the frequency of tetraploid cells (Fig. 4) that occurred in untreated SHR during this interval. These data show that the effectiveness of antihypertensive treatment in reducing aortic smooth muscle hypertrophy in SHR between 3 and 5 months of age was due to inhibition of cellular hypertrophy and hyperploidy, and not to inhibition of cellular hyperplasia.

Interrelationship between Blood Pressure, Animal Age, and Smooth Muscle Cell Hyperploidy

To explore further the possible relationship between blood pressure and development of tetraploidy, a linear regression analyses was done for these factors in untreated SHR and WKY rats. As observed previously (Owens and Schwartz, 1982), a significant linear relationship was observed ($r^2 = 0.36$, $P < 0.001$, $n = 65$), between the frequency of tetraploid cells and blood pressure. However, the r^2 value was relatively low, and data from the 3-month SHR group clearly did not fit this relationship, since blood pressure had peaked in these animals but ploidy levels had not. When data from this group were eliminated from the regression analysis, the correlation coefficient increased substantially ($r^2 = 0.60$, $P < 0.001$, $n = 59$). It is also important to note that, whereas tetraploidy increased by nearly 300% in SHR between 3 and 7 months old (Fig. 4), blood pressure did not change during this interval (Fig. 2). These observations emphasize the importance of an age-pressure (or time-pressure) component, and show that blood-pressure appears to peak much sooner than does the polyploid or hypertrophic response. This can be seen diagrammatically by comparing blood pressure data (Fig. 2) with the time-course of changes in ploidy (Fig. 4) and smooth muscle hypertrophy (Fig. 3). The relationship between these factors was explored further by multiple regression analysis between the frequency of tetraploid SMC, animal age, and systolic blood pressure. The multiple coefficient of determination (i.e., r^2) for this relationship in all untreated SHR and WKY rats was 0.77. The r^2 value for this same relationship for untreated SHR alone was 0.66. In contrast, this same analyses showed that age ($P < 0.001$) but not blood pressure ($P = 0.09$) was significantly related to the frequency of tetraploid cells in WKY.

Discussion

In previous studies (Owens et al., 1981; Owens and Schwartz, 1982), we demonstrated that the increased mass of smooth muscle in aortas of 5-month SHR compared to normotensive WKY rats was due to SMC hypertrophy not hyperplasia, and that cellular hypertrophy was accompanied by an increase in DNA ploidy. The studies presented here are the first, to my knowledge, to examine the effects of antihypertensive drug treatment on vascular SMC hypertrophy and hyperploidy in the SHR. Results showed that antihypertensive drug treatment of SHR for 2 months with a combination of reserpine, hydralazine, and chlorothiazide prevented further increases in polyploidism that normally occur in SHR with age, but did not reverse changes in ploidy that had already occurred. Likewise, drug treatment did not decrease ploidy levels in WKY rats below pretreatment levels in either the 3- to 5-month or 5- to 7-month treatment groups, suggesting that there were no strain differences in the response of tetraploid cells to drug treatment. However, in contrast to observations in SHR, treatment did not prevent the increase in tetraploidy that occurred in WKY rats between 3 and 5 months of age. Thus, antihypertensive treatment prevented the accelerated development of polyploidism associated with hypertension, but did not prevent increases in polyploidism that occur with age in normotensive rats.

Studies presented here confirm previous reports (Wolinsky, 1971; Warshaw et al., 1980; Ehrhart and Ferrario, 1981) demonstrating that increases in aortic medial smooth muscle mass can be prevented or reversed by antihypertensive drug treatment. The new observations in this study relate to the cellular mechanisms responsible for these reductions. The data presented here clearly demonstrated that reductions in medial smooth muscle content with drug treatment occurred without a corresponding decrease in SMC number; i.e., drug treatment prevented or reversed cellular hypertrophy but not cellular hyperplasia. This conclusion was independently confirmed in the 5- to 7-month SHR groups where microdensitometric analyses showed significant reductions in mean cellular protein content in cells from each respective ploidy class in drug-treated rats. Thus, whereas changes in cellular mass were decreased by decreasing blood pressure by antihypertensive treatment, changes in cellular ploidy were not.

The potential significance of a fixed change in SMC ploidy in the etiology of hypertension remains to be determined. Very little is known concerning possible functional alterations which may be associated with development of SMC polyploidism, although myocardial hypertrophy, which is also characterized by development of polyploidism (Sandriter and Scomazzoni, 1964; Brodsky and Uryvaeva, 1977) is associated with profound alterations in myosin isozymes and contractile properties (Alpert and Mulieri, 1982). Since ultimate control of cell function resides at the level of DNA, it is interesting to speculate that some of the functional alterations reported for hypertensive smooth muscle (Holloway and Bohr, 1973; Jones, 1973; Lais and Brody, 1975) may be related to development of SMC hyperploidy. The fixed change in ploidy observed in this study may relate to observations that treatment or reversal of chronic hypertension was not totally effective in reversing functional vascular alterations (Hamilton, 1975; Lundgren and Weiss, 1979).

It is important to note, however, that the studies presented here have been done exclusively in large vessels. Whereas studies have demonstrated that hypertrophy of smooth muscle occurs in resistance vessels of SHR (Warshaw et al., 1980; Lee et al., 1983), further studies are needed to determine the role of polyploidism in these vessels. Polyploid cells are present in mesenteric arterioles (unpublished observations), but we have not as yet determined whether their frequency is increased in hypertension. Furthermore, it is important to note that Lee et al. (1983) have presented morphometric evidence suggesting that smooth muscle cell hyperplasia, not hypertrophy, is principally responsible for medial hypertrophy in mesenteric arterioles of SHR. Their data also showed that hypertrophy of smooth muscle was present in small mesenteric arteries and arterioles but not in the superior mesenteric artery of 10- to 12-week-old SHR. Similarly, our data showed no hypertrophy of smooth muscle in aortas of 3-month-old SHR. Taken together, these data suggest the possibility that both the time course and nature of smooth muscle growth may differ between large and small vessels.

The effects of antihypertensive drug treatment on the smooth muscle and extracellular components of the aorta varied, depending on when rats were treated. For example, drug treatment of SHR from 3 to 5 months old was effective in reducing the extracellular volume of the aorta below pretreatment levels, but had no effect on extracellular volume in animals treated when 5–7 months old. Although we cannot directly compare data, the failure of drug treatment to decrease extracellular volume in the older treatment group in this study is consistent with studies by Wolinsky (1971) and others (Ehrhart and Ferrario, 1981), showing that increases in collagen and elastin content during hypertension were not readily reversed by treatment or reversal of hypertension. It is possible that loss of water or mucopolysaccharides may accout for all or part of the extracellular reductions observed in the younger treatment group, as observed by Tobian et al. (1969) in renovascular hypertension. Why drug treatment was more effective in decreasing aortic smooth muscle content in the older rats than in younger ones is not clear, especially since the fractional blood pressure reduction was greater in the younger group. However, if wall stress is an important determinant of vessel hypertrophy (Wolinsky, 1970), one possibility is that the stiffer elastic components in aortas of older animals (Yin et al., 1983) may absorb a greater proportion of the total wall stress than in the younger group, and thereby decrease the load on the SMC.

Results of the present investigation showing a 68% increase in smooth muscle content, but no significant difference in SMC number in 5-month-old SHR compared to WKY, have confirmed our previous findings (Owens and Schwartz, 1982) demonstrating that differences in aortic smooth muscle mass at this age were due to cellular hypertrophy without detectable hyperplasia. However, in 3-month SHR and WKY, no significant differences in either smooth muscle content or cell number were found, indicating that significant hypertrophic growth has not yet occurred at this age despite the fact that SHR already had established hypertension. An additional observation in these studies was that, although aortic medial SMC number was not different between SHR and WKY rats at either 3 or 5 months, cell number did increase in parallel in both strains during this age interval. These results thus extend previous observations by Olivetti et al. (1982), which showed that aortic SMC number increased in parallel in SHR and WKY between birth and 45 days of age. A somewhat surprising observation in these studies was that aortic medial SMC number continued to increase in SHR but not WKY that were between 5 and 7 months old (Fig. 5). Thus, chronic hypertension in SHR did appear to be associated with aortic SMC hyperplasia. Although no significant differences in thoracic aortic SMC number were observed between SHR and WKY rats at either 3 or 5 months, mean values were higher in SHR at both ages. Thus, it is possible that a small increase in aortic SMC number was present at all ages that was not detectable with the methods employed in these studies. However, our data clearly indicate that the major cellular growth response contributing to aortic medial hypertrophy in SHR was SMC hypertrophy, not hyperplasia.

Whereas other investigators have reported that SMC hyperplasia occurs in aortas of SHR (Jurukova et al., 1976; Seidel, 1979), previous studies were based on methods that did not clearly distinguish hypertrophic from hyperplastic cell growth. This distinction may be particularly important in understanding the relationship between accelerated atherogenesis and hypertension, since intimal smooth muscle growth in atherosclerosis occurs by cellular proliferation, not cellular hypertrophy and hyperploidy (Barrett et al., 1983; Thomas and Kim, 1983; Orekhov et al., 1983). Furthermore, our observation that anithypertensive drug treatment did not prevent the proliferation of SMC in SHR between 5 and 7 months old, despite normalization of blood pressure, may have important implications for assessing the beneficial effects of antihypertensive drug therapy on progression of cardiovascular disease (e.g., is effective control of blood pressure alone sufficient in assessing antihypertensive regimens?). Results in clinical studies have shown that, whereas antihypertensive treatment of humans is extremely effective in reducing mortality from "pressure-related" complications, such as congestive heart failure or stroke, treatment is not nearly as effective in reducing the incidence of atherosclerotic complications, particularly coronary artery disease (Mathisen et al., 1969; Kannel et al., 1984). Thus, it has remained unclear whether the progression of cardiovascular atherosclerosis is retarded or prevented by reduction of blood pressure to levels near normal.

Whereas drug treatment of SHR between 5 and 7 months old did not prevent SMC proliferation, it did prevent further development of SMC polyploidism and decreased SMC hypertrophy. Likewise, drug treatment had no effect on the parallel increases in aortic SMC number that occurred in both SHR and WKY rats between 3 and 5 months old, although it also prevented development of SMC hypertrophy and hyperploidy in SHR during this interval. The differential effects of drug treatment on SMC hypertrophy and hyperploidy, compared to cellular hyperplasia, clearly suggest that control of these growth processes is mediated by different factors. Furthermore, these observations, and findings that development of smooth muscle hypertrophy and hyperploidy occurred primarily after blood pressure had peaked (i.e., post 3 months) support the hypothesis that hypertrophic, but not hyperplastic, SMC growth represents a response to increased blood pressure or wall stress. Some caution must be used in interpreting drug treatment studies, however, since they did not distinguish whether the effects of drugs on hypertrophic SMC growth were the direct result of lowering of blood pressure or of some specific effect of one or more of the drugs on cellular growth. The latter seems unlikely, given the similarity of our findings to those of Wolinsky (1971), who demonstrated reversal of aortic medial hypertrophy in experimental renal hypertension following removal of renal artery clips, and Ehrhart and Ferrario (1981) who found that methyldopa was also effective in decreasing aortic medial hypertrophy. Data presented in this and previous studies (Owens and Schwartz, 1982, 1983) which showed a high degree of correlation between blood pressure, and the frequency of tetraploid smooth muscle cells in untreated SHR and WKY rats, are also consistent with a role for increased wall stress or blood pressure in mediation of hypertrophic cellular growth. However, our observations that large changes in aortic smooth muscle content, smooth muscle cell protein content, and polyploidism occur after blood pressure has plateaued, and that there is a high degree of correlation between age, blood pressure, and polyploidism emphasize the importance of a time-pressure component and suggest that both the severity and duration of hypertension may be important determinants of hypertrophic SMC growth.

The data presented here provide no direct evidence as to the nature of the stimulus for SMC proliferation in SHR between 5 and 7 months old. The finding that proliferation occurred despite lowering of blood pressure suggests that hyperplasia was not a direct response to increased blood pressure. However, the data do not exclude the possibility of mediation by hypertension-induced changes that occurred prior to initiation of drug treatment. One possibility is that changes in endothelial function (e.g., increased permeability) (Schwartz, 1977) that occurred before drug treatment may have persisted during a significant portion of the drug treatment period and resulted in accelerated SMC growth. An alternative possibility is that the increased SMC replication in SHR was mediated by factors independent of increased blood pressure. Studies by Bevan et al. (1975) and Rorive et al. (1980) have implicated a role for the sympathetic nervous system in mediation of SMC growth in hypertension. Whereas increased sympathetic output is a characteristic feature of the SHR (Trippodo and Frolich, 1981), our observations in this study that detectable aortic hyperplasia was not apparent in SHR before 7 months (Fig. 5, Table 2), and that treatment with a three-drug regimen including reserpine did not inhibit SMC proliferation, argue against a direct role for the sympathetic nervous system in the hyperplastic growth response. However, we cannot be certain that the treatment regimen utilized here was effective in inhibiting sympathetic function in the aorta. Finally, it should be noted that previous studies that have explored the possible mediating factors for accelerated SMC growth in hypertension have not clearly distinguished hyperplastic from hypertrophic growth. Data presented in this study showing differential effects of blood pressure lowering on cellular hypertrophy, hyperploidy, and hyperplasia clearly suggest that, in order to identify the mechanisms initiating SMC growth in hypertension, it is necessary to know the cellular nature of that growth.

I would like to thank Mary McCanna, Diane Singer, Susan Ramos and Larry Hawkey for their excellent technical assistance in performing these studies; Betty Ferguson for typing the manuscript; Drs. Brian Duling and Richard Murphy for their critical evaluation of the manuscript; and Dr. Donald Kaiser for his help in performing statistical analyses.

Supported by Grants R01 HL-29960 and P01 HL-19242 from the National Institutes of Health.

Address for reprints: Dr. Gary K. Owens, Department of Physiology, Box 449, School of Medicine, University of Virginia, Charlottesville, Virginia 22908.

Received December 12, 1983; accepted for publication January 10, 1985.

References

Alpert NR, Mulieri RA (1982) Heat, mechanics, and myosin ATPase in normal and hypertrophied heart muscle. Fed Proc **41:** 192–198

Barrett TB, Sampson P, Owens GK, Schwartz SM, Benditt EP (1983) Polyploid nuclei in human artery wall smooth muscle cells. Proc Natl Acad Sci USA **80:** 882–885

Berner PF, Somlyo AV, Somlyo AP (1981) Hypertrophy-induced increases of interediate filaments in vascular smooth muscle, J Cell Biol **88:** 96–101

Bevan RD (1976) An autoradiographic and pathological study of cellular proliferation in rabbit arteries correlated with an increase in arterial pressure. Blood Vessels **13:** 100–128

Bevan RD, Purdy RE, Su C, Bevan JA (1975) Evidence for an increase in adrenergic nerve function in blood vessels from experimental hypertensive rabbits. Circ Res **37:** 503–508

Brecher P, Chan CT, Franzblau C, Faris B, Chobanian AV (1978) Effects of hypertension and its reversal on aortic metabolism in the rat. Circ Res **43:** 561–569

Brodsky WY, Uryvaeva I (1977) Cell polyploidy: Its relation to tissue growth and function. Int Rev Cytol **50:** 275–332

Dean PN, Jett NH (1974) Mathematical analysis of DNA distributions derived from flow microfluorimetry. J Cell Biol **60:** 523–532

Ehrhart LA, Ferrario CM (1981) Collagen metabolism and reversal of aortic medial hypertrophy in spontaneously hypertensive rats treated with methyldopa. Hypertension **3:** 479–484

Fand SB (1970) Environmental conditions for optimal Feulgen hydrolysis. *In* Introduction to Quantitative Cytochemistry-II, edited by GL Wied, GF Bahr. New York, Academic Press, pp 209–211

Folkow B, Hallback M, Lundgren R, Sivertsson R, Weiss L (1973) Importance of adaptive changes in vascular design for establishment of primary hypertension, studied in man and in spontaneously hypertensive rats. Circ Res **32/33** (suppl I): 2–16

Freis ED, Ragan D, Pillsbury H, Mathews M (1972) Alteration in the course of hypertension in the spontaneously hypertensive rat. Circ Res **41:** 1–7

Furuyama M (1962) Histometrical investigations of arteries in reference to arterial hypertension. Tohoku J Exp Med **76:** 388–414

Gabella G (1979) Hypertrophic smooth muscle. IV. Myofilaments, intermediate filaments, and some mechanical properties. Cell Tissue Res **201:** 277–288

Gaub J, Auer G, Zetterberg A (1975) Quantitative cytochemical aspects of a combined feulgen-naphthol yellow staining procedure for the simultaneous determination of nuclear and cytoplasmic proteins and DNA in mammalian cells. Exp Cell Res **92:** 323–332

Hamilton TC (1975) Influence of antihypertensive drug treatment on vascular reactivity in spontaneously hypertensive rats. Br J Pharmacol **54:** 429–436

Holloway ET, Bohr DF (1973) Reactivity of vascular smooth muscle in hypertensive rats. Circ Res **23:** 678–685

Jones AW (1973) Altered ion transport in vascular smooth muscle from spontaneously hypertensive rats: Influences of aldosterone, norepinephrine and angiotensin. Circ Res **33:** 563–572

Jurukova Z, Hadjisky P, Renais J, Scebat L (1976) Aortic smooth muscle cells reaction in rat spontaneous hypertension. Pathol Europ **11:** 105–115

Kannel WB, Schwartz MJ, McNamar PM (1969) Blood pressure and the risk of coronary heart disease: The Framingham study. Dis Chest **56:** 43–52

Kannel WB, Doyle JT, Ostfield AM, Jenkins CD, Kuller L, Podell RN, Stamler J (1984) Optimal resources for primary prevention of atherosclerotic diseases. Circulation **70:** 157A–205A

Labarca C, Piegen K (1980) A simple, rapid, and sensitive DNA assay procedure. Anal Biochem **102:** 344–352

Lais LT, Brody MJ (1975) Mechanism of vascular hyper-responsiveness in the spontaneously hypertensive rat. Circ Res **36/37** (suppl I): 216–222

Lee RM, Forrest JB, Garfield RE, Daniel E (1983) Ultrastructural changes in mesenteric arteries from spontaneously hypertensive rats. Blood Vessels **20:** 72–91

Lowry OH, Rosebrough NJ, Farr A, Randall RJ (1951) Protein measurement with the Folin phenol reagent. J Biol Chem **193:** 265–275

Lundgren Y, Weiss L (1979) Cardiovascular design after reversal of long-standing renal hypertension in rats. Clin Sci **57:** 195–215

Lundgren Y, Hallback M, Weiss L, Folkow B (1974) Rate and extent of adaptive cardiovascular changes in rats during experimental renal hypertension. Acta Physiol Scand **91:** 103–115

Mathison HS, Loken H, Brox D, Steinbeck KO (1969) Prognosis in long term treated and untreated essential hypertension. Acta Med Scand **185:** 253–258

Mendenhall W (1979) Introduction to Probability and Statistics, ed 6. Boston, Duxbury Press

Mulvany MJ, Hansen PK, Aalkjaer C (1978) Direct evidence that the greater contractility of resistance vessels in spontaneously hypertensive rats is associated with a narrowed lumen, a thickened media, and an increased number of smooth muscle cell layers. Circ Res **43:** 854–864

Olivetti G, Melissar M, Marchetti G, Anversa P (1982) Quantitative structural changes of the rat thoracic aorta in early spontaneous hypertension. Circ Res **51:** 19–26

Owens GK, Schwartz SM (1982) Alterations in vascular smooth muscle mass in the spontaneously hypertensive rat. Role of cellular hypertrophy, hyperploidy, and hyperplasia. Circ Res **51:** 280–289

Owens GK, Schwartz SM (1983) Vascular smooth muscle cell hypertrophy and hyperploidy in the Goldblatt hypertensive rat. Circ Res **53:** 491–501

Owens GK, Rabinovitch PS, Schwartz SM (1981) Smooth muscle cell hypertrophy versus hyperplasia in hypertension. Proc Natl Acad Sci USA **78:** 7759–7763

Orekhov AN, Kosykh VA, Repin VS, Smirnov VN (1983) Cell proliferation in normal and atherosclerotic human aorta. I. Flow cytometric determination of cellular deoxyribonucleic acid content. Lab Invest **48:** 395–398

Rorive GL, Carlier PJ, Foidart JM (1980) Hyperplasia of rat arterial smooth muscle cells associated with development and reversal of renal hypertension. Clin Sci **59:** 335s–338s

Ross R, Glomset J (1976) The pathogenesis of atherosclerosis. N Engl J Med **295:** 369–377

Sandriter W, Scomazzoni G (1964) Deoxyribonucleic acid content and dry weight of normal and hypertrophic heart muscle fibres. Nature **202:** 100–101

Schwartz SM (1977) Hypertension, endothelial injury and atherosclerosis. Cardiovasc Med **2:** 991–1001

Seidel CL (1979) Aortic actomyosin content of maturing normal and spontaneously hypertensive rats. Am J Physiol **237:** 434–439

Thomas WA, Kim DN (1983) Biology of disease, atherosclerosis as a hyperplastic and/or neoplastic process. Lab Invest **48:** 245–255

Tobian L, Olson R, Chesley G (1969) Water content of arteriolar wall in renovascular hypertension. Am J Physiol **216:** 22–24

Trippodo NC, Frolich ED (1981) Similarities of genetic (spontaneous) hypertension: Man and rat. Circ Res **48:** 309–319

Warshaw DM, Root DT, Halpern W (1980) Effects of antihypertensive drug therapy on the morphology and mechanics of resistance arteries from spontaneously hypertensive rats. Blood Vessels **17:** 257–270

Weibel ER, Bolender RP (1973) Stereological techniques for electron microscopic morphometry. *In* Principles and Techniques of Electron Microscopy, vol 3, edited by MA Hayat. New York, Van Nostrand Reinhold Company, pp 237–296

Wolinsky H (1970) Response of the rat aortic media to hypertension. Circ Res **26:** 507–522

Wolinsky H (1971) Effects of hypertension and its reversal on the thoracic aorta of male and female rats. Circ Res **28:** 622–637

Wolinsky H, Daly MM (1970) A method for the isolation of intima-media samples from arteries. Proc Soc Exp Biol Med **135:** 364–368

Yin FCP, Spurgeon HA, Kallman CH (1983) Age-associated alterations in viscoelastic properties of canine aortic strips. Circ Res **53:** 464–472

INDEX TERMS: Spontaneously hypertensive rats • Smooth muscle cell • Smooth muscle cell hypertrophy and hyperploidy • Smooth muscle cell hyperplasia • Antihypertensive drug treatment

The Significance of the Late Fall in Myocardial P_{CO_2} and Its Relationship to Myocardial pH after Regional Coronary Occlusion in the Dog

Shukri F. Khuri, Robert A. Kloner, Stephanie A. Karaffa, William Marston, Arthur D. Taylor, N.C. Joseph Lai, Donald E. Tow, and Ernest M. Barsamian

From the Departments of Surgery, Medicine and Nuclear Medicine, West Roxbury Veterans Administration Medical Center, Brigham and Women's Hospital, and Harvard Medical School, Boston, Massachusetts

SUMMARY. After acute regional coronary occlusion, myocardial tissue P_{CO_2}, as measured by mass spectrometry, rises, reaches a peak, and then gradually falls. This late fall in myocardial tissue P_{CO_2} could be due to (1) a gradual increase in tissue blood flow (and hence improved carbon dioxide washout), (2) a gradual comsumption of tissue biocarbonate, (3) a gradual reduction in the production of carbon dioxide due to progressive cellular damage, or (4) an artifact caused by the continued presence of the mass spectrometer probe in the ischemic tissue. To determine which of these four mechanisms is responsible for the late fall in myocardial tissue P_{CO_2}, we subjected 27 anesthetized open-chest dogs to 3-hour occlusion of the left anterior descending coronary artery. Both myocardial tissue P_{CO_2} and intramyocardial hydrogen ion concentration were measured in the myocardial segment supplied by the left anterior descending coronary artery. Ten dogs (group 1) were killed after the occlusion (occlusion I), and 11 dogs (group 2) underwent reocclusion (occlusion II) at the same site after a 45-minute period of reflow. Regional myocardial blood flow was measured periodically by the intramural injection of ^{127}Xe. Changes in myocardial tissue P_{CO_2} and hydrogen ion concentration were related to ultrastructural changes in the tissues adjacent to the myocardial tissue P_{CO_2} probe. Regional myocardial blood flow remained unchanged throughout the 3-hour occlusion, ruling out increased carbon dioxide washout as a cause for its late fall. Tissue hydrogen ion concentration, as measured by a new lead glass electrode, correlated well with myocardial tissue P_{CO_2}, with the reduction in regional myocardial blood flow, and with ischemic damage assessed histologically. Myocardial hydrogen ion concentration also exhibited a late fall after the occlusion, from a peak of 199.8 ± 27.8 nmol/liter to 91.9 ± 12.1 nmol/liter (mean ± SEM). This ruled out consumption of tissue bicarbonate as the cause for the late fall in myocardial tissue P_{CO_2}. Peak rise in myocardial tissue P_{CO_2} after occlusion II (71.2 ± 7.9 mm Hg) was significantly lower than peak myocardial tissue P_{CO_2} after occlusion I (116.7 ± 13.9 mm Hg, $P < 0.001$). The difference between these latter two values, as well as the magnitude of fall in myocardial tissue P_{CO_2} during occlusion I, related directly to the degree of histological damage observed. In six additional experiments (group 3), peak myocardial tissue P_{CO_2} in myocardial segments supplied by normal (unoccluded) coronary arteries remained unchanged over 3 hours, and hydrogen ion concentration in segments supplied by an occluded left anterior descending coronary artery exhibited a late fall, even in the absence of a mass spectrometer probe. We conclude that, following regional coronary occlusion, there is a late fall in both myocardial tissue P_{CO_2} and hydrogen ion concentration; this late fall probably is a reflection of progressive cellular damage which does not reverse after a 45-minute period of reflow. Myocardial tissue P_{CO_2} and hydrogen ion concentration curves following coronary occlusion reflect the metabolic viability of the ischemic myocardium. **(*Circ Res 56: 537–547, 1985*)**

ACCUMULATION of hydrogen ions, lactate, and carbon dioxide, are important features of regional myocardial ischemia (Opie, 1976). Until recently, there have been no reliable techniques for the quantification of interstitital accumulation of carbon dioxide in the ischemic myocardium. In 1972, Brantigan, Gott, and Martz described the mass spectrometer technique for measurement of myocardial oxygen (P_{MO_2}) and carbon dioxide (P_{MCO_2}) tension. Utilizing this technique, we have demonstrated that the magnitude of rise in P_{MCO_2} following regional coronary artery occlusion correlated well with the degree of underlying ischemic damage assessed by intramural ST segment changes (Khuri et al., 1975), and by changes in regional blood flow and tissue histology (Khuri et al., 1979a).

Our studies with the mass spectrometer have shown that after regional coronary occlusion, P_{MCO_2} rises, reaches a peak in 20–30 minutes and then falls gradually. This late fall in P_{MCO_2} has not been observed during global myocardial ischemia (McGregor et al., 1974; Lange et al., 1983). Neither did Case et al. (1979b), who utilized a different P_{MCO_2} measuring system, observe such a fall during regional ischemia. Since we had observed this late fall, invariably, in all the regional occlusion experiments we had performed, we elected to examine this phenomenon further, aided by a new tissue pH electrode that we had evaluated in our laboratory (Khuri et al., 1979b).

Thus, the purpose of this study is to describe the changes in $Pmco_2$ during 3 hours of regional myocardial ischemia, to relate these changes to changes in hydrogen ion concentration, and to postulate a reason for the late fall in $Pmco_2$ following regional coronary occlusion.

Methods

Twenty-seven adult mongrel dogs of both sexes weighing 15–20 kg were anesthetized with pentobarbital (30 mg/kg), intubated, and placed on a Harvard respiratory breathing room air. Tidal volume and ventilatory rate were adjusted to yield normal arterial blood gases and pH measured with an IL model 713 pH/blood gas analyzer. Arterial pressure was monitored continuously through a catheter placed in the left femoral artery and attached to a Gould-Statham P23ID pressure transducer. The external jugular vein was cannulated and used for administration of fluids and drugs. A left thoracotomy through the 5th intercostal space was performed, the pericardium was split, and the heart was suspended in a pericardial cradle. The left anterior descending coronary artery (LAD) or one of its branches was dissected and prepared for occlusion at a later time. In the myocardial segment supplied by the portion of the LAD to be occluded (which was identified by epicardial cyanosis following a transient 5-second occlusion), measurements of regional myocardial oxygen and carbon dioxide (Pmo_2 and $Pmco_2$), regional myocardial hydrogen ion concentration ([H+]), and regional myocardial blood flow (RMBF) were made. Arterial blood gases and pH were analyzed at 1-hour intervals throughout each experiment to ascertain their stability.

Measurements of Regional Myocardial Gas Tensions

The Medspect II mass spectrometer (Chemetron Inc.) was used to monitor Pmo_2 and $Pmco_2$ throughout each experiment. The mass spectrometer probe, described previously (Brantigan et al., 1972), consisted of Teflon-coated 22-gauge stainless steel tubing with a 19-mm sensing tip. The probe was inserted in the left ventricular wall after making a small epicardial nick; it was advanced gently to lie parallel to and midway between the epicardial and the endocardial surfaces. The other end of the probe was attached to a cannula connecting it to the mass spectrometer. The vacuum exerted by the mass spectrometer withdrew gas molecules across the Teflon membrane at a rate of 5×10^{-6} ml/sec. A constant readout of the tissue gas tensions in mm Hg was displayed on the mass spectrometer and the output was recorded on a multichannel recorder (Grass Instruments).

The mass spectrometer probe was calibrated before and after each experiment in a water tonometer into which known gas mixtures of oxygen, nitrogen, and carbon dioxide were bubbled at 37°C. The initial and 95% in vitro response times of the probe were 0.5 and 5.5 minutes for oxygen and 0.7 and 6 minutes for CO_2, respectively.

Measurement of Intramyocardial pH

A miniature steel-jacketed glass electrode developed in our laboratory in conjunction with Ingold Electrodes, Inc. was utilized for the continuous measurement of intramural pH (Khuri et al., 1979b). The details of the electrode are illustrated in Figure 1. The electrode is steel-jacketed for more rigidity; its sensing glass membrane is 4 mm long and 1 mm in outside diameter. It is conical in shape and rounded at the tip to ensure minimal tissue damage during insertion. Each electrode was tested in vitro for its Nernstian response in buffer of pH 4.00 and 7.00 at 25°C. The in vitro reproducibility of each electrode was determined as the difference in electromotive force (emf) potential voltage readings in pH 7.00 buffer at 1-minute intervals after an in-between reading in pH 4.00 buffer. The electrodes utilized had a reproducibility which was within 0.5 mV, or 0.008 pH unit. The 95% in vitro response time to a step change in pH was 30 seconds.

STEEL-JACKETED MUSCLE/TISSUE pH ELECTRODE

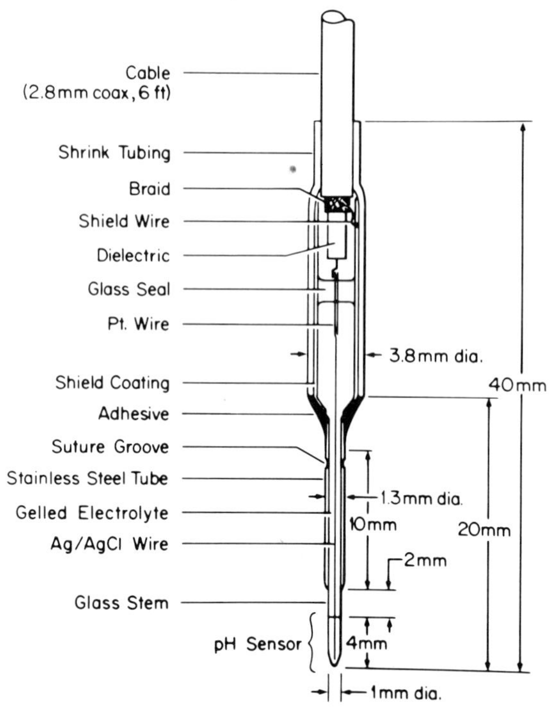

FIGURE 1. *Details of the miniature glass electrode utilized in the study.*

The electrode was inserted into the myocardium through a minute epicardial incision and then advanced until the sensing surface was at a level within the myocardial wall closest to the level of the adjacent mass spectrometer probe. The electrode was then fixed to the surface of the heart with a fine epicardial suture. A silver chloride reference electrode, 40 mm long and 2 mm in outside diameter, was placed in a subcutaneous pocket through the edge of the thoractomy incision, i.e., at a site remote from the ischemic myocardium. [With this system, the placement of the reference electrode at a site remote from the ischemic myocardium does not affect the magnitude of fall in pH during regional ischemia (Khuri et al., 1984).] Both the pH and the reference electrodes were connected to a Corning model 610A pH meter via shielded coaxial cables. The output from the pH meter was recorded on a multichannel recorder (model D7 Polygraph, Grass Instruments). Since all these experiments were performed at constant normothermic myocardial temperatures, hydrogen ion concentration, expressed as $[H^+]$ in nanomoles per liter (nmol/liter), was calculated from the pH in accordance with the formula $pH = -\log [H^+]$ (Davenport, 1967).

To correct for the difference in response time between the mass spectrometer probe and the pH electrode, we developed an in vitro response curve for each, by placing them first in a solution of known pH and Pco_2 and then moving into another solution with a different pH and Pco_2. The difference in the 95% response time between the probe and the electrode was then calculated from these curves and used as the basis for the correction.

Measurement of Regional Myocardial Flow (RMBF)

RMBF in the area adjacent to the mass spectrometer probe was measured using the washout of the radioactivity of Xenon-127 injected into the myocardium, as described previously (Khuri et al., 1980). Briefly, a 23-gauge right-angled needle attached to #50 P.E. tubing was inserted intramurally and fixed to the epicardium with a fine suture. A scintillation single-probe detector with a 2-inch in diameter sodium iodide crystal and a straight-bore lead collimator was suspended over the site of insertion of the needle and connected to a rate-meter. For each RMBF determination, 0.1 ml of saline containing approximately 200 μCi of ^{127}Xe was injected and flushed with 0.15 ml of saline. The ^{127}Xe washout curve was recorded on a multichannel recorder (Grass Instruments) and later transcribed onto a semilog paper so that its half time could be determined. RMBF was then calculated according to the formula:

$$\text{RMBF (ml/100 g per min)} = \frac{(0.693)\ (0.7)\ (100)}{T_{1/2}},$$

where 0.693 is the natural logarithm of 2, $T_{1/2}$ is the half-time expressed in minutes, and 0.7 is the partition coefficient of xenon gas between tissue and blood (Ingvar and Lassen, 1961). To ensure that RMBF is determined at the same level within the myocardial wall as that of the $Pmco_2$ probe, the exact depth of the latter was determined after its insertion into the myocardium by echocardiography (Ekoline 20, Smith Kline Instrument Co.), and the xenon needle was bent so that the distance between the tip and right angle of the needle was equal to the depth of the probe. The needle then was inserted around 5 mm away from the probe.

Experimental Protocol

The 27 dogs studied were divided into three experimental groups. Group 1 experiments were performed first. In this group of 10 dogs, the LAD was occluded for 3 hours; the animal then was killed, and histological damage was assessed, as described below. Throughout each experiment, continuous measurements of blood pressure, heart rate, Pmo_2, $Pmco_2$ and $[H^+]$ were made; regional myocardial blood flow as determined before and 10, 30, 90, and 165 minutes after the occlusion.

On the basis of data obtained from group 1, group 2 experiments were performed in 11 dogs. In this group, the LAD was occluded for 3 hours (occlusion I), the occlusion totally released for a period of 45 minutes, and the LAD reoccluded at the same site (occlusion II). When the $Pmco_2$ during occlusion II started to decline, after reaching a peak level, the animal was killed and the histological damage was assessed. The same continuous hemodynamic and metabolic measurements were made in group 2 as in group 1. During occlusion I, regional myocardial blood flow was measured at 10, 30, 90, and 165 minutes into the occlusion; during occlusion II, it was measured when the $Pmco_2$ peaked before the animal was killed.

Group 3 experiments were performed in six dogs to investigate whether the changes in $Pmco_2$ and $[H^+]$ observed in groups 1 and 2 were caused by the continued presence of the mass spectrometer probe per se in the ischemic tissue. In this group, no $Pmco_2$ probes were placed in segments supplied by the LAD. Instead, one $Pmco_2$ probe was placed in a remote segment supplied by the circumflex coronary artery, and a single pH electrode was placed in a segment supplied by the LAD. All six dogs underwent a 3-hour occlusion of the LAD. After the peak $[H^+]$ was reached in three dogs (nearly 40 minutes into the LAD occlusion), a second pH electrode was placed in the ischemic area supplied by the occluded LAD, and was kept until the end of the experiment. RMBF was not determined in this group, and no histological studies were performed. Blood pressure and heart rate were recorded continuously.

Assessment of Histological Damage

At the end of each experiment, three tissue samples, each 2 × 1 × 1 mm, were obtained from the myocardium 1–2 mm away from the distal end, the middle, and the proximal end of the sensing surface of the mass spectrometer probe. Three other similar tissue samples were obtained from the myocardium 1–2 mm away from the sensing tip of the pH electrode. All tissue samples were immersed in 3% glutaraldehyde for 3 hours, after which they were washed in cacodylate buffer and postfixed with cold 1% osmic acid for 1 hour. Then, the tissue cubes were dehydrated in graded alcohol. Subsequently, over a period of 24 hours, they were placed successively in propylene oxide and 1:1 mixture of propylene oxide and Epon 812. At the end of the 24-hour period, they were embedded in Epon 812. Sections (1 μm thick) were cut and stained with toluidine-blue. The severity of ischemic injury was graded according to the following criteria: 0, normal myocardial cell; 1+, clumping of nuclear chromatin alone, or with occasional vacuoles plus myocardial relaxation as manifested by wide I-bands; 2+, further clumping of nuclear chromatin plus intramyofibrillar edema and more vacuoles; 3+, marked intracellular edema, numerous vacuoles, and the sarcolemmal membrane lifted off the myofilaments by the intracellular edema; and 4+, severe swelling and architectural disruption. The histological sections were examined and graded by one observer (RAK) who had no previous knowledge of the associated changes in myocardial gas tensions. For each mass spectrometer probe, the average value of the three histological sections were obtained and expressed as mean ischemic score (MIS). The methodology utilized in the assessment of histological damage is similar to that which we reported previously (Kloner et al., 1974, 1977a, 1977b; Khuri et al., 1979a).

Analysis of Data

We calculated a rate-pressure product, using the mean blood pressure and heart rate. All summary data were expressed as mean ± SEM. Linear regression was used to establish the relationships between parameters which exhibited a biological continuum. Data representing nonbiological continuum were analyzed by multivariate analysis. Where applicable, Student's *t*-test for paired and unpaired data was used to evaluate the significance of changes observed.

TABLE 1
Summary of Data Obtained in Group 2

	Baseline	At $Pmco_{2\,max}$ (occlusion 1)	3 hr post occlusion I	45 min post reflow	At $Pmco_{2\,max}$ (occlusion II)
HR (beats/min)	115 ± 6	130 ± 5	121 ± 7	109 ± 8	97 ± 8*
Mean BP (mm Hg)	136 ± 7	130 ± 4	131 ± 7	121 ± 8	121 ± 6
Rate pressure product	19885 ± 1477	17390 ± 1089	16149 ± 1516	13385 ± 1891	10851 ± 1164*
Pmo_2 (mm Hg)	23 ± 4.3	2.6 ± 1.2	3.8 ± 1.9	49.7 ± 11.3	4.5 ± 2.1
$Pmco_2$ (mm Hg)	38.2 ± 1.8	116.7 ± 13.9	63.7 ± 5.7	33 ± 2.7	71.2 ± 7.9*
$[H^+]$ (nmol/liter)	46.9 ± 4.5	184.6 ± 34.9	89.6 ± 14	44.3 ± 2.5	95.8 ± 13.6*
RMBF (ml/100 g per min)	60.5 ± 4.3	9.7 ± 1.4	11.7 ± 2.2	Not measured	10.5 ± 1.5

Results are expressed as mean ± SEM. $Pmco_{2\,max}$ = peak value during occlusion.
* When compared to occlusion 1, differences are significant (P = or <0.001).

To determine whether the $Pmco_2$ values obtained postocclusion reflected a level of CO_2 accumulation over and above that which would be expected on the basis of decreased washout only, we utilized a mathematical model which predicted the postocclusion $Pmco_2$ assuming no change in the rate of CO_2 production between the pre- and the postocclusion states. Hence, under the assumption of a constant preocclusion rate of CO_2 production (C_0) following a step change in coronary flow from Q_1 ml/min to a reduced but steady flow of Q ml/min, the concentration of CO_2 at time T [C(T)] was predicted by

$$C(T) = \left[C_0 - \frac{M + QC_i}{Q}\right]e^{-\frac{Q}{V}T} + \frac{M + QC_i}{Q}$$

where C_i = concentration of CO_2 in the coronary arterial blood,

$$M = C_0Q_1 - C_iQ_1 = Q_1(C_0 - C_i),$$

and V is the CO_2 space in the myocardium modeled as a well-mixed compartment of 75 cm^3.

Results

In all three groups, heart rate and mean blood pressure did not change significantly throughout the initial 3-hour coronary occlusion. Data obtained in groups 1 and 3 were similar to those obtained in group 2, and are shown in Table 1. In group 2, heart rate (but not mean BP) during occlusion II was significantly lower than during the initial 3-hour occlusion. Consequently, there was a significant difference in rate-pressure product between the two occlusions (Table 1).

Myocardial Gas Tension Changes

During the initial 3-hour LAD occlusion in groups 1 and 2, $Pmco_2$ rose to peak and then invariably fell, in all the animals studied. Pmo_2 fell to a nadir and remained unchanged. A typical curve obtained is shown in the upper panel of Figure 2, and data are summarized in Tables 1 and 2. In group 2, following the release of occlusion I, $Pmco_2$ rose continuously throughout the whole period of reflow, reaching a peak level which was significantly higher than preocclusion value (P = 0.005). Following occlusion II, Pmo_2 fell again and was not significantly different from the nadir value during occlusion I (Fig. 2, lower panel; Table 1). Following occlusion II, $Pmco_{2max}$ was significantly lower than $Pmco_{2max}$ during occlusion I, but was not significantly different from the $Pmco_2$ value recorded 3 hours after occlu-

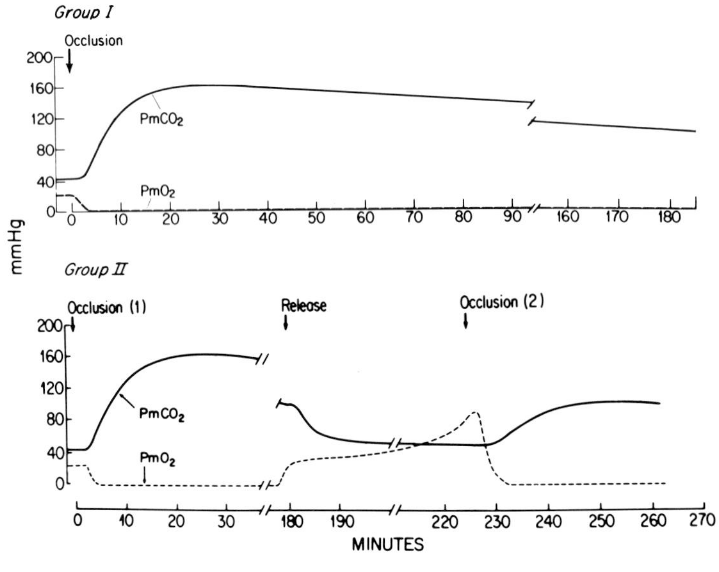

FIGURE 2. *Myocardial gas tension (Pmo_2 and $Pmco_2$) curves recorded in the course of a typical experiment in group 1 (upper panel) and group 2 (lower panel). In group 1, the animal was killed at the end of a 3-hour occlusion of the LAD. In group 2, the 3-hour occlusion was released, 45 minutes of reflow were allowed, and the occlusion was reinstituted; the animal was killed after $Pmco_2$ reached its peak during occlusion II.*

TABLE 2
Summary of [H^+], Pmo_2 and $Pmco_2$ Data Obtained in Group 1

	Pmo_2	$Pmco_2$	[H^+]
Stabilization time after probe or electrode insertion	43.2 ± 2.9 min	43.2 ± 2.9 min	12 ± 3.4 min
Baseline value	16.2 ± 1.3 mm Hg	52.8 ± 3.3 mm Hg	45.6 ± 2.0 nmol/liter
Time of initial change after CO*	1.0 ± 0.1 min	2.7 ± 0.3 min	14 ± 0.8 sec
Peak or nadir value reached after CO	0.2 ± 2.0 mm Hg	190.8 ± 22.0 mm Hg†	199.8 ± 27.8 nmol/liter
Time at which peak or nadir value was reached	9.4 ± 2.5 min	28.1 ± 4.4 min	37.7 ± 5.2 min
Value at 3 hr into the CO	0.2 ± 3.0 mm Hg	84.4 ± 7.1 mm Hg‡	91.9 ± 12.1 nmol/liter

Results are expressed as mean ± SEM.
* CO = coronary occlusion.
† $Pmco_{2max}$.
‡ $Pmco_{2(3\ hr)}$.

sion I (Table 1). For each of the two occlusions in group 2, the time of initial rise of $Pmco_2$ and its maximal rate of rise ($\Delta Pmco_2/\Delta t_{max}$), as well as $Pmco_{2max}$ and the time it took to reach $Pmco_{2max}$, are all shown in Figure 3 and summarized in Table 3. Note that the differences between both occlusions in all four parameters were highly significant. To determine whether, in group 2, the fall in $Pmco_{2max}$ during occlusion II was causally related to the fall in rate pressure product (Table 1), the difference in $Pmco_{2max}$ between occlusions I and II was correlated to the difference in rate-pressure product between the two occlusions. A poor linear correlation between both parameters was observed (r = 0.027), suggesting that the fall in $Pmco_{2max}$ during occlusion II was not primarily due to the reduction in rate-pressure product.

In group 3, Pmo_2 and $Pmco_2$ recorded from six probes placed in segments supplied by a normal circumflex coronary artery remained unchanged throughout the 3-hour LAD occlusion (Table 4).

Changes in Myocardial [H^+] and Their Relationship to $Pmco_2$, RMBF, and Tissue Histology

Changes in [H^+] throughout the 3-hour occlusion were similar to the changes in $Pmco_2$ in that both parameters rose after the occlusion, reached a peak, and then fell gradually throughout the rest of the occlusion (Tables 1 and 2). The rise and subsequent fall in [H^+] was highly significant (P = 0.0005). In group 2, mean peak [H^+] during occlusion II was also significantly lower than during occlusion I (P = 0.005), but not significantly different from the mean [H^+] recorded 3 hours after occlusion I (Table 1). In group 3, myocardial [H^+] was determined in a segment supplied by an occluded LAD in the absence of a mass spectrometer probe. Data from these experiments, shown in Table 4, were no different from [H^+] data obtained in groups 1 and 2. In the three animals in this group in which a second pH electrode was placed in the ischemic segment nearly 40 minutes after occlusion, only a fall in [H^+] was observed (Table 4).

Because of the difference in response time between the mass spectrometer probe and the pH electrode, the initial rise in [H^+] following coronary occlusion was observed significantly earlier (P < 0.001) than the initial rise in $Pmco_2$ (Table 2). Correcting for the difference in response times between the pH electrode and the $Pmco_2$ probe, cumulative data were calculated from the [H^+] and the $Pmco_2$ curves just before the occlusion, and at 5-minute intervals throughout the occlusion. These data are

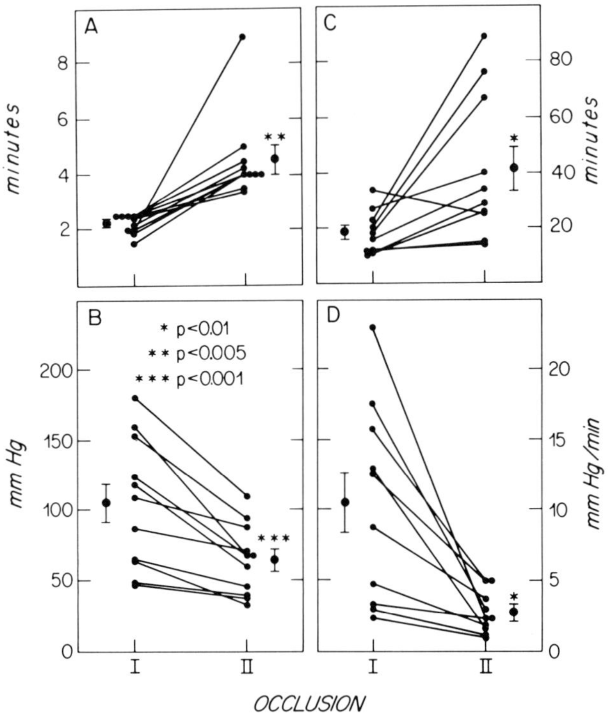

FIGURE 3. *Differences in the characteristics of $Pmco_2$ curves between occlusions I and II (group 2). Each line connects the values from one dog. The mean ± SEM during the two occlusions is shown on either side of the individual sets of data. All differences between means were statistically significant. Panel A: the time of initial rise in $Pmco_2$ following occlusion. Panel B: the maximal value of $Pmco_2$ reached during the occlusion ($Pmco_{2max}$). Panel C: the time following occlusion at which $Pmco_{2max}$ was reached. Panel D: the maximal rate of rise of $Pmco_2$ following the occlusion ($\Delta Pmco_{2max}/\Delta t$).*

TABLE 3
Differences in the Characteristics of the $Pmco_2$ Curves between the Two Coronary Occlusions in Group 2

	Occlusion I	Occlusion II	P
Time of initial $Pmco_2$ rise following CO* (min)	2.4 ± 0.13	4.55 ± 0.51	<0.005
$\Delta Pmco_2/\Delta t_{max}$ (mm Hg/min)	10.4 ± 2.2	2.7 ± 0.4	<0.005
Minutes after CO at which point c was reached	8.2 ± 0.6	11.1 ± 0.7	<0.02
Minutes after CO at which $Pmco_{2max}$ was reached	18.3 ± 24.4	41.4 ± 8.4	<0.01
$Pmco_{2max}$ (mm Hg)	116.7 ± 13.9	63.7 ± 5.7	<0.001

Results are expressed as mean ± SEM.
* Coronary occlusion.

shown in Figure 4. $[H^+]$ and $Pmco_2$ at these points in time were compared within each experiment by linear regression analysis. The correlation coefficients ranged from 0.77 to 0.99 and averaged 0.89. P was <0.001 for all correlations.

There was a direct linear relationship in group 1 between the peak rise in $[H^+]$ following the occlusion and the mean ischemic score assessed histologically (Fig. 5A). A linear relationship was also observed between peak $[H^+]$ and the fall in regional myocardial blood flow (Fig. 5B).

Regional Myocardial Blood Flow

RMBF data in group 1 are shown in Figure 4. Before occlusion, RMBF was 61.9 ± 10.6 ml/100 g per min. At 10, 30, 90, and 165 minutes into the occlusion, it was 11.6 ± 5.3, 10.6 ± 3.1, 11.1 ± 3.6, and 11.6 ± 4.3 ml/100 g per min, respectively. The fall in RMBF following the occlusion was highly significant ($P < 0.001$), but there were no significant differences between the RMBF values obtained throughout the occlusion. In group 2, there was no significant difference between RMBF during occlusion II and mean RMBF during occlusion I (Table 1).

Relationship of $Pmco_2$ and Pmo_2 Changes to the Degree of Histological Damage

Since the mean ischemic score (MIS) was not a biological continuum, this relationship was elucidated by grouping $Pmco_2$ and Pmo_2 values over three ranges of MIS. The difference between the maximal $Pmco_2$ value reached during the occlusion and the value reached at the end of a 3-hour occlusion ($Pmco_{2max} - Pmco_{2(3hr)}$) represented the magnitude of late fall in $Pmco_2$. During the first occlusion, there was a direct relationship between the magnitude of rise and the magnitude of late fall in the $Pmco_2$ and the degree of histological damage observed (Fig. 6). In group 2, two additional direct relationships were noted (Fig. 7). The magnitude of rise in Pmo_2 after the release of occlusion I (probably a manifestation of a reactive hyperemic response) related directly to the degree of underlying ischemia assessed both by $Pmco_{2max}$ during occlusion I (r =

TABLE 4
$[H^+]$ and Myocardial Gas Tensions Data in Group 3

Experiment no.	$[H^+]$* in LAD (ischemic) area: Before CO	40 min post-CO	180 min post-CO	Pmo_2† in CCX (normal) area: Before CO	40 min post-CO	180 min post-CO	$Pmco_2$† in CCX (normal) area: Before CO	40 min post-CO	180 min post-CO
1	78	759	204	25.5	27.6	23.7	53.6	40.5	35.8
2	117	1288	1096	25.5	26.9	28.8	44.2	38.7	34.3
3‡	68	126	89	14.2	15.2	15.9	59.1	50.2	50.6
		166	87						
4‡	55	295	145	23.8	24.1	25.3	39.3	39.5	45.3
		389	126						
5	115	389	380	29.4	30.1	30.1	50.1	38.9	52.0
6‡	56	245	162	43.0	44.4	45.8	37.1	39.7	39.2
		776	186						
Mean	81.5	492.6	275.0	26.9	28.1	28.3	47.2	41.2	42.9
SEM	11.4	126.2	106.7	3.8	3.9	4.1	3.5	1.8	3.4

LAD = left anterior descending coronary artery. CCX = circumflex coronary artery. CO = coronary occlusion.
* nmol/liter.
† mm Hg.
‡ In experiments 3, 4, and 6, a second pH electrode was inserted in the ischemic area after a peak in $[H^+]$, recorded by first pH electrode, was reached.

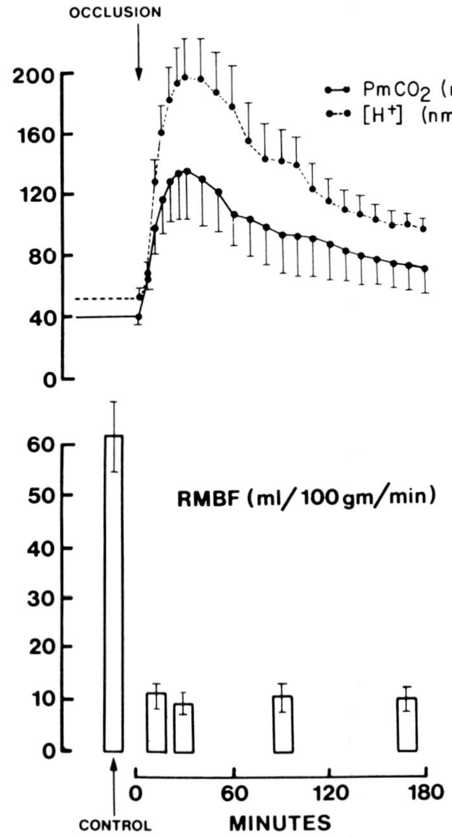

Figure 4. *Upper panel: Pm_{CO_2} and myocardial tissue [H^+] cumulative data (mean ± SEM) obtained at 5-minute intervals after a 3-hour occlusion of the LAD in 10 dogs (group 1). Lower panel: RMBF in the segment supplied by the LAD. Flow was determined before and 10, 30, 90, and 165 minutes after LAD occlusion. There were no significant differences between the values obtained after the occlusion.*

0.90, $P < 0.001$) and by the histological MIS ($P < 0.01$) (Fig. 7, upper panels). Similarly, the difference between Pm_{CO_2max} during occlusion I and Pm_{CO_2max} during occlusion II related directly to the degree of underlying myocardial ischemic damage ($P < 0.05$) (Fig. 7, lower panels).

Observed vs. Predicted Postocclusion Pm_{CO_2}

Figure 8 compares the observed postocclusion Pm_{CO_2} values (at the points in time during which RMBF measurements were made) to those predicted assuming a constant rate of CO_2 production equal to the preocclusion rate. The highly significant differences between both curves indicated that CO_2 production had increased following the occlusion. Note that, in the predicted curve, no significant difference in Pm_{CO_2} was observed between 30 and 165 minutes postocclusion. In contrast, a highly significant fall in the observed Pm_{CO_2} was noted during this period, confirming a decrease in Pm_{CO_2} production which occurred beyond 30 minutes of occlusion.

Discussion

Source and Measurement of Tissue Carbon Dioxide in Regional Myocardial Ischemia

In regional ischemia there is a reduction in both substrate (oxygen) and blood flow to certain segments of the myocardium, resulting in altered metabolic pathways (Scheuer and Brachfeld, 1966; Opie, 1976). Experimental studies on the beating heart in situ have shown that, even with total occlusion of a coronary artery, tissue flow in the center of the ischemic zone is never totally interrupted, and oxidative metabolism continues, albeit at a very slow rate (Opie, 1976). Anaerobic metabolism predominates and results in accumulation of H^+, lactate, and CO_2, among other metabolic products (Opie, 1976). The CO_2 measured in an ischemic segment is thus the result of production of CO_2 and its decreased washout. Two processes are thought to lead to CO_2 production in regional ischemia: (1) retention of respiratory CO_2 (since, in contrast to anoxic states, there is a continued but reduced provision of oxygen) (Opie, 1976; Gevers, 1977) and (2) buffering of H^+ with bicarbonate (Khuri et al., 1975; Gevers, 1977). Although the relative contribution of these

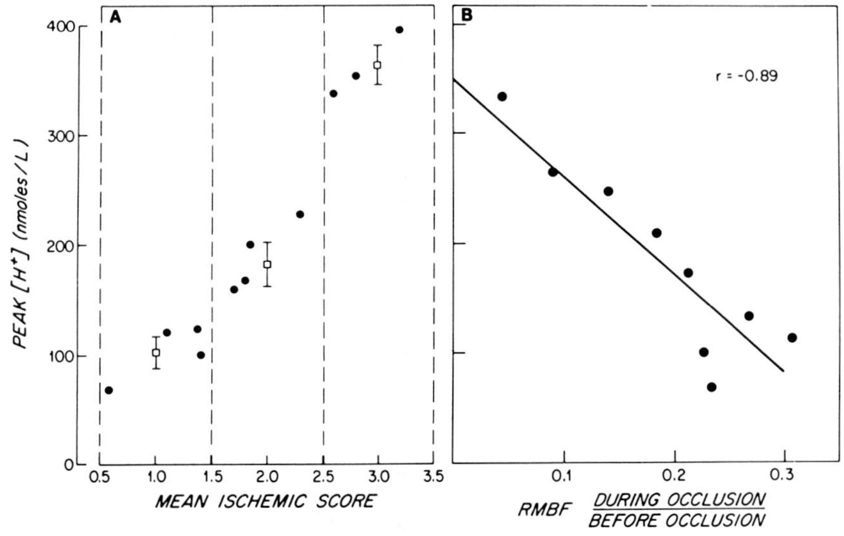

Figure 5. *Panel A: relationship of peak [H^+] during occlusion I (group 1) to the degree of ischemia as assessed histologically. The more severe the ischemia, the higher was the peak [H^+]. Within the three ranges of mean ischemic scores shown, cumulative peak [H^+] values (mean ± SEM, illustrated by open squares) were significantly different from each other ($P < 0.01$). Panel B: relationship of peak [H^+] during the same occlusion to RMBF expressed as a ratio of the preocclusion value.*

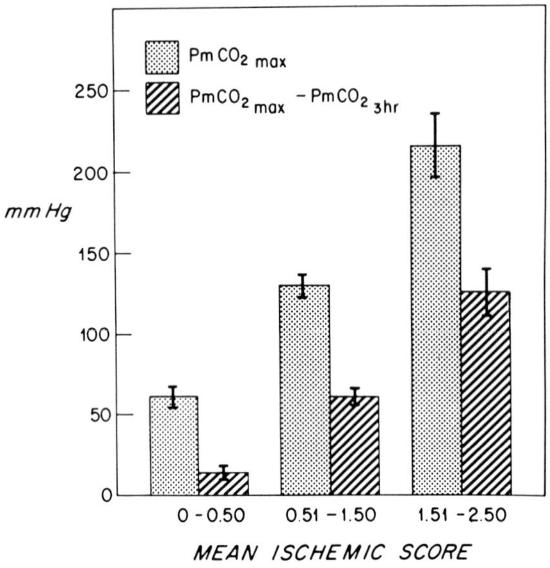

FIGURE 6. *Relationship of ultrastructural ischemic damage, assessed by mean ischemic score, to the magnitude of rise ($Pmco_{2max}$) and late fall ($Pmco_{2max}$ − $Pmco_{2(3hr)}$) of $Pmco_2$ following a 3-hour LAD occlusion. The barographs represent mean ± SEM. Differences between the respective means, analyzed by one-way analysis of variance, were all statistically significant ($P < 0.01$).*

two processes to the overall CO_2 production has not been investigated, it is accepted that the source of CO_2 is closely linked to the source of $[H^+]$ in the ischemic process. Gevers (1977) has postulated a

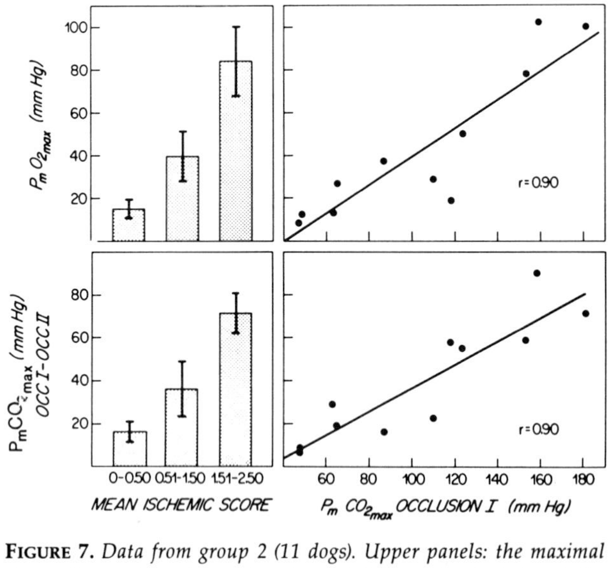

FIGURE 7. *Data from group 2 (11 dogs). Upper panels: the maximal rise in Pmo_2 after release of occlusion I (Pmo_{2max}) reflected well the degree of ischemia during that occlusion, as assessed by $Pmco_{2max}$ and mean ischemic score. Differences between the three barographs analyzed by one-way analysis of variance were statistically significant ($P < 0.01$) and the correlation coefficient of the regression analysis was 0.90 ($P < 0.001$). Lower panels: the difference between $Pmco_{2max}$ during occlusion I and $Pmco_{2max}$ during occlusion II correlated well with the degree of myocardial ischemia incurred during occlusion I and assessed by $Pmco_{2max}$ ($r = 0.90$); there was also a direct relationship between this difference and the mean ischemic score ($P < 0.05$).*

number of sources for the H^+ in the ischemic process, the most important of which is the breakdown of ATP. Other sources that he has postulated include continued mitochondrial respiration with CO_2 production and subsequent cytoplasmic acidification, hydrolysis of triglycerides, and increased glycogen turnover. Chance and Mela (1966) have postulated that H^+ can also be produced by the increased uptake of Ca^{++} in the ischemic state.

The sources of H^+ in regional ischemia are theoretically sources of CO_2, pending the availability of tissue bicarbonate. Since CO_2 is freely diffusible across cell membrane, measuring it in the extracellular tissue space should be fairly representative of the overall CO_2 pool in the ischemic myocardium. Brantigan et al. (1972) first described a Teflon probe-mass spectrometer system for the on-line measurement of tissue Pco_2. Utilizing this system, we have shown that during regional myocardial ischemia the magnitude of rise in $Pmco_2$ correlated with intramural S-T segment changes (Khuri et al., 1975), with reduction in regional myocardial blood flow, and with histological evidence of ischemia (Khuri et al., 1979a). The measurement of $Pmco_2$ with mass spectrometry has been useful not only in quantifying the degree of regional myocardial ischemia, but also in assessing the efficacy of pharmacological interventions in ameliorating ischemic damage (Hillis, 1979, 1981; Rude, 1980).

Our experiments with the mass spectrometer (Khuri et al., 1975, 1979a) have consistently shown what the present study demonstrates—namely, that, after acute coronary ligation in the canine heart in situ, $Pmco_2$ rises, reaches a peak, and then gradually declines. Case described a different method for the measurement of $Pmco_2$ which employed what was essentially a miniature Sevringhaus electrode (Coon, 1976; Case, 1979a). Utilizing this electrode, he observed a rise in $Pmco_2$ 9.6 ± 0.7 seconds (mean ± SEM) after regional coronary occlusion (Case, 1979b). He stated that he did not observe a subsequent fall in $Pmco_2$ with prolonged occlusions, although his observations in that study did not extend beyond 15 minutes postocclusion (Case, 1979b).

Quantification of Regional Myocardial Ischemia by Measurement of Tissue pH

Benzing, Gebert, and Strohm were the first to utilize glass microelectrodes to monitor intramural pH changes in the dog myocardium during ischemia (Benzing et al., 1971; Gebert et al., 1971). Similar observations were made by Hicks et al. in 1976. Cobb and Poole-Wilson (1980) have described a new membrane tissue electrode with which they assessed the severity of acidosis in myocardial ischemia. These groups demonstrated prompt and significant regional pH changes in response to coronary occlusion, but they did not attempt to compare the magnitude of these changes to other quantitative parameters of myocardial ischemia. Walters et al.

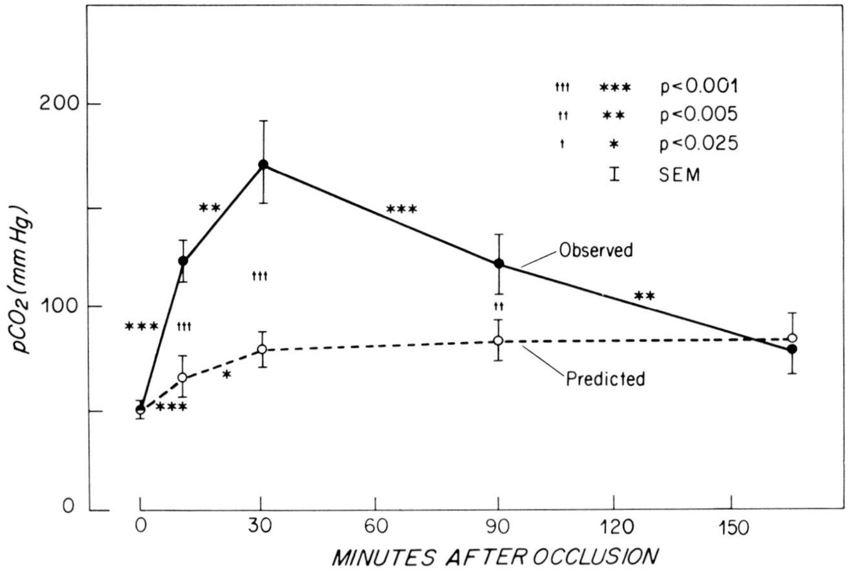

FIGURE 8. *Observed and predicted Pm_{CO_2} values (mean ± SEM) in 12 dogs undergoing a 3-hour coronary occlusion in which reliable regional myocardial blood flow measurements were made before and 10, 30, 90, and 165 minutes after coronary occlusion. The solid lines connect the Pm_{CO_2} values as measured by the mass spectrometer. The dotted lines connect the Pm_{CO_2} values predicted on the basis of a constant preocclusion rate of CO_2 production. A two-factor analysis of variance showed a highly significant difference within and between the observed and predicted values (F-ratio was 12.2 for the columns, 25.9 for the rows, and 6.22 for the interaction). The levels of significance between and within the two sets of data, as calculated by paired t-test, are shown.*

(1979) have described a miniature glass electrode housed in a 21-gauge needle for the measurement of intramyocardial pH. They did not relate their interstitial pH measurements to regional myocardial blood flow or to tissue histology, but they did demonstrate that these measurements reflected intracellular metabolism during elective arrest of the heart.

In the present study, we utilized a new glass electrode which we developed in our laboratory in conjunction with Ingold Electrodes, Inc. We assessed the ability of this electrode to quantify regional myocardial ischemia in a manner similar to our previous assessment of the Pm_{CO_2} probe (Khuri et al., 1979a). Changes in the extracellular $[H^+]$ in the ischemic myocardium related directly to the degree of histological damage incurred (Fig. 5A), to the magnitude of fall in regional myocardial blood flow (Fig. 5B), and to the magnitude of rise in Pm_{CO_2} ($r = 0.89$). These data prompt us to conclude that changes in intramyocardial pH can be as reliable as changes in Pm_{CO_2} in reflecting the degree of underlying ischemic damage.

Because of differences in methodology and response time between the mass spectrometer probe and the pH electrode, the exact temporal relationship between Pm_{CO_2} and $[H^+]$ changes following coronary occlusion cannot be elicited in this study. Furthermore, the temporal differences observed between the Pm_{CO_2} and the $[H^+]$ curves (Table 2) may not be due only to differences in the methods used to generate them. They may also reflect differences in solubility and diffusibility in the extracellular space between H^+ and CO_2. For example, peak $[H^+]$ was reached well after peak Pm_{CO_2}, although the pH electrode had a faster response time. This, in itself, may reflect a more rapid washout of CO_2 due to its increased diffusibility in the extracellular space. It is clear, however, that elucidating the exact temporal and causal relationships between Pm_{CO_2} and myocardial $[H^+]$ during regional ischemia will have to await the development of a newer, more compatible measuring system.

Possible Causes for the Late Fall in Pm_{CO_2} Following Regional Coronary Occlusion

The late decline in Pm_{CO_2} observed during the occlusion can be theorized to be due to one or more of the following four mechanisms: (1) a gradual increase in tissue blood flow (and, hence, improved CO_2 washout) through the opening of new collateral channels; (2) a gradual consumption of tissue bicarbonate, since Pm_{CO_2} produced in ischemia is thought to be due, at least in part, to the buffering of hydrogen ions by bicarbonate; (3) an artifact caused by the continued presence of the mass spectrometer probe, as suggested by Case et al. Since the probe aspirates the gases from the surrounding tissues, albeit at a very slow rate, it may cause tissue depletion of CO_2 and, hence, a late fall in the Pm_{CO_2} curve; (4) a gradual reduction in the production of both H^+ and CO_2 due to progressive cellular damage.

Evidence against the Blood Flow, Bicarbonate Consumption, and CO_2 Depletion Factors as Causes for the Late Fall in Pm_{CO_2}

To determine whether the late fall in Pm_{CO_2} following coronary occlusion related to a late improvement in the rate of washout, regional myocardial blood flow was measured from the washout curves of ^{127}Xe injected intramurally at sites adjacent to the mass spectrometer probes. Regional myocardial blood flow at 10, 30, 90, and 165 minutes after occlusion remained essentially unchanged, and no improvement in ^{127}Xe washout was demonstrated (Fig. 4). Other investigtors, utilizing the microsphere technique, also demonstrated no significant increase in collateral blood flow up to 6 hours after coronary occlusion in the dog (Opie, 1976).

In the present study, myocardial $[H^+]$ following

coronary occlusion exhibited a pattern similar to that of $Pmco_2$; it rose soon after the onset of the 3-hour occlusion, reached a peak, and then gradually declined (Fig. 4). Within each study, the correlation coefficient between $Pmco_2$ and $[H^+]$ averaged 0.89. During occlusion II in group 2, both $Pmco_2$ and $[H^+]$ peaked at significantly lower levels than during occlusion I (Table 3). These observations rule out the possibility of the consumption of tissue bicarbonate as the cause for the late decline in $Pmco_2$ during prolonged coronary occlusion. Had this been the case, the $Pmco_2$ and $[H^+]$ curves would not have been similar, and a poor correlation between both parameters would have been observed.

The possibility of the late fall in $Pmco_2$ being due to depletion of tissue CO_2 as a result of the continuous sampling by the mass spectrometer was ruled out in group 3 experiments. Here, the continued presence of the probe in normal myocardial segments supplied by unoccluded coronary arteries, under stable conditions of blood pressure and heart rate, resulted in stable measurements over a period of at least 3 hours (Table 4). Furthermore, as demonstrated in Table 4, a late fall in $[H^+]$ in the ischemic segment was demonstrated, even in the absence of a mass spectrometer probe, and the addition of another pH electrode late after the occlusion demonstrated only a fall in $[H^+]$.

Evidence in Favor of Progressive Cellular Damage as the Cause for the Late Fall in $Pmco_2$

By excluding the above three factors as causes for the late fall in $Pmco_2$, the fourth possible cause remains: decreased production of CO_2 secondary to progressive cellular damage. To postulate this, it is important to demonstrate an initial increase in the rate of postocclusion CO_2 production as compared to the preocclusion rate, since one may argue that the rise in $Pmco_2$ observed following coronary occlusion could be a manifestation of a steady state reduction in coronary flow without any net increase in the rate of CO_2 production per se. To address this issue, we used a mathematical model which predicted for each experiment the postocclusion $Pmco_2$ values had the preocclusion rate of $Pmco_2$ production remained unchanged. Since RMBF was measured before and at 10, 30, 90, and 165 minutes after the coronary occlusion in group 1, predicted values could be calculated at four postocclusion points in time. As shown in Figure 8, the $Pmco_2$ values observed at 10, 30, and 90 minutes following occlusion were significantly higher than those predicted on the basis of a steady state reduction in coronary flow alone. At 165 minutes, the observed $Pmco_2$ was no different from the predicted value, indicating that between 30 and 165 minutes after the occlusion, a significant decrease in $Pmco_2$ production had occurred.

Two additional observations made in this study suggested that the late fall in $Pmco_2$ following coronary occlusion was due to progressive cellular damage leading to a gradual reduction in the production of H^+ and CO_2. (1) The magnitude of fall in $Pmco_2$ following its peak ($Pmco_{2\,max} - Pmco_{2\,(3hr)}$) was directly related to the degree of ischemic damage as assessed histologically at the end of a 3-hour coronary occlusion (Fig. 6). (2) Following a 3-hour occlusion and 45 minutes of reflow, a second occlusion of the LAD resulted in a significantly lower peak $Pmco_2$ value compared to the first occlusion. In fact, peak values of $Pmco_2$ and $[H^+]$ during occlusion II were not significantly different from their corresponding values prior to release of occlusion I. Since RMBF did not change significantly between both occlusions, these observations, along with the data shown in Table 3, suggest that a certain population of myocardial cells had been damaged during the first occlusion, and that this damage was not reversed during the 45-minute period of reflow. Hence, when occlusion II was made, a smaller population of viable cells was left to produce H^+ and CO_2 resulting in significantly lower peak concentrations of these metabolites. This loss of cellular metabolic viability is confirmed by the direct relationship observed between the difference in peak $Pmco_2$ values during both occlusions and the degree of underlying ultrastructural ischemic damage (Fig. 7). The more that ultrastructural damage was observed, the wider was the difference in peak $Pmco_2$ between the two occlusions.

The observed late fall in $Pmco_2$ which occurs beyond 30 minutes of coronary occlusion seems to be a manifestation of regional and not necessarily of global myocardial ischemia. McGregor et al. (1974), utilizing the mass spectrometer, recorded intramyocardial Pco_2 in in the dog during cardiopulmonary bypass. After aortic clamping, they observed a significant rise in $Pmco_2$, but they failed to observe a decline in $Pmco_2$ after 66 minutes of normothermic global ischemia. Data from our laboratory (Lange et al., 1983) in which $Pmco_2$ did not fall, even after 2 hours of global normothermic anoxic arrest, confirm the findings of McGregor et al. and underscore the difference between the $Pmco_2$ curves obtained during regional and global ischemia. This difference may be a manifestation of (1) an increased myocardial demand in the beating as opposed to the arrest heart, and (2) an improved washout in the localized ischemic region provided by surrounding unoccluded coronary arteries. The difference in the $Pmco_2$ curves between both states may also reflect metabolic differences already outlined by Opie (1976).

In conclusion, this study demonstrates that the late fall in $Pmco_2$ following regional coronary occlusion in the dog is accompanied by a late fall in myocardial $[H^+]$, as well, and that it most likely is a reflection of progressive cellular damage leading to a decrease in the production of hydrogen ion and CO_2. $Pmco_2$ and myocardial pH curves following regional coronary occlusion allow the quantification of underlying ischemic damage and reflect the metabolic viability of the ischemic myocardium.

We wish to thank Dr. Eugene Braunwald for reviewing the manuscript, and also thank Kathy Kearns, Carol McDevitt, Clare Smith, Donna Kantarges, and David Bromley for their secretarial help.

Supported by the Veterans Administration, and also, in part, by Grant HL 23140 from the National Heart, Lung, and Blood Institutes, National Institutes of Health, Bethesda, Maryland, and with funds contributed in part by the Massachusetts Heart Association.

This work was performed during Dr. Koner's tenure as an Established Investigator of the American Heart Association.

Address for reprints: Shukri F. Khuri, M.D., Chief, Surgical Service, Veterans Administration Medical Center, West Roxbury, Massachusetts 02132

Received August 2, 1983; accepted for publication January 2, 1985.

References

Benzing H, Gebert G, Strohm M (1971) Extracellular acid-base changes in the dog myocardium during hypoxia and local ischemia, measured by means of glass microelectrodes. Cardiology **56:** 85–88

Brantigan JW, Gott, VL, Martz MN (1972) A teflon membrane for measurement of blood and intramyocardial gas tensions by mass spectroscopy. J Appl Physiol **32:** 276–282

Case RB, Felix A, Wachter M (1979a) Measurement of myocardial P_{CO_2} with a microelectrode: Its relation to coronary sinus P_{CO_2}. Am J Physiol **236:** H29–H34

Case RB, Felix A, Castellana F (1979b) Rate of rise of myocardial P_{CO_2} during early myocardial ischemia in the dog. Circ Res **45:** 324–330

Chance B, Melna M (1966) Intramitochondrial pH changes in cation accumulation. Proc Natl Acad Sci USA **55:** 1243–1251

Cobbe SM, Poole-Wilson PA (1980) The time onset and severity of acidosis in myocardial ischemia. J Mol Cell Cardiol **12:** 745–760

Coon R, Lai NCJ, Kampine JP (1976) Evaluation of a dual function pH and P_{CO_2} in vivo sensor. J Appl Physiol **40:** 625–629

Davenport HW (1967) The ABC of Acid-Base Chemistry, Chicago, The University of Chicago Press

Gebert G, Benzing H, Strohm M (1971) Changes in the interstitial pH of dog myocardium in response to local ischemia, hypoxia, hyper- and hypocapnia, measured continuously by means of glass microelectroes. Pflugers Arch **329:** 72–81

Gevers W (1977) Generation of protons by metabolic processes in heart cells. J Mol Cell Cardiol **9:** 867–874

Hicks GL, Hill A, DeWeese JA (1976) Monitoring of midmyocardial and subendocardial pH in normal and ischemic ventricles. J Thorac Cardiovasc Surg **72:** 52–56

Hillis LD, Khuri SF, Braunwald E, Kloner RA, Tow DE, Barsamian E, Maroko P (1979) Assessment of the efficacy of interventions to limit ischemic injury by direct measurement of intramural carbon dioxide tension after coronary artery occlusion in the dog. J Clin Invest **63:** 99–107

Hillis LD, Davis C, Khuri SF (1981) The effect of nitroglycerin and nitroprusside on intramural carbon dioxide tension during acute experimental myocardial ischemia in dogs. Circ Res **48:** 372–378

Ingvar DH, Lassen NA (1961) Quantitative determination of regional cerebral blood flow in man. Lancet **2:** 806–807

Khuri SF, Flaherty JT, O'Riordan JB, Pitt B, Brawley RL, Donahoo JS, Gott VL (1975) Changes in intramyocardial ST segment voltage and gas tensions with regional ischemia in the dog. Circ Res **37:** 455–463

Khuri SF, Kloner RA, Hillis LD, Tow DE, Barsamian EM, Maroko PR, Braunwald E (1979a) Intramural P_{CO_2}: A reliable index of the severity of myocardial ischemic injury. Am J Physiol **237:** H253–H259

Khuri SF, Kloner RA, Karaffa S, Couch N, Lai NCJ, Carlson N, Tow DE (1979b) A new intramural pH electrode for the assessment of myocardial ischemia (abstr). Circulation 59 (suppl II): 96

Khuri SF, Karaffa S, Kloner RA, Barsamian EM, Yasuda T, Tow DE (1980) Determination of intramyocrdial blood flow with Xenon-127. J Thorac Cardiovasc Surg **80:** 262–270

Khuri SF, Marston W, Josa M, Crowe W, Zierler M, Lange R, Miller W (1984) First report of intramyocardial pH in man: I. Methodology and initial results. Med Instrum **18:** 167–171

Kloner RA, Ganot EC, Whalen DA, Jennings RB (1974) Effect of a transient period of ischemia on myocardial cells. II. Fine structure during the first few minutes of reflow. Am J Pathol **74:** 399–422

Kloner RA, Fishbein MC, Cotran RS, Braunwald E, Maroko PR (1979a) The effect of propranolol on microvascular injury in acute myocardial ischemia. Circulation **55:** 872–880

Kloner RA, Fishbein MC, MacLean D, Braunwald E, Maroko PR (1977b) Effect of hyaluronidase during the early phase of acute myocardial ischemia: An ultrastructural and morphometric analysis. Am J Cardiol **40:** 43–49

Lange R, Koner RA, Zierler M, Carlson N, Seiler M, Khuri SF (1983) Time course of ischemic alterations during normo- and hypothermic arrest and its reflection by on-line monitoring of tissue pH. J Thorac Cardiovasc Surg **86:** 418–434

McGregor DC, Wilson GJ, Holness DE, Lixfield W, Yasui H, Tanaka S, Silver MD, Gustensen J (1974) Intramyocardial carbon dioxide tensions: A guide to the safe period of anoxic arrest of the heart. J Thorac Cardiovasc Surg **68:** 101–107

Opie LH (1976) Effects of regional ischemia on metabolism of glucose and fatty acids. Circ Res **38** (supppl I): 52–68

Rude RE, Kloner RA, Maroko PR, Khuri SF, Karaffa S, DeBoer LW, Braunwald E (1980) Effects of amrinone on experimental acute myocardial ischemic injury. Cardiovasc Res **14:** 419–427

Scheuer J, Brachfeld N (1966) Myocardial uptake and fractional distribution of palmitate-1-C^{14} by the ischemic dog heart. Metabolism **15:** 945–954

Walters FJM, Chin B, Wilson GJ, Steward DJ, Domenech RJ, McGregor DC (1979) Intramyocardial pH as an index of myocardial metabolism during cardiac surgery. J Thorac Cardiovasc Surg **78:** 319–30.

INDEX TERMS: Regional myocardial ischemia • Myocardial gas tensions • Myocardial pH

Transmural Distribution of Isomyosin in Rabbit Ventricle during Maturation Examined by Immunofluorescence and Staining for Calcium-Activated Adenosine Triphosphatase

Brenda R. Eisenberg, Joy A. Edwards, and Radovan Zak

From the Department of Physiology, Rush Medical College, and Department of Medicine, University of Chicago, Chicago, Illinois

SUMMARY. Mammalian ventricle contains two major isomyosins, V_1 and V_3, which differ in the primary structure of their heavy chains (HC$\alpha\alpha$ and HC$\beta\beta$, respectively) and in their adenosine triphosphatase activity. The distribution of the HCα isomyosin in the left ventricle of the rabbit was followed as a function of age and transmural location. HCα was detected with a monoclonal antibody found to be specific for the hinge region of V_1 myosin molecules when viewed in the electron microscope after low-angle rotary shadowing. Frozen sections were observed with indirect immunofluorescence developed to this anti-HCα hinge antibody. Serial sections were observed with the histochemical assay for calcium-activated myosin adenosine triphosphatase, using preincubation at various pH levels. Results show that all the ventricular myocytes in baby rabbits (2 weeks) are stained by the HCα-antibody from the epi- to endocardium. The isomyosin content of myocytes varies through the epi- to endocardium of the right ventricular wall of the adult (1-year-old) rabbit, with the HCα form predominating in the outer epicardial third of the wall and the lowest amount of HCα in the middle third of the wall. A mixture of stained and unstained myocytes is seen in the endo- and subendocardial regions. The spatial distribution of HCα in 4-month-old rabbits varies between that of the baby and adult. There is good agreement between myocyte classifications made by histochemical and antibody staining methods. A rabbit ventricular myocyte with HCα detected by antibody has high adenosine triphosphatase activity, and a myocyte without HCα has a low adenosine triphosphatase activity. Myocytes with similar staining properties appear in large clusters, long strands, and major anatomical regions. However, heterogeneous myocytes are also seen connected by an intercalated disc. **(*Circ Res 56: 548–555, 1985*)**

MYOSIN in cross-striated muscles belongs to a multigene family composed of approximately eight variants which differ in their structure and enzymatic properties. The divergence among isomyosins is reflected both in their heavy chains (HC) and light chains (reviewed in Zak and Galhotra, 1983). In the heart, two subclasses of myosin can be demonstrated; atrial and ventricular (Hoh et al., 1978). In the ventricle, the α and β HC associate in the cell as two homodimers of HC$\alpha\alpha$ and HC$\beta\beta$, and one heterodimer HC $\alpha\beta$, called V_1, V_3, and V_2, respectively (Hoh et al., 1978; Everett et al., 1983a, 1983b). The HCα is very similar, if not identical, to the one present in atria, and the HCβ is similar to the form present in slow skeletal muscle (Sinha et al., 1984).

Ventricular isomyosins have been detected in all mammalian species examined. Their relative content in the ventricle differs depending on animal species (Lompre et al., 1981; Clark et al., 1982). Thus, in hearts of small animals, such as a mouse, the V_1 isoform predominates, but in large animals, e.g., human, the V_3 variant is most common. The proportions of the ventricular isomyosins vary depending on the age of the animal (Lompre et al., 1981; Clark et al., 1982; Martin et al., 1983), hemodynamic load (Lompre et al., 1979; Gorza et al., 1981; Litten et al., 1982), and a variety of hormones and nutritional factors, of which the thyroid hormone is the most potent (Morkin et al., 1983).

At the cellular level, the isomyosin composition of a ventricle has been analyzed by the immunofluorescence technique (Samuel et al., 1983). In those hearts that have been found to contain all three isomyosins, e.g., the 8-week-old rat, the isomyosin distribution within the population of myocytes was found to be heterogeneous. Some cells react only with anti V_1 or V_3 antibodies, whereas others react with both. Of particular interest is the fact that myocytes of different isomyosin content were found in cells directly connected by an intercalated disc (Sartore et al., 1981). Considering that neighboring cells in the myocardium have similar electrical and mechanical properties, the heterogeneity in isomyosin content of individual cells poses a great challenge as far as the identification of factors determining cardiac phenotype is concerned.

In this paper, we report a comparison of two histological techniques which localize the V_1 and V_3

isomyosins. First, we use a monoclonal antibody specific for HCα. One drawback of the immunofluorescence technique is that, although it is very sensitive to small amounts of antigen, it is not very quantitative. Progress has been made recently in differentiation between the V_1 and V_3 isozymes by a second histochemical method which is based on differential pH lability of ATPase activity of individual isomyosins, and which may suffer less from the problem of the threshold phenomenon. We have examined the effect of age and transmural location on the presence of the HCα in rabbit cardiac tissue so that the work being done may be related to the kind of myosin being expressed.

Methods

Three New Zealand white rabbits were used at each selected stage of maturity: baby animals weighing under 500 g (about 2 weeks old), young animals of 2.5–3 kg (approximately 4 months), and adults of 4–5 kg (approximately 1 year). All animals were anesthetized with sodium pentobarbitol, the thoracic cavity opened, and the ventricles injected with 1 mEq/ml KCl to stop the heart in diastole. The heart was then removed and the left ventricle trimmed free.

Tissue was excised from the region midway between the apex and the base of the ventricle, and segments were carefully oriented so that a transmural surface was in the sectioning plane. The segments were attached to a slice of cork with embedding medium and frozen in isopentane slush that had been precooled in liquid nitrogen. Serial sections (6 μm thick) were cut on an Ames Cryostat (Miles) at −20°C. Some sections were stained with periodic acid Schiff's stain (PAS) for glycogen, or NADH tetrazolium reductase for mitochondrial enzymes. In addition, alternate sections were stained for immunofluorescence or ATPase, as described below. All sections were stored at −20°C and were used within 24 hours.

The monoclonal antibody mcAb 37 reacts specifically with rabbit myosin HCα with the purity specified by radioimmunoassay (RIA) (Chizzonite et al., 1982). Myosin preparation consisting of pure heterodimers of HCα or HCβ were obtained from hyperthyroid or PTU-treated rabbits. Antibody (60 μg/ml) and myosin (144 μg/ml) were mixed in 33% glycerol and 0.3 M ammonium formate buffer at pH 7.3 (Claviez et al., 1983). The tagged molecules were immediately sprayed onto freshly cleaved mica at room temperature, and, after rotary shadowing with platinum/palladium at an angle of 7° and coating with carbon, were observed in the electron microscope (Pullman, 1978). Micrographs of at least 300 molecules were printed at 80,000×, and each molecule was classified as having two, one, or zero antibodies bound to it. The location of the antibody on the myosin was noted.

Indirect immunofluorescence to the HCα antibody was performed on sections picked up on coverslips coated with poly-*l*-lysine at pH 8.5 and air-dried to prevent detachment (Wolosowick and DeMey, 1982); these sections then were washed in 0.01 M phosphate-buffered saline (PBS) containing 0.02% NaN_3 and 2% heat-inactivated fetal calf serum (Gibco) to block nonspecific antibody binding. The sections were incubated for 45–60 minutes at room temperature with the final dilution of monoclonal antibody (mc Ab 37) of 1:1000 which was selected empirically for maximal signal with minimal nonspecific background binding. Sections were rinsed with phosphate-buffered saline (PBS) and stained for 1 hour with fluorescein-labeled rabbit anti-rat IgG (Cappel Laboratories, Inc.). Aliquots of antibody were refrigerated, and aliquots of labeled IgG solutions were frozen to ensure standardized immunostaining. Sections were again rinsed with PBS and mounted on slides with glycerol:PBS (9:1) containing 0.1% phenylenediamine to protect against fading (Johnson and Araujo, 1981). A control was designed to give a positive reaction by using an incubation with rat serum to replace the first incubation of fetal calf serum. Other controls were run, omitting the antibody or the fluorescein label, and were always negative. Fluorescein-stained slides were stored in the dark at 4°C until viewed within 3 days with a Nikon microscope equipped with epifluorescent illumination (excitation filter of B2, wavelength 460–490, barrier filter 515).

Frozen sections alternating with those used for the antibody localization were stained for ATPase (myosin adenosine triphosphatase, Ca^{++}-activated, EC 3.6.1.3.) activity (p32 in Dubowitz and Brooke, 1973). The acidic preincubation solution consisted of 50 mM sodium acetate and 30 mM sodium barbital, with a pH of 4.2, 4.4, or 4.6, adjusted with 1 M HCl. Basic preincubation solutions consisted of 100 mM 2-amino-2-methyl-*l*-propanol and 18 mM $CaCl_2 \cdot 2H_2O$, with a pH of 10.1, 10.2, 10.3, or 10.4, adjusted with 1 M NaOH (Thornell and Forsgren, 1982). Sections were viewed and photographed with a Zeiss Photomicroscope III using bright field illumination.

The proportion of the ventricular wall occupied by myocytes containing HCα was estimated from slides stained by the ATPase reactions at pH 10.2, which always correlated with the bright immunofluorescence. The stereological method of linear integration was used where a length ratio estimates a volume fraction (Eq. 2.23, Weibel, 1979). The ratio of length of the test line lying over the cells dark with the ATPase stain to that over light cells, L_α:L_β, is equal to the ratio of the volume of HCα- to HCβ-containing cells. A micrometer was used in the eyepiece of the light microscope at a magnification of 3.5 to measure lengths in two noncontiguous frozen sections. The lengths L_α and L_β were measured at five different locations with sufficient number of fields to cover the entire ventricular wall in each section. In addition, the transmural width and the position of the dark (HCα) cells from the endocardial surface was measured so that the gradient of cell types from the epicardium to endocardium could be determined.

Results

Specificity of the Antibody

We assign differential ATPase staining to a specific isomyosin by comparing adjacent frozen sections, one preincubated at alkaline pH and reacted for ATPase, and the other identified by a fluorescent tag to the anti-HCα antibody. The specificity of the monoclonal antibody (Chizzonite et al., 1982) was confirmed by immuno-electronmicroscopy by direct observation of myosin molecules of known heavy chain composition (Fig. 1). Of the 300 HCα myosin molecules counted, 23% had a pair of antibodies bound at the hinge in the tail, 7% had a single antibody bound at the hinge, and 67% had no bound antibody (Fig. 1, upper panels). Only 3% had bind-

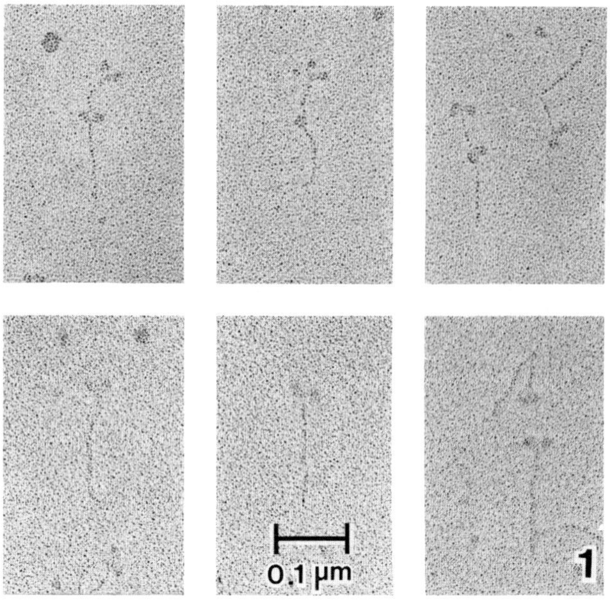

FIGURE 1. *Upper panels show V_1 myosin molecules of the heterodimer HCα from rabbits tagged with monoclonal antibody mcAb 37. The location of the bound antibody is at the hinge region in the tail, as seen in the upper right panel where one tagged myosin lies next to another bent at the hinge. Lower panels show untagged heterodimers of HCβ V_3 myosin molecules. Bar length = 0.1 μm.*

ing at a location other than the hinge. Of 300 HCβ myosin molecules counted, 98% had no bound antibody (Fig. 1, lower panels).

In frozen sections stained by immunofluorescence (Fig. 2A), the A-band appears bright when reacted with anti-HCα antibody. However, nonspecific binding is not seen elsewhere in the tissue.

ATPase Activity

Myocytes from rat ventricle have different intensities of ATPase staining, depending upon the duration, temperature, and pH of the preincubation solutions (Weisberg et al., 1982; Carlsson et al., 1982). In the rat ventricle, incubation at various pH levels presumably inhibits the V_1, V_2, and V_3 isomyosins differentially in both the alkaline and acid range, making it possible to estimate the isomyosin composition of the myocyte. The A-band appears dark when staining reveals a high level of Ca^{++}-activated ATPase (Fig. 2B). The staining reaction seen in the baby rabbits confirmed that the ATPase activity was correctly assigned to HCα. Acid preincubation affected all the isomyosins equally, inactivating enzymes below pH 4.6 (data not shown). However, in the range, pH 10.1–10.3, differential staining of HCα was possible by the ATPase histochemical method (Fig. 3). At a given pH preincubation, the appearance of the stain varied from one animal to another. Thus, in one animal, the sharpest division into dark and light cells occurred at pH 10.2, and in another it was at pH 10.3. In all animals there were several alkaline preincubations that gave grey, intermediately stained cells (see Fig. 3C). It is possible that these represent the ATPase activity derived from the V_2 heterodimer, HCαβ. However, the grey level could also have arisen from numerous other technical sources. We did not take special precautions to control such factors as section thickness, substrate levels, temperature, and so on, which makes it awkward to utilize the histochemical method to determine ATPase activity, quantitatively (see discussion by Weisberg et al., 1982). It therefore is difficult to make absolute estimates of ATPase activity with this assay.

HCα Myosin Distribution with Age

Baby (2-week-old) rabbits contain 50% HCα, as determined by native state electrophoresis, and by the age of 1 year, contain over 95% HCβ (Everett et al., 1983b). This shift in isomyosin content should be reflected in the staining patterns obtained with both ATPase activity and immunofluorescent reactions in serial sections. In the baby, the ventricle appears uniformly bright with the fluorescent tag to anti-HCα and uniformly dark when stained by the Ca^{++}-activated ATPase after an alkaline preincuba-

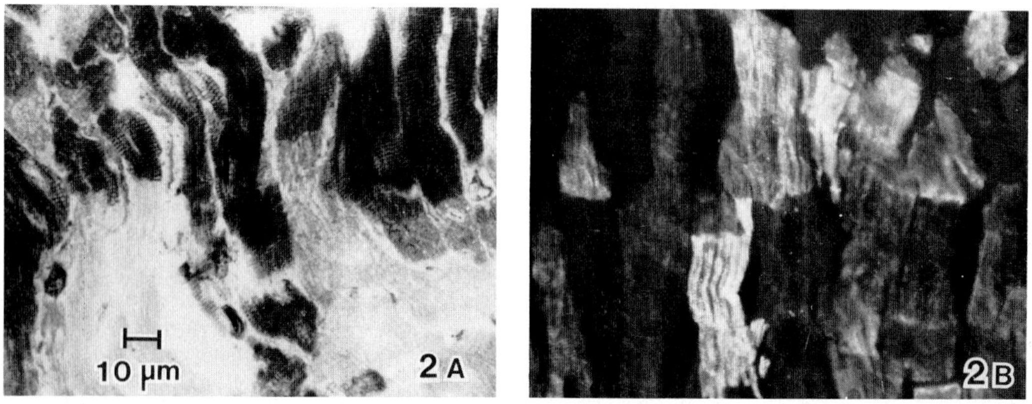

FIGURE 2. *Frozen sections in the mid-wall region of a 4-month-old rabbit. In Figure 2A, the A-band is stained dark with ATPase reaction at pH 10.2, and in Figure 2B, the A-band is bright with immunofluorescence staining of myocytes with anti-HCα. Myocytes containing HCα and high ATPase are seen directly coupled to nonstaining myocytes. Bar = 10 μm.*

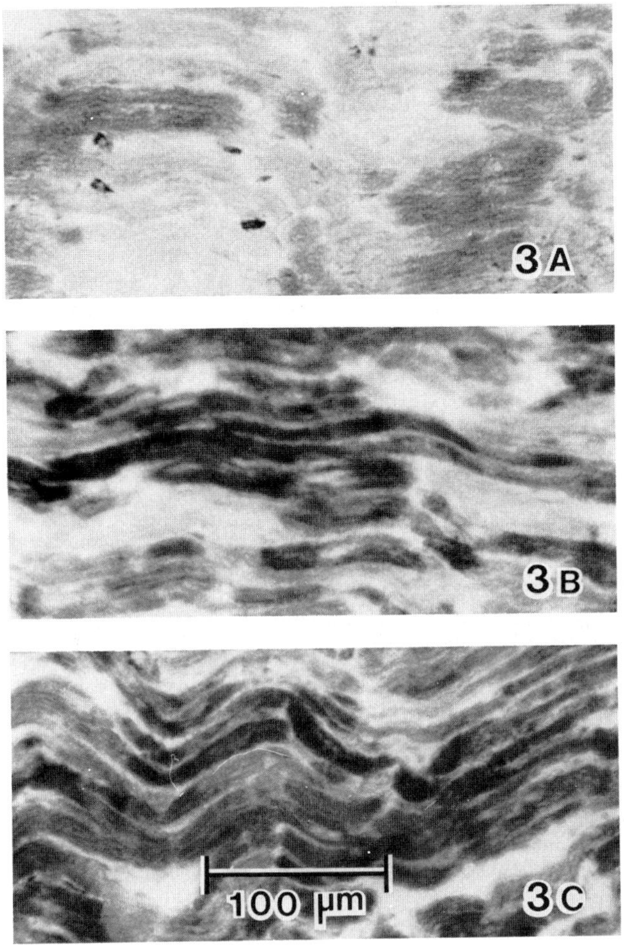

FIGURE 3. *Frozen sections through the mid-wall region of the left ventricular wall of an adult rabbit (wt 5 kg) stained with the ATPase reaction run after preincubations at different pH levels [at pH 10.3 (panel A), pH 10.2 (panel B), and pH 10.1 (panel C)]. In the alkaline preincubation (panels A–C), there is differential staining between myocytes. All myocytes were dark at pH 9.4, and all myocytes were light at pH 4.2, except for smooth muscle in the wall of the blood vessels, which was still stained dark at pH 4.2 (not shown). Bar = 100 μm.*

tion. The young (4-month-old) rabbits show a patchy appearance, with some myocytes containing HCα and others containing none. This is seen as a mixture of dark and light myocytes when stained with Ca^{++}-activated ATPase after alkaline preincubation (Fig. 4A), and as mixture of bright and dim myocytes when reacted for anti-HCα (Fig. 4B). By either method, the adult animals show even smaller numbers of cells staining for HCα content, and many of these are near blood vessels (Fig. 4, C and D).

Transmural Distribution of Ventricular Isomyosins

Transmural sections were obtained from oriented blocks of tissue, permitting the study of this anatomical variable. Histochemical stains for glycogen and mitochondrial content showed uniform distribution across the ventricular wall, in all animals. Baby rabbits stain uniformly bright with anti-HCα immunofluorescence (Fig. 5A), and darkly with the alkaline-preincubated ATPase reaction (Fig. 5D), as expected, since their isomyosin content is almost entirely HCα. In the adult animals weighing over 4 kg, there is a marked transmural gradient with both immunofluorescence (Fig. 5C) and ATPase staining (Fig. 5F), with an epicardial zone comprised of HCα myocytes. The endocardial region is predominantly unstained and is, therefore, HCβ. In the mid-wall region, there are some myocytes of each kind. Groups, strands, or clusters of similar stained cells are often contiguous. However, myocytes with different staining patterns are also seen directly connected (Fig. 2), as has been reported by Sartore et al. (1981). The 4-month-old (2-kg) rabbits have a marked predominance of HCα myocytes in the epicardial region, but the mid- and endocardial zones have large patches of tissue that stain for V_1 with both the fluorescent anti-HCα and dark, alkaline ATPase reactions.

The morphometric method of linear integration was used to determine the volume of the ventricular wall occupied by HCα-containing myocytes which stain dark with the ATPase reaction after the alkaline preincubation. This analysis was not repeated on the immunofluorescent sections because of problems with variance in the absolute intensity of the stain when fresh, compounded by long-term fading during storage. In the baby animals (2 weeks), 100% of the tissue volume is occupied by myocytes expressing HCα (n = 3 rabbits). In the young rabbits (4 months), 61 ± 7% of the tissue volume has HCα myocytes (mean ± SD, n = 3 rabbits). In adults, 49 ± 7% of the tissue volume has HCα myocytes (n = 3 rabbits). In all cases, the HCα-staining myocytes were found in the entire epicardial zone (defined as the outer third of the transmural wall thickness). Both HCα and HCβ myocytes are dispersed throughout the mid-wall and endocardium of young and adult rabbits. In some cases, we observed a concentration of HCα myocytes just away from the walls of larger blood vessels (Fig. 4, C and D), although we did not attempt a quantitative estimation.

Discussion

We have evaluated transmural distribution of HCα myosin in ventricles of rabbits of different ages by immunofluorescence and histochemical assessment of ATPase. Both techniques gave similar results. All ventricular myocytes of baby rabbits contain HCα myosin, in agreement with native state electrophoretic analysis done in our laboratory (Everett et al., 1983a). As the animal ages, HCα myosin is eliminated from some cells, with resulting cellular heterogeneity and a transmural pattern of isomyosin distribution. In the epicardial region of adult animals, most of the myocytes stain positively for HCα

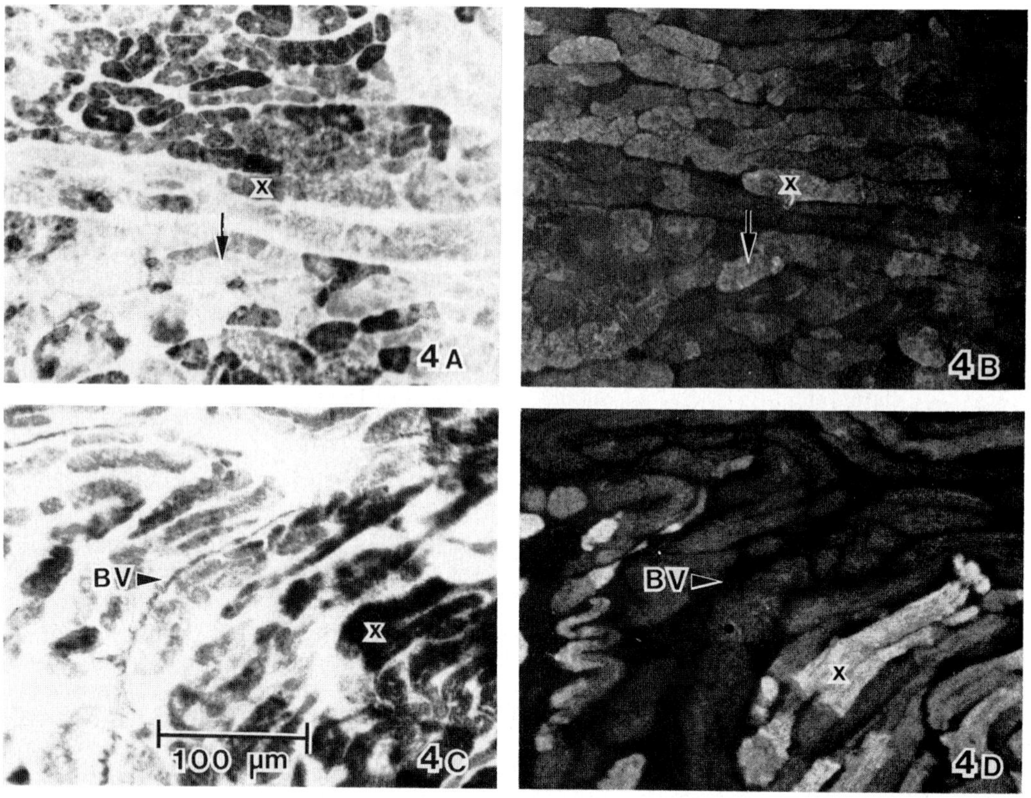

FIGURE 4. *Pairs of adjacent sections stained for ATPase after pH 10.2 preincubation (left panels) and with immunofluorescence of anti-HCα (right panels). Panels A and B: 4-month-old rabbit, (2.5 kg); panels C and D: adult rabbit (5 kg). Myocytes adjacent to the bloodvessel (BV) usually express HCβ, whereas those slightly further away express HCα. Sections probably through the same myocyte, marked by ×, are dark (high ATPase) and bright (HCα), respectively. Note that in panel C, the cell marked × shortened during processing for ATPase reactivity, but did not shorten, in panel D, during immuno-staining. In some places, adjacent section probably passes through different cells (arrow) because the section thickness is comparable to the cell diameter. Bar = 100 µm.*

myosin, while the midportion and the endocardium contain a substantial number of cells which do not.

The trend that we detected toward loss of HCα myosin with maturity agrees, in general, with previous immunofluorescence study (Sartore et al., 1981) and myosin analysis by native gel electrophoresis (Hoh et al., 1978; Everett et al., 1983a). However, our data indicate consistently more heterogeneity in the hearts of adult animals than would be predicted from densitometric scans of electrophoretically separated isomyosins. This lack of correlation between histochemical and electrophoretic analysis has also been seen in isolated rat myocytes, in which only traces of V_2 and V_3 isomyosin were detected electrophoretically, whereas about half of the isolated cells stained positively with anti-V_3 antibody (Samuel et al., 1983). These combined data indicate that the observed quantitative discrepancies are not a result of sampling error (the native state electrophoresis is usually performed with 10-mg samples of tissue), but, rather, results from method sensitivity.

The biological significance of regional distribution and of cellular heterogeneity of isomyosin distribution in the heart is presently unknown. This is not surprising, since the regional stresses and strains within the heart have not been described; the mechanical properties of the V_1 and V_3 isomyosin have recently been reported (Pagani and Julian, 1984). It has been established, however, that the V_1 isomyosin, which is dimer of heavy chains α, has about three times higher ATPase activity (Pope et al., 1980) than the HCβ dimer in V_3. The correlation between the shortening velocity and ATPase activity in the heart is less clear-cut than in studies of skeletal muscles (Barany, 1967). Nevertheless, the maximum velocity of shortening of the ventricular myocardium varies between animal species (Schwartz et al., 1981), as well as in the heart of a single animal (Hamrell and Low, 1978), in parallel with the Ca^{++}-activated myosin ATPase.

Whether any correlation between shortening velocity and isomyosin pattern applies to the regional heterogeneity seen in our study remains to be established. It is clear that the heterogeneity is in some cases small, such as in the case of human ventricle (Gorza et al., 1984), or it is absent altogether, such as in the hearts of young rabbits or hyperthyroid animals which contain solely V_1 isomyosin, and in hearts in the hypothyroid state, which lose all V_1 at

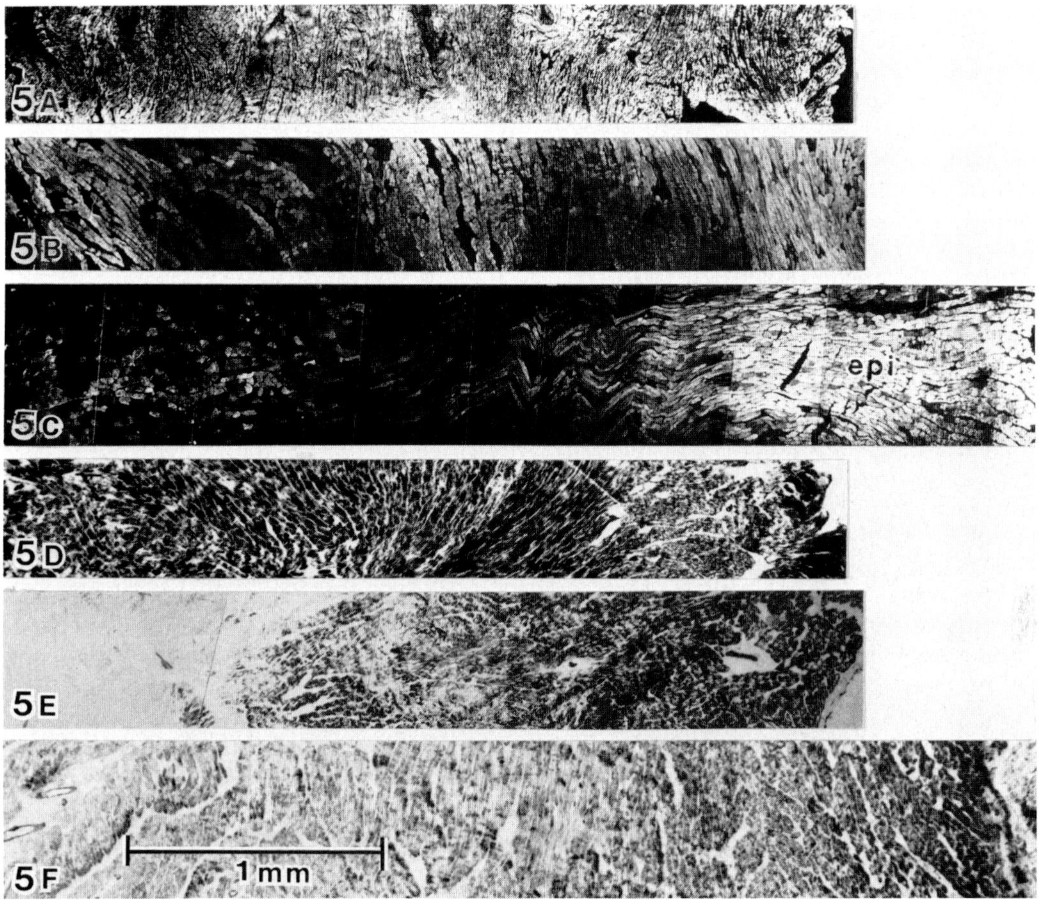

FIGURE 5. *Typical transmural sections through the left ventricle of the rabbit midway between the apex and the base. Photomicrographs from the endocardium (left) to the epicardium (right) showing the transmural distribution of the HCα myosin (panels A, B, and C) and high ATPase activity at pH 10.2 (panels D, E, and F). In the ventricle of baby (2-week-old) rabbits (panels A and D), all the myocytes are HCα and high ATPase. In the ventricle of the 4-month-old rabbits (panels B and E), there are large regions of both myosins and levels of ATPase activity present. In the ventricle of adult rabbits (panels C and F), there is a transmural gradient, with the epicardium being predominantly of the HCα myocyte type, the mid- to subendocardium being predominantly HCβ, and the endocardium being mixed. Sections from animals of the same age are not necessarily from serial sections. Bar = 1 mm.*

the expense of V_3 isomyosin (Sartore et al., 1981). Also, because the immunofluorescence technique is not a quantitative one and is sufficiently sensitive to detect minute amounts of reactive material, the amount of myosin contributing to the apparent heterogeneity might be quite small. Moreover our method does not allow us to determine whether there is co-expression of HCβ in HCα cells. This could account for some of the apparent discrepancies between the isomyosin content determined from tissue extracts (Everett et al., 1983a) and those determined in the present study.

Isomyosin type is regulated by mechanical demands and a variety of humoral factors. If we understood this epigenetic regulation, we might also understand why regions of the heart are anatomically and functionally different. The heart has a complex architecture, with myocyte columns spiralling upward and outward from the apex to the base (Streetor, 1979). Thus, the myocyte orientation varies with anatomical location from apex to base and from endo- to epicardial surface, the same route followed by a depolarizing wave initiated via the Purkinje conduction system. The longest-lasting action potentials are found in the endocardial myocytes and the shortest are found in the epicardial myocytes, which give rise to the inversion of the T-wave seen in the electrocardiogram (Cohen et al., 1976). The mechanical result is that force is first generated in the endocardial myocytes, and that the epicardial layers have the briefest contraction. The endocardial layer is thought to do more work in a normal cycle, but when the ventricles are stretched, the epicardial layers are recruited, and may contribute to the increased tension described by Starling (Ford and Forman, 1974). The sarcomere length also varies with anatomical location, the greatest length being found in the midwall and the shortest near the epicardium (Yoran et al., 1973; Grimm et al., 1980).

Although regional specialization of function exists, myocyte diversity is not readily seen with conventional anatomical techniques. Electron microscopic studies using quantitative ultrastructural analysis have not shown differences in cell size and subcellular contents within the rabbit ventricle (Anversa et al., 1971). However, stresses induced in the rat by renal hypertension which produce hypertrophy increase cell size more in the epicardial layers, and resulting transmural gradients become evident in mitochondrial-to-myofibrillar ratio and in the T-system surface density (Anversa et al., 1978). Regional regulation of electrical properties in the epicardial myocytes has also been seen in the rat during hypertrophy (Keung and Aronson, 1981).

Regional work loads might be assessed by regional oxygen consumption and metabolic profiles. Recent studies based on the transmural pH profile have suggested that, normally, the metabolism and energy balance is uniform, and that only during ischemia when the balance between supply and demand are perturbed do transmural gradients occur (Watson et al., 1984), and result in the greatest ischemic damage in the subendocardial zone (Moir, 1972). Metabolic gradients were suggested by earlier histochemical reports of a gradient in the glycogen content transmurally (Jideiken, 1964), but have not been confirmed by our histochemical stains for glycogen and for mitochondrial content.

Cellular heterogeneity might also be the result of a noncoordinated change of cellular phenotype during maturation. In this case, heterogeneity between two adjacent cells expressing different amounts of an isomyosin might depend on a stage of genetic reprogramming reflecting the different lineage of each myocyte, rather than on microenvironmental signals.

We thank Darlene Bruner for her excellent assistance with the microscopy.

Research was supported by grants from the American Heart Association (B.R.E.), by a Basic Research Science Grant (J.A.E.), by U.S. Public Health Service Grants HL 16627 and HL 20592 from the National Heart, Lung, and Blood Institute, and by a grant from the Muscular Dystrophy Association of America (R.Z.).

Address for reprints: Dr. Brenda R. Eisenberg, Physiology Department, Rush Medical College, 1750 West Harrison Street, Chicago, Illinois 60612.

Received September 4, 1984; accepted for publication January 18, 1985.

References

Anversa P, Vitalli-Mazza L, Visioli O, Marchetti G (1971) Experimental cardiac hypertrophy: A quantitative ultrastructural study in the compensatory stage. J Mol Cell Cardiol **3:** 213–227

Anversa P, Loud AV, Giacomelli F, Weiner J (1978) Absolute morphometric study of myocardial hypertrophy in experimental hypertension. II. Ultrastructure of myocytes and interstitium. Lab Invest **38:** 597–609

Barany M (1967) ATPase activity of myosin correlated with speed of muscle shortening. J Gen Physiol **50:** 197–216

Carlsson E, Kjorell U, Thornell L-E (1982) Differentiation of the myofibrils and intermediate filament system during postnatal development in the rat heart. Eur J Cell Biol **27:** 62–73

Chizzonite RA, Everett AW, Clark WA, Jakovcic S, Rabinowitz M, Zak R (1982) Isolation and characterization of two molecular variants of myosin heavy chain from rabbit ventricle. J Biol Chem **257:** 2056–2065

Clark WA, Chizzonite RA, Everett AW, Rabinowitz M, Zak R (1982) Species correlations between cardiac isomyosins: A comparison of electrophoretic and immunological properties. J Biol Chem **257:** 5449–5454

Claviez M, Pagh K, Maruta H, Baltes W, Fisher P, Gerisch G (1982) Electron microscopic mapping of monoclonal antibodies on the tail region of dictyostelium myosin. EMBO J **1:** 1017–1022

Cohen IS, Giles W, Noble D (1976) Cellular basis for the T wave of the electrocardiogram. Nature **262:** 657–661

Dubowitz V, Brooke MH (1973) Muscle Biopsy: A Modern Approach. London, Saunders

Everett AW, Chizzonite RA, Clark WA, Zak R (1983a) Relationship of changes in molecular forms of myosin heavy chain to endogenous levels of thyroid hormone during postnatal growth. Perspect Cardiovasc Res **8:** 83–92

Everett AW, Clark WA, Chizzonite RA, Zak R (1983b) Change in synthesis rates of α- and β-myosin heavy chains in rabbit heart after treatment with thyroid hormone. J Biol Chem **258:** 2421–2425

Ford LE, Forman R (1974) Tetanized cardiac muscle. *In* The Physiological Basis of Starling's Law of the Heart. Amsterdam, Ciba Foundation Elsevier, pp 137–150

Gorza L, Pauletto P, Pessina AL, Sartore S, Schiaffino S (1981) Isomyosin distribution in normal and pressure-overloaded rat ventricular myocardium. A immunohistochemical study. Circ Res **49:** 1003–1009

Gorza L, Mercadier JJ, Schwartz K, Thornell LE, Sartore S, Schiaffino S (1984) Myosin types in the human heart: An immunofluorescence study of normal and hypertrophied atrial and ventricular myocardium. Circ Res **54:** 694–702

Grimm AF, Lin H, Grimm BR (1980) Left ventricular free wall and intraventricular pressure-sarcomere length distributions. Am J Physiol **8:** H101–H107

Hamrell BB, Low RB (1978) The relationship of mechanical V_{max} to myosin ATPase activity in rabbit and marmot ventricular muscle. Pflugers Arch **377:** 119–124

Hoh JFY, McGrath PA, Hale PT (1978) Electrophoretic analysis of multiple forms of rat cardiac myosin: Effects of hypophysectomy and thyroxine replacement. J Mol Cell Cardiol **10:** 1053–1075

Jedeikin LA (1964) Regional distribution of glycogen and phosphorylase in the ventricles of the heart. Circ Res **14:** 202–211

Johnson GD, Araujo GMCN (1981) A simple method of reducing the fading of immuno-fluorescence during microscopy. J Immunol Meth **43:** 349–350

Keung ECH, Aronson RS (1981) Non-uniform electrophysiological properties and electronic interaction in hypertrophied rat myocardium. Circ Res **49:** 150–158

Litten RL, Martin BJ, Low RB, Alpert NR (1982) Altered myosin isozyme pattern from pressure-overloaded and thyrotoxic hypertrophied rabbit heart. Circ Res **50:** 856–865

Lompre A-M, Schwartz K, d'Albis A, Lacombe G, Van Thiem N, Swynghedauw B (1979) Myosin isozyme redistribution in chronic heart overload. Nature **282:** 105–107

Lompre AM, Mercadier JJ, Wisnewsky C, Bouveret P, Pantaloni C, D'Albis A, Schwartz K (1981) Species- and age-dependent changes in the relative amounts of cardiac myosin isoenzymes in mammals. Develop Biol **84:** 286–290

Martin AF, Haithcoap JL, Dowell RP (1983) Redistribution of ventricular myosin isoenzymes in neonatal and adult rat heart in response to a chronic pressure overload. Perspect Cardiovasc Res **7:** 359–371

Moir TW (1972) Subendocardial distribution of coronary blood flow and the effect of antianginal drugs. Circ Res **30:** 621–627

Morkin E, Flink IL, Goldman S (1983) Biochemical and physiological effects of thyroid hormone on cardiac performance. Prog Cardiovasc Dis **25:** 435–464

Pagani ED, Julian FJ (1984) Rabbit papillary muscle myosin isozymes and the velocity of muscle shortening. Circ Res **54:** 586–594

Pope B, Hoh JFY, Weeds A (1980) The ATPase activity of rat

cardiac myosin isoenzymes. FEBS Lett **118:** 205–208

Pullman JM (1978) The assembly of myosin on polysomes. Thesis, University of Chicago.

Samuel JL, Rappaport L, Mercadier JJ, Lompre AM, Sartore S, Tribani C, Schiaffino S, Schwartz K (1983) Distribution of myosin isozymes within single cardiac cells: A immunohistochemical study. Circ Res **52:** 200–209

Sartore S, Gorza L, Bormioli SP, Libera LD, Schiaffino S (1981) Myosin types and fiber types in cardiac muscle. I. Ventricular myocardium. J Cell Biol **88:** 226–233

Schwartz K, Lecarpentier Y, Martin JL, Lompre AM, Mercadier JJ, Swynghedauw B (1981) Myosin isoenzymic distribution correlates with speed of myocardial contraction. J Mol Cell Cardiol **13:** 1071–1075

Sinha AM, Friedman DJ, Nigro JM, Jakovcic S, Rabinowitz M, Umeda PK (1984) Expression of rabbit ventricular α-myosin heavy chain messenger RNA sequences in atrial muscle. J Biol Chem **259:** 6674–6680

Streetor DD (1979) Gross morphology and fiber geometry of the heart. *In* Handbook of Physiology, vol 1, sec 2, The Cardiovascular System, edited by RM Berne, N Sperelakis, SR Geiger. Washington, D.C., The American Physiological Society, pp 61–112

Thornell LE, Forsgren S (1982) Myocardial cell heterogeneity in the human heart with respect to myosin ATPase activity. Histochem J **14:** 479–490

Watson RM, Markle DR, Ro YM, Goldstein SR, McGuire DA, Peterson JI, Patterson RE (1984) Transmural pH gradient in canine myocardial ischemia. Am J Physiol **24:** H232–H238

Weibel ER (1979) Stereological Methods. I. Practical Methods for Biological Morphometry. New York, Academic Press

Weisberg A, Winegrad S, Tucker M, McClellan G (1982) Histochemical detection of specific isozymes of myosin in rat ventricular cells. Circ Res **51:** 802–809

Wolosewick J, DeMey J (1982) Localization of tubulin and actin in polyethylene glycol embedded rat seminiferous epithelium. Biol Cell **44:** 85–88

Yoran C, Covell JW, Ross J (1973) Structural basis for the ascending limb of left ventricular function. Circ Res **32:** 297–303

Zak R, Galhotra SS (1983) Contractile and regulatory proteins. *In* Cardiac Metabolism, edited by AJ Drake-Holland, MIM Nobel. Chichester, J Wiley & Sons, pp 339–364

INDEX TERMS: Isomyosin • ATPase activity • Transmural gradients • Left ventricle

Fibrosis, Lipids, and Calcium in Human Atherosclerotic Plaque

In Vitro Differentiation from Normal Aortic Walls by Ultrasonic Attenuation

Eugenio Picano, Luigi Landini, Alessandro Distante, Antonio Benassi, Roberta Sarnelli, and Antonio L'Abbate

From the Istituto di Fisiologia Clinica, C.N.R., Pisa, and the Facoltà di Ingegneria, the Istituto di Patologia Medica I, and the Istituto di Anatomia Patologica, Università di Pisa, Pisa, Italy

SUMMARY. This study was designed to determine whether attenuation of ultrasound by the aortic wall is potentially useful in characterizing the atherosclerotic lesion. Measurements were made on fresh specimens taken from a human aorta at autopsy. Four hundred different sites, 4 mm in diameter each, corresponding to the dimension of the ultrasonic beam at the focal zone, were ultrasonically analyzed and histologically studied. Attenuation of ultrasound in each site was assessed by Fourier analysis of the echo produced by a specular reflector placed behind the specimen. Two parameters were measured over the range 7–11 MHz: the integrated attenuation index (per cm), and slope (per cm per MHz) of the best fit straight line relating attenuation and frequency. Histological examination—performed for each of the 400 sites where attenuation had been measured—identified four subsets (100 samples each): normal aortic walls, fibrous plaques, fibrofatty plaques, and calcified plaques. Results obtained from ultrasonic and histological analyses showed that the integrated attenuation index was lowest in normal walls (24 ± 2.1, mean ± SE) and progressively increased in fibrous (32 ± 3.1), fibrofatty (82 ± 6.5), and calcific (185 ± 8.7) subsets (all intergroup differences were significant, except for the normal vs. fibrous comparison). The slope value was significantly lower in the fibrous than in the normal subsets: (10^{-3}) 31.9 ± 4.5 vs. (10^{-3}) 99.5 ± 9.1, respectively. Values of fibrofatty and calcific plaques overlapped: (10^{-3}) 383 ± 21 vs. (10^{-3}) 320 ± 23, respectively. Both were significantly different from normal and fibrous groups. Thus, alterations in ultrasonic indices related to attenuation characterize the different pathological patterns of atherosclerosis in the human arterial wall, providing a distinction between normal specimens and fibrous, fibrofatty, and calcified plaques. **(*Circ Res 56: 556–562, 1985*)**

RECENT information has linked the biochemical profile of atherosclerotic plaque (that is, the relative amounts of fibrous, lipid, and calcific constituents) to its biological activity and clinical relevance. "Unfortunately, however, at our present stage of technology and knowledge, it is virtually impossible to evaluate the quantities of these major components in any given plaque in the human subject at any specific time, short of surgical removal or examination at autopsy" (Wissler, 1984).

In the recent past, ultrasonic tissue characterization has proved useful in the study of many pathological situations (Linzer, 1979; Chivers, 1981). Therefore, we decided to study atherosclerotic disease with this new emerging tool. Encouraging data have been recently obtained in vitro, using backscattered signals as a means of differentiating normal, fibrofatty, and calcific formalin-fixed human aortic walls, both with narrow (Picano et al., 1983a) and broadband (Picano et al., 1983b) transducers. Identification of attenuation properties of normal and diseased arterial tissue could provide additional useful information, since such properties are also based on intrinsic characteristics of the tissue and could be, at least theoretically, measured in vivo exploiting reflected ultrasound (Kuc and Schwartz, 1979; Fink et al., 1983).

The aim of this study was to measure in vitro attenuation properties of human fresh aortic walls—normal, and with different degrees of atherosclerosis. Four hundred aortic regions from human autoptic aortas were studied in vitro: 100 normal walls, 100 fibrous, 100 fibrofatty, and 100 calcified plaques. Atherosclerotic disease was independently assessed, after ultrasonic measurements, by histological examination performed on each site. Quantitative indices of ultrasonic attenuation were derived from the frequency dependence of the ultrasonic attenuation characterizing each arterial region over the range 7–11 MHz.

Methods

Experimental Procedure

Specimens of fresh arterial wall were taken from human aortas at autopsy and were selected to consist of diseased regions containing three district kinds of lesion (fibrotic, fibrofatty, and calcified), along with regions—whenever possible—of relatively normal tissue. In order to deal with potential problems of methodology related to the time after death at which the tissues were harvested and examined by ultrasound and the temperature of the tissue during the examination (Mimbs et al., 1979), sampling was performed only when the interval from death to excision ranged between 10 and 15 hours, and the ultrasonic examination was started immediately after excision and performed in a water bath at a constant temperature of 20°C.

Excised samples of aorta were cut down the anterior midline, opened flat, and mounted on a squared, metallic, hollow-rimmed sample holder with pins along its periphery and placed in a distilled water bath. This device provided stabilization of the tissue sample and avoided interference with ultrasonic measurements.

Once the ultrasonic studies were over, the tissue was removed from the water bath, and thickness was measured by means of a micrometer (for each of the sites studied ultrasonically) before histological preparation.

For each pathological subset, the first 100 consecutive sites acquired were considered for analysis.

Ultrasonic Characterization

Measurements were made by employing the system described in Figure 1. It consists of a single transducer acting as transmitter and receiver of the echo produced by a specular reflector lodged behind the specimen under study. In this approach, the amplitude of the echo that has passed twice through the specimen is measured. The electrical source consisted of a broadband pulser-receiver (Panametric model 5052PR).

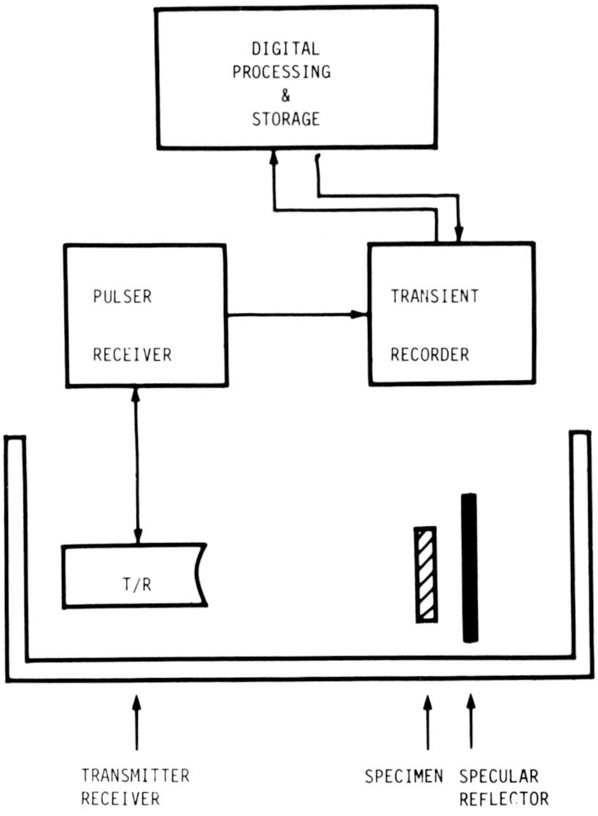

FIGURE 1. *Experimental system employed.*

A small-diameter focused transducer (Aerotech, model gamma, 15 MHz nominal frequency, 0.5 cm in diameter, 8 cm focal distance, 4 mm in diameter at the focal zone) was used. The ultrasonic beamwidth (evaluated at −3 dB) was determined with pulsed broadband signal by means of a metallic Rayleigh reflector. To achieve broadband characteristics, we designed this transducer to operate over the frequency range of 4–14 MHz on the left tail of the frequency response of the 15 MHz center frequency quartz plate. Before tissue was placed in the path of the ultrasonic beam, we measured the response characteristics of the system by employing the substitution technique of Schwan and Carstensen (1952). Both the sample holder and the specular reflector were placed in the focal zone of the ultrasonic beam. The mounted tissue sample was analyzed ultrasonically at 16 discrete sites. A square matrix of the 16 sites (4 × 4) was obtained for each specimen, every point being 2 mm apart from the other. For each point, four measurements were obtained with micrometer displacement of the transducer, with the aim to minimize phase cancellation effects (Mimbs et al., 1979). The average measurement of the four was taken as representative of that site. Data collection was performed automatically. Under control of a timing unit, broadband ultrasonic pulses are digitized by a transient recorder (Tektronik, model 7912 AD, conversion rate 10 nsec, 9 bits of amplitude resolution). Data from the transient recorder were continuously transferred to a minicomputer (HP-1000) for the analysis.

Ultrasonic Indices

The transfer function ($H_{(f)}$) of each specimen was estimated by the ratio of the Fourier transforms of the two signals received, respectively, in the presence and absence of the interposed tissue. The $\ln|H_{(f)}|$ was evaluated according to the following relationship (Kak and Dines, 1978):

$$\ln|H_{(f)}| = \ln T - 2\,\alpha_{(f)}\cdot X \qquad (1)$$

where $\alpha_{(f)}$ describes the signal loss due both to absorption and scattering of ultrasound within the specimen, X is the thickness of the sample, and T represents the product of the amplitude transmission coefficients for the water-tissue and tissue-water interfaces. The attenuation coefficient of the water has been neglected.

The range where $\ln|H_{(f)}|$ is a linear function of the frequency (7–11 MHz) has been previously assessed (unpublished data). Over the range 7–11 MHz, two indices were derived:

1. The integral value of $\ln|H_{(f)}|$ normalized for the thickness of the specimen (*integrated attenuation index*: A). Such an index is supposed to assess both intimal and internal signal losses due to atherosclerosis. The normalization for the thickness is made on both components contributing to $\ln|H_{(f)}|$ (see Eq. 1): internal loss (which is thickness dependent) and surface reflection loss (which is thickness independent, and therefore should not be normalized). From the practical point of view, however, it is impossible to discriminate—by analyzing the received signal—one contribution from the other. Therefore, the

normalization procedure introduces an approximation which can be considered reasonable, if it is assumed that a negligible loss in signal occurs due to the reflection at the water-specimen interface (Mimbs et al., 1977).

2. The slope of the least square straight line regression fit to (1/X) ln | $H_{(f)}$ | (*slope index*: S). Such an index is supposed to be independent of the amplitude transmission coefficients (Kak and Dines, 1978) (ln A = 0).

Equation 1 is based on the assumption that phase cancellation effects are insignificant. This is an obvious oversimplification, which can be considered reasonable, however, when a broadband-focused transducer with a small surface is employed.

Pathological Characterization

Four hundred aortic regions, 4 mm in diameter, equivalent to the dimension of the transducer focal zone, were independently studied, after ultrasonic measurements, by histology. Weigert-Van Gieson stain was employed. According to generally accepted criteria (Robbins and Cotran, 1979), four pathological subsets were identified, each consisting of 100 samples: normal aortic walls, fibrous plaques (i.e., with wall thickened by connective tissue), fibrofatty plaques (usually characterized by a fibrous cap and a lipid core), and calcified plaques (where calcification of the atheromata occurs).

It must be pointed out that each ultrasonically studied aortic region had a diameter of 4 mm, and every point was 2 mm apart from the others. Therefore, a half overlap of the focal zone (corresponding to approximately 30% overlap in two adjacent areas) was made. This is necessary for an accurate acoustical mapping of the specimen. If no overlap had been made, a significant area of the aortic specimen would not have been sampled at all. A greater overlap would have been useful for the acoustical mapping, but this would have made more difficult the correlation with histological data.

Statistical Methods

For both indices employed, the mean value and standard error of each pathological subset were measured. Differences were tested for significance by analysis of variance, with subgroup analysis by Newmann-Keuls test (Wiener, 1971).

TABLE 1
Value of Integrated Attenuation Index in the Four Subsets

	A	Comparison			
	(per cm)	NL	FI	FA	CL
NL	24 ± 2.1		NS	*	*
FI	32 ± 3.1			*	*
FA	82 ± 6.5				*
CL	185 ± 8.7				

NS = not significant. NL = normal arterial wall tissue, FI = fibrous arterial wall tissue, FA = fibrofatty arterial wall tissue, CL = calcified specimen.
* $P < 0.01$.

Results

Changes in Ultrasonic Integrated Attenuation Index Associated with Atherosclerosis

Figure 2 illustrates the relative values of the integrated attenuation index for normal and atherosclerotic arterial walls; a statistically significant difference is obtained between fibrous, fibrofatty, and calcified specimens (Table 1).

In Figure 3, a complete ultrasonic matrix (1 pixel = 1 acquisition) is shown for a specimen of each subset, together with a typical histological appearance. A pictorial tridimensional representation (256 levels) is adopted for the matrix display. Normal and pathological specimens are different, both for the absolute height value and, also, for the matrix pattern; i.e., normal specimens have points in the matrix very similar in intensity among them, whereas pathological specimens, on the contrary, show a highly inhomogeneous pattern.

In Figures 4 and 5, the best fit straight line for the ln | $H_{(f)}$ | is shown for each of the 16 discrete sites of two specimens [one mostly fibrous (Figs. 4a and 5a) the other mostly fibrofatty (Figs. 4b and 5b)]. It is apparent that both the absolute value and the slope of the best fit straight line help to differentiate fibrous from fibrofatty samples.

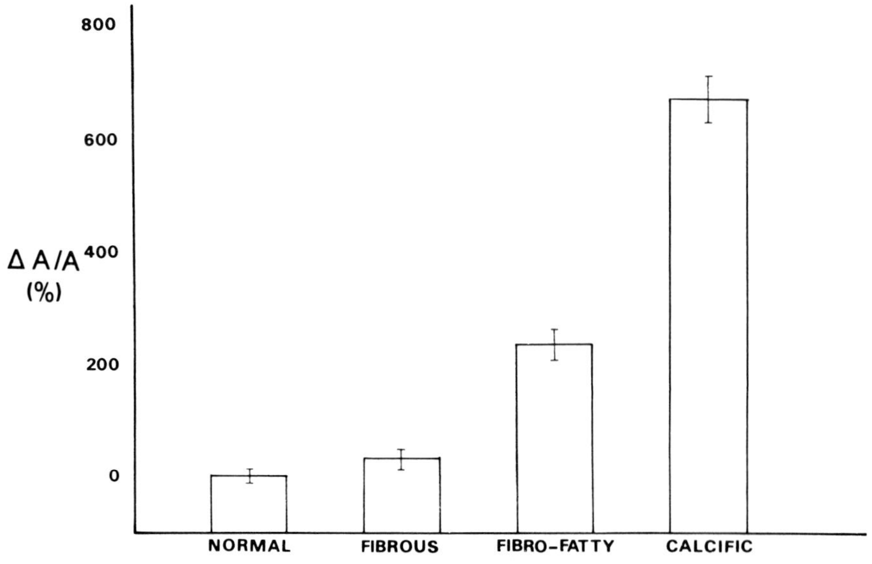

FIGURE 2. *Ultrasonic attenuation of normal and atherosclerotic fresh aortic walls. Index of attenuation is integrated attenuation over 7–11 MHz (A), as described in the text. It has been expressed as fractional attenuation difference (ΔA/A). ΔA/A represents the fractional difference between the value of A in a particular pathological subset and the average value of A in the normal group. Each bar represents the mean value ± SE of the aortic regions studied for each group.*

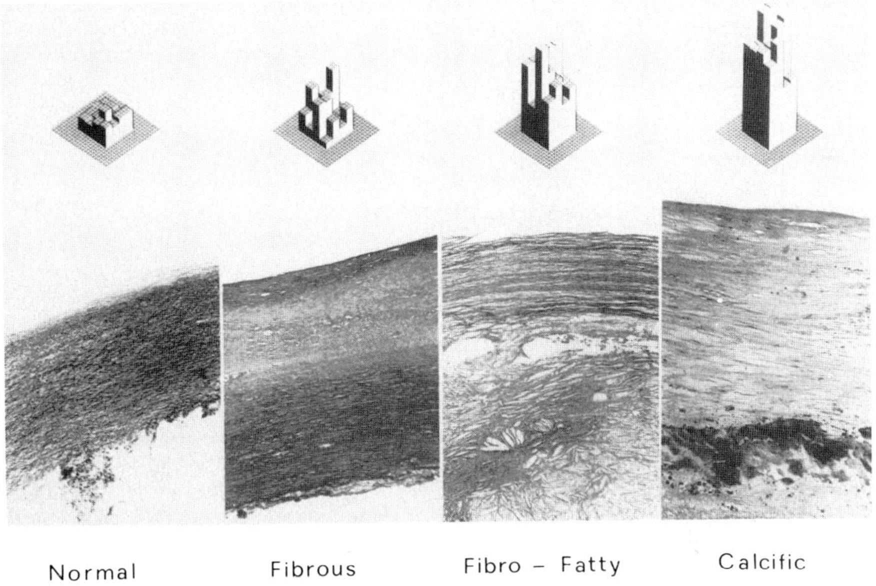

FIGURE 3. *Pictorial three-dimensional display (by 4 × 4 matrix) of four specimens: normal, fibrous, fibrofatty, and calcific. For each specimen, 16 different values of A were measured and displayed. In the lower panel, the histological slice shown (Weigert-Van Gieson, 32×) is a typical one out of the 16 slices, perpendicular to the tissue surface, performed for each specimen.*

Changes in Slope Index Associated with Atherosclerosis

Figure 6 illustrates the value of the slope index in the four subsets of normal and pathological specimens. This index can also differentiate between normal and fibrous specimens; however, there is a substantial overlap between fibrofatty and calcified samples (Table 2).

In Figure 7, the complete ultrasonic matrix (16 points) of four specimens (one for each subset) is shown.

Discussion

The results of this study indicate that alterations in ultrasonic attenuation may characterize the different pathological patterns of atherosclerosis in the arterial wall, providing a distinction between normal specimens and fibrous, fibrofatty, calcified plaques. Such alterations in ultrasonic attenuation may reflect intrinsic changes in biochemical and mechanical properties of atherosclerotic tissue.

The biochemistry of the atheroma documents an increase in at least three structural components potentially responsible for increased attenuation of the plaque: collagen, lipids, and calcium.

Fibrous plaques show a slightly higher attenuation, but in a nonstatistically significant way, compared with normal aortic walls. This finding is in agreement with the well-known fact that collagen is an important determinant of acoustic attenuation in soft tissues (Fields and Dunn, 1973; O'Donnel et al., 1979). However, the slope index—which is relatively independent from the angle of incidence of interrogating beam with the tissue, and reflects only the internal contribution of the sample to attenuation—has lower values in the fibrous than in the normal subset. This implies that a relevant compo-

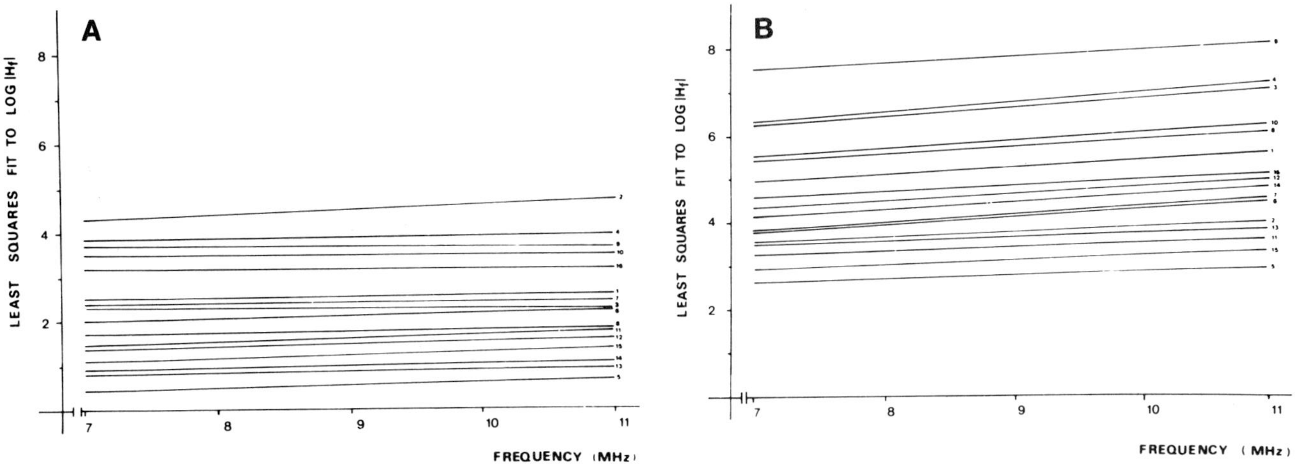

FIGURE 4. *Panel A: attenuation-frequency best fit straight line in the 16 sites of a single aortic specimens (fibrous plaque). Panel B: attenuation-frequency best fit straight line in the 16 sites of a single specimen (fibrofatty plaque).*

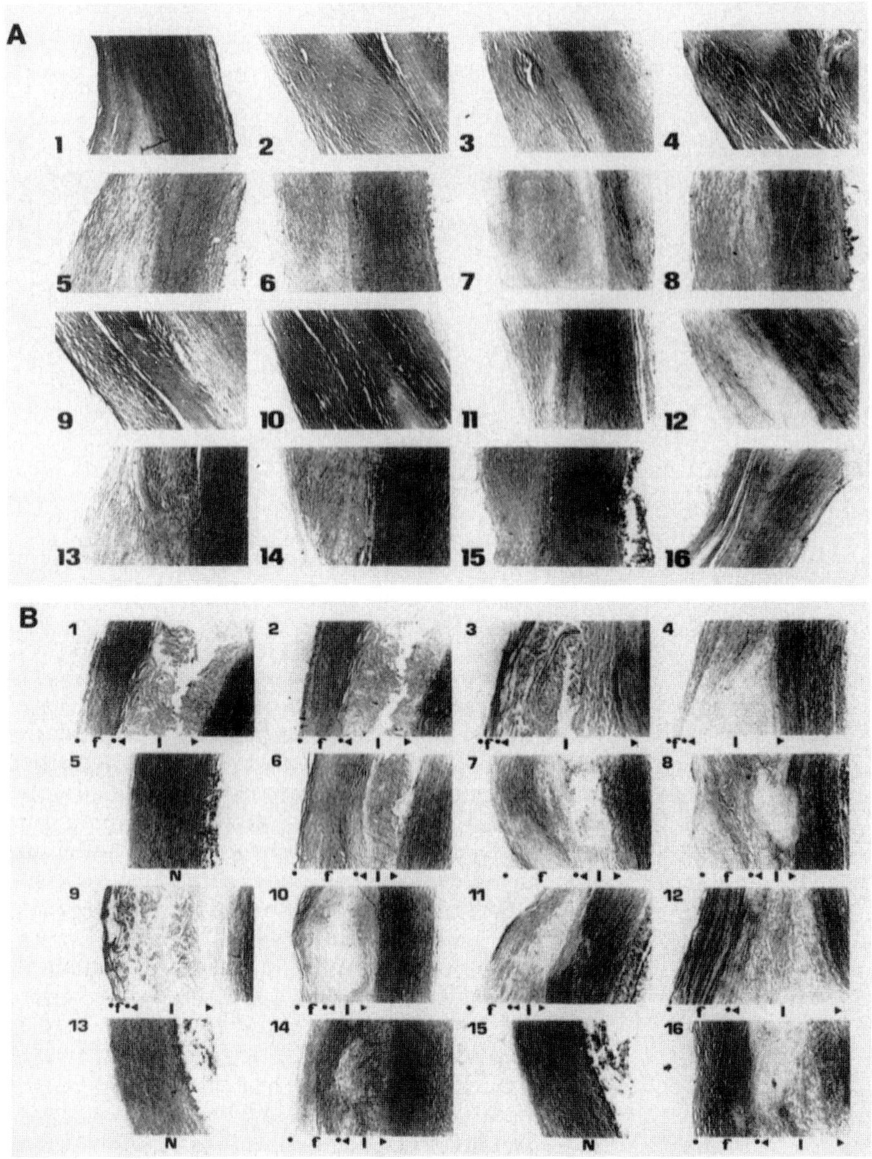

FIGURE 5. *Panel A: histological appearance (Weigert-Gieson, 16×) for each of the 16 sites ultrasonically studied and displayed in Figure 4A. Panel B: histological appearance (Weigert-Van Gieson, 16×) for each of the 16 sites ultrasonically studied and displayed in Figure 4B. Most sites are "fibrofatty," with different relative components of fibrous (f) and lipoidal (l) tissue. Two sites (panel B, no. 5 and no. 15) are completely normal; they have the lower absolute value in attenuation among the 16 sites, and also a less steep slope (see Fig. 6). The corresponding ultrasonic measurement at each site is shown in Figure 4B.*

nent of the overall attenuation measured by integrated attenuation index is due to surface (as opposed to internal) contribution of the sample. This surface contribution may recognize a morphological substrate in the fact that atherosclerosis (particularly in the uncomplicated phase of fibrous plaque) is primarily a disease of the intima (the first reflecting interface of the sample, which determines the surface contribution to attenuation). Only in its more advanced stages (fibrofatty and calcified samples), the atherosclerotic process involves the deeper layers of the wall and is therefore detectable with a significant increase in the slope index, which is sensitive only to internal contributions.

The increased attenuation in fibrofatty samples, compared to fibrous ones, could seem surprising, at least at first sight. Adipose tissue has a very low attenuation value among various tissues of the body, higher only than blood (Fields and Dunn, 1973). In other situations where pathology is characterized by a change in relative proportions of fibrous and adipose tissue (as in breast pathology), the increase in relative amount of fibrous tissue is known to determine an overall increase in attenuation (Kobayashi, 1979). In the atherosclerotic plaque, on the contrary, the increase in fat component raises the attenuation, also with a distinctly peculiar pattern of the slope. A possible explanation could be that—in the plaque—the increase in fat component is also determined by cholesterol crystals [the high reflectivity of which was documented (Glancy et al., 1980)] and not by amorphous adipose tissue only. A significant deposition of cholesterol crystals was indeed seen by histology in 53% of fibrofatty samples. Another possible explanation could be that, in fibrofatty plaques, an acoustic interface is present inside the arterial wall, due to the impedance step between the fibrous cap and the lipidic core. Both such additional

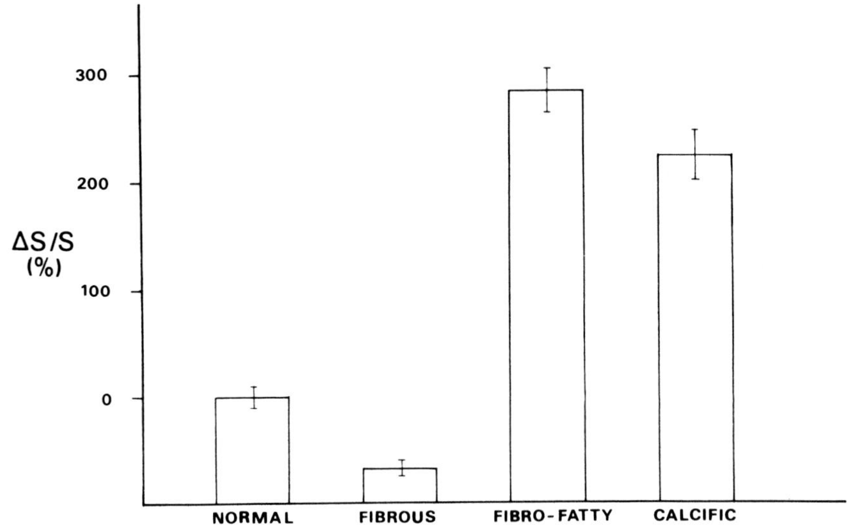

FIGURE 6. *Slope of the ultrasonic attenuation (S) of normal and atherosclerotic aortic walls. It has been expressed as fractional attenuation difference ($\Delta S/S$). $\Delta S/S$ represents the fractional difference between the value of S in a particular pathological subset compared to the average value of A in the normal group. Each bar represents the mean value (expressed as a percentage) ± SE of the 100 aortic regions studied for each group.*

interface and the accumulation of cholesterol crystals could lead to an increase in the reradiative loss of the signal, with a resulting increased attenuation.

As compared to fibrofatty specimens, a further increase in integrated attenuation index takes place in calcified specimens. This is not surprising, since calcium salts have by far the highest impedance among biological materials (Fields and Dunn, 1973).

Phase Cancellation Problems

Our measurements were made with phase-sensitive transducers. Phase cancellation effects due to the inhomogeneous nature of biological samples are a well-known potential source of error. The optimal solution to overcome such problems would be the use of a phase-insensitive acoustoelectric receiver (Busse and Miller, 1981); however, the use of a focused broadband transducer with a small diameter can substantially minimize phase cancellation artifacts, providing an adequate approach for studies in vitro. In fact, in a study performed in our laboratory (Landini et al., in press), phase cancellation effects [measured by means of statistical indexes, following the method of Mimbs et al. (1977)] were demonstrated to be: (1) minimized by employing focused small diameter transducers, (2) less evident with the 0.5 cm than with the 1.2 cm diameter focused transducer, and (3) less important in normal than in pathological specimens.

The recorded inhomogeneity of the matrix pattern, apparently more pronounced in pathological specimens as compared to normal ones (Figs. 3 and 9), has two possible explanations, one biological, the other methodological. This highly inhomogeneous pattern may reflect the spotty nature of the disease, whose only constant feature, from the pathologist's point of view, is variability (McMillan, 1982). For instance, even in the same fibrofatty plaque, the relative amounts of fibrosis and fat deposition can vary from point to point (Fig. 5b), and histology is unable to quantify properly such subtle gradations.

TABLE 2
Slope Values in the Four Subsets

	S (per cm per MHz)	Comparison NL	FI	FA	CL
NL	(10^{-3}) 99.5 ± 9.1		*	†	†
FI	(10^{-3}) 31.9 ± 4.5			†	†
FA	(10^{-3}) 383 ± 21				NS
CL	(10^{-3}) 320 ± 23				

NS = not significant.
* $P < 0.05$.
† $P < 0.01$.

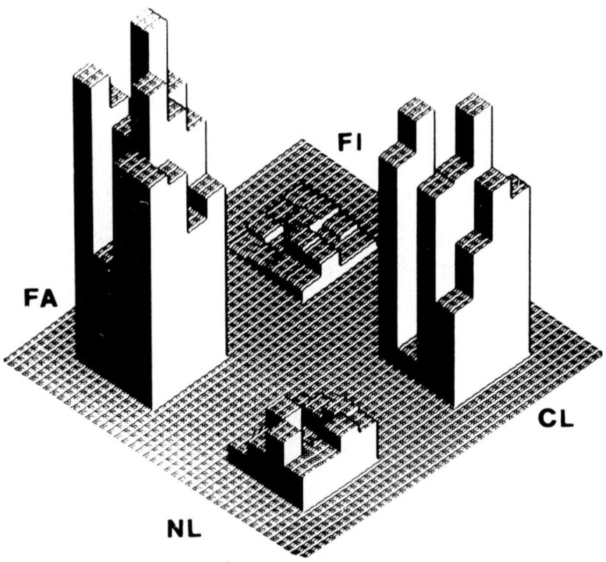

FIGURE 7. *Pictorial three-dimensional display (256 levels) of four specimens: normal (NL), fibrous (FI), fibrofatty (FA), and calcific (CL). For each specimen, 16 different values of S were measured and displayed (4 × 4 matrix). For each pixel displayed, a histological sampling was made (16 for each three-dimensional plot). It is apparent that, with this index, there is a substantial overlap between fibrofatty and calcific specimens.*

The other possible explanation is that phase cancellation effects, due to structural variations inside the tissue, are most prominent in pathological specimens (Landini et al., in press) where internal inhomogeneities should be, on the average, more pronounced than in normal aortic walls.

Conclusions

Results of the present study demonstrate that it is possible to measure ultrasonic attenuation indices which characterize different types of atherosclerotic material. Even if ultrasound attenuation is not suitable, per se, for in vivo application, identification of attenuation properties of normal and diseased arterial tissue can be helpful in many ways. First, more basic data than those currently available are needed for a better understanding of the interaction between ultrasound and arterial tissue: this is a prerequisite for any development in the direction of ultrasonic characterization of atherosclerosis. Furthermore, there is the possibility that additional developments (e.g., measurements of ultrasonic attenuation based on backscattered signals) ultimately may permit the use in vivo of the approach employed (Flax et al., 1983). Of course, the feasibility of these various methods in the case of atherosclerosis remains to be evaluated, in a way similar to that done for attenuation in myocardium (Johnston et al., 1982).

It may be possible to utilize attenuation measurements as an experimental, or potentially clinical, tool, to characterize the nature of atherosclerotic plaque in the noninvasive, nondestructive fashion.

We are very grateful to Daniela Banti for the preparation of the manuscript, Alessandro Mazzarisi and Marco Salvadori for technical help, Dr. Claudio Michelassi for statistical advice, and Daniela Grossi Frediani for secretarial assistance.

This work has been partially supported by C.N.R. (Consiglio Nazionale delle Ricerche), Project Tecnologie Biomediche e Sanitarie, Subproject Ultrasounds.

Dr. Eugenio Picano is recipient of the A.R.MED. Research Fellowship for Ultrasonic Diagnosis of Atherosclerosis.

Drs. Picano and Benassi are affiliated with the Istituto di Fisiologia Clinica, Dr. Landini with the Facoltà di Ingegneria, Drs. Distante and L'Abbate with the Istituto di Patologia Medica I, and Dr. Sarnelli with the Istituto di Anatomia Patologica.

Address for reprints: Dr. Eugenio Picano, Istituto di Fisiologia Clinica, C.N.R., Via Savi, 8, Pisa, Italy.

Received May 9, 1984; accepted for publication November 30, 1984.

References

Busse LJ, Miller JG (1981) Response characteristics of a finite aperture, phase insensitive ultrasonic receiver based upon the acoustoelectric effect. J Acoust Soc Am **70:** 1370–1376

Chivers RC (1981) Tissue characterization. Ultrasound Med Biol **7:** 1–20

Fields S, Dunn F (1973) Correlation of echographic visualizability of tissue with biological composition and physiological state. J Acoust Soc Am **54:** 809–812

Fink M, Hottier F, Berger G, Perrin J (1983) In vivo attenuation estimation in reflection mode. *In* Ultrasound '82, edited by RA Lersky, P Morley. Oxford, Pergamon Press, pp 117–122

Flax SW, Pele NJ, Glover GH, Gutmann FD, McLachlan M (1983) Spectral characterization and attenuation measurements in ultrasound. Ultrasonic Imaging **5:** 95–101

Glancy J, Goddard J, Pearson D (1980) In vitro demonstration of cholesterol crystals, high echogenicity relative to protein particles. J Clin Ultrasound **8:** 827–829

Johnston PH, Lewis JT, Miller JG (1982) A comparison of methods of estimating attenuation using backscattered ultrasound (abstr). Ultrasonic Imaging **4:** 177

Kak AC, Dines KA (1978) Signal processing of broadband pulsed ultrasound: Measurements of attenuation of soft biological tissues. IEEE Trans Biomed Eng **25:** 321–344

Kobayashi T (1979) Correlation of ultrasonic attenuation with connective tissue content in breast cancers. *In* Bureau of Standards, Special Publication 525. Washington D.C., U.S. Government Printing Office, pp 93–99

Kuc R, Schwartz M (1979) Estimating the acoustic attenuation coefficient slope for liver from reflected ultrasound signals. IEEE Trans Sonics Ultrasound **SU-26:** 353–362

Landini L, Picano E, Sarnelli R (in press) Attenuation measurements in atherosclerotic tissues: Problems with phase cancellation artifacts. Med Biol Eng Comput

Linzer M, ed (1979) Ultrasonic tissue characterization. II. National Bureau of Standards, Special Publication 525. Washington, D.C., U.S. Government Printing Office

McMillan GC (1982) Commentary. *In* Noninvasive techniques for assessment of atherosclerosis in peripheral, carotid, and coronary arteries, edited by TF Budinger, AS Berson, I Ringqvist, MB Mock, JT Watson, RS Powell. New York, Raven Press, pp 21–22

Mimbs JW, Yuhas DE, Miller JG, Weiss AN, Sobel BE (1977) Detection of myocardial infarction in vitro based on altered attenuation of ultrasound. Circ Res **41:** 192–198

Mimbs JW, O'Donnel M, Miller JG, Sobel BE (1979) Changes in Ultrasonic attenuation indicative of early myocardial ischemic injury. Am J Physiol **236:** M340–M344

O'Donnel M, Mimbs JW, Miller JG (1979) The relationship between collagen and ultrasonic attenuation in myocardial tissue. J Acoust Soc Am **65:** 512–517

Picano E, Landini L, Distante A, Benassi A, Bevilacqua G, L'Abbate A (1983a) In vitro differentiation of human atherosclerotic aortic walls by backscattered ultrasound (abstr). J Am Coll Cardiol **1:** 670

Picano E, Landini L, Distante A, Sarnelli R, Benassi A, L'Abbate A (1983b) Different degrees of atherosclerosis detected by backscattered ultrasound: An in vitro study on fixed human aortic walls. J Clin Ultrasound **11:** 375–379

Robbins SL, Cotran RS (1979) Pathological Basis of Disease, ed 2, chap 14, Blood Vessels. Philadelphia, WB Saunders, pp 593–642

Schwan HP, Carstensen EL (1952) Ultrasonic aids in diathermy experiments. Electronics **25:** 216–220

Wiener BJ (1971) Statistical Principles in Experimental Design, ed 2. New York, McGraw-Hill, p 196–198

Wissler RW (1984) Principles of the pathogenesis of atherosclerosis. *In* Heart Disease: A textbook of Cardiovascular Medicine, edited by E. Braunwald. Philadelphia, W.B. Saunders, pp 1183–1204

INDEX TERMS: Atherosclerosis • Tissue characterization • Ultrasound attenuation

Differential Effects of Central Angiotensin II and Substance P on Sympathetic Nerve Activity in Conscious Rats

Implications for Cardiovascular Adaptation to Behavioral Responses

Thomas Unger, Hans Becker, Margaret Petty, Gudrun Demmert, Bernhard Schneider, Detlev Ganten, and Rudolf E. Lang

From the Department of Pharmacology, University of Heidelberg, and German Institute for High Blood Pressure Research, Heidelberg, Federal Republic of Germany

SUMMARY. The centrally induced effects of angiotensin II and substance P on the cardiovascular system and on neuronal efferent activity of the splanchnic, renal, and adrenal nerves were investigated in chronically instrumented conscious rats. The pressor responses to substance P injected into the lateral brain ventricle were accompanied by marked and short latency increases in heart rate, cardiac output, splanchnic, renal, and adrenal nerve activity, and a rise in plasma noradrenaline and adrenaline. Behaviorally, an arousal-type reaction was observed. In contrast, the pressor responses to intracerebroventricular angiotensin II were associated with initial decreases in heart rate, cardiac output, splanchnic, renal, and adrenal nerve activity, and a fall in plasma noradrenaline at the time of the maximal blood pressure increase. In some but not all animals, a second blood pressure peak associated with increases in heart rate and splanchnic nerve activity was observed after several minutes. Incomplete chronic sinoaortic baroreceptor deafferentiation prevented the angiotensin II-induced fall in heart rate but not the initial fall in splanchnic nerve activity. The decreases in splanchnic nerve activity also occurred in diabetes insipidus rats and persisted in Long Evans rats after vascular vasopressin receptor blockade with $d(CH_2)_5AVP$, despite marked reductions of the pressor responses in both groups. Peripheral α-adrenoceptor blockade with prazosin or ganglion blockade with hexamethonium inhibited the central angiotensin II pressor responses only in combination with vasopressin receptor blockade. On the other hand, either sympatholytic drug, alone, abolished the pressor responses in the diabetes insipidus rats. This indicates that in intact conscious rats the central pressor effects of angiotensin II are initiated by vasopressin release but become dependent on the sympathetic nervous system when vasopressin is absent or not effective. When rats were allowed to drink in response to angiotensin II, a further sharp rise in blood pressure occurred, together with increases in heart rate and splanchnic nerve activity. The results demonstrate fundamental differences in the mechanisms by which central pressor peptides can influence cardiovascular and autonomic function. It is conceivable that the distinct sympathetic response patterns to central angiotensin II and substance P receptor stimulation form part of a specific cardiovascular adjustment to the individual behavioral reactions, such as drinking, as in the case of angiotensin II, or arousal within the central processing of pain, as in the case of substance P. **(*Circ Res 56: 563–575, 1985*)**

THE octapeptide angiotensin (AII), a circulating vasopressor hormone, increases blood pressure not only by its effects on peripheral target organs but also by a direct action on the brain. The centrally mediated effects of AII include stimulation of vasopressin (AVP), oxytocin, and adrenocorticotropic hormone (ACTH) release from the pituitary gland, and induction of drinking behavior [for review, see Severs and Daniels-Severs (1973), Fitzsimons (1980), and Lang et al. (1983a)]. AII-sensitive sites can be reached from inside and outside the blood-brain barrier; these include the subfornical organ, the AV3V region, and the area postrema [for review, see Ferrario et al. (1972), Buckley and Jandhyala (1977), Ganten and Stock (1978), and Brody and Johnson (1980)].

The possible physiological and pathophysiological significance of the central effects of AII was underlined by the discovery of an active renin angiotensin system in the brain and its increased activity in the hypertensive state (Ganten et al., 1983). However, despite a wealth of experimental data, the hemodynamic consequences of central AII receptor stimulation are still not fully understood. Evidence has been presented that sympathetic stimulation, the release of AVP, and interference with the baroreceptor reflex can contribute to the central pressor actions of this peptide, but there is still uncertainty as to the relative significance and mutual interactions of these mechanisms. Investigations into the role of the sympathetic nervous system have yielded contradictory results. Increased, unchanged, or even decreased sympathetic activity has been reported, depending on species, site of injection, and location of the sympathetic nerves from which the responses were recorded (Aars and Akre, 1968; Morrison and Pickford, 1969; Ferrario et al., 1972; Fukiyama, 1972; Severs and Daniels-Severs, 1973; Mann et al., 1982; Tobey et al., 1983; Stein et al., 1984). A differential regional involvement of sympathetic nerves in anesthetized dogs and cats has already been implied by Fukiyama (1972), Tobey et al. (1983), and Stein et al. (1984). A major reason for the discrepancies in the literature may be the fact that in none of the previous studies was sympathetic nerve activity assessed directly in conscious animals.

Substance P is a neuropeptide that exerts a variety of actions on the central and peripheral nervous system. It has been shown to stimulate neuronal activity and modulate synaptic transmission, and it may be a neurotransmitter involved in the processing of pain [for review, see Pernow (1983)]. Substance P has pressor actions when administered into the brain ventricular system [for review, see Pernow (1983)] and into the anterior and posterior hypothalamus (Unger et al., 1983). In contrast to AII, this peptide does not release AVP (Unger et al., 1981) and is not dipsogenic in the rat. Based on pharmacological evidence, it has been suggested that the central pressor actions of substance P are mediated by sympathetic stimulation (Unger et al., 1981; Petty and Reid, 1982).

In the present investigation, we compared the effects of central AII and substance P receptor stimulation after intracerebroventricular (icv) peptide injection on efferent splanchnic, renal, adrenal, and femoral nerve activity in rats. Particular attention was paid to the following questions: (1) How do the peptide-induced changes in these sympathetic nerves correlate with general changes in sympathetic activity, as evidenced by circulating catecholamines and the effect of pharmacological interference with the sympathetic nervous system? (2) Is the sympathetic response to central AII influenced by the concomitant release of AVP, and do changes in sympathetic activity gain importance for the central AII pressor actions in the absence of AVP? (3) What is the influence of the baroreceptor reflex on the sympathetic response to AII? (4) Is the sympathetic response modified by AII-induced drinking?

Our results provide evidence for distinct cardiovascular and sympathetic response patterns to centrally acting pressor peptides in awake animals. Substance P causes an arousal reaction with generalized sympatho-adrenal stimulation; AII, on the other hand, elicits a more complex reaction with uniform initial decreases in splanchnic, renal, and adrenal nerve activity and subsequent sympathetic stimulation in some animals, the latter being present in all animals if they are allowed to drink following the AII injection.

Methods

Experimental Animals and Procedures

Experiments were performed in conscious male Wistar rats (WI) weighing between 300 and 350 g (Thomae, Biberach, FRG). In experiment 5, male rats of the Brattleboro strain homozygous for hereditary hypothalamic diabetes insipidus (DI), together with Long Evans rats (LE), their genetic controls, were used. Both strains have been bred in Heidelberg since 1972.

Animals were kept under controlled conditions, with respect to temperature, humidity, and light period. For icv injections, chronic cannulas (PP20, Portex Corp.) were implanted into the lateral brain ventricle 1–2 weeks before, and arterial and venous catheters were inserted into the femoral artery and vein 1 or 2 days before the acute experiments. The surgical procedures have been described

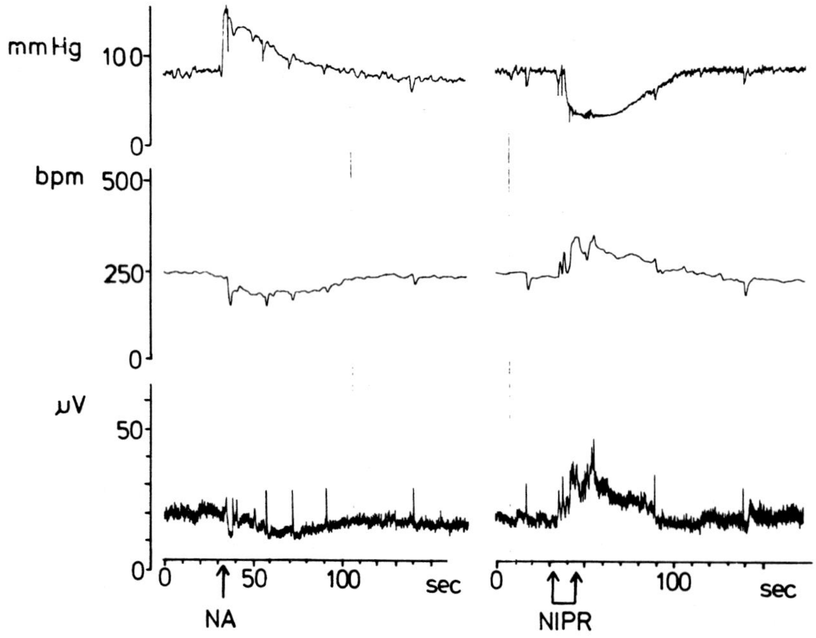

FIGURE 1. *Responses in mean arterial blood pressure (mm Hg), heart rate (beats/min), and mean rectified splanchnic nerve activity (µV) to 1 µg noradrenaline (NA), iv, and 1 µg sodium nitroprusside (NIPR), iv.*

previously (Unger et al., 1981). Measurements of mean arterial blood pressure (MAP) and heart rate were performed via the arterial line with a Statham P23Db pressure transducer, Gould Brush pressure coupler, and Gould Brush 2400 recorder.

Measurements of efferent sympathetic nerve activity were performed with chronic bipolar electrodes implanted 1 or 2 days before recording, using a modification of the method of Ricksten and Thoren (1980), as has been described elsewhere in detail (Unger et al., 1984). Splanchnic, renal, and adrenal nerve activities were recorded from separate groups of animals. The results are expressed in microvolts and represent mean rectified sympathetic nerve activity. The background level was defined as nerve activity measured 30 minutes after the animal was killed. A 24- to 36-hour recovery period was allowed after surgery until nerve recordings were performed in the animals' home cages. The animals were first challenged with intravenous injections of either 1 μg phenylephrine or noradrenaline and 1 μg sodium nitroprusside. Only those preparations showing the appropriate sympathetic responses (Fig. 1) were used in the experiments. At the time of recording, the rats had resumed their regular eating, drinking, and grooming habits, and did not exhibit any signs of stress or pain. In one experiment (experiment 7), nerve recordings were done under α-chloralose anaesthesia (50 mg/kg, iv) 1 day after surgery.

Experiment 1: Effect of icv AII on Blood Pressure, Heart Rate, Splanchnic Nerve Activity (SpNA), Renal Nerve Activity (RNA), and Adrenal Nerve Activity (ANA) in Conscious Rats

Rats (n = 10) were injected icv with 1-10-100 ng AII. Injections commenced after a 1-hour stabilization period. The next dose was given when blood pressure, heart rate, and SpNA had returned to control levels, with a minimum interval of 60 minutes between two injections. The injection volume was 5 μl (1 μl AII solution flushed with 4 μl 0.9% NaCl). An additional group of rats (n = 6) was injected with vehicle alone, to serve as controls. A second group of rats (n = 6) was injected icv with 100 ng AII. Blood pressure, heart rate, and RNA were recorded. A third group of rats (n = 4) was injected icv with 100 ng AII, as described above, and blood pressure, heart rate, and ANA were recorded. Rats were not allowed to drink during this experiment.

Experiment 2: Effect of icv Substance P on Blood Pressure, Heart Rate, and Splanchnic, Renal, and Adrenal Nerve Activity in Conscious Rats

Rats (n = 6) were injected icv with 1 μg substance P. Blood pressure, heart rate, SpNA (n = 6), RNA (n = 6), and ANA (n = 4) were recorded as described above.

Experiment 3: Effect of icv AII and Substance P on Cardiac Output in Conscious Rats

Rats instrumented with chronic brain cannulas and femoral artery catheters were implanted with a Thermistor probe (Mesecke), (external diameter, 0.6 mm) in the aortic arch, and a jugular vein cannula (PP25) with the tip lying at the entrance of the right atrium. The surgical procedures have been described previously in detail (Rascher et al., 1983). Following a recovery period of at least 4 hours after surgery, cardiac output was determined by computed automatic calculation of the dilution curve (HMV BN 7905, Hoyer Co.), after a bolus injection of 0.2 ml 0.9% NaCl at room temperature (20°–22°C) had been administered into the right atrium.

The animals were divided into three groups and injected icv with 100 ng AII (n = 6), 1 μg substance P (n = 6), or vehicle (n = 6). Blood pressure and heart rate were recorded and cardiac output was determined before, and 0.5, 2.5, 5, 10, and 15 minutes after the central injections.

Experiment 4: Effects of icv AII and Substance P on Plasma Catecholamines in Conscious Rats

Rats were prepared with chronic brain cannulas and arterial and venous catheters, and were injected icv with 100 ng AII (n = 8) or 10 μg substance P (n = 8), respectively. Control groups (n = 8 each) received icv injections of the vehicle. The 10-μg dose of substance P was found to produce slightly greater pressor responses than the 1-μg dose used in the previous experiments, but otherwise produced similar reactions (Unger et al., 1981). Blood (400 μl) was sampled through an extension of the arterial catheter from outside the cage 1 minute after AII, icv, and 5 minutes after substance P, icv. Sampling procedures and sample processing have been described previously in detail (Unger et al., 1984). Plasma noradrenaline and adrenaline concentrations were assayed by a modified radioenzymatic method (Da Prada and Zürcher, 1976).

Experiment 5: Blood Pressure, Heart Rate, and Splanchnic Nerve Activity after AII, icv, in LE and DI rats—Effect of Pharmacological Interference with Peripheral AVP Receptors and the Sympathetic Nervous System

LE rats (n = 6) were prepared for SpNA recording, and AII (100 ng) was injected icv, as described above. In a second group (n = 6), the experiment commenced with an intravenous (iv) bolus injection of 100 ng AVP. After blood pressure had returned to control levels, 10 μg/kg of the vascular AVP receptor antagonist $d(CH_2)_5AVP$ was injected iv, and the iv AVP injection was repeated to test for peripheral AVP receptor blockade. Five minutes later, AII (100 ng) was injected icv. In some animals, the peripheral AVP injection was repeated once again when the AII pressor response had subsided, to ensure continuous peripheral AVP receptor blockade during the experiment. DI rats (n = 11) were prepared for SpNA recording, as described above. AII (100 ng) was injected icv, and blood pressure, heart rate, and SpNA were recorded. Before the AII injection, rats were allowed to drink ad libitum to ensure adequate hydration.

The second part of this experiment was designed to investigate the role of the sympathetic nervous system for the central pressor responses to AII in the absence of AVP-mediated vasoconstriction.

Groups of DI (n = 10) and LE (n = 8) rats were prepared for blood pressure recording only. In the DI rats, experiments were performed on two consecutive days. On day 1, the animals were injected icv with 100 ng AII. After return of blood pressure to control levels, an infusion of prazosin (100 μg/kg per min) was started. Ten minutes later, the rats received an iv injection of 1 μg phenylephrine to test the degree of peripheral α_1-adrenoceptor blockade, and the icv injection of AII was repeated. On the second day, the animals were pretreated iv with hexamethonium (9 mg/kg bolus injection, followed by an infusion of 600 μg/kg per min), and were injected icv with 100 μg AII 10 minutes after the infusion was begun. Rats were allowed to drink during the stabilization period before AII injections. In the LE rats, as in DI rats, experiments were performed on days 1 and 2. On day 3, the animals were injected iv with 10 μg/kg of the vascular AVP receptor antagonist $d(CH_2)_5AVP$ after an initial control injection with 100 ng AII, icv. Blockade of the peripheral vascular AVP receptors was tested with 100 ng AVP, iv, and 5 minutes later, the icv injection of AII was repeated. When blood pressure had returned to control levels, a prazosin infusion was started as on the first day, and the icv AII injection was repeated under combined AVP and α_1-adrenoceptor blockade.

Experiment 6: Effect of icv AII on Blood Pressure, Heart Rate, and Splanchnic Nerve Activity in Conscious Chronically Baroreceptor-Denervated Rats

To investigate the possibility that the AII-induced changes in sympathetic discharge were due to baroreceptor reflex activation, we performed baroreceptor denervation (n = 6) by bilateral sinoaortic deafferentiation (SAD) according to the method of Krieger (1964) 4 weeks before the experiment, as described previously (Rascher et al., 1983). The area of carotid bifurcation was exposed in sham-operated controls (n = 6). The animals were prepared for SpNA recordings as described above. The experiment was started with iv injections of 1 μg phenylephrine and 1 μg sodium nitroprusside to test the completeness of SAD. Rats then were injected with 100 ng AII, icv, as described above.

Experiment 7: Effect of icv AII on Blood Pressure, Heart Rate, and Splanchnic and Femoral Nerve Activity (FNA) in α-Chloralose Anesthetized Rats

Rats (n = 6) were prepared for SpNA recordings as described above. In a second group (n = 6), the inguinal area contralateral to the side where the femoral catheters had been inserted was exposed. Usually, three branches of the femoral nerve could be isolated in the vicinity of the femoral artery and vein. The branch yielding the best signal was used. Tests with phenylephrine and sodium nitroprusside for sympathetic activity yielded weak but measurable responses. Since the recorded nerve activity was dominated by bursts originating from motor fibers within the nerve bundle, the injections of AII (100 ng, icv) were performed in both groups under α-chloralose anesthesia 1 day after surgery. The SpNA recordings in this experiment served as control for the effect of anesthesia on the central AII effects, since recordings of sympathetic nerve activity in the other experiments all were done in conscious animals.

Experiment 8: Effect of AII-Induced Drinking on Blood Pressure, Heart Rate, and Splanchnic Nerve Activity in Rats

Rats (n = 6) were prepared for SpNA recording as described above. A small pot filled with tap water was placed into the cage and the animals were allowed to drink during the experiment. AII (100 ng) was injected icv as usual. Blood pressure, heart rate, and SpNA were recorded for 1 hour after the central application of AII.

Drugs

Angiotensin II (AII) and substance P were purchased from Bachem, Bubendorf, Switzerland, arginine vasopressin (AVP) was from Serva, Heidelberg, FRG, phenylephrine was from Sigma, München, FRG, and sodium nitroprusside was from Merck, Darmstadt, FRG. The vascular AVP antagonist $d(CH_2)_5AVP$ was kindly provided by Dr. M. Manning, Toledo, Ohio, and prazosin was provided by Pfizer, Karlsruhe, FRG. Hexamethonium bromide was purchased from Serva, Heidelberg, FRG. All drugs except prazosin were dissolved in isotonic saline and diluted to the appropriate concentrations before use. Prazosin was dissolved in a solution containing 5% glycerol and 5% glucose.

Statistics

Results are reported as means ± SEM. For statistical evaluation, Student's t-test was used for paired and unpaired observations, and BMDP7D analysis of variance (ANOVA) with Bonferroni's method of multiple pairwise comparison was used, when appropriate. A significance level of $P < 0.05$ was accepted.

Results

Experiment 1

Effect of icv AII on Blood Pressure, Heart Rate, SpNA, RNA, and ANA (Table 1, Figs. 2–4)

The icv injection of AII at doses of 1, 10, and 100 ng increased blood pressure with a latency of 15–20 seconds after the injection, and a maximum after 1–

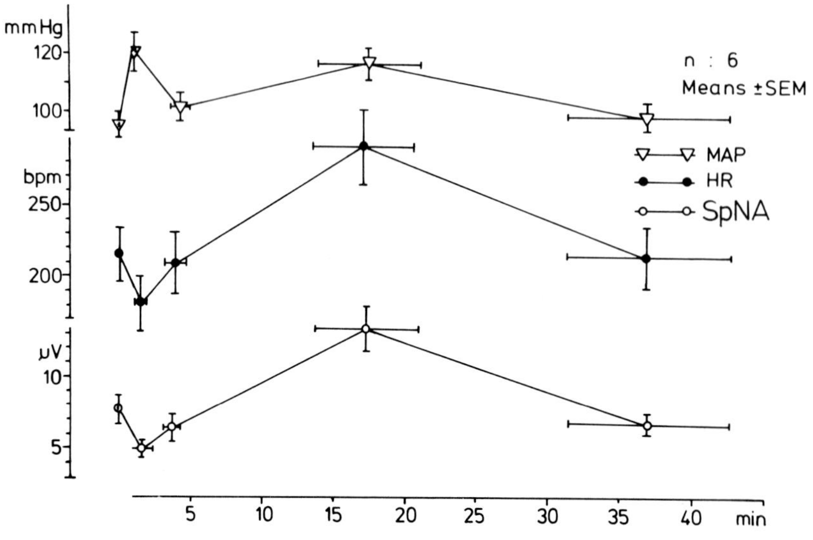

FIGURE 2. *Biphasic responses in mean arterial blood pressure (MAP, mm Hg), heart rate (HR, beats/min), and mean rectified splanchnic nerve activity (SpNA, μV) to 10 ng AII, icv, in a group of conscious rats (n = 6). Note the time course of events with the rapid initial fall in heart rate and nerve activity and the late increase with a maximum about 17 minutes after the AII injection. The latter was not seen in all animals tested (n = 10).*

TABLE 1
Effect of icv AII on Blood Pressure, Heart Rate, and Efferent Sympathetic Nerve Activity in Conscious Rats

Dose		Responses: Baseline	Responses: Maximal response	Responses: % Change in nerve activity	Time: Latency (sec)	Time: Max (min)	Time: Return (min)
			Splanchnic nerve				
1 ng	MAP	93.3 ± 4.4	+17.5 ± 2.1*		15 ± 2	1.9 ± 0.4	11.8 ± 2.5
n = 10	HR	235 ± 17	−12 ± 21		30 ± 14	2.1 ± 0.3	4.8 ± 0.7
	SpNA	7.8 ± 1.1	−1.9 ± 1	(−24)	21 ± 5	2.0 ± 0.4	3.7 ± 0.6
10 ng	MAP	95.5 ± 5.0	+25.0 ± 2.6*		15 ± 2.2	1.2 ± 0.1	20.2 ± 4.8
	HR	218 ± 19	−38 ± 6*		21.7 ± 4	1.6 ± 0.4	7.5 ± 1.1
	SpNA	7.9 ± 1.0	−4.8 ± 0.6†	−60	26 ± 8	1.7 ± 0.8	5.3 ± 1.2
100 ng	MAP	100.0 ± 5.0	+22.5 ± 2.1†		18 ± 5	1.4 ± 0.1	29.5 ± 3.7
	HR	220 ± 23	−42 ± 3†		25 ± 7	4.9 ± 1.4	14.8 ± 3.5
	SpNA	8.1 ± 0.9	−3.5 ± 0.7†	−43	18 ± 3	6.6 ± 3.3	11.5 ± 1.9
			Renal nerve				
100 ng	MAP	90.0 ± 3.4	+28.3 ± 5.3*		23 ± 2	1.1 ± 0.2	
n = 6	HR	220 ± 25	−62 ± 13†		25 ± 8	4.3 ± 1.6	
	RNA	13.0 ± 1.6	−4.7 ± 1.1†	−36	30 ± 5	2.6 ± 1.0	
			Adrenal nerve				
100 ng	MAP	86.3 ± 6.3	+30.0 ± 2.04*		30 ± 1	1.0 ± 0.1	
n = 4	HR	283 ± 35	−55 ± 5‡		40 ± 7	5.8 ± 1.6	
	ANA	14.3 ± 0.9	−2.5 ± 0.7‡	−18	53 ± 8	5.8 ± 0.5	

Results are expressed as means ± SEM; MAP, mean arterial blood pressure (mm Hg); HR, heart rate (beats/min); SpNA: splanchnic nerve activity (μV); RNA, renal nerve activity (μV); ANA: adrenal nerve activity (μV).
* $P < 0.001$, † $P < 0.01$, ‡ $P < 0.05$, when compared with control values before AII injection.

2 minutes. In some animals, a second smaller peak was noted after 13–17 minutes. The initial peak was accompanied by a fall in heart rate and a marked decrease in SpNA of −24% after 1 ng, −60% after 10 ng, and −43% after 100 ng AII. The second peak, if present, usually was associated with increases in heart rate and SpNA, as shown in Figure 2. Control injections of the vehicle (0.9% NaCl) did not produce any significant changes of the parameters measured.

The fall in sympathetic activity associated with the initial pressor peak was also observed in the renal and adrenal nerves (Table 1). Representative recordings are shown in Figures 3 and 4.

Experiment 2

Effect of icv Substance P on Blood Pressure, Heart Rate, and Splanchnic, Renal, and Adrenal Nerve Activity (Table 2; Figs. 3 and 4)

The icv injection of 1 μg substance P increased blood pressure with a latency of about 1 minute, the

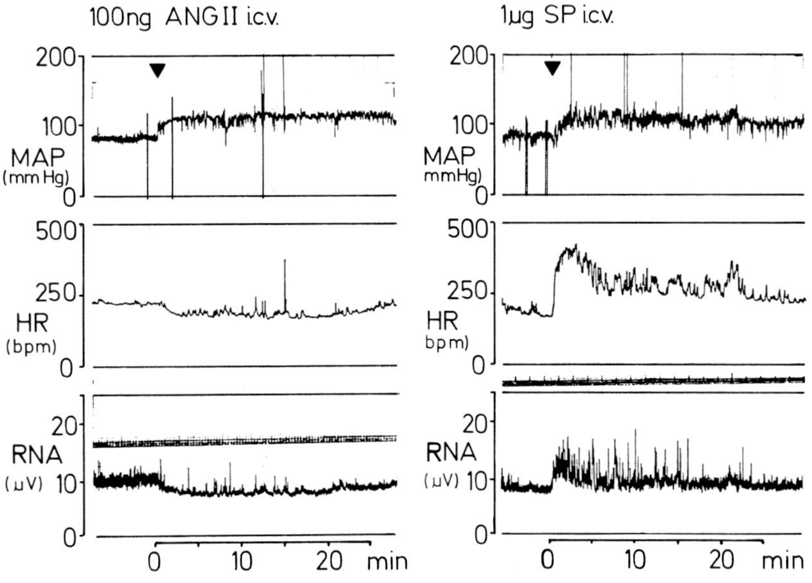

FIGURE 3. *Representative recordings of the changes in mean arterial blood pressure (MAP), heart rate (HR), and mean rectified renal nerve activity (RNA) after central AII and substance P injections in conscious rats.*

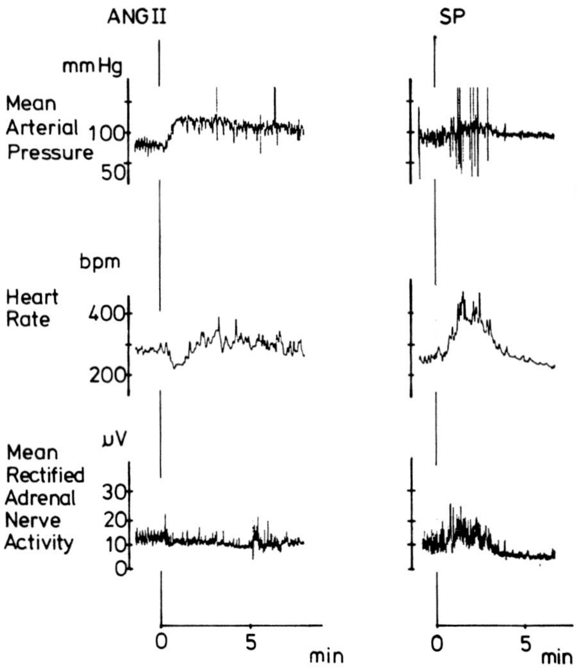

FIGURE 4. *Representative recordings of the changes in blood pressure (MAP), heart rate (HR), and adrenal nerve activity (ANA) after icv injections of AII (100 ng) and substance P (1 μg) in conscious rats.*

peak was reached after about 5 minutes. This response was accompanied by a marked rise in heart rate, SpNA, RNA, and ANA. Representative recordings are shown in Figures 3 and 4. In all instances, the rises in heart rate and sympathetic nerve activity preceded the blood pressure increases. A behavioral arousal reaction, with enhanced locomotion, grooming, and scratching, was usually associated with the pressor response.

Experiment 3

Effect of icv AII, and Substance P on Cardiac Output (Table 3)

After the injection of 100 ng AII, icv, cardiac output tended to fall; however, this change did not achieve statistical significance until 2.5 minutes had elapsed. The calculated total peripheral resistance was increased throughout the observation period. In contrast, substance P (1 μg icv) produced an early increase in cardiac output (30 seconds), which was no longer significant after 5 minutes. The calculated total peripheral resistance remained unchanged throughout the observation period.

Experiment 4

Effects of icv AII and Substance P on Plasma Catecholamines (Fig. 5)

Plasma catecholamines, measured at the time of the respective pressor peaks, were influenced differently by the two peptides. After the injection of 100 ng AII, icv, noradrenaline was reduced by 34% and adrenaline remained unchanged, compared to saline-injected controls. Substance P (10 μg icv) increased noradrenaline by 65% and adrenaline by 302%.

Experiment 5

Blood Pressure, Heart Rate, and Splanchnic Nerve Activity after icv AII, in LE and DI Rats: Effects of Peripheral Interference with AVP Receptors and α_1-Adrenoceptors, and of Ganglion Blockade (Table 4; Fig. 6)

Injection of 100 ng AII, icv, produced the same pattern of changes in LE rats as observed in WI rats

TABLE 2
Effect of icv Substance P (1 μg) on Blood Pressure, Heart Rate, and Efferent Sympathetic Nerve Activity in Conscious Rats

		Responses			Time		
		Baseline	Maximal response	% Change in nerve activity	Latency (sec)	Max (min)	Return (min)
				Splanchic nerve			
$n = 6$	MAP	88.3 ± 4.0	+29.2 ± 3.6*		54 ± 18	5.3 ± 0.3	25.7 ± 4.3
	HR	292 ± 39	+128 ± 14*		48 ± 12	5.3 ± 0.9	26.2 ± 4.1
	SpNA	8.0 ± 1.2	+6.8 ± 0.6*	+85	36 ± 6	4.8 ± 0.9	24.8 ± 3.8
				Renal nerve			
$n = 6$	MAP	85.0 ± 3.9	+24.2 ± 2.7*		55 ± 5	3.8 ± 0.5	
	HR	268 ± 26	+145 ± 27*		35 ± 5	2.8 ± 0.5	
	RNA	13.3 ± 1.7	+19.5 ± 6.7*	+147	35 ± 5	2.3 ± 0.5	
				Adrenal nerve			
$n = 4$	MAP	92.5 ± 1.4	+23.8 ± 3.8*		53 ± 14	3.8 ± 0.3	
	HR	273 ± 21	+168 ± 20*		29 ± 11	2.6 ± 0.5	
	ANA	10.8 ± 1.5	+6.8 ± 1.4*	+63	33 ± 10	2.6 ± 0.2	

Results are expressed as means ± SEM; abbreviations as defined in footnote to Table 1.
* $P < 0.001$, compared with control values before substance P injection.

TABLE 3
Effect of icv AII and Substance P on Cardiac Output and Total Peripheral Resistance in Conscious Rats ($n = 6$)

		Responses to AII/SP					
		Control before injection	30 sec	2.5 min	5 min	10 min	15 min after injection
AII (100 ng)	MAP	96.4 ± 2.7	+26.0 ± 2.8‡	+27.3 ± 3.5‡	+23.7 ± 3.2‡	+18.3 ± 3.9‡	+18.0 ± 3.7‡
	CO	120.8 ± 11.2	−16.3 ± 7.8	−27.2 ± 5.6*	−22.0 ± 4.1	−19.1 ± 6.2	−21.6 ± 3.0
	TPR	086 ± 0.08	0.06 ± 0.2†	+0.7 ± 0.2†	+0.5 ± 0.1†	+0.5 ± 0.2†	+0.4 ± 0.1†
SP (1 μg)	MAP	80.4 ± 8.3	+19.0 ± 1.3‡		+16.0 ± 2.6‡	+6.7 ± 2.4*	+4.0 ± 1.6
	CO	154.8 ± 25.7	+106.6 ± 31.8†		+37.6 ± 16.2	+9.9 ± 18.7	+4.2 ± 11.5
	TPR	0.56 ± 0.09	−0.15 ± 0.01		−0.04 ± 0.05	−0.02 ± 0.06	−0.02 ± 0.06
Saline	MAP	82.0 ± 7.5	+1.7 ± 1.7	+1.7 ± 1.0	+0.7 ± 1.0	−0.3 ± 1.3	−2.0 ± 2.3
	CO	142.7 ± 17.0	+2.0 ± 10.7	+0.8 ± 9.8	−0.3 ± 9.8	+4.5 ± 7.9	−3.3 ± 7.9
	TPR	0.58 ± 0.07	−0.02 ± 0.02	−0.02 ± 0.02	−0.02 ± 0.02	−0.02 ± 0.03	−0.02 ± 0.02

Results are expressed as means ± SEM; MAP, mean arterial blood pressure (mm Hg), CO, cardiac output (ml/min); TPR, total peripheral resistance (mm Hg·min/ml); Statistics: ANOVA with Bonferroni's multiple pairwise comparison.
* $P < 0.05$, † $P < 0.01$, ‡ $P < 0.001$.

in the previous experiments. Intravenous pretreatment with the vascular AVP receptor antagonist $d(CH_2)_5AVP$ abolished the pressor responses to 100 ng AVP, iv (43.4 ± 4.8 mm Hg vs. 1.3 ± 0.8 mm Hg). The pressor responses to 100 ng AII, icv, were reduced from 22.0 ± 2.0 mm Hg in the control group to 14.2 ± 0.8 mm Hg in the AVP antagonist-pretreated group, whereas the corresponding changes in heart rate and SpNA were not significantly different between the two groups (Fig. 6). In the DI rats, the pressor response to 100 ng AII, icv, was 11.4 ± 2.7 mm Hg (Fig. 6). The changes in heart rate and SpNA were not uniform. In 9 of 11 animals, a decrease in heart rate (−54.4 ± 9.9 beats/min) and a dramatic fall in SpNA (−9.0 ± 2.2 μV) were observed, whereas, in two animals, heart rate increased by +30 and +40 beats/min and SpNA increased by +10 and +13 μV.

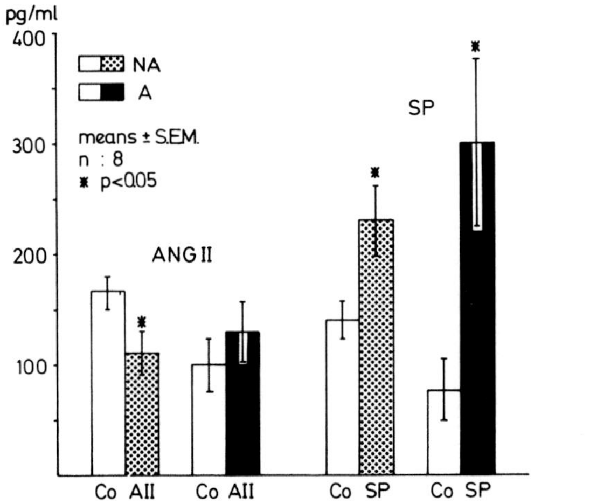

FIGURE 5. *Effect of icv injections of 100 ng AII (left) and 10 μg substance P (right) on plasma catecholamines in conscious rats. NA, noradrenaline; A, adrenaline; Co, control vehicle injections; ANG II, angiotensin II; SP, substance P.*

The effects of peripheral vascular AVP receptor, α_1-adrenoceptor, and ganglion blockade are summarized in Table 4. At the time of the icv AII injection, the pressor responses to iv AVP were completely blocked in the $d(CH_2)_5AVP$-pretreated animals, as were the pressor responses to iv phenylephrine after prazosin pretreatment. In the LE rats, peripheral AVP receptor blockade reduced the pressor responses to 100 ng AII by 60%, whereas peripheral α_1-adrenoceptor blockade did not have a significant effect, and ganglion blockade even potentiated the AII pressor responses. However, combined pretreatment with $d(CH_2)_5AVP$ and prazosin completely prevented the central AII pressor responses. In the DI rats, prazosin or hexamethonium each practically eliminated the central pressor responses to AII.

Experiment 6

Effect of icv AII on Blood Pressure, Heart Rate, and Splanchnic Nerve Activity in Conscious Chronically Baroreceptor-Denervated (SAD) Rats (Table 5; Figs. 7 and 8)

In the SAD rats, the heart rate and SpNA responses to iv phenylephrine and iv sodium nitroprusside were markedly reduced but not totally abolished, compared to sham-operated controls, indicating that the denervation was not complete (Table 5). After injection of 100 ng AII, icv, the pressor responses were potentiated to 49.2 ± 10.3 mm Hg ($p < 0.05$) in the SAD rats, whereas heart rate remained unaltered. The fall in SpNA persisted in the same magnitude as in the sham-operated controls (−3.83 ± 0.84 μV, Fig. 7). A representative recording is shown in Figure 8.

TABLE 4
Effect of Blockade of Peripheral α_1-Adrenoceptors, Vascular AVP Receptors, and of Ganglion Blockade on the Pressor Responses to 100 ng AII, icv, in Conscious Rats

	Blood pressure responses						
	Day 1				Day 2		
	Baseline MAP	AII, icv	Prazosin, iv	AII Prazosin, iv	Baseline MAP	Hexamethonium, iv	AII, icv Hexamethonium, iv
LE $n = 8$	88 ± 5	+24 ± 3	−14 ± 2	+20 ± 2	83 ± 7	−22 ± 2	+47 ± 9*
DI $n = 10$	90 ± 4	+7 ± 2	−15 ± 1	+2 ± 1†	88 ± 3	−24 ± 2	+1 ± 1†

	—Blood pressure responses, Day 3					
	Baseline MAP	AII, icv	$(CH_2)_5$AVP, iv	AII, icv $d(CH_2)_5$AVP, iv	Prazosin, iv	AII, icv $(CH_2)_5$AVP + prazosin, iv
LE $n = 8$	88 ± 4	+25 ± 4	−8 ± 2	+10 ± 2†	−13 ± 2	±0

Results are expressed as means ± SEM; MAP, mean arterial blood pressure (mm Hg); LE, Long Evans rats; DI, diabetes insipidus rats. Doses were: AII, 100 ng, icv; prazosin, 100 μg/kg per min, iv; hexamethonium, 12 mg/kg + 600 μg/kg per min, iv.
* $P < 0.05$; † $P < 0.01$, compared with AII control injections.

Experiment 7

Effect of icv AII on Blood Pressure, Heart Rate, and Splanchnic and Femoral Nerve Activity (FNA) in α-Chloralose-Anesthetized Rats (Table 6)

Under α-chloralose anesthesia, the central effects of AII on blood pressure and heart rate were shortened and reduced, compared to those in conscious rats (cf Table 1). The fall in SpNA was reduced but present in all animals. In contrast, FNA was found to increase in four of six rats tested, being unchanged in the two remaining animals. The onset of the increase in FNA was later than the onset of the pressor response (Table 6).

Experiment 8

Effect of AII-Induced Drinking on Blood Pressure, Heart Rate, and Splanchnic Nerve Activity in Rats (Fig. 9)

When rats were allowed to drink after an icv injection of 100 ng AII, a further rise in blood pressure (+12.5 ± 1.1 mm Hg) of rapid onset was observed in all animals. Heart rate and SpNA, both of which decreased immediately after the AII injection, recovered quickly, and rose to above control levels during the drinking response (+120.0 ± 18.9 beats/min and +2.83 ± 0.57 μV, respectively). A representative recording is shown in Figure 9.

Discussion

Differences between AII and Substance P

A consistent and unexpected feature of this study was the initial fall in splanchnic, renal, and adrenal sympathetic nerve activity immediately after the central injection of AII in conscious rats. A generalized sympathetic stimulation must therefore be ruled out as an initiating factor for the central pressor action of this peptide in rats. The additional finding of a decrease in heart rate and plasma noradrenaline at the time of the AII-induced pressor peak, and the

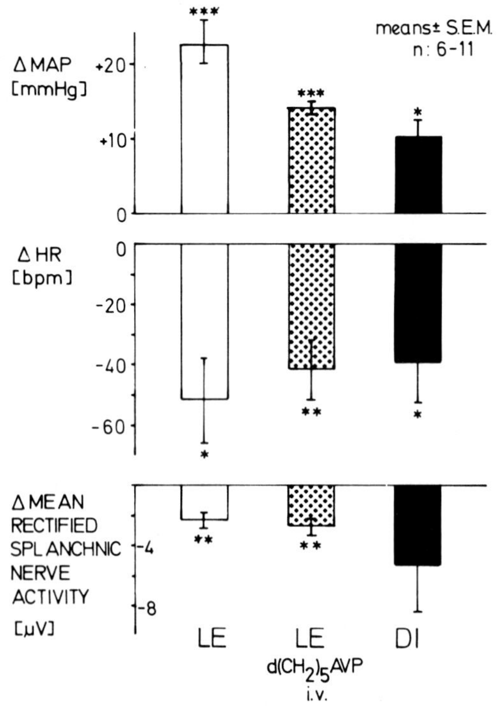

FIGURE 6. *Maximum responses in blood pressure (MAP), heart rate (HR), and splanchnic nerve activity to 100 ng AII, icv, in conscious Long Evans (LE) rats ($n = 6$ each group) and diabetes insipidus (DI) rats ($n = 11$). The columns in the middle depict the respective changes in LE rats after intravenous (iv) pretreatment with the vascular vasopressin receptor antagonist $d(CH_2)_5$ AVP. *$P < 0.05$, **$P < 0.01$, ***$P < 0.001$.*

TABLE 5

Effect of Chronic Sinoaortic Deafferentiation (SAD) on Blood Pressure, Heart Rate, and Sympathetic Nerve Responses to iv Phenylephrine and Sodium Nitroprusside in Conscious Rats

		SAD			Sham		
		Baseline	Response	Response per mm Hg Δ MAP	Baseline	Response	Response per mm Hg Δ MAP
PE (1 μg iv)	MAP	97.0 ± 1.2	+51.0 ± 7.3*		106.7 ± 3.8	+35.8 ± 1.5	
	HR	324.0 ± 17.8	−48.0 ± 2.0†	0.94	302 ± 21.8	−88.0 ± 4.9	2.46
	SpNA	9.2 ± 0.6	−1.6 ± 0.4*	0.03	12.8 ± 1.4	−4.3 ± 1.2	0.12
NIPR (1 μg, iv)	MAP	99.1 ± 1.0	−55.0 ± 1.6*		105.8 ± 4.0	−42.5 ± 5.0	
	HR	310.0 ± 22.6	+74.2 ± 17.8*	1.35	270.0 ± 22.2	+118.3 ± 14.5	2.78
	SpNA	9.4 ± 0.9	+2.9 ± 1.2*	0.05	12.0 ± 1.2	+11.0 ± 2.7	0.26

Results are expressed as means ± SEM; $n = 6$ per group. MAP, mean arterial blood pressure (mm Hg); HR, heart rate (beats/min); SNA, splanchnic nerve activity (μV); PE, phenylephrine; NIPR, sodium nitroprusside.
* $P < 0.05$, † $P < 0.01$, compared with sham-operated group.

fact that pharmacological interference with the sympathetic nervous system in the periphery had little influence on the pressor response to AII (prazosin), or even potentiated it (hexamethonium), support this conclusion.

The response pattern to AII was in contrast with that observed after substance P. Central pressor effects comparable to AII were associated with marked increases in heart rate, SpNA, RNA, ANA, and circulating catecholamines. Together with previous findings that the substance P-induced blood pressure increases could be completely prevented by peripheral α_1-adrenoceptor blockade (Unger et al., 1981), or antagonized by ganglionic blockade (Petty and Reid, 1982), this result indicates that substance P increases blood pressure centrally by a

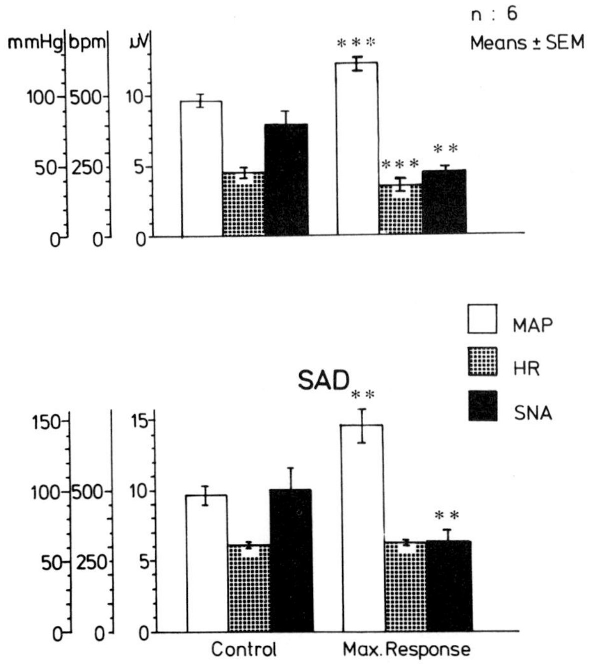

FIGURE 7. *Responses in mean arterial blood pressure (MAP), heart rate (HR), and mean rectified splanchnic nerve activity (SpNA) to 100 ng AII, icv, in sham-operated (top) and chronically sinoaortic-denervated (SAD, bottom) conscious rats. **P < 0.01, ***P < 0.001.*

generalized sympathetic stimulation. When applied directly to the hypothalamus, SP causes a rise in blood pressure (Unger et al., 1983) and augments hypothalamic blood flow (Klugman et al., 1980). The latter effect was abolished by a variety of procedures, including central chemical sympathectomy with 6-hydroxydopamine, central adrenoceptor or cholinoreceptor blockade, or destruction of a so-called intracerebral noradrenergic pathway.

It is therefore, conceivable that some neuropeptides such as SP could exert their central cardiovascular actions by changing blood flow in discrete cardiovascular control centers of the brain, thereby changing the function of, e.g., hypothalamic circuits, whereas such a mechanism seems less likely for angiotensin.

In contrast to AII, SP has not been found to release AVP when applied centrally (Unger et al., 1981), although increases in vasopressinergic neuron activity in the nucleus supraopticus after intraventricular injection of SP have been reported (Clarke et al., 1980). However, we have observed a selective dose-dependent release of the stress-related (Lang et al., 1983b) neurohormone oxytocin from the pituitary gland after icv injections of substance P (Unger et al., 1983).

Differences between the two peptides were also found with respect to their effects on cardiac output and total peripheral resistance. AII decreased cardiac output and increased total peripheral resistance, whereas substance P produced a short-lasting initial rise in cardiac output.

Thus, in agreement with previous results obtained in mongrel dogs by Ferrario et al. (1972) and Brosnihan et al. (1979), central AII increases blood pressure in the rat by a rise in total peripheral resistance, rather than by an increase in cardiac output as was observed with substance P.

Evidence for Sympathetic Activation following Central AII

Our finding of reduced abdominal sympathetic activity appears to be at variance with a number of

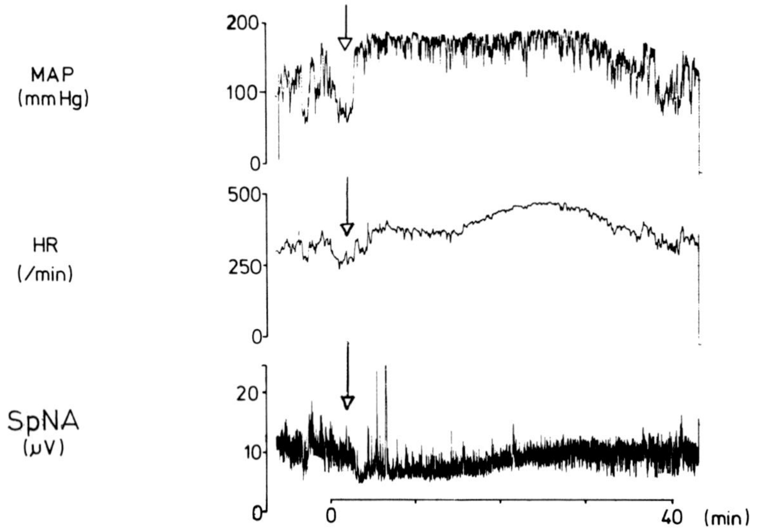

FIGURE 8. *Representative recording of the changes in mean arterial blood pressure (MAP), heart rate (HR), and mean rectified splanchnic nerve activity (SpNA) after injection of 100 ng AII, icv, in a conscious rat 4 weeks after sinoaortic denervation (SAD). Note the lability of the basal blood pressure and the marked pressor response associated with a rise in heart rate and a fall in SpNA.*

previous reports, including our own, in several species including the rat, rabbit, cat, dog, and monkey, in which neurally mediated vasoconstriction was postulated to be responsible for at least part of the increase in blood pressure after central administration of AII [for review, see Severs and Daniels-Severs (1973), Brody and Johnson (1980), and Schölkens et al. (1983)].

However, most of these discrepancies can be explained by the lack of directly obtained data on sympathetic nerve activity in conscious animals, and by factors such as anesthesia, dose, and route of administration of AII, time of measurements or sampling, and different species used in the various experiments. For instance, in the dog, not only do the central AII-sensitive sites appear to be different from those in rats, but also the sympathetic contribution to the central AII pressor effects may be greater (Severs and Daniels-Severs, 1973). Even in this species, direct measurements of sympathetic activity following central AII application are scarce, and have yielded contradictory results. Whereas Fukiyama (1972) observed an initial, nonsustained excitation of SpNA and RNA, with a subsequent fall in RNA following intravertebral arterial infusion of AII in anesthetized mongrel dogs, Ferrario et al. (1972) reported variable changes in SpNA (increase or no change) and a decrease of renal nerve discharge in the same experimental model.

The decrease in RNA which occurred in these experiments and in our own study could help to explain two consistently observed phenomena following central AII receptor stimulation, namely, the suppression of plasma renin activity (Reid and Day, 1977) and the increase in sodium excretion (Severs et al., 1971; Brooks and Malvin, 1982).

Recently, Tobey et al. (1983) compared renal and splenic nerve activity after intracarotid and icv administration of AII in anesthetized cats, and found differential changes in sympathetic outflow, depending on the site of application. The increase in nerve discharge was confined to the splenic nerve, and there was little or no change of activity in the renal nerve. They concluded that discrete and nonuniform effects on sympathetic activity with alterations in visceral blood flow distribution contributed to the central pressor responses to AII.

In the rat, conclusions regarding a sympathetic

TABLE 6

Effect of icv AII (100 ng) on Blood Pressure, Heart Rate, and Splanchnic and Femoral Nerve Activity in α-Chloralose Anesthetized Rats

		Responses			Time		
		Baseline	Maximal response	% Change in nerve activity	Latency (sec)	Max (min)	Return (min)
				Splanchnic nerve			
$n = 6$	MAP	71.7 ± 6.4	+17.5 ± 4.8†		13 ± 2	1.8 ± 0.4	4.2 ± 1.0
	HR	305.0 ± 31.1	−38.3 ± 18.5		23 ± 8	1.4 ± 0.4	3.3 ± 0.9
	SpNA	8.2 ± 1.0	−1.3 ± 0.2†	−16%	20 ± 5	1.0 ± 0.4	3.2 ± 1.0
				Femoral nerve			
$n = 6$	MAP	95.0 ± 3.7	+11.7 ± 2.1†		17 ± 3	2.0 ± 0.3	14.0 ± 2.9
	HR	318.3 ± 31.6	−26.0 ± 8.7*		28 ± 8	2.4 ± 0.6	9.3 ± 3.3
	FNA	8.5 ± 1.4	+3.3 ± 1.7	(+39%)	60 ± 38	2.4 ± 1.2	4.7 ± 1.7

Results are expressed as means ± SEM. MAP, mean arterial blood pressure (mm Hg); HR, heart rate (beats/min); SpNA, splanchnic nerve activity (μV); FNA, femoral nerve activity.

* $P < 0.05$; † $P < 0.01$, compared with control values before AII injection.

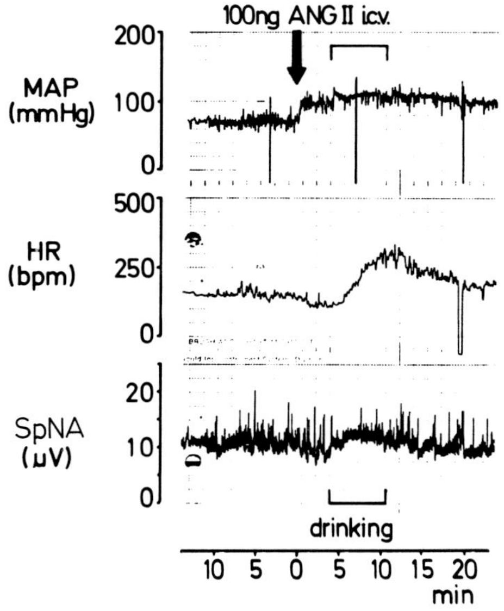

FIGURE 9. *Representative recording of the changes in mean arterial blood pressure (MAP), heart rate (HR), and mean rectified splanchnic nerve activity (SpNA) after injection of 100 ng AII, icv, and during AII-induced drinking.*

contribution to the central pressor action of AII have been based on circumstantial evidence from ablation experiments, pharmacological interference with the sympathetic nervous system, plasma catecholamine determinations, or measurements of regional blood flow (see reviews cited above), but not on direct measurements of sympathetic nerve activity. The results were not unequivocal. For instance, the combination of adrenalectomy and sympathetic nerve destruction by 6-hydroxydopamine abolished only part of the pressor response (Falcon et al., 1978), as did peripheral α-adrenoceptor blockade (Unger et al., 1981), whereas peripheral ganglionic blockade with hexamethonium caused little or no change (Brody and Johnson, 1980), or even increased the pressor response (Severs et al., 1970; Lappe and Brody, 1984), as was also found in this study. Further, peripheral sympathectomy with 6-hydroxydopamine did not attenuate the pressor peak following icv AII. This effect was found to be due to increased sensitivity to circulating AVP (Hoffman et al., 1977). On the other hand, when increased sympathetic tone was inferred on the basis of increased regional vascular resistances following central AII, the data were either obtained after infusion of the peptide into the carotid artery with mixed central and direct peripheral vascular effects of the peptide (Lappe and Brody, 1984), or the data were not adequately controlled for other vasoconstrictor mechanisms, such as circulating AVP, and reference to the exact time course of the initial events following the central AII application.

Specificity of the Central Effects of AII on Sympathetic Activity

From our data, it seems that the initial decrease in SpNA, RNA, and ANA is a specific feature of the central response to AII. However, this effect could also be brought about by factors not directly related to AII receptor stimulation in the brain. First, there could have been leakage of the peptide from the CSF into the circulation, giving rise to a systemic AII pressor response with reflexly inhibited sympathetic tone and heart rate. Second, the reduced sympathetic nerve activity could be a baroreceptor reflex-mediated event to counteract the rise in blood pressure, as pointed out by Ferrario et al. (1972). The first possibility has been addressed in the past by us and other investigators (Severs and Daniels-Severs, 1973; Schelling et al., 1980) and can be excluded, since penetration of peptides such as AII and saralasin from the cerebrospinal fluid into the blood occurs only at considerably higher doses and has never been detected immediately, but only after a lag time of several minutes following peptide application into the lateral brain ventricle (Schelling et al., 1980). Moreover, we have found previously that peripheral blockade of vascular AII receptors with saralasin (10 μg/kg per min, iv)—which leads to a reduction of more than 60% of the pressor responses to 100 ng AII injected iv—does not affect the pressor responses to the same dose of AII-injected icv (Unger et al., unpublished observation).

The second possibility of a baroreceptor reflex-mediated event cannot be ruled out entirely, but appears unlikely on the basis of the data obtained in this study. First, there was no correlation between the increase in blood pressure and the fall in SpNA, as one might have expected if the latter was reflex mediated. Second, the fall in SpNA, but not in heart rate, persisted in the chronically baroreceptor-denervated animals, despite a marked attenuation of the reflex SpNA responses to blood pressure increases by phenylephrine and decreases by sodium nitroprusside. Third, the fall in SpNA persisted to the same degree after complete blockade of vascular AVP receptors, and was present in most DI rats, despite a significant reduction of the pressor responses to AII. Finally, comparable centrally evoked pressor responses to substance P (this study) and to AVP (Unger et al., in press) were not associated with decreases, but with marked increases in SpNA, RNA, and ANA.

Other cardiovascular reflexes, for instance, those mediated by cardiac mechanoreceptors (Bishop et al., 1984), must be considered as well. It is conceivable that the increase in arterial blood pressure induced a distension of the cardiac ventricles and activated their receptors with subsequent sympathetic inhibition. To exclude this possibility, one would have to study the sympathetic responses to central AII, while at the same time preventing any blood pressure increase. This experiment was not completed in the present study, since our preliminary attempts showed that all manuevers to prevent the central pressure response to AII also simultaneously markedly altered blood pressure, heart rate, and sympathetic activity prior to the administration of the peptide. These complex responses precluded a comparison with the original preparation.

Nevertheless, even if mediated in part by cardiovascular reflex activation such as the heart rate response, the initial decrease in sympathetic activity of the splanchnic, renal, and adrenal regions appears to be specific for AII, when compared to other centrally acting pressor peptides such as substance P or AVP.

Hemodynamic Implications

The question regarding the hemodynamic consequences of this finding remains to be investigated further. Reduced sympathetic tone within nerves controlling distinct vascular areas does not necessarily mean vasodilation and increased blood flow, if, as with AII, a pressor hormone is released simultaneously into the circulation. On the other hand, the fact that the reduction of sympathetic activity occurs in the absence of AVP-induced vasoconstriction, as seen in the $d(CH_2)_5AVP$-treated LE rats and in DI rats, indicates that this effect is independent of AVP and could give rise to regionally increased blood flow. It is also possible that central AII selectively increases the sympathetic drive to other vascular territories, e.g., the skeletal muscle or the skin. Increased vascular resistance in these regions could account for the persistence of (reduced) pressor responses in the absence of AVP-mediated vasoconstriction, as has been observed here and in a number of previous studies [see Severs et al. (1970), Hutchinson et al. (1976), Haack and Möhring (1978), and Unger et al. (1981)]. Accordingly, in these cases, peripheral interference with the sympathetic nervous system by ganglionic blockade or α_1-adrenoceptor blockade completely abolished the central pressor responses to AII. This demonstrates the total dependence of the pressor response on the integrity of the sympathetic nervous system, when AVP is absent or not effective.

It could be interpreted that the increase in femoral nerve activity, together with the fall in splanchnic nerve activity that we observed in anesthetized rats, supports the idea of a regionally restricted sympathetic stimulation by central AII. However, this finding must be interpreted with caution for the following reasons: first, the sympathetic component within the femoral nerve bundle was small compared to its motor and sensory fibers (a fact which precluded testing of the FNA responses in conscious animals); second, the increase in femoral nerve activity did not occur in all animals tested; third, the rise in blood pressure had a shorter latency than the corresponding increase in FNA.

With respect to the changes observed upon drinking, one could speculate that stimulation of central AII receptors not only gives rise to drinking behavior itself, but also initiates the drinking response with a behavioral ("appetitive behavior," exploration) and hemodynamic (blood pressure increase) adjustment. The act of drinking which then ensues, changes the hemodynamic situation to a typical "drinking pattern" with further increases in blood pressure, increases in heart rate, and recruitment of additional sympathetic nerves in areas in which the nerve activity was initially suppressed. The additional rise in blood pressure, induced by drinking, has previously also been reported by Falcon et al. (1978). Since we observed the "drinking pattern" as such also in the DI rats upon spontaneous drinking, it appears to be independent of the original stimulus. Interestingly, a late marked increase in SpNA upon icv AII injections was also observed in some but not all animals in the absence of drinking. This response was usually associated with a second smaller peak in blood pressure and with tachycardia, but never with the initial pressor peak. Thus, it appears, that late activation of initially suppressed sympathetic nerves can help to maintain the pressor response to central AII, even in the absence of drinking.

Substance P, on the other hand, initiates a behavioral hemodynamic and neuronal pattern which has more similarities to the classical defense-type reaction described by (among others) Folkow and Rubinstein (1965), after electrical stimulation of distinct hypothalamic areas in the cat. This could be plausible on the basis of the involvement of this peptide in central pain processing.

In conclusion, we have described two distinct hemodynamic and neuronal patterns following the injection of equipressor doses of AII and substance P into the lateral brain ventricle of conscious rats. The pressor responses to substance P were associated with behavioral arousal, together with increases in heart rate, cardiac output, and a generalized sympatho-adrenal stimulation. The AII response pattern was more complex, with an initial decrease in heart rate and splanchnic, renal, and adrenal sympathetic nerve activity, followed by a rise in heart rate and splanchnic discharge during water ingestion. The cardiovascular and sympathetic response pattern produced by central AII could thus be considered as a prerequisite for the drinking reaction, one of the many ways in which this peptide contributes to body fluid homeostasis, whereas the response pattern to substance P could be instrumental in adjusting the organism to react to unpleasant stimuli such as pain.

We are indebted to Drs. R. Dietz and A. Schömig for measuring plasma catecholamines. The secretarial help of B. Hess is gratefully acknowledged.

This work was supported by a grant from the Deutsche Forschungsgemeinschaft within the SFB 90 "Cardiovasculäres System."

Address for reprints and correspondence: Thomas Unger, M.D., German Institute for High Blood Pressure Research and Department of Pharmacology, University of Heidelberg, Im Neuenheimer Feld 366, D-6900 Heidelberg, FRG.

Received March 6, 1984; accepted for publication January 2, 1985.

References

Aars H, Akre S (1968) Effect of angiotensin on sympathetic nerve activity. Acta Physiol Scand **74:** 134–141

Bishop VS, Malliani A, Thoren P (1984) Cardiac mechanoreceptors. *In* Handbook of Physiology, The Cardiovascular System III, chap 15. Washington, D.C., American Physiological Society, pp 497–555
Brody MJ, Johnson AK (1980) Role of the anteroventral third ventricle region in fluid and electrolyte balance, arterial pressure regulation, and hypertension. *In* Frontiers in Neuroendocrinology, edited by WF Ganong, L Martini. New York, Raven Press, pp 249–292
Brooks VL, Malvin RL (1982) Intracerebroventricular infusions of angiotensin II increases sodium excretion. Proc Soc Exp Biol Med **169:** 532–537
Broshnihan KB, Berti GA, Ferrario CM (1979) Hemodynamics of central infusion of angiotensin II in normal and sodium-depleted dogs. Am J Physiol **6:** H139–H145
Buckley JP, Jandhyala BS (1977) Central cardiovascular effects of angiotensin. Life Sci **20:** 1485–1493
Clarke G, Kirby PJC, Thomson A (1980) Effects on vasopressinergic and oxytocinergic neurons of intraventricular substance P. J Physiol (Lond) **307:** 59P–60P
Falcon II JC, Phillips MI, Hoffman WE, Brody MJ (1978) Effects of intraventricular angiotensin II mediated by the sympathetic nervous system. Am J Physiol **235:** H392–H399
Ferrario CM, Gildenberg PL, McCubbin JW (1972) Cardiovascular effects of angiotensin mediated by the central nervous system. Circ Res **30:** 257–262
Fitzsimons JT (1980) Angiotensin stimulation of the central nervous system. Rev Physiol Biochem Pharmacol **87:** 117–167
Folkow B, Rubinstein EH (1965) Behavioural and autonomic patterns evoked by stimulation of the lateral hypothalamic area in the cat. Acta Physiol Scand **65:** 292–299
Fukiyama K (1972) Central action of angiotensin and hypertension-increased central vasomotor outflow by angiotensin. Jpn Circ J **36:** 599–602
Ganten D, Stock G (1978) Humoral and neurohormonal aspects of blood pressure regulation: focus on angiotensin. Klin Wochenschr **56** (suppl I): 31–41
Ganten D, Hermann K, Bayer C, Unger T, Lang RE (1983) Angiotensin synthesis in the brain and increased turnover in hypertensive rats. Science **221:** 869–871
Haack D, Möhring J (1978) Vasopressin-mediated blood pressure response to intraventricular injection of angiotensin II in the rat. Pflugers Arch **373:** 167–173
Hoffman WE, Phillips MI, Schmid PG, Falcon J, Weet JF (1977) Antidiuretic hormone release and the pressor response to central angiotensin II and cholinergic stimulation. Neuropharmacology **16:** 463–472
Hutchinson JS, Schelling P, Möhring J, Ganten D (1976) Pressor action of centrally perfused angiotensin II in rats with hereditary hypothalamic diabetes insipidus. Endocrinology **99:** 819–823
Klugman KP, Lembeck F, Markowitz S, Mitchell G, Rosendorff C (1980) Substance P increases hypothalamic blood flow via an indirect adrenergic-cholinergic interaction. Br J Pharmacol **71:** 623–629
Krieger EM (1964) Neurogenic hypertension in the rat. Circ Res **15:** 511–521
Lang RE, Unger T, Rascher W, Ganten D (1983a) Brain angiotensin. *In* Handbook of Psychopharmacology, vol 16, edited by L Iversen, SD Iversen, SH Snyder. New York, Plenum, pp 307–361
Lang RE, Heil JWE, Ganten D, Hermann K, Unger T, Rascher W (1983b) Oxytocin unlike vasopressin is a stress hormone in the rat. Neuroendocrinology **37:** 314–316
Lappe RW, Brody MJ (1984) Mechanisms of the central pressor action of angiotensin II in conscious rats. Am J Physiol **246:** R-56–R-62
Mann JFE, Rascher W, Schömig A, Buu T, Kuchel O, Boucher R, Genest J (1982) Contribution of the sympathetic nervous system to the centrally-induced pressor action of angiotensin II in rats. Clin Exp Pharmacol Physiol **9:** 193–201
Morrison JFB, Pickford M (1969) The absence of central sympathetic stimulation by low doses of angiotensin in the cat (abstr). J Physiol (Lond) **202:** 37P
Pernow B (1983) Substance P. Pharmacol Rev **35:** 85–141
Petty MA, Reid JL (1982) The cardiovascular effects of centrally administered substance P in the anaesthetized rabbit. Eur J Pharmacol **82:** 9–14
Rascher W, Lang RE, Ganten D, Meffle H, Taubitz M, Unger T, Gross F (1983) Vasopressin in deoxycorticosterone acetate hypertension of rats: A hemodynamic analysis. J Cardiovasc Pharmacol **5:** 418–425
Reid IA, Day RP (1977) Interactions and properties of some components of the renin-angiotensin system. *In* Central Actions of Angiotensin and Related Hormones, edited by JP Buckley, CM Ferrario. New York, Pergamon Press, pp 255–270
Ricksten SE, Thoren P (1980a) Reflex inhibition of sympathetic activity during volume load in awake normotensive and spontaneously hypertensive rats. Acta Physiol Scand **110:** 77–82
Schelling P, Ganten U, Sponer G, Unger T, Ganten D (1980b) Components of the renin-angiotensin system in the cerebrospinal fluid of rats and dogs with special consideration of the origin and the fate of angiotensin II, Neuroendocrinology **31:** 297–308
Schölkens BA, Jung W, Lang RE, Racher W, Unger T, Ganten D (1983) The role of neuropeptides in central mechanisms of blood pressure regulation. *In* Endocrinology of Hypertension, edited by F Mantero, EG Biglieri, CRW Edwards. New York, Academic Press, pp 339–362
Severs WB, Daniels-Severs AE (1973) Effects of angiotensin on the central nervous system. Pharmacol Rev **25:** 415–449
Severs WB, Summy-Long J, Taylor JS, Connor JD (1970) A central effect of angiotensin: Release of pituitary pressor material. J Pharmacol Exp Ther **174:** 27–34
Severs WB, Daniels-Severs A, Summy-Long J, Radio GJ (1971) Effects of centrally administered angiotensin II on salt and water excretion. Pharmacology **6:** 242–252
Stein RD, Stephenson RB, Weaver LC (1984) Central actions of angiotensin II oppose baroreceptor-induced sympathoinhibition. Am J Physiol **246:** R13–R19
Tobey JC, Fry HK, Mizejewski CS, Fink GD, Weaver LC (1983) Differential sympathetic responses initiated by angiotensin and sodium chloride. Am J Physiol **68:** R60–R68
Unger T, Rascher W, Schuster C, Pavlovitch R, Schömig A, Dietz R, Ganten D (1981) Central blood pressure effects of substance P and angiotensin II: Role of the sympathetic nervous system and vasopressin. Eur J Pharmacol **71:** 33–42
Unger T, Becker H, Ganten D, König M, Lang RE, Petty MA (1983) Central cardiovascular actions of substance P. *In* Substance P, edited by P Skrabanek, D Powell. Dublin, Boole Press, pp 73–74
Unger T, Becker H, Dietz R, Ganten R, Lang RE, Rettig R, Schömig A, Schwab NA (1984) Antihypertensive effect of the GABA receptor agonist muscimol in spontaneously hypertensive rats: Role of the sympatho-adrenal axis. Circ Res **54:** 30–37
Unger T, Rohmeiss P, Becker H, Ganten D, Lang RE, Petty M (in press) Sympathetic activation following central vasopressin receptor stimulation in conscious rats. J Hypertension

INDEX TERMS: Angiotensin II • Substance P • Sympathetic nerve activity • Central blood pressor regulation • Vasopressin • Behavior

Effect of Membrane Depolarization on Binding of [^{3}H]Nitrendipine to Rat Cardiac Myocytes

Frank J. Green, Barbara B. Farmer, Gail L. Wiseman, Mimi J.L. Jose, and August M. Watanabe
From the Departments of Medicine and Pharmacology, and the Krannert Institute of Cardiology, Indiana University School of Medicine, Indianapolis, Indiana

SUMMARY. Binding of the dihydropyridine calcium antagonist [^{3}H]nitrendipine was studied in cardiac myocytes incubated in normal and high potassium buffer so that we might examine the voltage dependence of dihydropyridine binding. Hearts were obtained from adult male Wistar rats, and isolated calcium tolerant myocytes were dissociated by enzymatic dispersion. Cells in 5.6 mM extracellular potassium showed specific binding of [^{3}H]nitrendipine with K_D 587 ± 50 (mean ± SE) pM and maximum receptor density, B_{max}, 10.8 ± 1.3 fmol/mg wet weight. Cells depolarized in 50 mM potassium showed no change in K_D, 661 ± 77 pM, but approximate doubling of B_{max} 25.6 ± 3.7 fmol/mg wet weight. Binding equilibrium was reached within 5 minutes at 37°C, and the K_D determined by kinetic analysis was in good agreement with K_D determined by saturation experiments. Unlabeled nitrendipine and nifedipine completely inhibited [^{3}H]nitrendipine binding with slope factors less than one, whereas verapamil and diltiazem only partially inhibited binding with slope factors substantially less than one. As a function of increasing extracellular potassium concentration from 2.4–54.1 mM, the number of nitrendipine-binding sites increased gradually 115%. Aconitine also produced a 58% increase in binding sites over a concentration range of 1–30 μg/ml. The potassium-induced changes in number of binding sites occurred rapidly and were rapidly reversible with changes in extracellular potassium concentration. There was no change in the number of [^{3}H]nitrendipine-binding sites as a function of potassium or aconitine concentration in dead or digitonin-treated myocytes. We conclude that nitrendipine receptor density in viable myocytes is voltage dependent, but we detect no change in K_D as a function of voltage. **(*Circ Res 56: 576–585, 1985*)**

THE calcium channel in cardiac tissue has been the subject of intense scrutiny during the past decade (Reuter, 1983; Hagiwara and Byerly, 1981; Tsien, 1983). Recent advances in electrophysiological techniques, including voltage-clamp studies and gigaseal recordings of membrane patches in isolated cardiac cells, have increased our understanding of the kinetics of the calcium channel and its response to depolarization, adrenergic agonists, cyclic adenosine monophosphate analogs, cAMP-dependent protein kinase, and calcium antagonists (Reuter, 1983; Lee and Tsien, 1983; Fenwick et al., 1982; Osterrieder et al., 1982). Several investigators have observed that the calcium channel exists in one open and two closed states. When it is open, it admits a current of uniform amplitude, which suggests that there is no intermediate conductance through the channel. Depolarization of the membrane increases the probability of channel opening (Fenwick et al., 1982; Reuter, 1982, 1983). Recently, calcium channel behavior has been characterized as having three gating modes, comprised of periods of no opening of the channel, brief openings, or prolonged openings and only brief closings (Hess et al., 1984).

The interaction of calcium channel antagonists with the channel recently has been further delineated. Verapamil, diltiazem, and nitrendipine block both inward and outward current flow through the channel, and this is interpreted to be consistent with channel blockade. The fact that inward current can be restored by increasing extracellular calcium concentrations suggests that unblocked calcium channels are available for recruitment. The half-time of the decay of inward current is more rapid in the presence of calcium antagonists, and this has been interpreted to be consistent with binding of the drugs to open channels (Lee and Tsien, 1983). Recently, it has been noted that the effects of three dihydropyridine calcium channel antagonists, nisoldipine, nitrendipine, and nicardipine, on the calcium channel current, are augmented at less negative resting membrane potentials. This evidence of voltage dependence has been interpreted in terms of the modulated receptor hypothesis (Hondeghem and Katzung, 1984) and suggests that these drugs bind to inactivated channels as well (Sanguinetti and Kass, 1984). The concept that dihydropyridines act by sterically plugging the channel is being modified in favor of a model in which binding of the dihydropyridine stabilizes the channel in a mode in which no openings occur (Hess et al., 1984; Janis et al., 1984).

Particular interest in the dihydropyridine class of calcium antagonists has been sparked by the observations that [^{3}H]nitrendipine and [^{3}H]nimodipine bind to high-affinity receptors in membranes of a variety of tissues, including brain, myocardium, ileal and vascular smooth muscle, and skeletal muscle (Belleman et al., 1981; Gould et al., 1982; Glossman et al., 1982; Murphy and Snyder, 1982; Bolger et al., 1982; Ehlert et al., 1982a, 1982b; Yamamura et al., 1982; Williams and Tremble, 1982; DePover et al., 1982, 1983a, 1983b; Fairhurst et al., 1983; Fosset et al., 1983; Sarmiento et al., 1983). In most of these studies, the measured equilibrium dissociation constant, K_D, has ranged between 0.11 and 0.4 nM. A second site of lower affinity with K_D of 67 nM has been reported (Belleman, 1981). In addition, specific binding of [^{3}H]nitrendipine (Marsh et al., 1983) and of [^{3}H]nimodipine (DePover et al., 1983a) has been described in intact cells. The interaction of dihydropyridines with these sites is stereospecific, and correlation of pharmacological potency with order of binding affinity has been established in ileal smooth muscle (Bolger et al., 1982). In myocardium, however, it is well recognized that the K_D of the dihydropyridine receptor for [^{3}H]nitrendipine is two to three orders of magnitude lower than the concentration of nitrendipine which produces half-maximal pharmacological effects (Millard et al., 1983; Lee and Tsien, 1983). Because the effect of nitrendipine on calcium channel current is voltage dependent, a model has been proposed which postulates an increase in the affinity of the calcium channel for nitrendipine at less negative membrane potentials (Sanguinetti and Kass, 1984). Alternatively, the pharmacological IC_{50} of nitrendipine for depression of contractility has been correlated with a second class of binding sites with lower affinity in cultured chick myocytes (Marsh et al., 1983) and in canine cardiac sarcolemma (Vaghy et al., 1984).

Competition between labeled dihydropyridines and unlabeled calcium channel antagonists of other chemical classes have disclosed apparent different sites of action of these drugs in myocardial membranes. Verapamil and D600 only partially inhibit [^{3}H]nitrendipine binding, increase the half-time of association and dissociation, and cause a maximum 4-fold increase in the equilibrium dissociation constant, K_D, without changing the maximum number of receptor sites in rat cerebral cortex and myocardial homogenates (Ehlert et al., 1982b). This interaction is postulated to be consistent with negative heterotropic cooperativity. In contrast, diltiazem has been observed to inhibit [^{3}H]nitrendipine binding partially at 0°C, whereas at 25°C and 37°C, partial or no inhibition, or actual enhancement, of binding occurs (Murphy and Snyder, 1982; Ehlert et al., 1982a, 1982b; Yamamura et al., 1982; Ferry and Glossman, 1982; DePover et al., 1982). In brain membranes, diltiazem decreases the rate of dissociation of [^{3}H]nitrendipine from its receptor (Ferry and Glossman, 1982; Yamamura et al., 1982). In myocardial membranes, diltiazem has been reported to increase [^{3}H]nitrendipine- and [^{3}H]nimodipine-binding sites without changing receptor affinity (Millard et al., 1982; DePover et al., 1982, 1983b). In rabbit ventricular membranes, a diltiazem-induced increase in receptor affinity has been noted (Janis et al., 1984). In addition, diltiazem, in small concentrations that depress myocardial contractility only slightly, has been shown to potentiate the negative inotropic effects of nimodipine in isolated rat hearts (DePover et al., 1983b). These observations are consistent with allosteric modulation of the dihydropyridine-binding site by verapamil, but the mechanism of interaction with diltiazem appears to be more complex.

We studied [^{3}H]nitrendipine binding to intact polarized and depolarized ventricular myocytes in order to relate specific binding to changes in membrane voltage. We were interested in the following questions. What is the relationship between binding of [^{3}H]nitrendipine to high-affinity sites and membrane potential of the cell? If changes in [^{3}H]nitrendipine binding occur in response to alterations in membrane potential, are they reversible? Do calcium channel antagonists compete with [^{3}H]nitrendipine with different potency in polarized and depolarized cells? Does diltiazem increase the number of [^{3}H]-nitrendipine-binding sites in intact cells?

Methods

Myocyte Preparation

Adult male Wistar rats weighing 250–300 g were injected with 500 U sodium heparin, intraperitoneally, and were killed 30 minutes later. Following a blow to the cranium, cervical dislocation was performed, and the hearts were rapidly excised and placed in ice-cold physiological saline solution. The aorta was transected adjacent to the innominate artery, cannulated, and subjected to retrograde perfusion at a constant pressure of 60 cm water with Krebs-Henseleit solution containing compounds of the following millimolar concentrations: NaCl, 118; KCl, 4.74; KH_2PO_4, 0.93; $MgSO_4$, 1.2; $NaHCO_3$, 25; glucose, 10; and $CaCl_2$, 2.5. The buffer was equilibrated with 95% O_2/5% CO_2 for 30 minutes. Calcium-tolerant myocytes were isolated enzymatically by a previously described method (Farmer et al., 1983). Briefly, following 20 minutes of perfusion at constant pressure with Krebs-Henseleit buffer containing 2.5 mM calcium, the hearts were subjected to perfusion with buffer devoid of calcium at a constant flow rate of 7.5–8 ml/min for 3.5–4.5 minutes. Next, Krebs-Henseleit buffer containing 0.1% collagenase, 0.1% bovine serum albumin, and 50 μM calcium was introduced via stopcock, and perfusion continued 5 minutes. The ventricles were then cut down, two vertical slashes were made toward but not including the apex, and the tissue then was immersed in Krebs-Henseleit buffer containing 0.1% collagenase (Worthington type I or Sigma type I), 2% bovine serum albumin, and 50 μM calcium and was shaken gently (Labline Orbit Shaker) for four 5-minute periods, each followed by sieving to harvest eluted cells. The cells were suspended and centrifuged twice in Krebs-Henseleit medium containing 50 μM calcium and 2% bovine serum albumin before final suspension in Krebs-Henseleit medium containing 1.8 mM calcium. Dead myocytes were prepared by chilling myocytes at 4°C for

24–48 hours. In selected experiments, myocytes were made permeable by the addition of digitonin, 5 μg/ml.

Membrane Vesicles

Canine cardiac membrane vesicles were prepared as previously described by Jones et al. (1979).

Buffer

The myocytes were incubated in buffer with various concentrations of extracellular potassium, $[K^+]_o$. For $[K^+]_o$ of 5.6, buffer constituents were the same as in the Krebs-Henseleit buffer used for final suspension. For selected experiments, buffer containing $[K^+]_o$ of 2.5, 50, and 80 mM was created by adjusting KCl and increasing or reducing NaCl appropriately to maintain constant osmolarity. In addition, we also conducted experiments in which *N*-2-hydroxyethylpiperazine-*N'*-2-ethanesulfonic acid (HEPES), 10 mM, or morpholinopropane sulfonic acid (MOPS), 20 mM, was substituted for $NaHCO_3$, with added NaCl to maintain constant osmolarity. Bicarbonate buffer was gassed with 95% O_2, 5% CO_2 to maintain pH 7.4, while Good buffers were gassed with 100% O_2, and pH was adjusted to 7.4 with 6 N NaOH.

Equilibrium-Binding Studies

Saturation of [^{3}H]nitrendipine [5 methyl-^{3}H]-1,4-dihydro-2,6-dimethyl-4-(3-nitrophenyl)-3, 5-pyridine-decarboxylic acid ethyl methyl ester]-binding sites in myocytes was examined at 37°C after 30 minutes of incubation. All binding studies were performed in the dark. Myocytes from one preparation were divided and suspended in each buffer at a concentration of 2–5 mg wet weight per ml. Binding reactions were terminated by adding various volumes of cold buffer that contained the identical $[K^+]_o$, and were maintained at a temperature of 4°C. Cold buffer was also used for washing filtered samples. Three experimental designs were used for equilibrium studies. Method 1: identical 2- to 3-ml volumes of cells were incubated with [^{3}H]nitrendipine, 50–1200 pM, in the absence or presence of unlabeled nitrendipine, 1 μM, and 200 μl-aliquots then were sampled in triplicate for measurement of total and nonspecific binding, respectively. Method 2: identical 3-ml volumes of cells were incubated with [^{3}H]nitrendipine. After 30 minutes, triplicate and duplicate 200-μl aliquots were taken for measurement of total binding and total counts, respectively. Unlabeled nitrendipine, 40 μM, was added in a volume of 50 μl to yield a final concentration of 1 μM. The suspension was incubated for 30 more minutes, and triplicate 200-μl aliquots were taken for measurement of nonspecific binding. For both methods 1 and 2, each sample aliquot was immersed for 15 minutes in a 5-ml volume of buffer. The 5-ml volumes then were filtered over Whatman GF/C filters and washed three times with 5 ml of buffer. Both methods gave comparable values for nonspecific binding. Method 3: triplicate 400-μl volumes of cells were incubated with ascending concentrations of [^{3}H]nitrendipine in a final volume of 500 μl in the presence and absence of unlabeled nitrendipine, 1 μM. After 30 minutes of incubation at 37°C, the reaction was terminated by the addition of 10 ml of buffer. After 15 minutes, the 10-ml volume was filtered over Whatman GF/C glass fiber filters and washed three times with 5 ml of buffer.

We determined that the 15-minute immersion in cold buffer prior to filtration caused a net decrease in total and nonspecific binding without changing specific binding. For instance, at equilibrium in 400 pM [^{3}H]nitrendipine, 0.5 mg wet weight of cells filtered immediately after immersion yielded total binding, 1716, nonspecific binding, 1066, and specific binding, 650 counts/min, whereas 15 minutes of immersion before filtering gave 1086, 499, and 587 counts/min, respectively. Thus, the percent specific binding increased, with little change in the absolute number of counts specifically bound.

Competition studies were conducted as in method 3, using a fixed concentration of [^{3}H]nitrendipine, approximately 700 pM, and ascending concentrations of unlabeled competitor. Nitrendipine and nifedipine were initially diluted in absolute ethanol to make a 1 mM solution before further dilution in 0.9% NaCl. Verapamil and diltiazem were diluted in 0.9% NaCl.

[^{3}H]Nitrendipine binding in myocytes was examined over a range of $[K^+]_o$ from 2.4–54.1 mM, and over a range of concentrations of aconitine, 1–300 μg/ml. Aconitine was dissolved in absolute ethanol in a concentration of 3 mg/ml before further dilution in buffer with $[K^+]_o$ of 5.6 mM. To create a range of potassium concentrations, we used buffer containing $[K^+]_o$ of 2.5 mM and combined varying volumes of two buffers containing $[K^+]_o$ of 5.6 and 80 mM in flasks. Aliquots of cells then were added to the flasks containing each concentration of potassium or aconitine, with final cell concentration 2–5 mg wet weight per ml in a final volume of 3 ml. From these flasks, 400-μl cell samples were incubated in triplicate with [^{3}H]-nitrendipine, 700 pM, in the absence and presence of unlabeled nitrendipine, 1 μM, as in method 3. To terminate the reaction, 10 ml buffer with the identical $[K^+]_o$ or aconitine concentration was added, and 15 minutes later the 10-ml volume was filtered over Whatman GF/C glass fiber filters and washed three times with 5 ml of buffer.

For reversibility studies, the cell preparation was divided, and cells were suspended at 25 mg wet weight per ml in approximately 2 ml of buffer containing $[K^+]_o$ of either 5.6 or 50 mM. They were incubated with a free [^{3}H]nitrendipine concentration of approximately 600 pM, in the absence and presence of unlabeled nitrendipine, 1 μM. After 30 minutes, 500-μl aliquots of cells were removed and diluted in 5 ml of the buffer with either the identical or opposite $[K^+]_o$, with [^{3}H]nitrendipine and unlabeled nitrendipine concentrations maintained as in the first incubation. These suspensions were incubated at 37°C, and at various time points triplicate 200-μl aliquots were removed and immersed in 5 ml of buffer, 4°C, having the same $[K^+]_o$ as the second incubation. After 15 minutes, these 5-ml volumes were filtered and washed 3 times with 5 ml of buffer, 4°C.

Kinetic Studies

Preliminary studies showed that association and dissociation were complete within 10 minutes. Association time course studies were initiated with the addition of [^{3}H]-nitrendipine following 5 minutes of incubation at 37°C. Triplicate 200-μl aliquots were obtained at various times and each was immersed in 5 ml of buffer at 4°C for 15 minutes before rapid filtration and washing with three 5-ml aliquots of buffer. Nonspecific binding was determined by parallel incubation which included unlabeled nitrendipine, 1 μM. To determine the dissociation time course, cells were incubated 1 hour with [^{3}H]nitrendipine, triplicate 200-μl aliquots were taken for total binding at time 0, then unlabeled nitrendipine was added and subsequent triplicate 200-μl aliquots were obtained at various times.

Membrane Saturation Studies

The experiments were performed in Tris-HCl buffer containing compounds of the following millimolar concentrations: Trizma base, 50; $MgCl_2$, 9; with concentrated HCl added to yield pH 7.5. In addition, 20 mM MOPS buffer (as described above) was used. Membrane vesicles in concentrations of 13–15 μg protein/ml were incubated in 5-ml volumes of buffer in triplicate in the presence of ascending concentrations of [^{3}H]nitrendipine for 45 minutes. Each incubation volume was rapidly filtered over Whatman GF/C glass fiber filters and washed three times with 5 ml cold buffer. Nonspecific binding was defined as that occurring in the presence of 1 μM unlabeled nitrendipine.

Filters were placed in scintillation vials, 7 ml of scintillation cocktail (New England Nuclear formula 947 or 963) were added, and the counts per minute were determined in a Beckman LS 7500 scintillation counter at 47% efficiency.

Materials

[^{3}H]Nitrendipine was purchased from New England Nuclear. Crystalline nitrendipine was the gift of the Miles Institute of Preclinical Pharmacology and crystalline nifedipine was the gift of Pfizer Laboratories Division. Verapamil was donated by Knoll Pharmaceutical Company, and diltiazem by Marion Laboratories, Inc. Aconitine, MOPS free acid, and Trizma base were purchased from Sigma Chemical Co., HEPES free acid was purchased from Calbiochem-Behring, and all other chemicals used were of highest reagent grade commercially available.

Calculations

Saturation data were subjected to Scatchard analysis (Scatchard, 1949), and linear regression was performed to yield the equilibrium dissociation constant, K_D, and maximum receptor concentration, B_{max}. Cell density was determined by measurement of dry weight and conversion to wet weight as previously described (Farmer, 1983). B_{max} in picomoles per liter was then converted to density per mg wet weight of cells. Analysis of time courses and competition data was done using standard equations (Manalan et al., 1981; Fairhurst et al., 1983; Cheng and Prusoff, 1973):

$$\ln \frac{[RL]_{eq}}{[RL]_{eq} - [RL]_T} = K_{OBS}t \quad (1)$$

$$K_{OBS} = K_1[L] + K_{-1} \quad (2)$$

$$K_{-1} = \frac{0.693}{T_{1/2}} \quad (3)$$

$$K_i = \frac{IC_{50}}{1 + \frac{[L]}{K_D}} \quad (4)$$

Paired *t*-tests were used to compare time course and equilibrium data in polarized and depolarized cells using STATPAK (Western Michigan University) on a PDP-11 computer (Digital Equipment Corporation). Comparison of competition data in polarized and depolarized cells was done with one-way analysis of variance of repeated observations. Comparison of binding in cells after sequential incubation in two $[K^+]_o$ was done using the Bonferroni *t*-test.

Results

The myocyte preparation yielded adult rat ventricular myocytes which had initial viability greater than 75% as assessed by rod-shaped morphology criteria. This has correlated well with a low rate of succinate oxidation in the absence of digitonin (Farmer et al., 1983). The cells tolerated extracellular calcium concentration, $[Ca^{++}]_o$, of 1.8 mM. Viability remained 61 ± 2% (mean ± SE) at the conclusion of each experiment. These adult cells were used the same day for experimentation. The isolated cells did not spontaneously contract either in $[K^+]_o$ of 5.6 or 50 mM. We have concluded from biochemical data previously described (Farmer et al., 1983) that the cells have impermeable membranes and therefore that varying $[K^+]_o$ above 5.6 mM should cause depolarization of the cells.

Figure 1 depicts results from one representative [^{3}H]nitrendipine saturation experiment in polarized and depolarized cells. Specific binding was saturable and ranged from 48 ± 2.5% to 33 ± 2.5% (mean ± SE) in polarized cells and 65 ± 1.8% to 45 ± 2.9% in depolarized cells. In the inset is a Scatchard analysis of the two saturation curves. In polarized myocytes, K_D was 962 pM and B_{max} 44.3 pM or 13.6 fmol/mg

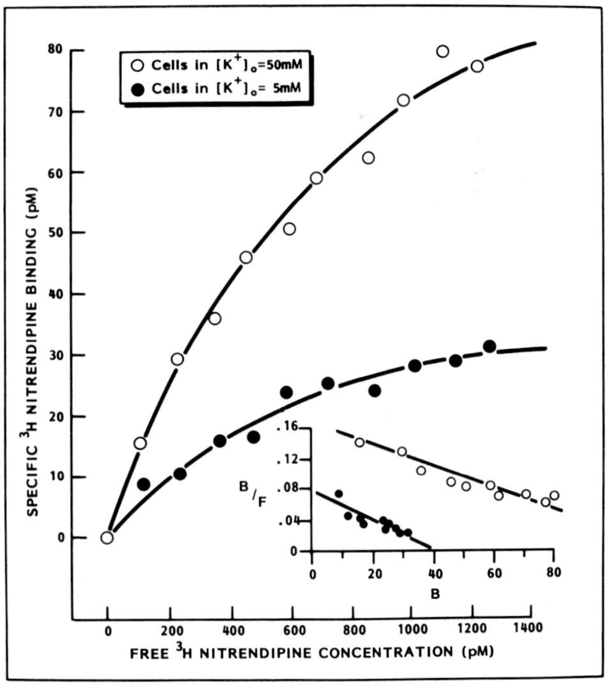

FIGURE 1. *Saturation of binding of [^{3}H]nitrendipine to polarized and depolarized intact adult rat cardiac myocytes. Specific binding, defined as that displaced by 1 μM unlabeled nitrendipine, is plotted vs. free [^{3}H]nitrendipine concentration. Inset is Scatchard analysis in which B represents the concentration of bound [^{3}H]nitrendipine, and F represents the concentration of free [^{3}H]nitrendipine. Points are means of triplicate determinations from one representative experiment. For this experiment, in polarized myocytes (●), K_D was 962 pM and total receptor concentration, B_{max}, was 44.3 pM or 13.6 fmol/mg wet weight. In depolarized myocytes (○), K_D was 845 pM, and B_{max}, 131 pM or 40.1 fmol/mg wet weight.*

TABLE 1
Specific Binding of [^{3}H]Nitrendipine

Preparation	n	$[K^+]_o$	K_D (pM)	B_{max}
Intact myocytes	18	5.6	587 ± 50	10.8 ± 1.3*
		50	661 ± 77	25.6 ± 3.7
Dead myocytes	4	5.6	543 ± 126	17.8 ± 3.4*
		50	565 ± 173	19.2 ± 3.9
Canine cardiac membrane vesicles	1	5.6	483	857†
		50	389	782

See text for description of preparation. Values are expressed as mean ± SE. The increase in B_{max} in live cells in $[K^+]_o$ of 50 mM is significant, $P < 0.0001$.
* fmol/mg wet weight.
† fmol/mg protein.

wet weight. In depolarized myocytes, K_D was 845 pM and B_{max} 131 pM or 40.1 fmol/mg wet weight. Although the K_D was not significantly changed in the depolarized myocytes, the B_{max} increased strikingly. Results from 18 experiments in live myocytes are shown in Table 1. In polarized myocytes, the mean K_D was 587 ± 50 pM and B_{max} was 10.8 ± 1.3 fmol/mg wet weight. In depolarized myocytes, the mean K_D was 661 ± 77 pM and B_{max} was 25.6 ± 3.7 fmol/mg wet weight. There was no significant difference between the K_D in polarized and depolarized myocytes, but the increase in B_{max} in depolarized myocytes was highly significant ($P < 0.0001$) by paired t-test.

If this phenomenon of increased number of binding sites is related to depolarization of membranes, then cells which have no resting potential should not exhibit changes in binding characteristics when extracellular potassium concentration is changed. We examined dead cell preparations as assessed by morphological evidence of 100% irreversible contracture. These results are also shown in Table 1. In $[K^+]_o$ of 5.6 mM, K_D was 543 ± 126 pM and B_{max}, 17.8 ± 3.4 fmol/mg wet weight. In $[K^+]_o$ of 50 mM, these values were unchanged: K_D was 565 ± 173 pM, and B_{max}, 19.2 ± 3.9 fmol/mg wet weight. We also performed a parallel experiment in which we incubated canine myocardial membrane vesicles in each MOPS buffer. In $[K^+]_o$ of 5.6 mM, K_D was 483 pM with B_{max}, 857 fmol/mg protein and in $[K^+]_o$ of 50 mM, K_D, 389 pM and B_{max}, 782 fmol/mg protein. These results were comparable to our results in membrane vesicles incubated in Tris-HCl buffer, in which we observed K_D of 314 ± 28 pM and B_{max}, 823 ± 82 fmol/mg protein.

We performed time course studies of [^{3}H]nitrendipine binding to myocytes in both $[K^+]_o$. We found association and dissociation to be monophasic and complete within 5 minutes at 37°C. In polarized myocytes, K_1 was 9.725 ± 1.7 × 10^8 M/min and K_{-1} was 0.37 ± 0.04/min. The mean K_D from these five experiments was 436 ± 102 pM. In depolarized myocytes, K_1 was 12.056 ± 1.9 × 10^8 M/min and K_{-1} was 0.36 ± 0.03/min, with K_D 315 ± 39 pM. There was no difference in dead myocytes. These K_D are in good agreement with equilibrium determinations of K_D.

We wished to see whether [^{3}H]nitrendipine binding was maximal at any particular membrane voltage in order to relate binding to channel activation state. We examined changes in [^{3}H]nitrendipine binding as a function of increasing $[K^+]_o$, and this is shown in Figure 2. Specifically bound [^{3}H]nitrendipine more than doubled as $[K^+]_o$ was increased from 2.4 mM to 54.1 mM. In $[K^+]_o$ of 4.5 mM, [^{3}H]nitrendipine binding in 48-hour-old dead myocytes was 44% greater than in live cells from the same preparation, but it was less than that observed in depolarized live cells. Because we were concerned about a possible time-related loss in binding sites, we treated live cells acutely with digitonin, 5 μg/ml, to abolish membrane potential, and compared binding in these cells with live cells from the same preparation. It is apparent, in Figure 2, that digitonin-treated cells bind as much [^{3}H]nitrendipine at 4.5 mM $[K^+]_o$ as depolarized live cells, and there is no further change at higher $[K^+]_o$.

To verify further that the increase in [^{3}H]nitrendipine-binding sites was due to depolarization, we treated cells in $[K^+]_o$ of 5.6 mM with ascending concentrations of aconitine, a sodium channel-activating drug (Peper and Trautwein, 1967; Catterall, 1977); these results are shown in Figure 3. As aconitine concentration was increased from 1–30 μg/ml, [^{3}H]nitrendipine specifically bound in the presence of a free [^{3}H]nitrendipine concentration of 700 pM increased to 158 ± 6% of control. Again, aconitine did not change specific binding in dead cells (data not shown). It should be noted that cells exposed to aconitine, 300 μg/ml, were also exposed to 10% ethanol, which by itself caused a 9% decrease in specific binding below that seen in 5.4 mM $[K^+]_o$ alone.

If the potassium-induced change in [^{3}H]nitrendipine receptor density is the result of differences in membrane voltage, then this change should be rapidly reversible if $[K^+]_o$ is changed. The reversibility of this depolarization-induced binding is depicted

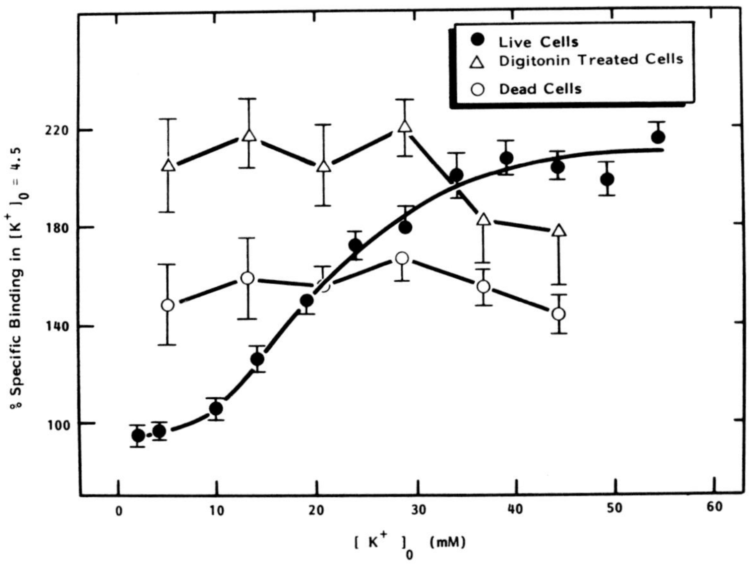

FIGURE 2. *[³H]Nitrendipine binding in live, dead, and digitonin-treated adult rat cardiac myocytes as a function of $[K^+]_o$. Binding is expressed as a percent of the specific binding which occurred in the presence of $[K^+]_o = 4.5$ mM. Live cells, n = 9; dead cells, n = 5; digitonin-treated cells, n = 4. Points represent mean ± SE.*

in Table 2. These figures were obtained after 30 minutes of incubation in the second medium. It can be seen that cells initially and subsequently incubated in $[K^+]_o$ of 5.6 mM bound the same amount of [³H]nitrendipine as did cells that were initially incubated in $[K^+]_o$ of 50 mM prior to incubation in $[K^+]_o$ of 5.6 mM. Cells initially incubated in $[K^+]_o$ of 5.6 mM before incubation in $[K^+]_o$ of 50 mM bound the same amount of [³H]nitrendipine as cells incubated in $[K^+]_o$ of 50 mM for both incubations. However, there was a significant difference between the number of [³H]nitrendipine sites in cells finally incubated in $[K^+]_o$ of 50 mM and in those finally incubated in $[K^+]_o$ of 5.6 mM ($P < 0.01$). Because the number of [³H]nitrendipine-binding sites correlated with the $[K^+]_o$ of the second but not the first incubation, it can be concluded that this change in numbers of binding sites is reversible. Subsequently, we examined the time course of the change in [³H]-nitrendipine binding after the cells were placed in the second $[K^+]_o$ and found that binding equilibrated within 1 minute (data not shown). Because of technical limitations, earlier time points could not be examined.

We examined competition of [³H]nitrendipine with unlabeled nitrendipine, nifedipine, verapamil, and diltiazem. In Figure 4, we have depicted competition of unlabeled calcium channel antagonists with [³H]nitrendipine in polarized and depolarized cells. There is no difference in the IC_{50} of nitrendipine in the two $[K^+]_o$. It can be observed that the curves are slightly shallow and, indeed, the slope factor for these mean determinations is less than one. We suspect that a second lower affinity site is being revealed. The IC_{50} of nifedipine is slightly but not significantly greater than that observed with nitrendipine, there is no difference in nifedipine competition in polarized and depolarized cells, and the slope factors are also less than one.

Unlabeled verapamil only partially inhibited [³H]-

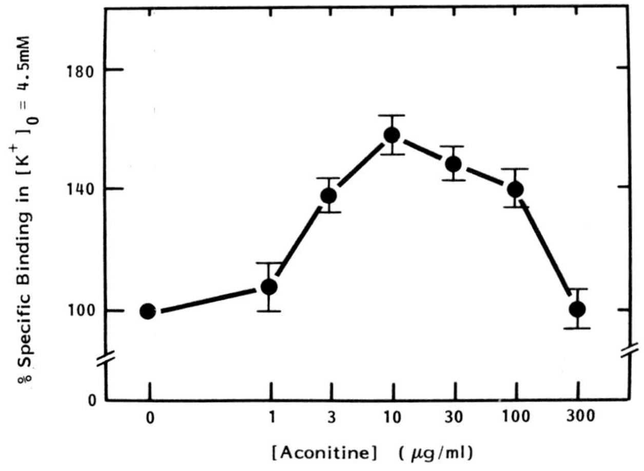

FIGURE 3. *[³H]Nitrendipine binding in live adult rat cardiac myocytes as a function of aconitine concentration. Binding is expressed as a percent of the specific binding which occurred in the presence of $[K^+]_o = 4.5$ mM and in the absence of aconitine, n = 9.*

TABLE 2
Reversibility of Potassium-Induced Changes in [³H]Nitrendipine Binding

First $[K^+]_o$ (mM)	Second $[K^+]_o$ (mM)	Specifically bound [³H]nitrendipine (fmol/mg wet wt)
5.6	5.6	6.4 ± 0.1
	50	14.1 ± 0.9
50	5.6	6.4 ± 1.0
	50	13.5 ± 1.1

See text for description of method. Values are expressed as mean ± SE. Cells were incubated at 37°C for 30 minutes in the first $[K^+]_o$ in the presence of [³H]nitrendipine, 700 pM, and in the presence or absence of unlabeled nitrendipine, 1 µM. Aliquots of the cells were then diluted 10-fold in either second $[K^+]_o$ with drug concentrations maintained constant. After 30 minutes of additional incubation at 37°C, specific [³H]nitrendipine binding was determined.

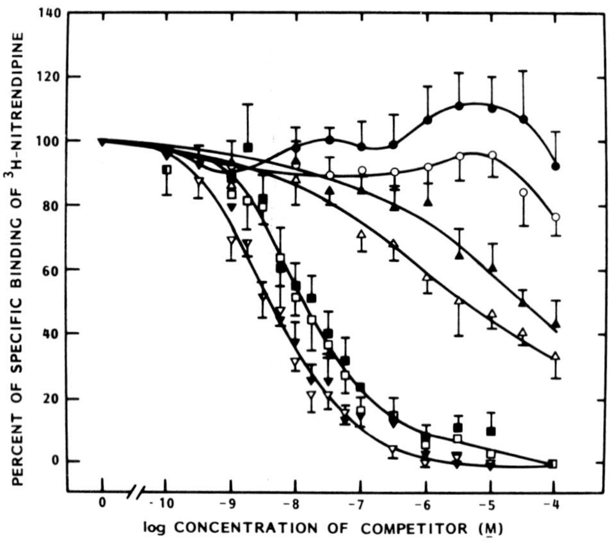

FIGURE 4. *Competition of unlabeled nitrendipine, nifedipine, verapamil, and diltiazem with [³H]nitrendipine in polarized and depolarized adult rat cardiac myocytes. Data points represent mean ± SE of results from 7–10 experiments with each competitor. Closed symbols represent results in polarized myocytes. Open symbols represent results in depolarized myocytes.* ▼ ▽ *Nitrendipine, n = 10;* ■ □ *nifedipine, n = 7;* ▲ △ *verapamil, n = 8;* ● ○ *diltiazem, n = 8.*

nitrendipine, and there was sometimes greater inhibition of binding in depolarized than in polarized cells. Overall, the differences in these eight experiments were not significant. Whereas partial inhibition of binding can be seen at concentrations as low as 1 nM, IC_{50} for these means of eight experiments was approximately 10 μM. In several experiments, partial inhibition was less than 50% at 10^{-4} M. The mean slope factor for these eight experiments was much less than one.

The competition of diltiazem with [³H]nitrendipine exhibited remarkable variability. In most experiments in both polarized and depolarized myocytes, diltiazem weakly inhibited [³H]nitrendipine binding. In a total of 4 out of 10 experiments, however, we noted an increase of up to 70% in specific binding in polarized but not depolarized myocytes. Because of the inconsistency of this phenomenon in the myocytes, there was no significant difference overall in the ability of diltiazem to inhibit [³H]nitrendipine binding in polarized and depolarized myocytes. Diltiazem inhibited much less than 50% of [³H]nitrendipine binding. The average slope factors and K_i for each competitor are summarized in Table 3.

Discussion

Our experiments document the presence of a high-affinity binding site for nitrendipine in both polarized and depolarized myocytes. In membranes, the K_D we observed ranged between 314 and 483 pM, in good agreement with the results obtained by others (Glossman et al., 1982; Murphy and Snyder, 1982; Ehlert et al., 1982a, 1982b; Bolger et al., 1982; DePover et al., 1982). The K_D we observed in cells was slightly higher, comparable to that reported by DePover (DePover et al., 1983a). The possibility of a second site of lower affinity and higher capacity has previously been raised, both in work in membranes (Belleman et al., 1981; Vaghy et al., 1984), and in cells (Marsh et al., 1983). We have chosen to confine our inquiry to the high-affinity site.

We have observed, for the first time, a significant increase in the number of [³H]nitrendipine-binding sites with depolarization of live cells. This can be demonstrated not only as a function of potassium concentration, but also as a function of aconitine concentration. It is apparent that this increase in binding sites approaches a maximum in $[K^+]_o$ of 54.1 mM. In addition, this phenomenon is rapidly reversible with changes in extracellular potassium concentration. These observations are consistent with voltage-dependent binding of [³H]nitrendipine in these cardiac myocytes.

Because nitrendipine is a putative calcium channel label, these voltage-dependent changes in binding may occur as a result of changes in the state of activation of the calcium channel. Previous work in

TABLE 3
Competition of Unlabeled Calcium Antagonists with [³H]Nitrendipine in Intact Myocytes

Competitor	$[K^+]_o$	K_i (nM)	Slope factor
Nitrendipine (*n* = 10)	5.6	2.0 ± 0.35	0.58 ± 0.07
	50	1.9 ± 0.47	0.73 ± 0.11
Nifedipine (*n* = 7)	5.6	6.0 ± 1.7	0.62 ± 0.09
	50	4.8 ± 1.0	0.76 ± 0.09
Verapamil (*n* = 8)	5.6	8317 ± 2580	0.22 ± 0.06
	50	2329 ± 889	0.21 ± 0.03
Diltiazem (*n* = 8)	5.6	Inhibition less than 50%	−0.0305 ± 0.09
	50		0.067 ± 0.04

Values are expressed as mean ± SE.

isolated myocytes suggested that the channel exists in either a fully open or possibly two closed states, and that opening occurs in bursts (Reuter, 1982). The probability that channel opening will occur increases with depolarization (Reuter, 1982). Recent observations of an increase in the apparent rate of calcium channel inactivation during the first membrane depolarization in the presence of nitrendipine suggested that nitrendipine binds to the channel in the open state (Lee and Tsien, 1983; Sanguinetti and Kass, 1984). Subsequently, voltage-dependent effects of nisoldipine, nitrendipine, and nicardipine have been noted, and these results suggested that nitrendipine binds predominantly to inactivated channels (Sanguinetti and Kass, 1984). Moreover, recent studies of nifedipine in frog ventricular muscle have suggested that once depolarization of the membrane occurs, photoinactivation of nifedipine does not result in unblocking of the channel until a brief period of repolarization occurs (Morad et al., 1983). Our data suggest that the number of binding sites of [^{3}H]nitrendipine is greatest under conditions of prolonged depolarization in which a large proportion of calcium channels is inactivated. Taken together, these observations support the concept of state-dependent binding of nitrendipine to the myocardial calcium channel and indicate that nitrendipine binds not only to open but to inactivated channels, as well.

The binding affinity of nisoldipine and nitrendipine in depolarized myocardium has been predicted to increase by three orders of magnitude over that affinity observed in polarized myocardium (Sanguinetti and Kass, 1984). This observation might help to explain the discrepancy between the K_D of the [^{3}H]nitrendipine receptor in myocardium and the half-maximal concentration, IC_{50}, of nitrendipine which produces negative inotropic effects (Millard et al., 1983) and reduces sarcolemmal calcium influx (Lee and Tsien, 1983). We were unable to demonstrate any difference in K_D between polarized and depolarized cells, however, even though the modulated receptor hypothesis would have predicted a higher K_D in polarized cells. It is possible that occupancy of a low affinity receptor correlates with pharmacological effect (Marsh et al., 1983; Vaghy et al., 1984) or that there is unusual coupling of the pharmacological effect to receptor occupancy. It is also possible that membrane depolarization may open access to a channel-associated receptor without changing receptor affinity (Starmer et al., 1984).

We found that nitrendipine and nifedipine completely inhibited binding of [^{3}H]nitrendipine, with a slope factor less than 1, comparable to cultured cell data (Marsh et al., 1983). We concur that there may be lower affinity sites detected by these competition studies. Our results demonstrate no difference in the potency of these calcium antagonists in polarized vs. depolarized cells. Verapamil only partially inhibited binding, and this is in agreement with observations in membranes (Ehlert et al., 1982a,b). Verapamil was previously reported to have a K_D of 8 nM for a lower affinity site in cells (Marsh et al., 1983), but our observations pertain to the higher affinity site, at which verapamil competed slightly at 1 nM and to a greater extent at micromolar concentrations. Diltiazem weakly competed for [^{3}H]nitrendipine-binding sites, and in only one experiment did this exceed 50% inhibition of specific binding. We observed diltiazem-induced enhancement of [^{3}H]nitrendipine binding at 37°C in polarized but not depolarized myocytes. This phenomenon in membranes has been well described, and has been ascribed to changes in the rate of dissociation of the ligand in brain (Yamamura, 1982; Ferry and Glossman, 1982) and in myocardium (Janis et al., 1984) and to increases in the number of receptors in myocardium (DePover et al., 1982; Millard et al., 1982). Given that membranes have no electrical potential, it is unclear to us why depolarized cells did not exhibit the same enhancement of [^{3}H]nitrendipine binding. Our results on diltiazem-nitrendipine interactions are in contrast with those obtained in embryonic chick ventricular cells, in which no interaction was observed (Marsh et al., 1983).

If we assume 4.4×10^4 cells per mg wet weight, our maximum nitrendipine receptor density was 160,000 sites per polarized cell and 382,000 sites per depolarized cell. These are greater than estimates of 2,000–10,000 channels/cell based on electrophysiological studies of cultured neonatal rat cardiac cells (Reuter, 1983). One other study in isolated adult rat cardiac myocytes estimated 10^6 sites/cell (DePover et al., 1983a). Studies in cultured embryonic chick ventricular cells measured 51 fmol/mg protein (Marsh et al., 1983). This can be compared with 61 and 147 fmol/mg protein in these rat heart cells in $[K^+]_o$ of 5.6 and 50 mM, respectively. Discrepancies in binding data may be the result of different methods of converting concentrations of receptors in solution to density per milligram of tissue or number of sites per cell. It is more difficult to reconcile the binding data with the electrophysiological data. It is unlikely that multiple nitrendipine molecules bind to one channel. Our cells are from adult rats and are not cultured. By contrast, electrophysiological estimates were from cultured neonatal rat cells. It is possible that age-related differences in density or binding sites exist. In addition, cultured cells may have binding characteristics different from those of freshly isolated cells that have been recently exposed to enzymatic digestion (Glossman et al., 1982).

Observations in subcellular fractions of myocytes also provide a possible explanation for the increase in the number of [^{3}H]nitrendipine-binding sites in depolarized myocytes. Subfractions of cardiac sarcoplasmic reticulum have been isolated by selective calcium oxalate loading and discontinuous sucrose density gradient centrifugation (Jones and Cala, 1981). Three fractions which demonstrate increased calcium uptake in the presence of the alkaloid ryanodine have particularly high concentrations of

[3H]nitrendipine-binding sites (Williams and Jones, 1983), and these findings have subsequently been confirmed in a different preparation technique (DePover et al., 1983a). Thus, there may be intracellular binding sites for [3H]nitrendipine which are not detected by electrophysiological study (DePover et al., 1983a).

Although [3H]nitrendipine binding sites do not copurify with sarcolemmal markers such as Na^+,K^+-ATPase, and muscarinic cholinergic and β-adrenergic receptors, the cellular location of [3H]nitrendipine-binding sites is still unclear. The ryanodine-sensitive fraction of sarcoplasmic reticulum that is collected at the 1.0 M:1.5 M sucrose interface has high concentrations of a 55,000-dalton calcium-binding protein (Jones and Cala, 1981; Campbell et al., 1983). This protein cross-reacts with antiserum to calsequestrin, a skeletal muscle protein localized to terminal cisternae (Jorgensen et al., 1982; Campbell et al., 1983). There is evidence that this cardiac calsequestrin is also located in junctional sarcoplasmic reticulum (Campbell et al., 1983; Jorgensen et al., 1984). It is possible that this membrane fraction contains dyads and triads of sarcolemmal T-tubules and sarcoplasmic reticulum. It is also possible that there are calcium release channels in sarcoplasmic reticulum membranes which are detected as nitrendipine-binding sites. Recently, a dihydropyridine analog has been used as a photoaffinity label of a 32,000-dalton membrane protein found to be enriched in ryanodine-sensitive membrane fractions from canine myocardium (Campbell et al., 1984). Similar studies have isolated a 41,000-dalton protein in intestinal smooth muscle membrane (Venter et al., 1983). These studies may aid future attempts to localize these binding sites within the myocardial cell.

High levels of nonspecific binding remain a problem for cellular binding studies using [3H]nitrendipine. It is interesting that multiple washings of isolated cells with consequent removal of albumin have been observed to reduce nonspecific binding (DePover et al., 1983). We have had improved results by allowing our samples to equilibrate in a large volume of ice cold buffer for 15 minutes. Time course studies have indicated that this reduces total and nonspecific binding without changing specific binding. High nonspecific binding still hampers investigation of a possible second lower affinity binding site (DePover et al., 1983a).

Our results suggest that radioligand-binding studies in cells may be of value in correlating alterations in nitrendipine binding with manipulations that are known to modulate the calcium channel. Contrary to hypotheses generated from electrophysiological studies, we did not detect a difference in the affinity of receptor sites in polarized and depolarized cells, but depolarization did increase the number of nitrendipine-binding sites. Our estimates of receptor density, taken together with others, suggest that there may be more [3H]nitrendipine-binding sites per cell than sarcolemmal calcium channels, as predicted by electrophysiological measurements of sarcolemmal calcium current.

We thank Terri Butcher and Stevie Rolfe for expert preparation of this manuscript.

Supported in part by the Herman C. Krannert Fund; by Grants HL18795, HL06308, and HL07182 from the National Heart, Lung, and Blood Institute of the National Institutes of Health; and by the American Heart Association, Indiana Affiliate. This work was completed while Dr Green was a Squibb Cardiovascular Fellow.

Address for reprints: Frank J. Green, M.D., Krannert Institute of Cardiology, 1001 West 10th Street, Indianapolis, Indiana 46202.

Received November 3, 1983; accepted for publication January 16, 1985.

References

Belleman P, Ferry D, Lubbecke F, Glossman H (1981) [3H]Nitrendipine, a potent calcium antagonist, binds with high affinity to cardiac membranes. Arzneimforsch **31:** 2064–2067

Bolger GT, Gengo PJ, Luchowski EM, Siegel H, Triggle DJ, Janis RA (1982) High affinity binding of a calcium channel antagonist to smooth and cardiac muscle. Biochem Biophys Res Commun **104:** 1604–1609

Cachelin AB, dePeyer JE, Kokubun S, Reuter H (1983) Ca^{2+} channel modulation by 8-bromocyclic AMP in cultured heart cells. Nature 304:462–464

Campbell KP, MacLennon DH, Jorgensen AO, Mintzer MC (1983) Purification and characterization of calsequestrin from canine cardiac sarcoplasmic reticulum and identification of the 53,000 dalton glycoprotein. J Biol Chem **258:** 1197–1204

Campbell KP, Lipschutz GM, Denney GH (1984) Direct photoaffinity labelling of the high affinity nitrendipine-binding site in subcellular membrane fractions isolated from canine myocardium. J Biol Chem **259:** 5384–5387

Catterall WA (1977) Activation of the action potential Na^+ ionophore by neurotoxins. An allosteric model. J Biol Chem **252:** 8669–8676

Cheng YC, Prusoff WH (1973) Relationship between the inhibition constant (K_i) and the concentration of inhibitor which causes 50 percent inhibition (I_{50}) of an enzymatic reaction. Biochem Pharmacol **22:** 3099–3108

DePover A, Matlib MA, Lee SW, Dube GP, Grupp IL, Grupp G, Schwartz A (1982) Specific binding of [3H]nitrendipine to membranes from coronary arteries and heart in relation to pharmacological effects. Paradoxical stimulation by diltiazem. Biochem Biophys Res Commun **108:** 110–117

DePover A, Lee SW, Matlib MA, Whitmer K, Davis BA, Powell T, Schwartz A (1983a) 3H-nimodipine specific binding to cardiac myocytes and subcellular fractions. Biochem Biophys Res Commun **113:** 185–191

DePover A, Grupp IL, Grupp G, Schwartz A (1983b) Diltiazem potentiates the negative inotropic action of nimodipine in heart. Biochem Biophys Res Commun **114:** 922–929

Ehlert FJ, Itoga E, Roeske WR, Yamamura HI (1982a) The interaction of 3H-nitrendipine with receptors for calcium antagonists in the cerebral cortex and heart of rats. Biochem Biophys Res Commun **104:** 937–943

Ehlert FJ, Roeske WR, Itoga E, Yamamura HI (1982b) The binding of 3H-nitrendipine to receptors for calcium channel antagonists in the heart, cerebral cortex, and ileum of rats. Life Sci **30:** 2191–2202

Fairhurst AS, Thayer SA, Colker JE, Beatty DE (1983) A calcium antagonist drug binding site in skeletal muscle sarcoplasmic reticulum: Evidence for a calcium channel. Life Sci **32:** 1331–1339

Farmer BB, Mancina M, Williams ES, Watanabe AM (1983) Isolation of calcium tolerant myocytes from adult rat hearts: Review of the literature and description of a method. Life Sci **33:** 1–18

Fenwick EM, Marty A, Neher E (1982) Sodium and calcium channels in bovine chromaffin cells. J Physiol (Lond) **331:** 599–635

Ferry DR, Glossman H (1982) Evidence for multiple receptor sites within a putative calcium channel. Naunyn Schmiedebergs Arch Pharmacol **321:** 80–83

Fosset M, Jaimovich E, Delpont E, Lazdunski M (1983) ^{3}H-nitrendipine receptors in skeletal muscle: Properties and preferential localization in transverse tubules. J Biol Chem **258:** 6086–6092

Glossman H, Ferry DR, Lubbecke F, Mewes R, Hofmann F (1982) Calcium channels: Direct identification with radioligand binding studies. Trends Pharmacol Sci **3:** 431–437

Gould RJ, Murphy KMM, Snyder SH (1982) ^{3}H-Nitrendipine labelled calcium channels discriminate inorganic calcium agonists and antagonists. Proc Natl Acad Sci USA **79:** 3656–3660

Hagiwara S, Byerly L (1981) Calcium channel. Annu Rev Neurosci **4:** 69–125

Henry PD (1980) Comparative pharmacology of calcium antagonists: Nifedipine, verapamil, and diltiazem. Am J Cardiol **46:** 1047–1058

Hess P, Lansman JB, Tsien RW (1984) Different modes of Ca channel gating behavior favored by dihydropyridine Ca agonists and antagonists. Nature **311:** 538–544

Hondeghem LM, Katzung BG (1984) Antiarrythmic agents: the modulated receptor mechanism of action of sodium and calcium channel-blocking drugs. Annu Rev Pharmacol Toxicol **24:** 387–423

Janis RA, Sarmiento JG, Maurer SC, Bolger GT, Triggle DJ (1984) Characteristics of the binding of ^{3}H-nitrendipine to rabbit ventricular membranes: modification by other Ca^{2+} channel antagonists and by the Ca^{2+} channel agonist BAY K 8644. J Pharmacol Exp Ther **231:** 8–15

Jones LR, Cala S (1981) Biochemical evidence for functional heterogeneity of cardiac sarcoplasmic reticulum vesicles. J Biol Chem **256:** 11809–11818

Jones LR, Besch HR Jr, Fleming JW, McConnaughey MM, Watanabe AM (1979) Separation of vesicles of cardiac sarcolemma from vesicles of sarcoplasmic reticulum. J Biol Chem **254:** 530–539

Jorgensen AO, Kalnins V, MacLennan DH (1979) Localization of sarcoplasmic reticulum proteins in rat skeletal muscle by immunofluorescence. J Cell Biol **80:** 372–384

Jorgensen AO, McLeod AG, Campbell KP, Denney GH (1984) Evidence for the presence of calsequestrin in both peripheral and interior regions of sheep Purkinje fibers. Circ Res **55:** 267–270

Lee KS, Tsien RW (1983) Mechanism of calcium channel blockade by verapamil, D600, diltiazem, and nitrendipine in single dialyzed heart cells. Nature **302:** 790–794

Manalan AS, Besch HR Jr, Watanabe AM (1981) Characterization of [^{3}H] (±) carazolol binding to beta-adrenergic receptors: Application to study of beta-adrenergic receptor subtypes in canine ventricular myocardium and lung. Circ Res **49:** 326–336

Marsh JD, Loh E, Lachance D, Barry WH, Smith TW (1983) Relationship of binding in a calcium channel blocker to inhibition of contraction in intact cultured embryonic chick ventricular cells. Circ Res **53:** 539–543

Millard RW, Grupp G, Grupp IL, DiSalvo J, DePover A, Schwartz A (1983) Chronotropic, inotropic, and vasodilator actions of diltiazem, nifedipine, and verapamil: A comparative study of physiological responses and membrane receptor activity. Circ Res **52** (suppl I): 29–39

Morad M, Goldman YE, Trentham DR (1983) Rapid photochemical inactivation of Ca^{2+}-antagonists shows that Ca^{2+} entry directly activates contraction in frog heart. Nature **304:** 635–638

Murphy KM, Snyder SH (1982) Calcium antagonist receptor binding sites labelled with ^{3}H-nitrendipine. Eur J Pharmacol **77:** 201–202

Osterrieder W, Brum G, Hescheler J, Trautwein W, Flockerzi V, Hofmann F (1983) Injection of subunits of cyclic AMP-dependent protein kinase into cardiac myocytes modulates Ca^{2+} current. Nature **298:** 576–578

Peper, Trautwein W (1967) The effect of aconitine on the membrane current in cardiac muscle. Pflugers Arch **296:** 328–336

Reuter H (1983) Calcium channel modulation by neurotransmitters, enzymes, and drugs. Nature **301:** 569–574

Reuter H, Stevens CF, Tsien RW, Yellen G (1982) Properties of single calcium channels in cardiac cell culture. Nature **297:** 501–504

Sanguinetti MC, Kass RS (1984) Voltage-dependent block of calcium channel current in the calf cardiac Purkinje fiber by dihydropyridine calcium channel antagonists. Circ Res **55:** 336–348

Sarmiento JG, Jarvis RA, Colvin RA, Triggle DJ, Katz AM (1983) Binding of the calcium channel blocker nitrendipine to its receptor in purified sarcolemma from canine cardiac ventricle. J Mol Cell Cardiol **15:** 135–137

Scatchard G (1949) The attractions of proteins for small molecules and ions. Ann NY Acad Sci **51:** 660–672

Starmer CF, Grant AO, Strauss HC (1984) Mechanisms of use-dependent block of sodium channels in excitable membranes by local anesthetics. Biophys J **46:** 15–27

Tsien RW (1983) Calcium channels in excitable cell membranes. Annu Rev Physiol **45:** 341–358

Vaghy PL, Grupp IL, Grupp G, Williams JS, Balwierczak JL, Schwartz A (1984) Dihydropyridine binding to high and low affinity sites in canine cardiac sarcolemma correlates with positive and negative inotropic effects (abstr). Circulation **70** (suppl II): 70

Venter JC, Fraser CM, Schaber JS, Jung CY, Bolger G, Triggle DJ (1983) Molecular properties of the slow inward calcium channel: molecular weight determinations by radiation inactivation and covalent affinity labeling. J Biol Chem **258:** 9344–9348

Williams LT, Jones LR (1983) Specific binding of the calcium antagonist, ^{3}H-nitrendipine, to subcellular fractions isolated from canine myocardium: Evidence for high affinity binding to ryanodine-sensitive sarcoplasmic reticulum vesicles. J Biol Chem **258:** 5344–5347

Williams LT, Tremble P (1982) Binding of a calcium antagonist, ^{3}H-nitrendipine, to high affinity sites in bovine aortic smooth muscle and canine cardiac membranes. J Clin Invest **70:** 209–212

Yamamura HI, Schoemaker H, Boles RL, Roeske WR (1982) Diltiazem enhancement of ^{3}H-nitrendipine binding to calcium channel associated drug receptor sites in rat brain synaptosomes. Biochem Biophys Res Commun **108:** 640–646

INDEX TERMS: Calcium channel • Calcium antagonists • Cardiac myocytes

Optimal Arterial Resistance for the Maximal Stroke Work Studied in Isolated Canine Left Ventricle

Kenji Sunagawa, W. Lowell Maughan, and Kiichi Sagawa

From the Department of Biomedical Engineering, and Department of Medicine, The Johns Hopkins University, School of Medicine, Baltimore, Maryland

SUMMARY. In a previous analysis of ventricular arterial interaction (Sunagawa et al., 1983), we represented the left ventricle as an elastic chamber which periodically increases its volume elastance to a value equal to the slope of the linear end-systolic pressure-volume relationship. Similarly, the arterial load property was represented by an effective elastance which is the slope of the arterial end-systolic pressure-stroke volume relationship. Since the maximal transfer of potential energy from one elastic chamber to another occurs when they have equal elastance, we hypothesized that the left ventricle would do maximal external work if the ventricular elastance and the effective arterial elastance were equal. We tested this hypothesis in 10 isolated canine left ventricles, ejecting into a simulated arterial impedance, by extensively altering arterial resistance and finding the optimal resistance that maximized left ventricular stroke work under various combinations of end-diastolic volume, contractility, heart rate, and arterial compliance. Each of these parameters was set at one of three levels while others were at control. The optimal resistance varied only slightly with arterial compliance, whereas it varied widely with contractility and heart rate. We thus determined that the ratio of the optimal effective arterial elastance to the given ventricular elastance remained nearly unity. This result supports the hypothesis that the left ventricle does maximal external work to the arterial load when the ventricular and arterial elastances are equalized. **(*Circ Res 56: 586–595, 1985*)**

THE purpose of the cardiovascular system is to provide adequate blood flow to peripheral tissues and thus support the normal function of these tissues. Whereas adequate cardiac output for peripheral perfusion can be achieved by multiple combinations of ventricular contractility and loading conditions, it is likely that the cardiovascular control system uses a unique combination of ventricular contractility, heart rate, and arterial impedance characteristics which optimizes ventricular performance from an energetics point of view. This question of optimum coupling can be answered by studying the energy-related ventricular variables that generate adequate cardiac output, to determine whether some are maximized (or optimized in some other way) at a certain combination of arterial impedance and ventricular contraction characteristics. The list of energy-related ventricular variables includes stroke work, mean or peak stroke power, and the myocardial oxygen cost of these variables.

The mean stroke power output of the normal excised feline left or right ventricle was found to be maximum when the ventricle was loaded with normal arterial impedance (Elzinga et al., 1980). Also, in the cat right ventricle, pump efficiency (defined as the ratio of external stroke work to total theoretically usable energy) was found to be maximum at normal pulmonary arterial impedance (Piene and Sund, 1982). However, it is not known how multiple combinations of changes in end-diastolic volume, ventricular contractility, heart rate, and arterial resistance and compliance, which probably vary under physiological conditions, affect ventricular performance and energetic variables.

In a recent analysis (Sunagawa et al., 1983), we predicted that maximal stroke work results when the end-systolic elastances of the ventricle and arterial load are equal. The purpose of this study was to test this prediction. We decided that external stroke work was the coupling variable to be optimized, because perfusion of vital organs (such as brain, heart, and kidney) requires both adequate stroke volume and adequate arterial pressure, which can be integratively accounted for by the stroke work. In order to cover a wide range of physiological coupling conditions between the ventricle and the arterial system, we varied left ventricular end-diastolic volume, ventricular contractility, heart rate, or arterial compliance independently, at three levels, and combined each of these changes with changes in arterial resistance at multiple levels. By analyzing the stroke work data determined under these conditions, we did arrive, as predicted, at a simple unifying notion of the optimal ventriculoarterial coupling in terms of the relative magnitude of ventricular end-systolic elastance and arterial effective volume elastance.

Because the present analysis with an isolated heart preparation deals only with the fundamental mechanics of ventriculoarterial coupling, our criterion for design optimization may not necessarily be valid for a normally functioning animal which responds to various environmental stimuli. In such a circumstance, the criterion for optimizing circulatory system control probably is multi-factorial, and undoubtedly varies dynamically with the nature of given stimuli. The validity also may not hold for pathological circumstances, where physiological principles are likely to be compromised or distorted.

Methods

Preparation

The surgical preparation of an isolated canine ventricle has been described elsewhere (Suga and Sagawa, 1977; Sunagawa et al., 1982a). Briefly, in each experiment we used a pair of mongrel dogs (20–22 kg), anesthetized with sodium pentobarbital (30 mg/kg, iv). The chest of the heart donor was opened under artificial ventilation, and the subclavian artery and right atrium were cannulated and connected to the femoral arteries and veins, respectively, of a support dog. After ligation of the azygous vein, superior and inferior venae cavae, brachiocephalic artery, descending aorta, and pulmonary hili, the heart was removed from the chest. The pericardium was removed, the left and right ventricles were vented, and the chordae tendinae were cut. A thin balloon mounted on a plastic adaptor was placed in the left ventricle and the adaptor was sewn into the mitral valve annulus. The balloon adaptor then was connected to a ventricular volume control servo-pump system (Suga and Sagawa, 1977; Sunagawa et al., 1982b). A constant volume of tap water filled the pump and balloon. Therefore, absolute volume changes in the balloon were precisely controlled and measured by the volume servo-pump. A disc oxygenator (Pemco model 7109) was placed in parallel with the support dog so that oxygenated blood could be received either from the support dog or from the oxygenator, as desired. Coronary arterial pressure was measured by a catheter placed via the brachiocephalic trunk in the aortic root. A servo-controlled perfusion pump (Harvard Apparatus model 1215) maintained mean coronary arterial pressure at 100 mm Hg throughout the experiment. Coronary arterial blood temperature was maintained at approximately 37°C with a heat exchanger. The left ventricular pressure was measured in the balloon with a catheter tip micromanometer (Millar model PC-380). Ventricular pressure-volume loops were monitored on-line on an X-Y storage oscilloscope and photographed with a Polaroid camera.

Impedance-Loading System

We used a modified version of the impedance loading system for the isolated canine ventricle previously reported by Sunagawa et al. (1982c). Basic characteristics and performance are essentially the same as those of the previous one. Briefly, we simulated the arterial afterload system with a 3-element (Westerhof et al., 1971) Windkessel model, and the preload system with a simple dc pressure source coupled with a filling resistance in series (Fig. 1). In the original impedance-loading system, we programmed these simulation models on an analog computer and calculated the instantaneous flow out of or into the ventricle that should occur in response to the instantaneous ventricular pressure measured in the isolated heart. In the new impedance-loading system, we digitally calculated the instantaneous flow every 2 msec with a high-performance 16-bit microprocessor (Intel 8086/8087) by feeding digitized instantaneous ventricular pressure to pre- and afterloading system models. The calculated instantaneous flow as then numerically integrated with respect to time, and the integral was used as the command signal to the volume servo-pump through a 12-bit digital to analog converter. Compared with the analog computer-based system, arterial impedance generated by this system is much more precise and reliable. With the loading system, the ejection pattern and stroke volume of a given left ventricle depended on its interaction with the afterload system parameters (R_c, R, and C) set in the arterial model. To calculate external stroke work on-line digitally, ventricular pressure was integrated with respect to volume over each cardiac cycle and recorded on a chart recorder as an analog signal. Ventricular pressure and volume and aortic pressure of the isolated heart preparation were recorded simultaneously with arterial pressure of the support dog, on the same chart recorder.

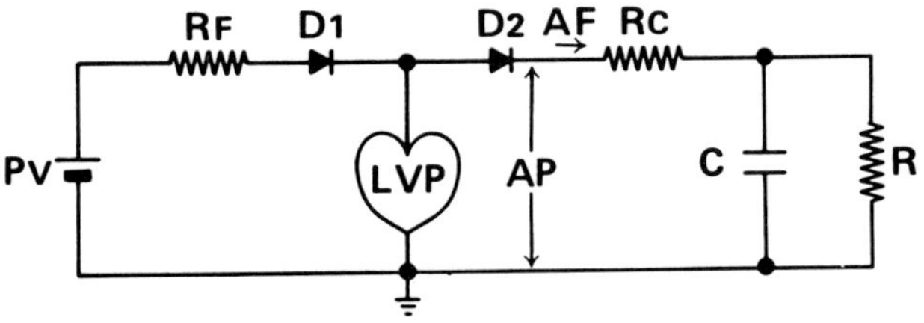

FIGURE 1. *An electrical analogue of the 3-element Windkessel arterial model (Westerhof et al., 1971). R_c = characteristic impedance; C = arterial compliance; R = arterial resistance.*

Protocols

Protocol 1: Effect of End-Diastolic Volume on Optimal Arterial Resistance

In eight ventricles, we changed end-diastolic volume at three different levels (i.e., 35, 30, and 25 ml) under a constant inotropic background. At each end-diastolic volume, we obtained multiple pressure-volume loops as shown in panel A of Figure 2 by successively decreasing arterial resistance (R in panel B of Fig. 1) to 79.4% of the preceding test R value. The initial R value was always set at 8.0 mm Hg/ml sec. Repeating the constant fractional reduction in arterial resistance 11 times yielded the smallest resistance of 0.8 mm Hg/sec ml, which is one-tenth of the starting value. With this 10-fold reduction in arterial resistance, the ventricle changed stroke volume over a wide range. At each resistance value, we waited for the ventricle to reach a steady state, and only the steady state during the subsequent 10 seconds was used for analysis. Panel B of Figure 2 shows a typical strip chart recording from one entire sequence. Heart rate was maintained at 120 beats/min by right atrial pacing. Arterial compliance and characteristic impedance were fixed at their control values, 0.4 ml/mm Hg and 0.2 mm Hg/ml sec, respectively (Sunagawa et al., 1982c).

Protocol 2: Effect of Changes in Contractility on the Optimal Arterial Resistance

We measured ventricular contractility from the slope (E_{es}) of the end-systolic pressure-volume relationship, which was determined by applying linear regression analysis on the left upper corners of the pressure-volume loops, as shown in Figure 2A. In seven ventricles, we changed contractility of the left ventricle at three levels by

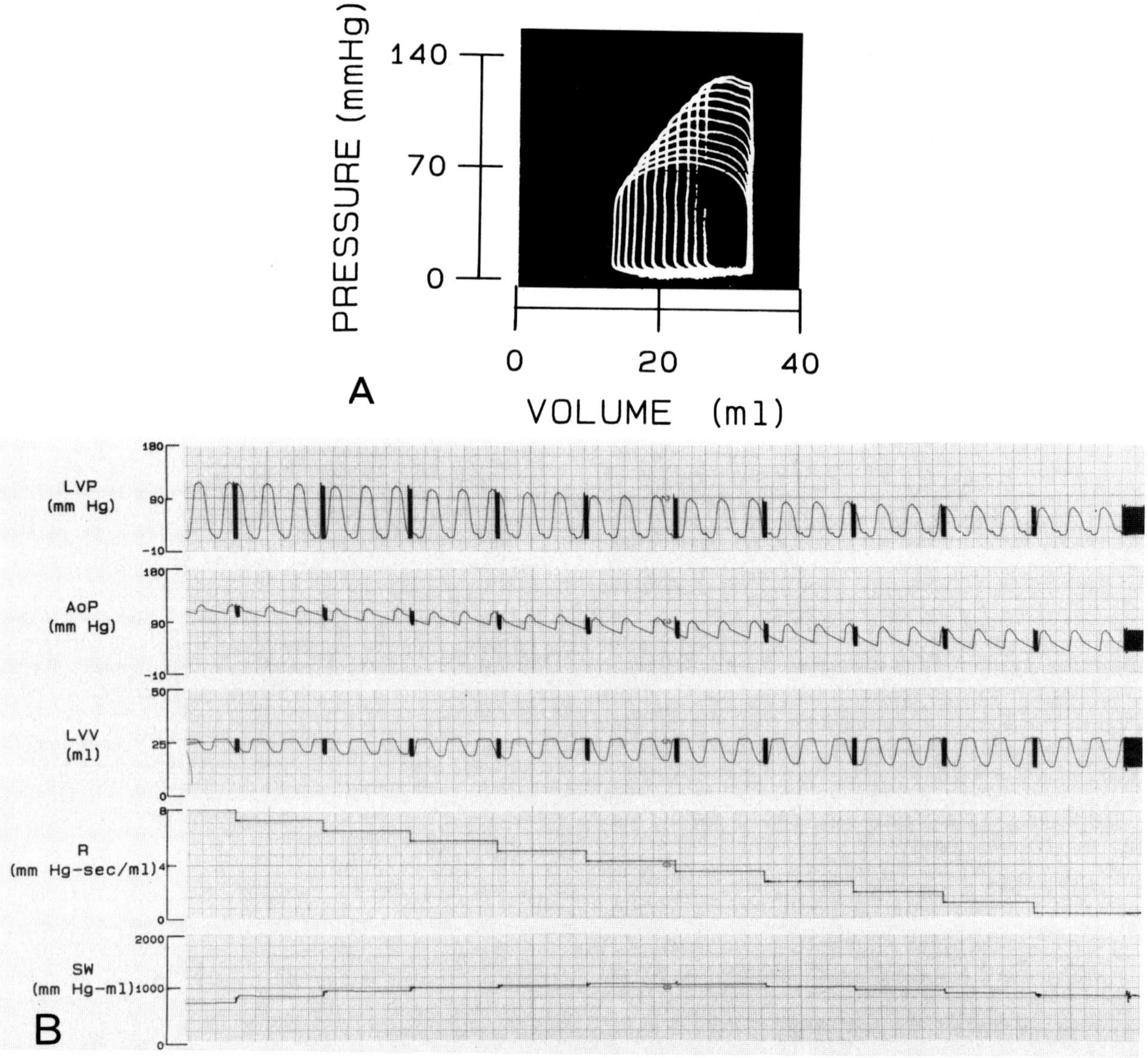

FIGURE 2. *Panel A: example of a typical left ventricular pressure-volume loop diagram. Under a constant end-diastolic volume, we obtained these multiple loops by varying arterial resistance stepwise from 8 to 0.8 mmHg/sec per ml while maintaining ventricular contractility, heart rate, and arterial properties (i.e., arterial compliance and characteristic impedance) constant. Panel B: chart recording of left ventricular pressure (LVP), aortic pressure (AoP), left ventricular volume (LVV), arterial resistance (R), and calculated external stroke work (SW).*

intracoronary infusion of dobutamine, starting at 10 μg/min and titrating to a 20% increase in E_{es}. At each level of contractility, we obtained multiple pressure-volume loops by reducing arterial resistance stepwise, as described in protocol 1, while maintaining end-diastolic volume constant at 35 ml. Heart rate, arterial compliance, and characteristic impedance were also fixed at their control values throughout this protocol. When dobutamine increased heart rate above the paced rate (120 beats/min), the pacing rate was increased so that the chronotropic intervention would not occur.

Protocol 3: Effect of Changes in Heart Rate on the Optimal Arterial Resistance

Seven ventricles were paced at three different heart rates: 120, 140, and 160 beats/min. At each heart rate, we obtained multiple pressure-volume loops by reducing arterial resistance stepwise, as described in protocol 1. End-diastolic volume was fixed at 35 ml. Arterial compliance and characteristic impedance were maintained constant at their control values throughout this protocol.

Protocol 4: Effect of Changes in Arterial Compliance on the Optimal Arterial Resistance

In seven ventricles, we set the arterial compliance to three different values, 0.2, 0.4, and 0.8 ml/mm Hg, under a constant inotropic background. At each compliance value, we obtained multiple pressure-volume loops by reducing arterial resistance stepwise, as described in protocol 1, while maintaining characteristic impedance and heart rate constant at their control values. End-diastolic volume was fixed at 35 ml.

Data Analysis

To test the significance of effects of changes in end-diastolic volume, contractility, heart rate, and arterial compliance on the magnitude of external stroke work and the optimal arterial resistance, we used repeated-measure

TABLE 1

Effects of End-Diastolic Volume, Contractility, Heart Rate, and Arterial Compliance on the Slope (E_{es}) and Volume Axis Intercept (V_0) of Ventricular End-Systolic Pressure-Volume Relationship

	End-diastolic volume (ml)			Contractility			Heart rate (beats/min)			Arterial compliance (ml/mm Hg)		
	25	30	35	Low	Med	High	120	140	160	0.2	0.4	0.8
E_{es} (mm Hg/ml)	5.6±1.3	5.4±1.2	5.2±0.7	4.1±1.1*	5.8±1.9*	7.5±2.3*	4.5±0.9	4.9±0.8	4.6±0.4	5.0±0.4	4.8±0.3	4.8±0.6
V_0 (ml)	7.3±2.3	7.0±2.2	6.2±2.8	5.4±3.5	4.3±2.6	3.2±2.9	5.4±2.7	4.9±2.5	5.4±3.5	5.4±3.7	4.7±3.7	4.4±3.3

Data are presented in mean ± SEM values.
* $P < 0.001$.

analysis of variance. Our criterion for statistical significance was a P value below 0.05.

Results

Table 1 summarizes the slope (E_{es}) and volume axis intercept (V_o) of the end-systolic pressure-volume relationship under these four protocols. E_{es} was altered only when contractility was changed. Figure 3 summarizes the effects of end-diastolic volume (panel A), contractility (panel B), heart rate (panel C), and arterial compliance (panel D) on the external stroke work vs. arterial resistance relationship. In all experimental conditions, the stroke work was 50–69% of the maximal value with the initial, largest arterial resistance of 8 mm Hg/sec per ml. The stroke work increased rapidly with the decrease in arterial resistance. There was always one optimal arterial resistance at which the stroke work peaked. When arterial resistance was further decreased toward 0.8

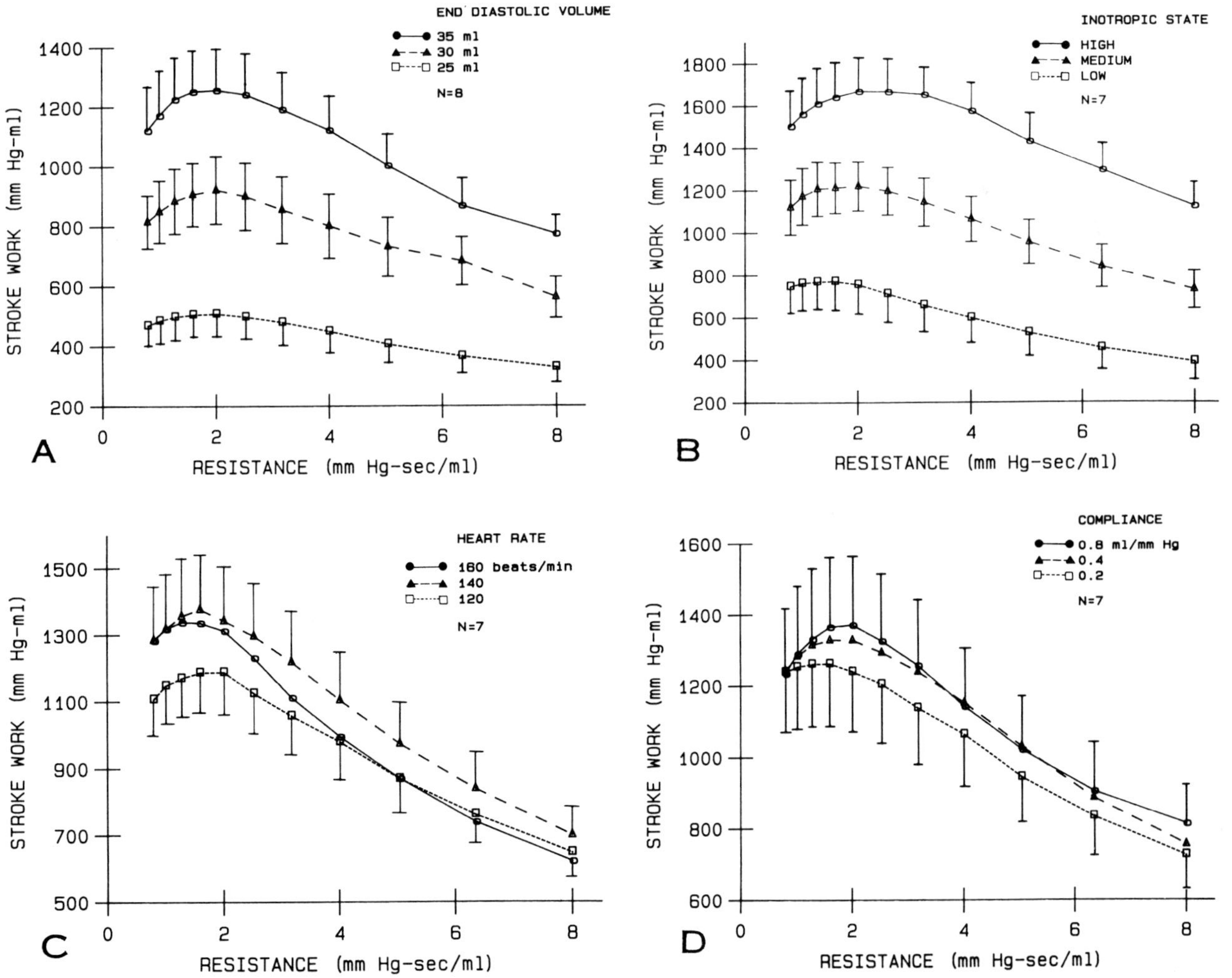

FIGURE 3. *Effects of changes in arterial resistance on the stroke work under various end-diastolic volumes (panel A), contractilities (panel B), heart rates (panel C), and compliances (panel D). Stroke work is calculated on-line as the developed pressure-volume area per cardiac cycle. Stroke work reached its peak value as the arterial resistance decreased from 8 to a certain value. Further reductions of arterial resistance decreased stroke work.*

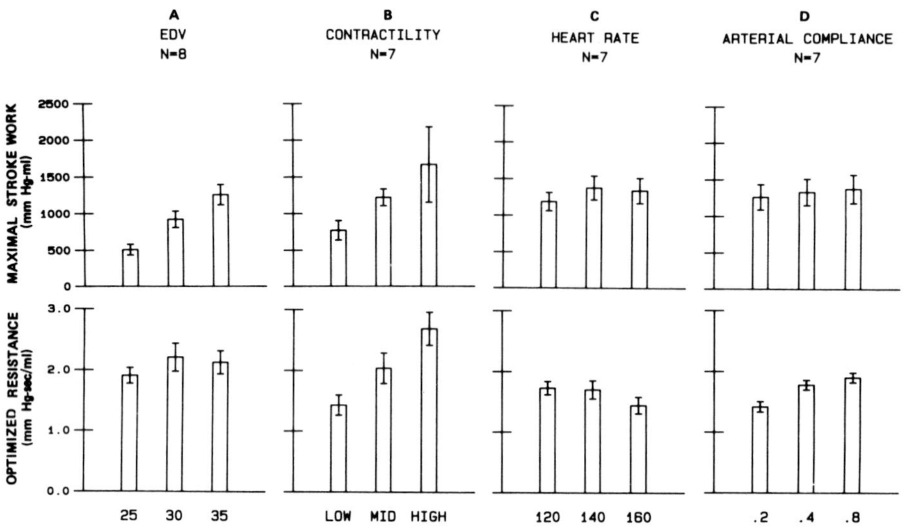

FIGURE 4. *Top panel: effects of changes in end-diastolic volume (panel A), contractility (panel B), heart rate (panel C), and compliance (panel D) on the maximal stroke work. Maximal stroke work was increased with increases in end-diastolic volume and contractility. Changes in heart rate or compliance did not alter the maximal stroke work. Bottom panel: effects of changes in end-diastolic volume (panel A), contractility (panel B), heart rate (panel C), and compliance (panel D) on the optimal arterial resistance. The optimal arterial resistance remained constant despite changes in end-diastolic volume, but was increased with increases in contractility. Increases in heart rate tended to decrease the optimal arterial resistance. A small increase in optimum resistance occurred with increased arterial compliance.*

mm Hg/sec per ml, the stroke work started decreasing again, although it did not decrease to the same level obtained with the largest resistance (panel B, Fig. 2). By increasing end-diastolic volume, the stroke work could be increased at any given arterial resistance (panel A, Fig. 3). Optimal resistance did not change significantly. Increases in contractility increased the stroke work by any given arterial resistance (panel B). Unlike the effect of changes in end-diastolic volume, however, the optimal arterial resistance became larger with increases in contractility (panel B). As shown in panels C and D of Figure 3, there was no consistent relationships between heart rate and the optimal arterial resistance or between arterial compliance and the optimal arterial resistance.

Influences of changes in end-diastolic volume, contractility, heart rate, and arterial compliance, specifically, on the maximal external stroke work and optimal arterial resistance are summarized in Figure 4. Maximal stroke work increased significantly ($P < 0.0001$) with increases in end-diastolic volume. However, optimal arterial resistance did not change significantly. Increases in contractility altered the maximal stroke work ($P < 0.0001$) with concomitant increases in the optimal arterial resistance ($P < 0.0001$). Alterations in heart rate did not change the maximal stroke work. The optimal arterial resistance tended to decrease with increases in heart rate, although this trend was not statistically significant (panel C). Increases in arterial compliance did slightly increase ($P < 0.01$) the maximal stroke work (panel D). Although quantitatively small, the optimal resistance significantly increased ($P < 0.01$) with increases in arterial compliance (panel D).

Discussion

We have shown that increases in end-diastolic volume increased the maximal stroke work without changing the optimal arterial resistance, whereas increases in contractility, which increased the maximal stroke work, did increase the optimal arterial resistance. The optimal arterial resistance tended to decrease with increases in heart rate, although it was statistically insignificant. In order to clarify the general rule that determines the optimal arterial resistance, we have used the framework of analysis that was previously proposed for prediction of stroke volume under variable ventriculoarterial coupling conditions (Sunagawa et al., 1983).

Analysis of Optimal Loading by a Framework of Ventriculoarterial Coupling

The end-systolic pressure-volume relationship is approximately linear over a physiological range, and is relatively insensitive to changes in loading conditions (Suga et al., 1973, 1979; Suga and Sagawa, 1974). This relationship is illustrated in the left panels of Figure 5. The mechanical characteristics of the arterial system can be represented by the relationship of arterial end-systolic pressure to stroke volume (P_{es}-SV relationship) as shown in the third right panel of Figure 5. The greater the stroke volume ejected into the arterial system, the greater the generated P_{es} will be. In the fourth, righthand panel of Figure 5, the volume axis is simply reversed, so that the stroke volume is plotted with zero reference to some specified end-diastolic volume for the left ventricle. The equilibrium SV when the ventricle is coupled with the arterial system can be obtained from the intersection between these two P_{es}-LVV relationship lines (bottom panel). Although this coupling framework is extremely simple, stroke volumes predicted by this method were indeed very close to experimentally determined stroke volumes (Sunagawa et al., 1983).

In this coupling framework, the arterial system was treated as if it were an elastic chamber with a

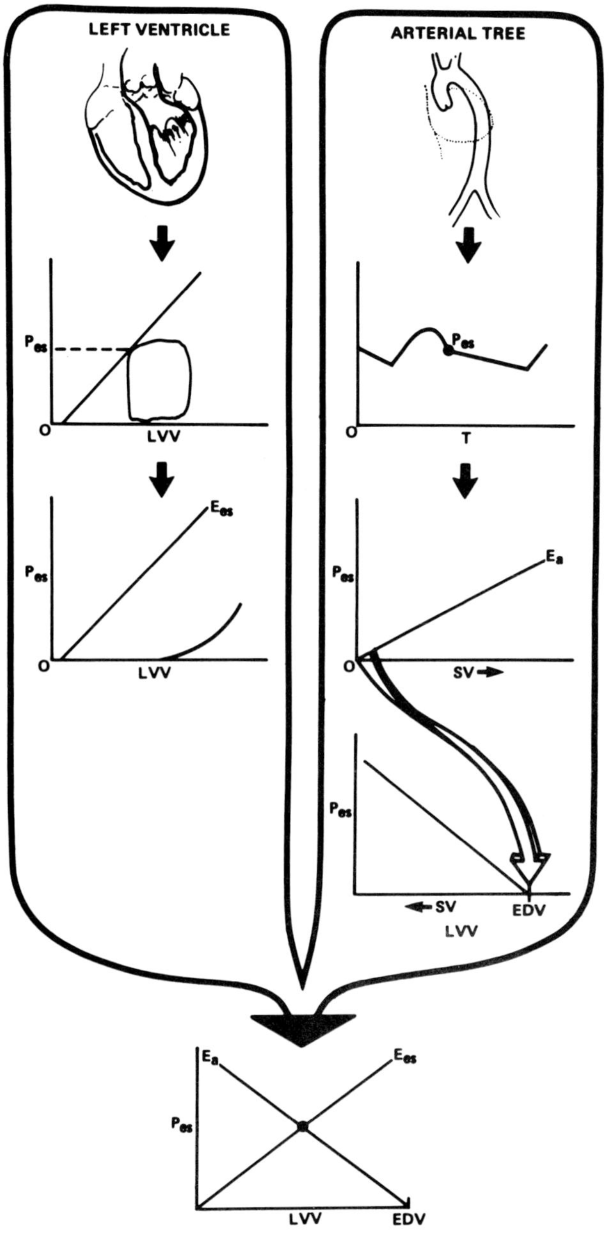

FIGURE 5. *A schematic illustration of the framework of analysis for coupling the ventricle with the arterial load. The mechanical characteristics of the left ventricle are expressed by the end-systolic pressure (P_{es}) vs. volume (LVV) relationship (left middle panel). The mechanical characteristics of the arterial system is expressed by the arterial end-systolic pressure (P_{es}) vs. stroke volume (SV) relationship (right middle panel) which can be transformed into the P_{es}-LVV relationship. The equilibrium end-systolic pressure and volume when the ventricle is coupled with the arterial system are obtained from the intersection between these two P_{es}-LVV relationship lines (bottom panel).*

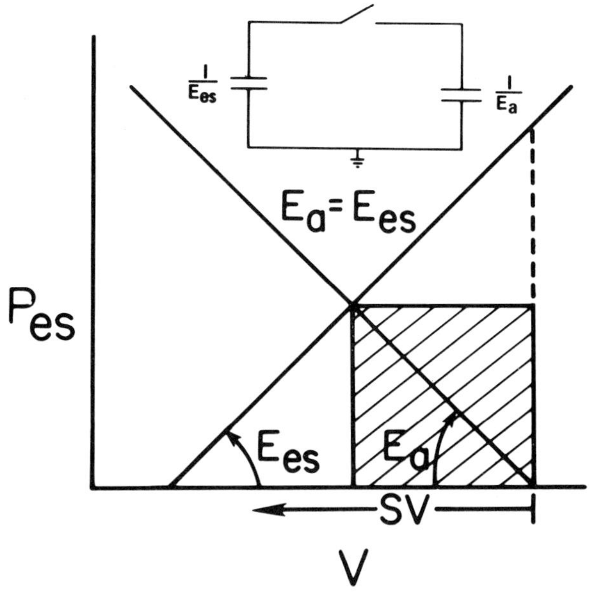

FIGURE 6. *Schematic representation of ventriculoarterial coupling on the pressure-volume plane. The shaded area represents the maximal stroke work under optimal coupling when the slopes of both ventricular and arterial P_{es}-SV relationships are the same. Under the optimal condition, the stroke volume is 50% of the effective preload (i.e., V_{ed}-V_o). The inset represents ventricular end-systolic elastance and effective arterial elastance by two electrical capacitors which are coupled by a switch at the moment of end systole. See text and Appendix 2 for further explanation.*

volume elastance E_a (Appendix 1), just as we treated the ventricle as an elastic chamber with an end-systolic volume elastance E_{es}. With such representations, one can predict analytically (see Appendix 2) or intuitively, from the diagram in Figure 6, that mechanical energy transferred from the ventricular elastance to the arterial elastance will become maximal when the slopes of the ventricular and arterial P_{es}-SV relationships, E_{es} and E_a, are equal to one another. Under this optimally loaded condition, an *effective* ejection fraction defined as the ratio of stroke volume to the *effective* end-diastolic volume would be 50%. To test these predictions, we directly determined the optimal slope E_a of the arterial P_{es}-SV relationship in each of four different protocols by calculating the ratio of the arterial end-systolic pressure to the stroke volume when the arterial resistance was optimal, The P_{es} was measured as the arterial pressure at the end of ejection. As shown in the bottom panel of Figure 7, the ratio of the optimal E_a thus calculated to the E_{es} of a given ventricle was quite close to unity, despite a wide variety of end-diastolic volumes, contractilities, heart rates, and arterial compliances. The effective ejection fraction in all the optimized conditions was also found to be nearly 50%, as shown in the top panel of Figure 7. Therefore, our hypothesis that the arterial elastance will be equal to ventricular elastance when the external stroke is maximal was shown to be valid.

Figure 8 further clarifies our points by plotting the experimentally determined average relationships between end-systolic pressure and stroke volume of both the ventricle and the arterial system in each protocol. Changes in end-diastolic volume did not change the ventricular end-systolic pressure-volume relationship (panel A). Therefore, there were no substantial differences in arterial elastance which

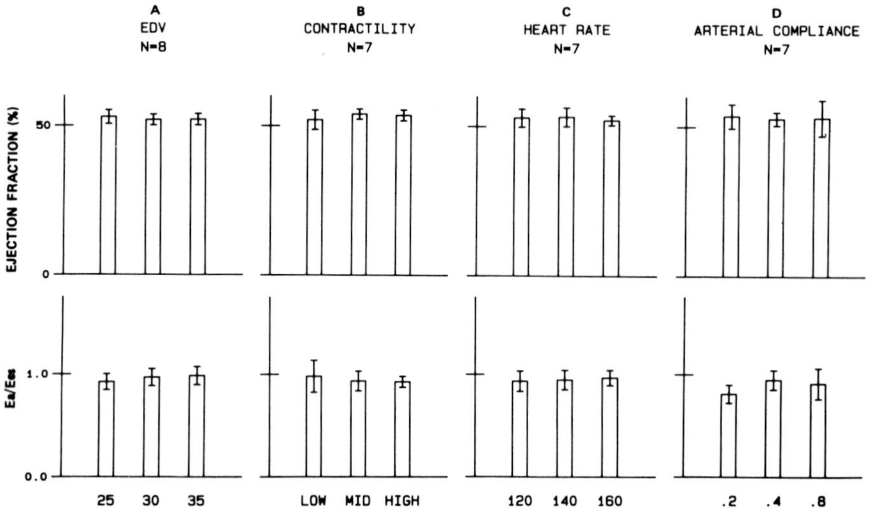

FIGURE 7. *Top panel: effects of changes in end-diastolic volume, contractility, heart rate, and arterial compliance on the effective ejection fraction at the optimal arterial resistance are shown in panels A, B, C, and D, respectively. The effective ejection fraction remains close to 50% irrespective of changes in loading conditions. Bottom panel: effects of changes in end-diastolic volume, contractility, heart rate, and arterial compliance on the ratio of E_a at the optimal arterial resistance to E_{es} are shown in panels A, B, C, and D, respectively. The E_a/E_{es} ratio remains close to unity, irrespective of these changes in loading conditions.*

maximized the stroke work. Changes in contractility changed the ventricular elastance. The maximal stroke work resulted when the arterial volume elastance was increased in parallel with the increases in ventricular volume elastance (panel B of Fig. 8). Changes in heart rate or compliance in the range presently studied did not significantly affect the ventricular end-systolic pressure-volume relationship. Therefore, the arterial elastance that maximized stroke work also remained unaltered (panels C and D of Fig. 8).

Influences of changes in preload, arterial compliance, contractility, and heart rate on the optimal arterial resistance, rather than elastance, can also be predicted quantitatively with this framework of analysis. If we approximate the end-systolic pressure by mean arterial pressure, the effective arterial elastance E_a can be approximated by the ratio of total resistance to cardiac cycle length (Appendix 1). With this approximation, the total resistance that maximizes stroke work is determined simply as the product of E_{es} and cardiac cycle length T (Eq. 9 in Appendix 3). Because this simplified formula ($R_{T,opt} = E_{es}$ T) for optimal resistance contains neither preload nor physical compliance of the arterial system, it suggests that changes in end-diastolic volume or arterial compliance would not affect the optimal resistance at all. If, on the other hand, the ventricular contractility increases, a larger arterial resistance is required for the optimal condition. All these predictions were found to be consistent with the experimental data. The optimal resistance formula also leads to a prediction that a mere increase in heart rate, which slightly shortens T without a change in E_{es}, would slightly decrease the optimal arterial resistance. This prediction was also substantiated, although the decrease in optimal resistance was not statistically significant. Had we extended the heart rate change to a much lower range, (e.g., between 120 and 60 beats/min), we might have seen significant changes in the optimal arterial resistance.

Only a few studies in the literature have addressed

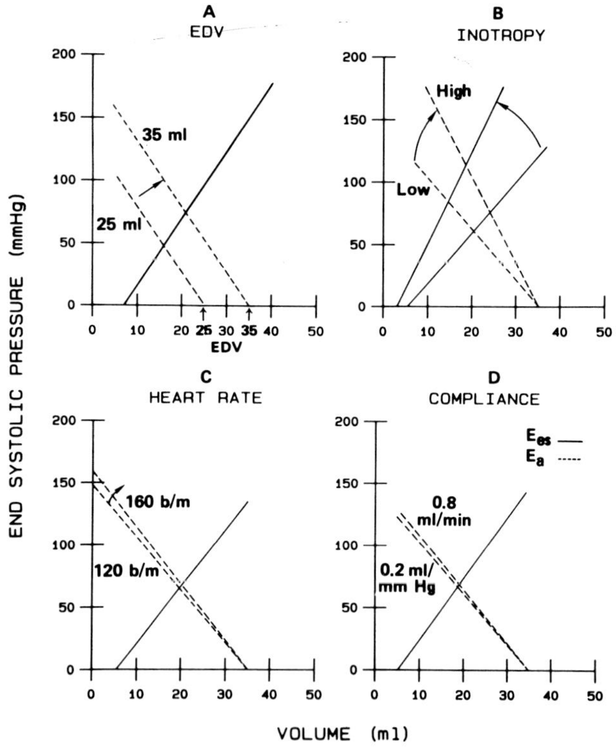

FIGURE 8. *Panel A: effects of changes in end-diastolic volume on the optimal ventricular loading. Changes in end-diastolic volume did not alter the ventricular end-systolic pressure-volume relationship. Therefore, the optimal loading was achieved with the same arterial elastance value. Panel B: effects of changes in contractility on the optimal ventricular loading. The slope of ventricular end-systolic pressure-volume relationship was increased with increases in contractility. The arterial elastance needed to be increased by increasing arterial resistance to similar extents, to obtain the optimal loading conditions. Panel C: the slope of the ventricular end-systolic pressure-volume relationship was not influenced significantly with changes in heart rate. The arterial elastance remained practically unaltered to obtain the optimal loading conditions. Panel D: the ventricular end-systolic pressure-volume relationship was not influenced by changes in arterial compliance. Therefore, the arterial elastance remained unaltered to obtain the optimal loading conditions.*

the effect of changing arterial compliance alone on stroke work output of the left ventricle. Elzinga and Westerhof (1973) coupled a hydraulic model of arterial impedance with isolated cat hearts and determined the effect of multiple combinations of arterial resistance and compliance on left ventricular pressure and outflow and aortic pressure. From these data, Noble (1979) calculated the relationship of mean power output (stroke work times heart rate per minute) to mean aortic pressure under two different arterial compliance values (Fig. 4.6 of the cited reference). When the compliance value was set at 8% of the normal, the maximum stroke work was reduced to less than one-half of control. This drastic effect of compliance may appear to be contradictory to the very small effect observed in our study. In fact, the seemingly large difference comes from the extremely large reduction of arterial compliance down to 8% of normal, used in Elzinga and Westerhof's experiment, as opposed to the more physiological magnitude of compliance changes (to 50% and 200% of normal) in the present experiment. The data from the same cat heart suggest (although we cannot be sure, because not enough information was provided) that when the compliance was decreased to 37% of control, the stroke work did not fall by more than 10%. Therefore, those authors demonstrated that a large reduction in arterial compliance *can* markedly reduce flow and work output from the left ventricle, whereas we showed that more physiological magnitudes of arterial compliance change do not cause such a drastic effect.

Nature's Design for Ventriculoarterial Matching

The analysis described in the previous section validated the prediction from our previous study that ventricular stroke work will be maximized when the ventricular and arterial elastances are matched in magnitude (Sunagawa et al., 1983). Whether the maximum external stroke work is really the crucial criterion that an organism uses for optimizing the operation of the cardiovascular system in physiological circumstances is an entirely different question, and one which remains to be answered.

It is well known that the physiological value of the ejection fraction in many animal species, including man, is approximately 50% or slightly larger. Considering the fact that V_o is negligibly small relative to the end-diastolic volume in vivo, the average ejection fraction of 47% observed in anesthetized dogs (Tsakiris et al., 1969) may be regarded as supportive evidence for the theory that maximal external work may be the optimization criterion in intact animals as well.

It is notable, however, that the decrease in the external work with mild deviations of arterial resistance from the optimum value is rather slight, as evidenced by the flatness of the work curves around the maximum region (Fig. 3). Over the same range of arterial resistance, the ventricular ejection fraction can change much more significantly. Therefore, the 50% ejection fraction observed under the optimal matching could occur for a totally different reason, and does not prove that the maximal external work is used as the optimization criterion.

Any hypothesis concerning physiological matching of cardiac performance with arterial load must eventually be tested and validated in an intact animal under various physiological conditions. Needless to say, our study with isolated hearts does not mimick the in vivo situation. Nevertheless, the information from the present study attests to the compatability of our hypothesis with the basic mechanical property of the ventricular pump. We believe that the hypothesis will be useful in interpreting other data from intact animals.

Limitations

In this investigation, we maintained coronary arterial pressure constant throughout the experiments, regardless of the ventricular loading conditions. In the real ventriculoarterial coupled system, coronary arterial pressure is determined as the result of hydraulic interactions of the ventricle with the arterial impedance. Because coronary arterial pressure can modulate the ESPVR if it falls below a critical level (Sunagawa et al., 1982a), the optimal matching will be determined in a somewhat more complex manner than analyzed here. Therefore, the proposed framework is valid only when the ventricle is operating, as it normally does, in a range of arterial pressures over which the ESPVR is insensitive to changes in coronary perfusion pressure.

In this analysis, we used the 3-element Windkessel model (Westerhof et al., 1971) to approximate arterial input impedance. Although this arterial model does not reproduce the fluctuations of impedance modulus over the high frequency range, due to wave reflections, the frequency spectrum of the impedance of the Windkessel model simulates the average characteristics of the impedance of the natural arterial tree reasonably well. Specifically, the similarity is better in the low-frequency range than in the high-frequency range. The fact that most of the oscillatory power of ventricular ejection resides in the first several harmonics suggests that the similarity of the impedance spectrum in the low-frequency range is more crucial than that in the high-frequency range. Therefore, we believe that the 3-element Windkessel model served the purpose of our analysis as a reasonable first approximation of the arterial input impedance. Influences of wave reflections in the natural arterial system on the optimal ventricular loading should be investigated in further studies.

Appendix 1

The slope (E_a) of the arterial end-systolic pressure vs. stroke volume relationship of the arterial system is determined by various factors. The following derivation of E_a, which is first a general form, and then

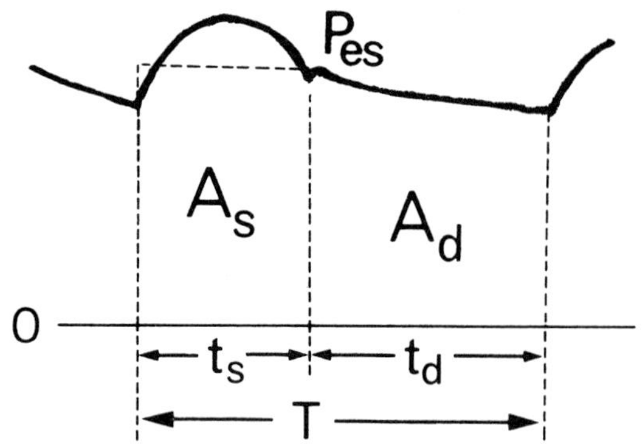

FIGURE 9. *A schematic diagram of aortic pressure curve. The total area A_T under the aortic pressure curve over one cardiac cycle T is divided into A_s, the area over the systolic duration t_s, and A_d, the area over the diastolic duration t_d.*

an approximation, will allow one to grasp the nature of E_a.

With reference to the afterload circuit of the model in Figure 1 and the schematic arterial pressure curve in Figure 9, mean arterial flow ($\overline{AF}$) averaged over the duration (T) of one cardiac cycle is obtained as

$$\overline{AF} = \frac{\overline{AP}}{R_c + R} \tag{1}$$

where $\overline{AF}$ and $\overline{AP}$ are aortic flow and arterial pressure averaged over one cardiac cycle. Since mean arterial flow equals SV/T, and mean arterial pressure equals the total area $A_T(= A_s + A_d)$ under the arterial pressure curve (Fig. 9) over one cardiac cycle divided by T, Equation 1 can be rewritten as

$$\frac{SV}{T} = \frac{A_T/T}{R_c + R}. \tag{2}$$

Therefore, stroke volume can be related to A_T and $R_c + R$ as

$$SV = A_T/(R_c + R). \tag{3}$$

The end-systolic pressure can be slightly different from the end-ejection pressure. However, if we disregard this small difference and denote both the end-ejection pressure and the end-systolic pressure by P_{es}, the diastolic pressure area A_d in Figure 9 can be approximated by

$$A_d{}^* = P_{es}\tau[1 - \exp(-t_d/\tau)] \tag{4}$$

where t_d is the duration of "arterial diastole" and is the time constant of the diastolic arterial pressure decay, which is equal to the product of the arterial resistance (R) and compliance (C). The asterisk indicates that Equation 4 is an approximation of the true A_d. Approximating the systolic pressure area (A_s) by the rectangle shown in Figure 9 yields an approximation of A_s as

$$A_s{}^* = P_{es}t_s \tag{5}$$

where t_s is the ejection time. Adding Equations 4 and 5 yields an approximation of $A_T(= A_s + A_d)$ as

$$A\,* = P\ \{t + \tau[1 - \exp(-\ t\ /\tau)]\}$$

The asterisk will be dropped hereafter. Substituting the approximate A_T described by Equation 6 into the true A_T in Equation 3 yields an approximated P_{es} – SV relationship of the arterial system

$$P_{es} = \frac{R_c + R}{t_s + \tau[1 - \exp(-\ t_d/\tau)]} SV \tag{7}$$

and

$$E_a = \frac{R_c + R}{t_s + \tau[1 - \exp(-\ t_d/\tau)]} \tag{8}$$

If we further approximate the end-systolic pressure by mean arterial pressure, P_{es} can be described as:

$$P_{es} \simeq \overline{AP} = \frac{SV}{T} R_T \tag{9}$$

where $R_T = R_c + R$. The effective arterial elastance E_a defined as the slope of the P_{es} vs. SV relationship can then be first approximated by

$$E_a \simeq P_{es}/SV = R_T/T. \tag{10}$$

This approximation indicates that the effective arterial volume elastance can be increased either by increasing the total arterial resistance or by decreasing the cardiac cycle length, whereas compliance has little effect unless it is changed excessively.

Appendix 2

The two capacitances in the inset of Figure 6 represent the reciprocal of ventricular end-systolic volume elastance E_{es} and the reciprocal of *effective* arterial elastance E_a. Suppose that just before end systole, the right side capacitance is momentarily shunted to the ground, and at end-systole the switch momentarily closes to couple the two capacitances. Part of the energy stored in the ventricular capacitance will be transferred to the arterial capacitance, bringing the pressures in the two capacitances to an equilibrium. The energy received (W_A) by the effective arterial elastance at end systole is:

$$W_A = E_a SV^2/2. \tag{11}$$

The amount of volume shift from the left ventricle to the arterial system (i.e., SV) is simply determined by the ratio of E_{es} to the sum of E_{es} and E_a as,

$$SV = \frac{E_{es}}{E_{es} + E_a}(V_{ed} - V_o) \tag{12}$$

where V_{ed} and V_o are the end-diastolic volume and the volume axis intercept of the ventricular end-systolic pressure-volume relationship, respectively. Substituting SV in Equation 12 into Equation 11 yields,

$$W_A = \frac{E_a E_{es}^2 (V_{ed} - V_o)^2}{2(E_{es} + E_a)^2}. \tag{13}$$

By differentiating Equation 13 with respect to E_a, one can show that W_A becomes maximal when E_{es}

equals E_a. Figure 6 illustrates this condition and the resultant maximal external stroke work of the left ventricle by the shaded area.

When $E_a = E_{es}$, Equation 12 simplifies to describe the optimized stroke volume as

$$SV_{opt} = (V_{ed} - V_o)/2, \quad (14)$$

namely, SV is 50% of effective preload (i.e., $V_{ed} - V_o$) in the optimally loaded condition.

Appendix 3

Substituting $E_a = E_{es}$ of Equation 10 and rearranging it yields

$$R_{T,opt} = E_{es}T, \quad (15)$$

which states that the optimal arterial resistance $R_{T,opt}$ is proportional to E_{es} and cardiac cycle length T.

We gratefully acknowledge the excellent technical assistance of Kenneth Rent.

This study was supported in part by research grants from the National Institutes of Health, HL-14903 and Ischemic Heart Disease SCOR HL-17655.

Kenji Sunagawa's current address is Research Institute of Angiocardiology and Cardiovascular Clinic, Kyushu University Medical School, Fukuoka, Japan.

Address for reprints: Kiichi Sagawa, M.D., Department of Biomedical Engineering, The Johns Hopkins University, School of Medicine, 720 Rutland Avenue, Baltimore, Maryland 21205.

Received July 30, 1984; accepted for publication January 16, 1985.

References

Elzinga G, Westerhof N (1973) Pressure and flow generated by the left ventricle against different impedances. Circ Res **32:** 178–186

Elzinga G, Piene H, Jong JP (1980) Left and right ventricular pump function and consequences of having two pumps in one heart. A study on the isolated cat heart. Circ Res **46:** 564–574

Noble MI (1979) The Cardiac Cycle. Oxford, Blackwell Scientific Publications, p 100

Piene H, Sund T (1982) Does normal pulmonary impedance constitute the optimum load for the right ventricle? Am J Physiol **242:** H154–H160

Suga H, Sagawa K (1974) Instantaneous pressure-volume relationships and their ratio in the excised, supported canine left ventricle. Circ Res **35:** 117–125

Suga H, Sagawa K (1977) End-diastolic and end-systolic ventricular volume clamper for isolated canine heart. Am J Physiol **233:** H267–H275

Suga H, Sagawa K, Shoukas AA (1973) Load independence of the instantaneous pressure volume ratio of the canine left ventricle and effects of epinephrine and heart rate on the ratio. Circ Res **32:** 314–332

Suga H, Kitabatake A, Sagawa K (1979) End-systolic pressure determines stroke volume from fixed end-diastolic volume in the isolated canine left ventricle under a constant contractile state. Circ Res **44:** 238–249

Sunagawa K, Maughan WL, Freisinger G, Guzman PA, Chang M, Sagawa K (1982a) Effect of coronary arterial pressure on left ventricular end-systolic pressure-volume relationship. Circ Res **50:** 727–734

Sunagawa K, Lim K, Burkhoff D, Sagawa K (1982b) Microprocessor control of a ventricular pump. Ann Biomed Eng **10:** 145–159

Sunagawa K, Burkhoff D, Lim K, Sagawa K (1982c) Impedance loading servo pump system for excised canine ventricle. Am J Physiol **243:** H346–H350

Sunagawa K, Maughan WL, Burkhoff D, Sagawa K (1983) Left ventricular interaction with arterial load studied in isolated canine ventricle. Am J Physiol **245:** H773–H780

Tsakiris AG, Donald OE, Sturm RE, Wood EH (1969) Volume, ejection fraction, and internal dimensions of left ventricle determined by biplane videometry. Fed Proc **28:** 1358–1368

Westerhof N, Elzinga G, Sipkema P (1971) An artificial arterial system for pumping hearts. J Appl Physiol **31:** 776–781

INDEX TERMS: Ventriculoarterial coupling • Impedance matching • Maximal external work • Optimal effective arterial elastance • Optimized ejection fraction

Transient Analysis of the Canine Cerebrovascular Response to Carbon Dioxide

David A. Wilson, Richard J. Traystman, and Carlos E. Rapela

From the Department of Physiology and Pharmacology, Bowman Gray School of Medicine, Wake Forest University, Winston-Salem, North Carolina, and Department of Anesthesiology and Critical Care Medicine, The Johns Hopkins University, School of Medicine, Baltimore, Maryland

SUMMARY. Cerebral venous outflow and carbon dioxide transients were studied during five different transitional states: (1) on and off 10% carbon dioxide breathing, (2) on and off hyperventilation, (3) on 7% carbon dioxide breathing, (4) on 10% carbon dioxide breathing initiated from 7% carbon dioxide breathing, and (5) on 10% carbon dioxide breathing initiated during intracarotid papaverine infusion, in pentobarbital anesthetized, paralyzed, mechanically ventilated dogs. Plots of the temporal relationships between these variables indicated that cerebral blood flow is closely related with cerebral venous carbon dioxide tension but not arterial carbon dioxide tension. The rate at which flow changed upon transition from one steady state to another was phase dependent, in that longer times were required to establish stable conditions in the on phase than in the off phase. The magnitude of the maximum rates of change in cerebral blood flow achieved during transition was influenced both by the size of the forcing function and the level of flow present at the time the response was initiated. Directional changes had no effect upon the maximum rate of the flow change as long as equivalent-sized forcing functions were employed and the initial blood flow levels were similar between responses. However, faster flow transients could be produced by increasing either of the latter two factors. These findings are consistent with the hypothesis that it is either tissue carbon dioxide tension or cerebral venous carbon dioxide tension that is the important variable regulated by cerebral blood flow. The rate-limiting factor in the response appears to be carbon dioxide delivery rate and not the rate of carbon dioxide diffusion. **(*Circ Res 56: 596–605, 1985*)**

CARBON DIOXIDE (CO_2) is intimately involved in the regulation of cerebral blood flow (CBF). Steady state studies have shown that the cerebrovascular effects of CO_2 are mediated locally (Kontos et al., 1977), as opposed to mediation via brain stem centers (Shalit et al., 1967). However, there are relatively few studies of the time-dependent factors which ultimately must be considered in any hypothesis regarding the local regulatory mechanism. Such factors include smooth muscle response time, and transport-dependent and diffusion-related phenomenon, as well as the time-dependent influences of the physical and metabolic buffer mechanisms. A traditional method of investigating control mechanisms is to use the so-called "black box" approach, i.e., a known input variable is driven to change in either a step or sinusoidal manner and the mechanisms output response is evaluated (Cunningham et al., 1965; Lambertsen et al., 1965; Gelfand and Lambertsen, 1973; and Tuteur et al., 1976). With this method of analysis, the effects of initial load level and forcing function amplitude are varied and used to derive information about the mechanisms' control characteristics. In part, the absence of this information is due to a lack of suitable methods for measuring CBF in the non-steady state. Of those studies that have been attempted, the results are contradictory. One group (Shapiro et al., 1966) reported that CBF becomes dissociated from arterial carbon dioxide tension (Pa_{CO_2}) when driven by a step increase in inspired CO_2. In their studies, CBF was found to correlate more closely with cerebral venous carbon dioxide tension (Pv_{CO_2}) than with Pa_{CO_2}. However, another group (Severinghaus and Lassen, 1967) measured CBF during step hypocapnia and observed that CBF and Pa_{CO_2} were closely allied, whereas CBF and Pv_{CO_2} were dissociated. The findings of the former group were taken to suggest that tissue carbon dioxide tension (Pt_{CO_2}) is the predominant variable regulating cerebral vessel tone, whereas the findings of the latter group suggest that cerebral vessels are insensitive to CO_2 within the tissue and are more strongly influenced by intravascular CO_2. Although the discrepancies between these two studies have not been fully resolved, other data (Nilsson et al., 1975; Tuteur et al., 1976) seem to support the latter interpretation.

We have observed that CBF increases relatively more slowly than does end-tidal CO_2 (Pe_{CO_2}) during the onset phase of hypercapnia and parallels Pe_{CO_2} during the offset phase of hypercapnia. Flow transients produced in this manner are asymetrical and phase dependent, requiring a longer time to achieve steady state conditions in the onset than offset phases. Since P_{ECO_2} reflects Pa_{CO_2}, our initial observations appeared to be inconsistent with the concept that cerebral vessels sense intravascular CO_2 predominantly.

The purpose of this study was to evaluate the temporal relationships between Pa_{CO_2}, Pv_{CO_2}, and CBF more closely. These relationships were studied under conditions in which the effects of initial load level (initial CBF), forcing function amplitude (differing degrees of hypercapnia), and direction of change, could be analyzed.

Methods

General

Mongrel dogs of both sexes, (17–22 kg) were anesthetized with sodium pentobarbital (Nembutal, 35 mg/kg, iv). A surgical level of anesthesia was maintained throughout the experiments by giving supplemental doses of anesthesia (30–60 mg). Flaxidil (1 mg/kg, iv) was used as the paralytic agent. Rectal temperature was monitored by a Tele-thermometer (Yellow Springs Instrument Co.) and maintained around 38°C with a heating pad. Temperature measurements were recorded for later determination of blood gas correction factors. End-tidal percent CO_2 was monitored continuously (Beckman Instruments Co.).

Surgical Preparation

Arterial blood pressure was measured from a cannula placed in an omocervical artery. The femoral veins were cannulated bilaterally to return the cerebral venous effluent and to administer anesthetic and paralytic agents. All animals were tracheotomized and mechanically ventilated. In a number of experiments, blood volume was deliberately altered to maintain the mean arterial blood pressure rigorously at a constant value throughout the altered CO_2 state. In these experiments, the femoral arteries were cannulated bilaterally with large bore polyvinyl tubes and attached to a feedback actuated Harvard infusion-withdrawal pump.

Cerebral Blood Flow Measurement

The technique used to measure cerebral venous outflow has been described previously (Rapela and Green, 1964). The confluence of the cerebral sinuses was cannulated and the lateral sinuses and occipital emissary veins were occluded with bone wax to prevent communication between intracranial and extracranial venous circulations. From the confluence of the sinuses, blood then passed through a calibrated electromagnetic flow probe before being returned to the dog via the femoral vein. With this technique, approximately 50–70% of the mass of the brain is drained at the confluence of the sagittal and straight sinuses. All pressures were referred to a common zero-reference plane set at the level of the right atrium. Cerebral venous outflow pressure was measured upstream from the flow probe. Brain perfusion pressure was estimated as systemic arterial pressure minus cerebral venous outflow pressure. Intracranial vascular resistance was calculated by dividing brain perfusion pressure by cerebral venous outflow.

The verification procedures for measuring CBF utilizing this venous outflow technique have been described in detail elsewhere (Traystman and Rapela, 1975). In addition, the viability and responsivity of the cerebral vasculature to hypercapnia (Traystman and Rapela, 1975), hypoxia (Traystman et al., 1978), and the ability to autoregulate (Rapela and Green, 1964) using this technique have been previously demonstrated.

To assess the transient response of the flow measuring system, the response time of the flowmeter (Carolina Medical Electronics, model 332R) and Grass polygraph recorder was determined for a step input voltage representing an 80 ml/min full scale deflection from zero flow conditions. The 90% response time was 730 msec when the Grass driver amplifier was set to give a 0.5 output-to-input signal ratio at 15 Hz.

Blood Gas Analysis

Arterial and cerebral venous blood samples (1 ml) were drawn 60 seconds before changing inspired CO_2, and at predetermined intervals throughout the procedure. Arterial blood samples were collected from an omocervical artery catheter, whereas cerebral venous blood samples were drawn directly from the cerebral venous outflow line. Blood gases (P_{CO_2} and P_{O_2}) and pH measurements were made with a model PHM73 pH/blood gas meter and combined BMS 3MK2 blood gas microsystem (Radiometer). The microsystem was calibrated with standard phosphate buffers (6.841 and 7.383 pH units), humidified 5%, and 10% CO_2-containing gas mixtures, and 0% and 12% O_2-containing gas mixtures. All measurements were body temperature corrected.

Protocols

During surgical preparation, all animals were mechanically ventilated from one side of a Harvard apparatus dual cylinder ventilator (Harvard model 618). Normocapnic blood gas levels were maintained by adjusting tidal volume with the respiratory rate held constant at about 15 breaths per minute. Before generating any transients, the tidal volume of both ventilator cylinders was tripled. Normocapnic blood gases were maintained in this hyperventilated state by adding a blended mixture of CO_2 and room air to the inlet port of the cylinder used for ventilation. In all instances, the second cylinder was preequilibrated with the gas mixture used for generating the transient. Step changes in Pa_{CO_2} were produced by rapidly switching the animal's source of inspired air to the equilibrated cylinder. This technique of normocapnic-hyperventilation was found to produce significantly faster P_{CO_2} transients than by administering CO_2 gas mixtures to normally ventilated animals.

Step Hypercapnia

In 12 animals, step hypercapnia was produced by switching the animal from a normocapnic gas mixture to a gas mixture containing 10% CO_2, 21% O_2, and 69% N_2. CBF was recorded continuously. Paired arterial and cerebral venous blood samples were drawn at predetermined times before and after the fractional concentration of CO_2 in the inspired air ($F_{I_{CO_2}}$) was changed. Hypercapnia was maintained for 10 minutes, at which time the animal was switched back to the normocapnic gas mixture. Blood gas samples were again collected periodically for 10 minutes while CBF was measured continuously.

Step Hypocapnia—Step Hypercapnia

In seven animals, arterial P_{CO_2} was decreased stepwise by hyperventilation with room air. Eight minutes were allowed for the CBF and P_{CO_2} transients to stabilize before returning FI_{CO_2} to the normocapnic level. The CBF transient was characterized during the return to normocapnia in four of the seven animals. In five of the seven animals, step hypercapnia was produced after the animals became normocapnic. The step hypercapnia was produced by ventilating with a 7–8% CO_2 gas mixture. This fractional CO_2 mixture was predicted to cause an equal, but directionally opposite, change in $Paco_2$ against which the transient generated during step hypocapnia could be compared.

Step Increases in $Paco_2$ after Raising CBF with a Previous Episode of Hypercapnia

In 15 animals, two step increments in $Paco_2$ were produced by administering two different CO_2 gas mixtures sequentially. The goal of these experiments was to generate two equal magnitude increases in CBF from differing baseline values. It was assumed that the relationship between $Paco_2$ and CBF was linear within the 30–80 mm Hg $Paco_2$ range (Reivich, 1964), and therefore anticipated that two equal magnitude increases in $Paco_2$ would elicit two CBF transients with equal magnitude CBF changes. However, in the course of the series, it was determined that two equal magnitude changes in $Paco_2$ do not produce equal magnitude changes in CBF because the CO_2-CBF relationship is not linear. Thus the CO_2 concentration of the initial gas mixture was reduced from 8 to 7% CO_2. A challenge with 10.2% CO_2 in 21% oxygen and 68.8% nitrogen was always used to obtain the second CBF transient.

Step Increases in $Paco_2$ after Raising Initial CBF by Intra-arterial Papaverine Infusion

A solution containing 5 mg papaverine (6,7-dimethoxy-1-veratryl quinoline hydrochloride; Sigma Chemical Co.) per milliliter saline was infused bilaterally into the common carotid arteries at rates sufficient to elevate CBF above baseline levels. The dose-rate of infusion ranged from 38 mg/kg·min to 330 mg/kg·min. Adequate time was allowed for CBF to stabilize at the elevated rate before increasing FI_{CO_2}. A step hypercapnia, induced by 10.2% CO_2, was then superimposed upon the papaverine infusion. An 8- to 10-minute stabilization period was used, throughout which arterial and cerebral venous blood gases and CBF were measured. The CBF and CO_2 transients collected in these studies were compared to those obtained in animals administered 10% CO_2 without previous vasodilation to determine the effect of initial blood flow rate on CBF transient response time.

Characterization and Analysis of the CO_2 and Cerebral Blood Flow Transients

The CO_2 transients were sampled intermittently. To obtain a continuous transient, the measured Pco_2 was plotted as a function of time and a smooth curve drawn through the points. CO_2 response half-time measurements were taken from the smoothed transient. The CBF response half-time value was taken from a smoothed tracing of the original record. This procedure minimized the fluctuations in CBF due to cerebral venous blood sampling, and facilitated calculation of the instantaneous rate of change in CBF ($d\dot{Q}/dt$) over small time intervals. Four characteristics of the CBF transient were measured: (1) the time required to induce 5% of the total change in CBF ($t_{0.05}$), (2) the time required to induce 50% of the total change in CBF ($t_{0.50}$), (3) the time required to induce 90% of the total change in CBF ($t_{0.90}$), (4) maximum instantaneous rate of change in CBF ($d\dot{Q}/dt_{max}$). $t_{0.05}$ was taken as the estimate of the time delay between the onset of CO_2 breathing and the first change in blood flow. $t_{0.50}$ was used as a common point for comparing CBF and the CO_2 rates of change. Stability time was estimated from $t_{0.90}$. $d\dot{Q}/dt$ was estimated from the first derivative of the CBF transient using a three-point numerical averaging technique. $d\dot{Q}/dt_{max}$ was considered to be the best indicator of cerebral vessel responsivity to tissue CO_2.

Correlational Analysis

Dispersion Analysis

As a first approximation, the degree of dispersion, that is the difference between the half-times of the CO_2 and CBF transients, was evaluated to establish cause and effect relationships. This analysis procedure assumes a proportional stimulus-response relationship. Thus, assuming there are no time-dependent processes acting upon the relationship, the rate of change in CBF would be expected to resemble that of the effective stimulus and to exhibit a similar half-time.

Momentary Correlation Analysis

Deductions based solely upon dispersion analysis techniques are limited by the assumption of a proportional stimulus-response relationship. However, this limitation can be overcome by comparing transients generated in both the onset and offset phases of a pulse, against one another. If it can be assumed that the stimulus-response relationship is not altered between the onset and offset phases, then the correlation of the CBF transient on the CO_2 transient responsible for initiating the effect should give identical relationships in both phases of the pulse.

To evaluate moment-to-moment relationships between CBF and $Paco_2$ and between CBF and $Pvco_2$, the Pco_2 at each sample time was plotted against the CBF present at the time of sampling. A smooth line was then drawn through the points of each relationship. Hysteresis-like phenomena were taken to suggest "loose," or distant coupling between the two variables, whereas the absence of hysteresis-like phenomenon was taken to indicate "tight," or close coupling between the two variables.

Statistical Analysis

A major portion of the experiments performed in this study were performed to investigate the origin of the dispersion between the various CO_2 and CBF transients following a step change in inspired CO_2 concentration. Significant differences between dispersion times of transients of differing types were determined using a paired *t*-test to test for a difference in $t_{0.50}$ characteristics. In comparing transients of the same type, either a paired *t*-test or Student's *t*-test was used to analyze the differences in $t_{0.50}$, depending upon whether or not the control transient was generated within the same preparation.

Multivariate statistical procedures (Draper and Smith, 1966; Snedecor and Cochran, 1967) were applied in some protocols to aid in interpreting the data after it was realized that other factors affecting the test characteristic could not be adequately controlled. In these experiments, the multivariate analysis aided in assessing the contribution of the uncontrolled variable to the outcome of the results.

Results

Transients Produced by Means of a Step Increase in Pa_{CO_2}

Figure 1 shows the dynamic relationship between CBF and CO_2 transients during the onset of hypercapnia. In 12 transients, generated in 10 animals, there was a short lag period (0.23 ± 0.01 min) that preceded the initial CBF change. During this time, Pa_{CO_2} was increasing, but CBF was not. CBF became stable at 5.06 ± 1.23 minutes with $t_{0.50}$ occurring 2.03 ± 0.12 minutes after the onset of CO_2 breathing. The $t_{0.50}$ values for the Pa_{CO_2} and Pv_{CO_2} transients were 0.39 ± 0.05 and 1.36 ± 0.11 minutes, respectively. The Pv_{CO_2} and CBF half-times were significantly different, as were the Pa_{CO_2} and CBF half-times.

$d\dot{Q}/dt_{max}$ occurred 0.98 ± 0.42 minute after CO_2 exposure. The peak was closely related to the minimum venous-arterial P_{CO_2} difference that occurred 0.5 minute after the inspired CO_2 was increased. In most experiments, the CBF transient displayed a second period of acceleration 2 minutes after the onset of hypercapnia. This second peak was always of lesser magnitude than the first, and for the remainder of the CO_2 breathing period, the CBF transient decelerated until steady state conditions were established. Arterial blood pressure was held constant at a mean value of 109 ± 3 mm Hg.

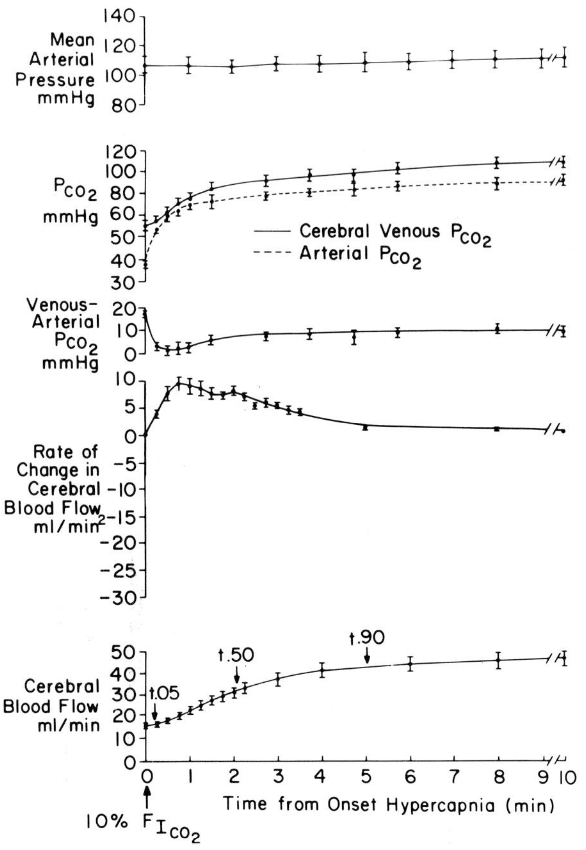

FIGURE 1. *The temporal relationships between arterial P_{CO_2}, cerebral venous P_{CO_2}, and cerebral blood flow during the onset phase of 10% $F_{I_{CO_2}}$ breathing. Mean ± SE; n = 12.*

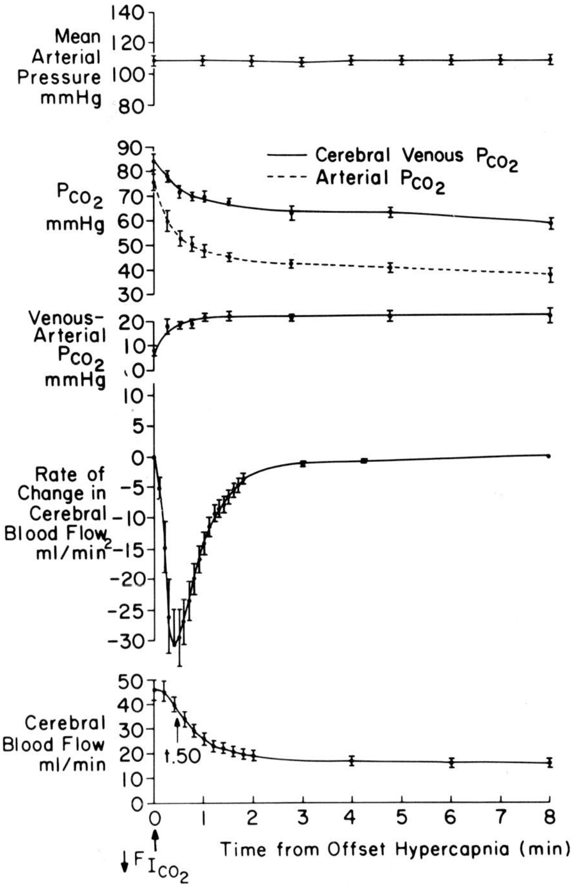

FIGURE 2. *The temporal relationships between arterial P_{CO_2}, cerebral venous P_{CO_2}, and cerebral blood flow during the offset phase of 10% $F_{I_{CO_2}}$ breathing. Mean ± SE; n = 15.*

The dynamic relationship between CBF and P_{CO_2} in the offset phase of hypercapnia is shown in Figure 2. After a short lag period, CBF changed at a rate that quickly exceeded (39 ± 5 ml/min^2) that measured in the onset phase (11 ± 1 ml/min^2) and resulted in a shorter half-time of response (0.66 ± 0.06 min). Differing rates for the Pa_{CO_2} forcing function could not account for the differing rates of change seen in the CBF transient on the two phases. Mean arterial blood pressure was 109 ± 3 mm Hg in the offset phase.

The momentary correlations of CBF on Pa_{CO_2} and Pv_{CO_2} from a representative experiment are shown in Figure 3. In the onset phase, Pa_{CO_2} increased rapidly, with CBF following at a slower rate. A similar lag occurred between Pa_{CO_2} and CBF on the offset phase of hypercapnia. In each experiment, the momentary correlation between Pv_{CO_2} and CBF demonstrated less hysteresis than did the arterial P_{CO_2} and CBF relation. Generally, in the offset phase, Pv_{CO_2} fell more rapidly than did CBF for the first 0.5–1.0 minute. The pattern then became reversed, and small changes in Pv_{CO_2} were accompanied by large changes in CBF. After CBF achieved

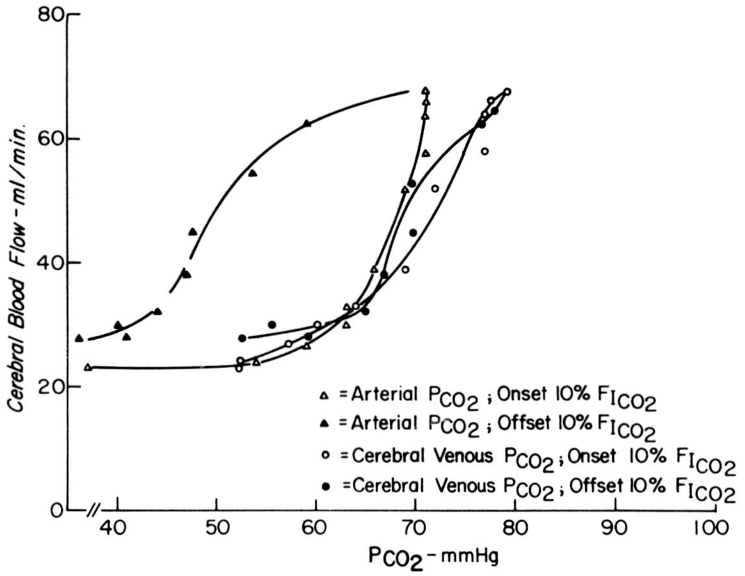

FIGURE 3. *The momentary correlation between arterial* P_{CO_2} *and cerebral blood flow and between cerebral venous* P_{CO_2} *and cerebral blood flow during the onset and offset phases of 10%* $F_{I_{CO_2}}$ *breathing.*

a near steady state, P_{VCO_2} continued to decrease slowly.

Transients Produced by Means of a Step-Decrease in Pa_{CO_2}

Figure 4 shows the temporal relationships between the P_{CO_2} and CBF transient for the two phases of hypocapnia. In both phases, a reasonable approximation to the CBF transient could be made by assuming that the rate of change in CBF was a single exponential. The rate constants were 0.77 minute in the hypocapnic-going direction and 0.74 minute in the normocapnic-going direction. In comparison, arterial P_{CO_2} changed in both phases in a manner that could be characterized by a double exponential function. The rate constants were 0.21 minute and 1.78 minutes for the fast and slow components, respectively. In the normocapnic-going direction, the rate constants for the two Pa_{CO_2} components were 0.22 and 5.1 minutes.

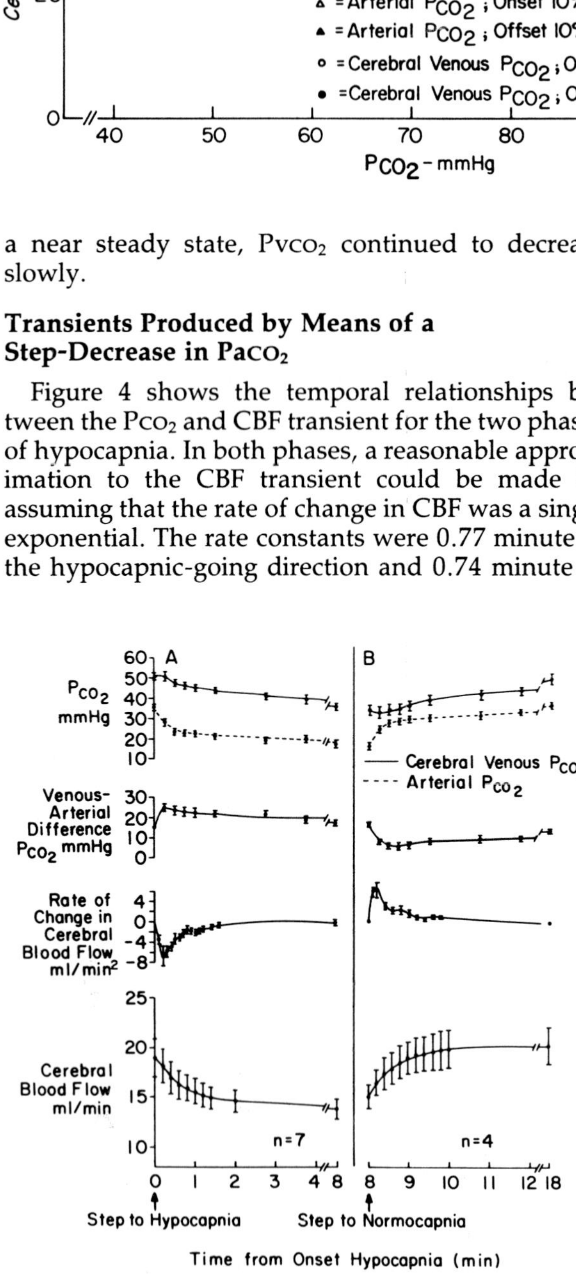

FIGURE 4. *The temporal relationships between arterial* P_{CO_2}*, cerebral venous* P_{CO_2} *and cerebral blood flow transients during the onset (panel A; n = 7) and offset (panel B; n = 7) phases of hypocapnia. Mean ± SE.*

Figure 5 shows the momentary correlation of CBF on the two CO_2 transients. In this experiment, the closed loop formed by the Pa_{CO_2}-CBF correlation demonstrated that a similar level of CBF was associated with the same Pa_{CO_2} for both phases of the pulse. The P_{VCO_2}-CBF relation tended to be more open than the loops encountered in experiments where 10% CO_2 was used to generate the transients. Higher CBF levels occurred for the levels of P_{VCO_2} on the return limb than on the hypocapnic-going limb.

Table 1 shows the results from five experiments in which a step hypercapnia was produced after the

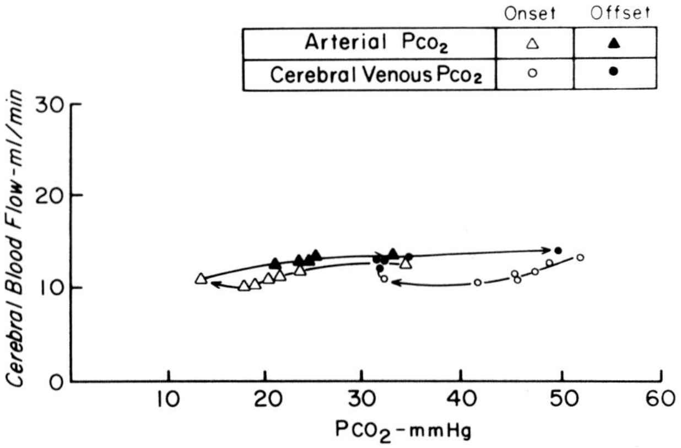

FIGURE 5. *The momentary correlation between arterial* P_{CO_2} *and cerebral blood flow and between cerebral venous* P_{CO_2} *and cerebral blood flow during the onset and offset phases of hypocapnia.*

TABLE 1
The Effect of Differing Directional Changes in Arterial P_{CO_2} on the Response Characteristics of Cerebral Blood Flow Transients Initiated from Normocapnia

	Arterial P_{CO_2}			Cerebral blood flow				
	Initial (mm Hg)	Final (mm Hg)	Final-initial (mm Hg)	Initial (ml/min)	Final (ml/min)	Final-initial (ml/min)	$d\dot{Q}/dt_{max}$ (ml/min^2)	CBF $t_{0.50}$ (min)
Step to hypocapnia from normocapnia	36 ± 3.7	16.8 ± 4.6	19.9 ± 4.2	20.5 ± 4.1	15.1 ± 2.0	5.4 ± 2.6*	−7.2 ± 2.3	0.47 ± 0.14*
Step to hypercapnia from normocapnia	37.6 ± 4.6	56.7 ± 5.8	19.1 ± 1.8	19.2 ± 3.2	35.8 ± 11.5	16.6 ± 8.8	7.6 ± 2.2	1.41 ± 0.34

Results are expressed as mean ± SE; $n = 5$.
* Significantly different from step to hypercapnia.

animals became normocapnic from a previously induced hypocapnic episode. There was no significant difference in $d\dot{Q}/dt_{max}$ produced by forcing Pa_{CO_2} in either the hypercapnic or hypocapnic directions; thus the shorter halftime for the hypocapnic CBF transient was the result of the smaller magnitude change in CBF.

Transients Produced by Step Increases in Arterial P_{CO_2} after Initial Cerebral Blood Flow was Raised by Moderate Hypercapnia

The initial steady state levels of Pa_{CO_2} and CBF in 15 responses, from 15 dogs, were 36.6 ± 9 mm Hg and 19 ± 1 ml/min, respectively. The change in Pa_{CO_2} averaged 17.0 ± 0.9 mm Hg during step A (step to moderate hypercapnia) and 15.1 ± 1.0 mm Hg during step B (step to hypercapnia). There was no significant difference between the mean change in Pa_{CO_2} for the two steps. CBF was raised by 12 ± 2ml/min during step A and 17 ± 2 ml/min in step B. Due to the nonlinear nature of the CO_2-CBF curves, the magnitude of the change in CBF was significantly different for the two steps.

Table 2 shows that the abrupt increase in Pa_{CO_2} during step A was sufficient to disperse the Pa_{CO_2} and CBF transients and the Pa_{CO_2} and Pv_{CO_2} transients, but was not sufficient to disperse the Pv_{CO_2} and CBF transients. Similarly, there was no significant difference between the half-times for Pv_{CO_2} and CBF in step B, but Pa_{CO_2} and Pv_{CO_2}, as well as Pa_{CO_2} and CBF half-times, were significantly dispersed. There was no significant difference in the half-times for the Pa_{CO_2} transients in the two FI_{CO_2} steps. Pv_{CO_2} tended to increase at a faster rate during step B than during step A, but no statistical difference could be shown, due to the slow transient which occurred in one experiment. In this animal, the Pa_{CO_2} transient was slower in step B than in step A, and probably accounts for the lengthened Pv_{CO_2} half-times. The CBF transient increased at a significantly faster rate during FI_{CO_2} step A, as indicated by both the shorter half-time and greater absolute rates of change.

Equal magnitude increases in Pa_{CO_2} for steps A and B were expected to produce equal magnitude increases in CBF. However, the average increase in CBF per mm Hg increases in Pa_{CO_2} was 0.740 ± 0.40 and 1.21 ± 0.60 ml/min per mm Hg for the two steps, respectively. The average difference (0.47 ± 0.63) was significant. Since CBF changes of unequal magnitude could influence the method of comparing response rate between the two steps, multiple regression analysis was applied to the data to establish the contribution of initial CBF to the increase in CBF response rate. For the multiple regression model, data from the 15 experiments were pooled. Each step was considered to be a separate experiment. The only factors considered to

TABLE 2
Non-steady State Arterial P_{CO_2}, Cerebral Venous P_{CO_2}, and Cerebral Blood Flow Characteristics for Two Sequentially Produced Step Increases in Inspired CO_2 Concentration

Step A				Step B			
Half-time			$d\dot{Q}/dt_{max}$ (ml/min^2)	Half-time			$d\dot{Q}/dt_{max}$ (ml/min^2)
Pa_{CO_2} (min)	Pv_{CO_2} (min)	CBF (min)		Pa_{CO_2} (min)	Pv_{CO_2} (min)	CBF (min)	
0.50 ± 0.30	1.60 ± 0.53*	1.57 ± 0.51*†	6.3 ± 2.8	0.52 ± 0.29	1.31 ± 0.30*	1.20 ± 0.30*†‡	11.9 ± 1.22‡

Results are expressed as mean ± SE; $n = 15$.
* Half-time significantly different from the Pa_{CO_2} half-time.
† Half-time not significantly different from the Pv_{CO_2} half-time.
‡ Significantly different from step B.

affect $d\dot{Q}/dt_{max}$ were initial CBF rate and the change in CBF that occurred. No consideration was given to the factors responsible for the change in CBF. The purpose of the analysis was to determine whether the outcome of the results presented in Table 2 were significantly affected by differing magnitude changes in CBF between the two steps. The results indicated that a substantial portion of the variability in the maximum rate of change in CBF was attributable to both differing initial CBF rate and response magnitude. When the variation attributed to differing response magnitudes was held constant, the relationship between initial CBF and $d\dot{Q}/dt$ was significant at the 0.001 percentile level.

Figure 6 shows the dynamic relationship between Pa_{CO_2}, Pv_{CO_2}, and CBF for six selected experiments. In these animals, change in CBF during step B was within ±30% of that produced during step A. Two points are illustrated. First, the figure shows that the time course for the rate of change in CBF in the two $F_{I_{CO_2}}$ steps was significantly increased in those animals whereby the criteria for comparing rate constants held, i.e., where the change in CBF was approximately equal for the two steps. Second, when $F_{I_{CO_2}}$ was increased to 7–8%, the cerebral venous P_{CO_2} measured 15 seconds after the onset of the step change indicated a transient decrease before rising. In 13 of the 15 animals for which complete Pv_{CO_2} transients were available, the decrease in Pv_{CO_2} was significant (2 ± 2 mm Hg). The Pv_{CO_2} measurement taken 15 seconds after the onset of 10% CO_2 breathing was not significant. Analysis of the CBF transient 15 second after the step change indicated CBF was significantly increased in both step A and step B.

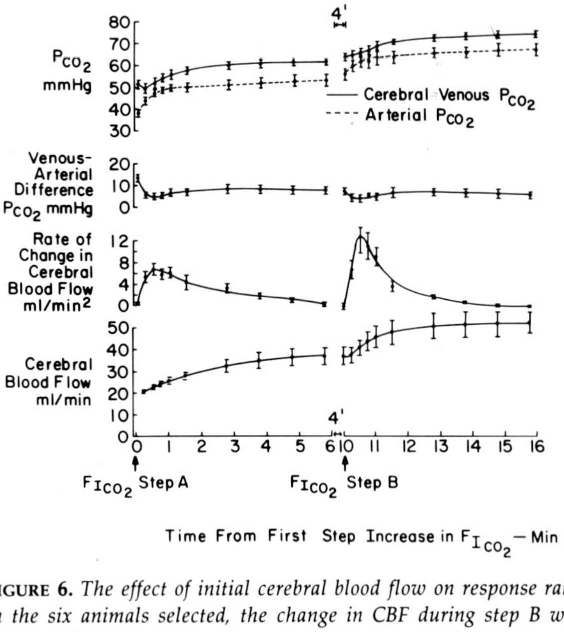

FIGURE 6. *The effect of initial cerebral blood flow on response rate. In the six animals selected, the change in CBF during step B was within 30% of the change that occurred during step A. Step A = 7–8% $F_{I_{CO_2}}$; step B = 10% $F_{I_{CO_2}}$.*

Studies Utilizing Intra-arterial Papaverine Infusion to Increase Initial Cerebral Blood Flow

In seven dogs, papaverine infusion raised initial CBF by an average of 9 ± 2 ml/min (from 17 ± 7 to 26 ± 8 ml/min) while decreasing Pa_{CO_2} 2 ± 2 mm Hg (from 7 ± 2 to 35 ± 3 mm Hg). The arteriovenous P_{CO_2} difference was not significantly altered in the higher blood flow state (15 ± 3 vs. 13 ± 1 mm Hg), because a significant increase in cerebral metabolism (from 1.55 ± 0.17 to 1.83 ± 0.17 ml/O_2 per min) accompanied papaverine infusion.

During 10% CO_2 breathing, arterial P_{CO_2} rose from 35 ± 3 to 68 ± 3 mm Hg and CBF increased from 26 ± 8 to 50 ± 14 ml/min. Although the control group (animals administered 10% CO_2 without previous dilation) tended toward larger magnitude changes in CBF during CO_2 inhalation than did the papaverine-infused group, no significant difference could be demonstrated between groups. The differing magnitude changes in CBF may have resulted from the higher Pa_{CO_2} achieved by the control group during hypercapnia. Nevertheless, the mean half-time of 0.99 ± 0.38 minute for CBF transients generated in the group receiving papaverine to increase initial CBF was significantly shorter than the 2.03 ± 0.42 minute half-time for CBF transients initiated without previous vasodilation. Moreover, $d\dot{Q}/dt_{max}$ was significantly greater in the group dilated with papaverine (18 ± 3 ml/min²) than in the untreated control group (11 ± 1 ml/min²).

Discussion

The findings of the present study show: (1) CBF is more closely correlated with cerebral venous P_{CO_2} than with large artery P_{CO_2}, (2) the rapidity of the CBF response to hypercapnia is influenced by multiple factors, including initial blood flow rate and forcing function amplitude, but is independent of the direction of CO_2 change. These studies provide new evidence which we believe will aid in clarifying the controversy over the appropriate stimulus for the cerebrovascular response to CO_2. Moreover, they provide additional insight into the physical factors involved in the response. This discussion will focus on the relative significance of the time-related factors that contribute to the observed dispersion of CO_2 and CBF transients.

Methodological Considerations

Three previous attempts (Shapiro et al., 1966; Severinghaus and Lassen, 1967; and Tuteur et al., 1976) have been made to evaluate the transient responses of the cerebral circulation to a step change in arterial P_{CO_2}. Each of these studies employed the reciprocal arteriovenous oxygen difference technique to estimate relative changes in CBF. However, as Zierler (1961) pointed out, if the arterial and venous oxygen concentrations are not stable, or if blood flow or the rate of tissue uptake are unsteady, then the arteriovenous difference can be affected unpredictably. Whereas we believe these studies were valid in their approach, their methodological limitations must clearly be kept in mind. The cerebral venous outflow technique utilized in the present study requires no assumptions regarding steady state. It provides a direct, continuous measurement of CBF, and thus seems optimally suited to the study of CBF transients.

Origins of the Differing Dynamic Response Characteristics for Cerebral Blood Flow and CO_2 Transients

Step Hypercapnia

Lag. The initial changes in CBF always lagged behind the Pa_{CO_2} transient. This initial delay appears to be a pure transport delay originating from the transit time for blood passing from the lung to the brain. Previous studies have shown the lung-to-carotid artery circulation time in cats is 6 seconds (Nims and Marshall, 1938), 5–6 seconds in awake dogs (Bouvert et al., 1965), and 4–10 seconds in man (Dejours, 1962; Cunningham et al., 1965). Thus, assuming a lung-to-carotid artery appearance time of from 4–10 seconds and a carotid artery-to-jugular bulb appearance time of 6–7 seconds, the lung-to-brain lag should have a range of from 10–17 seconds. The average 14-second initial lag in CBF measured in the present study is within this range.

An alternative explanation for the initial delay is in the time required for cerebral vessels to respond to a change in pH or P_{CO_2} of their environment. Data from previous studies however, tend to discount such an explanation. Both Wahl and coworkers (1970) and Purves and Cragg (1976) have shown that pial arteries begin to dilate within 2–7 seconds after the close application of acidic mock cerebral spinal fluid. Greenberg and Reivich (1977) reported that intervals up to 75 seconds long may, in some instances, be required for pial vessels to respond to a change in perivascular fluid pH, but that most vessels develop a maximum response within the first 10 seconds. The latter group attributed the wide variation in vessel response times to an inability to control accurately the distances between the injecting pipette and the vessel under study. Consequently, their conclusion was that the time course for a change in vessel diameter closely resembles the time course of the change in perivascular fluid pH.

Dispersion. Several possibilities exist to explain the 1.4-minute difference between Pa_{CO_2} and CBF transients half-times. The most probable of these are that: (1) the combination of a highly permeable vessel wall and a large tissue solubility for CO_2 allows for complete equilibration of CO_2 between the blood and tissue phases as the hypercapnic blood passes into the smaller diameter brain vessels, and/or (2) the non-proportional nature of the stimulus-response relationship tends to lengthen the difference in half-times used to characterize dispersion.

An important distinction must therefore be made between the P_{CO_2} in large systemic arteries and the P_{CO_2} in smaller arteries and arterioles. If gaseous exchange occurs freely in the larger brain vessels and is not limited by diffusion processes, the loss of CO_2 to the surrounding tissue will reduce arteriolar P_{CO_2} as it raises tissue P_{CO_2}. The result is a small transmural gradient across the arteriolar wall. Such an acute reduction in Pa_{CO_2} at the small arteries level may account for the dispersion between CBF and CO_2 transients, since it has been shown that smaller cerebral vessels are more responsive to CO_2 than are larger cerebral vessels (Wei et al., 1980). Supporting this concept, a smaller difference was measured between the half-time for the Pv_{CO_2} and CBF transient than was measured for the Pa_{CO_2} and CBF transient. The momentary correlation plot indicated that a similar level of CBF occurred for the same Pv_{CO_2} in both phases of hypercapnia. In contrast, a higher flow was measured for any given Pa_{CO_2} in the offset phase than for the same Pa_{CO_2} in the onset phase of hypercapnia.

To interpret these findings, consideration must be given to the concept of tissue P_{CO_2} and how tissue P_{CO_2} might be expected to change in the onset of CO_2 breathing. Ponten and Siesjo (1966) measured P_{CO_2} in arterial and cerebral venous blood, and in cisternal cerebral spinal fluid (CSF) and on the surface of the cat cortex. CSF P_{CO_2} was found to exceed the average of the arterial and cerebral venous P_{CO_2} by 0.5 to 1 mm Hg. Measured cortical P_{CO_2} gave identical values. The relation was found to hold true for hypocapnia, normocapnia, and hypercapnia, as long as sufficient time was allowed for steady state equilibration between FI_{CO_2} alterations.

Ponten and Siesjo (1965) have also reported the results of measured cortical surface P_{CO_2} ("tissue P_{CO_2}") changes in spontaneously breathing cats abruptly exposed to 7% CO_2. The halftime for the tissue P_{CO_2} transient was about 1.5 minutes, with equilibrium achieved 5–10 minutes after the onset of CO_2 breathing. At the end of the CO_2 administration, the marked increase in ventilation caused tissue P_{CO_2} to return to its pre-hypercapnic control value within 1 minute. Similar findings have been demonstrated by Krnjevic et al. (1964). The values are nearly identical to the 1.60 ± 0.53 min Pv_{CO_2} half-time reported in the present study for dogs hyperventilated with 7% CO_2 and appear to be compatible with the Pv_{CO_2} half-times measured in spontaneously breathing dog (Lambertsen et al., 1965). In view of the fact that Pv_{CO_2} and CBF transients closely resemble one another during onset hypercapnia and that Pv_{CO_2} appears to reflect tissue P_{CO_2} in the nonsteady state, these findings are interpreted as strongly suggesting that the tissue exerts an influence on the rate of change in CBF induced by arterial P_{CO_2}. By this concept it is the P_{CO_2} of the tissue that is important in determining cerebral vascular resistance. Presumably, this effect is mediated through the action of extracellular fluid (ECF $[H^+]$) (Kontos et al., 1977).

Step Hypocapnia

CBF transients elicited by abrupt decreases in Pa_{CO_2} to hypocapnic levels appear to closely resemble the Pa_{CO_2} transient, whereas cerebral venous P_{CO_2} continues to change after CBF has stabilized. Whereas these results have led others to conclude that perivascular P_{CO_2} is more important in determining cerebrovascular tone than is tissue P_{CO_2} (Severinghaus and Lassen, 1967), there appears to be no basis for distinguishing between these two variables solely on the closeness of the Pa_{CO_2} and CBF transients. In the present studies, when Pa_{CO_2} was abruptly increased from normocapnia by an amount equivalent to that used to induce hypocapnia, the absolute maximum rate of change in CBF achieved was the same as that induced for a decreasing change in Pa_{CO_2}. As previously discussed, in the hypercapnic-going direction, the CBF transient closely correlated with Pv_{CO_2}. If the rate of change transient reflects the vascular response to the impact of Pa_{CO_2} change, then the shorter half-time for the hypocapnic-going CBF transient might suggest that the CBF transient is restricted by a limited degree of reduction in blood flow, thereby invalidating the dispersion correlation procedure.

It is well known that normobaric-hyperventilation increases the concentration of lactic acid in cerebral tissue (Plum and Posner, 1967; Leusen et al., 1967). The resultant shift in extracellular pH limits the amount by which hyperventilation can decrease CBF. It is uncertain whether the lactic acid concentration rises as a consequence of the raised extracellular pH or a relative ischemia or both (Siesjo et al., 1974). The data of MacMillan and Siesjo (1973) seem to establish that the increased lactate production during marked hypocapnia is of hypoxic origin. Moreover, Winn et al. (1981) have also implicated increased adenosine release as a factor which further prevents vasoconstriction in severe hypocapnia. It is clear that further decreases in CBF can be achieved by increasing the amount of dissolved oxygen in plasma during hyperbaric conditions (Plum et al., 1968). Thus the limitation imposed on the excursion of the CBF transient could make the CBF transient appear more rapid than would be apparent if the vascular response to the change in Pa_{CO_2} were allowed to develop unrestricted.

It remains to be shown whether or not compensatory changes in metabolism are activated within the time-frame of the response. Folbergrova et al. (1975) have presented evidence showing the enzymatic changes necessary to account for intracellular buffering developed within 15 seconds after a change in Pa_{CO_2}. Extracellular buffering appears to occur over a longer period of time and may not explain the limited change in CBF (Siesjo et al., 1972).

The Influence of Initial Cerebral Blood Flow

Two previous studies have reported that CBF stabilizes earlier in the offset phase than in the onset phase (Shapiro et al., 1966; Tuteur et al., 1976). Both groups attributed this disparity to spontaneous changes in ventilation. However, a similar observation was made in the present study when ventilation was controlled. Thus, keeping in mind the limitations associated with the arteriovenous O_2 methodology, it seems appropriate to pursue alternative explanations for this phenomenon. Both groups studied human subjects and allowed minute ventilation to change spontaneously in response to inhaled CO_2. Consequently, differing arterial forcing functions were produced for the two phases of hypercapnia which could readily account for the differences in response time. In the present investigation, ventilation was held constant, yet the CBF transients changed at a rate that was more than two times faster upon the return to normocapnia from 10% CO_2 breathing than when 10% CO_2 was used to induce hypercapnia from normocapnia. To account for this phenomenon, it was hypothesized that the CBF response to Pa_{CO_2} is a blood flow-limited process. In this hypothesis, it is differences between CO_2 delivery and CO_2 clearance rates that are responsible for the asymmetries of the response.

For a purely diffusion-limited vascular bed, two CBF transients initiated from differing initial volume flow rates should display similar rate characteristics provided equal magnitude changes in Pa_{CO_2} are produced. If, however, the addition of CO_2 to the tissue is rate-limited by blood flow, then a faster rate of change should be observed in transients initiated from elevated volume flows, because larger quantities of CO_2 would be presented to the tissue per unit time interval.

In the present study, the effect of initial CBF on cerebrovascular CO_2 response rate was studied by two different means to produce the initial elevation in flow. The results of both investigations support the concept that the response is flow limited rather than diffusion limited, but neither study is conclusive due to technical limitations. In the group administered two levels of CO_2, the test criteria assumes that there is a linear relationship between CBF and Pa_{CO_2}. This condition was not met. Although faster CBF transients were associated with smaller increments in Pa_{CO_2} at higher initial Pa_{CO_2} levels, it may still be argued that the differing response rates were attributable to nonlinearities in the steady state CBF-CO_2 response curve. To exclude this possibility, Pa_{CO_2} was incremented over similar portions of the CBF-CO_2 relationship using intra-arterial papaverine to produce the flow change. The studies were confounded by the observation that papaverine vasodilation increases cerebral oxygen consumption. Previous studies (Fujishima et al., 1971; Edvinsson and MacKenzie, 1977; and Dahlgren and Siejo, 1981), as well as our own observations, indicate that barbiturate anesthesia curtails cerebral CO_2 responsiveness. Presumably, these effects are brought about by changes in cerebral metabolism, but direct effects have been documented as well (Edvinsson and McCulloch, 1981). Despite these complications, it seems unlikely to us that an 18% increase in $CMRO_2$ can fully account for the 2-fold increase in response rate observed in the present study. Thus, we maintain that the major factor affecting cerebrovascular response rate was the elevated initial blood flow, that is, CO_2 delivery, and not cerebral metabolism.

We wish to acknowledge the excellent technical assistance of Bill Brooks in performing these experiments, and thank Janet Wolfe and Candace Berryman for their aid in preparing the manuscript.

Supported by U.S. Public Health Service, National Institutes of Health Grants HL 05392, NS 11953, and NS 20020, and by grants from the North Carolina Heart Association.

Address for reprints: David A. Wilson, Ph.D., Anesthesiology and Critical Care Medicine, Johns Hopkins Hospital, Blalock 1404, 600 N. Wolfe Street, Baltimore, Maryland 21205.

Received April 6, 1983; revised manuscript received August 13, 1984; accepted for publication January 18, 1985.

References

Bouvert P, Flandrois R, Puccinelli R, Dejours P (1965) Etude du role des chemorecepteurs arteriels dans la regulation de la respiration pulmonaire chez le chien eveille. Arch Intern Pharmacodyn **157:** 253–271

Cunningham DJ, Lloyd BB, Miller JP, Young JM (1965) The time course of human ventilation after transient changes in Pa_{CO_2}. J Physiol (Lond) **179:** 68P

Dahlgren N, Siesjo BK (1981) Effects of indomethacin on cerebral blood flow and oxygen consumption in barbiturate-anesthetized normocapnic and hypercapnic rats. J Cereb Blood Flow Metabol **1:** 109–115

Dejours P (1962) Chemoreflexes in breathing. Physiol Rev **42:** 335

Draper NR, Smith H (1966) Applied Regression Analysis. New York, John Wiley

Edvinsson L, MacKenzie ET (1977) Amine mechanisms in the cerebral circulation. Pharmacol Rev **28:** 275–348

Edvinsson L, McCulloch JC (1981) Effects of pentobarbital on contractile responses of feline cerebral arteries. J Cereb Blood Flow Metabol **1:** 437–440

Folbergrova J, Norberg K, Quistorff B, Siesjo BK (1975) Carbohydrate and amino acid metabolism in rat cerebral cortes in moderate and extreme hypercapnia. J Neurochem **25:** 457–462

Fujishima M, Scheinberg P, Busto R, Reinmuth OM (1971) The relation between cerebral oxygen consumption and cerebral vascular reactivity to carbon dioxide. Stroke **2:** 251–257

Gelfand R, Lambertsen CJ (1973) Dynamic respiratory response to abrupt change in inspired CO_2 at normal and high P_{O_2}. J Appl Physiol **35:** 903–913

Greenberg JH, Reivich M (1977) Response time of cerebral arterioles to alterations in extravascular fluid pH. Microvasc Res **14:** 383–393

Kontos HA, Raper J, Patterson JL (1977) Analysis of vasoactivity of local pH, P_{CO_2} and bicarbonate on pial vessels. Stroke **8:** 358–360

Krnjevic K, Randic M, Siesjo BK (1964) Cortical CO_2 tension and neuronal excitability. J Physiol (Lond) **176:** 105–122

Lambertsen CJ, Gelfand R, Kemp RA (1965) Dynamic response characteristics of several CO_2-reactive components of the respiratory control system. *In* Cerebrospinal Fluid and the Regulation of Ventilation, edited by C McC Brooks, FF Kao, BB Lloyd. Oxford, Blackwell, pp 211–240

Leusen I, Lacroix E, Demeester G (1967) Lactate and pyruvate in the brain of rats during changes in acid-base balance. Arch Int Physiol Biochim **75:** 310–324

MacMillan V, Siejo BK (1973) The influence of hypocapnia upon intracellular pH and upon some carbohydrate substrates, amino acids and organic phosphates in the brain. J Neurochem **21:** 1283–1299

Nilsson B, Norberg K, Nordstrom C, Siesjo BK (1975) Influence of hypoxia and hypercapnia on CBF in rats. *In* Blood Flow and Metabolism in the Brain, edited by M Harper, B Jennett, D Miller, J Rowan. New York, Churchill-Livingstone, pp 9.19–9.21

Nims LF, Marshall C (1938) Blood pH in vivo. I. Changes due to respiration. Yale J Biol Med **10:** 445–448

Plum F, Posner JB (1967) Blood and cerebrospinal fluid lactate during hyperventilation. Am J Physiol **212:** 864–870

Plum F, Posner JB, Smith WW (1968) Effect of hyperbaric-hyperoxic hyperventilation on blood, brain and CSF lactate. Am J Physiol **215:** 1240–1244

Ponten U, Siesjo BK (1965) Brain tissue carbon dioxide changes and cerebral blood flow measurements. Acta Neurol Scand [suppl 14]: 129–134

Ponten U, Siesjo BK (1966) Gradients of CO_2 tension in the brain. Acta Physiol Scand **67:** 129–140

Purves MJ, Cragg PA (1976) The use of microelectrodes for the measurement of perivascular fluid pH on the surface of the medulla of the cat. *In* The Cerebral Vessel Wall, edited by J Cervo's-Navarro, E Betz, F Matakas, R Wiillanweker. New York, Raven Press, pp 97–106

Rapela CE, Green HD (1964) Autoregulation of canine cerebral blood flow. Circ Res **14/15** (suppl I): 205–211

Reivich M (1964) Arterial P_{CO_2} and cerebral hemodynamics. Am J Physiol **206:** 25–35

Severinghaus JW, Lassen N (1967) Step hypocapnia to separate arterial from tissue P_{CO_2} in the regulation of cerebral blood flow. Circ Res **20:** 272–278

Shalit MN, Reinmuth OM, Shimojyo S, Scheinberg P (1967) Carbon dioxide and cerebral circulatory control. II. The effects of brainstem lesions. Arch Neurol **17:** 342–353

Shapiro W, Wasserman AJ, Patterson JL (1966) Mechanism and pattern of human cerebrovascular regulation after rapid changes in blood CO_2 tension. J Clin Invest **45:** 913–922

Siesjo BK, Folbergrova J, Messeter K (1972) Acid-base and energy metabolism of the brain in hypercapnia and hypocapnia. *In* CO_2 and Metabolism. New York, Springer-Verlag

Siesjo BK, Johannson H, Ljunggren B, Norberg K (1974) Brain dysfunction in cerebral hypoxia and ischemia. *In* Brain Dysfunction in Metabolic Disorders, vol 53, edited by F Plum. New York, Raven Press, p 75

Snedecor GW, Cochran GW (1967) Statistical Methods. Ames, Iowa, The Iowa State University Press

Traystman RJ, Rapela CE (1975) Effect of sympathetic nerve stimulation on cerebral and cephalic blood flow in dogs. Circ Res **36:** 620–630

Traystman RJ, Fitzgerald RS, Luscutoff SC (1978) Cerebral circulatory responses to arterial hypoxia in normal and chemodenervated dogs. Circ Res **42:** 649–657

Tuteur P, Reivich M, Goldberg HI, Cooper ES, West JW, McHenry LC Jr, Cherniack N (1976) Transient responses of cerebral blood flow and ventilation to changes in Pa_{CO_2} in normal subjects and patients with cerebrovascular disease. Stroke **7:** 584–590

Wahl M, Deetjen P, Thurau K, Ingvar DH, Lassen NA (1970) Micropuncture evaluation of the importance of perivascular pH for the arteriolar diameter on the brain surface. Pflugers Arch **316:** 152–163

Wei EP, Kontos HA, Patterson JL (1980) Dependence of pial arteriolar response to hypercapnia on vessel size. Am J Physiol **238:** H697–H703

Winn HR, Rubio R, Berne RM (1981) Brain adenosine concentration during hypoxia in rats. Am J Physiol **241:** H235–H242

Zierler K (1961) Theory of the use of arteriovenous concentration differences for measuring metabolism in steady and non-steady states. J Clin Invest **40:** 2111–2125

INDEX TERMS: Cerebral blood flow • Cerebrovascular response time • Blood gases • Carbon dioxide • Transient analysis • Blood flow limitation • Hypercapnia • Hypocapnia

BRIEF COMMUNICATIONS

Failure of Atriopeptin II to Cause Arterial Vasodilation in the Conscious Rat

Rodney W. Lappe, Jos F.M. Smits, Joy A. Todt, Jacques J.M. Debets, and Robert L. Wendt

From the Department of Experimental Therapeutics, Wyeth Laboratories, Inc., Philadelphia, Pennsylvania, and the Department of Pharmacology, Rijksuniversiteit Limberg, Maastricht, The Netherlands

SUMMARY. The cardiovascular actions of the synthetic natriuretic peptide, atriopeptin II, were examined in conscious unrestrained spontaneously hypertensive rats and normotensive Wistar-Kyoto rats. The animals were chronically instrumented with miniaturized pulsed Doppler flow probes to allow measurement of regional blood flow, or with an electromagnetic flow probe on the ascending aorta to facilitate the measurement of cardiac output in the conscious rat. Intravenous infusion of increasing doses of atriopeptin II (0.25–4 μg/kg per min) caused a dose-dependent fall in mean arterial pressure in the hypertensive and normotensive rats. Blood flow in the renal, mesenteric, and hindquarters vascular beds was markedly decreased during the infusion of atriopeptin II, and regional vascular resistance was significantly increased in both groups of rats. Heart rate was significantly elevated (47 ± 14 beats/min) in the spontaneously hypertensive rats during atriopeptin II infusion, but no change in heart rate was observed in the Wistar rats. In the hypertensive rats, atriopeptin II caused a marked dose-dependent decrease in cardiac output (maximal decrease = −39 ± 4%) and stroke volume (maximal decrease = −48 ± 4%). Central venous pressure and left atrial pressure were also significantly reduced during atriopeptin II infusion. Total peripheral resistance was increased over the infusion protocol by 26 ± 3%. These data suggest that atriopeptin II infusion markedly attenuated cardiac output in the conscious spontaneously hypertensive rats. Total and regional vascular resistances were increased, possibly through reflex compensatory mechanisms, to maintain arterial pressure in the face of decreased cardiac output. Also, similar changes in regional vascular resistance were observed in normotensive and hypertensive rats, suggesting that these responses were not confined to the spontaneously hypertensive rat. **(*Circ Res 56: 606–612, 1985*)**

IT has long been thought that an endogenous "natriuretic factor" was involved in the regulation of sodium excretion. Recently, atrial extracts have been demonstrated to contain several peptides [atrial natriuretic factor (ANF)] which possess powerful natriuretic and diuretic properties (deBold et al., 1981; deBold, 1981; Keller, 1982). Partially purified extracts containing ANF were also found to relax isolated vascular smooth muscle (Currie et al., 1983; Kleinert et al., 1984) and antagonize the vasoconstrictor actions of norepinephrine and angiotensin II in vitro (Kleinert et al., 1984; Camargo et al., 1984). With the subsequent purification, sequencing, and synthesis of ANF by several groups (Flynn et al., 1983; Currie et al., 1983; Thibault et al., 1983; Atlas et al., 1984; Misono et al., 1984), more precise investigation of the vascular and renal actions of these peptides has been possible. Synthetic ANF was found to be a potent natriuretic agent and reduced arterial pressure (Currie et al., 1983; Atlas et al., 1984; Seymour et al., 1984), thus producing results similar to those reported when atrial extracts were used. The depressor actions of synthetic ANF were thought to be mediated through peripheral vasodilation. Synthetic ANF has been demonstrated to relax isolated vascular smooth muscle (Currie et al., 1983; Winquist et al., 1984), and injections of ANF caused a prolonged decrease in renal vascular resistance without affecting hindlimb blood flow or arterial pressure in anesthetized rats (Oshima et al., 1984). Similarly, bolus injections of ANF in conscious rats reduced arterial pressure and caused a sustained increase in renal blood flow, whereas blood flow in other vascular beds (heart, brain, skeletal muscle, gut) were not significantly altered (Koike et al., 1984). These data suggested ANF may cause selective vasodilation of the kidney. However, other investigators have reported conflicting results. Bolus intravenous administration of ANF failed to increase renal blood flow in conscious normotensive rats (M. J. Brody, unpublished data) and increased vascular resistance in isolated perfused rat kidneys (Atlas et al., 1984). In addition, continuous infusion of synthetic ANF failed to alter renal blood flow significantly in anesthetized dogs (Seymour et al., 1985). Thus, the vascular actions of ANF have become an area of controversy. Unfortunately, the actions of ANF were examined only after bolus administration of the peptide in all but one (Seymour et al., 1984) of the above studies. The hemodynamic effects of ANF were not studied during continuous infusion.

The present study was designed to examine the cardiovascular action of the synthetic ANF, atriopeptin II (APII), in conscious rats, as described by Currie et al. (1984). Spontaneously hypertensive rats (SHR) and normotensive Wistar Kyoto rats were chronically instrumented to allow continuous measurement of systemic blood pressure, heart rate, and regional blood flow. In addition, in a separate group of SHR, cardiac output, central venous pressure, and left atrial pressure were monitored in the conscious rats. Changes in the hemodynamic parameters were recorded during the steady state period of continuous infusions of APII.

Methods

Regional Blood Flow

Spontaneously hypertensive rats (SHR) and Wistar-Kyoto rats (WKY), approximately 18–21 weeks old, were chronically instrumented with miniaturized pulsed Doppler flow probes to allow measurement of renal, mesenteric, and hindquarters blood flow. The methods employed have been previously described (Haywood et al., 1982). In brief, rats were anesthetized with sodium pentobarbital (50 mg/kg, ip) and atropine (0.5 mg/kg). Through a midline incision the right renal artery, superior mesenteric artery and the left iliac artery were cleared of connective tissue. A small pulsed Doppler flow probe was placed around each artery and secured in place. The leads from the flow probes were exteriorized at the base of the skull, where they were soldered into a small head plug and cemented to the skull.

Cannulae (P.E. 10 fused to P.E. 50) were also inserted into the abdominal aorta and the inferior vena cava via the midline incision to facilitate the measurement of arterial pressure and allow administration of the natriuretic peptide. The cannulas were secured to the peritoneal wall, exteriorized in the scapular region, and sealed when not in use. Rats were allowed to recover for at least 4 days before experiments were begun.

On the day of the experiment, stable baseline hemodynamic parameters were recorded and increasing doses of APII (0.25, 0.5, 1.0, 2.0, and 4.0 μg/kg per min) or saline (0.625, 1.25, 2.5, 5, and 10 μl/min) were infused intravenously into WKY and SHR. The dose was increased at 15-minute intervals over the entire dose range. Hemodynamic measurements were made after a steady state condition was obtained with each infusion rate. Changes in mean arterial pressure, heart rate, and renal, mesenteric and hindquarters blood flow during ANF infusion in WKY and SHR were compared with responses in saline-infused rats using a one-way analysis of variance and a Student-Newman Kuels nonpaired *t*-test.

Cardiac Output

In additional separate experiments, the effects of APII on blood pressure and cardiac output were examined in conscious SHR. Rats were prepared as described by Smith and Hutchins (1978) and Smits et al. (1984). In brief, SHR were anesthetized with sodium pentobarbital (60 mg/kg, ip). The trachea was intubated and the rats were artificially ventilated (60 strokes/min 2.5 ml tidal volume). A thoracotomy was performed in the 3rd right intercostal space. The ascending aorta was carefully isolated and an electromagnetic flow probe (Skalar; 2.3–2.5 mm i.d.) was placed around the vessel. The cable was fixed to the ribs, tunneled subcutaneously to the neck where the connector was sutured to the skin. After the SHR had recovered for 4–6 days, cardiac output was monitored with a Skalar M 400 sinewave flowmeter. Cannulas were inserted into the femoral artery and vein and advanced into the abdominal aorta and inferior vena cava; respectively. The cannulas were exposed at the base of the skull.

In a separate group of SHR, changes in central venous pressure and left atrial pressure were monitored during APII administration. Central venous pressure was monitored through a cannula that was inserted into the femoral vein with the tip advanced 9 cm so that it lay in the thoracic section of the inferior vena cava (Smits et al., 1982). Left atrial pressure was measured directly through a catheter implanted in the left atrium. Prior to surgery, two small rims of Silastic adhesive were formed on a 10-cm piece of Silastic (602-135) tubing. The rats were anesthetized and artifically respirated as previously described. A thoracotomy was performed in the 4th left intercostal space, and a miniature hemostat was placed on the left atrial appendage. The catheter was inserted into the left atrium through a small incision and attached with a 5-0 silk ligature, tied between the Silastic rims. The catheter was exteriorized at the neck. The rats were allowed to recover for 2–3 days. On the day of the experiment, control levels for central venous pressure and left atrial pressure were taken to be 3 cm above the cage floor.

In these experiments, we employed the same experimental protocol described above. Increasing doses of APII were infused intravenously for 15-minute periods and changes in mean arterial pressure, heart rate, cardiac output, central venous pressure, and left atrial pressure were recorded during the steady state at each infusion level. Arterial blood samples were collected before and after the last infusion rate of APII for hematocrit determination. Responses were compared to preinfusion control values by Student's *t*-test.

All data in this study are presented as the means ± SEM. Statistical significance was accepted if $P < 0.05$. All synthetic APII used in these studies was purchased from BaChem Inc. The peptide purity was found to be of greater than 97%, by high pressure liquid chromatography (HPLC).

Results

Regional Blood Flow

Baseline measurements of mean arterial pressure (MAP) (159 ± 3 vs. 168 ± 8 mm Hg) and heart rate (328 ± 14 vs. 348 ± 16 beats/min) in the SHR were similar in APII- and saline-treated groups, respectively. WKY had significantly lower MAP than the SHR, but heart rates were similar in the two groups of rats. There were no differences between the respective MAP (113 ± 2 vs. 118 ± 6 mm Hg) and heart rate (364 ± 11 vs. 326 ± 12 beats/min) values in the APII- and saline-treated WKY rats.

The hemodynamic effects of APII and saline were markedly different in the conscious SHR (Fig. 1).

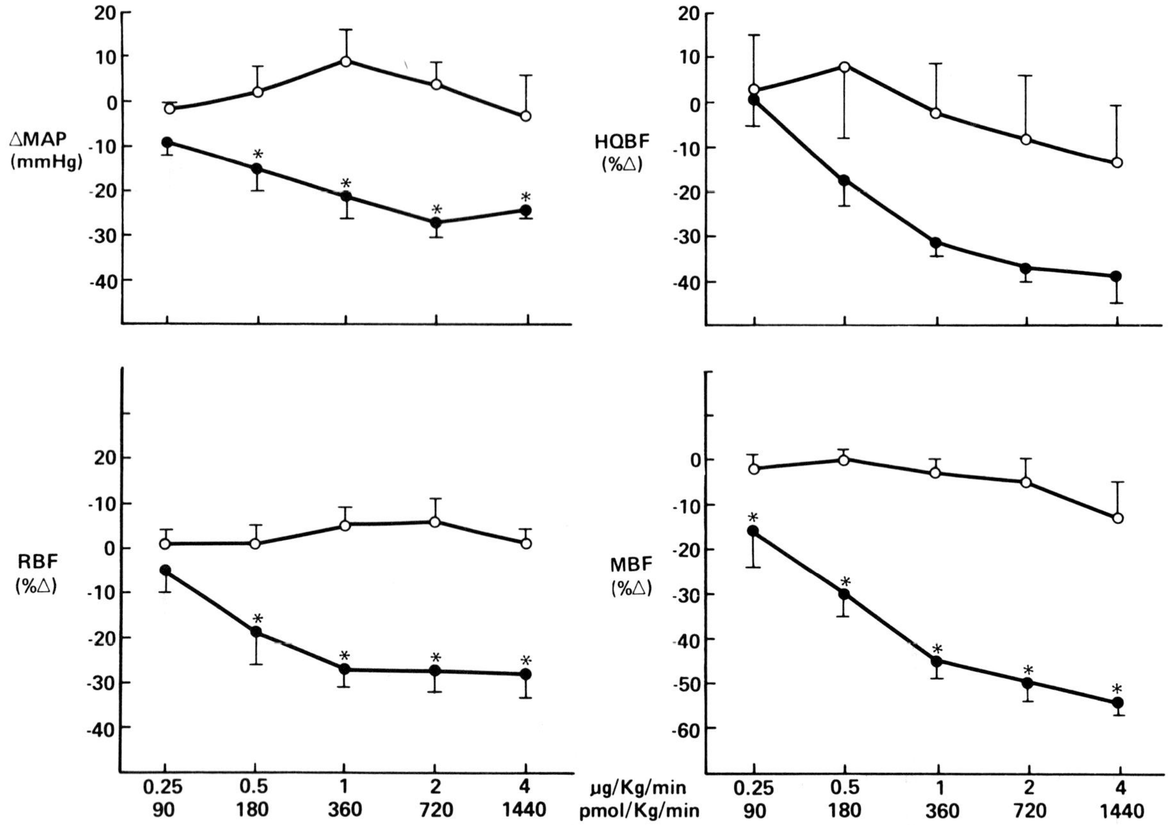

FIGURE 1. *Changes in mean arterial pressure (MAP) and renal (RBF), mesenteric (MBF), and hindquarters (HQBF) blood flow in conscious SHR during the infusion of APII (closed circles) or saline (open circles). *P < 0.05, comparison to response in saline-treated SHR; % Δ = percent change from preinfusion baseline.*

Saline infusion failed to cause a significant alteration in MAP, heart rate, or renal, mesenteric, or hindquarters blood flow from baseline. However, APII infusion caused a dose-dependent fall in MAP and all three regional blood flows. With each increasing dose of APII, MAP fell rapidly to a steady state level within 5–7 minutes and remained stable for the duration of the infusion period. Heart rate was significantly elevated in the SHR during APII infusion (maximal Δ = 47 ± 14 beats/min), but these responses were not dose-related. Maximal depressor responses (−27 ± 3 mm Hg) were observed during the infusion of APII at 2 µg/kg per min. Similar to MAP, renal and mesenteric blood flow were also significantly reduced by APII infusion in the SHR. A transient increase in renal blood flow was initially observed immediately after the lowest infusion of APII was begun, but this response lasted only 30–45 seconds. Blood flow quickly returned to control levels, and no indication of increased renal blood flow was observed during the remainder of the experimental protocol. The maximal fall in regional blood flow was greater in the mesenteric vascular bed (−54 ± 3%) than in the renal vascular bed (−28 ± 5%). Interestingly, maximal reductions in renal blood flow were observed during APII infusions of 1 µg/kg per min. Increasing doses failed to reduce renal blood flow further. Hindquarter blood flow was also markedly reduced. However, due to variable responses in the saline-infused SHR, the effects of APII on hindquarters blood flow failed to achieve statistical significance.

In the normotensive WKY, saline infusion again failed to cause significant changes in baseline MAP or regional blood flow parameters (Fig. 2). However, APII produced significant dose-dependent reductions in MAP, as well as in renal, mesenteric, and hindquarter blood flow. The decreases in renal, mesenteric, and hindquarters blood flow were of a magnitude similar to those observed in SHR during the infusion of APII. However, unlike that in SHR, no significant change in heart rate was observed in the WKY during APII infusion.

Regional vascular resistance was increased significantly in the renal, mesenteric, and hindquarters vascular beds in both SHR and WKY during APII infusion (Fig. 3). Vasoconstrictor responses in the renal and mesenteric vascular beds were similar in SHR and WKY during APII infusion. However, significantly greater increases in hindquarter vascular resistance were observed in WKY, compared to SHR. Depressor responses were also consistently greater in SHR than WKY.

Cardiac Output

The APII infusion protocol was repeated in a separate group of conscious SHR chronically instrumented with an electromagnetic flowprobe on the

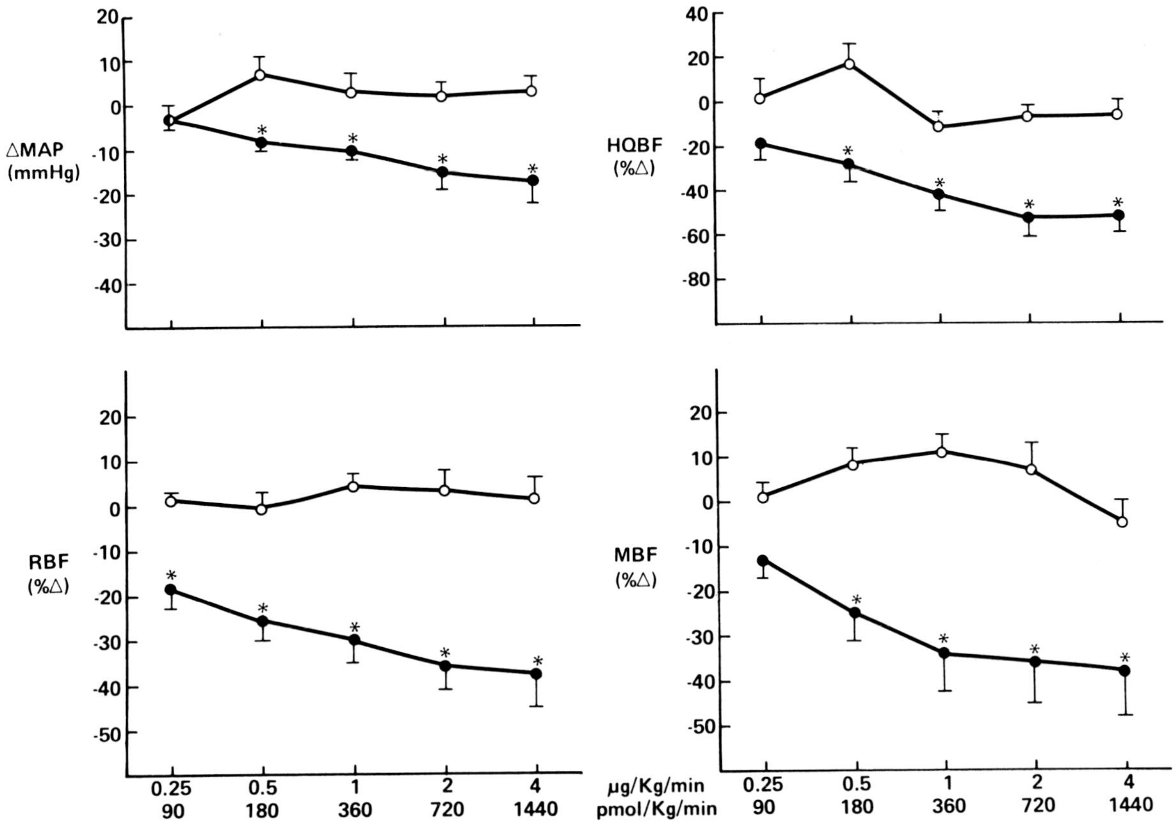

FIGURE 2. *Changes in mean arterial pressure (MAP) and renal (RBF), mesenteric (MBF), and hindquarters (HQBF) blood flow in conscious WKY during the infusion of APII (closed circles) or saline (open circles). *$P < 0.05$, comparison to responses in saline-treated WKY; % Δ = percent change from preinfusion baseline.*

ascending aorta. APII again caused a dose-dependent fall in MAP, which was accompanied by a significant tachycardia (Table 1). Reductions in cardiac output (−13 ± 3%) and stroke volume (−18 ± 4%) were observed during the lowest infusion of APII (0.25 μg/kg per min) and continued to fall with increasing doses of APII. During the highest dose of APII (4 μg/kg per min), cardiac output and stroke volume were reduced by 39 ± 4% and 48 ± 4%, respectively. Total peripheral resistance (TPR), on the other hand, was increased during the infusion of APII. Dose-related increases in TPR of 10 ± 3% to 26 ± 3% were observed during the infusion protocol. In a separate group of SHR, central venous pressure and left atrial pressure fell significantly during the lowest infusion rate of APII and continued to fall in a dose-dependent fashion with increasing doses of APII (Table 1). Also, hematocrit was increased slightly from a preinfusion level of 46.4 ± 1.1 vol% by 2.3 ± 1 vol% (5 ± 2.5%) at the end of the infusion protocol.

Discussion

In the present study, the dose-dependent depressor actions of APII in the conscious SHR were mediated through suppression of cardiac output, rather than through reductions in peripheral vascular resistance. In fact, total and regional vascular resistances increased during APII infusion in SHR. Essentially similar hemodynamic changes were observed during APII infusion in conscious WKY rats.

The fall in cardiac output during APII apparently was due to marked reductions in venous filling pressure in both right and left atria, rather than to a direct cardiac depressant action of APII. The fall in central venous pressure and, particularly, left atrial pressure could account entirely for the observed changes in stroke volume and cardiac output in the present study. APII could reduce venous return via reductions in plasma volume caused by the diuretic actions of APII or by direct venodilator effects similar to those of sodium nitroprusside (Winquist et al., 1984). However, only a small increase in hematocrit (5 ± 2.5%), an index of plasma volume, was observed over the entire infusion period. In addition, cardiac output began to fall immediately after each dose of APII, reaching a steady state level within 5–8 minutes. Thus, the rapid onset of the response and the relatively small change in hematocrit would suggest that reduction of plasma volume could not solely account for the precipitous fall in cardiac output observed after APII. Rather, it would appear that APII caused venodilation in the conscious rats. Synthetic ANF has been demonstrated to relax rabbit facial veins but was weakly active in relaxing the phasic contractions of rat portal veins in vitro (Winquist et al., 1984). Interestingly, the rabbit facial vein

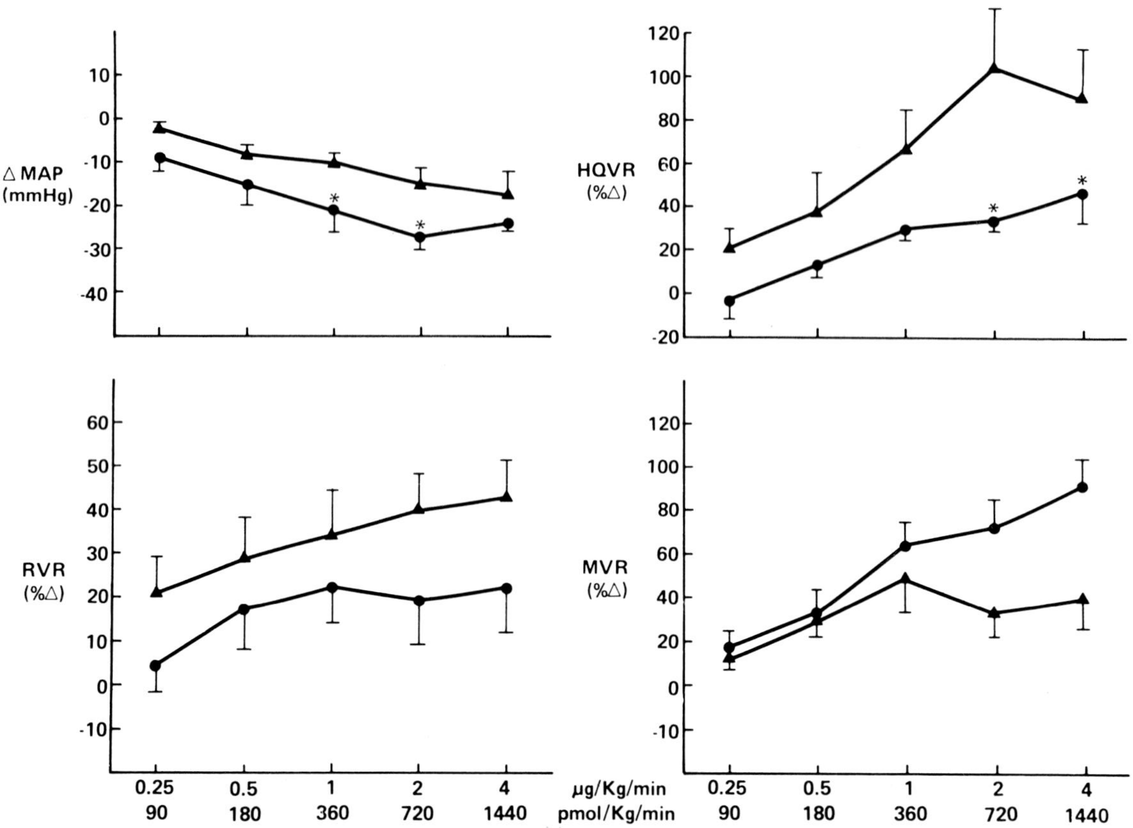

FIGURE 3. *Comparisons of the effects of APII on mean arterial pressure (MAP) and renal (RVR), mesenteric (MVR) and hindquarters (HQVR) vascular resistance in conscious SHR (●) and WKY (▲). *P < 0.05, comparison to responses in WKY; % Δ = percent change from preinfusion baseline.*

appeared to resemble arterioles more closely than other venous tissues, in its smooth muscle composition and intrinsic tone (Winquist et al., 1984), and may not accurately represent venous responses to ANF. The fall in central venous pressure in the present study would suggest that peripheral venous tone was reduced in the intact rat by APII. In addition, since left atrial pressure fell more than central venous pressure, it was possible that APII may also reduce pulmonary vascular resistance.

Interestingly, other investigators (Koike et al., 1984) did not observe reductions in cardiac output after ANF in conscious rats. However, ANF was administered by intravenous bolus, and cardiac output was not measured continuously with an electromagnetic flow probe. Rather, microsphere techniques were employed by Koike et al. (1984). It is possible that the mode of administration could effect the cardiovascular actions of ANF. Owing to an apparent short plasma half-life, the diuretic effects

TABLE 1
Hemodynamic Effects of APII in Conscious SHR (*n* = 7)*

Infusion (µg/kg/min)	MAP (mmHg)	HR (b/min)	CO (ml/min)	SV (µl)	TPR (mmHg/ml)	CVP† (mmHg)	LAP† (mmHg)
Baseline	148 ± 4	356 ± 9	78.4 ± 5	220 ± 14	1.92 ± 0.1	1.0 ± 0.3	4.6 ± 0.5
0.25	−9 ± 5	+40 ± 8*	−9.8 ± 2.2*	−46 ± 3*	0.18 ± 0.06*	−0.5 ± 0.2*	−1.2 ± 0.2*
0.5	−19 ± 5*	+49 ± 17*	−16.5 ± 1.9*	−66 ± 9*	0.19 ± 0.05*	−0.8 ± 0.1*	−1.8 ± 0.2*
1.0	−28 ± 6*	+61 ± 13*	−23.2 ± 2.2*	−87 ± 8*	0.28 ± 0.06*	−1.2 ± 0.1*	−2.0 ± 0.1*
2.0	−29 ± 4*	+66 ± 10*	−25.5 ± 2.0*	−95 ± 7*	0.39 ± 0.06*	−1.4 ± 0.1*	−2.4 ± 0.2*
4.0	−33 ± 6*	+65 ± 11*	−30.3 ± 2.5*	−105 ± 7*	0.49 ± 0.05*	−1.5 ± 0.3*	−2.5 ± 0.1*

MAP = mean arterial pressure; HR = heart rate; CO = cardiac output; SV = stroke volume; TPR = total peripheral resistance; CVP = central venous pressure; LAP = left atrial pressure.

* Data are presented as the maximal changes in the respective parameters from baseline measurements.

† Measurements taken in separate group of conscious SHR.

‡ $P < 0.05$, comparison to baseline values.

of injected ANF are of relatively short duration (deBold, 1981). Similarly, only minor or transient reductions in cardiac output may occur in conscious rats after bolus administration of ANF. Without continuous measurement of cardiac output, such changes could go undetected. However, Ackermann et al. (1984), using thermodilution techniques, were able to demonstrate a small but significant reduction in cardiac output in anesthetized rats after bolus administration of atrial extracts. In the present experiment, sustained reductions in cardiac output were observed at each infusion rate of APII, indicating that with continuous infusion, the suppression of cardiac output and stroke volume could be maintained.

APII failed to reduce total or regional vascular resistance in the conscious SHR and WKY. To the contrary, increases in renal, mesenteric, and hindquarters vascular resistance were consistently recorded, with little variability observed in the dose-dependent reductions in the regional blood flow caused by APII. Similar responses to APII infusion have also been observed in normotensive Sprague-Dawley rats (unpublished observation). These findings suggest that the vasoconstrictor effects of APII infusion are not confined to one particular strain of rat.

It could be argued that other natriuretic peptides may elicit somewhat different responses, and that the present study is applicable only to APII, a 23-amino acid peptide. However, limited studies to date with equi-molar infusions of rat atrial natriuretic peptide (28 amino acids, Ba Chem, Inc.) also demonstrate increased regional vascular resistance in the conscious SHR (data not shown). Thus it would appear that atrial natriuretic peptides in general possess similar cardiovascular actions in the conscious rat. Likewise, it is doubtful that impurities in the synthetic APII could be responsible for the cardiovascular responses of the peptide. All studies were performed with APII purchased from Ba Chem, Inc., and the samples were found to be 97% pure by HPLC analysis.

It is doubtful that regional vascular resistance was increased through direct vasoconstrictor actions of APII. Several studies have demonstrated that ANF possesses potent vasorelaxant properties in isolated vascular smooth muscle (Currie et al., 1983; Winquist et al., 1984; Kleinert et al., 1984). Similarly, intrarenal administration of APII reduced renal vascular resistance in anesthetized rats (Oshima et al., 1984; Seymour et al., 1985). ANF did, however, increase renal vascular resistance in isolated perfused kidneys, but only if all vasoconstrictor agents were removed from the perfusate. (Camargo et al., 1984; Atlas et al., 1984).

APII may, indeed, cause measurable vasodilator responses in the rat at much lower concentrations. However, at the doses examined in the present study, the vasodilator actions of ANF may have been obscured by reflex neural vasoconstrictor responses. With the progressive fall in cardiac output and arterial pressure stimulating baroreflex mechanisms, increased sympathetic vasoconstrictor tone could mask any moderate ANF-induced vasodilation. Humoral mechanisms could also be involved. A fall in renal perfusion pressure may stimulate renin release in the conscious rats, resulting in increased vascular resistance. However, ANF has been reported to inhibit renin release directly (Atlas et al., 1984), suggesting that the renin-angiotensin system may not be involved in increasing vascular resistance during APII infusion. Similarly, ANF has been reported to inhibit the release of vasopressin (Januszewicz, unpublished data), suggesting that increased plasma levels of this vasoconstrictor peptide may not contribute to the cardiovascular actions of APII. The precise vasoconstrictor mechanism is, as yet, unknown, and further studies are necessary to define possible reflex mechanisms involved in the cardiovascular responses to APII infusion.

The doses of APII used in the present study were chosen to cover a drug range which elicited minimal to marked depressor effects on arterial pressure during acute infusion in the conscious rat. Also, the diuretic and natriuretic threshold for the synthetic APII in our laboratories was found to occur between 0.12 and 0.24 μg/kg per min in anesthetized assay rats (unpublished observation). Thus, lower infusion rates were not examined in the conscious instrumented rats. It would be of interest, however, to determine whether chronic infusion of very low doses of ANF would eventually elicit cardiovascular responses similar to those observed in the present study. Regardless, the present study clearly indicates that even at moderate infusion levels, APII decreased cardiac output and increased peripheral resistance while lowering arterial pressure in the conscious rat.

Drs. Lappe and Wendt and Ms. Todt are affiliated with Wyeth Laboratories, USA, and Dr. Smits and Mr. Debets, with Rijksuniversiteit Limberg, The Netherlands.

Address for reprints: Dr. Rodney W. Lappe, Dept. of Experimental Therapeutics, Wyeth Laboratories, Inc., P.O. Box 8299, Philadelphia, Pennsylvania 19101

Received November 19, 1984; accepted for publication January 3, 1985.

References

Ackermann U, Irizawa TG, Milojevic S, Sonnenberg H (1984) Cardiovascular effects of atrial extracts in anesthetized rats. Can J Physiol Pharmacol **62:** 819–826

Atlas SA, Kleinert HD, Camargo MJ, Januszewicz A, Sealey JE, Laragh JH, Schilling JW, Lewicki JA, Johnson LK, Maack T (1984) Purification, sequencing and synthesis of natriuretic and vasoactive rat atrial peptide. Nature **309:** 717–722

Atlas SA, Marion D, Kleinert HD, Camargo MJ, Laragh JH, Vougham ED, Maack T (1984) Inhibition of aldosterone and renin release by synthetic atrial natriuretic factor (abstr). Circulation **70** (suppl II): 332

Camargo MJ, Kleinert HD, Atlas SA, Sealey JE, Laragh JH, Maack T (1984) Ca-dependent hemodynamic and natriuretic effects of atrial extract in isolated rat kidney. Am J Physiol **246:** F447–F456

Currie MG, Geller DM, Cole BR, Boylan JG, Sheng WY, Holmberg SW, Needleman P (1983) Bioactive cardiac substances: Potent vasorelaxant activity in mammalian atria. Science *221:* 71–73

Currie MG, Geller DM, Cole BR, Siegel NR, Fok FK, Adams SP, Eubanks SR, Galluppi GR, Needleman P (1984) Purification and sequence analysis of bioactive atrial peptides (atriopeptins). Science **223:** 67–69

deBold AJ (1981) Tissue fractionation studies on the relationship between an atrial natriuretic factor and specific atrial granules. Can J Physiol Pharmacol **60:** 324–330

deBold AJ, Borenstein HB, Veress AT, Sonnenberg H (1981) A rapid and potent natriuretic response to intravenous injection of atrial myocardial extract in rats. Life Sci **28:** 89–94

Flynn TG, deBold ML, deBold AJ (1983) The amino acid sequence of an atrial peptide with potent diuretic and natriuretic properties. Biochem Biophys Res Commun **117:** 859–865

Haywood JR, Shaffer RA, Fastenow C, Fink GD, Brody MJ (1981) Regional blood flow measurement in the conscious rat with a pulsed Doppler flowmeter. Am J Physiol **241:** H273–H278

Keller R (1982) Atrial natriuretic factor has a direct, prostaglandin-independent action on kidneys. Can J Physiol Pharmacol **60:** 1078–1082

Kleinert HD, Maack T, Atlas SA, Januszewicz A, Sealey JE, Laragh JH (1984) Atrial natriuretic factor inhibits angiotensin-, norepinephrine-, and potassium-induced vascular contractility. Hypertension **6** (suppl 1): 143–147

Koike H, Sada T, Miyamoto M, Oizumi K, Sugiyama M, Inagami T (1984) Atrial natriuretic factor selectively increases renal blood flow in conscious spontaneously hypertensive rats. Eur J Pharamcol **104:** 391–392

Misono KS, Fukumi H, Grammer RT, Inagami T (1984) Rat atrial natriuretic factor: Complete amino acid sequence and disulfide linkage essential for biological activity. Biochem Biophys Res Commun **119:** 524–528

Oshima T, Currie MG, Geller DM, Needleman P (1984) An atrial peptide is a potent renal vasodilator substance. Circ Res **54:** 612–616

Seymour AA, Blaine EH, Mazack EK, Smith SG, Stabilito II, Haley AB, Napier MA, Whinnery MK, Nutt RF (1985) Renal and systemic effects of synthetic atrial natriuretic factor. Life Sci **39:** 33–44

Smith TL, Hutchins PM (1979) Central hemodynamics in the developmental stage of spontaneous hypertension in the unanesthetized rat. Hypertension **1:** 508–517

Smits JFM, Coleman TG, Smith TL, Kasbergen CM, Van Essen H, Struyker-Boudier HAJ (1982) Antihypertensive effect of propranolol in conscious spontaneously hypertensive rats: Central hemodynamics, plasma volume and renal function during β-blockade with propranolol. J Cardiovasc Pharmacol **4:** 903–914

Thibault G, Garcia R, Cantin M, Genest J (1983) Atrial natriuretic factor characterization and partial purification. Hypertension **5** (suppl I): 75–80

Winquist RJ, Faison EP, Nutt RF (1984) Vasodilator profile of synthetic atrial natriuretic factor. Eur J Pharmacol **102:** 169–173

INDEX TERMS: Atrial natriuretic peptide • Cardiac output • Regional vascular resistance • Vasoactive peptides

Effects of Acetylcholine on Action Potential Characteristics of Atrial and Ventricular Myocardium after Bilateral Cervical Vagotomy in the Cat

Richard J. Kovacs and John C. Bailey

From the Krannert Institute of Cardiology, Department of Medicine, Indiana University School of Medicine, Indianapolis, Indiana

SUMMARY. Acetylcholine, the parasympathetic neurotransmitter, shortens the action potential duration of cat atrial muscle cells, but not ventricular muscle cells. In mammalian species, atrial tissue receives a richer cholinergic nerve supply than ventricular tissue. To determine whether chronic withdrawal of cholinergic tone might influence the subsequent response of these tissues to cholinergic stimulation, we examined the effect of acetylcholine on the action potentials of atrial and ventricular myocytes from cats with intact vagi and cats after chronic bilateral cervical vagotomy. Following bilateral cervical vagotomy, physostigmine (10^{-6} M) failed to alter atrial tension development or action potential duration. Acetylcholine produced shortening of the action potential duration in atrial muscle from cats with intact vagi and in cats following bilateral cervical vagotomy. However, the degree of shortening produced by acetylcholine after bilateral cervical vagotomy was significantly greater ($P < 0.001$). In ventricular muscle from cats with intact vagi, acetylcholine did not alter action potential duration. In ventricular muscle from cats after bilateral cervical vagotomy, acetylcholine shortened the action potential duration. Maximal effect was seen at a concentration of 10^{-5} M where acetylcholine shortened action potential duration at 90% repolarization from a control value of 179 ± 4 to 150 ± 7 msec. Atropine (10^{-6} M) reversed the effects of acetylcholine. Addition of propranolol (10^{-6} M) to the superfusate or pretreatment of the animals with reserpine (2 mg/kg, ip) 24 hours before sacrifice failed to alter the response of ventricular muscle cells to acetylcholine. We conclude that after bilateral cervical vagotomy, acetylcholine produces an exaggerated effect on atrial action potential duration, and produces a direct effect on the action potential duration of ventricular myocytes. These effects are mediated through muscarinic cholinergic receptors. **(*Circ Res 56: 613–620, 1985*)**

THE effects of muscarinic cholinergic stimulation on transmembrane action potential characteristics in the mammalian heart are different in atrial and ventricular myocardium. Early in vitro microelectrode studies proved exogenous acetylcholine capable of producing direct effects on the action potential characteristics of atrial myocytes, but not ventricular myocytes, in several mammalian species (Hoffman and Cranefield, 1960). Histological studies available at that time failed to identify significant parasympathetic input to the ventricle (Nonidez, 1939, 1943). These findings led to the conclusion that vagal input to the mammalian ventricle was both anatomically and functionally of little significance.

Subsequently, anatomic (Jacobowitz et al., 1967; Kent et al., 1974), biochemical (Roskoski et al., 1974; Brown, 1976; Fields et al., 1978), and electrophysiological (for a review, see Rardon and Bailey, 1983a) evidence has been advanced suggesting a role for the parasympathetic nervous system in the regulation of ventricular electrical function. Despite the demonstration of all the elements necessary for parasympathetic influence in both atria and ventricle, the physiological basis for the difference in response to muscarinic cholinergic stimulation is not known. Since atrial myocardium receives a denser supply of parasympathetic input than the ventricle, it is possible that the observed difference in responsiveness to cholinergic stimuli is a function of the density of innervation. If so, alterations in the extent of cholinergic innervation may produce a change in the response of the tissue to cholinergic agonists. The following experiments tested the hypothesis that a chronic withdrawal of vagal input to the heart might influence the subsequent responsiveness of atrial and ventricular myocardium to acetylcholine applied in vitro.

Methods

Adult cats of either sex weighing 2.5–5 kg were utilized for these experiments. One group of cats served as nonoperated control animals, a second group underwent bilateral cervical vagotomy, and a third group underwent a sham operation. Cats undergoing bilateral cervical vagotomy were anesthetized with sodium secobarbital (30 mg/kg, ip); ECG lead I was monitored during surgery. Under sterile conditions the cervical vagi were isolated bilaterally and stimulated electrically through bipolar electrodes with a 10-V square wave 4 msec long, at a frequency of 10 Hz. The development of sinus slowing or atrioventricular (AV) block with vagal stimulation was demonstrated prior to nerve sectioning. A 5-mm segment of the vagosympathetic trunk was excised, a tracheostomy performed, and the wound closed. Sham-operated animals underwent an identical procedure, but the vagosympathetic trunks were left intact. Animals received a single dose of benzathine penicillin, 50,000 U/kg, intramuscularly, at the time of surgery.

Forty-eight to 72 hours after surgery, the animals were again anesthetized with secobarbital and their hearts rapidly removed and placed in cool, oxygenated Tyrode's solution. Atrial trabeculae from either the right or left atrium and right ventricular papillary muscles of less than 1 mm in diameter and less than 4 mm long, and left ventricular muscle strips of similar dimension, were excised and pinned to the wax bottom of a Lucite muscle chamber. The chamber was superfused with Tyrode's solution, gassed with a mixture of 95% O_2–5% CO_2, and maintained at a temperature of 37 ± 0.5°C. The composition of the Tyrode's solution was (in mM): Na^+, 141; K^+, 4.0; Cl^-, 127; Ca^{++}, 2.0; HCO_3^-, 22; $H_2PO_4^-$, 0.9; Mg^{++}, 0.5; and glucose, 5.5.

Tissues were paced electrically through stainless steel bipolar electrodes placed on the endocardium. Stimuli, 4 msec in duration, at an intensity of 1.5 times the diastolic threshold, were applied. Atrial fibers were paced at a cycle length of 700 msec and ventricular fibers at a cycle length of 1000 msec. Transmembrane action potentials were recorded by standard microelectrode techniques. Action potentials were displayed on a 5100 series Tektronix oscilloscope, and photographed with a Tektronix Polaroid oscilloscope camera. Single microelectrode impalements were maintained for the duration of each experiment.

Tension was recorded from atrial trabeculae. One end of the atrial muscle was pinned to the floor of the tissue bath, and the opposite end was attached by means of a stainless steel hook to a Gould Statham UC-3 strain gauge transducer fitted with a UL-5 arm. The strain gauge was mounted on a micromanipulator allowing fine adjustment of tissue length. Isometric tension was measured at the apex of the length active tension curve. Strain gauge output was amplified by a custom-designed amplifier and derivative circuit and was displayed on a Hewlett-Packard 7402A strip chart recorder as developed tension and the first derivative of developed tension with time, dT/dt. Tension in the atrial muscle and changes in tension are expressed in absolute terms or as a percentage of control.

Experiments were begun after stable tension and/or action potential characteristics were maintained for at least 20 minutes. Drugs were administered into the tissue bath via a sidearm with a Harvard constant infusion pump.

To test for evidence of denervation in vitro, the response of atrial tissue to physostigmine (10^{-6} M) was examined. Previous work has shown that bilateral cervical vagotomy depletes tissue stores of acetylcholine within 48 hours (Brown, 1976). Physostigmine inhibits the hydrolysis of acetylcholine and has been utilized previously by this laboratory to provide a muscarinic cholinergic stimulus that is dependent on the presence of endogenous acetylcholine (Bailey et al., 1979; Mirro et al., 1980a, 1980b). We compared the atrial contractile response to physostigmine in cats with intact vagi, and in cats that had undergone bilateral cervical vagotomy. In addition, action potentials were recorded both from cats with intact vagi and cats after bilateral cervical vagotomy during exposure to physostigmine.

Atrial and ventricular muscle from cats with intact vagi and cats after bilateral cervical vagotomy (BCV) was exposed to increasing concentrations of acetylcholine in the superfusate, and the responses were assessed. In separate experiments, the same concentration range of acetylcholine was applied in a random fashion. After all acetylcholine concentrations had been administered, atropine was applied concomitant with the highest concentration of acetylcholine.

The contribution of endogenously released catecholamines to the observed action potential changes was examined in two ways. In some experiments, the tissue was exposed to propranolol (10^{-6} M) either before or after exposure to acetylcholine. This concentration of propranolol produces adrenergic blockade, but not direct membrane effects (Wit et al., 1975). In separate experiments, cats after bilateral cervical vagotomy were pretreated with reserpine, 2 mg/kg, intraperitoneally, 24 hours before sacrifice. This dose has been shown to deplete tissue norepinephrine stores, as measured by a spectrofluorometric method (Dahlstrom and Haggendahl, 1966). In addition, this dose of reserpine produces catecholamine depletion sufficient to render tissues insensitive to superfusion with 10^{-4} M tyramine, as previously shown (Rardon and Bailey, 1983b).

To assess any possible role for changes in tissue levels of acetylcholinesterase, we superfused the atrial and ventricular myocardium from cats with intact vagi, and cats after bilateral cervical vagotomy, with solutions containing carbamylcholine, a choline ester not hydrolyzed by acetylcholinesterase. Responses to carbamylcholine and acetylcholine were compared to determine whether the rate of hydrolysis of the agonist contributed to the observed results.

Statistical comparison of dose responses in animals with intact vagi and animals after bilateral cervical vagotomy was made by a two-way analysis of variance with repeated measures. When the analysis of variance was significant, comparison of values from animals with intact vagi to animals after bilateral cervical vagotomy was made by a *t*-test adjusted for multiple comparison (Wallenstein, 1980). Paired *t*-tests were used if only one measurement was compared to the control value.

Drugs used included atropine sulfate, acetylcholine chloride, physostigmine sulfate, *dl*-propranolol hydrochloride, carbamylcholine, and tyramine hydrochloride, all purchased from Sigma Chemical Company. Reserpine was obtained from CIBA. Fresh solutions of each drug were prepared daily.

Results

No significant differences were observed between the responses of sham-operated cats or non-operated cats to the conditions of any of the experiments. Data from these two groups have been pooled and will hereafter be referred to as the group of cats with intact vagi. In atrial muscle from cats with intact vagi, physostigmine (10^{-6} M) produced a reduction in developed tension of 30 ± 8% (266 ± 50 mg to 188 ± 43 mg, $n = 7$, $P < 0.01$), and a decrease in the rate of developed tension of 33% (1814 ± 320 mg/sec to 1214 ± 415 mg/sec, $n = 7$, $P < 0.01$). After bilateral cervical vagotomy, physostigmine (10^{-6} M) produced no significant change in developed tension (238 ± 82 mg to 227 ± 67 mg, $n = 21$) or in the rate of developed tension (1100 ± 415 mg/sec to 1207 ± 320 mg/sec, $n = 21$). A reduction in atrial contractility of greater than 10% with physostigmine (10^{-6} M) was interpreted as an incomplete vagotomy. This occurred in less than 5% of the animals operated, and data from these animals were discarded.

In atria from cats with intact vagi, 10 minutes of exposure to physostigmine (10^{-6} M) increased resting membrane potential by 3 ± 1 mV and shortened action potential duration at 50% and 90% repolarization by 17 ± 5 msec and 31 ± 8 msec, respectively ($n = 6$). Action potential amplitude and $\dot{V}_{max}$ were unaffected by physostigmine. After bilateral cervical vagotomy, 10 minutes of exposure to physostigmine (10^{-6} M) produced no changes in atrial fiber resting membrane potential, action potential duration, action potential amplitude, or $\dot{V}_{max}$ ($n = 6$). In ventricular tissue from either cats with intact vagi ($n = 5$) or cats after bilateral cervical vagotomy ($n = 6$), physostigmine (10^{-6} M) failed to alter action potential duration, resting potential, action potential amplitude, or $\dot{V}_{max}$.

The effects of exogenously applied acetylcholine were studied in atrial tissue from cats with intact vagi and cats after bilateral cervical vagotomy. In cats with intact vagi, acetylcholine increased resting membrane potential and shortened action potential duration. The effects of acetylcholine after bilateral cervical vagotomy were qualitatively similar, but the degree of action potential duration shortening was greater than in animals with intact vagi. No significant differences were observed in the magnitude of response between left and right atria, so data from these experiments were pooled. Table 1 summarizes data from a series of these experiments. Membrane hyperpolarization occurred in response to acetylcholine in both groups. There were no significant differences between groups in the amount of hyperpolarization produced by acetylcholine. In cats after bilateral cervical vagotomy, acetylcholine produced a greater degree of shortening of the action potential duration measured at 50% and 90% repolarization. Figure 1 compares action potential duration responses in the two groups. Application of 10^{-8} M acetylcholine to fibers from cats after bilateral cervical vagotomy and from normally innervated cats failed to elicit a significant degree of action potential shortening.

Desensitization of the atrial tissue to the effects of acetylcholine did not occur with superfusion of a given concentration for up to 30 minutes. Randomizing the order of the applied concentrations of acetylcholine failed to alter the magnitude of the response to a given concentration of the agent. In all experiments, 10^{-6} M atropine reversed the effects of acetylcholine, indicating that the observed effects were mediated through muscarinic cholinergic receptors.

The action potential characteristics of ventricular myocardium prior to the administration of any drugs were similar in the control animals and animals after bilateral cervical vagotomy. No statistically significant differences were observed between the two groups in action potential amplitude, action potential duration at 50% and 90% repolarization, resting potential, or $\dot{V}_{max}$. Right ventricular papillary muscles or left ventricular muscle strips from control animals showed no changes in any of the measured action potential characteristics on exposure to exogenous acetylcholine (10^{-7} to 10^{-5} M). In right ventricular papillary muscles and left ventricular muscle strips from cats after bilateral cervical vagotomy, acetylcholine shortened action potential duration at both 50% and 90% repolarization (Fig. 2). The effects of acetylcholine were concentration dependent, with effects first apparent at a concentration of 10^{-7} M. Application of doses of acetylcholine greater than 10^{-5} M failed to elicit a greater response. Acetylcholine did not affect resting membrane po-

TABLE 1
Action Potential Characteristics in Cat Atria

	Acetylcholine concentration				
	0	10^{-7} M	10^{-6} M	10^{-5} M	10^{-5} M + atropine 10^{-6} M
Cats with intact vagi (n = 6)					
APA (mV)	100 ± 6	101 ± 6	101 ± 6	100 ± 6	99 ± 3
RP (mV)	76 ± 8	77 ± 7	78 ± 7	80 ± 7	76 ± 6
APD_{50} (msec)	62 ± 6	59 ± 7	52 ± 6*	37 ± 5*	66 ± 7
APD_{90} (msec)	138 ± 6	132 ± 12	114 ± 15*	94 ± 13*	140 ± 10
$\dot{V}_{max}$ (V/sec)	240 ± 100	260 ± 115	200 ± 92	240 ± 94	225 ± 90
Cats after bilateral cervical vagotomy (n = 6)					
AP (mV)	98 ± 3	99 ± 5	98 ± 3	96 ± 7	99 ± 9
RP (mV)	77 ± 6	76 ± 5	79 ± 5	78 ± 6	73 ± 5
APD_{50} (msec)	63 ± 5	56 ± 6	25 ± 3*	14 ± 2*	57 ± 5
APD_{90} (msec)	146 ± 7	132 ± 11	75 ± 7*	37 ± 5*	135 ± 10
$\dot{V}_{max}$ (V/sec)	200 ± 70	200 ± 70	200 ± 70	200 ± 83	190 ± 85

Results are expressed as means ± SE. APA = action potential amplitude; RP = resting potential; APD_{50} and APD_{90} = action potential duration at 50% and 90% repolarization, respectively.
* Significantly different from acetylcholine concentration = 0, $P < 0.01$.

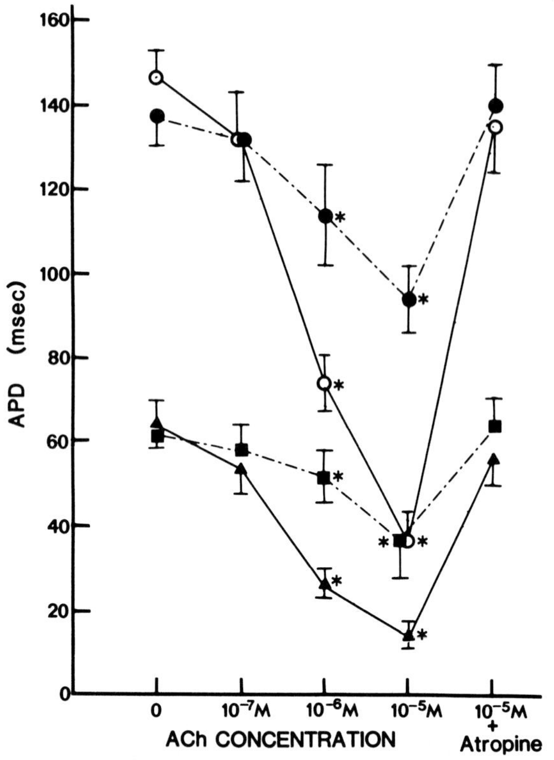

Figure 1. *Comparison of action potential duration shortening produced in atria from animals with intact vagi (●, ■), and animals after bilateral cervical vagotomy (BCV) (○, ▲). Action potential duration (APD) is plotted as function of acetylcholine (ACh) concentration. The upper pair of curves represents values for APD at 90% repolarization, and the lower pair of curves represents values for APD at 50% repolarization. An (*) indicates a significant ($P < 0.01$) difference from the value for APD at 0 concentration of ACh within that group. Differences in the response to ACh between the two groups were analyzed by two-way ANOVA with repeated measures. There is a significant difference in APD response to ACh between cats with intact vagi and cats after BCV when measured at 90% repolarization (interaction $F = 7.88$, $P < 0.001$) and 50% repolarization (interaction $F = 16.4$, $P < 0.001$). This exaggerated effect of ACh is graphically illustrated by the increased steepness of the curve for animals after BCV.*

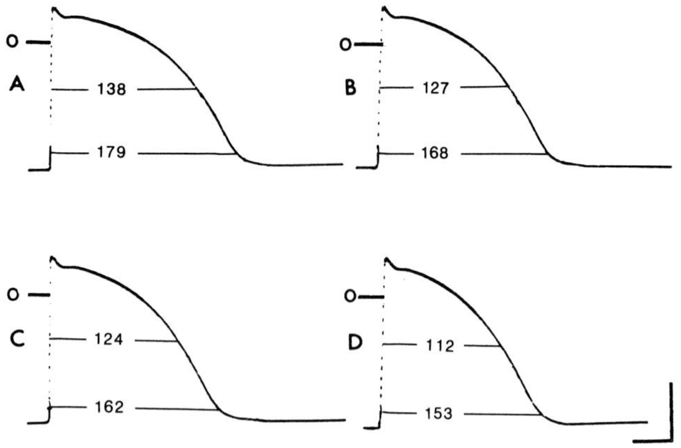

Figure 2. *The effect of ACh on action potentials in ventricular muscle from a cat after BCV. The preparation is paced at a cycle length of 1000 msec. Values for APD at 50% and 90% repolarization are shown within each action potential. Panel A shows the control action potential. Panel B: application of 10^{-7} M ACh. Panel C: application of 10^{-6} M ACh. Further shortening occurs with the application of 10^{-5} M ACh in panel D. Vertical calibration bar equals 40 mV. Horizontal calibration bar equals 50 msec.*

tential, action potential amplitude, or $\dot{V}_{max}$ in these cells. Data from right ventricular papillary muscles ($n = 6$) and left ventricular muscle strips ($n = 5$) were pooled and are presented in Table 2. Atropine 10^{-6} M reversed the effects of acetylcholine in both right and left ventricular myocytes.

The role of endogenous catecholamines in the altered responsiveness of ventricular myocardium to acetylcholine after bilateral cervical vagotomy was tested in two ways. Ventricular fibers were exposed to acetylcholine in the presence of 10^{-6} M propranolol. This concentration of propranolol had no effect on the measured action potential characteristics of ventricular muscle from cats after bilateral cervical vagotomy, and failed to attenuate the action potential shortening produced by acetylcholine ($n = 4$) (Table 3). In separate experiments, endogenous catecholamines were depleted by the administration of reserpine 24 hours before sacrifice. Ventricular myocytes from these animals showed no alteration in action potential characteristics, compared to animals not treated with reserpine, and showed no action potential changes in response to superfusion with tyramine (10^{-4} M). Pretreatment with reserpine failed to ablate the action potential duration shortening produced by acetylcholine ($n = 7$) (Table 3).

In atrial tissue from cats with intact vagi, carbamylcholine (10^{-7} to 10^{-5} M) produced action potential duration shortening equivalent to that produced by acetylcholine. Furthermore, in cats after bilateral cervical vagotomy, carbamylcholine produced a greater degree of action potential duration shortening in a manner virtually identical to acetylcholine (Fig. 3). In ventricular tissue from cats with intact vagi, carbamylcholine (10^{-7} M to 10^{-5} M) produced no effects on action potential duration. In cats after bilateral cervical vagotomy, carbamylcholine produced action potential duration shortening that was not significantly different to that produced by acetylcholine (Fig. 4).

Discussion

Our present experiments indicate that chronic vagotomy alters the response of both atrial and ventricular muscle to cholinergic stimuli. These responses are mediated through muscarinic cholinergic receptors, and are direct effects—that is, effects independent of the level of adrenergic tone. Vagal stimulation or the application of muscarinic cholinergic agonists alters the contractile (Webb, 1950; Sarnoff et al., 1960) and electrical (Hoffman and Suckling, 1953) properties of the mammalian atrium. More recently, vagal stimulation or muscarinic cholinergic agonists have been shown to alter the mechanical (DeGeest et al., 1965; Levy et al.,

TABLE 2
Action Potential Characteristics in Cat Ventricle

	Acetylcholine concentration				
	0	10^{-7} M	10^{-6} M	10^{-5} M	10^{-5} M + atropine 10^{-6} M
	Cats with intact vagi (n = 11)				
APA (mV)	108 ± 5	107 ± 6	109 ± 3	109 ± 4	108 ± 5
RP (mV)	81 ± 3	81 ± 3	81 ± 2	82 ± 3	82 ± 3
APD_{50} (msec)	127 ± 5	129 ± 3	125 ± 5	122 ± 8	128 ± 6
APD_{90} (msec)	175 ± 6	180 ± 6	176 ± 8	170 ± 8	178 ± 9
$\dot{V}_{max}$ (V/sec)	207 ± 58	202 ± 64	205 ± 53	202 ± 64	187 ± 63
	Cats after bilateral cervical vagotomy (n = 11)				
APA (mV)	106 ± 6	107 ± 7	105 ± 9	106 ± 9	108 ± 9
RP (mV)	82 ± 3	81 ± 4	82 ± 5	81 ± 6	82 ± 5
APD_{50} (msec)	140 ± 7	133 ± 6	114 ± 6*	106 ± 7*	134 ± 4
APD_{90} (msec)	179 ± 4	172 ± 4	160 ± 3*	150 ± 7*	169 ± 6
$\dot{V}_{max}$ (V/sec)	210 ± 60	210 ± 60	211 ± 50	204 ± 60	203 ± 51

Results are expressed as means ± SE. See Table 1 for explanation of abbreviations.
* Significantly different from acetylcholine concentration = 0, $P < 0.01$.

1966; Daggett et al., 1967) and electrical (for a review, see Rardon and Bailey, 1983a) properties of the mammalian ventricle. In vitro electrophysiological studies have shown that acetylcholine may act either indirectly by antagonizing the effects of catecholamines (Inui and Imamura, 1977; Bailey et al., 1979; Biegon and Pappano, 1980), or directly, independent of the presence of adrenergic tone (Rardon and Bailey, 1983b). Although ventricular myocytes show no changes in action potential characteristics with muscarinic cholinergic stimulation, in specialized ventricular conducting tissue, acetylcholine affects automaticity and conduction (Bailey et al., 1972; Tse et al., 1976; Gadsby et al., 1978). The effects of acetylcholine on the action potentials of Purkinje fibers appear to be species dependent and variable. Microelectrode studies have shown the action potentials of Purkinje fibers to prolong (Carmeliet and Ramon, 1980; Lipsius and Gibbons, 1980), show no change (Bailey et al., 1979), or shorten (Gadsby et al., 1978; Mubagwa and Carmeliet, 1983), on exposure to acetylcholine. Stimulation of vagal nerves in the experimental animal alters ventricular refractoriness (Blair et al., 1980; Martins and Zipes, 1980), and vagal tone may exert a significant effect on ventricular refractoriness in man, as well (Prystowsky et al., 1981). Conversely, ablation of specific parasympathetic fibers to the heart can eliminate the effects of truncal vagal stimulation on atrial and ventricular contractile response (Randall et al., 1983). Thus, either augmentation or withdrawal of vagal input can influence cardiac function.

After complete interruption of vagal input, a rapid decrease in the biochemical markers of parasympathetic activity occurs (Brown, 1976; Lund et al., 1978, 1979). The fact that the application of physostigmine to atrial tissue following bilateral cervical vagotomy produces no effect provides a physiological correlate for the observation that vagotomy depletes tissue stores of acetylcholine.

After bilateral cervical vagotomy, the effect of acetylcholine on atrial action potential duration is exaggerated. We define exaggerated to mean that, although the threshold concentration necessary to elicit a response does not appear to be changed, the magnitude of the response is increased. This is in contrast to the classical supersensitivity of denervated structures to neurotransmitters, in which the threshold concentration is decreased, but the maximum effect is unchanged (Cannon and Rosenblueth, 1936).

No conclusions can be rendered from these experiments concerning the changes in ionic currents

TABLE 3
Action Potential Duration Shortening Produced by Acetylcholine in Cat Ventricle after Bilateral Cervical Vagotomy

	Acetylcholine concentration							
	0		10^{-7} M		10^{-6} M		10^{-5} M	
	APD_{50}	APD_{90}	APD_{50}	APD_{90}	APD_{50}	APD_{90}	APD_{50}	APD_{90}
BCV (n = 11)	140 ± 4	179 ± 4	133 ± 6	172 ± 4	114 ± 6	160 ± 3	106 ± 7	150 ± 7
BCV + 10^{-6} M propranolol (n = 4)	136 ± 8	180 ± 7	130 ± 7	175 ± 8	118 ± 9	160 ± 5	105 ± 10	115 ± 10
BCV + reserpine (n = 7)	147 ± 6	175 ± 10	138 ± 5	169 ± 4	120 ± 7	155 ± 8	109 ± 6	145 ± 8

All results are expressed in msec, means ± SE. BCV = Bilateral cervical vagotomy.

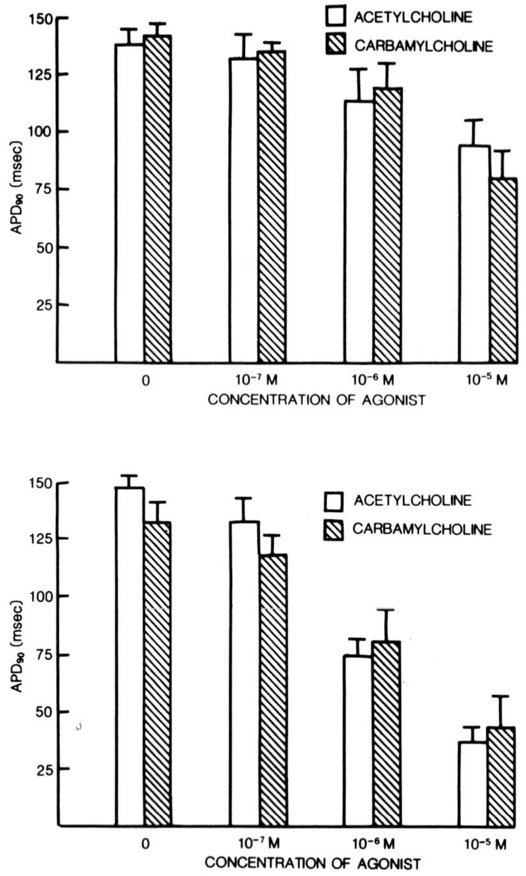

FIGURE 3. *A comparison of the effect of carbamylcholine, a nonhydrolyzed choline ester, and ACh on atrial action potential duration. The top panel illustrates values from cats with intact vagi. There is no significant difference in the action potential duration shortening produced by the two drugs. The bottom panel illustrates values from cats after BCV. Note first that there is an exaggerated response to each cholinergic agonist when compared to the cats with intact vagi. In addition, there is no significant difference in the action potential duration shortening produced by the two drugs in cats after BCV.*

responsible for the observed change in action potential duration of atrial and ventricular muscle. However, the effects of acetylcholine on normally innervated atrial muscle are mediated through an increase in membrane potassium conductance (Trautwein et al., 1956); thus an exaggerated effect of acetylcholine could be expected to be mediated through this mechanism. It is interesting to note that the hyperpolarization of resting membrane potential produced by acetylcholine was not significantly changed after bilateral cervical vagotomy. The dissociation of these two manifestations of altered potassium conductance may suggest that altered sensitivity to acetylcholine is not simply an amplification of the normal increase in potassium flux seen in cholinergic stimulation.

Previous studies have shown that enhanced sensitivity to acetylcholine may be seen in the presence of simultaneous adrenergic stimulation (Levy, 1971; Inui and Imamura, 1977; Bailey et al., 1979; Biegon and Pappano, 1980). Although the results of our ventricular experiments could be due to this type of interaction, the effects of acetylcholine remained intact with β-receptor blockade in vitro, or with depletion of endogenous catecholamines prior to sacrifice. These results lead us to conclude that the observed effects of acetylcholine in the ventricle were due to direct effects of muscarinic cholinergic stimulation. The demonstration of direct muscarinic cholinergic effects on action potential duration in ventricular muscle is important in further defining the functional significance of parasympathetic innervation of the ventricle. Despite multiple lines of evidence demonstrating vagal input to mammalian ventricle, direct effects of muscarinic cholinergic agonists on ventricular action potential characteristics have been demonstrated in only one species, the guinea pig (Ochi and Hino, 1978). Our data suggest that, at least under the specific conditions of our experiments, the cellular and subcellular components necessary to translate muscarinic cholinergic stimuli into a direct effect on cellular action potentials exist in mammalian ventricular myocardium.

Altered sensitivity to acetylcholine after bilateral cervical vagotomy could occur through several mechanisms. Decreased hydrolysis of acetylcholine

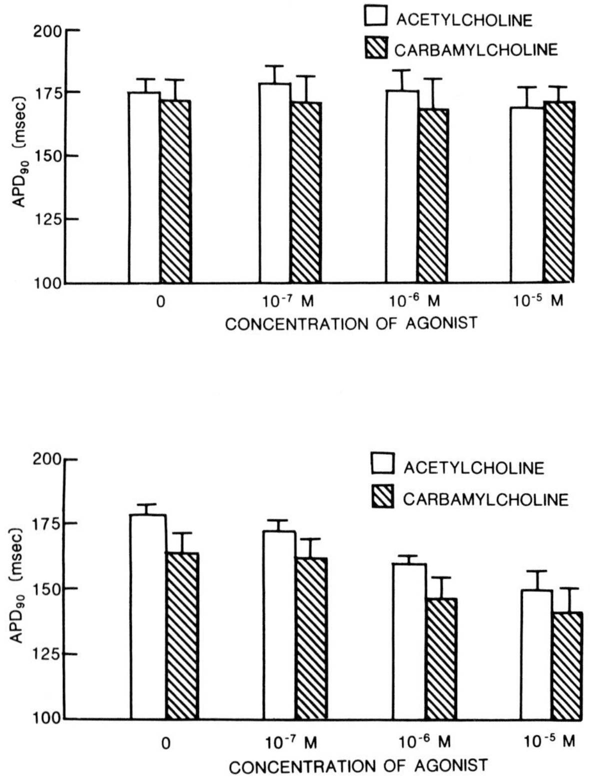

FIGURE 4. *A comparison of the effect of carbamylcholine and acetylcholine on ventricular action potential duration. Top panel illustrates values from cats with intact vagi. Neither agonist produces a significant effect on APD. The bottom panel illustrates values from cats after BCV. Both agonists shorten APD. There was no statistically significant difference in the APD shortening produced by the two drugs in cats after BCV.*

following bilateral cervical vagotomy could increase the functional concentration of acetylcholine at its receptor and produce a greater physiological response. This possibility is unlikely, due to the fact that carbamylcholine produces the same exaggerated effects on action potential duration as does acetylcholine. Thus, the effects of muscarinic cholinergic agonists after bilateral cervical vagotomy are not dependent on the rate of hydrolysis of acetylcholine.

Complications related to the surgical procedure could be the cause for altered sensitivity to acetylcholine after bilateral cervical vagotomy. Two possible complications of a neck dissection, hypothyroidism and hypoxia, have been shown to alter the number of muscarinic cholinergic receptors in the heart as measured by radioligand-binding techniques (Sharma and Banerjee, 1977; Crockatt et al., 1981). It is unlikely that the consequences of a surgical procedure other than vagotomy are responsible for our results, however, since sham-operated animals responded to acetylcholine in a manner identical to nonoperated animals.

Denervation supersensitivity following vagal transection is another possible mechanism. Organs become supersensitive to their neurotransmitters after denervation (Cannon, 1949). Although this is an attractive hypothesis, data from other investigators would argue against this interpretation of our experiments. The denervated mammalian heart shows supersensitivity to exogenous catecholamines (Cooper, 1965; Spann et al., 1966; Dempsey and Cooper, 1968). However, both total cardiac denervation and selective parasympathectomy of the heart fail to produce supersensitivity to the effects of acetylcholine on contractility or heart rate in vivo (Jacobs et al., 1974; Hageman et al., 1975; Priola and Spurgeon, 1977). The heart may be an exception to Cannon's "law of denervation," since extrinsic cardiac denervation does not alter the intrinsic postganglionic parasympathetic neurons (Priola et al., 1977; Priola and Spurgeon, 1977), leaving the heart decentralized but not denervated with respect to this limb of the autonomic nervous system. Bilateral cervical vagotomy also decentralizes the heart from parasympathetic influence, leaving the intrinsic nerves intact. A failure to denervate the heart does not completely eliminate supersensitivity as an explanation for our results, however, since organs can show an increase in sensitivity to neurotransmitter following decentralization (Cannon and Rosenblueth, 1936).

Denervation or decentralization supersensitivity might be expected to be due to an increase in muscarinic receptor number or affinity at the cell surface. Although chronic exposure to cholinergic agonists has been shown to decrease the receptor number in cultured cells (Halvorson and Nathanson, 1981), receptor numbers have not been determined in the heart following withdrawal of cholinergic tone. In addition, simple determination of receptor numbers may not be sufficient to determine whether the receptors are capable of mediating a physiological response at the cell level. Thus, chronic bilateral cervical vagotomy in the cat could alter responsiveness to acetylcholine at the level of the receptor, at the level of receptor effector coupling, or at both levels.

We wish to acknowledge the excellent technical assistance of David Mendel and the excellent secretarial work of Carmen Mason and Christy Jones.

Supported in part by the Herman C. Krannert Fund, and by Grants HL06308 and HL07182 from the National Heart, Lung, and Blood Institute, National Institutes of Health.

Dr. Kovacs is a U.S. Public Health Service Trainee in Cardiology.

Address for reprints: John C. Bailey, M.D., Indiana University School of Medicine, Krannert Institute of Cardiology, 1001 W. 10th Street, Indianapolis, Indiana 46202.

Received April 24, 1984; accepted for publication December 20, 1984.

References

Bailey JC, Greenspan K, Elizari MV, Anderson GJ, Fisch C (1972) Effects of acetylcholine on automaticity and conduction in the proximal portion of the His-Purkinje specialized conduction system in the dog. Circ Res **30:** 210–216

Bailey JC, Watanabe AM, Besch HR Jr, Lathrop DA (1979) Acetylcholine antagonism of the electrophysiological effects of isoproterenol on canine cardiac Purkinje fibers. Circ Res **44:** 378–383

Biegon RL, Pappano AJ (1980) Dual mechanism for inhibition of calcium dependent action potentials by acetylcholine in avian ventricular muscle: Relationship to cyclic AMP. Circ Res **46:** 353–362

Blair RW, Shimizu T, Bishop VS (1980) The role of vagal afferents in the reflex control of the left ventricular refractory period in the cat. Circ Res **46:** 378–386

Brown OM (1976) Cat heart acetylcholine: Structural proof and distribution. Am J Physiol **231:** 781–785

Cannon WB (1949) The Supersensitivity of Denervated Structures. New York, Macmillan

Cannon WB, Rosenblueth A (1936) The sensitization of a sympathetic ganglion by preganglionic denervation. Am J Physiol **116:** 408–413

Carmeliet E, Ramon J (1980) Electrophysiological effects of acetylcholine in sheep cardiac Purkinje fibers. Pflugers Arch **387:** 197–205

Cooper T (1965) Physiologic and pharmacologic effects of cardiac denervation (abstr). Fed Proc **24:** 1428

Crockatt LH, Lund DD, Schmid PG, Roskoski R (1981) Hypoxia induced changes in parasympathetic neurochemical markers in guinea pig heart. J Appl Physiol **50:** 1017–1021

Daggett NM, Nugent CG, Cau PW, Powers PC, Harada Y (1967) Influence of vagal stimulation on ventricular contractility, O_2 consumption and coronary flows. Am J Physiol **212:** 8–18

Dahlstrom A, Haggendahl J (1966) Recovery of noradrenaline levels after reserpine compared with the lifespan of amine storage granules in rat and rabbit. J Pharm Pharmacol **18:** 750–751

DeGeest H, Levy MN, Zieske H, Lipman RI (1965) Depression of ventricular contractility by stimulation of the vagus nerves. Circ Res **17:** 222–225

Dempsey PJ, Cooper T (1968) Supersensitivity of the chronically denervated feline heart. Am J Physiol **215:** 1245–1249

Gadsby DC, Wit AL, Cranefield PF (1978) The effects of acetylcholine on the electrical activity of canine cardiac Purkinje fibers. Circ Res **43:** 29–35

Hageman GR, Urthaler F, James TN (1975) Absence of supersensitivity to acetylcholine in the extrinsically denervated sinus

node (abstr). Physiologist **18:** 236
Halvorsen SW, Nathanson NM (1981) In vivo regulation of muscarinic acetylcholine receptor number and function in embryonic chick heart. J Biol Chem **256:** 7941–7948
Hoffman BF, Cranefield PF (1960) Electrophysiology of the Heart. New York, McGraw-Hill
Hoffman BF, Suckling EE (1953) Cardiac cellular potentials: Effects of vagal stimulation and acetylcholine. Am J Physiol **173:** 312–320
Inui J, Imamura H (1977) Effects of acetylcholine on calcium-dependent electrical and mechanical response in the guinea pig papillary muscle partially depolarized by potassium. Naunyn Schmiedebergs Arch Pharmacol **299:** 1–7
Jacobowitz D, Cooper T, Barner H (1967) Histochemical and chemical studies of the localization of adrenergic and cholinergic nerves in normal and denervated cat hearts. Circ Res **20:** 289–298
Jacobs HK, Randall WC, Kaye MP (1974) Responses of the parasympathectomized canine heart to neurochemical stimulation (abstr). Physiologist **17:** 254
Kent KM, Epstein SE, Cooper T, Jacobowitz DM (1974) Cholinergic innervation of the canine and human ventricular conducting system. Circ Res **50:** 948–955
Levy MN (1971) Sympathetic-parasympathetic interactions in the heart. Circ Res **29:** 437–445
Levy MN, NG M, Martin P, Zieske H (1966) Sympathetic and parasympathetic interactions upon the left ventricle of the dog. Circ Res **19:** 5–10
Lipsius SL, Gibbons WR (1980) Acetylcholine lengthens action potentials of sheep cardiac Purkinje fibers. Am J Physiol **238:** H237–H243
Lund DD, Schmid PG, Kelley SD, Corry RJ, Roskoski R (1978) Choline acetyltransferase in rat heart after transplantation. Am J Physiol **235:** H367–H371
Lund DD, Schmid PG, Roskoski R (1979) Choline acetyltransferase activity in rat and guinea pig heart following vagotomy. Am J Physiol **236:** H620–H623
Martins JB, Zipes DP (1980) Effects of sympathetic and vagal nerves on recovery properties of the endocardium and epicardium of the canine left ventricle. Circ Res **46:** 100–110
Mirro MJ, Watanabe AM, Bailey JC (1980a) Electrophysiological effects of disopyramide and quinidine on guinea pig atria and canine cardiac Purkinje fibers. Circ Res **46:** 660–668
Mirro MJ, Manalan AS, Bailey JC, Watanabe AM (1980b) Anticholinergic effects of disopyramide and quinidine on guinea pig myocardium. Circ Res **47:** 855–865
Mubagwa K, Carmeliet E (1983) Effects of acetylcholine on electrophysiological properties of rabbit cardiac Purkinje fibers. Circ Res **53:** 740–751
Nonidez JF (1939) Studies on the innervation of the heart. Am J Anat **65:** 361–413
Nonidez JF (1943) The structure and innervation of the conductive system of the heart of the dog and rhesus monkey as seen with silver impregnation techniques. Am Heart J **26:** 577–597
Ochi R, Hino N (1978) Depression of slow inward current by acetylcholine in mammalian ventricular muscle. Proc Jpn Acad **54(B):** 474–477
Priola DV, Spurgeon HA (1977) Cholinergic sensitivity of the denervated canine heart. Circ Res **41:** 600–606
Priola DV, Spurgeon HA, Geis WF (1977) The intrinsic innervation of the canine heart: A functional study. Circ Res **40:** 50–56
Prystowsky EN, Jackman WM, Rinkenberger RL, Heger JJ, Zipes DP (1981) Effect of autonomic blockade on ventricular refractoriness and atrioventricular nodal conduction in humans. Circ Res **49:** 511–518
Randall WC, Thomas JX, Barber MJ, Rickenman LE (1983) Selective denervation of the heart. Am J Physiol **244:** H607–H613
Rardon DP, Bailey JC (1983a) Parasympathetic effects on electrophysiologic properties of cardiac ventricular tissue. J Am Coll Cardiol **2:** 1200–1209
Rardon DP, Bailey JC (1983b) Direct effects of cholinergic stimulation on ventricular automaticity in guinea pig myocardium. Circ Res **52:** 105–110
Roskoski R, Mayer HE, Schmid PG (1974) Choline acetyltransferase activity in guinea pig heart in vitro. J Neurochem **23:** 1197–1200
Sarnoff SJ, Brockman SK, Gilmore JP, Linden RJ, Mitchell JH (1960) Regulation of ventricular contraction: Influence of cardiac sympathetic and vagal nerve stimulation on atrial and ventricular dynamics. Circ Res **9:** 1108
Sharma VK, Banerjee SP (1977) Muscarinic cholinergic receptors in rat heart. J Biol Chem **252:** 7444–7446
Spann JF, Sonnenblick EH, Cooper T, Chidsey CA, Willman VL, Braunwald E (1966) Cardiac norepinephrine stores and the contractile state of heart muscle. Circ Res **19:** 317–325
Trautwein W, Kuffler SW, and Edwards C (1956) Changes in membrane characteristics of heart muscle during inhibition. J Gen Physiol **40:** 135–145
Tse WW, Han J, Yoon M (1976) Effect of acetylcholine on automaticity of canine Purkinje fibers. Am J Physiol **173:** 312–320
Wallenstein S, Zucker CL, Fleiss JL (1980) Some statistical methods useful in circulation research. Circ Res **47:** 1–9
Webb JL (1950) Action of acetylcholine on the rabbit auricle. Br J Pharmacol **5:** 335
Wit AL, Hoffman BF, Rosen MR (1975) Electrophysiology and pharmacology of cardiac arrhythmias. IX. Cardiac electrophysiologic effects of beta adrenergic stimulation and blockade. Am Heart J **90:** 521–533

INDEX TERMS: Acetylcholine • Vagus nerve • Electrophysiology • Muscarinic receptor

Comparative Vascular Pharmacology of the Atriopeptins

Korekiyo Wakitani, Takeshi Oshima, Arthur D. Loewy, Sandra W. Holmberg, Barbara R. Cole, Steven P. Adams, Kam F. Fok, Mark G. Currie, and Philip Needleman

From the Washington University School of Medicine, Departments of Pharmacology, Anatomy, and Neurobiology and Pediatrics, St. Louis, Missouri, and Monsanto Research Laboratories, St. Louis, Missouri

SUMMARY. The atriopeptins are potent relaxants of norepinephrine-constricted aortic strips or are dilators of renal blood vessels in isolated perfused rat kidneys that are constricted by norepinephrine. This vasorelaxant property of the atriopeptins requires the presence of phenylalanine arginine (i.e., atriopeptin II, III, or ser-leu-arg-arg atriopeptin III) residues in the carboxy terminus which are considerably more effective than atriopeptin I (the 21 amino acid peptide which lacks the phe-arg C-terminus) or the core peptide (residues 3–19). However, these artificially in vitro precontracted preparations do not accurately predict the vascular effectiveness of the atriopeptins in intact rats. Intravenous administration of the atriopeptins (including atriopeptin I) to anesthetized rats produces concentration-dependent hypotension, a selective decrease in renal resistance in low doses (determined with microspheres), and pronounced diuresis. At higher doses, atriopeptins increase blood flow in other vascular beds. On the other hand, in the anesthetized dog, injection (intraarterially) of the phe-arg-containing peptides produces a concentration-dependent increase in both renal blood flow and sodium excretion, whereas atriopeptin I is inactive. Although there is a species difference in responsiveness to atriopeptin I, these data demonstrate a direct correlation between the renal vasodilation and diuresis produced by this novel family of atrial peptides. **(*Circ Res 56: 621–627, 1985*)**

THE pioneering observation of deBold and his colleagues (1981) that intravenous administration of atrial extracts in rats resulted in pronounced natriuresis-diuresis elicited extensive interest in the isolation and characterization of the intrinsic substance causing the response. Within the course of several months, a number of laboratories reported the purification and amino acid sequence of a family of small peptides ranging in size from 19–33 amino acids which were derived from atrial extracts and which possessed biological activity (Flynn et al., 1983; Currie et al., 1984a; Kangawa and Matsuo, 1984; Geller et al., 1984; Napier et al., 1984; Misono et al., 1984; Seidah et al., 1984). All these peptides exhibited the same core sequence of 17 amino acids within a cystine disulfide bridge, but differed in their N- and C-termini. The high molecular weight peptide fraction was demonstrated to be the precursor of the more active low molecular peptides (Currie et al., 1984B; and Trippodo et al., 1984), and purification and sequence analysis indicated that the biologically active fragment was at the C-terminus (Geller et al., 1984; Thibault et al., 1984; Kangawa et al., 1984; Lazure et al., 1984). Oligonucleotide probes were prepared from the sequenced peptide and were utilized to clone the appropriate cDNA (Yamanaka et al., 1984; Maki et al., 1984; Oikawa et al., 1984; Seidman et al., 1984).

The natriuretic and diuretic effectiveness of these peptides has been extensively described. Another prominent biological effect of the atrial peptides is their ability to act as vasorelaxants when tested on isolated blood vessel segments (Currie et al., 1983; Geller et al., 1984; Currie et al., 1984a). Furthermore, the atrial peptides reduce renal resistance in blood autoperfused rat kidneys (Oshima et al., 1984) and in vivo in conscious trained unanesthetized dogs (Hintze et al., 1984).

Knowledge of the structure of the atrial peptides allowed the production of synthetic peptides for more extensive biological testing. The demonstration of reduced content of biologically active peptide in the atria of spontaneous hypertensive rats (Sonnenberg et al., 1983) or in syrian hamsters with cardiomyopathy (Chimoskey et al., 1984) implies that a deficiency of circulating atrial peptide may be related to the disease process and suggests the possibility for replacement therapy. In the present study, several of the naturally occurring peptides were subjected to structure-activity and dose-response analyses in a variety of in vitro and in vivo preparations. The selection of peptides for our study was based on our initial finding that there were two groups of substances that we had sequenced which had minor differences in length and which elicited different biological effects (Currie et al., 1984A; Geller et al., 1984). We termed the low molecular weight substances "atriopeptins" (AP) (Currie et al., 1984a). Atriopeptin I contains 21 amino acid residues possessing a core 17 amino acid ring enclosed within a cystine disulfide ring with an N-terminal ser-ser extension and a C-terminal asn-ser terminal. Atriopeptin I (API) relaxes intestinal smooth muscle strips, but is impotent on blood vessel segments (Currie et al., 1984a). In this study, we evaluated one N-terminal- and two C-terminal-extended atrial peptides that were isolated from rat atria. Atriopeptin II and III (APII and APIII) are vasodilators which contain 23 and 24 amino acid residues with a phe-arg or a phe-arg-tyr C-terminal extension of API, respectively. We also studied the N-terminal-extended peptide originally characterized by Flynn et al. (1983) which we term ser-leu-arg-arg-APIII (SLRR-APIII). From such quantitative and qualitative studies, the utility of exogenously administered atrial peptides for therapeutic advantage can be evaluated.

Methods

Materials

The atrial peptides studied were prepared by solid-phase peptide synthesis (Merrifield et al., 1963), and their structures were confirmed by amino acid analysis and verified by gas-phase sequence analysis.

Procedures

Smooth Muscle Preparations

Strips obtained from the thoracic aorta of anesthetized (pentobarbital) rabbits were continuously bathed by superfusion with Krebs-Henseleit media (10 ml/min). The strips were contracted with norepinephrine, and application of atriopeptins caused a concentration-dependent relaxation, as originally described (Currie et al., 1983, 1984).

Isolated Perfused Rat Kidney Preparation

Sprague-Dawley rats (300–500 g) were anesthetized with pentobarbital sodium (30 mg/kg, ip) and heparinized (1000 U/kg, iv). The renal artery was cannulated with PE 50 tubing (I.D., 0.59 mm), and the kidney was removed from the animal and attached to a non-recirculating perfusion system of oxygenated (O_2/CO_2-95%/5%) Krebs-Henseleit medium at 37°C flowing at 8 ml/min at a basal perfusion pressure of 60–80 mm Hg. With a constant flow of perfusion media, measurement of renal pressure provides an indication of renal resistance changes. Renal pressure was elevated to 140 mm Hg by the continuous infusion of 10 ng/ml of norepinephrine.

Rat Blood Pressure Experiments

Female Sprague-Dawley rats (200 g) were anesthetized with pentobarbital sodium (30 mg/kg, ip). The blood pressure was recorded with a Statham blood pressure transducer and a Beckman R511 recorded via a femoral artery cannula (PE50). The animals were maintained on a continuous infusion of 5% dextrose, 0.225% NaCl at 26 μl/min.

Microsphere Technique

Male Sprague-Dawley rats (350–450 g) were anesthetized with pentobarbital sodium (35 mg/kg, ip). The trachea was intubated and the rats were ventilated with a Harvard rat respirator. A cannula (tapered PE50 tubing) for microsphere injection was inserted into the right carotid artery and advanced into the left ventricle, with the location of the tip of cannula being confirmed by the pressure tracing and by autopsy. The jugular and femoral veins were cannulated for infusion of test materials and blood. The brachial and femoral arteries were cannulated for recording blood pressure and for withdrawing a reference blood sample. Blood pressure and heart rates (measured from the pulse pressure with a Grass 7P44 cardiotachometer) were recorded on a Grass model 7 polygraph.

Microsphere injections were performed according to the method described by Stanek et al. (1983, 1984). Dry carbonized microspheres (New England Nuclear) 16.0 ± 0.3 μm in diameter and labeled with ^{51}Cr or ^{57}Co, were suspended in an 84% dextrose solution containing several drops of 0.05% Tween 80, dispersed by ultrasonication, and mixed on a vortex shaker for 3 minutes before infusion. A 0.1-ml suspension of the ^{51}Cr microspheres was transferred to a 70-cm length of coiled PE-50 tubing, and the number of microspheres was determined by gamma counting (Tracor 1191 gamma counter). A coincidence loss of 11.5% was calculated for counts exceeding 100,000 counts/min, and the necessary corrections were made to compensate for this error. The microsphere coil then was connected to the left ventricular cannula and flushed with 0.5 ml heparinized-saline for 60 seconds with a Gilford infusion pump. A reference sample of blood (1 ml) was withdrawn at 1 ml/min beginning 10 seconds before microsphere injection was begun. Simultaneously, 0.5 ml of heparinized rat blood was infused intravenously to compensate for the blood loss. To minimize geometric counting error, the reference blood sample was mixed with 1.0 ml of a 20% hot gelatin solution and its radioactivity was determined. Then the atrial peptide was infused intravenously for 5 minutes, at which time the ^{57}Co microspheres were administered. At the end of the experiment, the rat was killed with an overdose of pentobarbital sodium, and the organs were excised, blotted on gauze, and placed into preweighed plastic tubes for counting of radioactivity. The blood samples were used as reference flows in the calculation of cardiac outputs and organ flow, as previously described (Stanek et al., 1984). A computer (VAX 11/780) was used to correct the counts for interaction between the two isotopes, as well as to calculate tissue flow (ml/min per g) and regional vascular resistance. Paired Student's t-test was used to determine the level of statistical significance, comparing the pretreatment data with the treatment data (at 5 minutes of atriopeptin infusion) for each rat. Thus, each value served as its own control, and P values were determined for five animals in each group.

Rat Diuresis Studies

Anesthetized (pentobarbital sodium, 30 mg/kg, ip) female rats (200 ± 20 g) were infused with 0.15 ml/min of a saline:5% dextrose mixture via a jugular vein cannula. After the animals were permitted 1 hour of equilibration time to recover from the catheter insertion and to allow volume expansion, urine was collected via a urethral catheter at 10-minute intervals. The peptides were administered intravenously as a bolus injection. The peak response to the administered peptide was exhibited in the first 10 minutes, and recovery was complete by the 30-minute collection. The diuretic response to the peptides was reported as the total volume collected in 30 minutes.

Canine Renal Function Experiments

Mongrel dogs (8–16 kg) were anesthetized with pentobarbital sodium (30 mg/kg, iv), and the trachea was intubated with a cuffed endotracheal tube connected to a Harvard respirator. Blood pressure (femoral artery cannulation) and heart rate were recorded on a Beckman recorder. A continuous infusion (1.2 ml/min) of saline was delivered into the cannulated brachial vein. The renal artery was exposed via a retroperitoneal incision, and renal blood flow was measured with a 2.5-mm (i.d.) electromagnetic flow probe (Carolina Instrument Flowmeter). A 22-gauge needle attached to PE-50 tubing was introduced into the right renal artery distal to the flow probe for infusions of peptide. The ureter was catheterized with PE-160 tubing (1.14 mm, i.d.) for urine collection at 5-minute intervals in a fraction collector. Urinary electrolytes were measured by flame photometry.

Results

Spasmolytic Properties of The Atrial Peptides

The relative potency of the atrial peptides as blood vessel relaxants is shown in Figure 1. The presence of the phe-arg C-terminus appears to be a critical determinant of vasorelaxant activity. Thus APII, APIII, and SLRR-APIII are extremely potent compounds. C-terminus truncation of either the arg (des arg-APII) or the phe-arg (API) decreases vascular potency, compared to APII, by 10- and 100-fold, respectively. The N- and C-terminal truncated core peptide (residues 3–19) is essentially inactive as a vascular relaxant, and it does not exhibit inhibitory activity against the active atriopeptins. SLRR-APIII (i.e., the N-terminal extension of APIII) facilitated the vascular spasmolytic activity.

Isolated Krebs-Perfused Rat Kidney

The isolated perfused rat kidney was employed for the quantitative and qualitative evaluation of the naturally occurring atrial peptides on renal vasculature, independent of any non-renal or plasma hydrolysis of the atriopeptins or neuronal or extrarenal hormonal influences. The advantage of using the perfused kidney over the isolated aorta strip is that changes in pressure in the intact organ directly reflect alterations in resistance vessels, and, furthermore, the kidney is a likely target organ for the atrial peptides. Consistent with the data obtained on the isolated rabbit aorta strips, the phe-arg-containing atrial peptides (APII, III, and SLRR-APIII) were potent renal vasodilator substances (Fig. 2). Loss of the C-terminal phe-arg residues (i.e., API and the 3–19 core peptide) caused a 90% reduction in potency.

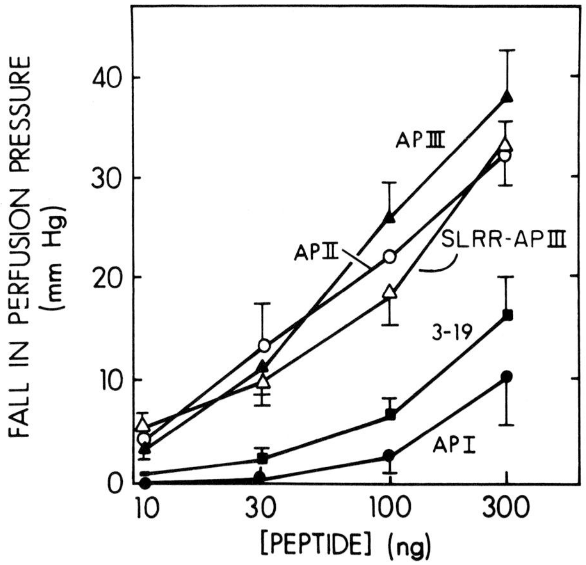

FIGURE 2. *Comparative vasodilator potency of the naturally occurring, low molecular weight atriopeptins in the isolated perfused rat kidney. The values represent the mean ± SEM (n = 5). For comparison, a 10-μg dose of glyceryltrinitrate (GTN) caused a 24 ± 7 mm Hg (n = 5) fall in renal perfusion pressure.*

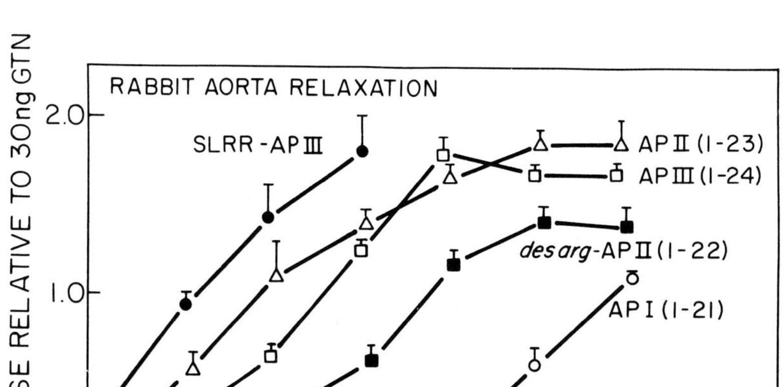

FIGURE 1. *The blood vessel relaxant potency of the atrial peptides. Rabbit thoracic aorta strips were precontracted with norepinephrine (2 × 10^{-9} M) and calibrated by performing a glyceryl trinitrate (GTN) dose-response curve. The atriopeptin responses were compared to the 30-ng GTN response (ED_{50}) which corrected for the differences in sensitivity between different aorta strips. The values are the mean ± SEM (n = 5). The following abbreviations were employed: GTN-glyceryl trinitrate (nitroglycerin); API (1-21)-atriopeptin I, the 21 amino acid peptide which serves as the basis for a comparative numbering and nomenclature system; APII and APIII are extensions of API containing phe-arg or phe-arg-tyr, respectively, added to the C-terminus of API. SLRR-APIII indicates atriopeptin III with tetrapeptide N-terminal extension of ser-leu-arg-arg; 3–19 indicates the 17 amino acid core peptide contained within the cystine disulfide ring thus lacking the ser-ser from the N-terminal and the asn-ser from the C-terminal of API; and des arg-APII (1–22), which lacks the arg C-terminal of APII.*

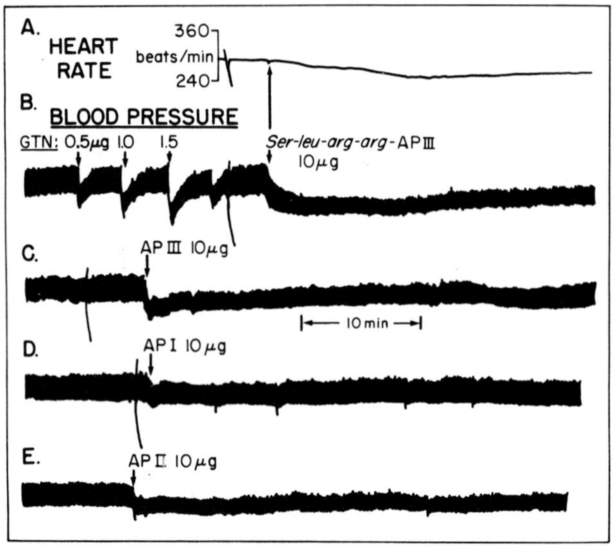

FIGURE 3. *Blood pressure tracings of pentobarbital-anesthetized rats treated with bolus injections (iv) of atrial peptide. Each blood pressure tracing is from a separate rat (200 g, female). In each case, a nitroglycerin (GTN) dose-response curve was performed to standardize the preparation. Tracing A represents the heart rate tracing obtained simultaneously with the blood pressure curve in tracing B, which indicated the vasodepressor response to SLRR-APIII that was associated with a modest bradycardia.*

Rat Blood Pressure Experiments

Intravenous administration of up to 50 μg/kg APIII to an unanesthetized, untrained, normal rat did not cause a change in blood pressure or heart rate. We subsequently found that the atriopeptins elicited a hypotensive effect in pentobarbital- anesthesized rats. The blood pressure tracing from four separate animals treated with nitroglycerin exhibited a dose-dependent but transient hypotension; however, bolus injections (iv) of the atrial peptides produced a sustained hypotensive response that was not accompanied by a tachycardia (Fig. 3). The atriopeptins tested produced a parallel dose-response curve requiring a threshold dose of 20 μg/kg (iv) to elicit a 10–18 mm Hg fall in blood pressure, and a maximum hypotensive effect was achieved with 300–500 μg/kg of the various atrial peptides. There was no significant quantitative difference in the potency of the initial hypotensive response to bolus injections of the atriopeptins (Table 1). However, structural features of the peptides clearly influenced the duration of the hypotensive response. SLRR-APIII, APIII, and APII (i.e., the phe-arg-containing peptides) were extremely long lasting, compared to nitroglycerin, and required more than an hour to recover to control (preinjection) blood pressure levels following a 50 μg/kg injection (iv) of the peptide (Table 1). On the other hand, the truncated peptides (lacking the phe-arg C-terminus) API and the 3–19 core peptide were more transient hypotensives, requiring 35 and 15 minutes, respectively to recover to control values (Table 1).

TABLE 1
The Comparative Vasodepressor Potency and Duration of Action of Atrial Peptides* in Pentobarbital-Anesthetized Rats

Peptide	*n*	Fall in blood pressure (mm Hg)	Duration of action (min)
SLRR-APIII	4	36 ± 9	68 ± 6
APIII	4	29 ± 7	77 ± 11
APII	5	40 ± 6	64 ± 13
API	4	30 ± 10	34 ± 9
3–19	4	31 ± 4	16 ± 2

* 50 μg/kg bolus iv injection. The duration of action represents the time required for the blood pressure to return to pretreatment control levels following the 50 μg/kg (iv) injection. The abbreviations are listed in the legend for Figure 1, and the values are the mean ± SEM.

Changes in Regional Blood Flow

We selected API, APIII, and SLRR-APIII, because of their varying N- and C-terminal extensions, for more extensive study of regional vascular changes as measured by microsphere studies in anesthetized rats. Use of anesthetized animals permits comparison to the blood pressure studies and reduces variability. We observed a blood flow for the whole organs of 0.5–1.5 ml/min for brain, stomach, spleen, skin (flow/10 g), skeletal muscle (flow/10 g), large intestine, and cecum; 4–5 ml/min for liver and heart (7% of cardiac output); 7 ml/min for each kidney (i.e., approximately 10% of the cardiac output to each kidney); and 9.5 ml/min for the small intestine. In these experiments, the first injection of ^{51}Cr microspheres was given before drug treatment, thereby permitting the animal to serve as its own control. Then the test compound was infused for 5 minutes, which permitted the development of a stable hemodynamic response, and during the peptide infusion, the ^{57}Co microspheres were injected. Table 2 presents the detailed analysis of the effect of a 5 μg/kg per min infusion of APIII on regional vascular blood flow per gram of tissue. This dose of peptide produced a 15 mm Hg fall in blood pressure, with little effect on cardiac output. The stomach and intestine exhibited a significant reduction in blood flow, but when the fall of blood pressure was taken into account, only slight changes in vascular resistance were noted, and the kidney was the only vascular bed which showed a significant reduction in resistance (Table 2). Infusion of a higher concentration of APIII (i.e., 30 μg/kg per min for 5 minutes) resulted in a greater fall in blood pressure, an enhanced renal blood flow, and a marked reduction in renal resistance (Table 3), as well as a significant decrease in brain, heart, and skin resistance (data not shown). In the anesthetized rat, API produced a selective renal vasodilation analogous to that achieved with APIII. SLRR-APIII at 1 μg/kg per min caused only renal vasodilation; however, at 5 μg/kg per min, a

TABLE 2
The Regional Blood Flow and Vascular Resistance of Pentobarbital-Anesthetized Rats after an Intravenous Infusion of APIII

	Tissue flow (ml/min per g)		Vascular resistance (mm Hg/min per g per ml)	
Regions	−APIII	+APIII	−APIII	+APIII
Brain	0.74 ± 0.13	0.78 ± 0.16	204 ± 48	185 ± 52
Heart	3.37 ± 0.43	3.19 ± 0.31	36 ± 3.2	36.1 ± 3.0
Stomach	0.40 ± 0.06	0.32 ± 0.05*	332 ± 31	366 ± 38
Small intestine	1.88 ± 0.21	1.60 ± 0.15*	75.4 ± 11.1	74.4 ± 11.1
Large intestine	0.64 ± 0.09	0.59 ± 0.08	214 ± 28	201 ± 22
Cecum	1.67 ± 0.33	1.39 ± 0.24	86.6 ± 16.1	89.2 ± 12.4
Kidney	4.41 ± 0.46	4.96 ± 0.41†	29.4 ± 2.0	22.9 ± 0.9†
Spleen	1.73 ± 0.49	1.03 ± 0.29	113 ± 36	194 ± 85
Liver	0.38 ± 0.04	0.37 ± 0.04	351 ± 52	332 ± 56
Skeletal M	0.052 ± 0.01	0.05 ± 0.01	3137 ± 630	3294 ± 791
Skin	0.057 ± 0.014	0.06 ± 0.01	2992 ± 741	2358 ± 357

The values obtained from the microsphere experiments are the means ± SEM for five animals (419 ± 9 g). Each animal served as its own control. The blood pressure was 127 ± 8 and 112 ± 7* mm Hg before and during the 5-minute infusion of APIII at 5 μg/kg per min. Neither the heart rate (392 beats/min control vs. 387 beats/min with APIII) nor the cardiac output (83 ± 12 ml/min control vs. 76 ± 10 ml/min with APIII) changed significantly during the infusion of the peptide.

* $P < 0.05$.

† $P < 0.01$ (paired *t*-test).

pronounced blood pressure reduction was elicited that blunted the increase in renal blood flow, although there also was a significant decrease in vascular resistance in the kidney (Table 3), as well as in skeletal muscle, brain, and skin (data not shown). Nitroglycerin (GTN) infusion was employed for comparison purposes, and a 5 μg/kg per min infusion significantly decreased vascular resistance nonselectively in the kidney (Table 3), and in brain, intestines, skeletal muscle, and skin (not shown).

Atriopeptin Diuresis in Rats

We previously demonstrated that API and APII, obtained by purification of rat atrial extracts, were natriuretic and diuretic in anesthetized rats (Currie et al., 1984), but only small amounts of material were available; thus, careful quantitative comparison was not practical. In view of the ability of API to produce a hypotensive response and renal vasodilation in anesthetized rats (comparable to the phe-arg-containing peptides), we performed a quantitative comparison with pure synthetic API and APIII. These experiments were facilitated by establishing volume expansion conditions which markedly reduced the variability between animals. We found that API produced a concentration-dependent diuresis following bolus intravenous injections of the peptide (Fig. 4). No response was produced by 0.1 μg API, and no tachyphylaxis was produced by the 3.3-μg dose, since it could be repeated at 40-minute intervals and elicited the same volume excretion as the previous dose. APIII produced a parallel but

TABLE 3
Comparative Effectiveness of Atrial Peptides as Renal Vasodilators in Pentobarbital-Anesthetized Rats

		Blood pressure (mm Hg)		Renal blood flow (ml/min per g)		Vascular resistance (mm Hg/min per g per ml)	
Peptide	Dose (μg/kg per min)	Control	Treated	Control	Treated	Control	Treated
APIII	5	127 ± 8	112 ± 7*	4.41 ± 0.48	4.96 ± 0.43*	29.4 ± 2.0	22.9 ± 0.9*
	30	137 ± 8	105 ± 8*	3.98 ± 0.34	5.32 ± 0.38*	41.8 ± 7.0	20.0 ± 1.8*
API	5	130 ± 5	113 ± 7*	3.91 ± 0.54	4.40 ± 0.37*	34.8 ± 3.9	27.1 ± 4.5*
	30	136 ± 6	104 ± 6*	3.94 ± 0.51	4.74 ± 0.59*	38.8 ± 8.1	24.7 ± 5.6*
SLRR-APIII	1	132 ± 6	123 ± 6*	4.27 ± 0.36	4.93 ± 0.35*	32.2 ± 4	25.5 ± 2.4*
	5	132 ± 10	74 ± 6*	3.40 ± 0.40	3.79 ± 0.43*	40.3 ± 3.9	20.1 ± 2.0*
GTN	5	137 ± 5	113 ± 7*	4.68 ± 0.49	5.09 ± 0.44	31.8 ± 5.5	22.8 ± 2.3*

Determined by microsphere technique. The values reported indicate the mean ± SEM from control ($n = 5$) after a 5-minute (iv) infusion.

* $P < 0.05$.

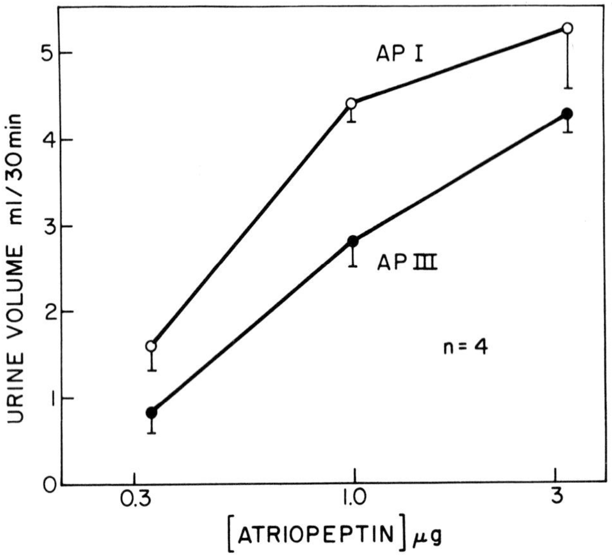

Figure 4. *Atriopeptin-induced diuresis in rats. The peptides were administered as bolus intravenous injections into 200 ± 20 g female rats. There was no cross-tolerance between peptides; thus, injection of two consecutive doses of 3.3 μg of API, followed by a 3.3-μg APIII dose, produced 6.17, 6.21, and 6.73 ml urine/30 min, respectively, when injected into a pentobarbital-anesthetized rat. The values are the means ± SEM (n = 4).*

slightly less potent concentration-dependent diuretic response (Fig. 4).

Renal Vascular and Natriuretic Response to Atrial Peptides in the Intact Dog

In the above microsphere experiments, the atrial peptides had to be administered intravenously to the anesthetized rats, and efforts to deliver the compounds directly into renal arteries would compromise measurement of renal resistance. We therefore performed structure-activity and dose-response curve analysis of the renal vasodilator and sodium excretory effect of atrial peptides in intact anesthetized dogs. When atrial peptides are administered directly into the renal artery of pentobarbital-anesthetized dogs, the phe-arg-containing atriopeptins are potent renal vasodilator (flowmeter measurements) and natriuretic ($U_{Na}V$) substances (Table 4). On the other hand, API was two to three orders of magnitude less potent than the other atrial peptides. A bolus injection of 100 nmol of API (the largest dose tested) caused a 13 ± 4 ml/min increase in renal blood flow and a 45 ± 20% increase in $U_{Na}V$. The N-terminal-extended peptide (SLRR-APIII) was about eight times as effective as APII and APIII (which were equipotent) in the canine kidney.

Table 4
Renal Vasodilator and Natriuretic Response of Canine Kidney in Vivo when Injected (ia) with AP in the Pentobarbital Sodium-Anesthetized Animal

Atrial peptide	Renal blood flow [Dose required to cause an increase of 15 ml/min (nmol)]	$U_{Na}V$ [Dose required to cause an increase of 200% (nmol)]	*n*
SLRR-APIII	0.40 ± 0.06	0.36 ± 0.4	7
APIII	3.0 ± 0.5	3.0 ± 0.6	7
APII	3.7 ± 0.8	6.0 ± 0.6	7
API	>100	>100	6

The control renal blood flow was 55–60 ml/min and the basal $U_{Na}V$ was 1.3–1.6 nEq/g per min.

Discussion

A primary finding in this paper is the renal selectivity of atriopepins in anesthetized rats. Under our experimental conditions, we could not detect significant reductions in the vascular resistance of other organs, except at high concentrations of infused atriopeptins. Utilizing the microsphere technique in anesthetized rats, others have demonstrated that partially purified rat atrial (but not ventricular) extract increases renal blood flow and causes a shift of blood flow from outer to inner cortex (Borenstein et al., 1983). However, such an extract would include a number of the low molecular weight peptides, and these experiments did not describe the blood flow distribution changes of the other vascular beds. Injection of the atrial peptides into tissues with high vascular tone, such as the isolated perfused kidney or aorta strips (Figs. 1 and 2) or the autoperfused rat kidney (Oshima et al., 1984), appears to result in a renal vasodilation with phe-arg-containing atriopeptins, but not with API. On the other hand, intravenous injection of the atrial peptide in anesthetized rats (with or without phe-arg in the C-terminus) causes a fall in blood pressure (Fig. 3), an increase in renal blood flow (Table 3), and diuresis (Fig. 4). The hypotensive effect of these agents was not abolished in nephrectomized rats (data not shown), suggesting that vascular beds (for example the venous bed) other than those analyzed are relaxed by the atriopeptins. We previously observed that both API and APII were effective in producing natriuresis and diuresis in anesthetized rats (Currie et al., 1984). The mechanisms underlying this paradox are unclear. Interestingly, in a preliminary report, administration of a rat atrial extract caused a fall in blood pressure in unanesthetized spontaneously hypertensive rats, but produced no effect in the normotensive Wistar-Kyoto control rats (Pegram et al., 1984). Others have found that the spontaneously hypertensive rat (but not the Wistar-Kyoto control) exhibited diminished atrial levels of stored natriuretic factor (Sonnenberg et al., 1983). Perhaps a reflex mechanism which blunts the hypotensive effects of the atrial peptides is abolished by anesthesia, and is suppressed in the spontaneous hypertensive rat.

Since it was impractical to study sodium excretion following intrarenal arterial injections in anesthetized rats, we studied some of the naturally occurring atriopeptins in anesthetized dogs. Intrarenal injection (ia) of the phe-arg-containing atriopeptins (SLRR-APIII, APII, and APII), but not API or the core peptide (residues 3–19), increased renal blood flow (electromagnetic flowmeter) and sodium excretion ($U_{Na}V$). We recently found that atriopeptin II and III but not API produced a renal vasodilation without altering coronary, mesenteric, or iliac flow, or blood pressure or heart rate in conscious dogs (Hintze et al., 1984). Thus, although there are differences in peptide structural recognition in at least two species, there is evidence that the atriopeptins preferentially dilate the renal vascular bed. Experiments using these species did not permit determination of the renal vascular site of action or the redistribution of the renal blood flow caused by the atrial peptides. However, our data in both species suggest that the natriuresis and diuresis produced by the atriopeptins directly reflect the vasodilator response. The utility of a renal selective vasodilator in renal vasospastic or excretory function disorders has obvious therapeutic potential.

We acknowledge the excellent technical assistance of A. Johnston, W.B. Sawyer, X.V. Nguyen, S.R. Eubanks, and M.E. Zupec.

Arthur D. Loewy is an Established Investigator of the American Heart Association.

Grant support: Monsanto.

Drs. Adams and Fok are affiliated with the Monsanto Research Laboratories.

Dr. Wakatani's current address is: Ono Research Institute, Osaka, Japan.

Dr. Oshima's current address is: Sankyo Biological Research Laboratories, Tokyo, Japan.

Address for reprints: Dr. Philip Needleman, Washington University School of Medicine, Department of Pharmacology, 660 South Euclid Avenue, St. Louis, Missouri 63110.

Received August 17, 1984; accepted for publication January 17, 1985.

References

Borenstein HB, Cupples WA, Sonnenberg H, Veress AT (1983) The effects of a natriuretic atrial extract on renal hemodynamics and urinary excretion in anaesthetized rats. J Physiol (Lond) **334:** 133–140

Chimoskey JE, Spielman WS, Brandt MA, Heidemann SR (1984) Cardiac atria of BI0 14.6 hamsters are deficient in natriuretic factor. Science **223:** 820–821

Currie MG, Geller DM, Cole BR, Boylan JG, Wu YS, Holmberg SW, Needleman P (1983) Bioactive cardiac substances: Potent vasorelaxant activity in mammalian atria. Science **221:** 71–73

Currie MG, Geller DM, Cole BR, Siegel NR, Fok KF, Adams SP, Eubanks SR, Galluppi G, Needleman P (1984a) Purification and sequence analysis of bioactive atrial peptides (atriopeptins). Science **223:** 67–69

Currie MG, Geller DM, Cole BR, Needleman P (1984b) Proteolytic activation of bioactive cardiac by in vitro trypsin cleavage. Proc Natl Acad Sci USA **81:** 1230–1233

deBold AJ, Borenstein HB, Veress AT, Sonnenberg H (1981) A rapid and potent natriuretic response to intravenous injection of atrial myocardial extracts in rats. Life Sci **28:** 89–94

Flynn TG, deBold ML, deBold AJ (1983) The amino acid sequence of an atrial peptide with potent diuretic and natriuretic properties. Biochem Biophys Res Commun **117:** 859–865

Geller DM, Currie MG, Wakatani K, Cole BR, Adams SP, Fok KF, Siegle NR, Eubanks SR, Galluppi GR, Needleman P (1984a) Atriopeptins: A family of potent biologically active peptides derived from mammalian atria. Biochem Biophys Res Commun **120:** 333–338

Geller DM, Currie MG, Siegel NR, Fok KF, Adams SP, Needleman P (1984b) The sequence of an atriopepitgen: A precursor of the bioactive atrial peptides. Biochem Biophys Res Commun **12:** 802–807

Hintze TH, Currie MG, Needleman P (1984) Atriopeptins: Renal specific vasodilators in conscious dogs. Am J Physiol In Press.

Kangawa K, Matsuo H (1984) Purification and complete amino acid sequence of α-human atrial natriuretic polypeptide (α-hANP). Biochem Biophys Res Commun **118:** 131–139

Kangawa K, Fukuda A, Minamino N, Matsuo H (1984) Purification and complete amino acid sequence of beta-rat atrial natriuretic polypeptide (β-rANP) of 5,000 daltons. Biochem Biophys Res Commun **119:** 933–940

Lazure C, Seidah NG, Chretien M, Thibault G, Garcia R, Cantin M, Genest J (1984) Atrial pronatriodilatin: A precursor for natriuretic factor and cardiodilation. FEBS Lett **172:** 80–86

Maki M, Takayanangi R, Misono KS, Pandey KN, Tibbets C, Inagami T (1984) Structure of rat atrial natriuretic factor precursor deduced from cDNA sequence. Nature **309:** 722–724

Merrifield RB (1963) Solid phase peptide synthesis. I. The synthesis of a tetrapeptide. J Am Chem Soc **85:** 2149–2154

Misono KS, Fukumi H, Grammer RT, Inagami T (1984) Rat atrial natriuretic factor: Complete amino acid sequence and disulfide linkage essential for biological activity. Biochem Biophys Res Commun **119:** 524–529

Napier MA, Dewey RS, Albers-Schonberg G, Bennett CD, Rodkey JA, Marsh EA, Whinnery M, Seymour AA, Blaine EH (1984) Isolation and sequence determination of peptide components of atrial natriuretic factor. Biochem Biophys Res Commun **120:** 981–988

Oikawa S, Imai M, Ueno A, Tanaka S, Noguchi T, Nakazato H, Kangawa K, Fukuda A, Matsuo H (1984) Cloning and sequence analysis of cDNA encoding a precursor for human atrial natriuretic polypeptide. Nature **309:** 724–726

Oshima T, Currie MG, Geller DM, Needleman P (1984) An atrial peptide is a potent renal vasodilator substance. Circ Res **54:** 612–616

Pegram BL, Trippodo NC, Cole FC, MacPhee AA (1984) Hypotensive effect of atrial natriuretic factor (rANF) in conscious Wistar-Kyoto and spontaneous hypertensive rats (abstr). Fed Proc **43:** 453

Seidah NG, Lazure C, Chretien M, Thibault G, Garcia R, Cantin M, Genest J, Nutt RF, Brady SF, Lyle TS, Paleveda WJ, Colton CD, Ciccarone TM, Veber DF (1984a) Amino acid sequence of homologous rat atrial peptides: Natriuretic activity of native and synthetic forms. Proc Natl Acad Sci USA **81:** 2640–2644

Seidman CE, Duby AD, Choi E, Graham RM, Haber E, Homcy C, Smith JA, Seidman JG (1984b) The structure of rat preproatrial natriuretic factor as defined by a complementary DNA clone. Science **225:** 324–326

Sonnenberg H, Milojevic S, Chong CK, Veress AT (1983) Atrial natriuretic factor. Reduced cardiac content in spontaneously hypertensive rats. Hypertension **5:** 672–675

Stanek KA, Smith TL, Murphy WR, Coleman TG (1983) Hemodynamic disturbances in the rat as a function of the number of microspheres injected. Am J Physiol **245:** H920–H923

Stanek KA, Neil JJ, Sawyer WB, Loewy AD (1984) Changes in regional blood flow and cardiac output after L-glutamate stimulation of A5 cell group. Am J Physiol **246:** H44–H51

Thibault G, Garcia R, Cantin M, Genest J, Lazure C, Seidah NG, Chretien M (1984) Primary structure of a high Mr form of rat atrial natriuretic factor. FEBS Lett **167:** 352–356

Trippodo NC, Ghai RD, MacPhee AA, Cole FE (1984) Atrial natriuretic factor: Atrial conversion of high to low molecular weight forms. Biochem Biophys Res Commun **119:** 282–288

Yamanaka M, Greenberg B, Johnsson L, Seihamer J, Brewer M, Friedmann T, Miller J, Atlas S, Laragh J, Lewicki J, Fiddes J (1984) Cloning and sequence analysis of the cDNA for the rat atrial natriuretic factor precursor. Nature **309:** 719–722

INDEX TERMS: Atriopeptins • Natriuresis • Vasodilation • Kidney • Diuresis

Errata

RE: Lipid Solubility Modulates pH Potentiation of Local Anesthetic Block of $\dot{V}_{max}$ Reactivation in Guinea Pig Myocardium (*Circ. Res. 55: 513–523, 1984*)

Following are corrections to errors that appeared in the above-referenced article:

p. 517 righthand column, line 18
musles should read muscles

p. 517 righthand column, line 38
pH = pK_a −2 should read pH = pK_a +2

p. 520 righthand column, lines 5–10

Scheme 1 (uncoupled) *should read* Scheme 1 (uncoupled)

$$\begin{array}{l} U + D_c \underset{l_c}{\overset{k_c}{\rightleftharpoons}} B_c \\ U + D_n \underset{l_n}{\overset{k_n}{\rightleftharpoons}} B_n \end{array} \qquad \begin{array}{l} U + D_c \underset{l_c}{\overset{k_c}{\rightleftharpoons}} B_c \\ \quad\;\; \updownarrow \\ U + D_n \underset{l_n}{\overset{k_n}{\rightleftharpoons}} B_n \end{array}$$

Scheme 2 (coupled) *should read* Scheme 2 (coupled)

$$\begin{array}{l} U + D_c \underset{l_c}{\overset{k_c}{\rightleftharpoons}} B_c \\ U + D_n \underset{l_n}{\overset{k_n}{\rightleftharpoons}} B_n \end{array} \qquad \begin{array}{l} U + D_c \underset{l_c}{\overset{k_c}{\rightleftharpoons}} B_c \\ \quad\;\; \updownarrow \qquad \updownarrow \\ U + D_n \underset{l_n}{\overset{k_n}{\rightleftharpoons}} B_n \end{array}$$

RE: M.J. Brunner, A.S. Greene, C.H. Kallman, and A.A. Shoukas. Interaction of Canine Carotid Sinus and Aortic Arch Baroreflexes in the Control of Total Peripheral Resistance (*Circ. Res. 55: 740–750, 1984*)

In our recently published paper, Equations 1 and 2 were reported incorrectly. Equation 1 should read:

$$AP = C_0 + C_1ISP + C_2ISP^2 + C_3ISP^3 + C_4AAP + C_5AAP^2 + C_6AAP^3 \quad (1)$$

and Equation 2 should read:

$$AP = C_0 + C_1ISP + C_2ISP^2 + C_3ISP^3 + C_4AAP + C_5AAP^2 + C_6AAP^3 + C_7(ISP * AAP) \quad (2)$$

The discussion on the derivative and the meaning of the coefficients are correct.

News from the American Heart Association

7320 Greenville Avenue, Dallas, Texas 75231
Telephone: 214 750-5300

1985-6 Research Awards Are Announced by Heart; 58 New EIs Are Included

Fifty-eight new Established Investigators were named by the American Heart Association for 1985–86, appointment beginning July 1, 1985. They will receive a total of $2,283,000 annually and will be continued for five years, subject to annual review.

Also approved were 217 continuing EI awards supported with $8,564,000.

Clinical Scientists

Clinical Scientist awards, given to "talented young clinically trained physicians" who wish investigative careers, were given to 12 new applicants and were continued for 36. They are supported with $523,000 for the new appointees; $1,665,000 for those continuing. The term is three years of full-time research training and may continue as the scientists begin to inaugurate independent research.

Last year there were 16 new clinical scientists but only 29 continued for a total of $1,695,600 in support. This year the total was 48 scientists supported at a cost of $2,188,000.

Medical Students

The Medical Student Research Fellowship Awards program, entering its second year, accepted 28 new students and continued 82 at a total cost of $1,045,000 in 25 schools. Last year, the first, $380,000 was given for the program for 40 students in 14 schools. The program is designed to encourage medical students to choose careers in research.

British-American Fellowships

Four British-American Research Fellowships were awarded with support of $108,000. British-American Fellowships are for one year and are given to "individuals who have had some research training but who wish to receive additional experience in Great Britain." They are supported jointly by AHA and the British Heart Foundation. Last year three Fellowships were given with support of $75,200.

The total support of all Fellowship awards for 1985–86 was $14,188,000 as opposed to $11,965,700 in the previous year. Grants-in-Aid for the year will be announced later.

Names of investigators given Fellowship awards and those continued another year are published in CIRCULATION (**71**, No. 4 (April) 1985).

Ambulatory ECG Standards Recommended by AHA Group

"Recommendations for Standards of Instrumentation and Practice in the Use of Ambulatory Electrocardiography," a Special Report by the Task Force of the Committee on Electrocardiography and Cardiac Electrophysiology of the AHA Council on Clinical Cardiology, has been published in CIRCULATION (**71**, March, 1985).

"The major value of ambulatory electrocardiographic recording," the Task Force said, "is the documentation of transient electrocardiographic events that may not be detected during the short recording periods available in the laboratories of hospitals and clinics. . ."

The Report then listed six clinical situations where ambulatory electrocardiographic recording (AECG) may be applied, made procedural recommendations, provided data on instrumentation, reported on computer-aided analysis, and discussed technicians and interpreters of the data. The Report also suggested requirements for the AECG report and noted new systems.

Members of the Task Force were L. Thomas Sheffield, M.D., chairman; Alan Berson, Ph.D., Deborah Bragg-Remschel, M.S., Paul C. Gillette, M.D., Russell E. Hermes, M.S., Lawrence Hinkle, M.D., Harold Kennedy, M.D., David M. Mirvis, M.D. and Charles Oliver, M.D.

Single reprint copies of the Report are available from AHA National Center, 7320 Greenville Ave., Dallas, TX 75231. (Ask for No. 72-206-A).

1.5 Million Heart Attacks Expected in U.S. in 1985

As many as 1.5 million Americans may have a heart attack in 1985 and about 550,000 of them will die, it was estimated in "Heart Facts," an annual publication of the American Heart Association. Data in the publication are based on 1982 provisional statistics of the National Center for Health Statistics, U.S. Public Health Service.

Other statistical projections for the U.S. in 1985 offered in Heart Facts include:

- 45 million will have one or more forms of heart or blood vessel disease.
- Stroke will afflict 1,900,000 persons.
- High blood pressure affects an estimated 37,990,000.
- Rheumatic heart disease afflicts 1,940,000 adults and 100,000 children.
- The cost of CVD is expected to reach $72.1 billion in 1985.
- The increase in number of coronary artery bypass operations slowed in 1982 (estimated 170,000 operations, an increase of less than 7 percent over 1981. This com-

pares with an increase of 16 per cent in 1981 and 20 per cent in 1980. The rate reduction was attributed to development of balloon angioplasty and use of streptokinase and other clot lysis medication.

- CV diseases remained the most widespread cause of death in the U.S.

Need for Research Funds Cited by AHA Executive

Excerpt from a recent speech by Dudley H. Haffner, Executive Vice President of AHA, to affiliate and national executives:

"In 1984, the National Center and the affiliates had a total of 832 grant applications which were ranked meritorious for funding through the peer review process but were not funded. These were 832 applications that should have been funded but lack of resources prevented us from doing so. This is not an issue of allocating a greater percent of current income to research; it's an issue of increasing the total dollar resources of the Association.

High Quality Research

"We must recognize that we do not always fund the best available research and that we must have a vehicle and a willingness for releasing research budgets to go wherever necessary in the organization to support the best research available."

Journal Supplements Offered as Monographs

"Central Alpha-Adrenergic Blood Pressure Regulating Mechanisms," a supplement to HYPERTENSION (September/October 1984) and "New Frontiers in Biology Related to Heart, Lung, and Blood Pressure," a supplement to CIRCULATION (November, 1984), have been issued as monographs by the Heart Association.

The first, Monograph No. 109 (73-095-A), 97 pages, was edited by William B. Abrams, M.D., F.A.C.P., and Charles B. Sweet, Ph.D. It records a symposium on central alpha-adrenergic blood pressure regulating mechanisms. Its price is $4.00.

The second, Monograph No. 108 (73-094-A), 94 pages, was edited by Drs. Claude Lenfant, director of NHLBI, and Jay Moskowitz. It records a symposium held to celebrate the 35th anniversary of NHLBI. Its price is $4.00.

Both monographs may be ordered from the AHA National Center, Dallas.

Board for Laser Surgery Formed to Set Standards

The American Board of Laser Surgery has been organized as a non-profit group to create and administer standards of qualification for physicians, surgeons, scientists, and paramedical personnel engaged in application of lasers to patient health.

Stanley Stellar, M.D., of St. Barnabas Medical Center, Livingston, NJ, is president, Billie Aronoff, M.D., vice president, John C. Fisher, Sc.D., secretary-treasurer, and Mary Cayton, R.N., assistant to the president.

"Because the use of these unique sources of light in medical applications crosses the borders of all recognized medical specialties," an organization statement said, "none of the existing specialty boards has been willing to adopt appropriate standards into its existing requirements for certification. As a result, the American Board of Laser Surgery was founded by 19 individuals from a variety of medical or surgical disciplines using lasers."

The group estimated that more than 5,000 practitioners in the United States and Canada use lasers and their number was growing rapidly.

The Board plans to hold its first examination in 1985 leading to certification of qualification in the theory and practice of laser surgery and therapy. Application is open to medical and paramedical persons who have attained board certification or equivalent in their specialties.

Inquiries may go to Dr. Stanley Stellar, president, American Board of Laser Surgery, St. Barnabas Medical Center, Old Short Hills Road, Livingston, NJ 07039. Tel. 1-201-533-5070.

HBP Control Conference Meets Chicago Apr. 28–30

The National Conference on High Blood Pressure Control will meet in the Palmer House, Chicago, April 28–30.

James A. Schoenberger, M.D., a former president of the American Heart Association (1980–81), is conference chairman. The conference, it was pointed out, provides one of the few forums for health professionals from various fields to exchange ideas on hypertension control. Previous meetings have attracted over 1,000 attendants.

Highlights of the program include a critique of the 1984 Joint National Committee Report on Detection, Evaluation, and Treatment of Hypertension, debates on the treatment of mild hypertension, and review of some results of blood pressure management in the past 12 years.

Inquiries may go to the National Conference on HBP Control, 2121 Wisconsin Ave., NW, Washington, DC 20007.

Name 4 New Members To NHLBI Council

Four new members have been appointed to the Advisory Council of the National Heart, Lung, and Blood Institute. They are:

Richard A. Carleton, M.D., chief, cardiology division, physician-in-chief and director, division of health education, Memorial Hospital, Pawtucket, RI. He is a member of AHA Councils on Clinical Cardiology and Epidemiology.

Eliot Corday, M.D., senior attending physician, Cedars Sinai Medical Center, Los Angeles.

Carl Franzblau, M.D., professor of biochemistry, Boston University School of Medicine and chairman, interdepartmental biochemistry program, Boston University Graduate School. He is a former AHA Established Investigator and is a Fellow of the AHA Council on Arteriosclerosis.

Charles D. Knight, Jr., M.D., resident, vascular surgery, Mayo Graduate School of Medicine, Rochester, MN.

The Council reviews applications for research and training support and reports to the President and Congress on the status of Institute of Health programs. It also makes recommendations on future programs.

AHA Briefs . . .

• **Modern Concepts of Cardiovascular Disease** for April is "Unstable Angina: Current Status" by Shahbudin H. Rahimtoola, M.D., of Los Angeles.

• Two scientists of the University of Texas Health Science Center, Dallas, who were given the AHA Research Achievement Award at the AHA 57th Scientific Sessions in Miami, have also been awarded Columbia University's 1984 Louisa Gross Horwitz prize. They are geneticists **Michael S. Brown, M.D. and Joseph L. Goldstein, M.D.**, who described the mechanism by which the body processes and accumulates cholesterol.

• **Dr. James E. Dalen**, chairman of the department of medicine, University of Massachusetts Hospital, has been named president-elect of the American College of Chest physicians. **Dr. Richard Dowling Briggs, Jr.**, of the University of Alabama, Birmingham, School of Medicine, is the current president.

• The AHA has prepared a 1984–85 **Board of Directors book** containing brief biographies of the 36 members of the Board.

• The AHA will supply one **recipe a month** to weekly and small daily newspapers, shoppers and corporate newsletters through 52 affiliates which have agreed to participate.

• The Swedish National Association against Heart and Chest Diseases will again award three one-year **research scholarships for study in Sweden**. Two awards will be made in cardiology and one in pneumology. Applicants should be non-Swedish cardiologists and pneumologists under 45 years-of-age. Applications before June 30, 1985, may go to the National Association against Heart and Chest Diseases, Kungsgatan 54, 111 35 Stockholm, Sweden.

• The **13th European Congress on Noninvasive Cardiovascular Dynamics** will be held April 22–25 in Brescia, Italy. C. Rusconi, M.D. is chairman. Inquiries may go to G. Orlando, M.D., S. Orsola Hospital, Via V. Emanuele 27, 25122 Brescia, Italy. Tel. 030147061.

• Three-dimensional **heart models** with removable parts to illustrate idiopathic hypertrophic subaortic stenosis (IHSS) and the Morrow operation have been created by an NHLBI artist for use by NHLBI surgeon Charles L. Macintosh, M.D. Models have also been created by artist Marion Wilcox to explain heart valve replacements and arterial bypass surgery to patients and staff.

• An International Symposium on the "**Sick Sinus Syndrome Today**," will be held in Milan, Italy, April 12–14. It is organized by the Cardiology department of the Ospedale Maggiore of Milan. Inquiries may go to OIC, Largo Corsia dei Servi, 11, 20122 Milano, Italy. Tel. (02) 70.84.19 and 70.83.57.

Meetings Calendar 1985

April 21–26: **Federation of American Societies for Experimental Biology.** Anaheim, CA. Inquiries: 9650 Rockville Pike, Bethesda, MD 20014.

April 28–30: **National Conference on High Blood Pressure Control.** Palmer House, Chicago. Inquiries: NCHBP, 1501 Wilson Blvd., Suite 600, Arlington, VA 22209. Tel. 1-202-944-3176.

April 29–May 1: **American Association for Thoracic Surgery.** Hilton Hotel, New Orleans. Inquiries: W. T. Maloney, 13 Elm St., Manchester, MA 01944.

April 29–May 4: **20th Annual Family Practice Symposium.** Medical College of Georgia, Augusta. Inquiries: Div. Cont. Ed., Medical College of Georgia, Augusta, GA 30912. Tel. 1-404-828-3967.

April 30–May 3: **Exercise and Heart Disease: Prevention and Rehabilitation: 8th Cardiac Rehabilitation Symposium.** Red Carpet Hotel, Milwaukee, WI. Sponsored by Univ. of Wis.—Milwaukee Clinical Campus, Mount Sinai Medical Center (CV Dis. Sect.). Inquiries: S. Z. Aslakson, CME, 465B WARF Bldg, 610 Walnut St., Madison, WI 53705. Tel. 1-608-263-2856.

May 1–2: **21st Annual Cardiovascular Symposium.** Hunt Memorial, Hartford, CT, Medical Society. Sponsored by Cardiology Section, St. Francis Hosp. and Medical Center. Inquiries R. M. Jeresaty, M.D., Cardiology, St. Francis Hosp./Medical Center, 114 Woodland St., Hartford, CT 06105. Tel. 1-289-548-4820.

May 3–4: **Perspectives on the Management of Chronic Congestive Heart Failure.** Baltimore, MD. Sponsored by Div. of Cardiology, University of Maryland School of Medicine. Inquiries: Program of Cont. Ed., University of Maryland School of Medicine, 10 S. Pine St., Rm. 300, Baltimore, MD 21201. Tel. 1-301-528-3956.

May 3–6: **Annual Meeting American Federation for Clinical Research, American Society for Clinical Investigation, and Association of American Physicians.** Sheraton Hotel, Washington, DC. Inquiries Slack Inc., 6900 Grove Rd., Thorofare, NJ 08086.

May 6–7: **Symposium on Leukotrienes in Cardiovascular and Pulmonary Function.** Philadelphia. Inquiries: Allen R. Lefer, Ph.D. Dept. Physiology, Jefferson Medical College, 1020 Locust St., Philadelphia, PA 19107.

May 8–10: **2nd Biennial Chicago Cardiovascular Symposium.** Chicago. Inquiries: Registrar, American College of Physicians, 4200 Pine St., Philadelphia, PA 19104.

May 9–11: **International Symposium on Myocardial Protection.** Westin Hotel, Boston. Sponsored by Boston University School of Medicine and the Heart Programs of Boston University Medical Center. Arthur J. Roberts, M.D., chairman. Inquiries: Boston Univ. School of Med., 80 E. Concord St., Boston, MA 02118. Tel. 1-617-247-5602.

May 10–11: **Critical Hemodynamic Diagnosis, Monitoring and Management.** Chattanooga, TN. (Also June 7–8, Akron, OH). Inquiries: See May 8–10 ACP.

May 12–15: **6th Annual Meeting, Society for Clinical Trials.** New Orleans. Inquiries: Curt Furberg, MD, SCT, 600 Wyndhurst Ave., Baltimore, MD 21210.

May 12–15: **Annual Meeting, American Thoracic Society.** Anaheim, CA. Slide and poster presentations. Inquiries: ATS, 1740 Broadway, New York, NY 10019. Tel. 1-212-245-8000, Ext. 570.

May 13–15: **International Symposium: Ultrasound Diag-**

nosis of Cerebrovascular Disease. Seattle. (May 10–12: Pre-symposium Basic Course in Cerebrovascular Ultrasound—Doppler and B-Scan). Sponsored by Institute of Applied Physiology and Medicine. Merrill P. Spencer, M.D., program chairman. Inquiries: Dept. Med. Ed., Inst. Applied Physiology and Med., 701 Sixteenth Ave., Seattle, WA 98122. Tel. 1-206-442-7330.

May 15–17: **Update in Infectious Diseases.** Philadelphia. Inquiries: See May 8–10 ACP.

May 15–17: **Clinical Approaches to Arterial Blood Gas Interpretation and Electrolytes.** Dallas. (Also May 31–June 1, Chicago and June 14–15, New York City). Inquiries: See May 8–10 ACP.

May 16–18: **Practical Applications of Echo and Doppler Techniques in Cardiology.** Cleveland Marriott Inn-Airport Hotel. Inquiries: Professional Medical Seminars, POB 5400, Sherman Oaks, CA 91413.

May 17–18: **Clinical Concerns in Hemodialysis Therapy**. Sheraton Harbor Island East Hotel, San Diego. Program Chairman, Richard A. Sherman, M.D. Sponsored by American Kidney Fund and Nephrology Society of New Jersey. Inquiries: Dr. R. A. Sherman, Academic Health Science Center, CN 19, New Brunswick, NJ 08903. Tel. 1-800-922-0130.

May 17–22: **UCSD-Anesthesiology Review.** Vacation Village, San Diego. Sponsored by Dept. Anesthesiology, University of California, San Diego School of Medicine. Inquiries: K. Naughton, Dept. Anesthesia (M-029), UCSD, La Jolla, CA 92093. Tel. 1-619-452-3865.

May 19–23: **6th Scientific Meeting Inter-American Society of Hypertension.** Cleveland. Inquiries: 6th Meeting IASH, Research Division FF2-49, 9500 Euclid Ave., Cleveland, OH 44106. Tel. 1-216-444-5837.

May 23–24: **Vascular Surgery 1985. Current State of the Art. 2nd International Vascular Symposium.** Waldorf-Astoria Hotel, New York City. John B. Chang, M.D., program chairman. Inquiries: A. J. Boehme, Long Island Jewish-Hillside Medical Center, New Hyde Park, NY 11042. Tel. 1-212-470-2114.

May 24–27: **7th Annual Meeting American Section of the International Society for Heart Research.** Houston. Inquiries: Dr. J. Allen, Dept. Cell Biophysics, Baylor College of Med., Houston, TX 77025.

May 25–27: **13th Annual Conference: Master Approach to Cardiovascular Problems.** Lake Buena Vista, FL. Sponsored by University of Miami School of Medicine; co-sponsored by AHA Council on Clinical Cardiology. Augustin Castellanos, M.D., program director. Inquiries: Y. Barcena, Univ. Miami Sch. Med., Cardiology (D-39), Box 016960, Miami, FL 33101. Tel. 1-305-549-7124/6975.

May 30–June 1: **Three Days in Cardiology.** Boston, Dr. Michael D. Freed program director. Sponsored by Children's Hospital, Boston. Cosponsored by the Council on Cardiovascular Diseases in the Young of the AHA. Inquiries: J. Cartier, Dept. Cardiology, the Children's Hospital, 300 Longwood Ave., Boston, MA 02115. Tel. 1-617-735-7893.

June 2–6: **2nd World Congress of Pediatric Cardiology.** New York City. Sponsors: American Academy of Pediatrics, American College of Cardiology, American Heart Association, Asian-Pacific Society of Cardiology, Asian Society of Pediatric Cardiology, Association of European Pediatric Cardiologists, Interamerican Society of Cardiology, International Society and Federation of Cardiology, New York Heart Association, Sociedad Latina de Cardiologia Pediatrica. Cosponsored by the Councils on Cardiovascular Diseases in the Young, and Cardiovascular Surgery of the AHA. Inquiries: V. Herlitz, 404 Park Ave. S., New York, NY 10016. Tel. 1-212-532-9400. Cable: HERLIMED.

June 10–12: **Surgery for Coronary Artery Disease.** Durham, NC. Sponsored by Duke University Medical Center and American College of Cardiology. R. H. Jones, M.D., program director. Inquiries: ACC, 9111 Georgetown Rd., Bethesda, MD 20814. Tel. 1-301-897-5400, Ext. 228.

June 10–13: **16th Annual Internal Medical Symposium.** Kiawah Island Inn, Kiawah Island, SC. Sponsored by the School of Medicine, Medical College of Georgia. Inquiries: Div. Cont. Ed., Medical College of Georgia, Augusta, GA 30912. Tel. 1-404-828-3867.

June 10–13: **Coronary Angiography 1985: New Developments in Diagnostic Techniques, PTCA, and Thrombolytic Therapy.** Boston. Dr. David C. Levin program director. Sponsored by The Harvard Medical School. Cosponsored by the Council on Cardiovascular Radiology of the AHA. Inquiries: Dept. Cont. Ed., Harvard Medical School, 25 Shattuck St., Boston, MA 02115. Tel. 1-617-732-6265.

June 17–18: **Today's Therapy in Nephrology**. Resorts International Hotel, Atlantic City, NJ. Sponsored by American Kidney Fund and Nephrology Society of New Jersey. Inquiries: See May 17–18, Dr. Sherman.

July 12: **Certifying Examination, Sub-Board of Pediatric Cardiology.** Chapel Hill, NC. Inquiries: American Board of Pediatrics, 111 Silver Cedar Court, Chapel Hill, NC 27514-1651.

July 15–18: **Clinical Cardiology.** Hilton Head Inn, Hilton Head Island, SC. Sponsored by the School of Medicine, Medical College of Georgia. Inquiries: See Med. Coll. of Georgia Div. Cont. Ed., June 10–13.

July 18–21: **Pulmonary Diseases.** Kiawah Island Inn, Kiawah Island, SC. Sponsored by School of Medicine, Medical College of Georgia. Inquiries: See Div. Cont. Ed., Med. Coll. of Georgia, June 10–13.

July 21–26: **37th Annual Meeting American Association of Clinical Chemistry.** Georgia World Congress Center, Atlanta. Inquiries: AACC, 1725 K St., NW, Washington, DC 20006. Tel. 1-202-857-0717.

July 22–26: **Interdisciplinary Symposium on Plant Flavonoids in Biology and Medicine.** Biochemical, Pharmacological, and Structure-Activity Relationships. Buffalo, NY. Inquiries: Dr. Elliott Middleton, Jr., Dept. Med., Buffalo General Hospital, 100 High St., Buffalo, NY 14203. Tel. 1-716-845-2985.

July 22–26: **Topics in Clinical Nuclear Medicine.** Colby College, Waterville, ME. Henry N. Wagner, Jr., M.D., course director. Inquiries: R. Kany, Colby College, Waterville, ME 04901. Tel. 1-207-873-3386.

July 24–28: **Critical Care Medicine.** Kiawah Island Inn, Kiawah Island, SC. Sponsored by School of Medicine, Medical College of Georgia. Inquiries: See Med. Coll. of Georgia, Div. Cont. Ed., June 10–13.

Oct. 11–12: **4th Southern Biomedical Engineering Conference.** Jackson MS. Inquiries: Dr. Barry W. Sauer, SBEC, Div. Cont. Health Prof. Ed., University of Mississippi Medical Center, 2500 N. State St., Jackson, MS 39216-4505.

Oct. 13–18: **Clinical Congress, American College of Surgeons.** Chicago. Inquiries: ACS, 55 East Erie St., Chicago, IL 60611.

Oct 25: **Annual Meeting, Society of Neurological Anesthesia and Neurological Supportive Care.** San Francisco. Inquiries: Society of Neurological Anesthesia, POB 238, Univ. of Virginia Medical Center, Charlottesville, VA 22908.

Nov. 11–14: **58th Annual Scientific Sessions, American Heart Association, Washington, DC. Inquiries: Coordinator Scientific Sessions, AHA, 7320 Greenville Ave., Dallas, TX 75231. Tel. for Abstracts: 1-214-750-5439; for housing and reservations 1-214-750-5425. Commercial Exhibits: 1-214-750-5388.**

Nov. 19–20: **Subspecialty Boards in Cardiovascular Disease.** Philadelphia. Inquiries: American Board of Internal Medicine, 3624 Market St., Philadelphia, PA 19104. Tel. 1-215-243-1500. (New date.)

1986

Jan 24–25: **Current Controversies and Techniques in Congenital Heart Surgery.** Baltimore, MD. (Immediately prior to Annual Meeting Society of Thoracic Surgeons, Washington, DC). Sponsored by Div. of Thoracic and Cardiovascular Surgery, University of Maryland School of Medicine. Inquiries: Program Cont. Ed., University of Maryland School of Medicine, 10 South Pine St., Suite 300, Baltimore, MD 21201. Tel. 301-528-3956.

Sept. 13–20: **Xth World Congress of Cardiology.** Washington, DC. Inquiries: Secretariat, 7320 Greenville Ave., Dallas, TX 75231. Tel. 1-214-750-5429. Cable Tencard, Dallas, TX.

Abroad

1985

May 1–3: **International Symposium on Neural Mechanisms and Cardiovascular Disease**. Santa Margharita Ligure, (near Genoa), Italy. Dr. C. Bartorelli, symposium president. Inquiries: A. Malliani, Istituto Ricerche Cardiovascolari, Via Bonfadini, 214, 20138 Milano, Italy. Tel. 02-5063984 (p.m.)

May 1–4: **Controversies in Heart Valve Replacement.** Hotel Rheinpark Plaza, Düsseldorf, West Germany. Sponsored by European Society of Cardiology and Working Group on Valvular Prostheses. Inquiries: Dr. D. Horstkotte, Dept. Med. B, Univ. Düsseldorf, Moorenstrasse 5, D-4000 Düsseldorf, Germany. Tel. 049-211-3118278. Telex: 8587348 uni d.

May 2–4: **International Congress on Advanced Age.** Villa Marigola, San Terenzo di Lenci (SP) (near La Spezia). Official languages Italian and English. Topics: Advanced age and medical, surgical, physiopathological, and social problems. Inquiries: D. Valentini, XIX U.S.I. Spezzino, Via XXIV Maggio, 139, I-19100 La Spezia. Tel. (0187)533503.

May 8–10: **4th Congress Southern African Hypertension Society.** Johannesburg, South Africa. Inquiries: Prof. Clive Rosendorff, Dept. Physiology, Univ. Witwatersrand Medical School, York Rd., Parktown 2193, South Africa.

May 10–12: **International Symposium on Sports Cardiology**. Knokke, Belgium. Inquiries: Dr. I. Bekaert, Alg. Ziekenhuis St. Jozef, Steenweg op Merksplas 44, 2300 Turnhout, Belgium. Tel. 014-4104-51.

May 18–June 2: **Multimodality General Radiology in Scandinavia.** Stockholm, Oslo, Bergen, Copenhagen. Sponsored by Radiology Dept., University of California, San Francisco. Inquiries: Travel Planners, Inc., POB 32366, San Antonio, TX, 78216. Tel. 1-512-341-8131.

May 20–22: **Two Dimensional and Doppler Echocardiography.** Bisceglie (Bari), Italy. Drs. Navin C. Nanda and Paolo Rizzon, directors. Cosponsored by Cardiology Division of Alabama in Birmingham and University of Bari. Inquiries: Secretariat, Inter Centre, Via Principe Amedeo, 93, 70122 Bari, Italy.

May 22: **Symposium on Coronary Arteriography.** Rotterdam, the Netherlands. Organized by Working Group on Coronary Blood Flow and Angina Pectoris, on behalf of the European Society of Cardiology. Inquiries: Prof. P. G. Hugenholtz, M.D., Thoraxcenter BD 406, Erasmus Univ., Rotterdam, POB 1738, 3000 DR Rotterdam, the Netherlands.

May 23–25: **Unstable Angina Revisited.** Rotterdam, the Netherlands. Organized by the Thoraxcenter of Erasmus University, Rotterdam, the Netherlands Interuniversitary Cardiological Institute, the Netherlands, and the Toronto General Hospital, Toronto, Canada. Inquiries: Prof. P.G. Hugenholtz, M.D., Thoraxcenter Bd 406, Erasmus University, Rotterdam. POB 1738, 3000 DR Rotterdam, the Netherlands.

June 1–8: **Frontiers in Imaging and Cardiopulmonary Diagnosis.** England. (Also in Scotland, June 9–15). Eric N. C. Milne, M.D., program director. Faculty from U.S.A., 3 British and 2 Scottish medical schools. Inquiries: Ryals, POB 610203, DFW Airport, Texas 75261, U.S.A. 214-659-9590.

June 8–20: **2nd Advanced Ten Day International Teaching Seminar on Epidemiology and Prevention.** Ireland. Sponsored by Council of Epidemiology and Prevention, International Society and Federation of Cardiology in cooperation with WHO. Inquiries: Rose Stamler, Room 1-615, 303 E. Chicago Ave., Chicago, IL 60611.

June 9–14: **International Congress of Angiology.** Athens, Greece. Inquiries: Prof. P. Balas, 17 Sisini St., 115 28 Athens (612) Greece. (New date).

June 10–11: **Advances in Internal Medicine.** Banff, Alberta, Canada. Inquiries: American College of Physicians, 4200 Pine St., Philadelphia, PA 19104.

June 11–14: **3rd International Symposium on Body Surface Mapping.** Nijmegen, the Netherlands. Inquiries: Dr. R. Th. van Dam, Dept. Cardiology, Geert Grooteplein Zuid 8, 6525 AG Nijmegen, the Netherlands.

June 16–20: **12th Symposium, International Society of Cerebral Blood Flow—"Brain: 85."** Ronneby Brunn Hotel. Lund, Sweden. Inquiries: K. Dahlgren, Dept. Clinical Neurophysiology, University Hospital, S-221 85 Lund, Sweden. Tel. +46-46-10-33-70.

June 16–21: **12th International Congress of Cardiology.** Vancouver, B.C., Canada. Inquiries: Dr. Henry Mizgala, Suite 1704, 1200 Alberni St., Vancouver, B.C., Canada V6E 1A6. Tel. 604-681-5226. Cable: Venuvan.

June 16–21: **International Symposium on the Biomechanics of Muscle** (14th Neuroelectric Society Meeting). Hotel Vraona Bay, Vravrona-Attica, Athens, Greece. Ivan Bourgeois, M.S., program chairman. Inquiries: Dr. A. Sances, Jr., Dept. Neurosurgery, Medical College of Wisconsin, 8700 W. Wisconsin Ave., Milwaukee, WI 53226. Tel. 1-414-257-5307.

June 20: **Doppler Ultrasound Techniques in Cardiology.** St. Bartholomew's Hospital, London, U.K. Inquiries: Biological Engineering Society, c/o Royal College of Surgeons, Lincoln's Inn Fields, London WC2A 3PN, United Kingdom.

June 23–26: **International Conference on Preventive Cardiology.** Sovincenter, Moscow, USSR. Sponsored by WHO, International Society and Federation of Cardiology. Official languages English and Russian. Inquiries: A. A. Stepanenko, International Conference on Prevention Cardiology, Institute of Preventive Cardiology, 10 Petroverigsky Lane 101837 Moscow, USSR. Telex 411355. Cable USSR MOSCOW K-62, Preventive Cardiology. Tel. 221-93-47.

June 26–28: **6th Symposium on Echocardiology With a Postgraduate Course on Doppler Cardiography.** Rotterdam, the Netherlands. Sponsored by Erasmus University Thoraxcenter. Inquiries: PG Med. Ed., Erasmus University, Rotterdam, PBO 1738, 3000 DR Rotterdam, the Netherlands. Tel. 010-635011/635013.

July 15–19: **4th Meeting, World Federation on Ultrasound in Medicine and Biology.** Sydney, Australia. Inquiries: WFUMB, POB 1441 GPO, Sydney, NSW, Australia 2001.

Aug. 3–17: **5th Annual Roentgen Revisited.** Postgraduate Radiology Course with NMR Symposium. Switzerland, Austria, Germany. Sponsored by University of California San Francisco Medical Center and Univeristy of Munich. Charles B. Higgins, M.D. course director. Inquiries: See May 18–June 2, Travel Planners.

Aug. 31–Sept. 7: **Diagnosis of Diseases of the Chest.** Italy. (Also in Greece, Sept. 8–14). 2nd Great Teachers Foundation International Postgraduate Medical Education Program. Eric N. C. Milne, M.D., program director. Inquiries: Ryals (see June 1–8 above).

Aug. 31–Sept. 7: **11th Congress of International Society of Hypertension.** Heidelberg, Federal Republic of Germany. Organized by German Institute of High Blood Pressure Research and German Hypertension League. Dr. Detlev Ganten, Congress chairman. Inquiries: GKV, Frankfurter Str. 57, D-6050 Offenbach 1, Heidelberg, FRGermany.

Sept. 1–6: **13th World Congress of Neurology.** Hamburg, Germany. Inquiries: Dr. T. Stober, Dept. Neurology, Faculty of Med., University of Saarland, D-6650 Homburg/ Saar, FRG.

Sept. 1–7: **3rd Postgraduate International Course on Pain Therapy.** Vicenza, Italy. Inquiries: Ruggiero Rizzi, M.D., Ospedale Generale Regionale, 36100 Vicenza, Italy.

Sept. 3–6: **European Nuclear Medicine Congress.** Barbican Centre, London, England. Incorporates 23rd Meeting Society of Nuclear Medicine, Europe, 8th Meeting European Nuclear Medicine Society, 13th Meeting British Nuclear Medicine Society. Inquiries: Congress, Institute of Nuclear Medicine, Middlesex Hospital Medical School, Mortimer St., London, W1N 8AA, United Kingdom. Tel. OI-631 1066.

Sept. 5–7: **1st Asian-Pacific Conference on Doppler and Echocardiography.** Tokyo. Inquiries: Pravin M. Shah, M.D., Coordinator for North America, Cardiology Section (691/111E), Wadsworth VA Medical Center, Wilshire & Sawtelle Blvds, Los Angeles, CA. Tel. 1-213-824-3126.

Sept. 7–9: **3rd International Brain Heart Conference.** Trier, Germany. Inquiries: Dr. T. Stober, Dept. Neurology, Faculty of Med. University of Saarland, D-6650, Homburg/Saar, Federal Republic of Germany.

Sept. 8–12: **1st International Congress on Hospital Laws, Procedures, and Ethics.** Tel Aviv, Israel. Judge Amnon Carmi, organizing chairman. Inquiries: Hospitalaw, 28 Ahad Ha'am St., POB 394, Tel Aviv 61003, Israel. Tel. 03-650862. Telex 33803 TLV. Cable PELTOURS TELAVIV.

Sept. 9–12: **8th Annual European Conference on Lipoproteins.** Evangelische Akademie, Tutzing (near Munich), West Germany. Apolipoprotein mutants and dyslipoproteinemias; cellular processing of lipoproteins. Sponsored by European Lipoprotein Club. Abstracts by May 1. Inquiries: Dr. J. Shepherd, Secretary European Lipoprotein Club, Dept. Pathological Biochemistry, Royal Infirmary, Glasgow, Scotland, G4 OSF.

Sept. 11–14: **4th European Conference on Mechanocardiography.** Budapest, Hungary. Organized by the European-African Div. of the International Society of Mechanocardiography and the Hungarian Society of Cardiology. Prof. J. Simonyi chairman scientific committee. Inquiries: Mechanocardiography Organizing Committee, Budapest, Pf 88, H-1450, Hungary.

Sept. 11–14: **Acute Brain Ischemia 1985: Medical and Surgical Therapy.** University of Siena, Italy. Satellite of 13th World Congress of Neurology, Sept. 1–6, Hamburg, Germany. Prof. Noè Battistini, organizer. Inquiries: GIBI S.a.s., M. P. Gerini, Via Orlona, 7, 00198 Rome, Italy.

Sept. 16–20: **International Symposium on Cardiogenic Reflexes.** University of Leeds, England. Organized by Dept. of CV Studies, Univ. Leeds, and Commission on CV Physiology of International Univ. of Physiological Sciences. Inquiries: Dr. R. Hainsworth, Dept. CV Studies, University of Leeds, Leeds LS2 93T, England.

Oct. 3–4: **Hemodynamics and Atherosclerosis.** Wellington, New Zealand. Inquiries: Dr. W.E. Stehbens, Dept. Pathology, Wellington Clinical School of Med., Wellington, 2, New Zealand.

Oct. 6–10: **7th International Symposium on Atherosclerosis.** Melbourne, Australia. Inquiries: Dr. P. J. Nestel, Baker Medical Research Inst., Commercial Rd., Prahran, Vic., Australia 3181.

Oct. 8–10: **1st Latin American Congress of Cardiac Pacing.** Buenos Aires, Argentina. Operated by Latin American Society of Cardiac Pacing and Argentine Chamber of Cardiac Pacing. Dr. Alejandro Dussaut, president organizing committee. Inquiries: Congresos Internacionales S.A., Moreno 854—9° piso, 1091 Buenos Aires, Argentina. Tel. 14-3216/3408/3283. Telex 22036 JECON AR.

Oct. 11–12: **2nd International Symposium on Hypertension in Children and Adolescents.** Heidelberg, FRG. Organized by Dept. of Pediatrics, Univ. of Heidelberg, and German Institute for High Blood Pressure Research. Inquiries: German Institute HBP Research, University of Heidelberg, Im Neuenheimer Feld 366, D-6900 Heidelberg, FRG.

Oct. 11–18: **Cell Biology of the Artery Wall.** Hayman Island, Great Barrier Reef, Australia. Satellite of 7th International Symposium on Arteriosclerosis, Oct. 6–10, Melbourne. Inquiries: Dr. Gordon H. Campbell, Dept. Anatomy, University of Melbourne, Parkville, 3052, Australia.

Oct. 20–22: **5th International Symposium on Rats with Spontaneous Hypertension and Related Studies.** Kyoto, Japan. Yukio Yamori, M.D., program director. Inquiries: 5th SHR Symposium, Shimane Medical University, Izumo 693, Japan. Tel. 0853-23-2111 Ext. 2375. Cable: WHOCOLLAB IZUMO.

Oct. 25–27: **International Symposium on Brain and Blood Pressure Control.** Kikai-Shinkoh Hall, Shiba Park, Tokyo, Japan. Dr. Keiji Nakamura organizing chairman. Abstracts by May 31. Inquiries: Brain and Blood Pressure, Dept. of Pharmacology, Nippon Roche Research Center, Kamakura 247, Japan. Tel. 0467-45-3191-Ext. 380 or 381. Telex 2222861 PANROCHE J.

Oct. 27–30: **3rd Asian Pacific Symposium on Cardiac Pacing and Electrophysiology.** Hilton Hotel, Melbourne, Australia. Sponsored by Cardiac Society of Australia and New Zealand under auspices of International Cardiac Pacing Society. Inquiries: 3rd Asian Pacific Symposium on Cardiac Pacing and Electrophysiology, Suite 3.5, Epworth Medical Centre, 62 Erin St., Richmond, Vic. 3131, Australia.

Nov. 28–30: **7th Biennial Congress of Cardiology.** Rawalpindi/Islamabad, Pakistan. Inquiries: Pakistan Cardiac Society, Brig. Muhammad Zulfiqar Ali Khan, AFIC/ NIHD, Rawalpindi, Pakistan. Tel. 64946, 61-31113, 61-33911.

1986

July 13–18: **30th International Congress of Physiological Sciences.** The University of British Columbia, Vancouver, Canada. Dr. H. McLennan, chairman program committee. Inquiries: IUPS, Suite 801, 750 Jervis St., Vancouver, B.C., Canada V6E 2A9. Tel. 604-681-5226. Telex 04-352848 VCR.

AHA Scientific Sessions Future Meeting Dates

1985	Washington, DC	Nov. 11–14
1986	Dallas, TX	Nov. 17–20
1987	Anaheim, CA	Nov. 16–19
1988	Locale not set	Nov. 14–17
1989	New Orleans	Nov. 13–16
1990	Dallas	Nov. 12–15

Xth World Congress of Cardiology, 1986

The Xth World Congress of Cardiology will be held in Washington, DC, Sept. 13–20, 1986. Official languages English, Spanish, and French. Inquiries: Secretariat, Xth World Congress Cardiology, 7320 Greenville Ave., Dallas, TX 75231. Tel. 214-750-5429. Cable: Tencard, Dallas.

Circulation Research MAY 1985 VOL. 56 NO. 5

An Official Journal of the American Heart Association

BRIEF REVIEWS

Molecular Characterization of Adrenergic Receptors

Charles J. Homcy and Robert M. Graham

From the Cellular and Molecular Research Laboratory, Cardiac Unit, Massachusetts General Hospital and Harvard Medical School, Boston, Massachusetts

THIS is an appropriate time to review progress in the area of adrenergic receptors, particularly in terms of research that aims at achieving an understanding of these proteins at the level of their molecular composition. The past decade has seen an explosion in the field of adrenergic receptor pharmacology, made possible to a large extent by the development of the radioligand-binding assay. Alterations in receptor number and affinity occurring under a variety of physiological conditions have now been documented. Numerous examples can be given, such as an increase in receptor number in hyperthyroidism (Williams et al., 1977; Tsai and Chen, 1978), decreased receptor number in hypothyroidism (Ciaraldi and Marinetti, 1975; Banerjee and Kung, 1977) or alterations in receptor-effector coupling seen in cases of abnormal thyroid hormone (Stiles and Lefkowitz, 1981) or steroid hormone levels (Davies et al., 1981). It is not often, however, that such studies can clearly define the mechanisms underlying the observed phenomena. In the simplest case, the receptor assay may pinpoint whether an observed alteration in the physiological response occurs at the receptor level or distal to it. In a few cases, unambiguous results indicate that the altered responsiveness to an adrenergic agonist is not at the receptor level. For example, a marked hyporesponsiveness to adrenergic agonists is apparent in the neonatal dog, despite the greater numbers of receptors, an unaltered affinity, and enhanced cyclase activation, as compared to the adult (Rockson et al., 1981). Less commonly, insights into underlying mechanisms can be gained. One of the best examples is the process of receptor desensitization, whereby the physiological response becomes attenuated on continuous exposure to an agonist (Harden, 1983). Not only has a loss of receptors from the cell surface been documented due to an apparent internalization of these receptors in some systems, but also an actual uncoupling of the receptor from its effector system, adenylate cyclase, has been observed as an early event in certain models. Application of the radioligand-binding assay to this problem has indicated that desensitization may be effected by different mechanisms, depending on the species and tissue type examined, or even through a combination of mechanisms. However, it is clear that a definitive understanding of how various components produce a transmembrane message, of the factors modulating or attenuating this activation, and of the stoichiometry of the interactive components will come only from their purification and reconstitution into artificial membrane systems.

α-Adrenergic Receptors

α-Adrenergic receptors are integral membrane proteins that, like other membrane-bound receptors, probably span the lipid bilayer. Much like β-adrenergic receptors, these receptor proteins mediate the actions of the sympathetic nervous system following interaction with endogenous catecholamines, norepinephrine and epinephrine (Mayer, 1980; Graham, 1981). Both α- and β-adrenergic receptors bind the endogenous catechols with comparable affinity. However, they are readily distinguished by their differing effector-coupled responses, by the opposing effects that they mediate in different tissues, and by their affinities for synthetic ligands, which can differ by as much as one million-fold (Graham, 1981). Further, whereas α- and β-adrenergic receptors have a number of similar biophysical and biochemical properties, as will be detailed below, there is now ample evidence to indicate that they are distinct proteins.

Classification of α-Adrenergic Receptors

α-Adrenergic receptors have been broadly classified into α_1 and α_2 subtypes (Graham, 1981, 1984). This classification was initially invoked on an anatomical basis, when it was realized that, in addition to the classical postjunctional (α_1) receptors that mediate responses such as vasoconstriction, there exist prejunctional (α_2) receptors (Langer, 1974). At the time of their classification, these prejunctional receptors were believed to modulate the release of norepinephrine from sympathetic nerve terminals by a negative feedback mechanism, although this conclusion at present is still controversial (McGrath, 1982; Kalsner, 1984). Subsequently, the availability of subtype selective compounds allowed the now widely accepted subdivision of α-adrenergic receptors to be made on the basis of their differential selectivity for a variety of adrenergic agonists and antagonists (Berthelson and Pettinger, 1977; McGrath, 1982; Bylund and U'Prichard, 1983).

Apart from prejunctional α_2-adrenergic receptors, there now is a large body of data implicating the existence of a postjunctional α-receptor, which can be activated by α_2-agonists to produce pressor responses in pithed animals and which is blocked by specific α_2-adrenergic antagonists such as yohimbine but not by α_1-antagonists, such as prazosin (Timmermans and van Zweiten, 1981, 1982; McGrath, 1982, 1983). That this postjunctional α_2-receptor also mediates vasoconstriction was first clearly demonstrated by Drew and Whiting (1979), when they reported that prazosin did not antagonize pressor responses to norepinephrine to the same degree as it attenuated responses to the α_1-adrenergic agonist, phenylephrine. Similarly, Jauering et al. (1978) found that norepinephrine responses in isolated human digital arteries, unlike visceral arteries, were resistant to blockade by prazosin. More recently, in vivo studies in the dog (Shepperson et al., 1982; Holtz et al., 1982) and in man (Van Brummelen et al., 1983; Elliot et al., 1983) support the existence of postjunctional α_2-adrenergic receptors.

Of particular interest is the finding that the combination of the selective α_2-antagonist, rauwolscine, plus the α_1-antagonist, prazosin, causes a greater shift of the norepinephrine vasoconstrictor dose-response curve to the right than is produced by the same dose of either antagonist alone (Alabster and Davey, 1984). This synergism implies that endogenous norepinephrine can interact with α_1- or α_2-adrenergic receptors and still elicit a partial biological effect, even after selective blockade of the alternate subtype. Analysis of such dose-response curves further indicates that α_1- and α_2-antagonists produce differential shifts of the curves. Rauwolscine has a greater effect on vasoconstrictor responses to lower concentrations of norepinephrine, whereas prazosin preferentially shifts the top part of the norepinephrine dose-response curve. These findings suggest that α_2-adrenergic receptors mediate vasoconstriction to blood-borne catecholamines at physiologically relevant concentrations. In contrast, vascular α_1-adrenergic receptors may be involved primarily in sympathetic neurotransmission mediated via norepinephrine, independent of the local environment (Alabster and Davey, 1984).

In addition to these differences, α_1- and α_2-adrenergic receptors appear to have divergent tissue distributions and functions (Graham, 1981, 1984; Bylund and U'Prichard, 1983), as well as distinct biochemical effector mechanisms (vide infra). Based largely on pharmacological studies, particularly in vascular tissue preparations, a number of other contrasting features of α_1- and α_2-adrenergic receptors have been noted that probably reflect differences in the receptor-coupled effector mechanisms or in the triggering of signal transduction by various agents, e.g., partial vs. full agonists. For example, the time course of α_2-adrenergic receptor-mediated pressor responses is generally slower in onset than that mediated by α_1-adrenergic receptors, a difference that cannot be readily dismissed due to solubility, diffusion, etc. (Docherty and McGrath, 1980). Other documented differences are the susceptibility of some α_1-adrenergic receptors (e.g., rat anococcygeus and vas deferens but not vascular postjunctional α_1 effects), and of some α_2-adrenergic effects (vascular postjunctional α_2 effects but not prejunctional α_2 effects) to calcium entry blockade or to the absence of extracellular calcium (McGrath, 1983). In contrast, both α_1- and α_2-adrenergic responses to non-phenylethanolamines, which are partial agonists (e.g., clonidine, xylazine, azepexole), are attenuated by calcium entry blockers, whereas those to phenylethanolamines, which are full agonists, are not (McGrath, 1983).

Such differences, the ability of pH changes and calcium entry blockers to distinguish separate components of α_1- and α_2-mediated responses (McGrath, 1983), and differences in the structure-activity requirements of α_1-adrenergic receptors for phenylethylamines and imidazolines (Ruffolo et al., 1983), have suggested subtypes of α-adrenergic receptors beyond the present α_1 and α_2 subdivision. A third or γ subtype of α-adrenergic receptor has been proposed (Hirst and Neild, 1981; Bevan, 1984), predicated on the finding that norepinephrine released after sympathetic nerve stimulation initiates membrane depolarization (excitatory junctional potentials) that is resistant to blockade by α-adrenergic antagonists. At present, however, the evidence implicating an additional subdivision of α-adrenergic receptors is largely inferential, and may be due to nuances of the particular tissue studied or to artifacts of the preparation (McGrath, 1983; Bevan, 1984).

Biochemical Mechanisms of Signal Transduction

α_1-Adrenergic Receptors

Although the mechanism(s) of signal transduction after α_1-adrenergic receptor activation remains elusive, recent studies have provided significant new insights (Fig. 1). In contrast to β-adrenergic and α_2-adrenergic receptors, which are coupled to the membrane-bound enzyme adenylate cyclase by guanine nucleotide regulatory proteins, activation of α_1-adrenergic receptors does not alter intracellular levels of cyclic adenosine 3',5'-monophosphate (cAMP).

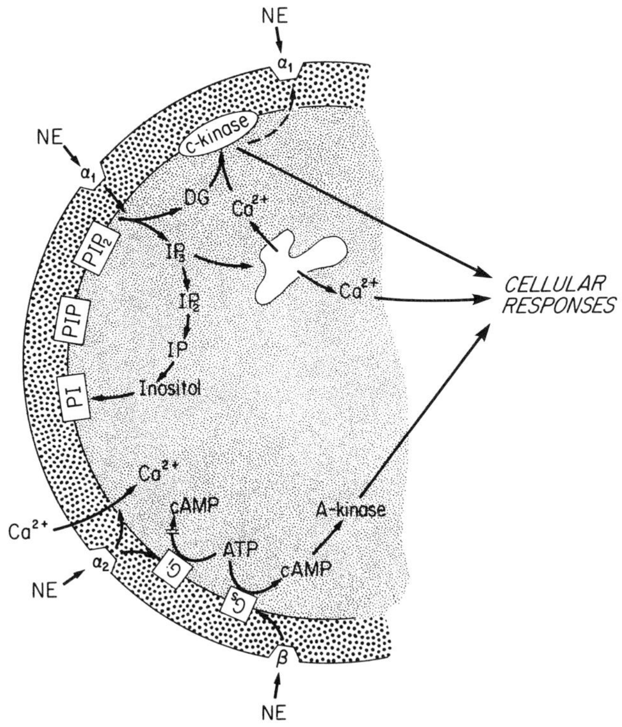

FIGURE 1. *α_1-, α_2- and β-Adrenergic receptor-coupled signal transduction mechanisms leading to cellular responses. Binding of an agonist to the α_1-receptor is postulated to activate an enzyme that hydrolyzes the phosphatidylinositol-4,5-bisphosphate (PIP_2) to form myo-inositol-1,4,5-trisphosphate (IP_3) and diacylglycerol (DG). Availability of IP_3 leads to intracellular Ca^{++} release, which can then activate cellular responses such as actin-myosin coupling or together with DG may promote protein kinase C (C-kinase) activation. C-Kinase activation may limit (broken line) further signal transduction via the α_1-adrenergic receptor. Resynthesis of PIP_2 involves the conversion of IP_3 to inositol by sequential removal of three phosphate groups to form inositol bisphosphate (IP_2), then inositol phosphate (IP), and finally inositol. The cytosine nucleotide derivative, cytosine diphosphate-diacylglycerol (not shown), combines with inositol to produce phosphatidylinositol (PI), which is phosphorylated to yield PIP and then PIP_2. Activation of α_2- or β-adrenergic receptors inhibits or stimulates, respectively, the membrane-bound enzyme adenylate cyclase (not shown); responses are mediated by independent inhibitory (G_i) and stimulatory (G_s) guanine nucleotide-binding regulatory proteins. Increased adenylate cyclase activity promotes the hydrolysis of adenosine triphosphate (ATP) to cyclic adenosine monophosphate (cAMP), which is then available to activate cAMP-dependent protein kinase (A-kinase).*

Rather, the mobilization of Ca^{++} from intracellular vesicles and/or the influx of extracellular Ca^{++} appears to be linked closely to activation of the α_1-receptor, as well as other calcium-mobilizing receptors, such as acetylcholine (muscarinic), vasopressin, angiotensin II, dopamine (D_2), histamine (H_1), thromboxane, thrombin, platelet-activating factor, and various chemoattractant and growth factor receptors. This change in intracellular Ca^{++} may be a primary biochemical mechanism in signal transduction, or may be secondary to the degradation of membrane phospholipids.

Initially, a phospholipid mechanism for signal transduction of calcium-mobilizing receptors was believed to involve the phosphodiesteratic cleavage of the membrane-bound phospholipid, phosphatidylinositol (PI), to yield diacylglycerol and a mixture of inositol 1:2-cyclic phosphate and inositol-1-phosphate (IP) (Michell, 1975). These compounds may increase intracellular Ca^{++} by an ionophore-like action. More recently, Berridge (1983) and, subsequently, Streb et al. (1983) and Joseph et al. (1984), have provided plausible evidence that activation of calcium-mobilizing receptors results in the breakdown of the polyphosphoinositide, phosphatidylinositol-4,5-bisphosphate (PIP_2) to release diacylglycerol and myo-inositol-1,4,5-trisphosphate (IP_3). Furthermore, IP_3 can selectively release Ca^{++} from nonmitochondrial vesicular stores [possibly endoplasmic reticulum (Joseph, 1984)]. On the basis of these observations, and the finding of appropriate temporal changes in IP_3, and considerations of the IP_3-induced Ca^{++} changes with respect to its kinetics, concentration-response, and specificity, several reports have postulated that IP_3 is the second messenger for the α_1-adrenergic (Joseph et al., 1984) and other calcium-mobilizing receptors (Streb et al., 1983).

There now have been similar findings with various types of cells, including insulin- and prolactin-secreting tumor cells, neutrophils, and vascular smooth muscle cells [for a review, see Joseph (1984)], as well as with the hepatocyte, pancreatic islet cell, and blow-fly salivary gland used in the studies mentioned above (Berridge, 1983; Streb et al., 1983; Joseph et al., 1984). Nevertheless, at least in rat hepatocytes, Kunos (1984) has questioned the role of IP_3 as a mediator of intracellular Ca^{++} release, because the breakdown of PIP_2 to IP_3 depends on extracellular Ca^{++} and requires a much higher concentration of agonist than is required for increases in phosphorylase activity or calcium release (Rhodes et al., 1983).

The enzymes involved in the PI-IP_3 cascade have not yet been clearly identified. Of particular interest is the enzyme catalyzing the hydrolysis of PIP_2 to IP_3, presumably a PIP_2-specific membrane-bound phosphodiesterase. Phospholipase C, a cytosolic enzyme, was initially thought to be an unlikely candidate for this reaction, as it is not membrane-bound and requires Ca^{++} for activation. However, Hoffmann et al. (1982) recently reported the isolation of two distinct PI-specific phospholipase C enzymes, one of which specifically hydrolyzed only PIP and PIP_2 after Ca^{++} depletion with EGTA. This finding suggests that cleavage of PIP and PIP_2 occurs prior to increases in Ca^{++} (Majerus et al., 1984). Further, once intracellular Ca^{++} rises, PI breakdown by the Ca^{++}-dependent phospholipase C may predominate, since PI is quantitatively the major potential substrate for this enzyme. A predominantly membrane-bound and Mg^{++}-dependent phosphatase, specific for IP_3, has more recently been isolated from rat liver (Joseph, 1984). This enzyme presumably catalyzes the degradation of IP_3 to IP_2, and may explain the observation that, following the rapid phase of IP_3-induced Ca^{++} release, there is a gradual reuptake of the divalent cation (Joseph, 1983). Thus, as would be expected for a "second messenger," the cell appears to possess enzymes capable of promoting both the production of IP_3 and its degradation to IP_2 and phosphate.

Another recent suggestion by several groups is that the mechanism of signal transduction for α_1-adrenergic receptors may involve more than one pathway (Joseph, 1983; Corvera and Garcia-Sainz, 1983; Bodnar et al., 1983; Morgan et al., 1983). In certain situations, responses to α_1-adrenergic agonists can be clearly dissociated from those of other Ca^{++}-mobilizing hormones, such as vasopressin and angiotensin II (Garcia-Sainz and Corvera, 1983). For example, in the isolated hepatocyte, the phorbol ester, 12-*O*-tetradecanoyl-phorbol-13-acetate (TPA) can attenuate the metabolic effects of α_1-adrenergic agonists without altering the responses to vasopressin or angiotensin II (Corvera and Garcia-Sainz, 1984).

The phorbol-ester, TPA, a diterpene tumor-promoting agent, activates the Ca^{++} and phospholipid-dependent enzyme "C-kinase," in vitro. This activation is believed to reflect the structural similarily between TPA and diacylglycerol (Nishizuka, 1984), which bind specifically and with high affinity to the enzyme. Diacylglycerol, as discussed above, is produced by the hydrolysis of PIP_2 and is felt to be the endogenous activator of C-kinase. This enzyme phosphorylates protein substrates at seryl and threonyl residues. As the covalent modification of proteins by phosphorylation is a common mechanism for their inactivation, it is likely that the selective attenuation of α_1-adrenergic responses by TPA (Corvera and Garcia-Sainz, 1984) is due to C-kinase-induced phosphorylation of a protein very proximal in the signal transduction pathway. Furthermore, as TPA stimulates the phosphorylation of insulin and somatomedin C receptors (Jacobs et al., 1983), the α_1-receptor protein may, itself, be phosphorylated by TPA.

At least two major mechanisms for signal transduction may, therefore, be operative. Initially, IP_3 is formed rapidly and leads to Ca^{++} mobilization. This response is probably common to all calcium-mobilizing receptors. Subsequently, with the availability of increased Ca^{++}, as well as diacylglycerol, protein kinase C may be activated and selectively limit α_1-adrenergic receptor-mediated responses.

Increased production of cyclic guanosine monophosphate (cGMP) has also been proposed as a mediator of α_1-receptor responses. However, the role of cGMP, as well as the mechanism which increases the level of this cyclic nucleotide, is still not clearly understood. Ca^{++} directly stimulates guanylate cyclase, although arachidonic acid peroxide and prostaglandin endoperoxide are more likely to be the in vivo activators of this enzyme (Graff et al., 1978).

Haslam et al. (1980) have suggested that cGMP may act as a negative messenger, as sodium nitroprusside, a potent vasodilator and platelet inhibitor, induces cGMP formation. Similarly, Schultz et al. (1977) have demonstrated that both sodium nitroprusside and the cGMP analog, 8-bromo-cGMP, cause smooth muscle relaxation, although α-adrenergic and muscarinic agonist-induced contraction is associated with enhanced levels of cGMP, as well as inositol phospholipid breakdown. Nishizuka (1984) has interpreted these findings to indicate that, in those cells where cGMP generation inhibits the transmission of "positive signals," cAMP and cGMP do not act antagonistically, but similarly inhibit receptor-induced degradation of inositol phospholipids and thereby act as a control mechanism to limit the "positive" or vasoconstrictor stimulus.

Whether the α_1-adrenergic receptor is coupled to its signal transduction mechanism by a guanine nucleotide-binding protein is presently unclear. Hoffman et al. (1980a) reported that guanine nucleotides decrease the ability of epinephrine to compete with the binding of [^{3}H]dihydroergocryptine to hepatic membrane α-adrenergic receptor sites. However, they interpreted this finding to indicate a nucleotide effect on the interaction of epinephrine—not with α_1-adrenergic receptors—but with the small population of hepatic membrane α_2-adrenergic receptors (Hoffman et al., 1980b; Geynet et al., 1981). In contrast, some evidence suggests, as would be expected for a receptor coupled to a guanine nucleotide regulatory protein, that guanine nucleotides decrease the binding of both [^{3}H]epinephrine and [^{3}H]norepinephrine to α_1-adrenergic receptors of rat liver membranes (El-Rafai et al., 1979; Geynet et al., 1980, 1981). Goodhardt et al. (1982) have also demonstrated agonist-specific regulation by guanine nucleotides in studies with the selective α_1-antagonist, [^{3}H]prazosin. The reason for these discrepant findings is not readily apparent. Nevertheless, it is of interest that a guanine nucleotide-binding protein has been implicated in the gating of Ca^{++} by receptors (Gomperts, 1983). Preliminary studies by Haslam and Davidson (1984) also suggest a role for guanine nucleotide-binding proteins in the activation of platelets by thrombin. Thus, guanine nucleotide-binding proteins, including G_i (vide infra) or perhaps G_o, the newest member of the "family" described very recently by Sternweiss (1984), may well be involved in the signal transduction pathways for the α_1-adrenergic and other Ca^{++}-mobilizing receptors.

α_2-Adrenergic Receptors

Activation of α_2-adrenergic receptors, such as muscarinic receptors in the heart (Watanabe et al., 1978; Jakobs et al., 1979) and opiate receptors in neuroblastoma-glioma (NG 108-15) cultured cells

(Sharma et al., 1977), inhibits the stimulation of adenylate cyclase and limits the availability of intracellular cAMP (Burns and Langley, 1975; Jacobs et al., 1976; Aktories et al., 1979; Cooper et al., 1979; Katada and Ui, 1981) (Fig. 1). Binding of ligands to α_2-adrenergic receptors and, in some tissues, responses to α_2-agonists, correlate with this inhibitory activity (Jacobs et al., 1976). Thus, like β-adrenergic (Fig. 1) and other cAMP-dependent receptors, such as those for dopamine (D_1 or D_2), histamine (H_1), ACTH, and prostaglandin E_2, signal transfer for α_2-adrenergic receptors may involve agonist-induced coupling to adenylate cyclase by a guanine nucleotide-binding protein. Additionally, GTP is required for α_2-agonist-induced inhibition of adenylate cyclase, GTP decreases the affinity for agonists at α_2-adrenergic receptors, and regulation of receptor affinity by guanine nucleotides correlates with agonist efficacy in modulating catalytic activity (Jakobs, 1979).

Despite these similarities, it is now clear that the coupling protein for α_2-adrenergic receptors, G_i, is distinct from that for adenylate cyclase-stimulating receptors, G_s (Yamamura et al., 1977; Cooper et al., 1979; Pinkett et al., 1980; Schlegel et al., 1980; Michel et al., 1981a; Smith and Limbird, 1982; Bokoch et al., 1984; Katada et al., 1984a, 1984b, 1984c). G_s and G_i are both multisubunit proteins with two common subunits, β (mol wt = 35,000) and γ (mol wt = 8,000). However, the molecular weights of the α-subunits differ: 45,000 daltons for G_s and 41,000 for G_i. Furthermore, the α-subunit of G_s ($G_s\ \alpha$) is a substrate for ADP-ribosylation by cholera enterotoxin, whereas $G_i\ \alpha$ is a substrate for ADP-ribosylation by islet-activating protein, a toxin secreted by *Bordetella pertussis* that eliminates or at least reduces the attenuating effects of α_2-adrenergic agonists on adenylate cyclase activity.

Details of this α_2-agonist-induced attenuation of adenylate cyclase remain unclear. However, Gilman (1984) has presented plausible evidence to implicate the following scheme. Activation of G_s-coupled receptors leads to a dissociation of the α and β subunit complex of G_s. In the absence of G_i-coupled receptor activation, $G_s\ \alpha$ is available to stimulate adenylate cyclase. However, when G_i-coupled receptors are activated, the α- and β-subunit complex of G_i dissociates. Since the concentration of G_i is greatly in excess of G_s, the homologous 35,000 dalton β-subunit of G_i released by this process prevents $G_s\ \alpha$-induced stimulation of adenylate cyclase by binding and thus inactivating $G_s\ \alpha$. According to this scheme, $G_i\ \alpha$ is a "passive bystander," acting as an anti-inhibitor of adenylate cyclase. It is also possible that $G_i\ \alpha$ plays an active role in the regulation of other α-adrenergic functions, just as guanine nucleotide-binding proteins have roles independent of an interaction with adenylate cyclase. For example, it has been suggested that insulin affects a plasma membrane kinase and cAMP phosphodiesterase through a specific guanine nucleotide regulatory protein (Heyworth et al., 1983a, 1983b). A particularly interesting system which also involves a guanine nucleotide-binding regulatory protein, termed transducin (Tc), is visual transduction. Upon absorption of light by the visual pigment of the retina, rhodopsin, which is embedded in specialized membrane regions of the photoreceptor, Tc (like G_s and G_i) exchanges GTP for GDP. The Tc-GTP complex thus formed activates a cGMP phosphodiesterase that, in turn, mediates the hydrolysis of cGMP (Fung et al., 1981; Baehr et al., 1982; Bitensky et al., 1978). Marked similarities have also been noted between the gene products of the *ras* gene, contained in a significant proportion of human tumor cell lines and chemically induced rodent tumors, and the guanine nucleotide-binding proteins responsible for inhibition and stimulation of adenylate cyclase (Newbold, 1984).

Such considerations call into question the possibility that not all α_2-adrenergic responses are mediated by inhibition of adenylate cyclase activity. Connolly and Limbird (1983), for example, have postulated that the effects of epinephrine on platelet function may result from the modulation of a Na^+-sensitive process, independent of the α_2-adrenergic receptor-adenylate cyclase system. Similarly, Ullrich and Wollheim (1984) have provided evidence that epinephrine inhibits insulin release from intact isolated rat pancreatic islet cells, at a step distal to the generation of cAMP. Finally, with respect to the classical α_2-adrenergic receptor of prejunctional sympathetic terminals, there is as yet no evidence to show that inhibition of adenylate cyclase decreases norepinephrine release. Electrophysiologically, stimulation of prejunctional α_2-receptors leads to hyperpolarization (Svensson et al., 1975; Taokimasa et al., 1981), a response that may be mediated by activation of the sodium pump, i.e., Na^+,K^+-ATPase, which would result in enhanced calcium efflux (Cohen et al., 1980), thereby limiting Ca^{++} availability for excitation-secretion coupling.

Solubilization, Purification and Biophysical Characterization

α_1-Adrenergic Receptors

To date, most studies directed at the solubilization and molecular characterization of the α_1-adrenergic receptor have employed rat hepatic plasma membranes. This tissue is particularly suitable for such studies because membranes can be obtained in highly purified form and the specific activity of hepatic α_1-adrenergic receptors is about 10-fold higher than in most other tissues. Also, α_1-adrenergic receptors are the predominant subtype in hepatic membranes, being about four times more abundant than α_2-adrenergic receptors.

Initial attempts to characterize the binding of solubilized rat hepatic α_1-adrenergic receptors with the nonselective antagonist [^{3}H]dihydroergocryptine were unsuccessful, probably due to the lipophilicity of this radioligand (Guellaen et al., 1979). Prelabeling with [^{3}H]dihydroergocryptine before solubilization, or use of the non-ionic detergent, digitonin, instead of the ionic detergent, Lubrol PX, did not enhance the identification of a solubilized receptor-protein (Guellaen et al., 1979). For this reason, Guellaen et al. (1979) covalently labeled the receptor with the irreversible antagonist [^{3}H]phenoxybenzamine before solubilization with Lubrol-PX and investigation of its biophysical properties.

Although, in general, the pharmacological specificity of [^{3}H]phenoxybenzamine binding to hepatic membranes correlates with the binding of the highly selective α_1-adrenergic antagonist [^{3}H]prazosin (Kunos et al., 1983), and with [^{3}H]dihydroergocryptine binding (U'Prichard, 1981), this radioligand also interacts covalently with a number of other monoaminergic receptors such as α_2-adrenergic (U'Prichard, 1981), muscarinic cholinergic (Blazso and Minker, 1980), opiate (Robson and Kosterlitz, 1979), and dopaminergic receptors (Lehmann and Langer, 1981), as well as with nonspecific plasma membrane sites (Kunos et al., 1983). It has been suggested that the specificity of [^{3}H]phenoxybenzamine can be enhanced by using very low concentrations of the radioligand (Kunos, 1984). However, identification of the extremely low concentrations of receptor sites present in most tissues then becomes problematic, given the relatively low specific activity (3.3–45 Ci/mmol) of this radioligand. An additional problem with the use of [^{3}H]phenoxybenzamine is that prelabeling of membrane receptors before solubilization precludes investigations of the binding characteristics of the solubilized protein, as its binding site has been irreversibly occupied by the radioprobe. Other investigators, therefore, have attempted to solubilize the membrane-bound receptor in active form.

Graham et al. (1982a, 1982b) investigated a number of both ionic and non-ionic detergents, using a variety of solubilization protocols and various detergent-to-protein ratios. Only the non-ionic detergent, digitonin, reproducibly released the membrane-bound receptors in a form that could be identified by a direct radioligand-binding assay. The binding characteristics of the digitonin-solubilized preparation were identical to that of hepatic membranes, and the binding of the α_1-selective radioligand [^{3}H]prazosin was of high affinity and saturable. When the specificity of [^{3}H]prazosin binding to the solubilized preparation was examined in competition studies with a variety of adrenergic ligands, affinities comparable to those determined with particulate preparations were observed, and the stereoisomeric potency ratio of agonists was closely maintained. These findings thus indicate that the α_1-adrenergic receptor-binding site of hepatic membranes can be solubilized with complete retention of its binding characteristics.

Digitonin has subsequently been used to solubilize membrane-bound α_1-adrenergic receptors from a variety of tissues and species, e.g., rat kidney and rabbit liver (Schwarz, Homcy, and Graham, unpublished observations). In addition, Wikberg et al. (1983) have since reported the successful solubilization of rat hepatic α_1-adrenergic receptors with digitonin.

With the ability to solubilize the α_1-adrenergic receptor in active form, its purification (70,000-fold) to apparent homogeneity (Fig. 2) has been achieved with sequential affinity and gel filtration chromatography (Graham et al., 1982b). The affinity step of this procedure required the synthesis of a novel analog of the highly selective α_1-adrenergic antagonist, prazosin, that could be immobilized on a solid-phase support.

Biophysical characterization of the purified receptor-protein has been confined to the evaluation of the receptor-protein detergent complex, as the hydrodynamic properties of digitonin preclude determination of protein-detergent stoichiometry. Nevertheless, the Stokes radius, sedimentation coefficient, and frictional ratio of the purified receptor-protein have been determined (Graham et al., 1982b). The values determined from these studies differ from those of the solubilized [^{3}H]phenoxybenzamine-binding protein reported by Guellaen et al. (1979). This difference may relate to the limitations of receptor identification by [^{3}H]phenoxybenzamine-labeling, discussed above, as well as to the divergent physical properties of the different detergents used in these studies, namely, Lubrol PX (Guellaen et al., 1979) vs. digitonin (Graham et al., 1982b).

The subunit characteristics of the α_1-adrenergic receptor have been investigated after [^{3}H]phenoxybenzamine labeling of the membrane receptor (Guellaen et al., 1982; Kunos et al., 1983), after purification (Graham et al., 1982b), and, more recently, after covalent labeling of membranes with high specific activity, selective photoaffinity α_1-probes (Seidman et al., 1984a, 1984b; Fredrik-Leeb-Lundberg et al., 1984). Subunit molecular weights (MW) were determined from gel electrophoresis studies. Guellaen et al. (1982) reported a subunit MW of 45,000 daltons for the [^{3}H]phenoxybenzamine-binding protein of rat hepatic membranes. Using [^{3}H]phenoxybenzamine of higher specific activity, Kunos et al. (1983) more recently reported the identification of a major 80,000 dalton band as well as a minor 58,000 subunit. Inasmuch as these studies were performed with membranes prepared in the presence of multiple protease inhibitors, it is likely that the 45,000 dalton peptide identified by Guellaen et al. (1982) in the absence of such inhibitors, is a proteolytic fragment. Similar considerations may also apply to the 59,000 dalton peptide identified after the purification of the α_1-adrenergic receptor-protein (Graham et al., 1982b). Nevertheless, this subunit retains hormone-binding activity, as specific [^{3}H]prazosin binding could be identified following elution and renaturation of the purified receptor-protein from polyacrylamide gels. Very recently, using high specific activity radioiodi-

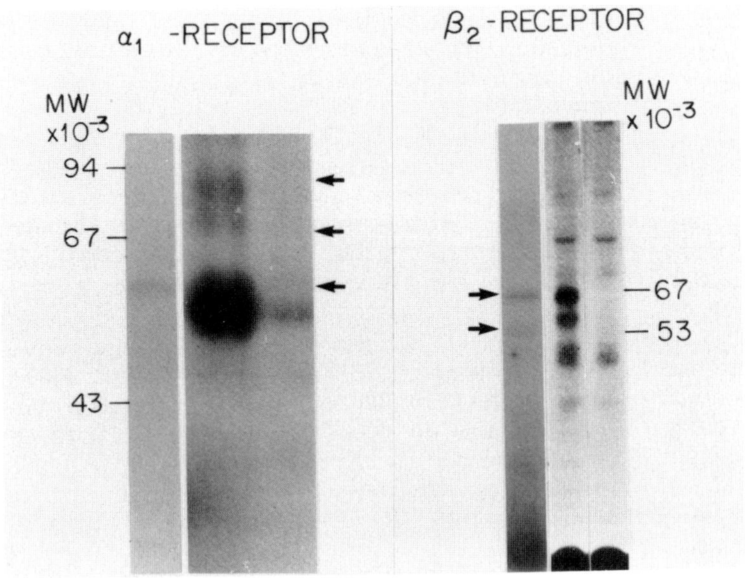

FIGURE 2. *Identification of α_1- and β_2-adrenergic receptors. Lane 1: α_1-adrenergic receptors from rat liver membranes were purified by sequential affinity chromatography with an analog of prazosin, 2-[4-(2-succinoyl/piperazin-1-yl]-4-amino-6,7-dimethoxyquinazoline (CP57,609), immobilized via an amide linkage to agarose, and by gel filtration chromatography after solubilization with the non-ionic detergent, digitonin. The resulting purified receptor was subjected to sodium dodecyl sulfate polyacrylamide gel electrophoresis (SDS-PAGE), and the receptor-protein was visualized by Coomassie blue staining (see Graham et al., 1982b, for details). A single 59,000 dalton molecular weight band is seen. However, as the purification procedure was performed in the absence of protease inhibitors, the possibility that the 59,000 dalton peptide is a proteolyte fragment cannot be excluded [see text for detailed discussion reproduced from Graham et al. (1982b) with permission of the publisher]. Lanes 2 and 3: rat hepatic membrane α_1-adrenergic receptors were labeled with a ^{125}I-p-azidobenzyl analog of the highly selective α_1-adrenergic antagonist, prazosin, in the absence (lane 2) or presence (lane 3) of unlabeled prazosin (10^{-7} M), solubilized, and were subjected to SDS-PAGE and autoradiography [reproduced from Seidman et al. (1984a) with permission of the publisher]. Arrows indicate specifically labeled bands at 77,000, 67,000, and 59,000 daltons. Lane 4: β_2-adrenergic receptors from bovine lung were purified and the receptor-protein was visualized by iodination of the protein, followed by SDS-PAGE and autoradiography (Insoft, 1984). Major bands at 67,000 and 53,000 daltons are visualized. Lanes 5 and 6: S49 lymphoma membrane β_2-adrenergic receptors were labeled with ^{125}I-azidobenylpindolol in the absence (lane 5) or presence (lane 6) of alprenolol (10^{-6} M). The autoradiogram shows specifically labeled peptides at 65,000 and 55,000 daltons. [Reproduced from Rashidbaigi et al. (1983) with permission of the publisher.] Molecular weight (MW) standards are shown.*

nated photoaffinity probes, Seidman et al. (1984a, 1984b) identified a subunit of approximately 80,000 daltons, as well as a 58,000–59,000 dalton species, in membrane preparations (Fig. 2).

From these studies, therefore, there appears to be general agreement that the α_1-adrenergic receptor from rat hepatic membranes, as well as other tissues (Fredrik-Leeb-Lundberg et al., 1984), contains a major subunit of approximately 80,000 daltons. The smaller 59,000 dalton peptide, which retains hormone-binding activity (Graham et al., 1982b), may be a proteolytic fragment. However, the possibility that this species is an integral part of the α_1-adrenergic receptor or is generated in vivo in the intact plasma membrane cannot be entirely excluded, as Seidman et al. (1984b) and Kunos (1984) were unable to prevent completely the identification of a 58,000–59,000 dalton protein, despite the use of the most stringent measures to prevent proteolysis. Since a molecular weight of 147,000–160,000 daltons has been reported for the holoreceptor (Graham et al., 1982b; Venter et al., 1984), it is probable that the α_1-adrenergic receptor contains more than one subunit.

Studies with the purified rat hepatic α_1-adrenergic receptor-protein indicate a resilient tertiary structure stabilized by a disulfide bond. This bond is critical for ligand binding but is inaccessible to solvent. Thus, complete binding activity can be recovered after lyophilization of the receptor-protein and renaturation out of guanidine (Graham et al., 1982a, 1982b; Homcy et al., 1982). Strong hydrophobic interactions are also likely, since full binding activity can be observed with urea solubilization (Homcy et al., 1982). The canine lung β_2-adrenergic receptor is similarly stabilized by hydrophobic interactions (Homcy and Sylvestre, 1982), although the binding site of both the membrane and purified forms of this receptor-protein contains a disulfide bond accessible to solvent (Homcy et al., 1982). Preliminary studies by Snavely and Insel (1983) suggest that α_1-adrenergic receptor sites of rat renal membranes may also contain sulfhydryl groups critical for ligand binding.

α_2-Adrenergic Receptor

Studies directed at the solubilization and molecular characterization of α_2-adrenergic receptors have employed platelets, almost exclusively, as the tissue source.

Smith and Limbird (1981) and Michel et al. (1981b) have solubilized platelet membranes with the non-ionic detergent, digitonin, which has permitted the identification of the receptor-protein by direct radioligand-binding assay. The digitonin-solubilized binding component could be identified with the α_2-selective antagonist, [^{3}H]yohimbine. Although the binding characteristics of the solubilized receptor were largely conserved with respect to the membrane-binding site, the affinity for agonists was reduced, and was no longer modulated by guanine nucleotides. In addition, solubilization of the platelet membranes after prelabeling with the agonist [^{3}H]epinephrine resulted in a complex sensitive to guanine nucleotides that sedimented more rapidly in sucrose gradients than unoccupied or antagonist-occupied receptors. These findings suggest that agonist occupancy stabilizes the receptor interaction with the inhibitory guanine nucleotide-binding regulatory protein, which is required for modulation of agonist affinity by guanine nucleotides. Thus, in the absence of agonist occupancy, solubilization presumably promotes an uncoupling of the membrane receptor from its effector-coupled component, and agonist affinity is no longer modulated by guanine nucleotides. These studies also provide some data on the biophysical properties of the α_2-adrenergic receptor. Thus, a sedimentation coefficient of 11.4–12.9S was observed for the unoccupied or antagonist-labeled receptor, and 13.4–14.6S for the agonist-prelabeled protein (Smith and Limbird, 1981; Michel et al., 1981b).

Partial purification of the digitonin-solubilized platelet α_2-adrenergic receptor has been reported. Smith and Limbird (1982) employed a wheat germ affinity resin, which successfully adsorbed the solubilized receptor. This finding provides evidence for the glycosylated nature of the protein, although co-solubilization of an unrelated but glycosylated protein in the same detergent micelle cannot be definitely excluded. Desorption was achieved with the carbohydrate *N*-acetyl-*O*-glucosamine. Regan et al. (1982, 1984) have reported a 200- to 600-fold purification of the human platelet α_2-adrenergic receptor by the use of an affinity column composed of a 3-benzazepine (SKF-101253) coupled to Sepharose CL-4B. However, the specificity of the protein purified with this affinity resin is not entirely clear. Thus, phentolamine, a nonselective α-adrenergic antagonist, was equal to yohimbine, an α_2-antagonist, in its ability to prevent adsorption of the solubilized receptor protein to the affinity resin, and was more effective than yohimbine in eluting the adsorbed protein from the column. The use of this affinity column for purification of α_2-adrenergic receptors from tissues containing both α-receptor subtypes may also be limited, as SKF-101253 has a relatively low selectivity (5-fold) for α_2- compared to α_1-adrenergic receptors.*

After partial affinity purification of solubilized platelets, Regan et al. (1984) covalently labeled the proteins obtained with the alkylating agent [^{3}H]-phenoxybenzamine. The molecular mass of the labeled proteins then was evaluated by sodium dodecyl sulfate gel electrophoresis and autoradiography and was found to be 61,000 daltons. In contrast, Venter et al. (1983) used target-size analysis by radiation inactivation to determine a molecular mass of 160,000 daltons for the holoreceptor in platelet membranes.

Atlas and Steer (1982) recently reported the synthesis and characterization of an affinity label, clonidine *p*-isothiocyanate, for the α_2-adrenergic receptor. Although this compound and a related radiolabeled photoaffinity probe (U'Prichard and Ensberger, 1983) have low affinity for the α_2-adrenergic receptor, it can be anticipated that related high affinity, high specific activity compounds will soon be available for more complete investigation of the molecular characteristics of this adrenergic receptor subtype.

Progress in β-Receptor Purification and Reconstitution

The β-adrenergic receptor is also an intrinsic membrane protein which requires detergents for its solubilization. When liberated into a detergent micelle, these molecules can be characterized and purified by biochemical techniques, including gel filtration and affinity chromatography. Haga et al. (1977) prelabeled the receptor with ^{125}I-hydroxybenzylpindolol before solubilization, thus allowing them to characterize the biophysical properties of the labeled receptor-detergent complex. However, such a technique is cumbersome, particularly in the presence of high levels of nonspecific ligand binding. Furthermore, a prelabeling technique does not permit the use of purification methods such as affinity chromatography which requires an unencumbered binding site to allow the receptor to interact with immobilized ligand. Although high concentrations of disrupting agents such as urea have been shown to liberate the receptor (Homcy and Sylvestre, 1982), digitonin, a sterol detergent similar to the bile acids, remains the most useful and effective agent for its solubilization. It appears to be the only non-ionic detergent that does not appreciably interfere with ligand binding (Caron and Lefkowitz, 1976). Problems with characterization of the solubilized receptor relate to the extremely low concentration of the receptor, typically 50 to 400 fmol/mg of membrane protein, or 1,000 to 10,000 copies/cell, usually in direct relation to cell surface area. After solubilization, concentrations in the pmol (10^{-12} M) range can be expected. This, together with the relatively high level of nonspecific binding of lipophilic ligands such as dihydroalprenolol, has made routine assay difficult. Successful solubilization of the β-receptor in a form assayable by direct binding assay

* *With a demethylated analog of the selective α_2-adrenergic antagonist yohimbine coupled to agarose (Graham et al., 1982c), partial purification (200-fold) of the digitonin-solubilized platelet-membrane receptor has also been achieved (Graham, Karnes, and Homcy, unpublished observations).*

was reported by Caron and Lefkowitz (1976). The solubilized receptor was extracted from frog erythrocyte membranes. These membranes could be readily prepared, and contained a receptor concentration as high as 1 pmol/mg (Caron and Lefkowitz, 1976). With the development of reliable solubilization and assay techniques, purification of the receptor protein became an attainable goal, although the task remained onerous. Two different affinity supports employing either alprenolol (Vacquelin et al., 1977; Shorr et al., 1981) or acebutolol (Homcy et al., 1983) have proved invaluable in isolating the solubilized receptor. Recently, this technique, coupled with high performance gel filtration chromatography, has enabled the entire purification protocol to be completed within a period of hours rather than days.

A perplexing observation was the initial description by several laboratories of multiple molecular weight forms, whether the receptor was identified by SDS gel electrophoresis after purification, or, for impure preparations, by the technique of photoaffinity labeling. It is valuable to review some of this data and then summarize the relevant points.

The initial studies which were successful in purifying the β-receptor used either avian or amphibian erythrocytes. These are nucleated and provide a rich source of receptors with concentrations as high as 1 pmol/mg membrane protein. Purification of the turkey erythrocyte β-receptor was first reported by Vacquelin et al. in 1977. Subsequently, Atlas and Levitzki (1978), utilizing a tritiated affinity label, a derivative of propranolol, visualized two bands of 37,000 and 41,000 daltons for the β_1-receptor of the turkey erythrocyte. For the β_2-receptor of the frog red blood cell, the laboratories of Caron and Lefkowitz have consistently reported a molecular weight for the hormone-binding subunit of approximately 58,000 daltons, with the peptide migrating as a rather diffuse band on SDS gels (Shorr et al., 1981). In contrast, the β_2-receptor from mammalian tissue, principally lung, was identified at several different weights of 64,000 (Benovic et al., 1983), 53,000 (Homcy et al., 1983) to 59,000 (Fraser and Venter, 1982) and 44,000 (Benovic et al., 1983) daltons. The affinity-purified β_2-receptor from canine lung was first reported to contain a major form of approximately 53,000 daltons (Homcy et al., 1983). However, over the past 2 years, this diversity in molecular weight is slowly disappearing, and the likelihood that it is an artifact produced by proteolysis is becoming clearer. Recently, Benovic et al. (1983) have described a principal molecular weight of 64,000–67,000 daltons from mammalian lung with lesser bands sometimes seen at 53,000–55,000 daltons. Rashidbaigi et al. (1983) have consistently reported visualization of 65,000 and 55,000 dalton bands for the photolabeled β_2-receptor of the S49 lymphoma cell (Fig. 2). With more careful attention to inhibiting proteolysis, as well as more rapid purification procedures, a principal band of 67,000 daltons for the β_2-receptor from calf lung, with a lesser band at 53,000 daltons, was also visualized (Insoft and Homcy et al., 1984) (Fig. 2). More recently, a preliminary report describes a principal band of 67,000 daltons for the β_2-receptor from liver (Graziano and Malbon et al., 1984). For the mammalian β_1-receptor, a principal molecular weight of 62,000–67,000 daltons is generally visualized, whether obtained by photoaffinity labeling of myocardial membranes (Stiles et al., 1982) or following purification of the receptor from fat cell membranes (Cubero and Malbon, 1984). The turkey red blood cell, identified as a β_1-receptor by its relative affinities for a variety of ligands, is anomalous, with two molecular weight forms of approximately 43,000 and 38,000 daltons being reported (Atlas and Levitzki, 1978; Shorr et al., 1982; Burgermeister et al., 1982).

In summary, both the mammalian β_1- and β_2-receptors, whether identified following purification or by photoaffinity labeling, consist of a principal band of 62,000–67,000 daltons. In addition, several laboratories have consistently visualized lower molecular weights of approximately 53,000–55,000 daltons, particularly for the β_2-receptor.

Although increasing information on the molecular weight of the hormone-binding subunit has become available, the structural and chemical properties of the intact receptor have not been well characterized. For comparison, in the case of the nicotinic acetylcholine receptor, it is known that a pentameric structure exists, with each of the four subunits (α, β, γ, and δ) (Changeux, 1981; Conti-Tronconi and Raftery, 1982) represented singly, except for the α-subunit, which contributes two polypeptide chains to the pentameric ring. In the case of the β-receptor, little information of this kind exists. Preliminary data based on hydrodynamic measurements of the intact receptor following receptor solubilization suggest that it contains the hormone-binding polypeptide in monomeric or perhaps dimeric form (Benovic et al., 1983; Cubero and Malbon, 1984). Since the receptor is a hydrophobic protein and does not behave as a globular structure in solution, its absolute mass cannot be directly calculated by comparing its mobility to soluble protein standards during gel exclusion chromatography or sedimentation velocity experiments. However, approximations of this type have indicated that the non-denatured receptor has a molecular weight ranging from 130,000–160,000 daltons consistent with a monomeric or possibly dimeric representation of the hormone-binding polypeptide, depending on the contribution of bound detergent to this measurement of overall mass (Haga et al., 1977, 1983; Cubero and Malbon, 1984).

Some data indicate that the receptor is a glycoprotein, such as the demonstration that the solubilized receptor can be immobilized on lectin affinity resins which are known to bind to specific carbohydrate residues (Stadel et al., 1981a), and that expression of the receptor on the cell surface is inhibited by the antibiotic tunicamycin which inhibits protein glycosylation (Doss et al., 1982). Since it is well known that the mobility of a protein during SDS-polyacrylamide gel electrophoresis can be affected by its state of glycosylation, it is possible that the minor subunit observed at 53,000–55,000 dalton and the broad 50,000–60,000 dalton band observed in frog β-receptor differ in carbohydrate rather than amino acid content. Differences in carbohydrate content might also contribute to the minor variations in mobility for receptor subtypes prepared from different species and cell lines (Stiles et al., 1984). Although the migration of a protein during SDS-gel electrophoresis is not only a function of its amino acid content, i.e., molecular weight, but also of its carbohydrate composition, the above studies nevertheless suggest that the mammalian β-adrenergic receptor consists of a single peptide of 62,000–67,000 daltons. This structure is generally observed despite the tissue of origin or the receptor subtype. In certain tissues from lower species, such as amphibian and avian erythrocytes, receptor proteins have consistently been documented to be of smaller molecular weight.

Several laboratories have now successfully incorporated these highly purified receptor preparations into lipid vesicles, thus providing a system in which individual components of hormone-sensitive adenylate cyclase can be reconstituted. Schramm and his colleagues laid the groundwork for these types of studies. They initially introduced a crude solubilized receptor preparation into membranes lacking receptor but containing G_S (the GTP-binding protein which couples receptor to adenylate cyclase) and cyclase catalytic activity (Citri and Schramm, 1980, 1982). More recently, Pederson and Ross (1982) and Brandt et al. (1983) successfully reconstituted partially purified β-receptor from turkey erythrocytes with G_S purified from rabbit liver, resulting in both hormone-mediated stimulation of adenylate cyclase activity and GTPase activity, the latter being a direct measurement of receptor-coupled G_S. Similarly Kelleher et al. (1983) reconstituted a highly purified β-receptor prepared from turkey erythrocytes into human erythrocyte membranes which lacked both receptor and catalytic activity, but which possessed the G_S coupling protein. A GTP-induced shift in agonist affinity, which was lacking in the solubilized receptor preparation, indicated that a functional linkage between the receptor protein and G_S was occurring. Previous to this work, Jeffery et al. (1980) had demonstrated similar results utilizing a crude detergent-solubilized receptor preparation. Recently, with purified β_2-receptor preparations which ran as single bands of approximately 65,000 daltons on SDS gels, Cerione et al. (1983) were able to reconstitute hormone-sensitive adenylate cyclase into erythrocytes from *Xenopus laevis* which contain G_S and catalytic activity, but lack endogenous receptors.

When considered together, the above studies indicate that the hormone-binding peptide contains all the necessary information to transduce a signal following the binding of an agonist hormone. Within a short period of time, it can be expected that such reconstitution experiments, utilizing purified receptor and cyclase components reconstituted within artificial lipid vesicles, will allow direct evaluation of the stoichiometry and kinetics of the reaction leading to cyclase activation following hormone binding. Furthermore, such approaches will allow definition of the role that the lipid bilayer plays in promoting and modulating these interactions.

Receptor Regulation

Much information and insight has accrued concerning the mechanisms of catecholamine-induced desensitization. Although a large body of experimental data has accumulated in this area, it is our aim to review only that work relating to the molecular mechanisms underlying these processes. We will limit the discussion to that form of desensitization, generally termed homologous, which indicates cellular refractoriness upon rechallenge with the same agonist used in the initial exposure. By way of introduction, a general scheme for catecholamine-specific desensitization can now be formulated (Harden, 1983). The receptor proteins probably are situated within the lipid bilayer as distinct species that interact with hormones and G_S, the guanylyl nucleotide-binding protein(s), which couples the receptor protein to the catalytic unit of adenylate cyclase. Upon binding agonist, there is a rapid conversion from the native form of the receptor to one incapable of forming a high affinity complex with G_S. It is postulated, but has not been proved, that this event is due to covalent modification of the receptor protein. Thereafter, the receptor protein probably is internalized and subsequently degraded or reprocessed, according to evidence from several laboratories. Chuang and Costa (1979) were the first to suggest this possibility, utilizing the frog erythrocyte as a model system to demonstrate that [^{3}H]-dihydroalpenolol (DHA)-binding sites appeared in the cytosol after exposure of the cells to isoproterenol. Later work suggested that a biochemical pathway similar to that mediating internalization of peptide hormone receptors might be involved; however, the details of these events still remain sketchy (Chuang, 1981). This process of internalization has subsequently been confirmed by others who have also demonstrated that the internalized β-receptors probably exist in a vesicular form which may eventually be degraded (Waldo et al., 1983). The early processes of uncoupling and internalization are rapid, beginning within 1–2 minutes after binding of agonsits, and are responsible for a loss of adenylate cyclase activation, and may also explain the apparent low affinity agonist binding seen in whole cell-binding assays. It has been suggested that this latter phenomenon is secondary to internalization of uncoupled receptors, thus precluding their binding of agonists. Hydrophilic catecholamines cannot freely cross the plasma membrane to compete with the binding of lipophilic ligands such as [^{3}H]dihydroalprenolol or [^{125}I]cyanopindolol. The subsequent slower loss of receptors as detected by ligand-binding experiments in intact cells may result from lysozymal degradation of the internalized species, a processing pathway that regulates the activity of a variety of membrane proteins.

The likelihood that each of these steps will eventually be dissected is underscored by recent work carried out by Stadel et al. (1983). Heterologous desensitization in the turkey erythrocyte β-receptor-adenylate cyclase system previously has been shown to be mediated through a cAMP-dependent pathway (Stadel et al., 1981b). Unlike the more common form of catecholamine-specific desensitization, which clearly does not depend on activation of cyclase catalytic activity and cannot be mimicked by agents which increase intracellular cAMP, the uncoupling of the receptor from cyclase can be produced by either of these interventions in the turkey erythrocyte. Furthermore, since receptor loss in the turkey erythrocyte does not occur, even at later stages of desensitization, the technique of photoaffinity labeling could be brought to bear to ascertain whether the hormone-binding subunit is physically altered under conditions that lead to receptor desensitization. After agonist exposure in the intact cells, the receptor was covalently labeled with [^{125}I]azidobenzylcarazolol, and a shift in its apparent molecular weight was observed. Since covalent modification of a protein can alter its behavior during SDS-gel electrophoresis, it was suggested that cAMP-dependent phosphorylation of the receptor might have occurred. Thereafter, the intact cell was desensitized during incubation with $^{32}P_i$ and the receptor protein was purified by affinity chromatography. Under these conditions, $^{32}P_i$ labeling of the receptor protein was detectable, and its migration on the gel coincided with that observed by photoaffinity labeling. Finally, purified cAMP-dependent protein kinase was shown to phosphorylate the purified β-receptor protein. Rashidbaigi et al. (1983) have recently carried out similar investigations in the mammalian S49 lymphoma line. During the early stages of desensitization before receptor loss has occurred, these investigators could not detect any alteration in the mobility of the photolabeled receptor on SDS gels. This suggests that phosphorylation of the receptor, to a significant extent, is not initiated during receptor uncoupling in this system as occurs in the turkey erythrocyte.

Although the mechanism of desensitization, as outlined above for the turkey erythrocyte β_1-receptor, does not appear to be the major pathway by which receptor function is modulated by agonists in mammalian cells, this work nevertheless emphasizes the potential insight to be gained through the scrutinizing of purified components as they become available. Such an approach is not limited to this kind of study, but should prove useful in demonstrating, for any particular pathophysiological state, whether an altered form of receptor protein is operative. For example, recently Vatner et al. (1984) have found, in a chronic canine model of severe left ventricular hypertrophy, that the affinity of the β-receptor protein for adrenergic ligands is significantly reduced and worsens as heart failure ensues. Since even antagonist binding demonstrates this alteration, it is possible that the receptor protein has been changed through a post-translational modification (e.g., phosphorylation) or a different gene product has been expressed consistent with gene polymorphism. Several examples of this latter mechanism clearly occur in the hypertrophied left ventricle, where isozymes of lactate dehydrogenase (LDH), myosin, and creatine phosphokinase are transcribed under these conditions.

Antibodies

The development of specific antibodies to the β-adrenergic receptor is a major goal of several laboratories, and would provide a valuable tool for investigating receptor regulation and structure. In the analysis of desensitization where receptor loss occurs as detected by ligand binding, anti-receptor antibodies not dependent on a functional binding site would allow an independent method of quantifying receptor metabolism. Homology between receptor subtypes could be addressed using antibodies to identify specific epitopes which might differ between two related polypeptides, e.g., between the β_1- and β_2-receptors. Although several groups have now successfully raised antibodies to the β-receptor protein, little substantive information has yet come from studies with these probes. Wrenn and Haber (1979) initially reported an antibody raised to a partially purified cardiac β_1-receptor preparation which distinguished between the β_1- and β_2-receptor subtypes. However, it appeared to be of generally low affinity. Couraud et al. (1981) and Fraser and Venter (1980) both have reported on the development of monoclonal antibodies to the β_1-adrenergic receptor of the turkey erythrocyte. However, on the basis of their titers, these antibodies were of such low affinity that their sensitivity was probably insufficient to permit them to be used successfully as probes of receptor structure or metabolism. Strader et al. (1983) also have recently obtained antisera raised to a partially purified β-receptor preparation which noncompetitively inhibits adenylate cyclase activation.

In addition to immunizing with the receptor protein itself, binding site-directed anti-receptor antibodies have been developed by employing the anti-idiotypic response to antibodies raised to the ligand, alprenolol. Anti-alprenolol antibodies are used which display binding characteristics similar to those of the β-receptor itself (Rockson et al., 1980). Immunization with these antibodies generates anti-idiotypic antiserum that contains antibodies directed against the binding site of the first antibody. Since the anti-ligand antibodies used as the immunogen were homologous to the biological receptor in their binding properties, the second antibody response might be expected to generate a set of anti-idiotypic antibodies that interacts with a similarly structured binding site within the receptor itself. Homcy et al. (1980) used this approach to generate an antisera which competitively inhibited both ligand binding and cyclase activation by isoproterenol to β-receptors from different species and tissue types. Similar work also had been carried out by Schreiber et al. (1980), although their antisera behaved in a somewhat anomalous manner, not clearly interacting directly with the ligand-binding site of the receptor.

Elicited polyclonal anti-idiotypic antiserum has the disadvantages that the serum response is often short-lived and that multiple antibodies of varying affinity are expressed. The development of monoclonal anti-idiotypic antibodies via somatic cell hybridization techniques should overcome these problems and permit the generation of sufficient quantities of antibody to be used routinely as laboratory reagents.

Directions for the Future

Although much progress has been made in the structural characterization of the β- and α-adrenergic receptors, there are wide gaps in our knowledge of how these receptors are arranged in the lipid bilayer and of the exact mechanisms through which they couple to effector proteins. What are the directions that will lead in the future to a clearer picture of how these membrane proteins work? If we list recent advances in the molecular characterization of another neurotransmitter receptor, the nicotinic acetylcholine receptor (Burgermeister et al., 1982; Changeux, 1981), then the power of the new approaches in molecular biology becomes readily apparent. Since this receptor could be found in much greater quantities, its purification in high yield was accomplished with relative ease. With large quantities of protein, monoclonal antibodies to defined epitopes were raised (Gullick and Lindstrom, 1983). Primary amino acid sequence data became available as well (Noda et al., 1982, 1983a, 1983b). With these tools in hand, the gene was eventually isolated and the receptor has now been cloned and expressed in active form (Mishina et al., 1984). Such tools, particularly site-specific antibodies, have allowed assignment of specific functions, e.g., ligand binding to a specific subunit of this receptor, one of four distinct polypeptide chains. Their arrangement as pentamers (the α subunit is represented twice) to form apparent pores within the membrane bilayer was determined when the purified receptor was reconstituted into synthetic phospholipid micelles. Recently, monoclonal antibodies raised to each of these subunits demonstrated that immunologically similar regions exist within the different subunits. This, together with primary amino acid sequence data, has led to the suggestion that the subunits may have evolved from a common precursor gene through the process of reduplication.

The availability of a cDNA clone and the eventual expression of the gene product in a bacterial system would have even greater implications for progress in the area of adrenergic receptors. These proteins exist in such small quantities that experiments aimed at addressing questions related to the stoichiometry between receptor and G_S, the effects of excess receptors, and the processing of the receptor protein may be more easily approached as cloning techniques allow for the expression of the receptor protein in larger quantity. Both the availability of cDNA probes and monoclonal antibodies to specific sites within the receptor subunit should allow insight into the evolution of the different adrenergic receptor genes. There is the possibility that an even greater diversity of receptor subtypes exists that could represent either gene polymorphism or allelic variation. These kinds of questions can be adequately addressed only after an appropriate cDNA probe is obtained. Furthermore, those factors, including heterologous and homologous hormonal control mechanisms which regulate expression of the receptor gene, can be studied to determine whether they mediate their effect at the transcriptional or translational level.

We thank D. Rollins, K. Taylor, and N. Roosa for assistance with the preparation of the manuscripts. We would also like to thank Janice Countaway, David Egan, Hans Hess, Robert Insoft, Christine Seidman, and Diana Sylvestre who participated in this research. In particular, we would like to thank Dr. Edgar Haber for his continued support and encouragement.

Studies reported here were based on research supported in part by Grants HL-19259, NS-19583, and AHA 83-1242, with funds from the Massachusetts Affiliate, and by a grant from the R.J. Reynolds Co. CJH and RMG are Established Investigators, American Heart Association (AHA 80-148 and 82-240).

Address for reprints: Dr. Charles J. Homcy, Cellular and Molecular Research Laboratory, Cardiac Unit, Massachusetts General Hospital, Boston, Massachusetts 02114.

References

Aktories K, Schultz G, Jakobs KH (1979) Inhibition of hamster fat cell adenylate cyclase by prostaglandin E_1 and epinephrine: Requirement for GTP and sodium ions. FEBS Lett **107:** 100–104

Alabster V, Davy M (in press) Precapillary vessels: Effects of the sympathetic nervous system and of catecholamines. J Cardiovasc Pharmacol

Atlas D, Levitzki A (1978) Tentative identification of beta-adrenoceptor subunits. Nature (Lond) **272:** 370–371

Atlas D, Steer ML (1982) Clonidine *p*-isothiocyanate, an affinity label for alpha-2 adrenergic receptors on human platelets. Proc Natl Acad Sci USA **79:** 1378–1382

Baehr W, Morita EA, Swanson RJ, Applebury ML (1982) Characterization of bovine rod outer segment G-protein. J Biol Chem **257:** 6452–6460

Banerjee SP, Kung LS (1977) Beta-adrenergic receptors in rat heart: Effects of thyroidectomy. Eur J Pharmacol **43:** 207–208

Benovic JL, Stiles GL, Lefkowitz RJ, Caron MG (1983) Photoaffinity labeling of mammalian beta-adrenergic receptors: Metal-dependent proteolysis explains apparent heterogeneity. Biochem Biophys Res Commun **110:** 504–511

Berridge MJ (1983) Rapid accumulation of inositol trisphosphate reveals that agonists hydrolyse polyphosphoinositides instead of phosphatidylinositol. Biochem J **212:** 849–858

Berthelson S, Pettinger WA (1977) A functional basis for classification of alpha-adrenergic receptors. Life Sci **21:** 595–606

Bevan JA (1984) The gamma-connection: Are we ready to throw out the alpha-adrenoceptor in sympathetic vasoconstriction? Trends Pharmacol Sci **2:** 53–55

Bitensky MW, Wheeler GL, Aloni B, Vetury S, Matuo Y (1978) Light- and GTP-activated photoreceptor phosphodiesterase: Regulation of a light activated GTPase and identification of rhodopsin as the phosphodiesterase binding site. Adv Cyclic Nucleotide Res **9:** 553–572

Blazso G, Minker E (1980) Alkylation of ganglionic cholinergic receptors with haloalkyl amines. ACTA Pharm Hung **50:** 137–144

Bodnar L, Hoopes MT, Gec M, Ito H, Roth GS, Baum BJ (1983) Multiple transduction mechanisms are likely involved in calcium-mediated exocrine secretory events in rat parotid cells. J Biol Chem **258:** 2774–2777

Bokoch GM, Katada T, Northup JK, Ui M, Gilman AG (1984) Purification and properties of the inhibitory guanine nucleotide-binding regulatory component of adenylate cyclase. J Biol Chem **259:** 3560–3567

Brandt DR, Asano T, Pedersen SE, Ross EM (1983) Reconstitution of catecholamine-stimulated guanosinetriphosphatase activity. Biochemistry **22:** 4357–4362

Burgermeister W, Hekman M, Helmreich EJM (1982) Photoaffinity labeling of the beta-adrenergic receptor with azide derivative of iodocyanopindolol. J Biol Chem **257:** 5306–5311

Burns TW, Langley PE (1975) The effect of alpha- and beta-adrenergic receptor stimulation and adenylate cyclase activity of human adipocytes. J Cyclic Nucleotide Res **1:** 321–328

Bylund DB, U'Prichard DC (1983) Characterization of alpha-1 and alpha-2 adrenergic receptors. Int Rev Neurobiol **24:** 343–431

Caron MG, Lefkowitz RJ (1976) Solubilization and characterization of the beta-adrenergic receptor binding site of frog erythrocytes. J Biol Chem **251:** 2374–2384

Cerione RA, Strulovici B, Benovic JL, Lefkowitz RJ, Caron MG (1983) Pure beta-adrenergic receptor: The single polypeptide confers catecholamine responsiveness to adenylate cyclase. Nature **306:** 562–566

Changeux JP (1981) The acetylcholine receptors: An "allosteric" membrane protein. Harvey Lecture **75:** 85–254

Chuang DM (1981) Inhibitors of transglutaminase prevent agonist-mediated internalization of beta-adrenergic receptors. J Biol Chem **256:** 8291–8293

Chuang DM, Costa E (1979) Evidence for internalization of the recognition site of beta-adrenergic receptors during receptor subsensitivity induced by (−)isoproterenol. Proc Natl Acad Sci USA **76:** 3024–3028

Ciaraldi TP, Mainetti GR (1975) Adrenergic receptors in rat heart and adipocytes and their modulation by thyroxine. Biochim Biophys Acta **54:** 334–346

Citri Y, Schramm M (1980) Resolution, reconstitution and kinetics of the primary action of a hormone receptor. Nature (Lond) **287:** 297–300

Citri Y, Schramm M (1982) Probing of the coupling site of the beta-adrenergic receptor. Competition between different forms of the guanylyl nucleotide binding protein for interaction with the receptor. J Biol Chem **257:** 13257–13262

Cohen J, Eckstein L, Gutman Y (1980) The mechanism of alpha-adrenergic inhibition of catecholamine release. Br J Pharmacol **71:** 135–142

Connolly TM, Limbird LE (1983) The influence of Na^+ on the alpha-2 adrenergic receptor system of human platelets. A method for removal of extraplatelet Na^+: Effect of Na^+ removal on aggregation, secretion, and cAMP accumulation. J Biol Chem **258:** 3907–3912

Conti-Tronconi BM, Raftery MA (1982) Nicotinic cholinergic receptor correlation of molecular structure with functional properties. Annu Rev Biochem **51:** 491–530

Cooper DMF, Schlegel W, Lin MC, Rodbell M (1979) The fat cell adenylate cyclase system. Characterization and manipulation of its bimodal regulation of GTP. J Biol Chem **254:** 8927–8931

Corvera S, García-Sáinz JA (1983) Hypothyroidism abolishes the glycogenolytic effect of vasopressin, angiotensin II and A23187 but not that of alpha-1 adrenergic amines in rat hepatocytes. FEBS Lett **153:** 366–368

Corvera S, García-Sáinz JA (1984) Phorbol esters inhibit alpha-1 adrenergic stimulation of glycogenolysis in isolated rat hepatocytes. Biochem Biophys Res Commun **119:** 1128–1133

Couraud PO, Delavier-Klutchko C, Durieu-Trautmann O, Strosberg AD (1981) Antibodies raised against beta-adrenergic receptors stimulate adenylate cyclase. Biochem Biophys Res Commun **99:** 1295–1302

Cubero A, Malbon C (1984) The fat cell beta-adrenergic receptor. Purification and characterization of a mammalian beta-1 adrenergic receptor. J Biol Chem **259:** 1344–1350

Davies AO, DeLean A, Lefkowitz RJ (1981) Myocardial beta-adrenergic receptors from adrenalectomized rats: Impaired formation of high affinity agonist receptor complexes. Endocrinology **108:** 720–722

Docherty JR, McGrath JC (1980) A comparison of pre- and post-junctional potencies of several alpha-adrenoceptor agonists in the cardiovascular system and anococcygeus muscle of the rat. Evidence for two types of post-junctional alpha-adrenoceptor. Naunyn Schmiedebergs Arch Pharmacol **312:** 107–116

Doss RC, Harden TK, Perkins JP (1982) Role of protein glycosylation in the synthetic processing of beta-adrenergic receptors. Fed Proc **41:** 1534

Drew GM, Whiting SB (1979) Evidence for two distinct types of postsynaptic alpha-adrenoceptor in vascular smooth muscle in vivo. Br J Pharmacol **67:** 207–215

Elliot HL, Jones CR, Vincent J, Reid JL (1983) Alpha-adrenoceptor antagonist action of RX781094 in man: Selective effects on alpha-2 adrenoceptors. Br J Clin Pharmacol **15:** 598P

El-Rafai MF, Blackmore PF, Exton JH (1979) Evidence for two alpha-adrenergic binding sites in liver plasma membranes. Studies with [^{3}H]epinephrine and [^{3}H]dihydroergocryptine. J Biol Chem **254:** 4375–4386

Fraser CM, Venter JC (1980) Monoclonal antibodies to beta-adrenergic receptors: Use in purification and molecular characterization of beta-receptors. Proc Natl Acad Sci USA **77:** 7034–7038, 1980.

Fraser CM, Venter JC (1982) The size of the mammalian lung beta-2 adrenergic receptor as determined by target size analysis and immunoaffinity chromatography. Biochem Biophys Res Commun **109:** 21–29

Fredrik-Leeb-Lundberg LM, Dickinson KEJ, Heald SL, Wikberg JES, Hagen PO, DeBernardis JF, Winn M, Arendsen DL, Lefkowitz MC, Caron MG (1984) Photoaffinity labeling of mammalian alpha-1 adrenergic receptors. Identification of the ligand binding subunit with a high affinity radioiodinated probe. J Biol Chem **259:** 2579–2587

Fung BKK, Hurley JB, Stryer L (1981) Flow of information in the light-triggered cyclic nucleotide cascade of vision. Proc Natl Acad Sci USA **78:** 152–156

Garcia-Sainz JA, Corvera S (1983) Alpha-1 adrenergic action: Only calcium? Trends Pharmacol Sci **12:** 489

Geynet P, Borsodi A, Ferry N, Hanoune J (1980) Proteolysis of rat liver plasma membranes cancels the guanine nucleotide sensitivity of agonist binding to the alpha-adrenoceptor. Biochem Biophys Res Commun **97:** 947–954

Geynet P, Ferry N, Borsodi A, Hanoune J (1981) Two distinct alpha-1 adrenergic receptor sites in rat liver: Differential binding of (−)-[^{3}H]norepinephrine, [^{3}H]prazosin and [^{3}H]dihydroergocryptine. Biochem Pharmacol **30:** 1665–1675

Gilman AG (1984) Guanine nucleotide-binding regulatory proteins and dual control of adenylate cyclase. J Clin Invest **73:** 1–4

Gomperts BD (1983) Involvement of guanine nucleotide-binding protein in the gating of Ca^{2+} by receptors. Nature **306:** 64–66

Goodhardt M, Ferry N, Geynet P, Hanoune J (1982) Hepatic alpha-1 adrenergic receptors show agonist-specific regulation by guanine nucleotides. Loss of nucleotide effect after adrenalectomy. J Biol Chem **257:** 11577–11583

Graff G, Stephenson JH, Glass DB, Haddox MK, Golberg ND (1978) Activation of soluble splenic cell guanylate cyclase by prostaglandin endoperoxides and fatty acid hydroperoxides. J Biol Chem **253:** 7662–7676

Graham RM (1981) The physiology and pharmacology of alpha and beta blockade. J Cardiovasc Med (Special Suppl., April): 7–22

Graham RM (1984) Alpha-adrenergic receptor involvement in antihypertensive therapy and circulatory homeostasis. Excerpta Med **29:** 51–62

Graham RM, Hess HJ, Homcy CJ (1982a) Solubilization and purification of the alpha-1 adrenergic receptor using a novel affinity resin. Proc Natl Acad Sci USA **79:** 2186–2190

Graham RM, Hess HJ, Homcy CJ (1982b) Biophysical characterization of the purified alpha-1 adrenergic receptor and identification of the hormone binding subunit. J Biol Chem **257:** 15174–15178

Graham RM, Hess HJ, Haber E, Homcy CJ (1982c) Antibodies to the alpha-1 and alpha-2 selective antagonists prazosin and yohimbine as probes of the alpha-adrenergic binding site. Hypertension **4** (suppl II): 183–187

Graziano MP, Malbon CC (1984) The hepatic beta-2 adrenergic receptor: purification and characterization (abstr). Fed Proc **43:** 541

Guellaen G, Aggerbeck M, Hanoune J (1979) Characterization and solubilization of the alpha-adrenoceptor of rat liver plasma membranes labeled with [^{3}H]phenoxybenzamine. J Biol Chem **254:** 10761–10768

Guellaen G, Goodhardt M, Barouki R, Hanoune J (1982) Subunit structure of rat liver alpha-1 adrenergic receptor. Biochem Pharmacol **31:** 2817–2820

Gullick WJ, Lindstrom JM (1983) Mapping of the binding of monoclonal antibodies to the acetylcholine receptor from torpedo californica. Biochemistry **22:** 3312–3320

Haga T, Haga K, Gilman AG (1977) Hydrodynamic properties of the beta-adrenergic receptor and adenylate cyclase from wild type and variant S49 lymphoma cells. J Biol Chem **252:** 5776–5782

Harden TK (1983) Agonist-induced desensitization of the beta-adrenergic receptor-linked adenylate cyclase. Pharmacol Rev **35:** 5–32

Haslam RJ, Davidson MML (1984) Roles of Ca^{2+}, GTP, diglyceride and protein phosphorylation in the secretion of 5-HT from permeabilized platelets (abstr). Fed Proc **43:** 736

Haslam RJ, Salama SE, Fox JEB, Lynham JA, Davidson MML (1980) *In* Platelets: Cellular Response Mechanisms and Their Biological Significance, (edited by A Rotman, FA Meyer, C Gitler, A Silderberg). New York, Wiley, pp 213–231

Heyworth CM, Rawal S, Houslay MD (1983a) Guanine nucleotides can activate the insulin-stimulated phophodiesterase in liver plasma membranes. FEBS Lett **154:** 87–91

Heyworth CM, Wallace AV, Houslay MD (1983b) Insulin and glucagon regulate the activation of two distinct membrane-bound cyclic AMP phosphodiesterases in hepatocytes. Biochem J **214:** 99–110

Hirst GDS, Neild TO (1981) Localization of specialized noradrenaline receptors at neuromuscular junctions on arterioles of the guinea-pig. J Physiol (Lond) **313:** 343–350

Hoffman BB, Mullikin-Kilpatrick D, Lefkowitz RJ (1980a) Heterogeneity or radioligand binding to alpha-adrenergic receptors. Analysis of guanine nucleotide regulation of agonist binding in relation to receptor subtypes. J Biol Chem **255:** 4645–4652

Hoffman BB, Dukes DF, Lefkowitz RJ (1980b) Alpha-adrenergic receptors in liver membranes: Delineation with subtype selective radioligands. Life Sci **28:** 265–272

Hoffman SL, Majerus PW (1982) Identification and properties of two distinct phosphatidylinositol-specific phospholipase C enzymes from sheep seminal vesicular glands. J Biol Chem **257:** 6461–6469

Holtz J, Saeed M, Sommer O, Bassenge E (1982) Norepinephrine constricts the canine coronary bed via postsynaptic alpha-2 adrenoceptors. Eur J Pharmacol **82:** 199

Homcy CJ, Sylvestre D (1982) Characterization of the mammalian beta-2 receptor in 8 M urea. Biochem Biophys Res Commun **108:** 504–509

Homcy CJ, Rockson SG, Haber E (1980) An antiidiotypic antibody that recognizes the beta-adrenergic receptor. J Clin Invest **69:** 1147–1154

Homcy CJ, Graham RM, Haber E, Hess HJ (1982) Characterization of the purified mammalian alpha- and beta-adrenergic receptors reveals homologous molecular properties (abstr). Clin Res **30:** 482A

Homcy CJ, Rockson SG, Countaway J, Egan D (1983) Purification and characterization of the mammalian beta-2 adrenergic receptor. Biochemistry **22:** 660–668

Insoft R, Homcy CJ (1984) Advances in the purification and characterization of the mammalian beta-2 adrenergic receptor (abstr). Fed Proc **43:** 1580

Jacobs KH, Saur W, Schultz G (1976) Reduction of adenylate cyclase activity in lysates of human platelets by the alpha-adrenergic component of epinephrine. J Cyclic Nucleotide Res **2:** 381–392

Jacobs S, Sahyoun NE, Saltiel AR, Cuatrecasas P (1983) Phorbol esters stimulate the phosphorylation of receptors for insulin and somatomedin C. Proc Natl Acad Sci USA **80:** 6211–6213

Jakobs KH (1979) Inhibition of adenylate cyclase by hormones and neurotransmitters. Mol Cell Endocrinol **16:** 147–156

Jakobs KH, Aktories K, Schultz G (1979) GTP dependent inhibition of cardiac adenylate cyclase by muscarinic cholinergic agonists. Naunyn Schmiedbergs Arch Pharmacol **310:** 113–119

Jauering RA, Moulds RFW, Shaw J (1978) The action of prazosin in human vascular preparations. Arch Int Pharmacodyn **231:** 81–89

Jeffery DR, Charlton RR, Venter JC (1980) Reconstitution of turkey erythrocyte beta-adrenergic receptors into human erythrocyte receptor membranes: Demonstration of guanine nucleotide regulation of agonist affinity. J Biol Chem **255:** 5015–5018

Joseph SK (1984) Inositol trisphosphate: An intracellular messenger produced by Ca^{2+} mobilizing hormones. Trends Biochem Sci **9:** 420–421

Joseph SK, Thomas AP, Williams RJ, Irvine RF, Williamson JR (1984) Myo-inositol-1,4,5-trisphosphate. A second messenger for the hormonal mobilization of intracellular Ca^{2+} in liver. J Biol Chem **259:** 3077–3081

Kalsner S (1984) The noradrenergic presynaptic receptor controversy (abstr) Fed Proc **43:** 1351

Katada T, Ui M (1981) Islet-activating protein. A modifier of receptor-mediated regulation of rat islet adenylate cyclase. J Biol Chem **256:** 8310–8317

Katada T, Bokoch GM, Northup JK, Ui M, Gilman AG (1984a) The inhibitory guanine nucleotide-binding regulatory component of adenylate cyclase. Properties and function of the purified protein. J Biol Chem **259:** 3568–3577

Katada T, Northup JK, Bokoch GM, Ui M, Gilman AG (1984b) The inhibitory guanine nucleotide-binding regulatory component of adenylate cyclase. Subunit dissociation and guanine nucleotide-dependent hormonal inhbition. J Biol Chem **259:** 3578–3595

Katada T, Bokoch GM, Smigel MD, Ui M, Gilman AG (1984c) The inhibitory guanine nucleotide-binding regulatory component of adenylate cyclase. Subunit dissociation and the inhibition of adenylate cyclase in S49 lymphoma cyc- and wild type membranes. J Biol Chem **259:** 3586–3595

Kelleher DJ, Rashidbaigi A, Ruoho AE, Johnson GL (1983) Rapid vesicle reconstitution of alprenolol-sepharose-purified beta-1 adrenergic receptors: Interaction of the purified receptor with N_S. J Biol Chem **258:** 12881–12885

Kunos G (1984) The hepatic alpha-1 adrenoceptor. Trends Pharmacol Sci **5:** 380–383

Kunos G, Kan WH, Greguski R, Venter JC (1983) Selective affinity labeling and molecular characterization of hepatic alpha-adrenergic receptors with [^{3}H]phenoxybenzamine. J Biol Chem **258:** 326–332

Langer SZ (1974) Presynaptic regulation of catecholamine release.

Biochem Pharmacol **23:** 1793–1800

Lehmann J, Lanager SZ (1981) Phenoxybenzamine blocks dopamine autoreceptors irreversibly: Implications for multiple dopamine receptor hypothesis. Eur J Pharmacol **75:** 247–254

Majerus PW, Neufeld EJ, Wilson DB (1984) Production of phosphoinositide-derived messengers. Cell **37:**701–703

Mayer SE (1980) *In* The Pharmacological Basis of Therapeutics, edited by A Gilman, LS Goodman. New York, Macmillan, pp 56–90

McGrath JC (1982) Evidence for more than one type of postjunctional alpha-adrenoceptor. Biochem Pharmacol **31:** 467–484

McGrath JC (1983) The variety of vascular alpha-adrenoceptors. Trends Pharmacol Sci **1:** 14–18

Michel T, Hoffman BB, Lefkowitz RJ (1981a) Stimulation and inhibition of adenylate cyclase in platelet lysates: Evidence for distinct regulatory intermediates (abstr). Clin Res **29:** 566A

Michel T, Hoffman BB, Lefkowitz RJ, Caron MG (1981b) Differential sedimentation of agonist- and antagonist-labelled platelet alpha-2 adrenergic receptors. Biochem Biophys Res Commun **100:** 1131–1136

Michell RH (1975) Inositol phospholipids and cell surface receptor function. Biochim Biophys Acta **415:** 81–147

Mishina M, Kurosaki T, Tobimatsu T, Yuuki Morimoto, Noda M, Yamamoto T, Terao M, Lindstrom J, Takahashi T, Kuno M, Numa S (1984) Expression of functional acetylcholine receptor from cloned cDNAs. Nature **307:** 604–608

Morgan NG, Blackmore PF, Exton JH (1983) Age-related changes in the control of hepatic cyclic AMP levels by alpha-1 and beta-2 adrenergic receptors in male rats. J Biol Chem **258:** 5103–5109

Newbold R (1984) Mutant *ras* proteins and cell transformation. Nature **310:** 628–629

Nishizuka Y (1984) The role of protein kinase C in cell surface signal transduction and tumour promotion. Nature **308:** 693–698

Noda M, Takahashi H, Tanabe T, Toyosato M, Furutani Y, Hirose T, Asai M, Inayama S, Miyata T, Numa S (1982) Primary structure of alpha-subunit precursor of *Torpedo californica* acetylcholine receptor deduced from cDNA sequence. Nature **299:** 793–797

Noda M, Takahashi H, Tanabe T, Toyosato M, Kikyotani S, Hirose T, Asai M, Takashima H, Inayama S, Miyata T, Numa S (1983a) Primary structures of beta- and delta-subunit precursors of *Torpedo californica* acetylcholine receptor deduced from cDNA sequences. Nature **301:** 251–255

Noda M, Takahashi H, Tanabe T, Toyosato M, Kikyotani S, Furutani Y, Hirose T, Takashima H, Inayama S, Miyata T, Numa S (1983b) Structural homology of *Torpedo californica* acetylcholine receptor subunits. Nature **302:** 528–532

Pedersen SE, Ross EM (1982) Functional reconstitution of beta-adrenergic receptors and the stimulatory GTP-binding protein of adenylate cyclase. Proc Natl Acad Sci USA **79:** 7228–7232

Pinkett MO, Jaworski CJ, Evain D, Anderson WB (1980) Limited proteolysis eliminates guanine nucleotide inhibition of cholergen-activated adenylate cyclase. Possible basis for proteolytic stimulation of cyclic AMP production. J Biol Chem **255:** 7716–7721

Rashidbaigi A, Ruoho AE, Green DA, Clark RB (1983) Photoaffinity labeling of the beta-adrenergic receptor from cultured lymphoma cells with [^{125}I]iodoazidobenzyl pindolol: Loss of the label with desensitization. Proc Natl Acad Sci USA **80:** 2849–2853

Regan JW, Barden N, Lefkowitz RJ, Caron MC, DeMarinis RM, Krog AJ, Holden KG, Mattews WD, Hieble JP (1982) Affinity chromatography of human platelet alpha-2 adrenergic receptors. Proc Natl Acad Sci USA **79:** 7223–7227

Regan JW, DeMarinis RM, Caron MG, Lefkowitz RJ (1984) Identification of the subunit-binding site of alpha-2 adrenergic receptors using [^{3}H]phenoxybenzamine. J Biol Chem **259:** 7864–7869

Rhodes D, Prpic' V, Exton JH, Blackmore PF (1983) Stimulation of phosphatidylinositol 4,5-bisphosphate hydrolysis in hepatocytes by vasopressin. J Biol Chem **258:** 2770–2773

Robson LE, Kosterlitz HW (1979) Specific protection of the binding sites of D-Ala^{2}-D-Leu^{4}-enkephalin (delta receptors) and dihydromorphine (mu receptors). Proc R Soc Lond [Biol] **205:** 425–432

Rockson SG, Homcy CJ, Haber E (1980) Anti-alprenolol antibodies in the rabbit. A new probe for the study of beta-adrenergic receptor interactions. Circ Res **46:** 808–813

Rockson SG, Homcy CJ, Quinn P, Marders W, Haber E, Vatner S (1981) Cellular mechanisms of impaired adrenergic responsiveness in neonatal dogs. J Clin Invest **67:** 319–327

Ruffolo RR, Rice PJ, Patil PN, Hamada A, Miller DD (1983) Differences in the applicability of the Easson-Stedman hypothesis to the alpha-1 and alpha-2 adrenergic effects of phenethylamines and imidazolines. Eur J Pharmacol **86:** 471–475

Schlegel W, Cooper DMF, Rodbell M (1980) Inhibition and activation of fat cell adenylate cyclase by GTP is mediated by structures of different size. Arch Biochem Biophys **201:** 678–682

Schreiber AB, Courand PO, Andre C, Vray B, Strosberg AD (1980) Anti-alprenolol anti-idiotypic antibodies bind to beta-adrenergic receptors and modulate catecholamine-sensitive adenylate cyclase. Proc Natl Acad Sci USA **77:** 7385–7389

Schultz KD, Schultz K, Schultz G (1977) Sodium nitroprusside and other smooth muscle-relaxants increase cyclic GMP levels in rat ductus deferens. Nature **265:** 750–751

Seidman CE, Hess HJ, Homcy CJ, Graham RM (1984a) Synthesis and characterization of a radioiodinated photoaffinity probe for the alpha-1 adrenergic receptor. Hypertension **6** (suppl I): 7–11

Seidman CE, Hess HJ, Homcy CJ, Graham RM (1984b) Photoaffinity labeling of the alpha-1 adrenergic receptor using an [^{125}I] arylazide analog of prazosin. Biochemistry **23:** 3765–3770

Sharma SK, Klee WA, Nirenberg M (1977) Opiate-dependent modulation of adenylate cyclase. Proc Natl Acad Sci USA **74:** 3365–3369

Shepperson NB, Duval N, Langer SZ (1982) Dopamine decreases mesenteric blood flow in the anaesthetised dog through the stimulation of postsynaptic alpha-2 adrenoceptors. Eur J Pharmacol **81:** 617–635

Shorr RGL, Lefkowitz RJ, Caron MG (1981) Purification of the beta-adrenergic receptor: Identification of the hormone binding subunit. J Biol Chem **256:** 5820–5826

Shorr RGL, Strohsacker MW, Lavin TN, Lefkowitz RJ, Caron MG (1982) The beta-1 adrenergic receptor of the turkey erythrocyte: Molecular heterogeneity revealed by purification and photoaffinity labeling. J Biol Chem **257:** 12341–12350

Smith SK, Limbird LE (1981) Solubilization of human platelet alpha-adrenergic receptors: Evidence that agonist occupancy of the receptor stabilizes receptor-effector interactions. Proc Natl Acad Sci USA **78:** 4026–4030

Smith SK, Limbird LE (1982) Evidence that human platelet alpha-adrenergic receptors coupled to inhibition of adenylate cyclase are not associated with the subunit of adenylate cyclase ADP-ribosylated by cholera toxin. J Biol Chem **257:** 10471-1:478

Snavely MD, Insel PA (1983) Different roles for thiol groups in renal alpha-1 and alpha-2 adrenergic receptors (abstr). Fed Proc **42:** 1876

Stadel JM, Shorr RGL, Limbird CE, Lefkowitz RJ (1981a) Evidence that the beta-adrenergic receptor-associated guanine nucleotide regulatory proten conveys guanosine 5′*O*-(3-thiotriphosphate)-dependent adenylate cyclase activity. J Biol Chem **256:** 8718–8723

Stadel JM, DeLean A, Mullikin-Kilpatrick DD, Sawyer DO, Lefkowitz RJ (1981b) Catecholamine-induced desensitization in turkey erythrocytes: cAMP mediated impairment of high affinity agonist binding alteration in receptor number. J Cyclic Nucleotide Res **7:** 37–47

Stadel JM, Nambi P, Shorr RGL, Sawyer DF, Caron MG, Lefkowitz RJ (1983) Catecholamine-induced desensitization of turkey erythrocyte adenylate cyclase is associated with phosphorylation of the beta-adrenergic receptor. Proc Natl Acad Sci USA **80:** 3178–3177

Sternweiss PC (in press) A novel guanine nucleotide-binding regulatory protein from brain. Fed Proc

Stiles GL, Lefkowitz RJ (1981) Thyroid hormone modulation of agonist-beta receptor interactions in the rat heart. Life Sci **28:** 2529–2536

Stiles GL, Strasser RH, Lavin TN, Jones LR, Caron MG, Lefkowitz RJ (1982) The cardiac beta-adrenergic receptor: Structural similarities of beta-1 and beta-2 receptor subtypes demonstrated by photoaffinity labeling. J Biol Chem **258:** 8443–8449

Stiles GL, Benovic JL, Caron MG, Lefkowitz RJ (1984) Mammalian beta-adrenergic receptors: Distinct glycoprotein populations containing high mannose or complex type carbohydrate chains. J Biol Chem **259:** 8655–8663

Strader CD, Pickel VM, Joh TH, Strohsacker MW, Shorr RGL, Lefkowitz RJ, Caron MG (1983) Antibodies to the beta-adrenergic receptor: Attenuation of catecholamine sensitive adenylate cyclase and demonstration of postsynaptic receptor localization in the brain. Proc Natl Acad Sci USA **80:** 1840–1844

Streb H, Irvine RF, Berridge MJ, Schulz I (1983) Release of Ca^{2-} from a nonmitochondrial intracellular store in pancreatic acinar cells by inositol-1,4,5,-trisphosphate. Nature **306:** 67–69

Svensson TH, Bunney BS, Aghajanian GK (1975) Inhibition of both noradrenergic and serotonergic neurons in brain by the alpha-adrenergic agonist clonidine. Brain Res **92:** 291–306

Taokimasa T, Morita K, North A (1981) Opiates and clonidine prolong calcium-dependent after-hyperpolarizations. Nature **294:** 162–163

Timmermans PBMWM, van Zweiten PA (1981) The postsynaptic alpha-2 adrenoreceptor. J Auton Pharmacol **1:** 171–183

Timmermans PBMWM, van Zweiten PA (1982) Alpha-2 adrenoceptors: Classification, localisation, mechanisms and targets for drugs. J Med Chem **25:** 1389–1401

Tsai JS, Chen A (1978) Effect of L-triiodothyronine on (−)-[^{3}H] dihydroalprenolol binding and cyclic AMP response to (−)adrenaline in cultured heart cells. Nature (Lond) **275:** 138–140

Ullrich S, Wollheim CB (1984) Islet cyclic AMP levels are not lowered during alpha-2 adrenergic inhibition of insulin release. Studies with epinephrine and forskolin. J Biol Chem **259:** 4111–4115

U'Prichard DC (1981) Direct binding studies of alpha-adrenoceptors. *In* Adrenoceptors and Catecholamine Action, part A, edited by G. Kunos. New York, Wiley, pp 131–179

U'Prichard DC, Ensberger P (1983) p-Azidoclonidine: A potential photoaffinity ligand for the alpha-2 adrenergic receptor. Society of Neurosciences, abstr. 325.3, abstract 1117, Boston

Vacquelin G, Geynet P, Hanoune J, Strosberg AD (1977) Isolation of adenylate cyclase-free, beta-adrenergic receptors from turkey erythrocyte membrane by affinity chromatography. Proc Natl Acad Sci USA **74:** 3710–3714

Van Brummelen P, Vermey P, Timmermans PBMWM, Van Zweiten PA (1983) Preliminary evidence for a postsynaptic alpha-2 adrenoceptor in the vasculature of the human forearm. Br J Clin Pharmacol **15:** 134P–135P

Vatner DE, Homcy CJ, Sit SP, Manders WT, Vatner SF (1984) Effects of pressure overload, left ventricular hypertrophy on beta-adrenergic receptors, and responsiveness to catecholamines. J Clin Invest **73:** 1473–1482

Venter JC, Schaber JS, U'Prichard DC, Fraser CM (1983) Molecular size of th human platelet alpha-2 adrenergic receptor as determined by radiation inactivation. Biochem Biophys Res Commun **116:** 1070–1075

Venter JC, Horne P, Eddy B, Greguski R, Fraser CM (1984) Alpha-1 adrenergic receptor structure. Mol Pharmacol **26:** 196–205

Waldo GL, Northup JK, Perkins JP, Harden TK (1983) Characterization of an altered membrane form of the beta-adrenergic receptor produced during agonist-induced desensitization. J Biol Chem **258:** 13900–13908

Watanabe AM, McConnaughey MM, Strawbridge RA, Fleming JW, Jones LR, Besch HR (1978) Muscarinic cholinergic receptor modulation of beta-adrenergic receptor affinity for catecholamines. J Biol Chem **253:** 4833–4836

Wikberg JES, Lefkowitz RJ, Caron MG (1983) Solubilization of rat liver alpha-1 adrenergic receptors. Agonist specific alteration in receptor binding affinity. Biochem Pharmacol **32:** 3171–3178

Williams LT, Lefkowitz RJ, Watamabe AM, Hathaway, Besch HR (1977) Thyroid hormone regulation of beta-adrenergic receptor number. J Biol Chem **252:** 2787–2789

Wrenn S, Haber E (1979) An antibody specific for the propranolol binding site of cardiac muscle. J Biol Chem **254:** 6577–6582

Yamamura H, Lad PM, Rodbell M (1977) GTP stimulates and inhibits adenylate cyclase in fat cell membranes through distinct regulatory processes. J Biol Chem **252:** 7964–7966

INDEX TERMS: Adrenergic receptors • Isolation • Molecular structure • Adenylate cyclase • Catecholamines

SPECIAL ARTICLES

Animal Models for Protecting Ischemic Myocardium: Results of the NHLBI Cooperative Study

Comparison of Unconscious and Conscious Dog Models

Keith A. Reimer and Robert B. Jennings

From the Department of Pathology, Duke Medical Center, Durham, North Carolina

Fred R. Cobb, Robert H. Murdock, and Joseph C. Greenfield, Jr.

From the Department of Medicine, Duke Medical Center, and Durham Veterans Administration Medical Center, Durham, North Carolina

Lewis C. Becker, Bernadine Healy Bulkley, and Grover M. Hutchins

From the Departments of Medicine and Pathology, The Johns Hopkins Medical Institutions, Baltimore, Maryland

Richard P. Schwartz, Jr., Kent R. Bailey, and Eugene R. Passamani

From the National Heart, Lung, and Blood Institute, Bethesda, Maryland

SUMMARY. The Animal Models for Protecting Ischemic Myocardium Study was undertaken for the purpose of developing reproducible animal models that could be used to assess interventions designed to limit infarct size. This paper describes the results obtained in an unconscious dog model and in a conscious dog model, developed in three participating laboratories. The unconscious dog model, involving reperfusion after 3 hours of ischemia in open-chest dogs, was intended to determine whether therapy followed by early reperfusion would limit infarct size more than reperfusion alone. The conscious dog model used chronically instrumented dogs and permanent coronary occlusion to better mimic myocardial infarction in man. In both models, the proximal circumflex artery was occluded, and the primary experimental endpoint was infarct size, as measured by histological techniques 3 days after the initial occlusion. Infarct size was analyzed in relation to baseline variables including the anatomic area at risk, collateral blood flow to the subepicardial zone of ischemia and hemodynamic determinants of myocardial metabolic demand. Most of the variation in infarct size in control dogs could be related to variation in the area at risk, collateral blood flow, and rate pressure product. Using multivariate analysis and groups of 15 dogs, an intervention that limited infarct size by 10–13% of the area at risk would have been detected 50% of the time. Larger treatment effects would be detected more readily, and smaller effects often would be missed, unless group sizes were larger. Two drugs, verapamil and ibuprofen, were evaluated in both models, with experimental group sizes averaging 13 and 20 dogs, in the unconscious and conscious models, respectively. Three of 15 verapamil-treated dogs in the unconscious model study had much smaller infarcts than expected from baseline parameters. With these exceptions, neither drug limited infarct size in either model. **(*Circ Res 56: 651–665, 1985*)**

WITH most potential therapies to protect ischemic myocardium, some studies have shown dramatically positive results, whereas others have shown no benefit. To achieve a better understanding of the major factors that determine infarct size and to develop two, well-characterized, standardized canine models of myocardial infarction, collaborative studies were undertaken in three independent laboratories, as a part of the NHLBI-sponsored Animal Models for Protecting Ischemic Myocardium (AMPIM) program.* The unconscious model studied at Duke (DU) was designed to determine whether therapy can reduce the amount of cell death developing in the

** The AMPIM (Animal Models for Protecting Ischemic Myocardium) study grew out of the Workshop on More Uniform Animal Models and Protocols for Assessment of Interventions to Protect Ischemic Myocardium held at the National Institutes of Health on January 24–25, 1978, which concluded that, while many promising animal models existed for studying protection of ischemic myocardium, more standardization of these models was required to improve comparability of results between different laboratories. The NHLBI recommended that three different coronary-occluded preparations be studied: (1) the rat, for relatively inexpensive and rapid screening of potentially useful treatments; (2) the anesthetized dog, for verification of effectiveness in a more physiological situation; and (3) the conscious dog, for testing the most promising agents under the most physiological conditions. Studies reported here were on anesthetized dogs (Duke Medical Center: Reimer et al.) and on conscious dogs (Duke Medical Center: Cobb et al.; and The Johns Hopkins University: Becker et al.). The NHLBI served as a data-coordinating center.*

open-chest dog heart as a consequence of 3 hours of ischemia. This model was viewed as intermediate, to screen for therapeutic effects. The conscious model studied at the Durham Veterans Administration Medical Center (DVA) and at The Johns Hopkins University (JH) was designed to test the effect of therapy following permanent occlusion. The conscious model was believed to simulate better the state of patients with acute myocardial infarction. To evaluate the precision and reproducibility of these experimental models, two agents, verapamil and ibuprofen, as well as a placebo control, were tested.

Methods

Animal Selection and Exclusion Criteria

Adult mongrel dogs of either sex, weighing 10–25 kg, were used. No beagles or pregnant animals were included. No dogs were accepted into the study with a hematocrit <35, clinically evident infection, or circulating heart worm filariae. Obese dogs also were avoided, and the thickness of subcutaneous fat was measured during thoracotomy. Dogs that were entered and that later were found to have heart worms were excluded from analysis. Data were collected, to the extent possible, on all dogs that died before termination of the study. However, infarct size was measured only in dogs that survived until sacrifice; dogs that died prematurely have been excluded.

Preparation for Study

Unconscious Model

Dogs were fasted overnight prior to study. They were anesthetized with 30–40 mg/kg of iv sodium pentobarbital, and additional doses were given as needed throughout the experiment. The dogs were intubated and ventilated at 200 ml/kg per min of room air. Aseptic surgical technique was used, and 1,000,000 units of penicillin were given im as a prophylaxis against infection. Catheters were placed in the femoral vein and artery. The arterial catheter was connected to a Statham model P23ID transducer to monitor blood pressure. Arterial blood gases were checked, and the ventilation rate and/or oxygen flow rate were adjusted to achieve physiological blood gas values (Po_2: 100–140 mm Hg, Pco_2: 32–40 mm Hg, and pH 7.37–7.47) before thoracotomy. A 6 to 8-cm thoracotomy then was performed in the 4th intercostal space and the heart was suspended in a temporary pericardial cradle. The proximal circumflex artery was isolated 1.5–2.0 cm from the origin and was encircled with a 00. silk suture so that the artery could be occluded with an atraumatic clamp. Two catheters were placed into the left atrium via the left atrial appendage to monitor pressure and inject microspheres. Fluid loss was replaced with saline at a continuous infusion rate of 2.5 ml/kg per hr.

Conscious Model

Dogs were anesthetized with thiamylal sodium (30–40 mg/kg, iv) and underwent left thoracotomy through the 4th intercostal space. Heparin-filled polyvinyl chloride catheters were positioned in the aortic root, the left atrium via the left atrial appendage, and a systemic vein. A mechanical adjustable snare type occluder was placed around the proximal left circumflex coronary artery above or below the first marginal branch, so that temporary occlusion resulted in cyanosis of at least 75% of the inferior wall. The catheters and snare were either exteriorized (JH) or positioned in a subcutaneous pocket at the back of the neck (DVA). Penicillin, 1,000,000 units, and streptomycin, 1.0 g, were given im for the first 4 postoperative days, and for at least 7 days were allowed for recovery from surgery. Dogs were fasted overnight prior to study, which was carried out in a noise-free, dimly lit room with the animal either lying on a padded table (DVA) or standing supported in a sling (JH). After exteriorization and/or flushing of the catheters, 30–40 minutes were allowed for the animals to adjust to the laboratory conditions. Morphine sulfate, 0.25 mg/kg, im, was given 30 minutes before occlusion, and an additional 0.25 mg/kg, iv, was given 20 minutes later. No additional analgesics were used.

In both models, heart rate and aortic and left atrial pressures were monitored continuously. A test dose of 0.6–1.0 ml of 0.05% Tween-80 was injected into the left atrial catheter to minimize subsequent hemodynamic reactions to microsphere injections containing Tween-80. No antiarrhythmic drugs were used in either the conscious or unconscious model. Dogs that developed ventricular fibrillation were excluded from analysis.

Coronary Occlusion

Unconscious Model

Coronary occlusion was performed suddenly, with an atraumatic Schwartz vascular clamp. The occlusion was maintained for 3 hours, and then was removed in one stage. The presence of reperfusion was confirmed by the appearance of an epicardial blush. The thoracotomy was closed in layers, and air was evacuated from the chest.

Conscious Model

Permanent coronary occlusion was produced by a sudden one-stage tightening of the snare occluder.

Randomization of Treatment Groups

In both models, dogs were randomized (Peto et al., 1976) into three treatment groups: verapamil, ibuprofen, or control (ibuprofen vehicle). Randomization was done 5 minutes after coronary occlusion by drawing a drug identification code number from a sealed envelope supplied by NIH. Drug infusion was begun 15 minutes after coronary occlusion. Because verapamil has hypotensive effects, the identity of vials containing this drug was not hidden. However, investigators were blinded with respect to ibuprofen vs. vehicle controls.

Drug Regimens

Verapamil was diluted from ampules containing 2.5 mg of drug/ml and was administered at an initial rate of 0.03 mg/kg per min for 5 minutes and then at 0.01 mg/kg per min for the 3 hours of occlusion in the unconscious model, and for 6 hours in the conscious model. The infusion rate was slowed by 20% if diastolic blood pressure decreased by more than 20 mm Hg below pretreatment values, or to less than 70 mm Hg, or if heart rate increased by more than 20 beats/min.

Ibuprofen or placebo was diluted from refrigerated ampules containing 50 mg of blinded drug/ml and was administered at an initial rate of 2.5 mg/kg per min for 5 minutes and then at 6.25 mg/kg per hour for the duration of coronary occlusion in the unconscious model, and for 24 hours in the conscious model. In the latter situation, a self-contained back pack with a Cormed battery powered infusion pump was used.

Measurements Recorded in Vivo

Hemodynamic measurements, including heart rate, systolic and diastolic blood pressure, mean left atrial pressure, and mean arterial pressure, were taken 5 minutes before occlusion and 10, 25, 105, and 180 minutes after occlusion. Measurements were repeated at 6 hours in the conscious model. Arterial blood gases were measured 10 minutes before and 10 minutes after occlusion in both models.

Measurements of Regional Myocardial Blood Flow

Myocardial blood flow was measured with microspheres (9 ± 1 μm) labeled with ^{46}Sc, ^{85}Sr, ^{95}Nb, or ^{141}Ce (Rivas et al., 1976; Jugdutt et al., 1979a; Reimer and Jennings, 1979a). Measurements were made 5 minutes before and 10 and 105 minutes after occlusion in *both* models, and at 6 hours after occlusion in the conscious model. Microspheres were obtained from stock solutions containing 10% dextran and 0.01–0.02% Tween-80. These solutions were agitated in an ultrasonic bath for 15 minutes and mixed on a Vortex agitator prior to injection. We determined flow, in each instance, by injecting approximately 2–3,000,000 microspheres into the left atrium over a 15-second period, followed by a 10-ml saline flush. A reference arterial blood flow sample was collected with a constant withdrawal pump beginning 5 seconds before sphere injection and continuing for 1.5 to 2.5 minutes, at a rate of 5–15 ml/min.

Postmortem Analyses

In both models, the experiment was terminated at 72 hours after reanesthesia and administration of 5000 units of iv heparin.

Myocardium at Risk

Unconscious Model. Myocardium at risk was assessed by postmortem dye injection of occluded and unoccluded coronary beds (Reimer and Jennings, 1979a). Catheters were placed in the unoccluded left main coronary artery and the proximal left circumflex artery. Both vessels were perfused simultaneously for approximately 3 minutes at identical pressures of 120–140 mm Hg at 37°C. The perfusion fluid was sodium phosphate buffer (8.8 × 10^{-2} mol dibasic and 0.18 × 10^{-2} mol monobasic sodium phosphate/liter, pH 8.25–8.6) plus 6% dextran (82,000 mol. wt., Sigma), to which either 1.0% triphenyltetrazolium chloride (TTC) (for perfusion of the previously occluded vascular bed) or 0.05% monastral blue dye (for perfusion of the remainder of the left ventricle) was added. The heart was then fixed by immersion in a large volume of phosphate-buffered formalin. The left ventricle was sectioned into eight transverse slices. The slices were weighed, and the apical surfaces photographed. The previously occluded vascular bed (area at risk) was identified and traced from enlarged projections of the photographic slide of each ventricular slice. The area at risk was measured by "cut-and-weigh" techniques using copies of these tracings as previously described (Reimer and Jennings, 1979a).

Conscious Model. The myocardium at risk was assessed by postmortem injection of the proximal left circumflex artery and the nonoccluded left main artery with barium sulfate suspended in gelatin, perfused at pressures of 120–140 mm Hg (Jugdutt et al., 1979a). The hearts were fixed in 10% formalin solution for 2–4 days. After x-rays had been taken, the heart was sectioned in eight transverse rings, and each was radiographed. The region supplied by the occluded vessel (risk region), was identified by x-rays of the whole left ventricle and rings, and marked on tracings of each ring. Occluded bed mass was determined by direct excision and weighing (DVA), or by planimetry of tracings of the four rings (JH).

Histological Analysis

The method of sampling for histological and blood flow analysis is shown in Figure 1. The basal half of the four composite slices, plus the apical half of the apical slice were used for histological analysis. Sections were stained with hematoxylin and eosin (and at DU with Heidenhain's variant of Mallory's connective tissue stain). Infarct size was determined for each slice and for the heart as a whole using cut-and-weigh techniques with copies of enlarged photographs or traced projections of these histological sections.

Regional Blood Flow

Flow measurements were made using the apical half of each of the top three composite slices (Fig. 1). The slices were divided into the following zones for regional myocardial blood flow analysis: (1) nonischemic zone, (2) central ischemic zone (central 50% of the vascular bed at risk), (3) septal border zone (septal 25% of the vascular bed at risk), and (4) lateral border zone (lateral 25% of vascular bed at risk). However, in the present paper, only the collateral flow of the central ischemic zone is reported and analyzed. Data from septal and lateral samples have been excluded to avoid misinterpretation of measurements from samples which may have contained nonischemic as well as ischemic myocardium. These regions were further subdivided into subendocardial, mid-myocardial, and subepicardial thirds. Regional myocardial blood flow was calculated by the formula,

$$Qm = \frac{Qr \times Cm}{Cr},$$

where Qm = myocardial blood flow (ml/min); Qr = reference blood flow (ml/min); Cm = counts/min in myocardial sample; Cr = counts/min in reference sample. The myocardial blood flow was expressed relative to the tissue sample weight (ml/min per g). Corrections were made for true and/or apparent microsphere loss (Reimer and Jennings, 1979b; Capurro et al., 1979; Jugdutt et al., 1979b; Murdock and Cobb, 1980). True and/or apparent microsphere loss was calculated by the following equation:

$$\%\ \text{apparent microsphere loss} = \frac{(MBF_{NI} - MBF_{PO})}{MBF_{NI}} \times 100,$$

where MBF_{PO} = preocclusion blood flow in individual samples of the region subjected to ischemia, MBF_{NI} = mean flow in nonischemic samples from the same layer. Ischemic blood flow measurements were then corrected for each sample using the following equation:

$$MBF_c = MBF_u \times \frac{100}{100 - \%\ \text{apparent microsphere loss}},$$

where MBF_c = corrected blood flow values, MBF_u = uncorrected blood flow values, and % apparent microsphere loss = the percent loss from preceding equation.

Data Analysis

The postmortem sampling procedures and quantitative analysis were done by individuals who did not know the treatment of any given dog. Data forms were submitted

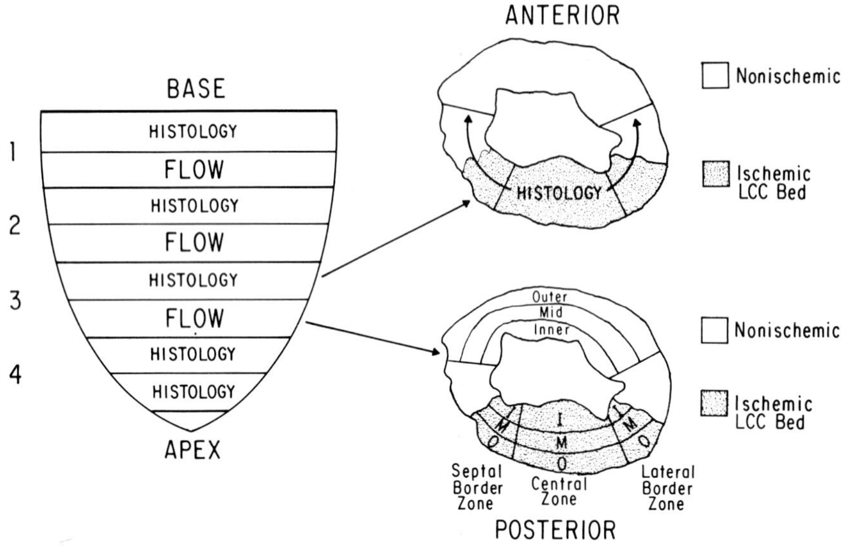

Figure 1. *The method of tissue sampling, common to each of the three participating laboratories, is illustrated. The left ventricle of each heart was divided into four slices of approximately equal thickness. Each of these slices was subdivided, with the apical half used for blood flow analysis and the basal half for histological evaluation of infarct size. [However, both halves of the fourth (apical) slice were used for histological analysis]. Histological sections were prepared from the entire circumferential extent of the infarct in each slice. These histological sections were cut from the center of each slice (specifically, from the apical surface of the basal half of each slice). The area of infarction in this plane was considered to be representative of the full thickness of each slice, for conversion of infarct surface area to infarct weight. Blood flow was measured in the nonischemic region, central ischemic zone (central 50% of the infarct), and septal and lateral border zones. Each of these regions was further subdivided into inner, middle, and outer thirds. The individual flow data illustrated in this paper is the arithmetic mean of blood flow measured in the three slices. Because of probable contamination of some septal and lateral border samples with nonischemic myocardium, data from these samples has not been included in this paper.*

to NIH, where all data were computerized for subsquent analysis. At the end of the study, the drug identification code was broken and data from all three laboratories were compared.

Comparisons of histological, hemodynamic, and flow measurements were made among treatments, between conscious model sites, and between models, using simple two-sample *t*-tests. When differences between pre- and post-treatment values were studied, these differences were computed for each animal and then compared by two-sample *t*-tests, as desired, among groups. Paired *t*-tests were used to determine whether any pre-post treatment differences existed.

Because of the major importance of area at risk, collateral flow, and cardiac metabolic demand in determining infarct size, these parameters were incorporated into the statistical analysis of infarct size, using rate pressure product as an index of metabolic demand.

Two methods were used to control for area at risk and collateral flow. The first was to relate infarct size to area at risk by expressing infarct size as a percent of area at risk. Infarct size (as % of area at risk) then was compared among treatments in an analysis of covariance using collateral blood flow as the covariate. This method has the advantage of simplicity and ease of interpretation, since the relationship can be displayed graphically using observed data. On the other hand, it makes an assumption that the relationship of infarct size to area at risk goes through the origin (i.e., that infarct size will be proportional to area at risk). The method also assumes that treatment effect will be proportional to area at risk. Moreover, this method permits incorporation of only one variable in addition to area at risk.

The second method used to control for baseline variables was to fit a multiple linear regression model with baseline variables as independent variables, and infarct size as the dependent variable. This method does not depend on the above-mentioned assumptions and permits simultaneous analysis of several independent variables. Treatment effects were entered into this multiple regression model as treatment-specific intercepts and coefficients for the independent variables. By estimating models both with and without treatment specific coefficients, it was possible to assess whether the regression equations were different for different treatment groups. Two multiple linear regression models were considered, an additive and a multiplicative model. In the additive model it was assumed that infarct size could be predicted by a linear combination of the three variables, area at risk, subepicardial collateral blood, and rate pressure product (RPP). In the multiplicative model, the three independent variables were area at risk, and the products of area at risk × subepicardial collateral and area at risk × RPP. Both models were estimated; the results were very similar. We present only the multiplicative analysis herein, based on the rationale that differences in collateral flow or RPP may have more of an effect on infarct size when area at risk is large than when it is small. (At the extreme, if area at risk is zero, flow differences should have virtually no effect on infarct size.)

Results

Animal Selection and Mortality (Table 1)

Unconscious Model

Fifty-one dogs were entered into the study and all were randomized. One dog was pregnant at the time of study and was excluded. In addition, two dogs had minimal reductions of coronary blood flow following occlusions, probably due to failure of the

TABLE 1
Selection, Survival, and General Characteristics of Dogs Studied by Site and Treatment*

Group	*n*	No. of exclusions pre-random	No. of exclusions post-random	Total inclusions	Deaths pre-Rx	Deaths post-Rx	*n* (% of randomized inclusions)	Dogs surviving study % Male	Dog wt (mean ± SD)	Hematocrit (mean ± SD)
DU										
Control			3	14	0	3	11 (79)	55	15 ± 2.8	40 ± 3.2
Verapamil			0	17	1	0	16 (94)	31	14 ± 2.5	40 ± 3.2
Ibuprofen			0	17	1	4	12 (71)	33	14 ± 2.3	39 ± 3.3
Total	51	0	3	48	2	7	39 (81)	38	14 ± 2.5	40 ± 3.2
JH										
Control			2	10	0	4	6 (60)	50	19 ± 0.8	44 ± 4.5
Verapamil			2	11	0	1	10 (91)	40	20 ± 2.4	43 ± 3.6
Ibuprofen			1	12	0	4	8 (67)	25	20 ± 2.0	42 ± 7.6
Total	38	0	5	33	0	9	24 (73)	38	20 ± 1.9	43 ± 5.2
DVA										
Control			1	14	0	0	14 (100)	57	20 ± 1.7	42 ± 3.7
Verapamil			4	11	0	0	11 (100)	64	19 ± 3.6	40 ± 2.1
Ibuprofen			1	15	0	2	13 (87)	85	19 ± 1.7	42 ± 3.6
Total	53	7	6	40	0	2	38 (95)	68	19 ± 2.5	41 ± 3.2
JH + DVA										
Control			3	24	0	4	20 (83)	55	20 ± 1.5	42 ± 4.0
Verapamil			6	22	0	1	21 (95)	52	19 ± 3.1	42 ± 3.2
Ibuprofen			2	27	0	6	21 (78)	62	20 ± 1.9	42 ± 5.3
Total	91	7	11	73	0	11	62 (85)	56	20 ± 2.3	42 ± 4.2

* The unconscious dog model was studied at Duke (DU), and the conscious model was studied at Johns Hopkins (JH) and the Durham VA hospital (DVA).

Schwartz clamp, and have been excluded. Nine dogs (19%) died prior to sacrifice. Of these, five developed ventricular fibrillation during the first hour of coronary occlusion (two during the first 15 minutes); one died 55 minutes after reperfusion, and the other three died of unknown cause (presumably ventricular fibrillation) during the 3 days between acute study and sacrifice. Thus, infarct size was analyzed in 39 of the dogs randomized. Of the dogs included in the final analysis, 38% were male, mean weight was 14 kg ± 2.5, and hematocrit was 40 ± 3.2%. There were no significant differences among treatment groups in these parameters.

Conscious Model

Ninety-one dogs were entered into the study, of which 84 were randomized. Seven dogs were excluded prior to randomization because of technical difficulties arising from the prior instrumentation. Eleven randomized dogs also were excluded for several reasons: four at DVA and two at JH for heart worms, two for occlusion failure at JH, one at each center for receiving incomplete therapy, and one at DVA because of failure to obtain histology. Nine of 33 (27%) of the remaining dogs studied at JH and two of 40 (5%) dogs at DVA died before sacrifice and have been excluded. All 11 deaths occurred 12 hours or more after occlusion. In the combined conscious study, infarct size was analyzed in 62 of the 84 randomized dogs. Of these dogs, 56% were male, mean weight was 20 ± 2.3 kg, and hematocrit was 42 ± 4.2%. Most of the dogs at DVA were male, and most at JH were female.

Comparison of Baseline Parameters by Model and Site (Tables 2–6)

Hemodynamic parameters measured 10 minutes after coronary occlusion and before treatment (baseline measurements) are listed in Tables 2 and 3. Comparison of the results from each study site showed some consistent hemodynamic differences between the unconscious and conscious models and between the JH and DVA conscious study sites. Mean heart rate was higher in the unconscious dogs (158 vs. 121 beats/min) and resulted in a higher rate-pressure product. Systolic and diastolic arterial pressures and left atrial pressures were similar in the two models. However, the mean systolic blood pressure and left atrial pressure were higher at JH compared to DVA. Within each study site, however, no significant hemodynamic differences between control and treatment groups were detected.

Despite the higher rate-pressure product, coronary blood flow to nonischemic myocardium was lower in the unconscious than conscious dogs (Tables 4 and 5). The reason for this paradox is unknown. A possible cause is reduced contractility in the unconscious model; however, indices of myocardial contractility were not measured. In addition, baseline central ischemic collateral blood flow was

TABLE 2
Hemodynamic Parameters—Unconscious Model

Experimental group	Heart rate		Systolic blood pressure		Diastolic blood pressure		Mean left atrial pressure		Rate pressure product (× 10^{-2})	
	10 min	105 min	10 min	105 min	10 min	105 min	10 min	105 min	10 min	105 min
Control	156±20	150±26	133±22	155±21*	96±20	115±15*	7.1±1.8	8.5±3.2	208±41	235±59
Verapamil	158±29	123±24†§	142±26	131±15†§	98±19	80±11†§	7.2±4.1	8.6±5.0*	230±81	164±48†§
Ibuprofen	159±27	145±30†	136±25	165±24†	100±33	127±14*	7.0±2.6	9.5±4.9*	217±57	242±72
All groups	158±26 ‖		138±24		98±24		7.1±3.1		220±64¶	

Results are expressed as mean ± SD. Heart rate is in beats/min, and all pressures are in mm Hg. Significant changes between the 10- and 105-minute measurements within a group, by paired *t*-analysis, are indicated by * $P<0.05$; † $P<0.01$. Significant differences between control and treated groups are indicated as ‡$P<0.05$, §$P<0.01$. Significant differences between the unconscious and conscious models are indicated by ‖ $P<0.05$, ¶ $P<0.01$. Hemodynamic parameters for all groups 5 minutes before coronary occlusion were: heart rate 156±27; systolic blood pressure 154±19; diastolic blood pressure 107±13; mean left atrial pressure 4.3±1.8; rate pressure product (× 10^{-2}) 241±53. Coronary occlusions had a significant effect on all of these parameters except heart rate.

lower in the unconscious dogs. The reason for this difference in collateral blood flow also is unknown. The sampling protocol was designed to prevent admixture of nonischemic and ischemic tissue, but we cannot be certain that the higher collateral flows in the conscious dogs was not due, in part, to such admixture. Another more likely reason for higher collateral flow in the conscious dogs is that snare placement around the circumflex artery induced collateral growth in some dogs. Finally, the smaller areas at risk at JH also may have contributed to the higher collateral flows. Baseline nonischemic and collateral coronary blood flow did not differ significantly between the JH and DVA groups. Within each study site, measurements of collateral coronary flow following randomization and treatment also did not differ between control and treatment groups.

The anatomic area at risk averaged 41% of the left ventricle in both unconscious and conscious models (Tables 6 and 7). However, the mean area at risk was smaller at JH (35%) than at DVA (45%), apparently due to use of a somewhat more distal occlusion site at JH. Again, within each study site, the area at risk was comparable in treatment groups.

Treatment Effects on Hemodynamic Parameters and Coronary Blood Flow

Unconscious Model

In the unconscious model, coronary occlusion caused a reduction in blood pressure but no change in heart rate (see footnote to Table 2). In the control group, the major hemodynamic change between 10 and 105 minutes after occlusion was an increase

TABLE 3
Hemodynamic Parameters—Conscious Model

Experimental group	Heart rate		Systolic blood pressure		Diastolic blood pressure		Mean left atrial pressure		Rate pressure product (×10^{-2})	
	10 min	105 min	10 min	105 min	10 min	105 min	10 min	105 min	10 min	105 min
JH										
Control	111±12	107±27	140±13	135±21	96±11	90±17	8.8±4.0	7.7±3.6	156±27	148±58
Verapamil	102±23	124±22*	145±23	144±19	96±18	92±19	8.4±2.3	7.3±2.4*	150±48	178±39*
Ibuprofen	125±34	112±22	151±18	153±19	103±22	100±15	11.0±8.8	7.8±3.4	189±57	170±45
All groups	112±26		145±19¶		98±18		9.4±5.5‖			
DVA										
Control	129±43	113±32	120±25	112±22	87±23	79±20	7.1±4.3	5.2±2.9	159±66	125±40*
Verapamil	132±27	132±23	128±23	113±10*	93±19	79±13*	7.0±6.4	4.4±3.6	172±60	151±34
Ibuprofen	121±35	104±28*	128±21	124±22	93±13	84±16	3.7±4.7	3.5±3.9	157±60	128±40
All groups	127±35		125±23		91±18		6.1±5.2			
Combined										
Control	123±37	111±30	126±23	119±24*	90±20	82±19*	7.6±4.2	6.0±3.3†	158±56	132±46
Verapamil	118±29	128±22‡	136±24	128±22	94±18	85±17*	7.7±4.8	5.8±3.4*	161±55	164±38‡
Ibuprofen	122±33	107±26*	137±23	134±25*	97±17	90±17*	7.1±7.7	5.6±4.2	170±59	143±45
All groups	121±33		133±23		94±18		7.5±5.5		163±56	

Units are as defined for Table 2. Statistical significance for various comparisons also is indicated—as defined for Table 2—except that ‖ $P<0.05$ and ¶ $P<0.01$ refers to comparison of JH vs. DVA results. Hemodynamic parameters for all groups 5 minutes prior to coronary occlusion were: heart rate 91±19; systolic blood pressure 136±22; diastolic blood pressure 85±16; mean left atrial pressure 4.1±3.2; rate pressure product (x 10^{-2}) 125±38. Coronary occlusion had a significant effect on all of these parameters except systolic blood pressure.

Table 4
Coronary Blood Flow (ml/min per g) in Nonischemic and Central Ischemic Zones—Unconscious Models

Experimental group	10 Minutes						105 Minutes					
	Nonischemic			Ischemic			Nonischemic			Ischemic		
	I	M	O	I	M	O	I	M	O	I	M	O
Control	1.02	1.06	0.98	0.03	0.09‖	0.18	1.13	1.18	1.03	0.05	0.10‖	0.22‖
	±0.31	±0.33	±0.31	±0.05	±0.10	±0.18	±0.35	±0.41	±0.41	±0.08	±0.15	±0.23
n	11	11	11	11	11	11	11	11	11	11	11	11
Verapamil	1.05	1.09‖	0.97	0.05	0.11‖	0.19¶	0.96¶	0.96¶*	0.93¶	0.04*‖	0.09	0.22*‖
	±0.43	±0.45	±0.39	±0.05	±0.07	±0.13	±0.50	±0.51	±0.43	±0.04	±0.09	±0.16
n	15	15	15	15	15	15	16	16	16	16	16	16
Ibuprofen	0.87¶	0.96‖	0.88‖	0.05‖	0.13‖	0.24‖	1.18	1.24*	1.07	0.04‖	0.12‖	0.33
	±0.22	±0.22	±0.18	±0.04	±0.12	±0.16	±0.38	±0.37	±0.32	±0.04	±0.16	±0.33
n	11	11	11	11	11	11	12	12	12	12	12	12
All groups	0.99¶	1.05¶	0.95¶	0.05¶	0.11¶	0.20¶						
	±0.34	±0.35	±0.31	±0.05	±0.09	±0.15						
n	37	37	37	37	37	37						

I = inner (subendocardial), M = middle, and O = outer (subepicardial) thirds of the myocardium. Statistical significance for various comparisons is indicated as defined for Table 2.

(partial recovery) in systolic and diastolic blood pressure (Table 2). Nonischemic and central ischemic collateral blood flow were unchanged between 10 and 105 minutes of coronary occlusion (Table 4). In the ibuprofen group, blood pressure also increased between 10 and 105 minutes (Table 2). Mean heart rate was moderately lower and left atrial pressure moderately higher in both control and treated groups at 105 vs. 10 minutes, but the changes were significant only in the ibuprofen group. Neither nonischemic nor central ischemic collateral flow was affected by ibuprofen (Table 4). In contrast, verapamil decreased heart rate and blood pressure and increased left atrial pressure (Table 2). The effects of verapamil on nonischemic and central ischemic collateral coronary blood flow were minor.

Conscious Model

In the conscious model, coronary occlusion caused increases in both heart rate and diastolic blood pressure (see footnote to Table 3), and arterial and left atrial pressure decreased between 10 and 105 minutes after occlusion. These effects were directionally opposite to those observed in the unconscious model. Between 10 and 105 minutes, nonischemic and central ischemic collateral blood flow did not change in the combined group (Table 5), but nonischemic flow decreased in the DVA group. Ibuprofen reduced heart rate in the conscious model, as it did in the unconscious model. Nonischemic coronary blood flow decreased between 10 and 105 minutes in the ibuprofen group at the DVA but not at JH, paralleling the observations in the control groups at the same sites. Ibuprofen did not significantly alter central ischemic collateral blood flow (10 vs. 105 min) at either conscious study site, but subepicardial collateral flow was higher prior to treatment in the ibuprofen group vs. controls studied at DVA. In the combined conscious verapamil groups, the only significant hemodynamic effects were slight reductions in diastolic arterial and left atrial pressures. However, the hemodynamic effects of verapamil differed between JH and DVA, the major effect at JH being an increased heart rate without a decrease in blood pressure, and the major effect at DVA was a decrease in pressure without change in heart rate. Nonischemic coronary blood flow was modestly increased after verapamil therapy, but central ischemic collateral blood flow was unchanged. Comparison of the overall response to verapamil in conscious vs. unconscious dogs indicated that the cardiodepressant effects of the drug were more pronounced in the unconscious model.

Analysis of Infarct Size Variability among Control Dogs

Unconscious Model

Infarct size (Table 6) in control dogs averaged 26% of the left ventricle, with a sizeable standard deviation (±14% of the LV). Much of this variation in infarct size could be related to variation in the anatomic area at risk ($r^2 = 0.77$) (Fig. 2A). When infarct size was normalized to the area at risk, infarct size averaged 60% ± 27% (SD) of the area at risk in the control group.

Central ischemic collateral flow varied considerably among dogs and this variation was greatest in the subepicardial region (0.20 ± 0.15 ml/min per g). In the unconscious control dogs, the relationship between infarct size (as a percent of the area at risk) and central ischemic subepicardial flow measured 10 minutes after coronary occlusion is shown in Figure 3A. About 50% of the variation in infarct

TABLE 5
Coronary Blood Flow (ml/min per g) in Nonischemic and Central Ischemic Zones—Conscious Model

Experimental group	10 Minutes						105 Minutes					
	Non-Ischemic			Ischemic			Non-Ischemic			Ischemic		
	I	M	O	I	M	O	I	M	O	I	M	O
JH												
Control	1.23	1.26	0.94	0.23	0.25	0.41	1.18	1.18	0.92	0.11	0.19	0.39
	±0.54	±0.53	±0.42	±0.42	±0.31	±0.36	±0.23	±0.28	±0.19	±0.19	±0.13	±0.14
n	6	6	6	6	6	6	6	6	6	6	6	6
Verapamil	1.10‖	1.26	1.00	0.28	0.34	0.42	1.38	1.55	0.134‡	0.13	0.21	0.40
	±0.28	±0.33	±0.33	±0.42	±0.40	±0.26	±0.35	±0.48	±0.46	±0.12	±0.21	±0.24
n	10	10	10	10	10	10	8	8	8	8	8	8
Ibuprofen	1.90	2.18	1.60	0.25	0.32	0.42	1.43	1.50	1.14	0.14	0.20	0.30
	±1.46	±1.97	±1.32	±0.37	±0.41	±0.40	±0.34	±0.36	±0.33	±0.21	±0.26	±0.22
n	8	8	8	8	8	8	6	6	6	6	6	6
All groups	1.40	1.57	1.18	0.26	0.31	0.42						
	±0.94	±1.22	±0.84	±0.39	±0.37	±0.32						
n	24	24	24	24	24	24						
DVA												
Control	1.45	1.46	1.28	0.10	0.18	0.30	1.15*	1.20*	1.09*	0.15	0.25	0.40*
	±0.70	±0.69	±0.60	±0.09	±0.13	±0.15	±0.39	±0.48	±0.53	±0.19	±0.21	±0.24
	14	14	14	14	14	14	14	14	14	14	14	14
Verapamil	1.49	1.50	1.41	0.10	0.19	0.32	1.50‡	1.73‡	1.68‡	0.07*	0.15*	0.33
	±0.39	±0.40	±0.38	±0.11	±0.13	±0.15	±0.43	±0.69	±0.65	±0.08	±0.10	±0.11
n	11	11	11	11	11	11	11	11	11	11	11	11
Ibuprofen	1.58	1.64	1.36	0.17	0.34	0.48	1.12†	1.20†	1.02*	0.32	0.41	0.48‡
	±0.73	±0.73	±0.55	±0.11	±0.24	±0.28	±0.44	±0.48	±0.38	±0.40	±0.33	±0.25
n	13	13	13	13	13	13	13	13	13	13	13	13
All groups	1.51	1.53	1.32	0.12	0.24	0.37						
	±0.63	±0.62	±0.52	±0.10	±0.19	±0.21						
n	38	38	38	38	38	38						
Combined												
Control	1.38	1.40	1.18	0.14	0.20	0.33	1.16	1.20	1.04	0.14	0.23	0.40
	±0.65	±0.64	±0.56	±0.23	±0.20	±0.23	±0.35	±0.42	±0.46	±0.18	±0.19	±0.21
n	20	20	20	20	20	20	20	20	20	20	20	20
Verapamil	1.31	1.39	1.61	0.19	0.26	0.37	1.45‡	1.65§	±1.54*§	0.09	0.18	0.36
	±0.39	±0.38	±0.38	±0.31	±0.30	±0.21	±0.39	±0.60	±0.59	±0.10	±0.16	±0.18
n	21	21	21	21	21	21	19	19	19	19	19	19
Ibuprofen	1.70	1.85	1.45	0.20	0.33	0.46	1.22*	1.30*	1.06*	0.27	0.35	0.42
	±1.05	±1.32	±0.90	±0.24	±0.31	±0.32	±0.43	±0.46	±0.26	±0.36	±0.32	±0.25
n	21	21	21	21	21	21	19	19	19	19	19	19
All groups	1.47	1.55	1.27	0.17	0.26	0.39						
	±0.76	±0.89	±0.66	±0.26	±0.27	±0.26						
n	62	62	62	62	62	62						

Abbreviations are as defined for Table 4. Statistical significance for various comparisons is indicated as defined for Table 3.

size, normalized to area at risk, was explained by the variation in subepicardial collateral flow ($r^2 = 0.53$). The rate-pressure product, an index of myocardial metabolic demand, did not contribute significantly to variation in infarct size in a univariate analysis (the correlation coefficient for infarct size/area at risk vs. the rate-pressure product was only 0.26). Based on the relationship illustrated in Figure 3A, and assuming group sizes of 15 dogs, a 13% (of area at risk) limitation of infarct size would be detected at a significance level of $P < 0.05$ about 50% of the time. Larger treatment effects would be

TABLE 6
Infarct Size and Area at Risk in Control and Treated Dogs—Unconscious Model

Experimental group	n	Infarct size (% of LV)	Area at risk (% of LV)	Infarct size (% of area at risk)
Control	11	26 ± 13.7	40 ± 8.3	60 ± 27.1
Verapamil	16	22 ± 8.4	42 ± 7.6	53 ± 20.7
Ibuprofen	12	23 ± 8.7	41 ± 4.5	56 ± 20.2
All groups	39		41 ± 7.9	

more readily detected and smaller effects probably would be missed.

When the multiple linear regression model was estimated (model 2) for control animals, the estimated regression equation (n = 11) was

$$IS = \underset{(0.13)}{-0.13} + AAR \times [\underset{(0.35)}{0.61} - (\underset{(0.44)}{0.94} \times CBF) + (\underset{(1.0)}{2.4} \times RPP/10^5)]$$

where IS = infarct size, AAR = area at risk, CBF = subepicardial collateral blood flow, and RPP = rate-pressure product. The numbers in parentheses are standard errors of the coefficients. The r^2 value was 0.90, and the residual standard deviation was 0.052 or 5.2% of the left ventricle. This model accounted for 90% of the variation in infarct size observed in the study; 77% of the variation was attributable to area at risk alone. Based on this multiple regression model, and assuming group sizes of 15 dogs per group, a 10% (of area at risk) limitation of infarct size would be detected at a significance level of $P <$ 0.05 about 50% of the time.

TABLE 7
Infarct Size and Area at Risk in Control and Treated Dogs—Conscious Model

Experimental group	n	Infarct size (% of LV)	Area at risk (% of LV)	Infarct size (% of area at risk)
JH				
Control	6	18 ± 11.6	36 ± 9.2	48 ± 26.3
Verapamil	10	15 ± 11.5	33 ± 9.4	41 ± 29.4
Ibuprofen	8	21 ± 13.3	38 ± 9.0	51 ± 27.6
All groups	24		35 ± 9.1*	
DVA				
Control	14	24 ± 14.3	46 ± 9.8	49 ± 21.9
Verapamil	11	21 ± 10.8	45 ± 5.0	45 ± 21.3
Ibuprofen	13	16 ± 11.7	44 ± 5.5	34 ± 22.7
All groups	38		45 ± 7.2	
Combined				
Control	20	22 ± 13.5	43 ± 10.6	49 ± 22.6
Verapamil	21	18 ± 11.3	39 ± 9.4	43 ± 24.9
Ibuprofen	21	18 ± 12.2	42 ± 7.4	40 ± 25.4
All groups	62		41 ± 9.2	

No significant differences were observed between control and treated groups.

* $P < 0.01$.

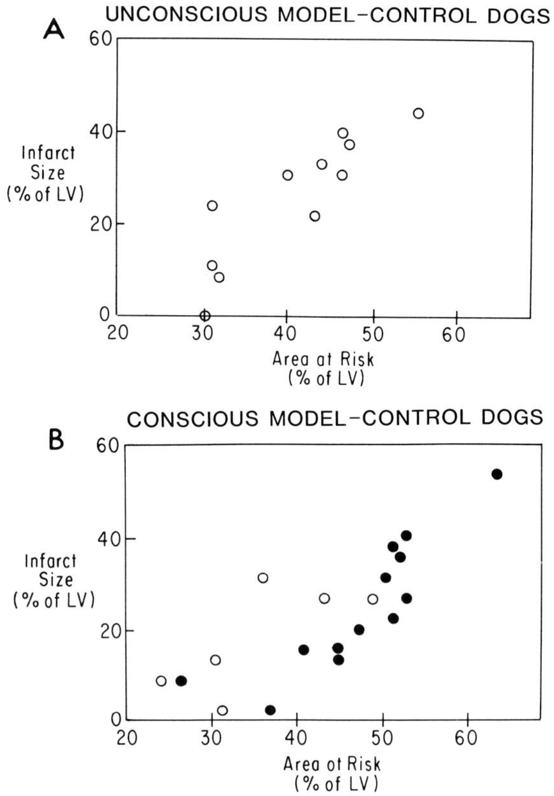

FIGURE 2. *The relationship between infarct size (% of LV) in control dogs and area at risk (% of LV) is illustrated for the unconscious (panel A) and conscious (panel B) models. For panel A, the linear correlation coefficient, r = 0.88 and for panel B, r = 0.81. Each point represents an individual dog. In panel B, open circles are from the study at JH (r = 0.76), solid points are from the DVA (r = 0.85).*

Conscious Model

Infarct size (Table 7) among control dogs (6 from JH and 13 from DVA) had about the same degree of variability observed in the unconscious model, averaging 22% ± 14% of the LV and 49% ± 23% of the area at risk. The relation between infarct size (as % of LV) and area at risk in the conscious study is illustrated in Figure 2B. As with the unconscious model, based on r^2 = 0.66, most (66%) of the variation in infarct size was related to the size of the area at risk. Infarct size (as % of LV) was slightly smaller at JH (18%) compared with DVA (22%), a difference which was clearly related to smaller areas at risk in the dogs studied at JH. Infarct size, normalized as % of area at risk, was similar at the two conscious dog study sites (48 and 49%, respectively).

As was observed with the unconscious model, conscious dogs showed a transmural gradient in central ischemic collateral blood flow, with considerable variation among dogs in the amount of collateral flow to the subepicardial region (0.40 ± 0.21 ml/min per g). As in the unconscious model, part of the variation in infarct size (normalized to area at risk) was accounted for by variation in central ischemic collateral blood flow r^2 = 0.40 and 0.18 at DVA and JH, respectively) (Fig. 3B). Based on the

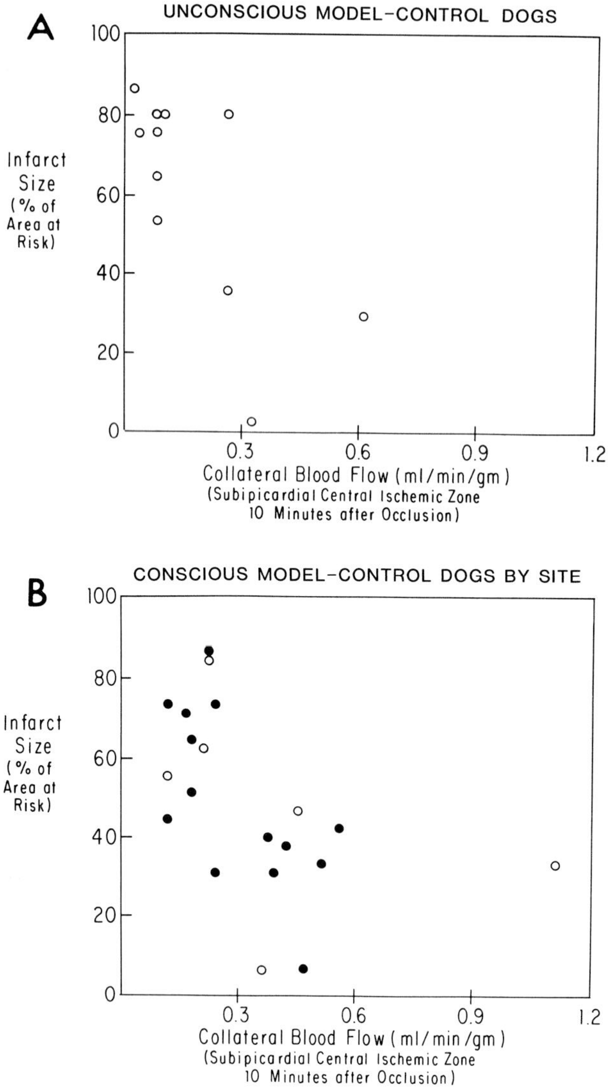

FIGURE 3. *The relationship between infarct size, normalized to area at risk, in control dogs and baseline central ischemic collateral blood flow is illustrated for the unconscious (panel A) and conscious (panel B) models. For panel A, the linear correlation coefficient, $r = -0.72$ and for panel B, $r = -0.49$. Each point represents an individual dog. In panel B, open circles are from the study at JH ($r = -0.43$), solid points are from the DVA ($r = -0.63$).*

relationship in Figure 3B and assuming group sizes of 15 dogs, a 13% (of area at risk) limitation of infarct size would be detectable at a significance level of $P < 0.05$ about 50% of the time.

In contrast to the unconscious model, the rate-pressure product was significantly related to infarct size/area at risk in the conscious model ($r^2 = 0.23$). When the multiple regression model was fit to conscious control dogs, the resulting equation ($n = 20$) was:

$$\text{IS} = \underset{(0.10)}{0.04} + \text{AAR} \times [\underset{(0.23)}{0.50} - (\underset{(0.32)}{0.59} \times \text{CBF}) + (\underset{(0.64)}{1.82} \times \text{RPP}/10^5)]$$

The regression had an $r^2 = 0.80$ with a residual standard deviation of 0.067 or 6.7% of LV. The model thus accounted for 80% of the variability in infarct size; 66% of the variability was accounted for by risk region alone. Based on the multiple regression relationship, and assuming group sizes of 15 dogs, a 13% (of area at risk) limitation of infarct size would be detected at a significance level of $P <$ 0.05 about 50% of the time.

Effects of Verapamil or Ibuprofen on Infarct Size and Ancillary Variables

Unconscious Model

The relationship between infarct size (as a percent of area at risk) and central ischemic subepicardial collateral blood flow is illustrated in Figure 4A. There was a trend toward protection with verapamil, in that at least three individual points were conspicuously below the relationship observed in control animals. However, by this method, comparison of regression lines of control animals vs. verapamil- or ibuprofen-treated dogs failed to show that either drug significantly limited infarct size.

The multiple regression equations for the ibuprofen- and verapamil-treated dogs were:

$$\text{IS} = \underset{(0.11)}{0.13} + \text{AAR} \times [\underset{(0.31)}{0.188} - (\underset{(0.17)}{1.14} \times \text{CBF}) + (\underset{(0.52)}{1.49} \times \text{RPP}/10^5)]$$

$$\text{Verapamil IS} = \underset{(0.10)}{0.04} + \text{AAR} \times [\underset{(0.25)}{0.041} - (\underset{(0.33)}{0.60} \times \text{CBF}) + (\underset{(0.53)}{1.48} \times \text{RPP}/10^5)]$$

The r^2 values for these equations were 0.88 and 0.49, respectively, and the residual standard deviations were 3.6 and 7.0, respectively. The equation for verapamil dogs was significantly different from that for control dogs, based either on an F-test comparing all four coefficients between treatments, or on a t-test comparing only the coefficients for area at risk. In the first case, the comparison of all four coefficients yielded $F(4,18) = 3.09$, $P = 0.042$.

Figure 5A is a plot of actual infarct size vs. infarct size predicted by the multiple regression model. A protective treatment effect in individual dogs is suggested by points falling below the line of identity. At least three verapamil dogs had infarct sizes markedly below the line of identity. The significant difference between control and verapamil-treated groups, using the above multiple regression analysis, clearly was due primarily to these three dogs. No clear effect of therapy occurred in most (12 of 15) of the dogs treated with this drug.

Conscious Model

The relationship between infarct size as a percent of area at risk and central ischemic subepicardial collateral blood flow is illustrated in Figure 4B. As in the unconscious model, comparison of regression lines of control dogs vs. verapamil- or ibuprofen-treated dogs by this method failed to show significant limitation of infarct size by either drug. It is of

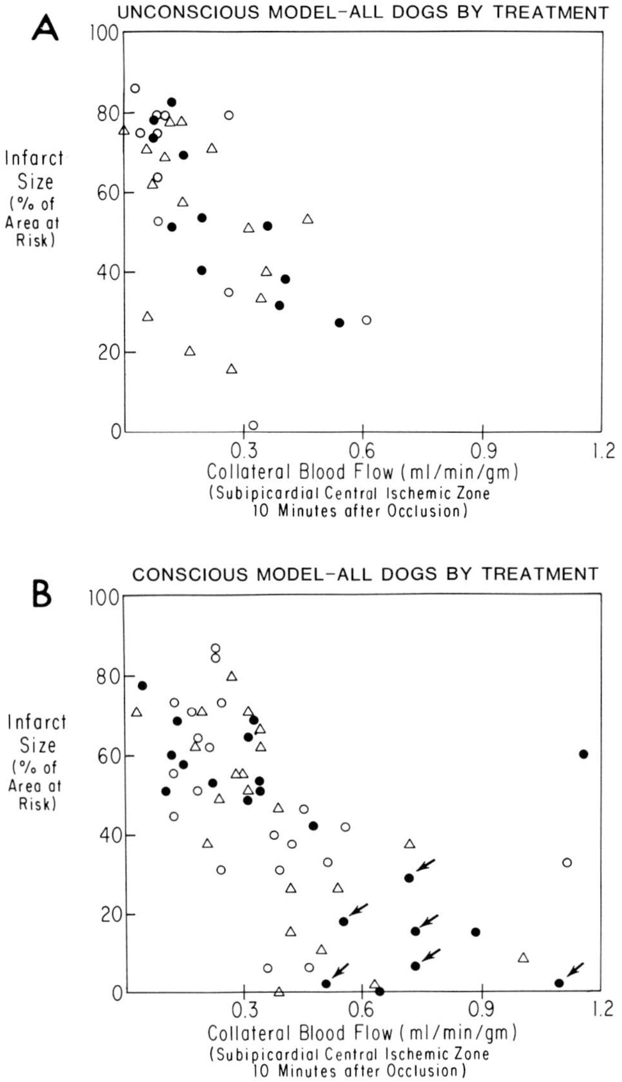

FIGURE 4. *The same relationship shown in Figure 3 is illustrated for control, but also for verapamil-treated, and ibuprofen-treated infarcts from the unconscious (panel A) and conscious (panel B) studies. Each point represents an individual dog. Open circles represent control dogs, triangles are verapamil-treated dogs, and solid points are ibuprofen-treated dogs. In panel A, the linear correlation coefficient for verapamil treated infarcts is $r = -0.38$ and for ibuprofen-treated infarcts is $r = -0.84$. The low r value for the verapamil group is due to three infarcts which were smaller than expected on the basis of baseline collateral flow. However, with these possible exceptions, neither verapamil nor ibuprofen altered the relationship between infarct size and subepicardial collateral flow. In panel B, data from JH and VA has been combined. For verapamil, $r = -0.67$ (JH $r = -0.79$ and DVA $r = -0.43$) and for ibuprofen, $r = -0.70$ (JH $r = -0.51$ and DVA $r = -0.81$). Neither therapy altered the relationship between infarct size and collateral blood flow. However, several ibuprofen-treated dogs at DVA (arrows) had relatively high baseline collateral blood flow and correspondingly small infarcts. Thus, an apparent protective effect with ibuprofen suggested in Table 7 clearly was due to random selection bias. Without the analysis of infarct size in relation to baseline collateral blood flow, an erroneous conclusion, that ibuprofen limited infarct size in the DVA study, could have been drawn.*

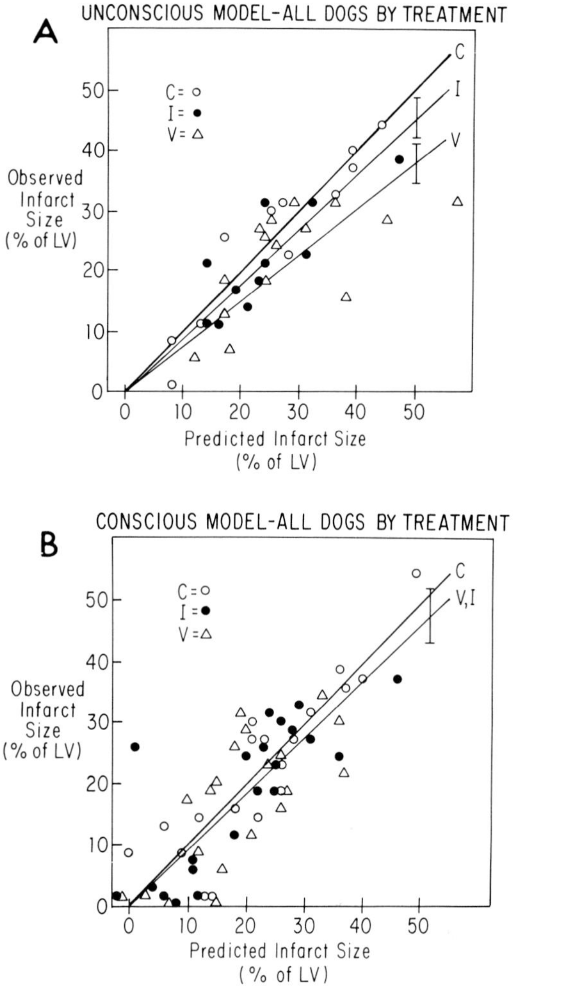

FIGURE 5. *The relationship between observed infarct size and predicted infarct size based on multiple regression analysis (statistical model 2) of control infarcts, relating infarct size to area at risk, subepicardial collateral flow, and rate pressure product, is illustrated for unconscious (panel A) and conscious (panel B) studies. Each point represents an individual dog. Open circles represent control dogs, triangles are verapamil-treated dogs, and solid points are ibuprofen-treated dogs. With this analysis, any point that was markedly below the line of identity would suggest limitation of infarct size in that individual dog. The control regression lines on panels A and B are the lines of identity. The regression lines for each treatment group are shown with brackets indicating the standard errors of the slope. The regression line for the verapamil-treated infarcts in the unconscious model (panel A) was significantly different from the control regression line. This difference is attributed to an apparent marked limitation of infarct size in three of the 15 dogs in this group. The drug did not have a marked effect in the remaining 12 dogs in this treatment group. In the ibuprofen-treated group, observed infarct size was not markedly different from predicted infarct size in any of the dogs. In the conscious study (panel B), the regression lines and standard errors for verapamil and ibuprofen groups were virtually identical; thus only a single line is shown. Neither treatment resulted in a regression line that differed significantly from the control regression line.*

particular interest to note that when infarct size is considered without regard to collateral flow (Table 5), the difference between control and treated groups at DVA (infarct size/area at risk = 49% vs. 34%) approached significance ($P < 0.1$). This tendency toward infarct limitation in the treated group was entirely explained by the chance selection of several dogs with unusually high baseline central ischemic collateral flows (measured prior to treatment) into this treatment group (Fig. 4B).

The multiple regression equations for ibuprofen and verapamil dogs were:

$$\text{Ibuprofin IS} = -0.22 + \text{AAR} \times [0.87 - (0.29 \times \text{CBF}) + (1.25 \times \text{RPP}/10^5)]$$
$$(0.10) \quad (0.24) \quad (0.14) \quad (0.64)$$

$$\text{Verapamil IS} = -0.04 + \text{AAR} \times [0.82 - (0.77 \times \text{flow}) + (0.02 \times \text{RPP}/10^5)]$$
$$(0.08) \quad (0.25) \quad (0.27) \quad (0.79)$$

The r^2 values were 0.71 and 0.62, and the residual standard deviations were 0.071 and 0.075, respectively, for ibuprofen and verapamil. There were no statistically significant differences among the three equations, based either on tests comparing all four regression coefficients or on t-tests comparing only the coefficient for area at risk.

Figure 5B displays actual infarct sizes plotted against the expected infarct size based on the multiple regression model. In this analysis, there were no treated animals which had infarct sizes markedly below the line of identity.

Discussion

Rationale of Models

Choice of Animal Species and Duration of Coronary Occlusion

Dogs were selected for study, in part, because of the past experience of the investigators involved, but also because canine myocardial infarcts resemble human infarcts in several respects. Most occur in the presence of some residual coronary perfusion via subepicardial collateral anastomoses (Becker et al., 1973; Wusten et al., 1974; Rivas et al., 1976; Williams et al., 1976; Reimer and Jennings, 1979a; Kuo et al., 1982), the location is related to the vascular distribution of the occluded artery(ies) (Reimer and Jennings, 1979a; Lee et al., 1981; Factor et al., 1981, 1982; Murdock et al., 1983), and the subendocardial zone is more susceptible than the subepicardial zone to infarction (Rivas et al., 1976; Reimer and Jennings, 1979a; Lee et al., 1981).

In the unconscious model, infarction was induced by a temporary (3-hour) occlusion of the proximal left circumflex artery, followed by reperfusion. In this model, some subepicardial myocardium is still viable at 3 hours, even without pharmacological therapy (Reimer and Jennings, 1979a) and a 10% limitation of infarct size can be achieved by reperfusion. Thus, an intervention that could at least delay cell death could increase the amount of myocardium that could be salvaged by reperfusion (Reimer and Jennings, 1979a, 1984). The occlusion was permanent in the awake models to produce a more prolonged period of ischemia and a more rigorous test of therapeutic efficacy.

Dose, Time of Initiation, Duration of Therapy

The initial loading dose and rate of verapamil infusion were selected to be the largest that did not cause marked detrimental hemodynamic changes. The dose of ibuprofen was chosen based on previous studies which had shown limitation of infarct size (Jugdutt et al., 1980). In both models, drug administration was begun 15 minutes after coronary occlusion to permit baseline measurements of postocclusion hemodynamic parameters and coronary collateral blood flow so that the effect of therapy on these potential determinants of infarct size could be observed.

In the unconscious model, therapy was continued throughout coronary occlusion and for 15–30 minutes after reperfusion. In the conscious model, verapamil and ibuprofen were discontinued after 6 and 24 hours of coronary occlusion, respectively. The decision to discontinue therapy at these times was based on the difficulty of maintaining chronic drug delivery and on previous studies that had shown limitation of infarct size following temporary therapy with ibuprofen (Lefer and Polansky, 1979; Jugdutt et al., 1980; Lefer and Crossley, 1980; Romson et al., 1980).

Choice of Experimental Endpoints: Methods of Measurement

Since our primary objective was to develop protocols to determine whether therapy can limit infarct size, the primary endpoint was the direct measurement of infarct size. Among published anatomic studies, gross staining techniques using triphenyl tetrazolium chloride (TTC) or nitroblue tetrazolium chloride (Lie et al., 1975; Fallon, 1979) have been used more commonly than histological techniques. Gross staining techniques have the advantage of being less time consuming and less expensive. However, we chose histological methods because positive staining of myocardium with TTC may not necessarily be synonymous with myocyte viability, and because resolution of the complex interdigitations between necrotic and viable areas can be done most reliably by histological evaluation. The decision to end the studies at 3 days was based on the progressively easier task of histological infarct sizing with passing time, balanced by the fact that infarct repair results in the gradual replacement of infarct by scar, which may not represent accurately the initial infarct size (Reimer and Jennings, 1979b).

Because infarct size varies considerably among untreated dogs, additional parameters that may influence infarct size must also be measured. Previous studies have shown that variation in infarct size in dogs is related to variation in (1) the size of the ischemic region (area at risk) (Lowe et al., 1978; Reimer and Jennings, 1979a; Jugdutt et al., 1979a;

Schaper, 1979), (2) collateral blood flow to the ischemic region (Rivas et al., 1976; Reimer and Jennings, 1979a; Jugdutt et al., 1979a; Schaper, 1979; Gottwick et al., 1981), and (3) myocardial metabolic demand which is determined in part by hemodynamic parameters, including heart rate, wall tension, and myocardial contractility (Schaper et al., 1979).

In this study, the area at risk of undergoing infarction was defined as the anatomic region supplied by the occluded coronary artery (Reimer and Jennings, 1979a; Jugdutt et al., 1979a; Lee et al., 1981), as distinguished from a "physiological" risk region (DeBoer et al., 1980), defined as the area with moderate or severe ischemia, based on the paucity of myocardial staining by dyes injected in vivo. The anatomic definition of area at risk was chosen in this study because (1) it is a baseline constant, determined by coronary anatomy, which cannot be altered by spontaneous or therapeutically induced fluctuation in collateral blood flow during an experiment, and (2) identification of an anatomic vascular region requires the identification of boundaries between two vascular regions but does not require the arbitrary distinction between severely vs. less severely ischemic myocardium based on a graded concentration of injected dyes or particles.

Two methods of identifying the anatomic area at risk were used: In the unconscious reperfusion model, in which collateral growth had not been induced, the area at risk could be identified by the boundary between the two different-colored dyes (Reimer and Jennings, 1979a). Precise sampling of ischemic and nonischemic areas for blood flow analysis was possible because vascular boundaries are seen directly on the ventricular slices. However, in the setting of permanent (3-day) coronary occlusions, new collaterals develop such that dyes in fluid suspension may readily cross the ischemic/nonischemic interface. Thus, in the conscious model, coronary arteries were injected postmortem with radioopaque material, and vascular bed boundaries were identified on radiographs of serial slices of the ventricle (Jugdutt et al., 1979a, 1979c, 1980; Lee et al., 1981; Murdock et al., 1983). The radiographic technique allows direct anatomic delineation of vascular bed boundaries, which are not influenced by collateral growth. The principle limitations of the radiographic techniques are the overlap of vasculature on two-dimensional representation of three-dimensional myocardial slices, and relative imprecision of using x-rays to guide the sampling of myocardium for blood flow analysis.

Tissue sampling for evaluation of collateral blood flow was designed with two major objectives: (1) to select central ischemic samples that were uncontaminated by nonischemic myocardium interdigitating with infarcted myocardium at the boundaries of the ischemic region, and (2) to measure the transmural distribution of collateral blood flow in the central ischemic zone.

Importance of Baseline Variables to Improve Precision and Prevent Erroneous Conclusions

Although, in a randomized study, baseline variables would tend to be balanced across treatments, it is important to control for them statistically in a "small" study in which 30% of the animals are excluded. Controlling for baseline variables improves precision of estimated effects while giving some protection against bias from imbalances in baseline factors due to treatment-dependent exclusions.

Analysis of the control infarcts at each of the three sites confirmed that the area at risk, collateral blood flow, and rate pressure product each were independent determinants of infarct size. Indeed, variation in the size of the area at risk accounted for over half the variation in infarct size (as % of LV), and when collateral flow and rate pressure product were included in the model, 90% of the variation among unconscious controls, and 80% of the variation among conscious control infarcts could be explained. The crucial importance of incorporating collateral blood flow into the analysis is best illustrated by the DVA results with ibuprofen. If infarct size had been evaluated alone, (e.g., based on Table 7), without respect to collateral blood flow, it could have been concluded erroneously that ibuprofen limited infarct size in the DVA arm of the study (but not at the other two sites). When collateral flow was taken into account, however (Fig. 4B), it was readily apparent that the smaller infarcts in the ibuprofen-treated group at DVA were due to the random selection into this group, of several dogs with unusually high native levels of collateral blood flow. Conversely, in the unconscious model, the positive verapamil treatment effect seen in 3 of 15 dogs was undetectable without adjustment for baseline variables. In comparison to area at risk or collateral blood flow, rate-pressure product was only a weak predictor of infarct size. However, it is recognized that determinants of myocardial metabolic rate and systolic blood pressure include not only heart rate and systolic blood pressure, but also contractility and cardiac size. Whether a more precise estimate of cardiac MVO_2 would have proven to be a better predictor of infarct size in this study is not known; only 10% of the variation in infarct size remained unaccounted for by the baseline parameters measured in this study.

Effect of Therapy with Verapamil or Ibuprofen on Infarct Size

Verapamil and ibuprofen were selected as the two drugs for study, because these drugs represented two general classes of drugs, with presumably different mechanisms of myocardial protection, which had previously shown considerable promise as possible therapies to limit infarct size.

The hypothesis that calcium antagonists protect ischemic myocardium has been tested in a large number of laboratories, using a variety of experimental models and different endpoints [see Reimer and Jennings, 1984 and 1985 (in press), for detailed review]. At least five studies have shown limitation of experimental infarct size with calcium antagonists when measured at times ranging from 6 hours to 2 days after coronary occlusion (Henry et al., 1978; DeBoer et al., 1980; Zamanis et al., 1982; Alps et al., 1983; Yellon et al., 1983; Melin et al., 1984). In contrast, several studies have failed to show salvage of ischemic myocardium with various calcium antagonists (Karlsberg et al., 1977; Geary et al., 1982; Alps et al., 1983; Reimer and Jennings, 1984). The reason(s) that calcium antagonists have shown protective effects in some studies but not in others is not known. These differences may have been due to differences among the individual drugs or the dose regimens used, to different responses to therapy among different animal models used, or to failure in many studies, to consider one or more of the important baseline determinants of infarct size.

The nonsteroidal anti-inflammatory agent, Ibuprofen, has been studied much less extensively than verapamil, but was selected because it has produced marked reduction of ischemic injury in cats (Lefer and Polansky, 1979; Lefer and Crossley, 1979), and because it had limited infarct size by over 50% in a conscious dog model (Jugdutt et al., 1980; Romson et al., 1980). Subsequent to the initiation of these studies, Romson et al. (1982a, 1982b), observed limitations of infarct size in an unconscious dog reperfusion model in which infarction was induced by 60 minutes of circumflex coronary occlusion. Chambers et al. (1983), concluded that flurbiprofen, a fluorinated derivative of ibuprofen, delayed the evolution of TTC evidence of infarction in unconscious dogs but did not limit ultimate infarct size.

The explanation for the discrepancies between those studies showing limitation vs. no limitation of infarct size with nonsteroidal anti-inflammatory agents is not known. However, none of the studies discussed above have made careful analyses of the relation between infarct size and collateral blood flow in treated and untreated dogs.

Conclusions

The goal of these studies was to establish experimental models which could be used to demonstrate reproducibly whether a particular therapy could limit experimental infarct size. Three major sources of variation in infarct size in either unconscious or conscious dogs have been confirmed; 90% of the variation in infarct size among control dogs was related to variation in anatomic area at risk, collateral blood flow, and the rate-pressure product. Methods for measuring these baseline parameters and for including them in the analysis of treatment effects have been standardized. Although neither verapamil nor ibuprofen were shown to limit infarct size, we estimate that by using groups of 15 dogs, and incorporating baseline predictors into the analysis, as little as 10–13% limitation of infarct size would be detected 50% of the time. Larger treatment effects would be more readily detected.

We wish to acknowledge technical assistance by the following individuals: Duke Medical Center: William R. Hamilton, Nancy J. Kramer, and Robert B. Kinney, M.D.; Durham VA Medical Center: Marjorie Grubb, Kirby Cooper, and Eric Fields; The Johns Hopkins Medical Center: Anthony F. DiPaula, John M. Nicklas, M.D., and Joe Zulty.

Supported in part by National Institutes of Health Contracts 1-HV92926 and 1-HV92923, and by Grants HL 27416, HL 18537, and 2P50 HL-17655.

Address for reprints: Dr. Keith A. Reimer, Department of Pathology, Duke Medical Center, Durham, North Carolina 27710.

Received August 6, 1984; accepted for publication January 17, 1985.

References

Alps BJ, Calder C, Wilson A (1983) The beneficial effect of nicardipinc compared with nifedipine and verapamil in limiting myocardial infarct size in baboons. Arzneimforsch Drug Res **33:** 868–876

Becker LC, Ferreira R, Thomas M (1973) Mapping of left ventricular blood flow with radioactive microspheres in experimental coronary artery occlusion. Cardiovasc Res **7:** 391–400

Capurro NL, Goldstein RE, Aamodt R, Smith HJ, Epstein SE (1979) Loss of microspheres from ischemic canine cardiac tissue. Circ Res **44:** 223–227

Chambers DE, Yellon DM, Hearse DJ, Downey JM (1983) Effects of Flurbiprofen in altering the size of myocardial infarcts in dogs: reduction or delay? Am J Cardiol **51:** 884–890

DeBoer LWV, Strauss HW, Kloner RA, Rude RE, Davis RF, Maroko PR, Braunwald EB (1980) Autoradiographic method for measuring the ischemic myocardium at risk: Effects of verapamil on infarct size after experimental coronary artery occlusion. Proc Natl Acad Sci USA **77:** 6119–6123

Factor SM, Okun EM, Kirk ES (1981) The histological lateral border of acute canine myocardial infarction: A function of microcirculation. Circ Res **48:** 640–649

Factor SM, Okun EM, Minase T, Kirk ES (1982) The microcirculation of the human heart. End-capillary loops with discrete perfusion fields. Circulation **66:** 1241–1248

Fallon JT (1979) Simplified method for histochemical demonstration of experimental myocardial infarct. Circulation **60:** 11–42

Geary GG, Smith GT, Suehiro GT, McNamara JJ (1982) Failure of nifedipine therapy to reduce myocardial infarct size in the baboon. Am J Cardiol **49:** 331–338

Gottwik M, Zimmer P, Wusten B, Hofmann M, Winkler B, Schaper W (1981) Experimental myocardial infarction in a closed-chest canine model: Observations of temporal and spatial evolution over 24 hours. Basic Res Cardiol **76:** 670–680

Henry PD, Shuchleib R, Borda LJ, Roberts R, Williamson JR, Sobel BE (1978) Effects of nifedipine on myocardial perfusion and ischemic injury in dogs. Circ Res **43:** 372–380

Jugdutt BI, Hutchins GM, Bulkley BH, Becker LC (1979a) Myocardial infarction in the conscious dog: Three dimensional mapping of infarct, collateral flow, and region at risk. Circulation **60:** 1141–1150

Jugdutt BI, Hutchins GM, Bulkley BH, Becker LC (1979b) The loss of radioactive microspheres from canine necrotic myocardium. Circ Res **45:** 746–756

Jugdutt BI, Hutchins GM, Bulkley BH, Becker LC (1980) Salvage of ischemic myocardium by ibuprofen during infarction in the conscious dog. Am J Cardiol **46:** 74–82

Karlsberg RP, Henry PD, Ahmed SA, Sobel BE, Roberts R (1977) Lack of protection of ischemic myocardium by verapamil in conscious dogs. Eur J Pharmacol **42:** 339–346

Kuo PT, Kostis JB, Moreyra AE (1982) Protection of myocardium by the compensatory mechanism of coronary collaterals after total occlusion of major coronary arteries shown in patients with familial hypercholesterolemia. Am Heart J **104:** 36–43

Lee JT, Ideker RE, Reimer KA (1981) Myocardial infarct size and location in relation to the coronary vascular bed at risk in man. Circulation **64:** 526–534

Lefer AM, Crossley K (1980) Mechanisms of the optimal protective effects of ibuprofen in acute myocardial ischemia. Adv Shock Res **3:** 133–141

Lefer AM, Polansky EW (1979) Beneficial effects of ibuprofen in acute myocardial ischemia. Cardiology **64:** 265–279

Lie JT, Pairolero PC, Holley KE, Titus JL (1975) Macroscopic enzyme-mapping: Verification of large, homogeneous, experimental myocardial infarcts of predictable size and location in dogs. J Thorac Cardiovasc Surg **69:** 599–605

Lowe JE, Reimer KA, Jennings RB (1978) Experimental infarct size as a function of the amount of myocardium at risk. Am J Pathol **90:** 363–379

Melin JA, Becker LC, Hutchins GM (1984) Protective effect of early and late treatment with nifedipine during myocardial infarction in the conscious dog. Circulation **69:** 131–141

Murdock RH Jr, Cobb FR (1980) Effects of infarcted myocardium on regional blood flow measurements to ischemic regions in canine heart. Circ Res **47:** 701–709

Murdock RH Jr, Harlan DM, Morris JJ III, Pryor WW Jr, Cobb FR (1983) Transitional blood flow zones between ischemic and non-ischemic myocardium in the awake dog. Analysis based on distribution of the intramural vasculature. Circ Res **52:** 451–459

Peto R, Pike MC, Armitage P, Breslow NE, Cox DR, Howard SV, Mantel N, McPherson K, Peto J, Smith PG (1976) Design and analysis of randomized clinical trials requiring prolonged observations of each patient: Introduction and design. Br J Cancer **34:** 585

Reimer KA, Jennings RB (1979a) The "wavefront phenomenon" of myocardial ischemic cell death. II. Transmural progression of necrosis within the framework of ischemic bed size (myocardium at risk) and collateral flow. Lab Invest **40:** 633–644

Reimer KA, Jennings RB (1979b) The changing anatomic reference base of evolving myocardial infarction. Underestimation of myocardial collateral blood flow and overestimation of experimental anatomic infarct size due to tissue edema, hemorrhage, and acute inflammation. Circulation **60:** 866–876

Reimer KA, Jennings RB (1984) Verapamil in two reperfusion models of myocardial infarction: Temporary protection of severely ischemic myocardium without limitation of ultimate infarct size. Lab Invest **51:** 655–666

Reimer KA, Jennings RB (in press) Effects of calcium channel blockers on myocardial preservation during experimental acute myocardial infarction. Am J Cardiol

Rivas F, Cobb FR, Bache RJ, Greenfield JC Jr (1976) Relationship between blood flow to ischemic regions and extent of myocardial infarction: Serial measurement of blood flow to ischemic regions in dogs. Circ Res **38:** 439–447

Romson JL, Bush LR, Haack DW, Lucchesi BR (1980) The beneficial effects of oral ibuprofen on coronary artery thrombosis and myocardial ischemia in the conscious dog. J Pharmacol Exp Ther **215:** 271–278

Romson JL, Bush LR, Jolly SR, Lucchesi BR (1982a) Cardioprotective effects of ibuprofen in experimental regional and global myocardial ischemia. J Cardiovasc Pharmacol **4:** 187–196

Romson JL, Hook BG, Rigot VH, Schork MA, Swanson DP, Lucchesi BR (1982b) The effect of ibuprofen on accumulation of Indium-III-labeled platelets and leukocytes in experimental myocardial infarction. Circulation **66:** 1002–1011

Schaper W (1979) Residual perfusion of acutely ischemic heart muscle. *In* The Pathophysiology of Myocardial Perfusion, edited by W Schaper. New York, Elsevier/North-Holland Biomedical Press, pp 345–378

Williams DO, Amsterdam EA, Miller RR, Mason DT (1976) Functional significance of coronary collateral vessels in patients with acute myocardial infarction: Relation to pump performance, cardiogenic shock and survival. Am J Cardiol **37:** 345–351

Wusten B, Flameng W, Schaper W, Carl M (1974) The distribution of myocardial flow. Part I: Effects of experimental coronary occlusion. Basic Res Cardiol **69:** 422–434

Yellon DM, Hearse DJ, Maxwell MP, Chambers DE, Downey JM (1983) Sustained limitation of myocardial necrosis 24 hours after coronary artery occlusion: Verapamil infusion in dogs with small myocardial infarcts. Am J Cardiol **51:** 1409–1413

Zamanis A, Verdetti J, de Leiris J (1982) Reduction of ischemia-induced myocardial necrosis in the rat with permanent coronary artery occlusion under the effect of diltiazem. J Mol Cell Cardiol **14:** 53–62

INDEX TERMS: Infarct size limitation • Reperfusion of ischemic myocardium • Verapamil • Ibuprofen

Coronary Venous Perfusion of the Ischemic Myocardium during Acute Coronary Artery Occlusion in Isolated Rat Hearts

Yuji Taira, Hideo Kanaide, and Motoomi Nakamura

From the Research Institute of Angiocardiology and Cardiovascular Clinic, Faculty of Medicine, Kyushu University, Fukuoka, Japan

SUMMARY. Effects of retrograde coronary venous perfusion on oxygen supply and energy metabolism of ischemic myocardium of the isolated perfused rat heart were examined by means of NADH fluorescence photography. Occlusion of the left coronary artery produced regional ischemia of the left ventricular free wall, as evidenced by the sharply demarcated increase in NADH fluorescence. During ischemia, a narrow area of minimal fluorescence (140 ± 10 μm), indicating sufficient oxygenation for oxidative phosphorylation, was observed around the epicardial coronary veins in the ischemic lesion. Retrograde perfusion was introduced through the coronary vein (left cardiac vein) that drained off the ischemic area, which resulted in a marked reduction of the area of increased NADH fluorescence in the epicardial surface. In the cross-sectional view, although the myocardium of the entire ischemic area induced by left coronary artery occlusion could be perfused by venous retroperfusion, the effect on reduction of the area of increased NADH fluorescence was seen only in the epicardial half of the myocardium. Retrograde coronary venous perfusion also resulted in a small increase in tension development ($P < 0.05$), a decrease in resting tension ($P < 0.01$), and partial preservation of myocardial high energy phosphate content ($P < 0.01$). We propose that coronary venous retroperfusion improves oxygenation, partially preserves oxidative phosphorylation in the epicardium, and improves contractile function in the ischemic region. **(*Circ Res 56: 666–675, 1985*)**

EXPERIMENTS involving retrograde perfusion on arterialization of the coronary veins were first reported by Pratt (1893), who was able to sustain the contraction of the cat heart for several hours by coronary sinus perfusion. Since then, attempts have been made to restore the impaired myocardial circulation in cases of ischemic heart disease. The first clinical application of this attempt was accomplished by Beck (1948). He performed a carotid-coronary sinus anastomosis or an aortocoronary sinus anastomosis, using a vein graft. However, the mortality with the procedure remained high. These studies have been overshadowed by the development of direct coronary artery revascularization (Berger and Stary, 1971). Recently, there is renewed interest in retrograde coronary venous perfusion, in selective situations such as diffuse coronary arteriosclerosis, and in cases of temporal support for patients with acute myocardial infarction. Recent efforts of Meerbaum et al. (1976) showed the usefulness of a synchronized diastolic retroperfusion system to decrease damage in the acutely ischemic myocardium.

There have been numerous studies on the usefulness of retrograde coronary venous perfusion; yet, metabolic events associated with the possible increase in oxygenation to the tissue are poorly understood. The objective of our study was to obtain evidence for direct oxygen delivery to the ischemic lesion, by retrograde coronary venous perfusion (RCVP), using NADH fluorescence photography (Barlow and Chance, 1976; Steenbergen et al., 1977; Harken et al., 1978). Nicotinamide adenine dinucleotide, reduced form (NADH), fluorescence increases when the oxygen supply is deficient, and, as a result, oxidative phosphorylation is inhibited (Chance, 1976). Fluorescence photography was used to determine the area involved by antegrade aortic perfusion and RCVP, and for this, a fluorescent dye was added to the perfusate.

Methods

Perfusion Technique

Male Wistar rats weighing 250–350 g were given free access to a commercial diet and tap water. Thirty minutes before excision of the hearts, 500 U of heparin were given intraperitoneally. The isolated hearts were perfused at a pressure of 80 cm H_2O by the Langendorff procedure (Langendorff, 1895), with a minor modification. The perfusate was Krebs-Ringer bicarbonate buffer solution containing 2.5 mM calcium and 5.5 mM glucose, aerated with a 95% O_2–5% CO_2 mixture for the aerobic perfusion and a 95% N_2–5% CO_2 mixture for the anaerobic perfusion. The perfusate was allowed to pass through the heart only once. The hearts were perfused at 30°C and were paced electrically at 200 beats/min. Under these conditions, we obtained a stable preparation for almost 60 minutes. Myocardial oxygen consumption under these conditions was 1.08 ± 0.08 mmol O_2/hr per g.

A strain gauge (SB-1T, Nihon Kohden) was attached via a nylon ligature to the ventricular apex for the measurement of tension development of the whole heart. At the start of each experiment, the resting tension was set at about 1 g.

To induce regional ischemia in the left ventricular wall, we surgically occluded the left coronary artery (LCA) at a point 5 mm from its origin, using the techniques developed by Selye et al. (1960).

Arterial and venous effluent Po_2 during the perfusion in aerobic, anaerobic, and LCA occlusions was measured with a Corning blood gas analyzer. Coronary flow rates (flow rates of venous effluent) were measured with a drop counter.

In all experiments, preconditioning of the preparation involved a 20-minute perfusion to wash out the red blood cells and to stabilize the heart rate and coronary flow.

Coronary Venous Retroperfusion

For retrograde coronary venous perfusion (RCVP), a polyethylene catheter, 300 μm in diameter, was inserted into the left cardiac vein (Halpern, 1953) via the right atrium. The distal end of the catheter was carefully located near the margin of the ischemic region, and retrograde flow rate through the catheter was controlled by a roller pump. To diminish the possible fluctuation of the flow rate, a 10-ml air space was made within the perfusion route. Since the outside diameter of the catheter was less than the inside diameter of the vein, obstruction of antegrade venous drainage of the perfusate from the heart during systole and resultant possible tissue edema was prevented (Farcot et al., 1978). Since coronary flow rates during the aerobic control period and during LCA ligation were 8.8 ± 0.3 ml/min and 5.7 ± 0.4 ml/min, respectively (indicating that there was a reduction of at least 3 ml/min during ischemia), retrograde flow rate was set at 3 or 5 ml/min; with these flow rate levels, there was no tissue edema. To monitor pressure in the retrograde-perfused vein, we punctured a branch of the vein near the ischemic margin, inserted a polyethylene catheter 300 μm in diameter, and connected it to a catheter-tip transducer (Millar; pc-350). For simultaneous determination of the area of arterial antegrade perfusion and the area of venous retrograde perfusion by fluorescence photography, fluorescein sodium (Wako-Junyaku) and thioflavin S (Chroma) were perfused from the aortic and venous roots, respectively.

Fluorescence Photographs

Photographs of NADH fluorescence were obtained by a system we developed in collaboration with the Union Giken Company, Osaka, Japan, the principles and the techniques of which were described initially by Barlow and Chance (1976). A Canon A-1 camera with a 50-mm focal length microlens and extension tube (FD-25) was used. Tashiba Y-45 and B-46 filters were placed before the camera lens to allow for transmission in the 440- to 500-nm region. NADH excitation was provided by two 300J xenon flash tubes (FS-403, Union Giken), one mounted on either side of the camera lens, to provide fairly uniform illumination on the left ventricular free wall. The xenon flash tubes were covered with Toshiba UV-D36C and UV-35 filters to provide 340–380 nm excitation. To avoid possible fluctuations of fluorescence during the cardiac cycle, the flash was synchronized to occur during diastole, with an electrical pacing spike as a trigger.

All heart preparations for the cross-sectional NADH fluorescence photography were immersed immediately in liquid nitrogen, and then freeze-dried. Cross-sectioning was performed with a razor blade, at a right angle to the long axis of the freeze-dried heart, at a level 10 mm from the apex. For detailed microscopic examinations of the cross-sectional distribution of NADH fluorescence, fluoromicrophotography was carried out with a reflected fluoromicroscope (Zeiss-standard 18F, filter set 01).

For the fluorescence photography of both thioflavin S (emission: 440 nm) and fluorescein sodium (emission: 530 nm), 340- to 380-nm wavelength was also used for excitation. Both thioflavin S and NADH emit at 440 nm.

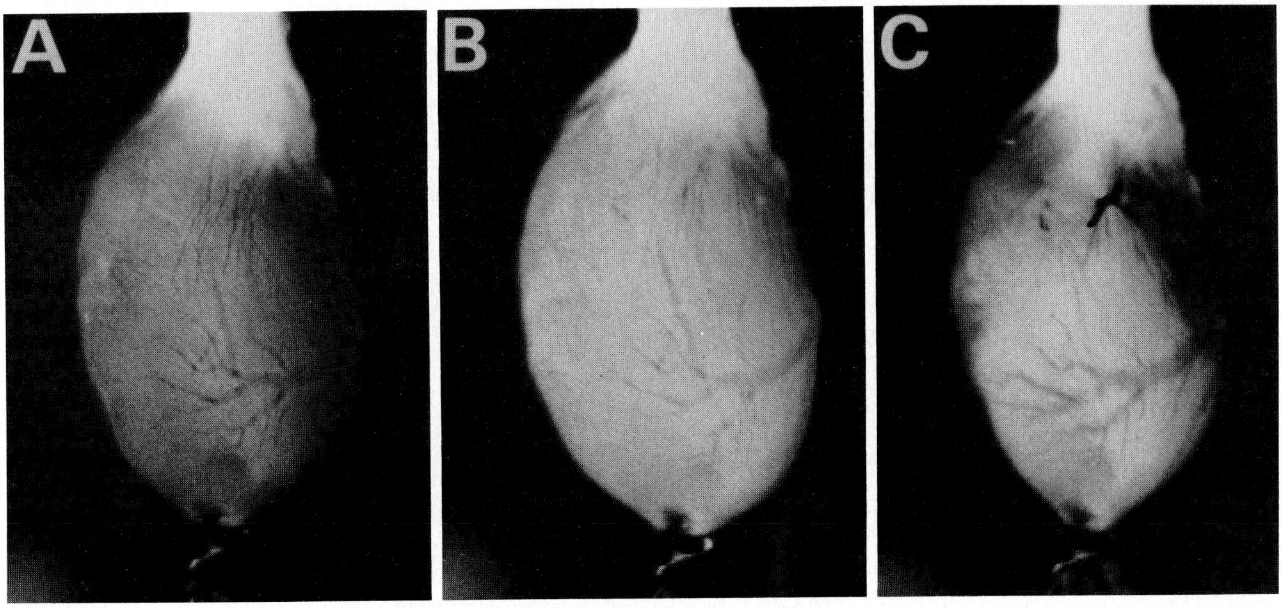

FIGURE 1. *Epicardial NADH fluorescence photographs under conditions of aerobic perfusion (panel A), hypoxia (panel B), and regional ischemia (panel C).*

When we examined the distribution of NADH and thioflavin S fluorescence in the same heart, NADH fluorescence was photographed before the venous retroperfusion of thioflavin S. The fluorescence intensity of thioflavin S is so high that the photographic condition required to detect the fluorescence of added dyes is not sensitive enough to be disturbed by NADH fluorescence of low intensity. Fluorescence of NADH and added dyes was clearly recorded in characteristic color (emission) on Kodak Tri X film (ASA 400, monochrome) and Kodak color negative film (ASA 400).

Biochemical Analysis

After 20 minutes of regional ischemia, with or without venous retrograde perfusion, the left ventricular free wall subjected to ischemia assessed by NADH fluorescence was quickly excised and frozen, using a Wollenberger's tong precooled in liquid nitrogen. In addition, the control left ventricular free wall was obtained from the heart perfused with aerobic solution for 20 minutes, following 20 minutes of perfusion for preconditioning (control). Tissue concentrations of adenosine 5'-triphosphate (ATP) and creatine phosphate (CP) were assayed according to the method of Lamprecht et al. (1975). Adenosine diphosphate (ADP) and adenosine monophosphate (AMP) were assayed by the procedures described by Jaworek et al. (1975). Tissue concentrations of nicotinamide adenine dinucleotide (NAD) and its reduced type (NADH) were assayed according to the method of Williamson and Corkey (1969).

Statistical Analysis

Results were expressed as mean ± SEM. Statistical significance was determined by analysis of variance. Values of $P < 0.05$ were considered significant.

Results

The Area of Increased NADH Fluorescence Induced by LCA Occlusion

All control photographs of each normoxic-preischemic heart showed uniform distributions of minimal NADH fluorescence (Fig. 1A). When the heart, initially perfused with aerobic perfusate (Fig. 1A), was perfused with an anaerobic one, the entire heart

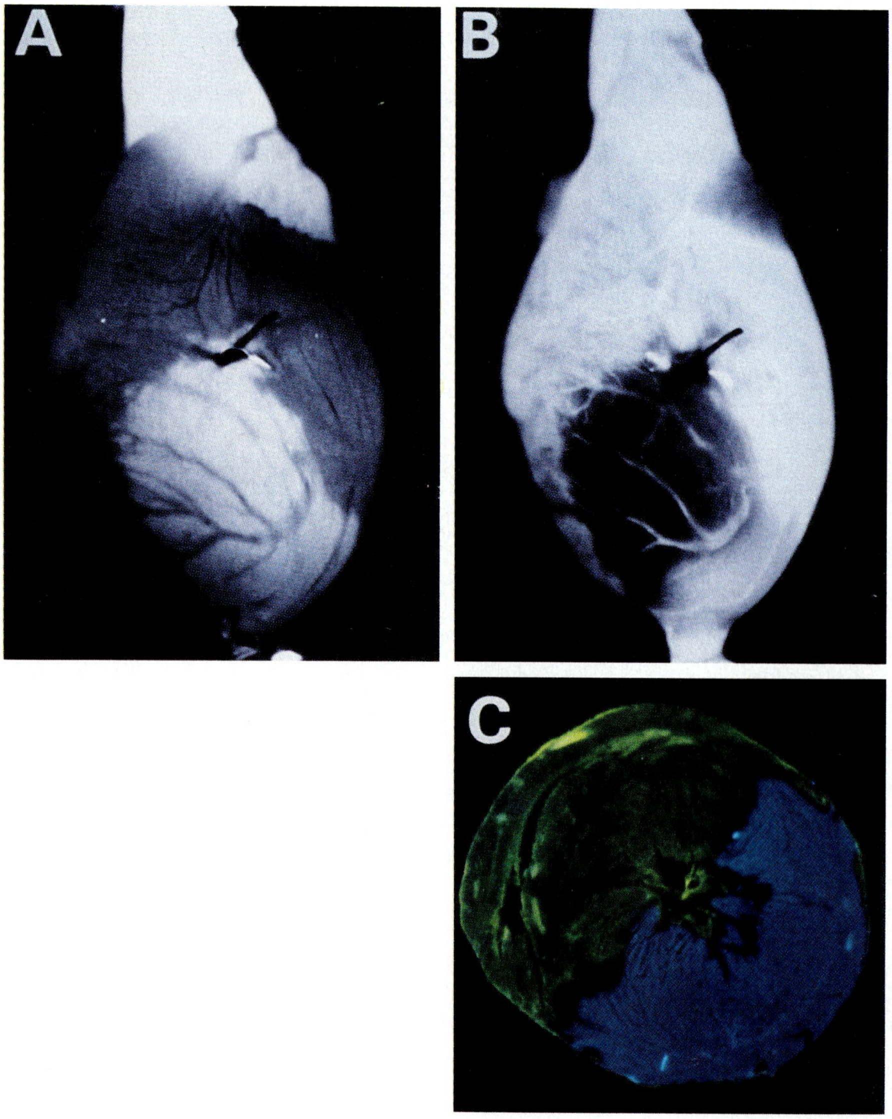

FIGURE 2. *Photographs of NADH fluorescence, indicating the area of ischemia lacking oxidative phosphorylation (panel A), the fluorescence of fluorescein sodium perfused via the aorta after occlusion, indicating the area of normal perfusion (panel B), and the cross-sectional fluorescence of both NADH (right: blue) and fluorescein sodium (left: green) (panel C). Panels A and B were taken from the same heart in which LCA ligation was carried out 5 mm from origin. Panel C: ligation of LCA was carried out at its origin.*

showed an increase of epicardial NADH fluorescence that was relatively uniform in intensity (Fig. 1B). Upon occlusion of LCA, increased NADH fluorescence was clearly visible distal to the occlusion (Fig. 1C). The ischemic myocardium showed a zone of NADH fluorescence relatively low in intensity around the epicardial vein, which was broader (1.4 times) than that observed under conditions of anaerobic perfusion. Figure 2A also shows a typical NADH fluorescence photograph of regional ischemia induced by LCA occlusion. In this experiment, the relatively distal portion of the LCA was ligated to demonstrate clearly the border between the ischemic and normal areas, in a photograph of the left ventricular free wall. Because of the minimum NADH fluorescence, both in and around the epicardial veins, the areas appeared distinctly as networks of dark lines in the ischemic area of increased fluorescence. When fluorescein sodium was perfused by admixture with the aortic perfusate following LCA ligation, we obtained a photograph of fluorescein sodium with a reversed impression of the NADH fluorescence photograph (Fig. 2B). The area of minimal NADH fluorescence in Figure 2A coincided with the area of fluorescein sodium in Figure 2B. The epicardial veins in the ischemic area clearly showed evidence of fluorescein sodium, which may have derived from the perfused normoxic area because the dye was absent in the ischemic area and was present only in the epicardial veins.

TABLE 1
Changes in Coronary Flow and Po_2 during Normoxia, Anoxia, and Regional Ischemia

	Normoxia	Anoxia	Regional ischemia
Coronary flow (ml/min)	8.8 ± 0.3	17.5 ± 0.5	5.7 ± 0.4
Arterial Po_2 (mm Hg)	595 ± 12	39 ± 2	597 ± 13
Effluent Po_2 (mm Hg)	273 ± 27	23 ± 2	251 ± 12

Figure 2C shows a cross-sectional fluorescence photograph of both NADH and fluorescein sodium perfused from the aorta during LCA occlusion. NADH fluorescence (blue color) demonstrates an anoxic area in regional ischemia, and fluorescein sodium (green color) demonstrates a perfusion area from the aorta. Between these two fluorescent areas, there was a narrow band of no fluorescence approximately 180 ± 30 μm wide. It is emphasized that the NADH fluorescence area was clearly demarcated, and transition from minimal to full NADH fluorescence was abrupt.

Cross-sectional fluoromicrophotographs of

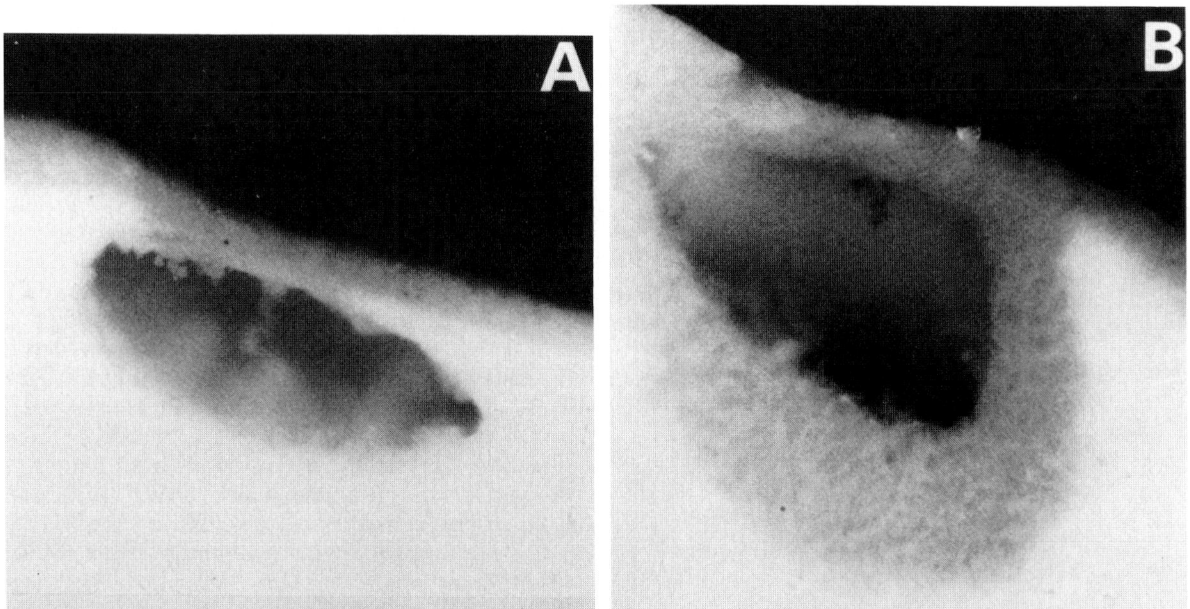

FIGURE 3. *Fluoromicrophotographs around the epicardial large vein under conditions of hypoxia (panel A) and regional ischemia (panel B) Panels A and B: cross-sectional views.*

NADH of the subepicardial myocardium in the perfusional anoxia and regional ischemia are shown in Figure 3. In cases of global anoxia, an increase in NADH fluorescence around the subepicardial vein was fairly uniform (Fig. 3A), whereas there was a narrow less-fluorescent zone (140 ± 10 μm in 10 heart experiments) around an epicardial vein of a size approximately equal to that in Figure 3A in regional ischemia (Fig. 3B).

Changes in coronary flow rate, arterial Po_2 in aerobic perfusion, hypoxic perfusion, and perfusion under LCA occlusion are shown in Table 1. There was an increase in coronary flow rate in cases of hypoxic perfusion and a decrease in regional ischemia. Venous effluent Po_2 in LCA occlusion was 251 ± 12 mm Hg, which is significantly lower than in aerobic control perfusion, but much higher than in cases of perfusional anoxia.

Effect of RCVP on Venous Pressure

Figure 4 shows changes in the pressure of the distal branch of the epicardial vein, under conditions of RCVP. The mean venous pressure in the aerobic control perfusion was 8.2 ± 0.2 mm Hg. Venous pressure decreased by LCA occlusion to 3.6 ± 0.4 mm Hg. During RCVP, there was a flow-dependent increase in the venous pressure. We observed an almost direct correlation between the RCVP flow rate and the venous pressure.

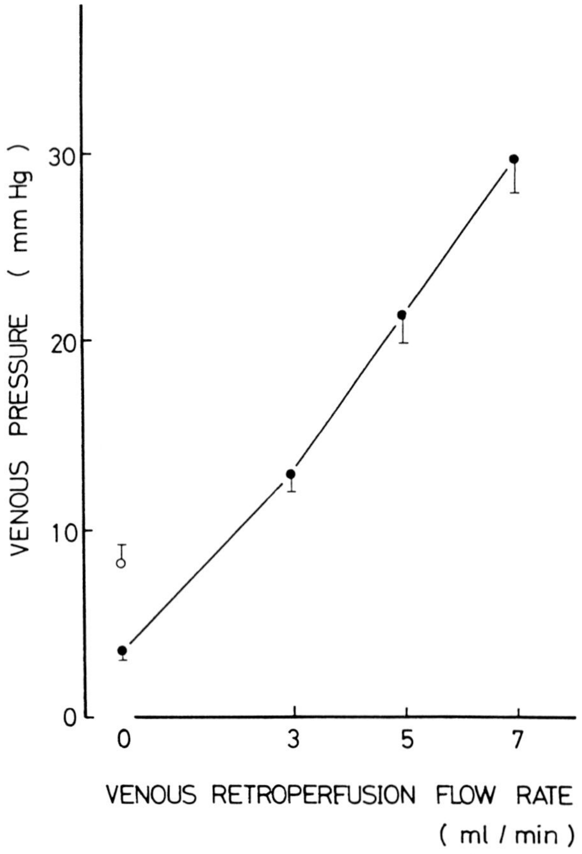

FIGURE 4. *Effect of coronary venous retroperfusion (RCVP) on the perfusion pressure of left cardiac vein.* ○: *aerobic control perfusion* ●: *during LCA occlusion (mean ± SEM of 10 heart preparations).*

Perfusion Area of RCVP

Assessment of the area perfused by RCVP (5 ml/min) during LCA occlusion was carried out by admixing thioflavin S with the venous-retroperfusate. We found that the area of increased NADH fluorescence (Fig. 5A) during occlusion coincided almost completely with the area perfused by RCVP (Fig. 5B). In the normally perfused normoxic area, however, only a network of large epicardial veins was stained with thioflavin S of RCVP (Fig. 5B). Thus, the dye had reached the normoxic area by RCVP, but it remained at the large epicardial veins and did not enter the smaller veins or capillaries and, as a result, no area of thioflavin S was observed in the normoxic area. A cross-sectional view of the distribution of the thioflavin S and fluorescein sodium, indicating the area of RCVP and the area of arterial antegrade perfusion, respectively, is shown in Figure 5C. The area of thioflavin S and the area of fluorescein sodium adjoined, and both the border zone and the overlapping of the two fluorescent dyes were negligible.

Effect of RCVP on the Area of Increased NADH Fluorescence during LCA Occlusion

Figure 6 represents a typical sequence of epicardial NADH fluorescence photographs taken during aerobic perfusion, LCA occlusion, and LCA occlusion with subsequent RCVP at 3 ml/min and 5 ml/min. When LCA of the aerobic perfused heart (Fig. 6A) was ligated at 5 mm from its origin, a sharply demarcated area of the increased NADH fluorescence, relatively uniform in intensity, was observed in the left ventricular free wall (Fig. 6B). Upon RCVP at 3 ml/min, a heterogeneous reduction in the intensity of NADH fluorescence occurred, especially around the epicardial veins, and the NADH fluorescence had a patchy appearance (Fig. 6C). When the RCVP flow rate was increased to 5 ml/min, reduction in the area and intensity of NADH fluorescence became more prominent (Fig. 6D).

Typical cross-sectional NADH fluorescence photographs of aerobic control, LCA occlusion, and LCA occlusion with subsequent RCVP (5 ml/min) of separate hearts are shown in Figure 7. There was minimal NADH fluorescence in the aerobic control heart (Fig. 7A). Upon LCA occlusion, a transmural involvement of an increase in NADH fluorescence was observed in the left ventricular free wall (Fig. 7B). In accordance with a heterogeneous reduction of increased epicardial surface NADH fluorescence, RCVP after LCA occlusion induced patchy areas of reduced intensity in NADH fluorescence in the left ventricular free wall, especially in the myocardium adjacent to the epicardium (Fig. 7C). These patchy areas were clearly demarcated from the surrounding areas with increased NADH fluorescence, because

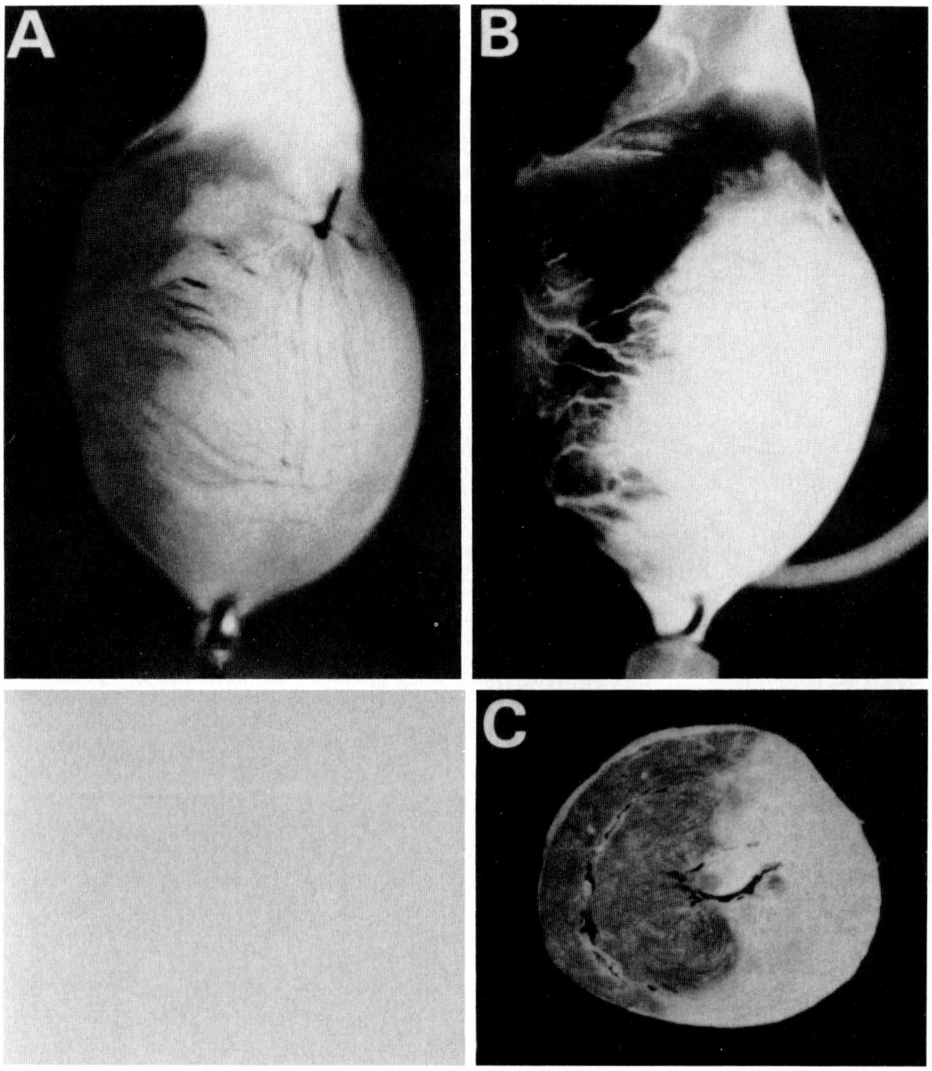

FIGURE 5. *NADH fluorescence photograph (panel A) indicates the area of ischemia lacking oxidative phosphorylation. Fluorescence photograph of thioflavin S (panel B) admixed with the buffer solution for retroperfusion indicates the area of RCVP. Panel C indicates the cross-sectional distribution of thioflavin S (right side), in the same heart.*

the intensities of the NADH fluorescence of these areas were almost equal to those of oxygenated areas of the heart. We divided the left ventricular wall into endo- and epicardium of an equal width by drawing a line along the midpoint between the endo- and epicardial margin. When the areas of increased NADH fluorescence in an epicardial half and an endocardial half of the myocardium of the left ventricular wall were measured separately (the values in the ischemic state prior to RCVP being about 50% for each), RCVP induced a decrease in the area of an increased NADH by 15% in the epicardial half ($P < 0.01$ vs. no-RCVP) and a negligible change in the endocardial half (Fig. 8).

Effects of RCVP during LCA Occlusion on the Myocardial Function and Metabolic Intermediates

Changes in developed tension and resting tension of aerobic control, and in LCA occlusion, with and without subsequent RCVP, are shown in Figure 9. LCA occlusion produced a rapid decrease in developed tension and a gradual increase in the resting tension. Subsequent RCVP resulted in prevention of these deleterious changes induced by LCA occlusion ($P < 0.05$ in developed tension, $P < 0.01$; resting tension).

Tissue concentrations of adenine nucleotides, creatine phosphate, and pyridine nucleotides after 20 minutes of regional ischemia, with or without RCVP (5 ml/min), are shown in Figure 10. Upon LCA ligation, myocardial stores of ATP, total adenine nucleotides, creatine phosphate (CP), and NAD^+ markedly decreased (vs. normal control; $P < 0.01$). RCVP had a significant preserving effect on the reduction of these constituents ($P < 0.01$). The myocardial concentrations of AMP and NADH which significantly increased during LCA occlusion (vs. normal control; $P < 0.01$), were partially prevented by RCVP (vs. no-RCVP, $P < 0.01$).

Discussion

In the present study, the effect of RCVP on myocardial oxygenation was evaluated by both epicar-

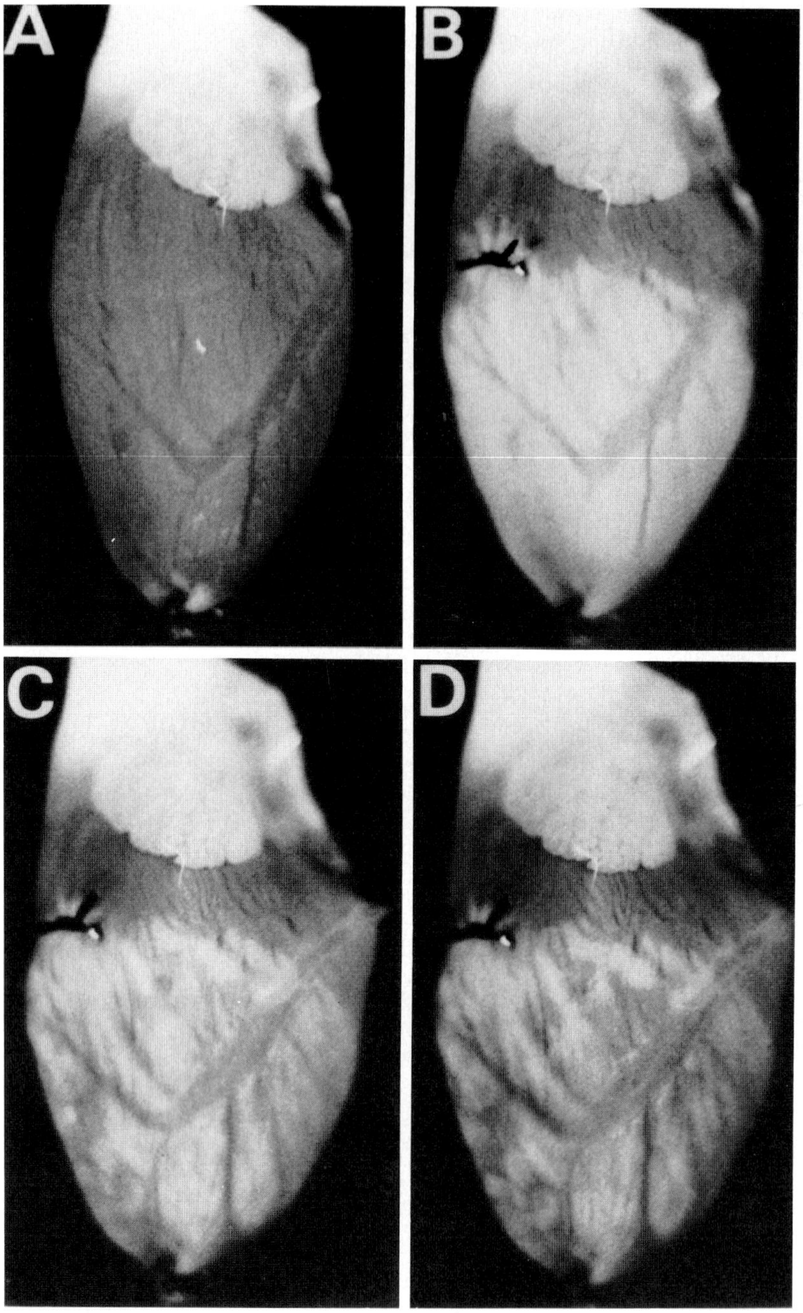

FIGURE 6. *A representative series of epicardial NADH fluorescence photographs under (panel A) aerobic perfusion, (panel B) LCA occlusion, (panel C) LCA occlusion with subsequent coronary venous retroperfusion at 3 mm/min, and (panel D) at 5 ml/min.*

dial and cross-sectional NADH fluorescence photography.

Barlow and Chance (1976) first used NADH fluorescence photography to evaluate regional ischemia. When most of the NADH fluorescence was attributed to mitochondrial NADH (Chance, 1976), there was a linear relation between increase of epicardial surface fluorescence and increase of tissue NADH content (Chance, 1976; Kanaide et al., 1982), and the oxidation-reduction potential of NADH was proportional to the state of phosphorylation (Owen and Wilson, 1974). If the intensity of NADH fluorescence under conditions of anaerobic perfusion was taken as 100%, and that of the aerobic perfusion as 0%, the increase in NADH fluorescence reportedly reached a 50% increase at approximately 10^{-8} M intracellular oxygen tension (Chance, 1976). Thus, it is well accepted that NADH fluorescence is an excellent indicator of tissue anoxia (Chance et al., 1965). In the present study, in addition to the surface fluorophotography, cross-sectional observations of the rapidly freeze-dried tissues were made, by both fluorophotography and fluoromicroscopy, to evaluate three-dimensional changes in the ischemic areas and the NADH fluorescence of the perfused rat hearts. The propriety of the freeze-drying technique was supported by the following findings obtained from preliminary studies: the global shapes of the

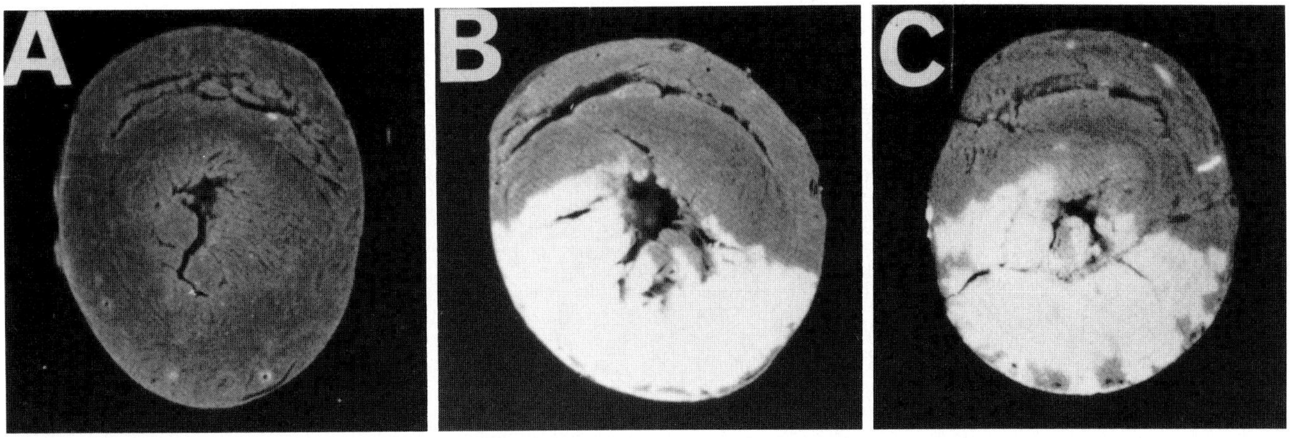

FIGURE 7. *Typical cross-sectional NADH fluorescence photographs in (panel A) aerobic perfusion, in (panel B) regional ischemia, and in (panel C) regional ischemia with coronary venous retroperfusion at 5 ml/min, in separate hearts.*

heart were not changed by freeze-drying and tissue concentrations of pyridine nucleotides before and after freeze-drying were equal.

In contrast to the homogeneous increase in surface NADH fluorescence in perfusional global anoxia, occlusion of LCA 5 mm from its origin under aerobic perfusion induced a nonfluorescent zone about 140 μm wide around the epicardial large veins in the ischemic region of increased NADH fluorescence. We mixed the fluorescent dye with aerobic-aortic perfusate and found that the epicardial large veins

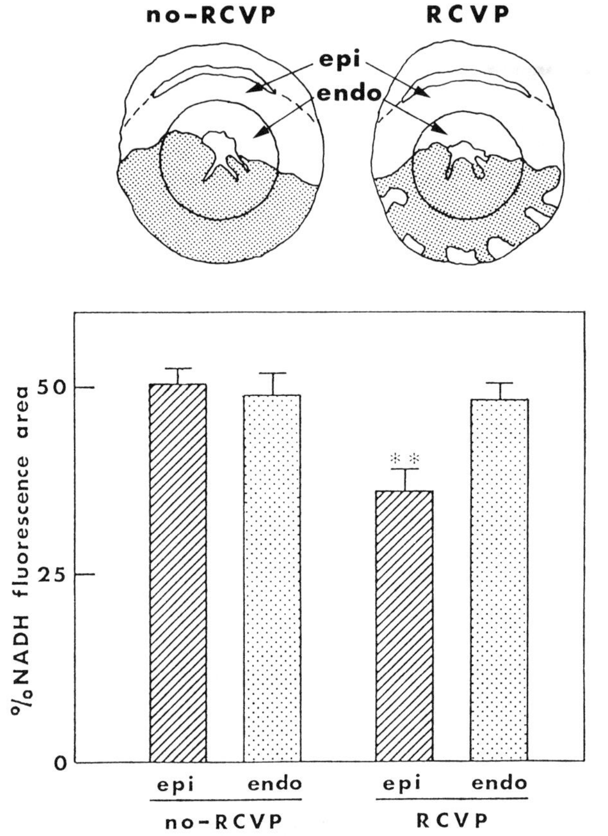

FIGURE 8. *Relative areas of increased NADH fluorescence in the epicardial half and endocardial half of the myocardium. The left ventricular wall was divided by drawing a line along the midpoint between endo- and epicardium. Percent NADH fluorescence area was calculated separately. Each column represents data on 10 heart preparations; no-RCVP: LCA occlusion only; RCVP: LCA occlusion with subsequent coronary venous retroperfusion (5 ml/min). **P < 0.01 vs. epicardial half in no-RCVP.*

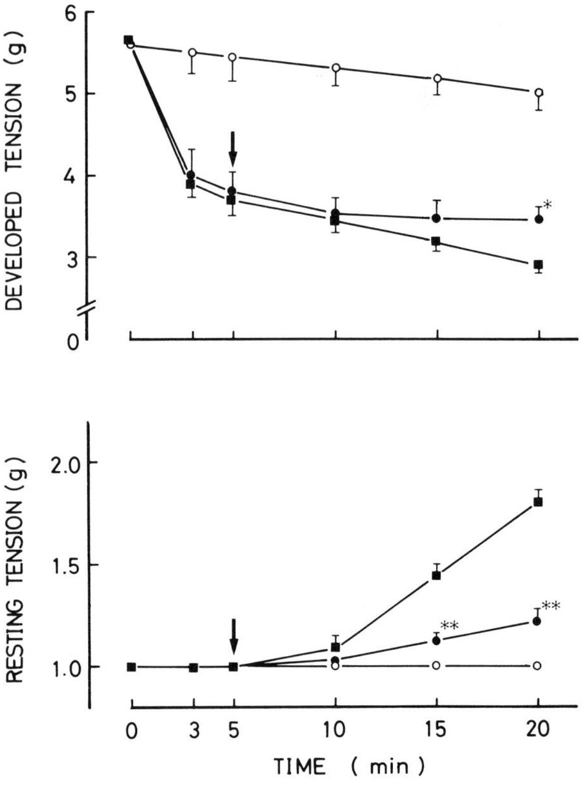

FIGURE 9. *Changes in developed tension (above) and resting tension (below) with aerobic perfusion (○), regional ischemia (■), and regional ischemia with subsequent coronary venous retroperfusion (●). Coronary venous retroperfusion was introduced (5 ml/min) at the time indicated by the arrow (↓). (n = 8 heart preparations in each group). *P < 0.05, **P < 0.01 vs. no-RCVP.*

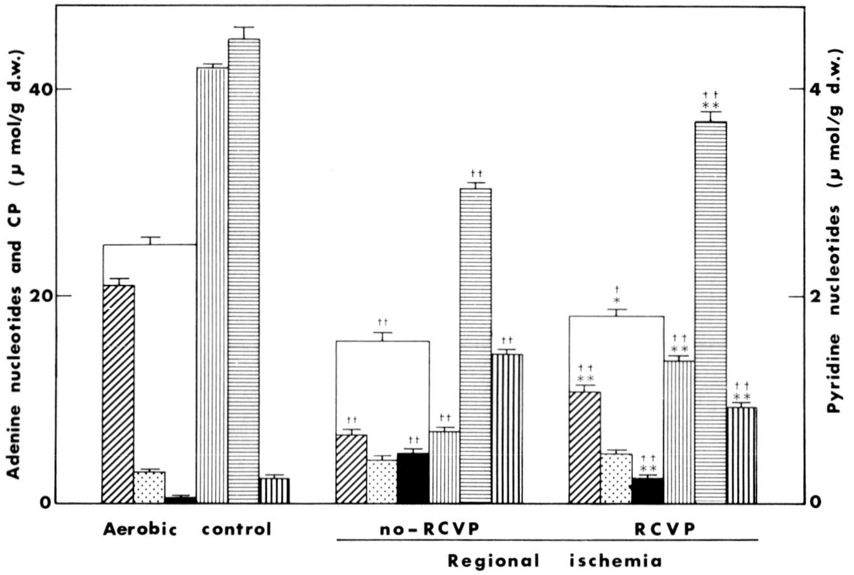

FIGURE 10. *Tissue concentration of high energy phosphates and pyridine nucleotides in left ventricular free wall of aerobic control and in regional ischemia, with and without subsequent coronary venous retroperfusion, ▨, ATP; ▩, ADP; ■, AMP; □, total adenine nucleotides; ▥, creatine phosphate; ▤, NAD; ▥, NADH; (n = eight heart preparations in each group). +P < 0.05, ++P < 0.01 vs. aerobic control; *P < 0.05, **P < 0.01 vs. no-RCVP.*

(left cardiac vein) in the ischemic area seem to drain away perfusate, not only from the ischemic area, but also from the area of normal perfusion. A narrow zone 140 μm wide around the epicardial veins, which receives an oxygen supply from these veins, may maintain myocardial oxygenation; hence, there would be no increase in NADH fluorescence. The maintenance of myocardial oxygenation may contribute to the preservation of a thin layer of intact myocardium adjacent to the epicardial large veins as reported in the studies of myocardial infarction in rats (Seyle et al., 1960; Fishbein et al., 1978).

The vascular system of the rat heart differs anatomically from those of dogs or humans. The left circumflex artery is poorly developed, and the left coronary artery is not accompanied by large veins (Selye et al., 1960). The drainage of most of the left ventricular free wall is through the left cardiac vein, which traverses the left ventricular surface and opens in the right atrium or right anterior vena cava without forming a coronary sinus (Halpern, 1953). In the present study, RCVP was carried out through the left cardiac vein cannulated with a fine polyethylene tube via the right atrium. The area of RCVP estimated by admixing thioflavin S with the retroperfusion fluid coincided fairly well with that of NADH fluorescence, both in the epicardial surface and cross-sectional views. These findings are similar to those of Gardner et al. (1974), who used ^{131}I macroaggregated albumin in retrograde perfusion to assess the effects of coronary circulation and concluded that the retrograde flow was largely distributed in the ischemic zone in the in situ dog heart.

Coronary venous retroperfusion under conditions of regional ischemia demonstrated the improvement of S-T changes in epicardial electrocardiograms (Bhayana et al., 1974) and a reduction in the infarcted area (Chiu and Mulder, 1975). Meerbaum et al. (1976) developed a synchronized diastolic coronary venous retroperfusion system with a ECG triggered balloon pumping unit, and noted the improvement of myocardial force, decrease in epicardial S-T elevation, and increase of O_2 uptake, as assessed from blood samples. Using ultrasonic crystals to measure myocardial contractility and an endocardial electrocardiogram to assess changes in the subendocardium, Gundry (1982) demonstrated the beneficial effect of coronary venous retroperfusion on myocardial contractility and also ECG changes in the subendocardium, both in normal and hypertrophied canine hearts. More recently, Meerbaum et al. (1982) applied hypothermic synchronized retroperfusion in the closed-chest dog after acute coronary occlusion and demonstrated a favorable effect on cardiac function after reperfusion. Despite the increasing number of reports indicating the beneficial effects of RCVP, its effect on the nutritional supply to the ischemic region has not been determined.

In the present study, oxygen delivery by RCVP to the ischemic area was assessed directly by NADH fluorescence photography. RCVP induced a marked reduction of the area of increased epicardial NADH fluorescence during LCA occlusion. Although the RCVP flow was distributed over the entire ischemic area, oxygen delivery and the resultant restoration of oxidative phosphorylation were limited to the epicardial half of the myocardium. Inhibition of diastolic tissue pressure reduction in the subendocardial myocardium in acute ischemia (Sabbah and Stein, 1982) or high rate of energy utilization and resultant high rate of oxygen consumption in the subendocardial myocardium in the reversible phase of ischemia (Dunn and Griggs, 1975), or both, may explain the insufficient oxygen supply to the subendocardial layer by RCVP.

When Chiu and Mulder (1975) included 15-μm microspheres in the retrograde perfusate and estimated flow distribution, only a small portion of retrograde flow, even in the excised heart, provided nutritional benefits to the ischemic lesion. Since the retroperfusion technique of their study is similar in principle to ours, the small microsphere flow increases in their study may be related to the patchy and modest epicardial increases in "oxygenation" in the present study.

Although we used a relatively low work heart with a high flow rate, and the perfusion medium for antegrade arterial perfusion and for RCVP was of low viscosity, RCVP resulted in a relatively modest increase in tension development, a decrease in resting tension, and a partial preservation of myocardial high energy phosphate content. Thus, we propose that RCVP improves oxygenation, partially preserves oxidative phosphorylation in the epicardium, and improves contractile function in the ischemic region.

Farcot et al. (1978) reported that, in addition to the oxygenation of the tissue, one of the important effects of RCVP is the acceleration of secretion of toxic metabolites in the ischemic lesion. This factor was not given attention in the present study.

We are grateful to M. Okada and R. Maeda for technical assistance, M. Funato of Union Giken Co. for help in the design and development of the fluorescence photography systems, M. Ohara for critical readings of the manuscript, and N. Hayashi and A. Nishi for secretarial services.

This study was supported by Grants-in-Aid 56570337, 57570354, and 544049 for Scientific Research from the Ministry of Education, Science and Culture, Japan.

Address for reprints: Hideo Kanaide, M.D., Research Institute of Angiocardiology, and Cardiovascular Clinic, Faculty of Medicine, Kyushu University, 3-1-1 Maidashi, Higashi-ku, Fukuoka 812, Japan.

Received June 27, 1983; accepted for publication December 28, 1984.

References

Barlow CH, Chance B (1976) Ischemic areas in perfused rat hearts: Measurement by NADH fluorescence photography. Science **193:** 909–910

Beck CS, Stanton E, Batinchok W, Leifer E (1948) Revascularization of the heart by graft of systemic artery into the coronary sinus. JAMA **137:** 436–442

Berger RL, Stary HC (1971) Assessment of operability by the saphenous vein bypass operation. N Engl J Med **285:** 248–252

Bhayana JN, Olsen BB, Byrne JP, Kolff WJ (1974) Reversal of myocardial ischemia by arterialization of the coronary vein. J Thorac Cardiovasc Surg **67:** 125–132

Chance B (1976) Pyridine nucleotide as an indicator of the oxygen requirements for energy-linked functions of mitochondria. Circ Res **38** (suppl I): 31–38

Chance B, Williamson JR, Jamieson D, Schoener B (1965) Properties and kinetics of reduced pyridine nucleotide fluorescence of the isolated in vivo rat heart. Biochem Z **341:** 357–377

Chiu CJ, Mulder DS (1975) Selective arterialization of coronary veins for diffuse coronary occlusion. J Thorac Cardiovasc Surg **70:** 177–182

Dunn RB, Griggs DM (1975) Transmural gradients in ventricular tissue metabolites produced by stopping coronary blood flow in the dog. Circ Res **37:** 438–445

Farcot JC, Meerbaum S, Lang TW, Kaplan L, Corday E (1978) Synchronized retroperfusion of coronary veins for circulatory support of jeopardized ischemic myocardium. Am J Cardiol **41:** 1191–1201

Fishbein MC, Maclean D, Maroko PR (1978) Experimental myocardial infarction in the rat. Am J Pathol **90:** 57–70

Gardner RS, Magovern GJ, Park SB, Dixon CM (1974) Arterialization of coronary veins in the treatment of myocardial ischemia. J Thorac Cardiovasc Surg **68:** 273–282

Gundry SR (1982) Modification of myocardial ischemia in normal and hypertrophied hearts utilizing diagnostic retroperfusion of the coronary veins. J Thorac Cardiovasc Surg **83:** 659–669

Halpern MG (1953) Extra coronary cardiac veins in rat. Am J Anat **92:** 309–329

Harken AH, Barlow CH, Harden WR, Chance B (1978) Two and three dimensional display of myocardial ischemic "border zone" in dogs. Am J Cardiol **42:** 954–959

Jaworek K, Gruber W, Bergmeyer HU (1975) Adenosine-5′-diphosphate and adenosine-5′-monophosphate. *In* Methods of Enzymatic Analysis, edited by HU Bergmeyer. New York, Academic Press, pp 2127–2131

Kanaide H, Yoshimura R, Makino N, Nakamura M (1982) Regional myocardial function and metabolism during acute coronary artery occlusion. Am J Physiol **242:** H980–H989

Lamprecht W, Stein P, Heinz F. Weisser H (1975) Creatine phosphate. *In* Methods of Enzymatic analysis, edited by HU Bergmeyer. New York, Academic Press, pp 1777–1781

Langendorff O (1895) Untersuchungen am uberlebenden getierherzen. Pfür Ges Physiol Menschen Tier **61:** 191–332

Meerbaum S, Lang TW, Osher JV, Hashimoto K, Lewis GW, Feldstein C, Corday E (1976) Diastolic retroperfusion of acutely ischemic myocardium. Am J Cardiol **37:** 588–598

Meerbaum S, Haendchen RV, Corday E, Povzhitkov M, Fishbein MC, Y-Rit J, Lang TW, Uchiyama T, Aosaki N (1982) Hypothermic coronary venous phased retroperfusion: A closed-chest treatment of acute regional myocardial ischemia. Circulation **65:** 1435–1445

Owen CS, Wilson DF (1974) Control of respiration by the mitochondrial phosphorylation state. Arch Biochem Biophys **161:** 581–591

Pratt FH (1893) The nutrition of the heart through the vessels of Thebesius and the coronary veins. Am J Physiol **1:** 86–103

Sabbah HN, Stein PD (1982) Effect of acute regional ischemia on pressure in the subepicardium and subendocardium. Am J Physiol **242:** H240–H244

Selye H, Bajusz S, Gransso S, Mendell P (1960) Simple technique for the surgical occlusion of coronary vessels in the rat. Angiology **11:** 398–407

Steenbergen C, Delleuw G, Barlow CH, Chance B, Williamson JR (1977) Heterogeneity of the hypoxic state in perfused rat heart. Circ Res **41:** 606–615

Williamson JR, Corkey BE (1969) Assays of intermediates of the citric acid cycle and related compounds by fluorometric enzyme methods. Methods Enzymol **13:** 434–514

INDEX TERMS: Myocardial ischemia • Coronary venous perfusion • NADH fluorescence photography • Energy metabolism

Inotropic Effect, Binding Properties, and Calcium Flux Effects of the Calcium Channel Agonist CGP 28392 in Intact Cultured Embryonic Chick Ventricular Cells

Stephane Laurent, Donghee Kim, Thomas W. Smith, and James D. Marsh

From the Cardiovascular Division, Brigham and Women's Hospital, and Departments of Medicine, Brigham and Womens Hospital and Harvard Medical School, Boston, Massachusetts

SUMMARY. CGP 28392 is a recently described dihydropyridine derivative with positive inotropic properties. To study the mechanism of action of this putative calcium channel agonist, we have related the effects of CGP 28392 on contraction (measured with an optical video system) and radioactive calcium uptake to ligand-binding studies in cultured, spontaneously beating chick embryo ventricular cells. CGP 28392 produced a concentration-dependent increase in amplitude and velocity of contraction ($EC_{50} = 2\times 10^{-7}$ M; maximum contractile effect = 85% of the calcium 3.6 mM response). Nifedipine produced a shift to the right of the concentration-effect curve for CGP 28392 without decreasing the maximum contractile response, suggesting competitive antagonism ($pA_2 = 8.3$). Computer analysis of displacement of [^{3}H]nitrendipine binding to intact heart cells by unlabeled CGP 28392 indicated a $K_D = 2.2 \pm 0.95 \times 10^{-7}$ M, in good agreement with the EC_{50} for the inotropic effect. CGP 28392 increased the rate of radioactive calcium influx (+39% at 10 seconds) without altering beating rate, while nifedipine decreased radioactive calcium influx and antagonized the CGP 28392-induced increase in calcium influx. Our results indicate that, in intact cultured myocytes, CGP 28392 acts as a calcium channel agonist and competes for the dihydropyridine-binding site of the slow calcium channel. In contrast to calcium channel blockers, CGP 28392 increases calcium influx and enhances the contractile state. **(*Circ Res 56: 676–682, 1985*)**

TRANSSARCOLEMMAL influx of calcium via the slow calcium channel appears to have an essential role in excitation-contraction coupling in cardiac and smooth muscle (Fabiato et al., 1979; Henry, 1980; Blinks et al., 1982; Reuter et al., 1982). Calcium channel-blocking agents, including verapamil, nifedipine, and diltiazem, have been developed, and possess negative inotropic and smooth muscle relaxant properties. Recently, CGP 28392 (4-[2-(difluormethoxy)phenyl]-1,4,5,7-tetrahydro-2-methyl-5-oxofuro[3,4-b]pyridine-3-carboxylic acid ethylester), a novel dihydropyridine derivative (Fig. 1) structurally similar to nifedipine, has been shown to have effects opposite to those of the calcium channel blockers (Preuss et al., 1984). Another dihydropyridine derivative, Bay k 8644, has been reported to have positive inotropic and vasoconstricting properties in the pentobarbital-anesthetized dog (Schramm et al., 1983). Schramm and colleagues have shown indirectly an increase in calcium influx in isolated rabbit aortic strips. CGP 28392 and Bay k 8644 have been referred to as calcium channel agonists.

We report here the effects of the calcium channel agonist CGP 28392 on cultured cardiac myocytes. To gain insights into the mechanism of the effects of CGP 28392 on the calcium channel in contracting myocardial tissue, we examined the pharmacological action of CGP 28392 in intact, spontaneously contracting cultured heart cells. This preparation obviates diffusion limitations inherent in isolated organ preparations and permits direct comparison of contractile function, binding properties, and calcium fluxes under similar conditions. Moreover, as reviewed by Reuter (1983), calcium channels, unlike sodium channels, are not functional in isolated membrane vesicles, and binding experiments should preferably be done in intact cells.

The preparation utilizes embryonic tissue, not intact heart, but basic cellular mechanisms observed in this preparation generally have been observed in mature hearts and in intact, loaded muscle, as well (Marsh, 1983).

Previous work done in this laboratory (Marsh et al., 1983) has shown two binding sites of differing affinities in intact myocardial cells for the dihydropyridine nitrendipine. Binding to the low-affinity site correlates well with the pharmacological negative inotropic effect of this drug. The relationships among inotropic effect, binding properties, and augmented calcium influx induced by CGP 28392 were examined in this study.

Methods

Tissue Culture

Primary monolayer cultures of beating chick embryo ventricular cells were prepared as previously described

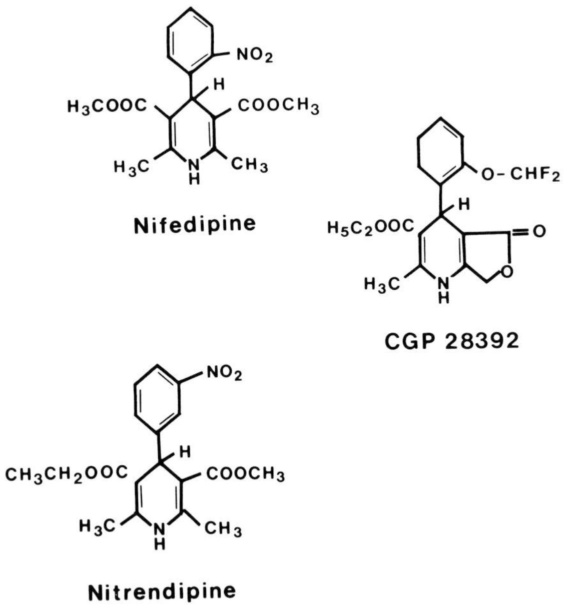

Figure 1. *Chemical structure of nifedipine, nitrendipine, and CGP 28392.*

(Marsh et al., 1982). Briefly, fragments of embryonic chick ventricles 10 days in ovo were dissociated by repeated cycles of trypsinization. The resulting cell suspensions were plated in 100-mm culture dishes and grown in culture medium consisting of a bicarbonate-buffered physiological salt solution containing 40% medium 199 (Gibco), 6% fetal calf serum (FCS), and 54% balanced salt solution containing glucose. Final concentrations (mM) in the culture medium were Na^+, 144; K^+, 4.0; Ca^{++}, 0.97; HCO_3^-, 18; Mg^{++}, 0.8; and Cl^-, 131. Cultures were incubated in a humidified 5% CO_2-95% air atmosphere at 37°C. Spontaneously and synchronously contracting confluent monolayers were present by 3 days in culture. For contractility and ion flux experiments, cells were grown on 25-mm circular glass coverslips.

Contractility Measurements

Measurements of the amplitude and velocity of contraction of individual cells in a spontaneously contracting monolayer at 3 days in culture were made with a phase contrast microscope-video motion detector system (Barry and Smith, 1982). The medium bathing cells during contractility measurements was culture medium containing 0.6 mM calcium. The pH of the buffer solution was maintained at 7.4 by continuously gassing the chamber with a 95% air-5% CO_2 gas mixture. A constant temperature of 37°C was maintained by enclosing the microscope in a thermostated Lucite box. After a 15-minute equilibration period, cells were superfused with solution containing either CGP 28392 (10^{-8}–10^{-5} M) or 3.6 mM Ca^{++}, and changes in the amplitude and velocity of motion of an individual cell were monitored. The first derivative with respect to time of the amplitude signal was obtained electronically and calibrated to indicate velocity of motion in μm/sec. For assessment of relaxation, the peak velocity of cell wall motion during relaxation was measured and compared to peak velocity of contraction. Only one cell from each coverslip was used. Observations were repeated in at least five different preparations. At the end of each experiment, after complete washout of CGP 28392, cells were exposed to 3.6 mM Ca^{++}. The change in the amplitude and velocity of contraction induced by CGP 28392 was expressed as a percent of the change produced by 3.6 mM Ca^{++}, a concentration that produces maximal contractile response (Miura et al., 1981). All solutions containing nifedipine were assiduously protected from light.

Calcium Fluxes

The procedures for estimating calcium fluxes have been described in detail by Biedert et al. (1979) and Barry and Smith (1982). For determination of calcium uptake, cells were exposed to medium containing ^{45}Ca (5 μCi/ml; [Ca^{++}] = 0.6 mM) for 10, 20, 30, or 60 seconds. Barry and Smith (1982) have shown that this period of exposure to ^{45}Ca labels the rapidly exchangeable calcium pool. After appropriate periods of labeling with ^{45}Ca in the presence or absence of CGP 28392, nifedipine, or both, cells were washed twice for 8 seconds each by gently agitating the glass coverslips sequentially in two 60-ml volumes of ice cold balanced salt solution containing no radiolabeled ions. Cells then were dissolved in medium containing 1% sodium dodecyl sulfate (SDS) and 10 mM sodium borate. Aliquots of the medium containing dissolved cells were assayed for radioactivity in a liquid scintillation spectrometer (Packard, model 3330).

Binding Studies

Marsh et al. (1983) confirmed observations from other laboratories that binding sites for [^{3}H]nitrendipine can be identified in heart homogenates and extended binding studies to intact cultured cells. In the present experiments, we studied the binding properties of CGP 28392 by examining the displacement of 0.5 nM [^{3}H]nitrendipine from specific binding sites by graded concentrations of unlabeled CGP 28392.

Cells were harvested by gentle scraping of the culture plates to suspend sheets of cells. Nine hundred microliters of cell suspension were added to 50 μl of [^{3}H]nitrendipine and 50 μl of buffered medium containing the desired amount of CGP 28392.

The medium in which experiments were conducted was identical to the physiological salt solution in which contractility experiments were conducted, except that medium for binding studies was buffered by 4 mM HEPES and contained 1% bovine serum albumin (BSA) rather than FCS. Incubation was for 15 minutes at 37°C in the dark. Binding was terminated by adding 10 ml of wash buffer (50 mM potassium phosphate, pH 7.5) at 37°C to the assay mixture, incubating 5 seconds, then rapidly filtering through a Whatman GF/C filter, followed by two rapid 5-ml washes with buffer at 37°C. Filters were dried and counted at 24% efficiency in a Packard liquid scintillation counter. Displacement curves were analyzed with the iterative, nonlinear least squares method of Munson and Rodbard (1980) on an IBM 370 computer to determine ligand affinity and number of binding sites.

Cell Density Correction

To normalize for cell density on each culture dish or coverslip, the monolayers were incubated in L-[4,5-^{3}H(N)] leucine (0.1 μCi/ml) for 24 hours before the experiment. [^{3}H]Leucine was incorporated into cell protein, and the ^{3}H counts permitted estimation of cell density on each glass coverslip. The relationship between radioactive counts and protein concentration (Lowry et al., 1951) allowed estimation of protein content of cells on each glass coverslip. Thus, simultaneous counting of ^3H and ^{45}Ca permitted normalization of calcium flux per milligram cell protein.

Materials

CGP 28392 was kindly provided by Dr. K. Scheibli of Ciba Geigy A.G., Basel, Switzerland, and nifedipine was obtained from Pfizer. Stock solutions of 10^{-3} M CGP 28392 and nifedipine were made up in 75% ethanol. For contractility and ^{45}Ca uptake studies, control medium contained the same percentage of ethanol present in final CGP 28392 or nifedipine solutions. [^{3}H]Nitrendipine (specific activity 88 Ci/mmol) and ^{45}Ca were obtained from New England Nuclear, and unlabeled nitrendipine was from Miles Laboratories. Other reagents were obtained from Fisher Scientific and were the highest grade commercially available. Tissue culture media were from sources previously described (Marsh et al., 1982).

Results

Effects on Contractility

Both amplitude and velocity of contraction of spontaneously beating myocytes were increased by CGP 28392, as illustrated in Figure 2. This inotropic effect was concentration dependent, and was not accompanied by a significant change in beating rate over the range from 10^{-8} to 10^{-5} M. The increase in contractile state had a rapid onset, reached plateau values within 3–5 minutes, and was fully reversible on washing CGP 28392 from the myocyte chamber with return to control levels within 5–10 minutes. The positive inotropic effect had its threshhold at 10^{-8} M CGP 28392. The maximum effect achieved at 10^{-5} M represented 85 ± 4% of the contractile response to $[Ca^{++}]_o$ = 3.6 mM. Log-logit transformation of the sigmoid concentration effect curve yielded an EC_{50} of 2×10^{-7} M for the increase in contractility produced by CGP 28392. The peak velocity of contraction and of relaxation were increased by CGP 28392 in a concentration-dependent fashion, but their ratio was unchanged, suggesting that relaxation was not directly altered over this range of concentrations (Miura et al., 1981).

To determine whether the calcium channel blocker nifedipine was able to antagonize the CGP 28392 response, we made additional contractility measurements. After 10 minutes of superfusion of myocytes with CGP 28392, the dihydropyridine calcium channel antagonist nifedipine was added to the superfusion medium. The decrease in contractility had a rapid onset and reached a plateau within 5–10 minutes. In Figure 3, the contractile state observed at equilibrium in the presence of nifedipine and CGP 28392 is expressed as a percentage of the Ca^{++} = 3.6 mM response. Under these conditions, nifedipine produced a shift to the right of the concentration-effect curve for CGP 28392. Contractile response to CGP 28392 in the presence of 3×10^{-4} M nifedipine was indistinguishable from that to 1×10^{-5} M CGP 28392 in the absence of nifedipine. Drug solubility limitations prohibited testing higher CGP 28392 concentrations in the presence of nifedipine to ensure a plateau in response, but we consider it unlikely that nifedipine would enhance CGP 28392 efficacy. The curve shift is roughly parallel, suggesting competitive pharmacological antagonism. The pA_2 was 8.31. These results indicate

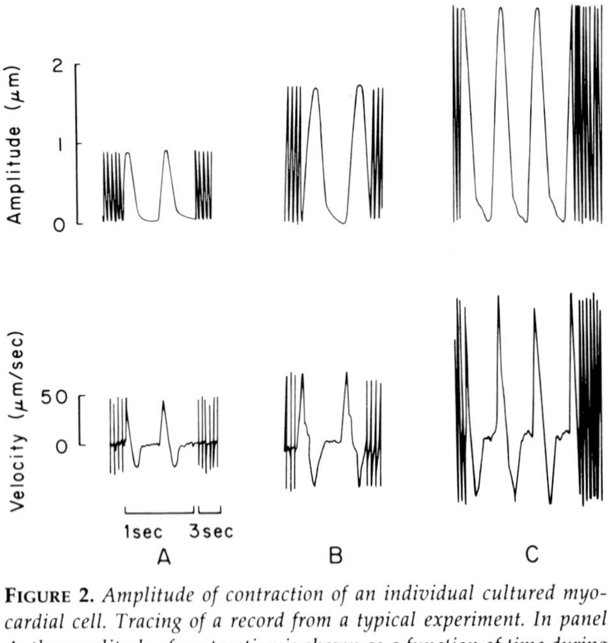

FIGURE 2. *Amplitude of contraction of an individual cultured myocardial cell. Tracing of a record from a typical experiment. In panel A, the amplitude of contraction is shown as a function of time during superfusion of the monolayer with medium containing 0.6 mM Ca^{++}. Panel B shows the response to 0.6 mM Ca^{++} + 0.3 μM CGP 28392. Control amplitude was then reestablished in 0.6 mM Ca^{++} solution. Panel C shows the amplitude of contraction when the medium was changed to 3.6 mM Ca^{++}. In 0.6 mM Ca^{++} medium, the increase in amplitude induced by CGP 28392 0.3 μM was 46% of the increase elicited by exposure to 3.6 mM Ca^{++} medium.*

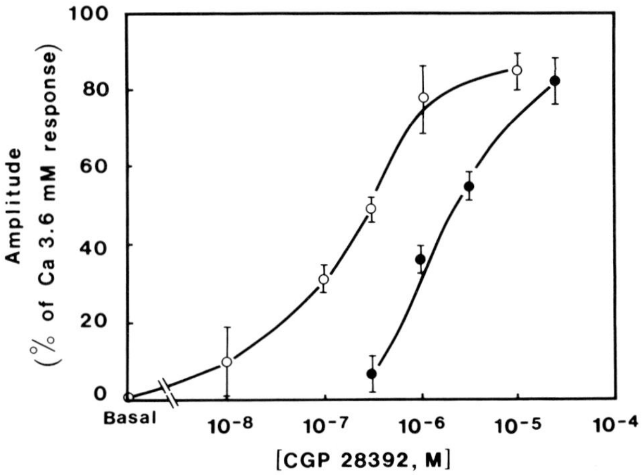

FIGURE 3. *Concentration-effect curve for increase in amplitude of contraction of cultured heart cells by CGP 28392. Percent maximal amplitude of contraction (100% response = response to 3.6 mM Ca^{++}) is plotted against CGP 28392 concentration. Each point is the mean ± SEM of the response of five different preparations to CGP 28392 alone (○) or CGP 28392 + nifedipine 10^{-8} M (●).*

that the novel calcium agonist CGP 28392 is able to increase contractility in cultured heart cells, and that this effect is antagonized by nifedipine.

Radioligand-Binding Experiments

Previous work from this laboratory demonstrated that [^{3}H]nitrendipine bound rapidly to intact cultured heart cells, reaching equilibrium at 5 minutes at 37°C; the binding was saturable and reversible with a K_D of 2.6×10^{-10} M for the high-affinity site and 1.9×10^{-8} M for the low-affinity site. Binding properties of CGP 28392 were studied by examining the displacement of 0.5 nM [^{3}H]nitrendipine from the dihydropyridine-binding site by graded concentrations of unlabeled CGP 28392. Binding was analyzed by fixing dissociation constants for nitrendipine at values previously determined (Marsh et al., 1983) and solving for dissociation constants for CGP 28392, B_{max}, and nonspecific binding. Analysis of four 16 to 18-point nitrendipine displacement curves indicated that CGP 28392 bound to a single class of sites with $K_D = 2.2 \pm 0.95 \times 10^{-7}$ M (mean ± SEM) and $B_{max} = 145 \pm 17$ fmol/mg protein. In each case, a single-site model for CGP 28392 binding was preferred over a two-site model ($P < 0.01$) (Fig. 4).

^{45}Ca Uptake

To determine whether the positive inotropic effect of CGP 28392 could be correlated with altered calcium influx via the slow calcium channel, we studied ^{45}Ca uptake in cultured heart cells in the presence and absence of a calcium channel antagonist. Cells were preincubated in HEPES-buffered medium (pH 7.4) containing 0.9 mM Ca^{++} for 5 minutes, then were incubated further in medium containing ^{45}Ca, with or without 10^{-6} M CGP 28392. In control cells, ^{45}Ca content increased with time. CGP 28392 at 10^{-6} M did not produce a measurable increase in ^{45}Ca influx under these conditions. Therefore, cells were preincubated in calcium-free solution continuing 0.1 mM EGTA, which has been shown to induce persistent slow channel activation (Garnier et al., 1969; Linden and Brooker, 1981) (see discussion below). Cells were incubated in calcium-free medium for 5 minutes, then were exposed to medium containing 0.9 mM Ca^{++}, ^{45}Ca tracer, and (1) 0.05% ethanol, (2) 10^{-6} M CGP 28392, (3) 10^{-5} M nifedipine, or (4) 10^{-6} M CGP 28392 + 10^{-5} M nifedipine. As shown in Figure 5, under these conditions CGP 28392 markedly increased the rate of calcium uptake such that ^{45}Ca influx observed at 10 seconds was 39% greater than that observed under control conditions. When 10^{-5} M nifedipine was added during the 5-minute preincubation in calcium-free medium, it lowered significantly the rate of ^{45}Ca uptake and ^{45}Ca content throughout the 30-second period. When 10^{-5} M nifedipine was present during the preincubation and calcium uptake period, the CGP 28392-induced augmentation of ^{45}Ca uptake was abolished. These results support the thesis that CGP 28392 augments Ca^{++} entry via the slow calcium channel, and that this contributes to the positive inotropic effect observed in cultured chick heart cells.

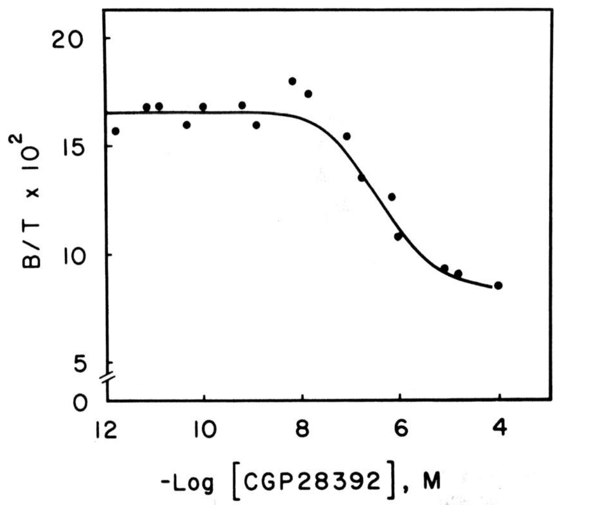

FIGURE 4. *Displacement of [^{3}H]nitrendipine by unlabeled CGP 28392. [^{3}H]Nitrendipine (0.5 nM for this experiment) and graded concentrations of CGP 28392 were incubated with intact cells for 15 minutes. Each point was measured in duplicate, and results agreed within 10%. The horizontal axis indicates the concentration of unlabeled CGP 28392 and the vertical axis the ratio of bound [^{3}H]nitrendipine to total [^{3}H]nitrendipine.*

Discussion

The monolayer preparation of spontaneously beating cultured chick embryo heart cells allows direct comparison among contractile function, bind-

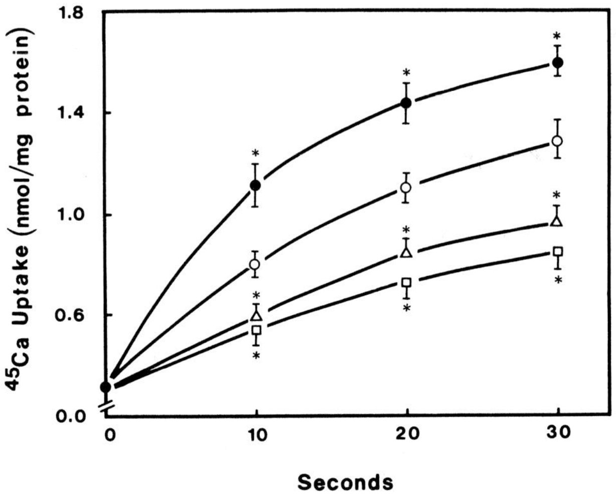

FIGURE 5. *Effect of CGP 28392 and nifedipine on ^{45}Ca uptake. Cells were incubated first in medium containing no calcium for 5 minutes, and then were exposed to medium containing 0.9 mM Ca^{++}, ^{45}Ca, and either (1) 0.03% ethanol (○); (2) 10^{-6} M CGP 28392 (●); (3) 10^{-5} M nifedipine (□), or (4) 10^{-6} M CGP 28392 + 10^{-5} M nifedipine (Δ). Statistical analysis was performed by means of an analysis of variance followed by Student's t-test for unpaired data. Each point is the mean ± SEM of seven determinations. * Significantly different from the corresponding control value ($P < 0.05$).*

ing properties, and Ca^{++} fluxes, studied under similar conditions. Moreover, the lack of major diffusion limitation inherent in isolated organ preparations and the lack of endogenous neuroeffectors simplify interpretation of the results.

CGP 28392 induced a rapid, sustained, and concentration-dependent increase in contractility. The relationship between CGP 28392 concentration and contractile response is sigmoidal, as shown in Figure 3, with a threshold at 10^{-8} M. The efficacy of this new compound in our cultured cell system was high, since the maximum response represents 85% of the 3.6 mM Ca^{++} response, which, in our experience, is the maximum response obtainable in this preparation (Miura et al., 1981). The efficacy of CGP 28392 was greater than that of isoproterenol, which at a saturating concentration of 10^{-6} M induced only 50 ± 5% of the 3.6 mM Ca^{++} response. However, the potency of CGP 28392 is lower than that of isoproterenol, since the EC_{50} values are respectively 2×10^{-7} and 1.3×10^{-8} M. The dihydropyridine calcium channel antagonist nifedipine antagonized the CGP 28392 contractile effect, suggesting a direct effect of CGP 28392 on the calcium channel or a closely related structure. However, the EC_{50} of CGP 28392 for the contractile effect was high, compared to the IC_{50} of 23 nM for nifedipine (Marsh et al., 1983). The lower affinity of CGP 28392 for the calcium channel site in our system suggested by this result was confirmed by binding experiments. The density and affinity of β-receptors and dihydropyridine-binding sites are age and species dependent (Renaud, et al., 1984), so extrapolation of relative efficacy to other systems must be considered cautiously.

The shift to the right in the concentration-contractile response curve for CGP 28392 produced by nifedipine is roughly parallel. This shift is consistent with competitive antagonism, although the present data do not exclude the possibility of spare calcium antagonist-binding sites and a noncompetitive interaction. The observation that the CGP 28392-[^{3}H]nitrendipine displacement curve is steep (N_H = 1.26 ± 0.09) is also consistent with the hypothesis that these structurally similar dihydropyridine derivatives interact with the same binding site according to the law of mass action.

There was a close relationship between the pharmacological effects and binding properties of CGP 28392, since the K_D obtained from the [^{3}H]nitrendipine displacement curve (2.2×10^{-7} M) and the EC_{50} from contractility experiments (2.0×10^{-7} M) done under comparable conditions were quite similar. Computer analysis of the [^{3}H]nitrendipine displacement curve indicated a single class of binding sites for CGP 28392 competing with nitrendipine. High (K_D = 0.3–3 nM) and low (K_D = 19–67 nM) -affinity sites have been described for the calcium channel antagonist nitrendipine in intact cells (Marsh et al., 1983) and guinea pig cardiac membrane fractions (Belleman et al., 1981) and for the calcium channel agonist BAY k 8644 in membranes from rabbit ventricles (Sarmiento et al., 1984). These high- and low-affinity sites have been suggested to mediate positive and negative inotropic effects induced by dihydropyridines (Grupp et al., 1984). Whether or not the calcium channel agonist-positive inotropic effect is mediated by a common dihydropyridine-binding site remains to be determined. This might be examined by comparing in the same preparation the binding properties and pharmacological effects of the recently described Ca^{++} channel agonists CGP 28392 and Bay k 8644.

To determine the effects of CGP 28392 on calcium influx via the slow calcium channel, we studied ^{45}Ca uptake by myocytes in the presence and absence of a dihydropyridine calcium channel antagonist. No measurable change in ^{45}Ca uptake was found in response to CGP 28392 (10^{-6} M) or nifedipine (10^{-5} M) in the presence of 0.9 mM Ca. Why CGP 28392 at the same concentration in 0.9 mM Ca^{++} medium was able to increase contractility, whereas no detectable change in ^{45}Ca uptake was found, is not clear. It is possible that, despite an increase in ^{45}Ca influx, ^{45}Ca content did not increase appreciably because of a compensating increase in ^{45}Ca efflux (Barry and Smith, 1982). It must also be recognized that it is difficult to measure true unidirectional transmembrane fluxes of calcium in intact cardiac tissue because of back diffusion of tracer, as discussed by Atwell et al. (1979) and Horres et al. (1979). Therefore, it appears that the CGP 28392-induced increase in ^{45}Ca influx is sufficient to induce a change in contractility, but small enough to escape detection by the method used. When the sensitivity of ^{45}Ca uptake was enhanced by preincubation in zero calcium medium, CGP 28392 clearly increased the measured ^{45}Ca uptake rate, whereas nifedipine decreased it. Nifedipine antagonized the CGP 28392-induced increment in ^{45}Ca uptake.

The interpretation of ^{45}Ca uptake experiments done after acute exposure to zero calcium medium must be viewed cautiously. Observations relevant to the interpretation of this experiment include the fact that prolonged slow channel activation was shown to occur when cardiac muscle was superfused with calcium-free solutions (Garnier et al., 1969; Linden and Brooker, 1981). It is of interest that, in frog ventricular strips, verapamil produced a dramatic reduction in the duration of long action potentials induced by low $[Ca^{++}]_o$, isoproterenol, or both (Linden and Brooker, 1981). Recent experiments in our own laboratory with spontaneously beating chick embryo ventricular cells confirm these findings in that superfusion of the cells with calcium-free medium enhanced dramatically the duration of the transmembrane action potential. The rate of isoproterenol-induced ^{45}Ca uptake was also enhanced after preincubation in calcium-free medium as compared to the rate of isoproterenol-induced ^{45}Ca uptake after 0.9 mM Ca^{++} preincubation (Kim et al., in preparation). Additional observations include the fact that when cells are superfused with calcium-free medium, they cease contracting; when normal calcium is restored in the superfusate, contractions return to baseline in less than 2 minutes (data not shown). Under these conditions, intracellular calcium content returns to 90% of control in 60 seconds. Thus, withdrawal of extracellular calcium for 5 minutes has no sustained effect on contractile performance. Since binding experiments are conducted over 15 minutes (equilibrium conditions), transient depression of contractility and Ca^{++} content would not be expected to alter equilibrium binding.

Although prolonged slow channel activation presumably ceases following the return of cells to medium containing 0.9 mM Ca^{++} plus ^{45}Ca, resumption of normal slow channel kinetics may be delayed by (1) the decreased intracellular calcium content and the increased intracellular sodium content (measured at the end of the calcium-free preincubation), and (2) the need for a 16- to 20-second period to equilibrate fully the extracellular space with the new calcium concentration (Barry and Smith, 1982). Thus, when cells are exposed to calcium-free medium, one may speculate that the slow channels open more frequently and/or stay open longer, that CGP 28392 interacts preferentially with this activated state, and that the slow channels maintain that property, at least in part, for the first 20 seconds of the subsequent exposure to 0.9 mM Ca^{++}.

In summary, our results demonstrate that CGP 28392 acts as a calcium channel agonist in that it increases nifedipine-sensitive ^{45}Ca uptake in intact cardiac cells. There is concomitant augmentation of contractility, and the drug appears to occupy the [^{3}H]nitrendipine-binding site at concentrations that produce contractile and ion flux effects. By enhancing calcium influx into the myocardial cell, CGP 28392 appears to augment the contractile state of the heart cell. Although another dihydropyridine derivative (Bay k 8644) has been shown in a preliminary report to enhance calcium uptake in vascular tissue (Anderson et al., 1984), we are not aware of other data directly demonstrating an increase in calcium influx by a calcium channel agonist in cardiac tissue. Our results are consistent with electrophysiological findings that the calcium channel agonist Bay k 8644 enhances calcium channel current in myocardial cells (Cohen and Chung, 1984; Hess et al., 1984). This novel class of compounds should be useful probes for the study of calcium channel properties. They may also be prototypes of clinically useful drugs that act by a mechanism different from other conventional or investigational inotropic agents.

Stephane Laurent is a recipient of fellowships from Ministere des Relations Exterieures (France) and Harvard-Arthur Sachs Foundation. This work was also supported by Grants HL 18003 and HL00691 from the National Heart, Lung, and Blood Institute, National Institutes of Health. Dr. Marsh is the recipient of a Clinical Investigator Award from the NIH.

Address for reprints: James D. Marsh, M.D., Cardiovascular Division, Brigham and Women's Hospital, 75 Francis Street, Boston, Massachusetts 02115.

Received August 8, 1984; accepted for publication January 24, 1985.

References

Anderson CL, Scriabine A, Janis RA (1984) Effects of a Ca^{2+} channel agonist (BAY k 8644) and antagonists (nitrendipine, nisoldipine, verapamil, and diltiazem) on Ca^{2+} uptake by rabbit aortic rings (abstr). Fed Proc **43:** 550a

Attwell D, Eisner D, Cohen I (1979) Voltage clamp and tracer flux data: Effects of a restricted extracellular space. Q Rev Biophys **12:** 213–261

Barry WH, Smith TW (1982) Mechanisms of transmembrane calcium movements in cultured chick embryo ventricular cells. J Physiol (Lond) **325:** 243–260

Belleman P, Ferry D, Lubbecke F, Glossman H (1981) [^{3}H]nitrendipine, a potent calcium antagonist, binds with high affinity to cardiac membranes. Arzneimforsch Drug Res **31:** 2064–2067

Biedert S, Barry WH, Smith TW (1979) Inotropic effects and change in sodium and calcium contents associated with inhibition of monovalent cation active transport by ouabain in cultured myocardial cells. J Gen Physiol **74:** 479–494

Blinks JR, Wier WG, Morgan JP, Hess P (1982) Regulation of intracellular [Ca^{++}] by cardiotonic drugs. *In* Advances in Pharmacology and Therapeutics II, vol 3, Cardio-renal and Cell Pharmacology, edited by H Yoshida, Y Hagihara, S Ebashi. Oxford, Pergamon, pp 205–216

Cohen CJ, Chung M (1984) A nifedipine derivative (Bay k 8644) that increases Ca currents in myocardial cells: A novel positive inotropic agent (abstr). Biophys J **45:** 394a

Fabiato A, Fabiato F (1979) Calcium and cardiac excitation-contraction coupling. Annu Rev Physiol **41:** 473–484

Garnier D, Rougier O, Gargouil YM, Coraboeuf E (1969) Analyse electrophysiologique du plateau des reponses myocardiques, mise en evidence d'un courant lent entrant en absence d'ions bivalents. Pflugers Arch **313:** 321–342

Grupp IL, Dube GP, Baik YH, Lathrop D, Grupp G, Schwartz A (1984) Effects of dihydropyridine Ca^{2+} agonist Bay K 8644 on porcine coronary artery, isolated rat hearts and canine Purkinje and trabecular action potentials (abstr). Fed Proc **43:** 937a

Henry PD (1980) Comparative pharmacology of calcium antagonists: Nifedipine, verapamil and diltiazem. Am J Cardiol **46:** 1047–1058

Hess P, Lansman JB, Tsien RW (1984) Different modes of Ca channel gating behaviour favored by dihydropyridine Ca agonist and antagonist. Nature **311:** 538–544

Horres CR, Aiton JF, Lieberman M (1979) Potassium permeability of embryonic avian heart cells in tissue culture. Am J Physiol **236:** C163–C170

Linden J, Brooker G (1982) Evidence for persistent activation of cardiac slow channels in low-calcium solutions. Am J Physiol **11:** H827–H833

Lowry DH, Rosebrough NJ, Farr AL, Randall RJ (1951) Protein measurement with the Folin phenol reagent. J Biol Chem **193:** 265–275

Marsh JD (1983) The cultured heart cell: A useful model for physiological and biochemical investigation. Int J Cardiol **3:** 465–468

Marsh JD, Barry WH, Smith TW (1982) Densitization to the inotropic effect of isoproterenol in cultured ventricular cells. J Pharmacol Exp Ther **223:** 60–67

Marsh JD, Loh E, LaChance D, Barry WH, Smith TW (1983) Relationship of binding of a calcium channel blocker to inhibition of contraction in intact cultured embryonic chick ventricular cells. Circ Res **53:** 539–543

Miura DS, Biedert S, Barry WH (1981) Effects of calcium overload on relaxation in cultured heart cells. J Mol Cell Cardiol **13:** 949–961

Munson PJ, Rodbard D (1980) Ligand: A versatile computerized approach for characterization of ligand-binding systems. Anal Biochem **107:** 220–239

Preuss KC, Brooks HL, Zyvoloski MG, Gross GJ, Warltier DC (1984) Hemodynamic effects of the dihydropyridine Ca^{++} agonist, CGP 28392 in conscious dogs (abstr). Fed Proc **43:** 551a

Renaud JF, Kazazoglou T, Schmidt A, Romey G, Lazdunski M (1984) Differentiation of receptor sites for [^{3}H]nitrendipine in chick hearts and physiologic relation to the slow Ca channel and excitation-contraction coupling. Eur J Biochem **139:** 673–681

Reuter H (1983) Calcium channel modulation by neurotransmitters, enzymes and drugs. Nature **301:** 569–574

Reuter H, Stevens CF, Tsien RW, Yellen G (1982) Properties of single calcium channels in cardiac cell culture. Nature **297:** 501–504

Sarmiento JG, Janis RA, Rampe D, Triggle DJ (1984) [^{3}H] Bay k 8644, a calcium channel agonist, binds to high and low affinity sites on membranes from cardiac muscle and brain (abstr). Fed Proc **43:** 448a

Schramm M, Thomas G, Towart R, Franckowiak G (1983) Novel dihydropyridines with positive inotropic action through activation of Ca^{2+} channels. Nature **303:** 535–537

INDEX TERMS: Calcium agonist • Contractility • [^{3}H]Nitrendipine binding • ^{45}Ca uptake • Cultured heart cells

Effects of Coronary Artery Occlusion and Reperfusion on Cardiac Cycle-Dependent Variation of Myocardial Ultrasonic Backscatter

Robert M. Glueck, Jack G. Mottley, James G. Miller, Burton E. Sobel, and Julio E. Pérez
From the Department of Medicine, Cardiovascular Division, and Department of Physics, Washington University, St. Louis, Missouri

SUMMARY. We have recently reported a systematic variation in integrated ultrasonic backscatter throughout the cardiac cycle in canine hearts. This study was performed to determine whether the pattern of such variation is modified systematically by ischemia. Measurements of integrated ultrasonic backscatter in selected regions of normal, ischemic, and reperfused hearts were compared in view of known differences in systolic function of myocardium in each of these regions. Integrated ultrasonic backscatter (3–7 MHz) gated to the first derivative of left ventricular pressure was measured at the apex, midwall, and base in 10 dogs and at the apex before and during transient ischemia and reperfusion in four dogs. Quantitative integrated ultrasonic backscatter was referenced to a steel reflector. Cyclic variation of integrated ultrasonic backscatter was greatest at the apex [peak to trough variation 5.5 ± 0.9 dB (mean ± SE)] with the maximum near end diastole (−52.9 ± 0.9 dB) and minimum near end systole (−58.4 ± 1.0 dB). Variation at the apex (5.5 ± 0.9 dB) and the midwall (4.3 ± 0.8 dB) was greater than at the base (0.5 ± 1.0 dB) ($P < 0.01$ for either region compared with base). Left anterior descending coronary occlusion for 10 minutes in four of 10 dogs reduced variation at the apex to 0.4 ± 1.5 dB ($P < 0.02$ compared with preocclusion). Reperfusion for 2 hours restored apical cyclic variation to 3.9 ± 1.7 dB, i.e., to values not significantly different from those before occlusion. Thus, regional differences in cyclic variation of integrated ultrasonic backscatter in the intact canine heart are blunted promptly by ischemia and restored substantially by reperfusion. These results suggest that quantitative ultrasonic interrogation may permit assessment with ultrasound of the intrinsic properties of myocardium modified by ischemia by analysis of physical properties of the tissue per se, rather than exclusively by assessment of geometrical changes. **(*Circ Res 56: 683–689, 1985*)**

ULTRASONIC tissue characterization has been undertaken to differentiate specific pathological entities by analysis of the interaction of ultrasound with myocardial tissue (Miller et al., 1976; Gramiak et al., 1979; Chivers, 1981). This approach differs from M-mode and two-dimensional echocardiography, which employ ultrasound to depict the shape and motion of cardiac structures (Feigenbaum, 1981). Approaches to ultrasonic characterization of cardiac tissue have included qualitative interpretation of the original (Wells and Halliwell, 1981; Bhandari and Nanda, 1981) or processed (Logan-Sinclair et al., 1981) two-dimensional image, stochastic analysis of A-mode amplitude (Green et al., 1981), and gray scale analysis (Skorton et al., 1983; Collins et al., 1983). Our laboratory has employed quantitative ultrasonic backscatter, which measures energy scattered by intramural tissue, and attenuation of transmitted ultrasound to characterize normal and diseased myocardium.

We have previously observed that ischemic injury in canine myocardium alters attenuation measured in vitro (Mimbs et al., 1977) and elevates backscatter measured both in vitro and in vivo in open and closed-chest preparations (Mimbs et al., 1981a; Cohen et al., 1982). Structural correlates of these findings include increased tissue collagen (Mimbs et al., 1980) and water content (Mimbs et al., 1981a). In addition, determination of quantitative backscatter and attenuation has detected doxorubicin-induced cardiomyopathic changes in rabbit heart (Mimbs et al., 1981b) and the naturally occurring cardiomyopathy of Syrian hamsters (Pérez et al., 1984).

We have recently demonstrated that myocardial backscatter varies systematically throughout the cardiac cycle in open and closed-chest dogs, with the highest values recorded at end diastole and the lowest at end systole (Barzilai et al., 1984). These and related observations suggested that quantitative ultrasonic backscatter can be used not only to detect changes in structural components of the heart but also to detect changes in its functional state. Accordingly, we undertook the present study to determine whether quantitative backscatter can detect normal regional gradations as well as serial changes in intrinsic properties of the tissue associated with functional abnormalities induced by myocardial ischemia and reperfusion.

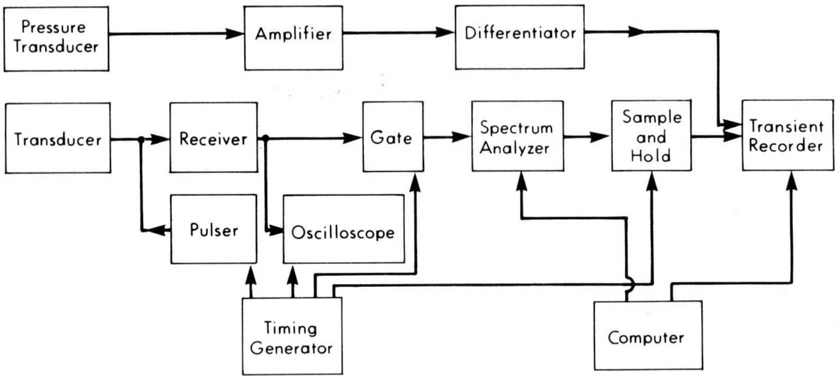

FIGURE 1. *Block diagram of data acquisition system.*

Methods

Ultrasonic measurements were made with the electronic equipment represented in the block diagram (Fig. 1). The pulser-receiver (Metrotek MP 215 pulser and MR101 receiver) launched broadband ultrasonic impulses from a 5-MHz focused transducer (Panametrics model V309) at the rate of 1000/sec. The transducer was mounted in a water-filled plexiglass holder fitted with a highly distensible latex balloon tip to avoid compression of subjacent myocardium. The transducer was held static at each site of interrogation by a clamp and ringstand assembly. The sample volume was defined by the ultrasonic beam width and an electronic gate triggered on the specular reflection of the epicardial surface which selected a 4-μsec portion of the backscattered RF signal, corresponding to a 3-mm-long cylinder of intramural myocardium. Signals from the sample volume were fed to an analog spectrum analyzer (Hewlett-Packard 8553) whose peak output was recorded at a rate of 500/sec by a Biomation 8100 recorder. Values from the spectrum analyzer were acquired for 2 seconds at each frequency from 3–7 MHz in 1-MHz steps under the control of a Hewlett-Packard model 9825 desk-top computer. Data acquisition for each cardiac cycle was triggered by the positive deflection of the first derivative of left ventricular pressure (dP/dt), a physiological event corresponding to the onset of mechanical systole. After compensation for a 50-msec time shift introduced by an electronic filter used in the differentiator, the data collected during each cardiac cycle were time renormalized into 32 windows, and the data gathered within each window were averaged. Integrated backscatter for each window was calculated as described below in the section entitled Data Analysis.

Dog Preparations

Ten mongrel dogs (15–25 kg) were anesthetized with sodium pentobarbital, 25 mg/kg, iv, and ventilated with a Harvard respirator. A left thoracotomy was performed in the 5th intercostal space, the pericardium was opened, and the heart was suspended in a pericardial cradle to minimize respiratory motion. The left atrium was incised, and a fluid-filled catheter connected to a Statham P23dB pressure transducer was inserted across the mitral valve into the left ventricle. The pressure pulse was differentiated with respect to time with a Honeywell model 132 differentiator with continuous display on an oscilloscope. End diastole was identified immediately before positive deflection of the dP/dt and end systole at the nadir of the negative deflection (Gleason and Braunwald, 1962).

Three regions of the free left ventricular wall were identified, as indicated in Figure 2. The base was considered to be the region adjacent to the bifurcation of the circumflex and left anterior descending coronary arteries, the midwall was taken to be approximately half-way between the circumflex coronary artery and the tip of the apex, and the apical region was identified as the region distal to the origin of the last diagonal branch of the left anterior descending coronary artery (LAD).

Backscatter measurements were obtained at five adjacent sites within each of the three regions, and the results were averaged. A Honeywell E for M mechanical scanner with a 3.5-MHz transducer was applied directly to the epicardium to record baseline two-dimensional echocardiograms from the four dogs which were to undergo transient ischemia. Normal regional backscatter recordings were obtained in all 10 dogs. A reversible snare was then used to occlude the LAD completely, just proximal to the last major diagonal branch, in four dogs. Ischemia of the apical region was confirmed by an immediate appearance of cyanosis and by repeat two-dimensional echocardiography which demonstrated apical dyskinesis. Segmental systolic wall thickening was quantified off-line from recorded two-dimensional echocardiograms with an image analysis computer using electronic calipers (Easy View II, Microsonics). Backscatter measurements and two-dimensional echocardiograms were repeated immediately before release of the snare 10 minutes after occlusion, and at 15, 30, 60, 90, and 120 minutes after reperfusion.

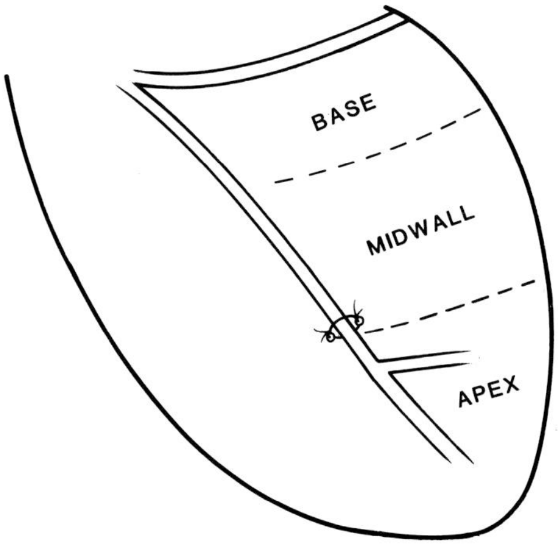

FIGURE 2. *Regions interrogated by ultrasonic backscatter in intact dog myocardium illustrating the site of temporary coronary occlusion.*

Data Analysis

Data from systole and diastole for each cardiac cycle at every site and frequency were fit to a time-renormalized cycle to permit comparisons of data gathered from different animals and different conditions. The systolic and diastolic phases of each cycle were divided into 16 equal time windows. The onset of systole and the onset of diastole were defined as the start of the upstroke and the nadir of the dP/dt, respectively. The backscatter data recorded during each phase were allocated among the 16 windows assigned to that phase, and the data corresponding to each window were then averaged. Thus, 50% of the time-renormalized cycle comprised data from systole and 50% data from diastole. The magnitude of the energy backscattered from tissue at each frequency from 3–7 MHz was referenced to the magnitude received from a planar stainless steel reflector placed in a water bath at the same distance from the transducer as was the tissue to obtain the backscatter transfer function (BSTF). Integrated backscatter was then calculated by averaging the BSTF over the range of frequencies employed. To highlight the magnitude of the cyclic variations, the time-average value of backscatter was offset to zero to obtain the relative integrated backscatter, which was averaged for all animals (Fig. 3).

To quantify regional cyclic variation, Fourier transforms of the relative integrated backscatter over the cardiac cycle were performed. The fundamental component, or that spectral component which exhibits one complete cycle over the cardiac period, was the only spectral component of appreciable amplitude. Thus, the peak-to-peak amplitude of the fundamental spectral component was chosen as an index to quantify the magnitude of the cyclic variation of backscatter (Fig. 4). Higher frequency components are present in the spectra, but were not of substantial amplitude and could have been affected by the time-renormalization process, and so were not included in the analysis.

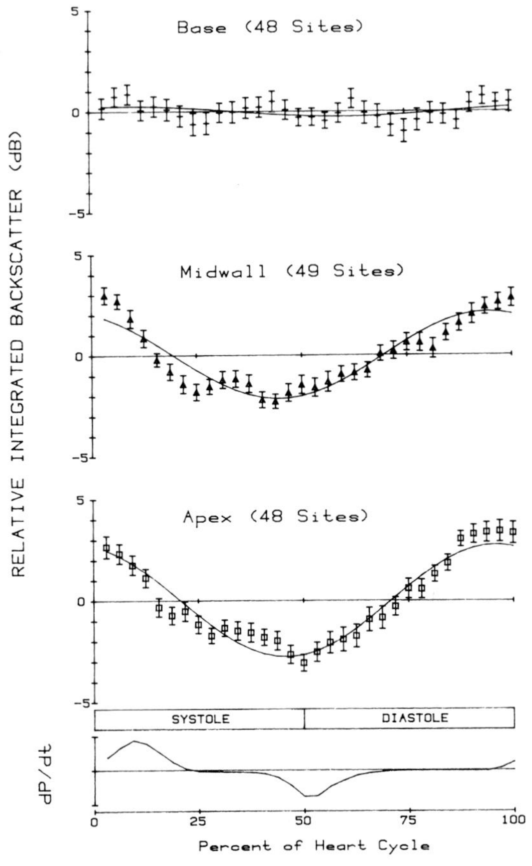

FIGURE 3. *Relative integrated backscatter in normal myocardium obtained throughout the cardiac cycle, measured at the base, midwall, and apex of the left ventricle in 10 dogs.*

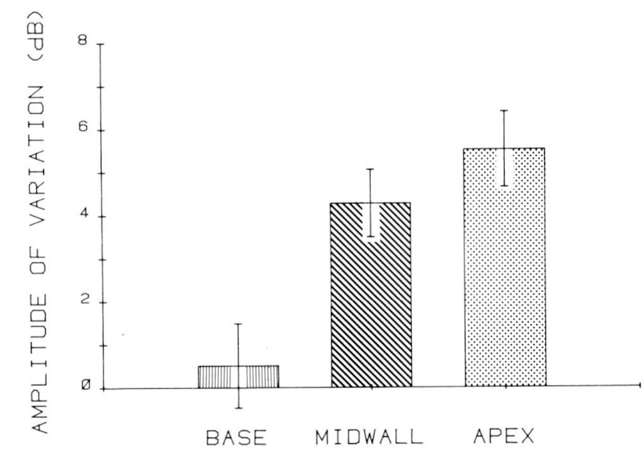

FIGURE 4. *Peak-to-peak amplitude (fundamental) of the systolic-to-diastolic variation of integrated backscatter in the three regions of normal myocardium.*

The standard errors of the amplitudes of variation were calculated from the amplitude of the fundamental of each animal's relative integrated backscatter. Statistical significance was determined with the use of *t*-tests modified for multiple comparisons (Bonferroni's procedure). (Wallenstein et al., 1980).

Results

Figure 3 depicts regional differences in relative integrated backscatter recorded throughout the cardiac cycle. At the apex and midwall, where a cyclic pattern was discernible, the lowest values for backscatter were recorded near end systole, and the highest near end diastole. The amplitude of the fundamental frequency for each region (Fig. 4) increased progressively from base (0.5 ± 1.0 dB; mean ± SE) to midwall (4.3 ± 0.8 dB) to apex (5.5 ± 0.9 dB). The difference in the magnitude of cyclic variation between the apex or midwall and the base was significant ($P < 0.01$, with allowance for multiple comparisons).

Despite marked regional differences in the pattern of cyclic variation, the absolute value of backscatter averaged over the cardiac cycle was similar for each area of the heart (apex = −55.6 ± 0.7 dB, midwall = −53.6 ± 0.9 dB, base = −53.8 ± 0.7 dB, P = NS for comparison of any two regions.)

Figure 5 depicts relative integrated backscatter measurements recorded throughout the cardiac cycle from the apical region of four dogs under control conditions (upper panel), after 10 minutes of ischemia (middle panel), and after 2 hours of reperfusion (lower panel). The amplitude of peak-

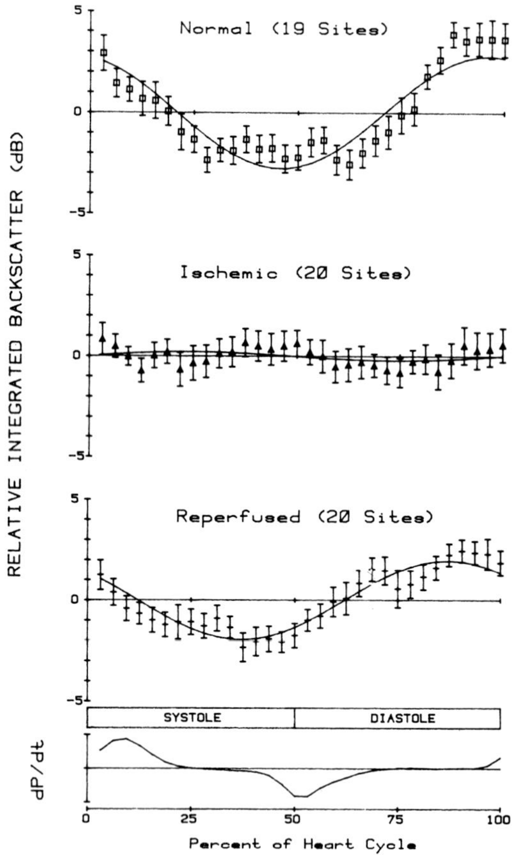

FIGURE 5. *Relative integrated backscatter obtained over the cardiac cycle at the apex of the left ventricle in four dogs under conditions of normal perfusion, after 10 minutes of ischemia, and after 2 hours of coronary reperfusion.*

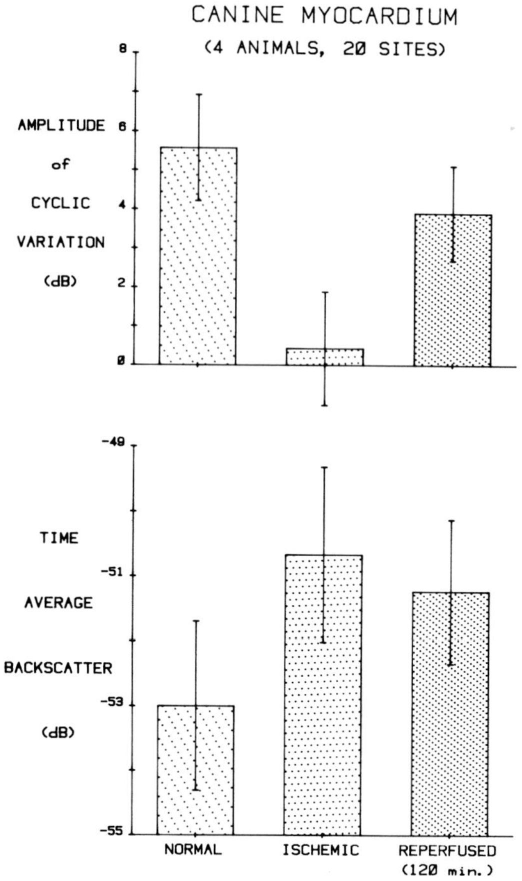

FIGURE 6. *Upper panel: peak-to-peak amplitude (fundamental) of the systolic-to-diastolic variation of integrated backscatter in the left ventricular apex under conditions of normal perfusion, after 10 minutes of ischemia, and after 2 hours of coronary reperfusion. Lower panel: time-averaged integrated backscatter (not gated) during the same time intervals as data shown in upper panel. The overlap among values is evident, and the differences were not significant.*

to-trough variation, which was 5.6 ± 1.4 dB under control conditions, diminished to only 0.4 ± 1.5 dB after 10 minutes of ischemia ($P < 0.02$, with Bonferroni's procedure), and returned to 3.9 ± 1.2 dB after 2 hours of reperfusion ($P =$ NS compared with control) (Fig. 6, upper panel). Although early recovery of the amplitude of cyclic variation after transient ischemia was substantial, the course of improvement was gradual and still incomplete after two hours of reperfusion (Fig. 7). Furthermore, although there were small increases in absolute time-average values of integrated backscatter during ischemia, and subsequently decreases during reperfusion, these were not significant in contrast to the amplitude of the cyclic variation (Fig. 6, lower panel).

Systolic wall thickening values before coronary occlusion averaged 63.4 ± 17.7%, compared with 2.2 ± 11.5% during coronary occlusion (SD; $P < 0.001$; $n = 20$). Two hours after reperfusion, wall thickening did not differ from control values (52.85 ± 26.8; $P =$ NS). Representative end-diastolic and end-systolic frames of apical four chamber echocardiograms are displayed in Figure 8. Recordings were obtained at times corresponding to the backscatter measurements presented in Figure 5. Normal symmetric contraction of the left ventricle under control conditions (panel A) was replaced by apical systolic bulging under conditions of ischemia (panel B). Substantial improvement in mechanical function was noted after 2 hours of reperfusion (panel C).

Discussion

The results obtained indicate that myocardial ischemia modifies the cardiac cycle-dependent variation of myocardial ultrasonic backscatter in intact canine hearts. Despite significant regional differences in cyclic variation, the absolute value of backscatter averaged over the cardiac cycle was similar throughout the heart. This suggests that the observed gradient in cyclic variation is due to regional heterogeneity in dynamic, not structural, scattering properties of the tissue. The progressive increase in the magnitude of cyclic variation from base to apex is parallel to a regional gradient in contractile function previously described by others in normal

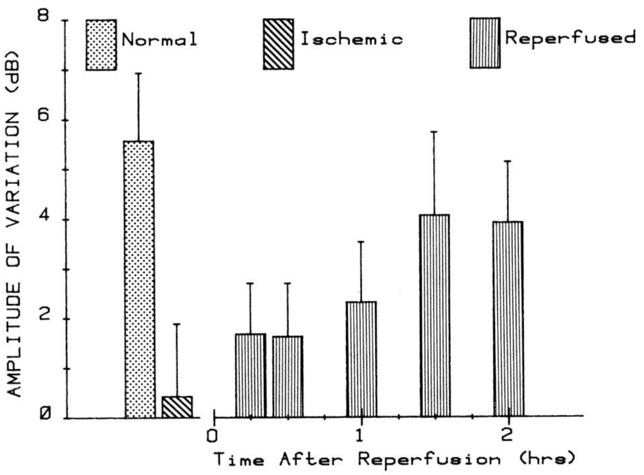

FIGURE 7. *Peak-to-peak amplitude (fundamental) of the systolic-to-diastolic variation of integrated backscatter at the left ventricular apex during normal perfusion, after 10 minutes of ischemia, and after 15, 30, 60, 90, and 120 minutes of coronary reperfusion.*

hearts of dogs and humans. Measurements performed with implanted ultrasonic crystals (LeWinter et al., 1975; Badke and Covell, 1979), biplane cineangiography (Kong et al., 1971; Liedtke et al., 1973), digital intravenous ventriculography (Slutsky et al., 1982), and two-dimensional echocardiography (Haendchen et al., 1983) have demonstrated an increase in magnitude of contractile activity from base to apex in the intact heart. The parallel increases in cardiac cycle-dependent regional variation in ultrasonic backscatter from base to apex are consistent with the hypothesis that the ultrasonic alterations are expressions of differences in myocardial fiber orientation. (Streeter et al., 1969).

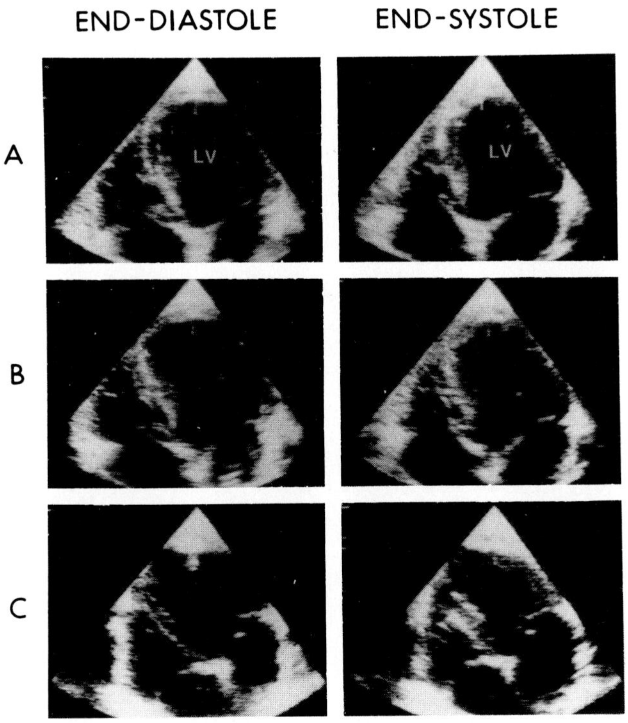

FIGURE 8. *Two-dimensional echocardiographic four chamber still-frames in a dog at end diastole and end systole under conditions of normal perfusion (panel A), after 10 minutes of ischemia (panel B), and after 2 hours of coronary reperfusion (panel C).*

The cardiac cycle-dependent variation of backscatter appears to be sensitive not only to the locus of the region within the heart, but also to changes in the myocardial properties induced by ischemia or reperfusion. Changes in the cardiac cycle-dependent variation of backscatter accompanied changes in local contractile function documented by simultaneous two-dimensional echocardiography. Ten minutes after LAD occlusion, apical four-chamber views of the apex demonstrated dyskinesis and loss of systolic thickening of the septum (Fig. 8B). At the same time, normal apical cyclic variation of backscatter was eliminated (Fig. 5). After release of the coronary occlusion, echocardiographically delineated apical function gradually improved, and was substantially, although not completely, restored 2 hours after the onset of reperfusion (Fig. 8C). Simultaneously, apical cyclic variation of ultrasonic backscatter returned to 70% of control values (Fig. 5, lower panel; Fig. 6, upper panel).

Based on the behavior of other indexes of intrinsic properties of myocardium, such as contractile performance, it is not surprising that the cyclic variation of backscatter was not fully restored 2 hours after release of a transient LAD occlusion. Indeed, the time course of observed changes in cyclic variation of backscatter are consistent with results of studies of the time course after transient ischemia of altered contractile function assessed with implanted ultrasonic crystals. Heyndrickx et al. (1975) found that velocity of myocardial shortening at the apex of conscious dogs was eliminated 5 minutes after LAD occlusion, and that it returned to approximately 50% of control velocity after 2 hours of reperfusion. Other investigators, using implanted ultrasonic crystals (Théroux et al., 1976; Kloner et al., 1981) and segment length gauges (Weiner et al., 1976), have found that the impairment of contractile function induced by brief ischemia exhibits prompt partial resolution, but that complete recovery requires more prolonged reperfusion.

Because the electronic gating arrangement employed in this study does not permit the precise tracking of the same sample volume of tissue, we cannot exclude possible displacement of the segment relative to the ultrasonic beam during a heart cycle. However, it is unlikely that cardiac wall motion per se was responsible for the cyclic variation of ultrasonic backscatter observed, in view of the absence of systematic differences in backscatter recorded at the apex when it was rendered ischemic in each animal, in spite of marked systolic bulging and diastolic retraction.

It is improbable that regional differences in myocardial perfusion account for the observed regional differences in cyclic variation of backscatter in normal hearts. Studies with radiolabeled microspheres have shown that blood flow is relatively evenly distributed throughout the normal left ventricle (Marcus et al., 1975, 1977). Radiotracer studies performed in isolated perfused canine hearts (Yipintsoi et al., 1973; Warltier et al., 1975; Mosca et al., 1981) and open-chest anesthetized dogs (Griggs and Nakamura, 1968) indicate that the endocardial-to-epicardial blood flow ratio in normal hearts does not exhibit significant regional differences. We cannot exclude the possibility that variations in myocardial blood flow changes throughout the cardiac cycle may have influenced our ultrasonic measurements. However, we have documented systematic changes in backscatter values in isolated, nonperfused skeletal amphibian muscle associated with contractile state (Glueck et al., 1984). Thus, changes in blood flow per se are not a necessary condition for the alteration in backscatter associated with a change in function.

With respect to transient ischemia and reperfusion, the discrepancy in time course between the gradual recovery of contractile activity and cyclic variation and the prompt restoration of perfusion after transient ischemia suggests that blood flow per se is not the primary determinant of the observed changes in cardiac cycle-dependent variation in backscatter. Using radiolabeled microspheres, Heyndrickx et al. (1978) found that transmural blood flow was 90% restored after 1 hour of reperfusion following 15 minutes of ischemia, but that systolic wall thickening recovered more slowly. Kerber and collaborators (1975), using a similar technique, demonstrated normal myocardial perfusion 30 minutes after release of a transient coronary occlusion, although mechanical function remained significantly impaired. Thus, the backscatter changes parallel those of myocardial systolic function more closely than they parallel changes in perfusion per se.

Our results do not define a relationship between the amplitude of the cyclic variation of ultrasonic backscatter and myocardial contractility. Although myocardial ischemia and reperfusion are characterized by disruption and restoration of segmental contractile function, these interventions are accompanied also by considerable mechanical alterations in the tissue that could influence the observed changes in backscatter. Nevertheless, it appears likely that both cyclic variation of backscatter and contractile function may reflect conformational changes of myocardial contractile elements. We have previously reported that measurements of ultrasonic backscatter and attenuation in excised canine myocardium are highly dependent on the angle between the interrogating beam and the predominant myofiber orientation (Mottley and Miller, 1982). Furthermore, cineangiographic and morphometric studies of the canine heart have demonstrated that myocardial fiber orientation varies systematically throughout the cardiac cycle, and that there are regional differences in the magnitude of this variation (Streeter et al., 1969; Meier et al., 1982). In addition, cyclic changes in the attenuation of contracting cardiac muscle may account in part for the observed systematic changes in backscatter. Thus, changes in myocardial fiber orientation as a result of altered contractile activity may provide one ultrastructural basis for the changes in cardiac cycle-dependent variation in ultrasonic backscatter manifest in myocardium subjected to ischemia.

We thank Joyce Kalayeh for preparation of the manuscript and Delbert McGraw for skillful technical assistance.

This work was supported in part by National Institutes of Health Grants HL17646 (SCOR in Ischemic Heart Disease), HL28998, RR00396, and Ella L. Buder and Ida Marie Peters Cardiovascular Research Scholar Award of the St. Louis Heart Association (Dr. Pérez).

Address for reprints: Julio E. Pérez, M.D., Cardiovascular Division, Box 8086, Washington University School of Medicine, 660 South Euclid Avenue, St. Louis, Missouri 63110.

Received October 3, 1983; accepted for publication February 8, 1985.

References

Badke FR, Covell JW (1979) Early changes in left ventricular regional dimensions and function during chronic volume overloading in the conscious dog. Circ Res **45:** 420–428

Barzilai B, Madaras E, Sobel BE, Miller JG, Pérez JE (1984) Effects of myocardial contraction on ultrasonic backscatter before and after ischemia. Am J Physiol **247:** H478–H483

Bhandari AK, Nanda NC (1982) Two-dimensional echocardiographic recognition of abnormal changes in the myocardium. Ultrasound Med Biol **8:** 663–671

Chivers RC (1981) Tissue characterization. Ultrasound Med Biol **7:** 1–20

Cohen RD, Mottley JG, Miller JG, Kurnik P, Sobel BE (1982) Detection of ischemic myocardiun in vivo through the chest wall by quantitative ultrasonic tissue characterization. Am J Cardiol **50:** 838–843

Collins SM, Skorton DJ, Olshansky B, Prasad NV, Melton HE (1983) Alteration of left ventricular wall gray level in two-dimensional echocardiograms due to cardiac contraction (abstr). Ultrasonic Imaging **5:** 183–184

Feigenbaum H (1981) Echocardiography, ed 3. Philadelphia, Lea & Febiger

Gleason WL, Braunwald E (1962) Studies on the first derivative of the ventricular pressure pulse in man. J Clin Invest **41:** 80–91

Glueck RM, Mottley JG, Pérez JE, Miller JG, Sobel BE (1984) Systematic changes in quantitative ultrasonic indexes caused by the contractile state of muscle (abstr). Clin Res **32:** 169A

Gramiak R, Waag RC, Schenk EA, Lee PL, Thomson K, MacIntosh P (1979) Ultrasonic detection of myocardial infarction by amplitude analysis. Radiology **130:** 713–720

Green SE, Joynt L, Fitzgerald PJ, Rubenson DS, Popp R (1982) In vivo ultrasonic tissue characterization of human intracardiac masses. Am J Cardiol **51:** 231–236

Griggs DM, Nakamura Y (1968) Effect of coronary constriction on myocardial distribution of iodoantipyrine-^{131}I. Am J Physiol **215:** 1082–1088

Haendchen RV, Wyatt HL, Maurer G, Zwehl W, Bear M, Meerbaum S, Corday E (1983) Quantitation of regional cardiac function by two-dimensional echocardiography. I. Patterns of contraction in the normal left ventricle. Circulation **67:** 1234–1235

Hess DS, Bache RJ (1976) Transmural distribution of myocardial blood flow during systole in the awake dog. Circ Res **38:** 5–15

Heyndrickx GR, Millar RW, McRitchie RJ, Maroko PR, Vatner S

(1975) Regional myocardial functional and electrophysiological alterations after brief coronary artery occlusion in conscious dogs. J Clin Invest **56:** 978–985
Heyndrickx GR, Baig H, Nellens P, Leusen I, Fishbein MC, Vatner S (1978) Depression of regional blood flow and wall thickening after brief coronary occlusions. Am J Physiol **234:** H653–H659
Kerber R, Marcus M, Ehrhardt J, Abboud F (1975) Correlation between myocardial dyskinesis and regional myocardial perfusion in experimental coronary occlusion and reperfusion (abstr). Clin Res **23:** 189
Kloner RA, DeBoer LWV, Darsee J, Ingwall JS, Braunwald D (1981) Recovery from prolonged abnormalities of canine myocardium salvaged from ischemic necrosis by coronary reperfusion. Proc Natl Acad Sci USA **78:** 7152–7156
Kong Y, Morris JJ, McIntosh HD (1971) Assessment of regional myocardial performance from biplane coronary cineangiograms. Am J Cardiol **27:** 529–537
LeWinter MM, Kent RS, Kroener JM, Carew T, Covell JW (1975) Regional differences in myocardial performance in the left ventricle of the dog. Circ Res **37:** 191–199
Liedtke AJ, Gault JH, Leaman DM, Blumenthal MS (1973) Geometry of left ventricular contraction in the systolic click syndrome. Characterization of a segmental myocardial abnormality. Circulation **67:** 27–35
Logan-Sinclair R, Wong CM, Gibson DG (1981) Clinical application of amplitude processing of echocardiographic images. Br Heart J **45:** 621–627
Marcus ML, Kerber RE, Ehrhardt J, Abboud FM (1975) Three-dimensional geometry of acutely ischemic myocardium. Circulation **52:** 254–263
Marcus ML, Kerber RE, Erhardt JC, Falsetti HL, Davis DM, Abboud FM (1977) Spatial and temporal heterogeneity of left ventricular perfusion in awake dogs. Am Heart J **94:** 748–754
Meier GD, Ziskin MC, Bove A (1982) Helical fibers in myocardium of dogs change their pitch as they contract. Am J Physiol **243:** H1–H12
Miller JG, Yuhas DE, Mimbs JW, Dierker SB, Busse LV, Laterra VV, Weiss AN, Sobel BE (1976) Ultrasonic tissue characterization: Correlation between biochemical and ultrasonic indices of myocardial injury. Proc IEEE Ultrasonics Symp **76** CH1120-5SU: 33–43
Mimbs JW, Yuhas DE, Miller JG, Weiss AN, Sobel BE (1977) Detection of myocardial infarction in vitro based on altered attenuation of ultrasound. Circ Res **41:** 192–198
Mimbs JW, O'Donnell M, Bauwens D, Miller JW, Sobel BE (1980) The dependence of ultrasonic attenuation and backscatter on collagen content in dog and rabbit hearts. Circ Res **47:** 49–58
Mimbs JW, Bauwens D, Cohen RD, O'Donnell M, Miller JG, Sobel BE (1981a) Effects of myocardial ischemia on quantitative ultrasonic backscatter and identification of responsible determinants. Circ Res **49:** 89–96
Mimbs JW, O'Donnell M, Miller JG, Sobel BE (1981b) Detection of cardiomyopathic changes induced by doxorubicin based on quantitative analysis of ultrasonic backscatter. Am J Cardiol **47:** 1056–1060
Mosca SM, Escudero E, Gelpi RJ, Kosoglov AT, Rinaldi GJ, Cingolani HE (1981) Myocardial flow distribution. Empty beating heart, ventricular fibrillation and cardiac arrest. Arch Int Physiol Biochem **89:** 357–364
Mottley JG, Miller JG (1982) Anisotropy of ultrasonic attenuation in canine heart and liver (abstr). Ultrasonic Imaging **4:** 180
Pérez JE, Barzilai B, Madaras E, Glueck RM, Saffitz JE, Johnston P, Miller JG, Sobel BE (1984) Applicability of ultrasonic tissue characterization for longitudinal assessment and differentiation of calcification and fibrosis in cardiomyopathy. J Am Coll Cardiol **4:** 88–95
Skorton DJ, Melton HE, Pandian NG, Nichols J, Koyanagi S, Marcus ML, Collins SM, Kerber RE (1983) Detection of acute myocardial infarction in closed-chest dogs by analysis of regional two-dimensional echocardiographic gray-level distributions. Circ Res **52:** 36–44
Slutsky RA, Gerber KH, Higgins CB (1982) Digital intravenous ventriculography: Analysis and validation of wall thickness changes during ischemia and inotropic stimulation in dogs. Am J Cardiol **50:** 874–880
Streeter DD, Spotnitz HM, Patel DP, Ross J, Sonnenblock EH (1969) Fiber orientation in the canine left ventricle during diastole and systole. Circ Res **24:** 339–347
Theroux P, Ross J, Franklin D, Kemper WS, Sasayama S (1976) Regional myocardial function in the conscious dog during acute coronary occlusion and response to morphine, propranolol, nitroglycerin and lidocaine. Circulation **53:** 302–314
Wallenstein S, Zucker CL, Fleiss JL (1980) Some statistical methods useful in circulation research. Circ Res **47:** 1–9
Warltier DC, Hardman HF, Laddu AR, Somani P, Gross GJ (1975) Myocardial distribution of coronary blood flow in the isolated supported heart preparation. Cardiovasc Res **9:** 634–639
Weiner JM, Apstein CS, Arthur JH, Pirzada FA, Hood WB (1976) Persistence of myocardial injury following brief periods of coronary occlusion. Cardiovasc Res **10:** 678–686
Wells PNT, Halliwell M (1981) Speckle in ultrasonic imaging. Ultrasonics **19:** 225–229
Yipintsoi T, Dobbs WA, Scanlon PD, Knopp TJ, Bassingthwaighte JB (1973) Regional distribution of diffusible tracers and carbonized microspheres in the left ventricle of isolated dog hearts. Circ Res **33:** 573–587

INDEX TERMS: Quantitative ultrasound • Ultrasonic tissue characterization • Myocardial performance • Myocardial ischemia and reperfusion

Viscoelastic Behavior of the Thoracic Aorta of Dogs and Rabbits

Brian J. Gentile and David R. Gross

From the Physiology and Applied Physics Laboratory, Department of Veterinary Physiology and Pharmacology, College of Veterinary Medicine, and the Texas Engineering Experiment Station, Texas A&M University, College Station, Texas

SUMMARY. Data are presented which demonstrate no correlation between atrial electrical activity and diameter changes in the descending thoracic aorta of dogs or rabbits. The experiments conducted included bypassing a segment of the descending thoracic aorta in dogs, and production of a variety of arrhythmias without the bypass in dogs and rabbits. We found no evidence of electrical stimulation-induced phasic activity as suggested by other authors. (***Circ Res 56: 690–695, 1985***)

TRUE understanding of many vascular diseases, characterization of detailed hemodynamics, and the design criteria for most, if not all, cardiovascular prosthetic devices, depend empirically on knowledge of normal and abnormal vascular mechanical behavior. Classically, the arterial tree has been described as being an elastic or viscoelastic conduit network (Bergel, 1961a, 1961b; Gow, 1972; Patel and Vaishnav, 1972; Dobrin, 1978). Bergel (1961b) has described the elastic properties of arteries in vitro in terms of the dynamic elastic modulus. Another dynamic elastic modulus using the frequency domain has been described by Cox (1975). Pseudoelasticity of arteries has been defined in vitro by Fung et al. (1979) using the stress-strain relationship of preconditioned arteries subjected to cyclic loading and unloading. The term pseudoelasticity indicates that, in spite of the inelastic, anisotropic, nonlinear properties of arteries, the concept of elasticity can be used if loading and unloading phenomena are separated and identified.

Mangel et al. (1982) suggested the possibility of sinoatrial node-controlled phasic aortic contractility. If true, the implications of these observations on the mechanical behavior of arteries are very significant. The existence of pacemaker-controlled phasic electrical stimulation of the vascular smooth muscle of major conduit arteries would have a significant impact on how we describe the mechanical properties of these vessels, since all of the current theories are based on passive elastic or viscoelastic models.

Most investigators have agreed that the primary function of vascular smooth muscle is to maintain vasomotor tone. Changes in tone may have significant effects on the viscoelastic properties of arteries (Gow, 1972; Dobrin, 1978; Cox, 1982). However, substantial evidence has been presented in support of rhythmic activity in a variety of vascular smooth muscle preparations. Nicoll and Webb (1955) and D'Agrosa (1970) have demonstrated active vasomotion in the form of peristaltic waves in bat wing arterioles and veins. Subcutaneous arterial strips from the dog's paw have shown spontaneous rhythmic activity in response to a variety of vasoactive agents (Johansson and Bohr, 1966). Superior mesenteric vein strips from the guinea pig have been described as being capable of spontaneous contractile activity when incubated in warm, modified Kreb's solution (Nakajima and Horn, 1967). Biamino and Kruckenberg (1969) showed that rhythmic contractions could be induced in helical aortic strips from rats by adding norepinephrine or by increasing external potassium ion concentration. Hermsmeyer (1979) observed spontaneous contractions and relaxations of isolated arterial muscle cells from the rat or chick at a rate of 5 beats/sec. Using a skinfold window preparation, Colantuoni et al. (1984) recently described rhythmic vasomotion in the arterial microvasculature of hamsters. Histamine-induced rhythmic contractions have been observed in swine carotid arteries (Stein and Driska, 1984). Our study was designed to test the hypothesis that the thoracic aorta behaves in a purely viscoelastic manner without a demonstrable active component.

Methods

Bypass Experiments

Three mongrel dogs were used in this series which included bypassing a segment of aorta, as done by Mangel et al. (1982). For the bypass procedure, the dogs were preanesthetized with acepromazine maleate (0.25 mg/kg, im) and anesthetized with sodium pentobarbital (20 mg/kg, iv). An airway was provided by means of an endotracheal tube, and the dogs were maintained with positive pressure ventilation after the thorax was opened. Physiological saline was administered intravenously at a rate of 200 ml/hr by means of a catheter inserted into the jugular vein. A high-fidelity catheter-tip manometer (Millar Mikro-tip model PC-350) was inserted into the carotid artery to the level of the aorta to measure blood pressure proximal to the bypass. A median sternotomy was used to enter the thoracic activity. A 5- to 8-cm segment of the descending thoracic aorta was isolated, and branches leading from this segment were ligated to prevent excessive backflow of blood into the bypassed segment. Change in aortic diameter (ΔD) was measured with an ultrasonic dimension gauge activated by a Metrotek MP203 pulser and a Metrotek MR101 receiver. A more detailed description of the dimension gauge system used has been given (Gross et al., 1981). Piezoelectric dimension gauge transducers with a frequency of 3.5 MHz were dipped in epoxy and attached to Dacron patches. These transducers were arranged across the diameter of the descending thoracic aorta, then connected to the dimension gauge system by flexible copper leads to measure ΔD. Alignment of the crystals was verified during the procedure, with an oscilloscope displaying the received ultrasonic signal.

The aorta was cross-clamped proximal to the bypass site. The bypass procedure was performed using two aortic perfusion cannulas that were joined with a tubing connector. Each cannula was secured in place with a snare. They were connected together while saline was instilled at the junction to prevent an air bubble from entering the arterial system. The aortic cross-clamp was then removed, and blood was shunted around the bypassed aortic segment. The dog was previously heparinized (150 units/kg, iv) to prevent blood clotting within the bypass tubing during the experiment. Half of the heparin dose was repeated every 30 minutes. Pressure in the bypass tubing was measured with a Statham P23dB strain transducer connected to a fluid-filled pressure tap in the shunt.

The pericardial sac was opened and transcardiac bipolar leads were attached to monitor the electrical activity of the heart. All measurements were recorded on a Gould Mark 200 eight-channel oscillograph throughout the experiment. Baseline measurements of the electrocardiogram (ECG), aortic pressure (Pao), bypass pressure (Pbp), and change in aortic diameter (ΔD) were made before the bypass was performed, and the same measurements were repeated after the bypass was in place and functioning.

Atrial Stimulation

Atrial stimulation was used to test for a conduction pathway between the atrium and the aorta. Two dogs were anesthetized with sodium pentobarbital (30 mg/kg) and surgery was performed, except for the bypass procedure, as previously described. In this experiment, the auricle of the right atrium was isolated and the positive electrode of a bipolar lead was attached to this appendage. The heart was stimulated with 0.5-, 1-, and 2-mV single stimuli while measurements of the ECG, Pao, and ΔD were made. The stimulating electrodes were then removed and the dogs were used in one or more of the following arrhythmia experiments.

Arrhythmia Production

Five dogs (including the two from the atrial pacing experiments) and five rabbits were used in these studies. Some of these animals were used for more than one perturbation. Rabbits were anesthetized with ketamine (75 mg/kg) and acepromazine maleate (0.75 mg/kg) mixed in the same syringe and given intramuscularly. A tracheostomy was performed, and the rabbits were mechanically ventilated. The jugular vein was cannulated for administration of fluids and additional anesthesia, as required. Rabbits were instrumented the same as the dogs for recording of ECG, aortic pressure, and ΔD. Following baseline recordings of Pao, ΔD, and ECG, a variety of perturbations were introduced to produce an assortment of arrhythmias. Ventricular tachycardia was produced during the rebound period after administration of acetylcholine (0.025 mg/kg), iv, in three dogs. Premature ventricular contraction(s) (PVC) were induced with topical application of methacholine, followed by mechanical stimulation in three dogs and three rabbits and by ventricular intramyocardial injection of formalin in two rabbits. Phenylephrine (0.02 mg/kg, iv) produced PVC in three dogs. Atrial flutter and/or fibrillation was induced by local administration of methacholine (1 mg/ml) and by then stimulating the sensitized atrial myocardium with the tip of a 25-gauge needle (five dogs). A complete atrioventricular conduction block was produced by the injection of 0.1–0.2 ml of 10% buffered neutral formalin into the base of the interventricular septum (three dogs and two rabbits). Techniques for the latter procedure have been described in detail by Guzman et al. (1959) and Steiner and Kovalik (1968). Atrial fibrillation was induced by interatrial septal injection of 0.1 ml of 10% buffered neutral formalin (one dog). The effects of these arrhythmias on the relationships between Pao, ΔD, and the electrical activity generated by the heart then were evaluated with respect to sinoatrial (SA) node control of aortic smooth muscle. After all of the experimental protocols

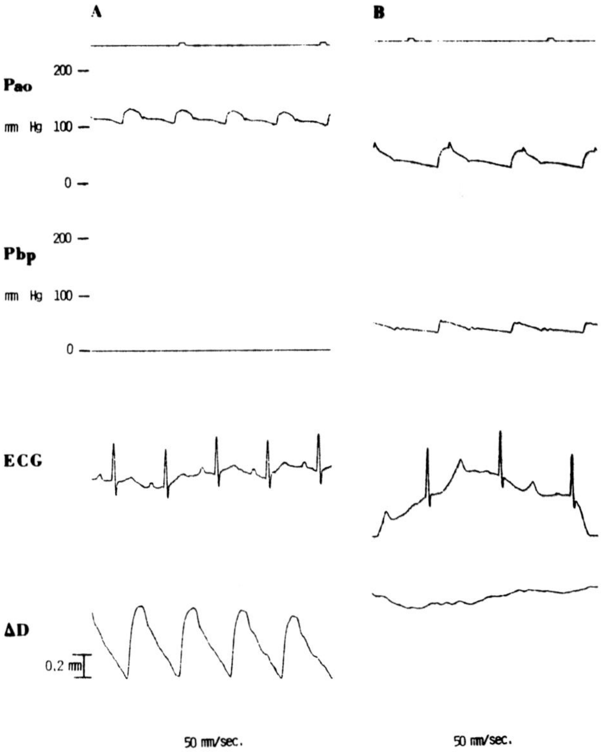

FIGURE 1. *Panel A: dog no. 1 baseline data for aortic pressure (Pao) measured proximal to the bypass, bypass pressure (Pbp) within the bypass tubing prior to opening the bypass, electrocardiogram (ECG), and change in aortic diameter (ΔD) before opening the by-pass. Panel B: same dog; recordings following bypass of a segment of the thoracic aorta. The diameter changes measured on the bypassed aortic segment no longer track the pressure waveforms. There is still electrical activity, but no indication of any organized diameter changes occurring. One-second time marks are indicated at the top of each panel. Paper speed is indicated in the lower portion of each panel.*

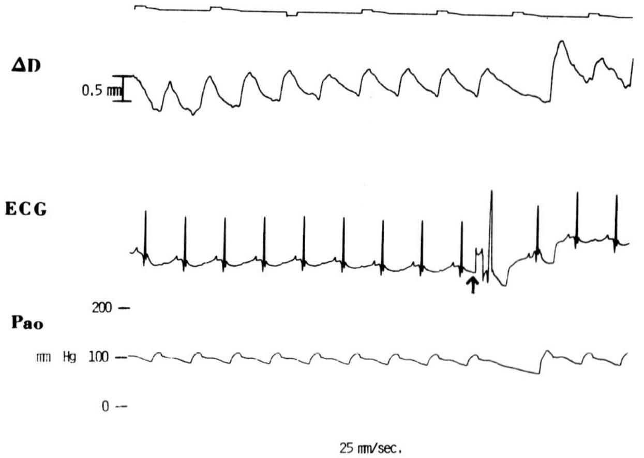

Figure 2. *Baseline recordings of ECG, change in aortic diameter (ΔD), and aortic pressure (Pao) from dog no. 4. A 1-mV stimulus (arrow) is applied to the right atrial appendage. Note that the impulse causing the deflection on the electrocardiogram is not accompanied by a corresponding change in aortic diameter. This observation suggests that electrical impulses from the heart do not control aortic contractility.*

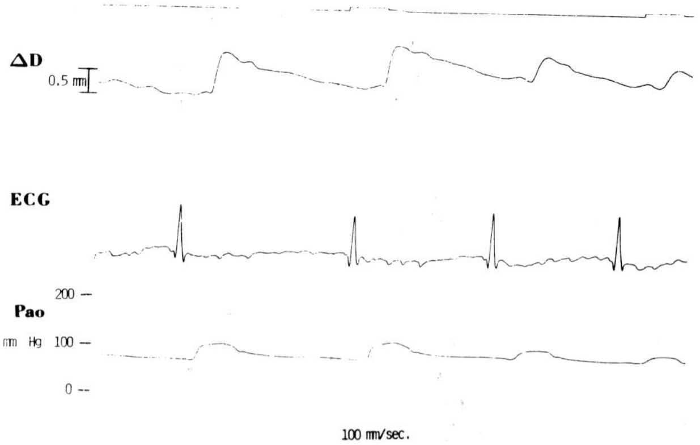

Figure 3. *Atrial fibrillation induced by mechanical stimulation of the right atrial appendage of dog no. 4 after sensitizing that area with 1 ml of methacholine (1 mg/ml). Change in aortic diameter (ΔD) is associated in a one-to-one relationship with the aortic pressure (Pao) waveform and not the intermittent F-waves on the electrocardiogram (ECG). This evidence suggests that there are no rhythmic aortic contractions controlled by electrical activity originating in the atria. Baseline recordings from this same dog are shown in Figure 2. The pressure waveform is recorded from a high-fidelity catheter-tipped manometer, but there may be some electronic "noise" in the diameter signal in this figure.*

had been completed, all animals were killed with an overdose of barbiturate.

Results

Bypass Experiment

Figure 1A shows baseline recordings of Pao, Pbp (before opening the bypass), ECG, and ΔD from dog no. 1. The aortic diameter changes coincided with the aortic pressure waveforms. Figure 1B shows representative recordings of Pao, Pbp, ECG, and ΔD after the bypass had been opened. No well-defined rhythmic aortic contractile activity, in synchrony with the pressure waves, was apparent. Although slight changes in aortic dimensions were recorded, these changes in the bypassed segment were attributed to movement transmitted by means of the direct tethering of the heart to the aorta. It was possible to detect visually this beat-by-beat movement during the experiment. The tethering of the perivascular connective tissue and the aortic side branches also played a role in the character of the movement seen. There was some baseline shifting of the ECG and ΔD signals, as shown in Figure 1B, due to positive pressure ventilation. Note the decrease in aortic pressure associated with the opening of the bypass. In Figure 1A, before the bypass was opened, there was no pressure in the bypass (Pbp); after it was opened, the pressure waveform was seen.

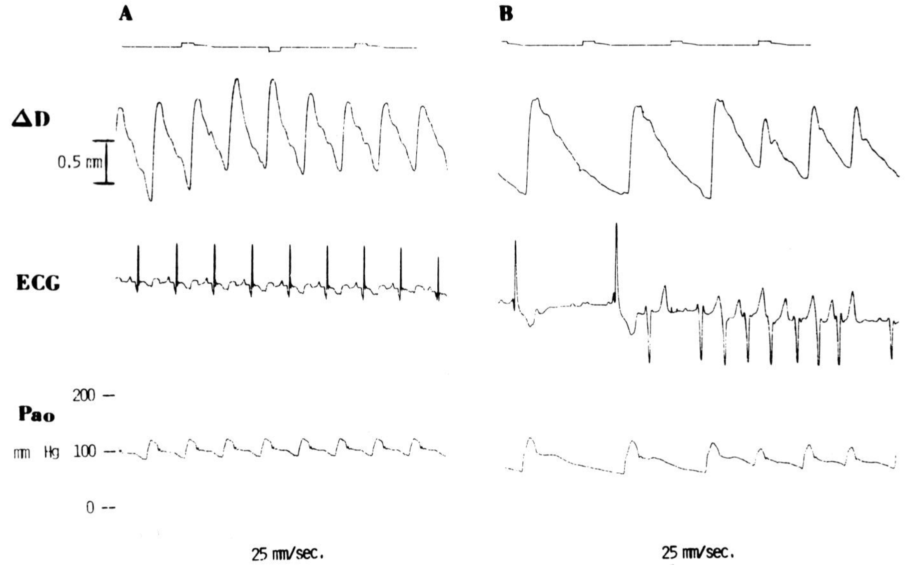

Figure 4. *Panel A: baseline recordings of ΔD, ECG, and Pao for dog no. 5. Panel B: ventricular tachycardia induced as a rebound phenomena following a bolus intravenous injection of acetylcholine (0.025 mg/kg) in the same dog. The character of the ΔD waveform is apparently determined by the pulse pressure, some tethering effects, and the viscoelastic nature of the aorta.*

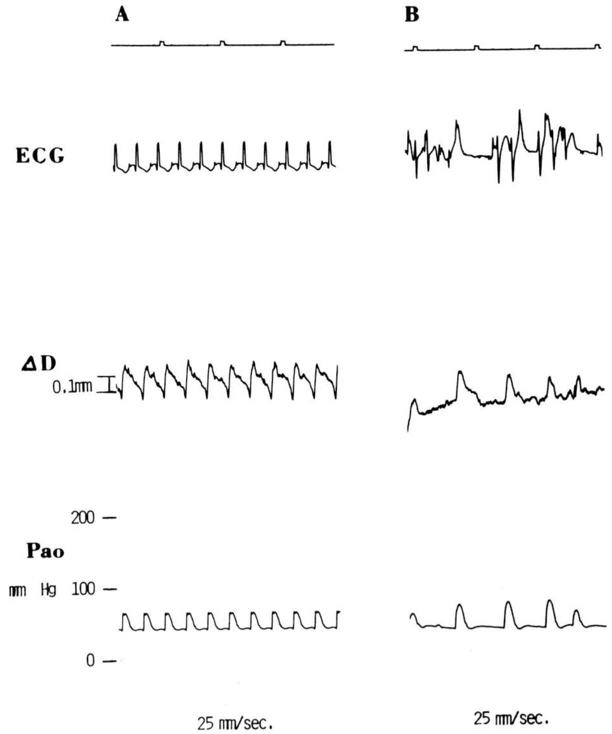

FIGURE 5. *Ventricular tachycardia in rabbit no. 4. Essentially the same response is seen in the dog illustrated in Figure 4. Baseline recordings are seen in panel A, and the response to mechanical stimulation of the left ventricle is shown in panel B. ECG is a bipolar lead with the positive electrode on the left atrial appendage.*

Atrial Stimulation

Figure 2 illustrates baseline measurements of ΔD, ECG, and Pao from dog 4. Application of a 1-mV stimulus to the right atrial appendage produced a deflection that registered on the ECG. There was no corresponding deflection in the ΔD. Transmission of any electrical signal originating on or near the heart would be expected to follow the same pathway to the aorta as an impulse originating in the SA

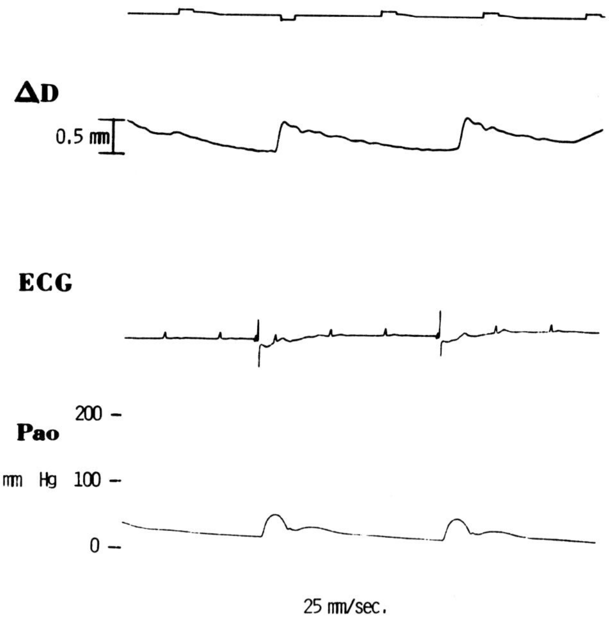

FIGURE 7. *Complete atrioventricular conduction block induced in dog no. 4 with 10% buffered neutral formalin injected into the interventricular septum. Changes in aortic diameter (ΔD) track the aortic pressure (Pao) waveforms and not the P-waves recorded on the ECG. This demonstrates that ΔD is unrelated to the electrical activity generated by the sinoatrial node, since the P-waves are not associated with corresponding deflections in ΔD. Baseline recordings from this dog are shown in Figure 3.*

node. If the SA node stimulus resulted in an aortic contraction, we would expect a response to the stimulus in the ΔD recordings. Similar negative results were obtained with 0.5- and 2-mV single stimuli.

Arrhythmia Production

The experiments conducted in this series were designed to demonstrate the effects of various induced arrhythmias on the relationships between

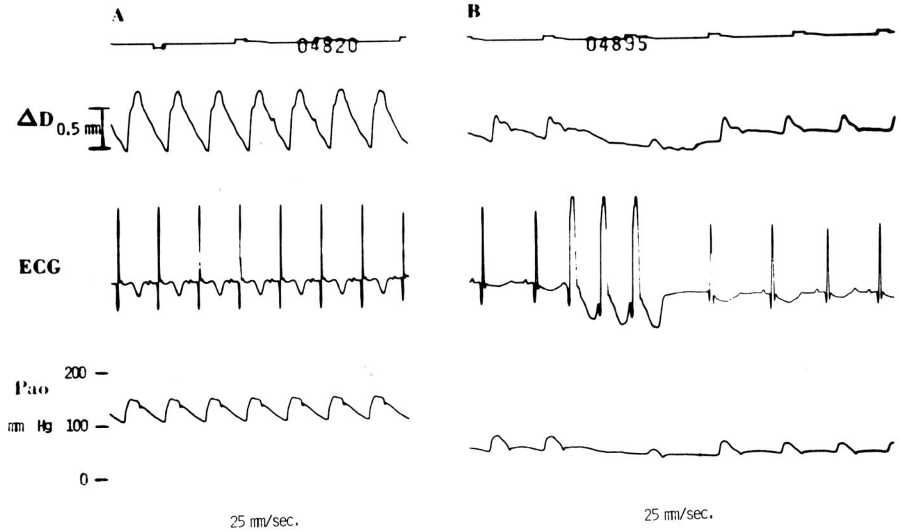

FIGURE 6. *Panel A: baseline recordings for dog no. 6. Panel B: premature ventricular contractions induced by injecting 0.2 ml of 10% buffered neutral formalin into the interventricular septum. The impulses causing the premature contractions do not stimulate aortic contractions. The change in diameter (ΔD) corresponds only to the Pao waveform, not to the ECG.*

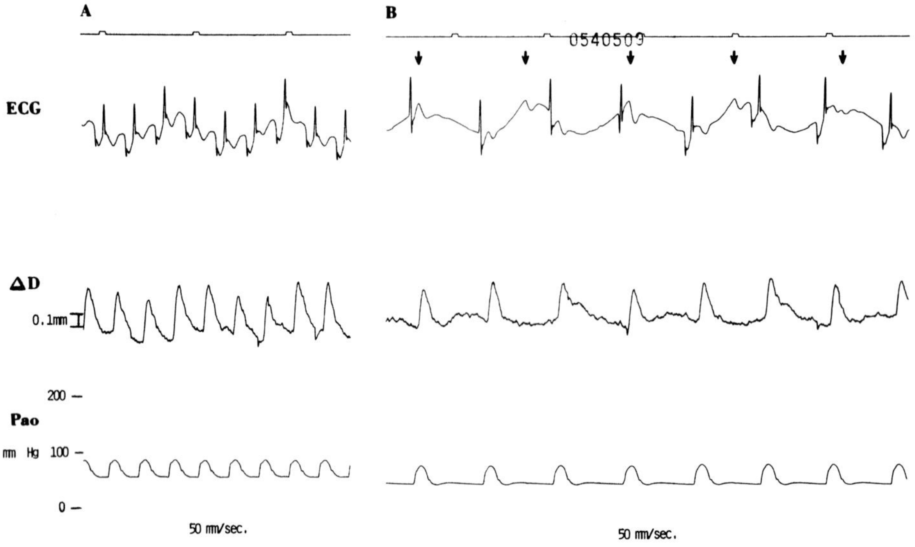

FIGURE 8. *Complete atrioventricular conduction block induced in rabbit no. 5 with a formalin injection into the AV node area. ECG is a bipolar lead with the positive electrode on the left atrial appendage. Note that the SA node rate (arrows indicate P-waves) is slower than the ventricular rate, but that Pao and ΔD are correlated with the ventricular contractions. Baseline recordings are seen in panel A, and AV block in panel B.*

ΔD, Pao, and the ECG. Figure 3 illustrates atrial fibrillation induced by mechanical stimulation of a methacholine-sensitized atrium (dog 4). Although there is no SA node activity, there are F-waves with the same amplitude as P-waves. The change in diameter corresponded to the aortic pressure waveform, not to any electrical activity from the atria; i.e., there was no correlation with the F-waves on the ECG.

Ventricular tachycardia, during the rebound period following the intravenous injection of acetylcholine, provided another example of the independence of ΔD from cardiac electrical activity (Fig. 4B). The ΔD is associated with only the Pao, not with electrical activity from the heart. Figure 4A shows the baseline values for this dog (no. 5). Figure 5 shows the same response to ventricular tachycardia seen in rabbit no. 4 after mechanical stimulation.

The recordings in Figure 6B (dog 6) demonstrate a definite lack of synchronicity between ventricular electrical activity of multifocal origin and the change in aortic diameter. Figure 6A shows baseline recordings from the same dog. Similar results were seen in two other dogs and two rabbits following intramyocardial formalin injections. In all five cases, the electrical activity generated by the heart had no apparent effect on the obviously pressure-dependent ΔD.

Representative recordings of a complete atrioventricular (AV) conduction block are shown in Figures 7 (dog no. 4) and 8 (rabbit no. 5). Again, there was no evidence of SA node-controlled rhythmic aortic contractile activity. Baseline values for dog no. 4 can be seen in Figure 3. In all cases of complete AV block (three dogs and two rabbits), ΔD was associated with the pressure waveform, not the P-wave.

Discussion

On the basis of these findings, we conclude that there is no SA node-controlled, active, beat-by-beat component of aortic mechanical behavior in dogs or rabbits. Peterson et al. (1960) found no evidence suggesting that the arteries undergo active contraction synchronous with the cardiac cycle. As they point out, such behavior would require a peculiar type of diastolic relaxation not in agreement with available data on temporal behavior of vascular smooth muscle. While doing these experiments, it was obvious to us that the large conduit blood vessels are well tethered to the beating heart and, with each heart beat, there was gross movement, especially in the longitudinal direction, separate from the diameter and longitudinal segment length movements associated with the pressure pulse. Any longitudinal movement of this nature would be translated into a dimension change in the experimental setup used by Mangel et al. (1982).

If there is beat-to-beat contraction of the aorta, it obviously is not stimulated by electrical signals starting at the SA node or other locations in the atria or ventricles. Figures 1–8 offer substantial documentation against this hypothesis.

Special thanks to E. Grazioli, C. Van, and T. Cooper for their constant cheerfulness in the face of never-ending revisions.

This work was supported, in part, by the Center for Comparative Medicine, Texas A&M University, and by National Institutes of Health Grant CA33531.

Address for reprints: D.R. Gross, D.V.M., Ph.D., Department of Veterinary Physiology and Pharmacology, College of Veterinary Medicine, Texas A&M University, College Station, Texas 77843.

Received August 16, 1984; accepted for publication January 25, 1985.

References

Bergel DH (1961a) The static elastic properties of the arterial wall. J Physiol (Lond) **156:** 445–457

Bergel DH (1961b) The dynamic elastic properties of the arterial wall. J Physiol (Lond) **156:** 458–469

Biamino G, Kruckenberg P (1969) Synchronization and conduction of excitation in the rat aorta. Am J Physiol **217:** 376–382

Colantuoni A, Bertuglia S, Intaglietta M (1984) Quantitation of rhythmic diameter changes in arterial microcirculation. Am J Physiol **246:** H508–H517

Cox RH (1975) Pressure dependence of the mechanical properties of arteries in vivo. Am J Physiol **229:** 1371–1375

Cox RH (1982) Mechanical properties of the coronary vascular wall and the contractile process. *In* The Coronary Artery, edited by Stanley Kalsner. New York, Oxford University Press, pp 59–90

D'Agrosa LS (1970) Patterns of venous vasomotion in the bat wing. Am J Physiol **218:** 530–535

Dobrin PB (1978) Mechanical properties of arteries. Physiol Rev **58:** 397–460

Fung YC, Fronek K, Patitucci P (1979) Pseudoelasticity of arteries and the choice of its mathematical expression. Am J Physiol **237:** H620–H631

Gow BS (1972) The influence of vascular smooth muscle on the viscoelastic properties of blood vessels. *In* Cardiovascular Fluid Dynamics, vol 2, edited by DH Bergel. London, Academic Press, pp 65–110

Gross DR, Hunter JF, Allert JA (1981) Pressure-diameter relationships in the coronary artery of intact, awake calves. J Biomech **14:** 613–620

Guzman SV, DeLeon AC, West JW, Bellet S (1959) Cardiac effects of isoproterenol, norepinephrine and epinephrine in complete A-V heart block during experimental acidosis and hyperkalemia. Circ Res **7:** 666–671

Hermsmeyer K (1979) Twitch-like contractions of isolated single arterial muscle cells. Fed Proc **38:** 1243

Johansson B, Bohr DF (1966) Rhythmic activity in smooth muscle from small subcutaneous arteries. Am J Physiol **210:** 801–806

Mangel A, Fahim M, Van Breeman C (1982) Control of vascular contractility by the cardiac pacemaker. Science **215:** 1627–1629

Nakajima A, Horn L (1967) Electrical activity of single vascular smooth muscle fibers. Am J Physiol **213:** 25–30

Nicoll PA, Webb RL (1955) Vascular patterns and active vasomotion as determiners of flow through minute vessels. Angiology **64:** 291–308

Patel DJ, Vaishnav RN (1972) The rheology of large blood vessels. *In* Cardiovascular Fluid Dynamics, vol 2, edited by DH Bergel. London, Academic Press, pp 1–64

Peterson LH, Jensen RE, Parnell J (1960) Mechanical properties of arteries in vivo. Circ Res **8:** 622–639

Stein PG, Driska SP (1984) Histamine-induced rhythmic contraction of hog carotid artery smooth muscle. Circ Res **55:** 480–485

Steiner C, Kovalik TW (1968) A simple technique for production of chronic complete heart block in dogs. J Appl Physiol **25:** 631–632

INDEX TERMS: Vascular rheology • Vascular viscoelasticity • Mechanical behavior • Aortic mechanics

The Effects of Antiarrhythmic Drugs, Stimulation Frequency, and Potassium-Induced Resting Membrane Potential Changes on Conduction Velocity and dV/dt_{max} in Guinea Pig Myocardium

Jack W Buchanan, Jr., Tomoaki Saito, and Leonard S. Gettes

From the Department of Medicine, University of North Carolina at Chapel Hill, Chapel Hill, North Carolina

SUMMARY. For one-dimensional propagation, a nonlinear relationship between $\dot{V}_{max}$ and conduction velocity is predicted by cable theory, and, under experimental conditions, $\dot{V}_{max}$ and conduction velocity may change in opposite directions. Using standard microelectrode techniques, we have measured $\dot{V}_{max}$ and conduction velocity in guinea pig papillary muscles exposed to tetrodotoxin and low sodium (agents expected primarily to decrease, directly, the rapid inward current), increased extracellular potassium (an agent which decreases the rapid inward current at least partially by inactivation mediated by depolarization of the resting membrane potential), and, over a wide range of stimulation frequencies, the antiarrhythmic drugs, quinidine, lidocaine, and procainamide. In all cases, except for the region of potassium-induced "supernormal conduction" between 5.4 and 9 mM, $\dot{V}_{max}$ and conduction velocity varied as predicted by one-dimensional cable theory; that is, changes in $\dot{V}_{max}$ were always proportional to changes in the square of conduction velocity. We conclude that the relationship between $\dot{V}_{max}$ and conduction velocity predicted by cable theory occurs experimentally in guinea pig papillary muscle subjected to commonly used antiarrhythmic drugs and other interventions expected to reduce the sodium inward current. This relationship may be useful in applying known effects of drugs on $\dot{V}_{max}$ to action potential propagation. **(*Circ Res 56: 696–703, 1985*)**

A MAJOR factor affecting the propagation of the cardiac impulse is the magnitude of the rapid sodium-dependent inward current. A decrease in this current would be expected to decrease both the maximum rate of rise of the action potential upstroke ($\dot{V}_{max}$) and conduction velocity. Because $\dot{V}_{max}$ can be measured under conditions of action potential propagation, models for the effects of agents modifying the sodium current have been constructed which utilize the known effects of these agents on $\dot{V}_{max}$. In addition, it has been assumed that the effects of antiarrhythmic drugs on conduction correlate directly with their effects on $\dot{V}_{max}$. In spite of these assumptions, it appears likely that neither the relationship between the sodium current and $\dot{V}_{max}$ (Cohen and Strichartz, 1977; Bean et al., 1982, 1983; Cohen et al., 1984) nor the relationship between $\dot{V}_{max}$ and conduction velocity (Hunter et al., 1975, Buchanan et al., 1982; Walton and Fozzard, 1983a, 1983b) is linear. There are even examples of conduction velocity increases in the presence of a decrease in $\dot{V}_{max}$ (Dominguez and Fozzard, 1970; Spear and Moore, 1974; Peon et al., 1978; Saito et al., 1978).

The cable equation for constant conduction velocity is

$$\frac{a}{2R_i\theta^2}\frac{d^2V}{dt^2} = C\frac{dV}{dt} + I_i,$$

where a is the radius, R_i is the specific resistivity of the intracellular fluid, θ is conduction velocity, V is the membrane potential, C is the membrane capacitance per unit area, I_i represents the sum of the instantaneous ionic currents per unit area of membrane, and t represents time. Although this equation must generally be solved numerically, a number of investigators have found that dV/dt varies approximately as θ^2, particularly for mathematical simulations which result in variations of the rapid sodium inward current (Hunter et al., 1975; Jack et al., 1975; Walton and Fozzard, 1983b).

The purpose of the present study was to determine whether commonly used antiarrhythmic drugs altered $\dot{V}_{max}$ and conduction velocity in ventricular muscle in a predictable fashion. To be more certain that the observed changes in $\dot{V}_{max}$ and conduction were mediated by changes in the sodium inward current, and were not just a fortuitous combination of other factors, we varied the sodium current by other well-established mechanisms, including blockade with tetrodotoxin, changing the chemical gradient for sodium by decreasing extracellular sodium concentration, and changing the electrical driving force for the rapid sodium-dependent inward current by depolarization with potassium.

We utilized guinea pig papillary muscles because suitably selected preparations have demonstrated one-dimensional propagation (Weidmann, 1970;

Spach et al., 1981; Buchanan, et al., 1983; Veenstra, et al., 1984). We then compared our results to those predicted from one-dimensional cable theory, i.e., that $\dot{V}_{max}$ should be proportional to the square of conduction velocity. We hoped that these studies would enhance our understanding of the changes in propagation caused by antiarrhythmic drugs and other agents which directly affect the sodium inward current, and would provide data useful in refining mathematical models of action potential propagation.

Portions of these results have been presented in abstract form (Saito et al., 1978; Buchanan et al., 1982; Buchanan and Gettes, 1983).

Methods

Guinea pig right ventricular papillary muscles were placed in a 3-ml chamber and superfused (2.5–3.0 ml/min) with control Tyrode's solution containing (mM) NaCl, 137; KCl, 5.4; $CaCl_2$, 1.8; $MgCl_2$, 1.05; $NaHCO_3$, 24.0; NaH_2PO_4, 0.42; and glucose, 5.0. The solution was gassed with 95% O_2 and 5% CO_2, the pH maintained between 7.35 and 7.4, and the bath temperature maintained at 37° ± 0.5°C. Suitable fibers were characterized by a lack of visible branching, by a diameter of 1.5 mm or less, and by a length at least 5 times the diameter. In most experiments, bipolar silver/silver chloride electrodes were used to stimulate the preparation at the cut end. In a few experiments, stimulation was obtained with a bipolar KCl-filled glass macroelectrode constructed by fusing two pieces of 1-mm glass tubing, pulled slightly by hand over a flame. A silver wire then was inserted into the shank of each pole of the electrode and chlorided. The type of stimulation electrode used appeared to have no effect on the results. Two separate microelectrode impalements were made in a line along the long axis of the preparation, and a common reference electrode was used. The signals obtained were amplified by negative capacitance compensation amplifiers (WP Instruments M-707 or Transidyne MPA-6), displayed on a storage oscilloscope (Tektronix 5113), and photographed by a Polaroid camera. Capacitance compensation was adjusted to provide the best reproduction of a 10-mV square wave attached to the input with the electrodes in the bath. In most cases, this corresponded to the maximum compensation which could be obtained without inducing oscillation. The signals were also sent to identical electronic differentiators which produced a linear response to beyond 500 V/sec. Conduction time was defined as the time between the peaks of the differentiated upstroke signals. We required that both impalements be maintained throughout an intervention and its control, in order to avoid inaccuracies in the measurement of interelectrode distance. Pilot studies showed that 10–15 minutes of exposure were necessary to obtain steady state conditions. Thus, all data reported were obtained at least 20 minutes after any change of the superfusing solution. In most cases, the time interval was greater than 30 minutes. In separate experiments, the following interventions were made: (1) various concentrations of tetrodotoxin ($n = 5$), (2) decreased extracellular sodium (substituted with tetramethylammonium chloride) ($n = 2$), (3) varying extracellular potassium ($n = 16$), (4) various concentrations of lidocaine ($n = 6$), (5) various concentrations of quinidine ($n = 4$), and (6) various concentrations of procainamide ($n = 3$).

The potassium variation was obtained by adding measured amounts from a 500 mM KCl/Tyrodes' stock solution to the perfusate. Osmotic compensation was not attempted. In two quinidine experiments, in two lidocaine experiments, and in two procainamide experiments, the stimulation frequency was varied between 0.1 and either 5 or 8 Hz at each drug concentration. In the experiments in which stimulation frequency was not varied, the driving rate was 0.5 Hz.

Presentation of Data and Statistics

For each experiment and group of experiments, $\dot{V}_{max}$ and the square of conduction velocity were normalized to their values at the slowest stimulation frequency tested during perfusion with the control solution. In each figure, the solid line represents the relationship that would be obtained were $\dot{V}_{max}$ proportional to the square of conduction velocity. The normalized results were plotted and a linear regression was performed. In addition, a *t*-test was performed to test the confidence with which each set of points actually describes the regression line obtained. Although Figures 6–8 show multiple panels for clarity, linear

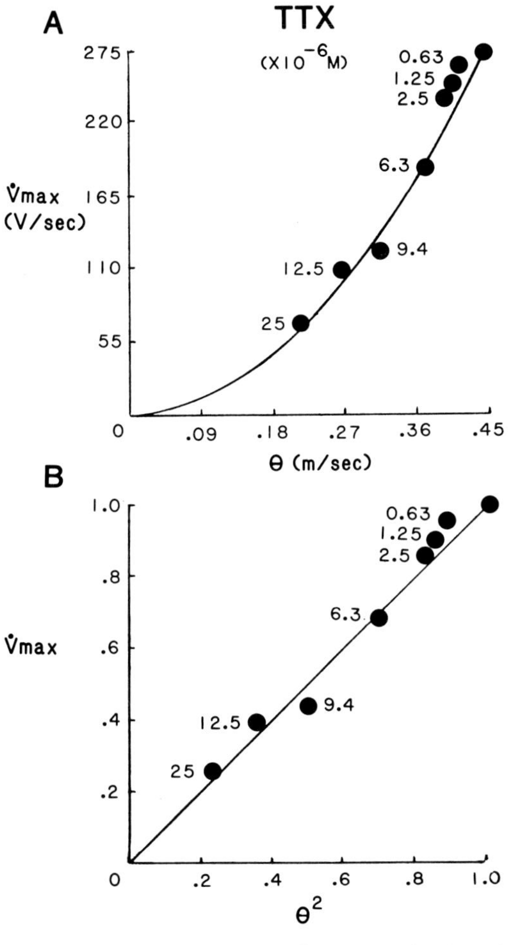

FIGURE 1. *The effect of tetrodotoxin on $\dot{V}_{max}$ and conduction velocity. Panel A shows a plot of the raw data from a single experiment. In panel B, and in the following figures, the data are normalized to control conditions, and $\dot{V}_{max}$ (ordinate) is plotted against the square of conduction velocity (abscissa). As can be seen, the results are well fit by the relationship that $\dot{V}_{max}$ is proportional to the square of conduction velocity (intercept 0.08, slope 0.98, r 0.992, $P < 0.001$).*

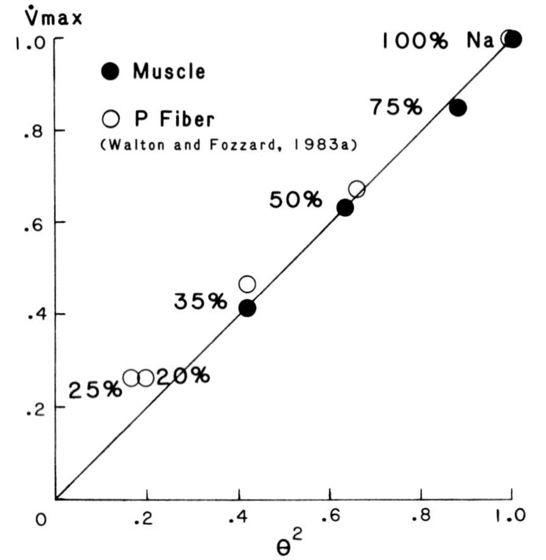

FIGURE 2. *The effect of decreased extracellular sodium on $\dot{V}_{max}$ and conduction velocity in guinea pig papillary muscle (closed circles). Also shown (open circles) is our plot of the mean results from five similar experiments in sheep Purkinje fibers reported by Walton and Fozzard (1983a). As can be seen, both in sheep Purkinje fibers (intercept 0.09, slope 0.909, r 0.999, $P < 0.001$) and in guinea pig ventricular muscle (intercept −0.04, slope 1.04, r 0.999, $P < 0.001$), lowering extracellular sodium concentration produces the relationship that $\dot{V}_{max}$ is proportional to the square of conduction velocity.*

regression was performed using all the data points in each figure. The slope, intercept, *r* value, and *P* value for these lines are given in the figure legends. In the ideal case, the intercept would be 0, and the slope and *r* value would be 1.

Results

Effects of Tetrodotoxin and Decreased Extracellular Sodium Concentration on $\dot{V}_{max}$ and Conduction Velocity

Figure 1 shows the effect of various concentrations of the sodium channel blocker, tetrodotoxin, on $\dot{V}_{max}$ and conduction. In panel A, $\dot{V}_{max}$ is plotted against conduction velocity, obtained by dividing the interelectrode spacing in millimeters by the conduction time in milliseconds. In panel B, and in subsequent figures, $\dot{V}_{max}$ and conduction velocity are normalized to the values obtained under control conditions, and the square of conduction velocity is plotted on the abscissa. In this and the following figures, the solid line represents the relationship which would be obtained if $\dot{V}_{max}$ were proportional to the square of conduction velocity. The figure shows that tetrodotoxin induces changes in $\dot{V}_{max}$ which are proportional to the square of the changes in conduction velocity. Similar results were obtained in three other experiments.

Figure 2 shows the results of substituting tetramethylammonium chloride (Walton and Fozzard, 1983a), mole for mole for extracellular sodium, in order to decrease the sodium current by changing the transmembrane concentration gradient for sodium. Similar results were obtained in one other experiment. Also shown is our plot of mean data obtained by Walton and Fozzard (1983a, 1983b) when several similar experiments were performed with sheep Purkinje fibers. The data for each intervention are well represented by the relationship that changes in $\dot{V}_{max}$ are proportional to the square of changes in conduction velocity.

Effects of Variations in Extracellular Potassium on $\dot{V}_{max}$ and Conduction Velocity

Table 1 shows the average results of 16 experiments in which $\dot{V}_{max}$ and conduction velocity were measured as extracellular potassium was raised in steps from 5.4–15 mM, and lowered to 2.0 mM. Figure 3 shows the results from a typical experiment. In panel A, data are normalized to 5.4 mM potassium. Increasing potassium first speeds, then slows, conduction, in spite of a consistent decrease in $\dot{V}_{max}$. In panel B, when the data are normalized to the point of maximum conduction velocity (8 mM potassium), values obtained from 8–15 mM are in excellent agreement with the relationship of $\dot{V}_{max}$ proportional to the square of conduction velocity. As has been shown previously (Gettes et al., 1985), similar results are seen when the average data from all 16 experiments are used (intercept 0.016, slope 1.03, *r* 0.958, $P < 0.001$). In the experiment shown in Figure 4, conduction velocity and $\dot{V}_{max}$ were first measured

TABLE 1
Effects of Potassium on $\dot{V}_{max}$ and Conduction Velocity in Guinea Pig Papillary Muscles

Potassium (mM)	*n*	RMP (mV)	$\dot{V}_{max}$ (V/sec)	$\dot{V}_{max}$ (%)	Conduction velocity (%)
2.0	4	−99.6 ± 2.3	273.0 ± 29.6	98.7 ± 1.5	88.0 ± 3.1
5.4	16	−86.2 ± 1.8	277.5 ± 35.0	100	100
7	7	−80.4 ± 2.1	276.7 ± 27.6	99.7 ± 2.1	105.9 ± 5.5
8	5	−76.7 ± 2.4	248.2 ± 45.0	89.4 ± 3.3	113.7 ± 6.8
9	7	−72.8 ± 1.9	247.4 ± 22.3	89.2 ± 5.0	107.5 ± 5.1
10	7	−71.1 ± 3.0	223.0 ± 46.9	80.3 ± 6.8	107.3 ± 4.3
11	6	−68.4 ± 1.6	198.7 ± 20.0	71.6 ± 6.6	104.6 ± 4.7
12	5	−64.8 ± 2.8	173.2 ± 11.7	62.4 ± 6.2	90.8 ± 2.4
13	2	−62.4	157.1	56.6	81.5
15	3	−57.1 ± 1.9	65.2 ± 16.8	23.5 ± 1.4	66.1 ± 9.7

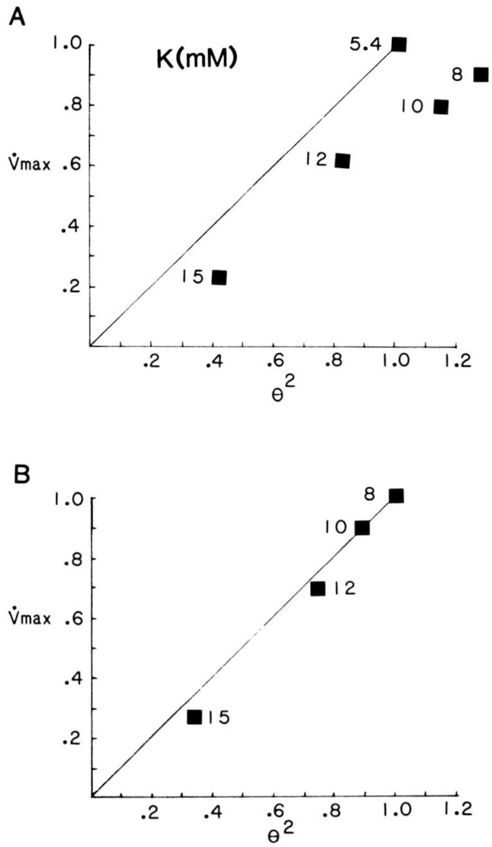

Figure 3. *The effects of various concentrations of extracellular potassium on* $\dot{V}_{max}$ *and conduction velocity in guinea pig papillary muscle. In this figure from a single experiment, as well as in the average data (Table 1), the effect of increasing potassium to increase conduction velocity in spite of a constant decrease in* $\dot{V}_{max}$ *is clearly seen (panel A). When the data are normalized to 8 mM potassium (panel B), further elevations in potassium produce the predicted changes in* $\dot{V}_{max}$ *and conduction velocity.*

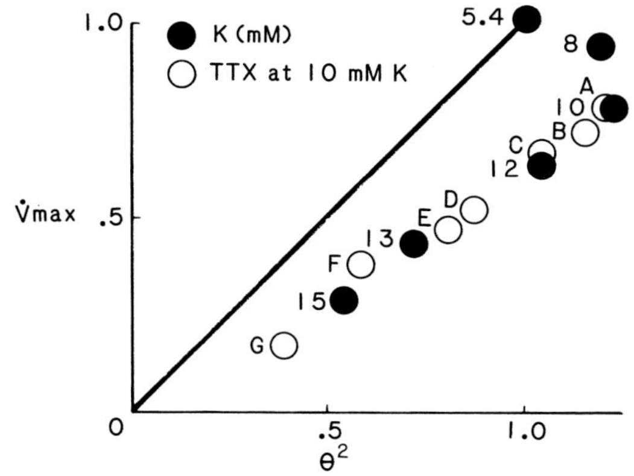

Figure 4. *Comparison of the effects of increased potassium and progressively increasing tetrodotoxin concentrations at 10 mM potassium. Points A–G represent tetrodotoxin levels of 0, 0.625, 1.25, 2.5, 3.75, 6.25, and 12.5 micromolar at 10 mM potassium. Note that increasing extracellular potassium concentration above 10 mM or adding tetrodotoxin at 10 mM potassium produces similar changes in* $\dot{V}_{max}$ *and conduction velocity.*

at six potassium levels between 5.4 and 15 mM. The extracellular potassium was then maintained at 10 mM, and six concentrations of tetrodotoxin were added to the test solution (points (B–G). The figure shows that the changes in $\dot{V}_{max}$ and conduction velocity fit the predicted relationship in both situations.

Effects of Various Concentrations of Antiarrhythmic Drugs on $\dot{V}_{max}$ and Conduction Velocity

Figure 5 shows the effects of various concentrations of quinidine and lidocaine on $\dot{V}_{max}$ and conduction velocity at a constant stimulation frequency of 0.5 Hz. Within the range tested, increasing concentrations of these drugs produce changes in $\dot{V}_{max}$ and conduction velocity which fit the predicted relationship.

Figures 6, 7, and 8 show the effects of several concentrations of lidocaine, quinidine, and procainamide, respectively, on $\dot{V}_{max}$ and the square of conduction velocity over a wide range of stimulation frequencies. Within each figure, all data are normalized to 0.1 Hz without drug. Each concentration of drug is displayed in a separate panel for clarity. The figures show that the changes in $\dot{V}_{max}$ are proportional to the square of changes in conduction velocity for all drugs at all tested stimulation frequencies. Similar results were obtained in each of two other experiments, for lidocaine and quinidine, and in one other experiment for procainamide, where both stimulation frequency and drug concentration were varied.

Discussion

It is generally accepted that, in tissues in which the rapid sodium inward current predominates, a decrease in this current will lead to some decrease in the maximum rate of rise of the action potential upstroke ($\dot{V}_{max}$), and, although this relationship may not be linear (Cohen and Strichartz, 1977; Bean et al., 1982, 1983; Cohen et al., 1984), the effects on $\dot{V}_{max}$ of agents that block the sodium inward current have been used to construct models of drug action (Hondeghem and Katzung, 1977, 1980). Whereas there has been a tacit assumption that decreases in $\dot{V}_{max}$ relate to decreases in conduction velocity, this relationship also need not be linear, and, in fact, experimental evidence (Walton and Fozzard 1983a, 1983b), as well as conventional cable theory (Hunter et al., 1975; Jack et al., 1975), predict that it is not. In addition, effects such as "supernormal conduction," which has been observed in the presence of a decrease in $\dot{V}_{max}$ (Dominguez and Fozzard, 1970; Spear and Moore, 1974), demonstrate that, under some circumstances, there is not a direct relationship between $\dot{V}_{max}$ and conduction velocity.

One-dimensional cable theory predicts that $\dot{V}_{max}$ should be approximately proportional to the square of conduction velocity (Hunter et al., 1975; Walton

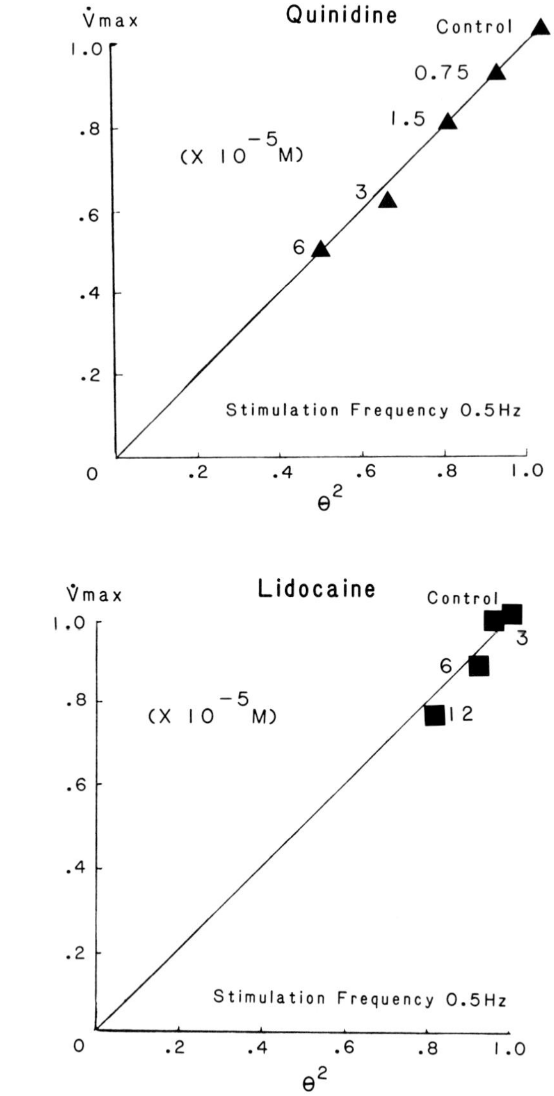

FIGURE 5. *Effects of four concentrations of quinidine and three concentrations of lidocaine on $\dot{V}_{max}$ and conduction velocity measured at a stimulation frequency of 0.5 Hz. Note that changes in $\dot{V}_{max}$ and conduction velocity are consistent with the predicted relationship (for quinidine: intercept −0.06, slope 1.08, r 0.991, P < 0.001; for lidocaine: intercept −0.11, slope 1.13, r 0.978, P < 0.001).*

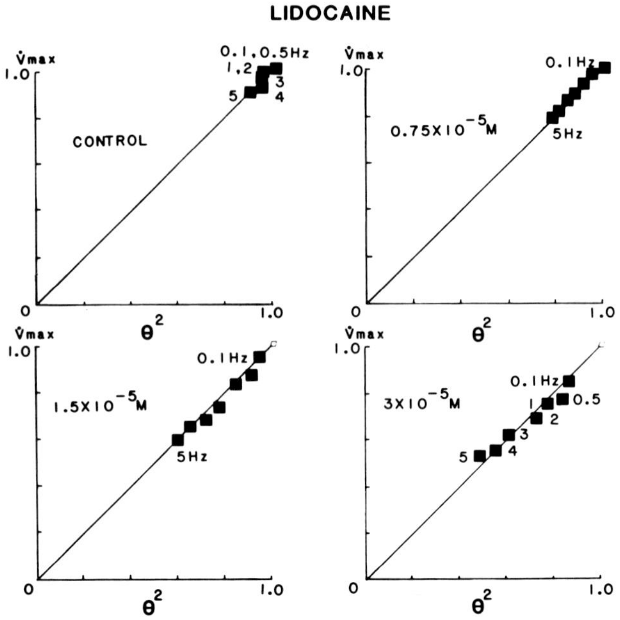

FIGURE 6. *Stimulus frequency-dependent effects of three concentrations of lidocaine on $\dot{V}_{max}$ and conduction velocity. All panels are normalized to 0.1 Hz without drug. Although both frequency-dependent and steady state effects of lidocaine are seen, all changes are consistent with the prediction that $\dot{V}_{max}$ is proportional to the square of conduction velocity (intercept 0.020, slope 0.968, r 0.984, P < 0.001).*

and Fozzard, 1983b). Using a ventricular muscle preparation which can be considered to show one-dimensional propagation (Weidmann, 1970; Spach et al., 1981; Buchanan, et al., 1983; Veenstra et al., 1984), we found the decrease in $\dot{V}_{max}$ to be proportional to the square of the decrease in conduction velocity in the presence of tetrodotoxin, a known sodium channel-blocking agent. Varying the sodium current by a different mechanism (i.e., modification of the driving force for sodium by decreasing its extracellular concentration) causes changes in $\dot{V}_{max}$ and conduction which also fit the theoretical relationship, not only in muscle, but also in Purkinje fibers (Walton and Fozzard, 1983b).

We confirmed the biphasic relationship of increasing extracellular potassium to first accelerate and then slow conduction velocity in spite of a constant decrease in $\dot{V}_{max}$ (Kagiyama et al., 1982). However, beyond the point of maximum velocity, the cable theory-predicted relationship between $\dot{V}_{max}$ and con-

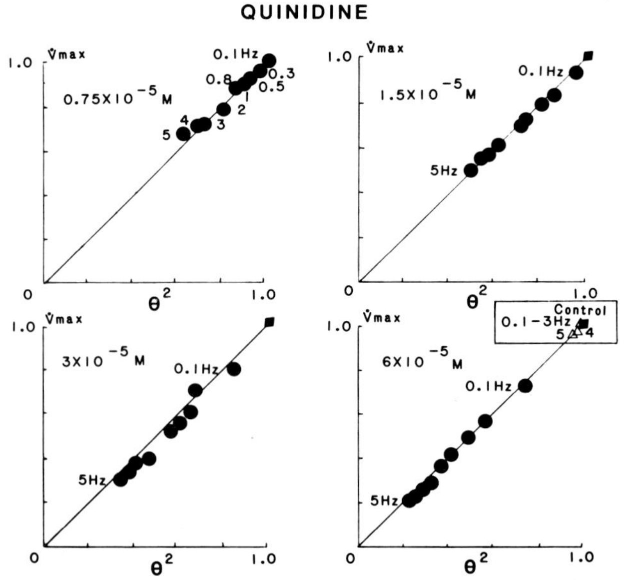

FIGURE 7. *Stimulus frequency-dependent effects of four concentrations of quinidine on $\dot{V}_{max}$ and conduction velocity. All panels are normalized to 0.1 Hz without drug, and the control is shown in the inset. Note that both steady state and stimulus frequency-dependent changes in $\dot{V}_{max}$ and conduction velocity are consistent with the predicted relationship (intercept −0.023, slope 1.02, r 0.996, P < 0.001).*

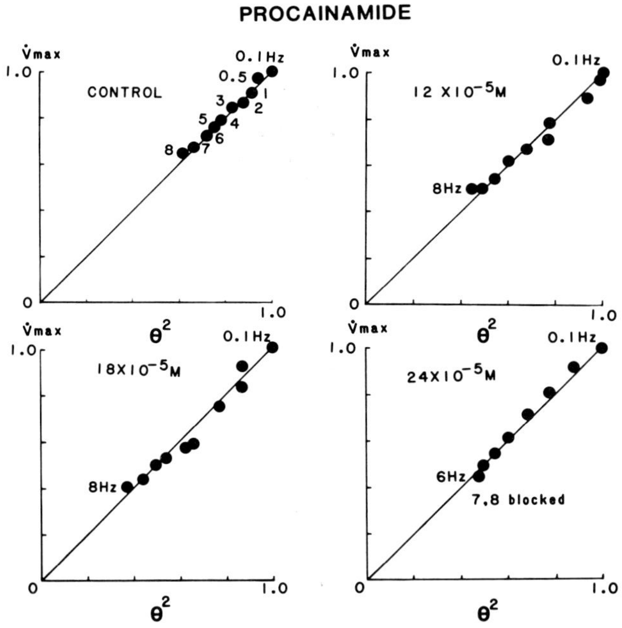

FIGURE 8. *Stimulus frequency-dependent effects of procainamide on $\dot{V}_{max}$ and conduction velocity. All panels are normalized to 0.1 Hz without drug. Note that, in spite of high drug concentrations, compared to the quinidine and lidocaine experiments, no change in $\dot{V}_{max}$ or conduction velocity was seen at the slowest stimulation frequency. Frequency-dependent effects are clearly seen. In all cases, the results are consistent with the relationship that $\dot{V}_{max}$ is proportional to the square of conduction velocity (intercept 0.014, slope 0.977, r 0.990, P < 0.001).*

duction velocity appears valid for increasing extracellular potassium. This effect is consistent with sodium current inactivation due to depolarization of the resting membrane potential, although the possibility that potassium has a direct effect on sodium channels (Kishida et al., 1979) cannot be ruled out. In either case, a direct action on the sodium inward current is likely to be present. The "supernormal" conduction seen at lower potassium concentrations does not fit the simple predicted relationship between $\dot{V}_{max}$ and conduction velocity. Although changes in cellular coupling could produce this effect, previous studies from our laboratory have shown little or no change in total internal longitudinal resistance over the pertinent potassium range. Dominguez and Fozzard (1970) postulated that potassium changes in this range cause a greater shift in resting membrane potential relative to threshold potential. Similar "supernormal conduction" seen when Purkinje fibers are depolarized during phase 3 (Spear and Moore, 1974; Peon et al., 1978) or phase 4 (Peon et al., 1978) are also most reasonably explained by this hypothesis. Using uniformly depolarized papillary muscle tips in a Vaseline gap (Imanishi and Surawicz, 1976), we have found relative changes in resting membrane potential and threshold potential similar to those postulated by the previous investigators (Gettes et al., 1985).

To determine, in addition, whether the effects of potassium above the region of supernormal conduction are consistent with a decrease in the sodium inward current, we compared the effects of potassium depolarization on $\dot{V}_{max}$ and conduction with those induced by tetrodotoxin, administered at the potassium level that showed the maximum conduction speeding. Under these conditions, the administration of either more potassium or TTX produced results consistent with the predicted relationship between $\dot{V}_{max}$ and conduction velocity.

Over the ranges tested, both the steady state (constant slow stimulation frequency) and stimulation frequency-dependent effects of lidocaine, quinidine, and procainamide are well fit by the relationship that changes in $\dot{V}_{max}$ are proportional to the square of changes in conduction velocity. Differences in the steady state and time (rate)-dependent characteristics of the individual drugs are seen in our results, and correspond to differences previously reported (Chen and Gettes, 1976; Hondeghem and Katzung, 1980).

As can be seen in the control panels of Figures 6–8, variations in stimulus frequency alone often caused variations in $\dot{V}_{max}$ and conduction velocity that appeared to fit the predicted relationship. Possible mechanisms for this effect include the time dependence of recovery from sodium current inactivation, a change in the electrical gradient due to slight membrane depolarization caused by an extracellular accumulation of potassium at rapid frequencies, or a change in the sodium concentration gradient due to the intracellular accumulation of sodium. In addition, it is quite possible that some of our interventions themselves result in the intracellular accumulation of sodium. All of these mechanisms involve direct modulation of the sodium inward current which would add to any effect of pharmacological channel blockade.

Models describing action potential propagation in one-dimensional cables have been constructed (Cooley and Dodge, 1966; Hunter et al., 1975; Sharp and Joyner, 1980), and progress is being made toward extending these models to realistic situations including three-dimensional propagation (Joyner et al., 1983). Since many of the assumptions inherent in these models have not been tested extensively, and some may be untestable by current experimental techniques, perhaps the results we have presented should be considered only as empirical observations of the effects of specific interventions on $\dot{V}_{max}$ and conduction velocity. On the other hand, even though we varied the sodium current by several different mechanisms, our results are well described by predictions of the most simple of models.

Recently, Walton and Fozzard (1983b) compared three different models for the action potential upstroke to their experimental observations concerning the effects of decreased extracellular sodium on action potential propagation in sheep Purkinje fibers. They found that the relationship between $\dot{V}_{max}$ and conduction velocity, as well as a number of other relationships, were model independent and arose from the cable theory relationships upon which all the models were based. Their results regarding $\dot{V}_{max}$ and conduction velocity are completely consistent with our own. The true complexity needed to adequately describe action potential propagation in various excitable tissues under the influence of important interventions will be determined only by further experimental observations and further mathematical simulations.

In spite of these unresolved theoretical considerations, our results indicate that, at least under the conditions of our experiments, information concerning the effects on action potential propagation in guinea pig papillary muscle of agents which primarily affect the sodium inward current can be inferred from a knowledge of the effects of these agents on $\dot{V}_{max}$, provided the squared relationship between the two is appreciated. Although the results of Bean et al. (1982, 1983) and Cohen et al. (1984) regarding the nonlinearity of the sodium current/$\dot{V}_{max}$ relationship were determined in rabbit Purkinje fibers at non-physiological temperatures, their results, combined with our own, may provide a useful qualitative model of the effect of sodium channel blockade on impulse propagation. If their results are ultimately shown to be correct for guinea pig papillary muscle under physiological conditions, an 80% reduction in available gNa would produce about a 35% reduction in $\dot{V}_{max}$ which would be associated with less than a 15% reduction in conduction velocity. An understanding of the $\dot{V}_{max}$/conduction velocity relationship, as well as the sodium channel/$\dot{V}_{max}$ relationship, may provide a link between models of sodium channel blockade at the cellular level and action potential propagation in cable-like structures and, ultimately, in the intact heart.

Supported by Grants P01 HL27430 and RO1 HL23624 from the National Heart, Lung, and Blood Institute, U.S. Public Health Service, and by a Grant-in-Aid from the North Carolina Affiliate, American Heart Association (JWB).

Address for reprints: Jack Buchanan, M.D., Division of Cardiology, University of North Carolina, 349 Clinical Sciences Bldg 229H, Chapel Hill, North Carolina 27514.

Received October 1, 1984; accepted for publication December 13, 1984.

References

Bean BP, Cohen CJ, Tsien RW (1982) Block of cardiac sodium channels by tetrodotoxin and lidocaine: Sodium current and $\dot{V}_{max}$ experiments. *In* Normal and Abnormal Conduction in the Heart. Biophysics Physiology, Pharmacology and Ultrastructure, edited by A Paes de Carvalho, BF Hoffman, M Lieberman. New York, Futura, pp 189–209

Bean BP, Cohen CJ, Tsien RM (1983) Lidocaine block of cardiac sodium channels. J Gen Physiol **81:** 613–642

Buchanan JW Jr, Gettes LS (1983) Steady state and rate dependent effects of antiarrhythmic drugs on $\dot{V}_{max}$ and conduction velocity in guinea pig papillary muscle (abstr). Circulation **68:** (suppl III): 295

Buchanan JW Jr, Saito T, Kagiyama Y, Hill JL, Gettes LS (1982) The relationship between upstroke velocity and conduction in guinea pig myocardium (abstr). Am J Cardiol **49:** 983

Chen CM, Gettes LS (1976) Combined effects of rate, membrane potential, and drugs on maximum rate of rise ($\dot{V}_{max}$) of action potential upstroke of guinea pig papillary muscle. Circ Res **38:** 464–469

Cohen CJ, Bean BP, Tsien RW (1984) Maximal upstroke velocity as an index of available sodium conductance: Comparison of maximal upstroke velocity and voltage clamp measurements of sodium current in rabbit Purkinje fibers. Circ Res **54:** 636–651

Cohen IS, Strichartz GR (1977) On the voltage-dependent action of tetrodotoxin. Biophys J **17:** 275–279

Cooley JW, Dodge FA Jr (1966) Digital computer solutions for excitation and propagation of the nerve impulse. Biophys J **6:** 583–599

Dominguez G, Fozzard HA (1970) Influence of extracellular K^+ concentration on cable properties and excitability of sheep cardiac Purkinje fibers. Circ Res **26:** 565–574

Geselowitz DB, Barr RC, Spach MS, Miller WT III (1982) The impact of adjacent isotropic fluids on electrograms from anisotropic cardiac muscle. Circ Res **51:** 602–613

Gettes LS, Buchanan JW Jr, Saito T, Kagiyama Y, Oshita S, Fujino T (1985) Studies concerned with slow conduction. *In* Cardiac Electrophysiology and Arrhythmias, edited by DP Zipes, J Jalife. Orlando, Grune & Stratton, pp 81–87

Hondeghem LM, Katzung BG (1977) Time- and voltage-dependent interactions of antiarrhythmic drugs with cardiac sodium channels. Biochim Biophys Acta **472:** 373–398

Hondeghem L, Katzung BG (1980) Test of a model of antiarrhythmic drug action: Effects of quinidine and lidocaine on myocardial conduction. Circulation **61:** 1217–1224

Hunter PJ, McNaughton PA, Noble D (1975) Analytical models of propagation in excitable cells. Prog Biophys Mol Biol **30:** 99–144

Imanishi S, Surawicz B (1976) Automatic activity in depolarized guinea pig ventricular myocardium: Characteristics and mechanisms. Circ Res **39:** 751–759

Jack JJB, Noble D, Tsien RW (1975) Electric current flow in excitable cells. Oxford, Clarendon Press

Joyner RW, Picone J, Veenstra R, Rawling D (1983) Propagation through electrically coupled cells: Effects of regional changes in membrane properties. Circ Res **53:** 526–534

Kagiyama Y, Hill JL, Gettes LS (1982) Interaction of acidosis and increased extracellular potassium on action potential characteristics and conduction in guinea pig ventricular muscle. Circ Res **51:** 614–623

Kishida H, Surawicz B, Fu LT (1979) Effects of K^+ and K^+-induced polarization on $(dV/dt)_{max}$, threshold potential, and membrane input resistance in guinea pig and cat ventricular myocardium. Circ Res **44:** 800–814

Peon J, Ferrier GR, Moe GK (1978) The relationship of excitability to conduction velocity in canine Purkinje tissue. Circ Res **43:** 125–135

Saito T (1982) Effect of extracellular potassium on resting membrane potential, threshold potential and $\dot{V}_{max}$. (in Japanese) Nichidai Igaku J **41:** 479–487

Saito T, Buchanan JW Jr, Gettes LS, Hill JL (1978) Determinants of conduction velocity in guinea pig papillary muscle at varying K^+ concentrations (abstr). Circulation **58:** (suppl II): 45

Sharp GH, Joyner RW (1980) Simulated propagation of cardiac action potentials. Biophys J **31:** 403–423

Spach MS, Miller WT III, Miller-Jones E, Warren RB, Barr RC (1979) Extracellular potentials related to intracellular action potentials during impulse conduction in anisotropic canine cardiac muscle. Circ Res **45:** 188–204

Spach MS, Miller WT III, Geselowitz DB, Barr RC, Kootsey JM, Johnson EA (1981) The discontinuous nature of propagation in normal canine cardiac muscle. Circ Res **48:** 39–54

Spear JR, Moore EN (1974) Supernormal excitability and conduction in the His-Purkinje system of the dog. Circ Res **35:** 782–792

Veenstra RD, Joyner RW, Rawling DA (1984) Purkinje and ventricular activation sequences of canine papillary muscle: Effects of quinidine and calcium on the Purkinje-ventricular conduction delay. Circ Res **54:** 500–515

Walton MK, Fozzard HA (1983a) Experimental study of the conducted action potential in cardiac Purkinje strands. Biophys J **44:** 1–8

Walton MK, Fozzard HA (1983b) The conducted action potential: Models and comparison to experiments. Biophys J **44:** 9–26

Weidmann S (1970) Electrical constants of trabecular muscle from mammalian heart. J Physiol (Lond) **210:** 1041–1054

INDEX TERMS: Sodium current • Antiarrhythmic drugs • $\dot{V}_{max}$ • Conduction velocity • Cable theory

Protection of Canine Cardiac Mitochondrial Function by Verapamil-Cardioplegia during Ischemic Arrest

Seung Boo Yoon, Jeanie B. McMillin-Wood, Lloyd H. Michael, Robert M. Lewis, and Mark. L. Entman

From the Department of Medicine, Section of Cardiovascular Sciences, The Methodist Hospital and Baylor College of Medicine, Houston, Texas

SUMMARY. Hemodynamic and mitochondrial function recover following 60 minutes of ischemic arrest and reperfusion in hearts pretreated with verapamil. The present study was carried out to determine whether verapamil prevents the onset of mitochondrial oxidative impairment after 60 minutes of ischemic arrest without reperfusion. Two preparations of mitochondria isolated following Polytron homogenization and subsequent treatment of the myofibrillar pellet with Nagarse were examined for phosphorylating respiration. The Polytron mitochondria were more sensitive to ischemic arrest than were the Nagarse mitochondria with either glutamate-malate (57% vs. 22% inhibition), succinate (+ rotenone) (41% vs. 14% inhibition), or palmitoylcarnitine (57% vs. 27% inhibition) as respiratory substrates. Verapamil pretreatment significantly increased oxidation of all substrates by the subsequently isolated Polytron mitochondria, but only succinate-supported respiration returned to control levels. In contrast, the small amount of respiratory inhibition exhibited by the Nagarse mitochondria after ischemic arrest was insensitive to verapamil pretreatment. We conclude that the Polytron preparation of mitochondria is more susceptible to ischemia than the Nagarse mitochondria, and this susceptibility correlates with a striking sensitivity to verapamil protection. In general, oxidation of NADH-linked substrates, including palmitoylcarnitine, is more affected by ischemic arrest than succinate, and only oxidation of the latter substrate is totally protected by verapamil. The beneficial action of verapamil on mitochondrial function occurs prior to reperfusion. The data suggest that alterations in calcium homeostasis occur during the ischemic period, as well as in the subsequent reperfusion period. **(*Circ Res 56: 704–708, 1965*)**

ISCHEMIC damage to the myocardium is expressed by hemodynamic abnormalities following introduction of coronary reflow. Although it is generally believed that cardiac injury is a direct consequence of a series of biochemical events occurring during the ischemic interval, other evidence suggests that reperfusion also may contribute to cellular injury either by exacerbation of sarcolemmal Ca^{++} entry (Whalen et al., 1974) or by introduction of oxygen free-radical toxicity (Jolly et al., 1984). However, since adequate cardiac perfusion is essential to recovery of cellular viability and mechanical function, pharmacological maneuvers have been designed to ameliorate the intolerance of cells to ischemic damage and reperfusion and, thus, eventual salvage of functioning myocardium. Ca^{++} overload and loss of cellular Ca^{++} homeostasis are believed to be involved in the progression to irreversible ischemic damage (Whalen et al., 1974). Therefore, therapeutic interventions include a class of drugs designated as organic Ca^{++} antagonists. These compounds, which include verapamil, diltiazem, and nifedipine, have been shown to inhibit the cell membrane slow Ca^{++} current and to prevent Ca^{++} overload which is thought to occur during reperfusion of the jeopardized myocardium. Work from our laboratory has demonstrated that a single bolus infusion of verapamil-KCl prior to a 60-minute ischemic arrest produces functional recovery of canine hearts on reperfusion, whereas this never occurs in control ischemic preparations (Pinsky et al., 1981). Mechanical recovery was also found to be associated with preservation of mitochondrial oxidative phosphorylation with either glutamate-malate or succinate (+ rotenone) as respiratory substrate. Moreover, the damage observed in mitochondria and the protection of isolated mitochondrial function after ischemia and reperfusion by verapamil pretreatment (Pinsky et al., 1981) were significant in a mitochondrial population prepared by Polytron homogenization, presumed to represent the mitochondria in the subsarcolemmal compartment (Palmer et al., 1977). Mitochondria isolated by Nagarse digestion (thought to represent intermyofibrillar mitochondria) (Palmer et al., 1977) were normal, and were not affected during the ischemic protocol in either the absence or presence of verapamil in the cardioplegic solution. These data were compatible with the protective effects of low Ca^{++} and Ca^{++}-blocking agents during global ischemia observed in other laboratories (Shine et al., 1978; Nayler et al., 1980). In some of the latter studies, however, data suggested that the Ca^{++}-

induced ischemic damage occurred predominantly during reperfusion (Whalen et al., 1974; Shine et al., 1978; Nayler et al., 1980), since that appears to be the time of maximal Ca^{++} influx (Whalen et al., 1974; Jennings, 1984). In some models, Ca^{++} protection is only required during reperfusion (Shine et al., 1978) when maximal mitochondrial loading occurs (Jennings, 1984). Since reperfusion was involved in all of our *initial* studies so that we might deduce the functional hemodynamic significance of the observed biochemical changes, these studies were carried out to determine whether verapamil prevents the onset of mitochondrial dysfunction during the 60-minute period of ischemic arrest in the absence of reperfusion and to compare this with our previous data (Pinsky et al., 1981), where reperfusion for 1 hour occurred before mitochondria were isolated. In addition, the potential protective effects of verapamil in the nonreperfused ischemic myocardium are described.

Methods

Thirty-five healthy mongrel dogs (18–28 kg) were anesthetized with pentobarbital sodium (30 mg/kg) and ventilated with a Harvard respiratory pump to maintain O_2 and CO_2 partial pressures within normal physiological limits. A left thoracotomy via the 5th intercostal space allowed exposure of the circumflex (CFX) coronary artery for placement of ligature 3 cm from the left main coronary artery. Before coronary ligation or cross-clamping of the aorta, a surface electrocardiogram was monitored, along with systemic arterial pressure, via a Statham P23 DB transducer.

Three groups of dogs were studied: (1) control, nonischemic, with hearts removed immediately after anesthesia and open chest ($n = 15$); (2) 60 minutes of ischemia produced by cross-clamp of aorta following prior infusion of the basic cardioplegic solution containing KCl ($n = 5$); (3) 60 minutes of ischemia produced by cross-clamp of aorta with prior infusion of the basic cardioplegic solution containing KCl and verapamil ($n = 9$).

Ischemia by Cross-Clamp (Groups 2 and 3)

Hearts were made ischemic by placing a noncrushing arterial clamp across the ascending aorta immediately distal to the aortic valve as previously described (Pinsky et al., 1981). There were no differences in cardiac function in any of the groups before cross-clamping.

Cardioplegic Solutions (Pinsky et al., 1981)

The basic solution was 5% dextrose containing 15 mEq KCl, 5 mEq sodium bicarbonate, and 100,000 U/liter heparin (group 2). Verapamil (1 micromolar) was added to the basic solution for group 3 experiments. All solutions were cooled to 4°C.

Cross-Clamp Protocol (Pinsky et al., 1981)

A 12-gauge needle was placed in the aorta between the aortic valve and the aortic clamp to perfuse the cardioplegic solution.

A 1-cm cut was made in the right ventricle for excess drainage resulting from the subsequent infusion. The solution was infused rapidly (250 ml in <5 min) into the aorta, and hence coronary vessels, until asystole. All hearts (groups 2 and 3) were ischemic for 60 minutes and were then removed immediately for mitochondrial isolation. Myocardial temperature was monitored throughout the procedure and was not different between groups 2 and 3. With cold infusion, temperature dropped to 14.5 ± 2°C and gradually rose throughout the 60-minute time period. The temperature range at 60 minutes was from 17.0–18.5°C. Time to ischemic arrest in groups 2 and 3 was not different.

Mitochondrial Isolation

Mitochondria were isolated from canine left ventricle as previously described (Palmer et al., 1977; Pinsky et al., 1981).

The myocardial tissue was homogenized using a Polytron tissue processor in a buffer solution containing 220 mM mannitol, 70 mM sucrose, 5 mM morpholinopropanesulfonic acid (MES), pH 7.4, 2 mM EGTA, and 0.2% bovine serum albumin (BSA). The homogenate was centrifuged at 600 *g*. The post 600 *g* supernatant was then centrifuged at 4500 *g* and the pellet, designated Polytron mitochondria, was resuspended in a buffer containing 220 mM mannitol, 70 mM sucrose, 5 mM MOPS, pH 7.4, at a protein concentration of 20–30 mg/ml. The post 600 *g* pellet was resuspended in homogenization buffer and treated briefly with Nagarse (5 mg/g wet weight) followed by centrifugation at 600 *g*. The mitochondria were then isolated by centrifugation at 4500 *g* of the post 600 *g* supernatant. These mitochondria, designated Nagarse mitochondria, were resuspended under the same conditions as the Polytron mitochondria. Mitochondrial protein was determined by the biuret method (Layne, 1957).

Mitochondrial respiration was measured at 30°C with a Yellow Springs Instrument oxygen monitor. The respiratory medium contained 80 mM KCl, 50 mM MOPS, pH 7.4, 5 mM potassium phosphate, 0.1% BSA, and 1 mM EGTA in a total volume of 2 ml. Respiratory substrates were added at the final concentrations of 10 mM glutamate-malate, 20 mM succinate, plus 5 μg rotenone/mg protein, and 0.2 mM palmitoylcarnitine. Each assay contained 2 mg protein; 100–200 nmol of ADP were added to initiate phosphorylating oxygen consumption (state 3 Qo_2). The respiratory control ratio (RCR) reflects the degree of coupling of respiration to ATP production and was obtained by dividing the rate of oxygen consumption in the presence of ADP by the rate of oxygen consumption following ATP synthesis.

The data were statistically analyzed by using the analysis of variance and the Tukey method for post-hoc comparisons, with the 0.05 probability level established for significance.

Results

Mitochondrial respiration with glutamate-malate following 60 minutes of KCl-cardioplegia was significantly decreased in both preparations of mitochondria (Table 1). The Nagarse preparation was less affected by 60 minutes of KCl cardioplegia than the Polytron mitochondria (22% vs. 57% inhibition). For the Polytron mitochondria, state 3 respiration following verapamil pretreatment (group 3) was significantly higher than rates measured following KCl cardioplegia (group 2), but not as high as control (group 1).

A similar pattern was apparent with succinate as

TABLE 1
Respiration in Polytron and Nagarse Mitochondria

Group	Glutamate-malate	Succinate (+rotenone)	Palmitoyl-carnitine
	I. Polytron mitochondria		
1	373 ± 23	271 ± 18	290 ± 22
2	160 ± 34*	157 ± 34*	123 ± 22*
3	238 ± 20†*	297 ± 25	207 ± 31†*
	II. Nagarse mitochondria		
1	455 ± 25	437 ± 27	339 ± 23
2	354 ± 28‡	376 ± 33	247 ± 30
3	333 ± 35‡	380 ± 34	264 ± 37

* $P < 0.05$ with respect to group 1 (Polytron mitochondria).
† $P < 0.05$ with respect to group 2 (Polytron mitochondria).
‡ $P < 0.05$ with respect to group 1 (Nagarse mitochondria).
Mitochondria were isolated as described in Methods. Groups 1, 2, and 3 refer to cardiac mitochondria isolated from control animals (no ischemic arrest), from animals following 60 minutes of ischemia without (group 2) and with (group 3) verapamil pretreatment. Oxygen consumption is expressed as ng-atoms/min per mg mitochondrial protein ± SEM.

TABLE 2
RCR in Polytron and Nagarse Mitochondria

Group	Glutamate-malate	Succinate (+rotenone)	Palmitoyl-carnitine
	I. Polytron mitochondria		
1	11.32 ± 0.86	3.60 ± 0.39	11.75 ± 1.38
2	3.78 ± 0.92*	1.93 ± 0.03*	3.85 ± 0.53*
3	6.90 ± 1.60†	4.14 ± 0.50†	9.55 ± 1.12†
	II. Nagarse mitochondria		
1	12.22 ± 0.79	3.80 ± 0.32	14.09 ± 1.27
2	5.10 ± 0.56‡	2.98 ± 0.57	4.40 ± 0.42‡
3	10.50 ± 1.62§	4.48 ± 0.46§	8.82 ± 1.13§

See Table 1—respiratory control index is expressed ± SEM.
* $P < 0.05$ with respect to group 1 (Polytron mitochondria).
† $P < 0.05$ with respect to group 2 (Polytron mitochondria).
‡ $P < 0.05$ with respect to group 1 (Nagarse mitochondria).
§ $P < 0.05$ with respect to group 2 (Nagarse mitochondria).

respiratory substrate (Table 1). In this case, Nagarse mitochondria demonstrated a trend toward decrease in respiration that was smaller (and not statistically significant) following KCl cardioplegia (group 2), compared to the Polytron preparation (14% vs. 41% inhibition for succinate). Inclusion of verapamil in the KCl basic solution produced a significant enhancement of the Polytron mitochondrial respiration so that group 3 did not differ from control (group 1) rates.

Since fatty acids represent a primary substrate for oxidative metabolism in the heart, the effects of ischemic cardioplegia on fatty acid oxidation was assessed in the presence of palmitoylcarnitine as the oxidative substrate (Table 1). The Polytron mitochondria were more affected by cardioplegic ischemia when compared to Nagarse mitochondria (57% inhibition vs. 27% inhibition), and the trend to reduced respiration in Nagarse mitochondria was not statistically significant. Verapamil inclusion significantly enhanced oxidation of palmitoylcarnitine by 50% (but did not return to control) in the Polytron preparation, but had no effects on the respiration in mitochondria isolated by Nagarse exposure. Thus, we conclude that, regardless of the respiratory substrate employed, the rates of phosphorylating respiration in the Polytron mitochondrial preparation are more sensitive to ischemic damage, and that this greater reduction in respiration is selectively affected by verapamil administration prior to the 60-minute arrest.

In contrast to the lack of significant differences in oxygen consumption between Nagarse mitochondria isolated following ischemic arrest in the presence and absence of verapamil, a significant elevation in the respiratory control ratios of both mitochondrial preparations is observed following verapamil pretreatment, with either glutamate or palmitoylcarnitine as respiratory substrates (Table 2). In the Polytron preparation, the increased respiratory control is a direct consequence of increased rates of phosphorylating respiration. However, the significant differences in respiratory control in the Nagarse mitochondria between groups 2 and 3 reflect an elevated respiratory rate subsequent to adenosine diphosphate (ADP) phosphorylation (state IV) with ischemic arrest alone. Verapamil pretreatment returns these rates toward control values in this mitochondrial preparation. Since 1 mM EGTA is present in the assay medium, it is not likely that the respiration observed at the end of adenosine triphosphate (ATP) synthesis is a result of any Ca^{++} influx-efflux cycling during the assay.

Discussion

Mitochondrial function is a useful biochemical index to assess myocardial damage following coronary occlusion (Whalen et al., 1974; Nayler et al., 1980; Pinsky et al., 1981). A decline in energy production by mitochondria in vivo is reflected by a decrease in tissue ATP content which correlates directly with recovery of cardiac function upon reperfusion (Reibel and Rovetto, 1979). By following mitochondrial Ca^{++} uptake and ADP:O_2 ratios subsequent to ischemia and reflow, Weishaar et al. (1979) have concluded that the degree of biochemical damage following reperfusion of the ischemic myocardium is determined by the degree of ischemia before onset of reperfusion.

In our previous studies, the protocol differed from that described here by a 1-hour reperfusion period preceding the isolation of the mitochondria in order to assess hemodynamic function (Pinsky et al., 1981). A similar pattern of mitochondrial function to that previously reported emerges from the present studies where the reperfusion portion of the protocol was omitted. The Polytron mitochondria continue to be more susceptible to alterations in function following 60 minutes of ischemic arrest than were the mitochondria prepared by Nagarse treatment. Furthermore, inclusion of verapamil in the basic cardioplegia partially (but not completely) restored respiratory activities of the Polytron mitochondria toward control levels when either glutamate or palmitoylcarnitine were respiratory substrates. Complete reversal of succinate-linked respiration was observed in the Polytron mitochondria when verapamil was present. When verapamil cardioplegia was followed by reperfusion (Pinsky et al., 1981), the Polytron mitochondrial preparation demonstrated oxidative function that was indistinguishable from control, suggesting that the residual dysfunction observed during ischemia with verapamil protection is potentially reversible during reperfusion.

The data from the two studies taken together suggest the following:

1. Subsarcolemmal mitochondria are more sensitive to ischemia, and this sensitivity correlates with a striking protective effect of verapamil not observed in the Nagarse mitochondria in measurement of oxygen consumption, although a significant improvement of respiratory control was noted. It is important to note that the mitochondria demonstrating the highest function in both control and ischemic state were those isolated with Nagarse in both this and previous studies (Palmer et al., 1977; Pinsky et al., 1981), so that proteolysis played no part in the observed dysfunction. The yield ratio of Polytron: Nagarse mitochondria was unchanged in ischemia so that there is no evidence of organelle redistribution, although mitochondrial yield was reduced in ischemia. The mitochondrial yield reduction varies with method of isolation. Since our intention was to select for the least contaminated mitochondrial fraction, it must be stated that we did not seek to maximize the yield. The significance of this finding is not known (Table 3).

2. Glutamate-malate- and palmitoylcarnitine-supported respiration are more sensitive to ischemia than succinate-linked respiration, although both are protected by verapamil to some extent. The marked sensitivity of NADH-linked oxidation to ischemia has been reported previously (Jennings et al., 1969; Pinsky et al., 1981), and is confirmed in the present studies by the greater depression in respiration with glutamate. The sensitivity of palmitate oxidation to ischemia may also reflect the NAD^+-dependent oxidation of β-hydroxy fatty acids in β-oxidation.

TABLE 3
Mitochondrial Yields from Control and Ischemic Hearts

Group	Nagarse	Polytron
1	22.06 ± 1.15	13.58 ± 1.25
2	9.42 ± 1.88*	6.08 ± 0.96*
3	13.09 ± 1.11*	8.13 ± 1.04*

Mitochondria were isolated as described in Methods. The yield is expressed as mg mitochondrial protein/g wet weight myocardium.

* $P < 0.05$ with respect to group 1.

Healy-Moore et al. (1980) have previously demonstrated augmented levels of hydroxy fatty acids in ischemia, and Bremer and Wojtczak (1972) have implicated the NAD^+-dependent dehydrogenase step as a sensitive index of reduced matrix nicotinamide adenine dinucleotide.

3. Differences observed in the presence and absence of reperfusion suggest that reperfusion appears to ameliorate any significant residual dysfunction found before reperfusion: (a) in mitochondrial function in hearts provided verapamil protection, or (b) in succinate (+ rotenone)-supported respiration of the Nagarse mitochondria, regardless of verapamil protection.

We suggest, therefore, that mitochondrial dysfunction in ischemia is a multifactorial process that is of great consequence in ischemic injury and functional recovery. One of these processes is ameliorated by verapamil, and is presumably related to Ca^{++} influx and occurs prior to reperfusion. In the past, we have postulated a mechanism (Entman et al., 1983) whereby ischemia induces depolarization of the cardiac cell resulting in Ca^{++} influx through the slow channel. The increased Ca^{++} influx results in elevated cellular Ca^{++} which is taken up in part by the mitochondria. In the presence of ischemia-augmented concentrations of metabolic amphiphiles (Wolkowicz et al., 1980) and/or lower pH (Wolkowicz et al., 1981), a phosphate-dependent Ca^{++} efflux from mitochondria ensues which is related to a decrease in the proton motive force necessary for oxidative phosphorylation. Although such events occur in vitro, their significance in vivo is highly speculative. If such a mechanism was pertinent in vivo, it is possible that the subsarcolemmal mitochondria are more sensitive because of their physical contiguity to the sarcolemma, whereas the deeper mitochondria are protected by the sarcoplasmic reticulum and other Ca^{++}-binding proteins.

It is clear that the results of these studies may be different from experimental protocols which involve occlusion-induced ischemia and reperfusion. Others have suggested that exacerbation of ischemic damage may be directly correlated with events which occur during the reperfusion period. Perfusion-related events involved in Ca^{++} overload or free-radical injury have been elegantly demonstrated in several ischemic models (Whalen et al., 1974; Shine et al., 1978; Jolly et al., 1984). However, the apparent effects of reperfusion must also be directly influenced by ischemic events which produce subsequent alterations in ionic permeabilities and membrane function (Weishaar et al., 1979). The present studies demonstrate that the beneficial action of the Ca^{++} channel blocker, verapamil, on mitochondrial function occurs prior to the reperfusion event, and that this action is suggestive of alterations in cellular Ca^{++} metabolism during the ischemic period in addition to that described during reperfusion (Whalen et al., 1974; Shine et al., 1978; Jennings, 1984).

These studies were supported by Grant HL 23161 from the National Institutes of Health.

Address for reprints: Dr. Mark L. Entman, Department of Medicine, Section of Cardiovascular Sciences, Baylor College of Medicine, Houston, Texas 77030.

Received August 24, 1984; accepted for publication January 31, 1985.

References

Bremer J, Wojtczak AB (1972) Factors controlling the rate of fatty acid β-oxidation in rat liver mitochondria. Biochim Biophys Acta **280:** 515–530

Entman ML, McMillin-Wood JB, Lewis RM, Wolkowicz PE, Michael LH (1983) Myocardial Cell Dysfunction and Death: Relationship of Energy Metabolism and Membrane Systems. *In* Factors of Influencing the Course of Myocardial Ischemia, edited by AM Gotto, Jr, ME DeBakey. Amsterdam, Elsevier Biomechanical Press, pp 39–54

Healy MK, Radloff JF, Hull FE, Sweely CC (1980) Incomplete fatty acid oxidation by ischemic heart: β-Hydroxy fatty acid production. Am J Physiol **239:** H257–H265

Jennings R (1984) Calcium Ions in Ischemia. *In* Calcium Antagonists and Cardiovascular Disease, edited by LH Opie. New York, Raven Press, pp 85–95

Jennings RD, Herdson PD, Sommers HM (1969) Structural and functional abnormalities in mitochondria isolated from ischemic dog myocardium. Lab Invest **20:** 548–557

Jolly SR, Kane WJ, Bailie MB, Abrams GD, Lucchesi BR (1984) Canine myocardial reperfusion injury: Its reduction by the combined administration of superoxide dismutase and catalase. Circ Res **54:** 277–285

Layne E (1957) Spectrophotometric and turbidimetric methods for measuring proteins. Methods Enzymol **3:** 447–454

Nayler WG, Ferrari R, Williams A (1980) The protective effects of pretreatment with verapamil, nifedipine, and propranolol on mitochondrial function in the ischemic and reperfused myocardium. Am J Cardiol **46:** 242–248

Palmer JW, Tandler B, Hoppel CL (1977) Biochemical properties of subsarcolemmal and intermyofibrillar mitochondria isolated from rat cardiac muscle. J Biol Chem **252:** 8731–8739

Pinsky W, Lewis R, McMillin-Wood J, Hara H, Hartley C, Gillette PC, Entman ML (1981) Myocardial protection from ischemic arrest: Potassium and verapamil cardioplegia. Am J Physiol **240:** H326–H355

Reibel DK, Rovetto MJ (1979) Myocardial adenosine salvage rates and restoration of ATP content following ischemia. Am J Physiol **237:** H247–H252

Shine KI, Douglas AM, Ricchiuti NV (1978) Calcium, strontium, and barium movements during ischemia and reperfusion in rabbit ventricle. Circ Res **43:** 712–720

Weishaar R, Tschurtschenthaler GV, Ashikawa K, Bing RJ (1979) The relationship of regional coronary blood flow to mitochondrial function during reperfusion of the ischemic myocardium. Cardiology **64:** 350–364

Whalen DA Jr, Hamilton DG, Ganote CE, Jennings RB (1974) Effect of a transient period of ischemia on myocardial cells. Am J Pathol **74:** 381–398

Wolkowicz PE, McMillin-Wood J (1980) Respiration-dependent calcium ion uptake by two preparations of cardiac mitochondria: Effects of palmitoyl-coenzyme A and palmitoylcarnitine on calcium ion cycling and nicotinamide nucleotide reduction state. Biochem J **186:** 257–266

Wolkowicz PE, McMillin-Wood J (1981) Glutamate-supported calcium movements in rat liver mitochondria: Effects of anions and pH. Arch Biochem Biophys **209:** 408–422

INDEX TERMS: Myocardial ischemia • Mitochondrial function • Verapamil • Myocardial preservation

Surface Densities of Diaphragmed Fenestrae and Transendothelial Channels in Different Murine Capillary Beds

Anthony J. Milici, Nancy L'Hernault, and George E. Palade
From the Department of Cell Biology, Yale University School of Medicine, New Haven, Connecticut

SUMMARY. Fenestrated capillaries are provided with two types of regular discontinuities: (1) fenestrae with negatively charged diaphragms, and (2) transendothelial channels fitted with two diaphragms, of which the luminal one is uncharged. These structures are expected to affect macromolecular exchanges on the basis of size and charge. We have detected variations in the surface density of fenestrations and transendothelial channels (normalized to 1 μm of capillary endothelial profiles in sections) in selected areas of different murine organs, i.e., kidney cortex, duodenal mucosa, and exocrine pancreas. The survey was limited to endothelial segments ≤400 nm thick, and covered a total length of endothelial profiles of 1180 μm, 730 μm, and 1189 μm in the exocrine pancreas, intestinal mucosa, and kidney cortex, respectively. At least 1000 transendothelial openings were recorded by scoring for easily recognizable fenestrations, transendothelial channels, and unknowns, the latter representing either of the above in grazing sections. The linear density of all transendothelial openings taken together was found to vary among the different capillary beds (kidney cortex > intestinal mucosa > exocrine pancreas). This same sequence was observed for the linear densities of fenestrations, transendothelial channels, and unknowns considered individually. The values obtained were as follows: kidney cortex, 1.35 fenestrations per μm, 0.25 transendothelial channels per μm, 0.52 unknowns per μm; intestinal mucosa, 0.92 fenestrations per μm, 0.10 transendothelial channels per μm, 0.38 unknowns per μm; exocrine pancreas, 0.58 fenestrations per μm, 0.04 transendothelial channels per μm, 0.27 unknowns per μm. The differences in distribution of transendothelial openings among fenestrated capillary beds probably reflect capillary permeability modulations connected with the functions of these various organs. **(*Circ Res 56: 709–717, 1985*)**

IN fenestrated capillaries, blood plasma-interstitial fluid exchanges of hydrophilic macromolecules involve fenestrae (with one diaphragm), and transendothelial channels (fitted with two diaphragms) in addition to plasmalemmal vesicles (Clementi and Palade, 1969; Simionescu et al., 1972; Venkatachalam and Karnovsky, 1972). Since diaphragmed fenestrae were the most numerous structures detected by transmission electron microscopy (TEM) in these vessels, and appeared to offer the least resistance to tracer egress, they were assumed to be the most important structural elements for the permeability properties of these capillaries. Moreover, when replicas of freeze-cleaved specimens of visceral capillaries were studied, it was generally assumed that all of the openings observed were diaphragmed fenestrae (Friederici, 1968; Simionescu et al., 1974). The importance of a precise identification of fenestrae and channels became evident only when electron-dense cationic probes were used to examine charge distribution on the luminal surface of endothelial cells. Such studies detected differentiated microdomains, generated by an uneven distribution of anionic sites on the luminal plasmalemma of pancreatic and intestinal capillaries (Simionescu et al., 1981), and found to coincide precisely and consistently with structures involved in blood-tissue exchanges, e.g., plasmalemmal vesicles, fenestrations, and transendothelial channels. The existence of differentiated microdomains led Simionescu et al. (1981) to propose that electrostatic charge repulsion would restrict the passage of anionic macromolecules through fenestral diaphragms past a certain molecular size, e.g., probably lower than that of plasma proteins, leaving the uncharged channels and plasmalemmal vesicles to function as a preferential pathway for the exchange of anionic macromolecules.

Information about differences in structure and charge-distribution among capillary beds is needed to help determine the factors that influence capillary permeability in the corresponding organs. If channels function in the exchange of plasma proteins, then variations in their surface density among capillary beds in different organs could account for local differences in vascular permeability. In this paper we present our observations on the heterogeneous distribution of transendothelial openings in the fenestrated capillaries found in the microvasculature of the exocrine pancreas, intestinal mucosa, and kidney cortex of the mouse.

Methods

Animals

Male Swiss albino mice (either Charles River Laboratory or Jackson Laboratory) weighing 20–25 g were used in all experiments. All animals were allowed access to food and water ad libitum.

Reagents

Cationized ferritin (CF) (mol wt 450,000–600,000, depending on ferric hydroxide content; pI determined to be ~8.6) was obtained from Miles laboratory and used directly after dilution with Dulbecco's phosphate-buffered saline supplemented with 14 mM glucose (PBSG).

Experimental Protocol

For morphological studies, a two-step procedure (blood removal followed by fixation in situ) was used.

1. Blood Removal

Under light ether anesthesia, a thoracotomy was performed, and a cannula, connected to a constant pressure perfusion apparatus, was inserted into the left ventricle. The blood then was removed by perfusing 30–40 ml of PBSG (prewarmed to 37°C) through the animal at a flow rate of 3.5 ml/min and at a pressure of 60–80 mm Hg, with the right ventricle cut open to allow easy outflow of the perfusate.

2. Perfusion Fixation

After blood removal, the whole animal was fixed in situ under identical perfusion conditions with 30–40 ml of 3% glutaraldehyde in 0.1 M sodium cacodylate buffer, pH 7.2.

In the experiments involving CF, the following steps were added after removal of the blood:

a. Perfusion with CF: The vasculature was perfused intermittently [(1 minute of flow, followed by a 3-minute wait) × 3] for 12 minutes, with about 9 ml of 0.5 mg/ml CF in PBSG at a flow rate of 3 ml/min.

b. Flush with 15 ml of PBSG, as in section 1, to remove unbound CF from the vasculature.

c. Perfusion fixation of the animal as in section 2.

3. Processing of Tissue

After fixation in situ, pancreas, intestine (duodenum), and kidney cortex specimens were removed and immersed in the same fixative for 90 minutes, followed by treatment for 90 minutes with 1% OsO_4 in acetate veronal buffer, pH 7.6, at 4°C. The specimens then were routinely processed, embedded, and sectioned for electron microscopy.

Morphometric Analysis

To determine the average vessel diameter, we examined 50 low magnification micrographs (~11,000×) for each organ, and determined the diameter of cross-sectioned vessels (or the maximum transverse diameter of obliquely sectioned vessels) with a map measurer. The values obtained were 4.56 ± 1.22 μm, 4.48 ± 1.47 μm, and 6.12 ± 1.77 μm for pancreas, intestine, and kidney, respectively.

To determine the extent of endothelial attenuation, we examined at least 30 micrographs of capillaries for each organ at an intermediate magnification (~20,000×). In determining the thickness of the endothelium, we used two cut-off points, i.e., ≤250 nm and ≤400 nm, and measured and recorded the lengths of endothelial profiles falling below these values (Fig. 1; Table 1). The fractional perimeter ≤250 nm represents the area of highest concentration of fenestrae and channels and describes further the variable degree of attenuation from one capillary bed to another.

To determine the number of transendothelial openings (TO) per micrometer length of endothelium, a minimum of eight blocks from three different animals were sectioned, and enough micrographs were taken to allow the identification of at least 1,000 transendothelial openings. The micrographs were of sufficiently high magnification (~34,000×) to ensure the easy identification of the following endothelial structures: transendothelial channels (C), fenestrations (F), plasmalemmal vesicles, and coated vesicles. All of the above structures were counted on and normalized per micron length of endothelium ≤400 nm thick for each capillary profile. Structures that could not be reliably identified as either channels or fenestrae (because of the local obliquity of the sections or because the sections included mostly the rims of these structures) were designated unknowns (U) (Table 2A). The linear density of fenestrae and channels from Table 2B can be expressed also per μm of total capillary profile by multiplying the total length of endothelium ≤400 nm by the inverse of the percent of attenuated endothelium from Table 1 and dividing the product into the number of the different structures observed.

Results

General Morphology

The general morphology of the endothelium was found to be the same in all visceral capillary beds examined and in agreement with observations already recorded in the literature (Bennet et al., 1959; Rhodin, 1962; Clementi and Palade, 1969). The endothelial cells have a perinuculear region ~3 μm thick, and around it a highly attenuated, plate-like periphery that measures 0.4 μm or less in thickness and occupies from 66–82% of the cells' area (Table 1). It is in these attenuated cytoplasmic plates that the endothelial cell is pierced by many transendothelial openings which represent two different structures: (1) fenestrae ~60 nm in diameter closed by a single fenestral diaphragm, and (2) transendothelial channels fitted with two (and occasionally three) stomatal diaphragms ~61 nm diameter, one at each end. The shape of transendothelial channels varies from cylindrical to barrel-shaped, and their length ranges from 20.2–115.9 nm (average: 37 nm).* The diaphragms of most channels are parallel to one another, but quite often one of the diaphragms is at an angle to its partner. In sections, channels often appear singly or in small groups. Occasionally, rows

** These dimensions represent numerical averages obtained from measuring 100 diaphragmed fenestrae and 100 transendothelial channels, all randomly located.*

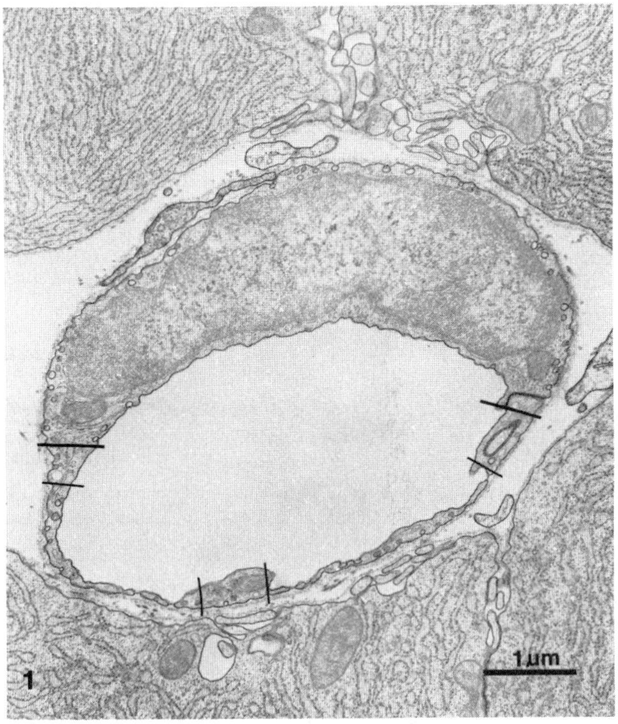

FIGURE 1. *This low magnification micrograph of a pancreatic blood capillary is representative of the vessels examined in this study. The attenuated endothelium found between the thick lines is less than 400 nm thick, whereas that between the thin lines is less than 250 nm thick.*

of more than three are encountered (Fig. 2), suggesting that channels—like fenestrae (Rhodin, 1962; Friederici, 1968, Simionescu et al., 1974)—are distributed in compact clusters. This type of distribution is in fact confirmed by scanning electron microscopy of the luminal aspect of the fenestrated capillaries of the renal cortex (Peters and Milici, 1983).

Morphometric Data

Micrographs of sectioned specimens were used to obtain data on the linear numerical density of diaphragmed fenestrations and transendothelial channels in the capillary beds indicated in Methods. Additional data were collected concerning: (1) the fraction of the endothelial perimeter ≤400 nm thick in which essentially all transendothelial openings are found (Table 1), (2) the fraction of the same perimeter ≤250 nm thick in which most, i.e., >95%, of the openings are located (Table 1), and (3) the distribution of anionic sites on the luminal aspect of the endothelium of the corresponding vessels. Such data provided the basis for subsequent comparisons of the capillary beds studied.

Diaphragmed fenestrae, transendothelial channels, and unknowns were counted on capillary profiles in each organ and normalized per micrometer of endothelial perimeter less than 400 nm thick (Fig. 3, Table 2). The absolute and relative linear densities of diaphragmed fenestrations and channels were found to vary from one capillary profile to another for each type of microvascular bed, but a consistent, characteristic pattern already emerged after we had examined 10–20 profiles. This pattern remained the same as the size of the sample was increased to 268, 190, and 291 profiles for pancreas, intestine, and kidney, respectively. The values for linear densities of fenestrations and channels were the lowest in pancreatic capillaries (0.58 and 0.04, respectively); they were higher in the capillaries of the intestinal mucosa (0.92 and 0.10, respectively), and the highest in the peritubular capillaries of the kidney cortex (1.35 and 0.25, respectively).

Linear densities were converted to surface densities, to make them more useful for physiological correlations. This conversion was done by assuming a section thickness of ~50 nm and by calculating on this basis the density of structures per square micrometer of attenuated endothelium.† The results are shown in Table 3.

The values for fenestrations and channels in Tables 2A and 3A exclude the contribution of unknowns. Since the latter actually represent either oblique sections through the former structures or sections, including mostly the rims of these openings, they must be taken into account to obtain better estimates. The percent of channels was determined in each capillary bed and expressed as percent of their total; the values obtained were 7.5% C/F+C in the pancreas, 10.4% C/F+C in the intestinal mucosa, and 18.6% C/F+C in the kidney cortex. These figures were multiplied by the number of unknowns to give corrected values for the linear and surface densities of channels and fenestrae (Tables 2B and 3B).

Since fenestrae and transendothelial channels are essentially restricted to endothelium less than 400 nm thick, and since we have already determined the corresponding fraction as a percent of total endothe-

TABLE 1
Percent of Attenuated Endothelium in Normal Sections of Capillary Walls

Microvascular bed	Endothelium ≤400 nm	Endothelium ≤250 nm	Sample size (µm)
Kidney cortex	82	72	638.48
Intestinal mucosa	66	53	518.21
Exocrine pancreas	78	53	417.11

† *To check the validity of the surface density estimates calculated in this fashion, we took freeze-fractured micrographs of the fenestrated portion of intestinal mucosal capillaries, cut them into 2 µm × 50 nm strips, counted TO on each strip, and summated the counts after eliminating overlaps between adjacent strips. The values obtained were as follows: TO per µm = 1.48 (counted on 60-µm length); TO per µm² = 26.54 ± 6.44 (counted on 22 µm² of endothelial cell surface). Thus, a correction factor for our estimates in Table 3 does not appear to be necessary, since the values obtained directly from the endothelial cell surface do not differ significantly from those estimated in Table 3.*

TABLE 2
Linear Density (and Corrected Values) of Selected Endothelial Structures

Type of opening	Microvascular beds		
	Exocrine pancreas	Intestinal mucosa	Kidney cortex
	A. Linear density		
No. of channels/μm	0.04	0.10	0.25
No. of fenestrations/μm	0.58	0.92	1.35
No. of unknowns/μm	0.27	0.38	0.52
Total no. of transendothelial openings/μm	0.90 (1061)*	1.40 (1020)*	2.11 (2513)*
No. of plasmalemmal vesicles/μm	3.15 (3863)*	1.34 (969)*	0.33 (381)*
No of coated vesicles/μm	0.12 (141)*	0.09 (62)*	0.05 (63)*
Length of endothelium examined ≤400 nm thick	1182 μm	729 μm	1189 μm
	B. Corrected values for the linear density of fenestrations and channels		
No. of channels/μm	0.06 (0.05)†	0.14 (0.09)†	0.31 (0.25)†
No. of fenestrations/μm	0.83 (0.65)†	1.26 (0.83)†	1.80 (1.48)†

* Numbers in parentheses = number counted for each structural unit.
† Numbers in parentheses = linear density of each structure per total endothelial profile (>400 nm + <400 nm).

lial perimeter and area, we can calculate surface densities as well as aggregate areas for each structure per total luminal endothelial surface in the capillaries of each of the microvasculatures studied. The results obtained for pancreas, intestine, and kidney were as follows (Table 4): channels, 0.28%, 0.51%, and 1.44%, respectively; fenestrations, 3.68%, 4.72%, and 8.35%, respectively.

Plasmalemmal vesicles (luminal, abluminal, and apparently free in the cytoplasm) and coated pits and vesicles also were counted, and their relative frequency was determined in the same attenuated regions that were examined for transendothelial openings. The number of plasmalemmal vesicles per micrometer of capillary endothelial perimeter was found to decrease from the pancreas (3.15) to the intestinal mucosa (1.34) to the kidney cortex (0.33). The number of coated vesicles per micrometer underwent a decrease in the same order, but the differences were not as great (Table 2A). However, the percentage of coated vesicles to plasmalemmal vesicles was greatest in the kidney (16.7%), decreased to approximately one-half this value in the intestine (6.7%), and to approximately one-quarter of this value in the pancreas (3.8%). These figures are valid for approximately 66–82% of the cell surface and are therefore low estimates for total endothelial cell surface, since both structures are also found in thicker (>400 nm) cytoplasmic areas.

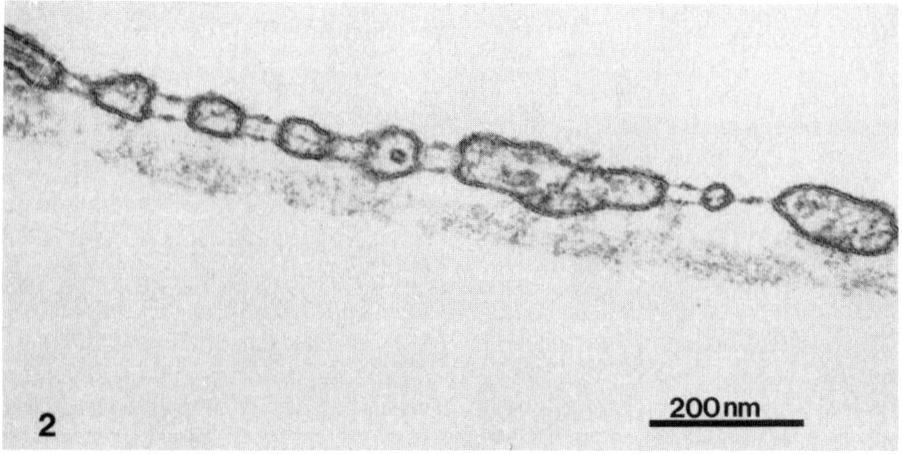

FIGURE 2. *Cluster of six transendothelial channels in a kidney peritubular capillary. Smaller clusters of transendothelial channels are routinely found in sections of endothelial cells in these capillaries.*

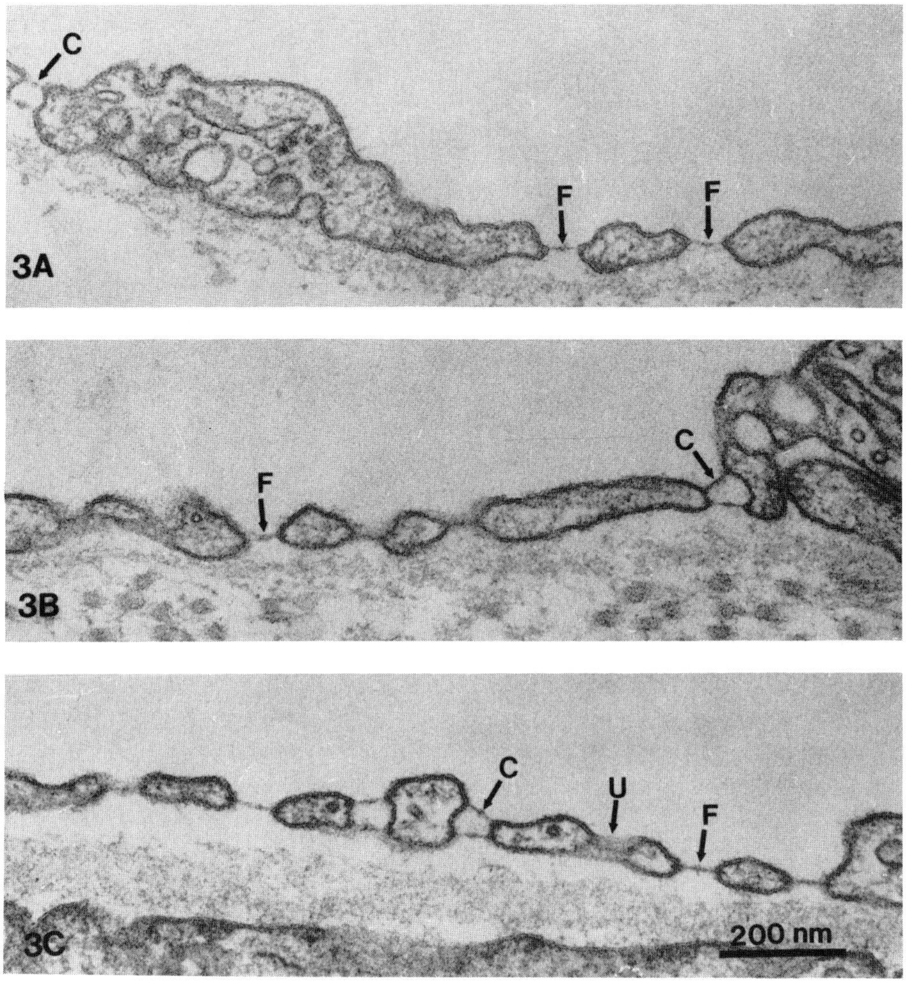

FIGURE 3. *Panel A = pancreatic capillary, panel B = intestinal mucosal capillary, and panel C = kidney peritubular capillary. Representative segments of blood capillaries, demonstrating the types of cell structures examined in this study. These structures were identified as either diaphragmed fenestrae (F) or transendothelial channels (C); equivocal appearances (caused by sectioning obliquely or too close to the rim of either fenestrae or channels) were classified as unknowns (U).*

Anionic Sites Distribution

We examined the distribution of anionic sites on the luminal plasmalemma, using CF, pI ~8.6, as a probe. In kidney peritubular capillaries, CF was found to bind to anionic sites on fenestral diaphragms and the luminal surface of the plasmalemma proper, while the luminal surfaces of the stomatal diaphragms of transendothelial channels and plasmalemmal vesicles were unlabeled (Fig. 4).

TABLE 3
Surface Density (and Corrected Values) of Transendothelial Openings*

Type of opening	Microvascular beds: Exocrine pancreas	Intestinal mucosa	Kidney cortex
A. Surface density			
No. of channels per μm^2	0.88	1.92	5.03
No. of fenestrations per μm^2	11.61	18.41	26.93
No. of unknowns per μm^2	5.47	7.65	10.31
Total no. of transendothelial openings per μm^2	17.95	27.98	42.27
Aggregate surface area of endothelium ≤400 nm thick	59.10 μm^2	36.45 μm^2	59.45 μm^2
B. Corrected values for the surface density of fenestrations and channels			
No. of channels per μm^2	1.28	2.72	6.22
No. of fenestrae per μm^2	16.67	25.26	36.05

* All measurements are per μm^2 assuming a section thickness of 50 nm.

TABLE 4
Percent of Total Endothelial Surface Occupied by Transendothelial Openings*

Type of opening	Microvascular bed		
	Exocrine pancreas	Intestinal mucosa	Kidney cortex
Channels	0.28%	0.51%	1.44%
Fenestrations	3.68%	4.72%	8.35%
Total	3.96%	5.23%	9.79%

* To calculate the percent of endothelial sample occupied by different openings, it was assumed that: (1) all openings were 60 nm in diameter, and (2) the thickness of the sections was 50 nm; corrected numerical values were taken from Table 2B, and the percent of endothelium surface occupied by either channels or fenestrae was arrived by the following formula:

$$\frac{(\text{Number of structures observed}) \cdot \pi\, r^2}{(\text{Total endothelium surface area})\dagger}$$

† Calculated from the data in Table 1 normalized to the entire capillary surface, as explained in the text.

This is identical to the binding pattern first reported by Simionescu et al. (1981)—and duplicated by ourselves—in the pancreas and intestine. Occasionally, CF was observed to emerge into the extravascular space through a transendothelial opening. The density of CF within such permeated openings was high enough to mask the presence of a diaphragm(s), if present, and thereby preclude accurate identification of such structures as either channels or fenestrations (Fig. 4).

Discussion

Morphometric Data

Our morphometric data can be compared at two different levels to findings already recorded in the literature. At the first level, the surface density of transendothelial openings (TO), i.e., the sum of fenestrae, channels, and unknowns established in this study, can be compared to the density of "fenestrae" obtained by other investigators on freeze-cleaved specimens of fenestrated capillaries. The corresponding studies did not differentiate between fenestrae and channels because of limited or no information available at that time on the latter. Our data (18 TO per μm^2 and 28 TO per μm^2 for pancreas and intestinal mucosa, respectively) are in reasonably close agreement with those obtained on the same vessels in rats by Simionescu et al. (1974) (15 F per μm^2 and 26 F per μm^2 for pancreas and intestinal mucosa, respectively). There has been no similar systematic investigation of the peritubular capillaries in the kidney cortex. Rhodin (1962), from a few randomly collected thin sections, estimated the surface density of fenestrations in murine kidney cortex capillaries to be ~30 per μm^2, which is less than the ~42 transendothelial openings per μm^2 found by us in our study. Friederici (1968) found ~60 fenestra-

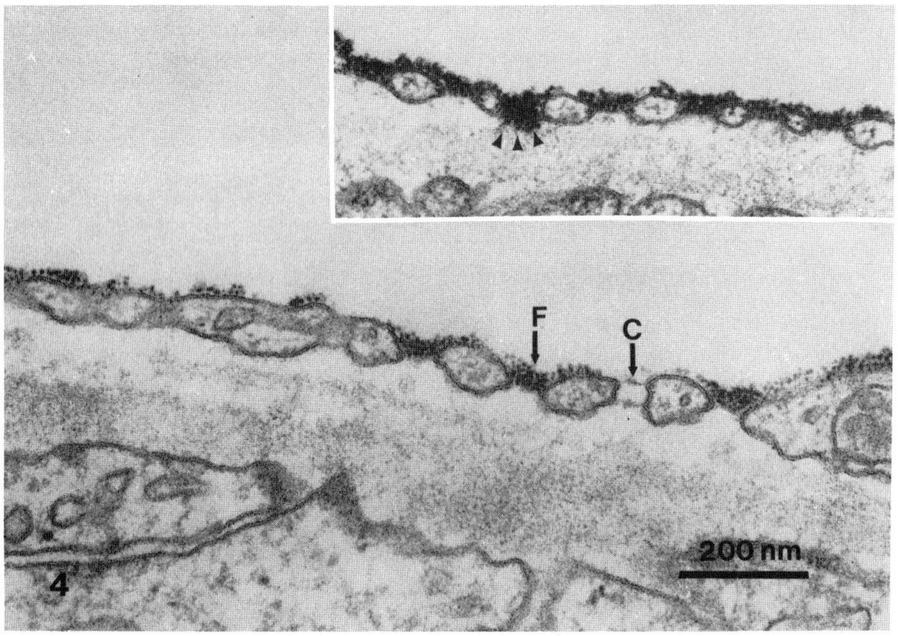

FIGURE 4. *The binding pattern of cationic ferritin (CF) to the luminal surface of the endothelium of peritubular capillaries. CF has a high affinity for the plasmalemma proper and for fenestral diaphragms (F), but the diaphragms of transendothelial channels (C) and plasmalemmal vesicles (not shown) do not have anionic sites detectable by CF binding. In the insert, an example of a CF aggregate passing into the extravascular space through a transendothelial opening is marked by arrowheads. CF density precludes an accurate identification of the structure as either a fenestration or channel.*

tions per μm^2 on freeze-cleaved capillaries of the renal medulla (papilla) in rats. The differences mentioned above may reflect differences in sample size and location within each organ.

At the second level of inquiry, transendothelial channels have been observed in the fenestrated capillaries of the intestinal mucosa (Clementi and Palade, 1969), kidney (Venkatachalam and Karnovsky, 1972), and pancreas (Simionescu et al., 1972), but their surface density relative to that of diaphragmed fenestrae was not determined until this study. Our morphometric data apply only to the attenuated regions ($\leq$400 nm thick) of the endothelium in the vascular beds examined, but these regions, which account for 66–82% of the total endothelial surface, comprise essentially all transendothelial openings, and are apparently of major importance for blood plasma-interstitial fluid exchanges. However, the data obtained allow an estimate of the surface density of transendothelial channels and fenestrae for the entire surface of the capillaries investigated (see Table 4).

In the specimens we have examined, all normally (or nearly normally) sectioned fenestrae appear to be provided with a diaphragm. Diaphragm-free fenestrae, as described by Casley-Smith et al. (1975) (about 50% of total) or as postulated by Clementi and Palade (1969) (a small fraction of total), have not been encountered in this study. The existence or absence of a diaphragm is difficult to ascertain in oblique sections cutting through part of the fenestral rim. Such appearances were counted as unknowns in our survey (see Table 2A), not as diaphragm-free fenestrae, and this may explain the differences between our findings and those of Casley-Smith et al. (1975).

Simionescu and coworkers (1981), using CF, examined the electrostatic binding of this cationic probe to the negatively charged ectodomains of proteoglycans and glycoproteins on the plasmalemma of pancreatic and intestinal capillaries. They observed a generally even distribution of anionic sites on the plasmalemma proper, and a high concentration of such sites on fenestral diaphragms; however, the luminal diaphragms of plasmalemmal vesicles and transendothelial channels in adjacent areas of fenestrated endothelium were not labeled with CF. This finding led them to postulate that fenestral diaphragms discriminate against anionic macromolecules past a certain size, and that transendothelial channels and plasmalemmal vesicles represent the preferential exchange pathways for negatively charged macromolecules. This postulate assumes that the second diaphragm of transendothelial channels is, like the first, not negatively charged. Neutral macromolecules are presumably selected on the basis of size alone, and all endothelial cell structures discussed above could be involved in their transport. These assumptions remain to be tested experimentally by using appropriate tracers, but they are compatible, at least in part, with findings already published on the permeability of the microvasculatures considered in this paper.

Physiological Implications

The assumption that anionic plasma proteins like albumin (7 nm dia, pI ~4.8) leave the blood preferentially through transendothelial channels implies that the surface density of the latter should correlate with the concentration of albumin in the pericapillary spaces. Plasma proteins are also expected to be transported by plasmalemmal vesicles, but in this case a correlation would be more difficult to establish because of unknown time factors involved in vesicular transport. Under normal circulatory conditions, the interactions between permeant macromolecules and interstitial components are expected to reach a steady state equilibrium. Accordingly, the lymph:plasma (L:P) ratios of such macromolecules can be assumed to reflect primarily their interactions with the endothelial barrier.

Data already on record indicate that the L:P ratio of albumin in the intestinal lymph (0.1)‡ and, presumably, in the interstitia of the intestinal mucosa, is considerably lower than the corresponding ratio for renal lymph (0.33) (Deen et al., 1976; Perry et al., 1983). In fact, the latter value ranges to as high as 0.7 (Pinter and O'Morchoe, 1970). Because of this difference in L:P ratios, it is tempting to postulate a correlation between the surface density of transendothelial channels and the differential degree of permeability to albumin between the intestinal mucosal and the renal cortical vascular beds. The postulate remains to be tested, however, by further work.

Data on the distribution and concentration of albumin in the interstitia of the kidney (especially cortex) have been obtained in a number of studies. For instance, the renal tissue volume for red blood cells, chylomicrons,§ and albumin were concomitantly determined by Pinter (1967), who found the albumin volume four times larger than that for red blood cells. The extravascular pool of albumin in this study was equivalent to 31% of the total albumin in the kidney. Other investigators (Källskog and Wolgast, 1973) have also arrived at the conclusion that there is a high concentration of albumin in the interstitia of the cortex, which may facilitate tubular readsorption of fluid and small solutes.‖

There is, however, no general agreement on this matter. Notwithstanding the relatively high L:P ratio

‡ *This value does vary, however, under different perfusion conditions.*

§ *The chylomicron volume was 2.65 larger than the RBC volume, presumably because the cells flow preferentially along a central column in blood capillaries.*

‖ *Spitzer and Windhager (1970) also found that the readsorping capacity of isolated proximal tubues can be increased to in vivo levels by adding 8% dextran (mol wt 110,000) to the incubation medium.*

for albumin, Deen et al. (1976) assumed that the convective reflection coefficient for this molecule and dextran (>7.2 nm dia) was essentially equal to 1, and that plasma proteins exert their entire osmotic pressure across the peritubular capillary walls. Moreover, by fluorescence microscopy (a qualitative procedure of undefined sensitivity), albumin was found supposedly restricted to within the renal microvasculature (Carone et al., 1967).

The influence of macromolecular charge on the permeability of fenestrated endothelia has been studied only in intestinal capillaries (Perry et al., 1983) by using neutral, cationic, and anionic dextrans of low molecular weight (mol wt ~25,000), as well as a series of lactate dehydrogenase (LDH) isoenzymes of similar size (mol wt 140,000, diameter 8.4 nm) but different pI levels (LDH1 = 5.2 through LDH5 = 8.3). The L:P ratio decreased from anionic > neutral > cationic dextrans, and a similar decrease was found in the L:P ratio of the cationic LDH isoenzymes when compared to those of their anionic counterparts (L:P for LDH5 ~0.18, L:P for LDH1 ~0.55). Since fenestral diaphragms are already known to bind (and thereby retard the passage of) cationic ferritin (molecular diameter 11 nm, pI 8.2–8.6) in these microvessels (Simionescu et al., 1981; this manuscript), the data collected by Perry et al. (1983) suggest that cationic molecules begin to be discriminated against by fenestral diaphragms, because of size restrictions, when they approach 8 nm in diameter. Horseradish peroxidase, diameter 5 nm, pI unspecified, but presumably above 8, was shown to exit through all fenestrae in the same vessels (Clementi and Palade, 1969).

The data on neutral and anionic LDH and dextrans are difficult to interpret in terms of our findings. Anionic and neutral LDH may leave the plasma preferentially via transendothelial channels and plasmalemmal vesicles. Threadlike, flexible, relatively small macromolecules, like the dextrans used (mol wt ~25,000), are expected to encounter fewer restrictions in moving across the endothelium than globular macromolecules of the same size. Neutral dextrans (Simionescu et al., 1972) appear to egress from the lumen of intestinal mucosal capillaries through both fenestrae and plasmalemmal vesicles, but the exit sites of anionic dextrans remain unknown. Perry and coworkers (1983) have proposed that the wall of the microvessels in the intestinal mucosa behaves as a positively charged barrier, in contradistinction to the other capillary walls so far investigated (Garby and Areekul, 1970; Rennke et al., 1975) which act as negatively charged barriers. It would be useful to determine whether exogenous, cationic probe molecules can contribute significantly to the creation of a cationic barrier upon adsorption to, or interaction with, anionic sites on the luminal surface of the endothelium.

Some of the physiological data discussed above appear to be in partial agreement with the different functions postulated for transendothelial channels and diaphragmed fenestrae, but more extensive and more reliable data are needed to define the molecular size beyond which the effect of macromolecular charge detectably influences endothelial permeability, and to identify the pathway followed by macromolecules of different charge across the endothelium of fenestrated capillaries. Even in the present state of knowledge, our findings suggest, however, that endothelial permeability can be modulated to a large extent by varying the absolute and relative surface density of transendothelial channels, diaphragmed fenestrae, and plasmalemmal vesicles in different microvascular beds.

The excellent technical assistance of Nancy Watrous and Hans Stukenbrok, the secretarial skills of Cindy Davis, and the photographic and graphic work of Pam Ossorio are gratefully acknowledged.

A portion of this work was presented in abstract form at the 23rd Annual Meeting of the American Society for Cell Biology (Milici and L'Hernault, 1983).

This work was supported by National Institutes of Health Grant HL 17080 to G.E.P. and by an American Heart Association/Connecticut Affiliate (Fairfield County Chapter) Fellowship to A.J.M.

Address for reprints: Dr. A.J. Milici, Department of Cell Biology, Yale University School of Medicine, P.O. Box 3333, 333 Cedar Street, New Haven, Connecticut 06510.

Received October 11, 1984; accepted for publication February 5, 1985.

References

Bennet HS, Luft JH, Hampton JC (1959) Morphological classification of vertebrate blood capillaries. Am J Physiol **196:** 381–390

Carone FA, Everett BA, Blondel NJ, Stolarczyk J (1967) Renal localization of albumin and its function in the concentrating mechanism. Am J Physiol **212:** 387–393

Casley-Smith J, O'Donoghue P, Crocker K (1975) The quantitative relationship between fenestrae in jejunal capillaries and connective tissue channels: Proof of "tunnel-capillaries." Microvasc Res **9:** 78–100

Clementi F, Palade GE (1969) Intestinal capillaries. I. Permeability to peroxidase and ferritin. J Cell Biol **41:** 33–58

Deen W, Ueki I, Brenner B (1976) Permeability of renal peritubular capillaries to neutral dextrans and endogenous albumin. Am J Physiol **231:** 283–291

Friederici HH (1968) The tridimensional ultrastructure of fenestrated capillaries. J Ultrastruct Res **23:** 444–456

Garby L, Areekul S (1970) Reflection coefficients of neutral and sulfate-substituted dextran molecules in the capillaries of the isolated rabbit ear. *In* Alfred Benzon Symposium. II. Capillary Permeability, edited by C Crone, N Lassen. New York, Academic Press, pp 560–563

Källskog O, Wolgast M (1973) Driving forces over the peritubular capillary membrane in the rat kidney during antidiuresis and saline expansion. Acta Physiol Scand **89:** 116–125

Milici AJ, L'Hernault N (1983) Variation in the number of fenestrations and channels between fenestrated capillary beds (abstr). J Cell Biol **97:** 336a

Perry MA, Benoit JN, Kvietys PR, Granger DN (1983) Restricted transport of cationic macromolecules across intestinal capillaries. Am J Physiol **245:** G568–G572

Peters KR, Milici AJ (1983) High resolution SEM of the luminal surface of a fenestrated capillary endothelium (abstr). J Cell Biol **97:** 336a

Pinter G (1967) Distribution of chylomicrons and albumin in dog kidney. J Physiol (Lond) **192:** 761–772

Pinter G, O'Morchoe C (1970) Turnover of interstitial albumin in the kidney. Experientia **26:** 265–266

Rennke H, Cotran R, Venkatachalam M (1975) Role of glomerular charge in glomerular permeability. J Cell Biol **67:** 638–646

Rhodin J (1962) The diaphragm of capillary endothelial fenestrations. J Ultrastruct Res **6:** 171–185

Simionescu M, Simionescu N, Palade GE (1974) Morphometric data on the endothelium of blood capillaries. J Cell Biol **60:** 128–152

Simionescu N, Simionescu M, Palade GE (1972) Permeability of intestinal capillaries. Pathway followed by dextran and glycogens. J Cell Biol **53:** 365–392

Simionescu N, Simionescu M, Palade GE (1981) Differentiated microdomains on the luminal surface of capillary endothelium: I. Preferential distribution of anionic sites. J Cell Biol **90:** 605–613

Spitzer A, Windhager E (1970) Effect of peritubular oncotic pressure changes on proximal tubular fluid reabsorption. Am J Physiol **218:** 1188–1193

Venkatachalam M, Karnovsky M (1972) Extravascular protein in the kidney. An ultrastructural study of its relation to renal peritubular capillary permeability using protein tracers. Lab Invest **27:** 435–444

INDEX TERMS: Endothelium • Fenestrae • Transendothelial channels • Capillary permeability

"Fade" of Hyperpolarizing Responses to Vagal Stimulation at the Sinoatrial and Atrioventricular Nodes of the Rabbit Heart

Joseph J. Salata and Jose Jalife
From the State University of New York, Upstate Medical Center, Syracuse, New York

SUMMARY. Previous studies have suggested that maintained vagal stimulation or acetylcholine infusion results in a fade of responses in the sinoatrial node but not in the atrioventricular node, implying different muscarinic receptor subtypes in the two regions. We investigated this hypothesis in 23 isolated rabbit atrial preparations made quiescent by continuous superfusion with verapamil (1 μg/ml). Transmembrane potentials were recorded simultaneously from cells in the sinoatrial pacemaker region and from the "N" region of the atrioventricular node. Postganglionic vagal stimulation was achieved by the application of trains of pulses (50–150 μsec; 10–20 V; 200 Hz). Simultaneous application of long-lasting (1–10 sec) vagal trains produced hyperpolarizations which were nearly identical for both nodal regions. Maximal hyperpolarizations ($\approx$ 24 mV for sinoatrial node; 26 mV for atrioventricular node) were reached about 500 msec after initiation of the vagal train. Thereafter, hyperpolarizations faded, following a biphasic time course, and thus displaying two different time constants, one fast (τ_{fast} = 580 msec for sinoatrial node; 550 msec for atrioventricular node), and one slow (τ_{slow} = 9.2 sec for both sinoatrial and atrioventricular nodes). Hyperpolarizations during brief (200-msec) but repetitive vagal trains also faded biphasically, but approached a steady state much more rapidly than responses to long-lasting trains. Recovery from hyperpolarization decay occurred rather slowly and was linear. Our results demonstrate that the membrane potential responses to vagal stimulation in the atrioventricular node are indistinguishable from those in the sinoatrial node, and suggest that similar muscarinic receptors are operative in both regions. These phenomena may play an important role in the response of the cardiac conducting system to direct or reflexly mediated vagal input. **(*Circ Res 56: 718–727, 1985*)**

A NUMBER of reports have noted a gradual decay or "fade" in the magnitude of cardiac responses to either sustained or brief repetitive cholinergic interventions. Sinoatrial (SA) rate and atrial contractile responses consistently have been shown to fade after reaching a maximum despite continued vagal stimulation (Chess and Caralesu, 1974; Jalife et al., 1980; Loeb et al., 1981; 1982; Martin et al., 1982; Martin, 1983). In vivo studies of atrioventricular (AV) conduction responses to maintained vagal stimulation have yielded variable results. Loeb et al. (1981) reported that, unlike heart period, AV conduction remained prolonged to the same extent throughout maintained vagal stimulation. They hypothesized that such effects might indicate a difference in muscarinic receptor subtypes between the SA and AV nodes.

In contrast, Martin (1983) found that "secondary" dromotropic responses in the AV node were dependent upon the "initial" magnitude of the response. When the initial response was large, there was a secondary, relatively rapid fading. At intermediate initial levels, there was no appreciable fade. If the initial dromotropic response was small, there was actually a secondary increase in conduction time. He suggested that some aspect of the mechanism responsible for secondary changes in chronotropic and inotropic responses was considerably different from that of the AV conduction response, but questioned the hypothesis invoking different receptor subtypes.

Previous in vitro studies from this laboratory (Jalife et al., 1980) demonstrated that hyperpolarizations of quiescent SA node preparations evoked by vagal stimulation or by exogenous acetylcholine (ACh) or carbamylcholine (CCh) decay with time despite maintained cholinergic influence. Similar findings were reported from responses in bullfrog sinus (Satow, 1968), bullfrog atrium (Tokimasa et al., 1980, 1981), guinea pig atrium (Baumgarten et al., 1984), and rabbit Purkinje fibers (Mubagwa and Carmeliet, 1983).

The present study was undertaken to determine whether the in vitro muscarinic responses of the AV node are the same as those of the SA node. Vagally induced membrane hyperpolarizations were used as a physiological indicator of muscarinic receptor activity. A preliminary report of these findings has appeared elsewhere in abstract form (Salata et al., 1983).

Methods

Isolated SA node-AV node preparations were obtained from 23 albino rabbits (1.5–3.0 kg), which were anesthetized with sodium pentobarbital (35 mg/kg, iv). Hearts were excised and quickly placed in oxygenated Tyrode's solution at 37°C. Dissection was performed in a manner similar to that described by Hoffman et al. (1959). The right atrium, together with both venae cavae, the interatrial septum, the upper portions of both the right ventricular free wall and interventricular septum were cut out. An incision was made starting at the inferior end of the right ventricular free wall, extending through the atrioventricular groove along the anterior border of the right atrium, and terminating with a longitudinal cut through the anterior wall of the superior vena cava. A second incision was made along the lateral border of the crista terminalis, extending inferiorly and then medially along the junction of the right atrial free wall and septum. Preparations then were pinned to a wax bottom Plexiglas tissue bath with the endocardial surface up. Equilibration was allowed for at least 1 hour while the preparation was superfused at a rate of 20 ml/min with a modified Tyrode's solution that was saturated with a mixture of 95% O_2 and 5% CO_2 and maintained at 37°C. The composition of the solution was (mM): NaCl, 130; KCl, 4; NaH_2PO_4, 1.2; $NaHCO_3$, 24; $CaCl_2$, 1.8; $MgCl_2$, 1.0; and dextrose, 5.6. Propranolol (4 μM) was added to eliminate any β-adrenergic effects due to release of norepinephrine.

A schematic diagram of the preparation is shown in Figure 1. Transmembrane potentials were recorded differentially from the primary pacemaker region (ME1) of the SA node and N-region (ME2) of the AV node using microelectrodes (20–30 MΩ) filled with 2.7 M KCl and connected to high input impedance amplifiers (WPI models 750 and KS-700). The electrical signals were displayed on a Tektronix 565 oscilloscope and photographed with a Grass C4 kymographic camera. The primary pacemaker region of the SA node and N-region of the AV node were identified by their characteristic action potential configurations and responses to vagal stimuli (cf. Cranefield et al., 1959; West and Toda, 1967). Postganglionic vagal nerve stimulation was performed by a technique modified from Vincenzi and West, (1963). Stimuli were applied through two pairs of Teflon-coated silver electrodes exposed only at the tips which were separated by 3–5 mm. The stimulating electrodes were positioned directly on the endocardial surface of the preparation, one pair near the cephalic portion of the SA node (VS1) and the other pair near the coronary sinus anterior to the AV node (VS2; Fig. 1). Final electrode positioning was determined by optimal responses to vagal stimulation at any given intensity (cf. West and Toda, 1967). Stimuli were generated by two P6i Frederick Haer units and consisted of trains of biphasic pulses, 50–150 μsec in duration, 10–20 V in amplitude, and at a frequency of 200 Hz. These pulses were subthreshold for cardiac cells but were of sufficient magnitude to stimulate postganglionic vagal nerve terminals (Jalife et al., 1983; Slenter et al., 1984).

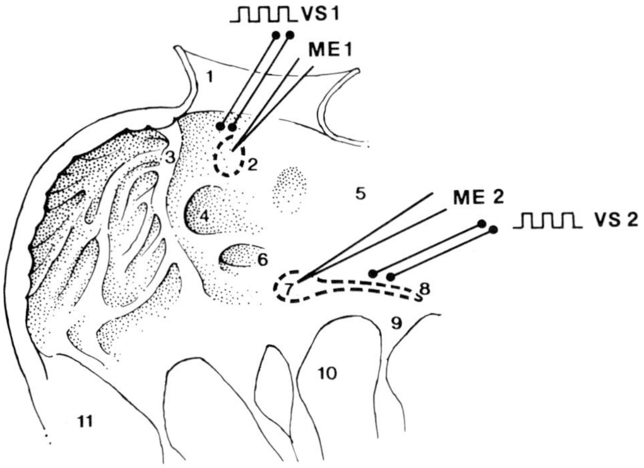

FIGURE 1. *Diagram of preparations: 1 = superior vena cava, 2 = sinoatrial node, 3 = crista terminalis, 4 = inferior vena cava, 5 = interatrial septum, 6 = coronary sinus, 7 = atrioventricular node, 8 = His bundle, 9 = septal cusp of tricuspide valve, 10 = interventricular septum, and 11 = right ventricular free wall. Microelectrode recording sites (ME) and bipolar electrodes for postganglionic vagal stimulation (VS) of the SA node (1) and AV node (2), respectively.*

Test vagal stimuli were applied while preparations were discharging spontaneously to assess the effects on SA nodal rate and on AV conduction or junctional pacemaker rate in order to (1) confirm that recordings were from the primary pacemaker region of the SA node and N-region of the AV node, (2) assure that satisfactory vagal effects were achieved, and (3) aid in positioning of the stimulating electrodes and optimize the stimulation parameters. Once the optimal vagal stimulation parameters were achieved, only the number of pulses and, thus, the duration of the vagal trains were altered to vary the intensity of the vagal stimulus.

After obtaining sufficient information from the spontaneously beating preparations, they were superfused with Tyrode's solution containing 2.2 μM verapamil for the remainder of the experiments. Most preparations became quiescent within 60 minutes after superfusion was initiated, and vagally induced hyperpolarizations could be studied without interference from spontaneous action potentials. In some preparations, it was necessary to cut away bordering myocardial tissue exhibiting subsidiary pacemaker activity which was refractory or less sensitive to verapamil. In 11 of 23 preparations, the AV node was carefully dissected free from surrounding tissue and was studied in isolation. The other 12 preparations were studied with both SA and AV nodes intact.

For analysis of the data, the following definitions were employed: latency is defined as the time interval between the onset of vagal stimulation and the onset of the induced hyperpolarization. During prolonged (200 msec or longer) vagal stimulation, the maximal membrane hyperpolarization (nadir) is defined as E_{max}, and the time interval from the onset of vagal stimulation to E_{max} is termed T_o. Thus T_o corresponds to the point in time at which E_{max} is achieved (see inset, Fig. 4).

TABLE 1
Hyperpolarizing Responses of SA and AV Node Cells to Postganglionic Vagal Stimulation

	RMP (mV)	E_{max} (mV)	T_o (msec)
SAN ($n = 7$)	−43.2 ± 1.1	24.4 ± 3.5	479 ± 46
AVN ($n = 14$)	−48.3 ± 3.1	26.0 ± 2.3	512 ± 51

Data expressed as mean ± SEM; vagal train durations 2–5 seconds. SAN: sinoatrial node; AVN: atrioventricular node; RMP: resting membrane potential; E_{max}: maximal membrane hyperpolarzation; T_o: time from onset of vagal stimulation to E_{max}. Analysis by Dunnett's method revealed no significant differences between SAN and AVN.

TABLE 2
Regression Analysis of Recovery Process during Twin Vagal Pulses

	Slope ($\%E_{max}$/sec)		Intercept ($\%E_{max}$)		
	Mean ± SEM	Range	Mean ± SEM	Range	*r*
SAN (*n* = 12)	7.4 ± 0.7	2.6–11.8	60.1 ± 4.7	24.8–79.8	0.94
AVN (*n* = 10)	7.7 ± 1.9	2.7–14.9	52.1 ± 6.4	30.5–78.1	0.97

No significant difference between the slopes of the regression lines for the SAN and AVN (Student's *t*-test). Abbreviations defined in footnote to Table 1.

Analysis of variance was used for statistical analysis of vagally induced changes in membrane potential (Table 1) and Dunnett's *t*-test (Steel and Torrie, 1960) was used for comparisons. Recovery from fade was studied via regression analysis (Table 2), and was compared in SA vs. AV nodes via Student's *t*-test.

The time constants for the fade of hyperpolarization were determined by curve peeling (Zierler 1981). The varying amplitude (E_t) of the hyperpolarizations was measured at time (t) after E_{max}, was expressed as a fraction of E_{max} and plotted on semilogarthmic coordinates as a function of time (Fig. 4). Straight lines were drawn by eye through the linear portions of the curve. The fast component was determined by subtracting the slow component from the total curve, and the time constants (τ) were determined from the resulting lines.

Results

Hyperpolarization in SA and AV Nodes

Previous studies have shown that vagal stimulation produces membrane hyperpolarization in quiescent SA nodal cells (Jalife and Moe, 1979; Jalife et al., 1980). Such hyperpolarization increases in amplitude and duration as a direct function of the vagal stimulus train duration.

In this study, we found that graded hyperpolarizations mediated by postganglionic vagal stimulation are also characteristic of cells within the AV node region. This is illustrated in Figure 2, which shows transmembrane potentials recorded from an N-cell in a quiescent AV node preparation with a resting potential of −50 mV. Six superimposed traces demonstrate the responses induced by postganglionic vagal trains consisting of 5, 10, 15, 25, and 30 pulses, from top to bottom, respectively. Hyperpolarizations began after a latency of about 80 msec following initiation of the vagal trains (arrow), and varied in amplitude between 4 and 21 mV, depending on vagal train duration. Longer vagal trains (not shown) produced increasingly greater hyperpolarizations, which, in this case, reached an E_{max} of 25 mV at an interval of 490 msec (T_o) after the onset of vagal stimulation. Similar results were observed in seven isolated AV node and seven combined SA-AV node preparations (Table 1). These results in the rabbit AV node were analogous to previous results in cat SA node-vagus nerve preparations (Jalife et al., 1980) and bullfrog sinus node preparations (Satow, 1968).

Study of vagally induced hyperpolarizations of the SA and AV nodes simultaneously in the same preparation substantiated the similarities of the re-

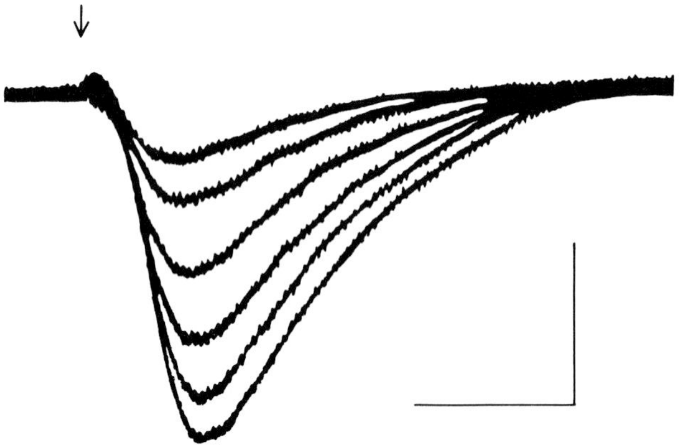

FIGURE 2. *Transmembrane potential recordings from an N-cell of an isolated AV node preparation. Six superimposed traces show progressively greater hyperpolarizations induced by submaximal vagal stimulus trains of 5, 10, 15, 20, 25, and 30 pulses (top to bottom). Arrow indicates onset of vagal trains. Calibrations are 400 msec and 10 mV. (Experiment of 6-17-82.)*

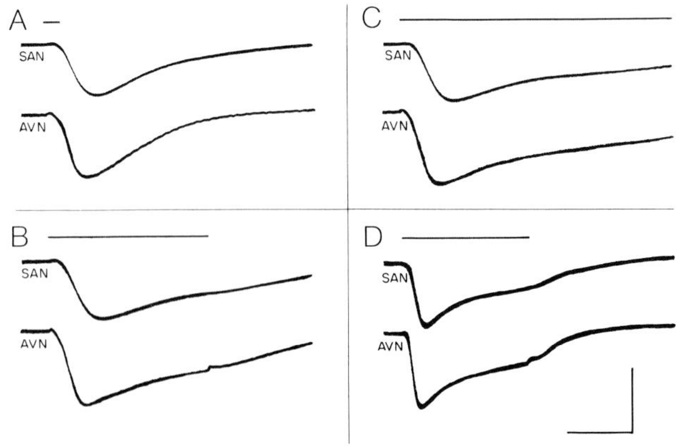

FIGURE 3. *Simultaneous transmembrane potential recordings from the SA node and AV node during vagal stimulation (top bars). Panel A: submaximal (100-msec) vagal train results in very similar responses in both the SA and AV nodes. Panel B: supramaximal (1-sec) vagal train produces maximal amplitude hyperpolarizations in both regions, which decay with time despite maintained vagal stimulation. Longer vagal trains (2 sec) in panels C and D further demonstrate the decay phenomenon. Note slower sweep speed in panel D. Scale: vertical: 20 mV; horizontal: A, B, C, = 400 msec, D = 1 sec. (Experiment of 5-5-83.)*

sponses in the two regions. Indeed, as shown by the example in Figure 3, the hyperpolarizations were found to be nearly identical. In panel A, a 100-msec vagal train (top horizontal bar) produced submaximal hyperpolarizations of 15 and 18 mV in the SA and AV nodes, respectively. A 1.0-second vagal train in panel B produced maximal responses with an E_{max} of 18 mV in the SA node and 22 mV in the AV node. T_o values were 320 and 260 msec, respectively. Most importantly, despite maintained vagal stimulation beyond attainment of E_{max}, the amplitude of the hyperpolarization in both regions was not maintained, but decayed gradually in a very similar biphasic manner. Application of a longer vagal train (2.0 sec) in panels C and D, further demonstrated this time-dependent decay process. Note that the time scale in panel D was reduced to illustrate better the biphasic nature of the decay.

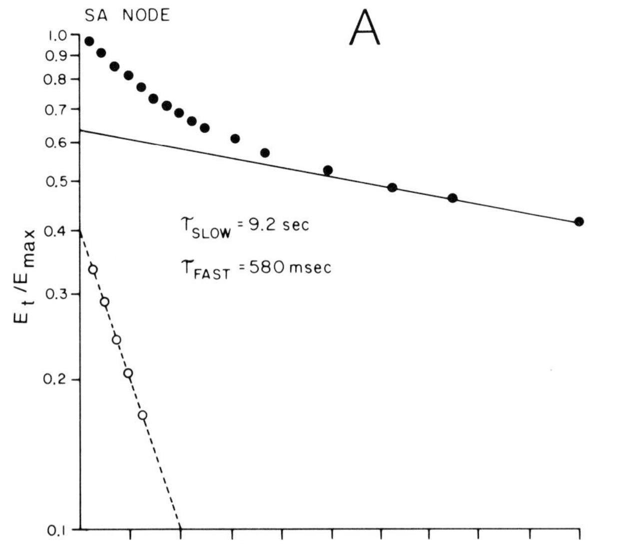

FIGURE 4. *Determination of time constants for the biphasic decay of vagally induced muscarinic responses of the SA node and AV node. Inset shows one example from an N-cell of the AV node to illustrate the method. The time of maximal hyperpolarization (E_{max}) is defined as T_o. Hyperpolarization amplitudes (E_t) were measured at increasing times (t) after T_o and plotted as a fraction of E_{max} on semilogarithmic coordinates. Data fit a biexponential process upon analysis by curve peeling. Time constants (τ) were determined from the lines drawn by eye, and the fast component (unfilled circles) was calculated after subtracting the slow component (solid line) from the total curve. Plotted data are means: SAN, n = 7; AVN, n = 14. (Inset: experiment of 6-14-83.)*

In the example of Figure 3, the E_{max}, T_o, and time course of decay of the SA nodal cell are slightly different from those in the AV node cell. Such minor variations were often seen within a given preparation. Yet, statistical analysis yielded no significant differences in any of the parameters recorded from the two regions (see Table 1 and Fig. 4).

Long Vagal Trains and Time Course of the Fade

Upon quantitative analysis (see Methods), the decay phenomenon in both SA and AV nodes was nearly identical. Figure 4 shows semilogarithmic plots of the mean membrane potential changes with time (E_t), expressed as a fraction of E_{max}. The top panel shows results from the SA node and the bottom panel those from the AV node. In either case, the data best fit a double exponential, and thus displayed two different time constants, one "fast" and one "slow." The fast time constants for the SA and AV nodes were nearly equal (580 vs. 550 msec), whereas the slow time constants were exactly the same (9.2 sec). Clearly, quantitative comparison of SA and AV node hyperpolarizing responses to prolonged vagal stimulation demonstrates that these responses are practically indistinguishable from each other.

The slow time constant has been estimated at 9.2 seconds using vagal trains of less than 5 seconds. Ideally, a time constant should be determined over several multiples of the suggested value. We attempted to analyze quantitatively the decay during long vagal trains (>5 sec) in these studies, but were unable to obtain satisfactory results in all but a few experiments. Typically, when the vagal train duration exceeded 5 seconds, the membrane potential of one or both regions (SA or AV node) became unstable. Subthreshold oscillations were common, and spontaneous action potentials appeared occasionally during and, often, after termination of such vagal trains (cf. Goto et al., 1983). In five experiments, the decay of the membrane potential followed a predictable time course during long vagal trains. One such AV node experiment is shown in Figure 5. The high vertical sensitivity resulted in a noisy trace due to the vagal stimulus throughout the recording. A 50-second vagal train produced a typical biphasic fade of the membrane potential response, which did not reach a steady state. Similar results were obtained in two other AV node and two SA node experiments. The estimated individual time con-

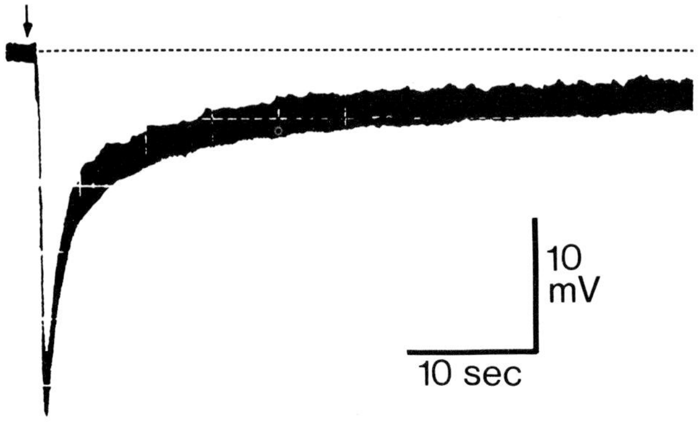

FIGURE 5. *Hyperpolarization of an AV node cell during a long vagal train (50 sec), which terminated just beyond the oscilloscope trace. Dotted line indicates resting membrane potential level of −50 mV. (Experiment of 9-26-84.)*

stants from these experiments ranged from 8–15 msec.

Brief but Repetitive Vagal Trains

Whereas the responses to a continuous vagal train of prolonged duration exhibit essentially the same time curve or decay in both the SA and AV nodes, such continuous vagal activity would not be expected to occur under physiological conditions. Rather, efferent vagal activity has been shown to occur in brief bursts as a result of baroreflex activation during the systolic pressure wave (Jewett, 1964). Therefore, we examined the hyperpolarizing responses produced by brief repetitive vagal stimulation. Figure 6 shows two examples of simultaneous responses of the SA and AV nodes to brief repetitive postganglionic vagal trains (200-msec duration) delivered at 1400- and 850-msec intervals (A and B, respectively). Hyperpolarization amplitude decreased in a biphasic manner that was similar to that demonstrated during continuous vagal stimulation. In the example of Figure 6, the return toward the resting membrane potential for each hyperpolarization was slower for the SA node than for the AV node and, as a result, each successive hyperpolarization was initiated from a more negative membrane potential (i.e., closer to the equilibrium potential for K). This might account in part for the smaller amplitude of the SA node hyperpolarizations in this experiment, and for the apparently more pronounced decay of successive responses in the SA node. As noted previously, such variations between the responses of the two nodal systems were not uncommon. However, no quantitative distinctions between the two regions could be made (see below and Fig. 7).

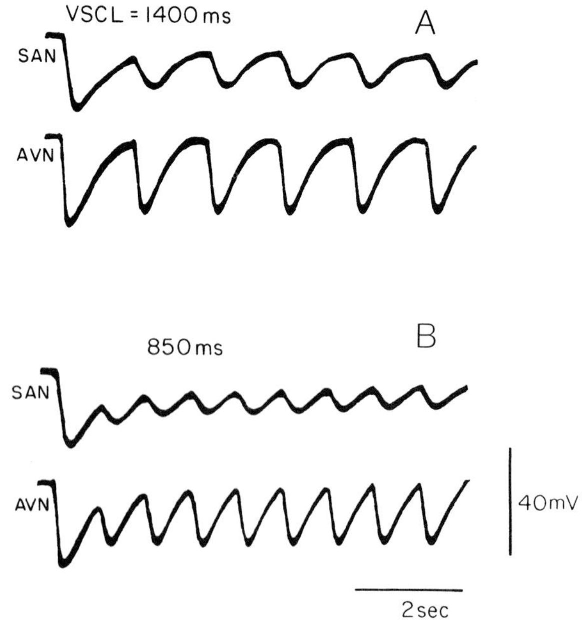

FIGURE 6. *Simultaneous responses of SA and AV nodes to repetitive supramaximal vagal stimuli at cycle lengths of 1400 and 850 msec. Representative traces show that decay occurs in a manner similar to that with continuous vagal stimulation. (Experiment of 5-6-83.)*

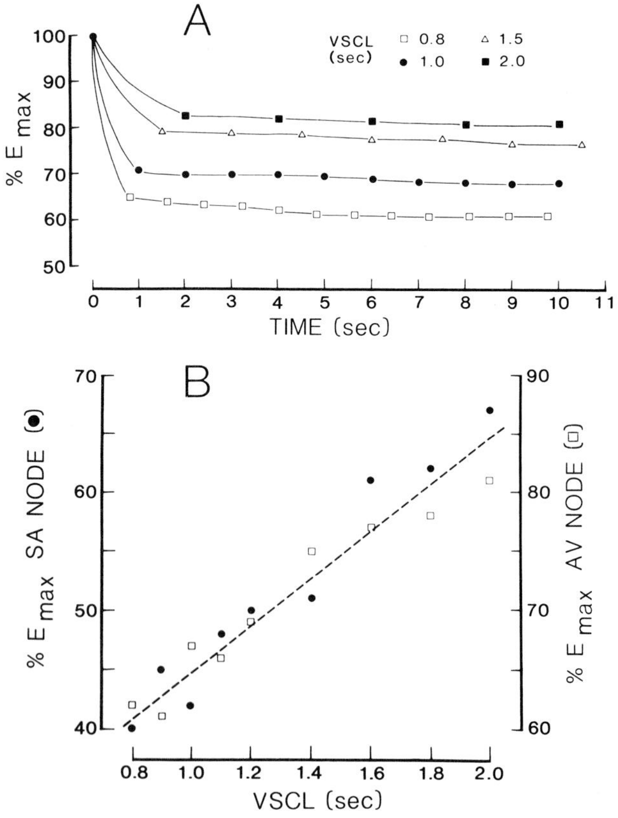

FIGURE 7. *Analysis of responses to repetitive supramaximal vagal stimuli at various cycle lengths. Panel A: the peak amplitude of each successive hyperpolarization, expressed as a percent of the initial hyperpolarization amplitude (E_{max}), is plotted on the ordinate as a function of time. Thus, the "envelope" of the responses is outlined for various vagal stimulus cycle lengths (VSCL). Panel B: the "steady state" amplitude of repetitive responses for the SA node (left ordinate; filled circles) and AV node (right ordinate; unfilled squares) is plotted as a function of the VSCL. See text for details. (Experiment of 5-6-83.)*

The results of Figure 6 suggest that, during repetitive application of brief vagal trains, the rates of fade in both SA and the AV nodes are dependent on the frequency of the trains. This suggestion is confirmed by the data presented in figure 7, which were taken from the same experiment as those in Figure 6. Figure 7A shows the time course of the "envelope" for the responses in the AV node. Brief vagal trains of constant duration (200 msec) were applied repetitively at various cycle lengths (VSCL). In this experiment, the fade of the responses was more rapid at shorter VSCL. In addition, the amplitude of subsequent responses to repetitive vagal trains appeared to approach a steady state value much more rapidly than the responses to continuous vagal stimulation (cf. Fig. 5).

The "steady state" amplitude of hyperpolarization, measured after 30 seconds of repetitive vagal stimulation and expressed as percent of the initial amplitude (E_{max}), is plotted in Figure 7B, as a function of the VSCL. This steady state amplitude increased with increasing VSCL in a linear manner. Furthermore, as evident from Figure 7B, the slopes of the lines for the SA and AV nodes were indistinguishable. Similar data were obtained in all experiments tested in this manner. Regression analysis yielded lines with slopes ($\%E_{max}$/sec) of 11.3 ± 1.9 (mean ± SEM; $n = 6$) and 9.0 ± 2.2 ($n = 5$) for the SA and AV nodes, respectively. These slopes were not significantly different from each other (Student's *t*-test).

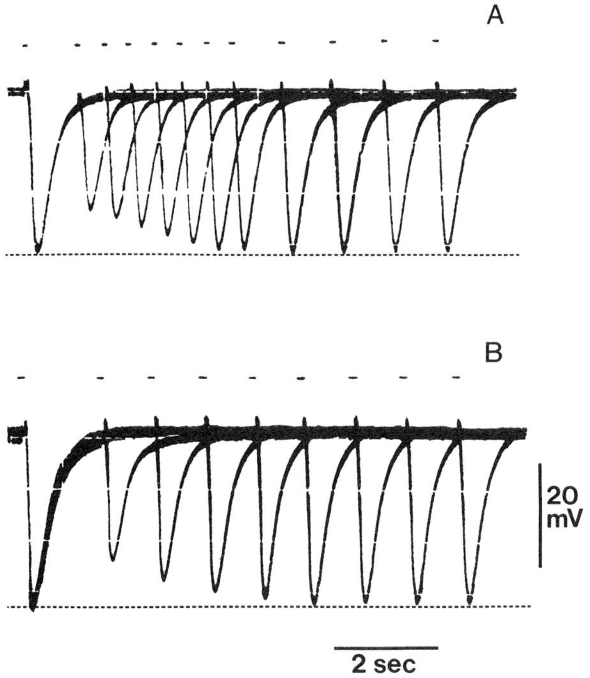

FIGURE 8. *Recovery of muscarinic response in the SA node (panel A) and AV node (panel B). Superimposed traces show responses to twin vagal stimulus trains (top bars; durations: 100 msec for A; 150 msec for B) at increasing coupling intervals. Dotted line drawn to demarcate approximate time of complete recovery. Regression analysis demonstrated that the recovery process under these conditions is best fit by a straight line (see text and Table 2). Data obtained from two separate experiments. (Panel A: experiment of 10-3-84; panel B: experiment of 9-26-84.)*

Recovery from the Fade

The observation that the rate of fade during repetitive vagal stimulation displayed a frequency dependence suggests that, at lower frequencies of vagal stimulation, there was more time for recovery from the process(es) responsible for the decay phenomenon. We studied the recovery process by applying twin vagal trains at either increasing or decreasing coupling intervals. Each vagal train was of sufficient duration to produce a hyperpolarization of maximal amplitude (E_{max}). Examples of separate experiments in the SA node (panel A) and AV node (panel B) are shown in Figure 8. Superimposed traces in each panel demonstrate the responses to twin vagal trains at increasing coupling intervals. Identical results were obtained using decreasing coupling intervals; therefore, no hysteresis was apparent. These results demonstrate that recovery of the muscarinic response is rather slow, and best fit by a linear time course upon regression analysis (Table 2). The slopes of the regression lines for the SA node and AV node are not significantly different.

Discussion

Membrane Hyperpolarization, Fading, and Recovery

We studied membrane potential responses simultaneously in the SA and AV node during postganglionic vagal stimulation as a physiological indicator of muscarinic receptor activation. The interaction of ACh with cardiac muscarinic receptors causes an increase in the membrane conductance to potassium ions (Harris and Hutter, 1956), resulting in hyperpolarization toward the potassium equilibrium potential. Hyperpolarizations of AV node cells increased in amplitude with increasing vagal train duration (Fig. 1), similar to SA nodal and atrial cell membrane responses in previous publications (Toda and West, 1967; Glitsch and Pott, 1978; Jalife and Moe, 1979; Jalife et al., 1980).

In this study, simultaneous application of long vagal trains of supramaximal intensity to both nodal regions, produced hyperpolarizations that reached a maximum and then decayed in a biphasic manner. In all cases, a maximal hyperpolarization was achieved in both nodes, leading to the assumption that a saturating concentration of ACh was present throughout the period of vagal stimulation. In this manner, it was possible to standardize the vagal influence on both regions and to demonstrate that their hyperpolarizing responses and time courses of decay were qualitatively and quantitatively the same (see Table 1 and Figs. 3 and 4). Indeed, maximal hyperpolarizations of about 24 and 26 mV were demonstrated for SA and AV nodes, respectively, and, in both cases, the decay phenomenon was described by a biexponential process yielding two time constants which were nearly identical for the two nodes.

Decay of membrane responses to prolonged muscarinic receptor activation has been described in a number of other cardiac tissue preparations from several species. Hyperpolarization in quiescent bullfrog sinus returned gradually toward the original resting potential, despite continued vagal stimulation (Satow, 1968). Similar results were obtained in kitten sinus node preparations during vagal stimulation or iontophoretic application of ACh (Jalife et al., 1980). Also, in bullfrog atrial muscle, effects on membrane potential, membrane conductance, and action potential amplitude and duration all were found to diminish gradually during prolonged exposure to ACh or CCh (Tokimasa et al., 1980). Moreover, holding clamp current in small SA node preparations has been shown to decline progressively with time in the continuous presence of ACh (Noma et al., 1979). More recent experiments have shown that prolonged exposure to ACh or CCh can result in a concentration-dependent biphasic decay of membrane hyperpolarization or action potential shortening in rabbit Purkinje fibers (Mubagwa and Carmeliet, 1983).

Some investigators have found a lack of decay of muscarinic response (Glitsch and Pott, 1978; Hartzell, 1979; Boyden et al., 1983). Glitsch and Pott (1978) reported that, for the most part, ACh-induced hyperpolarization in guinea pig atria did not dissipate with time. However, more recent experiments in the same preparation (Baumgarten et al., 1984) have indeed demonstrated a significant time-dependent decline in the hyperpolarization, particularly in the presence of high ACh concentrations (see Baumgarten et al., 1984; their Fig. 5).

In a recent study in anesthetized dogs (Martin, 1983), high frequencies of vagal stimulation produced large initial dromotropic responses that gradually decayed toward control. The time course of decay of the dromotropic responses was similar to that of the chronotropic responses found in earlier studies (Loeb et al., 1981; Martin et al., 1982), but was substantially slower than the slowest decay observed in our study (τ = 33 sec vs. 9.2 sec, respectively). This discrepancy may be related to different kinetic parameters being responsible for the fade in each experimental situation (see below), or to differences in the parameters measured, i.e., SA rate and AV conduction time vs. membrane hyperpolarizations.

During application of twin vagal trains at variable coupling intervals (Fig. 8), we found that recovery from hyperpolarization decay in both the SA and AV nodes occurs rather slowly and follows a linear time course. Furthermore, the mean slope of the linear recovery was essentially the same for both regions. A similar type of recovery for AV node conduction has been observed in vivo (Martin, 1976). In atrially paced dogs, two identical brief stimulus bursts were applied to either vagus separated by increasing time intervals. The change in AV nodal conduction time in response to the second stimulus burst was reduced maximally at a coupling interval of about 5 seconds, and it took about 50 seconds to recover completely. This time to recovery is about 10 times longer than that demonstrated in our experiments for the hyperpolarizing response (see Fig. 8). This suggests that, in addition to hyperpolarization, ACh-receptor interactions at the AV nodal cell membrane may trigger changes in other parameters [e.g., inhibition of slow inward current (Ten Eick et al., 1976)] which have slower kinetics and contribute to conduction delay.

Duration- and Frequency-Dependence of the Fade

Our results indicate that the magnitude and rate of decay of vagally induced membrane potential responses in both nodal structures were dependent on the duration and frequency of vagal stimulation (see Figs. 2 and 5). Other authors have demonstrated similar duration and/or frequency dependent effects of vagal stimulation on membrane hyperpolarization, chronotropic responses of the SA node and dromotropic responses of the AV node (Vincenzi and West, 1965; West and Toda, 1967; Chess and Calaresu, 1974; Jalife et al., 1980; Martin et al., 1982).

Although quantitatively different, our results are in general qualitative agreement with those of Martin et al. (1982) in that the pattern of the fade depends on the frequency of vagal stimulation. These results are also consistent with previous data in the isolated kitten sinus node (Jalife et al., 1980). In those experiments, hyperpolarization and negative chronotropic response faded gradually at vagal stimulus frequencies of 25 Hz or more. However, at lower frequencies, maximal hyperpolarization and chronotropic response were either achieved rapidly and maintained (12.5 Hz), or approached more gradually, never reaching a steady state (3.1 and 6.2 Hz). Likewise, in the present experiments, when low frequency vagal stimuli were used to stimulate postganglionic vagal terminals in the AV node region (not shown), the initial hyperpolarization was small and increased continuously for as long as the vagal train was applied.

The hyperpolarizing responses to brief repetitive vagal trains also fade following a biphasic time course (Fig. 6). However, in contrast to the responses to long-lasting stimulation (Fig. 5), the amplitude of brief hyperpolarizations reaches a steady state (Fig. 7) after 10–20 seconds of repetitive stimulation. This observation, together with the demonstration that both the rate of fade and the amplitude of the responses are functions of the interval between repetitive inputs (Figs. 7A and B), explains the reason for the recently demonstrated difference in the amplitude of the phase-response curve (PRC) to single vs. repetitive vagal stimulation (Jalife et al., 1983). Indeed, during repetitive vagal input, the PRC is usually reduced in amplitude in the steady state because the hyperpolarizing effect of the individual trains is diminished, especially at brief vagal train cycle lengths. Similar results would be expected for the phasic responses of AV conduction to repetitive vagal discharge (Jalife et al., 1983, 1984).

Different Receptor Subtypes?

Loeb et al. (1981) reported that during prolonged vagal stimulation in anesthetized dogs, chronotropic responses of the SA node decayed secondarily with time, but the negative dromotropic effect on AV nodal conduction remained nearly constant. They proposed a difference in the ability of muscarinic receptors at the SA and AV node to respond to prolonged activation by ACh, and suggested that different muscarinic receptor subtypes may exist between the SA and AV nodes. Our results and those of Martin (1983) indicate that the lack of decay of AV node responses might be due to frequency or ACh concentration dependence. Loeb et al. (1981) stimulated at only one vagal frequency, which may have been insufficient to demonstrate the fade in the AV node response.

Our findings show that the hyperpolarizing responses of the SA and AV nodes to vagal stimulation are both qualitatively and quantitatively identical. As such, these data do not support the contention that there are different muscarinic receptor subtypes in the two regions. However, muscarinic receptor subtypes have been classified, based on differences in binding affinities or kinetics (Barlow et al., 1976; Galper and Smith, 1978; Hulme et al., 1981), rather than physiological responses. It thus remains possible that different subtypes of muscarinic receptors exist in different cardiac regions or co-exist within a given region.

One final point in this regard deserves consideration. Equating changes in SA node pacemaker rate with those of AV node conduction time as quantitative indicators of muscarinic receptor activation (Loeb et al., 1981) may not be entirely valid. One must assume that these two different responses are modulated equally by the same effector mechanism, or at least by mechanisms having equal gain. Yet, AV node conduction has been found to be less sensitive to vagal influences than is sinus pacemaker activity (Spear and Moore, 1973) and the two systems exhibit different characteristic responses to vagal stimulation (de la Fuente et al., 1969, Jalife et al., 1982). Indeed, when conduction was monitored as a common parameter, i.e., during constant atrial drive, the response of the SA node to cholinergic stimulation was analogous to that of the AV node (West and Toda, 1967). However, since AV node conduction is dependent on the slow inward current, which was blocked in our study, we cannot exclude the possibility that the effect of ACh on this current does not fade.

Possible Mechanism of the Fade

A number of factors may contribute to the decay of responses observed in this study, including (1) a gradual reduction in the release of ACh from synaptic terminals, (2) a decrease in ACh concentration induced by an increase in the activity of cholinesterase, (3) a decrease in the effector response to a constant (saturated) level of receptor occupancy, (4) accumulation of potassium ions in the extracellular space secondary to an increase in potassium conductance, (5) a vagally induced time-dependent increase in inward current, which would tend to depolarize the membrane and oppose the hyperpolarizing response, and (6) desensitization of the postjunctional muscarinic receptors. Our results do not permit an extensive discussion in this regard. However, some of the proposed mechanisms appear to be unlikely, in the light of previous results from this and other laboratories. Indeed, the first two possibilities can be ruled out by the experiments of Jalife et al. (1980) in the kitten SA node in which iontophoretic application of exogenous ACh or CCh also demonstrated fade in the hyperpolarizing response. Similar results were obtained by Tokimasa et al. (1980, 1981) in the bullfrog atrium, and by Mubagwa and Carmeliet (1983) in Purkinje fibers.

The third possibility is also doubtful. A fade in the hyperpolarizing response has been observed even when brief vagal trains or ACh pulses are used to test the responsiveness after conditioning inputs of submaximal intensity (Jalife et al., 1980). In addition, it has been demonstrated that full response to ACh can take as long as 15 minutes to recover, whereas potential and conductance changes reach control values soon after removal of the drug (Tokimasa et al., 1981). With respect to the fourth possibility, potassium accumulation has been proposed to explain the fade in the muscarinic effects on membrane potential in guinea pig atrium and the transient depolarization beyond the resting potential upon washout (Glitsch and Pott, 1978; Baumgarten et al., 1984). Although potassium accumulation might contribute partly to the decay in the hyperpolarizing response in our preparations, recent experiments in Purkinje fibers (Mubagwa and Carmeliet, 1983) argue against this being a major factor in the development of the fade.

The data presented here are consistent with the last two postjunctional mechanisms listed above, namely the activation of a hyperpolarization-induced inward current, possibly i_H (Yanagihara et al., 1980), and the development of desensitization (Katz and Thesleff, 1957; Rang and Ritter, 1970; Jalife et al., 1980) of the muscarinic receptor at the SA and AV node membranes. Whether one or both of these mechanisms are responsible for the fade under our experimental conditions, remains to be determined.

Yet, it seems reasonable to speculate that the biphasic time course of the fade in our SA and AV node preparations might have resulted from at least two different kinetic constants of desensitization (see Clapham and Neher, 1984), and that these constants are identical in the two systems. It is also possible that the complex time course of the decay is the result of a combination of two completely different mechanisms. Thus, the fast initial decay might have resulted from rapid depolarization induced by activation of i_H (Yanagihara et al., 1980), whereas the slower decay could have been associated with muscarinic receptor desensitization.

We thank Victor A.J. Slenter for his help in some of the experiments, and Judith Hefferon for her invaluable technical assistance.

This work was supported by Grants HL29439 and HL06367 from the National Institutes of Health and by a Grant-in-Aid from the American Heart Association, with funds provided in part by the Upstate and Broome County New York Chapters.

J. Jalife is an Established Investigator of the American Heart Association.

J.J. Salata's present address is: University of Chicago, Departments of Medicine, Cardiology, Box 423, 950 East 59th Street, Chicago, Illinois 60637.

Address for reprints: Dr. Jose Jalife, Department of Pharmacology, SUNY/Upstate Medical Center, 766 Irving Avenue, Syracuse, New York 13210.

Received June 28, 1984; accepted for publication February 14, 1985.

References

Barlow RB, Berry KJ, Glenton PAM, Nikolaou NM, Soh KS (1976) A comparison of affinity constants for muscarine-sensitive ACh receptors in guinea pig atrial pacemaker cells at 29°C and 37°C. Br J Pharmacol **58:** 613–620

Baumgarten CM, Singer DH, Fozzard HA (1984) Intra- and extracellular potassium activities, acetylcholine and resting potential in guinea pig atria. Circ Res **54:** 65–73

Boyden PA, Cranefield PF, Gadsby DC, Wit AL (1983) The basis for the membrane potential of quiescent cells of the canine coronary sinus. J Physiol (Lond) **339:** 161–183

Chess GF, Calaresu FR (1974) A mathematical model of the vagus-heart period system in the cat. IEEE Trans Biomed Eng **21:** 21–27

Clapham DE, Neher E (1984) Substance P reduces acetylcholine-induced currents in isolated bovine chromaffin cells. J Physiol (Lond) **347:** 255–277

Cranefield PF, Hoffman BF, Paes de Carvalho A (1959) Effects of acetylcholine on single fibers of the atrioventricular node. Circ Res **7:** 19–23

De la Fuente D, Jedlicka J, Moe GK (1969) Time course of vagal effects on SA and AV nodes (abstr). Fed Proc **28:** 269

Galper JB, Smith TW (1978) Properties of muscarinic acetylcholine receptors in heart cell cultures. Proc Natl Acad Sci USA **75:** 5831–5835

Glitsch HG, Pott L (1978) Effects of acetylcholine and parasympathetic nerve stimulation on membrane potential in quiescent guinea-pig atria. J Physiol (Lond) **279:** 665–668

Goto J, Toyama J, Yamada K (1983) Effects of timing of vagal stimulation on the sinoatrial nodal cell discharge. J Electrocardiol **16:** 45–52

Harris EJ, Hutter OF (1956) The action of acetylcholine on the movements of potassium ions in the sinus venosus of the frog. J Physiol (Lond) **133:** 58P–59P

Hartzell HC (1979) Adenosine receptors in frog sinus venosus: Slow inhibitory potentials produced by adenine compounds and acetylcholine. J Physiol (Lond) **293:** 23–49

Hoffman BF, Paes de Carvalho A, De Mello WC, Cranefield PF (1959) Electrical activity of single fibers of the atrioventricular node. Circ Res **7:** 11–18

Hulme EC, Berrie CP, Birdsall NJM, Burgen ASV (1981) Two populations of binding sites for muscarinic antagonists in the rat heart. Eur J Pharmacol **73:** 137–142

Jalife J, Moe GK (1979) Phasic effects of vagal stimulation on pacemaker activity of the isolated sinus node of the young cat. Circ Res **45:** 595–607

Jalife J, Hamilton AJ, Moe GK (1980) Desensitization of the cholinergic receptor of the sinoatrial cell of the kitten. Am J Physiol **238:** H439–H448

Jalife J, Fraccola P, Moe GK (1982) Entrainment of the SA nodal pacemaker by brief vagal bursts in relation to AV conduction. *In* Cardiac Rate and Rhythm, edited by LN Bouman, HJ Jongsma. The Hague, Martinus Nihoff, pp 577–603

Jalife J, Slenter VAJ, Salata JJ, Michaels DC (1983) Dynamic vagal control of pacemaker activity in the mammalian sinoatrial node. Circ Res **52:** 642–656

Jalife J, Slenter VAJ, Salata JJ (1984) Dynamic vagus-SA node-AV node interactions as a mechanism of complex rhythm and conduction disturbances. Circulation **70** (suppl II): 420

Jewett JD (1964) Activity of single efferent fibers in the cervical vagus nerve of the dog, with special reference to possible cardioinhibitory fibers. J Physiol (Lond) **175:** 321–357

Katz B, Thesleff S (1957) A study of the "desensitization" produced by acetylcholine at the motor end-plate. J Physiol (Lond) **138:** 36–80

Loeb JM, Dalton DP, Moran JM (1981) Sensitivity differences of SA and AV node to vagal stimulation: Attenuation of vagal effects at SA node. Am J Physiol **241:** H684–H690

Loeb JM, De Tarnowsky JM, Johnsen JA (1982) Differential cholinergic sensitivity of sinus and AV nodes. Eur J Pharmacol **83:** 321–324

Martin P (1976) Depression of atrioventricular sensitivity in the dog by successive brief bursts of vagal stimulation. Circ Res **38:** 448–453

Martin P (1983) Secondary AV conduction responses during tonic vagal stimulation. Am J Physiol **245:** H584–H591

Martin P, Levy MN, Matsuda Y (1982) Fade of cardiac responses during tonic vagal stimulation. Am J Physiol **243:** H219–H225

Mubagwa K, Carmeliet E (1983) Effects of acetylcholine on electrophysiological properties of rabbit cardiac Purkinje fibers. Circ Res **53:** 740–751

Noma A, Pepper K, Trautwein W (1979) Acetylcholine-induced potassium current fluctuations in the rabbit sino-atrial node. Pflugers Arch **381:** 255–262

Rang HP, Ritter JM (1970) On the mechanism of desensitization at cholinergic receptors. Mol Pharmacol **6:** 357–382

Salata JJ, Slenter VAJ, Jalife J (1983) Biphasic decay of muscarinic response to acetylcholine in SA and AV nodes. Circulation **68** (suppl III): 154

Satow Y (1968) Hyperpolarization of the quiescent heart and inhibition of the heart beat by vagal impulses. Tahoku J Exp Med **94:** 241–256

Slenter VAJ, Salata JJ, Jalife J (1984) Vagal control of pacemaker periodicity and intranodal conduction in the rabbit sinoatrial node. Circ Res **54:** 436–446

Spear JF, Moore EN (1973) Influence of brief vagal and stellate nerve stimulation on pacemaker activity and conduction within the atrioventricular conduction system of the dog. Circ Res **32:** 27–41

Steel RGD, Torrie JH (1960) Principles and Procedures of Statistics. New York, McGraw-Hill

Ten Eick R, Nawrath H, McDonald TF, Trautwein W (1976) On the mechanism of the negative inotropic effect of acetylcholine. Pflugers Arch **361:** 207–213

Toda N, West TC (1967) Interactions of K, Na, and vagal stimulation in the S-A node of the rabbit. Am J Physiol **212:** 416–423

Tokimasa T, Hasuo H, Koketsu K (1980) Desensitization of the muscarinic receptor of bullfrog atrial muscle. Experientia **36:** 1200–1201

Tokimasa T, Hasuo H, Koketsu K (1981) Desensitization of the muscarinic receptor of atrium in bullfrogs. Jpn J Physiol **31:** 83–97

Vincenzi FF, West TC (1963) Release of autonomic mediators in cardiac tissue by direct subthreshold electrical stimulation. J Pharmacol Exp Ther **141:** 185–194

Vincenzi FF, West TC (1965) Modification by calcium of the release of autonomic mediators in the isolated sinoatrial node. J Pharmacol Exp Ther **150:** 349–360

West TC, Toda T (1967) Response of the A-V node of the rabbit to stimulation of intracardiac cholinergic nerves. Circ Res **20:** 18–31

Yanagihara K, Noma A, Irisawa H (1980) Reconstruction of sinoatrial node pacemaker potential based on voltage clamp experiments. Jpn J Physiol **30:** 841–857

Zierler K (1981) A critique of compartmental analysis. Annu Rev Biophys Bioeng **10:** 531–562

INDEX TERMS: SA node • AV node • Vagal stimulation • Acetylcholine • Muscarinic receptor • Desensitization

The Mechanism by Which Adenosine and Cholinergic Agents Reduce Contractility in Rat Myocardium

Correlation with Cyclic Adenosine Monophosphate and Receptor Densities

Joel Linden, Cathy E. Hollen, and Amrat Patel

From the Cardiovascular Research Program, Oklahoma Medical Research Foundation, Oklahoma City, Oklahoma

SUMMARY. The adenosine analogue phenylisopropyladenosine decreased the basal and isoproterenol-stimulated contractile state of isolated rat left atria. The ED_{50} levels for both responses were similar, suggesting that direct and antiadrenergic effects may be mediated by the same receptor. Phenylisopropyladenosine decreased the cyclic adenosine monophosphate content of isolated atria and inhibited isoproterenol-stimulated adenylate cyclase activity in membranes prepared from atria and ventricles, but not as much as did methacholine. A maximally effective concentration of phenylisopropyladenosine or methacholine greatly reduced atrial contractility measured in the presence of either isoproterenol (1 μM) or Ro7-2956 (a phosphodiesterase inhibitor, 1 mM); however, in the presence of isoproterenol plus Ro7-2956, the contractile effects of phenylisopropyladenosine and methacholine were greatly attenuated. From the contractile data and cyclic adenosine monophosphate analyses, we conclude that direct and antiadrenergic contractile effects of both phenylisopropyladenosine and methacholine result primarily from their effects on cyclic adenosine monophosphate metabolism. The densities of adenosine, muscarinic, and β-adrenergic receptors in rat atrial membranes were found to be 30, 551, and 24 fmol/mg protein, respectively, based on equilibrium-binding assays conducted with ^{125}I-aminobenzyladenosine, [^{3}H]quinuclidinyl benzilate, and ^{125}I-labeled pindolol. The greater effectiveness of methacholine than phenylisopropyladenosine as a negative inotropic agent and an inhibitor of adenylate cyclase in atria may be related to the relative densities of muscarinic and adenosine receptors. **(*Circ Res 56: 728–735, 1985*)**

N^6-SUBSTITUTED adenosine derivatives retaining an unsubstituted ribose ring bind to alkylxanthine-sensitive "ribose-site" (R-site) extracellular receptors and bind poorly to internal sites which require an unsubstituted purine for binding to "purine-sites" [P-sites (Londos and Wolff, 1977)]. There are two types of extracellular R-site adenosine receptors designated R_i (A_1) which decrease adenylate cyclase activity, and R_a (A_2) which stimulate adenylate cyclase activity (Londos et al., 1980). In heart, adenosine reduces catecholamine-stimulated cyclic adenosine monophosphate (cAMP) accumulation and acts on an extracellular receptor which can be blocked by alkylxanthines—attributes which are characteristic of mediation by R_i receptors (Schrader et al., 1977; Belardinelli et al., 1982a). In mammalian ventricular preparations, adenosine alone scarcely attenuates basal tension development, but adenosine inhibits the positive inotropic effect exerted by β-adrenergic agents (Endoh and Yamashita, 1980). In contrast, in mammalian atria, adenosine produces a direct effect, i.e., it reduces basal contractility in the absence of catecholamines (Rockoff and Dobson, 1980; Evans et al., 1982).

The response of cardiac muscle to cholinergic muscarinic agents is strikingly similar to the response to adenosine. Direct effects observed in the absence of catecholamines are much more prominent in mammalian atria than ventricles, whereas large antiadrenergic responses are demonstrable in both atria and ventricles (Levy, 1971; Schwegler et al., 1976). Dobson (1983a) has asserted that the results of Degubareff and Sleator (1965) and Grossman and Furchgott (1964) suggest that antiadrenergic and direct effects of adenosine are different. However, the production of endogenous adenosine (Schrader et al., 1977) may affect the apparent potency of added adenosine. In this study, we have used adenosine deaminase to deaminate endogenous adenosine, and we have examined the contractile effects of the adenosine analogue *l*-N^6-(R-phenyl-isopropyl)-adenosine (PIA) which is resistant to deamination (Westerman and Stock, 1970). We have found that the potency of PIA for direct and antiadrenergic contractile effects on rat left atria is the same, and most or all of the contractile effects of PIA appear to be mediated by a reduction in cyclic adenosine monophosphate (cAMP). The greater effectiveness of methacholine than PIA as a negative inotropic agent and as an inhibitor of adenylate cyclase have been related to the greater density of muscarinic than adenosine receptors.

Methods

Ro7-2956 and *l*-pindolol were the kind gifts of Dr. P.F. Sorter of Hoffman-LaRoche and Drs. H. Weidmann and H. Friedly of Sandoz, respectively. PIA and adenosine deaminase were purchased from Boehringer Mannheim. 2′,5′-Dideoxyadenosine (dideoxyadenosine) was purchased from P-L Biochemicals. *l*-Isoproterenol hydrochloride (isoproterenol), atropine sulfate, phenylmethylsufonic fluoride, and benzamidine were purchased from Sigma. The radioligands ^{125}I-aminobenzyladenosine and ^{125}I-pindolol were prepared as described by Linden et al. (1984) and Barovsky and Brooker (1980), respectively. [^{3}H]Quinuclidinyl benzilate ([^{3}H]QNB) was purchased from New England Nuclear.

Contractility Studies

Left atria were obtained from pentobarbital-anesthetized 200- to 300-g male Sprague-Dawley rats and were stretched to a resting tension of 1 g between platinum hooks in buffer composed of (mM):NaCl, 120; KCl, 5; $MgSO_4$, 1.2; NaH_2PO_4, 1.2; dextrose, 10; $NaHCO_3$, 25; $CaCl_2$, 1.5; pH 7.4, 30°C. The buffer was gassed with 95% O_2, 5% CO_2, and the atria were stimulated through point electrodes with 10-msec monophasic pulses at two times the threshold for contractions at a rate of 2 pulses/sec. Tensions from as many as six atria were digitized simultaneously at 1-msec intervals (Trans Era analog-to-digital converter), and contractile parameters were computer monitored (Tektronix 4052) and stored on magnetic tape every 5 seconds. Some atria were pretreated with 10^{-7} M *l*-pindolol to block *β*-adrenergic receptors; all atria were pretreated with adenosine deaminase (0.2 U/ml).

cAMP and Protein Analyses

Atria were frozen between clamps precooled in liquid nitrogen and homogenized with a Polytron tissue disruptor in 2 ml of 0.1 N HCl. One milliliter of the homogenate was centrifuged at 10,000 *g* for 20 minutes. The supernatants were assayed for cAMP by automated Gammaflow radioimmunoassay (Brooker et al., 1976). Fifty-microliter aliquots of homogenates were assayed for protein by a modification of the procedure of Stowell et al. (1978). Samples of bovine serum albumin standards were added to 750 *μ*l of 0.2 N NaOH containing 0.1% (wt/vol) sodium dodecyl sulfate (SDS). To these solutions, 750 *μ*l of 0.4 N boric acid were added, followed by 1 ml of 0.1 mg/ml of fluorescamine in acetone. Fluorescence was measured at an excitation wavelength of 390 nm and an emission wavelength of 475 nm. The standard curve was fit to a quadratic equation.

Radioligand-Binding Assays

Ventricular or atrial muscle derived from rat hearts was homogenized for 10 seconds with a Polytron tissue disruptor in 50 volumes of ice-cold medium containing 10% sucrose and 0.01% phenylmethylsulfonic fluoride in HED (10 mM HEPES, 10 mM ethylenediamine tetraacetic acid, 1 mM dithiothreitol, and 0.1 mM benzamidine, pH 7.5). The homogenate was filtered through gauze and centrifuged at 20,000 *g* for 30 minutes. The pellet was resuspended in 50 volumes of ice-cold HED and centrifuged again. The pellet then was resuspended in 10 volumes of HED, diluted by 20% with glycerol, and frozen in aliquots at −70°C. For binding assays, 50 *μ*l of the membrane suspension were incubated with 50 *μ*l of radioligands in Tris buffer (50 mM Tris-Cl, 15 mM $MgCl_2$, pH 7.3, at 21°C) and in some cases, 5 U/ml adenosine deaminase. After 2 hours of incubation, the membranes were filtered over glass fiber filters (Gelman type A/E). Nonspecific binding to muscarinic and adenosine receptors was assessed by the addition of 1 *μ*M atropine and 10 *μ*M PIA, respectively.

Adenylate Cyclase Assays

Membranes prepared as described above were thawed and incubated for 20 minutes at room temperature with 10 U/ml adenosine deaminase, and, in some cases, 0.025% sodium dodecyl sulfate, to uncover latent enzyme activity. The membranes were diluted 10-fold with ice-cold 10 mM Tris-Cl (pH 7.9 at 4°C). Fifty microliters of membrane suspensions containing 10–20 *μ*g of protein were added to 50 *μ*l of an enzyme cocktail prepared in 100 mM Tris-Cl (pH 7.5 at 37°C) to make 100 *μ*l of a solution containing 0.5 mM Ro7-2956, 100 *μ*M guanidine triphosphate (GTP), 5 mM phosphoenolpyruvate, 20 U/ml pyruvate kinase, 100 *μ*M adenosine triphosphate (ATP), 2.5 mM $MgCl_2$, 100 *μ*M EDTA, 5 U/ml adenosine deaminase, and various drugs. The enzyme was incubated at 37°C for 10 minutes, and the assay was terminated by the addition of 250 *μ*l of 0.1 M $ZnSO_4$ and 250 *μ*l of 0.1 M Na_2CO_3. The assay was linear with time for at least 15 minutes at protein concentrations up to 100 *μ*g. After centrifugation at 1,500 *g* for 10 minutes, aliquots of the supernatants were acetylated and assayed for cAMP by automated radioimmunoassay (Brooker et al., 1979).

Results

Comparison of Direct and Antiadrenergic Effects of PIA

The direct effects of PIA on rat left atrial contractility were assessed after the addition of pindolol

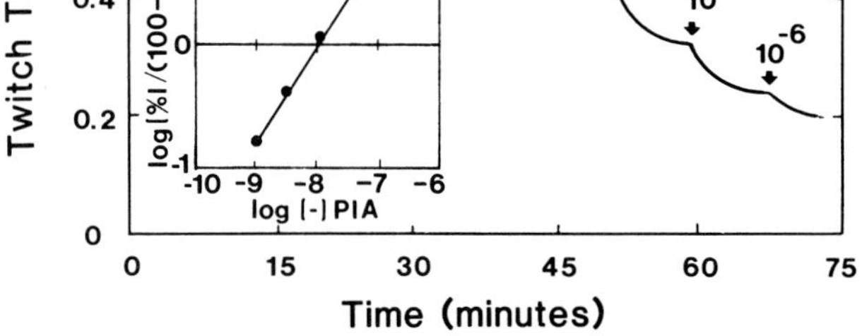

FIGURE 1. *Effect of PIA on rat left atrial contractility. Computer-monitored twitch tension (maximum-resting) of an isolated rat left atrium is plotted as a function of time. The arrows indicate the time of addition of 0.1 μM pindolol, 0.2 U/ml adenosine deaminase, and various cumulative concentrations of PIA. The ED_{50} of PIA was calculated from the x-axis intercept of the Hill plot shown in the inset; %I = percent of maximum PIA-induced contractile response.*

TABLE 1
Summary of the Direct and Antiadrenergic Effects of PIA on Rat Left Atrial Contractility

	PIA ED_{50} (nM)*	Twitch tension (g)†	Efficacy‡
No treatment	12.5 ± 2.3	0.52 ± 0.08	73.6 ± 3.8
Isoproterenol (1 μM)	9.9 ± 0.9	1.37 ± 0.16	87.2 ± 1.9§
Isoproterenol (10 nM)	12.0 ± 1.1	0.98 ± 0.10	84.1 ± 1.1§

Results are expressed as mean ± SEM; $n = 9$.

* ED_{50} values were derived from the x-axis intercepts of Hill plots as illustrated in Figure 1. Each atrium was treated with 6–8 cumulative doses of PIA ranging between 10^{-9} and 10^{-5} M at 10-minute intervals after a 15-minute pretreatment with the indicated drugs. None of the groups differed significantly from the others, based on the F-ratio after analysis of variance.

† Twitch tension measured just before addition of the first dose of PIA.

‡ Efficacy = % [(developed tension before PIA-developed tension after 10 μM PIA)/developed tension before PIA].

§ Greater than no treatment by the Dunnett test ($P < 0.05$).

and adenosine deaminase. These agents were added to counter the effects of endogenous norepinephrine and adenosine, respectively. The effects of PIA on a typical atrium are illustrated in Figure 1. Pindolol produced a small but variable (5–20%) decrease in contractility; adenosine deaminase had no effect. In a series of experiments, direct effects of cumulative doses of PIA on rat atrial contractility were compared to effects of PIA measured in the presence of isoproterenol, which increased contractility and elevated tissue levels of cAMP. The potency of PIA, i.e., the ED_{50} of the PIA-induced negative inotropic response calculated as shown in Figure 1, was not affected by the prior addition of the catecholamine (Table 1). The "P-site" agonist, dideoxyadenosine (10 μM), had no effect on rat atrial contractility in the absence or presence of isoproterenol (not shown).

Effect of Drugs which Modify cAMP Content on the Atrial Contractile Response to PIA and Methacholine

To assess the role of cAMP in mediating the contractile effects of PIA, the contractile response of atria to the most effective dose of PIA (1 μM) was measured in the presence of various other drugs which increase the tissue content of cAMP. PIA produced a large negative inotropic effect when added to atria alone, or when added after either 1 mM Ro7-2956 (86.5 ± 2.26%, $n = 3$) or isoproterenol (Table 2). However, the inotropic response to the purine was greatly attenuated in the presence of both Ro7-2956 and isoproterenol (Table 2). PIA produced a substantial decrease in the tissue content of cAMP in the presence of Ro7-2956 plus isoproterenol, but even in the presence of the purine, tissue

TABLE 2
Direct and Antiadrenergic Effects of PIA and Methacholine on Rat Left Atrial Contractility and cAMP Content

	cAMP (pmol/mg protein, $n = 10$)	cAMP (% decrease)	Contractility (% decrease, $n = 3$)
CON	7.5 ± 0.70		
PIA (1 μM)	5.8 ± 0.62*	33 ± 8.3	72 ± 6.2
MCh (0.3 μM)	5.9 ± 0.72*	31 ± 9.6	64 ± 4.1
MCh (10 μM)	4.6 ± 0.75*	39 ± 10	86 ± 1.4‡
ISO (1 μM)	16.7 ± 3.05		
ISO + PIA	9.5 ± 0.45*	43 ± 2.7	89 ± 1.2
ISO + 0.3 μM MCh	9.3 ± 0.36*	44 ± 2.2	83 ± 3.1
ISO + 10 μM MCh	7.0 ± 0.19*	58 ± 1.1	95 ± 0.3
ISO + Ro (1 mM)	39.6 ± 3.9		
ISO + Ro + PIA	24.0 ± 1.4*	39 ± 3.5	14 ± 1.1
ISO + Ro + 0.3 μM MCh	24.1 ± 1.5*	39 ± 3.8	9 ± 0.8
ISO + Ro + 10 μM MCh	15.1 ± 0.8†	62 ± 2.0	64 ± 4.8‡

Results are expressed as mean ± SEM. Statistical significance was assessed by the Tukey test at $P < 0.05$ (MCh = methacholine, ISO = isoproterenol, Ro = Ro7-2956).

* Significant effect by PIA or MCh.

† Less than PIA and 0.3 μM MCh.

‡ Greater than PIA and 0.3 μM MCh.

levels of cAMP remained substantially higher (3.2-fold) than basal levels. These data strongly suggest that the contractile effects of PIA are mediated primarily by a reduction of cAMP.

The effects of two doses of methacholine on rat atrial contractility and cAMP content are also summarized in Table 2. The ED_{50} of the cholinergic agent as a negative inotropic agent was 82 ± 11 nM ($n = 4$, not shown). A moderate dose of methacholine, 0.3 μM, produced effects similar to those of 1 μM PIA (Table 2). Large negative inotropic responses measured in the presence of Ro7-2956 alone or isoproterenol alone were greatly attenuated in the combined presence of Ro7-2956 and isoproterenol. However, unlike PIA the most effective dose of methacholine (10 μM) did produce a substantial negative inotropic response in the presence of both Ro7-2956 and isoproterenol, possibly because it was more effective than PIA at reducing the tissue content of cAMP.

Effects of PIA and Methacholine on Adenylate Cyclase Activity

The effects of PIA and methacholine on basal and isoproterenol-stimulated adenylate cyclase activity were assessed in rat ventricle and atrial membranes. If membranes were pretreated with a low concentration of sodium dodecyl sulfate, latent adenylate cyclase activity was unmasked, and the response of the enzyme to drugs was enhanced. Therefore, subsequent assays employed membranes which were pretreated with the detergent. PIA and methacholine produced small effects on the basal activity of adenylate cyclase; the isoproterenol-stimulated enzyme was inhibited to a greater extent (Table 3). Similar statistically significant effects of PIA and methacholine were observed with two additional batches of ventricular membranes. Since the effects of PIA and methacholine on atrial adenylate cyclase activity were quite small, experiments to assess the effects of these drugs on the enzyme in the presence of isoproterenol were repeated with four additional preparations of atrial membranes. PIA and methacholine reduced isoproterenol-stimulated adenylate cyclase activity by an average of 9.05 ± 1.41% and 17.8 ± 2.47%, respectively. Paired analysis of the mean data from these five experiments indicated that the PIA response differed significantly from the control and methacholine responses at $P < 0.01$.

The inhibitory effects of adenosine R-site agonists on adipocyte membranes have been reported to be amplified by sodium (Londos et al., 1981). Therefore, the adenylate cyclase activity of heart membranes was measured in response to the most effective concentrations of PIA, methacholine, and isoproterenol as a function of sodium concentration. Results obtained with a typical batch of membranes are illustrated in Figure 2. Similar results were obtained with three additional batches of membranes. PIA failed to decrease the basal activity of adenylate cyclase in the absence of sodium, although the isoproterenol-stimulated enzyme was inhibited by 7–10% in the absence of sodium. At NaCl concentra-

TABLE 3
Effect of Sodium Dodecyl Sulfate on Latent Adenylate Cyclase Activity in Single Batches of Rat Ventricle and Atrial Membranes*

Drug	cAMP (pmol/mg protein per 10 min) Without SDS	With SDS†
Ventricles (n = 3)		
Basal	900 ± 20	1340 ± 50
PIA (1 μM)	880 ± 20	1180 ± 10‡
MCh (10 μM)	720 ± 20‡	940 ± 60‡
ISO (10 μM)	2330 ± 70	4220 ± 80
ISO + PIA	2090 ± 100‡	3650 ± 120‡
ISO + MCh	2040 ± 40‡	3310 ± 30‡
Atria (n = 5)		
Basal	127 ± 5	158 ± 6
PIA	131 ± 3	159 ± 8
MCh	127 ± 3	140 ± 4‡
ISO	345 ± 7	472 ± 9
ISO + PIA	324 ± 4‡	438 ± 9‡
ISO + MCh	302 ± 7‡	395 ± 8‡

* Adenylate cyclase activity was assayed as described in Methods. The assay buffer contained 100 mM NaCl. Data are presented as means ± SEM; (MCh = methacholine; ISO = isoproterenol; SDS = sodium dodecyl sulfate).

† Membranes were pretreated with or without 0.025% SDS for 20 minutes at 21°C. The detergent was diluted 20-fold before initiation of the assay.

‡ Less than basal or ISO alone ($P < 0.05$) by the one-tailed Dunnett test. The three groups containing ISO were evaluated separately from the three groups that did not contain ISO.

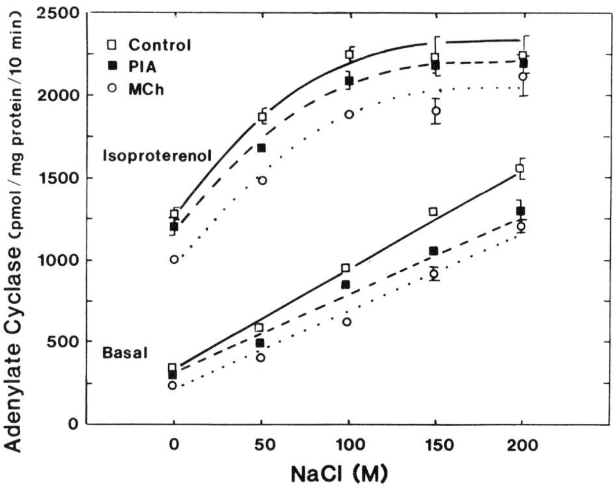

FIGURE 2. *Effects of PIA and methacholine on rat ventricular adenylate cyclase activity. Adenylate cyclase activity was measured using the cocktail described in Methods, supplemented with various concentrations of NaCl. Most effective concentrations of PIA (10 μM), methacholine (100 μM), and isoproterenol (10 μM) were used. Data represent the mean ± SEM, n = 5; standard errors smaller than the symbols are not shown.*

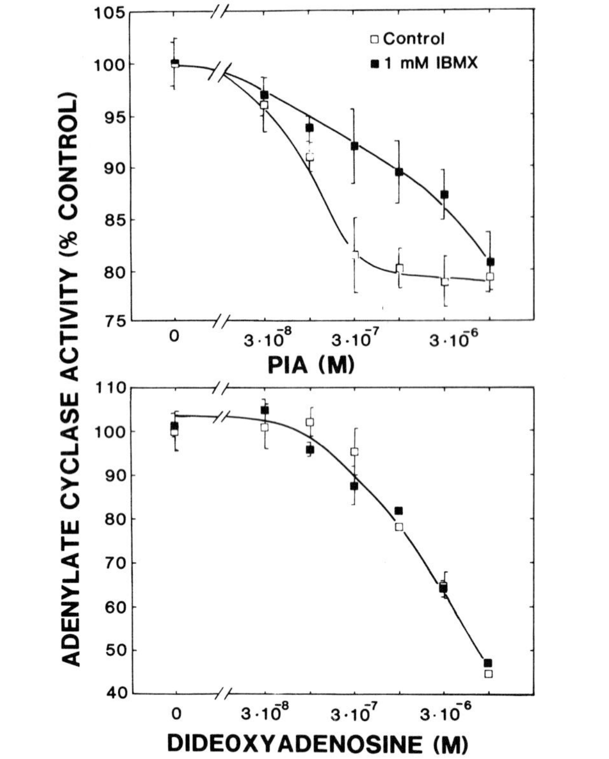

FIGURE 3. *Effects of IBMX on the dose-response curves of PIA and dideoxyadenosine for inhibition of adenylate cyclase in ventricular membranes. Enzyme activity was measured in the presence of 100 mM NaCl. 100% = 427 pmol cAMP formed/mg protein per 10 min. Data represent the mean ± SEM, n = 4; standard errors smaller than the symbols are not shown.*

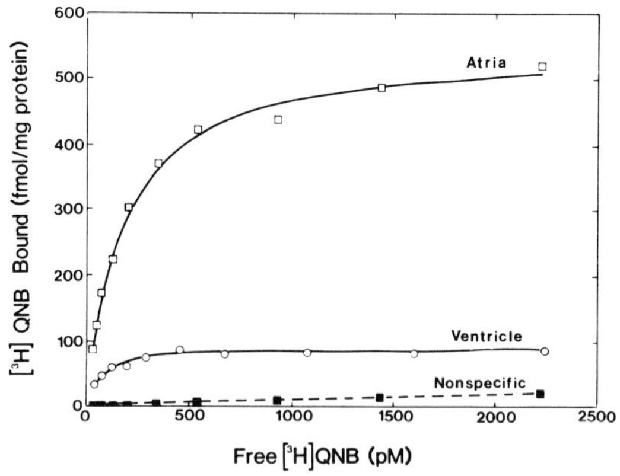

FIGURE 4. *Equilibrium [³H]QNB binding to rat atria and rat ventricle membranes. The open symbols represent specific (total − nonspecific) binding. Each data point represents the mean of three closely agreeing replicates. The curves represent computer-generated best fits to a single site-binding model.*

tions above 100 mM, 1 μM PIA reduced both basal and isoproterenol-stimulated enzyme activity 10–20%. Methacholine was more effective than PIA, decreasing enzyme activity 20–30%.

To determine whether the inhibitory effect of PIA on basal adenylate cyclase activity is receptor mediated, we used a known inhibitor of adenosine receptors, the methylxanthine IBMX (Schwabe and Trost, 1980). IBMX shifted the dose-response curve of PIA to the right, indicative of a competitive inhibitor (Fig. 3). In contrast, inhibition of adenylate cyclase produced by the "P-site" agonist dideoxyadenosine was not affected by IBMX. These data confirm that inhibition of basal ventricular adenylate cyclase activity is mediated by an R_i-receptor.

Quantification of Adenosine, Cholinergic-Muscarinic, and β-Adrenergic Receptors in Atrial and Ventricular Membranes

The density of various receptors was assessed in membranes prepared from atria and ventricles. The greatest discrepancy between atria and ventricles was in the density of muscarinic-cholinergic receptors assessed by [³H]QNB binding (Fig. 4). The results of equilibrium-binding assays using ¹²⁵I-aminobenzyladenosine, [³H]QNB, and ¹²⁵I-pindolol to label adenosine, muscarinic, and β-adrenergic receptors, respectively, are summarized in Table 4. There was a large excess of cholinergic-muscarinic receptors compared to adenosine or β-adrenergic receptors, particularly in atria.

TABLE 4
Equilibrium Binding of Various Radioligands to Membranes Derived from Rat Atria and Ventricles

	Radioligand (receptor)	R_T (fmol/mg protein)	Ratio of R_T (atria:ventricle)	K_D (nM)
Ventricle	¹²⁵I-Aminobenzyl-adenosine	23	1.3	9
Atria	(Adenosine)	30		3.0
Ventricle	[³H]QNB (Muscarinic)	88	6.3	0.07
Atria		551		0.18
Ventricle	¹²⁵I-Pindolol	10	2.4	0.022
Atria	(β-Adrenergic)	24		0.026

Six to 10 radioligand concentrations were used in each binding assay. The same preparation of membranes was used for all assays. Similar results were obtained in a second experiment using different membrane preparations.

Discussion

The results of this study indicate that the potency of the adenosine analogue PIA as a negative inotropic agent in rat left atria is the same, regardless of whether direct or antiadrenergic responses are measured. By "direct," we are referring to the tissue response in the absence of other drugs and in the presence of pindolol, a β-adrenergic receptor antagonist, which was added to counter the effects of any endogenous catecholamine released by sympathetic nerves contained in the isolated atria. By "antiadrenergic," we are referring to the response elicited by PIA after the prior addition of the catecholamine isoproterenol. These studies were conducted in the presence of adenosine deaminase in order to deaminate any endogenous adenosine released by the atria to inosine, which is inactive. As mentioned in the introduction, it has been suggested that direct and antiadrenergic effects of adenosine may be mediated by different receptors. However, these responses are probably influenced by the release of endogenous adenosine, as well as by adenosine uptake and degradation. This study, which indicates that the potency of PIA is equivalent for direct and antiadrenergic contractile effects, suggests that both responses may be mediated by the same receptor.

Our results also suggest that effects of PIA and methacholine on rat atrial contractility are mediated predominantly or entirely by inhibition of adenylate cyclase activity. If the atrial concentration of cAMP was elevated to a very high level by the combined addition of isoproterenol and Ro7-2956, the ability of PIA or a low dose (0.3 μM) of methacholine to reduce contractility was greatly attenuated. The adenylate cyclase inhibitors still lowered tissue levels of cAMP, but the cyclic nucleotide concentration remained well above the basal level. Possibly, this combination of drugs causes saturation of cAMP-dependent protein kinase by the cyclic nucleotide even after the addition of PIA or methacholine. At the most effective concentrations, methacholine was more effective than PIA at reducing the cAMP content of atria. A large dose of methacholine (10 μM) reduced the atrial content of cAMP to near the basal level and produced a substantial negative inotropic response, even in the presence of isoproterenol and Ro7-2956. However, we have shown previously that in the presence of both isoproterenol (0.1 μM) and IBMX (300 μM), even a high concentration of methacholine (20 μM) produced only a small negative inotropic effect (Linden and Brooker, 1979).

The results of this study indicate that PIA reduces rat atrial contractility, cAMP content and adenylate cyclase activity. Numerous other studies confirm that adenosine agonists produce negative inotropic in vitro effects in atria and ventricles through an extracellular receptor blocked by methylxanthines (see the introductory paragraphs). However, Seiteberger et al. (1984) have suggested that adenosine effects are not important under physiological conditions in anesthetized dogs. In contrast, adenosine does influence myocardial function in humans, and has been used successfully to treat paroxysmal supraventricular tachycardia, suggesting a physiologically important role by adenosine in man (DiMarco et al., 1983; Belhassen and Pelleg, 1984).

As in this study, Leung et al. (1983) demonstrated an adenosine receptor-mediated decrease in adenylate cyclase activity in membranes derived from guinea pig ventricles, but Schütz and Tuisl (1981) did not. We have found that receptor-mediated effects of adenosine on myocardial adenylate cyclase are small, about half the size of cholinergic effects, require high GTP (100 μM), are reduced or abolished by KCl extraction of heart membranes, and require the addition of adenosine deaminase to deaminate endogenous adenosine even in the absence of added ATP. Schütz and Tuisl (1981) used 10 μM GTP, extracted membranes with KCl, and did not add adenosine deaminase, whereas Leung et al. (1983) used 100 μM GTP, did not extract membranes with KCl, and did add adenosine deaminase. There are also conflicting data on the effects of adenosine on the cAMP content of intact hearts. Most investigators have found that adenosine agonists decrease the myocardial content of cAMP. cAMP was reduced by phenylisopropyladenosine in this study using rat atria. The cyclic nucleotide was also lowered by adenosine agonists in enzymatically dispersed embryonic chick heart cells and intact embryonic chick ventricles (Belardinelli et al., 1982b; Linden et al., 1984), in enzymatically dispersed rat heart cells (Hazeki and Ui, 1981), in perfused guinea pig hearts (Schrader et al., 1977; Belardinelli et al., 1982a), and perfused rat hearts (Dobson, 1978; Dobson, 1983b). In contrast, Schmitz et al. (1981) and Böhm et al. (1984) failed to detect statistically significant effects of adenosine on the cAMP content of guinea pig hearts. Possibly, these negative data result from the partial occupancy of adenosine receptors by endogenously released adenosine, since the addition of adenosine deaminase in some cases has been shown to increase myocardial contractility (Dobson, 1983a) and cAMP content (Hazeki and Ui, 1984).

Both acetylcholine (TenEick et al., 1976) and adenosine (Belardinelli and Isenberg, 1983; Jochem and Nawrath, 1983) have been reported to activate a potassium conductance in mammalian atria, but not ventricles. The latter investigators speculated that ventricular heart muscle may lack a receptor-controlled potassium conductance. These observations raise the possibility that cAMP mediates antiadrenergic effects observed in both atria and ventricles, whereas a cAMP-independent effect on potassium conductance may mediate direct contractile effects observed in atria. Alternatively, both direct and indirect effects of acetylcholine and adenosine may be mediated by cAMP. The results of this study favor the latter hypothesis. A mechanism by which cAMP may influence potassium conductance is suggested by the observation that cAMP enhances calcium pumping into the cardiac sarcoplasmic reticulum by increasing the phosphorylation of phospholamban (Kranias and Solaro, 1982). Since raising intracellular calcium activates a potassium conductance in nervous tissue (Meech, 1978) and Purkinje fibers (Isenberg, 1977), effects of acetylcholine and adenosine on potassium channel conductance may be secondary to reduced myocardial cAMP and increased diastolic levels of calcium.

The possibility that the contractile effects of adenosine and acetylcholine are mediated by inhibition of adenylate cyclase is supported by studies on the effects of phosphodiesterase inhibitors on the sensitivity of mammalian ventricles to inhibitors of adenylate cyclase. Direct effects of acetylcholine are minimal or absent in mammalian ventricles (Schwegler et al., 1976) and embryonic chick ventricles (Biegon et al., 1980), but acetylcholine inhibits the stimulatory effects of phosphodiesterase inhibitors in both mammalian ventricles (Meester and Hardman, 1967; Endoh and Honma, 1979) and embryonic chick ventricles (Biegon et al., 1980). Similarly, we have shown previously that although adenosine alone has no effects on slow Ca^{++}-dependent action potentials in embryonic chick ventricles, the stimulatory effects of Ro7-2956 in embryonic chick ventricles are inhibited by adenosine (Linden et al., 1982). Both cholinergic agents (Murad et al., 1962) and PIA (this report and Leung et al., 1983) can decrease the basal activity of adenylate cyclase measured in ventricular membranes. These data suggest that the absence of direct ventricular contractile effects by adenylate cyclase inhibitors may be a consequence of low basal levels of cAMP in a physiologically important pool in the ventricular myocardium, i.e., basal levels may be below the threshold for activation of cAMP-dependent protein kinase.

Both PIA and dideoxyadenosine were found to decrease adenylate cyclase activity in rat ventricle membranes, but only the effect of PIA was blocked by a methylxanthine (IBMX). Dobson (1983b) reported that adenosine reduced isoproterenol-stimulated but not basal rat ventricle adenylate cyclase activity. However, these responses were measured in the absence of adenosine deaminase and were not inhibited by theophylline. Therefore, they probably represent intracellular P-site rather than receptor-mediated R-site effects (Londos et al., 1978, 1981). P-site-mediated effects produced by dideoxyadenosine (this report) or by adenosine (Dobson, 1983b) are probably not related to the contractile effects of adenosine, which appear to be mediated by extracellular R-site receptors that can be blocked by alkylxanthines (Schrader et al., 1977; Belardinelli et al., 1982).

Methacholine was found to be more effective than PIA as a negative inotropic agent and as an inhibitor of adenylate cyclase activity. Also, the density of muscarinic receptors was found to be greater than the density of adenosine receptors in both rat atria and ventricles. Adenosine and muscarinic receptors probably are coupled to adenylate cyclase through a common guanine nucleotide-binding protein (Gilman, 1984). These data conform to a model in which the effectiveness of inhibitors of adenylate cyclase depends on receptor density. The probability of an interaction between agonist-occupied receptors and inhibitory guanine nucleotide-binding proteins is enhanced as receptor density increases.

We gratefully acknowledge the technical assistance of Sherri Lyman. George Mikos was instrumental in developing computer programs to monitor cardiac contractility. We also thank Kim Hauenstein for her help in preparing this manuscript.

This study was supported in part by Grant OK-83-17 from the American Heart Association. Ms. Hollen was the recipient of a Fleming Scholarship from the Oklahoma Medical Research Foundation.

Address for reprints: Dr. Joel Linden, Cardiovascular Research Program, Oklahoma Medical Research Foundation, 825 Northeast 13th Street, Oklahoma City, Oklahoma 73104.

Received August 13, 1984; accepted for publication February 14, 1985.

References

Barovsky K, Brooker G (1980) (−)[125]I-Iodopindolol, a new highly selective radioiodinated β-adrenergic receptor antagonist: Measurement of β-receptors on intact rat astrocytoma cells. J Cyclic Nucleotide Res **6:** 297–307

Belardinelli L, Isenberg C (1983) Increase in potassium conductance in isolated guinea pig atrial myocytes by adenosine and acetylcholine. Am J Physiol **244:** H734–H737

Belardinelli L, Fenton RA, West A, Linden J, Althaus JS, Berne RM (1982a) Extracellular action of adenosine and the antagonism by aminophylline on the atrioventricular conduction of isolated perfused guinea pig and rat hearts. Circ Res **51:** 569–579

Belardinelli L, Vogel S, Linden J, Berne RM (1982b) Antiadrenergic action of adenosine on ventricular myocardium in embryonic chick hearts. J Mol Cell Cardiol **14:** 291–294

Belhassen B, Pelleg A (1984) Acute management of paroxysmal supraventricular tachycardia: Verapamil, adenosine triphosphate or adenosine? Am J Cardiol **54:** 225–227

Biegon RL, Epstein PM, Pappano AJ (1980) Muscarinic antagonism of the effects of a phosphodiesterase inhibitor (methylisobutylxanthine) in embryonic chick ventricle. J Pharmacol Exp Ther **215:** 348–356

Böhm M, Brückner R, Hackbarth I, Haubitz B, Linhart R, Meyer W, Schmidt B, Schmidt W, Scholz H (1984) Adenosine inhibition of catecholamine-induced increase in force of contraction in guinea pig atrial and ventricular heart preparations. Evidence against a cyclic AMP- and cyclic GMP-dependent effect. J Pharmacol Exp Ther **230:** 483–492

Brooker G, Harper JF, Terasaki WL, Moylan RD (1979) Radioimmunoassay of cyclic AMP and cyclic GMP. Adv Cyclic Nucleotide Res **10:** 1–34

Brooker G, Terasaki WL, Price MG (1976) Gammaflo: A completely automated radioimmunoassay system. Science **194:** 270–276

DeGubareff T, Sleator WJ (1965) Effects of caffeine on mammalian atrial muscle and its interaction with adenosine and calcium. J Pharmacol Exp Ther **148:** 202–214

DiMarco JP, Sellers TD, Berne RM, West GA, Belardinelli L (1983) Adenosine: Electrophysiologic effects and therapeutic use for terminating paroxysmal supraventricular tachycardia. Circulation **6:** 1254–1263

Dobson JG Jr (1978) Reduction by adenosine of the isoproterenol-induced increase in cyclic adenosine 3′,5′-monophosphate formation and glycogen phosphorylase activity in rat heart muscle. Circ Res **43:** 785–792

Dobson JG Jr (1983a) Interaction between adenosine and inotropic interventions in guinea pig atria. Am J Physiol **245:** H475–H480

Dobson JG Jr (1983b) Mechanism of adenosine inhibition of catecholamine-induced responses in heart. Circ Res **52:** 151–160

Endoh H, Honma M (1979) Effects of papaverine and its interaction with isoprenaline and carbachol on the contractile force and cyclic nucleotide levels of the canine ventricular myocardium. Naunyn Schmiedebergs Arch Pharmacol **306:** 241–248

Endoh M, Yamashita S (1980) Adenosine antagonizes the positive inotropic action mediated via β-, but not α-adrenoceptors in the rabbit papillary muscle. Eur J Pharmacol **65:** 445–448

Evans DB, Schenden JA, Bristol JA (1982) Adenosine receptors mediating cardiac depression. Life Sci **31:** 2425–2432

Gilman AG (1984) G Proteins and dual control of adenylate cyclase. Cell **36:** 577–579

Grossman A, Furchgott RF (1964) The effects of various drugs on calcium exchange in the isolated guinea pig left auricle. J Pharmacol Exp Ther **145:** 162–172

Hazeki O, Ui M (1981) Modification by islet-activating protein of receptor-mediated regulation of cyclic AMP accumulation in isolated rat heart cells. J Biol Chem **256:** 2856–2862

Isenberg G (1977) Cardiac Purkinje fibers: The slow inward current component under the influence of modified $[Ca^{2+}]_i$. Pflugers Arch **371:** 61–69

Jochem G, Nawrath H (1983) Adenosine activates a potassium conductance in guinea-pig atrial heart muscle. Experientia **39:** 1347–1349

Kranias EG, Solaro RJ (1982) Phosphorylation of troponin I and phospholamban during catecholamine stimulation of rabbit heart. Nature **298:** 182–184

Leung E, Johnston CI, Woodcock EA (1983) Demonstration of specific receptors for adenosine in guinea pig myocardium. Clin Exp Pharmacol Physiol **10:** 325–329

Levy NM (1971) Sympathetic-parasympathetic interactions in the heart. Circ Res **29:** 437–445

Linden J, Brooker G (1979) The questionable role of cyclic guanosine 3′:5′-monophosphate in heart. Biochem Pharmacol **28:** 3351–3360

Linden J, Vogel S, Sperelakis N (1982) Sensitivity of Ca-dependent slow action potentials to methacholine is induced by phosphodiesterase inhibitors in embryonic chick ventricles. J Pharmacol Exp Ther **222:** 383–388

Linden J, Patel A, Sadek S (1985) [^{125}I]Aminobenzyladenosine, a new radioligand with improved specific binding to adenosine receptors in heart. Circ Res **56:** 279–284

Londos C, Wolff J (1977) Two distinct adenosine-sensitive sites on adenylate cyclase. Proc Natl Acad Sci USA **74:** 5482–5486

Londos C, Cooper DMF, Schlegel W, Rodbell M (1978) Adenosine analogs inhibit adipocyte adenylate cyclase by a GTP-dependent process: Basis for actions of adenosine and methylxanthines on cyclic AMP production and lipolysis. Proc Natl Acad Sci USA **75:** 5362–5366

Londos C, Cooper DMF, Wolff J (1980) Subclasses of external adenosine receptors. Proc Natl Acad Sci USA **77:** 2551–2554

Londos C, Cooper DMF, Rodbell M (1981) Receptor-mediated stimulation and inhibition of adenylate cyclase: The fat cell as a model system. Adv Cyclic Nucleotide Res **14:** 163–171

Londos C, Wolff J, Cooper DMF (1981) Adenosine as a regulator of adenylate cyclase. *In* Purinergic Receptors, edited by G Burnstock. London, Chapman and Hall, pp 287–323

Meech RW (1978) Calcium-dependent potassium activation in nervous tissues. Annu Rev Biophys Bioeng **7:** 1–18

Meester WD, Hardman HF (1967) Blockade of the positive inotropic actions of epinephrine and theophylline by acetylcholine. J Pharmacol Exp Ther **158:** 241–247

Murad F, Chi Y-M, Rall TW, Sutherland EW (1962) The effect of catecholamines and choline esters on the formation of adenosine 3′,5′-phosphate by preparations from cardiac muscle and liver. J Biol Chem **237:** 1233–1238

Rockoff JB, Dobson JG Jr (1980) Inhibition by adenosine of catecholamine-induced increase in rat atrial contractility. Am J Physiol **2398:** H365–H370

Schmitz W, Hackbarth I, Haubitz B, Linhart R, Meyer W, Scholz H (1981) Effect of adenosine and isoprenaline on force of contraction and on the C-AMP system in guinea-pig atria. Naunyn Schniedebergs Arch Pharmacol **316:** R34

Schrader J, Baumann G, Gerlach E (1977) Adenosine as inhibitor of myocardial effects of catecholamines. Pflugers Arch **372:** 29–35

Schütz W, Tuisl E (1981) Evidence against adenylate cyclase-coupled adenosine receptors in the guinea pig heart. Eur J Pharmacol **76:** 285–288

Schwabe U, Trost T (1980) Characterization of adenosine receptors in rat brain by (−)-[3H]-N^6-phenylisopropyladenosine. Naunyn Schmiedebergs Arch Pharmacol **313:** 179–187

Schwegler M, Reutter K, Shieber G, Jacob R (1976) Noncompetitive catecholamine antagonism of acetylcholine in the sympathectomized mammalian ventricular myocardium. Basic Res Cardiol **71:** 407–419

Seitelberger R, Schütz W, Schlappack O, Raberger G (1984) Evidence against the adenosine-catecholamine antagonism under in vivo conditions. Naunyn Schmiedebergs Arch Pharmacol **325:** 234–239

Stowell CP, Kuhlenschmidt TG, Hoppe CA (1978) A fluorescamine assay for submicrogram quantities of protein in the presence of triton X-100. Anal Biochem **85:** 522–580

TenEick R, Nawrath H, McDonald TF, Trautwein W (1976) On the mechanism of the negative inotropic effect of acetylcholine. Pflugers Arch **361:** 207–213

Westermann E, Stock K (1970) Inhibitors of lipolysis: Potency and mode of action of α- and β-adrenolytics, methoxamine derivatives, prostaglandin E_1, and phenylisopropyl adenosine. *In* Adipose Tissue, Regulatory and Metabolic Functions, edited by B Jeanrenaud, D Hepp. Stuttgart, Thieme, pp 47–54

INDEX TERMS: Heart • Adenosine receptors • Acetylcholine • Muscarinic receptors • β-Adrenergic receptors • Cyclic adenosine monophosphate • ^{125}I-Aminobenzyladenosine • [^{3}H]Quinuclidinylbenzilate • ^{125}I-Pindolol

Intramural Reentry as a Mechanism of Ventricular Tachycardia during Evolving Canine Myocardial Infarction

Jeffrey B. Kramer, Jeffrey E. Saffitz, Francis X. Witkowski, and Peter B. Corr
From the Departments of Medicine, Pathology, Pharmacology, and Surgery, Washington University School of Medicine, St. Louis, Missouri

SUMMARY. We evaluated the contribution of intramural electrical events in initiation and maintenance of ventricular tachycardia in 15 dogs 3–8 days after either permanent (n = 2) or transient (n = 13) coronary artery occlusion. Seven of the dogs (47%) demonstrated eight distinct monomorphic ventricular tachycardia patterns which were mapped by means of a recently designed computerized system capable of simultaneously detecting, storing, and assessing information from 232 individual cardiac sites. Using both epicardial and intramural electrodes, we found definitive evidence for intramural reentry in seven of the eight monomorphic tachycardias analyzed. Furthermore, five of these animals (71%) demonstrated microreentry, in which small epicardial conduction loops exited intermittently into nonrefractory subendocardium to initiate succeeding beats, while, in the remaining two dogs, ventricular tachycardia was due to macroreentry, during which the broad subendocardial wavefronts depolarizing the ventricle constituted the proximal (fast) reentry limbs. Detailed anatomical analysis of the resultant infarcts demonstrated the thin surviving epicardial tissue rim to be the site of conduction delay necessary for reentry, whereas "preferred pathways" of exit into the subendocardial plane occurred at the infarct borders and were of variable configuration. Successful interruption of these rhythms should accompany interference with the process of exit into nonrefractory subendocardial tissue.
(*Circ Res 56: 736–754, 1985*)

MALIGNANT ventricular arrhythmias frequently occur during the recovery phase of acute myocardial infarction (Moss, 1980) and contribute to the enhanced risk of sudden cardiac death in the weeks to months that follow the initial event (Moss et al., 1977; Moss, 1980). Therapeutic interventions to prevent or treat these lethal arrhythmias are currently empirical, nonspecific, and consequently often unsuccessful in reducing the risk of sudden cardiac death. Previous investigators have utilized a canine model wherein either permanent (El-Sherif et al., 1977) or transient coronary artery occlusion followed by reperfusion (Karagueuzian et al., 1979; Michelson et al., 1980) results in a high proportion of animals that are susceptible to induction of ventricular tachycardia with programmed electrical stimulation using protocols analogous to those employed clinically in patients with evolving myocardial infarction. Likewise, detailed pathological examination of these experimental infarcts demonstrates marked similarity to infarcts in patients with documented ventricular tachycardia and subsequent sudden cardiac death, in that both exhibit interdigitation of necrotic and apparently viable myocardial tissue (Ursell and Fenoglio, 1982). Although the time course of the anatomic and electrophysiological derangements is accelerated in experimental compared to human infarction, the sequence of infarct evolution is comparable, suggesting that the pathophysiological basis of arrhythmogenesis probably is analogous.

Several lines of evidence indicate that reentry is a likely mechanism for sustained ventricular tachycardia during evolving myocardial infarction. Induction of ventricular tachycardia by premature extrastimuli and the presence of continuous diastolic electrical activity recorded from regions bordering the infarct during the tachycardia (El-Sherif et al., 1977) suggest, albeit indirectly, a reentrant process. Furthermore, recent evidence utilizing epicardial mapping from multiple sites both in vivo (El-Sherif et al., 1981; Wit et al., 1982; Mehra et al., 1983; Cardinal et al., 1984) and in vitro (Richards et al., 1984), indicates that reentrant circuits overlying the infarct are the source of some, but not all, ventricular tachycardias. These studies have emphasized that reentry is initiated by functional conduction block occurring within the surviving epicardial tissue rim overlying the infarct, and that induction is related to the prematurity of the paced extrasystole. Although these findings have contributed substantially to our understanding of the genesis of ventricular tachycardia, there are several critical observations which indicate that "epicardial reentry" is not fully responsible for the ventricular tachycardias seen either clinically or experimentally. For example, since only epicardial or extremely limited intramural activation information is monitored in these studies, it is left implicit that the remaining, noninfarcted ventricle activates passively from the epicardium. Likewise, results from clinical epicardial and endocardial mapping studies clearly demonstrate that earliest activation occurs in the endocardium during ventricular tachycardia (Horowitz et al., 1980), and successful surgical interruption of these tachycardias occurs after ablation of endocardial regions (Wittig and Boineau, 1975; Josephson et al., 1979a). Epicardial reentry circuits in experimental animals are consistently associated with "large gaps" in the sequence of activation, despite extremely detailed and extensive epicardial recordings (Wit et al., 1982; Mehra et al., 1983; Cardinal et al., 1984). In addition, reentry has not been demonstrated in many of the sustained tachycardias. Experimental studies sometimes employ interventions to facilitate mapping which may artifactually alter the arrhythmogenic substrate, including cardiopulmonary bypass, ventriculotomy, pharmacological maneuvers to enhance arrhythmogenesis, and interference with the autonomic innervation of the heart. Finally, several fundamental observations, such as beat-to-beat variation in morphology of the QRS complex during the initial beats of a monomorphic tachycardia, have not been adequately explained. Thus, although disturbances in epicardial conduction contribute to the genesis of ventricular arrhythmias during evolving infarction, this likely constitutes only one element predisposing the heart to ventricular tachycardia.

The present investigation was performed to elucidate the role of epicardial and intramural activation in the genesis of monomorphic ventricular tachycardia. Specifically, two major questions were posed. First, what are the contributions of subendocardial and intramyocardial regions in the initiation and maintenance of monomorphic ventricular tachycardia? Second, what are the anatomic and electrophysiological substrates during evolving infarction that are responsible for monomorphic ventricular tachycardia, as well as what aspects might be potentially amenable to therapeutic manipulation?

Methods

Animal Preparation

Fifteen adult mongrel dogs were anesthetized with sodium pentobarbital (30 mg/kg intravenously), intubated, and artificially ventilated with a Harvard respirator. After antibiotic prophylaxis (300,000 U penicillin, intramuscularly), a limited sterile thoracotomy was performed through the 4th left intercostal space, a pericardial cradle was constructed, and the left anterior descending coronary artery was isolated immediately proximal to the first large diagonal branch. A snare consisting of polyethylene tubing (PE 190) was gradually lowered onto a suture surrounding the artery, and partial occlusion was maintained for 20 minutes, followed by complete occlusion (Harris, 1950). In 13 animals, the snare was released after 2 hours of total occlusion and the myocardium was reperfused, whereas in the remaining two dogs, the artery was permanently ligated. Lidocaine hydrochloride (2 mg/kg) was administered intravenously immediately before coronary occlusion and, in the reperfused group, again just prior to reperfusion. The chest then was closed in layers, and the residual pneumothorax was evacuated through a small thoracostomy tube. A sterile cannula was placed into the left external jugular vein and exteriorized through a posterior cervical incision, and the animals were returned to their cages for recovery.

Programmed Electrical Stimulation

Three to 8 days after myocardial infarction, the animals were reanesthetized (sodium pentobarbital, 30 mg/kg, intravenously) and, by the cardiac activation mapping system described below, were studied electrophysiologically. The lead II electrocardiogram and femoral arterial blood pressure were monitored in all dogs by a Gould (model 260) six-channel recorder, whereas five dogs had more extensive hemodynamic evaluation. The dogs were ventilated, the left chest reopened, and a pericardial cradle was constructed. A sock electrode array, consisting of 24–32 epicardial button electrodes fitted into a nylon mesh (details below), was placed around the heart and sewn gently to the atrioventricular groove (Fig. 1). Bipolar endocardial hook electrodes which were constructed from Teflon-coated stainless steel wires (diameter = 0.33 mm) were then inserted into peri-infarct pacing sites through an introducing needle, and programmed electrical stimulation was performed, utilizing a Bloom model DTU-101 programmable stimulator (Bloom Associates).

Pacing was performed with pulse width = 2 msec and at twice diastolic threshold current (0.5–5.0 mA). The protocol was similar to that used clinically (Josephson et al., 1978a), in that a train of eight paced beats (S_1's) at basic cycle lengths = 300, 250, or 220 msec was delivered, after which double premature stimuli (S_2 and S_3) were introduced at varying coupling intervals. The S_2–S_3 interval was lowered by 2-msec decrements until noncapture of S_3 resulted, at which time the S_1–S_2 coupling interval was narrowed. This sequence was repeated until either the heart became refractory to the S_2 stimulus, ventricular fibrillation ensued (followed by DC cardioversion), or

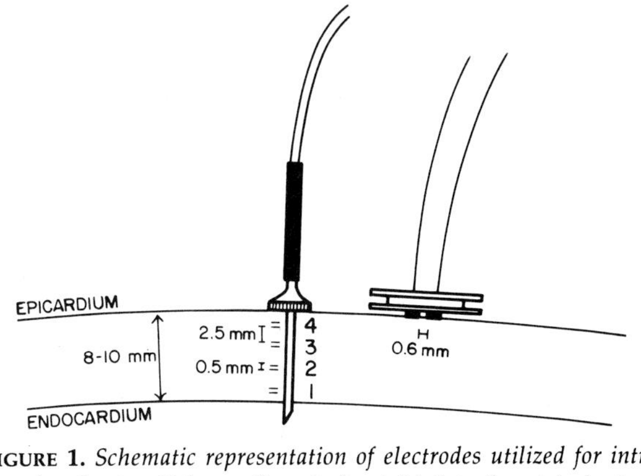

FIGURE 1. *Schematic representation of electrodes utilized for intramural and epicardial recordings during initiation of ventricular tachycardia. Plunge needles contain four bipolar pairs transmurally, determining four tangential activation planes, the outermost located 500 μm from the epicardial surface. Button electrodes were fixed to the heart by a nylon mesh sock.*

monomorphic ventricular tachycardia (uniform VT > 5 beats) appeared. If the S_2 stimulus consistently failed to capture the ventricle, or only polymorphic tachycardias resulted, the pacing protocol was repeated at the remaining basic cycle lengths until all three cycle lengths (S_1–S_1) had been tested. Finally, several alternative pacing sites were utilized in order to initiate monomorphic tachycardia, since the pacing location is known to be crucial in initiation of ventricular tachycardia (Michelson et al., 1981). Pacing protocols similar to this have been shown previously to induce tachycardias only in infarcted animals, never in the normal canine ventricle (Hamer et al., 1983). Once the animal had responded with monomorphic ventricular tachycardia or pacing from six sites resulted in only isolated or polymorphic extrasystoles, 50 plunge needles (details below) containing four bipolar electrode pairs per needle (200 sites) were inserted into the heart, concentrated within and at the border regions of the epicardial infarct zone. In the areas of interest, spacing between individual plunge needles averaged 5–10 mm. After a delay of at least 15 minutes, the pacing protocol was repeated until the responses observed prior to electrode placement were again elicited. Intramural and epicardial electrical activity was then recorded during the initiation of ventricular tachycardia. During and between pacing runs, warm (37°C) saline was intermittently applied topically to the heart to moisten the epicardium and prevent surface cooling. Body temperature was maintained at 37°C throughout the experiment.

Upon completion of the protocol, the animals were heparinized (2000 U, intravenously), and the hearts were arrested with intravenous injection of 3 M KCl. We then carefully removed each plunge and button electrode, and, in the resulting hole, placed a small stickpin bearing an identifying flag in order to facilitate accurate localization of the electrode positions. The heart was then excised, rinsed in normal saline, and the nylon mesh sock removed. A polyethylene catheter (PE 60) was placed into both coronary ostia, and the arterial tree was perfused with 10% sodium phosphate-buffered formalin. The heart was then immersed and fixed in formalin for subsequent histopathological analysis.

Hemodynamic Studies

To assess the effect of the plunge needle insertion on cardiac and peripheral hemodynamics, five of the infarcted dogs undergoing programmed stimulation had concomitant invasive hemodynamic monitoring. In addition to arterial blood pressure measurements, which were obtained in all of the studies, left atrial and left ventricular pressures were determined in these animals by insertion of a polyethylene (PE 50) catheter into each chamber, secured in place with a pursestring suture. The left ventricular cannula was placed in the basolateral aspect of the heart, distant from the zone of infarction. Cardiac output determinations were made with a Narcomatic (RT500) flowprobe placed around the ascending aorta just proximal to the origin of the innominate artery, and stroke work was calculated by the formula: $SW = CO/HR \times$ (mean BP-mean LAP) where CO is cardiac output, HR is heart rate, BP is blood pressure, and LAP is left arterial pressure. Hemodynamic parameters were then assessed before and at selected intervals after insertion of needle electrodes, and comparisons were evaluated by ANOVA.

Mapping System and Data Analysis

Details regarding the recently designed cardiac mapping system employed in the present study have been reported (Witkowski and Corr, 1984) and will be only briefly summarized. Electrical activity from multiple surface and intramyocardial locations was collected from arrays of electrodes as depicted in Figure 1. Epicardial electrodes were constructed from cylindrical Teflon buttons, pierced by two double-stranded stainless steel wires with soldered interfaces separated by 0.6 mm (Witkowski and Corr, 1984). These were held lightly onto the epicardial surface by a nylon mesh sock (Harrison et al., 1980), which maintained the button positions throughout each experiment. Intramural recordings were obtained from plunge electrodes which were fabricated from 50 μm in diameter Teflon-insulated tungsten wire contained within a 21-gauge straight needle, having an interpole spacing of 0.5 mm and an interpair distance of 2.5 mm (Witkowski and Corr, 1984). The most proximal of the four electrode pairs was located 500 μm from a small phenolic collar which rested on the epicardial surface. This design ensured that the endocardial-most electrode pair, located 8 mm from the epicardium, would lie within the left ventricular wall except in regions of extreme wall thinning, such as in the very center of a transmural infarct. For assessment of right ventricular activation, only the three epicardial-most pairs were consistently within the ventricular myocardium, so that the distal (endocardial-most) pair in these regions was ignored during electrogram analysis.

Two hundred thirty-two bipolar electrograms obtained during each cardiac activation were amplified, filtered from 40–500 Hz, sampled at a 2-kHz rate, and individually converted from analog to digital on 232 channels to yield true simultaneous data acquisition on all channels. Digital data were then stored in 12 parallel bits on a Sangamo-Weston Sabre IV high-density recorder, and subsequently analyzed off-line using a PDP 11-34 (Digital Equipment Corporation) computer system equipped with interactive high-resolution color graphics.

Map construction was performed in several automated steps to facilitate rapid and accurate analysis of the three-dimensional data. Initially, the electrocardiogram was scanned, and a time window was chosen to focus on depolarizations of interest, such as the initiating beats of ventricular tachycardia (Witkowski and Corr, 1984). Individual electrograms from each electrode site occurring within the critical window were automatically calibrated, displayed on a high-resolution Barco color monitor, and computer-generated activation times were derived, based on peak criteria (Durrer and Van Der Tweel, 1954; Gallagher et al., 1978). During review of each electrogram, the computer-chosen activation time was manually overridden in case of an overt error in analysis. Since signals from infarcted and peri-infarcted zones were often of low amplitude and poorly defined in configuration, an amplitude threshold of 0.25 mV was arbitrarily considered to indicate tissue activation by a depolarizing wavefront. This arbitrary cut-off was based on the observation that activity of lower amplitude was not consistently accompanied by activation of immediately adjacent electrodes to result in reasonable activation sequences. Conduction block between two electrodes was defined by any of three criteria: (1) intervening electrodes demonstrated no activation, (2) electrode recordings distal to a block demonstrated low-voltage electrotonic activity followed closely by a larger amplitude electrogram (Wit et al., 1982; Mehra et al., 1983), and (3) large temporal gaps between two electrodes occurred while adjacent electrodes in a less direct spatial path connecting them demonstrated sequential interval activation. For analysis of transmural conduction patterns, plunge electrodes which recorded activation at every electrode pair transmurally were considered to activate "antegrade" if the direction of activation was endocardium to epicardium, and "retrograde" if this pattern was reversed.

Following electrogram review, computer-generated and hand-drawn isochronal maps were obtained based on activation times, and then converted to the three-dimensional representations presented below. Epicardial maps were drawn, using activations derived from both surface electrodes and the most proximal plunge bipoles, located immediately beneath the epicardium. Subendocardial maps were derived from the distal plunge bipoles situated 8 mm below the epicardial surface in the left ventricle and 5.5 mm deep at right ventricular sites. The minimum speed of conduction along the mapped reentrant pathways was determined by direct measurements of interelectrode dimensions from the heart in question, as viewed from the epicardial surface. Path lengths were divided by the differences in activation times between the appropriate electrodes to yield conduction velocities in each limb of the reentrant loop.

Anatomical Studies

Anatomical studies were performed to delineate the relation of specific activation pathways to the three-dimensional topography of the infarcts. The morphological analyses were undertaken in four dogs without prior detailed knowledge of the electrophysiology underlying the arrhythmias. Intact, excised hearts, in which the surface and intramural positions of the epicardial and plunge electrodes were marked with stickpins, were fixed for several days in 10% sodium phosphate-buffered formalin. A large transmural block comprising most of the anterior free wall of the left ventricle and containing the electrode sites of interest was removed from the heart and cut transversely into 4–7 transmural blocks measuring up to 6 × 2 × 2 cm. The epicardial location of each pin was diagrammed carefully, the pins were removed, the left lateral transmural cut surface was marked with India ink, and the blocks were processed conventionally for light microscopy. Each block was sectioned subserially in its entirety in the apical-to-basal dimension. Sections were cut at 10 μm, and every 20th section was mounted on a slide and stained with hematoxylin and eosin, yielding five subserial sections per mm and a total of 350–450 sections per heart.

Infarct topography was reconstructed in three dimensions, and the precise epicardial surface and intramural locations of each electrode were determined by examining the subserial sections in an apical-to-basal sequence. Anatomically precise drawings of selected sections (40–50 per heart) were made with the use of an optical drawing tube attached to a conventional light microscope equipped with a 2× objective lens. With this system, a pen placed on paper at the side of the microscope is optically superimposed on the microscopic field of vision, thereby permitting accurate tracings of the structural elements of the section. For each section drawn, the outlines of the epicardial fibroadipose tissue, including coronary arteries, the myocardium, the borders delineating infarct from viable tissue, and the epicardial and transmural positions of each electrode, were traced. The tracings were drawn at a magnification of approximately 20× which permitted resolution of individual cardiac myocytes.

Results

Inducibility

Fifteen dogs survived either transient ($n = 13$) or permanent ($n = 2$) coronary artery occlusion and underwent detailed electrophysiological study with three-dimensional activation analysis between the 3rd and 8th postoperative day. In seven dogs (47%) monomorphic ventricular tachycardia (VT) was reproducibly elicited by the pacing protocol described previously, including the two animals with permanent coronary ligation (100%) and five of 13 with transient left atrial descending coronary artery (LAD) occlusion (38%). In these seven animals, eight distinct VT morphologies were evaluated in detail, and the tachycardia cycle lengths, durations, and modes of termination are summarized in Table 1. The cycle length of the ventricular tachycardias varied between 155 and 240 msec, and there was no correlation between the presence or absence of reperfusion and the cycle length of the tachycardia. The tachycardias were terminated by rapid burst pacing (cycle length, 90–140 msec) when the arrhythmia exceeded 10–15 seconds in duration, although spontaneous termination did occur, as did degeneration of ventricular fibrillation in two animals. In the latter two cases (dogs 2 and 3), attempted overdrive pacing during VT was unsuccessful and fibrillation ensued only after >30 seconds of monomorphic VT. Since activation analysis of these arrhythmias was concentrated on the early

TABLE 1
Characteristics of the Monomorphic Tachycardias Induced by Programmed Electrical Stimulation

Dog	Reperfusion	Cycle length VT (msec)	Duration of VT (sec)	Mode of VT termination	Mechanism	Initial polymophism
1	+	240	>10	Burst paced	Microreentry	+
2	+	155	>10	VF	Microreentry	+
3	+	160	>10	VF	Microreentry	+
4	−	160	>10	Burst paced	Microreentry	−
5A	−	240	2	Spontaneous	Macroreentry	−
5B		185	>10	Burst paced		−
6	+	160	>10	Burst paced	Macroreentry	+
7	+	155	>10	Burst paced	Microreentry	+

VT = ventricular tachycardia; VF = ventricular fibrillation; + or − indicates the presence or absence of each index in the respective animal.

beats of VT prior to a sustained drop in coronary perfusion pressure and associated ischemia, the mechanism responsible for induction of the tachycardia was attributed to the prior infarction, rather than to acute ischemia.

Validation of the plunge Electrode Procedures

Five dogs, three with monomorphic and two with polymorphic ventricular tachycardia, underwent hemodynamic assessment during the electrophysiological studies, using the full complement of needle electrodes. There were no significant alterations in heart rate, mean arterial blood pressure, mean left atrial pressure, mean left ventricular pressure, cardiac output, or stroke work, when assessed prior to and 5, 30, and 60 minutes after plunge needle insertion (Fig. 2). Furthermore, two of these five animals were studied for longer than 3 hours, and no hemodynamic deterioration occurred during either experiment.

Although there were often transient 5- to 10-minute periods following plunge insertion during which episodic multiform ventricular ectopic beats occurred, these always subsided by the time programmed stimulation was begun. Likewise, there were no instances, in any of the dogs studied, of failure to elicit monomorphic ventricular tachycardia subsequent to placement of the plunge electrodes in dogs that demonstrated this phenomenon prior to plunge needle insertion. Alternatively, there were no instances in which conversion to monomorphic ventricular tachycardia occurred in animals in which only polymorphic ventricular tachycardias was present before placement of the plunge electrodes. Figure 3 demonstrates the epicardial patterns and activation times of epicardial electrodes during normal sinus rhythm and with pacing in a dog which later demonstrated monomorphic VT. The activation times at the epicardial electrode sites are shown both immediately before insertion of the plunge electrodes, and 60 minutes later, for each map. Linear regression analysis of the two groups of activation times (Fig. 3), reveals a high correlation and a slope near 1. In the entire group of dogs studied, average values for linear regression slopes were 0.94 ± 0.03 (SEM) during sinus rhythm and 0.95 ± 0.03 with ventricular pacing, while correlation coefficients averaged 0.94 (sinus rhythm) and 0.97 (pacing).

Mechanisms of Ventricular Tachycardia

Two distinct variants of reentry were observed in the initiating beats of monomorphic ventricular tachycardia. In five animals with monomorphic ventricular tachycardia (71%), a microreentrant mechanism was present, in which an independently circulating epicardial reentrant loop intermittently exited down to the subendocardium after recovery of excitability and initiated broad wavefronts of conduction which resulted in complete ventricular depolarization. In the remaining two animals, maintenance of the tachycardia was attributable to macroreentry, wherein a fast limb of the reentry loop was subendocardial in origin, and a slow limb was epicardial. The fast subendocardial limb in the macroreentrant tachycardias was part of a broad wavefront which depolarized the entire ventricle, such that the reentry loop itself did not activate, independent of ventricular depolarization, but rather constituted a part of the overall activation sequence.

Microreentry

An example of the activation sequences during initiation of monomorphic ventricular tachycardia by a process of microreentry is illustrated in Figures

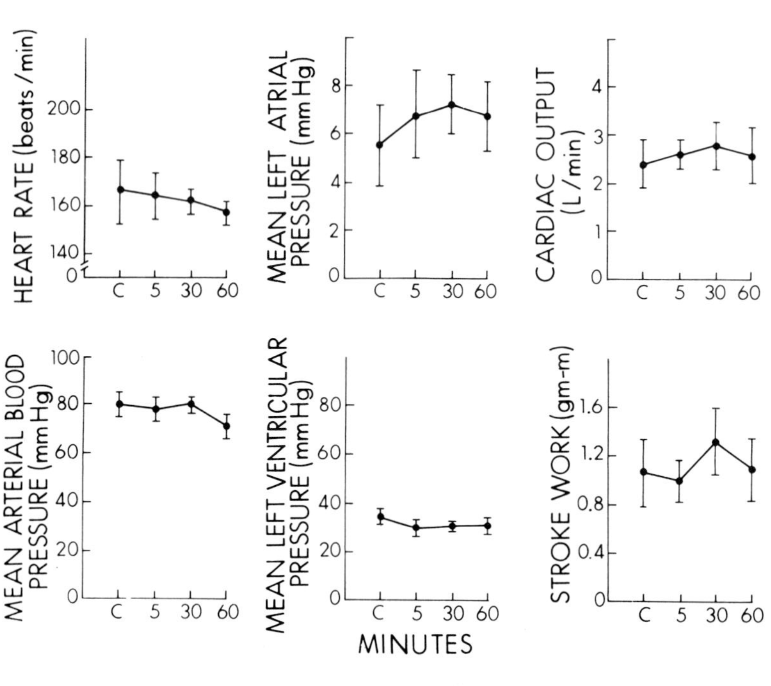

FIGURE 2. *Hemodynamic effects of plunge needle insertion. Values are means ± SEM for hemodynamic parameters from five open-chested, infarcted dogs undergoing concomitant electrophysiological study. For each dog, parameters were assessed before (C) and after (5 min, 30 min, 60 min) plunge needle insertion.*

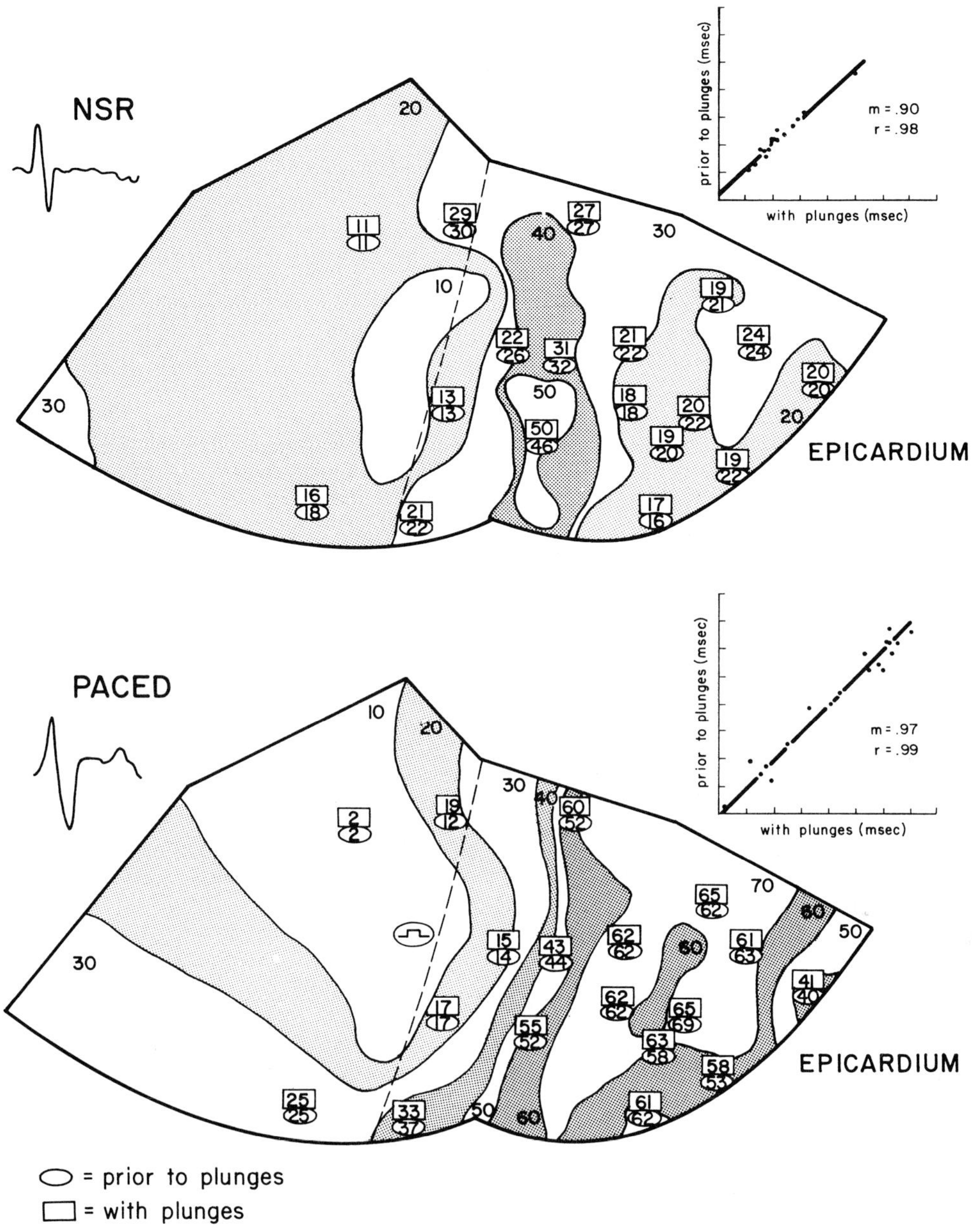

FIGURE 3. *Effects on conduction of plunge needle insertion. Epicardial maps in normal sinus rhythm (NSR) and with endocardial pacing from the right ventricle (⎍) are shown for infarct dog 2. Numbers represent activation times of surface electrodes before and 1 hour after insertion of 50 plunge needles and are referenced to the earliest epicardial activation. The corresponding plots are linear regression analyses of activation times in each case. m = least squares slope; r = correlation coefficient.*

4 through 8, in a dog (dog 2) with a previous infarct associated with coronary occlusion and reperfusion. The electrocardiogram in Figure 4 illustrates a run of ventricular tachycardia initiated by a train of extrastimuli (S_1's) followed by two premature extrastimuli (S_2 and S_3). The first four extrasystoles of the run (T_1 through T_4) are polymorphic, whereas the subsequent beats are of uniform morphology, occurring at a coupling interval at 155 msec. The activation maps in Figure 4 represent isochronal activation patterns in both the epicardial (upper) and subendocardial (lower) planes during the transition between the last premature paced beat (S_3, left side) and the first nonpaced extrasystole (T_1, right side) of this tachycardia. The origin of S_3 is the endocardial pacing site, activation reaching the subendocardium (*, Fig. 4) at a time defined as 0 msec. From this point, depolarization proceeds in two wavefronts (arrows) radially in the subendocardial plane around a large area of conduction block, ultimately activating the left lateral border of this zone within 120 msec. Synchronous with conduction in the subendocardial plane, depolarization also proceeds upward through ventricular muscle to the epicardium, as was documented by multiple plunge electrodes located within the left and right ventric-

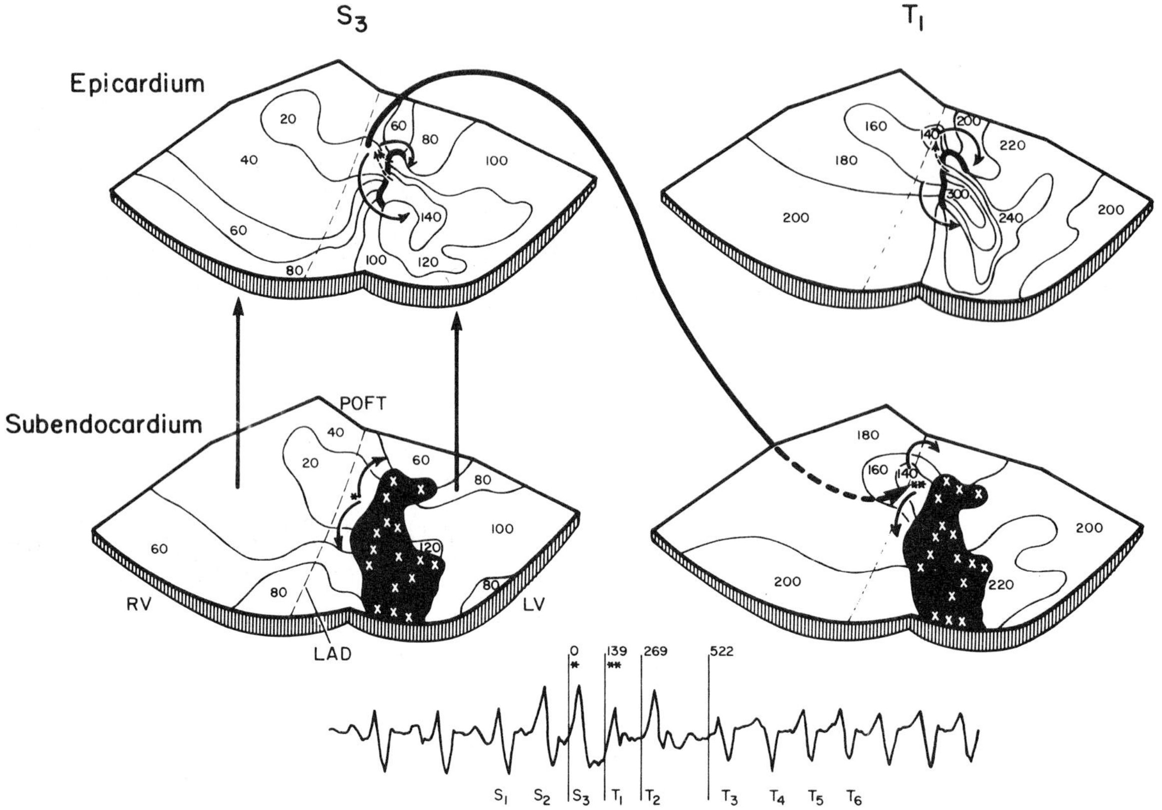

FIGURE 4. *S_3–T_1 transition (dog 2). Epicardial and subendocardial isochronal activation maps illustrating transitions between the last premature beat of a pacing train (S_3) and the first nonpaced extrasystole (T_1). Cardiac chambers and landmarks as are described in the lower left map. Each × within shaded areas corresponds to electrodes demonstrating conduction block within the given activation planes. On the electrocardiogram, vertical lines and numbers correspond to times of earliest subendocardial activation for each depolarization sequence illustrated, while asterisks represent the sites of subendocardial exit. See text for details.*

ular free walls along the routes of conduction (see below). Most of the noninfarcted ventricle during S_3, as well as in subsequent beats, is therefore depolarized antegrade, i.e., from endocardium to epicardium, along the wavefront of subendocardial conduction.

In the epicardium directly overlying the large region of subendocardial conduction block, however, activation cannot originate from immediately subjacent tissue. Thus, on the epicardial plane, the activation wavefront invades this zone from the area adjacent to the endocardial pacing site, but, during S_3, blocks in a front (heavy line; S_3, Fig. 4) located on the septal border of the zone. This block is functional in nature, as has been well demonstrated in previous studies (Wit et al., 1982; Mehra et al., 1983), and results in the conduction wavefront circulating around the basal and apical portions of this epicardial border zone. The wavefront ultimately enters this zone, overlying the silent subendocardium and mid-myocardium, but conduction is slow (crowded isochrones, S_3 epicardium) within this area, allowing for tissue proximal to the epicardial conduction block to recover excitability. This culminates in reentry into this region, not only on the epicardial surface (broken arrows, S_3 epicardium), but also retrogradely, from epicardium to the subendocardium after recovery of excitability (large arrow, Fig. 4). This reentry into the subendocardium occurs 139 msec after the initial S_3 activation at a site (**, Fig. 4) near to, but not identical with, the original pacing site, and marks the beginning of the following depolarization sequence, T_1.

The activation pattern of the first nonpaced extrasystole, T_1, is, at least in its initial phase, similar to that of S_3, and is diagrammed in Figures 4 (right half) and 5 (left half), the latter figure illustrating the transition to the second nonpaced beat, T_2. As was the case during S_3, subendocardial depolarization occurs in two broad wavefronts radially progressing around a sizable area of conduction block, whereas midmyocardial and epicardial muscle is passively activated along these fronts. On the epicardial plane, however, the delayed wavefront from the S_3 activation, which broke through and reentered retrogradely into adjacent nonrefractory subendocardium to initiate the T_1 depolarization sequence, also has conducted radially around a new line of epicardial conduction block (Fig. 5, T_1 epicardium). This new front on the epicardium was formed by the delayed depolarization during the S_3 beat, and resulted in delayed recovery of excitability. This

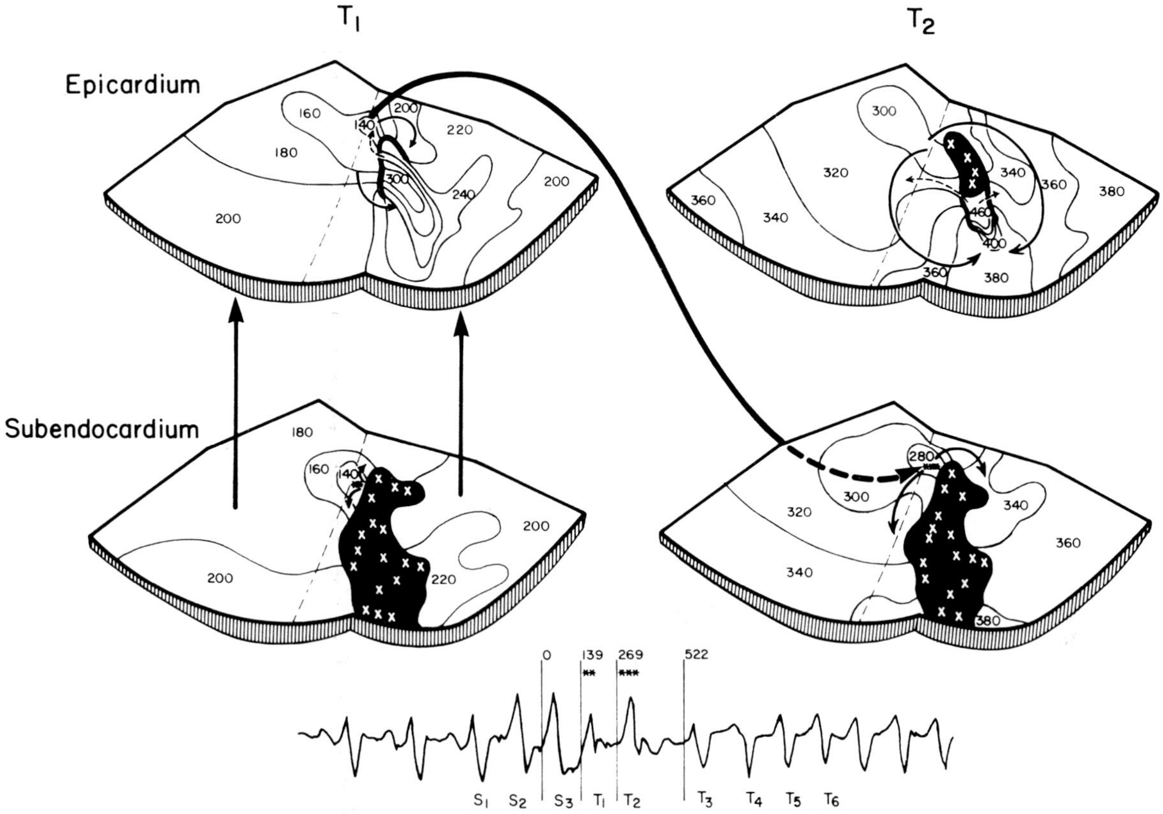

FIGURE 5. *T_1–T_2 transition (dog 2). Epicardial and subendocardial isochronal maps representing the transition between the first two nonpaced extrasystoles. See text for details.*

wavefront then enters the epicardial rim of tissue overlying the subendocardial silent zone, but due to its premature arrival, conducts even slower than during the S_3 beat. Again, this allows for the zone proximal to the epicardial block to recover, and it is reexcited (dashed arrows; T_1, Fig. 5) both in the epicardial plane and, via intramural pathways, in the subendocardium (***, Fig. 5). For the T_1 beat, exit into the subendocardium occurred 269 msec after the initial S_3 activation and coincided with the beginning of the T_2 depolarization sequence. Note that in the surface electrocardiogram in Figure 5, the onset of T_2 is coincident with the earliest subendocardial activation. Epicardial delay was so pronounced during the T_1 beat that the epicardial rim overlying the subendocardial silent region exhibited activation well after retrograde subendocardial excitation had occurred (300 msec isochrone). The similarity in QRS morphology between T_1 and T_2 is due to the fact that exit into the subendocardium occurred at the same location to begin both of these depolarization sequences.

The activation sequence of the second nonpaced extrasystole, T_2, is also illustrated in Figure 5. In its final stages, the activation sequence for T_2 differs from that of the previous two beats (S_3 and T_1), and ultimately results in a distinct activation pattern characteristic of the subsequent uniform beats of the monomorphic ventricular tachycardia. After exit of the T_1 depolarizing wavefront into the subendocardium (***), T_2 activation on this plane once again proceeds radially around the central electrically silent zone. As in previous beats, passive transmural conduction occurs in an antegrade fashion to depolarize the midmyocardium and epicardium in most of the noninfarcted ventricle. On the epicardial plane, the conduction wave which reentered tissue proximal to the conduction block during the latter stages of the T_1 beat, also circulates around the basal portion of the epicardial rim but, during T_2, blocks completely and cannot enter the basal portion of this zone (four blocked electrodes; T_2, Fig. 5 epicardium). This probably is a direct result of the extreme delay in epicardial activation observed during the preceding depolarization sequence (beat T_1), causing this zone to be refractory at a time when the circulating wavefront has arrived for the next depolarization. Instead, the conduction wavefront enters this zone at its apical aspect (400 msec isochrone), conducting very slowly in an apical-to-basal direction. After considerable delay, this conduction wave emerges from the slowly conducting epicardial rim and reenters nonrefractory tissue both in the epicardial plane and, conducting transmurally, into the subendocardium. Exit occurs at 522 msec in the right ventricle and slightly thereafter (554 msec) at the left lateral aspect of the infarct border to initiate the T_3 depolarization sequence (not shown). The sequence and timing of conduction in the epicardial zone overlying the infarct during T_2 accounts for the relatively long T_2–T_3 coupling interval, as well as for the change in extrasystole QRS morphology beginning with T_3.

The previous examples have illustrated the transition between three polymorphic extrasystoles preceding a run of monomorphic ventricular tachycardia, demonstrating that: (1) most of the ventricle depolarizes after the delayed epicardial conduction wave exits and then reenters into the subendocardium following the recovery of excitability, (2) an epicardial reentrant loop can circulate, independent of the broad wavefronts depolarizing the noninfarcted ventricle, an example of microreentry, and (3) initial polymorphism of monomorphic ventricular tachycardia is due to differing exit sites from regions of epicardial delay into nonrefractory subendocardium. The morphology of a given extrasystole is conditioned by the exit site of the preceding extrasystole. The former two principles are also characteristic of the stable monomorphic phase of this ventricular tachycardia, as shown in Figure 6, schematizing the transition between the fifth and sixth nonpaced extrasystoles (T_5 and T_6). Subendocardial T_5 activation commences (0 msec) at a right ventricular paraseptal location (*), followed by radial spread on this plane around the central subendocardial silent zone. Slightly later (39 msec), a second area of subendocardial activation begins on the lateral border of this zone, spreading radially in the opposite direction of the first wave, the two eventually meeting at the base of the heart. Again, transmural conduction in the normal myocardial regions is toward the epicardium, as documented by intramural electrodes. However, a broad wavefront of block occurs at the epicardial surface during T_5 (Fig. 6, T_5–epicardium) overlying the silent subendocardium and midmyocardium. Activation proceeds around this block via two separate circulating wavefronts, at the basal and apical borders of the epicardial rim, eventually entering this zone and conducting slowly through it. The basal circuit, activating in a clockwise fashion, exits from the epicardial rim, resulting in retrograde subendocardial activation at 133 msec (large arrow A, Fig. 6), initiating the T_6 depolarization sequence from the RV subendocardium (**). The other circulating wavefront, activating independently in a counterclockwise manner, exits into nonrefractory subendocardium (large arrow B, Fig. 6) slightly later (at 175 msec) at the lateral border of the subendocardial silent zone (***). Just as occurred during T_5, the subendocardial pattern of T_6 consists then of two colliding wavefronts originating from opposite ends of the infarct border. Transmural conduction proceeds in an antegrade

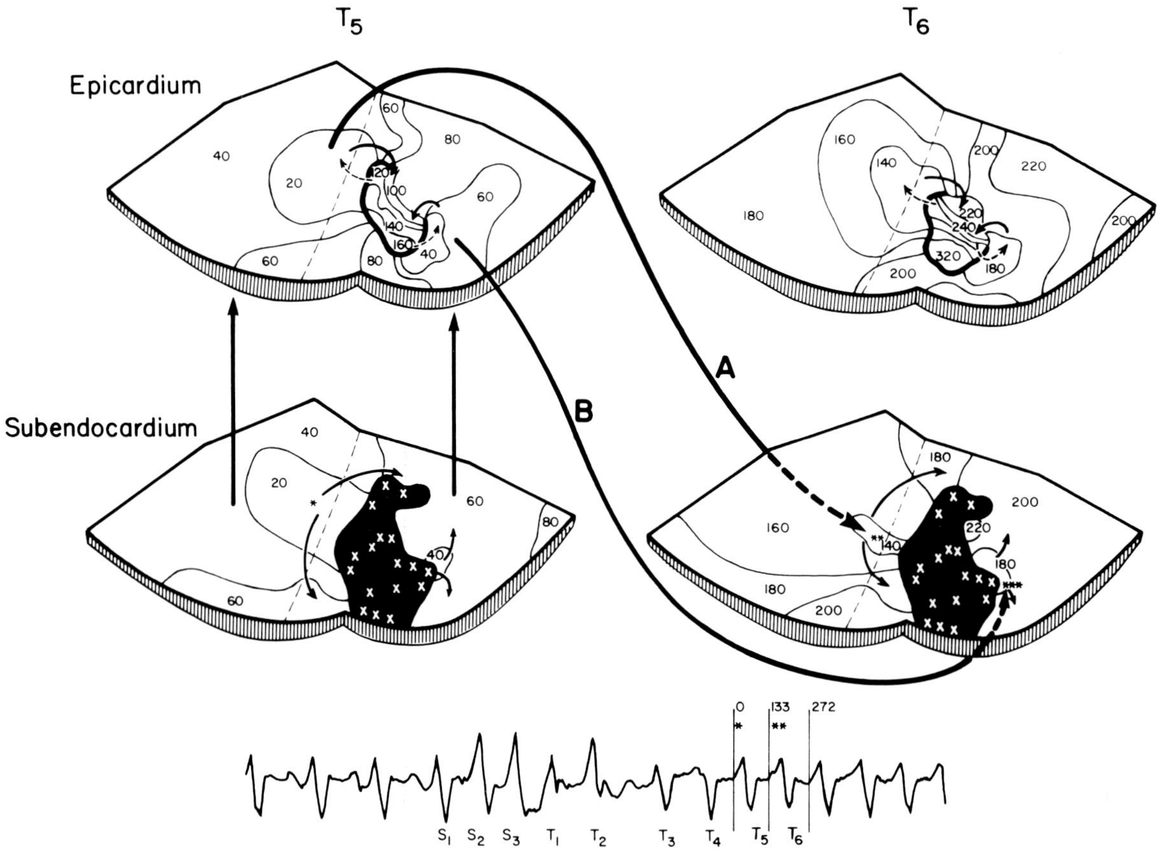

FIGURE 6. *T_5–T_6 transition (dog 2). Epicardial and subendocardial isochronal maps demonstrating interbeat transitions during the uniform phase of monomorphic VT. See text for details.*

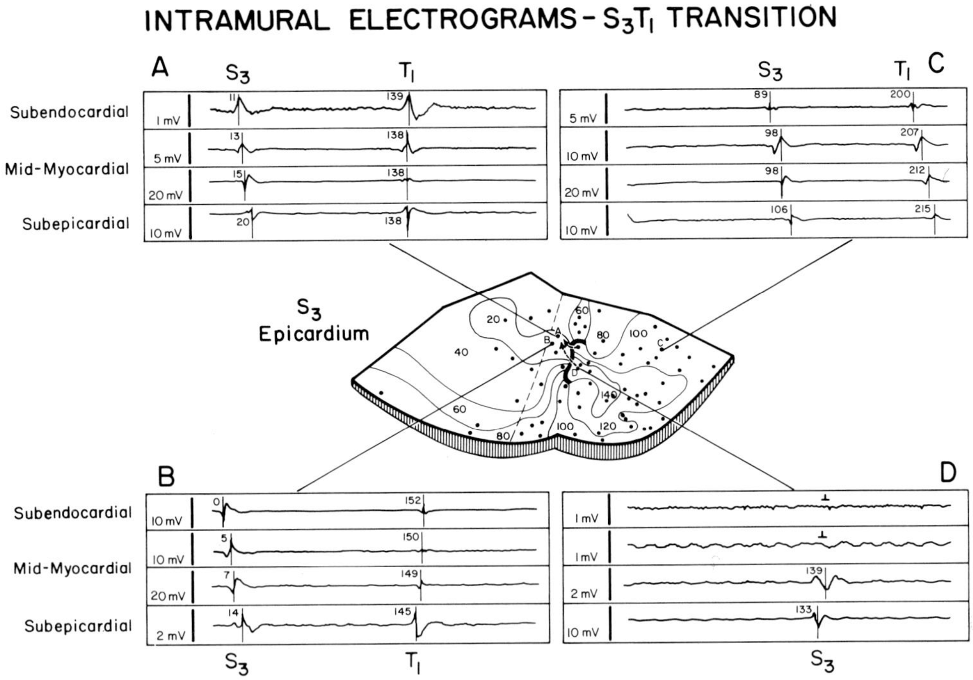

FIGURE 7. *Intramural electrograms (dog 2). Electrograms from four intramural plunge needles are shown for the S_3–T_1 transition illustrated in Figure 4. Dots on the map correspond to positions of epicardial and subepicardial electrodes utilized to determine the two activation sequences. A 250-msec time window is shown in each recording. Signals have been autocalibrated, and the amplitude calibration scale is displayed to the left of each electrogram. A vertical cursor marks the activation point of each electrogram and its time of activation (relative to the first subendocardial activation of S_3). See text for details.*

fashion along these wavefronts, except at the infarct borders, and delay in the epicardial region overlying the central silent zone allows for the two circulating loops to perpetuate. The T_5 and T_6 activation sequences are nearly identical.

The critical evidence supporting this mechanism of reentry is that transmural conduction during the ventricular tachycardia, as during sinus rhythm, generally proceeds in an antegrade direction except along certain "preferred pathways" of exit into the subendocardial plane. The findings are summarized in Figures 7 and 8. Bipolar intramural electrograms from four selected left ventricular electrodes are shown in Figure 7, for beats S_3 and T_1 of the ventricular tachycardia shown in Figure 4. Above each electrogram is the activation time relative to the first S_3 subendocardial activation (electrode B), and, in the center of the diagram, the position of each electrode used to construct the epicardial activation maps is displayed. Electrodes A, B, and C exhibit normal antegrade activation sequences during the S_3 beat (first column). Electrode D is located in tissue overlying the subendocardial silent zone and demonstrates conduction block at the two endocardial-most bipoles and late activation (133 msec) at the two epicardial-most sites. In the second (T_1) depolarization sequence, however (second column of electrograms), electrode A demonstrates nearly simultaneous transmural activation, whereas electrode B shows clear reverse activation from the subepicardium. These two electrodes, located in the zone of exit of the delayed epicardial impulse, are within the "preferred pathway" leading to transition between S_3 and T_1. In contrast, electrode C, situated well away from this zone on the noninfarcted lateral LV wall, again activates antegrade during the T_1 depolarization as it had during the previous sequence. The activation of electrode D is delayed and its T_1 depolarization is not shown.

Intramural activation information, such as that outlined in Figure 7, can be utilized to construct maps summarizing the directional behavior of transmural conduction. The three maps in Figure 8 represent the transmural activation sequence during normal sinus rhythm, as well as during the T_1 and T_5 beats of the ventricular tachycardia shown in Figures 4–6. Darkly shaded areas correspond to the regions of subendocardial conduction block, as in the previous diagrams, whereas each circle represents a plunge electrode position outside this zone which demonstrated transmural activation of the pattern indicated. During sinus rhythm, most of both ventricles activates antegradely, as expected. However, as the middle (T_1) map indicates, even though the majority of the noninfarcted ventricle activates normally from endocardium to epicardium, a discrete zone of reverse transmural activation corresponding to the pathway of transition between T_1 and T_2 is apparent (light shading). This is also the case during the T_5 beat, in which the two circulating epicardial loops were shown to maintain monomorphic VT (Fig. 6). In the lower map of Figure 8,

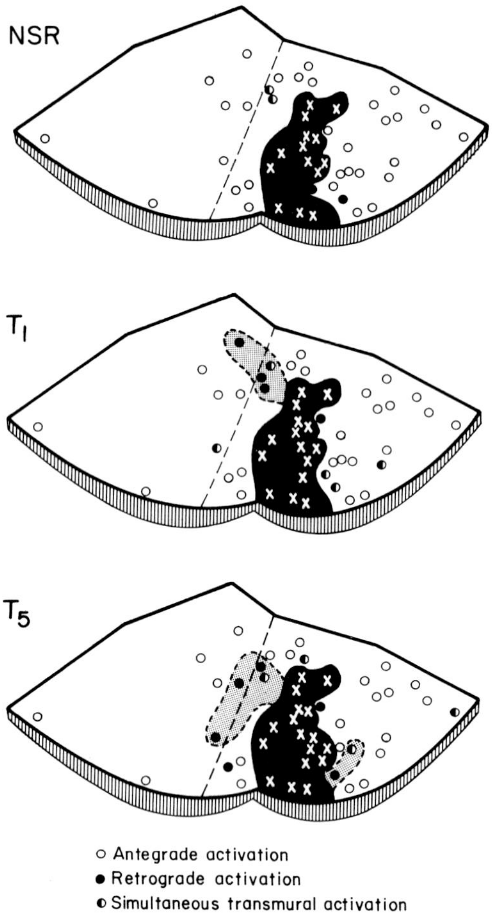

FIGURE 8. *Transmural activation patterns (dog 2). Directionality of transmural conduction is indicated at plunge electrode sites outside the region of subendocardial block (darkly shaded) for a sinus beat, as well as beats T_1 and T_5 described in Figures 4–7. ×'s correspond to electrodes demonstrating bidirectional subendocardial block.*

the two zones of exit (shaded) again correspond to discrete regions of retrograde transmural activation, whereas the remaining noninfarcted ventricle, for the most part, activates antegradely. The remaining electrodes which do not activate antegradely during the ectopic beats are either periseptal, where no endocardium connects the ventricles, or in peri-infarct regions. However these are only isolated retrograde events (Fig. 8). Thus, transmural activation is largely antegrade, except within the discreet pathways of exit.

Macroreentry

A distinct mechanism was discovered to be important in the initial beats of ventricular tachycardia in two animals (Figs. 9 and 10). The isochronal maps in Figure 9 summarize the transition between beats S_3 (the last paced beat), T_1, and T_2 (the initial spontaneous beats of monomorphic ventricular tachycardia) in an animal 6 days after permanent coronary artery ligation (dog 5). Unlike the previous example, in Figures 4–6, this tachycardia does not exhibit the initial polymorphism often preceding monomorphic ventricular tachycardia, but instead inscribes a uniform QRS pattern from the onset of the arrhythmia. The last premature paced beat, S_3, originates at the subendocardial base of the right ventricle (*) and activates, as in the previous tachycardia, radially around a large electrically silent zone and, at the same time, transmurally to more superficial myocardial layers. Whereas the subendocardium activates completely by 80 msec, the activation front on the epicardial plane invades the zone (epicardial rim) overlying the silent subendocardial region only to block in a large front at its septal aspect. The wavefront circumvents the block and enters the epicardial rim from both the apical and basolateral sides, conducting slowly within this zone, and eventually emerging on the lateral border (dashed arrows, epicardium—S_3), reentering tissue proximal to the block after recovery of its excitability. As in the previous example, transmural conduction proceeds retrograde and exit into the subendocardium occurs at 239 msec (**), corresponding to the beginning of the T_1 depolarization sequence. As is evident from this initial transition, the first nonpaced beat need not originate at a location near the pacing site. In this case, the exit site from this epicardial region was located on the opposite side of the pacing site, producing an activation sequence for T_1 which differs markedly from that shown for S_3, a finding also reflected in the differing QRS morphologies for the two beats.

The activation pattern for beat T_1 also begins in the subendocardial plane, proceeds around the area of conduction block in the subendocardium as two wavefronts, and conducts transmurally toward the epicardium. The depolarization wavefront on the epicardial plane appears similar to that on the subendocardial plane, but encounters conduction block along a broad front. Eventually, the two merging epicardial wavefronts enter the epicardial rim overlying the subendocardial silent zone at its septal side at 320 msec. Once within this epicardial zone, conduction is again very slow until exit into the subendocardium occurs (***, at 462 msec) at a site on the opposite side into which the impulse initially reentered the epicardium. The following extrasystole, T_2, then activated in a virtually identical fashion after subendocardial reentry had occurred, consistent with the observed monomorphic QRS configuration.

Several elements are common to the first and second examples of ventricular tachycardia presented, including: (1) rapid activation of the subendocardium around a central zone of block with passive antegrade transmural conduction, (2) significant conduction delay occurring within a limited region of the epicardial border tissue, and (3) exit from electrically isolated epicardial delay zones retrograde into the subendocardium resulting in initiation of the next sequential beat of the tachycardia. However, one important difference between the two

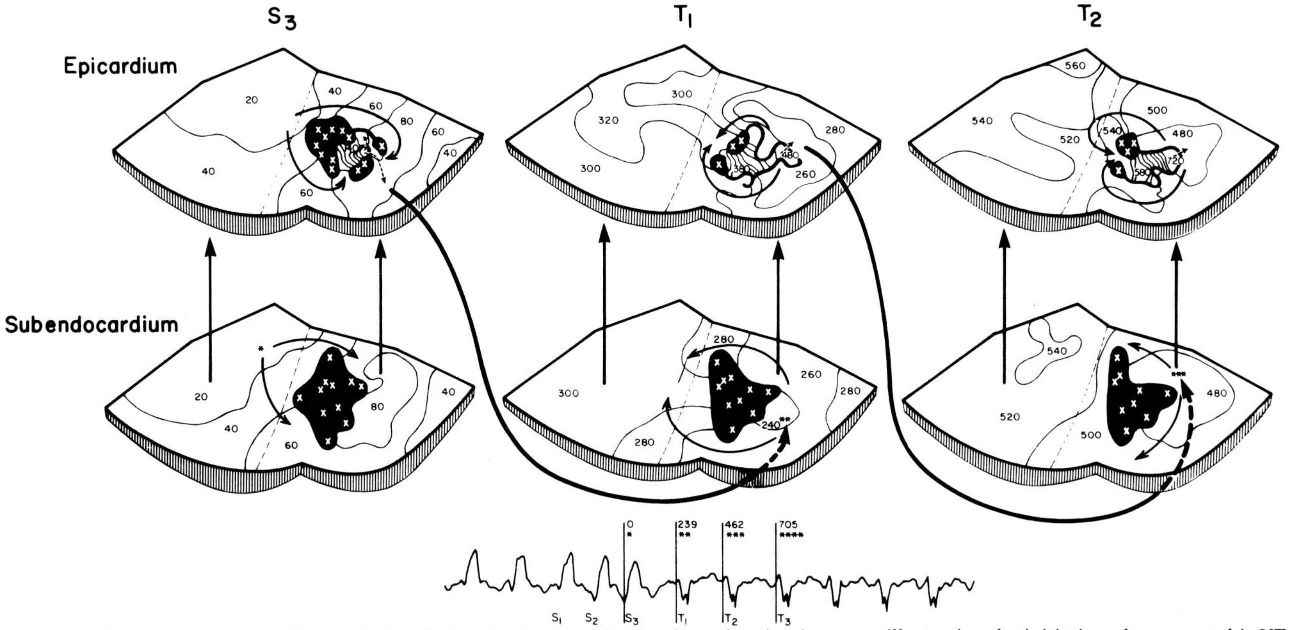

FIGURE 9. *S_3–T_1–T_2 transitions (dog 5). Epicardial and subendocardial isochronal activation maps illustrating the initiation of monomorphic VT following infarction due to coronary artery occlusion. See text for details.*

examples is the much larger extent of conduction block and therefore size of the epicardial circuit in the latter case (Fig. 9). This suggests two potential explanations for the reentry observed in Figure 9. First, as is the case in the earlier example (Figs. 4–6), the reentry loop itself could be epicardial, activating independent of the broad wavefronts depolarizing the remaining ventricle. Alternatively, the long epicardial circuits seen with beats T_1 and T_2 in Figure 9 could be, in part, reflections of fast subendocardial activation transmitted to the more superficial epicardial layers. In this case, the proximal limb of the reentrant loop would actually originate in the subendocardium part of the broad wavefront depolarizing most of the ventricle. Two lines of evidence suggest that the second explanation, macroreentry, is the mechanism which is important in the ventricular tachycardia shown in Figure 9. First, from direct measurements of interelectrode distances and path lengths along the perimeter of

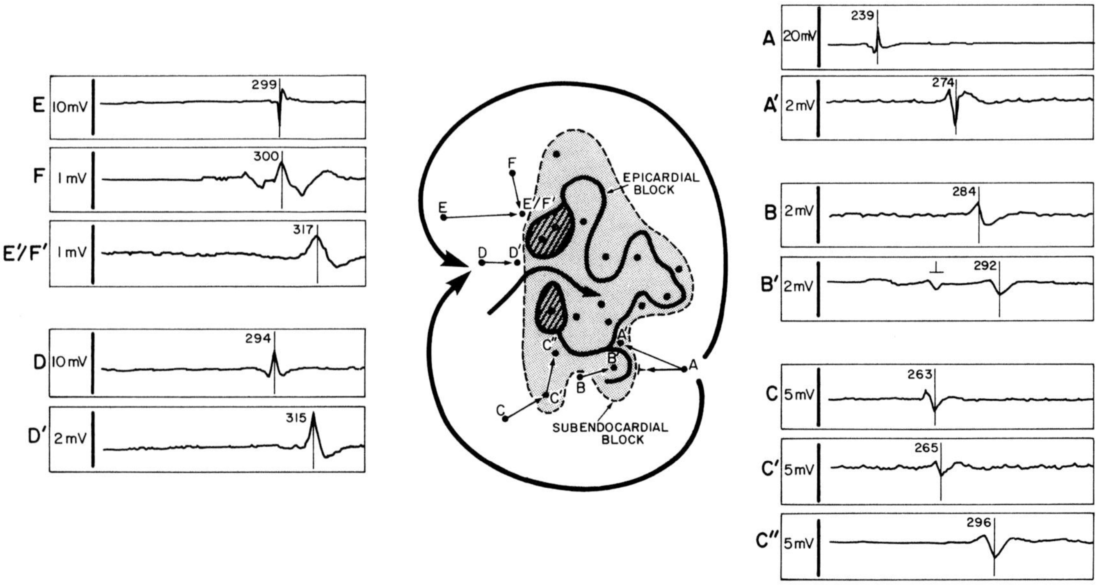

FIGURE 10. *Epicardial electrograms (dog 5). Epicardial electrograms from sites on the periphery of the zone of conduction block during beat T_1 are shown, demonstrating centripetal conduction along the apical and basal limbs of activation. Electrograms and associated activation times are displayed relative to the first subendocardial activation during beat S_3. See text for details.*

the epicardial conduction block illustrated in Figure 9, conduction velocities computed for the T_1 beat are 1.26 and 0.94 m/sec in the apical and basal limbs of the wavefront, respectively. This is much faster than 0.5 m/sec, the maximal epicardial conduction velocity determined in vivo and in vitro by several investigators (Roberts et al., 1979; Spear et al., 1983). Thus, it is unlikely that the "epicardial loops" seen in Figure 9 are truly spreading horizontally in that plane, except in the region without viable underlying subendocardial tissue, and the apparent fast epicardial conduction is due to transmitted subendocardial activation rather than tangential activation in the epicardial plane. Of course, the precise pathways of activation, and hence, conduction velocities, can only be estimated, despite the large number of electrodes located within this region, so that this argument alone might be insufficient to implicate a subendocardial component.

The other evidence implicating a macroreentrant mechanism lies in the fact that epicardial tissue immediately bordering the functional conduction block in Figure 9 is activated from noninfarcted zones showing antegrade transmural conduction, originating in the subendocardium. Electrograms recorded from several epicardial electrodes located along the proximal aspect of the reentry circuit during T_1 are shown in Figure 10. The map in the center illustrates the position of electrodes within the immediate vicinity of the reentrant loop. As was apparent from Figure 9, activation proceeded around the epicardial block from the left lateral infarct border and entered the epicardial zone of conduction delay at its septal margin. Unlike the example of microreentry (Figs. 4–8) in which the wavefront obtained early entrance into the epicardial rim, the timing of electrograms recorded during this beat indicates that its first access was 180° away from the earliest epicardial site, and once within the rim, it conducted slowly from the septal to lateral margin (large arrow, Fig. 10). Early access to the epicardial rim probably did not occur between electrodes, since activation within the rim was in the direction indicated. If the wavefront of conduction were circulating in the epicardial plane and exiting down to the subendocardium between successive beats, as was the case in the first ventricular tachycardia, it would be expected that conduction along the epicardial loop would exhibit *centrifugal* spread from the loop. However, as is clear from the electrograms in Figure 10, electrodes located on the perimeter of the loop instead show *centripetal* conduction, in which electrodes adjacent to the epicardial block, within the region overlying the subendocardial silent zone, are activated from "normal" tissue on the periphery. For instance, electrode A, located within a normally conducting region, activates prior to electrodes A′ and B′, which are immediately adjacent to the subepicardial block. In fact, conduction between electrodes A and B′ is blocked (B′ electrogram), and the latter electrode is activated only after the wave of conduction has spread first to electrode B, further along the "reentry loop" path. Since activation of the noninfarcted tissue on the periphery of the blocked zones occurs antegrade, from the subendocardium, it must be assumed that the proximal (fast) reentry limbs are actually subendocardial in origin. The transmural reflection of this fast conduction gives the appearance of fast conduction on the epicardial plane. Thus, the broad wavefronts of activation which depolarized the ventricles during T_1 participate in the reentry circuit and comprise its proximal (fast) limb.

Anatomical Correlations

Several important aspects of infarct histology and topography are summarized in Figure 11. By 3–8 days after myocardial infarction, the inflammatory and reparative processes are sufficiently advanced to permit precise delineation of the borders of the infarct. Viable cardiac myocytes were recognized easily by the presence of pink cytoplasm with cross striations and ovoid nuclei containing finely granular chromatin (panel F). Necrotic myocardium had been resorbed from the borders of the infarct, and these regions contained inflammatory cells and newly forming granulation tissue (panels A and E). The infarct core was composed of necrotic myocardium exhibiting typical advanced degenerative features (panel B). Necrotic muscle had also been resorbed along the endocardium underlying the transmural infarcts, and the endocardial borders consisted of a zone of fibro-inflammatory tissue. In numerous focal areas, endocardial necrosis was complete, and no viable muscle cells were observed (panel C). In many areas, however, a few viable muscle cells persisted in the subendocardium. These cells were loosely arranged in 1–3 discontinuous layers and appeared to be separated from each other by the local edema and inflammation (panel D). Although judged to be viable, the surviving endocardial myocytes displayed nuclear hyperchromicity and cytoplasmic eosinophilia indicative of some degree of injury.

An epicardial zone of viable myocardium was observed over each transmural infarct (Figs. 11–13). Both the epicardial and lateral borders of the infarcts were highly complex and convoluted, and were composed of extensive interdigitations with viable myocardium which created the impression of multiple "islands" of necrotic tissue when examined in two-dimensional tissue sections. In focal areas, necrosis extended fully to the epicardial fibro-adipose tissue, but these regions were small, and, when reconstructed in three-dimensions, were surrounded by interdigitating zones of viable muscle.

In order to define the precise anatomical substrate underlying the electrophysiological behavior observed during ventricular tachycardia, we examined

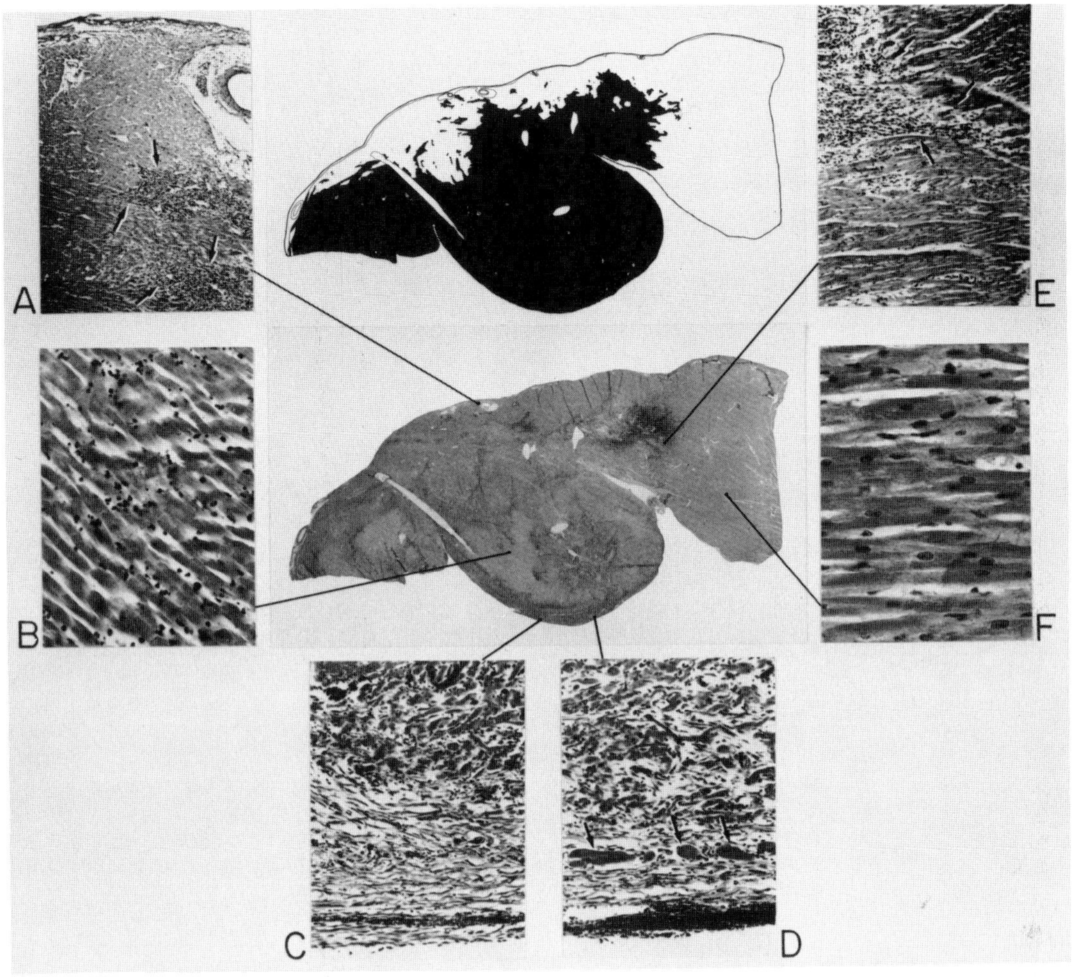

FIGURE 11. *A low magnification photomicrograph and corresponding tracing of a representative transmural section from a canine infarct. Infarcted tissue is indicated in black. Panels A–F illustrate histopathological features of selected regions within the infarct. Panels A and E: epicardial and left lateral borders, respectively, of the infarct illustrating distinct demarcation of viable myocardium and infarct (arrows); panel B: necrotic myocardium; panel C: complete subendocardial necrosis without surviving myocytes; panel D: surviving myocytes within the infarcted subendocardium (arrows), arranged in a discontinuous layer; panel F: viable myocardium.*

in detail the areas of abnormal activity described in the examples presented above. Specifically, we focused on the anatomical correlates of epicardial delay and the "preferred pathways" of exit found to be critical in determining the perpetuation of reentrant beats. Figure 12 illustrates tracings of histological sections from the infarcted heart described in Figures 4–8 (dog 2), showing initiation of monomorphic ventricular tachycardia by a microreentrant mechanism. Selected transmural slices from base to apex and the critical electrodes located along the routes of reentry are shown. Plunge electrodes A, B, and D of Figure 12 correspond to those used to record the electrograms shown in Figure 7. During the first two interbeat transitions of this arrhythmia, epicardial conduction was delayed in the region to the left of (distal to) the line of unidirectional conduction block (Figs. 4 and 5, S_3–T_1 and T_1–T_2) and exit from this zone into the paraseptal LV initiated the subsequent depolarization sequences. In Figure 12, the area of conduction delay occurred in the region of electrodes D, E, and F (panels 4–6), located within the thin rim of surviving epicardial tissue overlying the infarct. The wavefront progressed in an apical-to-basal direction until it gained access to viable subendocardium at the periphery of the infarct. Thus, during the S_3–T_1 and T_1–T_2 transitions, electrodes A and B (Fig. 12, panels 1 and 2) were located along the "preferred pathway" of exit into nonrefractory subendocardium. The viable epicardial rim widens as it approaches the edge of the infarct, resulting in nearly simultaneous transmural activation at electrode A and true retrograde conduction at electrode B (Fig. 7).

As illustrated in Figures 6 and 8, the regions of reentry during the uniform phase of this tachycardia are distinct from those just described for the S_3–T_1 and T_1–T_2 transitions. During the T_5–T_6 transition (Fig. 6), two small independent circuits circulated at either edge of the intramural silent zone, exiting

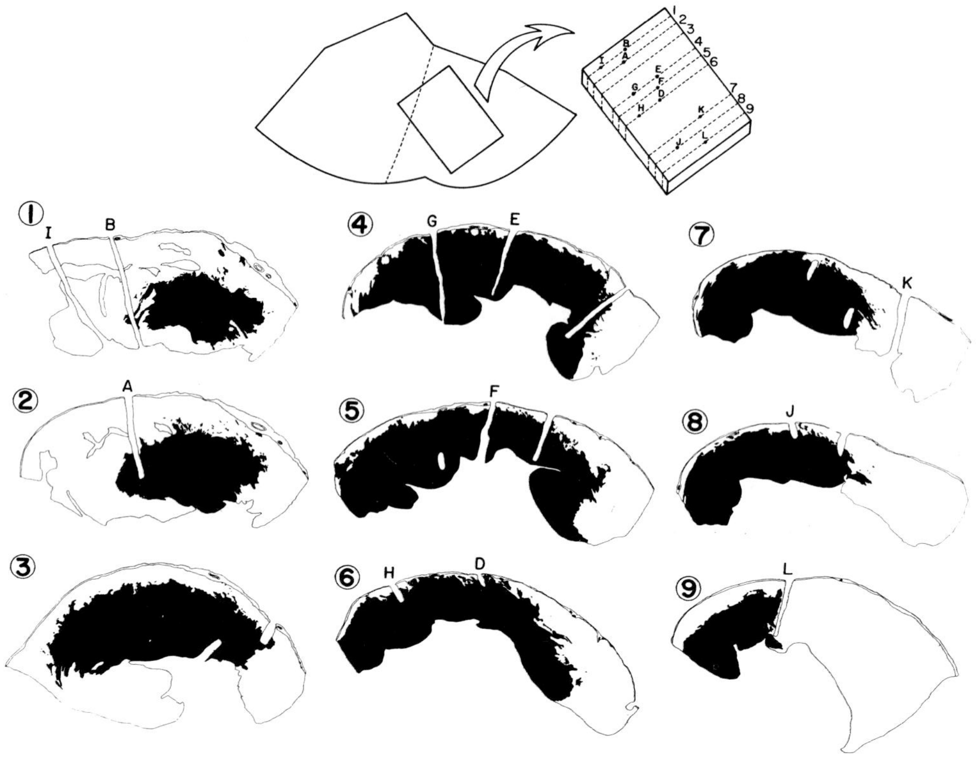

FIGURE 12. *Selected tracings of the transmural infarct of dog 2, corresponding to electrophysiological data presented in Figures 4–8. A large transmural block containing the infarct and electrodes of interest was excised from the heart (upper diagram). Tracings are arranged in a basal-(panel 1) to-apical (panel 9) sequence, and their relative positions in the excised tissue block are shown. Critical electrode positions are depicted as channels in the tracings and are labeled A through L. Additional electrode positions are illustrated but not labeled. Infarcted myocardium is indicated in black. See text for details regarding anatomical and electrophysiological correlations.*

asynchronously into the subendocardium. The anatomical regions in which this activity occurred are also shown in Figure 12. The clockwise (basal) circuit exhibited latest epicardial activity at electrode sites G and H (Fig. 12, panels 4 and 6), located at the viable rim of epicardium overlying the infarct, while the earliest subendocardial activation was situated at site I in the normal RV (Fig. 12, panel 1). Similarly, the latest epicardial electrogram in the counterclockwise (apical) circuit was recorded at electrode J (Fig. 12, panel 8), while early subendocardial activity, leading to the T_6 beat, occurred at electrode sites K and L (Fig. 12, panels 7 and 9). Thus, in both of these small circuits, delayed activation was localized to the thin rim of viable epicardium, whereas retrograde conduction initiating the subsequent beat occurred precisely at the infarct border—at the first access to viable subendocardium.

The correlation between infarct anatomy and electrical behavior during ventricular tachycardia was similar in the example of macroreentry presented in Figures 9 and 10 (dog 5). Figure 13 illustrates tracings of selected transmural sections from this animal. The latest epicardial activity during the S_3–T_1 transition (Fig. 9) was in the vicinity of electrode W (Fig. 13, panel 3), whereas the earliest subendocardial activation of the T_1 beat occurred at electrode X (Fig. 13, panel 6). Once again, late activations were recorded from epicardial tissue overlying necrotic myocardium, whereas the first access to viable subendocardium determined the site of T_1 initiation (**, Fig. 9). During this sequence, epicardial activation spread in a base-to-apex direction, but in the following sequence (T_1–T_2, Fig. 9), the horizontal direction of epicardial activation was apex-to-base. In this latter transition, late epicardial activation occurred again in the surviving epicardial rim (electrodes W and Y; Fig. 13, panels 3 and 4), and earliest subendocardial T_2 activation was located at the infarct edge (electrode Z, Fig. 13, panel 1). As is apparent from Figure 13 (panels 1–3), the epicardial border zone between electrodes W and Z becomes increasingly complex and develops extensive interdigitations of necrotic and viable tissue as it approaches the basolateral infarct edge. Thus, the wavefront traveling on the epicardial rim appears to gain access to the subendocardium within this complex border zone at the periphery of the infarct. Since transmural activation at the earliest site (electrode Z) actually progressed in an *antegrade* fashion, retrograde exit into the subendocardium must have preceded activation at electrode Z and presumably occurred along a convoluted oblique pathway in the highly irregular infarct border depicted in Figure 13 (panels 1–3). Thus, the "preferred pathway" from epicardium to endocardium may traverse a complex tissue channel

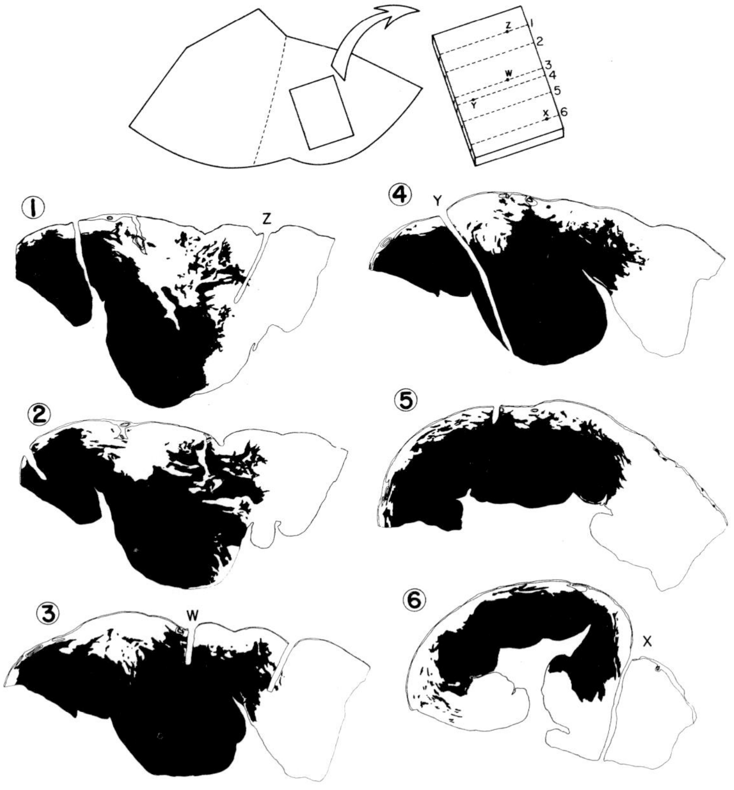

FIGURE 13. *Selected tracings of the transmural infarct of dog 5, corresponding to electrophysiological data presented in Figures 9 and 10. As in the previous diagram, a large transmural tissue block was excised from the ventricle and slices arranged from base (panel 1) to apex (panel 6). Actual electrode positions are depicted as channels labeled W through Z. See text for details.*

which is relatively inaccessible to detection by insertion of a limited number of plunge electrodes.

Discussion

Results of the present study demonstrate that intramural, and, in particular, subendocardial electrical activity mediates a key role in initiation and perpetuation of reentrant ventricular tachycardias resulting from canine myocardial infarction. In all seven dogs undergoing programmed electrical stimulation and three-dimensional isochronal activation mapping, reentrant rhythms were detected and found to involve active intramural participation. Most of these rhythms (71%) were due to a microreentrant mechanism in which continuous circus movement at the epicardial surface was found to conduct via preferential pathways to a subendocardial exit site, from which activation of the noninfarcted ventricle emanated. In these cases, subendocardial and intramural events, although not a part of the reentry circuit per se, were critical in transmitting the rapid impulse to the ventricle. In the remaining morphologies, the subendocardium was an integral component of the macroreentry loop itself, comprising the fast proximal limb which was then reflected to the epicardial surface. In both types of reentry, slow conduction was found anatomically to correspond to the surviving epicardial tissue overlying necrotic myocardium, whereas pathways of transition between successive sequences occurred invariably at the infarct periphery, at the earliest access to viable subendocardial tissue. The configuration of these borders is highly variable so that exit may occur along either a broad front (dog 2) or a relatively narrow one (dog 5).

Previous experimental efforts directed at delineating the mechanisms responsible for ventricular tachycardia during evolving infarction have focused on the characteristics of surviving epicardial muscle. Initial studies utilized the "composite electrode," which recorded delayed diastolic activity over a large region of surviving epicardium (El-Sherif et al., 1977; Kabell et al., 1982) and, later, involved sophisticated multi-site epicardial mapping procedures. The results of these studies indicated that reentrant loops develop entirely within the epicardial rim overlying the infarcted region (El-Sherif et al., 1981; Wit et al., 1982; Mehra et al., 1983). This concept has recently been extended by showing that interruption of activity in the epicardial loops, and termination of the tachycardias, occur when the diastolic portion of the circuit is subjected to cryothermal injury (El-Sherif et al., 1983; Gessman et al., 1983). Thus, although the importance of epicardial conduction delay during canine ventricular tachycardia has been appreciated, its precise role in overall ventricular activation has not. The computerized mapping system utilized in the present study was designed to circumvent the technical problems that have prevented adequate assessment of intramural events, in that information from multiple intramyocardial sites can be rapidly sampled, recorded, and analyzed. Furthermore, the large storage capacity for data from all 232 simultaneous locations allows for analysis and comparison of multiple sequences during initiation of ventricular tachycardia.

Analysis of intramural events was also made feasible by placement of multiple plunge needles into the myocardium. Although some investigators have alluded to changes in conduction due to insertion of plunge electrodes (Mehra et al., 1983), we assessed both hemodynamic performance and epicardial conduction patterns in dogs undergoing programmed stimulation and found no alterations over the course of each experiment. Furthermore, induction of ventricular tachycardia of a given morphology was reproducible before and after plunge electrode insertion, suggesting that the reentrant pathways involved in these arrhythmias were unaffected.

Three points regarding analysis of these data impact significantly on the subsequent conclusions. First, we elected to design and utilize plunge electrodes which recorded intramural activity at fixed distances from the epicardial surface, the result being that endocardial activation per se was not always directly assessed. Although the reported survival of endocardial Purkinje cells within canine infarcts (Karaguezian et al., 1980) suggests that some conduction along this thin layer underlying the infarct could occur, the patterns of subendocardial activation observed in the present study (Figs. 4, 5, 6, and 9) in each case implicate a radial, pincer-like activation pattern around a central area of conduction block. Subendocardial zones on the far border of a block are activated last, which is inconsistent with the existence of wavefronts progressing deep to this area of block and activating the far border. The overall histological appearance of subendocardial tissue within the infarct also is consistent with subendocardial block in this region, since extensive discontinuities appear within this subendocardial zone (Fig. 11). Furthermore, the mechanism presented is derived largely from the transmural activation pattern, indicating the relationship between areas of epicardial delay and adjacent myocardium. Even if present, Purkinje conduction deep to the zone of block would not alter the basic substrate of protected delay and retrograde exit. A second important consideration is the accuracy of plunge electrode localization critical for both isochronal and anatomical analyses. By the stickpin method, every attempt was made to duplicate the precise path taken by each electrode; however, small errors could result from disparity in the angles of entry into the myocardium. We feel, however, that the resolution afforded by this method allows for precise analysis of regional electrophysiological and anatomic detail. The other factor novel to our approach was the combined use of surface epicardial buttons and immediately subepicardial plunge electrode bipoles to evaluate "epicardial" conduction. The subepicardial plunge bipole was located only 500 μm from the epicardial surface and allowed recording of detailed intramural information at the infarct borders. On the other hand, the sock array was valuable in determining the effect of plunge electrodes on conduction (Fig. 3), and provided a concentrated electrode field over areas of gross infarction at the epicardial rim where detailed transmural information was somewhat less useful. Thus, the combined use of epicardial and subepicardial bipoles within this 500-μm region maximized our ability to detect zones of delay and their relationship to adjacent tissue.

Although the mechanisms defined in the present study differ substantially from previous descriptions, our findings are not inconsistent with previous data, but rather clarify several outstanding issues. For instance, the present data account for the disparate findings of micro- (Richards et al., 1983) and macro- (Mehra et al., 1983) reentry during ventricular tachycardia, since we found that either pattern can occur, dependent upon the extent of conduction block encountered at the epicardial rim. Thus, small fronts of conduction block will result in small loops and microreentry, whereas large fronts are circumvented by wavefronts propagating from fast subendocardial activation and result in macroreentry. As would be predictable from our proposed mechanisms, zones of early epicardial activation near the QRS onset should be relatively unresponsive to interruption by ablation (Wittig and Boineau, 1975; El-Sherif et al., 1983) since they may be distant from the endocardial site of origin, whereas late regions showing diastolic activity should be consistently vulnerable to ablation (El-Sherif et al., 1983; Gessman et al., 1983). Finally, although epicardial reentry has not been clearly documented in studies evaluating infarction due to reperfusion of the coronary artery (Wit et al., 1982), we found that intramural reentry was indeed important in the five dogs studied with this lesion, and was identical to the mechanism responsible for monomorphic ventricular tachycardia in the two dogs with permanent coronary occlusion.

The implications of these mechanisms for ventricular tachycardia in patients undergoing evolving myocardial infarction depend on the degree to which the experimental preparation approximates human pathophysiology. In addition to the electrophysiological and anatomic similarities between the two types of infarction, there are several aspects of the proposed mechanisms which also coincide with current clinical observations. First, earliest activity during clinical ventricular tachycardia is endocardial when concurrent endocardial and epicardial mapping is performed intraoperatively (Horowitz et al., 1980). Second, the success of surgical techniques which involve inactivation of these early endocardial sites, including endocardial resection (Josephson et al., 1979a) and encircling endocardial ventriculotomy (Guiraudon et al., 1978), is certainly compatible with the present findings. The results of endocardial ablation and isolation are difficult to explain on the basis of the previous notion of reentry confined to the epicardial surface. Third, the clinical observation that it is probable that a change in QRS morphology during clinical ventricular tachycardia is due to differing exit sites from a single reentrant loop (Josephson et at., 1979b) is entirely consistent with our proposed mechanisms, since the initial polymorphic beats of ventricular tachycardia are due to varying exit into the subendocardium from an epicardial circuit. Fourth, there is evidence for a protected reentrant loop during human ventricular tachycardia (Josephson et al., 1978b), which would again be consistent with our present observations. Despite these marked similarities between canine and human ventricular tachycardias, there might be dissimilarities as well, such as the location of human reentrant circuits, which could be septal, intramural, or endocardial.

Several critical questions remain from the observations presented. Although the data are very suggestive of the importance of intramural electrical events, the *requirement* for their participation in ventricular tachycardia is speculative. Only elimination of endocardial tissue from the process would definitively answer this question. Also, the role of the bundle branches and septum require direct evaluation, since clinical and experimental evidence (Spurrell et al., 1973; Klein et al., 1979; Cardinal et al., 1984) suggests that these sites may be critical under some circumstances. Several of the tachycardias analyzed in the present study originated from periseptal locations, implying that the presence of septal recordings might provide useful information about many tachycardias, particularly those arising from septal infarcts. Another question of considerable significance is the mechanism responsible for the highly malignant arrhythmias associated with nontransmural infarction, resulting in a relatively high risk of sudden death in that patient population (Cannom et al., 1976). Finally, it would seem feasible that pharmacological interruption of monomorphic ventricular tachycardia might result from agents which either increase endocardial refractoriness (and, hence, prevent exit into that plane), or, alternatively, which slow epicardial conduction such that delay might convert to block. Surgically, interruption of the reentrant path might include discreet excision of the "preferred pathways" of transmural reentry, following precise localization by mapping similar to that used in the present study.

We would like to thank Roosevelt Dean, Jr., for technical assistance, Marcie Hartstein and Vicki Friedman for design of the three-dimensional representations, Louise Schoelch for photographic assistance, and Jill Van Denburg and Elaine Zuzack for the epicardial socks. We also appreciate the assistance of Evelyn Kanter, who constructed the plunge electrodes, and Ava Ysaguirre, Kelly Ragsdale, and Barbara Donnelly for preparation of the manuscript. We are grateful to Dr. Burton E. Sobel for his advice and support throughout the project.

Research from the authors' laboratory was supported in part by National Institutes of Health Grant HL 17646, SCOR in Ischemic Heart Disease, Grant HL 28995, and by Grant RR 00396 from the Division of Research Resources. It was performed during Dr. Corr's tenure as an Established Investigator of the American Heart Association and with funds contributed in part by the Missouri Heart Affiliate.

Address for reprints: Dr. Peter B. Corr, Cardiovascular Division, Washington University School of Medicine, 660 South Euclid Avenue, Box 8086, St. Louis, Missouri 63110.

Received November 12, 1984; accepted for publication February 21, 1985.

References

Cannom DS, Levy W, Cohen LS (1976) The short- and long-term prognosis of patients with transmural and nontransmural myocardial infarction. Am J Med **61:** 452–458

Cardinal R, Savard P, Carson DL, Perry J-B, Page P (1984) Mapping of ventricular tachycardia induced by programmed stimulation in canine preparations of myocardial infarction. Circulation **70:** 136–148

Durrer D, Van Der Tweel LH (1954) Spread of activation in the left ventricular wall of the dog. II. Activation conditions at the epicardial surface. Am Heart J **47:** 192–203

El-Sherif N, Scherlag BJ, Lazarra R, Hope RR (1977) Reentrant ventricular arrhythmias in the late myocardial infarction period. I. Conduction characteristics in the infarction zone. Circulation **55:** 686–707

El-Sherif N, Smith RA, Evans K (1981) Canine ventricular arrhythmias in the late myocardial infarction period. 8. Epicardial mapping of reentrant circuits. Circ Res **49:** 255–265

El-Sherif N, Mehra R, Gough WB, Zeiler RH (1983) Reentrant ventricular arrhythmias in the late myocardial infarction period interruption of reentrant circuits by cryothermal techniques. Circulation **68:** 644–656

Gallagher JJ, Kasell J, Sealy WC, Pritchett ELC, Wallace AG (1978) Epicardial mapping in the Wolff-Parkinson-White syndrome. Circulation **57:** 854–866

Gessman LJ, Agarawal JB, Endo T, Helfant RH (1983a) Localization and mechanism of ventricular tachycardia by ice mapping 1 week after the onset of myocardial infarction in dogs. Circulation **68:** 657–666

Guiraudon G, Fontaine G, Frank R, Escande G, Etievent P, Cabrol C (1978) Encircling endocardial ventriculotomy: A new surgical treatment for life-threatening ventricular tachycardias resistant to medical treatment following myocardial infarction. Ann Thorac Surg **26:** 438–444

Hamer S, Karagueuzian HS, Sugi K, Mandel WJ, McCullen A, Zaher C, Peter CT (1983) Can programmed stimulation induce ventricular fibrillation in the normal canine ventricle? (abstr). J Am Coll Cardiol **83:** 594

Harris AS (1950) Delayed development of ventricular ectopic rhythms following experimental coronary occlusion. Circulation **1:** 1318–1328

Harrison L, Ideker RE, Smith WM, Klein GJ, Kassell J, Wallace AG, Gallagher JJ (1980) The sock electrode array: A tool for determining global epicardial activation during unstable arrhythmias. Pace **3:** 531–540

Horowitz LN, Josephson ME, Harken AH (1980) Epicardial and endocardial activation during sustained ventricular tachycardia in man. Circulation **61:** 1227–1238

Josephson ME, Horowitz LN, Farshidi A, Kastor JA (1978a) Recurrent sustained ventricular tachycardia. I. Mechanisms. Circulation **57:** 431–439

Josephson ME, Horowitz LN, Farshidi A, Spielman SR, Michelson EL, Greenspan AM (1978b) Sustained ventricular tachycardia: Evidence for protected localized reentry. Am J Cardiol **42:** 416–424

Josephson ME, Harken AH, Horowitz LN (1979a) Endocardial excision: A new surgical technique for the treatment of recurrent ventricular tachycardia. Circulation **60:** 1430–1439

Josephson ME, Horowitz LN, Farshidi A, Spielman SR, Michelson EL, Greenspan AM (1979b) Recurrent sustained ventricular tachycardia. 4. Pleomorphism. Circulation **59:** 459–468

Kabell G, Scherlag BJ, Hope RR, Lazzara R (1982) Patterns of interectopic activation recorded during pleomorphic ventricular tachycardia after myocardial infarction in the dog. Am J Cardiol **49:** 56–62

Karagueuzian HS, Fenoglio JJ Jr, Weiss MB, Wit AL (1979) Protracted ventricular tachycardia induced by premature stimulation of the canine heart after coronary artery occlusion and reperfusion. Circ Res **44:** 833–846

Karagueuzian HS, Fenoglio JJ Jr, Weiss MB, Wit AL (1980) Coronary occlusion and reperfusion: Effects on subendocardial cardiac fibers. Am J Physiol **238:** H581–H593

Klein GJ, Ideker RE, Smith WM, Harrison LA, Kasell J, Wallace AG, Gallagher JJ (1979) Epicardial mapping of the onset of ventricular tachycardia initiated by programmed stimulation in the canine heart with chronic infarction. Circulation **60:** 1375–1384

Mehra R, Zeiler R, Gough WB, El-Sherif N (1983) Reentrant ventricular arrhythmias in the late myocardial infarction period. 9. Electrophysiologic-anatomic correlation of reentrant circuits. Circulation **67:** 11–24

Michelson EL, Spear JF, Moore EN (1980) Electrophysiologic and anatomic correlates of sustained ventricular tachyarrhythmias in a model of chronic myocardial infarction. Am J Cardiol **45:** 583–590

Michelson EL, Spear JF, Moore EN (1981) Initiation of sustained ventricular tachyarrhythmias in a canine model of myocardial infarction: Importance of the site of stimulation. Circulation **63:** 776–784

Moss AJ (1980) Clinical significance of ventricular arrhythmias in patients with and without coronary artery disease. Prog Cardiovasc Dis **23:** 33–52

Moss AJ, DeCamilla J, Davis H (1977) Cardiac death in the first 6 months after myocardial infarction: Potential for mortality reduction in the early posthospital period. Am J Cardiol **39:** 816–820

Richards DA, Blake GJ, Spear JF, Moore EN (1984) Electrophysiologic substrate for ventricular tachycardia: Correlation of properties in vivo and in vitro. Circulation **69:** 369–381

Roberts RE, Hersh LT, Scher AM (1979) Influence of cardiac fiber concentration on wavefront voltage, conduction velocity, and tissue resistivity in the dog. Circ Res **44:** 701–712

Spear JF, Michelson EL, Moore EN (1983) Cellular electrophysiologic characteristics of chronically infarcted myocardium in dogs susceptible to sustained ventricular tachyarrhythmias. J Am Coll Cardiol **1:** 1099–1110

Spurrell RAJ, Sowton E, Deuchbar DC (1973) Ventricular tachycardia in 4 patients evaluated by programmed electrical stimulation of the heart and treated in 2 patients by surgical division of the anterior radiation of the left bundle-branch. Br Heart J **35:** 1014–1025

Ursell PC, Fenoglio JJ Jr (1982) Structural basis of ventricular tachycardia. *In*: Ventricular Tachycardia, edited by ME Josephson. Mount Kisco, New York, Futura Publishing Co., pp 151–178

Wit AL, Allessie MA, Bonke FIM, Lammers W, Smeets J, Fenoglio JJ Jr (1982) Electrophysiologic mapping to determine the mechanism of experimental ventricular tachycardia initiated by premature impulses. Am J Cardiol **49:** 166–185

Witkowski FX, Corr PB (1984) An automated simultaneous cardiac mapping system. Am J Physiol **247:** H661–H668

Wittig JH, Boineau JP (1975) Surgical treatment of ventricular arrhythmias using epicardial, transmural, and endocardial mapping. Ann Thorac Surg **20:** 117–126

INDEX TERMS: Ventricular tachycardia • Mapping • Myocardial infarction • Arrhythmias • Reentry

Effects of Propranolol on Atherogenesis in the Cholesterol-Fed Rabbit

Aram V. Chobanian, Peter Brecher, and Catherine Chan
From the Cardiovascular Institute, and Evans Department of Clinical Research, Boston University School of Medicine, Boston, Massachusetts

SUMMARY. These studies have examined the effects of *dl*-propranolol, *d*-propranolol, and metoprolol on aortic atherogenesis in the cholesterol-fed rabbit and have correlated the vascular effects of the drugs with their influence on blood pressure, plasma lipids and lipoproteins, arterial metabolism, and arterial permeability. *dl*-Propranolol, and, to a lesser extent, *d*-propranolol, used in clinically relevant doses of 5 mg/kg body weight per day, inhibited the development of aortic atherosclerosis in association with significant reductions in aortic free and esterified cholesterol content. No significant effects of the drugs on blood pressure or on the total amounts or types of circulating lipoproteins were apparent. Accumulation of cholesterol in the liver and adrenal gland was not influenced by propranolol. Aortic acyl CoA:cholesterol acyltransferase and lysosomal enzyme activities were reduced by propranolol administration, but the inhibition may have been secondary to the lesser degrees of atherosclerosis and cholesterol accumulation present. In vitro inhibition of acyl CoA:cholesterol acyltransferase activity by either *dl*- or *d*-propranolol was also observed, but occurred only at propranolol concentrations of 10^{-3} M or greater. Treatment with *dl*-propranolol had no significant effect on the rate of transport of labeled albumin across the isolated carotid artery of cholesterol-fed rabbits. Metoprolol administration (6.25 mg/kg body weight per day) had no significant influence on atherogenesis or arterial metabolism in this model. The results suggest that propranolol inhibits in part the development of atherosclerosis in the cholesterol-fed rabbit, and that the effect may be related to a direct action on the arterial wall.
(*Circ Res 56: 755–762, 1985*)

SEVERAL drugs affecting sympathetic nervous function and used clinically to lower blood pressure may also inhibit the development of atherosclerosis in normotensive animals in response to cholesterol feeding. Propranolol, a β-adrenergic blocker, has been reported to retard atherogenesis in the cholesterol-fed rabbit (Whittington-Coleman et al., 1973). Similar effects have been observed in both rats and rabbits with reserpine (Smith and Rossi, 1962; Deming, 1966; Whittington-Coleman et al., 1968), a centrally acting adrenergic inhibitor, and in rabbits with guanethidine (Whittington-Coleman and Carrier, 1970), a peripheral sympathetic blocker. The mechanism for any anti-atherogenic action of these drugs in the cholesterol-fed rabbit has not been delineated, although several possibilities exist, including effects of the drugs on blood pressure, the renin-angiotensin system, the amount or properties of plasma lipoproteins, platelet function, or on the arterial wall itself through some direct action.

The current study has been performed to investigate the effects of β-adrenergic blockade on blood pressure, plasma lipids and lipoproteins, arterial metabolism, arterial permeability, and atherogenesis in the cholesterol-fed rabbit. Three drugs were selected as pharmacological probes to examine the problem: *dl*-propranolol, which is a potent antagonist of both β_1- and β_2-receptor activity; *d*-propranolol, the optical isomer which has little β-blocking action except at high doses, but which has similar membrane-stabilizing activity as the racemic mixture; and metoprolol, a potent antagonist with membrane-stabilizing properties, but unlike propranolol, netroprolol has a weak inhibitory effect on the β_2-receptor, except at high doses.

Methods

Animals

Male New Zealand white rabbits (Charles River Breeding Laboratories) weighing between 1.5 and 2.0 kg were used in this study. Animals were housed individually with free access to food. The cholesterol-fed animals were fed a diet containing 2% cholesterol and 8% peanut oil for an 8-week period, while the control group received only commercial rabbit chow (Purina Co.).

We monitored systolic blood pressure every 2 weeks, using a tail cuff method developed in our laboratory (Kramsch et al., 1980). Measurements were made between 2 and 4 hours after drug administration. Unanesthetized rabbits were placed in a Styrofoam box with an opening for exposure of the tail. The tail was shaved, and the animal was acclimated to the box with head and eyes covered for 30 minutes before the measurements. A photoelectric sensing element was taped into place over the tail, and the systolic blood pressure was detected with an IITC MOD 59 preamplifier (Innovators in Instrumentation) and recorded by a Narco physiograph. The average of five consecutive measurements was used for the determinations. Values varied less than 10 mm Hg between measurements.

Materials

[1-^{14}C]-oleoyl CoA (specific activity 43.4 Ci/mol) and tri [1-^{14}C]-oleoyl glycerol (specific activity 44 Ci/mol) were obtained from New England Nuclear Corp. *P*-nitrophenyl-*N*-acetyl-β-glucosaminide and *p*-nitrophenyl-α-D-glucoside were obtained from Sigma Chemical Co. Egg yolk lecithin was a product of Lipid Products. *dl*-Propranolol and *d*-propranolol were kindly supplied by Ayerst Laboratories, and metoprolol was supplied by the Ciba-Geigy Company.

Drug Treatment

Three separate sets of experiments were performed to evaluate the effects of β-blocker therapy on aortic atherosclerosis. In an initial study, only the influence of daily *dl*-propranolol in cholesterol-fed rabbits was assessed. In the second investigation, four groups of animals were studied: control, cholesterol-fed, cholesterol-fed with *dl*-propranolol, and cholesterol-fed with *d*-propranolol treatment, and the effects of therapy on arterial lipid metabolism as well as atherogenesis were examined. The third set of experiments examined the influence of metoprolol in treated and untreated cholesterol-fed rabbits.

Propranolol or metoprolol was dissolved in sterile saline, and the pH was adjusted to 7.0. Each drug was administered once daily by intraperitoneal injection in a total volume of 1 ml beginning at the initiation of cholesterol feeding. The dose of *dl*- and *d*-propranolol was 5 mg daily, and of metoprolol, 6.25 mg daily. Paired cholesterol-fed rabbits were injected daily with the vehicle alone.

Plasma Lipids and Lipoproteins

Blood was obtained from the marginal ear vein at 1- to 2-week intervals. Previously described procedures were used for measuring plasma cholesterol (Rudel and Morris, 1973) and triglyceride (Fletcher, 1968). Plasma lipoproteins were analyzed after 4 weeks of cholesterol feeding in samples of blood drawn into EDTA after an overnight fast. Three milliliters of plasma were layered beneath a solution containing 0.195 M NaCl, 1 mM K_2 EDTA, and 0.04% sodium azide and centrifuged at 49,000 rpm for 17 hours at 4°C in a 60 Ti rotor. The very low density lipoprotein (VLDL) fraction obtained was washed once and analyzed by agarose gel electrophoresis (Brecher et al., 1983). Electrophoretic analysis of total plasma samples was also performed. Apoproteins were determined by polyacrylamide gel electrophoresis with 10% gels containing 0.1% sodium dodecyl sulfate. The lipoproteins were delipidated and the gels were stained as described previously (Brecher et al., 1983).

Tissue Preparation

Rabbits were killed by decapitation at the end of the 8th week of study. The entire aorta from the aortic valve to the bifurcation was removed quickly and transferred to ice-cold medium containing 0.25 M sucrose and 0.01 M Tris, pH 7.4. The adventitia was removed and the aorta opened along the mid-dorsal line to expose the intimal surface. Tracings of the intimal lesions were made, and representative lesions were examined on hematoxylin and eosin-stained sections by standard light microscopy. The segment of aorta between the aortic valve and celiac artery was weighed, minced, and homogenized in 10 volumes of sucrose-Tris buffer with a motor-driven, glass-glass homogenizer at 0–2°C. In the initial set of studies that examined the effects of *dl*-propranolol alone, the homogenates were assayed only for free and esterified cholesterol content. In the second and third group of experiments, a portion of the tissue homogenate was stored at −20°C for subsequent lipid determinations. The remaining material was centrifuged at 10,000 *g* for 10 minutes, and the supernatant was centrifuged again at 100,000 *g* for 45 minutes. The resulting microsomal fraction was washed once and resuspended in 0.25 M sucrose, 0.01 M Tris, pH 7.4, and frozen at −80°C for subsequent chemical and enzymatic studies. The 100,000 *g* supernatant was used for the lysosomal enzyme assays. Tissue homogenates of the left adrenal gland and a segment of the right anterior lobe of the liver were also prepared in buffer, and aliquots were used for subsequent lipid determinations.

Enzyme Assays

Acyl CoA:cholesterol acyltransferase activity (ACAT) was determined in aortic microsomes by measuring the rate of incorporation of [1-^{14}C]oleoyl CoA into cholesteryl-[^{14}C]oleate (Brecher and Chan, 1980). In the standard assay, 15–20 μg of protein were incubated for 25 minutes at 25°C in 0.2 ml of solution containing 0.1 M potassium phosphate buffer (pH 7.5), 20 μM dithiothreitol, 0.3% of bovine serum albumin, and 5 μM [1-^{14}C]oleoyl CoA. The reaction was terminated by adding 4 ml chloroform:methanol (2:1, vol/vol) containing unlabeled cholesteryl oleate and oleic acid (10 mg/liter) as carriers, and a lipid extract was obtained (Folch et al., 1957). Cholesteryl-[1-^{14}C]oleate was determined in the lipid extract by thin layer chromatography using hexane:diethyl ether:acetic acid (90:10:1, vol/vol/vol) as developing solvent. Enzymatic activity was expressed as pmol of cholesteryl[^{14}C]-oleate formed per min per mg of microsomal protein. In selected experiments, where the in vitro effect of *dl*- and *d*-propranolol on ACAT activity was examined, the drugs were added directly to the assay system before the reaction was initiated.

Neutral α-D-glucosidase activity was determined in aortic microsomes as described (Brecher and Chan, 1980).

We assayed *N*-acetyl-β-glucosaminidase (NAGA) activity in the 100,000 *g* supernatant by measuring the release of *p*-nitrophenol resulting from the hydrolysis of *p*-nitrophenol-*N*-acetyl-β-glucosaminide, using incubation conditions reported previously (Brecher et al., 1978). Enzymatic activity was expressed as nmol *p*-nitrophenol released per min per mg protein.

Acid lipase activity was measured in the 100,000 *g* supernatant of aortic homogenate according to a slight modification of our previously published procedure (Brecher et al., 1977). Triacylglycerol-phospholipid vesicles (1:5 molar ratio) were prepared by sonification of a mixture of 60 mg of egg yolk lecithin, 12.5 mg triolein, and 8.0 μCi tri[1-^{14}C]oleoyl glycerol and were employed as -substrate. The assay of lipolytic activity was performed in a total volume of 0.3 ml containing 75 μl of the vesicle preparation and 50–100 μl of enzyme solution in 0.15 M sodium acetate buffer (pH 4.0). The final concentrations of triolein and lecithin were 0.6 mM and 3.0 mM, respectively, and each assay tube contained 0.10 μCi [1-^{14}C]-triolein. Incubations were conducted at 37°C for 30 minutes, and the labeled free fatty acid formed was measured following solvent partition. Enzymatic activity was expressed as nmol free fatty acid released per min, per mg protein.

Chemical Analysis

The protein content of aortic homogenates was determined by a micro-Kjeldahl procedure. Protein was determined on the microsomal fraction and 100,000 *g* supernatant as described (Lowry et al., 1951).

Lipids were extracted from tissue homogenates (Folch et al., 1957). Free and esterified cholesterol were separated by thin layer chromatography and their content analyzed using a Transidyne RFT-II recording densitometer under conditions where a linear relationship between peak area and the amount of cholesterol was obtained (between 0.3 and 8.0 μg material).

Studies of Arterial Albumin Transport

The influence of *dl*-propranolol on albumin transport across rabbit common carotid artery was also examined in cholesterol-fed rabbits using an experimental system recently developed in our laboratory (Chobanian et al., 1983). Studies were performed after 8 weeks of cholesterol feeding in the presence or absence of daily propranolol treatment (see above). Rabbits were anesthetized and the left common carotid artery exposed. Its branches were ligated and Silastic catheters were inserted at both ends to allow continuous perfusion in a closed system with solution consisting of Dulbecco's modified Eagle's medium to which was added 10% fetal calf serum, *l*-glutamine, and papaverine. [^{125}I]Albumin (New England Nuclear Co.) was also added to the perfusion medium in concentration of 5 μCi/ml, and the solution was continuously recirculated through the carotid artery at approximately 50 mm Hg mean pressure. Blood samples were collected from a jugular venous catheter at intervals over a 4-hour period, and both the total ^{125}I radioactivity and that precipitated with trichloroacetic acid were determined. Radioactivity also was assayed in the intima-media preparation of the perfused carotid artery at the end of the study period. Four rabbits were used in each group.

Results were expressed as the mean ± SE. The data in Tables 1–3 were analyzed statistically by one-way analysis of variance for each variable. When differences were significant, intergroup comparisons were done by Neuman-Keuls test.

Results

Effects of *dl*-Propranolol in Cholesterol-Fed Rabbits

We performed pilot studies of groups of five cholesterol-fed rabbit treated for 8 weeks with either saline or *dl*-propranolol. Propranolol administration produced a marked decrease in total surface involvement of the aorta by visible atherosclerotic lesions, compared with the saline-treated controls, with disease in the propranolol group restricted primarily to the upper arch of the thoracic aorta and the regions surrounding the ostia of the intercostal vessels. The individual lesions in the treated and untreated groups appeared comparable when examined by light microscopy. Total aortic cholesterol content was reduced significantly by propranolol from 12.8 ± 0.6 to 4.9 ± 0.4 mg/g wet weight ($P < 0.05$).

TABLE 1
Effect of Chronic *dl*- or *d*-Propranolol Therapy on Body Weight, Blood Pressure, and Aortic and Heart Weights in the Rabbit

	Body wt (kg)	Blood pressure (mm Hg)	Heart/ body wt ($\times 10^{-3}$)	Aortic wt (g)
Control	2.7 ± 0.2	104 ± 7	1.9 ± 0.1	0.51 ± 0.08
Cholesterol-fed	2.9 ± 0.3	89 ± 6	1.9 ± 0.2	0.71 ± 0.10
Cholesterol-fed and *dl*-propranolol	2.5 ± 0.2	81 ± 6	1.8 ± 0.1	0.62 ± 0.08
Cholesterol-fed and *d*-propranolol	2.7 ± 0.3	88 ± 7	1.9 ± 0.1	0.67 ± 0.08

Results represent the means ± SE for six animals.

Plasma cholesterol levels did not differ significantly between the two groups.

Effects of *dl*- and *d*-Propranolol on Tissue Cholesterol and Aortic Enzyme Activity

On the basis of the above findings, a more extensive study was performed involving four groups of rabbits: chow-fed controls, cholesterol-fed controls, cholesterol-fed rabbits treated daily with *dl*-propranolol, and cholesterol-fed animals treated with *d*-propranolol. Body weights did not differ significantly in the four groups, and no undesirable side effects due to propranolol treatment were observed. The systolic blood pressures were somewhat lower in all cholesterol-fed groups than in the control animals (Table 1). However, neither *dl*- nor *d*-propranolol in the dosage used produced a significant change in the blood pressure of the animals, compared to their cholesterol-fed controls. The ratios of heart weight to body weight were similar in all groups studied.

A rapid increase in the mean plasma cholesterol level occurred in response to the cholesterol diet, with values exceeding 1000 mg/dl by 3 weeks, and further rises to levels between 2000 and 2500 mg/dl by the end of the study. There were no significant differences in plasma cholesterol or triglyceride between the cholesterol-fed groups.

As in the pilot studies, the rabbits receiving *dl*-propranolol had visible aortic atherosclerosis restricted primarily to the upper arch of the thoracic aorta and to the ostia of the intercostal arteries. Somewhat greater involvement was apparent in the *d*-propranolol group, but the latter still was not as widespread as the extensive disease present in the untreated cholesterol-fed animals.

The aortic cholesterol data reflected the changes apparent by visual inspection. Aortic free and ester cholesterol contents were significantly increased above control levels in the three cholesterol-fed groups (Table 2). However, both *dl*- and *d*-propranolol treatment significantly decreased free and ester aortic cholesterol accumulation, although the *d*-iso-

TABLE 2
Effects of *dl*- or *d*-Propranolol on Serum and Tissue Cholesterol Content in Control and Cholesterol-Fed Rabbits

	Serum cholesterol (mg/dl)	Aorta		Liver (mg/g wet wt)		Adrenal	
		Free	Ester	Free	Ester	Free	Ester
Control	77 ± 6	1.8 ± 0.2	ND	2.2 ± 0.1	2.2 ± 0.2	6.6 ± 0.5	124 ± 10
Cholesterol-fed	2120 ± 165	6.6 ± 0.5	10.6 ± 1.2	8.7 ± 3.7	46.2 ± 3.7	9.7 ± 0.8	251 ± 18
Cholesterol-fed and *dl*-propranolol	2320 ± 211	2.8 ± 0.2†	2.7 ± 0.3†	9.9 ± 0.7	49.3 ± 4.1	11.1 ± 0.9	251 ± 21
Cholesterol-fed and *d*-propranolol	2701 ± 231	3.3 ± 0.3*	6.7 ± 0.5†	8.4 ± 0.6	54.0 ± 4.3	10.8 ± 0.8	272 ± 23

Results represent the means ± SE for six animals. ND = not detectable.
* Significantly ($P < 0.05$) different from cholesterol-fed group.
† Significantly ($P < 0.01$) different from cholesterol-fed group.

mer appeared to have a lesser effect than the racemic mixture.

Marked increases in free and total esterified content of both adrenal gland and liver occurred in each of the cholesterol-fed groups (Table 2). Neither *dl*- nor *d*-propranolol had any significant influence on the accumulation of cholesterol in these organs, despite their effects on the aorta.

Enzymatic studies on aortic subcellular fractions from the four groups are summarized in Table 3. ACAT activity was increased 10-fold as a result of cholesterol feeding, but when *dl*-propranolol was also administered, the increase in aortic ACAT was attenuated. *d*-Propranolol treatment was not as effective in reducing aortic ACAT as the *dl*-isomer, and, in general, ACAT activity reflected aortic cholesterol content in all 3 cholesterol-fed groups. Neutral glucosidase activity, a microsomal marker enzyme, also was increased by cholesterol feeding, but the relative changes between the different groups were not clearly related to the incidence of atherosclerosis. Interestingly, if ACAT activity was expressed relative to glucosidase activity, the relative enhancement of ACAT activity was similar for the cholesterol-fed and cholesterol-fed plus *d*-propranolol groups. Lysosomal enzyme activity was assessed using NAGA and acid lipase as marker enzymes. Changes in the activities of both enzymes reflected the degree of atherosclerosis found for all groups treated. Acid lipase activity for the *d*-propranolol group was not measured.

Experiments were performed to determine if either *dl*- or *d*-propranolol influenced ACAT activity directly (Fig. 1). Addition of either compound to the in vitro assay system for ACAT over a wide range of concentrations resulted in a dose-dependent inhibition only at relatively high concentrations. A 50% inhibition was achieved at 10^{-3} M with both *dl*- and *d*-propranolol. No appreciable difference between the drugs was present at any concentration.

To determine whether propranolol treatment might alter the characteristics of the lipoproteins of cholesterol-fed rabbits, we performed a separate study to compare the d <1.006 g/ml fraction from cholesterol-fed controls and cholesterol-fed rabbits given *d*-propranolol. Plasma lipids were determined 4 weeks after initiating treatment. Plasma cholesterol and triglyceride were similar in both groups, with triglyceride levels less than 75 mg/100 ml in all rabbits from both groups. Over 75% of the total plasma cholesterol was localized in the d < 1.006 g/ml fraction. Figure 2A shows agarose gel electro-

TABLE 3
Effect of Propranolol Treatment on Microsomal and Lysosomal Enzymes of Rabbit Aorta

Treatment	ACAT (pmol/min per mg)	Neutral *d*-glucosidase	NAGA (nmol/min per mg)	Acid lipase
Control	4.0 ± 0.2	3.8 ± 0.2	1.6 ± 0.2	55 ± 2.0
Cholesterol-fed	43.1 ± 2.5	9.8 ± 0.8	8.2 ± 0.9	148 ± 5.1
Cholesterol-fed and *dl*-propranolol	14.2 ± 3.1†	6.0 ± 0.5†	3.7 ± 0.4†	78 ± 3.1†
Cholesterol-fed and *d*-propranolol	29.0 ± 3.4†	7.2 ± 0.4*	7.5 ± 0.3	

Results represent the means ± SE for six animals. ND = not detectable.
* Significantly ($P < 0.05$) different from cholesterol-fed group.
† Significantly ($P < 0.01$) different from cholesterol-fed group.

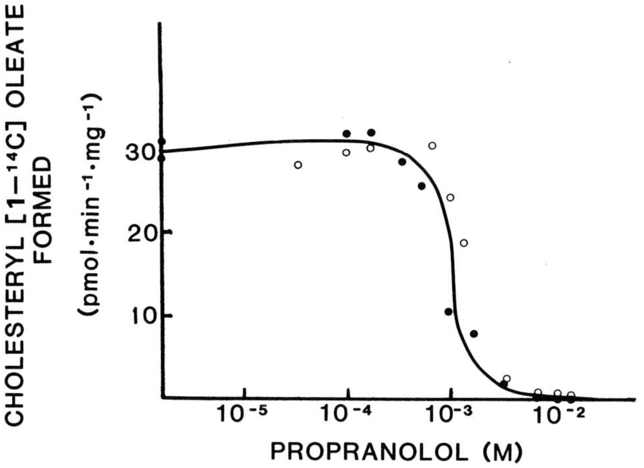

Figure 1. *In vitro effects of dl-propranolol (closed circles) and d-propranolol (open circles) on incorporation of [1-^{14}C]oleoyl CoA into cholesteryl-[^{14}C]oleate. The drug was added directly to the assay system prior to initiating the reaction.*

phoretograms of representative plasma samples from both groups, indicating that the major lipoproteins had a β migration typical of β-VLDL. The apoprotein profiles of the d < 1.006 g/ml fractions, determined using polyacrylamide gel electrophoresis (Fig. 2B), showed that in both groups, apo-B and apo-E were clearly the major apoproteins present. Collectively, the data in Figure 3 indicate that β-VLDL, the major lipoprotein of cholesterol-fed rabbits, also was the predominant cholesterol-containing particle in the *dl*-propranolol-treated group.

The studies of ^{125}I-albumin transport across the rabbit common carotid artery are summarized in Table 4. Comparisons were made between cholesterol-fed rabbits that were treated with saline or *dl*-propranolol for 8 weeks. As noted, no significant difference between the groups in the rate of appearance of ^{125}I-albumin into jugular venous blood was present during 4 hours of perfusions. Both groups showed significantly greater rates of albumin flux than control, chow-fed rabbits that we had previously studied (Chobanian et al., 1983).

Table 4
Effects of Propranolol Treatment on Appearance of ^{125}I Radioactivity in Jugular Venous Blood of Cholesterol-Fed Rabbits*

	Plasma ^{125}I radioactivity (dpm/ml per hr)
Cholesterol-fed	3850 ± 1225
Cholesterol-fed + propranolol (5 mg/kg per day)	5830 ± 2850

Values represent the means ± SE for four separate studies.
* After 4-hour perfusion of carotid artery with ^{125}I-labeled albumin.

Effects of Metoprolol Therapy

A separate set of experiments was performed to study the influence of metoprolol on atherogenesis and arterial metabolism. Comparisons were made between cholesterol-fed animals that received either metoprolol (6.25 mg/kg per day), intraperitoneally, or the saline vehicle. Heart rate was significantly lower in the metoprolol-treated animals (175 ± 14 beats/min), compared with either control (230 ± 7) or cholesterol-fed untreated rabbits (217 ± 8). Blood pressure appeared unaffected by metoprolol (87.3 ± 6.3 mm Hg in controls, 90.3 ± 8.4 in the cholesterol-fed untreated group, and 90.6 ± 7.1 with metoprolol therapy). Similarly, no significant differences in either aortic free or ester cholesterol, ACAT, or NAGA activity were present (Fig. 3).

Discussion

These studies demonstrate that propranolol inhibits the development of aortic atherosclerosis in cholesterol-fed rabbits and confirms the prior findings of Whittington-Coleman et al. (1973). Interestingly, *d*-propranolol which has minimal β-receptor-block-

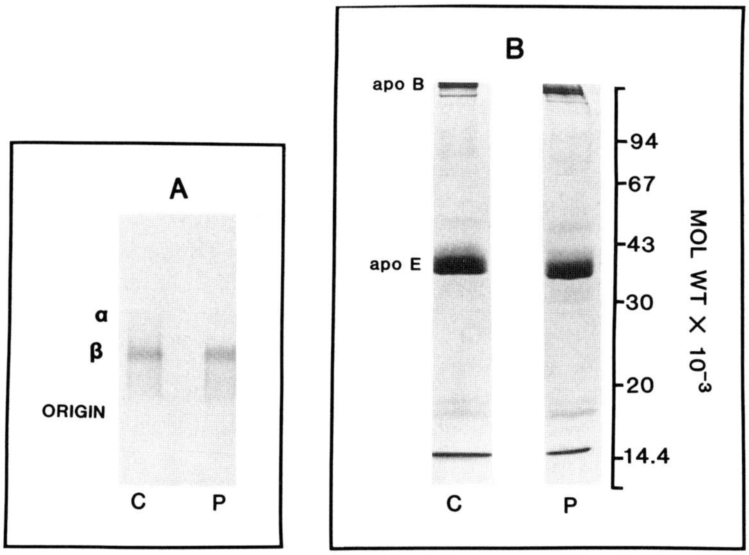

Figure 2. *Electrophoresis of plasma lipoproteins from cholesterol-fed control rabbits (C) and animals given dl-propranolol (P) for 4 weeks. Panel A: representative agarose gel electrophoretograms of plasma from control and propranolol treated animals. Panel B: sodium dodecyl sulfate-polyacrylamide gel electrophoresis of d<1.006 g/ml fractions from control and propranolol-treated animals.*

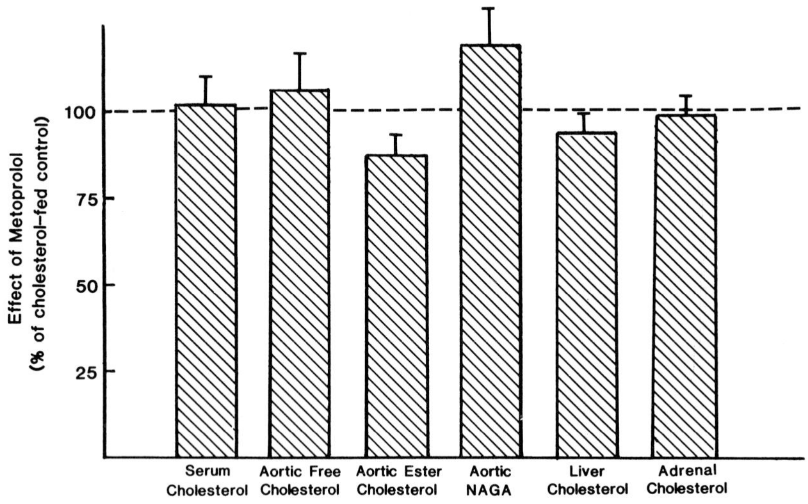

FIGURE 3. *Effects of metoprolol on serum and tissue cholesterol and aortic NAGA activity in the cholesterol-fed rabbit. The metoprolol data are presented as the percent of the values in cholesterol-fed controls. Eight animals are in each group. Error bars represent the coefficient of variation.*

ing effects, except at large doses, also appeared to have an anti-atherosclerotic action, although to a lesser extent than the racemic mixture. Metoprolol, on the other hand, appeared to have no influence on atherogenesis in this model, indicating that the propranolol response is not necessarily shared by all β-adrenergic inhibitors. Several possible explanations for these results need to be considered.

A blood pressure-lowering action or some other hemodynamic-related effect of propranolol could conceivably play a role in inhibiting atherosclerosis. Other antihypertensive medications, including guanethidine (Whittington-Coleman and Carrier, 1970), reserpine (Smith and Rossi, 1962; Deming, 1966), and the calcium channel blocker, nifedipine (Henry and Bentley, 1981), have been reported to have similar protective action in the cholesterol-fed rabbit. However, in the dosages that we used, which were based on the average amount of drug typically administered to human patients, no significant lowering of systolic blood pressure could be demonstrated beyond that induced by cholesterol feeding alone. In addition, metoprolol, which should be expected to have an influence on blood pressure or cardiac contractility similar to that of propranolol, offered no protection to the animals. Propranolol has been reported to produce a reduction in blood velocity in rhesus monkeys (Spence et al., 1977). Such an effect could potentially reduce sheer stress on the arterial endothelium, but its relationship to atherogenesis is unknown.

Sympathetic nervous function may influence the response of the arterial wall to potentially injurious stimuli such as hypertension or hyperlipoproteinemia. Sympathetic de-innervation of rabbit ear arteries has been shown to reduce both the growth of the artery and DNA synthesis in medial smooth muscle cells (Bevan and Tsuru, 1981). Furthermore, sympathetic de-innervation of cerebral arteries in the spontaneously hypertensive rat can minimize the expected increases in wall thickness and elevate markedly the risk of developing strokes (Sadoshima et al., 1981). Although it is appealing to consider that the effect of propranolol is somehow related to its influence on vascular sympathetic activity, the findings with *d*-propranolol and metoprolol would not support such an explanation.

We also examined the effects of propranolol on plasma lipid and lipoprotein levels and on the nature of the circulating lipoproteins. Although no influence on total plasma cholesterol and triglyceride levels in the rabbit had previously been noted, it was possible that some critical change in the lipoproteins themselves might be induced by the drug. In fact, we recently observed in another model, the alloxan-diabetic cholesterol-fed rabbit, that protection against atherosclerosis occurred despite even higher levels of total plasma cholesterol and triglyceride. Such protection appeared attributable to the formation of an unusual particle with properties of a chylomicron remnant which became the major circulating lipoprotein rather than β-VLDL (Brecher et al., 1983). In the current study, chemical and electrophoretic analysis of the d <1.006 g/ml lipoprotein fraction from *dl*-propranolol-treated rabbits indicated the presence of the β-VLDL particle characteristic of that typically found in cholesterol-fed rabbits. Recent work has shown that β-VLDL interacts with macrophages leading to cholesteryl ester accumulation in these cells (Goldstein et al., 1980; Mahley et al., 1980), and it has been suggested that β-VLDL particles also interact with cells within the vessel wall leading to foam cell formation (Pitas et al., 1983). The determinants thought to be necessary for the atherogenic properties of β-VLDL are a core of cholesteryl ester and the presence of apoprotein E on the surface. The presence of β-VLDL as the major cholesterol-carrying lipoprotein in propranolol-treated animals suggests that the effects of the drug on lesion development are not due to alterations in the properties of this potentially atherogenic lipoprotein.

We cannot exclude the possibility that some other important effect of propranolol on arterial lipid metabolism may have occurred. Prior in vitro studies have demonstrated that propranolol can inhibit several hydrolytic enzymes including rat liver phospholipase A_2 and phospholipase C (Matsuzawa and Hoestler, 1980), as well as platelet phospholipase A_2 (Vanderhoek and Feinstein, 1979). In addition, decreased phosphatidylcholine synthesis from ^{32}P-labeled phosphate has been reported with propranolol (Pappu and Hanser, 1982). The significance of these findings, however, is uncertain. In our own studies, the changes observed in aortic ACAT activity or in lysosomal enzymes reflected the degree of atherosclerosis and are probably not related to direct effects of propranolol.

Both *l*- and *d*-propranolol have effects on cell membranes which appear unrelated to their β-blocking action. Such membrane-stabilizing action has been reported for several tissues, including cardiac muscle (Langslet, 1970). Of particular interest with respect to atherogenesis is the action of propranolol on platelet aggregation. A marked reduction in sensitivity to platelet aggregation induced by adenosine diphosphate (ADP), epinephrine, collagen, and thrombin has been observed with both isomers in vitro (Weksler et al., 1977) while an inhibition of platelet aggregation and thromboxane synthesis in patients receiving long-term propranolol also has been noted (Campbell et al., 1981). However, metoprolol also appears to share membrane-stabilizing and platelet actions (Campbell et al., 1981), and it is unlikely that differences between the drugs can be explained on this basis.

Studies with erythrocyte membranes suggest that propranolol interacts with membrane protein (Singer, 1977) or lipid (Godin et al., 1976) and could conceivably influence a variety of properties of cells, including their permeability. We recently demonstrated, using a model of the isolated rabbit common carotid artery perfused in vivo, that cholesterol feeding of even brief duration markedly increased albumin flux across the vessel (Chobanian et al., 1983). We therefore considered whether propranolol might affect such transport. However, no significant effect of the drug on albumin transport could be demonstrated in this model after 8 weeks of cholesterol feeding. It is possible that shorter periods of study might be required to demonstrate such an effect. As noted, propranolol does not prevent entirely the development of atherosclerosis, and even mild changes in the arterial intima might cause profound effects on permeability.

Inhibition of plasma renin activity and circulating levels of angiotensin II also could theoretically be beneficial to the vasculature. High levels of angiotensin II, when associated with hypertension, may be vasculotoxic, particularly to small arteries and arterioles (Giese, 1973). Hypertensive patients with low plasma renin activity were reported to be relatively protected from developing myocardial infarcts or strokes (Brunner et al., 1972), but more recent clinical evidence has not supported this hypothesis (Kaplan, 1975). In addition, recent studies in cholesterol-fed rabbits do not support a role of renin on atherogenesis in this model (Overturf et al., 1981a, 1981b). In addition, metoprolol is a potent inhibitor of plasma renin activity and still afforded no protection against cholesterol feeding.

Other studies have demonstrated that the cholesterol-fed rabbit can be a useful model for studying the relationship between hyperlipoproteinemia and atherosclerosis, but the possibility exists that metabolic differences are present between rabbits and humans which might confound the interpretation of the data as related to their clinical relevance. For example, lipid deposition in reticuloendothelial tissue and a hemolytic anemia can occur frequently in the cholesterol-fed rabbit, but rarely if ever in hyperlipoproteinemic man. How such differences might influence our findings is unknown.

The recent observation that ablation of the sinoatrial node in male cynomolgus monkeys reduces the extent of coronary atherosclerosis after cholesterol feeding (Beere et al., 1984) raises the possibility that the effects of propranolol that we observed may somehow be related to its chronotropic action. We do not consider this to be likely in view of the beneficial effects of *d*-propranolol, which did not slow heart rate, and the lack of anti-atherosclerotic effect of metoprolol, which, however, reduced heart rate to an extent induced by *dl*-propranolol.

The clinical implications of our findings cannot be assessed by the current study, although major interest has developed recently in the long-term effects of antihypertensive drugs on coronary artery atherosclerosis and its complications. Some large clinical trials have suggested that mortality related to ischemic heart disease may not be reduced by drug therapy (VA Cooperative Study Group, 1970; Management Committee ATTMH, 1980) and that high-dose diuretic treatment may possibly increase coronary-related deaths (MRFIT Research Group, 1982). Also, diuretic drugs can have an adverse effect on plasma lipids and lipoproteins by increasing plasma low density lipoproteins (LDL) and VLDL, while some β-blockers may lower plasma high density lipoproteins (HDL) (Weidmann et al., 1983). On the other hand, propranolol has been shown to reduce the rate of reinfarction in patients surviving a myocardial infarct (BHAT Study Group, 1981). The current investigation provides no information regarding these issues. To our knowledge, the only published study examining the effects of propranolol on atherogenesis in primates was by Pick and associates using stumptail Macaque monkeys (Pick and Glick, 1977). Their findings were equivocal in that their initial results suggesting an anti-atherogenic action of propranolol could not be confirmed by their subsequent investigation.

In conclusion, these studies have demonstrated that propranolol has a potent atherosclerosis-inhibiting action in the cholesterol-fed rabbit which does not appear to be related to its antihypertensive or β-blocking properties. It has been suggested that this drug has a direct effect on the arterial wall, although the exact mechanism remains to be defined.

Supported by National Institutes of Health Grant HL 18318.

Address for reprints: Aram V. Chobanian, M.D., Boston University School of Medicine, 80 East Concord Street, Boston, Massachusetts 02118.

Received May 21, 1984; accepted for publication January 31, 1985.

References

Beere PA, Glagov S, Zarins CK (1984) Retarding effect of lowered heart rate on coronary atherosclerosis. Science **226:** 180–182

Beta-Blocker Heart Attack Study Group (1981) The β-blocker heart attack trial. JAMA **246:** 2973–2974

Bevan RD, Tsuru H (1981) Functional and structural changes in the rabbit ear artery after sympathetic denervation. Circ Res **49:** 478–485

Brecher P, Chan CT (1980) Properties of acyl CoA cholesterol acyltransferase in aortic microscomes from atherosclerotic rabbits. Biochim Biophys Acta **617:** 458–471

Brecher P, Pyun HY, Chobanian V (1977) Effect of atherosclerosis on lysosomal cholesterol esterase activity in rabbit aorta. J Lipid Res **18:** 154–163

Brecher P, Chan CT, Franzblau C, Faris B, Chobanian AV (1978) Effect of hypertension and its reversal on aortic metabolism in the rat. Circ Res **43:** 561–569

Brecher P, Chobanian AV, Small DM, Van Sickle W, Tercyak A, Lazzari A, Baler J (1983) Relationship of an abnormal plasma lipoprotein to protection from atherosclerosis in the cholesterol-fed diabetic rabbit. J Clin Invest **72:** 1553–1562

Brunner HR, Laragh JH, Baer J, Goodwin FT, Krakoff LR, Bard RH, Bühler FR (1972) Essential hypertension: Renin and aldosterone, heart attack and stroke. N Engl J Med **286:** 441–449

Campbell WB, Callahan KS, Johnson AR, Graham RM (1981) Anti-platelet activity of beta-adrenergic antagonists: Inhibition of thromboxane synthesis and platelet aggregation in patients receiving long-term propranolol treatment. Lancet **2:** 1382–1384

Chobanian AV, Menzoian JO, Shipman J, Heath K, Haudenschild CC (1983) Effects of endothelial denudation and cholesterol feeding on in vivo transport of albumin glucose, and water across rabbit carotid artery. Circ Res **53:** 805–814

Deming QB (1966) Hypertension and vascular disease. *In* Antihypertensive Therapy, edited by F Gross. New York, Springer-Verlag, p 111

Fletcher MJ (1968) A colorimetric method for estimating serum triglycerides. Clin Chim Acta **22:** 393–397

Folch J, Lees M, Sloane-Stanley GM (1957) A simple method for isolation and purification of total lipids from animal tissues. J Biol Chem **226:** 497–509

Giese J (1973) Renin, angiotensin, and hypertensive vascular damage. A review. Am J Med **55:** 315–332

Godin DV, Ng TW, Tuchek JM (1976) Studies on the interaction of propranolol with erythrocyte membranes. Biochim Biophys Acta **436:** 757–773

Goldstein SL, Ho YK, Brown MS, Innerarity TL, Mahley RW (1980) Cholesteryl ester accumulation in macrophages resulting from receptor-mediated uptake and degradation of hypercholesterolemic canine β-very low density lipoproteins. J Biol Chem **255:** 1839–1848

Henry PD, Bentley KI (1981) Suppression of atherogenesis in cholesterol-fed rabbit treated with nifedipine. J Clin Invest **68:** 1366–1369

Kaplan NM (1975) The prognostic implications of plasma renin in essential hypertension. JAMA **231:** 167–170

Kramsch DM, Aspen AJ, Apstein CS (1980) Suppression of experimental atherosclerosis by the Ca^{++}-antagonist lanthanum. J Clin Invest **65:** 967–981

Langslet A (1970) Membrane stabilization and cardiac effects of *dl*-propranolol, *d*-propranolol, and chlorpromazine. Eur J Pharmacol **13:** 6–14

Lowry OH, Rosebrough NJ, Farr AL, Randall RJ (1951) Protein measurement with the Folin phenol reagent. J Biol Chem **193:** 265–275

Mahley RW, Innerarity TL, Brown MS, Ho YK, Goldstein JL (1980) Cholesteryl ester synthesis in macrophages: Stimulation by β-very low density lipoproteins from cholesterol-fed animals of several species. J Lipid Res **21:** 970–980

Management Committee of the Australial Therapeutic Trial in Mild Hypertension (1980) The Australian therapeutic trial in mild hypertension. Lancet **1:** 1261–1267

Matsuzawa Y, Hoestler KY (1980) Inhibition of lysosomal phospholipase C by chloroquine and 4-4′-bis (diethylaminoethoxy)-α,β-diethyldiphenylethane. J Biol Chem **255:** 5190–5194

Multiple Risk Factor Intervention Trial Research Group (1982) Multiple risk factor intervention trial. Risk factor changes and mortality results. JAMA **248:** 1465–1477

Overturf ML, Aschenbrener C, Druilhet RE, Kirkendall WM (1981) Renin as a risk factor for atherogenesis: Effects of hypercholesterolemia and two-kidney one-clip hypertension in the rabbit. Atherosclerosis **38:** 97–119

Overturf ML, Sybers HD, Druilhet RE, Kirkendall WM (1981) Renin as a risk factor for atherosclerosis. II. Effects of hypercholesterolemia and hyporeninemia in the rabbit. Atherosclerosis **40:** 203–222

Pappu AS, Hanser G (1982) Phospholipid metabolism changes in rat tissues in vitro after injections of propranolol. J Pharmacol Exp Ther **222:** 109–115

Pick R, Glick G (1977) Effects of propranolol, minoxidil, and clofibrate on cholesterol-induced atherosclerosis in stumptail macaques (*Macaca arctoides*). Atherosclerosis **27:** 71–77

Pitas RE, Innerarity TL, Mahley RW (1983) Foam cells in explants of atherosclerotic aorta have receptors for β-very low density lipoproteins and modified low density lipoproteins. Arteriosclerosis **3:** 2–12

Rudel LL, Morris MD (1973) Determination of cholesterol using *o*-phthalaldehyde. J Lipid Res **14:** 364–366

Sadoshima S, Busija D, Brody M, Heistad D (1981) Sympathetic nerves protect against stroke in stroke-prone hypertensive rats. Hypertension **3:** I-124–I-127

Singer MA (1977) Interaction of dibucaine and propranolol with phospholipid bilayer membranes—Effect of alterations in fatty acyl composition. Biochem Pharmacol **26:** 51–57

Smith THG, Rossi GV (1962) The effect of reserpine and mecamylamine on experimental atheromatosis in the normotensive and hypertensive rat. J Pharmacol Exp Ther **135:** 367–373

Spence JD, Pesout AB, Melmon KL (1977) Effects of antihypertensive drugs on blood velocity in rhesus monkeys. Stroke **8:** 589–594

Vanderhoek JY, Feinstein MB (1979) Local anesthetics, chlorpromazine and propranolol inhibit stimulus-activation of phospholipase A2 in human platelets. Mol Pharmacol **16:** 171–180

Veterans Administration Cooperative Study Group on Antihypertensive Agents (1970) Results in patients with diastolic blood pressures averaging 90 through 114 mm Hg. JAMA **213:** 1143–1152

Weidmann P, Gerber A, Mordasa R (1983) Effects of antihypertensive therapy on serum lipoproteins. Hypertension **5:** III-120–III-131

Weksler BB, Gillick M, Pink J (1977) Effect of propranolol on platelet function. Blood **49:** 185–196

Whittington-Coleman PJ, Carrier O Jr (1970) Effects of agents altering vascular calcium in experimental atherosclerosis. Atherosclerosis **12:** 15–24

Whittington-Coleman PJ, Carrier O Jr, Clover Br (1968) The effects of reserpine in vasopressin and cholesterol induced atheromatous lesions. J Pharmacol Exp Ther **160:** 32–39

Whittington-Coleman PJ, Carrier O Jr, Douglas BH (1973) The effects of propranolol on cholesterol-induced atheromatous lesions. Atherosclerosis **18:** 337–345

INDEX TERMS: Atherogenesis • Propranolol • Arterial wall • β-Blocker

BRIEF COMMUNICATIONS

Acetylcholine Release from Rat Atria Can Be Regulated through an α_1-Adrenergic Receptor

Glenn T. Wetzel, David Goldstein, and Joan Heller Brown

From the Division of Pharmacology, University of California, San Diego, La Jolla, California

SUMMARY. Isolated superfused rat atria release [^{3}H]acetylcholine when depolarized with 57 mM potassium. The depolarization-induced overflow of [^{3}H]acetylcholine is markedly inhibited by micromolar concentrations of epinephrine and norepinephrine. The α_1-selective adrenergic agonist methoxamine also inhibits tritium overflow, but the α_2-selective adrenergic agonist clonidine and the β-adrenergic agonist isoproterenol do not. Prazosin, an selective α_1-adrenergic antagonist, blocks adrenergic inhibition of [^{3}H]acetylcholine overflow with a K_i of approximately 0.4 nM. Yohimbine has approximately one-hundredth the potency of prazosin for blocking adrenergic inhibition of [^{3}H]acetylcholine overflow. [^{3}H]Norepinephrine overflow from isolated rat atria is also inhibited by norepinephrine, but this effect is antagonized by yohimbine and not by prazosin. We suggest that the release of acetylcholine from cardiac parasympathetic neurons can be regulated through an α_1-adrenergic receptor, and that this mechanism may underly, at least in part, the relative lack of effects of prazosin on heart rate. **(*Circ Res 56: 763–766, 1985*)**

ACETYLCHOLINE (ACh) is the neurotransmitter of the cardiac vagus and is the chemical signal by which parasympathetic activity modulates heart rate, impulse conduction, and contractility. The activity of the vagus nerve is known to be controlled centrally, but the possibility that there is local modulation of ACh release from cardiac parasympathetic neurons has not been adequately explored. We recently found that ACh overflow from parasympathetic neurons in isolated rat atria was inhibited by the sympathetic neurotransmitter norepinephrine and by the sympathetic hormone epinephrine (Wetzel and Brown, 1985). Further studies with selective agonists and antagonists are reported here. These studies demonstrate that the adrenergic receptor regulating ACh release does not have the α_2-adrenergic characteristics typical of presynaptic receptors but, instead, has the pharmacological properties of an α_1-adrenergic receptor (Starke et al., 1975; Wikberg, 1978; Hoffman and Lefkowitz, 1980; Langer, 1981).

Methods

Right atria from adult male Sprague-Dawley rats were incubated with [^{3}H]choline to label acetylcholine stores, and [^{3}H]acetylcholine release was quantified as previously described (Wetzel and Brown, 1985). Briefly, labeled atria were superfused with oxygenated Krebs-Henseleit buffer, and [^{3}H]ACh release was stimulated by pulses of depolarization with buffer containing 57 mM K^+. The superfusate was counted directly to measure total ^{3}H overflow, or [^{3}H] ACh and [^{3}H]choline were separated and quantified by high voltage electrophoresis (Potter and Murphy, 1967). More than 95% of the ^{3}H overflow from artia stimulated by 57 mM K^+ depolarization was [^{3}H]ACh, whereas [^{3}H] ACh comprised only 17% of the ^{3}H overflow from unstimulated atria (Wetzel and Brown, 1985).

Eight individual atria were superfused in each experiment. The release of [^{3}H]ACh from each atrium was normalized by calculating the ratio of the K^+-stimulated ^{3}H overflow during two consecutive stimulation periods (S_1 and S_2). We tested the effects of adrenergic agonists on ^{3}H overflow by adding them to four of the atria just before beginning the S_2 stimulation period. The decrease in ^{3}H overflow produced by the catecholamines results in a decreased S_2:S_1 ratio compared to control atria. Ratios were compared statistically by the Mann-Whitney test. Antagonists were added 20 minutes before the adrenergic agonists.

Results and Discussion

The naturally occurring catecholamines epinephrine (EPI) and norepinephrine (NE) inhibit the K^+-stimulated overflow of ^{3}H by as much as 60%, decreasing the S_2:S_1 ratio to ~0.3 (Table 1). The catecholamine concentrations that give half-maximal inhibition are 2 μM and 6 μM for EPI and NE, respectively. In contrast, isoproterenol does not inhibit K^+-stimulated ^{3}H overflow (Table 1). These data indicate that NE inhibits ACh overflow through activation of an α- rather than a β-adrenergic receptor. This is supported by our previous observation that the effect of NE is blocked by yohimbine, an α-adrenergic receptor antagonist, but not by the β-adrenergic receptor antagonist propranolol (Wetzel and Brown, 1985).

α-Adrenergic receptors have been classified as α_1

TABLE 1
Effects of Adrenergic Agonists on [^{3}H]Acetylcholine Overflow from Rat Atria

	S_2:S_1				
μM	NE	EPI	ISO	Methoxamine	Clonidine
0	0.74	0.74	0.76	0.83	0.79
1	0.65	0.64			
10	0.48*	0.34*		0.78	0.79
100	0.36*	0.29*	0.75	0.50*	0.89
300				0.54*	

Adrenergic agonists, at the concentrations indicated, were added 6 minutes before the second (S_2) K^+ stimulation. None of the agonists affected the basal ^{3}H overflow in the period prior to K^+ stimulation. Decreased ^{3}H overflow during the S_2 K^+-stimulation period is indicated by a decreased S_2:S_1 ratio. The values given are means from 4–16 individual atria. Standard errors are between ±0.02 and ±0.08 for all experimental conditions.

* [^{3}H]ACh overflow significantly ($P < 0.001$) decreased in the

or α_2, based on their location and pharmacological properties (Wikberg, 1978; Hoffman and Lefkowitz, 1980; Langer, 1981). Although EPI and NE interact with both α_1 and α_2 receptors at similar concentrations (Starke et al., 1975; Wikberg, 1978; Snavely and Insel, 1982), other agonists show selectivity (i.e., greater relative potency) for one vs. the other receptor subtype. Methoxamine and clonidine are selective agonists at α_1- and α_2-adrenergic receptors, respectively (Wikberg, 1978; Hoffman and Lefkowitz, 1980; Langer, 1981; van Meel et al., 1981; Snavely and Insel, 1982). We find that methoxamine significantly decreases K^+-stimulated [^{3}H]ACh overflow from rat atria (S_2:S_1 = 0.50 ± 0.02) at a concentration of 100 μM. Methoxamine is a full agonist at α_1-receptors in guinea pig aorta (Wikberg, 1978), but apparently does not have full activity in our preparation, since its maximal effect does not equal that of norepinephrine. The selective partial α_2-agonist clonidine does not inhibit the K^+-stimulated overflow of [^{3}H]ACh at 10 or 100 μM (Table 1).

Another means of distinguishing α_1- and α_2-adrenergic receptors is through the use of specific antagonists. We originally assumed that the receptor regulating ACh release would be an α_2-adrenergic receptor, and therefore used yohimbine (10 μM) to block the effect of NE (Wetzel and Brown, 1985). Complete antagonist concentration-response curves (Fig. 1) reveal that prazosin, an antagonist with marked selectivity for the α_1-adrenergic receptor subtype (Hoffman and Lefkowitz, 1980; Langer, 1981; Snavely and Insel, 1982), is almost 100 times more potent than yohimbine. The K_i calculated for prazosin inhibition of the effect of NE on ^{3}H overflow is approximately 0.4 nM. This is nearly identical to the K_d of the cardiac α_1-adrenergic receptor for prazosin, as determined in radioligand-binding studies (Karliner et al., 1979; Williams et al., 1981). Thus, data with both agonists and antagonists suggest that the receptor mediating α-adrenergic inhibition of cardiac ACh release is an α_1-adrenergic receptor.

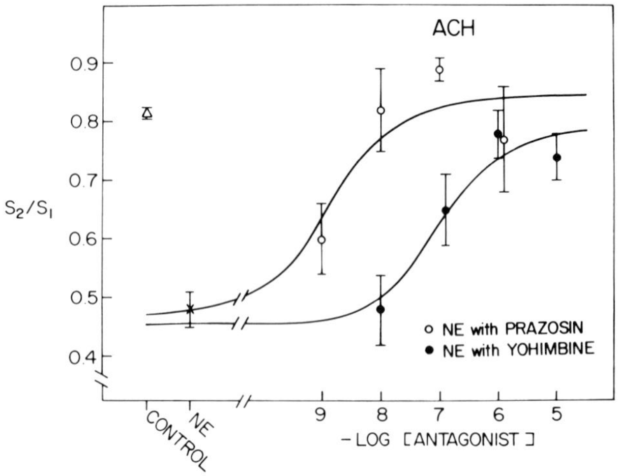

FIGURE 1. *Antagonism of the inhibitory effect of NE on [^{3}H]ACh overflow. The inhibitory effect of 10 μM NE on K^+-stimulated [^{3}H]ACh overflow was tested in the absence or presence of different concentrations of the selective α_1- and α_2-adrenergic antagonists prazosin and yohimbine. The antagonists were present during both the S_1 and S_2 stimulation periods. The S_2:S_1 ratio for all matching control stimulations in the presence of antagonist (53 atria) is also shown. Values are means ± SE for four atria. The IC_{50} values for prazosin and yohimbine are approximately 1 nM and 100 nM, giving K_i values of 0.4 nM and 40 nM when corrected for the concentration of NE according to the equation of Cheng and Prusoff (1973):*

$$K_i = \frac{IC_{50}}{1 + \frac{[NE]}{K_{act}}}.$$

It is well established that the release of NE from cardiac sympathetic neurons is regulated through a receptor with properties of an α_2-adrenergic receptor (Yamaguchi et al., 1977; van Meel et al., 1981; Rand et al., 1982; Fuder et al., 1983). We confirmed this in our preparation by comparing the effects of yohimbine and prazosin on ^{3}H overflow from atria prelabeled with [^{3}H]NE. The inhibitory effect of exogenous NE, and its blockade by the α_2-selective antagonist, yohimbine, are shown in Figure 2. Prazosin, at concentrations up to 10 μM, does not prevent noradrenergic inhibition of ^{3}H overflow from rat atria labeled with [^{3}H]NE (Fig. 2). Thus, yohimbine is more potent than prazosin at the adrenergic receptor modulating [^{3}H]NE overflow, whereas the converse is true at the adrenergic receptor modulating [^{3}H]ACh overflow. These data suggest that transmitter release from sympathetic and parasympathetic neurons in rat atria is regulated via pharmacologically distinct α-adrenergic receptors.

Several studies suggest that the chronotropic response to vagal nerve stimulation is modulated via presynaptic effects of catecholamines (Starke, 1972; Chassaing, 1983), but the physiological relevance of these experiments has been questioned by Lew and Angus (1983), who found no evidence for prejunctional α-receptors on vagal nerve endings. The effects of catecholamines on cardiac ACh release have been studied directly only in the perfused chicken heart, and in that preparation neither clonidine nor

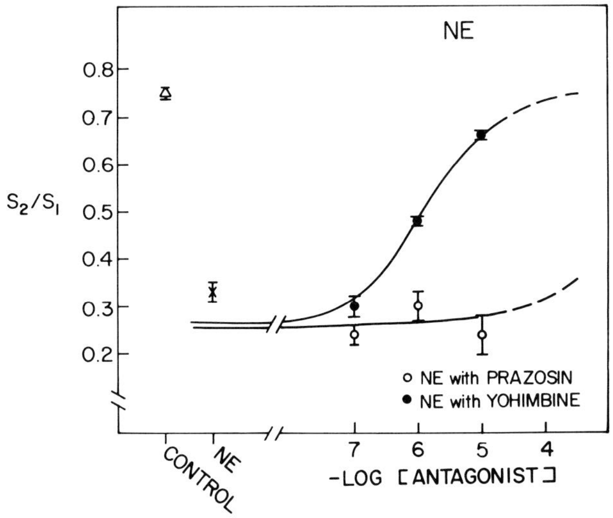

FIGURE 2. *Antagonism of the inhibitory effect of NE on [^{3}H]NE overflow. Atria were labeled by incubation with 0.2 μM [^{3}H]NE (10 μCi/ml). All subsequent procedures were the same as those described for [^{3}H]ACh overflow experiments. The inhibitory effect of 10 μM NE on K$^+$-stimulated ^{3}H overflow was determined in the absence or presence of different concentrations of prazosin and yohimbine. The antagonists were present during both the S_1 and S_2 stimulation periods. The S_2:S_1 ratio for all matching control stimulations in the presence of antagonist (32 atria) is also shown. To avoid the confounding effects of exogenous NE on [^{3}H]NE reuptake, we blocked the amine uptake system in all atria with 1 μM desmethylimipramine. This may raise the synaptic concentration of NE and thus the absolute concentration of yohimbine required for antagonism. Values are means ± SE for three or four atria.*

methoxamine inhibit ACh release (Loffelholz, 1981, Loffelholz et al., 1984). Our studies provide direct evidence that catecholamines inhibit ACh overflow from the mammalian heart. Whether adrenergic inhibition occurs physiologically, in response to local sympathetic nerve stimulation or epinephrine release from the adrenal, remains to be determined. The latter possibility appears less likely, since plasma epinephrine concentrations are generally below those needed to inhibit release.

The observation that catecholamines inhibit [^{3}H]ACh overflow from the rat heart is consistent with the finding that there is adrenergic regulation of ACh overflow from cholinergic neurons in the ileum (Paton and Vizi, 1969; Wikberg, 1978; Drew, 1978). In the ileum, however, it is an α_2-adrenergic receptor that modulates transmitter release, whereas our data indicate that release of ACh in the heart is regulated through an α_1-adrenergic receptor.

It is not possible to determine the precise location of the α_1-adrenergic receptor responsible for modulation of [^{3}H]ACh overflow. We have previously presented evidence that changes in K$^+$-stimulated ^{3}H overflow are unlikely to be secondary to muscarinic or adrenergic effects on atrial muscle activity or to changes in impulse transmission through parasympathetic ganglia (Wetzel and Brown, 1985). We have also ruled out the possibility that the effect of NE on ACh release is secondary to α-adrenergic receptor-mediated changes in prostaglandin formation (McDonough and Brown, in preparation). Norepinephrine could act by releasing other neuromodulators or transmitters from cardiac interneurons. The most parsimonious explanation, however, is that norepinephrine acts directly on α_1-adrenergic receptors located on the parasympathetic nerve endings.

The early notion that all postsynaptic adrenergic receptors are of the α_1-subtype, whereas presynaptic adrenergic receptors are of the α_2-subtype, has proven inadequate (McGrath, 1982). Indeed, several physiological studies suggest that α_1-adrenergic receptors may be present presynaptically in the rat heart (Kobinger and Pichler, 1980; Docherty, 1984). The physiological importance of presynaptic α_1-adrenergic receptors has been questioned because the primary regulation of norepinephrine release is clearly via α_2-receptors (Docherty, 1984). The possibility that α_1-adrenergic receptors play a significant physiological role by regulating the release of acetylcholine remains to be tested.

The parasympathetic nervous system predominates over the sympathetic nervous system in the control of heart rate (Levy, 1971). If the adrenergic receptor mechanism described here functions physiologically, it would provide a means for locally withdrawing this parasympathetic control by inhibiting ACh release when sympathetic tone is elevated. The ability of prazosin to block this adrenergic charge receptor mechanism, and thus disinhibit ACh release, may explain why antihypertensive therapy with prazosin does not cause tachycardia (Cavero and Roach, 1980; Hoffman and Lefkowitz, 1980). We postulate that adrenergic inhibition of ACh release may involve a mechanism by which heart rate is normally increased. The cardiac parasympathetic neuron may therefore be a novel site for sympathetic-parasympathetic antagonism (Levy, 1971) that bears consideration in the design of adrenergic antagonists for cardiovascular drug therapy.

We thank Dr. Patrick McDonough for carrying out some of the most recent experiments.

This work was supported by American Heart Association Grant 80-960. JHB is an Established Investigator of the American Heart Association.

Address for reprints: Dr. Joan Heller Brown, Department of Medicine, M-013 H, University of California, San Diego, La Jolla, California 92093.

Received November 9, 1984; accepted for publication January 23, 1985.

References

Cavero I, Roach A (1980) The pharmacology of prazosin, a novel antihypertensive agent. Life Sci **27:** 1525–1540

Chassaing C, Duchene-Marullaz P, Veyrac M (1983) Effects of catecholamines on cardiac chronotropic responses to vagal stimulation in the dog. Am J Physiol **245:** H721–724

Cheng Y, Prusoff W (1973) Relationship between the inhibition constant (K_i) and the concentration of an inhibitor that causes a 50% inhibition (I_{50}) of an enzymatic reaction. Biochem Pharmacol **22:** 3099–3108

Docherty JR (1984) An investigation of presynaptic α-adrenoceptor subtypes in the pithed rat heart and in the rat isolated vas deferens. Br J Pharmacol 82: 15–23

Drew GM (1978) Pharmacological characterization of the presynaptic α-adrenoceptors regulating cholinergic activity in the guinea pig ileum. Br J Pharmacol 64: 293–300

Fuder H, Muscholl E, Sperman R (1983) The determination of presynaptic pA_2 values of yohimbine and phentolamine on the perfused rat heart under conditions of negligible autoinhibition. Br J Pharmacol 79: 109–119

Hoffman B, Lefkowitz RJ (1980) Alpha-adrenergic receptor subtypes. N Engl J Med 302: 1390–1396

Karliner JS, Barnes P, Hamilton CA, Dollery CT (1979) Alpha$_1$-adrenergic receptors in guinea pig myocardium: Identification by binding of a new radioligand, [^{3}H]prazosin. Biochem Biophys Res Commun 90: 142–148

Kobinger W, Pilcher L (1980) Investigations into different types of post- and presynaptic alpha-adrenoceptors at cardiovascular sites in rats. Eur J Pharmacol 65: 393–402

Langer SZ (1981) Presynaptic regulation of the release of catecholamines. Pharmacol Rev 32: 337–362

Levy M (1971) Sympathetic-parasympathetic interactions in the heart. Circ Res 29: 437–445

Lew MJ, Angus J (1983) Clonidine and noradrenaline fail to inhibit vagal induced bradycardia. Naunyn Schmiedebergs Arch Pharmacol 323: 228–232

Loffelholz K (1981) Release of acetylcholine in the isolated heart. Am J Physiol 240: H431–440

Loffelholz K, Brehm R, Lindmar R (1984) Hydrolysis, synthesis and release of acetylcholine in the isolated heart. Fed Proc 43: 2603–2606

McGrath J (1982) Evidence for more than one type of postjunctional α-adrenoceptor. Br J Pharmacol 64: 293–300

Paton WDM, Vizi E (1969) The inhibitory action of noradrenaline and adrenaline on acetylcholine output by guinea pig ileum longitudinal muscle strips. Br J Pharmacol 35: 10–28

Potter LT, Murphy W (1967) Electrophoresis of acetylcholine, choline, and related compounds. Biochem Pharmacol 16: 1386–1388

Rand MJ, Yang C, Cole-Goodwin HM, McCulloch MW, Story DF (1982) The operation of autoregulatory feedback loops in noradrenergic transmission to cardiovascular effector tissues. J Cardiovasc Pharmacol 4: 541–545

Snavely MD, Insel PI (1982) Characterization of alpha-adrenergic receptor subtypes in the rat renal cortex. Mol Pharmacol 22: 532–546

Starke K (1972) Alpha sympathomimetic inhibition of adrenergic and cholinergic transmission in the rabbit heart. Naunyn Schmiedebergs Arch Pharmacol 274: 18–45

Starke K, Endo T, Taube HD (1975) Relative pre- and postsynaptic potencies of α-adrenoceptor agonists in the rabbit pulmonary artery. Naunyn Schmiedebergs Arch Pharmacol 291: 55–78

van Meel JCA, de Jong A, Timmermans P, van Zwieten P (1981) Selectivity of some alpha-adrenoceptor agonists for peripheral alpha$_1$- and alpha$_2$-adrenergic receptors in the normotensive rat. J Pharmacol Exp Ther 219: 760–767

Wetzel GT, Brown JH (1983) Relationships between choline uptake, acetylcholine synthesis and acetylcholine release in isolated rat atria. J Pharmacol Exp Ther 226: 343–348

Wetzel GT, Brown JH (1985) Presynaptic modulation of acetylcholine release from cardiac parasympathetic neurons. Am J Physiol 248: H33–H39

Wikberg J (1978) Pharmacological classification of adrenergic α-receptors in the guinea pig. Nature 273: 164–166

Williams RS, Dukes D, Lefkowitz RJ (1981) Subtype specificity of α-adrenergic receptors in rat heart. J Cardiovasc Pharmacol 3: 522–531

Yamaguchi N, de Champlain J, Nadeau R (1977) Regulation of norepinephrine release from cardiac sympathetic fibers in the dog by presynaptic α- and β-receptors. Circ Res 41: 108–117

INDEX TERMS: Acetylcholine release • α_1-Adrenergic receptor • Prazosin • Atria

News from the American Heart Association

7320 Greenville Avenue, Dallas, Texas 75231
Telephone: 214 750-5300

AHA Delegate Assembly Meets 1st Time in June For Session in Chicago

The 37th annual meeting of the AHA Delegate Assembly, the "democratic" voice for affiliates and Scientific Councils in AHA affairs, will meet for the first time apart from the Scientific Sessions when it will convene in Chicago for a June 21–22 session.

A Futures Conference will be held with the meeting to draft Association-wide and National Center long-range goals.

A Strategic Issues group was authorized by the Board of Directors to plan the Futures Conference. W.W. "Bill" Aston, treasurer of AHA is chairman. Other members of the Group are William B. Dulany, Esq., secretary of AHA, W. Virgil Brown, M.D., Bernadine Healy Bulkley, M.D., William Curtis, Oscar A. Gonzales, Henry Hunter, Mrs. Jeanne Ponteous, R.N., Kenneth I. Shine, M.D., and Anthony Starbird.

Because of the transition from a November to a June assembly, the committee appointments were extended from Nov. 1984 to June 1986.

Other Business

Other business of the Delegate Assembly will be the award of Gold Hearts, the highest AHA award for volunteer service, at a banquet. Up to six Howard W. Blakeslee Awards, given to print and broadcast journalists for outstanding reports on heart and blood vessel diseases, will also be presented.

11th Stroke Conference Feb. 19–22, San Diego

The 11th International Joint Conference on Stroke and Cerebral Circulation will be held Feb. 19–22, 1986 in Vacation Village, San Diego.

J. Donald Easton, M.D., of San Antonio, and Vladimir Hachinski, M.D., of London, Ont., Canada, will be conference chairmen.

The Conference is cosponsored by the AHA Stroke Council, Cerebrovascular Surgery Section of the American Association of Neurological Surgeons, Canadian Stroke Society of the Canadian Heart Foundation, the American Neurological Association and the Society for Vascular Surgery.

Inquiries may go to the Administrative Assistant, Scientific Sessions, AHA, Dallas, TX 75231. Tel. 1-214-750-5441.

Monograph Is Published on HBP Structure Changes

"Pathophysiology and Clinical Implications of Early Structural Changes (in Hypertension)" has been published as a supplement to HYPERTENSION (III **6** Nov–Dec, 1984) and is now available as AHA Monograph No. 110 (73-096A).

Guest editors of the publication are Björn Folkow, M.D., Margareta I. L. Nordlander, Ph.D., Bodo-Eckehard Strauer, F.A.C.C., and John Wikstrand, M.D., Ph.D.

In the preface the Editors explained that "despite the importance of structural adaptation within the cardiovascular system for the initiation and maintenance of primary hypertension, no meeting has previously been arranged to broadly consider these issues. Scientists who work in a wide range of disciplines, ranging from biophysics and experimental research in animals to clinical and epidemiological research, were invited to participate in this symposium because the so-called normal structural adaptation to an increased pressure load has wide-ranging consequences for all areas of cardiovascular research."

"Midnight Sun Symposium"

As the Editors explained, the symposium was arranged in collaboration with the Universities of Göteborg and Munich as a "Midnight Sun Symposium". Papers represent "state-of-the-art" reviews.

33 Papers

The 33 papers in the Monograph are grouped under the following topics:

Factors determining structural cardiovascular changes; regional structural differences and functional consequences; cardiovascular structural changes in human primary hypertension; regression of structural cardiovascular changes by antihypertensive therapy; and effects of intervention on long-term prognosis.

Kyoto Symposium on SHR Will Honor Dr. Okamoto

The 5th International Symposium on Rats with Spontaneous Hypertension (SHR) and Related Studies will be held in Kyoto, Japan, Oct. 20–22, to honor the 77th birthday ("Happy Year") of Dr. Koso Okamoto, the "father" of the SHR.

Official papers will be published in the JOURNAL OF HYPERTENSION, the official journal of the International Society of Hypertension, as a Festschrift in honor of Dr. Okamoto.

Dr. Yuko Yamori is president of the Symposium, the language for which will be English. Kyoto is honored as the "birthplace" of SHR and stroke-prone SHR which are widely used as genetic hypertensive models.

Main topic of the meeting will be contributions of hypertensive rats models in medicine—past, present, and future.

Inquires may go to: Secretariat, 5th SHR Symposium, Shimane Medical University, Izumo 693, Japan. Tel. 0853-23-2111, Ext. 2375. Cable: WHOCOLLAB IZUMO.

Satellite Meeting

A satellite symposium in Nagoya, Japan, Oct. 23–4 will be the International Symposium on Mechanisms and Treatment in Essential Hypertension—Calcium and Calcium Antagonists. Inquiries for this meeting with 20 invited speakers may go to Dr. Kyuzo Aoki, Hinokuchi-cho, Nishi-ku, Nagoya 467, Japan. Tel. 052-521-2121.

Over 16,600 Registered In '84 Scientific Sessions

Over 16,600 persons registered for the 57th AHA Scientific Sessions in Miami Beach, November, 1984, it was reported to the AHA Board of Directors.

Dr. Bernadine Healy Bulkley, chairman of the Committee on Scientific Sessions Program, also reported that 1,852 abstracts were presented out of the 5,750 submitted.

Abstracts for the 58th Sessions in Washington, DC, (Nov. 11–14), are due at the National Center in Dallas May 13.

LV Function Is Topic For Israel Symposium

An international symposium on Left Ventricular Function will be held at the Jerusalem Hilton, Israel, Dec. 1–4, under the auspices of the Universities of Tel Aviv and Massachusetts.

Co-chairmen of the meeting will be Drs. Jan J. Kellermann of Tel-Hashomer, Israel, and David Spodick of Worcester, MA.

Topics to be discussed include definition, exercise performance in impaired left ventricular function, prognostic value of left ventricular dysfunction, use of beta-blockers in patients with angina pectoris with low ejection, prophylaxis and rehabilitation of patients with congestive heart failure, influence of calcium antagonists in patients with left ventricular dysfunction, physical training in patients with left ventricular dysfunction, drug management of cardiac failure in patients with angina, adaptive mechanisms of physiological response to physical training with patients with impaired ventricular function.

Inquires may go to: Secretariat, POB 50006, Tel Aviv 61500, Israel. Tel. 03-654571. Telex 341171 KENS IL.

2 Councils Issue Report On Meeting in Snowmass

A report of the Joint Meeting of the AHA Councils of Circulation and Basic Science in August, 1984, at Snowmass was prepared by the Councils as follows:

"The AHA Councils on Circulation and Basic Science held a Joint Scientific Session at Snowmass on August 9–12, 1984. The Joint Session of the two Councils brought together prominent scientists for presentations and open discussions of a wide range of subjects."

The subjects were: "concepts regarding regulation of membrane excitability, the role of calcium in regulating myocyte function, the role of autonomic factors in congestive heart failure, current concepts about coronary pressure-flow relationships, the endothelium and vascular vasomotor control, new concepts of serotonergic regulation of the circulation, autonomic control of blood volume."

Also discussed were: "myocardial biochemistry and cardiac hypertrophy, the conceptual basis for metabolic imaging, new technologies in cardiovascular diagnosis, mechanisms for therapeutic induction of collaterals in the heart, recent advances in biochemistry of autonomic receptors, and the role of protein phosphorylation in the regulation of cardiac and smooth muscle function.

"Each of the major topics was covered by three to five presentations of new research data. The chairman of each of the major sesions, a senior investigator, then summarized the field for each session and indicated established facts as well as questions remaining and new directions for research. Small poster sessions were held in the afternoons. The emphasis for the entire program was on small group discussions and individual exchanges."

High Blood Pressure Month

For the 11th year May has been designated High Blood Pressure Month. This continues the campaign of the National High Blood Pressure Education Program of the U.S. National Heart, Lung, and Blood Institute to inform the public of the disease and its control.

AHA Briefs . . .

• **Modern Concepts of Cardiovascular Disease** for May is "Syncope: Evaluation and Treatment" by Peter J. Kudenchuk, M.D., and John H. McAnulty, M.D., of the Oregon Health Sciences University, Portland.

• **Current Concepts of Cerebrovascular Disease/Stroke** for May/June is "Calcium, Hypercalcemia, and Stroke," by Philip Gorelick, M.D., of Chicago and Louis Caplan, M.D., of Boston.

• The **Richard Bing Award** competition for young investigators (35 years or less) will be held at the 12th World Congress of the International Society for Heart Research in Melbourne, Australia, Feb. 9–13, 1986. Applications will be accepted up to Sept. 1, 1985. Inquiries may go to Dr. N.S. Dhalla, Dept. Physiology, Faculty of Medicine, University of Manitoba, Winnipeg, Canada R3E 0W3. The **Peter Harris Distinguished Scientist Award** will also be presented at the 12th World Congress. Nominations may be made to Dr. Dhalla.

• **"Practical Applications of Echo and Doppler Echocardiography, An Update,"** will be held at Cleveland Marriott Inn/Airport Hotel, Cleveland, May 16–18. Inquiries may to to Professional Medical Seminars, POB 5400, Sherman Oaks, CA 91413. Tel. 1-818-789-6497.

• **Dr. Mortimer B. Lipsett** has been named Director of the National Institute of Arthritis, Diabetes, and Digestive and Kidney Diseases, of the National Institutes of Health. Dr. Lipsett had been director of the National Institute of Child Health and Human Development.

• **Dr. Curt D. Furberg** has been named associate director for Clinical Applications and Prevention Program of the National Heart, Lung, and Blood Institute Division of Epidemiology and Clinical Applications. He was formerly chief of the Clinical Trials Branch.

• An **International Conference on Lipoprotein Deficiency Syndromes** will be held May 13–14 at the University of British Columbia, Vancouver, B.C., Canada, in connection with the 10th Canadian Lipoprotein Conference, Drs. Jiri Frehlich and Aubie Angel, chairmen. Inquiries may go to Dr. H. Pritchard, Dept. Pathology, University of British Columbia, 2211 Wesbrook Mall, Vancouver, B.C., Canada, V6T 1W5. Tel. 604-228-7109.

• **Dr. Dennis Johnsen** has been named director of the Primate Research Centers Program of the National Institutes of Health, succeeding Dr. Leo Whitehair. He was chief of the Veterinary Medicine and Surgery Section of the NIH Division of Research Services.

• **Drs. Henry M. Cathey and Robert E. Smith** have been named to the Board of Trustees of BioSciences Information Services (BIOSIS), publisher of BIOLOGICAL ABSTRACTS.

• The Division of Epidemiology and Clinical Applications of the National Heart, Lung, and Blood Institute has invited applications for **clinical centers for the studies of left ventricular dysfunction (SOLVOL)**. Applications are due by May 24. Two trials are planned: 1) the *prevention* trial to enroll 4,000 patients with low ejection fraction but not in need of treatment for heart failure; 2) the *treatment* trial will enroll 2,000 patients who need treatment. Each clinical center will study about 255 patients over three years and follow up two years more.

• **"Prevention of Bacterial Endocarditis,"** a statement for health professionals prepared by the AHA Committee on Rheumatic Fever and Infective Endocarditis of the Council of Cardiovascular Disease in the Young, is now available as a reprint from AHA affiliates and the National Center (71-005-C). The statement, an update of a 1977 publication, was originally published in the December, 1984, issue of CIRCULATION.

• The **12th International Congress of Electrocardiology** will be held June 16–19 in Minsk, USSR. Prof. M. Sidorenko is assistant chairman of the organizing committee. The **International Conference on Preventive Cardiology** will be held June 23–26 in Moscow. A.A. Stepanenko is secretary general. Inquiries may go to Garber Travel, POB 404-Dept. 91-5273, Brookline, MA 02146. Tel. 1-800-225-4570 (In Massachusetts: 1-617-787-0600).

Meetings Calendar 1985

May 15–17: **Clinical Approaches to Arterial Blood Gas Interpretation and Electrolytes.** Dallas. (Also May 31–June 1, Chicago and June 14–15, New York City). Inquiries: American College of Physicians, 4200 Pine St., Philadelphia, PA 19104.

May 16–18: **Practical Applications of Echo and Doppler Techniques in Cardiology.** Cleveland Marriott Inn-Airport Hotel. Inquiries: Professional Medical Seminars, POB 5400, Sherman Oaks, CA 91413.

May 17–18: **Clinical Concerns in Hemodialysis Therapy.** Sheraton Harbor Island East Hotel, San Diego. Program Chairman, Richard A. Sherman, M.D. Sponsored by American Kidney Fund and Nephrology Society of New Jersey. Inquiries: Dr. R. A. Sherman, Academic Health Science Center, CN 19, New Brunswick, NJ 08903. Tel. 1-800-922-0130.

May 17–22: **UCSD-Anesthesiology Review.** Vacation Village, San Diego. Sponsored by Dept. Anesthesiology, University of California, San Diego School of Medicine. Inquiries: K. Naughton, Dept. Anesthesia (M-029), UCSD, La Jolla, CA 92093. Tel. 1-619-452-3865.

May 19–23: **6th Scientific Meeting Inter-American Society of Hypertension.** Cleveland. Inquiries: 6th Meeting IASH, Research Division FF2-49, 9500 Euclid Ave., Cleveland, OH 44106. Tel. 1-216-444-5837.

May 23–24: **Vascular Surgery 1985. Current State of the Art. 2nd International Vascular Symposium.** Waldorf-Astoria Hotel, New York City. John B. Chang, M.D., program chairman. Inquiries: A. J. Boehme, Long Island Jewish-Hillside Medical Center, New Hyde Park, NY 11042. Tel. 1-212-470-2114.

May 24–27: **7th Annual Meeting American Section of the International Society for Heart Research.** Houston. Inquiries: Dr. J. Allen, Dept. Cell Biophysics, Baylor College of Med., Houston, TX 77025.

May 25–27: **13th Annual Conference: Master Approach to Cardiovascular Problems.** Lake Buena Vista, FL. Sponsored by University of Miami School of Medicine; co-sponsored by AHA Council on Clinical Cardiology. Augustin Castellanos, M.D., program director. Inquiries: Y. Barcena, Univ. Miami Sch. Med., Cardiology (D-39), Box 016960, Miami, FL 33101. Tel. 1-305-549-7124/6975.

May 30–June 1: **Three Days in Cardiology.** Boston, Dr. Michael D. Freed program director. Sponsored by Children's Hospital, Boston. Cosponsored by the Council on Cardiovascular Diseases in the Young of the AHA. Inquiries: J. Cartier, Dept. Cardiology, the Children's Hospital, 300 Longwood Ave., Boston, MA 02115. Tel. 1-617-735-7893.

June 2–6: **2nd World Congress of Pediatric Cardiology.** New York City. Sponsors: American Academy of Pediatrics, American College of Cardiology, American Heart Association, Asian-Pacific Society of Cardiology, Asian Society of Pediatric Cardiology, Association of European Pediatric Cardiologists, Interamerican Society of Cardiology, International Society and Federation of Cardiology, New York Heart Association, Sociedad Latina de Cardiologia Pediatrica. Cosponsored by the Councils on Cardiovascular Diseases in the Young, and Cardiovascular Surgery of the AHA. Inquiries: V. Herlitz, 404 Park Ave. S., New York, NY 10016. Tel. 1-212-532-9400. Cable: HERLIMED.

June 2–7: **Teaching Stress Management and Relaxation Skills Workshop.** (Also July 14–19; Nov. 10–15). LaCrosse Exercise Program, University of Wisconsin-La Crosse. Inquiries: Philip K. Wilson, University of Wisconsin-LaCrosse, WI 54601. Tel. 1-608-785-8686.

June 3–7: **Fitness and Weight Control Workshops** (also July 22–26). LaCrosse Exercise Program, University of Wisconsin-La Crosse. Inquiries: See June 2–7.

June 10–12: **Surgery for Coronary Artery Disease.** Durham, NC. Sponsored by Duke University Medical Center and American College of Cardiology. R. H. Jones, M.D., program director. Inquiries: ACC, 9111 Georgetown Rd., Bethesda, MD 20814. Tel. 1-301-897-5400, Ext. 228.

June 10–14: **Cardiac Rehabilitation Workshop.** (also July 15–19; Nov. 18–22). LaCrosse Exercise Program, University of Wisconsin-La Cross. Inquiries: See June 2–7.

June 10–13: **16th Annual Internal Medical Symposium.**

Kiawah Island Inn, Kiawah Island, SC. Sponsored by the School of Medicine, Medical College of Georgia. Inquiries: Div. Cont. Ed., Medical College of Georgia, Augusta, GA 30912. Tel. 1-404-828-3867.

June 10–13: **Coronary Angiography 1985: New Developments in Diagnostic Techniques, PTCA, and Thrombolytic Therapy.** Boston. Dr. David C. Levin program director. Sponsored by The Harvard Medical School. Cosponsored by the Council on Cardiovascular Radiology of the AHA. Inquiries: Dept. Cont. Ed., Harvard Medical School, 25 Shattuck St., Boston, MA 02115. Tel. 1-617-732-6265.

June 17–18: **Today's Therapy in Nephrology.** Resorts International Hotel, Atlantic City, NJ. Sponsored by American Kidney Fund and Nephrology Society of New Jersey. Inquiries: See May 17–18, Dr. Sherman.

June 24–29: **Advances in Nuclear Medicine, NMR, and Angioplasty for the Practicing Physicians Including 7th Nuclear Cardiology Symposium.** Sea Pines Plantation, Hilton Head Island, SC. Sponsored by Emory University School of Medicine, Dept. of Radiology, Div. of Nuclear Med. Inquiries: CME Emory Univ. School of Medicine, 1440 Clifton Rd., N.E., 110 WHSCAB, Atlanta, GA 30322. Tel. 1-404-329-5695.

July 12: **Certifying Examination, Sub-Board of Pediatric Cardiology.** Chapel Hill, NC. Inquiries: American Board of Pediatrics, 111 Silver Cedar Court, Chapel Hill, NC 27514-1651.

July 15–18: **Clinical Cardiology.** Hilton Head Inn, Hilton Head Island, SC. Sponsored by the School of Medicine, Medical College of Georgia. Inquiries: See Med. Coll. of Georgia Div. Cont. Ed., June 10–13.

July 18–21: **Pulmonary Diseases.** Kiawah Island Inn, Kiawah Island, SC. Sponsored by School of Medicine, Medical College of Georgia. Inquiries: See Div. Cont. Ed., Med. Coll. of Georgia, June 10–13.

July 21–24: **Nutrition in Cardiovascular Disease and Diabetes Mellitus. 26th Annual Meeting of American College of Nutrition.** Donaldson Brown Center for Continuing Education of Virginia Polytechnic Institute and State University, Blacksburg, VA. Inquiries: Mildred S. Seelig, M.D., M.P.H., F.A.C.N., American College of Nutrition, POB 831, White Plains, NY 10602. Tel. 1-914-948-4848.

July 21–26: **37th Annual Meeting American Association of Clinical Chemistry.** Georgia World Congress Center, Atlanta. Inquiries: AACC, 1725 K St., NW, Washington, DC 20006. Tel. 1-202-857-0717.

July 22–26: **Interdisciplinary Symposium on Plant Flavonoids in Biology and Medicine.** Biochemical, Pharmacological, and Structure-Activity Relationships. Buffalo, NY. Inquiries: Dr. Elliott Middleton, Jr., Dept. Med., Buffalo General Hospital, 100 High St., Buffalo, NY 14203. Tel. 1-716-845-2985.

July 22–26: **Topics in Clinical Nuclear Medicine.** Colby College, Waterville, ME. Henry N. Wagner, Jr., M.D., course director. Inquiries: R. Kany, Colby College, Waterville, ME 04901. Tel. 1-207-873-3386.

July 24–28: **4th International Symposium on Magnesium.** Magnesium in Cardiovascular Diseases, Open Heart and Other Surgery, Stress, Epidemiology, and Diagnosis. Donaldson Brown Center for Continuing Education, Virginia Polytechnic Institute and State University, Blacksburg, VA. Inquiries: See July 21–24.

July 24–28: **Critical Care Medicine.** Kiawah Island Inn, Kiawah Island, SC. Sponsored by School of Medicine, Medical College of Georgia. Inquiries: See Med. Coll. of Georgia, Div. Cont. Ed., June 10–13.

Aug. 27–30: **Research Conference on Regulation of Bile Acid Synthesis.** Given Institute of Pathobiology, Aspen, CO. Sponsored by American Gastroenterological Association. Inquiries: Bile Acid Research, 740 Krameria St., Denver, CO 80220.

Sept. 12–14: **International Symposium on Cardiovascular Surgery—1985. 15th Annual Symposium of Texas Heart Institute.** Houston. Inquiries: Medical Director, Texas Heart Institute, POB 20269, Houston, TX 77225. Tel. 1-713-791-2157.

Oct. 11–12: **4th Southern Biomedical Engineering Conference.** Jackson MS. Inquiries: Dr. Barry W. Sauer, SBEC, Div. Cont. Health Prof. Ed., University of Mississippi Medical Center, 2500 N. State St., Jackson, MS 39216-4505.

Oct. 13–18: **Clinical Congress, American College of Surgeons.** Chicago. Inquiries: ACS, 55 East Erie St., Chicago, IL 60611.

Oct 25: **Annual Meeting, Society of Neurological Anesthesia and Neurological Supportive Care.** San Francisco. Inquiries: Society of Neurological Anesthesia, POB 238, Univ. of Virginia Medical Center, Charlottesville, VA 22908.

Nov. 11–14: **58th Annual Scientific Sessions, American Heart Association, Washington, DC. Inquiries: Coordinator Scientific Sessions, AHA, 7320 Greenville Ave., Dallas, TX 75231. Tel. for Abstracts: 1-214-750-5439; for housing and reservations 1-214-750-5425. Commercial Exhibits: 1-214-750-5388.**

Nov. 19–20: **Subspecialty Boards in Cardiovascular Disease.** Philadelphia. Inquiries: American Board of International Medicine, 3624 Market St., Philadelphia, PA 19104. Tel. 1-215-243-1500. (New date.)

1986

Jan 24–25: **Current Controversies and Techniques in Congenital Heart Surgery.** Baltimore, MD. (Immediately prior to Annual Meeting Society of Thoracic Surgeons, Washington, DC). Sponsored by Div. of Thoracic and Cardiovascular Surgery, University of Maryland School of Medicine. Inquiries: Program Cont. Ed., University of Maryland School of Medicine, 10 South Pine St., Suite 300, Baltimore, MD 21201. Tel. 301-528-3956.

Sept. 14–19: **Xth World Congress of Cardiology.** Washington, DC. Inquiries: Secretariat, 7320 Greenville Ave., Dallas, TX 75231. Tel. 1-214-750-5429. Cable Tencard, Dallas, TX.

Abroad
1985

June 1–8: **Frontiers in Imaging and Cardiopulmonary Diagnosis.** England. (Also in Scotland, June 9–15). Eric N. C. Milne, M.D., program director. Faculty from U.S.A., 3 British and 2 Scottish medical schools. Inquiries: Ryals, POB 610203, DFW Airport, Texas 75261, U.S.A. 214-659-9590.

June 8–20: **2nd Advanced Ten Day International Teaching Seminar on Epidemiology and Prevention.** Ireland. Sponsored by Council of Epidemiology and Prevention, International Society and Federation of Cardiology in cooperation with WHO. Inquiries: Rose Stamler, Room 1-615, 303 E. Chicago Ave., Chicago, IL 60611.

June 9–14: **International Congress of Angiology.** Athens, Greece. Inquiries: Prof. P. Balas, 17 Sisini St., 115 28 Athens (612) Greece. (new date).

June 10–11: **Advances in Internal Medicine.** Banff, Alberta, Canada. Inquiries: American College of Physicians, 4200 Pine St., Philadelphia, PA 19104.

June 11–14: **3rd International Symposium on Body Surface Mapping.** Nijmegen, the Netherlands. Inquiries: Dr. R. Th. van Dam, Dept. Cardiology, Geert Grooteplein Zuid 8, 6525 AG Nijmegen, the Netherlands.

June 16–19: **12th International Congress of Electrocardiology.** Minsk, USSR. Prof. M. Sidorenko, organizing chairman. Inquiries: Garber Travel, POB 404-Dept. 91-5273, Brookline, MA 02146. Tel. 1-800-225-4570 (In Massachusetts: 617-787-0600.)

June 16–20: **12th Symposium, International Society of Cerebral Blood Flow—"Brain: 85."** Ronneby Brunn Hotel. Lund, Sweden. Inquiries: K. Dahlgren, Dept. Clinical Neurophysiology, University Hospital, S-221 85 Lund, Sweden. Tel. +46-46-10-33-70.

June 16–21: **12th International Congress of Cardiology.** Vancouver, B.C., Canada. Inquiries: Dr. Henry Mizgala, Suite 1704, 1200 Alberni St., Vancouver, B.C., Canada V6E 1A6. Tel. 604-681-5226. Cable: Venuvan.

June 16–21: **International Symposium on the Biomechanics of Muscle** (14th Neuroelectric Society Meeting). Hotel Vraona Bay, Vravrona-Attica, Athens, Greece. Ivan Bourgeois, M.S., program chairman. Inquiries: Dr. A. Sances, Jr., Dept. Neurosurgery, Medical College of Wisconsin, 8700 W. Wisconsin Ave., Milwaukee, WI 53226. Tel. 1-414-257-5307.

June 20: **Doppler Ultrasound Techniques in Cardiology.** St. Bartholomew's Hospital, London, U.K. Inquiries: Biological Engineering Society, c/o Royal College of Surgeons, Lincoln's Inn Fields, London WC2A 3PN, United Kingdom.

June 23–26: **International Conference on Preventive Cardiology.** Sovincenter, Moscow, USSR. Sponsored by WHO, International Society and Federation of Cardiology. Official languages English and Russian. Inquiries: A. A. Stepanenko, International Conference on Prevention Cardiology, Institute of Preventive Cardiology, 10 Petroverigsky Lane 101837 Moscow, USSR. Telex 411355. Cable USSR MOSCOW K-62, Preventive Cardiology. Tel. 221-93-47.

June 26–28: **6th Symposium on Echocardiology With a Postgraduate Course on Doppler Cardiography.** Rotterdam, the Netherlands. Sponsored by Erasmus University Thoraxcenter. Inquiries: PG Med. Ed., Erasmus University, Rotterdam, PBO 1738, 3000 DR Rotterdam, the Netherlands. Tel. 010-635011/635013.

July 15–19: **4th Meeting, World Federation on Ultrasound in Medicine and Biology.** Sydney, Australia. Inquiries: WFUMB, POB 1441 GPO, Sydney, NSW, Australia 2001.

Aug. 3–17: **5th Annual Roentgen Revisited.** Postgraduate Radiology Course with NMR Symposium. Switzerland, Austria, Germany. Sponsored by University of California San Francisco Medical Center and Univeristy of Munich. Charles B. Higgins, M.D. course director. Inquiries: See May 18–June 2, Travel Planners.

Aug. 31–Sept. 7: **Diagnosis of Diseases of the Chest.** Italy. (Also in Greece, Sept. 8–14). 2nd Great Teachers Foundation International Postgraduate Medical Education Program. Eric N. C. Milne, M.D., program director. Inquiries: Ryals (see June 1–8 above).

Aug. 31–Sept. 7: **11th Congress of International Society of Hypertension.** Heidelberg, Federal Republic of Germany. Organized by German Institute of High Blood Pressure Research and German Hypertension League. Dr. Detlev Ganten, Congress chairman. Inquiries: GKV, Frankfurter Str. 57, D-6050 Offenbach 1, Heidelberg, FRGermany.

Sept. 1–6: **13th World Congress of Neurology.** Hamburg, Germany. Inquiries: Dr. T. Stober, Dept. Neurology, Faculty of Med., University of Saarland, D-6650 Homburg/Saar, FRG.

Sept. 1–7: **3rd Postgraduate International Course on Pain Therapy.** Vicenza, Italy. Inquiries: Ruggiero Rizzi, M.D., Ospedale Generale Regionale, 36100 Vicenza, Italy.

Sept. 3–6: **European Nuclear Medicine Congress.** Barbican Centre, London, England. Incorporates 23rd Meeting Society of Nuclear Medicine, Europe, 8th Meeting European Nuclear Medicine Society, 13th Meeting British Nuclear Medicine Society. Inquiries: Congress, Institute of Nuclear Medicine, Middlesex Hospital Medical School, Mortimer St., London, W1N 8AA, United Kingdom. Tel. OI-631 1066.

Sept. 5–7: **1st Asian-Pacific Conference on Doppler and Echocardiography.** Tokyo. Inquiries: Pravin M. Shah, M.D., Coordinator for North America, Cardiology Section (691/111E), Wadsworth VA Medical Center, Wilshire & Sawtelle Blvds, Los Angeles, CA. Tel. 1-213-824-3126.

Sept. 7–9: **3rd International Brain Heart Conference.** Trier, Germany. Inquiries: Dr. T. Stober, Dept. Neurology, Faculty of Med. University of Saarland, D-6650, Homburg/Saar, Federal Republic of Germany.

Sept. 8–12: **1st International Congress on Hospital Laws, Procedures, and Ethics.** Tel Aviv, Israel. Judge Amnon Carmi, organizing chairman. Inquiries: Hospitalaw, 28 Ahad Ha'am St., POB 394, Tel Aviv 61003, Israel. Tel. 03-650862. Telex 33803 TLV. Cable PELTOURS TELAVIV.

Sept. 9–12: **8th Annual European Conference on Lipoproteins.** Evangelische Akademie, Tutzing (near Munich), West Germany. Apolipoprotein mutants and dyslipoproteinemias; cellular processing of lipoproteins. Sponsored by European Lipoprotein Club. Inquiries: Dr. J. Shepherd, Secretary European Lipoprotein Club, Dept. Pathological Biochemistry, Royal Infirmary, Glasgow, Scotland, G4 OSF.

Sept. 11–14: **4th European Conference on Mechanocardiography.** Budapest, Hungary. Organized by the European-African Div. of the International Society of Mechanocardiography and the Hungarian Society of Cardiology. Prof. J. Simonyi chairman scientific committee. Inquiries: Mechanocardiography Organizing Committee, Budapest, Pf 88, H-1450, Hungary.

Sept. 11–14: **Acute Brain Ischemia 1985: Medical and Surgical Therapy.** University of Siena, Italy. (Satellite of 13th World Congress of Neurology, Sept. 1–6, Hamburg, Germany.) Prof. Noè Battistini, organizer. Inquiries: GIBI S.a.s., M. P. Gerini, Via Orlona, 7, 00198 Rome, Italy.

Sept. 16–20: **International Symposium on Cardiogenic Reflexes.** University of Leeds, England. Organized by Dept. of CV Studies, Univ. Leeds, and Commission on CV Physiology of International Univ. of Physiological Sciences. Inquiries: Dr. R. Hainsworth, Dept. CV Studies, University of Leeds, Leeds LS2 93T, England.

Oct. 3–4: **Hemodynamics and Atherosclerosis.** Wellington, New Zealand. Inquiries: Dr. W.E. Stehbens, Dept. Pathology, Wellington Clinical School of Med., Wellington, 2, New Zealand.

Oct. 6–10: **7th International Symposium on Atherosclerosis.** Melbourne, Australia. Inquiries: Dr. P. J. Nestel, Baker Medical Research Inst., Commercial Rd., Prahran, Vic., Australia 3181.

Oct. 8–10: **1st Latin American Congress of Cardiac Pacing.** Buenos Aires, Argentina. Operated by Latin American Society of Cardiac Pacing and Argentine Chamber of Cardiac Pacing. Dr. Alejandro Dussaut, president organizing committee. Inquiries: Congresos Internacionales S.A., Moreno 854—9° piso, 1091 Buenos Aires, Argentina. Tel. 14-3216/3408/3283. Telex 22036 JECON AR.

Oct. 11–12: **2nd International Symposium on Hypertension in Children and Adolescents.** Heidelberg, FRG. Organized by Dept. of Pediatrics, Univ. of Heidelberg, and German Institute for High Blood Pressure Research. Inquiries: German Institute HBP Research, University of Heidelberg, Im Neuenheimer Feld 366, D-6900 Heidelberg, FRG.

Oct. 11–18: **Cell Biology of the Artery Wall.** Hayman Island, Great Barrier Reef, Australia. Satellite of 7th International Symposium on Arteriosclerosis, Oct. 6–10, Melbourne. Inquiries: Dr. Gordon H. Campbell, Dept. Anatomy, University of Melbourne, Parkville, 3052, Australia.

Oct. 14–18: **International Congress on Cardiac Doppler.** Pisa, Italy. (Tutorial sessions Oct. 14–15; Scientific Sessions Oct. 16–18). Prof. Luigi Donato and Dr. Merrill Spencer presidents. Inquiries: Istituto di Fisiologia Clinica, C.N.R., University of Pisa, Via Savi 8, 1-567100 Pisa, Italy. Tel. 050-47231/502109. Telex: 590549 IFCI.

Oct. 20–22: **5th International Symposium on Rats with Spontaneous Hypertension and Related Studies.**

Kyoto, Japan. Yukio Yamori, M.D., program director. Inquiries: 5th SHR Symposium, Shimane Medical University, Izumo 693, Japan. Tel. 0853-23-2111 Ext. 2375. Cable: WHOCOLLAB IZUMO.

Oct. 20–23: **3rd World Congress of Cardiac Rehabilitation.** Caracas, Venezuela. Sponsored by the International Society and Federation of Cardiology: Scientific Council on Rehabilitation of Cardiac Patients and AHA Council on Clinical Cardiology. Inquiries: Dr. Deyanira Almeida, Congreca C.A., POB 17422, Caracas 1015A, Venezuela.

Oct. 20–25: **Conference on Leukotrienes and Prostanoids in Health and Disease.** Jerusalem and Rehovot, Israel. Inquiries: Prof. Uriel Zor, Weizmann Institute of Science, Rehovot, Israel 76100. Tel. 1081 483557. Telex 361900. Cable: Weizinst.

Oct. 23–24: **International Symposium on Mechanisms and Treatment in Essential Hypertension: Calcium and Calcium Antagonists.** Hotel Nagoya Castle, Nagoya, Japan. (Satellite of 5th International Symposium on Rats with Spontaneous Hypertension, Oct. 20–22, Kyoto, Japan). Inquiries: Kyuzo Aoki, M.D., 2nd Dept. Internal Med., Nagoya City University Medical School, Mizuho-ku, Nagoya 467, Japan. Tel. 052-851-5511, Ext. 2204.

Oct. 25–27: **International Symposium on Brain and Blood Pressure Control.** Kikai-Shinkoh Hall, Shiba Park, Tokyo, Japan. Dr. Keiji Nakamura organizing chairman. Abstracts by May 31. Inquiries: Brain and Blood Pressure, Dept. of Pharmacology, Nippon Roche Research Center, Kamakura 247, Japan. Tel. 0467-45-3191-Ext. 380 or 381. Telex 2222861 PANROCHE J.

Oct. 27–30: **3rd Asian Pacific Symposium on Cardiac Pacing and Electrophysiology.** Hilton Hotel, Melbourne, Australia. Sponsored by Cardiac Society of Australia and New Zealand under auspices of International Cardiac Pacing Society. Inquiries: 3rd Asian Pacific Symposium on Cardiac Pacing and Electrophysiology, Suite 3.5, Epworth Medical Centre, 62 Erin St., Richmond, Vic. 3131, Australia.

Oct. 28–31: **1st International Congress on Food and Health.** Salsomaggiore Terme, Italy. Sponsored by International Association for Advancement of Biomedical Research, by Society of Medical Gastronomy, and Institute of Pharmacology of University of Pisa. Inquiries: ALM s.r.l., Via Lattuada, 26, 20135 Milan, Italy. Telex: 313063 HOTALM I.

Nov. 28–30: **7th Biennial Congress of Cardiology.** Rawalpindi/Islamabad, Pakistan. Inquiries: Pakistan Cardiac Society, Brig. Muhammad Zulfiqar Ali Khan, AFIC/NIHD, Rawalpindi, Pakistan. Tel. 64946, 61-31113, 61-33911.

Dec. 1–4: **International Symposium on Left Ventricular Dysfunction.** Jerusalem Hilton Hotel, Israel. Jan J. Kellermann, M.D., of Israel and David Spodick, M.D., of Worcester, MA co-chairmen. Under the auspices of the Universities of Tel Aviv and Massachusetts. Inquiries: POB 50006, Tel Aviv 61500, Israel. Tel. 03-654571. Telex 341171 KENS IL.

1986

Feb. 9–13: **12th World Congress of the International Society for Heart Research,** Melbourne, Australia. Inquiries: Dr. N.S. Dhalla, Dept. of Physiology, Faculty of Medicine, University of Manitoba, Winnipeg, Canada R3E OW3.

July 8–11: **8th Annual Meeting American Section of the International Society For Heart Research and Satellite Symposium on Heart Metabolism for the 30th International Congress of Physiological Sciences.** Winnipeg, Canada. Inquiries: Dr. R. E. Beamish, Experimental Cardiology Section, Dept. of Physiology, Faculty of Medicine, University of Manitoba, Winnipeg, Canada R3E 0W3.

July 13–18: **30th International Congress of Physiological Sciences.** The University of British Columbia, Vancouver, Canada. Dr. H. McLennan, chairman program committee. Inquiries: IUPS, Suite 801, 750 Jervis St., Vancouver, B.C., Canada V6E 2A9. Tel. 604-681-5226. Telex 04-352848 VCR.

AHA Scientific Sessions Future Meeting Dates

1985	Washington, DC	Nov. 11–14
1986	Dallas, TX	Nov. 17–20
1987	Anaheim, CA	Nov. 16–19
1988	Locale not set	Nov. 14–17
1989	New Orleans	Nov. 13–16
1990	Dallas	Nov. 12–15

Xth World Congress of Cardiology, 1986

The Xth World Congress of Cardiology will be held in Washington, DC, Sept. 14–19, 1986. Official languages English, Spanish, and French. Inquiries: Secretariat, Xth World Congress Cardiology, 7320 Greenville Ave., Dallas, TX 75231. Tel. 214-750-5429. Cable: Tencard, Dallas.

Circulation Research JUNE 1985 VOL. 56 NO. 6

An Official Journal of the American Heart Association

BRIEF REVIEWS

The Plasma Membrane Sodium-Hydrogen Exchanger and Its Role in Physiological and Pathophysiological Processes

Rex L. Mahnensmith and Peter S. Aronson

From the Departments of Medicine and Physiology, Yale University School of Medicine, New Haven, Connecticut

SUMMARY. The plasma membranes of most if not all vertebrate cells contain a transport system that mediates the transmembrane exchange of sodium for hydrogen. The kinetic properties of this transport system include a 1:1 stoichiometry, affinity for lithium and ammonium ion in addition to sodium and hydrogen, the ability to function in multiple 1:1 exchange modes involving these four cations, sensitivity to inhibition by amiloride and its analogues, and allosteric regulation by intracellular protons. The plasma membrane sodium-hydrogen exchanger plays a physiological role in the regulation of intracellular pH, the control of cell growth and proliferation, stimulus-response coupling in white cells and platelets, the metabolic response to hormones such as insulin and glucocorticoids, the regulation of cell volume, and the transepithelial absorption and secretion of sodium, hydrogen, bicarbonate and chloride ions, and organic anions. Preliminary evidence raises the possibility that the sodium-hydrogen exchanger may play a pathophysiological role in such diverse conditions as renal acid-base disorders, essential hypertension, cancer, and tissue or organ hypertrophy. Thus, future research on cellular acid-base homeostasis in general, and on plasma membrane sodium-hydrogen exchange in particular, will enhance our understanding of a great variety of physiological and pathophysiological processes. (*Circ Res 57: 773–788, 1985*)

FOR many years it was held that acid-base equivalents merely distributed passively across the plasma membrane of cells according to a Donnan equilibrium. Neutralization of acid produced from intermediary metabolism was presumed to rely first upon cytoplasmic and membrane buffer action, and, second, upon the diffusive movement of protons (H^+) out of the cell down an electrochemical gradient. With the advent of refined and reliable electrode techniques for actually measuring transmembrane voltage differences and intracellular H^+ activity, however, it has become clear that intracellular pH (pH_i) is maintained at a much higher value than predicted if protons were in Donnan equilibrium across the plasma membrane (Roos and Boron, 1981). Measurements from numerous vertebrate and invertebrate cell types have given pH_i values ranging from 6.8–7.3, whereas if H^+ were in electrochemical equilibrium across the membrane, pH_i would average 6.3–6.5, because the typical cell has a large interior-negative membrane potential. Thus, there is continual passive influx of H^+ into the cell, and/or passive efflux of hydroxyl (OH^-) or bicarbonate (HCO_3^-) ions out of the cell (Fig. 1). It is clear that maintenance of pH_i must depend upon an energy-requiring active H^+ extrusion (or OH^- accumulation) system.

One such mechanism for active H^+ extrusion that has been documented in the plasma membrane of a wide variety of cell types is a carrier-mediated Na^+-H^+ exchange (antiport, countertransport) system that catalyzes the coupled transmembrane exchange of sodium (Na^+) for H^+. In the intact cell, the plasma membrane Na^+-H^+ exchanger mediates the uphill extrusion of protons directly coupled to the downhill flux of Na^+ into the cell (Fig. 1). This antiport process is not directly dependent upon any exergenic chemical reaction, such as ATP hydrolysis; rather, energy for the uphill extrusion of H^+ is obtained exclusively from the steep inwardly directed Na^+ gradient, which is maintained by the primary active extrusion of Na^+ via the separate plasma membrane Na^+,K^+-ATPase system. Thus, Na^+-H^+ antiport is an example of secondary active transport.

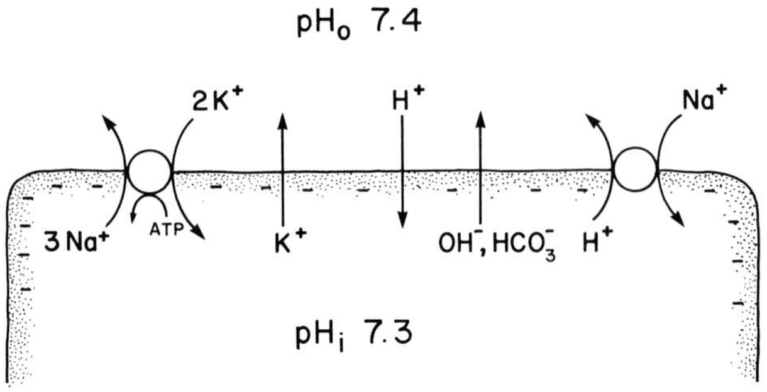

Figure 1. *Role of the Na^+-H^+ exchanger in cellular acid-base homeostasis.*

This transport system has been identified in virtually every type of cell that has been examined to determine its presence, including ova, sperm, erythrocytes, lymphocytes, skeletal muscle, cardiac muscle and Purkinje fibers, neurons, capillary endothelia, fibroblasts, renal tubular cells, intestinal and gall bladder epithelia, and a variety of cells in culture (Aronson, 1985). The principal physiological role of the Na^+-H^+ exchanger is to regulate intracellular pH. However, as a corollary of this role, the Na^+-H^+ exchanger has an important additional role as a signal-transducer for various stimuli that influence cell function by altering intracellular pH. Examples include sperm activation of oocytes, the initiation of cell growth and proliferation in response to serum growth factors, and certain actions of insulin and thrombin. Moreover, as a transporter of Na^+, this system plays a role in the regulation of cell volume. Finally, the Na^+-H^+ exchanger has an important role in mediating the net transport of acid-base equivalents and Na^+ across various epithelia, such as the renal proximal tubule and small intestine.

This review presents a current overview of the physiological roles subserved by the plasma membrane Na^+-H^+ exchanger in different animal cells. The intrinsic properties of the antiporter will be presented first, as these have bearing on the interpretation of the many investigations that pertain to its various roles in diverse cells and tissues. Of burgeoning interest is how this transport system might be regulated and how its state of activity might be important in certain pathophysiological states.

Properties of the Na^+-H^+ Exchanger

The distinctive nature of this transport system, like any other transport system, resides in its specific properties with regard to stoichiometry, selectivity for substrates, sensitivity to inhibitors, and capacity for regulation. The first clear-cut demonstration of directly coupled Na^+-H^+ exchange was made in microvillus membrane vesicles derived from the luminal membranes of rat intestinal mucosa and renal proximal tubular cells (Murer et al., 1976). In this experimental preparation, uphill ^{22}Na influx can be driven by an outward proton gradient, and outward extrusion of H^+ can be driven by an inward Na^+ gradient. In intact cellular preparations, the technique is essentially the same: Na^+-dependent H^+ extrusion can be assayed with intracellular H^+-sensitive microelectrodes, with pH-sensitive fluorescent dyes, or with nuclear magnetic resonance (NMR); and H^+-coupled Na^+ movements can be assayed isotopically or with intracellular Na^+-sensitive electrodes (see Nuccitelli and Deamer, 1982). The transport properties derived from these various approaches show remarkably close agreement.

Stoichiometry

Several observations indicate that the stoichiometry of the Na^+-H^+ antiport process is one-for-one. In a number of studies with intact cell systems, the net flux of Na^+ in one direction and the net flux of H^+ in the opposite direction have been directly quantified (Cala, 1980; Moolenaar et al., 1981b; Boron and Boulpaep, 1983; Grinstein et al., 1984). In each of these studies, the directly measured ratio of these fluxes did not differ significantly from 1.0. Second, in vesicle studies, maneuvers that alter the transmembrane electrical potential difference have no effect on Na^+ influx via this transport pathway (Murer et al., 1976; Kinsella and Aronson, 1980; Cohn et al., 1982; Knickelbein et al., 1983), and in intact cell systems, stimulating or inhibiting Na^+-H^+ antiport does not cause any measureable change in the transmembrane electrical potential difference (Aickin and Thomas, 1977; Cala, 1980; Deitmer and Ellis, 1980; Vigne et al., 1982; Grinstein et al., 1983), indicating that the operation of the Na^+-H^+ exchanger is electrically silent and must have a Na^+:H^+ coupling ratio close to 1.0. Third, when the transmembrane Na^+ gradient is thermodynamically balanced by an H^+ gradient of the same magnitude (i.e., when $Na_o^+/Na_i^+ = H_o^+/H_i^+$), the Na^+-H^+ exchanger is at equilibrium and mediates no net flux of Na^+ and H^+ (Moody, 1981; Kinsella and Aronson, 1982), which also implies that the exchange is electroneutral and that the coupling ratio is 1.0. A Na^+:H^+ coupling ratio of 1.0 is consistent with stoichiometries of 1:1, 2:2, 3:3, etc., but the interaction of external Na^+ and external H^+ with the Na^+-H^+ exchanger conforms to simple saturating Michaelis-Menten kinetics, with a Hill coefficient of 1.0 (Burnham et al., 1982; Aronson et al., 1983; Ives et al., 1983a; Gunther and Wright, 1983; Frelin et al., 1983; Paris and Pouyssegur, 1983; Grinstein et al., 1984). This is most consistent with the presence of only a single binding site for external Na^+ or H^+, and indicates that the stoichiometry of exchange is actually one Na^+ for one H^+.

Alternative Substrates and Modes

The Na^+-H^+ exchanger can operate in more than one mode with a narrow selection of monovalent cations. In addition to mediating Na^+-H^+ exchange in either direction, it can mediate Na^+-Na^+ exchange, and can bind and transport Li^+ under certain conditions. Thus, exchange of external Na^+ for internal H^+, external H^+ for internal Na^+, external Na^+ for internal Na^+, external Li^+ for internal H^+, and internal Li^+ for external H^+ have all been demonstrated (Murer et al., 1976; Kinsella and Aronson, 1980, 1981a; Deitmer and Ellis, 1980; Rindler and Saier, 1981; Moolenaar et al., 1981b; Aronson et al., 1982; Burnham et al., 1982; Paris and Pouyssegur, 1983; Gunther and Wright, 1983; Abercrombie and Roos, 1983). There is also evidence in microvillus membrane vesicles (Kinsella and Aronson, 1981a; Aronson et al., 1983; Gunther and Wright, 1983) that ammonium ion (NH_4^+) can share the Na^+-H^+ exchanger. Taken together, these observations suggest that the Na^+-H^+ exchanger has appreciable affinity for Li^+ and NH_4^+ in addition to Na^+ and H^+, and can function in multiple exchange modes involving these four cations, as illustrated schematically in Figure 2. In several preparations, the $K_{1/2}$ for interaction of external H^+ with the Na^+-H^+ exchanger is in the range, 10^{-8} to 10^{-7} M, far lower than the $K_{1/2}$ values (10^{-3} to 10^{-2} M) for Li^+, NH_4^+, and Na^+ (Aronson, 1985). The apparent selectivity sequence for binding of external cations is $H^+ \gg Li^+ > NH_4^+ \geq Na^+$; there is no appreciable affinity for K^+, Rb^+, Cs^+, or organic cations such as choline or tetramethylammonium (Aronson, 1985).

Given the model in Figure 2, one would predict that the plasma membrane Na^+-H^+ exchanger could mediate Na^+-Li^+ exchange. However, this has yet to be conclusively demonstrated. In erythrocytes, a one-for-one exchange of Na^+ for Li^+ is easily demonstrated, and this system has been well characterized as having many features in common with the Na^+-H^+ exchange system (Aronson, 1982; Funder et al., 1984). Specifically, both systems mediate electroneutral monovalent cation exchange, both systems are ATP-independent and ouabain-insensitive and are energized by the downhill cation gradients, both systems can transport Li^+ and actually have a higher affinity for Li^+ than for Na^+, and, both systems can operate in a Na^+-Na^+ exchange mode. Furthermore, external H^+ interacts competitively with the erythrocyte Na^+-Li^+ exchanger, just as Li^+ interacts competitively with the Na^+-H^+ exchanger

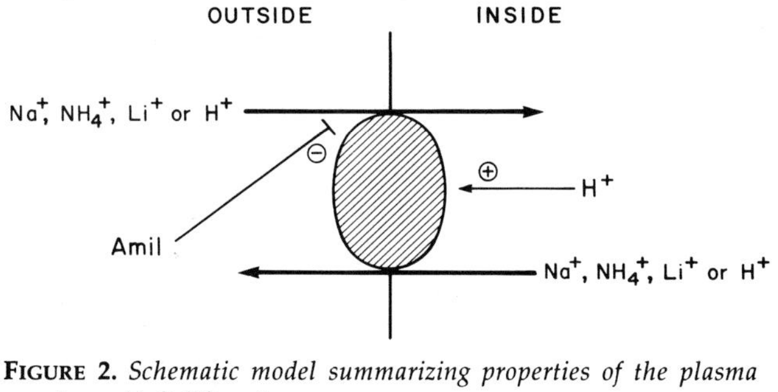

FIGURE 2. *Schematic model summarizing properties of the plasma membrane Na^+-H^+ exchanger.*

(Funder et al., 1984). Coupled Na^+-H^+ exchange has been demonstrated in mammalian erythrocytes (Dissing and Hoffman, 1982; Parker, 1983; Parker and Glosson, 1984), but whether the same antiport system that mediates Na^+-Li^+ exchange also mediates the Na^+-H^+ exchange in these erythrocytes is not yet clear.

Inhibitors

Sensitivity of the plasma membrane Na^+-H^+ exchanger to a variety of transport inhibitors has been evaluated. Ouabain, furosemide, disulfonic acid stilbene derivatives, and acetazolamide have no direct effects on this pathway (Kinsella and Aronson, 1980). The best inhibitors identified to date are the diuretic drug amiloride and its analogues. With the exception of one study (Ives et al., 1983a), amiloride has generally been found to be a purely competitive inhibitor with respect to external Na^+($K_i \sim 10^{-6}$ to 10^{-5} M) (Kinsella and Aronson, 1981b; Vigne et al., 1982; Paris and Pouyssegur, 1983), implying that amiloride interacts at or near the Na^+ transport site. Inhibition by this agent is immediate in onset and is rapidly reversible. Note that, compared to its effect on Na^+-H^+ exchangers, amiloride is 10–100 times more potent as an inhibitor of the Na^+ channels found in the apical membranes of such epithelia as the colon and the cortical collecting tubule of the kidney (Benos, 1982). The effects of amiloride as a diuretic employed clinically probably arise solely from inhibition of apical Na^+ channels in the distal nephron, rather than from inhibition of Na^+-H^+ exchange.

Nevertheless, amiloride has been employed extensively as an experimental probe of Na^+-H^+ exchange activity in various tissues. Inhibition of H^+ efflux or Na^+ influx along with inhibition of a particular cell function is often taken as evidence for a specific role of Na^+-H^+ exchange in that cell function. Although amiloride is useful and informative in this regard, it is not an ideal agent when employed in this manner, and such experiments need to be interpreted carefully. Because amiloride and Na^+ compete for access to the external transport site of the Na^+-H^+ exchanger, and because the K_m for Na^+ is quite low ($K_m \sim$ 3–50 mM), amiloride is not an effective inhibitor of Na^+-H^+ exchange in the presence of physiological Na^+ concentrations (140–150 mM) unless relatively high concentrations of the drug ($>10^{-4}$ to 10^{-3} M) are used. At these concentrations, amiloride may have additional effects, such as inhibiting paracellular cation permeability in epithelia (Balaban et al., 1979), and inhibiting Na^+,K^+-ATPase (Soltoff and Mandel, 1983). In addition, at high concentrations, amiloride can act as a weak base and nonspecifically alter transmembrane pH gradients (Dubinsky and Frizzell, 1983). Finally, high concentrations of amiloride can inhibit protein synthesis in cells and in cell-free systems, implying that, under certain circumstances, this drug has a direct toxic action (Leffert et al., 1982). In spite of these constraints, amiloride has been useful as an experimental probe of Na^+-H^+ exchange activity, particularly when used in the presence of lower than physiological Na^+ concentrations. Recently, amiloride analogues with substitution of the 5-amino group by alkyl or alkenyl groups have been found to be up to 100 times more potent than amiloride in inhibiting Na^+-H^+ exchangers (Vigne et al., 1984). These analogues should be more useful than amiloride for studying the functions of Na^+-H^+ exchangers under physiological conditions.

Other inhibitors of the Na^+-H^+ exchanger include the alkaloids, harmaline and quinidine, which are less specific than amiloride (Kinsella and Aronson, 1980; Parker, 1983), the carboxyl-activating reagent *N*-ethoxycarbonyl-2-ethoxy-1,2-dihydroquinoline (EEDQ) (Burnham et al., 1982), and the histidine-specific reagent diethylpyrocarbonate, an irreversible inhibitor (Grillo and Aronson, 1983). Whether any of these agents are useful for probing the function and roles of the Na^+-H^+ exchanger under physiological conditions is yet to be determined.

Regulation by Intracellular H^+

A general observation in most studies reviewed is that raising the internal H^+ concentration dramatically stimulates the rate of Na^+-H^+ exchange. Since this system is thermodynamically energized by the Na_o^+/Na_i^+ and H_i^+/H_o^+ gradients, it is predicted that as the outward H^+ gradient steepens in the face of an unchanging inward Na^+ gradient, the rate of antiport should increase proportionally. However, in renal microvillus membrane vesicles, the rate of Na^+ influx by Na^+-H^+ exchange has a greater than linear dependence on internal H^+ concentration (Aronson et al., 1982), and, in whole renal cells and in human lymphocytes, efflux of H^+ via Na^+-H^+ exchange shows a steeper dependence on internal pH than expected for a simple Michaelis-Menten process (Boron and Boulpaep, 1983; Grinstein et al., 1984). In view of the considerable data indicating that the stoichiometry of Na^+-H^+ exchange is one-for-one, these observations have led to the proposal that internal H^+ can allosterically activate the exchanger through an interaction that is independent of its role as a transportable ion (Aronson et al., 1982). The evidence in support of this concept derives from two observations: first, that raising the internal H^+ concentration actually stimulates Na^+-Na^+ exchange in vesicles, an effect opposite to that expected if internal H^+ were to interact (and compete) only at the internal transport site, and second, that raising internal H^+ stimulates net Na^+ efflux in exchange for external H^+, also an effect opposite to that expected if internal H^+ were interacting only at the transport site (Aronson et al., 1982). Conceptually, one explanation for the striking stimulatory effect of internal H^+ is that the transport system possesses one or more functional groups on its inner, cytoplasmic surface, the protonation of which causes activation of the exchanger.

This kinetic regulation of Na^+-H^+ exchange activity by internal protons has important consequences for the cell. Activation of Na^+-H^+ exchange by a falling cytoplasmic pH would greatly enhance the ability of plasma membrane Na^+-H^+ exchangers to extrude protons promptly, thereby protecting against intracellular acid loads. Conversely, this property is reflected by the existence of an apparent "activity threshold," because, as pH_i rises to or above a certain value, the rate of H^+ extrusion is sharply curtailed in most tissues. This kinetically protects against the generation of an intracellular alkalosis inasmuch as the average Na_o^+/Na_i^+ gradient of approximately 10 could theoretically drive pH_i 1.0 unit higher than extracellular pH if there were not some mechanism to prevent the system from reaching thermodynamic equilibrium. It appears that the kinetic dependence on internal H^+ activity is just such a "brake" for this system. Of interest in this regard is recent evidence that suggests that stimulation of the plasma membrane Na^+-H^+ exchanger by purified growth factors results from a shift in its sensitivity to intracellular pH (Moolenaar et al., 1983). Hence, altering the apparent affinity of the transporter for internal H^+ ions may be an important mechanism for physiological regulation of this transport system.

Possible Regulation by Intracellular Ca^{++}

In addition to the regulation of Na^+-H^+ exchange by internal pH, it has been proposed that antiport activity might also be importantly influenced by intracellular calcium (Ca^{++}) activity, perhaps through the mediation of calmodulin (Benos, 1982; Owen and Villereal, 1982a, 1982b). This hypothesis is founded on the observation in fibroblasts that elevations in free intracellular Ca^{++} induced by the calcium ionophore A23187 markedly stimulate amiloride-sensitive Na^+ influx, and that treatment of these cells with intracellular Ca^{++} antagonists or with calmodulin antagonists blocks activation of Na^+-H^+ exchange in a dose-dependent manner (Villereal, 1981; Owen and Villereal, 1982a, 1982b, 1983; Mix et al., 1984). Furthermore, in sea urchin eggs, fertilization is associated with an immediate rise in free intracellular Ca^{++} and a subsequent activation of Na^+-H^+ exchange (see next section). Since treatment of the unfertilized egg with A23187 also induces egg activation and Na^+-dependent H^+ extrusion, it has been proposed that intracellular Ca^{++} might be a modulator of Na^+-H^+ exchange in these cells (Whitaker and Steinhardt, 1982; Busa and Nuccitelli, 1984). However, some doubt has been cast upon the hypothesis that Ca^{++} is a regulator of Na^+-H^+ exchange activity. Treatment of either mouse neuroblastoma cells (Moolenaar et al., 1981a) or mouse fibroblast cells (Frelin et al., 1983) with a range of A23187 concentrations in the presence of external Ca^{++} does not modify the rate of amiloride-sensitive Na^+ uptake, nor does it trigger mitogenesis. Also, Grinstein et al. (1984) have reported that the Ca^{++} ionophore ionomycin does not activate Na^+-H^+ exchange in human lymphocytes, and preloading renal microvillus membrane vesicles with 10^{-7} to 10^{-3} M calcium has no significant effect on renal Na^+-H^+ exchange activity (Aronson et al., 1982). Thus, the exact interplay between intracellular Ca^{++} activity, calmodulin, and the Na^+-H^+ exchanger is uncertain.

An alternative mechanism for Ca^{++}-dependent regulation of the plasma membrane Na^+-H^+ exchanger is via the action of the calcium and phospholipid-dependent protein kinase (i.e., protein kinase C). In several different cell types, phorbol esters, which are relatively specific activators of protein kinase C, stimulate the rate of plasma membrane Na^+-H^+ exchange (Burns and Rozengurt, 1983; Moolenaar et al., 1984). If Na^+-H^+ exchange activity is regulated by protein kinase C-induced phosphorylation under physiological conditions, then it may be sensitive not only to changes in intracellular Ca^{++} activity, but also to changes in availability of diacylglycerol, a potent endogenous activator of protein kinase C (Berridge, 1984). Diacylglycerol is a product of phosphoinositide hydrolysis. Another such product is inositol triphosphate, which is known to stimulate the release of Ca^{++} from intracellular storage pools. Thus, receptor-mediated hydrolysis of phosphoinositides to diacylglycerol and inositol triphosphate may be an important mechanism for regulating activity of the Na^+-H^+ exchanger through the action of protein kinase C (Berridge, 1984).

Physiological Roles

In almost all animals cells, a steep inwardly directed Na^+ gradient is maintained across the plasma membrane due to the primary active extrusion of Na^+ from the cell via the Na^+,K^+-ATPase (sodium pump). Because Na_o^+/Na_i^+ exceeds H_o^+/H_i^+ under most physiological conditions, the net thermodynamic driving force acting on plasma membrane Na^+-H^+ exchangers generally favors the net exchange of external Na^+ for internal H^+. Thus, it is easy to conceptualize how this transport system could function in the protection of intracellular pH against intracellular acid loads, especially in light of the demonstrated ability of internal protons to activate proton extrusion. Of great interest are the recent observations that the plasma membrane Na^+-H^+ exchange system serves a variety of functions in addition to merely defending pH_i against acid loads. These roles can be broadly distinguished into three categories: (1) intracellular pH change is caused by activation of Na^+-H^+ exchange, and the ensuing pH_i rise is permissive or serves as a signal for generating a biological response; (2) changes in activity of plasma membrane Na^+-H^+ exchange alter the intracellular content of Na^+, as in cell volume regulation; and (3) plasma membrane Na^+-H^+ exchange participates in net transepithelial movement of Na^+ and H^+, as in the processes of acid secretion and Na^+ reabsorption by gallbladder, intestine, and kidney.

Regulation of Intracellular pH

Since the development of accurate means for intracellular pH and voltage measurements, there has been general agreement that H^+ activity is lower inside cells than would be predicted if H^+ were simply passively distributed in equilibrium with the membrane potential. In most cell systems studied to date, active H^+ extrusion is accomplished by a Na^+-coupled ion exchange mechanism, whereby downhill Na^+ influx is coupled either singly to H^+ efflux or Na^+ influx is coupled to Cl^- efflux and HCO_3^- influx (Roos and Boron, 1981). Which system is present or predominates in any given tissue appears to depend at first approximation on animal class and perhaps tissue type: with one exception, invertebrate cells seem to rely on the Na^+-dependent Cl^--HCO_3^- exchange system, whereas vertebrate cells appear to rely more on Na^+-H^+ exchange with or without an independently operating Cl^--HCO_3^- exchange. The systems are distinguished by external and internal ionic requirements and by their sensitivity to inhibitors: Na^+-H^+ exchange is inhibited by amiloride, and Cl^--HCO_3^- exchange but not Na^+-H^+ exchange is inhibited by disulfonic stilbene derivatives (DIDS, SITS).

For example, in the snail neuron (Thomas, 1977), the squid giant axon (Boron and Russell, 1983), and the giant barnacle muscle fiber (Boron et al., 1981), effective recovery of pH_i after the cell interior is acidified depends on the presence of external Na^+ and HCO_3^- and internal Cl^-. Based on experiments with either ion-sensitive electrodes or radioisotope tracers, the actual stoichiometry of ion fluxes appears to be 1 Na^+ in, 1 Cl^- out, and 2 equivalents of HCO_3^- in (Boron and Russell, 1983). The entire process is electroneutral and can be inhibited by SITS, a selective anion inhibitor, but not by amiloride. Although a Na^+-H^+ exchange may occur along with the Cl^--HCO_3^- exchange in these tissues, an independent Na^+-H^+ exchange has not been discerned. Unlike other tissues to be discussed, there is an absolute dependence on Cl^- and HCO_3^-, and deletion of any one ion prevents pH_i recovery. In another invertebrate preparation, the crayfish neuron, Moody (1981) found that regulation of pH_i occurs somewhat differently. In this case, two operations were needed to effect pH_i recovery: Na^+-H^+ exchange, and a Na^+-dependent Cl^--HCO_3^- exchange.

A more prominent role for Na^+-H^+ exchange in pH_i regulation has been documented in a variety of vertebrate cells. Aickin and Thomas (1977) recorded an intracellular pH of 7.07 in mouse skeletal muscle situated in buffered Ringers at pH_o 7.40. After intracellular acid loading, pH_i recovered spontaneously over about 30 minutes, and was associated with an influx of Na^+. Recovery of pH_i could be blocked more than 90% by removal of outside Na^+ or application of 10^{-4} M amiloride. A less active Cl^--HCO_3^- exchange process was also noted in this tissue, and it made a minor contribution to pH_i recovery. Other similar types of investigations in vertebrate skeletal muscle have documented that Na^+-H^+ exchange and Cl^--HCO_3^- exchange co-exist independently in the plasma membranes of this tissue (Roos and Boron, 1978; Abercrombie et al., 1983). Although both systems appear to function importantly toward pH_i recovery when the cell is acid loaded, activity of the amiloride-sensitive Na^+-H^+ exchanger appears to be more significant, particularly when the muscle cell is depolarized (Roos and Boron, 1978; Abercrombie et al., 1983).

Regulation of internal pH in mammalian cardiac tissue also depends importantly on Na^+-H^+ exchange. Ellis and Thomas (1976) were the first to document that both mammalian Purkinje tissue and ventricular muscle cells possess active mechanisms for pH_i maintenance. Resting intracellular pH was 7.27, and after cytoplasmic acidification, pH_i recovery was prompt. This recovery process was dependent upon external Na^+, was accompanied by Na^+ influx, was amiloride-sensitive, and was unaffected by Cl^- or HCO_3^- deletion or SITS addition (Deitmer and Ellis, 1980). This strongly suggests that Na^+-H^+ exchange is the chief if not sole pH_i regulator in this tissue. A similar conclusion was reached by Piwnica-Worms and Lieberman (1983), who investigated regulation of intracellular pH in spontaneously beating cardiac muscle cells in culture by using the pH-sensitive chromophore, 6-carboxyfluorescein. Significantly, either lowering external Na^+ from 144 mM to 0.8 mM or application of 1 mM amiloride caused a rapid cytosolic acidification. These data strongly imply that the Na^+-H^+ exchanger is continuously active in the contracting cardiac cell, where it compensates for the generation of metabolic acid or for the passive entry of H^+ or exit of HCO_3^- across the cell membrane. A Cl^--HCO_3^- exchange system that is independent of Na^+-H^+ antiport also exists in the Purkinje fiber (Vaughan-Jones, 1979). However, this anion transport system does not appear to play a major part in acid extrusion in the heart, but, rather, it may serve to facilitate Cl^- entry into the cell and thereby regulate intracellular Cl^- activity (Vaughan-Jones, 1979).

The Na^+-H^+ exchange system has been identified as the principal mechanism for pH_i regulation in a number of other tissues and cells. In such epithelia as the gallbladder (Weinman and Reuss, 1982) and the renal proximal tubule (Boron and Boulpaep, 1983), Na^+-H^+ exchange is the principal mechanism for controlling intracellular pH. Grinstein et al. (1984) have found that lymphocytes activate an amiloride-sensitive electroneutral Na^+-H^+ exchange following cytoplasmic acidification, and Betz (1983) has identified Na^+-H^+ exchange in isolated brain capillary endothelium from the rat. Finally, a variety of cultured animal cells possess a relatively quiescent Na^+-H^+ antiporter that is dramatically stimulated when the cell interior is acidified slightly, indicating a direct link between activity of the Na^+-H^+ exchanger and intracellular pH (Moolenaar et al., 1981b; 1983; Rindler and Saier, 1981; Vigne et al., 1982; Schuldiner and Rozengurt, 1982; Rothenberg et al., 1983; Paris and Pouyssegur, 1983; Frelin et al., 1983).

In general, acid-loaded cells recover only to the baseline pH_i and then seem to curtail H^+ transport sharply, even though the driving force for Na^+-H^+ exchange, the inwardly directed Na^+ gradient, still remains favorable for additional H^+ extrusion. This phenomenon probably reflects the kinetic sensitivity of the transport system to internal H^+ as discussed earlier (Aronson et al., 1982; Boron and Boulpaep, 1983). Thus, H^+ extrusion rates are dramatically increased as internal H^+ rises, and are dramatically slowed as internal H^+ falls in spite of a persistently steep thermodynamic driving force for continued H^+ extrusion. The physiological importance of this phenomenon resides in the fact that the cell must maintain its pH_i within narrowly defined limits for optimal enzyme and organelle functioning. If there were not a kinetic modulator for this system, and if activity depended solely on thermodynamic forces, the mechanism would be sluggish in defense of acid loads, and would tend to drive steady state pH_i to excessively alkaline values.

Intracellular pH as Mediator of Cell Response to Activating Stimuli

Cell Proliferation

Within the first few minutes after fertilization of an oocyte, there is a dramatic increase in DNA and protein synthesis, an increase in metabolic rate, and initiation of cell division (Whitaker and Steinhardt, 1982; Busa and Nuccitelli, 1984). One of the earliest events triggered by sperm-egg fusion is an increase in intracellular pH. In studies with sea urchin eggs, this cytoplasmic alkalinization appears to be due to an active proton extrusion process that is quiescent in the unfertilized egg but is activated 5–10 minutes after the fertilization event. Both the proton efflux and the increase in pH_i depend upon the presence of external Na^+ and have been linked to Na^+ influx; as well, these Na^+ and H^+ fluxes are amiloride-sensitive. Thus, it is postulated that activation of sea urchin eggs by sperm-egg fusion involves activation of Na^+-H^+ exchange, which is critical to further development. The subsequent alkalinization of the cytoplasm may act as a regulator of the biosynthetic events (Whitaker and Steinhardt, 1982; Busa and Nuccitelli, 1984). Of additional interest in this regard is that initiation of motility in sea urchin and rat sperm also appears to rely upon a Na^+-dependent H^+-efflux system and an associated rise in pH_i (Wong et al., 1981; Lee et al., 1982).

An even more convincing role for Na^+-H^+ antiport and alterations of cytoplasmic pH in the regulation of cell proliferation and growth has been documented with a variety of mammalian cells in culture. When quiescent cells in culture are stimulated to grow and divide by the application of serum, a dramatic and persistent increase in Na^+ influx occurs (Smith and Rozengurt, 1978). The cell growth response can be suppressed by either a reduction in external Na^+ (Smith and Rozengurt, 1978) or by the presence of amiloride (Koch and Leffert, 1979; Rozengurt and Mendoza, 1980; Moolenaar et al., 1982). Similarly, in a number of cultured cell preparations it has been observed that (1) serum-activated Na^+ influx is simultaneous with a rise in pH_i due to H^+ extrusion, (2) serum and purified growth factors stimulate a rise in pH_i, and this is strictly dependent on external Na^+; (3) the pH_i increase, like Na^+ influx, is inhibited by amiloride, and (4) the fluxes of Na^+ and H^+ are electroneutral (Moolenaar et al., 1981a, 1981b, 1982, 1983; Pouyssegur et al., 1982; Schuldiner and Rozengurt, 1982; Cassel et al., 1983; Paris and Pouyssegur, 1983; Frelin et al., 1983). Moreover, when mutant fibroblasts which specifically lack Na^+-H^+ exchange activity are exposed to mitogens, cytoplasmic pH does not rise and DNA synthesis is not activated to the same magnitude as in the wild type fibroblast (L'Allemain et al., 1984).

The biochemical steps by which the binding of growth factors to their membrane receptors is linked to activation of Na^+-H^+ exchange are unknown at present. In this regard, Villereal (1981) has suggested that the serum activation of Na^+-H^+ exchange seen in human fibroblasts might be secondary to an elevation in intracellular free Ca^{++} activity. When quiescent fibroblasts are activated by growth factors, there is a prompt mobilization of Ca^{++} from intracellular Ca^{++} storage pools, causing a rise in free intracellular Ca^{++} activity, as measured by quin-2 fluorescence (Mix et al., 1984); this occurs at the same time that Na^+-H^+ exchange activity is stimulated by serum. In the absence of serum growth factors, the calcium ionophore A23187 induces a dose-dependent increase in amiloride-sensitive Na^+ influx and cell proliferation (Villereal, 1981). Amiloride blocks serum-stimulated Na^+ influx but does not block Ca^{++} mobilization, suggesting that the serum-induced rise in Ca_i^{++} is an event that is independent of Na^+ influx; treatment with agents that block intracellular Ca^{++} mobilization or with agents that inactivate Ca^{++}-calmodulin complexes inhibits serum-stimulated Na^+ influx and blocks cell activation (Owen and Villereal, 1982a, 1982b). Therefore, it has been proposed that serum growth factors act primarily by mobilizing Ca^{++} from intracellular pools, and the consequent formation of Ca^{++}-calmodulin complexes then activates Na^+-H^+ exchange, causing a rise in pH_i. However, as discussed earlier, activation of Na^+-H^+ exchange by calcium ionophores is an inconsistent finding. Also as discussed earlier, the critical event may instead be a receptor-mediated hydrolysis of phosphophinositides to yield diacylglycerol, a potent stimulator of protein kinase C. A rise in Ca_i^{++} may not be necessary or sufficient for stimulation of Na^+-H^+ exchange via the mediation of protein kinase C (Moolenaar et al., 1984). It appears that, perhaps, as the result of protein kinase C-mediated phosphorylation, growth factors alter the proton modifier site of the Na^+-H^+ exchanger, resulting in an increased affinity for cytoplasmic H^+, and, thus, a shift in the curve for activation by internal H^+ (Moolenaar et al., 1983).

Whatever the precise biochemical steps that result in the activation of Na^+-H^+ exchange by serum growth factors, it is the resulting cytoplasmic alkalinization that is responsible, at least in part, for the subsequent biosynthetic and mitotic events. For example, the early phosphorylation of certain proteins that occurs with mitogen activation of quiescent fibroblasts is strongly influenced by pH_i and seems to be a limiting prerequisite for further activation of biosynthetic events (Pouyssegur et al., 1982). Likewise, a small rise in pH_i accelerates other critical operations within the cell, such as glycolysis (Fidelman et al., 1982; Moolenaar et al., 1983), DNA synthesis (Zetterberg and Engstrom, 1981; Gerson et al., 1982), and protein synthesis (Winkler et al., 1980). Mitosis can be induced in serum-starved fibroblasts simply by alkalinizing the cells, while serum-induced mitosis can be halted by a small acidification (Busa and Nuccitelli, 1984). Furthermore, mutant fibroblasts that lack Na^+-H^+ exchangers do not alkalinize when exposed to serum mitogens, and their rate of DNA synthesis and cell growth rises very slowly compared with wild type cells that possess Na^+-H^+ exchangers (L'Allemain et al., 1984). Thus, it is clear that an internal pH shift brought about by activation of Na^+-H^+ exchange is probably a critical feature of cell activation, but other regulatory signals are probably equally important and may not be related to pH_i shifts at all. This point has been emphasized by those workers who have demonstrated the parallel importance of internal Ca^{++} activity (Winkler et al., 1980; Mix et al., 1984) and by those investigators who have noted that the protein phosphorylation events induced by mitogens were only partially suppressible by inhibiting Na^+-H^+ exchange activity (Pouyssegur et al., 1982). Moreover, new DNA synthetic activity can occur upon cell exposure to growth factors in the absence of a pH_i rise, albeit at a much slower rate (L'Allemain et al., 1984). An interesting observation in this context is that the calcium-calmodulin interaction appears to be pH sensitive, such that a rise in pH from 7.0 to 7.5 might increase calcium binding to calmodulin by more than 60% (Busa and Nuccitelli, 1984).

This implies that calmodulin-mediated reactions might be pH_i sensitive and that activity of the Na^+-H^+ exchanger might have a modulating function for calmodulin-mediated responses. An alkaline pH_i shift might serve to amplify Ca^{++}-calmodulin signals involved in cell activation, and some calmodulin responses may depend upon this alkaline amplification. Furthermore, if Na^+-H^+ exchange itself is indeed modulated by a calmodulin-dependent mechanism, then an enhanced Ca^{++}-calmodulin interaction might serve to sustain Na^+-H^+ exchange activity in the face of a higher than normal pH_i.

Stimulus-Response Coupling in Neutrophils, Lymphocytes, and Platelets

Stimulus-response coupling in certain differentiated cells also appears to bear a relationship to activation of Na^+-H^+ exchange and subsequent cytoplasmic alkalinization. When mature lymphocytes are activated by exposure to bacterial lipopolysaccharide or concanavalin A, there is an abrupt rise in intracellular pH that is associated with a burst of RNA and protein synthesis, followed by a second higher and more protracted rise in pH_i that strongly correlates with the rate of RNA synthesis (Gerson et al., 1982, 1983). An early surge of amiloride-inhibitable Na^+ influx occurs during lymphocyte activation (Rosoff and Cantley, 1983), and lymphocyte activation and subsequent DNA synthesis can be inhibited by micromolar doses of amiloride, an effect due to inhibition of cation flux and not nonspecific toxicity (Heikkila et al., 1983; Rosoff and Cantley, 1983).

Similarly, activation of mammalian neutrophils by complement component C5a and by the synthetic chemotactic agent formyl-methionyl-leucyl-phenylalanine causes a significant increase in Na^+ influx and cytoplasmic pH (Naccache et al., 1977a; Molski et al., 1981). These events have been correlated with the functional ability of the neutrophil to migrate, degranulate, and generate antibacterial granular superoxides (Naccache et al., 1977b). Both the Na^+ influx and the rise in pH_i induced by f-met-leu-phe are amiloride-sensitive but DIDS-insensitive, suggesting that this response is mediated by Na^+-H^+ exchange (Molski et al., 1981).

Platelet activation by thrombin also appears to involve activation of plasma membrane Na^+-H^+ antiport (Horne et al., 1981; Greenberg-Sepersky and Simons, 1984). With the use of internalized pH-sensitive fluorescent indicators, it has been observed that thrombin stimulation of washed human platelets leads to a dose-dependent increase in ^{22}Na influx and a concomitant rise in cytoplasmic pH. The rise in pH_i produced by a saturating dose of thrombin is reduced 50% by 10^{-4} M amiloride and is prevented completely by 10^{-3} M amiloride. The secretion of serotonin by the platelet, which serves to attract and aggregate other platelets, is also thrombin-dependent and is partially inhibited by amiloride. The dose-response curve for thrombin-induced serotonin secretion is nearly identical to that of the thrombin-induced pH_i rise. Taken together, these data imply a primary role for Na^+-H^+ exchange in platelet activation by thrombin but do not exclude other parallel events. For example, activation of platelets and neutrophils also involves a rise in intracellular free Ca^{++}, and protein phosphorylations are prerequisite steps for the full physiological cellular response (Kaibuchi et al., 1983; Korchak et al., 1984). The relationships among Na^+ influx, elevation of pH_i, and these events are presently unclear.

Effects of Hormones

Rather convincing evidence has been presented which suggests that cytoplasmic alkalinization secondary to activation of Na^+-H^+ exchange is one of the early events mediating the action of insulin to stimulate glycolysis in frog skeletal muscle. The addition of insulin to muscle strips increases pH_i by 0.1 to 0.15 pH unit (Moore, 1981; Fidelman et al., 1982). The possibility that activation of plasma membrane Na^+-H^+ exchange is responsible for this rise in pH_i is suggested by the observations that the elevation in pH_i is associated with an increased influx of Na^+, that lowering extracellular Na^+ prevents the insulin-induced pH_i rise, and that both the insulin-induced Na^+ influx and the pH_i rise can be inhibited by 0.5 mM amiloride (Moore, 1981). That insulin stimulation of glycolysis results from the rise in pH_i per se is indicated by the findings that changes in glycolytic activity closely parallel the changes in pH_i produced by insulin, and that glycolysis is significantly reduced when the insulin-induced rise in pH_i is inhibited by amiloride or by lowering extracellular Na^+ (Fidelman et al., 1982). It was known earlier that glycolysis in cell-free extracts from rat diaphragm and in guinea pig leukocytes is increased by small increases in medium pH (Ui, 1966; Halperin et al., 1969). The likely explanation for this effect is that the activity of the rate-limiting enzyme of glycolysis, phosphofructokinase, is very sensitive to small changes in ambient pH and can be maximally stimulated by a pH elevation as small as 0.1–0.2 pH unit (Trivedi and Danforth, 1966).

Other hormones also appear to influence Na^+-H^+ exchange activity. For example, when rats are adrenalectomized, Na^+-H^+ exchange activity as measured in isolated renal microvillus membrane vesicles is diminished compared to control rats (Freiberg et al., 1982). In these adrenalectomized rats, Na^+-H^+ exchange activity can be restored by the administration of dexamethasone but not aldosterone. Hence, it appears that glucocorticoids but not mineralocorticoids stimulate renal Na^+-H^+ exchange activity. That this effect can be demonstrated in isolated membrane vesicles studied in vitro indicates that there has been an intrinsic change in the number or activity of the Na^+-H^+ exchangers in the membrane

(Freiberg et al., 1982). Stimulation of renal Na^+-H^+ exchange by glucocorticoids may explain the effect of these hormones to augment renal acid excretion (Wilcox et al., 1982). Whether glucocorticoids stimulate Na^+-H^+ exchange in other target tissues or whether changes in pH_i are important for mediating the metabolic effects of glucocorticoids is not known.

Preliminary investigations also indicate an interaction between thyroid hormone and Na^+-H^+ exchange activity. Induction of a hypothyroid state with thiouracil in rats causes a decrease in renal brush border Na^+-H^+ exchange activity (Kinsella and Sacktor, 1984). As thyroid extract is given back to hypothyroid animals, a dose-related increase in renal Na^+-H^+ exchange is observed. A physiological correlation is suggested by the fact that hypothyroidism in the intact rat is associated with urinary sodium and bicarbonate wasting (Michael et al., 1979). Again, it is not known to what extent changes in Na^+-H^+ exchange and pH_i may be important for mediating the effects of thyroid hormone on other tissues.

It is interesting to note that the three hormones just discussed—insulin, glucocorticoids and thyroid hormone—all are known to enhance the specific activity of Na^+,K^+-ATPase in a variety of target tissues (Edelman, 1974; Asano et al., 1976; Resh et al., 1980; Kaji et al., 1981). The increased specific activity of Na^+,K^+-ATPase induced by mineralocorticoids in certain target tissues appears to be secondary to stimulation of Na^+ entry into the cell via an increased number of Na^+ channels (Marver, 1984). Analogously, it is possible that insulin, glucocorticoids, and thyroid hormone stimulate Na^+,K^+-ATPase activity secondary to increased Na^+ entry via Na^+-H^+ exchange.

In addition, at least one hormone has been described that inhibits Na^+-H^+ exchange activity. Renal membrane vesicles isolated from parathyroidectomized dogs have enhanced Na^+-H^+ exchange (Cohn et al., 1983), and parathyroid hormone inhibits Na^+-H^+ exchange and reduces pH_i in cultured renal cells (Pollock et al., 1984). Inhibition of Na^+-H^+ exchange may explain the ability of parathyroid hormone to reduce the rate of proximal tubular acidification (Iino and Burg, 1979). It is not known whether alterations in Na^+-H^+ exchange and pH_i result from the action of parathyroid hormone in other target tissues such as bone.

Finally, it has been reported that angiotensin peptides stimulate amiloride-sensitive Na^+ influx in vascular smooth muscle cells (Smith and Brock, 1983). The possibility that this may represent an activation of plasma membrane Na^+-H^+ exchange has not been examined.

Cell Volume Regulation

In the steady state, most cells appear to maintain their cell volume through primary active extrusion of Na^+ via the Na^+,K^+-ATPase system (MacKnight and Leaf, 1977). However, when cells are exposed to anisotonic media, ouabain- insensitive ion flux pathways are activated, which restore cell volume to original size within minutes (Kregenow, 1981; Spring and Ericson, 1982). Based on specific ionic requirements and inhibitor sensitivity, two types of electroneutral transport mechanisms have been proposed to mediate the regulatory volume increase that occurs after cell shrinkage in hyperosmotic media: (1) a Na^+-K^+-$2Cl^-$ cotransport system that is inhibited by loop diuretics such as furosemide (Kregenow, 1981); (2) an amiloride-sensitive Na^+-H^+ antiport system, which when activated in parallel with Cl^--HCO_3^- antiport, results in net cellular gain of Na^+, Cl^-, and H_2O. Activation of Na^+-H^+ exchange by cell shrinkage has been described in salamander and dog erythrocytes, and *Necturus* gallbladder (Cala, 1980; Ericson and Spring, 1982; Parker, 1983). For example, after *Amphiuma* erythrocytes shrink in hypertonic media, cell re-expansion occurs within 3 hours with a dramatic increase in Na^+ influx that is amiloride-sensitive, and accompanied by an increase in intracellular pH and a decrease in medium pH (Cala, 1980). Similar volume-responsive sodium and proton movements are observed in dog erythrocytes (Parker, 1983) and in human lymphocytes (Grinstein et al., 1983). The process of cell volume regulation by gallbladder epithelial cells in hypertonic media appears to be much the same, although actual H^+ fluxes have not been measured (Ericson and Spring, 1982).

What actually activates Na^+-H^+ exchange at the initiation of regulatory volume increase is an open question. Evidence has been presented that cell shrinkage per se is not the trigger (Cala, 1980; Spring and Ericson, 1982). Alternative proposals have included a shrinkage-associated fall in intracellular pH (Cala, 1980) and/or a change in intracellular Ca^{++} (Cala, 1983). However, affirmative data for either one of these mechanisms are lacking, and measurements in hypertonically shrunken lymphocytes have failed to show any significant shift in pH_i or in free cytoplasmic Ca^{++} (Grinstein et al., 1983).

Transepithelial Ion Transport

Epithelial cells mediate the net transport of solutes and water from one extracellular compartment to another, and thereby play a determining role in the ionic composition and volume of extracellular fluids. Although the involvement of Na^+-H^+ exchange in transepithelial fluxes of Na^+ and H^+ would seem most obvious, this transport system also indirectly but importantly contributes to the transport of Cl^- and organic anions in several epithelia.

Studies both in isolated membranes vesicles (Murer et al., 1976; Kinsella and Aronson, 1980) and in isolated perfused tubules (Boron and Boulpaep, 1983) have clearly demonstrated the presence of Na^+-H^+ exchange across the luminal membrane of the renal proximal tubular cell. In the amphibian (Boron and Boulpaep, 1983), but not the mammalian proximal tubule (Ives et al., 1983b; Sabolic and Burckhardt, 1983), Na^+-H^+ exchange also occurs in the basolateral membrane. Along the mammalian proximal tubule, over 90% of the filtered bicarbonate load is reabsorbed and a lumen-acid transtubular pH gradient is generated. The role of luminal membrane Na^+-H^+ exchange in facilitating the process of H^+ secretion and HCO_3^- absorption along the mammalian proximal tubule is illustrated in Figure 3A. The "primary active" transport of Na^+ across the basolateral membrane via the Na,K-ATPase generates an inward electrochemical gradient for Na^+ across the luminal membrane. This Na^+ gradient then serves as the driving force for secondary active H^+ secretion via the Na^+-H^+ exchanger. Normally, luminal HCO_3^- acts as the principal acceptor for secreted H^+, with its eventual disappearance after conversion of H_2CO_3 to CO_2 and H_2O, a reaction catalyzed by carbonic anhydrase. The intracellular OH^- generated by H^+ secretion combines with CO_2 to form intracellular HCO_3^-, another reaction catalyzed by carbonic anhydrase. Thus, the net effect of active H^+ secretion by the Na^+-H^+ exchanger is to cause the intracellular accumulation of HCO_3^- against its electrochemical gradient. Hence, there is a large passive driving force for the exit of HCO_3^- across the basolateral membrane of the cell. As recently reviewed elsewhere, current evidence suggests that at least 80% of active H^+ secretion and HCO_3^- reabsorption in the proximal tubule takes place via the luminal membrane Na^+-H^+ exchanger (Aronson, 1983).

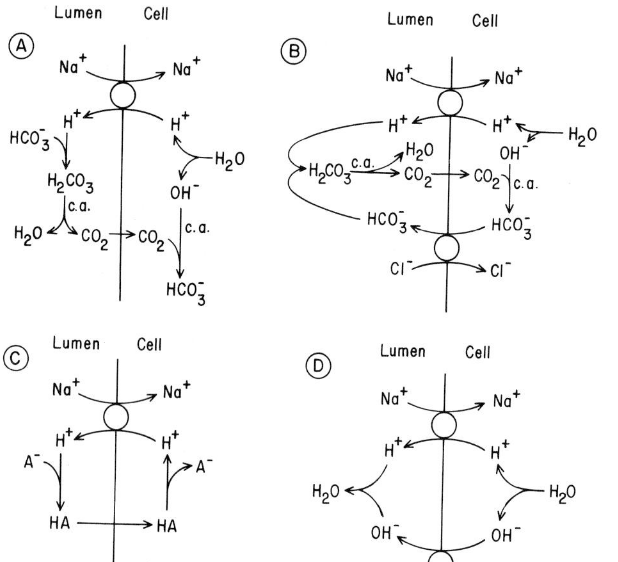

FIGURE 3. *Role of the Na^+-H^+ exchanger in facilitating active transport of HCO_3^- (part A), Cl^- (part B), and organic anions (parts C and D). See text for details. Abbreviations: c.a., carbonic anhydrase.*

The presence of luminal membrane Na^+-H^+ exchange has also been clearly demonstrated in the small intestine (Murer et al., 1976; Gunther and Wright, 1983; Knichelbein et al., 1983) and gall bladder (Weinman and Reuss, 1982). There is acidification of the luminal fluid in both the jejunum (Turnberg et al., 1970) and gall bladder (Whitlock and Wheeler, 1969). Thus, the model shown in Figure 3A is probably applicable to the process of H^+ secretion in these epithelia as well.

In other epithelia, such as pancreas (Swanson and Solomon, 1975) and choroid plexus (Wright, 1977), there is net secretion of HCO_3^-. In these cases, there is probably Na^+-H^+ exchange across the basolateral membrane of the cell and downhill exit of HCO_3^- across the luminal membrane.

When a Cl^--OH^- (or HCO_3^-) exchange system is present, Na^+-H^+ exchange can promote active transepithelial transport of Cl^-. For example, Figure 3B illustrates the case in which both Na^+-H^+ and Cl^--HCO_3^- exchangers are present on the luminal membrane of an epithelial cell. In this scheme, secondary active H^+ secretion via Na^+-H^+ exchange is driven by the luminal membrane Na^+ gradient and serves to maintain intracellular OH^- above the concentration at which it would be in electrochemical equilibrium across the luminal membrane. In the presence of CO_2, intracellular HCO_3^- is generated from OH^-, a reaction accelerated by carbonic anhydrase. The resulting electrochemical HCO_3^- gradient from cell to lumen then drives Cl^- uptake across the luminal membrane by Cl^--HCO_3^- exchange. Such tertiary active Cl^- accumulation elevates the intracellular Cl^- concentration above equilibrium so that there is a favorable driving force for passive Cl^- exit across the basolateral membrane. The simultaneous presence of Na^+-H^+ and Cl^--OH^- exchangers on the same membrane was first shown by Liedtke and Hopfer (1982) using luminal membrane vesicles from rat small intestine. Na^+-H^+ and Cl^--OH^- (or HCO_3^-) exchangers have subsequently been demonstrated in luminal membrane vesicles isolated from Necturus proximal tubule (Seifter and Aronson, 1984) and from rabbit ileum (Knickelbein et al., 1983), but not from rabbit or rat jejunum (Gunther and Wright, 1983; Cassano et al., 1984). Stimulation of Cl^- uptake by H^+ gradients has been observed in luminal membrane vesicles isolated from the rabbit proximal tubule, a finding interpreted to indicate the presence of Cl^--OH^- exchange in this preparation (Warnock and Yee, 1981). However, when adequate precautions are taken to avoid electrical coupling of Cl^- and H^+ fluxes through independent conductive pathways, actual Cl^--OH^- exchange cannot be documented in rabbit or rat renal microvillus membranes (Seifter et al., 1984; Sabolic and Burckhardt, 1983). Similarly, studies on the intact proximal tubule of the rabbit have failed to demonstrate measurable Cl^--OH^- exchange across the luminal membrane (Schwartz, 1983; Sasaki et al., 1984). Experiments employing ion-specific microelectrodes have documented the simultaneous presence of Na^+-H^+ and Cl^--OH^- (or HCO_3^-) exchangers in the apical membrane of the *Necturus* gall bladder (Reuss 1984), but there is dispute as to whether these exchangers contribute the major fraction of NaCl entry under basal conditions (Reuss 1984) or only during cell volume regulation (Ericson and Spring, 1982). Simultaneous Na^+-H^+ and Cl^--HCO_3^- exchange probably also occurs across the apical membrane of the mouse renal cortical thick ascending limb of Henle, although this has not yet been directly demonstrated (Friedman and Andreoli, 1982).

Clearly, double ion exchange is a commonly found but not ubiquitous mechanism for mediating Na^+-coupled Cl^- transport in diverse epithelia. It is interesting to note that in many of the epithelia in which this mechanism is found, such as the gall bladder, ileum, and renal cortical thick ascending limb, Na^+-coupled Cl^- transport is stimulated by CO_2 and is sensitive to inhibitors of carbonic anhydrase (Fisher et al., 1981; Heintze et al., 1981; Nellans et al., 1975; Friedman and Andreoli, 1982). These characteristics probably arise from the fact that at physiological pH values, Cl^- exchanges with HCO_3^- much more rapidly than with OH^- (Seifter and Aronson, 1984; Knicklebein et al., 1984). Thus, the generation of HCO_3^- from intracellular OH^- (Fig. 3B) may, under certain conditions, be rate-limiting for Na^+-coupled Cl^- transport occurring by the parallel operation of Na^+-H^+ and Cl^--HCO_3^- exchangers.

There are at least two mechanisms whereby Na^+-H^+ exchange can promote the transepithelial transport of organic anions. First, the processes of active H^+ secretion and HCO_3^- absorption resulting from luminal membrane Na^+-H^+ exchange can drive the net absorption of lipid-soluble weak acids that cross cell membranes predominantly by nonionic diffusion (Fig. 3C). This mechanism probably accounts for the absorption of organic anions such as glycodiazine, butyrate, propionate, and acetate in the mammalian proximal tubule (Ullrich et al., 1971). Similar mechanisms probably account for absorption of lipid-soluble weak acids in the jejunum (Jackson and Morgan, 1975) and for their secretion in the choroid plexus (Wright, 1977). A second mechanism for organic anion transport indirectly coupled to Na^+-H^+ exchange is shown in Figure 3D. In this case, the transport of organic anion across the luminal membrane occurs by a carrier-mediated process of OH^--anion exchange or H^+-anion cotransport. Such a mechanism probably contributes at least in part to urate reabsorption in the mammalian proximal tubule (Blomstedt and Aronson, 1980).

Pathophysiological Roles

To be sure, a clear-cut role for Na^+-H^+ exchange in any specific pathophysiological state is yet to be proved with certainty. Nevertheless, in view of the several important physiological roles of the plasma membrane Na^+-H^+ exchanger just discussed, it requires only a small leap of imagination to invoke a role for this transport system in various pathological states. A few examples will be described briefly.

Renal Acid-Base Disorders

As mentioned earlier, Na^+-H^+ exchange appears to be the principal mechanism for mediating H^+ secretion and HCO_3^- reabsorption in the proximal tubule. Factors affecting the number or activity of Na^+-H^+ exchangers in the proximal tubule may therefore influence the efficiency of reclamation of filtered bicarbonate, and may thereby contribute to determining the steady state concentration of plasma bicarbonate. For example, the elevated renal threshold for bicarbonate excretion during hypercapnia may result from the fact that elevating P_{CO_2} lowers intracellular pH (Struyvenberg et al., 1968), an effect leading to allosteric stimulation of the luminal membrane Na^+-H^+ exchanger by intracellular H^+ (Aronson et al., 1982). Another example is the increased number or activity of Na^+-H^+ exchangers in the luminal membranes of proximal tubular cells during potassium depletion (Seifter and Harris, 1984), an effect that may contribute to the maintenance of metabolic alkalosis in this disorder. Addi tional examples include the mild metabolic acidosis of hyperparathyroidism and the metabolic alkalosis of hyperglucocorticoid states. These two disorders may at least in part reflect the effects of parathyroid hormone and glucocorticoids to inhibit and stimulate, respectively, the number or activity of Na^+-H^+ exchangers in the luminal membrane of proximal tubular cells (Freiberg et al., 1982; Cohn et al., 1983).

Essential Hypertension

As recently reviewed elsewhere (Haddy, 1983; Parker and Berkowitz, 1983; Blaustein, 1984), several different alterations of transmembrane Na^+ transport in patients with hypertension have been described. One of the more consistent and reproducible findings has been an increased activity of the red cell transport system mediating Na^+-Li^+ exchange in certain subgroups of patients with essential hypertension and their first degree relatives (see Smith et al., 1984, for a comprehensive compilation of these data). Under physiological conditions in the absence of Li^+, the red cell Na^+-Li^+ exchanger mediates 1:1 Na^+-Na^+ exchange and, thus, has no impact on intracellular electrolyte content (Duhm and Becker, 1979). The role of abnormal Na^+-Li^+ countertransport in the pathogenesis of hypertension has therefore been obscure.

One possibility is that the transport system assayed for its Na^+-Li^+ exchange activity in red cells is really a Na^+-H^+ exchanger. As discussed above, the plasma membrane Na^+-H^+ exchanger has several features in common with the pathway mediating Na^+-Li^+ exchange in red cells, and Na^+-H^+ exchange has been demonstrated in human red cells

(Dissing and Hoffman, 1982).

Several mechanisms have been suggested by which increased activity of the plasma membrane Na^+-H^+ exchanger in cells other than erythrocytes could play a pathophysiological role in essential hypertension (Aronson, 1982; Funder et al., 1984). First, increased Na^+-H^+ exchange across the luminal membrane of cells in the proximal tubule or cortical thick ascending limb of Henle would tend to enhance Na^+ reabsorption and thereby cause a defect in renal salt excretion. By analogy with other abnormalities that tend to impair renal Na^+ excretion, such as chronic renal insufficiency or hyperaldosteronism, a defect of this type would require that the kidney be perfused at greater than normal arterial pressure in order to maintain salt balance (Guyton et al., 1974). In addition, the secondary release of natriuretic, digitalis-like, humoral factors could lead to an increase in peripheral vascular resistance (Hamlyn et al., 1982; Poston et al., 1982). In the steady state condition with sustained hypertension, "escape" from the primary defect in salt excretion would prevent a detectable increase in extracellular fluid volume. In addition, the expected tendency of augmented Na^+-H^+ exchange to generate metabolic alkalosis would be offset by inhibition of distal nephron H^+ secretion, which occurs by an ATP-driven H^+ pump, rather than by Na^+-H^+ exchange (Koeppen and Steinmetz, 1983). There is considerable evidence that a defect in renal salt excretion is a cause of essential hypertension in at least some patients (Haddy, 1980; de Wardener and MacGregor, 1982).

Increased activity of the plasma membrane Na^+-H^+ exchanger in vascular smooth muscle cells could alternatively play a pathophysiological role in essential hypertension. Blaustein (1977, 1984) has suggested that Na^+-Ca^{++} exchange across the plasma membrane is an important determinant of the steady state cytosolic concentration of Ca^{++} in vascular smooth muscle cells, and thus of steady state vessel wall tension. According to this view, any factor that elevates intracellular Na^+ will tend to elevate intracellular Ca^{++} and increase vascular tone. Thus, increased activity of the Na^+-H^+ exchanger in vascular smooth muscle could cause an elevated peripheral resistance by virtue of a rise in intracellular Na^+. In addition, it is likely that vascular tone is sensitive to changes in intracellular pH. For example, in a variety of vascular beds, hypercapnia induces vasodilation, probably secondary to a fall in intracellular pH (Shepherd, 1983). Thus, increased activity of the Na^+-H^+ exchanger in vascular smooth muscle might also lead to an elevated peripheral resistance by virtue of a rise in intracellular pH.

Cancer

As outlined previously, activation of plasma membrane Na^+-H^+ exchange is an early event in the response of cells to mitogenic growth factors. One such mitogenic substance known to activate Na^+-H^+ exchange is platelet-derived growth factor (PDGF) (Burns and Rozengurt, 1983; Cassel et al., 1983). PDGF-like molecules are produced by a number of transformed cell lines, including naturally occurring human tumors (Bowen-Pope et al., 1984). Moreover, the oncogene product of the simian sarcoma virus is extensively homologous with PDGF (Waterfield et al., 1983). Tumor promotors such as phorbol esters have been recently found to stimulate plasma membrane Na^+-H^+ exchange (Burns and Rozengurt, 1983). Thus, it appears likely that activation of plasma membrane Na^+-H^+ exchange plays an important part in oncogenic transformation.

Activation of plasma membrane Na^+-H^+ exchange could explain the high rates of lactic acid production by malignant tumors, as first described by Warburg 60 years ago. Glycolysis is limited by the availability of inorganic phosphate and adenosine diphosphate (ADP), and thus, by the rate of breakdown of adenosine triphosphate (ATP) to ADP and P_i by cellular ATPases (Racker, 1983). The increased Na^+ influx associated with enhanced Na^+-H^+ exchange in transformed cells could therefore promote glycolysis by stimulating the Na^+,K^+-ATPase, which is highly sensitive to changes in intracellular Na^+ concentration (Smith and Rozengurt, 1978). Furthermore, the elevation of intracellular pH resulting from activation of Na^+-H^+ exchange would also stimulate lactic acid production, inasmuch as the rate-limiting enzyme in glycolysis, phosphofructokinase, is extremely pH sensitive (Trivedi and Danforth, 1966).

Organ Growth and Hypertrophy

Another implication of the important role of Na^+-H^+ exchange in the response of cells to mitogenic stimuli is the possible involvement of this transport system in nonmalignant forms of cell growth and proliferation. For example, after loss of renal mass, the remaining renal tissue undergoes compensatory growth (Hayslett, 1979). Recent studies indicate that Na^+-H^+ exchange activity is enhanced in plasma membrane vesicles prepared from remnant renal tissue after renal ablation in the dog or rat (Cohn et al., 1982; Harris et al., 1984). Whether stimulation of Na^+-H^+ exchange is a general feature of such other examples of tissue growth and proliferation as cardiac or vascular smooth muscle hypertrophy remains to be examined. The possible effect of angiotensins to stimulate Na^+-H^+ exchange as noted earlier is of interest in this regard.

Conclusions

The plasma membrane Na^+-H^+ exchanger is a ubiquitous transport system that participates in diverse cell functions involving extrusion of H^+ from the cell or uptake of Na^+. Intracellular pH is probably the most important physiological factor regulating the Na^+-H^+ exchanger, a property that enables the antiporter to play a critical role in the regulation of intracellular pH. As a consequence of this role, the Na^+-H^+ exchanger functions as an important signal transducer for a broad spectrum of stimuli that alter cell function through changes in intracellular pH. As a transporter of Na^+, the antiporter participates in the regulation of cell volume. The plasma membrane Na^+-H^+ exchanger helps mediate the transport of not only Na^+ and H^+, but also Cl^- and organic anions across epithelia. The Na^+-H^+ exchanger thus plays a major role in determining the volume and ionic composition of the extracellular fluid and of various epithelial secretions.

Given the diversity of its physiological functions, it would not be surprising if the Na^+-H^+ exchanger participated in pathophysiological processes, as well. Very preliminary evidence raises the possibility that this may indeed be the case. Disorders of whole body acid-base balance have traditionally been considered to fall within the domain of nephrology. Clearly, the study of acid-base homeostasis at the cellular level is of great relevance to all disciplines. It is not altogether unreasonable to suggest that pharmacological manipulation of plasma membrane Na^+-H^+ exchange activity may eventually find clinical use in the treatment of a spectrum of diseases ranging from cancer to hypertension.

The excellent secretarial assistance of Carol Robinson is gratefully acknowledged. Critical review of the manuscript by F. Gregory Grillo and Peter Igarashi is also appreciated.

Support was provided by U.S. Public Health Service Grants AM-17433 and AM-33793, and an Established Investigatorship from the American Heart Association (P.S.A.).

Address for reprints: Peter S. Aronson, M.D., Department of Physiology, Yale University School of Medicine, 333 Cedar Street, New Haven, Connecticut 06510.

References

Abercrombie RF, Putnam RW, Roos A (1983) The intracellular pH of frog skeletal muscle: Its regulation in isotonic solutions. J Physiol (Lond) **345:** 175–187

Aickin CC, Thomas RC (1977) An investigation of the ionic mechanism of intracellular pH regulation in mouse soleus muscle fibers. J Physiol (Lond) **273:** 295–316

Aronson PS (1982) Red-cell sodium-lithium countertransport and essential hypertension. N Engl J Med **307:** 317

Aronson PS (1983) Mechanisms of active H^+ secretion in the proximal tubule. Am J Physiol **245:** F647–F659

Aronson PS (1985) Kinetic properties of the plasma membrane Na^+-H^+ exchanger. Annu Rev Physiol **47:** 545–560

Aronson PS, Nee J, Suhm MA (1982) Modifier role of internal H^+ in activating the Na-H exchanger in renal microvillus membrane vesicles. Nature **299:** 161–163

Aronson PS, Suhm MA, Nee J (1983) Interaction of external H^+ with Na-H exchanger in renal microvillus membrane vesicles. J Biol Chem **258:** 6767–6771

Asano Y, Liberman UA, Edelman IS (1976) Relationships between Na^+-dependent respiration and Na + K-adenosine triphosphatase activity in rat skeletal muscle. J Clin Invest **57:** 368–376

Balaban RS, Mandel LJ, Benos DJ (1979) On the cross-reactivity of amiloride and 2,4,6-triaminopyrimidine (TAP) for the cellular entry and tight junctional cation permeation pathways in epithelia. J Membr Biol **49:** 363–390

Benos DJ (1982) Amiloride: A molecular probe of sodium transport in tissues and cells. Am J Physiol **242:** C131–C145

Berridge MJ (1984) Inositol triphosphate and diacylglycerol as second messengers. Biochem J **220:** 345–360

Betz AL (1983) Sodium transport in capillaries isolated from rat brain. J Neurochem **41:** 1150–1157

Blaustein MP (1977) Sodium ions, calcium ions, blood pressure regulation, and hypertension: A reassessment and a hypothesis. Am J Physiol **232:** C165–C173

Blaustein MP (1984) Sodium transport and hypertension. Where are we going? Hypertension **6:** 445–453

Blomstedt JW, Aronson PS (1980) pH gradient-stimulated transport of urate and para-aminohippurate in dog renal microvillus membrane vesicles. J Clin Invest **65:** 931–934

Boron WF, Boulpaep EL (1983) Intracellular pH regulation in the renal proximal tubule of the salamander. Na-H exchange. J Gen Physiol **81:** 29–52

Boron WF, Russell JM (1983) Stoichiometry and ion dependencies of the intracellular pH regulating mechanism in squid giant axons. J Gen Physiol **81:** 373–399

Boron WF, McCormick WC, Roos A (1981) pH regulation in barnacle muscle fibers: Dependence on extracellular sodium and bicarbonate. Am J Physiol **240:** C80–C89

Bowen-Pope DF, Vogel A, Ross R (1984) Production of platelet-derived growth factor-like molecules and reduced expression of platelet-derived growth factor receptors accompany transformation by a wide spectrum of agents. Proc Natl Acad Sci USA **81:** 2396–2400

Burnham C, Munzesheimer C, Rabon E, Sachs G (1982) Ion pathways in renal brush border membranes. Biochim Biophys Acta **685:** 260–272

Burns CP, Rozengurt E (1983) Serum, platelet-derived growth factor, vasopressin and phorbol esters increase intracellular pH in Swiss 3T3 cells. Biochem Biophys Res Commun **116:** 931–938

Busa WB, Nuccitelli R (1984) Metabolic regulation via intracellular pH. Am J Physiol **246:** R409–R438

Cala PM (1980) Volume regulation by *Amphiuma* red blood cells. The membrane potential and its implications regarding the nature of ion flux pathways. J Gen Physiol **76:** 683–708

Cala PM (1983) Cell volume regulation by *Amphiuma* red blood cells. The role of Ca^{++} as a modulator of alkali metal/H^+ exchange. J Gen Physiol **82:** 761–784

Cassano G, Stieger B, Murer H (1984) Na/H- and Cl/OH-exchange in rat jejunal and rat proximal tubular brush border membrane vesicles. Pflugers Arch **400:** 309–317

Cassel D, Rothenberg P, Zhuang Y, Deuel TF, Glaser L (1983) Platelet-derived growth factor stimulates Na/H exchange and induces cytoplasmic alkalinization in NR6 cells. Proc Natl Acad Sci USA **80:** 6224–6228

Cohn DE, Hruska KA, Klahr S, Hammerman MR (1982) Increased Na-H exchange in brush border vesicles from dogs with renal failure. Am J Physiol **243:** F293–F299

Cohn DE, Klahr S, Hammerman MR (1983) Metabolic acidosis and parathyroidectomy increase Na-H exchange in brush border vesicles. Am J Physiol **245:** F217–F222

Deitmer JW, Ellis D (1980) Interaction between the regulation of the intracellular pH and sodium activity of sheep cardiac Purkinje fibers. J Physiol (Lond) **304:** 471–488

deWardener HE, MacGregor GA (1982) The natriuretic hormone and essential hypertension. Lancet **1:** 1450–1454

Dissing S, Hoffman JF (1982) Ouabain-insensitive Na efflux from human red blood cells stimulated by outside H, Na, or Li ions. J Gen Physiol **80:** 15a

Dubinsky WP Jr, Frizzell RA (1983) A novel effect of amiloride on H^+-dependent Na^+ transport. Am J Physiol **245:** C157–C159

Duhm J, Becker BF (1979) Studies on lithium transport across the red cell membrane. V. On the nature of the Na-dependent Li countertransport system of mammalian erythrocytes. J Membr Biol **51:** 263–286

Edelman IS (1974) Thyroid thermogenesis. N Engl J Med **290:** 1303–1308

Ellis D, Thomas RC (1976) Direct measurement of intracellular pH of mammalian cardiac muscle. J Physiol (Lond) **262:** 755–771

Ericson AC, Spring KR (1982) Volume regulation by *Necturus* gallbladder: Apical Na-H exchange and Cl-HCO_3 exchange. Am J Physiol **243:** C146–C150

Fidelman ML, Seeholzer SH, Walsh KB, Moore RD (1982) Intracellular pH mediates action of insulin on glycolysis in frog skeletal muscle. Am J Physiol **242:** C87–C93

Fisher RS, Persson B-E, Spring KR (1983) Epithelial cell volume regulation-bicarbonate dependence. Science **214:** 1357–1358

Freiberg JM, Kinsella J, Sacktor B (1982) Glucocorticoids increase the Na-H exchange and decrease the Na gradient dependent phosphate uptake systems in renal brush border membrane vesicles. Proc Natl Acad Sci USA **79:** 4932–4936

Frelin C, Vigne P, Lazdunski M (1983) The amiloride-sensitive Na^+/H^+ antiport in 3T3 fibroblasts. J Biol Chem **258:** 6272–6276

Friedman PA, Andreoli TE (1982) CO_2-stimulated NaCl absorption in the mouse renal cortical thick ascending limb of Henle. Evidence for synchronous Na/H and Cl/HCO_3 exchange in apical plasma membranes. J Gen Physiol **80:** 683–712

Funder J, Wieth JO, Jensen HE, Ibsen KK (1984) The sodium/lithium exchange mechanism in essential hypertension. Is it a sodium/proton exchanger? *In* Topics in Pathophysiology of Hypertension, edited by H Villarreal, MP Sambhi. Boston, Martinus Nijhoff, pp 147–161

Gerson DF, Kiefer H (1983) Intracellular pH and the cell cycle of mitogen-stimulated murine lymphocytes. J Cell Physiol **114:** 132–136

Gerson DF, Kiefer H, Eufe W (1982) Intracellular pH of mitogen-stimulated lymphocytes. Science **216:** 1009–1010

Greenberg-Sepersky SM, Simons ER (1984) Cation gradient dependence of the steps in thrombin stimulation of human platelets. J Biol Chem **259:** 1502–1508

Grillo FG, Aronson PS (1983) Inactivation of the renal Na-H exchanger by histidine-specific reagents (abstr). J Gen Physiol **82:** 27a

Grinstein S, Clarke CA, Rothstein A (1983) Activation of Na/H exchange in lymphocytes by osmotically induced volume changes and by cytoplasmic acidification. J Gen Physiol **82:** 619–638

Grinstein S, Cohen S, Rothstein A (1984) Cytoplasmic pH regulation in thymic lymphocytes by an amiloride-sensitive Na^+-H^+ antiport. J Gen Physiol **83:** 341–369

Gunther RD, Wright EM (1983) Na^+, Li^+, and Cl^- transport by brush border membranes from rabbit jejunum. J Membr Biol **74:** 85–94

Guyton AC, Coleman TG, Cowley AW Jr, Manning RD Jr, Norman RA Jr, Ferguson JD (1974) A systems analysis approach to understanding long-range arterial blood pressure control and hypertension. Circ Res **35:** 159–176

Haddy FJ (1980) Mechanism, prevention and therapy of sodium-dependent hypertension. Am J Med **69:** 746–758

Haddy FJ (1983) Abnormalities of membrane transport in hypertension. Hypertension **5** (suppl V): V66–V72

Halperin ML, Connors HP, Relman AS, Karnovsky ML (1969) Factors that control the effect of glycolysis in leukocytes. J Biol Chem **244:** 384–390

Hamlyn JM, Ringel R, Schaeffer J, Levinson PD, Hamilton BP, Kowarski AA, Blaustein MP (1982) A circulating inhibitor of (Na+K)ATPase associated with essential hypertension. Nature **300:** 650–652

Harris RC, Seifter JL, Brenner BM (1984) Uninephrectomy and dietary protein excess enhance Na-H exchange in rat renal brush border membrane vesicles. Kidney Int **25:** 302

Hayslett JP (1979) Functional adaptation to reduction in renal mass. Physiol Rev **59:** 137–164

Heikkila R, Iversen JG, Godol T (1983) Amiloride inhibits anti-Ig induction of proliferation in a human B-lymphoma cell population. Exp Cell Res **149:** 299–302

Heintze K, Peterson KU, Wood JR (1981) Effects of bicarbonate on fluid and electrolyte transport by guinea pig and rabbit gallbladder: Stimulation of absorption. J Membr Biol **62:** 175–181

Horne WC, Norman NE, Schwartz DB, Simons ER (1981) Changes in cytoplasmic pH and in membrane potential in thrombin stimulated human platelets. Eur J Biochem **120:** 295–302

Iino Y, Burg MB (1979) Effects of parathyroid hormone on bicarbonate absorption by proximal tubules in vitro. Am J Physiol **236:** F387–F391

Ives HE, Yee VJ, Warnock DG (1983a) Mixed type inhibition of the renal Na/H antiporter by Li and amiloride. J Biol Chem **258:** 9710–9716

Ives HE, Yee VJ, Warnock DG (1983b) Asymmetric distribution of the Na^+-H^+ antiporter in the renal proximal tubule epithelial cell. J Biol Chem **258:** 13513–13516

Jackson MJ, Morgan BN (1975) Relations of weak electrolyte transport and acid-base metabolism in rat small intestine in vitro. Am J Physiol **228:** 482–487

Kaibuchi K, Takai Y, Sawamura M, Hoshijima M, Kujikara T, Nishizuka Y (1983) Synergistic functions of protein phosphorylation and calcium mobilization in platelet activation. J Biol Chem **258:** 6701–6704

Kaji DM, Thakkar U, Kahn T (1981) Glucocorticoid-induced alterations in the sodium-potassium pump of the human erythrocyte. J Clin Invest **68:** 422–430

Kinsella JL, Aronson PS (1980) Properties of the Na-H exchanger in renal microvillus membrane vesicles. Am J Physiol **238:** F461–F469

Kinsella JL, Aronson PS (1981a) Interaction of NH_4 and Li with the renal microvillus membrane Na-H exchanger. Am J Physiol **241:** C220–C226

Kinsella JL, Aronson PS (1981b) Amiloride inhibition of the Na-H exchanger in renal microvillus membrane vesicles. Am J Physiol **241:** F374–F379

Kinsella JL, Aronson PS (1982) Determination of the coupling ratio for Na-H exchange in renal microvillus membrane vesicles. Biochim Biophys Acta **689:** 161–164

Kinsella JL, Sacktor B (1984) Thyroid hormones affect Na^+-H^+ exchange and Na-phosphate (P_i) co-transport in renal brush border membrane vesicles (abstr). Fed Proc **43:** 633

Knickelbein R, Aronson PS, Atherton W, Dobbins JW (1983) Sodium and chloride transport across rabbit ileal brush border. I. Evidence for Na-H exchange. Am J Physiol **245:** G504–G510

Knickelbein R, Aronson PS, Schron CM, Dobbins JW (1984) Na and Cl transport across rabbit ileal brush border: Mechanism of coupling (abstr). Fed Proc **43:** 299

Koch KS, Leffert HL (1979) Increased sodium ion flux is necessary to initiate rat hepatocyte proliferation. Cell **18:** 153–163

Koeppen BM, Steinmetz PR (1983) Basic mechanisms of urinary acidification. Med Clin N Am **67:** 753–770

Korchak HM, Vienne K, Rutherford LE, Wilkenfeld C, Finkelstein MC, Weissman G (1984) Stimulus response coupling in the human neutrophil. II. Temporal analysis of changes in cytosolic calcium and calcium efflux. J Biol Chem **259:** 4076–4082

Kregenow FM (1981) Osmoregulatory salt transporting mechanisms: Control of cell volume in anistonic media. Annu Rev Physiol **43:** 493–505

L'Allemain G, Paris S, Pouyssegur J (1984) Growth factor action and intracellular pH regulation in fibroblasts. Evidence for a major role of the Na/H antiport. J Biol Chem **259:** 5809–5815

Lee HC, Johnson C, Epel D (1983) Changes in internal pH associated with initiation of motility and acrosome reaction of sea urchin sperm. Dev Biol **95:** 31–45

Leffert HL, Koch KS, Fehlmann M, Keiser W, Lad PJ, Skelly H (1982) Amiloride blocks cell-free protein synthesis at levels attained inside cultured rat hepatocytes. Biochem Biophys Res Commun **108:** 738–745

Liedkte CM, Hopfer U (1982) Mechanism of Cl^- translocation across small intestinal brush-border membrane. II. Demonstration of Cl-OH exchange and Cl conductance. Am J Physiol **242:** G272–G280

MacKnight ADC, Leaf A (1977) Regulation of cellular volume. Physiol Rev **57:** 510–573

Marver D (1984) Evidence of corticosteroid action along the nephron. Am J Physiol **246:** F111–F123

Michael UF, Kelley J, Vaamonde CA (1979) Impaired renal bicarbonate reabsorption in the hypothyroid rat. Am J Physiol **236:** F536–F540

Mix LL, Dinerstein RJ, Villereal ML (1984) Mitogens and melittin stimulate an increase in intracellular free calcium concentration in human fibroblasts. Biochem Biophys Res Commun **119:** 69–75

Molski TFP, Naccache PH, Borgeat P, Sha'afi RI (1981) Similarities in the mechanisms by which formyl-methionyl-leucyl-phenylalanine, arachidonic acid, and leukotriene B_4 increase calcium and sodium influxes in rabbit neutrophils. Biochem Biophys Res Commun **103:** 227–232

Moody WJ Jr (1981) The ionic mechanism of intracellular pH regulation in crayfish neurones. J Physiol (Lond) **316:** 293–308

Moolenaar WH, Mummery CL, Van der Saag PT, de Laat SW (1981a) Rapid ionic events and the initiation of growth in serum-stimulated neuroblastoma cells. Cell **23:** 789–798

Moolenaar WH, Boonstra J,van der Saag PT, de Laat SW (1981b) Sodium/proton exchange in mouse neuroblastoma cells. J Biol Chem **256:** 12883–12887

Moolenaar WH, Yarden Y, de Laat SW, Schlessinger J (1982) Epidermal growth factor induces electrically silent Na^+ influx in human fibroblasts. J Biol Chem **257:** 8502–8506

Moolenaar WH, Tsien RY, Van der Saag PT, de Laat SW (1983) Na^+/H^+ exchange and cytoplasmic pH in the action of growth factors in human fibroblasts. Nature **304:** 645–648

Moolenaar WH, Tertoolen LGJ, de Laat SW (1984) Phorbol ester and diacylglycerol mimic growth factors in raising cytoplasmic pH. Nature **312:** 371–374

Moore RD (1981) Stimulation of Na:H exchange by insulin. Biophys J **33:** 203–210

Murer H, Hopfer U, Kinne R (1976) Sodium/proton antiport in brush border membrane vesicles isolated from rat small intestine and kidney. Biochem J **154:** 597–604

Naccache PH, Showell HJ, Becker EL, Sha'afi RI (1977a) Transport of sodium, potassium, and calcium across rabbit polymorphonuclear leukocyte membranes: Effect of chemotactic factor. J Cell Biol **73:** 428

Naccache PH, Showell HJ, Becker EL, Sha'afi RI (1977b) Changes in ionic movements across rabbit polymorphonuclear leukocyte membranes during lysosomal enzyme release. J Cell Biol **75:** 635–649

Nellans HN, Frizzell RA, Schultz SG (1975) Effect of acetazolamide on sodium and chloride transport by in vitro rabbit ileum. Am J Physiol **228:** 1808–1814

Nuccitelli R, Deamer DW (1982) Intracellular pH: Its Measurement, Regulation, and Utilization in Cellular Functions. New York, Alan R Liss Inc.

Owen NE, Villereal ML (1982a) Evidence for a role of calmodulin in serum stimulation of Na^+ influx in human fibroblasts. Proc Natl Acad Sci USA **79:** 3537–3541

Owen NE, Villereal ML (1982b) Effect of the intracellular Ca^{2+} antagonist TMB-8 on serum stimulated Na influx in human fibroblasts. Biochem Biophys Res Commun **109:** 762–768

Paris S, Pouyssegur J (1983) Biochemical characterization of the amiloride-sensitive Na^+/H^+ antiport in Chinese hamster lung fibroblasts. J Biol Chem **258:** 3503–3508

Parker JC (1983) Volume-responsive sodium movements in dog red blood cells. Am J Physiol **244:** C324–C330

Parker JC, Berkowitz LR (1983) Physiologically instructive genetic variants involving the human red cell membrane. Physiol Rev **63:** 261–313

Parker JC, Glosson PS (1984) Coupling of sodium extrusion to proton inflow in dog red blood cells (abstr). Fed Proc **43:** 1078

Piwnica-Worms D, Lieberman M (1983) Microfluorometric monitoring of pH_i in cultured heart cells: Na-H exchange. Am J Physiol **244:** C422–C428

Pollock AS, Strewler GJ, Warnock DG (1984) PTH decreases Na^+-H^+ antiporter activity in a cultured opossum kidney cell line (abstr). Clin Res **32:** 535A

Poston L, Sewell RB, Wilkinson SP, Richardson PJ, Williams R, Clarkson EM, MacGregor GA, de Wardener HE (1981) Evidence for a circulating sodium transport inhibitor in essential hypertension. Br Med J **282:** 847–849

Pouyssegur J, Chambard JC, Franchi A, Paris S, Van Obberghen-Schilling E (1982) Growth factor activation of an amiloride-sensitive Na^+/H^+ exchange system in quiescent fibroblasts: Coupling to ribosomal protein S6 phosphorylation. Proc Natl Acad Sci USA **79:** 3935–3939

Racker E (1983) Resolution and reconstitution of biological pathways from 1919 to 1984. Fed Proc **42:** 2899–2909

Resh MD, Nemenoff RA, Guidotti G (1980) Insulin stimulation of (Na,K)-adenosine triphosphatase-dependent $^{86}Rb^+$ uptake in rat adipocytes. J Biol Chem **255:** 10938–10945

Reuss L (1984) NaCl entry in Necturus gallbladder epithelium is mediated by Na/H and Cl/HCO_3 exchangers. Fed Proc **43:** 298

Rindler MJ, Saier MH Jr (1981) Evidence for Na/H antiport in cultured dog kidney cells (MDCK). J Biol Chem **256:** 10820–10825

Roos A, Boron WF (1978) Intracellular pH transients in rat diaphragm muscle measured with DMO. Am J Physiol **235:** C49–C54

Roos A, Boron WF (1981) Intracellular pH. Physiol Rev **61:** 296–434

Rosoff PM, Cantley LC (1983) Increasing the intracellular Na^+ concentration induces differentiation in a pre-B lymphocyte cell line. Proc Natl Acad Sci USA **80:** 7547–7550

Rothenberg P, Glaser L, Schlesinger P, Cassel D (1983) Activation of Na/H exchange by epidermal growth factor elevates intracellular pH in A431 cells. J Biol Chem **258:** 12644–12653

Rozengurt E, Mendoza S (1980) Monovalent ion fluxes and the control of cell proliferation in cultured fibroblasts. Ann NY Acad Sci **339:** 175–190

Sabolic I, Burckhardt G (1983) Proton pathways in rat renal brush-border and basolateral membranes. Biochim Biophys Acta **734:** 210–220

Sasaki S, Iino Y, Shiigai T, Takeuchi J (1984) Intracellular pH of isolated perfused rabbit proximal tubule: Effect of luminal Na and Cl. Kidney Int **25:** 282

Schuldiner S, Rozengurt E (1982) Na/H antiport in Swiss 3T3 cells: Mitogenic stimulation leads to cytoplasmic alkalinization. Proc Natl Acad Sci USA **79:** 7778–7782

Schwartz GJ (1983) Absence of Cl^--OH^- or Cl^--HCO_3^- exchange in the rabbit renal proximal tubule. Am J Physiol **245:** F462–F469

Seifter JL, Aronson PS (1984) Cl^- transport via anion exchange in *Necturus* renal microvillus membrane. Am J Physiol **247:** F888–F895

Seifter JL, Harris RC (1984) Chronic K depletion increases Na-H exchange in rat renal cortical brush-border membrane vesicles. Kidney Int **25:** 282

Seifter J, Knickelbein R, Aronson PS (1984) Absence of Cl-OH exchange and NaCl cotransport in rabbit renal microvillus membrane vesicles. Am J Physiol **247:** F753–F759

Shepherd JT (1983) Circulation to skeletal muscle. *In* Handbook of Physiology, sec II, vol III. Peripheral Circulation and Organ Blood Flow, part I, edited by JT Shepherd, FM Abboud. Washington, D.C., American Physiological Society, pp 319–370

Smith JB, Rozengurt E (1978) Serum stimulates the Na-K pump in quiescent fibroblasts by increasing Na entry. Proc Natl Acad Sci USA **75:** 5560–5564

Smith JB, Brock TA (1983) Analysis of angiotensin-stimulated sodium transport in cultured smooth muscle cells from rat aorta. J Cell Physiol **114:** 284–290.

Smith JB, Ash KO, Hunt SC, Hentschel MS, Sprowell W, Dadone MM, Williams RR (1984) Three red cell sodium transport systems in hypertensive and normotensive Utah adults. Hypertension **6:** 159–166

Soltoff SP, Mandel LJ (1983) Amiloride directly inhibits the Na,K-ATPase activity of rabbit kidney proximal tubules. Science **220:** 957–959

Spring KR, Ericson AC (1982) Epithelial cell volume modulation and regulation. J Membr Biol **69:** 167–176

Struyvenberg A, Morrison RD, Relman AS (1968) Acid-base

behavior of separated canine renal tubule cells. Am J Physiol **214:** 1155–1162
Swanson CH, Solomon AK (1975) Micropuncture analysis of the cellular mechanisms of electrolyte secretion by the in vitro rabbit pancreas. J Gen Physiol **65:** 22–45
Thomas RC (1977) The role of bicarbonate, chloride, and sodium ions in the regulation of intracellular pH in snail neurones. J Physiol (Lond) **273:** 317–338
Trivedi B, Danforth WH (1966) Effect of pH on the kinetics of frog muscle phosphofructokinase. J Biol Chem **241:** 4110–4114
Turnberg LA, Fordtran JS, Carter NW, Rector FC Jr (1970a) Mechanism of bicarbonate absorption and its relationship to sodium transport in the human jejunum. J Clin Invest **49:** 548–556
Turnberg LA, Bieberdorf FA, Morawski SG, Fordtran JS (1970b) Interrelationships of chloride, bicarbonate, sodium, and hydrogen transport in the human ileum. J Clin Invest **49:** 557–567
Ui M (1966) A role of phosphofructokinase in pH-dependent regulation of glycolysis. Biochim Biophys Acta **124:** 310–322
Ullrich KJ, Radtke HW, Rumrich G (1971) The role of bicarbonate and other buffers on isotonic fluid absorption in the proximal convolution of the rat kidney. Pflugers Arch **330:** 149–161
Vaughan-Jones RD (1979) Regulation of chloride in quiescent sheep heart Purkinje fibers studied using intracellular chloride and pH-sensitive microelectrodes. J Physiol (Lond) **295:** 111–137
Vigne P, Frelin C, Lazdunski M (1982) The amiloride sensitive Na/H exchange system in skeletal muscle cells in culture. J Biol Chem **257:** 9394–9400
Vigne P, Frelin C, Cragoe EJ Jr, Lazdunski M (1984) Structure-activity relationships of amiloride and certain of its analogues in relation to the blockade of the Na^+/H^+ exchange system. Mol Pharmacol **25:** 131–136
Villereal ML (1981) Sodium fluxes in human fibroblasts: Effect of serum, Ca^{++}, and amiloride. J Cell Physiol **107:** 359–369
Warnock DG, Yee VJ (1981) Chloride uptake by brush border membrane vesicles isolated from rabbit renal cortex: Coupling to proton gradients and K diffusion potentials. J Clin Invest **67:** 103–115
Waterfield MD, Scrace GT, Whittle N, Stroobant P, Johnsson A, Wasteson A, Westermark B, Heldin C-H, Huang JS, Deuel TF (1983) Platelet-derived growth factor is structurally related to the putative transforming protein p28 of simian sarcoma virus. Nature **304:** 35–39
Weinman SA, Reuss L (1982) Na^+-H^+ exchange at the apical membrane of *Necturus* gallbladder. Extracellular and intracellular pH studies. J Gen Physiol **80:** 299–321
Whitaker MJ, Steinhardt RA (1982) Ionic regulation of egg activation. Q Rev Biophys **15:** 593–666
Whitlock RT, Wheeler HO (1969) Hydrogen ion transport by isolated rabbit gallbladder. Am J Physiol **217:** 310–316
Wilcox CS, Cemerikic DA, Giebisch G (1982) Differential effects of acute mineralo- and glucocorticosteroid administration on renal acid elimination. Kidney Int **21:** 546–556
Winkler MM, Steinhardt RA, Grainger JL, Minning L (1980) Dual ionic controls for the activation of protein synthesis at fertilization. Nature **287:** 558–560
Wong PYD, Lee WM, Tsang AYF (1981) The effects of extracellular sodium on acid release and motility initiation in rat caudal epididymal spermatozoa in vitro. Exp Cell Res **131:** 97–104
Wright EM (1977) Effect of bicarbonate and other buffers on choroid plexus Na/K pump. Biochim Biophys Acta **468:** 486–489
Zetterberg A, Engström W (1981) Mitogenic effect of alkaline pH on quiescent serum-starved cells. Proc Natl Acad Sci USA **78:** 4334–4339

INDEX TERMS: Acid-base transport • Bicarbonate transport • Cell growth • Cell volume regulation • pH homeostasis • Stimulus-response coupling

CONTROVERSIES IN CARDIOVASCULAR RESEARCH

The following comments by Jos A.E. Spaan and by Francis J. Klocke et al. were invited in order to give each author the opportunity to respond to the alternate position in this controversy.

The Editor.

Response to the Article by Klocke et al. on *"Coronary Pressure-Flow Relationships: Controversial Issues and Probable Implications"* which appeared in *Circ. Res. 56: 310–323, 1985*

BOTH studies in the "Controversies" show that models play an important role in attempts to understand the physics of the coronary circulation. A model is a representation of and is supposed to be analogous to a different, more complex system. If the physics of the system is well understood and the boundary conditions are well defined, a model can be used as an analogous computer. Thus can the sailing characteristics of a mammoth tanker be designed by studies on a model no longer than a few meters. Unfortunately, in coronary physiology, there is as yet a dramatic lack in knowledge of anatomy and mechanical behavior of the microcirculation. Hence, models are used to test whether hypothetized mechanisms may indeed be operative at locations where observations are not yet possible. The chance that mechanisms are as hypothetized is greater, as more measured phenomena are being correctly described. Hence, an appraisal of these phenomena is important. In this respect, the two reviews are complementary.

To many researchers, but especially to clinicians, this discussion about models may seem very theoretical. However, the discussion has practical implications. This is clear from the different recommendations resulting from the two different papers in these "Controversies." According to the model based on intramyocardial compliance alone, the ratio between mean pressure and mean flow in the beating heart is an adequate index of vasomotor tone. If a waterfall element is thought to be essential, both the slope of the diastolic pressure-flow line and $P_{f=0}$ should be measured. In addition, a number of experimental requirements must be met.

Lumped Models

The models presented in both reviews are imperfect, in that they are discrete. Distributed quantities such as compliance are lumped into one or more capacitors. One has to be very careful with the physiological interpretation of model parameters estimated from fitting model equations to physiological data. In this context, I would like to point to a possible misinterpretation of the very valuable input impedance results of Klocke et al. The fit of the simple resistance-compliance model to the input impedance measured over a limited range of frequencies showed that vasodilation resulted in the increase of the compliance value. This could lead to the conclusion that the compliance per unit length decreases with increasing vascular tone. However, in the RC model, the distributed compliance is thought to be concentrated in one proximal compliance. Since the distributed resistance decreases with reduction of vascular tone, the vascular space represented by the lumped compliance may increase. Hence, even if compliance per unit length of all vessel types remain unaltered, the value of the lumped compliance would increase due to a reduction in resistance.

Nonlinearities and Time Constants

The study of the mechanics of the coronary circulation is hampered by nonlinearities. The nonlinear behavior of resistances and compliancies of the large and small coronary vessels has been emphasized in both reviews. As a result of these nonlinearities, a simplified model may be useful only under limited circumstances. Probably the "controversies" have been created by unjustified extrapolation from one set of experimental conditions to the other. In this respect, it is worth noting that Klocke et al. emphasized studies on the fully dilated coronary bed, whereas my own attention was directed primarily to autoregulation.

In the autoregulated coronary bed, the time constants for venous outflow and peripheral coronary pressure decay are of the order of seconds (Fig. 4 of my review). Hence, the constant-pressure technique for obtaining pressure-flow lines may be free of epicardial compliance effects, but steady state in the microcirculation and venes was not established in most, if any, studies on diastolic pressure flow lines in the autoregulated bed. Klocke and co-workers (1981) showed a measurement on the fully dilated bed (their Fig. 3) in which coronary flow was stable in about 0.5 second after a pressure step. A similar response has been shown by Dole et al. (1984).

(Because of the low $P_{f=0}$ value and large perfusion pressure before the pressure step, one has to assume that the coronary bed was dilated in that particular experiment.) As has been discussed in my review, this difference may be explained by higher resistance and compliance values in the autoregulated bed. However, the study by Downey et al. (1983) showed the presence of a time constant of 0.055, and a *possible* one of 3 seconds in the autoregulated heart. The first one is in agreement with the fast initial fall in the coronary peripheral pressure decay curve and the second one is in agreement with the microvascular time constant estimated from coronary venous flow curves.

Waterfall Pump Model

One has to admit that, under certain circumstances, arterial and venous flow may cease at an arterial venous pressure difference. Bellamy et al. (1984) have shown this for drastic interventions such as barium contracture and acetylcholine infusion in the isolated pig heart. The question is, however, whether such a situation occurs in a normal heart. From the steady state measurements of Figure 1 of the opposing paper, Klocke et al. show an intercept of 12 mm Hg. One has to note, however, that $P_{f=0}$ was obtained by extrapolation of the measured pressure-flow relation. Increased curvature at lower pressures could indicate that true $P_{f=0}$ may have been overestimated (Klocke et al., 1981). Great cardiac venous pressure has not been reported in Figure 1 but amounted to 6 mm Hg in Figure 3. In other words, the arteriovenous pressure difference at stopped flow in the fully dilated bed has come to less than 6 mm Hg.

One may wonder whether stopped flow pressure is identical to back pressure when blood is flowing (Burton, 1951; Dole et al., 1984). This is the assumption in the waterfall-pump model. Should a waterfall exist, waterfall pressure and/or anatomic location of the waterfall could be flow dependent. Especially the anatomic location deserves attention. Should back pressure to arterial flow equal $P_{f=0}$ then, judged by the value of $P_{f=0}$, the waterfall would be postcapillar in the fully dilated bed and precapillar in the autoregulated bed. At vasodilation, the anatomic location of the vascular collapse would move downstream from the arterioles to larger venules or venes. However, should the location of the hypothetical waterfall be able to migrate gradually from the arteriolar site to the veins, all types of vessels would be disposed to show the waterfall behavior at low intraluminal pressures. The ultimate consequence would be a bloodless microcirculation in the excised heart. This is not the case.

In their review, Klocke et al. acknowledge the growing evidence for the existence of a significant intramyocardial compliance. However, they uncouple its influence on coronary arterial pressure and flow by a waterfall mechanism. Because of the necessary introduction of the intramyocardial compliance in the model, it becomes very hard to prove that the high $P_{f=0}$ values in the autoregulated heart are due to a waterfall mechanism. It is required not only that $P_{f=0}$ be higher than right atrial pressure, but it must also be higher than intramyocardial blood pressure, which, in the model, is the pressure proximal to R_2 (Fig. 2 of opposing review). In the case of zero venous outflow, one may assume that intramyocardial blood pressure equals venous pressure. However, the time constant for coronary venous outflow in the autoregulated bed is in the order of 3 seconds. Hence, real steady state measurements require stabilization times of 6 or more seconds. The requirement of such a long stabilization time at constant vasomotor tone can never be met.

It is not clear how backflow is explained in the waterfall-pump model. Is this backflow due to a discharge of C_2 before the waterfall becomes active, or has the hydrodynamics of the waterfall element still to be defined? This is an important point. Figure 3 of the opposing review depicts backflow at constant arterial pressure just after the pressure step. Hence, some intramyocardial compliance must influence arterial flow within 0.2–0.4 second after the pressure step. It seems rational, therefore, to include an intramyocardial compliance just prior to the waterfall element.

Steady State Pressure Flow Lines

The upper curve in Figure 3 of the opposing paper is important in two respects. First, the data on the curve have been measured at true steady states. Second, the curve is clearly nonlinear at lower pressure. This is in contrast to the typical pressure-flow line in the arrested heart presented by Downey and Kirk (1975). In their study, the pressure-flow line was only curvilinear in the beating heart. This curvature was thought to be caused by a systolic waterfall pressure varying across the ventricular wall. One has to conclude that the linearity of their diastolic pressure-flow line was due to compensating effects. Now that the steady state diastolic pressure flow line appears to be curvilinear, important evidence needed for the systolic waterfall hypothesis has been eliminated.

Microvascular Studies and Lumped Models

It seems realistic to assume a gradual pressure decrease from arteries to arterioles (Lipowsky et al., 1978). It is important to note that local vessel collapse, required for a waterfall mechanism, has not been reported in studies on the microcirculation. In a study from Burton's group (Nichol et al., 1951), a report is given on observations in the microcirculation of the mesentery of the frog at pressures around arterial stopped flow pressure. They found continuation of movement of blood. Diameters of vessels were changing with, in general, the smaller vessels becoming thinner and the larger vessels thicker. They also reported: "though we were seldom fortunate enough to have the vessels which closed completely in the field of the microscope." Haack and Johnson (1983) reported a continuation of red cell motion in the microcirculation up to a minute after occlusion. Hence, "stopped flow" is an idealized situation that probably does not exist in the microcirculation. As long as blood moves through vessels, pressure differences across vessels will remain. The exchange of fluid between interstitial space and vascular space is mentioned only in passing in my review. It is not unlikely that transcapillary fluid transport plays a role in the phenomena discussed and in maintaining microvascular pressures at stopped arterial flow.

Since microvascular studies in the endocardium do not seem to be possible with the present techniques, we have to continue to use models in coronary research. For decades, models have been tested on pressure and flow measurements in the coronary artery alone. We should now move forward more carefully and validate our models on the basis of more extensive experimental information.

Address for reprints: Prof. Dr. Ir. J.A.E. Spaan, Laboratorium voor Fysiologie, Wassenaarseweg 62, P.O. Box 9604, 2300 RC Leiden, The Netherlands.

References

Bellamy RF, O'Benar JD (1984) Cessation of arterial and venous flow at a finite driving pressure in porcine coronary circulation. Am J Physiol **246:** H525–H531
Burton AC (1951) On the physical equilibrium of small blood vessels. Am J Physiol **164:** 319–329
Dole WP, Alexander GM, Campbell AB, Hixson EL, Bishop VS (1984) Interpretation and physiological significance of diastolic coronary artery pressure-flow relationship in the canine coronary bed. Circ Res **55:** 215–226
Downey JM, Kirk ES (1975) Inhibition of coronary blood flow by a vascular waterfall mechanism. Circ Res **36:** 753–760
Downey JM, Lee J, Chambers DE (1983) Location and magnitude of the coronary artery capacitance. *In* Mechanics of the Coronary Circulation, edited by RE Mates, RM Nerem, PD Stein. New York, American Society of Mechanical Engineers, pp 45–48
Haack DW, Johnson PC (1983) Blood flow in the microcirculation during acute arterial occlusion (abstr). Fed Proc **42:** 1001
Klocke FJ, Weinstein IR, Klocke JF, Ellis AK, Kraus DR, Mates RE, Canty JM, Anbar RD, Romanowski RR, Wallmeyer KW, Echt MP (1981) Zero-flow pressures and pressure-flow relationships during single long diastoles in the canine coronary bed before and during maximum vasodilation: Limited influence of capacitive efforts. J Clin Invest **68:** 970–980
Lipowsky HH, Kovalcheck S, Zweifach BW (1978) The distribution of blood rheological parameters in the microvasculature of cat mesentery. Circ Res **43:** 738–749
Nichol J, Girling F, Jerrard W, Claxton EB, Burton AC (1951) Fundamental instability of the small blood vessels and critical closing pressures in vascular beds. Am J Physiol **164:** 330–344

Jos A.E. Spaan
Departments of Physiology and Physiological Physics
Leiden University Medical Centre
Leiden
and of Mechanical Engineering
Delft University of Technology
Delft, The Netherlands

Response to the Article by Spaan on *"Coronary Diastolic Pressure-Flow Relation and Zero Flow Pressure Explained on the Basis of Intramyocardial Compliance"* which appeared in *Circ. Res. 56: 293–309, 1985*

DR. SPAAN provides an explanation for the observed diastolic pressure-flow behavior of the coronary circulation based on his model of an intramyocardial pump. We agree that the intramyocardial pump provides the most plausible explanation for the phasic pattern of coronary venous outflow, but question whether the model also suffices to explain diastolic inflow behavior.

The limited amount of experimental data available for the coronary circulation makes it necessary to employ relatively simple lumped parameter models when attempting to characterize its complex behavior. The inherent limitations of any such model hamper the evaluation of alternate explanations for experimental observations. Dr. Spaan has concentrated his modeling on the autoregulating coronary bed. His model presents difficulties in interpretation, since the time constant for autoregulation (Spaan and Laird, 1981) is apparently similar to the time constant for charging or discharging the intramyocardial capacitance. In studies of our own and others in the vasodilated bed, a constant inflow pressure has been used to separate resistive and reactive components of impedance. This procedure cannot be extended in a straightforward way to the autoregulating bed, even if inflow pressure is constant, because of time variations in resistance, capacitance, and probably $P_{f=0}$ as well.

As we understand Dr. Spaan's Appendix A, the "model" data in his Figure 7 are derived from an RCR simplification of the model shown in Figure 3, with ~2/3 of total coronary resistance being located upstream of the capacitive element. This characterization appears effectively to exclude the arterial-arteriolar capacitance demonstrated experimentally in the coronary bed (studies 1–5 in our Table 1 and the first two items in Dr. Spaan's Table 2). We also have reservation about the method of calculation and interpretation of "P_{cpi}" (Figs. 5 and 6). The monoexponential analysis of inflow pressure between 0.5 and 3 seconds neglects influences of slower components of the multiexponential decay following inflow occlusion in an autoregulating bed. Perhaps more importantly, we envision this pressure decay as being influenced by time- and pressure-dependent changes in resistance, capacitance and $P_{f=0}$.

We are surprised by the suggestion that the compliance of vasoconstricted arterial segments can be greater than that of vasodilated segments at the same pressure level. Our own experiments, as well as those of Lewi and Schaper (1971) and Downey et al. (1983) cited in our Table 1, suggest that capacitance is lower with tone present. We understand that panels B and C in Dr. Spaan's Figure 2 were obtained by differentiating the relationships between cross-sectional areas and external pressure in panel A. These relationships were themselves derived from measurements of circumference and tension (e.g., Fig. 5, Mulvany and Halpern, 1977). We have reservations about the appropriateness of the differentiation procedure for the activated (i.e., contracted) artery. In the study by Mulvany and Halpern (1977), tension-circumference data for the activated artery were obtained by stretching the passive artery to a given initial length and then exposing it isometrically to an activating solution. This procedure was repeated at different initial lengths to obtain the active tension-circumference relationship. It is not clear that the slope of an isometric relationship derived in this fashion is related to the compliance of the activated muscle. If one first activates a muscle, and then stretches it, the resulting tension-length curve will differ from the isometric relationship. Indeed, using a square-wave length perturbation, Mulvany and Halpern (1977) determined the dynamic stiffness, dT/dL, to be 56 $\Delta T_1/L_1$, where ΔT_1 is the active tension at length L_1. At any given length, this stiffness is considerably greater than the slope of the maximum measured tension-circumference relationship indicated by the data of Mulvany and Halpern (1977, Fig. 5).

Because presently available data do not allow unequivocal definition of the mechanisms underlying coronary pressure-flow behavior, Dr. Spaan's and our own models, as well as those proposed by other investigators, need to be evaluated in a variety of additional experimental circumstances. Dr. Spaan's theoretical and experimental contributions have importantly advanced the thinking and understanding of all of us working in the area. We look forward to continuing dialogue with him.

References

Downey JM, Lee J, Chambers DE (1983) Location and magnitude of the coronary artery capacitance. *In* Mechanics and Coronary Circulation, edited by ReMates, RM Nerem, PD Stein, New York, American Society of Mechanical Engineers, pp 45–48

Lewi PJ, Schaper WKA (1971) The estimation of coronary volume elasticity in the beating heart of the dog, Pflugers Arch **325:** 191–198

Mulvany MJ, Halpern W (1977) Contractile properties of small arterial resistance vessels in spontaneously hypertensive and normotensive rats. Circ Res **41:** 19–26

Spaan JAE, Laird J (1981) Coronary vasoconstriction in long diastoles (abstr). Circulation 64 (suppl IV): 39

Francis J. Klocke
Robert E. Mates
John M. Canty, Jr.
Avery K. Ellis

Hemodynamic Response to Normovolemic Polycythemia at Rest and during Exercise in Dogs

JoAnn Lindenfeld, John V. Weil, Victoria L. Travis, and Lawrence D. Horwitz
From the Division of Cardiology, University of Colorado Health Sciences Center, Denver, Colorado

SUMMARY. Very little is known about the influence of polycythemia on oxygen transport during exercise. We studied chronically instrumented dogs trained to run on a treadmill before and after their hematocrit had been increased by isolvolemic exchange transfusion with packed red blood cells. With normovolemic polycythemia, cardiac output fell in a linear fashion as hematocrit was increased to 65%, but these changes were balanced by an increasing oxygen content resulting in constant systemic oxygen transport. Oxgen consumption was unchanged both at rest and during exercise after induction of polycythemia. To investigate the effect of polycythemia on oxygen transport further, we measured both mixed venous Po_2 and lactate. Mixed venous Po_2 increased and lactate remained unchanged both at rest and in exercising polycythemic dogs. Thus, we conclude that, in conscious animals, systemic oxygen transport is well preserved with increasing hematocrit to at least 65%. **(*Circ Res 56: 793–800, 1985*)**

ALTHOUGH polycythemia is a fundamental mammalian response to hypoxemia, it has often been assumed to be detrimental. Whereas it would seem that the increased capacity of blood to carry oxygen might be useful, this may be negated by the fall in cardiac output which occurs with polycythemia. Indeed, previous studies in resting, anesthetized dogs concluded that systemic oxygen transport (cardiac output × oxygen content) is maximal at a normal hematocrit and falls with either anemia or polycythemia (Richardson and Guyton, 1959; Murray et al., 1962, 1963). The decreased systemic oxygen transport with polycythemia was due to a fall in cardiac output that exceeded the rise in oxygen content. The fall in cardiac output has been attributed to increased viscosity of the polycythemic blood which, in turn, could have increased vascular resistance and limited venous return (Guyton and Richardson, 1961). However, these studies were performed in barbiturate-anesthetized animals in which resting vascular resistances are abnormally high and reflexes blunted; both conditions might exaggerate the effects of viscosity. In addition, there are several reasons why polycythemia might not prove disadvantageous during exercise. Muscle pumps may overcome the effects of viscosity on venous return (Stegall, 1966), arterial vasodilation in exercising muscle might overcome the increased vascular resistance imposed by increased viscosity; and, finally, increased flow rates alone should decrease the effects of viscosity in both the venous and arterial beds (Whittaker and Winton, 1933). If so, polycythemia might not have a detrimental effect on systemic oxygen transport during exercise. Thus, we sought to determine the effects of polycythemia on systemic oxygen transport during exercise, using conscious, chronically instrumented dogs trained to run on a treadmill.

Methods

Surgical Techniques

In an initial series, 11 mongrel dogs weighing 22–37 kg were trained to run easily for several minutes on a level treadmill. Subsequently, a splenectomy was performed under sterile conditions, using halothane anesthesia to minimize large variations in hematocrit and blood volume in the dog (Barcroft and Florey, 1931; Vatner et al., 1974). The dogs were allowed to recover for a minimum of 7 days, after which each underwent a left thoracotomy with placement of 18-gauge polyvinyl catheters in the descending aorta, the main pulmonary artery, and the left atrium. A solid state pressure transducer (Konigsberg P 18) was placed through a stab incision in the apex of the left ventricle, and a Zepeda electromagnetic flow probe was placed around the ascending aorta. This surgery was followed by a recovery period of at least 2 weeks. Two days before each study, under light pentobarbital anesthesia, one external jugular vein was used to place a 14-gauge polyvinyl catheter used for infusion of packed red blood cells. All catheters were tunneled subcutaneously and exteriorized at the back of the neck.

Because high hematocrits could influence the accuracy of electromagnetic flow probe readings, in an additional eight dogs (24–36 kg), radioactive microspheres were used for study of cardiac output measurements. These dogs underwent the same surgical procedures, except the solid-state pressure transducer and flow probe were not placed during the thoracotomy.

Treadmill Training

Each dog was trained to run on a level treadmill at a speed between 5 and 9 miles/hr. No dog was run for more than 10 minutes, three times a week, to avoid conditioning effects.

Donor Blood

Blood was removed from anesthetized donor dogs via a 13-gauge steel needle placed in the apex of the left ventricle and drained into vacuum bottles containing either 5000 U of heparin or 60 ml of ACD for each 500 ml of whole blood and transferred to transfer packs and spun at 1200 *g* for 20 minutes to pack the red blood cells to a hematocrit of 75–80%. Donor blood was acquired within 24 hours of the study day and stored at 4°C in ACD. All packed blood cells were filtered through a blood filter prior to transfusion. Blood which demonstrated visible hemolysis was not used. Blood was warmed to body temperature just before transfusion. There was no evidence of major or minor transfusion reactions during these studies.

Hematocrit, Lactate, Blood Gases, and Oxygen Content

Hematocrits were drawn from the pulmonary artery catheter and were measured by the microhematocrit centrifuge method. No correction was made for trapped plasma. Blood lactate was measured by a standard technique (Henry, 1968). Blood gas tensions for oxygen, carbon dioxide, and measurement of pH were obtained using polarographic electrodes (Radiometer) calibrated against gases analyzed in our laboratory by the Scholander technique and against pH using glass electrodes calibrated with standard buffers. All blood gas values were corrected for temperature. Arterial oxygen content was measured with the Lex-O_2-Con device (Lexington Instruments) which, in our hands, agrees with Van Slyke measurements within 0.1 volume %.

Blood Volume

On the day before each study, 6 ml of whole blood were removed from each dog. Two milliliters of red blood cells were incubated with $Na_2{}^{51}CrO_4$ in N.I.H. A-ACD (ICSH panel) for 15 minutes at room temperature. The cells were washed three times in normal saline and rediluted in plasma to the original volume. After mixing, three small aliquots were taken to determine the total number of counts injected. The remaining blood was added to a preweighed syringe and reweighed to determine the total weight of the blood. The day of the study, we removed 2 ml of blood from the dog and determined its exact volume by using its weight and the specific gravity of blood at that hematocrit. Each sample was counted in a well-type γ-counter. Initial blood volume was then determined by the formula

$$\frac{\text{Total } ^{51}\text{Cr counts injected}}{\text{Blood volume}} = \frac{\text{counts per sample}}{\text{ml per sample}}.$$

Subsequent blood volumes were estimated by measuring all blood removed from the dog and counting aliquots of this blood to determine the total amount of ^{51}Cr removed. By knowing the total amount of ^{51}Cr injected initially and the amount removed, blood volume was determined at each level of the experiment without relabeling red blood cells by the formula

$$\frac{\text{Total } ^{51}\text{Cr counts remaining}}{\text{Blood volume}} = \frac{\text{counts/sample}}{\text{ml/sample}}.$$

To ensure further that normovolemia was maintained, all transfusions were isovolemic exchange transfusions, a method previously shown to maintain a constant blood volume (McGrath and Weil, 1978).

Cardiac Output and Pressure

In the dogs with electromagnetic flow probes stroke volume was calculated using the integral of the aortic flow signal (Horwitz, 1972). Cardiac output was determined by averaging stroke volume for at least six consecutive beats to reduce the effects of respiratory variation. Each electromagnetic flow probe was calibrated in vitro before insertion in each dog. Calibrations were made with normal saline at room temperature. Flow was assumed to be zero at end-diastole using an electromagnetic flowmeter (Zepeda, EDP2). We compared cardiac output obtained by electromagnetic flowmeter to those determined by microspheres over a hematocrit range of 35–66 and found the cardiac outputs by electromagnetic flow probe were not consistently different from those obtained by microsphere; thus, no correction was made for hematocrit.

All signals were recorded on an eight-channel Beckman dynagraph recorder. Mean arterial and left atrial pressures were measured through the implanted catheters with Statham P23Db manometers using the mid chest level as reference. Zero references were recorded both at rest and during exercise. Mean left atrial and aortic pressures were recorded continuously during exercise. A dose of 1 ml of 0.02% Tween-80 was injected before each study. If a reaction occurred, the studies were not begun for 30 minutes after heart rate and blood pressure had returned to normal.

In the microsphere studies, cardiac output was measured by microspheres, 15 ± 3 μm in diameter, (New England Nuclear) labeled with ^{46}Sc, ^{95}Nb, ^{103}Ru, ^{113}Sn, ^{51}Cr, and ^{153}Gd. The microspheres were suspended in 10% dextran and 0.02% Tween 80. At rest, after a steady withdrawal of blood was established from the descending aortic catheter with a Cole-Parmer Masterflex pump set at a single constant flow rate between 7 and 10 ml/min, microspheres were injected through the left atrial catheter, followed by a 7-ml flush of normal saline. Each injection contained 2–5 × 10^6 microspheres, depending on the activity of the nuclide. Arterial blood was collected directly into preweighed counting tubes. This collection of blood began 10 seconds before injection of microspheres and lasted for a total of 200 seconds. Before all injections, microspheres were continually agitated by vortex mixer for 1 minute. During exercise, two different microspheres were injected through the left atrial catheter, the first at approximately 3 minutes of exercise and the second microsphere 80 seconds later. Each injection was followed by a 7-ml flush of normal saline. Arterial blood was collected into counting tubes at a constant flow rate (7–10 ml/min) beginning 10 seconds before injection of the first microsphere and lasting for a total of 300 seconds. The interval for injection of the two microspheres was chosen to avoid overlap between the two microspheres. All cardiac output tubes were counted consecutively in a well-type γ-counter with appropriate energy levels for each nuclide. Each tube was counted for 4 minutes. Cardiac output was calculated by the formula:

$$CO = I(Qar/Iar),$$

where CO = cardiac output, I = total counts injected, Qar = the arterial withdrawal flow rate, and Iar = the total activity in the arterial sample collected (Archie et al., 1973; Fixler et al., 1976). "I" was calculated as the total counts in the preweighed microsphere syringe, minus the counts remaining in the syringe after injection. During exercise, the dogs continued to run at the same speed until the microspheres collections were completed. The two values for cardiac output during exercise showed no consistent or significant differences. Because they were obtained during steady state exercise, an average of the two values for cardiac output during exercise was used.

Study Design

In the group of 11 dogs in which cardiac output was measured by electromagnetic flow probe, hemodynamic measurements were made at rest and at 3 minutes of steady state exercise. Each dog was first studied at its baseline hematocrit, both at rest and during exercise. Isovolemic exchange transfusion then was performed, removing 200–400 ml of whole blood from the dog and replacing it with an equal volume of donor-packed red blood cells. Blood volume and hematocrit determinations were made at least one-half hour after each transfusion to assure normovolemia. At least 45 minutes after each transfusion, all measurements were repeated at rest, and exercise was again performed at precisely the same treadmill speed as during the control run. This procedure was repeated between four and six times on any one day at several levels of hematocrit. Exercise blood samples for arterial oxygen content, and for arterial and mixed venous Po_2, Pco_2, pH, and lactate were drawn within 15 seconds of the end of exercise. This protocol was so lengthy that we could not achieve high levels of hematocrit in a single day. Thus, in 4 of the 11 dogs, we studied only normal and very high hematocrits (64–70%). The dogs were studied at the initial hematocrit and then again after multiple exchange transfusions when the hematocrit reached at least 65%.

In the second group of eight dogs in which microspheres were used for cardiac output, the dogs were studied only at the normal hematocrit and then at a hematocrit of 64–70%. The study design differed in only two ways from the study done in animals with electromagnetic flow probes. Microspheres were injected for cardiac output measurements and blood samples for arterial oxygen content, arterial Po_2, Pco_2, pH, and for mixed venous oxygen content, and for mixed venous Po_2, Pco_2, and were drawn simultaneously after 3 minutes of exercise. The lactate samples (aorta, mixed venous) were drawn within 15 seconds of the end of exercise.

Control Studies

To control the effects of transfusion and time, and because of the nonrandom sequence of increasing hematocrits, we prepared three dogs as described above, including electromagnetic flow probes. All measurements were performed in the same way, and the study design was the same as described above. However, transfusions were different, in that 200–400 ml of whole blood were removed and an equal amount of donor *whole blood* was reinfused to keep both hematocrit and blood volume constant. Donor whole blood was first packed by centrifugation but then was resuspended in plasma to a normal hematocrit in these control studies to mimic exactly the blood preparation in the polycythemia studies.

Statistics

The group of 11 dogs studied with electromagnetic flow probes was divided into two groups for statistical analysis. Because each dog had different levels of hematocrit, in the group of seven animals studied at multiple hematocrits, each dog was tested for hematocrit effects, and the results were combined by a cumulative p-test (Fisher test) (Steel and Torie, 1960). For purposes of illustration, these dogs are grouped in hematocrit ranges of five points: that is, 35–40%, 40–45%, 45–50%, 50–55%, 55–60%. All dogs studied at only two hematocrit levels were analyzed by paired *t*-test (Steel and Torie, 1960).

In the eight dogs studied at two hematocrits, using cardiac output by radioactive microspheres, statistical analysis was performed by paired *t*-testing. The cumulative p-test (Fisher test) was used for evaluation of the control dogs.

Results

Heart Rate

No significant changes in heart rate were detected in dogs with polycythemia, at rest or during exercise, whether studied with electromagnetic flow probes (Fig. 1A) or radioactive microspheres (Fig. 1B).

Cardiac Output and Systemic Oxygen Transport

Cardiac output fell significantly in dogs with polycythemia both at rest and during exercise (Fig. 2). The fall in cardiac output occurred in a linear fashion as a function of hematocrit (Fig. 2A). Despite this fall in cardiac output, there were no significant changes in systemic oxygen transport (Fig. 3). Since heart rate did not change either at rest or during

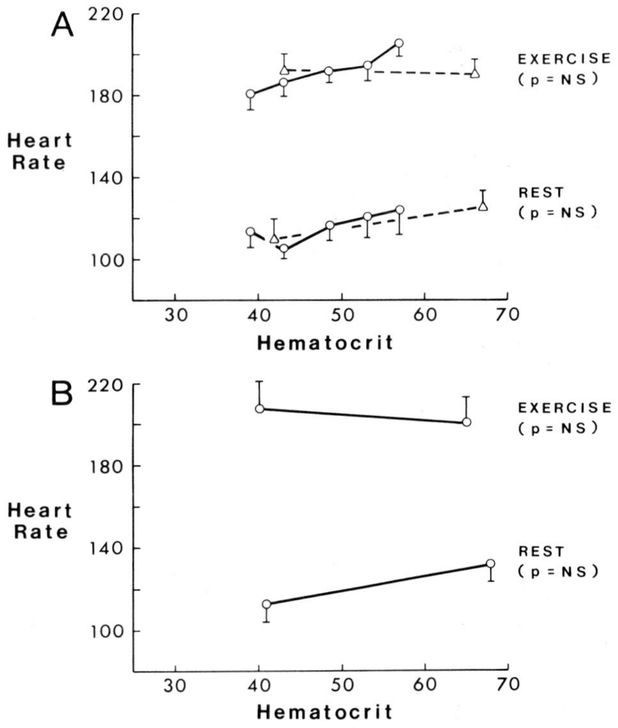

FIGURE 1. *Heart rate vs. hematocrit. Heart rate ± 1 SE (bar) as a function of hematocrit. Panel A is the group of 11 dogs with cardiac output measured by electromagnetic flow probe. (○ represents the seven dogs with sequential measurements. Δ represents four dogs studied only at normal and high hematocrits). Panel B is the group of eight dogs with cardiac output measured by radioactive microspheres.*

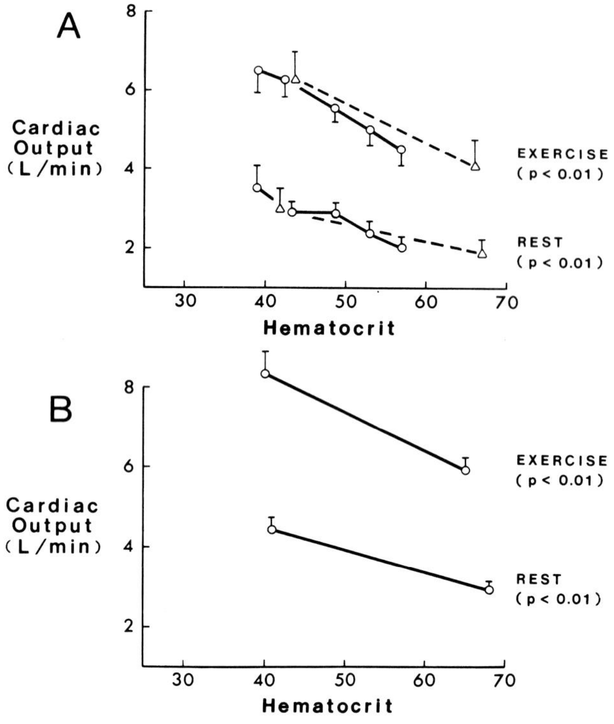

FIGURE 2. *Cardiac output vs. hematocrit. Cardiac output ± 1 SE (bar). See Figure 1.*

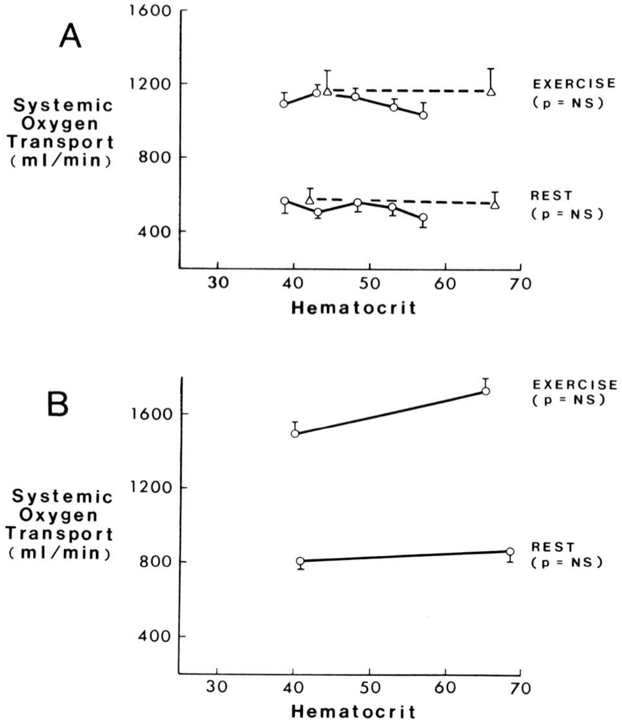

FIGURE 3. *Systemic oxygen transport vs. hematocrit. Systemic oxygen transport ± 1 SE (bar). See Figure 1.*

exercise, the fall in cardiac output in both groups of dogs was due entirely to a fall in stroke volume.

Arterial-Venous Oxygen Difference and Oxygen Consumption (Table 1)

Arterial-venous oxygen difference was measured in the group of eight dogs studied at two levels of hematocrit with radioactive microspheres. The arterial-venous oxygen difference increased after polycythemia, both at rest and during exercise, balancing the fall in cardiac output. There were no significant changes in oxygen consumption (AVO_2 difference × CO) with polycythemia.

Mean Arterial Pressure and Systemic Vascular Resistance

In the 11 dogs studied with electromagnetic flow probes, no significant changes were seen in mean aortic pressure with polycythemia (Fig. 4A). In the second group of dogs, there was a significant rise in aortic pressure only with exercise (Fig. 4B). Polycythemia led to a rise in systemic vascular resistance both at rest and during exercise (Fig. 5).

Mixed Venous Po_2 and Arterial and Mixed Venous Lactate (Table 2)

Mixed venous Po_2 levels were unchanged in the animals studied at several levels of hematocrit. However, in the two groups of dogs studied at just two levels of hematocrit, Po_2 levels in mixed venous blood were higher with polycythemia, both at rest and during exercise. Mixed venous Po_2 was lower during exercise than at rest ($P < 0.01$ for both control and polycythemia in all groups). Both arterial and mixed venous lactate levels were unaffected by polycythemia at rest or during exercise. Mixed venous and arterial lactate levels were not different at rest or with exercise. Resting lactates were significantly lower than exercise lactates before and after polycythemia ($P < 0.01$ in all groups).

Blood Volume

Blood volume as measured by ^{51}Cr labeling showed no significant changes in either of the groups of dogs studied with flow probes (1840 ± 135 vs. 1955 ± 173) or in the second group of dogs studied with microspheres (2153 ± 90 vs. 2240 ± 132) (mean ± SEM).

TABLE 1
Arterial-Venous Oxygen Difference and Oxygen Consumption

	Control	Polycythemia
AVO_2 difference (vol %)		
Rest	8.2 ± 0.4	10.5 ± 0.6*
Exercise	12.9 ± 0.4	17.0 ± 0.8†
O_2 consumption (ml/min)		
Rest	351 ± 23	295 ± 26
Exercise	1065 ± 89	997 ± 70

* $P < 0.05$.
† $P < 0.01$.

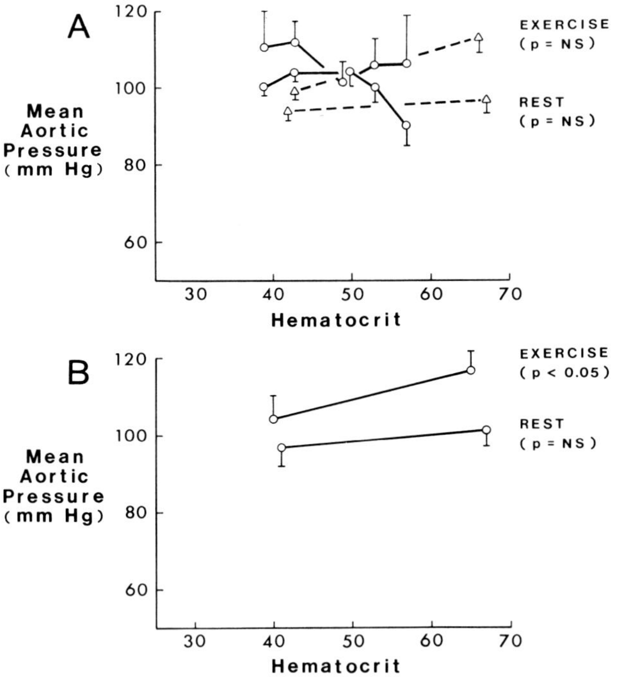

FIGURE 4. *Mean aortic pressure vs. hematocrit. Mean aortic pressure ± 1* SE *(bar). See Figure 1.*

Control Dogs (Table 3)

Three dogs underwent a control run followed by four exchange transfusions with whole blood leaving hematocrit unchanged. Cardiac output, measured by electromagnetic flow probe, did not increase in any animal.

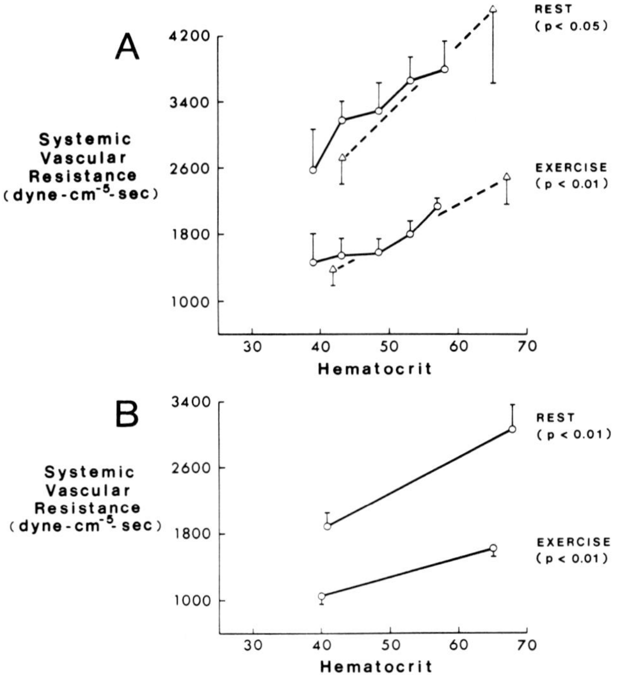

FIGURE 5. *Systemic vascular resistance vs. hematocrit. Systemic vascular resistance ± 1* SE *(bar). See Figure 1.*

Discussion

We found that acutely induced normovolemic polycythemia to hematocrits up to 68% caused to no decrement in systemic oxygen transport. Although cardiac output fell progressively with rising hematocrit, this was offset by comparable increases in oxygen content, and thus there was no change in systemic oxygen transport.

These results differ from most previous data, the bulk of which was collected in anesthetized dogs, and led to the conclusion that the optimal hematocrit for oxygen transport is the normal hematocrit, and that at higher hematocrits the fall in cardiac output leads to a fall in systemic oxygen transport (Richardson et al., 1959; Murray et al., 1963). Cardiac output fell much less with polycythemia in our study than in previous studies in anesthetized dogs. There are several possible reasons for this difference. In anesthetized, artificially ventilated animals, circulatory reflexes may be blunted or totally abolished (Kontos et al., 1965), and vascular resistance is often quite high (Murray et al., 1963). Thus, in previous studies, decreases in stroke volume with polycythemia may have been accentuated by the extremely high baseline systemic resistance. In many of these studies, only very high and very low hematocrit ranges were studied. Our particular interest was in hematocrits between 30% and 65%, a range that has not been carefully investigated. Others have speculated that the fall in cardiac output with polycythemia is due primarily to increased viscosity, leading to decreased venous return and, possibly, to an increased afterload (Guyton and Richardson, 1961). Viscosity does increase as hematocrit rises; however, several studies have shown that viscosity in vivo is lower than viscosity measured in vitro (Whittaker and Winton, 1933; Levy and Share, 1953; Djojosugito et al., 1970), and that the effects of hematocrit on viscosity are much less in vivo than in vitro. In particular, an elevation in hematocrit appears to have a negligible effect on in vivo viscosity in a vasodilated vascular bed in exercising muscle (Gustafsson et al., 1980). In the hematocrit range of our study (up to 68), in vivo viscosity changes are quite small (Whittaker and Winton, 1953; Gustafsson et al., 1980). In anesthetized animals with very high resting vascular resistances, viscosity may play a much more important role.

Only one previous study deals with polycythemia in the awake, exercising animal (Weisse et al., 1964). In that study, three dogs were studied during exercise—two had a fall in systemic oxygen transport with polycythemia and one had an increase. As in our study, these investigators found that the fall in cardiac output with polycythemia is much less in conscious animals than has been reported in anesthetized animals.

Normovolemia was maintained during this study because hypervolemia itself may increase cardiac output (Murray et al., 1963; Keroes et al., 1969).

TABLE 2
Mixed Venous Po_2 and Lactate

	Hematocrit				
	30–35	35–40	40–45	45–50	50–55
(n = 7)					
Mixed venous Po_2					
Rest	35 ± 3	34 ± 3	36 ± 1	35 ± 1	34 ± 3
Exercise	26 ± 2	28 ± 2	27 ± 1	28 ± 1	28 ± 2
Mixed venous lactate					
Rest	1.5 ± 0.4	1.4 ± 0.3	1.6 ± 0.2	1.6 ± 0.2	1.5 ± 0.2
Exercise	2.0 ± 0.3	1.8 ± 0.1	1.7 ± 0.2	1.7 ± 0.2	1.7 ± 0.3
		Control (Hct 42–43)		*Polycythemia (Hct 65–66)*	
(n = 4)					
Mixed venous Po_2					
Rest		38 ± 4		43 ± 3*	
Exercise		36 ± 2		38 ± 3*	
Mixed venous lactate					
Rest		1.0 ± 0.1		1.0 ± 0.2	
Exercise		1.7 ± 0.3		1.6 ± 0.3	
		Control (Hct 42–43)		*Polycythemia (Hct 65–68)*	
(n = 8)					
Mixed venous Po_2					
Rest		37 ± 2		42 ± 2†	
Exercise		30 ± 1		34 ± 1*	
Mixed venous lactate					
Rest		1.0 ± 0.1		0.9 ± 0.1	
Exercise		2.0 ± 0.6		1.7 ± 0.4	
Arterial lactate					
Rest		1.1 ± 0.1		0.9 ± 0.1	
Exercise		1.9 ± 0.5		1.8 ± 0.4	

* $P < 0.05$ compared to control.
† $P < 0.01$ compared to control.

Normovolemia was ensured by the process of isovolemic exchange transfusions (McGrath and Weil, 1978) and by blood volume measurements.

Systemic oxygen transport measures the amount of oxygen delivered to the body but may not indicate the adequacy of delivery relative to demand. To assess O_2 utilization, we measured Po_2 and lactate in the mixed venous blood. Mixed venous Po_2 was well preserved with rising hematocrit, and mixed venous lactate levels did not rise with induced polycythemia. Thus, it would appear that oxygen delivery to exercising muscle was intact during normovolemic polycythemia at this modest level of exercise.

Whether polycythemia improves exercise performance in humans has been the subject of several studies. The earliest studies concluded that both $\dot{V}O_{2max}$ and exercise capacity were improved one

TABLE 3
Hemodynamic Values in Three Dogs at Baseline and after Each of Four Exchange Transfusions

	Control	×1	×2	×3	×4
Cardiac output					
Rest	3.8 ± 0.3	3.2 ± 0.4	3.2 ± 0.7	3.2 ± 0.4	3.4 ± 0.7
Exercise	6.7 ± 1.1	6.3 ± 1.1	6.0 ± 1.1	6.4 ± 0.5	6.1 ± 0.9
Systemic oxygen transport					
Rest	61.3 ± 9	54.8 ± 1	56.7 ± 5	55.8 ± 3	57.4 ± 5
Exercise	111.7 ± 12	104.1 ± 13	105.0 ± 9	104.1 ± 7	101.3 ± 7

Values are expressed as a mean ± SE. 1×, 2×, 3×, 4× represent values after subsequent exchange transfusions. There are no significant differences.

day after reinfusion of autologous frozen red blood cells (Ekblom et al., 1972, 1976). These studies lacked control groups and blinded design. Subsequent studies (Videman and Rytomaa, 1977; Williams et al., 1978) reported that induced polycythemia ("blood doping") did not lead to significant improvements in exercise performance. However, these studies led to only very small changes in hemoglobin after blood reinfusion. Two recent studies with adequate controls suggest that polycythemia may indeed improve exercise performance. Horstman et al. (1980) used altitude to induce polycythemia in nine male volunteers and demonstrated an improved $\dot{V}O_{2max}$, systemic oxygen transport, and endurance time at high altitude, despite a fall in cardiac output. They concluded that polycythemia contributes to increased work capacity at high altitude. In another study of 11 highly trained runners, $\dot{V}O_{2max}$ and running time to exhaustion were significantly improved after infusion of 900 ml of autologous freeze-preserved red blood cells (Buick et al., 1980). No such improvements were seen in these same subjects before phlebotomy or with a sham infusion of 50 ml of saline. The results of both of these studies may have been influenced by an increase in total blood volume, so that it is difficult to separate the effects of an increase in hematocrit alone.

According to our results, for hematocrits as high as 68%, systemic oxygen transport is well preserved at rest and during exercise in spite of a lower cardiac output. The increase in mixed venous Po_2 following polycythemia supports the notion that systemic oxygen transport may actually improve. Our data are insufficient to determine whether or not there is an eventual fall-off in systemic oxygen transport when hematocrits are above 68%.

Our study fails to indicate the mechanism of the decrease in cardiac output with polycythemia. Previous investigators have suggested that increasing viscosity may be the cause (Guyton and Richardson, 1961). However, several factors suggest that this is not the case. Myocardial performance does not appear to be altered with polycythemia, and tachycardia is typically absent in polycythemia, suggesting that the cardiac output is not working with either a preload deficiency or an afterload burden (Horstman et al., 1980). Mean arterial pressures remain relatively constant at both rest and exercise, a finding described in previous studies (Weisse et al., 1966). Systemic oxygen transport also appears to be remarkably constant with increasing hematocrit. A major question remains as to whether it is homeostasis of mean arterial pressure, systemic oxygen transport, a combination of these, or a factor previously undefined, which modulates cardiac output with polycythemia.

We acknowledge the valuable technical assistance of Stephen Bell, Holly Coller, Jane Smoak, Eva Toyos, Rosann McCullough, and Laurie Fullerton, and thank Carole Becker for her careful preparation of the manuscript.

Supported by National Heart, Lung, and Blood Institute Grants HL 24763 and HL 14985.

Address for reprints: Dr. JoAnn Lindenfeld, Division of Cardiology, B-130, University of Colorado Health Sciences Center, 4200 East Ninth Avenue, Denver, Colorado 80262.

Received July 1, 1983; received in revised form October 29, 1984; accepted for publication January 31, 1985.

References

Archie JP Jr, Fixler DE, Ullyot DJ et al. (1973) Measurement of cardiac output with end organ trapping of radioactive microspheres. J Appl Physiol **35:** 148–154

Barcroft J, Florey H (1929) The effects of exercise on the vascular conditions in the spleen and the colon. J Physiol (Lond) **68:** 181–189

Buckberg GD, Luck JC, Payne DP, Hoffman JIE, Archie JP, Fixler DE (1971) Some sources of error in measuring regional blood flow with radioactive microspheres. J Appl Physiol **31:** 598–604

Buick FJ, Gledhill N, Froese AB et al. (1980) Effect of induced erythrocythemia on aeorbic work capacity. J Appl Physiol **48:** 636–642

Djojosugito AM, Folkow B, Oberg B, White SW (1970) A comparison of blood viscosity measured in vitro and in a vascular bed. Act Physiol Scand **78:** 70–84

Ekblom B, Goldbarg AN, Gullbring B (1972) Response to exercise after blood loss and reinfusion. J Appl Physiol **33:** 175–180

Ekblom B, Wilson G, Astrand PO (1980) Central circulation during exercise after venesection and reinfusion of red blood cells. J Appl Physiol **40:** 636–642

Fixler DE, Atkins JM, Mitchell J, Horwitz LD (1976) Blood flow to respiratory, cardiac and limb muscles in dogs during graded exercise. Am J Physiol **231:** 1515–1519

Gustafsson L, Appelgren L, Myrvold HE (1980) The effect of polycythemia on blood flow in working and non-working skeletal muscle. Acta Physiol Scand **109:** 143–148

Guyton AC, Richardson TQ (1961) Effect of hematocrit on venous return. Circ Res **9:** 157–164

Henry RJ (1968) Clinical Chemistry: Principles and Techniques. New York, Harper and Row, pp 664–666

Heymann MA, Payne BD, Hoffman JIE, Rudolph AM (1977) Blood flow measurements with radionuclide-labeled particles. Prog Cardiovasc Dis **20:** 55–79

Horstman D, Weiskopf R, Jackson RE (1980) Work capacity during a 3-week sojurn at 4,300 m: Effects of relative polycythemia. J Appl Physiol **49:** 311–318

Horwitz LD, Atkins JM, Leskin SJ (1972) Role of the Frank-Starling mechanism in exercise. Circ Research **31:** 868–875

International Committee for Standardization in Haematology (ICSH) (1971) Recommended methods for radioisotope red-cell survival studies. Br J Haematol **21:** 241–250

Keroes J, Ecker RR, Rapaport E (1969) Ventricular function curves in the exercising dog. Circ Res **25:** 557–567

Kontos HA, Mauck HP Jr, Richardson DW, Patterson JL Jr (1965) Mechanisms of circulatory responses to systemic hypoxia in the anesthetized dog. Am J Physiol **209:** 397–403

Levy ML, Share L (1953) The influence of erythrocyte concentration upon pressure-flow relationships in the dog's hind limb. Circ Res **1:** 247–255

McGrath RL, Weil JV (1978) Adverse effects of normovolemic polycythemia and hypoxia on hemodynamics in the dog. Circ Res **43:** 795–798

Murray JF, Gold P, Johnson BL Jr (1962) Systemic oxygen transport in induced normovolemic anemia and polycythemia. Am J Physiol **203:** 720–724

Murray JF, Gold P, Johnson BL Jr (1963) The circulatory effects of hematocrit variations in normovolemic and hypervolemic dogs. J Clin Invest **42:** 1150–1159

Richardson TQ, Guyton AC (1959) Effects of polycythemia and anemia on cardiac output and other circulatory factors. Am J Physiol **197:** 1167–1170

Steel RGD, Torrie JH (1960a) Principles and Procedures of Statistics. New York, McGraw-Hill, pp 350–351

Steel RGD, Torrie JH (1960b) Principles and Procedures of Statistics. New York, McGraw-Hill, pp 57–63

Stegall HF (1966) Muscle pumping in the dependent dog. Circ Res **19:** 180–190

Vatner SF, Higgins CB, Millard RW, Franklin D (1974) Role of the spleen in the peripheral vascular response to severe exercise in untethered dogs. Cardiovasc Res **8:** 276–282

Videman T, Rytomaa T (1977) Effect of blood removal and autotransfusion on heart rate response to a submaximal workload. J Sports Med **17:** 387–390

Weisse AB, Calton FM, Kuida H, Hecht HH (1964) Hemodynamic effects of normovolemic polycythemia at rest and during exercise. Am J Physiol **207:** 1361–1366

Weisse AB, Regan TJ, Nadimi M, Hellems HK (1966) Late circulatory adjustments to acute normovolemic polycythemia. Am J Physiol **211:** 1413–1418

Whittaker SFR, Winton FR (1933) The apparent viscosity of blood flowing in the isolated hind limb of the dog and its variation with corpuscular concentration. J Physiol (Lond) **78:** 339–369

Williams MH, Lindhjem M, Schuster R (1978) The effect of blood infusion upon endurance capacity and ratings of perceived exertion. Med Sci Sports **10:** 113–118

Williams MH, Wesseldine S, Somma T, Schuster R (1981) The effect of induced erythrocythemia upon 5-mile treadmill run time. Med Sci Sports **13:** 169–175

INDEX TERMS: Polycythemia • Systemic oxygen transport • Exercise

Vascular and Adrenal Receptors for Atrial Natriuretic Factor in the Rat

Ernesto L. Schiffrin, Lynn Chartier, Gaétan Thibault, Jean St-Louis, Marc Cantin, and Jacques Genest

From the Clinical Research Institute of Montreal, Montreal, Quebec, Canada

SUMMARY. Previous studies have shown that atrial natriuretic factor, a powerful vasorelaxant of precontracted vessels, inhibits the secretion of aldosterone stimulated by angiotensin II, adrenocorticotropic hormone, and potassium. We now report the presence of specific binding sites for atrial natriuretic factor in rat blood vessels (mesenteric and renal arteries) and adrenal capsules. Radioiodinated synthetic atrial natriuretic factor bound to a single class of high-affinity (K_D = 0.1 nM) low-capacity receptors in a particulate fraction from blood vessels and adrenals. Unrelated peptides did not displace atrial natriuretic factor. Fragments of atrial natriuretic factor displaced the labeled ligand with decreasing potency after cleavage at the N-terminal. The cleavage of the C-terminal tyrosine did not decrease the potency of atrial natriuretic factor, but further cleavage at the C-terminal dramatically reduced the affinity of the resulting peptides. The potency of the atrial natriuretic factor fragments in the radioligand assay was in proportion to their potency to inhibit aldosterone secretion by isolated rat glomerulosa cells. Our results suggest that these binding sites mediate the biological actions of atrial natriuretic factor in blood vessels and the adrenal, and that both receptors have similar specificities. **(*Circ Res 56: 801–807, 1985*)**

ATRIAL natriuretic factor (ANF) is a peptide identified recently in the atria of rats (De Bold et al., 1981; De Bold, 1982; Garcia et al., 1982) and other species (De Bold and Salerno, 1983; Nemeh and Gilmore, 1983; Trippodo et al., 1983). ANF has been purified (Thibault et al., 1983; Grammer et al., 1983), sequenced (Flynn et al., 1983; Currie et al., 1984; Seidah et al., 1984; Misono et al., 1984) and the cDNA sequence of its precursor determined (Maki et al., 1984; Yamanaka et al., 1984; Zivin et al., 1984). Studies by Currie et al. (1983) and Grammer et al. (1983) demonstrated that ANF was a powerful vasorelaxant. Garcia et al. (1984) and Kleinert et al. (1984) found that ANF blocked the response of vascular strips to angiotensin II and norepinephrine. We therefore investigated the effects of ANF on the response of another target tissue of angiotensin II, the adrenal glomerulosa. We found that ANF blocked the stimulation of aldosterone secretion by angiotensin II in vitro (Chartier et al., 1984a) and in vivo in conscious rats (Chartier et al., 1984b). ANF also blocked the aldosterone response to adrenocorticotropic hormone (ACTH) and potassium in vitro (Chartier et al., 1984a, 1984b). Atarashi et al. (1984) simultaneously reported similar effects on aldosterone production with an atrial extract. Thus ANF is not a selective blocker of any of these agents, but rather probably interferes with a common mechanism involved in the smooth muscle response to angiotensin II and norepinephrine and in the adrenal response to angiotensin II, ACTH, and potassium. In view of these results, we attempted to determine ANF binding sites in the vasculature and the adrenal capsules of the rat (Schiffrin et al., 1984). Finally, since recent results suggest that ANF may act as a calcium channel blocker (Camargo et al., 1984), we tested the cross-competition of ANF and calcium antagonists (nitrendipine, nifedipine, and verapamil) for the putative binding sites.

Methods

Materials

The nomenclature of ANF peptides is based on the sequence of the propeptide containing 128 amino acids (without the signal peptide) deduced from the rat cDNA sequence (Maki et al., 1984; Yamanaka et al., 1984; Zivin et al., 1984). Synthetic ANF (Arg 101-Tyr 126), previously termed ANF 8-33 or ANF 48-73 based on the then known structure of the precursor peptides (Chartier et al., 1984; Thibault et al., 1984a), has the following amino acid sequence (Seidah et al., 1984).

```
                    105                 110
NH2-Arg-Arg-Ser-Ser-Cys-Phe-Gly-Gly-Arg-Ile-Asp-Arg-Ile-
                     |________________________
                                              |
-Gly-Ala-Gln-Ser-Gly-Leu-Gly-Cys-Asn-Ser-Phe-Arg-Tyr-COOH
 115                     120                 125
```

Synthetic ANF was a generous gift of Dr. R.F. Nutt of Merck, Sharp and Dohme Research Laboratories. Atriopeptin II (ANF 103–124), III (ANF 103–126) and human ANF (99–126) were purchased from Peninsula Laboratories. ANF (96–126) and ANF (54–126) were obtained from rat atria during purification of ANF (101–126) (Seidah et al., 1984; Thibault et al., 1984a). N-terminal truncated peptides were produced from synthetic ANF by Edman degradation (Thibault et al., 1984b). C-terminal truncated peptides were obtained by treatment with various carboxypeptidases (Thibault et al., 1984b). The natriuretic and relaxant properties of these peptides have been defined (Thibault et al., 1984b).

ACTH was adrenocorticotropin 1-24 (Cortrosyn, Organon). Human angiotensin II (AII) and (Arg^8) vasopressin (AVP) were purchased from Peninsula.

Iodination of Atrial Natriuretic Factor

Synthetic ANF was iodinated with iodine-125 by a modification (Gutkowska et al., 1984) of the chloramine-T method (Greenwood and Hunter, 1963). Separation of radiolabeled ANF from free iodine was by immunoaffinity chromatography (Gutkowska et al., 1984) followed by C-18 reverse phase high pressure liquid chromatography. Specific activity measured by radioreceptor assay and self-displacement was approximately 1200–1300 Ci/mmol. ANF was also iodinated with iodine-127 and purified identically to ^{125}I-ANF. The mass of ^{127}I-ANF was determined by aminoacid analysis. The biological properties of ANF iodinated with iodine-127 were tested on aldosterone production by adrenal glomerulosa cells, on the precontracted chick rectum (Currie et al., 1983), and the rabbit aorta (Garcia et al., 1984).

Preparation of Membranes

Sprague-Dawley rats weighing 300 g were killed by decapitation. The atria, ventricles, renal arteries, mesentery, and adrenals were processed for the binding studies. The mesenteric vascular bed was isolated as described (Schiffrin and Genest, 1983; Schiffrin et al., 1983). The adrenal capsules were separated by manual compression. The tissues were then immersed in 0.25 M sucrose solution, finely minced with scissors, homogenized in a Polytron (Kinematica; setting 8, 10 seconds twice). The homogenate was centrifuged at 1,500 *g* for 10 minutes at 4°C; the supernatant was decanted and recentrifuged. The final supernatant was filtered through cheesecloth, then centrifuged at 104,000 *g* for 30 minutes. The pellet was resuspended in a 0.05 M Tris-HCl buffer, pH 7.4, containing 120 mM NaCl, 5 mM $MgCl_2$, 0.5 mM phenyl methyl sulfonyl fluoride (PMSF), 0.1% bacitracin, and 1 μM aprotinin. Proteins were measured by the Coomassie blue method (Spector, 1978). Next, bovine serum albumin was added at a concentration of 0.2%, and the membranes were diluted to a protein concentration of 0.25 to 1 mg/ml in the Tris-HCl buffer containing 0.2% albumin ("assay buffer").

^{125}I-ANF Binding Assay

The binding assay used 30–50 pM of labeled ANF and 10^{-13} to 10^{-6} M unlabeled ANF in competition experiments. In saturation experiments, increasing concentrations of ^{125}I-ANF (6–200 pM) were used, and nonspecific binding was determined by incubation in the presence of 1 μM unlabeled ANF for each point of saturation-binding curves. Incubation was done with 25–100 μg of receptor protein per tube, at 4°C for 60 minutes, since a plateau is achieved after 30 minutes. All assays were performed in duplicate. Separation of bound and free radioactivities was achieved by rapid filtration through polyethyleneimine-treated Whatman GF/C filters (Bruns et al., 1983) soaked with 0.5 ml of "assay buffer." The filters were washed twice with 3 ml of 0.9% NaCl, then were allowed to dry and were counted in a Rackgamma LKB counter with 65% efficiency. In studies in which nifedipine was used, tubes were protected from light.

[^{3}H]Nitrendipine Binding Assay

This assay was identical to the ANF-binding assay, except that tubes were protected from light. The assay buffer contained 5 mM $CaCl_2$. [^{3}H]nitrendipine was bought from New England Nuclear (specific activity 79.5 Ci/mmol). Nifedipine was kindly provided by Dr. David Frankel of Miles Laboratories, Canada.

Aldosterone Production by Isolated Rat Adrenal Cells

Isolated rat adrenal glomerulosa cells were prepared according to a modification of a technique previously described (Schiffrin et al., 1981). Briefly, male Sprague-Dawley rats weighing 250 g were killed by decapitation, and the adrenal glands were immediately removed and dissected free of fat. Capsules were separated from fasciculata-reticularis by compression. The capsules were minced and incubated for 40 minutes at 37°C in medium 199 with Hanks' salts (Gibco) with sodium bicarbonate (0.35 g/liter) containing 80 μg/ml Dispase (Boehringer Mannheim), 3 μg/ml deoxyribonuclease I (Sigma Chemical Co.), 2 mg/ml collagenase type I (Sigma), and 2% bovine serum albumin. The cells were dispersed mechanically, filtered through a 100-μm Nitex nylon filter (Tetko) and centrifuged at 200 *g* for 2 minutes. The cells were resuspended in medium 199 and preincubated for 2 hours at 37°C in a Dubnoff metabolic shaker in an atmosphere of 95% O_2 and 5% CO_2. After centrifugation, they were resuspended in the same medium and incubated in the presence of the agents to be tested for 90 minutes. At the end of the incubation, the cell suspension was centrifuged and the supernatant was decanted into glass tubes and frozen at −20°C until assayed for aldosterone by radioimmunoassay (Schiffrin et al., 1981).

Analysis of Data

Binding data was analyzed by computer assisted nonlinear regression analysis using the LIGAND program (Munson and Rodbard, 1980) for determination of density and affinity of binding sites. The ALLFIT program (De Léan et al., 1979), based on the four-parameter logistic equation, was used to calculate the concentration of unlabeled ANF and related peptides inhibiting binding by 50% (IC_{50}) in competition experiments. The inhibition constant (K_I) was calculated according to the method of Cheng and Prusoff (1973): $K_I = IC_{50}/[1 + (\text{concentration of radioligand}/K_D \text{ radioligand})]$.

Results

Specific binding of ^{125}I-ANF was found in the vasculature (mesenteric and renal arteries) and the adrenal capsule of the rat (Fig. 1). Binding was saturable. A one-site model provided the best fit for the binding data. No statistically significant improvement of the fit was obtained with a two-site model. The density of binding sites (B_{max}) calculated from competition curves was 95 ± 7 fmol/mg protein with a K_D of 82 ± 7 pM in the mesenteric arteries ($n = 5$). In saturation experiments a B_{max} of 68 ± 22 fmol/mg protein ($n = 2$) and K_D of 73 ± 11 pM were found. In renal arteries, the B_{max} detected was 23 ± 5 fmol/mg protein with a dissociation constant of 184 ± 86 pM ($n = 5$). In adrenal capsules, the B_{max} in competition studies was 130 ± 22 fmol/mg, and

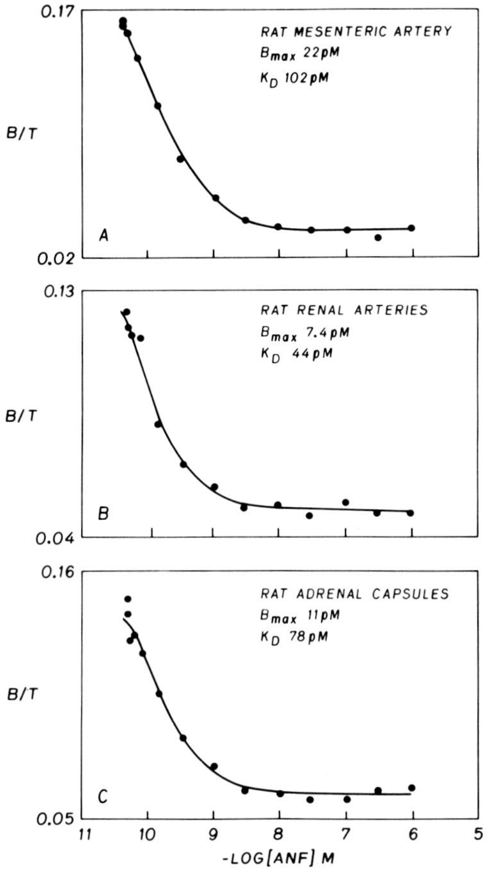

FIGURE 1. *Binding of ANF to membranes from rat mesenteric artery (panel A), renal arteries (panel B), and adrenal capsules (panel C). Binding of ^{125}I-ANF (50 pM) competing with unlabeled ANF is represented as bound/total vs. total ANF present (labeled plus unlabeled). Protein concentration was 0.25 to 1 mg/ml. Similar results were obtained in repeated experiments. B_{max} = density of binding sites. K_D = apparent equilibrium dissociation constant.*

the K_D was 107 ± 26 pM (n = 5). Saturation data showed a B_{max} of 90 ± 30 fmol/mg protein and K_D of 64 ± 5 pM (n = 5).

The similarity of data from competition and saturation experiments suggests that labeled and unlabeled ANF had similar behaviors in the binding assay. Indeed, we found that biological activity of ANF labeled with iodine-127 was conserved on the chick rectum and rabbit aorta by 70–100% (results not shown). On rat glomerulosa cells, ^{127}I-ANF was equipotent with unlabeled ANF in inhibiting basal aldosterone production (Fig. 2).

Binding of labeled ANF was also examined in membranes prepared from rat atria, ventricles, and decapsulated adrenals. Only in the decapsulated adrenals did specific binding occur, but affinity was one-thirtieth that in adrenal capsules.

Degradation of labeled ANF during incubation was examined by reverse phase high pressure liquid chromatography (HPLC) (Fig. 3). At 4°C and in the presence of bacitracin, PMSF, and aprotinin, more

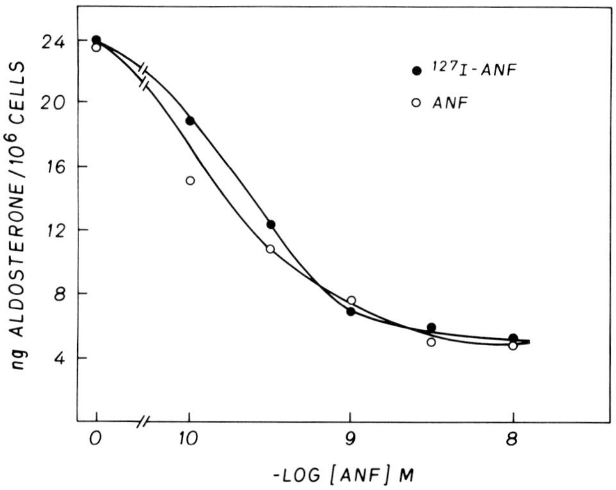

FIGURE 2. *Effect of synthetic unlabeled and ^{125}I-ANF on basal aldosterone production by rat adrenal glomerulosa cells.*

than 90% of the labeled peptide was intact after a 60-minute incubation with mesenteric or adrenal membranes. Ninety-two percent of labeled ANF incubated with adrenal membranes and separated by centrifugation was found to bind to these membranes on re-incubation, in agreement with the HPLC elution profile of labeled ANF after incubation (Fig. 3).

The specificity of binding to mesenteric and adrenal membranes was demonstrated by the absence of displacement of labeled ANF competing with unrelated peptides such as angiotensin II (AII), va-

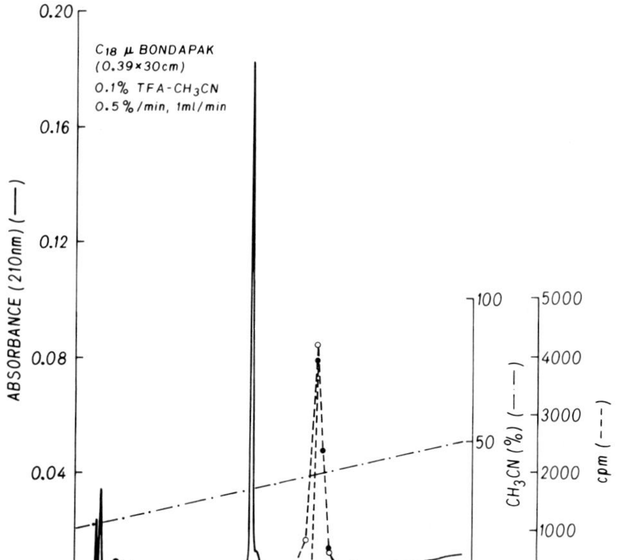

FIGURE 3. *Reverse phase high pressure liquid chromatography elution profile of unlabeled (continuous line) and labeled ANF, incubated (●) or not (○), with mesenteric artery membranes in the presence of protease inhibitors.*

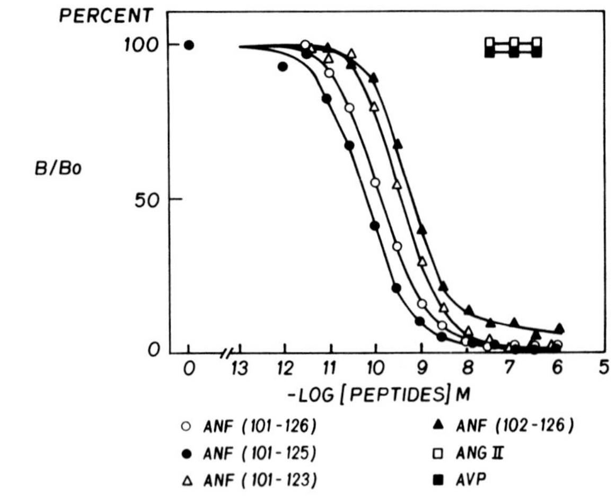

Figure 4. *Competition of unlabeled ANF, ANF fragments, and unrelated peptides with ^{125}I-ANF for binding to rat mesenteric artery. The concentration of ^{125}I-ANF was 0.05 nM and the protein concentration was 0.5 mg/ml. AII (ANG II) = angiotensin II, AVP = (Arg^8) vasopressin. Each point is the mean of 3–5 experiments.*

sopressin (AVP), or adrenocorticotropic hormone (ACTH) (10^{-7} to 10^{-6} M). ANF-related peptides displaced labeled ANF with varying affinity (Fig. 4; Table 1). The cleavage of the N-terminal arginine of synthetic ANF (101–126) resulted in a peptide (ANF 102–126) which was less potent both in the mesenteric artery and the adrenal preparation by a factor of 4. Loss of the second arginine at the N-terminal end (ANF 103–126 or atriopeptin III) resulted in a dramatic loss of activity, by a factor of 20 in both preparations. Further splitting at the N-terminal end resulted in slight or no further loss of potency. The C-terminal tyrosine was unimportant for binding

Table 1
Comparison of Potency of ANF Peptides in the Mesenteric and Adrenal Radioligand-Binding Assay

	K_I (pmol/liter)	
ANF peptides	Mesenteric artery	Adrenal capsules
rANF (101–126)	95	105
rANF (101–125)	50	70
rANF (101–124)	253	267
rANF (101–123)	268	262
rANF (101–121)	309	400
rANF (102–126)	395	529
rANF (103–126)	2022	2151
rANF (103–125)	1472	686
rANF (103–123)	882	1983
rANF (104–126)	745	595
rANF (105–126)	853	358
rANF (54–126)	89	71
rANF (96–126)	78	70
hANF (99–126)	123	129

rANF = rat ANF; hANF = human ANF. The concentration of ^{125}I-ANF was 0.05 nM. Results are means of 3–5 experiments. K_I was calculated according to the formula of Cheng and Prusoff (1973).

Table 2
Potency of ANF Peptides to Inhibit Aldosterone Production and Binding of Labeled ANF to Adrenal Membranes

ANF peptide	Aldosterone production (% of control)*	K_I (pmol/liter)
ANF (101–126)	26.6	105
ANF (101–125)	5.8	70
ANF (101–123)	49.0	262
ANF (103–123)	100.0	1983

* The concentration of ANF peptides was 1 nM.

and, if anything, affinity of the resulting ANF (101–125) was up to 50% higher. Further splitting at the C-terminal end produced a decrease in binding affinity. ANF (101–124), ANF (101–123), and ANF (101–121) were equipotent in both preparations, and about one-third as potent as ANF (101–126). Interestingly, human synthetic ANF (99–126) was slightly less potent in both preparations than the synthetic rat peptide. ANF (101–125) appears to contain the minimum core sequence active in these radioligand assays. The correlation coefficient of the K_I of these peptides in the mesenteric artery and adrenal capsule preparations was 0.93, suggesting that the adrenal and vascular receptors are identical.

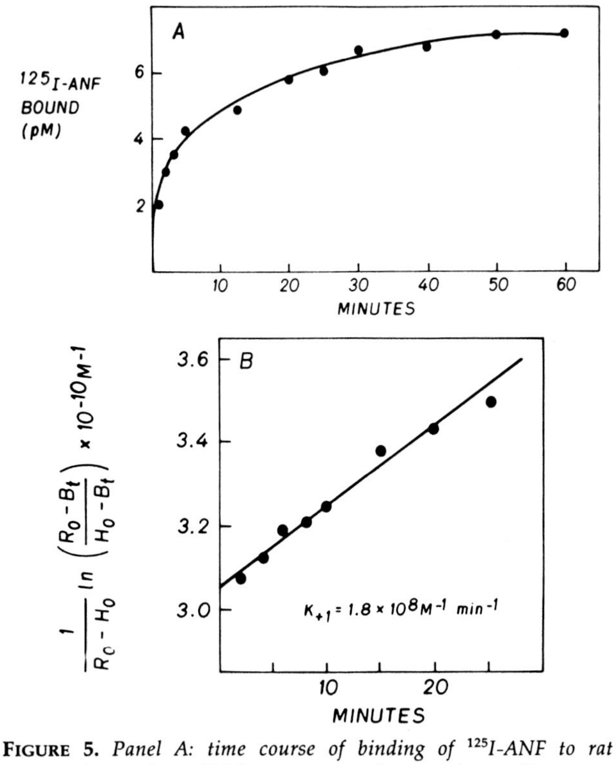

Figure 5. *Panel A: time course of binding of ^{125}I-ANF to rat mesenteric arteries at 4°C in a representative experiment. Concentration of ^{125}I-ANF was 0.07 nM with 0.5 mg/ml protein. Panel B: association rate constant for binding of ^{125}I-ANF to mesenteric artery membranes. The data from the experiment shown in panel A was fitted to the second-order rate equation to obtain K_{+1}. $R_o = B_{max}$ = density of binding sites determined in a simultaneous competition curve (14 pM). H_o = total hormone present. B_t = ANF bound at time (t). Similar results were found in two other experiments.*

The inhibitory potency of four of these peptides on basal aldosterone secretion agreed with the data from the radioligand-binding experiments on adrenal capsular particulate fraction, as shown in Table 2. This suggests that, indeed, these binding sites are involved in mediating the effects of ANF, at least on the adrenal glomerulosa.

The kinetics of binding of ANF were examined in association and dissociation experiments in membranes from mesenteric and adrenal capsules. On mesenteric artery membranes, the association rate constant at 4°C obtained by fitting the data to the second-order rate equation was 1.8×10^8 M/min (Fig. 5). The dissociation rate constant at 4°C estimated by fitting the binding data to the pseudo-first order rate equation was 0.01/min (Fig. 6). The K_D at 4°C calculated from kinetic data was between 55 and 130 pM, in agreement with that obtained from steady state experiments. In adrenal capsules, kinetic data obtained (not shown) were similar, and kinetically determined K_D agreed with the apparent equilibrium dissociation constant obtained by Scatchard analyses or from competition experiments.

The possibility that one of the mechanisms involved in the actions of ANF is an interference with calcium movements (Camargo et al., 1984) prompted us to test the hypothesis that ANF may be an endogenous ligand of the receptors for calcium channel blockers. Neither nifedipine nor verapamil displaced labeled ANF in competition experiments with adrenal membranes. Unlabeled ANF did not compete with [^{3}H]nitrendipine for binding to the particulate fraction from adrenal capsules. The K_I of nifedipine in this assay was 3.1 nM and that of verapamil 8.8 μM (Fig. 7).

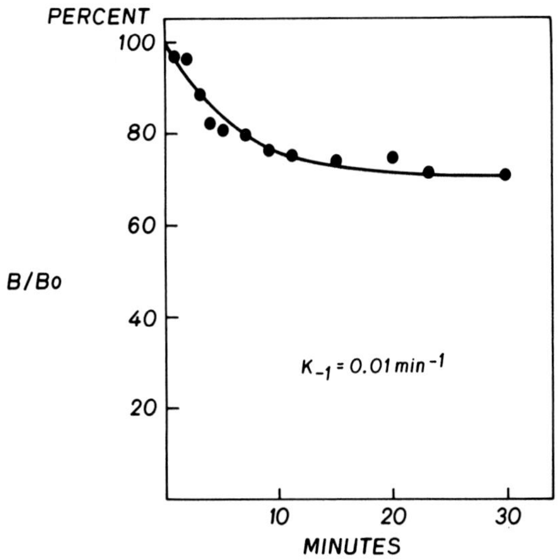

FIGURE 6. *Dissociation of ^{125}I-ANF (0.07 nM) from rat mesenteric arteries. Unlabeled ANF, 1 μM (final concentration), was added at time 0, after incubation to steady state. The binding data were fitted to the pseudo-first order rate equation to obtain K_{-1}. Similar results were found in two other experiments.*

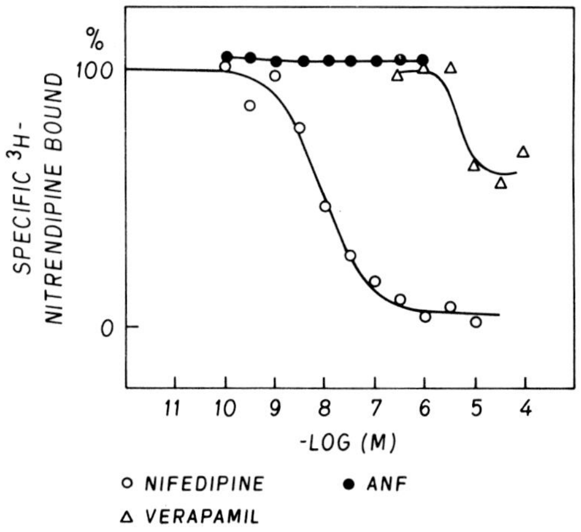

FIGURE 7. *Competition of ANF, nifedipine, and verapamil with [^{3}H]-nitrendipine, for binding to rat adrenal capsular membranes. Concentration of [^{3}H]nitrendipine was 1.4 nM and that of proteins was 1 mg/ml.*

Discussion

Our results demonstrate the presence of specific high-affinity low-capacity receptors for atrial natriuretic factor in the vasculature (renal and mesenteric vessels) and the adrenal capsule of the rat. Low-affinity specific binding was detectable in rat decapsulated adrenals, and no specific binding was detected in membranes from rat atria or ventricles. These results, together with the evidence that ANF is vasorelaxant (Currie et al., 1983; Grammer et al., 1983; Garcia et al., 1984) and inhibits the stimulated secretion of aldosterone (Atarashi et al., 1984, Chartier et al., 1984a, 1984b), suggests that the high-affinity binding sites we describe are involved in biological effects of ANF in these target organs. This hypothesis is further supported by the correlation which exists between the potency of ANF-related peptides to displace ANF from adrenal membranes and the potency of these peptides to inhibit basal aldosterone secretion. Taken together, our results lead us to propose a general bioregulatory role of ANF affecting the vasculature, the kidney, and adrenals. The generalized effects which resemble some of the actions of calcium blockers support the hypothesis that ANF may exert its effects by modulation of calcium fluxes. However, receptors for ANF are specific, and our results argue against a possible role of ANF as a putative endogenous ligand of receptors for calcium channel blockers.

The data obtained with ANF fragments suggest that ANF (101–125) contains the minimal core sequence of the peptide with potent biological activity on these preparations, since further cleavage at the C- or N-terminal amino acids reduces the potency from 3- to 10-fold. The result of the cleavage of the C-terminal tyrosine is interesting in that the potency of the resulting peptide is slightly increased, both on the binding assay and on the inhibition of aldosterone production, in agreement with the findings on natriuresis and relaxation of the chick rectum (Thibault et al., 1984b). The only important discrepancy between the binding and the effects on natriuresis and smooth muscle relaxation, resides in the actions of ANF (102–126). This peptide is as potent as ANF (101–126) on natriuresis and chick rectum relaxation (Thibault et al., 1984b), and relaxation of the precontracted rabbit aorta (Garcia et al., 1985). Since the synthetic ANF is more potent in the radioligand-binding assay than in the dispersed glomerulosa cells (Chartier et al., 1984a, 1984b), these findings may result from differences in the rate of degradation in the bioassays (at 37°C) and the radioligand-binding assay (performed at 4°C in the presence of protease inhibitors). A similar explanation may apply to the surprising potency in both radioligand-binding assays (vascular and adrenal) of ANF (101–121), which is inactive on natriuresis and of intermediate potency on the chick rectum (Thibault et al., 1984b) or the norepinephrine-contracted rabbit aorta (Garcia et al., 1985).

During the final preparation of this publication, a report by Napier et al. (1984) demonstrated the presence of specific membrane receptors for ANF in rabbit aorta and rabbit and rat kidney cortex. The results in the rabbit are in close agreement with those we have obtained in the rat, and suggest that there may be similarities across species. Degradation of ANF during incubation may, however, be different in the rabbit and rat vasculature (Napier et al., 1984).

In summary, we demonstrate the presence of vascular and adrenal binding sites for atrial natriuretic factor which mediate its effects on these target organs. Furthermore, our results indicate that vascular and adrenal binding sites for ANF have the same specificities for ANF fragments, and are probably similar receptors.

Presented at the 57th Scientific Sessions, American Heart Association, Miami, November 1984.

We thank Mario Deslongchamps, Lyne Poissant, and Josée Bilodeau for excellent technical help. Dr. R.F. Nutt of Merck, Sharp, and Dohme Research Laboratories (West Point, Penn.) graciously provided us with synthetic ANF.

This work was supported by grants from the Medical Research Council of Canada (MA 8018 to E.L.S. and the Multidisciplinary Group on Hypertension to G.T., M.C., and J.G.), and by the National Research Council of Canada.

Address for reprints: Ernesto L. Schiffrin, M.D., Ph.D., Clinical Research Institute of Montreal, 110 Pine Avenue West, Montreal, Quebec H2W 1R7, Canada.

Received December 10, 1984; accepted for publication February 27, 1985.

References

Atarashi K, Mulrow PJ, Franco-Saenz R, Snajdar R, Rapp J (1984) Inhibition of aldosterone production by an atrial extract. Science **224:** 992–994

Bruns RF, Lawson-Wendling K, Pugsley TA (1983) A rapid filtration assay for soluble receptors using polyethylenimine-treated filters. Anal Biochem **132:** 74–81

Camargo NJF, Kleinert HD, Atlas SA, Sealy JE, Laragh JH, Maack T (1984) Ca-dependent hemodynamic and natriuretic effects of atrial extract in isolated rat kidney. Am J Physiol **246:** F447–F456

Chartier L, Schiffrin EL, Thibault G (1984a) Effects of atrial natriuretic factor (ANF)-related peptides on aldosterone secretion by adrenal glomerulosa cells: Critical role of the intramolecular disulphide bond. Biochem Biophys Res Commun **122:** 171–174

Chartier L, Schiffrin EL, Thibault G, Garcia R (1984b) Atrial natriuretic factor inhibits the effect of angiotensin II, ACTH and potassium on aldosterone secretion in vitro and angiotensin II-induced steroidogenesis in vivo. Endocrinology **115:** 2026–2028

Cheng Y, Prusoff W (1973) Relationship between the inhibition constant (K_I) and the concentration of inhibitor which causes 50 percent inhibition (IC_{50}) of an enzymatic reaction. Biochem Pharmacol **22:** 3099–3108

Currie MG, Geller DM, Cole BR, Boylan JG, Sheng WY, Holmberg SW, Needleman P (1983) Bioactive cardiac substances: Potent vasorelaxant activity in mammalian atria. Science **221:** 71–73

Currie MG, Geller DM, Cole BR, Seigel NR, Fok KF, Adams SP, Eubank SR, Galluppi GR, Needleman P (1984) Purification and sequence analysis of bioactive atrial peptides (atriopeptins). Science **222:** 67–69

De Bold AJ (1982) Tissue fractionation studies on the relationship between an atrial natriuretic factor and specific atrial granules. Can J Physiol Pharmacol **60:** 324–330

De Bold A, Salerno TA (1983) Natriuretic activity of extracts from hearts of different species and from various rat tissues. Can J Physiol Pharmacol **61:** 127–130

De Bold AJ, Borenstein HB, Veress AT, Sonnenberg H (1981) A rapid and potent natriuretic response to intravenous injection of atrial myocardial extract in rats. Life Sci **28:** 89–94

De Léan A, Munson PJ, Rodbard D (1978) Simultaneous analysis of families of sigmoidal curves: Application to bioassay, radioligand assay and physiological dose-response curves. Am J Physiol **235:** E97–E102

Flynn TG, De Bold ML, De Bold AJ (1983) The aminoacid sequence of an atrial peptide with potent diuretic and natriuretic properties. Biochem Biophys Res Commun **117:** 859–865

Garcia R, Cantin M, Thibault G, Ong H, Genest J (1982) Relationship of specific granules to the natriuretic and diuretic activity of rat atria. Experientia **38:** 1071–1073

Garcia R, Thibault G, Cantin M, Genest J (1984) Effects of a purified atrial natriuretic factor on rat and rabbit vascular strips and vascular beds. Am J Physiol **247:** R34–R39

Garcia R, Thibault G, Seidah NG, Lazure C, Cantin M, Genest J, Chrétien M (1985) Structure activity relationships of atrial natriuretic factor (ANF) II. Effect of chain length modifications on vascular reactivity. Biochem Biophys Res Commun **126:** 178–184

Grammer RT, Fukumi H, Inagami T, Misono KS (1983) Rat atrial natriuretic factor. Purification and vasorelaxant activity. Biochem Biophys Res Commun **116:** 696–703

Greenwood FC, Hunter WM (1963) The preparation of ^{131}I-labelled human growth hormone of high specific radioactivity. Biochem J **89:** 114–123

Gutkowska J, Thibault G, Januszewicz P, Cantin M, Genest J (1984) Direct radioimmunoassay of atrial natriuretic factor. Biochem Biophys Res Commun **122:** 593–601

Kleinert HD, Maack T, Atlas SA, Januszewicz A, Sealy JE, Laragh JH (1984) Atrial natriuretic factor inhibits angiotensin-, norepinephrine- and potassium-induced vascular contractility. Hypertension **6** (Suppl I): I-143–I-147

Maki M, Takayanagi R, Misono KS, Pandley KN, Tibbetts C, Inagami T (1984) Structure of the rat atrial natriuretic factor precursor deduced from cDNA sequence. Nature **309:** 722–724

Misono KS, Fukumi H, Grammer RT, Inagami T (1984) Rat atrial natriuretic factor: Complete amino acid sequence and disulfide linkage essential for biological activity. Biochem Biophys Res Commun **119:** 524–529

Munson PJ, Rodbard D (1980) Ligand: a versatile computerized approach for characterization of ligand-binding system. Anal Biochem **107:** 220–239

Napier MA, Vandlen RL, Albers- Schonberg G, Nutt RF, Brady S, Lyle T, Winquist R, Faison EP, Heinel LA, Blaine EH (1984) Specific membrane receptors for atrial natriuretic factor in renal and vascular tissues. Proc Natl Acad Sci USA **81:** 5946–5950

Nemeh MN, Gilmore JP (1983) Natriuretic activity of human and monkey atria. Circ Res **53:** 420–423

Schiffrin EL, Genest J (1983) ^{3}H-vasopressin binding to the rat mesenteric artery. Endocrinology **113:** 409–411

Schiffrin EL, Lis M, Gutkowska J, Genest J (1981) Role of Ca^{2+} in response of adrenal glomerulosa cells to angiotensin II, ACTH, K^+ and ouabain. Am J Physiol **241:** E42–E46

Schiffrin EL, Thomé FS, Genest J (1983) Vascular angiotensin II receptors in renal and DOCA-salt hypertensive rats. Hypertension **5** (Suppl V): V-16–V-21

Schiffrin EL, Chartier L, Thibault G, St-Louis J, Gutkowska J, Cantin M (1984) Vascular and adrenal binding sites for atrial natriuretic factor (abstr). Circulation **70** (Suppl II): 335A

Seidah NG, Lazure C, Chrétien M, Thibault G, Garcia R, Cantin M, Genest J, Nutt RF, Brady SF, Lyle TA, Paleveda WJ, Toltone CD, Ciccerone TM, Veber DF (1984) Aminoacid sequence of homologous rat atrial peptides: Natriuretic activity of native and synthetic forms. Proc Natl Acad Sci USA **81:** 2640–2644

Spector T (1978) Refinement of the Coomassie blue method of protein quantitation. Anal Biochem **86:** 142–146

Thibault G, Garcia R, Seidah NG, Lazure C, Cantin M, Chrétien M, Genest J (1983) Purification of three rat atrial natriuretic factors and their aminoacid composition. FEBS Lett **164:** 286–290

Thibault G, Garcia R, Cantin M, Genest J, Lazure C, Seidah NG, Chrétien M (1984a) Primary structure of a high M_r form of rat atrial natriuretic factor. FEBS Lett **167:** 352–356

Thibault G, Garcia R, Carrier F, Seidah NG, Lazure C, Chrétien M, Cantin M, Genest J (1984b) Structure-activity relationship of atrial natriuretic factor (ANF). I. Natriuretic activity and relaxation of intestinal smooth muscle. Biochem Biophys Res Commun **125:** 938–946

Trippodo NC, MacPhee AA, Cole FE (1983) Partially purified human and rat atrial natriuretic factor. Hypertension **5** (Suppl I) I-81–I-88

Yamanaka M, Greenberg B, Johnson L, Seilhamer J, Brewer M, Friedeman T, Miller J, Atlas S, Laragh J, Lewicki J, Fiddes J (1984) Cloning and sequence analysis of the cDNA for the rat atrial natriuretic factor precursor. Nature **309:** 719–722

Zivin RA, Condra JH, Dixon RAF, Seidah NG, Chrétien M, Nemer M, Chamberland M, Drouin J (1984) Molecular cloning and characterization of DNA sequences encoding rat and human atrial natriuretic factors. Proc Natl Acad Sci USA **81:** 6325–6329

INDEX TERMS: Rat mesenteric arteries • Renal arteries • Adrenal capsules • Atrial natriuretic factor

The Left Ventricular dP/dt_{max}-End-Diastolic Volume Relation in Closed-Chest Dogs

William C. Little
From the Division of Cardiology/Department of Medicine, University of Texas Health Science Center, San Antonio, Texas

SUMMARY. I investigated the relation of the maximum rate of left ventricular pressure rise to the end-diastolic volume and the comparison of the maximum rate of left ventricular pressure rise-end-diastolic volume relation to the end-systolic pressure-volume relation, using the time-varying elastance model. These studies were performed in 11 dogs chronically instrumented to measure left ventricular pressure and determine left ventricular volume from three orthogonal dimensions. During vena caval occlusions, the relations between the maximum rate of left ventricular pressure rise and end-diastolic volume were described by straight lines ($r = 0.97 \pm 0.01$, mean ± SD). Dobutamine increased the slope of the maximum rate of left ventricular pressure rise-end-diastolic volume relation to 358 ± 94% of control. This increase was greater than the 244 ± 61% increase in the slope of the end-systolic pressure-volume relation ($P < 0.005$). The volume intercepts of the maximum rate of left ventricular pressure rise-end-diastolic volume relation and end-systolic pressure-volume relation were similar and were not significantly altered by dobutamine. The ratio of the slope of the maximum rate of left ventricular pressure rise-end-diastolic volume relation to the slope of the end-systolic pressure-volume relation divided by the time from end-diastole to end-systole was similar before (2.2 ± 0.7) and after dobutamine (2.3 ± 0.7, P = NS). Angiotensin II did not significantly alter the maximum rate of left ventricular pressure rise-end-diastolic volume relation generated by caval occlusion. Thus, consistent with the predictions of the time-varying elastance model, the maximum rate of left ventricular pressure rise-end-diastolic volume relation generated by caval occlusions is linear, and its slope may be a sensitive load-independent measure of left ventricular contractile performance. **(*Circ Res 56: 808–815, 1985*)**

IT has been proposed that left ventricular (LV) systolic pump function can be modeled as a time-varying elastance (Suga and Sagawa, 1974; Sunagawa and Sagawa, 1982). In this model, the left ventricle is considered to behave as an elastic structure that stiffens in a predictable manner during systole. The LV pressure, P(t), at any time after the onset of contraction, t, is described by:

$$P(t) = E(t)\,(V(t) - V_o), \qquad (1)$$

where E(t) is the LV elastance at t, V(t) the LV volume at t, and V_o the minimal volume required for the LV to generate supra-atmospheric pressure. The LV elastance, E(t), reaches a maximum value, E_{max}, at time t_{max}, which has been termed end systole. This end-systolic pressure-volume relation,

$$P_{ES} = E_{max}\,(V_{ES} - V_o),$$

has been the subject of much investigation. E_{max}, the slope of the P_{ES}-V_{ES} relation, is a measure of the global inotropic state, and is relatively insensitive to changes in loading conditions in isolated canine hearts (Suga et al., 1973; Suga and Sagawa, 1974; Suga and Yamakoshi, 1977; Suga et al., 1979; Sagawa, 1978, 1981), conscious dogs (Sodums et al., 1984), and man (Grossman et al., 1977; Mehmel et al., 1981).

In isolated canine hearts, Suga and Sagawa (1974) demonstrated that E(t) can be normalized by considering E_{max} and t_{max}, so that:

$$E_N(t_N) = E(t)/E_{max},$$

where $t_N = t/t_{max}$ and $E_N(t_N)$ is a normalized elastance function that is similar for all ventricles. Thus, the LV elastance can be expressed as:

$$E(t) = E_{max}\,E_N(t_N). \qquad (2)$$

Although the P_{ES}-V_{ES} relation has been the subject of intense investigation, the more general time-varying elastance model has not been as widely studied in preparations other than the isolated heart. In addition to the P_{ES}-V_{ES} relation, the time-varying elastance model also has implications concerning the relation between the maximum rate of rise of LV pressure (dP/dt_{max}) and the end-diastolic volume (V_{ED}).

Derivation of the dP/dt_{max}-V_{ED} Relation from the Time-Varying Elastance Model

The time derivative of LV pressure (dP/dt) can be expressed in terms of LV elastance, as suggested by Sunagawa and Sagawa (1982), by differentiating Equation 1:

$$dP/dt = d(E(t)\,(V(t)-V_o))/dt.$$

Under normal conditions, dP/dt reaches its maximum value, dP/dt_{max}, during isovolumic contraction when V(t) is equal to V_{ED}. Thus,

$$dP/dt_{max} = [dE(t)/dt_{max}] (V_{ED} - V_o). \quad (3)$$

$dE(t)/dt_{max}$ can be evaluated by differentiating Equation 2,

$$dE/dt_{max} = (E_{max}/t_{max}) (dE_N/dt_{Nmax}).$$

Since E_N (t_N) appears to be relatively constant in all ventricles (Suga and Sagawa, 1974; Sunagawa and Sagawa, 1982), the maximum value of its derivative should also be a constant, k. Thus,

$$dE/dt_{max} = k\ E_{max}/t_{max}. \quad (4)$$

Therefore, the time-varying elastance model of the LV predicts that the dP/dt_{max}-V_{ED} relation should be linear (Eq. 3). Furthermore, the slope of this relation, or dE/dt_{max}, should be proportional to E_{max}/t_{max} (Eq. 4). Since E_{max} and t_{max} are both assumed to be independent of loading conditions, this relation should also be load independent. Since E_{max} increases in response to positive inotropic stimuli, while t_{max} decreases (Suga et al., 1973), the slope of the dP/dt_{max}-V_{ED} relation, which is proportional to their ratio, should be highly sensitive to changes in contractile function. The model also predicts that the volume intercept of the dP/dt_{max}-V_{ED} relation should be the same as the volume intercept (V_o) of the LV P_{ES}-V_{ES} relation.

This study was thus undertaken to evaluate the above predictions of the time-varying elastance model in intact, chronically instrumented dogs.

Methods

Instrumentation

Eleven healthy, adult mongrel dogs were instrumented by a slight modification of a previously described technique (Little et al., 1984; Sodums et al., 1984). A sterile left lateral thoracotomy was performed under anesthesia with halothane (1–2%) following induction with xylene (1 mg/kg) and sodium thiopental (6 mg/kg). The pericardium was opened wide. A micromanometer pressure transducer (Konigsberg Instruments) and a polyvinyl catheter for transducer calibration (i.d. 1.1 mm) were inserted through the LV apex. Three pairs of ultrasonic crystals (5 MHz) were implanted in the endocardium of the LV to measure the anterior-posterior, septal-lateral, and base-apex (long axis) dimensions. Hydraulic occluder cuffs were placed around the inferior and superior venae cavae.

Data Collection

All studies were performed after full recovery from the thoracotomy (10 days to 2 weeks), with the dogs lying on their right sides in a sling. The LV catheter was connected to a pressure transducer (Statham P23DB) calibrated with a mercury manometer. The signal from the micromanometer was adjusted to match that of the catheter. The transit time of 5 MHz sound between the crystal pairs was determined and converted to distance assuming a constant velocity of sound in blood of 1.55 m/msec. The first derivative of LV pressure (dP/dt) was obtained by electronically differentiating the micromanometer signal using an RC circuit with a linear frequency response to above 70 Hz. The analog signals were recorded on an eight-channel oscilligraph (Beckman Instruments) and digitized with an on-line analog-to-digital converter (Dual Control Systems) at 100 Hz and stored on a floppy disk memory system utilizing a computer system (Zobex).

Experimental Protocol

The dogs were sedated with fentanyl (0.03–0.06 mg/kg) in combination with droperidol (1.5–3.0 mg/kg) and intubated. To prevent reflex changes in heart rate, the dogs were treated with atropine sulfate (0.2 mg/kg, iv), and were ventilated with room air. To minimize the effect of fluctuations in intrathoracic pressure, all data were recorded during 12-second periods while the dogs were apneic, with the glottis held open by the endotracheal tube (Little et al., 1984).

The effect of dobutamine (10 μg/kg per min, iv) was assessed in six dogs. Data were recorded during a steady state, non-intervention period to obtain baseline values. The P_{ES}-V_{ES} and dP/dt_{max}-V_{ED} relations were then generated by sudden occlusion of the cavae. This caused a progressive fall in LV end-systolic pressure, volume, and dP/dt_{max} over a 12-second recording period (Fig. 1). Immediately after the recording period, the caval occlusion was released. After all parameters had returned to their baseline level, the caval occlusion was repeated. Then dobutamine was infused until a steady state had been achieved, and the caval occlusions were repeated.

In seven dogs, the effect of arterial vasoconstriction produced by the infusion of angiotensin II (0.5–2.5 μg/min) was assessed. In addition to atropine, these animals were also pretreated with propranolol (2 mg/kg, iv) to block β-adrenergically mediated changes in contractility. Two caval occlusions were performed before, and again after, the infusion of angiotensin II sufficient to raise the systolic arterial pressure by at least 40 mm Hg (Sodums et al., 1984).

Data Analysis

The stored digitized data were analyzed by computer algorithm (Sodums et al., 1984; Little et al., 1984). Baseline

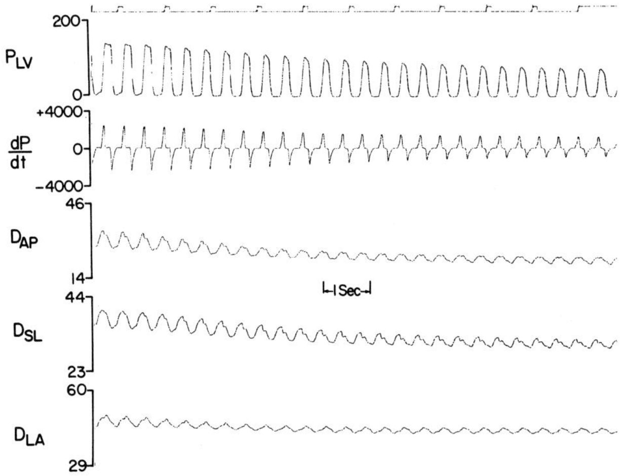

FIGURE 1. *Analog recording following caval occlusion. P_{LV} = LV pressure in mm Hg D_{AP} = anterior-posterior LV dimension in mm, D_{SL} = septal-lateral LV dimension in mm, D_{LA} = long axis dimension in mm.*

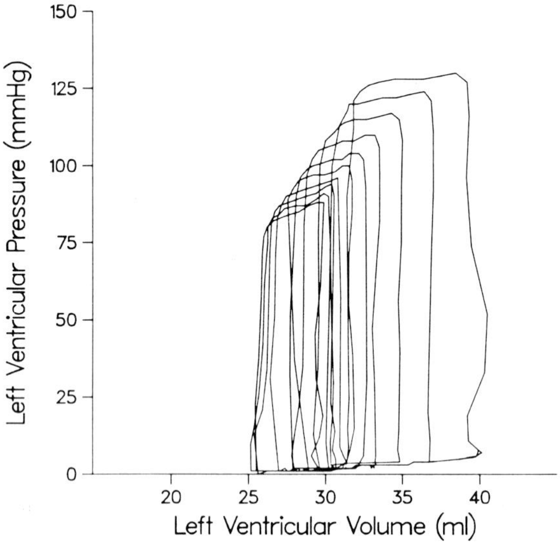

FIGURE 2. *Representative LV pressure-volume loops following caval occlusion. Only every other beat is displayed for clarity.*

TABLE 1
Effect of Dobutamine on Hemodynamic Parameters

	Control	Dobutamine
HR	168 ± 31	185 ± 28
P_{ES}	150 ± 32	160 ± 15
P_{ED}	8.1 ± 3.2	2.0 ± 2.1*
V_{ES}	36 ± 8.7	28 ± 8.8*
V_{EE}	35 ± 9.5	27 ± 8.6*
V_{ED} (ml)	48 ± 12	40 ± 12*
dP/dt_{max}	2232 ± 740	3581 ± 915*
dP/dt_{min}	−2470 ± 766	−3048 ± 431*

Results are expressed as mean ± SD; $n = 6$.
* $P < 0.05$, P_{ES} = LV end-systolic pressures (mm Hg); HR = heart rate; P_{ED} = LV end-diastolic pressure (mm Hg); V_{ES} = LV end-systolic volume (ml); V_{ED} = LV end-diastolic volume (ml); V_{EE} = LV end-ejection volume (ml); dP/dt_{max} = peak value of time derivative LV pressure (mm Hg/sec); dP/dt_{min} = peak negative value of dP/dt (mm Hg/sec).

hemodynamic values in each dog were obtained by averaging the data obtained during the 12-second steady state, non-intervention recording periods. End systole was defined as the time when the ratio of LV pressure to volume reached its maximum (Suga and Yamakoshi, 1977). End diastole was defined as the relative minima following the "a" wave of the high-fidelity LV pressure tracing. The time from end diastole to end systole was defined as t_{max}. End ejection was defined as peak negative dP/dt (dP/dt_{min}). The LV volume was calculated as a modified general ellipsoid using the equation:

$$V_{LV} = (\pi/6)\, D_{AP} D_{SL} D_{LA}$$

where V_{LV} = LV volume, D_{AP} = the anterior-posterior LV dimension, D_{SL} = the septal-lateral LV dimension, and D_{LA} = the long axis LV dimension. This method of volume calculation has been validated in our laboratory (Little et al., 1984; Sodums et al., 1984; Little and O'Rourke, 1985) and is similar to that used and validated by others (Olson et al., 1983), except that we determined endocardial dimensions directly; thus, the subtraction of LV wall thickness or volume was not necessary. This method gives a consistent measure of LV volume ($r > 0.97$, SEE < 2ml) despite changes in LV loading conditions and configuration.

Only caval occlusions that produced a fall in LV systolic pressure of at least 40 mm Hg, and that produced no extra systoles, were analyzed. The LV end-systolic pressure-volume data during the fall of LV pressure produced by the caval occlusions were fit to

$$P_{ES} = E_{max}(V_{ES} - V_o),$$

using the linear least square technique. The LV V_{ED} and dP/dt_{max} were fit to

$$dP/dt_{max} = (dE/dt_{max})\,(V_{ED} - V_o), \quad (3a)$$

where dE/dt_{max} is the slope of the relation and V_o is the volume intercept.

All results are summarized as the mean ± 1 SD, and the level of significance was $P < 0.05$. Multiple comparisons were performed by analysis of variance. Intergroup comparisons were performed by paired *t*-tests with an appropriate correction for the performance of multiple comparisons using the Bonferoni inequality (Glantz, 1981).

Postmortem Studies

At the conclusion of the experiments, the animals were killed and the hearts were examined to confirm the proper positioning of the instrumentation.

Results

A typical analog recording during a caval occlusion is shown in Figure 1. The LV pressure, dP/dt_{max}, and the three LV dimensions decline to-

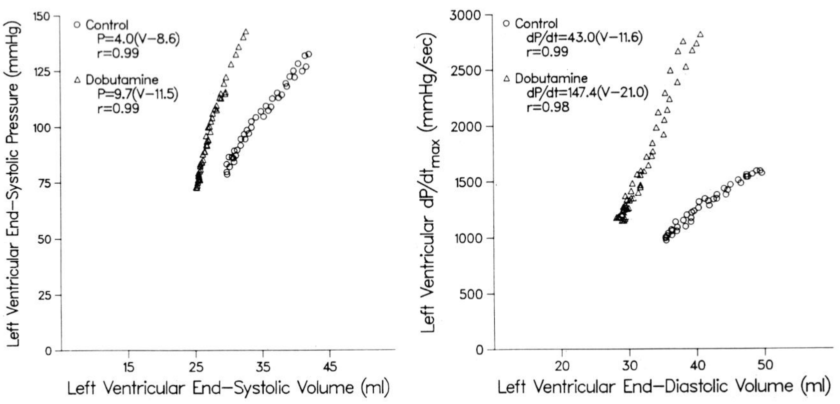

FIGURE 3. *Simultaneously determined LV P_{ES}-V_{ES} (left) and dP/dt_{max}-V_{ED} relations (right) during control and after dobutamine. Both relations are linear, and their slopes increase with dobutamine. The increase in slope of the dP/dt_{max}-V_{ED} is greater.*

TABLE 2
Effect of Dobutamine on the LV End-Systolic Pressure-Volume Relation

	Control				Dobutamine			
Dog	*n*	*r*	E_{max}	V_o	*n*	*r*	E_{max}	V_o
1	61	0.978	10.69	17.7	28	0.950	27.78	18.5
2	60	0.985	11.75	8.2	63	0.964	25.13	9.2
3	39	0.990	3.96	8.6	49	0.986	9.66	11.5
4	71	0.983	6.74	9.4	71	0.964	23.35	10.2
5	28	0.996	5.99	23.5	36	0.969	14.18	28.8
6	36	0.995	7.19	9.9	41	0.981	11.55	8.7
Mean			7.7	12.9			18.6	14.5
±SD			2.9	6.3			7.7	7.9
P vs. control							$P < 0.005$	NS

E_{max} = slope of P_{ES}-V_{ES} relation in mm Hg/ml, V_o = volume intercept of P_{ES}-V_{ES} relation in ml.

gether following caval occlusion. An example of the LV pressure-volume loops generated by the caval occlusion is shown in Figure 2. The infusion of dobutamine increased LV dP/dt$_{max}$, and decreased V_{ED} and V_{ES} (Table 1). The response of typical LV P_{ES}-V_{ES} and dP/dt$_{max}$-V_{ED} relations to the infusion of dopamine are shown in Figure 3. The individual regression information is shown in Tables 2 and 3. Both the P_{ES}-V_{ES} and dP/dt$_{max}$-V_{ED} relations were described by straight lines during control and after administration of dobutamine ($r = 0.97 \pm 0.01$). Dobutamine markedly increased the slopes of both the LV P_{ES}-V_{ES} and dP/dt$_{max}$-V_{ED} relations. The increase in the slope of the dP/dt$_{max}$-V_{ED} relation (dE/dt$_{max}$) (358 ± 94% of control) was greater than the increase in the slope of the P_{ES}-V_{ES} relation (244 ± 61% of control, $P < 0.005$) (Fig. 4). The ratios of dE/dt$_{max}$ to E_{max}/t_{max} were similar, 2.2 ± 0.7 during control and 2.3 ± 0.7 after dobutamine (P = NS). The volume intercepts of the control P_{ES}-V_{ES} and dP/dt$_{max}$-V_{ED} relations were similar (12.9 ± 6.3 and 9.4 ± 5.1 ml, P = NS) and were not altered significantly by dobutamine (14.5 ± 7.9 and 14.5 ± 8.9 ml, respectively, P = NS); although V_o increased in five of six animals.

Angiotensin II increased P_{ES} from 105 ± 23 to 191 ± 19 mm Hg ($P < 0.05$) and also increased V_{ED}, V_{ES}, dP/dt$_{max}$, and dP/dt$_{min}$ (Table 4). Because of the autonomic blockade, the heart rate was not altered, and t_{max} remained nearly constant. Consistent with our previous observations (Sodums et al., 1984), the infusion of angiotensin II shifted the P_{ES}-V_{ES} relation to the left, as manifest by a decrease of the volume intercept from 18.0 ± 7.9 to 11.7 ± 7.6 ml (Fig. 5; Table 5). The slope of the P_{ES}-V_{ES} relation also decreased somewhat in response to angiotensin II (9.5 ± 4.1 to 6.3 ± 2.2 mm Hg/ml, $P < 0.05$). In contrast, the dP/dt$_{max}$-V_{ED} relation was not altered as much by angiotensin II (Fig. 5; Table 6). Although the slope and volume intercept of the dP/dt$_{max}$-V_{ED} relation were slightly, but not significantly, decreased in response to angiotensin II, a single line described the dP/dt$_{max}$-V_{ED} relation before and after angiotensin II ($r = 0.982 \pm 0.010$) more adequately

TABLE 3
Effect of Dobutamine on the LV dP/dt$_{max}$-V$_{ED}$ Relation Determined Simultaneously with Table 2

	Control					Dobutamine				
Dog	*r*	dE/dt$_{max}$	V_o	t_{max}	dE/dt$_{max}$ / E_{max}/t_{max}	*r*	dE/dt$_{max}$	V_o	t_{max}	dE/dt$_{max}$ / E_{max}/t_{max}
1	0.968	64.9	12.2	200	1.2	0.953	199.0	13.6	180	1.3
2	0.975	95.4	1.0	200	1.6	0.978	315.0	7.1	150	1.9
3	0.985	43.0	11.6	220	2.4	0.983	147.4	21.0	160	2.4
4	0.971	71.1	6.2	190	2.0	0.961	333.3	13.1	140	2.0
5	0.955	77.3	15.5	210	2.7	0.969	332.0	28.1	140	3.3
6	0.989	11.3	10.1	200	3.2	0.978	266.6	4.0	130	3.0
Mean		77.8	9.4	203	2.2		265	14.5	150	2.3
±SD		±25.1	±5.1	±10	±0.7		±77.2	±8.9	±18	±0.7
P vs. control							$P < 0.001$	NS	$P < 0.001$	NS

dE/dt$_{max}$ = slope of dp/dt$_{max}$-V$_{ED}$ relation in mm Hg/ml·sec, V_o = volume intercept in ml, t_{max} = time from end diastole to end systole in msec.

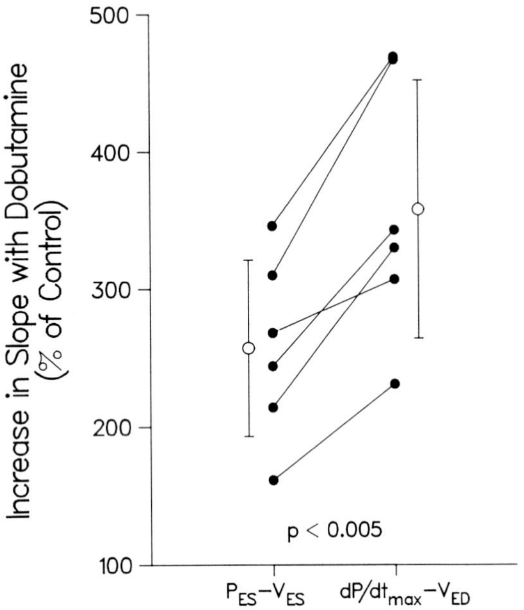

FIGURE 4. *Comparison of the effect of dobutamine on the slope of the P_{ES}-V_{ES} and dP/dt_{max}-V_{ED} relations.*

TABLE 4
Effect of Angiotension II on LV Pressure and Volumes

	Control	Angiotension II
HR	158 ± 13	153 ± 15
dP/dt_{max}	2298 ± 558	2585 ± 711*
dP/dt_{min}	−2398 ± 416	−2662 ± 281*
V_{ED}	46.6 ± 13.8	56.8 ± 17.5*
V_{EE}	28.3 ± 4.7	34.8 ± 5.5*
V_{ES}	28.7 ± 5.2	35.4 ± 6.2*
P_{ED}	4.3 ± 4.7	11.9 ± 10.3*
P_{ES}	105 ± 23	191 ± 19*
t_{max}	200 ± 31	197 ± 23

Results are expressed as mean ± SD; $n = 7$.

* $P < 0.05$, HR = heart rate (beats/min), dP/dt_{max} = peak rate of LV pressure rise (mm Hg); dP/dt_{min} = peak rate of LV pressure fall (mm Hg/sec); V_{ED} = LV end-diastolic volume (ml); V_{EE} = LV end-ejection volume (ml); V_{ES} = LV end-systolic volume (ml); P_{ED} = LV end-diastolic pressure (mm Hg); P_{ES} = LV end-systolic pressure (mm Hg); t_{max} = time from end diastole to end systole (msec).

than a single regression line described the simultaneously determined P_{ES}-V_{ES} relation ($r = 0.956 \pm 0.019$, $P < 0.05$). In one animal, the dP/dt_{max}-V_{ED} relation (Fig. 6) did not remain linear at the higher V_{ED} levels produced by angiotensin II infusion. At these higher V_{ED} levels, the relationship flattened out. Only the linear portion of this curve ($V_{ED} < 33$ ml) was subjected to linear regression analysis.

Discussion

This study investigated several predictions suggested by the time-varying elastance model of the LV concerning the dP/dt_{max}-V_{ED} relation and its link to the P_{ES}-V_{ES} relation. Most of the results are consistent with these predictions. First, the relation between LV dP/dt_{max} and the V_{ED} is described by a straight line during acute preload reductions produced by caval occlusion. The dP/dt_{max}-V_{ED} relation is relatively unchanged by increases in aortic pressure produced by vasoconstriction. In response to dobutamine, the slope of the dP/dt_{max}-V_{ED} relation is markedly increased (more so than the increase in E_{max}, the slope of the P_{ES}-V_{ES} relation), while the volume intercept of the relation is relatively unchanged. Also, consistent with the time-varying elastance model, the volume intercept of the dP/dt_{max}-V_{ED} relation is similar to the volume intercept of the P_{ES}-V_{ES} relation.

The simple time-varying elastance model of LV function does not account for any effect of the characteristics of ejection on the LV systolic pressure generated at any LV volume (Suga and Sagawa 1974; Sunagawa and Sagawa, 1982). However, the LV pressure generated at any volume may be reduced somewhat when the stroke volume, ejection fraction, maximal velocity of ejection, or flow at end-systole are markedly altered (Suga and Yamakoshi, 1977; Suga et al., 1977; Hunter et al., 1983; Weber et al., 1982; Shroff et al., 1983; Maughan et al., 1984). These factors may account for the shift of the LV P_{ES}-V_{ES} relation observed in this study and seen previously (Sodums et al., 1984) after the infusion of a vasoconstrictor. Interestingly, the LV dP/dt_{max}-V_{ED} relation was not shifted as much by

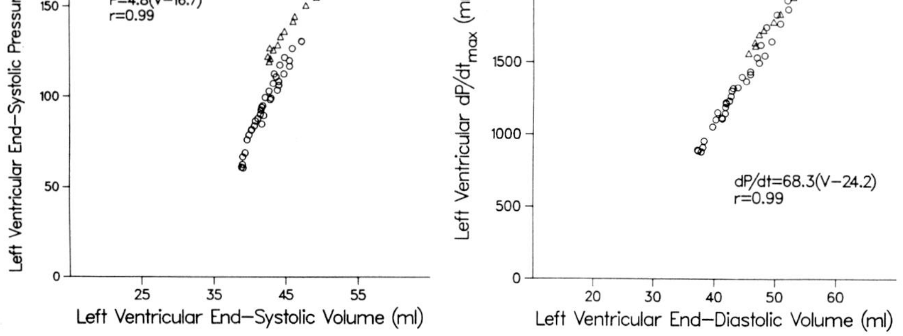

FIGURE 5. *Simultaneously determined P_{ES}-V_{ES} (left) and dP/dt_{max}-V_{ED} (right) relations before and after infusion of angiotensin II. Angiotension II shifts the P_{ES}-V_{ES} relation to the left, decreasing the volume intercept. The dP/dT_{max}-V_{ED} relation is well described by a single line both before and after angiotensin II. Data from, Dog 5, restudied 1 week after data reported in Table 5 were obtained.*

TABLE 5
Effect of Angiotensin II on the LV P$_{ES}$-V$_{ES}$ Relation

	Control				Angiotensin II				Control and angiotensin II			
Dog	*n*	*r*	E_{max}	V_o	*n*	*r*	E_{max}	V_o	*n*	*r*	E_{max}	V_o
2	22	0.995	9.11	9.3	35	0.994	7.87	6.3	57	0.983	8.94	8.6
5	19	0.982	8.53	28.1	21	0.990	6.41	20.1	40	0.929	9.02	28.5
7	21	0.992	6.77	11.1	10	0.957	4.51	1.9	31	0.970	8.65	13.3
8	56	0.960	17.30	25.4	59	0.948	9.81	20.9	115	0.963	11.87	23.4
9	9	0.962	6.74	25.1	53	0.967	3.16	14.3	62	0.960	3.83	18.4
10	43	0.988	5.77	14.3	47	0.990	5.90	11.4	87	0.968	7.49	17.4
11	17	0.988	12.38	12.4	19	0.998	6.64	2.1	36	0.927	13.94	12.9
Mean			9.5	18.0			6.3	11.7			9.1	17.5
±SD			±4.1	±7.9			±2.2	±7.6			±3.2	±6.8
P vs. control							$P < 0.05$	$P < 0.005$			NS	NS

Abbreviations as in Table 1.

vasoconstriction. This may indicate that the simple time-varying elastance model is a better descriptor of the isovolumic phase of LV contraction than during ejection, and that the dP/dt$_{max}$-V$_{ED}$ relation may be affected less by alterations of the arterial input characteristics than the P$_{ES}$-V$_{ES}$ relation. Under conditions different than those employed in this study, the predictions of the time-varying elastance model may not be as accurate. For example, if the stroke volume and rate of LV ejection were increased due to a slow heart rate or vasodilation, the simple time-varying elastance model may not be adequate because of a much greater deactivating effect of ejection flow (Suga and Yamakoshi, 1977; Hunter et al., 1983; Shroff et al., 1983).

In this study, the slope of the dP/dt$_{max}$-V$_{ED}$ relation, or dE/dt$_{max}$, was roughly proportional to E$_{max}$/t$_{max}$. The time-varying elastance model of the LV predicts that this portionality constant should be equal to the maximum value of dE$_N$/dt$_N$ which is similar in all ventricles. Suga and Sagawa (1974) evaluated E$_N$(t$_N$) in a series of isolated hearts. Figure 9 of their paper indicates that the maximum value of dE$_N$/dt$_N$ is approximately 1.4. This is somewhat lower than the ratio of dE/dt$_{max}$ to E$_{max}$/t$_{max}$ found in this study (2.2 ± 0.7 control and 2.3 ± 0.7 with dobutamine). However, the values obtained for dE/dt$_{max}$ and E$_{max}$/t$_{max}$ from Figure 3 of Suga and Sagawa's earlier study (1972) indicate that this ratio is approximately 2, in closer agreement with the observations of this study. The relationship between dE/dt$_{max}$ and E$_{max}$/t$_{max}$, and the similarity of the volume intercepts of the dP/dt$_{max}$-V$_{ED}$ and P$_{ES}$-V$_{ES}$ relations indicate that the time-varying elastance model provides a conceptual link between the events occurring during isovolumic contraction and at end systole.

The observation that the slope of the dP/dt$_{max}$-V$_{ED}$ relation (dE/dt$_{max}$) showed a greater increase in response to a positive inotropic stimulation than E$_{max}$

TABLE 6
Effect of Angiotensin II on the LV dp/dt$_{max}$-V$_{ED}$ Relation*

	Control			Angiotensin II			Control and angiotensin II		
Dog	*r*	dE/dt$_{max}$	V_o	*r*	dEdt/$_{max}$	V_o	*r*	dE/dt$_{max}$	V_o
2	0.996	66.1	14.2	0.987	62.1	2.7	0.990	65.6	4.4
5	0.996	77.0	23.1	0.990	81.7	22.4	0.986	87.2	24.8
7†	0.985	64.8	7.2	0.970	52.1	1.4	0.989	66.3	7.5
8	0.987	105.0	19.7	0.982	96.1	17.7	0.986	103.3	19.2
9	0.980	53.0	44.8	0.955	33.6	28.8	0.970	36.6	33.1
10	0.964	62.0	6.6	0.959	52.4	1.2	0.965	55.9	3.5
11	0.995	106.9	2.6	0.977	80.4	6.4	0.990	97.1	1.5
Mean		76.4	16.9		65.5	11.5		73.1	13.4
±SD		±21.6	±14.4		±21.6	±11.3		±23.9	±12.3
P vs. control					NS	NS		NS	NS

* Determined simultaneously with Table 5. Abbreviations as in Table 2.

† In animal 7, the LV dp/dt$_{max}$-V$_{ED}$ relation became nonlinear at high V$_{ED}$ (see Fig. 5). Only data from the linear portion (V$_{ED}$ <33 ml) were analyzed.

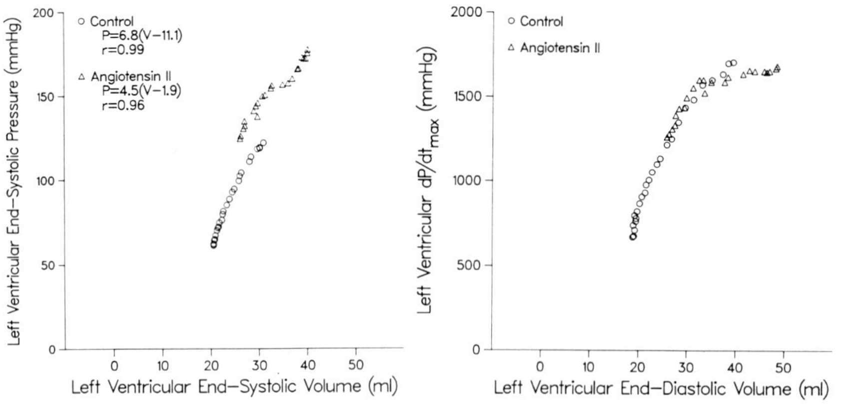

FIGURE 6. *In the same format as Figure 5, the LV P_{ES}-V_{ES} (right) and dP/dt_{max} (left) relations in dog 7 are shown. In this animal, the dP/dt_{max}-V_{Ed} relation flattened out at $V_{ED} > 33$ ml.*

is consistent with a previous observation of Suga et al. (1976). They compared the effects of baroreflex inotropic interventions on E_{max} and dP/dt_{max} in open-chest canine LV preparations contracting isovolumically at a constant volume. In their study, dP/dt_{max} showed greater changes than E_{max} in response to changes in contractility.

The results of this study are consistent with previous observations that dP/dt_{max} is preload dependent (Mason, 1969; Mahler et al., 1975; Wallace et al., 1963; Schmidt and Hoppe, 1978). These earlier studies assessed LV preload, using the LV end-diastolic pressure and not V_{ED}. Due to the nonlinear relation of LV end-diastolic pressure and V_{ED}, the dP/dt_{max}-V_{ED} relation cannot be directly deduced from these studies. Also, consistent with the observations of this study, Reeves et al. (1960) found in open-chest dogs that the relation between dP/dt_{max} and a measure of LV end-diastolic stretch was approximated by a straight line, whose slope was increased by epinephrine. Similarly, Quinones et al., (1976) reported that the ratio of dP/dt_{max} to the LV end-diastolic circumference increased in response to isoproterenol.

Most previous studies have found that dP/dt_{max} increases somewhat in response to elevations of arterial pressure. This increase in dP/dt_{max} can usually be attributed to an increase in the LV end-diastolic pressure and, thus, presumably, V_{ED} (Mason, 1969). However, Wallace et al., (1963) found, in a canine right-heart bypass preparation, that a sudden increase in aortic pressure increased dP/dt_{max} before the end-diastolic pressure increased. Others (Wildenthal et al., 1969; Furnival et al., 1970) have found that such sudden increases in aortic diastolic pressure do not alter dP/dt_{max} when it occurs prior to aortic valve opening.

Suga and Sagawa (1972) have derived the force-velocity relation from the time-varying elastance model. The force-velocity relation is related by appropriate scaling factors to the relation of E(t) to [dE(t)/dt]Et. Figure 3 of their paper shows an analog recording of dE(t)/dt obtained in an isolated heart as an intermediate step toward constructing a force-velocity relation. The peak value of dE(t)/dt or dE/dt_{max} in their figure is relatively constant during an increase in LV systolic pressure or an increase in V_{ED}, but increases in response to the infusion of positive inotropic agent, epinepherine. Since $dE(t)/dt_{max}$ is the slope of the dP/dt_{max}-V_{ED} relationship, our results are consistent with these observations of Suga and Sagawa (1972).

In one animal in this study, the dP/dt_{max}-V_{ED} relation became nonlinear at high V_{ED}. This may be a manifestation of the flat portion of the Frank-Starling relationship. The time-varying elastance model treats the ventricle as a perfectly elastic structure in which pressure and volume are linearly related at all volumes. It is clear that the real LV must have a limit above which further increase in volume will not result in a continued linear increase in dP/dt_{max} or LV systolic pressure. The dP/dt_{max}-V_{ED} relation may reach this limit sooner than the P_{ES}-V_{ES} relation, since V_{ED} is larger than V_{ES}. The observations of the linearity of the P_{ES}-V_{ES} relation and the data in the other animals in this study indicate that this limit is not usually reached in the physiological range of LV volumes.

The derivation of the dP/dt_{max}-V_{ED} relation described in the introduction depends on several assumptions that may not be completely accurate. First, LV volume may not be constant during isovolumic systole, as some volume is ejected into outwardly bulging mitral and aortic valves. Second, the volume correction factor (V_o) may not be constant early in systole (Suga and Sagawa, 1974). Finally, dP/dt_{max} may not always occur during isovolumic systole, but instead may in some circumstances be reached shortly after aortic valve opening. This is most likely to occur after vasodilation or when the LV systolic performance is depressed (Wildenthal et al., 1969; Quinones et al., 1976). However, the agreement of our results with the predictions of the time-varying elastance model (i.e., equations 3 and 4) suggests that these factors do not have a substantial effect under the conditions of this study.

The results of this study suggest that the LV dP/dt_{max}-V_{ED} relation is a sensitive, load-independent index of LV performance. However, before this can be applied, several limitations of this study must be considered. First, this study was performed after opening of the pericardium. Second, although the study was performed in close-chest animals, the conditions were carefully controlled. Measurements were obtained during periods of apnea to avoid the confounding influences of changes in intrathoracic pressure. The animals were treated with atropine to avoid the influences of alterations in heart rate during caval occlusion, and with atropine and propranolol to prevent reflex changes in contractility during angiotensin II administration. Finally, the dP/dt$_{max}$-V$_{ED}$ relations were generated by acute preload reduction. The effect of changing loading conditions by other methods and the variability of the relation over time remain to be determined.

In conclusion, this study demonstrates that in chronically instrumented dogs LV dP/dt$_{max}$ and the V$_{ED}$ are linearly related during caval occlusions. The relation is not altered by arterial vasoconstriction, and the slope of the dP/dt$_{max}$-V$_{ED}$ relation appears to be more sensitive to positive inotropic stimulation than E$_{max}$, the slope of the P$_{ES}$-V$_{ES}$ relation. These results are consistent with predictions of the time-varying elastance model of the LV and support its use as a conceptual framework for the understanding of LV systolic performance.

I thank Drs. Robert A. O'Rourke and Gregory L. Freeman for their review of the manuscript; Anna Fackenthall and Debbie Palmer for typing the manuscript, and James Colston, Danny Escobedo, James Galloway, and Don Watkins for expert technical assistance. I also thank Ayerst Laboratories for donating the propranolol.

Supported in part by grants from the Texas Affiliate of the American Heart Association, and the University of Texas Health Science Center.

Address for reprints: William C. Little, M.D., Division of Cardiology/Department of Medicine, University of Texas Health Science Center, 7703 Floyd Curl Drive, San Antonio, Texas 78284.

Received January 11, 1985; accepted for publication March 7, 1985.

References

Furnival CM, Linden RJ, Snow HM (1970) Inotropic changes in the left ventricle: The effect of changes in heart rate, aortic pressure and end-diastolic pressure. J Physiol (Lond) **211:** 359–387

Glantz SA (1981) Primer of Biostatistics. New York, McGraw-Hill

Grossman W, Braunwald E, Mann T, McLaurin LP, Green LW (1977) Contractile state of the left ventricle in man as evaluated from end-systolic pressure-volume relations. Circulation **56:** 845–852

Hunter WC, Janicki JS, Weber KT, Noordergraaf A (1983) Systolic mechanical properties of the left ventricle: Effects of volume and contractile state. Circ Res **52:** 319–327

Little WC, O'Rourke RA (1985) Effect of regional ischemia on the left ventricular end-systolic pressure-volume relation in chronically instrumented dogs. J Am Coll Cardiol **5:** 297–302

Little WC, Badke FR, O'Rourke RA (1984) Effect of right ventricular pressure on the left ventricular diastolic pressure-volume relationship in dogs without pericardia. Circ Res **54:** 718–730

Mahler F, Ross J Jr., O'Rourke RA, Covell JW (1975) Effects of changes in preload, afterload and inotropic state on ejection and isovolumic phase measures of contractility in the conscious dog. Am J Cardiol **35:** 626–634

Mason DT (1969) Usefulness and limitations of the rate of rise of intraventricular pressure (dp/dt) in the evaluation of myocardial contractility in man. Am J Cardiol **23:** 516–527

Maughan WL, Sunagawa K, Burkhoff, Sagawa K (1984) Effect of arterial impedance changes on the end-systolic pressure-volume relation. Circ Res **54:** 595–602

Mehmel HC, Stocknis B, Ruffmann K, von Olshausen K, Schuler G, Kubler (1981) The linearity of the end-systolic pressure-volume relationship in man and its sensitivity for assessment of left ventricular function. Circulation **63:** 1216–1222

Olsen CO, Tyson GS, Maier GW, Spratt JA, Davis JW, Rankin JA (1983) Dynamic ventricular interaction in the conscious dog. Circ Res **52:** 85–104

Quinones MA, Gaasch WH, Alexander JK (1976) Influence of acute changes in preload, afterload, contractile state and heart rate on ejection and isovolumic indices of myocardial contractility in man. Circulation **53:** 293–302

Reeves TJ, Hefner LL, Jones WB, Coghlan C, Prieto G, Carroll J (1960) The hemodynamic determinants of the rate of change in pressure in the left ventricle during isometric contraction. Am Heart J **60:** 745–761

Sagawa K (1978) The left ventricular pressure-volume diagram revisited. Circ Res **43:** 677–687

Sagawa K (1981) The end-systolic pressure-volume relation of the ventricle: Definition, modification and clinical use. Circulation **63:** 1223–1227

Schmidt HD, Hoppe H (1978) Preload dependence of dP/dt$_{max}$, V$_{CE\ max}$ and calculated V$_{max}$ compared to the inotropic sensitivity of these indices of cardiac contractility. Basic Res Cardiol **73:** 380–393

Shroff SG, Janicki JS, Weber KT (1983) Left ventricular systolic dynamics in terms of its chamber mechanical properties. Am J Physiol **245:** H110–H124

Sodums MT, Badke FR, Starling MR, Little WC, O'Rourke RA (1984) Evaluation of left ventricular contractile performance utilizing end-systolic pressure-volume relationships in conscious dogs. Circ Res **54:** 731–739

Suga H, Sagawa K (1972) Mathematical interrelationships between instantaneous ventricular pressure-volume ratio and myocardial force-velocity relation. Ann Biomed Eng **1:** 160–181

Suga H, Yamakoshi K (1977) Effects of stroke volume and velocity of ejection on end-systolic pressure of canine left ventricle. Circ Res **40:** 445–450

Suga H, Sagawa K (1974) Instantaneous pressure-volume relationships and the excised supported canine left ventricle. Circ Res **35:** 117–128

Suga H, Sagawa K, Shoukas AA (1973) Load independence of the instantaneous pressure-volume ratio of the canine left ventricle and effects of epinephrine and heart rate on the ratio. Circ Res **32:** 314–322

Suga H, Sagawa K, Kowtiuk DP (1976) Controls of ventricular contractility assessed by pressure-volume ratio, E$_{max}$. Cardiovasc Res **10:** 582–592

Suga H, Kitabatake A, Sagawa K (1979) End-systolic pressure determines stroke volume from fixed end-diastolic volume in the isolated canine left ventricle under a constant contractile state. Circ Res **44:** 238–249

Sunagawa K, Sagawa K (1982) Models of ventricular contraction based on time-varying elastance. CRC Crit Rev Biomed Eng **7:** 193–228

Wallace AG, Skinner S, Mitchell JH (1963) Hemodynamic determinants of the maximal rate of rise of left ventricular pressure. Am J Physiol **205:** 30–36

Weber KT, Janicki JS, Hunter WC, Shroff S, Pearlman ES, Fishman AP (1982) The contractile behavior of the heart and its functional coupling to the circulation. Prog Cardiovasc Dis **24:** 375–400

Wildenthal K, Mierzwiak DS, Mitchell JH (1969) Effect of sudden changes in aortic pressure on left ventricular dp/dt. Am J Physiol **216:** 185–190

INDEX TERMS: Left ventricular dP/dt • Pressure-volume relations • Left ventricular performance

Characterization of a Kininogenase from Rat Vascular Tissue Resembling Tissue Kallikrein

Hector Nolly, A. Guillermo Scicli, Gloria Scicli, and Oscar A. Carretero
From the Hypertension Research Division, Henry Ford Hospital, Detroit, Michigan

SUMMARY. A kininogenase resembling glandular kallikrein was partially purified from vascular tissue and characterized. Saline-perfused rat tail arteries and veins were homogenized in 0.25 M sucrose containing 10 mM Tris-HCl (pH 7.4). The homogenate was centrifuged at 105,000 *g* for 60 minutes, and a vascular kininogenase was purified from the supernatant by chromatofocusing, affinity chromatography on immobilized antibodies against rat urinary kallikrein, and gel filtration on Sephadex G-100. The inhibitory effects of antibodies against rat urinary kallikrein were tested with equivalent kinin-forming concentrations of rat urinary kallikrein and vascular kininogenase. Kininogenase activities of both enzymes were similarly inhibited by both polyclonal and monoclonal antibodies. Aprotinin (1,000 KIU) completely inhibited vascular kininogenase activity, while soybean trypsin inhibitor (100 μg) did not modify its kinin-forming activity. Vascular kininogenase and rat urinary kallikrein had the same elution volume when chromatographed on a Sephadex G-100 column, and had similar mobilities in 10% polyacrylamide gel electrophoresis. Kinins released by vascular kininogenase were identified as bradykinin by reverse-phase high performance liquid chromatography. Rat vascular kininogenase appears to be similar to glandular kallikrein. Kinins released locally by vascular kininogenase may contribute to the regulation of vascular tone. **(*Circ Res 56: 816–821, 1985*)**

KALLIKREINS are enzymes that generate kinins from protein substrates called kininogens (Webster, 1970). The ubiquity of these enzymes in different tissues, the potent vasodilator action of kinins, and their stimulatory effect upon prostaglandin synthesis in arteries are some of the data that support the postulated role of the kallikrein-kinin system in the regulation of vascular resistance. Tissue kallikreins have recently been found in brain, thyroid gland, intestine, stomach, and plasma (Rabito et al., 1980; Lawton et al., 1981; Uetsuju et al., 1982; Uchida et al., 1982; Chao et al., 1983; Schachter et al., 1983). One of us has previously reported the presence of a kininogenase in rat mesenteric arteries (Nolly and Lama, 1982). However, in this study, contamination with pancreatic kallikrein could not be excluded, since, in the rat, the pancreas is spread into part of the mesenteric region. In the present study, we have determined that a kinin-forming enzyme different from plasma kallikrein is also present in tail arteries and veins of the rat. We have partially purified this vascular kininogenase and defined some of its biochemical characteristics.

Methods

Reagents

The following materials were obtained from commercial sources: molecular weight markers, polybuffer anion exchanger (PBE 94), and polybuffer 74 (Pharmacia Fine Chemicals); captopril (Squibb); polyacrylamide (Eastman Kodak); all other reagents used were analytical grade. Aprotinin was a kind gift from G. Haberland, (A.G. Bayer, W. Germany).

Preparation of Tissue Extracts

One hundred male and female Sprague-Dawley rats (400–500 g) were used. After an animal was killed by decapitation, the ventral artery and veins of the tail were exposed proximally through small incisions and catheterized with P.E. 50 polyethylene tubing (Friedman et al., 1968). The tail was perfused through the artery with a buffered saline solution (pH 7.4) for 10–20 minutes at a flow rate of 1.0 ml/min until the effluent collected from the veins appeared visually free of blood. Subsequently, the vessels were removed, cleaned of any adherent fat and connective tissue, and placed in Petri dishes containing a saline solution. The tail vascular bed was washed by renewing the saline solution several times. Then, the vessels were cut into 1–2 mm rings and kept frozen at −70°C.

For the experiments, 600 mg of tail arteries, 800 mg of tail veins, or 4,200 mg of pooled tail vessels were used. The vessels were frozen and thawed four times. The tissue was suspended in three volumes of 0.25 M sucrose (pH 7.0) and homogenized on ice for four 15-second intervals with a Polytron homogenizer. The homogenate was centrifuged at 1,000 *g* for 10 minutes to eliminate debris. The supernatant was further centrifuged at 105,000 *g* for 60 minutes in a L-5 Beckman ultracentrifuge. This supernatant was dialyzed overnight at 4°C against 0.01 M Tris-HCl buffer (pH 7.0) for further purification. Kininogenase activity was also found in the pellet dissolved in 0.1% Triton X-100, but was much less than that present in the supernatant. Further purification was done using the supernatant.

Chromatofocusing on Polybuffer Anion Exchanger 94 (PBE 94)

The vascular extract was applied to a polybuffer exchanger 94 column (20 × 1 cm) equilibrated with 0.025 M imidazole-hydrochloride buffer (pH 7.4). A pH gradient between 7.0 and 4.0 was obtained by using polybuffer adjusted to pH 4.0. Proteins that were still bound to the gel after pH 4.0 were eluted with 0.1 M sodium acetate buffer, pH 3.5, 1 M NaCl. During acid elution, the pH was rapidly neutralized by collecting in equal volumes of 2 M Tris-HCl, pH 8.5. The fractions obtained after the sodium acetate elution were pooled in three major fractions of 10 ml each. The fractions were dialyzed against distilled water, concentrated by evaporating under a nitrogen stream at 37°C, and frozen at −70°C until assayed for kininogenase activity.

Affinity Chromatography on Immobilized Kallikrein Antibody

The γ-globulin fraction of the rabbit antiserum against rat kallikrein was purified by precipitation with 40% ammonium sulfate. The kallikrein antibodies of this fraction were further purified by adsorption to, and elution from, a rat glandular kallikrein CH-sepharose column. For this, glandular kallikrein was purified from rat submandibular gland by chromatography on DEAE-Sephadex, adsorption to and elution from a aprotinin-sepharose gel, isoelectric focusing, and gel filtration on high performance liquid chromatography (HPLC) with a TSK-250 column. One microgram of the purified enzyme released 1.1 μg of kinin per minute when incubated with semi-purified dog kininogen (Carretero et al., 1976). In 12% slab polyacrylamide gel electrophoresis, purified kallikrein (20 μg) showed a major and a minor band, both of which had kininogenase activity. One milligram of purified rat submandibular gland kallikrein was covalently bound to activated CH-sepharose (Pharmacia) as indicated by the manufacturer.

The kallikrein CH-sepharose gel was equilibrated with 0.1 M Tris-HCl, 0.5 M sodium chloride, pH 8.0, and mixed with the antikallikrein antibodies for 2 hours at room temperature and then overnight at 4°C. After the gel was washed to eliminate unbound material, the antikallikrein antibodies were eluted with 0.1 M acetic acid, pH 2.9. Purified kallikrein antibodies were coupled to activated CH-sepharose (Pharmacia), as suggested by the manufacturer. The antikallikrein-sepharose gel was equilibrated with 0.1 M sodium phosphate buffer, pH 7.4. The fraction containing kininogenase after chromatofocusing activity was dissolved in phosphate buffer and mixed with the antikallikrein-sepharose gel for 2 hours at room temperature, followed by 24 hours at 4°C. Nonbound proteins were separated by successive washings first with 0.1 M sodium phosphate buffer (pH 7.4), and then with 0.1 M sodium phosphate buffer (pH 6.0) containing 1 M NaCl. The kininogenase activity was eluted with 0.1 M sodium acetate buffer (pH 3.5) containing 1 M NaCl. Fractions (3 ml) were collected in equal volumes of 2 M Tris, pH 8.5. The samples then were dialyzed against distilled water, concentrated under a nitrogen stream, and frozen at −70°C until assayed for kininogenase activity.

Gel Filtration on Sephadex G-100 and Molecular Weight Determination

Two milliliters of the concentrated solution from the immunoaffinity chromatography step were applied to a Sephadex G-100 column (50 × 1 cm) equilibrated with 0.1 M phosphate buffer, pH 7.4. The column was eluted at a flow rate of 20 ml/hr. Fractions (4 ml) were collected, dialyzed against distilled water, and frozen at −70°C until assayed. Standards used for molecular weight determination were ovalbumin, chymotrypsinogen, and ribonuclease.

Discontinuous Polyacrylamide Gel Electrophoresis

Disc gel electrophoresis was performed in 10% polyacrylamide gels as described by Nustad and Pierce (1974). Each gel was cut into 2-mm slices, and each slice was homogenized in the presence of 1 ml of 0.1 M sodium phosphate buffer (pH 7.4), centrifuged at 4,000 *g* for 20 minutes, and the supernatant was saved for kininogenase assay.

High Performance Liquid Chromatography of Kinins

Identification of kinins liberated during kininogenase assay was carried out by comparing the elution volume of kinins generated by the vascular homogenate with that of synthetic bradykinin and lys-bradykinin during reverse-phase high performance liquid chromatography. Each kinin solution was injected into a C_{18} Bondapack column equilibrated with 10% acetonitrile in 0.05 M triethyl ammonium formate (TEAF), pH 4.4, and eluted with a linear gradient (10% to 20% acetonitrile in 0.05 M triethyl ammonium formate, TEAF, pH 4.4) with a flow rate of 1 ml/min.

Kininogenase Assay

Kinin-generating activity in tissue extracts and fractions were determined by incubation with partially purified dog kininogen by a method identical to that previously described (Carretero et al., 1976), except that the buffer was altered by the addition of captopril (10 μg/ml). Kinins were measured by RIA (Carretero et al., 1976).

Inhibition Studies

The effect of soybean trypsin inhibitor (SBTI) and aprotinin on vascular kininogenase activity was examined. SBTI was dissolved in 0.1 M Tris-HCl (5,000 μg/ml) and aprotinin was diluted with 0.1 M Tris-HCl (50,000 KIE/ml). The vascular kininogenase was preincubated with 20 μl of the aforementioned inhibitors for 60 minutes at 37°C. The final concentrations of inhibitors was 100 μg of SBTI and 1,000 KIE of aprotinin per ml of sample. The mixture was then incubated with kininogen for assay of kininogenase as described. The γ-globulin fraction of the rabbit antiserum against rat urinary kallikrein was diluted in 0.1 M Tris-HCl buffer (pH 7.4) to a final concentration of 20 mg/ml, and an aliquot containing 10 μg proteins

TABLE 1
Kininogenase Activity in Tail Arteries and Tail Veins

	Kininogenase activity		% Inhibition	
Blood vessel	pg/mg per hr	*n*	UKKAb	SBTI
Tail artery	605 ± 46	6	72	3
Tail vein	528 ± 23	8	87	5

Each experiment consisted of pooled arteries or veins (100 mg) from three to five rats; *n* = number of experiments; UKKAb = urinary kallikrein antibodies; SBTI = soybean trypsin inhibitor (100 μg/ml); mean values ± SE. Kininogenase activity is expressed per mg protein per hour of incubation.

TABLE 2
Purification of Vascular Kininogenase from Rat Tail Vessels

Total purification step	Protein (mg)	Total activity	Specific activity (μg BK/hr)	Purification factor (μg BK/mg per hr)	Yield (%)
Supernatant, 105,000 *g*	1.80	1.68	0.9	1	100
Chromatofocusing	1.08	2.12	2.0	2.1	125
Immunoaffinity	0.028	1.92	68.4	73.3	113
Gel filtration	0.022	1.60	72.7	77.9	95

was added to the samples of vascular kininogenase or urinary kallikrein and preincubated for 60 minutes at 37°C. As control, nonimmunized rabbit serum was used in the same concentration. After the preincubation period, the mixture was incubated with kininogen for assay of kininogenase activity. Monoclonal antibodies against rat glandular kallikrein were kindly provided by Dr. R. Savoy-Moore (Savoy-Moore et al., 1984). Subclones were propagated by intraperitoneal injection in mice. The ascites fluid containing monoclonal antibodies against kallikrein was used. As a control, we used normal mice serum diluted 1/400 with 0.1 M Tris-HCl, pH 7.4

Protein determination was done by the method of Bradford (1976), using bovine serum albumin as the standard. Protein concentration in column effluents was measured at 280 nm ($\mathring{A}_{280}$).

Rat urinary kallikrein was purified with a modification of a previously described method (Oza et al., 1976). In brief, proteins from rat urine obtained by ammonium sulfate precipitation were chromatographed on a DEAE A52 cellulose column. Fractions containing kininogenase activity were adsorbed to and eluted from a aprotinin-CH-sepharose. Further purification was performed by size exclusion in high performance liquid chromatography using a bio-sil TSK-250 column. Purified rat urinary kallikrein was homogeneous in 12% alkaline polyacrylamide gel electrophoresis and released 1.2 μg of kinin per μg protein per min when incubated with semipurified dog kininogen.

Rat plasma kallikrein was prepared from blood collected into 1/10 volumes of 0.1 M sodium citrate solution and centrifuged at 1500 *g* for 30 minutes at 4°C. Acetone was added to the plasma (17% vol/vol) for 18 hours at room temperature. The acetone was evaporated under a nitrogen stream. After correction for water loss, the preparation was kept at −20°C until needed.

Results

Table 1 shows the kininogenase activity of several preparations of tail arteries and veins. The mean values of kininogenase activity and the inhibition profile with kallikrein antibodies and soybean-trypsin inhibitor were similar for both types of blood vessel.

The results of the partial purification of rat vascular kininogenase are summarized in Table 2. Chromatofocusing resulted in a 2-fold increase in the specific activity, but total activity also increased after this step. With immunoaffinity, the specific activity increased up to 68-fold. After gel filtration, a 78-fold purification with 95% recovery was obtained. On chromatofocusing, vascular kininogenase and purified rat urinary kallikrein eluted together when pH reached 3.5 (Fig. 1). This indicates that their isoelectric point is below 4.0.

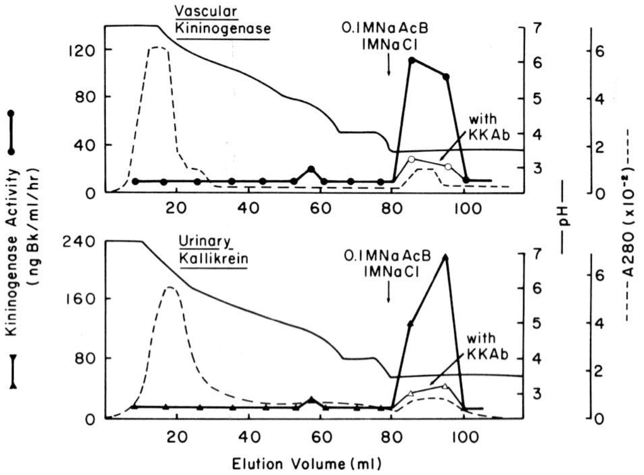

FIGURE 1. *Chromatofocusing on polybuffer anion exchanger 94 (PBE 94). Vascular kininogenase and urinary kallikrein were applied to a column of PBE 94 (20 × 1 cm) equilibrated with 0.025 M imidazole-HCl buffer (pH 7.4). When the pH was 4.0, the vascular kininogenase and urinary kallikrein were eluted with 0.1 M sodium acetate buffer, 1 M NaCl (pH 3.5). Fractions of 2 ml were collected over 2 ml of 2 M Tris-HCl, pH 8.5. Open circles and triangles indicates inhibition of the kininogenase activity by incubation with kallikrein antibodies.*

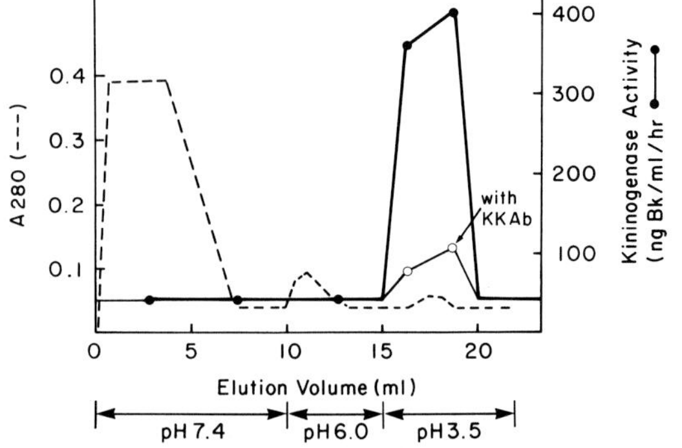

FIGURE 2. *Affinity chromatography of vascular extract on antikallikrein-CH-sepharose. The gel was equilibrated with 0.1 M sodium phosphate buffer (pH 7.4). Weakly bound proteins were eluted with 0.1 M sodium phosphate, 1 M NaCl (pH 6.0), and the vascular kininogenase was eluted with 0.1 M sodium acetate buffer, 1 M NaCl (pH 3.5). Open circles indicate inhibition of the kininogenase activity by incubation with kallikrein antibodies.*

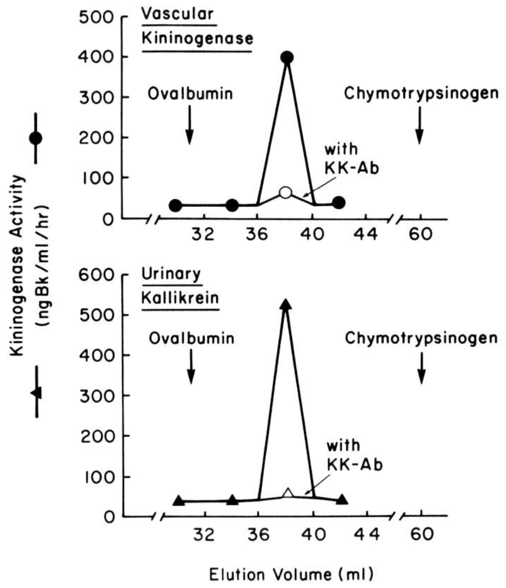

FIGURE 3. *Gel filtration of the purified vascular and urinary kininogenases on Sephadex G-100. The column was eluted at a flow rate of 20 ml/hr. Fractions of 4 ml were collected. Open circles and triangles indicate inhibition of the kininogenase activity by incubation with kallikrein antibodies.*

On immunoaffinity chromatography, the kininogenase activity was eluted in a single peak with 0.1 M sodium acetate buffer (pH 3.5), 1 M NaCl (Fig. 2). Vascular and urinary kininogenases also eluted in a single peak on gel filtration (Fig. 3). Kininogenase activity of both vascular and urinary kallikrein was inhibited by incubation with kallikrein antibodies. The apparent molecular weight of vascular kininogenase as calculated from the elution volume on the gel filtration column was 37,000 daltons (Fig. 4).

Mobility on disc polyacrylamide gel electrophoresis of both vascular kininogenase and urinary kallikrein was similar (Fig. 5).

The kininogenase activity of both vascular kininogenase and urinary kallikrein was completely inhibited (98 ± 2%) by aprotinin (not shown in the figure), whereas it was resistant to soybean trypsin inhibitor. In contrast, the kininogenase activity of trypsin and plasma was strongly inhibited by soybean trypsin inhibitor (Fig. 6). Kininogenase activity of both enzymes was inhibited to the same extent

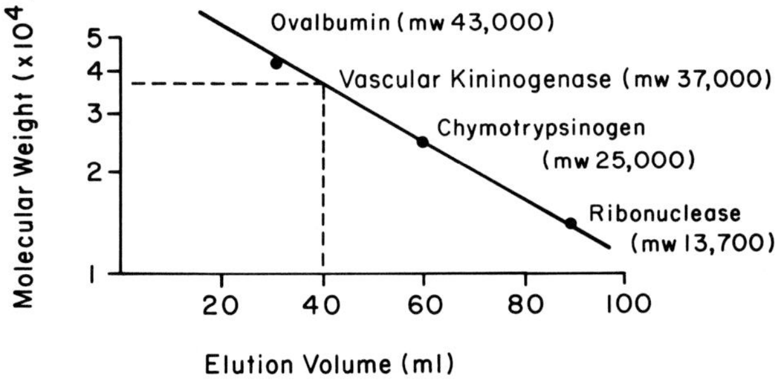

FIGURE 4. *Determination of the molecular weight of vascular kininogenase by gel filtration on a Sephadex G-100 column.*

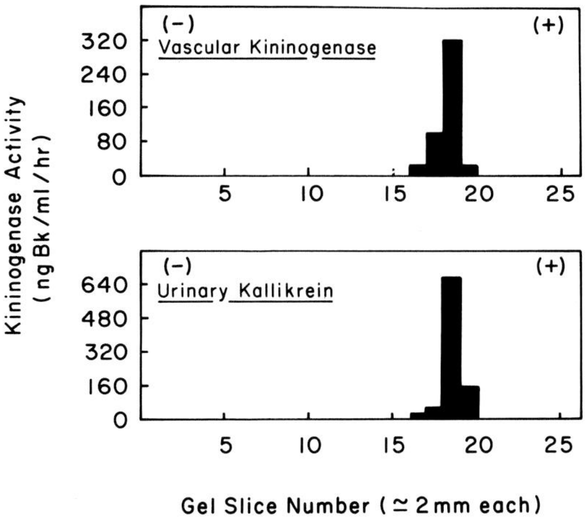

FIGURE 5. *Alkaline disc gel electrophoresis of the purified vascular kininogenase and of urinary kallikrein. Each slice (2 mm) was homogenized and centrifuged; the kininogenase activity was measured in the supernatant.*

by kallikrein antibodies. Nonimmunized rabbit serum had a negligible effect.

Identification of the reaction products by reverse phase HPLC showed that kinins generated by vascular kininogenase had the same elution volume as synthetic bradykinin (Fig. 7).

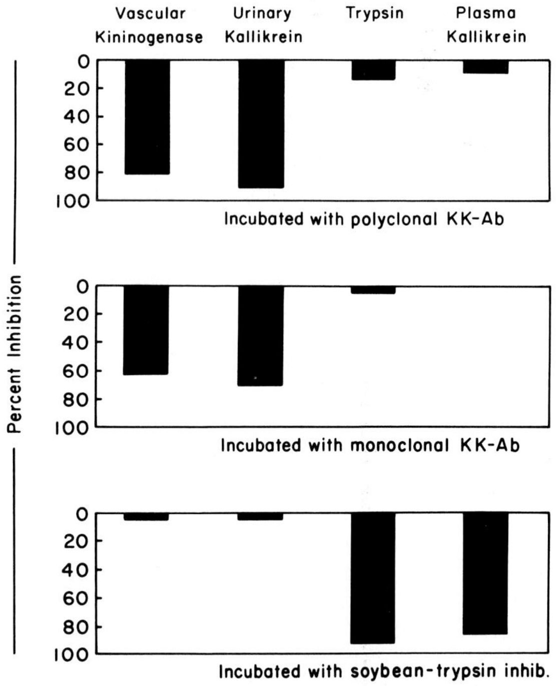

FIGURE 6. *Effect of kallikrein antibodies and soybean trypsin inhibitor on kinin-generating activity of vascular kininogenase, urinary kallikrein, trypsin, and rat plasma (plasma kallikrein). The different enzyme preparations were incubated for 60 minutes at 37°C, pH 8.5, with kallikrein antibody, nonimmunized rabbit serum, or soybean trypsin inhibitor, then kininogenase activity was measured. The values represent the mean of at least three determinations.*

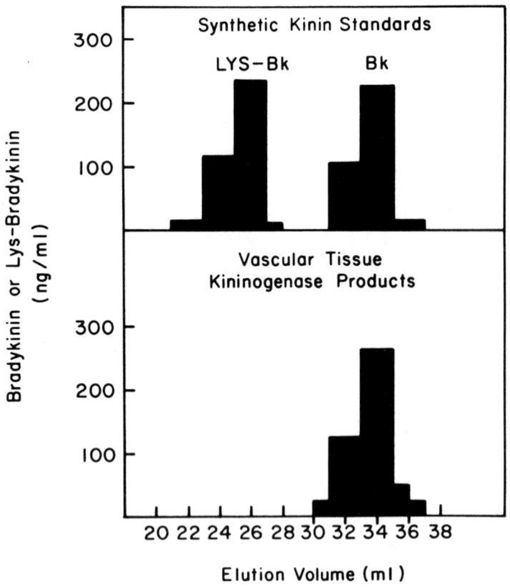

FIGURE 7. *Elution of synthetic kinin standards or kinin generated by the vascular extract. The column was equilibrated and eluted at a flow rate of 1.0 ml/min, as described in Methods. Kinin content of the fractions was measured by RIA. Upper: injection of a mixture of synthetic bradykinin (Bk) or Lys-bradykinin (LYS-Bk). Lower: injection of the kinin product of the vascular kininogenase.*

Discussion

The present study demonstrates that a kinin-forming enzyme is present in rat vascular tissue. Vascular kininogenase was purified by a series of chromatographic steps with a very high yield. This was unexpected, since the combination of these chromatographic steps usually results in much lower recoveries (Fiedler, 1979). Whereas we do not have an explanation for this high yield, it is possible that either activation of a proenzyme or separation from inhibitors may have occurred during purification. Chromatofocusing is likely to be an "activating" step, since it yielded 125% of the loaded activity. The insensitivity of the vascular kininogenase to SBTI readily distinguishes it from trypsin and plasma kallikrein. On the other hand, rat vascular kininogenase appears to be very similar to rat glandular kallikrein; both purified rat vascular kininogenase and urinary kallikrein had similar molecular weights, isoelectric points, electrophoretic mobilities, and inhibition profiles. Only bradykinin was released by vascular kallikrein. This is not surprising, since rat glandular kallikrein differ from similar enzymes from other species in that they generate bradykinin and not lys-bradykinin (Seki et al., 1972; Alhenc-gelas et al., 1981; Yamada and Erdos, 1982).

The similar behavior of both enzymes when reacted with rabbit antiserum against rat urinary kallikrein strengthens the contention that they are very similar if not identical. Vascular kininogenase and urinary kallikrein were strongly bound to kallikrein antiserum coupled to CH-sepharose, since they were not released when the gel was washed with buffer, pH 6.0, containing 1 M NaCl. The property of the vascular kininogenase to bind strongly to immobilized kallikrein antiserum was used for its partial purification from vascular tissue. The combination of chromatofocusing, gel filtration, and immunoaffinity chromatography resulted in a 70-fold purification. Due to the small amount of material available, the analytical techniques usually used to determine purity were not performed.

We do not know at this time the precise localization of vascular kininogenase within the vascular structures. Recently, it has been reported that mast cells from humans and rats have a kallikrein-like enzyme (Proud et al., 1982; Garret et al., 1984), and it has been clearly demonstrated that these cells are normally present around the arterioles, capillaries, venules, and beneath the endothelium in man and rats (McGovern, 1956; Robinson et al., 1978; Plonsky and Boyles, 1981).

In our experiments, the presence of mast cells cannot be ruled out, but recent studies have demonstrated that the kininogenase present in human mast cells is not immunologically cross-reactive with glandular kallikrein (Proud et al., 1982). In addition, the one present in rat mast cells is not inhibited by aprotinin (Garret et al., 1982; Garret et al., 1984). These two important differences should be taken into consideration when comparing them with the vascular kininogenase described here.

Although the precise cellular localization of vascular kininogenase is still unknown, it could be speculated that the enzyme may play a role in regulating local vascular resistance and, hence, blood flow, either directly or through kinin release. If the enzyme is located in the endothelial lining, it may participate in the regulation of phospholipase activity and local formation of arachidonic acid metabolites, either directly (Morita et al., 1984), or through kinin formation (Whorton et al., 1982). If the enzyme is located in smooth muscle, it may participate directly in regulation of vascular tone, and, if located in the adventitia, could have a role in regulating vascular permeability. Furthermore, a recent report (Cardin et al., 1984) suggests that low density lipoproteins are a substrate for tissue kallikrein; thus, tissue kallikrein may participate in low density lipoprotein metabolism within the vascular wall.

In summary, a protease(s) which resembles glandular kallikrein is present in vessels isolated from rat tails. This enzyme is present in an active form, and its isoelectric point, molecular weight, and immunological characteristics are similar to those of urinary kallikrein.

We would like to thank Pat Piejak for typing, and Dr. Robert Murray for editing the manuscript.

This work was supported in part by National Institutes of Health Grants HL 28982, and HL 15839

Dr. Nolly is an Established Investigator of the Argentine Council of Research (CONICET). His present address is: Universidad National

De Cuyo, School of Medicine, Department of Pathology, Mendoza, Argentina.

Address for reprints: Oscar A. Carretero, M.D., Henry Ford Hospital, Hypertension Research Division, 2799 West Grand Boulevard, Detroit, Michigan 48202.

Received December 14, 1984; accepted for publication February 27, 1985.

References

Alhenc-gelas F, Marchetti J, Allegrini J, Corvol P, Menard J (1981) Measurement of urinary kallikrein activity: Species differences in kinin production. Biochim Biophys Acta **677:** 477–488

Bradford MM (1976) A rapid and sensitive method for the quantitation of microgram quantities of protein utilizing the principle of protein-dye binding. Anal Biochem **72:** 248–254

Cardin AD, Witt KR, Chao J, Margolius HS, Donalson VH, Jackson RL (1984) Degradation of apolipoprotein B-100 of human plasma low density lipoproteins by tissue and plasma kallikreins. J Biol Chem **259:** 8522–8528

Carretero OA, Oza NB, Piwonska A, Ocholik T, Scicli AG (1976) Measurement of urinary kallikrein activity by kinin radioimmunoassay. Biochem Pharmacol **25:** 2265–2270

Chao J, Woodley C, Chao L, Margolius HS (1983) Identification of tissue kallikrein in brain and in the cell-free translation product encoded by brain mRNA. J Biol Chem **258:** 15173–15178

Fiedler F (1979) Enzymology of glandular kallikreins. *In* Handbook of Experimental Pharmacology; Bradykinin, Kallidin, and Kallikrein (Suppl), edited by EG Erdos. New York, Springer-Verlag, pp 103–161

Friedman SM, Sustafson B, Hamilton D, Friedman CL (1968) Compartments of sodium in a small artery. Can J Physiol Pharmacol **46:** 673–679

Garret JR, Kidd A, Kyriacou K, Smith RE (1982) New observations on the localization of kallikrein-like activity in human salivary parenchymal and mast cells by enzyme histochemistry. Histochem J **16:** 789–791

Garret JR, Smith RE, Kidd A, Kyriacou K, Grabske RJ (1984) Kallikrein-like activity in salivary glands using a new tripeptide substrate, including preliminary secretory studies and observations on mast cells. Histochem J **14:** 967–979

Lawton WJ, Proud D, Frech ME, Pierce JV, Keiser HS, Pisano JJ (1981) Characterization and origin of immunoreactive glandular kallikrein in rat plasma. Biochem Pharmacol **30:** 1731–1737

McGovern VJ (1956) Mast cells and their relationship to endothelial surfaces. J Pathol Bacteriol **71:** 1–6

Morita I, Kanayasu T, Murota S (1984) Kallikrein stimulates prostacyclin production in bovine vascular endothelial cells. Biochim Biophys Acta **792:** 304–309

Nolly H, Lama MC (1982) "Vascular kallikrein": A kallikrein-like enzyme present in vascular tissue of the cat. Clin Sci **63:** 249s–251s

Nustad K, Pierce JV (1974) Purification of rat urinary kallikrein and their specific antibody. Biochemistry **13:** 2312–2319

Oza NB, Amin VM, McGregor RK, Scicli AG, Carretero OA (1976) Isolation of rat urinary kallikrein and properties of its antibodies. Biochem Pharmacol **25:** 1607–1612

Plonsky LD, Boyles J (1981) Vascular associations of mast cells in the diaphragm. Microvasc Res **22:** 127–142

Proud D, Schulman ES, MacGlashan DW, Pierce JV, Newball HH (1982) Anaphylactic release of a kininogenase from purified human lung mast cells. Clin Res **30:** 165A

Rabito SF, Scicli AG, Carretero OA (1980) Immunoreactive glandular kallikrein in plasma. *In* Enzymatic Release of Vasoactive Peptides, edited by F Gross, HG Vogel. New York, Raven Press, pp 247–258

Robinson RW, Likar IN, Likar LJ (1978) Mast cells in normal, aged and discussed arteries. Monogr Atheroscler **8:** 73–116

Savoy-Moore RT, Carretero OA, Scicli AG (1984) Characterization and application of monoclonal antibodies against kallikrein (KK) (abstr). Fed Proc **43:** 359

Schachter M, Peret MW, Billing AG, Wheeler GD (1983) Immunolocalization of the protease kallikrein in the colon. J Histochem Cytochem **31:** 1255–1260

Seki T, Nakajama T, Erdos EG (1972) Colon kallikrein: Its relation to the plasma enzyme. Biochem Pharmacol **21:** 1227–1235

Uchida K, Kushino H, Kodama J, Hitomi Y, Niinobe M, Fujii S (1982) Rat thyroid kallikrein: Its purification and properties. Agents Actions [Suppl] **9:** 167–172

Uetsuji S, Yamamura M, Yamamoto M, Uchida K, Kushiro H, Kodama J, Fuji S (1982) Human stomach kallikrein. Agents Actions [Suppl] **9:** 137–142

Webster ME (1970) Kallikrein in glandular tissue. *In* Handbook of Experimental Pharmacology; Bradykinin, Kallidin and Kallikrein, edited by EG Erdos. New York, Springer-Verlag, pp 131–156

Whorton AR, Young SC, Data JL, Barchowsky A, Kent RS (1982) Mechanism of bradykinin-stimulated prostacyclin synthesis in porcine aortic endothelial cells. Biochim Biophys Acta **712:** 79–87

Yamada K, Erdos EG (1982) Kallikrein and prekallikrein of the isolated basolateral membrane of rat kidney. Kidney Int **22:** 331–337

INDEX TERMS: Kininogenases • Kallikrien-kinin system • Arterial wall • Kinins and blood pressure • Serine protease

Differences in Norepinephrine Activation and Diltiazem Inhibition of Calcium Channels in Isolated Rabbit Aorta and Mesenteric Resistance Vessels

Cynthia Cauvin, Scott Lukeman, John Cameron, Ok Hwang, and Cornelis van Breemen
From the Department of Pharmacology, University of Miami School of Medicine, Miami, Florida

SUMMARY. The mechanisms of norepinephrine stimulation of calcium ion entry in isolated rabbit aorta and mesenteric resistance vessels were studied through measurements of effects on calcium-45 influx, tension, and membrane potential. The resistance vessels were considerably less sensitive to norepinephrine than the aorta. The aorta exhibited complex dose-response curves for norepinephrine-stimulated calcium influx and contraction, whereas these were simple in the arterioles. Both vessels were depolarized with increasing concentrations of potassium. Norepinephrine did not depolarize the aorta, whereas it did depolarize the mesenteric resistance vessels. This result supports the contention that norepinephrine opens receptor-operated channels to induce calcium entry in the aorta, while it may activate potential sensitive calcium channels in the mesenteric resistance vessels. However, the maximum depolarization with norepinephrine (10^{-4} M) in the arterioles was completely blocked by 10^{-5} M diltiazem, whereas that induced by 80 mM potassium was unaltered by the diltiazem. Furthermore, 10^{-4} M norepinephrine was able to stimulate virtually the same contraction and calcium influx in 80 mM potassium-depolarized arterioles as in normal polarized tissues. These results are consistent with norepinephrine opening of receptor-operated channels to allow calcium entry in the rabbit mesenteric resistance vessels. That the behavior of norepinephrine-activated channels in the aorta is more complex than in the arterioles is further illustrated by a dramatically decreasing sensitivity of norepinephrine-stimulated calcium influx to diltiazem with increasing norepinephrine in the aorta but not in the arterioles. We have hypothesized that the complexity of the norepinephrine-stimulated calcium influx in the aorta compared to the resistance vessels may be related to the substantial release of intracellular calcium in the former, such that, as release of intracellular calcium is increased, sensitivity of norepinephrine-activated channels to diltiazem decreases. ***(Circ Res 56: 822–828, 1985)***

ORGANIC Ca^{++} antagonists demonstrate a remarkable degree of selectivity for particular tissues, even though their binding affinities to membranes isolated from these tissues are only minimally different (for reviews, see Flaim and Zelis, 1982; Merrill and Weiss, 1982; Cauvin et al., 1983; Janis and Triggle, 1984). For example, Towart (1981) has shown that nimodipine is 10,000 times more potent in relaxing the serotonin-contracted rabbit basilar artery than the saphenous artery. Similarly, diltiazem relaxes norepinephrine (NE)-constricted rabbit mesenteric resistance vessels at concentrations which are five orders of magnitude lower than those needed to inhibit aortic norepinephrine contractions (Cauvin et al., 1984). To explain such selectivity in the light of uniform binding constants, it is necessary to compare mechanisms of Ca^{++} mobilization in arteries possessing different sensitivities to Ca^{++} antagonist-induced relaxation. For this purpose, we chose the rabbit aorta and mesenteric resistance vessels. The latter should be a particularly interesting model, since human resistance vessels are extremely important Ca^{++} antagonist targets, whereas very little is known about their Ca^{++} regulation.

Saida and van Breemen (1983) established that intracellular Ca^{++} release is far less sensitive to blockade by diltiazem and nisoldipine than is stimulated Ca^{++} entry. Furthermore, in most blood vessels, Ca^{++} antagonists more potently inhibit Ca^{++} entry stimulated by electrical and potassium-induced depolarization than that activated by pharmacological agonists. In the present study, we have investigated mechanisms of stimulated Ca^{++} entry and intracellular release in the aorta and resistance vessels by recording their contractile tension, Ca^{++} fluxes, and membrane potentials. Moreover, differences in these phenomena in the two vessels are discussed in relationship to differences in the pattern of diltiazem sensitivity of the Ca^{++} influx pathways in the two vessel types. (Cauvin et al., 1984). Parts of this work have been presented in preliminary reports (van Breemen et al., 1982; van Breemen et al., 1983; Cauvin and van Breemen, 1983; Lukeman and van Breemen, 1983).

Methods

New Zealand white rabbits were stunned and exsanguinated; the thoracic aorta and mesenteric vascular bed were then removed. Vascular tissues were cleaned of fat and surrounding tissue while incubated in warmed (37°C), oxygenated (100% O_2), physiological salt solution (PSS) of the following composition (mM): NaCl (140), $MgCl_2$ (1), $CaCl_2$ (1.5), KCl (4.6), dextrose (10), HEPES buffer (5); pH = 7.4.

Contractions

For contraction studies, aortic rings were mounted as previously described (van Breemen et al., 1972). Isolated cylindrical segments (2 mm long) of fourth or fifth branches (≈200 μm i.d.) of the superior mesenteric artery were mounted in a manner adapted from Bevan and Osher (1972) and Mulvany and Halpern (1977). Two 40-μm tungsten wires (Westinghouse, Inc.) were passed through the lumen of the isolated mesenteric resistance vessel. One wire was fastened with screws to a fixed tissue mount. The other wire was pulled taut by parallel hooks that were attached to a strain gauge force transducer (U-gage, Shinko Co, Ltd.), the position of which could be adjusted with a micromanipulator. A resting tension of 25 mg was placed on the tissues, which were allowed to equilibrate for 1 hour. Concentration-response curves for NE were obtained in both vessel types by exchanging the bathing media with PSS containing successively higher concentrations of NE. Contractions in Ca^{++}-free solution were obtained by omitting Ca^{++} from the PSS and adding 2 mM EGTA; preincubation for 10 minutes in this solution was used for all contractions in Ca^{++}-free media.

^{45}Ca Flux Measurements

Unidirectional Ca^{++} influx measurements were made by a pulse labeling technique (Meisheri et al., 1981). After tissues were dissected and allowed to equilibrate in PSS for 2 hours, they were placed in ^{45}Ca-containing media (either PSS or experimental media) for 90 seconds, then were washed for 40 minutes (resistance vessels) or 45 minutes (aortae) in ice cold, vigorously gassed with a calcium-free PSS solution containing 2 mM EGTA. Tissues then were blotted gently, weighed (to 0.01 mg), and placed in 5 mM EDTA solution overnight. A scintillation cocktail containing toluene and Triton X-100 was added and the tissues were counted. Ca^{++} influx was then calculated using the specific activity of the labeling media. Experimental labeling media consisted of PSS with various NE concentrations, and NE-containing PSS plus various concentrations of diltiazem. In experiments in which inhibitory effects of diltiazem on Ca^{++} influx were determined, a 10-minute preincubation period in nonlabeled PSS plus the diltiazem was utilized. Concentrations at which diltiazem inhibited 50% of the NE-stimulated Ca^{++} influx (IC_{50}) were determined graphically from dose-response curves.

Membrane Potential Measurements

To determine membrane potential, short (<1 cm) cylindrical segments of aorta were cut open and pinned, intimal surface upward, in an 80-ml Lucite tissue bath. Segments of the mesenteric vascular bed were mounted intact for electrophysiological recording from resistance vessels. The tissues were continuously superfused with warmed, oxygenated PSS. Transmembrane potentials were recorded with standard glass microelectrodes filled with 3 M KCl that had tip resistances in the range of 40–90 MΩ. The microelectrodes were connected to dual differential preamplifiers with input impedences of 10^5 MΩ (WPI, KS 700). Amplifier output was displayed on a calibrated oscilloscope (Tektronix) for visual determination of membrane potential. No potentials were accepted unless the following criteria were fulfilled: (1) upon initial impalement, potential changes were abrupt and subsequent drift was less than 10 mV; (2) membrane potential remained stable for at least 30 seconds; (3) upon retraction, the potential returned abruptly to baseline; (4) electrode resistance before and after an impalement was identical. Electrode resistance was also checked during each impalement, and when it increased dramatically, the electrode was removed from the cell and resistance was checked again. If the resistance remained elevated, the electrode was assumed to be plugged and was discarded. Also, care was taken to balance DC offset potentials for each electrode in order to account for microelectrode tip potentials. At the end of the experiment, electrode tips were broken and tip potential was determined. These were always less than or equal to 6 mV. When feasible, electrode penetration was maintained during drug infusion. However, contraction induced by stimulatory agents often forced the microelectrode out of the cell. In either case, a series of at least 10 separate membrane potential determinations were carried out before and after each change in drug or ionic concentration.

Drugs

The following drugs were utilized in this study: norepinephrine (*l*-arterenol bitartrate; Sigma) and diltiazem (Marion).

Statistics

Values are given as means ± SE. To compare means, Student's *t*-test for unpaired data was utilized. ($P < 0.05$ considered significant). Unless otherwise indicated, values indicate the number of animals used.

Results

The first three figures illustrate marked differences in the way NE activates the rabbit aorta and mesenteric resistance vessels. In the aorta, the threshold for contraction is 3×10^{-9} M, but maximal contraction is not achieved until 10^{-5} M NE (Fig. 1). The shallow concentration response curve has a Hill coefficient of 0.7, which may indicate negative cooperativity, more than one operative receptor, or multiple contributing processes. At least two processes appear to be operational, as indicated by the concentration-response curves for NE-stimulated ^{45}Ca influx and the less NE-sensitive intracellular Ca^{++} release contractions (Fig. 1). The concentration response curve for NE-stimulated ^{45}Ca influx appears to be biphasic, which may be suggestive of two receptors activated or two ^{45}Ca influx processes. Receptor binding studies (Docherty et al., 1981), as well as our own previous work (Cauvin et al., 1982) indicate that only α_1-adrenoceptors are involved in NE activation of this vessel. In contrast, the mesenteric resistance vessels present a much simpler picture with similar, monophasic concentration-response curves for contraction and stimulated ^{45}Ca influx and very little responsiveness in the absence of external Ca^{++} (Fig. 2). The resistance vessels respond to NE concentrations of 3×10^{-7} through

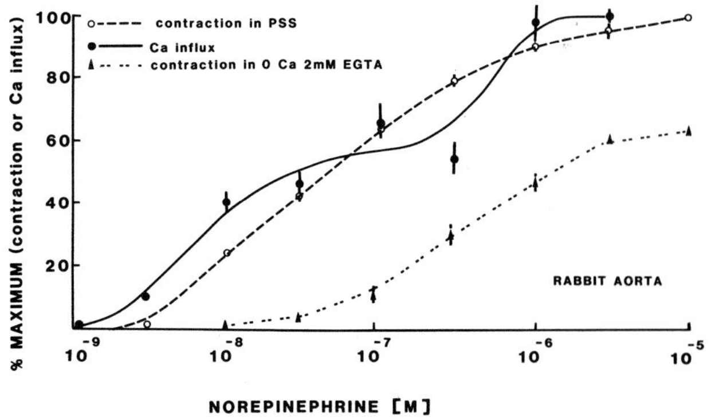

FIGURE 1. *Concentration-response curves for norepinephrine-induced contraction in normal physiological saline solution (PSS), stimulated calcium (^{45}Ca) influx, and contraction in calcium-free solution containing 2 mM EGTA in isolated rabbit aorta. Contraction values (n = 4–5; 2 tissues each) are expressed as means ± SEM. ^{45}Ca influx was calculated in μmol/kg wet weight. NE-stimulated ^{45}Ca influx was calculated by subtracting the ^{45}Ca influx in PSS from that obtained with NE. The maximum value of NE (10^{-5} M)-stimulated ^{45}Ca influx was 21 ± 2 μmol ^{45}Ca/kg in 90 seconds; NE stimulated ^{45}Ca influx significantly at all concentrations equal to or greater than 10^{-8} M (n = 4–5, 4–5 tissues each). These data have been presented in a preliminary report (van Breemen et al, 1982).*

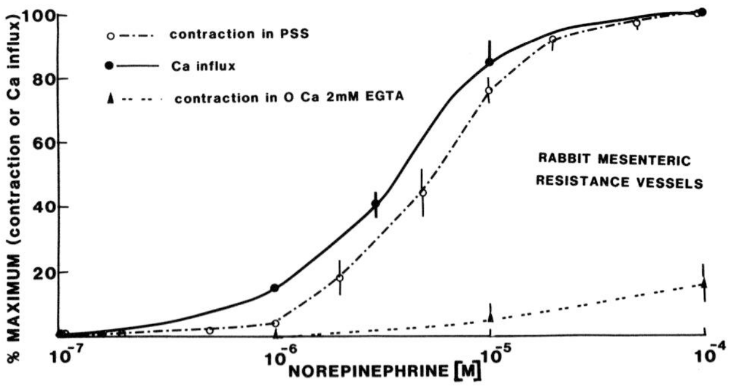

FIGURE 2. *Concentration-response curves for norepinephrine-induced contraction in calcium-free PSS containing 2 mM EGTA, and for stimulated ^{45}Ca influx in isolated rabbit mesenteric resistance vessels. Contractions values (n = 4–5) are expressed as means ± SEM. ^{45}Ca influx calculations were as described in Figure 1. NE stimulated ^{45}Ca influx significantly at all concentrations greater than or equal to 10^{-6} M (n = 4–5, 2–3 tissues each).*

10^{-4} M in a manner consistent with a single activating process, namely, stimulation of Ca^{++} influx, with little to no release of intracellular Ca^{++}.

We next examined the effects of NE on membrane potential (E_m) in the two artery types. Figure 3 illustrates that over the concentration range where NE activates the aorta, it causes no significant cell membrane depolarization. As expected, membrane depolarization was recorded in the aorta and mesenteric resistance vessels when the external K^+ concentration was raised (Fig. 3). However, in contrast to the lack of NE depolarization in the aorta, it caused marked depolarization of the mesenteric resistance vessels. Figure 4 shows the voltage-tension curves for NE and K^+ activation of the two vessels. The coupling of E_m and tension changes in the aorta, and mesenteric resistance vessels activated by elevated K^+ are fairly similar. The aorta begins to contract at a more polarized E_m than do the resistance vessels. Tension develops from 20–100% of maximum with a 16-mV change in E_m in the aorta compared to a 13-mV change in the mesenteric resistance vessels. The voltage-tension coupling relationship for depolarization induced by NE in the mesenteric resistance vessels has a markedly lower voltage threshold for tension development (−53 mV) as compared to that for K^+-induced tension development (−39 mV). The voltage change for which tension develops from 20–100% of maximum is 14 mV, which is very similar to that observed with K^+-induced depolarization and tension development.

From these data, it appeared likely that NE activated the rabbit aorta through pharmacomechanical coupling, while it activated the mesenteric resistance vessels through electromechanical coupling. To strengthen this conclusion, we performed a set of experiments similar to ones previously performed in rabbit aorta (Meisheri et al., 1981). In the rabbit

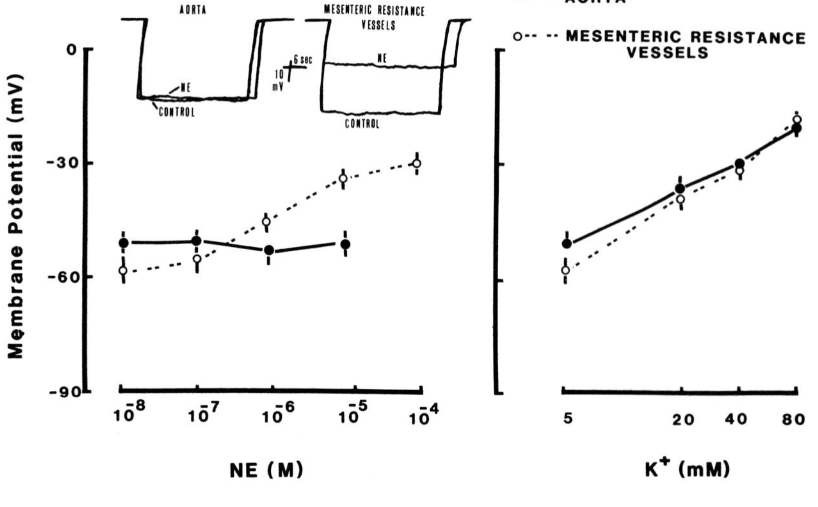

FIGURE 3. *Concentration-response curves for norepinephrine (NE)- and potassium (K^+)-induced changes in membrane potential in isolated rabbit aorta and mesenteric resistance vessels. Values are expressed as means ± SEM, and represent at least five determinations per animal for at least five animals. The insert at top left shows representative tracings from physiograph recordings of membrane potential measurements from the two vessel types. The membrane potentials recorded from tissues during steady state NE contractions are superimposed upon those recorded from tissues resting in PSS.*

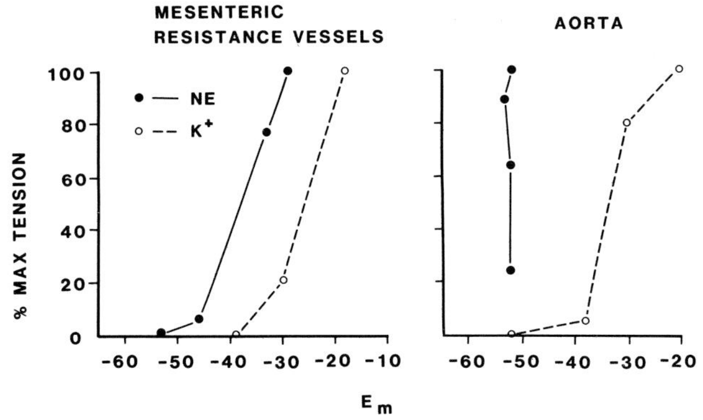

FIGURE 4. *Voltage-tension coupling curves for NE and K^+ activation of rabbit aorta and mesenteric resistance vessels.*

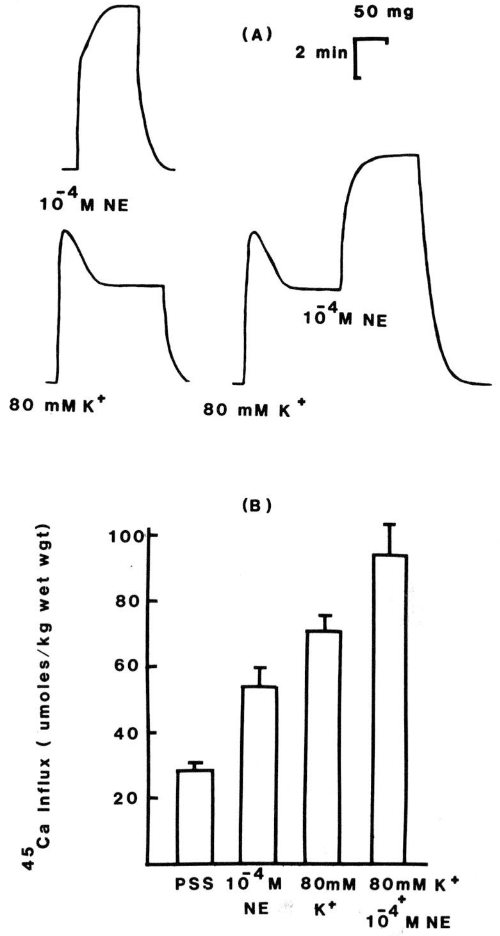

FIGURE 5. *Panel A: representative tracings of norepinephrine (NE)-induced contractions in normal polarized and in 80 mM K^+-depolarized rabbit mesenteric resistance vessels. Panel B: unidirectional Ca^{++} influx measured over a 90-second period in the indicated media. The Ca^{++} influx stimulated by the combination of 80 mM K^+ and 10^{-4} M NE was significantly ($P < 0.05$, $n = 8$) greater than that stimulated by the K^+ alone.*

aorta, 80 mM K^+ and 10^{-5} M NE were found to stimulate contraction and ^{45}Ca influx in an additive manner. Since these two modes of activation represented maximal stimulation of their respective activation mechanisms, the additivity suggested that these activation mechanisms were distinct, as has been verified by the lack of depolarization by NE in the aorta (Fig. 3). We expected to find the opposite result in the mesenteric resistance vessels, since NE activation is associated with depolarization in these tissues (Fig. 3). We found, however, that after depolarization of the mesenteric resistance vessels with 80 mM K^+, NE induced contraction and ^{45}Ca influx to nearly the same extent as in normal polarized tissues (Fig. 5). The contraction by NE in high K^+ was 92 ± 5% of that obtained in normal PSS. The ^{45}Ca influx stimulated by NE over 80 mM K^+ was 24 ± 8 μmol/kg wet tissue compared to 26 ± 5 μ mol/kg stimulated by NE over basal levels in ^{45}Ca-PSS. The stimulation of tension and ^{45}Ca influx by NE in the 80 mM K^+-depolarized tissues occurred in the absence of further depolarization by NE. These results led us to question whether NE-induced depolarization may be a secondary rather than primary event in excitation contraction coupling. To study this possibility, we determined the effects of the Ca^{++} entry blocker diltiazem (10^{-5} M) on NE and 80 mM K^+-induced depolarization in these vessels. This concentration of diltiazem has been shown to inhibit completely the ^{45}Ca influx stimulated by both these modes of activation in these vessels (Cauvin et al., 1984). The diltiazem had no significant effect on the resting E_m, or on the K^+ depolarization, but it completely inhibited the NE depolarization (Table 1).

The final comparison between the aorta and mesenteric resistance vessels was with regard to their patterns of diltiazem sensitivity of NE-stimulated ^{45}Ca influxes. We reported previously that NE-stimulated ^{45}Ca influx was more sensitive to diltiazem in the mesenteric resistance vessels for maximal activation (Cauvin et al., 1984). Figure 6 shows the IC_{50} for diltiazem inhibition of ^{45}Ca influx stimulated by varying [NE]. The aorta is variable in its sensitivity to diltiazem with variable [NE]; i.e., as the level of NE activation increases, the diltiazem sensitivity decreases. In contrast, the mesenteric resistance vessels maintain their high sensitivity to diltiazem throughout the effective NE concentration range.

TABLE 1
Membrane Potentials in Rabbit Mesenteric Resistance Vessels

Bathing medium	Membrane potential (mV)*
PSS	57 ± 2
PSS + 10^{-5} M diltiazem	54 ± 3
PSS + 10^{-4} M norepinephrine	29 ± 1
PSS + 10^{-5} M diltiazem + 10^{-4} M norepinephrine	53 ± 4
80 mM K^+	18 ± 3
80 mM K +10^{-5} M diltiazem	20 ± 1
80 mM K +10^{-4} M norepinephrine	19 ± 3

* Values are given as means ± SEM for at least five animals, with at least five determinations made per animal.

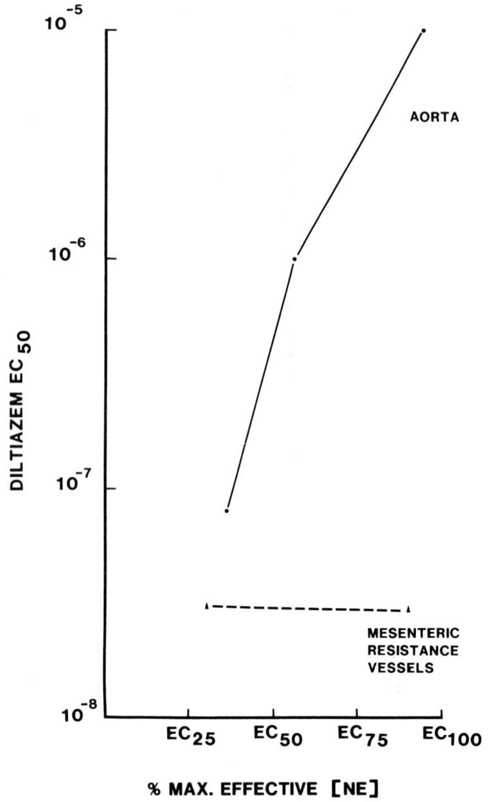

FIGURE 6. *The half-maximally effective diltiazem concentration (ordinate) in inhibiting ^{45}Ca influx stimulated by the various percent maximally effective concentrations of norepinephrine (abscissa) in isolated rabbit aorta and mesenteric resistance vessels.*

Discussion

The concept of pharmacomechanical coupling in smooth muscle has long been debated (Somlyo and Somlyo, 1968). Edman and Schild (1962) originally demonstrated that acetylcholine could cause a sustained contraction of uterine smooth muscle that was previously depolarized with a high K^+ solution, and that the contraction was dependent upon extracellular Ca^{++}. In 1964, Su et al. reported that perivascular nerve stimulation induced contraction of the rabbit pulmonary artery without depolarizing the smooth muscle membrane. Droogmans et al. (1977) later found that exogenously applied NE could produce maximal contraction of the rabbit ear artery without causing depolarization. These observations, along with the observation that the sustained phase of agonist-induced contraction of arteries generally is dependent upon extracellular Ca^{++} (Bohr, 1963; Hink, 1964; Flaim and Zelis, 1982; Cauvin et al., 1983; Loutzenhiser et al., in press), led to the hypothesis that NE could stimulate Ca^{++} entry into arterial smooth muscle through receptor-operated channels (ROC) rather than potential sensitive Ca^{++} channels [PSC (Bolton, 1979; van Breemen et al., 1979)]. However, in many arterial preparations, agonists have been found to produce at least some degree of depolarization (Casteels et al., 1977; Haeusler, 1978; Hermsmeyer et al., 1981; Mulvany et al., 1982; Harder and Hermsmeyer, 1983). Nevertheless, three further lines of evidence which support the hypothesis that NE could stimulate Ca^{++} entry through ROC in the isolated rabbit aorta are as follows: (1) ^{45}Ca influx stimulated by NE (10^{-5} M) is additive to that stimulated by 80 mM K^+ (Meisheri et al., 1981); (2) ^{45}Ca influx induced by 80 mM K^+ is selectively inhibited over that stimulated by 10^{-5} M NE when organic Ca^{++} antagonists (Meisheri et al., 1981; Cauvin et al., 1983) or dibutyryl cAMP (Meisheri and van Breemen, 1982) are employed to inhibit Ca^{++} entry; and (3) the ^{45}Ca influx stimulated by the new "Ca^{++} channel agonist" Bay K8644 is additive to that stimulated by 10^{-5} M NE, but not to that stimulated by 80 mM K^+ (Yamamoto et al., 1984). The final line of evidence that NE opens ROC in rabbit aorta is that it produces a tonic contraction that is dependent on Ca^{++} influx without producing membrane depolarization (see Fig. 3). It could be argued that the cells near the medial surface do not represent all aortic smooth muscle cells, and, hence, that our E_M measurements made from the intimal surface could have missed NE depolarization of cells near the adventitial surface. We feel that this is unlikely, since Mekata (1984) has shown that NE depolarized the muscle in the inner but not the outer regions of the rabbit carotid artery. Our results thus indicate that NE induces Ca^{++} entry in the rabbit aorta and its consequent tonic contraction through pharmacomechanical coupling.

In the rabbit aorta, the concentration-response curve for NE-induced contraction is very shallow. Possible explanations for this observation are the presence of more than one type of α-adrenoreceptor or the operation of multiple Ca^{++} delivery systems. It has been suggested that α_1-adrenoceptors activate intracellular Ca^{++} release while α_2-adrenoreceptors are linked to Ca^{++} channels (van Meel et al., 1981). This hypothesis was refuted, however, when it was found that the aortic NE contractions were initiated exclusively via α_1-adrenoreceptors (Cauvin et al., 1982). Nevertheless, it can be seen that the NE concentration ranges over which Ca^{++} release and influx are stimulated are not identical, intracellular Ca^{++} release being less sensitive to NE than Ca^{++} influx. The concentration-response curve for NE-stimulated Ca^{++} influx is also very shallow, with a second component of stimulated Ca^{++} influx becoming apparent at NE concentrations which induce intracellular Ca^{++} release. The absence of membrane depolarization during exposure of the aorta to NE rules out the possibility that the two Ca^{++} influx components are due to sequential opening of ROC and PSC; however, different open states of the ROC are possible, and may be an explanation for the drastic change in their sensitivity in aorta to diltiazem as NE concentrations are varied (see Fig. 6).

Excitation-contraction coupling mechanisms for NE activation of the rabbit mesenteric resistance vessels are apparently quite different from those in the aorta. Figure 2 shows for the full active NE concentration range that there is very little release of intracellular Ca^{++} in the rabbit mesenteric resistance vessels, whereas this phenomenon is substantial in the aorta. [This comparison for 10^{-5} M NE in the two vessels originally suggested this conclusion (Cauvin et al., 1984).] Moreover, NE depolarizes the plasmalemma in these vessels, while it has no effect on E_M in the aorta (Fig. 3). Hence, whereas NE appears to induce contraction through pharmacomechanical coupling in the aorta, it is not completely clear how it does so in the resistance vessels. The electromechanical relationship for NE-induced depolarization and contraction of these vessels has the same slope as that for K^+-induced depolarization and tension. The degree of E_M change associated with 80% of the tension development for NE and K^+ is similar to that reported by others for peripheral but not cerebral arteries, where the E_M changes are larger (see Hermsmeyer et al., 1981, for review). The threshold for tension development occurs at a more polarized E_M for NE than for K^+, suggesting that NE may modify the gating and conductance for PSC. The latter hypothesis may also explain why addition of NE to vessels which were depolarized already with 80 mM K^+, did not affect the E_M (Table 1), but still increased tension and stimulated ^{45}Ca influx to nearly the same extent as it did in normal polarized tissues (see Fig. 5). However, an alternative explanation for the increase in tension and Ca^{++} entry produced by NE under these conditions might be the opening of ionic channels similar to the ROC found in the rabbit aorta. Consistent with this possibility is the observation that diltiazem prevented NE- but not 80 mM K^+-induced depolarization. This observation is similar to that of Ito et al. (1978) who found that NE depolarization of the rabbit pulmonary artery was blocked by diltiazem. These results are unlikely to be due to specific α-adrenoceptor blockade, since diltiazem binds preferentially to Ca^{++} channels over α-adrenoceptors (Motulsky et al., 1983). The diltiazem may, however, inhibit both Ca^{++} and Na^+ entry (Aaronson and Jones, 1983) in these vessels, thereby preventing NE depolarization. Bolton and Kitamura (1983) have provided evidence to support the hypothesis that activation of muscarinic receptors in guinea pig intestional smooth muscle opens receptor-operated ionic channels, which can admit sufficient Ca^{++} to depolarize the cells and cause tension development. It is unclear at this time whether a similar conclusion can be reached in the rabbit mesenteric resistance vessels for NE activation.

One question that arises from this study is why NE depolarizes the mesenteric resistance vessels, but not the aorta. Droogmans et al. (1977) have suggested that the lack of NE-induced depolarization that they have found in the rabbit ear artery could be due to rectifying increases in other ion permeabilities (e.g. K^+), such that the overall effect of NE on the membrane potential would not change. The lack of NE-induced membrane depolarization that we found in the rabbit aorta does not agree with the results of Mekata (1979), who found a 21-mV depolarization by 10^{-5} g/ml noradrenaline (~6×10^{-5} M NE) in a PSS containing 2.5 mM Ca^{++}. The greater $[Ca^{++}]$ used by Mekata would produce greater Ca^{++} entry in this vessel (Lodge and van Breemen, in press) than that in 1.5 mM Ca^{++} used in the present study. This greater Ca^{++} entry may be responsible for the depolarization seen by Mekata, if the Ca^{++} entry were not fully electrically compensated for by other ion fluxes.

The final question we examined was how the differences observed between the activating mechanisms of the two arteries might be related to their differences in diltiazem sensitivity. ^{45}Ca influx stimulated by NE (10^{-5} M) in the rabbit aorta has been shown to be far less sensitive to diltiazem inhibition than that in the mesenteric resistance vessels (Cauvin et al., 1984). It may be suggested that the depolarization by NE observed in the mesenteric resistance vessels but not in the aorta sensitizes these arteries to diltiazem; however, there are two indirect arguments against this explanation. One is the fact that, at low NE concentrations, the aorta does not depolarize, yet its NE-stimulated Ca^{++} influx at these low concentrations is almost as sensitive to diltiazem as that in the resistance vessels (Cauvin et al., 1984). The other is that the ^{45}Ca influx induced by 10^{-5} M NE in the mesenteric resistance vessels is approximately 20 times more sensitive than that induced by 80 mM K^+. An alternative explanation proposed for the differences in diltiazem sensitivity of the NE-activated Ca^{++} channels in the two vessels is that their sensitivity to diltiazem may be inversely related to the process of intracellular Ca^{++} release (Cauvin et al., 1984). It is clear that when comparing agonist-induced contractions and their sensitivity to Ca^{++} antagonists among various vessels, this sensitivity appears to be inversely related to the release of intracellular Ca^{++} by that agonist in different vessels (see Cauvin et al., 1983, for review). Furthermore, the NE-stimulated Ca^{++} influx in the rabbit aorta at high concentrations of NE is much less sensitive to diltiazem than at low concentrations of NE, and is less sensitive than in the resistance vessels at all NE concentrations (Fig. 6). Since this pattern is inversely correlated to the pattern of intracellular Ca^{++} release in these arteries, it is possible that the Ca^{++} release process may perturb the cell membrane in a manner which affects the α-adrenoceptor-activated Ca^{++} channels. In light of the clinical importance of Ca^{++} antagonist selectivity, we feel that the latter hypothesis deserves further investigation.

Our thanks to Libby Blasdel and Maria-Isabel Martinez for typing the manuscript.

This work was supported by National Institutes of Health Grants

HL 29467 and HL 30412, and the American Heart Association, Florida Affiliate.

Address for reprints: Cynthia Cauvin, Ph.D., University of Miami School of Medicine, Department of Pharmacology (R-189), Miami, Florida 33101.

Received January 25, 1984; accepted for publication February 28, 1985.

References

Aaronson P, Jones A (1983) Effects of forskolin and diltiazem on polyionic fluxes in rabbit arterial smooth muscle (abstr). Fed Proc **42:** 398

Bevan JA, Osher JV (1972) A direct method for recording tension changes in the wall of small blood vessels in vitro. Agents and Actions **2:** 257–260

Bohr DF (1963) Vascular smooth muscle: Dual effect of calcium. Science **139:** 597–599

Bolton T (1979) Mechanisms of action of transmitters and other substances on smooth muscle. Physiol Rev **59:** 607–718

Bolton T, Kitamura K (1983) Evidence that ionic channels associated with the muscarinic receptor of smooth muscle may admit calcium. Br J Pharmacol **78:** 405–416

Casteels R, Kitamura K, Kuriyama H, Suzuki H (1977) Excitation-contraction coupling in the smooth muscle cells of the rabbit main pulmonary artery. J Physiol (Lond) **271:** 63–79

Cauvin C, van Breemen C (1983) Sensitivity of norepinephrine (NE) induced ^{45}Ca influx to diltiazem (Dilt) in rabbit aorta and mesenteric resistance vessels (mrv's) (abstr). Fed Proc **42:** 1348

Cauvin C, Loutzenhiser R, Hwang O, van Breemen C (1982) α_1-adrenoceptors induce Ca influx and intracellular Ca release in isolated rabbit aorta. Eur J Pharmacol **84:** 233–235

Cauvin C, Loutzenhiser R, van Breemen C (1983) Mechanisms of calcium antagonist-induced vasodilation. Annu Rev Pharmacol Toxicol **23:** 373–396

Cauvin C, Saida K, van Breemen C (1984) Extracellular Ca^{2+} dependence and diltiazem inhibition of contraction in rabbit conduit arteries and mesenteric resistance vessels. Blood Vessels **21:** 23–31

Docherty J, Constantine J, Starke J (1981) Smooth muscle of the rabbit aorta contains α_1-but not α_2-adrenoceptors. Naunyn Schmiedbergs Arch Pharmacol **317:** 5–7

Droogmans G, Raeymakers L, Casteels R (1977) Electro- and pharmacomechanical coupling in the smooth muscle cells of the rabbit ear artery. J Gen Physiol **70:** 129–148

Edman K, Schild H (1962) The need for calcium in contractile responses induced by acetylcholine and potassium in the rat uterus. J Physiol (Lond) **161:** 424–441

Flaim SF, Zelis R (eds) (1982) Calcium Blockers. Mechanisms of Action and Clinical Applications. Baltimore, Urban & Schwarzenberg

Haeusler G (1978) Relationship between noradrenaline-induced depolarization and contraction in vascular smooth muscle. Blood Vessels **15:** 46–54

Harder D, Hermsmeyer K (1983) Membrane mechanisms in arterial hypertension. Hypertension **5:** 404–408

Hermsmeyer K, Trapani A, Abel P (1981) Membrane potential-dependent tension in vascular smooth muscle. *In* Vasodilation, edited by P Vanhoutte, I Leusen Raven Press, pp 273–284

Hinke J (1964) Calcium requirements for noradrenaline and high potassium ion contraction in arterial smooth muscle. *In* Muscle, edited by W Paul, E Daniel, C Kay, G Monckton. New York, Pergamon, pp 269–284

Ito Y, Kuriyama H, Suzuki H (1978) The effects of diltiazem on the membrane and mechanical properties of vascular smooth muscles of the rabbit. Br J Pharmacol **64:** 503–510

Janis RA, Triggle DJ (1984) 1,4-dihydropyridine Ca^{2+} channel antagonists and activators: A comparison of binding characteristics and pharmacology. Drug Development Res **4:** 257–274

Lodge N, van Breemen C (in press) The mobilization of extracellularly bound Ca^{2+} during high K^+ and norepinephrine stimulation of the rabbit aorta. Blood Vessels

Loutzenhiser RD, Leijten PA, Saida K, van Breemen C (in press) Ca^{2+} compartments and Ca^{2+} mobilization during contraction of smooth muscle. *In* Calcium and Smooth Muscle Contractility, edited by A Grover, E Daniel. Humana Press

Lukeman S, van Breemen C (1983) Differential effects of calcium blockers on Ca influx and contractile tension in vascular smooth muscle (abstr). Fed Proc **42:** 1348

Meisheri KD, Hwang O, van Breemen C (1981) Evidence for two separate Ca^{2+} pathways in smooth muscle plasmalemma. J Membr Biol **59:** 19–25

Meisheri KD, van Breemen C (1982) Effects of β-adrenergic stimulation on Ca^{2+} movements in rabbit aortic smooth muscle: relationship with cyclic AMP. J Physiol (Lond) **331:** 429–441

Mekata F (1979) Studies of the electrical excitability of aorta smooth muscle of rabbit. J Physiol (Lond) **293:** 11–21

Mekata F (1984) Different electrical responses of outer and inner muscle of rabbit carotid artery to noradrenaline and nerves. J Physiol (Lond) **346:** 589–98

Merrill GF, Weiss HR eds (1982) Symposium on Calcium Entry Blockers, Adenosine and Neurohumors. Baltimore/Munich, Urgan & Schwarzenberg

Motulsky HJ, Snavely MD, Hughes RJ, Insel PA (1983) Interaction of verapamil and other Ca channel blockers with α_1- and α_2-adrenergic receptors. Circ Res **52:** 226–231

Mulvany MJ, Halpern W (1977) Contractile properties of small arterial resistance vessels in spontaneously hypertensive and normotensive rats. Circ Res **41:** 19–26

Mulvany MJ, Nilsson H, Flatman JA (1982) Role of membrane potential in the response of rat small mesenteric arteries to exogenous noradrenaline stimulation. J Physiol (Lond) **332:** 363–373

Saida K, van Breemen C (1983) Mechanism of Ca^{2+} antagonist induced vasodilation; intracellular actions. Circ Res **52:** 137–142

Somlyo AP, Somlyo AV (1968) Vascular smooth muscle. I. Normal structure pathology, biochemistry and biophysics. Pharmacol Rev **20:** 197–272

Su C, Bevan J, Ursillo RC (1964) Electrical quiescence of pulmonary artery smooth muscle during sympathomimetic stimulation. Circ Res **15:** 20–27

Towart R (1981) The selective inhibition of serotonin-induced contractions of rabbit cerebral vascular smooth muscle by calcium-antagonist dihydropyridines. An investigation of the mechanism of action of nimodipine. Circ Res **48:** 650–657

van Breemen C, Farinas BR, Gerba P, McNaughton D (1972) Excitation-contraction coupling in rabbit aorta studied by the lanthanum method for measuring cellular calcium influx. Circ Res **30:** 44–54

van Breemen C, Aaronson P, Loutzenhiser R (1979) Na-Ca interactions in mammalian smooth muscle. Pharmacol Rev **30:** 167–208

van Breemen C, Hwang O, Cauvin C (1982) Ca antagonist inhibition of norepinephrine stimulated Ca influx in vascular smooth muscle. *In* Calcium Modulators, edited by T Godfraind, A Albertini, R Paoletti. Amsterdam, Elsevier Biomedical Press, pp 185–198

van Breemen C, Lukeman S, Loutzenhiser R, Saida S, Cauvin C (1983) Ca^{2+} "channels" and Ca^{2+} antagonists in arterial smooth muscle. *In* Calcium Antagonists: The State of the Art & Role in Cardiovascular Disease, edited by B Hoffman. Philadelphia, College of Physicians of Philadelphia, pp 13–26

van Meel JCA, de Jonge A, Kalkman HO, Wilffert B, Timmermans PBMWM, van Zwieten, PA (1981) Organic and inorganic Calcium Antagonists reduce vasoconstriction in vivo mediated by postsynaptic α_2-adrenoceptors. Naunyn Schmiedbergs Arch Pharmacol **316:** 288–293

Yamamoto H, Hwang O, van Breemen C (1984) Bay K 8644 differentiates between potential- and receptor-operated Ca^{2+} channels. Eur J Pharmacol **102:** 555–557

INDEX TERMS: Norepinephrine • Membrane depolarization • Ca^{++} channels • Ca^{++} antagonists • Arteries and arterioles • Intracellular Ca^{++} • Ca^{++} influx

Cytoskeletal Features of Rat Aortic Cells during Development

An Electron Microscopic, Immunohistochemical, and Biochemical Study

Olivier Kocher, Omar Skalli, Daniel Cerutti, Francoise Gabbiani, and Giulio Gabbiani
From the University of Geneva, Department of Pathology, Geneva, Switzerland

SUMMARY. Actin, vimentin, desmin, and tropomyosin distribution in rat aortic endothelial and smooth muscle cells has been studied during development using fetal (18 to 20 days of gestation), and 5- and 14-day-, and 5-, and 12-week-old rats. Endothelial cells of newborn animals actively replicate and contain many actin stress fibers, whereas, in adult animals, replication is minimal and actin stress fibers are rare. The actin, vimentin, desmin, and tropomyosin content of smooth muscle cells increases gradually from fetal to adult animals. The number of desmin-containing cells also increases from 13% in fetal rats to 51% in adult rats. The β-actin isoform is predominant in fetal and newborn animals, but gradually the α-isoform becomes quantitatively the most important, as seen by bidimensional polyacrylamide gels. Several analogies exist between the features of developing smooth muscle and what is known for developing striated muscle cells. The evolution of cytoskeletal features from fetal to adult animals is remarkably the opposite of what takes place in: (1) rat aortic smooth muscle cells proliferating after an endothelial injury, (2) human arterial smooth muscle cells present in atheromas, and (3) actively growing rat aortic smooth muscle cells in vitro. Thus, the assumption that pathological or cultured smooth muscle cells are "dedifferentiated" is supported by our biochemical observations. **(*Circ Res 56: 829–838, 1985*)**

ALTHOUGH several features of embryonic and neonatal arterial endothelial (EC) and smooth muscle (SMC) cells are well documented (Stein et al., 1969; Gerrity and Cliff, 1975; Gerrity et al., 1975; Cliff, 1976; Schwartz and Benditt, 1977; Olivetti et al., 1980), little is known about their cytoskeletal composition. Quantitative and qualitative changes of cytoskeletal elements have been shown to represent useful markers for the study of differentiation phenomena (Moll et al., 1982; Osborn and Weber, 1982) and, in some cases, of pathological phenomena (Osborn and Weber, 1983; Rungger-Brändle and Gabbiani, 1983). Our laboratory has previously reported that during endothelial regeneration and smooth muscle proliferation in the rat aorta following an experimental endothelial injury, typical morphological and biochemical changes of cytoskeletal elements develop (Gabbiani et al., 1984; Kocher et al., 1984), which vary with the evolution of the lesions (Kocher et al., 1984). SMC of the human atheromatous plaque show a pattern of cytoskeletal composition similar to that of proliferating rat SMC (Gabbiani et al., 1984). We undertook the present study to learn more about the cytoskeletal features (and their evolution) of aortic EC and SMC in embryonic, neonatal, and adult rats and to compare these features with those previously described in the same cells of rats and humans under pathological conditions.

Methods

Experimental Procedures

A total of 190 fetal (18–20 days of gestation), 5- and 14-day-old, and 5- and 12-week-old female Wistar rats were used. The rats were killed by perfusion through the left ventricle of the heart with 0.9% NaCl when the aortas were used for biochemical studies (70 rats), and by enzymatic digestion (70 rats) with 2% paraformaldehyde when the aortas were used for immunofluorescent staining (40 rats) or with 2% glutaraldehyde when the aortas were processed for electron microscopy (10 rats). For the biochemical studies and SMC isolation, the aorta was opened on its dorsal aspect, the endothelium was gently scraped with a scalpel, and the media was carefully dissected from the adventitia under a magnifying glass with fine forceps (Kocher et al., 1984). The completeness of the dissections was controlled by light microscopic examination of hematoxylin and eosin or van Gieson elastin-stained sections, or of toluidine blue-stained sections of Epon-embedded tissue.

SMC were harvested from enzymatically dissociated rat aortic media according to the method described by Ives et al. (1978) for normal rabbit aorta. After 2 hours of digestion at 37°C in minimal Eagle medium (MEM), pH 7.4, containing 0.2% collagenase (*Clostridium histolyticum*, Sigma Chemical Co., type I, 125–250 U/mg), 0.05% elastase (pancreatopeptidase, Sigma Chemical Co.) type III, 70 U/mg), 0.1% soybean trypsin inhibitor (Boehringer Co, Mannheim), 25 mM HEPES (Sigma Chemical Co.), SMC were centrifuged at 300 *g*, washed, and resuspended in

MEM and were used for immunofluorescence or electrophoretic analysis. The percent of cell recovery was 32.5 ± 5.5 (mean of three experiments ± SE) in adult animals and 29.0 ± 4.0 (mean of three experiments) in newborn animals. In both cases, the dead cells (measured by Trypan blue dye exclusion) were less than 5%.

Electron Microscopy

The fetal aorta was fixed by immersion in glutaraldehyde (2% in 0.1 M cacodylate buffer, pH 7.4), and the same fixative was perfused through the left ventricle of the heart at a constant pressure of 30 mm of Hg for 5- and 14-day-old rats and of 100 mm of Hg for 5- and 12-week-old rats. The thoracic aorta was isolated and processed as previously described (Gabbiani et al., 1979). Sections 1 μm thick were cut on a Reichert ultramicrotome and stained with toluidine blue; from selected areas, thin sections were cut and examined with a Philips 300 or 400 electron microscope.

EC Thymidine Index, Density, and En Face Staining with Anti-Actin Antibodies (AAA)

Five-day-old (20) and 12-week-old (20) Wistar rats were used for this experiment. For the study of EC thymidine index and density, we followed essentially the protocol described by Schwartz and Benditt (1977). Each rat received intraperitoneally tritium-labeled thymidine ([^{3}H]-TdR, The Radiochemical Center, specific activity 5 Ci/mmol) dissolved in saline at the dose of 5 μCi of [^{3}H]TdR per 10 g body weight 3 times at 8-hour intervals. One hour after the third injection, perfusion with 2% glutaraldehyde in 0.1 M cacodylate buffer (pH 7.4) was carried out through the left ventricle of the heart for 10 minutes. Thoracic aortas were then isolated, cleaned, opened on the dorsal aspect, and cut into blocks, about 5 mm long, which were prepared for autoradiography on en face preparation, as previously described (De Chastonay et al., 1983). Cells were counted using a Zeiss light microscope equipped with a square-shaped reticulum in a 10× eyepiece and a 40× objective. Cell density was determined as the average number of cells (evaluated by counting nuclei) per unit area (= 0.04 mm^2) (Schwartz and Benditt, 1977; De Chastonay et al., 1983). Thymidine index was calculated as the number of labeled cells divided by the total number of cells (cell density × number of fields counted).

For the endothelial en face preparations stained with AAA, the above procedure was modified according to a method described previously (Gabbiani et al., 1983).

Immunofluorescent Staining for Vimentin and Desmin

Vimentin antibodies were raised in guinea pigs against the 57-kD band of a 7% preparative sodium dodecyl sulfate-polyacrylamide gel (SDS-PAGE) loaded with a Triton X-100 high-salt extract (Franke et al., 1979) of human embryo lung fibroblasts (Azzarone et al., 1983). Desmin antibodies were raised in rabbits against a 53-kD band of a 7% preparative SDS-PAGE loaded with chicken gizzard acetone powder highly enriched in desmin (Hubbard and Lazarides, 1979). An IgG fraction of both sera was obtained by passing them on a column of sepharose covalently linked with protein A (protein-A sepharose Cl-4B, Pharmacia). Affinity-purified antibodies were then prepared by passing these fractions through a column of ultrogel AcA22 (LKB Co.) covalently linked (Nagle et al., 1983), respectively, with pure vimentin from bovine lens (Geisler and Weber, 1981) or desmin from chicken gizzard (Geisler and Weber, 1980). For immunofluorescent staining, we used the indirect method (Gabbiani et al., 1981) with: (1) the antibody containing whole sera (a drop of 40 μl diluted 1:20), (2) IgG fractions (a drop of 40 μl containing 0.5 mg of protein/ml for antidesmin IgG and 0.9 mg/ml for antivimentin IgG), and most frequently (3) the affinity-purified antibodies (a drop of 40 μl containing 0.05 mg of protein/ml for antidesmin and 0.18 mg/ml of antivimentin antibodies). For the second step, we used goat antibodies to guinea pig and rabbit IgG (Behringwerke, both diluted 1:20 in PBS). To avoid cross-reactions, the second antibodies were passed on a solid immunoabsorbent made with glutaraldehyde-coupled rat IgG (Avrameas and Ternynck, 1969). Isolated SMC were cytocentrifuged with a Shandon cytocentrifuge (Shandon Scientific Co, Ltd.) at 125 *g*, fixed in methanol at −20°C for 5 minutes, and double stained with desmin and vimentin antibodies. For fetal, 5-day- and 14-day-old rats, we have pooled cells from five animals per determination, and, for 5-week-old rat, we have pooled cells from three rats per determination. Results are given as mean ± SE of at least three determinations. The percentage of cells positive for vimentin, desmin, or both were counted 3 times independently by two researchers without knowledge of the condition examined. Fragmented cells were excluded from the evaluation.

Photographs were taken with a Zeiss (Carl Zeiss, Inc.) photomicroscope equipped with epi-illumination and specific filters for fluorescein and rhodamine, generally using a plan apo-chromate ×63/1.4 objective on 640-T color slide film (3M Company).

DNA and Protein Determination, Sodium Dodecyl Sulfate Polyacrylamide Gels (SDS-PAGE), and Densitometry

We determined DNA content by the method of Burton (1968), and of protein content by the method of Bradford (1976). For SDS-PAGE, tissues or isolated cells were dissolved directly in sample buffer containing 1 mM phenylmethylsulfonylfluoride, sonicated (3 times, 20 seconds, at setting 7 of a Branson sonifier) and boiled for 3 minutes. We used 10% resolving gels (Laemmli, 1970) which were stained with Coomassie blue. For quantification of actin, vimentin, desmin, and tropomyosin, gels were scanned with a high-resolution laser beam densitometer built from readily obtainable precision optical, electronic, and mechanic components essentially according to Brayden and Halpern (1983) with few modifications. The densitometer was connected by means of an analog-to-digital converter to a computer (microcomputer based on the S-100 bus running under CP/M operating system, Digital Research Inc.) programmed for scanning and quantifying one-dimensional Coomassie blue or silver-stained gels and one-dimensional autoradiographic film profiles generated in gel electrophoresis of radioactive proteins or nucleic acids. The BASIC-program developed in our laboratory was based on previous work (Schumaker, 1978; Yakin et al., 1982): it corrects the baseline and minimizes the background noise. Areas of selected peaks are integrated and given as percentage of the total area of the scan. Raw densitometric data (Fig. 1a) are smoothed with a triangularly weighted average of neighboring samples with the same algorithm used by Yakin et al. (1982). Every density sample taken within the scanning line is replaced by the weighted mean of an area of a predetermined length (or

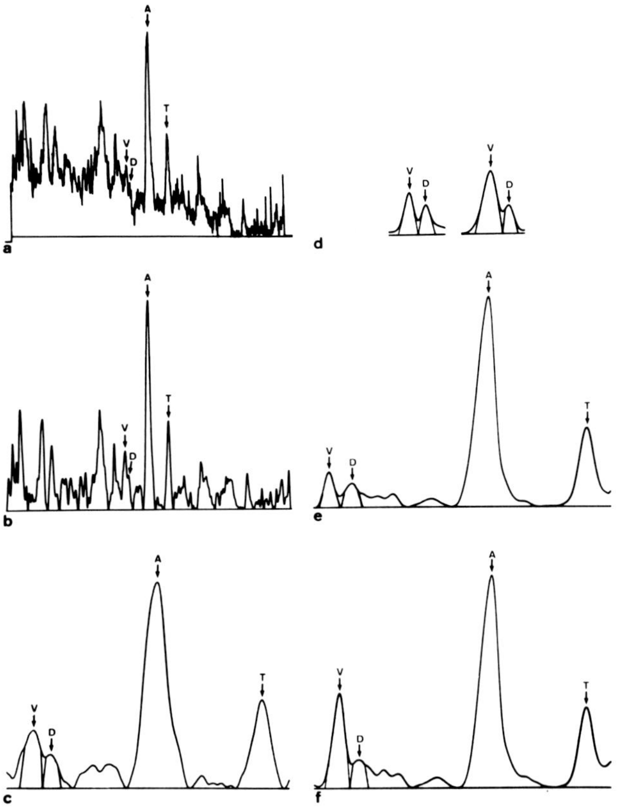

FIGURE 1. *Programmed background reduction and baseline correction on a densitometric profile obtained by scanning a Coomassie blue-stained SDS-PAGE of a total extract of 5-week-old rat aortic media. Panel a: sketch of the absorbance along the migration path of proteins. Panel b: profile developed from panel a, after processing by the program for smoothing and baseline evaluation. Panel c: automatic enlargement of the area under the profile in panel b from the vimentin (V) peak to the tropomyosin (T) peak and arbitrary tracing of the limits of vimentin and desmin (D) peaks. Panel d: enlargement of tracings obtained from gels in which pure vimentin is mixed together with pure desmin; left: 1 μg of vimentin plus 0.5 μg of desmin; right: 2 μg of vimentin plus 0.5 μg of desmin. The surface calculated in internal units of the computer is: Left: vimentin = 8200, desmin = 4150; and right: vimentin = 16500, desmin = 4200, thus showing that increasing the vimentin peak does not alter the surface of the desmin peak and that doubling the amount of vimentin results in doubling the peak area. Panel e: enlargement from the V-peak to the T-peak of a tracing of normal adult rat aortic media. Panel f: enlargement of the tracing of the same normal adult rat aortic media to which 2 μg of vimentin have been added. Here again, addition of vimentin to the preparation produces an increase of the peak area very close to the expected value, whereas the desmin peak does not change. Quantification of peak areas is given in Table 1. A = actin.*

window). The window size has been adjusted to provide the best noise filtration without modifying protein peaks. Baseline evaluation is derived from the method of Schumaker (1978) which breaks up the total profile into smaller regions; these are used to determine line segments giving the background. We use a window of predetermined length which moves along the total profile. For every point located in the middle of the window, we obtain a background which is equal to the minimal value in the window. The resulting background profile is subtracted from the smoothed profile, giving the final profile as shown in Figure 1b. Single peaks are integrated and given as a percentage of the total area of the scan. For determination of overlapping peaks, these are arbitrarily delimited by tracing a diagonal line connecting the presumed peak limit (in general, at a shoulder of the slope) with the baseline. For practical reasons, this is made on an enlargement of the relevant area (Fig. 1c represents an enlargement of the area containing the peaks of vimentin, desmin, actin, and tropomyosin in Fig. 1b). Care should be taken that the two lines delimiting each peak (here, vimentin and desmin) do not overlap. The delimited peaks are integrated and given as percentage of the total area of the scan.

Calibration experiments were done with purified cytoskeletal proteins (actin, vimentin, and desmin), alone, or mixed in different proportions, and by adding different amounts of each of these proteins to preparations of media of normal adult rats. In all cases, the addition of known amounts of actin, vimentin, and desmin, in the range of the amounts tested, resulted in linear increases of the areas of the peaks studied. Special care was taken in controlling the arbitrary delimitation of vimentin- and desmin-overlapping peaks by calculating the area of peaks under the tracing of known amounts of purified vimentin and desmin mixed together in different proportions (Fig. 1d) or added to preparations of media of normal adult rats (Figs. 1, e and f). The results thus obtained showed a good correlation between the area of peaks and the amounts of the two proteins charged on the gels. Table 1 shows an example of the results obtained by adding known amounts of vimentin to a preparation of normal adult rat aorta. In further control experiments, we verified that, over the concentration range studied, Coomassie blue staining is directly proportional to the amount of vimentin, actin, and desmin, and that the same amounts of these proteins stain with comparable intensity, thus allowing direct visual or densitometric comparison on the same gel. Results are expressed as means ± SEM. The number of samples utilized for each analysis is indicated in the tables. The evaluation of the results was done by means of Student's *t*-test and Bonferroni method (Wallenstein et al., 1980).

Bidimensional gels were performed according to the method of O'Farrel (1975) with minor modifications in sample preparation (Kelly and Cotman, 1978).

Results

Morphology, Thymidine Index, and Cell Density of EC

At electron microscopic examination, EC of newborn animals were in general similar to those of adult rats, as previously described (Schwartz and Benditt, 1972; Cliff, 1976). However, EC of newborn animals contained larger amounts of rough endoplasmic reticulum than did those of adult animals (Schwartz and Benditt, 1972), and, in addition, contained many cytoplasmic microfilament bundles, localized mainly at the abluminal periphery of the cell (Fig. 2), which showed dense areas distributed throughout their length. These bundles or "stress fibers" (Burridge, 1981; Gabbiani et al., 1983; White et al., 1983; Wong et al., 1983) were similar to those previously described by means of electron microscopy in aortic EC of hypertensive adult animals

TABLE 1
Densitometric Evaluation of Vimentin and Desmin in Preparations of Normal Adult Rat Aorta with or without Addition of Known Quantitites of Vimentin

	Vimentin		Desmin	
	% of total proteins	μg	% of total proteins	μg
Normal adult rat aorta	1.89 ± 0.24	0.95 ± 0.12	1.34 ± 0.06	0.67 ± 0.03
Normal adult rat aorta + 0.5 μg of vimentin	2.91 ± 0.17 (2.89)	1.46 ± 0.09 (1.45)	1.37 ± 0.05	0.69 ± 0.03
Normal adult rat aorta + 1 μg of vimentin	3.80 ± 0.30 (3.90)	1.90 ± 0.15 (1.95)	1.35 ± 0.06	0.68 ± 0.03
Normal adult rat aorta + 2 μg of vimentin	5.97 ± 0.24 (5.89)	2.99 ± 0.12 (2.95)	1.40 ± 0.10	0.70 ± 0.05

In all cases, 50 μg of proteins of normal adult rat aorta were loaded on the gel. Values in μg are calculated from the % of total proteins. The expected values are in parentheses.

(Gabbiani et al., 1975, 1979). After immunofluorescent staining of en face preparations in 5-day-old rats, stress fibers were very evident, averaging 3–4/cell, and being present in practically all EC (Fig. 3a). No differences in stress fibers distribution were seen in EC located close to the ostia of intercostal arteries compared to EC located in the ventral part of the aorta. Thymidine index in en face preparations of newborn rat EC was 0.130 ± 0.004 and cell density was 130 ± 2.4. In adult rats, endothelial cells contained stress fibers only exceptionally and preferentially in areas immediately below the ostia of intercostal arteries (Gabbiani et al., 1983), but showed a faint accumulation of actin at their periphery (Fig. 3c). Thymidine index was 0.007 ± 0.0007 and cell density was 75 ± 1.

Morphology of SMC

By means of electron microscopy, we examined the SMC of fetal, 5-day-, 14-day-, 5-week-, and 12-week-old rats. As previously described (Cliff, 1976; Gerrity and Cliff, 1975; Gerrity et al., 1975; Stein et al., 1969), fetal and newborn rat aortas contained 6–7 layers of SMC. In contrast to adult animals, they showed prominent endoplasmic reticulum and Golgi apparatus (Fig. 4a). In the extracellular space, elastic laminae were present but discontinuous, and very few collagen fibers were seen. In older rats, the appearance of SMC changed; in particular, they developed an important microfilamentous apparatus, distributed throughout the cytoplasm (Fig. 4b) whereas endoplasmic reticulum and Golgi apparatus became minor cytoplasmic components and were confined to the perinuclear space. Intermediate filaments were present at all times, distributed throughout the cytoplasm. With increasing age, the layers of SMC became separated by much wider elastic laminae, and collagen fibers increased in quantity, as previously described (Stein et al., 1969; Gerrity and Cliff, 1975; Gerrity et al., 1975; Cliff, 1976).

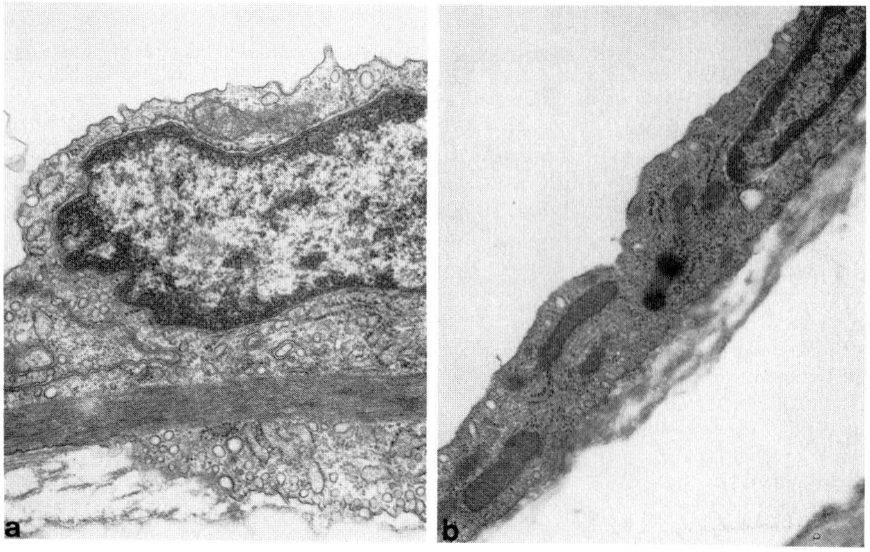

FIGURE 2. *Morphological features of aortic EC in newborn (panel a) and adult (panel b) rats. The EC in panel a contains, in addition to the usual organelles, a prominent band of microfilaments, running parallel and close to the abluminal surface. 22,000×.*

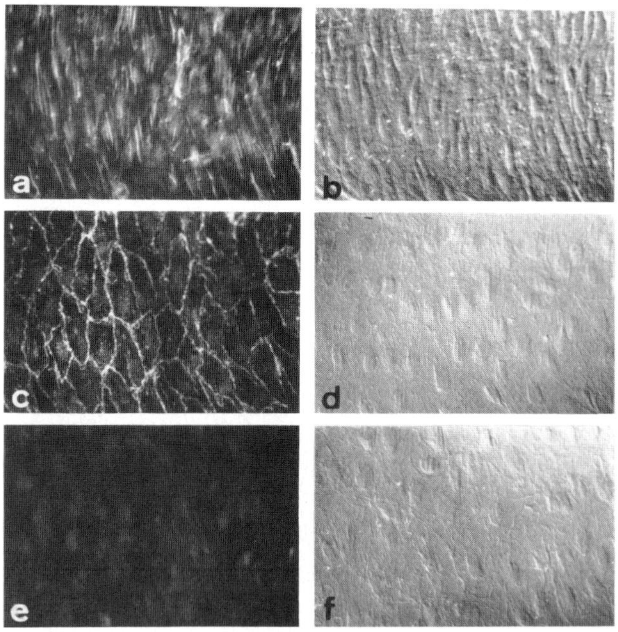

FIGURE 3. *Actin distribution in EC of newborn and adult rats. The en face preparation of EC in a newborn rat (panel a) shows the presence of many actin-positive intracellular stress fibers. These are absent in EC of an adult animal (panel c). Panel e shows a control en face preparation of EC in an adult animal incubated with normal human IgG instead of AAA. Panels b, d, and f are Nomarski optics micrographs corresponding to panels a, c, and e, respectively. Note that the cell density is higher in the newborn than in the adult animal; the EC of the adult animal also appears flatter than those of the newborn animal. 400×.*

Immunofluorescent and Biochemical Characterization of Cytoskeletal Elements in SMC

Double immunofluorescence staining with antivimentin and antidesmin antibodies was applied on isolated SMC from the media of fetal, 5-day-old, 14-day-old, and 5-week-old rats (Fig. 5). In fetal

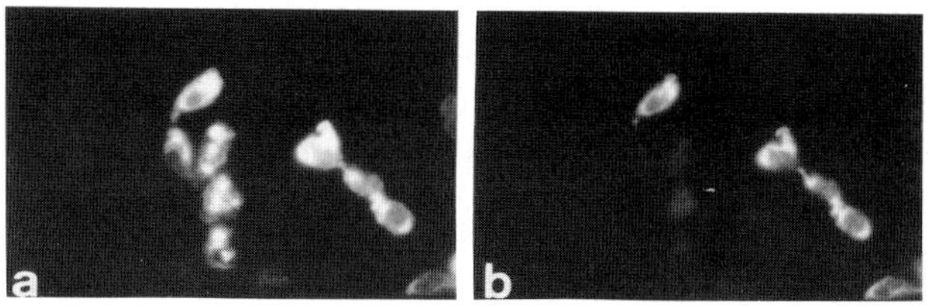

FIGURE 5. *Vimentin and desmin distribution in aortic SMC. After double immunofluorescent staining for vimentin (panel a) and desmin (panel b) in cytocentrifuged SMC isolated from a 5-week-old rat aortic media, all cells appear positive for vimentin, but only some are positive for desmin. 630×.*

rats, 87.0 ± 1.9% (mean ± SE) of the isolated cells showed a positive staining for vimentin alone, 13.2 ± 0.9% for both vimentin and desmin, and none for desmin alone. The same results were obtained with 5-day-old rats. In 14-day-old rats, 76.7 ± 2.3% of the cells showed a positive staining for vimentin alone and 22.7 ± 1.5% for both vimentin and desmin. In 5-week-old rats, 61.3 ± 1.1% of the isolated SMC showed positive staining for vimentin alone and 39.3 ± 1.4% for both vimentin and desmin. In all cases, none of the isolated SMC examined was positive for desmin alone. We knew from previous experiments (Kocher et al., 1984) that in adult (12-week-old) rat aortic media, 51% of the isolated cells were positive for vimentin alone, 48% for both vimentin and desmin, and only 1% for desmin alone.

For the biochemical studies, we first determined the DNA and protein content per mg of tissue in the aortic media of fetal, 5-day-old, 14-day-old, 5-week-old, and adult (12-week-old) rats, as well as the DNA and protein content in enzymatically isolated SMC from the media of 5-day- and 5-week-old rats. These procedures allowed us to calculate, after densitometric estimation of actin, vimentin, desmin, and tropomyosin on the gels as percentage of total pro-

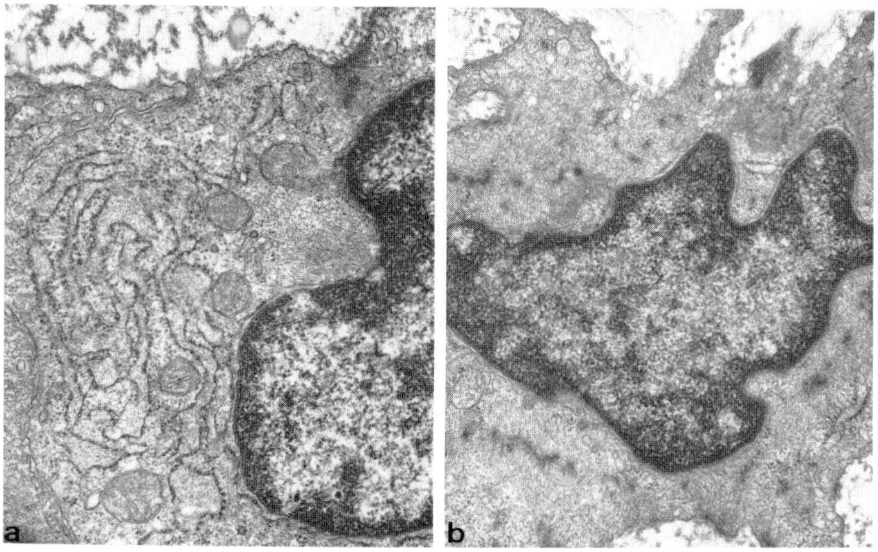

FIGURE 4. *Morphological features of aortic SMC in a newborn (panel a) and a 5-week-old (panel b) rat. The cytoplasm of the SMC in the newborn rat (panel a) contains a well-developed endoplasmic reticulum and Golgi apparatus and many mitochondria. Microfilaments are barely visible, whereas they become the major cytoplasmic component in cells of a 5-week-old animal (panel b). 22,000×.*

TABLE 2
Actin, Vimentin, Desmin and Tropomyosin Content of SMC in Developing and Adult Rat Aortic Media

	No. of samples	DNA*	Protein*	Actin†	Vimentin†	Desmin†	Tropomyosin†	Vimentin: actin	Desmin: actin	Tropomyosin: actin	Vimentin: desmin
Fetal	10	8.7±0.1	56.2±0.6	3.64±0.08	1.25±0.18	0.44±0.10	0.72±0.12	0.34±0.02	0.12±0.02	0.20±0.02	2.84±0.20
5 days	10	7.9±0.4	56.3±3.8	4.07±0.30	1.26±0.07	0.49±0.02	0.89±0.13	0.31±0.01	0.12±0.01	0.22±0.02	2.57±0.15
14 days	10	4.0±0.2	37.5±1.4	6.41±0.28	1.56±0.09	0.72±0.09	1.99±0.22	0.24±0.02	0.11±0.01	0.31±0.03	2.17±0.18
5 weeks	8	2.7±0.1	37.3±2.8	10.23±0.34	1.80±0.16	1.20±0.03	3.91±0.27	0.18±0.01	0.12±0.02	0.38±0.03	1.50±0.20
Adult	8	1.6±0.1	41.8±1.3	20.04±0.32	2.96±0.38	2.01±0.09	7.04±0.67	0.15±0.02	0.10±0.01	0.35±0.04	1.47±0.28

* μg/mg of tissue.
† pg/cell.

tein, the amounts of each of these proteins per cell. The results are summarized in Tables 2 and 3.

The quantity of DNA per mg of tissue (Table 2) was found to be 8.7 μg in fetal rat aortic media; it did not change significantly ($P > 0.05$) in 5-day-old the resules werrat aortic media in which it was 7.9 μg, but decreased progressively to 4.0 μg in 14-day-old rat aortic media, 2.7 μg in 5-week-old, and 1.6 μg in adult rats [see, for comparison, the results obtained by Stein et al. (1969) in 1- and 3-month-old rats].

The DNA content of isolated cells was similar in 5-day- and 5-week-old aortic SMC: 6.0 pg of DNA per cell (Table 3).

The protein content of the aortic media was about 56 μg protein/mg tissue in fetal and 5-day-old rat, decreased to 37.5 μg in 14-day-old and 5-week-old rats, and to 41.8 μg in adult rats (Table 2). In isolated cells, the protein content was 33.6 pg/cell in 5-day-old, and almost doubled to 54.9 pg/cell in 5-week-old rat SMC (Table 3). We know from previous experiments that SMC isolated from adult rat aorta contain, under our conditions, about 110 pg protein/cell (Kocher et al., 1984).

Actin, vimentin, desmin, and tropomyosin (identified by means of immunoblotting using antibodies against chicken gizzard tropomyosin, kindly supplied by Dr. W. Wnuk, Department of Biochemistry, University of Geneva, Geneva, Switzerland, data not shown) were estimated as percentage of total protein by densitometric analysis of SDS-PAGE, and the results were converted to amounts per cell according to the measurements of DNA and protein per milligram of tissue (Table 2). The vimentin:actin, desmin:actin, tropomyosin:actin, and vimentin:desmin ratios were also calculated (Table 2). Actin, as percentage of total protein in the aortic media, did not change between fetal (9.4 ± 0.2) and 5-day-old (9.5 ± 0.7) rats, but increased in 14-day- (11.4 ± 0.5) and 5-week- (12.7 ± 0.5) old rats, and then remained unchanged in adult rats (12.8 ± 0.2). Vimentin progressively decreased from fetal (3.23 ± 0.46) to adult (1.89 ± 0.24) rat aortic media. Desmin increased slightly but not significantly in all groups studied, whereas tropomyosin progressively increased from fetal (1.86 ± 0.02) to adult (4.5 ± 0.43) aortic media. The actin content per cell (Table II) did not change between fetal and 5-day-old rat ($P > 0.05$), but increased progressively from 5-day-old to adult rat with a significant difference between all the age groups. The changes were statistically significant, using both Student's t-test ($P < 0.001$ in every comparison) and the Bonferroni method. The vimentin content per cell did not change significantly between fetal and 14-day-old rats, and between 14-day- and 5-week-old rats, but increased significantly between 5-day- and 5-week-old rats ($P < 0.01$) and between 5-week-old and adult rats ($P < 0.001$). The desmin content per cell did not change significantly between fetal and 14-day-old rats, but increased progressively from 14-day-old to adult rats ($P < 0.001$ between the different age groups). The tropomyosin content per cell did not change from fetal to 5-day-old rats, but increased progressively from 5-day-old to adult rats ($P < 0.001$ between the different age groups). The vimentin:actin ratio decreased significantly from 5-day- to 14-day-old rats ($P < 0.001$), and from 14- to 5-week-old rats. There was no significant change of this ratio between fetal and 5-day-old rats, both of which had a high vimentin:actin ratio, and there also was no significant change between 5-week-old and adult rats, which, on the contrary, had a low vimentin:actin ratio compared to the other groups. The desmin:actin ratio did not change, under any of the conditions studied. Fetal and 5-day-old rat aortic

TABLE 3
DNA, Protein, and Actin Content of SMC Isolated from 5-Day-Old and 5-Week-Old Rat Aortic Media

	No. of samples	DNA*	Protein*	Actin*	Vimentin*	Desmin*	Tropomyosin*	Vimentin: actin	Desmin: actin	Tropomyosin: actin	Vimentin: Desmin
5 days	10	6.0±0.2	33.6±3.6	4.40±0.20	1.01±0.05	0.40±0.04	1.11±0.13	0.23±0.01	0.09±0.01	0.25±0.02	2.53±0.12
5 weeks	10	6.0±0.2	54.9±3.4	9.55±0.16	1.25±0.10	0.94±0.04	3.44±0.18	0.13±0.01	0.10±0.01	0.36±0.03	1.33±0.20

* pg/cell.

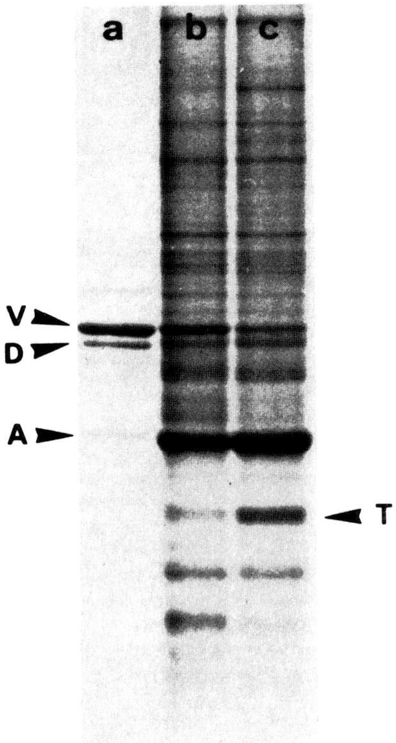

FIGURE 6. *Protein profile of isolated aortic SMC by means of SDS-PAGE. Panel a shows a cytoskeletal preparation of baby hamster kidney cells containing vimentin (V), desmin (D), and actin (A) as markers. SMC from 5-day-old (panel b) and 5-week-old (panel c) rats differ clearly in their content of vimentin, actin, and tropomyosin (T).*

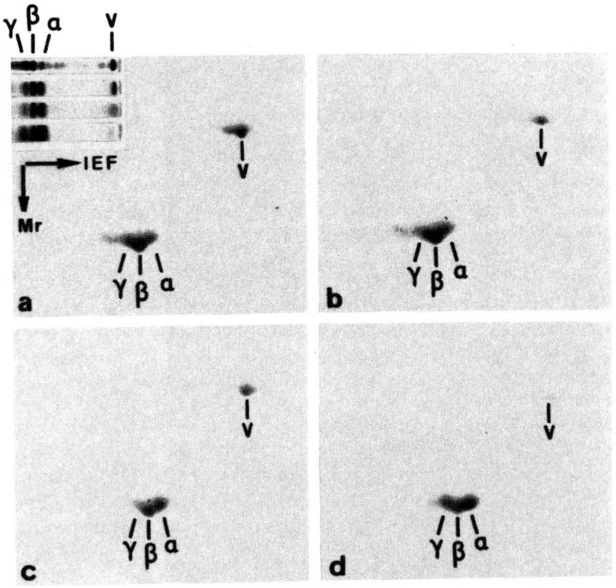

FIGURE 7. *Pattern of actin isoforms in developing rats. Bidimensional gels of total extracts of aortic media from fetal (panel a), 5-day- (panel b), 14-day- (panel c), and 5-week-old rats (panel d). In panels a and b, there is a clear predominance of the β-isoform. In panel c, the α- and β-isoforms show spots comparable in size, and in panel d, the α-isoform becomes predominant. Note that the intensity of the vimentin spot is decreasing with the age of the animal. The inset in panel a shows one-dimensional isoelectric focusing gel of the different preparations. They provide a clear distinction between the different actin types present.*

SMC had a low tropomyosin:actin ratio compared to 14-day-old, 5-week-old, and adult rat SMC. The vimentin:desmin ratio did not change between fetal and 5-day-old rats, but decreased progressively from 5-day-old to 5-week-old rat SMC. There was no difference in the vimentin:desmin ratio between 5-week-old and adult rat aortic SMC.

We controlled the results obtained with total extracts of media using enzymatically isolated SMC (from 5-day- and 5-week-old rats) (Fig. 6). The results were similar to those obtained in tissues (Table 3). Furthermore, we dissolved whole tissues and isolated cells in a buffer composed of Tris-HCl 50 mM, EGTA 5 mM, and KCl 100 mM containing 1% Triton X100, in order to recover cytoskeletal elements and to obtain gels with a low background. Under these conditions, the relative proportions of actin, vimentin, and desmin were similar to those obtained with whole tissue extracts (data not shown).

IEF, as well as bidimensional gel electrophoresis (Fig. 7), showed that the SMC of fetal and 5-day-old rats had a predominance of β-nonmuscle actin, whereas α- and γ-actins were present in small amounts. This tended to change in 14-day-old rat SMC which showed approximately equal amounts of α- and β-actins. Five-week-old rat VSMC showed a clear α-actin predominance and a decrease of the β-actin practically similar to the α-actin predominance previously described in the SMC of the adult rat aortic media (Gabbiani et al., 1981, 1984; Kocher et al., 1984).

Discussion

It is well accepted that arteries, aorta in particular, become less and less cellular during development, due to a relative increase of extracellular tissue (Stein et al., 1969; Gerrity and Cliff, 1975; Gerrity et al., 1975; Cliff, 1976; Schwartz and Benditt, 1977; Olivetti et al., 1980). EC and SMC have a high replicating activity during fetal and early neonatal life, but show a limited degree of replication in normal adult animals (Berry et al., 1972; Schwartz and Benditt, 1977). Developing SMC are ultrastructurally very similar to fibroblasts and only gradually acquire the features typical of adult cells (Hoyes et al., 1974; Gerrity and Cliff, 1975; Chamley-Campbell et al., 1979).

Our results agree with these previous findings, and furnish new information concerning the morphological and biochemical characteristics of developing aortic cells. Stress fibers, i.e., bundles of microfilaments such as those present in cultured cells, are common organelles in EC of developing animals, whereas they are rare in EC of adult animals (Gabbiani et al., 1983). In the aorta of adult animals, stress fibers are numerous only in EC located in areas submitted to turbulent flow (Gabbiani et al., 1983; Wong et al., 1983) or during pathological situations such as hypertension (Gabbiani et al., 1975; White et al., 1983) or regeneration after injury (Gabbiani et al., 1983). These conditions are characterized by an increased degree of replicating activity and cell density (Haudenschild and Schwartz, 1979; De Chastonay et al., 1983) which is also true for developing endothelial cells (Schwartz and Benditt, 1977; see our Results). However, previous studies have shown that stress fibers persist in vivo long after regeneration and replication have ceased (Gabbiani et al., 1983). Moreover, in vitro, the presence of stress fibers is probably related more to attachment to the substrate and isometric contraction than to replication and/or cell movement (Burridge, 1981; Herman et al., 1981). Further studies are needed in order to define the function of endothelial stress fibers, but it is noteworthy that these organelles are particularly numerous in vivo both in the normal aorta of developing rats and during pathological conditions such as hypertension (Gabbiani et al., 1975) and regeneration (Gabbiani et al., 1983) in adult animals.

It has been shown that in the developing rat aorta, SMC undergo two different phenomena. Early in life, hyperplasia is the most important phenomenon: between the first and the fifth day of life, the number of SMC in the aortic media doubles (Olivetti et al., 1980). The DNA synthesis drops progressively up to 1 year of age (Looker and Berry, 1972), and during that time, SMC undergo hypertrophy. According to our results, the amount of total protein per cell triples from the neonatal period to the adult state (see Results). For this reason, we have expressed our protein measurements as amounts of protein per cell, as well as ratios between two given proteins, in order to be able to understand how one protein is changing compared to the others.

The gradual increase of actin, tropomyosin, vimentin, and desmin content per cell in developing SMC correlates well with the previously described morphological changes accompanying SMC maturation (Hoyes et al., 1974; Gerrity and Cliff, 1975; Chamley-Campbell et al., 1979). It appears that the increase in actin (which, in adult SMC, becomes by far the most prevalent protein) is the major factor contributing to the classical morphological aspect of adult SMC. Concurrent with an increase of actin content, there is also a switch from the predominance of the β-isotype to the predominance of the α-isotype, typical of the adult vascular SMC (Gabbiani et al., 1981). Previous morphometric studies have indicated that the proportion of SMC cytoplasm occupied by myofilaments does not change between birth and 11 days of age, although the absolute volume of microfilaments increases with age (Olivetti et al., 1980). However, in 14-day-old rats, we see a significant increase in the actin content per cell, compared to both fetal and 5-day-old rats. These apparent discrepancies may be due to the difficulties of evaluating morphometrically the space occupied by various cytoplasmic filaments, or, alternatively, to the fact that at these periods an important proportion of actin is present in the form of oligomers or short filaments.

The present work, as well as previous studies (Gabbiani et al., 1981; Frank et al., 1982), have shown that SMC of the arterial wall are heterogeneous as far as their contents of vimentin and desmin are concerned. This heterogeneity is not apparent from ultrastructural studies (Gerrity and Cliff, 1975; Olivetti et al., 1980; this work). The functional significance of this SMC heterogeneity is presently not known.

Although quantification of proteins by means of immunocytochemistry and gel scanning should be interpreted with caution, our results suggest several general considerations. Vimentin and desmin represent an important component of SMC cytoplasm. From fetal to adult animals, the vimentin content per cell appears to increase about 2.3 times (this increase being less important than the increase of total cellular proteins), whereas desmin increases about 5 times. However, desmin increase probably reflects more an increase in the number of desmin positive cells than a real increase of desmin per cell. We have previously shown that, contrary to striated or cardiac muscle, adult aortic SMC contain large amounts of vimentin (Gabbiani et al., 1981). Our quantitative data show that, even in adult life, the rat aortic media contains vimentin as the prevalent intermediate filament protein. However, from fetal to adult life, the percentage of SMC containing desmin increases from 13 to 51. In striated and cardiac muscle cells, the appearance of α-actin isotype, as well as the appearance of desmin, coincides with the appearance of differentiated functions (Buckingham et al., 1982; Caplan et al., 1983). The same is true for aortic SMC with the exception that, in adult animals, there remains still a high proportion of vimentin-positive SMC (Gabbiani et al., 1981; Kocher et al., 1984; see Results). In the normal aorta of fetal and newborn rats (Berry et al., 1972; Olivetti et al., 1980) and in arterial intimal thickening after endothelial injury of adult rats (Björkerud and Bondjers, 1973; Clowes et al., 1983), the replicative activity of SMC is high, and most SMC contain only vimentin as judged by immunofluorescent staining (Kocher et al., 1984; see Results), suggesting that vimentin-positive SMC possess a higher mitotic potential than those also containing desmin during development as well as in adult life.

It is remarkable that during proliferation after endothelial injury in experimental animals and in human atheromatosis, SMC undergo a series of morphological and biochemical changes concerning their cytoskeletal elements which are practically the reverse of what we have described for developing SMC: (1) they lose microfilaments and acquire a prominent rough endoplasmic reticulum and Golgi apparatus (Ghidoni and O'Neal, 1967; Poole et al., 1971; Chamley-Campbell et al., 1979); (2) the actin content per cell decreases and there is a switch from the predominance of the α-isotype to the predominance of the β-isotype (Gabbiani et al., 1984; Kocher et al., 1984); (3) the number of vimentin-positive cells, as well as the content of vimentin per cell, increases (Gabbiani et al., 1981; Kocher et al., 1984); and (4) the number of desmin-positive cells decreases (we do not know about the content of desmin per cell) (Kocher et al., 1984). Similar changes are seen in actively replicating SMC in vitro (Gabbiani et al., 1984). These observations suggest that the term "dedifferentiation," which was based only on morphological features of pathological SMC (Fritz et al., 1970; Blose et al., 1975; Chamley et al., 1977), and hence was considered controversial (Chamley-Campbell et al., 1979), is supported by the biochemical changes of proliferating and atheromatous SMC, compared to their normal adult counterparts, at least as far as the cytoskeletal elements are concerned.

In conclusion, our study has illustrated the progressive changes of cytoskeletal components in developing rat aortic EC and SMC, and has indicated an analogy between the cytoskeletal features of SMC cells during early development and SMC during proliferation after an experimental lesion, atheromatous plaque formation, or active growth in vitro.

We thank Dr. R.B. Low, Department of Physiology and Biophysics, University of Vermont, Burlington, for giving us the plans for the construction of our laser beam densitometer.

Supported by the Swiss National Science Foundation, Grant 3.178-0.82, and by the Ernst and Lucie Schmidheiny Foundation.

Address for reprints: Dr. G. Gabbiani, University of Geneva, Department of Pathology, CMU, 1, rue Michel Servet, 1211 Geneva 4, Switzerland.

Received November 28, 1983; accepted for publication March 4, 1985.

References

Avrameas S, Ternynck T (1969) The cross-linking of proteins with glutaraldehyde and its use for the preparation of immunoadsorbents. Immunochemistry **6:** 53–66

Azzarone B, Failly-Crepin C, Daya- Grosjean L, Chaponnier C, Gabbiani G (1983) Abnormal behavior of cultured fibroblasts from nodule and nonaffected aponeurosis of Dupuytren's disease. J Cell Physiol **117:** 353–361

Berry CL, Looker T, Germain J (1972) The growth and development of the rat aorta. I. Morphological aspects. J Anat **113:** 1–16

Björkerud S, Bondjers G (1973) Arterial repair and atherosclerosis after mechanical injury. Part 5. Tissue response after induction of a large superficial transverse injury. Atherosclerosis **18:** 235–255

Blose SH, Lazarides E, Chacko SK (1975) Loss of differentiated phenotype in the progeny of aortic smooth muscle cells (abstr). J Cell Biol **67:** 34a

Bradford MM (1976) A rapid and sensitive method for the quantitation of microgram quantities of protein utilizing the principle of protein-dye binding. Anal Biochem **72:** 248–254

Brayden JE, Halpern W (1983) A high-spatial-resolution laser beam densitometer for quantitative analysis of polyacrylamide gels. Anal Biochem **130:** 9–13

Buckingham ME, Minty A, Alonso A, Caravatti M, Robert B, Cohen A, Bugaisky G, Daubas P, Weydert A (1982) Actin and myosin genes and their expression during skeletal muscle myogenesis. *In* Biochemistry of Differentiation and Morphogenesis, 33. Colloquium—Mosbach 1982, Berlin. Springer-Verlag, pp 22–33

Burridge K (1981) Are stress fibers contractile? Nature **294:** 691–692

Burton K (1968) Determination of DNA concentration with diphenylamine. Meth Enzymol **12** (part B): 163–166

Caplan AI, Fiszman MY, Eppenberger HM (1983) Molecular and cell isoforms during development. Science **221:** 921–927

Chamley JH, Campbell GR, McConnell JD, Gröschel-Stewart U (1977) Comparison of vascular smooth muscle cells from adult human, monkey and rabbit in primary culture and in subculture. Cell Tissue Res **177:** 503–522

Chamley-Campbell J, Campbell GR, Ross R (1979) Smooth muscle cell in culture. Physiol Rev **59:** 1–61

Cliff WJ (1976) Blood Vessels. Cambridge, Cambridge University Press

Clowes AW, Reidy MA, Clowes MM (1983) Kinetics of cellular proliferation after arterial injury. Smooth muscle growth in the absence of endothelium. Lab Invest **49:** 327–333

De Chastonay C, Gabbiani G, Elemer G, Hüttner I (1983) Remodeling of the rat aortic endothelial layer during experimental hypertension. Changes in replication rate, cell density, and surface morphology. Lab Invest **48:** 45–52

Frank ED, Tuszynski GP, Warren L (1982) Localization of vimentin and desmin in BHK 21/C13 cells and in baby hamster kidney. Exp Cell Res **139:** 235–247

Franke WW, Schmid E, Weber K, Osborn M (1979) HeLa cells contain intermediate-sized filaments of the prekeratin type. Exp Cell Res **118:** 95–109

Fritz KE, Jarmolych J, Daoud AS (1970) Association of DNA synthesis and apparent dedifferentiation of aortic smooth muscle cells in vitro. Exp Mol Pathol **12:** 354–362

Gabbiani G, Badonnel MC, Rona G (1975) Cytoplasmic contractile apparatus in aortic endothelial cells of hypertensive rats. Lab Invest **32:** 227–234

Gabbiani G, Elemer G, Guelpa Ch, Vallotton MB, Badonnel MC, Hüttner I (1979) Morphologic and functional changes of the aortic intima during experimental hypertension. Am J Pathol **96:** 399–422

Gabbiani G, Schmid E, Winter S, Chaponnier C, de Chastonay C, Vandekerckhove J, Weber K, Franke WW (1981) Vascular smooth muscle cells differ from other smooth muscle cells: Predominance of vimentin filaments and a specific α-type actin. Proc Natl Acad Sci USA **78:** 298–302

Gabbiani G, Gabbiani F, Lombardi D, Schwartz SM (1983) Organization of actin cytoskeleton in normal and regenerating arterial endothelial cells. Proc Natl Acad Sci USA **80:** 2361–2364

Gabbiani G, Kocher O, Bloom WS, Vanderkerckhove J, Weber K (1984) Actin expression in smooth muscle cells of rat aortic intimal thickening and human atheromatous plaque. J Clin Invest **73:** 148–152

Geisler N, Weber K (1980) Purification of smooth muscle desmin and a protein-chemical comparison of desmins from chicken gizzard and log stomach. Eur J Biochem **111:** 425–433

Geisler N, Weber K (1981) Isolation of polymerization-competent vimentin from porcine eye lens tissue. FEBS Lett **125:** 253–256

Gerrity RG, Cliff WJ (1975) The aortic tunica media of the developing rat. I. Quantitative stereologic and biochemical analysis. Lab Invest **32:** 585–600

Gerrity RG, Adams EP, Cliff WJ (1975) The aortic tunica media of the developing rat. II. Incorporation by medial cells of ^{3}H-proline into collagen and elastin: Autoradiographic and chemical studies. Lab Invest **32:** 601–609

Ghidoni JJ, O'Neal RM (1967) Recent advances in molecular pathology: A review. Ultrastructure of human atheroma. Exp Mol Pathol **7:** 378–400

Haudenschild CC, Schwartz SM (1979) Endothelial regeneration. II. Restitution of endothelial continuity. Lab Invest **41:** 407–418

Herman IM, Crisona NJ, Pollard TD (1981) Relation between cell activity and the distribution of cytoplasmic actin and myosin. J Cell Biol **90:** 84–91

Hoyes AD, Savage PEA, Hamilton RFD, Martin BGH (1974) Myodifferentiation in the carotid artery of the adult sheep: an ultrastructural study. Acta Anat **88:** 34–43

Hubbard BD, Lazarides E (1979) Copurification of actin and desmin from chicken smooth muscle and their copolymerization in vitro to intermediate filaments. J Cell Biol **80:** 166–182

Ives HE, Schultz GS, Galardy RE, Jamieson JD (1978) Preparation of functional smooth muscle cells from the rabbit aorta. J Exp Med **148:** 1400–1413

Kelly PT, Cotman CW (1978) Synaptic proteins. Characterization of tubulin and actin and identification of a distinct post-synaptic density polypeptide. J Cell Biol **79:** 173–183

Kocher O, Skalli O, Bloom WS, Gabbiani G (1984) The cytoskeleton of rat aortic smooth muscle cells. Normal conditions and experimental intimal thickening. Lab Invest **50:** 645–652

Laemmli UK (1970) Cleavage of structural proteins during the assembly of the head of bacteriophage T4. Nature **227:** 680–685

Looker T, Berry CL (1972) The growth and development of the rat aorta. II. Changes in nucleic acid and scleroprotein content. J Anat **113:** 17–34

Low RB, Chaponnier C, Gabbiani G (1981) Organization of actin in epithelial cells during regenerative and neoplastic conditions: Correlation of morphologic, immunofluorescent and biochemical findings. Lab Invest **44:** 359–367

Moll R, Franke WW, Schiller DL, Geiger B, Krepler R (1982) The catalog of human cytokeratins: patterns of expression in normal epithelia, tumors, and cultured cells. Cell **31:** 11–24

Nagle RB, McDaniel KM, Clark VA, Payne CM (1983) The use of antikeratin antibodies in the diagnosis of human neoplasms. Am J Clin Pathol **79:** 458–466

O'Farrel PH (1975) High resolution two-dimensional electrophoresis of proteins. J Biol Chem **250:** 4007–4021

Olivetti G, Anversa P, Melissari M, Loud AV (1980) Morphometric study of early postnatal development of the thoracic aorta in the rat. Circ Res **47:** 417–424

Osborn M, Weber K (1982) Intermediate filaments: Cell-type-specific markers in differentiation and pathology. Cell **31:** 303–306

Osborn M, Weber K (1983) Tumor diagnosis by intermediate filament typing: A novel tool for surgical pathology. Lab Invest **48:** 372–394

Poole JCF, Cromwell SB, Benditt EP (1971) Behavior of smooth muscle cells and formation of extracellular structures in the reaction of arterial walls to injury. Am J Pathol **62:** 391–414

Rungger-Brändle E, Gabbiani G (1983) The role of cytoskeletal and cytocontractile elements in pathological processes. Am J Pathol **110:** 359–392

Schumaker MF (1978) A program which automatically quantitates gel electrophoretic autoradiograms. Anal Biochem **91:** 375–393

Schwartz SM, Benditt EP (1972) Postnatal development of the aortic subendothelium in rats. Lab Invest **26:** 778–786

Schwartz SM, Benditt EP (1977) Aortic endothelial cell replication. I. Effects of age and hypertension in the rat. Circ Res **41:** 248–255

Stein O, Eisenberg S, Stein Y (1969) Aging of aortic smooth muscle cells in rats and rabbits. A morphologic and biochemical study. Lab Invest **21:** 386–397

Wallenstein S, Zucker CL, Fleiss JL (1980) Some statistical methods useful in circulation research. Circ Res **47:** 1–9

White GE, Gimbrone MA Jr, Fujiwara K (1983) Factors influencing the expression of stress fibers in vascular endothelial cells in situ. J Cell Biol **97:** 416–424

Wong AJ, Pollard TD, Herman IM (1983) Actin filament stress fibers in vascular endothelial cells in vivo. Science **219:** 867–869

Yakin HM, Kronberg H, Zimmer HG, Neuhoff V (1982) Photometric evaluation of slab gels. II: Delimitation and integration of peaks in one-dimensional electropherograms. Electrophoresis **3:** 244–254

INDEX TERMS: Actin • Vimentin • Desmin • Endothelium • Smooth muscle

Hyaluronidase Does Not Prevent Deterioration of Vascular Functional Integrity during Reperfusion after No-Flow Ischemia in Isolated Rabbit Hearts

Ronald G. Tilton, Peter A. Cole, Kenneth B. Larson, Charles Kilo, and Joseph R. Williamson

From the Departments of Pathology and Medicine and the Biomedical Computer Laboratory, Washington University School of Medicine, St. Louis, Missouri

SUMMARY. Effects of hyaluronidase on myocardial water content and distribution, and on coronary vascular hemodynamics and endothelial cell transport function were assessed in isolated rabbit hearts during 3.5 hours of reperfusion after 30 minutes of global, no-flow ischemia. In nonischemic control hearts, perfusion pressure, left ventricular end-diastolic pressure, maximum +dP/dt, and intravascular clearance of radiolabeled albumin remained constant during 5 hours of continuous perfusion, while the mean-transit time and vascular into extravascular space clearance of radiolabeled albumin increased 1.5× and 2.5× baseline, respectively. During reperfusion after 30 minutes of no flow, perfusion pressure increased 53% and interstitial fluid volume increased 2-fold, while left ventricular end-diastolic pressure and maximum +dP/dt returned to control levels. The rate of intravascular clearance of radiolabeled albumin decreased 38%, and the mean-transit time and vascular-into-extravascular space clearance of albumin increased ~3× and 5× baseline, respectively. Hyaluronidase blocked the ischemia-reperfusion-induced increases in total water content and in interstitial fluid volume and reduced the increases in perfusion pressure and mean-transit time of radiolabeled albumin by 40% and 45%, respectively, but did not prevent the increase in albumin vascular-into-extravascular space clearance and the decrease in albumin clearance from the coronary vasculature. These findings indicate that hyaluronidase does not prevent ischemia-reperfusion-induced increases in albumin permeation of the coronary vasculature, and suggest that its protective effect on ischemic myocardium is mediated, instead, by reducing interstitial edema and vascular resistance. **(*Circ Res 56: 839–850, 1985*)**

WHEREAS hyaluronidase has been reported by some investigators (Maroko et al., 1972; Maclean et al., 1976; Hillis et al., 1977; Rovetto, 1977; Kloner et al., 1977; Ribeiro et al., 1978) to have a protective effect on ischemic myocardium, no beneficial effects have been observed by others (Most et al., 1976; Cairns et al., 1982). Since hyaluronidase depolymerizes hyaluronic acid, a major mucopolysaccharide constituent of the cardiac interstitium, it has been postulated that this enzyme protects the heart by reducing tissue edema (de Oliveira and Levy, 1960) and by facilitating the diffusion of nutrients and metabolic waste products (Day, 1957). It also has been shown that hyaluronidase decreases coronary vascular resistance (Rovetto, 1977; Overholser and Harris, 1981; Sunnergren and Rovetto, 1983) and increases collateral blood flow (Askenazi et al., 1977; Rovetto, 1977). Thus, the improved metabolism of ischemic myocytes may be secondary to decreased interstitial edema and improved vascular hemodynamics. Since studies of the effect of hyaluronidase on vascular integrity have yielded conflicting results (Szabo and Magyar, 1958; Kloner et al., 1977, 1978), we undertook the present study to examine further the effect of this enzyme on tissue water content and distribution, on vascular hemodynamics, and on endothelial cell functional integrity during reperfusion following 30 minutes of global, no-flow ischemia.

Methods

Perfusion Techniques

Isovolumically beating, isolated hearts from male New Zealand rabbits (weighing 2–3 kg and heparinized intravenously with 2000 U of sodium heparin 10 minutes before sacrifice) were perfused retrograde via the aorta with no recirculation at a paced rate of 180–200 beats/min with Krebs-Henseleit (KH) buffer containing 1% dialyzed bovine serum albumin (BSA), 0.5% dialyzed polyvinylpyrrolidone (mol wt = 360,000), 3 mM pyruvate, 8 mM dextrose, and 100 mU/liter insulin (pork; regular iletin II). The KH buffer was filtered through 0.45-μm Gelman mini-capsule filters, warmed to 37°C, and oxygenated at pH 7.4 by dialysis against 95% O_2:5% CO_2 across thin-walled (0.009-inch) Silastic tubing (Dow Corning), which maintained arterial P_{O_2} constant at ~600 mm Hg. Perfusion pressure, left ventricular end-diastolic pressure (LVEDP), and left ventricular developed pressure (obtained from a left ventricle balloon) were recorded continuously with P23Db Statham pressure transducers and a Gould recorder, and maximum +dP/dt was obtained by differentiation of the left ventricular pressure signal. Hearts were perfused apex-up and were rinsed continuously over the surface and through the right ventricle and atrium to facilitate rapid removal of tracer that had passed through the coronary vasculature.

Preparation of Radiolabeled Tracers

Purified monomer albumin (20 mg) in phosphate-buffered saline was iodinated with 1 mCi ^{125}I as previously described (Tilton et al., 1983). Prior to use, ^{125}I-BSA was dialyzed extensively against KH buffer (pH 7.0, 4°C), filtered through 0.2-μm Acrodisc filters (Gelman Sciences), and vacuum concentrated with the use of collodion bags with a 25,000 molecular weight cut-off (Schleicher and Schuell). Radiolabeled ^{57}Co-EDTA was prepared by the technique employed by Bridge et al. (1982) for the preparation of ^{58}Co-EDTA. Before use, an aliquot was passed through a 2-cm column of Dowex 50 (Na^+ form) to remove free ^{57}Co completely.

Experimental Protocol

Nonischemic control hearts were perfused continuously for 5 hours under constant flow conditions; ischemic hearts were perfused for 1 hour prior to 30 minutes of global, no-flow ischemia, then reperfused at the same baseline flow rate for 3.5 hours. Chromatographically purified and dialyzed bovine testicular hyaluronidase (Sigma) in KH buffer (3 ml of 1000 U/ml), pH 7.4, was flushed into the coronary vasculature at the onset and for the duration of no-flow ischemia. In a separate series of control experiments ($n = 6$), 3000 U/ml hyaluronidase were flushed into the coronary vasculature at the onset of 10 minutes of no flow after 1 hour of baseline perfusion. These hearts were then reperfused for 4 hours. During periods of no flow, heart temperature was maintained at 37°C with heat lamps and surface rinses. Every 30 minutes during the perfusion, a 25-μl bolus of ^{125}I-BSA in KH buffer, pH 7.0, was injected into the proximal aorta, and the single passage of this tracer through the coronary vasculature was monitored with external-detection equipment as described previously (Tilton et al., 1983).

In selected experiments, ^{57}Co-EDTA in KH buffer was perfused during the terminal 10 minutes. Hearts were removed, rinsed with saline, trimmed, blotted dry, weighed, and sectioned (6–8 transmural left ventricular sections) before assay of ^{57}Co radioactivity by γ-spectrometry. Perfusate radioactivity was assayed similarly. Selected transmural left ventricular sections were dried to constant weight at 70°C for determination of water content.

γ-Spectrometry Data Analysis

The ^{57}Co-EDTA volume of distribution per g wet weight (V_{EDTA}) was calculated using

$$V_{EDTA} = \frac{C_{EDTA}\ (\text{heart})}{C_{EDTA}\ (\text{perfusate})}, \tag{1}$$

where C_{EDTA} (heart) and C_{EDTA} (perfusate) are, respectively, the specific ^{57}Co activities in each sample of heart (counts/min per g wet weight) and in perfusate (counts/min per ml KH buffer). Results of tissue assays were converted into ml/g dry weight, and these data, together with baseline estimates of vascular volume derived from the two-compartment-model analysis of residue-detection data, were used to estimate the specific interstitial fluid volume, which also was used for the calculations of convective transport (Eqs. 10 and 12). We calculated intracellular water content (ml/g dry weight) at the end of each experiment by subtracting V_{EDTA} (Eq. 1) from total water content determined gravimetrically.

Mathematical Model for Assessment of Radiolabeled Albumin Transport

The uptake and clearance of a bolus injection of ^{125}I-labeled albumin in these heart preparations were interpreted with a two-compartment model describing temporal changes of radiolabeled tracer distributions due to transport of the label within the vasculature and between the vascular and extravascular spaces. Components of the model and complete mathematical derivations have been described previously (Tilton et al., 1983), and only the principal equations used to interpret the experimental data are provided here. Conventional requirements are assumed to hold for the validity of tracer stimulus-response methods concerning stationarity and linearity (Perl, 1971). Tracer movements are interpreted in terms of diffusive and convective transport mechanisms operating simultaneously within a hypothetical membrane (of assumed negligible tracer content) separating albumin-accessible vascular and extravascular spaces; no specific morphological identity is assigned to this membrane. The model parameters and their numerical estimates from the experimental data represent global averages. Spatial uniformity of detection efficiency is assumed.

With the use of a parameter-estimation technique described below, the biexponential function

$$r(t) = A_1 e^{-\alpha_1 t} + A_2 e^{-\alpha_2 t} \tag{2}$$

is fitted to the experimental residue count-rate data. Here, t represents time elapsed after the instant the maximum count rate is observed after injection of the radiotracer bolus. The symbols A_1, A_2, α_1, and α_2 represent adjustable parameters and are related to the compartmental turnover-rate constants of the model, k_{01}, k_{12} and k_{21} according to

$$k_{01} = \alpha_1 - (\alpha_1 - \alpha_2)A_2/r_0, \tag{3a}$$

$$= \alpha_2 + (\alpha_1 - \alpha_2)A_1/r_0, \tag{3b}$$

$$k_{12} = \alpha_1\alpha_2/k_{01}, \tag{4}$$

and

$$k_{21} = (\alpha_1 + \alpha_2) - (k_{01} + k_{12}), \tag{5}$$

where $r_0 = r(t = 0)$, i.e., the peak count rate, whose instant of occurrence defines zero time. Parameter estimation was accomplished by utilizing an algorithm (Markham et al., 1976) based on maximum-likelihood estimation procedures for Poisson-distributed data (Sandor and Wilson, 1972; Snyder, 1973), which was implemented by maximizing the Poisson-distribution likelihood function having the biexponential intensity specified by Equation 2. This provided estimates of $\hat{A}_1$, $\hat{A}_2$, $\hat{\alpha}_1$, and $\hat{\alpha}_2$ of the intensity function, which were used in Equations 3–5, assuming stochastic independence of the variates, to obtain estimates of the turnover-rate constants. The k_{ij} in Equations 3–5 represent the fraction of the mass of tracer in compartment j that is transported, per unit time, into compartment i. Here, subscripts 1 and 2 denote, respectively, vascular space and extravascular space accessible to albumin; 0 denotes the surroundings external to both compartments 1 and 2.

An interpretation of the compartmental turnover-rate constants of the model is based on the following equations, which relate them to perfusate flow, to the compartmental albumin spaces, and to the practical membrane transport coefficients (Kedem and Katchalsky, 1961; House, 1974;

Perl, 1975):

$$k_{01} = \tilde{F}/\tilde{V}_1 \text{ (sec}^{-1}\text{)}, \quad (6)$$

$$k_{21} = [\gamma_1 P\tilde{S} + \tfrac{1}{2}(1 - \sigma)\tilde{J}_v]/\tilde{V}_1 \text{ (sec}^{-1}\text{)}, \quad (7)$$

and

$$k_{12} = [\gamma_2 P\tilde{S} - \tfrac{1}{2}(1 - \sigma)\tilde{J}_v]/\tilde{V}_2 \text{ (sec}^{-1}\text{)}. \quad (8)$$

In the above, $\tilde{F}$ is the measured specific perfusate flow, P is the surface area-averaged permeability coefficient, $\tilde{S}$ is the total membrane surface available for permeation, $\tilde{J}_v$ is the net systemic fluid-filtration volume flow, σ is the filtration-flow-averaged solvent-drag reflection coefficient (Perl, 1975), $\tilde{V}_1$ is the vascular compartment volume, $\tilde{V}_2$ is the extravascular albumin compartment volume, and γ_i is the thermodynamic activity coefficient of albumin in compartment i, for i = 1,2. The volume flow, $\tilde{J}_v$, is driven by an average pressure drop, due to combined hydraulic and osmotic effects, from compartment 1 to compartment 2. To allow comparison of results between preparations of different sizes, values of the global parameter estimates are computed and reported relative to the dry weight, W, of each heart; this normalization is indicated by tildes.

Simultaneous solution of Equations 7 and 8 yields

$$P\tilde{S} = \tfrac{1}{2}(\tilde{F}_{21} + \tilde{F}_{12})/\bar{\gamma} \text{ (cm}^3\text{/sec per g dry weight)} \quad (9)$$

for the specific (i.e., weight-normalized) permeability coefficient surface-area product and

$$\tilde{U} \triangleq \tfrac{1}{2}(1 - \sigma)\tilde{J}_v = \tfrac{1}{2}(\gamma_2\tilde{F}_{21} - \gamma_1\tilde{F}_{12})/\bar{\gamma}, \text{ (cm}^3\text{/sec per g dry weight)} \quad (10)$$

for the specific ultrafiltration parameter, $\tilde{U}$. For the above, we further define the unidirectional clearances (Perl, 1975) as

$$\tilde{F}_{21} \triangleq \gamma_1 P\tilde{S} + \tilde{U} = k_{21}\tilde{V}_1 \quad (11)$$

and

$$\tilde{F}_{12} \triangleq \gamma_2 P\tilde{S} - \tilde{U} = k_{12}\tilde{V}_2, \quad (12)$$

with

$$\bar{\gamma} \triangleq \tfrac{1}{2}(\gamma_1 + \gamma_2). \quad (13)$$

Since $\tilde{V}_2$, the specific extravascular space, is obtainable from the externally monitored radioalbumin count-rate history only in the special case when albumin ultrafiltration flux is zero, an independent estimate is required. For this reason, we report only the albumin forward unidirectional clearance, $\tilde{F}_{21}$ (Eq. 11), using baseline estimates of $\tilde{V}_1$. In certain experiments (see Experimental Protocol), estimates of $\tilde{V}_2$ were determined from ^{57}Co-EDTA equilibrium data at the end of the perfusion. For these experiments, estimates of the specific permeability coefficient surface-area product and the specific ultrafiltration coefficient were obtained by evaluation of Equations 9 and 10. Approximate values of the thermodynamic activity coefficients for bovine serum albumin have been derived previously (Tilton et al., 1983).

The mean of the distribution of radioalbumin transit times, $\bar{t}_{BSA}$, is related to the parameters of the intensity function of the model, by

$$\bar{t}_{BSA} = [(A_1/\alpha_1) + (A_2/\alpha_2)]/r_0 \quad (14)$$

as described previously (Tilton et al., 1983).

Statistical Analysis

Within Runs

From initial estimates of variance for perfusate flow, heart dry weight, peak count rate (r_0), and the four parameters of the intensity function computed by the maximum-likelihood algorithm, variance estimates were computed for each of the derived physiological parameters using the theory of error propagation (Eadie et al., 1971). Standard deviations were obtained as the positive square roots of the corresponding error propagation variances. Likewise, estimates of variance and standard deviation for $\bar{t}_{BSA}$ were obtained using error-propagation theory.

Between Runs

Means and standard deviations, as well as standard errors of the mean (for data presented graphically) were calculated for each parameter assessed for controls and ischemic groups at each perfusion time interval. A repeated-measures analysis of variance test (based on data obtained during the last 2 hours of reperfusion) was used to assess significant differences between nonischemic controls and the two groups of ischemic hearts. A comparison of the means of each group within each time interval during the last 2 hours of perfusion was performed with Tukey's studentized range test. Student's *t*-test for paired observations was used to evaluate significant differences between baseline values (mean of two recordings obtained at 30 and 45 minutes of perfusion) and values obtained during subsequent perfusion within each group of hearts. Student's *t*-test and χ^2 analysis were used to assess differences in total water content, and the former statistical test also was used in Tables 1 and 3.

Results

Heart Weight, Flow Rate, and Water Content

Heart weight (~1.0 g dry weight) and perfusate flow rate (~23 ml/min per g dry weight) did not differ significantly between the control and ischemic groups of hearts. The water content of hearts perfused continuously for 5 hours averaged 5.5 ± 0.3 ml/g dry weight (mean ± SD; Fig. 1). The water content was reduced to 4.2 ± 0.2 ml/g dry weight when control hearts were treated with 3000 U/ml hyaluronidase during a 10-minute no-flow period after the initial 60 minutes of perfusion. Untreated hearts reperfused for 3.5 hours following 30 minutes of ischemia contained 18% more water than control hearts ($t = 4.03$, $P < 0.005$) and 24% more water than hyaluronidase-treated, ischemic hearts ($t = 4.06$, $P < 0.005$). Although the mean water content of the hyaluronidase-treated ischemic group was only 5% less than that of untreated controls, the variance was over 2× that of controls. Thus, five hyaluronidase-treated ischemic hearts had appreciably less water, whereas two had more water than the untreated control group, so that the χ^2 for the difference between the two groups was statistically significant ($\chi^2 = 5.00$, $P < 0.025$).

Interstitial and Intracellular Fluid Volumes

After 5 hours of perfusion, the interstitial fluid volume of untreated control hearts averaged 1.76 ±

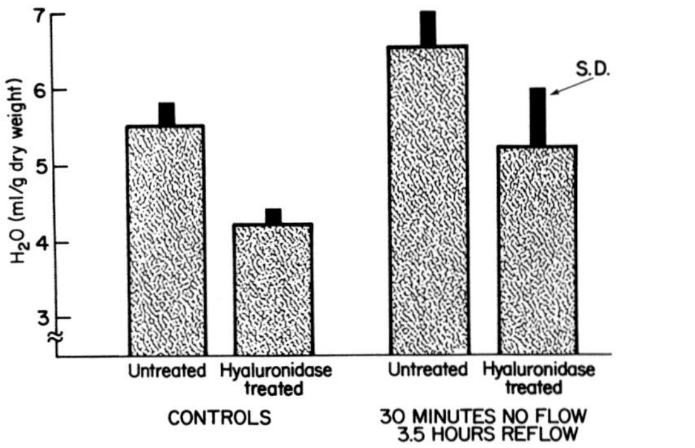

FIGURE 1. *Myocardial water content of control and ischemic hearts perfused with buffer for 5 hours. Values are expressed in ml/g dry weight and are determined gravimetrically at the end of the experiment. Untreated controls, n = 6; hyaluronidase-treated controls, n = 6; untreated ischemic hearts, n = 7; hyaluronidase-treated ischemic hearts, n = 9.*

0.76 ml/g dry weight, whereas that of hyaluronidase-treated control hearts averaged 0.95 ± 0.65 ml/g dry weight (Table 1). Reperfusion for 3.5 hours following 30 minutes of no flow was associated with a 90% increase in the interstitial fluid volume ($t = 2.97$, $P < 0.025$), compared to untreated controls, while hyaluronidase treatment during no flow completely blocked this increase. Intracellular water, which averaged 2.40 ± 0.84 ml/g dry weight at the end of untreated control perfusions, was decreased slightly in the untreated ischemic hearts; this difference, however, was not statistically significant. Hyaluronidase had no effect on the intracellular water content of control or ischemic hearts.

Physiological Pressure Data

Perfusion pressure (Fig. 2) was adjusted to ~43 mm Hg at the beginning of each experiment and, in controls, remained constant for the entire duration of perfusion. No significant differences were evident in baseline perfusion pressures of either group of

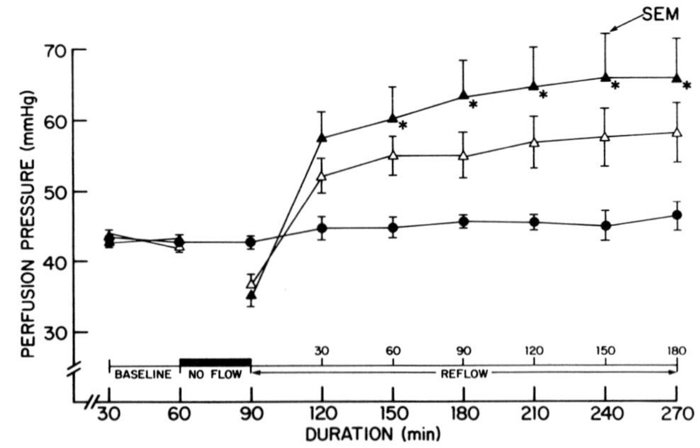

FIGURE 2. *Aortic perfusion pressure for nonischemic controls and during baseline and reperfusion following 30 minutes of global, no-flow ischemia (mm Hg; mean ± SEM). Solid circles denote nonischemic controls (n = 6); solid triangles, untreated hearts subjected to 30 minutes of no-flow ischemia (n = 7); open triangles, ischemic hearts treated with 1000 U/ml hyaluronidase during no flow (n = 9). Tukey's Studentized range test (compared to nonischemic controls during the last 2 hours of perfusion): *denotes P < 0.05.*

ischemic hearts compared to controls. After 1 minute of reperfusion following 30 minutes of global, no-flow ischemia, perfusion pressure was significantly lower than baseline in both groups of ischemic hearts. In untreated ischemic hearts, perfusion pressure was 40% above baseline values by 1 hour and 53% above baseline by 3 hours of reperfusion ($t = 4.32$, $P < 0.005$; compared to baseline). Instillation of 1000 U/ml hyaluronidase into the coronary vasculature at the onset and for the duration of no-flow injury partially blocked the perfusion pressure increases during reflow (pressure recordings reached levels 34% above baseline after 3 hours of reperfusion). A repeated-measures analysis of variance test indicated that during the last 2 hours of perfusion differences in perfusion pressure between each group of hearts were highly significant ($P < 0.0001$).

TABLE 1

Estimates of Interstitial* and Intracellular† Fluid Volumes after 5 Hours of Perfusion

Experiment	n	Interstitial fluid volume‡	Intracellular fluid volume‡
		Control perfusions	
Untreated	6	1.76 ± 0.76	2.40 ± 0.84
Hyaluronidase treated (3000 U/ml, 10 min)	3	0.95 ± 0.65	2.06 ± 0.48
		Ischemic perfusions	
Untreated	6	3.34 ± 1.06§	2.15 ± 0.81
Hyaluronidase treated (1000 U/ml, 30 min)	6	1.81 ± 0.69‖	2.49 ± 0.35

Results are expressed as mean ± SD; n = number of rabbit hearts evaluated.

* Calculated by subtracting baseline estimates of vascular volume obtained from external-detection data from V_{EDTA} (Eq. 1) obtained from ^{57}Co-EDTA equilibrium data at the end of the perfusion.

† Calculated as total water content determined gravimetrically at the end of the perfusion minus V_{EDTA}.

‡ ml/g dry weight.

§ Student's t-test (compared to nonischemic control perfusions). $P < 0.025$.

‖ Student's t-test (compared to untreated ischemic perfusions). $P < 0.025$.

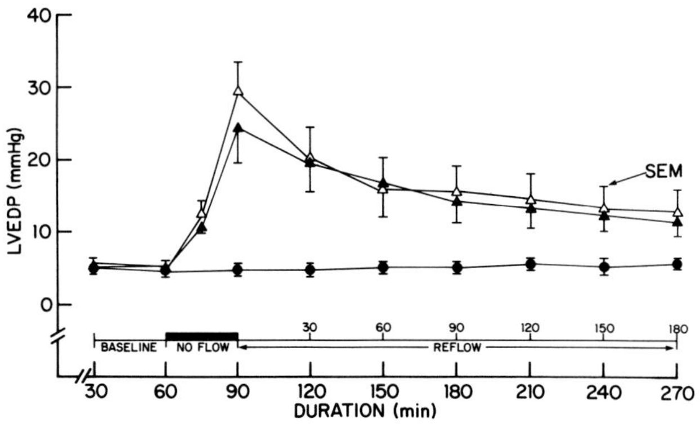

Figure 3. *LVEDP for nonischemic controls and hearts subjected to 30 minutes of no-flow ischemia (mm Hg; mean ± SEM). Solid circles denote nonischemic controls (n = 6); solid triangles, untreated hearts subjected to 30 minutes of no-flow ischemia (n = 7); open triangles, ischemic hearts treated with 1000 U/ml hyaluronidase during no flow (n = 9).*

A comparison of the means of each group at each time interval during the last 2 hours of perfusion indicated that only perfusion pressure of untreated ischemic hearts differed significantly from that of controls (Tukey's Studentized range test, $P < 0.05$).

LVEDP (Fig. 3), adjusted during baseline to ~5 mm Hg by filling the left ventricle balloon with KH buffer, remained constant in controls for the entire duration of perfusion. After 30 minutes of no-flow ischemia, LVEDP had increased to levels 4.6× above baseline in the untreated hearts and 5.5× above baseline in hyaluronidase-treated hearts. Differences between the two ischemic groups were not statistically significant at any time during no flow or reperfusion. During reperfusion, LVEDP decreased in both groups of ischemic hearts, remaining significantly elevated above control values during the last 2 hours of reperfusion when assessed with a repeated-measures analysis of variance test ($P < 0.0001$). Values at each time interval did not differ from controls when assessed with Tukey's Studentized range test.

Left ventricular developed pressure (Fig. 4) averaged 80 mm Hg during baseline, and in control perfusions remained constant. In both groups of ischemic hearts, developed pressure dropped promptly to 0 during no-flow ischemia; after 60 minutes of reperfusion, developed pressure had recovered to 95% of baseline in untreated hearts and 94% of baseline in hyaluronidase-treated hearts. Although differences between these groups were small and not significant when assessed with Tukey's Studentized range test, they were significant by the repeated-measures analysis of variance test ($P < 0.0001$).

The maximum rate of left ventricular pressure development, +dP/dt, for controls and for hearts subjected to ischemia and reperfusion is shown in Figure 5. Maximum +dP/dt averaged 1350 mm Hg/sec during baseline in controls and, except for a slight increase evident by 3 hours of perfusion, remained constant for 5 hours. In both groups of ischemic hearts, +dP/dt recovered ~50% by 10 minutes of reperfusion and returned to baseline and control values by 30 minutes of reperfusion. All three groups were similar to one another during the last 2 hours of perfusion (Tukey's Studentized range test).

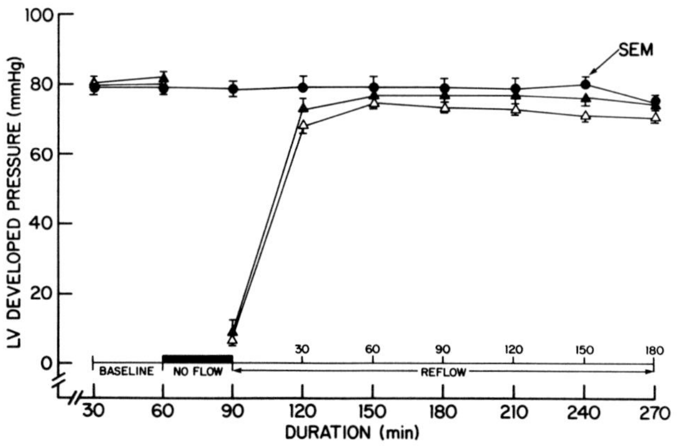

Figure 4. *Left ventricular developed pressure for nonischemic controls and hearts subjected to 30 minutes of no-flow ischemia (mm Hg; mean ± SEM). Developed pressure was calculated as end-systolic pressure minus LVEDP and was used as an index of maximal heart contraction. Solid circles denote nonischemic controls (n = 6); solid triangles, untreated hearts subjected to 30 minutes of no-flow ischemia (n = 7); open triangles, ischemic hearts treated with 1000 U/ml hyaluronidase during no flow (n = 9).*

^{125}I-BSA Time-Activity Curves

Figure 6 shows a representative series of time-activity curves generated after a bolus injection of ^{125}I-BSA into the proximal aorta every 30 minutes during 5 hours of perfusion. The maximum-likelihood estimate of the intensity function, r(t), was plotted as a solid curve for each run. The data were normalized to the peak count rate, r_0, and plotted for times during which the count rate decreased to 0.01% of the peak value. The curves exhibited peak

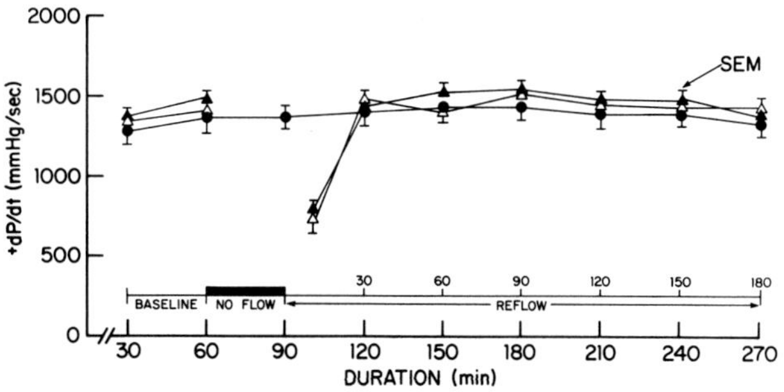

Figure 5. *Left ventricular maximum rate of pressure development, +dP/dt, for nonischemic controls and hearts subjected to 30 minutes of no-flow ischemia (mm Hg/sec; mean ± SEM). Solid circles denote nonischemic controls (n = 6); solid triangles, untreated hearts subjected to 30 minutes of no-flow ischemia (n = 7); open triangles, ischemic hearts treated with 1000 U/ml hyaluronidase during no flow (n = 9).*

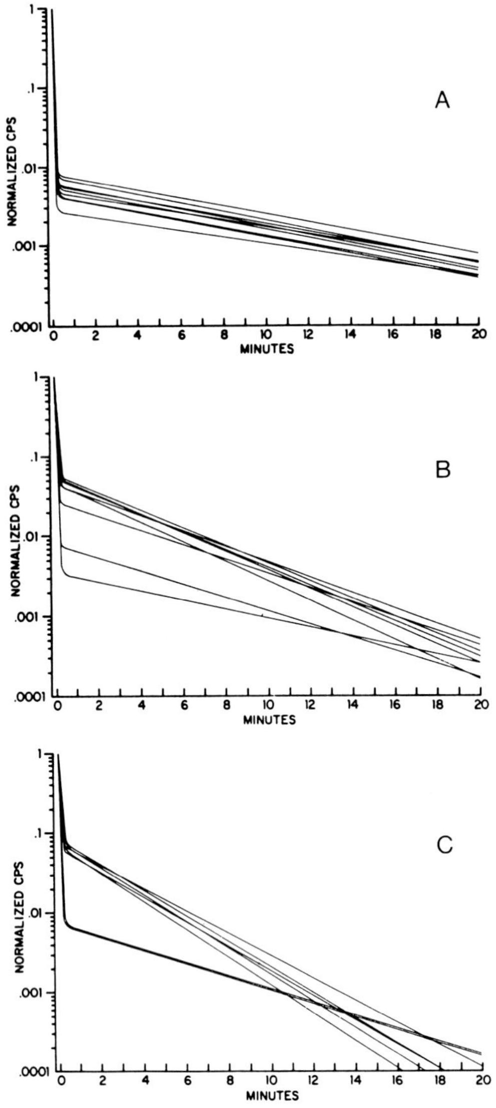

FIGURE 6. *Representative external-detection recordings of ^{125}I-BSA passage through the coronary vasculature and extravascular space every 30 minutes during 5 hours of perfusion in nonischemic controls (panel A) and during reperfusion after 30 minutes of no flow in untreated (panel B) and hyaluronidase-treated (panel C) hearts. The ordinate is a logarithmic scale of counts/sec normalized to the peak count rate, r_0. The abscissa is time elapsed since injection of the tracer bolus. The maximum-likelihood estimate of the intensity function r(t), is plotted as a solid line for each run. Two components of each recording include a rapid decrease in activity, followed by a slower monoexponential decrease to background (99.99% clearance). Progressive increases in the intercept, A_2, and the slope of the monoexponential portion of the curve, α_2, during reperfusion after ischemia are evident in panels B and C.*

activity rapidly as radiolabeled albumin entered the coronary circulation (and the detector field of view), and exhibited a rapid decrease in activity as ^{125}I-BSA was cleared from the vasculature. The terminal portion of each curve exhibited monoexponential disappearance of activity to background levels over 15–20 minutes. In nonischemic control perfusions (Fig. 6a), the y-intercepts, A_2, of the tails of the washout curves increased gradually with increasing duration of perfusion whereas the slopes, α_2, of the same portion of the curves remained relatively constant. During reperfusion after 30 minutes of no-flow ischemia in untreated (Fig. 6b) and hyaluronidase-treated (Fig. 6c) hearts, the y-intercepts of the tails of the washout curves increased progressively and the slopes became much steeper relative to baseline (and controls). The slope of the initial portion of the washout curve, α_1, decreased slightly, but similarly, in both groups of ischemic hearts during reperfusion.

Compartmental-Model Analysis of Radiolabeled Albumin External-Detection Data

Tracer turnover-rate constants (k_{01}, k_{12}, k_{21}) and estimates of ^{125}I-BSA vascular into extravascular space clearance ($\tilde{F}_{21}$) and mean-transit time ($\bar{t}_{BSA}$) are shown in Table 2 for 5-hour control perfusions and for untreated and hyaluronidase-treated hearts subjected to 30 minutes of no-flow ischemia and reperfusion. Baseline values for the rate constant k_{01} (clearance of tracer from the coronary vasculature) were similar for all groups of hearts and remained constant throughout the perfusion interval in nonischemic control experiments. Significant decreases in k_{01} compared to controls were observed after 2 hours of reperfusion in the hyaluronidase-treated ischemic hearts and after 3 hours of reflow in the untreated ischemic hearts (Tukey's Studentized range test, $P < 0.05$). The turnover-rate constants k_{12} (from extravascular into vascular space) and k_{21} (from vascular into extravascular space) were similar for nonischemic controls and both groups of ischemic hearts during baseline. Significant increases in k_{12} compared to control values were observed in hyaluronidase-treated ischemic hearts during the last 2 hours of reperfusion, while increases were significant only at the end of reflow in the untreated ischemic hearts. Whereas k_{21} increased significantly relative to baseline during the course of the perfusion in nonischemic controls ($t = 3.25$, $P < 0.025$), much larger increases were observed during reflow in both groups of ischemic hearts ($t = 7.96$, $P < 0.001$ and $t = 6.68$, $P < 0.001$ for untreated and hyaluronidase-treated hearts, respectively, compared to baseline). A repeated-measures analysis of variance test ($P < 0.0001$) and Tukey's Studentized range test ($P < 0.05$) indicated that k_{21} of both groups of ischemic hearts differed significantly from controls but not from each other during the last 2 hours of reperfusion.

Albumin vascular into extravascular space clearance, $\tilde{F}_{21}$, averaged 0.0033 ml/sec per g dry weight during baseline and increased 2.5× during 5 hours of continuous perfusion. Although this was a significant increase over baseline ($t = 2.85$, $P < 0.05$), it was much smaller than the 5.6-fold increase ob-

TABLE 2
Compartmental-Model Analysis of ^{125}I-BSA External Detection Data

Duration (min)	*n*	k_{01} (per sec)	k_{12} (10^{-3}/sec)	k_{21} (10^{-3}/sec)	$\tilde{F}_{21}$*	$\bar{t}_{BSA}$ (sec)
			Nonischemic control perfusions			
Baseline†	6	0.358 ± 0.074	1.91 ± 0.54	2.88 ± 0.82	3.29 ± 1.17	7.57 ± 1.79
90	6	0.378 ± 0.055	2.17 ± 0.20	3.86 ± 1.00	4.31 ± 1.67	7.58 ± 2.11
120	6	0.356 ± 0.060	2.07 ± 0.34	4.19 ± 1.33	4.64 ± 1.87	8.80 ± 2.61
150	6	0.361 ± 0.040	2.32 ± 0.61	4.55 ± 1.52	5.08 ± 2.31	8.25 ± 1.48
210	6	0.339 ± 0.053	2.39 ± 0.48	5.34 ± 1.92	6.00 ± 3.02	9.79 ± 2.65
270	6	0.348 ± 0.040	2.48 ± 0.91	7.29 ± 3.65	8.30 ± 5.02	11.57 ± 3.17
			30 Minutes of no flow			
Baseline	7	0.426 ± 0.091	1.99 ± 0.58	3.32 ± 0.85	3.15 ± 1.12	6.88 ± 1.33
(1)	7	0.405 ± 0.099	1.58 ± 0.40	4.02 ± 1.74	3.79 ± 2.19	9.35 ± 3.01
(30)	7	0.391 ± 0.095	3.08 ± 1.28	11.99 ± 7.95	11.55 ± 9.60	12.04 ± 3.78
(60)	6	0.371 ± 0.084	3.60 ± 1.50	15.63 ± 8.99‡	14.95 ± 11.26‡	14.90 ± 5.98‡
(120)	7	0.315 ± 0.056	3.69 ± 1.00	16.39 ± 4.54‡	15.05 ± 6.01‡	18.74 ± 4.38‡
(180)	7	0.264 ± 0.035‡	4.06 ± 1.09‡	18.93 ± 5.72‡	17.67 ± 7.54‡	22.12 ± 3.57‡
			30 Minutes of no flow + hyaluronidase			
Baseline	9	0.381 ± 0.035	2.56 ± 0.62	3.93 ± 1.48	3.30 ± 0.45	6.68 ± 1.05
(1)	8	0.398 ± 0.091	3.12 ± 0.83	7.21 ± 2.17	6.92 ± 1.27	8.92 ± 2.98
(30)	7	0.307 ± 0.033	5.00 ± 1.05	13.79 ± 5.35	12.79 ± 4.83	12.00 ± 2.30
(60)	9	0.325 ± 0.049	5.29 ± 1.16‡‖	16.14 ± 5.02‡	15.82 ± 4.94‡	12.48 ± 1.90
(120)	9	0.252 ± 0.052‡	5.67 ± 1.88‡‖	16.10 ± 7.45‡	15.96 ± 7.58‡	16.80 ± 3.25‡
(180)	8	0.232 ± 0.060‡	5.26 ± 1.10‡	15.13 ± 4.21‡	14.95 ± 4.39‡	17.20 ± 2.90‡‖

Results are expressed as mean ± SD; *n* = number of rabbit hearts evaluated for each time interval.
* μl/sec per g dry weight; calculated from Equation 11 using baseline estimates of $\tilde{V}_1$.
† Baseline denotes an average of two recordings during the first hour of perfusion. Parentheses indicate duration of reperfusion following 30 minutes of no-flow ischemia.
‡ $P < 0.05$ (compared to nonischemic control perfusions) and ‖ $P < 0.05$ (compared to untreated ischemic perfusions), by Tukey's Studentized range test.

served by the end of reperfusion of untreated ischemic hearts ($t = 5.81$, $P < 0.005$). Hyaluronidase was without effect on this parameter; a repeated-measures analysis of variance test using albumin clearance data collected during the last 2 hours of reperfusion confirmed that both groups of ischemic hearts differed significantly from controls ($P < 0.0001$) but not from each other ($P < 0.1$).

Baseline mean-transit times of radiolabeled albumin ($\bar{t}_{BSA}$) for all groups of hearts were similar (6.7–7.6 seconds), and in nonischemic controls, increased gradually as a function of the duration of perfusion by ~50% after 5 hours ($t = 4.62$, $P < 0.01$; compared to baseline). During reperfusion after ischemia, $\bar{t}_{BSA}$ increased much more rapidly in the untreated hearts and by 2 hours of reperfusion, was 2× that of controls (Tukey's studentized range test, $P < 0.05$). $\bar{t}_{BSA}$ of hyaluronidase-treated hearts also increased more rapidly than in nonischemic controls, but the increase was not as great as that of untreated ischemic hearts, and after 3 hours of reperfusion, differed significantly from that of the latter group (Tukey's Studentized range test, $P < 0.05$). Assessment of $\bar{t}_{BSA}$ during the last 2 hours of perfusion with a repeated-measures analysis of variance test indicated that differences between each group of hearts were highly significant ($P < 0.0001$).

Albumin Diffusive- and Convective-Transport Parameters

Estimates of diffusive- ($P\tilde{S}$, Equation 9) and convective- ($\tilde{U}$; Eq. 10) transport parameters for ^{125}I-

TABLE 3
Estimates of Diffusive- ($P\tilde{S}$) and Convective- ($\tilde{U}$) Transport Parameters* for ^{125}I-BSA after 5 Hours of Perfusion

	n	$P\tilde{S}$†	$\tilde{U}$†
Control	6	3.53 ± 1.31	0.36 ± 0.92
30 Min no flow	6	14.01 ± 6.52§	2.47 ± 1.85‡
30 Min no flow + hyaluronidase	6	11.29 ± 2.17‖	3.39 ± 2.34‡

Results are expressed as mean ± SD; *n* = number of rabbit hearts evaluated.
* Diffusive- and convective-transport parameters were calculated from Equations 9 and 10 utilizing baseline estimates of vascular volume derived from two-compartment model data fitting and estimates of interstitial fluid volume obtained by subtraction of vascular volume from the ^{57}Co-EDTA space determined at the end of the perfusion.
† μl/sec per g dry weight.
‡ $P < 0.05$; § $P < 0.005$; ‖ $P < 0.001$, by Student's *t*-test (compared to nonischemic controls).

BSA based on baseline estimates of vascular volume obtained from external detection and interstitial fluid volume obtained from ^{57}Co-EDTA equilibration data at the termination of selected experiments are shown in Table 3. After 5 hours of continuous perfusion, permeation of the vasculature by ^{125}I-BSA is accounted for primarily by diffusive transport (91%). After 3.5 hours of reperfusion following 30 minutes of ischemia, $P\tilde{S}$ was 4.0× that of nonischemic controls and ultrafiltration accounted for 15% of total albumin transport. In hyaluronidase-treated ischemic hearts, $P\tilde{S}$ was still 3.2× that of nonischemic controls and not different from that of the untreated ischemic group; ultrafiltration accounted for 23% of total albumin transport, but this was not statistically different from that of untreated ischemic hearts.

Discussion

These experiments confirm our previous observations that reperfusion of isolated hearts after 30 minutes of no-flow ischemia is associated with marked increases in total water content, extracellular fluid volume, vascular resistance, and vascular permeation by ^{125}I-BSA, while indices of left ventricular function, including developed pressure and maximum +dP/dt, rapidly return to preischemic baseline levels (Tilton et al., 1983, 1985). The significant increases in extracellular water and in albumin permeation across endothelium during reperfusion indicate that damage to vascular endothelium is an important, early consequence of ischemia and reperfusion, with functional sequelae that persist despite recovery of left ventricular function. Although the observations that hyaluronidase decreased the water content of ischemic tissue and partially blocked the vascular-resistance increases are consistent with previous reports (de Oliveira and Levy, 1960; Rovetto, 1977; Overholser and Harris, 1981; Sunnergren and Rovetto, 1983), the finding that hyaluronidase does not prevent ischemia-reperfusion-induced increases in albumin permeation is a new one which suggests that this enzyme does not protect endothelial cells from ischemic injury.

The possibility that hyaluronidase may have increased albumin leakage was ruled out in separate control experiments in which the enzyme was instilled at a concentration 3× that used in the earlier (30-minute no-flow) preparations for 10 minutes of no flow ($n = 6$). Additional controls ($n = 3$) were subjected to 10 minutes of no flow without hyaluronidase, and in both groups of hearts, perfusion pressure, LVEDP, left ventricular developed pressure, and +dP/dt rapidly returned to baseline values during reperfusion. Although 3000 U/ml hyaluronidase significantly decreased the water content of the treated hearts compared to untreated controls (Fig. 1), it had no effect on albumin permeation, which was similar for both groups of hearts after 5 hours of perfusion (unpublished observations). These results indicate that the chromatographically purified and dialyzed hyaluronidase used in these experiments did not alter coronary vascular permeability to albumin. This finding is consistent with that of Houck and Chang (1979), who reported that the increased vascular permeability sometimes associated with administration of hyaluronidase is due to a contaminant of the enzyme preparation and not to the enzyme itself.

Baseline estimates of k_{21} in this study predict very rapid albumin equilibration between the intravascular and extravascular compartments. Although the observation that albumin permeation of coronary vessels is higher in these experiments than in vivo is consistent with previous reports (Sutherland and Young, 1966; Young, 1968), the increased k_{21} does not necessarily imply vascular damage, but may be accounted for by shifts in pressure gradients across vessel walls when blood is replaced with a low-viscosity asanguineous perfusate.

Although pressure data remained constant, estimates of albumin permeation, $\tilde{F}_{21}$, and the mean-transit time of radiolabeled albumin increased significantly in hearts perfused continuously for 5 hours. Since perfusate flow rate and intravascular clearance of radiolabeled albumin (k_{01}) remained constant, increases in the vascular into extravascular space rate constant (k_{21}) for radiolabeled albumin accounted for the increases in $\tilde{F}_{21}$ (Eqs. 6 and 11). This increase could result from: (1) fluid shear stress damage (focal or diffuse) to endothelium induced by high perfusate flow rates, and/or (2) changes in pressure gradients across vessel walls (see discussion under "Myocardial Edema") resulting in increased ultrafiltration of albumin and water without any vascular damage or change in vascular porosity per se. In view of the absence of ultrastructural evidence of endothelial damage, we tend to favor the latter explanation. The finding that k_{12} does not increase in parallel with k_{21} is consistent with the observation that $\tilde{V}_2$ increases during the course of these perfusions, whereas $\tilde{V}_1$ remains constant.

Baseline estimates of vascular volume (Eq. 6) averaged ~1.0 ml/g dry weight in these experiments. We have reported previously that the weight of vascular fluid in isolated hearts was 15% of total heart weight (Tilton et al., 1983). This value, which was calculated using baseline $\tilde{V}_1$ estimates of ~0.8 ml/g dry weight, is consistent with the high vascularity of cardiac tissue and is in good agreement with data by Gonzalez et al. (1980). The slightly larger estimates of $\tilde{V}_1$ in this study probably are accounted for by the ~10% increase in perfusion pressure and flow rates, which would tend to dilate the vasculature. The fact that estimates of vascular volume obtained by external detection are larger, in general, than those based on gravimetric analysis is probably explained by the unavoidable loss of blood from the larger coronary vessels with the latter technique. This interpretation is supported by the finding that in equilibration experiments in which ^{125}I-BSA content of the heart is monitored by external detection, almost one half of the activity in the heart is lost within seconds of turning off the perfusion pump.

The significant increase in $\bar{t}_{BSA}$ during control perfusions may be due to an increase in the albumin volume of distribution (vascular and/or extravascular, the latter of which was increased) and/or to an increase in albumin ultrafiltration across coronary endothelium. The possibility that developing regions of low flow contribute to the prolonged mean-transit time of ^{125}I-BSA in control perfusions can be virtually excluded on the basis of the observation that k_{01} (the fractional rate of tracer clearance from the coronary vasculature) and α_1, the slope of the initial portion of the washout curve, remained constant for 5 hours.

Myocardial Edema

We elected to use asanguineous Krebs-Henseleit buffer to perfuse isolated rabbit hearts for convenience and to avoid difficulties associated with aggregation of cellular elements and/or hemolysis during 5 hours of perfusion. Although this results in significant increases in the myocardial water content of nonischemic control hearts relative to nonperfused hearts, evidence discussed below indicates that the increased water is localized primarily to the cardiac interstitium, and the increased extracellular fluid does not interfere with our ability to demonstrate marked increases in vascular leakage of albumin and in water content of the heart during reperfusion after ischemia. The increased water content may simply be the consequence of a downstream shift in the distribution of pressure gradients across vessel walls (due to the low perfusate viscosity), resulting in an increase in convective transport of water and small molecular weight solutes. This interpretation is consistent with the virtually normal ultrastructural appearance of endothelium of these hearts. It is noteworthy that maximum +dP/dt remained constant for the entire duration of perfusion, suggesting that the extracellular edema did not compromise myocardial contractility, and that the tissue was adequately oxygenated. In light of the fact that this is a "low-work" heart preparation, it might be anticipated that the deleterious effects of ischemia and reperfusion would be even more severe in working heart preparations or in vivo.

Several lines of evidence indicate that, under the conditions of these experiments, the increased water content of ischemic-reperfused hearts is localized primarily in the interstitium. First, 10-minute equilibration data obtained at the end of selected experiments indicated that the ^{57}Co-EDTA volume of distribution was increased markedly after ischemia and reperfusion in untreated hearts, and that this increased volume could be accounted for entirely by the increase in total water content without any change in intracellular water. Second, the decrease in total tissue water associated with hyaluronidase treatment during no flow was entirely accounted for by the decrease in interstitial fluid volume without any changes in the estimates of vascular and intracellular volumes. Third, as discussed above, the significant increase in $\bar{t}_{BSA}$ in the untreated ischemic hearts is attributable to an increase in the albumin volume of distribution (vascular and/or extravascular, both of which were increased) and to an increase in albumin ultrafiltration across coronary endothelium. Since hyaluronidase treatment did not affect diffusive or convective transport of albumin (Table 3), the reduction in $\bar{t}_{BSA}$ observed after 3 hours of reflow in hyaluronidase-treated ischemic hearts (compared to untreated ischemic hearts) must be attributed to a decrease in the albumin volume of distribution. This interpretation is consistent with the marked decrease in interstitial fluid volume shown in Table 1.

The increased $\bar{t}_{BSA}$ during reperfusion after ischemia may also be accounted for in part by the development of flow heterogeneity. This interpretation is supported by the observation that k_{01}, the rate of clearance of radiolabeled tracer from the coronary vasculature, was decreased by ~40% in both groups of ischemic hearts. It is of interest, however, that decreases in k_{01} were similar in the hyaluronidase-treated and untreated ischemic hearts, even though $\bar{t}_{BSA}$ of the former was significantly less than that of the latter at the end of the experiment.

Vascular Hemodynamic Changes

Although vascular hemodynamic changes, including increased vascular resistance and increased flow heterogeneity (leading ultimately to regions of no flow) during and following ischemia have long been recognized, the underlying pathophysiological mechanisms(s) responsible for these changes has not been fully elucidated. The hemodynamic changes may result from an increase in the intracellular water content of ischemic tissue. Endothelial cell swelling (Kloner et al., 1974; Armiger and Gavin, 1975) and capillary collapse and/or compression secondary to myocardial cell swelling (Hauschild et al., 1970) have been suggested as possible explanations for the failure of vascular reperfusion following ischemia. The possibility that the increased volume of extracellular fluid in the untreated, ischemic-reperfused hearts compressed vessels, producing regions of no reflow, appears unlikely in view of separate experiments in which colloidal carbon (dialyzed, filtered through 1.2-μm Acrodisc filters immediately before use) was infused during the terminal 15 seconds (unpublished observations). Hearts were removed from the perfusion chamber, fixed in 10% formalin, sectioned into ~10 transmural pieces, and examined for areas of myocardium that were not labeled with carbon. In continuously perfused (n =

1), as well as in ischemic-reperfused hearts ($n = 3$), myocardium was uniformly darkened, including subendocardial regions and papillary muscles. Although this technique cannot demonstrate regions of low flow, these results do suggest that significant areas of no flow did not develop during reperfusion after ischemia in this experimental model. These findings, together with the observation that myocardial contractility recovered completely during reperfusion, are consistent with the observations that 30 minutes of ischemia are minimum for the development of no reflow in the intact dog model (Kloner et al., 1974), as well as in isolated, buffer-perfused rat hearts (Humphrey et al., 1980, 1984). Furthermore, in the absence of blood cells in these experiments, complete collapse and/or compression of vessels by extravascular fluid would be necessary to produce regions of no flow, and this seems unlikely in view of the constant flow conditions employed.

Reduced myocardial perfusion during reflow after ischemia also has been attributed to intramyocardial tension generated by ischemic contracture of myocytes (Hearse et al., 1977; Gavin et al., 1978; Alanen et al., 1980; Humphrey et al., 1980). It is noteworthy, however, that the experimental protocol in those studies differed significantly from our experiments, in that the hearts were perfused under conditions of constant pressure rather than constant flow, reperfusion was absent or very brief (only a few seconds), and/or myocyte contractile function was markedly impaired. The observations in our experiments that k_{01} was not decreased at 1 minute reflow when LVEDP was increased maximally, and that during subsequent reperfusion, LVEDP decreased while the rate of intravascular clearance of tracer was prolonged suggest that the hemodynamic changes observed during reflow were independent of myocyte contracture. Furthermore, in view of evidence that placement of an isovolumic balloon in the left ventricle reduces no reflow associated with ischemic contracture (Humphrey et al., 1981), the isovolumic balloon in the left ventricle of our isolated heart preparations should minimize the development of such perfusion defects in our experiments. In any case, our observations that indices of myocyte function, including LVEDP, developed pressure, maximum +dP/dt, and intracellular water content returned to control levels during reperfusion, while indices of vascular function deteriorated, suggest that ischemic injury to the vasculature is independent of, and precedes that to, myocytes under the conditions of our experiments.

Intracellular water may indeed be increased early during reperfusion following brief periods of ischemia (Leaf, 1973; Whalen et al., 1974) and/or after ischemic intervals that result in irreversible membrane damage during reflow. However, the observations in our experiments that intracellular water content was not increased after 3.5 hours of reperfusion (Table 1) and that left ventricular function had recovered to baseline and control levels by 1 hour of reflow, suggest that any increase in intracellular water that might have occurred early in the course of reperfusion at a time when contractile function was still impaired was not substantial or was subsequently reversed during 3.5 hours of reperfusion. Although the observation that intracellular water content of ischemic hearts was not decreased suggests that little, if any, ^{57}Co-EDTA accessed myocytes, we cannot rule out the possibility that cell swelling of viable myocytes, which exclude ^{57}Co-EDTA, is balanced by ^{57}Co-EDTA penetration of a small number of lethally injured myocytes, resulting in no net change in intracellular volume.

It is of interest that estimates of vascular volume (Eq. 6) increased ~60% during reperfusion in both groups of ischemic hearts in the face of significant increases in perfusion pressure. Since flow rate was held constant in these experiments, dilation of the coronary vasculature proximal to sites of constriction or increased vascular resistance could account for the increase in vascular volume. This interpretation is consistent with evidence that most of the vascular volume is contained within large vessels (Green, 1950) and that 4 μM diltiazem prevents increases in both perfusion pressure and vascular volume (Tilton et al., 1985). Increased estimates of vascular volume observed during reflow could be accounted for by prolonged washout of radiolabeled tracer from the coronary vasculature and/or increased porosity of the vasculature, rather than an actual anatomical increase in vascular volume. For this reason and the fact that the possibility of flow heterogeneity after ischemia cannot be excluded, only baseline estimates of $\tilde{V}_1$ were used in calculations of albumin permeation (Eq. 11) during reperfusion.

The possibility that increases in vascular resistance in the ischemic-reperfused hearts accounted for the increases in k_{21} was excluded on the basis of several different lines of evidence. First, only one fifth of the total albumin transport in ischemic-reperfused hearts was attributable to ultrafiltration, which would be affected by changes in perfusion pressure. The remainder was accounted for by diffusion, which could not be influenced by pressure changes. Second, in a separate study (Tilton et al., 1985), 0.4 μM diltiazem decreased by one half the perfusion pressure increases observed during reflow after 30 minutes of ischemia, but did not reduce albumin permeation of the vasculature. Third, in a separate series of unpublished experiments in which aortic perfusion pressure was maintained at baseline levels (by decreasing the buffer flow rate) during reperfusion after 30 minutes of no-flow ischemia, albumin permeation was still significantly elevated over nonischemic controls. Only the difference in k_{21} between these constant pressure experiments (~4-fold increase) and the constant flow experiments (~5-fold increase) can be attributed to convective albumin transport.

Other Effects of Hyaluronidase

Since hyaluronidase was present within myocardium only during the no-flow period, its effect on tissue-water content probably is not mediated by an intravascular osmotic effect during reperfusion. Likewise, the observation that hyaluronidase decreased the tissue-water content of controls (in which the effects of the 10-minute ischemic incubation with hyaluronidase were completely reversible) indicates that hyaluronidase effects are not restricted to edema resulting from ischemia-reperfusion injury. These results are consistent with the report of Sunnergren and Rovetto (1983), who have shown that hyaluronidase significantly reduces the tissue-water content of buffer-perfused rat hearts, and that the reduction in water content could be accounted for by changes in extracellular-water content with no change in intracellular-water content.

Since there is no experimental evidence to suggest that hyaluronidase acts intracellularly, the ability of this enzyme to block increases in interstitial edema during reperfusion must be due, at least in part, to depolymerization of the large mucopolysaccharide matrix of the interstitium (Wolf et al., 1980). This would decrease the mass of extracellular matrix and increase the fluidity of the residual matrix relative to its normal gel-like consistency. These changes could render the interstitial matrix more compliant, which would tend to reduce vascular resistance and also facilitate permeation of the matrix by solutes. This interpretation is consistent with the observations of de Oliveira and Levy (1960), and further suggests a possible mechanism to account for the observed increases in collateral blood flow (Askenazi et al., 1977; Rovetto, 1977). These observations and interpretations also suggest that the increased vascular resistance observed during reflow cannot be attributed entirely to increased tissue edema, but must be due, at least in part, to vasoconstriction.

In conclusion, these findings indicate that hyaluronidase does not prevent ischemia-reperfusion-induced increases in albumin permeation of the coronary vasculature, and suggest that its protective effect on ischemic myocardium is mediated, instead, by reducing interstitial edema and vascular resistance.

We thank Sandy Brickey for her excellent secretarial assistance, and acknowledge the photographic assistance of Jeff Fulford.

This work was supported by National Institutes of Health Grants HL17646, HL12839, and RR00396 (Division of Research Resources), and by the Kilo Diabetes and Vascular Research Foundation.

Dr. Larson is affiliated with the Biomedical Computer Laboratory, and Dr. Kilo, with the Department of Medicine.

Address for reprints: Ronald G. Tilton, Ph.D., Department of Pathology, Washington University School of Medicine, 660 S. Euclid Avenue, St. Louis, Missouri 63110.

Received July 25, 1984; accepted for publication March 15, 1985.

References

Alanen K, Nevalainen TJ, Lipasti J (1980) Ischaemic contracture and myocardial perfusion in isolated rat heart. Virchows Arch [Pathol Anat] **385:** 143–149

Armiger LC, Gavin JB (1975) Changes in the microvasculature of ischemic and infarcted myocardium. Lab Invest **33:** 51–56

Askenazi J, Hillis D, Diaz PE, Davis MA, Braunwald E, Maroko PR (1977) The effects of hyaluronidase on coronary blood flow following coronary artery occlusion in the dog. Circ Res **40:** 566–571

Bridge JHB, Bersohn MM, Gonzalez F, Bassingthwaighte JF (1982) Synthesis and use of radio cobaltic EDTA as an extracellular marker in rabbit heart. Am J Physiol **242:** 671–676

Cairns JA, Holder DA, Tanser P, Missirlis E (1982) Intravenous hyaluronidase therapy for myocardial infarction in man: Double-blind trial to assess infarct size limitation. Circulation **65:** 764–771

Camilleri JP, Joseph D, Fabiani JN, Deloche A, Schlumberger M, Relland J, Carpentier A (1976) Microcirculatory changes following early reperfusion in experimental myocardial infarction. Virchows Arch [Pathol Anat] **369:** 315–333

Day TD (1957) The permeability of interstitial connective tissue and the nature of the interfibrillary substance. J Physiol (Lond) **117:** 1–8

de Oliveira JM, Levy MN (1960) Effect of hyaluronidase upon the water content of ischemic myocardium. Am Heart J **60:** 106–109

Eadie WT, Dryard D, James FE, Roos M, Saudolet B (1971) Statistical Methods in Experimental Physics. New York, American Elsevier

Gavin JB, Nevalainen TJ, Seelye RN, Webster VJ, Thomson RW (1978) An association between the onset of rigor and loss of vascular competence in early myocardial infarcts. Pathology **10:** 219–225

Gonzalez F, Harris C, Bassingthwaighte JB (1980) Volumes of distribution of intact rabbit hearts. Physiologist **23:** 78

Green HD (1950) Circulatory System: Physical Principles in Medical Physics, vol II. edited by O Glasser. Chicago, The Year Book Publishers, p 228

Hauschild U, Baghirzade MF, Kirsch U (1970) Compression of capillaries as a result of ischemia. Electronmicroscopic investigations on papillary myocardium of man and guinea pigs. Virchows Arch [Pathol Anat] **351:** 205–224

Hearse DJ, Garlick PB, Humphrey SM (1977) Ischemic contracture of the myocardium: Mechanisms and prevention. Am J Cardiol **39:** 986–993

Hillis LD, Fishbein MC, Braunwald E, Maroko PR (1977) The influence of the time interval between coronary artery occlusion and the administration of hyaluronidase on salvage of ischemic myocardium in dogs. Circ Res **41:** 26–31

Houck JC, Chang CM (1979) Permeability factor contaminating hyaluronidase preparations. Inflammation **3:** 447–451

House CR (1974) Water Transport in Cells and Tissues. London, Edward Arnold

Humphrey SM, Gavin JB, Herdson PB (1980) The relationship of ischemic contracture to vascular reperfusion in the isolated rat heart. J Mol Cell Cardiol **12:** 1397–1406

Humphrey SM, Thomson RW, Gavin JB (1981) The effect of an isovolumic left ventricle on the coronary vascular competence during reflow after global ischemia in the rat heart. Circ Res **49:** 784–791

Humphrey SM, Thomson RW, Gavin JB (1984) The influence of the no-reflow phenomenon on reperfusion and reoxygenation damage and enzyme release from anoxic and ischaemic isolated rat hearts. J Mol Cell Cardiol **16:** 915–930

Kedem O, Katchalsky A (1961) A physical interpretation of the phenomenological coefficients of membrane permeability. J Gen Physiol **45:** 143–179

Kloner RA, Ganote CE, Jennings RB (1974) The "no-reflow" phenomenon after temporary coronary occlusion in the dog. J Clin Invest **54:** 1496–1508

Kloner RA, Fishbein MC, Maclean D, Braunwald E, Maroko PR (1977) Effect of hyaluronidase during the early phase of acute myocardial ischemia: An ultrastructural and morphometric analysis. Am J Cardiol **40:** 43–49

Kloner RA, Braunwald E, Maroko PR (1978) Long-term preservation of ischemic myocardium in the dog by hyaluronidase. Circulation **58:** 220–226

Leaf A (1973) Cell swelling. A factor in ischemic tissue injury. Circulation **158:** 455–458

Maclean D, Fishbein MC, Maroko PR, Braunwald E (1976) Hya-

luronidase-induced reductions in myocardial infarct size. Science **194:** 199–200
Markham J, Snyder DL, Cox JR Jr (1976) A numerical implementation of the maximum-likelihood method of parameter estimation for tracer-kinetic data. Math Biosci **28:** 275–300
Maroko PR, Libby P, Bloor CM, Sobel BE, Braunwald E (1972) Reduction by hyaluronidase of myocardial necrosis following coronary artery occlusion. Circulation **46:** 430–437
Most AS, Capone RJ, Mastrofrancesco PA (1976) Failure of hyaluronidase to alter the early course of acute myocardial infarction in pigs. Am J Cardiol **38:** 28–33
Overholser KA, Harris TR (1981) Effects of hyaluronidase and protamine on resistance and transport after coronary flow reduction in heparinized dogs. J Pharmacol Exp Ther **217:** 62–69
Perl W (1971) Stimulus-response method for flows and volumes in slightly perturbed constant parameter systems. Bull Math Biophys **33:** 225–233
Perl W (1975) Convection and permeation of albumin between plasma and interstitium. Microvasc Res **10:** 83–94
Ribeiro LGT, Hillis LD, Louie EK, Davis MA, Maroko PR, Braunwald E (1978) A method for demonstrating the efficacy of interventions designed to limit infarct size following coronary occlusion: beneficial effect of hyaluronidase. Cardiovasc Res **12:** 334–340
Rovetto MJ (1977) Effect of hyaluronidase and methylprednisolone on myocardial function, glucose metabolism, and coronary flow in the isolated ischemic rat heart. Circ Res **41:** 373–379
Sandor T, Wilson GD (1972) Maximum likelihood estimation of parameters in multiexponential fits when data follow Poisson distribution. Comput Programs Biomed **2:** 111–117
Snyder DL (1973) Statistical analysis of dynamic tracer data. IEEE Trans Biomed Eng **20:** 11–20
Sunnergren KP, Rovetto MJ (1983) Hyaluronidase reversal of increased coronary vascular resistance in ischemic rat hearts. Am J Physiol **245:** H183–H188
Sutherland TM, Young DAB (1966) Increased permeability of the capillaries of the rat heart to plasma albumin with asphyxiation and with perfusion. J Physiol **183:** 112–122
Szabo G, Magyar S (1958) Effect of hyaluronidase on capillary permeability, lymph flow and passage of dye-labelled protein from plasma to lymph. Nature (Lond) **182:** 377–379
Tilton RG, Larson KB, Udell JR, Sobel BE, Williamson JR (1983) External detection of early microvascular dysfunction after no-flow ischemia followed by reperfusion in isolated rabbit hearts. Circ Res **52:** 210–225
Tilton RG, Williamson EK, Cole PA, Larson KB, Kilo C, Williamson JR (in press) Coronary vascular hemodynamic and permeability changes during reperfusion after no-flow ischemia in isolated, diltiazem-treated rabbit hearts. J Cardiovasc Pharmacol
Whalen DA, Hamilton DG, Ganote CE, Jennings RB (1974) Effect of a transient period of ischemia on myocardial cells. Am J Pathol **74:** 381–397
Wolf RA, Chaung LY, Muller JE, Kloner RA, Braunwald E (1980) Intravenous bovine testicular hyaluronidase depolymerizes myocardial hyaluronic acid in dogs with coronary artery occlusion. Circ Res **48:** 88–95
Young DAB (1968) Factors controlling the washout of the interstitial space of the isolated, perfused rat heart. J Physiol (Lond) **196:** 747–759

INDEX TERMS: Hyaluronidase • Ischemia • Reperfusion • External detection • Endothelium • Albumin permeation

The Electromotive Force of the Ventricular Free Wall and Papillary Muscle Preparations

Saburo Mashima, Kan Takayanagi, Georg Schmidt, and Akira Nozaki
From the Second Department of Internal Medicine, University of Tokyo, Tokyo, Japan

SUMMARY. The electromotive force of the ventricular tissues with different anatomy and activation patterns was studied. The left ventricular wall was perfused with Tyrode's solution from the circumflex branch of the left coronary artery and was stimulated first at an epicardial and then endocardial site to induce ectopic beats. The early QRS voltage was compared with the activated area at the same instant. In other experiments, the whole heart was perfused from the aorta, and the anterior papillary muscle of the right ventricle was introduced into a small separate chamber. Different locations were stimulated to induce longitudinal and transverse activation, and the remote potential was measured with leads in both directions. By means of a calibration system with artificial dipoles, the strength of the double layer was expressed in terms of mA·cm per unit area of the activation wave front. The results indicated that epicardial stimulation of the left ventricular wall produced voltage proportional to the activated area; the average moment was found to be 0.11 mA·cm per unit area. The potential curve produced by endocardial stimulation of the same preparation was characterized by an initial low-voltage phase, followed by a sharp upstroke. The right ventricular papillary muscle produced a larger double layer moment during activation in the longitudinal direction, but voltage due to transverse activation was several times smaller. **(*Circ Res 56: 851–856, 1985*)**

THE extracellular potential field of myocardial tissue was studied in our previous report (Mashima et al., 1978). Using the isolated dog heart, we determined the effectiveness of the activation wave front as a current generating the double layer in terms of mA·cm per unit area. Although our experiments measured the average amount of the double layer extending over layers of ventricular muscle, contributions from different portions probably vary, depending on local structures and activation patterns of the tissue. Some evidence indicates that the strength of the double layer depends on the local activation sequence with respect to the orientation of fibers (Corbin and Scher, 1977; Spach et al., 1979; Colli-Franzone et al., 1982). Whereas the direction of the fibers varies with muscle layers of different depths, the apical portion of the papillary muscle consists of nearly parallel fibers (Myerburg et al., 1978), which provides an opportunity for investigation of different patterns of the activation process. Patterns of activation in subendocardial layers of the ventricle containing specialized fibers may be different from those in subepicardial layers.

This work was undertaken to extend our previous studies to include different tissues and activation sequences. Utilizing preparations perfused from a coronary artery, we examined the effect of an activation wave on remote potential by stimulating the left ventricular wall at epi- and endocardial sites. The potential produced by the anterior papillary muscle of the right ventricle was measured during activation proceeding along and across the long axis of the preparation.

Methods

Twenty mongrel dogs were used in this study. The hearts were isolated and perfused with Tyrode's solution at 37°C. For experiments with the left ventricular wall, the circumflex branch of the left coronary artery was selectively perfused, and portions of the ventricle, perfused from other branches, including the right ventricle and interventricular septum, were removed. The free wall obtained from the left ventricle was supported by a stiff wire to make a plate-like configuration and was suspended in a cubic box filled with Tyrode's solution. Stimulating electrodes were attached to the midportion of the preparation at corresponding sites on the epicardial and endocardial surfaces.

The recording system is similar to that described in our previous paper (Mashima et al., 1978) and will be mentioned here only briefly. The preparation was immersed in Tyrode's solution in a cubic container (edge length, 12 cm). Five silver electrodes attached at each of the surfaces of the container were connected through equal resistors making a remote lead with a uniform lead field. The potential in the lead perpendicular to the preparation was amplified and observed on an oscilloscope with photographic recording, or was written directly with an ink-jet recorder (Nihon-Koden model RIJ 1108-4S). There were no significant differences in the results obtained by these two methods.

The local activation time was determined at many epicardial and endocardial sites. On the epicardial surface, a cross-shaped electrode holder with 80 electrodes, 20 on each of the four arms, was attached for the measurement of activation time. On the endocardial surface, a bipolar search electrode or one of the arms of the electrode holder described above was used. In addition, the intramural activation time was determined by electrode needles with 10 small electrodes having an interelectrode distance of 1.0 mm. The needles were inserted into the preparation at 8–14 locations successively around the stimulating electrodes. On the endocardial surface, deflections due to the activation of Purkinje fibers and the ventricular muscle were sometimes observed. In these instances, the latter was used for the determination of local activation time.

Within a short time after stimulation, the activation wave was confined to the inside of the preparation without breaking through the opposite surface. During this period, the area of the activation wave front was estimated by the activated area on the epi- or endocardial surface. Voltage and area measurements were performed at 5-msec intervals and were compared to calculate the average voltage per unit area of the activation wave front.

For experiments with papillary muscle, the whole heart was perfused from the aorta. The right coronary artery was ligated and the right ventricle was opened. The anterior papillary muscle of the right ventricle, which was perfused from the anterior descending branch, was exposed, and the valvular attachment was cut free after being ligated with a thread. As shown in Figure 1, the papillary muscle was introduced into a small cubic box (edge length, 19 mm), which had a hole 8 mm in diameter at the bottom. Longitudinal potential measurements were made with a lead from two loops of silver wire at the

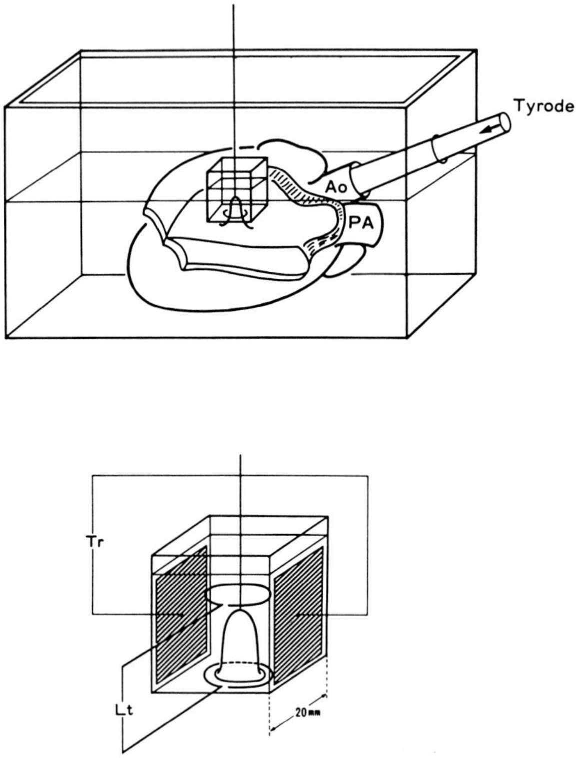

FIGURE 1. *Potential measurement of the right ventricular papillary muscle. The whole heart was perfused from the aorta, and the anterior papillary muscle of the right ventricle was introduced into a separate chamber. The lower panel is an enlarged view of the chamber with longitudinal and transverse leads for recording potential.*

bottom and at a height of 12 mm. The box had another pair of silver plates on the inside surface to form the transverse lead (Fig. 1). To activate the preparation longitudinally, a remote epicardial site outside the small box was stimulated electrically. To obtain transverse activation, two small pairs of stimulating electrodes were applied to the side of the muscle, at a site near the bottom and at about one-third the distance from the apex of the papillary muscle. On both occasions, local activation time was determined at many sites on the epicardial surface of the preparation to confirm nearly longitudinal or transverse directions of activation. With longitudinal activation, the area of the activation wave was considered as the transverse section of the muscle, which was calculated from the long and short diameters of the muscle at the level of the midpoint between the base and apex. The area of the transverse activation wave varied with time. The maximal value was estimated by multiplying the height of the muscle by thickness. Since the potential due to transverse activation usually was small, the peak voltage was compared with the maximal cross-sectional area estimated as stated above.

In order to express the effectiveness of the myocardial generator in terms of dipole moment in mA·cm, each measurement system was calibrated with artificial dipoles. The lead system for the left ventricular wall was calibrated with an artificial dipole placed at several locations within the region corresponding to the preparation. The effect was found to be nearly uniform over the region, with less than 10% errors. In the small box for the papillary muscle experiments, the transverse lead was also practically uniform, but the longitudinal lead showed slightly different sensitivity to dipoles of different locations. The average sensitivity to several dipole locations was used for this lead.

Because of the differences in the resistivity of Tyrode's solution and ventricular muscle, a dipole inserted into the tissue was more effective than that in the solution with the same moment. The ratio of their effectiveness was determined by comparison of a needle dipole inserted into the preparation and the same needle in the solution, as described previously (Mashima et al., 1978). For the papillary muscle, two directions of the needle, longitudinal and transverse, were examined. For the left ventricular preparation, the direction perpendicular to the wall was selected.

Results

Left Ventricular Wall

Examples of recorded potential curves are shown in Figure 2. The spread of activation from epicardial and endocardial sites is shown in Fig. 3, where the surface measurements (top) and intramural activation times (bottom) are shown. With epicardial stimulation, arrival of the activation at the endocardial surface was usually more than 30 msec after stimulation. The spread of activation was faster with endocardial stimulation, and the breakthrough at the epicardial surface was sometimes less than 20 msec after stimulation. However, the activation front was generally confined within the intramural region to 20 msec, and since measurements at the earlier time were susceptible to errors, the voltage

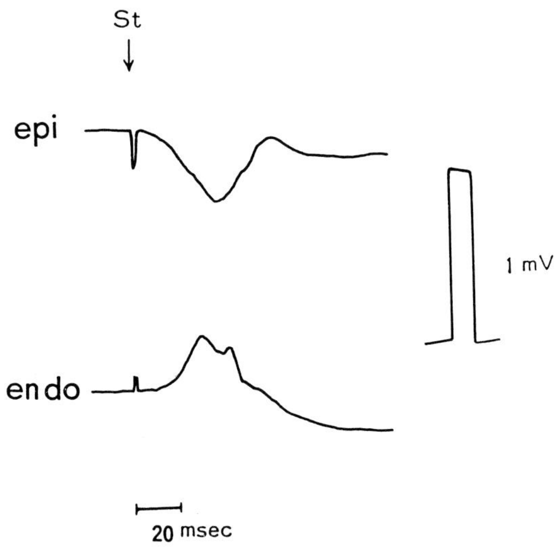

FIGURE 2. *Examples of potential curves caused by activation of left ventricular wall preparations. St = epi- or endocardial stimulation.*

was read at 20 msec after endocardial stimulation and at 20 and 30 msec after epicardial stimulation. At the same instants, the activated area on the corresponding surface was determined. Dividing the voltage by area, the strength of the double layer was expressed in terms of mV/cm^2. This value was compared with the effectiveness of an artificial dipole with known moment inserted into the preparation. Thus, the absolute moment of the double layer was obtained in terms of mA·cm per unit area of the activation wave front. The results are shown in Table 1. It can be seen that values at 20 and 30 msec after the epicardial stimulation are not significantly different. At 20 msec, endocardial activation produced a smaller voltage.

The potential curves in Figure 2 show that endocardial stimulation was characterized, as compared with epicardial stimulation, by initial low voltages, which were followed by a sharp rise. The timing of the sharp upstroke differed from preparation to preparation, ranging from 15–25 msec. Sometimes a delay of the upstroke was noticed after prolonged experimental procedures in the same preparation. Since an accurate area measurement was difficult at times before 20 msec, the amplitude of the voltage at 10 and 15 msec relative to the value at 20 msec standardized as unity was plotted as shown in Figure 4. The solid line indicates the curve of the square of elapsed time. Epicardial potentials were almost on the line; that is, the potential was nearly proportional to the square of time. In contrast, the endocardial potentials were significantly lower than the line in Figure 4. At 20 msec, the double layer moment due to endocardial stimulation was already about 60% that of epicardial stimulation (Table 1). Earlier voltages were even smaller.

Papillary Muscle

Figure 5 shows the activation time on the surface of two papillary muscle preparations. The left panel shows the longitudinal activation induced by a stimulus applied to a remote site, indicating that activation was not perfectly longitudinal. However, since the voltage in the longitudinal lead was due to the longitudinal component of the double layer, the voltage was compared with the cross-sectional area of the papillary muscle as the projection of the activation wave on the plane perpendicular to the long axis of the preparation. The preparation on the right-hand side in Figure 5 is an example of transverse activation. Even with stimulation of one location, the spread of activation was faster in the longitudinal direction and the activation on the whole proceeded in the transverse direction.

Figure 6 shows the potential curves of longitudinal and transverse leads, which were obtained during longitudinal activation of the preparation. In this experiment, activation was confined almost entirely within the papillary muscle between 55 and 65

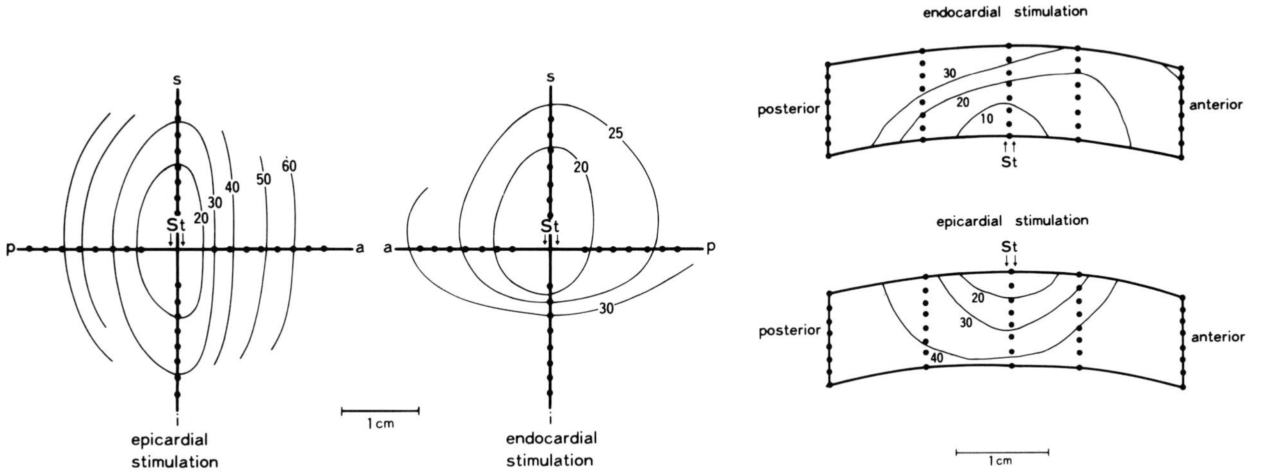

FIGURE 3. *Activation spread near the stimulation electrodes (St) in the left ventricular preparation. Left: epicardial and endocardial spread of activation. Right: intramural activation shown in the horizontal section. Dots indicate the location of electrodes.*

TABLE 1
Double Layer Moment of the Activation Wavefront Measured with Left Ventricular Free Wall and Anterior Papillary Muscle of the Right Ventricle

		No. of preparations	mA·cm per unit area
Left ventricular wall			
Epicardial stimulation	20 msec	13	0.10 ± 0.042
	30 msec	15	0.11 ± 0.039
Endocardial stimulation	20 msec	13	0.06 ± 0.031
Right ventricular papillary muscle			
Longitudinal activation	mean	9	0.17 ± 0.041
	peak	10	0.18 ± 0.044
Transverse activation		6	0.021 ± 0.009

Results are expressed as mean ± SD.

msec. Hence, the mean voltage during this period was measured as the representative value of the voltage. In addition, the peak voltage was used for calculation, since tapering of the preparation, as well as the width of the activation wave, may cause reduction of the voltage. For comparison with the peak voltage, the thickest cross-section of the preparation was used. The results are also shown in Table 1.

Transverse activation of the papillary muscle was usually induced by simultaneous stimulation of two locations, one at the base and the other near the apex. We used only those experiments in which variations of the activation time along the long axis on the line opposed to the stimulated side were within 5 msec. The peak voltage in the transverse lead was measured and compared with the projectional area of the preparation on the plane perpendicular to the lead. Hence, the results (Table 1) are not strictly from the simultaneous voltage and area measurements. However, it is obvious that transverse activation was associated with much smaller moment. At the same time, the longitudinal lead in Figure 7 also recorded certain deflections due to local longitudinal activation processes, indicating that activation was not completely transverse. The voltage in the longitudinal lead was quite small compared with the potential due to longitudinal activation.

Discussion

The electromotive force of ventricular tissue is based not only on the membrane potential of individual fibers, but also, on the mode of impulse conduction in tissue. So that the electromotive force associated with different structures and activation patterns could be investigated, special preparations were designed in this study. The isolated left ventricular wall was perfused from the circumflex artery to keep the intramural layers in active physiological condition. The anterior papillary muscle of the right ventricle was similarly perfused from the anterior

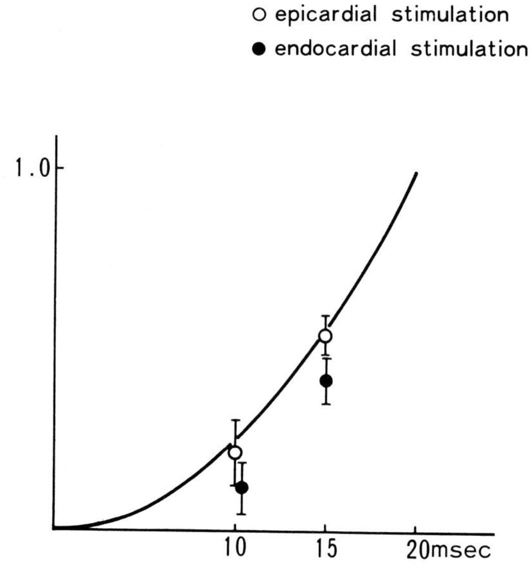

FIGURE 4. *Upstroke of the potential curves of epicardial (epi) and endocardial (endo) stimulation with standardization of the value at 20 msec as unity. A solid line indicates the square function of time.*

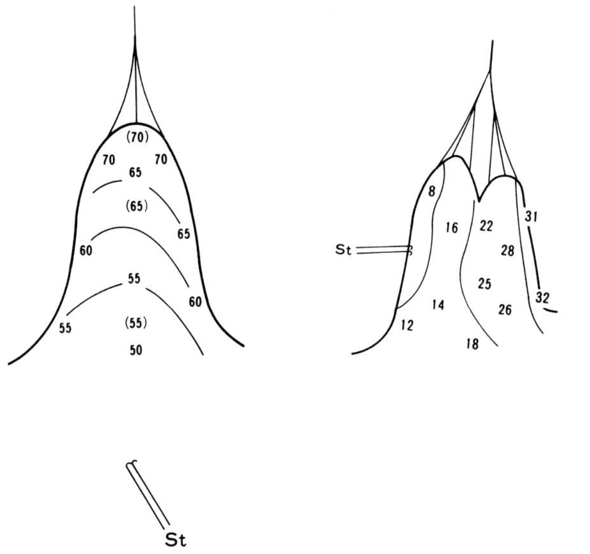

FIGURE 5. *Examples of the activation spread in two papillary muscle preparations stimulated at a remote site (left) and at the side of the preparation (right). Numbers indicate the time after the stimulus in msec.*

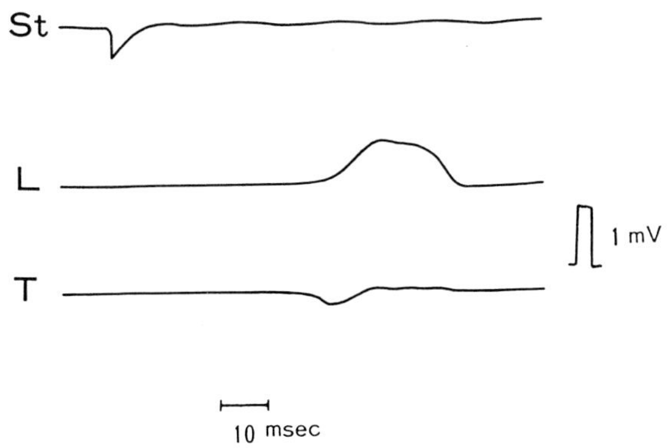

FIGURE 6. *Potential curves obtained in longitudinal and transverse leads during longitudinal activation of the papillary muscle.*

descending artery, and the potential measurements were performed in a separate chamber. Longitudinal and transverse leads in the chamber were practically insensitive to outside events, if the level of the solution was kept below the edge of the small box and there was no electrical connection to the outside solution over the edge.

The results of the experiments with the left ventricular wall indicated that epicardial stimulation produced a double layer with the moment of 0.11 mA·cm per unit area. Comparable values at 20 and 30 msec after stimulation indicate that the strength of the double layer was proportional to the activated area on the epicardial surface, which was in accord with our previous results (Mashima et al., 1978), and supported the view that the moment was representative of ventricular tissue with muscle conduction. The value 0.11 mA·cm was somewhat smaller than that of the previous study with the whole heart, but individual variations were rather large and the differences were not significant. A systematic difference may exist, as implied by the same values at 20 and 30 msec in this study. Differences in the preparations may be the cause.

With endocardial stimulation of the left ventricular wall, the activation spread was faster, probably due to the existence of the Purkinje network. However, the observed potential was not proportionally

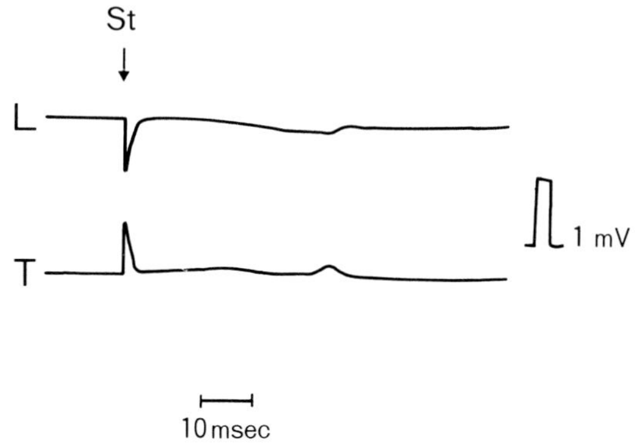

FIGURE 7. *Potential curves obtained in longitudinal and transverse leads during transverse activation of the papillary muscle.*

larger, at least not in the initial phase. Since the relation between the increase in voltage and the activation front area was not linear and differed from preparation to preparation, the moment at 20 msec listed in Table 1 did not appear to be general. Possible explanations of a smaller moment with endocardial stimulation include island-like activated areas on the endocardial surface in the initial phase, which would cause an overestimation of the activated area. Another possibility is a cancellation effect due to irregularities of the activation wave. Purkinje muscle junctions in deeper layers may create a local radial spread of activation, resulting in the cancellation of forward and backward forces. Opposite directions of activation were sometimes observed in intramural activation studies. This was, however, not a constant finding. Besides the existence of Purkinje fibers, the orientation of fibers in subendocardial layers was reported as mainly tangential (Myerburg et al., 1978). Such a structure produces, as indicated by the present experiments with papillary muscle, much smaller voltage in the direction perpendicular to the fiber orientation.

There have been controversies concerning the existence of "electrically silent" subendocardial layers of ventricular wall (Pipberger and Lopez, 1980), and quantitative evaluation of different layers has not been made. According to the present results, endocardial layers are not silent, but are less effective in generating extracellular potential. Configurations of the upstroke of the potential curve suggest that the effect of cancellation or irregularities of the activation process are more marked in the earlier phase. Later, the moment may grow to the level of the epicardial stimulation experiments, although this could not be confirmed due to the breakthrough of activation on the epicardial surface or the wavefront exceeding the measurement area.

The potential produced by longitudinal activation of the papillary muscle was found to be about 50% larger than that of epicardial activation of the left ventricular wall. Uniform orientation of fibers simulates the hypothetic thick fiber considered in our previous study (Mashima et al., 1978). Concerning the effectiveness of generating external potential, a fiber with a cross-sectional area of 1 cm^2 is equivalent to a dipole with a moment of M/r_i mA·cm, where M is the height of the action potential and r_i, intracellular resistivity. If the value 470 ohm·cm is used for r_i (Weidmann, 1970), the moment of the equivalent dipole is calculated to be about 0.21 mA·cm. The measured moment of the papillary muscle in this study amounted to 80% of the theoretical value, which seemed to be reasonable for tissue containing interstitial space.

Transverse activation of the papillary muscle is another extreme condition. Even the peak voltage in the transverse lead was generally small, and the moment of the activation wave was estimated as several times smaller than that of longitudinal activation. If the electromotive force of individual fibers is directed along the fiber, a zig-zag course of activation will cause cancellation between opposing forces. The number of branchings and angles with the long axis will determine the net moment of the transverse activation wave.

On the other hand, influences of the anisotropic structure of the myocardium on the electromotive force have received attention in recent years. Dependence of conduction velocity and extracellular potential on the direction of activation spread has been observed in different preparations (Roberts et al., 1979; Spach et al., 1981; Baruffi et al., 1978). For tissue composed of numerous fibers, the remote potential appears to depend on the total intracellular current flow in the direction of the recording lead (Mashima et al., 1978; Spach et al., 1979). In other words, the "effective internal resistance" (Spach et al., 1981) is a principal determinant of the conduction velocity and extracellular potential. With epicardial potential measurements, Roberts and Scher (1982) reported 6 times the internal resistivity in the transverse direction compared with the longitudinal direction. Clerc's (1976) data indicated similarly 9 times the resistivity in the transverse direction. Our results showed that extracellular potential with transverse activation was about one-eighth that with longitudinal activation. The conduction velocity was not accurately determined in this study. However, as shown in Figure 5, the conduction velocity is estimated to be more than twice as fast along the long axis of the preparation. In spite of complex branchings and electrical properties of fibers in three-dimensional living tissue, observed longitudinal and transverse r_i and conduction velocity seem to be related similarly as expected from the theory with regard to a single fiber, that conduction velocity is inversely proportional to the square root of internal resistivity (Hodgkin, 1954).

Previous studies usually are based on epicardial measurements or observations of excised myocardial strips. Methods of the present study are more physiological, freer from boundary effects and other restrictions, and are therefore suitable for evaluation of the net absolute electromotive force of myocardium as a tissue generator. Underlying cellular mechanisms await further studies, which could explain observed extracellular events.

This study was supported in part by Grant-in-Aid for Scientific Research 56480176 from the Japanese Ministry of Education.

Dr. Schmidt's present address is: I. Medizinische Klinik, Technische Universität, München, West Germany.

Address for reprints: Saburo Mashima, M.D., The Second Department of Internal Medicine, University of Tokyo, Tokyo 113, Japan.

Received June 19, 1984; accepted for publication February 21, 1985.

References

Baruffi S, Spaggiari S, Stille D, Musso E, Taccardi B (1978) The influence of fiber orientation in determining the features of cardiac electrical field. *In* Modern Electrocardiology, edited by Z Antaloczy. Amsterdam, Excerpta Medica, pp 89–92

Clerc L (1976) Directional differences of impulse spread in trabecular muscle from mammalian heart. J Physiol (Lond) **255:** 335–346

Colli-Franzone P, Guerri L, Viganotti C, Macchi E, Baruffi S, Spaggiari S, Taccardi B (1982) Potential field generated by oblique dipole layers modeling excitation wave fronts in the aisotropic myocardium. Circ Res **51:** 330–346

Corbin LV, Scher AM (1977) The canine heart as an electrocardiographic generator. Circ Res **41:** 58–67

Hodgkin AL (1954) A note on conduction velocity. J Physiol (Lond) **125:** 221–224

Mashima S, Harumi K, Murao S (1978) The magnitude of the electromotive force of canine ventricular myocardium. Circ Res **42:** 757–763

Myerburg RJ, Gelband H, Nilsson K, Castellanos A, Morales AR, Bassett AL (1978) The role of canine superficial ventricular muscle fibers in endocardial impulse distribution. Circ Res **42:** 27–35

Pipberger HV, Lopez EA (1980) "Silent" subendocardial infarcts: Fact or fiction? Am Heart J **100:** 597–599

Roberts DE, Scher AM (1982) Effect of tissue anisotropy on extracellular potential fields in canine myocardium in situ. Circ Res **50:** 342–351

Roberts DE, Hersh LT, Scher AM (1979) Influence of cardiac fiber orientation on wavefront voltage, conduction velocity, and tissue resistivity. Circ Res **44:** 701–712

Spach MS, Miller WT, Miller-Jones E, Warren RB, Barr RC (1979) Extracellular potentials related to intracellular action potentials during impulse conduction in anisotropic canine cardiac muscle. Circ Res **45:** 188–204

Spach MS, Miller WT, Geselowitz DB, Barr RC, Kootsey JM, Johnson EA (1981) The discontinuous nature of propagation in normal canine cardiac muscle. Circ Res **48:** 39–54

Weidmann S (1970) Electrical constants of trabecular muscle from mammalian heart. J Physiol (Lond) **210:** 1041–1054

INDEX TERMS: Ventricular activation sequence • Equivalent double layer • Subendocardial layer • Myocardial fiber orientation

Action Potential Prolongation and Induction of Abnormal Automaticity by Low Quinidine Concentrations in Canine Purkinje Fibers

Relationship to Potassium and Cycle Length

Dan M. Roden and Brian F. Hoffman

From the Departments of Medicine and Pharmacology, Vanderbilt University School of Medicine, Nashville, Tennessee, and Department of Pharmacology, Columbia University College of Physicians and Surgeons, New York, New York

SUMMARY. Marked QT prolongation with induction of polymorphous ventricular tachycardia ("Torsades de Pointes") is a well-described phenomenon during quinidine therapy, frequently occurring at low plasma quinidine concentrations, low serum potassium, and slow heart rates. We have therefore assessed the dose-electrophysiological effects of quinidine as a function of extracellular potassium and cycle length in canine Purkinje fibers, using standard microelectrode techniques. Quinidine (1 μM) prolonged action potential at 90% repolarization, while leaving phase zero upstroke slope ($\dot{V}_{max}$) unchanged at a cycle length 300–8000 msec; at 10 μM, $\dot{V}_{max}$ depression became evident. Increases in the action potential at 90% repolarization were most marked at long cycle lengths and low extracellular potassium (in contrast to $\dot{V}_{max}$ depression) and were partially reversed by tetrodotoxin (1 μM). The relationship between log of cycle length and action potential at 90% repolarization was linear (for cycle length 300–8000 msec) in the absence of quinidine. Quinidine increased the slope of this relationship in a concentration-related fashion, whereas increasing extracellular potassium shifted the curve rightward (without changing slope), regardless of the presence or absence of quinidine. Action potentials were also measured following pauses of 5–60 seconds. In the absence of quinidine, the action potential depolarization returned to its baseline value in a monoexponential fashion (time constant 36.0 ± 4.9 sec, mean ± SE, n = 10). In the presence of 1 μM quinidine, this return was better fit as a biexponential process (time constants 4.2 ± 1.2 and 40.7 ± 6.2 seconds, n = 14). At slow stimulation rates (cycle length greater than 4000 msec) in low extracellular potassium (2.7 mM), quinidine produced early afterdepolarizations in 7/14 (50%) of fibers at 1 μM and 14/18 (78%) at 10 μM. Early afterdepolarizations were eliminated by increasing stimulation rates, raising the extracellular potassium concentration to 5 mM, or adding tetrodotoxin. These data suggest that prolongation by quinidine of action potentials at 90% repolarization is multifactorial, with both a "tonic" prolonging effect and a prominent frequency-dependent action potential shortening effect. At long cycle lengths and low extracellular potassium, low quinidine concentrations consistently produced early afterdepolarizations. The parallels between this form of triggered activity and clinical arrhythmias induced by quinidine suggest that early afterdepolarizations may play a role in quinidine-induced Torsades de Pointes. **(*Circ Res 56: 857–867, 1985*)**

MARKED QT interval prolongation and induction of a distinctive polymorphous ventricular tachycardia ("Torsades de Pointes") is a well-described complication of quinidine therapy (Smith and Gallagher, 1980). This complication frequently occurs during the first few days of treatment, at low plasma quinidine concentrations, and without QRS widening (Selzer and Wray, 1964). A number of apparently predisposing factors have been described, including, commonly, hypokalemia and bradyarrhythmias (Smith and Gallagher, 1980; Roden et al., 1983). Conversely, potassium administration or increasing heart rate (by pacing or isoproterenol infusion) often reverses the arrhythmia. An obvious question, then, is how quinidine's dose-electrophysiological response relations in vitro are altered by changes in cycle length and potassium.

The relationship between cycle length and depression of maximal phase 0 upstroke slope ($\dot{V}_{max}$) produced by quinidine has long been recognized (Johnson and McKinnon, 1956). Depression is greatest as short cycle lengths and, presumably, reflects blockade of fast inward (sodium) channels. Depolarization by raising extracellular potassium concentration $[K^+]_o$ generally exaggerates the degree of depression. More recently action potential duration (APD) shortening produced by quinidine in some species has been attributed to the same action, viz., blockade of inward sodium channels (Carmeliet and Saikawa, 1982), with the resultant attenuation of the plateau window current described by Attwell et al. (1979). The selective sodium channel blocker tetrodotoxin produces similar effects, with shortening of action potential duration becoming apparent at concentrations lower than those producing decreases in $\dot{V}_{max}$ (Coraboeuf et al., 1979).

Action potential prolongation occurs when canine Purkinje fibers are exposed to quinidine and ventricular muscle repolarization (as assessed by QT duration) is also prolonged in patients receiving quinidine. Increased $[K^+]_o$ blunts this response in canine Purkinje fibers, whereas lowering $[K^+]_o$ exaggerates it (Wang and Parker, 1980). Colatsky (1982) attributed action potential prolongation by quinidine in rabbit Purkinje fibers to blockade of the delayed potassium rectifier (i_x). However the frequency dependence of the relationship among quinidine, potassium, and action potential duration has not been explored.

Studies of the effects of quinidine in vitro have generally used concentrations ≥10 μM (3 μg/ml) which produce obvious changes in $\dot{V}_{max}$. In fact, concentrations over 30 μM frequently produce irreversible depolarization and inexcitability (Weld et al., 1980). However, with few exceptions (Wang and Parker, 1980; Mirro et al., 1981), the effects of much lower concentrations have not been well studied. We therefore undertook an evaluation of the effects of changes in $[K^+]_o$ and cycle length on the electrophysiological actions of a range of quinidine concentrations in canine Purkinje fibers. We found that action potential prolongation was evident at quinidine concentrations lower than those depressing $\dot{V}_{max}$. This action potential prolongation, unlike $\dot{V}_{max}$ depression, was greatest at long cycle lengths and low $[K^+]_o$. Furthermore, at long cycle lengths and low $[K^+]_o$, abnormal automaticity resulting from early afterdepolarizations (EAD) was consistently triggered in the presence of such low quinidine concentrations.

Methods

Mongrel dogs (15–20 kg) were anesthetized with intravenous sodium pentobarbital (30 mg/kg), and the heart was excised and immersed in cold (6–8°C) Tyrode's solution (gassed with O_2-CO_2, 95%–5%) containing (in mM) NaCl (137), $NaHCO_3$ (12), dextrose (5.5), $MgCl_2$ (0.5), NaH_2PO_4 (1.8), KCl (4), and $CaCl_2$ (2.7). False tendons were removed from either ventricle, and mounted in a tissue bath. They were superfused at 15 ml/min with warmed Tyrode's (containing 5 mM KC1) which has been gassed with 95% O_2-5% CO_2. The pH of the perfusate in the bath was 7.35 and the temperature was 37 ± 0.5°C. Temperature was monitored throughout each experiment with a YS1 model 43 thermistor with a model 511 probe (1 mm in diameter). A valve interposed between Tyrode's reservoirs and heat exchanger allowed switching perfusates without disturbing the tissue bath. The dead space was approximately 7 ml (25 seconds).

A pair of Teflon-coated silver-silver chloride wires scraped bare at the ends was connected to a stimulator with isolated output for field stimulation of the tissue. Stimuli were 1–2 msec in duration and 1.5-2 times threshold. Purkinje fiber cells were impaled with glass microelectrodes selected for tip resistances of 10–30 MΩ and filled with 3 M KCl. The microelectrodes were connected through a silver-silver chloride junction to an operational amplifier with high input impedance and variable input capacitance neutralization. The tissue bath was grounded through a similar 3 M KCl-silver-silver chloride junction.

The signal from the operational amplifier was displayed on one channel of a Tektronix RS565A oscilloscope and on a Gould paper recorder (model 2200). The signal from the operational amplifier and a sawtooth signal (200 V/sec) triggered from the oscilloscope were differentiated, and the differentiated signal was displayed on a second channel (with a different time base) of the oscilloscope. The differentiator had a linear response in the 100–1000 V/sec range. The output of the differentiator also provided input to a peak hold circuit, which recorded the maximum signal in a preset "window" (selected to encompass $\dot{V}_{max}$). The peak hold output was recorded on the second channel of the paper recorder.

To record action potential characteristics, the oscilloscope was triggered by the stimulus timer (plus delay) and its screen photographed. The following parameters were derived from the photographs: takeoff potential, action potential amplitude (APA), overshoot, action potential duration at 50% of APA (APD_{50}) and at 90% of APA (APD_{90}), and, from the differentiated trace, $\dot{V}_{max}$. A 100-mV signal was used to calibrate the amplifier-oscilloscope-pen recorder before each experiment. A sawtooth signal generator was used to confirm the linear output of the differentiator and to calibrate the peak hold output to the paper record prior to each experiment. The paper record was used to quantify changes in action potential duration (as described below), to detect spontaneous automaticity (whether normal or abnormal), and, using the peak hold circuit output, to follow changes in $\dot{V}_{max}$ on a beat-to-beat basis.

After having been positioned in the bath, fibers were stimulated at a cycle length of 500–1000 msec. Following impalement, no measurements were made for at least 30 minutes. To study the cycle length and potassium dependence of quinidine's effects, the following approach was used. The tissue was stimulated at each of a range of cycle lengths, and action potentials were photographed after a stable configuration had been reached. With the protocol we used (serial doubling of cycle length), stable changes usually were achieved within 1 minute, although, at longer cycles, longer periods occasionally were required; this is consistent with reports of others (Colatsky and Hogan, 1980) who used somewhat different protocols. The cycle lengths used were (in order) 300, 500, 750, 1000, 2000, 4000, and 8000 msec. The perfusate then was switched to Tyrode's solution containing 2.7 mM KCl (without correction for osmolar changes), the tissue was stimulated at a cycle length of 500–1000 msec, and approximately 10 minutes was allowed to elapse (until the paper record showed the takeoff potential had stabilized at its more negative value). Action potentials were again photographed. The perfusate then was switched to Tyrode's with 5 mM KCl containing quinidine 0.1 μM. Action potentials were photographed after 30 minutes, the solution switched to Tyrode's with 2.7 mM KCl and quinidine 0.1 μM, and action potentials were rephotographed after 10 minutes (as above). The perfusate then was switched to Tyrode's with 5 mM KCl and 1.0 μM quinidine; the above sequence then was repeated for quinidine concentrations of 1.0 μM and 10 μM. Previous reports indicate that action potential characteristics could be expected to have reached near steady state values in 30 minutes (Mirro et al., 1981). As described below, dose-response information was analyzed only for impalements maintained in a single cell throughout the experiment. In some experiments, only the actions of a single concentration were examined (usually 1.0 or 10 μM), particularly to study in greater detail interventions affecting early afterdepolarizations (EAD). These included changes in cycle length and $[K^+]_o$ and the addition of tetrodotoxin or lidocaine.

The effects of pauses in stimulation on action potential duration were assessed in the following manner. Tissue was stimulated for at least 3 minutes at a cycle length of 1000 msec. The action potential was then recorded at fast paper speed (100 mm/sec), and the stimulator was then turned off for pauses of 5, 10, 30, or 60 seconds. Action potentials were recorded at fast paper speed for 4–8 seconds after the pause ended and then intermittently thereafter for the next 60–120 seconds. Since true action potential amplitude could not be measured from the paper recorder because of its poor frequency response characteristics, action potential durations were measured at takeoff plus 10 mV. Action potentials were excluded if, because of phase 4 depolarization, the takeoff potential had shifted more than 10 mV positive to the takeoff potential during stimulation at a cycle length of 1000 msec. Reinitiation of stimulation after a pause also precipitated EAD (particularly at 10 μM quinidine) in some fibers; these action potentials were also excluded from analysis. We recognize that this approach is not likely to detect changes with time constants under 1–2 seconds (e.g., in i_{x1}).

Quinidine sulfate was purchased from Aldrich. Refrigerated stock solutions of 2 mg (base)/ml and 80 μg/ml were added to Tyrode's solution to make up the final concentrations required (1 μM quinidine = 324 μg/liter). Similarly, tetrodotoxin (Sigma) was made up to a stock of 40 μg/ml (1 μM = 317 μg/liter).

Data Analysis

Two-way analysis of variance was used to analyze quinidine concentration-response data. If significant differences ($P < 0.05$) were detected, Duncan's multiple range test was used to analyze paired data. Standard linear regression techniques were used to analyze relationships between cycle length and APD_{90} and between pause duration and post-pause APD. Student's paired *t*-test was used to analyze differences between $[K^+]_o = 2.7$ mM and $[K^+]_o = 5$ mM at a given quinidine level or pause duration.

Post-pause action potentials were normalized to pre-pause baseline values. For pauses of 30–60 seconds, changes in action potential duration were sufficiently large to assess the time course of their return to baseline. Inspection of these time courses suggested that some were monoexponential and others appeared biexponential. Hence, the following approach was used to separate these possibilities. Each action potential duration vs. time plot was fitted to both mono- (2-parameter) and biexponential (4-parameter) declines using nonweighted nonlinear regression (Sheiner, 1981). For each fit, the degrees of freedom (df = number of data points—number of parameters) and the residual sum of squares [RSS = $\sum_{\text{(all data points)}}$ (predicted-observed values)^2] were calculated. The residual sum of squares of a more complex function (in this case, the biexponential fit) will always be smaller than the RSS of the simpler one. Recognizing this fact, the general linear test (Neter and Wasserman, 1974) allows selection between two models. The test statistic F with 2,df_{bi} (degrees of freedom) was calculated:

$$F = \frac{(RSS_{mono}\text{-}RSS_{bi})}{df_{mono}\text{-}df_{bi}} \Big/ \frac{(RSS_{bi})}{df_{bi}}$$

[note that $(df_{mono} - df_{bi}) = 2$]. If the biexponential model was "much" better, then $(RSS_{mono} - RSS_{bi})$ was large, making F larger. If this F was associated with a $P < 0.05$, the biexponential model was deemed more appropriate. If, on the other hand, there was no particular advantage to adding more exponential terms, $(RSS_{mono} - RSS_{bi})$ was small and the P (associated with the resultant F) >0.05; in this case, the monoexponential model was selected. The difference in proportions of monoexponential vs biexponential fits in the absence and presence of drug were assessed by χ^2 analysis.

All data are reported as mean ± SE.

Results

Action potentials recorded from the same cell at two quinidine concentrations and two cycle lengths (300 and 2000 msec) are presented in Figure 1. At 1 μM quinidine, APD_{90} was prolonged, particularly at the slower stimulation rate. In contrast, $\dot{V}_{max}$ was unaffected at 1 μM quinidine and, at 10 μM quinidine, $\dot{V}_{max}$ was depressed to a greater degree at the faster stimulation rate. Changes observed in experiments in which impalements were maintained in the same cell throughout ($n = 8$) are shown in Figure 2 at these cycle lengths. Statistically significant increases in APD_{90} were noted at quinidine concentrations as low as 1 μM, whereas no changes occurred in $\dot{V}_{max}$, overshoot, APA, takeoff potential, or APD_{50} until

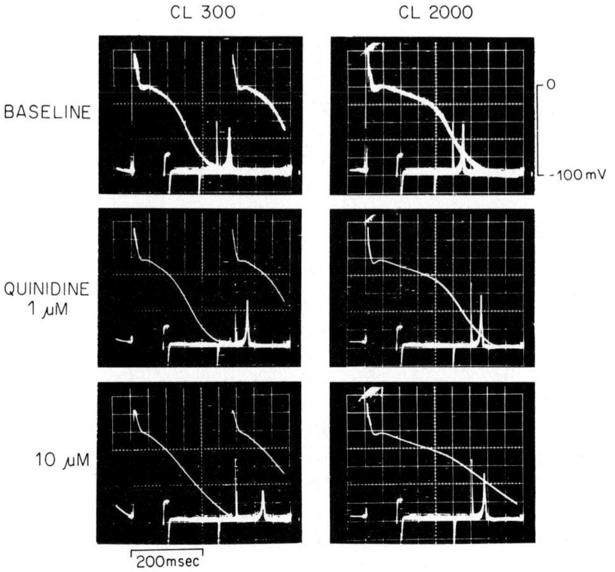

FIGURE 1. *Action potentials recorded from a single Purkinje cell in the absence of drug (top row) in 1 μM quinidine (middle row), and in 10 μM quinidine (bottom row). Cycle lengths were 300 msec (left) and 2000 msec (right), and $[K^+]_o$ was 2.7 mM. Calibrations for action potential measurement are shown. At the bottom of each photograph is the differentiated phase 0 trace, photographed at a faster sweep speed, offset on the time axis, and preceded by a 200 V/sec calibration.*

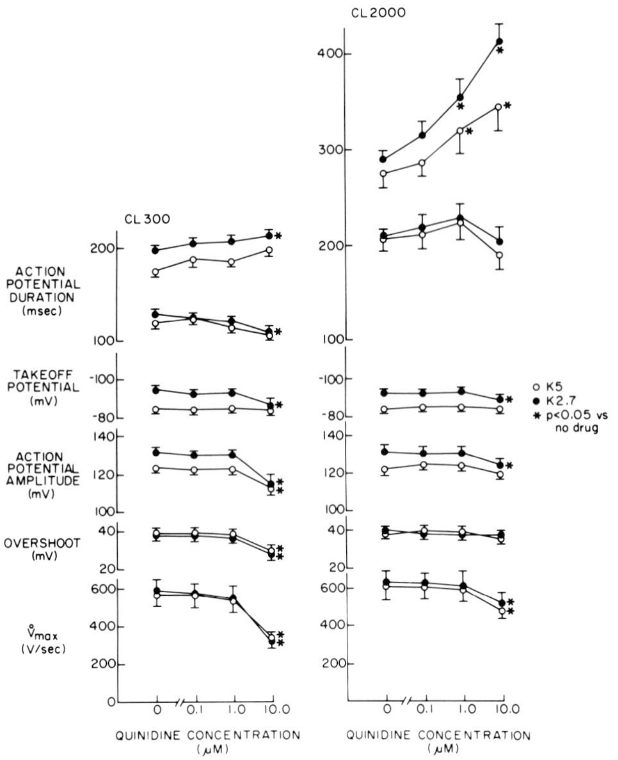

FIGURE 2. *Changes in action potential duration, takeoff potential, action potential amplitude, overshoot, and maximal phase 0 upstroke slope ($\dot{V}_{max}$) as a function of quinidine concentration. Action potential durations at both 50% and 90% repolarization are shown. Left panel: cycle length = 300 msec; right panel: 2000 msec. Open circles: $[K^+]_o$ = 5 mM; filled circles: $[K^+]_o$ = 2.7 mM (n = 8) * $P < 0.05$ compared to no drug.*

10 μM quinidine was used. APD_{50}, unlike APD_{90}, in fact shortened with 10 μM quinidine. Furthermore, the changes in $\dot{V}_{max}$, overshoot, APA, takeoff potential, and APD_{50} were greatest at the more rapid stimulation rate, whereas APD_{90} changes were greatest at the longer cycle length. With $[K^+]_o$ = 5 mM, takeoff potential at a cycle length of 300 msec rose insignificantly from −84.8 ± 2.0 mV at baseline to −83.8 ± 1.2 mV in 10 μM quinidine, while $\dot{V}_{max}$ fell from 570 ± 59 V/sec to 330 ± 32 V/sec, a 42% decrease. At a cycle length of 2000 msec, on the other hand, takeoff potential was similarly unchanged (−84 ± 1.9 mV vs. −84 ± 1.1 mV), but $\dot{V}_{max}$ fell from 605 ± 72 V/sec to 482 ± 48 V/sec, a 20% drop. With $[K^+]_o$ lowered to 2.7 mM, statistically significant changes in takeoff potential were observed in 10 μM quinidine. The accompanying decreases in $\dot{V}_{max}$ shown in Figure 2 may therefore represent both voltage- and drug-dependent effects. Our findings also suggest that the depolarization induced by raising $[K^+]_o$ was not sufficient to move into the steep portion of the takeoff potential-$\dot{V}_{max}$ plot, and that therefore the marked $\dot{V}_{max}$ decreases in this voltage range were due primarily to drug.

The relationship between cycle length and APD_{90} in these eight experiments is further analyzed in Figure 3. For the sake of clarity only the means at each cycle length are presented. In low $[K^+]_o$ (2.7 mM), data are presented only for cycle length ≤2000 msec, since, at slower rates in the presence of quinidine, these fibers developed either normal automaticity or EAD. It can be seen that the log (cycle length) vs. APD plot provided good linearization of the relationship between the two parameters with correlation coefficients at baseline of 0.77 and 0.84. [The data could also be plotted as the hyperbolic function (1/APD) = slope (1/cycle length) + intercept (Elharrar and Surawicz, 1983) with similar correlation coefficients (0.75 − 0.85). The asymptotic nature of the relationship is better appreciated in this way, but slope changes are more easily assessed by the log (cycle length) vs. APD linearization)]. With increasing quinidine concentrations, linearity was maintained (except perhaps an upward deviation at very long cycle lengths in quinidine 10 μM), but the slopes increased. Regardless of $[K^+]_o$, the

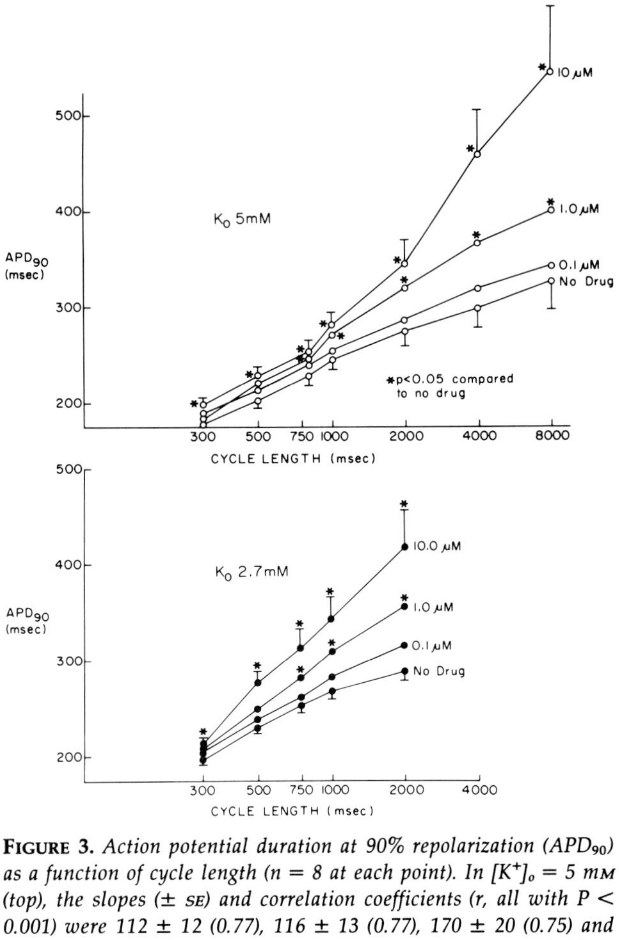

FIGURE 3. *Action potential duration at 90% repolarization (APD_{90}) as a function of cycle length (n = 8 at each point). In $[K^+]_o$ = 5 mM (top), the slopes (± SE) and correlation coefficients (r, all with $P <$ 0.001) were 112 ± 12 (0.77), 116 ± 13 (0.77), 170 ± 20 (0.75) and 246 ± 25 (0.81) for no drug and 0.1, 1, and 10 μM quinidine, respectively. In $[K^+]_o$ = 2.7 mM (bottom), the corresponding values were 111 ± 11 (0.84), 134 ± 16 (0.81), 182 ± 21 (0.82), and 243 ± 37 (0.73). In both cases, the slopes associated with 1 and 10 μM quinidine were significantly different from those at baseline. Raising $[K^+]_o$ shifted the plots rightward (in the absence or presence of quinidine) without altering slope. Standard error is also shown for individual data points in the absence of drug and in 10 μM quinidine.*

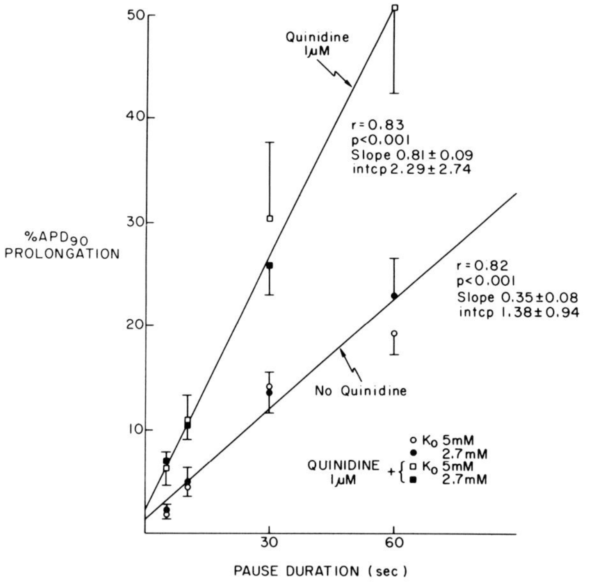

FIGURE 4. *Relationship between pause duration and resultant prolongation of action potential at 90% repolarization (APD_{90}). In the absence of drug, n = 6–9 at each point; with 1 μM quinidine, n = 5–6 at each point.*

slope at the baseline was 110–112 and rose to 242–246 at quinidine 10 μM. Both 1 and 10 μM quinidine produced statistically significant increases in slope. In contrast, the effect of raising $[K^+]_o$ was to shift the curves rightward, without changing the slope, suggesting that the mechanism of the APD prolongation induced by lowering $[K^+]_o$ was not the same as that produced by adding quinidine.

Figure 4 shows the relationship between the duration of a pause in stimulation and the duration of the first action potential following the pause (normalized to baseline). There was no significant difference in normalized APD change between high $[K^+]_o$(5 mM) and low $[K^+]_o$ (2.7 mM) at any pause duration, either in the drug-free state or in the presence of 1 μM quinidine. As is shown, there was an excellent correlation between pause duration and post-pause increase in normalized APD, in both the presence and absence of drug. However, a low concentration of quinidine markedly increased the slope of this relationship. Neither intercept differed significantly from zero. At longer pauses (≥ 30 sec), in the presence of 1 μM quinidine and low $[K^+]_o$ (2.7 mM), resumption of stimulation initiated EAD in 3/5 experiments.

Figure 5 illustrates the method of data analysis used to assign the return of APD to baseline and to a mono- or biexponential fit after a 30- or 60-second pause. In 10/11 experiments in the absence of drug, a monoexponential fit was sufficient, whereas, in one instance, the biexponential curve afforded a better fit. In contrast, a biexponential fit was required in 14/19 experiments in the presence of 1 μM quinidine ($P < 0.05$, χ^2). The time constants for these fits are shown in Table 1.

As shown in Figure 2, $\dot{V}_{max}$ was unchanged by 1 μM quinidine. However, as shown in Figure 6, the absence of quinidine markedly depressed $\dot{V}_{max}$ at rapid rates (42% at cycle length 300 msec), whereas, at cycle lengths of 4000–8000 msec, $\dot{V}_{max}$ depression was less (13–14%). When the interstimulus interval

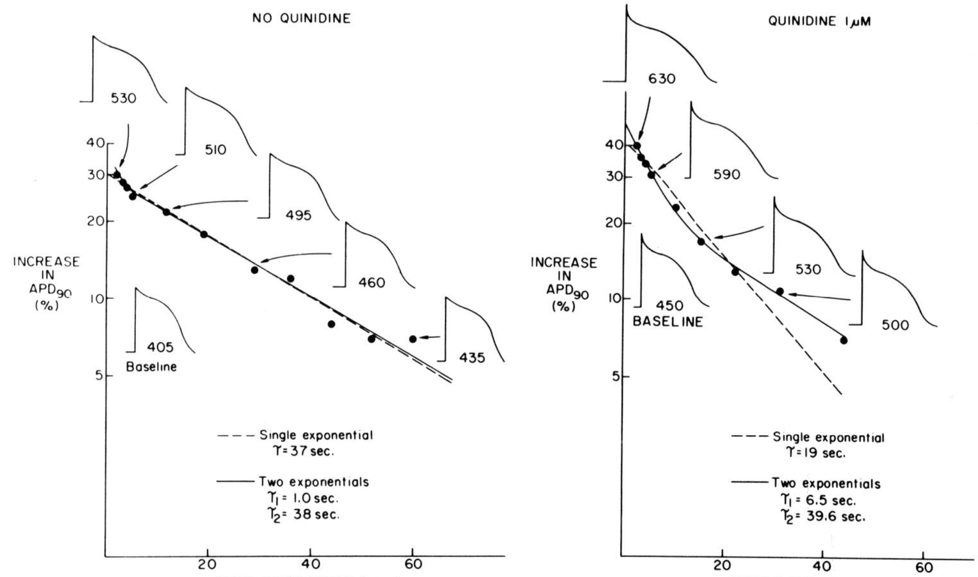

FIGURE 5. *Action potential at 90% repolarization (APD_{90}, normalized to pre-pause value) during resumption of stimulation (1 Hz) after a pause of 60 seconds. The curves were fit to both mono- and biexponential declines, and the method used to decide which was more appropriate is illustrated (see text for further details). Data shown here are from the same cell (in $[K^+]_o$ = 5 mM) after a 60-second pause at the baseline (left) and in 1 μM quinidine (right). Numbers under each action potential are the measured APD in msec. In the absence of drug, the residual sum of squares for the biexponential fit (4.62) provided no statistically significant improvement ($F_{2,7}$ = 2.02, $P > 0.05$) over that for the monoexponential fit (7.29). With 1 μM quinidine, however, the residual sum of squares for the biexponential fit (1.95) was significantly better ($F_{2,5}$ = 34.3, $P <$ 0.001) than that for the monoexponential fit (28.6).*

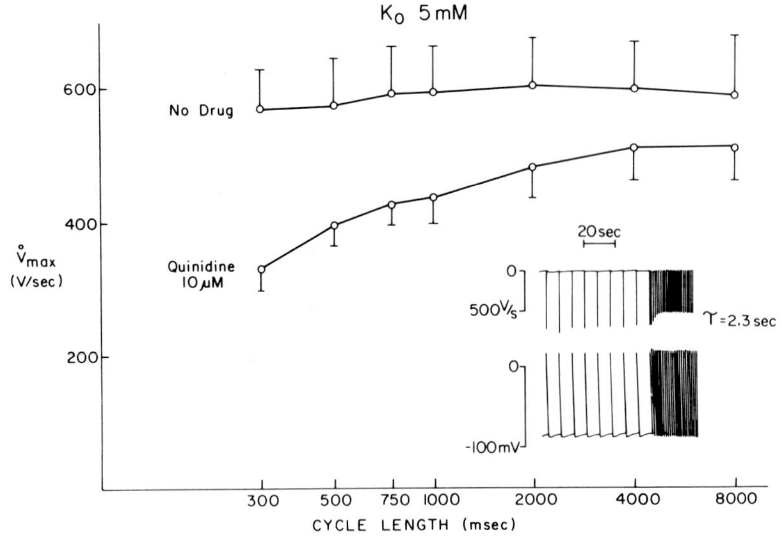

FIGURE 6. *Relations between maximal phase 0 upstroke slope ($\dot{V}_{max}$) and cycle length (n = 8 at each point). Inset: changes in $\dot{V}_{max}$ (top tracing) when interstimulus cycle length was changed from 8000 to 1000 msec. $\dot{V}_{max}$ declined exponentially to its new value with a time constant of 2.3 seconds in this experiment.*

was decreased from 8000–1000 msec in the presence of 10 μM quinidine, $\dot{V}_{max}$ declined to its new value (Fig. 6, inset) with a mean time constant of 4.6 ± 0.4 sec (n = 12), approximately the same as the "rapid component" of decline in normalized APD in the presence of quinidine in Table 1.

With low $[K^+]_o$ (2.7 mM), stimulation at long cycle lengths (>4000 msec) or normal automaticity at similar low rates frequently caused EAD (Fig. 7), the first of which arose during late phase 2/early phase 3 from a takeoff potential of −40 to −55 mV. The incidence of EAD under these conditions is shown in Figure 8. At 1 μM quinidine, multiple EAD were present in half of the experiments and, in 10 μM quinidine, in 14/18. An example of an EAD arising during phase 3 at a cycle length of 8000 msec is shown in Figure 9.

EAD were readily abolished by a number of interventions. Resumption of more rapid rates of stimulation was effective in each experiment. Raising $[K^+]_o$ to 5 mM was tried in 15 experiments and was always effective (upper panel, Fig. 10). Tetrodotoxin (TTX, middle panel, Fig. 10) was used in eight experiments: 0.1 μM abolished EAD in 1/6 attempts, and 1.0 μM did so in 7/7 attempts. Lidocaine (10 μM) also abolished EAD in 2/2 attempts (lower panel, Fig. 10). The changes in $\dot{V}_{max}$ and APD_{90} observed in association with abolition of EAD by TTX are shown in Figure 11. For these experiments, we used quinidine concentrations sufficient to cause EAD (1 μM in three cases and 10 μM in five) and TTX concentrations sufficient to abolish the EAD (0.1 μM in one case and 1.0 μM in seven). The ability of TTX to shorten APD_{90} was markedly dependent on cycle length, with the greatest change occurring at the longest cycle length. The slope of the log (cycle length) vs. APD_{90} plot was significantly lowered by the addition of tetrodotoxin. Conversely, $\dot{V}_{max}$ depression was not cycle length dependent.

In several fibers, 10 μM quinidine (in $[K^+]_o$ = 2.7 mM) produced a stable depolarized (−40 to −50 mV) level of resting potential. As illustrated in Figure 12, addition of tetrodotoxin (1 μM) or elevation of $[K^+]_o$ to 5 mM restored a normal resting potential. In

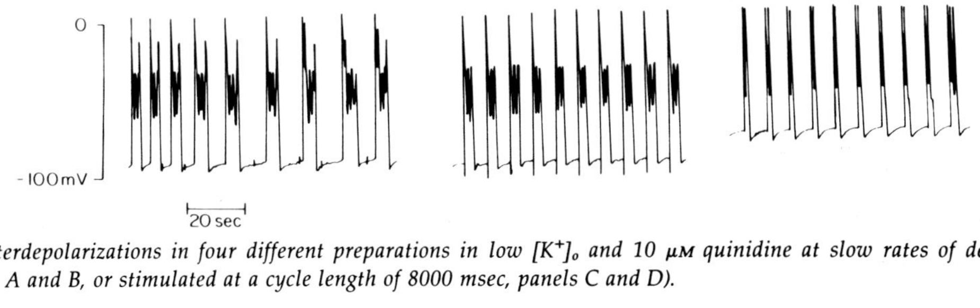

FIGURE 7. *Early afterdepolarizations in four different preparations in low $[K^+]_o$ and 10 μM quinidine at slow rates of depolarization (either spontaneous, panels A and B, or stimulated at a cycle length of 8000 msec, panels C and D).*

TABLE 1
Time Constants for the Return of APD to Baseline

	Monoexponential	Biexponential	
No drug	36.0 ± 4.9 (n = 10)	0.91	26.3
		(n = 1)	
Quinidine (1 M)	22.3 ± 2.1 (n = 5)	4.2 ± 1.2	40.7 ± 6.2
		(n = 14)	

contrast to changes shown in Figure 10, an interval of several minutes at the new conditions was required before the more negative resting potential was abruptly restored.

Discussion

We have shown that a low concentration of quinidine prolonged action potentials of canine Purkinje fibers and consistently triggered abnormal depolarizations in low $[K^+]_o$ at slow stimulation rates. A number of lines of evidence suggest that this action potential prolongation reflects a non-sodium channel-mediated effect, although, as outlined below, sodium channel blockade may well modulate these action potential changes. First, selective sodium channel blockade (by TTX) shortens APD (Coraboeuf et al., 1979). Second, the effects on APD that we observed were most prominent at slow stimulation rates whereas $\dot{V}_{max}$ changes were most evident with rapid stimulation. Third, Colatsky (1982) has shown that quinidine abolished i_x current tails in rabbit Purkinje fibers while it prolonged the action potential. Fourth, Nattel and Bailey (1983) have examined the time courses of quinidine-induced changes in phase 0, 2, and 3 slopes; they concluded that phase 3 slope changes were due to a mechanism different from that producing phase 0 and 2 changes. Our action potential findings complement those of other workers. Mirro et al. (1981) examined

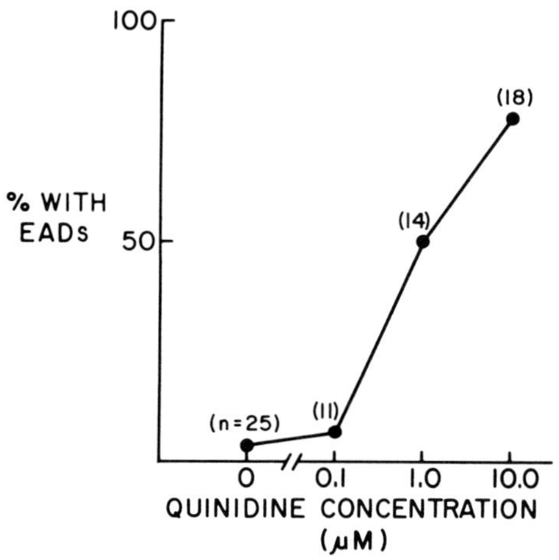

FIGURE 8. *Incidence of multiple early afterdepolarizations (EAD) in low $[K^+]_o$ (2.7 mM) and at long cycle lengths (>4000 msec) as a function of quinidine concentration. The figures at each point are the number of fibers evaluated.*

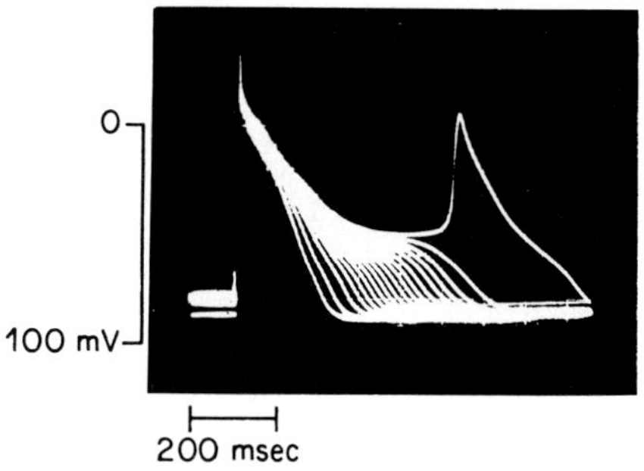

FIGURE 9. *Example of an early afterdepolarization. The preparation was initially driven at cycle length of 1000 msec (shortest action potential). The cycle length was then increased to 8000 msec, and successive action potentials were photographed. APD gradually increased and, after 128 seconds, an early afterdepolarization was triggered during repolarization.*

quinidine concentration-response relations in canine Purkinje fibers driven at a cycle length of 1000 msec in $[K^+]_o$ = 4 mM. They found 1 μM to be without effect, but 3 μM prolonged APD_{90} and depressed $\dot{V}_{max}$. On the othe hand, Wang and Parker (1980) found that $\dot{V}_{max}$ depression and APD_{90} shortening were the most prominent effects of quinidine up to concentrations of 20 μM without significant APD_{95} changes when fibers were driven at a cycle length of 800 msec in $[K^+]_o$ = 4 mM; lowering $[K^+]_o$ to 2 mM prolonged APD_{95} in 20 μM quinidine. APD_{50} changes were not significant in the study of Mirro et al. (1981), but the trend toward shortening at higher concentrations reported by Wang and Parker (1980) was found in our data. As discussed below, this change may reflect blockade of the window current.

The observation that the action potential-prolonging effect of quinidine was evident at a lower concentration than that depressing $\dot{V}_{max}$ has several potential implications. First, depression of $\dot{V}_{max}$ and resultant conduction slowing has been proposed as the major mechanism of quinidine's antiarrhythmic effect (Vaughan Williams, 1958; Wallace et al., 1966). However, action potential prolongation itself may be antiarrhythmic by decreasing dispersion of repolarization, i.e., by producing disproportionately greater increases in short action potentials. Whereas data in this study were collected from mid-false tendon, others have reported that quinidine exerts disproportionately greater effects on action potential in "post-gate" fibers, thereby reducing dispersion of repolarization (Wang and Parker, 1980). Hence, low concentrations of quinidine might be antiarrhythmic by such an effect on action potential duration without depressing $\dot{V}_{max}$. Second, this action (action potential prolongation without changes in $\dot{V}_{max}$) has been held to be a "class III" (amiodarone-like) effect (Vaughan Williams, 1975). The demonstration of APD and $\dot{V}_{max}$ effects with different dose-dependencies in this study underlines the difficulties with such classification schemes. Extrapolation from changes in parameters such as action potential duration or $\dot{V}_{max}$ to antiarrhythmic effects in vivo is not

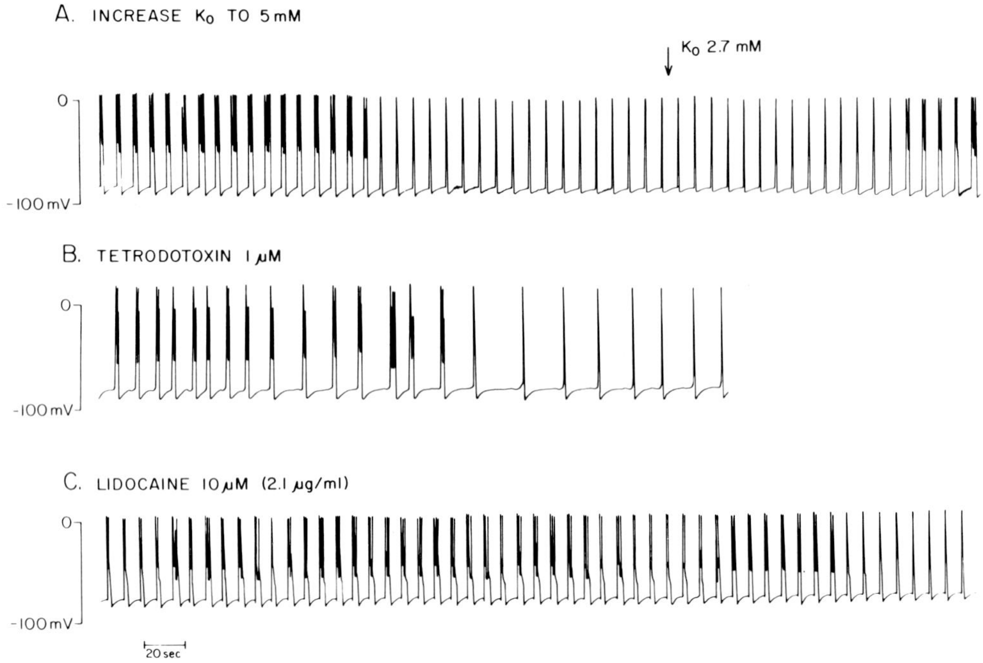

FIGURE 10. *Interventions altering early afterdepolarizations. In each experiment, the intervention was made at the beginning of the record (the time from intervention change to tissue bath being 25 seconds). As can be seen, raising $[K^+]_o$ or adding tetrodotoxin or lidocaine abolished EAD, and they recurred when $[K^+]_o$ was changed back to 2.7 mM (top).*

justified, as no data are available to link quinidine's antiarrhythmic effects in man to such a "class III" action.

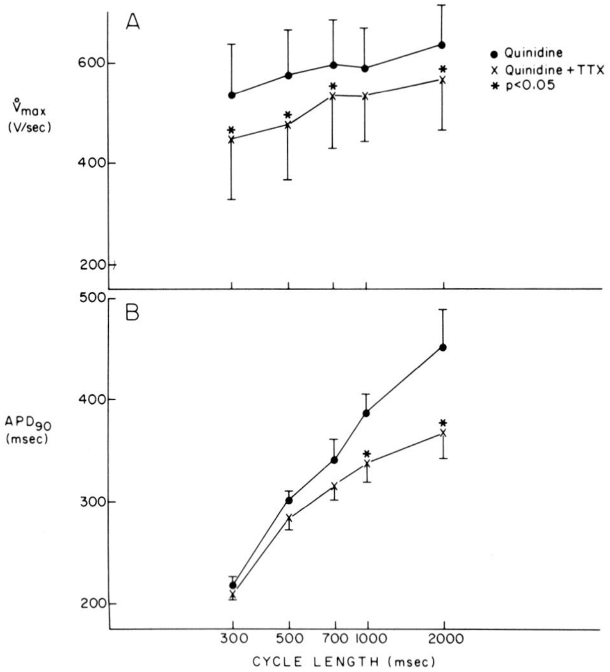

FIGURE 11. *Effects of adding tetrodotoxin (TTX) in the presence of quinidine on maximal phase 0 upstroke slope ($\dot{V}_{max}$, top panel) and action potential duration at 90% repolarization (APD_{90}, bottom) as a function of a cycle length (n = 8). The slope of the cycle length vs. APD_{90} plots decreased ($P < 0.05$) from 283 ± 35 ($r = 0.81$, $P < 0.001$) to 184 ± 26 ($r = 0.77$, $P < 0.001$) with the addition of TTX while $\dot{V}_{max}$ was slightly depressed but in a cycle length-independent fashion. See text for concentrations.*

We did not measure membrane ionic currents in this study. However, our findings do suggest an explanation for the APD changes induced by quinidine which is consistent with other reports. The observation that APD in Purkinje fibers lengthens after a pause and shortens exponentially thereafter has been made previously (Greenspan et al., 1967; Vick, 1971; Miller et al., 1971). The factors responsible are not completely understood. One possibility is activation of the Na^+-K^+ pump; pump current has been measured in small canine Purkinje fibers following pauses in stimulation, and its magnitude after resumption of stimulation followed an exponential decline with a fairly long (1.3 minute) time constant (Gadsby and Cranefield, 1979). Hence, with a long pause, the pump current would decline to a low value and the first action potential after such a pause would be correspondingly prolonged. The rate of return of APD to baseline would similarly be a function of pause duration. Other phenomena which might contribute to such APD changes include slow inactivation of fast channels (Gintant et al., 1984) or changes in i_x, which have been implicated as the major determinant of the duration of premature action potentials (Hauswirth et al., 1972). Changes in the slow inward current might also contribute, although Colatsky and Hogan (1980) suggested that the long time course of return to baseline was not mediated by changes in i_{si}.

Quinidine (1 μM) produced a characteristic alteration in the time course of APD changes following a pause: the long time constant was unaltered, but a more rapid component was superimposed. The time constant for this rapid process was similar to that for the development of $\dot{V}_{max}$ depression in 10

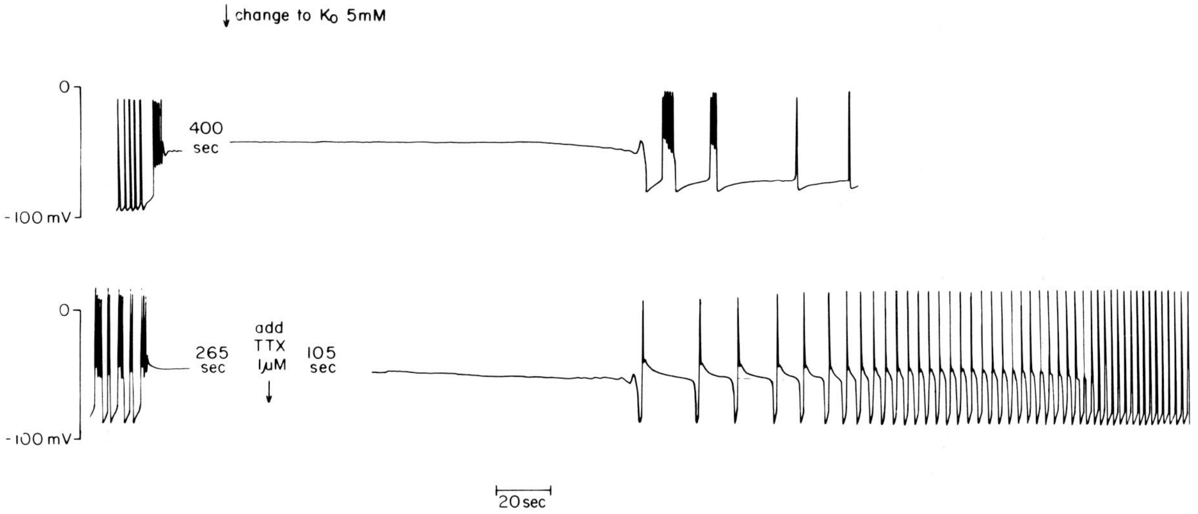

FIGURE 12. *Effects of increasing $[K^+]_o$ to 5 mM (top) or adding tetrodotoxin (bottom) in two fibers which became quiescent at a low transmembrane potential (−45 to −50 mV) in low $[K^+]_o$ (2.7 mM) plus 10 μM quinidine. Note that, in contrast to changes shown in Figure 10, restoration of a more normal transmembrane potential required several minutes under the new conditions.*

μM quinidine. This finding would be consistent with cycle length-dependent blockade of sodium channels by quinidine, not only during phase 0, but also during plateau when it would accelerate repolarization. Although data obtained in ovine Purkinje fibers (Carmeliet and Saikawa, 1982) suggest that quinidine does exert this action, we cannot be certain that the rapid phase of action potential shortening we observed actually represents this fast channel effect. For example, it is likely that the time course of onset of use-dependent fast channel blockade is concentration-dependent (Gintant et al., 1983) and that, at least under some conditions, $\dot{V}_{max}$ may not be linearly related to sodium conductance (Bean et al., 1982). Hence the correlation we found between time constants may be fortuitous; without more detailed measurements, we cannot offer alternative explanations for the change induced by quinidine in the time course of APD changes after a pause.

EAD were seen when action potential was markedly prolonged, i.e., when, in the presence of quinidine, stimulation rate was slowed and $[K^+]_o$ lowered. The recordings shown in Figure 12 suggest that, under these circumstances, changes in repolarizing currents were sufficient to enable the development of a stable, depolarized level of resting potential (Gadsby and Cranefield, 1977). These changes would include, as described above, a decrease in i_x induced by quinidine, a decrease in i_{K1} induced by lowering $[K^+]_o$, and possibly, a decrease in the pump current due to a reduction in stimulation rate. The use-dependent nature of quinidine's fast inward current-blocking properties would permit relative preservation of this depolarizing current at slow stimulation rates. Increasing stimulation rate would, by increasing pump current and decreasing fast inward current, reverse the tendency to develop such a stable depolarized level of resting potential. In keeping with this concept, interventions which increased outward current (raising $[K^+]_o$) or decreased inward current (adding TTX) restored a normal level of resting potential. A low level of resting potential can itself result in oscillatory activity (Hauswirth et al., 1969). Hence, quinidine-induced EAD might simply be a reflection of the marked APD increase seen in these experiments, although certain interventions (e.g. tetraethylammonium, Ito and Surawicz, 1981) can markedly prolong APD without without being associated with EAD. This oscillatory activity at a low level of resting potential has been attributed to time-dependent changes in i_x accompanied by small increases in background inward current (Hauswirth et al., 1969; Imanishi and Surawicz, 1976) or to increased sodium conductivity (Brown, 1981). Coraboeuf et al. (1980) reported abnormalities in the terminal phase of repolarization in false tendon Purkinje fibers exposed to low $[K^+]_o$ and acidosis. Such abnormalities, which, if sufficiently prominent, triggered EAD, were attributed to a decrease in background outward K^+ currents. In an accompanying computer simulation, the same workers (Coulombe et al., 1980) suggested that such repolarization abnormalities were most sensitive to small changes in time-independent outward K^+ currents, moderately sensitive to changes in i_{x1}, and insensitive to changes in i_{x2}. The computer simulation also suggested that the window current exerted an important facilitatory influence upon the development of EAD. This group of workers did not report APD itself but the data presented suggests that EAD developed when APD (measured at 90% repolarization) prolonged due to terminal phase 3 abnormalities. They also noted that shortening cycle length and raising $[K^+]_o$ also abolished EAD, and raised the possibility that these abnormalities could account for arrhythmias in the prolonged QT syndrome. We cannot conclude that quinidine-induced EAD and acidosis-induced EAD are due to the same underlying membrane derangement. However, our findings are consistent with the suggestion that the presence of an inward sodium current at long cycle lengths and reduction of outward potassium current(s) are important contributing factors to the generation of this rhythm abnormality.

Brachman et al. (1983) have reported that cesium administration to dogs triggered a bradycardia-dependent polymorphous ventricular tachycardia very closely resembling Torsades de Pointes. Since they and others (Damiano and Rosen, 1983) showed that cesium precipitated EAD at slow stimulation rates in canine Purkinje fibers, they suggested that EAD triggered Torsades de Pointes. They also showed that both the EAD and the in vivo arrhythmia were abolished by low doses of tetrodotoxin, suggesting that an "unblocked" window current facilitated the development of this rhythm disturbance. In contrast to our findings, cesium precipitated EAD at "usual" $[K^+]_o$ (4 mM); this difference may reflect the fact that cesium is thought to block i_{K1}, as well as pacemaker and pump currents (Isenberg, 1976), while leaving i_x unaffected. Cycle-length dependent EAD have also been reported after *N*-acetylprocainamide superfusion of canine Purkinje fibers (Dangman and Hoffman, 1981). It is of interest that this agent, the major metabolite of procainamide, did not depress $\dot{V}_{max}$ in vitro (Dangman and Hoffman, 1981) or conduction velocity in vivo (in dogs or patients) (Jaillon and Winkle, 1979; Jaillon et al., 1981). Furthermore, it can cause bradycardia-dependent polymorphic ventricular tachyarrhythmias in dogs (Dangman and Hoffman, 1981) and has been implicated in the development of Torsades de Pointes (Olshansky et al., 1982). Quinidine-induced EAD are triggered and reversed by the same alterations that can trigger and reverse Torsades de Pointes in patients (changes in $[K^+]_o$, cycle length). Hence, it is tempting to speculate that "idiosyncratic" arrhythmia induction by low plasma concentrations of quinidine is in fact a reflection of predictable changes modulated in an individual by cleft K^+, heart rate, and other factors such as autonomic tone (Malliani et al., 1980). The role of EAD in triggering these distinctive clinical arrhythmias requires further studies in intact hearts.

Supported in part by grants from the U.S. Public Health Service (GM31304 and HL05808) and a grant-in-aid from the American Heart Association (with funds contributed in part by the Tennessee affiliate). Dr. Roden is a recipient of the Clinician-Scientist Award of the American Heart Association.

Address for reprints: Dan M. Roden, M.D., Department of Pharmacology, Vanderbilt University School of Medicine, Nashville, Tennessee 37232.

Received January 12, 1984; accepted for publication March 7, 1985.

References

Attwell D, Cohen I, Eisner D, Ohba M, Ojeda C (1979) The steady state TTX-sensitive ("window") sodium current in cardiac Purkinje fibers. Pflugers Arch **379:** 137–142

Bean BP, Cohen CJ, Tsien RW (1982) Block of cardium sodium channels by TTX and lidocaine: Sodium current and $\dot{V}_{max}$ experiments. *In* Normal and Abnormal Conduction of the Heart in the Heart edited by BF Hoffman, M Lieberman, A Paes de Carvalho. Mt. Kisco, New York, Futura Publishing

Brachmann J, Scherlag BJ, Rosenshtraukh LV, Lazzara R (1983) Bradycardia-dependent triggered activity: relevance to drug-induced multiform ventricular tachycardia. Circulation **68:** 846–856

Brown B (1983) Early after depolarizations induced by batrachotoxin: Possible involvement of a sodium current (abstr). Fed Proc **42:** 581

Carmeliet E, Saikawa T (1982) Shortening of the action potential and reduction of pacemaker activity by lidocaine, quinidine, and procainamide in sheep cardiac Purkinje fibers. Circ Res **50:** 257–261

Colatsky TJ (1982) Mechanisms of action of lidocaine and quinidine on action potential duration in rabbit cardiac Purkinje fibers. Circ Res **50:** 17–27

Colatsky TJ, Hogan PM (1980) Effect of external calcium, calcium channel-blocking agents, and stimulation frequency on cycle length-dependent changes in canine cardiac action potential duration. Circ Res **46:** 543–552

Coraboeuf E, Deroubaix E, Coulombe A (1979) Effect of tetrodotoxin on action potentials of the conducting system in the dog heart. Am J Physiol **236:** H561–H567

Coraboeuf E, Deroubaix E, Coulombe A (1980) Acidosis-induced abnormal repolarization and repetitive activity in isolated dog Purkinje fibers. J Physiol (Paris) **76:** 97–106

Coulombe A, Coraboeuf E, Deroubaix E (1980) Computer simulation of acidosis-induced abnormal repolarization and repetitive activity in dog Purkinje fibers. J Physiol (Paris) **76:** 107–112

Damiano BP, Rosen MR (1983) The effects of pacing on early afterdepolarizations and triggered activity (abstr). Fed Proc **42:** 581

Dangman KH, Hoffman BF (1981) In vivo and in vitro antiarrhythmic and arrhythmogenic effects of *N*-acetyl procainamide. J Pharmacol Exp Ther **217:** 851–862

Elharrar V, Surawicz B (1983) Cycle length effect on restitution of action potential duration in dog cardiac fibers. Am J Physiol **244:** H782–H792

Gadsby DC, Cranefield PF (1977) Two levels of resting potential in cardiac Purkinje fibers. J Gen Physiol **70:** 725–746

Gadsby DC, Cranefield PF (1979) Direct measurement of changes in sodium pump current in canine cardiac Purkinje fibers. Proc Natl Acad Sci USA **76:** 1783–1787

Gintant GA, Hoffman BF, Naylor RE (1983) The influence of molecular form of local anesthetic-type antiarrhythmic agents on reduction of the maximum upstroke velocity of canine cardiac Purkinje fibers. Circ Res **52:** 735–746

Gintant GA, Datyner NB, Cohen IS (1984) Slow inactivation of tetrodotoxin-sensitive current in cardiac fibers (abstr). Biophys J **41:** 76a

Greenspan K, Edmands RE, Fisch C (1967) Effects of cycle-length alteration on canine cardiac action potentials. Am J Physiol **212:** 1416–1420

Hauswirth O, Noble D, Tsien RW (1969) The mechanism of oscillatory activity at low membrane potentials in cardiac Purkinje fibres. J Physiol (Lond) **200:** 255–265

Hauswirth O, Noble D, Tsien RW (1972) The dependence of plateau currents in cardiac Purkinje fibres on the interval between action potentials. J Physiol (Lond) **222:** 27–49

Imanishi S, Surawicz B (1976) Automatic activity in depolarized guinea pig ventricular myocardium. Circ Res **39:** 751–759

Isenberg G (1976) Cardiac Purkinje fibers: Cesium as a tool to block inward rectifying potassium currents. Plfugers Arch **365:** 99–106

Ito S, Surawicz B (1981) Effect of tetraethylammonium chloride on action potential in cardiac Purkinje fibers. Am J Physiol **241:** H139–H144

Jaillon P, Winkle RA (1979) Electrophysiologic comparative study of procainamide and *N*-acetylprocainamide in anesthetized dogs: Concentration-response relationships. Circulation **60:** 1385–1394

Jaillon P, Rubenson D, Peters F, Mason JW, Winkle RA (1981) Electrophysiologic effects of *N*-acetylprocainamide in human

beings. Am J Cardiol **47:** 1134–1140
Johnson EA, McKinnon MG (1956) The differential effect of quinidine and pyrilamine on the myocardial action potential at various rates of stimulation. J Pharmacol Exp Ther **117:** 237–244
Malliani A, Schwartz PJ, Zanchetti A (1980) Neural mechanisms in life-threatening arrhythmias. Am Heart J **100:** 705–715
Miller JP, Wallace AG, Feezor MD (1971) A quantitative comparison of the relation between the shape of the action potential and the pattern of stimulation in canine ventricular muscle and Purkinje fibers. J Mol Cell Cardiol **2:** 3–19
Mirro J, Watanabe AM, Bailey JC (1981) Electrophysiological effects of the optical isomers of disopyramide and quinidine in the dog. Circ Res **48:** 867–874
Nattel S, Bailey JC (1983) Time course of the electrophysiological effects of quinidine on canine cardiac Purkinje fibers: Concentration dependence and comparison with lidocaine and disopyramide. J Pharmacol Exp Ther **225:** 176–180
Neter J, Wasserman W (1974) Applied Linear Statistical Models. Homewood, Illinois, Richard D. Irwin, Inc., pp 87–89, 259–265
Olshansky B, Martins J, Hunt S (1982) *N*-acetylprocainamide causing Torsades de Pointes. Am J Cardiol **50:** 1439–1441
Roden DM, Woosley RL, Bernard Y, Bostick D, Primm RK (1983) Quinidine-induced long QT syndrome: Incidence and presenting features (abstr). Circulation **68** (suppl III): 276
Selzer A, Wray HW (1964) Quinidine syncope. Paroxysmal ventricular fibrillation occurring during treatment of chronic atrial arrhythmias. Circulation **30:** 17–26
Sheiner LB (1981) ELSFIT: A Program for Extended Least Squares Fit. San Francisco, University of California Press
Smith WM, Gallagher JJ (1980) "Les Torsades de Pointes": An unusual ventricular arrhythmia. Ann Int Med **93:** 578–584
Vaughan Williams EM (1958) The mode of action of quinidine on isolated rabbit atria interpreted from intracellular potential records. Br J Pharmacol **13:** 276–278
Vaughan Williams EM (1975) Classification of antidysrhythmic drugs. Pharmacol Ther B **1:** 115–138
Vick RL (1971) Action potential duration in canine Purkinje tissue: Effects of preceding excitation. J Electrocardiol **4:** 105–115
Wallace AG, Cline RE, Sealy WC, Young WG, Troyer WG (1966) Electrophysiologic effects of quinidine. Studies using chronically implanted electrodes in awake dogs with and without cardiac denervation. Circ Res **19:** 960–969
Wang CM, Parker CH (1980) Reassessment of the electrophysiologic effects of the antiarrhythmic agent quinidine canine Purkinje fibers. Life Sci **27:** 663–670
Weld FM, Rottman J, Bigger JT (1980) Quinidine toxicity: An electrophysiological evaluation in cardiac Purkinje fibers (abstr). Am J Cardiol **45:** 428

INDEX TERMS: Quinidine • Action potential duration • Early afterdepolarizations • Arrhythmogenesis

The Calcium Channel Blocker Nitrendipine Blocks Sodium Channels in Neonatal Rat Cardiac Myocytes

Atsuko Yatani and Arthur M. Brown

From the Department of Physiology and Biophysics, University of Texas Medical Branch, Galveston, Texas

SUMMARY. The dihydropyridine calcium channel blocker, nitrendipine, was studied for its effects on the sodium current of single cultured ventricular cells from neonatal rats. The patch-clamp method of recording whole cell currents was used, and sodium currents were isolated by suppressing potassium and calcium currents. Potassium currents were blocked by replacing potassium with cesium in the internal and external solutions and by adding tetraethylammonium chloride and 4-aminopyridine in the external solution; calcium current was blocked by replacing calcium with cobalt in the external solution. At low frequencies (0.1 Hz), nitrendipine reduced sodium currents without any significant change in the current-voltage relation. The block was dose dependent, and assuming a single occupancy model with complete block, had a half-maximum value of 3×10^{-6} M at a holding potential of −80 mV where half the sodium channels are activatable. This value is within the range of the K_d's that have been reported for low-affinity dihydropyridine-binding sites found in cardiac sarcolemmal vesicles. In the presence of nitrendipine, the inactivation curve was shifted to hyperpolarized potentials. The block was greater with pulse intervals shorter than 1000 msec, and repriming was prolonged in the presence of the drug. These effects are similar to those of local anesthetics of the tertiary amine class, such as lidocaine. The block was relieved by the dihydropyridine agonist Bay K8644. The results are interpreted as indicating that dihydropyridines react with sodium channels. **(*Circ Res 57: 868–875, 1985*)**

ELECTROPHYSIOLOGICAL studies have shown that Ca^{++} channel blockers affect other membrane currents as well. For example, the organic Ca^{++} channel blocker, D600, and the inorganic Ca^{++} channel blockers, Mn^{++} and La^{++}, reduce outward currents in Purkinje fibers (Kass and Tsien, 1975; Siegelbaum and Tsien, 1980). D600 and verapamil have recently been shown to block Na^+ channels in neuronal as well as cardiac cells (Galper and Catterall, 1979; Frelin et al., 1982). The lack of specificity is not restricted to Ca^{++} channel blockers. Organic Na^+ channel blockers such as the local anesthetic group of drugs have effects on K^+ currents (Weld and Bigger, 1976). Ca^{++} channels in neuronal cells are also blocked by what were thought to be Na^+ channel-specific drugs, such as veratridine, batrachotoxin, and other agents (Romey and Lazdunski, 1982).

Recently, a new group of Ca^{++} channel blockers, the 1,4-dihydropyridines (DHP), of which nifedipine and nitrendipine are examples, has been shown to block Ca^{++} currents (I_{Ca}) in some smooth muscle, with a very low half-maximal inhibition (IC_{50}) value (Triggle and Swamy, 1983; Fleckenstein, 1983). The DHP also block inactivated Ca^{++} channels in the heart with high potency, as well (Sanguinetti and Kass, 1984; Brown et al., 1984a; Bean, 1984). Receptor-binding studies have shown that DHP bind to a very high affinity (K_d of about 0.1 nM) site in plasma membranes of many excitable cells from tissues including heart, brain, and smooth muscle [for cardiac sarcolemmal vesicles, see Bellemann et al. (1981), Ehlert et al. (1982), Williams and Tremble (1982), DePover et al. (1982), Murphy and Snyder (1982); for cardiac cells, see Marsh et al. (1983)]. In addition, DHP bind to a lower affinity site in these tissues [K_d of about 100 nM (Bellemann et al., 1981; Marsh et al., 1983; Schwartz et al., 1984)]. At these concentrations DHP could have effects on other membrane currents as well as calcium currents. In the present paper, we examined the effects of nitrendipine on Na^+ currents (I_{Na}) in cultured cardiac cells from neonatal rat hearts. At micromolar concentrations, the drug blocked Na^+ channels. The block was voltage and use dependent, and had characteristics similar to the block of Na^+ channels produced by local anesthetics.

Methods

Culture of Neonatal Rat Heart Cells

Primary cardiac cell cultures were prepared from hearts of neonatal rats (1–3 days old) according to a modification of the method of Mark and Strasser (1966). Hearts were removed under sterile conditions and the ventricles were cut into small pieces. The tissue pieces were incubated at 37°C for 5 minutes in Ca^{++}-free Hanks' solution containing 0.5% trypsin (Sigma T-0134). The supernatant was removed and added to culture medium, DMEM-10 FCS to stop enzyme action. The cell suspensions were seeded on glass cover-slips which were put into 35 mM Falcon dishes containing the culture medium. The cultures were kept in an incubator at 37°C in an H_2O-saturated, 5% CO_2-95% O_2 air atmosphere.

Electrical Recording

Electrophysiological recordings were made with the whole-cell patch-clamp techniques as described by Hamill et al. (1981) and Fenwick et al. (1982). Patch pipettes (resistances 2–3 MΩ) were prepared as described by Hamill et al. (1981). In some experiments, series resistance (1 ~ MΩ) was compensated electronically by positive current feedback. Transient cancellation was used as described by Hamill et al. (1981). The experimental chamber was placed on a microscope stage, and external solutions superfused the 0.2 ml chamber volume at a rate of 2 ml/min by gravity. To suppress outward currents, the pipettes were filled with a Cs^+-rich solution of the following composition (mM): CsOH, 110; aspartic acid, 110; CsCl, 20; HEPES, 5; EGTA, 3; pH 7.3, with NaOH. Liquid junction potentials (<5 mV) measured between bath solution and pipette solution were compensated. To improve voltage control, Na^+ in the bath was decreased to 60 mM. The calcium current was suppressed by substitution of Co^{++} for Ca^{++} in the presence of Mg^{++}. Potassium currents were suppressed by replacing K^+ with Cs^+ and by adding tetraethylammonium chloride (TEA) and 4-aminopyridine (4-AP) (Isenberg, 1976; Keynon and Gibbons, 1979a, 1979b; Hagiwara and Byerly, 1981; Yatani et al., 1984). The bath solution contained (mM): NaCl, 60; CsCl, 5; TEA, 20; $MgCl_2$, 2.5; $CoCl_2$, 2; 4-AP, 5; glucose, 5.5; sucrose, 80; pH 7.4, with HCl. All experiments were performed at room temperature (20–22°C).

The current and voltage recorded in response to command pulses were monitored on a storage oscilloscope, digitized at 2 μsec/point, with a signal averager. The digitized records were stored on a digital tape recorder. Experimental curve fitting was accomplished with a PDP 11/70 computer using a modified Marquardt-Levenberg routine. In Figure 2, Student's *t*-test was used.

Drugs Used

Nitrendipine (3-ethyl-5-methyl-1,4-dihydro-2,6-dimethyl-4-[3-nitrophenyl]-3,5-pyridine carboxylate, and Bay K8644 (methyl 1,4-dihydro-2,6-dimethyl-3-nitro-4-[2-trifluoromethylphenyl]-pyridine-5-carboxylate were kindly supplied by Miles Institute for Preclinical Pharmacology. The drugs were dissolved in absolute ethanol. In some experiments, polyethylene glycol 400 was used. The final concentration of bath solvents was held constant at 0.1% for doses of nitrendipine up to 10^{-5} M. When nitrendipine was used at 10^{-4} M concentration, the solvent concentration rose to 1%.

Results

Cardiac myocytes prepared from neonatal rats 1–3 days old are spherical when first dispersed, and have a diameter of 10–20 μm. The geometry is therefore very favorable for voltage clamping. In addition, electron micrographs show that T-tubules are absent (Moses and Kasten, 1979). Electrically, the cells behave as a simple R-C circuit with a time constant <100 μsec (Lacerda et al., in preparation). The patch pipettes had tip resistances of 3 MΩ or less and the input resistance of the cells we used was ~10 GΩ. The peak I_{Na} were always less than 1000 pA, and the effect of the series resistance was therefore very small. The voltage clamp was judged to be adequate when the current records showed no abnormal deflections and the conductance-voltage relation showed the smooth progression illustrated by the current-voltage (I-V) curves (Fig. 1B). The I-V relations retained their shapes when peak I_{Na} differed by as much as 400–500%, which is further evidence that voltage control was satisfactory.

Effects of Nitrendipine on I-V Relations and Availability of Na Currents

Figure 1A shows families of I_{Na} obtained from a single spherical cultured neonatal rat cardiac cell, in the absence (a) and presence of nitrendipine 10^{-6} M (b), 10^{-5} M (c), and 10^{-4} M (d). The currents in 1A are produced by depolarizing voltage steps of 10-mV increments from −50 to −20 mV from a holding potential of −80 mV. Records were taken in control solution, and then 5 minutes after exposure to each drug concentration. The 10-msec test pulses were applied at a low frequency (0.1 Hz). The peak I_{Na} was measured as the maximum inward current displacement from the holding current level (zero current level), since the leakage current was negligibly small over the range explored (Fig. 1B). Nitrendipine produced a concentration-dependent decrease in I_{Na} without changing the I-V relations. Reduction of I_{Na} began at concentrations as low as 10^{-7} M. I_{Na} threshold and reversal potential (E_{Na}) remained unchanged. There were no changes in the waveform during the voltage clamp step (Fig. 6), and therefore development of block during the voltage step was either too fast or too slow to be detected. As we shall see later, one component of block develops

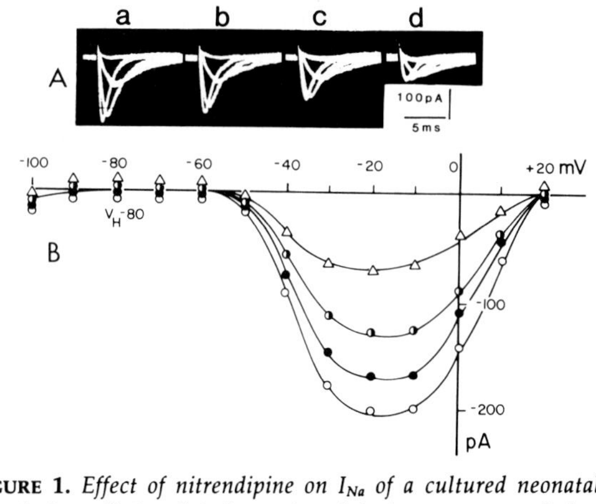

FIGURE 1. *Effect of nitrendipine on I_{Na} of a cultured neonatal rat ventricular cell. Panel A shows the original current traces before (a), and after superfusion with nitrendipine 10^{-6} M (b), 10^{-5} M (c) and 10^{-4} M (d). No correction for leak or capacitive currents was made in this display. Holding potential was −80 mV, and 10-msec depolarizing and hyperpolarizing pulses in 10-mV steps were applied at a frequency of 0.1 Hz. The membrane currents produced by depolarizing voltage steps of 10-mV increments from −50 to −20 mV are shown. Panel B shows the I-V curves for I_{Na} in the absence (○) and in the presence of nitrendipine 10^{-6} M (●), 10^{-5} M (◑), and 10^{-4} M (△).*

very slowly (Figs. 5 and 6). These effects were reversible and the current was restored to its control value after a 5- to 10-minute wash period. The solvent effects were tested and were found to be negligible.

For each concentration of drug, I-V relations before and after application were obtained using the same protocol shown in Figure 1. Percent reductions of peak I_{Na} obtained in solutions containing various concentrations of nitrendipine were collected and are plotted in Figure 2. Nitrendipine produced an inhibition of I_{Na} at concentrations as low as 10^{-7} M, which is approximately the concentration required for half-maximal inhibition of resting Ca^{++} channels in cardiac cells (Lee and Tsien, 1983; Brown et al., 1984a; Sanguinetti and Kass, 1984; Bean, 1984). Similar inhibition of I_{Ca} is also observed in neonatal rat cells (Yatani et al., in preparation).

A new dihydropyridine derivative (Bay K8644) has recently been shown to be a potent Ca^{++} channel agonist (Brown et al., 1984b), and it is inhibited by nitrendipine (Schramm et al., 1983a). Receptor-binding studies suggest that nitrendipine and other members of the dihydropyridine family bind to the same receptor and the receptor differs from other known receptors such as α- and β-adrenergic receptors (Schramm et al., 1983b).

We therefore examined the action of nitrendipine in combination with Bay K8644 (Fig. 2). The top panel in Figure 2 shows I_{Na} before (a), 5 minutes after 10^{-5} M nitrendipine was added (b), then after 5 minutes of exposure to nitrendipine (10^{-5} M) plus 10^{-7} M Bay K8644 containing solution (c). Bay K8644 partially reversed the nitrendipine-induced inhibition of I_{Na}. In this experiment, the membrane was clamped to −30 mV, 30 msec in duration, from a holding potential of −80 mV. Bay K8644 (10^{-7} M) alone did not induce a change of I_{Na}. At concentrations greater than 10^{-6} M, Bay K8644 increased I_{Na} in five of eight experiments. The question concerning a possible interaction of Bay K8644 with the Na^+ channel is currently being studied.

The block of Na^+ channels by nitrendipine was partly reversed by shifting the holding potential (−90 mV) to more negative values (−110 mV) (Fig. 3, inset). Thus, the interaction between nitrendipine block and Na^+ channel availability was examined over a range of potentials in the absence and presence of the drug. Figure 3 shows a representative steady state inactivation curve of a cultured neonatal rat heart cell. The extent of inactivation of I_{Na} was determined by a double-pulse protocol. The prepulse duration was 500 msec, which produces steady state inactivation of I_{Na} under control conditions, and the test potential was −30 mV and 4 msec long. The test I_{Na} current produced at the most hyperpolarized prepulse potential (I_{max}) was used to normalize the test I_{Na} that resulted from other conditioning pulse potentials. The curves were fitted using the equation for steady state inactivation developed by Hodgkin and Huxley (1952):

$$h_\infty = 1/[1 + \exp(V_m - V_h)/k]$$

where V_h is the midpotential and k is the slope of the curve. The mean control values for V_h and k in

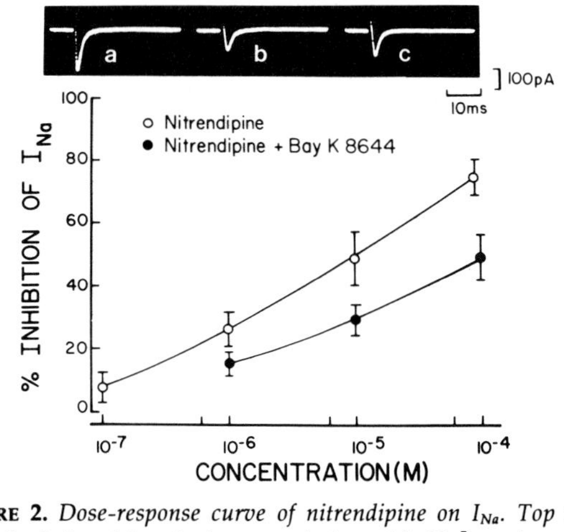

FIGURE 2. *Dose-response curve of nitrendipine on I_{Na}. Top traces show I_{Na} before (a) and after superfusion with 10^{-5} M nitrendipine (b) and after changing to 10^{-5} M nitrendipine containing Bay K8644, 10^{-7} M solution (c). The cell was clamped from a holding potential of −80 mV to −30 mV for 30 msec at 0.1 Hz. Percent inhibition values of maximum peak I_{Na} on the I-V curve corresponding to the control value were plotted vs. nitrendipine concentration, in the absence and presence of 10^{-7} M Bay K8644. The experimental protocol is identical to that described in Figure 1. Each point is mean ± SD value of at least six observations. $P < 0.05$ for 10^{-7} M nitrendipine vs. control. $P < 0.01$ for 10^{-6}, 10^{-5}, and 10^{-4} nitrendipine vs. control.*

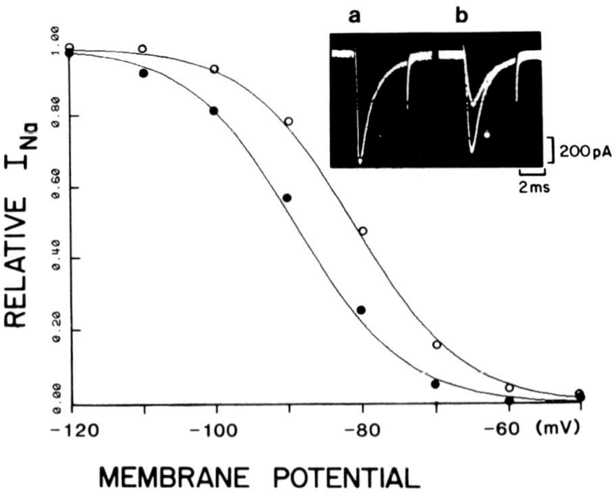

FIGURE 3. *Effects of nitrendipine (10^{-5} M) on the voltage dependence of I_{Na} availability. The conditioning pulses of 500 msec duration from a holding potential of −80 mV with a test voltage of −30 mV and 4 msec in duration were applied at 0.1 Hz. Solid lines are drawn according to $h_\infty = 1/[1 + \exp(V_m - V_h)/k]$. For the control (○), V_h = −81 mV, k = 7.3. With nitrendipine (●), V_h = −89 mV, k = 7.3. The normalization factor is 0.875: for control, I_{max} (control) is 873 pA and with nitrendipine, I_{max} (drug) = 764 pA. Inset: (a) I_{Na} elicited by a 4-msec depolarizing pulse to −30 mV from a holding potential of −90 mV; (b) in the presence of nitrendipine (10^{-5} M), I_{Na} was elicited as in (a), then holding potential was hyperpolarized to −110 mV (open circle).*

14 cells were −83 ± 7 mV and 7.3 ± 0.8 mV, respectively.

Nitrendipine shifted the inactivation curve to negative potentials with the same steepness factor as the control. I_{Na} was reduced by nitrendipine even with conditioning pulses up to −120 mV, although this is not apparent, since the points were normalized. Negative conditioning pulses of more than −120 mV showed no further effect on current size, suggesting that the effect of the holding potential on nitrendipine block may saturate at −120 mV. The corresponding V_h values in the absence and presence of nitrendipine (10^{-5} M) were −82 mV and −89 mV, respectively. The nitrendipine-induced shift of the inactivation curve was larger for high concentrations of the drug, and there was no consistent change in the k value. The shifts of the inactivation curve in various nitrendipine concentrations and the normalization factor [I_{max}(drugs)/I_{max}(control)] used for curve fitting are presented in Table 1.

Use-Dependent Action of Nitrendipine

Our result showing that nitrendipine shifted the inactivation curve in the hyperpolarizing direction resembled the effects of local anesthetics having a tertiary amine structure, such as lidocaine (Lee et al., 1981; Bean et al., 1983; Sanchez-Chapula et al., 1983). According to the modulated receptor hypothesis (Hille, 1977a, 1977b; Hondghem and Katzung, 1977, 1984) this indicates stronger binding to the inactivated state. According to the guarded gate hypothesis, this is due to retention of the drug by closed h gates (Starmer et al., 1984). In either case, it was of interest to examine use- or frequency-dependent effects. Thus, trains of 20 depolarizing clamp pulses (−80 to −30 mV for 50 msec) were applied at different pulse intervals, ranging from 1000 to 200 msec (Fig. 4). The cells were rested for 5 minutes before the train of pulses was applied. The top panels in Figure 4 show superimposed I_{Na} during the 1st and 20th pulse at a pulse interval of 300 msec. In the absence of drug (a), the first and 20th currents are about the same size. In the presence of nitrendipine (10^{-5} M), the first pulse elicited a current reduced to 65% of control, and by the 20th pulse, I_{Na} was reduced to 45% (b).

The development of use-dependent inhibition

TABLE 1

Nitrendipine-Induced Shifts of I_{Na} Availability

[Nitrendipine] M	k (mV)	Shift of V_h (mV)	Normalization factor [I_{max} (drug)/ I_{max} (control)]	*n*
10^{-7}	7.2 ± 1.0	−5.0 ± 2.4	0.98 ± 0.01	4
10^{-6}	7.3 ± 0.8	−8.3 ± 3.2	0.92 ± 0.02	4
10^{-5}	7.2 ± 1.0	−12.0 ± 5.0	0.87 ± 0.02	6

The dependence of test pulse I_{Na} on conditioning potential was obtained by the experimental protocol which is identical to that described in Figure 3. Results are expressed as mean ± SD; *n* = number of experiments.

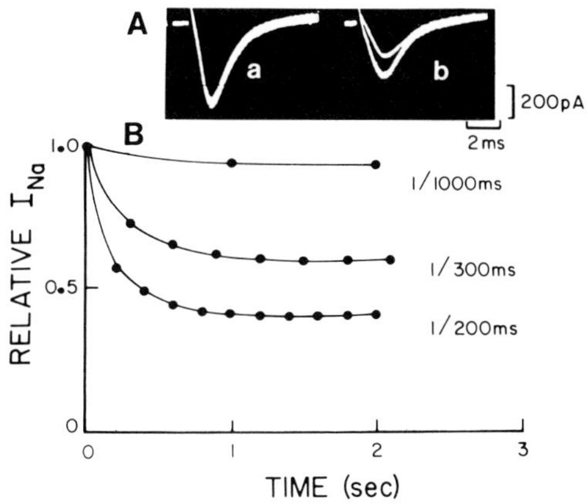

FIGURE 4. *Use-dependent effect of nitrendipine 10^{-5} M. Panel A: trains of 20 depolarizing pulses (−80 to −30 mV for 50 msec) were applied at an interval of 300 msec. The first and 20th I_{Na} were superimposed: (a) control, (b) in the presence of nitrendipine. Panel B: development of use-dependent block of I_{Na} in the presence of nitrendipine (10^{-5} M), at each pulse interval. I_{Na} relative to the first pulse was plotted. Voltage clamp steps of 50 msec from −80 mV to −30 mV were applied.*

during trains of pulses is shown in Figure 4B. In each of three pulse intervals, the inhibition of I_{Na} increased with each pulse, and the block was cumulative. This additional inhibition was gradually lost after the trains were stopped. The use-dependent block of I_{Na} in the presence of nitrendipine was obtained in four additional experiments. In five experiments, the additional use-dependent inhibition produced by nitrendipine (10^{-5} M) at pulse intervals of 300 and 200 msec was 28 ± 6% and 55 ± 8%, respectively, when compared to intervals of 10 seconds (0.1 Hz).

The accumulation of use-dependent block during a train of pulses indicates that the interval between pulses was not sufficiently long to allow recovery of the Na^+ channel from block. Therefore, the effects of nitrendipine (10^{-5} M) on recovery from inactivation were studied by using a double-pulse procedure. The time course of I_{Na} is shown in Figure 5A. Recovery at −90 mV was assessed by measuring I_{Na} in response to paired 50-msec depolarizing pulses to −30 mV, separated by a variable length of time. Each double-pulse sequence was followed by a 10-second rest period. The recovery curve was plotted as the relation of $I_{Na(test)}/I_{Na(conditioning)}$ (I_t/I_c) against the pulse interval. The same data shown in Figure 5A was plotted semilogarithmically [$\log(1-I_t/I_c)$] against the pulse interval in Figure 5B.

In the absence of nitrendipine, the time course was fitted by an exponential with a time constant (τ_r) of 40 msec. With nitrendipine (10^{-5} M), the recovery of I_{Na} was fitted by two exponentials. The first phase $\tau_1 = 50$ msec corresponds to the recovery tau in the absence of drug and its amplitude was reduced about 50%. The second phase was much slower, with a τ_2 of 220 msec. Similar prolongation of I_{Na} recovery was found in five additional experi-

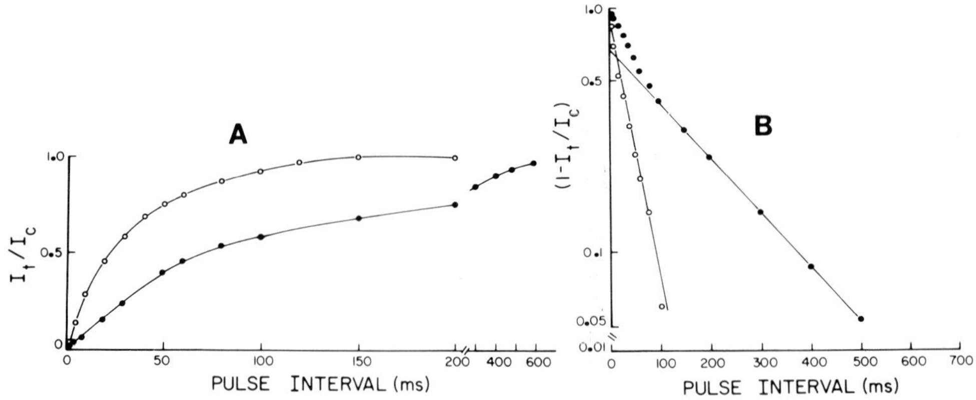

FIGURE 5. *Effects of nitrendipine (10^{-5} M) on the recovery of I_{Na}. I_{Na} was evoked by a test pulse at a varying interval after a 50-msec conditioning pulse. A pair of pulses from a holding potential of −90 mV to −30 mV was applied at 0.1 Hz. Panel A: I_{Na} during test pulse (I_t) was normalized by I_{Na} during and immediately preceding conditioning pulse (I_c). Panel B: same data as in panel A, but plotted semilogarithmically (○; control, ●; nitrendipine).*

ments with a recovery potential −80 or −100 mV. In each case, the fast taus were unchanged by the drug, although their amplitudes were reduced. The larger taus had values of 250 ± 30 msec for −80 mV (n = 3) and 180 ± 20 msec for −100 mV (n = 2).

To examine any possible interaction of nitrendipine with Na^+ channels when they are in the open state, 20 repetitive depolarizing clamp pulses from −80 to −20 mV, 1 msec in duration, were applied at 5 Hz. This protocol opens the channels but produces little inactivation. The cell was rested for 5 minutes before the test sequence was applied. In the control measurement, the relative I_{Na} did not vary from the first to the 20th pulse. With 10^{-5} M nitrendipine, the situation was nearly identical to the control, except that a reduction in the amplitude of the first test pulse of 50% was observed.

In addition, we compared the waveform of I_{Na} during depolarizing voltage pulses before and after exposure to nitrendipine, since drugs that bind to the open state of the channel have been shown to increase the inactivation rate of current through the channels (Coloquhoun and Hawkes, 1983). Figure 6a compares the time course of I_{Na}, before and after the application of nitrendipine (10^{-5} M). In b, the magnitudes of I_{Na} before and after the drug are normalized. Depolarizing pulses were applied to −10 mV for 5 msec at 0.1 Hz from a holding potential of −80 mV. As shown in Figure 6a, I_{Na} measured in the presence of the drug is reduced; however, the waveform, in particular the rate of inactivation, is not altered (see also Fig. 1).

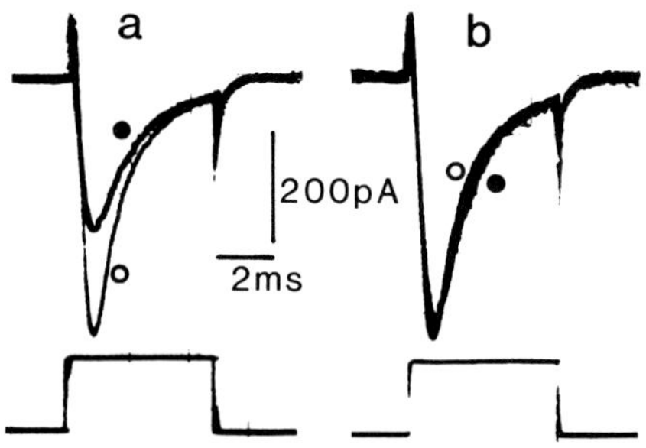

FIGURE 6. *Influence of nitrendipine (10^{-5} M) on rate of inactivation during depolarizing voltage pulse. Part a: current records response to voltage step to −30 mV from a holding potential of −90 mV, control (○) and in the presence of nitrendipine (●). Part b: current traces in control (○) and after nitrendipine (●) are scaled and superimposed to compare the inactivation time course of I_{Na}. Membrane currents during the 5-msec voltage steps are shown. I_{Na} of control and nitrendipine reached the same steady value during the pulse.*

Discussion

Our results show that the DHP Ca^{++} channel blocker nitrendipine also blocks Na^+ channels. The block occurs at concentrations that are required for full block of I_{Ca} (Lee and Tsien, 1983; Bean, 1984). These concentrations are also within the range of the concentrations at which low-affinity nitrendipine-binding sites in cardiac tissue are occupied (Bellemann et al., 1981; Schwartz et al., 1984). Nitrendipine action on Na^+ channels was both voltage and use dependent and the effects are similar to those of another group of Na^+ channel blockers, the local anesthetics (Lee et al., 1981; Bean et al., 1983; Sanchez-Chapula et al., 1983). Block to open channels was not observed, but it could have been so fast that a change in waveform might not have been detected. Effects such as those observed presently have been explained by the modulated receptor hypothesis of local anesthetic action (Hille, 1977a; 1977b; Hondeghem and Katzung, 1977, 1984) in which differing drug affinities for different channel conformations are assumed. The guarded gate hypothesis of Starmer et al. (1984) might be as reasonable; in this explanation, relief of block by hyperpolarization is explained by clearance of drug when the closed h gates are reopened. It should be noted that block to inactivated channels developed too slowly to be detected during the voltage clamp step. This is consistent with the recovery results and the superimposable waveforms shown in Figure 6.

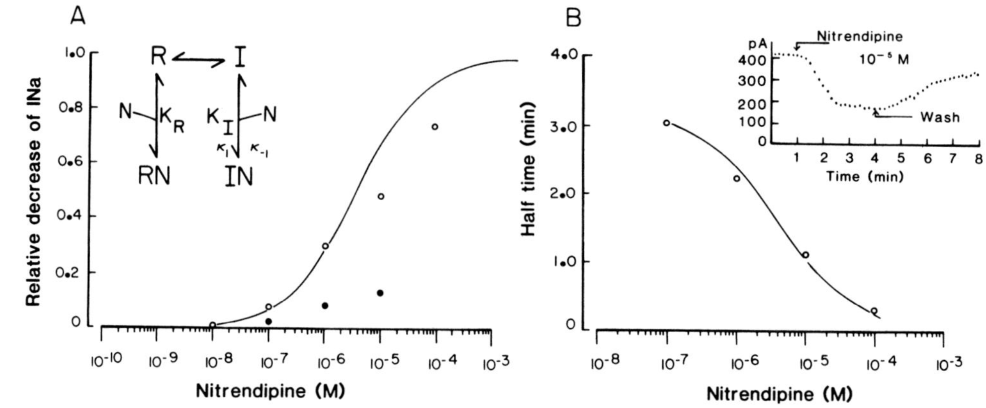

FIGURE 7. *Modulated receptor hypothesis for nitrendipine binding to* Na^+ *channels. R is rested state; RN is rested state with nitrendipine bound. I and IN are the corresponding forms of the inactivated state. One-to-one drug binding to the* Na^+ *channel is assumed, with different affinity for rested* (K_R) *and inactivated channels* (K_I). *Binding to open channels is omitted. Drug-associated channels differ from drug-free channels in that they do not conduct. Panel A: dose-response for block at holding potentials of −80 and −120 mV. The data at −80 mV are the same as in Figure 2 (○). At −120 mV, the data were the same as shown in Table 1 (●). Solid curve is best least squares fit to: Relative decrease of*

$$I_{Na} = \frac{[M]}{[M] + K_d},$$

where [M] is a drug concentration and K_d *is an apparent dissociation constant. Panel B: half-time of nitrendipine block determined by the same protocol as in inset. Points show mean value for four cells. Inset shows the time course of nitrendipine block with half-time of 1.2 minutes. Test pulse to −20 mV, 10 msec long, was applied from a holding potential of −80 mV at 0.1 Hz. Solid curve is best fit of* $1/[k_{-1} + N\cdot(1-h)\cdot k_1]$. $\tau = 1.443\, t_{1/2}$, *where* $t_{1/2}$ *is half time, was calculated. h is the fraction of channels in the rested state and N is the drug concentration.*

Figure 7 shows a simplified version of the modulated receptor model that can explain qualitatively the results obtained in the present study. According to the model (1) drugs bind to a receptor site on or very close to the sodium channel; (2) the affinity of the receptor for the drug is modulated by the channel state; rested (R) and inactivated (I); (3) drug-associated channels differ from drug-free channels in that they do not conduct, and their ability to activate is shifted to more negative potentials.

The concentration dependence of nitrendipine block at holding potentials of −120 mV and −80 mV is plotted in Figure 7A. At −80 mV, block clearly increased over the range of concentrations explored, and the data have been fit to a curve corresponding to 1:1 binding, with an apparent dissociation constant, K_d of 3×10^{-6} M. The K_d terms are used with the assumption that the efficacy is constant at the different holding potentials. The results were less clear when the membrane was hyperpolarized, but for purposes of exploring our hypothesis, the data were fit with the model and an apparent K_d of 2×10^{-5} M was obtained. Note that full block using our protocols was not produced even at concentrations as great as 10^{-4} M, but in spite of this the model fit was constrained to produce full block. Higher concentrations could not be used because, at very high concentrations, the effects of the DHP solvent, ethanol, or polyethylene glycol had to be considered. We checked for these effects and found them to be relatively insignificant at concentrations of 10^{-5} and 10^{-4} M. However, the effects would interfere at higher concentrations.

Although there is less block at higher concentrations than expected, the curve fits the data at lower concentrations. Following the development used by Bean et al. (1983), the apparent dissociation constant (K_{app}) that is determined by a mix of actual binding reactions is

$$K_{app} = \frac{1}{(h/K_R) + (1 - h)/K_I}$$

where h is the fraction of channels in rested state in the absence of drug, K_R is the dissociation constant for binding to rested state, and K_I is the dissociation constant for binding to the inactivated state. The data in Figure 7A are consistent with the predicted form. $K_R \gg K_I$, $K_I \approx (1\text{-}h)\, K_{app}$. In the experiment at −80 mV, h was about 0.5, and thus the observed apparent dissociation constant of 3×10^{-6} M would correct to a value of 1.62×10^{-6} M for binding to the inactivated state. The model in Figure 7 may also be used to evaluate the kinetics with which nitrendipine block developed. Assuming that the equilibration of channels between rested and inactivated states has occurred and that the binding reaction is rate-limiting, nitrendipine block will develop with the time constant of the second-order reaction; $\tau_{on} = 1/[k_{-1} + (1\text{-}h)\cdot N\cdot k_1]$, in which N is the nitrendipine concentration, k_1 the forward-rate constant, and k_{-1} the off-rate constant. The ratio k_{-1}/k_1 ($=K_I$) is determined from the fit to the equilibrium dose-response curve. The expression for the expected time constant can then be fit to the experimental data with k_{-1} as a free parameter (Bean, 1984).

As Figure 7B shows, the model accurately predicts the form of experimental data, and a value of 0.0002/sec is obtained for k_{-1}, which is roughly equal to the off-rate constant for the high affinity nitrendipine-binding site for cardiac membrane (Janis et al., 1984). The calculated on-rate constant for the IC_{50} effect is then two to three orders smaller than the on-rate constant for the high-affinity site. These results may be underestimates, however, since the values of hyperpolarizing shifts in the availability curve for I_{Na} that we have observed are underestimates. As Figure 7B shows, the prepulse duration should have been minutes, but such durations were not experimentally feasible. It should also be noted that use dependence of Ca^{++} channel block occurs, but seems not to be as prominent as the effect on Na^+ channels (Sanguinetti and Kass, 1984; Bean, 1984; Yatani et al., in preparation).

These observations, and the interaction with Bay K8644, constitute strong evidence that the effects on the Na^+ channels are due to an interaction of DHP with the Na^+ channel itself. It seems quite unlikely that the voltage-dependent effects on the Na^+ channels could be due only to absorption of DHP by membrane lipids. The fact that a component of the early phase of recovery of I_{Na} from inactivation persisted at very large concentrations also argues for a specific action of the drug on Na^+ channels. This has been confirmed in single-channel experiments (Kunze, Yatani, and Brown, manuscript in preparation). In this regard, it should be noted that Bay K8644 has a specific action on open Ca^{++} channels at concentrations of 10^{-5} M (Hess et al., 1984; Brown et al., 1984b). Nitrendipine also acts on Ca^{++} channels via the low-affinity sites (Yatani et al., unpublished work). It should be noted that, since Na^+ and Ca^{++} channels have a different voltage dependence of inactivation, there is a potential range (about −70 mV) in which most Na^+ channels are inactivated but very few Ca^{++} channels are inactivated. At these potentials, block of Na^+ channels by nitrendipine would be comparable to block of Ca^{++} channels. Thus nitrendipine will not be a selective blocker in all instances.

It has been shown that cardiac sarcolemmal vesicles have two saturable binding sites for DHP, one with a K_d of a fraction of a nanomolar, the other with a K_d of a fraction of a micromolar (Bellemann et al., 1981; Schwartz et al., 1984). The number of high-affinity sites is in reasonable agreement with estimates of Ca^{++} channel density (Yatani et al., unpublished work), but the number of low-affinity sites is one or more orders larger. The Na^+ channels may be included among these lower affinity sites. The low-affinity sites may also include the adenosine transporter (Glassmann, 1985), and this raises the possibility that effects of DHP on Na^+ channels could be secondary to effects on this molecule. It appears likely that the present results can be extended to the DHP class of Ca^{++} channel agonists such as Bay K8644. The fact that nitrendipine's effects were reduced by Bay K8644 would support the idea that DHP with Ca^{++} agonist actions bind to Na^+ channels, as well. The significance of these findings awaits further study, but suggests that Na^+ and Ca^{++} channels may contain some common structural features which operate in both types of channels. A similar conclusion could be drawn from the study of Romey and Lazdunski (1982).

The present results clearly have practical consequences. High doses of DHP Ca^{++} channel antagonists will have actions on cardiac I_{Na} in the heart, and the effects will be use-dependent. This is important clinically, since arrhythmias frequently involve cardiac tissue that is partially depolarized or is discharging at a fast rate.

We wish to thank Drs. D.L. Kunze, A. Lacerda, and J.M. Caffrey for comments, and S. Allison for typing the manuscript.

This work was supported in part by National Institutes of Health Grants HL25145 and HL16657.

Address for reprints: Arthur M. Brown, M.D., Professor and Chairman, Department of Physiology and Biophysics, University of Texas Medical Branch, Galveston, Texas 77550.

Received August 20, 1984; accepted for publication March 22, 1985.

References

Bean BP (1984) Nitrendipine block of cardiac calcium channels: High-affinity binding to the inactivated state. Proc Natl Acad Sci USA **81:** 6388–6392

Bean BP, Cohen CJ, Tsien RW (1983) Lidocaine block of cardiac sodium channels. J Gen Physiol **81:** 613–642

Belleman P, Ferry D, Lübbecke F, Glossmann H (1981) [^{3}H] Nitrendipine, a potent calcium antagonist, binds with high affinity to cardiac membranes. Arzneimittelforsch/Drug Res **31:** 2064–2067

Brown AM, Kunze DL, Yatani A (1984a) Agonist effect of a dihydropyridine Ca channel blocker on guinea-pig and rat ventricular myocytes. J Physiol (Lond) **357:** 59p

Brown AM, Kunze DL, Yatani A (1984b) The agonist effect of dihydropyridine on Ca channels. Nature **311:** 570–572

Coloquhoun D, Hawkes AG (1983) The principles of the stochastic interpretation of ion-channel mechanisms. *In* Single-Channel Recording, edited by B Sakmann, E Neher. pp 135–175

DePover A, Matlib MA, Lee SW, Dube GP, Grupp IL, Grupp G, Schwartz A (1982) Specific binding of [^{3}H]nitrendipine to membrane from coronary arteries and heart in relation to pharmacological effects. Paradoxical stimulation by diltiazem. Biochem Biophys Res Commun **108:** 110–117

Ehlert FJ, Itoga E, Roeske WR, Yamamura HI (1982) The interaction of [^{3}H]nitrendipine with receptors for calcium antagonists in the cerebral cortex and heart of rats. Biochem Biophys Res Commun **104:** 937–943

Fenwick EM, Marty A, Neher E (1982) Sodium and calcium channels in bovine chromaffin cells. J Physiol (Lond) **331:** 599–635

Fleckenstein A (1983) History of calcium antagonists. Circ Res **52** (suppl I): 3–16

Frelin C, Vigne P, Lazdunski M (1982) Biochemical evidence for pharmacological similarities between α-adrenoreceptors and voltage-dependent Na^+ and Ca^{++} channels. Biochem Biophys Res Commun **106:** 967–973

Galper JB, Catterall WA (1979) Inhibition of sodium channels by D600. Mol Pharmacol **15:** 174–178

Glossmann H (1985) Matter arising. Nature **317:** 503–504

Hagiwara S, Byerly L (1981) Calcium channel. Annu Rev Neurosci **4:** 69–125

Hamill OP, Marty A, Neher E, Sakmann B, Sigworth FJ (1981) Improved patch-clamp techniques for high-resolution current recording from cells and cell-free membrane patches. Pflugers Arch **391:** 85–100

Hess P, Lansman JB, Tsien RW (1984) Different modes of Ca channel gating behaviour favoured by dihydropyridine Ca agonists and antagonists. Nature **311:** 538–544

Hille B (1977a) The pH-dependent rate of action of local anesthetics on the node of Ranvier. J Gen Physiol **69:** 475–496

Hille B (1977b) Local anesthetics: Hydrophilic and hydrophobic pathways for the drug-receptor reaction. J Gen Physiol **69:** 497–515

Hodgkin AL, Huxley AF (1952) A quantitative description of membrane current and its application to conduction and excitation in nerve. J Physiol (Lond) **117:** 500–544

Hondeghem LM, Katzung BG (1977) Time- and voltage-dependent interactions of antiarrhythmic drugs with cardiac sodium channels. Biochim Biophys Acta **472:** 373–398

Hondeghem LM, Katzung BG (1984) Antiarrhythmic agents: The modulated receptor mechanism of action of sodium and calcium channel-blocking drugs. Annu Rev Pharmacol Toxicol **24:** 387–423

Isenberg G (1976) Cardiac Purkinje fibers: cesium as a tool to block inward rectifying potassium currents. Pflugers Arch **365:** 99–106

Janis RA, Sarmiento JG, Maurer SC, Bolger GT, Triggle DJ (1984) Characteristics of the binding of [^{3}H] nitrendipine to rabbit ventricular membranes: Modification by other Ca^{++} channel antagonist and by the Ca^{++} channel agonist Bay K8644. J Pharmacol Exp Ther **231:** 8–15

Kass RS, Tsien RW (1975) Multiple effects of calcium antagonists on plateau currents in cardiac Purkinje fibers. J Gen Physiol **66:** 169–192

Kenyon JL, Gibbons WR (1979a) Influence of chloride, potassium and tetraethylammonium on the early outward current of sheep cardiac Purkinje fibers. J Gen Physiol **73:** 117–138

Kenyon JL, Gibbons WR (1979b) 4-Aminopyridine and the early outward current of sheep cardiac Purkinje fibers. J Gen Physiol **73:** 139–157

Lee KS, Tsien RW (1983) Mechanism of calcium channel blockade by verapamil, D600, diltiazem and nitrendipine in single dialyzed heart cells. Nature **302:** 790–794

Lee KS, Hume JR, Giles W, Brown AM (1981) Sodium current depression by lidocaine and quinidine in isolated ventricular cells. Nature **291:** 325–327

Mark GE, Strasser FF (1966) Pacemaker activity and mitosis in cultures of newborn rat heart muscle cells. Exp Cell Res **44:** 217–233

Marsh JD, Loh E, Lachance D, Barry WH, Smith TW (1983) Relationship of binding of a calcium channel blocker to inhibition of contraction in intact cultured embryonic chick ventricular cells. Circ Res **53:** 539–543

Moses RL, Kasten FH (1979) T-tubes in cultured mammalian myocardial cells. Cell Tissue Res **203:** 173–180

Murphy KMM, Snyder SH (1982) Calcium antagonist receptor binding sites labeled with [^{3}H]nitrendipine. Eur J Pharmacol **77:** 201–202

Romey G, Lazdunski M (1982) Lipid-soluble toxins thought to be specific for Na^+ channels block Ca^{2+} channels in neuronal cells. Nature **297:** 79–80

Sanchez-Chapula J, Tsuda Y, Josephson I (1983) Voltage- and use-dependent effects of lidocaine on sodium current in rat single ventricular cells. Circ Res **52:** 557–565

Sanguinetti MC, Kass RS (1984) Voltage-dependent block of calcium channel current in the calf cardiac Purkinje fiber by dihydropyridine calcium channel antagonists. Circ Res **55:** 336–348

Schramm M, Thomas G, Towart R, Franckowiak G (1983a) Novel dihydropyridines with positive ionotropic action through activation of Ca^{2+} channels. Nature **303:** 535–537

Schramm M, Thomas G, Towart R, Franckowiak G (1983b) Activation of calcium channel by novel 1,4-dihydropyridines. A new mechanism for positive inotropics or smooth muscle stimulants. Arzneimittelforsch/Drug Res **33:** 1268–1272

Schwartz A, Grupp IL, Gupp G, Williams JS, Vaghy PL (1984) Effects of dihydropyridine calcium channel modulators in the heart: Pharmacological and Radioligand Binding Correlations. Biochem Biophys Res Commun **125:** 387–394

Siegelbaum SA, Tsien RW (1980) Calcium-activated outward current in calf cardiac Purkinje fibres. J Physiol (Lond) **299:** 485–506

Starmer CF, Grant AO, Strauss HC (1984) Mechanisms of use-dependent block of sodium channels in excitable membranes by local anesthetics. Biophys J **46:** 15–27

Triggle DJ, Swamy VC (1983) Calcium antagonists: some chemical-pharmacologic aspects. Circ Res **52** (suppl I): 17–28

Weld FM, Bigger JT (1976) The effect of lidocaine on diastolic transmembrane currents determining pacemaker depolarization in cardiac Purkinje fibers. Circ Res **38:** 203–208

Williams LT, Tremble P (1982) Binding of calcium antagonist, [^{3}H]nitrendipine, to high affinity sites in bovine aortic smooth muscle and canine cardiac membranes. J Clin Invest **70:** 209–212

Yatani A, Brown AM, Akaike N (1984) Effect of extracellular pH on sodium current in isolated single rat ventricular cells. J Membr Biol **78:** 163–168.

INDEX TERMS: Cultured cardiac myocytes • Voltage clamp • Sodium current • Nitrendipine

Interaction between a Normoxic and a Hypoxic Region of Guinea Pig and Ferret Papillary Muscles

Heinz Hofmann

From the Department of Physiology, University of Berne, Berne, Switzerland

SUMMARY. Papillary muscles were mounted in a three-compartment bath. The tip of the muscle was exposed to hypoxic and glucose-free solution. The other parts of the preparation were superfused with Tyrode's solution, building a free-flow border between hypoxic and normoxic superfusates. The normoxic part of the bath was subdivided by a rubber membrane so that current pulses could be applied between segments of the preparation. Signs of electrotonic interaction between normoxic and hypoxic parts were observed a few minutes after the onset of hypoxia. Transmembrane action potentials in the normoxic part retained their plateau, but progressively shortened. Those in the hypoxic tip showed an early phase of rapid repolarization followed by a plateau phase near the resting potential. Terminal repolarization in the two parts coincided for many minutes. After 35 minutes, fast propagated activity ceased in the tip and was replaced first by conducted slow responses, then by decremental conduction. At 50 minutes, cells near the borderline had resting potentials of either -76 ± 7 mV (SD, $n = 9$) in normoxic tissue or -16 ± 3 mV (SD, $n = 9$) in hypoxic tissue. Concurrently, subthreshold potentials no longer appeared to spread into the tip. Unipolar electrograms remained diphasic over the normoxic part but lost their negative deflection near the borderline, implying the absence of axial current flow into the hypoxic part. Furthermore, electrotonic potentials generated by current flow across the rubber membrane did not spread beyond a line of demarcation. Reduced nicotinamide adenine dinucleotide fluorescence increased in the hypoxic part, and appeared to correlate with the development of electrical decoupling. It is concluded that decoupling progresses gradually, but eventually results in a sharp borderline between regions of normoxic and hypoxic superfusion. **(*Circ Res 56: 876–883, 1985*)**

TRANSFORMATIONS in the border zone between surviving and perishing cardiac cells often are studied with whole hearts after ligation of a coronary artery (for references, see Janse and Kléber, 1981). The use of isolated muscles offers a less complicated geometrical arrangement to study propagated activity and passive electrical interaction during such a course of demarcation. However, this does not imply that a truly ischemic state exists within such an in vitro preparation as when metabolites, potassium ions and carbon dioxide accumulate. Nevertheless, some of the mechanisms resulting in progressive decoupling are generally thought to be common to both of these interventions with metabolism (Fozzard, 1975). Superfusion of isolated cat papillary muscles with hypoxic solutions reversibly shortens the monophasic action potential (Trautwein et al., 1954). In addition, hypoxia decreases electrical coupling between cardiac cells (Bredikis et al., 1976), contributing to the eventual failure of impulse conduction (Wojtczak, 1979). The present work deals with the time course of decoupling between a normoxic and a hypoxic region and provides evidence for the eventual isolation of surviving cells from their perishing neighbors.

Methods

Hearts were excised from ferrets or guinea pigs after halothane or ether anesthesia. Papillary muscles from the right ventricle were mounted in a double chamber, as shown in Figure 1. Their diameters ranged from 0.6–1.1 mm. The two compartments were separated by a 0.64-mm thick rubber membrane with a punched hole of a diameter that gently compressed the muscle. The preparations were stimulated by 20-μsec pulses at 3/sec through bipolar electrodes touching the base of the papillary muscle (upper chamber in Fig. 1). Activity propagated toward the tip (the end in which the chordae tendineae are inserted). Subthreshold square pulses of constant current, usually 30 msec in duration, were applied between the two compartments. The rubber membrane forced part of the current to enter and leave the inside of the fibers. Pulses of direct current depolarized the basal part and hyperpolarized the tip. All the electrical recordings were taken from the part of the bundle within the lower chamber. Membrane potentials were recorded between a bath ground (not shown in Fig. 1) and either one or two intracellular microelectrodes. Length constants were obtained from semi-logarithmic plots of the spatial decay of electrotonic potentials away from the rubber membrane (Weidmann, 1952; Kamiyama and Matsuda, 1966).

Tyrode's solution had the following composition (mM: NaCl, 137; KCl, 5.4; $NaHCO_3$, 11.9; $CaCl_2$, 1.8; $MgCl_2$, 0.5; NaH_2PO_4, 0.4; glucose, 20. It was gassed with 95% O_2 and 5% CO_2 (pH 7.2) and warmed to 35°C.

The preparations were kept in normoxic solution for at least 1 hour before action potentials were recorded at several points along the papillary muscle in the lower half-chamber. Only those preparations demonstrating a uniform action potential duration were employed for fur-

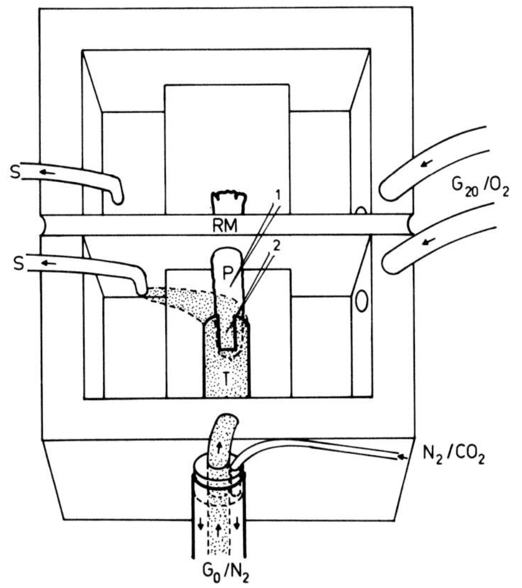

FIGURE 1. *Plastic double-chamber held in a rigid frame. The two parts were pressed against a rubber membrane (RM) by two screws, and the assembly was mounted into the cover of a thermostatically controlled bath. The tip of the papillary muscle was pulled from the upper part into the lower part of the chamber through a hole punched into the rubber membrane. The muscle within the lower chamber could be superfused partly by Tyrode's solution with a high glucose concentration (G_{20}/O_2; section P) and partly by hypoxic and glucose-free solution through tube T (G_0/N_2; stippled region). Back diffusion of atmospheric O_2 into hypoxic solution was prevented largely by the counterflow of N_2 through an outer polyethylene tube. Constant levels of the fluids were maintained by suction (S). Electrical connections are described in the text.*

ther experimentation. Papillary muscles from 17 guinea pigs and 21 ferrets were used.

After control data had been collected, the region of the muscle closest to the tendon (Fig. 1, stippled area) was superfused by glucose-free Tyrode's solution aerated with 95% N_2 and 5% CO_2. This gas mixture contained less than 0.1% O_2 as determined by gas chromatography (Carba Ltd. Berne). The Po_2 of the superfusate was less than 10 mm Hg as measured by polarography (Beckmann model 0260 oxygen analyzer). The flow rates of the hypoxic and normoxic solutions were 0.5 ml/min and 4 ml/min, respectively. A sharp division between the freely flowing solutions was visualized when India ink was added to the hypoxic solution (Fig. 1, dashed lines). The position of this limit varied by no more than ±50 μm during an experiment.

In eight additional experiments, the process of demarcation was followed by observing changes of the epifluorescence of reduced nicotinamide adenine dinucleotide (NADH) (Chapman, 1972). Incident light was delivered by a high-pressure Hg vapor light source (Leitz HBO, 200 W) with two quartz lenses and a transmission filter for UV light (UG 1). The surface of the muscle was observed through a Kodak 2C Wratten filter and a Wild M400 stereomicroscope at 50-fold magnification. Quantification of NADH fluorescence in superfused bundles with a gradient of Po_2 from the surface to the core would be of little additional value.

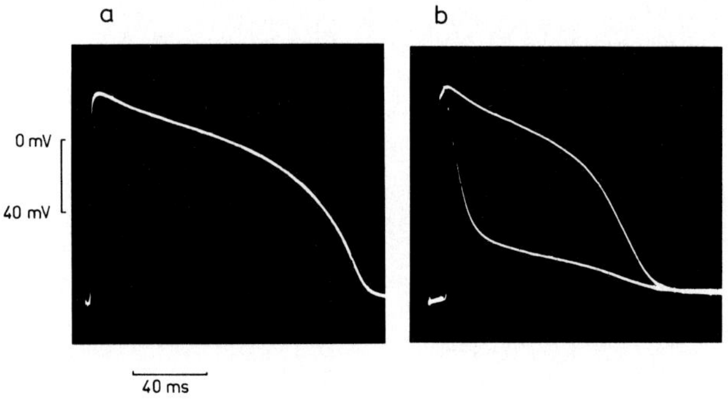

FIGURE 2. *Action potentials of a guinea pig papillary muscle. Panel 2a: record with the entire muscle in normoxic solution. Panel 2b: simultaneous records of a section of the muscle in the lower chamber obtained 10 minutes after the onset of hypoxic superfusion. The action potential with the lower plateau was from the hypoxic region (electrode 2 from stippled area in Fig. 1), whereas that with the higher plateau was recorded from the normoxic part (electrode 1 in Fig. 1).*

Results

Electrotonic Interaction between Normoxic and Hypoxic Fibers

Action potentials of guinea pig papillary muscles typically show a distinct plateau (Fig. 2). This plateau is lost and the action potentials become short and triangular when a papillary muscle is deprived of O_2 (Trautwein et al., 1954). Concomitantly, surface membrane resistance decreases (Vleugels et al., 1980). These changes also were observed in the present series of experiments after 10 minutes of global hypoxia (not illustrated). When only part of the preparation in the lower half-chamber was superfused by hypoxic solution, there were the expected signs of electrotonic coupling. Figure 2b shows simultaneous records taken after 10 minutes of localized hypoxia. The microelectrodes were positioned about 0.5 mm on both sides of the borderline, as indicated in Figure 1. It is noteworthy that, whereas the action potentials in both regions had the same duration, the levels of the plateau differed greatly. The normoxic action potential, 160 msec in duration before introduction of hypoxia (Fig. 2a), shortened to 130 msec but retained its general shape (Fig. 2b). The hypoxic action potential, after a phase of rapid repolarization, showed a prolonged but depressed plateau preceding final repolarization (Fig. 2b). Control resting potentials averaged −76 ± 7 mV (SD, $n = 9$). In the hypoxic region, only minor depolarization occurred over the first 25 minutes of hypoxia (<8 mV). However, the resting membrane potential consistently became more negative (by as much as 6 mV) immediately preceding the loss of propagated activity. Although there is no clear explanation, this may be related to the transitory improvement of excitability noted previously under conditions of ischemia (Scherlag et al., 1974; Kléber et al., 1978). When the resting potential in the hypoxic region had dropped to −60 mV, action potentials no longer exhibited a rapid phase of depolarization. Invading action potentials produced

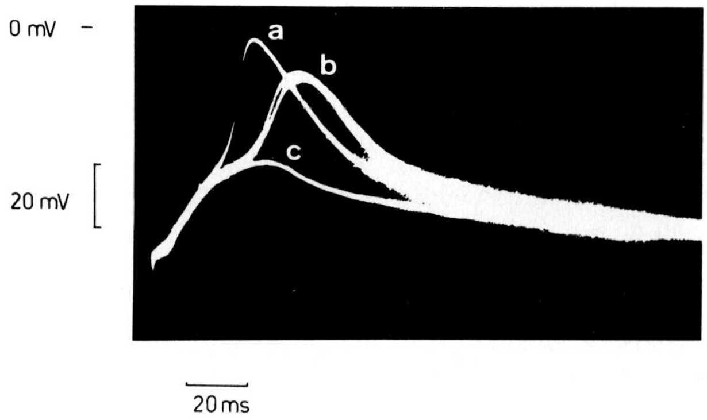

FIGURE 3. *Variability of responses from a ferret papillary muscle, 50 minutes after the onset of hypoxia. At a low rate of stimulation, 0.6/sec, there were signs of regenerative activity (trace a). At a slightly higher rate of stimulation, 0.7/sec, the records alternatively followed traces b and c. At 0.8/sec, only trace c could be recorded. The recording site was within the hypoxic region, 272 μm from the borderline; the resting potential was −74 mV.*

"slow responses" of the kind described by Wit et al. (1972), with a threshold near −35 mV. Their amplitudes depended critically upon stimulation frequency (Fig. 3; see also Wojtczak, 1979). The subsequent events are illustrated in Figure 4. At 35 minutes, propagated activity ceased within the hypoxic region. Only small amplitude potentials exhibiting spatial decrement ("electrotonic humps") remained. As long as decremental conduction persisted, reoxygenation resulted in recovery of excitability and action potentials of a normal configuration. This does not mean that full recovery from the hypoxic state could be achieved. Other parameters were not measured that indicate recovery of normal function, notably contractile strength.

A Biochemical Correlate of Hypoxia

The fluorescence of reduced nicotinamide adenine dinucleotide (NADH) is known to be a sensitive indicator of mitochondrial oxygen concentration. NADH has an absorption maximum at 340 nm and an emission peak at 463 nm (Jöbsis, 1964). The equilibrium between NAD^+ and NADH is shifted in favor of the fluorescent NADH when the oxygen concentration falls from 10^{-6} to 10^{-8} mol/liter (Chance, 1976). With a solubility coefficient of 0.02 ml O_2/ml of solution at 37°C (Mahler, 1978), this range corresponds to O_2 tensions of 1.0–0.01 mm Hg. Prolonged hypoxia and tissue degradation activate a glucohydrolase which irreversibly breaks down NAD^+ into adenine nucleotide (Klein et al., 1981). Thus, it seemed pertinent to explore the temporal correlation between the electrical events and NADH fluorescence under the conditions of the experiments.

Uniform autofluorescence was observed when both parts of the bundles were in well-oxygenated solution. This was attributed mainly to NADH. As judged by eye, the intensity of this fluorescence did not change markedly in the part of the bundle remaining well oxygenated. However, increasing brightness of fluorescence developed in the hypoxic region, starting at 5 minutes and peaking at approximately 18 minutes after withdrawal of O_2 and glucose (Fig. 5). The maximum fluorescence along the muscle did not coincide with the limit demarcated by India ink, but instead was clearly located within the hypoxic region, approximately 300 μm from the borderline. At the end of 2 hours, the hypoxic part was electrically unresponsive and the light intensity from the area of peak fluorescence now was distinctly less than control. The demarca-

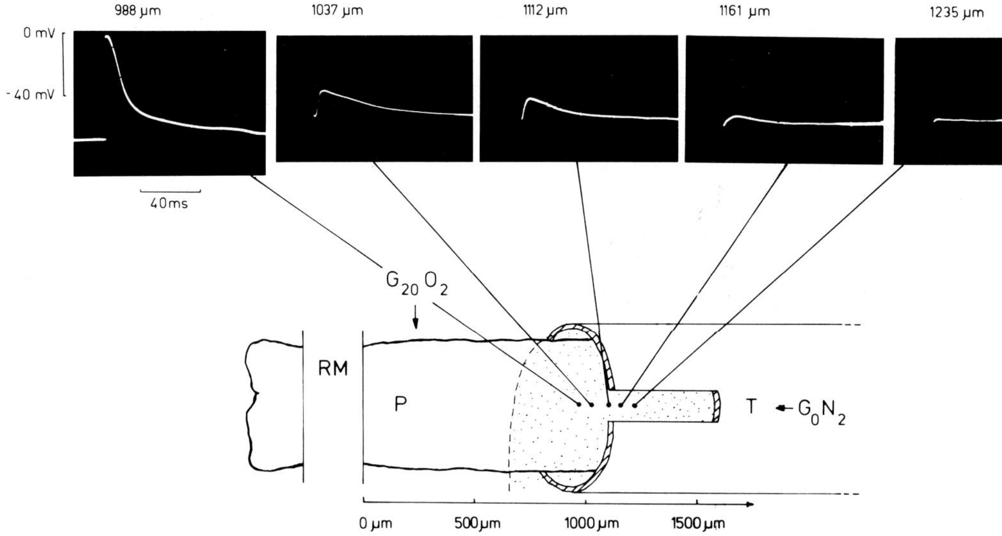

FIGURE 4. *Decremental conduction through the hypoxic region of a guinea pig papillary muscle (P), 35 minutes after the onset of hypoxia. Distances from the rubber membrane (RM) are indicated above each of the five records. The borderline between normoxic ($G_{20}O_2$) and hypoxic (G_0N_2) solution was 660 μm from the rubber membrane. The peak of the deflection recorded at 988 μm fell short of zero mV. With increasing distance into the hypoxic region, there was a graded response of decreasing amplitude. T denotes the polyethylene tube.*

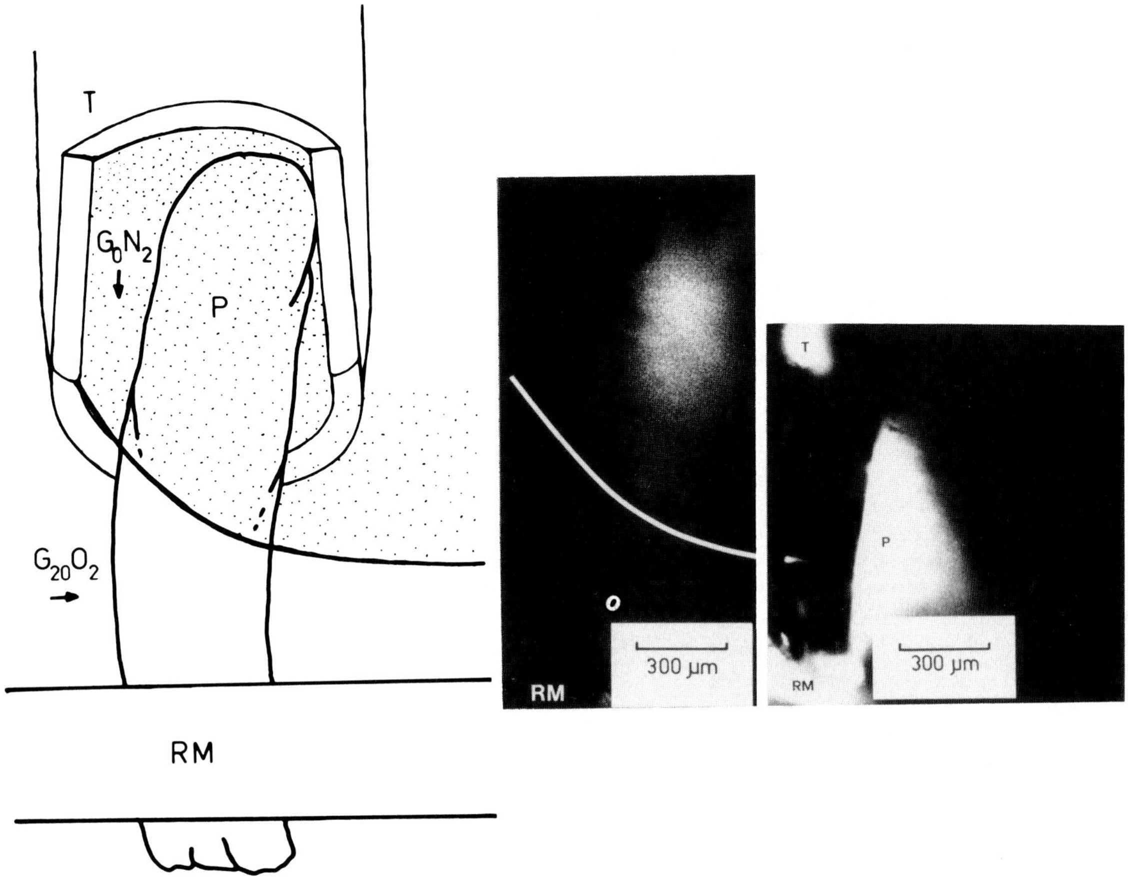

FIGURE 5. *Changes of autofluorescence. The drawing on the left shows the experimental arrangement with a ferret papillary muscle (P) inserted into a hole in a rubber membrane (RM) and loosely held by a polyethylene tube (T). The borderline between normoxic and hypoxic tissue is indicated. The photograph in the middle shows strong autofluorescence in the hypoxic part at 18 minutes. The fluorescence maximum was several hundred microns away from the borderline (white line) between normoxic and hypoxic solution. At the end of 2 hours (right photograph), there was no detectable fluorescence remaining in the hypoxic part, but autofluorescence of the normoxic part could be visualized by increasing the exposure time from 3 to 12 minutes. There was a sharp borderline of fluorescence between surviving and perishing tissue.*

tion was extremely sharp (transition zone <100 μm) and coincided with the region marked by India ink (see Fig. 5).

The State of Electrical Demarcation

Complete demarcation as judged by several criteria was reached between 50 and 90 minutes. Resting potentials lacked intermediate values between −76 ± 7 mV in the normoxic and 16 ± 3 mV (mean ± SD) in the hypoxic region. Cessation of all signs of electrotonic coupling within the hypoxic region was accompanied by reprolongation of action potentials in the normoxic region (Fig. 6).

Unipolar electrograms recorded between an indifferent electrode in the bath and an extracellular roving microelectrode touching the surface of the preparation allowed qualitative assessment of local circuit currents (for references, see Spach et al., 1971). Biphasic potentials would be expected as long as longitudinal current is arriving at and then departing from the microelectrode. Figure 7 indicates that indeed this was observed over the normoxic part of the muscle. However, only the positive deflection persisted, whereas the negative deflection was lost in the border region between hypoxic and normoxic muscle.

Figure 8 provides further evidence that high-resistance junctional membranes form at the borderline between normoxic and hypoxic tissue. The amplitude of intracellular voltage changes along the preparation was measured by applying subthreshold pulses of constant current across the rubber membrane. As expected, the spatial decay in normal Tyrode's solution could be fitted by an exponential, the average space constant (λ) being 780 ± 70 μm (n = 11) in ferret papillary muscle. With complete hypoxic demarcation, the voltage amplitude within the normoxic region near the borderline approached a constant value, indicating that little or no current passed from the normoxic region into the hypoxic section.

It should be mentioned that the same value of λ (0.67 mm) was used to draw both curves of Figure 8. An exponential equation nicely fitted the data (unfilled circles), while the line fitted to the filled circles was drawn on the assumption (Jack et al.,

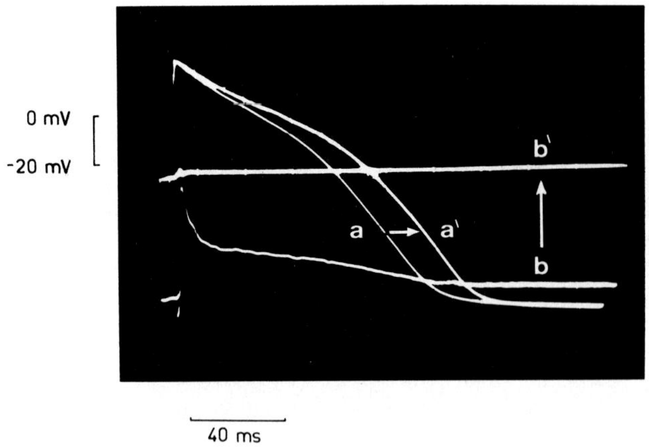

FIGURE 6. *Records from both sides of the demarcation zone in a guinea pig papillary muscle. Traces a and a': normoxic region, 226 μm from the borderline; b and b': hypoxic region 196 μm from the other side of the borderline. At 45 minutes, the normoxic action potential duration was relatively short (trace a) due to the adjacent hypoxic region. After 80 minutes, the normoxic action potential prolonged (a to a') and the resting potential in the hypoxic tip depolarized (b to b'). Prolongation from a to a' typically occurred during the loss of electrotonic interaction between the two regions.*

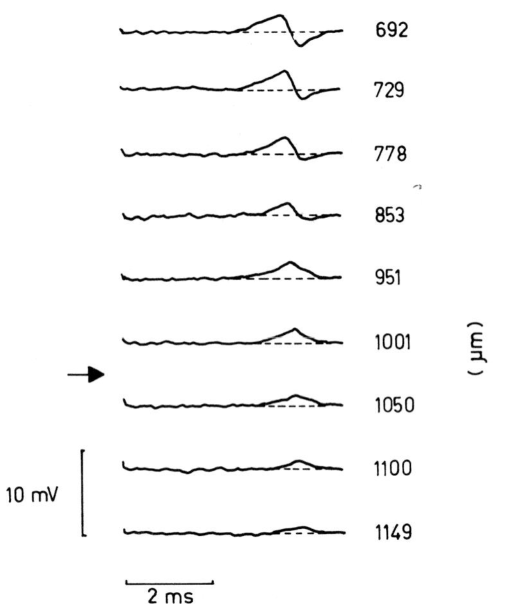

FIGURE 7. *Unipolar electrograms recorded between an indifferent bath electrode and the tip of a microelectrode touching the surface of a ferret papillary muscle, 80 minutes after the onset of hypoxia. Biphasic deflections were recorded over the normoxic part of the preparation, while the negative-going component was lost as the site of demarcation (arrow) was approached. Distances beyond the rubber membrane are indicated to the right of each record.*

1975; Eq. 4.10) that an infinite resistance terminated the cable at a distance of 0.53 mm (or 0.79 λ). By definition, λ is $\sqrt{r_m/r_i}$, where r_m is membrane resistance times unit length and r_i is internal longitudinal resistance per unit length. Since λ remained unchanged, it may be assumed that neither the membrane resistance nor the junctional resistance changed within the *normoxic* part as a result of demarcation.

Figure 9 shows the time course of electrotonic potentials at a distance of 0.22 mm (or 0.33 λ) from the rubber membrane (same experiment as in Fig. 8). For the case of an "infinite" cable immersed entirely in normoxic solution, Equation 3.24 by Jack et al. (1975) was used to fit the experimental time course (lower left). When demarcation was complete at a distance of 0.53 mm from the rubber membrane, the voltage-time course was fitted by Equation 4.12 of Jack et al. (lower right). It is noteworthy that the same time constant of the surface membrane (τ_m = 5.5 msec) provided a satisfactory fit in both instances. By definition, τ_m is R_m times C_m, where R_m

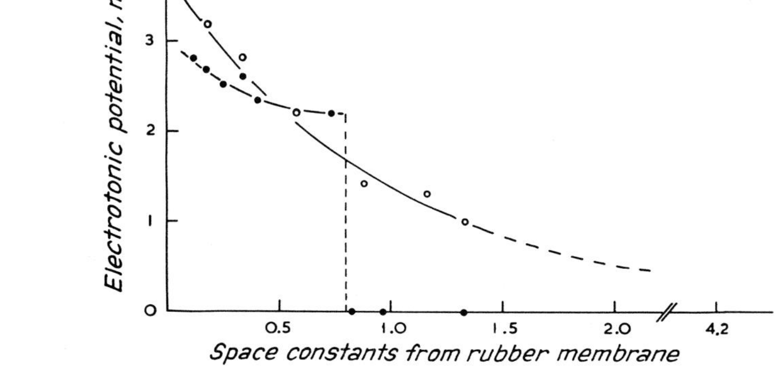

FIGURE 8. *Changes in spatial decay of electrotonic potentials during hypoxic demarcation in a ferret papillary muscle. Electrotonic potential amplitudes were recorded at various distances from the rubber membrane (RM) before the onset of hypoxia (unfilled circles) and 90 minutes after the onset of hypoxia (filled circles). The control values during normoxia were fitted by an exponential decay having a space constant (λ) of 0.67 mm. After 90 minutes of hypoxia, the amplitude of the electrotonic potentials reached an almost constant value as the line of demarcation was approached (here at a distance of 0.53 mm or 0.79 λ). This is typical of a cable sealed by a very high resistance. The strength of the hyperpolarizing current was reduced from 2.3 μA to 1.1 μA during hypoxic superfusion in order to remain within the linear region of the current-voltage relationship. Note that the preparation extended for 2.8 mm beyond the rubber membrane.*

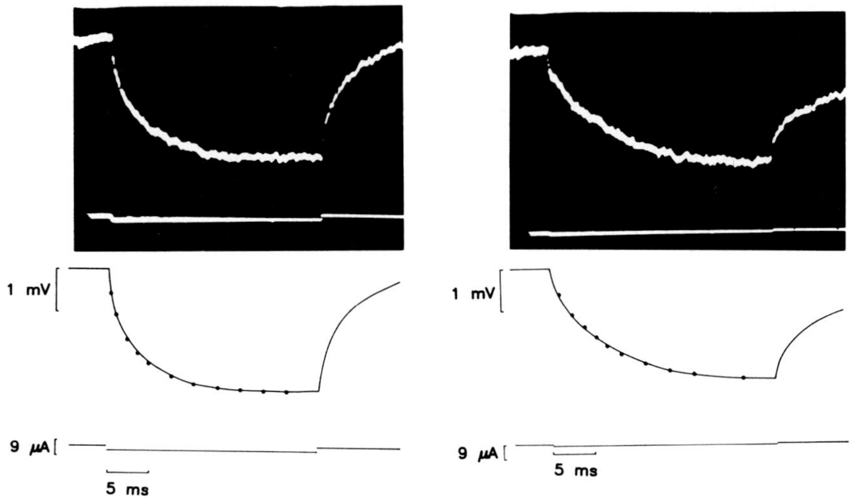

FIGURE 9. *Upper panel: time course of electrotonic potentials before the onset of hypoxia (left) and 90 minutes after the onset of hypoxia (right). Recordings were obtained 0.22 mm (or 0.33 λ) from the rubber membrane. Lower panel: tracings of experimental curves compared with calculated points assuming a cable of infinite length (left) or a cable terminated by a high resistance 0.53 mm (or 0.79 λ) from the rubber membrane (right). Strength of polarizing currents 2.3 and 1.1 μA, respectively. Same experiment as shown in Figure 8.*

is surface membrane resistance times cm^2 and C_m is surface membrane capacity per cm^2. An unchanged τ_m of the *normoxic* surface membrane would be expected if neither membrane resistance nor membrane capacitance of the surviving part of the bundle undergo changes as a result of demarcation.

Discussion

An in vitro model is presented which demonstrates the various stages of demarcation between a hypoxic and a normoxic region of a papillary muscle.

The Early Stages: Mutual Interactions

During the early stages of hypoxic injury, triangular action potentials within the hypoxic region prolonged and elevated, while action potentials in the adjacent normoxic region shortened (Fig. 2). This is consistent with the idea that neighboring parts of the cellular surface membranes interact if different time courses exist for their respective action potentials. However, a necessary condition for current to flow between regions of different membrane potentials is the presence of low-resistance junctional pathways. The kind of interactions demonstrated here by artificially creating different surface membrane properties are known to exist normally in certain regions of the heart. One such example concerns the atrioventricular (AV) node (Hoffman et al., 1958). The gradual change of its properties can be accounted for largely by electrotonic interaction between the typically nodal cells and both atrial and His bundle tissue (Kokubun et al., 1980). Another example of natural electrotonic interaction is the shortening of the terminal Purkinje fiber action potentials as the sites of contact with ventricular muscle are approached (Meyerburg et al., 1970). When freed from ventricular fibers (which have a much shorter action potential), the action potentials of terminal Purkinje fibers lengthen (Mendez et al., 1969). Analogously, when the central part of the AV node is freed from its connections with atrial and His bundle tissue, these cells become spontaneously active (Cranefield, 1983). Essential to all of these interactions between cells with different membrane properties is the presence of relatively low junctional resistances linked with relatively high surface membrane resistances. Appreciable electrotonic interactions result if surface membranes with different properties are separated by a distance on the order of one space constant.

The Metabolic State: Longitudinal and Radial Transitions

The gradual nature of decoupling also was supported by the time course and the longitudinal distribution of NADH fluorescence (Fig. 5). While decoupling proceeded, the region demonstrating adequate metabolism extended approximately 300 μm (~3 cell lengths) into the part of the bundle superfused by hypoxic solution. This agrees well with an observation reported for rabbit heart under conditions of local ischemia. Simson et al. (1979) ligated a branch of a coronary artery and demonstrated metabolically viable tissue for distances of 250–350 μm beyond the region irrigated by an intact microcirculation. These findings suggest that highly permeable junctional membranes allow cell-to-cell diffusion of metabolites into compromised tissue ["metabolic collaboration" (Gilula et al., 1972)].

In the radial direction, a gradient of O_2 tension is expected to exist between the bulk solution, surface fibers (from which electrical records were obtained), and fibers deeper within the bundle (for discussion of the general problem, see Tsacopoulos et al., 1981). Decoupling may well exist within the bundle even when surface regions remain coupled. Baumgarten et al. (1981) described heterogeneity of surface cell parameters in guinea pig papillary muscles when bulk Po_2 was maintained at 40 mm Hg. There was no evidence for such heterogeneity in the present series of experiments but this may have been due to the special precautions undertaken to keep the Po_2 low in the bulk solution (<10 mm Hg).

The Appearance of Decremental Conduction

One of the consequences of hypoxia is a drop in resting potential. The invading action potentials may still propagate in an all-or-nothing manner if sufficient inward current is provided by the "slow" and nonspecific Ca^{++}-Na^{+} channel (supposedly illustrated by Fig. 3a). Alternatively, they may conduct with decrement (Fig. 3c) or as electrotonic humps (Fig. 4). The conditions for an action potential to propagate safely along a *cable* are difficult to define precisely. Decremental conduction is expected when the inward membrane current available upon depolarization falls below a critical value. However, this critical value depends upon the entire "instantaneous" current-voltage relation, the nature and extent of cellular interactions, as well as of the kinetic properties of all membrane channels involved (see Noble, 1966).

Decremental conduction occurs whenever membrane resting potential and, hence, inward current decrease. For instance, premature atrial impulses are known to propagate decrementally when they arise in a region of short membrane action potential and invade a normal region at a time when recovery within the latter is not complete (Allessie et al., 1976). The phenomenon also is observed in canine Purkinje fibers when fast inward current is largely suppressed by ion-free sucrose solution (Jalife and Moe, 1981) and when ventricular trabeculae are partially depolarized by KCl (Rozanski et al., 1984).

Final Demarcation

At the end of 50–90 minutes of hypoxia, a sharp boundary was established between the normoxic and hypoxic muscle surfaces. This conclusion was supported (1) by the block of mutual electrotonic interaction at rest and during activity, (2) by the step-like fall in resting potential, (3) by the evolution of unipolar electrograms near the borderline, (4) by the alterations in the spatial decay of electrotonic potentials that indicated a "sealed end" for the "cable" in normoxic solution, and (5) by two distinct metabolic states suggested by the sharp boundary of autofluorescence. It seems reasonable to assume that the progressive establishment of the boundary during decoupling results from decreased cell-to-cell conductance (Wojtczak, 1979) which, in turn, might be consequent to cytoplasmic calcium accumulation (De Mello, 1975, 1979). A partial effect of low intracellular pH on cell coupling appears likely, but probably is of minor quantitative importance (Reber and Weingart, 1982). Judging by all criteria used in the present study, the transition between "surviving" and "perishing" tissue is gradual during the uncoupling process, but extremely sharp when demarcation is complete.

The possible existence of a "border zone" of intermediate injury during regional ischemia has spurred considerable controversy. Recent work has led to the conclusion that the boundary of an ischemic region may well correspond to the boundary of a single cell, not excluding the survival of islets of cells with sharp boundaries within perishing tissue [NADH fluorescence (Harken et al., 1978; Hearse et al., 1981); histological techniques (Factor et al., 1978; Kléber et al., 1978)]. The present results contribute strong evidence in favor of a sharp boundary when demarcation is complete, and appear to exclude the existence of surviving islands at the bundle's surface. They also show that surviving tissue maintains its typical values for intercellular resistance and membrane time constant, in spite of its immediate proximity to perishing tissue.

I wish to thank Dr. S. Weidmann for advice and guidance in carrying out the experiments, and Drs. M.L. Pressler and A.G. Kléber for reading the manuscript.

Address for reprints: Dr. Heinz Hofmann, Department of Ophthalmology, University of Zurich, CH-8091 Zürich, Switzerland.

Received September 1, 1982; received in revised form May 1, 1984; accepted for publication March 6, 1985.

References

Allessie MA, Bonke FIM, Schopman FJG (1976) Circus movement in rabbit atrial muscle as a mechanism of tachycardia. II. The role of nonuniform recovery of excitability in the occurrence of unidirectional block, as studied with multiple microelectrodes. Circ Res **39:** 168–177

Baumgarten CM, Cohen CJ, McDonald TF (1981) Heterogeneity of intracellular potassium activity and membrane potential in hypoxic guinea pig ventricle. Circ Res **49:** 1181–1189

Bredikis YY, Bukauskas FF, Mutskus KS (1976) Effect of hypoxia on cellular interaction in the myocardium. Translated from Byulleten' Éksperimental 'noi Biologii i Meditsiny **82:** 819–821

Chance B (1976) Pyridine nucleotide as an indicator of oxygen requirements for energy-linked functions of mitochondria. Circ Res **38** (suppl I): 31–38

Chapman JB (1972) Fluorometric studies of oxidative metabolism in isolated papillary muscle of the rabbit. J Gen Physiol **59:** 135–154

Cranefield PF (1983) Channels, cables, networks, and the cardiac impulse. Am J Physiol **245:** H901–H910

De Mello WC (1975) Effect of intracellular injection of calcium and strontium on cell communication in heart. J Physiol (Lond) **250:** 231–245

De Mello WC (1979) Effect of 2-4-dinitrophenol on intercellular communication in mammalian cardiac fibres. Pflugers Arch **380:** 267–276

Factor SM, Sonnenblick EH, Kirk ES (1978) The histologic border zone of acute myocardial infarction—islands or peninsulas? Am J Pathol **92:** 111–124

Fozzard HA (1975) Validity of myocardial infarction models. Circulation **51/52** (suppl III): 131–146

Gilula NB, Reeves OR, Steinbach A (1972) Metabolic coupling, ionic coupling and cell contacts. Nature **235:** 262–265

Harken AH, Barlow CH, Harden WR, Chance B (1978) Two and three dimensional display of myocardial ischemic "border zone" in dogs. Am J Cardiol **42:** 954–959

Hearse DJ, Yellon DM (1981) The "border zone" in evolving myocardial infarction: Controversy or confusion? Am J Cardiol **47:** 1321–1331

Hoffman BF, Paes de Carvalho A, De Mello WC (1958) Transmembrane potentials of single fibres of the atrio-ventricular node. Nature **181:** 66–67

Jack JJB, Noble D, Tsien RW (1975) Electric current flow in excitable cells. Oxford, Clarendon Press, pp 67–82

Jalife J, Moe GK (1981) Excitation, conduction, and reflection of

impulses in isolated bovine and canine cardiac Purkinje fibers. Circ Res **49:** 233–247
Janse MJ, Kléber AG (1981) Electrophysiological changes and ventricular arrhythmias in the early phase of regional myocardial ischemia. Circ Res **49:** 1069–1081
Jöbsis FF (1964) Basic processes in cellular respiration. *In* Handbook of Physiology, sec 3, vol I, edited by WO Fenn, H Rahn. Washington, D.C., American Physiological Society, pp 63–124
Kamiyama A, Matsuda K (1966) Electrophysiological properties of the canine ventricular fiber. Jpn J Physiol **16:** 407–420
Kléber AG, Janse MJ, van Capelle FJL, Durrer D (1978) Mechanism and time course of S-T and T-Q segment changes during acute regional myocardial ischemia in the pig heart determined by extracellular and intracellular recordings. Circ Res **42:** 603–613
Klein HH, Schaper J, Puschmann S, Nienaber C, Kreuzer H, Schaper W (1981) Loss of canine myocardial nicotinamide adenine dinucleotides determines the transition from reversible to irreversible ischemic damage of myocardial cells. Basic Res Cardiol **76:** 612–621
Kokubun S, Nishimura M, Noma A, Irisawa H (1980) The spontaneous action potential of rabbit atrioventricular node cells. Jpn J Physiol **30:** 529–540
Mahler M (1978) Diffusion and consumption of oxygen in the resting frog sartorius muscle. J Gen Physiol **71:** 533–557
Mendez C, Mueller WJ, Merideth J, Moe GK (1969) Interaction of transmembrane potentials in canine Purkinje fibers and at Purkinje fiber-muscle junctions. Circ Res **24:** 361–372
Meyerburg RJ, Stewart JW, Hoffman BF (1970) Electrophysiological properties of the canine peripheral A-V conduction system. Circ Res **26:** 361–378
Noble D (1966) Application of Hodgkin-Huxley equations to excitable tissue. Physiol Rev **46:** 1–50
Reber WR, Weingart R (1982) Ungulate cardiac Purkinje fibres: The influence of intracellular pH on the electrical cell-to-cell coupling. J Physiol (Lond) **328:** 87–104
Rozanski GJ, Jalife J, Moe GK (1984) Reflected reentry in nonhomogenous ventricular muscle as a mechanism of cardiac arrhythmias. Circulation **69:** 163–173
Scherlag BJ, El-Sherif N, Hope R, Lazzara R (1974) Characterization and localization of ventricular arrhythmias resulting from myocardial ischemia and infarction. Circ Res **35:** 372–383
Simson MB, Harden W, Barlow C, Harken AH (1979) Visualization of the distance between perfusion and anoxia along an ischemic border. Circulation **60:** 1151–1155
Spach MS, Barr RC, Serwer GS, Johnson EA, Kootsey JM (1971) Collision of excitation waves in the dog Purkinje system. Extracellular identification. Circ Res **29:** 499–511
Trautwein W, Gottstein U, Dudel J (1954) Der Aktionsstrom der Myokardfaser im Sauerstoffmangel. Pflugers Arch **260:** 40–56
Tsacopoulos M, Poitry S, Borsellino A (1981) Diffusion and consumption of oxygen in the superfused retina of the drone (*Apis mellifera*) in darkness. J Gen Physiol **77:** 601–628
Vleugels A, Vereecke J, Carmeliet E (1980) Ionic currents during hypoxia in voltage-clamped cat ventricular muscle. Circ Res **47:** 501–508
Weidmann S (1952) The electrical constants of Purkinje fibres. J Physiol (Lond) **118:** 348–360
Wit AL, Cranefield PF, Hoffman BF (1972) Slow conduction and reentry in the ventricular conducting system. II. Single and sustained circus movement in networks of canine and bovine Purkinje fibers. Circ Res **30:** 11–22
Wojtczak J (1979) Contractures and increase in internal longitudinal resistance of cow ventricular muscle induced by hypoxia. Circ Res **44:** 88–95

INDEX TERMS: Hypoxia • Electrotonic interaction • Demarcation • NADH fluorescence

Stimulation of Hypertrophy of Cultured Neonatal Rat Heart Cells through an α_1-Adrenergic Receptor and Induction of Beating through an α_1- and β_1-Adrenergic Receptor Interaction

Evidence for Independent Regulation of Growth and Beating

Paul Simpson

From the Cardiology Section, Veterans Administration Medical Center, and Cardiovascular Research Institute, Department of Medicine, University of California, San Francisco, California

SUMMARY. Catecholamines may be one of the molecular signals linking increased circulatory demand to myocardial hypertrophy, and I have found previously that norepinephrine stimulates hypertrophy of cultured neonatal rat heart muscle cells through an α_1-adrenergic receptor. Since catecholamine stimulation of contractility is believed to be under β-adrenergic control, I asked whether these cultured heart cells had dual pathways regulating growth and contractility through α- and β-adrenergic receptors, respectively. I examined the effect of adrenergic agents on hypertrophy and beating of myocytes in serum-free cultures. Hypertrophy was defined as an increase in myocyte surface area and in cell protein content, measured by a radioisotopic method, and chronotropic activity was examined visually. Norepinephrine and epinephrine were equipotent stimulants of hypertrophy and beating, increasing cell protein and area 1.5- to 2-fold, and the proportion of beating cells from 5% or less to 95%. Response maxima occurred 24–48 hours after exposure, and EC_{50} were 20–200 nM. Studies with other agonists (phenylephrine, methoxamine, clonidine, isoproterenol, dopamine) and antagonists (prazosin, terazosin, yohimbine, propranolol, betaxolol, ICI 118,551) indicated that hypertrophy was mediated through an α_1-adrenergic receptor, whereas the induction of beating required both α_1- and β_1-receptor activation. Hypertrophied cells with minimal beating were produced by α-stimulation, alone. In contrast, α- plus β-stimulation in the presence of cycloheximide to inhibit protein synthesis resulted in maximum beating but no hypertrophy. These findings imply that growth and beating can be regulated independently through separate cellular pathways. **(*Circ Res 56: 884–894, 1985*)**

EXPERIMENTS in vivo have raised the possibility that catecholamines may be one of the molecular signals linking increased circulatory demand to myocardial hypertrophy (Östman-Smith, 1981; Tarazi et al., 1982). In support of this hypothesis, I used neonatal rat heart cell cultures in which cell proliferation does not occur (Simpson and Savion, 1982) to show that norepinephrine (NE) stimulates myocyte (MC) hypertrophy, as quantified by MC volume, surface area, and protein content (Simpson et al., 1982). Recently, using these same methods and cultures maintained in serum-free medium, I found that NE-stimulated hypertrophy was mediated through an α_1-adrenergic receptor, as defined by experiments with NE, isoproterenol, and adrenergic antagonists (Simpson, 1983).

Since myocardial chronotropic and inotropic responses to adrenergic stimulation are believed to be primarily under the control of a β-receptor (Pollack, 1977; Scholz, 1980), the possibility was raised that there is a dual myocardial response to sympathetic activation: an increase in rate and contractility through a β-adrenergic receptor, and an increase in cell size through an α-adrenergic receptor. Alpha- and β-adrenergic receptors coexpressed on other types of cultured cells can be differentially regulated and can independently control separate metabolic pathways (Meier et al., 1983). Therefore, I asked whether stimulation of beating accompanied hypertrophy and whether these two processes were independently regulated through different receptors. I used serum-free cultures, which contain MCs with minimal growth and beating, and therefore are useful for studies of regulation (Simpson et al., 1982). Responses to both NE and epinephrine (EPI) were examined, since EPI had not been tested previously in this system. Hypertrophy was measured by a radioisotopic index of cell protein accumulation and by MC surface area, and chronotropic activity was observed visually.

The major findings are that an α_1-adrenergic receptor equipotently stimulated by NE and EPI controls hypertrophy, but that both α_1- and β_1-adrenergic activation are required for the development of beating. Furthermore, the growth response and the beating response can be dissociated, suggesting that they can be regulated independently.

Methods

Cell Culture

Single-cell cultures were prepared from hearts of day-old rats as described previously (Simpson and Savion, 1982; Simpson et al., 1982; Simpson, 1983). In summary, cells were obtained by brief, alternating cycles of room-temperature trypsinization and mechanical disaggregation. Cells were combined, washed, and preplated in the presence of 5% calf serum to reduce the number of contaminating nonmyocardial mesenchymal cells (NMCs). After 30 minutes, the still-suspended MCs were removed from the attached NMCs, counted (hemocytometer), and diluted to 260,000 viable (trypan blue-negative) cells/ml in culture medium with 5% serum. This cell suspension was distributed into 35-mm culture dishes (Falcon #3001; surface area, 800 mm^2) or 24-well culture trays (Falcon #3047; surface area, 200 mm^2/well), with a volume of 2 ml/dish or 1 ml/well. On culture day 1, after overnight attachment, the cultures were given 1 ml of serum-free medium containing transferrin and insulin (each 10 μg/ml). Medium was changed on day 4, and medium containing a radiolabeled amino acid was given on day 5 (see Experimental Protocol).

The standard culture medium was medium 199 (Hanks' salts) supplemented with 1.5 μM vitamin B_{12} and 50 U/ml penicillin. The medium until culture day 4 also contained 0.1 mM bromodeoxyuridine (BrdU) to prevent low-level NMC proliferation.

Cell yield was 3–5 million/heart, of which over 90% were viable. Plating efficiency was less in the 24-well trays than the 35-mm dishes, so that in both cases the total cell number on days 1–8 averaged 200 ± 40 (SD) per mm^2 surface area with 5–10% NMC (80 preparations).

Pure cultures of NMCs were obtained by scraping the cells in the preplates with a rubber spatula, allowing overnight reattachment, again scraping the cells, and combining and distributing them into culture vessels. The NMCs were maintained in medium with 5% serum without BrdU until the desired cell density was reached, then were switched to serum-free medium with transferrin and insulin for experiments. Differential trypsinization was used to remove the MCs from mixed cultures, leaving the NMCs attached in the dishes (Simpson et al., 1982).

All cultures were kept at 37°C in humidified air with sufficient CO_2 (about 1%) to maintain pH 7.3. Great care was taken to avoid alkaline medium, since catecholamines are unstable at high pH.

Experimental Protocol

The protocol has been described previously (Simpson et al., 1982; Simpson, 1983). In brief, 1 ml of fresh medium (without serum or BrdU, with transferrin and insulin) containing a radiolabeled amino acid (see Growth Measurements) was added to each dish or well on culture day 5. A few hours later, adrenergic agents or their diluent (control) were added in 20-μl aliquots, and cultures were taken subsequently for determination of protein, area, or beating, without an intervening change of medium.

Adrenergic agents were freshly prepared for each experiment as 10 mM stock solutions in 1 mM HCl and were serially diluted in medium 199 containing sufficient vitamin C to give a final concentration of 100 μM when added to the cultures. Under these conditions, NE concentration (radioenzymatic assay) through 48 hours remained at least 75% of that originally present (Simpson, 1983).

Growth Measurements

Cell number was determined by counting the cells using phase contrast microscopy, as described previously in detail (Simpson and Savion, 1982; Simpson et al., 1982).

Cell size was measured by protein content and surface area. Because cell numbers in these cultures are constant over time and are not changed by adrenergic agents, total cell protein per dish or well can be taken as an index of cell size (Simpson and Savion, 1982; Simpson et al., 1982; Simpson, 1983). Cell protein was measured in two ways. First, after rinsing, extraction, and dissolution as described below, protein was determined in quadruplicate by a modification of the method of Lowry et al. (1951), using crystalline bovine serum albumin as standard (Simpson et al., 1982).

Second, to increase sensitivity and reproductivity, a method employing asymptotic labeling with a radioactive amino acid was adapted from techniques described by others (Lee and Engelhardt, 1977; Ronning et al., 1979; Clark and Zak, 1981). The culture medium was brought to 0.1 μCi/ml (^{14}C) or 0.5 μCi/ml (^{3}H) with [U-^{14}C]phenylalanine, [ring-^{3}H]phenylalanine, or [U-^{14}C]tyrosine. Phenylalanine or tyrosine were used, since these amino acids are not metabolized by myocardial tissue (Morgan et al., 1971; McKee et al., 1978; Curfman et al., 1980). In two experiments, increasing medium phenylalanine from 303 μM to 1.303 mM with constant specific activity had no effect on the pattern of incorporation. Therefore, medium 199 which contained 303 μM phenylalanine and 255 μM tyrosine was used without modification. These concentrations are several-fold higher than those found in rat serum (Morgan et al., 1971) and should be sufficient to assure constant precursor specific activity during labeling in these sparse cultures [Rannels et al. (1982) and Results].

At intervals after the addition of isotope and adrenergic agents, cell protein, defined as material that was trichloroacetic acid (TCA)-insoluble and sodium dodecyl sulfate (SDS)-soluble, was taken for liquid scintillation counting. Labeling medium was removed, the attached cells were quickly rinsed with phosphate-buffered saline (PBS), treated with 10% TCA at 0°C for at least 1 hour, rinsed 3 times with TCA, and dissolved in 1 ml of 1% SDS at 37°C. The entire volume of SDS was quantitatively removed into glass vials and counted as a gel in a mixture of 8 ml of water and 10 ml of Aquasol II (New England Nuclear) or Fluorodyne (National Diagnostics) at an efficiency (internal standard) of 50–70% for ^{14}C and 20–30% for ^{3}H. Counting error was always less than 2% and usually less than 1%.

The PBS rinse and TCA extraction did not dislodge cells, as shown by cell counts before and after these procedures. In one experiment, it was found that neither the incubation medium nor the PBS rinse contained labeled protein. The incubation medium and PBS rinses were collected, adjusted to 10% TCA, and centrifuged (15,000 *g*, 0°C, 1 hour) in the presence of carrier protein; no TCA-precipitable counts were detected. TCA-soluble counts, presumed to represent primarily free intracellular amino acids, were just above background and were less than 5% of counts in TCA-insoluble material. As a measure of TCA extraction of soluble material, cells were loaded with ^{45}Ca. TCA removed over 98% of counts. Background was determined routinely on a dish or well containing dead cells, and was usually less than 30 counts/min. In most experiments, a group of 3–4 dishes or wells contained at least a mean of 1000 counts/min in the TCA-insoluble material, and the SD was less than 10% of the mean. By inhibiting incorporation of counts with cycloheximide, I obtained evidence that the TCA-insoluble, SDS-soluble material was protein (see Results). To estimate specific radioactivity, I measured the nmols of tyrosine in TCA-insoluble material (after hydrolysis in 6 N HCl) and in the culture medium on an amino acid analyzer.

MC surface area was determined as described previously (Simpson et al., 1982), except that planimetry of photomicrographs was not used. Instead, cell images collected with a video camera (Dage 650) fixed to the microscope (Zeiss IM 35) were projected on a monitor and traced with an LED cursor on a digitizing tablet (Hipad). Image analysis software (Bioquant II, R&M Biometrics) directed computation of MC area, calibrated against a stage micrometer and doubled to account for the surface in contact with the dish. All cells from randomly selected fields in two or three dishes were examined for each condition. Cell images were stored on ¾-inch videotape for later analysis, or cells were fixed with 2.5% glutaraldehyde, 0.1 M cacodylic acid (pH 7.4), and stored in PBS with 10% glycerol. Areas of videotaped living cells and of fixed cells were the same.

Beating Cells

As previously reported (Simpson et al., 1982), most MCs in serum-free cultures contract infrequently (1–4/min). In the present experiments, NE and EPI increased the proportion of beating cells, and this increase was quantified as follows. Dishes were removed from the incubator and immediately observed on a microscope stage maintained at 37°C. One hundred cells in each of five randomly selected fields were examined, and the number of MCs beating regularly (about 50–100/min) was recorded. This procedure was completed in less than 3 minutes, before a change in the medium pH indicator. Counting was repeated after several minutes, to give a total 10 fields (1000 cells) for each condition at each time point.

Materials

L-[U-^{14}C]phenylalanine (500 Ci/mol), L-[U-^{14}C]tyrosine (500 Ci/mol), and L-[2,3,4,5,6-^{3}H]phenylalanine (130 Ci/mol) were from Amersham. Medium 199 with Hanks' salts was made up by the UCSF Cell Culture Facility from Gibco powder. Hyclone calf serum was from Sterile Systems; porcine sodium insulin was from Lilly; and BrdU, human transferrin (#T2252), and cycloheximide were from Sigma. Sources of adrenergic agents were as follows: D-NE and D-EPI (Winthrop); prazosin (Pfizer); terazosin (Abbott); L-propranolol (Ayerst); clonidine (Boehringer Ingelheim); methoxamine (Burroughs); betaxolol (Synthe-Labo); ICI 118,551 (Imperial Chemical Industries); and L-NE, L-EPI, phenylephrine, dopamine, and catecholamine metabolites (Sigma). L-isomers were used except as specifically indicated.

Statistics

Group means were compared by analysis of variance and by Student-Neuman-Keuls test. Treated-to-control ratios, and percents of maximum effect were tested for deviation from unity and 100%, respectively, by computation of 95% and 99% confidence intervals (Zar, 1974).

Results

Stimulation of Hypertrophy through an α_1-Adrenergic Receptor

A representative time course experiment is shown in Figure 1. The total micrograms of cell protein measured by the Lowry technique did not change with time in control cells, but increased significantly to a plateau at about 2 days in NE-treated cells (Fig. 1, lower portion). TCA-insoluble counts increased progressively in both conditions to apparent asymptote at about 3 days after the addition of [^{14}C]-phenylalanine (Fig. 1, upper portion) or [^{14}C]tyrosine or [^{3}H]phenylalanine (not shown). Constant specific radioactivity of protein (counts/min per μg) suggested that equilibrium had been achieved, and this probability was supported by the specific radioactivity of tyrosine in the labeling medium and in the TCA-insoluble material at 3 days. For controls, there were 879 dpm/nmol tyrosine in the incubation medium and 919 dpm/nmol in TCA-insoluble material; for NE-treated cells, dpm/nmol were 931 in the medium and 1018 in protein. These data indicated approximately equal specific activities of tyrosine in the two compartments in both control and NE-

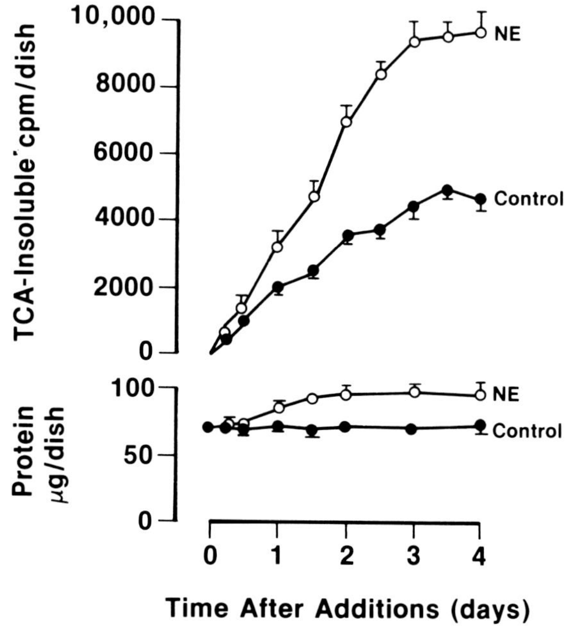

FIGURE 1. *Time course of accumulation of cell protein measured by the Lowry method in NE-treated and control cells and asymptotic labeling of TCA-insoluble material with a radioactive amino acid. Cells in serum-free medium were incubated on day 5 with [^{14}C]-phenylalanine (0.1 μCi/ml) and NE (2 μM) or diluent (control). Samples were taken at the indicated times for determination of counts in TCA-insoluble, SDS-soluble material (upper part of figure) and of total cell protein by the Lowry method (lower part). Each point is the mean ± SD of four dishes. NE was greater than control from 24 hours on (P < 0.01).*

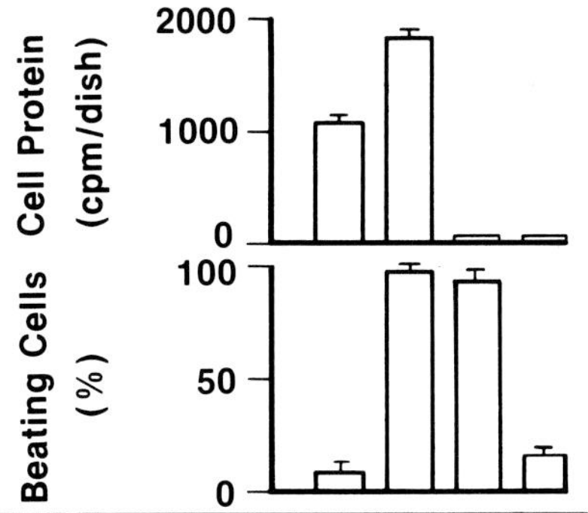

NE	2μM	0	+	+	+
Cycloheximide	5μM	0	0	+	+
Propranolol	2μM	0	0	0	+

FIGURE 2. *Induction of beating in the absence of growth. Cells were given [^{14}C]phenylalanine and diluents only (control), NE alone, NE plus cycloheximide, or NE plus cycloheximide plus propranolol. Beating cells and cell protein (TCA-insoluble counts/min) were measured after 1 day. Values are the mean ± SD for four dishes for protein and 10 microscopic fields of 100 cells each for beating cells. This is one of five similar experiments.*

treated cells. Incorporation of counts into TCA-insoluble, SDS-soluble material was reduced by about 95% in the presence of 5 μM (1.4 μg/ml) cycloheximide, an inhibitor of protein synthesis (Fig. 2), supporting the identification of this material as protein. Therefore, counts in TCA-insoluble material were used as an index of total cell protein.

Several experiments of the type shown in the upper portion of Figure 1 are summarized in Figure 3, with the TCA-insoluble counts plotted as the ratio of NE-treated to control. These data indicated that the stimulation of protein accumulation by NE occurred over the first 1–2 days after addition of NE, and reached a constant level of approximately 1.8 times control by 24–48 hours.

To determine whether the plateau phase of the NE effect shown in Figure 3 was due to time-dependent degradation of nutrients or NE, the cultures were used as a bioassay to test the growth-supporting ability of NE-treated and control media (Fig. 4). Media containing [^{14}C]phenylalanine and NE (2 μM) or diluent were collected at intervals up to 3 days after addition to cells, and frozen rapidly. One week later, these media were warmed and tested on a subsequent culture preparation. As shown in Figure 4, neither control nor NE media showed significant loss with age of the ability to support incorporation of [^{14}C]phenylalanine into protein, and the relative stimulation by NE did not change with medium age.

Using the radioisotopic technique of cellular hypertrophy, I determined dose-response relationships for the hypertrophic effect of NE, EPI, and other adrenergic agonists (Figs. 5 and 6). The L-isomers of

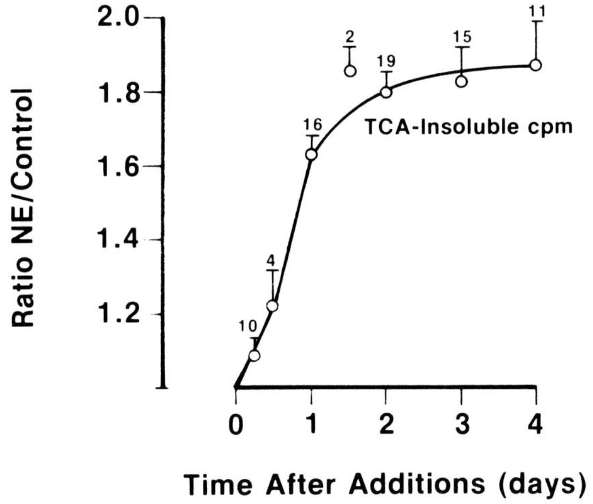

FIGURE 3. *Time-course of NE-stimulated increase in cell protein measured as TCA-insoluble counts/min. Results of several experiments of the type shown in Figure 1 are plotted as the NE:control ratio of TCA-insoluble counts/min. Cultures were incubated with [^{3}H]- or [^{14}C]phenylalanine or [^{14}C]tyrosine for 6 hours to 4 days. Each point is the mean ± SE of the indicated number of experiments, with a treated:control ratio obtained in each experiment from the means of at least four treated and four control dishes or wells. NE was greater than control at all time points (P < 0.05 at 6 and 12 hours, P < 0.01 from 24 hours).*

NE BIOASSAY

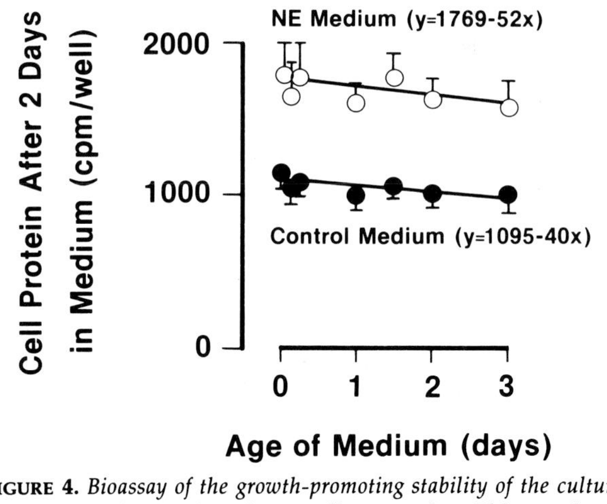

FIGURE 4. *Bioassay of the growth-promoting stability of the culture medium and of NE in the culture medium over time. This experiment involved two culture preparations. Cells in the first culture were incubated beginning on day 5 with [^{14}C]phenylalanine and NE (2 μM) or diluent (control). At the times indicated by Age of Medium on the Figure, NE-containing and control media were collected and pooled from 5–10 dishes or wells and rapidly frozen. These media were subsequently warmed and were added without modification to cells of the second culture preparation, and TCA-insoluble counts/min were determined after incubation for 2 days. Therefore, the total ages of the media at the time of protein measurement are those indicated on the horizontal axis, plus 2 days. Each point is the mean ± SD of 4–11 wells. The lines are drawn from the regression equations shown. There are no significant differences among the values for NE medium or for control medium. NE is different from control at all times (P < 0.01).*

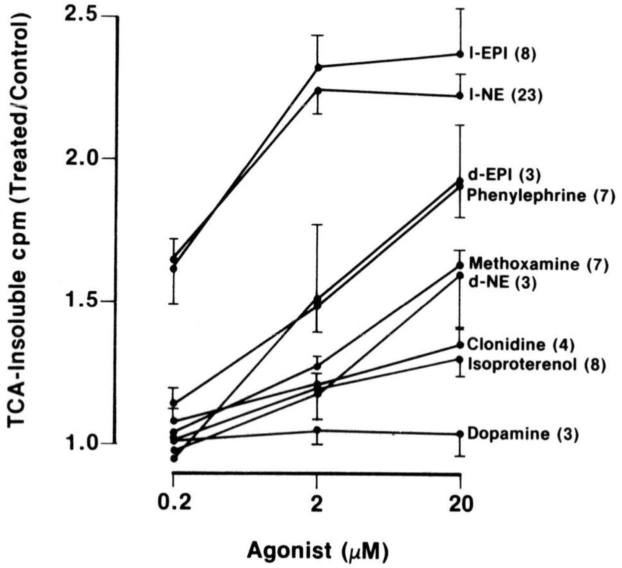

FIGURE 5. *Dose-response relationships for the hypertrophic effect of adrenergic agonists as measured by cell protein accumulation. Cultures were incubated with [^{14}C]phenylalanine or [^{14}C]tyrosine and adrenergic agonists (0.2–20 μM) or diluent (control). TCA-insoluble cpm were determined after 3 days. Each point is the mean ± SE for the number of experiments shown in parentheses. In each experiment, a treated-to-control ratio was calculated from the mean counts/min of at least four culture wells for control and for each concentration of agonist. At 0.2 μM, only phenylephrine ($P < 0.05$) and L-NE and L-EPI ($P < 0.01$) were different from control. At 2 μM, only D-EPI and dopamine were not different from control ($P < 0.05$), and at 20 μM only dopamine was the same as control.*

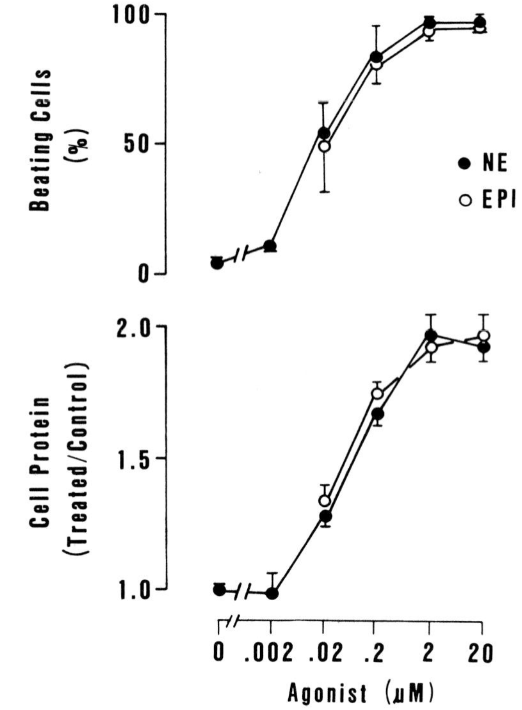

FIGURE 6. *NE and EPI have an equipotent trophic effect on growth and beating. Measurements were made 2–3 days after addition of 2 nM–20 μM NE (closed circles) or EPI (open circles). Values are mean ± SE of 6–8 experiments for beating cells (top panel) and 8–13 experiments for cell protein (bottom panel), except 2 nM was tested in two experiments only. There is significant stimulation of beating at 2 nM ($P < 0.01$) and of protein at 20 nM ($P < 0.01$).*

NE and EPI were equipotent, with maximum protein accumulation approximately twice control at 2 and 20 μM and an EC_{50} of 20–200 μM. The maximum effect produced by the other agonists (maximum concentration 20 μM) was considerably less, in the descending order D-EPI, phenylephrine, methoxamine, D-NE, clonidine, isoproterenol, dopamine (Fig. 5). The EC_{50} for these other agonists was at least 2 μM, or 10- to 100-fold higher than that for L-EPI and L-NE, assuming that the maximum response for these other agonists was reached at a concentration of 20 μM or greater (Fig. 5). The stimulation of protein content by 2 μM isoproterenol in 16 experiments was 1.15 ± 0.05 (SE) times control ($P < 0.01$), or 18% of the effect of 2 μM NE in the same experiments. For 2 μM clonidine, stimulation was 1.22 ± 0.04 (5) times control ($P < 0.01$), or 19% of the effect of NE in the same experiments.

Dopamine was the only agonist that was inactive up to 20 μM final concentration. Ascorbic acid has been reported to inhibit dopamine responses (Hadjiconstantinou and Neff, 1983). However, as shown in Table 1, removal of the extra 100 μM ascorbic acid used in the standard experimental protocol (leaving the 0.3 μM ascorbic acid present in unmodified medium 199) did not unmask a response to dopamine; it also did not reduce the response to EPI in this 1-day incubation.

Metabolites of NE and EPI (Graefe and Henseling, 1983) might accumulate during these long-term incubations, and their effect on growth was tested (Table 2). Of the compounds examined, only metanephrine and normetanephrine had a small effect on cell protein (1.16–1.20 times control, $P < 0.05$). DOMA, DOPEG, MOPEG, VMA, and vanillic acid were inactive at 20 μM. Adrenochrome was inactive

TABLE 1
Ascorbic Acid Does Not Modify the Hypertrophic Response to Dopamine Or EPI

Agent	Cell protein (counts/min per well) with ascorbic acid (100 μM)	
	Present	Absent
Control	1377 ± 31	1393 ± 77
Dopamine (2 μM)	1392 ± 162	1306 ± 69
EPI (2 μM)	2249 ± 28*	2319 ± 137*

Cells were labeled with [^{14}C]phenylalanine in the presence of the agents shown, and samples were taken after 1 day. An additional 100 μM ascorbic acid was or was not added to the incubation medium, as indicated. Values are mean ± SD for four wells.

* $P < 0.01$ vs. control; counts in the presence and absence of ascorbic acid are the same for each agent.

TABLE 2

The Effect of NE, EPI, and Their Metabolites and of Adrenergic Antagonists on Myocyte Protein Content

Agent	Cell protein (treated/control) with agent concentration of		
	0.2 μM	2 μM	20 μM
NE			2.01†
EPI			2.09†
Normetanephrine (NMN)			1.16*
Metanephrine (MN)			1.20*
3,4-Dihydroxymandelic acid (DOMA)			1.05
3,4-Dihydroxyphenylethylene glycol (DOPEG)			0.98
3-Methoxy-4-hydroxyphenyl-ethylene-glycol (MOPEG)			1.02
3-Methoxy-4-hydroxymandelic acid (VMA)			0.98
Vanillic acid			0.96
Adrenochrome	1.00	1.01	0.52†
Yohimbine	1.06	1.01	0.96
Terazosin	1.00	.98	0.96
Prazosin	.94	1.02	0.60†
Propranolol	1.04	.96	0.96
Betaxolol		1.01	1.07
ICI 118, 551		.99	0.97

TCA-insoluble, SDS-soluble material was taken for liquid scintillation counting after 3 days growth in the presence of [^{14}C]-phenylalanine and one of the agents listed, or diluent (control). Each ratio is the mean of at least two experiments; there were four treated and four control dishes or wells in each experiment. Toxicity of 20 μM adrenochrome and prazosin was indicated by dead cells and decreased cell numbers.

* $P < 0.05$, † $P < 0.01$ vs. control.

at 2 μM and toxic at 20 μM (Table 2), as indicated by dead cells and decreased cell numbers (not shown). Aged alkaline solutions of NE were inactive (not shown).

The effects of adrenergic antagonists on protein accumulation stimulated by NE or EPI are summarized in Figure 7, right panel. At 2 μM, there was 15% or less inhibition by propranolol (β_{1+2}), betaxolol (β_1), ICI 118,551 (β_2), or yohimbine (α_2), whereas terazosin (α_1) inhibited the protein response by a mean of 85%. Results with prazosin (α_1) were the same as with terazosin (not shown). Inhibition of the responses to phenylephrine and methoxamine was also obtained with prazosin and terazosin (not shown) but not with propranolol (Table 3). The antagonists alone had no effect on protein accumulation, except for 20 μM prazosin (Table 2), which had a toxic effect, as indicated by dead cells and decreased cell numbers (not shown).

In cultures not given BrdU, the protein response to NE was also inhibited by terazosin but not by propranolol (not shown). Neither NE nor EPI increased protein content of pure cultures of NMCs (Table 4). Protein contents were the same for control and for NE-treated NMCs left in the dishes of mixed cultures after removal of the MCs by differential trypsinization, and were less than 20% of total protein contents.

NE and EPI increased MC surface area, and this effect was inhibited by terazosin and by cycloheximide but not by propranolol (Table 5). Cycloheximide at 10 μM for 24 hours in the absence or presence of NE had no effect on cell numbers (not shown). The photomicrographs in Figure 8 illustrate hypertrophy stimulated by NE and NE plus propranolol.

The numbers of MCs and NMCs were stable over time and were not changed from control by any of

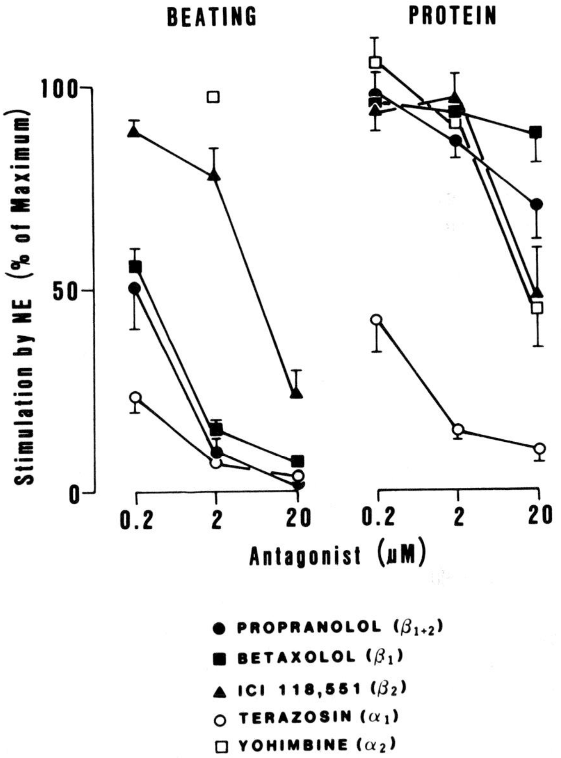

FIGURE 7. *Inhibition of NE-stimulated hypertrophy by an α_1-antagonist and of beating by an α_1- or β_1-antagonist. The stimulation of beating cells and of protein accumulation by NE plus antagonist, as a percentage of the maximum stimulation by NE alone in the same experiment, is plotted against the final concentration of antagonist. After 2–3 days in each experiment, at least 1000 cells were examined for beating, and 3–4 dishes or wells were taken for protein measurements. Each point is the mean ± SE. The number of separate experiments with each antagonist at 0.2, 2, and 20 μM for beating and protein, respectively, was as follows: propranolol, 4, 6, 6, and 8, 24, 8; betaxolol, 6, 8, 7, and 4, 6, 2; ICI 118,551, 6, 10, 10, and 7, 9, 7; terazosin, 3, 5, 4, and 9, 31, 18; yohimbine, 0, 2, 0, and 3, 3, 3. The maximum stimulation by NE was defined as the effect of 2 μM NE: an increase in the proportion of beating cells from 2.3 ± 0.6% to 94.4 ± 1.1% (25) and an increase in protein by 1.93 ± 0.05 (75) times control. Some of the experiments were done with 2 μM EPI; these did not differ from those with 2 μM NE and have been combined. For beating, ICI 118,551 was different from all other agents ($P < 0.01$) at all concentrations, as was yohimbine at 2 μM (the only concentration tested); terazosin showed greater inhibition than propranolol and betaxolol at 0.2 μM ($P < 0.01$), but was the same at 2 and 20 μM. For protein, terazosin was a more potent inhibitor than all other agents at all concentrations ($P < 0.01$).*

TABLE 3
Propranolol Inhibits Beating but Not Growth Stimulated by NE, EPI, Phenylephrine, and Methoxamine

Agent	Propranolol (2 μM)	Beating cells (%)	Cell protein (counts/min per dish)
Control	−	7.2 ± 2.4	2204 ± 298
NE (2 μM)	−	77.7 ± 10.4†	4220 ± 448†
NE (2 μM)	+	13.6 ± 2.3‡	3787 ± 389†
EPI (2 μM)	−	85.7 ± 7.2†	3950 ± 412†
EPI (2 μM)	+	13.6 ± 5.8‡	3687 ± 380†
Phenylephrine (20 μM)	−	29.1 ± 6.5†	3294 ± 464†
Phenylephrine (20 μM)	+	16.0 ± 6.3*‡	3265 ± 391†
Methoxamine (20 μM)	−	13.6 ± 5.2	3172 ± 341†
Methoxamine (20 μM)	+	9.4 ± 2.1	2970 ± 477*

Cells were incubated with [14C]phenylalanine and the agents listed, in the presence or absence of propranolol, as indicated. The proportion of beating cells and cell protein were determined 2 and 3 days after additions, respectively. Values are mean ± SD for 10 microscopic fields (beating) and four dishes (protein).

* $P < 0.05$, † $P < 0.01$ vs. control; ‡ $P < 0.01$ vs. same agent in the absence of propranolol; no symbol indicates no significant difference ($P > 0.05$).

the agents used in these experiments, with the exceptions noted in the legend to Table 2.

Induction of Beating through an α_1- and β_1-Adrenergic Receptor Interaction

Control cultures contained two populations of cells, according to beating observed under the microscope: a majority (95% or more) that beat sporadically at 0–4 times/min, and a minority that beat regularly at about 50–100 times/min. These cells were not otherwise different by phase contrast microscopy. As shown in Figures 9 and 10, treatment with NE induced a gradual increase in the population of cells beating regularly and rapidly, with a time course similar to that for the stimulation of growth (Fig. 3). The increase in the proportion of beating cells was not due to cell enlargement and establishment of contact with a small population of previously beating cells, since the NE- or EPI-stimulated increase was evident in sparse cultures with all cells clearly isolated, and since control cultures and NE plus propranolol-treated cultures did not exhibit rapid beating, even at densities sufficient to give cell contact. NE and EPI were equipotent, with an EC_{50} about 20 nM for stimulation of beating (Fig. 6). The effect of isoproterenol was significant ($P < 0.01$ vs. control) but averaged only 25% of the effect of NE (Figs. 9 and 10). Cultures treated with 2 μM clonidine had only 5% beating cells. Methoxamine had minimal effect on beating (Table 3). Beating induced by NE or EPI was inhibited a mean of 90% by 2 μM terazosin or propranolol [Figs. 7 (left panel), 9, and 10; Table 3]. The same result was obtained in cultures not given BrdU (not shown). Yohimbine had no inhibitory effect (Fig. 7). Antagonism by 2 μM betaxolol was greater than that produced by 2 μM ICI 118,551 (85% vs. 25% mean inhibition, $P < 0.01$) (Fig. 7). The antagonists alone did not influence beating (not shown). Cycloheximide did not prevent induction of beating by NE, but beating in the presence of NE plus cycloheximide was inhibited by propranolol (Fig. 2).

TABLE 4
NE and EPI Do Not Stimulate Growth in Pure Cultures of NMCs

Agent	Amino acid	Cell protein (counts/min per well) Control	Treated
NE (2 μM)	[14C]Phenylalanine	1334 ± 62	1373 ± 113
	[14C]Proline	1655 ± 258	1678 ± 272
EPI (2 μM)	[14C]Phenylalanine	1427 ± 138	1393 ± 101
	[14C]Proline	1673 ± 254	1530 ± 234

Pure NMC cultures were maintained in 24-well culture trays in medium with 5% serum until they were nearly confluent (4 days). They were then incubated in serum-free medium containing one of the indicated labeled amino acids plus NE, EPI, or diluent (control). Cell protein was measured after 3 days. Values are mean ± SD of 12 wells. There are no significant differences between treated and control groups.

Discussion

NE and EPI had a trophic effect on growth and beating of neonatal rat MCs in serum-free cultures. Hypertrophy was largely mediated through an α_1-adrenergic receptor, as shown by the experiments

TABLE 5
Cycloheximide and Terazosin, but Not Propranolol, Inhibit NE-Stimulated Hypertrophy Measured by MC Surface Area

Agent	Surface area (μm^2/cell)	Treated/control
Control	1921 ± 374	
Cycloheximide	1936 ± 462	1.01
EPI	3297 ± 530*	1.72
NE	3282 ± 651*	1.71
NE + cycloheximide	2082 ± 393	1.08
NE + propranolol	3314 ± 533*	1.73
NE + terazosin	1998 ± 341	1.04

Surface areas were measured 24 hours after the additions, all 2 μM final concentrations, except 10 μM cycloheximide. Values are mean ± SD, $n = 100$ cells from a representative experiment.

* $P < 0.01$ vs. control.

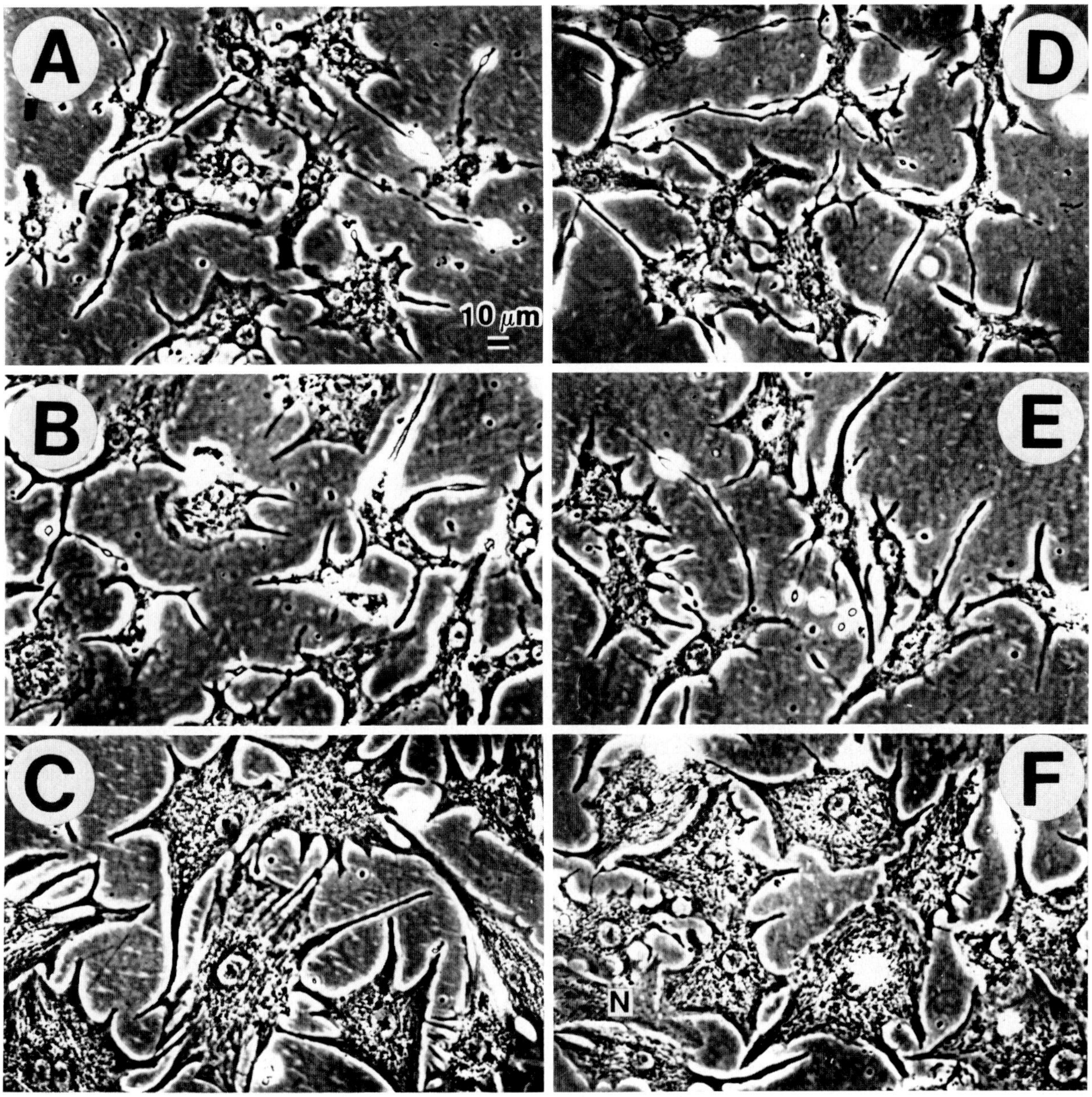

FIGURE 8. *Inhibition of NE-stimulated hypertrophy by cycloheximide and terazosin but not by propranolol. These are representative living MCs treated as follows: (A) control; (B) cycloheximide; (C) NE; (D) NE plus terazosin; (E) NE plus cycloheximide; (F) NE plus propranolol. Final concentrations were 2 μM, except cycloheximide (10 μM). Treatment time was 48 hours, except 24 hours in experiments with cycloheximide. All magnifications are identical; original was 128×. Note that cells treated with NE and with NE plus propranolol are equally large, and are clearly bigger than cells in the other four groups, which vary little among themselves. N = nonmyocardial mesenchymal cell (in F).*

summarized in Table 6. A 20% contribution of α_2, β_1, or β_2 stimulation cannot be excluded. These results confirm and extend my previous observations with NE (Simpson and Savion, 1982; Simpson, 1983), by defining the time course, agonist specificity, detailed dose-response relationship, and inhibition by cycloheximide of the hypertrophic response. In contrast, the development of chronotropic activity required both α_1- and β-receptor activation and was only 25% or less of the maximum NE or EPI effect with α- or β-receptor stimulation alone (Table 6). The predominant β-receptor subserving beating was probably of the β_1 subtype, judged by the greater inhibitory potency of betaxolol (β_1) than ICI 118,551 (β_2) (Stiles et al., 1983) and by the fact that NE and EPI were equipotent (Lands et al., 1967). A small population of β_2-receptors (Stiles et al., 1983) may have some role.

An important corollary to these results is that growth and beating can be regulated independently. Combined α and β stimulation with NE or EPI promoted parallel development of hypertrophy and beating. However, growth inhibition with cycloheximide did not prevent induction of beating by NE. Further, inhibition of beating with β-antagonists did not prevent stimulation of hypertrophy by NE or

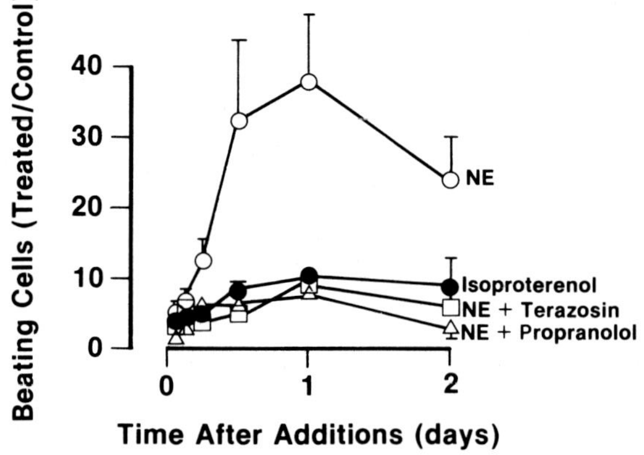

FIGURE 9. *Maximum induction of beating requires α- plus β-adrenergic stimulation. Cells were incubated with NE, isoproterenol, NE plus terazosin, or NE plus propranolol (all 2 μM). Each point is the mean ± SE for 4–8 experiments. At each time point in each experiment, 1000 treated and control cells in 10 fields from two dishes were examined; the proportion of cells beating regularly and rapidly was determined; and the result was expressed as the treated-to-control ratio. For the controls, the proportion of beating cells was 5.1 ± 4.0% n = 40 time points. At all time points, all treated groups had more beating cells than control ($P < 0.01$). NE was greater than the other groups from 6 hours on ($P < 0.01$). No differences were apparent among the other groups ($P > 0.05$). The frequency of beating in NE-treated cultures did not vary significantly between 12 and 48 hours.*

EPI. Therefore, under these conditions, growth and beating could be dissociated and were regulated through independent cellular pathways, even though α_1-receptor stimulation was necessary for both responses. These findings are diagrammed in Figure 11. Beating might stimulate growth under some circumstances, but this possibility was not tested.

The cellular pathways subserving growth and beating were not examined in this work, but the four types of cells defined in Table 7 should be useful for future study. The role of α_1-receptor activation in the induction of beating was not via stimulation of growth per se, as shown by the experiments with cycloheximide. The role of the α_1-receptor in this context might be control of energy metabolism (Keely et al., 1977; Clark et al., 1982), since adenosine triphosphate (ATP) generation is necessary for contractile activity in these cells (Pollack, 1977; Doorey and Barry, 1983). The manner in which the α_1-receptor stimulates hypertrophy is unknown. The role of β_1-receptor activation in beating might be through cyclic adenosine monophosphate (cAMP) accumulation, since cAMP is necessary for full expression of both chronotropic and inotropic activity (Pollack, 1977; Scholz, 1980). These and other hypothetical mechanisms require study.

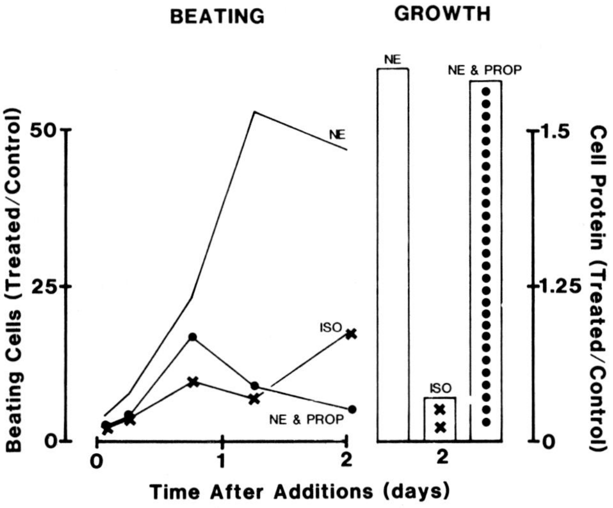

FIGURE 10. *α- or β-Adrenergic stimulation alone induces similar beating but dissimilar growth. The data in the left and right sides of this figure are from the same experiment. Cells were incubated with [^{14}C]phenylalanine, and NE, isoproterenol (ISO), or NE plus propranolol (PROP). Beating cells were determined at intervals after the start of incubation (as in the legend to Fig. 9), and the cells were taken after 2 days for measurement of protein (TCA-insoluble counts/min). The ratios shown reflect 1000 cells for beating and eight dishes for protein. For beating, there was no significant difference between isoproterenol and NE plus propranolol, and NE was greater than these groups ($P < 0.01$). For growth, NE and NE plus propranolol were the same and greater than control ($P < 0.01$), whereas isoproterenol was inactive ($P > 0.05$ vs. control).*

TABLE 6

Summary of the Effects of α- and β-Adrenergic Stimulation, Singly and in Combination, on Hypertrophy and the Induction of Beating

Stimulation	Hypertrophy (% of maximum)	Beating (% of maximum)
$\alpha_{1\&2}$ and $\beta_{1\&2}$		
NE or EPI	100	100
NE or EPI + cycloheximide	5	100
α_1 and β_{1+2}		
NE or EPI + yohimbine	95	95
α_2 and $\beta_{1\&2}$		
NE or EPI + terazosin	15	10
$\alpha_{1\&2}$		
NE or EPI + propranolol	85	10
α_2		
Clonidine	20	5
$\beta_{1\&2}$		
Isoproterenol	20	25
$\alpha_{1\&2}$ and β_1		
NE + ICI 118,551	95	75
$\alpha_{1\&2}$ and β_2		
NE + betaxolol	95	15

Hypertrophy and beating with selective α- and β-adrenergic stimulation are shown as approximate percentages of maximum, defined as that observed with combined α- and β-adrenergic stimulation with NE or EPI. Estimates are derived from the data given in the text and shown in the figures and tables, with all agents at 2 μM, except cycloheximide (5–10 μM). The maximum effect of NE or EPI was an increase in protein or area about 1.5- to 2-fold over control and an increase in beating cells from 2–5% in control to a mean 95%. Values are rounded to the nearest 5%.

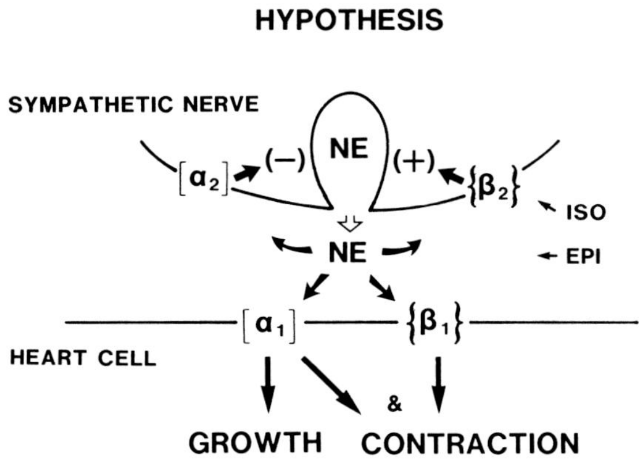

FIGURE 11. *A hypothesis to summarize the major findings of this study. The schematic diagram shows a sympathetic nerve terminal near a heart muscle cell. Nerve terminal α_2- and β_2-adrenergic receptors are believed to mediate inhibition and facilitation of NE release, respectively (Westfall et al., 1979; Dahlof, 1981; Langer, 1981). The results of this study suggest that growth is regulated by NE through an α_1-adrenergic receptor, whereas development of contractility requires both α_1- and β_1-adrenergic receptor stimulation. These two functions, growth and contraction, are hypothesized to be regulated through two largely independent cellular pathways, since they can be experimentally dissociated. Before innervation or after denervation, EPI from the circulation and/or from myocardial storage sites (Ellison and Hibbs, 1974; Spurgeon et al., 1974; Pollack, 1977) might replace NE, since EPI is equipotent to NE in the culture system. Since isoproterenol (ISO) does not stimulate growth in culture, it is proposed that its hypertrophic effect in vivo (Stanton et al., 1969) may be through facilitation of NE release (Mueller and Axelrod, 1968).*

The trophic effect of NE and EPI on chronotropic activity in these serum-free cultures may have a different mechanism from the well-known acute chronotropic effect of β stimulation in vivo (Pollack, 1977; Scholz, 1980) and in serum-supplemented cultures (Simpson and Savion, 1982), or from the acute chronotropic effect of α stimulation in culture (Hermsmeyer et al., 1982). This trophic effect on beating appears to be the opposite of the desensitization that might have been predicted with prolonged agonist exposure. Receptor numbers and affinities and the details of chronotropic and inotropic activity remain to be defined.

TABLE 7
Types of Myocardial Cells Produced by Adrenergic Receptor Stimulation in Serum-Free Culture

Stimulation	Cell Description
None or β	Small, nonbeating
α and β + cycloheximide	Small, beating
α_1	Large, nonbeating
α_1 and β_1	Large, beating

These cell populations are defined by the experiments summarized in Table 6. Beating and nonbeating refer to the proportion of cells showing regular chronotropic activity; nonbeating populations may include up to 25% beating cells, vs. almost 100% for NE or EPI. Small cells may have 20% hypertrophy, relative to 100% produced by NE or EPI. It is proposed that these four cell types will be useful in studies of growth and beating and their mediation by α- and β-receptor activation.

The hypothesis in Figure 11 summarizes the results in the context of a sympathetic nerve-MC junction. The EC_{50} for the trophic effects of NE (20–200 nM) are within the range of NE concentrations estimated for an active sympathetic nerve-vascular smooth muscle synapse (Bevan, 1978). The uncertain function of myocardial α_1-receptors and their potential role in growth control has been discussed previously (Simpson, 1983). Additional evidence for α-mediated cardiovascular growth regulation is the finding that an α-receptor stimulates proliferation of cultured rat aortic smooth muscle cells (Blaes and Boissel, 1983). α_2- and β_2-adrenergic receptors that are thought to mediate inhibition and facilitation of NE release, respectively (Fig. 11; Westfall et al., 1979; Dahlof, 1981; Langer, 1981), require consideration in testing the putative trophic functions of α_1-receptors. For example, hypertrophy induced by isoproterenol in vivo (Stanton et al., 1969) may be mediated indirectly, through increased release of myocardial NE (Mueller and Axelrod, 1968).

The equal potency of NE and EPI in the culture studies is important, and raises the possibility that the hormonal catecholamine might regulate MC growth before innervation or after denervation. EPI is stored extraneuronally in the myocardium (Ellison and Hibbs, 1974; Pollack, 1977), and these stores are relatively well-preserved after surgical or chemical denervation (Spurgeon et al., 1974).

I speculate that further study in the culture system may contribute to understanding certain phenomena in vivo. These phenomena include the improvement in myocardial function with dobutamine infusion in congestive cardiomyopathy (Liang et al., 1984), which might be analogous to the trophic β effect observed in this study. The excessive hypertrophy seen in hypertrophic cardiomyopathy (Perloff, 1981) and the inadequate hypertrophy in some patients with valvular heart disease or congestive cardiomyopathy (Benjamin et al., 1981; Grossman, 1983) might be explained by excessive or inadequate α-mediated growth, respectively. Pathological hypertrophy (Grossman et al., 1983) might be modeled as the hypertrophy produced by isolated α stimulation.

I thank Ann McGrath and Wesley Webb for technical assistance and Dr. Joel Karliner for review of the manuscript and support of my work.

*This work was presented in part at the 56th Scientific Session of The American Heart Association in Anaheim, California, November, 1983, and was published in abstract form in 1983 [Circulation **68** (suppl III): 169 and Clin Res 32: 72A].*

Dr. Simpson is a Research Associate of the Veterans Administration. These studies were supported by Grant HL 31113 from the U.S. Public Health Service, by a Grant-in-Aid from The American Heart Association, and with funds contributed in part by The AHA Alameda Chapter and The AHA Central Valley Chapter.

Address for reprints: Paul Simpson, M.D., VA Hospital 111C, 4150 Clement Street, San Francisco, California 94121.

Received December 30, 1983; accepted for publication January 31, 1985.

References

Benjamin IJ, Schuster EH, Bulkley BH (1981) Cardiac hypertrophy in idiopathic dilated congestive cardiomyopathy: A clinicopathologic study. Circulation **64:** 442–447

Bevan JA (1978) Norepinephrine and the presynaptic control of adrenergic transmitter release. Fed Proc **39:** 187–190

Blaes N, Boissel J-P (1983) Growth-stimulating effect of catecholamines on rat aortic smooth muscle cells in culture. J Cell Physiol **116:** 167–172

Clark WA Jr, Zak R (1981) Assessment of fractional rates of protein synthesis in cardiac muscle cultures after equilibrium labeling. J Biol Chem **256:** 4863–4870

Clark MG, Patten GS, Filsell OH (1982) Evidence for an α-adrenergic receptor-mediated control of energy production in heart. J Mol Cell Cardiol **14:** 313–321

Curfman GD, O'Hara DS, Hopkins BE, Smith TW (1980) Suppression of myocardial protein degradation in the rat during fasting. Circ Res **46:** 581–589

Dahlof C (1981) Studies on β-adrenoceptor mediated facilitation of sympathetic neurotransmission. Acta Physiol Scand Suppl **500:** 1–147

Doorey AJ, Barry WH (1983) The effects of inhibition of oxidative phosphorylation and glycolysis on contractility and high-energy phosphate content in cultured chick heart cells. Circ Res **53:** 192–201

Ellison JP, Hibbs RG (1974) Catecholamine-containing cells of the guinea pig heart: an ultrastructural study. J Mol Cell Cardiol **6:** 17–26

Graefe K-H, Henseling M (1983) Neuronal and extraneuronal uptake and metabolism of catecholamines. Gen Pharmacol **14:** 27–33

Grossman W, Carabello BA, Gunther S, Fifer MA (1983) Ventricular wall stress and the development of cardiac hypertrophy and failure. *In Perspectives in Cardiovascular Research,* vol 7, Myocardial Hypertrophy and Failure, edited by NR Alpert. New York, Raven Press, pp 1–18

Hadjiconstantinou M, Neff NH (1983) Ascorbic acid could be hazardous to your experiments: a commentary on dopamine receptor binding studies with speculation on a role for ascorbic acid in neuronal function. Neuropharmacology **22:** 939–943

Hermsmeyer K, Mason R, Griffen SH, Becker P (1982) Rat cardiac muscle single cell automaticity responses to α- and β-adrenergic agonists and antagonists. Circ Res **51:** 532–537

Keely SL, Corbin JD, Lincoln T (1977) *Alpha* adrenergic involvement in heart metabolism: Effects on adenosine cyclic 3'5'-monophosphate, adenosine cyclic 3'5'-monophosphate-dependent protein kinase, guanosine cyclic 3'5'-monophosphate, and glucose transport. Mol Pharmacol **13:** 965–975

Lands AM, Arnold A, McAuliff JP, Luduena FP, Brown TG Jr (1967) Differentiation of receptor systems activated by sympathomimetic amines. Nature **214:** 597–598

Langer SZ (1981) Presynaptic regulation of the release of catecholamines. Pharmacol Rev **32:** 337–362

Lee G T-Y, Engelhardt DL (1977) Protein metabolism during growth of vero cells. J Cell Physiol **92:** 293–301

Liang C-S, Sherman LG, Doherty JU, Wellington K, Lee VW, Hood WB Jr (1984) Sustained improvement of cardiac function in patients with congestive heart failure after short-term infusion of dobutamine. Circulation **69:** 113–119

Lowry OH, Rosebrough NJ, Farr AL, Randall RJ (1951) Protein measurement with the Folin phenol reagent. J Biol Chem **193:** 265–275

Mc Kee EE, Cheung JY, Rannels DE, Morgan HE (1978) Measurement of the rate of protein synthesis and compartmentation of heart phenylalanine. J Biol Chem **253:** 1030–1040

Meier KE, Snavely MD, Brown SL, Brown JH, Insel PA (1983) α_1- and β_2-Adrenergic receptor expression in the Madin-Darby canine kidney epithelial cell line. J Cell Biol **97:** 405–415

Morgan HE, Earl DCN, Broadus A, Wolpert EB, Giger KE, Jefferson LS (1971) Regulation of protein synthesis in heart muscle. I. Effect of amino acid levels on protein synthesis. J Biol Chem **246:** 2152–2162

Mueller RA, Axelrod J (1968) Abnormal cardiac norepinephrine storage in isoproterenol-treated rats. Circ Res **23:** 771–778

Östman-Smith I (1981) Cardiac sympathetic nerves as the final common pathway in the induction of adaptive cardiac hypertrophy. Clin Sci **61:** 265–272

Perloff JK (1981) Pathogenesis of hypertrophic cardiomyopathy: Hypotheses and speculations. Am Heart J **101:** 219–226

Pollack GH (1977) Cardiac pacemaking: An obligatory role of catecholamines? Science **196:** 731–738

Rannels DE, Wartell SA, Watkins CA (1982) The measurement of protein synthesis in biological systems. Life Sci **30:** 1679–1690

Ronning OW, Pettersen EO, Seglen PO (1979) Protein synthesis and protein degradation through the cell cycle of human NHIK 3025 cells in vitro. Exp Cell Res **123:** 63–72

Scholz H (1980) Effects of beta- and alpha-adrenoceptor activators and adrenergic transmitter releasing agents on the mechanical activity of the heart. *In* Adrenergic Activators and Inhibitors, Handbook of Experimental Pharmacology, 54/I, edited by L Szekeres. New York, Springer-Verlag, pp 651–733

Simpson P (1983) Norepinephrine-stimulated hypertrophy of cultured rat myocardial cells is an $alpha_1$ adrenergic response. J Clin Invest **72:** 732–738

Simpson P, Savion S (1982) Differentiation of rat myocytes in single cell cultures with and without proliferating nonmyocardial cells: Cross-striations, ultrastructure, and chronotropic response to isoproterenol. Circ Res **50:** 101–116

Simpson P, McGrath A, Savion S (1982) Myocyte hypertrophy in neonatal rat heart cultures and its regulation by serum and by catecholamines. Circ Res **51:** 787–801

Spurgeon HA, Priola DV, Montoya P, Weiss GK, Alter WA III (1974) Catecholamines associated with conductile and contractile myocardium of normal and denervated dog hearts. J Pharmacol Exp Ther **190:** 466–471

Stanton HC, Brenner G, Mayfield ED Jr (1969) Studies on isoproterenol-induced cardiomegaly in rats. Am Heart J **77:** 72–80

Stiles GL, Strasser RH, Lavin TN, Jones LR, Caron MG, Lefkowitz RJ (1983) The cardiac β-adrenergic receptor: structural similarities of β_1 and β_2 receptor subtypes demonstrated by photoaffinity labeling. J Biol Chem **258:** 8443–8449

Tarazi RC, Sen S, Saragoca M, Khairallah P (1982) The multifactorial role of catecholamines in hypertensive cardiac hypertrophy. Eur Heart J **3** (suppl A): 103–110

Westfall TC, Peach MJ, Tittermary V (1979) Enhancement of the electrically induced release of norepinephrine from the rat portal vein: Mediation by β_2-adrenoceptors. Eur J Pharmacol **58:** 67–74

Zar JH (1974) Biostatistical Analysis. Englewood Cliffs, N.J., Prentice-Hall

INDEX TERMS: Hypertrophy • Beating • Heart cell culture • α- and β-Adrenergic responses • Control of growth and differentiation

BRIEF COMMUNICATIONS

The Independent Effects of Oxygen Radical Scavengers on Canine Infarct Size

Reduction by Superoxide Dismutase but not Catalase

Steven W. Werns, Michael J. Shea, Edward M. Driscoll, Christopher Cohen, Gerald D. Abrams, Bertram Pitt, and Benedict R. Lucchesi

From The University of Michigan Medical School, Departments of Pharmacology, Pathology, and Internal Medicine (Division of Cardiology) Ann Arbor, Michigan

SUMMARY. Previous studies demonstrated a significant reduction of ultimate infarct size in the canine heart by the combined administration of superoxide dismutase plus catalase. This study was performed to assess the independent effects of each enzyme on ultimate infarct size due to ischemia/reperfusion. Dogs received 2-hour infusions of superoxide dismutase, catalase, or albumin (controls) via the left atrium beginning 15 minutes before and ending 15 minutes after a 90-minute occlusion of the left circumflex coronary artery. The dogs were killed 6 hours after reperfusion. After histochemical staining, infarct and risk area masses were calculated by gravimetric and planimetric analysis. Infarct size expressed as a percentage of the area at risk was: superoxide dismutase, 19 ± 5; catalase, 30 ± 5; and controls, 40 ± 3. Infarct size in the superoxide dismutase group, but not the catalase group, was significantly less than in controls ($P < 0.05$). No significant differences in hemodynamics or area at risk were observed that could explain the differences in infarct size. The results indicate that superoxide dismutase alone protects reperfused ischemic myocardium as well as does the combination of superoxide dismutase and catalase. The beneficial effect of superoxide dismutase and insignificant effect of catalase suggest that tissue damage during ischemia and reperfusion may be mediated largely by superoxide anion but not by hydrogen peroxide. **(*Circ Res 56: 895–898, 1985*)**

TISSUE injury resulting from a variety of causes is attributable to the toxic effects upon biological systems of reactive oxygen species, such as superoxide anion ($\cdot O_2^-$), hydrogen peroxide (H_2O_2), and hydroxyl radical ($\cdot OH$) (Freeman and Crapo, 1982). Studies of intestinal (Parks et al., 1982), cerebral (Demopoulous et al., 1980), and global cardiac (Shlafer et al., 1982; Gardner et al., 1983) ischemia implicate oxygen-free radicals in the development of ischemic tissue injury.

Previous experiments reported by this laboratory (Jolly et al., 1984) investigated the effects upon regional myocardial ischemia of the combined administration of superoxide dismutase (superoxide oxidoreductase EC 1.15.1.1) and catalase (H_2O_2:H_2O_2 oxidoreductase EC 1.11.1.6), enzymes which are endogenous scavengers of $\cdot O_2^-$ and H_2O_2, respectively. In a canine model of myocardial infarction, the combination achieved a 50% reduction of infarct size assessed 24 hours after a 90-minute circumflex coronary artery (LCX) occlusion followed by reperfusion. Although the results suggest that myocardial necrosis due to coronary occlusion and reperfusion may be limited by free radical scavengers, the relative importance of $\cdot O_2^-$ and H_2O_2 in the pathophysiological process could not be deduced. Therefore, this study was performed to determine the effect of either enzyme on the extent of myocardial injury after ischemia and reperfusion.

Methods

Detailed methods have been published previously (Romson et al., 1983). Briefly, male mongrel dogs (12–15 kg) were anesthetized with Dial-urethane (0.6 ml/kg, iv) and ventilated with room air. After thoracotomy, the proximal LCX was affixed with an electromagnetic flow probe and a critical stenosis of silk suture. Left atrial pressure, carotid artery pressure, LCX blood flow, and lead II ECG were recorded.

The treatment groups were: (1) bovine erythrocyte superoxide dismutase (SOD), 5 mg/kg (3,800 U/mg, Boehringer, or 3,000 U/mg, Sigma); (2) bovine liver catalase (CAT), 5 mg/kg (11,000 U/mg, Sigma); and (3) bovine serum albumin fraction V, 15 mg/kg (Calbiochem), dissolved in 60 ml of 0.9% sodium chloride. Albumin was selected as a nonspecific protein control for any osmotic effects of the enzymes. The solutions were infused via the left atrium at 0.5 ml/min starting 15 minutes before and ending 15 minutes after a 90-minute LCX occlusion. Reperfusion was initiated gradually over 30 minutes.

Six hours after onset of reperfusion, the heart was fibrillated electrically and excised. Using a dual perfusion technique previously described (Shea et al., 1984) followed by fixation in 10% formalin, infarct and risk area masses were calculated by both gravimetric and planimetric analysis.

Samples of triphenyltetrazolium chloride (TTC)-negative tissue along with the adjacent TTC-positive border were coded, fixed in 10% buffered formalin (pH 7.4, 37°C), embedded in paraffin, cut into 5-μm-thick sections, and stained with hematoxylin and eosin. A cardiac pathologist (G.D.A.), unaware of the treatment protocol, graded the samples on a semiquantitative scale for microscopic evidence of necrosis and leukocyte infiltration.

All data were expressed as mean ± SEM. Paired *t*-tests were used to analyze group differences in coronary blood flow (Armitage, 1971). Group comparisons of hemodynamic data were made by analysis of variance (Armitage, 1971) and Duncan's multiple range test (Duncan, 1955). Group comparisons of infarct data were made by analysis of variance (Armitage, 1971) and Scheffe's test (Neter and Wasserman, 1974). Differences were considered significant when $P < 0.05$.

Results

Dogs were excluded from analysis for heartworms or failure to develop objective evidence of regional ischemia upon LCX occlusion (no S-T segment change or epicardial cyanosis). Dogs were also excluded if more than two cardioversions were required to reverse ventricular fibrillation, or if a fatal arrhythmia occurred before 4 hours of reperfusion (4 CAT, 3 SOD, 1 control). One experiment (control) was terminated early because of a failure to develop LCX reflow and was excluded from analysis. The final groups consisted of 12 control, 10 CAT, and 8 SOD animals.

Reduction of Myocardial Infarct Size

Body weight, left ventricular mass, and area at risk as a percent of left ventricle for each group were not significantly different. By both gravimetric and planimetric analysis, infarct size in the SOD group was significantly smaller than controls ($P < 0.05$, Fig. 1). SOD reduced infarct size by greater than 50%, whether infarct mass was expressed as a percentage of the total left ventricle or area at risk. Infarct size in the CAT group, however, was not significantly different from controls ($P > 0.05$). As demonstrated in previous studies from this laboratory (Jolly and Lucchesi, 1983), gravimetric and planimetric analysis of IZ/LV, IZ/AR, and AR/LV (IZ = infarct zone, LV = left ventricle, AR = area at risk) were in close agreement. The planimetric (P) and gravimetric (G) determinations of IZ/AR were related as follows: $P = 0.89\ (G) + 1.29$, $r = 0.91$, $P < 0.001$, SEE 6.52, $n = 30$.

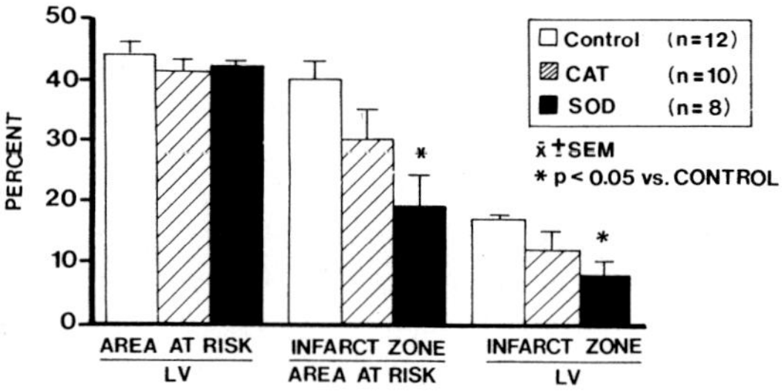

FIGURE 1. *Effect of superoxide dismutase (SOD) or catalase (CAT) on canine infarct size after a 90-minute occlusion and 6-hour reperfusion of the left circumflex coronary artery. Infarct size expressed both as percent of the left ventricle and percent of the area of risk was significantly reduced by SOD, but not CAT (P < 0.05 by ANOVA and Scheffe's test).*

Hemodynamic Parameters

Heart rate, mean arterial pressure, rate-pressure product, left atrial pressure, and LCX blood flow did not change significantly during the initial 15 minutes of albumin or enzyme infusion preceding LCX occlusion. There were also no significant intergroup differences in these parameters before, during, or after LCX occlusion (Table 1). The mean left atrial pressure rose 15 minutes after LCX occlusion by 3.3 mm Hg in controls, 3.1 mm Hg in the SOD group, and 3.0 mm Hg in the CAT group. For each group, the mean LCX flow 6 hours after reperfusion was significantly lower than preocclusion, but there were no differences among the groups (Table 1).

Histological Analysis of Risk Region

Histological examination of the border between the TTC-positive and -negative tissue confirmed the presence within the TTC-negative region of histo-

TABLE 1
Hemodynamic Data

	Time	Heart rate (beats/min)	Mean arterial pressure (mm Hg)	Rate pressure product (× 10^{-2})	LCX flow (ml/min)
Control	Preocclusion	134 ± 22*	102 ± 22	141 ± 55	23 ± 6
	End occlusion	131 ± 25	88 ± 27	120 ± 58	
	End reperfusion	178 ± 38	82 ± 17	164 ± 73	13 ± 4†
CAT	Preocclusion	134 ± 33	121 ± 16	165 ± 57	21 ± 7
	End occlusion	129 ± 20	99 ± 14	128 ± 34	
	End reperfusion	181 ± 49	88 ± 13	159 ± 45	10 ± 9†
SOD	Preocclusion	136 ± 22	123 ± 18	168 ± 45	28 ± 12
	End occlusion	132 ± 18	103 ± 23	137 ± 40	
	End reperfusion	155 ± 22	103 ± 20	160 ± 43	13 ± 6†

* Mean ± SEM.
† $P < 0.05$ vs. preocclusion.

logical signs of necrosis. The degree of leukocyte infiltration of infarcted tissue was quite variable, with no discernible difference between groups.

Discussion

This study demonstrates that a 2-hour infusion of superoxide anion scavenger, SOD, reduces by 50% the extent of myocardial injury after regional ischemia and reperfusion of 90 minutes and 6 hours, respectively. Using the same protocol and dose (5 mg/kg), a scavenger of hydrogen peroxide, catalase, had no significant effect. For the sample size of 10, the probabilities (type II error) of not detecting 50% or 40% reductions of infarct mass are approximately 15% or 30%.

In a previous study using the same duration of ischemia but longer reperfusion (24 hours), the same doses of SOD and CAT in combination also reduced infarct size by 50% (Jolly et al., 1984). Therefore, for the doses used, no additive or synergistic effects of the combination are apparent, although a larger dose of catalase might have a greater effect than the dose used in this study.

In vitro studies suggest that cellular damage, e.g., peroxidation of lipids by H_2O_2 and $\cdot O_2^-$, may be mediated by more toxic daughter species. Ferrous iron can catalyze reduction of H_2O_2 to hydroxyl radical, and neutrophil myeloperoxidase can catalyze the reaction of H_2O_2 with chloride to form hypochlorous acid (Fantone and Ward, 1982). The low pH of ischemic myocardium favors conversion of $\cdot O_2^-$ to the more reactive perhydroxyl radical ($\cdot HO_2^-$) (Freeman and Crapo, 1982). Since SOD should increase tissue H_2O_2 and CAT should decrease it, this study suggests that adequate endogenous pathways of H_2O_2 detoxification persist after ischemia, or that $\cdot HO_2^-$ is the predominant oxygen radical formed within ischemic myocardium.

Since SOD did not reduce myocardial oxygen demand, the inflammatory aspects of myocardial ischemia and anti-inflammatory properties of SOD merit consideration. Myocardial ischemia elicits an inflammatory response that includes activation of complement (Pinckard et al., 1979, 1980) and kinin (Torstila, 1978), release of chemotactic factor (Hartmann et al., 1977), migration of neutrophils (Mullane et al., 1984), and peroxidation of lipids (Rao and Mueller, 1983). Suppression of neutrophil infiltration of ischemic myocardium by anti-inflammatory drugs like ibuprofen (Romson et al., 1982) and nafazatrom (Shea et al., 1984), and granulocytopenic agents such as hydroxyurea (Mullane et al., 1984) and neutrophil antiserum (Romson et al., 1983), appears to reduce ischemic injury. SOD attenuates immunologically induced neutrophil accumulation, edema formation, and tissue destruction, possibly by suppressing generation of chemotactic lipids by $\cdot O_2^-$ (Fantone and Ward, 1982). Therefore, SOD may curtail injury to reperfused ischemic myocardium by preventing the inflammatory response to ischemia.

The growing recognition that oxygen radicals play a role in ischemic myocardial injury mandates reexamination of previously reported studies. For example, allopurinol's antiischemic characteristics have been ascribed to preservation of a purine pool for ATP synthesis (DeWall et al., 1971), but may reflect diminished $\cdot O_2^-$ generation by inhibition of xanthine oxidase (Gardner et al., 1983). Limitation of infarct size by mannitol was considered an osmolar effect on cell swelling, but quenching of hydroxyl radical may be the true mode of action (Magovern et al., 1984). The disparate effects on infarct size of cycloxygenase inhibitors may be a function of their differential abilities to inhibit $\cdot O_2^-$ release by neutrophils. For example, aspirin does not reduce infarct size or $\cdot O_2^-$ production by neutrophils, but ibuprofen decreases both (Flynn et al., 1984). Prostacyclin's suppressive influence on oxygen radical release by neutrophils (Fantone and Kinnes, 1983) may explain its limitation of infarct size by nonhemodynamic means (Melin and Becker, 1983).

Although animal data must be applied to human disease with caution, oxygen radical-mediated damage may be facilitated by current therapeutic approaches to acute myocardial infarction. Reperfusion of ischemic myocardium by streptokinase may increase the oxygen available to generate free radicals (Gauduel and Duvelleroy, 1984) and promote the formation of chemotactic factors from fibrin, complement, and kinin (Chesterman, 1978). An oxygen radical scavenger such as SOD, which has been applied to other inflammatory conditions, (Huber and Menander-Huber, 1980), might increase the amount of ischemic tissue salvaged by myocardial reperfusion and thereby improve the prognosis of patients with myocardial infarction.

We would like to express our appreciation to Dr. Michael A. Schork for his help in the statistical analysis of the data.

This study was supported by National Institutes of Health Grant HL-19782, and by a Grant-in-Aid from the American Heart Association of Michigan.

Dr. Werns is the recipient of a Physician Scientist Award (Grant HL-01409) from the National Institutes of Health, Heart, Lung, and Blood Institute, and is a Merck Fellow of the American College of Cardiology.

Dr. Shea is a Clinician-Scientist Awardee of the American Heart Association.

Address for reprints: Benedict R. Lucchesi, M.D., Department of Pharmacology, M6322 Medical Science Building I, The University of Michigan Medical School, Ann Arbor, Michigan 48109.

Received December 10, 1984; accepted for publication February 28, 1985.

References

Armitage P (1971) Statistical Methods in Clinical Research. Oxford, Blackwell, pp 116–118, 189–197

Chesterman CN (1978) Fibrinolysis and disseminated intravascular coagulation. *In* Fibrinolysis: Current Fundamental and Clinical Concepts, edited by PJ Gaffney, S Balkur-Ulutin. New York, Academic Press, pp 157–172

Demopoulos HB, Flamm ES, Pietronigro DD, Seligman ML (1980)

The free radical pathology and the microcirculation in the major central nervous system disorders. Acta Physiol Scand **492:** 91–119

DeWall RA, Vasko KA, Stanley EL, Kezdi P (1971) Responses of the ischemic myocardium to allopurinol. Am Heart J **82:** 362–370

Duncan DB (1955) Multiple range and multiple F-tests. Biometrics **11:** 1–42

Fantone JC, Ward PA (1982) Role of oxygen-derived free radicals and metabolites in leukocyte-dependent inflammatory reactions. Am J Pathol **107:** 397–418

Fantone JC, Kinnes DA (1983) Prostaglandin E_1 and prostaglandin I_2 modulation of superoxide production by human neutrophils. Biochem Biophys Res Commun **113:** 506–512

Flynn PJ, Becker WK, Vercellotti GM, Weisdorf DJ, Craddock PR, Hammerschmidt DE, Lillehei RC, Jacob HS (1984) Ibuprofen inhibits granulocyte responses to inflammatory mediators. Inflammation **8:** 33–44

Freeman BA, Crapo JD (1982) Free radicals and tissue injury. Lab Invest **47:** 412–426

Gardner TJ, Stewart JR, Casale AS, Downey JM, Chambers DE (1983) Reduction of myocardial ischemic injury with oxygen-derived free radical scavengers. Surgery **94:** 423–427

Gauduel Y, Duvelleroy MA (1984) Role of oxygen radicals in cardiac injury due to reoxygenation. J Mol Cell Cardiol **16:** 459–470

Hartmann JR, Robinson JA, Gunnar RM (1977) Chemotactic activity in the coronary sinus after experimental myocardial infarction: Effects of pharmacologic interventions on ischemic injury. Am J Cardiol **40:** 550–555

Huber W, Menander-Huber KB (1980) Orgotein. Clinics Rheum Dis **6:** 465–498

Jolly SR, Lucchesi BR (1983) Effect of BW755C in an occlusion-reperfusion model of ischemic myocardial injury. Am Heart J **106:** 8–13

Jolly SR, Kane WJ, Bailie MB, Abrams GD, Lucchesi BR (1984) Canine myocardial reperfusion injury: Its reduction by the combined administration of superoxide dismutase and catalase. Circ Res **54:** 277–285

Magovern GJ, Bolling SF, Casale AS, Bulkley BH, Gardner TJ (1984) The mechanism of mannitol in reducing ischemic injury: Hyperosmolarity or hydroxyl scavenger? Circulation **70** (suppl I): 91–95

Melin JA, Becker LC (1983) Salvage of ischemic myocardium by prostacyclin during experimental myocardial infarction. J Am Coll Cardiol **2:** 279–286

Mullane KM, Read N, Salmon JA, Moncada S (1984) Role of leukocytes in acute myocardial infarction in anesthetized dogs: Relationship to myocardial salvage by anti-inflammatory drugs. J Pharmacol Exp Ther **228:** 510–522

Neter J, Wasserman W (1974) Applied Linear Statistical Models. Homewood, Illinois, Richard Irwin

Parks DA, Bulkley GB, Granger DN, Hamilton SR, McCord JM (1982) Ischemic injury in the cat small intestine: Role of superoxide radicals. Gastroenterology **82:** 9–15

Pinckard RN, Olson MS, Giclas PC, Terry R, Boyer JT, O'Rourke RA (1975) Consumption of classical complement components by heart subcellular membranes in vitro and in patients after acute myocardial infarction. J Clin Invest **56:** 740–750

Pinckard RN, O'Rourke RA, Crawford MH, Grover FS, McManus LM, Ghidoni JJ, Storrs SB, Olson MS (1980) Complement localization and mediation of ischemic injury in baboon myocardium. J Clin Invest **66:** 1050–1056

Rao PS, Mueller HS (1983) Lipid peroxidation and acute myocardial ischemia. Adv Exp Med Biol **161:** 347–363

Romson JL, Hook BG, Rigot VH, Schork MA, Swanson DP, Lucchesi BR (1982) The effect of ibuprofen on accumulation of indium-111-labeled platelets and leukocytes in experimental myocardial infarction. Circulation **66:** 1002–1011

Romson JL, Hook BG, Kunkel SL, Abrams GD, Schork MA, Lucchesi BR (1983) Reduction of the extent of ischemic myocardial injury by neutrophil depletion in the dog. Circulation **67:** 1016–1023

Shea MJ, Murtagh JJ, Jolly SR, Abrams GD, Pitt B, Lucchesi BR (1984) Beneficial effects of nafazatrom on ischemic reperfused myocardium. Eur J Pharmacol **102:** 63–70

Shlafer M, Kane PF, Wiggins VY, Kirsh MM (1982) Possible role for cytotoxic oxygen metabolites in the pathogenesis of cardiac ischemic injury. Circulation **66** (suppl I): 85–92

Torstila I (1978) The plasma kinin system in acute myocardial infarction. Acta Med Scand [Suppl] **620:** 1–62

INDEX TERMS: Superoxide dismutase • Catalase • Myocardial ischemia • Myocardial infarction • Free radicals

Direct Observation of the "Oxygen Paradox" in Single Rat Ventricular Myocytes

Michael D. Stern, Ann M. Chien, Maurizio C. Capogrossi, Don J. Pelto, and Edward G. Lakatta

From the Cardiovascular Section, Gerontology Research Center, National Institute on Aging, National Institutes of Health, Baltimore, Maryland, and the Division of Cardiology, Johns Hopkins Medical Institutions, Baltimore, Maryland

SUMMARY. By phase contrast microscopy with video length tracking, we followed the sequence of morphological changes in individual isolated rat ventricular myocytes during anoxia followed by reoxygenation. Cells appeared normal during early anoxia. After a duration of anoxia T_1, which varied from 17–47 minutes in different cells, each cell *abruptly* contracted an average of 33% in length to an inert rectangular form presumed to be a rigor state. Cells which were reoxygenated before the onset of rigor showed normal morphology and an unchanged extent of shortening on field stimulation, compared to control. Cells that were reoxygenated after a time in the rigor state, T_2, either partially recovered to a shortened rectangular form capable of stimulated twitches or rounded up rapidly to a disordered hypercontracture form. The distribution of T_1 was the same for cells which recovered and which hypercontracted. In contrast, the outcome of reoxygenation depended markedly on T_2: all cells that were reoxygenated after less than 10 minutes of rigor recovered function, whereas all cells that spent more than 20 minutes in rigor hypercontracted when reoxygenated. The hypercontracture appears to be the cellular analog of the "oxygen paradox" in whole hearts. Its occurrence is reliably related to duration of rigor state but not to duration of hypoxia, because of marked cellular variability in the time of onset of rigor. (*Circ Res 56: 899–903, 1985*)

REFLOW of myocardium that has been ischemic for a prolonged period produces a characteristic histological picture of "contraction band necrosis" (Kloner et al., 1974). A similar phenomenon, the "oxygen paradox," is produced when an isolated heart that has been perfused anoxically and without glucose is reoxygenated (Hearse et al., 1975). The introduction of oxygen is associated with abrupt development of a patchy contracture state, with disruption of sarcolemmae and intercalated discs, contraction bands and Ca^{++} deposition in the mitochondria. On the basis of the timing of these events, it has been proposed (Ganote and Kaltenbach, 1979) that the primary event is a violent contracture, which produces cellular disruption, Ca^{++} loading, and enzyme release by a mechanical disruption of the intercellular attachments. Because isolated cardiac myocytes have no such attachments, the analog, if any, of the oxygen paradox in these cells would be of great interest.

Previous studies of hypoxia and reoxygenation in isolated cells have been performed in suspension or layers, sampled at discrete times (Acosta and Puckett, 1977; Acosta and Li, 1980; Altschuld et al., 1981; Cheung et al., 1982; Murphy et al., 1982; Hohl et al., 1982; Piper et al., 1984). The behavior of isolated myocytes under hypoxia is heterogeneous. Haworth et al. (1981) noted that the sarcomere lengths of hypoxic myocytes in suspension are bimodally distributed. As hypoxia is prolonged, there is an increase in the fraction of "short" cells and a decrease of "long" cells; the adenosine triphosphate (ATP) content of the suspension is proportional to the number of long cells. They proposed that an individual cell regulates its ATP level by means of anaerobic glycolysis until its energy reserves are exhausted; it then abruptly becomes ATP depleted and shortens to a rigor form. If this interpretation is correct, the averaging of cells in suspensions or dense layers might be quite misleading. We therefore undertook to observe, by direct phase contrast microscopy, the "histories" of individual myocytes during hypoxia and reoxygenation.

Methods

Isolated rat ventricular cells were prepared as previously described (Silver et al., 1983). Briefly, hearts from 6- to 7-month-old Wistar rats were perfused for 15 minutes with Krebs-Ringer bicarbonate buffer containing 0.1% collagenase type II (Worthington), 50 μM Ca^{++}, 10 mM glucose, at pH 7.4 and 37°C. The left ventricle was dissected free, minced, and the fragments pipetted gently and repeatedly. The supernatant extract was filtered through gauze and allowed to form a pellet by gravity. We washed the cells repeatedly with Spinner's medium (Gibco), progressively increasing concentrations of Ca^{++}, and resuspending them, finally, in Dulbecco's modified Eagle's medium containing 5% fetal calf serum and 1.8 mM Ca^{++}. This resulted in a cell suspension containing 60–75% rod-shaped Ca^{++}-tolerant myocytes. These were plated into 25-mm glass Petri dishes containing glass coverslips and

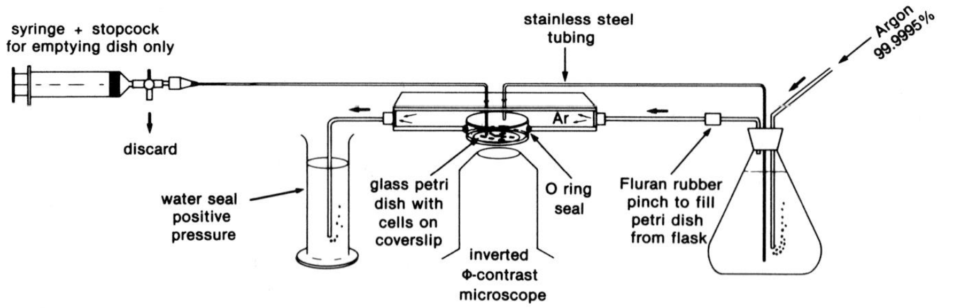

FIGURE 1. *Apparatus used to produce hypoxia in cells. Cells were in glass Petri dishes flushed by ultra-pure argon gas. The medium was exchanged for hypoxic medium (flask) by pinching the rubber segment of the gas line to raise pressure up in the flask, avoiding valves. During the hypoxic period, the liquid phase was left stationary, since the liquid is 30 times more susceptible to oxygen contamination than the gas phase because of relative solubilities.*

were incubated for 1 hour. The medium with unattached cells was then washed off and replaced with HEPES buffer containing (in mM): NaCl 137, KCl 5, $MgSO_4 \cdot 7\ H_2O$ 1.2, HEPES 20, glucose 15, $CaCl_2$ 1.5. Virtually all cells that remained attached to the coverslip were rod shaped, with regular sarcomere patterns, and contracted synchronously in response to field stimulation.

Attached cells were made hypoxic in glass Petri dishes (Fig. 1). The medium in the Petri dish was exchanged 10 times with glucose-free HEPES buffer with 1.5 mM Ca^{++} that had been equilibrated for 2 hours with ultra-pure argon gas (99.9995% Matheson). The upper part of the Petri dish was enclosed in a Lucite chamber flushed under positive pressure with argon pre-humidified by equilibration with the buffer flask. Gas was delivered through copper and glass tubing except for two 1-inch segments of low-oxygen permeability Fluran rubber to provide flexibility. The medium was exchanged through stainless steel tubing by partially occluding one of the rubber segments in the gas line to alter the pressure relationship between the flask and the chamber, avoiding valves. Measurements with a Clark oxygen electrode did not detect any oxygen in the gas or liquid phases; the dissolved P_{O_2} was estimated to be less than 0.5 torr at most. The system was maintained at 37°C for all experiments. The cells were viewed by phase contrast microscopy using a Leitz Diavert inverted microscope; the image was projected onto a Panasonic television camera, and the video signal was recorded on a Panasonic VHS cassette recorder. The cell length was monitored by a video edge tracking system (Instrumentation for Physiology and Medicine, San Diego) from the recorded image. Cells were reoxygenated by flushing the Lucite chamber with air. Cells were field stimulated before and after hypoxia by a Grass stimulator via platinum-iridium wires immersed at opposite sides of the Petri dish; stimulation was avoided during hypoxia to prevent electrolytic production of oxygen.

Results

When the above precautions were taken to ensure adequate hypoxia, cells were observed to undergo a highly reproducible sequence of events (Fig. 2). Initially, there was no alteration of light microscopic morphology or cell length. After a period of hypoxia which varied from cell to cell, ranging from 17–47 minutes, each cell underwent a smooth longitudinal collapse (Fig. 3A) which occurred abruptly, i.e., over about 10 seconds, to become an "R form," a short rectangular form with a faintly visible sarcomere pattern and an enhanced contrast of the myofibrillar structure. The cell length decreased by 32.5 ± 7.9% (mean ± SD, $n = 29$) on entering the R-form. Cells in the R-state remained perfectly inert, without motion or change of morphology, as long as hypoxia was maintained. We presume that the R-form is a rigor state, though this cannot be proven in the absence of ATP measurements on single cells. The initial period of hypoxia, measured from the completion of the last exchange of medium to the onset of the R-state, was defined as T_1, and varied in each cell and was unpredictable.

After onset of the R-state, hypoxia was continued for an additional time T_2, at which time air was blown into the space above the Petri dish. One

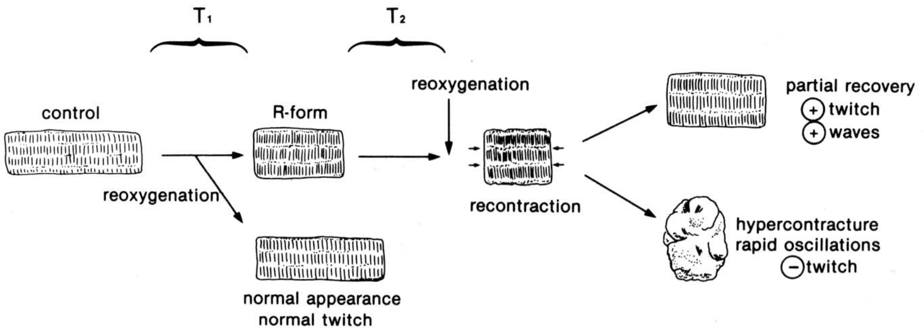

FIGURE 2. *Schematic of the morphological changes of a cell during hypoxia and reoxygenation. After a variable period of hypoxia, T_1, each cell abruptly shortened to an inert "R-form." After reoxygenation, all cells again "recontracted" briefly, and then either partially recovered to rectangular forms capable of twitching, or rounded up rapidly to hypercontracture forms.*

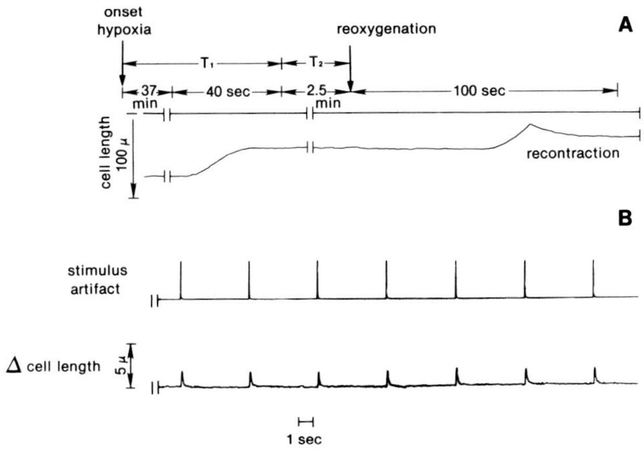

FIGURE 3. *The history of length of a cell (followed by video edge tracking) during the sequence shown in Figure 2. Panel A: cell length remained constant at 75 μm during the first 37 minutes of hypoxia, then abruptly decreased to 47 μm (note change in paper speed) in a period of seconds. One minute after reoxygenation (arrow), the cell underwent a transient "recontraction." The recontraction was quite marked in this cell; in most cells it was more subtle, but it occurred in all. Panel B: the same cell as in panel A, undergoing periodic field stimulation 5 minutes after reoxygenation. The upper trace represents the stimulus marker and the lower tracing shows the change in cell length during the stimulated twitch.*

minute after reoxygenation, all cells underwent a "recontraction," a brief longitudinal shortening, followed by a partial relaxation (Fig. 3A). The length of the cell at this point was close to that in the R-state or somewhat shorter.

Beyond this point, there were two possible outcomes. Some cells (17/29) underwent partial recovery. These cells, after a latent period of up to several minutes, began to display spontaneous wave-type contractions (Capogrossi and Lakatta, 1985). These often reached a frequency of one every 3–5 seconds before slowing down to a rate of 1–4/min, or ceasing altogether. Partially recovered cells remained rectangular and held constant lengths or elongated slowly, although never to control length. They reached a steady state which remained unchanged for at least an hour after reoxygenation. Most (68%) partially recovered cells produced a synchronous twitch contraction in response to field stimulation (Fig. 3B). Since the cells were short, and often located in an area far from the stimulating electrodes, it is possible that those which could not be field stimulated were nevertheless electrically intact.

The second possible outcome of reoxygenation was hypercontracture. These cells (12/29) exhibited rapid asynchronous oscillations (up to 4 Hz) and progressive contracture immediately following reoxygenation. Within 2 minutes, they had entirely rounded up into blebbed forms with absent sarcomere pattern and disordered myofibrils, shorter along the longitudinal axis than transversely. They were unresponsive to electrical stimulation and resembled in all respects the hypercontracted cells produced by massive Ca^{++} overload.

To determine the influence of the durations of the phases of hypoxia T_1 and T_2 on the occurrence of hypercontracture, we plotted the cumulative distributions of T_1 and T_2 with cells grouped retrospectively according to their outcome. The cumulative distribution of T_1 (Fig. 4A) is a "survival curve" with "death" defined as entry to the R-state. The times T_1 were distributed in the same way for cells which recovered and for those which hypercontracted; the mean T_1 was 32.7 ± 1.9 minutes (mean ± SEM) and 29.9 ± 2.3 minutes for the two groups, respectively (P = NS). The duration of hypoxia before development of rigor was thus not a determinant of the fate of the cell when reoxygenated. In contrast, the distributions of T_2, the duration of the rigor state before reoxygenation, differed markedly according to the outcome (Fig. 4B). The distribution of T_2 for the entire population was under the control of the ex-

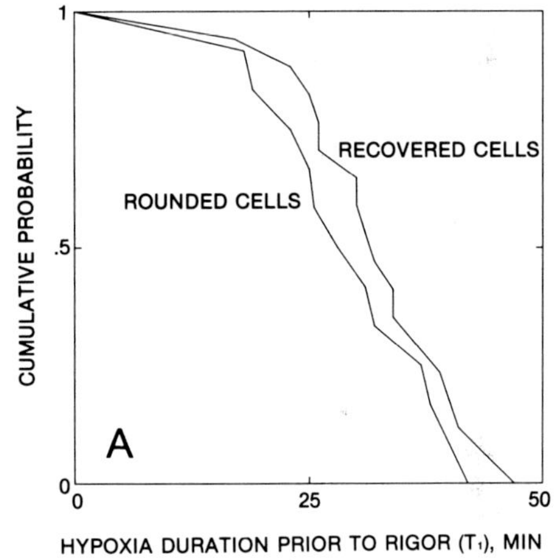

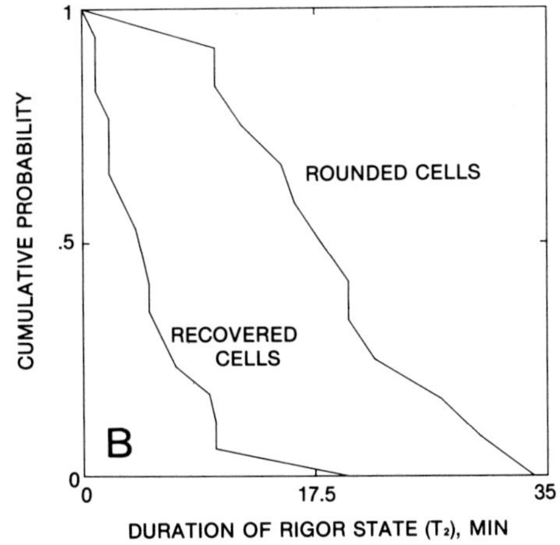

FIGURE 4. *Panel A: The cumulative distributions of T_1, the time between onset of hypoxia and transition to the R-form (presumed rigor state), for cells that either did or did not undergo hypercontracture when reoxygenated later. The ordinate is the probability that a hypoxic cell still shows normal morphology after duration T_1 of hypoxia. The distributions of T_1 were the same for cells that hypercontracted and for those that did not. Panel B: cumulative distributions of T_2, the time elapsed between onset of rigor and reoxygenation. The cells that underwent hypercontracture had markedly longer values of T_2 than those that did not.*

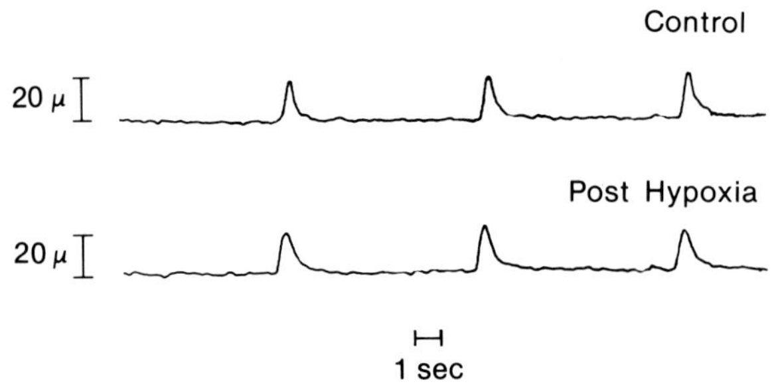

FIGURE 5. *Stimulated contractions, recorded by video edge tracking, of the same cell before and after 30 minutes of hypoxia followed by 5 minutes of reoxygenation. The cell did not enter the rigor state during this period, and function following hypoxia appeared unaltered.*

perimenter; the times of reoxygenation were chosen in an exponentially distributed manner to give a good sample of early reoxygenation times (i.e., short T_2's), in order to see the maximum degree of recovery possible in a cell that had passed through the R-state. Cells which recovered function were those which spent short times in the R-state: those which spent more than 20 minutes in the R-state invariably rounded up when reoxygenated, whereas cells that were reoxygenated within 10 minutes after onset of the R-state all recovered. The mean T_2 was 5.5 ± 1.2 minutes for cells which recovered function and 19.5 ± 2.2 minutes for cells which hypercontracted ($P < 0.001$, Student's *t*-test).

Figure 5 shows the extent of shortening during stimulated contractions of the same cell before and after 30 minutes of hypoxia, during which the cell did not enter the R-state. Cells that were reoxygenated during the T_1 period showed no morphological changes by light microscopy, and had contractile responses that were virtually superimposable on the control.

Discussion

Previous reports of the effects of anoxia on isolated cells have described a variety of apparently incompatible phenomena. Acosta and Puckett (1977), and Acosta and Li (1980) reported that 4 hours of anoxia without substrate produced enzyme leakage but no loss of viability in monolayers of cultured rat myocytes. Cheung et al. (1982) described progressive rounding up and loss of trypan blue exclusion when suspended rat myocytes were made hypoxic in the absence of glucose for longer than 15 minutes. Altschuld et al. (1981), Murphy et al. (1982), and Hohl et al. (1982) reported only a slow loss of viability (measured by trypan blue exclusion and enzyme retention) when myocytes were incubated anaerobically, but a rapid rounding up of anaerobic cells when they were reoxygenated. They proposed that this process is the cellular analog of the oxygen paradox. Since the resulting round cells remained "viable" by membrane permeability criteria, this provided support for the "mechanical" theory of the membrane damage which occurs upon reoxygenation of intact tissue. More recently, Piper et al. (1984) reported studies of myocytes attached to plastic Petri dishes in a nitrogen atmosphere. They described a progressive decrease of sarcomere length which correlated with a progressive fall in dish ATP levels. On reoxygenation, there was complete ultrastructural recovery. Only after an hour of anoxia were any rounded cells seen; after 2 hours, only 30% of cells were rounded, and there was no change in the number of rounded cells upon reoxygenation.

Our results show that anoxic and reoxygenation injury in cardiac myocytes is a "quantized" phenomenon, with each cell following its own timetable. This is in agreement with the inferences of Haworth et al. (1981) and Altschuld et al. (1981). The startling abruptness of the transition to the R-form may reflect the regenerative nature of the process: once myofilaments are activated by the lowering of ATP levels (generally thought to occur below 50 μM), they will rapidly consume the remaining ATP. We have confirmed the existence of a rapid hypercontracture in response to reoxygenation. In addition, we have shown for the first time that some cells which have entered a rigor state can partially recover function, including the ability to twitch in response to electrical stimulation, which implies relative intactness of sarcolemmal ionic permeabilities and energy production capability. While these cells remain markedly shortened and are clearly damaged, the outlook for their possible salvage is better than for the "viable rounded" cells or nonviable leaky cells which have been described previously.

The apparently inert R-form cell undergoes a time-dependent process which makes it vulnerable to hypercontracture at the time of reoxygenation. The nature of this process is conjectural. Although the hypercontracture itself resembles a Ca^{++} overload state, the nature of the damage when the rigor state is prolonged is probably complex, with sodium overload, failure of membrane repair, and oxidative radical damage each possibly contributing. It is noteworthy that in five preliminary experiments we have found that reducing extracellular calcium to 50 μM prevented the abrupt hypercontracture in cells with T_2 = 30 minutes, suggesting that calcium is important in the process.

It seems logical to identify the hypercontracture event with the oxygen paradox in whole hearts with the understanding that the damage produced is probably amplified by mechanical disruptions. However, the "recontraction" which occurs in all R-form cells at the time of reoxygenation might itself be sufficiently strong to produce mechanical disruption of intercellular attachments in intact hearts. Therefore, in using the isolated cell model to search for interventions to protect the myocardium against reflow injury, the effect of such interventions on all stages of the sequence shown in Figure 1 needs to be considered.

Our results differ from those of Piper et al. (1984),

with an apparently similar preparation, even after allowing for the effects of averaging over cellular inhomogeneity. They report no increase in rounded forms after reoxygenation. In addition, they observed continual rounding of cells during the second hour of hypoxia, at a time when all of our cells have entered the inert R-form. Because of the small number of cells which can be studied by continuous individual observation, we may have missed a "tail" of cells with long values of T_1. However, the 95% confidence limit for the fraction of cells in such a tail is only 10%, and the probability that the tail could contain the 30% of cells which were reported to round up during the second hour is less than 0.0001, given that we observed none. It seems likely, therefore, that the phenomena in their study differed from ours. The reasons for this difference are unclear, and might include difference in the age of the rats (ours were 3 months older) or their state of nutrition or glycogen stores. It is also possible that there was a difference in the degree of hypoxia. In whole tissues or dense cell suspensions, anoxia is achieved by consumption of oxygen by the cells; this mechanism is not available for sparse cells in a Petri dish. The concentration of oxygen at which cardiac myocytes become "anoxic" is not known. In isolated hepatocytes, cytochromes become fully oxygenated at a Po_2 of 3 torr (Jones and Kennedy, 1982), so it is possible that significant oxidative phosphorylation can take place even when the Po_2 is a fraction of a torr. We were unable to produce our results using plastic (polystyrene) Petri dishes and commercial USP nitrogen (99.5%). It is possible that outgassing of dissolved oxygen from the plastic substrate could influence the metabolic regulation of attached cells even when the supernatant contains insufficient oxygen to be detected with an oxygen electrode.

Further clarification of the biochemical basis of the states indicated in Figure 2 awaits the development of techniques for the measurement of ATP and ions in single cardiac cells under conditions of extreme hypoxia. The morphological sequence observed in this study underlines the importance of accounting for cellular heterogeneity in studies of reoxygenation injury. If the cellular heterogeneity seen in isolated cells exists in whole tissue, then the changes in contraction duration and strength after reoxygenation (Lakatta et al., 1975) may be due entirely to those cells which have passed through the rigor state and sustained permanent damage.

Supported in part by Grant HL 17655-11 of the National Heart, Lung, and Blood Institute.

Address for reprints: Dr. Edward G. Lakatta, Gerontology Research Center, Cardiovascular Section, National Institute on Aging, National Institutes of Health, Baltimore, Maryland 21224.

Received December 21, 1984; accepted for publication March 7, 1985.

References

Acosta D, Puckett M (1977) Ischemic myocardial injury in cultured heart cells: Preliminary observations on morphology and beating activity. In Vitro **13:** 818–823

Acosta D, Li CP (1980) Actions of extracellular acidosis on primary cultures of rat myocardial cells deprived of oxygen and glucose. J Mol Cell Cardiol **12:** 1459–1463

Altschuld RA, Hostetler JR, Brierley GP (1981) Response of isolated rat heart cells to hypoxia, reoxygenation, and acidosis. Circ Res **49:** 307–316

Capogrossi MC, Lakatta EG (1985) Frequency modulation and synchronization of spontaneous oscillations in cardiac cells. Am J Physiol **248:** H412–H418

Cheung JY, Thompson IG, Bonventre JV (1982) Effects of extracellular calcium removal and anoxia on isolated rat myocytes. Am J Physiol **243:** C184–C190

Ganote CE, Kaltenbach JP (1979) Oxygen-induced enzyme release: Early events and a proposed mechanism. J Mol Cell Cardiol **11:** 389–406

Haworth RA, Hunter DR, Berkoff HA (1981) Contracture in isolated adult rat heart cells: Role of Ca^{2+}, ATP, and compartmentation. Circ Res **49:** 1119–1128

Hearse DJ, Humphrey SM, Nayler WG, Slade A, Border D (1975) Ultrastructural damage associated with reoxygenation of the anoxic myocardium. J Mol Cell Cardiol **7:** 315–324

Hohl C, Ansel A, Altschuld RA, Brierlev GP (1982) Contracture of isolated rat heart cells on anaerobic to aerobic transition. Am J Physiol **242:** H1022–H1030

Jones DP, Kennedy FG (1982) Intracellular oxygen supply during hypoxia. Am J Physiol **243:** C247–C253

Kloner RA, Ganote CE, Whalen DA Jr, Jennings RB (1974) Effect of a transient period of ischemic on myocardial cells. Am J Pathol **74:** 399–422

Lakatta EG, Gerstenblith G, Angell CS, Shock NW, Weisfeldt ML (1975) Prolonged contraction duration in aged myocardium. J Clin Invest **55:** 61–68

Murphy MP, Hohl C, Brierlev GP, Altschuld RA (1982) Release of enzymes from adult rat heart myocytes. Circ Res **51:** 560–568

Piper HM, Schwartz P, Spahr R, Hutter JF, Spieckermann PG (1984) Absence of reoxygenation damage in isolated heart cells after anoxic injury. Pflugers Arch **401:** 71–76

Silver LH, Hemwall EL, Marino TA, Houser SR (1983) Isolation and morphology of calcium tolerant feline ventricular myocytes. Am J Physiol **245:** H891–H896

INDEX TERMS: Hypoxia • Cardiac myocytes • Hypercontracture • Oxygen • Paradox • Rigor

LETTERS TO THE EDITOR

Comments on
"Effects of Pericardial Effusates of Various Conductivities on Body-Surface Potential in Dogs: Documentation of the Eccentric Spheres Model"
which appeared in
Circ. Res. 55: 788–793

Kramer and colleagues have contributed important material on the effect of the composition of abnormal pericardial contents on electrocardiographic voltage (Kramer et al., 1984). They noted in passing that compression probably was not a part of the voltage reduction observed in fluids with conductivities either greater or less than that of blood. I wonder if the authors would care to comment on the work of Toney and Kolmen (1966), who used intrapericardial saline (among other substances) in animals with electrodes both on the endocardium and on the chest wall. Voltage reduction occurred in both electrodes during saline infusion at the point at which hemodynamic effects were first observed. The endocardial electrodes could not have been affected by any insulating effect of the physical presence of the fluid. However, their point was that both electrodes responded in tandem, and only after significant hemodynamic effects were observed.

These remarks are not meant to criticize a nice study, but, rather, to request amplification.

David H. Spodick
University of Massachusetts Medical School
Director
Division of Cardiology
St. Vincent Hospital
Worchester, Massachusetts 01604

References

Kramer DA, Hamlin RL, Weed HR (1984) Effects of pericardial effusates of various conductivities on body-surface potentials in dogs. Documentation of the eccentric spheres model. Circ Res **55:** 788–793

Toney JC, Kolmen SN (1966) Cardiac tamponade: Fluid and pressure effects on electrocardiographic changes. Proc Soc Exp Biol Med **121:** 642–648

Reply to the Preceding Letter

The question regarding the reduction in voltage at both sets of electrodes is founded (as was Toney and Kolmen's conclusion) on the premise that a dipole electrode pair "internal" to the added fluid in the pericardium is uneffected by the "surrounding" fluid medium. We believe that this generalized concept is unfounded in theory, and refer to research by Rudy and Plonsey (1980) which shows a theoretical effect on epicardial voltages when the conductivity of the surrounding lung layer is altered. Rudy and Plonsey's model demonstrates that in a modeled inhomogeneous torso, a change in the conductile parameter of an outer layer does indeed have an effect on the electrical field distribution of the source field in an internal layer. Although this reference would seem to refute the simplistic view of "insulated" layers expressed in Dr. Spodick's question, we can offer no direct explanation of Toney and Kolmen's result with regard to a modeled field theory explanation. However, several questions regarding Toney and Kolmen's experimental method might lead to an explanation of their findings.

1. Was the chest of the animal closed after the thoracotomy used to gain access to the pericardium? If not, it follows that normal internal current flow pathways have been disturbed during the experiments. It therefore would be quite possible that the data obtained did not reflect the actual in vivo conditions.

2. If heart compression did occur during these experiments, which is probable, based on the 55 mm of Hg pressure that was maintained in the pericardial sac, it would follow that the endocardial electrodes would move in closer proximity to one another, resulting in lower recorded voltages. This reduction in voltage would be difficult to distinguish from changes due to altered conductivities or activation sequences.

3. Although Toney and Kolmen reported that both electrodes responded in tandom, they did not say that this occurred only after significant hemodynamic effects were observed. Our review of the referenced work leads us to conclude that they conducted no control experiment using a high conductance liquid at low pericardial pressures and without hemodynamic effects. The inclusion of such data would have helped to reconcile the apparent discrepancy between their results and ours.

In conclusion, we feel that studies which attempt to reconcile ventricular activation with the distribution of body-surface potentials must take into account the field theory relationships between all layers of the subject in question, i.e., no layer or sets of layers may be considered to be independent of the remainder of the system.

Daniel A. Kramer
Herman R. Weed
Bio-Medical Engineering Center
Robert L. Hamlin
Department of Veterinary Physiology and Pharmacology
The Ohio State University
1900 Coffey Road
Columbus, Ohio 43210-1092

References

Rudy Y, Plonsey R (1980) A comparison of volume conductor and source geometry effects on body surface and epicardial potentials. Circ Res **46:** 283–291

Toney JC, Kolmen SN (1966) Cardiac tamponade: Fluid and pressure effects on electrocardiographic changes. Proc Soc Exp Biol Med **121:** 642–648

INDEX TERMS: Pericardial effusion • Pericardial conductivity

News from the American Heart Association

7320 Greenville Avenue, Dallas, Texas 75231
Telephone: 214 750-5300

AHA Research Committee Gives 5-Year Prospects, Notes More Funds Needed

The generation of additional funds to support Heart Association research was recommended by the National Research Committee in a recent report to the Board of Directors.

This would "allow the appropriate number of awards in existing (research) programs, an increase in the size of awards commensurate with inflation, and the development of new programs," the report said.

"Mechanisms to achieve this are under consideration within the Research Committee, the report went on," but the major portion of this increase in funds will have to come from an increase in the amount of money that can be made available for research."

EIs and Grants-in-Aid

The report noted studies which indicated that "the two well-established programs for supporting research, Established Investigators and Grants-in-Aid, are clearly accomplishing the goals for which they have been intended. The two newer programs, Clinician-Scientist Awards and Medical Student Research Fellowships, are reasonable responses to important needs in biomedical research. It is too early to gauge their degree of success, although preliminary responses are encouraging."

Gap is Seen

The report said that based on estimates of increased funds there is still "a significant gap between the amount of money available for the Established Investigatorships and Grants-in-Aid and the funds necessary for supporting all of the highly meritorious applications."

Need for Innovative Research

The Report pointed to a need for a research program that "will encourage experienced investigators to develop more innovative and consequently more risky research projects." It found there are problems in science that are not adequately addressed by existing programs within the research budgets of AHA or the National Heart, Lung, and Blood Institute.

Current procedures for grant applications and review favor the continuation of established lines of research over more innovative, high risk, high yield projects, the report noted.

Aging Equipment

"American research laboratories are aging," the report went on. "Equipment is becoming obsolete or simply unreliable. Laboratory research is very often limited not by ideas but by tools. There is the need to address the problem of equipment replacement or updating."

Support of new programs on a trial or test basis, the report suggested, might come from AHA reserves. It also called for new joint efforts by the affiliates and the National Center to support deserving research projects.

Strategic Issues Group Identifies Major Issues

The Strategic Issues Group, a new formation in the Heart Association, has identified five major sets of strategic issues—challenges, which are critical to its success, affecting the entire Association during the next 5 to 10 years.

They are: science, program and communications, fund raising, volunteer involvement, and management/operations.

The Group has been charged to plan the Futures Conferences to be held in conjunction with the Delegate Assembly—the first of which will be held in June in Chicago. It will also plan Futures Conferences expected to be held in conjunction with the General Assembly every third year.

The report, presented to the Board of Directors by the Strategic Issues group chairman, W.W. Aston, was based on 30 interviews and numerous studies and was reviewed by 55 volunteers and staff in four Group meetings. It will be further discussed by the General Assembly.

Biobehavioral Medicine Papers To Be Published

Papers delivered at the Conference on Biobehavioral Medicine and CVD are under review for publication in a scientific journal. The Conference was held Feb. 3–7 at Sea Island, GA, under the auspices of the American Heart Association and the National Heart, Lung, and Blood Institute.

Seventy-eight scientists, invited because of research contributions to behavioral medicine or cardiovascular research, discussed the following topics:

Relationship of biobehavioral medicine to hypertension; the relationship to coronary artery disease and stroke, and the relationship to sudden death.

Daily Task Forces

Task forces reviewed the evidence daily and discussed the significance of current information. They sought to establish what was scientific fact, what was applicable clinically, and what were the most promising directions for extension of research. A "Distinguished Panel," chosen by the AHA, reviewed the results to summarize the findings.

Three Issues

Dr. Kenneth I. Shine, AHA president-elect and chairman of the Conference, reported to the AHA Board of Directors on three issues: 1) the biological relationship between the central nervous system and heart disease; 2) environment and its impact on heart disease, (noting an inverse correlation between socioeconomic class and heart disease whereby lower socioeconomic groups suffer a greater risk of heart disease); and 3) personality and heart disease, saying there currently are no good ways of measuring what personality characteristics are associated with heart disease.

Among those participating in the Conference were Thomas J. Ryan, M.D., AHA President, and John Shepherd, M.D., D.Sc., a past President of AHA and Chairman of the Distinguished Panel.

Indications/Risks For Frozen Plasma

Caution in utilizing fresh frozen plasma (FFP), use of which has greatly increased, has been advised by a Consensus Development Conference Panel convened by the National Institutes of Health.

The panel, after meeting in September, 1984, concluded there was mounting evidence of potential risks (viral hepatitis and AIDS) in using FFP. Many patients, it said, can be managed more effectively and safely with alternative modalities.

"Appropriate use of FFP must be justified on clinical grounds," the panel statement said, "until better evidence is available... There is no justification for the use of FFP as a volume expander or as a nutritional source. Safer alternative therapies exist.

"FFP is indicated for some documented coagulation protein deficiencies as well as for selected patients who require massive transfusions," the panel stated. "It is indicated for patients with multiple coagulation defects as in liver disease, in conjunction with therapeutic plasma exchange for thrombotic thrombocytopenic purpura, for infants with protein-losing enteropathy, and for selected patients with other immune deficiencies. Its use in most other cases should be discouraged."

The panel called for research to develop safer FFP and for innovative educational efforts to encourage appropriate use.

The statement, available as a pamphlet from the U.S. Department of Health and Human Services, lists currently recommended clinical indications for FFP, gives the risks, notes the alternative therapies, discusses effectiveness, and offers directions for future research.

The Conference was sponsored by the National Heart, Lung, and Blood Institute, Office of Medical Applications of Research, NIH, and the Center for Drugs and Biologics of the FDA.

Correction

The article on research applications printed in February, 1985, CIRCULATION, CIRCULATION RESEARCH, and in March/April, 1985 STROKE, HYPERTENSION, and ARTERIOSCLEROSIS contained errors which are corrected below.

Research Applications Are Invited By Heart.

Applications for five programs of research awards in the cardiovascular field, including stroke, are invited by the American Heart Association.

Research Awards are:

ESTABLISHED INVESTIGATORSHIPS: 5-year awards to conduct independent research; 3 years postdoctoral research experience; ordinarily under age 40 at application; US citizenship or permanent visa required; stipend based on institutional standing, up to AHA maximum of $34,000 annually, plus fringe benefits. Deadline July 1.

CLINICIAN-SCIENTIST AWARDS: 3-year awards for rigorous fulltime research training of young clinically trained MDs—or with equivalent medical degrees; possible 2-year extension for initiation of investigative careers; ordinarily under age 35 at award activation; minimum 3 years post-MD clinical training; maximum 2 years relevant postdoctoral research at activation; MD/PhD graduates with clinical training but lacking relevant research training are eligible; US citizenship or permanent visa required; stipend $34,000 annually, plus fringe benefits—may be supplemented. Deadline July 1.

BRITISH-AMERICAN RESEARCH FELLOWSHIPS: A cooperative program with the British Heart Foundation for additional research training best available in British institutions; 1-year awards for US citizen physicians and scientists; ordinarily under age 35 at application; doctoral degree required; stipend $22,000 annually, plus $1,500 departmental grant, and travel allowances. Deadline July 1.

MEDICAL STUDENT RESEARCH FELLOWSHIPS: To encourage medical students to engage in fulltime research training for one or more years prior to graduation. Institutional 3-year award for accredited medical schools; 2 to 4 fellowships per year per institution; only 1 application per medical school; application initiated by institutional officer or faculty member responsible for conduct of program; stipend $8,000 per fellow, plus $1,500 annually for trainee-related expenses; medical students currently in MD/PhD program not eligible; not a scholarship. Deadline July 1.

GRANTS-IN-AID: 1- to 3-year research awards for projects broadly related to cardiovascular function and disease or related fundamental problems; proposals from talented, young investigators are encouraged; doctoral degree required at time of activation with very rare exceptions; $35,000 yearly maximum. Deadline October 1.

Statement of AHA Mission Adds Mention of Stroke

The American Heart 1977 Statement of its Mission—to reduce premature death and disability from cardiovascular disease—was broadened by the Board of Directors at its recent meeting to add the words: "and stroke."

This was approved to emphasize the AHA substantial involvement in the area of stroke.

The Board also approved regular review of the mission statement prior to the Futures Conference to be held every third year with the Delegate Assembly. This is to assure the statement's continued validity. The 1985 Futures Conference will be held in June with the General Assembly.

CV Nutrition Meeting Program for July 21–24

The 26th Annual Meeting of the American College of Nutrition, July 21–24, will focus on nutrition in cardiovascular disease and diabetes mellitus as well as advances in clinical nutrition. The meeting will be held at the Donaldson Brown Center for Continuing Education, Virginia Polytechnic Institute and State University, Blacksburg, VA.

Also meeting with the College will be the 4th International Symposium on Magnesium (July 23–28).

Topics To Discuss

Topics to be discussed include overview controversies on diet, arteries, and heart; evaluation of high fiber diet in hyperlipidemia; cholesterol and heart disease: rationale for dietary controls; are our diets so bad?; low fat, PUFA, and other oils in CVD (award lecture); role of triglycerides in vascular disease; low salt diet/potassium and hypertension.

In Diabetes

Also to be discussed: changing dietary concepts in diabetes, digestion, fates of fructose, other carbohydrates; lipid metabolism, exercise and type 2 diabetes mellitus; carbohydrates and metabolism in type 2 diabetes; glycemic index and hypertriglyceridemia in diabetes (award lecture); interrelations of Mg and lipids in CVD; insulin and Mg depletion: clinical consequences; carbohydrate craving of obese patients and diabetics.

There will also be a session on CVD and magnesium.

Inquires may go to Mildred S. Seelig, M.D., American College of Nutrition, POB 831, White Plains, NY 10602.

AHA Briefs . . .

- **Modern Concepts of Cardiovascular Disease** for June is "Primary Pulmonary Hypertension: Current Status," by Michael D. McGoon, M.D. and William D. Edwards, M.D., of Mayo Clinic.
- **Current Concepts of Cerebrovascular Disease/Stroke** for May/June is "Calcium, Hypercalcemia, and Stroke," by Philip Gorelick, M.D., of Chicago, and Louis Caplan, M.D., of Boston.
- **Former U.S. Senator Lister Hill,** who sponsored many of the nation's health laws, had died, aged 89, in Montgomery, AL. He was the son of Dr. Luther Leonidas Hill, believed to be the first surgeon to place sutures in the human heart.
- Two **cyclotrons**, the first at the National Institutes of Health, are planned for a new facility to be built to house them in Bethesda, MD. The cyclotrons produce short-lived radioactive isotopes for use in PET scanners, two of which have also been ordered.
- **Guy A. Zimmerman, M.D.,** of Utah has been selected as the first recipient of a new award to explore leukotrienes in heart disease. The award was given through the Heart Association by the pharmaceutical manufacturer Boehringer Ingelheim, Ltd. to note its centennial anniversary.
- **Six regional conferences** sponsored by the National High Blood Pressure Education Program for NHLBI and AHA to bring together health professionals involved in HBP programming, therapy, and research, have been authorized. Three have been scheduled: Los Angeles, Oct. 18; Orlando, FL, Oct. 30–Nov. 1; Wilmington, DE May 4–6, 1986.
- A nationwide conference, sponsored by AHA every six years to **update Emergency Cardiac Care and Cardiopulmonary Resuscitation standards and guidelines**, is scheduled for July 11–13 in Dallas. The AHA has issued a revised instructor's manual for basic life support (70-029-C), a loose-leaf source book.
- A **60-second radio health news and information program**, prepared by AHA, is now airing in 25 markets throughout the country. The "Help Your Heart," series will also be offered in six more markets in Georgia, and in Miami, FL.
- The AHA Council Affairs Committee has asked each of the 14 Scientific Councils to suggest **topics for research.** The suggestions will be forwarded to the Director of the National Heart, Lung, and Blood Institute. Last year the councils suggest nine new projects for CV research.
- The "Wise Giving Guide" has stated that the American Heart Association **meets the standards of the National Charities Information Bureau.**

Meetings Calendar 1985

June 17–21: **Symposium on the Temporomandibular Joint.** Maui, Hawaii. Sponsored by the University of California, San Francisco Dept. of Radiology. Dr. Clyde A. Helms, course program director. Inquiries: Dr. C. A. Helms, Dept. Radiology, University of California School of Medicine, San Francisco, CA 94143.

June 24–29: **Advances in Nuclear Medicine, NMR, and Angioplasty for Practicing Physicians, Including 7th Nuclear Cardiology Symposium.** Sea Pines Plantation, Hilton Head Island, SC. Sponsored by Emory University School of Medicine, Dept. of Radiology, Div. of Nuclear Med. Inquiries: CME Emory Univ. School of Medicine, 1440 Clifton Rd., N.E., 110 WHSCAB, Atlanta, GA 30322. Tel. 1-404-329-5695.

July 12: **Certifying Examination, Sub-Board of Pediatric Cardiology.** Chapel Hill, NC. Inquiries: American Board of Pediatrics, 111 Silver Cedar Court, Chapel Hill, NC 27514-1651.

July 14–19: **Teaching Stress Management and Relaxation Skills Workshop.** (Also Nov. 10–15). LaCrosse Exercise Program, University of Wisconsin-La Crosse. Inquiries: Philip K. Wilson, University of Wisconsin-LaCrosse, WI 54601. Tel. 1-608-785-8686.

July 15–18: **Clinical Cardiology.** Hilton Head Inn, Hilton Head Island, SC. Sponsored by the School of Medicine, Medical College of Georgia. Inquiries: Div. Cont. Ed., Medical College of Georgia, Augusta, GA 30912. Tel. 1-404-828-3867.

July 15–19: **Cardiac Rehabilitation Workshop.** (Also Nov. 18–22). La Crosse Exercise Program, University of Wisconsin. Inquiries: See July 14–19.

July 18–21: **Pulmonary Diseases.** Kiawah Island Inn, Kiawah Island, SC. Sponsored by School of Medicine, Medical College of Georgia. Inquiries: See Div. Cont. Ed., Med. Coll. of Georgia, July 15–18.

July 21–24: **Nutrition in Cardiovascular Disease and Diabetes Mellitus. 26th Annual Meeting of American College of Nutrition.** Donaldson Brown Center for Continuing Education of Virginia Polytechnic Institute and State University, Blacksburg, VA. Inquiries: Mildred S. Seelig, M.D., M.P.H., F.A.C.N., American College of

Nutrition, POB 831, White Plains, NY 10602. Tel. 1-914-948-4848.

July 21–26: **37th Annual Meeting American Association of Clinical Chemistry.** Georgia World Congress Center, Atlanta. Inquiries: AACC, 1725 K St., NW, Washington, DC 20006. Tel. 1-202-857-0717.

July 22–26: **Interdisciplinary Symposium on Plant Flavonoids in Biology and Medicine.** Biochemical, Pharmacological, and Structure-Activity Relationships. Buffalo, NY. Inquiries: Dr. Elliott Middleton, Jr., Dept. Med., Buffalo General Hospital, 100 High St., Buffalo, NY 14203. Tel. 1-716-845-2985.

July 22–26: **Fitness and Weight Control Workshop.** La Crosse Exercise Program, University of Wisconsin-La Crosse. Inquiries: See July 14–19.

July 22–26: **Topics in Clinical Nuclear Medicine.** Colby College, Waterville, ME. Henry N. Wagner, Jr., M.D., course director. Inquiries: R. Kany, Colby College, Waterville, ME 04901. Tel. 1-207-873-3386.

July 24–28: **4th International Symposium on Magnesium.** Magnesium in Cardiovascular Diseases, Open Heart and Other Surgery, Stress, Epidemiology, and Diagnosis. Donaldson Brown Center for Continuing Education, Virginia Polytechnic Institute and State University, Blacksburg, VA. Inquiries: See July 21–24.

July 24–28: **Critical Care Medicine.** Kiawah Island Inn, Kiawah Island, SC. Sponsored by School of Medicine, Medical College of Georgia. Inquiries: See Med. Coll. of Georgia, Div. Cont. Ed., July 15–18.

July 31–Aug. 2: **Interventional Radiology: An Update for Radiologic Technologists and Nurses.** Hyatt Regency Hotel, San Francisco. Ernest J. Ring, M.D., Robert Marco, Kathleen Marr, R.T., program directors. Sponsored by Dept. of Radiology, University of California San Francisco. Inquires: Dept. of Radiology, UCSF, San Francisco CA 94143.

Aug. 27–30: **Research Conference on Regulation of Bile Acid Synthesis.** Given Institute of Pathobiology, Aspen, CO. Sponsored by American Gastroenterological Association. Inquiries: Bile Acid Research, 740 Krameria St., Denver, CO 80220.

Sept. 12–14: **International Symposium on Cardiovascular Surgery—1985. 15th Annual Symposium of Texas Heart Institute.** Houston. Inquiries: Medical Director, Texas Heart Institute, POB 20269, Houston, TX 77225. Tel. 1-713-791-2157.

Sept. 30–Oct. 1: **2nd Annual Graduate Hospital Symposium: Acute Myocardial Infarction—Emerging Concepts of Pathogenesis and Treatment.** Philadelphia. Inquiries: M. Blob, Bockus Research Institute, The Graduate Hospital, Philadelphia, PA 19146. Tel. 1-215-893-2375.

Oct. 11–12: **4th Southern Biomedical Engineering Conference.** Jackson MS. Inquiries: Dr. Barry W. Sauer, SBEC, Div. Cont. Health Prof. Ed., University of Mississippi Medical Center, 2500 N. State St., Jackson, MS 39216-4505.

Oct. 13–18: **Clinical Congress, American College of Surgeons.** Chicago. Inquiries: ACS, 55 East Erie St., Chicago, IL 60611.

Oct. 19–20: **Head and Neck Radiology: Advanced Techniques in Diagnostic Imaging.** Hyatt Regency Hotel, San Francisco. William P. Dillon, M.D., and Gretchen A.W. Gooding, M.D., course directors. Sponsored by Radiology Research and Education Foundation, UCSF. Inquiries: Dept. Radiology, UCSF, San Francisco, CA 94143. Tel 1-415-666-5731.

Oct. 21–25: **Clinical Magnetic Resonance Imaging.** Hyatt Regency Hotel, San Francisco. Charles B. Higgins, M.D., Hedvig Hricak, Ph.D., program directors. Sponsored by UCSF Dept. of Radiology. Inquires: Dept. of Radiology, UCSF School of Medicine, San Francisco, CA 94143. Tel. 1-415-666-5731.

Oct 25: **Annual Meeting, Society of Neurological Anesthesia and Neurological Supportive Care.** San Francisco. Inquiries: Society of Neurological Anesthesia, POB 238, Univ. of Virginia Medical Center, Charlottesville, VA 22908.

Nov. 4–8: **Diagnostic Radiology Seminars.** Maui Marriott Hotel, Maui, Hawaii. Neil Chafetz, M.D. course director. Sponsored by UCSF Dept. of Radiology. Inquires: Radiology PG Education, UCSF Room C-324, Third and Parnassus, San Francisco, CA 94143. Tel. 1-415-666-5731 (7:30 AM–4:30 PM Pacific Time).

Nov. 11–14: **58th Annual Scientific Sessions, American Heart Association, Washington, DC. Inquiries: Coordinator Scientific Sessions, AHA, 7320 Greenville Ave., Dallas, TX 75231. Tel. for Abstracts: 1-214-750-5439; for housing and reservations 1-214-750-5425. Commercial Exhibits: 1-214-750-5388.**

Nov. 19–20: **Subspecialty Boards in Cardiovascular Disease.** Philadelphia. Inquiries: American Board of International Medicine, 3624 Market St., Philadelphia, PA 19104. Tel. 1-215-243-1500. (New date.)

1986

Jan 24–25: **Current Controversies and Techniques in Congenital Heart Surgery.** Baltimore, MD. (Immediately prior to Annual Meeting Society of Thoracic Surgeons, Washington, DC). Sponsored by Div. of Thoracic and Cardiovascular Surgery, University of Maryland School of Medicine. Inquiries: Program Cont. Ed., University of Maryland School of Medicine, 10 South Pine St., Suite 300, Baltimore, MD 21201. Tel. 301-528-3956.

Feb. 19–22: **11th International Joint Conference on Stroke and Cerebral Circulation.** Vacation Village, San Diego. Inquires: Admin. Assist., Scientific Sessions, AHA, Dallas, TX 75231. Tel. 1-214-750-5441.

July 10–12: **4th International Symposium on Mechanisms of Vasodilatation.** Rochester, MN. Satellite of International Congress of Physiological Sciences. Cerebral, coronary, and limb circulation. Paul M. Vanhoutte, M.D., chairman organizing committee. Abstracts by Oct. 30, 1985. Inquiries: J. Beckman, 942C Guggenheim Bldg., Mayo Clinic, Rochester, MN 55905.

Sept. 14–19: **Xth World Congress of Cardiology.** Washington, DC. Inquiries: Secretariat, 7320 Greenville Ave., Dallas, TX 75231. Tel. 1-214-750-5429. Cable Tencard, Dallas, TX.

Abroad
1985

June 23–26: **International Conference on Preventive Cardiology.** Sovincenter, Moscow, USSR. Sponsored by WHO, International Society and Federation of Cardiology. Official languages English and Russian. Inquiries: A. A. Stepanenko, International Conference on Prevention Cardiology, Institute of Preventive Cardiology, 10 Petroverigsky Lane 101837 Moscow, USSR. Telex 411355. Cable USSR MOSCOW K-62, Preventive Cardiology. Tel. 221-93-47.

June 26–28: **6th Symposium on Echocardiology With a Postgraduate Course on Doppler Cardiography.** Rotterdam, the Netherlands. Sponsored by Erasmus University Thoraxcenter. Inquiries: PG Med. Ed., Erasmus University, Rotterdam, PBO 1738, 3000 DR Rotterdam, the Netherlands. Tel. 010-635011/635013.

July 7–13: **8th International Congress of Neurological Surgery.** Toronto, Ont., Canada. Inquiries: World Federation of Neurosurgical Societies, Borgweg 12, Nijmegen, the Netherlands.

July 15–19: **4th Meeting, World Federation on Ultrasound in Medicine and Biology.** Sydney, Australia. Inquiries: WFUMB, POB 1441 GPO, Sydney, NSW, Australia 2001.

Aug. 3–17: **5th Annual Roentgen Revisited.** Postgraduate Radiology Course with NMR Symposium. Switzerland,

Austria, Germany. Sponsored by University of California San Francisco Medical Center and Univeristy of Munich. Charles B. Higgins, M.D. course director. Inquiries: Travel Planners Inc., POB 32366, San Antonio, TX 78216, U.S.A. Tel. 1-512-341-8131.

Aug. 31–Sept. 7: **Diagnosis of Diseases of the Chest.** Italy. (Also in Greece, Sept. 8–14). 2nd Great Teachers Foundation International Postgraduate Medical Education Program. Eric N. C. Milne, M.D., program director. Inquiries: Ryals POB 610203, DFW Airport, Texas 75261, U.S.A. Tel. 1-214-659-9590.

Aug. 31–Sept. 7: **11th Congress of International Society of Hypertension.** Heidelberg, Federal Republic of Germany. Organized by German Institute of High Blood Pressure Research and German Hypertension League. Dr. Detlev Ganten, Congress chairman. Inquiries: GKV, Frankfurter Str. 57, D-6050 Offenbach 1, Heidelberg, FRGermany.

Sept. 1–6: **13th World Congress of Neurology.** Hamburg, Germany. Inquiries: Dr. T. Stober, Dept. Neurology, Faculty of Med., University of Saarland, D-6650 Homburg/Saar, FRG.

Sept. 1–6: **13th World Federation of Neurology International Conference on Cerebrovascular Disease.** Salzburg, Austria. Inquires: Prof. Helmut Lechner, Chief, Clinic of Neurology and Psychiatry, University of Graz, Graz, Austria.

Sept. 1–7: **3rd Postgraduate International Course on Pain Therapy.** Vicenza, Italy. Inquiries: Ruggiero Rizzi, M.D., Ospedale Generale Regionale, 36100 Vicenza, Italy.

Sept. 3–6: **European Nuclear Medicine Congress.** Barbican Centre, London, England. Incorporates 23rd Meeting Society of Nuclear Medicine, Europe, 8th Meeting European Nuclear Medicine Society, 13th Meeting British Nuclear Medicine Society. Inquiries: Congress, Institute of Nuclear Medicine, Middlesex Hospital Medical School, Mortimer St., London, W1N 8AA, United Kingdom. Tel. OI-631 1066.

Sept. 5–7: **1st Asian-Pacific Conference on Doppler and Echocardiography.** Tokyo. Inquiries: Pravin M. Shah, M.D., Coordinator for North America, Cardiology Section (691/111E), Wadsworth VA Medical Center, Wilshire & Sawtelle Blvds, Los Angeles, CA. Tel. 1-213-824-3126.

Sept. 7–9: **3rd International Brain Heart Conference.** Trier, Germany. Inquiries: Dr. T. Stober, Dept. Neurology, Faculty of Med. University of Saarland, D-6650, Homburg/Saar, Federal Republic of Germany.

Sept. 8–12: **1st International Congress on Hospital Laws, Procedures, and Ethics.** Tel Aviv, Israel. Judge Amnon Carmi, organizing chairman. Inquiries: Hospitalaw, 28 Ahad Ha'am St., POB 394, Tel Aviv 61003, Israel. Tel. 03-650862. Telex 33803 TLV. Cable PELTOURS TELAVIV.

Sept. 9: **Workshop on Cardioembolic Stroke During 3rd International Brain/Heart Conference,** Sept. 7–9, Trier, Germany. Inquiries: David G. Sherman, M.D., and Robert G. Hart, M.D., co-chairmen, Dept. of Medicine, University of Texas Health Science Center, 7703 Floyd Curl Dr., San Antonio, TX 78284. Tel. 1-512-691-6521.

Sept. 9–12: **8th Annual European Conference on Lipoproteins.** Evangelische Akademie, Tutzing (near Munich), West Germany. Apolipoprotein mutants and dyslipoproteinemias; cellular processing of lipoproteins. Sponsored by European Lipoprotein Club. Inquiries: Dr. J. Shepherd, Secretary European Lipoprotein Club, Dept. Pathological Biochemistry, Royal Infirmary, Glasgow, Scotland, G4 OSF.

Sept. 11–14: **4th European Conference on Mechanocardiography.** Budapest, Hungary. Organized by the European-African Div. of the International Society of Mechanocardiography and the Hungarian Society of Cardiology. Prof. J. Simonyi chairman scientific committee. Inquiries: Mechanocardiography Organizing Committee, Budapest, Pf 88, H-1450, Hungary.

Sept. 11–14: **Acute Brain Ischemia 1985: Medical and Surgical Therapy.** University of Siena, Italy. (Satellite of 13th World Congress of Neurology, Sept. 1–6, Hamburg, Germany.) Prof. Noè Battistini, organizer. Inquiries: GIBI S.a.s., M. P. Gerini, Via Orlona, 7, 00198 Rome, Italy.

Sept. 16–19: **12th European Congress for Artificial Organs and Pre-Congress Meeting of the International Diabetes Federation.** Athens, Greece. (artificial endocrine pancreas, insulin delivery devices, pancreas and islet transplantation). Inquiries: Prof. S. Raptis, M.D., POB 14127, 11510 Athens, Greece.

Sept. 16–20: **International Symposium on Cardiogenic Reflexes.** University of Leeds, England. Organized by Dept. of CV Studies, Univ. Leeds, and Commission on CV Physiology of International Univ. of Physiological Sciences. Inquiries: Dr. R. Hainsworth, Dept. CV Studies, University of Leeds, Leeds LS2 93T, England.

Oct. 3–4: **Hemodynamics and Atherosclerosis.** Wellington, New Zealand. Inquiries: Dr. W.E. Stehbens, Dept. Pathology, Wellington Clinical School of Med., Wellington, 2, New Zealand.

Oct. 6–10: **7th International Symposium on Atherosclerosis.** Melbourne, Australia. Inquiries: Dr. P. J. Nestel, Baker Medical Research Inst., Commercial Rd., Prahran, Vic., Australia 3181.

Oct. 8–10: **1st Latin American Congress of Cardiac Pacing.** Buenos Aires, Argentina. Operated by Latin American Society of Cardiac Pacing and Argentine Chamber of Cardiac Pacing. Dr. Alejandro Dussaut, president organizing committee. Inquiries: Congresos Internacionales S.A., Moreno 854—9° piso, 1091 Buenos Aires, Argentina. Tel. 14-3216/3408/3283. Telex 22036 JECON AR.

Oct. 11–12: **2nd International Symposium on Hypertension in Children and Adolescents.** Heidelberg, FRG. Organized by Dept. of Pediatrics, Univ. of Heidelberg, and German Institute for High Blood Pressure Research. Inquiries: German Institute HBP Research, University of Heidelberg, Im Neuenheimer Feld 366, D-6900 Heidelberg, FRG.

Oct. 11–18: **Cell Biology of the Artery Wall.** Hayman Island, Great Barrier Reef, Australia. Satellite of 7th International Symposium on Arteriosclerosis, Oct. 6–10, Melbourne. Inquiries: Dr. Gordon H. Campbell, Dept. Anatomy, University of Melbourne, Parkville, 3052, Australia.

Oct. 14–18: **International Congress on Cardiac Doppler.** Pisa, Italy. (Tutorial sessions Oct. 14–15; Scientific Sessions Oct. 16–18). Prof. Luigi Donato and Dr. Merrill Spencer, presidents. Inquiries: Istituto di Fisiologia Clinica, C.N.R., University of Pisa, Via Savi 8, 1-567100 Pisa, Italy. Tel. 050-47231/502109. Telex: 590549 IFCI.

Oct. 20–22: **5th International Symposium on Rats with Spontaneous Hypertension and Related Studies.** Kyoto, Japan. Yukio Yamori, M.D., program director. Inquiries: 5th SHR Symposium, Shimane Medical University, Izumo 693, Japan. Tel. 0853-23-2111 Ext. 2375. Cable: WHOCOLLAB IZUMO.

Oct. 20–23: **3rd World Congress of Cardiac Rehabilitation.** Caracas, Venezuela. Sponsored by the International Society and Federation of Cardiology: Scientific Council on Rehabilitation of Cardiac Patients and AHA Council on Clinical Cardiology. Inquiries: Dr. Deyanira Almeida, Congresa C.A., POB 17422, Caracas 1015A, Venezuela.

Oct. 20–25: **Conference on Leukotrienes and Prostanoids in Health and Disease.** Jerusalem and Rehovot, Israel. Inquiries: Prof. Uriel Zor, Weizmann Institute of Science, Rehovot, Israel 76100. Tel. 1081 483557. Telex 361900. Cable: Weizinst.

Oct. 23–24: **International Symposium on Mechanisms and Treatment in Essential Hypertension: Calcium and Calcium Antagonists.** Hotel Nagoya Castle, Nagoya, Japan. (Satellite of 5th International Symposium on Rats with Spontaneous Hypertension, Oct. 20–22, Kyoto, Japan). Inquiries: Kyuzo Aoki, M.D., 2nd Dept. Internal Med., Nagoya City University Medical School, Mizuho-ku, Nagoya 467, Japan. Tel. 052-851-5511, Ext. 2204.

Oct. 25–27: **International Symposium on Brain and Blood**

Pressure Control. Kikai-Shinkoh Hall, Shiba Park, Tokyo, Japan. Dr. Keiji Nakamura, organizing chairman. Inquiries: Brain and Blood Pressure, Dept. of Pharmacology, Nippon Roche Research Center, Kamakura 247, Japan. Tel. 0467-45-3191-Ext. 380 or 381. Telex 2222861 PANROCHE J.

Oct. 27–30: **3rd Asian Pacific Symposium on Cardiac Pacing and Electrophysiology.** Hilton Hotel, Melbourne, Australia. Sponsored by Cardiac Society of Australia and New Zealand under auspices of International Cardiac Pacing Society. Inquiries: 3rd Asian Pacific Symposium on Cardiac Pacing and Electrophysiology, Suite 3.5, Epworth Medical Centre, 62 Erin St., Richmond, Vic. 3131, Australia.

Oct. 28–31: **1st International Congress on Food and Health.** Salsomaggiore Terme, Italy. Sponsored by International Association for Advancement of Biomedical Research, by Society of Medical Gastronomy, and Institute of Pharmacology of University of Pisa. Inquiries: ALM s.r.l., Via Lattuada, 26, 20135 Milan, Italy. Telex: 313063 HOTALM I.

Nov. 28–30: **7th Biennial Congress of Cardiology.** Rawalpindi/Islamabad, Pakistan. Inquiries: Pakistan Cardiac Society, Brig. Muhammad Zulfiqar Ali Khan, AFIC/NIHD, Rawalpindi, Pakistan. Tel. 64946, 61-31113, 61-33911.

Dec. 1–4: **International Symposium on Left Ventricular Dysfunction.** Jerusalem Hilton Hotel, Israel. Jan J. Kellermann, M.D., of Tel Aviv, Israel, and David Spodick, M.D., of Worcester, MA, co-chairmen. Under the auspices of the Universities of Tel Aviv and Massachusetts. Inquiries: POB 50006, Tel Aviv 61500, Israel. Tel. 03-654571. Telex 341171 KENS IL.

1986

Feb. 9–13: **12th World Congress of the International Society for Heart Research,** Melbourne, Australia. Inquiries: Dr. N.S. Dhalla, Dept. of Physiology, Faculty of Medicine, University of Manitoba, Winnipeg, Canada R3E OW3.

March 23–25: **2nd International Symposium on Holter Monitoring.** Jerusalem, Israel. V. Hombach, Cologne, and S. Stern, Jerusalem, co-chairmen. Inquiries: Prof. Shlomo Stern, c/o Stier Group, Ltd., 203 Dizengoff St., Tel Aviv 63115 Israel. Tel. (03) 224-153/4/5. Telex 35570 STI COIN IL.

April 23–25: **1st International Symposium on Cardiology.** Hospital de Clinicas, University of Buenos Aires, Argentina. Inquires: Dr. Luis D. Suŕez, Dean Funes 1075-(1231), Buenos Aires, Argentina. Tel. 821-6041.

July 8–11: **8th Annual Meeting American Section of the International Society For Heart Research and Satellite Symposium on Heart Metabolism for the 30th International Congress of Physiological Sciences.** Winnipeg, Canada. Inquiries: Dr. R. E. Beamish, Experimental Cardiology Section, Dept. of Physiology, Faculty of Medicine, University of Manitoba, Winnipeg, Canada R3E 0W3.

July 13–18: **30th International Congress of Physiological Sciences.** The University of British Columbia, Vancouver, Canada. Dr. H. McLennan, chairman program committee. Inquiries: IUPS, Suite 801, 750 Jervis St., Vancouver, B.C., Canada V6E 2A9. Tel. 604-681-5226. Telex 04-352848 VCR.

Sept. 14–17: **8th International Symposium on Microsurgical Anastomoses for Cerebral Ischemia.** Florence, Italy. Inquires: Rolando Gagliardi, M.D., Dept. of Neurosurgery, USL 10/D, Careggi Hospital, 50100 Florence, Italy.

Sept. 16–19: **12th European Congress for Artificial Organs. Pre-Congress Meeting of the International Diabetes Federation.** Athens, Greece. (artificial endocrine pancreas, insulin delivery devices, pancreas and islet transplantation). Inquiries: Prof. S. Raptis, M.D., POB 14127, 11510 Athens, Greece.

1987

Sept. 2–4: **International Conference on Management of Cardiac Arrhythmias.** London, England. Sponsored by the British Heart Foundation. Professor A. J. Camm and Dr. A. W. Nathan, members organizing committee. Inquiries: British Heart Foundation, 102 Gloucester Pl., London W1H 4DH England. Tel. 01-935-0185.

AHA Scientific Sessions Future Meeting Dates

1985	Washington, DC	Nov. 11–14
1986	Dallas, TX	Nov. 17–20
1987	Anaheim, CA	Nov. 16–19
1988	Locale not set	Nov. 14–17
1989	New Orleans	Nov. 13–16
1990	Dallas	Nov. 12–15

Xth World Congress of Cardiology, 1986

The Xth World Congress of Cardiology will be held in Washington, DC, Sept. 14–19, 1986. Official languages English, Spanish, and French. Inquiries: Secretariat, Xth World Congress Cardiology, 7320 Greenville Ave., Dallas, TX 75231. Tel. 214-750-5429. Cable: Tencard, Dallas.

Circulation Research

VOLUME 56 JANUARY–JUNE 1985

VOLUME AUTHOR INDEX

Abrams, G.D., 895
Adams, S.P., 621
Albala, A., 436
Alpert, N.R., 78
Antonetti, A., 331
Arend, L.J., 242
Aronson, P.S., 773
Aronstam, R.S., 392
Austen, K.F., 324

Baer, R.W., 11, 40
Bailey, J.C., 613
Bailey, K.R., 651
Ballermann, B.J., 324
Barry, W.H., 231
Barsamian, E.M., 537
Becker, H., 563
Becker, L.C., 651
Benassi, A., 556
Bersohn, M., 285
Bevan, J.A., 205
Bichet, D.G., 457
Bishop, V.S., 410, 517
Brayden, J.E., 205
Brecher, P., 755
Brenner, B.M., 324
Brown, A.M., 868
Brown, D.L., 359
Brown, J.H., 763
Bruner, C.A., 462
Brunton, L.L., 126
Buccafusco, J.J., 392
Buchanan, J.W., Jr., 696
Bulkley, B.H., 651
Burkhoff, D., 340
Buxton, I.L.O., 126

Calvin, J.E., Jr., 40
Cameron, J., 822
Cantin, M., 801
Canty, J.M., Jr., 791
Canty, J.M., Jr., 310
Capogrossi, M.C., 899
Carretero, O.A., 816
Carter, B.J., 109
Cauvin, C., 822
Cerutti, D., 829
Chambaret, J-P., 331
Chan, C., 755
Chandra, N., 20
Chartier, L., 801
Chen, Z., 351
Chien, A.M., 899
Chobanian, A.V., 755
Chung, H-M., 457
Chung, M., 87
Claes, V., 331
Clarkson, C.W., 496
Clemmons, D.R., 418
Clowes, A.W., 139
Cobb, F.R., 651
Cohen, C., 895
Cohen, C.J., 87
Cole, B.R., 621
Cole, P.A., 839
Cooper, C.L., 97
Corey, E.J., 324
Corr, P.B., 736
Covell, J.W., 31, 351
Currie, M.G., 621

Debets, J.J.M., 606
Demmert, G., 563
Distante, A., 556
Dole, W.P., 517
Driscoll, E.M., 895
Duckles, S.P., 109

Edwards, J.A., 548
Eisenberg, B.R., 548
Eisner, D.A., 452
Ellis, A.K., 310, 791
Elzinga, G., 252
Engler, R.L., 31
Entman, M.L., 704

Farmer, B.B., 576
Feigl, E.O., 486
Fenoglio, J.J. Jr., 436
Ferrier, G.R., 184
Fink, G.D., 462
Fok, K.F., 621
Fozzard, H.A., 475
Franz, M.R., 340
Freeman, G.L., 31
Furlan, R., 175

Gabbiani, F., 829
Gabbiani, G., 829
Ganten, D., 563
Gardner, P.I., 436
Genest, J., 801
Gentile, B.J., 690
Gettes, L.S., 696
Glantz, S.A., 40, 161
Glueck, R.M., 683
Goldstein, D., 763
Goresky, C.A., 57
Goulette, R.P., 78
Graham, R.M., 635
Grattan, M.T., 11
Green, F.J., 576
Greenfield, J.C., Jr., 651
Gross, D.R., 690
Guerci, A.D., 20
Guth, B., 351
Guyenet, P.G., 359
Guzzetti, S., 175

Haber, E., 72
Hanley, F.L., 11
Hasin, Y., 231
Hasser, E.M., 410
Hatt, P-Y., 331
Haywood, J.R., 410
Hill, M.L., 262
Hoffman, B.F., 857
Hoffman, J.I.E., 11
Hoffmeister, H.M., 220
Hofmann, H., 876
Hollen, C.E., 728
Holmberg, S.W., 621
Holubarsch, C., 78
Homcy, C., 72
Homcy, C.J., 635
Hondeghem, L.M., 496
Horwitz, L.D., 793
Hunter, W.C., 340
Hutchins, G.M., 651
Hwang, O., 822

Ito, B.R., 486
Izumi, F., 402

Jalife, J., 718
January, C.T., 475
Jennings, R.B., 262, 651
Johnson, A.K., 410
Jones, A.W., 507
Jose, M.J.L., 576

Kanaide, H., 666
Karaffa, S.A., 537
Katz, A.M., 370
Khaw, B.A., 72
Khuri, S.F., 537
Kilo, C., 839
Kim, D., 676
Kirby, M.L., 392
Klocke, F.J., 310, 791
Kloner, R.A., 537
Kluge, R., 457
Kobayashi, H., 402
Kocher, O., 829
Kovacs, R.J., 613
Kramer, J.B., 736

L'Abbate, A., 556
Lai, N.C.J., 537
Lakatta, E.G., 899
Lamers, J.M.J., 285
Landini, L., 556
Lang, R.E., 563
Langer, G.A., 146
Lappe, R.W., 606
Larson, K.B., 839
Laurent, S., 676
Lecarpentier, Y., 331
Levin, H., 20
Lew, W.Y.W., 351
LeWinter, M.M., 31
Lewis, R.A., 324
Lewis, R.M., 704
L'Hernault, N., 709
Linden, J., 279, 728
Lindenfeld, J., 793
Litten, R.Z., 78
Little, W.C., 808
Locke, E., 72

Loewy, A.D., 621
Lucchesi, B.R., 895
Lukas, A., 184
Lukeman, S., 822

Magnoni, M.S., 402
Mahnensmith, R.L., 773
Makielski, J.C., 475
Malik, K.U., 97
Malliani, A., 175
Mangiapane, M.L., 462
Marban, E., 133
Marsh, J.D., 676
Marston, W., 537
Martin, B.J., 78
Martin, J-L., 331
Mashima, S., 851
Mates, R.E., 310, 791
Maughan, W.L., 586
Mauser, M., 220
Mazet, F., 195
McCall, D., 370
McMahon, E.G., 427
McMillin-Wood, J.B., 704
Meiser, E., 377
Messina, L.M., 11
Michael, L.H., 704
Migus, A., 331
Milici, A.J., 709
Miller, J.G., 683
Moffat, M.P., 184
Mottley, J.G., 683
Mulieri, L.A., 78
Murdock, R.H., 651

Nakamura, M., 666
Needleman, P., 621
Nicholls, K.M., 457
Nienaber, C., 220
Nolly, H., 816
Nozaki, A., 851

Olsson, R.A., 517
Oshima, T., 621
Owens, G.K., 525

Pagani, M., 175
Palade, G.E., 709
Passamani, E.R., 651
Patel, A., 279, 728
Paul, R.J., 1, 427
Pelto, D.J., 899
Pérez, J.E., 683
Petty, M., 563
Phillips, M.I., 212
Picano, E., 556
Pitt, B., 895
Pizzinelli, P., 175

Rapela, C.E., 596
Reimer, K.A., 262, 651
Rich, T.L., 146
Rimoldi, O., 175
Roden, D.M., 857
Rose, C.P., 57
Rubanyi, G., 1, 117
Ruigrok, T.J.C., 285

Sadek, S., 279
Saffitz, J.E., 736
Sagawa, K., 340, 586
Saito, T., 696
Salata, J.J., 718
Sandrone, G., 175
Sarnelli, R., 556
Schaper, J., 262, 377
Schaper, W., 220
Schiffrin, E.L., 801
Schmidt, G., 851
Schneider, B., 563
Schrier, R.W., 457
Schwartz, R.P., Jr., 651
Schwartz, S.M., 139
Scicli, A.G., 816
Scicli, G., 816
Scott, J.A., 72
Shaffer, J.E., 97
Shapiro, M.D., 457
Shea, M.J., 895
Shi, A-Y., 20
Simpson, P., 884
Skalli, O., 829
Slinker B.K., 161
Smith, J.M., 507
Smith, T.W., 231, 676
Smits, J.F.M., 606
Sobel, B.E., 683
Spaan, J.A.E., 293, 789
Spielman, W.S., 242
Spray, D.C., 195
Stämmler, G., 377
Steenbergen, C., Jr., 262
Stenstrom, B., 212
Stern, M.D., 899
St-Louis, J., 801
Sunagawa, K., 586

Taira, Y., 666
Takayanagi, K., 851
Taylor, A.D., 537
Thibault, G., 801
Thomas, G., 87
Thompson, C.I., 242
Tilton, R.G., 839
Todt, J.A., 606
Tow, D.E., 537
Trabucchi, M., 402
Travis, V.L., 793
Traystman, R.J., 596
Tsitlik, J., 20

Uhlig, P.N., 11
Undesser, K.P., 410
Unger, T., 563
Ursell, P.C., 436

Valdeolmillos, M., 452
van Breemen, C., 822
van den Horn, G.J., 252
Vanhoutte, P.M., 117
Van Putten, V.J., 457

Wada, A., 402
Wakitani, K., 621
Watanabe, A.M., 576
Weil, J.V., 793
Weisfeldt, M.L., 20
Wendt, R.L., 606
Werns, S.W., 895
Westerhof, N., 252
Wetzel, G.T., 763
Wier, W.G., 133
Williams, C.L., 109
Williamson, J.R., 839
Wilson, D.A., 596
Wiseman, G.L., 576
Wit, A.L., 436
Witkowski, F.X., 736
Wittenberg, B.A., 195

Yamada, N., 517
Yatani, A., 868
Yoon, S.B., 704
Yue, D.T., 340

Zak, R., 548
Zimmer, L.J., 370

Circulation Research

VOLUME 56 JANUARY-JUNE 1985

VOLUME SUBJECT INDEX

A

Acetylcholine, 205
  action potential characteristics, 613
  muscarinic receptor density, 392
  regulation of release, 763
  sinoatrial node fade responses, 718
Acetylsalicylic acid, 1
Acid-base transport
  physiological processes, 773
Action potential
  duration and acetylcholine, 613
  90% repolarization, 857
  take-off, amplitude, and duration, 857
Action potential propagation, 696
Adenine nucleotide pool
  catabolites, 262
  ischemia with or without reperfusion, 262
Adenosine
  ATP synthesis, 220
  coronary blood flow, 517
  effect of dipyridamole, 242
  renal uptake, 242
Adenosine deaminase
  autoregulation, 517
  coronary blood flow, 517
  reactive hyperemia, 517
Adenosine receptors
  rat heart membranes, 728
Adenosine triphosphatase (ATPase)
  activity, staining, 548
Adenosine triphosphate
  ischemia and reperfusion, 262
Adenosine triphosphate synthesis
  adenosine, 220
  5-amino-4-imidazolcarboxamide riboside (AICAR), 220
  ribose, 220
Adenylate cyclase
  adrenergic receptors, 635
Adrenal capsules
  rat, 801
Adrenal nerve activity
  angiotensin II, 563
  substance P, 563
Adrenergic agonists
  clonidine, 763
  epinephrine, 763
  isoproterenol, 763
  methoxamine, 763
  norepinephrine, 763
  prazosin, 763
  yohimbine, 763
Adrenergic antagonists
  myocyte protein content, 884
Adrenergic control
  aging vs. young rats, 109
Adrenergic receptors
  acetylcholine regulation, 763
  alpha-adrenergic receptors, 635
  alpha- and beta-responses, 884
  antibodies to adrenergic receptors, 635
  beta-adrenergic receptors, 635
  molecular structure, 635
  physical properties, 635
  purification, 635
  reconstitution, 635
  regulation, 635
  signal transduction, 635
Adrenergic responsiveness
  postjunctional, 117
Adrenocorticotropic hormone (ACTH)
  aldosterone, 801
Aequorin luminescence, 133
  ryanodine, 452
  strophanthidin, 452
Afferents
  sympathetic, 175
  vagal, 175
Afterload pressures
  quantification of right ventricular with pulmonary vascular impedance, 40
AICAR
  5-amino-4-imidazolcarboxamide riboside, 220
  ATP synthesis, 220
Albumin transport
  mathematical assessment, 839
Aldosterone
  hypertensive rats, 427
Aminobenzyladenosines, 279
  ^{125}I-aminobenzyladenosine, 728
  N^6-4-aminobenzyladenosine, 728
Angiotensin II
  blood pressure control, 212
  brain, 212
  extracellular calcium depletion, 97
  left ventricular pressure-volume relation, 808
  mechanism of action, 97
  prostaglandin output, 97
  radioimmunoassay, 212
  renal vasoconstriction, 97
  sympathetic nerve activity, 563
  vascular tone, 97
Animal
  calf myocardial cells, 87
  cat, 205
  dog Purkinje fibers, 133
  dogs, 11, 31, 40, 57, 117, 242, 377
  dogs, conscious, 175, 651
  hamster, 377
  guinea pig, 87
  mice, 72, 377
  porcine, 1
  rabbit, 410
  rats, 78, 359, 377
    cultured myocardial cells, 370
    Fischer 344, 109
    injured carotid artery cell, 139
    spontaneously hypertensive, 402, 525
    Sprague-Dawley, 126
Animal models
  conscious and unconscious dogs, 651
  protecting ischemic myocardium, 651
Anisotropy, 427
Anoxia, 1
Antiarrhythmic drugs
  lidocaine, 696
  procainamide, 696
  quinidine, 696
  tetrodotoxin, 696
Aorta
  aortic mechanics, 690
  rat, 507
  thoracic aorta, 690
    diameter changes, 690
    electrical activity, 690
Aortic occlusion
  arterial pressure, 359
Area postrema
  baroreflex function, 410
Arrhythmias
  conduction in healed infarcts, 436
  ischemia-reperfusion, 184
  production in dogs, 690
  ventricular tachycardia, 736
Arrythmogenesis
  quinidine, 857
Arterial smooth muscle
  calcium-dependent potassium channel toxicity, 507
Arterial wall
  effect of cholesterol, 755
  kinins, 816
Arteries
  superior mesenteric, 822
Arterioles
  activation of calcium channels, 822
Arteriosclerosis, 139
Atherogenesis
  plasma lipids and lipoproteins, 755
Atherosclerosis, 418
  ultrasonic attenuation, 556
Atria
  acetylcholine release, 763
Atrial natriuretic factor
  angiotensin II, 801
  aldosterone production, 801
Atrial natiuretic peptide
  atriopeptin II, 606
Atriopeptins
  atriopeptin I, 621
  atriopeptin II, 621
    arterial vasodilation, 606
  atriopeptin III, 621
  ser-leu-arg-arg-atriopeptin III, 621
  renal effects, 621
Atrioventricular node
  vagal stimulation, 718
Automaticity
  depolarization-induced, 184
  potassium and cycle length relation, 857

Autoregulation
coronary, 517
quantification, 517

B

Baroreceptor reflexes, 359
Baroreceptors
aortic denervation, 486
Bay k 8644, 133, 868
a dihydropyridine, 87
positive inotropic effect, 87
Beating heart cells, 884
Behavior
angiotensin II
drinking, 563
substance P
arousal, 563
Behavioral responses
cardiovascular adaptation, 563
Binding studies
function of increasing radioligand, 324
ileum smooth muscle, 324
inhibition, 324
leukotriene C_4, 324
Biochemistry
cultured heart cells, 231
damage in cultured murine myocardial cells, 72
free radicals, 72
lipids, 755
lipoproteins, 755
plasma membrane Na^+-H^+ exchanger, 773
ventricular isomyosin distribution, 548
Blockade
alpha-adrenergic, 175
autonomic, 486
beta-adrenergic, 175
ganglionic, 175
muscarinic, 175
Blood gases
carbon dioxide transients, 596
Blood pressure
angiotensin II concentration, 462
Bradykinin
intracoronary injection, 175
prostaglandin output, 97
release by kallikrein, 816
Brain
hypothalmus, 212
pituitary, 212
Brainstem
cardiovascular neurons, 359
hypothalmic stimulation, 359
Brief Reviews
adrenergic receptors, 635
excitatory sodium currents in heart muscle, 475
plasma membrane Na^+-H^+ exchanger, 773
Bupivacaine, 496

C

Cable theory
conduction velocity and $\dot{V}_{max}$, 696
Calcium
accumulation on reperfusion, 262
agonists, 822
calcium-dependent fluxes, 507
cardiac glycosides and enhanced influx, 231
channel blockers, 97
channels, 133, 822
chloride channels, 507
contractility, 676
depletion, 97
effect of leukotriene binding, 324
entry and release, 133
excitation control, 507
handling in aldosterone-salt hypertensive rats, 427
influx, 822
intracellular, 822
intracellular antagonists, 97
overload, 285, 452
overload and ischemic damage, 704
paradox, 285
potassium channels, 507
ryanodine, 452
sensitivity in aortic smooth muscle, 427
sodium antiporter, 285
sodium-calcium exchange, 133, 231
sodium exchange, 285
transients, 133
uptake with CGP 28392, 676
Calcium agonist
CGP 28392, 676
Calcium antagonist
diltiazem, 822
nitrendipine, 576
Calcium channel
aorta and mesenteric resistance vessels, 822
binding of dihydropyridines, 576
diltiazem inhibition, 822
Calcium currents
dihydropyridine, 87
Calcium influx
norepinephrine, 822
Calcium ionophore
A23187, 205
Calcium overload
ischemia, 262
Calcium paradox, 285
Calcium sensitivity
response to KCl, 427
Calmodulin
inhibitors and prostaglandin output, 97
Capacitance
coronary, 310
diastolic relationships, 310
Carbon dioxide
cerebrovascular response rate, 596
Cardiac force-interval relationship, 340
Cardiac ischemia
calcium paradox, 285
reperfusion, 285
Cardiac malformations
histological examination, 392
Cardiac muscle, 87
Cardiac myocytes
morphological changes during anoxia, 899
Cardiac myocytes, dissociated
collagenase digestion, 195
rat ventricle, 195
Cardiac output
angiotensin II, 563
atriopeptin II, 606
polycythemia, 793
substance P, 563
systemic oxygen transport, 793
Cardiomechanics
anterior-posterior diameter, 161
contractile strength, 340
Frank-Starling mechanism, 351
heart-arterial interaction, 252
isolated volumic systole, 351
left ventricle, optimal power generation, 252
left ventricular volume, 161
postextrasystolic potentiation, 340
pulmonary artery constriction, 40
regional ventricular function, 351
right ventricular dynamic afterload, 40
ventricular afterload for maximal external work, 586
Cardiovascular neurons
selective deafferentation, 359
Catalase
infusion during occlusion, 895
Catecholamine kinetics, 457
Catecholamines, 635
Cation exchange
thallium effect on, 370
Cell cultures
control of growth and differentiation, 884
Cell growth
intracellular pH, 773
Cell injury, reversible
late reperfusion, 262
Cell membrane, 72
Cell volume regulation
sodium-hydrogen exchange, 773
Central nervous system
spinal cord, 212
Cerebral microvessels
alpha-adrenergic receptors, 402
CGP 2893
calcium channel agonist, 676
Chemical skinning
rat aortic rings, 427
Chick embryo heart cells, 286
Chick heart
tissue preparation and microsurgery, 392
Cholesterol
atherogenesis, 755
Cholinergic pathway, parasympathetic, 486
Cholinergic vasodilation, 205
Circuloventricular organs
subfornical, 462
Cirrhosis
norepinephrine, 457
Compliance
intramyocardial, 293
Conduction
body-surface potential, 904
Contractile strength
mathematical description, 340
postextrasystolic, 340
Contractility
amplitude and velocity, 676
CGP 28392 with calcium, 676
Contraction
normalization of developed force, 507
rested state, 87
Controversies in Cardiovascular Research, 293, 310
coronary, 293
intramyocardial compliance, 293
Coronary
arterial and overall volume, 293
arterial beta-adrenergic responsiveness, 117
autoregulation, 517
baroreflex control, 486
blood flow, 486
capacitance, 310

circulation and oxygen uptake, 57
compliance, 293
distensibility, 293
free radicals and ischemia, 895
inflow pressure, 310
input impedance, 310
intracoronary infusion, 517
ischemia, 839
ischemia of left ventricle, 351
occlusion and myocardial function, 666
peripheral pressure, 293
porcine artery, 1
pressure-flow relations in dogs, 11
pressure-flow relationships, 310
vasodilation, 486
venous flow and compliance, 293
venous retroperfusion, 666
waterfall model, 310
Coronary circulation
models of myocardial, 293
Coronary occlusion
carbon dioxide accumulation, 537
Coronary pressure
peripheral, 11
Coupling
stimulus-response, 773
ventriculoarterial, 586
Covaspheres
anti-myosin labeled, 72
Crossbridges, 78
Cultured heart cells
chick, 676
Cycle length
potassium concentration, 857
Cyclic adenosine monophosphate (cAMP)
effect of aminobenzyladenosine on heart cell cAMP, 728
radioimmunoassay, 279
Cytoskeletal features
development of rat endothelial and smooth muscle cells, 773

D

Defense reaction
vascular responses, 359
Demarcation
hypoxic and normoxic in myocardium, 876
Deoxycorticosterone acetate (DOCA)
hypertensive rats, 427
Desensitization
muscarinic receptor, 718
postjunctional mechanisms, 718
Desmin, 773
Desmosomes
morphological changes, 195
Development
heart, 392
Diameter
changes at various frequencies, 161
left ventricle, internal, 161
Diastole, 40
Digitalis
isotropic effects, 231
Dihydropyridines
Bay k 8644, 87, 133, 868
diltiazem, 576
nifedipine, 576
nitrendipine, 576
verapamil, 576
Dimensions
left ventricle, volume, 161
Dipole moments
right ventricular papillary muscle double layer, 851
Dipyridamole
renal uptake of adenosine, 242
Diuresis
atriopeptin in rats, 621
Dopamine
hypertrophic responses with ascorbic acid, 884
Dose-response curves
phenylephrine, 410
vasopressin, 410
Double layers, equivalent
right ventricular papillary muscle, 851
Drinking responses
subfornical organ, 462
Drug interactions
bupivacaine, lidocaine, and quinidine, 496
modulated receptor hypothesis, 496
Drug treatment, antihypertensive
chlorothiazide, 525
hydralazine, 525
reserpine, 525
Drugs
acetylcholine, 205
acetylsalicylic acid (aspirin), 1, 117
aconitine, 576
adenosine, 220, 242, 279
adenosine diphosphate, 220
adenosine monophosphate, 220
AICAR, 220
aminobenzyladenosine, 279
angiotensin II, 97, 212, 563, 808
arachidonic acid, 97
ascorbic acid, 507
atropine, 486
Bay k 8644 (dihydropyridine), 87, 133, 868
betaxolol, 884
bradykinin, 97, 175
bupivacaine, 496
calcium ionophore, A 23187, 205
calmidazolium, 97
catecholamine metabolites, 884
CGP 28392, 676
chlorothiazide, 525
clonidine, 402, 884
creatine kinase, 220
creatine phosphate, 220
dantrolene sodium, 97
deoxycorticosterone, 109
desmethylimipramine, 109
dihydroouabain, 231
diltiazem, 97, 507, 576, 822
dimethyl sulfoxide (DMSO), 71
dipyridamole, 242
dobutamine, 808
dopamine, 884
epinephrine, 884
fireflyluciferase, 220
glycine, 220
histamine, 1
hydralazine, 525
hypoxanthine, 220
ibuprofen, 651
ICI 118,551, 884
indomethacin, 1, 97, 117
inosine, 220
inosine monophosphate, 220
isobutylmethylxanthine (IBMX), 117
isoproterenol, 1, 117
lidocaine, 496, 696
mannitol, 72
mepacrine, 97
methoxamine, 884
metoprolol, 755
NAD^+, 220
nifedipine, 87, 576, 676, 801
nimodipine, 97
nisoldipine, 87
nitrendipine, 87, 133, 576, 676, 801, 868
nitrobenzyladenosine, 279
norepinephrine, 109, 402, 427, 507, 822, 884
norepinephrine, tritiated, 117
ouabain, 1, 231
papaverine, 1
phenoxybenzamine, 486
phentolamine, 1, 117, 402
phenylephrine, 410, 884
prazosin, 402, 884
procainamide, 696
propranolol, 1, 109, 117, 351, 486, 507, 755, 884
propylthiouracil, 78
prostacyclin, 117
prostaglandin E_2, 117
prostaglandin $F_{2\ alpha}$, 117
pyribenzamine, 1
quinidine, 496, 696, 857
reserpine, 525
ribose, 220
ryanodine, 97, 133, 452
[Sar^1,Ala^8]-angiotensin II, 97
sodium meclofenamate, 1
sodium nitroprusside, 1
strophanthidin, 452
terazosin, 884
tetrodotoxin, 109, 696, 857
theophylline, 242
TMB-8, 97
tranylcypromine, 117
trifluoperazine, 97
vasopressin, 410
verapamil, 576, 651, 801
W-7, 97

E

Early afterdepolarization
quinidine, 857
Ejection fraction, optimized, 586
Elastance
optimal effective arterial, 586
Electromotive force
papillary muscle preparations, 851
ventricular free wall, 851
ventricular tissue, 851
Electron microscopy
myocardial ultrastructure, 377
Electrophysiology
acetylcholine on action potential characteristics, 613
action potential duration, 857
acid-base transport, 773
anisotropy, 436
antiarrhythmic drugs, 696
arrhythmogenesis, 857
atrial pacing, 690
calcium channel agonist CGP 28392, 676
calcium channel inhibition, 822
calcium entry and release, 133
calcium overload, 452
calcium uptake, 87
cardiac, 475

cardiac sodium channels, 496
cardiac sodium currents, 868
cardiovascular neurons, 359
conduction, 436
conduction velocity, 696
early afterdepolarization, 857
electrocardiographic voltage, 857
electromotive force, 851
electrotonic interaction between normoxic and hypoxic fibers, 876
epicardial border zone of myocardial infarcts, 436
excitatory sodium currents, 475
fade responses in sinoatrial node, 718
inotropic effect of ryanodine, 452
ischemia and reperfusion, 184
maximum upstroke velocity, 495
membrane depolarization, 576
membrane potential, 231
monomorphic ventricular tachycardia, 736
positive inotropic dihydropyridines, 87
potassium channels, 87
potassium-induced depolarization, 822
resting membrane potential, 696
sodium channels, 475
sodium current, 696
stimulation in the presence of indomethacin, 117
stimulus-response coupling, 773
transmembrane potential, 436, 496
voltage clamp, 475
voltage-clamped cardiac muscle, 452
voltage clamp measurements, 87
Electrotonic interaction
hypxoic and normoxic fibers, 876
Endothelium
action stress fibers, 829
cell transport function, 839
morphology, 709
vasodilation, 205
Energy metabolism
high energy phosphates, 666
pyridine nucleotides, 666
Enzyme activity
metoprolol, 755
propranolol, 755
Enzymes
bovine superoxide dismutase, 72
myofibrillar ATPase, 78
Equilibrium binding
dihydropyridines on myocytes, 576
Errata, 286
carotid sinus and aortic arch baroreflexes in control of total peripheral resistance, 628
lipid solubility and pH potentiation, 628
Excitation-contraction coupling, 340
Excretion
water and urinary sodium 457
Exercise
polycythemia in dogs, 793
External detection
compartmental model of labeled albumin, 839
External power, 252

F

Fenestrae, 709
Ferrous sulfate
free radical formation, 72
Fiber orientation
transition from epicardium to endocardium, 31
Fiber orientation, myocardial, 851
Frank-Starling mechanism
segment shortening, 351
Free radicals
formation, role of ferrous ion, 72
oxygen-related damage in cultured murine cells, 72
radical scavenging agents and cellular injury, 72
superoxide dismutase, 895

G

Gamma-glutamyltransferase
brain capillary marker enzyme, 402
Gap junctions
morphological changes, 195
topology of cytoplasmic, 195
Geometry
left ventricle model shapes, 161
Glomerular function
rat renal glomeruli, 324
Glomerulonephritis
rat studies, 324
Graph fitting
pump function, 252
Growth factor
platelet, 418
platelet-derived, 139

H

Head-out water immersion
norepinephrine, 457
Heart
adenosine receptor determination, 279
calcium-depleted, 285
excitation-contraction coupling models, 340
oxygen transport, 57
ultrastructural morphometric analysis, 377
Heart cell culture
preparation, 884
Heart muscle
electrophysiology, 475
Hemodynamics
collateral blood flow, 11
left ventricular volume, 161
measurements after acute occlusion, 351
normovolemic polycythemia, 793
pulmonary, 40
regional blood flow, 606
regional blood flow measurements, 651
vasodilation, 606
High pressure liquid chromatography, 212
Histamine, 1
Histology
cardiac ganglionic cells, 392
degree of ischemic damage, 537
dog lung after microvascular injury, 40
isomyosin staining, 548
myocardial infarct, 895
tissue characterization, 556
Hodgkin-Huxley model
patch clamp, 475
voltage clamp, 475
Humans
morphometric analysis of myocardium, 377
Hyaluronidase
endothelial cell function, 839
tissue water content, 839
vascular hemodynamics, 839
Hypercapnia
carbon dioxide and cerebral blood flow, 596
Hypercontracture
oxygen paradox, 899
Hyperemia
myocardial reactive hyperemia, 517
Hyperkinesis, 351
Hyperoxia, 1
Hyperplasia
smooth muscle cell, 525
Hyperploidy
smooth muscle cell, 525
Hypertension
aldosterone-salt in the rat, 427
angiotensin II-induced, 462
Hypertrophy
alpha$_1$-adrenergic receptor stimulation, 884
smooth muscle cell, 525
Hypocapnia
cerebral blood flow and carbon dioxide, 596
Hypothesis
modulated receptor, 496
Hypothyroidism
rat myocardium, 78
Hypoxia, 1
electrical decoupling, 876

I

Ibuprofen
protection of ischemic myocardium, 651
Immunofluorescent staining
desmin, 829
vimentin, 829
Impedance
coronary input, 310
effects of lung hyperventilation, 40
heart rate and impedance, 40
loading system, 586
modeling, 310
reactive components, 310
stroke volume, 40
Indomethacin, 1
norepinephrine overflow, 117
Infarct
epicardial border zone, 436
size limitations, 651
Infarction
acute myocardial, 351
myocardial intramural reentry, 736
Inflammatory mediator, 324
Inotropy
calcium uptake, 676
effects of dihydroouabain, ouabain, potassium, 231
Intercalated disc, 195
Intracellular calcium
release from aorta, 822
Intracranial pressure
cardiopulmonary resuscitation, 20
Intramural reentry
ventricular tachycardia, 736
Intramyocardial compliance
diastolic pressure-flow and zero flow

pressure, 293
Intraventricular unloading
segment shortening, 351
Iodocyanopindolol
assay for labeled, 126
beta-adrenergic antagonist, 126
Ischemia, 436
adenine nucleotide pool, 262
animal models for protecting myocardium, 651
calcium overload, 262
cell volume regulation, 262
effect of elevated potassium levels, 184
free radical formation, 72
hemodynamic and mitochondrial function, 704
hyaluronidase, 839
myocardial calcium, 262
myocardial ultrasonic backscatter, 683
regional myocardial, 537
reperfusion, 895
reperfusion of myocardium, 651
segment shortening, 351
ultrastructure, 262
Isolated ventricle
postextrasystolic potentiation, 340
Isolation
adrenergic receptors, 635
Isometric force development
economy in rat myocardium, 78
Isomyosin
left ventricular presence, 548
rabbit cardiac tissue HCalpha, 548
transmural gradients, 548
V_1 and V_3 heavy chain structure, 548
Isoproterenol, 1
Isotope fluxes
chloride-36, 507
potassium-42, 507
sodium-24, 507

J

Junctions
gap, 195
intercellular, 195

K

Kallikrein-kinin system, 816
Kidney
excretory function disorders, 621
Kinetics
catecholamine, 457
Kininogenases
biological characteristics, 816
purification, 816
Kinins
blood pressure, 816

L

Laryngeal nerve stimulation, 359
Laser diffraction
experimental system, 331
kinetics of sarcomere relaxation, 331
mounting procedure, 331
Left ventricle
fiber direction and segment shortening, 31
isomyosins, 548
midwall of canine, 31
Left ventricle geometry, 161
Left ventricular pressure-time relations
derivation of time-varying elastance model, 808
Letter to the Editor, 285
electrocardiographic voltage, 904
Leukotrienes
binding, 324
LTC_4, 324
Lidocaine, 496
conduction velocity and $\dot{V}_{max}$, 696
Ligation
confluence of sinuses, 20
lateral ventricle, 20
right atrium, 20
thoracic subarachnoid, 20
Low potassium growth conditions, 286

M

Mapping
impulse propagation, 436
infarct activation maps, 436
isochronal activation maps, 736
normal sinus rhythm, 736
Marker enzymes
gamma-glutamyltransferase, 402
Matching, 252
Maximal external work, 586
Measurements
electromagnetic lever system, 331
force generation, 331
Mechanical restitution
potentiation, 340
Mechanics
aortic behavior, 690
Membrane potential, 133
Mesenteric arteries
rat, 801
Metabolism, cardiac
local regulatory mechanisms, 486
Metoprolol
atherogenesis, 755
Microcirculation
brain, 402
cerebral blood flow, 596
cerebral microvessels, 402
cerebrovascular response time, 596
coronary flow, 310
myocardial, 293
neuronal regulation, 402
Microspheres
measurement of collateral flow rates, 11
radionuclide-labeled, 11
Microsurgery
chick heart, 392
Microvascular studies
coronary circulation, 789
Migration
quiescent smooth muscle, 139
Mitochondria
function in ischemia, 704
Models
Hodgkin-Huxley, 475
Models of the coronary circulation
cross-sectional area and external pressure, 789
intramyocardial pump, 789
microvascular studies, 789
nonlinearities and time constants, 789
waterfall pump, 789
Modulated receptor hypothesis, 496
Molecular structure
adrenergic receptors, 635
Morphology
changes in desmosomes and gap junctions, 195
contrast microscopy, 899
fenestrated capillaries, 709
myocytes during anoxia, 899
video length tracking, 899
Morphometry
influence of sampling site, 377
ultrastructural, 377
volume densities, 377
Muscarinic receptor
atrioventricular node responses, 718
transmembrane cholinergic stimulation, 613
Muscarinic vasodilation, 205
Muscle
cardiac, 87, 452
Myocardial cells
cultured rat, 370
Myocardial edema
electrolyte effect, 262
Myocardial infarction
intramural reentry, 736
ischemia and reperfusion effects on size, 895
Myocardial pH, 537
Myocardium
fiber orientation, 31
ischemia, 683
ischemia and preservation, 704
reperfusion, 683
segment shortening, 31
Myocytes
distribution of beta-receptors, 126
preparation of rat cardiac, 576
Myosin
cardiac from mice, 72
distribution and age, 548
quantification of isoenzymes, 78

N

NADH fluorescence
hypoxia and electrical decoupling, 876
photography, 666
Natriuresis
atriopeptins, 621
Nerve stimulation
transmural, 109
Neural crest lesions
parasympathetic innervation, 392
Neurogenic control
alpha-adrenergic receptors, 402
angiotensin II, 563
arterial baroreflex function, 410
central blood pressure regulation, 563
embryonic chick crest ablation, 392
nerve recording, 410
neuronal regulation, 402
renal sympathetic nerves, 410
sinoaortic denervation, 410
substance P, 563
sympathetic nerve activity, 563
vasopressin and area postrema, 410
Neurogenic vasodilation, 205
Neuronal regulation, 402
Neurons
cardiovascular, 359
reticulospinal, 359
Nexus, 195
NHLBI Cooperative Study
animal models for protection of ischemic myocardium, 651
Nifedipine, 87
Nisoldipine, 87
Nitrendipine, 133, 867, 868
binding studies, 676

Nitrobenzyladenosines
N^6-4-nitrobenzyladenosine, 728
Norepinephrine
accumulation of tritiated, 109
calcium-response curves, 427
cirrhosis, 457
depolarization, 822
stimulation of effluxes, 507
Nucleotide uptake
renal function, 242

O

Oscillatory power, 252
Ouabain, 1
Oxygen
changes in vascular tone with change in bath, 1
hemodynamics and oxygen content, 57
intracellular sequestration, 57
limiting transfer rates, 57
outflow profiles in high and low consumption, 57
red cell pool effect on diffusion, 57
toxicity, 72
tracer uptake in coronary circulation, 57
transfer from blood to tissues, 57
transport in the heart, 57
Oxygen paradox
single heart cells, 899
Oxygen transport
systemic, cardiac output with polycythemia, 793
Pain, cardiac
excitatory reflexes, 175
Papaverine, 1
Peptides
vasoactive, 606
Pericardium
left ventricular diastolic pressure, 40
Peripheral coronary pressure, 11
Permeability
capillary, 709
Persantine, 242
pH homeostasis
bicarbonate transport, 773
pH potentiation
erratum, 628

P

Pharmacology
adrenergic neuroeffector function, 109
adrenergic receptor interaction, 884
adrenergic receptors, 635
alpha-receptor-stimulated ionic fluxes, 507
beta-adrenergic receptors, 126
beta-blockers, 755
coronary adrenergic responsiveness, 117
muscarinic receptors, 392
reduction of hypertension, 755
specific beta-antagonists, 126
sympathetic nervous function, 755
vascular, of atriopeptins, 621
Phentolamine, 1
alpha-adrenergic antagonist, 1
Phenylephrine
arterial pressure, 410
Piezelectric crystals
histological defects at site, 31
positioning as external long axis markers, 31
Platelet growth factor, 418
Polycythemia
normovolemic in dogs, 793
rest and exercise, 793
Positive end-expiratory pressure (PEEP)
left ventricular dimensions, 40
pulmonary hypertension, 40
Potassium
activation and concentration, 822
effect of extracellular concentration on vasoconstriction, 1
effect of thallium, 370
effects of normal and elevated levels on canine Purkinje tissues, 184
extracellular on sodium pump, 231
Potentials
body-surface, 904
transmembrane, 436
Potentiation
postextrasystolic, 340
Power output
right ventricular, 40
Prazosin
effect on heart rate, 763
Preparations
aminobenzyladenosines, 728
beating cells, 884
brain microvessels, 402
cultured chick heart cells, 676
cultured rat myocardial cells, 370
growth factors, 418
human Sm-C/IGF-I, 418
intact vascular vessel segments, 427
mitochondrial isolation, 704
Purkinje fiber-papillary muscle, 184
Purkinje fibers, 133
radiolabeled aminobenzyladenosines, 728
rat cultured cardiac myocytes, 868
rat dissociated cells, 195
rat heart cell culture, 884
skinned aortic rings, 427
tissue fixation, 377
tissue from perfused-fixed hearts, 377
ventricular cardiomyocytes, 126
ventricular membranes, 126
Pressor reflex, 175
Pressure
coronary artery, 293
diastolic pressure-flow curves, 293
flow relationships, 310
intracranial, 20
transmission of intrathoracic to intracranial space, 20
zero flow, 293, 310
Pressure-flow relations
steady state circumflex, 11
Pressure gradients
interarterial, 11
Pressure-volume relations
caval occlusion, 808
effect of angiotensin II, 808
Procainamide
conduction velocity and $\dot{V}_{max}$, 696
Propranolol, 1, 109
atherogenesis, 755
Prostaglandins
effect of calmodulin inhibitors on production, 97
endogenous, 117
6-keto-prostaglandin $F_{1\,alpha}$, 97
prostacyclin, 117
prostaglandin E_2, 97, 117
prostaglandin $F_{2\,alpha}$, 117
synthesis, 117
vascular synthesis, 1
Protein synthesis
alpha- and beta-adrenergic stimulation, 884
Pulmonary
artery constriction and right ventricular dynamic afterload, 40
Pump function graph fitting, 252
Pumps
intramyocardial, 310
waterfall, 310
Purkinje fibers
contraction, 133
papillary muscle preparations, 184
role of intracellular calcium release, 133
role of transsarcolemmal calcium entry, 133
sheep cardiac calcium overloaded, 452
superfusion in Tyrode's solution, 184
Pyribenzamine, 1
histamine antagonist, 1

Q

Quinidine
conduction velocity and $\dot{V}_{max}$, 696

R

Radiobinding assay, 126, 212, 279, 324, 676, 728, 801
Rat
cultured myocardial cells, 370
Receptors
adenosine, 279, 728
adrenal for atrial natriuretic factor, 801
adrenergic, Brief Review, 635
alpha-adrenergic, 402, 763
$alpha_1$- and $beta_1$-interaction, 884
$alpha_1$-induction of beating, 884
beta-adrenergic mechanisms, 1
cholinergic, 392
leukotriene degradation, 324
muscarinic, 392, 613, 718
sites for local anesthetic and antiarrhythmic drugs, 496
sympathetic alpha-receptor pathway, 486
vascular for atrial natriuretic factor, 801
Red cells
chromium-51 labeled, 57
pool effect on oxygen diffusion, 57
Reentry
ventricular tachycardia, 736
Reflex
baroreceptor, 359
baroreflex function and area postrema, 410
cartotid baroreflex, 486
ventrolateral medulla oblongata, 359
Regulation
cell volume, 773
central blood pressor, 563
Relaxation
cardiac, 331
sarcomere, 331
transmural, with and without endothelium, 205

Renal
glomerular filtration, 242
leukotriene C_4 receptors, 324
rabbit sympathetic nerves, 410
sodium-depleted dog, 242
vasoconstriction, 97
Renal arteries
rat, 801
Renal nerve activity
angiotensin II, 563
substance P, 563
Renal vein spiking
stimulation with norepinephrine, 109
Renin-angiotensin system
angiotensin II-induced hypertension, 462
Reperfusion
calcium activity, 262
ischemic myocardium, 262
left coronary artery side branch, 220
normal Tyrode's solution, 184
vascular function integrity, 839
Replication
smooth muscle cell somatomedin-like peptide, 418
Resistance
angiotensin II and substance P on total peripheral, 563
coronary vascular, 310
peripheral, 252
regional vascular, 606
source, 252
stroke work, 586
Resistance, total peripheral
erratum, 628
Response time, cerebrovascular, 596
Responses to Controversies in Cardiovascular Research
cross-sectional area and external pressure, 789
diastolic pressure flow behavior, 789
intramyocardial pump, 789
microvascular studies, 789
models of the coronary circulation, 789
nonlinearities and time constants, 789
waterfall pump, 789
Resuscitation
cardiopulmonary, 20
intracranial pressure, 20
Reticulospinal neurons, 359
Rheology
vascular, 690
Ribose
ATP synthesis, 220
Rigor state
cumulative probability, 899
hypoxia duration, 899
rounded vs. recovered cells, 899
Rostral ventrolateral medulla
electrophysiology, 359
vasopressor area, 359
Ryanodine
aequorin luminescence, 133
calcium overload, 452
effect on membrane potential, 133

S

Sarcolemma, 285
Sarcomere length
laser diffraction, 331
Sarcomere relaxation
lengthening and shortening, 331
peak velocity, 331
relaxation, 331
Saturation studies
membrane, 576
Segment shortening
acute ischemia, 35
Frank-Starling mechanism, 351
left ventricle, 351
Serine proteases
physical characteristics, 816
Sinoartic denervation, 410
Sinoatrial node
vagal stimulation, 718
Smooth muscle
angiotensin II, 801
developmental rat aortic cells, 829
norepinephrine response, 801
Smooth muscle cell
carotid artery, rat, 139
porcine aortic, 418
Sodium
channels, 475, 868
currents, 475, 868
Sodium channels
modulated receptor hypothesis for nitrendipine, 868
Sodium chloride, 42
Sodium current, 696
nitrendipine effect, 868
Sodium meclofenamate, 1
Sodium nitroprusside, 1, 117
Sodium potassium pump inhibition, 452
Sodium pump
extracellular potassium, 231
inhibition and inotropy, 231
thallium, 370
Sodium-calcium exchange, 133, 285
calcium reflux, 231
effect of glycosides, 231
Sodium-hydrogen exchanger
properties and stoichiometry, 773
Somatomedin
smooth muscle cell secretion, 418
somatomedin-C, 418
Sonomicrometer, 161
Special Article
models for protecting ischemic myocardium, 651
Splanchnic nerve activity
angiotensin II, 563
substance P, 563
Staining
en face with actin-actin antibodies, 829
immunofluorescent, 829
Stimuloresponse coupling
lymphocytes, 773
neutrophils, 773
platelets, 773
Strophanthidin
twitch tension, 452
Subendocardial layer, 851
Subfornical organ
angiotensin II in the rat, 462
drinking responses, 462
pressor responses, 462
Substance P
lateral brain ventricle, 563
neuronal efferent activity, 563
pressor responses, 563
Sulfidopeptide leukotrienes, 324
Superoxide dismutase
infusion during occlusion, 895
reperfused ischemic myocardium, 895
Systole, 40

T

Techniques
autofluorescence, 876
bypass experiments, 690
chemical skinning of vascular smooth muscle, 427
chromatofocusing, 816
computer analysis of competition, 126
contrast microscopy, 899
Doppler flow probe, 606
electron microscopy, 195, 377, 436, 829
extraction, rat brain tissue, 212
freeze fracture of dissociated cells, 195
gamma-spectrometry, 839
gel electrophoresis, 78, 816, 829
gel filtration, 212
gravimetric analysis of infarct size, 895
hemispherical crystals, 161
high pressure liquid chromatography, 212, 324, 801, 242, 816
histological and histochemical examination, 392
histology, 436
immunofluorescence, 829
immunoreactive somatomedin-like peptide content, 418
indicator-dilution curves, 242
laser diffraction, 331
experimental system
mounting procedure
leukotrienes, 324
mass spectrometry, 537
microsurgery, 392
morphometric analysis, 709
morphometric measurements, 377
muscarinc receptor-binding studies, 392
myocardial gas tension, 537
NADH fluorescence, 666, 876
nerve recording, 410
patch clamp, 868
pH electrode, 537
planimetric analysis of infarct size, 895
protein measurements, Lowry, 402
radiobinding assays, 126, 212, 279, 324, 676, 728, 801
sonomicrometry, 161
thallium scintigraphy, 370
thin section electron microscope studies, 195
tissue culture, 231
tissue preparation, 392
ultrasonic attenuation, 556
video length tracking, 899
voltage clamp, 87, 475
windkessel, 486
Tension
myocardial gas, 537
Tetrodotoxin
conduction velocity and $\dot{V}_{max}$, 696
Thallium scintigraphy
Myocardial, 370
Thallium uptake
cultured myocardial cells, 370
ouabain, 370
potassium, 370
Theophylline
glomerular filtration, 242
Thermodynamics
basal heat, 78
heat calculations, 78
recovery heat, 78

tension-independent and -dependent heat, 78
Thymidine
tritiated, 139
Tissue characterization
ultrasonic, 683
Tissue culture, 72
Total peripheral resistance
erratum, 628
Transendothelial channels
murine capillary beds, 709
Transient analysis
carbon dioxide and cerebral blood flow transients, 596
Transmural gradients
ventricular isomyosins, 548
Tranylcypromine
prostacyclin synthetase inhibitor, 117
Twitch tension
bupivacaine, lidocaine, quinidine, 496
strophanthidin, 452

U

Ultrasonic dimension gauge, 31
Ultrasound
characterization, 556
indices, 556
myocardial backscatter, 683
quantitative studies, 683
tissue characterization, 683
Ultrastructure
effect of reperfusion after ischemia, 262
ischemia damage, 537
myocardium
dogs, 377
hamsters, 377
humans, 377
mice, 377
rats, 377
ventricular muscle cells, 436
Upstroke velocity
maximum rate of rise of the action potential upstroke ($\dot{V}_{max}$), 696
Uric acid
increase with AICAR, 220

V

Vagotomy
acetylcholine, 613
Vagus nerve
bilateral cervical vagotomy, 613
Vascular resistance
coronary, 310
Vascular rheology, 690
Vascular smooth muscle
adrenergic nerve stimulation, 109
antihypertensive drug therapy, 525
calcium sensitivity, 427
cell hyperploidy, 525
cell hypertrophy, 525
chemically skinned aorta, 427
muscarinic receptors, 205
porcine, 1
Vascular tone
effects of oxygen, 1
Vasoconstriction
effect of extracellular potassium on coronary, 1
renal, 97
Vasodilation
atrial peptides, 621
carotid baroreceptor reflex, 486
cholinergic, 205
muscarinic, 205
neurogenic, 205
Vasomotor center
baroreceptor reflexes, 359
cardiovascular neurons, 359
electrophysiological location in the ventrolateral medulla oblongata, 359
Vasopressin
arterial pressure, 410
sympathetic nervous system, 563
Vasopressor
cardiovascular regulation, 359
Vasospasm
electrical stimulation, 117
presence of indomethacin, 117
Ventricular activation sequence
potential curves, 851
spread of activation, 851
Ventricular function
shortening data, 31
Ventricular tachycardia
myocardial infarction, 736
Ventricular tachycardia, polymorphous
"Torsades de Pointes," 857
quinidine therapy, 857
Verapamil, 704
protection of ischemic myocardium, 651
Vimentin
cytoskeletal protein, 829
Viscoelesticity
thoracic aorta of dogs and rabbits, 690
Voltage clamp
patch clamp techniques, 868
preparations for use with, 475
sodium currents, 475

W

Wall motion
canine left ventricle midwall, 31
Waterfall pump, 310
model of the coronary circulation, 789

Z

Zero flow pressure
capacitance, 310
collateral flow, 310